The Oxford Dictionary of
Quotations

SIXTH EDITION

Edited by **Elizabeth Knowles**

OXFORD

UNIVERSITY PRESS

OXFORD

UNIVERSITY PRESS

Great Clarendon Street, Oxford OX2 6DP

Oxford University Press is a department of the University of Oxford.
It furthers the University's objective of excellence in research, scholarship,
and education by publishing worldwide in

Oxford New York

Auckland Bangkok Buenos Aires Cape Town Chennai
Dar es Salaam Delhi Hong Kong Istanbul Karachi Kolkata
Kuala Lumpur Madrid Melbourne Mexico City Mumbai Nairobi
São Paulo Shanghai Taipei Tokyo Toronto

Oxford is a registered trade mark of Oxford University Press
in the UK and in certain other countries

Published in the United States
by Oxford University Press Inc., New York

First edition published 1941
Second edition published 1953
Third edition published 1979
Fourth edition published 1992
Fifth edition published 1999
Sixth edition published 2004

British Library Cataloguing in Publication Data

Data available

Library of Congress Cataloging in Publication Data

Data available

ISBN 0-19-860720-2

10 9 8 7 6 5 4 3 2 1

Designed by Jane Stevenson
Typeset in Photina and Argo
by Interactive Sciences Limited, Gloucester
Printed in Great Britain
by Biddles Limited, King's Lynn

Project team

Managing editor	Elizabeth Knowles
Associate editor	Susan Ratcliffe
Library research	Ralph Bates Marie G. Diaz
Reading programme	Jean Harker Verity Mason Helen Rappaport
Data capture	Susanne Charlett Richard Jones Muriel Ranivoalison
Proof-reading	Kim Allen Fabia Claris Carolyn Garwes Penny Trumble

Contents

Introduction

In this new sixth edition of the *Oxford Dictionary of Quotations*, the comprehensive nature of its coverage has been extended and sustained. Since the fifth edition appeared in 1999, the *Dictionary*, first published in 1941, has celebrated its diamond jubilee. The later part of this Introduction will look back at the history of the *Dictionary*, and we also reprint here the Introduction to the First Edition. Earlier editions provided the foundations of the current book, and these foundations are constantly added to with new material from the reading programme with which we monitor the language. Such new material includes not only high-profile utterances of the last few years (from 'axis of evil' to 'shock and awe'), but also, and excitingly, quotations from an earlier time which have acquired new resonance and currency.

A notable example of this occurred in the aftermath of '9/11', the terrorist attacks of 11 September, 2001, which destroyed the World Trade Center. In the debate on a possible invasion of Afghanistan, those opposed to intervention cited the words of John Quincy Adams, sixth President of the United States, who in 1821 gave it as his view that America 'goes not abroad in search of monsters to destroy'. A later President was also to be directly quoted. At an address in Washington National Cathedral, on 14 September 2001, George W. Bush stated that 'Today we feel what Franklin Roosevelt called the warm courage of national unity', reaching back to Roosevelt's first inaugural address of 4 March 1933.

At the end of the 20th century, events in the Balkans recalled Kipling's 19th-century war correspondent in *The Light that Failed*, who 'always opened his conversation with the news that there would be trouble in the Balkans in the spring.' What happened during the crumbling of the former Yugoslavia reminded us of the dreadful nature of civil war, but one aspect of its cruelty was highlighted over three centuries ago, when the Parliamentary General William Waller wrote to his Royalist counterpart (and old comrade) Ralph Hopton, 'With what a perfect hatred I detest this war without an enemy.' A few years later, another soldier of the time summed up the possible dangers of military victory. The Royalist Sir Jacob Astley, captured after a battle in 1646, said prophetically to his captors, 'Gentlemen, ye may now sit and play, for you have done all your work, if you fall not out among yourselves.'

It is fascinating to see similar ideas echoing across the centuries. 'The chief merit of language is clearness, and we know that nothing detracts so much from this as do unfamiliar terms,' said Galen, the Greek physician of the 2nd century AD. In 1665, John Bunyan (alluding to the Authorized Version of the Bible) wrote that 'Words easy to be understood do often hit the mark; when high and learned ones do only pierce the air.' Anxieties about heavy taxes might be thought of as a more recent concern, but it was the Roman Emperor Tiberius who pointed out to his provincial governors that 'It is the part of the good shepherd to shear his flock, not skin it.' (Tiberius would presumably have agreed with the words attributed to Jean-Baptiste Colbert, chief minister to Louis XIV of France, 'The art of taxation consists in so plucking the goose as to obtain the largest possible amount of feathers with the smallest possible amount of hissing.') The Machiavellian French cleric and statesman of the 17th century, the Cardinal de Retz, held the view that 'A man who does not trust himself will never really trust anybody.' Two centuries later we find in Goethe's *Faust* the line, 'Just trust yourself and you'll learn the art of living.' In the uncertain aftermath of the American Presidential election of 2000, when the exact nature of the vote in Florida was still being discussed, Bill Clinton commented, 'The American people have spoken . . . but it's going to take a little while to determine exactly what they said.' The remark would have been appreciated by the great 19th-century Conservative statesman, Lord Salisbury, who after a by-election in 1877 said wryly, 'One of the nuisances of the ballot is that when the oracle has spoken you never know what it means.'

Sometimes it is the precise wording of a quotation which is reworked. In 1931, Rudyard Kipling coined the phrase 'Power without responsibility.' In our own time, the Chilean writer Ariel Dorfman offers the revision: 'Responsibility without power, the fate of the secretary through the ages.'

The advisability of taking thought before committing oneself to a course is often pointed out. 'The closer these practical probabilities drive war toward the absolute . . . the more imperative the need not to take the first step without considering the last,' warned the Prussian military theorist Karl von Clausewitz. An earlier quotation, attributed to Edmund Burke, looks at the dangers of large-scale undertakings:

> Those who carry on great public schemes must be proof against the most fatiguing delays, the most mortifying disappointments, the most shocking insults, and, worst of all, the presumptuous judgements of the ignorant upon their designs.

We think of concern about the influence of spin-doctors to be a comparatively recent phenomenon, but John Buchan in *The Three Hostages* (1924) has a recognizable account of the process: 'Have you ever considered what a diabolical weapon that can be—using all the channels of modern publicity to poison and warp men's minds?' He described it as the most dangerous thing on earth, although happily in the long run (and having 'sown the world with mischief') self-defeating. Again, the accuracy of media reports is frequently criticized today, but it was in 1807 that Thomas Jefferson wrote, 'Nothing can now be believed which is seen in a newspaper. Truth itself becomes suspicious by being put into that polluted vehicle.'

Power has traditionally been seen as a dangerous commodity. 'Excessive dealings with tyrants are not good for the security of free states' said the Athenian statesman Demosthenes. In the sixteenth century, Thomas More warned that, 'Anyone who campaigns for public office becomes disqualified for holding any office at all.' On the other hand, Nathan Hale, the American revolutionary hanged as a spy by the British in 1776, thought that 'Every kind of service necessary to the public good becomes honourable by being necessary.' In the twentieth century Willy Brandt was determinedly optimistic: 'We want to risk more democracy.'

Some quotations reflect a personal passion. 'Good food is always a trouble and its preparation should be regarded as a labour of love,' said Elizabeth David in 1951, introducing her groundbreaking *French Country Cooking*. The English ceramic designer Susie Cooper pointed out, sensibly, the advantages of her chosen medium. 'Pottery . . . is a practical and lasting form of art. Not everyone can afford original paintings, but most people can afford pottery.' Another ceramic artist, Clarice Cliff, reflected, 'Colour seems to radiate happiness and the spirit of modern life and movement, and I cannot put too much of it in my designs to please women.' The sculptor Barbara Hepworth said of her own work, 'I rarely draw what I see—I draw what I feel in my own body.' The chemist Dorothy Hodgkin, a Nobel prizewinner, said of her early engagement in her subject, 'I was captured for life by chemistry and by crystals.' The French painter Paul Cézanne asserted, 'I will astonish Paris with an apple.'

A number of quotations bring the individuality (and story) of the speaker strongly to mind. 'I will not be triumphed over' said Cleopatra (according to the Roman historian Livy). 'Trifles make perfection, and perfection is no trifle' said Michelangelo (according to Samuel Smiles). Lord Melbourne, the Prime Minister who liked the Garter because there was 'no damned merit' about it, had a clear view of the management of higher education: 'Universities never reform themselves; everyone knows that.' Theodore Roosevelt likened the attempt to make an agreement with Colombia to trying to nail currant jelly to a wall. 'And the failure to nail currant jelly to the wall is not due to the nail. It's due to the currant jelly.' The explorer Ernest Shackleton thought that, 'Superhuman effort isn't worth a damn unless it achieves results.' Eleanor Roosevelt, speaking to the new President after the sudden death of her husband Franklin, said to Harry Truman, 'Is there anything we can do for you? For you are the one in trouble now.' The Canadian writer Robert MacNeil said of reading aloud to children, 'Parents can plant magic in a child's mind through certain words spoken with some thrilling quality of voice.'

The richness and diversity of the *Dictionary* is one of its great strengths, and abiding pleasures, but the book originally proposed would have been much less expansive. In 1915 there was an initial suggestion for 'an Oxford Dictionary of Poetry Quotations (not foreign quotations)', to be based on 'Oxford texts and the N.E.D. [now the *Oxford English Dictionary*]'.

The idea was not immediately followed up, and it was not until the 1930s that the project got under way. An assessment of what was wanted, in a letter of 1931, shows an extension of the original vision of 1915, highlighting especially familiar quotations from foreign languages and 'modern quotations that have not yet got into the books'. With major sources such as the Bible and Shakespeare, they would have to limit themselves to what was 'eminently *quotable* and constantly quoted'. The Classics were a particular consideration: if the book were not to be limited to English, it would seem illiterate to give 'a mere handful of classical tags'. It would however be essential to give translations. The question of overall organization was also debated, and the principle of A–Z author organization finally agreed.

There was a strong view that 'non-English quotations must be reduced to very narrow limits' (partly, it must be said, on grounds of extent and cost). A distinction was to be drawn between what a French scholar would quote in French, and 'that rather small number of French phrases which are almost current English (or have been)'. Latin should provide the bulk of the foreign quotations, with German, Italian, and Spanish being satisfied by a handful of tags. There was doubt too about the currency of classical Greek, with the question being asked 'Isn't it a fact that Greek has disappeared from the House of Commons?'

Consideration of the collection of material came with the warning that 'Even in English we shall have to guard against things quotable, as apart from things commonly quoted.' From a practical point of view it was thought risky to have texts read by people who were devoted to them. 'They probably quote, or think they quote, those texts to an abnormal extent.' The result would be a flood of material, and preparatory work that was 'vast or uneven'.

In conclusion, then, they were looking at a dictionary of quotations which would have a primarily literary base, and which would include quotations from major writers likely to be quoted in English by the literate and cultured person. The importance of the American market was somewhat grudgingly acknowledged ('We must consider the Americans lovingly'), but in reality this was more likely to mean American authors regarded as having honorary status in English literature, rather than a true reflection of American culture.

By the end of the 1930s, *the Oxford Dictionary of Quotations* was nearing publication. One problem, however, remained. In May 1941, an appeal was made to Cambridge, to the writer Bernard Darwin, noted for his knowledge and love of quotations, with the words 'Come over into Macedonia and help us' (Bible, Acts 16:9; Darwin had served in Macedonia during the First World War). It was explained that many months previously, in duty bound, they had asked the Vice-Chancellor, George Gordon, President of Magdalen, to write an Introduction to the *Dictionary*. According to the rueful explanation,

> With his customary charming politeness he said he would, but with his I fear equally customary press of business and, if I may be guilty of *scandalum magnum*, habit of postponement he has not delivered the goods.

The failure might have been predicted: according to the article on Gordon in the *Dictionary of National Biography*,

> It was hard to persuade him that even a lecture was fit to be printed; if he parted with the manuscript, he clung to the proof. Of anything much more than a lecture his friends learned to despair.

OUP sensibly did despair of Gordon's producing what was needed, and instead appealed to 'the sister University [to] come, as so often' to the rescue. Would Darwin write, and moreover write very quickly, the Introduction? If he would come over to Oxford as soon as possible he could be provided with a quiet room, the proofs of the book, and the factual Preface. They would 'gladly and thankfully' pay him fifteen guineas if at the end of six hours Darwin could produce an Introduction.

Darwin may have been flattered by the terms of the appeal ('You are the man . . . It's a great book, and we want a great Introduction'), or touched by its frankness ('We really are in a hole'). Whatever his reason, he accepted, and provided the Introduction which is reprinted here on pages xix–xxiv.

The *Dictionary* was published in October 1941, and generally extremely well received, the first printing of 20,000 being exhausted about a month after publication. For three months subsequently they struggled with wartime restrictions to get a reprint on to the market. This was 'the constantly recurring trouble with all our books nowadays'; a more individual difficulty is recorded in an exchange of correspondence with the famously litigious Lord Alfred Douglas.

Lord Alfred wrote to Humphrey Milford, Publisher to the Oxford University Press, in November 1941, to complain that he was represented in the *Dictionary* by two lines taken from his early nonsense verse. He was undecided as to whether this indicated deliberate rudeness or that the compiler was 'merely ignorant & illiterate'. The line on which the subsequent correspondence centred was 'The placid pug that paces in the park', from *The Placid Pug, and Other Rhymes*, by the Belgian Hare (London, 1906).

Milford, replying two days later, stated the general position, that the *Dictionary* was a collection of familiar quotations and not an anthology of chosen authors, good and bad, and then went on to the particular:

> I see a pug (not often, thank Heaven, in these days) and I at once
> think of your line and so do many other people. Therefore it naturally
> appears in a book of familiar quotations.

This was not an argument to appeal to Lord Alfred, and he found the letter 'singularly unconvincing'. The correspondence rumbled on, involving at one stage Lord Alfred's solicitors. It is possible to feel some sympathy for the solicitor whose instructions forced him to write,

> We are acting for Lord Alfred Douglas, who, as you must know, is one
> of the greatest living poets and has been so described by those best able
> to form an opinion and entitled to express it.

Today Lord Alfred is represented by the line

> I am the love that dare not speak its name.
> *Two Loves* (1896)

It is far from clear that he would have been happy with this sole evidence of his poetic mastery, but it is almost certainly the only line of his which today can be described as 'familiar'.

To return to the *Dictionary* as published in 1941. The book was, inevitably, Anglocentric, a feature reinforced by the arrangement of material. The quotations were organized in such separate sections as *Authors Writing in English*, *Book of Common Prayer*, *Holy Bible*, *Anonymous*, *Ballads*, *Nursery Rhymes*, *Quotations from Punch*, and *Foreign Quotations* (Latin, Greek, French, Italian, Spanish, and German have the language of origin; Russian, Norwegian, and Swedish appear only in translation). Opening the pages is rather like walking into a traditional study lined with leather-bound volumes.

The selection was pre-eminently a literary one: according to the prefatory note, 'The Compilers to the Reader', the writers most frequently quoted were Browning, Byron, Cowper, Dickens, Johnson, Kipling, Milton, Shakespeare, Shelley, Tennyson, and Wordsworth. Beyond the dominance of the canonical writers, room was also found for lesser figures. The Victorian writer Thomas Ashe (1836–89), whose poems according to the *Dictionary of National Biography* 'failed entirely to gain the ear of his generation' is represented by the plaintive line, 'Meet we no angels, Pansie?' The moderns were cautiously admitted: the single quotation from Virginia Woolf is the title of *A Room of One's Own*.

In his hastily compiled Introduction, Bernard Darwin had reflected that, 'It is difficult today not to deal in warlike metaphors', but in fact the text of the first *Dictionary* reflected little of the period leading up to the Second World War. Winston Churchill, outnumbered by his father Randolph, has a single quotation from 1906, 'It cannot in the opinion of His Majesty's Government be classified as slavery in the extreme acceptance of the word without some risk of terminological inexactitude.' George V's official last words, 'How is the Empire?' were there, but not the former Edward VIII's reference to 'the help and support of the woman I love' in his Abdication broadcast. The Prime Minister who had to deal with the Abdication Crisis, Stanley Baldwin, did not appear at all, although his warning that 'the bomber will always get through' was given in 1932. Franklin Roosevelt had a single quote: his assertion during his 1932 election campaign that, 'I pledge you—I pledge myself—to a new deal for the American people.' Neville Chamberlain was also absent: it should have been possible to record his mistaken 'I believe it is peace for our time' (returning from Munich in 1938), although the equally erroneous 'Hitler has missed the bus' of April 1940 did come too late for a book published in the autumn of 1941. There was in fact very little to indicate the coming storm, other than an item in the Addenda to German quotations, Hermann Goering's comment in a radio broadcast of 1936, 'Guns will make us powerful; butter will only make us fat.'

The novelist Norman Douglas once suggested that 'You can tell the ideals of a nation by its advertisements', and a number appeared in the *Dictionary*. Darwin's Introduction referred to what in 1941 was still a familiar advertising slogan, 'Pink pills for pale people', and the *Oxford English Dictionary* notes that the slogan for Kruschen salts, 'that Kruschen feeling', became a catchphrase of the 1920s to indicate a feeling of vigorous health. Health and concurrent good looks were in fact of particular concern, although some of the slogans seem to verge on the personal: for example, 'Good morning! Have you used Pears' soap?'. Wright's Coal Tar soap (corrected to Pears in the 2nd edition of 1953) has the somewhat surprising statement, 'He won't be happy till he gets it.'

Popular songs included soldiers' songs from the First World War ('Pack up your troubles in your old kit bag') and earlier music-hall favourites ('We don't want to fight, but by jingo, if we do'). There were a few precursors of larger entries in later editions: Irving Berlin was included for 'Alexander's Ragtime Band' (1911), but not for 'Let's face the music and dance' (1936). The possible dangers of social life (prefiguring Flanders and Swann's 'Have some madeira, m'dear' of the 1950s) were indicated by an anonymous limerick about a young lady of Kent who,

> When men asked her to dine,
> Gave her cocktails and wine,
> She knew what it meant—but she went!

The warm reception given to the *Dictionary* ensured that a second edition would follow, and in 1949 it was agreed that the time had come to start on a revision. There was already 'an immense accumulation of suggestions' which would have to be sorted through by a committee, and there were proposals for what could be dropped, including advertising slogans and lines from comic songs. Book titles and the opening lines of hymns were tags rather than quotes, and if they went so too could the opening words of Latin prayers. It was noted however that, 'No one has successfully solved what is and is not a quotation': a question which may still be debated today.

The ensuing discussion recognized that there was a point of view which 'would like to see all frivolities go' but felt that what was genuinely popular should keep its place. While it could be said that 'the post-first war jocularities which have by now completely faded out' (i.e., what was in 1941 the most topical and ephemeral should go), the 'frivolities of the '80s and '90s' had 'stood up to time much better': an interesting distinction which most quotations editors would find valid today. There were doubts about coverage of some of the 'canonical' authors, a comment on the Jane Austen entry running, 'I am not certain that the expert . . . is the best person to select from his author. To him all is familiar.'

A revision committee was set up, which was to go through the *Dictionary* considering existing matter for deletion or re-arrangement, and through addenda held for inclusion.

It was agreed that any item receiving two votes should be included.

Between April 1949 and August 1950, the committee met 17 times. Authors and texts identified for examination were quite diverse. At the first meeting, it was agreed to to get an outside opinion on the Addison entry, to look for additional quotations from Emily Brontë, and to examine Charles I's speech on the scaffold for quotable passages. The minutes of 5 May 1949 noted both Donne's prose and *The Wind in the Willows* as possible sources. Overall the coverage was still fairly Anglocentric—Roosevelt's speeches being an exception, although it was also agreed that the 'Foreign Section' needed thorough revision. It is noticeable however that reference to these items is made in the form 'French quotations' or 'German quotations': individual authors are not given. The meeting of 8 September was a key one, as it also made a momentous decision as to the organization of the material:

> It was then decided that reference would be facilitated if all the
> separate sections—including Greek—were to be incorporated into the
> main body of the book.

In other words, the overall author organization would be maintained, while entries like Anonymous, Ballads, and The Bible, would be incorporated into the alphabetic sequence.

The index would similarly be single-sequence with the exception of Greek: this would have its own index. It was also agreed that 'every key word' should be indexed: an over-ambitious plan which in August 1950 had to be rescinded when the extent (and cost) implications became apparent.

Another plan, which was wisely abandoned, was to include a section at the end of the text for quotations which had not been successfully sourced. By 1951 it was decided that any such should be held over to the next edition, although they made a last effort to verify outstanding problems. An appeal elicited this lament from Dorothy L. Sayers:

> Oh, dear . . . ! I never know where things come from. Nearly all are
> familiar, but I can't at the moment say where *any* of them come from.

The second edition of the *Oxford Dictionary of Quotations* was published in 1953, and is much more recognizably the *Dictionary* we know today. The single alphabetic sequence has already been described, and for the first time quotations were individually numbered through the page, providing the page number to quotation number (e.g. 223:11) which is still the form of reference today.

The content, however, was more reordered than substantially different. Items dropped were from the more ephemeral end of the scale: for example, 'Dr Brighton', as exemplifying Brighton's health-giving propensities, and the slogan 'Where's George? Gone to Lyonch' , which reflected the popularity of Lyons' Corner Houses in the 1920s. Key material added focused on Second World War quotations, especially reflected, of course, in the enhanced entry for Winston Churchill.

1979 was to present the first substantial revision of the *Dictionary* since the original compilation, and it was at this point that particular categories of material were excluded. Nursery rhymes were cut altogether, on the assumption that they were fully covered by Iona and Peter Opie's *Oxford Dictionary of Nursery Rhymes* (first published in 1951). Songs were also excluded:

> The rule of thumb, given to the revision team and followed by the
> editors, has been that if the words cannot be said without the tune
> (*a* tune, in the case of many hymns) coming to mind, they are not
> quotations in the same sense as others.

Advertisements, slogans, catchphrases, and other items from the world of 'broadcasting and other mass-media' were similarly to be avoided.

The existing text had been considered by the revision team. Each of the core members read the whole text (ten copies of the book with interleaved blank pages for comment were prepared). Suggestions for quotations to be added were circulated on specially prepared forms with a voting box for each item: the lists were then photocopied and distributed to the whole team, with three votes being considered necessary for inclusion. The aim was to compile a collection of popular (as distinct from familiar) quotations: the editors were particularly concerned that the book should not be:

> An anthology displaying the choice and taste of one man, or even of a
> small committee of the Press such as compiled the first edition of the
> *Dictionary*.

The result of their efforts was to return the collection firmly to its mainstream and literary tradition: quotations reflecting what we would think of now as the western canon rather than current affairs. (Although this was not necessarily their own view of their endeavours: according to the introduction, one of the revisers had commented on the necessity of clearing the 'huge snowdrifts of Wordsworth'). Perhaps more than any of the other editions it is a committee book, with fewer examples of the odd or quirky. The compilation's solid worth was to sustain the *Dictionary* for another thirteen years, until the publication of the fourth edition in 1992.

The fourth edition, the last to be compiled on paper, was notable for improving the coverage of non-English authors, thinkers, and public figures, both European and American. Scientists, like a number of women writers, began to make a long-delayed appearance, and current affairs were paid more attention. Existing material was re-evaluated and verified (songs and hymns, rightly, were allowed to 'make a welcome reappearance' as the then Editor put it), and quoted authors were given brief descriptions (for nationality and occupation) as well as dates.

This particular introduction underlines a trend that can be traced through the life of the *Dictionary*: the further we get from 1915, the clearer a particular social and cultural change becomes. In 1941, it could be assumed that the educated reader would have had a particular kind of education, following a monolithic classical curriculum (with possibly a nod to the 'Modern Side'). That is now a world away: our readers come to us from many and diverse educational and cultural backgrounds, and the notion of 'English-speaking culture' has to incorporate World English.

Another result of this, of course, is the identification of gaps which need to be addressed. The fifth edition, of 1999, for the first time gave proper place to the sacred texts of world religions other than Christianity. This was of course appropriate to a multicultural age, but it was fascinating to see how words and phrases from such sources were already permeating the English language. More contextual information was provided: because something is familiar to one section of our readership, we cannot necessarily assume that everyone will know it. We also responded to queries from readers by restoring proverbs and nursery rhymes (it has been clear from correspondence over the years that our readers expect to find this kind of material in the *Dictionary*).

The 1999 edition was also the first to be compiled online, and this fed back to the presentation of material: more navigational paths were provided for our readers, including a consciously generous system of cross-referencing. Particular categories of quotation, which in the main had previously been buried in the **Anonymous** section, were brought together in special category sections integrated into the main sequence: for example, **Advertising slogans** and **Newspaper headlines**.

The world of quotations is a kaleidoscopic one. What of the future?

The collection of quotations, and background material, will continue, and new information may be discovered relating even to apparently familiar sayings. The comment on T. E. Lawrence, 'Always backing into the limelight', is traditionally attributed to Lord Berners, but we now know that a similar comment was made by George Bernard Shaw, and recorded in a contemporary source. The diaries of the German diplomat, Count Harry Kessler, tell of a meeting with Shaw in November 1929. Lawrence had apparently complained that every move of his was followed by the Press, eliciting the Shavian response, 'You always hide just in the middle of the limelight.' The information came to light just too late to be fully covered by this edition.

What will perhaps be considered the most famous soundbite of 2003 ('Ladies and gentlemen, we got him'—Paul Bremer on the capture of Saddam Hussein) was uttered after the book went to Press. Topical material will always be a problem, not least because we have a devoted, and protective, readership. Those who care for the *Dictionary* are, rightly, concerned for its quality: less rightly, they may then extrapolate the view that the inclusion of topical or ephemeral material is somehow likely to devalue an adjacent quotation from classical literature. While having the charge of an iconic reference book is properly a serious responsibility, we still need to remember that we are publishing for our own times. A quotations collection published in 2004 needs to include the highest profile quotations of the recent past, though with the awareness that by the time the next edition is published some of them will be dropped. In the interim, however, we cannot tell people what they should remember, or refuse to answer questions which they may reasonably ask.

In compiling the new edition, we have once more drawn on the resources of Oxford Quotations Dictionaries: our published texts (and the research which lies behind them), and our growing database of new quotations derived from our reading programme. As always we have benefited from the generosity of readers who take the trouble to write to us with questions, comments, and suggestions. Colleagues in the Reference Department have again put forward quotations encountered in work and leisure. Among those to whom we are particularly grateful for contributions of material or solutions to particular questions, we would like to thank Matthew Carter, Margot Charlton, Mike Clark, Susie Dent, Henry Hardy, Antony Jay, Ian Linton, Kirk Marlow, Christopher Pelling, Nigel Rees, Ned Sherrin, Donald Smith, and Sarah Waldram. Finally, and most importantly, Susan Ratcliffe's editorial contribution has been of key importance in the preparation of this edition.

We know that the *Dictionary* must continue to be replanned and remade, and we face with resignation the fact that some future Editor will find a number of our choices as improbable as 'Meet we no angels, Pansie?' He or she, in their turn, will face difficulties: for example, grappling with the fact that the Authorized Version, although a main source for established phrases in the language, will no longer be the most familiar translation of the Bible to a new generation.

In his Introduction, Bernard Darwin envisaged typical readers of the *Dictionary* as 'friends by the fireside . . . indulging in a heated quoting-match', or as allies trying to solve a crossword puzzle. In 2004, readers are as likely to turn to it as a resource when trying to outdo a contestant on a television quiz show, solving a reference found while browsing the Net, or preparing for a presentation of their own. But although there are over sixty years, and infinite cultural and technological differences, between the worlds of the first and sixth editions, there is still a common thread: the fascination with words identified by Darwin in his opening sentence: 'Quotation brings to many people one of the intensest joys of living.' It is in response to this continuing fascination that we monitor the language and collect quotations. It is as always our aim to edit a text that for our own time will answer the key quotations questions, 'Who said that?' and 'What's been said about this?'

ELIZABETH KNOWLES

Oxford 2004

Introduction to the First Edition (1941)

By **Bernard Darwin**

Quotation brings to many people one of the intensest joys of living. If they need any encouragement they have lately received it from the most distinguished quarters. Mr Roosevelt quoted Longfellow to Mr Churchill; Mr Churchill passed the quotation on to us and subsequently quoted Clough on his own account. Thousands of listeners to that broadcast speech must have experienced the same series of emotions. When the Prime Minister said that there were some lines that he deemed appropriate we sat up rigid, waiting in mingled pleasure and apprehension. How agreeable it would be if we were acquainted with them and approved the choice! How flat and disappointing should they be unknown to us! A moment later we heard 'For though the tired waves, vainly breaking' and sank back in a pleasant agony of relief. We whispered the lines affectionately to ourselves, following the speaker, or even kept a word or two ahead of him in order to show our familiarity with the text. We were if possible more sure than ever that Mr Churchill was the man for our money. He had given his ultimate proofs by flattering our vanity. He had chosen what we knew and what, if we had thought of it, we could have quoted ourselves. This innocent vanity often helps us over the hard places in life; it gives us a warm little glow against the coldness of the world and keeps us snug and happy. It certainly does its full share in the matter of quotations. We are puffed up with pride over those that we know and, a little illogically, we think that everyone else must know them too. As to those which lie outside our line of country we say, with Jowett as pictured by some anonymous genius at Balliol, 'What I don't know isn't knowledge.' Yet here again we are illogical and unreasonable, for we allow ourselves to be annoyed by those who quote from outside our own small preserves. We accuse them in our hearts, as we do other people's children at a party, of 'showing off'. There are some departments of life in which we are ready to strike a bargain of mutual accommodation. The golfer is prepared to listen to his friend's story of missed putts, in which he takes no faintest interest, on the understanding that he may in turn impart his own heart-rending tale, and the bargain is honourably kept by both parties. The same rule does not apply to other people's quotations, which are not merely tedious but wound us in our tenderest spot. And the part played by vanity is perhaps worth pointing out because everybody, when he first plunges adventurously into this great work, ought in justice to the compilers to bear it in mind.

It is safe to say that there is no single reader who will not have a mild grievance or two, both as to what has been put in and what has been left out. In particular he will 'murmur a little sadly' over some favourite that is not there. I, for instance, have a small grievance. William Hepworth Thompson, sometime Master of Trinity, the author of many famous and mordant sayings on which I have been brought up, is represented by but a single one. Can it be, I ask myself, that this is due to the fact that an Oxford Scholar put several of the Master's sayings into his Greek exercise book but attributed them to one Talirantes? Down, base thought! I only mention this momentary and most unworthy suspicion to show other readers the sort of thing they should avoid as they would the very devil. It is not that of which any one of us is fondest that is entitled as of right to a place. As often as he feels ever so slightly aggrieved, the reader should say to himself, if need be over and over again, that this is not a private anthology, but a collection of the quotations which the public knows best. In this fact, moreover, if properly appreciated, there ought to be much comfort. 'My head' said Charles Lamb, 'has not many mansions nor spacious', and is that not true of most of us? If in this book there are a great many quotations that we do not know, there are also a great many that we do. There is that example of Clough with which I began. We may have to admit under cross-examination that we have only a rather vague acquaintance with Clough's poems, but we do know 'Say not the struggle'; and there on page so-and-so it is. Both we and the dictionary's compilers are thereupon seen to be persons of taste and discrimination.

If I may be allowed to harp a little longer on this string of vanity, it is rather amusing to imagine the varied reception given to this book by those who are quoted in it. They will consist largely of more or less illustrious shades, and we may picture them looking over one another's pale shoulders at the first copy of the dictionary to reach the asphodel. What jealousies there will be as they compare the number of pages respectively allotted to them! What indignation at finding themselves in such mixed company! Alphabetical order makes strange bedfellows. Dickens and Dibdin must get on capitally and convivially together, but what an ill-assorted couple are Mrs Humphrey Ward and the beloved Artemus of the same name! George Borrow may ask, 'Pray, who is this John Collins Bossidy?' Many readers may incidentally echo his question, and yet no man better merits his niche, for Mr Bossidy wrote the lines ending 'And the Cabots talk only to God', which have told the whole world of the blue blood of Boston. John Hookham Frere, singing of the mailed lobster clapping his broad wings, must feel his frivolity uncomfortably hushed for a moment by his next-door neighbour, Charles Frohman, on the point of going down with the *Lusitania*. And apropos of Frere, there rises before me the portentous figure of my great-great-grandfather, Erasmus Darwin. He was thought a vastly fine poet in his day and there is a family legend that he was paid a guinea a line for his too fluent verses. And yet he is deservedly forgotten, while those who parodied him in the Anti-Jacobin attain an equally well-deserved immortality. He was a formidable old gentleman, with something of the Johnson touch, but not without a sense of humour, and I do not think he will be greatly hurt.

The most famous poets must be presumed to be above these petty vanities, though it would be agreeable to think of Horace contemplating his array of columns and saying, 'I told you so—Exegi monumentum'. In any case the number of columns or pages does not constitute the only test. Another is the number of words in each line by which any particular quotation can be identified, and this gives me a chance of making my compliments to the ingenuity and fullness of the index. The searcher need never despair and should he draw blank under 'swings' he is pretty sure to find what he wants under 'roundabouts'. There is a little game to be played (one of the many fascinating games which the reader can devise for himself) by counting the number of 'key words' in each line and working out the average of fame to which any passage is entitled. Even a short time so spent shows unexpected results, likely to spread envy and malice among the shades. It might be imagined that Shakespeare would be an easy winner. It has been said that every drop of the Thames is liquid history and almost every line of certain passages of Shakespeare is solid quotation. Let us fancy that his pre-eminence is challenged, that a sweepstake is suggested, and that he agrees to be judged by 'To be or not to be'. It seems a sufficiently sound choice and is found to produce fifty-five key words in thirty-three lines. All the other poets are ready to give in at once; they cannot stand against such scoring as that and Shakespeare is about to pocket the money when up sidles Mr Alexander Pope. What, he asks, about that bitter little thing of his which he sent to Mr Addison? And he proves to be right, for in those two and twenty lines to Atticus there are fifty-two key words. I have not played this game nearly long enough to pronounce Pope the winner. Very likely Shakespeare or somebody else can produce a passage with a still higher average, but here at any rate is enough to show that it is a good game and as full of uncertainties as cricket itself.

Though the great poets may wrangle a little amongst themselves, they do not stand in need of anything that the dictionary can do for them. Very different is the case of the small ones, whose whole fame depends upon a single happy line or even a single absurd one. To them exclusion from these pages may virtually mean annihilation, while inclusion makes them only a little lower than the angels. Their anxiety must therefore be pitiful and their joy when they find themselves safe in the haven proportionately great. Sometimes that joy may be short-lived. Think of Mr Robert Montgomery, who was highly esteemed till the ruthless Macaulay fell upon him. With trembling hand he turns the pages and finds no less than four extracts from 'The Omnipresence of the Deity'. Alas! under his own letter M the traducer is waiting for him, and by a peculiar refinement of cruelty there are quoted no less than five of Lord Macaulay's criticisms on that very poem. This is a sad case; let us take a more cheerful one and still among the M's. Thomas Osbert Mordaunt has full recognition as the author of 'Sound, sound the clarion, fill the fife', after having for years had to endure the attribution of his lines to Sir Walter Scott, who in pure innocency put them at the head of a chapter. This to be sure was known already, but whoever heard the name of the author of 'We don't want to fight', the man who gave the word 'Jingo' to the world? We know that the Great McDermott sang it, but even he may not have known who wrote it, just as Miss Fotheringay did not know who wrote 'The Stranger'. Now G. W. Hunt comes into his kingdom and with him another who helped many thousands of soldiers on their way during the last war. Mr George H. Powell is fortunately still alive to enjoy the celebrity of 'Pack up your troubles in your old kit bag'. How many thousands, too, have sung 'Wrap me up in my tarpaulin jacket' without realizing that it was by Whyte Melville? To him, however, recognition is of less account. His place was already secure.

Among the utterers of famous sayings some seem to have been more fortunate than others. Lord Westbury, for instance, has always had the rather brutal credit of telling some wretched little attorney to turn the matter over 'in what you are pleased to call your mind'; but how many of us knew who first spoke of a 'blazing indiscretion' or called the parks 'the lungs of London'? We may rejoice with all these who, having for years been wronged, have come into their rights at last, but there are others with whom we can only sympathize. They must be contented with the fact that their sayings or their verses have been deemed worth recording, even though their names 'shall be lost for evermore'. The Rugby boy who called his headmaster 'a beast but a just beast' sleeps unknown, while through him Temple lives. He can only enjoy what the dynamiter Zero called 'an anonymous infernal glory'. So do the authors of many admirable limericks, though some of the best are attributed to a living divine of great distinction, who has not disclaimed such juvenile frolics. So again to those who have given us many household words from the advertisement hoardings, the beloved old jingle of 'the Pickwick, the Owl, and the Waverley pen', the alluring alliteration of 'Pink Pills for Pale People'. Let us hope that it is enough for them that they did their duty and sent the sales leaping upward.

So much for the authors without whom this book could never have been. Now for the readers and some of the happy uses to which they will put it. 'Hand me over the Burton's *Anatomy*', said Captain Shandon, 'and leave me to my abominable devices.' It was Greek and Latin quotations that he sought for his article, but fashion has changed and today it would rather be English ones. Here is one of the most obvious purposes for which the dictionary will be used. It cannot accomplish impossibilities. It will not prevent many an honest journalist from referring to 'fresh fields and pastures new' nor from describing a cup-tie as an example of 'Greek meeting Greek'. There is a fine old crusted tradition of misquoting not lightly to be broken and it might almost seem pedantry to deck these ancient friends in their true but unfamiliar colours. Misquoting may even be deemed an amiable weakness, since Dickens in one of his letters misquoted Sam Weller; but here at least is a good chance of avoiding it. There is likewise a chance of replenishing a stock grown somewhat threadbare. 'Well, you're a boss word', exclaimed Jim Pinkerton, when he lighted on 'hebdomadary' in a dictionary. 'Before you're very much older I'll have you in type as long as yourself.' So the hard-pressed writer in turning over these pages may find and note many excellent phrases against future contingencies, whether to give a pleasing touch of erudition or to save the trouble of thinking for himself. These, however, are sordid considerations, and the mind loves rather to dwell on fireside quoting-matches between two friends, each of whom thinks his own visual memory the more accurate. There are certain writers well adapted to this form of contest and among the moderns Conan Doyle must, with all respect to Mr Wodehouse, be assigned the first place. Sherlock Holmes scholars are both numerous and formidable; they set themselves and demand of others a high standard. It is one very difficult to attain since there often seems no reason why any particular remark should have been made on any particular occasion. This is especially true of Dr Watson. He was constantly saying that his practice was not very absorbing or that he had an accommodating neighbour, but when did he say which? Even the most learned might by a momentary blunder confuse 'A Case of Identity' with 'The Final Problem'. It would be dry work to plough through all the stories, even though the supreme satisfaction of being right should reward the search. Now a glance at the dictionary will dispose of an argument which would otherwise 'end only with the visit'.

It is incidentally curious and interesting to observe that two authors may each have the same power of inspiring devotion and the competitive spirit, and yet one may be, from the dictionary point of view, infinitely more quotable than the other. Hardly any prose writer, for instance, produces a more fanatical adoration than Miss Austen, and there are doubtless those who can recite pages of her with scarce a slip; but it is perhaps pages rather than sentences that they quote. Mr Bennet provides an exception, but generally speaking she is not very amenable to the treatment by scissors and paste. George Eliot, if we leave out Mrs Poyser, a professed wit and coiner of aphorisms, is in much poorer case. Another and a very different writer, Borrow, can rouse us to a frantic pitch of romantic excitement, but it is the whole scene and atmosphere that possess this magic and we cannot take atmosphere to pieces. These are but three examples of writers who do not seem to lend themselves to brief and familiar quotations. They have jewels in plenty, but these form part of a piece of elaborate ornament from which they cannot be detached without irreparable damage. The works of some writers may by contrast be said to consist of separate stones, each of which needs no setting and can sparkle on its own account. Dickens is an obvious and unique instance. Stevenson, too, has the gift of producing characters such as Prince Florizel and Alan Breck, John Silver and Michael Finsbury, whose words can stand memorable by themselves, apart from context and atmosphere. Those who share my love for Florizel will rejoice to observe that he has had some faithful friend among the compilers. As for Michael I cannot help feeling that he has been rather scurvily used, for 'The Wrong Box' is admirably suited to competition and even learned Judges of the Court of Appeal have been known, all unsuspected by their ignorant auditors, to bandy quotations from it on the Bench. Here, however, I taken leave to give any indignant reader a hint. Let him not cry too loudly before he is hurt! It is true that 'nothing like a little judicious levity' is not in the main body of the dictionary, but someone awoke just in time and it is among the addenda.

To return to those friends by the fireside whom I pictured indulging in a heated quoting-match, it may be that they will presently become allies and united to use the dictionary over a crossword puzzle. It is hardly too much to say that the setters of these problems should not use a quotation unless it is to be found in the dictionary. A crossword quotation should not be too simple, but it should be such that that hypothetical personage, the reasonable man, might have heard of it. The solver demands fair play, and the setter who takes a volume of verse at haphazard, finds a word that fits, and substitutes a blank for it, is not playing the game. There are solvers whose standard of sportsmanship is so high that they would as soon allow themselves to cheat at patience as have recourse to a book. We may admire though we cannot emulate this fine austere arrogance. It is the best fun to win unaided, but there is good fun too in ferreting out a quotation. It well repays the ardours of the chase. Moreover a setter of puzzles who oversteps honourable limits should be fought with his own weapons. He has palpably used books and this is an epoch of reprisals. Then let us use books today and hoist him with his own petard.

It is difficult today not to deal in warlike metaphors, but perhaps the truest and most perfect use of the dictionary is essentially peaceful. Reviewers are apt to say of a detective story that it is 'impossible to lay it down till the last page is reached'. It is rather for books of reference that such praise should be reserved. No others are comparable with them for the purposes of eternal browsing. They suggest all manner of lovely, lazy things, in particular the watching of a cricket match on a sunshiny day. We have only dropped in for half an hour, but the temptation to see just one more over before we go is irresistible. Evening draws on, the shadows of the fielders lengthen on the grass, nothing much is happening, a draw becomes every minute more inevitable, and still we cannot tear ourselves away. So it is with works of reference, even with the most arid, even with Bradshaw, whose vocabulary, as Sherlock Holmes remarked, is 'nervous and terse but limited.' Over the very next page of Bradshaw there may be hidden a Framlingham Admiral; adventure may always be in wait a little farther down the line. So, but a thousand times more so, is some exciting treasure-trove awaiting us over the next page of this dictionary. What it is we cannot guess, but it is for ever calling in our ears to turn over just one more. We have only taken down the book to look up one special passage, but it is likely enough that we shall never get so far. Long before we have reached the appropriate letter we shall have been waylaid by an earlier one, and shall have clean forgotten our original quest. Nor is this all, for, if our mood changes as we browse, it is so fatally, beautifully easy to change our pasture. We can play a game akin to that 'dabbing' cricket, so popular in private-school days, in which the batsman's destiny depended or was supposed to depend—for we were not always honest—on a pencil delivered with eyes tightly shut. We can close the book and open it again at random, sure of something that shall set us off again on a fresh and enchanting voyage of not too strenuous discovery.

Under this enchantment I have fallen deep. I have pored over the proofs so that only by a supreme effort of will could I lay them down and embark on the impertinent task of trying to write about them. I now send them back to their home with a sense of privation and loneliness. Here seems to me a great book. Then

> Deem it not all a too presumptuous folly,

this humble tribute to Oxford from another establishment over the way.

B.D.

May 1941

How to use the Dictionary

The sequence of entries is by alphabetical order of author, usually by surname but with occasional exceptions such as members of royal families (e.g. **Diana, Princess of Wales** and **Elizabeth II**) and Popes (**John Paul II**), or authors known by a pseudonym (**Saki**) or a nickname (**Caligula**). In general authors' names are given in the form by which they are best known, so that we have **Harold Macmillan** (not Lord Stockton), **George Eliot** (not Mary Ann Evans), and **H. G. Wells** (not Herbert George Wells). Collections such as **Anonymous**, the **Bible**, the **Book of Common Prayer**, the **Missal**, and so forth, are included in the alphabetical sequence. Some **Anonymous** quotations may be included in one of the special category sections (see below).

Author names are followed by dates of birth and death (where known) and brief descriptions; where appropriate, cross-references are then given to quotations about that author elsewhere in the text (*on Byron: see* **Lamb** 464:9). Cross-references are also made to other entries in which the author appears, e.g. '*see also* **Epitaphs** 309:7' and '*see also* **Lennon and McCartney**'. Within each author entry, quotations are separated by literary form (novels, plays, poems: see further below) and within each group arranged by order of title, 'a' and 'the' being ignored. Foreign-language text is given where the quotation is likely to be encountered in the language of origin.

Quotations from diaries, letters, and speeches are given in chronological order and usually follow the literary or published works quoted, with the form for which the author is best known taking precedence. Thus in the case of political figures, speeches appear first, just as poetry quotations precede those in prose for poets, and poetry quotations come second for an author regarded primarily as a novelist.

Quotations from secondary sources such as biographies and other writer's works, to which a date in the author's lifetime can be assigned, are arranged in sequence with diary entries, letters, and speeches. Other quotations from secondary sources and attributed quotations which cannot be so dated are arranged in alphabetical order of quotation text.

Within the alphabetical sequence there are a number of special category entries, such as **Advertising slogans**, **Catchphrases**, **Film lines**, **Misquotations**, and **Newspaper headlines and leaders**. Quotations in these sections are arranged alphabetically according to the first word of the quotation (ignoring 'a' and 'the'). A full list of the special categories is given on the Contents page.

Contextual information regarded as essential to a full appreciation of the quotation precedes the text in an italicized note; information seen as providing useful amplification follows in an italicized note. Each quotation is accompanied by a bibliographical note of the source from which the quotation is taken. Titles of published volumes (*Don Juan* by Byron and *David Copperfield* by Charles Dickens) appear in italics; titles of short stories and poems not published as volumes in their own right, and individual song titles, are given in roman type inside inverted commas ('Ode to a Nightingale' by John Keats and 'Both Sides Now' by Joni Mitchell).

All numbers in source references are given in arabic, with the exception of lower-case roman numerals denoting quotations from prefatory matter, whose page numbering is separate from the main text. The numbering itself relates to the beginning of the quotation, whether or not it runs on to another stanza or line in the original. Where possible, chapter numbers have been offered for prose works.

A date in brackets indicates first publication in volume form of the work cited. Unless otherwise stated, the dates thus offered are intended as chronological guides only and do not necessarily indicate the date of the text cited; where the latter is of significance, this has been stated. Where neither date of publication nor of composition is known, an approximate date (e.g. c.1625) may indicate the likely date of composition. Where there is a large discrepancy between date of composition (or performance) and of publication, in most cases the former only has been given (e.g. 'written 1725', 'performed 1622').

Spellings have been Anglicized and modernized except in those cases, such as **Burns** or **Chaucer**, where this would have been inappropriate; capitalization has been retained only for personifications; with rare exceptions, verse has been aligned with the left hand margin. Italic type has been used for all foreign-language originals.

Sub-headings have been used as a guide to novel titles under **Dickens,** for the names of books of the **Bible** (arranged canonically, not alphabetically), and for plays and poems under **Shakespeare**. **Anonymous** quotations are grouped by language.

Cross-references to specific quotations are used to direct the reader to another related item. In each case a reference is given to an author's name or to the title of a special category entry, followed by the page number and then the unique quotation number on that page ('see **Last words** 473:17, 'see **Tennyson** 779:11'). In some cases, the quotation may exist in two forms, or may depend on an earlier source not quoted in its own right; when this happens, the subordinate quotation is given directly below the quotation to which it relates. Authors who have their own entries are typographically distinguished by the use of bold (*'of William **Shakespeare**'*, *'by Mae **West**'*) in context or source notes.

Index

The most significant words from each quotation appear in the keyword index, allowing individual quotations to be traced. Both the keywords and the context lines following each keyword, including those in foreign languages, are in strict alphabetical order. Singular and plural nouns (with their possessive forms) are grouped separately; for 'some old lover's ghost' see **lover**; for 'at lovers' perjuries' see **lovers**. Variant forms of common words (fresshe/fresh, luve/love) are grouped under a single heading: **fresh, love**.

References are to the author's name (usually in abbreviated form, as AUST for Jane Austen) followed by the page number and the number of the unique quotation on the page. Thus AUST 39:18 means quotation number 18 on page 39, in the entry for Jane Austen.

Quotations

Aa

Peter Abelard 1079–1142
*French scholar, theologian, and philosopher, lover of **Héloise***

1 *O quanta qualia sunt illa sabbata,*
Quae semper celebrat superna curia.

O what their joy and glory must be,
Those endless sabbaths the blessèd ones see!
Hymnarius Paraclitensis bk. 1, pars altera 'Hymni Diurni' no. 29 'Sabbato. Ad Vesperas' (translated by J. M. Neale, 1854)

2 *Non enim facile de his quos plurimum diligimus turpitudinem suspicamur.*

For we do not easily expect evil of those whom we love most.
Historia Calamitatum Mearum ch. 6

Dannie Abse 1923–
Welsh-born doctor and poet

3 Are all men in disguise except those crying?
'Encounter at a Greyhound Bus Station' (1986)

4 I know the colour rose, and it is lovely,
But not when it ripens in a tumour;
And healing greens, leaves and grass, so springlike,
In limbs that fester are not springlike.
'Pathology of Colours' (1968)

5 So in the simple blessing of a rainbow,
In the bevelled edge of a sunlit mirror,
I have seen visible, Death's artifact
Like a soldier's ribbon on a tunic tacked.
'Pathology of Colours' (1968)

Accius 170–c.86 BC
Roman poet and dramatist

6 *Oderint, dum metuant.*
Let them hate, so long as they fear.
*often quoted by **Caligula**, according to Suetonius* Lives of the Caesars 'Caligula' sect. 30
from *Atreus*, in Cicero *De Officiis* bk. 1, ch. 28

Goodman Ace 1899–1982
American humorist

7 TV—a clever contraction derived from the words Terrible Vaudeville . . . we call it a medium because nothing's well done.
letter to Groucho Marx, in *The Groucho Letters* (1967)

Chinua Achebe 1930–
Nigerian novelist

8 The world is like a Mask dancing. If you want to see it well you do not stand in one place.
Arrow of God (1988)

Dean Acheson 1893–1971
American politician

9 I will undoubtedly have to seek what is happily known as gainful employment, which I am glad to say does not describe holding public office.
in *Time* 22 December 1952

10 Great Britain has lost an empire and has not yet found a role.
speech at the Military Academy, West Point, 5 December 1962, in *Vital Speeches* 1 January 1963

11 A memorandum is written not to inform the reader but to protect the writer.
in *Wall Street Journal* 8 September 1977

Lord Acton 1834–1902
British historian

12 Liberty is not a means to a higher political end. It is itself the highest political end.
The History of Freedom in Antiquity (1907), lecture delivered 26 February 1877

13 Power tends to corrupt and absolute power corrupts absolutely.
letter to Bishop Mandell Creighton, 3 April 1887, in Louise Creighton *Life and Letters of Mandell Creighton* (1904) vol. 1, ch. 13; see **Pitt** 596:3

Abigail Adams 1744–1818
*American letter writer, wife of John **Adams** and mother of John Quincy **Adams***

14 In the new code of laws which I suppose it will be necessary for you to make I desire you would remember the ladies, and be more generous and favourable to them than your ancestors. Do not put such unlimited power into the hands of the husbands. Remember all men would be tyrants if they could.
letter to John Adams, 31 March 1776, in Butterfield et al. (eds.) *The Book of Abigail and John Adams* (1975); see **Defoe** 261:18

15 It is really mortifying, sir, when a woman possessed of a common share of understanding considers the difference of education between the male and female sex, even in those families where education is attended to . . . Nay why should your sex wish for such a disparity in those whom they one day intend for companions and associates. Pardon me, sir, if I cannot help sometimes suspecting that this neglect arises in some measure from an ungenerous jealousy of rivals near the throne.
letter to John Thaxter, 15 February 1778, in *Adams Family Correspondence* vol. 2 (1963)

16 These are times in which a genius would wish to live. It is not in the still calm of life, or the repose of a pacific station, that great characters are formed . . . Great necessities call out great virtues.
letter to John Quincy Adams, 19 January 1780

17 A little of what you call frippery is very necessary towards looking like the rest of the world.
letter to John Adams, 1 May 1780

18 Patriotism in the female sex is the most disinterested of all virtues. Excluded from honours

and from offices, we cannot attach ourselves to the State or Government from having held a place of eminence . . . Yet all history and every age exhibit instances of patriotic virtue in the female sex; which considering our situation equals the most heroic of yours.
  letter to John Adams, 17 June 1782

Charles Francis Adams 1807–86
American lawyer and diplomat

1 It would be superfluous in me to point out to your lordship that this is war.
  of the situation in the United States during the American Civil War
  dispatch to Earl Russell, 5 September 1863, in C. F. Adams *Charles Francis Adams* (1900) ch. 17

Douglas Adams 1952–2001
English science fiction writer

2 The Answer to the Great Question Of . . . Life, the Universe and Everything . . . [is] Forty-two.
  The Hitch Hiker's Guide to the Galaxy (1979) ch. 27

Frank Adams and Will M. Hough

3 I wonder who's kissing her now.
  title of song (1909)

Franklin P. Adams 1881–1960
American journalist and humorist

4 When the political columnists say 'Every thinking man' they mean themselves, and when candidates appeal to 'Every intelligent voter' they mean everybody who is going to vote for them.
  Nods and Becks (1944)

5 Years ago we discovered the exact point, the dead centre of middle age. It occurs when you are too young to take up golf and too old to rush up to the net.
  Nods and Becks (1944)

6 Elections are won by men and women chiefly because most people vote against somebody rather than for somebody.
  Nods and Becks (1944); see **Fields** 318:22

Henry Brooks Adams 1838–1918
American historian

7 Politics, as a practice, whatever its professions, has always been the systematic organization of hatreds.
  The Education of Henry Adams (1907) ch. 1

8 Accident counts for much in companionship as in marriage.
  The Education of Henry Adams (1907) ch. 4; see **Ustinov** 806:3

9 Women have, commonly, a very positive moral sense; that which they will, is right; that which they reject, is wrong; and their will, in most cases, ends by settling the moral.
  The Education of Henry Adams (1907) ch. 6

10 All experience is an arch to build upon.
  The Education of Henry Adams (1907) ch. 6; see **Tennyson** 784:15

11 A friend in power is a friend lost.
  The Education of Henry Adams (1907) ch. 7

12 Sumner's mind had reached the calm of water which receives and reflects images without absorbing them; it contained nothing but itself.
  *of Charles **Sumner***
  The Education of Henry Adams (1907) ch. 13

13 Chaos often breeds life, when order breeds habit.
  The Education of Henry Adams (1907) ch. 16

14 A teacher affects eternity; he can never tell where his influence stops.
  The Education of Henry Adams (1907) ch. 20

15 Morality is a private and costly luxury.
  The Education of Henry Adams (1907) ch. 22

16 Symbol or energy, the Virgin had acted as the greatest force the Western world had ever felt, and had drawn man's activities to herself more strongly than any other power, natural or supernatural, had ever done.
  The Education of Henry Adams (1907) ch. 25

17 No one means all he says, and yet very few say all they mean, for words are slippery and thought is viscous.
  The Education of Henry Adams (1907) ch. 31

John Adams 1735–1826
*American statesman, 2nd President of the US; husband of Abigail **Adams** and father of John Quincy **Adams***
*see also **Last Words** 474:7*

18 The law, in all vicissitudes of government . . . will preserve a steady undeviating course; it will not bend to the uncertain wishes, imaginations, and wanton tempers of men . . . On the one hand it is inexorable to the cries of the prisoners; on the other it is deaf, deaf as an adder to the clamours of the populace.
  argument in defence of the British soldiers in the Boston Massacre Trials, 4 December 1770; see **Sidney** 735:18

19 There is danger from all men. The only maxim of a free government ought to be to trust no man living with power to endanger the public liberty.
  Notes for an Oration at Braintree (Spring 1772), in *Diary and Autobiography of John Adams* vol. 2 (1960)

20 A government of laws, and not of men.
  in *Boston Gazette* (1774) no. 7, 'Novanglus' papers; later incorporated in the Massachusetts Constitution (1780); see **Ford** 328:11

21 I agree with you that in politics the middle way is none at all.
  letter to Horatio Gates, 23 March 1776, in R. J. Taylor (ed.) *Papers of John Adams* 3rd series (1979) vol. 4

22 You bid me burn your letters. But I must forget you first.
  letter to Abigail Adams, 28 April 1776

23 Yesterday, the greatest question was decided which ever was debated in America, and a greater perhaps never was nor will be decided among

men. A resolution was passed without one
dissenting colony, 'that these United Colonies are,
and of right ought to be, free and independent
States.'
   letter to Abigail Adams, 3 July 1776

1 I must study politics and war that my sons may
have liberty to study mathematics and philosophy.
My sons ought to study mathematics and
philosophy, geography, natural history, naval
architecture, navigation, commerce, and
agriculture, in order to give their children a right
to study painting, poetry, music, architecture,
statuary, tapestry, and porcelain.
   letter to Abigail Adams, 12 May 1780

2 My country has in its wisdom contrived for me the
most insignificant office that ever the invention of
man contrived or his imagination conceived.
   of the vice-presidency
   letter to Abigail Adams, 19 December 1793

3 You and I ought not to die before we have
explained ourselves to each other.
   letter to Thomas Jefferson, 15 July 1813, in L. J. Cappon
   (ed.) *The Adams–Jefferson Letters* (1959) vol. 2

4 The fundamental article of my political creed is
that despotism, or unlimited sovereignty, or
absolute power, is the same in a majority of a
popular assembly, an aristocratic council, an
oligarchical junto, and a single emperor.
   letter to Thomas Jefferson, 13 November 1815, in P.
   Wilstach (ed.) *Correspondence of John Adams and Thomas
   Jefferson* (1925)

5 Liberty cannot be preserved without a general
knowledge among the people, who have a right
. . . and a desire to know; but besides this, they
have a right, an indisputable, unalienable,
indefeasible, divine right to that most dreaded and
envied kind of knowledge, I mean of the
characters and conduct of their rulers.
   A Dissertation on the Canon and Feudal Law (1765), in M. J.
   Kline (ed.) *Papers of John Adams* vol. 1 (1977)

6 The jaws of power are always opened to devour,
and her arm is always stretched out, if possible, to
destroy the freedom of thinking, speaking, and
writing.
   A Dissertation on the Canon and Feudal Law (1765), in
   Charles Francis Adams (ed.) *Works of John Adams* (1851)
   vol. 3

7 The happiness of society is the end of government.
   Thoughts on Government (1776)

8 Fear is the foundation of most governments.
   Thoughts on Government (1776)

John Quincy Adams 1767–1848
*American statesman, 6th President of the US; son of Abigail
Adams and John Adams*

9 Think of your forefathers! Think of your posterity!
   Oration at Plymouth 22 December 1802

10 *Fiat justitia, pereat coelum* [Let justice be done,
though heaven fall]. My toast would be, may our
country be always successful, but whether
successful or otherwise, always right.
   letter to John Adams, 1 August 1816, in A. Koch and W.

Peden (eds.) *The Selected Writings of John and John Quincy
Adams* (1946); see **Decatur** 261:1, **Mansfield** 511:6,
Mottoes 552:8, **Schurz** 672:6, **Watson** 823:2

11 Wherever the standard of freedom and
Independence has been or shall be unfurled, there
will her heart, her benedictions and her prayers
be. But she [America] goes not abroad in search of
monsters to destroy.
   speech to House of Representatives, 4 July 1821

Michael Adams
Canadian market researcher and writer

12 North of the 49th parallel we value equality;
south of it, they treasure freedom.
   Sex in the Snow (1997)

Samuel Adams 1722–1803
American revolutionary leader

13 What a glorious morning is this.
   *on hearing gunfire at Lexington, 19 April 1775;
   traditionally quoted as, 'What a glorious morning for
   America'*
   J. K. Hosmer *Samuel Adams* (1886) ch. 19

14 A nation of shopkeepers are very seldom so
disinterested.
   Oration in Philadelphia 1 August 1776 (the authenticity of
   this publication is doubtful); see **Napoleon** 557:4, **Smith**
   741:9

15 We cannot make events. Our business is wisely to
improve them . . . Mankind are governed more by
their feelings than by reason. Events which excite
those feelings will produce wonderful effects.
   J. N. Rakove *The Beginnings of National Politics* (1979) ch. 5

Sarah Flower Adams 1805–48
English hymn-writer

16 Nearer, my God, to thee,
Nearer to thee!
   'Nearer My God to Thee' in W. G. Fox *Hymns and Anthems*
   (1841)

Harold Adamson 1906–80
American songwriter

17 Comin' in on a wing and a pray'r.
   *words derived from the contemporary comment of a
   war pilot, speaking from a disabled plane to ground
   control*
   title of song (1943)

Jane Addams 1860–1935
American social worker

18 A conception of Democracy not merely as a
sentiment which desires the well-being of all men,
nor yet as a creed which believes in the essential
dignity and equality of all men, but as that which
affords a rule of living as well as a test of faith.
   Democracy and Social Ethics (1902)

19 The cure for the ills of Democracy is more
Democracy.
   Democracy and Social Ethics (1902); see **Smith** 741:14

1 The new growth in the plant swelling against the sheath, which at the same time imprisons and protects it, must still be the truest type of progress.
Democracy and Social Ethics (1902)

2 Perhaps I may record here my protest against the efforts, so often made, to shield children and young people from all that has to do with death and sorrow . . . Young people themselves often resent this attitude on the part of their elders; they feel set aside and belittled as if they were denied the common human experiences.
Twenty Years at Hull House (1910)

3 The common stock of intellectual enjoyment should not be difficult of access because of the economic position of him who would approach it.
Twenty Years at Hull House (1910)

Joseph Addison 1672–1719

English poet, dramatist, and essayist; co-founder of The Spectator
on Addison: see **Johnson** 424:25, **Pope** 602:29, **Tickell** 794:13; *see also* **Closing lines** 228:11, **Last words** 473:16

4 He more had pleased us, had he pleased us less.
of Abraham **Cowley**
An Account of the Greatest English Poets (1694)

5 'Twas then great Marlbro's mighty soul was proved.
The Campaign (1705) l. 279

6 And, pleased th' Almighty's orders to perform,
Rides in the whirlwind, and directs the storm.
The Campaign (1705) l. 291; see **Page** 581:13

7 And those who paint 'em truest praise 'em most.
The Campaign (1705) l. 476

8 'Tis not in mortals to command success,
But we'll do more, Sempronius; we'll deserve it.
Cato (1713) act 1, sc. 2, l. 43; see **Churchill** 221:11

9 'Tis pride, rank pride, and haughtiness of soul;
I think the Romans call it stoicism.
Cato (1713) act 1, sc. 4, l. 82

10 The pale, unripened beauties of the north.
Cato (1713) act 1, sc. 4, l. 135

11 The woman that deliberates is lost.
Cato (1713) act 4, sc. 1, l. 31; see **Proverbs** 622:9

12 Curse on his virtues! they've undone his country.
Such popular humanity is treason.
Cato (1713) act 4, sc. 1, l. 205

13   What pity is it
That we can die but once to serve our country!
Cato (1713) act 4, sc. 1, l. 258; see **Last words** 472:13

14 Content thyself to be obscurely good.
When vice prevails, and impious men bear sway,
The post of honour is a private station.
Cato (1713) act 4, sc. 1, l. 319

15 It must be so—Plato, thou reason'st well!—
Else whence this pleasing hope, this fond desire,
This longing after immortality?
Or whence this secret dread, and inward horror,
Of falling into naught?
Cato (1713) act 5, sc. 1, l. 1

16 Eternity! thou pleasing, dreadful thought!
Cato (1713) act 5, sc. 1, l. 10

17 I should think my self a very bad woman, if I had done what I do, for a farthing less.
The Drummer (1716) act 1, sc. 1

18 There is nothing more requisite in business than dispatch.
The Drummer (1716) act 5, sc. 1

19 Our Grubstreet biographers . . . watch for the death of a great man, like so many undertakers, on purpose to make a penny of him.
The Freeholder (1751) no. 35

20 Poetic fields encompass me around,
And still I seem to tread on classic ground.
Letter from Italy (1704)

21 A painted meadow, or a purling stream.
Letter from Italy (1704)

22 Music, the greatest good that mortals know,
And all of heaven we have below.
'A Song for St Cecilia's Day' (1694)

23 Should the whole frame of nature round him
    break,
In ruin and confusion hurled,
He, unconcerned, would hear the mighty crack,
And stand secure amidst a falling world.
translation of Horace *Odes* bk. 3, no. 3; see **Horace** 401:14,
Pope 602:24

24 A reader seldom peruses a book with pleasure until he knows whether the writer of it be a black man or a fair man, of a mild or choleric disposition, married or a bachelor.
The Spectator no. 1 (1 March 1711)

25 In all thy humours, whether grave or mellow,
Thou'rt such a touchy, testy, pleasant fellow;
Hast so much wit, and mirth, and spleen about
    thee,
There is no living with thee, nor without thee.
The Spectator no. 68 (18 May 1711); see **Martial** 515:3

26 As Sir Roger is landlord to the whole congregation, he keeps them in very good order, and will suffer nobody to sleep in it [the church] besides himself; for if by chance he has been surprised into a short nap at sermon, upon recovering out of it, he stands up, and looks about him; and if he sees anybody else nodding, either wakes them himself, or sends his servant to them.
The Spectator no. 112 (9 July 1711)

27 Sir Roger told them, with the air of a man who would not give his judgement rashly, that much might be said on both sides.
The Spectator no. 122 (20 July 1711)

28 I have often thought, says Sir Roger, it happens very well that Christmas should fall out in the Middle of Winter.
The Spectator no. 269 (8 January 1712)

29 A true critic ought to dwell rather upon excellencies than imperfections, to discover the concealed beauties of a writer, and communicate

to the world such things as are worth their observation.

The Spectator no. 291 (2 February 1712); see **Horace** 398:14

1 These widows, Sir, are the most perverse creatures in the world.

The Spectator no. 335 (25 March 1712)

2 Mirth is like a flash of lightning that breaks through a gloom of clouds, and glitters for a moment: cheerfulness keeps up a kind of day-light in the mind.

The Spectator no. 381 (17 May 1712)

3 The Knight in the triumph of his heart made several reflections on the greatness of the British Nation; as, that one Englishman could beat three Frenchmen; that we could never be in danger of Popery so long as we took care of our fleet; that the Thames was the noblest river in Europe; that London Bridge was a greater piece of work than any of the Seven Wonders of the World; with many other honest prejudices which naturally cleave to the heart of a true Englishman.

The Spectator no. 383 (20 May 1712)

4 Wide and undetermined prospects are as pleasing to the fancy, as the speculations of eternity or infinitude are to the understanding.

The Spectator no. 412 (23 June 1712)

5 Through all Eternity to Thee
A joyful Song I'll raise,
For oh! Eternity's too short
To utter all thy Praise.

The Spectator no. 453 (9 August 1712)

6 We have in England a particular bashfulness in every thing that regards religion.

The Spectator no. 458 (15 August 1712)

7 The spacious firmament on high,
With all the blue ethereal sky,
And spangled heavens, a shining frame,
Their great Original proclaim.

The Spectator no. 465 (23 August 1712) 'Ode'

8 In Reason's ear they all rejoice,
And utter forth a glorious voice,
For ever singing, as they shine:
'The hand that made us is divine.'

The Spectator no. 465 (23 August 1712) 'Ode'

9 A woman seldom asks advice before she has bought her wedding clothes.

The Spectator no. 475 (4 September 1712)

10 Our disputants put me in mind of the skuttle fish, that when he is unable to extricate himself, blackens all the water about him, till he becomes invisible.

The Spectator no. 476 (5 September 1712)

11 If we may believe our logicians, man is distinguished from all other creatures by the faculty of laughter.

The Spectator no. 494 (26 September 1712)

12 'We are always doing', says he, 'something for Posterity, but I would fain see Posterity do something for us.'

The Spectator no. 583 (20 August 1714)

13 There is sometimes a greater judgement shewn in deviating from the rules of art, than in adhering to them; and . . . there is more beauty in the works of a great genius who is ignorant of all the rules of art, than in the works of a little genius, who not only knows but scrupulously observes them.

The Spectator no. 592 (10 September 1714); see **Pope** 604:1

14 I remember when our whole island was shaken with an earthquake some years ago, there was an impudent mountebank who sold pills which (as he told the country people) were very good against an earthquake.

The Tatler no. 240 (21 October 1710)

George Ade 1866–1944
American humorist and dramatist

15 After being turned down by numerous publishers, he had decided to write for posterity.

Fables in Slang (1900)

16 R-E-M-O-R-S-E!
Those dry Martinis did the work for me;
Last night at twelve I felt immense,
Today I feel like thirty cents.
My eyes are bleared, my coppers hot,
I'll try to eat, but I cannot.
It is no time for mirth and laughter,
The cold, grey dawn of the morning after.

The Sultan of Sulu (1903) act 2

17 'Whom are you?' he asked, for he had attended business college.

'The Steel Box' in *Chicago Record* 16 March 1898

Konrad Adenauer 1876–1967
German statesman, first Chancellor of the Federal Republic of Germany

18 A thick skin is a gift from God.

in *New York Times* 30 December 1959

Adi Granth see Sikh Scriptures

Alfred Adler 1870–1937
Austrian psychologist and psychiatrist

19 The truth is often a terrible weapon of aggression. It is possible to lie, and even to murder, for the truth.

The Problems of Neurosis (1929) ch. 2

20 To be a human being means to possess a feeling of inferiority which constantly presses towards its own conquest . . . The greater the feeling of inferiority that has been experienced, the more powerful is the urge for conquest and the more violent the emotional agitation.

Heinz and Rowens Ansbacher (eds.) *The Individual Psychology of Alfred Adler* (1956) ch. 4, sect. 3

Polly Adler 1900–62
American writer

21 A house is not a home.

title of book (1954)

Theodor Adorno 1903–69
German philosopher, sociologist, and musicologist

1 It is barbarous to write a poem after Auschwitz.
  attributed

☐ Advertising slogans
see box opposite

Æ (George William Russell) 1867–1935
Irish poet and essayist

2 In ancient shadows and twilights
  Where childhood had strayed,
  The world's great sorrows were born
  And its heroes were made.
  In the lost boyhood of Judas
  Christ was betrayed.
  'Germinal' (1931)

Aeschylus c.525–456 BC
Greek tragedian

3 The rest, I keep silent: a great ox is treading on my tongue—but the house itself, if it got a voice, would speak very plainly.
  Agamemnon l. 35; see **Heaney** 377:22

4 Justice inclines her scales so that wisdom comes at the price of suffering.
  Agamemnon l. 250

5 Hell to ships, hell to men, hell to cities.
  of Helen (literally 'Ship-destroyer, man-destroyer, city-destroyer')
  Agamemnon l. 689

6 The sea is there—and who shall quench it?—nurturing the juices which yield much purple worth its weight in silver, wholly renewable, the dye of vestments; there is a remedy for these here with the gods' help, my lord, from our reserve: the house does not know how to be poor.
  Agamemnon l. 958

7 And from your city do not wholly banish fear,
  For what man living, freed from fear, will still be just?
  The Eumenides l. 698

8 Let war stay abroad; it makes no difficulty in coming, for the man who will have in him a strong desire for glory. I disapprove of a bird's battling in its own home.
  The Eumenides l. 863

9 Countless chuckles of the waves of the sea.
  Prometheus Bound l. 89

10 Everyone's quick to blame the alien.
  The Suppliant Maidens l. 972

11 The saying of the noble and glorious Aeschylus, who declared that his tragedies were large cuts taken from Homer's mighty dinners.
  Athenaeus *Deipnosophistae*

Aesop
Greek storyteller of the 6th century BC

12 Then one day there really was a wolf, but when the boy shouted they didn't believe him.
  'The Boy Who Cried Wolf'

13 Woe is me! I foolishly abandoned what I had in order to grab hold of a phantom, and thus I ended up losing both that phantom and what I had to begin with.
  'The Dog, the Meat, and the Reflection'

14 Oh, you aren't even ripe yet! I don't need any sour grapes.
  'The Fox and the Bunch of Grapes'

15 O raven, you do have a voice but no brains to go with it!
  'The Fox and the Raven'

16 While I see many hoof-marks going in, I see none coming out.
  'The Fox, the Lion, and the Footprints'; see **Horace** 399:2

17 Pray to the gods only when you're making some effort on your own behalf, otherwise your prayers are wasted.
  'Heracles and the Driver'

18 Since you rejected what was good in order to get something bad, you had better put up with it—or else something even worse might happen.
  'Jupiter and the Frogs', often known as 'King Log'

19 The wolf in sheep's clothing.
  title of fable

Herbert Agar 1897–1980
American poet and writer

20 The truth which makes men free is for the most part the truth which men prefer not to hear.
  A Time for Greatness (1942) ch. 7; see **Bible** 103:11

James Agate 1877–1947
British drama critic and novelist

21 Shaw's plays are the price we pay for Shaw's prefaces.
  diary, 10 March 1933

22 My mind is not a bed to be made and re-made.
  diary, 9 June 1943

23 A professional is a man who can do his job when he doesn't feel like it. An amateur is a man who can't do his job when he does feel like it.
  diary, 19 July 1945

Agathon b. c.445
Greek tragic poet

24 Even a god cannot change the past.
  literally 'The one thing which even God cannot do is to make undone what has been done'
  Aristotle *Nicomachaean Ethics* bk. 6; see **Butler** 176:22

25 One might perhaps say that this very thing is probable, that many things happen to men that are not probable.
  Aristotle *Art of Rhetoric* 1402a; see **Aristotle** 25:23

Advertising slogans

1 Access—your flexible friend.
Access credit card, 1981 onwards

2 An ace caff with quite a nice museum attached.
the Victoria and Albert Museum, February 1989

3 All human life is there.
the *News of the World*; used by Maurice Smelt in the late 1950s; see **James** 417:22

4 All the news that's fit to print.
motto of the *New York Times*, from 1896; coined by its proprietor Adolph S. Ochs (1858-1935)

5 American Express? . . . That'll do nicely, sir.
American Express credit card, 1970s

6 And all because the lady loves Milk Tray.
Cadbury's Milk Tray chocolates, 1968 onwards

7 Australians wouldn't give a XXXX for anything else.
Castlemaine lager, 1986 onwards

8 Beanz meanz Heinz.
Heinz baked beans, c.1967; coined by Maurice Drake

9 Beauty is power.
Helena **Rubinstein**'s Valaze Skin Food, 1904

10 Because I'm worth it.
advertising slogan for L'Oreal, from mid 1980s

11 Bovril . . . Prevents that sinking feeling.
Bovril, 1920; coined by H. H. Harris

12 . . . But I know a man who can.
Automobile Association, 1980s

13 Can you tell Stork from butter?
Stork margarine, from c.1956

14 Cool as a mountain stream.
Consulate menthol cigarettes, early 1960s onwards

15 A diamond is forever.
De Beers Consolidated Mines, 1940s onwards; coined by Frances Gerety; see **Loos** 491:19

16 Does she . . . or doesn't she?
Clairol hair colouring, 1950s

17 Don't be vague, ask for Haig.
Haig whisky, c.1936

18 Don't forget the fruit gums, Mum.
Rowntree's fruit gums, 1958-61; coined by Roger Musgrave (1929-)

19 Drinka Pinta Milka Day.
National Dairy Council, 1958; coined by Bertrand Whitehead

20 Dr Williams' pink pills for pale people.
patent medicine advertisement, from 1890

21 Even your closest friends won't tell you.
Listerine mouthwash, US, in *Woman's Home Companion* November 1923

22 Every picture tells a story.
advertisement for Doan's Backache Kidney Pills (early 1900s); see **Proverbs** 619:22

23 Full of Eastern promise.
Fry's Turkish Delight, 1950s onwards

24 The future's bright, the future's Orange.
slogan for Orange telecom company, mid 1990s

25 Go to work on an egg.
British Egg Marketing Board, from 1957; perhaps written by Fay Weldon or Mary Gowing

26 Guinness is good for you.
reply universally given to researchers asking people why they drank Guinness
adopted by Oswald Greene, c.1929; see **Advertising slogans** 8:5

27 Happiness is a cigar called Hamlet.
Hamlet cigars; see **Lennon** 480:11

28 Have a break, have a Kit-Kat.
Rowntree's Kit-Kat, from c.1955

29 Heineken refreshes the parts other beers cannot reach.
Heineken lager, 1975 onwards; coined by Terry Lovelock

30 High o'er the fence leaps Sunny Jim
'Force' is the food that raises him.
advertising slogan for breakfast cereal (1903); coined by Minnie Hanff (1880-1942)

31 Horlicks guards against night starvation.
Horlicks malted milk drink, 1930s

32 If you want to get ahead, get a hat.
the Hat Council, 1965

33 I liked it so much, I bought the company!
Remington Shavers, 1980; spoken by the company's new owner Victor Kiam (1926-2001)

34 I'm only here for the beer.
Double Diamond beer, 1971 onwards; coined by Ros Levenstein

35 It beats as it sweeps as it cleans.
Hoover vacuum cleaners, devised in 1919 by Gerald Page-Wood

36 It could be you.
British national lottery, from 1994

37 It's finger lickin' good.
Kentucky fried chicken, from 1958

38 It's good to talk.
British Telecom, from 1994

39 It's tingling fresh. It's fresh as ice.
Gibbs toothpaste; the first advertising slogan heard on British television, 22 September 1955

40 I was a seven-stone weakling.
Charles Atlas body-building, originally in US

41 Keep that schoolgirl complexion.
Palmolive soap, from 1917; coined by Charles S. Pearce

42 Kills all known germs.
Domestos bleach, 1959

43 Let the train take the strain.
British Rail, 1970 onwards

▶

▶ Advertising slogans *continued*

1 Let your fingers do the walking.
   Bell System Telephone Directory Yellow Pages, 1960s

2 The man you love to hate.
   billing for Erich von Stroheim in the film *The Heart of Humanity* (1918)

3 A Mars a day helps you work, rest and play.
   Mars bar, *c.*1960 onwards

4 The mint with the hole.
   Life-Savers, US, 1920; and for Rowntree's Polo mints, UK from 1947

5 My Goodness, My Guinness.
   Guinness stout, 1935; coined by Dicky Richards; see **Advertising slogans** 7:26

6 Never knowingly undersold.
   motto of the John Lewis Partnership, from *c.*1920; coined by John Spedan Lewis (1885-1963)

7 Nice one, Cyril.
   taken up by supporters of Cyril Knowles, Tottenham Hotspur footballer; the Spurs team later made a record featuring the line
   Wonderloaf, 1972

8 No manager ever got fired for buying IBM.
   IBM

9 Oxo gives a meal man-appeal.
   Oxo beef extract, *c.*1960

10 Persil washes whiter—and it shows.
   Persil washing powder, 1970s

11 Put a tiger in your tank.
   Esso petrol, 1964

12 Say it with flowers.
   Society of American Florists, 1917, coined by Patrick O'Keefe (1872-1934)

13 Sch . . . you know who.
   Schweppes mineral drinks, 1960s

14 Someone, somewhere, wants a letter from you.
   British Post Office, 1960s

15 Stop me and buy one.
   Wall's ice cream, from spring 1922; coined by Cecil Rodd

16 Tell Sid.
   privatization of British Gas, 1986

17 They come as a boon and a blessing to men,
   The Pickwick, the Owl, and the Waverley pen.
   advertisement by MacNiven and H. Cameron Ltd., current by 1879; almost certainly inspired by the following:

   It came as a boon and a blessing to men,
   The peaceful, the pure, the victorious PEN!
   J. C. Prince (1808-66) 'The Pen and the Press'

18 Things go better with Coke.
   Coca-Cola, 1963

19 Top people take *The Times*.
   The Times newspaper, from January 1959

20 *Vorsprung durch Technik.*
   Progress through technology.
   Audi motors, from 1986

21 We are the Ovaltineys,
   Little [*or* Happy] girls and boys.
   'We are the Ovaltineys' (song from *c.*1935); Ovaltine drink

22 We're number two. We try harder.
   Avis car rentals

23 We won't make a drama out of a crisis.
   Commercial Union insurance

24 Where's the beef?
   Wendy's Hamburgers, from January 1984; coined by Cliff Freeman; see **Mondale** 542:18

25 Worth a guinea a box.
   Beecham's pills, from *c.*1859, from the chance remark of a lady purchaser

26 You press the button, we do the rest.
   advertising slogan to launch Kodak camera 1888, coined by George Eastman (1854-1932)

27 You're never alone with a Strand.
   Strand cigarettes, 1960; coined by John May

Agesilaus 444-360 BC
Greek monarch, King of Sparta

28 Every honourable action has its proper time and season, or rather it is this propriety or observance which distinguishes an honourable action from its opposite.
   Plutarch *Lives* 'Agesilaus'

Spiro T. Agnew 1918-96
American Republican politician

29 I didn't say I wouldn't go into ghetto areas. I've been in many of them and to some extent I would have to say this: If you've seen one city slum you've seen them all.
   in *Detroit Free Press* 19 October 1968; see **Burton** 174:6

30 In the United States today, we have more than our share of the nattering nabobs of negativism.
   speech in San Diego, 11 September 1970

Agnolo di Tura b. *c.*1300
Sienese chronicler

31 No one wept for the dead, because everyone expected death itself.
   Rerum Italicarum scriptores; M. Meiss *Painting in Florence and Siena after the Black Death* (1951)

Maria, Marchioness of Ailesbury
d. 1902
British peeress

32 My dear, my dear, you never know when any beautiful young lady may not blossom into a Duchess!
   Duke of Portland *Men, Women, and Things* (1937) ch. 3; see **Mitford** 541:1

Alfred Ainger 1837–1904

English lecturer

1 No flowers, by request.
*summarizing the principle of conciseness for
contributors to the* Dictionary of National
Biography
   Supplement to the Dictionary of National Biography
   1901–1911 (1912)

Arthur Campbell Ainger 1841–1919

English schoolmaster

2 God is working his purpose out as year succeeds to
   year;
   God is working his purpose out and the time is
   drawing near;
   Nearer and nearer draws the time, the time that
   shall surely be,
   When the earth shall be filled with the glory of
   God as the waters cover the sea.
   'God is working his purpose out' (1894 hymn); **Bible**
   88:22

Jonathan Aitken 1942–

British Conservative politician

3 If it falls to me to start a fight to cut out the cancer
   of bent and twisted journalism in our country
   with the simple sword of truth and the trusty
   shield of British fair play, so be it.
   statement, London, 10 April 1995, in *The Times* 11 April
   1995

Max Aitken see Lord Beaverbrook

Mark Akenside 1721–70

English poet and physician

4 Mind, mind alone, bear witness, earth and
      heaven!
   The living fountains in itself contains
   Of beauteous and sublime.
   The Pleasures of Imagination (1744) bk. 1, l. 481

5   Nor ever yet
   The melting rainbow's vernal-tinctured hues
   To me have shone so pleasing, as when first
   The hand of science pointed out the path
   In which the sun-beams gleaming from the west
   Fall on the wat'ry cloud.
   The Pleasures of Imagination (1744) bk. 2, l. 103

Anna Akhmatova 1889–1966

Russian poet

6 All has been looted, betrayed, sold; black death's
   wing flashed ahead.
   'All has been Looted' (1921) (translated by Dmitri
   Obolensky)

7 As if I were a river
   The harsh age changed my course,
   Replaced one life with another,
   Flowing in a different channel
   And I do not recognize my shores.
   'As if I were a River' (1944) (translated by Amanda
   Haight)

8 It was a time when only the dead smiled, happy in
   their peace.
   Requiem (1935–40) (translated by Richard McKane)

9 I'd like to name the names of all that host
   but they snatched up the list and now it's lost.
   I've woven them a garment that's prepared
   out of poor words, those that I overheard,
   and will hold fast to every word and glance
   all of my days, even in new mischance.
   Requiem (1935–40) (translated by Stanley Kunitz and Max
   Hayward)

10 In the young century's cool nursery,
   In its chequered silence, I was born.
   'Willow' (1940)

Zoë Akins 1886–1958

American poet and dramatist

11 The Greeks had a word for it.
   title of play (1930)

William Alabaster 1567–1640

English divine and Latin poet

12 Tell them, my soul, the fears that make me quake:
   The smouldering brimstone and the burning lake,
   Life feeding death, death ever life devouring,
   Torments not moved, unheard, yet still roaring,
   God lost, hell found,—ever, never begun.
   Now bid me into flame from smoke to run!
   'Away, fear, with thy projects' (written 1597–8)

Alain (Émile-Auguste Chartier) 1868–1951

French poet and philosopher

13 *Rien n'est plus dangereux qu'une idée, quand on n'a
   qu'une idée.*
   Nothing is more dangerous than an idea, when
   you have only one idea.
   Propos sur la religion (1938) no. 74

Alain-Fournier (Henri Alban) 1886–1914

French novelist

14 *Mais quelqu'un est venu qui m'a enlevé à tous ces
   plaisirs d'enfant paisible. Quelqu'un a soufflé la bougie
   qui éclairait pour moi le doux visage maternel penché
   sur le repas du soir. Quelqu'un a éteint la lampe
   autour de laquelle nous étions une famille heureuse, à
   la nuit, lorsque mon père avait accroché les volets de
   bois aux portes vitrées. Et celui-là, ce fut Augustin
   Meaulnes, que les autres élèves appelèrent bientôt le
   grand Meaulnes.*
   But someone came and put an end to these mild
   and childish pleasures. Someone blew out the
   candle which illumined for me the sweet maternal
   face bent over the evening meal. Someone
   extinguished the lamp around which we had been
   a happy family group at night-time when my
   father had closed all the wooden shutters. And
   that someone was Augustin Meaulnes, whom in
   no time the other boys began to call le grand
   Meaulnes.
   Le Grand Meaulnes (1912) pt. 1, ch. 2 (translated by Frank
   Davison)

1 *Quand on a, disait-il, commis quelque lourde faute impardonnable, on songe parfois, au milieu d'une grande amertume: 'Il y a pourtant par le monde des gens qui me pardonneraient'. On imagine de vieilles gens, des grandparents pleins d'indulgence, qui sont persuadés à l'avance que tout ce que vous faites est bien fait.*

When you've done something inexcusable, you try to ease your conscience by telling yourself that someone, somewhere would forgive you. You think of old people, perhaps indulgent grandparents, who are convinced that whatever you do is right.
Le Grand Meaulnes (1912) pt. 1, ch. 14

2 *Notre aventure est finie. L'hiver de cette année est mort comme la tombe. Peut-être quand nous mourrons, peut-être la mort seule nous donnera la clef et la suite et la fin de cette aventure manquée.*

Our adventure is ended. The winter of this year is as dead as the grave. Perhaps when we come to die, death will provide the meaning and the sequel and the ending of this unsuccessful adventure.
Le Grand Meaulnes (1912) pt. 2, ch. 12

3 *Un homme qui a fait une fois un bond dans le paradis, comment pourrait-il s'accommoder ensuite de la vie de tout le monde?*

How can a man who has once strayed into Heaven ever hope to make terms with the earth!
Le Grand Meaulnes (1912) pt. 3, ch. 4

4 *C'est d'abord comme une voix tremblante qui, de très loin, ose à peine chanter sa joie . . . Cet air que je ne connais pas, c'est aussi une prière, une supplication au bonheur de ne pas être trop cruel, un salut et comme un agenouillement devant le bonheur.*

It is at first like some far-away tentative voice intimidated by an excess of joy . . . This melody, which I've never heard before, is a kind of prayer to happiness, an entreaty asking fate not to be too cruel, a salutation to happiness and at the same time a genuflexion.
Le Grand Meaulnes (1912) pt. 3, ch. 7

Edward Albee 1928–

American dramatist

5 Who's afraid of Virginia Woolf?
title of play (1962)

Prince Albert (Albert Francis Charles Augustus Emmanuel of Saxe-Coburg-Gotha) 1819–61

*German-born prince, British Consort of Queen **Victoria** from 1840*
*on Albert: see **Tennyson** 777:13, **Victoria** 809:9*

6 The works of art, by being publicly exhibited and offered for sale, are becoming articles of trade, following as such the unreasoning laws of markets and fashion; and public and even private patronage is swayed by their tyrannical influence.
speech at the Royal Academy Dinner, 3 May 1851, in *Addresses* (1857)

Scipione Alberti

7 *I pensieri stretti ed il viso sciolto* [Secret thoughts and open countenance] will go safely over the whole world.
letter from Henry Wotton to John Milton, 13 April 1638, prefixed to *Comus* in Milton *Poems* (1645 ed.)

Mary Alcock c.1742–98

English poet

8 A masquerade, a murdered peer,
His throat just cut from ear to ear—
A rake turned hermit—a fond maid
Run mad, by some false loon betrayed—
These stores supply the female pen,
Which writes them o'er and o'er again,
And readers likewise may be found
To circulate them round and round.
'A Receipt for Writing a Novel' l. 65

Louisa May Alcott 1832–88

American novelist
*see also **Opening lines** 574:10*

9 I am angry nearly every day of my life . . . but I have learned not to show it; and I still hope to learn not to feel it, though it may take me another forty years to do so.
Little Women (1868–9) ch. 8

Alcuin c.735–804

English scholar and theologian

10 *Nec audiendi qui solent dicere, Vox populi, vox Dei, quum tumultuositas vulgi semper insaniae proxima sit.*

And those people should not be listened to who keep saying the voice of the people is the voice of God, since the riotousness of the crowd is always very close to madness.
letter 164 in *Works* (1863) vol. 1; see **Pope** 605:22, **Proverbs** 633:37, **Sherman** 734:13

Richard Aldington 1892–1962

English poet, novelist, and biographer

11 Patriotism is a lively sense of collective responsibility. Nationalism is a silly cock crowing on its own dunghill.
The Colonel's Daughter (1931) pt. 1, ch. 6

Brian Aldiss 1925–

English science fiction writer

12 Keep violence in the mind
Where it belongs.
Barefoot in the Head (1969) 'Charteris'

Henry Aldrich 1647–1710

English scholar; Dean of Christ Church, Oxford, from 1689

13 If all be true that I do think,
There are five reasons we should drink;
Good wine—a friend—or being dry—
Or lest we should be by and by—

Or any other reason why.
'Reasons for Drinking' (1689)

Thomas Bailey Aldrich 1836–1907

American writer

1   The fair, frail palaces,
The fading alps and archipelagoes,
And great cloud-continents of sunset-seas.
'Miracles' (1874)

'Buzz' Aldrin (Edwin Eugene Aldrin Jnr)

1930–

American astronaut; second man on the moon after Neil **Armstrong**

2 Beautiful! Beautiful! Magnificent desolation.
of the lunar landscape
on the first moon walk, 20 July 1969

Alexander the Great 356–323 BC

Greek monarch, King of Macedon from 336 BC
see also **Diogenes** 274:18

3 If I were not Alexander, I would be Diogenes.
Plutarch *Parallel Lives* 'Alexander' ch. 14, sect. 3

4 Is it not worthy of tears that, when the number of
worlds is infinite, we have not yet become lords of
a single one?
*when asked why he wept on hearing from Anaxarchus
that there was an infinite number of worlds*
Plutarch *Moralia* 'On Tranquillity of the Mind'; see **Watts**
824:1

Alexander II ('the Liberator') 1818–81

Russian monarch, Tsar from 1855

5 Better to abolish serfdom from above than to wait
till it begins to abolish itself from below.
speech in Moscow, 30 March 1856

Cecil Frances Alexander 1818–95

Irish poet and hymn-writer

6 All things bright and beautiful,
All creatures great and small,
All things wise and wonderful,
The Lord God made them all.
'All Things Bright and Beautiful' (1848)

7 The rich man in his castle,
The poor man at his gate,
God made them, high or lowly,
And ordered their estate.
'All Things Bright and Beautiful' (1848)

8 Once in royal David's city
Stood a lowly cattle-shed,
Where a mother laid her baby
In a manger for his bed:
Mary was that mother mild,
Jesus Christ her little child.
'Once in royal David's city' (1848)

9 I bind unto myself to-day
The strong name of the Trinity,

By invocation of the same
The Three in One and One in Three.
'St Patrick's Breastplate' (1889); see **Patrick** 588:19

10 There is a green hill far away,
Without a city wall,
Where the dear Lord was crucified,
Who died to save us all.
'There is a green hill far away' (1848)

William Alexander, Lord Stirling

c.1567–1640
Scottish poet and courtier

11 The weaker sex, to piety more prone.
'Doomsday' 5th Hour (1637)

Alfonso 'the Wise' 1221–84

Spanish monarch, King of Castile and León from 1252

12 Had I been present at the Creation, I would have
given some useful hints for the better ordering of
the universe.
on studying the Ptolemaic system
attributed

Alfred the Great AD 849–899

English monarch, King of Wessex from AD 871

13 Ða ic ða gemunde hu sio lar Lædengeðiodes ær
ðissum afeallen wæs giond Angelcynn, ond ðeah
monige cuðon Englisc gewrit arædan, ða ongan ic on
gemang oðrum mislicum ond manigfealdum bisgum
ðisses kynerices ða boc wendan on Englisc ðe is
genemned on Læden Pastoralis, ond on Englisc
Hierdeboc, hwilum word be worde, hwilum andgit of
andgite.
When I recalled how knowledge of Latin had
previously decayed throughout England, and yet
many could still read things written in English, I
then began, amidst the various and multifarious
afflictions of this kingdom, to translate into
English the book which in Latin is called
Pastoralis, in English 'Shepherd-book', sometimes
word for word, sometimes sense for sense.
preface to the Anglo-Saxon version of St Gregory's *Pastoral
Care* (translated by S. Keynes and M. Lapidge, 1983)

Nelson Algren 1909–

American novelist

14 A walk on the wild side.
title of novel (1956)

15 Never play cards with a man called Doc. Never eat
at a place called Mom's. Never sleep with a
woman whose troubles are worse than your own.
in *Newsweek* 2 July 1956

Ali ibn-Abi-Talib c.602–661

Arab ruler, fourth Islamic caliph

16 He who has a thousand friends has not a friend to
spare,
And he who has one enemy will meet him
everywhere.
A Hundred Sayings

Muhammad Ali (Cassius Clay) 1942–

American boxer

1 I'm the greatest.
adopted as his catchphrase from 1962, in *Louisville Times* 16 November 1962

2 Float like a butterfly, sting like a bee.
summary of his boxing strategy (probably originated by his aide Drew 'Bundini' Brown)
G. Sullivan *Cassius Clay Story* (1964) ch. 8

3 I ain't got no quarrel with the Viet Cong.
refusing to be drafted to fight in Vietnam
at a press conference in Miami, Florida, February 1966

Abbé d'Allainval 1700–53

French dramatist

4 *L'embarras des richesses.*
The embarrassment of riches.
title of comedy (1726)

Fred Allen (John Florence Sullivan) 1894–1956

American humorist

5 Committee—a group of men who individually can do nothing but as a group decide that nothing can be done.
attributed

Lewis Allen (Abel Meeropol)

American teacher

6 Southern trees bear strange fruit,
Blood on the leaves and blood at the root,
Black bodies swinging in the Southern breeze,
Strange fruit hanging from the poplar trees.
'Strange Fruit' (1939), adapted and sung by Billie **Holiday**

William Allen see Last words

Woody Allen (Allen Stewart Konigsberg) 1935–

American film director, writer, and actor

7 That was the most fun I ever had without laughing.
of sex
Annie Hall (1977 film, with Marshall Brickman)

8 Don't knock masturbation. It's sex with someone I love.
Annie Hall (1977 film, with Marshall Brickman)

9 Is sex dirty? Only if it's done right.
Everything You Always Wanted to Know about Sex (1972 film)

10 If it turns out that there is a God, I don't think that he's evil. But the worst that you can say about him is that basically he's an underachiever.
Love and Death (1975 film)

11 My brain? It's my second favourite organ.
Sleeper (1973 film, with Marshall Brickman)

12 A fast word about oral contraception. I asked a girl to go to bed with me and she said 'no'.
Woody Allen Volume Two (Colpix CP 488) side 4, band 6

13 It's not that I'm afraid to die. I just don't want to be there when it happens.
Death (1975)

14 If only God would give me some clear sign! Like making a large deposit in my name at a Swiss bank.
'Selections from the Allen Notebooks' in *New Yorker* 5 November 1973

15 On bisexuality: It immediately doubles your chances for a date on Saturday night.
in *New York Times* 1 December 1975

16 I don't want to achieve immortality through my work . . . I want to achieve it through not dying.
Eric Lax *Woody Allen and his Comedy* (1975) ch. 12

Svetlana Alliluyeva 1925–

*Russian daughter of Joseph **Stalin***

17 He is gone, but his shadow still stands over all of us. It still dictates to us and we, very often, obey.
*of her father, Joseph **Stalin***
Twenty Letters to a Friend (1967)

William Allingham 1824–89

Irish poet

18 Up the airy mountain,
Down the rushy glen,
We daren't go a-hunting,
For fear of little men.
'The Fairies' (1850)

St Alphonsus (Alfonso Maria de' Liguori) 1696–1787

Italian theologian, founder of the Redemptorists

19 O Mother blest, whom God bestows
On sinners and on just,
What joy, what hope thou givest those
Who in thy mercy trust!
'O Mother Blest', translated by E. Vaughan

Joseph Alsop b. 1910

American journalist

20 Gratitude, like love, is never a dependable international emotion.
in *Observer* 30 November 1952

Robert Altman 1922–

American film director

21 What's a cult? It just means not enough people to make a minority.
in *Guardian* 11 April 1981

Luis Walter Alvarez 1911–88

American physicist

22 There is no democracy in physics. We can't say that some second-rate guy has as much right to opinion as Fermi.
D. S. Greenberg *The Politics of Pure Science* (1969)

St Ambrose c.339–397
French-born bishop of Milan
on Ambrose: see **Augustine** *37:3; see also* **Prayers** *611:7*

1 *Ubi Petrus, ibi ergo ecclesia.*

Where Peter is, there must be the Church.
'Explanatio psalmi 40' in *Corpus Scriptorum Ecclesiasticorum Latinorum* (1919) vol. 64

2 *Cum Romanum venio, ieiuno Sabbato; cum hic sum, non ieiuno: sic etiam tu, ad quam forte ecclesiam veneris, eius morem serva, si cuiquam non vis esse scandalum nec quemquam tibi.*

When I go to Rome, I fast on Saturday, but here [Milan] I do not. Do you also follow the custom of whatever church you attend, if you do not want to give or receive scandal.
St Augustine: Letters vol. 1 (translated by Sister W. Parsons, 1951) 'Letter 54 to Januarius'; see **Proverbs** 634:24

Leo Amery 1873–1955
British Conservative politician

3 For twenty years he has held a season-ticket on the line of least resistance and has gone wherever the train of events has carried him, lucidly justifying his position at whatever point he has happened to find himself.
of Herbert **Asquith**
in *Quarterly Review* July 1914

4 Speak for England.
to Arthur Greenwood in the House of Commons, 2 September 1939; see **Boothby** 145:2

5 I will quote certain other words. I do it with great reluctance, because I am speaking of those who are old friends and associates of mine, but they are words which, I think, are applicable to the present situation. This is what Cromwell said to the Long Parliament when he thought it was no longer fit to conduct the affairs of the nation: 'You have sat too long here for any good you have been doing. Depart, I say, and let us have done with you. In the name of God, go.'
speech, House of Commons, 7 May 1940; see **Cromwell** 252:2

Fisher Ames 1758–1808
American politician

6 A monarchy is a merchantman which sails well, but will sometimes strike on a rock, and go to the bottom; whilst a republic is a raft which would never sink, but then your feet are always in the water.
attributed to Ames, speaking in the House of Representatives, 1795; quoted by R. W. Emerson in *Essays* (2nd series, 1844) no. 7, but not traced in Ames's speeches

Kingsley Amis 1922–95
English novelist and poet

7 If there's one word that sums up everything that's gone wrong since the War, it's Workshop.
Jake's Thing (1979) ch. 14

8 His mouth had been used as a latrine by some small creature of the night, and then as its mausoleum.
Lucky Jim (1953) ch. 6

9 Alun's life was coming to consist more and more exclusively of being told at dictation speed what he knew.
The Old Devils (1986) ch. 7

10 Outside every fat man there was an even fatter man trying to close in.
One Fat Englishman (1963) ch. 3; see **Connolly** 240:5, **Orwell** 577:3

11 He was of the faith chiefly in the sense that the church he currently did not attend was Catholic.
One Fat Englishman (1963) ch. 8

12 Should poets bicycle-pump the human heart
Or squash it flat?
Man's love is of man's life a thing apart;
Girls aren't like that.
'A Bookshop Idyll' (1956); see **Byron** 180:15

13 We men have got love well weighed up; our stuff
Can get by without it.
Women don't seem to think that's good enough;
They write about it.
'A Bookshop Idyll' (1956)

14 Women are really much nicer than men:
No wonder we like them.
'A Bookshop Idyll' (1956)

15 Death has got something to be said for it:
There's no need to get out of bed for it;
Wherever you may be,
They bring it to you, free.
'Delivery Guaranteed' (1979)

16 The delusion that there are thousands of young people about who are capable of benefiting from university training, but have somehow failed to find their way there, is . . . a necessary component of the expansionist case . . . More will mean worse.
in *Encounter* July 1960

17 If you can't annoy somebody with what you write, I think there's little point in writing.
in *Radio Times* 1 May 1971

Anacharsis
Scythian prince of the 6th century BC

18 Written laws are like spiders' webs; they will catch, it is true, the weak and poor, but would be torn in pieces by the rich and powerful.
Plutarch *Parallel Lives* 'Solon' bk. 5, sect. 2; see **Shenstone** 732:24, **Swift** 766:27

Anatolius
8th-century hymn-writer

19 Fierce was the wild billow,
Dark was the night;
Oars laboured heavily,
Foam glimmered white;
Trembled the mariners,
Peril was nigh:
Then said the God of God,

'Peace! it is I.'
'Fierce was the wild billow' (translated by John Mason
Neale, 1862)

Hans Christian Andersen 1805-75

Danish novelist and writer of fairy stories

1 The Emperor's new clothes.
title of story in *Danish Fairy Legends and Tales* (1846)

2 'But the Emperor has nothing on at all!' cried a
little child.
Danish Fairy Legends and Tales (1846) 'The Emperor's New
Clothes'

3 And so they could see she was a real princess,
because she had felt the pea through twenty
mattresses and twenty eiderdowns.
Tales Told for Children (1835) 'The Princess and the Pea'

4 It doesn't matter about being born in a duckyard,
as long as you're hatched from a swan's egg!
Danish Fairy Legends and Tales (1846) 'The Ugly Duckling'

5 I never dreamt I should find so much happiness
when I was the ugly duckling!
Danish Fairy Legends and Tales (1846) 'The Ugly Duckling'

6 There sat the dog with eyes as big as millstones!
Tales Told for Children (1835) 'The Tinder-box'

Maxwell Anderson 1888-1959

American dramatist

7 But it's a long, long while
From May to December;
And the days grow short
When you reach September.
'September Song' (1938 song)

Maxwell Anderson 1888-1959 and Lawrence Stallings 1894-1968

American dramatists

8 What price glory?
title of play (1924)

Robert Anderson 1917-

American dramatist

9 Tea and sympathy.
title of play (1957)

Lancelot Andrewes 1555-1626

*English preacher and writer of sermons; bishop, successively,
of Chichester, Ely, and Winchester*

10 What shall become of me (said Righteousness)?
What use of Justice, if God will do no justice, if he
spare sinners? And what use of me (saith Mercy),
if he spare them not? Hard hold there was,
inasmuch as, *Perii, nisi homo moriatur* (said
Righteousness) I die, if he die not: And *Perii, nisi
Misericordiam consequatur* (said Mercy) if he die, I
die too.
Of the Nativity (1616) Sermon 11; see **Milton** 532:17

11 *Verbum infans*, the Word without a word, not able
to speak a word . . . He, that . . . taketh the vast

body of the main Sea, turns it to and fro, as a little
child, and rolls it about with the swaddling bands
of darkness; He, to come thus into clouts, himself!
Of the Nativity (1618) Sermon 12

12 It was no summer progress. A cold coming they
had of it, at this time of the year; just, the worst
time of the year, to take a journey, and specially a
long journey, in. The ways deep, the weather
sharp, the days short, the sun farthest off *in
solstitio brumali*, the very dead of Winter.
Of the Nativity (1622) Sermon 15; see **Eliot** 302:9

Norman Angell 1872-1967

English pacifist

13 The great illusion.
on the futility of war
title of book (1910), first published as 'Europe's Optical
Illusion' (1909)

Maya Angelou 1928-

American writer
see also **Dunbar** 291:15

14 Children's talent to endure stems from their
ignorance of alternatives.
I Know Why The Caged Bird Sings (1969) ch.17

15 You may shoot me with your words,
You may cut me with your eyes,
You may kill me with your hatefulness,
But still, like air, I'll rise.
'Still I Rise' (1978)

Paul Anka 1941-

Canadian singer and composer

16 I've lived a life that's full, I've travelled each and
ev'ry highway
And more, much more than this. I did it my way.
'My Way' (1969 song)

Anne, Princess Royal 1950-

British princess; daughter of **Elizabeth II**

17 I don't work that way . . . The very idea that all
children want to be cuddled by a complete
stranger, I find completely amazing.
on her work for Save the Children
in *Daily Telegraph* 17 January 1998

Anonymous
ENGLISH

18 An abomination unto the Lord, but a very present
help in time of trouble.
definition of a lie
an amalgamation of Proverbs 12.22 and Psalms 46.1,
often attributed to Adlai **Stevenson**; Bill Adler *The Stevenson
Wit* (1966); see **Bible** 84:14, **Book of Common Prayer**
136:24

19 Adam
Had 'em.
on the antiquity of microbes
noted as an example of a short poem

1 All human beings are born free and equal in dignity and rights.

Universal Declaration of Human Rights (1948) article 1

2 Along the electric wire the message came:
He is not better—he is much the same.

parodic poem on the illness of the Prince of Wales, later King Edward VII

F. H. Gribble *Romance of the Cambridge Colleges* (1913); sometimes attributed to Alfred Austin (1835–1913), Poet Laureate

3 Anyone here been raped and speaks English?

shouted by a British TV reporter in a crowd of Belgian civilians waiting to be airlifted out of the Belgian Congo, c.1960

Edward Behr *Anyone Here been Raped and Speaks English?* (1981)

4 Appeal from Philip drunk to Philip sober.

paraphrase of the words of an unidentified woman alluding to Philip II of Macedon (382–336 BC), in Valerius Maximus *Facta ac Dicta Memorabilia* (AD *c.*32) bk. 6, ch. 2

5 Back and side go bare, go bare,
Both foot and hand go cold:
But belly God send thee good ale enough,
Whether it be new or old.

Gammer Gurton's Needle (1575) act 2 'Song', the play being attributed to William Stevenson (*c.*1530–75) and also to John Still (1543–1608), the song possibly of earlier origin

6 A beast, but a just beast.

a schoolboy's description of Dr Temple, Headmaster of Rugby School

F.E. Kitchener *Rugby Memoir of Archbishop Temple 1857–1869* (1907) ch. 3

7 The best defence against the atom bomb is not to be there when it goes off.

contributor to *British Army Journal*, in *Observer* 20 February 1949

8 Bigamy is having one husband too many. Monogamy is the same.

Erica Jong *Fear of Flying* (1973) ch. 1 (epigraph)

9 Cathedral time is five minutes later than standard time.

order of service leaflet, Christ Church Cathedral, Oxford, 1990s

10 The cloud of unknowing.

title of mystical prose work (14th century)

11 Collapse of Stout Party.

supposed standard dénouement in Victorian humour

R. Pearsall *Collapse of Stout Party* (1975) introduction

12 A committee is a group of the unwilling, chosen from the unfit, to do the unnecessary.

various attributions (origin unknown)

13 A community in which power, wealth and opportunity are in the hands of the many not the few, where the rights we enjoy reflect the duties we owe . . . in which the enterprise of the market and the rigour of competition are joined with the forces of partnership and cooperation.

new Clause Four of the Labour Party constitution, passed at a special conference 29 April 1995; see **Anonymous** 19:15

14 A Company for carrying on an undertaking of Great Advantage, but no one to know what it is.

The South Sea Company Prospectus (1711), in Virginia Cowles *The Great Swindle* (1963) ch. 5

15 A contingency for the space shuttle has been declared.

Mission Control in Houston indicating that contact with the space shuttle Columbia had been lost

in *Sunday Times* 2 February 2003

16 [Death is] nature's way of telling you to slow down.

American life insurance proverb, in *Newsweek* 25 April 1960

17 Do not fold, spindle or mutilate.

Instruction on punched cards (found in this form in the 1950s, and in differing forms from the 1930s)

18 Do not stand at my grave and weep:
I am not there. I do not sleep.
I am a thousand winds that blow.
I am the diamond glints on snow.
I am the sunlight on ripened grain.
I am the gentle autumn's rain.
When you awaken in the morning's hush,
I am the swift uplifting rush
Of quiet birds in circled flight.
I am the soft stars that shine at night.
Do not stand at my grave and cry;
I am not there, I did not die.

quoted in letter left by British soldier Stephen Cummins when killed by the IRA, March 1989

origin uncertain; attributed to various authors

19 Earned a precarious living by taking in one another's washing.

attributed to Mark **Twain** by William **Morris**, in *The Commonweal* 6 August 1887

20 The eternal triangle.

book review title, in *Daily Chronicle* 5 December 1907

21 Every country has its own constitution; ours is absolutism moderated by assassination.

Ernst Friedrich Herbert, Count Münster, quoting 'an intelligent Russian', in *Political Sketches of the State of Europe, 1814–1867* (1868)

22 Everyman, I will go with thee, and be thy guide,
In thy most need to go by thy side.

spoken by Knowledge

Everyman (*c.*1509–19) l. 522

23 Expletive deleted.

in *Submission of Recorded Presidential Conversations to the Committee on the Judiciary of the House of Representatives by President Richard M. Nixon* 30 April 1974, appendix 1

24 Exterminate . . . the treacherous English, walk over General French's contemptible little army.

allegedly a copy of Orders issued by the Kaiser Wilhelm II but most probably fabricated by the British

annexe to BEF [British Expeditionary Force] Routine Orders of 24 September 1914, in Arthur Ponsonby *Falsehood in Wartime* (1928) ch. 10; see **Cromwell** 252:6

25 Faster than a speeding bullet! . . . Look! Up in the sky! It's a bird! It's a plane! It's Superman! Yes, it's Superman! Strange visitor from another planet . . . Who can change the course of mighty rivers,

bend steel with his bare hands, and who—
disguised as Clark Kent, mild-mannered reporter
for a great metropolitan newspaper—fights a
never ending battle for truth, justice and the
American way!
Superman (US radio show, 1940 onwards) preamble

1 The fault is great in man or woman
Who steals a goose from off a common;
But what can plead that man's excuse
Who steals a common from a goose?
in *The Tickler Magazine* 1 February 1821

2 Fee-fi-fo-fum
I smell the blood of an Englishman.
Be he alive or be he dead
I'll grind his bones to make my bread.
*versions of this rhyme exist from the early 15th
century in tales involving man-eating giants, and
survive in 'Jack the Giant-Killer' and 'Jack and the
Beanstalk'; see* **Nashe** 557:19, **Shakespeare** 701:2
Iona and Peter Opie *The Classic Fairy Tales* (1974)

3 A form of statuary which no careful father would
wish his daughter, or no discerning young man
his fiancée, to see.
on Jacob **Epstein**'s *sculptures for the former BMA
building in the Strand, London*
in *Evening Standard* 19 June 1908

4 A gentleman haranguing on the perfection of our
law, and that it was equally open to the poor and
the rich, was answered by another, 'So is the
London Tavern'.
Tom Paine's Jests (1794) no. 23; also attributed to John
Horne Tooke (1736–1812) in W. Hazlitt *The Spirit of the
Age* (1825) 'Mr Horne Tooke'; see **Mathew** 518:11

5 Good at a fight, but better at a play,
Godlike in giving, but—the devil to pay!
lines written on a cast from **Sheridan**'s *hand*
Thomas Moore *Memoirs of the Life of . . . Richard Brinsley
Sheridan* (1825) ch. 21

6 Great Chatham with his sabre drawn
Stood waiting for Sir Richard Strachan;
Sir Richard, longing to be at 'em,
Stood waiting for the Earl of Chatham.
'At Walcheren, 1809'; attributed to Joseph Jekyll
(1753–1837)

7 Have you heard? The Prime Minister has resigned
and Northcliffe has sent for the King.
joke circulating in 1919, *suggesting that Lord*
Northcliffe, **Lloyd George**'s *implacable enemy, would
succeed him as Prime Minister*
Hamilton Fyfe *Northcliffe, an Intimate Biography* (1930) ch.
16

8 He may be one of its [the Church's] buttresses, but
certainly not one of its pillars, for he is never
found within it.
of John Scott, Lord Eldon (1751–1838)
H. Twiss *Public and Private Life of Eldon* (1844) vol. 3 (later
attributed to Lord **Melbourne**)

9 He talked shop like a tenth muse.
on **Gladstone**'s *Budget speeches*
G. W. E. Russell *Collections and Recollections* (1898) ch. 12

10 He tickles this age that can
Call Tullia's ape a marmasyte

And Leda's goose a swan.
'Fara diddle dyno', in Thomas Weelkes *Airs or Fantastic
Spirits* (1608); reprinted in N. Ault *Elizabethan Lyrics*
(1925)

11 Hierusalem, my happy home
When shall I come to thee?
When shall my sorrows have an end,
Thy joys when shall I see?
'Hierusalem' (*c.*1600 hymn)

12 Hip young gunslinger.
New Musical Express *advertisement for a journalist
in* 1976, *answered by Julie* **Burchill**
Julie Burchill *I Knew I Was Right* (1998)

13 How different, how very different from the home
life of our own dear Queen!
*comment overheard at a performance of Cleopatra by
Sarah Bernhardt*
Irvin S. Cobb *A Laugh a Day* (1924) (probably apocryphal)

14 Icham of Irlaunde
Ant of the holy londe of irlonde
Gode sir pray ich ye
for of saynte charite,
come ant daunce wyt me,
in irlaunde.
fourteenth century

15 The idea that the PM gets integrated advice is
nonsense. You could not see a more *unjoined*
system. To say they have imported the White
House to No. 10—Washington to Downing
Street—is absolutely right.
*a senior Whitehall figure on the Blair administration,
January 2000*
Peter Hennessy *The Prime Minister: the Office and its Holders
since 1945* (2000)

16 I don't like the family Stein!
There is Gert, there is Ep, there is Ein.
Gert's writings are punk,
Ep's statues are junk,
Nor can anyone understand Ein.
rhyme current in the US in the 1920s; R. Graves and A.
Hodge *The Long Weekend* (1940) ch. 12

17 I feel no pain dear mother now
But oh, I am so dry!
O take me to a brewery
And leave me there to die.
parody of 'The Collier's Dying Child'; see **Farmer** 315:5

18 If you really want to make a million . . . the
quickest way is to start your own religion.
previously attributed to L. Ron Hubbard (1911–86) in B.
Corydon and L. Ron Hubbard Jr. *L. Ron Hubbard* (1987),
but attribution subsequently rejected by L. Ron Hubbard
Jr., who also dissociated himself from this book

19 I'm armed with more than complete steel—The
justice of my quarrel.
Lust's Dominion (1657) act 4, sc. 3 (attributed to **Marlowe**,
though of doubtful authorship)

20   In Affectionate Remembrance
                        of
              ENGLISH CRICKET,
        Which Died at The Oval
                        on
            29th August, 1882.

Deeply lamented by a large circle of
sorrowing friends and acquaintances.
R. I. P.
N. B.—The body will be cremated and
the ashes taken to Australia.
following England's defeat by the Australians
in *Sporting Times* September 1882

1 I saw my lady weep,
And Sorrow proud to be exalted so
In those fair eyes where all perfections keep.
Her face was full of woe;
But such a woe, believe me, as wins more hearts,
Than Mirth can do with her enticing parts.
lute song set by John Dowland, in *New Oxford Book of
Sixteenth-Century Verse* (1991)

2 It became necessary to destroy the town to save it.
*statement by unidentified US Army Major, referring
to Ben Tre in Vietnam*
in Associated Press Report, *New York Times* 8 February
1968

3 It's taking your face in your hands.
*on the dangers of sitting for one's portrait to John
Singer* **Sargent**
W. Graham Robertson *Time Was* (1931) ch. 21

4 Jacques Brel is alive and well and living in Paris.
title of musical entertainment (1968–72) which triggered
numerous imitations

5 Just when we thought it was safe to go back in the
water, the sharks are circling again.
*unidentified British Cabinet Minister on the
forthcoming report of the European Convention*
in *Daily Telegraph* 11 June 2003 (electronic edition); see
Clark 224:21, **Taglines for films** 771:6

6 Liberty is always unfinished business.
title of 36th Annual Report of the American Civil Liberties
Union, 1 July 1955–30 June 1956

7 Like Caesar's wife, all things to all men.
impartiality, as described by a newly-elected mayor
G. W. E. Russell *Collections and Recollections* (1898) ch. 30;
see **Caesar** 185:3

8 Little Englanders.
term applied to anti-imperialists
in *Westminster Gazette* 1 August 1895; in *Pall Mall Gazette*
16 September 1884 the phrase 'believe in a little England'
occurs

9 Lizzie Borden took an axe
And gave her mother forty whacks;
When she saw what she had done
She gave her father forty-one!
*after the acquittal of Lizzie Borden, in June 1893,
from the charge of murdering her father and
stepmother at Fall River, Massachusetts on 4 August
1892*
popular rhyme

10 Lloyd George knew my father,
My father knew Lloyd George.
two-line comic song, sung to the tune of 'Onward,
Christian Soldiers' and possibly by Tommy Rhys Roberts
(1910–75)

11 London, thou art of townes *A per se.*
'London' (poem of unknown authorship, previously
attributed to William Dunbar, *c.*1465–*c.*1530)

12 London, thou art the flower of cities all!
Gemme of all joy, jasper of jocunditie.
'London' l. 16

13 Love me little, love me long,
Is the burden of my song.
'Love me little, love me long' (1569–70)

14 CHILD: Mamma, are Tories born wicked, or do they
grow wicked afterwards?
MOTHER: They are born wicked, and grow worse.
G. W. E. Russell *Collections and Recollections* (1898) ch. 10

15 Medicine for the soul.
*inscription on the library of Ramses II at Thebes
(c.1292–1225 BC)*
Diodorus Siculus *Bibliotheca Historica* 60–30 BC

16 The ministry of all the talents.
*name given ironically to William Grenville's coalition
of 1806, and also applied to later coalitions*
G. W. Cooke *The History of Party* (1837) vol. 3

17 Miss Buss and Miss Beale
Cupid's darts do not feel.
How different from us,
Miss Beale and Miss Buss.
*of the Headmistress of the North London Collegiate
School and the Principal of the Ladies' College,
Cheltenham*
rhyme, *c.*1884

18 Most Gracious Queen, we thee implore
To go away and sin no more,
But if that effort be too great,
To go away at any rate.
epigram on Caroline of Brunswick, wife of **George IV**
letter from Francis Burton to Lord Colchester, 15 November
1820; in *Diary and Correspondence of Lord Colchester* (1861)
vol. 3

19 Multiplication is vexation,
Division is as bad;
The Rule of Three doth puzzle me,
And Practice drives me mad.
Lean's Collectanea vol. 4 (1904) (possibly 16th-century)

20 My name is George Nathaniel Curzon,
I am a most superior person.
of Lord **Curzon**
The Masque of Balliol (*c.*1870), in W. G. Hiscock *The Balliol
Rhymes* (1939); see **Beeching** 62:16, **Spring-Rice** 753:8

21 The nature of God is a circle of which the centre is
everywhere and the circumference is nowhere.
said to have been traced to a lost treatise of Empedocles;
quoted in the *Roman de la Rose*, and by St Bonaventura in
Itinerarius Mentis in Deum ch. 5, closing line

22 The nearest thing to death in life
Is David Patrick Maxwell Fyfe,
Though underneath that gloomy shell
He does himself extremely well.
on Lord **Kilmuir**
E. Grierson *Confessions of a Country Magistrate* (1972), said
to have been current on the Northern circuit in the late
1930s

23 No beauty she doth miss,
When all her robes are on;
But beauty's self she is,

When all her robes are gone.
'Madrigal', in F. Davison (ed.) *Poetical Rhapsody* (1602)

1 The noise, my dear! And the people!
of the retreat from Dunkirk, May 1940; the saying has also been attributed to Ernest Thesiger of the First World War
Anthony Rhodes *Sword of Bone* (1942) ch. 22

2 No more Latin, no more French,
No more sitting on a hard board bench.
No more beetles in my tea
Making googly eyes at me;
No more spiders in my bath
Trying hard to make me laugh.
children's rhyme for the end of term
Iona and Peter Opie *Lore and Language of Schoolchildren* (1959) ch. 13

3 Not so much a programme, more a way of life!
title of BBC television series, 1964

4 O God, if there be a God, save my soul, if I have a soul!
prayer of a common soldier before the battle of Blenheim, 1704
in *Notes and Queries* vol. 173, no. 15 (9 October 1937); quoted in John Henry Newman *Apologia pro Vita Sua* (1864)

5 Oh, the comfort—the inexpressible comfort of feeling safe with a person, having neither to weigh thoughts, nor measure words, but pouring them all out, just as they are, chaff and grain together; knowing that a faithful hand will take and sift them—keep what is worth keeping— and with the breath of kindness blow the rest away.
19th century saying, often attributed to George **Eliot** or Dinah Mulock Craik (1826–87)

6 One Cartwright brought a Slave from Russia, and would scourge him, for which he was questioned: and it was resolved, That England was too pure an Air for Slaves to breathe in.
'In the 11th of Elizabeth' (17 November 1568–16 November 1569), in John Rushworth *Historical Collections* (1680–1722) vol. 2; see **Cowper** 247:27

7 On Waterloo's ensanguined plain
Full many a gallant man was slain,
But none, by sabre or by shot,
Fell half so flat as Walter Scott.
*on Sir Walter **Scott**'s poem 'The Field of Waterloo' (1815)*
U. Pope-Hennessy *The Laird of Abbotsford* (1932) ch. 9

8 Peace, order, and good government.
British North America Act 1867 sect. 91, introduction

9 A place within the meaning of the Act.
usually taken to be a reference to the Betting Act 1853, sect. 2, which banned off-course betting on horse-races

10 The plan is called 'Shock and Awe', and its goal is 'the psychological destruction of the enemy's will to fight'.
in *New Yorker* 10 February 2003; see **Ullman** 804:7

11 Please do not shoot the pianist. He is doing his best.
printed notice in a dancing saloon
Oscar Wilde *Impressions of America* 'Leadville' (c.1882–3)

12 Please to remember the Fifth of November,
Gunpowder Treason and Plot.
We know no reason why gunpowder treason
Should ever be forgot.
traditional rhyme on the Gunpowder Plot (1605)

13 Prudence is the other woman in Gordon's life.
*of Gordon **Brown***
unidentified aide, quoted in BBC News online (Budget Briefing), 20 March 1998

14 Psychological flaws.
*on which, according to an unnamed source, Gordon **Brown** needed to 'get a grip'*
in *Observer* 18 January 1998; attributed to Alastair **Campbell** by Bernard **Ingham** in minutes of the Parliamentary Select Committee on Public Administration, 2 June 1998, but denied by Campbell in evidence to the Committee, 23 June 1998

15 *Puella Rigensis ridebat*
Quam tigris in tergo vehebat;
Externa profecta,
Interna revecta,
Risusque cum tigre manebat.

There was a young lady of Riga
Who smiled as she rode on a tiger;
They returned from the ride
With the lady inside,
And the smile on the face of the tiger.
variants exist from 1924 or earlier

16 The [*or* A] quick brown fox jumps over the lazy dog.
used by keyboarders to ensure that all letters of the alphabet are functioning
R. Hunter Middleton's introduction to *The Quick Brown Fox* (1945) by Richard H. Templeton Jr.

17 The rabbit has a charming face:
Its private life is a disgrace.
I really dare not name to you
The awful things that rabbits do.
'The Rabbit', in *The Week-End Book* (1925)

18 Raise the stone, and there thou shalt find me, cleave the wood and there am I.
Oxyrhynchus Papyri, in B. P. Grenfell and A. S. Hunt (eds.) *Sayings of Our Lord* (1897) Logion 5, l. 23

19 Say it ain't so, Joe.
'Shoeless' Joe Jackson and seven other Chicago players were charged with being bribed to lose the 1919 World Baseball Series
plea said to have been made by a boy as Jackson emerged from the hearing, September 1920

20 Says Tweed to Till—
'What gars ye rin sae still?'
Says Till to Tweed—
'Though ye rin with speed
And I rin slaw,
For ae man that ye droon
I droon twa'.
'Two Rivers' (traditional rhyme)

21 Science finds, industry applies, man conforms.
subtitle of guidebook to 1933 Chicago World's Fair

22 See the happy moron,
He doesn't give a damn,

I wish I were a moron,
My God! perhaps I am!
in *Eugenics Review* July 1929

1 Seven wealthy towns contend for HOMER dead
Through which the living HOMER begged his bread.
epilogue to *Aesop at Tunbridge; or, a Few Selected Fables in Verse* By No Person of Quality (1698); see **Heywood** 388:1

2 Since first I saw your face, I resolved to honour
and renown ye;
If now I be disdained, I wish my heart had never
known ye.
What? I that loved and you that liked, shall we
begin to wrangle?
No, no, no, my heart is fast, and cannot
disentangle.
song set by Thomas Ford in *Music of Sundry Kinds* (1607)

3 So cryptic as to be almost meaningless. If there is a meaning, it is doubtless objectionable.
banning the film The Seashell and the Clergyman (*1929*)
The British Board of Film Censors; J. C. Robertson *Hidden Cinema* (1989) ch. 1

4 So long as there shall but one hundred of us
remain alive, we will never subject ourselves to
the dominion of the English. For it is not glory, it
is not riches, neither is it honour, but it is freedom
alone that we fight and contend for, which no
honest man will lose but with his life.
to the Pope, asserting the independence of Scotland
'Declaration of Arbroath', a letter sent by the Scottish Parliament, 6 April 1320

5 So much chewing gum for the eyes.
small boy's definition of certain television programmes
James Beasley Simpson *Best Quotes of '50, '55, '56* (1957)

6 Sumer is icumen in,
Lhude sing cuccu!
Groweth sed, and bloweth med,
And springth the wude nu.
'Cuckoo Song' (*c.*1250), sung annually at Reading Abbey gateway and first recorded by John Fornset, a monk of Reading Abbey; see **Pound** 608:12

7 The Sun himself cannot forget
His fellow traveller.
on Sir Francis **Drake**
Wit's Recreations (1640) epigram no. 146

8 There is a lady sweet and kind,
Was never face so pleased my mind;
I did but see her passing by,
And yet I love her till I die.
found on the reverse of leaf 53 of 'Popish Kingdome or reigne of Antichrist', in Latin verse by Thomas Naogeorgus, and Englished by Barnabe Googe; printed in 1570; sometimes attributed to Thomas Forde

9 There is so much good in the worst of us,
And so much bad in the best of us,
That it hardly becomes any of us
To talk about the rest of us.
attributed, among others, to Edward Wallis Hoch (1849–1945) on the grounds of it having appeared in his Kansas publication, the *Marion Record*, though in fact disclaimed by him ('behooves' sometimes substituted for 'becomes')

10 There shall be a Scottish parliament.
first clause of the Scotland Act, 1998; see **Dewar** 266:9

11 This fictional account of the day-by-day life of an
English gamekeeper is still of considerable interest
to outdoor-minded readers, as it contains many
passages on pheasant raising, the apprehending of
poachers, ways to control vermin, and other
chores and duties of the professional gamekeeper.
Unfortunately one is obliged to wade through
many pages of extraneous material in order to
discover and savour these sidelights on the
management of a Midlands shooting estate, and in
this reviewer's opinion this book cannot take the
place of J. R. Miller's *Practical Gamekeeping*.
review of D. H. Lawrence *Lady Chatterley's Lover*; attributed to *Field and Stream, c.*1928

12 This is a rotten argument, but it should be good
enough for their lordships on a hot summer
afternoon.
annotation to a ministerial brief, said to have been read out inadvertently in the House of Lords
Lord Home *The Way the Wind Blows* (1976)

13 Though I yield to no one in my admiration for Mr
Coolidge, I do wish he did not look as if he had
been weaned on a pickle.
anonymous remark, in Alice Roosevelt Longworth *Crowded Hours* (1933) ch. 21

14 Too small to live in and too large to hang on a
watch-chain.
Chiswick House described by a guest
Cecil Roberts *And so to Bath* (1940) ch. 4

15 To secure for the workers by hand or by brain the
full fruits of their industry and the most equitable
distribution thereof that may be possible upon the
basis of the common ownership of the means of
production, distribution, and exchange.
Clause Four of the Labour Party's Constitution of 1918 (revised 1929); the commitment to common ownership of services was largely removed in 1995; see **Anonymous** 15:13

16 Weep you no more, sad fountains;
What need you flow so fast?
lute song (1603) set to music by John Dowland, in *New Oxford Book of Sixteenth-Century Verse* (1991)

17 We hold these truths to be self-evident, that all
men are created equal, that they are endowed by
their Creator with certain unalienable rights, that
among these are life, liberty and the pursuit of
happiness.
The American Declaration of Independence, 4 July 1776; see **Jefferson** 419:10

18 We want eight, and we won't wait.
on the construction of Dreadnoughts
George Wyndham, speech in *The Times* 29 March 1909

19 Western wind, when will thou blow,
The small rain down can rain?
Christ, if my love were in my arms
And I in my bed again!
'Western Wind' (published 1790) in *New Oxford Book of Sixteenth-Century Verse* (1991)

20 When I was a little boy, I had but a little wit,
'Tis a long time ago, and I have no more yet;

Nor ever ever shall, until that I die,
For the longer I live the more fool am I.
Wit and Mirth, an Antidote against Melancholy (1684 ed.)

1 Where is the man who has the power and skill
To stem the torrent of a woman's will?
For if she will, she will, you may depend on't;
And if she won't, she won't; so there's an end on't.
inscription on the pillar erected on the mount in the Dane John Field, Canterbury, in *Examiner* 31 May 1829

2 Whilst Adam slept, Eve from his side arose:
Strange his first sleep should be his last repose.
'The Consequence'

3 The whole is more than the sum of the parts.
traditional saying, probably deriving from Aristotle; see **Aristotle** 25:12

4 With a heart of furious fancies,
Whereof I am commander;
With a burning spear,
And a horse of air,
To the wilderness I wander.
'Tom o' Bedlam'

5 Would you like to sin
With Elinor Glyn
On a tigerskin?
Or would you prefer
To err
With her
On some other fur?
1907 rhyme, in A. Glyn *Elinor Glyn* (1955) bk. 2, sect. 30

6 Yet, if his majesty our sovereign lord
Should of his own accord
Friendly himself invite,
And say 'I'll be your guest tomorrow night',
How should we stir ourselves, call and command
All hands to work! . . .
But at the coming of the King of Heaven
All's set at six and seven:
We wallow in our sin.
Christ cannot find a chamber in the inn.
We entertain Him always like a stranger,
And as at first still lodge Him in the manger.
from Christ Church MS

7 You should make a point of trying every experience once, excepting incest and folk-dancing.
Arnold Bax (1883–1953), quoting 'a sympathetic Scot' in *Farewell My Youth* (1943)

8 You were a premature anti-Fascist.
interviewer for Yale Classics Department in 1946, on hearing that the young Bernard Knox had fought with the International Brigade in the Spanish Civil War
Bernard Knox 'Premature Anti-Fascist' (Bill Susman Lecture Series, New York, 1998)

FRENCH

9 *Ça ira.*
Things will work out.
refrain of 'Carillon national', popular song of the French Revolution (*c.*July 1790), translated by William Doyle; the phrase is believed to originate with Benjamin **Franklin**, who may have uttered it in 1776 when asked for news of the American Revolution

10 *Cet animal est très méchant,*
Quand on l'attaque il se défend.
This animal is very bad; when attacked it defends itself.
'La Ménagerie' (1868 song) by 'Théodore P. K.'

11 *Chevalier sans peur et sans reproche.*
Fearless, blameless knight.
description in contemporary chronicles of Pierre Bayard (1476–1524)

12 *Il y avait un jeune homme de Dijon,*
Qui n'avait que peu de religion.
Il dit: 'Quant à moi,
Je déteste tous les trois,
Le Père, et le Fils, et le Pigeon.'
There was a young man of Dijon,
Who had only a little religion,
He said: 'As for me,
I detest all the three,
The Father, the Son, and the Pigeon.'
The Norman Douglas Limerick Book (1969, privately printed, 1928, as *Some Limericks*) introduction

13 RIDDLE: *Je suis le capitaine de vingt-quatre soldats, et sans moi Paris serait pris?*
ANSWER: *A.*
RIDDLE: I am the captain of twenty-four soldiers, and without me Paris would be taken?
ANSWER: A [i.e. 'Paris' minus 'a' = *pris* taken].
the saying ' With twenty-six lead soldiers [the characters of the alphabet set up for printing] *I can conquer the world' may derive from this riddle, but probably arose independently*
Hugh Rowley *Puniana: or, Thoughts wise and otherwise* (1867)

14 *Laissez-nous-faire.*
Allow us to do [it].
remark dating from *c.*1664, in *Journal Oeconomique* Paris, April 1751: 'Monsieur Colbert assembled several deputies of commerce at his house to ask what could be done for commerce; the most rational and the least flattering among them answered him in one word: "Laissez-nous-faire"'; see **Argenson** 24:19, **Quesnay** 639:6

15 *L'amour est aveugle; l'amitié ferme les yeux.*
Love is blind; friendship closes its eyes.
proverbial saying; see **Proverbs** 625:43

16 *Le monde est plein de fous, et qui n'en veut pas voir*
Doit se tenir tout seul, et casser son miroir.
The world is full of fools, and he who would see none should live alone and smash his mirror.
adaptation from an original form attributed to Claude Le Petit (1640–65) in *Discours satiriques* (1686)

17 *L'ordre règne à Varsovie.*
Order reigns in Warsaw.
after the brutal suppression of an uprising, the newspaper *Moniteur* reported, 16 September 1831, '*L'ordre et la tranquillité sont entièrement rétablis dans la capitale* [Order and calm are completely restored in the capital]'; on the same day Count Sebastiani, minister of foreign affairs, declared: '*La tranquillité règne à Varsovie* [Peace reigns in Warsaw]'

18 *Nous n'irons plus aux bois, les lauriers sont coupés.*
We'll to the woods no more,
The laurels all are cut.
old nursery rhyme, quoted by Théodore de Banville in *Les*

Cariatides, les stalactites (1842–6); translated by A. E. Housman in *Last Poems* (1922) introductory

1 *Revenons à ces moutons.*

Let us get back to these sheep [i.e. 'Let us get back to the subject'].

Maistre Pierre Pathelin l. 1191 (often quoted as '*Retournons à nos moutons* [Let us return to our sheep]')

2 *Si le Roi m'avait donné,*
Paris, sa grand'ville,
Et qu'il me fallût quitter
L'amour de ma mie,
Je dirais au roi Henri:
'Reprenez votre Paris:
J'aime mieux ma mie, au gué,
J'aime mieux ma mie.'

If the king had given me Paris, his great city, and if I were required to give up my darling's love, I would say to King Henry: 'Take your Paris back; I prefer my darling, by the ford, I prefer my darling.'

popular song, attributed to Antoine de Navarre (1518–62); quoted in this form by Molière in *Le Misanthrope* act 1, sc. 2

3 *Toujours perdrix!*

Always partridge!

*attributed to a confessor of **Henri IV**, who rebuked the king for his sexual liaisons and thereafter was served nothing but partridge*

G. Büchmann *Geflügelte Worte* (1874 ed.)

4 *Tout passe, tout casse, tout lasse.*

Everything passes, everything perishes, everything palls.

Charles Cahier *Quelques six mille proverbes* (1856) no. 1718

GERMAN

5 *Arbeit macht frei.*

Work liberates.

words inscribed on the gates of Dachau concentration camp, 1933, and subsequently on those of Auschwitz

6 *Jedem das Seine.*

To each his own.

often quoted as 'Everyone gets what he deserves'

inscription on the gate of Buchenwald concentration camp, *c.*1937; see **Bold** 126:3

7 *Kommt der Krieg ins Land*
Gibt's Lügen wie Sand.

When war enters a country
It produces lies like sand.

epigraph to Arthur Ponsonby *Falsehood in Wartime* (1928)

GREEK

8 Let no one enter who does not know geometry [mathematics].

*inscription on **Plato**'s door, probably at the Academy at Athens*

Elias Philosophus *In Aristotelis Categorias Commentaria*; in A. Busse (ed.) *Commentaria in Aristotelem Graeca* (1900) vol. 18, pt. 1

9 Nothing in excess.

inscribed on the temple of Apollo at Delphi

variously ascribed to the Seven Wise Men

10 The very best thing for a person is health,
Second good looks and third honest wealth,

the fourth is to be in the prime of your life
With people around you who cause you no strife.

drinking song, quoted in Plato *Gorgias* 451e

11 Whenever God prepares evil for a man, He first damages his mind, with which he deliberates.

scholiastic annotation to Sophocles's *Antigone* l. 622; see **Proverbs** 635:3

LATIN

12 *Adeste, fideles,*
laeti triumphantes;
venite, venite in Bethlehem;
natum videte regem angelorum . . .
venite, adoremus Dominum.

O come, all ye faithful,
Joyful and triumphant,
O come ye, O come ye to Bethlehem;
Come and behold him,
Born the King of angels:
O come, let us adore him . . . Christ the Lord!

French or German hymn (*c.*1743) in *Murray's Hymnal* (1852); translation based on that of F. Oakeley (1841)

13 *Ave Caesar, morituri te salutant.*

Hail Caesar, those who are about to die salute you.

gladiators saluting the Roman Emperor

Suetonius *Lives of the Caesars* 'Claudius' ch. 21

14 *Ave verum corpus,*
natum ex Maria Virgine.

Hail the true body, born of the Virgin Mary.

Eucharistic hymn, probably dating from the 14th century

15 *Caveant consules ne quid res publica detrimenti capiat.*

Let the consuls see to it that no harm come to the state.

senatorial 'ultimate decree' in the Roman Republic; see Cicero *Pro Milone* ch. 70

16 *Cras amet qui nunquam amavit, quique amavit cras amet!*

Let those love now, who never loved before:
Let those who always loved, now love the more.

Pervigilium Veneris (translated by Thomas Parnell, 1722)

17 *Gaudeamus igitur,*
Juvenes dum sumus
Post jucundam juventutem,
Post molestam senectutem,
Nos habebit humus.

Let us then rejoice,
While we are young.
After the pleasures of youth
And the burdens of old age
Earth will hold us.

medieval students' song, traced to 1267, but revised in the 18th century

18 *Meum est propositum*
In taberna mori,
Ut sint vina proxima
Morientis ori.
Tunc cantabunt laetius
Angelorum chori:
'Sit Deus propitius
Huic potatori!'

I desire to end my days in a tavern drinking,

May some Christian hold for me the glass when I
   am shrinking;
That the Cherubim may cry, when they see me
   sinking,
'God be merciful to a soul of this gentleman's way
   of thinking.'
   The Arch-poet (fl. 1159–67) 'Estuans intrinsecus ira
   vehementi' (translated by Leigh Hunt)

1 *Omnia dispono solus meritos[que] corono. Quos scelus
exercet me judice poena coercet.*

I alone dispose of all things and crown the just.
Those who follow crime I judge and punish.
around the mandorla enclosing the figure of Christ
   inscription on the western portal of St-Lazare, Autun;
   carved by Gislebertus, c.1130

2   *Pereat, qui crastina curat!*
Mors aurem vellens 'vivite' ait, 'venio.'

Away with him who heeds the morrow! Death,
plucking the ear, cries: 'Live; I come!'
   Copa l. 37, formerly attributed to **Virgil**, (translated by H.
   Rushton Fairclough)

3 *Quidquid agis, prudenter agas, et respice finem.*

Whatever you do, do cautiously, and look to the
end.
   Gesta Romanorum no. 103

4 *Sic transit gloria mundi.*

Thus passes the glory of the world.
*said during the coronation of a new Pope, while flax is
burned to represent the transitoriness of earthly glory*
   used at the coronation of Alexander V in Pisa, 7 July 1409,
   but earlier in origin; see **Thomas à Kempis** 788:3

5 *Vox et praeterea nihil.*

A voice and nothing more.
describing a nightingale
   Plutarch *Moralia* sect. 233a, no. 15

OLD ENGLISH

6 *Hige sceal þe heardra, heorte þe cenre,*
mod sceal þe mare, þe ure mægen lytlað.

Thought shall be the harder, heart the keener,
courage the greater, as our might lessens.
   The Battle of Maldon (translated by R. K. Gordon, 1926)

7 *Hwæt! wē Gārdena in gēardagum*
þēodcyninga þrym gefrūnon,
hū ðā æþelingas ellen fremedon.

Listen!
             The fame of Danish kings
in days gone by, the daring feats
worked by those heroes are well known to us.
   Beowulf, translated by Kevin Crossley-Holland

8 *þæs oferēode, þisses swā mæg.*

That passed over, so may this.
   Deor

9 King Harold was killed and Earl Leofwine his
brother and Earl Gyrth his brother . . . and the
French remained masters of the field.
   Anglo-Saxon Chronicle for 1066

10 There was no single hide nor a yard of land nor
indeed was one ox or one cow or one pig left out,
that was not put down in his record.
*of William the Conqueror's commissioning of the
Domesday Book*
   Anglo-Saxon Chronicle for 1087

11 Men said openly that Christ slept and His saints.
*of England during the civil war between Stephen and
Matilda*
   Anglo-Saxon Chronicle for 1137

OLD NORSE

12 *Deyr fé, deyja frændr,*
deyr sjalfr et sama;
en orðstirr deyr aldrigi
hveims sér góðar getr.

Cattle die, kinsmen die,
the self must also die;
but glory never dies,
for the man who is able to achieve it.
   Hávamál ('Sayings of the High One'), c.10th century

13 The morning work has been unequal; I have spun
twelve ells of yarn, and you have killed Kjartan.
   Laxdæla Saga (c.12 century); the words of Gudrun

14 I did the worst to him I loved the most.
   Laxdæla Saga (c.12 century); the words of Gudrun

Jean Anouilh 1910–87
French dramatist
see also **Hellman** 380:11

15 *Dieu est avec tout le monde . . . Et, en fin de compte, il
est toujours avec ceux qui ont beaucoup d'argent et de
grosses armées.*

God is on everyone's side . . . And, in the last
analysis, he is on the side of those with plenty of
money and large armies.
   L'Alouette [The Lark] (1953); see **Bussy-Rabutin** 175:9,
   Voltaire 816:10

16 *Maintenant le ressort est bandé. Cela n'a plus qu'à se
dérouler tout seul. C'est cela qui est commode dans la
tragédie. On donne le petit coup de pouce pour que cela
démarre.*

The spring is wound up tight. It will uncoil of
itself. That is what is so convenient in tragedy.
The least little turn of the wrist will do the job.
Anything will set it going.
   Antigone (1944, translated by Lewis Galantiere, 1957)

17 *C'est propre, la tragédie. C'est reposant, c'est sûr.*
Tragedy is clean, it is restful, it is flawless.
   Antigone (1944, translated by Lewis Galantiere, 1957)

18 *Il y a l'amour bien sûr. Et puis il y a la vie, son
ennemie.*
There is love of course. And then there's life, its
enemy.
   Ardèle (1949)

19 *Vous savez bien que l'amour, c'est avant tout le don de
soi!*
You know very well that love is, above all, the gift
of oneself!
   Ardèle (1949)

20 *Mourir, mourir . . . Mourir ce n'est rien. Commence
donc par vivre. C'est moins drôle et c'est plus long.*

Dying is nothing. So start by living. It's less fun
and it lasts longer.
Roméo et Jeannette (1946) act 3

1 *Il y a aura toujours un chien perdu quelquepart qui
m'empêchera d'être heureux.*

There will always be a lost dog somewhere that
will prevent me from being happy.
La Sauvage [The Restless Heart] (1938) act 3

Christopher Anstey 1724–1805
English writer

2 If ever I ate a good supper at night,
I dreamed of the devil, and waked in a fright.
The New Bath Guide (1766) Letter 4 'A Consultation of the
Physicians'

3 You may go to Carlisle's, and to Almack's too;
And I'll give you my head if you find such a host,
For coffee, tea, chocolate, butter, and toast:
How he welcomes at once all the world and his
wife,
And how civil to folk he ne'er saw in his life.
The New Bath Guide (1766) Letter 13 'A Public Breakfast'

F. Anstey (Thomas Anstey Guthrie)
1856–1934
English writer

4 Drastic measures is Latin for a whopping.
Vice Versa (1882) ch. 7

Susan Brownell Anthony 1820–1906
American feminist and political activist

5 Join the union, girls, and together say, 'Equal Pay
for Equal Work!'
in *The Revolution* 8 October 1869

6 Marriage, to women as to men, must be a luxury,
not a necessity; an incident of life, not all of it.
speech, 1875

Minna Antrim 1861–1950
American writer

7 A fool bolts pleasure, then complains of moral
indigestion.
Naked Truth and Veiled Allusions (1902)

Apelles
Greek painter of the 4th century BC

8 *Nulla dies sine linea.*

Not a day without a line.
proverbial summary of his philosophy
Pliny the Elder *Historia Naturalis* bk. 35, sect. 36

Guillaume Apollinaire 1880–1918
French poet
on Apollinaire: see **Logue** 489:12

9 *Les souvenirs sont cors de chasse
Dont meurt le bruit parmi le vent.*

Memories are hunting horns

Whose sound dies on the wind.
'Cors de Chasse' (1912)

10 *Sous le pont Mirabeau coule la Seine.
Et nos amours, faut-il qu'il m'en souvienne?
La joie venait toujours après la peine.
Vienne la nuit, sonne l'heure,
Les jours s'en vont, je demeure.*

Under Mirabeau Bridge flows the Seine.
And our loves, must I remember them?
Joy always came after pain.
Let night come, ring out the hour,
The days go by, I remain.
'Le Pont Mirabeau' (1912)

11 When man wanted to make a machine that would
walk he created the wheel, which does not
resemble a leg.
Les Mamelles de Tirésias (1918)

12 *On ne peut pas porter partout le cadavre de son père.*

One can't carry one's father's corpse about
everywhere.
Les peintres cubistes (1965) 'Méditations esthétiques: Sur la
peinture' pt. 1

Edward Appleton 1892–1965
English physicist

13 I do not mind what language an opera is sung in
so long as it is a language I don't understand.
in *Observer* 28 August 1955

Thomas Gold Appleton 1812–84
American epigrammatist

14 Good Americans, when they die, go to Paris.
Oliver Wendell Holmes *The Autocrat of the Breakfast Table*
(1858) ch. 6; see **Proverbs** 621:4, **Wilde** 836:20

15 A Boston man is the east wind made flesh.
attributed

Arabian Nights Entertainments, or the Thousand and one Nights
A collection of stories written in Arabic

16 Who will change old lamps for new ones? . . . new
lamps for old ones?
'The History of Aladdin'

17 Open Sesame!
'The History of Ali Baba'

William Arabin 1773–1841
English judge

18 If ever there was a case of clearer evidence than
this of persons acting together, this case is that
case.
H. B. Churchill *Arabiniana* (1843)

19 Prisoner, God has given you good abilities, instead
of which you go about the country stealing ducks.
also attributed to a Revd Mr Alderson, in Frederick Pollock
Essays in the Law (1922)

1 They will steal the very teeth out of your mouth as you walk through the streets. *I know it from experience.*
on the citizens of Uxbridge
Sir W. Ballantine *Some Experiences of a Barrister's Life* (1882) vol. 1, ch. 6

Yasser Arafat 1929–
Palestinian statesman, President since 1996

2 Palestine is the cement that holds the Arab world together, or it is the explosive that blows it apart.
in *Time* 11 November 1974

Louis Aragon 1897–1982
French poet, essayist, and novelist

3 *Ô mois des floraisons mois des métamorphoses*
Mai qui fut sans nuage et Juin poignardé
Je n'oublierai jamais les lilas ni les roses
Ni ceux que le printemps dans ses plis a gardé.

O month of flowerings, month of metamorphoses,
May without cloud and June that was stabbed,
I shall never forget the lilac and the roses
Nor those whom spring has kept in its folds.
'Les lilas et les roses' (1940)

Diane Arbus 1923–71
American photographer

4 A photograph is a secret about a secret. The more it tells you the less you know.
Patricia Bosworth *Diane Arbus: a Biography* (1985)

John Arbuthnot 1667–1735
Scottish physician and pamphleteer

5 He [the writer] warns the heads of parties against believing their own lies.
The Art of Political Lying (1712)

6 Law is a bottomless pit.
The History of John Bull (1712) title of first pamphlet

7 Curle (who is one of the new terrors of Death) has been writing letters to every body for memoirs of his life.
letter to Jonathan Swift, 13 January 1733, in H. Williams (ed.) *The Correspondence of Jonathan Swift* vol. 4 (1965); see **Lyndhurst** 497:6, **Wetherell** 830:21

Archilochus
Greek poet of the 7th century BC

8 Not for me a tall and dandy captain with a shaven chin,
flaunting all affectedly his dainty lovelocks as he struts;
I'd prefer one short and bandy-legged, with a heart within
stout and good, and firmly planted on his feet, and full of guts.
E. Diehl (ed.) *Anthologia Lyrica Graeca* (3rd ed., 1949–52) vol. 1, no. 60, translated by A. R. Burn

9 The fox knows many things—the hedgehog one *big* one.
E. Diehl (ed.) *Anthologia Lyrica Graeca* (3rd ed., 1949–52) vol. 1, no. 103; see **Berlin** 70:3

Archimedes c.287–212 BC
Greek mathematician and inventor

10 Eureka! [I've got it!]
Vitruvius Pollio *De Architectura* bk. 9, preface, sect. 10

11 Give me but one firm spot on which to stand, and I will move the earth.
on the action of a lever
Pappus *Synagoge* bk. 8, proposition 10, sect. 11

Elizabeth Arden c.1880–1966
Canadian-born American businesswoman
*on Arden: see **Rubinstein** 658:4*

12 Nothing that costs only a dollar is worth having.
attributed; in *Fortune* October 1973

Robert Ardrey 1908–80
American dramatist and evolutionist

13 Not in innocence, and not in Asia, was mankind born.
African Genesis (1961)

Hannah Arendt 1906–75
American political philosopher

14 It was as though in those last minutes he was summing up the lessons that this long course in human wickedness had taught us—the lesson of the fearsome, word-and-thought-defying *banality of evil.*
of Adolf Eichmann, responsible for the administration of the Nazi concentration camps
Eichmann in Jerusalem (1963) ch. 15

15 Only crime and the criminal, it is true, confront us with the perplexity of radical evil; but only the hypocrite is really rotten to the core.
On Revolution (1963) ch. 2, pt. 5

16 The most radical revolutionary will become a conservative on the day after the revolution.
in *New Yorker* 12 September 1970

17 Under conditions of tyranny it is far easier to act than to think.
W. H. Auden *A Certain World* (1970)

Comte d'Argenson (Marc Pierre de Voyer d'Argenson) 1696–1764
French statesman; founder of the École Militaire, Paris

18 DESFONTAINES: I must live.
D'ARGENSON: I do not see the necessity.
on Desfontaines having produced a pamphlet satirizing D'Argenson, his benefactor
Voltaire *Alzire* (1736) 'Discours Préliminaire' footnote, in *Oeuvres Complètes Théâtre* (1877) vol. 2

Marquis d'Argenson (René Louis de Voyer d'Argenson) 1694–1757
French politician and political essayist

19 *Laisser-faire.*
No interference.
Mémoires et Journal Inédit du Marquis d'Argenson (1858 ed.) vol. 5; see **Anonymous** 20:14, **Quesnay** 639:6

Ludovico Ariosto 1474–1533
Italian poet and dramatist

1 *Natura il fece, e poi roppe la stampa.*
  Nature made him, and then broke the mould.
  Orlando Furioso (1532) canto 10, st. 84

Aristophanes c.450–c.385 BC
Greek comic dramatist

2 How about 'Cloudcuckooland'?
  naming the capital city of the Birds
  The Birds (414 BC) l. 819

3 This Second Logic then, I mean the Worse one,
  They teach to talk unjustly, and—prevail.
  The Clouds (423 BC) l. 113; see **Milton** 531:30

4 The old are in a second childhood.
  The Clouds (423 BC) l. 1417

5 But he was contented there, is contented here.
  on **Sophocles** (*there* = *on earth and* here = *in Hades*)
  The Frogs (405 BC) l. 82

6 Brekekekex koax koax.
  cry of the Frogs
  The Frogs (405 BC) l. 209 and *passim*

7 You have all the characteristics of a popular
  politician: a horrible voice, bad breeding and a
  vulgar manner.
  The Knights (424 BC) l. 217

8 Under every stone lurks a politician.
  *playing on the Greek proverb 'Under every stone lurks
  a scorpion'*
  Thesmophoriazusae l. 530

Aristotle 384–322 BC
Greek philosopher
on Aristotle: see **Dante** 255:17; *see also* **Ascham** 31:9, **Last
words** 472:9

9 Now, we may say that the most important
  subjects about which all men deliberate and
  deliberative orators harangue, are five in number,
  to wit: ways and means, war and peace, the
  defence of the country, imports and exports,
  legislation.
  The Art of Rhetoric bk. 1, 1359b 19–23

10 All use metaphors in conversation, as well as
   proper and appropriate words.
   The Art of Rhetoric bk. 3, 1404b 2

11 All men by nature desire knowledge.
   Metaphysics bk. 1, ch. 1, 980a 22

12 Whenever anything which has several parts is
   such that the whole is something over and above
   its parts, and not just the sum of them all, like a
   heap, then it always has some cause.
   Metaphysics 1045a 10f; see **Anonymous** 20:3

13 Every art and every investigation, and likewise
   every practical pursuit or undertaking, seems to
   aim at some good: hence it has been well said that
   the Good is That at which all things aim.
   Nicomachean Ethics bk. 1, 1094a 1–3

14 Therefore, the good of man must be the end [i.e.
   objective] of the science of politics.
   Nicomachean Ethics bk. 1, 1094b 6–7

15 The Good of man is the active exercise of his soul's
   faculties in conformity with excellence or virtue
   . . . Moreover this activity must occupy a complete
   lifetime; for one swallow does not make spring,
   nor does one fine day; and similarly one day or a
   brief period of happiness does not make a man
   supremely blessed and happy.
   Nicomachean Ethics bk. 1, 1098a 16–20

16 Now some think that all justice is of this sort,
   because that which is by nature is unchangeable
   and has everywhere the same force (as fire burns
   both here and in Persia), while they see change in
   the things recognized as just.
   Nicomachean Ethics bk. 5, 1134b 26

17 We make war that we may live in peace.
   Nicomachean Ethics bk. 10, 1177b 5–6 (translated by M.
   Ostwald); see **Vegetius** 808:9

18 Politicians also have no leisure, because they are
   always aiming at something beyond political life
   itself, power and glory, or happiness.
   Nicomachean Ethics bk. 10, 1177b 12–14

19 Even if our contact with eternal beings is slight,
   none the less because of its surpassing value this
   knowledge is a greater pleasure than our
   knowledge of everything around us.
   On the Parts of Animals bk. 1, ch. 5, 644b 31; see **Thomas
   Aquinas** 789:3

20 Tragedy is thus an imitation of an action that is
   worth serious attention, complete in itself and of
   some amplitude . . . by means of pity and fear
   bringing about the purgation of such emotions.
   Poetics ch. 6, 1449b 24–8

21 A whole is that which has a beginning, a middle,
   and an end.
   Poetics ch. 7, 1450b 26–7

22 So poetry is something more philosophical and
   more worthy of serious attention than history, for
   while poetry is concerned with universal truth,
   history treats of particular facts . . . The particular
   facts of the historian are what, say, Alcibiades did,
   or what happened to him.
   Poetics ch. 9, 1451b 5–6

23 Probable impossibilities are to be preferred to
   improbable possibilities.
   Poetics ch. 24, 1460a 26–7; see **Agathon** 6:25

24 Sophocles said that he drew men as they ought to
   be, whereas Euripides drew them as they are.
   Poetics ch. 25, 1460b 33–4

25 Man is by nature a political animal.
   *the literal meaning of the Greek is 'an animal which
   lives in cities'*
   Politics bk. 1, 1253a 2–3

26 He who is unable to live in society, or who has no
   need because he is sufficient for himself, must be
   either a beast or a god.
   Politics bk. 1, 1253a 27–9; see **Bacon** 44:13

1 Nature does nothing without purpose or uselessly.
Politics bk. 1, 1256b 20–21

2 For if liberty and equality, as is thought by some, are chiefly to be found in democracy, they will be best attained when all persons alike share in the government to the utmost.
Politics bk. 4, 1291b 35

3 Where some people are very wealthy and others have nothing, the result will be either extreme democracy or absolute oligarchy, or despotism will come from either of those excesses.
Politics bk. 4, 1296a 1–3

4 No tyrant need fear till men begin to feel confident in each other.
Politics bk. 5, 1314a

5 Whereas then a rattle is a suitable occupation for infant children, education serves as a rattle for young people when older.
Politics bk. 8, 1340b 29–31

6 *Amicus Plato, sed magis amica veritas.*
Plato is dear to me, but dearer still is truth.
Latin translation of a Greek original ascribed to Aristotle

7 When he was asked 'What is a friend?' he said 'One soul inhabiting two bodies.'
Diogenes Laertius *Lives of Philosophers* bk. 5, sect. 20

8 This realization, according to [Aristotle], is twofold. Either it is potential, as that of Hermes in the wax, provided the wax be adapted to receive the proper mouldings, or as that of the statue implicit in the bronze; or again it is determinate, which is the case with the completed figure of Hermes or the finished statue.
Diogenes Laertius *Lives of the Philosophers* bk. 5, sect. 33

Lewis Addison Armistead 1817–63
American army officer

9 Give them the cold steel, boys!
during the American Civil War, 1863
attributed

Harry Armstrong 1879–1951
American songwriter

10 There's an old mill by the stream, Nellie Dean,
Where we used to sit and dream, Nellie Dean.
And the waters as they flow
Seem to murmur sweet and low,
'You're my heart's desire; I love you, Nellie Dean.'
'Nellie Dean' (1905 song)

John Armstrong 1709–79
Scottish poet and physician

11   Much had he read,
Much more had seen; he studied from the life,
And in th'original perused mankind.
The Art of Preserving Health (1744) bk. 4, l. 231

12 'Tis not for mortals always to be blest.
The Art of Preserving Health (1744) bk. 4, l. 260

13 'Tis not too late tomorrow to be brave.
The Art of Preserving Health (1744) bk. 4, l. 460

Louis Armstrong 1901–71
American singer and jazz musician

14 If you still have to ask . . . shame on you.
when asked what jazz is
Max Jones et al. *Salute to Satchmo* (1970); see **Misquotations** 538:7

15 All music is folk music, I ain't never heard no horse sing a song.
in *New York Times* 7 July 1971

Neil Armstrong 1930–
American astronaut; first man on the moon

16 Houston, Tranquillity Base here. The Eagle has landed.
radio message as the lunar module touched down
in *The Times* 21 July 1969

17 That's one small step for a man, one giant leap for mankind.
landing on the moon
in *New York Times* 21 July 1969; interference in the transmission obliterated 'a'

Robert Armstrong 1927–
British civil servant; Head of the Civil Service, 1981–7

18 It contains a misleading impression, not a lie. It was being economical with the truth.
during the 'Spycatcher' trial in New South Wales
in *Daily Telegraph* 19 November 1986; see **Burke** 168:14, **Clark** 224:22, **Twain** 803:8

William Armstrong 1915–80
British civil servant, Head of the Civil Service 1968–74

19 The business of the Civil Service is the orderly management of decline.
in 1973: Peter Hennessy *Whitehall* (1990)

Arnald-Amaury d. 1225
French abbot of Citeaux

20 Kill them all; God will recognize his own.
when asked how the true Catholics could be distinguished from the heretics at the massacre of Béziers, 1209
Jonathan Sumption *The Albigensian Crusade* (1978)

Edwin Arnold 1832–1904
English poet and journalist

21 Nor ever once ashamed
So we be named
Press-men; Slaves of the Lamp; Servants of Light.
'The Tenth Muse' (1895) st. 18

George Arnold 1834–65
American humorist

22 The living need charity more than the dead.
'The Jolly Old Pedagogue' (1866)

Matthew Arnold 1822–88

English poet and essayist; son of Thomas **Arnold**

1 And we forget because we must
And not because we will.
'Absence' (1852)

2 A bolt is shot back somewhere in our breast,
And a lost pulse of feeling stirs again.
The eye sinks inward, and the heart lies plain,
And what we mean, we say, and what we would,
we know.
'The Buried Life' (1852) l. 84

3 The Sea of Faith
Was once, too, at the full, and round earth's shore
Lay like the folds of a bright girdle furled.
But now I only hear
Its melancholy, long, withdrawing roar,
Retreating, to the breath
Of the night-wind, down the vast edges drear
And naked shingles of the world.
'Dover Beach' (1867) l. 21

4 Ah, love, let us be true
To one another!
'Dover Beach' (1867) l. 29

5 And we are here as on a darkling plain
Swept with confused alarms of struggle and flight,
Where ignorant armies clash by night.
'Dover Beach' (1867) l. 35

6 Be neither saint nor sophist-led, but be a man.
Empedocles on Etna (1852) act 1, sc. 2, l. 136

7 Is it so small a thing
To have enjoyed the sun,
To have lived light in the spring,
To have loved, to have thought, to have done.
Empedocles on Etna (1852) act 1, sc. 2, l. 397

8 Because thou must not dream, thou needst not
then despair!
Empedocles on Etna (1852) act 1, sc. 2, l. 426

9 Come to me in my dreams, and then
By day I shall be well again!
For then the night will more than pay
The hopeless longing of the day.
'Faded Leaves' (1855) no. 5 (first published, 1852, as
'Longing')

10 Come, dear children, let us away;
Down and away below!
'The Forsaken Merman' (1849) l. 1

11 Now the great winds shorewards blow;
Now the salt tides seawards flow;
Now the wild white horses play,
Champ and chafe and toss in the spray.
'The Forsaken Merman' (1849) l. 4

12 Sand-strewn caverns, cool and deep,
Where the winds are all asleep;
Where the spent lights quiver and gleam;
Where the salt weed sways in the stream;
'The Forsaken Merman' (1849) l. 35

13 Where great whales come sailing by,
Sail and sail, with unshut eye,
Round the world for ever and aye.
'The Forsaken Merman' (1849) l. 43

14 Creep into thy narrow bed,
Creep, and let no more be said!
Vain thy onset! all stands fast.
Thou thyself must break at last.

Let the long contention cease!
Geese are swans, and swans are geese.
Let them have it how they will!
Thou art tired; best be still.
'The Last Word' (1867)

15 Calm soul of all things! make it mine
To feel, amid the city's jar,
That there abides a peace of thine,
Man did not make, and cannot mar.
'Lines written in Kensington Gardens' (1852)

16 He spoke, and loosed our heart in tears.
He laid us as we lay at birth
On the cool flowery lap of earth.
of William **Wordsworth**
'Memorial Verses, April 1850' (1852) l. 47

17 Ere the parting hour go by,
Quick, thy tablets, Memory!
'A Memory Picture' (1849)

18 With aching hands and bleeding feet
We dig and heap, lay stone on stone;
We bear the burden and the heat
Of the long day, and wish 'twere done.
Not till the hours of light return,
All we have built do we discern.
'Morality' (1852); see **Bible** 98:2

19 Say, has some wet bird-haunted English lawn
Lent it the music of its trees at dawn?
'Parting' (1852) l. 19

20 Hark! ah, the Nightingale!
The tawny-throated!
Hark! from that moonlit cedar what a burst!
What triumph! hark—what pain!
'Philomela' (1853) l. 1

21 Eternal Passion!
Eternal Pain!
of the nightingale
'Philomela' (1853) l. 31

22 Cruel, but composed and bland,
Dumb, inscrutable and grand,
So Tiberius might have sat,
Had Tiberius been a cat.
'Poor Matthias' (1885) l. 40

23 Her cabined ample Spirit,
It fluttered and failed for breath.
To-night it doth inherit
The vasty hall of death.
'Requiescat' (1853)

24 Not deep the Poet sees, but wide.
'Resignation' (1849) l. 214

25 Yet they, believe me, who await
No gifts from chance, have conquered fate.
'Resignation' (1849) l. 247

26 Not milder is the general lot
Because our spirits have forgot,
In action's dizzying eddy whirled,

The something that infects the world.
  'Resignation' (1849) l. 275

1 Coldly, sadly descends
  The autumn evening. The Field
  Strewn with its dank yellow drifts
  Of withered leaves, and the elms,
  Fade into dimness apace,
  Silent;—hardly a shout
  From a few boys late at their play!
  'Rugby Chapel, November 1857' (1867)

2 Go, for they call you, Shepherd, from the hill.
  'The Scholar-Gipsy' (1853) l. 1

3 All the live murmur of a summer's day.
  'The Scholar-Gipsy' (1853) l. 20

4 Tired of knocking at Preferment's door.
  'The Scholar-Gipsy' (1853) l. 35

5 Crossing the stripling Thames at Bab-lock-hithe.
  'The Scholar-Gipsy' (1853) l. 74

6 Rapt, twirling in thy hand a withered spray,
  And waiting for the spark from heaven to fall.
  'The Scholar-Gipsy' (1853) l. 119

7 The line of festal light in Christ-Church hall.
  'The Scholar-Gipsy' (1853) l. 129

8 Thou waitest for the spark from heaven! and we,
  Light half-believers in our casual creeds . . .
  Who hesitate and falter life away,
  And lose to-morrow the ground won to-day—
  Ah, do not we, Wanderer, await it too?
  'The Scholar-Gipsy' (1853) l. 171

9 O born in days when wits were fresh and clear,
  And life ran gaily as the sparkling Thames;
  Before this strange disease of modern life,
  With its sick hurry, its divided aims,
  Its heads o'ertaxed, its palsied hearts, was rife—
  Fly hence, our contact fear!
  'The Scholar-Gipsy' (1853) l. 201

10 Still nursing the unconquerable hope,
  Still clutching the inviolable shade.
  'The Scholar-Gipsy' (1853) l. 211

11 Resolve to be thyself: and know, that he
  Who finds himself, loses his misery.
  'Self-Dependence' (1852) l. 31

12 Others abide our question. Thou art free.
  We ask and ask: Thou smilest and art still,
  Out-topping knowledge.
  'Shakespeare' (1849)

13 And thou, who didst the stars and sunbeams
    know,
  Self-schooled, self-scanned, self-honoured, self-
    secure,
  Didst tread on Earth unguessed at.
  'Shakespeare' (1849)

14 Curled minion, dancer, coiner of sweet words!
  'Sohrab and Rustum' (1853) l. 458

15 No horse's cry was that, most like the roar
  Of some pained desert lion, who all day
  Hath trailed the hunter's javelin in his side,
  And comes at night to die upon the sand.
  'Sohrab and Rustum' (1853) l. 501

16 Truth sits upon the lips of dying men.
  'Sohrab and Rustum' (1853) l. 656

17 But the majestic river floated on,
  Out of the mist and hum of that low land,
  Into the frosty starlight.
  'Sohrab and Rustum' (1853) l. 875

18 The longed-for dash of waves is heard, and wide
  His luminous home of waters opens, bright
  And tranquil, from whose floor the new-bathed
    stars
  Emerge, and shine upon the Aral Sea.
  'Sohrab and Rustum' (1853) l. 889

19 For rigorous teachers seized my youth,
  And purged its faith, and trimmed its fire,
  Showed me the high, white star of Truth,
  There bade me gaze, and there aspire.
  'Stanzas from the Grande Chartreuse' (1855) l. 67

20 Wandering between two worlds, one dead,
  The other powerless to be born,
  With nowhere yet to rest my head,
  Like these, on earth I wait forlorn.
  'Stanzas from the Grande Chartreuse' (1855) l. 85

21 What helps it now, that Byron bore,
  With haughty scorn which mocked the smart,
  Through Europe to the Aetolian shore
  The pageant of his bleeding heart?
  That thousands counted every groan,
  And Europe made his woe her own?
  'Stanzas from the Grande Chartreuse' (1855) l. 133

22 Still bent to make some port he knows not where,
  Still standing for some false impossible shore.
  'A Summer Night' (1852) l. 68

23 The signal-elm, that looks on Ilsley downs,
  The Vale, the three lone weirs, the youthful
    Thames.
  'Thyrsis' (1866) l. 14

24 And that sweet City with her dreaming spires.
  of Oxford
  'Thyrsis' (1866) l. 19; see **Raphael** 642:11

25 So have I heard the cuckoo's parting cry,
  From the wet field, through the vext garden-trees,
  Come with the volleying rain and tossing breeze:
  'The bloom is gone, and with the bloom go I.'
  'Thyrsis' (1866) l. 57

26 Too quick despairer, wherefore wilt thou go?
  Soon will the high Midsummer pomps come on,
  Soon will the musk carnations break and swell.
  'Thyrsis' (1866) l. 61

27 For Time, not Corydon, hath conquered thee.
  'Thyrsis' (1866) l. 80

28 The foot less prompt to meet the morning dew,
  The heart less bounding at emotion new,
  And hope, once crushed, less quick to spring
    again.
  'Thyrsis' (1866) l. 138

29 Who saw life steadily, and saw it whole:
  The mellow glory of the Attic stage;

Singer of sweet Colonus, and its child.
of Sophocles
'To a Friend' (1849)

1 France, famed in all great arts, in none supreme.
'To a Republican Friend—Continued' (1849)

2 Yes! in the sea of life enisled,
With echoing straits between us thrown,
Dotting the shoreless watery wild,
We mortal millions live *alone*.
'To Marguerite—Continued' (1852) l. 1

3 A God, a God their severance ruled!
'To Marguerite—Continued' (1852) l. 22

4 And bade betwixt their shores to be
The unplumbed, salt, estranging sea.
'To Marguerite—Continued' (1852) l. 24

5 Nor bring, to see me cease to live,
Some doctor full of phrase and fame,
To shake his sapient head and give
The ill he cannot cure a name.
'A Wish' (1867)

6 And sigh that one thing only has been lent
To youth and age in common—discontent.
'Youth's Agitations' (1852)

7 Our society distributes itself into Barbarians,
Philistines, and Populace; and America is just
ourselves, with the Barbarians quite left out, and
the Populace nearly.
Culture and Anarchy (1869) preface

8 The pursuit of perfection, then, is the pursuit of
sweetness and light . . . He who works for
sweetness and light united, works to make reason
and the will of God prevail.
Culture and Anarchy (1869) ch. 1; see **Forster** 329:11, **Swift**
765:6

9 The men of culture are the true apostles of
equality.
Culture and Anarchy (1869) ch. 1

10 When I want to distinguish clearly the aristocratic
class from the Philistines proper, or middle class,
[I] name the former, in my own mind *the
Barbarians*.
Culture and Anarchy (1869) ch. 3

11 Marching where it likes, meeting where it likes,
bawling what it likes, breaking what it likes—to
this vast residuum we may with great propriety
give the name of Populace.
of the working class
Culture and Anarchy (1869) ch. 3

12 Hebraism and Hellenism—between these two
points of influence moves our world.
Culture and Anarchy (1869) ch. 4

13 No man, who knows nothing else, knows even his
Bible.
Culture and Anarchy (1869) ch. 5

14 Nothing could moderate, in the bosom of the great
English middle class, their passionate, absorbing,
almost blood-thirsty clinging to life.
Essays in Criticism First Series (1865) preface

15 Whispering from her towers the last
enchantments of the Middle Age . . . Home of lost
causes, and forsaken beliefs, and unpopular
names, and impossible loyalties!
of Oxford
Essays in Criticism First Series (1865) preface; see
Beerbohm 63:4

16 The gloom, the smoke, the cold, the strangled
illegitimate child! . . . And the final touch,—short,
bleak and inhuman: *Wragg is in custody*.
*prompted by a newspaper report of the murder of her
illegitimate child by a girl named Wragg*
Essays in Criticism First Series (1865) 'The Function of
Criticism at the Present Time'

17 I am bound by my own definition of criticism: *a
disinterested endeavour to learn and propagate the best
that is known and thought in the world*.
Essays in Criticism First Series (1865) 'The Function of
Criticism at the Present Time'

18 Philistinism!—We have not the expression in
English. Perhaps we have not the word because
we have so much of the thing.
Essays in Criticism First Series (1865) 'Heinrich Heine'

19 The great apostle of the Philistines, Lord
Macaulay.
Essays in Criticism First Series (1865) 'Joubert'

20 The absence, in this country, of any force of
educated literary and scientific opinion.
Essays in Criticism First Series (1865) 'The Literary
Influence of Academies'

21 In poetry, no less than in life, he is 'a beautiful
and ineffectual angel, beating in the void his
luminous wings in vain'.
Essays in Criticism Second Series (1888) 'Shelley' (quoting
from his own essay on Byron in the same work)

22 More and more mankind will discover that we
have to turn to poetry to interpret life for us, to
console us, to sustain us. Without poetry, our
science will appear incomplete; and most of what
now passes with us for religion and philosophy
will be replaced by poetry.
Essays in Criticism Second Series (1888) 'The Study of
Poetry'

23 The difference between genuine poetry and the
poetry of Dryden, Pope, and all their school, is
briefly this: their poetry is conceived and
composed in their wits, genuine poetry is
conceived and composed in the soul.
Essays in Criticism Second Series (1888) 'Thomas Gray'

24 Poetry is at bottom a criticism of life.
Essays in Criticism Second Series (1888) 'Wordsworth'

25 His expression may often be called bald . . . but it
is bald as the bare mountain tops are bald, with a
baldness full of grandeur.
Essays in Criticism Second Series (1888) 'Wordsworth'

1 I am past thirty, and three parts iced over.
   Howard Foster Lowry (ed.) *The Letters of Matthew Arnold to Arthur Hugh Clough* (1932) 12 February 1853

2 Terms like grace, new birth, justification . . . terms, in short, which with St Paul are literary terms, theologians have employed as if they were scientific terms.
   Literature and Dogma (1873) ch. 1

3 The true meaning of religion is thus not simply morality, but morality touched by emotion.
   Literature and Dogma (1873) ch. 1

4 Conduct is three-fourths of our life and its largest concern.
   Literature and Dogma (1873) ch. 1

5 But there remains the question: what righteousness really is. The method and secret and sweet reasonableness of Jesus.
   Literature and Dogma (1873) ch. 12

6 So we have the Philistine of genius in religion— Luther; the Philistine of genius in politics— Cromwell; the Philistine of genius in literature— Bunyan.
   Mixed Essays (1879) 'Lord Falkland'

7 Wordsworth says somewhere that wherever Virgil seems to have composed 'with his eye on the object', Dryden fails to render him. Homer invariably composes 'with his eye on the object', whether the object be a moral or a material one: Pope composes with his eye on his style, into which he translates his object, whatever it is.
   On Translating Homer (1861) Lecture 1

8 Of these two literatures [French and German], as of the intellect of Europe in general, the main effort, for now many years, has been a *critical* effort; the endeavours, in all branches of knowledge—theology, philosophy, history, art, science—to see the object as in itself it really is.
   On Translating Homer (1861) Lecture 2

9 He [the translator] will find one English book and one only, where, as in the *Iliad* itself, perfect plainness of speech is allied with perfect nobleness; and that book is the Bible.
   On Translating Homer (1861) Lecture 3

10 Nothing has raised more questioning among my critics than these words—noble, the grand style . . . I think it will be found that the grand style arises in poetry, when a noble nature, poetically gifted, treats with simplicity or with severity a serious subject.
   On Translating Homer. Last Words (1862)

11 Have something to say, and say it as clearly as you can. That is the only secret of style.
   G. W. E. Russell *Collections and Recollections* (1898) ch. 13

Samuel James Arnold 1774–1852
English organist and composer

12 England, home and beauty.
   'The Death of Nelson' (1811 song)

Thomas Arnold 1795–1842
*English historian and educator; Headmaster of Rugby School from 1828; father of Matthew **Arnold***

13 My object will be, if possible, to form Christian men, for Christian boys I can scarcely hope to make.
   on appointment to the Headmastership of Rugby School
   letter to Revd John Tucker, 2 March 1828; Arthur Penrhyn Stanley *The Life and Correspondence of Thomas Arnold* (1844) vol. 1, ch. 2

14 What we must look for here is, 1st, religious and moral principles: 2ndly, gentlemanly conduct: 3rdly, intellectual ability.
   address to the praepostors [prefects] of Rugby School
   Arthur Penrhyn Stanley *The Life and Correspondence of Thomas Arnold* (1844) vol. 1, ch. 3

15 As for rioting, the old Roman way of dealing with that is always the right one; flog the rank and file, and fling the ringleaders from the Tarpeian rock.
   from an unpublished letter written before 1828, quoted by Matthew **Arnold** in *Cornhill Magazine* August 1868 'Anarchy and Authority'

16 It is quite awful to watch the strength of evil in such young minds, and how powerless is every effort against it. It would give the vainest man alive a very fair notion of his own insufficiency, to see how little he can do and how his most earnest addresses are as a cannon ball on a bolster.
   David Newsome *Godliness and Good Learning* (1961)

17 My love for any place, or person, or institution, is exactly the measure of my desire to reform them.
   David Newsome *Godliness and Good Learning* (1961); **Tusa** 803:1

Raymond Aron 1905–
French sociologist and political journalist

18 *La pensée politique, en France, est rétrospective ou utopique.*
   Political thought, in France, is retrospective or utopian.
   The Opium of the Intellectuals (1955) ch. 1

Antonin Artaud 1896–1948
French actor, director, and dramatic theorist

19 *Il faut nous laver de la littérature. Nous voulons être hommes avant tout, être humains.*
   We must wash literature off ourselves. We want to be men above all, to be human.
   Les Oeuvres et les Hommes (unpublished MS, 17 May 1922)

Lev A. Artsimovich 1909–73
Russian physicist

20 The joke definition according to which 'Science is the best way of satisfying the curiosity of individuals at government expense' is more or less correct.
   in *Novy Mir* January 1967

21 If one proposed to the Royal Society a two-wheeled vehicle for personal transportation, they would immediately conclude that it was impossible because it is clearly and absolutely unstable.

on the conservatism of scientific bodies
attributed

Roger Ascham 1515-68

English scholar, writer, and courtier

1 I said . . . how, and why, young children, were sooner allured by love, than driven by beating, to attain good learning.
The Schoolmaster (1570) preface

2 There is no such whetstone, to sharpen a good wit and encourage a will to learning, as is praise.
The Schoolmaster (1570) bk. 1

3 Mark all mathematical heads which be only and wholly bent on these sciences, how solitary they be themselves, how unfit to live with others, and how unapt to serve the world.
The Schoolmaster (1570) bk. 1

4 To laugh, to lie, to flatter, to face
Four ways in court to win men grace.
The Schoolmaster (1570) bk. 1

5 Learning teacheth more in one year than experience in twenty.
The Schoolmaster (1570) bk. 1

6 We know by experience itself, that . . . we find out but a short way, by long wandering.
The Schoolmaster (1570) bk. 1

7 *Inglese Italianato, è un diavolo incarnato*, that is to say, you remain men in shape and fashion, but become devils in life and condition.
of Englishmen travelling in Italy
The Schoolmaster (1570) bk. 1

8 What toys, the daily reading of such a book, may work in the will of a young gentleman, or a young maid . . . wise men can judge, and honest men do pity.
of Malory's Le Morte D'Arthur *as unsuitable reading for the young*
The Schoolmaster (1570) bk. 1

9 He that will write well in any tongue, must follow this counsel of Aristotle, to speak as the common people do, to think as wise men do; and so should every man understand him, and the judgement of wise men allow him.
Toxophilus (1545) 'To all gentlemen and yeomen of England'

John Ashcroft 1942-

American Republican politician, Attorney General of the US since 2001

10 We may never know why he turned his back on our country and our values, but we cannot ignore that he did. Youth is not absolution for treachery.
on John Walker Lindh, an American who fought for the Taliban
in *Newsweek* 28 January 2002

Daisy Ashford 1881-1972

English child author

11 Mr Salteena was an elderly man of 42.
The Young Visiters (1919) ch. 1

12 I am not quite a gentleman but you would hardly notice it but can't be helped anyhow.
The Young Visiters (1919) ch. 1

13 Bernard always had a few prayers in the hall and some whiskey afterwards as he was rarther pious but Mr Salteena was not very addicted to prayers so he marched up to bed.
The Young Visiters (1919) ch. 3

14 It was a sumpshous spot all done up in gold with plenty of looking glasses.
The Young Visiters (1919) ch. 5

15 Oh I see said the Earl but my own idear is that these things are as piffle before the wind.
The Young Visiters (1919) ch. 5

16 My life will be sour grapes and ashes without you.
The Young Visiters (1919) ch. 8

Isaac Asimov 1920-92

Russian-born biochemist and science fiction writer

17 The three fundamental Rules of Robotics . . . One, a robot may not injure a human being, or, through inaction, allow a human being to come to harm . . . Two . . . a robot must obey the orders given it by human beings except where such orders would conflict with the First Law . . . three, a robot must protect its own existence as long as such protection does not conflict with the First or Second Laws.
I, Robot (1950) 'Runaround'

18 When, however, the lay public rallies around an idea that is denounced by distinguished but elderly scientists and supports that idea with great fervour and emotion—the distinguished but elderly scientists are then, after all, probably right.
*corollary to Arthur C. **Clarke**'s law; see **Clarke** 225:2*
Arthur C. Clarke 'Asimov's Corollary' in K. Frazier (ed.) *Paranormal Borderlands of Science* (1981)

19 The first law of dietetics seems to be: if it tastes good, it's bad for you.
attributed

Anne Askew 1521-46

English martyr

20 Like as the armèd knight
Appointed to the field,
With this world will I fight,
And faith shall be my shield . . .

I am not she that list
My anchor to let fall,
For every drizzling mist
My ship substantial.
'The Ballad which Anne Askew made and sang when she was in Newgate' (1546)

Herbert Asquith, Earl of Oxford and Asquith 1852–1928

*British Liberal statesman; Prime Minister, 1908–16; husband of Margot **Asquith***
*on Asquith: see **Telegrams** 776:6*

1 We had better wait and see.
  phrase used repeatedly in speeches in 1910, referring to the rumour that the House of Lords was to be flooded with new Liberal peers to ensure the passage of the Finance Bill
   Roy Jenkins *Asquith* (1964)

2 We shall never sheathe the sword which we have not lightly drawn until Belgium recovers in full measure all and more than all that she has sacrificed, until France is adequately secured against the menace of aggression, until the rights of the smaller nationalities of Europe are placed upon an unassailable foundation, and until the military domination of Prussia is wholly and finally destroyed.
   speech at the Guildhall, London, 9 November 1914, in The Times *10 November 1914*

3 Youth would be an ideal state if it came a little later in life.
   in Observer *15 April 1923*

4 It is fitting that we should have buried the Unknown Prime Minister by the side of the Unknown Soldier.
  *of Andrew **Bonar Law***
   Robert Blake *The Unknown Prime Minister* (1955)

5 [The War Office kept three sets of figures:] one to mislead the public, another to mislead the Cabinet, and the third to mislead itself.
   Alistair Horne *Price of Glory* (1962) ch. 2

Margot Asquith 1864–1945

*British political hostess; wife of Herbert **Asquith***

6 Kitchener is a great poster.
   More Memories (1933) ch. 6

7 The *t* is silent, as in *Harlow*.
  to Jean Harlow, who had been mispronouncing 'Margot'
   T. S. Matthews *Great Tom* (1973) ch. 7

8 Lord Birkenhead is very clever but sometimes his brains go to his head.
   in Listener *11 June 1953 'Margot Oxford' by Lady Violet Bonham Carter*

9 He can't see a belt without hitting below it.
  *of **Lloyd George***
   in Listener *11 June 1953 'Margot Oxford' by Lady Violet Bonham Carter*

Mary Astell 1668–1731

English poet and feminist

10   Their sophistry I can control
  Who falsely say that women have no soul.
   'Ambition' (written 1684) l. 7

11 Happy am I who out of danger sit,
  Can see and pity them who wade thro it;

Need take no thought my treasure to dispose,
What I ne'er had I cannot fear to lose.
   'Awake my Lute' l. 18

12 Our opposers usually miscall our quickness of thought, fancy and flash, and christen their own heaviness by the specious names of judgement and solidity; but it is easy to retort upon them the reproachful ones of dullness and stupidity.
   An Essay in Defence of the Female Sex (1696)

13 Fetters of gold are still fetters, and the softest lining can never make them so easy as liberty.
   An Essay in Defence of the Female Sex (1696); see **Bacon** 43:11

14 If all men are born free, how is it that all women are born slaves?
   Some Reflections upon Marriage (1706 ed.) preface

15 If marriage be such a blessed state, how comes it, may you say, that there are so few happy marriages? Now in answer to this, it is not to be wondered that so few succeed; we should rather be surprised to find so many do, considering how imprudently men engage, the motives they act by, and the very strange conduct they observe throughout.
   Some Reflections upon Marriage (1700) preface

16 'Tis less to be wondered at that women marry off in haste, for if they took time to consider and reflect upon it, they seldom would.
   Some Reflections upon Marriage (1700)

Jacob Astley 1579–1652

English soldier and royalist

17 O Lord! thou knowest how busy I must be this day: if I forget thee, do not thou forget me.
  prayer before the Battle of Edgehill, 1642
   Philip Warwick *Memoires* (1701)

18 Gentlemen, ye may now sit and play, for you have done all your work, if you fall not out among yourselves.
  to enemy officers, after being captured at Stow-on-the-Wold, 1646
   R. Field *Stow-on-the-Wold, 1646* (1992)

Nancy Astor 1879–1964

American-born British Conservative politician
*see also **Churchill** 222:20*

19 I married beneath me, all women do.
   in Dictionary of National Biography 1961–1970 *(1981)*

Brooks Atkinson 1894–1984

American journalist and critic

20 After each war there is a little less democracy to save.
   Once Around the Sun (1951) 7 January

David Attenborough 1926–

English naturalist and broadcaster

21 I'm not over-fond of animals. I am merely astounded by them.
   in Independent *14 January 1995*

Clement Attlee 1883–1967

British Labour statesman; Prime Minister, 1945–51
see also de Gaulle 262:6

1 The voice we heard was that of Mr Churchill but the mind was that of Lord Beaverbrook.
  speech on radio, 5 June 1945; Francis Williams *A Prime Minister Remembers* (1961)

2 A period of silence on your part would be welcome.
  letter to Harold Laski, 20 August 1945; Francis Williams *A Prime Minister Remembers* (1961)

3 Few thought he was even a starter
There were many who thought themselves smarter
But he ended PM
CH and OM
An earl and a knight of the garter.
  describing himself in a letter to Tom Attlee, 8 April 1956
  Kenneth Harris *Attlee* (1982)

4 [Russian Communism is] the illegitimate child of Karl Marx and Catherine the Great.
  speech at Aarhus University, 11 April 1956, in *The Times* 12 April 1956

5 Democracy means government by discussion, but it is only effective if you can stop people talking.
  speech at Oxford, 14 June 1957, in *The Times* 15 June 1957

6 A monologue is not a decision.
  to Winston Churchill, who had complained that a matter had been raised several times in Cabinet
  Francis Williams *A Prime Minister Remembers* (1961) ch. 7

7 If the King asks you to form a Government you say 'Yes' or 'No', not 'I'll let you know later!'
  Kenneth Harris *Attlee* (1982)

Margaret Atwood 1939–

Canadian novelist

8 The threshold of a new house is a lonely place.
  The Handmaid's Tale (1985)

9 Nobody dies from lack of sex. It's lack of love we die from.
  The Handmaid's Tale (1986)

10 Everyone has neuroses, but the artist has a way of working them out (art).
  letter to Charles Pachter, 28 December 1968; Nathalie Cook *Margaret Atwood* (1998)

11 People put down Canadian literature and ask us why there isn't a *Moby Dick*. The reason there isn't a *Moby Dick* is that if a Canadian did a *Moby Dick*, it would be done from the point of view of the whale.
  in *Saturday Night* November 1972

12 I tried for the longest time to find out what *deconstructionism* was. Nobody was able to explain it to me clearly. The best answer I got was from a writer, who said, 'Honey, it's bad news for you and me.'
  in an interview, December 1986; Earl G. Ingersoll (ed.) *Margaret Atwood: Conversations* (1990)

Henriette Auber 1773–1862

English hymn-writer

13 Our blest Redeemer, ere he breathed
His tender last farewell,
A Guide, a Comforter, bequeathed
With us to dwell.

He came in tongues of living flame,
To teach, convince, subdue;
All-powerful as the wind he came,
As viewless too.
  'Our blest Redeemer, ere he breathed' (1829 hymn)

John Aubrey 1626–97

English antiquary and biographer

14 The Bishop sometimes would take the key of the wine-cellar, and he and his chaplain [Lushington] would go and lock themselves in and be merry. Then first he lays down his episcopal hat—*There lies the Doctor*. Then he puts off his gown—*There lies the Bishop*. Then 'twas, *Here's to thee, Corbet*, and *Here's to thee, Lushington*.
  Brief Lives 'Richard Corbet'

15 How these curiosities would be quite forgot, did not such idle fellows as I am put them down.
  Brief Lives 'Venetia Digby'

16 He was wont to say that if he had read as much as other men, he should have known no more than other men.
  Brief Lives 'Thomas Hobbes'

17 As they were reading of inscribing and circumscribing figures, said he, I will show you how to inscribe a triangle in a quadrangle. Bring a pig into the quadrangle and I will set the college dog at him, and he will take the pig by the ear, then I come and take the dog by the tail and the hog by the tail, and so there you have a triangle in a quadrangle; *quod erat faciendum*.
  Brief Lives 'Ralph Kettel'

18 And when he saw the cheese-cakes:—'What have we here, *crinkum crankum*?'
  Brief Lives 'Ralph Kettel'

19 His harmonical and ingenious soul did lodge in a beautiful and well proportioned body. He was a spare man.
  Brief Lives 'John Milton'

20 Oval face. His eye a dark grey. He had auburn hair. His complexion exceeding fair—he was so fair that they called him *the lady of* Christ's College.
  Brief Lives 'John Milton'

21 He pronounced the letter R (*littera canina*) very hard—a certain sign of a satirical wit.
  Brief Lives 'John Milton'

22 Sciatica: he cured it, by boiling his buttock.
  Brief Lives 'Sir Jonas Moore'

23 She was when a child much against the Bishops, and prayed to God to take them to him, but afterwards was reconciled to them. Prayed aloud,

as the hypocritical fashion then was, and was overheard.
  Brief Lives 'Katherine Philips'

1 Sir Walter, being strangely surprised and put out of his countenance at so great a table, gives his son a damned blow over the face. His son, as rude as he was, would not strike his father, but strikes over the face the gentleman that sat next to him and said 'Box about: 'twill come to my father anon'.
  Brief Lives 'Sir Walter Raleigh'

2 He was a handsome, well-shaped man: very good company, and of a very ready and pleasant smooth wit.
  Brief Lives 'William Shakespeare'

3 Anno 1670, not far from Cirencester, was an apparition; being demanded whether a good spirit or a bad? returned no answer, but disappeared with a curious perfume and most melodious twang. Mr W. Lilly believes it was a fairy.
  Miscellanies (1696) 'Apparitions'

Auctoritates Aristotelis

A compilation of medieval propositions drawn from diverse classical and other sources (ed. J. Hamesse, 1974)

4 *Consuetudo est altera natura.*
  Habit is second nature.

5 *Contra negantem principia non est disputandum.*
  You cannot argue with someone who denies the first principles.

6 *Deus et natura nihil faciunt frustra.*
  God and nature do nothing in vain.

7 *Ignorantia excusat peccatum.*
  Ignorance excuses from sin.

8 *Melius est esse quam non esse.*
  It is better to be than not to be.

9 *Natura dat unicuique quod sibi conveniens est.*
  Nature gives to each what is appropriate.

10 *Natura desiderat semper quod melius est.*
  Nature always desires what is better.

11 *Non est idem bonus homo et bonus civis.*
  A good man and a good citizen are not the same thing.

12 *Omnes homines naturaliter scire desiderant.*
  All men naturally desire to know.

13 *Oportet inquisitores veritatis non esse inimicos.*
  There should be no enmity among seekers after truth.

14 *Parentes plus amant filios quam e converso.*
  Parents love their children more than children love their parents.

15 *Signum scientis est posse docere.*
  The touchstone of knowledge is the ability to teach.

16 *Silentium mulieri praestat ornatum.*
  Silence is a woman's finest ornament.

17 *Tempus est mensura motus rerum mobilium.*
  Time is the measure of movement.

W. H. Auden 1907-73

English poet
*on Auden: see **Orwell** 577:25*

18 Blessed Cecilia, appear in visions
  To all musicians, appear and inspire:
  Translated Daughter, come down and startle
  Composing mortals with immortal fire.
  Anthem for St Cecilia's Day (1941) pt. 1

19 I'll love you, dear, I'll love you
  Till China and Africa meet
  And the river jumps over the mountain
  And the salmon sing in the street,

  I'll love you till the ocean
  Is folded and hung up to dry
  And the seven stars go squawking
  Like geese about the sky.
  'As I Walked Out One Evening' (1940)

20 The glacier knocks in the cupboard,
  The desert sighs in the bed,
  And the crack in the teacup opens
  A lane to the land of the dead.
  'As I Walked Out One Evening' (1940)

21   Make intercession
  For the treason of all clerks.
  'At the Grave of Henry James' (1945); see **Benda** 66:9

22 August for the people and their favourite islands.
  title of poem (1936)

23 The desires of the heart are as crooked as corkscrews
  Not to be born is the best for man.
  'Death's Echo' (1937); see **Sophocles** 746:17

24 Happy the hare at morning, for she cannot read
  The Hunter's waking thoughts.
  Dog beneath the Skin (with Christopher **Isherwood**, 1935) act 2, sc. 2

25 To save your world you asked this man to die:
  Would this man, could he see you now, ask why?
  'Epitaph for the Unknown Soldier' (1955)

26 When he laughed, respectable senators burst with laughter,
  And when he cried the little children died in the streets.
  'Epitaph on a Tyrant' (1940); see **Motley** 551:14

27 Altogether elsewhere, vast
  Herds of reindeer move across
  Miles and miles of golden moss,
  Silently and very fast.
  'The Fall of Rome' (1951)

28 Stop all the clocks, cut off the telephone,
  Prevent the dog from barking with a juicy bone,
  Silence the pianos and with muffled drum
  Bring out the coffin, let the mourners come.
  'Funeral Blues' (1936)

29 He was my North, my South, my East and West,
  My working week and my Sunday rest,
  My noon, my midnight, my talk, my song;

I thought that love would last for ever: I was
  wrong.
'Funeral Blues' (1936)

1 To us he is no more a person
now but a whole climate of opinion.
'In Memory of Sigmund Freud' (1940) st. 17

2 The mercury sank in the mouth of the dying day.
What instruments we have agree
The day of his death was a dark cold day.
'In Memory of W. B. Yeats' (1940) pt. 1

3 You were silly like us; your gift survived it all:
The parish of rich women, physical decay,
Yourself. Mad Ireland hurt you into poetry.
'In Memory of W. B. Yeats' (1940) pt. 2

4 For poetry makes nothing happen: it survives
In the valley of its saying where executives
Would never want to tamper.
'In Memory of W. B. Yeats' (1940) pt. 2

5 Earth, receive an honoured guest:
William Yeats is laid to rest.
Let the Irish vessel lie
Emptied of its poetry.
'In Memory of W. B. Yeats' (1940) pt. 3

6 In the nightmare of the dark
All the dogs of Europe bark,
And the living nations wait,
Each sequestered in its hate;

Intellectual disgrace
Stares from every human face,
And the seas of pity lie
Locked and frozen in each eye.
'In Memory of W. B. Yeats' (1940) pt. 3

7 Time that with this strange excuse
Pardoned Kipling and his views,
And will pardon Paul Claudel,
Pardons him for writing well.
'In Memory of W. B. Yeats' (1940) pt. 3

8 In the deserts of the heart
Let the healing fountain start,
In the prison of his days
Teach the free man how to praise.
'In Memory of W. B. Yeats' (1940) pt. 3

9 Look, stranger, at this island now.
title of poem (1936)

10 The leaping light for your delight discovers,
Stand stable here
And silent be,
That through the channels of the ear
May wander like a river
The swaying sound of the sea.
'Look, stranger, at this island now' (1936)

11 Lay your sleeping head, my love,
Human on my faithless arm.
'Lullaby' (1940)

12 About suffering they were never wrong,
The Old Masters: how well they understood
Its human position; how it takes place
While someone else is eating or opening a window
  or just walking dully along.
'Musée des Beaux Arts' (1940)

13 They never forgot
That even the dreadful martyrdom must run its
  course
Anyhow in a corner, some untidy spot
Where the dogs go on with their doggy life and
  the torturer's horse
Scratches its innocent behind on a tree.
'Musée des Beaux Arts' (1940)

14 To the man-in-the-street, who, I'm sorry to say,
Is a keen observer of life,
The word 'Intellectual' suggests straight away
A man who's untrue to his wife.
New Year Letter (1941) l. 1277 n.

15 This is the Night Mail crossing the Border,
Bringing the cheque and the postal order,
Letters for the rich, letters for the poor,
The shop at the corner, the girl next door.
Pulling up Beattock, a steady climb:
The gradient's against her, but she's on time.
Past cotton-grass and moorland boulder,
Shovelling white steam over her shoulder.
'Night Mail' (1936) pt. 1

16 Letters of thanks, letters from banks,
Letters of joy from girl and boy,
Receipted bills and invitations
To inspect new stock or to visit relations,
And applications for situations,
And timid lovers' declarations,
And gossip, gossip from all the nations.
'Night Mail' (1936) pt. 3

17 And make us as Newton was, who in his garden
  watching
The apple falling towards England, became aware
Between himself and her of an eternal tie.
'O Love, the interest itself' (1936)

18 Private faces in public places
Are wiser and nicer
Than public faces in private places.
Orators (1932) dedication

19 Out on the lawn I lie in bed,
Vega conspicuous overhead.
'Out on the lawn I lie in bed' (1936)

20 O what is that sound which so thrills the ear
Down in the valley drumming, drumming?
Only the scarlet soldiers, dear,
The soldiers coming.
'O what is that sound' (1936)

21 O it's broken the lock and splintered the door,
O it's the gate where they're turning, turning;
Their boots are heavy on the floor
And their eyes are burning.
'O what is that sound' (1936)

22 Some thirty inches from my nose
The frontier of my Person goes,
And all the untilled air between
Is private pagus or demesne.
Stranger, unless with bedroom eyes
I beckon you to fraternize,
Beware of rudely crossing it:
I have no gun, but I can spit.
'Prologue: the Birth of Architecture' (1966) postscript

1 My Dear One is mine as mirrors are lonely.
  'The Sea and the Mirror' (1944) pt. 2 (Miranda)

2 I and the public know
  What all schoolchildren learn,
  Those to whom evil is done
  Do evil in return.
  'September 1, 1939' (1940)

3 But who can live for long
  In an euphoric dream;
  Out of the mirror they stare,
  Imperialism's face
  And the international wrong.
  'September 1, 1939' (1940)

4 All I have is a voice
  To undo the folded lie,
  The romantic lie in the brain
  Of the sensual man-in-the-street
  And the lie of Authority
  Whose buildings grope the sky:
  There is no such thing as the State
  And no one exists alone;
  Hunger allows no choice
  To the citizen or the police;
  We must love one another or die.
  'September 1, 1939' (1940)

5 A shilling life will give you all the facts.
  title of poem (1936)

6 Each year brings new problems of Form and
    Content,
  new foes to tug with: at Twenty I tried to
  vex my elders, past Sixty it's the young whom
  I hope to bother.
  'Shorts I' (1969)

7 A poet's hope: to be,
  like some valley cheese,
  local, but prized elsewhere.
  'Shorts II' (1976)

8 Harrow the house of the dead; look shining at
  New styles of architecture, a change of heart.
  'Sir, No Man's Enemy' (1930)

9 To-morrow for the young the poets exploding like
    bombs,
  The walks by the lake, the weeks of perfect
    communion;
  To-morrow the bicycle races
  Through the suburbs on summer evenings: but
    to-day the struggle.
  'Spain 1937' (1937) st. 20

10 The stars are dead; the animals will not look:
  We are left alone with our day, and the time is
    short and
  History to the defeated
  May say Alas but cannot help or pardon.
  'Spain 1937' (1937) st. 23

11 To ask the hard question is simple.
  title of poem (1933)

12 Was he free? Was he happy? The question is
    absurd:
  Had anything been wrong, we should certainly
    have heard.
  'The Unknown Citizen' (1940)

13 The sky is darkening like a stain;
  Something is going to fall like rain,
  And it won't be flowers.
  'The Witnesses' (1935) l. 67

14 All sin tends to be addictive, and the terminal
  point of addiction is what is called damnation.
  A Certain World (1970) 'Hell'

15 Man is a history-making creature who can neither
  repeat his past nor leave it behind.
  The Dyer's Hand (1963) 'D. H. Lawrence'

16 When I find myself in the company of scientists, I
  feel like a shabby curate who has strayed by
  mistake into a drawing room full of dukes.
  The Dyer's Hand (1963) 'The Poet and the City'

17 Some books are undeservedly forgotten; none are
  undeservedly remembered.
  The Dyer's Hand (1963) 'Reading'

18 Art is born of humiliation.
  Stephen Spender World Within World (1951) ch. 2

19 LSD? Nothing much happened, but I did get the
  distinct impression that some birds were trying to
  communicate with me.
  George Plimpton (ed.) The Writer's Chapbook (1989)

20 My face looks like a wedding-cake left out in the
  rain.
  Humphrey Carpenter W. H. Auden (1981) pt. 2, ch. 6

21 Nothing I wrote in the thirties saved one Jew from
  Auschwitz.
  attributed

Émile Augier 1820–89

French poet and dramatist

22 MARQUIS: *Mettez un canard sur un lac au milieu des
  cygnes, vous verrez qu'il regrettera sa mare et finira
  par y retourner.*
  MONTRICHARD: *La nostalgie de la boue!*

  MARQUIS: Put a duck on a lake in the midst of
  some swans, and you'll see he'll miss his pond and
  eventually return to it.
  MONTRICHARD: Longing to be back in the mud!
  Le Mariage d'Olympe (1855) act 1, sc. 1

St Augustine of Hippo AD 354–430

Roman Christian theologian
*on Augustine: see **Isidore** 414:11; see also **Prayers** 611:7*

23 The works of Creation are described as being
  completed in six days, the same formula for a day
  being repeated six times. The reason for this is that
  six is the number of perfection.
  The City of God bk. 9, ch. 30

24 *Tu excitas, ut laudare te delectet, quia fecisti nos, ad te
  et inquietum est cor nostrum, donec requiescat in te.*
  You stir man to take pleasure in praising you,
  because you have made us for yourself, and our
  heart is restless until it rests in you.
  Confessions (AD 397–8) bk. 1, ch. 1

25 *Nondum amabam, et amare amabam . . . quaerebam
  quid amarem, amans amare.*

I loved not yet, yet I loved to love . . . I sought what I might love, loving to love.
Confessions (AD 397–8) bk. 3, ch. 1

1 *Et illa erant fercula, in quibus mihi esurienti te inferebantur sol et luna.*
And these were the dishes wherein to me, hunger-starven for thee, the sun and moon were served up.
Confessions (AD 397–8) bk. 3, ch. 6

2 *Da mihi castitatem et continentiam, sed noli modo.*
Give me chastity and continency—but not yet!
Confessions (AD 397–8) bk. 8, ch. 7

3 When he was reading, he drew his eyes along over the leaves, and his heart searched into the sense, but his voice and tongue were silent.
of St Ambrose
Confessions (AD 397–8) bk. 6, ch. 3

4 *Tolle lege, tolle lege.*
Take up and read, take up and read.
Confessions (AD 397–8) bk. 8, ch. 12

5 *Sero te amavi, pulchritudo tam antiqua et tam nova, sero te amavi! et ecce intus eras et ego foris, et ibi te quaerebam.*
Too late came I to love thee, O thou Beauty both so ancient and so fresh, yea too late came I to love thee. And behold, thou wert within me, and I out of myself, where I made search for thee.
Confessions (AD 397–8) bk. 10, ch. 27

6 *Continentiam iubes; da quod iubes et iube quod vis.*
You command continence; give what you command, and command what you will.
Confessions (AD 397–8) bk. 10, ch. 29

7 Poetry is devil's wine.
Contra Academicos

8 *Securus iudicat orbis terrarum.*
The verdict of the world is conclusive.
Contra Epistulam Parmeniani bk. 3 ch. 24

9 *Salus extra ecclesiam non est.*
There is no salvation outside the church.
De Baptismo contra Donatistas bk. 4, ch. 17, sect. 24; see **Cyprian** 254:14, 254:16

10 I have, however, often observed this fact of human behaviour, that with certain people, when sexuality is repressed avarice seems to grow in its place.
De Bono Viduitatis sect. 26

11 *Audi partem alteram.*
Hear the other side.
De Duabus Animabus contra Manicheos ch. 14

12 Hence, a devout Christian must avoid astrologers and all impious soothsayers, especially when they tell the truth, for fear of leading his soul into error by consorting with demons and entangling himself with the bonds of such association.
De Genesi ad Litteram bk. 2, ch. 17, sect. 37; see **Misquotations** 537:15

13 *Dilige et quod vis fac.*
Love and do what you will.
often quoted as 'Ama et fac quod vis'
In Epistolam Joannis ad Parthos (AD 413) tractatus 7, sect. 8

14 *Multi quidem facilius se abstinent ut non utantur, quam temperent ut bene utantur.*
To many, total abstinence is easier than perfect moderation.
On the Good of Marriage (AD 401) ch. 21

15 *Martyres veros non faciat poena sed causa.*
True martyrdom is not determined by the penalty suffered, but by the cause.
Epistle 89 in Alois Goldbacher *S. Aureli Augustini Hipponensis Episcopi Epistulae* (1895) vol. 2

16 *Cum dilectione hominum et odio vitiorum.*
With love for mankind and hatred of sins.
often quoted as 'Love the sinner but hate the sin'
letter 211 in J.-P. Migne (ed.) *Patrologiae Latinae* (1845) vol. 33; see **Pope** 602:18

17 *Roma locuta est; causa finita est.*
Rome has spoken; the case is concluded.
traditional summary of words found in *Sermons* (Antwerp, 1702) no. 131, sect. 10

18 *De vitiis nostris scalam nobis facimus, si vitia ipsa calcamus.*
We make ourselves a ladder out of our vices if we trample the vices themselves underfoot.
sermon no. 176 ('On the Ascension of the Lord' no. 1) in J.-P. Migne (ed.) *Patrologiae Latinae* (1845) vol. 38

19 It is a singing to the praise of God. If you praise God, and do not sing, you utter no hymn. If you sing, and praise no God, you utter no hymn. If you praise anything which does not pertain to the praise of God, though in singing you praise, you utter no hymn.
defining a hymn
note to Psalm 148; J. R. Watson *The English Hymn: a Critical and Historical Study* (1997) ch. 1

Augustus 63 BC–AD 14
first Roman emperor

20 Quintilius Varus, give me back my legions.
on Varus' loss of three legions in battle with Germanic tribes, AD 9
Suetonius *Lives of the Caesars* 'Divus Augustus' sect. 23

21 *Festina lente.*
Make haste slowly.
Suetonius *Lives of the Caesars* 'Divus Augustus' sect. 25; see **Proverbs** 625:50

22 He could boast that he inherited it brick and left it marble.
referring to the city of Rome
Suetonius *Lives of the Caesars* 'Divus Augustus' sect. 28

23 That they would pay at the Greek Kalends.
meaning never; the Greeks did not use calends in reckoning time
Suetonius *Lives of the Caesars* 'Divus Augustus' sect. 87

Aung San Suu Kyi 1945–

Burmese political leader

1 It's very different from living in academia in Oxford. We called someone vicious in the *Times Literary Supplement*. We didn't know what vicious was.

on returning to Burma (Myanmar)
   in *Observer* 25 September 1988 'Sayings of the Week'

Marcus Aurelius AD 121–180

Roman emperor from AD 161

2 Nowhere can a man find a quieter or more untroubled retreat than in his own soul.
   Meditations bk. 4, sect. 3

3 Everything is fitting for me, my universe, which fits thy purpose. Nothing in its good time is too early or too late for me; everything is fruit for me which thy seasons, Nature, bear; from thee, in thee, to thee, are all things. The poet sings 'Dear city of Cecrops', and you will not say 'Dear city of God'?
   Meditations bk. 4, sect. 23

4 Time is a violent torrent; no sooner is a thing brought to sight than it is swept by and another takes its place, and this too will be swept away.
   Meditations bk. 4, sect. 43

5 Be like a headland of rock on which the waves break incessantly: but it stands fast and around it the seething of the waters sinks to rest.
   Meditations bk. 4, sect. 49

6 Nothing happens to anybody which he is not fitted by nature to bear.
   Meditations bk. 5, sect. 18

7 Sexual intercourse . . . is merely internal attrition and the spasmodic excretion of mucus.
   Meditations bk 6, sect. 13

8 Every instant of time is a pinprick of eternity. All things are petty, easily changed, vanishing away.
   Meditations bk. 6, sect. 36

9 He who sees what is now has seen all things, whatsoever comes to pass from everlasting and whatsoever shall be unto everlasting time.
   Meditations bk. 6, sect. 37

10 To change your mind and to follow him who sets you right is to be nonetheless the free agent that you were before.
   Meditations bk. 8, sect. 16

11 Mankind have been created for the sake of one another. Either instruct them, therefore, or endure them.
   Meditations bk. 8, sect. 59

12 Whatever befalls you was prepared for you beforehand from eternity, and the thread of causes was spinning from everlasting both your existence and this which befalls you.
   Meditations bk. 10, sect. 5

13 Man, you have been a citizen in this world city, what does it matter whether for five years or fifty?
   Meditations bk. 12, sect. 36

Decius Magnus Ausonius C.AD 309–392

Roman poet

14 *Nemo bonus Britto est.*
   No good man is a Briton.
   Epigrams 119

Jane Austen 1775–1817

English novelist
on Austen: see **Harding** 371:9, **Mitford** 540:16, **Scott** 674:27; *see also* **Borrowed titles** 146:14, **Clarke** 225:9

15 Miss Bates stood in the very worst predicament in the world for having much of the public favour; and she had no intellectual superiority to make atonement for herself, or frighten those who might hate her, into outward respect.
   Emma (1816) ch. 3

16 An egg boiled very soft is not unwholesome.
   Emma (1816) ch. 3

17 One half of the world cannot understand the pleasures of the other.
   Emma (1816) ch. 9

18 With men he can be rational and unaffected, but when he has ladies to please, every feature works.
   Emma (1816) ch. 13

19 The folly of people's not staying comfortably at home when they can! . . . five dull hours in another man's house, with nothing to say or to hear that was not said and heard yesterday, and may not be said and heard again tomorrow . . . four horses and four servants taken out for nothing but to convey five idle, shivering creatures into colder rooms and worse company than they might have had at home.
   Emma (1816) ch. 13

20 The sooner every party breaks up the better.
   Emma (1816) ch. 25

21 Surprises are foolish things. The pleasure is not enhanced, and the inconvenience is often considerable.
   Emma (1816) ch. 26

22 One has no great hopes from Birmingham. I always say there is something direful in the sound.
   Emma (1816) ch. 36

23 One of Edward's Mistresses was Jane Shore, who has had a play written about her, but it is a tragedy and therefore not worth reading.
   The History of England (written 1791)

24 Nothing can be said in his vindication, but that his abolishing Religious Houses and leaving them to the ruinous depredations of time has been of infinite use to the landscape of England in general.
   The History of England (written 1791)

25 It was too pathetic for the feelings of Sophia and myself—we fainted Alternately on a Sofa.
   Love and Freindship (written 1790) 'Letter the 8th'

26 She was nothing more than a mere good-tempered, civil and obliging young woman; as

such we could scarcely dislike her—she was only an Object of Contempt.
Love and Freindship (written 1790) 'Letter the 13th'

1 There is not one in a hundred of either sex who is not taken in when they marry. Look where I will, I see that it *is* so; and I feel that it *must* be so, when I consider that it is, of all transactions, the one in which people expect most from others, and are least honest themselves.
Mansfield Park (1814) ch. 5

2 We do not look in great cities for our best morality.
Mansfield Park (1814) ch. 9

3 A large income is the best recipe for happiness I ever heard of. It certainly may secure all the myrtle and turkey part of it.
Mansfield Park (1814) ch. 22

4 Shakespeare one gets acquainted with without knowing how. It is part of an Englishman's constitution. His thoughts and beauties are so spread abroad that one touches them everywhere, one is intimate with him by instinct.
Mansfield Park (1814) ch. 34

5 Let other pens dwell on guilt and misery. I quit such odious subjects as soon as I can.
Mansfield Park (1814) ch. 48

6 'Oh! it is only a novel! . . . only Cecilia, or Camilla, or Belinda:' or, in short, only some work in which the most thorough knowledge of human nature, the happiest delineation of its varieties, the liveliest effusions of wit and humour are conveyed to the world in the best chosen language.
Northanger Abbey (1818) ch. 5

7 Oh! who can ever be tired of Bath?
Northanger Abbey (1818) ch. 10

8 Where people wish to attach, they should always be ignorant. To come with a well-informed mind, is to come with an inability of administering to the vanity of others, which a sensible person would always wish to avoid. A woman especially, if she have the misfortune of knowing any thing, should conceal it as well as she can.
Northanger Abbey (1818) ch. 14

9 From politics, it was an easy step to silence.
Northanger Abbey (1818) ch. 14

10 A country like this, where . . . every man is surrounded by a neighbourhood of voluntary spies, and where roads and newspapers lay every thing open.
Northanger Abbey (1818) ch. 34

11 Sir Walter Elliot, of Kellynch-hall, in Somersetshire, was a man who, for his own amusement, never took up any book but the Baronetage; there he found occupation for an idle hour, and consolation in a distressed one.
Persuasion (1818) ch. 1

12 She had been forced into prudence in her youth, she learned romance as she grew older—the natural sequel of an unnatural beginning.
Persuasion (1818) ch. 4

13 She ventured to hope he did not always read only poetry; and to say, that she thought it was the misfortune of poetry, to be seldom safely enjoyed by those who enjoyed it completely; and that the strong feelings which alone could estimate it truly, were the very feelings which ought to taste it but sparingly.
Persuasion (1818) ch. 11

14 'My idea of good company, Mr Elliot, is the company of clever, well-informed people, who have a great deal of conversation; that is what I call good company.' 'You are mistaken,' said he gently, 'that is not good company, that is the best.'
Persuasion (1818) ch. 16

15 Men have had every advantage of us in telling their own story. Education has been theirs in so much higher a degree; the pen has been in their hands.
Persuasion (1818) ch. 23; see **Hardy** 371:15

16 All the privilege I claim for my own sex . . . is that of loving longest, when existence or when hope is gone.
Persuasion (1818) ch. 23

17 It was, perhaps, one of those cases in which advice is good or bad only as the event decides.
Persuasion (1818) ch. 23

18 It is a truth universally acknowledged, that a single man in possession of a good fortune, must be in want of a wife.
Pride and Prejudice (1813) ch. 1; see **Burney** 169:23

19 She was a woman of mean understanding, little information, and uncertain temper.
Pride and Prejudice (1813) ch. 1

20 May I ask whether these pleasing attentions proceed from the impulse of the moment, or are the result of previous study?
Pride and Prejudice (1813) ch. 14

21 Mr Collins had only to change from Jane to Elizabeth—and it was soon done—done while Mrs Bennet was stirring the fire.
Pride and Prejudice (1813) ch. 15

22 In his library he had been always sure of leisure and tranquillity; and though prepared . . . to meet with folly and conceit in every other room in the house, he was used to be free of them there.
Pride and Prejudice (1813) ch. 15

23 From this day you must be a stranger to one of your parents.—Your mother will never see you again if you do *not* marry Mr Collins, and I will never see you again if you *do*.
Pride and Prejudice (1813) ch. 20

24 Without thinking highly either of men or matrimony, marriage had always been her object; it was the only honourable provision for well-educated young women of small fortune, and however uncertain of giving happiness, must be their pleasantest preservative from want.
Pride and Prejudice (1813) ch. 22

1 What is the difference in matrimonial affairs, between the mercenary and the prudent move? Where does discretion end, and avarice begin?
Pride and Prejudice (1813) ch. 27

2 Loss of virtue in a female is irretrievable . . . one false step involves her in endless ruin.
Pride and Prejudice (1813) ch. 47

3 Are the shades of Pemberley to be thus polluted?
Pride and Prejudice (1813) ch. 56

4 You ought certainly to forgive them as a Christian, but never to admit them in your sight, or allow their names to be mentioned in your hearing.
Pride and Prejudice (1813) ch. 57

5 For what do we live, but to make sport for our neighbours, and laugh at them in our turn?
Pride and Prejudice (1813) ch. 57

6 An annuity is a very serious business.
Sense and Sensibility (1811) vol. 1, ch. 2

7 On every formal visit a child ought to be of the party, by way of provision for discourse.
Sense and Sensibility (1811) vol. 2, ch. 6

8 A man who has nothing to do with his own time has no conscience in his intrusion on that of others.
Sense and Sensibility (1811) vol. 2, ch. 9

9 A person and face, of strong, natural, sterling insignificance, though adorned in the first style of fashion.
Sense and Sensibility (1811) vol. 2, ch. 11

10 It is not time or opportunity that is to determine intimacy; it is disposition alone. Seven years would be insufficient to make some people acquainted with each other, and seven days are more than enough for others.
Sense and Sensibility (1811) vol. 2, ch. 12

11 To be so bent on marriage, to pursue a man merely for the sake of situation, is a sort of thing that shocks me; I cannot understand it. Poverty is a great evil; but to a woman of education and feeling it ought not, it cannot be the greatest.
The Watsons (c.1804)

12 I would rather be teacher at a school (and I can think of nothing worse) than marry a man I did not like.
The Watsons (c.1804)

13 We met . . . Dr Hall in such very deep mourning that either his mother, his wife, or himself must be dead.
letter to Cassandra Austen, 17 May 1799, in R. W. Chapman (ed.) *Jane Austen's Letters* (1952)

14 How horrible it is to have so many people killed!— And what a blessing that one cares for none of them!
letter to Cassandra Austen, 31 May 1811, after the battle of Albuera, 16 May 1811, in R. W. Chapman (ed.) *Jane Austen's Letters* (1952)

15 I suppose all the world is sitting in judgement upon the Princess of Wales's letter. Poor woman, I shall support her as long as I can, because she *is* a woman and because I hate her husband.
letter to Martha Lloyd, 16 February 1813; *Selected Letters* (1985)

16 3 or 4 families in a country village is the very thing to work on.
letter to Anna Austen, 9 September 1814, in R. W. Chapman (ed.) *Jane Austen's Letters* (1952)

17 I think I may boast myself to be, with all possible vanity, the most unlearned and uninformed female who ever dared to be an authoress.
letter, 11 December 1815, in R. W. Chapman (ed.) *Jane Austen's Letters* (1952)

18 What should I do with your strong, manly, spirited sketches, full of variety and glow?—How could I possibly join them on to the little bit (two inches wide) of ivory on which I work with so fine a brush, as produces little effect after much labour?
letter to J. Edward Austen, 16 December 1816, in R. W. Chapman (ed.) *Jane Austen's Letters* (1952)

19 Single women have a dreadful propensity for being poor—which is one very strong argument in favour of matrimony.
letter to Fanny Knight, 13 March 1817, in R. W. Chapman (ed.) *Jane Austen's Letters* (1952)

20 He and I should not in the least agree of course, in our ideas of novels and heroines;—pictures of perfection as you know make me sick and wicked.
letter to Fanny Knight, 23 March 1817, in R. W. Chapman (ed.) *Jane Austen's Letters* (1952)

21 I am going to take a heroine whom no-one but myself will much like.
on starting Emma
J. E. Austen-Leigh *A Memoir of Jane Austen* (1926 ed.)

22 When I asked if there was anything she wanted, her answer was that she wanted nothing but death.
of Jane Austen in her last illness
Cassandra Austen, letter to Fanny Knight, July 1817, in R. W. Chapman (ed.) *Jane Austen's Letters* (1952)

J. L. Austin 1911–60
English philosopher

23 In such cases we should not know what to say. This is when we say 'words fail us' and mean this literally. We should need new words. The old ones just would not fit. They aren't meant to cover this kind of case.
on being asked how one might describe the predicament of the character in **Kafka**'s Metamorphosis *who wakes to find himself transformed into a giant cockroach; see* **Kafka** 440:18
Isaiah Berlin 'Austin and the Early Beginnings of Oxford Philosophy' in *Essays on J. L. Austin* (1973)

24 When asked to state his 'criterion' of philosophical correctness, [he] replied that, well, if you could get a collection of 'more or less cantankerous colleagues' all to accept something after argument, that, he thought, would be 'a bit of a criterion'.
G. J. Warnock 'Saturday Mornings' in *Essays on J. L. Austin* (1973)

Earl of Avon see Anthony Eden

Revd Awdry (Wilbert Vere Awdry) 1911–97
English writer of children's books

1 You've a lot to learn about trucks, little Thomas. They are silly things and must be kept in their place. After pushing them about here for a few weeks you'll know almost as much about them as Edward. Then you'll be a Really Useful Engine.
Thomas the Tank Engine (1946)

2 I should like my epitaph to say, 'He helped people see God in the ordinary things of life, and he made children laugh.'
in *Independent* 22 March 1997, obituary

Alan Ayckbourn 1939–
English dramatist

3 My mother used to say, Delia, if S-E-X ever rears its ugly head, close your eyes before you see the rest of it.
Bedroom Farce (1978) act 2

4 This place, you tell them you're interested in the arts, you get messages of sympathy.
Chorus of Disapproval (1986) act 2

5 If you gave Ruth a rose, she'd peel all the petals off to make sure there weren't any greenfly. And when she'd done that, she'd turn round and say, do you call that a rose? Look at it, it's all in bits.
Table Manners (1975) act 1, sc. 2

A. J. Ayer 1910–89
English philosopher

6 The criterion which we use to test the genuineness of apparent statements of fact is the criterion of verifiability. We say that a sentence is factually significant to any given person, if, and only if, he knows how to verify the proposition which it purports to express—that is, if he knows what observations would lead him, under certain conditions, to accept the proposition as being true, or reject it as being false.
Language, Truth, and Logic (1936) ch. 1

7 If now I . . . say 'Stealing money is wrong,' I produce a sentence which has no factual meaning—that is, expresses no proposition which can be either true or false. It is as if I had written 'Stealing money!!'—where the shape and thickness of the exclamation marks show, by a suitable convention, that a special sort of moral disapproval is the feeling which is being expressed.
Language, Truth, and Logic (1936) ch. 6

8 We offer the theist the same comfort as we gave to the moralist. His assertions cannot possibly be valid, but they cannot be invalid either. As he says nothing at all about the world, he cannot justly be accused of saying anything false, or anything for which he has insufficient grounds. It is only when the theist claims that in asserting the existence of a transcendent god he is expressing a genuine proposition that we are entitled to disagree with him.
Language, Truth, and Logic (1936) ch. 6

9 Why should you mind being wrong if someone can show you that you are?
attributed

Ayesha fl. 1492
Moorish princess, mother of the last Sultan of Granada

10 You do well to weep as a woman over what you could not defend as a man.
reproach to her son Boabdil (Muhammad XI), who had surrendered Granada to Ferdinand and Isabella
traditional attribution; Washington Irving *The Alhambra* (1832; rev. ed. 1851) ch. 18

Pam Ayres 1947–
English writer of humorous verse

11 Medicinal discovery,
It moves in mighty leaps,
It leapt straight past the common cold
And gave it us for keeps.
'Oh no, I got a cold' (1976)

Robert Aytoun 1570–1638
Scottish poet and courtier

12 I loved thee once. I'll love no more,
Thine be the grief, as is the blame;
Thou art not what thou wast before,
What reason I should be the same?
'To an Inconstant Mistress'

W. E. Aytoun 1813–65
Scottish lawyer and writer of ballads

13 'He is coming! he is coming!'
Like a bridegroom from his room,
Came the hero from his prison
To the scaffold and the doom.
'The Execution of Montrose' (1849) st. 14

14 The grim Geneva ministers
With anxious scowl drew near,
As you have seen the ravens flock
Around the dying deer.
'The Execution of Montrose' (1849) st. 17

15 The deep, unutterable woe
Which none save exiles feel.
'The Island of the Scots' (1849) st. 12

16 The earth is all the home I have,
The heavens my wide roof-tree.
'The Wandering Jew' (1867) l. 49

Bb

Charles Babbage 1792–1871

English mathematician and inventor; pioneer of machine computing

1 Improvements succeeded each other so rapidly, that machines which had never been finished were abandoned in the hands of their makers, because new improvements had superseded their utility.
　On the Economy of Manufactures (1832)

2 Every moment dies a man,
　Every moment 1¹⁄₁₆ is born.
　　parody of **Tennyson**'s 'Vision of Sin', in an unpublished letter to the poet, in *New Scientist* 4 December 1958; see **Tennyson** 784:21

Isaac Babel 1894–1940

Russian short-story writer

3 A phrase is born into the world both good and bad at the same time. The secret lies in a slight, an almost invisible twist. The lever should rest in your hand, getting warm, and you can only turn it once, not twice.
　Guy de Maupassant (1932)

4 No iron can stab the heart with such force as a full stop put just at the right place.
　Guy de Maupassant (1932)

5 On Sabbath eves I am oppressed . . . O the rotted Talmuds of my childhood! O the dense melancholy of memories!
　Red Cavalry (1926) 'Gedali' (translated by Walter Morison)

6 Beyond the window, night stands like a black column . . . A shadowy radiance lies on the earth, and hanging from the bushes are necklaces of gleaming fruit.
　Red Cavalry (1926) 'Pan Apolek' (translated by Walter Morison)

7 The bee of sorrow had stung his heart.
　Red Cavalry (1926) 'Pan Apolek' (translated by Walter Morison)

8 Both of us looked on the world as a meadow in May—a meadow traversed by women and horses.
　Red Cavalry (1926) 'The Story of a Horse' (translated by Walter Morison)

Lauren Bacall 1924–

American actress

9 I think your whole life shows in your face and you should be proud of that.
　in *Daily Telegraph* 2 March 1988

Johann Sebastian Bach 1685–1750

German composer
on Bach: see **Beecham** 62:13, **Beethoven** 63:11, **Fry** 336:19

10 There is nothing to it. You only have to hit the right notes at the right time and the instrument plays itself.
　when complimented on his organ playing
　　K. Geiringer *The Bach Family* (1954)

Francis Bacon 1561–1626

English lawyer, courtier, philosopher, and essayist
on Bacon: see **Jonson** 436:9, **Strachey** 761:22, **Walton** 821:5; see also **Last words** 471:14

11 For all knowledge and wonder (which is the seed of knowledge) is an impression of pleasure in itself.
　The Advancement of Learning (1605) bk. 1, ch. 1, sect. 3

12 So let great authors have their due, as time, which is the author of authors, be not deprived of his due, which is further and further to discover truth.
　The Advancement of Learning (1605) bk. 1, ch. 4, sect. 12

13 If a man will begin with certainties, he shall end in doubts; but if he will be content to begin with doubts, he shall end in certainties.
　The Advancement of Learning (1605) bk. 1, ch. 5, sect. 8

14 [Knowledge is] a rich storehouse for the glory of the Creator and the relief of man's estate.
　The Advancement of Learning (1605) bk. 1, ch. 5, sect. 11

15 Antiquities are history defaced, or some remnants of history which have casually escaped the shipwreck of time.
　The Advancement of Learning (1605) bk. 2, ch. 2, sect. 1

16 Poesy was ever thought to have some participation of divineness, because it doth raise and erect the mind, by submitting the shows of things to the desires of the mind; whereas reason doth buckle and bow the mind unto the nature of things.
　The Advancement of Learning (1605) bk. 2, ch. 4, sect. 2

17 The knowledge of man is as the waters, some descending from above, and some springing from beneath; the one informed by the light of nature, the other inspired by divine revelation.
　The Advancement of Learning (1605) bk. 2, ch. 5, sect. 1

18 They are ill discoverers that think there is no land, when they can see nothing but sea.
　The Advancement of Learning (1605) bk. 2, ch. 7, sect. 5

19 Words are the tokens current and accepted for conceits, as moneys are for values.
　The Advancement of Learning (1605) bk. 2, ch. 16, sect. 3

20 A dance is a measured pace, as a verse is a measured speech.
　The Advancement of Learning (1605) bk. 2, ch. 16, sect. 5

21 But men must know, that in this theatre of man's life it is reserved only for God and angels to be lookers on.
　The Advancement of Learning (1605) bk. 2, ch. 20, sect. 8

1 Did not one of the fathers in great indignation call poesy *vinum daemonum*?

vinum daemonum = *the wine of devils*

The Advancement of Learning (1605) bk. 2, ch. 22, sect. 13; see **Augustine** 37:7

2 All good moral philosophy is but an handmaid to religion.

The Advancement of Learning (1605) bk. 2, ch. 22, sect. 14

3 It is in life as it is in ways, the shortest way is commonly the foulest, and surely the fairer way is not much about.

The Advancement of Learning (1605) bk. 2, ch. 23, sect. 45

4 Alonso of Aragon was wont to say in commendation of old age, that age appears to be best in four things,—old wood best to burn, old wine to drink, old friends to trust, and old authors to read.

Apophthegms New and Old (1625) no. 97

5 That all things are changed, and that nothing really perishes, and that the sum of matter remains exactly the same, is sufficiently certain.

Cogitationes de Natura Rerum Cogitatio 5 in J. Spedding (ed.) The Works of Francis Bacon vol. 5 (1858)

6 *Antiquitas saeculi juventus mundi.*

Ancient times were the youth of the world.

De Dignitate et Augmentis Scientiarum (1623) bk. 1 (translated by Gilbert Watts, 1640)

7 *Divitiae bona ancilla, pessima domina.*

Riches are a good handmaid, but the worst mistress.

De Dignitate et Augmentis Scientiarum (1623) bk. 6, ch. 3, pt. 3 'The Antitheta of Things' no. 6 (translated by Gilbert Watts, 1640)

8 *Nil moderatum vulgo gratum est.*

No term of moderation takes place with the vulgar.

De Dignitate et Augmentis Scientiarum (1623) bk. 6, ch. 3, pt. 3 'The Antitheta of Things' no. 30 (translated by Gilbert Watts, 1640)

9 *Silentium, stultorum virtus.*

Silence is the virtue of fools.

De Dignitate et Augmentis Scientiarum (1623) bk. 6, ch. 3, pt. 3 'The Antitheta of Things' no. 31 (translated by Gilbert Watts, 1640)

10 I hold every man a debtor to his profession.

The Elements of the Common Law (1596) preface

11 Why should a man be in love with his fetters, though of gold?

Essay of Death para. 4 in The Remaines of . . . Lord Verulam (1648); see **Astell** 32:13

12 He is the fountain of honour.

An Essay of a King (1642); attribution doubtful; see **Bagehot** 47:16

13 Prosperity is the blessing of the Old Testament, adversity is the blessing of the New.

Essays (1625) 'Of Adversity'

14 The pencil of the Holy Ghost hath laboured more in describing the afflictions of Job than the felicities of Solomon.

Essays (1625) 'Of Adversity'

15 Prosperity doth best discover vice, but adversity doth best discover virtue.

Essays (1625) 'Of Adversity'

16 I had rather believe all the fables in the legend, and the Talmud, and the Alcoran, than that this universal frame is without a mind.

Essays (1625) 'Of Atheism'

17 A little philosophy inclineth man's mind to atheism, but depth in philosophy bringeth men's minds about to religion.

Essays (1625) 'Of Atheism'

18 They that deny a God destroy man's nobility; for certainly man is of kin to the beasts by his body; and, if he be not of kin to God by his spirit, he is a base and ignoble creature.

Essays (1625) 'Of Atheism'

19 Virtue is like a rich stone, best plain set.

Essays (1625) 'Of Beauty'

20 There is no excellent beauty that hath not some strangeness in the proportion.

Essays (1625) 'Of Beauty'

21 He said it that knew it best.

referring to **Demosthenes**

Essays (1625) 'Of Boldness'; see **Demosthenes** 263:19

22 In civil business; what first? boldness; what second and third? boldness: and yet boldness is a child of ignorance and baseness.

Essays (1625) 'Of Boldness'; see **Danton** 256:14, **Demosthenes** 263:19

23 Boldness is an ill keeper of promise.

Essays (1625) 'Of Boldness'

24 Houses are built to live in and not to look on; therefore let use be preferred before uniformity, except where both may be had.

Essays (1625) 'Of Building'

25 Light gains make heavy purses.

Essays (1625) 'Of Ceremonies and Respects'

26 He that is too much in anything, so that he giveth another occasion of satiety, maketh himself cheap.

Essays (1625) 'Of Ceremonies and Respects'

27 Books will speak plain when counsellors blanch.

Essays (1625) 'Of Counsel'

28 [Some] there be that can pack the cards and yet cannot play well; so there are some that are good in canvasses and factions, that are otherwise weak men.

Essays (1625) 'Of Cunning'

29 In things that are tender and unpleasing, it is good to break the ice by some whose words are of less weight, and to reserve the more weighty voice to come in as by chance.

Essays (1625) 'Of Cunning'

30 I knew one that when he wrote a letter he would put that which was most material in the postscript, as if it had been a bymatter.

Essays (1625) 'Of Cunning'; see **Steele** 754:17

31 Nothing doth more hurt in a state than that cunning men pass for wise.

Essays (1625) 'Of Cunning'

1 Men fear death as children fear to go in the dark; and as that natural fear in children is increased with tales, so is the other.
Essays (1625) 'Of Death'

2 Revenge triumphs over death; love slights it; honour aspireth to it; grief flieth to it.
Essays (1625) 'Of Death'

3 It is as natural to die as to be born; and to a little infant, perhaps, the one is as painful as the other.
Essays (1625) 'Of Death'

4 Death . . . openeth the gate to good fame, and extinguisheth envy.
Essays (1625) 'Of Death'

5 If you dissemble sometimes your knowledge of that you are thought to know, you shall be thought, another time, to know that you know not.
Essays (1625) 'Of Discourse'

6 I knew a wise man that had it for a by-word, when he saw men hasten to a conclusion. 'Stay a little, that we may make an end the sooner.'
Essays (1625) 'Of Dispatch'

7 To choose time is to save time.
Essays (1625) 'Of Dispatch'

8 Riches are for spending.
Essays (1625) 'Of Expense'

9 A man ought warily to begin charges which once begun will continue.
Essays (1625) 'Of Expense'

10 There is little friendship in the world, and least of all between equals.
Essays (1625) 'Of Followers and Friends'

11 Chiefly the mould of a man's fortune is in his own hands.
Essays (1625) 'Of Fortune'

12 If a man look sharply, and attentively, he shall see Fortune: for though she be blind, yet she is not invisible.
Essays (1625) 'Of Fortune'

13 It had been hard for him that spake it to have put more truth and untruth together, in a few words, than in that speech: 'Whosoever is delighted in solitude is either a wild beast, or a god.'
Essays (1625) 'Of Friendship'; see **Aristotle** 25:26

14 A crowd is not company, and faces are but a gallery of pictures, and talk but a tinkling cymbal, where there is no love.
Essays (1625) 'Of Friendship'

15 It redoubleth joys, and cutteth griefs in halves.
Essays (1625) 'Of Friendship'

16 Cure the disease and kill the patient.
Essays (1625) 'Of Friendship'

17 God Almighty first planted a garden; and, indeed, it is the purest of human pleasures.
Essays (1625) 'Of Gardens'

18 Nothing is more pleasant to the eye than green grass kept finely shorn.
Essays (1625) 'Of Gardens'

19 If a man be gracious and courteous to strangers, it shows he is a citizen of the world.
Essays (1625) 'Of Goodness, and Goodness of Nature'

20 The inclination to goodness is imprinted deeply in the nature of man: insomuch, that if it issue not towards men, it will take unto other living creatures.
Essays (1625) 'Of Goodness, and Goodness of Nature'

21 Men in great place are thrice servants: servants of the sovereign or state, servants of fame, and servants of business.
Essays (1625) 'Of Great Place'

22 It is a strange desire to seek power and to lose liberty.
Essays (1625) 'Of Great Place'

23 The rising unto place is laborious, and by pains men come to greater pains; and it is sometimes base, and by indignities men come to dignities. The standing is slippery, and the regress is either a downfall, or at least an eclipse.
Essays (1625) 'Of Great Place'

24 Severity breedeth fear, but roughness breedeth hate. Even reproofs from authority ought to be grave, and not taunting.
Essays (1625) 'Of Great Place'

25 All rising to great place is by a winding stair.
Essays (1625) 'Of Great Place'

26 As the births of living creatures at first are ill-shapen, so are all innovations, which are the births of time.
Essays (1625) 'Of Innovations'

27 He that will not apply new remedies must expect new evils; for time is the greatest innovator.
Essays (1625) 'Of Innovations'

28 The speaking in a perpetual hyperbole is comely in nothing but in love.
Essays (1625) 'Of Love'

29 It has been well said that 'the arch-flatterer with whom all the petty flatterers have intelligence is a man's self.'
Essays (1625) 'Of Love'

30 He that hath wife and children hath given hostages to fortune; for they are impediments to great enterprises, either of virtue or mischief.
Essays (1625) 'Of Marriage and the Single Life'; see **Lucan** 495:3

31 A single life doth well with churchmen, for charity will hardly water the ground where it must first fill a pool.
Essays (1625) 'Of Marriage and the Single Life'

32 Wives are young men's mistresses, companions for middle age, and old men's nurses.
Essays (1625) 'Of Marriage and the Single Life'

33 He was reputed one of the wise men that made answer to the question when a man should marry? 'A young man not yet, an elder man not at all.'
Essays (1625) 'Of Marriage and the Single Life'; see **Punch** 637:4

1 It is generally better to deal by speech than by letter.
Essays (1625) 'Of Negotiating'

2 New nobility is but the act of power, but ancient nobility is the act of time.
Essays (1625) 'Of Nobility'

3 Nobility of birth commonly abateth industry.
Essays (1625) 'Of Nobility'

4 The joys of parents are secret, and so are their griefs and fears.
Essays (1625) 'Of Parents and Children'

5 Children sweeten labours, but they make misfortunes more bitter.
Essays (1625) 'Of Parents and Children'

6 Fame is like a river, that beareth up things light and swollen, and drowns things weighty and solid.
Essays (1625) 'Of Praise'

7 Age will not be defied.
Essays (1625) 'Of Regimen of Health'

8 Revenge is a kind of wild justice, which the more man's nature runs to, the more ought law to weed it out.
Essays (1625) 'Of Revenge'

9 A man that studieth revenge keeps his own wounds green.
Essays (1625) 'Of Revenge'

10 Defer not charities till death; for certainly, if a man weigh it rightly, he that doth so is rather liberal of another man's than of his own.
Essays (1625) 'Of Riches'

11 The four pillars of government . . . (which are religion, justice, counsel, and treasure).
Essays (1625) 'Of Seditions and Troubles'

12 The surest way to prevent seditions (if the times do bear it) is to take away the matter of them.
Essays (1625) 'Of Seditions and Troubles'

13 Money is like muck, not good except it be spread.
Essays (1625) 'Of Seditions and Troubles'; see **Proverbs** 626:35

14 The remedy is worse than the disease.
Essays (1625) 'Of Seditions and Troubles'

15 The French are wiser than they seem, and the Spaniards seem wiser than they are.
Essays (1625) 'Of Seeming Wise'

16 Studies serve for delight, for ornament, and for ability.
Essays (1625) 'Of Studies'

17 To spend too much time in studies is sloth.
Essays (1625) 'Of Studies'

18 They perfect nature and are perfected by experience.
Essays (1625) 'Of Studies'

19 Read not to contradict and confute, nor to believe and take for granted, nor to find talk and discourse, but to weigh and consider.
Essays (1625) 'Of Studies'

20 Some books are to be tasted, others to be swallowed, and some few to be chewed and digested.
Essays (1625) 'Of Studies'

21 Reading maketh a full man; conference a ready man; and writing an exact man.
Essays (1625) 'Of Studies'

22 Histories make men wise; poets, witty; the mathematics, subtile; natural philosophy, deep; moral, grave; logic and rhetoric, able to contend.
Essays (1625) 'Of Studies'

23 There is a superstition in avoiding superstition.
Essays (1625) 'Of Superstition'

24 Suspicions amongst thoughts are like bats amongst birds, they ever fly by twilight.
Essays (1625) 'Of Suspicion'

25 There is nothing makes a man suspect much, more than to know little.
Essays (1625) 'Of Suspicion'

26 Neither is money the sinews of war (as it is trivially said).
Essays (1625) 'Of the True Greatness of Kingdoms'; see **Cicero** 223:20

27 Neither will it be, that a people overlaid with taxes should ever become valiant and martial.
Essays (1625) 'Of the True Greatness of Kingdoms'

28 Travel, in the younger sort, is a part of education; in the elder, a part of experience. He that travelleth into a country before he hath some entrance into the language, goeth to school, and not to travel.
Essays (1625) 'Of Travel'

29 What is truth? said jesting Pilate; and would not stay for an answer.
Essays (1625) 'Of Truth'; see **Bible** 104:1

30 A mixture of a lie doth ever add pleasure.
Essays (1625) 'Of Truth'

31 It is not the lie that passeth through the mind, but the lie that sinketh in, and settleth in it, that doth the hurt.
Essays (1625) 'Of Truth'

32 The inquiry of truth, which is the love-making, or wooing of it, the knowledge of truth, which is the presence of it, and the belief of truth, which is the enjoying of it, is the sovereign good of human nature.
Essays (1625) 'Of Truth'

33 All colours will agree in the dark.
Essays (1625) 'Of Unity in Religion'

34 It was prettily devised of Aesop, 'The fly sat upon the axle-tree of the chariot-wheel and said, what a dust do I raise.'
Essays (1625) 'Of Vain-Glory'

35 In the youth of a state arms do flourish; in the middle age of a state, learning; and then both of them together for a time; in the declining age of a state, mechanical arts and merchandise.
Essays (1625) 'Of Vicissitude of Things'

1 Be so true to thyself as thou be not false to others.
Essays (1625) 'Of Wisdom for a Man's Self'; see
Shakespeare 684:20

2 It is the nature of extreme self-lovers, as they will
set a house on fire, and it were but to roast their
eggs.
Essays (1625) 'Of Wisdom for a Man's Self'

3 It is the wisdom of the crocodiles, that shed tears
when they would devour.
Essays (1625) 'Of Wisdom for a Man's Self'

4 Young men are fitter to invent than to judge, fitter
for execution than for counsel, and fitter for new
projects than for settled business.
Essays (1625) 'Of Youth and Age'

5 God forbid that we should give out a dream of our
own imagination for a pattern of the world.
The Great Instauration (1620) translated by J Spedding

6 For they thought generally that he was a Prince
as ordained, and sent down from heaven to unite
and put to an end the long dissensions of the two
houses; which although they had had, in the
times of Henry the Fourth, Henry the Fifth, and a
part of Henry the Sixth on the one side, and the
times of Edward the Fourth on the other, lucid
intervals and happy pauses; yet they did ever
hang over the kingdom, ready to break forth into
new perturbations and calamities.
History of King Henry VII (1622) para. 3 in J. Spedding (ed.)
The Works of Francis Bacon vol. 6 (1858)

7 I have rather studied books than men.
*A Letter of Advice . . . to the Duke of Buckingham, When he
became Favourite to King James* (1661)

8 I have taken all knowledge to be my province.
'To My Lord Treasurer Burghley' (1592) in J. Spedding
(ed.) *The Letters and Life of Francis Bacon* vol. 1 (1861)

9 Universities incline wits to sophistry and
affectation.
Valerius Terminus of the Interpretation of Nature ch. 26 in
Letters and Remains of the Lord Chancellor Bacon (collected by
Robert Stephens, 1734)

10 *Nam et ipsa scientia potestas est.*
For also knowledge itself is power.
Meditationes Sacrae (1597) 'Of Heresies'; see **Proverbs**
624:45

11 I would live to study, and not study to live.
Memorial of Access to King James I (c.1622) in *Letters,
Speeches, Charges, Advices, etc. of Francis Bacon* (1763)

12 God's first Creature, which was Light.
New Atlantis (1627)

13 The end of our foundation is the knowledge of
causes, and secret motions of things; and the
enlarging of the bounds of human Empire, to the
effecting of all things possible.
New Atlantis (1627)

14 *Subtilitas naturae subtilitatem sensus et intellectus
multis partibus superat.*
The subtlety of nature is greater many times over
than the subtlety of the senses and understanding.
Novum Organum (1620) bk. 1, Aphorism 10 (translated by
J. Spedding)

15 *Quod enim mavult homo verum esse, id potius credit.*
For what a man would like to be true, that he
more readily believes.
Novum Organum (1620) bk. 1, Aphorism 49 (translated by
J. Spedding); see **Caesar** 185:2

16 *Magna ista scientiarum mater.*
That great mother of sciences.
of natural philosophy
Novum Organum (1620) bk. 1, Aphorism 80 (translated by
J. Spedding)

17 *Vim et virtutem et consequentias rerum inventarum
notare juvat; quae non in aliis manifestius occurrunt,
quam in illis tribus quae antiquis incognitae, et
quarum primordia, licet recentia, obscura et ingloria
sunt: Artis nimirum Imprimendi, Pulveris
Tormentarii, et Acus Nauticae. Haec enim tria rerum
faciem et statum in orbe terrarum mutaverunt.*
It is well to observe the force and virtue and
consequence of discoveries, and these are to be
seen nowhere more conspicuously than in those
three which were unknown to the ancients, and of
which the origins, though recent, are obscure and
inglorious; namely, printing, gunpowder, and the
mariner's needle [compass] . . . these three have
changed the whole face and state of things
throughout the world.
Novum Organum (1620) bk. 1, Aphorism 129 (translated
by J. Spedding); see **Carlyle** 192:3

18 *Natura enim non imperatur, nisi parendo.*
Nature cannot be ordered about, except by
obeying her.
Novum Organum (1620) bk. 1, Aphorism 129 (translated
by J. Spedding)

19 Books must follow sciences, and not sciences
books.
Resuscitatio (1657) 'Proposition touching Amendment of
Laws'

20 Wise nature did never put her precious jewels into
a garret four stories high: and therefore . . .
exceeding tall men had ever very empty heads.
J. Spedding (ed.) *The Works of Francis Bacon* vol. 7 (1859)
'Additional Apophthegms' no. 17

21 Hope is a good breakfast, but it is a bad supper.
J. Spedding (ed.) *The Works of Francis Bacon* vol. 7 (1859)
'Apophthegms contained in *Resuscitatio*' no. 36; see
Proverbs 622:31

22 Anger makes dull men witty, but it keeps them
poor.
often attributed to Queen **Elizabeth I** *from a misreading
of the text*
J. Spedding (ed.) *The Works of Francis Bacon* vol. 7 (1859)
'Baconiana'

23 The world's a bubble; and the life of man
Less than a span.
The World (1629)

24 Who then to frail mortality shall trust,
But limns the water, or but writes in dust.
The World (1629)

25 What is it then to have or have no wife,
But single thraldom, or a double strife?
The World (1629)

1 What then remains, but that we still should cry,
Not to be born, or being born, to die?
The World (1629)

2 There be three things which make a nation great
and prosperous: a fertile soil, busy workshops,
easy conveyance for men and goods from place to
place.
attributed; S. Platt (ed.) *Respectfully Quoted* (1989)

Francis Bacon 1909–92

Irish painter

3 Champagne for my real friends, real pain for my
sham friends.
in the 1950s; Michael Peppiatt *Francis Bacon* (1996)

4 What I see is a marvellous painting. But how are
you going to make it? And, of course, as I don't
know how to make it, I rely then on chance and
accident making it for me.
David Sylvester (ed.) *Interviews with Francis Bacon: the
brutality of fact* (ed. 3, 1987)

Roger Bacon c.1220–c.1292

English philosopher, scientist, Franciscan friar

5 If in other sciences we should arrive at certainty
without doubt and truth without error, it behoves
us to place the foundations of knowledge in
mathematics.
Opus Majus bk. 1, ch. 4

Lord Baden-Powell see Mottoes 552:4

Karl Baedeker 1801–59

German publisher

6 Oxford is on the whole more attractive than
Cambridge to the ordinary visitor; and the
traveller is therefore recommended to visit
Cambridge first, or to omit it altogether if he
cannot visit both.
Great Britain (1887) Route 30 'From London to Oxford'

7 The traveller need have no scruple in limiting his
donations to the smallest possible sums, as
liberality frequently becomes a source of
annoyance and embarrassment.
Northern Italy (1895) 'Gratuities'

8 PASSPORTS. On arrival at a Syrian port the
traveller's passport is sometimes asked for, but an
ordinary visiting-card will answer the purpose
equally well.
Palestine and Syria (1876) 'Passports and Custom House'

Joan Baez 1941–

American singer and songwriter

9 The only thing that's been a worse flop than the
organization of non-violence has been the
organization of violence.
Daybreak (1970) 'What Would You Do If?'; see **Péguy**
591:6

Walter Bagehot 1826–77

English economist and essayist
see also **Disraeli** 275:10

10 A constitutional statesman is in general a man of
common opinion and uncommon abilities.
Biographical Studies (1881) 'Sir Robert Peel'

11 He believes, with all his heart and soul and
strength, that there *is* such a thing as truth; he
has the soul of a martyr with the intellect of an
advocate.
Biographical Studies (1881) 'Mr Gladstone'

12 Capital must be propelled by self-interest; it cannot
be enticed by benevolence.
Economic Studies (1880) ch. 2

13 The mystic reverence, the religious allegiance,
which are essential to a true monarchy, are
imaginative sentiments that no legislature can
manufacture in any people.
The English Constitution (1867) 'The Cabinet'

14 In such constitutions [as England's] there are two
parts . . . first, those which excite and preserve the
reverence of the population—the *dignified* parts . . .
and next, the *efficient* parts—those by which it, in
fact, works and rules.
The English Constitution (1867) 'The Cabinet'

15 No orator ever made an impression by appealing
to men as to their plainest physical wants, except
when he could allege that those wants were
caused by some one's tyranny.
The English Constitution (1867) 'The Cabinet'

16 The Crown is, according to the saying, the
'fountain of honour'; but the Treasury is the
spring of business.
The English Constitution (1867) 'The Cabinet'; see **Bacon**
43:12

17 A cabinet is a combining committee—a *hyphen*
which joins, a *buckle* which fastens, the legislative
part of the state to the executive part of the state.
The English Constitution (1867) 'The Cabinet'

18 It has been said that England invented the phrase,
'Her Majesty's Opposition'; that it was the first
government which made a criticism of
administration as much a part of the polity as
administration itself. This critical opposition is the
consequence of cabinet government.
The English Constitution (1867) 'The Cabinet'; see **Hobhouse**
391:3

19 *The Times* has made many ministries.
The English Constitution (1867) 'The Cabinet'

20 The great qualities, the imperious will, the rapid
energy, the eager nature fit for a great crisis are
not required—are impediments—in common
times.
The English Constitution (1867) 'The Cabinet'

21 We often want, at the sudden occurrence of a
grave tempest, to change the helmsman—to
replace the pilot of the calm by the pilot of the
storm.
The English Constitution (1867) 'The Cabinet'

1 It has been said, not truly, but with a possible approximation to truth, that in 1802 every hereditary monarch was insane.
The English Constitution (1867) 'Checks and Balances'

2 The soldier—that is, the great soldier—of to-day is not a romantic animal, dashing at forlorn hopes, animated by frantic sentiment, full of fancies as to a love-lady or a sovereign; but a quiet, grave man, busied in charts, exact in sums, master of the art of tactics, occupied in trivial detail; thinking, as the Duke of Wellington was said to do, *most* of the shoes of his soldiers; despising all manner of *éclat* and eloquence; perhaps, like Count Moltke, 'silent in seven languages'.
The English Constitution (1867) 'Checks and Balances'

3 The finest brute votes in Europe.
view of 'a cynical politician'; sometimes attributed to **Disraeli**
The English Constitution (1867) 'The House of Commons'

4 The order of nobility is of great use, too, not only in what it creates, but in what it prevents. It prevents the rule of wealth—the religion of gold. This is the obvious and natural idol of the Anglo-Saxon.
The English Constitution (1867) 'The House of Lords'

5 The House of Commons lives in a state of perpetual potential choice: at any moment it can choose a ruler and dismiss a ruler. And therefore party is inherent in it, is bone of its bone, and breath of its breath.
The English Constitution (1867) 'The House of Commons'

6 An Opposition, on coming into power, is often like a speculative merchant whose bills become due. Ministers have to make good their promises, and they find a difficulty in so doing.
The English Constitution (1867) 'The House of Commons'

7 A severe though not unfriendly critic of our institutions said that 'the cure for admiring the House of Lords was to go and look at it.'
The English Constitution (1867) 'The House of Lords'

8 Nations touch at their summits.
The English Constitution (1867) 'The House of Lords'

9 As soon as we see that England is a disguised republic we must see too that the classes for whom the disguise is necessary must be tenderly dealt with.
The English Constitution (1867) 'Its History'

10 It is nice to trace how the actions of a retired widow and an unemployed youth become of such importance.
of Queen **Victoria** *and the future* **Edward VII**
The English Constitution (1867) 'The Monarchy'

11 Women—one half the human race at least—care fifty times more for a marriage than a ministry.
The English Constitution (1867) 'The Monarchy'

12 Royalty is a government in which the attention of the nation is concentrated on one person doing interesting actions. A Republic is a government in which that attention is divided between many, who are all doing uninteresting actions.

Accordingly, so long as the human heart is strong and the human reason weak, Royalty will be strong because it appeals to diffused feeling, and Republics weak because they appeal to the understanding.
The English Constitution (1867) 'The Monarchy'

13 Throughout the greater part of his life George III was a kind of 'consecrated obstruction'.
The English Constitution (1867) 'The Monarchy'

14 There are arguments for not having a Court, and there are arguments for having a splendid Court; but there are no arguments for having a mean Court.
The English Constitution (1867) 'The Monarchy'

15 The Queen . . . must sign her own death-warrant if the two Houses unanimously send it up to her.
The English Constitution (1867) 'The Monarchy'

16 Above all things our royalty is to be reverenced, and if you begin to poke about it you cannot reverence it . . . Its mystery is its life. We must not let in daylight upon magic.
The English Constitution (1867) 'The Monarchy (continued)'

17 The Sovereign has, under a constitutional monarchy such as ours, three rights—the right to be consulted, the right to encourage, the right to warn.
The English Constitution (1867) 'The Monarchy (continued)'

18 The only fit material for a constitutional king is a prince who begins early to reign—who in his youth is superior to pleasure—who in his youth is willing to labour—who has by nature a genius for discretion. Such kings are among God's greatest gifts, but they are also among His rarest.
The English Constitution (1867) 'The Monarchy' (continued)

19 It is an inevitable defect, that bureaucrats will care more for routine than for results.
The English Constitution (1867) 'On Changes of Ministry'

20 The worst families are those in which the members never really speak their minds to one another; they maintain an atmosphere of unreality, and everyone always lives in an atmosphere of suppressed ill-feeling.
The English Constitution (ed. 2, 1872) introduction

21 No real English gentleman, in his secret soul, was ever sorry for the death of a political economist.
Estimates of some Englishmen and Scotchmen (1858) 'The First Edinburgh Reviewers'

22 Writers, like teeth, are divided into incisors and grinders.
Estimates of some Englishmen and Scotchmen (1858) 'The First Edinburgh Reviewers'

23 To a great experience one thing is essential, an experiencing nature.
Estimates of some Englishmen and Scotchmen (1858) 'Shakespeare—the Individual'

24 One of the greatest pains to human nature is the pain of a new idea.
Physics and Politics (1872) 'The Age of Discussion'

25 The most melancholy of human reflections, perhaps, is that, on the whole, it is a question whether the benevolence of mankind does most good or harm.

> *Physics and Politics* (1872) 'The Age of Discussion'

1 Civilized ages inherit the human nature which was victorious in barbarous ages, and that nature is, in many respects, not at all suited to civilized circumstances.

> *Physics and Politics* (1872) 'The Age of Discussion'

2 The truth is that the propensity of man to imitate what is before him is one of the strongest parts of his nature.

> *Physics and Politics* (1872) 'Nation-Making'

3 One of the most common defects of half-instructed minds is to think much of that in which they differ from others, and little of that in which they agree with others.

> *on the evils of sectarianism*
> in *Economist* 11 June 1870

4 A great Premier must add the vivacity of an idle man to the assiduity of a very laborious one.

> in *The Economist* 2 January 1875

5 In every country the extreme party is most irritated against the party which comes nearest to itself, but does not go so far.

> in *The Economist* 2 January 1875

6 Small sciences are the labours of our manhood; but the round universe is the plaything of the boy.

> in *National Review* January 1856 'Edward Gibbon'

7 The great breeding people had gone out and multiplied; colonies in every clime attest our success; French is the *patois* of Europe; English is the language of the world.

> in *National Review* January 1856 'Edward Gibbon'

8 The purchaser [of a newspaper] desires an article which he can appreciate at sight; which he can lay down and say, 'An excellent article, very excellent; exactly *my own* sentiments.'

> in *National Review* July 1856 'The Character of Sir Robert Peel'

9 He describes London like a special correspondent for posterity.

> in *National Review* 7 October 1858 'Charles Dickens'

10 To be commonly above others, still more to think yourself above others, is to be below them every now and then, and sometimes much below.

> in *National Review* July 1859 'John Milton'

11 Wordsworth, Tennyson and Browning; or, pure, ornate, and grotesque art in English poetry.

> in *National Review* November 1864, essay title

Abdul Baha 1844–1921
*Persian co-founder (with his father **Baha'ullah**) of the Baha'i faith*

12 In this century, which is the century of light and the revelation of mysteries . . . it is well established that mankind and womankind as parts of composite humanity are coequal and that no difference in estimate is allowable, for all are human.

> at a woman's suffrage meeting in New York, 1912; *The Promulgation of Universal Peace* (2nd ed., 1982)

13 Today, humanity is bowed down with trouble, sorrow and grief, no one escapes; the world is wet with tears; but, thank God, the remedy is at our doors. Let us turn our hands away from the world of matter and live in the spiritual world.

> *Paris Talks* (1912) November 22

Baha'ullah 1817–92
*Persian co-founder (with his son Abdul **Baha**) of the Baha'i faith*

14 No man shall attain the shores of the ocean of true understanding except he be detached from all that is in heaven and earth.

> *The Book of Certitude*

Bahya ibn Paquda fl. 1080
Spanish-born Jewish philosopher

15 We are obliged to serve God both outwardly and inwardly. Outward service is expressed in the duties of the members, such as prayer, fasting, almsgiving, learning and teaching the Torah . . . all of which can be wholly performed by man's physical body. Inward service, however, is expressed in the duties of the heart, in the heart's assertion of the unity of God, in belief in him and in his Book, in constant obedience to him and fear of him, in humility before him, love for him and complete reliance upon him, submission to him and abstinence from the things hateful to him.

> *The Duties of the Heart* introduction

16 You should know, O man, that the greatest enemy you have in the world is your inclination.

> *The Duties of the Heart* Gate 5, ch. 5

David Bailey 1938–
English photographer
*see also **Sayings** 740:5*

17 It takes a lot of imagination to be a good photographer. You need less imagination to be a painter, because you can invent things. But in photography everything is so ordinary; it takes a lot of looking before you learn to see the ordinary.

> interview in *The Face* December 1984

Philip James Bailey 1816–1902
English poet

18 We should count time by heart-throbs.

> *Festus* (1839) sc. 5

19 America, thou half-brother of the world;
With something good and bad of every land.

> *Festus* (1839) sc. 10

Bruce Bairnsfather see Cartoon captions

Henry Williams Baker 1821–77

English clergyman and hymn-writer

1 Lord, thy word abideth,
  And our footsteps guideth;
  Who its truth believeth
  Light and joy receiveth.
  'Lord, thy word abideth' (1861 hymn)

2 The King of love my shepherd is,
  Whose goodness faileth never;
  I nothing lack if I am his
  And he is mine for ever . . .
  Perverse and foolish oft I strayed,
  But yet in love he sought me,
  And on his shoulder gently laid,
  And home, rejoicing, brought me.
  'The King of love my shepherd is' (1868 hymn)

3 O praise ye the Lord, all things that give sound;
  Each jubilant chord re-echo around;
  Loud organs, his glory forth tell in deep tone,
  And, sweet harp, the story of what he hath done.
  'O praise ye the Lord!' (1875 hymn)

Michael Bakunin 1814–76

Russian revolutionary and anarchist

4 The urge for destruction is also a creative urge!
  Jahrbuch für Wissenschaft und Kunst (1842) 'Die Reaktion in Deutschland' (under the pseudonym 'Jules Elysard')

5 Everything will pass, and the world will perish but the Ninth Symphony will remain.
  of **Beethoven**'s *Ninth Symphony*
  Edmund Wilson *To The Finland Station* (1940)

James Baldwin 1924–87

American novelist and essayist

6 Children have never been very good at listening to their elders, but they have never failed to imitate them. They must, they have no other models.
  Nobody Knows My Name (1961) 'Fifth Avenue, Uptown: a letter from Harlem'

7 Anyone who has ever struggled with poverty knows how extremely expensive it is to be poor.
  Nobody Knows My Name (1961) 'Fifth Avenue, Uptown: a letter from Harlem'

8 Freedom is not something that anybody can be given; freedom is something people take and people are as free as they want to be.
  Nobody Knows My Name (1961) 'Notes for a Hypothetical Novel'

9 Money, it turned out, was exactly like sex, you thought of nothing else if you didn't have it and thought of other things if you did.
  in *Esquire* May 1961 'Black Boy looks at the White Boy'

10 It comes as a great shock around the age of 5, 6 or 7 to discover that the flag to which you have pledged allegiance, along with everybody else, has not pledged allegiance to you. It comes as a great shock to see Gary Cooper killing off the Indians and, although you are rooting for Gary Cooper, that the Indians are you.
  speaking for the proposition that 'The American Dream is at the expense of the American Negro'
  speech at the Cambridge Union, England, 17 February 1965; in *New York Times Magazine* 7 March 1965

11 If they take you in the morning, they will be coming for us that night.
  in *New York Review of Books* 7 January 1971 'Open Letter to my Sister, Angela Davis'

Stanley Baldwin 1867–1947

British Conservative statesman; Prime Minister, 1923–4, 1924–9, 1935–7

on Baldwin: see **Beaverbrook** 60:11, **Churchill** 222:2, **Curzon** 254:10, **Trevelyan** 798:13; *see also* **Kipling** 457:8

12 They [parliament] are a lot of hard-faced men who look as if they had done very well out of the war.
  J. M. Keynes *Economic Consequences of the Peace* (1919) ch. 5

13 A platitude is simply a truth repeated until people get tired of hearing it.
  speech in the House of Commons, 29 May 1924

14 There are three classes which need sanctuary more than others—birds, wild flowers, and Prime Ministers.
  in *Observer* 24 May 1925

15 I think it is well also for the man in the street to realize that there is no power on earth that can protect him from being bombed. Whatever people may tell him, the bomber will always get through. The only defence is in offence, which means that you have to kill more women and children more quickly than the enemy if you want to save yourselves.
  speech in the House of Commons, 10 November 1932

16 Since the day of the air, the old frontiers are gone. When you think of the defence of England you no longer think of the chalk cliffs of Dover; you think of the Rhine. That is where our frontier lies.
  speech in the House of Commons, 30 July 1934

17 I shall be but a short time tonight. I have seldom spoken with greater regret, for my lips are not yet unsealed. Were these troubles over I would make a case, and I guarantee that not a man would go into the lobby against us.
  on the Abyssinian crisis
  speech in the House of Commons, 10 December 1935; see **Misquotations** 538:10

18 This House today is a theatre which is being watched by the whole world. Let us conduct ourselves with that dignity which His Majesty is showing in this hour of his trial.
  speech on the abdication of **Edward VIII**, House of Commons, 10 December 1936

19 Once I leave, I leave. I am not going to speak to the man on the bridge, and I am not going to spit on the deck.
  resignation statement to the Cabinet, 28 May 1937

1 Do not run up your nose dead against the Pope or the NUM!

R. A. Butler *The Art of Memory* (1982) 'Iain Macleod'; see **Macmillan** 504:8

Arthur James Balfour 1848–1930

British Conservative statesman; Prime Minister, 1902–5

on Balfour: see **Churchill** *220:20,* **Churchill** *222:7,* **Lloyd George** *487:13*

2 It is unfortunate, considering that enthusiasm moves the world, that so few enthusiasts can be trusted to speak the truth.

letter to Mrs Drew, 19 May 1891; L. March-Phillips and B. Christian (eds.) *Some Hawarden Letters* (1917) ch. 7

3 The tyranny of majorities may be as bad as the tyranny of Kings . . . and I do not think that any rational or sober man will say that what is justifiable against a tyrannical King may not under certain circumstances be justifiable against a tyrannical majority.

watching the Belfast march past of Ulster Loyalists in 1893

in *Times* 5 April 1893

4 When it comes I shall not be sorry. Only let us have separation as well as Home Rule: England cannot afford to go on with the Irishmen in her Parliament.

Wilfrid Scawen Blunt *The Land War in Ireland* (1912)

5 His Majesty's Government view with favour the establishment in Palestine of a national home for the Jewish people, and will use their best endeavours to facilitate the achievement of this object, it being clearly understood that nothing shall be done which may prejudice the civil and religious rights of existing non-Jewish communities in Palestine, or the rights and political status enjoyed by Jews in any other country.

known as the 'Balfour Declaration'

letter to Lord Rothschild 2 November 1917

6 I make it a rule never to stare at people when they are in obvious distress.

on being asked what he thought of the behaviour of the German delegation at the signing of the Treaty of Versailles

Max Egremont *Balfour* (1980)

7 Zionism, be it right or wrong, good or bad, is rooted in age-long traditions, in present need, in future hopes, of far profounder import than the desires and prejudices of the seven hundred thousand Arabs who now inhabit that ancient land.

in August 1919; Max Egremont *Balfour* (1980)

8 Christianity, of course . . . but why journalism?

replying to Frank Harris, who had claimed that 'all the faults of the age come from Christianity and journalism'

Margot Asquith *Autobiography* (1920) vol. 1, ch. 10

9 I thought he was a young man of promise, but it appears he is a young man of promises.

of Winston **Churchill**

Winston Churchill *My Early Life* (1930) ch. 17

10 I am more or less happy when being praised, not very uncomfortable when being abused, but I have moments of uneasiness when being explained.

K. Young *A. J. Balfour* (1963)

Ballads

11 There was a youth, and a well-beloved youth,
And he was an esquire's son,
He loved the bailiff's daughter dear,
That lived in Islington.

'The Bailiff's Daughter of Islington'

12 All in the merry month of May,
When green buds they were swellin',
Young Jemmy Grove on his death-bed lay,
For love of Barbara Allen.

'Barbara Allen's Cruelty'

13 O mother, mother, make my bed,
O make it saft and narrow:
My love has died for me to-day,
I'll die for him to-morrow.

'Barbara Allen's Cruelty'

14 It fell about the Lammastide,
When the muir-men win their hay
The doughty Douglas bound him to ride
Into England, to drive a prey.

'Battle of Otterburn'

15 There were twa sisters sat in a bour;
Binnorie, O Binnorie!
There came a knight to be their wooer,
By the bonnie milldams o' Binnorie.

'Binnorie'

16 Ye Highlands and ye Lawlands,
O where hae ye been?
They hae slain the Earl of Murray,
And hae laid him on the green.

'The Bonny Earl of Murray'

17 He was a braw gallant,
And he played at the gluve;
And the bonny Earl of Murray,
O he was the Queen's luve!

O lang will his Lady
Look owre the Castle Downe,
Ere she see the Earl of Murray
Come sounding through the town!

'The Bonny Earl of Murray'

18 Is there any room at your head, Sanders?
Is there any room at your feet?
Or any room at your twa sides,
Where fain, fain I would sleep?

There is na room at my head, Margaret,
There is na room at my feet;
My bed it is the cold, cold grave;
Among the hungry worms I sleep.

'Clerk Sanders'

19 She hadna sailed a league, a league,
A league but barely three,

Till grim, grim grew his countenance
And gurly grew the sea.
'The Daemon Lover'

1 'What hills are yon, yon pleasant hills,
The sun shines sweetly on?'—
'O yon are the hills o' Heaven,' he said,
'Where you will never won.'
'The Daemon Lover'

2 Let me have length and breadth enough,
And under my head a sod;
That they may say when I am dead,
—*Here lies bold Robin Hood!*
'The Death of Robin Hood'

3 There were three lords drinking at the wine
On the dowie dens o' Yarrow;
They made a compact them between
They would go fight tomorrow.
'Dowie Dens of Yarrow'

4 O well's me o' my gay goss-hawk,
That he can speak and flee!
He'll carry a letter to my love,
Bring another back to me.
'The Gay Goss Hawk'

5 I am a man upon the land,
I am a selkie in the sea;
When I am far and far from land,
My home it is the Sule Skerry.
'The Great Selkie of Sule Skerry'

6 I wish I were where Helen lies,
Night and day on me she cries;
O that I were where Helen lies,
On fair Kirkconnell lea!

Curst be the heart that thought the thought,
And curst the hand that fired the shot,
When in my arms burd Helen dropt,
And died to succour me!
'Helen of Kirkconnell'

7 Blair Atholl's mine, Jeanie,
Little Dunkeld is mine, lassie,
St Johnston's bower, and Huntingtower,
And all that's mine is thine, lassie.
'Huntingtower'

8 Where are your eyes that looked so mild
When my poor heart you first beguiled?
Why did you run from me and the child?
Och, Johnny, I hardly knew ye!
'Johnny, I hardly knew Ye'

9 I was but seven years auld
When my mither she did die;
My father married the ae warst woman
The warld did ever see.

For she has made me the laily worm
That lies at the fit o' the tree
And my sister Masery she's made
The machrel of the sea.

An' evry Saturday at noon
The machrel comes to me
An' she takes my laily head
An' lays it on her knee;
An' she kaims it wi' a siller kaim

An' washes 't in the sea.
'The Laily Worm and the Machrel'

10 'What gat ye to your dinner, Lord Randal, my
Son?
What gat ye to your dinner, my handsome young
man?'
'I gat eels boil'd in broo'; mother, make my bed
soon,
For I'm weary wi' hunting, and fain wald lie
down.'
'Lord Randal'

11 This ae nighte, this ae nighte,
—*Every nighte and alle,*
Fire and fleet and candle-lighte,
And Christe receive thy saule.
fleet = *corruption of* flet, *meaning house-room*
'Lyke-Wake Dirge'

12 From Brig o' Dread when thou may'st pass,
—*Every nighte and alle,*
To Purgatory fire thou com'st at last;
And Christe receive thy saule.
'Lyke-Wake Dirge'

13 If ever thou gavest meat or drink,
—*Every nighte and alle,*
The fire sall never make thee shrink
And Christe receive thy saule.
'Lyke-Wake Dirge'

14 When captains courageous whom death could not
daunt,
Did march to the siege of the city of Gaunt,
They mustered their soldiers by two and by three,
And the foremost in battle was Mary Ambree.
'Mary Ambree'

15 For in my mind, of all mankind
I love but you alone.
'The Nut Brown Maid'

16 For I must to the greenwood go
Alone, a banished man.
'The Nut Brown Maid'

17 Marie Hamilton's to the kirk gane
Wi' ribbons on her breast;
The King thought mair o' Marie Hamilton
Than he listen'd to the priest.
'The Queen's Maries'

18 Yestreen the Queen had four Maries,
The night she'll hae but three;
There was Marie Seaton, and Marie Beaton,
And Marie Carmichael, and me.
'The Queen's Maries'

19 'O what is longer than the wave?
And what is deeper than the sea?

What is greener than the grass?
And what is more wicked than a woman once
was?'

'Love is longer than the wave,
And hell is deeper than the sea.

Envy's greener than the grass,
And the de'il more wicked than a woman e'er
was.'

As soon as she the fiend did name,

He flew awa' in a bleezing flame.
'Riddles Wisely Expounded'

1 There are twelve months in all the year,
As I hear many men say,
But the merriest month in all the year
Is the merry month of May.
'Robin Hood and the Widow's Three Sons'

2 Fight on, my men, sayes Sir Andrew Bartton,
I am hurt but I am not slain;
Ile lay mee downe and bleed a while
And then Ile rise and fight againe.
'Sir Andrew Bartton'

3 The king sits in Dunfermline town
Drinking the blude-red wine.
'Sir Patrick Spens'

4 To Noroway, to Noroway,
To Noroway o'er the faem;
The king's daughter o' Noroway,
'Tis thou must bring her hame.
'Sir Patrick Spens'

5 I saw the new moon late yestreen
Wi' the auld moon in her arm;
And if we gang to sea master,
I fear we'll come to harm.
'Sir Patrick Spens'

6 O lang, lang may the ladies sit,
Wi' their fans into their hand,
Before they see Sir Patrick Spens
Come sailing to the strand!
'Sir Patrick Spens'

7 Half-owre, half-owre to Aberdour,
'Tis fifty fathoms deep;
And there lies good Sir Patrick Spens,
Wi' the Scots lords at his feet!
'Sir Patrick Spens'

8 And she has kilted her green kirtle
A little abune her knee;
And she has braided her yellow hair
A little abune her bree.
'Tam Lin'

9 But what I ken this night, Tam Lin,
Gin I had kent yestreen,
I wad ta'en out thy heart o' flesh,
And put in a heart o' stane.
'Tam Lin'

10 She's mounted on her milk-white steed,
She's ta'en true Thomas up behind.
'Thomas the Rhymer'

11 And see ye not yon braid, braid road,
That lies across the lily leven?
That is the Path of Wickedness,
Though some call it the Road to Heaven.
'Thomas the Rhymer'

12 It was mirk, mirk night, there was nae starlight,
They waded thro' red blude to the knee;
For a' the blude that's shed on the earth
Rins through the springs o' that countrie.
'Thomas the Rhymer'

13 There were three ravens sat on a tree,
They were as black as they might be.

The one of them said to his make,
'Where shall we our breakfast take?'
'The Three Ravens'

14 God send every gentleman
Such hounds, such hawks, and such leman.
leman = *sweetheart*
'The Three Ravens'

15 As I was walking all alane,
I heard twa corbies making a mane:
The tane unto the tither did say,
'Where sall we gang and dine the day?'

'—In behint yon auld fail dyke
I wot there lies a new-slain knight;
And naebody kens that he lies there
But his hawk, his hound, and his lady fair.

'His hound is to the hunting gane,
His hawk to fetch the wild-fowl hame,
His lady's ta'en anither mate,
So we may make our dinner sweet.

'Ye'll sit on his white hause-bane,
And I'll pike out his bonny blue e'en:
Wi' ae lock o' his gowden hair
We'll theek our nest when it grows bare.'
corbies = *ravens*; fail = *turf*; hause = *neck*; theek
= *thatch*
'The Twa Corbies'

16 The wind doth blow to-day, my love,
And a few small drops of rain;
I never had but one true love;
In cold grave she was lain.

I'll do as much for my true-love
As any young man may;
I'll sit and mourn all at her grave
For a twelvemonth and a day.
'The Unquiet Grave'

17 O waly, waly, up the bank,
And waly, waly, doun the brae,
And waly, waly, yon burn-side,
Where I and my Love wont to gae!
'Waly, Waly'

18 O waly, waly, gin love be bonnie
A little time while it is new!
But when 'tis auld it waxeth cauld,
And fades awa' like morning dew.
'Waly, Waly'

19 But had I wist, before I kist,
That love had been sae ill to win,
I had locked my heart in a case o' gowd,
And pinned it wi' a siller pin.

And O! if my young babe were born,
And set upon the nurse's knee;
And I mysel' were dead and gane,
And the green grass growing over me!
'Waly, Waly'

20 Tom Pearse, Tom Pearse, lend me your grey mare,
All along, down along, out along, lee.
For I want for to go to Widdicombe Fair,
Wi' Bill Brewer, Jan Stewer, Peter Gurney, Peter
Davey, Dan'l Whiddon, Harry Hawk,
Old Uncle Tom Cobbleigh and all.

Old Uncle Tom Cobbleigh and all.
'Widdicombe Fair'

J. G. Ballard 1930-
British writer

1 A car crash harnesses elements of eroticism, aggression, desire, speed, drama, kinaesthetic factors, the stylizing of motion, consumer goods, status—all these in one event. I myself see the car crash as a tremendous sexual event really: a liberation of human and machine libido (if there is such a thing).
interview in *Penthouse* September 1970

2 Some refer to it as a cultural Chernobyl. I think of it as a cultural Stalingrad.
of Euro Disney
in *Daily Telegraph* 2 July 1994; see **Mnouchkine** 541:7

Whitney Balliett 1926-
American writer

3 A critic is a bundle of biases held loosely together by a sense of taste.
Dinosaurs in the Morning (1962) introductory note

4 The sound of surprise.
title of book on jazz (1959)

Pierre Balmain 1914-82
French couturier

5 The trick of wearing mink is to look as though you were wearing a cloth coat. The trick of wearing a cloth coat is to look as though you are wearing mink.
in *Observer* 25 December 1955

Honoré de Balzac 1799-1850
French novelist

6 *L'homme n'est ni bon ni méchant, il naît avec des instincts et des aptitudes.*
Man is neither good nor bad; he is born with instincts and abilities.
La Comédie Humaine (1842) vol. 1, foreword

7 *Affreuse condition de l'homme! il n'y a pas un de ses bonheurs qui ne vienne d'une ignorance quelconque.*
How frightful is man's condition! There is not one of his joys which does not come from some ignorance or other.
Eugénie Grandet (1833) 'Portraits of Bourgeois' (translated by Sylvia Raphael)

8 *La modestie, ou mieux la crainte, est une des premières vertus de l'amour.*
Modesty, or rather a fear of being unworthy, is one of the first virtues aroused by love.
Eugénie Grandet (1833) 'Provincial Love' (translated by Sylvia Raphael)

9 *La haine est un tonique, elle fait vivre, elle inspire la vengeance; mais la pitié tue, elle affaiblit encore notre faiblesse.*
Hatred is a tonic, it makes one live, it inspires vengeance; but pity kills, it makes our weakness weaker.
La Peau de Chagrin [The Wild Ass's Skin] (1831) ch. 1

10 *Le despotisme fait illégalement de grandes choses, la liberté ne se donne même pas la peine d'en faire légalement de très petites.*
Despotism accomplishes great things illegally; liberty doesn't even go to the trouble of accomplishing small things legally.
La Peau de Chagrin [The Wild Ass's Skin] (1831) ch. 3

11 If I'm not a genius, I'm done for.
letter to his sister Laure, 1819; Graham Robb *Balzac* (1994) ch. 3

12 I am not deep, but I am very wide, and it takes time to walk round me.
letter to Countess Maffei, 1837

George Bancroft 1800-91
American scholar and diplomat

13 Calvinism [in Switzerland] . . . established a religion without a prelate, a government without a king.
History of the United States (1855 ed.) vol. 3, ch. 6

Tallulah Bankhead 1903-68
American actress

14 Cocaine habit-forming? Of course not. I ought to know. I've been using it for years.
Tallulah (1952)

15 I'm as pure as the driven slush.
in *Saturday Evening Post* 12 April 1947

16 I read Shakespeare and the Bible and I can shoot dice. That's what I call a liberal education.
attributed

17 They used to shoot her through gauze. You should shoot me through linoleum.
on Shirley Temple
attributed

Joseph Banks 1743-1820
English botanist

18 Who knows but that England may revive in New South Wales when it has sunk in Europe.
letter to Governor Hunter, 30 March 1797

Théodore Faullain de Banville 1823-91
French poet

19 *Jeune homme sans mélancolie,*
Blond comme un soleil d'Italie,
Garde bien ta belle folie.
Young man untroubled by melancholy, fair as an Italian sun, take good care of your fine carelessness.
'A Adolphe Gaiffe' (1856)

20 LICENCES POÉTIQUES. *Il n'y en a pas.*
POETIC LICENCE. There's no such thing.
Petit traité de poésie française (1872) ch. 4

Imamu Amiri Baraka (Everett LeRoi Jones)
1934–
American poet and dramatist

1 A man is either free or he is not. There cannot be any apprenticeship for freedom.
in *Kulchur* Spring 1962 'Tokenism'

2 God has been replaced, as he has all over the West, with respectability and airconditioning.
Midstream (1963)

Yevgeny Baratynsky 1800–44
Russian poet

3 Providence has given human wisdom the choice between two fates: either hope and agitation, or hopelessness and calm.
'Two Fates' (1823) (translated by Dmitri Obolensky)

Anna Laetitia Barbauld 1743–1825
English poet and literary editor

4 If e'er thy breast with freedom glowed,
And spurned a tyrant's chain,
Let not thy strong oppressive force
A free-born mouse detain.
'The Mouse's Petition to Doctor Priestley Found in the Trap where he had been confined all Night' (1773) l. 9

5 Beware, lest in the worm you crush
A brother's soul you find.
'The Mouse's Petition' (1773) l. 33

6 Yes, injured Woman! rise, assert thy right!
'The Rights of Woman' (written *c*.1795, published 1825) l. 1

Mary Barber c.1690–1757
Irish poet

7 What is it our mammas bewitches
To plague us little boys with breeches?
'Written for My Son, and Spoken by Him at His First Putting on Breeches' (1731) l. 1

8 A husband's first praise is a Friend and Protector:
Then change not these titles for Tyrant and Hector.
'Conclusion of a Letter to the Revd Mr C—' (1734) l. 67

John Barbour c.1320–95
Scottish poet

9 Storys to rede ar delitabill,
Suppos that thai be nocht bot fabill.
The Bruce (1375) bk. 1, l. 1

10 A! fredome is a noble thing!
Fredome mayse man to haiff liking.
The Bruce (1375) bk. 1, l. 225

Alexander Barclay c.1475–1552
Scottish poet and priest

11 Thy bread is black, of ill sapour and taste,
And hard as flint because thou none should waste,
That scant be thy teeth able it to break.
Dip it in pottage if thou no shift can make,
And though white and brown be both at one price,
With brown shalt thou feed lest white might make thee nice.
The lords will alway that people note and see
Between them and servants some diversity,
Though it to them turn to no profit at all;
If they have pleasure, the servant shall have small.
Eclogues (1514) no. 2, l. 790

R. H. Barham ('Thomas Ingoldsby')
1788–1845
English clergyman

12 Though I've always considered Sir Christopher Wren,
As an architect, one of the greatest of men;
And, talking of Epitaphs,—much I admire his,
'Circumspice, si Monumentum requiris';
Which an erudite Verger translated to me,
'If you ask for his Monument, Sir-come-spy-see!'
The Ingoldsby Legends (First Series, 1840) 'The Cynotaph'; see **Epitaphs** 311:6

13 What *was* to be done?—'twas perfectly plain
That they could not well hang the man over again;
What *was* to be done?—The man was dead!
Nought *could* be done—nought could be said;
So—my Lord Tomnoddy went home to bed!
The Ingoldsby Legends (First Series, 1840) 'Hon. Mr Sucklethumbkin's Story'

14 The Jackdaw sat on the Cardinal's chair!
Bishop, and abbot, and prior were there;
Many a monk, and many a friar,
Many a knight, and many a squire,
With a great many more of lesser degree,—
In sooth a goodly company;
And they served the Lord Primate on bended knee.
The Ingoldsby Legends (First Series, 1840) 'The Jackdaw of Rheims'

15 And six little Singing-boys,—dear little souls!
In nice clean faces, and nice white stoles.
The Ingoldsby Legends (First Series, 1840) 'The Jackdaw of Rheims'

16 He cursed him in sleeping, that every night
He should dream of the devil, and wake in a fright.
The Ingoldsby Legends (First Series, 1840) 'The Jackdaw of Rheims'

17 Never was heard such a terrible curse!
But what gave rise
To no little surprise,
Nobody seemed one penny the worse!
The Ingoldsby Legends (First Series, 1840) 'The Jackdaw of Rheims'

18 Heedless of grammar, they all cried, 'That's him!'
The Ingoldsby Legends (First Series, 1840) 'The Jackdaw of Rheims'

19 Here's a corpse in the case with a sad swelled face,
And a 'Crowner's Quest' is a queer sort of thing!
in later editions: 'a Medical Crowner's a queer sort of thing!'
The Ingoldsby Legends (First Series, 1840) 'A Lay of St Gengulphus'

1 Now haste ye, my handmaidens, haste and see
How he sits there and glowers with his head on
   his knee!
   The Ingoldsby Legends (First Series, 1840) 'The Legend of
   Hamilton Tighe'

2 But wherever they live, or whenever they die
They'll never get rid of young Hamilton Tighe.
   The Ingoldsby Legends (First Series, 1840) 'The Legend of
   Hamilton Tighe'

3 A servant's too often a negligent elf;
—If it's business of consequence, DO IT YOURSELF!
   The Ingoldsby Legends (Second Series, 1842) 'The Ingoldsby
   Penance!—Moral'

Sabine Baring-Gould 1834–1924

English clergyman

4 Onward, Christian soldiers,
Marching as to war,
With the cross of Jesus
Going on before.
   'Onward, Christian Soldiers' (1864 hymn)

5 Through the night of doubt and sorrow
Onward goes the pilgrim band,
Singing songs of expectation,
Marching to the Promised Land.
   'Through the night of doubt and sorrow' (1867 hymn);
   translated from the Danish of B. S. Ingemann (1789–1862)

Frederick R. Barnard

6 One picture is worth ten thousand words.
   in *Printers' Ink* 10 March 1927

Julian Barnes 1946–

English novelist

7 The land of embarrassment and breakfast.
of Britain
   Flaubert's Parrot (1984) ch. 7

8 Do not imagine that Art is something which is
designed to give gentle uplift and self-confidence.
Art is not a *brassière*. At least, not in the English
sense. But do not forget that *brassière* is the French
for life-jacket.
   Flaubert's Parrot (1984) ch. 10

9 Books say: she did this because. Life says: she did
this. Books are where things are explained to you;
life is where things aren't.
   Flaubert's Parrot (1984) ch. 13

10 All novelists know their art proceeds by
indirection. When tempted by didacticism, the
writer should imagine a spruce sea-captain eyeing
the storm ahead, bustling from instrument to
instrument in a catherine wheel of gold braid,
expelling crisp orders down the speaking tube. But
there is nobody below decks; the engine-room was
never installed, and the rudder broke off centuries
ago.
   A History of the World in 10½ Chapters (1989) 'Parenthesis'

11 Does history repeat itself, the first time as tragedy,
the second time as farce? No, that's too grand, too
considered a process. History just burps, and we
taste again that raw-onion sandwich it swallowed
centuries ago.
   A History of the World in 10½ Chapters (1989)
   'Parenthesis'; see **Marx** 516:16, **Proverbs** 622:22

12 Love is just a system for getting someone to call
you darling after sex.
   Talking It Over (1991) ch. 16

Peter Barnes 1931–

English dramatist

13 CLAIRE: How do you know you're . . . God?
EARL OF GURNEY: Simple. When I pray to Him I find
I'm talking to myself.
   The Ruling Class (1969) act 1, sc. 4

William Barnes 1801–86

English poet

14 An' there vor me the apple tree
Do leän down low in Linden Lea.
   Hwomely Rhymes (1859) 'My Orcha'd in Linden Lea'

15 But still the neäme do bide the seäme—
'Tis Pentridge—Pentridge by the river.
   Hwomely Rhymes (1859) 'Pentridge by the River'

Richard Barnfield 1574–1627

English poet

16 The waters were his winding sheet, the sea was
   made his tomb;
Yet for his fame the ocean sea, was not sufficient
   room.
on the death of Sir John Hawkins
   The Encomion of Lady Pecunia (1598) 'To the Gentlemen
   Readers'

17 My flocks feed not, my ewes breed not,
My rams speed not, all is amiss:
Love in dying, Faith is defying,
Heart's renying, causer of this.
   'The Unknown Shepherd's Complaint' in Nicholas Ling
   (ed.) *England's Helicon* (1600)

18 Man's life is well comparèd to a feast,
Furnished with choice of all variety;
To it comes Time; and as a bidden guest
He sets him down, in pomp and majesty;
The three-fold Age of man the waiters be.
Then with an earthen voider (made of clay)
Comes Death, and takes the table clean away.
   'Man's life' (1598)

Phineas T. Barnum 1810–91

American showman
see also **Lincoln** 485:16

19 There's a sucker born every minute.
   attributed

Amelia E. Barr 1831–1919

American writer and journalist

20 The fate of love is that it always seems too little or
too much.
   The Belle of Bolling Green (1904) ch. 4

J. M. Barrie 1860–1937

Scottish writer and dramatist
*on Barrie: see **Guedalla** 365:11, **Hope** 396:5*

1 His lordship may compel us to be equal upstairs, but there will never be equality in the servants' hall.

> *The Admirable Crichton* (performed 1902, published 1914) act 1

2 When the first baby laughed for the first time, the laugh broke into a thousand pieces and they all went skipping about, and that was the beginning of fairies.

> *Peter Pan* (1928) act 1

3 Every time a child says 'I don't believe in fairies' there is a little fairy somewhere that falls down dead.

> *Peter Pan* (1928) act 1

4 To die will be an awfully big adventure.

> *Peter Pan* (1928) act 3; see **Last words** 474:15

5 Do you believe in fairies? Say quick that you believe! If you believe, clap your hands!

> *Peter Pan* (1928) act 4

6 That is ever the way. 'Tis all jealousy to the bride and good wishes to the corpse.

> *Quality Street* (performed 1901, published 1913) act 1

7 Charm . . . it's a sort of bloom on a woman. If you have it, you don't need to have anything else; and if you don't have it, it doesn't much matter what else you have.

> *What Every Woman Knows* (performed 1908, published 1918) act 1

8 There are few more impressive sights in the world than a Scotsman on the make.

> *What Every Woman Knows* (performed 1908, published 1918) act 2

9 The tragedy of a man who has found himself out.

> *What Every Woman Knows* (performed 1908, published 1918) act 4

Sebastian Barry 1955–

Irish writer and dramatist

10 Do you not feel that this island is moored only lightly to the sea-bed, and might be off for the Americas at any moment?

> *Prayers of Sherkin* (1991)

Ethel Barrymore 1879–1959

American actress

11 For an actress to be a success, she must have the face of a Venus, the brains of a Minerva, the grace of Terpsichore, the memory of a Macaulay, the figure of Juno, and the hide of a rhinoceros.

> George Jean Nathan *The Theatre in the Fifties* (1953)

Karl Barth 1886–1968

Swiss Protestant theologian

12 Men have never been good, they are not good and they never will be good.

> *Christian Community* (1948)

13 He will not be like an ant which has foreseen everything in advance, but like a child in a forest, or on Christmas Eve: one who is always rightly astonished by events, by the encounters and experiences which overtake him.

> *of the justified man*
> *Church Dogmatics* (1936)

Roland Barthes 1915–80

French writer and critic

14 What the public wants is the image of passion, not passion itself.

> *Mythologies* (1957) 'Le monde où l'on catche'

15 I think that cars today are almost the exact equivalent of the great Gothic cathedrals: I mean the supreme creation of an era, conceived with passion by unknown artists, and consumed in image if not in usage by a whole population which appropriates them as a purely magical object.

> *Mythologies* (1957) 'La nouvelle Citroën'

Bernard Baruch 1870–1965

American financier and presidential adviser

16 Let us not be deceived—we are today in the midst of a cold war.

> *'cold war' was suggested to him by H. B. Swope, former editor of the* New York World
>> speech to South Carolina Legislature, 16 April 1947; in *New York Times* 17 April 1947

17 To me old age is always fifteen years older than I am.

> in *Newsweek* 29 August 1955

18 Vote for the man who promises least; he'll be the least disappointing.

> Meyer Berger *New York* (1960)

19 A political leader must keep looking over his shoulder all the time to see if the boys are still there. If they aren't still there, he's no longer a political leader.

> in *New York Times* 21 June 1965

Jacques Barzun 1907–

American historian and educationist

20 If it were possible to talk to the unborn, one could never explain to them how it feels to be alive, for life is washed in the speechless real.

> *The House of Intellect* (1959) ch. 6

Matsuo Basho 1644–94

Japanese poet

21 Early autumn—
rice field, ocean,
one green.

> translated by Lucien Stryk

22 Friends part
forever—wild geese
lost in cloud.

> translated by Lucien Stryk

23 How pleasant—
just once *not* to see

Fuji through mist.
  translated by Lucien Stryk

1 Old pond,
  leap-splash—
  a frog.
    translated by Lucien Stryk

2 Rainy days—
  silkworms droop
  on mulberries.
    translated by Lucien Stryk

3 Under the cherry—
  blossom soup,
  blossom salad.
    translated by Lucien Stryk

4 You, the butterfly—
  I, Chuang Tzu's
  dreaming heart.
    translated by Lucien Stryk; see **Chuang Tzu** 219:2

5 Days and months are travellers of eternity. So are
  the years that pass by.
    The Narrow Road to the Deep North, translated by Nobuyuki
    Yuasa

William Basse d. c.1653

English poet

6 The first men that our Saviour dear
  Did choose to wait upon him here,
  Blest fishers were; and fish the last
  Food was, that he on earth did taste:
  I therefore strive to follow those
  Whom he to follow him hath chose.
    'The Angler's Song' (1653)

7 Renownèd Spenser, lie a thought more nigh
  To learnèd Chaucer, and rare Beaumont lie
  A little nearer Spenser, to make more room
  For Shakespeare, in your threefold, fourfold tomb.
    'On Mr Wm. Shakespeare' (1633)

Thomas Bastard 1566–1618

English poet

8 Age is deformed, youth unkind,
  We scorn their bodies, they our mind.
    Chrestoleros (1598) bk. 7, epigram 9

Edgar Bateman and George Le Brunn

British songwriters

9 Wiv a ladder and some glasses,
  You could see to 'Ackney Marshes,
  If it wasn't for the 'ouses in between.
    'If it wasn't for the 'Ouses in between' (1894 song)

H. M. Bateman see Cartoon captions 198:5

Katherine Lee Bates 1859–1929

American writer and educationist

10 America! America!
  God shed His grace on thee
  And crown thy good with brotherhood
  From sea to shining sea!
    'America the Beautiful' (1893)

Charles Baudelaire 1821–67

French poet and critic

11 *Le poète est semblable au prince des nuées
  Qui hante la tempête et se rit de l'archer;
  Exilé sur le sol, au milieu des huées,
  Ses ailes de géant l'empêchent de marcher.*

  The poet is like the prince of the clouds, who rides
  out the tempest and laughs at the archer. But
  when he is exiled on the ground, amidst the
  clamour, his giant's wings prevent him from
  walking.
    Les fleurs du mal (1857) 'L'Albatross'—'Spleen et idéal'
    no. 2

12 *Hypocrite lecteur,—mon semblable,—mon frère.*
  Hypocrite reader—my likeness—my brother.
    Les fleurs du mal (1857) 'Au Lecteur'

13 *La nature est un temple où de vivants piliers
  Laissent parfois sortir de confuses paroles;
  L'homme y passe à travers des forêts de symboles
  Qui l'observent avec des regards familiers.*

  Nature is a temple, where, from living pillars,
  confused words are sometimes allowed to escape;
  here man passes, through forests of symbols,
  which watch him with looks of recognition.
    Les fleurs du mal (1857) 'Correspondances' no. 4

14 *Là, tout n'est qu'ordre et beauté,
  Luxe, calme et volupté.*

  Everything there is simply order and beauty,
  luxury, peace and sensual indulgence.
    Les fleurs du mal (1857) 'L'Invitation au voyage'—'Spleen
    et idéal' no. 56

15 *Quelle est cette île triste et noire? C'est Cythère,
  Nous dit-on, un pays fameux dans les chansons,
  Eldorado banal de tous les vieux garçons.
  Regardez, après tout, c'est un pauvre terre.*

  What sad, black isle is that? It's Cythera, so they
  say, a land celebrated in song, the banal Eldorado
  of all the old fools. Look, after all, it's a land of
  poverty.
    Les fleurs du mal (1857) 'Un voyage à Cythère'—'Les fleurs
    du mal' no. 121

16 *Nous voulons, tant ce feu nous brûle le cerveau,
  Plonger au fond du gouffre, Enfer ou Ciel, qu'importe?
  Au fond de l'Inconnu pour trouver du nouveau!*

  We want, this fire so burns our brain tissue,
  to drown in the abyss—heaven or hell,
  who cares? Through the unknown, we'll find the
    new.
    Les fleurs du mal (1857) 'Le voyage' no. 126 (translated by
    Robert Lowell)

17 What happened on the 2nd of December
  physically depoliticized me. You can no longer talk
  of generally held ideas. That the whole of Paris is
  Orleanist is beyond dispute, but that doesn't
  concern me. If I had voted, I could only have
  voted for myself.
    letter to Narcisse Ancelle, 5 March 1852; in *Selected Letters
    of Charles Baudelaire* (tr. Rosemary Lloyd, 1986)

1 *Il y a dans tout changement quelque chose d'infâme et d'agréable à la fois, quelque chose qui tient de l'infidelité et du déménagement. Cela suffit à expliquer la Révolution Française.*

There is in all change something at once sordid and agreeable, which smacks of infidelity and household removals. This is sufficient to explain the French Revolution.

Journaux intimes (1887) 'Mon coeur mis à nu' no. 4 (translated by Christopher Isherwood)

2 *La croyance au progrès est une doctrine de paresseux, une doctrine de Belges. C'est l'individu qui compte sur ses voisins pour faire sa besogne.*

Belief in progress is a doctrine of idlers and Belgians. It is the individual relying upon his neighbours to do his work.

Journaux intimes (1887) 'Mon coeur mis à nu' no. 9 (translated by Christopher Isherwood)

3 *Il faut épater le bourgeois.*

One must astonish the bourgeois.

attributed; also attributed to Privat d'Anglemont (c.1820–59) in the form 'Je les ai épatés, les bourgeois [I flabbergasted them, the bourgeois]'

Jean Baudrillard 1929–
French sociologist and cultural critic

4 To love someone is to isolate him from the world, wipe out every trace of him, dispossess him of his shadow, drag him into a murderous future. It is to circle around the other like a dead star and absorb him into a black light.

Fatal Strategies (1983)

Yehuda Bauer 1926–
Czech-born Israeli historian

5 I come from a people who gave the ten commandments to the world. Time has come to strengthen them by three additional ones, which we ought to adopt and commit ourselves to: thou shalt not be a perpetrator; thou shalt not be a victim; and thou shalt never, but never, be a bystander.

speech to the German Bundestag, 1998, quoted in his own speech to the Stockholm International Forum on the Holocaust, 26 July 2000

L. Frank Baum 1856–1919
American writer

6 The road to the City of Emeralds is paved with yellow brick.

The Wonderful Wizard of Oz (1900) ch. 2; see **Harburg** 371:5

Beverley Baxter 1891–1964
British journalist and Conservative politician

7 Beaverbrook is so pleased to be in the Government that he is like the town tart who has finally married the Mayor!

Henry Channon Chips: the Diaries (1967) 12 June 1940

John Bayley 1925–
English academic

8 It is rather like falling from stair to stair in a series of bumps.

*on his wife Iris **Murdoch**'s progressive loss of memory from Alzheimer's disease*

in an interview, Daily Telegraph 8 February 1997

Thomas Haynes Bayly 1797–1839
English poet and dramatist

9 Oh! no! we never mention her,
Her name is never heard;
My lips are now forbid to speak
That once familiar word.

'Oh! No! We Never Mention Her' (1844)

Beachcomber see J. B. Morton

Todd Beamer see Last words 472:19

James Beattie 1735–1803
Scottish philosopher and poet

10 Some deemed him wondrous wise, and some
    believed him mad.

The Minstrel bk. 1 (1771) st. 16

11 Fancy a thousand wondrous forms descries
More wildly great than ever pencil drew,
Rocks, torrents, gulfs, and shapes of giant size,
And glittering cliffs on cliffs, and fiery ramparts
    rise.

The Minstrel bk. 1 (1771) st. 53

12 In the deep windings of the grove, no more
The hag obscene, and grisly phantom dwell;
Nor in the fall of mountain-stream, or roar
Of winds, is heard the angry spirit's yell.

The Minstrel bk. 2 (1774) st. 48

David Beatty 1871–1936
British Admiral of the Fleet, 1916–19

13 There's something wrong with our bloody ships today.

at the Battle of Jutland, 1916

Winston Churchill The World Crisis 1916–1918 (1927) pt. 1

Topham Beauclerk 1739–80
English dandy

14 Then he does not wear them out in practice.

on hearing that a certain person was 'a man of good principles'

James Boswell The Life of Samuel Johnson (1791) 14 April 1778

Pierre-Augustin Caron de Beaumarchais 1732–99
French dramatist

15 *Aujourd'hui ce qui ne vaut pas la peine d'être dit, on le chante.*

Today if something is not worth saying, people sing it.

Le Barbier de Séville (1775) act 1, sc. 2

1 *Je me presse de rire de tout, de peur d'être obligé d'en pleurer.*

I hurry to laugh at everything, for fear of having to weep at it.

Le Barbier de Séville (1775) act 1, sc. 2

2 *Boire sans soif et faire l'amour en tout temps, madame, il n'y a que ça qui nous distingue des autres bêtes.*

Drinking when we are not thirsty and making love all year round, madam; that is all there is to distinguish us from other animals.

Le Mariage de Figaro (1785) act 2, sc. 21

3 *Parce que vous êtes un grand seigneur, vous vous croyez un grand génie! . . . Vous vous êtes donné la peine de naître, et rien de plus.*

Because you are a great lord, you believe yourself to be a great genius! . . . You took the trouble to be born, but no more.

Le Mariage de Figaro (1785) act 5, sc. 3

Francis Beaumont 1584–1616

English poet and dramatist

4 Nose, nose, jolly red nose,
Who gave thee this jolly red nose? . . .
Nutmegs and ginger, cinnamon and cloves,
And they gave me this jolly red nose.

The Knight of the Burning Pestle (c.1607) act 1

5   What things have we seen,
Done at the Mermaid! heard words that have been
So nimble, and so full of subtil flame,
As if that every one from whence they came,
Had meant to put his whole wit in a jest,
And had resolved to live a fool, the rest
Of his dull life.

'Letter to Ben Jonson'

6 Here are sands, ignoble things,
Dropt from the ruined sides of kings;
Here's a world of pomp and state,
Buried in dust, once dead by fate.

'On the Tombs in Westminster Abbey'

Francis Beaumont 1584–1616 and John Fletcher 1579–1625

English dramatists
see also John Fletcher

7 Those have most power to hurt us that we love.

The Maid's Tragedy (written 1610–11) act 5

8 PHILASTER: Oh, but thou dost not know
What 'tis to die.
BELLARIO: Yes, I do know, my Lord:
'Tis less than to be born; a lasting sleep;
A quiet resting from all jealousy,
A thing we all pursue; I know besides,
It is but giving over of a game,
That must be lost.

Philaster (written 1609) act 3

9 There is no other purgatory but a woman.

The Scornful Lady (1616) act 3

10 It would talk: Lord how it talk't!

The Scornful Lady (1616) act 4

Lord Beaverbrook (Max Aitken, Lord Beaverbrook) 1879–1964

Canadian-born British newspaper proprietor and Conservative politician
on Beaverbrook: see **Attlee** 33:1, **Baxter** 59:7, **Kipling** 457:8

11 The Flying Scotsman is no less splendid a sight when it travels north to Edinburgh than when it travels south to London. Mr Baldwin denouncing sanctions was as dignified as Mr Baldwin imposing them.

in *Daily Express* 29 May 1937

12 He did not seem to care which way he travelled providing he was in the driver's seat.
of Lloyd George

The Decline and Fall of Lloyd George (1963) ch. 7

13 Now who is responsible for this work of development on which so much depends? To whom must the praise be given? To the boys in the back rooms. They do not sit in the limelight. But they are the men who do the work.

in *Listener* 27 March 1941

14 I ran the paper [*Daily Express*] purely for propaganda, and with no other purpose.

evidence to Royal Commission on the Press, 18 March 1948, in A. J. P. Taylor *Beaverbrook* (1972)

15 With the publication of his Private Papers in 1952, he committed suicide 25 years after his death.
of Earl Haig

Men and Power (1956)

16 Our cock won't fight.
to Winston Churchill of Edward VIII, during the abdication crisis of 1936

Frances Donaldson *Edward VIII* (1974) ch. 22

17 I have had two masters and one of them betrayed me.
of Bonar Law and Churchill

A. J. P. Taylor, letter, 16 December 1973; *Letters to Eva* (1991)

18 Who's in charge of the clattering train?
habitual question about an organization

A. Chisholm and M. Davie *Beaverbrook* (1992)

Carl Becker 1873–1945

American historian

19 The significance of man is that he is that part of the universe that asks the question, What is the significance of Man? He alone can stand apart imaginatively and, regarding himself and the universe in their eternal aspects, pronounce a judgement: The significance of man is that he is insignificant and is aware of it.

Progress and Power (1936) ch. 3

Samuel Beckett 1906–89

Irish dramatist, novelist, and poet

1 It is suicide to be abroad. But what is it to be at home, Mr Tyler, what is it to be at home? A lingering dissolution.
All That Fall (1957)

2 We could have saved sixpence. We have saved fivepence. (*Pause*) But at what cost?
All That Fall (1957)

3 I shall state silence more competently than ever a better man spangled the butterflies of vertigo.
A Dream of Fair to Middling Women (written 1932)

4 CLOV: Do you believe in the life to come?
HAMM: Mine was always that.
Endgame (1958)

5 Let us pray to God . . . the bastard! He doesn't exist!
Endgame (1958)

6 Perhaps my best years are gone . . . but I wouldn't want them back. Not with the fire that's in me now.
Krapp's Last Tape (1959)

7 There is no use indicting words, they are no shoddier than what they peddle.
Malone Dies (1958)

8 If I had the use of my body I would throw it out of the window.
Malone Dies (1958)

9 The sun shone, having no alternative, on the nothing new.
Murphy (1938)

10 His writing is not *about* something; it is that something itself.
Our Exagmination Round the Factification for Incamination of Work in Progress (1929)

11 To find a form that accommodates the mess, that is the task of the artist now.
Proust (1961)

12 Where I am, I don't know, I'll never know, in the silence you don't know, you must go on, I can't go on, I'll go on.
The Unnamable (1959)

13 Nothing to be done.
Waiting for Godot (1955) act 1

14 There's a man all over for you, blaming on his boots the faults of his feet.
Waiting for Godot (1955) act 1

15 One of the thieves was saved. (*Pause*) It's a reasonable percentage.
Waiting for Godot (1955) act 1

16 ESTRAGON: Charming spot. Inspiring prospects. Let's go.
VLADIMIR: We can't.
ESTRAGON: Why not?
VLADIMIR: We're waiting for Godot.
Waiting for Godot (1955) act 1

17 Nothing happens, nobody comes, nobody goes, it's awful!
Waiting for Godot (1955) act 1

18 He can't think without his hat.
Waiting for Godot (1955) act 1

19 All my lousy life I've crawled about in the mud! And you talk to me about scenery!
Waiting for Godot (1955) act 2

20 VLADIMIR: That passed the time.
ESTRAGON: It would have passed in any case.
VLADIMIR: Yes, but not so rapidly.
Waiting for Godot (1955) act 1

21 We are not saints, but we have kept our appointment. How many people can boast as much?
Waiting for Godot (1955) act 2

22 We all are born mad. Some remain so.
Waiting for Godot (1955) act 2

23 They give birth astride of a grave, the light gleams an instant, then it's night once more.
Waiting for Godot (1955) act 2

24 Habit is a great deadener.
Waiting for Godot (1955) act 2

25 Ever tried. Ever failed. No matter. Try again. Fail again. Fail better.
Worstward Ho (1983)

26 Time like a last oozing, so precious and worthless together.
letter to Kay Boyle, 23 August 1973; James Knowlson *Damned to Fame* (1996)

27 I couldn't have done it otherwise, gone on I mean. I could not have gone on through the awful wretched mess of life without having left a stain upon the silence.
Deirdre Bair *Samuel Beckett* (1978)

28 Even death is unreliable: instead of zero it may be some ghastly hallucination, such as the square root of minus one.
attributed

William Beckford 1759–1844

English writer and collector
on Beckford: see **Borges** 145:6

29 When he was angry, one of his eyes became so terrible, that no person could bear to behold it; and the wretch upon whom it was fixed, instantly fell backward, and sometimes expired. For fear, however, of depopulating his dominions and making his palace desolate, he but rarely gave way to his anger.
Vathek (1782; 3rd ed., 1816) opening para.

30 He did not think, with the Caliph Omar Ben Adalaziz, that it was necessary to make a hell of this world to enjoy Paradise in the next.
Vathek (1782; 3rd ed., 1816) para. 2

31 I am not over-fond of resisting temptation.
Vathek (1782; 3rd ed., 1816) para. 215

Thomas Lovell Beddoes 1803–49

English poet and dramatist

1 If thou wilt ease thine heart
Of love and all its smart,
Then sleep, dear, sleep.
  Death's Jest Book 1825–8 (1850) act 2, sc. 2 'Dirge'

2 But wilt thou cure thine heart
Of love and all its smart,
Then die, dear, die.
  Death's Jest Book 1825–8 (1850) act 2, sc. 2 'Dirge'

3 I have a bit of FIAT in my soul,
And can myself create my little world.
  Death's Jest Book 1825–8 (1850) act 5, sc. 1, l. 39

4 King Death hath asses' ears.
  Death's Jest Book 1825–8 (1850) act 5, sc. 4, l. 245

5 If there were dreams to sell,
What would you buy?
Some cost a passing bell;
Some a light sigh,
That shakes from Life's fresh crown
Only a rose-leaf down.
If there were dreams to sell,
Merry and sad to tell,
And the crier rung the bell,
What would you buy?
  'Dream-Pedlary' (written 1830, published 1851)

The Venerable Bede AD 673–735

English historian and scholar; monk of Jarrow

6 If history records good things of good men, the
thoughtful hearer is encouraged to imitate what is
good.
  Ecclesiastical History of the English People preface

7 *Talis, inquiens, mihi videtur, rex, vita hominum
praesens in terris, ad conparationem eius, quod nobis
incertum est, temporis, quale cum te residente ad
caenam cum ducibus ac ministris tuis tempore
brumali, . . . adveniens unus passerum domum
citissime, pervolaverit; qui cum per unum ostium
ingrediens, mox per aliud exierit. Ipso quidem
tempore, quo intus est, hiemis tempestate non
tangitur, sed tamen parvissimo spatio serenitatis ad
momentum excurso, mox de hieme in hiemem
regrediens, tuis oculis elabitur. Ita haec vita hominum
ad modicum apparet; quid autem sequatur, quidve
praecesserit, prorsus ignoramus.*

'Such,' he said, 'O King, seems to me the present
life of men on earth, in comparison with that time
which to us is uncertain, as if when on a winter's
night you sit feasting with your ealdormen and
thegns,—a single sparrow should fly swiftly into
the hall, and coming in at one door, instantly fly
out through another. In that time in which it is
indoors it is indeed not touched by the fury of the
winter, but yet, this smallest space of calmness
being passed almost in a flash, from winter going
into winter again, it is lost to your eyes.
Somewhat like this appears the life of man; but of
what follows or what went before, we are utterly
ignorant.'
  Ecclesiastical History of the English People (translated by B.
  Colgrave, 1969) bk. 2, ch. 13

Harry Bedford and Terry Sullivan

British songwriters

8 I'm a bit of a ruin that Cromwell knocked about a
bit.
  'It's a Bit of a Ruin that Cromwell Knocked about a Bit'
  (1920 song; written for Marie Lloyd)

Barnard Elliott Bee 1823–61

American Confederate general

9 There is Jackson with his Virginians, standing like
a stone wall. Let us determine to die here, and we
will conquer.
  *referring to General T. J. ('Stonewall') Jackson at the
  battle of Bull Run, 21 July, 1861 (in which Bee
  himself was killed)*
  B. Perley Poore *Perley's Reminiscences* (1886) vol. 2, ch. 7

Thomas Beecham 1879–1961

English conductor

10 Like two skeletons copulating on a corrugated tin
roof.
  describing the harpsichord
  Harold Atkins and Archie Newman *Beecham Stories* (1978)

11 The musical equivalent of the Towers of St
Pancras Station.
  of Elgar's 1st Symphony
  Neville Cardus *Sir Thomas Beecham* (1961) p. 113

12 There are two golden rules for an orchestra: start
together and finish together. The public doesn't
give a damn what goes on in between.
  Harold Atkins and Archie Newman *Beecham Stories* (1978)

13 Too much counterpoint; what is worse, Protestant
counterpoint.
  of J. S. Bach
  in *Guardian* 8 March 1971

14 Why do we have to have all these third-rate
foreign conductors around—when we have so
many second-rate ones of our own?
  L. Ayre *Wit of Music* (1966) p. 70

H. C. Beeching 1859–1919

English clergyman

15 Not when the sense is dim,
But now from the heart of joy,
I would remember Him:
Take the thanks of a boy.
  In a Garden and Other Poems (1895) 'Prayers'

16 First come I; my name is Jowett.
There's no knowledge but I know it.
I am Master of this college:
What I don't know isn't knowledge.
  The Masque of Balliol (composed by and current among
  members of Balliol College in the late 1870s) in W. G.
  Hiscock (ed.) *The Balliol Rhymes* (1939); see **Anonymous**
  17:20, **Spring-Rice** 753:8

Max Beerbohm 1872–1956

English critic, essayist, and caricaturist
on Beerbohm: see Shaw 727:24; see also Telegrams 776:4,
Telegrams 776:9

1 Mankind is divisible into two great classes: hosts and guests.
   And Even Now (1920) 'Hosts and Guests'

2 I was not unpopular [at school] . . . It is Oxford that has made me insufferable.
   More (1899) 'Going Back to School'

3 Enter Michael Angelo. Andrea del Sarto appears for a moment at a window. Pippa passes.
   Seven Men (1919) 'Savonarola Brown' act 3

4 The fading signals and grey eternal walls of that antique station, which, familiar to them and insignificant, does yet whisper to the tourist the last enchantments of the Middle Age.
   Zuleika Dobson (1911) ch. 1; see **Arnold** 29:15

5 The dullard's envy of brilliant men is always assuaged by the suspicion that they will come to a bad end.
   Zuleika Dobson (1911) ch. 4

6 Women who love the same man have a kind of bitter freemasonry.
   Zuleika Dobson (1911) ch. 4

7 The Socratic manner is not a game at which two can play.
   Zuleika Dobson (1911) ch. 15

8 Fate wrote her a most tremendous tragedy, and she played it in tights.
   of Caroline of Brunswick, wife of **George IV**
   The Yellow Book (1894) vol. 3

Ethel Lynn Beers 1827–79

American poet

9 All quiet along the Potomac to-night,
   No sound save the rush of the river,
   While soft falls the dew on the face of the dead—
   The picket's off duty forever.
   'The Picket Guard' (1861) st. 6; see **McClellan** 500:11

Ludwig van Beethoven 1770–1827

German composer
on Beethoven: see Bakunin 50:5

10 *Muss es sein? Es muss sein.*
   Must it be? It must be.
   String Quartet in F Major, Opus 135, epigraph

11 The immortal god of harmony.
   of J. S. **Bach**
   letter to Breitkopf und Härtel, 22 April 1801; Michael Hamburger (ed.) *Beethoven: Letters, Journals and Correspondence* (1951)

Brendan Behan 1923–64

Irish dramatist

12 PAT: He was an Anglo-Irishman.
   MEG: In the blessed name of God what's that?

PAT: A Protestant with a horse.
   Hostage (1958) act 1

13 Meanwhile I'll sing that famous old song, 'The Hound that Caught the Pubic Hare'.
   Hostage (1958) act 1

14 When I came back to Dublin, I was courtmartialled in my absence and sentenced to death in my absence, so I said they could shoot me in my absence.
   Hostage (1958) act 1

15 We're here because we're queer
   Because we're queer because we're here.
   Hostage (1958) act 3; see **Military sayings** 526:17

16 *on being asked 'What was the message of your play'*
   after a performance of The Hostage:
   Message? Message? What the hell do you think I am, a bloody postman?
   Dominic Behan *My Brother Brendan* (1965); see **Goldwyn** 356:7

17 There's no such thing as bad publicity except your own obituary.
   Dominic Behan *My Brother Brendan* (1965); see **Proverbs** 614:24

Aphra Behn 1640–89

English dramatist, poet, and novelist

18 Oh, what a dear ravishing thing is the beginning of an Amour!
   The Emperor of the Moon (1687) act 1, sc. 1

19 Love ceases to be a pleasure, when it ceases to be a secret.
   The Lover's Watch (1686) 'Four o' Clock. General Conversation'

20 All I ask, is the privilege for my masculine part the poet in me . . . If I must not, because of my sex, have this freedom . . . I lay down my quill, and you shall hear no more of me.
   preface to *The Lucky Chance* (1686)

21 Since man with that inconstancy was born,
   To love the absent, and the present scorn,
   Why do we deck, why do we dress
   For such a short-lived happiness?
   Why do we put attraction on,
   Since either way 'tis we must be undone?
   Lycidus (1688) 'To Alexis, in Answer to his Poem against Fruition'

22 I owe a duty, where I cannot love.
   The Moor's Revenge (1677) act 3, sc. 3

23 Be just, my lovely swain, and do not take
   Freedoms you'll not to me allow;
   Or give Amynta so much freedom back
   That she may rove as well as you.

   Let us then love upon the honest square,
   Since interest neither have designed.
   For the sly gamester, who ne'er plays me fair,
   Must trick for trick expect to find.
   Poems upon Several Occasions (1684) 'To Lysander, on some Verses he writ, and asking more for his Heart than 'twas worth'

1 A brave world, Sir, full of religion, knavery, and change: we shall shortly see better days.
  The Roundheads (1682) act 1, sc. 1

2 Variety is the soul of pleasure.
  The Rover pt. 2 (1681) act 1; see **Cowper** 247:30

3 Come away; poverty's catching.
  The Rover pt. 2 (1681) act 1

4 Money speaks sense in a language all nations understand.
  The Rover pt. 2 (1681) act 3

5 Do you not daily see fine clothes, rich furniture, jewels and plate are more inviting than beauty unadorned?
  The Rover pt. 2 (1681) act 4

6 The soft, unhappy sex.
  The Wandering Beauty (1698) para. 1

John Hay Beith see Ian Hay

Lord Belhaven 1656–1708
Scottish politician

7 Good God! What, is this an entire surrender?
  culmination of a speech opposing the Union with England
  speech in the Scottish Parliament, 2 November 1706

Alexander Graham Bell 1847–1922
Scottish inventor of the telephone

8 Mr Watson—come here—I want to see you.
  to his assistant, Thomas Watson; the first words spoken on the telephone, 10 March 1876
  James Mackay *Sounds Out of Silence* (1997) ch. 6

Clive Bell 1881–1964
English art critic

9 Art and Religion are, then, two roads by which men escape from circumstance to ecstasy. Between aesthetic and religious rapture there is a family alliance. Art and Religion are means to similar states of mind.
  Art (1914) pt. 2, ch. 1

10 I will try to account for the degree of my aesthetic emotion. That, I conceive, is the function of the critic.
  Art (1914) pt. 3, ch. 3

11 Only reason can convince us of those three fundamental truths without a recognition of which there can be no effective liberty: that what we believe is not necessarily true; that what we like is not necessarily good; and that all questions are open.
  Civilization (1928) ch. 5

George Bell 1883–1958
English clergyman, Bishop of Chichester

12 The policy is obliteration, openly acknowledged. This is not a justifiable act of war.
  of the saturation bombing of Berlin
  speech, House of Lords, 9 February 1944

Gertrude Bell 1868–1926
English traveller, archaeologist, and government servant

13 The world of adventure and of enterprise, dark with hurrying storms, glittering in raw sunlight, an unanswered question and unanswerable doubt hidden in the fold of every hill.
  on travel in the desert
  Syria: The Desert and the Sown (1907)

14 I feel at times like the Creator about the middle of the week. He must have wondered what it was going to be like, as I do.
  creating Iraq, at the Cairo Conference 1921; attributed

Francis Bellamy 1856–1931
American clergyman and editor

15 I pledge allegiance to the flag of the United States of America and to the republic for which it stands, one nation under God, indivisible, with liberty and justice for all.
  The Pledge of Allegiance to the Flag (1892)

St Robert Bellarmine 1542–1621
Italian cardinal and theologian

16 Nobody can remember more than seven of anything.
  reason for omitting the eight beatitudes from his catechism
  John Bossy *Christianity in the West 1400–1700* (1985)

Hilaire Belloc 1870–1953
British poet, essayist, historian, novelist, and Liberal politician

17 Child! do not throw this book about;
  Refrain from the unholy pleasure
  Of cutting all the pictures out!
  Preserve it as your chiefest treasure.
  A Bad Child's Book of Beasts (1896) dedication

18 I shoot the Hippopotamus
  With bullets made of platinum,
  Because if I use leaden ones
  His hide is sure to flatten 'em.
  A Bad Child's Book of Beasts (1896) 'The Hippopotamus';
  see **Forster** 329:6

19 And mothers of large families (who claim to
      common sense)
  Will find a Tiger well repay the trouble and
      expense.
  A Bad Child's Book of Beasts (1896) 'The Tiger'

20 Believing Truth is staring at the sun
  Which but destroys the power that could perceive.
  So naught of our poor selves can be at one
  With burning Truth, nor utterly believe.
  'Believing Truth is staring at the sun' (1938)

21 Physicians of the Utmost Fame
  Were called at once; but when they came
  They answered, as they took their Fees,
  'There is no Cure for this Disease.'
  Cautionary Tales (1907) 'Henry King'

22 And always keep a-hold of Nurse
  For fear of finding something worse.
  Cautionary Tales (1907) 'Jim'

1 Sir! you have disappointed us!
We had intended you to be
The next Prime Minister but three:
The stocks were sold; the Press was squared;
The Middle Class was quite prepared.
But as it is! . . . My language fails!
Go out and govern New South Wales!
Cautionary Tales (1907) 'Lord Lundy'

2 Matilda told such Dreadful Lies,
It made one Gasp and Stretch one's Eyes.
Cautionary Tales (1907) 'Matilda'

3 For every time She shouted 'Fire!'
They only answered 'Little Liar!'
Cautionary Tales (1907) 'Matilda'

4 A Trick that everyone abhors
In Little Girls is slamming Doors.
Cautionary Tales (1907) 'Rebecca'

5 She was not really bad at heart,
But only rather rude and wild:
She was an aggravating child.
Cautionary Tales (1907) 'Rebecca'

6 Of Courtesy, it is much less
Than Courage of Heart or Holiness,
Yet in my Walks it seems to me
That the Grace of God is in Courtesy.
'Courtesy' (1910)

7 Here richly, with ridiculous display,
The Politician's corpse was laid away.
While all of his acquaintance sneered and slanged
I wept: for I had longed to see him hanged.
'Epitaph on the Politician Himself' (1923)

8 I said to Heart, 'How goes it ?' Heart replied:
'Right as a Ribstone Pippin!' But it lied.
'The False Heart' (1910)

9 I'm tired of Love: I'm still more tired of Rhyme.
But Money gives me pleasure all the time.
'Fatigued' (1923)

10 Strong brother in God and last companion, Wine.
'Heroic Poem upon Wine' (1926)

11 Remote and ineffectual Don
That dared attack my Chesterton.
'Lines to a Don' (1910)

12 Whatever happens we have got
The Maxim Gun, and they have not.
The Modern Traveller (1898) pt. 6

13 The Llama is a woolly sort of fleecy hairy goat,
With an indolent expression and an undulating
throat
Like an unsuccessful literary man.
More Beasts for Worse Children (1897) 'The Llama'

14 The Microbe is so very small
You cannot make him out at all.
But many sanguine people hope
To see him through a microscope.
More Beasts for Worse Children (1897) 'The Microbe'

15 Oh! let us never, never doubt
What nobody is sure about!
More Beasts for Worse Children (1897) 'The Microbe'

16 Lord Finchley tried to mend the Electric Light
Himself. It struck him dead: And serve him right!

It is the business of the wealthy man
To give employment to the artisan.
More Peers (1911) 'Lord Finchley'

17 Like many of the Upper Class
He liked the Sound of Broken Glass.
New Cautionary Tales (1930) 'About John'; see **Waugh**
824:4

18 A smell of burning fills the startled Air—
The Electrician is no longer there!
'Newdigate Poem' (1910)

19 The accursed power which stands on Privilege
(And goes with Women, and Champagne, and
Bridge)
Broke—and Democracy resumed her reign:
(Which goes with Bridge, and Women and
Champagne).
'On a Great Election' (1923)

20 I am a sundial, and I make a botch
Of what is done much better by a watch.
'On a Sundial' (1938)

21 When I am dead, I hope it may be said:
'His sins were scarlet, but his books were read.'
'On His Books' (1923)

22 Pale Ebenezer thought it wrong to fight,
But Roaring Bill (who killed him) thought it right.
'The Pacifist' (1938)

23 The great hills of the South Country
They stand along the sea;
And it's there walking in the high woods
That I could wish to be,
And the men that were boys when I was a boy
Walking along with me.
'The South Country' (1910)

24 When I am living in the Midlands
That are sodden and unkind . . .
And the great hills of the South Country
Come back into my mind.
'The South Country' (1910)

25 Do you remember an Inn,
Miranda?
Do you remember an Inn?
'Tarantella' (1923)

26 And the fleas that tease in the High Pyrenees
And the wine that tasted of the tar?
'Tarantella' (1923)

27 Balliol made me, Balliol fed me,
Whatever I had she gave me again:
And the best of Balliol loved and led me.
God be with you, Balliol men.
'To the Balliol Men Still in Africa' (1910)

28 There's nothing worth the wear of winning,
But laughter and the love of friends.
Verses (1910) 'Dedicatory Ode'

29 Is there no Latin word for Tea? Upon my soul, if I
had known that I would have let the vulgar stuff
alone.
On Nothing (1908) 'On Tea'

30 Gentlemen, I am a Catholic . . . If you reject me on
account of my religion, I shall thank God that He

has spared me the indignity of being your representative.

speech to voters of South Salford, 1906, in R. Speaight *Life of Hilaire Belloc* (1957) ch. 10

Saul Bellow 1915-

American novelist

see also **Opening lines** 574:13

1 It is sometimes necessary to repeat what we all know. All mapmakers should place the Mississippi in the same location, and avoid originality.

Mr Sammler's Planet (1969)

2 Art has something to do with the achievement of stillness in the midst of chaos. A stillness which characterizes prayer, too, and the eye of the storm . . . an arrest of attention in the midst of distraction.

George Plimpton *Writers at Work* (1967) 3rd series

3 A novel is balanced between a few true impressions and the multitude of false ones that make up most of what we call life. It tells us that for every human being there is a diversity of existences, that the single existence is itself an illusion in part . . . it promises us meaning, harmony, and even justice.

speech on receiving the Nobel Prize, 1976

in *The American Scholar* Summer 1977, no. 46

Du Belloy (Pierre-Laurent Buirette du Belloy) 1725-75

French dramatist

4 *Plus je vis d'étrangers, plus j'aimai ma patrie.*

The more foreigners I saw, the more I loved my homeland.

Le Siège de Calais (1765) act 2, sc. 3

Robert Benchley 1889-1945

American humorist

see also **Film lines** 319:23, **Telegrams** 776:10

5 The biggest obstacle to professional writing is the necessity for changing a typewriter ribbon.

Chips off the old Benchley (1949) 'Learn to Write'

6 The surest way to make a monkey of a man is to quote him.

My Ten Years in a Quandary (1936)

7 In America there are two classes of travel—first class, and with children.

Pluck and Luck (1925)

8 It took me fifteen years to discover that I had no talent for writing, but I couldn't give it up because by that time I was too famous.

Nathaniel Benchley *Robert Benchley* (1955) ch. 1

Julien Benda 1867-1956

French philosopher and novelist

9 *La trahison des clercs.*

The treachery of the intellectuals.

title of book (1927)

Peter Benenson 1921-

British founder of Amnesty International

10 Better to light a candle than curse the darkness.

at a Human Rights Day ceremony, 10 December 1961; see **Proverbs** 615:29

Stephen Vincent Benét 1898-1943

American poet and novelist

11 I have fallen in love with American names,
The sharp, gaunt names that never get fat,
The snakeskin-titles of mining-claims,
The plumed war-bonnet of Medicine Hat,
Tucson and Deadwood and Lost Mule Flat.

'American Names' (1927)

12 I shall not rest quiet in Montparnasse.
I shall not lie easy at Winchelsea.
You may bury my body in Sussex grass,
You may bury my tongue at Champmédy.
I shall not be there, I shall rise and pass.
Bury my heart at Wounded Knee.

'American Names' (1927)

13 And kept his heart a secret to the end
From all the picklocks of biographers.

of Robert E. **Lee**

John Brown's Body (1928)

14 We thought we were done with these things but we were wrong.
We thought, because we had power, we had wisdom.

'Litany for Dictatorships' (1935)

William Rose Benét 1886-1950

American poet

15 Blake saw a treeful of angels at Peckham Rye,
And his hands could lay hold on the tiger's terrible heart.
Blake knew how deep is Hell, and Heaven how high,
And could build the universe from one tiny part.

'Mad Blake' (1918); see **Blake** 123:3

Judah Benjamin 1811-84

American politician and lawyer

16 The gentleman will please remember that when his half-civilized ancestors were hunting the wild boar in Silesia, mine were princes of the earth.

in reply to a taunt by a Senator of German descent

B. Perley Poore *Perley's Reminiscences* (1886)

Tony Benn (Anthony Wedgwood Benn) 1925-

British Labour politician

17 Not a reluctant peer but a persistent commoner.

at a Press Conference, 23 November 1960

18 Some of the jam we thought was for tomorrow, we've already eaten.

attributed, 1969; see **Carroll** 195:10

1 Office is something that builds up a man only if he is somebody in his own right.
*on seeing Harold **Wilson**, who had recently resigned as Prime Minister*
diary, 12 April 1976

2 It is as wholly wrong to blame Marx for what was done in his name, as it is to blame Jesus for what was done in his.
Alan Freeman *The Benn Heresy* (1982) 'Interview with Tony Benn'

3 A faith is something you die for; a doctrine is something you kill for: there is all the difference in the world.
in *Observer* 16 April 1989 'Sayings of the Week'

4 *questions habitually asked by Tony Benn on meeting somebody in a position of power:*
What power have you got? Where did you get it from? In whose interests do you exercise it? To whom are you accountable? How do we get rid of you?
'The Independent Mind', lecture at Nottingham, 18 June 1993

5 If you file your waste-paper basket for 50 years, you have a public library.
in *Daily Telegraph* 5 March 1994

6 A quotation is what a speaker wants to say— unlike a soundbite which is all that an interviewer allows you to say.
letter to Antony Jay, August 1996

George Bennard 1873–1958
American Methodist minister and hymn-writer

7 I will cling to the old rugged cross,
And exchange it some day for a crown.
'The Old Rugged Cross' (1913 hymn)

Alan Bennett 1934–
English dramatist and actor

8 The real solvent of class distinction is a proper measure of self-esteem—a kind of unselfconsciousness. Some people are at ease with themselves, so the world is at ease with them. My parents thought this kind of ease was produced by education . . . they didn't see that what disqualified them was temperament—just as, though educated up to the hilt, it disqualifies me. What keeps us in our place is embarrassment.
Dinner at Noon (BBC television, 1988)

9 I don't want to give you the idea I'm trying to hide anything, or that anything unorthodox goes on between my wife and me. It doesn't. Nothing goes on at all . . . No foreplay. No afterplay. And fuck all in between.
Enjoy (1980) act 1

10 I have never understood this liking for war. It panders to instincts already catered for within the scope of any respectable domestic establishment.
Forty Years On (1969) act 1

11 Memories are not shackles, Franklin, they are garlands.
Forty Years On (1969) act 2

12 Standards are always out of date. That is what makes them standards.
Forty Years On (1969) act 2

13 Sapper, Buchan, Dornford Yates, practitioners in that school of Snobbery with Violence that runs like a thread of good-class tweed through twentieth-century literature.
Forty Years On (1969) act 2

14 We started off trying to set up a small anarchist community, but people wouldn't obey the rules.
Getting On (1972) act 1

15 To be Prince of Wales is not a position. It is a predicament.
The Madness of King George (1995 film); in the 1992 play *The Madness of George III* the line was 'To be heir to the throne . . .'

16 People always complain about muck raking biographers saying 'Leave us our heroes.' 'Leave us our villains' is just as important.
*of an attempt to rehabilitate **Haig***
diary, 11 February 1996

Arnold Bennett 1867–1931
English novelist

17 His opinion of himself, having once risen, remained at 'set fair'.
The Card (1911) ch. 1

18 'What great cause is he identified with?' 'He's identified . . . with the great cause of cheering us all up.'
The Card (1911) ch. 12

19 The price of justice is eternal publicity.
Things that have Interested Me (2nd series, 1923) 'Secret Trials'

20 A cause may be inconvenient, but it's magnificent. It's like champagne or high heels, and one must be prepared to suffer for it.
The Title (1918) act 1

21 Being a husband is a whole-time job. That is why so many husbands fail. They cannot give their entire attention to it.
The Title (1918) act 1

22 Journalists say a thing that they know isn't true, in the hope that if they keep on saying it long enough it *will* be true.
The Title (1918) act 1

23 Literature's always a good card to play for Honours.
The Title (1918) act 3

Jill Bennett 1931–90
*English actress; former wife of John **Osborne***

24 Never marry a man who hates his mother, because he'll end up hating you.
in *Observer* 12 September 1982 'Sayings of the Week'

A. C. Benson 1862–1925
English writer

25 Land of Hope and Glory, Mother of the Free, How shall we extol thee who are born of thee?

Wider still and wider shall thy bounds be set;
God who made thee mighty, make thee mightier
   yet.

'Land of Hope and Glory' written to be sung as the Finale
to **Elgar**'s *Coronation Ode* (1902)

Stella Benson 1892–1933

English novelist

1 Call no man foe, but never love a stranger.
   This is the End (1917)

Henry A. Bent 1926–

American chemist

2 The important point is not the bigness of
   Avogadro's number but the bigness of Avogadro.
   *Avogadro's number is equal to 6.023×10^{23} (named
   after the Italian chemist and physicist Amedeo
   Avogadro (1776–1856), who in 1811 formulated a
   law for deriving molecular weights)*
   The Second Law (1965)

Jeremy Bentham 1748–1832

English philosopher

3 Right . . . is the child of law: from real laws come
   real rights; but from imaginary laws, from laws of
   nature, fancied and invented by poets,
   rhetoricians, and dealers in moral and intellectual
   poisons, come imaginary rights, a bastard brood of
   monsters.
   Anarchical Fallacies in J. Bowring (ed.) *Works* vol. 2 (1843)

4 Natural rights is simple nonsense: natural and
   imprescriptible rights, rhetorical nonsense—
   nonsense upon stilts.
   Anarchical Fallacies in J. Bowring (ed.) *Works* vol. 2 (1843)

5 The greatest happiness of the greatest number is
   the foundation of morals and legislation.
   *Bentham claimed to have acquired the 'sacred truth'
   either from Joseph **Priestley** or Cesare Beccaria
   (1738–94)*
   The Commonplace Book in J. Bowring (ed.) *Works* vol. 10
   (1843); see **Hutcheson** 410:19

6 The Fool had stuck himself up one day, with great
   gravity, in the King's throne; with a stick, by way
   of a sceptre, in one hand, and a ball in the other:
   being asked what he was doing? he answered
   '*reigning*'. Much of the same sort of reign, I take it
   would be that of our Author's [Blackstone's]
   Democracy.
   A Fragment on Government (1776) ch. 2, para. 34, footnote
   (e)

7 All punishment is mischief: all punishment in
   itself is evil.
   Principles of Morals and Legislation (1789) ch. 13, para. 2

8 The question is not, Can they reason? nor, Can
   they talk? but, Can they suffer?
   Principles of Morals and Legislation (1789) ch. 17

9 Every law is contrary to liberty.
   Principles of the Civil Code (1843)

10 He rather hated the ruling few than loved the
   suffering many.
   of James Mill
   H. N. Pym (ed.) *Memories of Old Friends, being Extracts from
   the Journals and Letters of Caroline Fox* (1882) p. 113, 7
   August 1840

11 Prose is when all the lines except the last go on to
   the end. Poetry is when some of them fall short of
   it.
   M. St. J. Packe *The Life of John Stuart Mill* (1954) bk. 1,
   ch. 2

Edmund Clerihew Bentley 1875–1956

English writer

12 The Art of Biography
   Is different from Geography.
   Geography is about Maps,
   But Biography is about Chaps.
   Biography for Beginners (1905) introduction

13 What I like about Clive
   Is that he is no longer alive.
   There is a great deal to be said
   For being dead.
   Biography for Beginners (1905) 'Clive'

14 Sir Humphrey Davy
   Abominated gravy.
   He lived in the odium
   Of having discovered Sodium.
   Biography for Beginners (1905) 'Sir Humphrey Davy'

15 John Stuart Mill,
   By a mighty effort of will,
   Overcame his natural *bonhomie*
   And wrote 'Principles of Political Economy'.
   Biography for Beginners (1905) 'John Stuart Mill'

16 Sir Christopher Wren
   Said, 'I am going to dine with some men.
   If anybody calls
   Say I am designing St Paul's.'
   Biography for Beginners (1905) 'Sir Christopher Wren'

17 George the Third
   Ought never to have occurred.
   One can only wonder
   At so grotesque a blunder.
   More Biography (1929) 'George the Third'

Eric Bentley 1916–

American dramatist and writer

18 Ours is the age of substitutes: instead of language,
   we have jargon; instead of principles, slogans;
   and, instead of genuine ideas, Bright Ideas.
   in *New Republic* 29 December 1952

Richard Bentley 1662–1742

English classical scholar

19 I hold it as certain, that no man was ever written
   out of reputation but by himself.
   William Warburton (ed.) *The Works of Alexander Pope*
   (1751) vol. 4

1 It is a pretty poem, Mr Pope, but you must not call it Homer.
*when pressed by **Pope** to comment on 'My Homer'* [i.e. his translation of **Homer**'s Iliad]
John Hawkins (ed.) *The Works of Samuel Johnson* (1787) vol. 4 'The Life of Pope'

2 It would be port if it could.
on claret
R. C. Jebb *Bentley* (1902) ch. 12

Lloyd Bentsen 1921–

American Democratic politician

3 *responding to Dan Quayle's claim to have 'as much experience in the Congress as Jack **Kennedy** had when he sought the presidency':*
Senator, I served with Jack Kennedy. I knew Jack Kennedy. Jack Kennedy was a friend of mine. Senator, you're no Jack Kennedy.
in the vice-presidential debate, 5 October 1988

Pierre-Jean de Béranger 1780–1857

French poet

4 *Nos amis, les ennemis.*
Our friends, the enemy.
'L'Opinion de ces demoiselles' (written 1815) in *Chansons de De Béranger* (1832)

5 *Il était un roi d'Yvetot*
Peu connu dans l'histoire.
There was a king of Yvetot
Little known to history.
'Le Roi d'Yvetot' (written 1813) in *Chansons de De Béranger* (1832)

Henri Bergson 1859–1941

French philosopher

6 The present contains nothing more than the past, and what is found in the effect was already in the cause.
L'Évolution créatrice [Creative Evolution] (1907) ch. 1

7 *L'élan vital.*
The vital spirit.
L'Évolution créatrice [Creative Evolution] (1907) ch. 2 (section title)

8 Only those ideas which least belong to us can be adequately expressed in words.
Time and Free Will (1910) ch. 2

George Berkeley 1685–1753

Irish philosopher and Anglican bishop
*on Berkeley: see **Byron** 181:25, **Johnson** 428:22, **Smith** 743:10*

9 They are neither finite quantities, or quantities infinitely small, nor yet nothing. May we not call them the ghosts of departed quantities?
*on **Newton**'s infinitesimals*
The Analyst (1734) sect. 35

10 [Tar water] is of a nature so mild and benign and proportioned to the human constitution, as to warm without heating, to cheer but not inebriate.
Siris (1744) para. 217; see **Cowper** 248:6

11 Truth is the cry of all, but the game of the few.
Siris (1744) para. 368

12 The same principles which at first lead to scepticism, pursued to a certain point bring men back to common sense.
Three Dialogues between Hylas and Philonous (1734) Dialogue 3

13 We have first raised a dust and then complain we cannot see.
A Treatise Concerning the Principles of Human Knowledge (1710) introduction, sect. 3

14 All the choir of heaven and furniture of earth—in a word, all those bodies which compose the mighty frame of the world—have not any subsistence without a mind.
A Treatise Concerning the Principles of Human Knowledge (1710) pt. 1, sect. 6

15 Westward the course of empire takes its way;
The first four acts already past,
A fifth shall close the drama with the day:
Time's noblest offspring is the last.
'On the Prospect of Planting Arts and Learning in America' (1752) st. 6.

Irving Berlin (Israel Baline) 1888–1989

American songwriter

16 Must you dance ev'ry dance
With the same fortunate man?
You have danced with him since the music began.
Won't you change partners and dance with me?
'Change Partners' (1938 song) in *Carefree*

17 Heaven—I'm in Heaven—And my heart beats so that I can hardly speak;
And I seem to find the happiness I seek
When we're out together dancing cheek-to-cheek.
'Cheek-to-Cheek' (1935 song) in *Top Hat*

18 God bless America,
Land that I love,
Stand beside her and guide her
Thru the night with a light from above.
From the mountains to the prairies,
To the oceans white with foam,
God bless America,
My home sweet home.
'God Bless America' (1939 song)

19 There may be trouble ahead,
But while there's moonlight and music and love and romance,
Let's face the music and dance.
'Let's Face the Music and Dance' (1936 song) in *Follow the Fleet*

20 A pretty girl is like a melody
That haunts you night and day.
'A Pretty Girl is like a Melody' (1919 song)

21 The song is ended (but the melody lingers on).
title of song (1927)

22 There's no business like show business.
title of song in *Annie Get Your Gun* (1946)

23 I'm dreaming of a white Christmas,
Just like the ones I used to know,

Where the tree-tops glisten
And children listen
To hear sleigh bells in the snow.
'White Christmas' (1942 song) in *Holiday Inn*

1 Listen, kid, take my advice, never hate a song that
has sold half a million copies.
to Cole **Porter**, *of the song 'Rosalie'*
Philip Furia *Poets of Tin Pan Alley* (1990)

Isaiah Berlin 1909–97
British philosopher

2 Injustice, poverty, slavery, ignorance—these may
be cured by reform or revolution. But men do not
live only by fighting evils. They live by positive
goals, individual and collective, a vast variety of
them, seldom predictable, at times incompatible.
Four Essays on Liberty (1969) 'Political Ideas in the
Twentieth Century'

3 There exists a great chasm between those, on one
side, who relate everything to a single central
vision . . . and, on the other side, those who
pursue many ends, often unrelated and even
contradictory . . . The first kind of intellectual and
artistic personality belongs to the hedgehogs, the
second to the foxes.
The Hedgehog and the Fox (1953) sect. 1; see **Archilochus**
24:9

4 Liberty is liberty, not equality or fairness or justice
or human happiness or a quiet conscience.
Two Concepts of Liberty (1958)

5 Few new truths have ever won their way against
the resistance of established ideas save by being
overstated.
Vico and Herder (1976)

6 Rousseau was the first militant lowbrow.
in *Observer* 9 November 1952

Hector Berlioz 1803–69
French composer

7 Time is a great teacher but unfortunately it kills
all its pupils.
attributed; in *Almanach des lettres françaises et étrangères*
(1924) 11 May

J. D. Bernal 1901–71
Irish-born physicist

8 Men will not be content to manufacture life: they
will want to improve on it.
The World, the Flesh and the Devil (1929)

Georges Bernanos 1888–1948
French novelist and essayist

9 The wish for prayer is a prayer in itself.
Journal d'un curé de campagne (1936) ch. 2

10 Hell, madam, is to love no more.
Journal d'un curé de campagne (1936) ch. 2

Bernard of Chartres d. c.1130
French philosopher

11 We are like dwarfs on the shoulders of giants, so
that we can see more than they, and things at a
greater distance, not by virtue of any sharpness of
sight on our part, or any physical distinction, but
because we are carried high and raised up by their
giant size.
John of Salisbury *The Metalogicon* (1159) bk. 3, ch. 4,
quoted in R. K. Merton *On the Shoulders of Giants* (1965)
ch. 9; see **Coleridge** 233:24, **Newton** 561:15

St Bernard of Clairvaux 1090–1153
French theologian, monastic reformer, and abbot
see also **Caswall** 199:3

12 You will find something more in woods than in
books. Trees and stones will teach you that which
you can never learn from masters.
Epistles no. 106; see **Shakespeare** 680:26, **Wordsworth**
850:12

13 I am a kind of chimaera of my age, neither cleric
nor layman.
Epistles no. 250

14 *Liberavi animam meam.*
I have freed my soul.
Epistles no. 371

15 In the cloister, under the eyes of the brethren who
read there, what profit is there in those ridiculous
monsters, in that marvellous and deformed
beauty, that beautiful deformity? To what purpose
are those unclean apes, those fierce lions, those
monstrous centaurs, those half-men, those striped
tigers, those fighting knights, those hunters
winding their horns. Many bodies are there seen
under one head, or again, many heads to a single
body. Here is a four-footed beast with a serpent's
tail; there, a fish with a beast's head. Here again
the forepart of a horse trails half a goat behind it,
or a horned beast bears the hind quarters of a
horse. In short so many and so marvellous are the
varieties of diverse shapes on every hand, that we
are more tempted to read in the marble than in
our books, and to spend the whole day in
wondering at these things rather than in
meditating the law of God. For God's sake, if men
are not ashamed of these follies, why at least do
they not shrink from the expense?
letter to William, Abbot of St-Thierry, c.1125

16 I spoke; and at once the Crusaders have multiplied
to infinity. Villages and towns are now deserted.
You will scarcely find one man for every seven
women. Everywhere you see widows whose
husbands are still alive.
of the effects of his preaching the Second Crusade
letter to Pope Eugenius III, 1146

17 Will the light only shine if it is in a candelabrum
of gold or silver?
on Pope Urban II's conferring the title of Lux Mundi
[light of the world] *on the abbey of Cluny*
attributed

Claude Bernard 1813–78

French physiologist

1 Observation is a passive science, experimentation an active science.
   An Introduction to the Study of Experimental Medicine (1865, translated by Henry Copley Green, 1949)

2 [The science of life] is a superb and dazzlingly lighted hall which may be reached only by passing through a long and ghastly kitchen.
   An Introduction to the Study of Experimental Medicine (1865, translated by Henry Copley Green, 1949)

Bill Bernbach 1911–82

American advertising executive

3 A great ad campaign will make a bad product fail faster. It will get more people to know it's bad.
   Bill Bernbach said (1989)

Eric Berne 1910–70

American psychiatrist

4 Games people play: the psychology of human relationships.
   title of book (1964)

5 Human life [as] . . . a process of filling in time until the arrival of death, or Santa Claus, with very little choice, if any, of what kind of business one is going to transact during the long wait, is a commonplace but not the final answer.
   Games People Play (1964) ch. 18

Lord Berners 1883–1950

English composer, artist, and writer

6 He's always backing into the limelight.
   of T. E. Lawrence
   oral tradition

Tim Berners-Lee 1955–

English computer scientist

7 It was always difficult to predict how fast it was going to take off or whether it would crash. We just kept our fingers crossed.
   referring to the early days of the World Wide Web
   in *CIO* December 1999

Yogi Berra 1925–

American baseball player

8 The future ain't what it used to be.
   attributed

9 If people don't want to come out to the ball park, nobody's going to stop 'em.
   of baseball games
   attributed

10 It ain't over till it's over.
   comment on National League pennant race, 1973, quoted in many versions

11 It was déjà vu all over again.
   attributed

Wendell Berry 1934–

American poet and novelist

12 I come into the peace of wild things
   who do not tax their lives with forethought
   of grief. I come into the presence of still water.
   And I feel above me the day-blind stars
   waiting with their light.
   'The Peace of Wild Things' (1968)

13 Our hair
   turns white with our ripening
   as though to fly away in some
   coming wind, bearing the seed
   of what we know.
   'Ripening' (1980)

14 Radiances know him. Grown lighter
   than breath, he is set free
   in our remembering. Grown brighter
   than vision, he goes dark
   into the life of the hill
   that holds his peace.
   'Three Elegiac Poems' (1969)

John Berryman 1914–72

American poet

15   People will take balls,
   Balls will be lost always, little boy,
   And no one buys a ball back.
   'The Ball Poem' (1948)

16 We must travel in the direction of our fear.
   'A Point of Age' (1942)

17 Life, friends, is boring. We must not say so . . .
   And moreover my mother taught me as a boy
   (repeatedly) 'Ever to confess you're bored
   means you have no
   Inner Resources.' I conclude now I have no
   inner resources, because I am heavy bored.
   77 Dream Songs (1964) no. 14

18 I seldom go to films. They are too exciting,
   said the Honourable Possum.
   77 Dream Songs (1964) no. 53

Pierre Berton 1920–

Canadian writer

19 The march of social progress is like a long and straggling parade, with the seers and prophets at its head and a smug minority bringing up the rear.
   The Smug Minority (1968)

20 Somebody who knows how to make love in a canoe.
   definition of a Canadian
   in *Toronto Star, Canadian Magazine* 22 December 1973

Charles Best fl. 1602

English poet

21 Look how the pale Queen of the silent night
   Doth cause the Ocean to attend upon her,
   And he, as long as she is in his sight,

With his full tide is ready her to honour.
'Of the Moon' (1602) in N. Ault (ed.) *Elizabethan Lyrics from the Original Texts* (1925)

Theobald von Bethmann Hollweg
1856–1921
German statesman, Chancellor 1909–17

1 Just for a word 'neutrality'—a word which in wartime has so often been disregarded—just for a scrap of paper, Great Britain is going to make war on a kindred nation who desires nothing better than to be friends with her.
summary of a report by Sir Edward Goschen to Sir Edward **Grey**
  British Documents on Origins of the War 1898–1914 (1926)
  vol. II; *The Diary of Edward Goschen 1900–1914* (1980)
  Appendix B discusses the contentious origins of this
  statement

John Betjeman 1906–84
English poet

2 He sipped at a weak hock and seltzer
As he gazed at the London skies
Through the Nottingham lace of the curtains
Or was it his bees-winged eyes?

He rose, and he put down *The Yellow Book.*
He staggered—and, terrible-eyed,
He brushed past the palms on the staircase
And was helped to a hansom outside.
  'The Arrest of Oscar Wilde at the Cadogan Hotel' (1937)

3 And girls in slacks remember Dad,
And oafish louts remember Mum,
And sleepless children's hearts are glad,
And Christmas-morning bells say 'Come!'
Even to shining ones who dwell
Safe in the Dorchester Hotel.

And is it true? And is it true,
This most tremendous tale of all,
Seen in a stained-glass window's hue,
A Baby in an ox's stall?
The Maker of the stars and sea
Become a Child on earth for me?
  'Christmas' (1954)

4 Oh! Chintzy, Chintzy cheeriness,
Half dead and half alive!
  'Death in Leamington' (1931)

5 Spirits of well-shot woodcock, partridge, snipe
Flutter and bear him up the Norfolk sky.
  'Death of King George V' (1937)

6 Old men who never cheated, never doubted,
Communicated monthly, sit and stare
At the new suburb stretched beyond the run-way
Where a young man lands hatless from the air.
  'Death of King George V' (1937)

7 Phone for the fish-knives, Norman
As Cook is a little unnerved;
You kiddies have crumpled the serviettes
And I must have things daintily served.
  'How to get on in Society' (1954)

8 Milk and then just as it comes dear?
I'm afraid the preserve's full of stones;

Beg pardon, I'm soiling the doileys
With afternoon tea-cakes and scones.
  'How to get on in Society' (1954)

9 The Church's Restoration
In eighteen-eighty-three
Has left for contemplation
Not what there used to be.
  'Hymn' (1931)

10 Think of what our Nation stands for,
Books from Boots' and country lanes,
Free speech, free passes, class distinction,
Democracy and proper drains.
Lord, put beneath Thy special care
One-eighty-nine Cadogan Square.
  'In Westminster Abbey' (1940)

11 Stony seaboard, far and foreign,
Stony hills poured over space,
Stony outcrop of the Burren,
Stones in every fertile place,
Little fields with boulders dotted,
Grey-stone shoulders saffron-spotted,
Stone-walled cabins thatched with reeds,
Where a Stone Age people breeds
The last of Europe's stone age race.
  'Ireland with Emily' (1945)

12 Belbroughton Road is bonny, and pinkly bursts
    the spray
Of prunus and forsythia across the public way.
  'May-Day Song for North Oxford' (1945); see **Songs**
  747:15

13 Gaily into Ruislip Gardens
Runs the red electric train,
With a thousand Ta's and Pardon's
Daintily alights Elaine;
Hurries down the concrete station
With a frown of concentration,
Out into the outskirt's edges
Where a few surviving hedges
Keep alive our lost Elysium—rural Middlesex
    again.
  'Middlesex' (1954)

14 Official designs are aggressively neuter,
The Puritan work of an eyeless computer.
  'The Newest Bath Guide' (1974)

15 Pam, I adore you, Pam, you great big
    mountainous sports girl,
Whizzing them over the net, full of the strength of
    five.
  'Pot Pourri from a Surrey Garden' (1940)

16 The gas was on in the Institute,
The flare was up in the gymn,
A man was running a mineral line,
A lass was singing a hymn,
When Captain Webb the Dawley man,
Captain Webb from Dawley,
Came swimming along in the old canal
That carries the bricks to Lewley.
  'A Shropshire Lad' (1940)

17 Come, friendly bombs, and fall on Slough!
It isn't fit for humans now,
There isn't grass to graze a cow.

Swarm over, Death!
'Slough' (1937)

1 Miss J. Hunter Dunn, Miss J. Hunter Dunn,
Furnish'd and burnish'd by Aldershot sun.
'A Subaltern's Love-Song' (1945)

2 Love-thirty, love-forty, oh! weakness of joy,
The speed of a swallow, the grace of a boy,
With carefullest carelessness, gaily you won,
I am weak from your loveliness, Joan Hunter
Dunn.
Miss Joan Hunter Dunn, Miss Joan Hunter Dunn,
How mad I am, sad I am, glad that you won.
'A Subaltern's Love-Song' (1945)

3 By roads 'not adopted', by woodlanded ways,
She drove to the club in the late summer haze.
'A Subaltern's Love-Song' (1945)

4 The dread of beatings! Dread of being late!
And, greatest dread of all, the dread of games!
Summoned by Bells (1960) ch. 7

5 Broad of Church and 'broad of Mind',
Broad before and broad behind,
A keen ecclesiologist,
A rather dirty Wykehamist.
'The Wykehamist' (1931)

6 Ghastly good taste, or a depressing story of the rise
and fall of English architecture.
title of book (1933)

Bruno Bettelheim 1903–90
Austrian-born American psychologist

7 The most extreme agony is to feel that one has
been utterly forsaken.
Surviving and other essays (1979)

Aneurin Bevan 1897–1960
British Labour politician
*on Bevan: see **Bevin** 74:7*

8 This island is made mainly of coal and surrounded
by fish. Only an organizing genius could produce a
shortage of coal and fish at the same time.
speech at Blackpool 24 May 1945, in *Daily Herald* 25 May
1945

9 No amount of cajolery, and no attempts at ethical
or social seduction, can eradicate from my heart a
deep burning hatred for the Tory Party . . . So far
as I am concerned they are lower than vermin.
speech at Manchester, 4 July 1948, in *The Times* 5 July
1948

10 The language of priorities is the religion of
Socialism.
speech at Labour Party Conference in Blackpool, 8 June
1949, in *Report of the 48th Annual Conference* (1949)

11 He does not talk the language of the 20th century
but that of the 18th. He is still fighting Blenheim
all over again. His only answer to a difficult
situation is send a gun-boat.
*of Winston **Churchill***
speech at Labour Party Conference, Scarborough, 2
October 1951, in *Daily Herald* 3 October 1951

12 We know what happens to people who stay in the
middle of the road. They get run down.
in *Observer* 6 December 1953

13 Damn it all, you can't have the crown of thorns
and the thirty pieces of silver.
on his position in the Labour Party, c.1956
Michael Foot *Aneurin Bevan* (1973) vol. 2, ch. 13

14 I am not going to spend any time whatsoever in
attacking the Foreign Secretary . . . If we complain
about the tune, there is no reason to attack the
monkey when the organ grinder is present.
during a debate on the Suez crisis
in the House of Commmons, 16 May 1957

15 If you carry this resolution you will send Britain's
Foreign Secretary naked into the conference
chamber.
*speaking against a motion proposing unilateral nuclear
disarmament by the UK at Labour Party Conference
in Brighton, 3 October 1957*
in *Daily Herald* 4 October 1957

16 I know that the right kind of leader for the Labour
Party is a desiccated calculating machine who
must not in any way permit himself to be swayed
by indignation. If he sees suffering, privation or
injustice he must not allow it to move him, for
that would be evidence of the lack of proper
education or of absence of self-control. He must
speak in calm and objective accents and talk about
a dying child in the same way as he would about
the pieces inside an internal combustion engine.
*generally taken as referring to Hugh **Gaitskell**,
although Bevan specifically denied it in an interview
with Robin Day on 28 April 1959*
Michael Foot *Aneurin Bevan* (1973) vol. 2, ch. 11

17 This so-called affluent society is an ugly society
still. It is a vulgar society. It is a meretricious
society. It is a society in which priorities have
gone all wrong.
speech in Blackpool, 29 November 1959

18 I read the newspapers avidly. It is my one form of
continuous fiction.
in *The Times* 29 March 1960

19 I stuffed their mouths with gold.
*of his handling of the consultants during the
establishment of the National Health Service*
Brian Abel-Smith *The Hospitals 1800-1948* (1964) ch. 29

20 Listening to a speech by Chamberlain is like
paying a visit to Woolworth's: everything in its
place and nothing above sixpence.
Michael Foot *Aneurin Bevan* (1962) vol. 1, ch. 8

William Henry Beveridge 1879–1963
British economist

21 Ignorance is an evil weed, which dictators may
cultivate among their dupes, but which no
democracy can afford among its citizens.
Full Employment in a Free Society (1944) pt. 7

22 Want is one only of five giants on the road of
reconstruction . . . the others are Disease,
Ignorance, Squalor and Idleness.
Social Insurance and Allied Services (1942) pt. 7

Ernest Bevin 1881–1951

British Labour politician and trade unionist
on Bevin: see Foot 327:26

1 The most conservative man in this world is the British Trade Unionist when you want to change him.
speech, 8 September 1927, in *Report of Proceedings of the Trades Union Congress* (1927)

2 I hope you will carry no resolution of an emergency character telling a man with a conscience like Lansbury what he ought to do . . . It is placing the Executive in an absolutely wrong position to be taking your conscience round from body to body to be told what you ought to do with it.
of the Labour politician George Lansbury (1859–1940); often quoted as 'hawking his conscience round the Chancelleries of Europe'
in *Labour Party Conference Report* (1935)

3 There never has been a war yet which, if the facts had been put calmly before the ordinary folk, could not have been prevented . . . The common man, I think, is the great protection against war.
speech in the House of Commons, 23 November 1945

4 My [foreign] policy is to be able to take a ticket at Victoria Station and go anywhere I damn well please.
in *Spectator* 20 April 1951

5 If you open that Pandora's Box, you never know what Trojan 'orses will jump out.
on the Council of Europe
Roderick Barclay *Ernest Bevin and the Foreign Office* (1975) ch. 3

6 I didn't ought never to have done it. It was you, Willie, what put me up to it.
to Lord Strang, after officially recognizing Communist China
C. Parrott *Serpent and Nightingale* (1977) ch. 3

7 *on the observation that Aneurin Bevan was sometimes his own worst enemy:*
Not while I'm alive 'e ain't!
also attributed to Bevin of Herbert Morrison
Roderick Barclay *Ernest Bevin and the Foreign Office* (1975)

Bhagavadgita

Hindu poem composed between the 2nd century BC and the 2nd century AD and incorporated into the Mahabharata
textual translations are those of J. Mascaro, 1978

8 As the Spirit of our mortal body wanders on in childhood, and youth and old age, the Spirit wanders on to a new body: of this the sage has no doubts.
ch. 2, v. 13

9 If any man thinks he slays, and if another thinks he is slain, neither knows the ways of truth. The Eternal in man cannot kill: the Eternal in man cannot die.
He is never born, and he never dies. He is in Eternity, he is for evermore. Never-born and eternal, beyond times gone or to come, he does not die when the body dies.
ch. 2, v. 19; see **Emerson** 306:10, **Upanishads** 805:6

10 As a man leaves an old garment and puts on one that is new, the spirit leaves his mortal body and puts on one that is new.
ch. 2, v. 22

11 Invisible before birth are all beings and after death invisible again. They are seen between two unseens. Why in this truth find sorrow?
ch. 2, v. 28

12 Set thy heart upon thy work but never upon its reward. Work not for a reward: but never cease to do thy work.
Do thy work in the peace of Yoga and, free from selfish desires, be not moved in success or in failure. Yoga is evenness of mind—a peace that is ever the same.
ch. 2, v. 47

13 When in recollection he withdraws all his senses from the attractions of the pleasures of sense, even as a tortoise withdraws all its limbs, then his is a serene wisdom.
ch. 2, v. 58

14 And do thy duty, even if it be humble, rather than another's, even if it be great. To die in one's duty is life: to live in another's is death.
ch. 3, v. 35

15 I [Krishna] am all-powerful Time which destroys all things, and I have come here to slay these men. Even if thou does not fight, all the warriors facing thee shall die.
ch. 11, v. 32; see **Oppenheimer** 573:17

16 Only by love can men see me, and know me, and come unto me.
He who works for me, who loves me, whose End Supreme I am, free from attachment to all things, and with love for all creation, he in truth comes unto me.
ch. 11, v. 54

17 God dwells in the heart of all beings, Arjuna: thy God dwells in thy heart. And his power of wonder moves all things—puppets in a play of shadows—whirling them onwards on the stream of time.
ch. 18, v. 61

18 Leave all things behind, and come unto me for thy salvation. I will make thee free from the bondage of sins. Fear no more.
ch. 18, v. 66

Benazir Bhutto 1953–

Pakistani stateswoman; Prime Minister 1988–90 and 1993–96

19 Every dictator uses religion as a prop to keep himself in power.
interview on *60 Minutes*, CBS-TV, 8 August 1986

The Bible (Authorized Version, 1611)

many phrases derive from **Tyndale**'s *translation of the early 16th century*

see also **Book of Common Prayer** (Psalms)

1 Upon the setting of that bright Occidental Star, Queen Elizabeth of most happy memory.
   The Epistle Dedicatory

2 The appearance of Your Majesty, as of the Sun in his strength.
   The Epistle Dedicatory

3 Translation it is that openeth the window, to let in the light; that breaketh the shell, that we may eat the kernel; that putteth aside the curtain, that we may look into the most holy place; that removeth the cover of the well, that we may come by the water.
   The Translators to the Reader

OLD TESTAMENT: GENESIS

4 In the beginning God created the heaven and the earth. And the earth was without form, and void; and darkness was upon the face of the deep. And the Spirit of God moved upon the face of the waters.
   And God said, Let there be light: and there was light.
   Genesis ch. 1, v. 1; see **Byron** 181:22

5 And the evening and the morning were the first day.
   Genesis ch. 1, v. 5

6 And God saw that it was good.
   Genesis ch. 1, v. 10

7 And God made two great lights; the greater light to rule the day, and the lesser light to rule the night.
   Genesis ch. 1, v. 16

8 And God said, Let us make man in our image, after our likeness: and let them have dominion over the fish of the sea, and over the fowl of the air, and over the cattle, and over all the earth and over every creeping thing that creepeth upon the earth.
   Genesis ch. 1, v. 26

9 Male and female created he them.
   Genesis ch. 1, v. 27

10 Be fruitful, and multiply, and replenish the earth, and subdue it.
   Genesis ch. 1, v. 28

11 And the Lord God formed man of the dust of the ground, and breathed into his nostrils the breath of life; and man became a living soul.
   And the Lord God planted a garden eastward in Eden.
   Genesis ch. 2, v. 7

12 And out of the ground made the Lord God to grow every tree that is pleasant to the sight, and good for food; the tree of life also in the midst of the garden, and the tree of knowledge of good and evil.
   Genesis ch. 2, v. 9

13 But of the tree of the knowledge of good and evil, thou shalt not eat of it: for in the day that thou eatest thereof thou shalt surely die.
   Genesis ch. 2, v. 17

14 It is not good that the man should be alone; I will make him an help meet for him.
   Genesis ch. 2, v. 18

15 And the Lord God caused a deep sleep to fall upon Adam, and he slept: and he took one of his ribs, and closed up the flesh instead thereof;
   And the rib, which the Lord God had taken from man, made he a woman.
   Genesis ch. 2, v. 21

16 This is now bone of my bones, and flesh of my flesh: she shall be called Woman, because she was taken out of Man.
   Genesis ch. 2, v. 23; see **Milton** 534:3

17 Therefore shall a man leave his father and his mother, and shall cleave unto his wife: and they shall be one flesh.
   Genesis ch. 2, v. 24

18 Now the serpent was more subtil than any beast of the field.
   Genesis ch. 3, v. 1

19 Ye shall be as gods, knowing good and evil.
   Genesis ch. 3, v. 5

20 And they sewed fig leaves together, and made themselves aprons.
   And they heard the voice of the Lord God walking in the garden in the cool of the day.
   Genesis ch. 3, v. 7

   And made themselves breeches.
   Genesis ch. 3, v. 7 in the Geneva Bible, 1560, known for that reason as the 'Breeches Bible'

21 The woman whom thou gavest to be with me, she gave me of the tree, and I did eat.
   Genesis ch. 3, v. 12

22 What is this that thou hast done?
   Genesis ch. 3, v. 13

23 The serpent beguiled me, and I did eat.
   Genesis ch. 3, v. 13

24 It shall bruise thy head, and thou shalt bruise his heel.
   Genesis ch. 3, v. 15

25 In sorrow thou shalt bring forth children.
   Genesis ch. 3, v. 16

26 In the sweat of thy face shalt thou eat bread.
   Genesis ch. 3, v. 19

27 For dust thou art, and unto dust shalt thou return.
   Genesis ch. 3, v. 19; see **Longfellow** 490:18

28 Am I my brother's keeper?
   Genesis ch. 4, v. 9

29 The voice of thy brother's blood crieth unto me from the ground.
   Genesis ch. 4, v. 10

30 My punishment is greater than I can bear.
   Genesis ch. 4, v. 13

1 And the Lord set a mark upon Cain.
Genesis ch. 4, v. 15

2 And Cain went out from the presence of the Lord, and dwelt in the land of Nod, on the east of Eden.
Genesis ch. 4, v. 16

3 And Enoch walked with God: and he was not; for God took him.
Genesis ch. 5, v. 24

4 And all the days of Methuselah were nine hundred sixty and nine years: and he died.
Genesis ch. 5, v. 27

5 There were giants in the earth in those days; and also after that, when the sons of God came in unto the daughters of men, and they bare children to them, the same became mighty men which were of old, men of renown.
Genesis ch. 6, v. 4

6 There went in two and two unto Noah into the Ark, the male and the female.
Genesis ch. 7, v. 9

7 But the dove found no rest for the sole of her foot.
Genesis ch. 8, v. 9

8 For the imagination of man's heart is evil from his youth.
Genesis ch. 8, v. 21

9 While the earth remaineth, seedtime and harvest, and cold and heat, and summer and winter, and day and night shall not cease.
Genesis ch. 8, v. 22

10 At the hand of every man's brother will I require the life of man.
Genesis ch. 9, v. 5

11 Whoso sheddeth man's blood, by man shall his blood be shed.
Genesis ch. 9, v. 6

12 I do set my bow in the cloud, and it shall be for a token of a covenant between me and the earth. And it shall come to pass, when I bring a cloud over the earth, that the bow shall be seen in the cloud.
Genesis ch. 9, v. 13

13 Even as Nimrod the mighty hunter before the Lord.
Genesis ch. 10, v. 9

14 Let there be no strife, I pray thee, between thee and me . . . for we be brethren.
Genesis ch. 13, v. 8

15 An horror of great darkness fell upon him.
Genesis ch. 15, v. 12

16 Thou shalt be buried in a good old age.
Genesis ch. 15, v. 15

17 His [Ishmael's] hand will be against every man, and every man's hand against him.
Genesis ch. 16, v. 12

18 Now Abraham and Sarah were old and well stricken in age; and it ceased to be with Sarah after the manner of women.
Genesis ch. 18, v. 11

19 Shall not the Judge of all the earth do right?
Genesis ch. 18, v. 25

20 But his [Lot's] wife looked back from behind him, and she became a pillar of salt.
Genesis ch. 19, v. 26

21 Take now thy son, thine only son Isaac, whom thou lovest.
Genesis ch. 22, v. 2

22 My son, God will provide himself a lamb.
Genesis ch. 22, v. 8

23 Behold behind him a ram caught in a thicket by his horns.
Genesis ch. 22, v. 13

24 Esau selleth his birthright for a mess of pottage.
Genesis ch. 25: chapter heading in Geneva Bible, 1560

25 Esau was a cunning hunter, a man of the field; and Jacob was a plain man, dwelling in tents.
Genesis ch. 25, v. 27

26 And he sold his birthright unto Jacob.
Genesis ch. 25, v. 33

27 Behold, Esau my brother is a hairy man, and I am a smooth man.
Genesis ch. 27, v. 11

28 The voice is Jacob's voice, but the hands are the hands of Esau.
Genesis ch. 27, v. 22

29 Thy brother came with subtilty, and hath taken away thy blessing.
Genesis ch. 27, v. 35

30 And he dreamed, and behold a ladder set up on the earth, and the top of it reached to heaven: and behold the angels of God ascending and descending on it.
Genesis ch. 28, v. 12

31 Surely the Lord is in this place; and I knew it not.
Genesis ch. 28, v. 16

32 This is none other but the house of God, and this is the gate of heaven.
Genesis ch. 28, v. 17

33 And Jacob served seven years for Rachel; and they seemed unto him but a few days, for the love he had to her.
Genesis ch. 29, v. 20

34 The Lord watch between me and thee, when we are absent one from another.
Genesis ch. 31, v. 49

35 I will not let thee go, except thou bless me.
Genesis ch. 32, v. 26

36 For I have seen God face to face, and my life is preserved.
Genesis ch. 32, v. 30

37 Now Israel loved Joseph more than all his children, because he was the son of his old age; and he made him a coat of many colours.
Genesis ch. 37, v. 3

38 Behold, your sheaves stood round about, and made obeisance to my sheaf.
Genesis ch. 37, v. 7

1 Behold, this dreamer cometh.
Genesis ch. 37, v. 19

2 Some evil beast hath devoured him.
Genesis ch. 37, v. 20

3 And she caught him by his garment, saying, Lie with me; and he left his garment in her hand, and fled.
Genesis ch. 39, v. 12

4 And the lean and the ill favoured kine did eat up the first seven fat kine.
Genesis ch. 41, v. 20

5 And the thin ears devoured the seven good ears.
Genesis ch. 41, v. 24

6 Jacob saw that there was corn in Egypt.
Genesis ch. 42, v. 1

7 Ye are spies; to see the nakedness of the land ye are come.
Genesis ch. 42, v. 9

8 My son shall not go down with you; for his brother is dead, and he is left alone: if mischief befall him by the way in which ye go, then shall ye bring down my grey hairs with sorrow to the grave.
Genesis ch. 42, v. 38

9 Ye shall eat the fat of the land.
Genesis ch. 45, v. 18

10 See that ye fall not out by the way.
Genesis ch. 45, v. 24

11 Few and evil have the days of the years of my life been.
Genesis ch. 47, v. 9

12 Unstable as water, thou shalt not excel.
Genesis ch. 49, v. 4

EXODUS

13 She took for him an ark of bulrushes, and daubed it with slime.
Exodus ch. 2, v. 3

14 Who made thee a prince and a judge over us?
Exodus ch. 2, v. 14

15 I have been a stranger in a strange land.
Exodus ch. 2, v. 22

16 Behold, the bush burned with fire, and the bush was not consumed.
Exodus ch. 3, v. 2

17 Put off thy shoes from off thy feet, for the place whereon thou standest is holy ground.
Exodus ch. 3, v. 5

18 And Moses hid his face; for he was afraid to look upon God.
Exodus ch. 3, v. 6

19 A land flowing with milk and honey.
Exodus ch. 3, v. 8

20 I AM THAT I AM.
Exodus ch. 3, v. 14

21 The Lord God of your fathers, the God of Abraham, the God of Isaac, and the God of Jacob.
Exodus ch. 3, v. 15

22 But I am slow of speech, and of a slow tongue.
Exodus ch. 4, v. 10

23 I know not the Lord, neither will I let Israel go.
Exodus ch. 5, v. 2

24 And I will harden Pharaoh's heart, and multiply my signs and my wonders in the land of Egypt.
Exodus ch. 7, v. 3

25 Aaron's rod swallowed up their rods.
And he hardened Pharaoh's heart, that he hearkened not.
Exodus ch. 7, v. 12

26 Let my people go.
Exodus ch. 7, v. 16

27 Stretch out thine hand toward heaven, that there may be darkness over the land of Egypt, even darkness which may be felt.
Exodus ch. 10, v. 21

28 Your lamb shall be without blemish.
Exodus ch. 12, v. 5

29 And they shall eat the flesh in that night, roast with fire, and unleavened bread; and with bitter herbs they shall eat it.
Eat not of it raw, nor sodden at all with water, but roast with fire; his head with his legs, and with the purtenance thereof.
Exodus ch. 12, v. 8

30 Ye shall eat it in haste; it is the Lord's passover.
Exodus ch. 12, v. 11

31 For I will pass through the land of Egypt this night, and will smite all the firstborn in the land of Egypt, both man and beast.
Exodus ch. 12, v. 12

32 And Pharaoh rose up in the night, he, and all his servants, and all the Egyptians; and there was a great cry in Egypt; for there was not a house where there was not one dead.
Exodus ch. 12, v. 30

33 And they spoiled the Egyptians.
Exodus ch. 12, v. 36

34 And the Lord went before them by day in a pillar of a cloud, to lead them the way; and by night in a pillar of fire, to give them light.
Exodus ch. 13, v. 21

35 The Lord is a man of war.
Exodus ch. 15, v. 3

36 Would to God we had died by the hand of the Lord in the land of Egypt, when we sat by the flesh pots, and when we did eat bread to the full.
Exodus ch. 16, v. 3

37 I am the Lord thy God, which have brought thee out of the land of Egypt, out of the house of bondage.
Thou shalt have no other gods before me.
Thou shalt not make unto thee any graven image, or any likeness of any thing that is in heaven above, or that is in the earth beneath, or that is in the water under the earth.
Exodus ch. 20, v. 2

1 I the Lord thy God am a jealous God, visiting the iniquity of the fathers upon the children unto the third and fourth generation of them that hate me.
Exodus ch. 20, v. 5; see **Book of Common Prayer** 131:7, **French** 333:12

2 Thou shalt not take the name of the Lord thy God in vain.
Exodus ch. 20, v. 7

3 Remember the sabbath day, to keep it holy.
Six days shalt thou labour, and do all thy work:
But the seventh day is the sabbath of the Lord thy God: in it thou shalt not do any work.
Exodus ch. 20, v. 8

4 For in six days the Lord made heaven and earth, the sea, and all that in them is, and rested the seventh day: wherefore the Lord blest the sabbath day, and hallowed it.
Exodus ch. 20, v. 11

5 Honour thy father and thy mother: that thy days may be long upon the land which the Lord thy God giveth thee.
Thou shalt not kill.
Thou shalt not commit adultery.
Thou shalt not steal.
Thou shalt not bear false witness against thy neighbour.
Thou shalt not covet thy neighbour's house, thou shalt not covet thy neighbour's wife, nor his manservant, nor his maidservant, nor his ox, nor his ass, nor any thing that is thy neighbour's.
Exodus ch. 20, v. 12; see **Book of Common Prayer** 131:9

6 Life for life,
Eye for eye, tooth for tooth, hand for hand, foot for foot,
Burning for burning, wound for wound, stripe for stripe.
Exodus ch. 21, v. 23

7 And thou shalt put in the breastplate of judgement the Urim and the Thummim.
sacred symbols worn on the breastplate of the high priest
Exodus ch. 28, v. 30

8 These be thy gods, O Israel.
Exodus ch. 32, v. 4

9 I will not go up in the midst of thee; for thou art a stiffnecked people: lest I consume thee in the way.
Exodus ch. 33, v. 3

10 There shall no man see me and live.
Exodus ch. 33, v. 20

LEVITICUS

11 And the swine, though he divide the hoof, and be cloven-footed, yet he cheweth not the cud; .
Leviticus ch. 11, v. 7

12 Let him go for a scapegoat into the wilderness.
Leviticus ch. 16, v. 10

13 Ye shall therefore keep my statutes and my judgments: which if a man do, he shall live in them: I am the Lord.
Leviticus ch. 18, v. 5; see **Talmud** 772:15

14 Thou shalt love thy neighbour as thyself.
Leviticus ch. 19, v. 18; see **Bible** 98:8

NUMBERS

15 The Lord bless thee, and keep thee:
The Lord make his face shine upon thee, and be gracious unto thee:
The Lord lift up his countenance upon thee, and give thee peace.
Numbers ch. 6, v. 24

16 These are the names of the men which Moses sent to spy out the land.
Numbers ch. 13, v. 16

17 And there we saw the giants, the sons of Anak, which come of the giants: and we were in our own sight as grasshoppers, and so we were in their sight.
Numbers ch. 13, v. 33

18 And Israel smote him with the edge of the sword, and possessed his land.
Numbers ch. 21, v. 24

19 He whom thou blessest is blessed, and he whom thou cursest is cursed.
Numbers ch. 22, v. 6

20 God is not a man, that he should lie.
Numbers ch. 23, v. 19

21 What hath God wrought!
quoted by Samuel Morse in the first electric telegraph message, 24 May 1844
Numbers ch. 23, v. 23

22 I called thee to curse mine enemies, and, behold, thou hast altogether blessed them these three times.
Numbers ch. 24, v. 10

23 Be sure your sin will find you out.
Numbers ch. 32, v. 23

DEUTERONOMY

24 I call heaven and earth to witness against you this day.
Deuteronomy ch. 4, v. 26

25 Remember that thou wast a servant in the land of Egypt, and that the Lord thy God brought thee out thence through a mighty hand and by a stretched out arm.
Deuteronomy ch. 5, v. 15

26 Hear, O Israel: The Lord our God is one Lord.
Deuteronomy ch. 6, v. 4; see **Siddur** 735:12

27 If there arise among you a prophet, or a dreamer of dreams . . . Thou shalt not hearken.
Deuteronomy ch. 13, v. 1

28 If thy brother, the son of thy mother, or thy son, or thy daughter, or the wife of thy bosom, or thy friend, which is as thine own soul, entice thee secretly . . . Thou shalt not consent.
Deuteronomy ch. 13, v. 6

29 The secret things belong unto the Lord our God.
Deuteronomy ch. 29, v. 29

1 I have set before you life and death, blessing and cursing: therefore choose life that both thou and thy seed may live.
Deuteronomy ch. 30, v. 19

2 He found him in a desert land, and in the waste howling wilderness; he led him about, he instructed him, he kept him as the apple of his eye.
Deuteronomy ch. 32, v. 10

3 For they are a very froward generation, children in whom is no faith.
Deuteronomy ch. 32, v. 20

4 I will heap mischiefs upon them; I will spend mine arrows upon them.
Deuteronomy ch. 32, v. 23

5 The eternal God is thy refuge, and underneath are the everlasting arms.
Deuteronomy ch. 33, v. 27

6 No man knoweth of his [Moses's] sepulchre unto this day.
Deuteronomy ch. 34, v. 6

JOSHUA

7 As I was with Moses, so I will be with thee: I will not fail thee, nor forsake thee.
Joshua ch. 1, v. 5

8 Be strong and of a good courage; be not afraid, neither be thou dismayed: for the Lord thy God is with thee, whithersoever thou goest.
Joshua ch. 1, v. 9

9 This line of scarlet thread.
Joshua ch. 2, v. 18

10 All the Israelites passed over on dry ground.
Joshua ch. 3, v. 17

11 When the people heard the sound of the trumpet, and the people shouted with a great shout, that the wall fell down flat, so that the people went up into the city.
Joshua ch. 6, v. 20

12 Let them live; but let them be hewers of wood and drawers of water unto all the congregation.
Joshua ch. 9, v. 21

13 Sun, stand thou still upon Gibeon; and thou, Moon, in the valley of Ajalon.
Joshua ch. 10, v. 12

14 I am going the way of all the earth.
Joshua ch. 23, v. 14

JUDGES

15 He delivered them into the hands of spoilers.
Judges ch. 2, v. 14

16 Then Jael Heber's wife took a nail of the tent, and took an hammer in her hand, and went softly unto him, and smote the nail into his temples, and fastened it into the ground: for he was fast asleep and weary.
Judges ch. 4, v. 21

17 I arose a mother in Israel.
Judges ch. 5, v. 7

18 The stars in their courses fought against Sisera.
Judges ch. 5, v. 20

19 He asked water, and she gave him milk; she brought forth butter in a lordly dish.
Judges ch. 5, v. 25

20 At her feet he bowed, he fell, he lay down.
Judges ch. 5, v. 27

21 The mother of Sisera looked out at a window, and cried through the lattice, Why is his chariot so long in coming? why tarry the wheels of his chariots?
Judges ch. 5, v. 28

22 The Lord is with thee, thou mighty man of valour.
Judges ch. 6, v. 12 (spoken to Gideon)

23 The Spirit of the Lord came upon Gideon, and he blew a trumpet.
Judges ch. 6, v. 34

24 The host of Midian was beneath him in the valley.
Judges ch. 7, v. 8

25 Is not the gleaning of the grapes of Ephraim better than the vintage of Abi-ezer?
Judges ch. 8, v. 2

26 Faint, yet pursuing.
Judges ch. 8, v. 4

27 Let fire come out of the bramble and devour the cedars of Lebanon.
Judges ch. 9, v. 15

28 Then said they unto him, Say now Shibboleth: and he said Sibboleth: for he could not frame to pronounce it right. Then they took him, and slew him.
Judges ch. 12, v. 6

29 Out of the eater came forth meat, and out of the strong came forth sweetness.
Judges ch. 14, v. 14

30 If ye had not plowed with my heifer, ye had not found out my riddle.
Judges ch. 14, v. 18

31 He smote them hip and thigh.
Judges ch. 15, v. 8 (Samson)

32 With the jawbone of an ass, heaps upon heaps, with the jaw of an ass have I slain a thousand men.
Judges ch. 15, v. 16

33 The Philistines be upon thee, Samson.
Judges ch. 16, v. 9

34 He wist not that the Lord was departed from him.
Judges ch. 16, v. 20

35 He did grind in the prison house.
Judges ch. 16, v. 21

36 The dead which he slew at his death were more than they which he slew in his life.
Judges ch. 16, v. 30

37 In those days there was no king in Israel, but every man did that which was right in his own eyes.
Judges ch. 17, v. 6

38 From Dan even to Beer-sheba.
Judges ch. 20, v. 1

1 The people arose as one man.
Judges ch. 20, v. 8

RUTH

2 Intreat me not to leave thee, or to return from following after thee: for whither thou goest, I will go; and where thou lodgest, I will lodge: thy people shall be my people, and thy God my God: Where thou diest, will I die, and there will I be buried: the Lord do so to me, and more also, if ought but death part thee and me.
Ruth ch. 1, v. 16

I SAMUEL

3 All the increase of thy house shall die in the flower of their age.
I Samuel ch. 2, v. 33

4 The Lord called Samuel: and he answered, Here am I.
I Samuel ch. 3, v. 4

5 Speak, Lord; for thy servant heareth.
I Samuel ch. 3, v. 9

6 The ears of every one that heareth it shall tingle.
I Samuel ch. 3, v. 11

7 Quit yourselves like men, and fight.
I Samuel ch. 4, v. 9

8 And she named the child I-chabod, saying, The glory is departed from Israel.
I Samuel ch. 4, v. 21; see **Browning** 161:28

9 And the asses of Kish Saul's father were lost. And Kish said to Saul his son, Take now one of the servants with thee, and arise, go seek the asses.
I Samuel ch. 9, v. 3; see **Milton** 534:18

10 Is Saul also among the prophets?
I Samuel ch. 10, v. 11

11 God save the king.
I Samuel ch. 10, v. 24

12 A man after his own heart.
I Samuel ch. 13, v. 14

13 I did but taste a little honey with the end of the rod that was in mine hand, and, lo, I must die.
I Samuel ch. 14, v. 43

14 To obey is better than sacrifice, and to hearken than the fat of rams.
I Samuel ch. 15, v. 22

15 For rebellion is as the sin of witchcraft.
I Samuel ch. 15, v. 23

16 For the Lord seeth not as man seeth: for man looketh on the outward appearance, but the Lord looketh on the heart.
I Samuel ch. 16, v. 7

17 Now he was ruddy, and withal of a beautiful countenance, and goodly to look to.
I Samuel ch. 16, v. 12 (David)

18 I know thy pride, and the naughtiness of thine heart.
I Samuel ch. 17, v. 28

19 Let no man's heart fail because of him.
I Samuel ch. 17, v. 32

20 Go, and the Lord be with thee.
I Samuel ch. 17, v. 37

21 And he took his staff in his hand and chose him five smooth stones out of the brook.
I Samuel ch. 17, v. 40

22 Am I a dog, that thou comest to me with staves?
I Samuel ch. 17, v. 43

23 Saul hath slain his thousands, and David his ten thousands.
I Samuel ch. 18, v. 7; see **Porteus** 607:21

24 David therefore departed thence, and escaped to the cave Adullam: and when his brethren and all his father's house heard it, they went down thither to him.
And every one that was in distress, and every one that was in debt, and every one that was discontented, gathered themselves unto him.
I Samuel ch. 22, v. 1; see **Bright** 151:12

25 And Saul said, God hath delivered him into mine hand.
I Samuel ch. 23, v. 7

26 Behold, I have played the fool, and have erred exceedingly.
I Samuel ch. 26, v. 21

II SAMUEL

27 The beauty of Israel is slain upon thy high places: how are the mighty fallen!
Tell it not in Gath, publish it not in the streets of Askelon; lest the daughters of the Philistines rejoice, lest the daughters of the uncircumcised triumph.
Ye mountains of Gilboa, let there be no dew, neither let there be rain, upon you, nor fields of offerings: for there the shield of the mighty is vilely cast away.
II Samuel ch. 1, v. 19 (David's lament for Saul and Jonathan)

28 Saul and Jonathan were lovely and pleasant in their lives, and in their death they were not divided: they were swifter than eagles, they were stronger than lions.
Ye daughters of Israel, weep over Saul, who clothed you in scarlet, with other delights, who put on ornaments of gold upon your apparel.
II Samuel ch. 1, v. 23

29 I am distressed for thee, my brother Jonathan: very pleasant hast thou been unto me: thy love to me was wonderful, passing the love of women.
How are the mighty fallen, and the weapons of war perished!
II Samuel ch. 1, v. 26

30 And David danced before the Lord with all his might.
II Samuel ch. 6, v. 14

31 Set ye Uriah in the forefront of the hottest battle.
II Samuel ch. 10, v. 15

32 The poor man had nothing, save one little ewe lamb.
II Samuel ch. 12, v. 3

1 Thou art the man.
   II Samuel ch. 12, v. 7

2 While the child was yet alive, I fasted and wept
   . . . But now he is dead, wherefore should I fast?
   can I bring him back again? I shall go to him but
   he shall not return to me.
   II Samuel ch. 12, v. 22

3 For we needs must die, and are as water spilt on
   the ground, which cannot be gathered up again;
   neither doth God respect any person.
   II Samuel ch. 14, v. 14

4 Come out, come out, thou bloody man, and thou
   man of Belial.
   II Samuel ch. 16, v. 7

5 And the king was much moved, and went up to
   the chamber over the gate, and wept: and as he
   went, thus he said, O my son Absalom, my son,
   my son Absalom! would God I had died for thee, O
   Absalom, my son, my son!
   II Samuel ch. 18, v. 33

6 By my God have I leaped over a wall.
   II Samuel ch. 22, v. 30; see **Book of Common Prayer**
   134:18

7 David . . . the sweet psalmist of Israel.
   II Samuel ch. 23, v. 1

8 Went in jeopardy of their lives.
   II Samuel ch. 23, v. 17

I KINGS

9 And Zadok the priest took an horn of oil out of the
   tabernacle, and anointed Solomon. And they blew
   the trumpet; and all the people said, God save king
   Solomon.
   I Kings ch. 1, v. 39

10 Then will I cut off Israel out of the land which I
   have given them; and this house, which I have
   hallowed for my name, will I cast out of my sight;
   and Israel shall be a proverb and a byword among
   all people.
   I Kings ch. 9, v. 7

11 And when the queen of Sheba had seen all
   Solomon's wisdom . . . there was no more spirit in
   her.
   I Kings ch. 10, v. 4

12 Behold, the half was not told me.
   I Kings ch. 10, v. 7

13 Once in three years came the navy of Tharshish,
   bringing gold, and silver, ivory, and apes, and
   peacocks.
   I Kings ch. 10, v. 22; see **Masefield** 517:12

14 But king Solomon loved many strange women.
   I Kings ch. 11, v. 1

15 My little finger shall be thicker than my father's
   loins.
   I Kings ch. 12, v. 10

16 My father hath chastised you with whips, but I
   will chastise you with scorpions.
   I Kings ch. 12, v. 11

17 To your tents, O Israel: now see to thine own
   house, David.
   I Kings ch. 12, v. 16

18 He slept with his fathers.
   I Kings ch. 14, v. 20

19 He went and dwelt by the brook Cherith, that is
   before Jordan.
   And the ravens brought him bread and flesh in
   the morning, and bread and flesh in the evening;
   and he drank of the brook.
   I Kings ch. 17, v. 5 (Elijah)

20 An handful of meal in a barrel, and a little oil in a
   cruse.
   I Kings ch. 17, v. 12

21 How long halt ye between two opinions?
   I Kings ch. 18, v. 21

22 He is talking, or he is pursuing, or he is in a
   journey, or peradventure he sleepeth, and must be
   awaked.
   I Kings ch. 18, v. 27

23 There is a sound of abundance of rain.
   I Kings ch. 18, v. 41

24 There ariseth a little cloud out of the sea, like a
   man's hand.
   I Kings ch. 18, v. 44

25 He girded up his loins, and ran before Ahab.
   I Kings ch. 18, v. 46

26 He himself went a day's journey into the
   wilderness, and came and sat down under a
   juniper tree.
   I Kings ch. 19, v. 4

27 But the Lord was not in the wind: and after the
   wind an earthquake; but the Lord was not in the
   earthquake:
   And after the earthquake a fire: but the Lord was
   not in the fire: and after the fire a still small voice.
   I Kings ch. 19, v. 11

28 Elijah passed by him, and cast his mantle upon
   him.
   I Kings ch. 19, v. 19

29 A vineyard, which was in Jezreel.
   I Kings ch. 21, v. 1

30 And Ahab spake unto Naboth, saying, Give me
   thy vineyard, that I may have it for a garden of
   herbs, because it is near unto my house.
   I Kings ch. 21, v. 2

31 Hast thou found me, O mine enemy?
   I Kings ch. 21, v. 20

32 I saw all Israel scattered upon the hills, as sheep
   that have not a shepherd.
   I Kings ch. 22, v. 17

33 Feed him with bread of affliction and with water of
   affliction, until I come in peace.
   I Kings ch. 22, v. 27

34 And a certain man drew a bow at a venture, and
   smote the king of Israel between the joints of the
   harness.
   I Kings ch. 22, v. 34

II KINGS

1 Elijah went up by a whirlwind into heaven. And Elisha saw it, and he cried, My father, my father, the chariot of Israel, and the horsemen thereof.
II Kings ch. 2, v. 11

2 The spirit of Elijah doth rest on Elisha.
II Kings ch. 2, v. 15

3 Go up, thou bald head.
II Kings ch. 2, v. 23 (the children to Elisha)

4 Is it well with the child? And she answered, It is well.
II Kings ch. 4, v. 26

5 There is death in the pot.
II Kings ch. 4, v. 40

6 He shall know that there is a prophet in Israel.
II Kings ch. 5, v. 8

7 Are not Abana and Pharpar, rivers of Damascus, better than all the waters of Israel?
II Kings ch. 5, v. 12 (Naaman)

8 I bow myself in the house of Rimmon.
II Kings ch. 5, v. 18

9 Whence comest thou, Gehazi?
II Kings ch. 5, v. 25

10 Is thy servant a dog, that he should do this great thing?
II Kings ch. 8, v. 13

11 Is it peace? And Jehu said, What hast thou to do with peace? turn thee behind me.
II Kings ch. 9, v. 18

12 The driving is like the driving of Jehu, the son of Nimshi; for he driveth furiously.
II Kings ch. 9, v. 20

13 She painted her face, and tired her head, and looked out at a window.
II Kings ch. 9, v. 30 (Jezebel)

14 Had Zimri peace, who slew his master?
II Kings ch. 9, v. 31

15 Who is on my side? who?
II Kings ch. 9, v. 32

16 They found no more of her than the skull, and the feet, and the palms of her hands.
II Kings ch. 9, v. 35

17 Thou trustest upon the staff of this bruised reed, even upon Egypt, on which if a man lean, it will go into his hand, and pierce it.
II Kings ch. 18, v. 21

I CHRONICLES

18 For we are strangers before thee, and sojourners, as were all our fathers: our days on the earth are as a shadow, and there is none abiding.
I Chronicles ch. 29, v. 15

19 He died in a good old age, full of days, riches, and honour.
I Chronicles ch. 29, v. 28

NEHEMIAH

20 Every one with one of his hands wrought in the work, and with the other hand held a weapon.
Nehemiah ch. 4, v. 17

ESTHER

21 And if I perish, I perish.
Esther ch. 4, v. 16

22 Yet all this availeth me nothing, so long as I see Mordecai the Jew sitting at the king's gate.
Esther ch. 5, v. 13

23 So they hanged Haman on the gallows that he had prepared for Mordecai.
Esther ch. 7, v. 10

24 Thus shall it be done to the man whom the king delighteth to honour.
Esther ch. 6, v. 9

JOB

25 And the Lord said unto Satan, Whence comest thou? Then Satan answered the Lord, and said, From going to and fro in the earth, and from walking up and down in it.
Job ch. 1, v. 7

26 Doth Job fear God for naught?
Job ch. 1, v. 9

27 The Lord gave, and the Lord hath taken away; blessed be the name of the Lord.
Job ch. 1, v. 21

28 All that a man hath will he give for his life.
Job ch. 2, v. 4

29 And he took him a potsherd to scrape himself withal.
Job ch. 2, v. 8

30 Curse God, and die.
Job ch. 2, v. 9

31 Let the day perish wherein I was born, and the night in which it was said, There is a man child conceived.
Job ch. 3, v. 3

32 For now should I have lain still and been quiet, I should have slept: then had I been at rest, With kings and counsellors of the earth, which built desolate places for themselves.
Job ch. 3, v. 13

33 There the wicked cease from troubling, and there the weary be at rest.
Job ch. 3, v. 17

34 Wherefore is light given to him that is in misery, and life unto the bitter in soul?
Job ch. 3, v. 20

35 Then a spirit passed before my face; the hair of my flesh stood up.
Job ch. 4, v. 15

36 Shall mortal man be more just than God? shall a man be more pure than his maker?
Job ch. 4, v. 17

37 Man is born unto trouble, as the sparks fly upward.
Job ch. 5, v. 7

38 My days are swifter than a weaver's shuttle.
Job ch. 7, v. 6

1 He shall return no more to his house, neither shall his place know him any more.
   Job ch. 7, v. 10

2 Let me alone, that I may take comfort a little, Before I go whence I shall not return, even to the land of darkness and the shadow of death.
   Job ch. 10, v. 20

3 A land . . . where the light is as darkness.
   Job ch. 10, v. 22

4 Canst thou by searching find out God?
   Job ch. 11, v. 7

5 No doubt but ye are the people, and wisdom shall die with you.
   Job ch. 12, v. 2

6 With the ancient is wisdom; and in length of days understanding.
   Job ch. 12, v. 12

7 Though he slay me, yet will I trust in him: but I will maintain mine own ways before him.
   Job ch. 13, v. 15

8 Man that is born of a woman is of few days, and full of trouble.
   He cometh forth like a flower, and is cut down: he fleeth also as a shadow, and continueth not.
   Job ch. 14, v. 1; see **Book of Common Prayer** 133:16

9 Miserable comforters are ye all.
   Job ch. 16, v. 2

10 I also could speak as ye do: if your soul were in my soul's stead.
   Job ch. 16, v. 4

11 I am escaped with the skin of my teeth.
   Job ch. 19, v. 20

12 I know that my redeemer liveth, and that he shall stand at the latter day upon the earth:
   And though after my skin worms destroy this body, yet in my flesh shall I see God.
   Job ch. 19, v. 25

13 Ye should say, Why persecute we him, seeing the root of the matter is found in me?
   Job ch. 19, v. 28

14 But where shall wisdom be found?
   Job ch. 28, v. 12

15 The price of wisdom is above rubies.
   Job ch. 28, v. 18

16 I was eyes to the blind, and feet was I to the lame.
   Job ch. 29, v. 15

17 For I know that thou wilt bring me to death, and to the house appointed for all living.
   Job ch. 30, v. 23

18 I am a brother to dragons, and a companion to owls.
   Job ch. 30, v. 29

19 Great men are not always wise.
   Job ch. 32, v. 9

20 Who is this that darkeneth counsel by words without knowledge?
   Job ch. 38, v. 2

21 Where wast thou when I laid the foundations of the earth? declare, if thou hast understanding.
   Job ch. 38, v. 4

22 When the morning stars sang together, and all the sons of God shouted for joy.
   Job ch. 38, v. 7

23 Hath the rain a father? or who hath begotten the drops of dew?
   Job ch. 38, v. 28

24 Canst thou bind the sweet influences of Pleiades, or loose the bands of Orion?
   Job ch. 38, v. 31

25 He saith among the trumpets, Ha, ha; and he smelleth the battle afar off, the thunder of the captains, and the shouting.
   Job ch. 39, v. 25

26 Behold now behemoth, which I made with thee; he eateth grass as an ox.
   Job ch. 40, v. 15

27 He is the chief of the ways of God: he that made him can make his sword to approach unto him.
   Job ch. 40, v. 19

28 The shady trees cover him with their shadow; the willows of the brook compass him about.
   Job ch. 40, v. 22

29 Canst thou draw out leviathan with an hook?
   Job ch. 41, v. 1

30 I have heard of thee by the hearing of the ear: but now mine eye seeth thee.
   Job ch. 42, v. 5

31 So the Lord blessed the latter end of Job more than his beginning.
   Job ch. 42, v. 12

PROVERBS

32 Surely in vain the net is spread in the sight of any bird.
   Proverbs ch. 1, v. 17; see **Proverbs** 623:35

33 For whom the Lord loveth he correcteth.
   Proverbs ch. 3, v. 12

34 Length of days is in her right hand; and in her left hand riches and honour.
   Proverbs ch. 3, v. 16

35 Her ways are ways of pleasantness, and all her paths are peace.
   Proverbs ch. 3, v. 17; see **Spring-Rice** 753:7

36 Wisdom is the principal thing; therefore get wisdom: and with all thy getting get understanding.
   Proverbs ch. 4, v. 7

37 The path of the just is as the shining light, that shineth more and more unto the perfect day.
   Proverbs ch. 4, v. 18

38 For the lips of a strange woman drop as an honeycomb, and her mouth is smoother than oil:
   But her end is bitter as wormwood, sharp as a two-edged sword.
   Her feet go down to death; her steps take hold on hell.
   Proverbs ch. 5, v. 3

1 Go to the ant thou sluggard; consider her ways, and be wise.
Proverbs ch. 6, v. 6

2 How long wilt thou sleep, O sluggard? When wilt thou arise out of thy sleep?
So shall thy poverty come as one that travelleth, and thy want as an armed man.
Yet a little sleep, a little slumber, a little folding of the hands to sleep.
Proverbs ch. 6, v. 9

3 Can a man take fire in his bosom, and his clothes not be burned?
Proverbs ch. 6, v. 27

4 Come, let us take our fill of love until the morning: let us solace ourselves with loves.
For the goodman is not at home, he is gone a long journey.
Proverbs ch. 7, v. 18

5 He goeth after her straightway, as an ox goeth to the slaughter.
Proverbs ch. 7, v. 22

6 Wisdom hath builded her house, she hath hewn out her seven pillars.
Proverbs ch. 9, v. 1; see **Borrowed titles** 146:17

7 Stolen waters are sweet, and bread eaten in secret is pleasant.
Proverbs ch. 9, v. 17; see **Proverbs** 631:24

8 A wise son maketh a glad father: but a foolish son is the heaviness of his mother.
Proverbs ch. 10, v. 1

9 The destruction of the poor is their poverty.
Proverbs ch. 10, v. 15

10 He that is surety for a stranger shall smart for it.
Proverbs ch. 11, v. 15

11 As a jewel of gold in a swine's snout, so is a fair woman which is without discretion.
Proverbs ch. 11, v. 22

12 A virtuous woman is a crown to her husband.
Proverbs ch. 12, v. 4

13 A righteous man regardeth the life of his beast: but the tender mercies of the wicked are cruel.
Proverbs ch. 12, v. 10

14 Lying lips are abomination to the Lord.
Proverbs ch. 12, v. 22; see **Anonymous** 14:18

15 Hope deferred maketh the heart sick: but when the desire cometh, it is a tree of life.
Proverbs ch. 13, v. 12; see **Proverbs** 622:29

16 The way of transgressors is hard.
Proverbs ch. 13, v. 15

17 The desire accomplished is sweet to the soul.
Proverbs ch. 13, v. 19

18 He that spareth his rod hateth his son.
Proverbs ch. 13, v. 24; see **Proverbs** 631:12

19 Even in laughter the heart is sorrowful.
Proverbs ch. 14, v. 13

20 In all labour there is profit.
Proverbs ch. 14, v. 23

21 Righteousness exalteth a nation.
Proverbs ch. 14, v. 34

22 A soft answer turneth away wrath.
Proverbs ch. 15, v. 1; see **Proverbs** 631:2

23 A merry heart maketh a cheerful countenance.
Proverbs ch. 15, v. 13

24 Better is a dinner of herbs where love is, than a stalled ox and hatred therewith.
Proverbs ch. 15, v. 17; see **Proverbs** 615:18

Better is a mess of pottage with love, than a fat ox with evil will.
Proverbs ch. 15, v. 17 in Matthew's Bible (1535)

25 A word spoken in due season, how good is it!
Proverbs ch. 15, v. 23

26 Pride goeth before destruction, and an haughty spirit before a fall.
Proverbs ch. 16, v. 18; see **Proverbs** 629:40

27 He that is slow to anger is better than the mighty; and he that ruleth his spirit than he that taketh a city.
Proverbs ch. 16, v. 32

28 He that repeateth a matter separateth very friends.
Proverbs ch. 17, v. 9

29 A friend loveth at all times, and a brother is born for adversity.
Proverbs ch. 17, v. 17

30 A merry heart doeth good like a medicine.
Proverbs ch. 17, v. 22

31 A wounded spirit who can bear?
Proverbs ch. 18, v. 14

32 There is a friend that sticketh closer than a brother.
Proverbs ch. 18, v. 24; see **Kipling** 455:20

33 Wine is a mocker, strong drink is raging.
Proverbs ch. 20, v. 1

34 Every fool will be meddling.
Proverbs ch. 20, v. 3

35 Even a child is known by his doings.
Proverbs ch. 20, v. 11

36 The hearing ear, and the seeing eye, the Lord hath made even both of them.
Proverbs ch. 20, v. 12

37 It is naught, it is naught, saith the buyer: but when he is gone his way, then he boasteth.
Proverbs ch. 20, v. 14

38 It is better to dwell in a corner of the housetop, than with a brawling woman in a wide house.
Proverbs ch. 21, v. 9

39 A good name is rather to be chosen than great riches.
Proverbs ch. 22, v. 1

40 Train up a child in the way he should go: and when he is old, he will not depart from it.
Proverbs ch. 22, v. 6

41 Remove not the ancient landmark, which thy fathers have set.
Proverbs ch. 22, v. 28

1 Look not thou upon the wine when it is red, when it giveth his colour in the cup . . . At the last it biteth like a serpent, and stingeth like an adder.
Proverbs ch. 23, v. 31

2 The heart of kings is unsearchable.
Proverbs ch. 25, v. 3

3 A word fitly spoken is like apples of gold in pictures of silver.
Proverbs ch. 25, v. 11

4 Whoso boasteth himself of a false gift is like clouds and wind without rain.
Proverbs ch. 25, v. 14

5 Withdraw thy foot from thy neighbour's house; lest he be weary of thee, and so hate thee.
Proverbs ch. 25, v. 17

6 If thine enemy be hungry, give him bread to eat; and if he be thirsty, give him water to drink. For thou shalt heap coals of fire upon his head, and the Lord shall reward thee.
Proverbs ch. 25, v. 21

7 As cold waters to a thirsty soul, so is good news from a far country.
Proverbs ch. 25, v. 25

8 Answer not a fool according to his folly, lest thou also be like unto him. Answer a fool according to his folly, lest he be wise in his own conceit.
Proverbs ch. 26, v. 4

9 As a dog returneth to his vomit, so a fool returneth to his folly.
Proverbs ch. 26, v. 11; see **Proverbs** 617:49

10 Seest thou a man wise in his own conceit? There is more hope of a fool than of him.
Proverbs ch. 26, v. 12

11 The sluggard is wiser in his own conceit than seven men that can render a reason.
Proverbs ch. 26, v. 16

12 Boast not thyself of to morrow; for thou knowest not what a day may bring forth.
Proverbs ch. 27, v. 1

13 Open rebuke is better than secret love.
Proverbs ch. 27, v. 5

14 Faithful are the wounds of a friend.
Proverbs ch. 27, v. 6

15 A continual dropping in a very rainy day and a contentious woman are alike.
Proverbs ch. 27, v. 15

16 The wicked flee when no man pursueth: but the righteous are bold as a lion.
Proverbs ch. 28, v. 1

17 He that maketh haste to be rich shall not be innocent.
Proverbs ch. 28, v. 20

18 A fool uttereth all his mind.
Proverbs ch. 29, v. 11

19 Where there is no vision, the people perish.
Proverbs ch. 29, v. 18

20 Give me neither poverty nor riches; feed me with food convenient for me.
Proverbs ch. 30, v. 8

21 There be three things which are too wonderful for me, yea, four which I know not:
The way of an eagle in the air; the way of a serpent upon a rock; the way of a ship in the midst of the sea; and the way of a man with a maid.
Proverbs ch. 30, v. 18

22 Give strong drink unto him that is ready to perish, and wine unto those that be of heavy hearts.
Proverbs ch. 31, v. 6

23 Who can find a virtuous woman? for her price is far above rubies.
Proverbs ch. 31, v. 10

24 Strength and honour are her clothing; and she shall rejoice in time to come.
Proverbs ch. 31, v. 25; *quoted by the Archbishop of Canterbury at funeral of Queen* **Elizabeth** *the Queen Mother, 9 April 2002, from the New Revised Standard Version; see below:*
Strength and dignity are her clothing, and she laughs at the time to come.
Proverbs ch. 31, v. 25

ECCLESIASTES

25 Vanity of vanities, saith the Preacher, vanity of vanities; all is vanity.
What profit hath a man of all his labour which he taketh under the sun?
One generation passeth away, and another generation cometh.
Ecclesiastes ch. 1, v. 2; see **Bible** 115:7

26 All the rivers run into the sea; yet the sea is not full.
Ecclesiastes ch. 1, v. 7

27 All things are full of labour; man cannot utter it: the eye is not satisfied with seeing, nor the ear filled with hearing.
Ecclesiastes ch. 1, v. 8

28 The thing that hath been, it is that which shall be; and that which is done is that which shall be done: and there is no new thing under the sun.
Ecclesiastes ch. 1, v. 9; see **Proverbs** 632:21

29 All is vanity and vexation of spirit.
Ecclesiastes ch. 1, v. 14

30 He that increaseth knowledge increaseth sorrow.
Ecclesiastes ch. 1, v. 18

31 Wisdom excelleth folly, as far as light excelleth darkness.
Ecclesiastes ch. 2, v. 13

32 To every thing there is a season, and a time to every purpose under the heaven:
A time to be born, and a time to die; a time to plant, and a time to pluck up that which is planted;
A time to kill, and a time to heal; a time to break down, and a time to build up;
A time to weep, and a time to laugh; a time to mourn, and a time to dance;

A time to cast away stones, and a time to gather stones together; a time to embrace, and a time to refrain from embracing;
A time to get, and a time to lose; a time to keep, and a time to cast away;
A time to rend, and a time to sew; a time to keep silence, and a time to speak;
A time to love, and a time to hate; a time of war, and a time of peace.
Ecclesiastes ch. 3, v. 1; see **Proverbs** 632:10

1 For that which befalleth the sons of men befalleth beasts; even one thing befalleth them: as the one dieth, so dieth the other; yea, they have all one breath; so that a man hath no preeminence above a beast: for all is vanity.
Ecclesiastes ch. 3, v. 19

2 Wherefore I praised the dead which are already dead more than the living which are yet alive.
Ecclesiastes ch. 4, v. 2

3 A threefold cord is not quickly broken.
Ecclesiastes ch. 4, v. 12; see **Burke** 166:6

4 God is in heaven, and thou upon earth: therefore let thy words be few.
Ecclesiastes ch. 5, v. 2

5 The sleep of a labouring man is sweet.
Ecclesiastes ch. 5, v. 12; see **Bunyan** 164:24

6 As the crackling of thorns under a pot, so is the laughter of a fool.
Ecclesiastes ch. 7, v. 6

7 Better is the end of a thing than the beginning thereof.
Ecclesiastes ch. 7, v. 8

8 Say not thou, What is the cause that the former days were better than these? for thou dost not enquire wisely concerning this.
Ecclesiastes ch. 7, v. 10

9 In the day of prosperity be joyful, but in the day of adversity consider.
Ecclesiastes ch. 7, v. 14

10 God hath made man upright; but they have sought out many inventions.
Ecclesiastes ch. 7, v. 29

11 There is no man that hath power over the spirit to retain the spirit; neither hath he power in the day of death; there is no discharge in that war.
Ecclesiastes ch. 8, v. 8

12 A man hath no better thing under the sun, than to eat, and to drink, and to be merry.
Ecclesiastes ch. 8, v. 15; see **Bible** 88:26, **Bible** 100:32, **Proverbs** 618:36

13 A living dog is better than a dead lion.
Ecclesiastes ch. 9, v. 4; see **Proverbs** 625:35

14 Go thy way, eat thy bread with joy, and drink thy wine with a merry heart; for God now accepteth thy works.
Ecclesiastes ch. 9, v. 7

15 Whatsoever thy hand findeth to do, do it with thy might; for there is no work, nor device, nor

knowledge, nor wisdom, in the grave, whither thou goest.
Ecclesiastes ch. 9, v. 10

16 The race is not to the swift, nor the battle to the strong.
Ecclesiastes ch. 9, v. 11; see **Davidson** 258:5, **Page** 581:13, **Proverbs** 630:3

17 He that diggeth a pit shall fall into it.
Ecclesiastes ch. 10, v. 8

18 Woe to thee, O land, when thy king is a child, and thy princes eat in the morning!
Ecclesiastes ch. 10, v. 16; see **Shakespeare** 716:29

19 Wine maketh merry: but money answereth all things.
Ecclesiastes ch. 10, v. 19

20 Cast thy bread upon the waters: for thou shalt find it after many days.
Ecclesiastes ch. 11, v. 1

21 In the place where the tree falleth, there it shall be.
Ecclesiastes ch. 11, v. 3; see **Proverbs** 614:33

22 He that observeth the wind shall not sow; and he that regardeth the clouds shall not reap.
Ecclesiastes ch. 11, v. 4

23 Truly the light is sweet, and a pleasant thing it is for the eyes to behold the sun.
Ecclesiastes ch. 11, v. 7

24 Rejoice, O young man, in thy youth; and let thy heart cheer thee in the days of thy youth.
Ecclesiastes ch. 11, v. 9

25 Remember now thy Creator in the days of thy youth, while the evil days come not, nor the years draw nigh, when thou shalt say, I have no pleasure in them;
While the sun, or the light, or the moon, or the stars, be not darkened, nor the clouds return after the rain:
In the day when the keepers of the house shall tremble, and the strong men shall bow themselves, and the grinders cease because they are few, and those that look out of the windows be darkened,
And the doors shall be shut in the streets, when the sound of the grinding is low, and he shall rise up at the voice of the bird, and all the daughters of music shall be brought low;
Also when they shall be afraid of that which is high, and fears shall be in the way, and the almond tree shall flourish, and the grasshopper shall be a burden, and desire shall fail: because man goeth to his long home, and the mourners go about the streets:
Or ever the silver cord be loosed, or the golden bowl be broken, or the pitcher be broken at the fountain, or the wheel broken at the cistern.
Then shall the dust return to the earth as it was: and the spirit shall return unto God who gave it.
Ecclesiastes ch. 12, v. 1

26 Of making many books there is no end; and much study is a weariness of the flesh.
Ecclesiastes ch. 12, v. 12

1 Fear God, and keep his commandments: for this is the whole duty of man.
For God shall bring every work into judgement, with every secret thing, whether it be good, or whether it be evil.
Ecclesiastes ch. 12, v. 13

SONG OF SOLOMON

2 The song of songs, which is Solomon's.
Let him kiss me with the kisses of his mouth: for thy love is better than wine.
Song of Solomon ch. 1, v. 1

3 I am black, but comely, O ye daughters of Jerusalem,
as the tents of Kedar, as the curtains of Solomon.
Song of Solomon ch. 1, v. 5

4 A bundle of myrrh is my wellbeloved unto me; he shall lie all night betwixt my breasts.
Song of Solomon ch. 1, v. 13

5 I am the rose of Sharon, and the lily of the valleys.
Song of Solomon ch. 2, v. 1

6 Rise up, my love, my fair one, and come away.
For, lo, the winter is past, the rain is over and gone;
The flowers appear on the earth; the time of the singing of birds is come, and the voice of the turtle is heard in our land.
Song of Solomon ch. 2, v. 10

7 Take us the foxes, the little foxes, that spoil the vines.
Song of Solomon ch. 2, v. 15

8 My beloved is mine, and I am his: he feedeth among the lilies.
Until the day break, and the shadows flee away.
Song of Solomon ch. 2, v. 16

9 By night on my bed I sought him whom my soul loveth.
Song of Solomon ch. 3, v. 1

10 Behold, thou art fair, my love; behold, thou art fair; thou hast doves' eyes within thy locks: thy hair is as a flock of goats, that appear from mount Gilead.
Thy teeth are like a flock of sheep that are even shorn, which came up from the washing; whereof every one bear twins, and none is barren among them.
Thy lips are like a thread of scarlet, and thy speech is comely: thy temples are like a piece of a pomegranate within thy locks.
Thy neck is like the tower of David builded for an armoury, whereon there hang a thousand bucklers, all shields of mighty men.
Thy two breasts are like two young roes that are twins, which feed among the lilies.
Song of Solomon ch. 4, v. 1

11 Thou art all fair, my love; there is no spot in thee.
Song of Solomon ch. 4, v. 7

12 A garden inclosed is my sister, my spouse; a spring shut up, a fountain sealed.
Song of Solomon ch. 4, v. 12

13 Awake, O north wind; and come, thou south; blow upon my garden, that the spices thereof may flow out. Let my beloved come into his garden, and eat his pleasant fruits.
Song of Solomon ch. 4, v. 16

14 I sleep, but my heart waketh: it is the voice of my beloved that knocketh, saying, Open to me, my sister, my love, my dove, my undefiled.
Song of Solomon ch. 5, v. 2

15 The watchmen that went about the city found me, they smote me, they wounded me; the keepers of the walls took away my veil from me.
I charge you, O daughters of Jerusalem, if ye find my beloved, that ye tell him, that I am sick of love.
What is thy beloved more than another beloved, O thou fairest among women?
Song of Solomon ch. 5, v. 7

16 His hands are as gold rings set with the beryl: his belly is as bright ivory overlaid with sapphires.
His legs are as pillars of marble, set upon sockets of fine gold: his countenance is as Lebanon, excellent as the cedars.
His mouth is most sweet: yea, he is altogether lovely. This is my beloved, and this is my friend, O daughters of Jerusalem.
Song of Solomon ch. 5, v. 14

17 Who is she that looketh forth as the morning, fair as the moon, clear as the sun, and terrible as an army with banners?
Song of Solomon ch. 6, v. 10

18 Return, return, O Shulamite; return, return, that we may look upon thee.
Song of Solomon ch. 6, v. 13

19 How beautiful are thy feet with shoes, O prince's daughter!
Song of Solomon ch. 7, v. 1

20 Thy navel is like a round goblet, which wanteth not liquor: thy belly is like an heap of wheat set about with lilies.
Song of Solomon ch. 7, v. 2

21 Thy neck is as a tower of ivory; thine eyes like the fishpools in Heshbon.
Song of Solomon ch. 7, v. 4

22 Set me as a seal upon thine heart, as a seal upon thine arm: for love is strong as death; jealousy is cruel as the grave.
Song of Solomon ch. 8, v. 6

23 Many waters cannot quench love, neither can the floods drown it: if a man would give all the substance of his house for love, it would utterly be contemned.
Song of Solomon ch. 8, v. 7

24 Make haste, my beloved, and be thou like to a roe or to a young hart upon the mountains of spices.
Song of Solomon ch. 8, v. 14

ISAIAH

25 The daughter of Zion is left as a cottage in a vineyard, as a lodge in a garden of cucumbers, as a besieged city.
Isaiah ch. 1, v. 8

1 Though your sins be as scarlet, they shall be as white as snow.
Isaiah ch. 1, v. 18

2 They shall beat their swords into plowshares, and their spears into pruninghooks: nation shall not lift up sword against nation, neither shall they learn war any more.
Isaiah ch. 2, v. 4; see **Rendall** 645:7. Micah ch. 4, v. 3, Joel ch. 3, v. 10 have same image

3 What mean ye that ye beat my people to pieces, and grind the faces of the poor?
Isaiah ch. 3, v. 15

4 My well-beloved hath a vineyard in a very fruitful hill.
Isaiah ch. 5, v. 1

5 And he looked that it should bring forth grapes, and it brought forth wild grapes.
Isaiah ch. 5, v. 2

6 And he looked for judgement, but behold oppression; for righteousness, but behold a cry.
Isaiah ch. 5, v. 7

7 Woe unto them that join house to house, that lay field to field, till there be no place.
Isaiah ch. 5, v. 8

8 Woe unto them that call evil good, and good evil.
Isaiah ch. 5, v. 20

9 For all this his anger is not turned away, but his hand is stretched out still.
Isaiah ch. 5, v. 25

10 In the year that king Uzziah died I saw also the Lord sitting upon a throne, high and lifted up, and his train filled the temple.
Above it stood the seraphims: each one had six wings; with twain he covered his face, and with twain he covered his feet, and with twain he did fly.
And one cried unto another, and said, Holy, holy, holy, is the Lord of hosts: the whole earth is full of his glory.
Isaiah ch. 6, v. 1

11 Then said I, Woe is me! for I am undone; because I am a man of unclean lips, and I dwell in the midst of a people of unclean lips.
Isaiah ch. 6, v. 5

12 Then flew one of the seraphims unto me, having a live coal in his hand, which he had taken with the tongs from off the altar.
And he laid it upon my mouth, and said, Lo, this hath touched thy lips.
Isaiah ch. 6, v. 6

13 Whom shall I send, and who will go for us? Then said I, Here am I; send me.
Isaiah ch. 6, v. 8

14 Then said I, Lord, how long?
Isaiah ch. 6, v. 11

15 Behold, a virgin shall conceive, and bear a son, and shall call his name Immanuel.
Butter and honey shall he eat, that he may know to refuse the evil, and choose the good.
Isaiah ch. 7, v. 14

16 Sanctify the Lord of hosts himself; and let him be your fear, and let him be your dread.
And he shall be for a sanctuary; but for a stone of stumbling and for a rock of offence to both the houses of Israel.
Isaiah ch. 8, v. 13

17 The people that walked in darkness have seen a great light: they that dwell in the land of the shadow of death, upon them hath the light shined.
Thou hast multiplied the nation, and not increased the joy: they joy before thee according to the joy in harvest, and as men rejoice when they divide the spoil.
Isaiah ch. 9, v. 2; see **Scottish Metrical Psalms** 675:7

18 For unto us a child is born, unto us a son is given: and the government shall be upon his shoulder: and his name shall be called Wonderful, Counsellor, The mighty God, The everlasting Father, The Prince of Peace.
Of the increase of his government and peace there shall be no end.
Isaiah ch. 9, v. 6

19 The zeal of the Lord of hosts will perform this.
Isaiah ch. 9, v. 7

20 And there shall come forth a rod out of the stem of Jesse, and a branch shall grow out of his roots:
And the spirit of the Lord shall rest upon him, the spirit of wisdom and understanding, the spirit of counsel and might, the spirit of knowledge and of the fear of the Lord.
Isaiah ch. 11, v. 1

21 The wolf also shall dwell with the lamb, and the leopard shall lie down with the kid; and the calf and the young lion and the fatling together; and a little child shall lead them.
Isaiah ch. 11, v. 6

22 And the lion shall eat straw like the ox.
And the sucking child shall play on the hole of the asp, and the weaned child shall put his hand on the cockatrice' den.
They shall not hurt nor destroy in all my holy mountain: for the earth shall be full of the knowledge of the Lord, as the waters cover the sea.
Isaiah ch. 11, v. 7

23 And the wild beasts of the islands shall cry in their desolate houses, and dragons in their pleasant palaces.
Isaiah ch. 13, v. 22

24 How art thou fallen from heaven, O Lucifer, son of the morning!
Isaiah ch. 14, v. 12

25 Watchman, what of the night? Watchman, what of the night?
The watchman said, The morning cometh, and also the night.
Isaiah ch. 21, v. 11

26 Let us eat and drink; for to morrow we shall die.
Isaiah ch. 22, v. 13; see **Bible** 86:12, **Bible** 100:32, **Proverbs** 618:36

1 In this mountain shall the Lord of hosts make unto all people a feast of fat things, a feast of wine on the lees, of fat things full of marrow, of wine on the lees well refined.
Isaiah ch. 25, v. 6

2 He will swallow up death in victory; and the Lord God will wipe away tears from off all faces.
Isaiah ch. 25, v. 8

3 For precept must be upon precept, precept upon precept; line upon line, line upon line; here a little, and there a little.
Isaiah ch. 28, v. 10

4 We have made a covenant with death, and with hell are we at agreement.
Isaiah ch. 28, v. 15; see **Garrison** 340:10

5 The bread of adversity, and the waters of affliction.
Isaiah ch. 30, v. 20

6 This is the way, walk ye in it.
Isaiah ch. 30, v. 21

7 And a man shall be as an hiding place from the wind, and a covert from the tempest; as rivers of water in a dry place, as the shadow of a great rock in a weary land.
Isaiah ch. 32, v. 2

8 And thorns shall come up in her palaces, nettles and brambles in the fortresses thereof: and it shall be an habitation of dragons, and a court for owls.
Isaiah ch. 34, v. 13

9 The wilderness and the solitary place shall be glad for them; and the desert shall rejoice, and blossom as the rose.
Isaiah ch. 35, v. 1

10 Strengthen ye the weak hands, and confirm the feeble knees.
Isaiah ch. 35, v. 3

11 Then shall the lame man leap as an hart, and the tongue of the dumb sing: for in the wilderness shall waters break out, and streams in the desert.
Isaiah ch. 35, v. 6

12 They shall obtain joy and gladness, and sorrow and sighing shall flee away.
Isaiah ch. 35, v. 10

13 Set thine house in order: for thou shalt die, and not live.
Isaiah ch. 38, v. 1

14 I shall go softly all my years in the bitterness of my soul.
Isaiah ch. 38, v. 15

15 Comfort ye, comfort ye my people, saith your God. Speak ye comfortably to Jerusalem, and cry unto her, that her warfare is accomplished.
Isaiah ch. 40, v. 1

16 The voice of him that crieth in the wilderness, Prepare ye the way of the Lord, make straight in the desert a highway for our God.
Every valley shall be exalted, and every mountain and hill shall be made low: and the crooked shall be made straight, and the rough places plain:

And the glory of the Lord shall be revealed, and all flesh shall see it together: for the mouth of the Lord hath spoken it.
Isaiah ch. 40, v. 3; see **Bible** 94:10

17 The voice said, Cry. And he said, What shall I cry? All flesh is grass, and all the goodliness thereof is as the flower of the field:
The grass withereth, the flower fadeth: because the spirit of the Lord bloweth upon it: surely the people is grass.
Isaiah ch. 40, v. 6; see **Bible** 112:3

18 He shall feed his flock like a shepherd: he shall gather the lambs with his arm, and carry them in his bosom, and shall gently lead those that are with young.
Isaiah ch. 40, v. 11

19 The nations are as a drop of a bucket, and are counted as the small dust of the balance: behold, he taketh up the isles as a very little thing.
Isaiah ch. 40, v. 15

20 Have ye not known? have ye not heard? hath it not been told you from the beginning?
Isaiah ch. 40, v. 21

21 But they that wait upon the Lord shall renew their strength: they shall mount up with wings as eagles; they shall run, and not be weary; and they shall walk, and not faint.
Isaiah ch. 40, v. 31

22 A bruised reed shall he not break, and the smoking flax shall he not quench.
Isaiah ch. 42, v. 3

23 Woe unto him that striveth with his maker! Let the potsherd strive with the potsherds of the earth. Shall the clay say to him that fashioneth it, What makest thou?
Isaiah ch. 45, v. 9

24 I have chosen thee in the furnace of affliction.
Isaiah ch. 48, v. 10

25 O that thou hadst hearkened to my commandments! then had thy peace been as a river, and thy righteousness as the waves of the sea.
Isaiah ch. 48, v. 18

26 There is no peace, saith the Lord, unto the wicked.
Isaiah ch. 48, v. 22

27 Can a woman forget her sucking child, that she should not have compassion on the son of her womb? yea, they may forget, yet will I not forget thee.
Isaiah ch. 49, v. 15

28 How beautiful upon the mountains are the feet of him that bringeth good tidings, that publisheth peace; that bringeth good tidings of good, that publisheth salvation; that saith unto Zion, Thy God reigneth!
Isaiah ch. 52, v. 7

29 For they shall see eye to eye, when the Lord shall bring again Zion.

Break forth into joy, sing together, ye waste places of Jerusalem: for the Lord hath comforted his people, he hath redeemed Jerusalem.
Isaiah ch. 52, v. 8

1 Who hath believed our report? and to whom is the arm of the Lord revealed?
Isaiah ch. 53, v. 1

2 He is despised and rejected of men; a man of sorrows, and acquainted with grief: and we hid as it were our faces from him; he was despised, and we esteemed him not.
Surely he hath borne our griefs, and carried our sorrows.
Isaiah ch. 53, v. 3

3 But he was wounded for our transgressions, he was bruised for our iniquities: the chastisement of our peace was upon him; and with his stripes we are healed.
All we like sheep have gone astray; we have turned every one to his own way; and the Lord hath laid on him the iniquity of us all.
He was oppressed, and he was afflicted, yet he opened not his mouth: he is brought as a lamb to the slaughter, and as a sheep before her shearers is dumb, so he openeth not his mouth.
Isaiah ch. 53, v. 5

4 He was cut off out of the land of the living.
Isaiah ch. 53, v. 8

5 He was numbered with the transgressors; and he bare the sin of many, and made intercession for the transgressors.
Isaiah ch. 53, v. 12

6 Ho, every one that thirsteth, come ye to the waters, and he that hath no money; come ye, buy, and eat; yea, come, buy wine and milk without money and without price.
Wherefore do ye spend money for that which is not bread? and your labour for that which satisfieth not?
Isaiah ch. 55, v. 1

7 Seek ye the Lord while he may be found, call ye upon him while he is near.
Isaiah ch. 55, v. 6

8 For my thoughts are not your thoughts, neither are your ways my ways, saith the Lord.
Isaiah ch. 55, v. 8

9 Instead of the thorn shall come up the fir tree, and instead of the brier shall come up the myrtle tree.
Isaiah ch. 55, v. 13

10 I will give them an everlasting name, that shall not be cut off.
Isaiah ch. 56, v. 5

11 Mine house shall be called an house of prayer for all people.
Isaiah ch. 56, v. 7; see **Bible** 98:4

12 The righteous perisheth, and no man layeth it to heart.
Isaiah ch. 57, v. 1

13 Peace to him that is far off, and to him that is near.
Isaiah ch. 57, v. 19

14 Is not this the fast that I have chosen? to loose the bands of wickedness, to undo the heavy burdens, and to let the oppressed go free, and that ye break every yoke?
Isaiah ch. 58, v. 6

15 Then shall thy light break forth as the morning, and thine health shall spring forth speedily.
Isaiah ch. 58, v. 8

16 They make haste to shed innocent blood.
Isaiah ch. 59, v. 7

17 Arise, shine; for thy light is come, and the glory of the Lord is risen upon thee.
Isaiah ch. 60, v. 1

18 The Spirit of the Lord God is upon me . . . To bind up the brokenhearted, to proclaim liberty to the captives, and the opening of the prison to them that are bound;
To proclaim the acceptable year of the Lord, and the day of vengeance of our God; to comfort all that mourn.
Isaiah ch. 61, v. 1

19 To give unto them beauty for ashes, the oil of joy for mourning, the garment of praise for the spirit of heaviness.
Isaiah ch. 61, v. 3

20 All our righteousnesses are as filthy rags; and we all do fade as a leaf.
Isaiah ch. 64, v. 6

21 Stand by thyself, come not near to me; for I am holier than thou.
Isaiah ch. 65, v. 5

22 For, behold, I create new heavens and a new earth.
Isaiah ch. 65, v. 17

JEREMIAH

23 Can a maid forget her ornaments, or a bride her attire?
Jeremiah ch. 2, v. 32

24 This people hath a revolting and a rebellious heart.
Jeremiah ch. 5, v. 23

25 The prophets prophesy falsely, and the priests bear rule by their means; and my people love to have it so: and what will ye do in the end thereof?
Jeremiah ch. 5, v. 31

26 They have healed also the hurt of the daughter of my people slightly, saying, Peace, peace; when there is no peace.
Jeremiah ch. 6, v. 14

27 The harvest is past, the summer is ended, and we are not saved.
Jeremiah ch. 8, v. 20

28 Is there no balm in Gilead?
Jeremiah ch. 8, v. 22

1 Can the Ethiopian change his skin, or the leopard his spots?

Jeremiah ch. 13, v. 23; see **Proverbs** 625:4

2 Woe is me, my mother, that thou hast borne me a man of strife and a man of contention to the whole earth!

Jeremiah ch. 15, v. 10

3 The heart is deceitful above all things, and desperately wicked.

Jeremiah ch. 17, v. 9

4 As the partridge sitteth on eggs, and hatcheth them not; so he that getteth riches, and not by right, shall leave them in the midst of his days.

Jeremiah ch. 17, v. 11

5 Behold, I will make thee a terror to thyself, and to all thy friends.

Jeremiah ch. 20, v. 4

LAMENTATIONS

6 How doth the city sit solitary, that was full of people!

Lamentations ch. 1, v. 1

7 Is it nothing to you, all ye that pass by? behold, and see if there be any sorrow like unto my sorrow.

Lamentations ch. 1, v. 12

8 And I said, My strength and my hope is perished from the Lord:
Remembering mine affliction and my misery, the wormwood and the gall.

Lamentations ch. 3, v. 18

9 It is good for a man that he bear the yoke in his youth.

Lamentations ch. 3, v. 27

10 He giveth his cheek to him that smiteth him.

Lamentations ch. 3, v. 30

11 O Lord, thou hast seen my wrong: judge thou my cause.

Lamentations ch. 4, v. 59

EZEKIEL

12 As is the mother, so is her daughter.

Ezekiel ch. 16, v. 44; see **Proverbs** 625:20

13 The fathers have eaten sour grapes, and the children's teeth are set on edge.

Ezekiel ch. 18, v. 2

14 When the wicked man turneth away from his wickedness that he hath committed, and doeth that which is lawful and right, he shall save his soul alive.

Ezekiel ch. 18, v. 27

15 The king of Babylon stood at the parting of the ways.

Ezekiel ch. 21, v. 21

16 The hand of the Lord was upon me, and carried me out in the spirit of the Lord, and set me down in the midst of the valley which was full of bones.

Ezekiel ch. 37, v. 1

17 Can these bones live?

Ezekiel ch. 37, v. 3

18 Again he said unto me, Prophesy upon these bones, and say unto them, O ye dry bones, hear the word of the Lord.

Ezekiel ch. 37, v. 4

DANIEL

19 To you it is commanded, O peoples, nations, and languages,
That at what time ye hear the sound of the cornet, flute, harp, sackbut, psaltery, dulcimer, and all kinds of music, ye fall down and worship the golden image that Nebuchadnezzar the king hath set up:
And whoso falleth not down and worshippeth shall the same hour be cast into the midst of a burning fiery furnace.

Daniel ch. 3, v. 4

20 Shadrach, Meshach, and Abed-nego, ye servants of the most high God, come forth and come hither.

Daniel ch. 3, v. 26

21 In the same hour came forth fingers of a man's hand, and wrote over against the candlestick upon the plaister of the wall of the king's palace.

Daniel ch. 5, v. 5

22 And this is the writing that was written, MENE, MENE, TEKEL, UPHARSIN.
This is the interpretation of the thing: MENE; God hath numbered thy kingdom, and finished it.
TEKEL; Thou art weighed in the balances and art found wanting.
PERES; Thy kingdom is divided, and given to the Medes and Persians.

Daniel ch. 5, v. 25

23 Now, O king, establish the decree, and sign the writing, that it be not changed, according to the law of the Medes and Persians, which altereth not.

Daniel ch. 6, v. 8

24 The Ancient of days did sit, whose garment was white as snow, and the hair of his head like the pure wool: his throne was like the fiery flame, and his wheels as burning fire.
A fiery stream issued and came forth from behind him: thousand thousands ministered unto him, and ten thousand times ten thousand stood before him: the judgement was set, and the books were opened.

Daniel ch. 7, v. 9

25 O Daniel, a man greatly beloved.

Daniel ch. 10, v. 11

26 Many shall run to and fro, and knowledge shall be increased.

Daniel ch. 12, v. 4

HOSEA

27 Like people, like priest.

Hosea ch. 4, v. 9; see **Proverbs** 625:21

28 They have sown the wind, and they shall reap the whirlwind.

Hosea ch. 8, v. 7; see **Proverbs** 632:37

29 I drew them . . . with bands of love.

Hosea ch. 11, v. 4

JOEL

1 That which the palmerworm hath left hath the locust eaten.
Joel ch. 1, v. 4

2 I will restore to you the years that the locust hath eaten, the cankerworm, and the caterpillar, and the palmerworm, my great army which I sent among you.
Joel ch. 2, v. 25

3 And it shall come to pass afterward, that I will pour out my spirit upon all flesh; and your sons and your daughters shall prophesy, your old men shall dream dreams, your young men shall see visions.
Joel ch. 2, v. 28

4 Multitudes, multitudes in the valley of decision: for the day of the Lord is near in the valley of decision.
Joel ch. 3, v. 14

AMOS

5 Can two walk together, except they be agreed?
Amos ch. 3, v. 3

6 Shall there be evil in a city, and the Lord hath not done it?
Amos ch. 3, v. 6

7 I have overthrown some of you, as God overthrew Sodom and Gomorrah, and ye were as a firebrand plucked out of the burning.
Amos ch. 4, v. 11

MICAH

8 But thou, Bethlehem Ephratah, though thou be little among the thousands of Judah, yet out of thee shall he come forth unto me that is to be ruler in Israel.
Micah ch. 5, v. 2

9 What doth the Lord require of thee, but to do justly, and to love mercy, and to walk humbly with thy God?
Micah ch. 6, v. 8

NAHUM

10 Woe to the bloody city! it is all full of lies and robbery; the prey departeth not.
Nahum ch. 3, v. 1

HABAKKUK

11 Write the vision, and make it plain upon tables, that he may run that readeth it.
Habakkuk ch. 2, v. 2

ZEPHANIAH

12 Woe to her that is filthy and polluted, to the oppressing city!
Zephaniah ch. 3, v. 1

HAGGAI

13 Ye have sown much, and bring in little; ye eat but ye have not enough . . . and he that earneth wages earneth wages to put it into a bag with holes.
Haggai ch. 1, v. 6

MALACHI

14 But unto you that fear my name shall the Sun of righteousness arise with healing in his wings.
Malachi ch. 4, v. 2; see **Wesley** 828:24

APOCRYPHA

15 The first wrote, Wine is the strongest. The second wrote, The king is strongest. The third wrote, Women are strongest: but above all things Truth beareth away the victory.
I Esdras ch. 3, v. 10

16 Great is Truth, and mighty above all things.
I Esdras ch. 4, v. 41; see **Bible** 115:19

17 Nourish thy children, O thou good nurse; stablish their feet.
II Esdras ch. 2, v. 25

18 For the world has lost his youth, and the times begin to wax old.
II Esdras ch. 14, v. 10

19 I shall light a candle of understanding in thine heart, which shall not be put out.
II Esdras ch. 14, v. 25; see **Last words** 471:4

20 The ear of jealousy heareth all things.
Wisdom of Solomon ch. 1, v. 10

21 Let us crown ourselves with rosebuds, before they be withered.
Wisdom of Solomon ch. 2, v. 8

22 Through envy of the devil came death into the world.
Wisdom of Solomon ch. 2, v. 24

23 But the souls of the righteous are in the hand of God, and there shall no torment touch them.
In the sight of the unwise they seemed to die: and their departure is taken for misery,
And their going from us to be utter destruction: but they are in peace.
For though they be punished in the sight of men, yet is their hope full of immortality.
And having been a little chastised, they shall be greatly rewarded: for God proved them, and found them worthy for himself.
Wisdom of Solomon ch. 3, v. 1

24 And in the time of their visitation they shall shine, and run to and fro like sparks among the stubble.
Wisdom of Solomon ch. 3, v. 7

25 He, being made perfect in a short time, fulfilled a long time.
Wisdom of Solomon ch. 4, v. 13

26 We fools accounted his life madness, and his end to be without honour:
How is he numbered among the children of God, and his lot is among the saints!
Wisdom of Solomon ch. 5, v. 4

27 Even so we in like manner, as soon as we were born, began to draw to our end.
Wisdom of Solomon ch. 5, v. 13

28 For the hope of the ungodly . . . passeth away as the remembrance of a guest that tarrieth but a day.
Wisdom of Solomon ch. 5, v. 14

29 And love is the keeping of her laws; and the giving heed unto her laws is the assurance of incorruption.
Wisdom of Solomon ch. 6, v. 18

1 For the same things uttered in Hebrew, and translated into another tongue, have not the same force in them: and not only these things, but the law itself, and the prophets, and the rest of the books, have no small difference, when they are spoken in their own language.
Ecclesiasticus: The Prologue

2 For the Lord is full of compassion and mercy, long-suffering, and very pitiful, and forgiveth sins, and saveth in time of affliction.
Ecclesiasticus ch. 2, v. 11

3 We will fall into the hands of the Lord, and not into the hands of men: for as his majesty is, so is his mercy.
Ecclesiasticus ch. 2, v. 18

4 Be not curious in unnecessary matters: for more things are shewed unto thee than men understand.
Ecclesiasticus ch. 3, v. 23

5 Be not ignorant of any thing in a great matter or a small.
Ecclesiasticus ch. 5, v. 15

6 A faithful friend is the medicine of life.
Ecclesiasticus ch. 6, v. 16

7 Laugh no man to scorn in the bitterness of his soul.
Ecclesiasticus ch. 7, v. 11

8 Miss not the discourse of the elders.
Ecclesiasticus ch. 8, v. 9

9 Open not thine heart to every man.
Ecclesiasticus ch. 8, v. 19

10 Forsake not an old friend; for the new is not comparable to him; a new friend is as new wine; when it is old, thou shalt drink it with pleasure.
Ecclesiasticus ch. 9, v. 10

11 Many kings have sat down upon the ground; and one that was never thought of hath worn the crown.
Ecclesiasticus ch. 11, v. 5

12 Judge none blessed before his death.
Ecclesiasticus ch. 11, v. 28; see **Solon** 745:13

13 He that toucheth pitch shall be defiled therewith.
Ecclesiasticus ch. 13, v. 1; see **Proverbs** 621:51

14 For how agree the kettle and the earthen pot together?
Ecclesiasticus ch. 13, v. 2

15 When a rich man is fallen, he hath many helpers: he speaketh things not to be spoken, and yet men justify him: the poor man slipped, and yet they rebuked him too; he spake wisely, and could have no place.
Ecclesiasticus ch. 14, v. 22

16 When thou hast enough, remember the time of hunger.
Ecclesiasticus ch. 18, v. 25

17 Be not made a beggar by banqueting upon borrowing.
Ecclesiasticus ch. 18, v. 33

18 He that contemneth small things shall fall by little and little.
Ecclesiasticus ch. 19, v. 1

19 A merchant shall hardly keep himself from doing wrong.
Ecclesiasticus ch. 26, v. 29

20 Many have fallen by the edge of the sword: but not so many as have fallen by the tongue.
Ecclesiasticus ch. 28, v. 18

21 And weigh thy words in a balance, and make a door and bar for thy mouth.
Ecclesiasticus ch. 28, v. 25

22 Envy and wrath shorten the life.
Ecclesiasticus ch. 30, v. 24

23 Leave off first for manners' sake.
Ecclesiasticus ch. 31, v. 17

24 Wine is as good as life to a man, if it be drunk moderately: what life is then to a man that is without wine? for it was made to make men glad.
Ecclesiasticus ch. 31, v. 27

25 Leave not a stain in thine honour.
Ecclesiasticus ch. 33, v. 22

26 Honour a physician with the honour due unto him for the uses which ye may have of him: for the Lord hath created him.
Ecclesiasticus ch. 38, v. 1

27 He that sinneth before his Maker, let him fall into the hand of the physician.
Ecclesiasticus ch. 38, v. 15

28 The wisdom of a learned man cometh by opportunity of leisure: and he that hath little business shall become wise.
Ecclesiasticus ch. 38, v. 24

29 How can he get wisdom . . . whose talk is of bullocks?
Ecclesiasticus ch. 38, v. 25

30 Let us now praise famous men, and our fathers that begat us.
Ecclesiasticus ch. 44, v. 1

31 Such as did bear rule in their kingdoms.
Ecclesiasticus ch. 44, v. 3

32 Such as found out musical tunes, and recited verses in writing:
Rich men furnished with ability, living peaceably in their habitations.
Ecclesiasticus ch. 44, v. 5

33 There be of them, that have left a name behind them.
Ecclesiasticus ch. 44, v. 8

34 And some there be, which have no memorial . . . and are become as though they had never been born . . .
But these were merciful men, whose righteousness hath not been forgotten . . .
Their seed shall remain for ever, and their glory shall not be blotted out.
Their bodies are buried in peace; but their name liveth for evermore.
Ecclesiasticus ch. 44, v. 9

1 As the flower of roses in the spring of the year, as lilies by the rivers of waters, and as the branches of the frankincense tree in the time of summer.
Ecclesiasticus ch. 50, v. 8

2 Get learning with a great sum of money, and get much gold by her.
Ecclesiasticus ch. 51, v. 28

3 It is a foolish thing to make a long prologue, and to be short in the story itself.
II Maccabees ch. 2, v. 32

4 When he was at the last gasp.
II Maccabees ch. 7, v. 9

NEW TESTAMENT: ST MATTHEW

5 There came wise men from the east to Jerusalem, Saying, Where is he that is born King of the Jews? for we have seen his star in the east, and are come to worship him.
St Matthew ch. 2, v. 1

6 They presented unto him gifts; gold, and frankincense, and myrrh.
St Matthew ch. 2, v. 11

7 They departed into their own country another way.
St Matthew ch. 2, v. 12

8 In Rama was there a voice heard, lamentation, and weeping, and great mourning, Rachel weeping for her children, and would not be comforted, because they are not.
St Matthew ch. 2, v. 18; referring to Jeremiah ch. 31, v. 15

9 Repent ye: for the kingdom of heaven is at hand.
St Matthew ch. 3, v. 2

10 The voice of one crying in the wilderness, Prepare ye the way of the Lord, make his paths straight.
St Matthew ch. 3, v. 3; see **Bible** 89:16

11 John had his raiment of camel's hair, and a leathern girdle about his loins; and his meat was locusts and wild honey.
St Matthew ch. 3, v. 4

12 O generation of vipers, who hath warned you to flee from the wrath to come?
St Matthew ch. 3, v. 7

13 And now also the axe is laid unto the root of the trees.
St Matthew ch. 3, v. 10

14 This is my beloved Son, in whom I am well pleased.
St Matthew ch. 3, v. 17

15 Man shall not live by bread alone, but by every word that proceedeth out of the mouth of God.
St Matthew ch. 4, v. 4, echoing Deuteronomy ch. 8, v. 3; see **Proverbs** 625:52

16 Thou shalt not tempt the Lord thy God.
St Matthew ch. 4, v. 7, echoing Deuteronomy ch. 6, v. 16

17 The devil taketh him up into an exceeding high mountain, and sheweth him all the kingdoms of the world, and the glory of them.
St Matthew ch. 4, v. 8

18 Angels came and ministered unto him.
St Matthew ch. 4, v. 11

19 Follow me, and I will make you fishers of men.
St Matthew ch. 4, v. 19

20 Blessed are the poor in spirit: for theirs is the kingdom of heaven.
Blessed are they that mourn: for they shall be comforted.
Blessed are the meek: for they shall inherit the earth.
Blessed are they which do hunger and thirst after righteousness: for they shall be filled.
Blessed are the merciful: for they shall obtain mercy.
Blessed are the pure in heart: for they shall see God.
Blessed are the peacemakers: for they shall be called the children of God.
St Matthew ch. 5, v. 3; see **Smith** 742:2

21 Ye are the salt of the earth: but if the salt have lost his savour, wherewith shall it be salted?
St Matthew ch. 5, v. 13

22 Ye are the light of the world. A city that is set on an hill cannot be hid.
St Matthew ch. 5, v. 14

23 Let your light so shine before men, that they may see your good works.
St Matthew ch. 5, v. 16

24 Think not that I am come to destroy the law, or the prophets: I am come not to destroy, but to fulfil.
St Matthew ch. 5, v. 17

25 Except your righteousness shall exceed the righteousness of the scribes and Pharisees, ye shall in no case enter into the kingdom of heaven.
St Matthew ch. 5, v. 20

26 Whosoever shall say, Thou fool, shall be in danger of hell fire.
St Matthew ch. 5, v. 22

27 Till thou hast paid the uttermost farthing.
St Matthew ch. 5, v. 26

28 Swear not at all; neither by heaven; for it is God's throne:
Nor by the earth; for it is his footstool.
St Matthew ch. 5, v. 34

29 Resist not evil: but whosoever shall smite thee on thy right cheek, turn to him the other also.
St Matthew ch. 5, v. 39

30 Whosoever shall compel thee to go a mile, go with him twain.
St Matthew ch. 5, v. 41

31 He maketh his sun to rise on the evil and on the good, and sendeth rain on the just and on the unjust.
St Matthew ch. 5, v. 45; see **Bowen** 148:9

32 For if ye love them which love you, what reward have ye? do not even the publicans the same?
St Matthew ch. 5, v. 46

33 Be ye therefore perfect, even as your Father which is in heaven is perfect.
St Matthew ch. 5, v. 48

1 When thou doest alms, let not thy left hand know what thy right hand doeth.
That thine alms may be in secret: and thy Father which seeth in secret himself shall reward you openly.
St Matthew ch. 6, v. 3

2 Use not vain repetitions, as the heathen do: for they think that they shall be heard for their much speaking.
St Matthew ch. 6, v. 7

3 After this manner therefore pray ye: Our Father which art in heaven, Hallowed be thy name.
Thy kingdom come. Thy will be done in earth, as it is in heaven.
Give us this day our daily bread.
And forgive us our debts, as we forgive our debtors.
And lead us not into temptation, but deliver us from evil: For thine is the kingdom, and the power, and the glory, for ever. Amen.
St Matthew ch. 6, v. 9; see **Book of Common Prayer** 127:18, **Missal** 539:7

4 Lay not up for yourselves treasures upon earth, where moth and rust doth corrupt, and where thieves break through and steal:
But lay up for yourselves treasures in heaven.
St Matthew ch. 6, v. 19

5 Where your treasure is, there will your heart be also.
St Matthew ch. 6, v. 21

6 No man can serve two masters . . . Ye cannot serve God and mammon.
St Matthew ch. 6, v. 24; see **Proverbs** 635:45

7 Is not the life more than meat, and the body than raiment?
Behold the fowls of the air: for they sow not, neither do they reap, nor gather into barns.
St Matthew ch. 6, v. 25

8 Which of you by taking thought can add one cubit unto his stature?
St Matthew ch. 6, v. 27

9 Consider the lilies of the field, how they grow; they toil not, neither do they spin:
And yet I say unto you, That even Solomon in all his glory was not arrayed like one of these.
St Matthew ch. 6, v. 28

10 Seek ye first the kingdom of God, and his righteousness; and all these things shall be added unto you.
St Matthew ch. 6, v. 33

11 Take therefore no thought for the morrow: for the morrow shall take thought for the things of itself. Sufficient unto the day is the evil thereof.
St Matthew ch. 6, v. 34; see **Proverbs** 631:33

12 Judge not, that ye be not judged.
St Matthew ch. 7, v. 1; see **Proverbs** 624:34

13 Why beholdest thou the mote that is in thy brother's eye, but considerest not the beam that is in thine own eye?
St Matthew ch. 7, v. 3

14 Neither cast ye your pearls before swine.
St Matthew ch. 7, v. 6; see **Proverbs** 618:5

15 Ask, and it shall be given you; seek, and ye shall find; knock, and it shall be opened unto you.
St Matthew ch. 7, v. 7; see **Proverbs** 630:26

16 Every one that asketh receiveth; and he that seeketh findeth.
St Matthew ch. 7, v. 8

17 Or what man is there of you, whom if his son ask bread, will he give him a stone?
St Matthew ch. 7, v. 9

18 Therefore all things whatsoever ye would that men should do to you, do ye even so to them: for this is the law and the prophets.
St Matthew ch. 7, v. 12

19 Wide is the gate, and broad is the way, that leadeth to destruction, and many there be that go in thereat.
St Matthew ch. 7, v. 13

20 Strait is the gate, and narrow is the way, which leadeth unto life, and few there be that find it.
St Matthew ch. 7, v. 14

21 Beware of false prophets, which come to you in sheep's clothing, but inwardly they are ravening wolves.
St Matthew ch. 7, v. 15

22 Do men gather grapes of thorns, or figs of thistles?
St Matthew ch. 7, v. 16

23 By their fruits ye shall know them.
St Matthew ch. 7, v. 20

24 The winds blew, and beat upon that house; and it fell not: for it was founded upon a rock.
St Matthew ch. 7, v. 25

25 Every one that heareth these sayings of mine, and doeth them not, shall be likened unto a foolish man, which built his house upon the sand:
And the rain descended, and the floods came, and the winds blew, and beat upon that house; and it fell: and great was the fall of it.
St Matthew ch. 7, v. 27

26 For he taught them as one having authority, and not as the scribes.
St Matthew ch. 7, v. 29

27 Lord I am not worthy that thou shouldest come under my roof.
St Matthew ch. 8, v. 8; see **Missal** 539:10

28 I am a man under authority, having soldiers under me: and I say to this man, Go, and he goeth; and to another, Come, and he cometh; and to my servant, Do this, and he doeth it.
St Matthew ch. 8, v. 9

29 I have not found so great faith, no, not in Israel.
St Matthew ch. 8, v. 10

30 But the children of the kingdom shall be cast out into outer darkness: there shall be weeping and gnashing of teeth.
St Matthew ch. 8, v. 12

1 The foxes have holes, and the birds of the air have nests; but the Son of man hath not where to lay his head.
St Matthew ch. 8, v. 20

2 Let the dead bury their dead.
St Matthew ch. 8, v. 22; see **Longfellow** 490:20, **Proverbs** 625:9

3 The whole herd of swine ran violently down a steep place into the sea, and perished in the waters.
St Matthew ch. 8, v. 32

4 He saw a man, named Matthew, sitting at the receipt of custom: and he saith unto him, Follow me. And he arose and followed him.
St Matthew ch. 9, v. 9

5 Why eateth your Master with publicans and sinners?
St Matthew ch. 9, v. 11

6 They that be whole need not a physician, but they that are sick.
St Matthew ch. 9, v. 12

7 I am not come to call the righteous, but sinners to repentance.
St Matthew ch. 9, v. 13

8 Neither do men put new wine into old bottles.
St Matthew ch. 9, v. 17; see **Proverbs** 635:43

9 Thy faith hath made thee whole.
St Matthew ch. 9, v. 22

10 The maid is not dead, but sleepeth.
St Matthew ch. 9, v. 24

11 He casteth out devils through the prince of the devils.
St Matthew ch. 9, v. 34

12 The harvest truly is plenteous, but the labourers are few.
St Matthew ch. 9, v. 37

13 Go rather to the lost sheep of the house of Israel.
St Matthew ch. 10, v. 6

14 Freely ye have received, freely give.
St Matthew ch. 10, v. 8

15 When ye depart out of that house or city, shake off the dust of your feet.
St Matthew ch. 10, v. 14

16 Be ye therefore wise as serpents, and harmless as doves.
St Matthew ch. 10, v. 16

17 The disciple is not above his master, nor the servant above his lord.
St Matthew ch. 10, v. 24

18 Are not two sparrows sold for a farthing? and one of them shall not fall on the ground without your Father.
The very hairs of your head are all numbered.
Fear ye not therefore, ye are of more value than many sparrows.
St Matthew ch. 10, v. 29; see **Bible** 100:31

19 I came not to send peace, but a sword.
St Matthew ch. 10, v. 34

20 A man's foes shall be they of his own household.
St Matthew ch. 10, v. 36

21 He that findeth his life shall lose it: and he that loseth his life for my sake shall find it.
St Matthew ch. 10, v. 39

22 Whosoever shall give to drink unto one of these little ones a cup of cold water only in the name of a disciple, verily I say unto you, he shall in no wise lose his reward.
St Matthew ch. 10, v. 42

23 Art thou he that should come, or do we look for another?
St Matthew ch. 11, v. 3

24 What went ye out into the wilderness to see? A reed shaken with the wind?
But what went ye out for to see? A man clothed in soft raiment? . . .
But what went ye out for to see? A prophet? yea, I say unto you, and more than a prophet.
St Matthew ch. 11, v. 7

25 We have piped unto you, and ye have not danced; we have mourned unto you, and ye have not lamented.
St Matthew ch. 11, v. 17

26 Wisdom is justified of her children.
St Matthew ch. 11, v. 19

27 Come unto me, all ye that labour and are heavy laden, and I will give you rest.
Take my yoke upon you, and learn of me; for I am meek and lowly in heart: and ye shall find rest unto your souls.
For my yoke is easy, and my burden is light.
St Matthew ch. 11, v. 28

28 He that is not with me is against me.
St Matthew ch. 12, v. 30 and St Luke ch. 11, v. 23

29 The blasphemy against the Holy Ghost shall not be forgiven unto men.
St Matthew ch. 12, v. 31

30 The tree is known by his fruit.
St Matthew ch. 12, v. 33; see **Proverbs** 633:18

31 Out of the abundance of the heart the mouth speaketh.
St Matthew ch. 12, v. 34; see **Proverbs** 629:13

32 Every idle word that men shall speak, they shall give account thereof in the day of judgement.
St Matthew ch. 12, v. 36

33 An evil and adulterous generation seeketh after a sign.
St Matthew ch. 12, v. 39

34 Behold, a greater than Solomon is here.
St Matthew ch. 12, v. 42

35 When the unclean spirit is gone out of a man, he walketh through dry places, seeking rest, and findeth none.
Then he saith, I will return into my house from whence I came out; and when he is come, he findeth it empty, swept, and garnished.
St Matthew ch. 12, v. 43

1 Then goeth he, and taketh with himself seven other spirits more wicked than himself, and they enter in and dwell there: and the last state of that man is worse than the first.
St Matthew ch. 12, v. 45

2 Behold my mother and my brethren!
St Matthew ch. 12, v. 49

3 Behold, a sower went forth to sow;
And when he sowed, some seeds fell by the wayside, and the fowls came and devoured them up:
Some fell upon stony places, where they had not much earth: and forthwith they sprung up, because they had no deepness of earth:
And when the sun was up, they were scorched; and because they had no root, they withered away.
And some fell among thorns; and the thorns sprang up and choked them:
But other fell into good ground, and brought forth fruit, some an hundredfold, some sixtyfold, some thirtyfold.
St Matthew ch. 13, v. 3

4 He also that received the seed among the thorns is he that heareth the word; and the care of this world, and the deceitfulness of riches, choke the word, and he becometh unfruitful.
St Matthew ch. 13, v. 22

5 The kingdom of heaven is like to a grain of mustard seed, which a man took, and sowed in his field:
Which indeed is the least of all seeds: but when it is grown, it is the greatest among herbs, and becometh a tree, so that the birds of the air come and lodge in the branches thereof.
St Matthew ch. 13, v. 31

6 The kingdom of heaven is like unto a merchant man, seeking goodly pearls:
Who, when he had found one pearl of great price, went and sold all that he had, and bought it.
St Matthew ch. 13, v. 45

7 A prophet is not without honour, save in his own country, and in his own house.
St Matthew ch. 13, v. 57; see **Proverbs** 629:44

8 In the fourth watch of the night Jesus went unto them, walking on the sea.
St Matthew ch. 14, v. 25

9 Be of good cheer; it is I; be not afraid.
St Matthew ch. 14, v. 27

10 O thou of little faith, wherefore didst thou doubt?
St Matthew ch. 14, v. 31

11 Not that which goeth into the mouth defileth a man; but that which cometh out of the mouth, this defileth a man.
St Matthew ch. 15, v. 11

12 They be blind leaders of the blind. And if the blind lead the blind, both shall fall into the ditch.
St Matthew ch. 15, v. 14; see **Proverbs** 634:27

13 Truth, Lord: yet the dogs eat of the crumbs which fall from their masters' table.
St Matthew ch. 15, v. 27

14 When it is evening, ye say, It will be fair weather: for the sky is red.
St Matthew ch. 16, v. 2

15 Ye can discern the face of the sky; but can ye not discern the signs of the times?
St Matthew ch. 16, v. 3

16 Thou art Peter, and upon this rock I will build my church; and the gates of hell shall not prevail against it.
St Matthew ch. 16, v. 18

17 Get thee behind me, Satan.
St Matthew ch. 16, v. 23

18 If ye have faith as a grain of mustard seed, ye shall say unto this mountain, Remove hence to yonder place; and it shall remove.
St Matthew ch. 17, v. 20; see **Proverbs** 619:41

19 Except ye be converted, and become as little children, ye shall not enter into the kingdom of heaven.
St Matthew ch. 18, v. 3

20 Whoso shall receive one such little child in my name receiveth me.
But whoso shall offend one of these little ones which believe in me, it were better for him that a millstone were hanged about his neck, and that he were drowned in the depth of the sea.
St Matthew ch. 18, v. 5

21 If thine eye offend thee, pluck it out, and cast it from thee: it is better for thee to enter into life with one eye, rather than having two eyes to be cast into hell fire.
St Matthew ch. 18, v. 9

22 For where two or three are gathered together in my name, there am I in the midst of them.
St Matthew ch. 18, v. 20

23 Lord, how oft shall my brother sin against me, and I forgive him? till seven times?
Jesus saith unto him I say not unto thee, Until seven times: but Until seventy times seven.
St Matthew ch. 18, v. 21

24 What therefore God hath joined together, let not man put asunder.
St Matthew ch. 19, v. 6; see **Book of Common Prayer** 133:11

25 If thou wilt be perfect, go and sell that thou hast, and give to the poor, and thou shalt have treasure in heaven.
St Matthew ch. 19, v. 21

26 He went away sorrowful: for he had great possessions.
St Matthew ch. 19, v. 22

27 It is easier for a camel to go through the eye of a needle, than for a rich man to enter into the kingdom of God.
St Matthew ch. 19, v. 24. See also St Luke ch. 18, v. 24

28 With men this is impossible; but with God all things are possible.
St Matthew ch. 19, v. 26; see **Proverbs** 614:18

1 But many that are first shall be last; and the last shall be first.
St Matthew ch. 19, v. 30

2 These last have wrought but one hour, and thou hast made them equal unto us, which have borne the burden and heat of the day.
St Matthew ch. 20, v. 12

3 I will give unto this last, even as unto thee.
Is it not lawful for me to do what I will with mine own?
St Matthew ch. 20, v. 14

4 It is written, My house shall be called the house of prayer; but ye have made it a den of thieves.
St Matthew ch. 21, v. 13; see **Bible** 90:11

5 For many are called, but few are chosen.
St Matthew ch. 22, v. 14; see **Proverbs** 626:10

6 Render therefore unto Caesar the things which are Caesar's; and unto God the things that are God's.
St Matthew ch. 22, v. 21; see **Crashaw** 250:17

7 For in the resurrection they neither marry, nor are given in marriage.
St Matthew ch. 22, v. 30

8 Thou shalt love the Lord thy God with all thy heart, and with all thy soul, and with all thy mind.
This is the first and great commandment.
And the second is like unto it, Thou shalt love thy neighbour as thyself.
St Matthew ch. 22, v. 38; see **Bible** 78:14

9 Woe unto you, scribes and Pharisees, hypocrites! for ye pay tithe of mint and anise and cummin, and have omitted the weightier matters of the law, judgement, mercy, and faith: these ought ye to have done, and not to leave the other undone.
St Matthew ch. 23, v. 23

10 Ye blind guides, which strain at a gnat, and swallow a camel.
St Matthew ch. 23, v. 24

11 Ye are like unto whited sepulchres, which indeed appear beautiful outward, but are within full of dead men's bones, and of all uncleanness.
St Matthew ch. 23, v. 27

12 O Jerusalem, Jerusalem, thou that killest the prophets, and stonest them which are sent unto thee, how often would I have gathered thy children together, even as a hen gathereth her chickens under her wings, and ye would not!
St Matthew ch. 23, v. 37

13 Ye shall hear of wars and rumours of wars: see that ye be not troubled: for all these things must come to pass but the end is not yet.
St Matthew ch. 24, v. 6

14 For nation shall rise against nation, and kingdom against kingdom.
St Matthew ch. 24, v. 7

15 When ye therefore shall see the abomination of desolation, spoken of by Daniel the prophet, stand in the holy place.
St Matthew ch. 24, v. 15, referring to Daniel ch. 12, v. 11

16 Wheresoever the carcase is, there will the eagles be gathered together.
St Matthew ch. 24, v. 28; see **Proverbs** 634:41

17 Heaven and earth shall pass away, but my words shall not pass away.
St Matthew ch. 24, v. 35

18 For as in the days that were before the flood they were eating and drinking, marrying and giving in marriage, until the day that Noe entered into the ark,
And knew not until the flood came, and took them all away; so shall also the coming of the Son of Man be.
St Matthew ch. 24, v. 38

19 One shall be taken, and the other left.
St Matthew ch. 24, v. 40

20 Watch therefore: for ye know not what hour your Lord doth come.
St Matthew ch. 24, v. 42

21 Well done, thou good and faithful servant: thou hast been faithful over a few things, I will make thee a ruler over many things: enter thou into the joy of thy lord.
St Matthew ch. 25, v. 21

22 Lord, I knew thee that thou art an hard man, reaping where thou hast not sown, and gathering where thou hast not strawed.
St Matthew ch. 25, v. 24

23 Unto every one that hath shall be given, and he shall have abundance: but from him that hath not shall be taken away even that which he hath.
St Matthew ch. 25, v. 29

24 And he shall set the sheep on his right hand, but the goats on the left.
St Matthew ch. 25, v. 33

25 For I was an hungred, and ye gave me meat: I was thirsty and ye gave me drink: I was a stranger, and ye took me in:
Naked, and ye clothed me: I was sick, and ye visited me: I was in prison, and ye came unto me.
St Matthew ch. 25, v. 35

26 Inasmuch as ye have done it unto one of the least of these my brethren, ye have done it unto me.
St Matthew ch. 25, v. 40

27 There came unto him a woman having an alabaster box of very precious ointment, and poured it on his head, as he sat at meat.
St Matthew ch. 26, v. 7

28 To what purpose is this waste?
For this ointment might have been sold for much, and given to the poor.
St Matthew ch. 26, v. 8 (St John ch. 12, v. 5 attributes this to Judas Iscariot)

29 What will ye give me, and I will deliver him unto you? And they covenanted with him [Judas Iscariot] for thirty pieces of silver.
St Matthew ch. 26, v. 15

30 It had been good for that man if he had not been born.
St Matthew ch. 26, v. 24

1 Jesus took bread, and blessed it, and brake it, and gave it to the disciples, and said, Take, eat; this is my body.
St Matthew ch. 26, v. 26

2 This night, before the cock crow, thou shalt deny me thrice.
St Matthew ch. 26, v. 34 (to St Peter)

3 Though I should die with thee, yet will I not deny thee.
St Matthew ch. 26, v. 35 (St Peter)

4 If it be possible, let this cup pass from me.
St Matthew ch. 26, v. 39

5 What, could ye not watch with me one hour?
St Matthew ch. 26, v. 40

6 Watch and pray, that ye enter not into temptation: the spirit indeed is willing but the flesh is weak.
St Matthew ch. 26, v. 41

7 Friend, wherefore art thou come?
St Matthew ch. 26, v. 50

8 All they that take the sword shall perish with the sword.
St Matthew ch. 26, v. 52; see **Proverbs** 622:12

9 Thy speech bewrayeth thee.
Then began he [St Peter] to curse and to swear, saying, I know not the man. And immediately the cock crew.
St Matthew ch. 26, v. 73

10 He [Pilate] took water, and washed his hands before the multitude, saying, I am innocent of the blood of this just person: see ye to it.
St Matthew ch. 27, v. 24

11 His blood be on us, and on our children.
St Matthew ch. 27, v. 25

12 He saved others; himself he cannot save.
St Matthew ch. 27, v. 42

13 Eli, Eli, lama sabachthani? . . . My God, my God, why hast thou forsaken me?
St Matthew ch. 27, v. 46; see **Book of Common Prayer** 134:26

14 And, lo, I am with you alway, even unto the end of the world.
St Matthew ch. 28, v. 20

ST MARK

15 The sabbath was made for man, and not man for the sabbath.
St Mark ch. 2, v. 27

16 How can Satan cast out Satan?
St Mark ch. 3, v. 23; see **Sorley** 748:13

17 If a house be divided against itself, that house cannot stand.
St Mark ch. 3, v. 25; see **Lincoln** 484:16, **Proverbs** 622:34

18 He that hath ears to hear, let him hear.
St Mark ch. 4, v. 9

19 With what measure ye mete, it shall be measured to you.
St Mark ch. 4, v. 24

20 My name is Legion: for we are many.
St Mark ch. 5, v. 9

21 Jesus, immediately knowing in himself that virtue had gone out of him, turned him about in the press, and said, Who touched my clothes?
St Mark ch. 5, v. 30

22 I see men as trees, walking.
St Mark ch. 8, v. 24

23 For what shall it profit a man, if he shall gain the whole world, and lose his own soul?
St Mark ch. 8, v. 36; see **Bolt** 126:16

24 Lord, I believe; help thou mine unbelief.
St Mark ch. 9, v. 24

25 Suffer the little children to come unto me, and forbid them not: for of such is the kingdom of God.
St Mark ch. 10, v. 14

26 Beware of the scribes, which love to go in long clothing, and love salutations in the marketplaces,
And the chief seats in the synagogues, and the uppermost rooms at feasts:
Which devour widows' houses, and for a pretence make long prayers.
St Mark ch. 12, v. 38

27 And there came a certain poor widow, and she threw in two mites.
St Mark ch. 12, v. 42

28 Watch ye therefore: for ye know not when the master of the house cometh . . . Lest coming suddenly he find you sleeping.
St Mark ch. 13, v. 35

29 Go ye into all the world, and preach the gospel to every creature.
St Mark ch. 16, v. 15

ST LUKE

30 Hail, thou that art highly favoured, the Lord is with thee: blessed art thou among women.
St Luke ch. 1, v. 28 (the angel to the Virgin Mary); see **Prayers** 611:1

31 And Mary said,
My soul doth magnify the Lord,
And my spirit hath rejoiced in God my Saviour.
For he hath regarded the low estate of his handmaiden: for, behold, from henceforth all generations shall call me blessed.
St Luke ch. 1, v. 46, known as the Magnificat; see **Bible** 115:10

Tell out my soul, the greatness of the Lord.
St Luke ch. 1, v. 47 in *The New English Bible*

32 He hath shewed strength with his arm; he hath scattered the proud in the imagination of their hearts.
He hath put down the mighty from their seats, and exalted them of low degree.
He hath filled the hungry with good things; and the rich he hath sent empty away.
St Luke ch. 1, v. 51 (the Magnificat)

33 To give light to them that sit in darkness and in the shadow of death, to guide our feet into the way of peace.
St Luke ch. 1, v. 79

1 And it came to pass in those days, that there went out a decree from Caesar Augustus, that all the world should be taxed.
St Luke ch. 2, v. 1

2 She brought forth her firstborn son, and wrapped him in swaddling clothes, and laid him in a manger; because there was no room for them in the inn.
And there were in the same country shepherds abiding in the field, keeping watch over their flock by night.
And, lo, the angel of the Lord came upon them, and the glory of the Lord shone round about them: and they were sore afraid.
St Luke ch. 2, v. 7

3 Behold, I bring you good tidings of great joy.
St Luke ch. 2, v. 10 (the angel to the shepherds)

4 Glory to God in the highest, and on earth peace, good will toward men.
St Luke ch. 2, v. 14 (the angels to the shepherds); see **Missal** 536:16

5 But Mary kept all these things, and pondered them in her heart.
St Luke ch. 2, v. 19

6 Lord, now lettest thou thy servant depart in peace, according to thy word.
St Luke ch. 2, v. 29 (Simeon); see **Bible** 115:12

7 A light to lighten the Gentiles, and the glory of thy people Israel.
St Luke ch. 2, v. 32 (Simeon)

8 Yea, a sword shall pierce through thy own soul also.
St Luke ch. 2, v. 35 (Simeon to the Virgin Mary)

9 Wist ye not that I must be about my Father's business?
St Luke ch. 2, v. 49

10 And the devil, taking him up into a high mountain, shewed unto him all the kingdoms of the world in a moment of time.
St Luke ch. 4, v. 5

11 Physician, heal thyself.
St Luke ch. 4, v. 23; see **Proverbs** 629:22

12 Master, we have toiled all the night, and have taken nothing: nevertheless at thy word I will let down the net.
St Luke ch. 5, v. 5 (St Peter)

13 No man . . . having drunk old wine straightway desireth new: for he saith, The old is better.
St Luke ch. 5, v. 39

14 Woe unto you, when all men shall speak well of you!
St Luke ch. 6, v. 26

15 Love your enemies, do good to them which hate you.
St Luke ch. 6, v. 27

16 Give, and it shall be given unto you; good measure, pressed down, and shaken together, and running over, shall men give into your bosom.
St Luke ch. 6, v. 38

17 Her sins, which are many, are forgiven; for she loved much.
St Luke ch. 7, v. 47

18 No man, having put his hand to the plough, and looking back, is fit for the kingdom of God.
St Luke ch. 9, v. 62

19 For the labourer is worthy of his hire.
St Luke ch. 10, v. 7; see **Proverbs** 624:46

20 I beheld Satan as lightning fall from heaven.
St Luke ch. 10, v. 18

21 Blessed are the eyes which see the things which ye see:
For I tell you, that many prophets and kings have desired to see those things which ye see, and have not seen them; and to hear those things which ye hear, and have not heard them.
St Luke ch. 10, v. 23

22 A certain man went down from Jerusalem to Jericho, and fell among thieves.
St Luke ch. 10, v. 30

23 He passed by on the other side.
St Luke ch. 10, v. 31

24 He took out two pence, and gave them to the host, and said unto him, Take care of him; and whatsoever thou spend more, when I come again, I will repay thee.
St Luke ch. 10, v. 35

25 Go, and do thou likewise.
St Luke ch. 10, v. 37

26 But Martha was cumbered about much serving, and came to him, and said, Lord, dost thou not care that my sister hath left me to serve alone? bid her therefore that she help me.
St Luke ch. 10, v. 40

27 Mary hath chosen that good part, which shall not be taken away from her.
St Luke ch. 10, v. 42

28 When a strong man armed keepeth his palace, his goods are in peace. But when a stronger than he shall come upon him, and overcome him, he taketh from him all his armour wherein he trusted, and divideth his spoils.
St Luke ch. 11, v. 21

29 No man, when he hath lighted a candle, putteth it in a secret place, neither under a bushel, but on a candlestick, that they which come in may see the light.
St Luke ch. 11, v. 33

30 Woe unto you, lawyers! for ye have taken away the key of knowledge.
St Luke ch. 11, v. 52

31 Are not five sparrows sold for two farthings, and not one of them is forgotten before God?
St Luke ch. 12, v. 6; see **Bible** 96:18

32 Soul, thou hast much goods laid up for many years; take thine ease, eat, drink, and be merry.
St Luke ch. 12, v. 19; see **Bible** 86:12, **Bible** 88:26

1 Thou fool, this night thy soul shall be required of thee.
St Luke ch. 12, v. 20

2 Let your loins be girded about, and your lights burning.
St Luke ch. 12, v. 35

3 When thou art bidden of any man to a wedding, sit not down in the highest room; lest a more honourable man than thou be bidden of him; And he that bade thee and him come and say to thee, Give this man place; and thou begin with shame to take the lowest room.
St Luke ch. 14, v. 8

4 Friend, go up higher.
St Luke ch. 14, v. 10

5 For whosoever exalteth himself shall be abased; and he that humbleth himself shall be exalted.
St Luke ch. 14, v. 11; St Matthew ch. 23, v. 12 is similar

6 They all with one consent began to make excuse . . . I pray thee have me excused.
St Luke ch. 14, v. 18

7 I have married a wife, and therefore I cannot come.
St Luke ch. 14, v. 20

8 Go out quickly into the streets and lanes of the city, and bring in hither the poor, and the maimed, and the halt, and the blind.
St Luke ch. 14, v. 21

9 Go out into the highways and hedges, and compel them to come in.
St Luke ch. 14, v. 23

10 For which of you, intending to build a tower, sitteth not down first, and counteth the cost, whether he have sufficient to finish it?
St Luke ch. 14, v. 28

11 Leave the ninety and nine in the wilderness.
St Luke ch. 15, v. 4

12 Rejoice with me; for I have found my sheep which was lost.
St Luke ch. 15, v. 6

13 Joy shall be in heaven over one sinner that repenteth, more than over ninety and nine just persons, which need no repentance.
St Luke ch. 15, v. 7

14 The younger son gathered all together, and took his journey into a far country, and there wasted his substance with riotous living.
St Luke ch. 15, v. 13

15 He would fain have filled his belly with the husks that the swine did eat: and no man gave unto him.
And when he came to himself, he said, How many hired servants of my father's have bread enough and to spare, and I perish with hunger!
St Luke ch. 15, v. 16

16 I will arise and go to my father, and will say unto him, Father, I have sinned against heaven, and before thee,

And am no more worthy to be called thy son: make me as one of thy hired servants.
St Luke ch. 15, v. 18

17 Bring hither the fatted calf, and kill it.
St Luke ch. 15, v. 23

18 This my son was dead, and is alive again; he was lost, and is found.
St Luke ch. 15, v. 24

19 And the Lord commended the unjust steward, because he had done wisely: for the children of this world are in their generation wiser than the children of light.
St Luke ch. 16, v. 8

20 Make to yourselves friends of the mammon of unrighteousness; that, when ye fail, they may receive you into everlasting habitations.
St Luke ch. 16, v. 9

21 He that is faithful in that which is least is faithful also in much.
St Luke ch. 16, v. 10

22 There was a certain rich man, which was clothed in purple and fine linen, and fared sumptuously every day:
And there was a certain beggar named Lazarus, which was laid at his gate, full of sores,
And desiring to be fed with the crumbs which fell from the rich man's table: moreover the dogs licked his sores.
And it came to pass that the beggar died, and was carried by the angels into Abraham's bosom.
St Luke ch. 16, v. 19

23 Between us and you there is a great gulf fixed.
St Luke ch. 16, v. 26

24 The kingdom of God is within you.
St Luke ch. 17, v. 21

25 Remember Lot's wife.
St Luke ch. 17, v. 32

26 Men ought always to pray, and not to faint.
St Luke ch. 18, v. 1

27 God, I thank thee, that I am not as other men are.
St Luke ch. 18, v. 11

28 God be merciful to me a sinner.
St Luke ch. 18, v. 13

29 Out of thine own mouth will I judge thee.
St Luke ch. 19, v. 22

30 If these should hold their peace, the stones would immediately cry out.
St Luke ch. 19, v. 40

31 If thou hadst known, even thou, at least in this thy day, the things which belong unto thy peace! but now they are hid from thine eyes.
St Luke ch. 19, v. 42

32 And when they heard it, they said, God forbid.
St Luke ch. 20, v. 16

33 He shall show you a large upper room furnished.
St Luke ch. 22, v. 12

34 I am among you as he that serveth.
St Luke ch. 22, v. 27

1 Nevertheless, not my will, but thine, be done.
St Luke ch. 22, v. 42

2 And the Lord turned, and looked upon Peter.
St Luke ch. 22, v. 61

3 For if they do these things in a green tree, what shall be done in the dry?
St Luke ch. 23, v. 31

4 Father, forgive them: for they know not what they do.
St Luke ch. 23, v. 34

5 Lord, remember me when thou comest into thy kingdom.
St Luke ch. 23, v. 42 (the Penitent Thief)

6 To day shalt thou be with me in paradise.
St Luke ch. 23, v. 43 (to the Penitent Thief)

7 Father, into thy hands I commend my spirit.
St Luke ch. 23, v. 46; see **Book of Common Prayer** 135:19

8 He was a good man, and a just.
St Luke ch. 23, v. 50 (Joseph of Arimathea)

9 Why seek ye the living among the dead?
St Luke ch. 24, v. 5

10 Their words seemed to them as idle tales.
St Luke ch. 24, v. 11

11 Abide with us: for it is toward evening, and the day is far spent.
St Luke ch. 24, v. 29; see **Lyte** 497:9

12 Did not our heart burn within us, while he talked with us by the way?
St Luke ch. 24, v. 32 (the disciples on the road to Emmaus)

13 He was known of them in breaking of bread.
St Luke ch. 24, v. 35

14 They gave him a piece of a broiled fish, and of an honeycomb.
St Luke ch. 24, v. 42

ST JOHN

15 In the beginning was the Word, and the Word was with God, and the Word was God.
St John ch. 1, v. 1; see **Missal** 539:12

16 All things were made by him; and without him was not any thing made that was made.
St John ch. 1, v. 3

17 And the light shineth in darkness; and the darkness comprehended it not.
St John ch. 1, v. 5

18 There was a man sent from God, whose name was John.
St John ch. 1, v. 6

19 He was not that Light, but was sent to bear witness of that Light.
That was the true Light, which lighteth every man that cometh into the world.
St John ch. 1, v. 8

20 He was in the world, and the world was made by him, and the world knew him not.
He came unto his own, and his own received him not.
St John ch. 1, v. 10

21 And the Word was made flesh, and dwelt among us, (and we beheld his glory, the glory as of the only begotten of the Father,) full of grace and truth.
St John ch. 1, v. 14; see **Missal** 539:13

22 No man hath seen God at any time.
St John ch. 1, v. 18

23 I baptize with water: but there standeth one among you, whom ye know not;
He it is, who coming after me is preferred before me, whose shoe's latchet I am not worthy to unloose.
St John ch. 1, v. 26 (St John the Baptist)

24 Behold the Lamb of God, which taketh away the sin of the world.
St John ch. 1, v. 29; see **Missal** 539:9

25 Can there any good thing come out of Nazareth?
St John ch. 1, v. 46

26 Behold an Israelite indeed, in whom is no guile!
St John ch. 1, v. 47

27 Woman, what have I to do with thee? mine hour is not yet come.
St John ch. 2, v. 4

28 Every man at the beginning doth set forth good wine; and when men have well drunk, then that which is worse: but thou hast kept the good wine until now.
St John ch. 2, v. 10

29 When he had made a scourge of small cords, he drove them all out of the temple.
St John ch. 2, v. 15

30 Verily, verily, I say unto thee, Except a man be born again, he cannot see the kingdom of God.
St John ch. 3, v. 3

31 The wind bloweth where it listeth, and thou hearest the sound thereof, but canst not tell whence it cometh, and whither it goeth.
St John ch. 3, v. 8

32 God so loved the world, that he gave his only begotten Son, that whosoever believeth in him should not perish, but have everlasting life.
St John ch. 3, v. 16

33 Men loved darkness rather than light, because their deeds were evil.
St John ch. 3, v. 19

34 God is a Spirit: and they that worship him must worship him in spirit and in truth.
St John ch. 4, v. 24

35 Except ye see signs and wonders, ye will not believe.
St John ch. 4, v. 48

36 Rise, take up thy bed, and walk.
St John ch. 5, v. 8

37 He was a burning and a shining light.
St John ch. 5, v. 35

38 Search the scriptures; for in them ye think ye have eternal life: and they are which testify of me.
St John ch. 5, v. 39

1 There is a lad here, which hath five barley loaves, and two small fishes: but what are they among so many?
St John ch. 6, v. 9

2 Gather up the fragments that remain, that nothing be lost.
St John ch. 6, v. 12

3 Verily, verily, I say unto you . . . my Father giveth you the true bread from heaven.
For the bread of God is he which cometh down from heaven, and giveth life to the world.
St John ch. 6, v. 32

4 I am the bread of life: he that cometh to me shall never hunger; and he that believeth on me shall never thirst.
St John ch. 6, v. 35

5 Him that cometh to me I will in no wise cast out.
St John ch. 6, v. 37

6 Verily, verily, I say unto you, He that believeth on me hath everlasting life.
St John ch. 6, v. 47

7 It is the spirit that quickeneth.
St John ch. 6, v. 63

8 And the scribes and the Pharisees brought unto him a woman taken in adultery.
St John ch. 8, v. 3

9 He that is without sin among you, let him first cast a stone at her.
St John ch. 8, v. 7

10 Neither do I condemn thee: go, and sin no more.
St John ch. 8, v. 11

11 And ye shall know the truth, and the truth shall make you free.
St John ch. 8, v. 32

12 Ye are of your father the devil, and the lusts of your father ye will do. He was a murderer from the beginning, and abode not in the truth, because there is no truth in him. When he speaketh a lie, he speaketh of his own: for he is a liar, and the father of it.
St John ch. 8, v. 44

13 The night cometh, when no man can work.
St John ch. 9, v. 4

14 He is of age; ask him: he shall speak for himself.
St John ch. 9, v. 21

15 One thing I know, that, whereas I was blind, now I see.
St John ch. 9, v. 25

16 I am the door.
St John ch. 10, v. 9

17 I am the good shepherd: the good shepherd giveth his life for the sheep.
St John ch. 10, v. 11

18 The hireling fleeth, because he is an hireling, and careth not for the sheep.
St John ch. 10, v. 13

19 Other sheep I have, which are not of this fold.
St John ch. 10, v. 16

20 Though ye believe not me, believe the works.
St John ch. 10, v. 38

21 I am the resurrection, and the life.
St John ch. 11, v. 25

22 Jesus wept.
St John ch. 11, v. 35; see **Hugo** 408:2

23 It is expedient for us, that one man should die for the people.
St John ch. 11, v. 50 (Caiaphas)

24 The poor always ye have with you.
St John ch. 12, v. 8

25 Lord, dost thou wash my feet?
St John ch. 13, v. 6 (St Peter)

26 That thou doest, do quickly.
St John ch. 13, v. 27

27 Let not your heart be troubled.
St John ch. 14, v. 1

28 In my Father's house are many mansions . . . I go to prepare a place for you.
St John ch. 14, v. 2

29 I am the way, the truth, and the life: no man cometh unto the Father, but by me.
St John ch. 14, v. 6

30 Have I been so long time with you, and yet hast thou not known me, Philip?
St John ch. 14, v. 9

31 Judas saith unto him, not Iscariot.
St John ch. 14, v. 22

32 Peace I leave with you, my peace I give unto you: not as the world giveth, give I unto you.
St John ch. 14, v. 27

33 Greater love hath no man than this, that a man lay down his life for his friends.
St John ch. 15, v. 13; see **Joyce** 437:23, **Thorpe** 793:21

34 Ye have not chosen me, but I have chosen you.
St John ch. 15, v. 16

35 It is expedient for you that I go away: for if I go not away, the Comforter will not come unto you.
St John ch. 16, v. 7

36 I have yet many things to say unto you, but ye cannot bear them now.
St John ch. 16, v. 12

37 A little while, and ye shall not see me: and again, a little while, and ye shall see me, because I go to the Father.
St John ch. 16, v. 16

38 In the world ye shall have tribulation: but be of good cheer; I have overcome the world.
St John ch. 16, v. 33

39 While I was with them in the world, I kept them in thy name: those that thou gavest me I have kept, and none of them is lost but the son of perdition.
St John ch. 17, v. 12

40 Put up thy sword into the sheath.
St John ch. 18, v. 11 (to St Peter)

1 Pilate saith unto him, What is truth?
St John ch. 18, v. 38; see **Bacon** 45:29

2 Now Barabbas was a robber.
St John ch. 18, v. 40; see **Campbell** 187:22

3 A place called the place of a skull, which is called in the Hebrew Golgotha.
St John ch. 19, v. 17

4 And Pilate wrote a title and put it on the cross. And the writing was, JESUS OF NAZARETH THE KING OF THE JEWS.
St John ch. 19, v. 19

5 What I have written I have written.
St John ch. 19, v. 22 (Pilate)

6 Woman, behold thy son! . . .
Behold thy mother!
St John ch. 19, v. 26 (to the Virgin Mary and, traditionally, St John)

7 I thirst.
St John ch. 19, v. 28

8 It is finished.
St John ch. 19, v. 30; see **Bible** 115:16

9 The first day of the week cometh Mary Magdalene early, when it was yet dark, unto the sepulchre, and seeth the stone taken away from the sepulchre.
St John ch. 20, v. 1

10 So they ran both together: and the other disciple did outrun Peter, and came first to the sepulchre.
St John ch. 20, v. 4

11 They have taken away my Lord, and I know not where they have laid him.
St John ch. 20, v. 13 (St Mary Magdalene)

12 Jesus saith unto her, Woman, why weepest thou? whom seekest thou? She supposing him to be the gardener saith unto him, Sir, if thou have borne him hence, tell me where thou hast laid him, and I will take him away.
St John ch. 20, v. 15

13 Touch me not.
St John ch. 20, v. 17 (to St Mary Magdalene); see **Bible** 115:17

14 Except I shall see in his hands the print of the nails, and put my finger into the print of the nails, and thrust my hand into his side, I will not believe.
St John ch. 20, v. 25 (St Thomas)

15 Be not faithless, but believing.
St John ch. 20, v. 27 (to St Thomas)

16 Thomas answered and said unto him, My Lord and my God.
St John ch. 20, v. 28

17 Thomas, because thou hast seen me, thou hast believed: blessed are they that have not seen, and yet have believed.
St John ch. 20, v. 29

18 Simon Peter saith unto them, I go a fishing.
St John ch. 21, v. 3

19 Simon, son of Jonas, lovest thou me more than these? . . . Feed my lambs.
St John ch. 21, v. 15

20 Feed my sheep.
St John ch. 21, v. 16

21 Lord, thou knowest all things; thou knowest that I love thee.
St John ch. 21, v. 17 (St Peter)

22 When thou wast young, thou girdedst thyself, and walkedst whither thou wouldest: but when thou shalt be old, thou shalt stretch forth thy hands, and another shall gird thee, and carry thee whither thou wouldest not.
St John ch. 21, v. 18 (to St Peter)

23 Peter, turning about, seeth the disciple whom Jesus loved following; which also leaned on his breast at supper, and said Lord, which is he that betrayeth thee?
St John ch. 21, v. 20 (tradionally St John)

24 Jesus saith unto him, If I will that he tarry till I come, what is that to thee?
St John ch. 21, v. 22 (to St Peter, of St John)

ACTS OF THE APOSTLES

25 Ye men of Galilee, why stand ye gazing up into heaven?
Acts of the Apostles ch. 1, v. 11

26 And suddenly there came a sound from heaven as of a rushing mighty wind, and it filled all the house where they were sitting.
And there appeared unto them cloven tongues like as of fire.
Acts of the Apostles ch. 2, v. 2

27 Parthians, and Medes, and Elamites, and the dwellers in Mesopotamia, and in Judaea, and Cappadocia, in Pontus, and Asia,
Phrygia, and Pamphylia, in Egypt, and in the parts of Libya about Cyrene, and strangers of Rome, Jews and proselytes,
Cretes and Arabians, we do hear them speak in our tongues the wonderful works of God.
Acts of the Apostles ch. 2, v. 9

28 And all that believed were together, and had all things common.
Acts of the Apostles ch. 2, v. 44

29 Silver and gold have I none; but such as I have give I thee.
Acts of the Apostles ch. 3, v. 6

30 Walking, and leaping, and praising God.
Acts of the Apostles ch. 3, v. 8

31 It is not reason that we should leave the word of God, and serve tables.
Acts of the Apostles ch. 6, v. 2

32 The witnesses laid down their clothes at a young man's feet, whose name was Saul.
Acts of the Apostles ch. 7, v. 58

33 Saul was consenting unto his death.
Acts of the Apostles ch. 8, v. 1

1 Thy money perish with thee, because thou hast thought that the gift of God may be purchased with money.
> Acts of the Apostles ch. 8, v. 20 (to Simon Magus)

2 Saul, Saul, why persecutest thou me?
> Acts of the Apostles ch. 9, v. 4

3 It is hard for thee to kick against the pricks.
> Acts of the Apostles ch. 9, v. 5

4 The street which is called Straight.
> Acts of the Apostles ch. 9, v. 11

5 Dorcas: this woman was full of good works.
> Acts of the Apostles ch. 9, v. 36

6 He fell into a trance,
And saw heaven opened, and a certain vessel descending unto him, as it had been a great sheet knit at the four corners, and let down to the earth: Wherein were all manner of four-footed beasts of the earth, and wild beasts, and creeping things, and fowls of the air.
> Acts of the Apostles ch. 10, v. 10

7 What God hath cleansed, that call not thou common.
> Acts of the Apostles ch. 10, v. 15

8 God is no respecter of persons.
> Acts of the Apostles ch. 10, v. 34

9 He was eaten of worms, and gave up the ghost.
> Acts of the Apostles ch. 12, v. 23

10 The gods are come down to us in the likeness of men.
> Acts of the Apostles ch. 14, v. 11

11 We also are men of like passions with you.
> Acts of the Apostles ch. 14, v. 15

12 Come over into Macedonia, and help us.
> Acts of the Apostles ch. 16, v. 9

13 What must I do to be saved?
> Acts of the Apostles ch. 16, v. 30

14 The Jews which believed not, moved with envy, took unto them certain lewd fellows of the baser sort, and gathered a company, and set all the city on an uproar.
> Acts of the Apostles ch. 17, v. 5

15 Those that have turned the world upside down are come hither also;
Whom Jason hath received: and these all do contrary to the decrees of Caesar, saying that there is another king, one Jesus.
> Acts of the Apostles ch. 17, v. 6

16 What will this babbler say?
> Acts of the Apostles ch. 17, v. 18

17 For all the Athenians and strangers which were there spent their time in nothing else, but either to tell, or to hear some new thing.
> Acts of the Apostles ch. 17, v. 21

18 Ye men of Athens, I perceive that in all things ye are too superstitious.
For as I passed by, and beheld your devotions, I found an altar with this inscription, TO THE UNKNOWN GOD. Whom therefore ye ignorantly worship, him declare I unto you.
> Acts of the Apostles ch. 17, v. 22

19 God that made the world and all things therein, seeing that he is Lord of Heaven and earth, dwelleth not in temples made with hands.
> Acts of the Apostles ch. 17, v. 24

20 For in him we live, and move, and have our being.
> Acts of the Apostles ch. 17, v. 28

21 We have not so much as heard whether there be any Holy Ghost.
> Acts of the Apostles ch. 19, v. 2

22 All with one voice about the space of two hours cried out, Great is Diana of the Ephesians.
> Acts of the Apostles ch. 19, v. 34

23 I go bound in the spirit unto Jerusalem.
> Acts of the Apostles ch. 20, v. 22

24 It is more blessed to give than to receive.
> Acts of the Apostles ch. 20, v. 35; see **Proverbs** 623:44

25 But Paul said, I am a man which am a Jew of Tarsus, a city in Cilicia, a citizen of no mean city.
> Acts of the Apostles ch. 21, v. 39

26 And the chief captain answered, With a great sum obtained I this freedom. And Paul said, But I was free born.
> Acts of the Apostles ch. 22, v. 28

27 A conscience void of offence toward God, and toward men.
> Acts of the Apostles ch. 24, v. 16

28 I appeal unto Caesar.
> Acts of the Apostles ch. 25, v. 11

29 Hast thou appealed unto Caesar? unto Caesar shalt thou go.
> Acts of the Apostles ch. 25, v. 12

30 Paul, thou art beside thyself; much learning doth make thee mad.
> Acts of the Apostles ch. 26, v. 24

31 For this thing was not done in a corner.
> Acts of the Apostles ch. 26, v. 26

32 Almost thou persuadest me to be a Christian.
> Acts of the Apostles ch. 26, v. 28

33 I would to God, that not only thou, but also all that hear me this day, were both almost, and altogether such as I am, except these bonds.
> Acts of the Apostles ch. 26, v. 29

ROMANS

34 Without ceasing I make mention of you always in my prayers.
> Romans ch. 1, v. 9

35 I am debtor both to the Greeks, and to the Barbarians; both to the wise, and to the unwise.
> Romans ch. 1, v. 14

36 The just shall live by faith.
> Romans ch. 1, v. 17

37 Worshipped and served the creature more than the Creator.
> Romans ch. 1, v. 25

1 Patient continuance in well doing.
Romans ch. 2, v. 7

2 A law unto themselves.
Romans ch. 2, v. 14

3 Let God be true, but every man a liar.
Romans ch. 3, v. 4

4 Let us do evil, that good may come.
Romans ch. 3, v. 8

5 For all have sinned, and come short of the glory of God.
Romans ch. 3, v. 23

6 For where no law is, there is no transgression.
Romans ch. 4, v. 15

7 Who against hope believed in hope, that he might become the father of many nations.
Romans ch. 4, v. 18 (of Abraham)

8 Hope maketh not ashamed; because the love of God is shed abroad in our hearts by the Holy Ghost which is given unto us.
Romans ch. 5, v. 5

9 Where sin abounded, grace did much more abound.
Romans ch. 5, v. 20

10 Shall we continue in sin, that grace may abound? God forbid. How shall we, that are dead to sin, live any longer in sin?
Romans ch. 6, v. 1

11 We also should walk in newness of life.
Romans ch. 6, v. 4

12 Christ being raised from the dead dieth no more; death hath no more dominion over him.
For in that he died, he died unto sin once: but in that he liveth, he liveth unto God.
Romans ch. 6, v. 9; see **Thomas** 789:6

13 The wages of sin is death.
Romans ch. 6, v. 23

14 Is the law sin? God forbid. Nay, I had not known sin, but by the law.
Romans ch. 7, v. 7

15 For the good that I would I do not: but the evil which I would not, that I do.
Romans ch. 7, v. 19; see **Ovid** 580:13

16 O wretched man that I am! who shall deliver me from the body of this death?
Romans ch. 7, v. 24

17 They that are after the flesh do mind the things of the flesh; but they that are after the Spirit the things of the Spirit.
For to be carnally minded is death.
Romans ch. 8, v. 5

18 For ye have not received the spirit of bondage again to fear; but ye have received the Spirit of adoption, whereby we cry, Abba, Father.
Romans ch. 8, v. 15

19 We are the children of God:
And if the children, then heirs; heirs of God, and joint-heirs with Christ.
Romans ch. 8, v. 16

20 For we know that the whole creation groaneth and travaileth in pain together until now.
Romans ch. 8, v. 22

21 All things work together for good to them that love God.
Romans ch. 8, v. 28

22 If God be for us, who can be against us?
Romans ch. 8, v. 31

23 For I am persuaded, that neither death, nor life, nor angels, nor principalities, nor powers, nor things present, nor things to come,
Nor height, nor depth, nor any other creature, shall be able to separate us from the love of God, which is in Christ Jesus our Lord.
Romans ch. 8, v. 38

24 Shall the thing formed say to him that formed it, Why hast thou made me thus?
Hath not the potter power over the clay, of the same lump to make one vessel unto honour, and another unto dishonour?
Romans ch. 9, v. 20

25 I beseech you therefore, brethren, by the mercies of God, that ye present your bodies a living sacrifice, holy, acceptable unto God.
Romans ch. 12, v. 1

26 Rejoice with them that do rejoice, and weep with them that weep.
Romans ch. 12, v. 15

27 Mind not high things, but condescend to men of low estate. Be not wise in your own conceits.
Romans ch. 12, v. 16

28 Vengeance is mine; I will repay, saith the Lord.
Romans ch. 12, v. 19

29 Be not overcome of evil, but overcome evil with good.
Romans ch. 12, v. 21

30 Let every soul be subject unto the higher powers
. . . the powers that be are ordained of God.
Romans ch. 13, v. 1

31 Render therefore to all their dues: tribute to whom tribute is due; custom to whom custom; fear to whom fear; honour to whom honour.
Owe no man anything, but to love one another: for he that loveth another hath fulfilled the law.
Romans ch. 13, v. 7

32 Now it is high time to awake out of sleep: for now is our salvation nearer than when we believed.
The night is far spent, the day is at hand: let us therefore cast off the works of darkness, and let us put on the armour of light.
Romans ch. 13, v. 11

33 Make not provision for the flesh, to fulfil the lusts thereof.
Romans ch. 13, v. 14

34 Doubtful disputations.
Romans ch. 14, v. 1

35 Let every man be fully persuaded in his own mind.
Romans ch. 14, v. 5

1 Salute one another with an holy kiss.
Romans ch. 16, v. 16

I CORINTHIANS

2 The foolishness of preaching to save them that believe.
I Corinthians ch. 1, v. 21

3 For the Jews require a sign, and the Greeks seek after wisdom.
I Corinthians ch. 1, v. 22

4 We preach Christ crucified, unto the Jews a stumbling-block, and unto the Greeks foolishness.
I Corinthians ch. 1, v. 23

5 God hath chosen the foolish things of the world to confound the wise; and God hath chosen the weak things of the world to confound the things which are mighty.
I Corinthians ch. 1, v. 27

6 I have planted, Apollos watered; but God gave the increase.
I Corinthians ch. 3, v. 6

7 Stewards of the mysteries of God.
I Corinthians ch. 4, v. 1

8 We are made a spectacle unto the world, and to angels.
I Corinthians ch. 4, v. 9

9 Absent in body, but present in spirit.
I Corinthians ch. 5, v. 3

10 Know ye not that a little leaven leaveneth the whole lump?
I Corinthians ch. 5, v. 6

11 Christ our passover is sacrificed for us:
Therefore let us keep the feast, not with the old leaven, neither with the leaven of malice and wickedness; but with the unleavened bread of sincerity and truth.
I Corinthians ch. 5, v. 7

12 Your body is the temple of the Holy Ghost.
I Corinthians ch. 6, v. 19

13 It is better to marry than to burn.
I Corinthians ch. 7, v. 9; see **Proverbs** 615:31

14 The unbelieving husband is sanctified by the wife.
I Corinthians ch. 7, v. 14

15 The fashion of this world passeth away.
I Corinthians ch. 7, v. 31

16 Knowledge puffeth up, but charity edifieth.
I Corinthians ch. 8, v. 1

17 Who goeth a warfare any time at his own charges? who planteth a vineyard, and eateth not of the fruit thereof?
I Corinthians ch. 9, v. 7

18 I am made all things to all men.
I Corinthians ch. 9, v. 22

19 Know ye not that they which run in a race run all, but one receiveth the prize.
I Corinthians ch. 9, v. 24

20 Now they do it to obtain a corruptible crown; but we an incorruptible.

I therefore so run, not as uncertainly; so fight I, not as one that beateth the air.
But I keep under my body, and bring it into subjection; lest that by any means, when I have preached to others, I myself should be a castaway.
I Corinthians ch. 9, v. 25

21 All things are lawful for me, but all things are not expedient.
I Corinthians ch. 10, v. 23

22 For the earth is the Lord's and the fulness thereof.
I Corinthians ch. 10, v. 26; see **Book of Common Prayer** 135:5

23 Doth not even nature itself teach you, that if a man have long hair, it is a shame unto him?
But if a woman have long hair, it is a glory to her.
I Corinthians ch. 11, v. 14

24 Now there are diversities of gifts, but the same Spirit.
I Corinthians ch. 12, v. 4

25 Though I speak with the tongues of men and of angels, and have not charity, I am become as sounding brass, or a tinkling cymbal.
And though I have the gift of prophecy, and understand all mysteries, and all knowledge; and though I have all faith; so that I could remove mountains; and have not charity, I am nothing.
And though I bestow all my goods to feed the poor, and though I give my body to be burned, and have not charity, it profiteth me nothing.
Charity suffereth long, and is kind; charity envieth not; charity vaunteth not itself, is not puffed up,
Doth not behave itself unseemly, seeketh not her own, is not easily provoked, thinketh no evil;
Rejoiceth not in iniquity, but rejoiceth in the truth;
Beareth all things, believeth all things, hopeth all things, endureth all things.
Charity never faileth: but whether there be prophecies, they shall fail; whether there be tongues, they shall cease; whether there be knowledge, it shall vanish away.
For we know in part, and we prophesy in part.
But when that which is perfect is come, then that which is in part shall be done away.
When I was a child, I spake as a child, I understood as a child, I thought as a child: but when I became a man, I put away childish things.
For now we see through a glass, darkly; but then face to face: now I know in part; but then shall I know even as also I am known.
And now abideth faith, hope, charity, these three; but the greatest of these is charity.
I Corinthians ch. 13, v. 1

26 If the trumpet give an uncertain sound, who shall prepare himself to the battle?
I Corinthians ch. 14, v. 8

27 Except ye utter by the tongue words easy to be understood, how shall it be known what is spoken? for ye shall speak into the air.
I Corinthians ch. 14, v. 9; see **Bunyan** 164:12

28 Let all things be done decently and in order.
I Corinthians ch. 14, v. 40

1 Last of all he was seen of me also, as of one born
out of due time.
For I am the least of the apostles, that am not
meet to be called an apostle, because I persecuted
the church of God.
But by the grace of God I am what I am.
I Corinthians ch. 15, v. 8

2 I laboured more abundantly than they all: yet not
I, but the grace of God which was with me.
I Corinthians ch. 15, v. 10

3 If in this life only we have hope in Christ, we are
of all men most miserable.
I Corinthians ch. 15, v. 19

4 But now is Christ risen from the dead, and become
the first fruits of them that slept.
For since by man came death, by man came also
the resurrection of the dead.
For as in Adam all die, even so in Christ shall all
be made alive.
I Corinthians ch. 15, v. 20

5 The last enemy that shall be destroyed is death.
I Corinthians ch. 15, v. 26

6 If after the manner of men I have fought with
beasts at Ephesus, what advantageth it me, if the
dead rise not? let us eat and drink; for to morrow
we die.
I Corinthians ch. 15, v. 32; see **Bible** 86:12, **Bible** 88:26,
Bible 100:32

7 Evil communications corrupt good manners.
I Corinthians ch. 15, v. 33; see **Proverbs** 619:25

8 One star differeth from another star in glory.
I Corinthians ch. 15, v. 41

9 So also is the resurrection of the dead. It is sown in
corruption; it is raised in incorruption.
I Corinthians ch. 15, v. 42

10 The first man is of the earth, earthy.
I Corinthians ch. 15, v. 47

11 Behold, I shew you a mystery; We shall not all
sleep, but we shall all be changed,
In a moment, in the twinkling of an eye, at the
last trump; for the trumpet shall sound, and the
dead shall be raised incorruptible, and we shall be
changed.
For this corruptible must put on incorruption, and
this mortal must put on immortality.
I Corinthians ch. 15, v. 51

12 O death, where is thy sting? O grave, where is thy
victory?
I Corinthians ch. 15, v. 55: see **Military sayings** 526:15

II CORINTHIANS

13 Our sufficiency is of God;
Who also hath made us able ministers of the new
testament; not of the letter, but of the spirit: for
the letter killeth, but the spirit giveth life.
II Corinthians ch. 3, v. 5

14 We have this treasure in earthen vessels.
II Corinthians ch. 4, v. 7

15 We know that if our earthly house of this
tabernacle were dissolved, we have a building of

God, an house not made with hands, eternal in
the heavens.
II Corinthians ch. 5, v. 1; see **Browning** 158:24

16 For he saith, I have found thee in a time accepted,
and in the day of salvation have I succoured thee:
behold, now is the accepted time; behold, now is
the day of salvation.
II Corinthians ch. 6, v. 2

17 As having nothing, and yet possessing all things.
II Corinthians ch. 6, v. 10

18 God loveth a cheerful giver.
II Corinthians ch. 9, v. 7

19 For ye suffer fools gladly, seeing ye yourselves are
wise.
II Corinthians ch. 11, v. 19

20 Are they Hebrews? so am I. Are they Israelites? so
am I. Are they the seed of Abraham? so am I.
Are they ministers of Christ? (I speak as a fool) I
am more.
II Corinthians ch. 11, v. 22

21 Of the Jews five times received I forty stripes save
one.
Thrice was I beaten with rods, once was I stoned,
thrice I suffered shipwreck, a night and a day have
I been in the deep;
In weariness and painfulness, in watchings often,
in hunger and thirst, in fastings often, in cold and
nakedness.
Beside those things that are without, that which
cometh upon me daily, the care of all the
churches.
II Corinthians ch. 11, v. 24

22 In journeyings often, in perils of waters, in perils
of robbers, in perils by mine own countrymen, in
perils by the heathen, in perils of the city, in perils
in the wilderness, in perils in the sea, in perils
among false brethren.
II Corinthians ch. 11, v. 26

23 I knew a man in Christ above fourteen years ago
(whether in the body, I cannot tell; or whether
out of the body, I cannot tell: God knoweth)—
such an one caught up to the third heaven.
II Corinthians ch. 12, v. 2

24 There was given to me a thorn in the flesh, the
messenger of Satan to buffet me.
II Corinthians ch. 12, v. 7

25 My strength is made perfect in weakness.
II Corinthians ch. 12, v. 9

GALATIANS

26 The right hands of fellowship.
Galatians ch. 2, v. 9

27 It is written, that Abraham had two sons, the one
by a bondmaid, the other by a freewoman.
But he who was of the bondwoman was born after
the flesh; but he of the freewoman was by
promise.
Which things are an allegory.
Galatians ch. 4, v. 22

28 Ye are fallen from grace.
Galatians ch. 5, v. 4

1 But the fruit of the Spirit is love, joy, peace, longsuffering, gentleness, goodness, faith, Meekness, temperance.
Galatians ch. 5, v. 22

2 Be not deceived; God is not mocked: for whatsoever a man soweth, that shall he also reap.
Galatians ch. 6, v. 7; see **Proverbs** 614:40

3 Let us not be weary in well doing: for in due season we shall reap, if we faint not.
Galatians ch. 6, v. 9; 'Be not weary in well doing' in II Thessalonians ch. 3, v. 13

4 Ye see how large a letter I have written unto you with mine own hand.
Galatians ch. 6, v. 11

EPHESIANS

5 [Christ] came and preached peace to you which were afar off, and to them that were nigh.
Ephesians ch. 2, v. 17

6 Unto me, who am less than the least of all saints, is this grace given, that I should preach among the Gentiles the unsearchable riches of Christ.
Ephesians ch. 3, v. 8

7 I bow my knees unto the Father of our Lord Jesus Christ,
Of whom the whole family in heaven and earth is named,
That he would grant you, according to the riches of his glory, to be strengthened with might by his Spirit in the inner man.
Ephesians ch. 3, v. 14

8 The love of Christ, which passeth knowledge.
Ephesians ch. 3, v. 19

9 Now unto him that is able to do exceeding abundantly above all that we ask or think, according to the power that worketh in us,
Unto him be glory in the church by Christ Jesus throughout all ages, world without end. Amen.
Ephesians ch. 3, v. 20

10 I therefore, the prisoner of the Lord, beseech you that ye walk worthy of the vocation wherewith ye are called.
Ephesians ch. 4, v. 1

11 He gave some, apostles; and some, prophets; and some, evangelists; and some, pastors and teachers;
For the perfecting of the saints, for the work of the ministry, for the edifying of the body of Christ:
Till we all come in the unity of the faith, and of the knowledge of the Son of God, unto a perfect man, unto the measure of the stature of the fulness of Christ:
That we henceforth be no more children, tossed to and fro, and carried about with every wind of doctrine, by the sleight of men, and cunning craftiness, whereby they lie in wait to deceive.
Ephesians ch. 4, v. 11

12 We are members one of another.
Ephesians ch. 4, v. 25

13 Be ye angry and sin not: let not the sun go down upon your wrath.
Ephesians ch. 4, v. 26; see **Proverbs** 627:22

14 Fornication, and all uncleanness, or covetousness, let it not be once named among you, as becometh saints;
Neither filthiness, nor foolish talking, nor jesting, which are not convenient.
Ephesians ch. 5, v. 3

15 Let no man deceive you with vain words: for because of these things cometh the wrath of God upon the children of disobedience.
Ephesians ch. 5, v. 6

16 See then that ye walk circumspectly, not as fools, but as wise,
Redeeming the time, because the days are evil.
Ephesians ch. 5, v. 15

17 Be not drunk with wine, wherein is excess; but be filled with the Spirit;
Speaking to yourselves in psalms and hymns and spiritual songs, singing and making melody in your heart to the Lord.
Ephesians ch. 5, v. 18

18 Ye fathers, provoke not your children to wrath.
Ephesians ch. 6, v. 4

19 Not with eyeservice, as menpleasers.
Ephesians ch. 6, v. 6

20 Put on the whole armour of God.
Ephesians ch. 6, v. 11

21 For we wrestle not against flesh and blood, but against principalities, against powers, against the rulers of the darkness of this world, against spiritual wickedness in high places.
Wherefore take unto you the whole armour of God, that ye may be able to withstand in the evil day, and having done all, to stand.
Stand therefore, having your loins girt about with truth, and having on the breastplate of righteousness;
And your feet shod with the preparation of the gospel of peace;
Above all, taking the shield of faith, wherewith ye shall be able to quench all the fiery darts of the wicked.
Ephesians ch. 6, v. 12

PHILIPPIANS

22 For me to live is Christ, and to die is gain.
Philippians ch. 1, v. 21

23 Having a desire to depart, and to be with Christ; which is far better.
Philippians ch. 1, v. 23

24 Let this mind be in you, which was also in Christ Jesus:
Who, being in the form of God, thought it not robbery to be equal with God:
But made himself of no reputation, and took upon him the form of a servant and was made in the likeness of men.
Philippians ch. 2, v. 5

25 God hath also highly exalted him, and given him a name which is above every name:

That at the name of Jesus every knee should bow, of things in heaven, and things in earth, and things under the earth.

Philippians ch. 2, v. 9; see **Noel** 565:6

1 Work out your own salvation with fear and trembling.

Philippians ch. 2, v. 12

2 If any other man thinketh that he hath whereof he might trust in the flesh, I more:
Circumcised the eighth day, of the stock of Israel, of the tribe of Benjamin, an Hebrew of the Hebrews; as touching the law, a Pharisee.

Philippians ch. 3, v. 4

3 But what things were gain to me, those I counted loss for Christ.

Philippians ch. 3, v. 7

4 Forgetting those things which are behind, and reaching forth unto those things which are before, I press toward the mark.

Philippians ch. 3, v. 13

5 Whose God is their belly, and whose glory is in their shame.

Philippians ch. 3, v. 19

6 Rejoice in the Lord alway: and again I say, Rejoice.

Philippians ch. 4, v. 4

7 The peace of God, which passeth all understanding, shall keep your hearts and minds through Christ Jesus.

Philippians ch. 4, v. 7; see **James I** 417:6

8 Whatsoever things are true, whatsoever things are honest, whatsoever things are just, whatsoever things are pure, whatsoever things are lovely, whatsoever things are of good report; if there be any virtue and if there be any praise, think on these things.

Philippians ch. 4, v. 8

9 I can do all things through Christ which strengtheneth me.

Philippians ch. 4, v. 13

COLOSSIANS

10 For by him were all things created, that are in heaven, and that are in earth, visible and invisible, whether they be thrones, or dominions, or principalities, or powers.

Colossians ch. 1, v. 16; see **Milton** 533:16

11 Set your affection on things above, not on things on the earth.

Colossians ch. 3, v. 2

12 Ye have put off the old man with his deeds:
And have put on the new man, which is renewed in knowledge after the image of him that created him:
Where there is neither Greek nor Jew, circumcision nor uncircumcision, Barbarian, Scythian, bond nor free: but Christ is all, and in all.

Colossians ch. 3, v. 9

13 Husbands, love your wives, and be not bitter against them.

Colossians ch. 3, v. 19

14 Let your speech be alway with grace, seasoned with salt.

Colossians ch. 4, v. 6

I THESSALONIANS

15 We give thanks to God always for you all, making mention of you in our prayers;
Remembering without ceasing your work of faith and labour of love, and patience of hope in our Lord Jesus Christ.

I Thessalonians ch. 1, v. 2

16 Study to be quiet, and to do your own business.

I Thessalonians ch. 4, v. 11

17 But let us, who are of the day, be sober, putting on the breastplate of faith and love; and for an helmet, the hope of salvation.

I Thessalonians ch. 5, v. 8

18 Rejoice evermore. Pray without ceasing. In everything give thanks.

I Thessalonians ch. 5, v. 16

19 Prove all things; hold fast that which is good.

I Thessalonians ch. 5, v. 21

II THESSALONIANS

20 If any would not work, neither should he eat.

II Thessalonians ch. 3, v. 10; see **Proverbs** 623:17

I TIMOTHY

21 Sinners; of whom I am chief.

I Timothy ch. 1, v. 15

22 A bishop then must be blameless, the husband of one wife, vigilant, sober, of good behaviour, given to hospitality, apt to teach;
Not given to wine, no striker, not greedy of filthy lucre; but patient, not a brawler, not covetous.

I Timothy ch. 3, v. 2

23 Refuse profane and old wives' fables, and exercise thyself rather unto godliness.

I Timothy ch. 4, v. 7

24 Use a little wine for thy stomach's sake.

I Timothy ch. 5, v. 23

25 For we brought nothing into this world, and it is certain we can carry nothing out.

I Timothy ch. 6, v. 7

26 The love of money is the root of all evil.

I Timothy ch. 6, v. 10; see **Proverbs** 626:33

27 Fight the good fight of faith, lay hold on eternal life.

I Timothy ch. 6, v. 12; see **Monsell** 543:7

II TIMOTHY

28 For God hath not given us the spirit of fear; but of power, and of love, and of a sound mind.

II Timothy ch. 1, v. 7

29 Hold fast the form of sound words.

II Timothy ch. 1, v. 13

30 Be instant in season, out of season.

II Timothy ch. 4, v. 2

1 I have fought a good fight, I have finished my
course, I have kept the faith.
II Timothy ch. 4, v. 7

TITUS

2 Unto the pure all things are pure.
Titus ch. 1, v. 15; see **Lawrence** 474:18, **Proverbs** 633:15

HEBREWS

3 God, who at sundry times and in divers manners
spake in time past unto the fathers by the
prophets,
Hath in these last days spoken unto us by his Son,
whom he hath appointed heir of all things, by
whom he also made the worlds:
Who being the brightness of his glory, and the
express image of his person, and upholding all
things by the word of his power, when he had by
himself purged our sins, sat down on the right
hand of the Majesty on high.
Hebrews ch. 1, v. 1

4 Without shedding of blood is no remission.
Hebrews ch. 9, v. 22

5 It is a fearful thing to fall into the hands of the
living God.
Hebrews ch. 10, v. 31

6 Faith is the substance of things hoped for, the
evidence of things not seen.
Hebrews ch. 11, v. 1

7 For he looked for a city which hath foundations,
whose maker and builder is God.
Hebrews ch. 11, v. 10

8 These all died in faith, not having received the
promises, but having seen them afar off, and were
persuaded of them, and embraced them, and
confessed that they were strangers and pilgrims on
the earth.
Hebrews ch. 11, v. 13

9 Of whom the world was not worthy.
Hebrews ch. 11, v. 38

10 Wherefore seeing we also are compassed about
with so great a cloud of witnesses, let us lay aside
every weight, and the sin which doth so easily
beset us, and let us run with patience the race
that is set before us,
Looking unto Jesus the author and finisher of our
faith; who for the joy that was set before him
endured the cross, despising the shame, and is set
down at the right hand of God.
Hebrews ch. 12, v. 1

11 Whom the Lord loveth he chasteneth.
Hebrews ch. 12, v. 6

12 The spirits of just men made perfect.
Hebrews ch. 12, v. 23

13 Let brotherly love continue.
Hebrews ch. 13, v. 1

14 Be not forgetful to entertain strangers: for thereby
some have entertained angels unawares.
Hebrews ch. 13, v. 2

15 Jesus Christ the same yesterday, and to day, and
for ever.
Hebrews ch. 13, v. 8

16 For here have we no continuing city, but we seek
one to come.
Hebrews ch. 13, v. 14

17 To do good and to communicate forget not.
Hebrews ch. 13, v. 16

JAMES

18 Let patience have her perfect work.
James ch. 1, v. 4

19 Blessed is the man that endureth temptation: for
when he is tried, he shall receive the crown of life.
James ch. 1, v. 12

20 Every good gift and every perfect gift is from
above, and cometh down from the Father of lights,
with whom is no variableness, neither shadow of
turning.
James ch. 1, v. 17

21 Be swift to hear, slow to speak, slow to wrath:
For the wrath of man worketh not the
righteousness of God.
Wherefore lay apart all filthiness and superfluity of
naughtiness, and receive with meekness the
engrafted word, which is able to save your souls,
For if any be a hearer of the word, and not a doer,
he is like unto a man beholding his natural face in
a glass:
For he beholdeth himself, and goeth his way, and
straightway forgetteth what manner of man he
was.
James ch. 1, v. 19

22 But be ye doers of the word, and not hearers only,
deceiving your own selves.
James ch. 1, v. 22

23 If any man among you seem to be religious, and
bridleth not his tongue, but deceiveth his own
heart, this man's religion is vain.
James ch. 1, v. 26

24 Pure religion and undefiled before God and the
Father is this, To visit the fatherless and widows in
their affliction, and to keep himself unspotted from
the world.
James ch. 1, v. 27

25 Faith without works is dead.
James ch. 2, v. 20

26 How great a matter a little fire kindleth.
James ch. 3, v. 5

27 The tongue can no man tame; it is an unruly evil.
James ch. 3, v. 8

28 Doth a fountain send forth at the same place sweet
water and bitter?
James ch. 3, v. 11

29 For what is your life? It is even a vapour, that
appeareth for a little time, and then vanisheth
away.
James ch. 4, v. 14

30 Ye have heard of the patience of Job.
James ch. 5, v. 11

31 Let your yea be yea; and your nay, nay.
James ch. 5, v. 12

1 The effectual fervent prayer of a righteous man availeth much.

James ch. 5, v. 16

I PETER

2 Jesus Christ: Whom having not seen, ye love; in whom, though now ye see him not, yet believing, ye rejoice with joy unspeakable and full of glory.

I Peter ch. 1, v. 7

3 All flesh is as grass, and all the glory of man as the flower of grass. The grass withereth, and the flower thereof falleth away.

I Peter ch. 1, v. 24; see **Bible** 89:17

4 As newborn babes, desire the sincere milk of the word, that ye may grow thereby:
If so be ye have tasted that the Lord is gracious.

I Peter ch. 2, v. 2

5 But ye are a chosen generation, a royal priesthood, an holy nation, a peculiar people.

I Peter ch. 2, v. 9

6 Abstain from fleshly lusts, which war against the soul.

I Peter ch. 2, v. 11

7 Honour all men. Love the brotherhood. Fear God. Honour the king.

I Peter ch. 2, v. 17

8 For what glory is it, if, when ye be buffeted for your faults, ye shall take it patiently? but if, when ye do well, and suffer for it, ye take it patiently, this is acceptable with God.

I Peter ch. 2, v. 20

9 Ye were as sheep going astray; but are now returned unto the Shepherd and Bishop of your souls.

I Peter ch. 2, v. 25

10 The ornament of a meek and quiet spirit.

I Peter ch. 3, v. 4

11 Giving honour unto the wife, as unto the weaker vessel.

I Peter ch. 3, v. 7

12 Not rendering evil for evil, or railing for railing: but contrariwise blessing.

I Peter ch. 3, v. 9

13 The end of all things is at hand.

I Peter ch. 4, v. 7

14 Charity shall cover the multitude of sins.

I Peter ch. 4, v. 8; see **Proverbs** 616:34

15 Be sober, be vigilant; because your adversary the devil, as a roaring lion, walketh about, seeking whom he may devour.

I Peter ch. 5, v. 8

II PETER

16 And the day star arise in your hearts.

II Peter ch. 1, v. 19

17 The dog is turned to his own vomit again.

II Peter ch. 2, v. 22

I JOHN

18 If we say that we have no sin, we deceive ourselves, and the truth is not in us.

I John ch. 1, v. 8

19 But whoso hath this world's good, and seeth his brother have need, and shutteth up his bowels of compassion from him, how dwelleth the love of God in him?

I John ch. 3, v. 17

20 He that loveth not knoweth not God; for God is love.

I John ch. 4, v. 8

21 There is no fear in love; but perfect love casteth out fear.

I John ch. 4, v. 18; see **Connolly** 240:7

22 If a man say, I love God, and hateth his brother, he is a liar: for he that loveth not his brother whom he hath seen, how can he love God whom he hath not seen?

I John ch. 4, v. 20

III JOHN

23 He that doeth good is of God: but he that doeth evil hath not seen God.

III John v. 11

REVELATION

24 John to the seven churches which are in Asia: Grace be unto you, and peace, from him which is, and which was, and which is to come.

Revelation ch. 1, v. 4

25 Behold, he cometh with clouds; and every eye shall see him, and they also which pierced him: and all kindreds of the earth shall wail because of him. Even so, Amen.
I am Alpha and Omega, the beginning and the ending, saith the Lord.

Revelation ch. 1, v. 7

26 I was in the Spirit on the Lord's day, and heard behind me a great voice as of a trumpet.

Revelation ch. 1, v. 10

27 What thou seest, write in a book, and send it unto the seven churches which are in Asia.

Revelation ch. 1, v. 11

28 Being turned, I saw seven golden candlesticks.

Revelation ch. 1, v. 12

29 His head and his hairs were white like wool, as white as snow; and his eyes were as a flame of fire;
And his feet like unto fine brass, as if they burned in a furnace; and his voice as the sound of many waters.
And he had in his right hand seven stars: and out of his mouth went a sharp two-edged sword: and his countenance was as the sun shineth in his strength.
And when I saw him, I fell at his feet as dead.

Revelation ch. 1, v. 14

30 I am he that liveth, and was dead; and, behold, I am alive for evermore, Amen; and have the keys of hell and of death.

Revelation ch. 1, v. 18

1 I have somewhat against thee, because thou hast left thy first love.
Revelation ch. 2, v. 4

2 Be thou faithful unto death, and I will give thee a crown of life.
Revelation ch. 2, v. 10

3 I will not blot out his name out of the book of life.
Revelation ch. 3, v. 5

4 I will write upon him my new name.
Revelation ch. 3, v. 12

5 I know thy works, that thou art neither cold nor hot: I would thou wert cold or hot.
So then, because thou art lukewarm, and neither cold nor hot, I will spew thee out of my mouth.
Revelation ch. 3, v. 15

6 Behold, I stand at the door, and knock.
Revelation ch. 3, v. 20

7 And he that sat was to look upon like a jasper and a sardine stone: and there was a rainbow round about the throne, in sight like unto an emerald.
Revelation ch. 4, v. 3

8 And before the throne there was a sea of glass like unto crystal: and in the midst of the throne, and round about the throne, were four beasts full of eyes before and behind.
Revelation ch. 4, v. 6

9 They were full of eyes within: and they rest not day and night, saying, Holy, holy, holy, Lord God Almighty, which was, and is, and is to come.
Revelation ch. 4, v. 8; see **Book of Common Prayer** 131:22, **Missal** 539:6

10 Thou hast created all things, and for thy pleasure they are and were created.
Revelation ch. 4, v. 11

11 Who is worthy to open the book, and to loose the seals thereof?
Revelation ch. 5, v. 2

12 The four beasts and four and twenty elders fell down before the Lamb, having every one of them harps, and golden vials full of odours, which are the prayers of saints.
Revelation ch. 5, v. 8

13 He went forth conquering, and to conquer.
Revelation ch. 6, v. 2

14 And I looked, and behold a pale horse: and his name that sat on him was Death.
Revelation ch. 6, v. 8

15 The kings of the earth, and the great men, and the rich men, and the chief captains, and the mighty men, and every bondman, and every free man, hid themselves in the dens and in the rocks of the mountains;
And said to the mountains and rocks, Fall on us, and hide us from the face of him that sitteth upon the throne, and from the wrath of the Lamb:
For the great day of his wrath is come; and who shall be able to stand?
Revelation ch. 6, v. 15

16 A great multitude, which no man could number, of all nations, and kindreds, and people, and tongues, stood before the throne, and before the Lamb.
Revelation ch. 7, v. 9

17 And all the angels stood round about the throne, and about the elders and the four beasts, and fell before the throne on their faces, and worshipped God.
Revelation ch. 7, v. 11

18 And one of the elders answered, saying unto me, What are these which are arrayed in white robes? and whence came they?
Revelation ch. 7, v. 13

19 These are they which came out of great tribulation, and have washed their robes, and made them white in the blood of the Lamb.
Revelation ch. 7, v. 14; see **Lindsay** 486:4

20 They shall hunger no more, neither thirst any more; neither shall the sun light on them, nor any heat.
Revelation ch. 7, v. 16

21 God shall wipe away all tears from their eyes.
Revelation ch. 7, v. 17

22 And when he had opened the seventh seal, there was silence in heaven about the space of half an hour.
Revelation ch. 8, v. 1

23 And the name of the star is called Wormwood.
Revelation ch. 8, v. 11

24 And in those days shall men seek death, and shall not find it; and shall desire to die, and death shall flee from them.
Revelation ch. 9, v. 6

25 And there were stings in their tails.
Revelation ch. 9, v. 10

26 It was in my mouth sweet as honey: and as soon as I had eaten it, my belly was bitter.
Revelation ch. 10, v. 10

27 And there appeared a great wonder in heaven; a woman clothed with the sun, and the moon under her feet, and upon her head a crown of twelve stars.
Revelation ch. 12, v. 1

28 And there was war in heaven: Michael and his angels fought against the dragon; and the dragon fought and his angels.
Revelation ch. 12, v. 7

29 Who is like unto the beast? who is able to make war with him?
Revelation ch. 13, v. 4

30 And that no man might buy or sell, save he that had the mark, or the name of the beast, or the number of his name.
Revelation ch. 13, v. 17

31 Let him that hath understanding count the number of the beast: for it is the number of a man; and his number is Six hundred threescore and six.
Revelation ch. 13, v. 18

1 And I heard a voice from heaven, as the voice of many waters, and as the voice of a great thunder: and I heard the voice of harpers harping with their harps:
And they sung as it were a new song . . . and no man could learn that song but the hundred and forty and four thousand, which were redeemed from the earth.
Revelation ch. 14, v. 2

2 Babylon is fallen, is fallen, that great city.
Revelation ch. 14, v. 8

3 And the smoke of their torment ascendeth up for ever and ever: and they have no rest day or night, who worship the beast and his image.
Revelation ch. 14, v. 11

4 Blessed are the dead which die in the Lord from henceforth: Yea, saith the Spirit, that they may rest from their labours; and their works do follow them.
Revelation ch. 14, v. 13

5 And I saw as it were a sea of glass mingled with fire.
Revelation ch. 15, v. 2

6 Behold, I come as a thief.
Revelation ch. 16, v. 15

7 And he gathered them together into a place called in the Hebrew tongue Armageddon.
Revelation ch. 16, v. 16

8 I will shew unto thee the judgement of the great whore that sitteth upon many waters.
Revelation ch. 17, v. 1

9 And upon her forehead was a name written, MYSTERY, BABYLON THE GREAT, THE MOTHER OF HARLOTS AND ABOMINATIONS OF THE EARTH.
Revelation ch. 17, v. 5

10 And a mighty angel took up a stone like a great millstone, and cast it into the sea, saying, Thus with violence shall that great city Babylon be thrown down, and shall be found no more at all.
Revelation ch. 18, v. 21

11 And I saw heaven opened, and behold a white horse; and he that sat upon him was called Faithful and True.
Revelation ch. 19, v. 11

12 And he hath on his vesture and on his thigh a name written, KING OF KINGS, AND LORD OF LORDS.
Revelation ch. 19, v. 16

13 And he laid hold on the dragon, that old serpent, which is the Devil, and Satan, and bound him a thousand years.
Revelation ch. 20, v. 2

14 And I saw a great white throne.
Revelation ch. 20, v. 11

15 And the sea gave up the dead which were in it; and death and hell delivered up the dead which were in them: and they were judged every man according to their works.
Revelation ch. 20, v. 13

16 And I saw a new heaven and a new earth: for the first heaven and the first earth were passed away; and there was no more sea.
And I John saw the holy city, new Jerusalem, coming down from God out of heaven, prepared as a bride adorned for her husband.
Revelation ch. 21, v. 1

17 And God shall wipe away all tears from their eyes; and there shall be no more death, neither sorrow, nor crying, neither shall there be any more pain: for the former things are passed away.
And he that sat upon the throne said, Behold, I make all things new. And he said unto me, Write: for these words are true and faithful.
Revelation ch. 21, v. 4; see **Pound** 608:14

18 I will give unto him that is athirst of the fountain of the water of life freely.
Revelation ch. 21, v. 6

19 The street of the city was pure gold.
Revelation ch. 21, v. 21

20 And the gates of it shall not be shut at all by day: for there shall be no night there.
Revelation ch. 21, v. 25

21 And he shewed me a pure river of water of life, clear as crystal, proceeding out of the throne of God and of the Lamb.
Revelation ch. 22, v. 1

22 And the leaves of the tree were for the healing of the nations.
Revelation ch. 22, v. 2

23 And, behold, I come quickly.
Revelation ch. 22, v. 12

24 For without are dogs, and sorcerers, and whoremongers, and murderers, and idolaters, and whosoever loveth and maketh a lie.
Revelation ch. 22, v. 15

25 Amen. Even so, come, Lord Jesus.
Revelation ch. 22, v. 20

VULGATE

26 *Dominus illuminatio mea, et salus mea, quem timebo?*
The Lord is the source of my light and my safety, so whom shall I fear?
Psalm 26, v. 1; see **Book of Common Prayer** 135:13, **Mottoes** 552:7

27 *Asperges me hyssopo, et mundabor; lavabis me, et super nivem dealbabor.*
You will sprinkle me with hyssop, and I shall be made clean; you will wash me and I shall be made whiter than snow.
Psalm 50, v. 9 (Psalm 51, v. 7 in the Authorized Version); see **Book of Common Prayer** 137:12

28 *Cantate Domino canticum novum, quia mirabilia fecit.*
Sing to the Lord a new song, because he has done marvellous things.
Psalm 97, v. 1 (Psalm 98, v. 1 in the Authorized Version); see **Book of Common Prayer** 140:13

1 *Jubilate Deo, omnis terra; servite Domino in laetitia.*

Sing joyfully to God, all the earth; serve the Lord with gladness.

Psalm 99, v. 2 (Psalm 100, v. 2 in the Authorized Version); see **Book of Common Prayer** 140:17

2 *Beatus vir qui timet Dominum, in mandatis ejus volet nimis!*

Happy is the man who fears the Lord, who is only too willing to follow his orders.

Psalm 111, v. 1 (Psalm 112, v. 1 in the Authorized Version)

3 *Non nobis, Domine, non nobis; sed nomini tuo da gloriam.*

Not unto us, Lord, not unto us; but to thy name give glory.

Psalm 113 (second part), v. 1 (Psalm 115, v. 1 in the Authorized Version); see **Book of Common Prayer** 142:3

4 *Laudate Dominum, omnes gentes; laudate eum, omnes populi.*

Praise the Lord, all nations; praise him, all people.

Psalm 116, v. 1 (Psalm 117, v. 1 in the Authorized Version)

5 *Nisi Dominus aedificaverit domum, in vanum laboraverunt qui aedificant eam.*
Nisi Dominus custodierit civitatem, frustra vigilat qui custodit eam.

Unless the Lord has built the house, its builders have laboured in vain. Unless the Lord guards the city, the watchman watches in vain.

Psalm 126, v. 1 (Psalm 127, v. 1 in the Authorized Version); see **Book of Common Prayer** 143:1, **Mottoes** 552:12

6 *De profundis clamavi ad te, Domine; Domine, exaudi vocem meam.*

Up from the depths I have cried to thee, Lord; Lord, hear my voice.

Psalm 129, v. 1 (Psalm 130, v. 1 in the Authorized Version); see **Book of Common Prayer** 143:6

7 *Vanitas vanitatum, dixit Ecclesiastes; vanitas vanitatum, et omnia vanitas.*

Vanity of vanities, said the preacher; vanity of vanities, and everything is vanity.

Ecclesiastes ch. 1, v. 2; see **Bible** 85:25, **Ménage** 521:12

8 *Rorate, coeli, desuper, et nubes pluant Justum; aperiatur terra, et germinet Salvatorem.*

Drop down dew, heavens, from above, and let the clouds rain down righteousness; let the earth be opened, and a saviour spring to life.

Isaiah ch. 45, v. 8

9 *Benedicite, omnia opera Domini, Domino; laudate et superexaltate eum in secula.*

Bless the Lord, all the works of the Lord; praise him and exalt him above all things for ever.

Daniel ch. 3, v. 57; see **Book of Common Prayer** 128:3

10 *Magnificat anima mea Dominum; Et exsultavit spiritus meus in Deo salutari meo.*

My soul doth magnify the Lord: and my spirit hath rejoiced in God my Saviour.

St Luke ch. 1, v. 46; see **Bible** 99:31

11 *Esurientes implevit bonis, et divites dimisit inanes.*

He hath filled the hungry with good things: and the rich he hath sent empty away.

St Luke ch. 1, v. 53; see **Bible** 99:32

12 *Nunc dimittis servum tuum, Domine, secundum verbum tuum in pace.*

Lord, now lettest thou thy servant depart in peace: according to thy word.

St Luke ch. 2, v. 29; see **Bible** 100:6

13 *Pax Vobis.*

Peace be unto you.

St Luke ch. 24, v. 36

14 *Quo vadis?*

Where are you going?

St John ch. 16, v. 5

15 *Ecce homo.*

Behold the man.

St John ch. 19, v. 5

16 *Consummatum est.*

It is achieved.

St John ch. 19, v. 30; see **Bible** 104:8

17 *Noli me tangere.*

Do not touch me.

St John ch. 20, v. 17; see **Bible** 104:13

18 *Sicut modo geniti infantes, rationabile, sine dolo lac concupiscite.*

After the fashion of newborn babes, desire the sincere milk of the word.

I Peter ch. 2, v. 2; see **Bible** 112:4

19 *Magna est veritas, et praevalet.*

Great is truth, and it prevails.

III Esdras ch. 4, v. 41; see **Bible** 92:16, **Brooks** 154:9

Isaac Bickerstaffe 1733–c.1808

Irish dramatist

20 Perhaps it was right to dissemble your love,
But—why did you kick me downstairs?

'An Expostulation' (1789); see **Carroll** 194:5

21 There was a jolly miller once,
Lived on the river Dee;
He worked and sang from morn till night;
No lark more blithe than he.

Love in a Village (a comic opera with music by Thomas Arne, 1762) act 1, sc. 2

22 And this the burthen of his song,
For ever used to be,
I care for nobody, not I,
If no one cares for me.

Love in a Village (1762) act 1, sc. 2

E. H. Bickersteth 1825–1906

English clergyman

23 Peace, perfect peace, in this dark world of sin?
The Blood of Jesus whispers peace within.

Songs in the House of Pilgrimage (1875) 'Peace, perfect peace'

Ambrose Bierce 1842–c.1914
American writer

1 ALLIANCE, *n*. In international politics, the union of two thieves who have their hands so deeply inserted in each other's pocket that they cannot separately plunder a third.
The Cynic's Word Book (1906)

2 APPLAUSE, *n*. The echo of a platitude.
The Cynic's Word Book (1906)

3 BATTLE, *n*. A method of untying with the teeth a political knot that would not yield to the tongue.
The Cynic's Word Book (1906)

4 CALAMITY, *n*. . . . Calamities are of two kinds: misfortune to ourselves, and good fortune to others.
The Cynic's Word Book (1906)

5 CONSERVATIVE, *n*. A statesman who is enamoured of existing evils, as distinguished from the Liberal, who wishes to replace them with others.
The Cynic's Word Book (1906)

6 HISTORY, *n*. An account, mostly false, of events, mostly unimportant, which are brought about by rulers, mostly knaves, and soldiers, mostly fools.
The Cynic's Word Book (1906)

7 PEACE, *n*. In international affairs, a period of cheating between two periods of fighting.
The Devil's Dictionary (1911)

8 PREJUDICE, *n*. A vagrant opinion without visible means of support.
The Devil's Dictionary (1911)

9 SAINT, *n*. A dead sinner revised and edited.
The Devil's Dictionary (1911)

Roger Bigod, Earl of Norfolk 1245–1306
English peer, Marshal of England, 1270–1301

10 EDWARD I: By God, earl, you shall either go or hang.
BIGOD: By God, O King, I will neither go nor hang!
on the King's requiring the barons to invade France through Gascony while he himself took command in Flanders, 24 February 1297
Harry Rothwell (ed.) *The Chronicle of Walter of Guisbrough* Camden Society Series 3, vol. 89 (1957)

Steve Biko 1946–77
South African anti-apartheid campaigner

11 The liberal must understand that the days of the Noble Savage are gone; that the blacks do not need a go-between in this struggle for their own emancipation. No true liberal should feel any resentment at the growth of black consciousness. Rather, all true liberals should realize that the place for their fight for justice is within their white society. The liberals must realize that they themselves are oppressed if they are true liberals and therefore they must fight for their own freedom and not that of the nebulous 'they' with whom they can hardly claim identification. The liberal must apply himself with absolute dedication to the idea of educating his white brothers.
'Black Souls in White Skins?' (written 1970), in *Steve Biko—I Write What I Like* (1978); see **Dryden** 287:30

Josh Billings (Henry Wheeler Shaw) 1818–85
American humorist

12 Love iz like the meazles; we kant have it bad but onst, and the latter in life we hav it the tuffer it goes with us.
Josh Billings' Wit and Humour (1874)

Maeve Binchy 1940–
Irish novelist

13 It's not perfect, but to me on balance Right Now is a lot better than the Good Old Days.
in *Irish Times* 15 November 1997

Laurence Binyon 1869–1943
English poet

14 They shall grow not old, as we that are left grow old.
Age shall not weary them, nor the years condemn.
At the going down of the sun and in the morning
We will remember them.
regularly recited as part of the ritual for Remembrance Day parades
'For the Fallen' (1914)

15 Now is the time for the burning of the leaves.
'The Ruins' (1942)

Bion c.325–c.255 BC
Greek popular philosopher, born in Olbia, Scythia

16 Boys throw stones at frogs for fun, but the frogs don't die for 'fun', but in sober earnest.
Plutarch *Moralia*

Nigel Birch 1906–81
British Conservative politician

17 My God! They've shot our fox!
on hearing of the resignation of Hugh Dalton, Labour Chancellor of the Exchequer, after the leak of Budget secrets
comment, 13 November 1947; Harold Macmillan *Tides of Fortune* (1969) ch. 3

Lord Birkenhead see F. E. Smith

Earle Birney 1904–
Canadian poet

18 We French, we English, never lost our civil war,
endure it still, a bloodless civil bore;
no wounded lying about, no Whitman wanted.
It's only by our lack of ghosts we're haunted.
'Can.Lit.' (1962)

Augustine Birrell 1850–1933

British essayist

1 That great dust-heap called 'history'.
  Obiter Dicta (1884) 'Carlyle'; see **Trotsky** 800:19

Harrison Birtwistle 1934–

English composer and clarinettist

2 You can't stop. Composing's not voluntary, you know. There's no choice, you're not free. You're landed with an idea and you have responsibility to that idea.
  in *Observer* 14 April 1996 'Sayings of the Week'

Billy Bishop 1894–1956

Canadian fighter pilot

3 This flying is the most wonderful invention. A man ceases to be human up there. He feels that nothing is impossible.
  letter to his parents from Netheravon, England, 1 September 1915; W. Arthur Bishop *The Courage of the Early Morning* (1965)

Elizabeth Bishop 1911–79

American poet

4 The state with the prettiest name,
  the state that floats in brackish water,
  held together by mangrove roots.
  'Florida' (1946)

5 This iceberg cuts its facets from within.
  Like jewelry from a grave
  it saves itself perpetually and adorns
  only itself.
  'The Imaginary Iceberg' (1946)

6 Topography displays no favourites; North's as
  near as West.
  More delicate than the historians' are the map-
  makers' colours.
  'The Map' (1946)

7 The armoured cars of dreams, contrived to let
  us do
  so many a dangerous thing.
  'Sleeping Standing Up' (1946)

8 Lullaby.
  Let nations rage,
  let nations fall.
  The shadow of the crib makes an enormous cage
  upon the wall.
  'Songs for a Coloured Singer' (1946)

9 If she speaks of a chair you can practically sit on
  it.
  of Marianne **Moore**
  notebook, *c.*1934/5; D. Kalstone *Becoming a Poet* (1989)

10 I am overcome by my own amazing sloth . . . Can you please forgive me and believe that it is really because I want to do something well that I don't do it at all?
  letter to Marianne Moore, 25 February 1937

11 I am sorry for people who can't write letters. But I suspect also that you and I . . . love to write them

because it's kind of like working without really doing it.
  letter to Kit and Ilse Barker, 5 September 1953

Otto von Bismarck 1815–98

German statesman
on Bismarck: see **Taylor** 774:13, **Tenniel** 775:14

12 If the Princess can leave the Englishwoman at home and become a Prussian, then she may be a blessing to the country.
  on the marriage of Victoria, Princess Royal, to Prince Frederick William of Prussia
  letter, *c.*1857; Hannah Pakula *An Uncommon Woman: The Empress Frederick* (1996)

13 The secret of politics? Make a good treaty with Russia.
  in 1863, when first in power
  A. J. P. Taylor *Bismarck* (1955) ch. 7

14 Politics is the art of the possible.
  in conversation with Meyer von Waldeck, 11 August 1867, in H. Amelung *Bismarck-Worte* (1918); see **Butler** 175:18, **Galbraith** 338:7, **Medawar** 520:5

15 Let us . . . put Germany in the saddle! She will know well enough how to ride!
  in 1867; Alan Palmer *Bismarck* (1976) ch. 9

16 We will not go to Canossa.
  during his quarrel with Pope Pius IX regarding papal authority over German subjects, in allusion to the Emperor Henry IV's submission to Pope Gregory VII at Canossa in Modena in 1077
  speech to the Reichstag, 14 May 1872

17 Not worth the healthy bones of a single Pomeranian grenadier.
  of possible German involvement in the Balkans; see **Harris** 374:1
  speech to the Reichstag, 5 December 1876

18 Whoever speaks of Europe is wrong, [it is] a geographical concept.
  marginal note on a letter from the Russian Chancellor Gorchakov, November 1876; see **Metternich** 523:11

19 I do not regard the procuring of peace as a matter in which we should play the role of arbiter between different opinions . . . more that of an honest broker who really wants to press the business forward.
  speech to the Reichstag, 19 February 1878, in Ludwig Hahn (ed.) *Fürst Bismarck. Sein politisches Leben und Wirken* vol. 3 (1881)

20 This policy cannot succeed through speeches, and shooting-matches, and songs; it can only be carried out through blood and iron.
  speech in the Prussian House of Deputies, 28 January 1886, in *Fürst Bismarck als Redner. Vollständige Sammlung der parlamentarischen Reden* (1885–91) vol. 15; in a speech on 30 September 1862, Bismarck had used the form 'Iron and blood' (in *Fürst Bismarck. Sein politisches Leben und Wirken* (1878) vol. 4)

21 I am bored; the great things are done. The German *Reich* is made.
  *c.*1888; A. J. P. Taylor *Bismarck* (1955) ch. 4

1 Jena came twenty years after the death of Frederick the Great; the crash will come twenty years after my departure if things go on like this.
*to Kaiser **Wilhelm II** at their last meeting in 1895*
A. J. P. Taylor *Bismarck* (1955) ch. 10

2 If there is ever another war in Europe, it will come out of some damned silly thing in the Balkans.
attributed by Herr Ballen and quoted by Winston S. **Churchill** in the House of Commons, 16 August 1945

3 A lath of wood painted to look like iron.
*describing Lord **Salisbury***
attributed, but vigorously denied by Sidney Whitman in *Personal Reminiscences of Prince Bismarck* (1902) ch. 14

4 The old Jew! That is the man.
*of **Disraeli** at the Congress of Berlin*
attributed

5 A statesman . . . must wait until he hears the steps of God sounding through events; then leap up and grasp the hem of his garment.
A. J. P. Taylor *Bismarck* (1955) ch. 5

James Black 1924-
British analytical pharmacologist; winner of the Nobel prize for medicine

6 In the culture I grew up in you did your work and you did not put your arm around it to stop other people from looking—you took the earliest possible opportunity to make knowledge available.
on modern scientific research
in *Daily Telegraph* 11 December 1995

Valentine Blacker 1728-1823
Irish soldier

7 Put your trust in God, my boys, and keep your powder dry.
*often attributed to Oliver **Cromwell** himself*
'Oliver's Advice' in E. Hayes *Ballads of Ireland* (1856) vol. I; see **Proverbs** 629:49

William Blackstone 1723-80
English jurist

8 Man was formed for society.
Commentaries on the Laws of England (1765) introduction, sect. 2; see **Aristotle** 25:26

9 The king never dies.
Commentaries on the Laws of England (1765) bk. I, ch. 7

10 The royal navy of England hath ever been its greatest defence and ornament; it is its ancient and natural strength; the floating bulwark of the island.
Commentaries on the Laws of England (1765) bk. I, ch. 13; see **Coventry** 244:14

11 That the king can do no wrong, is a necessary and fundamental principle of the English constitution.
Commentaries on the Laws of England (1765) bk. 3, ch. 17

12 It is better that ten guilty persons escape than one innocent suffer.
Commentaries on the Laws of England (1765) bk. 4, ch. 27

Cherie Blair 1954-
British lawyer

13 I am not Superwoman. The reality of my daily life is that I'm juggling a lot of balls in the air . . . and sometimes some of the balls get dropped.
personal statement, 10 December 2002; in *The Times* 11 December 2002

Robert Blair 1699-1746
Scottish poet

14 Oft, in the lone church-yard at night I've seen,
The schoolboy with a satchel in his hand,
Whistling aloud to keep his courage up . . .
Sudden he starts! and hears, or thinks he hears,
The sound of something purring at his heels;
Full fast he flies, and dares not look behind him,
Till out of breath, he overtakes his fellows.
The Grave (1743) l. 57; see **Coleridge** 233:7

Tony Blair 1953-
British Labour statesman; Prime Minister since 1997
*on Blair: see **Short** 735:8*

15 Labour is the party of law and order in Britain today. Tough on crime and tough on the causes of crime.
as Shadow Home Secretary
speech at the Labour Party Conference, 30 September 1993

16 Ask me my three main priorities for Government, and I tell you: education, education and education.
speech at the Labour Party Conference, 1 October 1996; see **Michelet** 524:5

17 We are not the masters. The people are the masters. We are the servants of the people . . . What the electorate gives, the electorate can take away.
*addressing Labour MPs on the first day of the new Parliament, 7 May 1997; see **Burke** 168:22*
in *Guardian* 8 May 1997

18 She was the People's Princess, and that is how she will stay . . . in our hearts and in our memories forever.
*on hearing of the death of **Diana**, Princess of Wales, 31 August 1997*
in *The Times* 1 September 1997

19 This is not a time for sound bites.
of the final stage of the Northern Irish negotiations
Belfast, 8 April 1998, in *Irish Times* 11 April 1998

20 This is not a battle betweeen the United States and terrorism, but between the free and democratic world and terrorism. We therefore here in Britain stand shoulder to shoulder with our American friends in this hour of tragedy and we, like them, will not rest until this evil is driven from our world.
in Downing Street, London, 11 September 2001

21 The state of Africa is a scar on the conscience of the world.
speech to Labour Party Conference, 2 October 2001

1 PRESENTER: [Is Britain] prepared to send troops to commit themselves, to pay the blood price?
TONY BLAIR: Yes. What is important though is that at moments of crisis they [the USA] . . . need to know, 'Are you prepared to commit, are you prepared to be there when the shooting starts?'
interview on BBC2 *Hotline to the President* 8 September 2002

2 This is not the time to falter.
speech in the House of Commons, 18 March 2003

Eubie Blake (James Hubert Blake) 1883–1983
American ragtime pianist

3 If I'd known I was gonna live this long, I'd have taken better care of myself.
on reaching the age of 100
in *Observer* 13 February 1983 'Sayings of the Week'

William Blake 1757–1827
English poet
on Blake: see **Benét** 66:15

4 When Sir Joshua Reynolds died
All Nature was degraded:
The King dropped a tear into the Queen's ear;
And all his pictures faded.
Annotations to The Works of Sir Joshua Reynolds 'When Sir Joshua Reynolds died' (c.1808)

5 To see a world in a grain of sand
And a heaven in a wild flower,
Hold infinity in the palm of your hand
And eternity in an hour.
'Auguries of Innocence' (c.1803) l. 1

6 A robin red breast in a cage
Puts all Heaven in a rage.
'Auguries of Innocence' (c.1803) l. 5

7 A dog starved at his master's gate
Predicts the ruin of the State.
A horse misused upon the road
Calls to Heaven for human blood.
Each outcry of the hunted hare
A fibre from the brain does tear.
A skylark wounded in the wing,
A cherubim does cease to sing.
'Auguries of Innocence' (c.1803) l. 9

8 He who shall hurt the little wren
Shall never be beloved by men
He who the ox to wrath has moved
Shall never be by woman loved.
'Auguries of Innocence' (c.1803) l. 29

9 The caterpillar on the leaf
Repeats to thee thy mother's grief.
Kill not the moth nor butterfly,
For the Last Judgement draweth nigh.
'Auguries of Innocence' (c.1803) l. 37

10 A truth that's told with bad intent
Beats all the lies you can invent.
'Auguries of Innocence' (c.1803) l. 53

11 Man was made for joy and woe;
And when this we rightly know
Thro' the world we safely go.
'Auguries of Innocence' (c.1803) l. 56

12 The strongest poison ever known
Came from Caesar's laurel crown.
'Auguries of Innocence' (c.1803) l. 97

13 If the Sun and Moon should doubt,
They'd immediately go out.
To be in a passion you good may do,
But no good if a passion is in you.
'Auguries of Innocence' (c.1803) l. 109

14 The whore and gambler, by the State
Licensed, build that nation's fate.
The harlot's cry from street to street
Shall weave old England's winding sheet.
'Auguries of Innocence' (c.1803) l. 113

15 Every night and every morn
Some to misery are born,
Every morn and every night
Some are born to sweet delight.
Some are born to sweet delight,
Some are born to endless night.
'Auguries of Innocence' (c.1803) l. 119

16 God appears and God is Light
To those poor souls who dwell in night
But does a human form display
To those who dwell in realms of day.
'Auguries of Innocence' (c.1803) l. 129

17 Does the eagle know what is in the pit?
Or wilt thou go ask the mole:
Can wisdom be put in a silver rod?
Or love in a golden bowl?
The Book of Thel (1789) plate i 'Thel's Motto'

18   Everything that lives,
Lives not alone, nor for itself.
The Book of Thel (1789) plate 3, l. 26

19 The Vision of Christ that thou dost see
Is my vision's greatest enemy;
Thine has a great hook nose like thine,
Mine has a snub nose like to mine.
The Everlasting Gospel (c.1818) (a) l. 1

20 Both read the Bible day and night,
But thou read'st black where I read white.
The Everlasting Gospel (c.1818) (a) l. 13

21 Was Jesus gentle, or did he
Give any marks of gentility?
When twelve years old he ran away
And left his parents in dismay.
The Everlasting Gospel (c.1818) (b) l. 1

22 Was Jesus humble or did he
Give any proofs of humility
Boast of high things with humble tone
And give with charity a stone.
The Everlasting Gospel (c.1818) (d) l. 1

23 Humility is only doubt
And does the sun and moon blot out
Rooting over with thorns and stems
The buried soul and all its gems
This life's dim windows of the soul
Distorts the heavens from pole to pole
And leads you to believe a lie

When you see with, not through, the eye.
The Everlasting Gospel (c.1818) (d) l. 99

1 Was Jesus chaste? or did he
Give any lessons of chastity?
The morning blushed fiery red:
Mary was found in adulterous bed.
The Everlasting Gospel (c.1818) (e) l. 1

2 Jesus was sitting in Moses' chair,
They brought the trembling woman there.
Moses commands she be stoned to death,
What was the sound of Jesus breath?
He laid His hand on Moses' Law:
The ancient Heavens, in silent awe
Writ with curses from pole to pole,
All away began to roll.
The Everlasting Gospel (c.1818) (e) l. 7

3 I am sure this Jesus will not do
Either for Englishman or Jew.
The Everlasting Gospel (c.1818) (f) l. 1

4 Mutual Forgiveness of each vice,
Such are the Gates of Paradise.
For the Sexes: The Gates of Paradise 'Mutual Forgiveness of
each Vice' [prologue]

5 Truly, my Satan, thou art but a dunce,
And dost not know the garment from the man;
Every harlot was a virgin once,
Nor can'st thou ever change Kate into Nan.

Tho' thou art worshipped by the names divine
Of Jesus and Jehovah, thou art still
The Son of Morn in weary Night's decline,
The lost traveller's dream under the hill.
For the Sexes: The Gates of Paradise 'To the Accuser who is
The God of This World' [epilogue]

6 Wisdom is sold in the desolate market where none
come to buy.
The Four Zoas 'Night the Second'

7 I must create a system, or be enslaved by another
man's.
I will not reason and compare: my business is to
create.
Jerusalem (1815) 'Chapter 1' (plate 10, l. 20)

8   Near mournful
Ever weeping Paddington.
Jerusalem (1815) 'Chapter 1' (plate 12, l. 27)

9 The fields from Islington to Marybone,
To Primrose Hill and Saint John's Wood
Were builded over with pillars of gold;
And there Jerusalem's pillars stood.
Jerusalem (1815) 'To the Jews' (plate 27, l. 1) "The fields
from Islington to Marybone"

10 Pancras and Kentish-town repose
Among her golden pillars high
Among her golden arches which
Shine upon the starry sky.
Jerusalem (1815) 'To the Jews' (plate 27, l. 9) "The fields
from Islington to Marybone"

11 For a tear is an intellectual thing;
And a sigh is the sword of an Angel King
And the bitter groan of the martyr's woe

Is an arrow from the Almighty's bow!
Jerusalem (1815) 'To the Deists' (plate 52, l. 25) "I saw a
Monk of Charlemaine"

12 He who would do good to another, must do it in
minute particulars
General good is the plea of the scoundrel,
hypocrite and flatterer:
For Art and Science cannot exist but in minutely
organized particulars.
Jerusalem (1815) 'Chapter 3' (plate 55, l. 60)

13 I give you the end of a golden string;
Only wind it into a ball:
It will lead you in at Heaven's gate,
Built in Jerusalem's wall.
Jerusalem (1815) 'To the Christians' (plate 77) "I give you
the end of a golden string"

14 England! awake! awake! awake!
Jerusalem thy sister calls!
Why wilt thou sleep the sleep of death,
And close her from thy ancient walls?
Jerusalem (1815) 'To the Christians' (plate 77) "England!
awake! . . . "

15 And now the time returns again:
Our souls exult, and London's towers,
Receive the Lamb of God to dwell
In England's green and pleasant bowers.
Jerusalem (1815) 'To the Christians' (plate 77)

16 I care not whether a man is good or evil; all that I
care
Is whether he is a wise man or a fool. Go! put off
holiness
And put on Intellect.
Jerusalem (1815) 'Chapter 4' (plate 91, l. 54)

17   May God us keep
From Single vision and Newton's sleep!
'Letter to Thomas Butts, 22 November 1802'

18 O why was I born with a different face?
Why was I not born like the rest of my race?
'Letter to Thomas Butts, 16 August 1803'

19 Without contraries is no progression. Attraction
and repulsion, reason and energy, love and hate,
are necessary to human existence.
The Marriage of Heaven and Hell (1790–3) 'The Argument'

20 Energy is Eternal Delight.
The Marriage of Heaven and Hell (1790–3) 'The voice of the
Devil'

21 The reason Milton wrote in fetters when he wrote
of Angels and God, and at liberty when of Devils
and Hell, is because he was a true Poet, and of the
Devil's party without knowing it.
The Marriage of Heaven and Hell (1790–3) 'The voice of the
Devil' (note)

22 The road of excess leads to the palace of wisdom.
The Marriage of Heaven and Hell (1790–3) 'Proverbs of Hell'

23 Prudence is a rich, ugly, old maid courted by
Incapacity.
The Marriage of Heaven and Hell (1790–3) 'Proverbs of Hell'

24 He who desires but acts not, breeds pestilence.
The Marriage of Heaven and Hell (1790–3) 'Proverbs of Hell'

25 A fool sees not the same tree that a wise man sees.
The Marriage of Heaven and Hell (1790–3) 'Proverbs of Hell'

1 Eternity is in love with the productions of time.

The Marriage of Heaven and Hell (1790–3) 'Proverbs of Hell'

2 Bring out number weight and measure in a year of dearth.

The Marriage of Heaven and Hell (1790–3) 'Proverbs of Hell'

3 If the fool would persist in his folly he would become wise.

The Marriage of Heaven and Hell (1790–3) 'Proverbs of Hell'

4 Prisons are built with stones of Law, brothels with bricks of Religion.

The Marriage of Heaven and Hell (1790–3) 'Proverbs of Hell'

5 The pride of the peacock is the glory of God.
The lust of the goat is the bounty of God.
The wrath of the lion is the wisdom of God.
The nakedness of woman is the work of God.

The Marriage of Heaven and Hell (1790–3) 'Proverbs of Hell'

6 The tygers of wrath are wiser than the horses of instruction.

The Marriage of Heaven and Hell (1790–3) 'Proverbs of Hell'

7 Damn braces: Bless relaxes.

The Marriage of Heaven and Hell (1790–3) 'Proverbs of Hell'

8 Exuberance is beauty.

The Marriage of Heaven and Hell (1790–3) 'Proverbs of Hell'

9 Sooner murder an infant in its cradle than nurse unacted desires.

The Marriage of Heaven and Hell (1790–3) 'Proverbs of Hell'

10 Truth can never be told so as to be understood, and not be believed.

The Marriage of Heaven and Hell (1790–3) 'Proverbs of Hell'

11 How do you know but every bird that cuts the airy way
Is an immense world of delight, closed by your senses five?

The Marriage of Heaven and Hell (1790–3) 'A Memorable Fancy' plate 7

12 Then I asked: 'Does a firm persuasion that a thing is so, make it so?'
He replied: 'All Poets believe that it does, and in ages of imagination this firm persuasion removed mountains; but many are not capable of a firm persuasion of anything.'

The Marriage of Heaven and Hell (1790–3) 'A Memorable Fancy' plates 12–13

13 If the doors of perception were cleansed everything would appear to man as it is, infinite.

The Marriage of Heaven and Hell (1790–3) 'A Memorable Fancy' plate 14

14 I was in a printing house in Hell, and saw the method in which knowledge is transmitted from generation to generation.

The Marriage of Heaven and Hell (1790–3) 'A Memorable Fancy' plates 15–17

15 And did those feet in ancient time
Walk upon England's mountains green?
And was the holy Lamb of God
On England's pleasant pastures seen?

And did the Countenance Divine
Shine forth upon our clouded hills?
And was Jerusalem builded here

Among these dark Satanic mills?

Bring me my bow of burning gold:
Bring me my arrows of desire:
Bring me my spear: O clouds, unfold!
Bring me my chariot of fire.

I will not cease from mental fight,
Nor shall my sword sleep in my hand,
Till we have built Jerusalem,
In England's green and pleasant land.

Milton (1804–10) preface 'And did those feet in ancient time'

16 Mock on, mock on Voltaire, Rousseau:
Mock on, mock on: tis all in vain!
You throw the sand against the wind,
And the wind blows it back again.

MS Note-Book

17 The atoms of Democritus
And Newton's particles of light
Are sands upon the Red sea shore,
Where Israel's tents do shine so bright.

MS Note-Book

18 He has observed the golden rule
Till he's become the golden fool.

MS Note-Book

19 To forgive enemies H— does pretend,
Who never in his life forgave a friend.

MS Note-Book

20 The errors of a wise man make your rule
Rather than the perfections of a fool.

MS Note-Book

21 Great things are done when men and mountains meet;
This is not done by jostling in the street.

MS Note-Book

22 He who binds to himself a joy
Doth the winged life destroy;
But he who kisses the joy as it flies
Lives in Eternity's sunrise.

MS Note-Book 'Several Questions Answered'—"He who binds to himself a joy"

23 What is it men in women do require?
The lineaments of gratified desire.
What is it women do in men require?
The lineaments of gratified desire.

MS Note-Book 'Several Questions Answered'—"What is it men in women do require"

24 The sword sung on the barren heath,
The sickle in the fruitful field:
The sword he sung a song of death,
But could not make the sickle yield.

MS Note-Book

25 Never pain to tell thy love
Love that never told can be;
For the gentle wind does move
Silently, invisibly.

MS Note-Book

26 Piping down the valleys wild,
Piping songs of pleasant glee,
On a cloud I saw a child,

And he laughing said to me.
'Pipe a song about a Lamb!'
So I piped with merry cheer.
'Piper pipe that song again;'
So I piped: he wept to hear.
Songs of Innocence (1789) introduction

1 When my mother died I was very young,
And my father sold me while yet my tongue
Could scarcely cry ''weep! 'weep! 'weep! 'weep!''
So your chimneys I sweep, and in soot I sleep.
Songs of Innocence (1789) 'The Chimney Sweeper'

2 To Mercy, Pity, Peace, and Love,
All pray in their distress.
Songs of Innocence (1789) 'The Divine Image'

3 For Mercy has a human heart,
Pity a human face,
And Love, the human form divine,
And Peace, the human dress.
Songs of Innocence (1789) 'The Divine Image'; see **Blake**
122:22

4 Then cherish pity, lest you drive an angel from
your door.
Songs of Innocence (1789) 'Holy Thursday'

5 Little Lamb who made thee?
Dost thou know who made thee?
Gave thee life and bid thee feed.
By the stream and o'er the mead;
Gave thee clothing of delight,
Softest clothing woolly bright;
Gave thee such a tender voice,
Making all the vales rejoice!
Songs of Innocence (1789) 'The Lamb'

6 My mother bore me in the southern wild,
And I am black, but O! my soul is white;
White as an angel is the English child:
But I am black as if bereaved of light.
Songs of Innocence (1789) 'The Little Black Boy'

7 When the voices of children are heard on the
green
And laughing is heard on the hill.
Songs of Innocence (1789) 'Nurse's Song'

8 Can I see another's woe,
And not be in sorrow too?
Can I see another's grief,
And not seek for kind relief?
Songs of Innocence (1789) 'On Another's Sorrow'

9 Hear the voice of the Bard!
Who present, past, and future, sees.
Songs of Experience (1794) introduction

10 Ah, Sun-flower! weary of time,
Who countest the steps of the Sun;
Seeking after that sweet golden clime
Where the traveller's journey is done.

Where the Youth pined away with desire,
And the pale Virgin shrouded in snow:
Arise from their graves and aspire,
Where my Sun-flower wishes to go.
Songs of Experience (1794) 'Ah, Sun-flower!'

11 Love seeketh not itself to please,
Nor for itself hath any care;

But for another gives its ease,
And builds a Heaven in Hell's despair.
Songs of Experience (1794) 'The Clod and the Pebble'

12 Love seeketh only Self to please,
To bind another to its delight,
Joys in another's loss of ease,
And builds a Hell in Heaven's despite.
Songs of Experience (1794) 'The Clod and the Pebble'

13 Am not I
A fly like thee?
Or art not thou
A man like me?
Songs of Experience (1794) 'The Fly'

14 My mother groaned! my father wept.
Into the dangerous world I leapt:
Helpless, naked, piping loud;
Like a fiend hid in a cloud.
Songs of Experience (1794) 'Infant Sorrow'

15 Children of the future age,
Reading this indignant page:
Know that in a former time
Love! sweet love! was thought a crime.
Songs of Experience (1794) 'A Little Girl Lost'

16 I was angry with my friend;
I told my wrath, my wrath did end.
I was angry with my foe:
I told it not, my wrath did grow.
Songs of Experience (1794) 'A Poison Tree'

17 In the morning glad I see,
My foe outstretched beneath the tree
Songs of Experience (1794) 'A Poison Tree'

18 O Rose, thou art sick!
The invisible worm
That flies in the night,
In the howling storm:

Has found out thy bed
Of crimson joy:
And his dark secret love
Does thy life destroy.
Songs of Experience (1794) 'The Sick Rose'

19 Tyger Tyger, burning bright,
In the forests of the night;
What immortal hand or eye,
Could frame thy fearful symmetry?
Songs of Experience (1794) 'The Tiger'

20 What the hand dare seize the fire?

And what shoulder, and what art,
Could twist the sinews of thy heart?
And when thy heart began to beat,
What dread hand? and what dread feet?
Songs of Experience (1794) 'The Tiger'

21 When the stars threw down their spears
And watered heaven with their tears:
Did he smile his work to see?
Did he who made the Lamb make thee?
Songs of Experience (1794) 'The Tiger'

22 Cruelty has a human heart,
And Jealousy a human face;
Terror the human form divine,

And Secrecy the human dress.
'A Divine Image'; etched but not included in *Songs of Experience* (1794); see **Blake** 122:3

1 Vision or Imagination is a Representation of what Eternally Exists, Really and Unchangeably.
A Vision of the Last Judgement (1810) in *MS Note-Book*

2 What it will be questioned when the sun rises do you not see a round disc of fire somewhat like a guinea O no no I see an innumerable company of the heavenly host crying Holy, Holy, Holy is the Lord God Almighty.
A Vision of the Last Judgement (1810) in *MS Note-Book*; see **Bible** 113:9

3 A tree filled with angels, bright wings bespangling every bough like stars.
Blake's first vision on Peckham Rye as a boy; see **Benét** 66:15
Alexander Gilchrist *The Life of William Blake* (1863)

Susanna Blamire 1747–94
English poet

4 I've gotten a rock, I've gotten a reel,
I've gotten a wee bit spinning-wheel;
An' by the whirling rim I've found
How the weary, weary warl goes round.
'I've Gotten a Rock, I've Gotten a Reel' (*c*.1790) l. 1

5 Should we miss but a tree where we used to be playing,
Or find the wood cut where we sauntered a-Maying,—
If the yew-seat's away, or the ivy's a-wanting,
We hate the fine lawn and the new-fashioned planting.
Each thing called improvement seems blackened with crimes,
If it tears up one record of blissful old times.
'When Home We Return' (*c*.1790) l. 7

Jean Joseph Louis Blanc 1811–82
French utopian socialist

6 In the Saint-Simonian doctrine, the problem of the distribution of benefits is resolved by this famous saying: *To each according to his ability; to each ability according to its fruits.*
Blanc cites Saint-Simon in order to disagree with his ideas
Organisation du travail (1841 ed.); see **Marx** 516:13, **Morelly** 549:1

Lesley Blanch 1907–
British writer

7 She was an Amazon. Her whole life was spent riding at breakneck speed towards the wilder shores of love.
of Jane Digby El Mezrab (1807–81)
The Wilder Shores of Love (1954) pt. 2, ch. 1

Danny Blanchflower 1926–93
English footballer

8 The great fallacy is that the game is first and last about winning. It is nothing of the kind. The game

is about glory, it is about doing things in style and with a flourish, about going out and beating the lot, not waiting for them to die of boredom.
attributed, 1972

Arthur Bliss 1891–1975
English composer

9 What is called the serenity of age is only perhaps a euphemism for the fading power to feel the sudden shock of joy or sorrow.
As I Remember (1970) foreword

Philip Paul Bliss 1838–76
American evangelist

10 Hold the fort, for I am coming.
suggested by a flag message from General **Sherman**; see **Sherman** 734:14
Gospel Hymns and Sacred Songs (1875) no. 14

Hans Blix 1928–
Swedish diplomat

11 We have not found any smoking guns.
of weapons inspections in Iraq
in *Newsweek* 20 January 2003

12 You can put up a sign on the door, 'beware of the dog', without having a dog.
in *Guardian* (online edition) 18 September 2003

Karen Blixen see Isak Dinesen

Alexander Blok 1880–1921
Russian poet

13 When rowan leaves are dank and rusting
And rowan berries red as blood,
When in my palm the hangman's thrusting
The final nail with bony thud . . .
Then, through the blood and weeping, stretches
My dying sight to space remote;
I see upon the river's reaches
Christ sailing to me in a boat.
'Autumn Love' (1907) (translated by Maurice Bowra)

14 The wind plays up; snow flutters down.
Twelve men are marching through the town.
'The Twelve' (1918) (translated by Jon Stallworthy and Peter France)

15 Caps tilted, fag drooping, every one
looks like a jailbird on the run.
'The Twelve' (1918) (translated by Jon Stallworthy and Peter France)

16 So they march with sovereign tread
Behind them limps the hungry dog,
and wrapped in wild snow at their head
carrying a blood-red flag—
soft-footed where the blizzard swirls,
invulnerable where bullets crossed—
crowned with a crown of snowflake pearls,
a flowery diadem of frost,
ahead of them goes Jesus Christ.
'The Twelve' (1918) (translated by Jon Stallworthy and Peter France)

Reginald Blomfield 1856–1942

English architect

1 Architecture should be at the head of the arts, not at the foot of the professions.
   R. N. Shaw and T. G. Jackson (eds.) *Architecture* (1892)

Judy Blume 1938–

American writer

2 Are you there God? It's me, Margaret.
   I just told my mother I want a bra.
   Please help me grow God. You know where.
   I want to be like everyone else.
   Are You There God? It's Me, Margaret (1970)

Edmund Blunden 1896–1974

English poet

3 All things they have in common being so poor,
   And their one fear, Death's shadow at the door.
   'Almswomen' (1920)

4 I am for the woods against the world,
   But are the woods for me?
   'The Kiss' (1931)

5 I have been young, and now am not too old;
   And I have seen the righteous forsaken,
   His health, his honour and his quality taken.
   This is not what we were formerly told.
   'Report on Experience' (1929); see **Book of Common Prayer** 136:1

6 This was my country and it may be yet,
   But something flew between me and the sun.
   'The Resignation' (1928)

David Blunkett 1947–

British Labour politician, Minister for Education, 1997–2001; Home Secretary from 2001

7 I don't use or recognize the term 'bog standard' but what I do recognize is the critical importance of honesty about what some children, in some schools, have had to put up with over the years.
   at Labour spring conference, 17 February 2001; see **Campbell** 186:18

8 They should go back home and re-create their countries which we have freed from tyranny, whether it is Kosovo or now Afghanistan. I have no sympathy whatsoever with young men in their twenties who do not.
   on asylum seekers
   in *Observer* 22 September 2002

Wilfrid Scawen Blunt 1840–1922

English poet

9 To the Grafton Gallery to look at . . . the Post-Impressionist pictures sent over from Paris . . . The drawing is on the level of that of an untaught child of seven or eight years old, the sense of colour that of a tea-tray painter, the method that of a schoolboy who wipes his fingers on a slate after spitting on them . . . These are not works of art at all, unless throwing a handful of mud against a wall may be called one. They are the works of idleness and impotent stupidity, a pornographic show.
   My Diaries (1920) 15 November 1910

Gebhard Lebrecht Blücher 1742–1819

Prussian field marshal

10 *Was für Plunder!*
   What rubbish!
   of London, as seen from the Monument in June 1814
   Evelyn Princess Blücher *Memoirs of Prince Blücher* (1932); see **Misquotations** 539:2

Robert Bly 1926–

American poet

11 Terror just before death,
   Shoulders torn, shot
   From helicopters, the boy
   Tortured with the telephone generator,
   'I felt sorry for him
   And blew his head off with a shotgun.'
   These instants become crystals,
   Particles
   The grass cannot dissolve. Our own gaiety
   Will end up
   In Asia, and in your cup you will look down
   And see
   Black Starfighters.
   We were the ones we intended to bomb!
   'Driving Through Minnesota During the Hanoi Bombings' (1968)

12 Alive, we are like a sleek black water beetle.
   Skating across still water in any direction
   We choose, and soon to be swallowed
   Suddenly from beneath.
   'Night' (1962)

13 Every modern male has, lying at the bottom of his psyche, a large, primitive being covered with hair down to his feet. Making contact with this Wild Man is the step the Eighties male or the Nineties male has yet to take.
   Iron John (1990)

Ronald Blythe 1922–

English writer

14 An industrial worker would sooner have a £5 note but a countryman must have praise.
   Akenfield (1969)

15 With full-span lives having become the norm, people may need to learn how to be aged as they once had to learn how to be adult.
   The View in Winter (1979)

Boccaccio 1313–75

Italian writer, poet, and humanist

16 *E infinite volte avvenne che, andando due preti con una croce per alcuno, si misero tre o quatro bare, da'portatori portate, di dietro a quella: e, dove un morto credevano avere i preti a seppilire, n'avevano sei o otto e tal fiate pii.*

And times without number it happened that two priests would be on their way to bury someone, holding a cross before them, only to find that bearers carrying three or four additional biers would fall in behind them; so that whereas the priests had thought they only had one burial to attend to, they in fact had six or eight, and sometimes more.

during the Black Death

Decameron (1348-58) introduction

1 *Fosse grandissime nelle quali a centinaia si mettevano i sopravegnenti; e in quelle stivati, come si mettono le mercantie nelle navi a suolo a suolo.*

They dug for each graveyard a huge trench, in which they laid the corpses as they arrived by hundreds at a time, piling them up tier upon tier as merchandise is stowed in a ship.

Decameron (1348-58) introduction

2 *In tanto che molto volte nelle cose da lui fatte si truova che il visivo denso degli uomini vi prese errore, quello credendo esser vero che era dipinto.*

Mortal sight was often puzzled, face to face with his creations, and took the painted thing for the actual object.

of the painting of Giotto (c.1267-1337)

Decameron (1348-58) bk. 6

John Ernest Bode 1816-74
English clergyman

3 O Jesus, I have promised
To serve thee to the end;
Be thou for ever near me,
My Master and my Friend.

'O Jesus, I have promised' (1869 hymn); written for the confirmation of Bode's three children

4 O let me hear thee speaking
In accents clear and still,
Above the storms of passion,
The murmurs of self-will.

'O Jesus, I have promised' (1869 hymn)

Ivan F. Boesky 1937-
American businessman

5 Greed is all right . . . Greed is healthy. You can be greedy and still feel good about yourself.

commencement address, Berkeley, California, 18 May 1986; see **Film lines** 319:9

Boethius C.AD 476-524
Roman statesman and philosopher

6 *Nam in omni adversitate fortunae infelicissimum est genus infortunii, fuisse felicem.*

For in every ill-turn of fortune the most unhappy sort of unfortunate man is the one who has been happy.

De Consolatione Philosophiae bk. 2, prose 4; see **Chaucer** 213:8, **Dante** 255:18, **Tennyson** 780:17

Louise Bogan 1897-1970
American poet

7 Women have no wilderness in them,
They are provident instead,
Content in the tight hot cell of their hearts
To eat dusty bread.

'Women' (1923)

Humphrey Bogart see **Catchphrases** 200:3, **Film lines** 319:10, **Film lines** 319:13, **Film lines** 320:13, **Telegrams** 776:8

John B. Bogart 1848-1921
American journalist

8 When a dog bites a man, that is not news, because it happens so often. But if a man bites a dog, that is news.

often attributed to Charles A. Dana

F. M. O'Brien The Story of the [New York] Sun (1918) ch. 10

Niels Bohr 1885-1962
Danish physicist

9 Anybody who is not shocked by this subject has failed to understand it.

of quantum mechanics

attributed; in Nature 23 August 1990

10 Never express yourself more clearly than you think.

Abraham Pais Einstein Lived Here (1994)

11 One of the favourite maxims of my father was the distinction between the two sorts of truths, profound truths recognized by the fact that the opposite is also a profound truth, in contrast to trivialities where opposites are obviously absurd.

S. Rozental Niels Bohr (1967)

Nicolas Boileau 1636-1711
French critic and poet

12 *Enfin Malherbe vint, et, le premier en France, Fit sentir dans les vers une juste cadence.*

At last came Malherbe, and he was the first in France to give poetry a proper flow.

L'Art poétique (1674) canto 1, l. 131

13 *Un sot trouve toujours un plus sot qui l'admire.*

A fool can always find a greater fool to admire him.

L'Art poétique (1674) canto 1, l. 232

14 *Qu'en un lieu, qu'en un jour, un seul fait accompli Tienne jusqu'à la fin le théâtre rempli.*

Let a single completed action, all in one place, all in one day, keep the theatre packed to the end of your play.

L'Art poétique (1674) canto 3, l. 45

15 *Si j'écris quatre mots, j'en effacerai trois.*

Of every four words I write, I strike out three.

Satire (2). A M. Molière (1665)

Eavan Boland 1944-

Irish poet

1 Imagine how they stood there, what they stood
  with
  that their possessions may become our power.
  Cardboard. Iron. Their hardships parcelled in
  them.
  'The Emigrant Irish' (1987)

2 I think of what great art removes:
  Hazard and death, the future and the past.
  'From the painting *Back from Market* by Chardin' (1967)

Alan Bold 1943-

Scottish poet

3 This happened near the core
  Of a world's culture. This
  Occurred among higher things.
  This was a philosophical conclusion.
  Everybody gets what he deserves.
  'June 1967 at Buchenwald' (1969); see **Anonymous** 21:6

4 Scotland, land of the omnipotent No.
  'A Memory of Death' (1969)

5 Our job is to try
  To change things.
  After Hiroshima
  You ask a poet to sing.
  'Recitative' (1965)

Henry St John, Lord Bolingbroke

1678-1751

English politician

6 They make truth serve as a stalking-horse to error.
  Letters on the Study and Use of History (1752) No. 4, pt. 1

7 They [Thucydides and Xenophon] maintained the
  dignity of history.
  Letters on the Study and Use of History (1752) No. 5, pt. 2

8 Nations, like men, have their infancy.
  On the Study of History letter 5, in *Works* (1809) vol. 3

9 Truth lies within a little and certain compass, but
  error is immense.
  Reflections upon Exile (1716)

10 What a world is this, and how does fortune banter
  us!
  letter to Jonathan Swift, 3 August 1714, in Harold
  Williams (ed.) *Correspondence of Jonathan Swift* (1963) vol. 2

11 The great mistake is that of looking upon men as
  virtuous, or thinking that they can be made so by
  laws.
  comment (c.1728), in Joseph Spence *Observations,
  Anecdotes, and Characters* (1820, ed. J. M. Osborn, 1966)
  Anecdote 882

12 The greatest art of a politician is to render vice
  serviceable to the cause of virtue.
  comment (c.1728), in Joseph Spence *Observations,
  Anecdotes, and Characters* (1820, ed. J. M. Osborn, 1966)
  Anecdote 882

Heinrich Böll 1917-85

German novelist and short-story writer

13 *Bald kann in einer Sekunde sein, bald kann in einem
  Jahr sein. Bald ist ein furchtbares Wort. Dieses Bald
  drückt die Zukunft zusammen, es macht sie klein, ind
  es gibt nichts Gewisses, gar nichts Gewisses, es ist die
  absolute Unsicherheit. Bald ist nichts und Bald ist
  vieles. Bald ist alles. Bald ist der Tod.*

  Soon can mean in one second, Soon can mean in
  one year. Soon is a terrible word. This Soon
  compresses the future, shrinks it, offers no
  certainty, no certainty whatever, it stands for
  absolute uncertainty. Soon is nothing and Soon is
  a lot. Soon is everything. Soon is death . . .
  The Train was on Time (1949)

14 *Die Freude wäscht vieles ab, so wie das Leid vieles
  abwäscht.*

  Happiness washes away many things, just as
  suffering washes away many things.
  The Train was on Time (1949)

Robert Bolt 1924-95

English dramatist
*see also **Borrowed titles** 146:13*

15 This country's planted thick with laws from coast
  to coast—Man's laws, not God's—and if you cut
  them down—and you're just the man to do
  it—d'you really think you could stand upright in
  the winds that would blow then?
  A Man for All Seasons (1960) act 1

16 It profits a man nothing to give his soul for the
  whole world . . . But for Wales—!
  A Man for All Seasons (1960) act 2; see **Bible** 99:23

Edmund Bolton c.1575-c.1633

English poet

17 The withered primrose by the mourning river,
  The faded summer's sun from weeping fountains,
  The light-blown bubble vanished for ever,
  The molten snow upon the naked mountains,
  Are emblems that the treasures we up-lay
  Soon wither, vanish, fade, and melt away.
  'A Palinode' (1600)

Elizabeth Patterson Bonaparte

1785-1879

*American-born wife of Jérôme Bonaparte, youngest brother of
Napoleon*

18 Even quarrels with one's husband are preferable
  to the ennui of a solitary existence.
  Eugene L. Didier *The Life and Letters of Madame Bonaparte*
  (1879)

Laetitia Bonaparte 1750-1836

*French mother of **Napoleon***

19 *Pourvu que ça dure!*
  Let's hope it lasts!
  *on her son **Napoleon** becoming Emperor, 1804*
  attributed, possibly apocryphal

Andrew Bonar Law 1858–1923

Canadian-born British Conservative statesman, Prime Minister 1922–3
on Bonar Law: see **Asquith** *32:4,* **Beaverbrook** *60:17*

1 There are things stronger than parliamentary majorities. I can imagine no length of resistance to which Ulster will not go, in which I shall not be ready to support them.
   at a Unionist meeting at Blenheim in 1912
   Robert Blake *The Unknown Prime Minister* (1955)

2 In war it is necessary not only to be active but to seem active.
   letter to Asquith, 1916; Robert Blake *The Unknown Prime Minister* (1955)

3 If I am a great man, then all great men are frauds.
   Lord Beaverbrook *Politicians and the War* (1932)

St Bonaventura (Giovanni di Fidanza) 1221–74

Italian Franciscan theologian

4 Reason is the natural image of the Creator.
   Itinerarium Mentis in Deum

Carrie Jacobs Bond 1862–1946

American songwriter

5 When you come to the end of a perfect day.
   'A Perfect Day' (1910 song)

David Bone 1874–1959

Scottish naval officer and writer

6 It's 'Damn you, Jack — I'm all right!' with you chaps.
   Brassbounder (1910) ch. 3

Dietrich Bonhoeffer 1906–45

German Lutheran theologian and martyr

7 I have come to the conclusion that I have made a mistake in coming to America. I must live through this difficult period of our national history with the Christian people of Germany. I shall have no right to participate in the reconstruction of Christian life in Germany after the war if I do not share the trials of this time with my people.
   letter to Reinhold Niebuhr, July 1939

8 In me there is darkness, but with you there is light.
   prayer written for fellow-prisoners in a Nazi prison, 1943
   Letters and Papers from Prison (1971)

9 It is the nature, and the advantage, of strong people that they can bring out the crucial questions and form a clear opinion about them. The weak always have to decide between alternatives that are not their own.
   Widerstand und Ergebung (Resistance and Submission, 1951) 'Ein paar Gedanken über Verschiedenes'

10 Jesus is there only for others . . . God in human form! not . . . in the Greek divine-human form of

'man in himself', but 'the man for others', and therefore the crucified.
   Widerstand und Ergebung (Resistance and Submission, 1951) 'Entwurf einer Arbeit'

The Book of Common Prayer 1662

11 It hath been the wisdom of the Church of England, ever since the first compiling of her Publick Liturgy, to keep the mean between the two extremes, of too much stiffness in refusing, and of too much easiness in admitting any variation from it.
   The Preface

12 There was never any thing by the wit of man so well devised, or so sure established, which in continuance of time hath not been corrupted.
   The Preface Concerning the Service of the Church

13 Dearly beloved brethren, the Scripture moveth us in sundry places to acknowledge and confess our manifold sins and wickedness; and that we should not dissemble nor cloke them before the face of Almighty God our heavenly Father; but confess them with an humble, lowly, penitent, and obedient heart.
   Morning Prayer Sentences of the Scriptures

14 I pray and beseech you, as many as are here present, to accompany me with a pure heart, and humble voice, unto the throne of the heavenly grace.
   Morning Prayer Sentences of the Scriptures

15 We have erred, and strayed from thy ways like lost sheep. We have followed too much the devices and desires of our own hearts.
   Morning Prayer General Confession

16 We have left undone those things which we ought to have done; And we have done those things which we ought not to have done; And there is no health in us.
   Morning Prayer General Confession

17 Restore thou them that are penitent; According to thy promises declared unto mankind in Christ Jesu our Lord. And grant, O most merciful Father, for his sake; That we may hereafter live a godly, righteous, and sober life.
   Morning Prayer General Confession

18 And forgive us our trespasses, As we forgive them that trespass against us.
   Morning Prayer The Lord's Prayer; see **Bible** 95:3, **Missal** 539:7

19 Glory be to the Father, and to the Son: and to the Holy Ghost; As it was in the beginning, is now, and ever shall be: world without end. Amen.
   Morning Prayer Gloria; see **Missal** 536:13

20 We praise thee, O God: we acknowledge thee to be the Lord.
   All the earth doth worship thee: the Father everlasting.
   To thee all Angels cry aloud: the Heavens, and all the Powers therein.
   To thee Cherubin, and Seraphin: continually do cry,

Holy, Holy, Holy: Lord God of Sabaoth;
Heaven and earth are full of the Majesty: of thy Glory.
The glorious company of the Apostles: praise thee.
The goodly fellowship of the Prophets: praise thee.
The noble army of Martyrs: praise thee.

Morning Prayer Te Deum; see **Prayers** 611:7

1 When thou hadst overcome the sharpness of death: thou didst open the Kingdom of Heaven to all believers.

Morning Prayer Te Deum

2 Day by day: we magnify thee;
And we worship thy Name: ever world without end.
Vouchsafe, O Lord: to keep us this day without sin.
O Lord, have mercy upon us: have mercy upon us.
O Lord, let thy mercy lighten upon us: as our trust is in thee.
O Lord, in thee have I trusted: let me never be confounded.

Morning Prayer Te Deum; see **Prayers** 611:8

3 O all ye Works of the Lord, bless ye the Lord.

Morning Prayer Benedicite

4 O ye Waters that be above the Firmament, bless ye the Lord.

Morning Prayer Benedicite

5 O ye Showers, and Dew, bless ye the Lord: praise him, and magnify him for ever.
O ye Winds of God, bless ye the Lord: praise him, and magnify him for ever.

Morning Prayer Benedicite

6 O ye Dews, and Frosts, bless ye the Lord: praise him, and magnify him for ever.
O ye Frost and Cold, bless ye the Lord: praise him and magnify him for ever.
O ye Ice and Snow, bless ye the Lord: praise him and magnify him for ever.
O ye Nights, and Days, bless ye the Lord: praise him, and magnify him for ever.

Morning Prayer Benedicite

7 O let the Earth bless the Lord: yea, let it praise him, and magnify him for ever.

Morning Prayer Benedicite

8 O all ye Green Things upon the Earth, bless ye the Lord: praise him, and magnify him for ever.

Morning Prayer Benedicite

9 O ye Whales, and all that move in the Waters, bless ye the Lord: praise him, and magnify him for ever.

Morning Prayer Benedicite

10 I believe in God the Father Almighty, Maker of heaven and earth:
And in Jesus Christ his only Son our Lord, Who was conceived by the Holy Ghost, Born of the Virgin Mary, Suffered under Pontius Pilate, Was crucified, dead, and buried, He descended into hell; The third day he rose again from the dead, He ascended into heaven, And sitteth on the right hand of God the Father Almighty; From thence he shall come to judge the quick and the dead.

I believe in the Holy Ghost; The holy Catholic Church; The Communion of Saints; The Forgiveness of sins; The Resurrection of the body, And the life everlasting. Amen.

Morning Prayer The Apostles' Creed; see **Book of Common Prayer** 131:10, **Missal** 536:19

11 Give peace in our time, O Lord.

Morning Prayer Versicle

12 O God, who art the author of peace and lover of concord, in knowledge of whom standeth our eternal life, whose service is perfect freedom; Defend us thy humble servants in all assaults of our enemies.

Morning Prayer The Second Collect, for Peace

13 Grant that this day we fall into no sin, neither run into any kind of danger.

Morning Prayer The Third Collect, for Grace

14 In Quires and Places where they sing, here followeth the Anthem.

Morning Prayer rubric following Third Collect

15 Endue her plenteously with heavenly gifts; grant her in health and wealth long to live.

Morning Prayer Prayer for the Queen's Majesty

16 Almighty God, the fountain of all goodness.

Morning Prayer Prayer for the Royal Family

17 Almighty and everlasting God, who alone workest great marvels; Send down upon our Bishops, and Curates, and all Congregations committed to their charge, the healthful Spirit of thy grace; and that they may truly please thee, pour upon them the continual dew of thy blessing.

Morning Prayer Prayer for the Clergy and People

18 Almighty God, who hast given us grace at this time with one accord to make our common supplications unto thee; and dost promise, that when two or three are gathered together in thy Name thou wilt grant their requests: Fulfil now, O Lord, the desires and petitions of thy servants, as may be most expedient for them.

Morning Prayer Prayer of St Chrysostom

19 O God, from whom all holy desires, all good counsels, and all just works do proceed; Give unto thy servants that peace which the world cannot give.

Evening Prayer Second Collect

20 Lighten our darkness, we beseech thee, O Lord; and by thy great mercy defend us from all perils and dangers of this night.

Evening Prayer Third Collect

21 Whosoever will be saved: before all things it is necessary that he hold the Catholic Faith.

At Morning Prayer Athanasian Creed 'Quicunque vult'

22 And the Catholic Faith is this: That we worship one God in Trinity, and Trinity in Unity;
Neither confounding the Persons: nor dividing the Substance.

At Morning Prayer Athanasian Creed 'Quicunque vult'

1 There are not three incomprehensibles, nor three uncreated: but one uncreated, and one incomprehensible.

At Morning Prayer Athanasian Creed 'Quicunque vult'

2 Perfect God, and perfect Man: of a reasonable soul and human flesh subsisting;
Equal to the Father, as touching his Godhead: and inferior to the Father, as touching his Manhood.

At Morning Prayer Athanasian Creed 'Quicunque vult'

3 Have mercy upon us miserable sinners.

The Litany

4 From all evil and mischief; from sin, from the crafts and assaults of the devil; from thy wrath, and from everlasting damnation,
Good Lord, deliver us.

The Litany

5 From envy, hatred, and malice, and from all uncharitableness,
Good Lord, deliver us.

The Litany

6 From all the deceits of the world, the flesh, and the devil,
Good Lord, deliver us.

The Litany

7 From lightning and tempest; from plague, pestilence, and famine; from battle and murder, and from sudden death,
Good Lord, deliver us.

The Litany

8 By thine Agony and bloody Sweat; by thy Cross and Passion; by thy precious Death and Burial; by thy glorious Resurrection and Ascension; and by the coming of the Holy Ghost,
Good Lord, deliver us.

The Litany

9 In all time of our tribulation; in all time of our wealth; in the hour of death, and in the day of judgement,
Good Lord, deliver us.

The Litany

10 That it may please thee to illuminate all Bishops, Priests, and Deacons, with true knowledge and understanding of thy Word; and that both by their preaching and living they may set it forth, and show it accordingly;
We beseech thee to hear us, good Lord.

The Litany

11 That it may please thee to strengthen such as do stand; and to comfort and help the weak-hearted; and to raise up them that fall; and finally to beat down Satan under our feet;
We beseech thee to hear us, good Lord.

The Litany

12 That it may please thee to preserve all that travel by land or by water, all women labouring of child, all sick persons, and young children; and to shew thy pity upon all prisoners and captives;
We beseech thee to hear us, good Lord.

The Litany; see **Swift** 766:13

13 Defend, and provide for, the fatherless children, and widows, and all that are desolate and oppressed.

The Litany

14 That it may please thee to give and preserve to our use the kindly fruits of the earth, so as in due time we may enjoy them;
We beseech thee to hear us, good Lord.

The Litany

15 O God, merciful Father, that despisest not the sighing of a contrite heart, not the desire of such as be sorrowful; Mercifully assist our prayers that we make before thee in all our troubles and adversities, whensoever they oppress us.

The Litany

16 O God, whose nature and property is ever to have mercy and to forgive, receive our humble petitions; and though we be tied and bound with the chain of our sins, yet let the pitifulness of thy great mercy loose us; for the honour of Jesus Christ, our Mediator and Advocate.

Prayers . . . upon Several Occasions A prayer

17 O God, the Creator and Preserver of all mankind, we humbly beseech thee for all sorts and conditions of men.

Prayers . . . upon Several Occasions 'Collect or Prayer for all Conditions of Men'

18 We pray for the good estate of the Catholick Church; that it may be so guided and governed by thy good Spirit, that all who profess and call themselves Christians may be led into the way of truth.

Prayers . . . upon Several Occasions 'Collect or Prayer for all Conditions of Men'

19 We commend to thy fatherly goodness all those, who are any ways afflicted, or distressed, in mind, body, or estate; that it may please thee to comfort and relieve them, according to their several necessities, giving them patience under their sufferings, and a happy issue out of all their afflictions.

Prayers . . . upon Several Occasions 'Collect or Prayer for all Conditions of Men'

20 We bless thee for our creation, preservation, and all the blessings of this life; but above all, for thine inestimable love in the redemption of the world by our Lord Jesus Christ; for the means of grace, and for the hope of glory.

Thanksgivings General Thanksgiving

21 O God our heavenly Father, who by thy gracious providence dost cause the former and the latter rain to descend upon the earth, that it may bring forth fruit for the use of man; We give thee humble thanks that it hath pleased thee, in our great necessity, to send us at the last a joyful rain upon thine inheritance, and to refresh it when it was dry.

Thanksgivings For Rain

22 Almighty God, give us grace that we may cast away the works of darkness, and put upon us the armour of light, now in the time of this mortal life, in which thy Son Jesus Christ came to visit us in great humility.

Collects The first Sunday in Advent

1 Blessed Lord, who hast caused all holy Scriptures to be written for our learning; Grant that we may in such wise hear them, read, mark, learn, and inwardly digest them, that by patience, and comfort of thy holy Word, we may embrace, and ever hold fast the blessed hope of everlasting life.

Collects The second Sunday in Advent

2 That whereas, through our sins and wickedness, we are sore let and hindered in running the race that is set before us, thy bountiful grace and mercy may speedily help and deliver us.

Collects The fourth Sunday in Advent

3 O Lord, we beseech thee mercifully to receive the prayers of thy people which call upon thee; and grant that they may both perceive and know what things they ought to do, and also may have grace and power faithfully to fulfil the same.

Collects The first Sunday after the Epiphany

4 O God, who knowest us to be set in the midst of so many and great dangers, that by reason of the frailty of our nature we cannot always stand upright; Grant to us such strength and protection, as may support us in all dangers, and carry us through all temptations.

Collects The fourth Sunday after the Epiphany

5 Almighty God, who seest that we have no power of ourselves to help ourselves; Keep us both outwardly in our bodies, and inwardly in our souls; that we may be defended from all adversities which may happen to the body, and from all evil thoughts which may assault and hurt the soul.

Collects The second Sunday in Lent

6 We humbly beseech thee, that, as by thy special grace preventing us thou dost put into our minds good desires, so by thy continued help we may bring the same to good effect.

Collects Easter-Day

7 Grant us so to put away the leaven of malice and wickedness, that we may alway serve thee in pureness of living and truth.

Collects The first Sunday after Easter

8 O Almighty God, who alone canst order the unruly wills and affections of sinful men; Grant unto thy people, that they may love the thing which thou commandest, and desire that which thou dost promise; that so, among the sundry and manifold changes of the world, our hearts may surely there be fixed, where true joys are to be found.

Collects The fourth Sunday after Easter

9 We beseech thee, leave us not comfortless; but send to us thine Holy Ghost to comfort us, and exalt us unto the same place whither our Saviour Christ is gone before.

Collects Sunday after Ascension Day

10 God, who as at this time didst teach the hearts of thy faithful people, by the sending to them the light of thy Holy Spirit; Grant us by the same Spirit to have a right judgement in all things.

Collects Whit-Sunday

11 Because through the weakness of our mortal nature we can do no good thing without thee, grant us the help of thy grace, that in keeping of thy commandments we may please thee, both in will and deed.

Collects The first Sunday after Trinity

12 O God, the protector of all that trust in thee, without whom nothing is strong, nothing is holy; Increase and multiply upon us thy mercy; that, thou being our ruler and guide, we may so pass through things temporal, that we finally lose not the things eternal.

Collects The fourth Sunday after Trinity

13 Grant, O Lord, we beseech thee, that the course of this world may be so peaceably ordered by thy governance, that thy Church may joyfully serve thee in all godly quietness.

Collects The fifth Sunday after Trinity

14 O God, who hast prepared for them that love thee such good things as pass man's understanding; Pour into our hearts such love toward thee, that we, loving thee above all things, may obtain thy promises, which exceed all that we can desire.

Collects The sixth Sunday after Trinity

15 Lord of all power and might, who art the author and giver of all good things; Graft in our hearts the love of thy Name, increase in us true religion, nourish us with all goodness, and of thy great mercy keep us in the same.

Collects The seventh Sunday after Trinity

16 Pour down upon us the abundance of thy mercy; forgiving us those things whereof our conscience is afraid.

Collects The twelfth Sunday after Trinity

17 O God, forasmuch as without thee we are not able to please thee; Mercifully grant, that thy Holy Spirit may in all things direct and rule our hearts.

Collects The nineteenth Sunday after Trinity

18 Grant, we beseech thee, merciful Lord, to thy faithful people pardon and peace, that they may be cleansed from all their sins, and serve thee with a quiet mind.

Collects The one and twentieth Sunday after Trinity

19 Lord, we beseech thee to keep thy household the Church in continual godliness.

Collects The two and twentieth Sunday after Trinity

20 Grant that those things which we ask faithfully we may obtain effectually.

Collects The three and twentieth Sunday after Trinity

21 Stir up, we beseech thee, O Lord, the wills of thy faithful people; that they, plenteously bringing forth the fruit of good works, may of thee be plenteously rewarded.

Collects The five and twentieth Sunday after Trinity

1 Give us grace, that, being not like children carried away with every blast of vain doctrine, we may be established in the truth of thy holy Gospel.
Collects St Mark's Day

2 O Almighty God, who hast knit together thine elect in one communion and fellowship, in the mystical body of thy Son Christ our Lord; Grant us grace so to follow thy blessed Saints in all virtuous and godly living, that we may come to those unspeakable joys, which thou hast prepared for them that unfeignedly love thee.
Collects All Saints' Day

3 And if any of those be an open and notorious evil liver, or have done any wrong to his neighbours by word or deed, so that the Congregation be thereby offended; the Curate, having knowledge thereof, shall call him and advertise him, that in any wise he presume not to come to the Lord's Table.
Holy Communion introductory rubric

4 Until he have openly declared himself to have truly repented and amended his former naughty life.
Holy Communion introductory rubric

5 The Table, at the Communion-time having a fair white linen cloth upon it, shall stand in the Body of the Church, or in the Chancel.
Holy Communion introductory rubric

6 Almighty God, unto whom all hearts be open, all desires known, and from whom no secrets are hid; Cleanse the thoughts of our hearts by the inspiration of thy Holy Spirit, that we may perfectly love thee, and worthily magnify thy holy Name.
Holy Communion The Collect

7 I the Lord thy God am a jealous God, and visit the sins of the fathers upon the children unto the third and fourth generation of them that hate me.
the phrase 'sins of the fathers' is also used in the Douay/Rheims Bible (1609) in Numbers ch. 14, v. 18
Holy Communion The Ten Commandments; see **Bible** 78:1

8 Incline our hearts to keep this law.
Holy Communion The Ten Commandments (response)

9 Thou shalt do no murder.
Holy Communion The Ten Commandments; see **Bible** 78:5

10 I believe in one God the Father Almighty, Maker of heaven and earth, And of all things visible and invisible:
And in one Lord Jesus Christ, the only-begotten Son of God, Begotten of his Father before all worlds, God of God, Light of Light, Very God of very God, Begotten, not made, Being of one substance with the Father, By whom all things were made.
Holy Communion Nicene Creed; see **Book of Common Prayer** 128:10, **Missal** 536:19

11 And I believe in the Holy Ghost, the Lord and giver of life, Who proceedeth from the Father and the Son, Who with the Father and the Son together is worshipped and glorified, Who spake

by the Prophets. And I believe one Catholick and Apostolick Church.
Holy Communion Nicene Creed; see **Missal** 536:19

12 Let us pray for the whole state of Christ's Church militant here in earth.
Holy Communion Prayer for the Church Militant

13 We humbly beseech thee most mercifully to accept our alms and oblations, and to receive these our prayers, which we offer unto thy Divine Majesty; beseeching thee to inspire continually the universal Church with the spirit of truth, unity, and concord: And grant, that all they that do confess thy holy Name may agree in the truth of thy holy Word, and live in unity, and godly love.
Holy Communion Prayer for the Church Militant

14 Grant unto her [the Queen's] whole Council, and to all that are put in authority under her, that they may truly and indifferently minister justice.
Holy Communion Prayer for the Church Militant

15 Give grace, O heavenly Father, to all Bishops and Curates, that they may both by their life and doctrine set forth thy true and lively Word.
Holy Communion Prayer for the Church Militant

16 We most humbly beseech thee of thy goodness, O Lord, to comfort and succour all them, who in this transitory life are in trouble, sorrow, need, sickness, or any other adversity. And we also bless thy holy Name for all thy servants departed this life in thy faith and fear.
Holy Communion Prayer for the Church Militant

17 Ye that do truly and earnestly repent you of your sins, and are in love and charity with your neighbours, and intend to lead a new life, following the commandments of God, and walking from henceforth in his holy ways; Draw near with faith, and take this holy Sacrament to your comfort; and make your humble confession to Almighty God, meekly kneeling upon your knees.
Holy Communion The Invitation

18 We do earnestly repent, And are heartily sorry for these our misdoings; The remembrance of them is grievous unto us; The burden of them is intolerable.
Holy Communion General Confession

19 Hear what comfortable words our Saviour Christ saith unto all that truly turn to him.
Holy Communion Comfortable Words (preamble)

20 Lift up your hearts.
Holy Communion versicles and responses; see **Missal** 536:22

21 It is meet and right so to do.
Holy Communion versicles and responses

22 It is very meet, right, and our bounden duty, that we should at all times, and in all places, give thanks unto thee, O Lord, Holy Father, Almighty, Everlasting God.
Therefore with Angels and Archangels, and with all the company of heaven, we laud and magnify thy glorious Name; evermore praising thee, and saying, Holy, holy, holy, Lord God of hosts,

heaven and earth are full of thy glory: Glory be to thee, O Lord most High.

Holy Communion Hymn of Praise; see **Bible** 113:9, **Missal** 539:6

1 Almighty God, our heavenly Father, who of thy tender mercy didst give thine only Son Jesus Christ to suffer death upon the cross for our redemption; who made there (by his one oblation of himself once offered) a full, perfect, and sufficient sacrifice, oblation, and satisfaction, for the sins of the whole world.

Holy Communion Prayer of Consecration

2 Who, in the same night that he was betrayed, took Bread; and, when he had given thanks, he brake it, and gave it to his disciples, saying, Take, eat, this is my Body which is given for you: Do this in remembrance of me. Likewise after supper he took the Cup; and, when he had given thanks, he gave it to them, saying, Drink ye all of this; for this is my Blood of the New Testament, which is shed for you and for many for the remission of sins: Do this, as oft as ye shall drink it, in remembrance of me.

Holy Communion Prayer of Consecration

3 Although we be unworthy, through our manifold sins, to offer unto thee any sacrifice, yet we beseech thee to accept this our bounden duty and service; not weighing our merits, but pardoning our offences.

Holy Communion First Prayer of Oblation

4 We are very members incorporate in the mystical body of thy Son, which is the blessed company of all faithful people; and are also heirs through hope of thy everlasting kingdom.

Holy Communion Second (alternative) Prayer of Oblation

Father of all, We give you thanks and praise, that when we were still far off you met us in your Son and brought us home. Dying and living, he declared your love, gave us grace, and opened the gate of glory.

Alternative Service Book Post-Communion prayer

5 The blessing of God Almighty, the Father, the Son, and the Holy Ghost, be amongst you and remain with you always.

Holy Communion The Blessing

6 Assist us mercifully, O Lord, in these our supplications and prayers, and dispose the way of thy servants towards the attainment of everlasting salvation; that, among all the changes and chances of this mortal life, they may ever be defended by thy most gracious and ready help.

Holy Communion Collects after the Offertory

7 Prevent us, O Lord, in all our doings with thy most gracious favour, and further us with thy continual help; that in all our works, begun, continued, and ended in thee, we may glorify thy holy Name.

Holy Communion Collects after the Offertory

8 Those things, which for our unworthiness we dare not, and for our blindness we cannot ask,

vouchsafe to give us, for the worthiness of thy Son Jesus Christ our Lord.

Holy Communion Collects after the Offertory

9 It is expedient that Baptism be administered in the vulgar tongue.

Public Baptism of Infants introductory rubric

10 O merciful God, grant that the old Adam in this Child may be so buried, that the new man may be raised up in him.

Public Baptism of Infants Invocation of blessing on the child

11 It is your part and duty also . . . to walk answerably to your Christian calling, and as becometh the children of light.

Baptism of Such as are of Riper Years Priest's final address

12 QUESTION: Who gave you this Name?
ANSWER: My Godfathers and Godmothers in my Baptism; wherein I was made a member of Christ, the child of God, and an inheritor of the kingdom of heaven.

Catechism

13 I should renounce the devil and all his works, the pomps and vanity of this wicked world, and all the sinful lusts of the flesh.

Catechism

14 QUESTION: What dost thou chiefly learn by these Commandments?
ANSWER: I learn two things: my duty towards God, and my duty to my Neighbour.

Catechism

15 My duty towards my Neighbour, is to love him as myself, and to do to all men, as I would they should do unto me.

Catechism

16 To submit myself to all my governors, teachers, spiritual pastors and masters.

Catechism

17 To keep my hands from picking and stealing, and my tongue from evil-speaking, lying, and slandering.

Catechism

18 Not to covet nor desire other men's goods; but to learn and labour truly to get mine own living, and to do my duty in that state of life, unto which it shall please God to call me.

Catechism

19 QUESTION: How many Sacraments hath Christ ordained in his Church?
ANSWER: Two only, as generally necessary to salvation, that is to say, Baptism, and the Supper of the Lord.
QUESTION: What meanest thou by this word *Sacrament?*
ANSWER: I mean an outward and visible sign of an inward and spiritual grace.

Catechism

20 Our help is in the name of the Lord;
Who hath made heaven and earth.

Order of Confirmation

1 Lord, hear our prayers.
And let our cry come unto thee.
Order of Confirmation

2 Defend, O Lord, this thy Child [*or* this thy Servant]
with thy heavenly grace, that he may continue
thine for ever; and daily increase in thy holy Spirit
more and more, until he come unto thy
everlasting kingdom.
Order of Confirmation

3 If any of you know cause, or just impediment,
why these two persons should not be joined
together in holy Matrimony, ye are to declare it.
This is the first [*second*, or *third*] time of asking.
Solemnization of Matrimony The Banns

4 Dearly beloved, we are gathered together here in
the sight of God, and in the face of this
congregation, to join together this Man and this
Woman in holy Matrimony.
Solemnization of Matrimony Exhortation

5 Which holy estate Christ adorned and beautified
with his presence, and first miracle that he
wrought, in Cana of Galilee; and is commended of
Saint Paul to be honourable among all men: and
therefore not by any to be enterprised, nor taken
in hand, unadvisedly, lightly, or wantonly, to
satisfy men's carnal lusts and appetites, like brute
beasts that have no understanding.
Solemnization of Matrimony Exhortation

6 First, It was ordained for the procreation of
children, to be brought up in the fear and nurture
of the Lord, and to the praise of his holy Name.
Solemnization of Matrimony Exhortation

7 If any man can shew any just cause, why they
may not lawfully be joined together, let him now
speak, or else hereafter for ever hold his peace.
Solemnization of Matrimony Exhortation

8 Wilt thou have this Woman to thy wedded wife, to
live together after God's ordinance in the holy
estate of Matrimony? Wilt thou love her, comfort
her, honour, and keep her in sickness and in
health; and, forsaking all other, keep thee only
unto her, so long as ye both shall live?
Solemnization of Matrimony Betrothal

9 I N. take thee M. to my wedded husband, to have
and to hold from this day forward, for better for
worse, for richer for poorer, in sickness and in
health, to love, cherish, and to obey, till death us
do part, according to God's holy ordinance; and
thereto I give thee my troth.
*the man having used the words 'I plight thee my
troth' and not having promised 'to obey'; the woman
may also omit the promise 'to obey'*
Solemnization of Matrimony Betrothal

10 With this Ring I thee wed, with my body I thee
worship, and with all my worldly goods I thee
endow.
Solemnization of Matrimony Wedding

All that I am I give to you, and all that I have I
share with you.
Alternative Service Book

11 Those whom God hath joined together let no man
put asunder.
Solemnization of Matrimony Wedding; see **Bible** 97:24

12 Forasmuch as M. and N. have consented together
in holy wedlock, and have witnessed the same
before God and this company, and thereto have
given and pledged their troth either to other, and
have declared the same by giving and receiving of
a Ring, and by joining of hands; I pronounce that
they be Man and Wife together.
Solemnization of Matrimony Minister's Declaration

13 Peace be to this house, and to all that dwell in it.
The Visitation of the Sick

14 Unto God's gracious mercy and protection we
commit thee.
The Visitation of the Sick

15 The Office ensuing is not to be used for any that
die unbaptized, or excommunicate, or have laid
violent hands upon themselves.
The Burial of the Dead introductory rubric

16 Man that is born of a woman hath but a short
time to live, and is full of misery.
The Burial of the Dead First Anthem; see **Bible** 83:8

17 In the midst of life we are in death.
The Burial of the Dead First Anthem; see **Mumford** 554:1

18 Forasmuch as it hath pleased Almighty God of his
great mercy to take unto himself the soul of our
dear brother here departed, we therefore commit
his body to the ground; earth to earth, ashes to
ashes, dust to dust; in sure and certain hope of the
Resurrection to eternal life, through our Lord
Jesus Christ; who shall change our vile body, that
it may be like unto his glorious body, according to
the mighty working, whereby he is able to subdue
all things to himself.
The Burial of the Dead Interment

19 Blessed is the man that hath not walked in the
counsel of the ungodly, nor stood in the way of
sinners: and hath not sat in the seat of the
scornful.
Psalm 1, v. 1

20 Why do the heathen so furiously rage together:
and why do the people imagine a vain thing?
Psalm 2, v. 1

21 Thou shalt bruise them with a rod of iron: and
break them in pieces like a potter's vessel.
Psalm 2, v. 9

22 Blessed are all they that put their trust in him.
Psalm 2, v. 12

23 Stand in awe, and sin not: commune with your
own heart, and in your chamber, and be still.
Psalm 4, v. 4

24 Lord, lift thou up: the light of thy countenance
upon us.
Psalm 4, v. 7

25 I will lay me down in peace, and take my rest.
Psalm 4, v. 9

26 Make thy way plain before my face.
Psalm 5, v. 8

1 Let them perish through their own imaginations.
Psalm 5, v. 11

2 I am weary of my groaning; every night wash I
my bed: and water my couch with my tears.
Psalm 6, v. 6

3 Away from me, all ye that work vanity.
Psalm 6, v. 8

4 Out of the mouth of very babes and sucklings hast
thou ordained strength, because of thine enemies.
Psalm 8, v. 2; see **Proverbs** 629:14

5 What is man, that thou art mindful of him: and
the son of man, that thou visitest him?
Thou madest him lower than the angels: to crown
him with glory and worship.
Psalm 8, v. 4

6 Up, Lord, and let not man have the upper hand.
Psalm 9, v. 19

7 He that said in his heart, Tush, I shall never be
cast down: there shall no harm happen unto
me.
Psalm 10, v. 6

8 Upon the ungodly he shall rain snares, fire and
brimstone, storm and tempest: this shall be their
portion to drink.
Psalm 11, v. 7

9 How long wilt thou forget me, O Lord, for ever:
how long wilt thou hide thy face from me?
Psalm 13, v. 1

10 The fool hath said in his heart: There is no God.
They are corrupt, and become abominable in their
doings: there is none that doeth good, no not one.
Psalm 14, v. 1

11 They are all gone out of the way, they are
altogether become abominable.
Psalm 14, v. 4

12 Lord, who shall dwell in thy tabernacle: or who
shall rest upon thy holy hill?
Even he, that leadeth an uncorrupt life: and doeth
the thing which is right, and speaketh the truth
from his heart.
He that hath used no deceit in his tongue, nor
done evil to his neighbour: and hath not slandered
his neighbour.
Psalm 15, v. 1

13 He that sweareth unto his neighbour, and
disappointeth him not: though it were to his own
hindrance.
He that hath not given his money upon usury:
nor taken reward against the innocent.
Whoso doeth these things: shall never fall.
Psalm 15, v. 5

14 The lot is fallen unto me in a fair ground: yea, I
have a goodly heritage.
Psalm 16, v. 7

The lines are fallen unto me in pleasant places.
Psalm 16, v. 6 in Authorized Version of the Bible

15 Thou shalt not leave my soul in hell: neither shalt
thou suffer thy Holy One to see corruption.
Psalm 16, v. 11

16 He rode upon the cherubims, and did fly: he came
flying upon the wings of the wind.
Psalm 18, v. 10

17 At the brightness of his presence his clouds
removed: hailstones, and coals of fire.
Psalm 18, v. 12

18 With the help of my God I shall leap over the wall.
Psalm 18, v. 29; see **Bible** 81:6

19 The heavens declare the glory of God: and the
firmament sheweth his handy-work.
Psalm 19, v. 1

20 There is neither speech nor language: but their
voices are heard among them.
Their sound is gone out into all lands: and their
words into the ends of the world.
In them hath he set a tabernacle for the sun:
which cometh forth as a bridegroom out of his
chamber, and rejoiceth as a giant to run his
course.
Psalm 19, v. 3

21 The statutes of the Lord are right, and rejoice the
heart: the commandment of the Lord is pure, and
giveth light unto the eyes.
Psalm 19, v. 8

22 The judgements of the Lord are true, and
righteous altogether.
More to be desired are they than gold, yea, than
much fine gold: sweeter also than honey, and the
honey-comb.
Psalm 19, v. 10; see **Lincoln** 485:11

23 Let the words of my mouth, and the meditation of
my heart: be alway acceptable in thy sight,
O Lord: my strength, and my redeemer.
Psalm 19, v. 14

24 Some put their trust in chariots, and some in
horses: but we will remember the Name of the
Lord our God.
Psalm 20, v. 7

25 They intended mischief against thee: and
imagined such a device as they are not able to
perform.
Psalm 21, v. 11

26 My God, my God, look upon me; why hast thou
forsaken me: and art so far from my health, and
from the words of my complaint?
O my God, I cry in the day-time, but thou hearest
not: and in the night-season also I take no rest.
Psalm 22, v. 1

27 But as for me, I am a worm, and no man: a very
scorn of men, and the out-cast of the people.
All they that see me laugh me to scorn: they shoot
out their lips, and shake their heads, saying,
He trusted in God, that he would deliver him: let
him deliver him, if he will have him.
Psalm 22, v. 6

28 Many oxen are come about me: fat bulls of Basan
close me in on every side.
Psalm 22, v. 12

1 I am poured out like water, and all my bones are out of joint: my heart also in the midst of my body is even like melting wax.

Psalm 22, v. 14

2 They pierced my hands and my feet; I may tell all my bones: they stand staring and looking upon me.
They part my garments among them: and cast lots upon my vesture.

Psalm 22, v. 17

3 The Lord is my shepherd: therefore can I lack nothing.
He shall feed me in a green pasture: and lead me forth beside the waters of comfort.

Psalm 23, v. 1; see **Herbert** 385:2, **Scottish Metrical Psalms** 675:4, and below:

The Lord is my shepherd; I shall not want.
He maketh me to lie down in green pastures: he leadeth me beside the still waters.

Bible (Authorized Version, 1611) Psalm 23, v. 1

4 Yea, though I walk through the valley of the shadow of death, I will fear no evil: for thou art with me; thy rod and thy staff comfort me.
Thou shalt prepare a table before me against them that trouble me: thou hast anointed my head with oil, and my cup shall be full.
But thy loving-kindness and mercy shall follow me all the days of my life: and I will dwell in the house of the Lord for ever.

Psalm 23, v. 4; see **Scottish Metrical Psalms** 675:4

5 The earth is the Lord's, and all that therein is: the compass of the world, and they that dwell therein.

Psalm 24, v. 1

6 Lift up your heads, O ye gates, and be ye lift up, ye everlasting doors: and the King of glory shall come in.
Who is the King of glory: it is the Lord strong and mighty, even the Lord mighty in battle.

Psalm 24, v. 7

7 Even the Lord of hosts, he is the King of glory.

Psalm 24, v. 10

8 O remember not the sins and offences of my youth.

Psalm 25, v. 6

9 Deliver Israel, O God: out of all his troubles.

Psalm 25, v. 21

10 Examine me, O Lord, and prove me: try out my reins and my heart.

Psalm 26, v. 2

11 I will wash my hands in innocency, O Lord: and so will I go to thine altar;
That I may shew the voice of thanksgiving: and tell of all thy wondrous works.

Psalm 26, v. 6

12 My foot standeth right: I will praise the Lord in the congregation.

Psalm 26, v. 12

13 The Lord is my light, and my salvation; whom then shall I fear: the Lord is the strength of my life; of whom then shall I be afraid?

Psalm 27, v. 1; see **Bible** 114:26

14 Teach me thy way, O Lord: and lead me in the right way, because of mine enemies.

Psalm 27, v. 13

15 I should utterly have fainted: but that I believe verily to see the goodness of the Lord in the land of the living.

Psalm 27, v. 15

16 The voice of the Lord breaketh the cedar-trees: yea, the Lord breaketh the cedars of Libanus.
He maketh them also to skip like a calf: Libanus also, and Sirion, like a young unicorn.

Psalm 29, v. 5

17 The Lord shall give strength unto his people: the Lord shall give his people the blessing of peace.

Psalm 29, v. 10

18 Heaviness may endure for a night, but joy cometh in the morning.

Psalm 30, v. 5

19 Into thy hands I commend my spirit.

Psalm 31, v. 6; see **Bible** 102:7

20 Blessed is the man unto whom the Lord imputeth no sin: and in whose spirit there is no guile.
For while I held my tongue: my bones consumed away through my daily complaining.

Psalm 32, v. 2

21 Great plagues remain for the ungodly: but whoso putteth his trust in the Lord, mercy embraceth him on every side.

Psalm 32, v. 11

22 Sing unto the Lord a new song: sing praises lustily unto him with a good courage.

Psalm 33, v. 3

23 O taste and see, how gracious the Lord is: blessed is the man that trusteth in him.

Psalm 34, v. 8

24 The lions do lack, and suffer hunger: but they who seek the Lord shall want no manner of thing that is good.

Psalm 34, v. 10

25 Keep thy tongue from evil: and thy lips, that they speak no guile.
Eschew evil, and do good: seek peace, and ensue it.

Psalm 34, v. 13

26 They rewarded me evil for good: to the great discomfort of my soul.

Psalm 35, v. 12

27 O deliver my soul from the calamities which they bring on me, and my darling from the lions.

Psalm 35, v. 17

28 Fret not thyself because of the ungodly.

Psalm 37, v. 1

1 I have been young, and now am old: and yet saw I never the righteous forsaken, nor his seed begging their bread.
Psalm 37, v. 25; see **Blunden** 124:5

2 I myself have seen the ungodly in great power: and flourishing like a green bay-tree.
Psalm 37, v. 36

3 I held my tongue, and spake nothing: I kept silence, yea, even from good words; but it was pain and grief to me.
Psalm 39, v. 3

4 Lord, let me know mine end, and the number of my days: that I may be certified how long I have to live.
Psalm 39, v. 5

5 For man walketh in a vain shadow, and disquieteth himself in vain: he heapeth up riches, and cannot tell who shall gather them.
Psalm 39, v. 7

6 I waited patiently for the Lord: and he inclined unto me, and heard my calling.
He brought me also out of the horrible pit, out of the mire and clay: and set my feet upon the rock, and ordered my goings.
Psalm 40, v. 1

7 In the volume of the book it is written of me, that I should fulfil thy will, O my God.
Psalm 40, v. 10

8 Thou art my helper and redeemer: make no long tarrying, O my God.
Psalm 40, v. 21

9 Blessed is he that considereth the poor and needy: the Lord shall deliver him in the time of trouble.
Psalm 41, v. 1

10 Yea, even mine own familiar friend, whom I trusted: who did also eat of my bread, hath laid great wait for me.
Psalm 41, v. 9

. . . hath lifted up his heel against me.
Psalm 41, v. 9 in the Authorized Version of the Bible

11 Like as the hart desireth the water-brooks: so longeth my soul after thee, O God.
My soul is a thirst for God, yea, even for the living God.
Psalm 42, v. 1; see **Tate** 773:12

As the hart panteth after the water brooks, so panteth my soul after thee, O God.
My soul thirsteth for God, the living God.
Psalm 42, v. 1 in the Authorized Version of the Bible

12 Why art thou so full of heaviness, O my soul: and why art thou so disquieted within me?
Psalm 42, v. 6

13 One deep calleth another, because of the noise of the water-pipes: all thy waves and storms are gone over me.
Psalm 42, v. 9

14 I will say unto the God of my strength, Why hast thou forgotten me: why go I thus heavily, while the enemy oppresseth me?

My bones are smitten asunder as with a sword: while mine enemies that trouble me cast me in the teeth;
Namely, while they say daily unto me: Where is now thy God?
Psalm 42, v. 11

15 Give sentence with me, O God, and defend my cause against the ungodly people: O deliver me from the deceitful and wicked man.
Psalm 43, v. 1

16 O send out thy light and thy truth, that they may lead me: and bring me unto thy holy hill, and to thy dwelling.
And that I may go unto the altar of God, even unto the God of my joy and gladness: and upon the harp will I give thanks unto thee, O God, my God.
Psalm 43, v. 3

17 O put thy trust in God: for I will yet give him thanks, which is the help of my countenance, and my God.
Psalm 43, v. 6

18 We have heard with our ears, O God, our fathers have told us: what thou hast done in their time of old.
Psalm 44, v. 1

19 My heart is inditing of a good matter: I speak of the things which I have made unto the King.
My tongue is the pen: of a ready writer.
Psalm 45, v. 1

20 Thou hast loved righteousness, and hated iniquity: wherefore God, even thy God, hath anointed thee with the oil of gladness above thy fellows.
Psalm 45, v. 8

21 Kings' daughters were among thy honourable women: upon thy right hand did stand the queen in a vesture of gold, wrought about with divers colours.
Psalm 45, v. 10

22 The King's daughter is all glorious within: her clothing is of wrought gold.
Psalm 45, v. 14

23 Instead of thy fathers thou shalt have children: whom thou mayest make princes in all lands.
Psalm 45, v. 17

24 God is our hope and strength: a very present help in trouble. Therefore will we not fear, though the earth be moved: and though the hills be carried into the midst of the sea.
Psalm 46, v. 1; see **Anonymous** 14:18

25 The heathen make much ado, and the kingdoms are moved: but God hath shewed his voice, and the earth shall melt away.
The Lord of hosts is with us: the God of Jacob is our refuge.
Psalm 46, v. 6

26 He maketh wars to cease in all the world: he breaketh the bow, and knappeth the spear in sunder, and burneth the chariots in the fire.

Be still then, and know that I am God: I will be exalted among the heathen, and I will be exalted in the earth.
Psalm 46, v. 9

1 O clap your hands together, all ye people: O sing unto God with the voice of melody.
Psalm 47, v. 1

2 He shall subdue the people under us: and the nations under our feet.
Psalm 47, v. 3

3 God is gone up with a merry noise: and the Lord with the sound of the trump.
Psalm 47, v. 5

4 For lo, the kings of the earth: are gathered, and gone by together.
They marvelled to see such things: they were astonished, and suddenly cast down.
Psalm 48, v. 3

5 Thou shalt break the ships of the sea: through the east-wind.
Psalm 48, v. 6

6 Walk about Sion, and go round about her: and tell the towers thereof.
Mark well her bulwarks, set up her houses: that ye may tell them that come after.
Psalm 48, v. 11

7 Man will not abide in honour: seeing he may be compared unto the beasts that perish.
Psalm 49, v. 12

8 All the beasts of the forest are mine: and so are the cattle upon a thousand hills.
Psalm 50, v. 10

9 Thinkest thou that I will eat bulls' flesh: and drink the blood of goats?
Psalm 50, v. 13

10 Wash me throughly from my wickedness: and cleanse me from my sin.
For I acknowledge my faults: and my sin is ever before me.
Against thee only have I sinned, and done this evil in thy sight.
Psalm 51, v. 2

11 Behold, I was shapen in wickedness: and in sin hath my mother conceived me.
Psalm 51, v. 5

12 Thou shalt purge me with hyssop, and I shall be clean: thou shalt wash me, and I shall be whiter than snow.
Thou shalt make me hear of joy and gladness: that the bones which thou hast broken may rejoice.
Psalm 51, v. 7; see **Bible** 114:27

13 Make me a clean heart, O God: and renew a right spirit within me.
Cast me not away from thy presence: and take not thy holy Spirit from me.
O give me the comfort of thy help again: and stablish me with thy free Spirit.
Psalm 51, v. 10

14 Deliver me from blood-guiltiness, O God.
Psalm 51, v. 14

15 Thou shalt open my lips, O Lord: and my mouth shall shew thy praise.
For thou desirest no sacrifice, else would I give it thee: but thou delightest not in burnt-offerings.
The sacrifice of God is a troubled spirit: a broken and contrite heart, O God, shalt thou not despise.
O be favourable and gracious unto Sion: build thou the walls of Jerusalem.
Psalm 51, v. 15

16 O that I had wings like a dove: for then would I flee away, and be at rest.
Psalm 55, v. 6

17 It was even thou, my companion: my guide, and mine own familiar friend.
We took sweet counsel together: and walked in the house of God as friends.
Psalm 55, v. 14

18 The words of his mouth were softer than butter, having war in his heart: his words were smoother than oil, and yet they be very swords.
Psalm 55, v. 22

19 Thou tellest my flittings; put my tears into thy bottle: are not these things noted in thy book?
Psalm 56, v. 8

20 Under the shadow of thy wings shall be my refuge, until this tyranny be over-past.
Psalm 57, v. 1

21 God shall send forth his mercy and truth: my soul is among lions.
And I lie even among the children of men, that are set on fire: whose teeth are spears and arrows, and their tongue a sharp sword.
Set up thyself, O God, above the heavens: and thy glory above all the earth.
Psalm 57, v. 4

22 They have laid a net for my feet, and pressed down my soul: they have digged a pit before me, and are fallen into the midst of it themselves.
Psalm 57, v. 7

23 Awake up, my glory; awake, lute and harp: I myself will awake right early.
Psalm 57, v. 9

24 They are as venomous as the poison of a serpent: even like the deaf adder that stoppeth her ears;
Which refuseth to hear the voice of the charmer: charm he never so wisely.
Psalm 58, v. 4

25 Gilead is mine, and Manasses is mine: Ephraim also is the strength of my head; Judah is my law-giver;
Philistia, be thou glad of me.
Psalm 60, v. 7

26 Moab is my wash-pot; over Edom will I cast out my shoe.
Psalm 60, v. 8

27 Their delight is in lies; they give good words with their mouth, but curse with their heart.
Psalm 62, v. 4

1 As for the children of men, they are but vanity:
   the children of men are deceitful upon the
   weights, they are altogether lighter than vanity
   itself.
   O trust not in wrong and robbery, give not
   yourselves unto vanity: if riches increase, set
   not your heart upon them.
   Psalm 62, v. 9

2 God spake once, and twice I have also heard the
   same: that power belongeth unto God;
   And that thou, Lord, art merciful: for thou
   rewardest every man according to his work.
   Psalm 62, v. 11

3 My soul thirsteth for thee, my flesh also longeth
   after thee: in a barren and dry land where no
   water is.
   Psalm 63, v. 2

4 These also that seek the hurt of my soul: they
   shall go under the earth.
   Let them fall upon the edge of the sword: that they
   may be a portion for foxes.
   Psalm 63, v. 10

5 Thou, O God, art praised in Sion: and unto thee
   shall the vow be performed in Jerusalem.
   Thou that hearest the prayer: unto thee shall all
   flesh come.
   Psalm 65, v. 1

6 Thou that art the hope of all the ends of the earth,
   and of them that remain in the broad sea.
   Who in his strength setteth fast the mountains:
   and is girded about with power.
   Who stilleth the raging of the sea: and the noise of
   his waves, and the madness of the people.
   Psalm 65, v. 5

7 Thou crownest the year with thy goodness: and
   thy clouds drop fatness.
   They shall drop upon the dwellings of the
   wilderness: and the little hills shall rejoice on
   every side.
   The folds shall be full of sheep: the valleys also
   shall stand so thick with corn, that they shall
   laugh and sing.
   Psalm 65, v. 12

8 God be merciful unto us, and bless us: and shew
   us the light of his countenance, and be merciful
   unto us;
   That thy way may be known upon earth: thy
   saving health among all nations.
   Let the people praise thee, O God: yea, let all the
   people praise thee.
   Psalm 67, v. 1

9 Then shall the earth bring forth her increase: and
   God, even our own God, shall give us his blessing.
   Psalm 67, v. 6

10 Let God arise, and let his enemies be scattered: let
    them also that hate him flee before him.
    Psalm 68, v. 1

11 O sing unto God, and sing praises unto his name:
    magnify him that rideth upon the heavens, as it
    were upon an horse; praise him in his name JAH,
    and rejoice before him.

He is a Father of the fatherless, and defendeth the
cause of the widows: even God in his holy
habitation.
He is the God that maketh men to be of one mind
in an house, and bringeth the prisoners out of
captivity: but letteth the runagates continue in
scarceness.
O God, when thou wentest forth before the people:
when thou wentest through the wilderness,
The earth shook, and the heavens dropped at the
presence of God.
   Psalm 68, v. 4

12 The Lord gave the word: great was the company
    of the preachers.
    Kings with their armies did flee, and were
    discomfited: and they of the household divided the
    spoil.
    Though ye have lien among the pots, yet shall ye
    be as the wings of a dove: that is covered with
    silver wings, and her feathers like gold.
    Psalm 68, v. 11

13 Why hop ye so, ye high hills? this is God's hill, in
    which it pleaseth him to dwell.
    Psalm 68, v. 16

14 Thou art gone up on high, thou hast led captivity
    captive, and received gifts for men.
    Psalm 68, v. 18

15 The zeal of thine house hath even eaten me.
    Psalm 69, v. 9

16 Thy rebuke hath broken my heart; I am full of
    heaviness: I looked for some to have pity on me,
    but there was no man, neither found I any to
    comfort me.
    They gave me gall to eat: and when I was thirsty
    they gave me vinegar to drink.
    Psalm 69, v. 21

17 Let their habitation be void: and no man to dwell
    in their tents.
    Psalm 69, v. 26

18 Let them be wiped out of the book of the living:
    and not be written among the righteous.
    Psalm 69, v. 29

19 Let them be ashamed and confounded that seek
    after my soul: let them be turned backward and
    put to confusion that wish me evil.
    Let them for their reward be soon brought to
    shame: that cry over me, There, there.
    Psalm 70, v. 2

20 I am become as it were a monster unto many: but
    my sure trust is in thee.
    Psalm 71, v. 6

21 Cast me not away in the time of age: forsake me
    not when my strength faileth me.
    Psalm 71, v. 8

22 The mountains also shall bring peace: and the
    little hills righteousness unto the people.
    Psalm 72, v. 3

23 His dominion shall be also from the one sea to the
    other: and from the flood unto the world's end.
    They that dwell in the wilderness shall kneel
    before him: his enemies shall lick the dust.

The Kings of Tharsis and of the isles shall give presents: the kings of Arabia and Saba shall bring gifts.
All kings shall fall down before him: all nations shall do him service.
Psalm 72, v. 8

1 He shall live, and unto him shall be given of the gold of Arabia.
Psalm 72, v. 15

2 Then thought I to understand this: but it was too hard for me.
Until I went into the sanctuary of God: then understood I the end of these men.
Psalm 73, v. 15

3 O deliver not the soul of thy turtle-dove unto the multitude of the enemies: and forget not the congregation of the poor for ever.
Psalm 74, v. 20

4 For promotion cometh neither from the east, nor from the west: nor yet from the south.
Psalm 75, v. 7

5 In Jewry is God known: his Name is great in Israel.
At Salem is his tabernacle: and his dwelling in Sion.
Psalm 76, v. 1

6 I have considered the days of old: and the years that are past.
Psalm 77, v. 5

7 Hear my law, O my people: incline your ears unto the words of my mouth.
I will open my mouth in a parable: I will declare hard sentences of old;
Which we have heard and known: and such as our fathers have told us.
Psalm 78, v. 1

8 Not to be as their forefathers, a faithless and stubborn generation: a generation that set not their heart aright, and whose spirit cleaveth not stedfastly unto God.
Psalm 78, v. 9

9 He divided the sea, and let them go through: he made the waters to stand on an heap.
Psalm 78, v. 14

10 He rained down manna also upon them for to eat: and gave them food from heaven.
So man did eat angels' food: for he sent them meat enough.
Psalm 78, v. 25

11 So the Lord awaked as one out of sleep: and like a giant refreshed with wine.
Psalm 78, v. 66

12 Turn us again, O God: shew the light of thy countenance, and we shall be whole.
Psalm 80, v. 3

13 Sing we merrily unto God our strength: make a cheerful noise unto the God of Jacob.
Take the psalm, bring hither the tabret: the merry harp with the lute.

Blow up the trumpet in the new-moon: even in the time appointed, and upon our solemn feast-day.
Psalm 81, v. 1

14 I have said, Ye are gods: and ye are all children of the most Highest.
But ye shall die like men: and fall like one of the princes.
Psalm 82, v. 6

15 O how amiable are thy dwellings: thou Lord of hosts!
My soul hath a desire and longing to enter into the courts of the Lord: my heart and my flesh rejoice in the living God.
Yea, the sparrow hath found her an house, and the swallow a nest where she may lay her young: even thy altars, O Lord of hosts, my King and my God.
Psalm 84, v. 1; see **Scottish Metrical Psalms** 675:5

16 Blessed is the man whose strength is in thee: in whose heart are thy ways.
Who going through the vale of misery use it for a well: and the pools are filled with water.
They will go from strength to strength.
Psalm 84, v. 5

17 For one day in thy courts: is better than a thousand.
I had rather be a door-keeper in the house of my God: than to dwell in the tents of ungodliness.
Psalm 84, v. 10

18 Wilt thou not turn again, and quicken us: that thy people may rejoice in thee?
Psalm 85, v. 6

19 Mercy and truth are met together: righteousness and peace have kissed each other.
Truth shall flourish out of the earth: and righteousness hath looked down from heaven.
Psalm 85, v. 10

20 Very excellent things are spoken of thee: thou city of God.
Psalm 87, v. 2

21 Lord, thou hast been our refuge: from one generation to another.
Before the mountains were brought forth, or ever the earth and the world were made: thou art God from everlasting, and world without end.
Psalm 90, v. 1

22 For a thousand years in thy sight are but as yesterday: seeing that is past as a watch in the night.
As soon as thou scatterest them they are even as a sleep: and fade away suddenly like the grass.
In the morning it is green, and groweth up: but in the evening it is cut down, dried up, and withered.
Psalm 90, v. 4

23 The days of our age are threescore years and ten; and though men be so strong that they come to fourscore years: yet is their strength then but labour and sorrow; so soon passeth it away, and we are gone.
Psalm 90, v. 10

1 So teach us to number our days: that we may apply our hearts unto wisdom.

Psalm 90, v. 12

2 For he shall deliver thee from the snare of the hunter and from the noisome pestilence.
He shall defend thee under his wings, and thou shalt be safe under his feathers: his faithfulness and truth shall be thy shield and buckler.

Psalm 91, v. 3

3 Thou shalt not be afraid for any terror by night: nor for the arrow that flieth by day;
For the pestilence that walketh in darkness: nor for the sickness that destroyeth in the noon-day.
A thousand shall fall beside thee, and ten thousand at thy right hand: but it shall not come nigh thee.

Psalm 91, v. 5

4 For thou, Lord, art my hope: thou hast set thine house of defence very high.
There shall no evil happen unto thee: neither shall any plague come nigh thy dwelling.
For he shall give his angels charge over thee: to keep thee in all thy ways.
They shall bear thee in their hands: that thou hurt not thy foot against a stone.
Thou shalt go upon the lion and adder: the young lion and the dragon shalt thou tread under thy feet.

Psalm 91, v. 9

5 With long life will I satisfy him: and shew him my salvation.

Psalm 91, v. 16

6 The Lord is King, and hath put on glorious apparel: the Lord hath put on his apparel, and girded himself with strength.
He hath made the round world so sure: that it cannot be moved.

Psalm 93, v. 1

7 The floods are risen, O Lord, the floods have lift up their voice: the floods lift up their waves.
The waves of the sea are mighty, and rage horribly: but yet the Lord, who dwelleth on high, is mightier.
Thy testimonies, O Lord, are very sure: holiness becometh thine house for ever.

Psalm 93, v. 4

8 He that planted the ear, shall he not hear: or he that made the eye, shall he not see?

Psalm 94, v. 9

9 O come, let us sing unto the Lord: let us heartily rejoice in the strength of our salvation.
Let us come before his presence with thanksgiving: and shew ourselves glad in him with psalms.

Psalm 95, v. 1

10 In his hand are all the corners of the earth: and the strength of the hills is his also.
The sea is his, and he made it: and his hands prepared the dry land.
O come, let us worship and fall down: and kneel before the Lord our Maker.

For he is the Lord our God: and we are the people of his pasture, and the sheep of his hand.
To-day if ye will hear his voice, harden not your hearts: as in the provocation, and as in the day of temptation in the wilderness;
When your fathers tempted me: proved me, and saw my works.
Forty years long was I grieved with this generation, and said It is a people that do err in their hearts, for they have not known my ways;
Unto whom I sware in my wrath: that they should not enter into my rest.

Psalm 95, v. 4

11 Ascribe unto the Lord the honour due unto his Name: bring presents, and come into his courts.
O worship the Lord in the beauty of holiness: let the whole earth stand in awe of him.

Psalm 96, v. 8

12 The Lord is King, the earth may be glad thereof: yea, the multitude of the isles may be glad thereof.

Psalm 97, v. 1

13 O sing unto the Lord a new song: for he hath done marvellous things.
With his own right hand, and with his holy arm: hath he gotten himself the victory.

Psalm 98, v. 1; see **Bible** 114:28

14 Praise the Lord upon the harp: sing to the harp with a psalm of thanksgiving.
With trumpets also, and shawms: O shew yourselves joyful before the Lord the King.

Psalm 98, v. 6

15 With righteousness shall he judge the world: and the people with equity.

Psalm 98, v. 10

16 The Lord is King, be the people never so impatient: he sitteth between the cherubims, be the earth never so unquiet.

Psalm 99, v. 1

17 O be joyful in the Lord, all ye lands: serve the Lord with gladness, and come before his presence with a song.
Be ye sure that the Lord he is God: it is he that hath made us, and not we ourselves; we are his people, and the sheep of his pasture.

Psalm 100, v. 1; see **Bible** 115:1

18 I am become like a pelican in the wilderness: and like an owl that is in the desert.
I have watched, and am even as it were a sparrow: that sitteth alone upon the house-top.

Psalm 102, v. 6

19 Thou, Lord, in the beginning hast laid the foundation of the earth: and the heavens are the work of thy hands.
They shall perish, but thou shalt endure: they all shall wax old as doth a garment;
And as a vesture shalt thou change them, and they shall be changed: but thou art the same, and thy years shall not fail.

Psalm 102, v. 25

1 Praise the Lord, O my soul: and forget not all his benefits.

Psalm 103, v. 2

2 The Lord is full of compassion and mercy: long-suffering, and of great goodness.
He will not alway be chiding: neither keepeth he his anger for ever.

Psalm 103, v. 8

3 For look how high the heaven is in comparison of the earth: so great is his mercy also toward them that fear him.
Look how wide also the east is from the west: so far hath he set our sins from us.
Yea, like as a father pitieth his own children: even so is the Lord merciful unto them that fear him.
For he knoweth whereof we are made: he remembereth that we are but dust.

Psalm 103, v. 11

4 The days of man are but as grass: for he flourisheth as a flower of a field.
For as soon as the wind goeth over it, it is gone: and the place thereof shall know it no more.

Psalm 103, v. 15

5 Who layeth the beams of his chambers in the waters: and maketh the clouds his chariot, and walketh upon the wings of the wind.
He maketh his angels spirits: and his ministers a flaming fire.
He laid the foundations of the earth: that it never should move at any time.
Thou coveredst it with the deep like as with a garment: the waters stand in the hills.

Psalm 104, v. 3

6 Thou hast set them their bounds which they shall not pass: neither turn again to cover the earth.
He sendeth the springs into the rivers: which run among the hills.
All beasts of the field drink thereof: and the wild asses quench their thirst.
Beside them shall the fowls of the air have their habitation: and sing among the branches.

Psalm 104, v. 9

7 He bringeth forth grass for the cattle: and green herb for the service of men;
That he may bring food out of the earth, and wine that maketh glad the heart of man: and oil to make him a cheerful countenance, and bread to strengthen man's heart.
The trees of the Lord also are full of sap: even the cedars of Libanus which he hath planted.

Psalm 104, v. 14

8 The high hills are a refuge for the wild goats: and so are the stony rocks for the conies.
He appointed the moon for certain seasons: and the sun knoweth his going down.

Psalm 104, v. 18

9 Thou makest darkness that it may be night: wherein all the beasts of the forest do move.
The lions roaring after their prey: do seek their meat from God.

Psalm 104, v. 20

10 There go the ships, and there is that Leviathan: whom thou hast made to take his pastime therein.

Psalm 104, v. 26

11 The earth shall tremble at the look of him: if he do but touch the hills, they shall smoke.

Psalm 104, v. 32

12 He had sent a man before them: even Joseph, who was sold to be a bond-servant;
Whose feet they hurt in the stocks: the iron entered into his soul.

Psalm 105, v. 17

13 The king sent, and delivered him: the prince of the people let him go free.
He made him lord also of his house: and ruler of all his substance;
That he might inform his princes after his will: and teach his senators wisdom.

Psalm 105, v. 20

14 Yea, they thought scorn of that pleasant land: and gave no credence to his word;
But murmured in their tents: and hearkened not unto the voice of the Lord.

Psalm 106, v. 24

15 Thus were they stained with their own works: and went a whoring with their own inventions.

Psalm 106, v. 38

16 Such as sit in darkness, and in the shadow of death: being fast bound in misery and iron.

Psalm 107, v. 10

17 Their soul abhorred all manner of meat: and they were even hard at death's door.

Psalm 107, v. 18

18 They that go down to the sea in ships: and occupy their business in great waters;
These men see the works of the Lord: and his wonders in the deep.

Psalm 107, v. 23

19 They reel to and fro, and stagger like a drunken man: and are at their wit's end.
So when they cry unto the Lord in their trouble: he delivereth them out of their distress.
For he maketh the storm to cease: so that the waves thereof are still.
Then are they glad, because they are at rest: and so he bringeth them unto the haven where they would be.

Psalm 107, v. 27

20 The Lord said unto my Lord: Sit thou on my right hand, until I make thine enemies thy footstool.

Psalm 110, v. 1

21 Thou art a Priest for ever after the order of Melchisedech.

Psalm 110, v. 4

22 The fear of the Lord is the beginning of wisdom: a good understanding have all they that do thereafter; the praise of it endureth for ever.

Psalm 111, v. 10

23 A good man is merciful, and lendeth: and will guide his words with discretion.

For he shall never be moved: and the righteous shall be had in everlasting remembrance.
Psalm 112, v. 5

1 He maketh the barren woman to keep house: and to be a joyful mother of children.
Psalm 113, v. 8

2 When Israel came out of Egypt: and the house of Jacob from among the strange people,
Judah was his sanctuary: and Israel his dominion.
The sea saw that, and fled: Jordan was driven back.
The mountains skipped like rams: and the little hills like young sheep.
Psalm 114, v. 1

3 Not unto us, O Lord, not unto us, but unto thy Name give the praise.
Psalm 115, v. 1; see **Bible** 115:3

4 They have mouths, and speak not: eyes have they, and see not.
They have ears, and hear not: noses have they, and smell not.
They have hands, and handle not: feet have they, and walk not: neither speak they through their throat.
Psalm 115, v. 5

5 The snares of death compassed me round about: and the pains of hell gat hold upon me.
Psalm 116, v. 3

6 And why? thou hast delivered my soul from death: mine eyes from tears, and my feet from falling.
Psalm 116, v. 8

7 I said in my haste, All men are liars.
Psalm 116, v. 10

8 I will pay my vows now in the presence of all his people: right dear in the sight of the Lord is the death of his saints.
Psalm 116, v. 13

9 The right hand of the Lord hath the pre-eminence: the right hand of the Lord bringeth mighty things to pass.
Psalm 118, v. 16

10 The same stone which the builders refused: is become the head-stone in the corner.
This is the Lord's doing: and it is marvellous in our eyes.
This is the day which the Lord hath made: we will rejoice and be glad in it.
Psalm 118, v. 22

11 Blessed be he that cometh in the Name of the Lord: we have wished you good luck, ye that are of the house of the Lord.
Psalm 118, v. 26

12 The law of thy mouth is dearer unto me: than thousands of gold and silver.
Psalm 119, v. 72

13 Thy word is a lantern unto my feet: and a light unto my paths.
Psalm 119, v. 105

14 Woe is me that I am constrained to dwell with Mesech: and to have my habitation among the tents of Kedar.
Psalm 120, v. 4

15 I labour for peace, but when I speak unto them therof: they make them ready to battle.
Psalm 120, v. 6

16 I will lift up mine eyes unto the hills: from whence cometh my help.
My help cometh even from the Lord: who hath made heaven and earth.
He will not suffer thy foot to be moved: and he that keepeth thee will not sleep.
Behold, he that keepeth Israel: shall neither slumber nor sleep.
The Lord himself is thy keeper: the Lord is thy defence upon thy right hand;
So that the sun shall not burn thee by day: neither the moon by night.
Psalm 121, v. 1; see **Scottish Metrical Psalms** 675:6

17 The Lord shall preserve thy going out, and thy coming in: from this time forth for evermore.
Psalm 121, v. 8

18 I was glad when they said unto me: We will go into the house of the Lord.
Our feet shall stand in thy gates: O Jerusalem.
Jerusalem is built as a city: that is at unity in itself.
For thither the tribes go up, even the tribes of the Lord.
Psalm 122, v. 1

19 O pray for the peace of Jerusalem: they shall prosper that love thee.
Peace be within thy walls: and plenteousness with thy palaces.
Psalm 122, v. 6

20 If the Lord himself had not been on our side, now may Israel say: if the Lord himself had not been on our side, when men rose up against us;
They had swallowed us up quick: when they were so wrathfully displeased at us.
Psalm 124, v. 1

21 Our soul is escaped even as a bird out of the snare of the fowler: the snare is broken, and we are delivered.
Our help standeth in the Name of the Lord: who hath made heaven and earth.
Psalm 124, v. 6; see **Book of Common Prayer** 132:20

22 The hills stand about Jerusalem: even so standeth the Lord round about his people, from this time forth for evermore.
Psalm 125, v. 2

23 When the Lord turned again the captivity of Sion: then were we like unto them that dream.
Then was our mouth filled with laughter: and our tongue with joy.
Psalm 126, v. 1

24 Turn our captivity, O Lord: as the rivers in the south.
They that sow in tears: shall reap in joy.
He that now goeth on his way weeping, and

beareth forth good seed: shall doubtless come again with joy, and bring his sheaves with him.
Psalm 126, v. 5

1 Except the Lord build the house: their labour is but lost that build it.
Except the Lord keep the city: the watchman waketh but in vain.
Psalm 127, v. 1; see **Bible** 115:5

2 Like as the arrows in the hand of the giant: even so are the young children.
Happy is the man that hath his quiver full of them: they shall not be ashamed when they speak with their enemies in the gate.
Psalm 127, v. 5

3 Thy wife shall be as the fruitful vine: upon the walls of thine house.
Thy children like the olive-branches: round about thy table.
Psalm 128, v. 3

4 Many a time have they fought against me from my youth up: may Israel now say.
Psalm 129, v. 1

5 But they have not prevailed against me.
The plowers plowed upon my back: and made long furrows.
Psalm 129, v. 2

6 Out of the deep have I called unto thee, O Lord: Lord, hear my voice.
O let thine ears consider well: the voice of my complaint.
If thou, Lord, wilt be extreme to mark what is done amiss: O Lord, who may abide it?
Psalm 130, v. 1; see **Bible** 115:6

7 My soul fleeth unto the Lord: before the morning watch, I say, before the morning watch.
Psalm 130, v. 6

8 Lord, I am not high-minded: I have no proud looks.
I do not exercise myself in great matters: which are too high for me.
Psalm 131, v. 1

9 Behold, how good and joyful a thing it is: brethren, to dwell together in unity!
Psalm 133, v. 1

10 He smote divers nations: and slew mighty kings;
Sehon king of the Amorites, and Og the king of Basan: and all the kingdoms of Canaan;
And gave their land to be an heritage: even an heritage unto Israel his people.
Psalm 135, v. 10

11 O give thanks unto the Lord, for he is gracious: and his mercy endureth for ever.
Psalm 136, v. 1; see **Milton** 529:28

12 By the waters of Babylon we sat down and wept: when we remembered thee, O Sion.
As for our harps, we hanged them up: upon the trees that are therein.
Psalm 137, v. 1

13 How shall we sing the Lord's song: in a strange land?

If I forget thee, O Jerusalem: let my right hand forget her cunning.
Psalm 137, v. 4

14 O Lord, thou hast searched me out, and known me: thou knowest my down-sitting, and mine up-rising; thou understandest my thoughts long before.
Psalm 139, v. 1

15 Such knowledge is too wonderful and excellent for me: I cannot attain unto it.
Psalm 139, v. 5

16 If I climb up into the heaven, thou art there: if I go down to hell, thou art there also.
If I take the wings of the morning: and remain in the uttermost parts of the sea;
Even there also shall thy hand lead me: and thy right hand shall hold me.
Psalm 139, v. 7

17 I will give thanks unto thee, for I am fearfully and wonderfully made.
Psalm 139, v. 13

18 Thine eyes did see my substance, yet being imperfect: and in thy book were all my members written;
Which day by day were fashioned: when as yet there were none of them.
Psalm 139, v. 15

19 Try me, O God, and seek the ground of my heart: prove me, and examine my thoughts.
Psalm 139, v. 23

20 Let the lifting up of my hands be an evening sacrifice.
Set a watch, O Lord, before my mouth: and keep the door of my lips.
Psalm 141, v. 2

21 Let the ungodly fall into their own nets together: and let me ever escape them.
Psalm 141, v. 11

22 Enter not into judgement with thy servant: for in thy sight shall no man living be justified.
Psalm 143, v. 2

23 Save me, and deliver me from the hand of strange children: whose mouth talketh of vanity, and their right hand is a right hand of iniquity.
That our sons may grow up as the young plants: and that our daughters may be as the polished corners of the temple.
Psalm 144, v. 11

24 The Lord upholdeth all such as fall: and lifteth up all those that are down.
Psalm 145, v. 14

25 Thou givest them their meat in due season.
Thou openest thine hand: and fillest all things living with plenteousness.
Psalm 145, v. 15

26 O put not your trust in princes, nor in any child of man: for there is no help in them.
Psalm 146, v. 2

1 The Lord looseth men out of prison: the Lord giveth sight to the blind.
Psalm 146, v. 7

2 The Lord careth for the strangers; he defendeth the fatherless and widow: as for the way of the ungodly, he turneth it upside down.
Psalm 146, v. 9

3 A joyful and pleasant thing it is to be thankful. The Lord doth build up Jerusalem: and gather together the out-casts of Israel.
He healeth those that are broken in heart: and giveth medicine to heal their sickness.
He telleth the number of the stars: and calleth them all by their names.
Psalm 147, v. 1

4 He hath no pleasure in the strength of an horse: neither delighteth he in any man's legs.
Psalm 147, v. 10

5 He giveth snow like wool: and scattereth the hoar-frost like ashes.
He casteth forth his ice like morsels: who is able to abide his frost?
Psalm 147, v. 16

6 Praise the Lord upon earth: ye dragons, and all deeps;
Fire and hail, snow and vapours: wind and storm, fulfilling his word.
Psalm 148, v. 7

7 Young men and maidens, old men and children, praise the Name of the Lord: for his Name only is excellent, and his praise above heaven and earth.
Psalm 148, v. 12

8 Let the saints be joyful with glory: let them rejoice in their beds.
Let the praises of God be in their mouth: and a two-edged sword in their hands;
To be avenged of the heathen: and to rebuke the people;
To bind their kings in chains: and their nobles with links of iron.
Psalm 149, v. 5; see **Macaulay** *499:4*

9 Praise him upon the well-tuned cymbals: praise him upon the loud cymbals.
Let every thing that hath breath: praise the Lord.
Psalm 150, v. 5

10 Be pleased to receive into thy Almighty and most gracious protection the persons of us thy servants, and the Fleet in which we serve.
Forms of Prayer to be Used at Sea First Prayer

11 That we may be . . . a security for such as pass on the seas upon their lawful occasions.
Forms of Prayer to be Used at Sea First Prayer

12 We therefore commit his body to the deep, to be turned into corruption, looking for the resurrection of the body (when the Sea shall give up her dead).
Forms of Prayer to be Used at Sea At the Burial of their Dead at Sea

13 Come, Holy Ghost, our souls inspire,
And lighten with celestial fire.

Thou the anointing Spirit art,
Who dost thy seven-fold gifts impart.
Ordering of Priests 'Veni, Creator Spiritus'; translation by Bishop John Cosin, 1627, from the *c.*9th century original, possibly by Rabanus Maurus (776–856)

14 Holy Scripture containeth all things necessary to salvation.
Articles of Religion (1562) no. 6

15 Man is very far gone from original righteousness.
Articles of Religion (1562) no. 9

16 It is a thing plainly repugnant to the Word of God, and the custom of the Primitive Church, to have publick Prayer in the Church, or to minister the Sacraments in a tongue not understood of the people.
Articles of Religion (1562) no. 24

17 The sacrifices of Masses, in the which it was commonly said, that the Priest did offer Christ for the quick and the dead, to have remission of pain or guilt, were blasphemous fables, and dangerous deceits.
Articles of Religion (1562) no. 31

18 The Bishop of Rome hath no jurisdiction in this Realm of England.
Articles of Religion (1562) no. 37

19 It is lawful for Christian men, at the commandment of the Magistrate, to wear weapons, and serve in the wars.
Articles of Religion (1562) no. 37

20 The Riches and Goods of Christians are not common, as touching the right, title, and possession of the same, as certain Anabaptists do falsely boast.
Articles of Religion (1562) no. 38

21 A Man may not marry his Mother.
A Table of Kindred and Affinity

John Wilkes Booth 1838–65
American actor and assassin
see also **Last words** *474:9*

22 *Sic semper tyrannis!* The South is avenged.
having shot President **Lincoln**, *14 April 1865*
in *New York Times* 15 April 1865; the second part of the statement does not appear in any contemporary source, and is possibly apocryphal; see **Mottoes** 552:18

Paul Booth

23 Who put the colours in the rainbow?
Who put the salt into the sea?
Who put the cold into the snowflake?
Who made you and me?
Who put the hump upon the camel?
Who put the neck on the giraffe? . . .
God made all of these.
'Who put the colours in the rainbow?'

William Booth 1829–1912
British religious leader; founder of the Salvation Army, 1878
on Booth: see **Lindsay** *486:4*

24 The submerged tenth.
defined by Booth as 'three million men, women, and

*children, a vast despairing multitude in a condition
nominally free, but really enslaved'*
In Darkest England (1890) pt. 1, title of ch. 2

Frances Boothby fl. 1670
English dramatist

1 I'm hither come, but what d'ye think to say?
A woman's pen presents you with a play:
Who smiling told me I'd be sure to see
That once confirmed, the house would empty be.
Marcelia (1670) prologue

Robert Boothby 1900–86
British Conservative politician

2 *You* speak for Britain!
*to Arthur Greenwood, acting Leader of the Labour
Party, after Neville **Chamberlain** had failed to
announce an ultimatum to Germany; perhaps taking
up an appeal already voiced by Leo **Amery***
Harold Nicolson, diary, 2 September 1939; see **Amery** 13:4

James H. Boren 1925–
American bureaucrat

3 Guidelines for bureaucrats: (1) When in charge,
ponder. (2) When in trouble, delegate. (3) When
in doubt, mumble.
in *New York Times* 8 November 1970

Jorge Luis Borges 1899–1986
Argentinian writer

4 The universe (which others call the Library) is
composed of an indefinite, perhaps an infinite
number of hexagonal galleries.
Ficciones (1956) 'The Library of Babel'

5 On those remote pages [of the *Celestial Emporium
of Benevolent Knowledge*] it is written that animals
are divided into (a) those that belong to the
Emperor, (b) embalmed ones, (c) those that are
trained, (d) suckling pigs, (e) mermaids, (f)
fabulous ones, (g) stray dogs, (h) those that are
included in this classification, (i) those that
tremble as if they were mad, (j) innumerable ones,
(k) those drawn with a very fine camel's hair
brush, (l) others, (m) those that have just broken a
flower vase, (n) those that resemble flies from a
distance.
Other Inquisitions (1966)

6 The original is unfaithful to the translation.
*of Henley's translation of **Beckford**'s* Vathek
Sobre el 'Vathek' de William Beckford (1943)

7 For one of those gnostics, the visible universe was
an illusion or, more precisely, a sophism. Mirrors
and fatherhood are abominable because they
multiply it and extend it.
Tlön, Uqbar, Orbis Tertius (1941)

8 The Falklands thing was a fight between two bald
men over a comb.
application of a proverbial phrase
in *Time* 14 February 1983

Cesare Borgia see Mottoes 552:2

George Borrow 1803–81
English writer

9 There are no countries in the world less known by
the British than these selfsame British Islands.
Lavengro (1851) preface

10 There's night and day, brother, both sweet things;
sun, moon, and stars, brother, all sweet things:
there's likewise a wind on the heath. Life is very
sweet, brother; who would wish to die?
Lavengro (1851) ch. 25

11 Let no one sneer at the bruisers of England—what
were the gladiators of Rome, or the bull-fighters of
Spain, in its palmiest days, compared to England's
bruisers?
Lavengro (1851) ch. 26

12 A losing trade, I assure you, sir: literature is a
drug.
Lavengro (1851) ch. 30

13 Fear God, and take your own part.
The Romany Rye (1857) ch. 16

☐ **Borrowed titles**
see box overleaf

Pierre Bosquet 1810–61
French general

14 *C'est magnifique, mais ce n'est pas la guerre.*
It is magnificent, but it is not war.
*on the charge of the Light Brigade at Balaclava, 25
October 1854*
Cecil Woodham-Smith *The Reason Why* (1953) ch. 12

John Collins Bossidy 1860–1928
American oculist

15 And this is good old Boston,
The home of the bean and the cod,
Where the Lowells talk to the Cabots
And the Cabots talk only to God.
verse spoken at Holy Cross College alumni dinner in
Boston, Massachusetts, 1910, in *Springfield Sunday
Republican* 14 December 1924

Jacques-Bénigne Bossuet 1627–1704
French preacher

16 *L'Angleterre, ah, la perfide Angleterre, que le rempart
de ses mers rendait inaccessible aux Romains, la foi du
Sauveur y est abordée.*
England, ah, faithless England, which the
protection afforded by its seas rendered
inaccessible to the Romans, the faith of the
Saviour spread even there.
first sermon on the feast of the Circumcision, in *Oeuvres de
Bossuet* (1816) vol. 11; see **Ximénèz** 852:20

Borrowed titles

1 Across the river and into the trees.
novel (1950) by Ernest **Hemingway**; see **Last words**
472:20

2 Brave new world.
novel (1932) by Aldous **Huxley**; see **Shakespeare** 719:7

3 By Grand Central Station I sat down and wept.
book (1945) by Elizabeth Smart (1913-86); see **Book of Common Prayer** 143:12

4 The catcher in the rye.
novel (1951) by J. D. **Salinger**; see **Burns** 170:17, **Salinger** 664:1

'You know that song "If a body catch a body comin' through the rye"? I'd like—'
'It's "If a body *meet* a body coming through the rye"!' old Phoebe said.
The Catcher in the Rye (1951) ch. 22

5 An evil cradling.
book (1992) by Brian **Keenan**; see **Koran** 459:17

6 Far from the madding crowd.
novel (1874) by Thomas **Hardy**; see **Gray** 361:7

7 For whom the bell tolls.
novel (1940) by Ernest **Hemingway**; see **Donne** 282:2

8 The glittering prizes.
novel (1976) by Frederic **Raphael**; see **Smith** 742:1

9 The golden bough.
book (1890-1915) by James George Frazer (1854-1941); from William Pitt's 1743 translation:

A mighty tree, that bears a golden bough.
Virgil *Aeneid* bk. 6

10 The grapes of wrath.
novel (1939) by John **Steinbeck**; see **Howe** 405:15

11 The heart is a lonely hunter.
novel (1940) by Carson McCullers (1917-67)

My heart is a lonely hunter that hunts on a lonely hill.
Fiona McLeod (William Sharp) (1855-1905) 'The Lonely Hunter' (1896) st. 6

12 The last enemy.
book (1942) by Richard Hillary (1919-43); see **Bible** 108:5

13 A man for all seasons.
play (1960) by Robert **Bolt**; see **Whittington** 834:7

14 Pride and prejudice.
novel (1813) by Jane **Austen**; see **Burney** 169:23

15 Remembrance of things past.
translation by C. K. Scott-Moncrieff and S. Hudson of *À la recherche du temps perdu* (1913-27) by Marcel **Proust**; see **Shakespeare** 723:1

16 Ring of bright water.
book (1960) by Gavin Maxwell (1914-69); see **Raine** 640:17

17 The seven pillars of wisdom.
book (1926) by T. E. **Lawrence**; see **Bible** 84:6

18 The singer not the song.
novel (1959) by Audrey Erskine Lindop

The singer not the song.
West Indian calypso

19 Two solitudes.
novel (1945) by Hugh MacLennan (1907-90); see **Rilke** 649:1

James Boswell 1740-95

*Scottish lawyer; biographer of Samuel **Johnson***
on Boswell: see **Macaulay** *498:1,* **Walpole** *819:15*

20 I think there is a blossom about me of something more distinguished than the generality of mankind.
Boswell's London Journal (ed. F. A. Pottle, 1950) 20 January 1763

21 I am, I flatter myself, completely a citizen of the world. In my travels through Holland, Germany, Switzerland, Italy, Corsica, France, I never felt myself from home.
Journal of a Tour to the Hebrides (ed. F. A. Pottle, 1936) 14 August 1773

22 We [Boswell and Johnson] are both *Tories*; both convinced of the utility of monarchical power, and both lovers of that reverence and affection for a sovereign which constitute loyalty, a principle which I take to be absolutely extinguished in Britain.
Journal of a Tour to the Hebrides (ed. F. A. Pottle, 1936) 13 September 1773

23 A page of my Journal is like a cake of portable soup. A little may be diffused into a considerable portion.
Journal of a Tour to the Hebrides (ed. F. A. Pottle, 1936) 13 September 1773

24 I have never yet exerted ambition in rising in the state. But sure I am, no man has made his way better to the best company.
Journal of a Tour to the Hebrides (ed. F. A. Pottle, 1936) 16 September 1773

25 JOHNSON: Well, we had a good talk.
BOSWELL: Yes, Sir; you tossed and gored several persons.
The Life of Samuel Johnson (1791) Summer 1768

26 A man, indeed, is not genteel when he gets drunk; but most vices may be committed very genteelly: a man may debauch his friend's wife genteelly: he may cheat at cards genteelly.
The Life of Samuel Johnson (1791) 6 April 1775

Horatio Bottomley 1860–1933

British newspaper proprietor and financier

1 *reply to a prison visitor who asked if he were sewing:*
No, reaping.
S. T. Felstead *Horatio Bottomley* (1936) ch. 16

2 What poor education I have received has been
gained in the University of Life.
speech at the Oxford Union, 2 December 1920; Beverley
Nichols 25 (1926) ch. 7

Lucien Bouchard 1938–

Canadian lawyer and politician, Premier of Quebec 1996–2001

3 Canada is divisible because it's not a real country.
Canada is two nations, two peoples, two territories
and this one is ours and we're keeping it!
*when asked, after the 1995 Quebec referendum on
independence, why he felt no guilt about having
Quebec separate from the rest of Canada*
statement at a press conference, January 1996

Dion Boucicault (Dionysius Lardner Boursiquot) 1820–90

Irish dramatist

4 Men talk of killing time, while time quietly kills
them.
London Assurance (1841) act 2, sc. 1; see **Sitwell** 739:1

Antoine Boulay de la Meurthe 1761–1840

French statesman

5 *C'est pire qu'un crime, c'est une faute.*
It is worse than a crime, it is a blunder.
*on hearing of the execution of the Duc d'Enghien,
captured in Baden by Napoleon's forces, in 1804*
C.-A. Sainte-Beuve *Nouveaux Lundis* (1870) vol. 12

Harold Edwin Boulton 1859–1935

British songwriter

6 Devon, glorious Devon!
'Glorious Devon' (1902)

7 Speed, bonnie boat, like a bird on the wing,
'Onward,' the sailors cry;
Carry the lad that's born to be king,
Over the sea to Skye.
'Skye Boat Song' (1908)

Matthew Boulton 1728–1809

British engineer

8 I sell here, Sir, what all the world desires to
have—POWER.
*speaking to **Boswell** of his engineering works*
James Boswell *Life of Samuel Johnson* (1791) 22 March
1776

Henri Bourassa 1868–1952

Canadian journalist and Liberal politician

9 We have in our country the patriotism of
Ontarians, the patriotism of Quebecers and the
patriotism of westerners . . . but there is no
Canadian patriotism, and there will not be a
Canadian nation as long as we do not have a
Canadian patriotism.
speech, the Canadian Club of Toronto, 22 January 1907

F. W. Bourdillon 1852–1921

English poet

10 The night has a thousand eyes,
And the day but one.
Among the Flowers (1878) 'Light'; see **Lyly** 497:4

Paul Bourget 1852–1935

French writer

11 *Il faut vivre comme on pense, sinon tôt ou tard on finit
par penser comme on a vécu.*
We had better live as we think, otherwise sooner
or later we shall end up by thinking as we have
lived.
Le Démon de Midi (1914)

12 *La pensée est à la littérature ce que la lumière est à la
peinture.*
Ideas are to literature what light is to painting.
La Physiologie de l'Amour Moderne (1890)

Louis Bousquet

French songwriter

13 *Nous en rêvons la nuit, nous y pensons le jour,
Ce n'est que Madelon, mais pour nous, c'est l'amour.*
We dream of her by night, we think of her by day,
It's only Madelon, but for us, it's love.
'Quand Madelon' (1914), French soldiers' song of the First
World War

E. E. Bowen 1836–1901

English schoolmaster

14 Forty years on, when afar and asunder
Parted are those who are singing to-day.
'Forty Years On' (Harrow School Song, published 1886)

Elizabeth Bowen 1899–1973

British novelist and short-story writer, born in Ireland

15 My family got their position and drew their power
from a situation that shows an inherent wrong. In
the grip of that situation, England and Ireland
each turned to the other a closed, harsh, distorted
face—a face that, in each case, their lovers would
hardly know.
Bowen's Court (afterword, ed. 2, 1964)

16 The innocent are so few that two of them seldom
meet—when they do, their victims lie strewn
around.
The Death of the Heart (1938) pt. 1, ch. 8

17 It is about five o'clock in an evening that the first
hour of spring strikes—autumn arrives in the
early morning, but spring at the close of a winter
day.
The Death of the Heart (1938) pt. 2, ch. 1

1 There is no end to the violations committed by children on children, quietly talking alone.
   The House in Paris (1935) pt. 1, ch. 2

2 Fate is not an eagle, it creeps like a rat.
   The House in Paris (1935) pt. 2, ch. 2

3 Jealousy is no more than feeling alone against smiling enemies.
   The House in Paris (1935) pt. 2, ch. 8

4 She could not conceive of her country emotionally: it was a way of living, an abstract of several landscapes, or an oblique frayed island, moored at the north but with an air of being detached and washed out west from the British coast.
   The Last September (1929)

5 I could wish that the English kept history in mind more, that the Irish kept it in mind less.
   'Notes on Eire' 9 November 1949

6 A high altar on the move.
   of Edith **Sitwell**
   V. Glendinning *Edith Sitwell* (1981) ch. 25

Lord Bowen 1835–94
English judge

7 The man on the Clapham omnibus.
   the average man
   in *Law Reports* (1903); attributed

8 When I hear of an 'equity' in a case like this, I am reminded of a blind man in a dark room—looking for a black hat—which isn't there.
   John Alderson Foote *Pie-Powder* (1911)

9 The rain, it raineth on the just
   And also on the unjust fella:
   But chiefly on the just, because
   The unjust steals the just's umbrella.
   Walter Sichel *Sands of Time* (1923) ch. 4: see **Bible** 94:31

David Bowie (David Jones) 1947–
English rock musician

10 Ground control to Major Tom.
   'Space Oddity' (1969 song)

11 We have created a child who will be so exposed to the media that he will be lost to his parents by the time he is 12.
   in *Melody Maker* 22 January 1972

12 The 1970s for me started the 21st century—it was the beginning of a true pluralism in social attitudes.
   An Earthling at 50 ITV programme; in *Sunday Times* 12 January 1997

William Lisle Bowles 1762–1850
English clergyman and poet

13 The cause of Freedom is the cause of God!
   A Poetical Address to the Right Honourable Edmund Burke (1791) l. 78

Maurice Bowra 1898–1971
English scholar and literary critic

14 I'm a man more dined against than dining.
   John Betjeman *Summoned by Bells* (1960) ch. 9; see **Shakespeare** 700:19

Boy George 1961–
English pop singer and songwriter

15 Sex has never been an obsession with me. It's just like eating a bag of crisps. Quite nice, but nothing marvellous. Sex is not simply black and white. There's a lot of grey.
   in *Sun* 21 October 1982

Mary Elizabeth Braddon 1837–1915
English novelist

16 It is worse than a crime, Violet; it is an impropriety.
   Vixen (1879) vol. 2, ch. 15

John Bradford c.1510–55
English Protestant martyr

17 But for the grace of God there goes John Bradford.
   on seeing a group of criminals being led to their execution; usually quoted as 'There but for the grace of God go I'
   in *Dictionary of National Biography* (1917–)

F. H. Bradley 1846–1924
English philosopher

18 Metaphysics is the finding of bad reasons for what we believe upon instinct; but to find these reasons is no less an instinct.
   Appearance and Reality (1893) preface

19 The world is the best of all possible worlds, and everything in it is a necessary evil.
   Appearance and Reality (1893) preface

20 Where everything is bad it must be good to know the worst.
   Appearance and Reality (1893) preface

Omar Bradley 1893–1981
American general

21 The way to win an atomic war is to make certain it never starts.
   speech on Armistice Day, 1948

22 We have grasped the mystery of the atom and rejected the Sermon on the Mount.
   speech on Armistice Day, 1948
   Collected Writings (1967) vol. 1

23 The world has achieved brilliance without wisdom, power without conscience. Ours is a world of nuclear giants and ethical infants.
   speech on Armistice Day, 1948
   Collected Writings (1967) vol. 1

Don Bradman 1908–2001
Australian cricketer

1 Bowl fast, bowl faster. When you play Test cricket you don't give Englishmen an inch. Play it tough, all the way. Grind them into the dust.
  Jack Fingleton *Batting from Memory* (1981)

John Bradshaw 1602–59
*English judge at the trial of **Charles I***

2 Rebellion to tyrants is obedience to God.
  suppositious epitaph; Henry S. Randall *Life of Thomas Jefferson* (1865) vol. 3, appendix 4; see **Mottoes** 552:16

Anne Bradstreet c.1612–72
English-born American poet

3 Thou ill-form'd offspring of my feeble brain,
  Who after birth did'st by my side remain,
  Till snatched from thence by friends, less wise than true
  Who thee abroad expos'd to public view,
  Made thee in rags, halting to th' press to trudge,
  Where errors were not lessened (all may judge)
  At thy return my blushing was not small,
  My rambling brat (in print) should mother call.
  'The Author to her Book' (1650)

4 I am obnoxious to each carping tongue,
  Who says my hand a needle better fits,
  A poet's pen, all scorn, I should thus wrong;
  For such despite they cast on female wits:
  If what I do prove well, it won't advance,
  They'll say it's stolne, or else, it was by chance.
  'The Prologue' (1650)

5 Let Greeks be Greeks, and Women what they are,
  Men have precedency, and still excel.
  'The Prologue' (1650)

6 This mean and unrefinèd stuff of mine,
  Will make your glistering gold but more to shine.
  'The Prologue' (1650)

7 Authority without wisdom is like a heavy axe without an edge, fitter to bruise than polish.
  The Tenth Muse (1650) 'Meditations Divine and Moral'

Ernest Bramah (Ernest Bramah Smith) 1868–1942
English writer

8 'Your insight is clear and unbiased,' said the gracious Sovereign. 'But however entrancing it is to wander unchecked through a garden of bright images, are we not enticing your mind from another subject of almost equal importance?'
  Kai Lung's Golden Hours (1922) ch. 10

9 It is a mark of insincerity of purpose to spend one's time in looking for the sacred Emperor in the low-class tea-shops.
  The Wallet of Kai Lung (1900)

James Bramston c.1694–1744
English clergyman and poet

10 What's not destroyed by Time's devouring hand?
  Where's Troy, and where's the Maypole in the Strand?
  The Art of Politics (1729) l. 71

Louis D. Brandeis 1856–1941
American jurist

11 If we would guide by the light of reason, we must let our minds be bold.
  Jay Burns Baking Co. v. Bryan (1924) (dissenting)

12 Fear of serious injury alone cannot justify suppression of free speech and assembly. Men feared witches and burned women. It is the function of speech to free men from the bondage of irrational fears.
  in *Whitney v. California* (1927)

13 The greatest dangers to liberty lurk in insidious encroachment by men of zeal, well-meaning but without understanding.
  dissenting opinion in *Olmstead v. United States* (1928)

Willy Brandt 1913–92
German statesman, Chancellor of West Germany 1969–74

14 We want to risk more democracy.
  speech to parliament after his election as Chancellor, 28 October 1969

15 Where mass hunger reigns, we cannot speak of peace.
  World Armament and World Hunger (1986)

Joseph Brant (Thayendanegea) 1742–1807
American-born Canadian Mohawk leader

16 I bow to no man for I am considered a prince among my own people. But I will gladly shake your hand.
  *on being presented to **George III***
  attributed

Georges Braque 1882–1963
French painter

17 Art is meant to disturb, science reassures.
  Le Jour et la nuit: Cahiers 1917–52

18 Truth exists; only lies are invented.
  Le Jour et la nuit: Cahiers 1917–52

Richard Brathwaite c.1588–1673
English poet

19 To Banbury came I, O profane one!
  Where I saw a Puritane-one
  Hanging of his cat on Monday
  For killing of a mouse on Sunday.
  Barnabee's Journal (1638) pt. 1, st. 4

John W. Bratton and James B. Kennedy
British songwriters

20 If you go down in the woods today
  You're sure of a big surprise

If you go down in the woods today
You'd better go in disguise
For every Bear that ever there was
Will gather there for certain because,
Today's the day the Teddy Bears have their Picnic.
'The Teddy Bear's Picnic' (1932 song)

Werner von Braun 1912–77
German-born American rocket engineer

1 Don't tell me that man doesn't belong out there.
Man belongs wherever he wants to go—and he'll
do plenty well when he gets there.
on space
in *Time* 17 February 1958

2 Basic research is what I am doing when I don't
know what I am doing.
R. L. Weber *A Random Walk in Science* (1973)

Bertolt Brecht 1898–1956
German dramatist
see also **Hare** 373:8

3 Terrible is the temptation to be good.
The Caucasian Chalk Circle (1948)

4 Hesitating doesn't matter if only you win out.
The Good Woman of Setzuan (1938) prologue

5 The aim of science is not to open the door to
infinite wisdom, but to set a limit to infinite error.
The Life of Galileo (1939) sc. 9

6 ANDREA: Unhappy the land that has no heroes! . . .
GALILEO: No. Unhappy the land that needs heroes.
The Life of Galileo (1939) sc. 13

7 One observes, they have gone too long without a
war here. Where is morality to come from in such
a case, I ask? Peace is nothing but slovenliness,
only war creates order.
Mother Courage (1939) sc. 1

8 Because I don't trust him, we are friends.
Mother Courage (1939) sc. 3

9 The finest plans are always ruined by the littleness
of those who ought to carry them out, for the
Emperors can actually do nothing.
Mother Courage (1939) sc. 6

10 War always finds a way.
Mother Courage (1939) sc. 6

11 Don't tell me peace has broken out, when I've just
bought some new supplies.
Mother Courage (1939) sc. 8

12 The resistible rise of Arturo Ui.
title of play (1941)

13 Oh, the shark has pretty teeth, dear,
And he shows them pearly white.
Just a jackknife has Macheath, dear
And he keeps it out of sight.
The Threepenny Opera (1928) prologue

14 Food comes first, then morals.
The Threepenny Opera (1928) act 2, sc. 3

15 What is robbing a bank compared with founding a
bank?
The Threepenny Opera (1928) act 3, sc. 3

16 Who built Thebes of the seven gates?
In the books you will find the names of kings.
Did the kings haul up the lumps of rock? . . .
Where, the evening that the wall of China was
finished
Did the masons go?
'Questions From A Worker Who Reads' (1935)

17 Would it not be easier
In that case for the government
To dissolve the people
And elect another?
*on the uprising against the Soviet occupying forces in
East Germany in 1953*
'The Solution' (1953)

18 Truly, I'm living in a time of darkness.
'To Those Born Later' (1939)

19 Yes, we went, as often changing countries as
changing shoes
Through the wars of the classes, despairing
Each time we found an abuse, and no sense of
outrage.
'To Those Born Later' (1939)

Gerald Brenan 1894–1987
British travel writer and novelist

20 Those who have some means think that the most
important thing in the world is love. The poor
know that it is money.
Thoughts in a Dry Season (1978); see **Baldwin** 50:7

21 Religions are kept alive by heresies, which are
really sudden explosions of faith. Dead religions do
not produce them.
Thoughts in a Dry Season (1978)

22 You can't get at the truth by writing history; only
the novelist can do that.
in *Times Literary Supplement* 28 November 1986

Sydney Brenner 1927–
British scientist

23 A modern computer hovers between the
obsolescent and the nonexistent.
attributed in *Science* 5 January 1990

Jane Brereton (née Hughes) 1685–1740
English poet

24 The picture, placed the busts between,
Adds to the thought much strength:
Wisdom and Wit are little seen,
But Folly's at full length.
'On Mr Nash's Picture at Full Length, between the Busts of
Sir Isaac Newton and Mr Pope' (1744)

Nicholas Breton c.1545–1626
English writer and poet

25 We rise with the lark and go to bed with the lamb.
The Court and Country (1618) para. 8

26 I wish my deadly foe, no worse
Than want of friends, and empty purse.
'A Farewell to Town' (1577)

1 Come little babe, come silly soul,
Thy father's shame, thy mother's grief,
Born as I doubt to all our dole,
And to thy self unhappy chief.
'A Sweet Lullaby' (1597)

Aristide Briand 1862–1932
French statesman

2 The high contracting powers solemnly declare . . .
that they condemn recourse to war and renounce
it . . . as an instrument of their national policy
towards each other . . . The settlement or the
solution of all disputes or conflicts of whatever
nature or of whatever origin they may be which
may arise . . . shall never be sought by either side
except by pacific means.
draft, 20 June 1927, later incorporated into the Kellogg
Pact, 1928, in *Le Temps* 13 April 1928

Percy Williams Bridgeman 1882–1961
American physicist

3 The scientific method, as far as it is a method, is
nothing more than doing one's damnedest with
one's mind, no holds barred.
Reflections of a Physicist (1955)

Edward Bridges 1892–1969
*British civil servant, Cabinet Secretary and Head of the Civil
Service*

4 I confidently expect that we shall continue to be
grouped with mothers-in-law and Wigan Pier as
one of the recognized objects of ridicule.
of civil servants
Portrait of a Profession (1950)

Robert Bridges 1844–1930
English poet

5 All my hope on God is founded.
'All my hope on God is founded' (1899 hymn)

6 When men were all asleep the snow came flying,
In large white flakes falling on the city brown,
Stealthily and perpetually settling and loosely
lying,
Hushing the latest traffic of the drowsy town.
'London Snow' (1890)

John Bright 1811–89
English Liberal politician and reformer

7 The angel of death has been abroad throughout
the land; you may almost hear the beating of his
wings.
on the effects of the war in the Crimea
speech in the House of Commons, 23 February 1855

8 A gigantic system of outdoor relief for the
aristocracy of Great Britain.
of British foreign policy
speech at Birmingham, 29 October 1858; G. Barnett Smith
Life and Speeches of John Bright (1881) vol. 1 ch. 16

9 I am for 'Peace, retrenchment, and reform', the
watchword of the great Liberal party 30 years
ago.
speech at Birmingham, 28 April 1859, in *The Times* 29
April 1859; the phrase occurs earlier as

An immense yellow banner . . . 'Peace!
Retrenchment!! Reform!!'
Samuel Warren *Ten Thousand a Year* (1841) bk. 7, ch. 1

10 My opinion is that the Northern States will
manage somehow to muddle through.
during the American Civil War
Justin McCarthy *Reminiscences* (1899) vol. 1, ch. 5

11 England is the mother of Parliaments.
speech at Birmingham, 18 January 1865, in *The Times* 19
January 1865

12 The right hon Gentleman . . . has retired into what
may be called his political Cave of Adullam—and
he has called about him every one that was in
distress and every one that was discontented.
*referring to Robert Lowe, leader of the dissident Whigs
opposed to the Reform Bill of 1866*
speech in the House of Commons, 13 March 1866; see
Bible 80:24

13 Force is not a remedy.
speech to the Birmingham Junior Liberal Club, 16
November 1880, in *The Times* 17 November 1880

14 The knowledge of the ancient languages is mainly
a luxury.
letter in *Pall Mall Gazette* 30 November 1886

Anthelme Brillat-Savarin 1755–1826
French jurist and gourmet

15 Tell me what you eat and I will tell you what you
are.
Physiologie du Goût (1825) aphorism no. 4; see **Feuerbach**
317:4

16 The discovery of a new dish does more for human
happiness than the discovery of a star.
Physiologie du Goût (1825) aphorism no. 9

17 Cooking is the most ancient of the arts, for Adam
was born hungry.
Physiologie du Goût (1825) pt. 1

Vera Brittain 1893–1970
English writer

18 Meek wifehood is no part of my profession;
I am your friend, but never your possession.
'Married Love' (1926)

19 Politics are usually the executive expression of
human immaturity.
Rebel Passion (1964)

Paul Broca 1824–80
French surgeon

20 The great regions of the mind correspond to the
great regions of the brain.
at the Société Anatomique, August 1861

Russell Brockbank see Cartoon captions

Joseph Brodsky 1940-96

Russian-born American poet

1 As a form of moral insurance, at least, literature is much more dependable than a system of beliefs or a philosophical doctrine.
  'Uncommon Visage', Nobel lecture 1987, in *On Grief and Reason* (1996)

Tom Brokaw 1940-

American journalist

2 We don't just have egg on our face. We have omelette all over our suits.
  on the networks' premature calls of a win in Florida in the presidential election, first to Al **Gore** *and then to George W.* **Bush**
  in *Atlanta Constitution-Journal* 9 November 2000 (online edition)

Alexander Brome 1620-66

English poet

3 I have been in love, and in debt, and in drink,
  This many and many a year.
  Songs and Other Poems (2nd ed., 1664) pt. 1 'The Mad Lover'

4 Come, blessed peace, we once again implore,
  And let our pains be less, or power more.
  Songs and Other Poems (1661) 'The Riddle' (written 1644)

Jacob Bronowski 1908-74

Polish-born mathematician and humanist

5 The world can only be grasped by action, not by contemplation . . . The hand is the cutting edge of the mind.
  The Ascent of Man (1973) ch. 3

6 The essence of science: ask an impertinent question, and you are on the way to a pertinent answer.
  The Ascent of Man (1973) ch. 4

7 The wish to hurt, the momentary intoxication with pain, is the loophole through which the pervert climbs into the minds of ordinary men.
  The Face of Violence (1954) ch. 5

8 Therapy has become what I think of as the tenth American muse.
  attributed

Charlotte Brontë 1816-55

English novelist; daughter of Patrick **Brontë**, *sister of Emily* **Brontë**
see also **Opening lines** 575:23

9 Conventionality is not morality. Self-righteousness is not religion. To attack the first is not to assail the last. To pluck the mask from the face of the Pharisee, is not to lift an impious hand to the Crown of Thorns.
  Jane Eyre (2nd ed., 1848) preface

10 As his curate, his comrade, all would be right . . . There would be recesses in my mind which would be only mine, to which he never came; and sentiments growing there, fresh and sheltered, which his austerity could never blight, nor his measured warrior-march trample down. But as his wife . . . forced to keep the fire of my nature continually low, to compel it to burn inwardly and never utter a cry . . . *this* would be unendurable.
  Jane Eyre (1847) ch. 34

11 Reader, I married him.
  Jane Eyre (1847) ch. 38

12 Of late years an abundant shower of curates has fallen upon the North of England.
  Shirley (1849) ch. 1

13 Be a governess! Better be a slave at once!
  Shirley (1849) ch. 13

14 It is rustic all through. It is moorish, and wild, and knotty as a root of heath.
  on the setting of Emily **Brontë**'s *Wuthering Heights*
  in Charlotte's preface to the 1850 edition

15 We wove a web in childhood,
  A web of sunny air;
  We dug a spring in infancy
  Of water pure and fair;
  We sowed in youth a mustard seed,
  We cut an almond rod;
  We are now grown up to riper age—
  Are they withered in the sod?
  'We wove a web in childhood' (written 1835)

16 I shall soon be 30—and I have done nothing yet . . . I feel as if we were all buried here.
  letter to Ellen Nussey, 24 March 1845; *The Letters of Charlotte Brontë* (1995) vol. I

17 You are not to suppose any of the characters in *Shirley* intended as literal portraits . . . We only suffer reality to *suggest*, never to *dictate*.
  letter to Ellen Nussey, 16 November 1849, in Elizabeth Gaskell *The Life of Charlotte Bronte* (1857) ch. 18

Emily Brontë 1818-48

English novelist and poet; daughter of Patrick **Brontë**, *sister of Charlotte* **Brontë**
on Brontë: see **Brontë** 152:14; *see also* **Closing lines** 228:16

18 No coward soul is mine,
  No trembler in the world's storm-troubled sphere:
  I see Heaven's glories shine,
  And faith shines equal, arming me from fear.
  'No coward soul is mine' (1846)

19 Oh! dreadful is the check—intense the agony—
  When the ear begins to hear, and the eye begins to see;
  When the pulse begins to throb, the brain to think again;
  The soul to feel the flesh, and the flesh to feel the chain.
  'The Prisoner' (1846)

20 Cold in the earth—and fifteen wild Decembers,
  From those brown hills, have melted into spring.
  'Remembrance' (1846)

21 My love for Linton is like the foliage in the woods; time will change it, I'm well aware, as winter

changes the trees—My love for Heathcliff resembles the eternal rocks beneath:—a source of little visible delight, but necessary.

Wuthering Heights (1847) ch. 9

Patrick Brontë 1777-1861

English clergyman, born in Ireland, perpetual curate of Haworth, Yorkshire from 1820; father of Charlotte **Brontë** *and Emily* **Brontë**

1 Charlotte has been writing a book, and it is much better than likely.

to his younger daughters, on first reading Jane Eyre; *in a letter of August 1850, Mrs Gaskell gives the wording as 'Charlotte has been writing a book—and it is better than I expected'*

Elizabeth Gaskell *The Life of Charlotte Brontë* (1857)

2 No quailing, Mrs Gaskell! no drawing back!

apropos her undertaking to write the life of Charlotte **Brontë**

letter from Mrs Gaskell to Ellen Nussey, 24 July 1855, in J. A. V. Chapple and A. Pollard (eds.) *The Letters of Mrs Gaskell* (1966) no. 257

Frances Brooke 1724-89

Canadian novelist and writer

3 The road from Quebec to Montreal is almost a continued street, the villages being numerous, and so extended along the banks of the river St. Lawrence as to leave scarce a space without houses in view; except where here or there a river, wood, or mountain intervenes, as if to give a more pleasing variety to the scene.

The History of Emily Montague (1769)

Henry Brooke 1703-83

Irish poet and dramatist

4 For righteous monarchs, Justly to judge, with their own eyes should see; To rule o'er freemen, should themselves be free.

Earl of Essex (performed 1750, published 1761) act 1; see **Johnson** 432:16

Rupert Brooke 1887-1915

English poet

on Brooke: see **Cornford** 243:11, **James** 418:14, **Leavis** 478:4

5 Blow out, you bugles, over the rich Dead! There's none of these so lonely and poor of old, But, dying, has made us rarer gifts than gold. These laid the world away; poured out the red Sweet wine of youth; gave up the years to be Of work and joy, and that unhoped serene, That men call age; and those that would have been, Their sons, they gave, their immortality.

'The Dead' (1914)

6 . . . The cool kindliness of sheets, that soon Smooth away trouble; and the rough male kiss Of blankets.

'The Great Lover' (1914)

7 Fish say, they have their stream and pond; But is there anything beyond?

'Heaven' (1915)

8 Just now the lilac is in bloom, All before my little room.

'The Old Vicarage, Grantchester' (1915)

9 Unkempt about those hedges blows An English unofficial rose.

'The Old Vicarage, Grantchester' (1915)

10 Curates, long dust, will come and go On lissom, clerical, printless toe; And oft between the boughs is seen The sly shade of a Rural Dean.

'The Old Vicarage, Grantchester' (1915)

11 God! I will pack, and take a train, And get me to England once again! For England's the one land, I know, Where men with Splendid Hearts may go.

'The Old Vicarage, Grantchester' (1915)

12 For Cambridge people rarely smile, Being urban, squat, and packed with guile.

'The Old Vicarage, Grantchester' (1915)

13 Stands the Church clock at ten to three? And is there honey still for tea?

'The Old Vicarage, Grantchester' (1915)

14 Now, God be thanked Who has matched us with His hour, And caught our youth, and wakened us from sleeping, With hand made sure, clear eye, and sharpened power, To turn, as swimmers into cleanness leaping.

'Peace' (1914)

15 If I should die, think only this of me: That there's some corner of a foreign field That is for ever England. There shall be In that rich earth a richer dust concealed; A dust whom England bore, shaped, made aware, Gave, once, her flowers to love, her ways to roam, A body of England's, breathing English air, Washed by the rivers, blest by suns of home.

And think, this heart, all evil shed away, A pulse in the eternal mind, no less Gives somewhere back the thoughts by England given; Her sights and sounds; dreams happy as her day; And laughter, learnt of friends; and gentleness, In hearts at peace, under an English heaven.

'The Soldier' (1914)

16 History repeats itself; historians repeat one another.

letter to Geoffrey Keynes, 4 June 1906; see **Proverbs** 622:22

Anita Brookner 1928-

British novelist and art historian

17 Good women always think it is their fault when someone else is being offensive. Bad women never take the blame for anything.

Hotel du Lac (1984) ch. 7

18 They were reasonable people, and no one was to be hurt, not even with words.

Hotel du Lac (1984) ch. 9

1 I have reached the age when a woman begins to perceive that she is growing into the person she least plans to resemble: her mother.
  Incidents in the Rue Laugier (1995) ch. 1

2 They were privileged children . . . they would always expect to be greeted with smiles.
  Lewis Percy (1989) ch. 9

3 Dr Weiss, at forty, knew that her life had been ruined by literature.
  A Start in Life (1981) ch. 1

Gwendolyn Brooks 1917–2000

American poet

4 Exhaust the little moment. Soon it dies.
  And be it gash or gold it will not come
  Again in this identical disguise.
  'Exhaust the little moment' (1949)

5 Abortions will not let you forget.
  You remember the children you got that you did
    not get . . .
  'The Mother' (1945)

6 The time
  cracks into furious flower. Lifts its face
  all unashamed. And sways in wicked grace.
  'The Second Sermon on the Warpland' (1968)

J. Brooks

7 A four-legged friend, a four-legged friend,
  He'll never let you down.
  sung by Roy Rogers about his horse Trigger
  'A Four Legged Friend' (1952)

Phillips Brooks 1835–93

American clergyman

8 O little town of Bethlehem,
  How still we see thee lie!
  Above thy deep and dreamless sleep
  The silent stars go by.
  Yet in thy dark streets shineth
  The everlasting light;
  The hopes and fears of all the years
  Are met in thee to-night.
  'O Little Town of Bethlehem' (1868 hymn)

Thomas Brooks 1608–80

English Puritan divine

9 For (*magna est veritas et praevalebit*) great is truth, and shall prevail.
  The Crown and Glory of Christianity (1662); see **Bible** 115:19

Robert Barnabas Brough 1828–60

English satirical writer

10 My Lord Tomnoddy is thirty-four;
  The Earl can last but a few years more.
  My Lord in the Peers will take his place:
  Her Majesty's councils his words will grace.
  Office he'll hold and patronage sway;
  Fortunes and lives he will vote away;
  And what are his qualifications?—ONE!
  He's the Earl of Fitzdotterel's eldest son.
  Songs of the Governing Classes (1855) 'My Lord Tomnoddy'

Lord Brougham 1778–1868

Scottish lawyer and politician; Lord Chancellor
*on Brougham: see **Melbourne** 520:18*

11 All we see about us, King, Lords, and Commons, the whole machinery of the State, all the apparatus of the system, and its varied workings, end in simply bringing twelve good men into a box.
  in the House of Commons, 7 February 1828

12 The schoolmaster is abroad! and I trust more to the schoolmaster, armed with his primer, than I do to the soldier in full military array, for upholding and extending the liberties of his country.
  sometimes quoted as 'Look out, gentlemen, the schoolmaster is abroad!', which Brougham is said to have used in a speech at the Mechanics' Instute, London, in 1825
  in the House of Commons, 29 January 1828

13 Education makes a people easy to lead, but difficult to drive; easy to govern, but impossible to enslave.
  attributed

Haywood Hale Broun 1918–

American actor

14 Sports do not build character. They reveal it.
  attributed; James Michener Sports in America (1976)

Heywood Broun 1888–1939

American journalist

15 Men build bridges and throw railroads across deserts, and yet they contend successfully that the job of sewing on a button is beyond them. Accordingly, they don't have to sew buttons.
  Seeing Things at Night (1921) 'Holding a Baby'

16 Posterity is as likely to be wrong as anybody else.
  Sitting on the World (1924) 'The Last Review'

17 Everybody favours free speech in the slack moments when no axes are being ground.
  in New York World 23 October 1926

18 Just as every conviction begins as a whim so does every emancipator serve his apprenticeship as a crank. A fanatic is a great leader who is just entering the room.
  in New York World 6 February 1928

Christy Brown 1932–81

Irish writer

19 Painting became everything to me . . . Through it I made articulate all that I saw and felt, all that went on inside the mind that was housed within my useless body like a prisoner in a cell.
  My Left Foot (1954)

Gordon Brown 1951–

British Labour politician, Chancellor of the Exchequer from 1997
on Brown: see **Anonymous** 18:13, **Anonymous** 18:14

1 Ideas which stress the growing importance of international cooperation and new theories of economic sovereignty across a wide range of areas—macroeconomics, the environment, the growth of post neo-classical endogenous growth theory and the symbiotic relationships between growth and investment in people and infrastructure.
New Labour Economics speech, September 1994, 'winner' of the ironic Plain English No Nonsense Award for 1994

2 It is about time we had an end to the old Britain, where all that matters is the privileges you were born with, rather than the potential you actually have.
speech, 25 May 2000

3 I'm a father, that's what matters most. Nothing matters more.
on the birth of his son John
in *Observer* 19 October 2003

H. Rap Brown (Hubert Geroid Brown) 1943–

American Black Power leader

4 I say violence is necessary. It is as American as cherry pie.
speech at Washington, 27 July 1967, in *Washington Post* 28 July 1967

Henry Box Brown b. 1815

American escaped slave

5 I entered the world a slave—in the midst of a country whose most honoured writings declare that all men have a right to liberty.
Narrative of the Life of Henry Box Brown (1851)

John Brown 1715–66

English clergyman and writer

6 I have seen some extracts from Johnson's Preface to his 'Shakespeare' . . . No feeling nor pathos in him! Altogether upon the high horse, and blustering about Imperial Tragedy!
letter to Garrick, 27 October 1765, in *The Private Correspondence of David Garrick* (1831) vol. 1

John Brown 1800–59

American abolitionist
on Brown: see **Songs** 747:13; see also **Last words** 474:4

7 Now, if it is deemed necessary that I should forfeit my life for the furtherance of the ends of justice, and mingle my blood further with the blood of my children, and with the blood of millions in this slave country whose rights are disregarded by wicked, cruel, and unjust enactments, I say let it be done.
last speech to the court, 2 November 1859, in *The Life, Trial and Execution of Captain John Brown* (1859)

8 I, John Brown, am now quite certain that the crimes of this guilty land will never be purged away but with blood.
written on the day of his execution, 2 December 1859, in R. J. Hinton *John Brown and His Men* (1894) ch. 12

Joseph Brown 1821–94

American politician; Confederate Governor of Georgia during the Civil War

9 I entered into this Revolution to contribute my mite to sustain the rights of states and prevent the consolidation of the Government, and I am *still* a rebel . . . no matter who may be in power
refusing to accept the Confederate President Jefferson Davis's call for a day of national fasting
in 1863; Geoffrey C. Ward *The Civil War* (1991)

Lew Brown (Louis Brownstein) 1893–1958

American songwriter

10 Life is just a bowl of cherries.
title of song (1931)

T. E. Brown 1830–97

Manx schoolmaster and poet

11 A garden is a lovesome thing, God wot!
'My Garden' (1893)

Thomas Brown 1663–1704

English satirist

12 A little before you made a leap into the dark.
Letters from the Dead to the Living (1702) 'Answer to Mr Joseph Haines'; see **Last words** 471:19

13 I do not love thee, Dr Fell.
The reason why I cannot tell;
But this I know, and know full well,
I do not love thee, Dr Fell.
written while an undergraduate at Christ Church, Oxford, of which Dr Fell was Dean
A. L. Hayward (ed.) *Amusements Serious and Comical by Tom Brown* (1927); see **Martial** 514:17, **Watkyns** 822:16

Cecil Browne 1932–

American businessman

14 But not so odd
As those who choose
A Jewish God,
But spurn the Jews.
reply to verse by William Norman Ewer; see **Ewer** 313:9

Sir Thomas Browne 1605–82

English writer and physician

15 He who discommendeth others obliquely commendeth himself.
Christian Morals (1716) pt. 1, sect. 34

16 As for that famous network of Vulcan, which enclosed Mars and Venus, and caused that unextinguishable laugh in heaven, since the gods themselves could not discern it, we shall not pry into it.
The Garden of Cyrus (1658) ch. 2

1 Life itself is but the shadow of death, and souls departed but the shadows of the living: all things fall under this name. The sun itself is but the dark *simulacrum*, and light but the shadow of God.
The Garden of Cyrus (1658) ch. 4

2 Flat and flexible truths are beat out by every hammer; but Vulcan and his whole forge sweat to work out Achilles his armour.
The Garden of Cyrus (1658) ch. 5

3 The quincunx of heaven runs low, and 'tis time to close the five ports of knowledge.
The Garden of Cyrus (1658) ch. 5

4 All things began in order, so shall they end, and so shall they begin again; according to the ordainer of order and mystical mathematics of the city of heaven.
The Garden of Cyrus (1658) ch. 5

5 Nor will the sweetest delight of gardens afford much comfort in sleep; wherein the dullness of that sense shakes hands with delectable odours; and though in the bed of Cleopatra, can hardly with any delight raise up the ghost of a rose.
The Garden of Cyrus (1658) ch. 5

6 Though Somnus in Homer be sent to rouse up Agamemnon, I find no such effects in these drowsy approaches of sleep. To keep our eyes open longer were but to act our Antipodes. The huntsmen are up in America, and they are already past their first sleep in Persia. But who can be drowsy at that hour which freed us from everlasting sleep? or have slumbering thoughts at that time, when sleep itself must end, and as some conjecture all shall awake again?
The Garden of Cyrus (1658) ch. 5

7 Old mortality, the ruins of forgotten times.
Hydriotaphia (Urn Burial, 1658) Epistle Dedicatory

8 With rich flames and hired tears they solemnized their obsequies.
Hydriotaphia (Urn Burial, 1658) ch. 3

9 Men have lost their reason in nothing so much as their religion, wherein stones and clouts make martyrs.
Hydriotaphia (Urn Burial, 1658) ch. 4

10 Were the happiness of the next world as closely apprehended as the felicities of this, it were a martyrdom to live.
Hydriotaphia (Urn Burial, 1658) ch. 4

11 The long habit of living indisposeth us for dying.
Hydriotaphia (Urn Burial, 1658) ch. 5

12 What song the Syrens sang, or what name Achilles assumed when he hid himself among women, though puzzling questions, are not beyond all conjecture.
Hydriotaphia (Urn Burial, 1658) ch. 5

13 But to subsist in bones, and be but pyramidally extant, is a fallacy in duration.
Hydriotaphia (Urn Burial, 1658) ch. 5

14 Generations pass while some trees stand, and old families last not three oaks.
Hydriotaphia (Urn Burial, 1658) ch. 5

15 To be nameless in worthy deeds exceeds an infamous history.
Hydriotaphia (Urn Burial, 1658) ch. 5

16 The iniquity of oblivion blindly scattereth her poppy, and deals with the memory of men without distinction to merit perpetuity.
Hydriotaphia (Urn Burial, 1658) ch. 5

17 The night of time far surpasseth the day, and who knows when was the equinox?
Hydriotaphia (Urn Burial, 1658) ch. 5

18 Man is a noble animal, splendid in ashes, and pompous in the grave.
Hydriotaphia (Urn Burial, 1658) ch. 5

19 Ready to be any thing, in the ecstasy of being ever.
Hydriotaphia (Urn Burial, 1658) ch. 5

20 At my devotion I love to use the civility of my knee, my hat, and hand.
Religio Medici (1643) pt. 1, sect. 3

21 Many from . . . an inconsiderate zeal unto truth, have too rashly charged the troops of error, and remain as trophies unto the enemies of truth.
Religio Medici (1643) pt. 1, sect. 6

22 A man may be in as just possession of truth as of a city, and yet be forced to surrender.
Religio Medici (1643) pt. 1, sect. 6

23 As for those wingy mysteries in divinity and airy subtleties in religion, which have unhinged the brains of better heads, they never stretched the *pia mater* of mine; methinks there be not impossibilities enough in religion for an active faith.
Religio Medici (1643) pt. 1, sect. 9

24 I love to lose myself in a mystery, to pursue my reason to an *O altitudo!*
Religio Medici (1643) pt. 1, sect. 9

25 Who can speak of eternity without a solecism, or think thereof without an ecstasy? Time we may comprehend, 'tis but five days elder than ourselves.
Religio Medici (1643) pt. 1, sect. 11

26 I have often admired the mystical way of Pythagoras, and the secret magic of numbers.
Religio Medici (1643) pt. 1, sect. 12

27 We carry within us the wonders we seek without us: there is all Africa and her prodigies in us.
Religio Medici (1643) pt. 1, sect. 15; see **Pliny** 598:4

28 All things are artificial, for nature is the art of God.
Religio Medici (1643) pt. 1, sect. 16

29 Obstinacy in a bad cause, is but constancy in a good.
Religio Medici (1643) pt. 1, sect. 25

30 Persecution is a bad and indirect way to plant religion.
Religio Medici (1643) pt. 1, sect. 25

31 Not wrung from speculations and subtleties, but from common sense, and observation; not picked

from the leaves of any author, but bred among the weeds and tares of mine own brain.
Religio Medici (1643) pt. 1, sect. 36

1 I am not so much afraid of death, as ashamed thereof; 'tis the very disgrace and ignominy of our natures, that in a moment can so disfigure us that our nearest friends, wife, and children, stand afraid and start at us.
Religio Medici (1643) pt. 1, sect. 40

2 Certainly there is no happiness within this circle of flesh, nor is it in the optics of these eyes to behold felicity; the first day of our Jubilee is death.
Religio Medici (1643) pt. 1, sect. 44

3 He forgets that he can die who complains of misery, we are in the power of no calamity, while death is in our own.
Religio Medici (1643) pt. 1, sect. 44

4 All places, all airs make unto me one country: I am in England, everywhere, and under any meridian.
Religio Medici (1643) pt. 2, sect. 1

5 If there be any among those common objects of hatred I do condemn and laugh at, it is that great enemy of reason, virtue and religion, the multitude, that numerous piece of monstrosity, which taken asunder seem men, and the reasonable creatures of God; but confused together, make but one great beast, and a monstrosity more prodigious than Hydra.
Religio Medici (1643) pt. 2, sect. 1

6 This trivial and vulgar way of coition; it is the foolishest act a wise man commits in all his life, nor is there any thing that will more deject his cooled imagination, when he shall consider what an odd and unworthy piece of folly he hath committed.
Religio Medici (1643) pt. 2, sect. 9

7 Sure there is music even in the beauty, and the silent note which Cupid strikes, far sweeter than the sound of an instrument. For there is music wherever there is a harmony, order or proportion; and thus far we may maintain the music of the spheres; for those well-ordered motions, and regular paces, though they give no sound unto the ear, yet to the understanding they strike a note most full of harmony.
Religio Medici (1643) pt. 2, sect. 9

8 We all labour against our own cure, for death is the cure of all diseases.
Religio Medici (1643) pt. 2, sect. 9

9 For the world, I count it not an inn, but an hospital, and a place, not to live, but to die in.
Religio Medici (1643) pt. 2, sect. 11

10 There is surely a piece of divinity in us, something that was before the elements, and owes no homage unto the sun.
Religio Medici (1643) pt. 2, sect. 11

11 We term sleep a death, and yet it is waking that kills us, and destroys those spirits which are the house of life.
Religio Medici (1643) pt. 2, sect. 12

12 Half our days we pass in the shadow of the earth; and the brother of death exacteth a third part of our lives.
S. Wilkin (ed.) *Sir Thomas Browne's Works* (1835) vol. 4, p. 355 'On Dreams'

13 That children dream not in the first half year, that men dream not in some countries, are to me sick men's dreams, dreams out of the ivory gate, and visions before midnight.
S. Wilkin (ed.) *Sir Thomas Browne's Works* (1835) vol. 4 'On Dreams'

William Browne 1692–1774
English physician and writer

14 The King to Oxford sent a troop of horse,
For Tories own no argument but force:
With equal skill to Cambridge books he sent,
For Whigs admit no force but argument.
reply to Trapp's epigram on **George I**, in J. Nichols *Literary Anecdotes* vol. 3 (1812); see **Trapp** 798:4

Elizabeth Barrett Browning 1806–61
English poet; wife of Robert **Browning**
on Browning: see **Fitzgerald** 323:18

15 Some people always sigh in thanking God.
Aurora Leigh (1857) bk. 1, l. 445

16 The works of women are symbolical.
We sew, sew, prick our fingers, dull our sight,
Producing what? A pair of slippers, sir,
To put on when you're weary.
Aurora Leigh (1857) bk. 1, l. 456

17   We have hearts within,
Warm, live, improvident, indecent hearts.
Aurora Leigh (1857) bk. 3, l. 461

18 Nay, if there's room for poets in this world
A little overgrown (I think there is)
Their sole work is to represent the age,
Their age, not Charlemagne's.
Aurora Leigh (1857) bk. 5, l. 200

19 And Camelot to minstrels seemed as flat
As Fleet Street to our poets.
Aurora Leigh (1857) bk. 5, l. 212

20 The devil's most devilish when respectable.
Aurora Leigh (1857) bk. 7, l. 105

21 Earth's crammed with heaven,
And every common bush afire with God.
Aurora Leigh (1857) bk. 7, l. 821

22 And kings crept out again to feel the sun.
'Crowned and Buried' (1844) st. 11

23 Do ye hear the children weeping, O my brothers,
Ere the sorrow comes with years?
'The Cry of the Children' (1844) st. 1

24 And lips say, 'God be pitiful,'
Who ne'er said, 'God be praised.'
'The Cry of the Human' (1844) st. 1

25 I tell you, hopeless grief is passionless.
'Grief' (1844)

26 Or from Browning some 'Pomegranate', which, if cut deep down the middle,

Shows a heart within blood-tinctured, of a veined
humanity.
'Lady Geraldine's Courtship' (1844) st. 41

1 'Yes,' I answered you last night;
'No,' this morning, sir, I say.
Colours seen by candle-light
Will not look the same by day.
'The Lady's Yes' (1844)

2 What was he doing, the great god Pan,
Down in the reeds by the river?
'A Musical Instrument' (1862)

3 How do I love thee? Let me count the ways.
I love thee to the depth and breadth and height
My soul can reach, when feeling out of sight
For the ends of Being and ideal Grace.
Sonnets from the Portuguese (1850) no. 43

4 I love thee with the breath,
Smiles, tears, of all my life!—and if God choose,
I shall but love thee better after death.
Sonnets from the Portuguese (1850) no. 43

5 Thou large-brained woman and large-hearted
man.
'To George Sand—A Desire' (1844)

Frederick 'Boy' Browning 1896–1965

British soldier

6 I think we might be going a bridge too far.
*expressing reservations about the Arnhem 'Market
Garden' operation to Field Marshal* **Montgomery**
on 10 September 1944; R. E. Urquhart *Arnhem* (1958)

Robert Browning 1812–89

English poet; husband of Elizabeth Barrett **Browning**
on Browning: see **Bagehot** 49:11, **Browning** 157:26, **Wilde**
835:26, **Wilde** 836:4

7 The high that proved too high, the heroic for earth
too hard,
The passion that left the ground to lose itself in the
sky,
Are music sent up to God by the lover and the
bard;
Enough that he heard it once: we shall hear it
by-and-by.
'Abt Vogler' (1864) st. 10

8 . . . I feel for the common chord again . . .
The C Major of this life.
'Abt Vogler' (1864) st. 12

9 Ah, but a man's reach should exceed his grasp,
Or what's a heaven for?
'Andrea del Sarto' (1855) l. 97

10 Still, what an arm! and I could alter it:
But all the play, the insight and the stretch—
Out of me, out of me!
'Andrea del Sarto' (1855) l. 115

11 One who never turned his back but marched
breast forward,
Never doubted clouds would break,
Never dreamed, though right were worsted,
wrong would triumph,

Held we fall to rise, are baffled to fight better,
Sleep to wake.
Asolando (1889) 'Epilogue'

12 Greet the unseen with a cheer!
Asolando (1889) 'Epilogue'

13 There spoke up a brisk little somebody,
Critic and whippersnapper, in a rage
To set things right.
Balaustion's Adventure (1871) l. 306

14 Just when we are safest, there's a sunset-touch,
A fancy from a flower-bell, some one's death,
A chorus-ending from Euripides.
'Bishop Blougram's Apology' (1855) l. 182

15 The grand Perhaps!
'Bishop Blougram's Apology' (1855) l. 190

16 Our interest's on the dangerous edge of things.
The honest thief, the tender murderer,
The superstitious atheist, demirep
That loves and saves her soul in new French
books.
'Bishop Blougram's Apology' (1855) l. 395

17 You, for example, clever to a fault,
The rough and ready man who write apace,
Read somewhat seldomer, think perhaps even less.
'Bishop Blougram's Apology' (1855) l. 420

18 He said true things, but called them by wrong
names.
'Bishop Blougram's Apology' (1855) l. 996

19 Shrewd was that snatch from out the corner
South
He graced his carrion with, God curse the same!
'The Bishop Orders his Tomb' (1845) l. 18

20 And have I not Saint Praxed's ear to pray
Horses for ye, and brown Greek manuscripts,
And mistresses with great smooth marbly limbs?
—That's if ye carve my epitaph aright.
'The Bishop Orders his Tomb' (1845) l. 73

21 And then how I shall lie through centuries,
And hear the blessed mutter of the mass,
And see God made and eaten all day long,
And feel the steady candle-flame, and taste
Good strong thick stupefying incense-smoke!
'The Bishop Orders his Tomb' (1845) l. 80

22 Boot, saddle, to horse, and away!
'Boot and Saddle' (1842)

23 And I turn the page, and I turn the page,
Not verse now, only prose!
'By the Fireside' (1855) st. 2

24 When earth breaks up and heaven expands,
How will the change strike me and you
In the house not made with hands?
'By the Fireside' (1855) st. 27; see **Bible** 108:15

25 Oh, the little more, and how much it is!
And the little less, and what worlds away!
'By the Fireside' (1855) st. 39

26 Setebos, Setebos, and Setebos!
'Thinketh, He dwelleth i' the cold o' the moon.
'Caliban upon Setebos' (1864) l. 24; see **Shakespeare**
718:25

1 'Let twenty pass, and stone the twenty-first,
 Loving not, hating not, just choosing so.
 'Caliban upon Setebos' (1864) l. 102

2 Dauntless the slug-horn to my lips I set,
 And blew. *'Childe Roland to the Dark Tower came.'*
 'Childe Roland to the Dark Tower Came' (1855) st. 34; see
 Shakespeare 701:2

3 We loved, sir—used to meet:
 How sad and bad and mad it was—
 But then, how it was sweet!
 'Confessions' (1864) st. 9

4 Stung by the splendour of a sudden thought.
 'A Death in the Desert' (1864) l. 59

5 . . . Progress, man's distinctive mark alone,
 Not God's, and not the beasts': God is, they are,
 Man partly is and wholly hopes to be.
 'A Death in the Desert' (1864) l. 586

6 Open my heart and you will see
 Graved inside of it, 'Italy'.
 'De Gustibus' (1855) pt. 2, l. 43

7   'Tis well averred,
 A scientific faith's absurd.
 'Easter-Day' (1850) l. 123

8 Karshish, the picker-up of learning's crumbs,
 The not-incurious in God's handiwork.
 'An Epistle . . . of Karshish' (1855)

9 Beautiful Evelyn Hope is dead!
 'Evelyn Hope' (1855)

10 If you get simple beauty and naught else,
 You get about the best thing God invents.
 'Fra Lippo Lippi' (1855) l. 217

11   This world's no blot for us,
 Nor blank; it means intensely, and means good:
 To find its meaning is my meat and drink.
 'Fra Lippo Lippi' (1855) l. 313

12 This is our master, famous calm and dead,
 Borne on our shoulders.
 'A Grammarian's Funeral' (1855) l. 27

13 Yea, but we found him bald too, eyes like lead,
 Accents uncertain:
 'Time to taste life,' another would have said,
 'Up with the curtain!'
 'A Grammarian's Funeral' (1855) l. 53

14 He said, 'What's time? Leave Now for dogs and
 apes!
 Man has Forever.'
 'A Grammarian's Funeral' (1855) l. 83

15 That low man seeks a little thing to do,
 Sees it and does it:
 This high man, with a great thing to pursue,
 Dies ere he knows it.
 That low man goes on adding one to one,
 His hundred's soon hit:
 This high man, aiming at a million,
 Misses an unit.
 'A Grammarian's Funeral' (1855) l. 113

16 He settled *Hoti*'s business—let it be!
 Properly based *Oun*—
 Gave us the doctrine of the enclitic *De*,

Dead from the waist down.
 'A Grammarian's Funeral' (1855) l. 129

17 Oh, to be in England
 Now that April's there,
 And whoever wakes in England
 Sees, some morning, unaware,
 That the lowest boughs and the brushwood sheaf
 Round the elm-tree bole are in tiny leaf,
 While the chaffinch sings on the orchard bough
 In England—now!
 'Home-Thoughts, from Abroad' (1845); see **cummings**
 253:8

18 That's the wise thrush; he sings each song twice
 over,
 Lest you should think he never could recapture
 The first fine careless rapture!
 'Home-Thoughts, from Abroad' (1845)

19 Nobly, nobly Cape Saint Vincent to the North-west
 died away;
 Sunset ran, one glorious blood-red, reeking into
 Cadiz Bay.
 'Home-Thoughts, from the Sea' (1845)

20 'Here and here did England help me: how can I
 help England?'—say,
 Whoso turns as I, this evening, turn to God to
 praise and pray,
 While Jove's planet rises yonder, silent over Africa.
 'Home-Thoughts, from the Sea' (1845)

21   'With this same key
 Shakespeare unlocked his heart,' once more!
 Did Shakespeare? If so, the less Shakespeare he!
 'House' (1876); see **Wordsworth** 849:26

22 How they brought the good news from Ghent to
 Aix.
 title of poem (1845)

23 I sprang to the stirrup, and Joris, and he;
 I galloped, Dirck galloped, we galloped all three.
 'How they brought the Good News from Ghent to Aix'
 (1845) l. 1

24 A man can have but one life and one death,
 One heaven, one hell.
 'In a Balcony' (1855) l. 13

25   I count life just a stuff
 To try the soul's strength on, educe the man.
 'In a Balcony' (1855) l. 651

26 'You're wounded!' 'Nay,' the soldier's pride
 Touched to the quick, he said:
 'I'm killed, Sire!' And his chief beside,
 Smiling the boy fell dead.
 'Incident of the French Camp' (1842) st. 5

27 Ignorance is not innocence but sin.
 The Inn Album (1875) canto 5

28 The swallow has set her six young on the rail,
 And looks sea-ward.
 'James Lee's Wife' (1864) pt. 3, st. 1

29 Who knows but the world may end tonight?
 'The Last Ride Together' (1855) st. 2

30 Had I said that, had I done this,
 So might I gain, so might I miss.

Might she have loved me? just as well
She might have hated, who can tell!
'The Last Ride Together' (1855) st. 4

1 'Tis an awkward thing to play with souls,
And matter enough to save one's own.
'A Light Woman' (1855) st. 12

2 Just for a handful of silver he left us,
Just for a riband to stick in his coat.
deploring **Wordsworth***'s abandoning of his radical
views*
'The Lost Leader' (1845)

3 We that had loved him so, followed him,
honoured him,
Lived in his mild and magnificent eye,
Learned his great language, caught his clear
accents,
Made him our pattern to live and to die!
Shakespeare was of us, Milton was for us,
Burns, Shelley, were with us—they watch from
their graves!
'The Lost Leader' (1845)

4 Never glad confident morning again!
'The Lost Leader' (1845)

5 Kentish Sir Byng stood for his King,
Bidding the crop-headed Parliament swing.
'Marching Along' (1842)

6 Marched them along, fifty-score strong,
Great-hearted gentlemen, singing this song.

God for King Charles! Pym and such carles
To the Devil that prompts 'em their treasonous
parles!
'Marching Along' (1842)

7 A tap at the pane, the quick sharp scratch
And blue spurt of a lighted match,
And a voice less loud, through its joys and fears,
Than the two hearts beating each to each!
'Meeting at Night' (1845)

8 Ah, did you once see Shelley plain,
And did he stop and speak to you
And did you speak to him again?
How strange it seems, and new!
'Memorabilia' (1855)

9 That's my last Duchess painted on the wall,
Looking as if she were alive.
'My Last Duchess' (1842) l. 1

10   She had
A heart—how shall I say?—too soon made glad,
Too easily impressed; she liked whate'er
She looked on, and her looks went everywhere.
'My Last Duchess' (1842) l. 21

11 Never the time and the place
And the loved one all together!
'Never the Time and the Place' (1883)

12   What's come to perfection perishes.
Things learned on earth, we shall practise in
heaven:
Works done least rapidly, Art most cherishes.
'Old Pictures in Florence' (1855) st. 17

13 Dante, who loved well because he hated,
Hated wickedness that hinders loving.
'One Word More' (1855) st. 5

14 Measure your mind's height by the shade it casts!
Paracelsus (1835) pt. 3, l. 821

15 I give the fight up: let there be an end,
A privacy, an obscure nook for me.
I want to be forgotten even by God.
Paracelsus (1835) pt. 5, l. 363

16 Round the cape of a sudden came the sea,
And the sun looked over the mountain's rim:
And straight was a path of gold for him,
And the need of a world of men for me.
'Parting at Morning' (1849)

17 It was roses, roses, all the way.
'The Patriot' (1855)

18 The air broke into a mist with bells.
'The Patriot' (1855)

19 Sun-treader, life and light be thine for ever!
of **Shelley**
Pauline (1833) l. 151

20 Rats!
They fought the dogs and killed the cats,
And bit the babies in the cradles,
And ate the cheeses out of the vats,
And licked the soup from the cooks' own ladles,
Split open the kegs of salted sprats,
Made nests inside men's Sunday hats,
And even spoiled the women's chats
By drowning their speaking
With shrieking and squeaking
In fifty different sharps and flats.
'The Pied Piper of Hamelin' (1842) st. 2

21 So munch on, crunch on, take your nuncheon,
Breakfast, supper, dinner, luncheon!
'The Pied Piper of Hamelin' (1842) st. 7

22 The year's at the spring
And day's at the morn;
Morning's at seven;
The hill-side's dew-pearled;
The lark's on the wing;
The snail's on the thorn:
God's in his heaven—
All's right with the world!
Pippa Passes (1841) pt. 1, l. 221; see **Proverbs** 620:48

23 All service ranks the same with God—
With God, whose puppets, best and worst,
Are we: there is no last nor first.
Pippa Passes (1841) epilogue

24 That moment she was mine, mine, fair,
Perfectly pure and good.
'Porphyria's Lover' (1842) l. 36

25   All her hair
In one long yellow string I wound
Three times her little throat around,
And strangled her. No pain felt she;
I am quite sure she felt no pain.
'Porphyria's Lover' (1842) l. 38

1 Fear death?—to feel the fog in my throat,
The mist in my face.
'Prospice' (1864)

2 I was ever a fighter, so—one fight more,
The best and the last!
I would hate that death bandaged my eyes, and
forbore,
And bade me creep past.
No! let me taste the whole of it, fare like my peers
The heroes of old,
Bear the brunt, in a minute pay glad life's arrears
Of pain, darkness and cold.
'Prospice' (1864)

3 Grow old along with me!
The best is yet to be,
The last of life, for which the first was made.
'Rabbi Ben Ezra' (1864) st. 1

4 Fancies that broke through language and escaped.
'Rabbi Ben Ezra' (1864) st. 25

5 Time's wheel runs back or stops: potter and clay
endure.
'Rabbi Ben Ezra' (1864) st. 27

6 O lyric Love, half-angel and half-bird.
The Ring and the Book (1868–9) bk. 1, l. 1391

7   So, Pietro craved an heir,
(The story always old and always new).
The Ring and the Book (1868–9) bk. 2, l. 213

8   Go practise if you please
With men and women: leave a child alone
For Christ's particular love's sake!
The Ring and the Book (1868–9) bk. 3, l. 88

9 In the great right of an excessive wrong.
The Ring and the Book (1868–9) bk. 3, l. 1055

10 Faultless to a fault.
The Ring and the Book (1868–9) bk. 9, l. 1175

11 White shall not neutralize the black, nor good
Compensate bad in man, absolve him so:
Life's business being just the terrible choice.
The Ring and the Book (1868–9) bk. 10, l. 1235

12 Gr-r-r—there go, my heart's abhorrence!
Water your damned flowerpots, do!
If hate killed men, Brother Lawrence,
God's blood, would not mine kill you!
'Soliloquy of the Spanish Cloister' (1842) st. 1

13 There's a great text in Galatians,
Once you trip on it, entails
Twenty-nine distinct damnations,
One sure, if another fails.
'Soliloquy of the Spanish Cloister' (1842) st. 7

14 Sidney's self, the starry paladin.
Sordello (1840) bk. 1, l. 69

15 Still more labyrinthine buds the rose.
Sordello (1840) bk. 1, l. 476

16   Any nose
May ravage with impunity a rose.
Sordello (1840) bk. 6, l. 881

17 And the sin I impute to each frustrate ghost
Is—the unlit lamp and the ungirt loin,

Though the end in sight was a vice, I say.
'The Statue and the Bust' (1863 revision) l. 246

18 Oh Galuppi, Baldassaro, this is very sad to find!
I can hardly misconceive you; it would prove me
deaf and blind;
But although I take your meaning, 'tis with such
a heavy mind!
'A Toccata of Galuppi's' (1855) st. 1

19 Hark, the dominant's persistence till it must be
answered to!
'A Toccata of Galuppi's' (1855) st. 8

20 Then they left you for their pleasure: till in due
time, one by one,
Some with lives that came to nothing, some with
deeds as well undone,
Death stepped tacitly and took them where they
never see the sun.
'A Toccata of Galuppi's' (1855) st. 10

21 In you come with your cold music till I creep
through every nerve.
'A Toccata of Galuppi's' (1855) st. 11

22 Dust and ashes, dead and done with, Venice spent
what Venice earned.
'A Toccata of Galuppi's' (1855) st. 12

23 What of soul was left, I wonder, when the kissing
had to stop?
'A Toccata of Galuppi's' (1855) st. 14

24 Dear dead women, with such hair, too—what's
become of all the gold
Used to hang and brush their bosoms? I feel chilly
and grown old.
'A Toccata of Galuppi's' (1855) st. 15

25 I would that you were all to me,
You that are just so much, no more.
'Two in the Campagna' (1855) st. 8

26   I pluck the rose
And love it more than tongue can speak—
Then the good minute goes.
'Two in the Campagna' (1855) st. 10

27 What's become of Waring
Since he gave us all the slip?
Waring (1842) pt. 1, l. 1

28 Ichabod, Ichabod,
The glory is departed!
Waring (1842) pt. 6, l. 99; see **Bible** 80:8

29 Let's contend no more, Love,
Strive nor weep:
All be as before, Love,
—Only sleep!
'A Woman's Last Word' (1855) st. 1

30 Ay, dead! and were yourself alive, good Fitz,
How to return your thanks would pass my wits.
Kicking you seems the common lot of curs—
While more appropriate greeting lends you grace:
Surely to spit there glorifies your face—
Spitting from lips once sanctified by Hers.
rejoinder to Edward **Fitzgerald**, who had 'thanked God
my wife was dead'
in Athenaeum 13 July 1889; see **Fitzgerald** 323:18

1 When it was written, God and Robert Browning knew what it meant; now only God knows.
on Sordello
attributed; see **Klopstock** 458:1

Lenny Bruce 1925–66
American comedian

2 The liberals can understand everything but people who don't understand them.
John Cohen (ed.) *The Essential Lenny Bruce* (1967)

3 I'll die young, but it's like kissing God.
on his drug addiction
attributed

Robert Bruce 1554–1631
Scottish minister and laird of Kinnaird

4 Now, God be with you, my children: I have breakfasted with you and shall sup with my Lord Jesus Christ this night.
Robert Fleming *The Fulfilling of the Scripture* (3rd ed., 1693)

Cathal Brugha 1874–1922
Irish nationalist

5 Don't you realize that, if you sign this thing, you will split Ireland from top to bottom?
to **de Valera**, *December 1921, on the Treaty*
Jim Ring *Erskine Childers* (1996)

Beau Brummell (George Bryan Brummell) 1778–1840
English dandy

6 Who's your fat friend?
referring to the Prince of Wales, later **George IV**
Capt. Jesse *Life of George Brummell* (1844) vol. I

7 [Brummell] used to say that, whether it was summer or winter, he always liked to have the morning well-aired before he got up.
Charles Macfarlane *Reminiscences of a Literary Life* (1917) ch. 27

8 No perfumes, but very fine linen, plenty of it, and country washing.
Memoirs of Harriette Wilson (1825) vol. I

Gro Harlem Brundtland 1939–
Norwegian stateswoman; Prime Minister 1981, 1986–89, and 1990–96

9 I do not know of any environmental group in any country that does not view its government as an adversary.
in *Time* 25 September 1989

Frank Bruno 1961–
English boxer

10 Boxing's just show business with blood.
in *Guardian* 20 November 1991

11 Know what I mean, Harry?
supposed to have been said in interview with sports commentator Harry Carpenter, possibly apocryphal

William Jennings Bryan 1860–1925
American Democratic politician

12 You shall not press down upon the brow of labour this crown of thorns, you shall not crucify mankind upon a cross of gold.
opposing the gold standard
speech at the Democratic National Convention, Chicago, 1896, in *The First Battle. A Story of the Campaign of 1896* (1896) vol. I, ch. 10

Bill Bryson 1951–
American travel writer

13 I had always thought that once you grew up you could do anything you wanted—stay up all night or eat ice-cream straight out of the container.
The Lost Continent (1989)

14 What an odd thing tourism is. You fly off to a strange land, eagerly abandoning all the comforts of home, and then expend vast quantities of time and money in a largely futile attempt to recapture the comforts that you wouldn't have lost if you hadn't left home in the first place.
Neither Here Nor There (1991)

Zbigniew Brzezinski 1928–
American politician

15 Russia can be an empire or a democracy, but it cannot be both.
in *Foreign Affairs* March/April 1994 'The Premature Partnership'

Martin Buber 1878–1965
Austrian-born religious philosopher and Zionist

16 Through the Thou a person becomes I.
I and Thou (1923)

John Buchan (Lord Tweedsmuir) 1875–1940
Scottish novelist and brother of O. **Douglas**; *Governor-General of Canada, 1935–40*

17 There may be Peace without Joy, and Joy without Peace, but the two combined make Happiness.
Memory-Hold-the-Door (1940) ch. 5

18 It's a great life if you don't weaken.
Mr Standfast (1919) ch. 5

19 Have you ever considered what a diabolical weapon that can be—using all the channels of modern publicity to poison and warp men's minds? It is the most dangerous thing on earth . . . Happily, in the long run it defeats itself, but only after it has sown the world with mischief.
The Three Hostages (1924) ch. 4

20 An atheist is a man who has no invisible means of support.
H. E. Fosdick *On Being a Real Person* (1943) ch. 10

Frank Buchman 1878–1961

American evangelist; founder of the Moral Re-Armament movement

1 I thank heaven for a man like Adolf Hitler, who built a front line of defence against the anti-Christ of Communism.
  in *New York World-Telegram* 26 August 1936

2 There is enough in the world for everyone's need, but not enough for everyone's greed.
  Remaking the World (1947)

Georg Büchner 1813–37

German dramatist

3 *Wer am Meisten geniesst, betet am Meisten.*
  Enjoy yourself—that's the best way to pray.
  Danton's Death (1835) act 1, sc. 5

4 *Das ist der einzige Unterschied, den ich zwischen den Menschen herausbringen kann. Jeder handelt seiner Natur gemäss d.h. er tut, was ihm wohltut.*
  That's the only difference between men that I've been able to discover. Everyone acts according to his nature—in other words he does what does him good.
  Danton's Death (1835) act 1, sc. 6

5 *Der verfluchte Satz: etwas kann nicht zu nichts werden! und ich bin etwas, das ist der Jammer! Die Schöpfung hat sich so breit gemacht, da ist nichts leer, Alles voll gewimmels. Das Nichts hat sich ermordet, die Schöpfung ist seine wunde.*
  That damned argument: something cannot become nothing, there's the misery. Creation has become so broad, there's no emptiness. Everything is packed and swarming. The void has destroyed itself; creation is its wound.
  Danton's Death (1835) act 3, sc. 7

Gene Buck (Edward Eugene Buck) 1885–1957 and Herman Ruby 1891–1959

6 That Shakespearian rag,—
  Most intelligent, very elegant.
  'That Shakespearian Rag' (1912 song); see **Eliot** 303:15

John Sheffield, 1st Duke of Buckingham and Normanby 1648–1721

English poet and politician

7 Learn to write well, or not to write at all.
  'An Essay upon Satire' (1689)

George Villiers, 2nd Duke of Buckingham 1628–87

English courtier and writer

8 The world is made up for the most part of fools and knaves, both irreconcilable foes to truth.
  The Dramatic Works (1715) vol. 2 'To Mr Clifford On his Humane Reason'

9 What a devil is the plot good for, but to bring in fine things?
  The Rehearsal (1672) act 3, sc. 1

10 Ay, now the plot thickens very much upon us.
  The Rehearsal (1672) act 3, sc. 2

H. J. Buckoll 1803–71

English clergyman; master at Rugby School from 1826

11 Lord, dismiss us with Thy blessing,
  Thanks for mercies past receive.
  Pardon all, their faults confessing;
  Time that's lost may all retrieve.
  Psalms and Hymns for the Use of Rugby School Chapel (1850) 'Lord, Dismiss us with Thy Blessing'

J. B. Buckstone 1802–79

English comedian and dramatist

12 And we won't go home till morning.
  Billy Taylor (performed 1829) act 1, sc. 2

Comte de Buffon (George-Louis Leclerc) 1707–88

French naturalist

13 Style is the man himself.
  Discours sur le style (address given to the Académie Française, 25 August 1753); see **Proverbs** 631:30

14 Genius is only a greater aptitude for patience.
  Hérault de Séchelles *Voyage à Montbar* (1803); **Carlyle** 192:4

Edward Bullard 1907–80

English geophysicist

15 Rutherford was a disaster. He started the 'something for nothing' tradition . . . the notion that research can always be done on the cheap . . . The war taught us differently. If you want quick and effective results you must put the money in.
  P. Grosvenor and J. McMillan *The British Genius* (1973); see **Rutherford** 661:20

Arthur Buller 1874–1944

British botanist and mycologist

16 There was a young lady named Bright,
  Whose speed was far faster than light;
  She set out one day
  In a relative way
  And returned on the previous night.
  'Relativity' in *Punch* 19 December 1923

Gerald Bullett 1894–1958

British writer

17 My Lord Archbishop, what a scold you are!
  And when your man is down how bold you are!
  Of charity how oddly scant you are!
  How Lang, O Lord, how full of Cantuar!
  *on the role of Cosmo Gordon Lang, Archbishop of Canterbury, in the abdication of **Edward VIII***
  composed c.1936

Bernhard von Bülow 1849–1929

German statesman, Chancellor of Germany 1900–9

1 We desire to throw no one into the shade [in East Asia], but we also demand our own place in the sun.
> in the Reichstag, 6 December 1897, in *Graf Bülows Reden* (1903); see **Wilhelm II** 837:18

Edward Robert Bulwer, Earl of Lytton
see **Owen Meredith**

Edward George Bulwer-Lytton (1st
Baron Lytton) 1803–73

British novelist and politician

2 From the petty droppings of the well of manners, the fossilized incrustations of national character are formed.
> *England and the English* (1833) vol. 1, ch. 2

3 Here Stanley meets,—how Stanley scorns, the glance!
The brilliant chief, irregularly great,
Frank, haughty, rash,—the Rupert of Debate!
> *on Edward Stanley, 14th Earl of **Derby***
> *The New Timon* (1846) pt. 1, sect. 3, l. 202; see **Disraeli** 275:7

4 Out-babying Wordsworth and out-glittering Keats.
> *on **Tennyson***
> *The New Timon* (1846) pt. 2, sect. 1, l. 62

5 Beneath the rule of men entirely great
The pen is mightier than the sword.
> *Richelieu* (1839) act 2, sc. 2, l. 307; see **Burton** 174:5, **Proverbs** 629:19

6 In science, read, by preference, the newest works; in literature, the oldest.
> *Caxtoniana* (1863) 'Hints on Mental Culture'

7 There is no man so friendless but what he can find a friend sincere enough to tell him disagreeable truths.
> *What will he do with it?* (1857) vol. 1, bk. 3, ch. 15

Alfred 'Poet' Bunn c.1796–1860

English theatrical manager and librettist

8 I dreamed that I dwelt in marble halls
With vassals and serfs at my side.
> *The Bohemian Girl* (1843) act 2 'The Gipsy Girl's Dream'

Basil Bunting 1900–85

English poet

9 Praise the green earth. Chance has appointed her home, workshop, larder, middenpit.
Her lousy skin scabbed here and there by cities provides us with name and nation.
> 'Attis: or, Something Missing' (1931) pt. 1

10 Dance tiptoe, bull,
black against may.
Ridiculous and lovely
chase hurdling shadows
morning into noon.
> 'Briggflatts' (1965) pt. 1

Luis Buñuel 1900–83

Spanish film director
*see also **Film titles** 322:3*

11 Thanks to God, I am still an atheist.
> in *Le Monde* 16 December 1959

John Bunyan 1628–88

English writer and Nonconformist preacher
*on Bunyan: see **Arnold** 30:6; see also **Opening lines** 574:5*

12 Words easy to be understood do often hit the mark; when high and learned ones do only pierce the air.
> *The Holy City* (1665) 'The Epistle to Four Sorts of Readers' 'To the Learned Reader'; see **Bible** 107:27

13 The name of the slough was Despond.
> *The Pilgrim's Progress* (1678) pt. 1

14 CHRISTIAN: Gentlemen, Whence came you, and whither do you go?
FORMALIST AND HYPOCRISY: We were born in the land of Vainglory, and we are going for praise to Mount Sion.
> *The Pilgrim's Progress* (1678) pt. 1

15 It is an hard matter for a man to go down into the valley of Humiliation . . . and to catch no slip by the way.
> *The Pilgrim's Progress* (1678) pt. 1

16 A foul Fiend coming over the field to meet him; his name is Apollyon.
> *The Pilgrim's Progress* (1678) pt. 1

17 It beareth the name of Vanity-Fair, because the town where 'tis kept, is lighter than vanity.
> *The Pilgrim's Progress* (1678) pt. 1; see **Book of Common Prayer** 138:1

18 Hanging is too good for him, said Mr Cruelty.
> *The Pilgrim's Progress* (1678) pt. 1

19 Yet my great-grandfather was but a water-man, looking one way, and rowing another: and I got most of my estate by the same occupation.
> *The Pilgrim's Progress* (1678) pt. 1; see **Burton** 174:1

20 They are for religion when in rags and contempt; but I am for him when he walks in his golden slippers, in the sunshine and with applause.
> *The Pilgrim's Progress* (1678) pt. 1

21 A castle, called Doubting Castle, the owner whereof was Giant Despair.
> *The Pilgrims Progress* (1678) pt.1

22 Now Giant Despair had a wife, and her name was Diffidence.
> *The Pilgrim's Progress* (1678) pt. 1

23 They came to the Delectable Mountains.
> *The Pilgrim's Progress* (1678) pt. 1

24 Sleep is sweet to the labouring man.
> *The Pilgrim's Progress* (1678) pt. 1; see **Bible** 86:5

25 Then I saw that there was a way to Hell, even from the gates of heaven.
> *The Pilgrim's Progress* (1678) pt. 1

26 So I awoke, and behold it was a dream.
> *The Pilgrim's Progress* (1678) pt. 1

1 A man that could look no way but downwards,
with a muckrake in his hand.
The Pilgrim's Progress (1684) pt. 2; see **Roosevelt** 654:10

2 One leak will sink a ship, and one sin will destroy
a sinner.
The Pilgrim's Progress (1684) pt. 2

3 He that is down needs fear no fall,
He that is low no pride.
He that is humble ever shall
Have God to be his guide.
The Pilgrim's Progress (1684) pt. 2 'Shepherd Boy's Song'

4 Difficulties, lions, or Vanity-Fair, he feared not at
all: 'twas only sin, death, and Hell that was to
him a terror.
of Mr Fearing
The Pilgrim's Progress (1684) pt. 2

5 A man there was, tho' some did count him mad,
The more he cast away, the more he had.
The Pilgrim's Progress (1684) pt. 2

6 Mercy . . . laboured much for the poor . . . an
ornament to her profession.
The Pilgrim's Progress (1684) pt. 2

7 Who would true valour see,
Let him come hither;
One here will constant be,
Come wind, come weather.
There's no discouragement
Shall make him once relent
His first avowed intent
To be a pilgrim.
Who so beset him round
With dismal stories,
Do but themselves confound—
His strength the more is.
The Pilgrim's Progress (1684) pt. 2

8 The last words of Mr Despondency were, Farewell
night, welcome day. His daughter went through
the river singing, but none could understand what
she said.
The Pilgrim's Progress (1684) pt. 2

9 I am going to my Fathers, and tho' with great
difficulty I am got hither, yet now I do not repent
me of all the trouble I have been at to arrive
where I am. My sword, I give to him that shall
succeed me in my pilgrimage, and my courage
and skill to him that can get it. My marks and
scars I carry with me, to be a witness for me, that
I have fought his battles, who will now be my
rewarder.
Mr Valiant-for-Truth
The Pilgrim's Progress (1684) pt. 2

10 So he passed over, and the trumpets sounded for
him on the other side.
Mr Valiant-for-Truth
The Pilgrim's Progress (1684) pt. 2

11 I have formerly lived by hearsay and faith, but
now I go where I shall live by sight, and shall be
with Him in whose company I delight myself.
Mr Standfast
The Pilgrim's Progress (1684) pt. 2

Samuel Dickinson Burchard 1812–91
American Presbyterian minister

12 We are Republicans and don't propose to leave
our party and identify ourselves with the party
whose antecedents are rum, Romanism, and
rebellion.
speech at the Fifth Avenue Hotel, New York, 29 October
1884, in *New York World* 30 October 1884

Julie Burchill 1960–
English journalist and writer
see also **Anonymous** 16:12

13 Now, at last, this sad, glittering century has an
image worthy of it: a wandering, wondering girl,
a silly Sloane turned secular saint, coming home
in her coffin to RAF Northolt like the good soldier
she was.
in *Guardian* 2 September 1997

James Bland Burges 1752–1824
English poet

14 Pandora's box, whence flew dispersed
All the dire mischiefs which mankind have cursed.
The Dragon Knight (1816) canto 7

Anthony Burgess 1917–93
English novelist and critic
see also **Opening lines** 574:27

15 A clockwork orange.
title of novel (1962)

16 He said it was artificial respiration, but now I find
I am to have his child.
Inside Mr Enderby (1963) pt. 1, ch. 4

17 The US presidency is a Tudor monarchy plus
telephones.
George Plimpton (ed.) *Writers at Work* (4th Series, 1977)

Gelett Burgess 1866–1951
American humorist and illustrator

18 I never saw a Purple Cow,
I never hope to see one;
But I can tell you, anyhow,
I'd rather see than be one!
The Burgess Nonsense Book (1914) 'The Purple Cow'

19 Ah, yes! I wrote the 'Purple Cow'—
I'm sorry, now, I wrote it!
But I can tell you anyhow,
I'll kill you if you quote it!
The Burgess Nonsense Book (1914) 'Confessional'

Lord Burghley see William Cecil

John William Burgon 1813–88
English clergyman; Dean of Chichester from 1876

20 Match me such marvel, save in Eastern clime,—
A rose-red city—half as old as Time!
Petra (1845) l. 131; see **Plomer** 598:12, **Rogers** 652:12

John Burgoyne 1722–92

English general and dramatist

1 You have only, when before your glass, to keep pronouncing to yourself nimini-pimini—the lips cannot fail of taking their plie.

plie = *curve*

The Heiress (1786) act 3, sc. 2

Edmund Burke 1729–97

Irish-born Whig politician and man of letters

on Burke: see **Goldsmith** *355:5,* **Johnson** *432:12,* **Paine** *582:14,* **Paine** *582:15; see also* **Misquotations** *538:4*

2 The conduct of a losing party never appears right: at least it never can possess the only infallible criterion of wisdom to vulgar judgements—success.

Letter to a Member of the National Assembly (1791)

3 Those who have been once intoxicated with power, and have derived any kind of emolument from it, even though for but one year, can never willingly abandon it.

Letter to a Member of the National Assembly (1791)

4 Tyrants seldom want pretexts.

Letter to a Member of the National Assembly (1791)

5 You can never plan the future by the past.

Letter to a Member of the National Assembly (1791)

6 The king, and his faithful subjects, the lords and commons of this realm,—the triple cord, which no man can break.

A Letter to a Noble Lord (1796); see **Bible** 86:3

7 Many have been taught to think that moderation, in a case like this, is a sort of treason.

Letter to the Sheriffs of Bristol (1777)

8 Between craft and credulity, the voice of reason is stifled.

Letter to the Sheriffs of Bristol (1777)

9 Liberty too must be limited in order to be possessed.

Letter to the Sheriffs of Bristol (1777)

10 Nothing in progression can rest on its original plan. We may as well think of rocking a grown man in the cradle of an infant.

Letter to the Sheriffs of Bristol (1777)

11 Among a people generally corrupt, liberty cannot long exist.

Letter to the Sheriffs of Bristol (1777)

12 There is, however, a limit at which forbearance ceases to be a virtue.

Observations on a late Publication on the Present State of the Nation (2nd ed., 1769)

13 It is a general popular error to imagine the loudest complainers for the public to be the most anxious for its welfare.

Observations on a late Publication on the Present State of the Nation (2nd ed., 1769)

14 It is the nature of all greatness not to be exact; and great trade will always be attended with considerable abuses.

On American Taxation (1775)

15 Falsehood has a perennial spring.

On American Taxation (1775)

16 To tax and to please, no more than to love and to be wise, is not given to men.

On American Taxation (1775); see **Proverbs** 628:30

17 I have in general no very exalted opinion of the virtue of paper government.

On Conciliation with America (1775)

18 The concessions of the weak are the concessions of fear.

On Conciliation with America (1775)

19 When we speak of the commerce with our colonies, fiction lags after truth; invention is unfruitful, and imagination cold and barren.

On Conciliation with America (1775)

20 The use of force alone is but *temporary*. It may subdue for a moment; but it does not remove the necessity of subduing again; and a nation is not governed, which is perpetually to be conquered.

On Conciliation with America (1775)

21 Nothing less will content me, than *whole America*.

On Conciliation with America (1775)

22 All Protestantism, even the most cold and passive, is a sort of dissent. But the religion most prevalent in our northern colonies is a refinement on the principle of resistance; it is the dissidence of dissent, and the Protestantism of the Protestant religion.

On Conciliation with America (1775)

23 I do not know the method of drawing up an indictment against an whole people.

On Conciliation with America (1775)

24 It is not, what a lawyer tells me I *may* do; but what humanity, reason, and justice, tells me I ought to do.

On Conciliation with America (1775)

25 Freedom and not servitude is the cure of anarchy; as religion, and not atheism, is the true remedy for superstition.

On Conciliation with America (1775)

26 Every human benefit, every virtue and every prudent act, is founded on compromise.

On Conciliation with America (1775)

27 Instead of a standing revenue, you will have therefore a perpetual quarrel.

On Conciliation with America (1775)

28 Parties must ever exist in a free country.

On Conciliation with America (1775)

29 Slavery they can have anywhere. It is a weed that grows in every soil.

On Conciliation with America (1775)

30 Deny them this participation of freedom, and you break that sole bond, which originally made, and must still preserve the unity of the empire.

On Conciliation with America (1775)

31 It is the love of the people; it is their attachment to their government, from the sense of the deep stake they have in such a glorious institution, which

gives you your army and your navy, and infuses into both that liberal obedience, without which your army would be a base rabble, and your navy nothing but rotten timber.
On Conciliation with America (1775)

1 Magnanimity in politics is not seldom the truest wisdom; and a great empire and little minds go ill together.
On Conciliation with America (1775)

2 By adverting to the dignity of this high calling, our ancestors have turned a savage wilderness into a glorious empire: and have made the most extensive, and the only honourable conquests; not by destroying, but by promoting the wealth, the number, the happiness of the human race.
On Conciliation with America (1775)

3 No passion so effectually robs the mind of all its powers of acting and reasoning as fear.
On the Sublime and Beautiful (1757) pt. 2, sect. 2

4 Custom reconciles us to everything.
On the Sublime and Beautiful (1757) pt. 4, sect. 18

5 I flatter myself that I love a manly, moral, regulated liberty as well as any gentleman.
Reflections on the Revolution in France (1790)

6 Whenever our neighbour's house is on fire, it cannot be amiss for the engines to play a little on our own.
Reflections on the Revolution in France (1790)

7 A state without the means of some change is without the means of its conservation.
Reflections on the Revolution in France (1790)

8 Make the Revolution a parent of settlement, and not a nursery of future revolutions.
Reflections on the Revolution in France (1790)

9 People will not look forward to posterity, who never look backward to their ancestors.
Reflections on the Revolution in France (1790)

10 Those who attempt to level never equalize.
Reflections on the Revolution in France (1790)

11 Whatever each man can separately do, without trespassing upon others, he has a right to do for himself; and he has a right to a fair portion of all which society, with all its combinations of skill and force, can do in his favour.
Reflections on the Revolution in France (1790)

12 Government is a contrivance of human wisdom to provide for human *wants*. Men have a right that these wants should be provided for by this wisdom.
Reflections on the Revolution in France (1790)

13 I thought ten thousand swords must have leapt from their scabbards to avenge even a look that threatened her with insult.
of *Marie-Antoinette*
Reflections on the Revolution in France (1790)

14 The age of chivalry is gone.— That of sophisters, economists, and calculators, has succeeded; and the glory of Europe is extinguished for ever.
Reflections on the Revolution in France (1790)

15 This barbarous philosophy, which is the offspring of cold hearts and muddy understandings.
Reflections on the Revolution in France (1790)

16 In the groves of *their* academy, at the end of every vista, you see nothing but the gallows.
Reflections on the Revolution in France (1790); see **Horace** 399:21

17 Kings will be tyrants from policy when subjects are rebels from principle.
Reflections on the Revolution in France (1790)

18 Learning will be cast into the mire, and trodden down under the hoofs of a swinish multitude.
Reflections on the Revolution in France (1790)

19 Because half a dozen grasshoppers under a fern make the field ring with their importunate chink, whilst thousands of great cattle, reposed beneath the shadow of the British oak, chew the cud and are silent, pray do not imagine that those who make the noise are the only inhabitants of the field.
Reflections on the Revolution in France (1790)

20 Man is by his constitution a religious animal; atheism is against not only our reason, but our instincts.
Reflections on the Revolution in France (1790); see **Aristotle** 25:25

21 A perfect democracy is therefore the most shameless thing in the world.
Reflections on the Revolution in France (1790)

22 Society is indeed a contract . . . it becomes a partnership not only between those who are living, but between those who are living, those who are dead, and those who are to be born.
Reflections on the Revolution in France (1790)

23 Nobility is a graceful ornament to the civil order. It is the Corinthian capital of polished society.
Reflections on the Revolution in France (1790)

24 Superstition is the religion of feeble minds.
Reflections on the Revolution in France (1790)

25 He that wrestles with us strengthens our nerves, and sharpens our skill. Our antagonist is our helper.
Reflections on the Revolution in France (1790)

26 Our patience will achieve more than our force.
Reflections on the Revolution in France (1790)

27 By hating vices too much, they come to love men too little.
Reflections on the Revolution in France (1790)

28 We begin our public affections in our families. No cold relation is a zealous citizen.
Reflections on the Revolution in France (1790)

29 Good order is the foundation of all good things.
Reflections on the Revolution in France (1790)

30 Every politician ought to sacrifice to the graces; and to join compliance with reason.
Reflections on the Revolution in France (1790)

31 Never, no never, did Nature say one thing and Wisdom say another.
Third Letter . . . on the Proposals for Peace with the Regicide Directory (1797)

1 Ambition can creep as well as soar.
   Third Letter . . . on the Proposals for Peace . . . (1797)

2 And having looked to government for bread, on the very first scarcity they will turn and bite the hand that fed them.
   Thoughts and Details on Scarcity (1800)

3 To complain of the age we live in, to murmur at the present possessors of power, to lament the past, to conceive extravagant hopes of the future, are the common dispositions of the greatest part of mankind.
   Thoughts on the Cause of the Present Discontents (1770)

4 I am not one of those who think that the people are never in the wrong. They have been so, frequently and outrageously, both in other countries and in this. But I do say, that in all disputes between them and their rulers, the presumption is at least upon a par in favour of the people.
   Thoughts on the Cause of the Present Discontents (1770)

5 The power of the crown, almost dead and rotten as Prerogative, has grown up anew, with much more strength, and far less odium, under the name of Influence.
   Thoughts on the Cause of the Present Discontents (1770)

6 We must soften into a credulity below the milkiness of infancy to think all men virtuous. We must be tainted with a malignity truly diabolical, to believe all the world to be equally wicked and corrupt.
   Thoughts on the Cause of the Present Discontents (1770)

7 When . . . [people] imagine that their food is only a cover for poison, and when they neither love nor trust the hand that serves it, it is not the name of the roast beef of old England that will persuade them to sit down to the table that is spread for them.
   Thoughts on the Cause of the Present Discontents (1770)

8 When bad men combine, the good must associate; else they will fall, one by one, an unpitied sacrifice in a contemptible struggle.
   Thoughts on the Cause of the Present Discontents (1770); see **Misquotations** 538:4

9 Of this stamp is the cant of *Not men, but measures*; a sort of charm by which many people get loose from every honourable engagement.
   Thoughts on the Cause of the Present Discontents (1770); see **Canning** 189:9, **Goldsmith** 355:20

10 It is therefore our business carefully to cultivate in our minds, to rear to the most perfect vigour and maturity, every sort of generous and honest feeling that belongs to our nature. To bring the dispositions that are lovely in private life into the service and conduct of the commonwealth;
   Thoughts on the Cause of the Present Discontents (1770)

11 So to be patriots, as not to forget we are gentlemen.
   Thoughts on the Cause of the Present Discontents (1770)

12 Laws, like houses, lean on one another.
   A Tract on the Popery Laws (planned *c.*1765) ch. 3, pt. 1 in *The Works* vol. 5 (1812)

13 In all forms of Government the people is the true legislator.
   A Tract on the Popery Laws ch. 3, pt. 1 in *The Works* vol. 5 (1812)

14 Falsehood and delusion are allowed in no case whatsoever: But, as in the exercise of all the virtues, there is an economy of truth.
   Two Letters on the Proposals for Peace with the Regicide Directory (1796) pt. 1; see **Armstrong** 26:18

15 All men that are ruined are ruined on the side of their natural propensities.
   Two Letters on the Proposals for Peace with the Regicide Directory (9th ed., 1796)

16 Example is the school of mankind, and they will learn at no other.
   Two Letters on the Proposals for Peace with the Regicide Directory (9th ed., 1796)

17 The greater the power, the more dangerous the abuse.
   speech on the Middlesex Election, 7 February 1771, in *The Speeches* (1854)

18 Your representative owes you, not his industry only, but his judgement; and he betrays, instead of serving you, if he sacrifices it to your opinion.
   speech, 3 November 1774, in *Speeches at his Arrival at Bristol* (1774)

19 People crushed by law have no hopes but from power. If laws are their enemies, they will be enemies to laws; and those, who have much to hope and nothing to lose, will always be dangerous, more or less.
   letter to Charles James Fox, 8 October 1777, in *The Correspondence of Edmund Burke* vol. 3 (1961)

20 Bad laws are the worst sort of tyranny.
   Speech at Bristol, previous to the Late Election (1780)

21 Individuals pass like shadows; but the commonwealth is fixed and stable.
   speech, House of Commons, 11 February 1780

22 The people are the masters.
   speech, House of Commons, 11 February 1780; see **Blair** 118:17

23 Not merely a chip of the old 'block', but the old block itself.
   on the younger **Pitt**'s *maiden speech, February 1781*
   N. W. Wraxall *Historical Memoirs of My Own Time* (1904 ed.) pt. 2

24 Every other conqueror of every other description has left some monument, either of state or beneficence, behind him. Were we to be driven out of India this day, nothing would remain to tell that it had been possessed, during the inglorious period of our dominion, by anything better than the orang-outang or the tiger.
   speech on Fox's East India Bill, House of Commons, 1 December 1783

25 Your governor [Warren Hastings] stimulates a rapacious and licentious soldiery to the personal search of women, lest these unhappy creatures should avail themselves of the protection of their sex to secure any supply for their necessities.
   speech on Fox's East India Bill, House of Commons, 1 December 1783

1 The people never give up their liberties but under some delusion.

> speech at County Meeting of Buckinghamshire, 1784, attributed in E. Latham *Famous Sayings* (1904), with 'except' substituted for 'but'

2 Religious persecution may shield itself under the guise of a mistaken and over-zealous piety.

> speech, 18 February 1788, in E. A. Bond (ed.) *Speeches . . . in the Trial of Warren Hastings* (1859) vol. 1

3 An event has happened, upon which it is difficult to speak, and impossible to be silent.

> speech, 5 May 1789, in E. A. Bond (ed.) *Speeches . . . in the Trial of Warren Hastings* (1859) vol. 2

4 At last dying in the last dyke of prevarication.

> speech, 7 May 1789, in E. A. Bond (ed.) *Speeches . . . in the Trial of Warren Hastings* (1859) vol. 2

5 Old religious factions are volcanoes burnt out.

> speech on the Petition of the Unitarians, 11 May 1792, in *The Works* vol. 5 (1812); see **Disraeli** 276:8

6 Dangers by being despised grow great.

> speech on the Petition of the Unitarians, 11 May 1792, in *The Works* vol. 5 (1812)

7 There is but one law for all, namely, that law which governs all law—the law of our Creator, the law of humanity, justice, equity, the law of nature and of nations.

> speech, 28 May 1794, in E. A. Bond (ed.) *Speeches . . . in the Trial of Warren Hastings* (1859) vol. 4

8 The cold neutrality of an impartial judge.

> J. P. Brissot *To his Constituents* (1794) 'Translator's Preface' (written by Burke)

9 The silent touches of time.

> letter to William Smith, 29 January 1795, in *The Correspondence of Edmund Burke* vol. 8 (1969)

10 Somebody has said, that a king may make a nobleman but he cannot make a gentleman.

> letter to William Smith, 29 January 1795, in *The Correspondence of Edmund Burke* vol. 8 (1969)

11 His virtues were his arts.

> inscription on the pedestal of the statue of the Marquis of Rockingham in Wentworth Park

12 Those who carry on great public schemes must be proof against the most fatiguing delays, the most mortifying disappointments, the most shocking insults, and, worst of all, the presumptuous judgements of the ignorant upon their designs.

> attributed; Benjamin Ward Richardson 'A Biographical Dissertation' ch. 4 in Edwin Chadwick *The Health of Nations* (1887)

Johnny Burke 1908–64

American songwriter

13 Every time it rains, it rains
Pennies from heaven.
Don't you know each cloud contains
Pennies from heaven?

> 'Pennies from Heaven' (1936 song)

14 Like Webster's Dictionary, we're Morocco bound.

> *The Road to Morocco* (1942 film) title song

Thomas E. Burnett Jnr see Last words

472:10

Fanny Burney (Mme d'Arblay) 1752–1840

English novelist and diarist

15 A little alarm now and then keeps life from stagnation.

> *Camilla* (1796) bk. 3, ch. 11

16 There is nothing upon the face of the earth so insipid as a medium. Give me love or hate! a friend that will go to jail for me, or an enemy that will run me through the body!

> *Camilla* (1796) bk. 3, ch. 12

17 It's a delightful thing to think of perfection; but it's vastly more amusing to talk of errors and absurdities.

> *Camilla* (1796) bk. 3, ch. 12

18 Vice is detestable; I banish all its appearances from my coteries; and I would banish its reality, too, were I sure I should then have any thing but empty chairs in my drawing-room.

> *Camilla* (1796) bk. 5, ch. 6

19 The cure of a romantic first flame is a better surety to subsequent discretion, than all the exhortations of all the fathers, and mothers, and guardians, and maiden aunts in the universe.

> *Camilla* (1796) bk. 5, ch. 6

20 O, we all acknowledge our faults, now; 'tis the mode of the day: but the acknowledgement passes for current payment; and therefore we never amend them.

> *Camilla* (1796) bk. 6, ch. 2

21 No man is in love when he marries. He may have loved before; I have even heard he has sometimes loved after: but at the time never. There is something in the formalities of the matrimonial preparations that drive away all the little cupidons.

> *Camilla* (1796) bk. 6, ch. 10

22 Travelling is the ruin of all happiness! There's no looking at a building here after seeing Italy.

> *Cecilia* (1782) bk. 4, ch. 2

23 'The whole of this unfortunate business,' said Dr Lyster, 'has been the result of PRIDE AND PREJUDICE.'

> *Cecilia* (1782) bk. 10, ch. 10

24 'Do you come to the play without knowing what it is?' 'O yes, Sir, yes, very frequently; I have no time to read play-bills; one merely comes to meet one's friends, and show that one's alive.'

> *Evelina* (1778) Letter 20

25 The freedom with which Dr Johnson condemns whatever he disapproves is astonishing.

> *Diary and Letters of Madame D'Arblay* (1842) pt. 2 (23 August 1778)

26 The delusive seduction of martial music.

> Joyce Hemlow et al. (eds.) *Journals and Letters of Fanny Burney* vol. 5 (1975) 'Paris Journal'

27 Such a set of tittle tattle, prittle prattle visitants! Oh dear! I am so sick of the ceremony and fuss of

these fall lall people! So much dressing—chit chat—complimentary nonsense—In short, a country town is my detestation.

diary, 17 July 1768, in *Early Journals and Letters of Fanny Burney* (ed. L. E. Troide, 1988) vol. 1

1 O! how short a time does it take to put an end to a woman's liberty!

of a wedding

diary, 20 July 1768, in *Early Journals and Letters of Fanny Burney* (ed. L. E. Troide, 1988) vol. 1

John Burns 1858–1943

British Liberal politician

2 The Thames is liquid history.

to an American who had compared the Thames disparagingly with the Mississippi

in *Daily Mail* 25 January 1943

Robert Burns 1759–96

Scottish poet

see also: **Last words** 471:11

3 O thou! whatever title suit thee,
Auld Hornie, Satan, Nick, or Clootie.
'Address to the Deil' (1786)

4 Address to the unco guid.
title of poem, 1787

5 Then gently scan your brother man,
Still gentler sister woman;
Tho' they may gang a kennin wrang,
To step aside is human.
'Address to the Unco Guid' (1787)

6 Ae fond kiss, and then we sever;
Ae fareweel, and then for ever!
'Ae fond Kiss' (1792)

7 Flow gently, sweet Afton, among thy green braes,
Flow gently, I'll sing thee a song in thy praise.
'Afton Water' (1792)

8 Should auld acquaintance be forgot
And never brought to mind?
'Auld Lang Syne' (1796)

9 We'll tak a cup o' kindness yet,
For auld lang syne.
'Auld Lang Syne' (1796)

10 Auld Scotland has a raucle tongue.
raucle *meaning 'rash, impetuous'*
'The Author's Earnest Cry' (1786)

11 Freedom and Whisky gang thegither!
'The Author's Earnest Cry and Prayer' (1786) l. 185

12 Ay waukin, Oh,
Waukin still and weary:
Sleep I can get nane,
For thinking on my dearie.
'Ay Waukin O' (1790)

13 Ye banks and braes o' bonny Doon,
How can ye bloom sae fresh and fair;
How can ye chant, ye little birds,
And I sae weary fu' o' care!
'The Banks o' Doon' (1792)

14 And my fause luver stole my rose,
But ah! he left the thorn wi' me.
'The Banks o' Doon' (1792)

15 Thou minds me o' departed joys,
Departed, never to return.
'The Banks o' Doon' (1792)

16 O saw ye bonnie Lesley,
As she gaed o'er the border?
She's gane, like Alexander,
To spread her conquests farther.

To see her is to love her,
And love but her for ever;
For Nature made her what she is
And never made anither!
'Bonnie Lesley' (1798)

17 Gin a body meet a body
Comin thro' the rye,
Gin a body kiss a body
Need a body cry?
'Comin thro' the rye' (1796)

18 Contented wi' little and cantie wi' mair,
Whene'er I forgather wi' Sorrow and Care,
I gie them a skelp, as they're creeping alang,
Wi' a cog o' gude swats and an auld Scotish sang.
'Contented wi' little' (1796)

19 Th' expectant wee-things, toddlin', stacher through
To meet their Dad, wi' flichterin' noise an' glee.
'The Cotter's Saturday Night' (1786) st. 3

20 They never sought in vain that sought the Lord aright.
'The Cotter's Saturday Night' (1786) st. 6

21 The healsome porritch, chief of Scotia's food.
'The Cotter's Saturday Night' (1786) st. 11

22 The sire turns o'er, wi' patriarchal grace,
The big ha'-Bible, ance his father's pride.
'The Cotter's Saturday Night' (1786) st. 12

23 From scenes like these old Scotia's grandeur springs,
That makes her loved at home, revered abroad:
Princes and Lords are but the breath of kings,
'An honest man's the noblest work of God.'
'The Cotter's Saturday Night' (1786) st. 19; see **Pope** 605:9

24 I wasna fou, but just had plenty.
'Death and Dr Hornbook' (1787) st. 3

25 On ev'ry hand it will allow'd be,
He's just—nae better than he shou'd be.
'A Dedication to G[avin] H[amilton]' (1786) l. 25

26 There's threesome reels, there's foursome reels,
There's hornpipes and strathspeys, man,
But the ae best dance e'er cam to the land
Was, the deil's awa wi' th'Exciseman.
'The Deil's awa wi' th'Exciseman' (1792)

27 Perhaps it may turn out a sang;
Perhaps, turn out a sermon.
'Epistle to a Young Friend' (1786) st. 1

28 I waive the quantum o' the sin;
The hazard of concealing;

But och! it hardens a' within,
And petrifies the feeling!
'Epistle to a Young Friend' (1786) st. 6

1 An atheist-laugh's a poor exchange
For Deity offended!
'Epistle to a Young Friend' (1786) st. 9

2 Gie me ae spark o' Nature's fire,
That's a' the learning I desire.
'Epistle to J. L[aprai]k' (1786) st. 13

3 For thus the royal mandate ran,
When first the human race began,
'The social, friendly, honest man,
Whate'er he be,
'Tis he fulfils great Nature's plan,
And none but he.'
'To the same [John Lapraik]' st. 15

4 The rank is but the guinea's stamp,
The man's the gowd for a' that!
'For a' that and a' that' (1790)

5 A man's a man for a' that.
'For a' that and a' that' (1790)

6 Green grow the rashes, O,
Green grow the rashes, O;
The sweetest hours that e'er I spend,
Are spent among the lasses, O.
'Green Grow the Rashes' (1787); see **Songs** 747:11

7 Auld nature swears, the lovely dears
Her noblest work she classes, O;
Her prentice han' she tried on man,
An' then she made the lasses, O.
'Green Grow the Rashes' (1787)

8 O, gie me the lass that has acres o' charms,
O, gie me the lass wi' the weel-stockit farms.
'Hey for a Lass wi' a Tocher' (1799)

9 Here, some are thinkin' on their sins,
An' some upo' their claes.
'The Holy Fair' (1786) st. 10

10 There's some are fou o' love divine;
There's some are fou o' brandy.
'The Holy Fair' (1786) st. 27

11 O L--d thou kens what zeal I bear,
When drinkers drink, and swearers swear,
And singin' there, and dancin' here,
Wi' great an' sma';
For I am keepet by thy fear,
Free frae them a'.
But yet—O L--d—confess I must—
At times I'm fash'd wi' fleshly lust . . .
O L--d—yestreen—thou kens—wi' Meg—
Thy pardon I sincerely beg!
O may 't ne'er be a living plague,
To my dishonour!
And I'll ne'er lift a lawless leg
Again upon her.
'Holy Willie's Prayer' (1785)

12 There's death in the cup—so beware!
'Inscription on a Goblet' (published 1834)

13 It was a' for our rightfu' King
We left fair Scotland's strand.
'It was a' for our Rightfu' King' (1796)

14 Corn rigs, an' barley rigs,
An' corn rigs are bonnie.
'It was upon a Lammas Night' (1796)

15 John Anderson my jo, John,
When we were first acquent,
Your locks were like the raven,
Your bonny brow was brent.
'John Anderson my Jo' (1790)

16 I once was a maid, tho' I cannot tell when,
And still my delight is in proper young men.
'The Jolly Beggars' (1799) l. 57, also known as 'Love and Liberty—A Cantata'

17 Partly wi' LOVE o'ercome sae sair,
And partly she was drunk.
'The Jolly Beggars' (1799) l. 183

18 A fig for those by law protected!
LIBERTY's a glorious feast!
Courts for cowards were erected,
Churches built to please the PRIEST.
'The Jolly Beggars' (1799) l. 254

19 Life is all a VARIORUM,
We regard not how it goes;
Let them cant about DECORUM,
Who have characters to lose.
'The Jolly Beggars' (1799) l. 270

20 Some have meat and cannot eat,
Some can not eat that want it:
But we have meat and we can eat,
Sae let the Lord be thankit.
'The Kirkudbright Grace' (1790), also known as 'The Selkirk Grace'

21 I've seen sae mony changefu' years,
On earth I am a stranger grown:
I wander in the ways of men,
Alike unknowing and unknown.
'Lament for James, Earl of Glencairn' (1793)

22 May coward shame distain his name,
The wretch that dares not die!
'McPherson's Farewell' (1788)

23   Nature's law,
That man was made to mourn!
'Man was made to Mourn' (1786) st. 4

24 Man's inhumanity to man
Makes countless thousands mourn!
'Man was made to Mourn' (1786) st. 7

25 O Death! the poor man's dearest friend,
The kindest and the best!
'Man was made to Mourn' (1786) st. 11

26 Go fetch to me a pint o' wine,
An' fill it in a silver tassie.
'My Bonnie Mary' (1790)

27 My heart's in the Highlands, my heart is not here;
My heart's in the Highlands a-chasing the deer;
Chasing the wild deer, and following the roe,
My heart's in the Highlands, wherever I go.
'My Heart's in the Highlands' (1790)

28 My love she's but a lassie yet.
title of poem, 1787

1 The minister kiss'd the fiddler's wife,
An' could na preach for thinkin' o't.
'My Love She's but a Lassie yet' (1790)

2 The wan moon sets behind the white wave,
And time is setting with me, Oh.
'Open the door to me, Oh' (1793)

3 O whistle, an' I'll come to you, my lad:
O whistle, an' I'll come to you, my lad:
Tho' father and mither should baith gae mad,
O whistle, and I'll come to you, my lad.
'O Whistle, an' I'll come to you, my Lad' (1788); see
Fletcher 327:11

4 O, my Luve's like a red, red rose
That's newly sprung in June;
O my Luve's like the melodie
That's sweetly play'd in tune.
'A Red Red Rose' (1796), derived from various folk-songs

5 Scots, wha hae wi' Wallace bled,
Scots, wham Bruce has aften led,
Welcome to your gory bed,—
Or to victorie.

Now's the day, and now's the hour;
See the front o' battle lour;
See approach proud Edward's power,
Chains and slaverie.
'Robert Bruce's March to Bannockburn' (1799), also
known as 'Scots, Wha Hae'

6 Liberty's in every blow!
Let us do—or die!!!
'Robert Bruce's March to Bannockburn' (1799)

7 Good Lord, what is man! for as simple he looks,
Do but try to develop his hooks and his crooks,
With his depths and his shallows, his good and his
evil,
All in all he's a problem must puzzle the devil.
'Sketch' inscribed to Charles James Fox (1800)

8 This day Time winds th'exhausted chain,
To run the twelvemonth's length again.
'Sketch. New Year's Day. To Mrs Dunlop' (1789)

9 His ancient, trusty, drouthy crony,
Tam lo'ed him like a vera brither;
They had been fou for weeks thegither.
'Tam o' Shanter' (1791) l. 42

10 Kings may be blest, but Tam was glorious,
O'er a' the ills o' life victorious!
'Tam o' Shanter' (1791) l. 57

11 But pleasures are like poppies spread,
You seize the flow'r, its bloom is shed;
Or like the snow falls in the river,
A moment white—then melts for ever.
'Tam o' Shanter' (1791) l. 59

12 Nae man can tether time or tide.
'Tam o' Shanter' (1791) l. 67

13 Inspiring, bold John Barleycorn,
What dangers thou canst make us scorn!
Wi' tippenny, we fear nae evil;
Wi' usquebae, we'll face the devil!
'Tam o' Shanter' (1791) l. 105

14 As Tammie glowr'd, amaz'd, and curious,
The mirth and fun grew fast and furious.
'Tam o' Shanter' (1791) l. 143

15 Tam tint his reason a' thegither,
And roars out—'Weel done, Cutty-sark!'
'Tam o' Shanter' (1791) l. 185

16 Ah Tam! ah Tam! thou'll get thy fairin'!
In hell they'll roast thee like a herrin!
'Tam o' Shanter' (1791) l. 201

17 A man may drink and no be drunk;
A man may fight and no be slain;
A man may kiss a bonnie lass,
And aye be welcome back again.
'There was a Lass' (1788)

18 Fair fa' your honest, sonsie face,
Great chieftain o' the puddin'-race!
Aboon them a' ye tak your place,
Painch, tripe, or thairm:
Weel are ye wordy o' a grace
As lang's my arm.
'To a Haggis' (1787)

19 O wad some Pow'r the giftie gie us
To see oursels as others see us!
It wad frae mony a blunder free us,
And foolish notion.
'To a Louse' (1786)

20 Wee, sleekit, cow'rin', tim'rous beastie,
O what a panic's in thy breastie!
Thou need na start awa sae hasty,
Wi' bickering brattle!
I wad be laith to rin an' chase thee,
Wi' murd'ring pattle!
'To a Mouse' (1786)

21 I'm truly sorry Man's dominion
Has broken Nature's social union,
An' justifies that ill opinion
Which makes thee startle,
At me, thy poor, earth-born companion,
An' fellow-mortal!
'To a Mouse' (1786)

22 The best laid schemes o' mice an' men
Gang aft a-gley.
'To a Mouse' (1786); see **Proverbs** 615:16

23 Come, Firm Resolve, take thou the van,
Thou stalk o' carl-hemp in man!
And let us mind, faint heart ne'er wan
A lady fair;
Wha does the utmost that he can,
Will whyles do mair.
'To Dr Blacklock' (1800)

24 Some rhyme a neebor's name to lash;
Some rhyme (vain thought!) for needfu' cash;
Some rhyme to court the countra clash,
An' raise a din;
For me, an aim I never fash;
I rhyme for fun.
'To J. S[mith]' (1786) st. 5

25 An' fareweel dear, deluding woman,
The joy of joys!
'To J. S[mith]' (1786) st. 14

1 Their sighan', cantan', grace-proud faces,
  Their three-mile prayers, and half-mile graces.
  'To the Rev. John M'Math' (1808)

2 We labour soon, we labour late,
  To feed the titled knave, man;
  And a' the comfort we're to get,
  Is that ayont the grave, man.
  'The Tree of Liberty' (1838)

3 His lockèd, lettered, braw brass collar,
  Shew'd him the gentleman and scholar.
  'The Twa Dogs' (1786) l. 13

4 An' there began a lang digression
  About the lords o' the creation.
  'The Twa Dogs' (1786) l. 45

5 Rejoiced they were na men, but dogs.
  'The Twa Dogs' (1786) l. 236

6 All in this mottie, misty clime,
  I backward mus'd on wasted time,
  How I had spent my youthfu' prime
  An' done nae-thing,
  But stringing blethers up to rhyme
  For fools to sing.
  'The Vision' (1785)

7 What can a young lassie, what shall a young
    lassie,
  What can a young lassie do wi' an auld man?
  'What can a Young Lassie do wi' an Auld Man' (1792)

8 It is the moon, I ken her horn,
  That's blinkin in the lift sae hie;
  She shines sae bright to wyle us hame,
  But by my sooth she'll wait a wee!
  'Willie Brew'd a Peck o' Maut' (1790)

9 The Poetic Genius of my country found me as the
  prophetic bard Elijah did Elisha—at the plough;
  and threw her inspiring mantle over me. She bade
  me sing the loves, the joys, the rural scenes and
  rural pleasures of my native soil, in my native
  tongue; I tuned my wild, artless notes, as she
  inspired.
  preface to *Poems* (1787 2nd ed.)

Aaron Burr 1756–1836
American politician

10 Law is whatever is boldly asserted and plausibly
   maintained.
   James Parton *The Life and Times of Aaron Burr* (1857);
   attributed

William S. Burroughs 1914–97
American novelist
see also **Last words** 473:4

11 Junk is the ideal product . . . the ultimate
   merchandise. No sales talk necessary. The client
   will crawl through a sewer and beg to buy.
   The Naked Lunch (1959) introduction

12 The face of 'evil' is always the face of total need.
   The Naked Lunch (1959) introduction

13 In homosexual sex you know exactly what the
   other person is feeling, so you are identifying with

the other person completely. In heterosexual sex
you have no idea what the other person is feeling.
Victor Bockris *With William Burroughs: A Report from the
Bunker* (1981) 'On Men'

Benjamin Hapgood Burt 1880–1950
American songwriter

14 One evening in October, when I was one-third
     sober,
   An' taking home a 'load' with manly pride;
   My poor feet began to stutter, so I lay down in the
     gutter,
   And a pig came up an' lay down by my side;
   Then we sang 'It's all fair weather when good
     fellows get together,'
   Till a lady passing by was heard to say:
   'You can tell a man who "boozes" by the
     company he chooses'
   And the pig got up and slowly walked away.
   'The Pig Got Up and Slowly Walked Away' (1933 song)

15 When you're all dressed up and no place to go.
   title of song (1913)

Nat Burton

16 There'll be bluebirds over the white cliffs of Dover,
   Tomorrow, just you wait and see.
   'The White Cliffs of Dover' (1941 song)

Richard Burton 1821–90
English explorer, anthropologist, and translator

17 Don't be frightened; I am recalled. Pay, pack, and
   follow at convenience.
   *note to his wife, 19 August 1871, on being replaced
   as British Consul to Damascus*
   Isabel Burton *Life of Captain Sir Richard F. Burton* (1893)
   vol. I, ch. 21

Robert Burton 1577–1640
English clergyman and scholar
see also **Closing lines** 228:6

18 All my joys to this are folly,
   Naught so sweet as Melancholy.
   The Anatomy of Melancholy (1621–51) 'The Author's
   Abstract of Melancholy'

19 I write of melancholy, by being busy to avoid
   melancholy.
   The Anatomy of Melancholy (1621–51) 'Democritus to the
   Reader'

20 They lard their lean books with the fat of others'
   works.
   The Anatomy of Melancholy (1621–51) 'Democritus to the
   Reader'

21 A loose, plain, rude writer . . . I call a spade a
   spade.
   The Anatomy of Melancholy (1621–51) 'Democritus to the
   Reader'

22 I had not time to lick it into form, as she [a bear]
   doth her young ones.
   The Anatomy of Melancholy (1621–51) 'Democritus to the
   Reader'

1 Like watermen, that row one way and look another.
   The Anatomy of Melancholy (1621–51) 'Democritus to the Reader'; see **Bunyan** 164:19

2 All poets are mad.
   The Anatomy of Melancholy (1621–51) 'Democritus to the Reader'; see **Wordsworth** 849:20

3 What, if a dear year come or dearth, or some loss? And were it not that they are loath to lay out money on a rope, they would be hanged forthwith, and sometimes die to save charges.
   The Anatomy of Melancholy (1621–51) pt. 1, sect. 2, member 3, subsect. 12

4 I may not here omit those two main plagues, and common dotages of human kind, wine and women, which have infatuated and besotted myriads of people. They go commonly together.
   The Anatomy of Melancholy (1621–51) pt. 1, sect. 2, member 3, subsect. 13

5 *Hinc quam sit calamus saevior ense patet.*
   From this it is clear how much the pen is worse than the sword.
   The Anatomy of Melancholy (1621–51) pt. 1, sect. 2, member 4, subsect. 4; see **Bulwer-Lytton** 164:5, **Proverbs** 629:19

6 See one promontory (said Socrates of old), one mountain, one sea, one river, and see all.
   The Anatomy of Melancholy (1621–51) pt. 1, sect. 2, member 4, subsect. 7

7 One was never married, and that's his hell: another is, and that's his plague.
   The Anatomy of Melancholy (1621–51) pt. 1, sect. 2, member 4, subsect. 7

8 The gods are well pleased when they see great men contending with adversity.
   The Anatomy of Melancholy (1621–51) pt. 2, sect. 3, member 1, subsect. 1

9 Who cannot give good counsel? 'tis cheap, it costs them nothing.
   The Anatomy of Melancholy (1621–51) pt. 2, sect. 3, member 3, subsect. 1

10 What is a ship but a prison?
   The Anatomy of Melancholy (1621–51) pt. 2, sect. 3, member 4, subsect. 1; see **Johnson** 427:23

11 All places are distant from Heaven alike.
   The Anatomy of Melancholy (1621–51) pt. 2, sect. 3, member 4, subsect. 1

12 'Let me not live,' saith Aretine's Antonia, 'if I had not rather hear thy discourse than see a play!'
   The Anatomy of Melancholy (1621–51) pt. 3, sect. 1, member 1, subsect. 1

13 To enlarge or illustrate this power and effect of love is to set a candle in the sun.
   The Anatomy of Melancholy (1621–51) pt. 3, sect. 2, member 1, subsect. 2; see **Sidney** 735:17, **Young** 857:7

14 No cord nor cable can so forcibly draw, or hold so fast, as love can do with a twined thread.
   The Anatomy of Melancholy (1621–51) pt. 3, sect. 2, member 1, subsect. 2

15 To these crocodile's tears they will add sobs, fiery sighs, and sorrowful countenance, pale colour, leanness.
   The Anatomy of Melancholy (1621–51) pt. 3, sect. 2, member 2, subsect. 4

16 Diogenes struck the father when the son swore.
   The Anatomy of Melancholy (1621–51) pt. 3, sect. 2, member 5, subsect. 5

17 One religion is as true as another.
   The Anatomy of Melancholy (1621–51) pt. 3, sect. 4, member 2, subsect. 1

Wilhelm Busch 1832–1908
German satirical poet and illustrator

18 *Ach, das war ein schlimmes Ding,*
   Wie es Max und Moritz ging!
   Drum ist hier, was sie getrieben,
   Abgemalt und aufgeschrieben.

   Oh, that was a bad business,
   What happened to Max and Moritz!
   Which is why their doings are here
   Pictured and written down.
   Max und Moritz (1865)

19 *Vater werden ist nicht schwer*
   Vater sein dagegen sehr.

   Becoming a father isn't difficult,
   But it's very difficult to be a father.
   Julchen (1877)

Hermann Busenbaum 1600–68
German theologian

20 *Cum finis est licitus, etiam media sunt licita.*
   The end justifies the means.
   Medulla Theologiae Moralis (1650); literally 'When the end is allowed, the means also are allowed'; see **Proverbs** 618:41

Barbara Bush 1925–
*American wife of George **Bush**; First Lady, 1989–93*

21 Somewhere out in this audience may even be someone who will one day follow in my footsteps, and preside over the White House as the President's spouse. I wish him well!
   remarks at Wellesley College Commencement, 1 June 1990

George Bush 1924–
*American Republican statesman; 41st President of the US, 1989–93; father of George W. **Bush***

22 Oh, the vision thing.
   responding to the suggestion that he turn his attention from short-term campaign objectives and look to the longer term.
   in *Time* 26 January 1987

23 Read my lips: no new taxes.
   campaign pledge on taxation
   in *New York Times* 19 August 1988

24 I'm President of the United States, and I'm not going to eat any more broccoli!
   in *New York Times* 23 March 1990

1 And now, we can see a new world coming into view. A world in which there is the very real prospect of a new world order.
  speech, in *New York Times* 7 March 1991

2 [It is] time to turn our attention to pressing challenges like ... how to make American families more like the Waltons and a little bit less like the Simpsons.
  speech, Neenah, Wisconsin, 27 July 1992

George W. Bush 1946-
*American Republican statesman; 43rd President of the US from 2001; son of George **Bush***
see also **Page** 581:13

3 We will make no distinction between terrorists who committed these acts and those who harbour them.
  after the terrorist attacks of 11 September
  televised address, 12 September 2001

4 Today we feel what Franklin Roosevelt called the warm courage of national unity. This unity against terror is now extending across the world.
  address in Washington National Cathedral, 14 September 2001, at the day of mourning for those killed in the terrorist attacks of 11 September
  in *Times* 15 September 2001; see **Roosevelt** 653:14

5 This crusade, this war on terrorism is going to take a while.
  the President later retracted his use of the word 'crusade'
  at a White House press conference, 16 September 2001

6 States like these ... constitute an axis of evil, arming to threaten the peace of this world.
  of Iraq, Iran, and North Korea
  State of the Union address, in *Newsweek* 11 February 2002

Comte de Bussy-Rabutin 1618-93
French soldier and poet

7 *L'amour vient de l'aveuglement,*
  L'amitié de la connaissance.
  Love comes from blindness,
  Friendship from knowledge.
  Histoire Amoureuse des Gaules: Maximes d'Amour (1665) pt. 1; see **Proverbs** 625:43

8 *L'absence est à l'amour ce qu'est au feu le vent;*
  Il éteint le petit, il allume le grand.
  Absence is to love what wind is to fire;
  It extinguishes the small, it kindles the great.
  Histoire Amoureuse des Gaules: Maximes d'Amour (1665) pt. 2; see **Francis** 332:7, **La Rochefoucauld** 469:18

9 As you know, God is usually on the side of the big squadrons against the small.
  letter to the Comte de Limoges, 18 October 1677, in *Lettres de ... Comte de Bussy* (1697) vol. 4; see **Anouilh** 22:15, **Proverbs** 629:45, **Tacitus** 770:13, **Voltaire** 816:10

Joseph Butler 1692-1752
English bishop and theologian

10 It has come, I know not how, to be taken for granted, by many persons, that Christianity is not so much as a subject of inquiry; but that it is, now at length, discovered to be fictitious.
  The Analogy of Religion (1736) 'Advertisement'

11 But to us, probability is the very guide of life.
  The Analogy of Religion (1736) 'Introduction'

12 Everything is what it is, and not another thing.
  preface to *Fifteen Sermons preached at the Rolls Chapel* (ed. 2, 1729)

13 Things and actions are what they are, and the consequences of them will be what they will be: why then should we desire to be deceived?
  Fifteen Sermons preached at the Rolls Chapel (1726) no. 7

14 Sir, the pretending to extraordinary revelations and gifts of the Holy Ghost is a horrid thing—a very horrid thing.
  to John **Wesley**, 16 August 1739; John Wesley *Journal* (ed. N. Curnock) note

Nicholas Murray Butler 1862-1947
American President of Columbia University, 1901-45

15 An expert is one who knows more and more about less and less.
  Commencement address at Columbia University (attributed)

R. A. ('Rab') Butler 1902-82
British Conservative politician

16 REPORTER: Mr Butler, would you say that this [Anthony Eden] is the best Prime Minister we have?
  R. A. BUTLER: Yes.
  interview at London Airport, 8 January 1956; R. A. Butler *The Art of the Possible*

17 I think a Prime Minister has to be a butcher and know the joints. That is perhaps where I have not been quite competent, in knowing all the ways that you can cut up a carcass.
  in *Listener* 28 June 1966

18 Politics is the Art of the Possible. That is what these pages show I have tried to achieve—not more—and that is what I have called my book.
  The Art of the Possible (1971); see **Bismarck** 117:14

19 In politics you must always keep running with the pack. The moment that you falter and they sense that you are injured, the rest will turn on you like wolves.
  Dennis Walters *Not Always with the Pack* (1989)

Samuel Butler 1612-80
English poet

20 He'd run in debt by disputation,
  And pay with ratiocination.
  Hudibras pt. 1 (1663), canto 1, l. 77

21 For rhetoric he could not ope
  His mouth, but out there flew a trope.
  Hudibras pt. 1 (1663), canto 1, l. 81

22 A Babylonish dialect
  Which learned pedants much affect.
  Hudibras pt. 1 (1663), canto 1, l. 93

1 What ever sceptic could inquire for;
For every why he had a wherefore.
Hudibras pt. 1 (1663), canto 1, l. 131

2 He knew what's what, and that's as high
As metaphysic wit can fly.
Hudibras pt. 1 (1663), canto 1, l. 149

3 Such as take lodgings in a head
That's to be let unfurnished.
Hudibras pt. 1 (1663), canto 1, l. 159

4 And still be doing, never done:
As if Religion were intended
For nothing else but to be mended.
Hudibras pt. 1 (1663), canto 1, l. 202

5 Compound for sins, they are inclined to,
By damning those they have no mind to.
Hudibras pt. 1 (1663), canto 1, l. 213

6 The trenchant blade, Toledo trusty,
For want of fighting was grown rusty,
And eat into it self, for lack
Of some body to hew and hack.
Hudibras pt. 1 (1663), canto 1, l. 357

7 For rhyme the rudder is of verses,
With which like ships they steer their courses.
Hudibras pt. 1 (1663), canto 1, l. 457

8 Great actions are not always true sons
Of great and mighty resolutions.
Hudibras pt. 1 (1663), canto 1, l. 877

9 Cleric before, and Lay behind;
A lawless linsy-woolsy brother,
Half of one order, half another.
Hudibras pt. 1 (1663), canto 3, l. 1226

10 Learning, that cobweb of the brain,
Profane, erroneous, and vain.
Hudibras pt. 1 (1663), canto 3, l. 1339

11 She that with poetry is won,
Is but a desk to write upon.
Hudibras pt. 2 (1664), canto 1, l. 591

12 Love is a boy, by poets styled,
Then spare the rod, and spoil the child.
Hudibras pt. 2 (1664), canto 1, l. 843; see **Proverbs** 631:12

13 Oaths are but words, and words but wind.
Hudibras pt. 2 (1664), canto 2, l. 107

14 For truth is precious and divine
Too rich a pearl for carnal swine.
Hudibras pt. 2 (1664) canto 2, l. 263

15 Doubtless the pleasure is as great
Of being cheated, as to cheat.
As lookers-on feel most delight,
That least perceive a juggler's sleight;
And still the less they understand,
The more th' admire his sleight of hand.
Hudibras pt. 2 (1664), canto 3, l. 1

16 What makes all doctrines plain and clear?
About two hundred pounds a year.
And that which was proved true before,
Prove false again? Two hundred more.
Hudibras pt. 3 (1680), canto 1, l. 1277

17 He that complies against his will,
Is of his own opinion still.
Hudibras pt. 3 (1680), canto 3, l. 547; see **Proverbs** 621:45

18 For Justice, though she's painted blind,
Is to the weaker side inclined.
Hudibras pt. 3 (1680), canto 3, l. 709

19 For money has a power above
The stars and fate, to manage love.
Hudibras pt. 3 (1680) 'The Lady's Answer to the Knight'
l. 131

20 All love at first, like generous wine,
Ferments and frets, until 'tis fine;
But when 'tis settled on the lee,
And from th' impurer matter free,
Becomes the richer still, the older,
And proves the pleasanter, the colder.
Genuine Remains (1759) 'Miscellaneous Thoughts'

21 The law can take a purse in open court,
Whilst it condemns a less delinquent for't.
Genuine Remains (1759) 'Miscellaneous Thoughts'

Samuel Butler 1835–1902

English novelist

22 It has been said that though God cannot alter the
past, historians can; it is perhaps because they can
be useful to Him in this respect that He tolerates
their existence.
Erewhon Revisited (1901) ch. 14; see **Agathon** 6:24

23 All animals, except man, know that the principal
business of life is to enjoy it.
The Way of All Flesh (1903) ch. 19

24 The advantage of doing one's praising for oneself
is that one can lay it on so thick and exactly in the
right places.
The Way of All Flesh (1903) ch. 34

25 Young as he was, his instinct told him that the
best liar is he who makes the smallest amount of
lying go the longest way.
The Way of All Flesh (1903) ch. 39

26 'Tis better to have loved and lost than never to
have lost at all.
The Way of All Flesh (1903) ch. 67; see **Tennyson** 779:1

27 It was very good of God to let Carlyle and Mrs
Carlyle marry one another and so make only two
people miserable instead of four.
*Letters between Samuel Butler and Miss E. M. A. Savage
1871–1885* (1935) 21 November 1884

28 All progress is based upon a universal innate
desire on the part of every organism to live beyond
its income.
Notebooks (1912) ch. 1

29 The history of art is the history of revivals.
Notebooks (1912) ch. 8

30 An apology for the Devil: It must be remembered
that we have only heard one side of the case. God
has written all the books.
Notebooks (1912) ch. 14

31 A definition is the enclosing a wilderness of idea
within a wall of words.
Notebooks (1912) ch. 14

1 To live is like to love — all reason is against it, and all healthy instinct for it.
   Notebooks (1912) ch. 14

2 The public buys its opinions as it buys its meat, or takes in its milk, on the principle that it is cheaper to do this than to keep a cow. So it is, but the milk is more likely to be watered.
   Notebooks (1912) ch. 17

3 You can do very little with faith, but you can do nothing without it.
   Notebooks (1912) ch. 20

4 The three most important things a man has are, briefly, his private parts, his money, and his religious opinions.
   Further Extracts from Notebooks (1934)

5 Jesus! with all thy faults I love thee still.
   Further Extracts from Notebooks (1934)

6 Conscience is thoroughly well-bred and soon leaves off talking to those who do not wish to hear it.
   Further Extracts from Notebooks (1934)

7 Yet meet we shall, and part, and meet again
   Where dead men meet, on lips of living men.
   'Not on sad Stygian shore' (1904)

8 Dusty, cobweb-covered, maimed, and set at naught,
   Beauty crieth in an attic, and no man regardeth.
   O God! O Montreal!
   'Psalm of Montreal', in *Spectator* 18 May 1878

William Butler 1535–1618
English physician

9 Doubtless God could have made a better berry, but doubtless God never did.
   of the strawberry
   Izaak Walton *The Compleat Angler* (3rd ed., 1661) pt. 1, ch. 5

A. S. Byatt 1936–
English novelist

10 Didactic rushes of information were a great shortcoming in returning travellers.
   Angels and Insects (1992) 'Morpho Eugenia'

11 That is the main thing, to be alive. As long as you are alive, everything is surprising, rightly seen.
   Angels and Insects (1992) 'Morpho Eugenia'

12 What literature can and should do is change the people who teach the people who don't read the books.
   interview in *Newsweek* 5 June 1995

13 They are inhabitants of urban jungles, not of the real wild. They don't have the skills to tell ersatz magic from the real thing.
   of adult readers of J. K. Rowling's Harry Potter
   in *New York Times* 7 July 2003

14 Ms. Rowling's magic world has no place for the numinous.
   in *New York Times* 7 July 2003

William Byrd 1543–1623
English composer

15 The exercise of singing is delightful to Nature, and good to preserve the health of man. It doth strengthen all parts of the breast, and doth open the pipes.
   Psalms, Sonnets and Songs (1588)

John Byrom 1692–1763
English poet

16 I am content, I do not care,
   Wag as it will the world for me.
   'Careless Content' (1773)

17 Christians, awake! Salute the happy morn,
   Whereon the Saviour of the world was born.
   Hymn (*c.*1750)

18 Some say, that Signor Bononcini,
   Compared to Handel's a mere ninny;
   Others aver, that to him Handel
   Is scarcely fit to hold a candle.
   Strange! that such high dispute should be
   'Twixt Tweedledum and Tweedledee.
   'On the Feuds between Handel and Bononcini' (1727)

19 God bless the King, I mean the Faith's Defender;
   God bless—no harm in blessing—the Pretender;
   But who Pretender is, or who is King,
   God bless us all—that's quite another thing.
   'To an Officer in the Army, Extempore, Intended to allay the Violence of Party-Spirit' (1773)

Lord Byron 1788–1824
English poet
on Byron: see **Arnold** 28:21, **Lamb** 464:9; see also **Campbell** 187:22

20 Proud Wellington, with eagle beak so curled,
   That nose, the hook where he suspends the world!
   'The Age of Bronze' (1823) st. 13

21 For what were all these country patriots born?
   To hunt, and vote, and raise the price of corn?
   'The Age of Bronze' (1823) st. 14

22 Year after year they voted cent per cent
   Blood, sweat, and tear-wrung millions—why? for rent!
   'The Age of Bronze' (1823) st. 14; see **Churchill** 221:5

23 Did'st ever see a gondola? . . .
   It glides along the water looking blackly,
   Just like a coffin clapt in a canoe.
   Beppo (1818) st. 19

24 In short, he was a perfect cavaliero,
   And to his very valet seemed a hero.
   Beppo (1818) st. 33; see **Cornuel** 243:15

25 His heart was one of those which most enamour us,
   Wax to receive, and marble to retain.
   Beppo (1818) st. 34

26 Our cloudy climate, and our chilly women.
   Beppo (1818) st. 49

1 A pretty woman as was ever seen,
Fresh as the Angel o'er a new inn door.
Beppo (1818) st. 57

2 Where the virgins are soft as the roses they twine,
And all, save the spirit of man, is divine.
The Bride of Abydos (1813) canto 1, st. 1

3 Such was Zuleika, such around her shone
The nameless charms unmarked by her alone—
The light of love, the purity of grace,
The mind, the Music breathing from her face,
The heart whose softness harmonized the whole,
And oh! that eye was in itself a Soul!
The Bride of Abydos (1813) canto 1, st. 6

4   I have looked out
In the vast desolate night in search of him;
And when I saw gigantic shadows in
The umbrage of the walls of Eden, chequered
By the far-flashing of the cherubs' swords,
I watched for what I thought his coming: for
With fear rose longing in my heart to know
What 'twas which shook us all—but nothing
    came.
Cain (1821) act 1, sc. 1, l. 266

5 Adieu, adieu! my native shore
Fades o'er the waters blue.
Childe Harold's Pilgrimage (1812–18) canto 1, st. 13

6 Lo! where the Giant on the mountain stands,
His blood-red tresses deep'ning in the sun,
With death-shot glowing in his fiery hands,
And eye that scorcheth all it glares upon.
Childe Harold's Pilgrimage (1812–18) canto 1, st. 39

7 Here all were noble, save Nobility.
Childe Harold's Pilgrimage (1812–18) canto 1, st. 85

8 Cold is the heart, fair Greece! that looks on thee,
Nor feels as lovers o'er the dust they loved;
Dull is the eye that will not weep to see
Thy walls defaced, thy mouldering shrines
    removed
By British hands.
Childe Harold's Pilgrimage (1812–18) canto 2, st. 15

9 None are so desolate but something dear,
Dearer than self, possesses or possessed
A thought, and claims the homage of a tear.
Childe Harold's Pilgrimage (1812–18) canto 2, st. 24

10 Dark Sappho! could not verse immortal save
That breast imbued with such immortal fire?
Could she not live who life eternal gave?
Childe Harold's Pilgrimage (1812–18) canto 2, st. 39

11 Fair Greece! sad relic of departed worth!
Immortal, though no more! though fallen, great!
Childe Harold's Pilgrimage (1812–18) canto 2, st. 73

12 Hereditary bondsmen! know ye not
Who would be free themselves must strike the
    blow?
Childe Harold's Pilgrimage (1812–18) canto 2, st. 76

13 What is the worst of woes that wait on age?
What stamps the wrinkle deeper on the brow?
To view each loved one blotted from life's page,
And be alone on earth, as I am now.
Childe Harold's Pilgrimage (1812–18) canto 2, st. 98

14 Once more upon the waters! yet once more!
And the waves bound beneath me as a steed
That knows his rider.
Childe Harold's Pilgrimage (1812–18) canto 3, st. 2

15 The wandering outlaw of his own dark mind.
Childe Harold's Pilgrimage (1812–18) canto 3, st. 3

16   Years steal
Fire from the mind as vigour from the limb;
And life's enchanted cup but sparkles near the
    brim.
Childe Harold's Pilgrimage (1812–18) canto 3, st. 8

17 Where rose the mountains, there to him were
    friends;
Where rolled the ocean, thereon was his home;
Where a blue sky, and glowing clime, extends,
He had the passion and the power to roam.
Childe Harold's Pilgrimage (1812–18) canto 3, st. 13

18 The very knowledge that he lived in vain,
That all was over on this side the tomb,
Had made Despair a smilingness assume.
Childe Harold's Pilgrimage (1812–18) canto 3, st. 16

19 There was a sound of revelry by night,
And Belgium's capital had gathered then
Her beauty and her chivalry, and bright
The lamps that shone o'er fair women and brave
    men;
A thousand hearts beat happily; and when
Music arose with its voluptuous swell,
Soft eyes looked love to eyes which spake again,
And all went merry as a marriage bell;

But hush! hark! a deep sound strikes like a rising
    knell!
Childe Harold's Pilgrimage (1812–18) canto 3, st. 21

20 On with the dance! let joy be unconfined;
No sleep till morn, when Youth and Pleasure meet
To chase the glowing Hours with flying feet.
Childe Harold's Pilgrimage (1812–18) canto 3, st. 22

21 He rushed into the field, and, foremost fighting,
    fell.
Childe Harold's Pilgrimage (1812–18) canto 3, st. 23

22   But life will suit
Itself to Sorrow's most detested fruit,
Like to the apples on the Dead Sea's shore,
All ashes to the taste.
Childe Harold's Pilgrimage (1812–18) canto 3, st. 34

23 Quiet to quick bosoms is a hell.
Childe Harold's Pilgrimage (1812–18) canto 3, st. 42

24 To fly from, need not be to hate, mankind.
Childe Harold's Pilgrimage (1812–18) canto 3, st. 69

25 I live not in myself, but I become
Portion of that around me; and to me,
High mountains are a feeling, but the hum
Of human cities torture.
Childe Harold's Pilgrimage (1812–18) canto 3, st. 72

26 His love was passion's essence:—as a tree
On fire by lightning, with ethereal flame
Kindled he was, and blasted.
Childe Harold's Pilgrimage (1812–18) canto 3, st. 78

1 Sapping a solemn creed with solemn sneer.
of Edward **Gibbon**
  Childe Harold's Pilgrimage (1812–18) canto 3, st. 107

2 I have not loved the world, nor the world me;
I have not flattered its rank breath, nor bowed
To its idolatries a patient knee.
  Childe Harold's Pilgrimage (1812–18) canto 3, st. 113

3 I stood in Venice, on the Bridge of Sighs:
A palace and a prison on each hand.
  Childe Harold's Pilgrimage (1812–18) canto 4, st. 1

4   I stood
Among them, but not of them; in a shroud
Of thoughts which were not their thoughts.
  Childe Harold's Pilgrimage (1812–18) canto 3, st. 113

5 The moon is up, and yet it is not night;
Sunset divides the sky with her—a sea
Of glory streams along the Alpine height
Of blue Friuli's mountains; Heaven is free
From clouds, but of all colours seems to be
Melted to one vast Iris of the West,
Where the day joins the past eternity.
  Childe Harold's Pilgrimage (1812–18) canto 4, st. 27

6 Italia! oh Italia! thou who hast
The fatal gift of beauty.
  Childe Harold's Pilgrimage (1812–18) canto 4, st. 42

7 Oh Rome! my country! city of the soul!
  Childe Harold's Pilgrimage (1812–18) canto 4, st. 78

8 Alas! our young affections run to waste,
Or water but the desert.
  Childe Harold's Pilgrimage (1812–18) canto 4, st. 120

9 Of its own beauty is the mind diseased.
  Childe Harold's Pilgrimage (1812–18) canto 4, st. 122

10 Time, the avenger! unto thee I lift
My hands, and eyes, and heart, and crave of thee
  a gift.
  Childe Harold's Pilgrimage (1812–18) canto 4, st. 130

11 But I have lived, and have not lived in vain:
My mind may lose its force, my blood its fire,
And my frame perish even in conquering pain;
But there is that within me which shall tire
Torture and Time, and breathe when I expire.
  Childe Harold's Pilgrimage (1812–18) canto 4, st. 137

12 *There* were his young barbarians all at play,
There was their Dacian mother— he, their sire,
Butchered to make a Roman holiday.
  Childe Harold's Pilgrimage (1812–18) canto 4, st. 141

13 A ruin—yet what ruin! from its mass
Walls, palaces, half-cities, have been reared.
  Childe Harold's Pilgrimage (1812–18) canto 4, st. 143

14 While stands the Coliseum, Rome shall stand;
When falls the Coliseum, Rome shall fall;
And when Rome falls—the World.
  Childe Harold's Pilgrimage (1812–18) canto 4, st. 145

15   The Lord of the unerring bow,
The God of life, and poesy, and light.
  Childe Harold's Pilgrimage (1812–18) canto 4, st. 161

16 Oh! that the desert were my dwelling-place,
With one fair spirit for my minister,

17 There is a pleasure in the pathless woods,
There is a rapture on the lonely shore,
There is society, where none intrudes,
By the deep sea, and music in its roar:
I love not man the less, but nature more.
  Childe Harold's Pilgrimage (1812–18) canto 4, st. 178

18 Roll on, thou deep and dark blue Ocean—roll!
Ten thousand fleets sweep over thee in vain;
Man marks the earth with ruin—his control
Stops with the shore.
  Childe Harold's Pilgrimage (1812–18) canto 4, st. 179

19 Without a grave, unknelled, uncoffined, and
  unknown.
  Childe Harold's Pilgrimage (1812–18) canto 4, st. 179

20 Dark-heaving;—boundless, endless, and
  sublime—
The image of eternity.
of the sea
  Childe Harold's Pilgrimage (1812–18) canto 4, st. 183

21 The glory and the nothing of a name.
  'Churchill's Grave' (1816)

22 Such hath it been—shall be—beneath the sun
The many still must labour for the one.
  The Corsair (1814) canto 1, st. 8

23 There was a laughing devil in his sneer,
That raised emotions both of rage and fear;
And where his frown of hatred darkly fell,
Hope withering fled, and Mercy sighed farewell!
  The Corsair (1814) canto 1, st. 9

24 Deep in my soul that tender secret dwells,
Lonely and lost to light for evermore,
Save when to thine my heart responsive swells,
Then trembles into silence as before.
  The Corsair (1814) canto 1, st. 14 'Medora's Song'

25   The spirit burning but unbent,
May writhe, rebel—the weak alone repent!
  The Corsair (1814) canto 2, st. 10

26 Oh! too convincing—dangerously dear—
In woman's eye the unanswerable tear!
  The Corsair (1814) canto 2, st. 15

27   And she for him had given
Her all on earth, and more than all in heaven!
  The Corsair (1814) canto 3, st. 17

28 He left a Corsair's name to other times,
Linked with one virtue, and a thousand crimes.
  The Corsair (1814) canto 3, st. 24

29 Slow sinks, more lovely ere his race be run,
Along Morea's hills the setting sun;
Not, as in northern climes, obscurely bright,
But one unclouded blaze of living light.
  'The Curse of Minerva' (1812) l. 1 and *The Corsair* (1814)
  canto 3, st. 1

30 A land of meanness, sophistry, and mist.
of Scotland
  'The Curse of Minerva' (1812) l. 138

31 Each breeze from foggy mount and marshy plain
Dilutes with drivel every drizzly brain,

Till, burst at length, each wat'ry head o'erflows,
Foul as their soil, and frigid as their snows.
of Scotland
'The Curse of Minerva' (1812) l. 139

1 The Assyrian came down like the wolf on the fold,
And his cohorts were gleaming in purple and
   gold;
And the sheen of their spears was like stars on the
   sea,
When the blue wave rolls nightly on deep Galilee.
'The Destruction of Sennacherib' (1815) st. 1

2 For the Angel of Death spread his wings on the
   blast,
And breathed in the face of the foe as he passed.
'The Destruction of Sennacherib' (1815) st. 3

3 And Coleridge, too, has lately taken wing,
But, like a hawk encumbered with his hood,
Explaining metaphysics to the nation—
I wish he would explain his explanation.
Don Juan (1819–24) canto 1, dedication st. 2

4 The intellectual eunuch Castlereagh.
Don Juan (1819–24) canto 1, dedication st. 11

5 My way is to begin with the beginning.
Don Juan (1819–24) canto 1, st. 7

6 But—Oh! ye lords of ladies intellectual,
Inform us truly, have they not hen-pecked you
   all?
Don Juan (1819–24) canto 1, st. 22

7 Married, charming, chaste, and twenty-three.
Don Juan (1819–24) canto 1, st. 59

8 What men call gallantry, and gods adultery,
Is much more common where the climate's sultry.
Don Juan (1819–24) canto 1, st. 63

9 Christians have burnt each other, quite persuaded
That all the Apostles would have done as they did.
Don Juan (1819–24) canto 1, st. 83

10 He thought about himself, and the whole earth,
Of man the wonderful, and of the stars,
And how the deuce they ever could have birth;
And then he thought of earthquakes, and of wars,
How many miles the moon might have in girth,
Of air-balloons, and of the many bars
To perfect knowledge of the boundless skies;
And then he thought of Donna Julia's eyes.
Don Juan (1819–24) canto 1, st. 92

11 A little still she strove, and much repented,
And whispering 'I will ne'er consent'—consented.
Don Juan (1819–24) canto 1, st. 117

12 'Twas strange that one so young should thus
   concern
His brain about the action of the sky;
If *you* think 'twas philosophy that this did,
I can't help thinking puberty assisted.
Don Juan (1819–24) canto 1, st. 93

13 Sweet is revenge—especially to women.
Don Juan (1819–24) canto 1, st. 124

14 Pleasure's a sin, and sometimes sin's a pleasure.
Don Juan (1819–24) canto 1, st. 133

15 Man's love is of man's life a thing apart,
'Tis woman's whole existence.
Don Juan (1819–24) canto 1, st. 194; see **Amis** 13:12

16 A panoramic view of hell's in training,
After the style of Virgil and of Homer,
So that my name of Epic's no misnomer.
Don Juan (1819–24) canto 1, st. 200

17 Prose poets like blank-verse, I'm fond of rhyme,
Good workmen never quarrel with their tools.
Don Juan (1819–24) canto 1, st. 201

18 So for a good old-gentlemanly vice,
I think I must take up with avarice.
Don Juan (1819–24) canto 1, st. 216

19 There's nought, no doubt, so much the spirit
   calms
As rum and true religion.
Don Juan (1819–24) canto 2, st. 34

20 A solitary shriek, the bubbling cry
Of some strong swimmer in his agony.
Don Juan (1819–24) canto 2, st. 53

21 Let us have wine and women, mirth and laughter,
Sermons and soda-water the day after.
Don Juan (1819–24) canto 2, st. 178

22 Man, being reasonable, must get drunk;
The best of life is but intoxication.
Don Juan (1819–24) canto 2, st. 179

23 They looked up to the sky, whose floating glow
Spread like a rosy ocean, vast and bright;
They gazed upon the glittering sea below,
Whence the broad moon rose circling into sight;
They heard the wave's splash, and the wind so
   low,
And saw each other's dark eyes darting light
Into each other—and, beholding this,
Their lips drew near, and clung into a kiss.
Don Juan (1819–24) canto 2, st. 185

24 And thus they form a group that's quite antique,
Half naked, loving, natural, and Greek.
Don Juan (1819–24) canto 2, st. 194

25 Alas! the love of women! it is known
To be a lovely and a fearful thing!
Don Juan (1819–24) canto 2, st. 199

26 In her first passion woman loves her lover,
In all the others all she loves is love.
Don Juan (1819–24) canto 3, st. 3

27 Love and marriage rarely can
combine,
Although they both are born in the same clime;
Marriage from love, like vinegar from wine—
A sad, sour, sober beverage—by time
Is sharpened from its high celestial flavour,
Down to a very homely household savour.
Don Juan (1819–24) canto 3, st. 5

28 Think you, if Laura had been Petrarch's wife,
He would have written sonnets all his life?
Don Juan (1819–24) canto 3, st. 8

29 All tragedies are finished by a death,
All comedies are ended by a marriage;
The future states of both are left to faith.
Don Juan (1819–24) canto 3, st. 9

1 Dreading that climax of all human ills,
The inflammation of his weekly bills.
Don Juan (1819–24) canto 3, st. 35

2 ... He was the mildest mannered man
That ever scuttled ship or cut a throat.
Don Juan (1819–24) canto 3, st. 41

3 But Shakespeare also says, 'tis very silly
'To gild refinèd gold, or paint the lily.'
Don Juan (1819–24) canto 3, st. 76; see **Shakespeare** 699:10

4 The isles of Greece, the isles of Greece!
Where burning Sappho loved and sung,
Where grew the arts of war and peace,
Where Delos rose, and Phoebus sprung!
Eternal summer gilds them yet,
But all, except their sun, is set!
Don Juan (1819–24) canto 3, st. 86 (1)

5 The mountains look on Marathon—
And Marathon looks on the sea;
And musing there an hour alone,
I dreamed that Greece might still be free.
Don Juan (1819–24) canto 3, st. 86 (3)

6 For what is left the poet here?
For Greeks a blush—for Greece a tear.
Don Juan (1819–24) canto 3, st. 86 (6)

7 Earth! render back from out thy breast
a remnant of our Spartan dead!
Of the three hundred grant but three,
To make a new Thermopylae!
Don Juan (1819–24) canto 3, st. 86 (7)

8 Milton's the prince of poets—so we say;
A little heavy, but no less divine.
Don Juan (1819–24) canto 3, st. 91

9 A drowsy frowzy poem, called the 'Excursion',
Writ in a manner which is my aversion.
Don Juan (1819–24) canto 3, st. 94

10 We learn from Horace, Homer sometimes sleeps;
We feel without him: Wordsworth sometimes
wakes.
Don Juan (1819–24) canto 3, st. 98; see **Horace** 398:15

11 Ave Maria! 'tis the hour of prayer!
Ave Maria! 'tis the hour of love!
Don Juan (1819–24) canto 3, st. 103; see **Prayers** 611:1

12 Now my sere fancy 'falls into the yellow
Leaf,' and imagination droops her pinion,
And the sad truth which hovers o'er my desk
Turns what was once romantic to burlesque.
Don Juan (1819–24) canto 4, st. 3; see **Byron** 183:1,
Shakespeare 707:8

13 And if I laugh at any mortal thing,
'Tis that I may not weep.
Don Juan (1819–24) canto 4, st. 4

14 'Whom the gods love die young' was said of yore.
And many deaths do they escape by this.
Don Juan (1819–24) canto 4, st. 12; see **Menander** 521:13

15 I've stood upon Achilles' tomb,
And heard Troy doubted; time will doubt of Rome.
Don Juan (1819–24) canto 4, st. 101

16 When amatory poets sing their loves
In liquid lines mellifluously bland,

And pair their rhymes as Venus yokes her doves.
They little think what mischief is in hand.
Don Juan (1819–24) canto 5, st. 1

17 And is this blood, then, formed but to be shed?
Can every element our elements mar?
And air—earth—water—fire live—and we dead?
We, whose minds comprehend all things?
Don Juan (1819–24) canto 5, st. 39

18 ... That all-softening, overpowering knell,
The tocsin of the soul—the dinner bell.
Don Juan (1819–24) canto 5, st. 49

19 Why don't they knead two virtuous souls for life
Into that moral centaur, man and wife?
Don Juan (1819–24) canto 5, st. 158

20 There is a tide in the affairs of women,
Which, taken at the flood, leads—God knows
where.
Don Juan (1819–24) canto 6, st. 2; see **Shakespeare** 698:21

21 A lady of a 'certain age', which means
Certainly aged.
Don Juan (1819–24) canto 6, st. 69

22 'Let there be light!' said God, and there was light!'
'Let there be blood!' says man, and there's a sea!
Don Juan (1819–24) canto 7, st. 41; see **Bible** 75:4

23 Read your own hearts and Ireland's present story,
Then feed her famine fat with Wellesley's glory.
Don Juan (1819–24) canto 8, st. 125

24 That water-land of Dutchmen and of ditches.
Don Juan (1819–24) canto 10, st. 63

25 When Bishop Berkeley said 'there was no matter',
And proved it—'twas no matter what he said.
Don Juan (1819–24) canto 11, st. 1

26 And, after all, what is a lie? 'Tis but
The truth in masquerade.
Don Juan (1819–24) canto 11, st. 37

27 'Tis strange the mind, that very fiery particle,
Should let itself be snuffed out by an article.
on **Keats** '*who was killed off by one critique*'
Don Juan (1819–24) canto 11, st. 60

28 For talk six times with the same single lady,
And you may get the wedding dresses ready.
Don Juan (1819–24) canto 12, st. 59

29 Merely innocent flirtation,
Not quite adultery, but adulteration.
Don Juan (1819–24) canto 12, st. 63

30 Now hatred is by far the longest pleasure;
Men love in haste, but they detest at leisure.
Don Juan (1819–24) canto 13, st. 4; see **Proverbs** 626:17

31 Cervantes smiled Spain's chivalry away.
Don Juan (1819–24) canto 13, st. 11

32 The English winter—ending in July,
To recommence in August.
Don Juan (1819–24) canto 13, st. 42

33 Society is now one polished horde,
Formed of two mighty tribes, the *Bores* and *Bored*.
Don Juan (1819–24) canto 13, st. 95

34 Of all the horrid, hideous notes of woe,
Sadder than owl-songs or the midnight blast,

Is that portentous phrase, 'I told you so.'
Don Juan (1819–24) canto 14, st. 50

1 'Tis strange—but true; for truth is always strange;
Stranger than fiction.
Don Juan (1819–24) canto 14, st. 101; see **Proverbs**
633:20

2 All present life is but an Interjection,
An 'Oh!' or 'Ah!' of joy or misery,
Or a 'Ha! ha!' or 'Bah!'—a yawn, or 'Pooh!'
Of which perhaps the latter is most true.
Don Juan (1819–24) canto 15, st. 1

3 A lovely being, scarcely formed or moulded,
A rose with all its sweetest leaves yet folded.
Don Juan (1819–24) canto 15, st. 43

4 'Tis wonderful what fable will not do!
'Tis said it makes reality more bearable:
But what's reality? Who has its clue?
Philosophy? No; she too much rejects.
Religion? Yes; but which of all her sects?
Don Juan (1819–24) canto 15, st. 89

5 How little do we know that which we are!
How less what we may be!
Don Juan (1819–24) canto 15, st. 99

6 The worlds beyond this world's perplexing waste
Had more of her existence for in her
There was a depth of feeling to embrace
Thoughts, boundless, deep, but silent too as space.
Don Juan (1819–24) canto 16, st. 48

7 The mind can make
Substance, and people planets of its own
With beings brighter than have been, and give
A breath to forms which can outlive all flesh.
'The Dream' (1816) st. 1

8 I'll publish, right or wrong:
Fools are my theme, let satire be my song.
English Bards and Scotch Reviewers (1809) l. 5

9 A man must serve his time to every trade
Save censure—critics all are ready made.
Take hackneyed jokes from Miller, got by rote,
With just enough of learning to misquote.
English Bards and Scotch Reviewers (1809) l. 63

10 Each country Book-club bows the knee to Baal,
And, hurling lawful Genius from the throne,
Erects a shrine and idol of its own.
English Bards and Scotch Reviewers (1809) l. 138

11 Who, both by precept and example, shows
That prose is verse, and verse is merely prose,
Convincing all by demonstration plain,
Poetic souls delight in prose insane;
And Christmas stories tortured into rhyme,
Contain the essence of the true sublime.
of **Wordsworth**
English Bards and Scotch Reviewers (1809) l. 241

12 Be warm, but pure; be amorous, but be chaste.
English Bards and Scotch Reviewers (1809) l. 306

13 The petrifactions of a plodding brain.
English Bards and Scotch Reviewers (1809) l. 416

14 Then let Ausonia, skilled in every art
To soften manners, but corrupt the heart,

Pour her exotic follies o'er the town,
To sanction Vice, and hunt Decorum down.
Ausonia = *Italy*
English Bards and Scotch Reviewers (1809) l. 618

15 Let simple Wordsworth chime his childish verse,
And brother Coleridge lull the babe at nurse.
English Bards and Scotch Reviewers (1809) l. 917

16 And glory, like the phoenix midst her fires,
Exhales her odours, blazes, and expires.
English Bards and Scotch Reviewers (1809) l. 959

17 Dusky like night, but night with all her stars,
Or cavern sparkling with its native spars;
With eyes that were a language and a spell,
A form like Aphrodite's in her shell,
With all her loves around her on the deep,
Voluptuous as the first approach of sleep.
'The Island' (1823) canto 2, st. 7

18 Friendship is Love without his wings!
'L'Amitié est l'amour sans ailes' (written 1806, published
1831)

19 So he has cut his throat at last!—He! Who?
The man who cut his country's long ago.
on Castlereagh's suicide, c.1822
'Epigram on Lord Castlereagh'

20 Sorrow is knowledge: they who know the most
Must mourn the deepest o'er the fatal truth,
The Tree of Knowledge is not that of Life.
Manfred (1817) act 1, sc. 1, l. 10

21 How beautiful is all this visible world!
How glorious in its action and itself!
But we, who name ourselves its sovereigns, we,
Half dust, half deity, alike unfit
To sink or soar, with our mixed essence make
A conflict of its elements, and breathe
The breath of degradation and of pride.
Manfred (1817) act 1, sc. 2, l. 37

22 I linger yet with nature, for the night
Hath been to me a more familiar face
Than that of man; and in her starry shade
Of dim and solitary loveliness
I learned the language of another world.
Manfred (1817) act 3, sc. 4, l. 2

23 Old man! 'tis not so difficult to die.
Manfred (2nd ed., 1819) act 3, sc. 4, l. 151

24 You have deeply ventured;
But all must do so who would greatly win.
Marino Faliero (1821) act 1, sc. 2

25 'Tis done—but yesterday a King!
And armed with Kings to strive—
And now thou art a nameless thing:
So abject—yet alive!
'Ode to Napoleon Bonaparte' (1814) st. 1

26 The arbiter of others' fate
A suppliant for his own!
'Ode to Napoleon Bonaparte' (1814) st. 5

27 The Cincinnatus of the West.
of George **Washington**
'Ode to Napoleon Bonaparte' (1814) st. 19

28 It is not in the storm nor in the strife
We feel benumbed, and wish to be no more,

But in the after-silence on the shore,
When all is lost, except a little life.
'On hearing that Lady Byron was ill' (written 1816)

1 My days are in the yellow leaf;
The flowers and fruits of love are gone;
The worm, the canker, and the grief
Are mine alone!
'On This Day I Complete my Thirty-Sixth Year' (1824); see
Byron 181:12, **Shakespeare** 707:8

2 My hair is grey, but not with years,
Nor grew it white
In a single night,
As men's have grown from sudden fears.
The Prisoner of Chillon (1816) st. 1

3 Remember thee! Aye, doubt it not;
Thy husband too shall think of thee;
By neither shalt thou be forgot,
Thou false to him, thou fiend to me!
reply to Lady Caroline **Lamb** *who had written*
'Remember me!' in a book belonging to Byron
'Remember Thee! Remember Thee!' (1813)

4 She walks in beauty, like the night
Of cloudless climes and starry skies;
And all that's best of dark and bright
Meet in her aspect and her eyes:
Thus mellowed to that tender light
Which heaven to gaudy day denies.
'She Walks in Beauty' (1815) st. 1

5 A mind at peace with all below,
A heart whose love is innocent!
'She Walks in Beauty' (1815)

6 Born in the garret, in the kitchen bred,
Promoted thence to deck her mistress' head.
'A Sketch from Private Life' (1816)

7 Eternal spirit of the chainless mind!
Brightest in dungeons, Liberty! thou art.
'Sonnet on Chillon' (1816)

8 So, we'll go no more a-roving
So late into the night,
Though the heart be still as loving,
And the moon be still as bright.
'So we'll go no more a-roving' (written 1817)

9 There's not a joy the world can give like that it
takes away.
'Stanzas for Music' (1816)

10 Oh, talk not to me of a name great in story;
The days of our youth are the days of our glory;
And the myrtle and ivy of sweet two-and-twenty
Are worth all your laurels, though ever so plenty.
'Stanzas Written on the Road between Florence and Pisa,
November 1821'

11 I knew it was love, and I felt it was glory.
'Stanzas Written on the Road between Florence and Pisa,
November 1821'

12 I am ashes where once I was fire.
'To the Countess of Blessington' (written 1823)

13 Still I can't contradict, what so oft has been said,
'Though women are angels, yet wedlock's the
devil.'
'To Eliza' (1806)

14 And when we think we lead, we are most led.
The Two Foscari (1821) act 2, sc. 1, l. 361

15 The angels all were singing out of tune,
And hoarse with having little else to do,
Excepting to wind up the sun and moon,
Or curb a runaway young star or two.
The Vision of Judgement (1822) st. 2

16 And when the gorgeous coffin was laid low,
It seemed the mockery of hell to fold
The rottenness of eighty years in gold.
on the burial of **George III**
The Vision of Judgement (1822) st. 10

17 In whom his qualities are reigning still,
Except that household virtue, most uncommon,
Of constancy to a bad, ugly woman.
The Vision of Judgement (1822) st. 12

18 As he drew near, he gazed upon the gate
Ne'er to be entered more by him or Sin,
With such a glance of supernatural hate,
As made Saint Peter wish himself within;
He pattered with his keys at a great rate,
And sweated through his apostolic skin:
Of course his perspiration was but ichor,
Or some such other spiritual liquor.
The Vision of Judgement (1822) st. 25

19 Yet still between his Darkness and his Brightness
There passed a mutual glance of great politeness.
The Vision of Judgement (1822) st. 35

20 Satan met his ancient friend
With more hauteur, as might an old Castilian
Poor noble meet a mushroom rich civilian.
The Vision of Judgement (1822) st. 36

21 And when the tumult dwindled to a calm,
I left him practising the hundredth psalm.
The Vision of Judgement (1822) st. 106

22 When we two parted
In silence and tears,
Half broken-hearted
To sever for years,
Pale grew thy cheek and cold,
Colder thy kiss.
'When we two parted' (1816)

23 If I should meet thee
After long years,
How should I greet thee?—
With silence and tears.
'When we two parted' (1816)

24 Near this spot are deposited the remains of one
who possessed beauty without vanity, strength
without insolence, courage without ferocity, and
all the virtues of Man, without his vices.
'Inscription on the Monument of a Newfoundland Dog'
(1808)

25 The man is mad, Sir, mad, frightful as a
Mandrake, and lean as a rutting Stag, and all
about a bitch not worth a Bank token.
of the Revd Robert Bland
letter to John Cam Hobhouse, 16 November 1811; in L. A.
Marchand (ed.) *Byron's Letters and Journals* vol. 2 (1973)

1 My Princess of Parallelograms.

of his future wife Annabella Milbanke, a keen amateur mathematician; Byron explains: 'Her proceedings are quite rectangular, or rather we are two parallel lines prolonged to infinity side by side but never to meet'

letter to Lady Melbourne, 18 October 1812; in L. A. Marchand (ed.) *Byron's Letters and Journals* vol. 2 (1973)

2 The place is very well and quiet and the children only scream in a low voice.

letter to Lady Melbourne, 21 September 1813, in L. A. Marchand (ed.) *Byron's Letters and Journals* vol. 3 (1974)

3 We have progressively improved into a less spiritual species of tenderness—but the seal is not yet fixed though the wax is preparing for the impression.

of his relationship with Lady Frances Webster

letter to Lady Melbourne, 14 October 1813; in L. A. Marchand (ed.) *Byron's Letters and Journals* vol. 3 (1974)

4 I by no means rank poetry high in the scale of intelligence—this may look like affectation—but it is my real opinion—it is the lava of the imagination whose eruption prevents an earthquake.

letter to Annabella Milbanke, 29 November 1813, in L. A. Marchand (ed.) *Byron's Letters and Journals* vol. 3 (1974)

5 I prefer the talents of action—of war—of the senate—or even of science—to all the speculations of those mere dreamers of another existence.

letter to Annabella Milbanke, 29 November 1813, in L. A. Marchand (ed.) *Byron's Letters and Journals* vol. 3 (1974)

6 What is hope? nothing but the paint on the face of Existence; the least touch of truth rubs it off, and then we see what a hollow-cheeked harlot we have got hold of.

letter to Thomas Moore, 28 October 1815, in L. A. Marchand (ed.) *Byron's Letters and Journals* vol. 4 (1975)

7 Like other parties of the kind, it was first silent, then talky, then argumentative, then disputatious, then unintelligible, then altogethery, then inarticulate, and then drunk.

letter to Thomas Moore, 31 October 1815, in L. A. Marchand (ed.) *Byron's Letters and Journals* vol. 4 (1975)

8 Wordsworth—stupendous genius! damned fool! These poets run about their ponds though they cannot fish.

fragment of a letter to James Hogg, recorded in the diary of Henry Crabb Robinson, 1 December 1816; in L. A. Marchand (ed.) *Byron's Letters and Journals* vol. 5 (1976)

9 Love in this part of the world is no sinecure.

letter to John Murray from Venice, 27 December 1816, in L. A. Marchand (ed.) *Byron's Letters and Journals* vol. 5 (1976)

10 I hate things all *fiction* . . . there should always be some foundation of fact for the most airy fabric and pure invention is but the talent of a liar.

letter to John Murray from Venice, 2 April 1817; in L. A. Marchand (ed.) *Byron's Letters and Journals* vol. 5 (1976)

11 Without means, without connection, without character . . . he beat them all, in all he ever attempted.

of Richard Brinsley Sheridan

letter to Thomas Moore, 1 June 1818, in L. A. Marchand (ed.) *Byron's Letters and Journals* vol. 6 (1978)

12 Is it not *life*, is it not *the thing*?—Could any man have written it—who has not lived in the world?—and tooled in a post-chaise? in a hackney coach? in a gondola? Against a wall? in a court carriage? in a *vis-à-vis*?—on a table?—and under it?

of Don Juan

letter to Douglas Kinnaird, 26 October 1819; in L. A. Marchand (ed.) *Byron's Letters and Journals* vol. 6 (1978)

13 The reading or non-reading a book—will never keep down a single petticoat.

letter to Richard Hoppner, 29 October 1819, in L. A. Marchand (ed.) *Byron's Letters and Journals* vol. 6 (1978)

14 Such writing is a sort of mental masturbation—he is always f—gg—g his *imagination*.—I don't mean that he is indecent but viciously soliciting his own ideas into a state which is neither poetry nor any thing else but a Bedlam vision produced by raw pork and opium.

of Keats

letter to John Murray, 9 November 1820; in L. A. Marchand (ed.) *Byron's Letters and Journals* vol. 7 (1979)

15 I awoke one morning and found myself famous.

on the instantaneous success of Childe Harold

Thomas Moore *Letters and Journals of Lord Byron* (1830) vol. 1

16 You should have a softer pillow than my heart.

to his wife, who had rested her head on his breast

E. C. Mayne (ed.) *The Life and Letters of Anne Isabella, Lady Noel Byron* (1929) ch. 11

Cc

James Branch Cabell 1879–1958

American novelist and essayist

17 The optimist proclaims that we live in the best of all possible worlds; and the pessimist fears this is true.

The Silver Stallion (1926) bk. 4, ch. 26

Caecilius Statius d. after 166 BC

Roman comic dramatist, born in Gaul

18 *Serit arbores, quae alteri saeclo prosint.*

He plants the trees to serve another age.

Synephebi; quoted in Cicero 'De Senectute'

Augustus Caesar see Augustus

Irving Caesar 1895–1996

American songwriter

19 Picture you upon my knee,
Just tea for two and two for tea.

'Tea for Two' (1925 song)

Julius Caesar 100–44 BC

Roman general and statesman
see also **Plutarch** 598:16

1 *Gallia est omnis divisa in partes tres.*
Gaul as a whole is divided into three parts.
De Bello Gallico bk. 1, sect. 1

2 Men are nearly always willing to believe what
they wish.
De Bello Gallico bk. 3, sect. 18; see **Bacon** 46:15

3 Caesar's wife must be above suspicion.
*divorcing his wife Pompeia after unfounded allegations
were made against her*
oral tradition, based on Plutarch *Parallel Lives* 'Julius
Caesar' ch. 10, sect. 9; see **Proverbs** 616:21

4 Caesar had rather be first in a village than second
at Rome.
Francis Bacon *The Advancement of Learning* pt. 2, ch. 23,
sect. 36; based on Plutarch
I should rather be first among these people than
second at Rome.
Parallel Lives 'Julius Caesar' ch. 11

5 Thou hast Caesar and his fortune with thee.
Plutarch *Parallel Lives* 'Julius Caesar' ch. 38, sect. 3
(translated by T. North, 1579; literally 'You are carrying
Caesar, and his fortune is in the same boat')

6 *Iacta alea est.*
The die is cast.
*at the crossing of the Rubicon, the boundary beyond
which he was forbidden to lead his army*
Suetonius *Lives of the Caesars* 'Divus Julius' sect. 32;
originally spoken in Greek, Plutarch *Parallel Lives* 'Pompey'
ch. 60, sect. 2

7 *Veni, vidi, vici.*
I came, I saw, I conquered.
inscription displayed in Caesar's Pontic triumph, according
to Suetonius *Lives of the Caesars* 'Divus Julius' sect. 37; or,
according to Plutarch *Parallel Lives* 'Julius Caesar' ch. 50,
sect. 2, written in a letter by Caesar, announcing the
victory of Zela, 47 BC, which concluded the Pontic
campaign

8 *Et tu, Brute?*
You too, Brutus?
traditional rendering of Suetonius; see **Shakespeare** 697:10
Some have written that when Marcus Brutus
rushed at him, he said in Greek, 'You too, my
child?'
Suetonius *Lives of the Caesars* 'Divus Julius' sect. 82

John Cage 1912–

American composer, pianist, and writer

9 I have nothing to say
and I am saying it and that is
poetry.
'Lecture on nothing' (1961)

James Cagney see Misquotations 539:5

James M. Cain 1892–1977

American novelist

10 The postman always rings twice.
title of novel (1934)

Pedro Calderón de La Barca 1600–81

Spanish dramatist and poet

11 *. . . Aun en sueños
no se pierde el hacer bien.*
Even in dreams good works are not wasted.
La Vida es Sueño (1636) 'Segunda Jornada' l. 2146

12 *¿Qué es la vida? Un frenesí.
¿Qué es la vida? Una ilusión,
una sombra, una ficción,
y el mayor bien es pequeño;
que toda la vida es sueño,
y los sueños, sueños son.*
What is life? a frenzy. What is life? An illusion, a
shadow, a fiction. And the greatest good is of
slight worth, as all life is a dream, and dreams are
dreams.
La Vida es Sueño (1636) 'Segunda Jornada' l. 2183; see
Montaigne 544:18

Caligula (Gaius Julius Caesar Germanicus) AD 12–41

Roman emperor from AD 37
see also **Accius** 1:6

13 *Utinam populus Romanus unam cervicem haberet!*
Would that the Roman people had but one neck!
Suetonius *Lives of the Caesars* 'Gaius Caligula' sect. 30

14 *Ita feri ut se mori sentiat.*
Strike him so that he can feel that he is dying.
Suetonius *Lives of the Caesars* 'Gaius Caligula' sect. 30

James Callaghan 1912–

British Labour statesman; Prime Minister 1976–9
see also **Misquotations** 537:8

15 You cannot now, if you ever could, spend your
way out of a recession.
speech at Labour Party Conference, 28 September 1976

16 You never reach the promised land. You can
march towards it.
in a television interview, 20 July 1978

17 I had known it was going to be a 'winter of
discontent'.
television interview, 8 February 1979; in *Daily Telegraph* 9
February 1979; see **Newspaper headlines** 562:24

18 It's the first time in recorded history that turkeys
have been known to vote for an early Christmas.
*in the debate resulting in the fall of the Labour
government, when the pact between Labour and the
Liberals had collapsed, and the Scottish and Welsh
Nationalists had also withdrawn their support*
in the House of Commons, 28 March 1979

19 There are times, perhaps once every thirty years,
when there is a sea-change in politics. It then does
not matter what you say or what you do. There is
a shift in what the public wants and what it
approves of. I suspect there is now such a sea-
change—and it is for Mrs Thatcher.
during the election campaign of 1979
Kenneth O. Morgan *Callaghan* (1997)

Callimachus c.305–c.240 BC
Greek poet and scholar

1 Someone spoke of your death, Heraclitus. It
  brought me
Tears, and I remembered how often together
We ran the sun down with talk.
  R. Pfeiffer (ed) *Callimachus* (1949–53) Epigram 2;
  translated by Peter Jay; see **Cory** 244:3

2 I abhor, too, the roaming lover, nor do I drink
from every well; I loathe all things held in
common.
  R. Pfeiffer (ed.) *Callimachus* (1949–53) Epigram 28; see
  Horace 401:9

3 A great book is like great evil.
  R. Pfeiffer (ed.) *Callimachus* (1949–53) Fragment 465; see
  Proverbs 621:15

4 I sing nothing that is not attested.
  fragment 617, translated by C. A. Trypanis

Charles Alexandre de Calonne 1734–1802
French statesman

5 *Madame, si c'est possible, c'est fait; impossible? cela
se fera.*
Madam, if a thing is possible, consider it done; the
impossible? that will be done.
  in J. Michelet *Histoire de la Révolution Française* (1847) vol.
  I, pt. 2, sect. 8; see **Military sayings** 526:6, **Nansen** 556:5

C. S. Calverley (born Blayds) 1831–84
English writer

6 The farmer's daughter hath soft brown hair;
(*Butter and eggs and a pound of cheese*)
And I met with a ballad, I can't say where,
Which wholly consisted of lines like these.
  'Ballad' (1872)

7 O Beer! O Hodgson, Guinness, Allsopp, Bass!
Names that should be on every infant's tongue!
  'Beer' (1861)

8 Life is with such all beer and skittles;
They are not difficult to please
About their victuals.
  'Contentment' (1872)

9 For I've read in many a novel that, unless they've
  souls that grovel,
Folks *prefer* in fact a hovel to your dreary marble
  halls.
  'In the Gloaming' (1872); see **Bunn** 164:8

10 How Eugene Aram, though a thief, a liar, and a
  murderer,
Yet, being intellectual, was amongst the noblest of
  mankind.
  'Of Reading' (1861); see **Hood** 394:24

Italo Calvino 1923–85
Italian novelist and short-story writer

11 The gaze of dogs who don't understand and who
don't know that they may be right not to
understand.
  Il Barone Rampante [The Baron in the Trees] (1957) ch. 10

12 Revolutionaries are more formalistic than
conservatives.
  Il Barone Rampante [The Baron in the Trees] (1957) ch. 28

Helder Camara 1909–99
Brazilian priest

13 When I give food to the poor they call me a saint.
When I ask why the poor have no food they call
me a communist.
  attributed

Pierre, Baron de Cambronne 1770–1842
French general

14 *La Garde meurt, mais ne se rend pas.*
The Guards die but do not surrender.
*attributed to Cambronne when called upon to
surrender at Waterloo, 1815, but later denied by him*
  H. Houssaye *La Garde meurt et ne se rend pas* (1907); an
  alternative version is that he replied:
  Merde!
  Shit!
  attributed, known in French as the '*mot de Cambronne*'

Lord Camden 1714–94
British Whig politician; Lord Chancellor, 1766–70

15 Taxation and representation are inseparable . . .
whatever is a man's own, is absolutely his own;
no man hath a right to take it from him without
his consent either expressed by himself or
representative; whoever attempts to do it,
attempts an injury; whoever does it, commits a
robbery; he throws down and destroys the
distinction between liberty and slavery.
*on the taxation of Americans by the British
parliament*
  speech in the House of Lords, 10 February 1766; see **Otis**
  579:11

Julia Margaret Cameron 1815–79
English photographer

16 I longed to arrest all beauty that came before me.
  Annals of my Glass House 1874

Alastair Campbell 1957–
*British journalist, Press Secretary to the Prime Minister
1997–2003*
see also **Anonymous** 18:14

17 Labour spin doctors aren't supposed to like Tory
MPs. But Alan Clark was an exceptional man.
  in *Mirror* 8 September 1999

18 The day of the bog-standard comprehensive is
over.
  press briefing, 12 February 2001; see **Blunkett** 124:7

19 It was grim, it was grim for me, grim for TB and
there is this huge stuff about trust.
  diary, 1 June 2003, as reported to the **Hutton** inquiry; in
  Guardian (online ed.) 20 August 2003

Jane Montgomery Campbell 1817–78

English hymn-writer

1 We plough the fields, and scatter
The good seed on the land,
But it is fed and watered
By God's almighty hand;
He sends the snow in winter,
The warmth to swell the grain,
The breezes and the sunshine,
And soft refreshing rain.
    'We plough the fields, and scatter' (1861 hymn);
    translated from the German of Matthias Claudius
    (1740–1815)

Mrs Patrick Campbell (Beatrice Stella Tanner) 1865–1940

English actress
on Campbell: see **Woollcott** 845:14

2 The deep, deep peace of the double-bed after the
hurly-burly of the chaise-longue.
    on her recent marriage
    Alexander Woollcott *While Rome Burns* (1934) 'The First
    Mrs Tanqueray'

3 It doesn't matter what you do in the bedroom as
long as you don't do it in the street and frighten
the horses.
    Daphne Fielding *The Duchess of Jermyn Street* (1964) ch. 2

Roy Campbell 1901–57

South African poet

4   Giraffes!—a People
Who live between the earth and skies,
Each in his lone religious steeple,
Keeping a lighthouse with his eyes.
    'Dreaming Spires' (1946)

5 You praise the firm restraint with which they
    write—
I'm with you there, of course:
They use the snaffle and the curb all right,
But where's the bloody horse?
    'On Some South African Novelists' (1930)

Thomas Campbell 1777–1844

Scottish poet

6 There was silence deep as death,
And the boldest held his breath
For a time.
    'Battle of the Baltic' (1809)

7 Let us think of them that sleep,
Full many a fathom deep,
By thy wild and stormy steep,
Elsinore!
    'Battle of the Baltic' (1809)

8 O leave this barren spot to me!
Spare, woodman, spare the beechen tree.
    'The Beech-Tree's Petition' (1800); see **Morris** 549:11

9 To-morrow let us do or die!
    'Gertrude of Wyoming' (1809) pt. 3, st. 37

10 On the green banks of Shannon, when Sheelah
    was nigh,

No blithe Irish lad was so happy as I;
No harp like my own could so cheerily play,
And wherever I went was my poor dog Tray.
    'The Harper' (1799)

11 On Linden, when the sun was low,
All bloodless lay the untrodden snow,
And dark as winter was the flow
Of Iser, rolling rapidly.
    'Hohenlinden' (1802)

12 'Tis the sunset of life gives me mystical lore,
And coming events cast their shadows before.
    Lochiel's Warning (1801)

13 A chieftain to the Highlands bound
Cries, 'Boatman, do not tarry!
And I'll give thee a silver pound
To row us o'er the ferry.'
    'Lord Ullin's Daughter' (1809)

14 O, I'm the chief of Ulva's isle
And this Lord Ullin's daughter.
    'Lord Ullin's Daughter' (1809)

15 'Tis distance lends enchantment to the view,
And robes the mountain in its azure hue.
    Pleasures of Hope (1799) pt. 1, l. 7; see **Proverbs** 617:44

16 Hope, for a season, bade the world farewell,
And Freedom shrieked—as Kosciuszko fell!
    Pleasures of Hope (1799) pt. 1, l. 381

17 What millions died—that Caesar might be great!
    Pleasures of Hope (1799) pt. 2, l. 174

18 What though my wingèd hours of bliss have been,
Like angel-visits, few and far between?
    Pleasures of Hope (1799) pt. 2, l. 375

19 An original something, fair maid, you would
    win me
To write—but how shall I begin?
For I fear I have nothing original in me—
Excepting Original Sin.
    'To a Young Lady, Who Asked Me to Write Something
    Original for Her Album' (1843)

20 Ye Mariners of England
That guard our native seas,
Whose flag has braved, a thousand years
The battle and the breeze.
    'Ye Mariners of England' (1801)

21 With thunders from her native oak
She quells the floods below.
    'Ye Mariners of England' (1801)

22 Now Barabbas was a publisher.
alteration of Bible verse; also attributed, wrongly, to
Byron
    attributed, in Samuel Smiles *A Publisher and his Friends:*
    Memoir and Correspondence of the late John Murray (1891)
    vol. 1, ch. 14; see **Bible** 104:2

Thomas Campion 1567–1620

English poet and musician

23 My sweetest Lesbia let us live and love,
And though the sager sort our deeds reprove,
Let us not weigh them: Heav'n's great lamps do
    dive

Into their west, and straight again revive,
But soon as once set is our little light,
Then must we sleep one ever-during night.
> A Book of Airs (1601) no. 1 'My sweetest Lesbia'
> (translation of Catullus Carmina no. 5); see **Catullus** 202:13

1 When to her lute Corinna sings,
Her voice revives the leaden strings,
And both in highest notes appear,
As any challenged echo clear.
But when she doth of mourning speak,
Ev'n with her sighs the strings do break.
> A Book of Airs (1601) no. 6

2 Follow your Saint, follow with accents sweet;
Haste you, sad notes, fall at her flying feet.
> A Book of Airs (1601) no. 10

3 Good thoughts his only friends,
His wealth a well-spent age,
The earth his sober inn
And quiet pilgrimage.
> A Book of Airs (1601) no. 18

4 There is a garden in her face
Where roses and white lilies grow;
A heavenly paradise is that place,
Wherein all pleasant fruits do flow.
There cherries grow, which none may buy
Till 'Cherry ripe' themselves do cry.
> The Fourth Book of Airs (c.1617) no. 7; music by Richard
> Alison, who published the song in An Hour's Recreation in
> Music (1606)

5 Rose-cheeked Laura, come;
Sing thou smoothly with thy beauty's
Silent music, either other
Sweetly gracing.
> 'Rose-cheeked Laura' (1602)

6 Kind are her answers,
But her performance keeps no day;
Breaks time, as dancers
From their own music when they stray.
> The Third Book of Airs (1617) no. 7

Albert Camus 1913–60

French novelist, dramatist, and essayist
see also Opening lines 574:7

7 *Intellectuel = celui qui se dédouble.*
An intellectual is someone whose mind watches
itself.
> Carnets, 1935–42 (1962)

8 *La politique et le sort des hommes sont formés par des
hommes sans idéal et sans grandeur.*
Politics and the fate of mankind are formed by
men without ideals and without greatness.
> Carnets, 1935–42 (1962)

9 *Vous savez ce qu'est le charme: une manière de
s'entendre répondre oui sans avoir posé aucune
question claire.*
You know what charm is: a way of getting the
answer yes without having asked any clear
question.
> The Fall (1956)

10 *Nous sommes tous des cas exceptionnels. Nous
voulons tous faire appel de quelque chose! Chacun*
*exige d'être innocent, à tout prix, même si, pour cela,
il faut accuser le genre humain et le ciel.*
We are all special cases. We all want to appeal
against something! Everyone insists on his
innocence, at all costs, even if it means accusing
the rest of the human race and heaven.
> The Fall (1956)

11 *Nous nous confions rarement à ceux qui sont
meilleurs que nous.*
We seldom confide in those who are better than
ourselves.
> The Fall (1956)

12 *Je vais vous dire un grand secret, mon cher.
N'attendez pas le jugement dernier. Il a lieu tous les
jours.*
I'll tell you a great secret, my friend. Don't wait for
the last judgement. It happens every day.
> The Fall (1956)

13 *Sisyphe, prolétaire des dieux, impuissant et révolté,
connaît toute l'entendue de sa misérable condition:
c'est à elle qu'il pense pendant sa descente. La
clairvoyance qui devait faire son tourment consomme
du même coup sa victoire. Il n'est pas de destin que ne
se surmonte par le mépris.*
Sisyphus, proletarian of the gods, powerless and
rebellious, knows the whole extent of his wretched
condition; it is what he thinks of during his
descent. The lucidity that was to constitute his
torture at the same time crowns his victory. There
is no fate that cannot be surmounted by scorn.
> The Myth of Sisyphus (1942) (translated by Justin O'Brien)

14 *L'honnêteté n'a pas besoin des règles.*
Integrity has no need of rules.
> The Myth of Sisyphus (1942)

15 *La lutte elle-même vers les sommets suffit à remplir un
cœur d'homme. Il faut imaginer Sisyphe heureux.*
The struggle itself towards the heights is enough
to fill a human heart. One must imagine that
Sisyphus is happy.
> The Myth of Sisyphus (1942)

16 *Qu'est-ce qu'un homme révolté ? Un homme qui dit
non.*
What is a rebel? A man who says no.
> The Rebel (1951)

17 *Toutes les révolutions modernes ont abouti à un
renforcement de l'État.*
All modern revolutions have ended in a
reinforcement of the State.
> The Rebel (1951)

18 *Tout révolutionnaire finit en oppresseur ou en
hérétique.*
Every revolutionary ends as an oppressor or a
heretic.
> The Rebel (1951)

19 When the imagination sleeps, words are emptied
of their meaning.
> Resistance, Rebellion and Death (1961) 'Reflections on the
> Guillotine'

20 One sometimes sees more clearly in the man who
lies than in the man who tells the truth. Truth,

like the light, blinds. Lying, on the other hand, is a beautiful twilight, which gives to each object its value.

attributed; Lord Trevelyan *Diplomatic Channels* (1973)

1 What I know most surely about morality and the duty of man I owe to sport.

often quoted as ' . . . I owe to football'

Herbert R. Lottman *Albert Camus* (1979)

2 Without work, all life goes rotten, but when work is soulless, life stifles and dies.

attributed; E. F. Schumacher *Good Work* (1979)

Elias Canetti 1905–94

Bulgarian-born writer and novelist

3 All the things one has forgotten scream for help in dreams.

Die Provinz der Menschen (1973)

George Canning 1770–1827

British Tory statesman; Prime Minister, 1827

4 In matters of commerce the fault of the Dutch
Is offering too little and asking too much.
The French are with equal advantage content,
So we clap on Dutch bottoms just twenty per cent.

dispatch, in cipher, to the English ambassador at the Hague, 31 January 1826

Sir Harry Poland *Mr Canning's Rhyming 'Dispatch' to Sir Charles Bagot* (1905)

5 A steady patriot of the world alone,
The friend of every country but his own.

on the Jacobin

'New Morality' (1821) l. 113; see **Disraeli** 276:16, **Overbury** 579:16

6 And finds, with keen discriminating sight,
Black's not so black;—nor white so very white.

'New Morality' (1821) l. 199

7 Give me the avowed, erect and manly foe;
Firm I can meet, perhaps return the blow;
But of all plagues, good Heaven, thy wrath can send,
Save me, oh, save me, from the candid friend.

'New Morality' (1821) l. 207

8 Pitt is to Addington
As London is to Paddington.

'The Oracle' (c.1803)

9 Away with the cant of 'Measures not men'!—the idle supposition that it is the harness and not the horses that draw the chariot along. If the comparison must be made, if the distinction must be taken, men are everything, measures comparatively nothing.

speech on the Army estimates, 8 December 1802, in *Speeches of . . . Canning* (1828) vol. 2; the phrase 'measures not men' may be found as early as 1742 (in a letter from Chesterfield to Dr Chevenix, 6 March); see **Burke** 168:9, **Goldsmith** 355:20

10 I called the New World into existence, to redress the balance of the Old.

speech on the affairs of Portugal, in House of Commons 12 December 1826

11 You well know how soon one of these stupendous masses, now reposing on their shadows in perfect stillness, would upon any call of patriotism or of necessity, assume the likeness of an animated thing, instinct with life and motion: how soon it would ruffle, as it were its swelling plumage, how quickly it would put forth all its beauty and its bravery, collect its scattered elements of strength and waken its dormant thunder . . . Such is England herself; while apparently passive and motionless, she silently concentrates the power to be put forth on an adequate occasion.

on the men-of-war lying at anchor in the harbour

speech at Plymouth, 12 December 1823; in R. W. Seton-Watson *Britain in Europe 1789–1914* (1945)

Brendan Cannon 1973–

Australian rugby player

12 It was like witnessing a car accident, you know it's about to happen but you don't want it to happen.

*on watching Jonny **Wilkinson**'s winning drop goal in the Rugby World Cup final, Sydney, 22 November 2003*

in *Weekend Australian* (online ed.) 23 November 2003

Hughie Cannon 1877–1912

American songwriter

13 Won't you come home Bill Bailey, won't you come home?

'Bill Bailey, Won't You Please Come Home' (1902 song)

Moya Cannon 1956–

Irish poet

14 Our windy, untidy loft
where old people had flung up old junk
they'd thought might come in handy
ploughs, ladles, bears, lions, a clatter of heroes.

'The Stars' (1997)

Eric Cantona 1966–

French footballer

15 When seagulls follow a trawler, it is because they think sardines will be thrown into the sea.

to the media at the end of a press conference, 31 March 1995

Robert Capa 1913–54

Hungarian-born American photojournalist

16 If your pictures aren't good enough, you aren't close enough.

Russell Miller *Magnum: Fifty years at the Front Line of History* (1997)

Truman Capote 1924–84

American writer and novelist
*on Capote: see **Vidal** 810:2*

17 Other voices, other rooms.

title of novel (1948)

Al Capp (Alfred Gerard Caplin) 1907–79

American cartoonist

1 A product of the untalented, sold by the
unprincipled to the utterly bewildered.
of abstract art
  in *National Observer* 1 July 1963; see **Zappa** 858:6

Francesco Caracciolo 1752–99

Neapolitan diplomat

2 In England there are sixty different religions, and
only one sauce.
  attributed

Ethna Carbery 1866–1902

Irish poet

3 I met the Love-Talker one eve in the glen,
  He was handsomer than any of our handsome
    young men,
  His eyes were blacker than the sloe, his voice
    sweeter far
  Than the crooning of old Kevin's pipes beyond in
    Coolnagar.
  'The Love-Talker' (1902)

4 Oh, Kathaleen Ní Houlihan, your road's a thorny
    way,
  And 'tis a faithful soul would walk the flints with
    you for aye,
  Would walk the sharp and cruel flints until his
    locks grew grey.
  'The Passing of the Gael' (1902)

5 Young Rody MacCorley goes to die
  On the Bridge of Toome today.
  'Rody MacCorley' (1902)

Ernesto Cardenal 1925–

Nicaraguan poet

6 While classes exist no one is free
  We are not born to be slaves
  or to be masters.
  We are born to be brothers and sisters.
  What is capitalism but buying and selling of
    people?
  'Canto Nacional' (1972) translated by Dinah Livingstone

7 When you get the nomination, the prize, the
    promotion,
  think of the ones who died.
  When you are at the reception, delegation,
    commission,
  think of the ones who died.
  When you have won the election and the crowd
    congratulates you,
  think of the ones who died.
  'For Those Dead Our Dead' translated by Dinah Livingstone

8 When they asked Joan of Arc at her trial whether
  God loved the English, she replied: 'God does not
  love the English *in* France.' And this is the mystery
  of our vocation. God also loves the man who is

dictator of Nigaragua, but he does not love him *as*
the dictator of Nigaragua.
of Anastasio **Somoza**
  Vida en el Amor (1970) 'Will of God' translated by Dinah
  Livingstone

Neville Cardus 1889–1975

English critic and writer

9 If everything else in this nation of ours were lost
but cricket—her Constitution and the laws of
England of Lord Halsbury—it would be possible to
reconstruct from the theory and practice of cricket
all the eternal Englishness which has gone to the
establishment of that Constitution and the laws
aforesaid.
  Cricket (1930)

Richard Carew 1555–1620

English poet

10 Will you have all in all for prose and verse? Take
the miracle of our age, Sir Philip Sidney.
  William Camden *Remains concerning Britain* (1614) 'The
  Excellency of the English Tongue'

Thomas Carew c.1595–1640

English poet and courtier

11 He that loves a rosy cheek,
  Or a coral lip admires,
  Or, from star-like eyes, doth seek
  Fuel to maintain his fires;
  As old Time makes these decay,
  So his flames must waste away.
  'Disdain Returned' (1640)

12 The Muses' garden with pedantic weeds
  O'erspread, was purged by thee; the lazy seeds
  Of servile imitation thrown away,
  And fresh invention planted.
  'An Elegy upon the Death of Dr John Donne' (1640)

13 Here lies a king, that ruled as he thought fit
  The universal monarchy of wit.
  'An Elegy upon the Death of Dr John Donne' (1640)

14 The purest soul that e'er was sent
  Into a clayey tenement.
  'Epitaph On the Lady Mary Villiers' (1640)

15 Good to the poor, to kindred dear,
  To servants kind, to friendship clear,
  To nothing but herself severe.
  'Inscription on the Tomb of Lady Mary Wentworth' (1640)

16 So though a virgin, yet a bride
  To every Grace, she justified
  A chaste polygamy, and died.
  'Inscription on the Tomb of Lady Mary Wentworth' (1640)

17 Give me more love or more disdain;
  The torrid or the frozen zone:
  Bring equal ease unto my pain;
  The temperate affords me none.
  'Mediocrity in Love Rejected' (1640)

18 Though a stranger to this place,
  Bewail in theirs thine own hard case:

For thou perhaps at thy return
Mayst find thy darling in an urn.
'On the Lady Mary Villiers' (1640)

1 Ask me no more where Jove bestows,
When June is past, the fading rose;
For in your beauty's orient deep
These flowers, as in their causes, sleep.
'A Song' (1640)

2 Ask me no more whither doth haste
The nightingale when May is past;
For in your sweet dividing throat
She winters and keeps warm her note.
'A Song' (1640)

3 Ask me no more if east or west
The Phoenix builds her spicy nest;
For unto you at last she flies,
And in your fragrant bosom dies.
'A Song' (1640)

4 When thou, poor excommunicate
From all the joys of love, shalt see
The full reward and glorious fate
Which my strong faith shall purchase me,
Then curse thine own inconstancy.
'To My Inconstant Mistress' (1640)

George Carey 1935–

English Anglican churchman; Archbishop of Canterbury
1991–2002

5 We must recall that the Church is always 'one
generation away from extinction.'
Working Party Report *Youth A Part: Young People and the
Church* (1996) foreword

Henry Carey c.1687–1743

English comic dramatist and songwriter
see also **Songs** 747:7

6 Let your little verses flow
Gently, sweetly, row by row;
Let the verse the subject fit,
Little subject, little wit.
'Namby-Pamby: or, A Panegyric on the New Versification'
(1725)

7 As an actor does his part,
So the nurses get by heart
Namby-pamby's little rhymes,
Little jingle, little chimes.
'Namby-Pamby' (1725)

8 Of all the girls that are so smart
There's none like pretty Sally,
She is the darling of my heart,
And she lives in our alley.
'Sally in our Alley' (1729)

Jane Carlyle (née Welsh) 1801–66

Scottish wife of Thomas **Carlyle**
on Carlyle: see **Butler** 176:27

9 I am not at all the sort of person you and I took
me for.
letter to Thomas Carlyle, 7 May 1822, in C. R. Sanders et
al. (eds.) *Collected Letters of Thomas and Jane Welsh Carlyle*
(1970) vol. 2

Thomas Carlyle 1795–1881

Scottish historian and political philosopher
on Carlyle: see **Butler** 176:27, **Clough** 229:13

10 A witty statesman said, you might prove anything
by figures.
Chartism (1839) ch. 2

11 Surely of all 'rights of man', this right of the
ignorant man to be guided by the wiser, to be,
gently or forcibly, held in the true course by him,
is the indisputablest.
Chartism (1839) ch. 6

12 In epochs when cash payment has become the
sole nexus of man to man.
Chartism (1839) ch. 6

13 The 'golden-calf of self-love.'
Critical and Miscellaneous Essays (1838) 'Burns'

14 The foul sluggard's comfort: 'It will last my time.'
Critical and Miscellaneous Essays (1838) 'Count Cagliostro.
Flight Last'

15 Thou wretched fraction, wilt thou be the ninth
part even of a tailor?
Critical and Miscellaneous Essays (1838) 'Francia'; see
Proverbs 627:35

16 What is all knowledge too but recorded
experience, and a product of history; of which,
therefore, reasoning and belief, no less than action
and passion, are essential materials?
Critical and Miscellaneous Essays (1838) 'On History'

17 History is the essence of innumerable biographies.
Critical and Miscellaneous Essays (1838) 'On History'

18 A well-written Life is almost as rare as a well-
spent one.
Critical and Miscellaneous Essays (1838) 'Jean Paul Friedrich
Richter'

19 There is no life of a man, faithfully recorded, but is
a heroic poem of its sort, rhymed or unrhymed.
Critical and Miscellaneous Essays (1838) 'Sir Walter Scott'

20 Under all speech that is good for anything there
lies a silence that is better. Silence is deep as
Eternity; speech is shallow as Time.
Critical and Miscellaneous Essays (1838) 'Sir Walter Scott'

21 To the very last he [Napoleon] had a kind of idea;
that, namely, of *La carrière ouverte aux talents*, The
tools to him that can handle them.
Critical and Miscellaneous Essays (1838) 'Sir Walter Scott'
(*La carrière . . .* Career open to the talents)

22 It can be said of him, when he departed, he took a
man's life along with him.
Critical and Miscellaneous Essays (1838) 'Sir Walter Scott'

23 This idle habit of 'accounting for the moral sense'
. . . The moral sense, thank God, is a thing you
will never 'account for' . . . By no greatest
happiness principle, greatest nobleness principle,
or any principle whatever, will you make that in
the least clearer than it already is.
Critical and Miscellaneous Essays (1838) 'Shooting Niagara:
and After?'

24 It is the Age of Machinery, in every outward and
inward sense of that word.
Critical and Miscellaneous Essays (1838) 'Signs of the Times'

1 The Bible-Society . . . is found, on inquiry, to be
. . . a machine for converting the Heathen.
Critical and Miscellaneous Essays (1838) 'Signs of the Times'

2 Thought, he [Dr Cabanis] is inclined to hold, is still
secreted by the brain; but then Poetry and
Religion (and it is really worth knowing) are 'a
product of the smaller intestines'!
Critical and Miscellaneous Essays (1838) 'Signs of the Times'

3 The three great elements of modern civilization,
Gunpowder, Printing, and the Protestant Religion.
Critical and Miscellaneous Essays (1838) 'The State of
German Literature'; see **Bacon** 46:17

4 'Genius' (which means transcendent capacity of
taking trouble, first of all).
History of Frederick the Great (1858–65) bk. 4, ch. 3; see
Buffon 163:14, **Proverbs** 620:35

5 A whiff of grapeshot.
History of the French Revolution (1837) vol. 1, bk. 5, ch. 3

6 History a distillation of rumour.
History of the French Revolution (1837) vol. 1, bk. 7, ch. 5

7 The difference between Orthodoxy or My-doxy and
Heterodoxy or Thy-doxy.
History of the French Revolution (1837) vol. 2, bk. 4, ch. 2;
see **Warburton** 821:8

8 The seagreen Incorruptible.
describing **Robespierre**
History of the French Revolution (1837) vol. 2, bk. 4, ch. 4

9 France was long a despotism tempered by
epigrams.
History of the French Revolution (1837) vol. 3, bk. 7, ch. 7

10 Aristocracy of the Moneybag.
History of the French Revolution (1837) vol. 3, bk. 7, ch. 7

11 Worship is transcendent wonder.
On Heroes, Hero-Worship, and the Heroic (1841) 'The Hero
as Divinity'

12 I hope we English will long maintain our *grand
talent pour le silence.*
On Heroes, Hero-Worship, and the Heroic (1841) 'The Hero
as King'

13 In books lies the *soul* of the whole Past Time; the
articulate audible voice of the Past, when the body
and material substance of it has altogether
vanished like a dream.
On Heroes, Hero-Worship, and the Heroic (1841) 'The Hero
as Man of Letters'

14 The true University of these days is a collection of
books.
On Heroes, Hero-Worship, and the Heroic (1841) 'The Hero
as Man of Letters'

15 Adversity is sometimes hard upon a man; but for
one man who can stand prosperity, there are a
hundred that will stand adversity.
On Heroes, Hero-Worship, and the Heroic (1841) 'The Hero
as Man of Letters'

16 Maid-servants, I hear people complaining, are
getting instructed in the 'ologies'.
Inaugural Address at Edinburgh, 2 April 1866, on being
installed as Rector of the University

17 A Parliament speaking through reporters to
Buncombe and the twenty-seven millions mostly
fools.
Latter-Day Pamphlets (1850) 'Parliaments'; see **Walker**
817:14

18 The Dismal Science.
on political economy
Latter-Day Pamphlets (1850) 'The Present Time'

19 Little other than a redtape talking-machine, and
unhappy bag of parliamentary eloquence.
describing himself
Latter-Day Pamphlets (1850) 'The Present Time'

20 Transcendental moonshine.
*on the influence of a romantic imagination in
motivating Sterling to enter the priesthood*
The Life of John Sterling (1851) pt. 1, ch. 15

21 There is always hope in a man that actually and
earnestly works: in Idleness alone is there
perpetual despair.
Past and Present (1843) bk. 3, ch. 11

22 Captains of industry.
Past and Present (1843) bk. 4, ch. 4 (title)

23 He who first shortened the labour of copyists by
device of *Movable Types* was disbanding hired
armies, and cashiering most Kings and Senates,
and creating a whole new democratic world: he
had invented the art of printing.
Sartor Resartus (1834) bk. 1, ch. 5

24 Man is a tool-using animal . . . Without tools he is
nothing, with tools he is all.
Sartor Resartus (1834) bk. 1, ch. 5; see **Franklin** 332:20

25 Whoso has sixpence is sovereign (to the length of
sixpence) over all men; commands cooks to feed
him, philosophers to teach him, kings to mount
guard over him,—to the length of sixpence.
Sartor Resartus (1834) bk. 1, ch. 5

26 Language is called the garment of thought:
however, it should rather be, language is the
flesh-garment, the body, of thought.
Sartor Resartus (1834) bk. 1, ch. 11

27 The end of man is an action and not a thought,
though it were the noblest.
Sartor Resartus (1834) bk. 2, ch. 6

28 The everlasting No.
Sartor Resartus (1834) bk. 2, ch. 7 (title)

29 Be no longer a chaos, but a world, or even
worldkin. Produce! Produce! Were it but the
pitifullest infinitesimal fraction of a product,
produce it in God's name! 'Tis the utmost thou
hast in thee: out with it, then.
Sartor Resartus (1834) bk. 2, ch. 9

30 Does it not stand on record that the English Queen
Elizabeth, receiving a deputation of eighteen
tailors, address them with a 'Good morning,
gentlemen both!'
Sartor Resartus (1834) bk. 3, ch. 11, quoting an imaginary
work by Diogenes Teufelsdröctch; see **Proverbs** 627:35

31 What a sad want I am in of libraries, of books to
gather facts from! Why is there not a Majesty's

library in every county town? There is a Majesty's jail and gallows in every one.
> diary, 18 May 1832

1 A good book is the purest essence of a human soul.
> speech in support of the London Library, 24 June 1840, in F. Harrison *Carlyle and the London Library* (1907)

2 'Gad! she'd better!'
> *on hearing that Margaret Fuller 'accept[ed] the universe'*
> William James *Varieties of Religious Experience* (1902) lecture 2

3 Macaulay is well for a while, but one wouldn't *live* under Niagara.
> R. M. Milnes *Notebook* (1838)

4 Cobden is an inspired bagman, who believes in a calico millennium.
> T. W. Reid *Life, Letters and Friendships of Richard Monckton* (1890) vol. 1, ch. 10

5 If Jesus Christ were to come to-day, people would not even crucify him. They would ask him to dinner, and hear what he had to say, and make fun of it.
> D. A. Wilson *Carlyle at his Zenith* (1927)

Stokely Carmichael 1941–98
American Black Power leader

6 The only position for women in SNCC is prone.
> *response to a question about the position of women*
> at a Student Nonviolent Coordinating Committee conference, November 1964

Stokely Carmichael 1941–98 and Charles Vernon Hamilton 1929–
American Black Power leaders

7 The adoption of the concept of Black Power is one of the most legitimate and healthy developments in American politics and race relations in our time. . . . It is a call for black people in this country to unite, to recognize their heritage, to build a sense of community. It is a call for black people to begin to define their own goals, to lead their own organizations and to support those organizations. It is a call to reject the racist institutions and values of this society.
> *Black Power* (1967)

Andrew Carnegie 1835–1919
American industrialist and philanthropist
see also **Proverbs** 620:31

8 The man who dies . . . rich dies disgraced.
> in *North American Review* June 1889 'Wealth'

9 The world's civilization started from the day on which everyone received reward for labour.
> *Autobiography* (1920)

Dale Carnegie 1888–1955
American writer and lecturer

10 How to win friends and influence people.
> title of book (1936)

Julia A. Carney 1823–1908

11 Little drops of water,
Little grains of sand,
Make the mighty ocean
And the beauteous land.
> 'Little Things' (1845)

Caroline of Ansbach 1683–1737
*German-born Queen of Great Britain and Ireland from 1727, wife of **George II***
see also **George II** 343:2

12 My dear firstborn is the greatest ass, and the greatest liar, and the greatest *canaille*, and the greatest beast in the whole world, and I heartily wish he was out of it.
> *of her eldest son, Frederick, Prince of Wales, father of **George III***
> in *Dictionary of National Biography* (1917–)

Joseph Edwards Carpenter 1813–85
English poet and songwriter

13 What are the wild waves saying
Sister, the whole day long,
That ever amid our playing,
I hear but their low lone song?
> 'What are the Wild Waves Saying?' (1850 song)

Emily Carr 1871–1945
Canadian artist

14 You come into the world alone and you go out of the world alone yet it seems to me you are more alone while living than even going and coming.
> *Hundreds and Thousands: The Journals of Emily Carr* (1966) 16 July 1933

15 A picture equals a movement in space.
> *Hundreds and Thousands: The Journals of Emily Carr* (1966) August 1935

J. L. Carr 1912–
English novelist

16 *You* have not had thirty years' experience . . . *You* have had one year's experience 30 times.
> *The Harpole Report* (1972)

Lewis Carroll (Charles Lutwidge Dodgson) 1832–98
English writer and logician

17 'What is the use of a book', thought Alice, 'without pictures or conversations?'
> *Alice's Adventures in Wonderland* (1865) ch. 1

18 'Curiouser and curiouser!' cried Alice.
> *Alice's Adventures in Wonderland* (1865) ch. 2

19 How doth the little crocodile
Improve his shining tail,
And pour the waters of the Nile
On every golden scale!
> *Alice's Adventures in Wonderland* (1865) ch. 2; see **Watts** 823:6

1 How cheerfully he seems to grin,
How neatly spreads his claws,
And welcomes little fishes in
With gently smiling jaws!
Alice's Adventures in Wonderland (1865) ch. 2

2 EVERYBODY has won, and all must have prizes.
Alice's Adventures in Wonderland (1865) ch. 3

3 'I'll be judge, I'll be jury,' said cunning old Fury;
'I'll try the whole cause, and condemn you to
death.'
Alice's Adventures in Wonderland (1865) ch. 3

4 'You are old, Father William,' the young man
said,
'And your hair has become very white;
And yet you incessantly stand on your head—
Do you think, at your age, it is right?'
Alice's Adventures in Wonderland (1865) ch. 5; see **Southey**
749:9

5 'I have answered three questions, and that is
enough,'
Said his father; 'don't give yourself airs!
Do you think I can listen all day to such stuff?
Be off, or I'll kick you downstairs!'
Alice's Adventures in Wonderland (1865) ch. 5; see
Bickerstaffe 115:20

6 'If everybody minded their own business,' said the
Duchess in a hoarse growl, 'the world would go
round a good deal faster than it does.'
Alice's Adventures in Wonderland (1865) ch. 6

7 Speak roughly to your little boy,
And beat him when he sneezes;
He only does it to annoy,
Because he knows it teases.
Alice's Adventures in Wonderland (1865) ch. 6

8 This time it vanished quite slowly, beginning with
the end of the tail, and ending with the grin,
which remained some time after the rest of it had
gone.
the Cheshire Cat
Alice's Adventures in Wonderland (1865) ch. 6

9 'Then you should say what you mean,' the March
Hare went on. 'I do,' Alice hastily replied; 'at
least—at least I mean what I say—that's the same
thing, you know.' 'Not the same thing a bit!' said
the Hatter. 'Why, you might just as well say that
"I see what I eat" is the same thing as "I eat what
I see!" '
Alice's Adventures in Wonderland (1865) ch. 7

10 Twinkle, twinkle, little bat!
How I wonder what you're at!
Up above the world you fly!
Like a teatray in the sky.
Alice's Adventures in Wonderland (1865) ch. 7; see **Taylor**
774:16

11 'Take some more tea,' the March Hare said to
Alice, very earnestly. 'I've had nothing yet,' Alice
replied in an offended tone, 'so I can't take more.'
'You mean you can't take *less*,' said the Hatter:
'it's very easy to take *more* than nothing.'
Alice's Adventures in Wonderland (1865) ch. 7

12 Off with her head!
the Queen of Hearts
Alice's Adventures in Wonderland (1865) ch. 8

13 Everything's got a moral, if you can only find it.
Alice's Adventures in Wonderland (1865) ch. 9

14 Take care of the sense, and the sounds will take
care of themselves.
Alice's Adventures in Wonderland (1865) ch. 9; see **Proverbs**
631:37

15 'That's nothing to what I could say if I chose,' the
Duchess replied.
Alice's Adventures in Wonderland (1865) ch. 9

16 'That's the reason they're called lessons,' the
Gryphon remarked: 'because they lessen from day
to day.'
Alice's Adventures in Wonderland (1865) ch. 9

17 'Will you walk a little faster?' said a whiting to a
snail,
'There's a porpoise close behind us, and he's
treading on my tail.'
Alice's Adventures in Wonderland (1865) ch. 10

18 Will you, won't you, will you, won't you, will you
join the dance?
Alice's Adventures in Wonderland (1865) ch. 10

19 'Tis the voice of the Lobster: I heard him declare
'You have baked me too brown, I must sugar my
hair.'
Alice's Adventures in Wonderland (1865) ch. 10; see **Watts**
823:12

20 Soup of the evening, beautiful Soup!
Alice's Adventures in Wonderland (1865) ch. 10

21 'Where shall I begin, please your Majesty?' he
asked. 'Begin at the beginning,' the King said,
gravely, 'and go on till you come to the end: then
stop.'
Alice's Adventures in Wonderland (1865) ch. 12

22 'That's not a regular rule: you invented it just
now.'
'It's the oldest rule in the book,' said the King.
'Then it ought to be Number One,' said Alice.
Alice's Adventures in Wonderland (1865) ch. 12

23 No! No! Sentence first—verdict afterwards.
Alice's Adventures in Wonderland (1865) ch. 12

24 What a comfort a Dictionary is!
Sylvie and Bruno Concluded (1893)

25 'Twas brillig, and the slithy toves
Did gyre and gimble in the wabe;
All mimsy were the borogoves,
And the mome raths outgrabe.
'Beware the Jabberwock, my son!
The jaws that bite, the claws that catch!'
Through the Looking-Glass (1872) ch. 1

26 And as in uffish thought he stood,
The Jabberwock, with eyes of flame,
Came whiffling through the tulgey wood,
And burbled as it came!
One, two! One, two! And through and through
The vorpal blade went snicker-snack!
He left it dead, and with its head

He went galumphing back.
'And hast thou slain the Jabberwock?
Come to my arms, my beamish boy!
O frabjous day! Callooh! Callay!'
He chortled in his joy.
Through the Looking-Glass (1872) ch. 1

1 Curtsey while you're thinking what to say. It saves time.
Through the Looking-Glass (1872) ch. 2

2 Now, *here*, you see, it takes all the running *you* can do, to keep in the same place. If you want to get somewhere else, you must run at least twice as fast as that!
Through the Looking-Glass (1872) ch. 2

3 Speak in French when you can't think of the English for a thing.
Through the Looking-Glass (1872) ch. 2

4 If you think we're wax-works, you ought to pay, you know. Wax-works weren't made to be looked at for nothing. Nohow!
Through the Looking-Glass (1872) ch. 4

5 'Contrariwise,' continued Tweedledee, 'if it was so, it might be; and if it were so, it would be: but as it isn't, it ain't. That's logic.'
Through the Looking-Glass (1872) ch. 4

6 The Walrus and the Carpenter
Were walking close at hand;
They wept like anything to see
Such quantities of sand:
'If this were only cleared away,'
They said, 'it would be grand!'

'If seven maids with seven mops
Swept it for half a year,
Do you suppose,' the Walrus said,
'That they could get it clear?'
'I doubt it,' said the Carpenter,
And shed a bitter tear.
Through the Looking-Glass (1872) ch. 4

7 'The time has come,' the Walrus said,
'To talk of many things:
Of shoes—and ships—and sealing wax—
Of cabbages—and kings—
And why the sea is boiling hot—
And whether pigs have wings.'
Through the Looking-Glass (1872) ch. 4

8 But answer came there none—
And this was scarcely odd because
They'd eaten every one.
Through the Looking-Glass (1872) ch. 4; see **Scott** 673:2

9 'You know,' he said very gravely, 'it's one of the most serious things that can possibly happen to one in a battle—to get one's head cut off.'
Through the Looking-Glass (1872) ch. 4

10 The rule is, jam to-morrow and jam yesterday—but never jam today.
Through the Looking-Glass (1872) ch. 5; see **Benn** 66:18

11 'It's a poor sort of memory that only works backwards,' the Queen remarked.
Through the Looking-Glass (1872) ch. 5

12 Why, sometimes I've believed as many as six impossible things before breakfast.
Through the Looking-Glass (1872) ch. 5

13 With a name like yours, you might be any shape, almost.
Through the Looking-Glass (1872) ch. 6

14 They gave it me,—for an un-birthday present.
Through the Looking-Glass (1872) ch. 6

15 'There's glory for you!' 'I don't know what you mean by "glory",' Alice said. 'I meant, "there's a nice knock-down argument for you!"' 'But "glory" doesn't mean "a nice knock-down argument",' Alice objected. 'When *I* use a word,' Humpty Dumpty said in a rather scornful tone, 'it means just what I choose it to mean—neither more nor less.'
Through the Looking-Glass (1872) ch. 6

16 'The question is,' said Humpty Dumpty, 'which is to be master—that's all.'
Through the Looking-Glass (1872) ch. 6; see **Shawcross** 727:28

17 You see it's like a portmanteau—there are two meanings packed up into one word.
Through the Looking-Glass (1872) ch. 6

18 'I can repeat poetry as well as other folk if it comes to that—' 'Oh, it needn't come to that!' Alice hastily said.
Through the Looking-Glass (1872) ch. 6

19 The little fishes of the sea,
They sent an answer back to me.
The little fishes' answer was
'We cannot do it, Sir, because—'
Through the Looking-Glass (1872) ch. 6

20 He's an Anglo-Saxon Messenger—and those are Anglo-Saxon attitudes.
Through the Looking-Glass (1872) ch. 7

21 The other Messenger's called Hatta. I must have *two* you know—to come and go. One to come, and one to go.
Through the Looking-Glass (1872) ch. 7

22 'There's nothing like eating hay when you're faint' . . . 'I didn't say there was nothing *better*,' the King replied, 'I said there was nothing *like* it.'
Through the Looking-Glass (1872) ch. 7

23 'I'm sure nobody walks much faster than I do!' 'He can't do that,' said the King, 'or else he'd have been here first.'
Through the Looking-Glass (1872) ch. 7

24 It's as large as life, and twice as natural!
Through the Looking-Glass (1872) ch. 7

25 It's my own invention.
the White Knight
Through the Looking-Glass (1872) ch. 8

26 I'll tell thee everything I can:
There's little to relate.
I saw an aged, aged man,
A-sitting on a gate.
Through the Looking-Glass (1872) ch. 8

27 He said, 'I look for butterflies
That sleep among the wheat:

I make them into mutton-pies,
And sell them in the street.'
Through the Looking-Glass (1872) ch. 8

1 Or madly squeeze a right-hand foot
Into a left-hand shoe.
Through the Looking-Glass (1872) ch. 8

2 No admittance till the week after next!
Through the Looking-Glass (1872) ch. 9

3 It isn't etiquette to cut any one you've been
introduced to. Remove the joint.
Through the Looking-Glass (1872) ch. 9

4 Un-dish-cover the fish, or dishcover the riddle.
Through the Looking-Glass (1872) ch. 9

5 What I tell you three times is true.
The Hunting of the Snark (1876) 'Fit the First: The Landing'

6 He would answer to 'Hi!' or to any loud cry,
Such as 'Fry me!' or 'Fritter-my-wig!'
The Hunting of the Snark (1876) 'Fit the First: The Landing'

7 His intimate friends called him 'Candle-ends',
And his enemies, 'Toasted-cheese'.
The Hunting of the Snark (1876) 'Fit the First: The Landing'

8 'What's the good of *Mercator's* North Poles and
Equators,
Tropics, Zones and Meridian lines?'
So the Bellman would cry: and the crew would
reply,
'They are merely conventional signs!'
The Hunting of the Snark (1876) 'Fit the Second: The
Bellman's Speech'

9 But the principal failing occurred in the sailing,
And the Bellman, perplexed and distressed,
Said he *had* hoped, at least, when the wind blew
due East,
That the ship would *not* travel due West!
The Hunting of the Snark (1876) 'Fit the Second: The
Bellman's Speech'

10 But oh, beamish nephew, beware of the day,
If your Snark be a Boojum! For then
You will softly and suddenly vanish away,
And never be met with again!
The Hunting of the Snark (1876) 'Fit the Third: The Baker's
Tale'

11 They sought it with thimbles, they sought it with
care;
They pursued it with forks and hope;
They threatened its life with a railway-share;
They charmed it with smiles and soap.
The Hunting of the Snark (1876) 'Fit the Fifth: The Beaver's
Lesson'

12 For the Snark *was* a Boojum, you see.
The Hunting of the Snark (1876) 'Fit the Eighth: The
Vanishing'

13 I never loved a dear Gazelle—
Nor anything that cost me much:
High prices profit those who sell,
But why should I be fond of such?
Phantasmagoria (1869) 'Theme with Variations'; see **Moore**
547:20

14 He thought he saw an Elephant,
That practised on a fife:
He looked again, and found it was

A letter from his wife.
'At length I realize,' he said,
'The bitterness of life!'
Sylvie and Bruno (1889) ch. 5

15 He thought he saw a Rattlesnake
That questioned him in Greek,
He looked again and found it was
The Middle of Next Week.
'The one thing I regret,' he said,
'Is that it cannot speak!'
Sylvie and Bruno (1889) ch. 6

16 Long and painful experience has taught me one
great principle in managing business for other
people, viz., if you want to inspire confidence, *give*
plenty of statistics.
C. L. Dodgson *Three Years in a Curatorship by One Whom It
Has Tried* (1886)

William Herbert Carruth 1859–1924

17 Some call it evolution,
And others call it God.
'Each In His Own Tongue' (1908)

Edward Carson 1854–1935
British lawyer and politician

18 I now enter into compact with you, and with the
help of God you and I joined together . . . will yet
defeat the most nefarious conspiracy that has ever
been hatched against a free people . . . We must be
prepared . . . the morning Home Rule passes,
ourselves to become responsible for the
government of the Protestant Province of Ulster.
speech at Craigavon, 23 September 1911

19 From the day I first entered parliament up to the
present, devotion to the union has been the
guiding star of my political life.
in *Dictionary of National Biography* (1917–)

Rachel Carson 1907–64
American zoologist

20 Over increasingly large areas of the United States,
spring now comes unheralded by the return of the
birds, and the early mornings are strangely silent
where once they were filled with the beauty of
bird song.
The Silent Spring (1962)

Angela Carter 1940–92
English novelist

21 Comedy is tragedy that happens to *other* people.
Wise Children (1991) ch. 4

22 If *Miss* means respectably unmarried, and *Mrs*
respectably married, then *Ms* means nudge,
nudge, wink, wink.
'The Language of Sisterhood' in Christopher Ricks (ed.) *The
State of the Language* (1980); see **Monty Python's Flying
Circus** 546:6

Henry Carter d. 1806

23 True patriots we; for be it understood,
We left our country for our country's good . . .

And none will doubt but that our emigration
Has proved most useful to the British nation.
*prologue, written for, but not recited at, the opening of
the Playhouse, Sydney, New South Wales, 16
January 1796, when the actors were principally
convicts*

> A. W. Jose and H. J. Carter (eds.) *The Australian
> Encyclopaedia* (1927); previously attributed to George
> Barrington (b. 1755); see **Fitzgeffrey** 322:23

Howard Carter 1874–1939

English archaeologist

1 Yes, wonderful things.
*when asked what he could see on first looking into the
tomb of Tutankhamun, 26 November 1922; his
notebook records the words as 'Yes, it is wonderful'*

> *The Tomb of Tut-ankh-amen* (1933)

James Earl 'Jimmy' Carter 1924–

*American Democratic statesman, 39th President of the US,
1977–81*

2 I'm Jimmy Carter, and I'm going to be your next
president.
I'll Never Lie to You (1976); see **Gore** 357:1

3 I've looked on a lot of women with lust. I've
committed adultery in my heart many times. This
is something that God recognizes I will do—and I
have done it—and God forgives me for it.
in Playboy November 1976

Sydney Carter 1915–2004

English folk-song writer

4 It's God they ought to crucify
Instead of you and me,
I said to the carpenter
A-hanging on the tree.
'Friday Morning' (1967)

5 I danced in the morning
When the world was begun
And I danced in the moon
And the stars and the sun
And I came down from heaven
And I danced on the earth—
At Bethlehem I had my birth.
Dance then wherever you may be,
I am the Lord of the Dance, said he,
And I'll lead you all, wherever you may be
And I'll lead you all in the dance, said he.
'Lord of the Dance' (1967)

6 One more step along the world I go.
'One More Step'

Jacques Cartier 1491–1557

French navigator and explorer

7 *J'estime mieux que autrement, que c'est la terre que
Dieu donne à Caïn.*
I am rather inclined to believe that this is the land
God gave to Cain.
*on discovering the northern shore of the Gulf of St
Lawrence (now Labrador and Quebec) in 1534; after*

the murder of Abel, Cain was exiled to the desolate
land of Nod (*see* **Bible** 76:2)

> La Première Relation; H. P. Biggar (ed.) *The Voyages of
> Jacques Cartier* (1924)

Henri Cartier-Bresson 1908–

French photographer and artist

8 The decisive moment.
title of book (1952); see **Retz** 645:11

9 To me, photography is the simultaneous
recognition, in a fraction of a second, of the
significance of an event as well as of a precise
organisation of forms which give that event its
proper expression.
The Decisive Moment (1952)

Barbara Cartland 1901–2000

English writer

10 After forty a woman has to choose between losing
her figure or her face. My advice is to keep your
face, and stay sitting down.
Libby Purves 'Luncheon à la Cartland'; in *The Times* 6
October 1993; similar remarks have been attributed since
c.1980

□ Cartoon captions

see box overleaf

John Cartwright 1740–1824

English political reformer

11 One man shall have one vote.
The People's Barrier Against Undue Influence (1780) ch. 1
'Principles, maxims, and primary rules of politics' no. 68

Elizabeth Tanfield Cary 1585–1639

English woman of letters, poet, and dramatist

12 I know I could enchain him with a smile:
And lead him captive with a gentle word,
I scorn my look should ever man beguile,
Or other speech, than meaning to afford.
The Tragedy of Mariam (1613)

Joyce Cary 1888–1957

Irish novelist and short-story writer

13 Sara could commit adultery at one end and weep
for her sins at the other, and enjoy both
operations at once.
The Horse's Mouth (1944)

Giovanni Jacopo Casanova see Last
words 472:7

Roger Casement 1864–1916

Irish nationalist; executed for treason in 1916
on Casement: see **Yeats** 854:10

14 Self-government is our right, a thing born in us at
birth, a thing no more to be doled out to us, or
Continued

Cartoon captions

1 Fog in Channel—Continent isolated.

> newspaper placard in cartoon, *Round the Bend with Brockbank* (1948) by the British cartoonist Russell Brockbank (1913–); the phrase 'Continent isolated' was quoted as already current by John Gunther *Inside Europe* (1938)

2 It's a naïve domestic Burgundy without any breeding, but I think you'll be amused by its presumption.

> caption in *New Yorker* 27 March 1937, by James **Thurber**

3 MOTHER: It's broccoli, dear.
CHILD: I say it's spinach, and I say the hell with it.

> cartoon caption in *New Yorker* 8 December 1928

4 It's our *own* story *exactly*! He bold as a hawk, she soft as the dawn.

> caption in *New Yorker* 25 February 1939, by James **Thurber**; see **Lover** 493:13

5 The man who . . .

> *illustrating social gaffes resulting from snobbery*
> opening words of the caption for a series of cartoons (first appearing in 1912) by H. M. Bateman (1887–1970)

6 No son—they're not the same—devolution takes longer.

> *father to his son, who is reading a book on evolution*
> caption to cartoon by Scottish cartoonist Ewen Bain (1925–89) in *Scots Independent* January 1978

7 On the Internet, nobody knows you're a dog.

> cartoon caption in *New Yorker* 5 July 1993, by the American cartoonist Peter Steiner (1940–)

8 The price of petrol has been raised by a penny. Official.

> *a torpedoed sailor with oil-stained face lying on a raft; the message was intended to be a warning against wasting petrol, but it was taken by some as suggesting that lives were being put at risk for profit*
> caption in *Daily Mirror* 3 March 1942; cartoon by Philip Zec (1909–83) and caption by 'Cassandra' (William Connor, 1909–67).

9 We have met the enemy and he is us.

> *the cartoon-strip character, Pogo the opossum, looking at litter under a tree; used as an Earth Day poster in 1971*
> Pogo cartoon, 1970, by the American cartoonist Walt Kelly (1913–73); see **Perry** 593:5

10 Well, if I called the wrong number, why did you answer the phone?

> caption in *New Yorker* 5 June 1937, by James **Thurber**

11 Well, if you knows of a better 'ole, go to it.

> *Old Bill and a friend in a shellhole under fire*
> caption in *Fragments from France* (1915), by the British cartoonist Bruce Bairnsfather (1888–1959)

Roger Casement *continued*

withheld from us, by another people than the right to life itself—than the right to feel the sun, or smell the flowers, or to love our kind.

> statement at the conclusion of his trial, the Old Bailey, London, 29 June 1916

12 Where all your rights become only an accumulated wrong; where men must beg with bated breath for leave to subsist in their own land, to think their own thoughts, to sing their own songs, to garner the fruits of their own labours . . . then surely it is a braver, a saner and truer thing, to be a rebel in act and deed against such circumstances as these than tamely to accept it as the natural lot of men.

> statement at the conclusion of his trial, the Old Bailey, London, 29 June 1916

Johnny Cash 1932–2003
American singer and songwriter

13 It was a real slow walk in a real sad rain.

> 'Drive On' (1993)

A. M. Cassandre 1901–68
French illustrator

14 A good poster is a visual telegram.

> attributed

Mary Cassatt 1844–1926
American artist

15 Why do people so love to wander? I think the civilized parts of the world will suffice for me in the future.

> letter to Louisine Havemeyer, 11 February 1911

Hugh Casson 1910–
English architect

16 We have now to plan no longer for soft little animals pottering about on their own two legs, but for hard steel canisters hurtling about with these same little animals inside them.

> C. Williams-Ellis *Around the World in 90 Years* (1978)

Barbara Castle 1910–2002
British Labour politician

17 I will fight for what I believe in until I drop dead. And that's what keeps you alive.

> in *Guardian* 14 January 1998

Ted Castle 1907–79
British journalist

18 In place of strife.

> *title of Government White Paper, 17 January 1969, suggested by Castle to his wife, Barbara* **Castle***, then Secretary of State for Employment*
> Barbara Castle, diary, 15 January 1969

Fidel Castro 1927–

Cuban statesman, Prime Minister 1959–76 and President since 1976

1 *La historia me absolverá.*

History will absolve me.
title of pamphlet (1953)

2 Capitalism is using its money; we socialists throw it away.
in *Observer* 8 November 1964 'Sayings of the Week'

Edward Caswall 1814–78

English hymn-writer

3 Jesu, the very thought of Thee
With sweetness fills the breast.
translation of 'Jesu dulcis memoria, dans vera cordis gaudia', *usually attributed to St* **Bernard**
'Jesu, the very thought of thee' (1849 hymn)

4 My God, I love Thee; not because
I hope for heaven thereby.
'My God, I Love Thee' (1849 hymn); translation of '*O deus ego amo te, nec amo te ut salves me*'; usually attributed to St Francis Xavier (1506–52)

5 See, amid the winter's snow,
Born for us on earth below,
See, the Lamb of God appears,
Promised from eternal years!

Hail, thou ever-blessèd morn!
Hail, redemption's happy dawn!
Sing through all Jerusalem:
Christ is born in Bethlehem!
'See, amid the winter's snow' (1858 hymn)

6 When morning gilds the skies.
Title of hymn (1854)

☐ Catchphrases

see box overleaf
see also **Laurel** 470:8

A Catechism of Christian Doctrine 1898

Popularly known as the 'Penny Catechism'

7 Who made you? God made me.
Why did God make you? God made me to know Him, love him, and serve Him in this world, and to be happy with Him for ever in the next.
ch. 1

Willa Cather 1873–1947

American novelist

8 Oh, the Germans classify, but the French arrange!
Death Comes For the Archbishop (1927)

9 Where there is great love there are always miracles.
Death Comes for the Archbishop (1927)

10 Men travel faster now, but I do not know if they go to better things.
Death Comes for the Archbishop (1927)

11 That is happiness: to be dissolved into something complete and great.
on her gravestone in Jaffrey, New Hampshire
My Ántonia (1918) bk 1, ch 2

12 Winter lies too long in country towns; hangs on until it is stale and shabby, old and sullen.
My Ántonia (1918) bk 2, ch 7

13 I like trees because they seem more resigned to the way they have to live than other things do.
O Pioneers! (1913) pt. 2, ch. 4

14 I tell you there is such a thing as creative hate!
The Song of the Lark (1915)

Catherine the Great 1729–96

Russian monarch, Empress from 1762

15 *Moi, je serai autocrate: c'est mon métier. Et le bon Dieu me pardonnera: c'est son métier.*

I shall be an autocrat: that's my trade. And the good Lord will forgive me: that's his.
attributed; see **Last words** 471:9

Cato the Elder (or 'the Censor') 234–149 BC

Roman statesman, orator, and writer

16 *Delenda est Carthago.*

Carthage must be destroyed.
words concluding every speech Cato made in the Senate
Pliny the Elder *Naturalis Historia* bk. 15, ch. 74

17 A farm is like a man—however great the income, if there is extravagance but little is left.
On Agriculture bk 2, sect. 6

18 Even though work stops, expenses run on.
On Agriculture bk 39, sect. 2

19 *Rem tene; verba sequentur.*

Grasp the subject, the words will follow.
Caius Julius Victor *Ars Rhetorica* 'De inventione'

Carrie Chapman Catt 1859–1947

American feminist

20 No written law has ever been more binding than unwritten custom supported by popular opinion.
speech at Senate hearing on woman's suffrage, 13 February 1900
Why We Ask for the Submission of an Amendment (1900)

21 When a just cause reaches its flood-tide . . . whatever stands in the way must fall before its overwhelming power.
speech at Stockholm, Is Woman Suffrage Progressing? (1911)

Catullus c.84–c.54 BC

Roman poet
on Catullus: see **Tennyson** 777:1

22 *Cui dono lepidum novum libellum
Arido modo pumice expolitum?*

To whom shall I give my nice new little book polished dry with pumice?
Carmina no. 1

Continued

Catchphrases

1 CECIL: After you, Claude.
CLAUDE: No, after you, Cecil.
> *ITMA* (BBC radio programme, 1939–49), written by Ted Kavanagh (1892–1958)

2 And now for something completely different.
> *Monty Python's Flying Circus* (BBC TV programme, 1969–74)

3 Anyone for tennis?
> said to be typical of drawing-room comedies, much associated with Humphrey Bogart (1899–1957); perhaps from George Bernard Shaw 'Anybody on for a game of tennis?' *Misalliance* (1914)

4 Are you sitting comfortably? Then I'll begin.
sometimes 'Then we'll begin'
> *Listen with Mother* (BBC radio programme for children, 1950–82), used by Julia Lang (1921–)

5 The butler did it!
a solution for detective stories
> Nigel Rees, in *Sayings of the Century* (1984), quotes a correspondent who recalls hearing it at a cinema *c.*1916 but the origin of the phrase has not been traced

6 Can I do you now, sir?
spoken by 'Mrs Mopp'
> *ITMA* (BBC radio programme, 1939–49), written by Ted Kavanagh (1892–1958)

7 Can you hear me, mother?
> used by Sandy Powell (1900–82)

8 Come on! Come on!
> habitual adjuration by Jeremy **Paxman** to contestants on *University Challenge* on BBC2 (1994–)

9 The day war broke out.
customary preamble to radio monologues in the role of a Home Guard
> used by Robb Wilton (1881–1957) from *c.*1940

10 Didn't she [*or* he *or* they] do well?
> used by Bruce Forsyth (1928–) in 'The Generation Game' on BBC Television, 1973 onwards

11 Does my bum look big in this?
> used by Arabella Weir in *The Fast Show* on BBC Television 1994–97

12 Don't forget the diver.
spoken by 'The Diver'; based on 'a memory of the pier at New Brighton where Tommy Handley used to go as a child . . . A man in a bathing suit . . . whined "Don't forget the diver, sir."'
> *ITMA* (BBC radio programme, 1939–49), written by Ted Kavanagh (1892–1958)

13 Don't have nightmares. Do sleep well.
> habitual closing words for BBC1's *Crimewatch* (1984–), spoken by Nick Ross

14 Eat my shorts!
> *The Simpsons* (American TV series, 1990–), created by Matt Groening

15 Ee, it was agony, Ivy.
> *Ray's a Laugh* (BBC radio programme, 1949–61), written by Ted Ray (1906–77)

16 Evening, all.
> opening words spoken by Jack Warner as Sergeant Dixon in *Dixon of Dock Green* (BBC television series, 1956–76), written by Ted Willis (1918–)

17 Everybody wants to get inta the act!
> used by Jimmy Durante (1893–1980)

18 An everyday story of country folk.
> introduction to *The Archers* (BBC radio serial, 1950 onwards), written by Geoffrey Webb and Edward J. Mason

19 George—don't do that.
> used by Joyce **Grenfell** as a recurring line in monologues about a nursery school, from the 1950s

20 Give him the money, Barney.
> *Have a Go!* (BBC radio quiz programme, 1946–67), used by Wilfred Pickles (1904–78)

21 A good idea—son.
> *Educating Archie*, 1950–3 BBC radio comedy series, written by Eric Sykes (1923–) and Max Bygraves (1922–)

22 Good morning, sir—was there something?
> used by Sam Costa in radio comedy series *Much-Binding-in-the-Marsh*, written by Richard Murdoch (1907–90) and Kenneth Horne (1900–69), started 2 January 1947

23 Goodnight, children . . . everywhere.
closing words normally spoken by 'Uncle Mac' in the 1930s and 1940s
> on *Children's Hour* (BBC Radio programme); written by Derek McCulloch (1892–1978)

24 Have you read any good books lately?
> used by Richard Murdoch in radio comedy series *Much-Binding-in-the-Marsh*, written by Richard Murdoch (1907–90) and Kenneth Horne (1900–69), started 2 January 1947

25 Hello, good evening, and welcome.
> used by David **Frost** in 'The Frost Programme' on BBC Television, 1966 onwards

26 Here come de judge.
> from the song-title 'Here comes the judge' (1968); written by Dewey 'Pigmeat' Markham, Dick Alen, Bob Astor, and Sarah Harvey

27 Here's one I made earlier.
culmination to directions for making a model out of empty yoghurt pots, coat-hangers, and similar domestic items
> children's BBC television programme *Blue Peter*, 1963 onwards

28 He shoots! He scores!
> used by Foster William Hewitt (1902–85), Canadian broadcaster, at ice-hockey games; first said over the radio 4 April 1933 at the game between the Toronto Maple Leafs and the Boston Bruins

29 I didn't get where I am today without . . . .
> used by the manager C. J. in BBC television series *The Fall and Rise of Reginald Perrin*, 1976–80); based on David Nobbs *The Death of Reginald Perrin* (1975)

▶

▶ Catchphrases *continued*

1 I don't like this game, let's play another game— let's play doctor and nurses.

phrase first used by Bluebottle in 'The Phantom Head-Shaver' in *The Goon Show* (BBC radio series) 15 October 1954, written by Spike **Milligan**; the catchphrase was often 'I do not like this game'

2 I don't mind if I do.

spoken by 'Colonel Chinstrap'

ITMA (BBC radio programme, 1939–49), written by Ted Kavanagh (1892–1958)

3 I go—I come back.

spoken by 'Ali Oop'

ITMA (BBC radio programme, 1939–49), written by Ted Kavanagh (1892–1958)

4 I have a cunning plan.

Baldrick's habitual overoptimistic promise in *Blackadder II* (1987 television series), written by Richard Curtis and Ben Elton (1959–)

5 I'm Bart Simpson: who the hell are you?

The Simpsons (American TV series, 1990–), created by Matt Groening

6 I'm in charge.

used by Bruce Forsyth (1928–) in 'Sunday Night at the London Palladium' on ITV, 1958 onwards

7 I'm worried about Jim.

frequent line in *Mrs Dale's Diary*, BBC radio series 1948–69

8 It all depends what you mean by . . .

habitually used by C. E. M. Joad (1891–1953) when replying to questions on 'The Brains Trust' (formerly 'Any Questions'), BBC radio (1941–8)

9 It's a good thing.

customary form of approbation in the areas of home decorating and cooking from US businesswoman Martha Stewart (1941–)

10 It's being so cheerful as keeps me going.

spoken by 'Mona Lott'

ITMA (BBC radio programme, 1939–49), written by Ted Kavanagh (1892–1958)

11 I've arrived and to prove it I'm here!

Educating Archie, 1950–3 BBC radio comedy series, written by Eric Sykes (1923–) and Max Bygraves (1922–)

12 I've started so I'll finish.

said when a contestant's time runs out while a question is being put

Magnus Magnusson (1929–) *Mastermind*, BBC television (1972–97)

13 Just like that!

used by Tommy Cooper (1921–84)

14 Keep on truckin'.

used by Robert Crumb (1943–) in cartoons from *c.*1972

15 Left hand down a bit!

The Navy Lark (BBC radio series, 1959–77), written by Laurie Wyman

16 Let's be careful out there.

Hill Street Blues (television series, 1981 onwards), written by Steven Bochco and Michael Kozoll

17 Meredith, we're in!

originating in a stage sketch by Fred Kitchen (1872–1950), *The Bailiff* (1907); J. P. Gallagher *Fred Karno* (1971) ch. 9

18 Mind my bike!

used by Jack Warner (1895–1981) in the BBC radio series *Garrison Theatre*, 1939 onwards

19 Nice to see you—to see you, nice.

used by Bruce Forsyth (1928–) in 'The Generation Game' on BBC Television, 1973 onwards

20 Oh, calamity!

used by Robertson Hare (1891–1979)

21 Ohhh, I don't *believe* it!

Victor Meldrew in *One Foot in the Grave* (BBC television series, 1989–), written by David Renwick

22 Once again we stop the mighty roar of London's traffic.

In Town Tonight (BBC radio series, 1933–60) preamble

23 Pass the sick bag, Alice.

used by John **Junor**; in *Sunday Express* and elsewhere, from 1980 or earlier

24 Phone a friend.

advice to contestants by Chris Tarrant, host of the ITV quiz show *Who Wants to be a Millionaire* (1998–)

25 Seriously, though, he's doing a grand job!

popularized by David **Frost** in 'That Was The Week That Was', on BBC Television, 1962–3; originally deriving from a sketch written for Roy Kinnear

26 Shome mishtake, shurely?

in *Private Eye* magazine, 1980s

27 So farewell then . . .

frequent opening of poems by 'E. J. Thribb' in Private Eye magazine, usually as an obituary

1970s onwards

28 Take me to your leader.

from science-fiction stories

29 The truth is out there.

The X Files (American television series, 1993–), created by Chris Carter

30 Very interesting . . . but stupid.

Rowan and Martin's Laugh-In (American television series, 1967–73), written by Dan Rowan (1922–87) and Dick Martin (1923–)

31 The weekend starts here.

Ready, Steady, Go, British television series, *c.*1963

32 We have ways of making you talk.

perhaps originating in the line 'We have ways of making men talk' in *Lives of a Bengal Lancer* (1935 film), written by Waldemar Young et al.

33 What's up, Doc?

Bugs Bunny cartoons, written by Tex Avery (1907–80) from *c.*1940

34 Who loves ya, baby?

used by Telly Savalas (1926–) in American TV series *Kojak* (1973–8)

▶

▶ Catchprases *continued*

1 Without hesitation, deviation, or repetition.
instruction for contestants' monologues on the panel show Just a Minute *(BBC Radio, 1967–)*

2 You are the weakest link . . . goodbye.
catchphrase used by Anne Robinson on the television game-show The Weakest Link *(2000–)*

3 You bet your sweet bippy.
Rowan and Martin's Laugh-In (American television series, 1967–73), written by Dan Rowan (1922–87) and Dick Martin (1923–)

4 You might very well think that. I couldn't possibly comment.
the Chief Whip's habitual response to questioning House of Cards *(televised 1990); written by Michael Dobbs (1948–)*

5 You're going to like this . . . not a lot . . . but you'll like it!
used by Paul Daniels (1938–) in his conjuring act, especially on television from 1981 onwards

6 You rotten swines. I told you I'd be deaded.
phrase first used by Bluebottle in 'Hastings Flyer' in The Goon Show *(BBC radio series) 3 January 1956, written by Spike* **Milligan**

7 Your starter for ten.
phrase often used by Bamber Gascoigne (1935–) in University Challenge *(ITV quiz series, 1962–87)*

8 You silly twisted boy.
phrase first used in 'The Dreaded Batter Pudding Hurler' in The Goon Show *(BBC radio series) 12 October 1954, written by Spike* **Milligan**

Catullus *continued*

9   *Namque tu solebas*
Meas esse aliquid putare nugas.

For you used to think my trifles were worth something.
Carmina no. 1

10 *Plus uno maneat perenne saeclo.*

May it live and last for more than a century.
Carmina no. 1

11 *Lugete, O Veneres Cupidinesque,*
Et quantum est hominum venustiorum.
Passer mortuus est meae puellae,
Passer, deliciae meae puellae.

Mourn, you powers of Charm and Desire, and all you who are endowed with charm. My lady's sparrow is dead, the sparrow which was my lady's darling.
Carmina no. 3; see **Millay** *526:21*

12 *Qui nunc it per iter tenebricosum*
Illuc, unde negant redire quemquam.

Now he goes along the darksome road, thither whence they say no one returns.
Carmina no. 4

13 *Vivamus, mea Lesbia, atque amemus,*
Rumoresque senum severiorum
Omnes unius aestimemus assis.
Soles occidere et redire possunt:
Nobis cum semel occidit brevis lux
Nox est perpetua una dormienda.

Let us live, my Lesbia, and let us love, and let us reckon all the murmurs of more censorious old men as worth one farthing. Suns can set and come again: for us, when once our brief light has set, one everlasting night is to be slept.
Carmina no. 5; see **Campion** *187:23,* **Jonson** *435:18, 435:20*

14 *Da mi basia mille, deinde centum,*
Dein mille altera, dein secunda centum,
Deinde usque altera mille, deinde centum.

Give me a thousand kisses, then a hundred, then another thousand, then a second hundred, then yet another thousand, then a hundred.
Carmina no. 5

15 *Miser Catulle, desinas ineptire,*
Et quod vides perisse perditum ducas.

Poor Catullus, drop your silly fancies, and what you see is lost let it be lost.
Carmina no. 8

16 *Paene insularum, Sirmio, insularumque Ocelle.*

Sirmio, bright eye of peninsulas and islands.
Carmina no. 31; see **Tennyson** *777:1*

17 *Nam risu inepto res ineptior nulla est.*

For there is nothing sillier than a silly laugh.
Carmina no. 39; see **Chesterfield** *215:7,* **Congreve** *238:15*

18 *Iam ver egelidos refert tepores.*

Now Spring restores balmy warmth.
Carmina no. 46

19 *Gratias tibi maximas Catullus*
Agit pessimus omnium poeta,
Tanto pessimus omnium poeta,
Quanto tu optimus omnium's patronum.

Catullus gives you warmest thanks,
And he the worst of poets ranks;
As much the worst of bards confessed,
As you of advocates the best.
letter of thanks to **Cicero**
Carmina no. 49 (translated by Sir William Marris)

20 *Ille mi par esse deo videtur,*
Ille, si fas est, superare divos,
Qui sedens adversus identidem te
Spectat et audit
Dulce ridentem, misero quod omnis
Eripit sensus mihi.

Like a god he seems to me, above the gods, if so may be, who sitting often close to you may see and hear you sweetly laughing, which snatches away all the senses from poor me.
Carmina no. 51 (a translation of Sappho); see **Sappho** *666:14*

1 *Caeli, Lesbia nostra, Lesbia illa,*
Illa Lesbia, quam Catullus unam
Plus quam se atque suos amavit omnes,
Nunc in quadriviis et angiportis
Glubit magnanimos Remi nepotes.

O Caelius, our Lesbia, that Lesbia whom Catullus
once loved uniquely, more than himself and more
than all his own, now at the crossroads and in the
alleyways has it off with the high-minded
descendants of Remus.
  Carmina no. 58

2 *Ut flos in saeptis secretus nascitur hortis,*
Ignotus pecori, nullo contusus aratro,
Quem mulcent aurae, firmat sol, educat imber;
Multi illum pueri, multae optavere puellae.

As a flower grows concealed in an enclosed
garden, unknown to the cattle, bruised by no
plough, and which the breezes caress, the sun
makes strong, and the rain brings out; many boys
and many girls long for it.
  Carmina no. 62

3 *Sed mulier cupido quod dicit amanti,*
In vento et rapida scribere oportet aqua.

But what a woman says to her lusting lover it is
best to write in wind and swift-flowing water.
  Carmina no. 70

4 *Desine de quoquam quicquam bene velle mereri,*
Aut aliquem fieri posse putare pium.

Give up wanting to deserve any thanks from
anyone, or thinking that anybody can be grateful.
  Carmina no. 73

5 *Siqua recordanti benefacta priora voluptas*
Est homini, cum se cogitat esse pium.

If a man can take any pleasure in recalling the
thought of kindnesses done, when he thinks that
he has been a true friend.
  Carmina no. 76

6 *Difficile est longum subito deponere amorem.*
Difficile est, verum hoc qualubet efficias.

It is difficult suddenly to lay aside a long-cherished
love. It is difficult; but you should accomplish it,
one way or another.
  Carmina no. 76

7 *Si vitam puriter egi.*

If I have led a pure life.
  Carmina no. 76

8 *O di, reddite mi hoc pro pietate mea.*

O gods, grant me this in return for my piety.
  Carmina no. 76

9 *Odi et amo: quare id faciam, fortasse requiris.*
Nescio, sed fieri sentio et excrucior.

I hate and I love: why I do so you may well ask. I
do not know, but I feel it happen and am in
agony.
  Carmina no. 85

10 *Multas per gentes et multa per aequora vectus*
Advenio has miseras, frater, ad inferias,
Ut te postremo donarem munere mortis
Et mutam nequiquam alloquerer cinerem . . .

Nunc tamen interea haec prisco quae more parentum
Tradita sunt tristi munere ad inferias,
Accipe fraterno multum manantia fletu,
Atque in perpetuum, frater, ave atque vale.

By many lands and over many a wave
I come, my brother, to your piteous grave,
To bring you the last offering in death
And o'er dumb dust expend an idle breath . . .
Yet take these gifts, brought as our fathers bade
For sorrow's tribute to the passing shade;
A brother's tears have wet them o'er and o'er;
And so, my brother, hail, and farewell evermore!
  Carmina no. 101 (translated by Sir William Marris); see
  Tennyson 777:1

11 *At non effugies meos iambos.*

But you shall not escape my iambics.
  R. A. B. Mynors (ed.) *Catulli Carmina* (1958) Fragment 3

Charles Causley 1917-
English poet and schoolmaster

12 Watch where he comes walking
Out of the Christmas flame,
Dancing, double-talking:
Herod is his name.
  'Innocents' Song' (1961)

13 Timothy Winters comes to school
With eyes as wide as a football-pool,
Ears like bombs and teeth like splinters:
A blitz of a boy is Timothy Winters.
  'Timothy Winters' (1957)

Constantine Cavafy 1863–1933
Greek poet

14 Body, remember not only how much you were
    loved,
not only the beds you lay on,
but also those desires glowing openly
in eyes that looked at you,
trembling for you in voices.
  'Body, Remember' (1918)

15 When you set out for Ithaka
ask that your way be long.
  'Ithaka' (1911) (translated by E. Keeley and P. Sherrard)

16 Ithaka gave you the splendid journey.
Without her you would not have set out.
She hasn't anything else to give you.
  'Ithaka' (1911)

17 What are we waiting for, gathered in the market-
    place?
The barbarians are to arrive today.
  'Waiting for the Barbarians' (1904) (translated by E.
  Keeley and P. Sherrard)

18 And now, what will become of us without the
    barbarians?
Those people were a kind of solution.
  'Waiting for the Barbarians' (1904)

19 New places you will not find, you will not find
    another sea
The city will follow you.
  'The Town' (1911) (translated by E. Keeley and P.
  Sherrard)

Edith Cavell 1865–1915

English nurse, executed by the Germans for assisting in the escape of British soldiers from occupied Belgium

1 Standing, as I do, in view of God and eternity, I realize that patriotism is not enough. I must have no hatred or bitterness towards anyone.
   on the eve of her execution
      in *The Times* 23 October 1915

Margaret Cavendish (Duchess of Newcastle) c.1624–74

English woman of letters

2 Greek, Latin poets, I could never read,
   Nor their historians, but our English Speed;
   I could not steal their wit, nor plots out take;
   All my plays' plots, my own poor brain did make.
   Plays (1662) 'To the Readers'

3 Marriage is the grave or tomb of wit.
   Plays (1662) 'Nature's Three Daughters' pt. 2, act 5, sc. 20

4 If Nature had not befriended us with beauty, and other good graces, to help us to insinuate our selves into men's affections, we should have been more enslaved than any other of Nature's creatures she hath made.
   Sociable Letters (1664)

5 But for the most part, women are not educated as they should be, I mean those of quality; oft their education is only to dance, sing, and fiddle, to write complimental letters, to read romances, to speak some languages that is not their native . . . their parents take more care of their feet than their head, more of their words than their reason.
   Sociable Letters (1664)

Count Cavour (Camillo Benso di Cavour) 1810–61

Italian statesman

6 We are ready to proclaim throughout Italy this great principle: a free church in a free state.
   speech, 27 March 1861, in William de la Rive *Reminiscences of the Life and Character of Count Cavour* (1862) ch. 13

William Caxton c.1421–91

first English printer

7 The worshipful father and first founder and embellisher of ornate eloquence in our English, I mean Master Geoffrey Chaucer.
   Caxton's edition (c.1478) of Chaucer's translation of Boethius *De Consolacione Philosophie* epilogue

8 It is notoriously known through the universal world that there be nine worthy and the best that ever were. That is to wit three paynims, three Jews, and three Christian men. As for the paynims they were . . . the first Hector of Troy . . . the second Alexander the Great; and the third Julius Caesar . . . As for the three Jews . . . the first was Duke Joshua . . . the second David, King of Jerusalem; and the third Judas Maccabaeus . . .

And sith the said Incarnation . . . was first the noble Arthur . . . The second was Charlemagne or Charles the Great . . . and the third and last was Godfrey of Bouillon.
   Thomas Malory *Le Morte D'Arthur* (1485) prologue

9 I, according to my copy, have done set it in imprint, to the intent that noble men may see and learn the noble acts of chivalry, the gentle and virtuous deeds that some knights used in those days.
   Thomas Malory *Le Morte D'Arthur* (1485) prologue

Nicolae Ceauşescu 1918–89

Romanian Communist statesman, first President of the Socialist Republic of Romania 1974–89

10 Fidel Castro is right. You do not quieten your enemy by talking with him like a priest, but by burning him.
   at a Communist Party meeting 17 December 1989
      in *Guardian* 11 January 1990

Lord Edward Cecil 1867–1918

British soldier and civil servant

11 An agreement between two men to do what both agree is wrong.
   definition of a compromise
      letter, 3 September 1911; Kenneth Rose *The Later Cecils* (1975) ch. 7

Lord Hugh Cecil 1869–1956

British Conservative politician and clergyman, Provost of Eton

12 There is no more ungraceful figure than that of a humanitarian with an eye to the main chance.
   in *The Times* 24 June 1901

13 The two dangers which beset the Church of England are good music and bad preaching.
   Kenneth Rose *The Later Cecils* (1975)

Robert Cecil 1563–1612

English courtier and statesman, son of William Cecil, Lord Burghley

14 Rest content, and give heed to one that hath sorrowed in the bright lustre of a court, and gone heavily even on the best-seeming fair ground . . . I know it bringeth little comfort on earth; and he is, I reckon, no wise man that looketh this way to Heaven.
   letter to John Harington; Algernon Cecil *A Life of Robert Cecil* (1915) ch. 12

William Cecil (Lord Burghley) 1520–98

English courtier and politician, father of Robert Cecil
on Cecil: see Elizabeth I 304:2, Elizabeth I 304:9, Elizabeth I 304:10

15 What! all this for a song?
   to Queen Elizabeth I, on being ordered to make a gratuity of £100 to Spenser in return for some poems
      Edmund Spenser *The Faerie Queene* (1751) 'The Life of Mr Edmund Spenser' by Thomas Birch

Paul Celan 1920–70

German poet

1 A man lives in the house he plays with his vipers
   he writes
   he writes when it grows dark to Deutschland your
      golden hair Margareta
   Your ashen hair Shulamith we shovel a grave in
      the air there you won't lie too cramped.
   'Deathfugue' (written 1944)

2 He shouts play death more sweetly this Death is a
      master from Deutschland
   he shouts scrape your strings darker you'll rise
      then as smoke to the sky
   you'll have a grave then in the clouds there you
      won't lie too cramped.
   'Deathfugue' (written 1944)

3 *Der Tod ist ein Meister aus Deutschland.*
   Death is a master from Germany.
   'Deathfugue' (written 1944)

4 There's nothing in the world for which a poet will
      give up writing, not even when he is a Jew and
      the language of his poems is German.
   letter to relatives, 2 August 1948

Susannah Centlivre c.1669–1723

English actress and dramatist

5 For he or she, who drags the marriage chain,
   And finds in spouse occasion to complain,
   Should hide their frailties with a lover's care,
   And let th'ill-judging world conclude 'em fair;
   Better th'offence ne'er reach the offender's ear.
   For they who sin with caution, whilst concealed,
   Grow impudently careless, when revealed.
   The Artifice (1722) act 5, sc. 3

6 The real Simon Pure.
   A Bold Stroke for a Wife (1718) act 5, sc. 1

7 Nothing to be done without a bribe I find, in love
      as well as law.
   The Perjured Husband (1700) act 3, sc. 2

8 The carping malice of the vulgar world; who think
      it a proof of sense to dislike every thing that is writ
      by Women.
   The Platonic Lady (1707) dedication

Cervantes (Miguel de Cervantes Saavedra)

1547–1616

Spanish novelist
on Cervantes: see **Byron** 181:31

9 *El Caballero de la Triste Figura.*
   The Knight of the Doleful Countenance.
   Don Quixote (1605) pt. 1, ch. 19

10 *El pan comido y la compañía deshecha.*
   With the bread eaten up, up breaks the company.
   Don Quixote (1605) pt. 2, ch. 7

11 *No todos podemos ser frailes, y muchos son los
   caminos por donde lleva Dios a los suyos al cielo:
   religión es la caballería.*

We cannot all be friars, and many are the ways by
which God leads his own to eternal life. Knight-
errantry *is* religion.
*to Sancho, on his asking whether, to get to heaven, we
ought not all to become monks*
   Don Quixote (1605) pt. 2, ch. 8

12 *Es un entreverado loco, lleno de lúcidos intervalos.*
   He's a muddle-headed fool, with frequent lucid
   intervals.
   Don Quixote (1605) pt. 2, ch. 18 (Don Lorenzo of Don
   Quixote)

13 *Dos linajes solos hay en el mundo, como decía una
   abuela mía, que son el tener y el no tener.*
   There are only two families in the world, as a
   grandmother of mine used to say: the haves and
   the have-nots.
   Don Quixote (1605) pt. 2, ch. 20

14 *Digo, paciencia y barajar.*
   What I say is, patience, and shuffle the cards.
   Don Quixote (1605) pt. 2, ch. 23

15 *La diligencia es madre de la buena ventura y la pereza,
   su contrario, jamás llegó al término que pide un buen
   deseo.*
   Diligence is the mother of good fortune, and
   idleness, its opposite, never led to good intention's
   goal.
   Don Quixote (1605) pt. 2, ch. 43

16 *Bien haya el que inventó el sueño, capa que cubre
   todos los humanos pensamientos, manjar que quita la
   hambre, agua que ahuyenta la sed, fuego que calienta
   el frío, frío que templa el ardor, y, finalmente, moneda
   general con que todas las cosas se compran, balanza y
   peso que iguala al pastor con el rey y al simple con el
   discreto.*
   Blessings on him who invented sleep, the mantle
   that covers all human thoughts, the food that
   satisfies hunger, the drink that slakes thirst, the
   fire that warms cold, the cold that moderates heat,
   and, lastly, the common currency that buys all
   things, the balance and weight that equalizes the
   shepherd and the king, the simpleton and the
   sage.
   Don Quixote (1605) pt. 2, ch. 68

17 *Morir cuerdo, y vivir loco.*
   To die in wisdom, having lived in folly.
   Don Quixote's epitaph
   Don Quixote (1605) pt. 2, ch. 74

18 *Los buenos pintores imitan la naturaleza, pero los
   malos la vomitan.*
   Good painters imitate nature, bad ones spew it up.
   El Licenciado Vidriera in Novelas Ejemplares (1613)

19 *Puesto ya el pie en el estribo.*
   With one foot already in the stirrup.
   apprehending his own imminent death
   Los Trabajos de Persiles y Sigismunda (1617) preface

Paul Cézanne 1839–1906

French painter

1 Treat nature in terms of the cylinder, the sphere, the cone, all in perspective.
  letter to Emile Bernard, 1904; Emile Bernard *Paul Cézanne* (1925)

2 I will astonish Paris with an apple.
  Gustave Geffroy *Claude Monet: His Life, His Times, His Works* (1894)

3 Monet is only an eye, but what an eye!
  attributed

John Chalkhill c.1600–42

English poet

4 Oh, the gallant fisher's life,
  It is the best of any
  'Tis full of pleasure, void of strife,
  And 'tis beloved of many.
  'Piscator's Song', in Izaak Walton *The Compleat Angler* (1653–76)

Jason Chamberlain fl. 1811

American clergyman

5 Morals and manners will rise or decline with our attention to grammar.
  inaugural address, University of Vermont, 1811

Joseph Chamberlain 1836–1914

British Liberal politician, father of Neville Chamberlain

6 In politics, there is no use looking beyond the next fortnight.
  letter from A. J. Balfour to 3rd Marquess of Salisbury, 24 March 1886; A. J. Balfour *Chapters of Autobiography* (1930) ch. 16; see **Wilson** 840:7

7 Provided that the City of London remains, as it is at present, the clearing-house of the world, any other nation may be its workshop.
  speech at the Guildhall, 19 January 1904, in *The Times* 20 January 1904; see **Disraeli** 275:5

8 The day of small nations has long passed away. The day of Empires has come.
  speech at Birmingham, 12 May 1904, in *The Times* 13 May 1904

9 We are not downhearted. The only trouble is we cannot understand what is happening to our neighbours.
  referring to a constituency which had remained unaffected by an electoral landslide
  speech at Smethwick, 18 January 1906, in *The Times* 19 January 1906

Neville Chamberlain 1869–1940

British Conservative statesman; Prime Minister, 1937–40, son of Joseph Chamberlain
*on Chamberlain: see **Bevan** 73:20*

10 In war, whichever side may call itself the victor, there are no winners, but all are losers.
  speech at Kettering, 3 July 1938, in *The Times* 4 July 1938

11 How horrible, fantastic, incredible it is that we should be digging trenches and trying on gas-masks here because of a quarrel in a far away country between people of whom we know nothing.
  on Germany's annexation of the Sudetenland
  radio broadcast, 27 September 1938, in *The Times* 28 September 1938

12 This is the second time in our history that there has come back from Germany to Downing Street peace with honour. I believe it is peace for our time.
  speech from 10 Downing Street, 30 September 1938, in *The Times* 1 October 1938; see **Disraeli** 276:17, **Russell** 661:13

13 This morning, the British Ambassador in Berlin handed the German government a final Note stating that, unless we heard from them by eleven o'clock that they were prepared at once to withdraw their troops from Poland, a state of war would exist between us. I have to tell you now that no such undertaking has been received, and that consequently this country is at war with Germany.
  radio broadcast, 3 September 1939

14 Whatever may be the reason—whether it was that Hitler thought he might get away with what he had got without fighting for it, or whether it was that after all the preparations were not sufficiently complete—however, one thing is certain—he missed the bus.
  speech at Central Hall, Westminster, 4 April 1940, in *The Times* 5 April 1940

Haddon Chambers 1860–1921

English dramatist

15 The long arm of coincidence.
  Captain Swift (1888) act 2

Jack Chambers 1931–78

Canadian painter

16 When you are interested in life more than you are in painting, then your paintings can come to life.
  William Withrow *Contemporary Painting in Canada* (1972)

William Chambers 1726–96

British architect

17 In the constructive part of architecture, the ancients were no great proficients.
  Treatise on Decorative Civil Architecture (ed. 3, 1791)

Nicolas-Sébastien Chamfort 1741–94

French writer

18 *La plus perdue de toutes les journées est celle où l'on n'a pas ri.*
  Of all days, the one most surely wasted is the one on which one has not laughed.
  Maximes et Pensées (1796) ch. 1

19 *Voulez-vous voir à quel point chaque état de la société corrompt les hommes? Examinez ce qu'ils sont quand ils en ont éprouvé plus long-temps l'influence, c'est-à-dire dans la vieillesse. Voyez ce que c'est qu'un vieux*

courtisan, un vieux prêtre, un vieux juge, un vieux procureur, un vieux chirurgien.

If you would find to what extent each condition of society can corrupt a man, examine what he is when he has undergone that influence for the longest possible time, that is to say, when he is old. See what an old courtier is like, an old priest, an old judge, an old solicitor, an old surgeon.

> *Maximes et Pensées* (1796) ch. 2

1 *Vivre est une maladie dont le sommeil nous soulage toutes les 16 heures. C'est un palliatif. La mort est le remède.*

Living is an illness to which sleep provides relief every sixteen hours. It's a palliative. The remedy is death.

> *Maximes et Pensées* (1796) ch. 2

2 *Des qualités trop supérieures rendent souvent un homme moins propre à la société. On ne va pas au marché avec des lingots; on y va avec de l'argent ou de la petite monnaie.*

Qualities too elevated often unfit a man for society. We don't take ingots with us to market; we take silver or small change.

> *Maximes et Pensées* (1796) ch. 3

3 *En amour, tout est vrai, tout est faux; et c'est la seule chose sur laquelle on ne puisse pas dire une absurdité.*

In love, everything is true, everything is false; and it is the one subject on which one cannot express an absurdity.

> *Maximes et Pensées* (1796) ch. 6

4 *L'amour, tel qu'il existe dans la société, n'est que l'échange de deux fantaisies et le contact de deux épidermes.*

Love, in the form in which it exists in society, is nothing but the exchange of two fantasies and the superficial contact of two bodies.

> *Maximes et Pensées* (1796) ch. 6

5 *Je dirais volontiers des métaphysiciens ce que Scaliger disait des Basques, on dit qu'ils s'entendent, mais je n'en crois rien.*

I am tempted to say of metaphysicians what Scaliger used to say of the Basques: they are said to understand one another, but I don't believe a word of it.

> *Maximes et Pensées* (1796) ch. 7

6 *On n'est point un homme d'esprit pour avoir beaucoup d'idées, comme on n'est pas un bon Général poue avoir beaucoup de soldats.*

A man is not necessarily intelligent because he has plenty of ideas, any more than he is a good general because he has plenty of soldiers.

> *Maximes et Pensées* (1796) ch. 7

7 *Les pauvres sont les nègres de l'Europe.*

The poor are Europe's blacks.

> *Maximes et Pensées* (1796) ch. 8

8 *Sois mon frère, ou je te tue.*

Be my brother, or I kill you.

his interpretation of 'Fraternité ou la mort [Fraternity or death]'

> P. R. Anguis (ed.) *Oeuvres Complètes* (1824) vol. 1 'Notice

Historique sur la Vie et les Écrits de Chamfort'; see **Political slogans** 601:1

9 *La postérité n'est pas autre chose qu'un public qui succède à un autre: or, vous voyez ce que c'est le public d'à présent.*

Posterity is no more than one public which follows another. Now, you see what the public is today!

> *Caractère et anecdotes* (1953) vol. 2, p. 99

John Chandler 1806-76

English clergyman

10 Conquering kings their titles take
From the foes they captive make.

> hymn (1837); translation from a Latin original: '*Victis sibi cognomina sumant tyranni gentibus . . .*'

Raymond Chandler 1888-1959

American writer of detective fiction

11 It was a blonde. A blonde to make a bishop kick a hole in a stained glass window.

> *Farewell, My Lovely* (1940) ch. 13

12 A big hard-boiled city with no more personality than a paper cup.

of Los Angeles

> *The Little Sister* (1949) ch. 26

13 I let go of her wrists, closed the door with my elbow and slid past her. It was like the first time. 'You ought to carry insurance on those,' I said.

> *The Little Sister* (1949) ch. 34

14 Crime isn't a disease, it's a symptom. Cops are like a doctor that gives you aspirin for a brain tumour.

> *The Long Good-Bye* (1953) ch. 47

15 Down these mean streets a man must go who is not himself mean, who is neither tarnished nor afraid.

> in *Atlantic Monthly* December 1944 'The Simple Art of Murder'

16 If my books had been any worse, I should not have been invited to Hollywood, and if they had been any better, I should not have come.

> letter to Charles W. Morton, 12 December 1945, in Dorothy Gardiner and Katherine S. Walker *Raymond Chandler Speaking* (1962)

17 Would you convey my compliments to the purist who reads your proofs and tell him or her that I write in a sort of broken-down patois which is something like the way a Swiss waiter talks, and that when I split an infinitive, God damn it, I split it so it will stay split.

> letter to Edward Weeks, 18 January 1947, in F. MacShane *Life of Raymond Chandler* (1976) ch. 7

18 When in doubt have a man come through the door with a gun in his hand.

> attributed

Coco Chanel (Gabrielle Bonheur) 1883-1971

French couturière

19 Passion always goes, and boredom stays.

> Frances Kennett *Coco: the Life and Loves of Gabrielle Chanel* (1989)

1 You ask if they were happy. This is not a characteristic of a European. To be contented—that's for the cows.
  A. Madsen *Coco Chanel* (1990) ch. 35

2 Youth is something very new: twenty years ago no one mentioned it.
  Marcel Haedrich *Coco Chanel, Her Life, Her Secrets* (1971)

Henry ('Chips') Channon 1897–1958
American-born British Conservative politician and diarist

3 What is more dull than a discreet diary? One might just as well have a discreet soul.
  diary, 26 July 1935

4 There is nowhere in the world where sleep is so deep as in the libraries of the House of Commons.
  diary, 15 January 1939

Charlie Chaplin (Charles Spencer Chaplin) 1889–1977
English film actor and director

5 All I need to make a comedy is a park, a policeman and a pretty girl.
  My Autobiography (1964) ch. 10

6 Words are cheap. The biggest thing you can say is 'elephant'.
  on the universality of silent films
  B. Norman *The Movie Greats* (1981)

Arthur Chapman 1873–1935
American poet

7 Out where the handclasp's a little stronger,
  Out where the smile dwells a little longer,
  That's where the West begins.
  Out Where the West Begins (1916)

George Chapman c.1559–1634
English scholar, poet, and dramatist

8   An Englishman,
  Being flattered, is a lamb; threatened, a lion.
  Alphonsus, Emperor of Germany (1654) act 1

9 Man is a torch borne in the wind; a dream
  But of a shadow, summed with all his substance.
  Bussy D'Ambois (1607–8) act 1, sc. 1

10 Who to himself is law, no law doth need,
  Offends no law, and is a king indeed.
  Bussy D'Ambois (1607–8) act 2, sc. 1

11   Oh my fame,
  Live in despite of murder!
  Bussy D'Ambois (1607–8) act 5, sc. 3

12 There is no danger to a man, that knows
  What life and death is; there's not any law,
  Exceeds his knowledge; neither is it lawful
  That he should stoop to any other law,
  He goes before them, and commands them all,
  That to himself is a law rational.
  The Conspiracy of Charles, Duke of Byron (1608) act 3, sc. 3

13 Come, come, dear Night, Love's mart of kisses,
  Sweet close of his ambitious line,

The fruitful summer of his blisses,
  Love's glory doth in darkness shine.
  O come, soft rest of cares, come Night,
  Come naked Virtue's only tire,
  The reapèd harvest of the light,
  Bound up in sheaves of sacred fire.
  Hero and Leander (1598)

14 We have watered our houses in Helicon.
  occasionally misread 'We have watered our horses in Helicon', following an 1814 edition
  May-Day (1611) act 3, sc. 3

15 For one heat, all know, doth drive out another,
  One passion doth expel another still.
  Monsieur D'Olive (1606) act 5, sc. 1

16 I am ashamed the law is such an ass.
  Revenge for Honour (1654) act 3, sc. 2; see **Dickens** 271:15

17 They're only truly great who are truly good.
  Revenge for Honour (1654) act 5, sc. 2, last line

18 A poem, whose subject is not truth, but things like truth.
  The Revenge of Bussy D'Ambois (1613) dedication

19 Danger, the spur of all great minds.
  The Revenge of Bussy D'Ambois (1613) act 5, sc. 1

20 And let a scholar all Earth's volumes carry,
  He will be but a walking dictionary.
  The Tears of Peace (1609) l. 530

John Jay Chapman 1862–1933
American essayist and poet

21 The present in New York is so powerful that the past is lost.
  Emerson and Other Essays (rev. ed. 1909), preface

Charles I 1600–49
*British monarch, King of England, Scotland, and Ireland from 1625, son of **James I** and father of **Charles II***
*on Charles I: see **Marvell** 515:18; see also **Last words** 473:15*

22 Never make a defence or apology before you be accused.
  letter to Lord Wentworth, 3 September 1636, in Sir Charles Petrie (ed.) *Letters of King Charles I* (1935)

23 I see all the birds are flown.
  *after attempting to arrest five members of the Long Parliament (**Pym**, Hampden, Haselrig, Holles, and Strode)*
  in the House of Commons, 4 January 1642

24 Sweet-heart, now they will cut off thy father's head. Mark, child, what I say: they will cut off my head, and perhaps make thee a king. But mark what I say: you must not be a king, so long as your brothers Charles and James do live.
  said to Prince Henry
  Reliquiae Sacrae Carolinae (1650)

25 You manifestly wrong even the poorest ploughman, if you demand not his free consent.
  The King's Reasons for declining the jurisdiction of the High Court of Justice, 21 January 1649, in S. R. Gardiner *Constitutional Documents of the Puritan Revolution* (1906 ed.)

26 As to the King, the laws of the land will clearly instruct you for that . . . For the people; and truly

I desire their liberty and freedom, as much as any body: but I must tell you, that their liberty and freedom consists in having the government of those laws, by which their life and their goods may be most their own; 'tis not for having share in government [sirs] that is nothing pertaining to 'em. A subject and a sovereign are clean different things.

speech on the scaffold, 30 January 1649; J. Rushworth *Historical Collections* pt. 4, vol. 2 (1701)

1 If I would have given way to an arbitrary way, for to have all laws changed according to the power of the sword, I needed not to have come here; and therefore I tell you (and I pray God it be not laid to your charge) that I am the martyr of the people.

speech on the scaffold, 30 January 1649; J. Rushworth *Historical Collections* pt. 4, vol. 2 (1701)

2 I die a Christian, according to the profession of the Church of England, as I found it left me by my father.

speech on the scaffold, 30 January 1649; J. Rushworth *Historical Collections* pt. 4, vol. 2 (1701)

3 I go from a corruptible to an incorruptible crown, where no disturbance can be, no disturbance in the world.

speech on the scaffold, 30 January 1649; J. Rushworth *Historical Collections* pt. 4, vol. 2 (1701)

Charles II 1630–85

British monarch, King of England, Scotland and Ireland from 1660, son of Charles I

on Charles: see Defoe 261:25, Epitaphs 309:14, Rochester 651:14, Sellar and Yeatman 676:22; see also Last words 472:18

4 Better than a play.

on the debates in the House of Lords on Lord Ross's Divorce Bill, 1670

A. Bryant *King Charles II* (1931)

5 He [Charles II] said once to myself, he was no atheist, but he could not think God would make a man miserable only for taking a little pleasure out of the way.

Bishop Gilbert Burnet *History of My Own Time* (1724) vol. 1, bk. 2, p. 93

6 He [Lauderdale] told me, the king spoke to him to let that [Presbytery] go, for it was not a religion for gentlemen.

Bishop Gilbert Burnet *History of My Own Time* (1724) vol. 1, bk. 2

7 His nonsense suits their nonsense.

said of Woolly, afterwards Bishop of Clonfert ('a very honest man, but a very great blockhead') who had gone from house to house trying to persuade Nonconformists to go to church

Bishop Gilbert Burnet *History of My Own Time* (1724) vol. 1, bk. 2

8 I am sure no man in England will take away my life to make you King.

to his brother James

William King *Political & Literary Anecdotes* (1818)

9 I am weary of travelling and am resolved to go abroad no more. But when I am dead and gone I know not what my brother will do: I am much afraid that when he comes to wear the crown he will be obliged to travel again.

on the difference between himself and his brother (later James II)

attributed

10 It is upon the navy under the good Providence of God that the safety, honour, and welfare of this realm do chiefly depend.

'Articles of War' preamble (probably a popular paraphrase); Geoffrey Callender *The Naval Side of British History* (1952) pt. 1, ch. 8

11 This is very true: for my words are my own, and my actions are my ministers'.

*reply to Lord **Rochester**'s epitaph on him*

Thomas Hearne: *Remarks and Collections* (1885–1921) 17 November 1706; see **Epitaphs** 309:14

12 He had been, he said, an unconscionable time dying; but he hoped that they would excuse it.

Lord Macaulay *History of England* (1849) vol. 1, ch. 4

Charles V 1500–58

Spanish monarch, Holy Roman Emperor, 1519–56; King of Spain from 1516

13 To God I speak Spanish, to women Italian, to men French, and to my horse—German.

attributed; Lord Chesterfield *Letters to his Son* (ed. Dobrée, 1932) vol. 4

Charles, Prince of Wales 1948–

Heir apparent to the British throne; son of Elizabeth II and former husband of Diana, Princess of Wales

14 *when asked if he was 'in love':*
Yes . . . whatever that may mean.

after the announcement of his engagement

interview, 24 February 1981; see **Duffy** 291:7

15 A monstrous carbuncle on the face of a much-loved and elegant friend.

on the proposed extension to the National Gallery

speech to the Royal Institute of British Architects, 30 May 1984, in *The Times* 31 May 1984; see **Spencer** 750:16

16 I just come and talk to the plants, really—very important to talk to them, they respond I find.

television interview, 21 September 1986

Pierre Charron 1541–1603

French philosopher and theologian

17 The true science and study of man is man.

De la Sagesse (1601) bk. 1, preface; see **Pope** 604:32

Salmon Portland Chase 1808–73

American lawyer and politician

18 The Constitution, in all its provisions, looks to an indestructible Union composed of indestructible States.

decision in Texas v. White, 1868, in *Cases Argued and Decided in the Supreme Court of the United States* (1926) bk. 19

François-René Chateaubriand (Vicomte de Chateaubriand) 1768–1848

French writer and diplomat

1 *L'écrivain original n'est pas celui qui n'imite personne, mais celui que personne ne peut imiter.*

The original writer is not he who refrains from imitating others, but he who can be imitated by none.

Le Génie du Christianisme (1802) pt. 2, bk. 1, ch. 3

2 *Les moments de crise produisentun redoublement de vie chez les hommes.*

Moments of crisis produce in man a redoubling of life.

Mémoires d'outre-tombe (1849–50)

Geoffrey Chaucer c.1343–1400

English poet

on Chaucer: see **Caxton** 204:7, **Dryden** 290:9, 290:10, **Dunbar** 292:3, **Lydgate** 496:18, **Spenser** 752:20, **Ward** 821:9

line references are to The Riverside Chaucer (ed. F. N. Robinson, 1987)

3 Ful craftier to pley she was
Than Athalus, that made the game
First of the ches, so was his name.
The Book of the Duchess l. 662

4 Whan that Aprill with his shoures soote
The droghte of March hath perced to the roote.
The Canterbury Tales 'The General Prologue' l. 1

5 And smale foweles maken melodye,
That slepen al the nyght with open ye
(So priketh hem nature in hir corages),
Thanne longen folk to goon on pilgrimages.
The Canterbury Tales 'The General Prologue' l. 9

6   He loved chivalrie,
Trouthe and honour, fredom and curteisie.
The Canterbury Tales 'The General Prologue' l. 45

7 He was a verray, parfit gentil knyght.
The Canterbury Tales 'The General Prologue' l. 72

8 He was as fressh as is the month of May.
The Canterbury Tales 'The General Prologue' l. 92

9 Curteis he was, lowely, and servysable,
And carf biforn his fader at the table.
The Canterbury Tales 'The General Prologue' l. 99

10 Hire gretteste ooth was but by Seinte Loy.
The Canterbury Tales 'The General Prologue' l. 120

11 Ful weel she soong the service dyvyne,
Entuned in hir nose ful semely;
And Frenssh she spak ful faire and fetisly,
After the scole of Stratford atte Bowe,
For Frenssh of Parys was to hire unknowe.
The Canterbury Tales 'The General Prologue' l. 122

12 She wolde wepe, if that she saugh a mous
Kaught in a trappe, if it were deed or bledde.
Of smale houndes hadde she that she fedde
With rosted flessh, or milk and wastel-breed.
But soore wepte she if oon of hem were deed.
The Canterbury Tales 'The General Prologue' l. 144

13 Of smal coral aboute hire arm she bar
A peire of bedes, gauded al with grene,

And theron heng a brooch of gold ful sheene,
On which ther was first write a crowned A,
And after *Amor vincit omnia.*
The Canterbury Tales 'The General Prologue' l. 158; see **Virgil** 814:10

14 He yaf nat of that text a pulled hen,
That seith that hunters ben nat hooly men.
The Canterbury Tales 'The General Prologue' l. 177

15 Somwhat he lipsed, for his wantownesse,
To make his Englissh sweete upon his tonge.
The Canterbury Tales 'The General Prologue' l. 264

16 A Clerk there was of Oxenford also,
That unto logyk hadde longe ygo.
As leene was his hors as is a rake,
And he was nat right fat, I undertake,
But looked holwe, and therto sobrely.
The Canterbury Tales 'The General Prologue' l. 285

17 For hym was levere have at his beddes heed
Twenty bookes, clad in blak or reed,
Of Aristotle and his philosophie
Than robes riche, or fithele, or gay sautrie.
But al be that he was a philosophre,
Yet hadde he but litel gold in cofre.
The Canterbury Tales 'The General Prologue' l. 293

18 And gladly wolde he lerne and gladly teche.
The Canterbury Tales 'The General Prologue' l. 308

19 Nowher so bisy a man as he ther nas,
And yet he semed bisier than he was.
The Canterbury Tales 'The General Prologue' l. 321

20 For he was Epicurus owene sone.
The Canterbury Tales 'The General Prologue' l. 336

21 Housbondes at chirche dore she hadde fyve,
Withouten oother compaignye in youthe—
But thereof nedeth nat to speke as nowthe.
The Canterbury Tales 'The General Prologue' l. 460

22 This noble ensample to his sheep he yaf,
That first he wroghte, and afterward he taughte.
The Canterbury Tales 'The General Prologue' l. 496

23 If gold ruste, what shall iren do?
The Canterbury Tales 'The General Prologue' l. 500

24 But Cristes loore and his apostels twelve
He taughte; but first he folwed it hymselve.
The Canterbury Tales 'The General Prologue' l. 527

25 His nosethirles blake were and wyde.
A swerd and a bokeler bar he by his syde.
His mouth as greet was as a greet forneys.
He was a janglere and a goliardeys,
And that was moost of synne and harlotries.
The Canterbury Tales 'The General Prologue' l. 557

26 A Somonour was ther with us in that place,
That hadde a fyr-reed cherubynnes face,
For saucefleem he was, with eyen narwe.
As hoot he was and lecherous as a sparwe.
The Canterbury Tales 'The General Prologue' l. 623

27 Wel loved he garleek, oynons, and eek lekes,
And for to drynken strong wyn, reed as blood.
The Canterbury Tales 'The General Prologue' l. 634

1 His walet, biforn him in his lappe,
Bretful of pardoun, comen from Rome al hoot.
The Canterbury Tales 'The General Prologue' l. 686

2 He hadde a croys of latoun ful of stones,
And in a glas he hadde pigges bones.
But with thise relikes, whan that he fond
A povre person dwellynge upon lond,
Upon a day he gat hym moore moneye
Than that the person gat in monthes tweye;
And thus, with feyned flaterye and japes,
He made the person and the peple his apes.
The Canterbury Tales 'The General Prologue' l. 699

3 O stormy peple! Unsad and evere untrewe!
The Canterbury Tales 'The Clerk's Tale' l. 995

4 Grisilde is deed, and eek hire pacience,
And bothe atones buryed in Ytaille;
For which I crie in open audience
No wedded man so hardy be t'assaille
His wyves pacience in trust to fynde
Grisildis, for in certein he shal faille.
The Canterbury Tales 'The Clerk's Tale: Lenvoy de Chaucer'
l. 1177

5 Ye archewyves, stondeth at defense,
Syn ye be strong as is a greet camaille;
Ne suffreth nat that men yow doon offense.
And sklendre wyves, fieble as in bataille,
Beth egre as is a tygre yond in Ynde;
Ay clappeth as a mille, I yow consaille.
The Canterbury Tales 'The Clerk's Tale: Lenvoy de Chaucer'
l. 1195

6 Be ay of chiere as light as leef on lynde,
And lat hym care, and wepe, and wrynge, and
waille!
The Canterbury Tales 'The Clerk's Tale: Lenvoy de Chaucer'
l. 1211

7 Love wol nat been constreyned by maistrye.
When maistrie comth, the God of Love anon
Beteth his wynges, and farewel, he is gon!
Love is a thyng as any spirit free.
The Canterbury Tales 'The Franklin's Tale' l. 764

8 Wommen, of kynde, desiren libertee,
And nat to been constreyned as a thral;
And so doon men, if I sooth seyen shal.
The Canterbury Tales 'The Franklin's Tale' l. 768

9 Til that the brighte sonne loste his hewe;
For th'orisonte hath reft the sonne his lyght—
This is as muche to seye as it was nyght.
The Canterbury Tales 'The Franklin's Tale' l. 1016

10 Trouthe is the hyeste thyng that man may kepe.
The Canterbury Tales 'The Franklin's Tale' l. 1479

11 And therefore, at the kynges court, my brother,
Ech man for hymself, ther is noon oother.
The Canterbury Tales 'The Knight's Tale' l. 1181

12 And whan a beest is deed he hath no peyne;
But man after his deeth moot wepe and pleyne.
The Canterbury Tales 'The Knight's Tale' l. 1319

13 The bisy larke, messager of day.
The Canterbury Tales 'The Knight's Tale' l. 1491

14 For pitee renneth soone in gentil herte.
The Canterbury Tales 'The Knight's Tale' l. 1761

15 The smylere with the knyf under the cloke.
The Canterbury Tales 'The Knight's Tale' l. 1999

16 Up roos the sonne, and up roos Emelye.
The Canterbury Tales 'The Knight's Tale' l. 2273

17 What is this world? what asketh men to have?
Now with his love, now in his colde grave.
The Canterbury Tales 'The Knight's Tale' l. 2777

18 She is mirour of alle curteisye.
The Canterbury Tales 'The Man of Law's Tale' l. 166

19 Lat take a cat, and fostre hym wel with milk
And tendre flessh, and make his couche of silk,
And lay hym seen a mous go by the wal,
Anon he weyveth milk and flessh and al,
And every deyntee that is in that hous,
Swich appetit hath he to ete a mous.
The Canterbury Tales 'The Manciple's Tale' l. 175

20 Kepe wel they tonge, and thenk upon the crowe.
The Canterbury Tales 'The Manciple's Tale' l. 362

21 And what is bettre than wisedoom? Womman.
And
what is bettre than a good womman? Nothyng.
The Canterbury Tales 'The Tale of Melibee' l. 1107

22 She was a prymerole, a piggesnye,
For any lord to leggen in his bedde,
Or yet for any good yeman to wedde.
The Canterbury Tales 'The Miller's Tale' l. 3268

23 Derk was the nyght as pich, or as the cole,
And at the wyndow out she putte hir hole,
And Absolon, hym fil no bet ne wers,
But with his mouth he kiste hir naked ers
Ful savourly, er he were war of this.
Abak he stirte, and thoughte it was amys,
For wel he wiste a womman hath no berd.
He felte a thyng al rough and long yherd,
And seyde, 'Fy! allas! what have I to do?'
'Tehee!' quod she, and clapte the wyndow to.
The Canterbury Tales 'The Miller's Tale' l. 3730

24 For certein, whan that Fortune list to flee,
Ther may no man the cours of hire withholde.
The Canterbury Tales 'The Monk's Tale' l. 1995

25 Ful wys is he that kan hymselven knowe!
The Canterbury Tales 'The Monk's Tale' l. 2139

26 Redeth the grete poete of Ytaille
That highte Dant, for he kan al devyse
Fro point to point; nat o word wol he faille.
The Canterbury Tales 'The Monk's Tale' l. 2460

27 His coomb was redder than the fyn coral,
And batailled as it were a castel wal;
His byle was blak, and as the jeet it shoon;
Lyk asure were his legges and his toon;
His nayles whitter than the lylye flour,
And lyk the burned gold was his colour,
This gentil cok hadde in his governaunce
Sevene hennes for to doon al his plesaunce,
Whiche were his sustres and his paramours,
And wonder lyk to hym, as of colours;
Of whiche the faireste hewed on hir throte
Was cleped fair damoysele Pertelote.
The Canterbury Tales 'The Nun's Priest's Tale' l. 2859

1 Mordre wol out; that se we day by day.
The Canterbury Tales 'The Nun's Priest's Tale' l. 3052; see **Proverbs** 627:5

2 Whan that the month in which the world bigan,
That highte March, whan God first maked man.
The Canterbury Tales 'The Nun's Priest's Tale' l. 3187

3 And on a Friday fil al this meschaunce.
The Canterbury Tales 'The Nun's Priest's Tale' l. 3341

4 Thanne peyne I me to strecche forth the nekke,
And est and west upon the peple I bekke.
The Canterbury Tales 'The Pardoner's Prologue' l. 395

5 O wombe! O bely! O stynkyng cod
Fulfilled of dong and of corrupcioun!
The Canterbury Tales 'The Pardoner's Tale' l. 534

6 And lightly as it comth, so wol we spende.
The Canterbury Tales 'The Pardoner's Tale' l. 781

7 Yet in oure asshen olde is fyr yreke.
The Canterbury Tales 'The Reeve's Prologue' l. 3882

8 The gretteste clerkes been noght wisest men.
The Canterbury Tales 'The Reeve's Tale' l. 4054

9 So was hir joly whistle wel ywet.
The Canterbury Tales 'The Reeve's Tale' l. 4155

10 Thou lookest as thou woldest fynde an hare,
For evere upon the ground I se thee stare.
The Canterbury Tales 'Prologue to Sir Thopas' l. 696

11 He hadde a semely nose.
The Canterbury Tales 'Sir Thopas' l. 729

12 'By God,' quod he, 'for pleynly, at a word,
Thy drasty rymyng is nat worth a toord!'
The Canterbury Tales 'Sir Thopas' l. 929

13 Experience, though noon auctoritee
Were in this world, is right ynogh for me
To speke of wo that is in mariage.
The Canterbury Tales 'The Wife of Bath's Prologue' l. 1

14 Yblessed be god that I have wedded fyve!
Welcome the sixte, whan that evere he shal.
For sothe, I wol nat kepe me chaast in al.
Whan myn housbonde is fro the world ygon,
Som Cristen man shall wedde me anon.
The Canterbury Tales 'The Wife of Bath's Prologue' l. 44

15 And after wyn on Venus moste I thynke,
For al so siker as cold engendreth hayl,
A likerous mouth moste han a likerous tayl.
The Canterbury Tales 'The Wife of Bath's Prologue' l. 464

16 But—Lord Crist!—what that it remembreth me
Upon my yowthe, and on my jolitee,
It tikleth me aboute myn herte roote.
Unto this day it dooth myn herte boote
That I have had my world as in my time.
The Canterbury Tales 'The Wife of Bath's Prologue' l. 469

17 And for to se, and eek for to be seye
Of lusty folk.
The Canterbury Tales 'The Wife of Bath's Prologue' l. 552

18 But yet I hadde alwey a coltes tooth.
Gat-tothed I was, and that bicam me weel.
The Canterbury Tales 'The Wife of Bath's Prologue' l. 602

19 Of which mayde anon, maugree hir heed,
By verray force, he rafte hire maydenhed.
The Canterbury Tales 'The Wife of Bath's Tale' l. 887

20 Wommen desiren to have sovereynetee
As wel over hir housbond as hir love.
The Canterbury Tales 'The Wife of Bath's Tale' l. 1038

21   Venus clerk Ovide,
That hath ysowen wonder wide
The grete god of Loves name.
The House of Fame l. 1487

22 And as for me, though that I konne but lyte,
On bokes for to rede I me delyte,
And to hem yive I feyth and ful credence,
And in myn herte have hem in reverence
So hertely, that ther is game noon
That fro my bokes maketh me to goon,
But yt be seldom on the holyday,
Save, certeynly, whan that the month of May
Is comen, and that I here the foules synge,
And that the floures gynnen for to sprynge,
Farewel my bok and my devocioun!
The Legend of Good Women 'The Prologue' l. 29

23   Of al the floures in the mede,
Thanne love I most thise floures white and rede,
Swiche as men callen daysyes in our toun.
The Legend of Good Women 'The Prologue' l. 41

24 That wel by reson men it calle may
The 'dayesye,' or elles the 'ye of day,'
The emperice and flour of floures alle.
The Legend of Good Women 'The Prologue' l. 183

25 And she was fayr as is the rose in May.
The Legend of Good Women 'Cleopatra' l. 613

26 That lyf so short,
the craft so long to lerne,
Th'assay so hard, so sharp the conquerynge.
The Parliament of Fowls l. 1; see **Hippocrates** 389:9, **Proverbs** 614:32

27 Thou shalt make castels thanne in Spayne
And dreme of joye, all but in vayne.
The Romaunt of the Rose l. 2573

28 O blynde world, O blynde entencioun!
How often falleth al the effect contraire
Of surquidrie and foul presumpcioun;
For kaught is proud, and kaught is debonaire.
This Troilus is clomben on the staire,
And litel weneth that he moot descenden;
But alday faileth thing that fooles wenden.
Troilus and Criseyde bk. 1, l. 211

29 For evere it was, and evere it shal byfalle,
That Love is he that alle thing may bynde,
For may no man fordon the lawe of kynde.
Troilus and Criseyde bk. 1, l. 236

30 But love a womman that she woot it nought,
And she wol quyte it that thow shalt nat fele;
Unknowe, unkist, and lost, that is unsought.
Troilus and Criseyde bk. 1, l. 807

31 O wynd, O wynd, the weder gynneth clere.
Troilus and Criseyde bk. 2, l. 2

32 Ye knowe ek that in forme of speche is chaunge
Withinne a thousand yeer, and wordes tho
That hadden pris, now wonder nyce and straunge
Us thinketh hem, and yet thei spake hem so.
Troilus and Criseyde bk. 2, l. 22

1 So longe mote ye lyve, and alle proude,
Til crowes feet be growe under youre yë.
Troilus and Criseyde bk. 2, l. 402

2 And we shall speek of the somwhat, I trowe,
Whan thow art gon, to don thyn eris glowe!
Troilus and Criseyde bk. 2, l. 1021

3 God loveth, and to love wol nought werne,
And in this world no lyves creature
Withouten love is worth, or may endure.
Troilus and Criseyde bk. 3, l. 12

4 It is nought good a slepyng hound to wake.
Troilus and Criseyde bk. 3, l. 764; see **Proverbs** 625:6

5 For I have seyn of a ful misty morwe
Folowen ful ofte a myrie someris day.
Troilus and Criseyde bk. 3, l. 1060

6 Right as an aspes leef she gan to quake.
Troilus and Criseyde bk. 3, l. 1200

7 And as the newe abaysed nyghtyngale,
That stynteth first whan she bygynneth to synge.
Troilus and Criseyde bk. 3, l. 1233

8 For of fortunes sharpe adversitee
The worst kynde of infortune is this,
A man to han ben in prosperitee,
And it remembren, whan it passed is.
Troilus and Criseyde bk. 3, l. 1625; see **Boethius** 125:6, **Dante** 255:18

9 Oon ere it herde, at tother out it wente.
Troilus and Criseyde bk. 4, l. 434

10 But manly sette the world on six and sevene;
And if thow deye a martyr, go to hevene!
Troilus and Criseyde bk. 4, l. 622

11 For tyme ylost may nought recovered be.
Troilus and Criseyde bk. 4, l. 1283

12 Ye, fare wel al the snow of ferne yere!
Troilus and Criseyde bk. 5, l. 1176

13 Ek gret effect men write in place lite;
Th' entente is al, and nat the lettres space.
Troilus and Criseyde bk. 5, l. 1629

14 Go, litel bok, go, litel myn tragedye,
Ther God thi makere yet, er that he dye,
So sende myght to make in som comedye!
But litel bok, no makyng thow n'envie,
But subgit be to alle poesye;
And kis the steppes, where as thow seest pace
Virgile, Ovide, Omer, Lucan, and Stace.

And for ther is so gret diversite
In Englissh and in writyng of oure tonge,
So prey I God that non myswrite the,
Ne the mysmetre for defaute of tonge;
And red wherso thow be, or elles songe,
That thow be understonde, God I biseche!
Troilus and Criseyde bk. 5, l. 1786; see **Stevenson** 760:19

15 And whan that he was slayn in this manere,
His lighte goost ful blisfully is went
Up to the holughnesse of the eighthe spere,
In convers letyng everich element;
And ther he saugh, with ful avysement
The erratik sterres, herkenyng armonye
With sownes ful of hevenyssh melodie.

And down from thennes faste he gan avyse
This litel spot of erthe, that with the se
Embraced is, and fully gan despise
This wrecched world, and held al vanite
To respect of the pleyn felicite
That is in hevene above.
Troilus and Criseyde bk. 5, l. 1811

16 O yonge, fresshe folkes, he or she,
In which that love up groweth with youre age.
Repeyreth hom fro worldly vanyte,
And of youre herte up casteth the visage
To thilke God that after his ymage
Yow made, and thynketh al nys but a faire,
This world that passeth soone as floures faire.
And loveth hym the which that right for love
Upon a crois, our soules for to beye,
First start, and roos, and sit in hevene above;
For he nyl falsen no wight, dar I seye,
That wol his herte al holly on hym leye.
And syn he best to love is, and most meke,
What nedeth feynede loves for to seke?
Troilus and Criseyde bk. 5, l. 1835

17 Lo here, of payens corsed olde rites!
Lo here, what alle hire goddes may availle!
Lo here, thise wrecched worldes appetites!
Lo here, the fyn and guerdoun for travaille
Of Jove, Appollo, of Mars, of swich rascaille!
Troilus and Criseyde bk. 5, l. 1849

18 O moral Gower, this book I directe
To the.
Troilus and Criseyde bk. 5, l. 1856

19 Flee fro the prees, and dwelle with sothfastnesse.
'Truth: Balade de Bon Conseyle' l. 1

20 Forth, pilgrim, forth! Forth, beste, out of thy stal!
Know thy contree, look up, thank God of al;
Hold the heye wey, and lat thy gost thee lede,
And trowth thee shal delivere, it is no drede.
'Truth: Balade de Bon Conseyle' l. 18

Anton Chekhov 1860–1904
Russian dramatist and short-story writer

21 If a lot of cures are suggested for a disease, it means that the disease is incurable.
The Cherry Orchard (1904) act 1 (translated by Elisaveta Fen)

22 The Lord God has given us vast forests, immense fields, wide horizons; surely we ought to be giants, living in such a country as this.
The Cherry Orchard (1904) act 2 (translated by Elisaveta Fen)

23 To begin to live in the present, we must first atone for our past and be finished with it, and we can only atone for it by suffering, by extraordinary, unceasing exertion.
The Cherry Orchard (1904) act 2 (translated by Elisaveta Fen)

24 MEDVEDENKO: Why do you wear black all the time?
MASHA: I'm in mourning for my life, I'm unhappy.
The Seagull (1896) act 1

25 NINA: Your play's hard to act, there are no living people in it.

TREPLEV: Living people! We should show life neither as it is nor as it ought to be, but as we see it in our dreams.

The Seagull (1896) act 1

1 Women can't forgive failure.

The Seagull (1896) act 2

2 I'm a seagull. No, that's wrong. Remember you shot a seagull? A man happened to come along, saw it and killed it, just to pass the time. A plot for a short story.

The Seagull (1896) act 4

3 Man must work by the sweat of his brow whatever his class, and that should make up the whole meaning and purpose of his life and happiness and contentment.

The Three Sisters (1901) act 1 (translated by Elisaveta Fen)

4 People who don't even notice whether it's summer or winter are lucky! If I lived in Moscow I don't think I'd care what the weather was like.

The Three Sisters (1901) act 2 (translated by Elisaveta Fen)

5 Life isn't finished for us yet! We're going to live! . . . Maybe, if we wait a little longer, we shall find out why we live, why we suffer.

The Three Sisters (1901) act 4 (translated by Elisaveta Fen)

6 Forests keep disappearing, rivers dry up, wild life's become extinct, the climate's ruined and the land grows poorer and uglier every day.

Uncle Vanya (1897) act 1

7 When a woman isn't beautiful, people always say, 'You have lovely eyes, you have lovely hair.'

Uncle Vanya (1897) act 3

8 A writer must be as objective as a chemist: he must abandon the subjective line; he must know that dung-heaps play a very reasonable part in a landscape, and that evil passions are as inherent in life as good ones.

letter to M. V. Kiselev, 14 January 1887, in L. S. Friedland (ed.) *Anton Chekhov: Letters on the Short Story . . .* (1964)

9 Medicine is my lawful wife and literature is my mistress. When I get tired of one I spend the night with the other.

letter to A. S. Suvorin, 11 September 1888, in L. S. Friedland (ed.) *Anton Chekhov: Letters on the Short Story . . .* (1964)

10 Brevity is the sister of talent.

letter to Alexander Chekhov, 11 April 1889, in L. S. Friedland (ed.) *Anton Chekhov: Letters on the Short Story . . .* (1964)

11 I couldn't stand a happiness that went on morning noon and night . . . I promise to be a splendid husband, but give me a wife who, like the moon, does not rise every night in my sky.

on being urged to marry

letter, 23 March 1895; Donald Rayfield *Anton Chekhov* (1997)

12 Between 'God exists' and 'There is no God' lies a whole enormous field which a true sage has great difficulty in crossing. But a Russian knows only one of these two extremes and the middle between them doesn't interest him, which is why he knows

nothing or very little . . . A good man's indifference is as good as any religion.

diary, 1897; Donald Rayfield *Anton Chekhov* (1997)

13 Women deprived of the company of men pine, men deprived of the company of women become stupid.

Notebooks (1921)

14 Love, friendship, respect do not unite people as much as common hatred for something.

Notebooks (1921)

15 If in the first act you have hung a pistol on the wall, then in the following one it should be fired. Otherwise don't put it there.

I. Ya. Gurlyand 'Reminiscences of A. P. Chekhov, in *Teatr i iskusstvo* 11 July 1904

Mary Chesnut 1823–86

American diarist and Confederate supporter

16 Atlanta is gone. That agony is over. There is no hope but we will try to have no fear.

after the fall of Atlanta to **Sherman**'s *army in* 1864

Geoffrey C. Ward *The Civil War* (1991) ch. 4

Lord Chesterfield (Philip Dormer Stanhope, Earl of Chesterfield) 1694–1773

English writer and politician

on Chesterfield: see **Johnson** 427:14, 427:18, **Walpole** 819:19; *see also* **Last words** 471:15

17 Unlike my subject will I frame my song,
It shall be witty and it sha'n't be long.

epigram on 'Long' Sir Thomas Robinson in the *Dictionary of National Biography* (1917–) vol. 17

18 In scandal, as in robbery, the receiver is always thought as bad as the thief.

Advice to his Son (1775) 'Rules for Conversation: Private Scandal'

19 In matters of religion and matrimony I never give any advice; because I will not have anybody's torments in this world or the next laid to my charge.

Letters to Arthur Charles Stanhope, Esq. (1817) 12 October 1765

20 Religion is by no means a proper subject of conversation in a mixed company.

Letters . . . to his Godson and Successor (1890) Letter 142

21 Cunning is the dark sanctuary of incapacity.

Letters . . . to his Godson and Successor (1890) 'Letter . . . to be delivered after his own death'

22 Parsons are very like men, and neither the better nor the worse for wearing a black gown.

Letters to his Son (1774) 5 April 1746

23 The knowledge of the world is only to be acquired in the world, and not in a closet.

Letters to his Son (1774) 4 October 1746

24 An injury is much sooner forgotten than an insult.

Letters to his Son (1774) 9 October 1746

25 Courts and camps are the only places to learn the world in.

Letters to his Son (1774) 2 October 1747

1 Take the tone of the company that you are in.
Letters to his Son (1774) 16 October 1747

2 Do as you would be done by is the surest method that I know of pleasing.
Letters to his Son (1774) 16 October 1747

3 I recommend to you to take care of minutes: for hours will take care of themselves.
Letters to his Son (1774) 6 November 1747; see **Lowndes** 494:20

4 Advice is seldom welcome; and those who want it the most always like it the least.
Letters to his Son (1774) 29 January 1748

5 Wear your learning, like your watch in a private pocket: and do not merely pull it out and strike it, merely to show that you have one.
Letters to his Son (1774) 22 February 1748

6 Speak of the moderns without contempt, and of the ancients without idolatry.
Letters to his Son (1774) 27 February 1748

7 In my mind, there is nothing so illiberal and so ill-bred, as audible laughter.
Letters to his Son (1774) 9 March 1748; see **Catullus** 202:17, **Congreve** 238:15

8 Women, then, are only children of a larger growth.
Letters to his Son (1774) 5 September 1748; see **Dryden** 287:24

9 It must be owned, that the Graces do not seem to be natives of Great Britain; and I doubt, the best of us here have more of rough than polished diamond.
Letters to his Son (1774) 18 November 1748

10 Idleness is only the refuge of weak minds.
Letters to his Son (1774) 20 July 1749

11 Putting moral virtues at the highest, and religion at the lowest, religion must still be allowed to be a collateral security, at least, to virtue; and every prudent man will sooner trust to two securities than to one.
Letters to his Son (1774) 8 January 1750

12 It is commonly said, and more particularly by Lord Shaftesbury, that ridicule is the best test of truth.
Letters to his Son (1774) 6 February 1752; see **Shaftesbury** 678:6

13 Knowledge may give weight, but accomplishments give lustre, and many more people see than weigh.
Maxims, in *Letters to his Son* (3rd ed., 1774) vol. 4

14 The chapter of knowledge is a very short, but the chapter of accidents is a very long one.
letter to Solomon Dayrolles, 16 February 1753, in M. Maty (ed.) *Miscellaneous Works* vol. 2 (1778) no. 79

15 I . . . could not help reflecting in my way upon the singular ill-luck of this my dear country, which, as long as ever I remember it, and as far back as I have read, has always been governed by the only two or three people, out of two or three millions, totally incapable of governing, and unfit to be trusted.
in *The World* 7 October 1756; M. Maty (ed.) *Miscellaneous Works* vol. 2 (1778) 'Miscellaneous Pieces' no. 45

16 Tyrawley and I have been dead these two years; but we don't choose to have it known.
James Boswell *Life of Samuel Johnson* (1934 ed.) vol. 2, 3 April 1773

17 The pleasure is momentary, the position ridiculous, and the expense damnable.
of sex
attributed

G. K. Chesterton 1874–1936
English essayist, novelist, and poet
on Chesterton: see **Epitaphs** *311:3; see also* **Telegrams** *776:1*

18 Are they clinging to their crosses, F. E. Smith?
satirizing F. E. **Smith***'s response to the Welsh Disestablishment Bill*
'Antichrist' (1915)

19 Talk about the pews and steeples
And the Cash that goes therewith!
But the souls of Christian peoples . . .
Chuck it, Smith!
'Antichrist' (1915)

20 The gallows in my garden, people say,
Is new and neat and adequately tall.
I tie the noose on in a knowing way
As one that knots his necktie for a ball;
But just as all the neighbours—on the wall—
Are drawing a long breath to shout 'Hurray!'
The strangest whim has seized me . . . . After all
I think I will not hang myself today.
'Ballade of Suicide' (1915)

21 I tell you naught for your comfort,
Yea, naught for your desire,
Save that the sky grows darker yet
And the sea rises higher.
The Ballad of the White Horse (1911) bk. 1

22 For the great Gaels of Ireland
Are the men that God made mad,
For all their wars are merry,
And all their songs are sad.
The Ballad of the White Horse (1911) bk. 2

23 The thing on the blind side of the heart,
On the wrong side of the door,
The green plant groweth, menacing
Almighty lovers in the Spring;
There is always a forgotten thing,
And love is not secure.
The Ballad of the White Horse (1911) bk. 3

24 When fishes flew and forests walked
And figs grew upon thorn,
Some moment when the moon was blood
Then surely I was born.

With monstrous head and sickening cry
And ears like errant wings,
The devil's walking parody
On all four-footed things.
'The Donkey' (1900)

25 Fools! For I also had my hour;
One far fierce hour and sweet:
There was a shout about my ears,

And palms before my feet.
'The Donkey' (1900)

1 They died to save their country and they only
saved the world.
'English Graves' (1922)

2 Why do you rush through the fields in trains,
Guessing so much and so much.
Why do you flash through the flowery meads,
Fat-head poet that nobody reads;
And why do you know such a frightful lot
About people in gloves and such?
'The Fat White Woman Speaks' (1933); an answer to
Frances Cornford; see **Cornford** 243:10

3 From all that terror teaches,
From lies of tongue and pen,
From all the easy speeches
That comfort cruel men,
From sale and profanation
Of honour and the sword,
From sleep and from damnation,
Deliver us, good Lord!
'A Hymn' (1915)

4 White founts falling in the courts of the sun,
And the Soldan of Byzantium is smiling as they
run.
'Lepanto' (1915)

5 The cold queen of England is looking in the glass;
The shadow of the Valois is yawning at the Mass.
'Lepanto' (1915)

6 The last and lingering troubadour to whom the
bird has sung,
That once went singing southward when all the
world was young.
'Lepanto' (1915)

7 Strong gongs groaning as the guns boom far,
Don John of Austria is going to the war.
'Lepanto' (1915)

8 The folk that live in Liverpool, their heart is in
their boots;
They go to hell like lambs, they do, because the
hooter hoots.
'Me Heart' (1914)

9 Before the Roman came to Rye or out to Severn
strode,
The rolling English drunkard made the rolling
English road.
A reeling road, a rolling road, that rambles round
the shire,
And after him the parson ran, the sexton and the
squire;
'The Rolling English Road' (1914)

10 A merry road, a mazy road, and such as we did
tread
The night we went to Birmingham by way of
Beachy Head.
'The Rolling English Road' (1914)

11 For there is good news yet to hear and fine things
to be seen,
Before we go to Paradise by way of Kensal Green.
'The Rolling English Road' (1914)

12 Smile at us, pay us, pass us; but do not quite
forget.
For we are the people of England, that never have
spoken yet.
'The Secret People' (1915)

13 We only know the last sad squires ride slowly
towards the sea,
And a new people takes the land: and still it is not
we.
'The Secret People' (1915)

14 God made the wicked Grocer
For a mystery and a sign,
That men might shun the awful shops
And go to inns to dine.
'The Song Against Grocers' (1914)

15 He keeps a lady in a cage
Most cruelly all day,
And makes her count and calls her 'Miss'
Until she fades away.
'The Song Against Grocers' (1914)

16 Tea, although an Oriental,
Is a gentleman at least;
Cocoa is a cad and coward,
Cocoa is a vulgar beast.
'Song of Right and Wrong' (1914)

17 Lancashire merchants whenever they like
Can water the beer of a man in Klondike
Or poison the meat of a man in Bombay;
And that is the meaning of Empire Day.
'Songs of Education: II Geography' (1922)

18 And Noah he often said to his wife when he sat
down to dine,
'I don't care where the water goes if it doesn't get
into the wine.'
'Wine and Water' (1914)

19 An adventure is only an inconvenience rightly
considered. An inconvenience is only an
adventure wrongly considered.
All Things Considered (1908) 'On Running after one's Hat'

20 Literature is a luxury; fiction is a necessity.
The Defendant (1901) 'A Defence of Penny Dreadfuls'

21 The rich are the scum of the earth in every
country.
The Flying Inn (1914) ch. 15

22 We make our friends; we make our enemies; but
God makes our next-door neighbour.
Heretics (1905) ch. 14

23 Bigotry may be roughly defined as the anger of
men who have no opinions.
Heretics (1905) ch. 20

24 After the first silence the small man said to the
other: 'Where does a wise man hide a pebble?'
And the tall man answered in a low voice: 'On the
beach.'
The small man nodded, and after a short silence
said: 'Where does a wise man hide a leaf?'
And the other answered: 'In the forest.'
The Innocence of Father Brown (1911)

1 One sees great things from the valley; only small things from the peak.
The Innocence of Father Brown (1911)

2 Thieves respect property. They merely wish the property to become their property that they may more perfectly respect it.
The Man who was Thursday (1908) ch. 4

3 Tradition means giving votes to the most obscure of all classes, our ancestors. It is the democracy of the dead.
Orthodoxy (1908) ch. 4

4 Democrats object to men being disqualified by the accident of birth; tradition objects to their being disqualified by the accident of death.
Orthodoxy (1908) ch. 4

5 All conservatism is based upon the idea that if you leave things alone you leave them as they are. But you do not. If you leave a thing alone you leave it to a torrent of change.
Orthodoxy (1908) ch. 7

6 It isn't that they can't see the solution. It is that they can't see the problem.
The Scandal of Father Brown (1935)

7 They say travel broadens the mind; but you must have the mind.
'The Shadow of the Shark' (1921)

8 Lying in bed would be an altogether perfect and supreme experience if only one had a coloured pencil long enough to draw on the ceiling.
Tremendous Trifles (1909)

9 Hardy went down to botanize in the swamp, while Meredith climbed towards the sun. Meredith became, at his best, a sort of daintily dressed Walt Whitman: Hardy became a sort of village atheist brooding and blaspheming over the village idiot.
The Victorian Age in Literature (1912)

10 He could not think up to the height of his own towering style.
*of **Tennyson***
The Victorian Age in Literature (1912) ch. 3

11 The Christian ideal has not been tried and found wanting. It has been found difficult; and left untried.
What's Wrong with the World (1910) pt. 1 'The Unfinished Temple'

12 The prime truth of woman, the universal mother . . . that if a thing is worth doing, it is worth doing badly.
What's Wrong with the World (1910) pt. 4 'Folly and Female Education'

13 To be clever enough to get all that money, one must be stupid enough to want it.
The Wisdom of Father Brown (1914)

14 Journalism largely consists in saying 'Lord Jones Dead' to people who never knew that Lord Jones was alive.
The Wisdom of Father Brown (1914)

15 Democracy means government by the uneducated, while aristocracy means government by the badly educated.
in *New York Times* 1 February 1931, pt. 5

16 When men stop believing in God they don't believe in nothing; they believe in anything.
widely attributed, although not traced in his works; first recorded as 'The first effect of not believing in God is to believe in anything' in Emile Cammaerts *Chesterton: The Laughing Prophet* (1937)

Maurice Chevalier 1888–1972
French singer and actor

17 Considering the alternative, it's not too bad at all.
on being asked what he felt about the advancing years, on his seventy-second birthday
Michael Freedland *Maurice Chevalier* (1981)

Joseph Benedict 'Ben' Chifley 1885–1951
Australian Labor statesman; Prime Minister 1945–9

18 We have a great objective—the light on the hill—which we aim to reach by working for the betterment of mankind not only here but anywhere we may give a helping hand.
speech to the Annual Conference of the New South Wales branch of the Australian Labor Party, 12 June 1949

Lydia Maria Child 1802–80
American abolitionist and suffragist

19 We first crush people to the earth, and then claim the right of trampling on them forever, because they are prostrate.
An Appeal on Behalf of That Class of Americans Called Africans (1833)

20 Woman stock is rising in the market. I shall not live to see women vote, but I'll come and rap at the ballot box.
letter to Sarah Shaw, 3 August 1856

Erskine Childers 1870–1922
British writer and Irish nationalist
see also **Last words** 471:6

21 The riddle of the sands.
title of novel (1903)

William Chillingworth 1602–44
English scholar

22 The Bible and the Bible only is the religion of Protestants.
The Religion of Protestants (1637)

23 I once knew a man out of courtesy help a lame dog over a stile, and he for requital bit his fingers.
The Religion of Protestants (1637)

Jacques Chirac 1932–

French statesman; Prime Minister 1974–6 and 1986–8, President since 1995

1 For its part, France wants you to take part in this great undertaking.
on European Monetary Union
speech to both Houses of Parliament, 15 May 1996

2 You have been very rude, and I have never been spoken to like this before.
to Tony Blair at the EU enlargement summit in Brussels
in *Guardian* online 29 October 2002

3 It is not well-brought-up behaviour. They missed a good opportunity to keep quiet.
criticizing the support from Central and Eastern European states for the Anglo-American stance on Iraq
in *The Times* 19 February 2003

4 This deserved victory is also a victory for Europe.
message to Tony Blair, on England winning the Rugby World Cup final, Sydney, 22 November 2003
in *Weekend Australian* (online ed.) 23 November 2003

Thomas O. Chisholm 1866–1960

5 Great is thy faithfulness! Great is thy faithfulness!
Morning by morning new mercies I see;
All I have needed thy hand has provided.
Great is thy faithfulness, Lord, unto me.
'Great is thy faithfulness' (hymn)

Rufus Choate 1799–1859

American lawyer and politician

6 Its constitution the glittering and sounding generalities of natural right which make up the Declaration of Independence.
letter to the Maine Whig State Central Committee, 9 August 1856, in S. G. Brown *The Works of Rufus Choate with a Memoir of his Life* (1862) vol. 1; see **Emerson** 307:17

Duc de Choiseul 1719–85

French politician

7 A minister who moves about in society is in a position to read the signs of the times even in a festive gathering, but one who remains shut up in his office learns nothing.
Jack F. Bernard *Talleyrand* (1973)

Noam Chomsky 1928–

American linguistics scholar

8 The notion 'grammatical' cannot be identified with 'meaningful' or 'significant' in any semantic sense. Sentences (1) and (2) are equally nonsensical, but . . . only the former is grammatical.
(1) Colourless green ideas sleep furiously.
(2) Furiously sleep ideas green colourless.
Syntactic Structures (1957) ch. 2

9 The empiricist view is so deep-seated in our way of looking at the human mind that it almost has the character of a superstition.
radio discussion, in *Listener* 30 May 1968

10 As soon as questions of will or decision or reason or choice of action arise, human science is at a loss.
television interview, in *Listener* 6 April 1978

11 The Internet is an élite organization; most of the population of the world has never even made a phone call.
on the limitations of the World Wide Web
in *Observer* 18 February 1996

Jean Chrétien 1934–

Canadian Liberal statesman; Prime Minister 1993–2003

12 Leadership means making people feel good.
in *Toronto Star* 7 June 1984

13 The art of politics is learning to walk with your back to the wall, your elbows high, and a smile on your face. It's a survival game played under the glare of lights.
Straight from the Heart (1985)

Agatha Christie 1890–1976

English writer of detective fiction

14 War settles *nothing* . . . to *win* a war is as disastrous as to lose one!
An Autobiography (1977) pt. 10

15 He [Hercule Poirot] tapped his forehead. 'These little grey cells. It is "up to them".'
The Mysterious Affair at Styles (1920) ch. 10

16 I'm a sausage machine, a perfect sausage machine.
G. C. Ramsey *Agatha Christie* (1972)

David Christy 1802–c.68

17 Cotton is King; or, the economical relations of slavery.
title of book, 1855

Chuang Tzu (Zhuangzi) c.369–286 BC

Chinese philosopher

18 Without them [feelings] there would not be I. And without me who will experience them? They are right near by. But we don't know what causes them. It seems there is a True Lord who does so, but there is no indication of his existence.
Chuang Tzu ch. 2

19 When one is at ease with himself, one is near Tao.
Chuang Tzu ch. 2

20 The sage harmonizes the right and wrong and rests in natural equalization. This is called following two courses at the same time.
Chuang Tzu ch. 2

21 The universe and I exist together, and all things and I are one.
Chuang Tzu ch. 2

1 The sage has the sun and moon by his side. He grasps the universe under the arm. He blends everything into a harmonious whole, casts aside whatever is confused or obscured, and regards the humble as honourable.
Chuang Tzu ch. 2

2 Once I, Chang Chou, dreamed that I was a butterfly and was happy as a butterfly. I was conscious that I was quite pleased with myself but I did not know that I was Chou. Suddenly I awoke and there I was, visibly Chou. I do not know whether it was Chou dreaming that he was a butterfly or the butterfly dreaming that it was Chou.
Chuang Tzu ch. 2; see **Basho** 58:4

3 If the Universe is hidden in the universe itself, then there can be no escape from it. This is the great truth of things in general.
Chuang Tzu ch. 6

4 Tao has reality and evidence but no action or physical form. It may be transmitted but cannot be received. It may be obtained but cannot be seen. It is based in itself, rooted in itself. Before heaven and earth came into being, Tao existed by itself from all time.
Chuang Tzu ch. 6

5 Those who are contented and at ease when the occasion comes and live in accord with the course of Nature cannot be affected by sorrow or joy. This is what the ancients called release from bondage. Those who cannot release themselves are so because they are bound by material things.
Chuang Tzu ch. 6

6 Do not be the possessor of fame. Do not be the storehouse of schemes. Do not take over the function of things. Do not be the master of knowledge [to manipulate things]. Personally realize the infinite to the highest degree and travel in the realm of which there is no sign. Exercise fully what you have received from Nature without any subjective viewpoint. In one word; be absolutely vacuous.
Chuang Tzu ch. 7

7 The mind of the perfect man is like a mirror. It does not lean forward or backward in its response to things. It responds to things but conceals nothing of its own. Therefore it is able to deal with things without injury to [its reality].
Chuang Tzu ch. 7

Mary, Lady Chudleigh (née Leigh)
1656–1710
English poet

8 'Tis hard we should be by the men despised,
Yet kept from knowing what would make us
    prized;
Debarred from knowledge, banished from the
    schools,
And with the utmost industry bred fools.
The Ladies Defence (1701)

9 Wife and Servant are the same,
But only differ in the name.
Poems (1703) 'To the Ladies'

10 Then shun, oh! shun that wretched state
And all the fawning flatterers hate:
Value yourselves, and men despise
You must be proud if you'll be wise.
on marriage
Poems (1703) 'To the Ladies'

Francis Pharcellus Church see
Newspaper headlines 562:25

Charles Churchill 1731–64
English poet

11 Though by whim, envy, or resentment led,
They damn those authors whom they never read.
The Candidate (1764) l. 57

12 The danger chiefly lies in acting well;
No crime's so great as daring to excel.
An Epistle to William Hogarth (1763) l. 51

13   Be England what she will,
With all her faults, she is my country still.
The Farewell (1764) l. 27; see **Cowper** 247:28

14 It can't be Nature, for it is not sense.
The Farewell (1764) l. 200

15 England—a happy land we know,
Where follies naturally grow.
The Ghost (1763) bk. 1, l. 111

16 And adepts in the speaking trade
Keep a cough by them ready made.
The Ghost (1763) bk. 2, l. 545

17 Just to the windward of the law.
The Ghost (1763) bk. 3, l. 56

18 . . . He for subscribers baits his hook,
And takes your cash; but where's the book?
No matter where; wise fear, you know,
Forbids the robbing of a foe;
But what, to serve our private ends,
Forbids the cheating of our friends?
satirizing Samuel **Johnson**
The Ghost (1763) bk. 3, l. 801

19 A joke's a very serious thing.
The Ghost (1763) bk. 4, l. 1386

20 Happy, thrice happy now the savage race,
Since Europe took their gold, and gave them
    grace!
Pastors she sends to help them in their need,
Some who can't write, with others who can't
    read.
Gotham (1764) bk. 1, l. 67

21 Old-age, a second child, by Nature cursed
With more and greater evils than the first,
Weak, sickly, full of pains; in ev'ry breath
Railing at life, and yet afraid of death.
Gotham (1764) bk. 1, l. 215

22 Keep up appearances; there lies the test;
The world will give thee credit for the rest.

Outward be fair, however foul within;
Sin if thou wilt, but then in secret sin.
Night (1761) l. 311

1 Stay out all night, but take especial care
That Prudence bring thee back to early prayer
As one with watching and with study faint,
Reel in a drunkard, and reel out a saint.
Night (1761) l. 321

2 Grave without thought, and without feeling gay.
on pretentious poets
The Prophecy of Famine (1763) l. 60

3   No merit but mere knack of rhyme,
Short gleams of sense, and satire out of time.
The Prophecy of Famine (1763) l. 81

4 Apt Alliteration's artful aid.
The Prophecy of Famine (1763) l. 86

5 He sickened at all triumphs but his own.
of Thomas Franklin, Professor of Greek at Cambridge University
The Rosciad (1761) l. 64

6 To mischief trained, e'en from his mother's womb,
Grown old in fraud, tho' yet in manhood's bloom.
Adopting arts, by which gay villains rise,
And reach the heights, which honest men despise;
Mute at the bar, and in the senate loud,
Dull 'mongst the dullest, proudest of the proud;
A pert, prim prater of the northern race,
Guilt in his heart, and famine in his face.
of Alexander Wedderburn, later Lord Loughborough
The Rosciad (1761) l. 69

7 Ne'er blushed unless, in spreading Vice's snares,
She blundered on some virtue unawares.
The Rosciad (1761) l. 137

8 Learned without sense, and venerably dull.
of Arthur Murphy
The Rosciad (1761) l. 592

9 But, spite of all the criticizing elves,
Those who would make us feel, must feel
   themselves.
The Rosciad (1761) l. 961

10 Where he falls short, 'tis Nature's fault alone;
Where he succeeds, the merit's all his own.
of the actor, Thomas Sheridan
The Rosciad (1761) l. 1025

Lord Randolph Churchill 1849–94

British Conservative politician

11 The forest laments in order that Mr Gladstone may
perspire.
on Gladstone's hobby of felling trees
   speech on Financial Reform, delivered in Blackpool, 24
   January 1884, in F. Banfield (ed.) *Life and Speeches of Lord
   Randolph Churchill* (1884)

12 I decided some time ago that if the G. O. M. went
for Home Rule, the Orange card would be the one
to play. Please God it may turn out the ace of
trumps and not the two.
G. O. M. = Grand Old Man (Gladstone)
   letter to Lord Justice FitzGibbon, 16 February 1886, in
   Robert Rhodes James *Lord Randolph Churchill* (1959) ch. 8

13 Ulster will fight; Ulster will be right.
   public letter, 7 May 1886, in R. F. Foster *Lord Randolph
   Churchill* (1981)

14 An old man in a hurry.
on Gladstone
   address to the electors of South Paddington, 19 June 1886;
   in W. S. Churchill *Lord Randolph Churchill* (1906) vol. 2

15 All great men make mistakes. Napoleon forgot
Blücher, I forgot Goschen.
*when Lord Randolph suddenly resigned the position of
Chancellor of the Exchequer in 1886, Goschen had
been appointed in his place*
   Leaves from the Notebooks of Lady Dorothy Nevill (1907)

16 I never could make out what those damned dots
[decimal points] meant.
   W. S. Churchill *Lord Randolph Churchill* (1906) vol. 2

Winston Churchill 1874–1965

*British Conservative statesman; Prime Minister, 1940–5,
1951–5*
*on Churchill: see **Attlee** 33:1, **Balfour** 51:9, **Bevan** 73:11, **de
Valera** 266:4, **Murrow** 555:6; see also **Johnson** 432:10*

17 It cannot in the opinion of His Majesty's
Government be classified as slavery in the extreme
acceptance of the word without some risk of
terminological inexactitude.
   speech in the House of Commons, 22 February 1906

18 He is one of those orators of whom it was well
said, 'Before they get up, they do not know what
they are going to say; when they are speaking,
they do not know what they are saying; and
when they have sat down, they do not know what
they have said.'
of Lord Charles Beresford
   speech in the House of Commons, 20 December 1912

19 Business carried on as usual during alterations on
the map of Europe.
on the self-adopted 'motto' of the British people
   speech at Guildhall, 9 November 1914, *Complete Speeches*
   (1974) vol. 3

20 The difference between him and Arthur is that
Arthur is wicked and moral, Asquith is good and
immoral.
comparing H. H. Asquith with Arthur Balfour
   E. T. Raymond *Mr Balfour* (1920)

21 The whole map of Europe has been changed . . .
but as the deluge subsides and the waters fall
short we see the dreary steeples of Fermanagh and
Tyrone emerging once again.
   speech in the House of Commons, 16 February 1922

22 Anyone can rat, but it takes a certain amount of
ingenuity to re-rat.
*on rejoining the Conservatives twenty years after
leaving them for the Liberals, c.1924*
   Kay Halle *Irrepressible Churchill* (1966)

23 I remember, when I was a child, being taken to
the celebrated Barnum's circus, which contained
an exhibition of freaks and monstrosities, but the
exhibit on the programme which I most desired to
see was the one described as 'The Boneless

Wonder'. My parents judged that that spectacle would be too revolting and demoralizing for my youthful eyes, and I have waited 50 years to see the boneless wonder sitting on the Treasury Bench.

of Ramsay MacDonald

speech in the House of Commons, 28 January 1931

1 [The Government] go on in strange paradox, decided only to be undecided, resolved to be irresolute, adamant for drift, solid for fluidity, all-powerful to be impotent.

speech in the House of Commons, 12 November 1936

2 Dictators ride to and fro upon tigers which they dare not dismount. And the tigers are getting hungry.

letter, 11 November 1937, in *Step by Step* (1939); see **Proverbs** 622:14

3 The utmost he [Neville Chamberlain] has been able to gain for Czechoslovakia and in the matters which were in dispute has been that the German dictator, instead of snatching his victuals from the table, has been content to have them served to him course by course.

speech in the House of Commons, 5 October 1938

4 I cannot forecast to you the action of Russia. It is a riddle wrapped in a mystery inside an enigma.

radio broadcast, 1 October 1939, in *Into Battle* (1941)

5 I have nothing to offer but blood, toil, tears and sweat.

speech in the House of Commons, 13 May 1940; see **Byron** 177:22

6 What is our policy? . . . to wage war against a monstrous tyranny, never surpassed in the dark, lamentable catalogue of human crime.

speech in the House of Commons, 13 May 1940

7 What is our aim? . . . Victory, victory at all costs, victory in spite of all terror; victory, however long and hard the road may be; for without victory, there is no survival.

speech in the House of Commons, 13 May 1940

8 We shall not flag or fail. We shall go on to the end. We shall fight in France, we shall fight on the seas and oceans, we shall fight with growing confidence and growing strength in the air, we shall defend our island, whatever the cost may be. We shall fight on the beaches, we shall fight on the landing grounds, we shall fight in the fields and in the streets, we shall fight in the hills; we shall never surrender.

speech in the House of Commons, 4 June 1940

9 Let us therefore brace ourselves to our duty, and so bear ourselves that, if the British Empire and its Commonwealth lasts for a thousand years, men will still say, 'This was their finest hour.'

speech in the House of Commons, 18 June 1940

10 Never in the field of human conflict was so much owed by so many to so few.

on the Battle of Britain

speech in the House of Commons, 20 August 1940

11 No one can guarantee success in war, but only deserve it.

letter to Lord Wavell, 26 November 1940, in *The Second World War* vol. 2 (1949) ch. 27; see **Addison** 4:8

12 Give us the tools and we will finish the job.

radio broadcast, 9 February 1941, in *Complete Speeches* (1974) vol. 6

13 When I warned them [the French Government] that Britain would fight on alone whatever they did, their generals told their Prime Minister and his divided Cabinet, 'In three weeks England will have her neck wrung like a chicken.' Some chicken! Some neck!

speech to Canadian Parliament, 30 December 1941, in *Complete Speeches* (1974) vol. 6

14 A medal glitters, but it also casts a shadow.

a reference to the envy caused by the award of honours in 1941; Kenneth Rose *King George V* (1983) p. 7

15 Now this is not the end. It is not even the beginning of the end. But it is, perhaps, the end of the beginning.

on the Battle of Egypt

speech at the Mansion House, London, 10 November 1942, in *The End of the Beginning* (1943)

16 We make this wide encircling movement in the Mediterranean, having for its primary object the recovery of the command of that vital sea, but also having for its object the exposure of the underbelly of the Axis, especially Italy, to heavy attack.

speech in the House of Commons, 11 November 1942; see **Misquotations** 538:17

17 National compulsory insurance for all classes for all purposes from the cradle to the grave.

radio broadcast, 21 March 1943, in *Complete Speeches* (1974) vol. 7

18 There is no finer investment for any community than putting milk into babies.

radio broadcast, 21 March 1943, in *Complete Speeches* (1974) vol. 7

19 The empires of the future are the empires of the mind.

speech at Harvard, 6 September 1943, in *Onwards to Victory* (1944)

20 From Stettin in the Baltic to Trieste in the Adriatic an iron curtain has descended across the Continent.

'iron curtain' *previously had been applied by others to the Soviet Union or her sphere of influence, e.g. Ethel Snowden* Through Bolshevik Russia (1920), *Dr* **Goebbels** Das Reich (25 February 1945), *and by Churchill himself in a cable to President* **Truman** (4 June 1945)

speech at Westminster College, Fulton, Missouri, 5 March 1946, in *Complete Speeches* (1974) vol. 7

21 Democracy is the worst form of Government except all those other forms that have been tried from time to time.

speech in the House of Commons, 11 November 1947

22 This is the sort of English up with which I will not put.

Ernest Gowers *Plain Words* (1948) 'Troubles with Prepositions'

1 Naval tradition?. Monstrous. Nothing but rum, sodomy, prayers, and the lash.
often quoted as 'rum, sodomy, and the lash', as in Peter Gretton Former Naval Person *(1968)*
Harold Nicolson, diary, 17 August 1950

2 The candle in that great turnip has gone out.
*in reply to the comment 'One never hears of **Baldwin** nowadays — he might as well be dead'*
Harold Nicolson: *Diaries and Letters 1945-62* (1968) diary 17 August 1950

3 To jaw-jaw is always better than to war-war.
speech at White House, 26 June 1954, in *New York Times* 27 June 1954

4 I have never accepted what many people have kindly said—namely, that I inspired the nation . . . It was the nation and the race dwelling all round the globe that had the lion's heart. I had the luck to be called upon to give the roar. I also hope that I sometimes suggested to the lion the right place to use his claws.
speech at Westminster Hall, 30 November 1954

5 I have taken more out of alcohol than alcohol has taken out of me.
Quentin Reynolds *By Quentin Reynolds* (1964) ch. 11

6 In defeat unbeatable: in victory unbearable.
*of Lord **Montgomery***
Edward Marsh *Ambrosia and Small Beer* (1964) ch. 5

7 Like a powerful graceful cat walking delicately and unsoiled across a rather muddy street.
*of **Balfour**'s moving from **Asquith**'s Cabinet to that of **Lloyd George***
Great Contemporaries (1937)

8 *of the career of Lord **Curzon**:*
The morning had been golden; the noontide was bronze; and the evening lead. But all were solid, and each was polished till it shone after its fashion.
Great Contemporaries (1937)

9 Courage is rightly esteemed the first of human qualities because as has been said, it is the quality which guarantees all others.
Great Contemporaries (1937)

10 Headmasters have powers at their disposal with which Prime Ministers have never yet been invested.
My Early Life (1930) ch. 2

11 Mr Gladstone read Homer for fun, which I thought served him right.
My Early Life (1930) ch. 2

12 It is a good thing for an uneducated man to read books of quotations.
My Early Life (1930) ch. 9

13 In war: resolution. In defeat: defiance. In victory: magnanimity. In peace: goodwill.
The Second World War vol. 1 (1948) epigraph, which according to Edward Marsh in *A Number of People* (1939), occurred to Churchill shortly after the conclusion of the First World War

14 The loyalties which centre upon number one are enormous. If he trips he must be sustained. If he makes mistakes they must be covered. If he sleeps he must not be wantonly disturbed. If he is no good he must be pole-axed. But this last extreme process cannot be carried out every day; and certainly not in the days just after he has been chosen.
The Second World War (1949) vol. 2, ch. 1

15 If Hitler invaded hell I would make at least a favourable reference to the devil in the House of Commons.
The Second World War (1950) vol. 3, ch. 20

16 I did not suffer from any desire to be relieved of my responsibilities. All I wanted was compliance with my wishes after reasonable discussion.
The Second World War (1951) vol. 4, ch. 5

17 Jellicoe was the only man on either side who could lose the war in an afternoon.
The World Crisis (1927) pt. 1, ch. 5

18 The ability to foretell what is going to happen tomorrow, next week, next month, and next year. And to have the ability afterwards to explain why it didn't happen.
describing the qualifications desirable in a prospective politician
B. Adler *Churchill Wit* (1965)

19 I am fond of pigs. Dogs look up to us. Cats look down on us. Pigs treat us as equals.
attributed, in M. Gilbert *Never Despair* (1988)

20 NANCY ASTOR: If I were your wife I would put poison in your coffee!
CHURCHILL: And if I were your husband I would drink it.
Consuelo Vanderbilt Balsan *Glitter and Gold* (1952)

21 A remarkable example of modern art. It certainly combines force with candour.
on the notorious 80th birthday portrait by Graham Sutherland, later destroyed by Lady Churchill
Martin Gilbert *Churchill: A Life* (1991)

22 The only recorded instance in history of a rat swimming *towards* a sinking ship.
of a former Conservative who proposed to stand as a Liberal
Leon Harris *The Fine Art of Political Wit* (1965)

23 A sheep in sheep's clothing.
*of Clement **Attlee***
Lord Home *The Way the Wind Blows* (1976) ch. 6; see **Gosse** 357:8

24 Take away that pudding—it has no theme.
Lord Home *The Way the Wind Blows* (1976) ch. 16

Count Galeazzo Ciano 1903–44
*Italian fascist politician; son-in-law of **Mussolini***

25 *La vittoria trova cento padri, e nessuno vuole riconoscere l'insuccesso.*
Victory has a hundred fathers, but defeat is an orphan.
literally 'no-one wants to recognise defeat as his own'
Diary (1946) vol. 2, 9 September 1942

Colley Cibber 1671–1757

English dramatist

1 Oh! how many torments lie in the small circle of a wedding-ring!
The Double Gallant (1707) act 1, sc. 2

2 Off with his head—so much for Buckingham.
Richard III (1700) act 4 (adapted from Shakespeare); see **Shakespeare** 716:31

3 Perish the thought!
Richard III (1700) act 5 (adapted from Shakespeare)

4 Conscience avaunt, Richard's himself again:
Hark! the shrill trumpet sounds, to horse, away,
My soul's in arms, and eager for the fray.
Richard III (1700) act 5 (adapted from Shakespeare)

5 Stolen sweets are best.
The Rival Fools (1709) act 1, sc. 1; see **Proverbs** 631:23

Cicero (Marcus Tullius Cicero) 106–43 BC

Roman orator and statesman
on Cicero: see **Catullus** 202:19, **Dickens** 269:7; see also **Misquotations** 537:5

6 *Dicit enim tamquam in Platonis* πολιτεία, *non tamquam in Romuli faece sententiam.*
For he delivers his opinions as though he were living in Plato's Republic rather than among the dregs of Romulus.
of M. Porcius Cato, the Younger
Ad Atticum bk. 2, letter 1, sect. 8

7 *Sed nescio quo modo nihil tam absurde dici potest quod non dicatur ab aliquo philosophorum.*
There is nothing so absurd but some philosopher has said it.
De Divinatione bk. 2, ch. 119

8 *Vulgo enim dicitur: Iucundi acti labores.*
For it is commonly said: completed labours are pleasant.
De Finibus bk. 2, ch. 105

9 *Salus populi suprema est lex.*
The good of the people is the chief law.
De Legibus bk. 3, ch. 8; see **Selden** 676:9

10 '*Ipse dixit.*' '*Ipse*' *autem erat Pythagoras.*
'He himself said', and this 'himself' was Pythagoras.
De Natura Deorum bk. 1, ch. 10

11 *Summum bonum.*
The highest good.
De Officiis bk. 1, ch. 5

12 For of all gainful professions, nothing is better, nothing more pleasing, nothing more delightful, nothing better becomes a well-bred man than agriculture.
De Officiis bk. 1, ch. 42

13 *Cedant arma togae, concedant laurea laudi.*
Let war yield to peace, laurels to paeans.
De Officiis bk. 1, ch. 77

14 *Mens cuiusque is est quisque.*
The spirit is the true self.
De Republica bk. 6, ch. 26

15 *Quousque tandem abutere, Catilina, patientia nostra?*
How long will you abuse our patience, Catiline?
In Catilinam Speech 1, ch. 1

16 *O tempora, O mores!*
Oh, the times! Oh, the manners!
In Catilinam Speech 1, ch. 1

17 *Abiit, excessit, evasit, erupit.*
He departed, he withdrew, he strode off, he broke forth.
In Catilinam Speech 2, ch. 1

18 *Civis Romanus sum.*
I am a Roman citizen.
In Verrem Speech 5, ch. 147; see **Kennedy** 449:5, **Palmerston** 584:20

19 *Quod di omen avertant.*
May the gods avert this omen.
Third Philippic ch. 35

20 *Nervos belli, pecuniam infinitam.*
The sinews of war, unlimited money.
Fifth Philippic ch. 5; see **Bacon** 45:26, **Farquhar** 315:20

21 *Silent enim leges inter arma.*
Laws are silent in time of war.
Pro Milone ch. 11

22 *Cui bono?*
To whose profit?
Pro Roscio Amerino ch. 84 and *Pro Milone* ch. 12, sect. 32, quoting L. Cassius Longinus Ravilla

23 *Id quod est praestantissimum maximeque optabile omnibus sanis et bonis et beatis, cum dignitate otium.*
The thing which is the most outstanding and chiefly to be desired by all healthy and good and well-off persons, is leisure with honour.
Pro Sestio ch. 98

24 *Errare mehercule malo cum Platone . . . quam cum istis vera sentire.*
I would rather be wrong, by God, with Plato . . . than be correct with those men.
on Pythagoreans
Tusculanae Disputationes bk. 1, ch. 39

25 *O fortunatam natam me consule Romam!*
O happy Rome, born when I was consul!
Juvenal *Satires* poem 10, l. 122

26 *Laudandum adulescentum, ornandum, tollendum.*
The young man should be praised, decorated, and got rid of.
*of Octavian, the future Emperor **Augustus***
referred to in a letter from Decimus Brutus to Cicero; *Epistulae ad Familiares* bk. 11, sect. 20

E. M. Cioran 1911–95

Romanian-born French philosopher

27 Without the possibility of suicide, I would have killed myself long ago.
in *Independent* 2 December 1989

28 I do nothing, granted. But I see the hours pass—which is better than trying to fill them.
in *Guardian* 11 May 1993

Claire Clairmont 1798–1879

English lover of Byron and stepsister of Mary Shelley

1 I shall ever remember the gentleness of your manners and the wild originality of your countenance.

> letter to Lord Byron, 16 April 1816; M. K. Stocking (ed.)
> *The Clairmont Correspondence* (1995)

John Clare 1793–1864

English poet

2 When badgers fight and everyone's a foe.

> 'Badger' (written *c.*1836)

3 He could not die when the trees were green,
For he loved the time too well.

> 'The Dying Child'

4 My life hath been one chain of contradictions,
Madhouses, prisons, whore-shops.

> 'Child Harold' (written 1841) l. 146

5 They took me from my wife, and to save trouble
I wed again, and made the error double.

> 'Child Harold' (written 1841) l. 152

6   God hath often saw
Things here too dirty for the light of day;
For in a madhouse there exists no law
Now stagnant grows my too refinèd clay;
I envy birds their wings to fly away.

> 'Child Harold' (written 1841) l. 158

7 Pale death, the grand physician, cures all pain;
The dead rest well who lived for joys in vain.

> 'Child Harold' (written 1841) l. 215

8 When words refuse before the crowd
My Mary's name to give,
The muse in silence sings aloud:
And there my love will live.

> 'Child Harold' (written 1841) l. 513

9 Hopeless hope hopes on and meets no end,
Wastes without springs and homes without a friend.

> 'Child Harold' (written 1841) l. 1018

10 A quiet, pilfering, unprotected race.

> 'The Gipsy Camp' (1841)

11 I am—yet what I am, none cares or knows;
My friends forsake me like a memory lost:
I am the self-consumer of my woes.

> 'I Am' (1848)

12 I long for scenes where man hath never trod
A place where woman never smiled or wept
There to abide with my Creator God
And sleep as I in childhood sweetly slept,
Untroubling and untroubled where I lie
The grass below, above, the vaulted sky.

> 'I Am' (1848)

13 The present is the funeral of the past,
And man the living sepulchre of life.

> 'The present is the funeral of the past' (written 1845)

14 Summers pleasures they are gone like to visions every one
And the cloudy days of autumn and of winter cometh on

I tried to call them back but unbidden they are gone
Far away from heart and eye and for ever far away.

> 'Remembrances'

Edward Hyde, Earl of Clarendon 1609–74

English statesman and historian

15 Without question, when he first drew the sword,
he threw away the scabbard.

of Hampden

> *The History of the Rebellion* (1703, ed. W. D. Macray, 1888)
> vol. 3, bk. 7, sect. 84; see **Proverbs** 635:6

16 He had a head to contrive, a tongue to persuade,
and a hand to execute any mischief.

of Hampden

> *The History of the Rebellion* (1703, ed. W. D. Macray, 1888)
> vol. 3, bk. 7, sect. 84; see **Gibbon** 345:7

17 He . . . would, with a shrill and sad accent,
ingeminate the word *Peace, Peace*.

of Falkland

> *The History of the Rebellion* (1703, ed. W. D. Macray, 1888)
> vol. 3, bk. 7, sect. 233

18 So enamoured on peace that he would have been
glad the King should have bought it at any price.

of Falkland

> *The History of the Rebellion* (1703, ed. W. D. Macray, 1888)
> vol. 3, bk. 7, sect. 233

19 He will be looked upon by posterity as a brave bad man.

of Cromwell

> *The History of the Rebellion* (1703, ed. W. D. Macray, 1888)
> vol. 6, bk. 15

Claribel (Mrs Charlotte Alington Barnard) 1840–69

English writer of ballads

20 I cannot sing the old songs
I sang long years ago,
For heart and voice would fail me,
And foolish tears would flow.

> 'The Old Songs' (1865)

Alan Clark 1928–99

British Conservative politician, son of Kenneth Clark
on Clark: see **Campbell** 18:14

21 There are no true friends in politics. We are all
sharks circling, and waiting, for traces of blood to
appear in the water.

> diary, 30 November 1990

22 Our old friend economical . . . with the *actualité*.

under cross-examination at the Old Bailey during the
Matrix Churchill case

> in *Independent* 10 November 1992; see **Armstrong** 26:18

23 Safe is spelled D-U-L-L. Politics has got to be a fun
activity, otherwise people turn their back on it.

> in *Daily Telegraph* 25 January 1997

Kenneth Clark 1903-83

*English art historian, father of Alan **Clark***

1 It's a curious fact that the all-male religions have produced no religious imagery—in most cases have positively forbidden it. The great religious art of the world is deeply involved with the female principle.

Civilisation (1969) ch. 7

Arthur C. Clarke 1917-

English science fiction writer

2 When a distinguished but elderly scientist states that something is possible, he is almost certainly right. When he states that something is impossible, he is very probably wrong.

Profiles of the Future (1962) ch. 2; see **Asimov** 31:18

3 Any sufficiently advanced technology is indistinguishable from magic.

Profiles of the Future (1962) ch. 2

4 How inappropriate to call this planet Earth when it is clearly Ocean.

in *Nature* 8 March 1990

5 The only genuine consciousness-expanding drug.

of science fiction

letter claiming coinage in *New Scientist* 2 April 1994

Austin Clarke 1896-1974

Irish poet, dramatist, and novelist

6 For the house of the planter
Is known by the trees.

'The Planter's Daughter' (1929)

7 And O! She was the Sunday
In every week.

'The Planter's Daughter' (1929)

Grant Clarke 1891-1931 and Edgar Leslie 1885-1976

8 He'd have to get under, get out and get under
And fix up his automobile.

He'd Have to Get Under—Get Out and Get Under (1913 song)

James Stanier Clarke c.1765-1834

English clergyman, chaplain and private secretary to Prince Leopold of Coburg

9 Perhaps when you again appear in print you may choose to dedicate your volumes to Prince Leopold: any historical romance, illustrative of the history of the august House of Coburg, would just now be very interesting.

letter to Jane Austen, 27 March 1816, in R. W. Chapman (ed.) *Jane Austen's Letters* (1952)

John Clarke d. 1658

10 He that would thrive
Must rise at five;
He that hath thriven
May lie till seven.

Paraemiologia Anglo-Latina (1639) 'Diligentia'

Claudian 370-c.404

Alexandrian-born Roman poet

11 *Erret, et extremos alter scrutetur Hiberos:*
Plus habet hic vitae, plus habet ille viae.

Let who will be a wanderer and explore farthest Spain: such may have more of a journey: this man has more of a life.

of the old man of Verona who never left his home

De Sene Veronensi

Appius Claudius Caecus fl. 312-279 BC

Roman censor, orator, and prose writer

12 *Faber est suae quisque fortunae.*

Each man is the smith of his own fortune.

Sallust *Ad Caesarem Senem de Re Publica Oratio* ch. 1, sect. 2; see **Proverbs** 619:17

Matthias Claudius 1740-1815

German poet

13 *'s ist leider Krieg—und ich begehre*
Nicht schuld daran zu sein!

Alas, it is war, and I have no wish to carry the guilt for it.

Warsong

14 *Was sollt ich machen, wenn im Schlaf mit Grämen*
Und blutig, bleich und blass,
Die Geister Erschlagnen zu mir kämen,
Und vor mir weinten, was?

What should I do if in fretful sleep
The ghosts of the slaughtered were to appear,
Bloody, pale, and wan, and weep
In front of me, what should I do?

Warsong

Karl von Clausewitz 1780-1831

Prussian soldier and military theorist

15 Everything is very simple in war, but the simplest thing is difficult. These difficulties accumulate and produce a friction which no man can imagine exactly who has not seen war.

On War (1832-4) bk. 1, ch. 7, tr. J. J. Graham

16 The closer these practical probabilities drive war toward the absolute, the more the belligerent states are involved and drawn into its vortex, the clearer appear the connections between its separate actions, and the more imperative the need not to take the first step without considering the last.

On War (1832-4) bk. 8, ch. 3, tr. M. Howard and P. Paret

17 War is nothing but a continuation of politics with the admixture of other means.

commonly rendered as 'War is the continuation of politics by other means'

On War (1832-4) bk. 8, ch. 6, sect. B

Henry Clay 1777–1852
American politician
*on Clay: see **Glascock** 351:13*

1 If you wish to avoid foreign collision, you had
better abandon the ocean.
> speech in the House of Representatives, 22 January 1812,
> in C. Colton *The Life, Correspondence and Speeches of Henry
> Clay* (1864) vol. 5

2 The gentleman [Josiah Quincy] can not have
forgotten his own sentiment, uttered even on the
floor of this House, 'peaceably if we can, forcibly if
we must'.
> speech in Congress, 8 January 1813, in C. Colton (ed.) *The
> Works of Henry Clay* (1904) vol. 1; see **Quincy** 639:9

3 The arts of power and its minions are the same in
all countries and in all ages. It marks a victim;
denounces it; and excites the public odium and
the public hatred, to conceal its own abuses and
encroachments.
> speech in the Senate, 14 March 1834, in C. Colton (ed.)
> *The Works of Henry Clay* (1904) vol. 5

4 I had rather be right than be President.
> *to Senator Preston of South Carolina, 1839*
> attributed; S. W. McCall *Life of Thomas Brackett Reed* (1914)
> ch. 14

5 It has been my invariable rule to do all for the
Union. If any man wants the key of my heart, let
him take the key of the Union, and that is the key
to my heart.
> speech in Norfolk, 22 April 1844; Robert V. Rimini *Henry
> Clay* (1991)

Philip 'Tubby' Clayton 1885–1972
Australian-born British clergyman, founder of Toc H

6 CHAIRMAN: What is service?
CANDIDATE: The rent we pay for our room on
earth.
> *admission ceremony of Toc H, a society founded after
> the First World War to provide Christian fellowship
> and social service*
> Tresham Lever *Clayton of Toc H* (1971)

Eldridge Cleaver 1935–98
American political activist

7 Too much agreement kills a chat.
> *Soul on Ice* (1968) 'Letters from Prison'

8 What we're saying today is that you're either part
of the solution or you're part of the problem.
> speech in San Francisco, 1968, in R. Scheer *Eldridge
> Cleaver, Post Prison Writings and Speeches* (1969)

John Cleland 1710–89
English writer

9 Truth! stark naked truth, is the word.
> *Memoirs of a Woman of Pleasure* a.k.a. *Fanny Hill* (1749)
> vol. 1

Georges Clemenceau 1841–1929
French statesman; Prime Minister of France, 1906–9, 1917–20
*see also **Sayings** 670:9*

10 War is too serious a matter to entrust to military
men.
> attributed to Clemenceau, e.g. in Hampden Jackson
> *Clemenceau and the Third Republic* (1946), but also to Briand
> and Talleyrand; see **de Gaulle** 262:6

11 My home policy: I wage war; my foreign policy: I
wage war. All the time I wage war.
> speech to French Chamber of Deputies, 8 March 1918, in
> *Discours de Guerre* (1968)

12 It is easier to make war than to make peace.
> speech at Verdun, 20 July 1919, in *Discours de Paix* (1938)

13 What do you expect when I'm between two men
of whom one [Lloyd George] thinks he is Napoleon
and the other [Woodrow Wilson] thinks he is
Jesus Christ?
> *to André Tardieu, on being asked why he always gave
> in to **Lloyd George** at the Paris Peace Conference,
> 1918*
> James Lees-Milne *Harold Nicolson* (1980) vol. 1, ch. 7, letter
> from Nicolson to his wife, 20 May 1919

Clement XIII 1693–1769
Italian cleric; Pope 1758–69

14 *Sint ut sunt aut non sint.*
Let them be as they are or not be at all.
> *replying to a request for changes in the constitutions
> of the Society of Jesus*
> J. A. M. Crétineau-Joly *Clément XIV et les Jésuites* (1847)

Cleopatra 69–30 BC
Egyptian monarch, Queen from 47 BC

15 I will not be triumphed over.
> Livy *Ab Urbe Condita* bk. 133 (fragment 54)

Grover Cleveland 1837–1908
*American Democratic statesman; 22nd and 24th President of
the US 1885–9 and 1893–7*

16 I have considered the pension list of the republic a
roll of honour.
> Veto of Dependent Pension Bill, 5 July 1888, in *A
> Compilation of the Messages and Papers of the Presidents* vol.
> 11 (1897)

17 The lessons of paternalism ought to be unlearned
and the better lesson taught that, while the people
should patriotically and cheerfully support their
government, its functions do not include the
support of the people.
> inaugural address, 4 March 1893, in *New York Times* 5
> March 1893

Harlan Cleveland 1918–
American government official

18 The revolution of rising expectations.
> phrase coined, 1950; Arthur Schlesinger *A Thousand Days*
> (1965) ch. 16

John Cleveland 1613–58

English poet
see also **Epitaphs** 310:7

1 Had Cain been Scot, God would have changed his
 doom
 Nor forced him wander, but confined him home.
 'The Rebel Scot' (1647)

Clarice Cliff 1899–1972

English ceramic artist

2 Women today want continual change, they will
 have colour and plenty of it. Colour seems to
 radiate happiness and the spirit of modern life and
 movement, and I cannot put too much of it into
 my designs to please women.
 in 1930; Leonard Griffin *Clarice Cliff: the Art of the Bizarre*
 (1999)

Hillary Rodham Clinton 1947–

American lawyer, wife of Bill **Clinton**, *First Lady of the US*
1993–2001

3 I am not standing by my man, like Tammy
 Wynette. I am sitting here because I love him, I
 respect him, and I honour what he's been through
 and what we've been through together.
 interview on *60 Minutes*, CBS-TV, 27 January 1992

4 I could have stayed home and baked cookies and
 had teas. But what I decided was to fulfil my
 profession, which I entered before my husband
 was in public life.
 comment on questions raised by rival Democratic
 contender Edmund G. Brown Jr.; in *Albany Times-Union* 17
 March 1992

5 The great story here . . . is this vast right-wing
 conspiracy that has been conspiring against my
 husband since the day he announced for
 president.
 interview on *Today* (NBC television), 27 January 1998

William Jefferson ('Bill') Clinton 1946–

American Democratic statesman; 42nd President of the US
1993–2001; husband of Hillary Rodham **Clinton**

6 I experimented with marijuana a time or two. And
 I didn't like it, and I didn't inhale.
 in *Washington Post* 30 March 1992

7 The comeback kid!
 description of himself after coming second in the New
 Hampshire primary in the 1992 presidential election
 (since 1952, no presidential candidate had won the
 election without first winning in New Hampshire)
 Michael Barone and Grant Ujifusa *The Almanac of American*
 Politics 1994

8 I did not have sexual relations with that woman.
 television interview, in *Daily Telegraph* 27 January 1998

9 It depends on what the meaning of 'is' is.
 videotaped evidence to the grand jury; tapes broadcast
 21 September 1998
 in *Guardian* 22 September 1998

10 The American people have spoken—but it's going
 to take a little while to determine exactly what
 they said.
 on the US presidential election
 in *Mail on Sunday* 12 November 2000; see **Salisbury** 664:6

Lord Clive 1725–74

British general; Governor of Bengal
on Clive: see **Bentley** 68:13

11 By God, Mr Chairman, at this moment I stand
 astonished at my own moderation!
 reply during Parliamentary cross-examination, 1773
 G. R. Gleig *The Life of Robert, First Lord Clive* (1848) ch. 29

12 I feel that I am reserved for some end or other.
 when his pistol twice failed to fire, while attempting to
 take his own life
 G. R. Gleig *The Life of Robert, First Lord Clive* (1848) ch. 1

☐ **Closing lines**
see box overleaf

Arthur Hugh Clough 1819–61

English poet
on Clough: see **Swinburne** 769:7

13 Rome, believe me, my friend, is like its own Monte
 Testaceo,
 Merely a marvellous mass of broken and castaway
 wine-pots.
 Amours de Voyage (1858) canto 1, pt. 2

14 I do not like being moved: for the will is excited;
 and action
 Is a most dangerous thing: I tremble for something
 factitious,
 Some malpractice of heart and illegitimate
 process;
 We are so prone to these things with our terrible
 notions of duty.
 Amours de Voyage (1858) canto 2, pt. 11

15 Whither depart the souls of the brave that die in
 the battle,
 Die in the lost, lost fight, for the cause that
 perishes with them?
 Amours de Voyage (1858) canto 5, pt. 6

16 Sesquipedalian blackguard.
 The Bothie of Tober-na-Vuolich (1848) pt. 2, l. 223

17 Good, too, Logic, of course; in itself, but not in fine
 weather.
 The Bothie of Tober-na-Vuolich (1848) pt. 2, l. 249

18 Grace is given of God, but knowledge is bought in
 the market.
 The Bothie of Tober-na-Vuolich (1848) pt. 4, l. 159

19 Afloat. We move: Delicious! Ah,
 What else is like the gondola?
 Dipsychus (1865) sc. 5

20 This world is bad enough may-be;
 We do not comprehend it;
 But in one fact can all agree
 God won't, and we can't mend it.
 Dipsychus (1865) sc. 5

Continued

Closing lines

1 After all, tomorrow is another day.
   Margaret **Mitchell** *Gone with the Wind* (1936)

2 *L'amor che muove il sole e l'altre stelle.*
   The love that moves the sun and the other stars.
   Dante Alighieri *Divina Commedia* 'Paradiso'

3 And so I betake myself to that course, which is
   almost as much as to see myself go into my
   grave—for which, and all the discomforts that
   will accompany my being blind, the good God
   prepare me!
   Samuel **Pepys** *Diary* 31 May 1669

4 And they lived happily ever after.
   traditional ending to a fairy story
   recorded (with slight variations) from the 1850s

5 And when they buried him the little port
   Had seldom seen a costlier funeral.
   Alfred, Lord **Tennyson** 'Enoch Arden' (1864)

6 Be not solitary, be not idle.
   Robert **Burton** *The Anatomy of Melancholy* (1621–51)

7 The creatures outside looked from pig to man,
   and from man to pig, and from pig to man
   again, but already it was impossible to say
   which was which.
   George **Orwell** *Animal Farm* (1945)

8 *Das Ewig-Weibliche zieht uns hinan.*
   Eternal Woman draws us upward.
   Johann Wolfgang von **Goethe** *Faust* pt. 2 (1832)
   'Hochgebirg'

9 For it is the dawn that has come, as it has come
   for a thousand centuries, never failing. But when
   that dawn will come, of our emancipation, from
   the fear of bondage and the bondage of fear,
   why, that is a secret.
   Alan **Paton** *Cry, The Beloved Country* (1948)

10   For ne'er
   Was flattery lost on poet's ear:
   A simple race! they waste their toil
   For the vain tribute of a smile.
   Sir Walter **Scott** *The Lay of the Last Minstrel* (1805)
   canto 4

11 From hence, let fierce contending nations know
   What dire effects from civil discord flow.
   Joseph **Addison** *Cato* (1713)

12 The gladsome light of Jurisprudence.
   Edward **Coke** *The First Part of the Institutes of the Laws of
   England* (1628) 'Epilogus'

13 Goddess, allow this aged man his right,
   To be your beadsman now that was your knight.
   George **Peele** *Polyhymnia* (1590) 'Sonnet'

14 He will be looked upon by posterity as a brave
   bad man.
   of **Cromwell**
   Edward Hyde, Earl of **Clarendon** *The History of the
   Rebellion* (1703)

15 *Hört ihr das Glöckchen klingeln? Kniet nieder—Man
   bringt die Sakramente einem sterbenden Gotte.*
   Do you hear the little bell tinkle? Kneel down.
   They are bringing the sacraments to a dying
   god.
   Heinrich **Heine** *Zur Geschichte der Religion und Philosophie
   in Deutschland* (1834) bk. 2

16 I lingered round them, under that benign sky:
   watched the moths fluttering among the heath
   and hare-bells; listened to the soft wind
   breathing through the grass; and wondered how
   any one could ever imagine unquiet slumbers for
   the sleepers in that quiet earth.
   Emily **Brontë** *Wuthering Heights* (1847)

17 'Justice' was done, and the President of the
   Immortals (in Aeschylean phrase) had ended his
   sport with Tess.
   Thomas **Hardy** *Tess of the D'Urbervilles* (1891)

18 Learn to write well, or not to write at all.
   John Sheffield, 1st Duke of **Buckingham** 'An Essay upon
   Satire' (1689)

19 Oh my grief, I've lost him surely. I've lost the
   only Playboy of the Western World.
   John Millington **Synge** *The Playboy of the Western World*
   (1907) act 3

20 The proletarians have nothing to lose but their
   chains. They have a world to win. WORKING MEN
   OF ALL COUNTRIES, UNITE!
   *commonly rendered as 'Workers of the world,
   unite!'*
   Karl **Marx** and Friedrich **Engels** *The Communist Manifesto*
   (1848)

21 Silent, upon a peak in Darien.
   John **Keats** 'On First Looking into Chapman's Homer'
   (1817)

22 So that, in the end, there was no end.
   Patrick **White** *The Tree of Man* (1955)

23 They hand in hand, with wandering steps and
   slow,
   Through Eden took their solitary way.
   John **Milton** *Paradise Lost* (1667)

24 *Zwei Seelen und ein Gedanke,
   Zwei Herzen und ein Schlag!*
   Two souls with but a single thought,
   Two hearts that beat as one.
   Friedrich Halm *Der Sohn der Wildnis* (1842) act 2;
   translated by Maria Lovell as *Ingomar the Barbarian*
   (1854)

Arthur Hugh Clough *continued*

1 I drive through the street, and I care not a d–mn;
The people they stare, and they ask who I am;
And if I should chance to run over a cad,
I can pay for the damage if ever so bad.
Dipsychus (1865) sc. 5

2 My pleasure of thought is the pleasure of thinking
How pleasant it is to have money, heigh ho!
How pleasant it is to have money.
Dipsychus (1865) sc. 5

3 And almost every one when age,
Disease, or sorrows strike him,
Inclines to think there is a God,
Or something very like Him.
Dipsychus (1865) sc. 6

4 Thou shalt have one God only; who
Would be at the expense of two?
'The Latest Decalogue' (1862); see **Bible** 77:37

5 Thou shalt not kill; but need'st not strive
Officiously to keep alive.
'The Latest Decalogue' (1862)

6 Do not adultery commit;
Advantage rarely comes of it.
'The Latest Decalogue' (1862)

7 Thou shalt not steal; an empty feat,
When it's so lucrative to cheat.
'The Latest Decalogue' (1862)

8 Thou shalt not covet; but tradition
Approves all forms of competition.
'The Latest Decalogue' (1862)

9 'Tis better to have fought and lost,
Than never to have fought at all.
'Peschiera' (1854); see **Tennyson** 779:1

10 Say not the struggle naught availeth,
The labour and the wounds are vain,
The enemy faints not, nor faileth,
And as things have been, things remain.
'Say not the struggle naught availeth' (1855)

11 If hopes were dupes, fears may be liars.
'Say not the struggle naught availeth' (1855)

12 In front the sun climbs slow, how slowly,
But westward, look, the land is bright.
'Say not the struggle naught availeth' (1855)

13 What shall we do without you? Think where we
are. Carlyle has led us all out into the desert, and
he has left us there.
parting words to Ralph Waldo **Emerson**, 15 *July*
1848
E. E. Hale *James Russell Lowell and his Friends* (1889) ch. 9

Kurt Cobain 1967-94

American rock singer, guitarist, and songwriter
see also **Young** 857:24

14 I'd rather be dead than cool.
'Stay Away' (1991 song)

Thomas W. Cobb fl. 1820

American politician

15 If you persist, the Union will be dissolved. You
have kindled a fire which all the waters of the
ocean cannot put out, which seas of blood can
only extinguish.
*to James Tallmadge, on his amendment to the bill to
admit Missouri to the Union as a slave state in 1820*
Robert V. Remini *Henry Clay* (1991) ch. 11

William Cobbett 1762-1835

English political reformer and radical journalist

16 Free yourselves from the slavery of the tea and
coffee and other slop-kettle.
Advice to Young Men (1829) letter 1, sect. 31

17 From a very early age, I had imbibed the opinion,
that it was every man's duty to do all that lay in
his power to leave his country as good as he had
found it.
Political Register 22 December 1832

18 Nouns of number, or multitude, such as Mob,
Parliament, Rabble, House of Commons,
Regiment, Court of King's Bench, Den of Thieves,
and the like.
English Grammar (1817) letter 17 'Syntax as Relating to
Pronouns'

19 But what is to be the fate of the great wen of all?
The monster, called . . . 'the metropolis of the
empire'?
of London
Rural Rides: The Kentish Journal in *Cobbett's Weekly Political
Register* 5 January 1822, vol. 40

Alison Cockburn (née Rutherford) 1713-94

Scottish poet and songwriter

20 I've seen the smiling of Fortune beguiling,
I've felt all its favours and found its decay;
Sweet was its blessing, kind its caressing,
But now it is fled, fled far, far away.
'The Flowers of the Forest' (1765); see **Elliot** 305:14

21 O fickle Fortune, why this cruel sporting?
Why thus torment us poor sons of day?
Nae mair your smiles can cheer me, nae mair
your frowns can fear me,
For the flowers of the forest are a' wade away.
*wade = weeded (often quoted as 'For the flowers of
the forest are withered away')*
'The Flowers of the Forest' (1765)

Bruce Cockburn 1945-

Canadian singer and songwriter

22 Got to kick at the darkness 'til it bleeds daylight.
'Lovers in a Dangerous Time' (1984 song)

Claud Cockburn 1904-81

British writer and journalist

23 Small earthquake in Chile. Not many dead.
winning entry for a dullest headline competition at
The Times
In Time of Trouble (1956) ch. 10

Jean Cocteau 1889–1963

French dramatist and film director

1 History is a combination of reality and lies. The reality of History becomes a lie. The unreality of the fable becomes the truth.
Journal d'un inconnu (1953) 'De la prééminence des fables'

2 Life is a horizontal fall.
Opium (1930)

3 Victor Hugo was a madman who thought he was Victor Hugo.
Opium (1930)

4 Being tactful in audacity is knowing how far one can go too far.
Le Rappel à l'ordre (1926) 'Le Coq et l'Arlequin'

5 If it has to choose who is to be crucified, the crowd will always save Barabbas.
Le Rappel à l'ordre (1926) 'Le Coq et l'Arlequin'

6 My method is simple: not to bother about poetry. It must come of its own accord. Merely whispering its name drives it away.
on 26 August 1945; *Professional Secrets* (1972)

George M. Cohan 1878–1942

American songwriter, dramatist, and producer

7 Over there, over there,
Send the word, send the word over there
That the Yanks are coming, the Yanks are coming,
The drums rum-tumming everywhere.
So prepare, say a prayer,
Send the word, send the word to beware.
We'll be over, we're coming over
And we won't come back till it's over, over there.
'Over There' (1917 song)

8 I'm a Yankee Doodle Dandy,
A Yankee Doodle, do or die;
A real live nephew of my Uncle Sam's,
Born on the fourth of July.
I've got a Yankee Doodle sweetheart,
She's my Yankee Doodle joy.
Yankee Doodle came to London,
Just to ride the ponies;
I am the Yankee Doodle Boy.
'Yankee Doodle Boy' (1904 song); see **Songs** 748:11

9 I don't care what you say about me, as long as you say *something* about me, and as long as you spell my name right.
to a newspaperman who wanted some information about Broadway Jones *in 1912*
John McCabe *George M. Cohan* (1973)

Leonard Cohen 1934–

Canadian singer and writer

10 Some say that no one ever leaves Montreal, for that city, like Canada itself, is designed to preserve the past, a past that happened somewhere else.
The Favourite Game (1963) bk. 2, ch. 19

11 A woman watches her body uneasily, as though it were an unreliable ally in the battle for love.
The Favourite Game (1963) bk. 3, ch. 8

12 I don't consider myself a pessimist. I think of a pessimist as someone who is waiting for it to rain. And I feel soaked to the skin.
in *Observer* 2 May 1993 'Sayings of the Week'

Aston Cokayne 1608–84

English poet

13 Sydney, whom we yet admire
Lighting our little torches at his fire.
Funeral Elegies, no. 1 'On the Death of my very good Friend Mr Michael Drayton' (1658)

Edward Coke 1552–1634

English jurist

14 How long soever it hath continued, if it be against reason, it is of no force in law.
The First Part of the Institutes of the Laws of England (1628) bk. 1, ch. 10, sect. 80

15 Reason is the life of the law, nay the common law itself is nothing else but reason.
The First Part of the Institutes of the Laws of England (1628) bk. 2, ch. 6, sect. 138

16 Law . . . is the perfection of reason.
The First Part of the Institutes of the Laws of England (1628) bk. 2, ch. 6, sect. 138

17 The gladsome light of Jurisprudence.
The First Part of the Institutes of the Laws of England (1628) 'Epilogus'

18 For a man's house is his castle, *et domus sua cuique est tutissimum refugium* [and each man's home is his safest refuge].
The Third Part of the Institutes of the Laws of England (1628) ch. 73; see **Proverbs** 618:45

19 Six hours in sleep, in law's grave study six,
Four spend in prayer, the rest on Nature fix.
translation of a quotation from Justinian *The Pandects* (or *Digest*) bk. 2, ch. 4 'De in Jus Vocando'; see **Jones** 434:11

20 They [corporations] cannot commit treason, nor be outlawed, nor excommunicate, for they have no souls.
The Reports of Sir Edward Coke (1658) vol. 5, pt. 10 'The case of Sutton's Hospital'; see **Proverbs** 617:11, **Thurlow** 794:4

21 Magna Charta is such a fellow, that he will have no sovereign.
on the Lords' Amendment to the Petition of Right, 17 May 1628
J. Rushworth *Historical Collections* (1659) vol. 1

Jean-Baptiste Colbert 1619–83

*French statesman; chief minister to **Louis XIV** 1665–83*

22 It is a 'beautiful maxim' that it is necessary to save five *sous* on unessential things, and to pour out millions when it is a question of your glory.
letter to Louis XIV, 1666

23 The art of taxation consists in so plucking the goose as to obtain the largest possible amount of feathers with the smallest possible amount of hissing.
attributed

David Coleman 1926–

British sports commentator

1 He just can't believe what isn't happening to him.
   in *Guardian* 24 December 1980 'Sports Quotes of the Year'

Hartley Coleridge 1796–1849

English poet; eldest son of Samuel Taylor **Coleridge**

2 But what is Freedom? Rightly understood,
   A universal licence to be good.
   'Liberty' (1833)

3 She is not fair to outward view
   As many maidens be;
   Her loveliness I never knew
   Until she smiled on me.
   Oh! then I saw her eye was bright,
   A well of love, a spring of light.
   'She is not fair' (1833)

Mary Coleridge 1861–1907

English poet, novelist, and essayist

4 Egypt's might is tumbled down
   Down a-down the deeps of thought;
   Greece is fallen and Troy town,
   Glorious Rome hath lost her crown,
   Venice' pride is nought.

   But the dreams their children dreamed
   Fleeting, unsubstantial, vain
   Shadowy as the shadows seemed
   Airy nothing, as they deemed,
   These remain.
   'Egypt's might is tumbled down' (1908); see **Shakespeare**
   711:28

Samuel Taylor Coleridge 1772–1834

English poet, critic, and philosopher, father of Hartley **Coleridge**

on Coleridge: see **Byron** 180:3, **Byron** 182:15, **Hazlitt** 376:10, **Hunt** 410:1, **Lamb** 465:7, **Shelley** 729:20

5 O softly tread, said Christabel.
   'Christabel' (1816) pt. 1, l. 164

6 Behold! her bosom and half her side—
   A sight to dream of, not to tell!
   'Christabel' (1816) pt. 1, l. 252

7 A little child, a limber elf,
   Singing, dancing to itself,
   A fairy thing with red round cheeks,
   That always finds, and never seeks,
   Makes such a vision to the sight
   As fills a father's eyes with light.
   'Christabel' (1816) pt. 2, conclusion, l. 656

8 I see them all so excellently fair,
   I see, not feel, how beautiful they are!
   'Dejection: an Ode' (1802) st. 2

9 O Lady! we receive but what we give,
   And in our life alone does Nature live.
   'Dejection: an Ode' (1802) st. 4

10 Ah! from the soul itself must issue forth
   A light, a glory, a fair luminous cloud
   Enveloping the Earth—

And from the soul itself must there be sent
A sweet and potent voice, of its own birth,
Of all sweet sounds the life and element!
   'Dejection: an Ode' (1802) st. 4

11 For hope grew round me, like the twining vine,
   And fruits, and foliage, not my own, seemed mine.
   'Dejection: an Ode' (1802) st. 6

12 But oh! each visitation
   Suspends what nature gave me at my birth,
   My shaping spirit of imagination.
   'Dejection: an Ode' (1802) st. 6; see **Coleridge** 233:21

13 And the Devil did grin, for his darling sin
   Is pride that apes humility.
   'The Devil's Thoughts' (1799)

14 And what if all animated nature
   Be but organic harps diversely framed,
   That tremble into thought, as o'er them sweeps,
   Plastic and vast, one intellectual breeze,
   At once the soul of each, and god of all?
   'The Eolian Harp' (1796) l. 44

15 What is an Epigram? a dwarfish whole,
   Its body brevity, and wit its soul.
   'Epigram' (1809)

16 O, lift one thought in prayer for S. T. C.;
   That he who many a year with toil of breath
   Found death in life, may here find life in death.
   'Epitaph for Himself' (1834)

17 Forth from his dark and lonely hiding-place
   (Portentous sight!) the owlet Atheism,
   Sailing on obscene wings athwart the noon,
   Drops his blue-fringèd lids, and holds them close,
   And hooting at the glorious sun in Heaven,
   Cries out, 'Where is it?'
   'Fears in Solitude' (1798)

18 The frost performs its secret ministry,
   Unhelped by any wind.
   'Frost at Midnight' (1798) l. 1

19   Sea, and hill, and wood,
   With all the numberless goings-on of life,
   Inaudible as dreams!
   'Frost at Midnight' (1798) l. 11

20   The thin blue flame
   Lies on my low-burnt fire, and quivers not;
   Only that film, which fluttered on the grate,
   Still flutters there, the sole unquiet thing
   'Frost at Midnight' (1798) l. 13

21   For I was reared
   In the great city, pent 'mid cloisters dim,
   And saw nought love but the sky and stars.
   But *thou*, my babe! shalt wander like a breeze
   By lakes and sandy shores, beneath the crags
   Of ancient mountain, and beneath the clouds,
   Which image in their bulk both lakes and shores
   And mountain crags.
   'Frost at Midnight' (1798) l. 51

22 Therefore all seasons shall be sweet to thee.
   'Frost at Midnight' (1798) l. 65

23   Whether the eave-drops fall
   Heard only in the trances of the blast,

Or if the secret ministry of frost
Shall hang them up in silent icicles,
Quietly shining to the quiet moon.
'Frost at Midnight' (1798) l. 70

1 O struggling with the darkness all the night,
And visited all night by troops of stars.
'Hymn before Sunrise, in the Vale of Chamouni' (1809)
l. 30

2 On awaking he . . . instantly and eagerly wrote
down the lines that are here preserved. At this
moment he was unfortunately called out by a
person on business from Porlock.
'Kubla Khan' (1816) preliminary note; see **Smith** 743:5

3 In Xanadu did Kubla Khan
A stately pleasure-dome decree:
Where Alph, the sacred river, ran
Through caverns measureless to man
Down to a sunless sea.
So twice five miles of fertile ground
With walls and towers were girdled round.
'Kubla Khan' (1816)

4 A savage place! as holy and enchanted
As e'er beneath a waning moon was haunted
By woman wailing for her demon-lover!
And from this chasm, with ceaseless turmoil
seething,
As if this earth in fast thick pants were breathing,
A mighty fountain momently was forced.
'Kubla Khan' (1816)

5 It was a miracle of rare device,
A sunny pleasure-dome with caves of ice.
'Kubla Khan' (1816)

6 And 'mid this tumult Kubla heard from far
Ancestral voices prophesying war!
'Kubla Khan' (1816)

7 A damsel with a dulcimer
In a vision once I saw:
It was an Abyssinian maid,
And on her dulcimer she played,
Singing of Mount Abora.
'Kubla Khan' (1816)

8 And all who heard should see them there,
And all should cry, Beware! Beware!
His flashing eyes, his floating hair!
Weave a circle round him thrice,
And close your eyes with holy dread,
For he on honey-dew hath fed,
And drunk the milk of Paradise.
'Kubla Khan' (1816)

9 All thoughts, all passions, all delights,
Whatever stirs this mortal frame,
All are but ministers of Love,
And feed his sacred flame.
'Love' (1800)

10 With Donne, whose muse on dromedary trots,
Wreathe iron pokers into true-love knots.
Rhyme's sturdy cripple, fancy's maze and clue,
Wit's forge and fire-blast, meaning's press and
screw.
'On Donne's Poetry' (1818)

11 It is an ancient Mariner,
And he stoppeth one of three.
'By thy long grey beard and glittering eye,
Now wherefore stopp'st thou me?'
'The Rime of the Ancient Mariner' (1798) pt. 1

12 He holds him with his glittering eye—
The Wedding-Guest stood still.
'The Rime of the Ancient Mariner' (1798) pt. 1

13 The Wedding-Guest sat on a stone:
He cannot choose but hear.
'The Rime of the Ancient Mariner' (1798) pt. 1

14 The Wedding-Guest here beat his breast,
For he heard the loud bassoon.
'The Rime of the Ancient Mariner' (1798) pt. 1

15 And ice, mast-high, came floating by,
As green as emerald.
'The Rime of the Ancient Mariner' (1798) pt. 1

16 'God save thee, ancient Mariner!
From the fiends that plague thee thus!—
Why look'st thou so?'—With my cross-bow
I shot the Albatross.
'The Rime of the Ancient Mariner' (1798) pt. 1

17 Nor dim nor red, like God's own head,
The glorious Sun uprist.
'The Rime of the Ancient Mariner' (1798) pt. 2

18 We were the first that ever burst
Into that silent sea.
'The Rime of the Ancient Mariner' (1798) pt. 2

19 As idle as a painted ship
Upon a painted ocean.
'The Rime of the Ancient Mariner' (1798) pt. 2

20 Water, water, everywhere,
And all the boards did shrink;
Water, water, everywhere,
Nor any drop to drink.
The very deep did rot: O Christ!
That ever this should be!
Yes, slimy things did crawl with legs
Upon the slimy sea.
'The Rime of the Ancient Mariner' (1798) pt. 2

21 *Her* lips were red, *her* looks were free,
Her locks were yellow as gold:
Her skin was white as leprosy,
The Night-mare LIFE-IN-DEATH was she,
Who thicks man's blood with cold.
'The Rime of the Ancient Mariner' (1798) pt. 3

22 The Sun's rim dips; the stars rush out;
At one stride comes the dark.
'The Rime of the Ancient Mariner' (1798) pt. 3

23 The hornèd Moon, with one bright star
Within the nether tip.
'The Rime of the Ancient Mariner' (1798) pt. 3; see
Wordsworth 845:18

24 I fear thee, ancient Mariner!
I fear thy skinny hand!
And thou art long, and lank, and brown,
As is the ribbed sea-sand.
'The Rime of the Ancient Mariner' (1798) pt. 4

25 Alone, alone, all, all alone,
Alone on a wide wide sea!

And never a saint took pity on
My soul in agony.
'The Rime of the Ancient Mariner' (1798) pt. 4

1 And a thousand thousand slimy things
Lived on; and so did I.
'The Rime of the Ancient Mariner' (1798) pt. 4

2 A spring of love gushed from my heart,
And I blessed them unaware.
'The Rime of the Ancient Mariner' (1798) pt. 4

3 Oh Sleep! it is a gentle thing,
Beloved from pole to pole.
To Mary Queen the praise be given!
She sent the gentle sleep from Heaven,
That slid into my soul.
'The Rime of the Ancient Mariner' (1798) pt. 5

4 Sure I had drunken in my dreams,
And still my body drank.
'The Rime of the Ancient Mariner' (1798) pt. 5

5 We were a ghastly crew.
'The Rime of the Ancient Mariner' (1798) pt. 5

6 It ceased; yet still the sails made on
A pleasant noise till noon,
A noise like of a hidden brook
In the leafy month of June,
That to the sleeping woods all night
Singeth a quiet tune.
'The Rime of the Ancient Mariner' (1798) pt. 5

7 Like one, that on a lonesome road
Doth walk in fear and dread,
And having once turned round walks on,
And turns no more his head;
Because he knows, a frightful fiend
Doth close behind him tread.
'The Rime of the Ancient Mariner' (1798) pt. 6; see **Blair**
118:14

8 No voice; but oh! the silence sank
Like music on my heart.
'The Rime of the Ancient Mariner' (1798) pt. 6

9 I pass, like night, from land to land;
I have strange power of speech.
'The Rime of the Ancient Mariner' (1798) pt. 7

10 He prayeth well, who loveth well
Both man and bird and beast.

He prayeth best, who loveth best
All things both great and small.
'The Rime of the Ancient Mariner' (1798) pt. 7

11 He went like one that hath been stunned,
And is of sense forlorn:
A sadder and a wiser man,
He rose the morrow morn.
'The Rime of the Ancient Mariner' (1798) pt. 7

12 So for the mother's sake the child was dear,
And dearer was the mother for the child.
'Sonnet to a Friend Who Asked How I Felt When the Nurse
First Presented My Infant to Me' (1797)

13 Well, they are gone, and here must I remain,
This lime-tree bower my prison!
'This Lime-Tree Bower my Prison' (1800) l. 1

14 When the last rook
Beat its straight path along the dusky air.
'This Lime-Tree Bower my Prison' (1800) l. 68

15 A charm
For thee, my gentle-hearted Charles, to whom
No sound is dissonant which tells of life.
of Charles **Lamb**
'This Lime-Tree Bower my Prison' (1800) l. 74

16 Work without hope draws nectar in a sieve,
And hope without an object cannot live.
'Work without Hope' (1828)

17 He who begins by loving Christianity better than
Truth will proceed by loving his own sect or
church better than Christianity, and end by loving
himself better than all.
Aids to Reflection (1825) 'Moral and Religious Aphorisms'
no. 25

18 Evidences of Christianity! I am weary of the word.
Make a man feel the want of it; rouse him, if you
can, to the self-knowledge of his need of it; and
you may safely trust it to his own Evidence.
Aids to Reflection (1825) 'Conclusion'

19 If a man could pass through Paradise in a dream,
and have a flower presented to him as a pledge
that his soul had really been there, and if he found
the flower in his hand when he awoke—Aye! and
what then?
Anima Poetae (E. H. Coleridge ed., 1895)

20 Until you understand a writer's ignorance,
presume yourself ignorant of his understanding.
Biographia Literaria (1817) ch. 12

21 The primary imagination I hold to be the living
Power and prime Agent of all human Perception,
and as a repetition in the finite mind of the eternal
act of creation in the infinite I AM.
Biographia Literaria (1817) ch. 13

22 That willing suspension of disbelief for the
moment, which constitutes poetic faith.
Biographia Literaria (1817) ch. 14

23 Our *myriad-minded* Shakespeare.
Footnote. Ἀνὴρ μυριόνους, a phrase which I have
borrowed from a Greek monk, who applies it to a
Patriarch of Constantinople.
Biographia Literaria (1817) ch. 15

24 The dwarf sees farther than the giant, when he
has the giant's shoulder to mount on.
The Friend (1818) vol. 2 'On the Principles of Political
Knowledge'; see **Bernard** 70:11, **Newton** 561:15

25 Iago's soliloquy— the motive-hunting of
motiveless malignity.
The Literary Remains of Samuel Taylor Coleridge (1836) bk. 2
'Notes on the Tragedies of Shakespeare: Othello'

26 State policy, a cyclops with one eye, and that in
the back of the head!
On the Constitution of the Church and State (1839)

27 Reviewers are usually people who would have
been poets, historians, biographers, &c., if they
could; they have tried their talents at one or at the
other, and have failed; therefore they turn critics.
Seven Lectures on Shakespeare and Milton (delivered
1811-12, published 1856) Lecture 1; see **Disraeli** 277:22

1 You abuse snuff! Perhaps it is the final cause of the human nose.
Table Talk (1835) 4 January 1823

2 To see him act, is like reading Shakespeare by flashes of lightning.
of Edmund Kean
Table Talk (1835) 27 April 1823

3 Prose = words in their best order;—poetry = the *best* words in the best order.
Table Talk (1835) 12 July 1827

4 The man's desire is for the woman; but the woman's desire is rarely other than for the desire of the man.
Table Talk (1835) 23 July 1827

5 Poetry is certainly something more than good sense, but it must be good sense at all events; just as a palace is more than a house, but it must be a house, at least.
Table Talk (1835) 9 May 1830

6 Swift was *anima Rabelaisii habitans in sicco*—the soul of Rabelais dwelling in a dry place.
Table Talk (1835) 15 June 1830

7 In politics, what begins in fear usually ends in folly.
Table Talk (1835) 5 October 1830

8 If men could learn from history, what lessons it might teach us! But passion and party blind our eyes, and the light which experience gives is a lantern on the stern, which shines only on the waves behind us!
Table Talk (1835) 18 December 1831

9 That passage is what I call the sublime dashed to pieces by cutting too close with the fiery four-in-hand round the corner of nonsense.
Table Talk (1835) 20 January 1834 (on lines excluded from his own poem *Limbo*, written 1817)

10 Shakespeare . . . is of no age—nor of any religion, or party or profession. The body and substance of his works came out of the unfathomable depths of his own oceanic mind.
Table Talk (1835) 15 March 1834

11 Bygone images and scenes of early life have stolen into my mind, like breezes blown from the spice-islands of Youth and Hope—those twin realities of this phantom world!
Table Talk (1835) 10 July 1834

12 Summer has set in with its usual severity.
Alfred Ainger (ed.) *Letters of Charles Lamb* (1888) vol. 2, letter to Vincent Novello, 9 May 1826

Colette (Sidonie-Gabrielle Colette) 1873–1954
French novelist

13 *Le monde des émotions qu'on nomme, à la légère, physiques.*
The world of the emotions that are so lightly called physical.
Le Blé en herbe (1923)

14 *Son enfance, son adolescence lui avaient appris la patience, l'espoir, le silence, le maniement aisé des armes et des vertus des prisonniers.*

Her childhood, then her adolescence, had taught her patience, hope, silence and the easy manipulation of the weapons and virtues of all prisoners.
Chéri (1920) pt. 2 (translated by Janet Flanner, 1930)

15 *Allons acheter des cartes à jouer, du bon vin, des marques de bridge, des aiguilles à tricoter, tous les bibelots qu'il faut pour boucher un grand trou, tout ce qu'il faut pour déguiser le monstre—la vieille femme.*
Let's buy a pack of cards, good wine, bridge scores, knitting needles, all the paraphernalia needed to fill an enormous void, everything needed to hide that horror—the old woman.
Chéri (1920) pt. 2 (translated by Janet Flanner, 1930)

16 *Les femmes libres ne sont pas des femmes.*
Free women are not women at all.
Claudine à Paris (1901)

17 *Si on voulait être sincère, on avouerait qu'il y a l'amour bien nourri, et l'amour mal nourri. Et le reste c'est de la littérature.*
If we want to be sincere, we must admit that there is a well-nourished love and an ill-nourished love. And the rest is literature.
La Fin de Chéri (1926) (translated by Viola Gerard Garvin)

Mary Collier c.1690–c.1762
English washerwoman and poet

18 Though we all day with care our work attend, Such is our fate, we know not when 'twill end. When evening's come, you homeward take your way;
We, till our work is done, are forced to stay.
The Woman's Labour (1739)

19 So the industrious bees do hourly strive To bring their loads of honey to the hive; Their sordid owners always reap the gains, And poorly recompense their toils and pains.
The Woman's Labour (1739)

20 The greatest heroes that the world can know, To *women* their original must owe.
'The Three Wise Sentences, from the First Book of Esdras' (1740) l. 132

William Collingbourne d. 1484
English landowner; conspirator against Richard III

21 The Cat, the Rat, and Lovell our dog Rule all England under a hog.
referring to Sir William Catesby (d. 1485), Sir Richard Ratcliffe (d. 1485), Lord Lovell (1454–c.1487), whose crest was a dog, and King Richard III, whose emblem was a wild boar
Robert Fabyan *The Concordance of Chronicles* (ed. H. Ellis, 1811)

Lord Collingwood 1748–1810
English admiral

22 Now, gentlemen, let us do something today which the world may talk of hereafter.
before the Battle of Trafalgar, 21 October 1805
G. L. Newnham Collingwood (ed.) *A Selection from the Correspondence of Lord Collingwood* (1828) vol. 1

R. G. Collingwood 1889–1943

English philosopher and archaeologist

1 Perfect freedom is reserved for the man who lives by his own work and in that work does what he wants to do.

    Speculum Mentis (1924); see **Gill** 349:10

Charles Collins

English songwriter

2 Any old iron, any old iron,
    Any any old old iron?
    You look neat
    Talk about a treat,
    You look dapper from your napper to your feet.
    Dressed in style, brand new tile,
    And your father's old green tie on,
    But I wouldn't give you tuppence for your old
        watch chain;
    Old iron, old iron?

    'Any Old Iron' (1911 song, with E. A. Sheppard and Fred Terry); the second line often sung 'Any any any old iron?'

3 My old man said, 'Follow the van,
    Don't dilly-dally on the way!'
    Off went the cart with the home packed in it,
    I walked behind with my old cock linnet.
    But I dillied and dallied, dallied and dillied,
    Lost the van and don't know where to roam.
    You can't trust the 'specials' like the old time
        'coppers'
    When you can't find your way home.

    'Don't Dilly-Dally on the Way' (1919 song, with Fred Leigh); popularized by Marie Lloyd

Michael Collins 1890–1922

Irish revolutionary

4 That volley which we have just heard is the only speech which it is proper to make over the grave of a dead Fenian.

    at the funeral of Thomas Ashe, who had died in prison while on hunger strike

    Glasnevin cemetery, 30th September 1917

5 Think—what I have got for Ireland? Something which she has wanted these past seven hundred years. Will anyone be satisfied at the bargain? Will anyone? I tell you this—early this morning I signed my death warrant. I thought at the time how odd, how ridiculous—a bullet may just as well have done the job five years ago.

    on signing the treaty establishing the Irish Free State; he was shot from ambush in the following year

    letter, 6 December 1921, in T. R. Dwyer *Michael Collins and the Treaty* (1981) ch. 4

6 We've been waiting seven hundred years, you can have the seven minutes.

    arriving at Dublin Castle for the handover by British forces on 16 January 1922, and being told that he was seven minutes late

    Tim Pat Coogan *Michael Collins* (1990); attributed

7 My own fellow-countrymen won't kill me.

    before leaving for Cork where he was ambushed and killed, 20 August 1922

    James Mackay *Michael Collins* (1996)

8 I found out that those fellows we put on the spot were going to put a lot of us on the spot, so we got in first.

    of the elimination of undercover British Intelligence officers (the 'Cairo Gang') in 1920

    Diana Norman *Terrible Beauty* (1987)

Tim Collins 1960–

British soldier

9 I expect you to rock their world. Wipe them out if that is what they choose. But if you are ferocious in battle remember to be magnanimous in victory.

    speech to the men under his command on arrival in Iraq, 20 March 2003

William Collins 1721–59

English poet

10 To fair Fidele's grassy tomb
    Soft maids and village hinds shall bring
    Each opening sweet of earliest bloom,
    And rifle all the breathing spring.

    'Dirge' (1744); occasionally included in 18th-century performances of Shakespeare's *Cymbeline*

11 Now air is hushed, save where the weak-eyed bat,
    With short shrill shriek flits by on leathern wing,
    Or where the beetle winds
    His small but sullen horn,
    As oft he rises 'midst the twilight path,
    Against the pilgrim borne in heedless hum.

    'Ode to Evening' (1747)

12 How sleep the brave, who sink to rest,
    By all their country's wishes blest!

    'Ode Written in the Year 1746' (1748)

13 By fairy hands their knell is rung,
    By forms unseen their dirge is sung.

    'Ode Written in the Year 1746' (1748)

14 With eyes up-raised, as one inspired,
    Pale Melancholy sate retired,
    And from her wild sequestered seat,
    In notes by distance made more sweet,
    Poured thro' the mellow horn her pensive soul.

    'The Passions, an Ode for Music' (1747)

15 Love of peace, and lonely musing,
    In hollow murmurs died away.

    'The Passions, an Ode for Music' (1747)

16 Too nicely Jonson knew the critic's part,
    Nature in him was almost lost in Art.

    'Verses addressed to Sir Thomas Hanmer' (1743)

George Colman, the Elder 1732–94 and David Garrick 1717–79

English dramatists

17 Love and a cottage! Eh, Fanny! Ah, give me indifference and a coach and six!

    The Clandestine Marriage (1766) act 1; see **Keats** 444:1

George Colman, the Younger 1762–1836

English dramatist

1 Oh, London is a fine town,
A very famous city,
Where all the streets are paved with gold,
And all the maidens pretty.
   The Heir at Law (performed 1797, published 1808) act 1,
   sc. 2

2 Says he, 'I am a handsome man, but I'm a gay
deceiver.'
   Love Laughs at Locksmiths (1808) act 2; see **Proverbs**
   625:44

3 My father was an eminent button maker . . . but I
had a soul above buttons . . . I panted for a liberal
profession.
   New Hay at the Old Market (1795) sc. 1

4 Johnson's style was grand and Gibbon's elegant;
the stateliness of the former was sometimes
pedantic, and the polish of the latter was
occasionally finical. Johnson marched to kettle-
drums and trumpets; Gibbon moved to flute and
hautboys: Johnson hewed passages through the
Alps, while Gibbon levelled walks through parks
and gardens.
   Random Records (1830) vol. 1

5 As the lone Angler, patient man,
At Mewry-Water, or the Banne,
Leaves off, against his placid wish,
Impaling worms to torture fish.
   The Lady of the Wreck (1813) canto 2, st. 18

6 And, on the label of the stuff,
He wrote this verse;
Which one would think was clear enough,
And terse:—
When taken,
To be well shaken.
   'The Newcastle Apothecary' (1797)

John Robert Colombo 1936–

Canadian writer

7 Canada could have enjoyed:
English government,
French culture,
and American know-how.

Instead it ended up with:
English know-how,
French government,
and American culture.
   'O Canada' (1965)

Charles Caleb Colton c.1780–1832

English clergyman and writer

8 When you have nothing to say, say nothing.
   Lacon (1820) vol. 1, no. 183

9 Examinations are formidable even to the best
prepared, for the greatest fool may ask more than
the wisest man can answer.
   Lacon (1820) vol. 1, no. 322

10 If you would be known, and not know, vegetate in
a village; if you would know, and not be known,
live in a city.
   Lacon (1820) vol. 1, no. 334

11 Man is an embodied paradox, a bundle of
contradictions.
   Lacon (1820) vol. 1, no. 408

St Colum Cille ?521–597

Irish cleric and missionary, founder of Iona

12 To every cow her calf, to every book its copy.
   traditionally attributed

Betty Comden 1919– and Adolph Green 1915–

13 New York, New York,—a helluva town.
   New York, New York (1945 song)

14 The party's over, it's time to call it a day.
   'The Party's Over' (1956); see **Crosland** 252:12

Henry Steele Commager 1902–

American historian

15 It was observed half a century ago that what is a
stone wall to a layman, to a corporate lawyer is a
triumphant arch. Much the same might be said of
civil rights and freedoms. To the layman the Bill of
Rights seems to be a stone wall against the misuse
of power. But in the hands of a congressional
committee, or often enough of a judge, it turns out
to be so full of exceptions and qualifications that it
might be a whole series of arches.
   'The Right to Dissent' in *Current History* October 1955; see
   Dunne 292:12

Denis Compton 1918–97

British cricketer

16 I couldn't bat for the length of time required to
score 500. I'd get bored and fall over.
   *to Brian Lara, who had recently scored 501 not out, a
   world record in first-class cricket*
   in *Daily Telegraph* 27 June 1994

Ivy Compton-Burnett 1884–1969

English novelist

17 Time has too much credit . . . It is not a great
healer. It is an indifferent and perfunctory one.
Sometimes it does not heal at all. And sometimes
when it seems to, no healing has been necessary.
   Darkness and Day (1951) ch. 7; see **Proverbs** 633:2

18 Being cruel to be kind is just ordinary cruelty with
an excuse made for it . . . And it is right that it
should be more resented, as it is.
   Daughters and Sons (1937) ch. 6

19 Well, of course, people are only human . . . But it
really does not seem much for them to be.
   A Family and a Fortune (1939) ch. 2

20 People don't resent having nothing nearly as
much as too little.
   A Family and a Fortune (1939) ch. 4

1 There are different kinds of wrong. The people sinned against are not always the best.
  The Mighty and their Fall (1961) ch. 7

2 A leopard does not change his spots, or change his feeling that spots are rather a credit.
  More Women than Men (1933) ch. 4

3 My point is that it [wickedness] is not punished, and that is why it is natural to be guilty of it. When it is likely to be punished, most of us avoid it.
  in *Orion* (1945) 'A Conversation between I. Compton-Burnett and M. Jourdain'

4 There's not much to say. I haven't been at all deedy.
  on being asked about herself
  in *The Times* 30 August 1969

Auguste Comte 1798–1857

French philosopher

5 M. Comte used to reproach his early English admirers with maintaining the 'conspiracy of silence' concerning his later performances.
  J. S. Mill *Auguste Comte and Positivism* (1865)

Prince de Condé (the Great Condé) 1621–86

French general

6 *Silence! Voilà l'ennemi!*
  Hush! Here comes the enemy!
  as the Jesuit preacher Louis Bourdaloue mounted the pulpit at St Sulpice
  P. M. Lauras *Bourdaloue: sa vie et ses oeuvres* (1881) vol. 2

Marquis de Condorcet 1743–94

French philosopher

7 As one meditates about the nature of the moral sciences one really cannot avoid the conclusion that since, like the physical sciences, they rest upon observation of the facts, they ought to follow the same methods, acquire a language no less exact and precise, and so attain to the same degree of certainty. If some being alien to our species were to set himself to study us he would find no difference between these two studies, and would examine human society as we do that of bees or beavers.
  Discours prononcé dans l'Académie Française 21 February 1782; A. Condorcet O'Connor and M. F. Arago (eds.) *Oeuvres de Condorcet* vol. 1 (1847–9)

Confucius (K'ung Fu-tzu) 551–479 BC

Chinese philosopher
textual translations are those of Wing-Tsit Chan, 1963

8 Is it not a pleasure to learn and to repeat or practice from time to time what has been learned? Is it not delightful to have friends coming from afar? Is one not a superior man if he does not feel hurt even though he does not feel recognized?
  Analects ch. 1, v. 1

9 When a man's father is alive, look at the bent of his will. When his father is dead, look at his conduct. If for three years [of mourning] he does not change from the way of his father, he may be called filial.
  Analects ch. 1, v. 11

10 A ruler who governs his state by virtue is like the north polar star, which remains in its place while all the other stars revolve around it.
  Analects ch. 2, v. 1

11 At fifteen my mind was set on learning. At thirty my character had been formed. At forty I had no more perplexities. At fifty I knew the Mandate of Heaven. At sixty I was at ease with whatever I heard. At seventy I could follow my heart's desire without transgressing moral principles.
  Analects ch. 2, v. 4

12 A man who reviews the old so as to find out the new is qualified to teach others.
  Analects ch. 2, v. 11

13 The superior man is broadminded but not partisan; the inferior man is partisan but not broadminded.
  Analects ch. 2, v. 14

14 A superior man in dealing with the world is not for anything or against anything. He follows righteousness as the standard.
  Analects ch. 4, v. 10

15 The Way of our Master is none other than conscientiousness and altruism.
  the 'one thread' of Confucius' doctrines
  Analects ch. 4, v. 15

16 The superior man understands righteousness; the inferior man understands profit.
  Analects ch. 4, v. 16

17 Man is born with uprightness. If one loses it he will be lucky if he escapes with his life.
  Analects ch. 6, v. 17

18 The man of wisdom delights in water; the man of humanity delights in mountains. The man of wisdom is active; the man of humanity is tranquil. The man of wisdom enjoys happiness; the man of humanity enjoys long life.
  Analects ch. 6, v. 21

19 The superior man extensively studies literature and restrains himself with the rules of propriety. Thus he will not violate the Way.
  Analects ch. 6, v. 25

20 I transmit but do not create. I believe in and love the ancients.
  Analects ch. 7, v. 1

21 Set your will on the Way. Have a firm grasp on virtue. Rely on humanity. Find recreation in the arts.
  Analects ch. 7, v. 6

22 Let a man be stimulated by poetry, established by the rules of propriety, and perfected by music.
  Analects ch. 8, v. 8

23 I have never yet seen anyone whose desire to build up his moral power was as strong as sexual desire.
  Analects ch. 9, v. 17; translated by Arthur Waley

1 The commander of three armies may be taken away but the will of even a common man may not be taken away from him.
Analects ch. 9, v. 25

2 If we are not yet able to serve man, how can we serve spiritual beings? . . . If we do not yet know about life how can we know about death?
Analects ch. 11, v. 11

3 To go too far is the same as not to go far enough.
Analects ch. 11, v. 15

4 No state can exist without the confidence of the people.
Analects ch. 12, v. 7

5 The way of the superior man is threefold, but I have not been able to attain it. The man of wisdom has no perplexities; the man of humanity has no worry; the man of courage has no fear.
Analects ch. 14, v. 30

6 It is the word altruism. Do not do to others what you do not want them to do to you.
replying to Tzu-hung's question 'Is there one word which can serve as the guiding principle for conduct throughout life?'
Analects ch. 15, v. 23

7 It is man that can make the Way great, and not the Way that can make man great.
Analects ch. 15, v. 28

8 In education there should be no class distinction.
Analects ch. 15, v. 38

9 By nature men are alike. Through practice they have become far apart.
Analects ch. 17, v. 2

10 Only the most intelligent and the most stupid do not change.
Analects ch. 17, v. 3

11 Does Heaven say anything? The four seasons run their course and all things are produced. Does Heaven say anything?
Analects ch. 17, v. 19

12 Women and servants are most difficult to deal with. If you are familiar with them, they cease to be humble. If you keep a distance from them, they resent it.
Analects ch. 17, v. 25

William Congreve 1670–1729

English dramatist

13 It is the business of a comic poet to paint the vices and follies of human kind.
The Double Dealer (1694) epistle dedicatory

14 Retired to their tea and scandal, according to their ancient custom.
The Double Dealer (1694) act 1, sc. 1

15 There is nothing more unbecoming a man of quality than to laugh; Jesu, 'tis such a vulgar expression of the passion!
The Double Dealer (1694) act 1, sc. 4; see **Catullus** 202:17, **Chesterfield** 215:7

16 Tho' marriage makes man and wife one flesh, it leaves 'em still two fools.
The Double Dealer (1694) act 2, sc. 3

17 See how love and murder will out.
The Double Dealer (1694) act 4, sc. 6; see **Proverbs** 627:5

18 No mask like open truth to cover lies,
As to go naked is the best disguise.
The Double Dealer (1694) act 5, sc. 6

19 Invention flags, his brain goes muddy,
And black despair succeeds brown study.
An Impossible Thing (1720)

20 I am always of the opinion with the learned, if they speak first.
Incognita (1692)

21 Has he not a rogue's face? . . . a hanging-look to me . . . has a damned Tyburn-face, without the benefit o' the Clergy.
Love for Love (1695) act 2, sc. 7

22 I came upstairs into the world; for I was born in a cellar.
Love for Love (1695) act 2, sc. 7

23 I know that's a secret, for it's whispered every where.
Love for Love (1695) act 3, sc. 3

24 He that first cries out stop thief, is often he that has stolen the treasure.
Love for Love (1695) act 3, sc. 14

25 Women are like tricks by sleight of hand,
Which, to admire, we should not understand.
Love for Love (1695) act 4, sc. 21

26 A branch of one of your antediluvian families, fellows that the flood could not wash away.
Love for Love (1695) act 5, sc. 2

27 Aye, 'tis well enough for a servant to be bred at an University. But the education is a little too pedantic for a gentleman.
Love for Love (1695) act 5, sc. 3

28 Nay, for my part I always despised Mr Tattle of all things; nothing but his being my husband could have made me like him less.
Love for Love (1695) act 5, sc. 11

29 Music has charms to sooth a savage breast.
The Mourning Bride (1697) act 1, sc. 1

30 Heaven has no rage, like love to hatred turned,
Nor Hell a fury, like a woman scorned.
The Mourning Bride (1697) act 3, sc. 8; see **Proverbs** 622:19

31   Is he then dead?
What, dead at last, quite, quite for ever dead!
The Mourning Bride (1697) act 5, sc. 11

32 In my conscience I believe the baggage loves me, for she never speaks well of me herself, nor suffers any body else to rail at me.
The Old Bachelor (1693) act 1, sc. 1

33 Man was by Nature Woman's cully made:
We never are, but by ourselves, betrayed.
The Old Bachelor (1693) act 3, sc. 1

34 Bilbo's the word, and slaughter will ensue.
The Old Bachelor (1693) act 3, sc. 7

1 If this be not love, it is madness, and then it is pardonable.
The Old Bachelor (1693) act 3, sc. 10

2 Eternity was in that moment.
The Old Bachelor (1693) act 4, sc. 7

3 Now am I slap-dash down in the mouth.
The Old Bachelor (1693) act 4, sc. 9

4 SHARPER: Thus grief still treads upon the heels of pleasure:
Married in haste, we may repent at leisure.
SETTER: Some by experience find those words misplaced:
At leisure married, they repent in haste.
The Old Bachelor (1693) act 5, sc. 1; see **Byron** 181:30, **Proverbs** 626:17

5 Courtship to marriage, as a very witty prologue to a very dull play.
The Old Bachelor (1693) act 5, sc. 10

6 I could find it in my heart to marry thee, purely to be rid of thee.
The Old Bachelor (1693) act 5, sc. 10

7 They come together like the Coroner's Inquest, to sit upon the murdered reputations of the week.
The Way of the World (1700) act 1, sc. 1

8 Ay, ay, I have experience: I have a wife, and so forth.
The Way of the World (1700) act 1, sc. 3

9 I always take blushing either for a sign of guilt, or of ill breeding.
The Way of the World (1700) act 1, sc. 9

10 Say what you will, 'tis better to be left than never to have been loved.
The Way of the World (1700) act 2, sc. 1; see **Tennyson** 779:1, **Proverbs** 633:7

11 Here she comes i' faith full sail, with her fan spread and streamers out, and a shoal of fools for tenders.
The Way of the World (1700) act 2, sc. 4

12 WITWOUD: Madam, do you pin up your hair with all your letters?
MILLAMANT: Only with those in verse, Mr Witwoud. I never pin up my hair with prose.
The Way of the World (1700) act 2, sc. 4

13 Beauty is the lover's gift.
The Way of the World (1700) act 2, sc. 4

14 A little disdain is not amiss; a little scorn is alluring.
The Way of the World (1700) act 3, sc. 5

15 O, nothing is more alluring than a levee from a couch in some confusion.
The Way of the World (1700) act 4, sc. 1

16 Don't let us be familiar or fond, nor kiss before folks, like my Lady Fadler and Sir Francis: nor go to Hyde-Park together the first Sunday in a new chariot, to provoke eyes and whispers, and then never be seen there together again; as if we were proud of one another the first week, and ashamed of one another ever after . . . Let us be very strange and well-bred: Let us be as strange as if

we had been married a great while, and as wellbred as if we were not married at all.
The Way of the World (1700) act 4, sc. 5

17 These articles subscribed, if I continue to endure you a little longer, I may by degrees dwindle into a wife.
The Way of the World (1700) act 4, sc. 5

18 I hope you do not think me prone to any iteration of nuptials.
The Way of the World (1700) act 4, sc. 12

19 Careless she is with artful care,
Affecting to seem unaffected.
'Amoret'

20 Music alone with sudden charms can bind
The wand'ring sense, and calm the troubled mind.
'Hymn to Harmony'

21 Would I were free from this restraint,
Or else had hopes to win her;
Would she could make of me a saint,
Or I of her a sinner.
'Pious Selinda Goes to Prayers' (song)

22 For 'tis some virtue, virtue to commend.
'To Sir Godfrey Kneller'

23 I confess freely to you, I could never look long upon a monkey, without very mortifying reflections.
letter to John Dennis, 10 July 1695

Gerry Conlon 1954–
Northern Irish member of the Guildford Four, the first to be released from prison

24 The life sentence goes on. It's like a runaway train that you can't just get off.
of life after his conviction was quashed by the Court of Appeal
in *Irish Post* 13 September 1997

James M. Connell 1852–1929
Irish socialist songwriter

25 The people's flag is deepest red;
It shrouded oft our martyred dead.
'The Red Flag' (1889) in H. E. Piggott *Songs that made History* (1937) ch. 6

26 Then raise the scarlet standard high!
Within its shade we'll live or die.
Tho' cowards flinch and traitors sneer,
We'll keep the red flag flying here.
'The Red Flag' (1889) in H. E. Piggott *Songs that made History* (1937) ch. 6

Billy Connolly 1942–
Scottish comedian

27 Marriage is a wonderful invention; but, then again, so is a bicycle repair kit.
Duncan Campbell *Billy Connolly* (1976)

1 I don't want a Stormont. I don't want a wee pretendy government in Edinburgh.
on the prospective Scottish Parliament; often quoted as 'a wee pretendy Parliament'
  interview on *Breakfast with Frost* (BBC TV), 9 February 1997

Cyril Connolly 1903–74
English writer

2 Whom the gods wish to destroy they first call promising.
  Enemies of Promise (1938) ch. 13; see **Proverbs** 635:5

3 There is no more sombre enemy of good art than the pram in the hall.
  Enemies of Promise (1938) ch. 14

4 The Mandarin style . . . is beloved by literary pundits, by those who would make the written word as unlike as possible to the spoken one. It is the style of those writers whose tendency is to make their language convey more than they mean or more than they feel, it is the style of most artists and all humbugs.
  Enemies of Promise (1938) ch. 20

5 Imprisoned in every fat man a thin one is wildly signalling to be let out.
  The Unquiet Grave (1944) pt. 2; see **Orwell** 577:3

6 Our memories are card-indexes consulted, and then put back in disorder by authorities whom we do not control.
  The Unquiet Grave (1944) pt. 3

7 Perfect fear casteth out love.
  remark to Philip Toynbee during the Blitz
  in *Observer* 1 December 1974; obituary notice by Toynbee; see **Bible** 112:21

8 It is closing time in the gardens of the West and from now on an artist will be judged only by the resonance of his solitude or the quality of his despair.
  in *Horizon* December 1949–January 1950

James Connolly 1868–1916
Irish labour leader and nationalist; executed after the Easter Rising, 1916

9 The worker is the slave of capitalist society, the female worker is the slave of that slave.
  The Re-conquest of Ireland (1915)

10 The time for Ireland's battle is NOW, the place for Ireland's battle is HERE.
  in *The Workers' Republic* 22 January 1916

Jimmy Connors 1952–
American tennis player

11 New Yorkers love it when you spill your guts out there. Spill your guts at Wimbledon and they make you stop and clean it up.
  at Flushing Meadow
  in *Guardian* 24 December 1984 'Sports Quotes of the Year'

Joseph Conrad (Teodor Josef Konrad Korzeniowski) 1857–1924
Polish-born English novelist
*see also **Spenser** 751:21, **Opening lines** 575:11*

12 As I waited I thought that there's nothing like a confession to make one look mad; and that of all confessions a written one is the most detrimental all round. Never confess! Never, never!
  Chance (1913) ch. 7

13 The conquest of the earth, which mostly means the taking it away from those who have a different complexion or slightly flatter noses than ourselves, is not a pretty thing when you look into it.
  Heart of Darkness (1902) ch. 1

14 We live, as we dream—alone.
  Heart of Darkness (1902) ch. 1

15 Exterminate all the brutes!
  Heart of Darkness (1902) ch. 2

16 The horror! The horror!
  Heart of Darkness (1902) ch. 3

17 Mistah Kurtz—he dead.
  Heart of Darkness (1902) ch. 3

18 A man that is born falls into a dream like a man who falls into the sea. If he tries to climb out into the air as inexperienced people endeavour to do, he drowns.
  Lord Jim (1900) ch. 20

19 To the destructive element submit yourself, and with the exertions of your hands and feet in the water make the deep, deep sea keep you up.
  Lord Jim (1900) ch. 20

20 My task which I am trying to achieve is by the power of the written word, to make you hear, to make you feel—it is, before all, to make you *see*. That—and no more, and it is everything.
  The Nigger of the Narcissus (1897) preface

21 Action is consolatory. It is the enemy of thought and the friend of flattering illusions.
  Nostromo (1904) pt. 1, ch. 6

22 It's only those who do nothing that make no mistakes, I suppose.
  Outcast of the Islands (1896) pt. 3, ch. 2

23 The terrorist and the policeman both come from the same basket.
  The Secret Agent (1907) ch. 4

24 Only in men's imagination does every truth find an effective and undeniable existence. Imagination, not invention, is the supreme master of art, as of life.
  Some Reminiscences (1912) ch. 1

25 The scrupulous and the just, the noble, humane, and devoted natures; the unselfish and the intelligent may begin a movement—but it passes away from them. They are not the leaders of a revolution. They are its victims.
  Under Western Eyes (1911) pt. 2, ch. 3

1 A belief in a supernatural source of evil is not necessary; men alone are quite capable of every wickedness.

   Under Western Eyes (1911) pt. 2, ch. 4

2 I remember my youth and the feeling that will never come back any more—the feeling that I could last for ever, outlast the sea, the earth, and all men; the deceitful feeling that lures us on to joys, to perils, to love, to vain effort—to death; the triumphant conviction of strength, the heat of life in the handful of dust, the glow in the heart that with every year grows dim, grows cold, grows small, and expires—and expires, too soon, too soon—before life itself.

   Youth (1902); see **Eliot** 303:9

3 For me, writing—*the only possible writing*—is just simply the conversion of nervous force into phrases.

   letter, October 1903

Shirley Conran 1932-
English writer

4 Life is too short to stuff a mushroom.

   Superwoman (1975)

Henry Constable 1562-1613
English poet

5 I did not know that thou wert dead before;
I did not feel the grief I did sustain;
The greater stroke astonisheth the more;
Astonishment takes from us sense of pain.
I stood amazed when others' tears begun,
And now begin to weep when they have done.

   'To Sir Philip Sidney's Soul' (1595)

John Constable 1776-1837
English painter

6 The sound of water escaping from mill-dams, etc., willows, old rotten planks, slimy posts, and brickwork . . . those scenes made me a painter and I am grateful.

   letter to John Fisher, 23 October 1821, in C. R. Leslie *Memoirs of the Life of John Constable* (1843) ch. 5

7 A gentleman's park—is my aversion. It is not beauty because it is not nature.

   of Fonthill

   letter to John Fisher, 7 October 1822, in *Correspondence* (1968) vol. 6

8 In Claude's landscape all is lovely—all amiable— all is amenity and repose;—the calm sunshine of the heart.

   lecture, 2 June 1836, in C. R. Leslie *Memoirs of the Life of John Constable* (1843) ch. 18

9 There is nothing ugly; *I never saw an ugly thing in my life*: for let the form of an object be what it may,—light, shade, and perspective will always make it beautiful.

   C. R. Leslie *Memoirs of the Life of John Constable* (1843) ch. 17

Benjamin Constant (Henri Benjamin Constant de Rebecque) 1767-1834
French novelist, political philosopher, and politician

10 Art for art's sake, with no purpose, for any purpose perverts art. But art achieves a purpose which is not its own.

   *describing a conversation with Crabb Robinson about the latter's work on **Kant**'s aesthetics*

   Journal intime 11 February 1804, in *Revue Internationale* 10 January 1887; see **Cousin** 244:12

Constantine the Great C.AD 288-337
Roman emperor from AD 306

11 *In hoc signo vinces.*
In this sign shalt thou conquer.

   traditional form of Constantine's vision (AD 312), reported in Greek

   τούτῳ νίκα.
By this, conquer.

   Eusebius *Life of Constantine* bk. 1, ch. 28

Constitution of the United States 1787
the first ten amendments are known as the Bill of Rights

12 He shall from time to time give to the Congress information of the state of the Union, and recommend to their consideration such measures as he shall judge necessary and expedient.

   article 2, sect. 3 'President shall communicate to Congress'

13 Congress shall make no law respecting an establishment of religion, or prohibiting the free exercise thereof; or abridging the freedom of speech, or of the press; or the right of the people peaceably to assemble, and to petition the government for a redress of grievances.

   First Amendment (1791)

14 A well-regulated militia, being necessary to the security of a free State, the right of the people to keep and bear arms, shall not be infringed.

   Second Amendment (1791)

15 Excessive bail shall not be required, nor excessive fines imposed, nor cruel and unusual punishment inflicted.

   Eighth Amendment (1791)

A. J. Cook 1885-1931
English labour leader; Secretary of the Miners' Federation of Great Britain, 1924-31

16 Not a penny off the pay, not a second on the day.

   often quoted with 'minute' substituted for 'second'

   speech at York, 3 April 1926, in *The Times* 5 April 1926

Eliza Cook 1818-89
English poet

17 Better build schoolrooms for 'the boy',
Than cells and gibbets for 'the man'.

   'A Song for the Ragged Schools' (1853)

James Cook 1728–79
English explorer

1 Ambition leads me not only farther than any other man has been before me, but as far as I think it possible for man to go.
   diary 30 January 1774

Robin Cook 1946–
British Labour politician

2 Our foreign policy must have an ethical dimension and must support the demands of other people for the democratic rights on which we insist for ourselves.
   mission statement by the new Foreign Secretary, 12 May 1997
   in *The Times* 13 May 1997

3 Why is it now so urgent that we should take military action to disarm a military capacity that has been there for 20 years, and which we helped to create?
   resigning from the government over Iraq
   speech in the House of Commons, 17 March 2003

Calvin Coolidge 1872–1933
American Republican statesman; 30th President of the US 1923–9
on Coolidge: see **Anonymous** *19:13,* **Lippmann** *486:13,* **Parker** *586:8*

4 There is no right to strike against the public safety by anybody, anywhere, any time.
   telegram to Samuel Gompers, 14 September 1919

5 Civilization and profits go hand in hand.
   speech in New York, 27 November 1920, in *New York Times* 28 November 1920

6 The chief business of the American people is business.
   speech in Washington, 17 January 1925, in *New York Times* 18 January 1925

7 That man has offered me unsolicited advice for six years, all of it bad.
   in 1928, when asked to support the Presidential nomination of his eventual successor Herbert **Hoover**
   Donald R. McCoy *Calvin Coolidge: the Quiet President* (1967)

8 *when asked by Mrs Coolidge what a sermon had been about:*
   'Sins,' he said. 'Well, what did he say about sin?' 'He was against it.'
   John H. McKee *Coolidge: Wit and Wisdom* (1933); perhaps apocryphal

9 They hired the money, didn't they?
   on war debts incurred by England and others
   John H. McKee *Coolidge: Wit and Wisdom* (1933)

10 Nothing in the world can take the place of persistence. Talent will not; nothing is more common than unsuccessful men with talent. Genius will not; unrewarded genius is almost a proverb. Education will not; the world is full of educated derelicts. Persistence and determination are omnipotent. The slogan 'press on' has solved and always will solve the problems of the human race.
   attributed in the programme of a memorial service for Coolidge in 1933

Duff Cooper, Lord Norwich 1890–1954
British Conservative politician, diplomat, and writer

11 Your two stout lovers frowning at one another across the hearth rug, while your small, but perfectly formed one kept the party in a roar.
   letter to Lady Diana Manners, later his wife, October 1914; in Artemis Cooper *Durable Fire* (1983)

Elizabeth Cooper fl. 1730
English writer and dramatist

12 Regularity and Decorum. 'Tis what we women-authors, in particular, have been thought greatly deficient in; and I should be concerned to find it an objection not to be removed.
   preface to *The Rival Widows* (1735)

Susie Cooper 1902–95
English ceramic designer and manufacturer

13 Pottery . . . is a practical and lasting form of art. Not everyone can afford original paintings, but most people can afford pottery.
   in *Evening Sentinel* 16 September 1971

14 The space you leave behind is as important as the space you fill.
   Ann Eatwell and Andrew Casey (eds.) *Susie Cooper: a Pioneer of Modern Design* (2002)

Wendy Cope 1945–
English poet

15 Making cocoa for Kingsley Amis.
   title of poem (1986)

16 I used to think all poets were Byronic—
   Mad, bad and dangerous to know.
   And then I met a few. Yes it's ironic—
   I used to think all poets were Byronic.
   They're mostly wicked as a ginless tonic
   And wild as pension plans.
   'Triolet' (1986); see **Lamb** 464:9

Aaron Copland 1900–90
American composer, pianist, and conductor

17 The whole problem can be stated quite simply by asking, 'Is there a meaning to music?' My answer to that would be, 'Yes.' And 'Can you state in so many words what the meaning is?' My answer to that would be, 'No.'
   What to Listen for in Music (1939)

Richard Corbet 1582–1635
English poet and prelate; Chaplain to James I

18 Farewell, rewards and Fairies,
   Good housewives now may say,
   For now foul sluts in dairies
   Do fare as well as they.
   'The Fairies' Farewell'

1 Who of late for cleanliness,
Finds sixpence in her shoe?
'The Fairies' Farewell'

2 By which we note the Fairies
Were of the old profession;
Their songs were Ave Marys,
Their dances were procession.
'The Fairies' Farewell'

3 I wish thee all thy mother's graces,
Thy father's fortunes, and his places.
I wish thee friends, and one at Court,
Not to build on, but support;
To keep thee, not in doing many
Oppressions, but from suffering any.
'To his Son, Vincent Corbet'

Pierre Corneille 1606–84
French dramatist
*on Corneille: see **Johnson** 433:7*

4 *A vaincre sans péril, on triomphe sans gloire.*
To conquer without risk is to triumph without glory.
Le Cid (1637) act 2, sc. 2

5 *Faites votre devoir et laissez faire aux dieux.*
Do your duty, and leave the outcome to the Gods.
Horace (1640) act 2, sc. 8

6 *Un premier mouvement ne fut jamais un crime.*
A first impulse was never a crime.
Horace (1640) act 5, sc. 3; see **Montrond** 545:17

Ralph Cornes

7 Computers are anti-Faraday machines. He said he couldn't understand anything until he could count it, while computers count everything and understand nothing.
in *Guardian* 28 March 1991

Bernard Cornfeld 1927–
American businessman

8 Do you sincerely want to be rich?
stock question to salesmen
C. Raw et al. *Do You Sincerely Want to be Rich?* (1971)

Frances Cornford (née Darwin) 1886–1960
*English poet; wife of Francis M. **Cornford***

9 How long ago Hector took off his plume,
Not wanting that his little son should cry,
Then kissed his sad Andromache goodbye —
And now we three in Euston waiting-room.
'Parting in Wartime' (1948)

10 O fat white woman whom nobody loves,
Why do you walk through the fields in gloves . . .
Missing so much and so much?
'To a Fat Lady seen from the Train' (1910); see **Chesterton** 216:2

11 A young Apollo, golden-haired,
Stands dreaming on the verge of strife,
Magnificently unprepared

For the long littleness of life.
*of Rupert **Brooke***
'Youth' (1910)

Francis M. Cornford 1874–1943
*English academic; husband of Frances **Cornford***

12 Every public action, which is not customary, either is wrong, or, if it is right, is a dangerous precedent. It follows that nothing should ever be done for the first time.
Microcosmographia Academica (1908) ch. 7

13 Another sport which wastes unlimited time is comma-hunting. Once start a comma and the whole pack will be off, full cry, especially if they have had a literary training . . . But comma-hunting is so exciting as to be a little dangerous. When attention is entirely concentrated on punctuation, there is some fear that the conduct of business may suffer, and a proposal get through without being properly obstructed on its demerits. It is therefore wise, when a kill has been made, to move at once for adjournment.
Microcosmographia Academica (1908) ch. 8

14 That branch of the art of lying which consists in very nearly deceiving your friends without quite deceiving your enemies.
of propaganda
Microcosmographia Academica (1922 ed.)

Mme Cornuel 1605–94
French society hostess

15 No man is a hero to his valet.
Lettres de Mlle Aïssé à Madame C (1787) Letter 13 'De Paris, 1728'; see **Byron** 177:24, **Proverbs** 627:41

Coronation Service 1689

16 We present you with this Book, the most valuable thing that this world affords. Here is wisdom; this is the royal Law; these are the lively Oracles of God.
The Presenting of the Holy Bible; L. G. Wickham Legge *English Coronation Records* (1901)

Correggio (Antonio Allegri Correggio) c.1489–1534
Italian painter

17 *Son pittore ancor io!*
I, too, am a painter!
on seeing Raphael's St Cecilia at Bologna, c.1525
L. Pungileoni *Memorie Istoriche de . . . Correggio* (1817) vol. 1

Gregory Corso 1930–
American poet

18 O God, and the wedding! All her family and her friends
and only a handful of mine all scroungy and bearded
just wait to get at the drinks and food.
'Marriage' (1960)

William Cory (born Johnson) 1823–92

English poet; assistant master at Eton College, 1845–72

1 Jolly boating weather,
And a hay harvest breeze,
Blade on the feather,
Shade off the trees
Swing, swing together
With your body between your knees.
'Eton Boating Song' in *Eton Scrap Book* (1865); E. Parker
Floreat (1923)

2 Nothing in life shall sever
The chain that is round us now.
'Eton Boating Song' in *Eton Scrap Book* (1865); E. Parker
Floreat (1923)

3 They told me, Heraclitus, they told me you were
dead,
They brought me bitter news to hear and bitter
tears to shed.
I wept as I remembered how often you and I
Had tired the sun with talking and sent him down
the sky.
'Heraclitus' (1858); translation of Callimachus 'Epigram
2'; see **Callimachus** 186:1

4 Your chilly stars I can forgo,
This warm kind world is all I know.
'Mimnermus in Church' (1858)

Bill Cosby 1937–

American comedian and actor

5 The heart of marriage is memories.
Love and Marriage (1989)

Charles Cotton 1630–87

English poet

6 The shadows now so long do grow,
That brambles like tall cedars show,
Molehills seem mountains, and the ant
Appears a monstrous elephant.
'Evening Quatrains' (1689) st. 3

John Cotton 1584–1652

English-born New England puritan preacher and theologian

7 If you pinch the sea of its liberty, though it be
walls of stone or brass, it will beat them down.
'Limitations of Government'; Perry Miller *The American
Puritans* (1956)

8 There is never peace where full liberty is not
given, nor never stable peace where more than
full liberty is granted.
'Limitations of Government'; Perry Miller *The American
Puritans* (1956)

Baron Pierre de Coubertin 1863–1937

French sportsman and educationist

9 The important thing in life is not the victory but
the contest; the essential thing is not to have won
but to have fought well.
speech at a government banquet in London, 24 July 1908,
in T. A. Cook *Fourth Olympiad* (1909)

Émile Coué 1857–1926

French psychologist
on Coué: see **Inge** 413:3

10 Every day, in every way, I am getting better and
better.
to be said 15 to 20 times, morning and evening
De la suggestion et de ses applications (1915)

Douglas Coupland 1961–

Canadian writer

11 Generation X: tales for an accelerated culture.
title of book (1991)

Victor Cousin 1792–1867

French philosopher

12 We must have religion for religion's sake, morality
for morality's sake, as with art for art's sake . . .
the beautiful cannot be the way to what is useful,
or to what is good, or to what is holy; it leads only
to itself.
Du Vrai, du beau, et du bien [Sorbonne lecture, 1818]
(1853) pt. 2; see **Constant** 241:10

Jacques Cousteau 1910–97

French naval officer and underwater explorer
see also **Epitaphs** 309:2

13 Mankind has probably done more damage to the
earth in the 20th century than in all of previous
human history.
'Consumer Society is the Enemy' in *New Perspectives
Quarterly* Summer 1996

Thomas Coventry 1578–1640

English judge

14 The dominion of the sea, as it is an ancient and
undoubted right of the crown of England, so it is
the best security of the land . . . The wooden walls
are the best walls of this kingdom.
wooden walls = ships
speech to the Judges, 17 June 1635, in J. Rushworth
Historical Collections (1680) vol. 2; see **Blackstone** 118:10,
Themistocles 787:20

Noël Coward 1899–1973

English dramatist, actor, and composer

15 Dance, dance, dance, little lady!
Leave tomorrow behind.
'Dance, Little Lady' (1928 song)

16 Don't let's be beastly to the Germans
When our Victory is ultimately won.
'Don't Let's Be Beastly to the Germans' (1943 song)

17 There's sand in the porridge and sand in the bed,
And if this is pleasure we'd rather be dead.
'The English Lido' (1928)

18 I believe that since my life began
The most I've had is just
A talent to amuse.
'If Love Were All' (1929 song)

1 I'll see you again,
Whenever spring breaks through again.
'I'll See You Again' (1929 song)

2 Mad about the boy.
title of song (1932)

3 Mad dogs and Englishmen
Go out in the midday sun.
The Japanese don't care to,
The Chinese wouldn't dare to,
The Hindus and Argentines sleep firmly from
twelve to one,
But Englishmen detest a siesta.
'Mad Dogs and Englishmen' (1931 song)

4 Don't put your daughter on the stage, Mrs
Worthington,
Don't put your daughter on the stage.
'Mrs Worthington' (1935 song)

5 Poor little rich girl.
title of song (1925)

6 Someday I'll find you,
Moonlight behind you,
True to the dream I am dreaming.
'Someday I'll Find You' (1930 song)

7 The Stately Homes of England,
How beautiful they stand,
To prove the upper classes
Have still the upper hand.
'The Stately Homes of England' (1938 song); see **Hemans**
381:1

8 There are bad times just around the corner,
There are dark clouds travelling through the sky
And it's no good whining
About a silver lining
For we know from experience that they won't roll
by.
'There are Bad Times Just Around the Corner' (1953
song); see **Proverbs** 619:4

9 I believe we should all behave quite differently if
we lived in a warm, sunny climate all the time.
Brief Encounter (1945)

10 Very flat, Norfolk.
Private Lives (1930) act 1

11 Extraordinary how potent cheap music is.
Private Lives (1930) act 1

12 Certain women should be struck regularly, like
gongs.
Private Lives (1930) act 3

13 Dear 338171 (May I call you 338?).
letter to T. E. Lawrence, 25 August 1930

14 Just say the lines and don't trip over the furniture.
advice on acting
D. Richards *The Wit of Noël Coward* (1968)

15 Television is for appearing on, not looking at.
D. Richards *The Wit of Noël Coward* (1968)

16 Two wise acres and a cow.
of Edith **Sitwell**, *Osbert* **Sitwell**, *and Sacheverell Sitwell*
John Pearson *Façades* (1978) ch. 10; see **Political slogans**
601:10

Abraham Cowley 1618–67

English poet and essayist
on Cowley: see **Addison** 4:4, **Dryden** 290:11, **Pope** 605:21

17 The thirsty earth soaks up the rain,
And drinks, and gapes for drink again.
The plants suck in the earth, and are
With constant drinking fresh and fair.
'Drinking' (1656)

18 Fill all the glasses there, for why
Should every creature drink but I,
Why, man of morals, tell me why?
'Drinking' (1656)

19 God the first garden made, and the first city Cain.
Essays, in Verse and Prose (1668) 'The Garden'; see **Cowper**
247:26

20 Hence, ye profane; I hate ye all;
Both the great vulgar, and the small.
Essays, in Verse and Prose (1668) 'Of Greatness' (translation
of Horace *Odes* bk. 3, no. 1); see **Horace** 401:9

21 This only grant me, that my means may lie
Too low for envy, for contempt too high.
Essays, in Verse and Prose (1668) 'Of Myself'

22 Acquaintance I would have, but when't depends
Not on the number, but the choice of friends.
Essays, in Verse and Prose (1668) 'Of Myself'

23 Love in her sunny eyes does basking play;
Love walks the pleasant mazes of her hair;
Love does on both her lips for ever stray;
And sows and reaps a thousand kisses there.
In all her outward parts Love's always seen;
But, oh, he never went within.
The Mistress: or . . . Love Verses (1647) 'The Change'

24 The world's a scene of changes, and to be
Constant, in Nature were inconstancy.
The Mistress: or . . . Love Verses (1647) 'Inconstancy'

25 Lukewarmness I account a sin
As great in love as in religion.
The Mistress: or . . . Love Verses (1647) 'The Request'

26   The stings,
The crowd, and buzz, and murmurings
Of this great hive, the city.
The Mistress: or . . . Love Verses (1647) 'The Wish'

27 Nothing so soon the drooping spirits can raise
As praises from the men, whom all men praise.
'Ode upon a Copy of Verses of My Lord Broghill's' (1663)

28 Poet and Saint! to thee alone are given
The two most sacred names of earth and Heaven.
'On the Death of Mr Crashaw' (1656)

29 Ye fields of Cambridge, our dear Cambridge, say,
Have ye not seen us walking every day?
Was there a tree about which did not know
The love betwixt us two?
'On the Death of Mr William Hervey' (1656)

30 Life is an incurable disease.
'To Dr Scarborough' (1656) st. 6

Hannah Cowley (née Parkhouse) 1743–1809

English dramatist

1 Five minutes! Zounds! I have been five minutes too late all my life-time!
   The Belle's Stratagem (1780) act 1, sc. 1

2 Vanity, like murder, will out.
   The Belle's Stratagem (1780) act 1, sc. 4

3 But what is woman?—only one of Nature's agreeable blunders.
   Who's the Dupe? (1779) act 2; see **Nietzsche** 564:4

William Cowper 1731–1800

English poet

4 No voice divine the storm allayed,
   No light propitious shone;
   When snatched from all effectual aid,
   We perished, each alone:
   But I beneath a rougher sea,
   And whelmed in deeper gulfs than he.
   'The Castaway' (written 1799) l. 61

5 Grief is itself a med'cine.
   'Charity' (1782) l. 159

6 He found it inconvenient to be poor.
   of a burglar
   'Charity' (1782) l. 189

7 A tale should be judicious, clear, succinct;
   The language plain, and incidents well linked;
   Tell not as new what ev'ry body knows,
   And new or old, still hasten to a close.
   'Conversation' (1782) l. 235

8 The pipe with solemn interposing puff,
   Makes half a sentence at a time enough;
   The dozing sages drop the drowsy strain,
   Then pause, and puff—and speak, and pause again.
   'Conversation' (1782) l. 245

9 Pernicious weed! whose scent the fair annoys,
   Unfriendly to society's chief joys.
   on tobacco
   'Conversation' (1782) l. 251

10 His wit invites you by his looks to come,
   But when you knock it never is at home.
   'Conversation' (1782) l. 303

11 . . . Thousands, careless of the damning sin,
   Kiss the book's outside who ne'er look within.
   on oath-taking
   'Expostulation' (1782) l. 388

12 The man that hails you Tom or Jack,
   And proves by thumps upon your back
   How he esteems your merit,
   Is such a friend, that one had need
   Be very much his friend indeed
   To pardon or to bear it.
   'Friendship' (1782) l. 169

13 Damned below Judas; more abhorred than he was.
   'Hatred and vengeance, my eternal portion' (written c.1774)

14 Man disavows, and Deity disowns me.
   'Hatred and vengeance, my eternal portion' (written c.1774)

15 Men deal with life, as children with their play,
   Who first misuse, then cast their toys away.
   'Hope' (1782) l. 127

16 Could he with reason murmur at his case,
   Himself sole author of his own disgrace?
   'Hope' (1782) l. 316

17 And differing judgements serve but to declare
   That truth lies somewhere, if we knew but where.
   'Hope' (1782) l. 423

18 John Gilpin was a citizen
   Of credit and renown,
   A train-band captain eke was he
   Of famous London town.
   'John Gilpin' (1785) l. 1

19 My sister and my sister's child,
   Myself and children three,
   Will fill the chaise; so you must ride
   On horseback after we.
   'John Gilpin' (1785) l. 13

20 O'erjoy'd was he to find
   That, though on pleasure she was bent,
   She had a frugal mind.
   'John Gilpin' (1785) l. 30

21 Beware of desperate steps. The darkest day
   (Live till tomorrow) will have passed away.
   'The Needless Alarm' (written c.1790) l. 132

22 No dancing bear was so genteel,
   Or half so dégagé.
   'Of Himself' (written 1752)

23 God moves in a mysterious way
   His wonders to perform;
   He plants his footsteps in the sea,
   And rides upon the storm.
   Olney Hymns (1779) 'Light Shining out of Darkness'

24 Ye fearful saints fresh courage take,
   The clouds ye so much dread
   Are big with mercy, and shall break
   In blessings on your head.
   Olney Hymns (1779) 'Light Shining out of Darkness'

25 Behind a frowning providence
   He hides a smiling face.
   Olney Hymns (1779) 'Light Shining out of Darkness'

26 Hark, my soul! it is the Lord;
   'Tis thy Saviour, hear his word;
   Jesus speaks, and speaks to thee;
   'Say, poor sinner, lov'st thou me?'
   Olney Hymns (1779) 'Lovest Thou Me?'

27 There is a fountain filled with blood
   Drawn from Emmanuel's veins,
   And sinners, plunged beneath that flood,
   Lose all their guilty stains.
   Olney Hymns (1779) 'Praise for the Fountain Opened'

28 Oh! for a closer walk with God,
   A calm and heav'nly frame;
   A light to shine upon the road
   That leads me to the Lamb!
   Olney Hymns (1779) 'Walking with God'

1 My dog! what remedy remains,
  Since, teach you all I can,
  I see you, after all my pains,
  So much resemble man!
  'On a Spaniel called Beau, killing a young bird' (written
  1793)

2 Toll for the brave—
  The brave! that are no more:
  All sunk beneath the wave,
  Fast by their native shore.
  'On the Loss of the Royal George' (written 1782)

3 His sword was in the sheath,
  His fingers held the pen,
  When Kempenfeld went down
  With twice four hundred men.
  'On the Loss of the Royal George' (written 1782)

4 Oh, fond attempt to give a deathless lot
  To names ignoble, born to be forgot!
  'On Observing Some Names of Little Note Recorded in the
  Biographia Britannica' (1782)

5 Thy morning bounties ere I left my home,
  The biscuit, or confectionary plum.
  'On the Receipt of My Mother's Picture out of Norfolk'
  (1798) l. 60

6 Me howling winds drive devious, tempest-tossed,
  Sails ripped, seams op'ning wide, and compass
  lost.
  'On the Receipt of My Mother's Picture out of Norfolk'
  (1798) l. 102

7 I shall not ask Jean Jacques Rousseau,
  If birds confabulate or no.
  'Pairing Time Anticipated' (1795)

8 The poplars are felled, farewell to the shade
  And the whispering sound of the cool colonnade.
  'The Poplar-Field' (written 1784)

9 Oh, laugh or mourn with me the rueful jest,
  A cassocked huntsman and a fiddling priest!
  'The Progress of Error' (1782) l. 110

10 Himself a wand'rer from the narrow way,
  His silly sheep, what wonder if they stray?
  'The Progress of Error' (1782) l. 118

11 Remorse, the fatal egg by pleasure laid.
  'The Progress of Error' (1782) l. 239

12 As creeping ivy clings to wood or stone,
  And hides the ruin that it feeds upon,
  So sophistry, cleaves close to, and protects
  Sin's rotten trunk, concealing its defects.
  'The Progress of Error' (1782) l. 285

13 How much a dunce that has been sent to roam
  Excels a dunce that has been kept at home.
  'The Progress of Error' (1782) l. 415

14 Thou god of our idolatry, the press . . .
  Thou fountain, at which drink the good and wise;
  Thou ever-bubbling spring of endless lies;
  Like Eden's dread probationary tree,
  Knowledge of good and evil is from thee.
  'The Progress of Error' (1782) l. 461

15 Laugh at all you trembled at before.
  'The Progress of Error' (1782) l. 592

16 The disencumbered Atlas of the state.
  of the statesman
  'Retirement' (1782) l. 394

17 He likes the country, but in truth must own,
  Most likes it, when he studies it in town.
  'Retirement' (1782) l. 573

18   Philologists, who chase
  A panting syllable through time and space,
  Start it at home, and hunt it in the dark,
  To Gaul, to Greece, and into Noah's ark.
  'Retirement' (1782) l. 691

19 'Till authors hear at length, one gen'ral cry,
  Tickle and entertain us, or we die.
  The loud demand from year to year the same,
  Beggars invention and makes fancy lame.
  'Retirement' (1782) l. 707

20 Admirals extolled for standing still,
  Or doing nothing with a deal of skill.
  'Table Talk' (1782) l. 192

21 Freedom has a thousand charms to show,
  That slaves, howe'er contented, never know.
  'Table Talk' (1782) l. 260

22 Stamps God's own name upon a lie just made,
  To turn a penny in the way of trade.
  'Table Talk' (1782) l. 420 (Perjury)

23 I sing the sofa.
  The Task (1785) bk. 1 'The Sofa' l. 1

24 Thus first necessity invented stools,
  Convenience next suggested elbow-chairs,
  And luxury the accomplished sofa last.
  The Task (1785) bk. 1 'The Sofa' l. 86

25 The nurse sleeps sweetly, hired to watch the sick,
  Whom, snoring, she disturbs.
  The Task (1785) bk. 1 'The Sofa' l. 89

26 God made the country, and man made the town.
  The Task (1785) bk. 1 'The Sofa' l. 749; see **Cowley**
  245:19, **Proverbs** 620:45

27 Slaves cannot breathe in England, if their lungs
  Receive our air, that moment they are free;
  They touch our country, and their shackles fall.
  The Task (1785) bk. 2 'The Timepiece' l. 40; see
  Anonymous 18:6

28 England, with all thy faults, I love thee still—
  My country!
  The Task (1785) bk. 2 'The Timepiece' l. 206; see **Churchill**
  219:13

29 There is a pleasure in poetic pains
  Which only poets know.
  The Task (1785) bk. 2 'The Timepiece' l. 285

30 Variety's the very spice of life,
  That gives it all its flavour.
  The Task (1785) bk. 2 'The Timepiece' l. 606; see **Behn**
  64:2, **Proverbs** 633:35

31 I was a stricken deer, that left the herd
  Long since.
  The Task (1785) bk. 3 'The Garden' l. 108; see **Shakespeare**
  687:9

32 Great contest follows, and much learned dust
  Involves the combatants.
  The Task (1785) bk. 3 'The Garden' l. 161

1 Defend me, therefore, common sense, say I,
From reveries so airy, from the toil
Of dropping buckets into empty wells,
And growing old in drawing nothing up!
The Task (1785) bk. 3 'The Garden' l. 187

2   Newton, childlike sage!
Sagacious reader of the works of God.
The Task (1785) bk. 3 'The Garden' l. 252

3   Detested sport,
That owes its pleasures to another's pain.
of hunting
The Task (1785) bk. 3 'The Garden' l. 326

4 Studious of laborious ease.
The Task (1785) bk. 3 'The Garden' l. 361

5 To combat may be glorious, and success
Perhaps may crown us; but to fly is safe.
The Task (1785) bk. 3 'The Garden' l. 686

6 Now stir the fire, and close the shutters fast,
Let fall the curtains, wheel the sofa round,
And, while the bubbling and loud-hissing urn
Throws up a steamy column, and the cups,
That cheer but not inebriate, wait on each,
So let us welcome peaceful evening in.
The Task (1785) bk. 4 'The Winter Evening' l. 34; see
Berkeley 69:10

7 'Tis pleasant through the loopholes of retreat
To peep at such a world; to see the stir
Of the great Babel, and not feel the crowd.
The Task (1785) bk. 4 'The Winter Evening' l. 88

8 I crown thee king of intimate delights,
Fire-side enjoyments, home-born happiness.
The Task (1785) bk. 4 'The Winter Evening' l. 139

9 A Roman meal . . .
. . . a radish and an egg.
The Task (1785) bk. 4 'The Winter Evening' l. 168

10 The slope of faces, from the floor to th' roof,
(As if one master-spring controlled them all),
Relaxed into a universal grin.
of the theatre
The Task (1785) bk. 4 'The Winter Evening' l. 202

11 Shaggy, and lean, and shrewd, with pointed ears
And tail cropped short, half lurcher and half cur.
The Task (1785) bk. 5 'The Winter Morning Walk' l. 45

12 But war's a game, which, were their subjects wise,
Kings would not play at.
The Task (1785) bk. 5 'The Winter Morning Walk' l. 187

13   Knowledge dwells
In heads replete with thoughts of other men;
Wisdom in minds attentive to their own.
The Task (1785) bk. 6 'The Winter Walk at Noon' l. 89

14 Knowledge is proud that he has learned so much;
Wisdom is humble that he knows no more.
The Task (1785) bk. 6 'The Winter Walk at Noon' l. 96

15 Nature is but a name for an effect,
Whose cause is God.
The Task (1785) bk. 6 'The Winter Walk at Noon' l. 223

16 A cheap but wholesome salad from the brook.
The Task (1785) bk. 6 'The Winter Walk at Noon' l. 304

17 I would not enter on my list of friends
(Tho' graced with polished manners and fine sense,
Yet wanting sensibility) the man
Who needlessly sets foot upon a worm.
The Task (1785) bk. 6 'The Winter Walk at Noon' l. 560

18 Public schools 'tis public folly feeds.
'Tirocinium' (1785) l. 250

19 The parson knows enough who knows a duke.
'Tirocinium' (1785) l. 403

20   As a priest,
A piece of mere church furniture at best.
'Tirocinium' (1785) l. 425

21   Tenants of life's middle state,
Securely placed between the small and great.
'Tirocinium' (1785) l. 807

22 He has no hope that never had a fear.
'Truth' (1782) l. 298

23 But what is man in his own proud esteem?
Hear him, himself the poet and the theme;
A monarch clothed with majesty and awe,
His mind his kingdom and his will his law.
'Truth' (1782) l. 403

24 I am monarch of all I survey,
My right there is none to dispute;
From the centre all round to the sea
I am lord of the fowl and the brute.
'Verses Supposed to be Written by Alexander Selkirk'
(1782)

25 Oh! I could thresh his old jacket till I made his
pension jingle in his pockets.
on Samuel **Johnson**'s *inadequate treatment of* Paradise
Lost
letter to the Revd William Unwin, 31 October 1779; J.
King and C. Ryskamp (eds.) *Letters and Prose Writings of
William Cowper* vol. 1 (1979)

26 Our severest winter, commonly called the spring.
letter to the Revd William Unwin, 8 June 1783, in J. King
and C. Ryskamp (eds.) *Letters and Prose Writings of William
Cowper* vol. 2 (1981)

George Crabbe 1754–1832
English poet

27 'What is a church?'—Our honest sexton tells,
''Tis a tall building, with a tower and bells.'
The Borough (1810) Letter 2 'The Church' l. 11

28 Virtues neglected then, adored become,
And graces slighted, blossom on the tomb.
The Borough (1810) Letter 2 'The Church' l. 133

29   The Town small-talk flows from lip to
lip;
Intrigues half-gathered, conversation-scraps,
Kitchen-cabals, and nursery-mishaps.
The Borough (1810) Letter 3 'The Vicar' l. 70

30 Habit with him was all the test of truth,
'It must be right: I've done it from my youth.'
The Borough (1810) Letter 3 'The Vicar' l. 138

31 There anchoring, Peter chose from man to hide,
There hang his head, and view the lazy tide

In its hot slimy channel slowly glide;
Where the small eels that left the deeper way
For the warm shore, within the shallows play;
Where gaping mussels, left upon the mud,
Slope their slow passage to the fallen flood;—
Here dull and hopeless he'd lie down and trace
How sidelong crabs had scrawled their crooked
    race.
    The Borough (1810) Letter 22 'Peter Grimes' l. 185

1 He nursed the feelings these dull scenes produce,
And loved to stop beside the opening sluice;
Where the small stream, confined in narrow
    bound,
Ran with a dull, unvaried, sad'ning sound;
Where all presented to the eye or ear,
Oppressed the soul! with misery, grief, and fear.
    The Borough (1810) Letter 22 'Peter Grimes' l. 199

2 Lo! the poor toper whose untutored sense,
Sees bliss in ale, and can with wine dispense;
Whose head proud fancy never taught to steer,
Beyond the muddy ecstasies of beer.
    'Inebriety' (in imitation of Pope, 1775) pt. 1, l. 132; see
    Pope 604:23

3 With awe, around these silent walks I tread;
These are the lasting mansions of the dead.
    'The Library' (1808) l. 105

4 Lo! all in silence, all in order stand,
And mighty folios first, a lordly band;
Then quartos their well-ordered ranks maintain,
And light octavos fill a spacious plain;
See yonder, ranged in more frequented rows,
A humbler band of duodecimos.
    'The Library' (1808) l. 128

5 Fashion, though Folly's child, and guide of fools,
Rules e'en the wisest, and in learning rules.
    'The Library' (1808) l. 167

6 Coldly profane and impiously gay.
    'The Library' (1808) l. 265

7 The murmuring poor, who will not fast in peace.
    'The Newspaper' (1785) l. 158

8 A master passion is the love of news.
    'The Newspaper' (1785) l. 279

9 Our farmers round, well pleased with constant
    gain,
Like other farmers, flourish and complain.
    'The Parish Register' (1807) pt. 1, l. 273

10 The one so worn as you behold,
So thin and pale—is yet of gold.
    *these lines were printed by Crabbe's son from a paper
    which he had found wrapped round his mother's
    wedding-ring (with 'ring' instead of 'one')*
    'A Ring to Me Cecilia Sends' (written *c.*1813–14)

11 That all was wrong because not all was right.
    Tales (1812) 'The Convert' l. 313

12 He tried the luxury of doing good.
    Tales of the Hall (1819) 'Boys at School' l. 139

13 'The game,' said he, 'is never lost till won.'
    Tales of the Hall (1819) 'Gretna Green' l. 334

14 The face the index of a feeling mind.
    Tales of the Hall (1819) 'Lady Barbara' l. 124

15 Secrets with girls, like loaded guns with boys,
Are never valued till they make a noise.
    Tales of the Hall (1819) 'The Maid's Story' l. 84

16 Yes, thus the Muses sing of happy swains,
Because the Muses never knew their pains:
They boast their peasants' pipes, but peasants now
Resign their pipes and plod behind the plough.
    The Village (1783) bk. 1, l. 21

17 I grant indeed that fields and flocks have charms,
For him that gazes or for him that farms.
    The Village (1783) bk. 1, l. 39

18   I paint the cot,
As truth will paint it, and as bards will not.
    The Village (1783) bk. 1, l. 53

19 Where Plenty smiles—alas! she smiles for few,
And those who taste not, yet behold her store,
Are as the slaves that dig the golden ore,
The wealth around them makes them doubly
    poor.
    The Village (1783) bk. 1, l. 136

20 The cold charities of man to man.
    The Village (1783) bk. 1, l. 245

21 A potent quack, long versed in human ills,
Who first insults the victim whom he kills;
Whose murd'rous hand a drowsy bench protect,
And whose most tender mercy is neglect.
    The Village (1783) bk. 1, l. 282

Maurice James Craig 1919–
Irish poet and architectural historian

22 O the bricks they will bleed and the rain it will
    weep
And the damp Lagan fog lull the city to sleep;
It's to hell with the future and live on the past:
May the Lord in His mercy be kind to Belfast.
    based on the traditional refrain 'May God in His
    mercy look down on Belfast'
    'Ballad to a Traditional Refrain' (1974)

Hart Crane 1899–1932
American poet

23 Stars scribble on our eyes the frosty sagas,
The gleaming cantos of unvanquished space.
    'Cape Hatteras' (1930)

24 Cowslip and shad-blow, flaked like tethered foam
Around bared teeth of stallions, bloomed that
    spring.
    'Cape Hatteras' (1930)

25 We have seen
The moon in lonely alleys make
A grail of laughter of an empty ash can.
    'Chaplinesque' (1926)

26 The apple on its bough is her desire,—
Shining suspension, mimic of the sun.
    'Garden Abstract' (1926)

27 Ah, madame! truly it's not right
When one isn't the real Gioconda,
To adapt her methods and deportment
For snaring the poor world in a blue funk.
    'Locutions des Pierrots' (1933)

1   So the 20th Century—so
whizzed the Limited—roared by and left
three men, still hungry on the tracks, ploddingly
watching the tail lights wizen and converge,
   slipping
gimleted and neatly out of sight.
  'The River' (1930)

2 O Sleepless as the river under thee,
Vaulting the sea, the prairies' dreaming sod,
Unto us lowliest sometime sweep, descend
And of the curveship lend a myth to God.
  'To Brooklyn Bridge' (1930)

3 You who desired so much—in vain to ask—
Yet fed your hunger like an endless task,
Dared dignify the labor, bless the quest—
Achieved that stillness ultimately best,

Being, of all, least sought for: Emily, hear!
  'To Emily Dickinson' (1927)

Stephen Crane 1871–1900
American writer

4 The red badge of courage.
  title of novel (1895)

Thomas Cranmer 1489–1556
English Anglican prelate and martyr; Archbishop of
Canterbury from 1553
on Cranmer: see **Henry VIII** *382:5*

5 This was the hand that wrote it [his recantation],
therefore it shall suffer first punishment.
  at the stake, Oxford, 21 March 1556
    John Richard Green *A Short History of the English People*
    (1874) ch. 7, sect. 2

Richard Crashaw c.1612–49
English poet
on Crashaw: see **Cowley** *245:28*

6 Lord, what is man? Why should he cost thee
So dear? What had his ruin lost thee?
Lord, what is man, that thou hast overbought
So much a thing of nought?
  'Caritas Nimia, or The Dear Bargain' (1648)

7 *Nympha pudica Deum vidit, et erubuit.*
The conscious water saw its God, and blushed.
  literally, 'the chaste nymph saw . . .'; the translation
  above is attributed to **Dryden**, *when a schoolboy*
    Epigrammata Sacra (1634) 'Aquae in vinum versae [Water
    changed into wine]'; the translation is discussed in *Notes*
    and Queries 4th series (1869) vol. 4

8 Love's passives are his activ'st part.
The wounded is the wounding heart.
  'The Flaming Heart upon the Book of Saint Teresa' (1652)
  l. 73

9 By all the eagle in thee, all the dove.
  'The Flaming Heart upon the Book of Saint Teresa' (1652)
  l. 95

10 Love, thou art absolute sole Lord
Of life and death.
  'Hymn to the Name and Honour of the Admirable Saint
  Teresa' (1652) l. 1

11 Poor World (said I) what wilt thou do
To entertain this starry stranger?
Is this the best thou canst bestow?
A cold, and not too cleanly, manger?
Contend, ye powers of heav'n and earth
To fit a bed for this huge birth.
  'Hymn of the Nativity' (1652)

12 Welcome, all wonders in one sight!
Eternity shut in a span.
  'Hymn of the Nativity' (1652)

13 Lo here a little volume, but large book.
  'On a Prayer book' (1646)

14 It is love's great artillery
Which here contracts itself and comes to lie
Close couched in your white bosom.
  'On a Prayer book' (1646)

15 I would be married, but I'd have no wife,
I would be married to a single life.
  'On Marriage' (1646)

16 Two walking baths; two weeping motions;
Portable, and compendious oceans.
  'Saint Mary Magdalene, or The Weeper' (1652) st. 19

17 All is Caesar's; and what odds
So long as Caesar's self is God's?
  Steps to the Temple (1646) 'Mark 12'; see **Bible** 98:6

18 And when life's sweet fable ends,
Soul and body part like friends;
No quarrels, murmurs, no delay;
A kiss, a sigh, and so away.
  'Temperance' (1652)

19 Whoe'er she be,
That not impossible she
That shall command my heart and me.
  'Wishes to His (Supposed) Mistress' (1646)

Julia Crawford c.1800–c.55
Irish poet and composer

20 Kathleen Mavourneen! the grey dawn is breaking,
The horn of the hunter is heard on the hill.
  'Kathleen Mavourneen' in *Metropolitan Magazine*, London
  (1835)

Robert Crawford 1959–
Scottish poet

21 In Scotland we live between and across languages.
  Identifying Poets (1993)

Crazy Horse (Ta-Sunko-Witko) c.1849–77
Sioux chief

22 One does not sell the earth upon which the people
walk.
  Dee Brown *Bury My Heart at Wounded Knee* (1970) ch. 12

Donald Creighton 1902–79
Canadian historian

23 The historian's first task is the elucidation of
character.
  Towards the Discovery of Canada (1972)

Mandell Creighton 1843–1901

English prelate

1 No people do so much harm as those who go about doing good.

   in *The Life and Letters of Mandell Creighton* by his wife (1904) vol. 2

Michel Guillaume Jean de Crèvecoeur 1735–1813

French-born immigrant to America

2 What then is the American, this new man? He is either a European, or the descendant of a European, hence that strange mixture of blood, which you will find in no other country . . . Here individuals of all nations are melted into a new race of men, whose labours and posterity will one day cause great changes in the world.

   Letters from an American Farmer (1782)

Ranulphe Crewe 1558–1646

English judge

3 And yet time hath his revolution; there must be a period and an end to all temporal things, *finis rerum*, an end of names and dignities and whatsoever is terrene; and why not of De Vere? Where is Bohun, where's Mowbray, where's Mortimer? Nay, which is more and most of all, where is Plantagenet? They are entombed in the urns and sepulchres of mortality. And yet let the name and dignity of De Vere stand so long as it pleaseth God.

   speech in Oxford Peerage Case, 22 March 1626; in *Dictionary of National Biography* (1917–) vol. 5

Francis Crick 1916–

English biophysicist

4 We have discovered the secret of life!
on the discovery of the structure of DNA, 1953
   James D. Watson *The Double Helix* (1968)

5 'You' your joys and your sorrows, your memories and ambitions, your sense of personal identity and free will, are in fact no more than the behaviour of a vast assembly of nerve cells and their associated molecules.

   The Astonishing Hypothesis: The Scientific Search for the Soul (1994) ch. 1

6 Almost all aspects of life are engineered at the molecular level, and without understanding molecules we can only have a very sketchy understanding of life itself.

   What Mad Pursuit (1988) ch. 5

Francis Crick 1916–   and **James D. Watson** 1928–

English biophysicist; American biologist

7 It has not escaped our notice that the specific pairing we have postulated immediately suggests a possible copying mechanism for the genetic material.
proposing the double helix as the structure of DNA, and hence the chemical mechanism of heredity
   in *Nature* 25 April 1953

Quentin Crisp 1908–99

English writer

8 There was no need to do any housework at all. After the first four years the dirt doesn't get any worse.

   The Naked Civil Servant (1968) ch. 15

9 An autobiography is an obituary in serial form with the last instalment missing.

   The Naked Civil Servant (1968) ch. 29

Julian Critchley 1930–2000

British Conservative politician and journalist

10 The only safe pleasure for a parliamentarian is a bag of boiled sweets.

   in *Listener* 10 June 1982

Richmal Crompton (Richmal Crompton Lamburn) 1890–1969

English writer of books for children

11 I'll thcream and thcream and thcream till I'm thick. I can.
Violet Elizabeth's habitual threat
   Still—William (1925) ch. 8

Oliver Cromwell 1599–1658

English soldier and statesman; Lord Protector from 1653
on Cromwell: see **Arnold** 30:6, **Blacker** 118:7, **Clarendon** 224:19, **Dryden** 288:10, **Milton** 535:10, **Pope** 605:11; see also **Last words** 473:6, **Misquotations** 538:20

12 A few honest men are better than numbers.

   letter to William Spring, September 1643, in Thomas Carlyle *Oliver Cromwell's Letters and Speeches* (2nd ed., 1846)

13 I would rather have a plain russet-coated captain that knows what he fights for, and loves what he knows, than that which you call 'a gentleman' and is nothing else.

   letter to William Spring, September 1643, in Thomas Carlyle *Oliver Cromwell's Letters and Speeches* (2nd ed., 1846)

14 Cruel necessity.
*on the execution of **Charles I***
   Joseph Spence *Anecdotes* (1820)

15 It has pleased God to bless our endeavours at Drogheda . . . I believe we put to the sword the whole number of the defendants.

   letter to Bradshaw, September 1649

16 I beseech you, in the bowels of Christ, think it possible you may be mistaken.

   letter to the General Assembly of the Kirk of Scotland, 3 August 1650, in Thomas Carlyle *Oliver Cromwell's Letters and Speeches* (1845)

1 The dimensions of this mercy are above my thoughts. It is, for aught I know, a crowning mercy.

> letter to William Lenthall, Speaker of the Parliament of England, 4 September 1651, in Thomas Carlyle *Oliver Cromwell's Letters and Speeches* (1845)

2 You have sat too long here for any good you have been doing. Depart, I say, and let us have done with you. In the name of God, go!

> addressing the Rump Parliament, 20 April 1653; oral tradition, based on Bulstrode Whitelock *Memorials of the English Affairs* (1732 ed.); see **Amery** 13:5

3 Take away that fool's bauble, the mace.

> at the dismissal of the Rump Parliament, 20 April 1653; in Bulstrode Whitelock *Memorials of the English Affairs* (1732 ed.); see **Misquotations** 538:19

4 It's a maxim not to be despised, 'Though peace be made, yet it's interest that keeps peace.'

> speech to Parliament, 4 September 1654, in Thomas Carlyle *Oliver Cromwell's Letters and Speeches* (1845)

5 Necessity hath no law. Feigned necessities, imaginary necessities . . . are the greatest cozenage that men can put upon the Providence of God, and make pretences to break known rules by.

> speech to Parliament, 12 September 1654, in Thomas Carlyle *Oliver Cromwell's Letters and Speeches* (1845); see **Proverbs** 627:13

6 Your poor army, those poor contemptible men, came up hither.

> speech to Parliament, 21 April 1657, in Thomas Carlyle *Oliver Cromwell's Letters and Speeches* (1845); see **Anonymous** 15:24

7 You have accounted yourselves happy on being environed with a great ditch from all the world besides.

> speech to Parliament, 25 January 1658, in Thomas Carlyle *Oliver Cromwell's Letters and Speeches* (1845)

8 Hell or Connaught.

> *summary of the choice offered to the Catholic population of Ireland, transported to the western counties to make room for settlers*
> traditionally attributed

Bing Crosby 1903–77
American singer and film actor
see also **Epitaphs** 310:9

9 Where the blue of the night
Meets the gold of the day,
Someone waits for me.

> 'Where the Blue of the Night meets the Gold of the Day' (1931 song, with Roy Turk and Fred Ahlert)

Anthony Crosland 1918–77
British Labour politician

10 Total abstinence and a good filing system are not now the right signposts to the socialist Utopia; or at least, if they are, some of us will fall by the wayside.

> *The Future of Socialism* (1956)

11 If it's the last thing I do, I'm going to destroy every fucking grammar school in England. And Wales, and Northern Ireland.

> *c.1965, while Secretary of State for Education and Science*
> Susan Crosland *Tony Crosland* (1982)

12 The party's over.

> *cutting back central government's support for rates, as Minister of the Environment in the 1970s*
> Anthony Sampson *The Changing Anatomy of Britain* (1982); see **Comden** 236:14

Amanda Cross (Carolyn G. Heilbrun)
1926–2003
American crime writer and academic

13 In former days, everyone found the assumption of innocence so easy; today we find fatally easy the assumption of guilt.

> *Poetic Justice* (1970)

Douglas Cross
American songwriter

14 I left my heart in San Francisco
High on a hill it calls to me.
To be where little cable cars climb half-way to the stars,
The morning fog may chill the air—
I don't care!

> 'I Left My Heart in San Francisco' (1954 song)

Richard Assheton, Lord Cross 1823–1914
British Conservative politician

15 I hear a smile.

> *when the House of Lords laughed at his speech in favour of Spiritual Peers*
> G. W. E. Russell *Collections and Recollections* (1898) ch. 29

Richard Crossman 1907–74
British Labour politician
on Crossman: see **Dalton** 255:1

16 While there is death there is hope.

> *on the death of Hugh* **Gaitskell** *in 1963; according to Crossman, this was a favourite phrase of Harold* **Laski**
> Tam Dalyell *Dick Crossman* (1989)

17 The Civil Service is profoundly deferential — 'Yes, Minister! No, Minister! If you wish it, Minister!'

> *Diaries of a Cabinet Minister* vol. 1 (1975) 22 October 1964

Samuel Crossman 1624–83
English clergyman

18 My song is love unknown,
My saviour's love for me,
Love to the loveless shown,
That they might lovely be.
O, who am I,
That for my sake
My Lord should take
Frail flesh and die?

> 'My song is love unknown' (1664); set to music as a hymn from 1868, and by John Ireland in 1919

Crowfoot c.1830-90

Blackfoot chief

1 A little while and I will be gone from among you, whither I cannot tell. From nowhere we came, into nowhere we go. What is life? It is a flash of a firefly in the night. It is a breath of a buffalo in the winter time. It is as the little shadow that runs across the grass and loses itself in the sunset.

  attributed farewell to his people, 25 April 1890; John Peter Turner *The North-West Mounted Police: 1873-93* (1950); see **Haggard** 367:6

Aleister Crowley 1875-1947

English diabolist

2 Do what thou wilt shall be the whole of the Law.

  Book of the Law (1909) l. 40; see **Rabelais** 639:17

Ralph Cudworth 1617-88

English Puritan divine and scholar

3 Some who are far from atheists, may make themselves merry with that conceit of thousands of spirits dancing at once upon a needle's point.

  The True Intellectual System of the Universe (1678)

Richard Cumberland 1631-1718

English divine

4 It is better to wear out than to rust out.

  George Horne *The Duty of Contending for the Faith* (1786); see **Proverbs** 615:32

e. e. cummings (Edward Estlin Cummings) 1894-1962

American poet

5 anyone lived in a pretty how town
  (with up so floating many bells down)
  spring summer autumn winter
  he sang his didn't he danced his did.

  50 Poems (1949) no. 29

6 'next to of course god america i
  love you land of the pilgrims' and so forth oh
  say can you see by the dawn's early my
  country 'tis of centuries come and go
  and are no more what of it we should worry
  in every language even deafanddumb
  thy sons acclaim your glorious name by gorry
  by jingo by gee by gosh by gum.

  is 5 (1926) p. 62

7 Humanity i love you because
  when you're hard up you pawn your
  intelligence to buy a drink.

  'La Guerre' no. 2 (1925)

8 o to be a metope
  now that triglyph's here.

  'Memorabilia' (1926); see **Browning** 159:17

9 a politician is an arse upon
  which everyone has sat except a man.

  1 x 1 (1944) no. 10

10 plato told
  him: he couldn't

believe it (jesus
told him; he
wouldn't believe
it) lao

tsze
certainly told
him, and general
(yes

mam)
sherman.

  1 x 1 (1944) no. 13

11 pity this busy monster, manunkind,
  not. Progress is a comfortable disease.

  1 x 1 (1944) no. 14

12 We doctors know
  a hopeless case if—listen: there's a hell
  of a good universe next door; let's go.

  1 x 1 (1944) no. 14

13 when man determined to destroy
  himself he picked the was
  of shall and finding only why
  smashed it into because.

  1 x 1 (1944) no. 26

14 i like my body when it is with your
  body. It is so quite new a thing.
  Muscles better and nerves more.

  'Sonnets–Actualities' no. 8 (1925)

15 the Cambridge ladies who live in furnished souls
  are unbeautiful and have comfortable minds.

  'Sonnets–Realities' no. 1 (1923)

William Thomas Cummings 1903-45

American priest

16 There are no atheists in the foxholes.

  Carlos P. Romulo *I Saw the Fall of the Philippines* (1943) ch. 15

Allan Cunningham 1784-1842

Scottish poet

17 A wet sheet and a flowing sea,
  A wind that follows fast
  And fills the white and rustling sail
  And bends the gallant mast.

  'A Wet Sheet and a Flowing Sea' (1825)

18 It's hame and it's hame, hame fain wad I be,
  O, hame, hame, hame to my ain countree!

  'It's hame and It's hame', in James Hogg *Jacobite Relics of Scotland* (1819) vol. 1; in his notes, Hogg says he took it from R. H. Cromek's *Remains of Nithsdale and Galloway Song* (1810) and supposes that it owed much to Cunningham

J. V. Cunningham 1911-

American poet

19 And all's coherent.
  Search in this gloss
  No text inherent:
  The text was loss.
  The gain is gloss.

  'To the Reader' (1947)

Mario Cuomo 1932–
American Democratic politician

1 You campaign in poetry. You govern in prose.
   in *New Republic*, Washington, DC, 8 April 1985

Don Cupitt 1934–
British theologian

2 Christmas is the Disneyfication of Christianity.
   in *Independent* 19 December 1996

Marie Curie 1867–1934
Polish-born French physicist

3 In science, we must be interested in things, not in persons.
   to an American journalist, c.1904, after she and her husband Pierre had shared the Nobel Prize for Physics with A.-H. Becquerel
   Eve Curie *Madame Curie* (1937)

John Philpot Curran 1750–1817
Irish judge

4 The condition upon which God hath given liberty to man is eternal vigilance; which condition if he break, servitude is at once the consequence of his crime, and the punishment of his guilt.
   speech on the right of election of the Lord Mayor of Dublin, 10 July 1790, in Thomas Davis (ed.) *Speeches* (1845)

5 Like the silver plate on a coffin.
   describing Robert Peel's smile
   quoted by Daniel O'Connell, House of Commons, 26 February 1835

Edwina Currie 1946–
British Conservative politician

6 I wasn't even in the index.
   on the omission of their affair from John Major's autobiography
   in *The Times* 28 September 2002

John Curtin 1885–1945
Australian Labor statesman; Prime Minister 1941–5

7 Australia looks to America, free of any pangs as to our traditional links or kinship with the United Kingdom.
   of the threat from Japan, and British reluctance to recall Australian troops from the Middle East
   in *Herald* (Melbourne) 27 December 1941

Michael Curtiz 1888–1962
Hungarian-born American film director

8 Bring on the empty horses!
   while directing The Charge of the Light Brigade (1936 *film*)
   David Niven *Bring on the Empty Horses* (1975) ch. 6

Lord Curzon 1859–1925
British Conservative politician; Viceroy of India 1898–1905
on Curzon: see **Anonymous** 17:20, **Churchill** 222:8, **Nehru** 558:8

9 When a group of Cabinet Ministers begins to meet separately and to discuss independent action, the death-tick is audible in the rafters.
   in November 1922, shortly before the fall of **Lloyd George**'s *Coalition Government*
   David Gilmour *Curzon* (1994)

10 Not even a public figure. A man of no experience. And of the utmost insignificance.
   of Stanley **Baldwin**, *appointed Prime Minister in 1923 in succession to* **Bonar Law**
   Harold Nicolson *Curzon: the Last Phase* (1934)

11 Dear me, I never knew that the lower classes had such white skins.
   supposedly said by Curzon when watching troops bathing during the First World War
   K. Rose *Superior Person* (1969)

12 Gentlemen do not take soup at luncheon.
   E. L. Woodward *Short Journey* (1942) ch. 7

Astolphe Louis Léonard, Marquis de Custine 1790–1857
French writer and traveller

13 This empire, vast as it is, is only a prison to which the emperor holds the key.
   of Russia
   La Russie en 1839; at Peterhof, 23 July 1839

St Cyprian C.AD 200–258
Roman writer and martyr; Bishop of Carthage

14 He cannot have God for his father who has not the church for his mother.
   De Ecclesiae Catholicae Unitate sect. 6; see **Augustine** 37:9

15 *Fratres nostros non esse lugendos arcessitione dominica de saeculo liberatos, cum sciamus non amitti sed praemitti.*
   Our brethren who have been freed from the world by the summons of the Lord should not be mourned, since we know that they are not lost but sent before.
   De Mortalite ch. 20 (ed. M. L. Hannam, 1933); see **Norton** 565:16, **Rogers** 652:11

16 There cannot be salvation for any, except in the Church.
   Epistle Ad Pomponium, De Virginibus sect. 4; see **Augustine** 37:9, **Cyprian** 254:14

Dd

Hugh Dalton 1887–1962
British Labour politician

1 He is loyal to his own career but only incidentally to anything or anyone else.
of Richard **Crossman**
diary, 17 September 1941

Tam Dalyell 1932–
Scottish-born Labour politician

2 Under the new Bill, shall I still be able to vote on many matters in relation to West Bromwich but not West Lothian, as I was under the last Bill, and will my right hon. Friend [James Callaghan, MP for Cardiff] be able to vote on many matters in relation to Carlisle but not Cardiff?
formulation of the 'West Lothian question', identifying the constitutional anomaly that would arise if devolved assemblies were established for Scotland and for Wales but not for England
in the House of Commons, 3 November 1977

Samuel Daniel 1563–1619
English poet and dramatist

3 And look, how Thames, enriched with many a
   flood . . .
Glides on, with pomp of waters, unwithstood,
Unto the ocean.
The Civil Wars (1595) bk. 2, st. 7

4 Custom that is before all law, Nature that is above all art.
A Defence of Rhyme (1603)

5 Men do not weigh the stalk for that it was,
When once they find her flower, her glory, pass.
Delia (1592) Sonnet 32

6 Fresh shalt thou see in me the wounds thou
   madest,
Though spent thy flame, in me the heat
   remaining;
I that have loved thee thus before thou fadest,
My faith shall wax, when thou art in thy waning.
The world shall find this miracle in me,
That fire can burn when all the matter's spent.
Delia (1592) Sonnet 33

7 Care-charmer Sleep, son of the sable Night,
Brother to Death, in silent darkness born.
Delia (1592) Sonnet 54; see **Fletcher** 327:9, **Shelley** 731:11

8 Tiring thy wits and toiling to no end,
But to attain that idle smoke of praise.
Musophilus (1599) l. 1

9 And who, in time, knows whither we may vent
The treasure of our tongue, to what strange
   shores
This gain of our best glory shall be sent,
T'enrich unknowing nations with our stores?
What worlds in th'yet unformed Occident

May come refined with th'accents that are ours?
Musophilus (1599) l. 957

10   But years hath done this wrong,
To make me write too much, and live too long.
Philotas (1605) 'To the Prince' (dedication) l. 108

11   Princes in this case
Do hate the traitor, though they love the treason.
The Tragedy of Cleopatra (1594) act 4, sc. 1; see **Dryden** 288:5

Dante Alighieri 1265–1321
Italian poet
on Dante: see **Browning** 160:13

12 *Nel mezzo del cammin di nostra vita*
Mi ritrovai per una selva oscura
che la diritta via era smarrita.
In the middle of the journey of our life I came to myself within a dark wood where the straight way was lost.
Divina Commedia 'Inferno' canto 1, l. 1

13 PER ME SI VA NELLA CITTÀ DOLENTE,
PER ME SI VA NELL' ETERNO DOLORE,
PER ME SI VA TRA LA PERDUTA GENTE . . .
LASCIATE OGNI SPERANZA VOI CH'ENTRATE!
Through me is the way to the sorrowful city.
Through me is the way to eternal suffering.
Through me is the way to join the lost people . . .
Abandon all hope, you who enter!
inscription at the entrance to Hell
Divina Commedia 'Inferno' canto 3, l. 1

14 *Non ragioniam di lor, ma guarda, e passa.*
Let us not speak of them, but look, and pass on.
Divina Commedia 'Inferno' canto 3, l. 51

15 *Il gran rifiuto.*
The great refusal.
Divina Commedia 'Inferno' canto 3, l. 60

16 *Onorate l'altissimo poeta.*
Honour the greatest poet.
Divina Commedia 'Inferno' canto 4, l. 80

17 *Il maestro di color che sanno.*
The master of those who know.
of **Aristotle**
Divina Commedia 'Inferno' canto 4, l. 131

18 . . . *Nessun maggior dolore,*
Che ricordarsi del tempo felice
Nella miseria.
There is no greater pain than to remember a happy time when one is in misery.
Divina Commedia 'Inferno' canto 5, l. 121; see **Boethius** 125:6, **Tennyson** 780:17

19 *Noi leggiavamo un giorno per diletto*
Di Lancialotto, come amor lo strinse:
Soli eravamo, e sanza alcun sospetto.
One day, we were reading for pleasure about Lancelot, and how love constrained him: we were alone and completely unsuspecting.
Divina Commedia 'Inferno' canto 5, l. 127

20 *Galeotto fu il libro e chi lo scrisse:*
Quel giorno più non vi leggemmo avante.

A Galeotto [a pander] was the book and writer too: that day we did not read any more.
Divina Commedia 'Inferno' canto 5, l. 137

1 *Siete voi qui, ser Brunetto?*

Are *you* here, Advocate Brunetto?
of Brunetto Latini, an old and respected friend of Dante, encountered in hell
Divina Commedia 'Inferno' canto 15, l. 30

2 *La cara e buona imagine paterna.*

The dear and kindly paternal image.
Divina Commedia 'Inferno' canto 15, l. 83

3 *Considerate la vostra semenza:*
Fatti non foste a viver come bruti,
Ma per seguir virtute e conoscenza.

Consider your origins: you were not made to live as brutes, but to follow virtue and knowledge.
Divina Commedia 'Inferno' canto 26, l. 118

4 *E quindi uscimmo a riveder le stelle.*

Thence we came forth to see the stars again.
Divina Commedia 'Inferno' canto 34, l. 139

5 *O dignitosa coscienza e netta,*
Come t'è picciol fallo amaro morso!

O pure and noble conscience, how bitter a sting to thee is a little fault!
Divina Commedia 'Purgatorio' canto 3, l. 8

6 *Che ti fa ciò che quivi pispiglia?*
Vien dietro a me, e lascia dir le genti.

What is it to thee what they whisper there? Come after me and let the people talk.
Divina Commedia 'Purgatorio' canto 5, l. 12

7 *O vana gloria dell'umane posse*
Com'poco verde in su la cima dura
se non è giunta dall'etati grosse!

Credette Cimabue nella pittura
tener lo campo, ed ora ha Giotto il grido
si che la fama di colui è oscura.

O vain renown of human enterprise, no longer lasting than the greenery of the trees, unless succeeded by an uncouth age.
In painting Cimabue was thought to hold the field; now Giotto has the palm, so that he has obscured the other's fame.
Divina Commedia 'Purgatorio' canto 11, l. 91

8 *Non è il mondan romore altro che un fiato*
di vento, ch'or vien quinci ed or qien quindi,
e muta nome perchè muta lato.

The reputation which the world bestows is like the wind, that shifts now here now there, its name changed with the quarter whence it blows.
Divina Commedia 'Purgatorio' canto 11, l. 100

9 　　　　　*Men che dramma*
Di sangue m'è rimaso, che no tremi;
Conosco i segni dell' antica fiamma.

Less than a drop of blood remains in me that does not tremble; I recognize the signals of the ancient flame.
Divina Commedia 'Purgatorio' canto 30, l. 46; see **Virgil** 812:1

10 *Puro e disposto a salire alle stelle.*

Pure and ready to mount to the stars.
Divina Commedia 'Purgatorio' canto 33, l. 145

11 *E'n la sua volontade è nostra pace.*

In His will is our peace.
Divina Commedia 'Paradiso' canto 3, l. 85

12 *Tu proverai sì come sa di sale*
Lo pane altrui, e com'è duro calle
Lo scendere e'l salir per l'altrui scale.

You shall find out how salt is the taste of another man's bread, and how hard is the way up and down another man's stairs.
Divina Commedia 'Paradiso' canto 17, l. 58

13 *L'amor che muove il sole e l'altre stelle.*

The love that moves the sun and the other stars.
Divina Commedia 'Paradiso' canto 33, l. 145

Georges Jacques Danton 1759–94
French revolutionary

14 *De l'audace, et encore de l'audace, et toujours de l'audace!*

Boldness, and again boldness, and always boldness!
speech to the Legislative Committee of General Defence, 2 September 1792, in *Le Moniteur* 4 September 1792; see **Bacon** 43:22

15 Thou wilt show my head to the people: it is worth showing.
to his executioner, 5 April 1794
Thomas Carlyle *History of the French Revolution* (1837) vol. 3, bk. 6, ch. 2

Joe Darion 1917–2001
American songwriter

16 Dream the impossible dream.
'The Impossible Dream' (1965 song)

George Darley 1795–1846
Irish-born poet

17 O blest unfabled Incense Tree,
That burns in glorious Araby.
'Nepenthe' (1835) l. 147

Bill Darnell
Canadian environmentalist

18 Make it a *green* peace.
at a meeting of the Don't Make a Wave Committee, which preceded the formation of Greenpeace
in Vancouver, 1970; Robert Hunter *The Greenpeace Chronicle* (1979); see **Hunter** 410:11

Clarence Darrow 1857–1938
American lawyer

19 I do not consider it an insult, but rather a compliment to be called an agnostic. I do not pretend to know where many ignorant men are sure—that is all that agnosticism means.
speech at the trial of John Thomas Scopes for teaching

Darwin's theory of evolution in school, 15 July 1925, in
The World's Most Famous Court Trial (1925) ch. 4

1 I would like to see a time when man loves his
fellow man and forgets his colour or his creed. We
will never be civilized until that time comes. I
know the Negro race has a long road to go. I
believe that the life of the Negro race has been a
life of tragedy, of injustice, of oppression. The law
has made him equal, but man has not.

speech in Detroit, 19 May 1926

2 When I was a boy I was told that anybody could
become President. I'm beginning to believe it.

Irving Stone *Clarence Darrow for the Defence* (1941)

Charles Darwin 1809–82

*English natural historian; grandson of Erasmus **Darwin**,
father of Francis **Darwin***

3 The highest possible stage in moral culture is
when we recognize that we ought to control our
thoughts.

The Descent of Man (1871) ch. 4

4 False views, if supported by some evidence, do
little harm, for everyone takes a salutary pleasure
in proving their falseness.

The Descent of Man (1871) ch. 21

5 A hairy quadruped, furnished with a tail and
pointed ears, probably arboreal in its habits.

on man's probable ancestors

The Descent of Man (1871) ch. 21

6 Man with all his noble qualities . . . still bears in
his bodily frame the indelible stamp of his lowly
origin.

The Descent of Man (1871), closing words

7 I have called this principle, by which each slight
variation, if useful, is preserved, by the term of
Natural Selection.

On the Origin of Species (1859) ch. 3

8 We will now discuss in a little more detail the
Struggle for Existence.

On the Origin of Species (1859) ch. 3

9 The expression often used by Mr Herbert Spencer
of the Survival of the Fittest is more accurate
[than 'Struggle for Existence'], and is sometimes
equally convenient.

On the Origin of Species (1869 ed.) ch. 3; see **Spencer** 750:8

10 From the war of nature, from famine and death,
the most exalted object which we are capable of
conceiving, namely, the production of the higher
animals, directly follows.

On the Origin of Species (1859) ch. 3

11 There is a grandeur in this view of life.

On the Origin of Species (1859) ch. 14

12 What a book a devil's chaplain might write on the
clumsy, wasteful, blundering, low, and horridly
cruel works of nature!

letter to J. D. Hooker, 13 July 1856, in *Correspondence of
Charles Darwin* vol. 6 (1990)

13 Animals, whom we have made our slaves, we do
not like to consider our equal.

Notebook B (1837–8) in P. H. Barrett et al. (eds.) *Charles
Darwin's Notebooks 1836-1844* (1987)

14 He who understands baboon [will] would do more
towards metaphysics than Locke.

Notebook M (16 August 1838) in P. H. Barrett et al. (eds.)
Charles Darwin's Notebooks 1836-1844 (1987)

15 With me the horrid doubt always arises whether
the convictions of man's mind which has been
developed from the mind of the lower animals, are
of any value or at all trustworthy.

Francis Darwin (ed.) *The Life and Letters of Charles Darwin*
(1887) ch. 3

Erasmus Darwin 1731–1802

*English physician; grandfather of Charles **Darwin**, great-
grandfather of Francis **Darwin***

16 A fool . . . is a man who never tried an experiment
in his life.

F. V. Barry (ed.) *Maria Edgeworth: Chosen Letters* (1931) To
Sophy Ruxton, 9 March 1792

17 No, Sir, because I have time to think before I
speak, and don't ask impertinent questions.

*when asked if he found his stammering very
inconvenient*

'Reminiscences of My Father's Everyday Life', an appendix
by Francis Darwin to his edition of Charles Darwin
Autobiography (1877)

Francis Darwin 1848–1925

*English botanist; son of Charles **Darwin**, great-grandson of
Erasmus **Darwin***

18 In science the credit goes to the man who
convinces the world, not to the man to whom the
idea first occurs.

in *Eugenics Review* April 1914 'Francis Galton'

Charles D'Avenant 1656–1714

English dramatist and political economist

19 Custom, that unwritten law,
By which the people keep even kings in awe.

Circe (1677) act 2, sc. 3

William D'Avenant 1606–68

English dramatist and poet

20 In every grave make room, make room!
The world's at an end, and we come, we come.

The Law against Lovers (1673) act 3, sc. 1 'Viola's Song'

21 Had laws not been, we never had been blamed;
For not to know we sin is innocence.

'The Philosopher's Disquisition directed to the Dying
Christian' (1672) st. 76

22 For I must go where lazy Peace
Will hide her drowsy head;
And, for the sport of kings, increase
The number of the dead.

'The Soldier Going to the Field' (1673); see **Somerville**
745:21, **Surtees** 764:12

23 The lark now leaves his wat'ry nest
And, climbing, shakes his dewy wings.

'Song: The Lark' (1638)

Elizabeth David 1913–92

British cook and writer

1 Good food is always a trouble and its preparation should be regarded as a labour of love.
   French Country Cooking (1951) introduction

2 The cooking of the Mediterranean shores, endowed with all the natural resources, the colour and flavour of the South, is a blend of tradition and brilliant improvisation. The Latin genius flashes from the kitchen pans.
   Mediterranean Food (1950) introduction

3 In Europe, spices were the jewels and furs and brocades of the kitchen and the still-room.
   Spices, Salt and Aromatics in the English Kitchen (1970) preface

John Davidson 1857–1909

Scottish poet

4 A runnable stag, a kingly crop.
   'A Runnable Stag' (1906)

5 In anguish we uplift
A new unhallowed song:
The race is to the swift,
The battle to the strong.
   'War Song' (1899) st. 1; see **Bible** 86:16

John Davies 1569–1626

English poet

6 Wedlock, indeed, hath oft compared been
To public feasts where meet a public rout,
Where they that are without would fain go in
And they that are within would fain go out.
   'A Contention Betwixt a Wife, a Widow, and a Maid for Precedence' (1608) l. 193

7 Skill comes so slow, and life so fast doth fly,
We learn so little and forget so much.
   'Nosce Teipsum' (1599) st. 19

8 For this, the wisest of all moral men
Said *he knew nought, but that he nought did know*;
And the great mocking master mocked not then,
When he said, *Truth was buried deep below*.
   'Nosce Teipsum' (1599) st. 20; see **Milton** 534:22, **Socrates** 744:24

9 I know my life's a pain and but a span,
I know my sense is mocked in every thing;
And to conclude, I know myself a man,
Which is a proud and yet a wretched thing.
   'Nosce Teipsum' (1599) st. 45

10 This wondrous miracle did Love devise,
For dancing is love's proper exercise.
   'Orchestra, or a Poem of Dancing' (1596) st. 18

11 What makes the vine about the elm to dance
With turnings, windings, and embracements round?
What makes the lodestone to the north advance
His subtle point, as if from thence he found
His chief attractive virtue to redound?
Kind nature first doth cause all things to love;
Love makes them dance, and in just order move.
   'Orchestra, or a Poem of Dancing' (1596) st. 56

12 Since all the world's great fortune and affairs
Forward and backward rapt and whirlèd are,
According to the music of the spheres;
And Chance herself her nimble feet upbears
On a round slippery wheel, that rolleth aye.
And turns all states with her imperious sway;
   'Orchestra, or a Poem of Dancing' (1596) st. 60

13 Learn then to dance, you that are princes born,
And lawful lords of earthly creatures all;
Imitate them, and thereof take no scorn,
(For this new art to them is natural)
And imitate the stars celestial.
For when pale death your vital twist shall sever,
Your better parts must dance with them forever.
   'Orchestra, or a Poem of Dancing' (1596) st. 61

Robertson Davies 1913–95

Canadian novelist

14 A great many complimentary things have been said about the faculty of memory, and if you look in a good quotation book you will find them neatly arranged.
   The Enthusiasms of Robertson Davies (1990)

15 I see Canada as a country torn between a very northern, rather extraordinary, mystical spirit which it fears and its desire to present itself to the world as a Scotch banker.
   The Enthusiasms of Robertson Davies (1990)

Ron Davies 1946–

British Labour politician

16 It was a moment of madness for which I have subsequently paid a very, very heavy price.
   of the episode on Clapham Common leading to his resignation as Welsh Secretary
   interview with BBC Wales and HTV, 30 October 1998

Scrope Davies c.1783–1852

English conversationalist

17 Babylon in all its desolation is a sight not so awful as that of the human mind in ruins.
   Addison, in The Spectator no. 421 (3 July 1712), *also remarked of 'a distracted person' that 'Babylon in ruins is not so melancholy a spectacle'*
   letter to Thomas Raikes, May 1835, in *A Portion of the Journal kept by Thomas Raikes* (1856) vol. 2; see **Doyle** 284:15

W. H. Davies 1871–1940

Welsh poet

18 And hear the pleasant cuckoo, loud and long—
The simple bird that thinks two notes a song.
   'April's Charms' (1916)

19 A rainbow and a cuckoo's song
May never come together again;
May never come
This side the tomb.
   'A Great Time' (1914)

20 It was the Rainbow gave thee birth,
And left thee all her lovely hues.
   'Kingfisher' (1910)

1 What is this life if, full of care,
We have no time to stand and stare.
'Leisure' (1911)

2 Come, lovely Morning, rich in frost
On iron, wood and glass.
'Silver Hours' (1932)

3 Sweet Stay-at-Home, sweet Well-content,
Thou knowest of no strange continent:
Thou hast not felt thy bosom keep
A gentle motion with the deep.
'Sweet Stay-At-Home' (1913)

Bette Davis see Epitaphs 311:5, Film lines 319:3, Film lines 319:6, Film lines 320:22

Jefferson Davis 1808-89

American statesman; President of the Confederate states 1861-5
on Davis: see Yancey 853:3

4 If the Confederacy fails, there should be written on its tombstone: *Died of a Theory*.
in 1865; Geoffrey C. Ward *The Civil War* (1991) ch. 5

Sammy Davis Jnr. 1925-90

American entertainer

5 Being a star has made it possible for me to get insulted in places where the average Negro could never *hope* to go and get insulted.
Yes I Can (1965) pt. 3, ch. 23

Thomas Davis 1814-45

Irish poet and nationalist
on Davis: see Ferguson 316:17

6 But the land of their heart's hope they never saw more,
For in far, foreign fields, from Dunkirk to Belgrade
Lie the soldiers and chiefs of the Irish Brigade.
'The Battle-Eve of the Brigade' (1846)

7 And then I prayed I yet might see
Our fetters rent in twain,
And Ireland, long a province, be
A Nation once again.
'A Nation Once Again' (1846)

8 Come in the evening, or come in the morning,
Come when you're looked for, or come without warning.
'The Welcome' (1846)

9 But—hark!—some voice like thunder spake:
The West's awake! the West's awake!
'The West's Asleep' (1846)

10 This country of ours is no sandbank, thrown up by some recent caprice of earth. It is an ancient land, honoured in the archives of civilisation, traceable into antiquity by its piety, its valour, and its sufferings. Every great European race has sent its stream to the river of Irish mind.
Literary and Historical Essays (1846)

11 If we live influenced by wind, and sun, and tree, and not by the passions and deeds of the past, we are a thriftless and hopeless people.
Literary and Historical Essays (1846)

Michael Davitt 1846-1905

Irish nationalist

12 An Englishman of the strongest type moulded for an Irish purpose.
of Charles Stewart Parnell
The Fall of Feudalism in Ireland (1906)

Richard Dawkins

English biologist

13 [Natural selection] has no vision, no foresight, no sight at all. If it can be said to play the role of watchmaker in nature, it is the *blind* watchmaker.
The Blind Watchmaker (1986) ch. 1; see **Paley** 583:4

14 However many ways there may be of being alive, it is certain that there are vastly more ways of being dead.
The Blind Watchmaker (1986) ch. 1

15 The essence of life is statistical improbability on a colossal scale.
The Blind Watchmaker (1986) ch. 11

16 They are in you and in me; they created us, body and mind; and their preservation is the ultimate rationale for our existence . . . they go by the name of genes, and we are their survival machines.
The Selfish Gene (1976) ch. 2

17 Science offers the best answers to the meaning of life. Science offers the privilege of understanding before you die why you were ever born in the first place.
in *Break the Science Barrier with Richard Dawkins* (Channel Four television programme) 1 September 1996

Christopher Dawson 1889-1970

English historian of ideas and social culture

18 As soon as men decide that all means are permitted to fight an evil, then their good becomes indistinguishable from the evil that they set out to destroy.
The Judgement of the Nations (1942)

Lord Dawson of Penn 1864-1945

British physician to King George V

19 The King's life is moving peacefully towards its close.
bulletin, drafted on a menu card at Buckingham Palace on the eve of the king's death, 20 January 1936, in Kenneth Rose *King George V* (1983) ch. 10

Robin Day 1923-

British broadcaster
on Day: see Howerd 406:4

20 Television . . . thrives on unreason, and unreason thrives on television . . . [Television] strikes at the emotions rather than the intellect.
Grand Inquisitor (1989)

Stockwell Burt Day 1950–

Canadian Progressive Conservative politician

1 God's law is clear. Standards of education are not set by government, but by God, the Bible, the home and the school.
   Alberta Report, 1984

Moshe Dayan 1915–81

Israeli statesman and general

2 War is the most exciting and dramatic thing in life. In fighting to the death you feel terribly relaxed when you manage to come through.
   in *Observer* 13 February 1972 'Sayings of the Week'

C. Day-Lewis 1904–72

English poet and critic

3 Do not expect again a phoenix hour,
   The triple-towered sky, the dove complaining,
   Sudden the rain of gold and heart's first ease
   Traced under trees by the eldritch light of
      sundown.
   'From Feathers to Iron' (1935)

4 Tempt me no more; for I
   Have known the lightning's hour,
   The poet's inward pride,
   The certainty of power.
   The Magnetic Mountain (1933) pt. 3, no. 24

5 And when the Treaty emptied the British jails,
   A haggard woman returned and Dublin went wild
      to greet her.
   But still it was not enough: an iota
   Of compromise, she cried, and the Cause fails.
   'Remembering Con Markievicz' (1970)

6 It is the logic of our times,
   No subject for immortal verse—
   That we who lived by honest dreams
   Defend the bad against the worse.
   'Where are the War Poets?' (1943)

James Dean see Film titles 322:10

John Dean 1938–

American lawyer and White House counsel during the Watergate affair

7 We have a cancer within, close to the Presidency, that is growing.
   from the [Nixon] Presidential Transcripts, 21 March 1973

Seamus Deane 1940–

Irish poet and novelist

8 Meningitis. It was a word you had to bite on to say it. It had a fright and a hiss in it.
   Reading in the Dark (1996)

9 The doctor came and gave her pills and medicines. She'd take them and become calmer, but her grief just collected under the drugs like a thrombosis.
   Reading in the Dark (1996)

Percy Dearmer 1867–1936

English clergyman

10 He who would valiant be
   'Gainst all disaster,
   Let him in constancy
   Follow the Master.
   'He who would valiant be', hymn after John Bunyan; see
   Bunyan 165:7

11 Jesu, good above all other,
   Gentle Child of gentle Mother,
   In a stable born our Brother,
   Give us grace to persevere.
   'Jesu, good above all other' (1906 hymn)

Simone de Beauvoir 1908–86

French novelist and feminist

12 It is not in giving life but in risking life that man is raised above the animal; that is why superiority has been accorded in humanity not to the sex that brings forth but to that which kills.
   The Second Sex (1949) vol. 1, pt. 2, ch. 1

13 One is not born a woman: one becomes one.
   The Second Sex (1949) vol. 2, pt. 1, ch. 1

14 Few tasks are more like the torture of Sisyphus than housework, with its endless repetition . . . The housewife wears herself out marking time: she makes nothing, simply perpetuates the present.
   The Second Sex (1949) pt. 5, ch. 1

Louis de Bernières 1954–

British novelist and short-story writer

15 The human heart likes a little disorder in its geometry.
   Captain Corelli's Mandolin (1994) ch. 26

Edward de Bono 1933–

British writer and physician

16 Some people are aware of another sort of thinking which . . . leads to those simple ideas that are obvious only after they have been thought of . . . the term 'lateral thinking' has been coined to describe this other sort of thinking; 'vertical thinking' is used to denote the conventional logical process.
   The Use of Lateral Thinking (1967) foreword

Eugene Victor Debs 1855–1926

American socialist

17 When great changes occur in history, when great principles are involved, as a rule the majority are wrong. The minority are right.
   speech at his trial for sedition in Cleveland, Ohio, 11 September 1918; in *Speeches* (1928); see **Dillon** 274:12

18 While there is a lower class, I am in it; while there is a criminal element, I am of it; while there is a soul in prison, I am not free.
   speech at his trial for sedition in Cleveland, Ohio, 14 September 1918; in *Liberator* November 1918

Stephen Decatur 1779–1820

American naval officer

1 Our country! In her intercourse with foreign nations, may she always be in the right; but our country, right or wrong.
  Decatur's toast at Norfolk, Virginia, April 1816, in A. S. Mackenzie *Life of Stephen Decatur* (1846) ch. 14; see **Adams** 3:10, **Schurz** 672:6

Daniel Defoe 1660–1731

English novelist and journalist

2 We must distinguish between a man of polite learning and a mere scholar: the first is a gentleman and what a gentleman should be; the last is a mere book-case, a bundle of letters, a head stuffed with the jargon of languages, a man that understands every body but is understood by no body.
  The Complete English Gentleman (written 1728–9) ch. 5

3 Pleasure is a thief to business.
  The Complete English Tradesman (1725) vol. 1, ch. 9

4 The soul is placed in the body like a rough diamond, and must be polished, or the lustre of it will never appear.
  An Essay Upon Projects (1697) 'Of Academies: An Academy for Women'

5 Why then should women be denied the benefits of instruction? If knowledge and understanding had been useless additions to the sex, God almighty would never have given them capacities.
  An Essay Upon Projects (1697) 'Of Academies: An Academy for Women'

6 Things as certain as death and taxes, can be more firmly believed.
  History of the Devil (1726) bk. 2, ch. 6; see **Franklin** 332:19

7 Vice came in always at the door of necessity, not at the door of inclination.
  Moll Flanders (1721)

8 Give me not poverty lest I steal.
  Review vol. 8, no. 75 (15 September 1711); later incorporated into *Moll Flanders* (1721)

9 He told me . . . that mine was the middle state, or what might be called the upper station of low life, which he had found by long experience was the best state in the world, the most suited to human happiness.
  Robinson Crusoe (1719)

10 I never saw them afterwards, or any sign of them, except three of their hats, one cap, and two shoes that were not fellows.
  Robinson Crusoe (1719, ed. J. D. Crowley, 1972) (on his shipmates)

11 It happened one day, about noon, going towards my boat, I was exceedingly surprised with the print of a man's naked foot on the shore, which was very plain to be seen in the sand. I stood like one thunderstruck, or as if I had seen an apparition.
  Robinson Crusoe (1719)

12 My man Friday.
  Robinson Crusoe (1719)

13 My island was now peopled, and I thought my self very rich in subjects; and it was a merry reflection which I frequently made, how like a king I looked.
  Robinson Crusoe (1719)

14 In trouble to be troubled
  Is to have your trouble doubled.
  The Farther Adventures of Robinson Crusoe (1719, ed. G. Aitken, 1895)

15 Necessity makes an honest man a knave.
  The Serious Reflections of Robinson Crusoe (1720) ch. 2

16 The best of men cannot suspend their fate:
  The good die early, and the bad die late.
  'Character of the late Dr S. Annesley' (1697)

17 We loved the doctrine for the teacher's sake.
  'Character of the late Dr S. Annesley' (1697)

18 Nature has left this tincture in the blood,
  That all men would be tyrants if they could.
  The History of the Kentish Petition (1712–13) addenda, l. 11

19 Actions receive their tincture from the times,
  And as they change are virtues made or crimes.
  A Hymn to the Pillory (1703) l. 29

20 Fools out of favour grudge at knaves in place.
  The True-Born Englishman (1701) introduction, l. 7

21 Wherever God erects a house of prayer,
  The Devil always builds a chapel there;
  And 'twill be found, upon examination,
  The latter has the largest congregation.
  The True-Born Englishman (1701) pt. 1, l. 1; see **Proverbs** 634:38

22 In their religion they are so uneven,
  That each one goes his own by-way to heaven.
  The True-Born Englishman (1701) pt. 1, l. 104

23 From this amphibious ill-born mob began
  That vain, ill-natured thing, an Englishman.
  The True Born Englishman (1701) pt.1, l. 132

24 Your Roman-Saxon-Danish-Norman English.
  The True-Born Englishman (1701) pt. 1, l. 139

25 His lazy, long, lascivious reign.
  of **Charles II**
  The True-Born Englishman (1701) pt. 1, l. 236

26 Great families of yesterday we show,
  And lords whose parents were the Lord knows who.
  The True-Born Englishman (1701) pt. 1, l. 374

27 And of all plagues with which mankind are curst,
  Ecclesiastic tyranny's the worst.
  The True-Born Englishman (1701) pt. 2, l. 299

28 When kings the sword of justice first lay down,
  They are no kings, though they possess the crown.
  Titles are shadows, crowns are empty things,
  The good of subjects is the end of kings.
  The True-Born Englishman (1701) pt. 2, l. 313

Edgar Degas 1834–1917

French artist

29 Art is vice. You don't marry it legitimately, you rape it.
  Paul Lafond *Degas* (1918)

Charles de Gaulle 1890–1970

French soldier and statesman; President of France, 1959–69
see also **Opening lines** 575:27

1 France has lost a battle. But France has not lost the war!

proclamation, 18 June 1940, in *Discours, messages et déclarations du Général de Gaulle* (1941)

2 Faced by the bewilderment of my countrymen, by the disintegration of a government in thrall to the enemy, by the fact that the instutions of my country are incapable, at the moment, of functioning, I General de Gaulle, a French soldier and military leader, realize that I now speak for France.

speech in London, 19 June 1940

3 Since they whose duty it was to wield the sword of France have let it fall shattered to the ground, I have taken up the broken blade.

speech, 13 July 1940, in *Discours et Messages* (1942)

4 *Je vous ai compris.*

I have understood you.

speech to French colonists at Algiers, 4 June 1958, in *Discours et Messages* vol. 3 (1970); by 1962 Algeria had achieved independence

5 Yes, it is Europe, from the Atlantic to the Urals, it is Europe, it is the whole of Europe, that will decide the fate of the world.

speech to the people of Strasbourg, 23 November 1959, in *Le Monde* 24 November 1959

6 Politics are too serious a matter to be left to the politicians.

replying to **Attlee**'s *remark that 'De Gaulle is a very good soldier and a very bad politician'*

Clement Attlee *A Prime Minister Remembers* (1961) ch. 4; see **Clemenceau** 226:10

7 *Europe des patries.*

A Europe of nations.

widely associated with De Gaulle, c.1962, and taken as encapsulating his views, although perhaps not coined by him

J. Lacouture *De Gaulle: the Ruler* (1991)

8 How can you govern a country which has 246 varieties of cheese?

Ernest Mignon *Les Mots du Général* (1962)

9 Since a politician never believes what he says, he is quite surprised to be taken at his word.

Ernest Mignon *Les Mots du Général* (1962)

10 Treaties, you see, are like girls and roses: they last while they last.

speech at Elysée Palace, 2 July 1963, in André Passeron *De Gaulle parle 1962–6* (1966)

11 *Vive Le Québec Libre.*

Long Live Free Quebec.

speech in Montreal, 24 July 1967, in *Discours et messages* (1970)

12 The sword is the axis of the world and its power is absolute.

Vers l'armée de métier (1934) 'Comment?' Commandement 3

13 And now she is like everyone else.

on the death of his daughter, who had been born with Down's syndrome

Jean Lacouture *De Gaulle* (1965)

14 One does not put Voltaire in the Bastille.

when asked to arrest **Sartre**, *in the 1960s*

in *Encounter* June 1975

Thomas Dekker 1570–1641

English dramatist

15 That great fishpond (the sea).

The Honest Whore (1604) pt. I, act I, sc. 2

16   The best of men
That e'er wore earth about him, was a sufferer,
A soft, meek, patient, humble, tranquil spirit,
The first true gentleman that ever breathed.

The Honest Whore (1604) pt. I, act I, sc. 2

17 Art thou poor, yet hast thou golden slumbers?
O sweet content!
Art thou rich, yet is thy mind perplexed?
O, punishment!
Dost thou laugh to see how fools are vexed
To add to golden numbers, golden numbers?
O, sweet content, O, sweet, O, sweet content!
Work apace, apace, apace, apace;
Honest labour bears a lovely face;
Then hey nonny, nonny; hey nonny, nonny.

Patient Grissil (1603) act I, sc. I

18 Golden slumbers kiss your eyes,
Smiles awake you when you rise:
Sleep, pretty wantons, do not cry,
And I will sing a lullaby:
Rock them, rock them, lullaby.

Patient Grissil (1603) act 4, sc. 2

19 Prince I am not, yet I am nobly born.

The Shoemaker's Holiday (1600) sc. 7

Walter de la Mare 1873–1956

English poet and novelist

20 Ann, Ann!
Come! quick as you can!
There's a fish that *talks*
In the frying-pan.

'Alas, Alack' (1913)

21 Oh, no man knows
Through what wild centuries
Roves back the rose.

'All That's Past' (1912)

22 He is crazed with the spell of far Arabia,
They have stolen his wits away.

'Arabia' (1912)

23 But beauty vanishes; beauty passes;
However rare—rare it be;

'Epitaph' (1912)

24 Look thy last on all things lovely,
Every hour.

'Fare Well' (1918)

25 Hi! handsome hunting man
Fire your little gun.

Bang! Now the animal
Is dead and dumb and done.
Nevermore to peep again, creep again, leap again,
Eat or sleep or drink again, Oh, what fun!
'Hi!' (1930)

1 Three jolly gentlemen,
In coats of red,
Rode their horses
Up to bed.
'The Huntsmen' (1913)

2 'Is there anybody there?' said the Traveller,
Knocking on the moonlit door;
And his horse in the silence champed the grasses
Of the forest's ferny floor.
'The Listeners' (1912)

3 'Tell them I came, and no one answered,
That I kept my word,' he said.
'The Listeners' (1912)

4 Ay, they heard his foot upon the stirrup,
And the sound of iron on stone,
And how the silence surged softly backward,
When the plunging hoofs were gone.
'The Listeners' (1912)

5 What is the world, O soldiers?
It is I:
I, this incessant snow,
This northern sky;
Soldiers, this solitude
Through which we go
Is I.
'Napoleon' (1906)

6 Softly along the road of evening,
In a twilight dim with rose,
Wrinkled with age, and drenched with dew,
Old Nod, the shepherd, goes.
'Nod' (1912)

7 Slowly, silently, now the moon
Walks the night in her silver shoon.
'Silver' (1913)

8 Behind the blinds I sit and watch
The people passing—passing by;
And not a single one can see
My tiny watching eye.
'The Window' (1913)

Shelagh Delaney 1939-
English dramatist

9 Women never have young minds. They are born
three thousand years old.
A Taste of Honey (1959) act 1, sc. 2

Frederick Delius 1862-1934
English composer, of German and Scandinavian descent

10 It is only that which cannot be expressed
otherwise that is worth expressing in music.
in *Sackbut* September 1920 'At the Crossroads'

11 No artist should ever marry . . . if ever you do
have to marry, marry a girl who is more in love
with your art than with you.
Eric Fenby *Delius as I Knew Him* (1936)

Michael Dell 1965-
American computer executive

12 Sometimes, it's better not to listen when people
tell you that something can't be done. I didn't ask
for permission or approval. I just went ahead and
did it.
*referring to the foundation of Dell Computers, a
highly-successful direct sales operation that went
counter to traditional industry marketing methods*
Direct from Dell (2000)

Agnes de Mille 1908-93
American dancer and choreographer

13 The truest expression of a people is in its dances
and its music. Bodies never lie.
in *New York Times Magazine* 11 May 1975

Democritus c.460-c.370 BC
Greek philosopher

14 By convention there is colour, by convention
sweetness, by convention bitterness, but in reality
there are atoms and space.
fragment 125

Demosthenes c.384-c.322 BC
Greek orator and Athenian statesman

15 What worse change can any one bring against an
orator than that his words and his sentiments do
not tally?
On the Crown

16 You, Athenians, possessing unsurpassed
resources—fleet, infantry, cavalry, revenue—have
never to this very day employed them aright, and
yet you carry on war with Philip exactly as a
barbarian boxes. The barbarian, when struck,
always clutches the place; hit him on the other
side and there go his hands. He neither knows nor
cares how to parry a blow or how to watch his
adversary.
First Philippic ch. 40

17 Excessive dealings with tyrants are not good for
the security of free states.
Second Philippic ch. 21

18 There is one safeguard known generally to the
wise, which is an advantage and security to all,
but especially to democracies against despots—
suspicion.
Second Philippic ch. 24

19 When asked what was first in oratory, [he] replied
to his questioner, 'action,' what second, 'action,'
and again third, 'action'.
Cicero *Brutus* ch. 37, sect. 142

Jack Dempsey 1895–1983
American boxer

1 Honey, I just forgot to duck.
*to his wife, on losing the World Heavyweight title, 23
September 1926; after a failed attempt on his life in
1981, Ronald **Reagan** quipped 'I forgot to duck'*
J. and B. P. Dempsey *Dempsey* (1977)

Catherine Deneuve 1943–
French actress

2 Sexuality is such a part of life, but sexuality in the
movies—I have a hard time finding it.
in *Première* April 1993

Deng Xiaoping 1904–97
*Chinese Communist statesman; from 1977 paramount leader
of China*

3 It doesn't matter if a cat is black or white, as long
as it catches mice.
in the early 1960s; in Daily Telegraph *20 February 1997,
obituary*

John Denham 1615–69
English poet

4 Thames, the most loved of all the Ocean's sons,
By his old sire, to his embraces runs,
Hasting to pay his tribute to the Sea,
Like mortal life to meet eternity.
'Cooper's Hill' (1642)

5 Youth, what man's age is like to be doth show;
We may our ends by our beginnings know.
'Of Prudence' (1668) l. 225

6 Old Mother Wit, and Nature gave
Shakespeare and Fletcher all they have;
In Spenser, and in Jonson, Art,
Of slower Nature got the start.
'On Mr Abraham Cowley' (1667)

7 Such is our pride, our folly, or our fate,
That few, but such as cannot write, translate.
'To Richard Fanshaw' (1648)

Lord Denman 1779–1854
English politician and lawyer; Lord Chief Justice, 1832–50

8 Trial by jury itself, instead of being a security to
persons who are accused, will be a delusion, a
mockery, and a snare.
*on a case involving the fraudulent omission of sixty
names from the list of jurors in Dublin*
speech in the House of Lords, 4 September 1844; in E. W.
Cox (ed.) *Reports of Cases in Criminal Law* (1846) vol. 1

Lord Denning 1899–1999
British judge

9 The Treaty [of Rome] is like an incoming tide. It
flows into the estuaries and up the rivers. It
cannot be held back.
in 1975; Anthony Sampson *The Essential Anatomy of
Britain* (1992)

10 To every subject of this land, however powerful, I
would use Thomas Fuller's words over three
hundred years ago, 'Be ye never so high, the law
is above you.'
in a High Court ruling against the Attorney-General,
January 1977

11 The keystone of the rule of law in England has
been the independence of judges. It is the only
respect in which we make any real separation of
powers.
The Family Story (1981)

12 We shouldn't have all these campaigns to get the
Birmingham Six released if they'd been hanged.
They'd have been forgotten and the whole
community would be satisfied.
in *Spectator* 18 August 1990

John Dennis 1657–1734
English critic, poet, and dramatist

13 A man who could make so vile a pun would not
scruple to pick a pocket.
in *The Gentleman's Magazine* (1781) editorial note

14 The great design of art is to restore the decays that
happened to human nature by the fall, by
restoring order.
The Grounds of Criticism in Poetry (1704) ch. 2

15 Damn them! They will not let my play run, but
they steal my thunder!
*on hearing his new thunder effects used at a
performance of* Macbeth, *following the withdrawal of
one of his own plays after only a short run*
William S. Walsh *A Handy-Book of Literary Curiosities*
(1893)

Christine de Pisan 1364–c.1430
Italian writer, resident in France from 1369

16 Where true love is, it showeth; it will not feign.
'The Epistle of Othea to Hector'

Thomas De Quincey 1785–1859
English essayist and critic

17 The burden of the incommunicable.
Confessions of an English Opium Eater (1856 ed.) pt. 1

18 Oxford Street, stony-hearted stepmother, thou that
listenest to the sighs of orphans, and drinkest the
tears of children.
Confessions of an English Opium Eater (1822, ed. 1856) pt. 1

19 A duller spectacle this earth of ours has not to
show than a rainy Sunday in London.
Confessions of an English Opium Eater (1822, ed. 1856) pt. 2

20 Thou hast the keys of Paradise, oh just, subtle,
and mighty opium!
Confessions of an English Opium Eater (1822, ed. 1856) pt. 2

21 Books, we are told, propose to *instruct* or to *amuse.*
Indeed! . . . The true antithesis to knowledge, in
this case, is not *pleasure*, but *power.* All that is

literature seeks to communicate power; all that is not literature, to communicate knowledge.

De Quincey adds that he is indebted for this distinction to 'many years' conversation with Mr **Wordsworth**'

Letters to a Young Man whose Education has been Neglected no. 3, in the London Magazine January–July 1823

1 Murder considered as one of the fine arts.

title of essay in Blackwood's Magazine February 1827

2 If once a man indulges himself in murder, very soon he comes to think little of robbing; and from robbing he comes next to drinking and sabbath-breaking, and from that to incivility and procrastination.

'On Murder Considered as One of the Fine Arts' (Supplementary Paper) in Blackwood's Magazine November 1839

3 There is first the literature of *knowledge*, and secondly, the literature of *power*.

review of the Works of Pope (1847 ed.) in North British Review August 1848, vol. 9

Edward Stanley, 14th Earl of Derby
1799–1869

British Conservative statesman; Prime Minister, 1852, 1858–9, 1866–8

on Derby: see **Bulwer-Lytton** 164:3, **Disraeli** 275:7

4 The duty of an Opposition [is] very simple . . . to oppose everything, and propose nothing.

quoting 'Mr Tierney, a great Whig authority' in the House of Commons, 4 June 1841

5 Meddle and muddle.

summarizing Lord John **Russell**'s foreign policy Speech on the Address, House of Lords, 4 February 1864

Jacques Derrida 1930–
Algerian-born French philosopher and critic

6 Il n'y a pas de hors-texte.

There is nothing outside of the text.

Of Grammatology (1967)

7 Il y a plus affaire à interpréter les interprétations qu'à interpréter les choses. Montaigne

We need to interpret interpretations more than to interpret things. Montaigne.

Writing and Difference (1967) 'Structure, Sign and Play in the Discourse of the Human Sciences' translated by Alan Bass: epigraph; see **Montaigne** 545:3

René Descartes 1596–1650
French philosopher and mathematician

on Descartes: see **Ryle** 662:4

8 La lecture de tous les bons livres est comme une conversation avec les plus honnêtes gens des siècles passés, qui en ont été les auteurs, et même une conversation étudiée en laquelle ils nous découvrent que les meilleures de leurs pensées.

The reading of good books is like a conversation with the best men of past centuries—in fact like a prepared conversation, in which they reveal only the best of their thoughts.

Le Discours de la méthode (1637) pt. 1

9 Le bon sens est la chose du monde la mieux partagée, car chacun pense en être bien pourvu.

Common sense is the best distributed commodity in the world, for every man is convinced that he is well supplied with it.

Le Discours de la méthode (1637) pt. 1

10 Car ce n'est pas assez d'avoir l'esprit bon, mais le principal est de l'appliquer bien.

For it is not enough to have a good mind; the main thing is to use it well.

Le Discours de la méthode (1637) pt. 1

11 Je pense, donc je suis.

I think, therefore I am.

usually quoted as, 'Cogito, ergo sum', from the 1641 Latin edition

Le Discours de la méthode (1637) pt. 4

12 Agnoscam fieri non posse ut existam talis naturae qualis sum, nempe ideam Dei in me habens, nisi revera Deus etiam existeret, Deus, inquam, ille idem cujus idea in me est.

I could not possibly exist with the nature I actually have, that is, one endowed with the idea of God, unless there really is a God; the very God, I mean, of whom I have an idea.

Meditationes (ed. 2, 1642) pt. 3

13 Repugnare ut detur vacuum sive in quo nulla plane sit res.

It is contrary to reason to say that there is a vacuum or space in which there is absolutely nothing.

Principia Philosophiae (1644) pt. 2, sect. 16 (translated by E. S. Haldane and G. R. T. Ross)

Camille Desmoulins 1760–94
French revolutionary

14 My age is that of the *bon Sansculotte Jésus*; an age fatal to Revolutionists.

reply given at his trial

Thomas Carlyle History of the French Revolution (1837) bk. 6, ch. 2

Philippe Néricault Destouches
1680–1754
French dramatist

15 Les absents ont toujours tort.

The absent are always in the wrong.

L'Obstacle imprévu (1717) act 1, sc. 6

Buddy De Sylva 1895–1950 and **Lew Brown** 1893–1958

16 The moon belongs to everyone,
The best things in life are free,
The stars belong to everyone,
They gleam there for you and me.

'The Best Things in Life are Free' (1927 song); see **Proverbs** 615:15

Eamonn de Valera 1882–1975

American-born Irish statesman; Taoiseach 1937–48, 1951–4, and 1957–9, and President of the Republic of Ireland 1959–73
on de Valera: see Lloyd George 488:2

1 Whenever I wanted to know what the Irish people wanted, I had only to examine my own heart and it told me straight off what the Irish people wanted.
speech in Dáil Éireann, 6 January 1922

2 Further sacrifice of life would now be in vain . . . Military victory must be allowed to rest for the moment with those who have destroyed the Republic.
message to the Republican armed forces, 24 May 1923

3 That Ireland which we dreamed of would be the home of a people who valued material wealth only as a basis of right living, of a people who were satisfied with frugal comfort and devoted their leisure to the things of the spirit; a land whose countryside would be bright with cosy homesteads, whose fields and villages would be joyous with sounds of industry, the romping of sturdy children, the contests of athletic youths, the laughter of comely maidens; whose firesides would be the forums of the wisdom of serene old age.
St Patrick's Day broadcast, 17 March 1943

4 Mr Churchill is proud of Britain's stand alone, after France had fallen, and before America had entered the war. Could he not find in his heart the generosity to acknowledge that there is a small nation that stood alone, not for one year or two, but for several hundred years, against aggression; that endured spoliation, famines, massacres in endless succession; that was clubbed many times into insensibility but each time, on returning consciousness, took up the fight anew; a small nation that could never be got to accept defeat and has never surrendered her soul?
radio broadcast, 16 May 1945

Edward De Vere, Earl of Oxford see Oxford

Robert Devereux, Earl of Essex see Essex

Bernard De Voto 1897–1955

American writer

5 The proper union of gin and vermouth is a great and sudden glory; it is one of the happiest marriages on earth, and one of the shortest lived.
in *Harper's Magazine* December 1949

Peter De Vries 1910–93

American novelist and humorist

6 Gluttony is an emotional escape, a sign something is eating us.
Comfort Me With Apples (1956)

7 It is the final proof of God's omnipotence that he need not exist in order to save us.
The Mackerel Plaza (1958) ch. 1

8 The value of marriage is not that adults produce children but that children produce adults.
The Tunnel of Love (1954) ch. 8

Donald Dewar 1937–2000

Scottish Labour politician; First Minister for Scotland from 1999

9 'There shall be a Scottish parliament.' Through long years, those words were first a hope, then a belief, then a promise. Now they are a reality.
at the official opening of the Scottish Parliament
speech, 1 July 1999; see **Anonymous** 19:10

10 We look forward to the time when this moment will be seen as a turning point: the day when democracy was renewed in Scotland, when we revitalised our place in this our United Kingdom.
at the official opening of the Scottish Parliament
speech, 1 July 1999

James Dewar 1842–1923

Scottish physicist

11 Minds are like parachutes. They only function when they are open.
attributed

Lord Dewar 1864–1930

British industrialist

12 [There are] only two classes of pedestrians in these days of reckless motor traffic—the quick, and the dead.
George Robey *Looking Back on Life* (1933) ch. 28

George Dewey 1837–1917

American naval officer

13 You may fire when you are ready, Gridley.
to the captain of his flagship at Manila, 1 May 1898, in *Autobiography* (1913) ch. 15

Sergei Diaghilev 1872–1929

Russian ballet impresario

14 *Étonne-moi.*
Astonish me.
to Jean Cocteau
Wallace Fowlie (ed.) *Journals of Jean Cocteau* (1956) ch. 1

15 Tchaikovsky thought of committing suicide for fear of being discovered as a homosexual, but today, if you are a composer and *not* homosexual, you might as well put a bullet through your head.
Vernon Duke *Listen Here!* (1963)

Diana, Princess of Wales 1961–97

*British princess, former wife of **Charles**, Prince of Wales*
*on Diana: see **Blair** 118:18, **Duffy** 291:7, **Elizabeth II** 305:4,*
***John** 422:13, **Spencer** 750:14*

1 I'd like to be a queen in people's hearts but I don't see myself being Queen of this country.
  interview on *Panorama*, BBC1 TV, 20 November 1995

2 There were three of us in this marriage, so it was a bit crowded.
  interview on *Panorama*, BBC1 TV, 20 November 1995

Diane de Poitiers 1499–1566

French mistress of Henry II of France

3 *Adieu doulx baisers colombins.*
  Adieu ce qu'en secret faisons
  Quand entre nous deux nous jouons.

  Farewell sweet kisses, pigeon-wise,
  With lip and tongue; farewell again
  The secret sports betwixt us twain.
  'To Henry II Upon His Leaving for a Trip' (*c*.1552)

Porfirio Diaz 1830–1915

Mexican revolutionary and statesman; President of Mexico, 1877–80, 1884–1911

4 Poor Mexico, so far from God and so close to the United States.
  attributed

Charles Dibdin 1745–1814

English songwriter and dramatist

5 Did you ever hear of Captain Wattle?
  He was all for love, and a little for the bottle.
  'Captain Wattle and Miss Roe' (1797)

6 For a soldier I listed, to grow great in fame,
  And be shot at for sixpence a-day.
  'Charity' (1791)

7 In every mess I finds a friend,
  In every port a wife.
  'Jack in his Element' (1790)

8 But the standing toast that pleased the most
  Was—The wind that blows, the ship that goes,
  And the lass that loves a sailor!
  'The Lass that Loves a Sailor' (1811)

9 Here, a sheer hulk, lies poor Tom Bowling,
  The darling of our crew.
  'Tom Bowling' (1790)

Thomas Dibdin 1771–1841

English songwriter

10 Oh! what a snug little Island,
  A right little, tight little Island!
  'The Snug Little Island' (1833)

Charles Dickens 1812–70

English novelist
*on Dickens: see **Bagehot** 49:9*

BARNABY RUDGE

11 Something will come of this. I hope it mayn't be human gore.
  Simon Tappertit
    Barnaby Rudge (1841) ch. 4

12 There are strings . . . in the human heart that had better not be wibrated.
  Mr Tappertit
    Barnaby Rudge (1841) ch. 22

BLEAK HOUSE

13 Jarndyce and Jarndyce still drags its dreary length before the Court, perennially hopeless.
    Bleak House (1853) ch. 1

14 This is a London particular . . . A fog, miss.
    Bleak House (1853) ch. 3

15 Telescopic philanthropy.
    Bleak House (1853) ch. 4, chapter heading

16 The wind's in the east . . . I am always conscious of an uncomfortable sensation now and then when the wind is blowing in the east.
  Mr Jarndyce
    Bleak House (1853) ch. 6

17 He wos wery good to me, he wos!
  Jo
    Bleak House (1853) ch. 11

18 He is celebrated, almost everywhere, for his Deportment.
  Caddy Jellyby of Mr Turveydrop
    Bleak House (1853) ch. 14

19 You are a human boy, my young friend. A human boy. O glorious to be a human boy! . . .
  O running stream of sparkling joy
  To be a soaring human boy!
  Mr Chadband
    Bleak House (1853) ch. 19

20 Jobling, there *are* chords in the human mind.
  Mr Guppy
    Bleak House (1853) ch. 20

21 'It is,' says Chadband, 'the ray of rays, the sun of suns, the moon of moons, the star of stars. It is the light of Terewth.'
    Bleak House (1853) ch. 25

22 It's my old girl that advises. She has the head. But I never own to it before her. Discipline must be maintained.
  Mr Bagnet
    Bleak House (1853) ch. 27

23 The one great principle of the English law is, to make business for itself.
    Bleak House (1853) ch. 39

24 Dead, your Majesty, Dead, my lords and gentlemen. Dead, Right Reverends and Wrong Reverends of every Order. Dead, men and women,

born with heavenly compassion in your hearts.
And dying thus around us, every day.
on the death of Jo
> *Bleak House* (1853) ch. 47

1 I call them the Wards in Jarndyce. They are caged
up with all the others. With Hope, Joy, Youth,
Peace, Rest, Life, Dust, Ashes, Waste, Want, Ruin,
Despair, Madness, Death, Cunning, Folly, Words,
Wigs, Rags, Sheepskin, Plunder, Precedent,
Jargon, Gammon, and Spinach!
Miss Flite's birds
> *Bleak House* (1853) ch. 60

THE CHIMES

2 O let us love our occupations,
Bless the squire and his relations,
Live upon our daily rations,
And always know our proper stations.
> *The Chimes* (1844) 'The Second Quarter'

A CHRISTMAS CAROL

3 'Bah,' said Scrooge. 'Humbug!'
> *A Christmas Carol* (1843) stave 1

4 I am the Ghost of Christmas Past.
> *A Christmas Carol* (1843) stave 2

5 'God bless us every one!' said Tiny Tim, the last of
all.
> *A Christmas Carol* (1843) stave 3

6 It *was* a turkey! He could never have stood upon
his legs, that bird. He would have snapped 'em off
short in a minute, like sticks of sealing-wax.
> *A Christmas Carol* (1843) stave 5

DAVID COPPERFIELD

7 I am a lone lorn creetur . . . and everythink goes
contrairy with me.
Mrs Gummidge
> *David Copperfield* (1850) ch. 3

8 I'd better go into the house, and die and be a
riddance!
Mrs Gummidge
> *David Copperfield* (1850) ch. 3

9 She's been thinking of the old 'un!
Mr Peggotty of Mrs Gummidge
> *David Copperfield* (1850) ch. 3

10 Barkis is willin'.
> *David Copperfield* (1850) ch. 5

11 I live on broken wittles—and I sleep on the coals.
The Waiter
> *David Copperfield* (1850) ch. 5

12 Experientia does it—as papa used to say.
Mrs Micawber
> *David Copperfield* (1850) ch. 11; see **Tacitus** 770:14

13 I have known him come home to supper with a
flood of tears, and a declaration that nothing was
now left but a jail; and go to bed making a
calculation of the expense of putting bow-windows
to the house, 'in case anything turned up,' which
was his favourite expression.
of Mr Micawber
> *David Copperfield* (1850) ch. 11

14 Annual income twenty pounds, annual
expenditure nineteen nineteen six, result
happiness. Annual income twenty pounds, annual
expenditure twenty pounds nought and six, result
misery.
Mr Micawber
> *David Copperfield* (1850) ch. 12

15 Mr. Dick had been for upwards of ten years
endeavouring to keep King Charles the First out of
the Memorial; but he had been constantly getting
into it, and was there now.
> *David Copperfield* (1850) ch. 14

16 The mistake was made of putting some of the
trouble out of King Charles's head into my head.
Mr Dick
> *David Copperfield* (1850) ch. 17

17 We are so very 'umble.
Uriah Heep
> *David Copperfield* (1850) ch. 17

18 I only ask for information.
Miss Rosa Dartle
> *David Copperfield* (1850) ch. 20

19 It was as true . . . as taxes is. And nothing's truer
than them.
Mr Barkis
> *David Copperfield* (1850) ch. 21; see **Franklin** 332:19

20 What a world of gammon and spinnage it is,
though, ain't it!
Miss Mowcher
> *David Copperfield* (1850) ch. 22

21 Other things are all very well in their way, but
give me Blood!
Mr Waterbrook
> *David Copperfield* (1850) ch. 25

22 I assure you she's the dearest girl.
Mr Traddles
> *David Copperfield* (1850) ch. 27

23 Accidents will occur in the best-regulated families.
> *David Copperfield* (1850) ch. 28 (Mr Micawber); see
> **Proverbs** 614:1

24 He told me, only the other day, that it was
provided for. That was Mr Micawber's expression,
'Provided for.'
Mr Traddles
> *David Copperfield* (1850) ch. 28

25 'People can't die, along the coast,' said Mr
Peggotty, 'except when the tide's pretty nigh out.
They can't be born, unless it's pretty nigh in—not
properly born, till flood. He's a going out with the
tide.'
> *David Copperfield* (1850) ch. 30

26 Mrs Crupp had indignantly assured him that there
wasn't room to swing a cat there; but, as Mr Dick
justly observed to me, sitting down on the foot of
the bed, nursing his leg, 'You know, Trotwood, I
don't want to swing a cat. I never do swing a cat.
Therefore, what does that signify to *me*!'
> *David Copperfield* (1850) ch. 35

1 It's only my child-wife.
of Dora
   David Copperfield (1850) ch. 44

2 Circumstances beyond my individual control.
Mr Micawber
   David Copperfield (1850) ch. 49

3 I'm Gormed—and I can't say no fairer than that!
Mr Peggotty
   David Copperfield (1850) ch. 63

DOMBEY AND SON

4 He's tough, ma'am, tough is J.B. Tough, and
devilish sly!
Major Bagstock
   Dombey and Son (1848) ch. 7

5 Papa! What's money?
Paul Dombey
   Dombey and Son (1848) ch. 8

6 There was no light nonsense about Miss Blimber
. . . she was dry and sandy with working in the
graves of deceased languages. None of your live
languages for Miss Blimber. They must be dead—
stone dead—and then Miss Blimber dug them up
like a Ghoul.
   Dombey and Son (1848) ch. 11

7 If I could have known Cicero, and been his friend,
and talked with him in his retirement at Tusculum
(beau-ti-ful Tusculum), I could have died
contented.
Mrs Blimber
   Dombey and Son (1848) ch. 11

8 In the Proverbs of Solomon you will find the
following words, 'May we never want a friend in
need, nor a bottle to give him!' When found,
make a note of.
Captain Cuttle
   Dombey and Son (1848) ch. 15

9 What the waves were always saying.
   Dombey and Son (1848) title of ch. 16

10 Cows are my passion.
Mrs Skewton
   Dombey and Son (1848) ch. 21

11 If you could see my legs when I take my boots off,
you'd form some idea of what unrequited affection
is.
Mr Toots
   Dombey and Son (1848) ch. 48

GREAT EXPECTATIONS

12 Your sister is given to government.
Joe Gargery
   Great Expectations (1861) ch. 7

13 'He calls the knaves, Jacks, this boy,' said Estella
with disdain, before our first game was out.
   Great Expectations (1861) ch. 8

14 In the little world in which children have their
existence, whosoever brings them up, there is
nothing so finely perceived and so finely felt, as
injustice.
   Great Expectations (1861) ch. 8

15 Her bringing me up by hand, gave her no right to
bring me up by jerks.
   Great Expectations (1861) ch. 8

16 It is a most miserable thing to feel ashamed of
home.
   Great Expectations (1861) ch. 14

17 On the Rampage, Pip, and off the Rampage, Pip;
such is Life!
Joe Gargery
   Great Expectations (1861) ch. 15

18 He wishes me most particular to write *what larks*.
He says you will understand.
message from Joe Gargery to Pip
   Great Expectations (1861) ch. 27

HARD TIMES

19 Now, what I want is, Facts . . . Facts alone are
wanted in life.
Mr Gradgrind
   Hard Times (1854) bk. 1, ch. 1

20 People mutht be amuthed. They can't be alwayth
a learning, nor yet they can't be alwayth a
working, they an't made for it.
Mr Sleary
   Hard Times (1854) bk. 3, ch. 8

LITTLE DORRIT

21 Whatever was required to be done, the
Circumlocution Office was beforehand with all the
public departments in the art of perceiving—HOW
NOT TO DO IT.
   Little Dorrit (1857) bk. 1, ch. 10

22 There's milestones on the Dover Road!
Mr F.'s Aunt
   Little Dorrit (1857) bk. 1, ch. 23

23 As to marriage on the part of a man, my dear,
Society requires that he should retrieve his
fortunes by marriage. Society requires that he
should gain by marriage. Society requires that he
should found a handsome establishment by
marriage. Society does not see, otherwise, what he
has to do with marriage.
Mrs Merdle
   Little Dorrit (1857) bk. 1, ch. 33

24 Father is rather vulgar, my dear. The word Papa,
besides, gives a pretty form to the lips. Papa,
potatoes, poultry, prunes, and prism, are all very
good words for the lips: especially prunes and
prism.
Mrs General
   Little Dorrit (1857) bk. 2, ch. 5

25 Once a gentleman, and always a gentleman.
Rigaud
   Little Dorrit (1857) bk. 2, ch. 28

MARTIN CHUZZLEWIT

26 Affection beaming in one eye, and calculation
shining out of the other.
Mrs Todgers
   Martin Chuzzlewit (1844) ch. 8

1 Charity and Mercy. Not unholy names, I hope?
Mr Pecksniff
   Martin Chuzzlewit (1844) ch. 9

2 Here's the rule for bargains: 'Do other men, for they would do you.' That's the true business precept.
Jonas Chuzzlewit
   Martin Chuzzlewit (1844) ch. 11

3 'Mrs Harris,' I says, 'leave the bottle on the chimley-piece, and don't ask me to take none, but let me put my lips to it when I am so dispoged.'
Mrs Gamp
   Martin Chuzzlewit (1844) ch. 19

4 Some people . . . may be Rooshans, and others may be Prooshans; they are born so, and will please themselves. Them which is of other naturs thinks different.
Mrs Gamp
   Martin Chuzzlewit (1844) ch. 19

5 Brought reg'lar and draw'd mild.
Mrs Gamp on her 'half a pint of porter'
   Martin Chuzzlewit (1844) ch. 25

6 He'd make a lovely corpse.
Mrs Gamp
   Martin Chuzzlewit (1844) ch. 25

7 'Sairey,' says Mrs Harris, 'sech is life. Vich likeways is the hend of all things!'
Mrs Gamp
   Martin Chuzzlewit (1844) ch. 29

8 'The Ankworks package . . . I wish it was in Jonadge's belly, I do,' cried Mrs Gamp; appearing to confound the prophet with the whale in this miraculous aspiration.
   Martin Chuzzlewit (1844) ch. 40

9 'Who deniges of it?' Mrs Gamp enquired.
   Martin Chuzzlewit (1844) ch. 49

10 No, Betsey! Drink fair, wotever you do!
Mrs Gamp
   Martin Chuzzlewit (1844) ch. 49

11 The words she spoke of Mrs Harris, lambs could not forgive . . . nor worms forget.
Mrs Gamp
   Martin Chuzzlewit (1844) ch. 49

12 Farewell! Be the proud bride of a ducal coronet, and forget me! . . . Unalterably, never yours, Augustus.
Augustus Moddle
   Martin Chuzzlewit (1844) ch. 54

NICHOLAS NICKLEBY

13 United Metropolitan Improved Hot Muffin and Crumpet Baking and Punctual Delivery Company.
   Nicholas Nickleby (1839) ch. 2

14 EDUCATION.—At Mr Wackford Squeers's Academy, Dotheboys Hall, at the delightful village of Dotheboys, near Greta Bridge in Yorkshire, Youth are boarded, clothed, booked, furnished with pocket-money, provided with all necessaries, instructed in all languages living and dead, mathematics, orthography, geometry, astronomy, trigonometry, the use of the globes, algebra, single stick (if required), writing, arithmetic, fortification, and every other branch of classical literature. Terms, twenty guineas per annum. No extras, no vacations, and diet unparalleled.
   Nicholas Nickleby (1839) ch. 3

15 He had but one eye, and the popular prejudice runs in favour of two.
Mr Squeers
   Nicholas Nickleby (1839) ch. 4

16 Here's richness!
Mr Squeers
   Nicholas Nickleby (1839) ch. 5

17 Subdue your appetites my dears, and you've conquered human natur.
Mr Squeers
   Nicholas Nickleby (1839) ch. 5

18 C-l-e-a-n, clean, verb active, to make bright, to scour. W-i-n, win, d-e-r, der, winder, a casement. When the boy knows this out of the book, he goes and does it.
Mr Squeers
   Nicholas Nickleby (1839) ch. 8

19 As she frequently remarked when she made any such mistake, it would be all the same a hundred years hence.
Mrs Squeers
   Nicholas Nickleby (1839) ch. 9

20 There are only two styles of portrait painting; the serious and the smirk.
Miss La Creevy
   Nicholas Nickleby (1839) ch. 10

21 Sir, My pa requests me to write to you, the doctors considering it doubtful whether he will ever recuvver the use of his legs which prevents his holding a pen.
Fanny Squeers
   Nicholas Nickleby (1839) ch. 15

22 I pity his ignorance and despise him.
Fanny Squeers
   Nicholas Nickleby (1839) ch. 15

23 'It's very easy to talk,' said Mrs Mantalini. 'Not so easy when one is eating a demnition egg,' replied Mr Mantalini; 'for the yolk runs down the waistcoat, and yolk of egg does not match any waistcoat but a yellow waistcoat, demmit.'
   Nicholas Nickleby (1839) ch. 17

24 Language was not powerful enough to describe the infant phenomenon.
   Nicholas Nickleby (1839) ch. 23

25 The unities, sir . . . are a completeness—a kind of universal dovetailedness with regard to place and time.
Mr Curdle
   Nicholas Nickleby (1839) ch. 24

1 She's the only sylph I ever saw, who could stand upon one leg, and play the tambourine on her other knee, like a sylph.
Mr Crummles
Nicholas Nickleby (1839) ch. 25

2 Bring in the bottled lightning, a clean tumbler, and a corkscrew.
The Gentleman in the Small-clothes
Nicholas Nickleby (1839) ch. 49

3 All is gas and gaiters.
The Gentleman in the Small-clothes
Nicholas Nickleby (1839) ch. 49

4 My life is one demd horrid grind!
Mr Mantalini
Nicholas Nickleby (1839) ch. 64

5 He has gone to the demnition bow-wows.
Mr Mantalini
Nicholas Nickleby (1839) ch. 64

THE OLD CURIOSITY SHOP

6 Codlin's the friend, not Short.
Codlin
The Old Curiosity Shop (1841) ch. 19

7 I never nursed a dear Gazelle, to glad me with its soft black eye, but when it came to know me well, and love me, it was sure to marry a market-gardener.
Dick Swiveller
The Old Curiosity Shop (1841) ch. 56; see **Moore** 547:20

8 It was a maxim with Foxey—our revered father, gentlemen—'Always suspect everybody.'
Sampson Brass
The Old Curiosity Shop (1841) ch. 66

OLIVER TWIST

9 Please, sir, I want some more.
Oliver
Oliver Twist (1838) ch. 2

10 Known by the *sobriquet* of 'The artful Dodger'.
Oliver Twist (1838) ch. 8

11 There is a passion for hunting something deeply implanted in the human breast.
Oliver Twist (1838) ch. 10

12 I only know two sorts of boys. Mealy boys, and beef-faced boys.
Mr Grimwig
Oliver Twist (1838) ch. 14

13 Oh, Mrs Corney, what a prospect this opens! What a opportunity for a jining of hearts and house-keepings!
Bumble
Oliver Twist (1838) ch. 27

14 This ain't the shop for justice.
The Artful Dodger
Oliver Twist (1838) ch. 43

15 'If the law supposes that,' said Mr Bumble . . . 'the law is a ass—a idiot.'
Bumble
Oliver Twist (1838) ch. 51; see **Chapman** 208:16

16 Strike them all dead! What right have they to butcher me?
Fagin
Oliver Twist (1838) ch. 52

OUR MUTUAL FRIEND

17 A literary man—*with* a wooden leg.
Mr Boffin, of Silas Wegg
Our Mutual Friend (1865) bk. 1, ch. 5

18 Professionally he declines and falls, and as a friend he drops into poetry.
Mr Boffin, of Silas Wegg
Our Mutual Friend (1865) bk. 1, ch. 5

19 Meaty jelly, too, especially when a little salt, which is the case when there's ham, is mellering to the organ.
Silas Wegg
Our Mutual Friend (1865) bk. 1, ch. 5

20 There is in the Englishman a combination of qualities, a modesty, an independence, a responsibility, a repose, combined with an absence of everything calculated to call a blush into the cheek of a young person, which one would seek in vain among the Nations of the Earth.
Mr Podsnap
Our Mutual Friend (1865) bk. 1, ch. 11

21 I think . . . that it is the best club in London.
Mr Twemlow, on the House of Commons
Our Mutual Friend (1865) bk. 2, ch. 3

22 A slap-up gal in a bang-up chariot.
Our Mutual Friend (1865) bk. 2, ch. 8

23 He'd be sharper than a serpent's tooth, if he wasn't as dull as ditch water.
Fanny Cleaver
Our Mutual Friend (1865) bk. 3, ch. 10

24 I want to be something so much worthier than the doll in the doll's house.
Bella
Our Mutual Friend (1865) bk. 4, ch. 5

PICKWICK PAPERS

25 He had used the word in its Pickwickian sense . . . He had merely considered him a humbug in a Pickwickian point of view.
Mr Blotton
Pickwick Papers (1837) ch. 1

26 Kent, sir—everybody knows Kent—apples, cherries, hops, and women.
Jingle
Pickwick Papers (1837) ch. 2

27 I wants to make your flesh creep.
The Fat Boy
Pickwick Papers (1837) ch. 8

28 'It's always best on these occasions to do what the mob do.' 'But suppose there are two mobs?' suggested Mr Snodgrass. 'Shout with the largest,' replied Mr Pickwick.
Pickwick Papers (1837) ch. 13

29 Battledore and shuttlecock's a wery good game, when you an't the shuttlecock and two lawyers

the battledores, in which case it gets too excitin' to be pleasant.
Mr Weller
Pickwick Papers (1837) ch. 20

1 Be wery careful o' vidders all your life.
Mr Weller
Pickwick Papers (1837) ch. 20

2 Poverty and oysters always seem to go together.
Sam Weller
Pickwick Papers (1837) ch. 22

3 A double glass o' the inwariable.
Mr Weller
Pickwick Papers (1837) ch. 33

4 It's my opinion, sir, that this meeting is drunk, sir!
Mr Stiggins
Pickwick Papers (1837) ch. 33

5 'Do you spell it with a "V" or a "W"?' inquired the judge. 'That depends upon the taste and fancy of the speller, my Lord,' replied Sam [Weller].
Pickwick Papers (1837) ch. 34

6 'Little to do, and plenty to get, I suppose?' said Sergeant Buzfuz, with jocularity. 'Oh, quite enough to get, sir, as the soldier said ven they ordered him three hundred and fifty lashes,' replied Sam. 'You must not tell us what the soldier, or any other man, said, sir,' interposed the judge; 'it's not evidence.'
Pickwick Papers (1837) ch. 34; see **Proverbs** 634:13

7 A good uniform must work its way with the women, sooner or later.
The Gentleman in Blue
Pickwick Papers (1837) ch. 37

8 'And a bird-cage, sir,' says Sam. 'Veels vithin veels, a prison in a prison.'
Pickwick Papers (1837) ch. 40

9 The have-his-carcase, next to the perpetual motion, is vun of the blessedest things as wos ever made.
Sam Weller
Pickwick Papers (1837) ch. 43

10 Anythin' for a quiet life, as the man said wen he took the sitivation at the lighthouse.
Sam Weller
Pickwick Papers (1837) ch. 43; see **Middleton** 524:8

11 'Never . . . see . . . a dead postboy, did you?' inquired Sam . . . 'No,' rejoined Bob, 'I never did.' 'No!' rejoined Sam triumphantly. 'Nor never vill; and there's another thing that no man never see, and that's a dead donkey.'
Pickwick Papers (1837) ch. 51

SKETCHES BY BOZ

12 Minerva House . . . where some twenty girls . . . acquired a smattering of everything, and a knowledge of nothing.
Sketches by Boz (1839) Tales, ch. 3 'Sentiment'

A TALE OF TWO CITIES

13 It was the best of times, it was the worst of times, it was the age of wisdom, it was the age of

foolishness, it was the epoch of belief, it was the epoch of incredulity, it was the season of Light, it was the season of Darkness, it was the spring of hope, it was the winter of despair, we had everything before us, we had nothing before us, we were all going direct to Heaven, we were all going direct the other way.
A Tale of Two Cities (1859) bk. 1, ch. 1

14 I pass my whole life, miss, in turning an immense pecuniary Mangle.
Mr Lorry
A Tale of Two Cities (1859) bk. 1, ch. 4

15 A likely thing . . . If it was ever intended that I should go across salt water, do you suppose Providence would have cast my lot in an island?
Miss Pross
A Tale of Two Cities (1859) bk. 1, ch. 4

16 If you must go flopping yourself down, flop in favour of your husband and child, and not in opposition to 'em.
Jerry Cruncher
A Tale of Two Cities (1859) bk. 2, ch. 1

17 'It is possible—that it may not come, during our lives . . . We shall not see the triumph.' 'We shall have helped it,' returned madame.
Monsieur and Madame Defarge
A Tale of Two Cities (1859) bk. 2, ch. 16

18 There might be medical doctors . . . a cocking their medical eyes.
A Tale of Two Cities (1859) bk. 3, ch. 9 (Jerry Cruncher)

19 It is a far, far better thing that I do, than I have ever done; it is a far, far better rest that I go to, than I have ever known.
Sydney Carton's thoughts on the scaffold
A Tale of Two Cities (1859) bk. 3, ch. 15

20 My faith in the people governing is, on the whole, infinitesimal; my faith in The People governed is, on the whole, illimitable.
speech at Birmingham and Midland Institute, 27 September 1869, in K. J. Fielding (ed.) Speeches of Charles Dickens (1960)

Emily Dickinson 1830–86

American poet
on Dickinson: see **Crane** 250:3

21 After great pain, a formal feeling comes.
'After great pain, a formal feeling comes' (1862)

22 Because I could not stop for Death—
He kindly stopped for me—
The Carriage held but just Ourselves—
And Immortality.
'Because I could not stop for Death' (c.1863)

23 Since then—'tis Centuries—and yet
Feels shorter than the Day
I first surmised the Horses Heads
Were toward Eternity.
'Because I could not stop for Death' (c.1863)

24 What fortitude the Soul contains,
That it can so endure

The accent of a coming Foot—
The opening of a Door.
'Elysium is as far as to' (c.1882)

1 There interposed a Fly—
With Blue—uncertain stumbling Buzz—
Between the light—and me—
And then the Windows failed—and then
I could not see to see.
'I heard a Fly buzz—when I died' (c.1862)

2 There is no Frigate like a Book
To take us Lands away
Nor any Coursers like a Page
Of prancing Poetry.
'A Book (2)' (c.1873)

3 The Bustle in a House
The Morning after Death
Is solemnest of industries
Enacted upon Earth—

The Sweeping up the Heart
And putting Love away
We shall not want to use again
Until Eternity.
'The Bustle in a House' (c.1866)

4 Heaven is what I cannot reach
The apple on the tree
'Forbidden Fruit' (c.1861)

5 Parting is all we know of heaven,
And all we need of hell.
'My life closed twice before its close'

6 The Soul selects her own Society—
Then—shuts the Door—
To her divine Majority—
Present no more.
'The Soul selects her own Society' (c.1862)

7 Success is counted sweetest
By those who ne'er succeed.
To comprehend a nectar
Requires sorest need.
'Success is counted sweetest' (1859)

8 There's a certain Slant of light,
Winter Afternoons—
That oppresses like the Heft
Of Cathedral Tunes—
'There's a certain Slant of light' (c.1861)

9 They shut me up in prose—
As when a little girl
They put me in the closet—
Because they liked me 'still'.
'They shut me up in prose' (c.1862)

10 This is my letter to the world
That never wrote to me.
'This is my letter to the world' (c.1862)

11 This quiet Dust was Gentlemen and Ladies
And Lads and Girls—
Was laughter and ability and Sighing
And Frocks and Curls.
'This quiet Dust was Gentlemen and Ladies' (c.1864)

12 Will you tell me my fault, frankly as to yourself,
for I had rather wince, than die. Men do not call

the surgeon to commend the bone, but to set it,
Sir.
letter to T. W. Higginson, July 1862

13 Friday I tasted life. It was a vast morsel. A Circus
passed the house—still I feel the red in my mind
though the drums are out. The Lawn is full of
south and the odors tangle, and I hear to-day for
the first time the river in the tree.
letter to Mrs J. G. Holland, May 1866, in T. H. Johnson
(ed.) *The Letters of Emily Dickinson* vol. 2 (1958)

John Dickinson 1732–1808
American politician

14 We have counted the cost of this contest, and find
nothing so dreadful as voluntary slavery . . . Our
cause is just, our union is perfect.
*declaration of reasons for taking up arms against
England, presented to Congress, 8 July 1775*
C. J. Stillé *The Life and Times of John Dickinson* (1891) ch. 5

15 Then join hand in hand, brave Americans all,—
By uniting we stand, by dividing we fall.
'The Liberty Song' (1768), in *The Writings of John Dickinson*
vol. 1 (1895); see **Proverbs** 633:34

Paul Dickson 1939–
American writer

16 Rowe's Rule: the odds are five to six that the light
at the end of the tunnel is the headlight of an
oncoming train.
in *Washingtonian* November 1978; see **Lowell** 494:16

Denis Diderot 1713–84
French philosopher and man of letters

17 *Et des boyaux du dernier prêtre
Serrons le cou du dernier roi.*
And [with] the guts of the last priest
Let's shake the neck of the last king.
Dithrambe sur fête de rois; see **Meslier** 523:7

18 Poetry wants something enormous, barbarous,
savage.
Discours de la poésie dramatique (1758)

19 There are two sorts of laws, those of absolute
equity and universality, and the bizarre ones
which owe their autonomy only to blindness or to
the force of circumstance. The latter merely cover
the man who is breaking them with a passing
disgrace, which time then transfers to the judges
and the nations, on whom it remains forever.
Oeuvres romanesques (ed. H. Bénac, revised L. Perol, 1981)
translated by Peter France

20 The first vows sworn by two creatures of flesh and
blood were made at the foot of a rock that was
crumbling to dust; they called as witness to their
constancy a heaven which never stays the same
for one moment; everything within them and
around them was changing, and they thought
their hearts were exempt from vicissitudes.
Children!
Oeuvres romanesques (ed. H. Bénac, revised L. Perol, 1981)
translated by Peter France

1 *L'esprit de l'escalier.*
Staircase wit.
the witty riposte one thinks of only when one has left the drawing-room and is already on the way downstairs
Paradoxe sur le Comédien (written 1773–8, published 1830)

2 See this egg. It is with this that all the schools of theology and all the temples of the earth are to be overturned.
on how life develops from an insensitive mass
Le Rêve de d'Alembert (written 1769, published 1830) pt. 1

3 Oh Richardson! thou singular genius.
Isaac D'Israeli Curiosities of Literature (1849 ed.)

Joan Didion 1934-
American writer

4 Was there ever in anyone's life span a point free in time, devoid of memory, a night when choice was any more than the sum of all the choices gone before?
Run River (1963) ch. 4

5 When we start deceiving ourselves into thinking not that we want something or need something, not that it is a pragmatic necessity for us to have it, but that it is a *moral imperative* that we have it, then is when we join the fashionable madmen, and then is when the thin whine of hysteria is heard in the land, and then is when we are in bad trouble.
Slouching towards Bethlehem (1968) 'On Morality'

John G. Diefenbaker 1895-1979
Canadian Progressive Conservative statesman; Prime Minister 1957–63

6 There can be no dedication to Canada's future without a knowledge of its past.
in *Toronto Star* 9 October 1964

Howard Dietz 1896-1983
American songwriter

7 *Ars gratia artis.*
Art for art's sake.
motto of Metro-Goldwyn-Mayer film studios, apparently intended to say 'Art is beholden to the artists'
Bosley Crowthier The Lion's Share (1957); see **Constant** 241:10

Wentworth Dillon, Lord Roscommon c.1633-85
Irish poet and critic

8 Men ever had, and ever will have leave,
To coin new words well suited to the age:
Words are like leaves, some wither every year,
And every year a younger race succeeds.
Art of Poetry (1680) l. 73; see **Horace** 398:2

9 But words once spoke can never be recalled.
Art of Poetry (1680) l. 438; see **Horace** 399:14

10 Choose an author as you choose a friend.
Essay on Translated Verse (1684) l. 96

11 Immodest words admit of no defence,
For want of decency is want of sense.
Essay on Translated Verse (1684) l. 113

12 The multitude is always in the wrong.
Essay on Translated Verse (1684) l. 183; see **Debs** 260:17, **Ibsen** 412:10

Ernest Dimnet 1866-1954
French priest, writer, and lecturer

13 [The word moral] is gradually getting to resemble the word *righteous* . . . But, for all that, moral is not preaching, it is beauty of a rare kind.
What We Live By (1932) pt. 1

14 Architecture, of all the arts, is the one which acts the most slowly, but the most surely, on the soul.
What We Live By (1932) pt. 2, ch. 12

Isak Dinesen (Karen Blixen) 1885-1962
Danish novelist and short-story writer

15 A herd of elephant . . . pacing along as if they had an appointment at the end of the world.
Out of Africa (1937) pt. 1, ch. 1

16 The giraffe, in their queer, inimitable, vegetative gracefulness . . . a family of rare, long-stemmed, speckled gigantic flowers slowly advancing.
Out of Africa (1937) pt. 1, ch. 1

17 What is man, when you come to think upon him, but a minutely set, ingenious machine for turning, with infinite artfulness, the red wine of Shiraz into urine?
Seven Gothic Tales (1934) 'The Dreamers'

Diogenes c.400-c.325 BC
Greek Cynic philosopher
*on Diogenes: see **Alexander** 11:3*

18 Alexander . . . asked him if he lacked anything.
'Yes,' said he, 'that I do: that you stand out of my sun a little.'
Plutarch Parallel Lives 'Alexander' ch. 14, sect. 4 (translated by T. North, 1579)

19 I am looking for a man.
on his reason for taking around a lamp in daylight; the context implies 'a good man', but often quoted as 'an honest man'
Diogenes Laertius Lives of the Philosophers

20 To get practice in being refused.
on being asked why he was begging for alms from a statue
Diogenes Laertius Lives of the Philosophers

Dionysius of Halicarnassus fl. 30-7 BC
Greek historian, resident in Rome from 30 BC

21 History is philosophy from examples.
Ars Rhetorica ch. 11, sect. 2

Pseudo-Dionysius fl. 6th century
unidentified author of theological and Neoplatonist works

22 The most holy mysteries are set forth in two modes: one by means of similar and sacred representations akin to their nature, and the other through unlike forms designed with every possible discordance and difference.

The Celestial Hierarchies

Paul Dirac 1902–84
British theoretical physicist

1 It is more important to have beauty in one's equations than to have them fit experiment . . . It seems that if one is working from the point of view of getting beauty in one's equations, and if one has a really sound insight, one is on a sure line of progress. If there is not complete agreement between the results of one's work and experiment, one should not allow oneself to be too discouraged, because the discrepancy may well be due to minor features that are not properly taken into account and that will get cleared up with further developments of the theory.

in *Scientific American* May 1963

Walt Disney 1901–66
American animator and film producer

2 I don't know, fellows, I guess I'm getting too old for animation.
on seeing rushes from The Jungle Book *(1967 film)*
Richard Schickel *The Disney Version* (1986)

3 Fancy being remembered around the world for the invention of a mouse!
during his last illness
Leonard Mosley *Disney's World* (1985)

Benjamin Disraeli, Lord Beaconsfield
1804–81
British Tory statesman and novelist; Prime Minister, 1868, 1874–80
on Disraeli: see **Salisbury** 664:2, **Salisbury** 664:8

4 Though I sit down now, the time will come when you will hear me.
maiden speech in the House of Commons, 7 December 1837

5 The Continent will [not] suffer England to be the workshop of the world.
speech, House of Commons, 15 March 1838; see **Chamberlain** 206:7

6 Thus you have a starving population, an absentee aristocracy, and an alien Church, and in addition the weakest executive in the world. That is the Irish Question.
speech, House of Commons, 16 February 1844

7 The noble Lord is the Prince Rupert of Parliamentary discussion.
of Edward Stanley, later Lord **Derby**
speech, House of Commons, 24 April 1844; see **Bulwer-Lytton** 164:3

8 The right hon. Gentleman caught the Whigs bathing, and walked away with their clothes.
on Sir Robert **Peel**'s *abandoning protection in favour of free trade, traditionally the policy of the Whig Opposition*
speech, House of Commons, 28 February 1845

9 Protection is not a principle, but an expedient.
speech, House of Commons, 17 March 1845

10 A Conservative Government is an organized hypocrisy.
Bagehot, *quoting Disraeli in* The English Constitution *(1867) 'The House of Lords', elaborated on the theme with the words 'so much did the ideas of its "head" differ from the sensations of its "tail" '*
speech, House of Commons, 17 March 1845

11 He traces the steam-engine always back to the tea-kettle.
of Robert **Peel**
speech, House of Commons, 11 April 1845

12 Justice is truth in action.
speech, House of Commons, 11 February 1851

13 I read this morning an awful, though monotonous, manifesto in the great organ of public opinion, which always makes me tremble: Olympian bolts; and yet I could not help fancying amid their rumbling terrors I heard the plaintive treble of the Treasury Bench.
speech, House of Commons, 13 February 1851

14 These wretched colonies will all be independent, too, in a few years, and are a millstone round our necks.
letter to Lord Malmesbury, 13 August 1852, in W. Monypenny and G. Buckle *Life of Benjamin Disraeli* vol. 3 (1914) ch. 12

15 Petulance is not sarcasm, and . . . insolence is not invective.
speech, House of Commons, 16 December 1852

16 England does not love coalitions.
speech, House of Commons, 16 December 1852

17 Finality is not the language of politics.
speech, House of Commons, 28 February 1859

18 It was a melancholy day for human nature when that stupid Lord Anson, after beating about for three years, found himself again at Greenwich. The circumnavigation of our globe was accomplished, but the illimitable was annihilated and a fatal blow [dealt] to all imagination.
written 1860, in *Reminiscences* (ed. H. and M. Swartz, 1975) ch. 6

19 You are not going, I hope, to leave the destinies of the British Empire to prigs and pedants.
speech, House of Commons, 5 February 1863

20 Party is organized opinion.
speech at Oxford, 25 November 1864, in *The Times* 26 November 1864

21 I hold that the characteristic of the present age is craving credulity.
speech at Oxford, 25 November 1864, in *The Times* 26 November 1864

22 Man, my Lord, is a being born to believe.
speech at Oxford, 25 November 1864, in *The Times* 26 November 1864

1 Is man an ape or an angel? Now I am on the side of the angels.
   speech at Oxford, 25 November 1864, in *The Times* 26 November 1864

2 Assassination has never changed the history of the world.
   speech, House of Commons, 1 May 1865

3 I had to prepare the mind of the country, and . . . to educate our party.
   speech at Edinburgh, 29 October 1867, in *The Times* 30 October 1867

4 Change is inevitable in a progressive country. Change is constant.
   speech at Edinburgh, 29 October 1867, in *The Times* 30 October 1867

5 There can be no economy where there is no efficiency.
   Address to his Constituents, 1 October 1868, in *The Times* 3 October 1868

6 We have legalized confiscation, consecrated sacrilege, and condoned high treason.
   speech, House of Commons, 27 February 1871

7 I believe that without party Parliamentary government is impossible.
   speech at Manchester, 3 April 1872, in *The Times* 4 April 1872

8 You behold a range of exhausted volcanoes.
   of the Treasury Bench
   speech at Manchester, 3 April 1872, in *The Times* 4 April 1872; see **Burke** 169:5

9 Increased means and increased leisure are the two civilizers of man.
   speech at Manchester, 3 April 1872, in *The Times* 4 April 1872

10 A University should be a place of light, of liberty, and of learning.
   speech, House of Commons, 11 March 1873

11 An author who speaks about his own books is almost as bad as a mother who talks about her own children.
   at a banquet given in Glasgow on his installation as Lord Rector, 19 November 1873, in *The Times* 20 November 1873

12 Upon the education of the people of this country the fate of this country depends.
   speech, House of Commons, 15 June 1874

13 He is a great master of gibes and flouts and jeers.
   *of the Marquess of **Salisbury***
   speech, House of Commons, 5 August 1874

14 Mr Gladstone not only appeared but rushed into the debate . . . the new members trembled and fluttered like small birds when a hawk is in the air.
   *of **Gladstone** in the House of Commons, 15 March 1875*
   letter to Queen Victoria, March 1875; Roy Jenkins *Gladstone* (1995)

15 Coffee house babble.
   on the Bulgarian Atrocities, 1876
   in R. W. Seton-Watson *Britain in Europe 1789–1914* (1955)

16 Cosmopolitan critics, men who are the friends of every country save their own.
   speech at Guildhall, 9 November 1877, in *The Times* 10 November 1877; see **Canning** 189:5, **Overbury** 579:16

17 Lord Salisbury and myself have brought you back peace—but a peace I hope with honour.
   speech on returning from the Congress of Berlin, 16 July 1878, in *The Times* 17 July 1878; see **Chamberlain** 206:12, **Russell** 661:13

18 A series of congratulatory regrets.
   describing Lord Harrington's Resolution on the Berlin Treaty
   at a banquet, Knightsbridge, 27 July 1878; in *The Times* 29 July 1878

19 A sophistical rhetorician, inebriated with the exuberance of his own verbosity.
   *of **Gladstone***
   in *The Times* 29 July 1878

20 I admit that there is gossip . . . But the government of the world is carried on by sovereigns and statesmen, and not by anonymous paragraph writers . . . or by the hare-brained chatter of irresponsible frivolity.
   speech at Guildhall, London, 9 November 1878, in *The Times* 11 November 1878

21 One of the greatest of Romans, when asked what were his politics, replied, *Imperium et Libertas.* That would not make a bad programme for a British Ministry.
   speech at Mansion House, London, 10 November 1879
   Here the two great interests Imperium & Libertas, res olim insociabiles (saith Tacitus), began to incounter each other.
   Winston Churchill (*c.*1620–88) *Divi Britannici* (1675); see **Tacitus** 769:21

22 The key of India is London.
   speech, House of Commons, 4 March 1881

23 Take away that emblem of mortality.
   on being offered an air cushion to sit on, 1881
   Robert Blake *Disraeli* (1966) ch. 32

24 No it is better not. She would only ask me to take a message to Albert.
   *on his death-bed, declining a proposed visit from Queen **Victoria***
   Robert Blake *Disraeli* (1966) ch. 32

25 I will not go down to posterity talking bad grammar.
   while correcting proofs of his last Parliamentary speech, 31 March 1881
   Robert Blake *Disraeli* (1966) ch. 32

26 No Government can be long secure without a formidable Opposition.
   Coningsby (1844) bk. 2, ch. 1

27 A government of statesmen or of clerks? Of Humbug or Humdrum?
   Coningsby (1844) bk. 2, ch. 4

28 Conservatism discards Prescription, shrinks from Principle, disavows Progress; having rejected all respect for antiquity, it offers no redress for the present, and makes no preparation for the future.
   Coningsby (1844) bk. 2, ch. 5

1 'A sound Conservative government,' said Taper, musingly. 'I understand: Tory men and Whig measures.'
Coningsby (1844) bk. 2, ch. 6

2 Youth is a blunder; Manhood a struggle; Old Age a regret.
Coningsby (1844) bk. 3, ch. 1

3 It seems to me a barren thing this Conservatism— an unhappy cross-breed, the mule of politics that engenders nothing.
Coningsby (1844) bk. 3, ch. 5; see **Power** 610:7

4 Where can we find faith in a nation of sectaries?
Coningsby (1844) bk. 4, ch. 13

5 Man is only truly great when he acts from the passions.
Coningsby (1844) bk. 4, ch. 13

6 With words we govern men.
Contarini Fleming (1832) pt. 1, ch. 21

7 Read no history: nothing but biography, for that is life without theory.
Contarini Fleming (1832) pt. 1, ch. 23; see **Emerson** 307:2

8 The practice of politics in the East may be defined by one word—dissimulation.
Contarini Fleming (1832) pt. 5, ch. 10

9 His Christianity was muscular.
Endymion (1880) ch. 14

10 An insular country, subject to fogs, and with a powerful middle class, requires grave statesmen.
Endymion (1880) ch. 37

11 As for our majority . . . one is enough.
Endymion (1880) ch. 64

12 'Sensible men are all of the same religion.' 'And pray what is that?' . . . 'Sensible men never tell.'
Endymion (1880) ch. 81; see **Shaftesbury** 678:4

13 The sweet simplicity of the three per cents.
Endymion (1880) ch. 91; see **Stowell** 761:20

14 I believe they went out, like all good things, with the Stuarts.
Endymion (1880) ch. 99

15 Time is the great physician.
Henrietta Temple (1837) bk. 6, ch. 9; see **Proverbs** 633:2

16 They mean well; their feelings are strong, but their hearts are in the right place.
The Infernal Marriage (1834) pt. 1, 1 (of the Furies)

17 The blue ribbon of the turf.
of the Derby
Lord George Bentinck (1852) ch. 26

18 A Protestant, if he wants aid or advice on any matter, can only go to his solicitor.
Lothair (1870) ch. 27

19 London: a nation, not a city.
Lothair (1870) ch. 27

20 The gondola of London.
a hansom cab
Lothair (1870) ch. 27

21 When a man fell into his anecdotage it was a sign for him to retire from the world.
Lothair (1870) ch. 28

22 You know who the critics are? The men who have failed in literature and art.
Lothair (1870) ch. 35; see **Coleridge** 233:27

23 'Two nations; between whom there is no intercourse and no sympathy; who are as ignorant of each other's habits, thoughts, and feelings, as if they were dwellers in different zones, or inhabitants of different planets; who are formed by a different breeding, are fed by a different food, are ordered by different manners, and are not governed by the same laws.' 'You speak of—' said Egremont, hesitatingly, 'THE RICH AND THE POOR.'
Sybil (1845) bk. 2, ch. 5; see **Foster** 330:8

24 Mr Kremlin himself was distinguished for ignorance, for he had only one idea,—and that was wrong.
Sybil (1845) bk. 4, ch. 5; see **Johnson** 429:10

25 I was told that the Privileged and the People formed Two Nations.
Sybil (1845) bk. 4, ch. 8

26 The Youth of a Nation are the trustees of Posterity.
Sybil (1845) bk. 6, ch. 13

27 That fatal drollery called a representative government.
Tancred (1847) bk. 2, ch. 13

28 A majority is always the best repartee.
Tancred (1847) bk. 2, ch. 14

29 The East is a career.
Tancred (1847) bk. 2, ch. 14

30 London is a modern Babylon.
Tancred (1847) bk. 5, ch. 5

31 There is no act of treachery or meanness of which a political party is not capable; for in politics there is no honour.
Vivian Grey (1826) bk. 4 ch. 1

32 Experience is the child of Thought, and Thought is the child of Action. We cannot learn men from books.
Vivian Grey (1826) bk. 5, ch. 1

33 All power is a trust . . . from the people, and for the people, all springs, and all must exist.
Vivian Grey (1826) bk. 6, ch. 7; see **Dryden** 287:3

34 All Paradise opens! Let me die eating ortolans to the sound of soft music!
The Young Duke (1831) bk. 1, ch. 10; see **Smith** 744:8

35 'The age of chivalry is past,' said May Dacre. 'Bores have succeeded to dragons.'
The Young Duke (1831) bk. 2, ch. 5

36 Damn your principles! Stick to your party.
*attributed to Disraeli and believed to have been said to Edward **Bulwer-Lytton***
E. Latham *Famous Sayings and their Authors* (1904)

37 Everyone likes flattery; and when you come to Royalty you should lay it on with a trowel.
*to Matthew **Arnold***
G. W. E. Russell *Collections and Recollections* (1898) ch. 23

1 I am dead; dead, but in the Elysian fields.
to a peer, on his elevation to the House of Lords
W. Monypenny and G. Buckle *Life of Benjamin Disraeli* vol.
5 (1920) ch. 13

2 I have climbed to the top of the greasy pole.
on becoming Prime Minister
W. Monypenny and G. Buckle *Life of Benjamin Disraeli* vol.
4 (1916) ch. 16

3 I never deny; I never contradict; I sometimes
forget.
*said to Lord Esher of his relations with Queen **Victoria***
Elizabeth Longford *Victoria R. I* (1964) ch. 27

4 Never complain and never explain.
J. Morley *Life of William Ewart Gladstone* (1903) vol. 1; see
Fisher 322:15, **Hubbard** 406:10

5 The palace is not safe when the cottage is not
happy.
Robert Blake *Disraeli* (1966)

6 Palmerston is now seventy. If he could prove
evidence of his potency in his electoral address
he'd sweep the country.
*to the suggestion that capital could be made from one
of Palmerston's affairs*
Hesketh Pearson *Dizzy* (1951); attributed, probably
apocryphal

7 Pray remember, Mr Dean, no dogma, no Dean.
W. Monypenny and G. Buckle *Life of Benjamin Disraeli* vol.
4 (1916) ch. 10

8 The school of Manchester.
*describing the free trade politics of Cobden and **Bright***
Robert Blake *Disraeli* (1966) ch. 10

9 There are three kinds of lies: lies, damned lies and
statistics.
attributed to Disraeli in Mark Twain *Autobiography* (1924)
vol. 1; anonymous versions of this occur earlier, e.g. in
Economic Journal June 1892

10 We came here for fame.
*to John **Bright**, in the House of Commons*
Robert Blake *Disraeli* (1966) ch. 4

11 When I want to read a novel, I write one.
W. Monypenny and G. Buckle *Life of Benjamin Disraeli* vol.
6 (1920) ch. 17; see **Punch** 637:17

Isaac D'Israeli 1766–1848
*British literary historian; father of Benjamin **Disraeli***

12 He wreathed the rod of criticism with roses.
of Pierre Bayle
Curiosities of Literature (9th ed., 1834) vol. 1

William Chatterton Dix 1837–98
English clergyman

13 Alleluia! sing to Jesus,
His the sceptre, his the throne;
Alleluia! his the triumph,
His the victory alone:
Hark! the songs of peaceful Zion
Thunder like a mighty flood;
Jesus, out of every nation,
Hath redeemed us by his blood.
'Alleluia! sing to Jesus' (1867 hymn)

14 As with gladness men of old
Did the guiding star behold.
'As with gladness men of old' (1861 hymn)

Henry Austin Dobson 1840–1921
English poet, biographer, and essayist

15 All passes. Art alone
Enduring stays to us;
The Bust outlasts the throne,—
The Coin, Tiberius.
'Ars Victrix' (1876); translation of Gautier's 'L'Art'; see
Gautier 341:2

16 Fame is a food that dead men eat,—
I have no stomach for such meat.
'Fame is a Food' (1906)

17 The ladies of St James's!
They're painted to the eyes;
Their white it stays for ever,
Their red it never dies:
But Phyllida, my Phyllida!
Her colour comes and goes;
It trembles to a lily, —
It wavers to a rose.
'The Ladies of St James's' (1883)

18 Time goes, you say? Ah no!
Alas, Time stays, *we* go.
'The Paradox of Time' (1877)

Ken Dodd 1931–
British comedian

19 Freud's theory was that when a joke opens a
window and all those bats and bogeymen fly out,
you get a marvellous feeling of relief and elation.
The trouble with Freud is that he never had to
play the old Glasgow Empire on a Saturday night
after Rangers and Celtic had both lost.
in *Guardian* 30 April 1991; quoted in many, usually much
contracted, forms since the mid-1960s

Philip Doddridge 1702–51
English Nonconformist divine

20 Ye servants of the Lord,
Each in his office wait,
Observant of his heavenly word
And watchful at his gate.
Hymns (1755) 'The active Christian'

21 O God of Bethel, by whose hand
Thy people still are fed,
Who through this weary pilgrimage
Hast all our fathers led.
Hymns (1755) 'O God of Bethel'

Bubb Dodington, Lord Melcombe
1691–1762
English politician

22 Love thy country, wish it well,
Not with too intense a care,
'Tis enough, that when it fell,
Thou its ruin didst not share.
'Ode' (written 1761) in Joseph Spence *Anecdotes* (1820)

Aelius Donatus

Roman grammarian of the 4th century AD

1 *Pereant, inquit, qui ante nos nostra dixerunt.*

Confound those who have said our remarks before
us.

St Jerome *Commentary on Ecclesiastes* bk 1; J.-P. Migne
Patrologiae Latinae vol. 23

J. P. Donleavy 1926–

Irish-American novelist

2 I got disappointed in human nature as well and
gave it up because I found it too much like my
own.

A Fairy Tale of New York (1973)

3 When you don't have any money, the problem is
food. When you have money, it's sex. When you
have both it's health.

The Ginger Man (1955) ch. 5

John Donne 1572–1631

English poet and divine

on Donne: see **Carew** 190:12, **Coleridge** 232:10, **James I**
417:6, **Jonson** 436:7, **McEwan** 501:14, **Walton** 821:4

Verse dates are those of composition

4 And new philosophy calls all in doubt,
The element of fire is quite put out;
The sun is lost, and th'earth, and no man's wit
Can well direct him, where to look for it.

An Anatomy of the World: The First Anniversary (1611)
l. 205

5 She, she is dead; she's dead; when thou know'st
this,
Thou know'st how dry a cinder this world is.

An Anatomy of the World: The First Anniversary (1611)
l. 427

6 Love built on beauty, soon as beauty, dies.

Elegies 'The Anagram' (*c.*1595)

7 No spring, nor summer beauty hath such grace,
As I have seen in one autumnal face.

Elegies 'The Autumnal' (*c.*1600)

8 Whoever loves, if he do not propose
The right true end of love, he's one that goes
To sea for nothing but to make him sick.

Elegies 'Love's Progress' (*c.*1600)

9 . . . The straight Hellespont between
The Sestos and Abydos of her breasts.

Elegies 'Love's Progress' (*c.*1600)

10 By our first strange and fatal interview,
By all desires which thereof did ensue.

Elegies 'On His Mistress' (*c.*1600)

11 Nurse, O my love is slain; I saw him go
O'er the white Alps, alone; I saw him, I,
Assailed, fight, taken, stabbed, bleed, fall, and die.

Elegies 'On His Mistress' (*c.*1600)

12 We easily know
By this these angels from an evil sprite,
They set our hairs, but these our flesh upright.

Elegies 'To His Mistress Going to Bed' (*c.*1595)

13 License my roving hands, and let them go,
Behind, before, above, between, below.
O my America, my new found land,
My kingdom, safeliest when with one man
manned.

Elegies 'To His Mistress Going to Bed' (*c.*1595)

14 Hail, Bishop Valentine, whose day this is,
All the air is thy Diocese.

'An Epithalamion . . . on the Lady Elizabeth and Count
Palatine being Married on St Valentine's Day' (1613)

15 The household bird, with the red stomacher.

'An Epithalamion . . . on the Lady Elizabeth and Count
Palatine . . .' (1613)

16 Clothed in her virgin white integrity.

'A Funeral Elegy' (1610) l. 75

17 At the round earth's imagined corners, blow
Your trumpets, angels, and arise, arise
From death, you numberless infinities
Of souls, and to your scattered bodies go.

Holy Sonnets (1609) no. 4 (ed. J. Carey, 1990)

18 All whom war, dearth, age, agues, tyrannies,
Despair, law, chance, hath slain.

Holy Sonnets (1609) no. 4 (ed. J. Carey, 1990)

19 Death be not proud, though some have called thee
Mighty and dreadful, for thou art not so,
For, those, whom thou think'st, thou dost
overthrow,
Die not, poor death, nor yet canst thou kill me.

Holy Sonnets (1609) no. 6 (ed. J. Carey, 1990)

20 One short sleep past, we wake eternally,
And death shall be no more; Death thou shalt die.

Holy Sonnets (1609) no. 6 (ed. J. Carey, 1990)

21 Batter my heart, three-personed God; for, you
As yet but knock, breathe, shine, and seek to
mend.

Holy Sonnets (after 1609) no. 10 (ed. J. Carey, 1990)

22 Take me to you, imprison me, for I
Except you enthral me, never shall be free,
Nor ever chaste, except you ravish me.

Holy Sonnets (after 1609) no. 10 (ed. J. Carey, 1990)

23 I am a little world made cunningly
Of elements, and an angelic sprite.

Holy Sonnets (after 1609) no. 15 (ed. J. Carey, 1990)

24 What if this present were the world's last night?

Holy Sonnets (after 1609) no. 19 (ed. J. Carey, 1990)

25 As thou
Art jealous, Lord, so I am jealous now,
Thou lov'st not, till from loving more, thou free
My soul; who ever gives, takes liberty:
O, if thou car'st not whom I love
Alas, thou lov'st not me.

'A Hymn to Christ, at the Author's last going into
Germany' (1619)

26 Seal then this bill of my divorce to all.

'A Hymn to Christ, at the Author's last going into
Germany' (1619)

27 To see God only, I go out of sight:
And to 'scape stormy days, I choose
An everlasting night.

'A Hymn to Christ, at the Author's last going into
Germany' (1619)

1 Since I am coming to that holy room,
Where, with thy choir of saints for evermore,
I shall be made thy music; as I come
I tune the instrument here at the door,
And what I must do then, think now before.
'Hymn to God my God, in my Sickness' (1623)

2 Wilt thou forgive that sin where I begun,
Which is my sin, though it were done before?
Wilt thou forgive those sins, through which I run
And do them still: though still I do deplore?
When thou hast done, thou hast not done,
For, I have more.
'A Hymn to God the Father' (1623)

3 Immensity cloistered in thy dear womb,
Now leaves his well-beloved imprisonment.
La Corona (1609) 'Nativity'

4 Think then, my soul, that death is but a groom,
Which brings a taper to the outward room.
Of the Progress of the Soul: The Second Anniversary (1612)
l. 85

5   Her pure and eloquent blood
Spoke in her cheeks, and so distinctly wrought,
That one might almost say, her body thought.
Of the Progress of the Soul: The Second Anniversary (1612)
l. 244

6 I sing the progress of a deathless soul.
'The Progress of the Soul' (1601) st. 1

7 Great Destiny the commissary of God.
'The Progress of the Soul' (1601) st. 4

8 So, of a lone unhaunted place possessed,
Did this soul's second inn, built by the guest,
This living buried man, this quiet mandrake, rest.
'The Progress of the Soul' (1601) st. 16

9 Nature's great masterpiece, an elephant,
The only harmless great thing.
'The Progress of the Soul' (1601) st. 39

10   On a huge hill,
Cragged, and steep, Truth stands, and he that will
Reach her, about must, and about must go.
Satire no. 3 (1594–5) l. 79

11 Air and angels.
title of poem, Songs and Sonnets

12 Twice or thrice had I loved thee,
Before I knew thy face or name;
So in a voice, so in a shapeless flame,
Angels affect us oft, and worshipped be.
Songs and Sonnets 'Air and Angels'

13   Just such disparity
As is 'twixt air and angels' purity,
'Twixt women's love, and men's will ever be.
Songs and Sonnets 'Air and Angels'

14 All other things, to their destruction draw,
Only our love hath no decay;
This, no tomorrow hath, nor yesterday,
Running it never runs from us away,
But truly keeps his first, last, everlasting day.
Songs and Sonnets 'The Anniversary'

15 Come live with me, and be my love,
And we will some new pleasures prove

Of golden sands, and crystal brooks,
With silken lines, and silver hooks.
Songs and Sonnets 'The Bait'; see **Marlowe** 513:16, **Ralegh** 640:18

16 A naked thinking heart, that makes no show,
Is to a woman, but a kind of ghost.
Songs and Sonnets 'The Blossom' l. 27

17 For God's sake hold your tongue, and let me love.
Songs and Sonnets 'The Canonization'

18 Dear love, for nothing less than thee
Would I have broke this happy dream,
It was a theme
For reason, much too strong for fantasy.
Songs and Sonnets 'The Dream' ('Dear love, for nothing less than thee')

19 So, if I dream I have you, I have you,
For, all our joys are but fantastical.
Songs and Sonnets 'The Dream' ('Image of her whom I love')

20 Where, like a pillow on a bed,
A pregnant bank swelled up, to rest
The violet's reclining head,
Sat we two, one another's best.
Songs and Sonnets 'The Ecstasy'

21 But O alas, so long, so far
Our bodies why do we forbear?
They're ours, though they're not we, we are
The intelligencies, they the sphere.
Songs and Sonnets 'The Ecstasy'

22 So must pure lovers' souls descend
T'affections, and to faculties,
Which sense may reach and apprehend,
Else a great prince in prison lies.
Songs and Sonnets 'The Ecstasy'

23 So, so, break off this last lamenting kiss,
Which sucks two souls, and vapours both away,
Turn thou ghost that way, and let me turn this,
And let our selves benight our happiest day.
We asked none leave to love; nor will we owe
Any, so cheap a death, as saying, Go.
Songs and Sonnets 'The Expiration'

24 Oh wrangling schools, that search what fire
Shall burn this world, had none the wit
Unto this knowledge to aspire,
That this her fever might be it?
Songs and Sonnets 'A Fever'

25 Whoever comes to shroud me, do not harm
Nor question much
That subtle wreath of hair, which crowns my
arm;
The mystery, the sign you must not touch,
For 'tis my outward soul,
Viceroy to that, which then to heaven being gone,
Will leave this to control,
And keep these limbs, her provinces, from
dissolution.
Songs and Sonnets 'The Funeral'

26 I wonder by my troth, what thou, and I
Did, till we loved, were we not weaned till then?
But sucked on country pleasures, childishly?
Or snorted we in the seven sleepers den?
Songs and Sonnets 'The Good-Morrow'

1 And now good morrow to our waking souls,
Which watch not one another out of fear.
Songs and Sonnets 'The Good-Morrow'

2 Stand still, and I will read to thee
A lecture, love, in love's philosophy.
Songs and Sonnets 'A Lecture in the Shadow'

3 Love is a growing or full constant light;
And his first minute, after noon, is night.
Songs and Sonnets 'A Lecture in the Shadow'

4 If yet I have not all thy love,
Dear, I shall never have it all.
Songs and Sonnets 'Lovers' Infiniteness'

5 I long to talk with some old lover's ghost,
Who died before the god of love was born.
Songs and Sonnets 'Love's Deity'

6 'Tis the year's midnight, and it is the day's.
Songs and Sonnets 'A Nocturnal upon St Lucy's Day'

7 The world's whole sap is sunk:
The general balm th'hydroptic earth hath drunk.
Songs and Sonnets 'A Nocturnal upon St Lucy's Day'

8 When my grave is broke up again
Some second guest to entertain,
(For graves have learnt that woman-head
To be to more than one a bed)
And he that digs it, spies
A bracelet of bright hair about the bone,
Will he not let us alone?
Songs and Sonnets 'The Relic'

9 Go, and catch a falling star,
Get with child a mandrake root,
Tell me, where all past years are,
Or who cleft the Devil's foot,
Teach me to hear mermaids singing.
Songs and Sonnets 'Song: Go and catch a falling star'

10 And swear
No where
Lives a woman true and fair.
Songs and Sonnets 'Song: Go and catch a falling star'

11 Sweetest love, I do not go,
For weariness of thee,
Nor in hope the world can show
A fitter love for me;
But since that I
Must die at last, 'tis best,
To use my self in jest
Thus by feigned deaths to die.
Songs and Sonnets 'Song: Sweetest love, I do not go'

12 Busy old fool, unruly sun,
Why dost thou thus,
Through windows, and through curtains call on
us?
Must to thy motions lovers' seasons run?
Songs and Sonnets 'The Sun Rising'

13 Love, all alike, no season knows, nor clime,
Nor hours, days, months, which are the rags of
time.
Songs and Sonnets 'The Sun Rising'

14 This bed thy centre is, these walls thy sphere.
Songs and Sonnets 'The Sun Rising'

15 I am two fools, I know,
For loving, and for saying so
In whining poetry.
Songs and Sonnets 'The Triple Fool'

16 I have done one braver thing
Than all the Worthies did,
And yet a braver thence doth spring,
Which is, to keep that hid.
Songs and Sonnets 'The Undertaking'

17 So let us melt, and make no noise,
No tear-floods, nor sigh-tempests move,
'Twere profanation of our joys
To tell the laity our love.
Songs and Sonnets 'A Valediction: forbidding mourning'

18 Thy firmness makes my circle just,
And makes me end, where I begun.
Songs and Sonnets 'A Valediction: forbidding mourning'

19   O more than moon,
Draw not up seas to drown me in thy sphere,
Weep me not dead, in thine arms, but forbear
To teach the sea what it may do too soon.
Songs and Sonnets 'A Valediction: of Weeping'

20 Sir, more than kisses, letters mingle souls.
'To Sir Henry Wotton' (1597–8)

21 And seeing the snail, which everywhere doth
roam,
Carrying his own house still, still is at home,
Follow (for he is easy paced) this snail,
Be thine own palace, or the world's thy gaol.
'To Sir Henry Wotton' (1597–8)

22 Whensoever my affliction assails me, methinks I
have the keys of my prison in mine own hand,
and no remedy presents itself so soon to my heart,
as mine own sword.
on suicide
Biathanatos (1608)

23 We have a winding sheet in our mother's womb,
which grows with us from our conception, and we
come into the world, wound up in that winding
sheet, for we come to seek a grave.
Death's Duel (1632)

24 That which we call life, is but *hebdomada mortium*,
a week of death, seven days, seven periods of our
life spent in dying, a dying seven times over; and
there is an end.
Death's Duel (1632)

25 There we leave you, in that blessed dependancy,
to hang upon him that hangs upon the Cross,
there bathe in his tears, there suck at his wounds,
and lie down in peace in his grave, till he
vouchsafe you a resurrection, and an ascension
into that Kingdom, which he hath prepared for
you, with the inestimable price of his incorruptible
blood. Amen.
Death's Duel (1632)

26 My God, my God, thou art a direct God, may I not
say a literal God, a God that wouldst be
understood literally and according to the plain

sense of all that thou sayest? But thou art also . . .
a figurative, a metaphorical God too.

Devotions upon Emergent Occasions (1624) 'Expostulation
XIX'

1 But I do nothing upon my self, and yet I am mine
own Executioner.

Devotions upon Emergent Occasions (1624) 'Meditation XII'

2 No man is an Island, entire of it self; every man is
a piece of the Continent, a part of the main; if a
clod be washed away by the sea, Europe is the
less, as well as if a promontory were, as well as if a
manor of thy friends or of thine own were; any
man's death diminishes me, because I am involved
in Mankind; And therefore never send to know for
whom the bell tolls; it tolls for thee.

Devotions upon Emergent Occasions (1624) 'Meditation XVII'

3 From this I testify her holy cheerfulness, and
religious alacrity, (one of the best evidences of a
good conscience), that as she came to this place,
God's house of Prayer . . . she ever hastened her
family, and her company hither, with that
cheerful provocation, For God's sake let's go, For
God's sake let's be there at the Confession.

A Sermon of Commemoration of the Lady Danvers [mother of
George Herbert] (1627)

4 This love of place and precedency rocks us in our
cradles, it lies down with us in our graves.

LXXX Sermons (1640) 19 December 1619

5 [Death] comes equally to us all, and makes us all
equal when it comes. The ashes of an Oak in the
Chimney, are no epitaph of that Oak, to tell me
how high or how large that was; It tells me not
what flocks it sheltered while it stood, nor what
men it hurt when it fell.

LXXX Sermons (1640) 8 March 1621/2

6 When a whirlwind hath blown the dust of the
Churchyard into the Church, and the man sweeps
out the dust of the Church into the Churchyard,
who will undertake to sift those dusts again, and
to pronounce, This is the Patrician, this is the
noble flower, and this the yeomanly, this the
Plebeian bran.

LXXX Sermons (1640) 8 March 1621/2

7 A day that hath no *pridie*, nor *postridie*, yesterday
doth not usher it in, nor tomorrow shall not drive
it out. *Methusalem*, with all his hundreds of years,
was but a mushroom of a night's growth, to this
day, And all the four Monarchies, with all their
thousands of years, and all the powerful Kings and
all the beautiful Queens of this world, were but as
a bed of flowers, some gathered at six, some at
seven, some at eight, All in one Morning, in
respect of this Day.

LXXX Sermons (1640) 30 April 1626 'Eternity'

8 I throw myself down in my Chamber, and I call in,
and invite God, and his Angels thither, and when
they are there, I neglect God and his Angels, for
the noise of a fly, for the rattling of a coach, for
the whining of a door.

LXXX Sermons (1640) 12 December 1626 'At the Funeral
of Sir William Cokayne'

9 A memory of yesterday's pleasures, a fear of
tomorrow's dangers, a straw under my knee, a
noise in mine ear, a light in mine eye, an
anything, a nothing, a fancy, a chimera in my
brain, troubles me in my prayer. So certainly is
there nothing, nothing in spiritual things, perfect
in this world.

LXXX Sermons (1640) 12 December 1626 'At the Funeral
of Sir William Cokayne'

10 There is nothing that God hath established in a
constant course of nature, and which therefore is
done every day, but would seem a Miracle, and
exercise our admiration, if it were done but once.

LXXX Sermons (1640) Easter Day, 25 March 1627

11 Man is but earth; 'Tis true; but earth is the centre.
That man who dwells upon himself, who is always
conversant in himself, rests in his true centre.

LXXX Sermons (1640) Christmas Day, 1627

12 Poor intricated soul! Riddling, perplexed,
labyrinthical soul!

LXXX Sermons (1640) 25 January 1628/9

13 They shall awake as Jacob did, and say as Jacob
said, *Surely the Lord is in this place*, and *this is no
other but the house of God, and the gate of heaven*,
And into that gate they shall enter, and in that
house they shall dwell, where there shall be no
Cloud nor Sun, no darkness nor dazzling, but one
equal light, no noise nor silence, but one equal
music, no fears nor hopes, but one equal
possession, no foes nor friends, but one equal
communion and identity, no ends nor beginnings,
but one equal eternity.

XXVI Sermons (1660) 29 February 1627/8

14 John Donne, Anne Donne, Un-done.

*in a letter to his wife, on being dismissed from the
service of his father-in-law, Sir George More*

Izaak Walton *The Life of Dr Donne* (first printed in *LXXX
Sermons*, 1640)

Ariel Dorfman 1942–

Chilean writer

15 Responsibility without power, the fate of the
secretary through the ages.

Reader (1995) act 1; see **Kipling** 457:8, **Stoppard** 761:8

16 In my other jurisdictions I kept a lid on that—
making men vanish like that—it's no good. It
drives the women out of their minds. Even if you
give them a finger to bury, but when there's just
nothing . . . They go crazy. And then the world
does.

Widows (1981) act 1, sc. 2

Fedor Dostoevsky 1821–81

Russian novelist

17 If you were to destroy in mankind the belief in
immortality, not only love but every living force
maintaining the life of the world would at once be
dried up.

The Brothers Karamazov (1879–80) bk. 2, ch. 6

1 Beauty is mysterious as well as terrible. God and devil are fighting there, and the battlefield is the heart of man.

　The Brothers Karamazov (1879–80) bk. 3, ch. 3

2 If the devil doesn't exist, but man has created him, he has created him in his own image and likeness.

　The Brothers Karamazov (1879–80) bk. 5, ch. 4

3 Too high a price is asked for harmony; it's beyond our means to pay so much to enter. And so I hasten to give back my entrance ticket . . . It's not God that I don't accept, Alyosha, only I most respectfully return Him the ticket.

　The Brothers Karamazov (1879–80) bk. 5, ch. 4

4 Imagine that you are creating a fabric of human destiny with the object of making men happy in the end, giving them peace and rest at last, but that it was essential and inevitable to torture to death only one tiny creature . . . and to found that edifice on its unavenged tears, would you consent to be the architect on those conditions?

　The Brothers Karamazov (1879–80) bk. 5, ch. 4

5 Men reject their prophets and slay them, but they love their martyrs and honour those whom they have slain.

　The Brothers Karamazov (1879–80) bk. 6, ch. 3

6 Power is given only to him who dares to stoop and take it . . . one must have the courage to dare.

　Crime and Punishment (1866) pt. 5, ch. 4 (translated by David Magarshak)

7 I wanted to murder, for my own satisfaction . . . At that moment I did not care a damn whether I would become the benefactor of someone, or would spend the rest of my life like a spider catching them all in my web and sucking the living juices out of them.

　Crime and Punishment (1866) pt. 5, ch. 4 (translated by David Magarshak)

8 Some new sorts of microbes were attacking the bodies of men, but these microbes were endowed with intelligence and will . . . Men attacked by them became at once mad and furious.

　Crime and Punishment (1866) epilogue (translated by Constance Garnett)

9 To crush, to annihilate a man utterly, to inflict on him the most terrible punishment so that the most ferocious murderer would shudder at it beforehand, one need only give him work of an absolutely, completely useless and irrational character.

　House of the Dead (1862) pt. 1, ch. 1 (translated by Constance Garnett)

10 Petersburg, the most abstract and premeditated city on earth.

　Notes from Underground (1864) pt. 1, ch. 2 (translated by Andrew R. McAndrew)

11 In despair there are the most intense enjoyments, especially when one is very acutely conscious of the hopelessness of one's position.

　Notes from Underground (1864) pt. 1, ch. 2 (translated by Andrew R. McAndrew)

12 What man wants is simply *independent* choice, whatever that independence may cost and wherever it may lead.

　Notes from Underground (1864) pt. 1, ch. 7 (translated by Constance Garnett)

Lord Alfred Douglas 1870–1945

English poet and intimate of Oscar **Wilde**

13 I am the Love that dare not speak its name.

　'Two Loves' (1896)

Gavin Douglas c.1475–1522

Scottish poet and prelate

14 And all small fowlys singis on the spray:
Welcum the lord of lycht and lamp of day.

　Eneados (1553) bk. 12, prologue l. 251

James Douglas, Earl of Morton c.1516–81

Scottish courtier

15 Here lies he who neither feared nor flattered any flesh.

　of John **Knox**, *said as he was buried, 26 November 1572*

　George R. Preedy *The Life of John Knox* (1940) ch. 7

Keith Douglas 1920–44

English poet

16 And all my endeavours are unlucky explorers come back, abandoning the expedition.

　'On Return from Egypt, 1943–4' (1946)

17 Remember me when I am dead
And simplify me when I'm dead.

　'Simplify me when I'm Dead' (1941)

18 But she would weep to see today
how on his skin the swart flies move;
the dust upon the paper eye
and the burst stomach like a cave.

For here the lover and killer are mingled
who had one body and one heart.
And death, who had the soldier singled
has done the lover mortal hurt.

　'Vergissmeinnicht, 1943'

Norman Douglas 1868–1952

Scottish-born novelist and essayist

19 To find a friend one must close one eye. To keep him—two.

　Almanac (1941)

20 You can tell the ideals of a nation by its advertisements.

　South Wind (1917) ch. 6

21 Many a man who thinks to found a home discovers that he has merely opened a tavern for his friends.

　South Wind (1917) ch. 20

O. Douglas (Anna Buchan) 1877–1948
Scottish writer, sister of John Buchan

1 It is wonderful how much news there is when people write every other day; if they wait for a month, there is nothing that seems worth telling.
   Penny Plain (1920)

2 I know heaps of quotations, so I can always make quite a fair show of knowledge.
   The Setons (1917)

Alec Douglas-Home see Lord Home

Frederick Douglass c.1818–95
American former slave and civil rights campaigner

3 Every tone [of the songs of the slaves] was a testimony against slavery, and a prayer to God for deliverance from chains.
   Narrative of the Life of Frederick Douglass (1845) ch. 2

4 The life of the nation is secure only while the nation is honest, truthful, and virtuous.
   speech on the 23rd anniversary of Emancipation in the District of Columbia, Washington DC, April 1885

Lorenzo Dow 1777–1834
American divine

5 You will be damned if you do—And you will be damned if you don't.
   on the Calvinist doctrine of 'Particular Election'
   Reflections on the Love of God (1836) ch. 6

Ernest Dowson 1867–1900
English poet

6 I have forgot much, Cynara! gone with the wind,
   Flung roses, roses, riotously, with the throng,
   Dancing, to put thy pale, lost lilies out of mind;
   But I was desolate and sick of an old passion,
   Yea, all the time, because the dance was long:
   I have been faithful to thee, Cynara! in my
      fashion.
   'Non Sum Qualis Eram' (1896) (also known as 'Cynara');
   see **Horace** 402:6

7 They are not long, the weeping and the laughter,
   Love and desire and hate.
   'Vitae Summa Brevis' (1896)

8 They are not long, the days of wine and roses.
   'Vitae Summa Brevis' (1896)

Arthur Conan Doyle 1859–1930
Scottish-born writer of detective fiction

9 Singularity is almost invariably a clue. The more featureless and commonplace a crime is, the more difficult is it to bring it home.
   The Adventures of Sherlock Holmes (1892) 'The Boscombe Valley Mystery'

10 It is my belief, Watson, founded upon my experience, that the lowest and vilest alleys in London do not present a more dreadful record of sin than does the smiling and beautiful countryside.
   The Adventures of Sherlock Holmes (1892) 'The Copper Beeches'

11 A man should keep his little brain attic stocked with all the furniture that he is likely to use, and the rest he can put away in the lumber room of his library, where he can get it if he wants it.
   The Adventures of Sherlock Holmes (1892) 'The Five Orange Pips'

12 It is quite a three-pipe problem, and I beg that you won't speak to me for fifty minutes.
   The Adventures of Sherlock Holmes (1892) 'The Red-Headed League'

13 You see, but you do not observe.
   The Adventures of Sherlock Holmes (1892) 'Scandal in Bohemia'

14 The giant rat of Sumatra, a story for which the world is not yet prepared.
   The Case-Book of Sherlock Holmes (1927) 'The Sussex Vampire'

15 Of all ruins that of a noble mind is the most deplorable.
   His Last Bow (1917) 'The Dying Detective'; see **Davies** 258:17

16 Good old Watson! You are the one fixed point in a changing age.
   His Last Bow (1917) title story

17 'Excellent,' I cried. 'Elementary,' said he.
   The Memoirs of Sherlock Holmes (1894) 'The Crooked Man'; see **Misquotations** 537:11

18 Ex-Professor Moriarty of mathematical celebrity . . . is the Napoleon of crime, Watson.
   The Memoirs of Sherlock Holmes (1894) 'The Final Problem'

19 'Is there any other point to which you would wish to draw my attention?'
   'To the curious incident of the dog in the night-time.'
   'The dog did nothing in the night-time.'
   'That was the curious incident,' remarked Sherlock Holmes.
   The Memoirs of Sherlock Holmes (1894) 'Silver Blaze'

20 What one man can invent another can discover.
   The Return of Sherlock Holmes (1905) 'The Dancing Men'

21 I didn't think there was a soul in England who didn't know Godfrey Staunton, the back three-quarter, Cambridge, Blackheath, and five Internationals. Good Lord! Mr Holmes where *have* you lived.
   The Return of Sherlock Holmes (1905) 'The Missing Three-Quarter'

22 You live in a different world to me, Mr Overton, a sweeter and a healthier one. My ramifications stretch out into many sections of society, but never, I am happy to say, into amateur sport, which is the best and soundest thing in England.
   The Return of Sherlock Holmes (1905) 'The Missing Three-Quarter'

23 Detection is, or ought to be, an exact science, and should be treated in the same cold and unemotional manner. You have attempted to

tinge it with romanticism, which produces much the same effect as if you worked a love-story or an elopement into the fifth proposition of Euclid.
The Sign of Four (1890) ch. 1

1 How often have I said to you that when you have eliminated the impossible, whatever remains, *however improbable*, must be the truth?
The Sign of Four (1890) ch. 6

2 You know my methods. Apply them.
The Sign of Four (1890) ch. 6

3 It is the unofficial force—the Baker Street irregulars.
The Sign of Four (1890) ch. 8

4 London, that great cesspool into which all the loungers and idlers of the Empire are irresistibly drained.
A Study in Scarlet (1888) ch. 1

5 It is a capital mistake to theorize before you have all the evidence. It biases the judgement.
A Study in Scarlet (1888) ch. 3

6 Where there is no imagination there is no horror.
A Study in Scarlet (1888) ch. 5

7 From the astrologer came the astronomer, from the alchemist the chemist, from the mesmerist the experimental psychologist. The quack of yesterday is the professor of tomorrow.
Tales of Terror and Mystery (1922) 'The Leather Funnel'

8 The vocabulary of 'Bradshaw' is nervous and terse, but limited.
The Valley of Fear (1915) ch. 1

9 Mediocrity knows nothing higher than itself, but talent instantly recognizes genius.
The Valley of Fear (1915) ch. 1

10 What of the bow?
The bow was made in England,
Of true wood, of yew wood,
The wood of English bows.
The White Company (1891) 'Song of the Bow'

Francis Doyle 1810–88
English poet

11 Last night, among his fellow roughs,
He jested, quaffed, and swore.
'The Private of the Buffs' (1866)

Margaret Drabble 1939–
English novelist

12 Lord knows what incommunicable small terrors infants go through, unknown to all. We disregard them, we say they forget, because they have not the words to make us remember . . . By the time they learn to speak they have forgotten the details of their complaints, and so we never know. They forget so quickly we say, because we cannot contemplate the fact that they never forget.
The Millstone (1965)

13 England's not a bad country . . . It's just a mean, cold, ugly, divided, tired, clapped-out, post-

imperial, post-industrial slag-heap covered in polystyrene hamburger cartons.
A Natural Curiosity (1989)

14 Perhaps the rare and simple pleasure of being seen for what one is compensates for the misery of being it.
A Summer Bird-Cage (1963) ch. 7

Francis Drake c.1540–96
English sailor and explorer
on Drake: see **Anonymous** 19:7

15 There must be a beginning of any great matter, but the continuing unto the end until it be thoroughly finished yields the true glory.
dispatch to Francis Walsingham, 17 May 1587, in *Navy Records Society* vol. 11 (1898)

16 The singeing of the King of Spain's Beard.
on the expedition to Cadiz, 1587
Francis Bacon *Considerations touching a War with Spain* (1629)

17 I must have the gentleman to haul and draw with the mariner, and the mariner with the gentleman . . . I would know him, that would refuse to set his hand to a rope, but I know there is not any such here.
J. S. Corbett *Drake and the Tudor Navy* (1898) vol. 1, ch. 9

18 There is plenty of time to win this game, and to thrash the Spaniards too.
when news of the Armada was brought while he was playing bowls on Plymouth Hoe
attributed, in *Dictionary of National Biography* (1917–) vol. 5

Joseph Rodman Drake 1795–1820
American poet

19 Forever float that standard sheet!
Where breathes the foe but falls before us,
With Freedom's soil beneath our feet,
And Freedom's banner streaming o'er us?
'The American Flag' in *New York Evening Post*, 29 May 1819 (also attributed to Fitz-Greene Halleck)

Michael Drayton 1563–1631
English poet

20 Ill news hath wings, and with the wind doth go,
Comfort's a cripple and comes ever slow.
The Barons' Wars (1603) canto 2, st. 28

21 The mind is free, whate'er afflict the man,
A King's a King, do Fortune what she can.
The Barons' Wars (1603) canto 5, st. 36

22 Thus when we fondly flatter our desires,
Our best conceits do prove the greatest liars.
The Barons' Wars (1603) canto 6, st. 94

23 Since there's no help, come let us kiss and part,
Nay, I have done: you get no more of me,
And I am glad, yea glad with all my heart,
That thus so cleanly, I myself can free,
Shake hands for ever, cancel all our vows,
And when we meet at any time again,

Be it not seen in either of our brows,
That we one jot of former love retain.
Idea (1619) Sonnet 61

1 That shire which we the Heart of England well
 may call.
of Warwickshire
 Poly-Olbion (1612–22) Song 13, l. 2

2 But when the bowels of the earth were sought,
And men her golden entrails did espy,
This mischief then into the world was brought,
This framed the mint which coined our misery.

Then lofty pines were by ambition hewn,
And men sea-monsters swam the brackish flood
In wainscot tubs to seek out worlds unknown,
For certain ill to leave assurèd good.
The Shepherd's Garland (1593) Eclogue 8

3 For that fine madness still he did retain
Which rightly should possess a poet's brain.
on Marlowe
 'To Henry Reynolds, of Poets and Poesy' (1627) l. 109

4 Next these, learn'd Jonson, in this list I bring,
Who had drunk deep of the Pierian spring.
 'To Henry Reynolds, of Poets and Poesy' (1627) l. 129; see
 Pope 604:2

5 These poor half-kisses kill me quite.
 'To His Coy Love' (1619)

6 Fair stood the wind for France
When we our sails advance,
Nor now to prove our chance
Longer will tarry.
 To the Cambro-Britons (1619) 'Agincourt'

William Drennan 1754–1820
Irish writer of patriotic verse

7 Nor one feeling of vengeance presume to defile
The cause, or the men, of the Emerald Isle.
 Erin (1795) st. 3

John Drinkwater 1882–1937
English poet and dramatist

8 　　　　Deep is the silence, deep
On moon-washed apples of wonder.
 'Moonlit Apples' (1917)

William Driver 1803–86
American sailor

9 I name thee Old Glory.
saluting a new flag hoisted on his ship, the Charles
Doggett
 attributed

Henry Drummond 1851–97
Scottish theological writer

10 There are reverent minds who ceaselessly scan the
fields of Nature and the books of Science in search
of gaps—gaps which they will fill up with God. As
if God lived in gaps?
 The Ascent of Man (1894) ch. 10

Thomas Drummond 1797–1840
*British government official; Under-secretary of State for
Ireland, 1835–40*

11 Property has its duties as well as its rights.
 letter to the Earl of Donoughmore, 22 May 1838, in R.
 Barry O'Brien *Thomas Drummond . . . Life and Letters* (1889)

William Drummond of Hawthornden
1585–1649
Scottish poet

12 Phoebus, arise,
And paint the sable skies,
With azure, white, and red.
 'Song: Phoebus, arise' (1614)

13 　　　　A morn
Of bright carnations did o'erspread her face.
 'Sonnet: Alexis here she stayed' (1614)

14 In all nations it is observed that there are some
families fatal to the ruin of the Commonwealth
and some persons fatal to the ruin of the house
and race of which they are descended.
 Agnes Mure *Scottish Pageant* (1946) vol. 1

John Dryden 1631–1700
English poet, critic, and dramatist
*on Dryden: see **Arnold** 29:23, **Arnold** 30:7, **Johnson** 425:3,
Macaulay 498:24; see also **Crashaw** 250:7*

15 In pious times, ere priestcraft did begin,
Before polygamy was made a sin.
 Absalom and Achitophel (1681) pt. 1, l. 1

16 Then Israel's monarch, after Heaven's own heart,
His vigorous warmth did, variously, impart
To wives and slaves: and, wide as his command,
Scattered his Maker's image through the land.
 Absalom and Achitophel (1681) pt. 1, l. 7

17 Whate'er he did was done with so much ease,
In him alone, 'twas natural to please.
 Absalom and Achitophel (1681) pt. 1, l. 27

18 Plots, true or false, are necessary things,
To raise up commonwealths and ruin kings.
 Absalom and Achitophel (1681) pt. 1, l. 83

19 Of these the false Achitophel was first,
A name to all succeeding ages curst.
For close designs and crooked counsels fit,
Sagacious, bold, and turbulent of wit,
Restless, unfixed in principles and place,
In power unpleased, impatient of disgrace;
A fiery soul, which working out its way,
Fretted the pigmy body to decay.
 Absalom and Achitophel (1681) pt. 1, l. 150

20 A daring pilot in extremity;
Pleased with the danger, when the waves went
 high
He sought the storms; but for a calm unfit.
 Absalom and Achitophel (1681) pt. 1, l. 159

21 Great wits are sure to madness near allied,
And thin partitions do their bounds divide.
 Absalom and Achitophel (1681) pt. 1, l. 163

22 Why should he, with wealth and honour blest,
Refuse his age the needful hours of rest?

Punish a body which he could not please;
Bankrupt of life, yet prodigal of ease?
And all to leave what with his toil he won
To that unfeathered two-legged thing, a son.
Absalom and Achitophel (1681) pt. 1, l. 165

1 In friendship false, implacable in hate:
Resolved to ruin or to rule the state.
Absalom and Achitophel (1681) pt. 1, l. 173

2 The people's prayer, the glad diviner's theme,
The young men's vision and the old men's dream!
Absalom and Achitophel (1681) pt. 1, l. 238

3 All empire is no more than power in trust.
Absalom and Achitophel (1681) pt. 1, l. 411; see **Disraeli**
277:33

4 Better one suffer, than a nation grieve.
Absalom and Achitophel (1681) pt. 1, l. 416

5 But far more numerous was the herd of such
Who think too little and who talk too much.
Absalom and Achitophel (1681) pt. 1, l. 533

6 A man so various that he seemed to be
Not one, but all mankind's epitome.
Stiff in opinions, always in the wrong;
Was everything by starts, and nothing long.
But, in the course of one revolving moon:
Was chemist, fiddler, statesman, and buffoon.
Absalom and Achitophel (1681) pt. 1, l. 545

7 In squandering wealth was his peculiar art:
Nothing went unrewarded, but desert.
Beggared by fools, whom still he found too late:
He had his jest, and they had his estate.
Absalom and Achitophel (1681) pt. 1, l. 559

8 Youth, beauty, graceful action seldom fail:
But common interest always will prevail:
And pity never ceases to be shown
To him, who makes the people's wrongs his own.
Absalom and Achitophel (1681) pt. 1, l. 723

9 For who can be secure of private right,
If sovereign sway may be dissolved by might?
Nor is the people's judgement always true:
The most may err as grossly as the few.
Absalom and Achitophel (1681) pt. 1, l. 779

10 Never was patriot yet, but was a fool.
Absalom and Achitophel (1681) pt. 1, l. 968

11 Beware the fury of a patient man.
Absalom and Achitophel (1681) pt. 1, l. 1005

12 Free from all meaning, whether good or bad,
And in one word, heroically mad.
Absalom and Achitophel (1681) pt. 2, l. 416

13 Rhyme is the rock on which thou art to wreck.
Absalom and Achitophel (1681) pt. 2, l. 486

14 Happy, happy, happy, pair!
None but the brave,
None but the brave,
None but the brave deserves the fair.
Alexander's Feast (1697) l. 4; see **Proverbs** 628:5

15 Drinking is the soldier's pleasure;
Rich the treasure;
Sweet the pleasure;
Sweet is pleasure after pain.
Alexander's Feast (1697) l. 57

16 Fallen from his high estate,
And welt'ring in his blood:
Deserted at his utmost need
By those his former bounty fed;
On the bare earth exposed he lies,
With not a friend to close his eyes.
Alexander's Feast (1697) l. 78

17 War, he sung, is toil and trouble;
Honour but an empty bubble.
Never ending, still beginning,
Fighting still, and still destroying,
If the world be worth thy winning,
Think, oh think, it worth enjoying.
Alexander's Feast (1697) l. 97

18 Sighed and looked, and sighed again.
Alexander's Feast (1697) l. 120

19 Revenge, revenge! Timotheus cries.
Alexander's Feast (1697) l. 131

20 Let old Timotheus yield the prize,
Or both divide the crown:
He raised a mortal to the skies;
She drew an angel down.
of 'Divine Cecilia'
Alexander's Feast (1697) l. 177

21 Errors, like straws, upon the surface flow;
He who would search for pearls must dive below.
All for Love (1678) prologue

22 My love's a noble madness.
All for Love (1678) act 2, sc. 1

23   Give, you gods,
Give to your boy, your Caesar,
The rattle of a globe to play withal,
This gewgaw world, and put him cheaply off:
I'll not be pleased with less than Cleopatra.
All for Love (1678) act 2, sc. 1

24 Men are but children of a larger growth;
Our appetites as apt to change as theirs,
And full as craving too, and full as vain.
All for Love (1678) act 4, sc. 1; see **Chesterfield** 215:8

25 By viewing nature, nature's handmaid art,
Makes mighty things from small beginnings grow:
Thus fishes first to shipping did impart,
Their tail the rudder, and their head the prow.
Annus Mirabilis (1667) st. 155

26 An horrid stillness first invades the ear,
And in that silence we the tempest fear.
Astraea Redux (1660) l. 7

27 Death, in itself, is nothing; but we fear,
To be we know not what, we know not where.
Aureng-Zebe (1675) act 4, sc. 1

28 None would live past years again,
Yet all hope pleasure in what yet remain;
And, from the dregs of life, think to receive,
What the first sprightly running could not give.
Aureng-Zebe (1675) act 4, sc. 1

29 Refined himself to soul, to curb the sense
And made almost a sin of abstinence.
'The Character of a Good Parson' (1700) l. 10

30 I am as free as nature first made man,
Ere the base laws of servitude began,

When wild in woods the noble savage ran.
The Conquest of Granada (1670) pt. 1, act 1, sc. 1

1 Forgiveness to the injured does belong;
But they ne'er pardon, who have done the wrong.
The Conquest of Granada (1670) pt. 2, act 1, sc. 2

2 Thou strong seducer, opportunity!
The Conquest of Granada (1670) pt. 2, act 4, sc. 3

3 Bold knaves thrive without one grain of sense,
But good men starve for want of impudence.
Constantine the Great (1684) epilogue

4 He trudged along unknowing what he sought,
And whistled as he went, for want of thought.
Cymon and Iphigenia (1700) l. 84

5 She hugged the offender, and forgave the offence.
Cymon and Iphigenia (1700) l. 367; see **Augustine** 37:16,
Dryden 288:20

6 Of seeming arms to make a short essay,
Then hasten to be drunk, the business of the day.
Cymon and Iphigenia (1700) l. 407

7 His colours laid so thick on every place,
As only showed the paint, but hid the face.
Epistle 'To my honoured friend Sir Robert Howard' (1660)
l. 75

8 Better to hunt in fields, for health unbought,
Than fee the doctor for a nauseous draught.
The wise, for cure, on exercise depend;
God never made his work, for man to mend.
Epistle 'To my honoured kinsman John Driden' (1700)
l. 92

9 Even victors are by victories undone.
Epistle 'To my honoured kinsman John Driden' (1700)
l. 164

10 For he was great, ere fortune made him so.
on the death of Oliver **Cromwell**
Heroic Stanzas (1659) st. 6

11 And doomed to death, though fated not to die.
The Hind and the Panther (1687) pt. 1, l. 8

12 For truth has such a face and such a mien
As to be loved needs only to be seen.
The Hind and the Panther (1687) pt. 1, l. 33

13 My manhood, long misled by wandering fires,
Followed false lights.
The Hind and the Panther (1687) pt. 1, l. 72

14 Good life be now my task: my doubts are done;
(What more could fright my faith than Three in
One?)
The Hind and the Panther (1687) pt. 1, l. 75

15 Reason to rule, but mercy to forgive:
The first is law, the last prerogative.
The Hind and the Panther (1687) pt. 1, l. 261

16 Either be wholly slaves or wholly free.
The Hind and the Panther (1687) pt. 2, l. 285

17 Much malice mingled with a little wit
Perhaps may censure this mysterious writ.
The Hind and the Panther (1687) pt. 3, l. 1

18 For present joys are more to flesh and blood
Than a dull prospect of a distant good.
The Hind and the Panther (1687) pt. 3, l. 364

19 By education most have been misled;
So they believe, because they so were bred.
The priest continues what the nurse began,
And thus the child imposes on the man.
The Hind and the Panther (1687) pt. 3, l. 389

20 T'abhor the makers, and their laws approve,
Is to hate traitors and the treason love.
The Hind and the Panther (1687) pt. 3, l. 706; see **Augustine**
37:16, **Dryden** 288:5

21 For those whom God to ruin has designed,
He fits for fate, and first destroys their mind.
The Hind and the Panther (1687) pt. 3, l. 1093; see
Anonymous 21:11, **Proverbs** 635:5

22 And love's the noblest frailty of the mind.
The Indian Emperor (1665) act 2, sc. 2; see **Shadwell**
677:21

23 Repentance is the virtue of weak minds.
The Indian Emperor (1665) act 3, sc. 1

24 For all the happiness mankind can gain
Is not in pleasure, but in rest from pain.
The Indian Emperor (1665) act 4, sc. 1

25 That fairy kind of writing which depends only
upon the force of imagination.
King Arthur (1691) dedication

26 War is the trade of kings.
King Arthur (1691) act 2, sc. 2

27 Fairest Isle, all isles excelling,
Seat of pleasures, and of loves;
Venus here will choose her dwelling,
And forsake her Cyprian groves.
King Arthur (1691) act 5 'Song of Venus'; see **Wesley**
829:8

28 Ovid, the soft philosopher of love.
Love Triumphant (1694) act 2, sc. 1

29 Thou tyrant, tyrant Jealousy,
Thou tyrant of the mind!
Love Triumphant (1694) act 3, sc. 1 'Song of Jealousy'

30 All human things are subject to decay,
And, when fate summons, monarchs must obey.
MacFlecknoe (1682) l. 1

31 The rest to some faint meaning make pretence,
But Shadwell never deviates into sense.
Some beams of wit on other souls may fall,
Strike through and make a lucid interval;
But Shadwell's genuine night admits no ray,
His rising fogs prevail upon the day.
MacFlecknoe (1682) l. 19

32 Thy genius calls thee not to purchase fame
In keen iambics, but mild anagram:
Leave writing plays, and choose for thy command
Some peaceful province in Acrostic Land.
There thou mayest wings display and altars raise,
And torture one poor word ten thousand ways.
MacFlecknoe (1682) l. 203

33 I am resolved to grow fat and look young till forty,
and then slip out of the world with the first
wrinkle and the reputation of five-and-twenty.
The Maiden Queen (1668) act 3, sc. 1

34 I am to be married within these three days;
married past redemption.
Marriage à la Mode (1672) act 1, sc. 1

1 We loathe our manna, and we long for quails.
   The Medal (1682) l. 131

2 But treason is not owned when 'tis descried;
   Successful crimes alone are justified.
   The Medal (1682) l. 207

3 Whatever is, is in its causes just.
   Oedipus (with Nathaniel Lee, 1679) act 3, sc. 1

4 But love's a malady without a cure.
   Palamon and Arcite (1700) bk. 2, l. 110

5 Fool, not to know that love endures no tie,
   And Jove but laughs at lovers' perjury.
   Palamon and Arcite (1700) bk. 2, l. 148; see **Ovid** 579:22,
   Proverbs 624:33

6 And Antony, who lost the world for love.
   Palamon and Arcite (1700) bk. 2, l. 607

7 Repentance is but want of power to sin.
   Palamon and Arcite (1700) bk. 3, l. 813

8 Like pilgrims to th'appointed place we tend;
   The world's an inn, and death the journey's end.
   Palamon and Arcite (1700) bk. 3, l. 887

9 A virgin-widow, and a *mourning bride*.
   Palamon and Arcite (1700) bk. 3, l. 927

10 But 'tis the talent of our English nation,
   Still to be plotting some new reformation.
   'The Prologue at Oxford, 1680' (prologue to Nathaniel Lee
   Sophonisba, 2nd ed., 1681)

11 So poetry, which is in Oxford made
   An art, in London only is a trade.
   'Prologue to the University of Oxon . . . at the Acting of *The
   Silent Woman*' (1673)

12 And this unpolished rugged verse I chose
   As fittest for discourse and nearest prose.
   Religio Laici (1682) l. 453

13 A very merry, dancing, drinking,
   Laughing, quaffing, and unthinking time.
   The Secular Masque (1700) l. 39

14 Joy ruled the day, and Love the night.
   The Secular Masque (1700) l. 81

15 All, all of a piece throughout;
   Thy chase had a beast in view;
   Thy wars brought nothing about;
   Thy lovers were all untrue.
   'Tis well an old age is out,
   And time to begin a new.
   The Secular Masque (1700) l. 92

16 For secrets are edged tools,
   And must be kept from children and from fools.
   Sir Martin Mar-All (1667) act 2, sc. 2

17 From harmony, from heavenly harmony
   This universal frame began:
   From harmony to harmony
   Through all the compass of the notes it ran,
   The diapason closing full in Man.
   A Song for St Cecilia's Day (1687) st. 1

18 What passion cannot Music raise and quell?
   A Song for St Cecilia's Day (1687) st. 2

19 The soft complaining flute.
   A Song for St Cecilia's Day (1687) st. 4

20 The trumpet shall be heard on high,
   The dead shall live, the living die,
   And Music shall untune the sky.
   A Song for St Cecilia's Day (1687) 'Grand Chorus'

21   There is a pleasure sure,
   In being mad, which none but madmen know!
   The Spanish Friar (1681) act 1, sc. 1

22 And, dying, bless the hand that gave the blow.
   The Spanish Friar (1681) act 2, sc. 2

23 Mute and magnificent, without a tear.
   Threnodia Augustalis (1685) st. 2

24 Freedom which in no other land will thrive,
   Freedom an English subject's sole prerogative.
   Threnodia Augustalis (1685) st. 10

25   Wit will shine
   Through the harsh cadence of a rugged line.
   'To the Memory of Mr Oldham' (1684)

26 Thou youngest virgin-daughter of the skies,
   Made in the last promotion of the blest.
   'To the pious Memory of . . . Mrs Anne Killigrew' (1686)
   l. 1

27 And he, who servilely creeps after sense,
   Is safe, but ne'er will reach an excellence.
   Tyrannic Love (1669) prologue

28 All delays are dangerous in war.
   Tyrannic Love (1669) act 1, sc. 1

29 Happy the man, and happy he alone,
   He, who can call to-day his own:
   He who, secure within, can say,
   Tomorrow do thy worst, for I have lived today.
   translation of Horace *Odes* bk. 3, no. 29; see **Horace** 402:2,
   Smith 744:1

30 Not Heaven itself upon the past has power;
   But what has been, has been, and I have had my
      hour.
   translation of Horace *Odes* bk. 3, no. 29

31 I can enjoy her while she's kind;
   But when she dances in the wind,
   And shakes the wings, and will not stay,
   I puff the prostitute away.
   of Fortune
   translation of Horace *Odes* bk. 3, no. 29

32 Look round the habitable world! how few
   Know their own good; or knowing it, pursue.
   translation of Juvenal *Satires* no. 10

33 She knows her man, and when you rant and
      swear,
   Can draw you to her *with a single hair*.
   translation of Persius *Satires* no. 5, l. 246

34 Arms, and the man I sing, who, forced by fate,
   And haughty Juno's unrelenting hate,
   Expelled and exiled, left the Trojan shore.
   translation of Virgil *Aeneid* (*Aeneis*, 1697) bk. 1, l. 1; see
   Virgil 810:15

35 We must beat the iron while it is hot, but we may
   polish it at leisure.
   Aeneis (1697) dedication

1 Every age has a kind of universal genius, which inclines those that live in it to some particular studies.
An Essay of Dramatic Poesy (1668)

2 The famous rules, which the French call *Des Trois Unitez*, or, the Three Unities, which ought to be observed in every regular play; namely, of Time, Place, and Action.
An Essay of Dramatic Poesy (1668)

3 A thing well said will be wit in all languages.
An Essay of Dramatic Poesy (1668)

4 He was naturally learn'd; he needed not the spectacles of books to read Nature: he looked inwards, and found her there . . . He is many times flat, insipid; his comic wit degenerating into clenches, his serious swelling into bombast. But he is always great.
on Shakespeare
An Essay of Dramatic Poesy (1668)

5 He invades authors like a monarch; and what would be theft in other poets, is only victory in him.
on Ben Jonson
An Essay of Dramatic Poesy (1668)

6 If by the people you understand the multitude, the *hoi polloi*, 'tis no matter what they think; they are sometimes in the right, sometimes in the wrong: their judgement is a mere lottery.
An Essay of Dramatic Poesy (1668)

7 [Shakespeare] is the very Janus of poets; he wears almost everywhere two faces; and you have scarce begun to admire the one, ere you despise the other.
Essay on the Dramatic Poetry of the Last Age (1672)

8 What judgement I had increases rather than diminishes; and thoughts, such as they are, come crowding in so fast upon me, that my only difficulty is to choose or reject; to run them into verse or to give them the other harmony of prose.
Fables Ancient and Modern (1700) preface

9 'Tis sufficient to say, according to the proverb, that here is God's plenty.
of Chaucer
Fables Ancient and Modern (1700) preface

10 [Chaucer] is a perpetual fountain of good sense.
Fables Ancient and Modern (1700) preface

11 One of our late great poets is sunk in his reputation, because he could never forgive any conceit which came in his way; but swept like a drag-net, great and small. There was plenty enough, but the dishes were ill-sorted; whole pyramids of sweetmeats, for boys and women; but little of solid meat for men.
on Abraham Cowley
Fables Ancient and Modern (1700) preface

12 Sure the poet . . . spewed up a good lump of clotted nonsense at once.
Notes and Observations on the Empress of Morocco [by Elkanah Settle] (1674) 'The First Act'

13 How easy it is to call rogue and villain, and that wittily! But how hard to make a man appear a fool, a blockhead, or a knave, without using any of those opprobrious terms! To spare the grossness of the names, and to do the thing yet more severely, is to draw a full face, and to make the nose and cheeks stand out, and yet not to employ any depth of shadowing.
Of Satire (1693)

14 A man may be capable, as Jack Ketch's wife said of his servant, of a plain piece of work, a bare hanging; but to make a malefactor die sweetly was only belonging to her husband.
Of Satire (1693)

15 Cousin Swift, you will never be a poet.
Samuel Johnson *Lives of the English Poets* (1779–81) 'Dryden'

Alexander Dubček 1921–92
Czechoslovak statesman; First Secretary of the Czechoslovak Communist Party, 1968–9

16 In the service of the people we followed such a policy that socialism would not lose its human face.
in *Rudé Právo* 19 July 1968; a resolution by the party group in the Ministry of Foreign Affairs, 1968, referred to Czechoslovakian foreign policy acquiring 'its own defined face'; in *Rudé Právo* 14 March 1968

Joachim Du Bellay 1522–60
French poet

17 *France, mère des arts, des armes et des lois.*
France, mother of arts, of warfare, and of laws.
Les Regrets (1558) sonnet no. 9

18 *Heureux qui comme Ulysse a fait un beau voyage*
Ou comme celui-là qui conquit la toison,
Et puis est retourné, plein d'usage et raison,
Vivre entre ses parents le reste de son âge!
Happy he who like Ulysses has made a great journey, or like that man who won the Fleece and then came home, full of experience and good sense, to live the rest of his time among his family!
Les Regrets (1558) Sonnet no. 31

19 *Plus que le marbre dur me plaît l'ardoise fine,*
Plus mon Loire Gaulois, que le Tibre Latin,
Plus mon petit Lyré, que le mont Palatin,
Et plus que l'air marin la douceur angevine.
I love thin slate more than hard marble, my Gallic Loire more than the Latin Tiber, my little Liré more than the Palatine Hill, and more than the sea air the sweetness of Anjou.
Les Regrets (1558) Sonnet no. 31

W. E. B. Du Bois 1868–1963
American social reformer and political activist

20 One thing alone I charge you. As you live, believe in life!
last message, written 26 June, 1957, and read at his funeral, 1963, in *Journal of Negro History* April 1964

21 The problem of the twentieth century is the problem of the colour line—the relation of the

darker to the lighter races of men in Asia and
Africa, in America and the islands of the sea.
The Souls of Black Folk (1905) ch. 2

1 Herein lies the tragedy of the age: not that men
are poor . . . not that men are wicked . . . but that
men know so little of men.
The Souls of Black Folk (1905) ch. 12

Stephen Duck 1705–56
English poet and clergyman

2 Let those who feast at ease on dainty fare,
Pity the reapers, who their feasts prepare.
'The Thresher's Labour' (1730)

3 Like Sisyphus, our work is never done;
Continually rolls back the restless stone.
'The Thresher's Labour' (1730)

Mme Du Deffand (Marie de Vichy-Chamrond) 1697–1780
French literary hostess

4 *La distance n'y fait rien; il n'y a que le premier pas
qui coûte.*
The distance is nothing; it is only the first step
that is difficult.
*commenting on the legend that St Denis, carrying his
head in his hands, walked two leagues*
letter to Jean Le Rond d'Alembert, 7 July 1763, in Gaston
Maugras *Trois mois à la cour de Frédéric* (1886); see
Proverbs 624:13

Helen, Lady Dufferin 1807–67
Irish writer

5 Is the cabin still left standing? Has the rich man
need of all?
Is the children's birthplace taken now within the
new park wall?
'The Emigrant Ship'

George Duffield 1818–88
American Presbyterian minister

6 Stand up!—stand up for Jesus!
Ye soldiers of the Cross.
'Stand Up, Stand Up for Jesus' (1858 hymn); the opening
line inspired by the dying words of the American
evangelist, Dudley Atkins Tyng; see **Last words** 473:21

Carol Ann Duffy 1965–
English poet

7 Whatever 'in love' means,
true love is talented.
Someone vividly gifted in love has gone.
on the death of **Diana**, *Princess of Wales*
'September, 1997' (1997); see **Charles** 209:14

Charles Gavan Duffy 1816–1903
Irish nationalist and (later) Australian politician

8 I am still an Irish rebel to the backbone and the
spinal marrow, a rebel for the same reason that

John Hampden and Algernon Sidney, George
Washington and Charles Carrol of Carrolltown,
were rebels—because tyranny had supplanted the
law.
arriving in Australia in 1856
Cyril Pearl *The Three Lives of Gavan Duffy* (1979)

Georges Duhamel 1884–1966
French novelist

9 I have too much respect for the idea of God to
make it responsible for such an absurd world.
Le désert de Bièvres (1937)

John Foster Dulles 1888–1959
American international lawyer and politician

10 The ability to get to the verge without getting into
the war is the necessary art . . . We walked to the
brink and we looked it in the face.
in *Life* 16 January 1956; see **Stevenson** 758:17

Alexandre Dumas ('Dumas père') 1802–70
French novelist and dramatist

11 *Cherchons la femme.*
Let us look for the woman.
*attributed to Joseph Fouché (1763–1820) in the form
'Cherchez la femme'*
Les Mohicans de Paris (1854–5) passim

12 *Tous pour un, un pour tous.*
All for one, one for all.
Les Trois Mousquetaires [The Three Musketeers] (1844)
ch. 9

Alexandre Dumas ('Dumas fils') 1824–95
French writer

13 All generalizations are dangerous, even this one.
attributed

Daphne Du Maurier see Opening lines 574:31

Charles François du Périer Dumouriez 1739–1823
French general

14 The courtiers who surround him have forgotten
nothing and learnt nothing.
*of Louis XVIII, at the time of the Declaration of
Verona, September 1795; quoted by* **Napoleon** *in his
Declaration to the French on his return from Elba,
1815*
Examen impartial d'un Écrit intitulé Déclaration de Louis XVIII
(1795); see **Talleyrand** 771:18

Paul Lawrence Dunbar 1872–1906
American poet

15 I know why the caged bird sings!
adopted by Maya **Angelou** *as the title of her
autobiography, 1969*
'Sympathy' st. 3; see **Webster** 826:11

William Dunbar c.1465–c.1513

Scottish poet and priest
see also **Anonymous** 17:11

1 All women of us suld have honouring,
 Service and love above all other thing.
  'In Praise of Women'

2 I that in heill wes and gladnes
 Am trublit now with gret seiknes
 And feblit with infirmitie:
 Timor mortis conturbat me.
 Timor . . . = *The fear of death troubles me;* makaris
 = *makers, i.e. poets*
  'Lament for the Makaris'

3 He hes done petuously devour,
 The noble Chaucer, of makaris flour,
 The Monk of Bery, and Gower, all three;
 Timor mortis conturbat me.
  'Lament for the Makaris'

4 All love is lost but upon God alone.
  'The Merle and the Nightingale' st. 2

Isadora Duncan see **Last words** 471:1

Henry Dundas 1742–1811

Scottish-born politician

5 When it is said that no alternative is left to the
 New Englanders but to starve or rebel, this is not
 the fact, for there is another way, to submit.
 *the word 'starvation' was said to have been coined in
 relation to this speech, and Dundas became known as
 'Starvation Dundas'*
  in the House of Commons, 1775

Ian Dunlop 1940–

British art historian

6 The shock of the new: seven historic exhibitions of
 modern art.
  title of book (1972)

Helen Dunmore 1952–

British poet and novelist

7 That killed head straining through the windscreen
 with its frill of bubbles in the eye-sockets
 is not trying to tell you something—
 it is telling you something.
  'Poem on the Obliteration of 100,000 Iraqi Soldiers'
  (1994)

Douglas Dunn 1942–

Scottish poet

8 In a country like this
 Our ghosts outnumber us . . .
  'At Falkland Palace' (1988)

9 My poems should be Clyde-built, crude and sure,
 With images of those dole-deployed
 To honour the indomitable Reds,
 Clydesiders of slant steel and angled cranes;
 A poetry of nuts and bolts, born, bred,

Embattled by the Clyde, tight and impure.
  'Clydesiders' (1974)

10 They ruined us. They conquered continents.
 We filled their uniforms. We cruised the seas.
 We worked their mines and made their histories.
 You work, we rule, they said. We worked; they
 ruled.
 They fooled the tenements. All men were fooled.
  'Empires' (1979)

11 I am light with meditation, religiose
 And mystic with a day of solitude.
  'Reading Pascal in the Lowlands' (1985)

Finlay Peter Dunne 1867–1936

American humorous writer

12 A law, Hinnissey, that might look like a wall to
 you or me wud look like a triumphal arch to
 th'expeeryenced eye iv a lawyer.
  'Mr Dooley on the Power of the Press' in *American Magazine*
  no. 62 1906; see **Commager** 236:15

Sean Dunne 1956–97

Irish poet

13 The country wears their going like a scar,
 Today their relatives save to support and
 Send others in planes for the new diaspora.
  'Letter from Ireland' (1991)

John Dunning, Lord Ashburton 1731–83

English lawyer and politician

14 The influence of the Crown has increased, is
 increasing, and ought to be diminished.
  resolution passed in the House of Commons, 6 April 1780

Richard Duppa 1770–1831

English artist and writer

15 In language, the ignorant have prescribed laws to
 the learned.
  Maxims (1830) no. 252

Marguerite Duras 1914–96

French writer

16 *C'est ma référence majeure, la peur. Faire peur, c'est
 le mal.*
 Fear is my main point of reference. Causing fear is
 what constitutes evil.
  Emily L. (1987)

17 Men like women who write. Even though they
 don't say so. A writer is a foreign country.
  Practicalities (1987) 'The M. D. Uniform'

18 In heterosexual love there's no solution. Man and
 woman are irreconcilable, and it's the doomed
 attempt to do the impossible, repeated in each new
 affair, that lends heterosexual love its grandeur.
  Practicalities (1990) 'Men'

Paul Durcan 1944–

Irish poet

19 Poetry's another word
 For losing everything

Except purity of heart.
'Christmas Day' (1996)

1   Some of us made it
To the forest edge, but many of us did not
Make it, although their unborn children did—
Such as you whom the camp commandant branded
Sid Vicious of the Sex Pistols. Jesus, break his fall:
There—but for the clutch of luck—go we all.
'The Death by Heroin of Sid Vicious' (1980)

Ray Durem 1915-63

American poet

2 Some of my best friends are white boys.
when I meet 'em
I treat 'em
just the same as if they was people.
'Broadminded' (written 1951)

Albrecht Dürer 1471-1528

German painter and engraver

3 He that would be a painter must have a natural turn thereto. Love and delight therein are better teachers of the Art of Painting than compulsion is.
Third Book of Human Proportions (written c.1512-3) introduction; William Martin Conway *Literary remains of Albrecht Dürer* (1889)

John George Lambton, Lord Durham 1792-1840

English Whig politician

4 £40,000 a year a moderate income—such a one as a man *might jog on with.*
Herbert Maxwell (ed.) *The Creevey Papers* (1903) vol. 2, from a letter from Mr Creevey to Miss Elizabeth Ord, 13 September 1821

5 I expected to find a contest between a government and a people: I found two nations warring in the bosom of a single state.
of Canada
Report of the Affairs of British North America (1839)

Leo Durocher 1906-91

American baseball coach

6 I called off his players' names as they came marching up the steps behind him . . . All nice guys. They'll finish last. Nice guys. Finish last.
casual remark at a practice ground in the presence of a number of journalists, July 1946, generally quoted as 'Nice guys finish last'
Nice Guys Finish Last (1975) pt. 1

Lawrence Durrell 1912-90

English novelist, poet, and travel writer

7 I love to feel events overlapping each other, crawling over one another like wet crabs in a basket.
Balthazar (1958) pt. 1

8 No history much? Perhaps. Only this ominous Dark beauty flowering under veils,

Trapped in the spectrum of a dying style:
A village like an instinct left to rust,
Composed around the echo of a pistol-shot.
'Sarajevo' (1951)

Ian Dury 1942-2000

British rock singer and songwriter

9 Sex and drugs and rock and roll.
title of song (1977)

10 I could be the catalyst that sparks the revolution.
I could be an inmate in a long term institution
I could lean to wild extremes I could do or die,
I could yawn and be withdrawn and watch them gallop by,
What a waste, what a waste, what a waste, what a waste.
'What a Waste' (1978 song)

Andrea Dworkin 1946-

American feminist and writer

11 Seduction is often difficult to distinguish from rape. In seduction, the rapist bothers to buy a bottle of wine.
speech to women at Harper & Row, 1976; in *Letters from a War Zone* (1988)

Edward Dyer d. 1607

English poet

12 Silence augmenteth grief, writing increaseth rage,
Staled are my thoughts, which loved and lost, the wonder of our age.
previously attributed to Fulke **Greville**
'Elegy on the Death of Sir Philip Sidney' (1593)

13 My mind to me a kingdom is.
Such perfect joy therein I find
That it excels all other bliss
That world affords or grows by kind.
Though much I want which most would have,
Yet still my mind forbids to crave.
'In praise of a contented mind' (1588), attributed

John Dyer 1700-58

Welsh clergyman and poet

14 The care of sheep, the labours of the loom,
And arts of trade, I sing.
The Fleece (1757) bk. 1, l. 1

15   Industry,
Which dignifies the artist, lifts the swain,
And the straw cottage to a palace turns.
The Fleece (1757) bk. 3, l. 332

16 But transient is the smile of fate:
A little rule, a little sway,
A sunbeam in a winter's day,
Is all the proud and mighty have
Between the cradle and the grave.
Grongar Hill (1726) l. 88

17 The town and village, dome and farm,
Each give each a double charm,
As pearls upon an Ethiop's arm.
Grongar Hill (1726) l. 111

1 The pilgrim oft
At dead of night, mid his orison hears
Aghast the voice of Time, disparting tow'rs.
The Ruins of Rome (1740) l. 38

John Dyer

English poet

2 And he that will this health deny,
Down among the dead men let him lie.
'Down among the Dead Men' (*c*.1700)

Bob Dylan (Robert Zimmerman) 1941–

American singer and songwriter

3 How many roads must a man walk down
Before you can call him a man? . . .
The answer, my friend, is blowin' in the wind,
The answer is blowin' in the wind.
'Blowin' in the Wind' (1962 song)

4 They're selling postcards of the hanging.
'Desolation Row' (1965)

5 Praise be to Nero's Neptune
The Titanic sails at dawn
And everybody's shouting
'Which Side Are You On?'
And Ezra Pound and T. S. Eliot
Fighting in the captain's tower
While calypso singers laugh at them
And fishermen hold flowers.
'Desolation Row' (1965 song)

6 Don't think twice, it's all right.
title of song (1963)

7 I saw ten thousand talkers whose tongues were all
broken,
I saw guns and sharp swords, in the hands of
young children . . .
And it's a hard rain's a gonna fall.
'A Hard Rain's A Gonna Fall' (1963 song)

8 Money doesn't talk, it swears.
'It's Alright, Ma (I'm Only Bleeding)' (1965 song)

9 She takes just like a woman, yes, she does
She makes love just like a woman, yes, she does
And she aches just like a woman
But she breaks like a little girl.
'Just Like a Woman' (1966 song)

10 How does it feel
To be on your own
With no direction home
Like a complete unknown
Like a rolling stone?
'Like a Rolling Stone' (1965 song)

11 She knows there's no success like failure
And that failure's no success at all.
'Love Minus Zero / No Limit' (1965 song)

12 Hey! Mr Tambourine Man, play a song for me.
I'm not sleepy and there is no place I'm going to.
'Mr Tambourine Man' (1965 song)

13 Ah, but I was so much older then,
I'm younger than that now.
'My Back Pages' (1964 song)

14 Señor, señor, do you know where we're headin'?
Lincoln County Road or Armageddon?
'Señor (Tale of Yankee Power)' (1978 song)

15 All that foreign oil controlling American soil.
'Slow Train' (1979 song)

16 The times they are a-changin'.
title of song (1964)

17 Come mothers and fathers,
Throughout the land
And don't criticize
What you can't understand.
'The Times They Are A-Changing' (1964 song)

18 But I can't think for you
You'll have to decide,
Whether Judas Iscariot
Had God on his side.
'With God on our Side' (1963 song)

Esther Dyson

American businesswoman

19 The important thing to remember is that this is
not a new form of life. It is just a new activity.
of the Internet
in *New York Times* 7 July 1996 'The Cyber-Maxims of
Esther Dyson'

James Dyson 1947–

English inventor and businessman

20 After the idea, there is plenty of time to learn the
technology.
Against the Odds (1997)

Ee

Amelia Earhart 1898–1937

American aviator

21 Courage is the price that Life exacts for granting
peace,
The soul that knows it not, knows no release
From little things.
'Courage' (1927)

22 The best mascot is a good mechanic.
Mary S. Lovell *The Sound of Wings* (1989)

23 Would you *mind* if I flew the Atlantic?
to her husband George Putnam; George P. Putnam *Soaring
Wings* (1939)

Clint Eastwood see Film lines 319:8

Abba Eban 1915–

Israeli diplomat

24 History teaches us that men and nations behave
wisely once they have exhausted all other
alternatives.
speech in London, 16 December 1970, in *The Times* 17
December 1970

Arthur Eddington 1882–1944
British astrophysicist

1 We do not argue with the critic who urges that the stars are not hot enough for this process; we tell him to go and find a hotter place.
on the formation of heavier elements by nuclear reactions
> The Internal Constitution of the Stars (1926)

2 Let us draw an arrow arbitrarily. If as we follow the arrow we find more and more of the random element in the world, then the arrow is pointing towards the future; if the random element decreases the arrow points towards the past . . . I shall use the phrase 'time's arrow' to express this one-way property of time which has no analogue in space.
> The Nature of the Physical World (1928) ch. 4

3 If an army of monkeys were strumming on typewriters they *might* write all the books in the British Museum.
> The Nature of the Physical World (1928); see **Wilensky** 837:17

4 If someone points out to you that your pet theory of the universe is in disagreement with Maxwell's equations—then so much the worse for Maxwell's equations. If it is found to be contradicted by observation—well, these experimentalists do bungle things sometimes. But if your theory is found to be against the second law of thermodynamics I can give you no hope; there is nothing for it but to collapse in deepest humiliation.
> The Nature of the Physical World (1928) ch. 14

5 I am standing on the threshold about to enter a room. It is a complicated business. In the first place I must shove against an atmosphere pressing with a force of fourteen pounds on every square inch of my body. I must make sure of landing on a plank travelling at twenty miles a second round the sun— a fraction of a second too early or too late, the plank would be miles away. I must do this whilst hanging from a round planet, head outward into space, and with a wind of aether blowing at no one knows how many miles a second through every interstice of my body.
> The Nature of the Physical World (1928) ch. 15

6 I ask you to look both ways. For the road to a knowledge of the stars leads through the atom; and important knowledge of the atom has been reached through the stars.
> Stars and Atoms (1928) Lecture 1

7 Science is one thing, wisdom is another. Science is an edged tool, with which men play like children, and cut their own fingers.
> attributed in Robert L. Weber *More Random Walks in Science* (1982)

Mary Baker Eddy 1821–1910
American religious leader and founder of the Christian Science movement

8 Jesus of Nazareth was the most scientific man that ever trod the globe. He plunged beneath the material surface of things, and found the spiritual cause.
> Science and Health with Key to the Scriptures (1875)

9 Disease is an experience of so-called mortal mind. It is fear made manifest on the body.
> Science and Health with Key to the Scriptures (1875)

Anthony Eden, Earl of Avon 1897–1977
British Conservative statesman; Prime Minister, 1955–7
*on Eden: see **Muggeridge** 553:9*

10 We are in an armed conflict; that is the phrase I have used. There has been no declaration of war.
on the Suez crisis
> speech in the House of Commons, 1 November 1956

11 Long experience has taught me that to be criticized is not always to be wrong.
during the Suez crisis
> speech at Lord Mayor's Guildhall banquet; in *Daily Herald* 10 November 1956

Clarissa Eden 1920–
*British wife of Anthony **Eden***

12 For the past few weeks I have really felt as if the Suez Canal was flowing through my drawing-room.
> speech at Gateshead, 20 November 1956

Marriott Edgar 1880–1951
British actor and writer

13 There's a famous seaside place called Blackpool,
That's noted for fresh air and fun,
And Mr and Mrs Ramsbottom
Went there with young Albert, their son.
> 'The Lion and Albert' (1932)

Maria Edgeworth 1767–1849
English-born Irish novelist

14 Well! some people talk of morality, and some of religion, but give me a little snug property.
> The Absentee (1812) ch. 2

15 It was her settled purpose to make the Irish and Ireland ridiculous and contemptible to Lord Colambre; to disgust him with his native country; to make him abandon the wish of residing on his own estate. To confirm him an absentee was her object.
> The Absentee (1812) ch. 7

16 We cannot judge either of the feelings or of the character of men with perfect accuracy, from their actions or their appearance in public; it is from their careless conversation, their half-finished sentences, that we may hope with the greatest probability of success to discover their real character.
> Castle Rackrent (1800) preface

17 To be sure a love match was the only thing for happiness, where the parties could any way afford it.
> Castle Rackrent (1800) 'Continuation of Memoirs'

1 Business was his aversion; pleasure was his business.
  The Contrast (1804) ch. 2

2 What a misfortune it is to be born a woman! . . . Why seek for knowledge, which can prove only that our wretchedness is irremediable? If a ray of light break in upon us, it is but to make darkness more visible; to show us the new limits, the Gothic structure, the impenetrable barriers of our prison.
  Leonora (1806) Letter 1

3 Man is to be held only by the *slightest* chains, with the idea that he can break them at pleasure, he submits to them in sport.
  Letters for Literary Ladies (1795) 'Letters of Julia and Caroline' no. 1

Richard Lovell Edgeworth 1744–1817
*Irish landowner and writer, father of Maria **Edgeworth***

4 We hear from good authority that the King was much pleased with Castle Rackrent—he rubbed his hands and said what—what—I know something now of my Irish subjects.
  letter to D. A. Beaufort, 26 April 1800

Thomas Alva Edison 1847–1931
American inventor

5 Genius is one per cent inspiration, ninety-nine per cent perspiration.
  said *c.*1903, in *Harper's Monthly Magazine* September 1932; see **Buffon** 163:14

6 For most of my life I refused to work at any problem unless its solution seemed to be capable of being put to commercial use.
  interview, in *New York Sun* February 1917

James Edmeston 1791–1867
English architect and hymn-writer

7 Lead us, Heavenly Father, lead us
  O'er the world's tempestuous sea;
  Guard us, guide us, keep us, feed us,
  For we have no help but Thee;
  Yet possessing every blessing,
  If our God our Father be.
  'Lead us, heavenly Father, lead us' (1821)

John Maxwell Edmonds see Epitaphs
311:17

St Edmund of Abingdon c.1175–1240
English scholar and churchman, Archbishop of Canterbury from 1233

8 Study as if you were to live for ever; live as if you were to die tomorrow.
  John Crozier *St Edmund of Abingdon* (1982)

Edward III 1312–77
English monarch, King from 1327
*see also **Mottoes** 552:9*

9 Also say to them, that they suffre hym this day to wynne his spurres, for if god be pleased, I woll this journey be his, and the honoure therof.
  speaking of the Black Prince at Crécy, 1346; commonly quoted as 'Let the boy win his spurs'
    The Chronicle of Froissart (translated by Sir John Bourchier, Lord Berners, 1523–5) ch. 130

Edward VII 1841–1910
British monarch, King of the United Kingdom from 1901
on Edward: see 562:21

10 I thought everyone must know that a *short* jacket is always worn with a silk hat at a private view in the morning.
  to Frederick Ponsonby, who had proposed accompanying him in a tailcoat
    Philip Magnus *Edward VII* (1964) ch. 19

Edward VIII, afterwards Duke of Windsor 1894–1972
British monarch, King of the United Kingdom, 1936
*on Edward: see **Beaverbrook** 60:16, **George V** 343:10, **Hardie** 371:7, **Mary** 517:8, **Mary** 517:9, **Newspaper headlines** 562:16*

11 These works brought all these people here. Something should be done to get them at work again.
  speaking at the derelict Dowlais Iron and Steel Works, 18 November 1936
    in *Western Mail* 19 November 1936; see **Misquotations** 538:18

12 At long last I am able to say a few words of my own . . . you must believe me when I tell you that I have found it impossible to carry the heavy burden of responsibility and to discharge my duties as King as I would wish to do without the help and support of the woman I love.
  radio broadcast following his abdication, 11 December 1936, in *The Times* 12 December 1936

13 The thing that impresses me most about America is the way parents obey their children.
  in *Look* 5 March 1957

Jonathan Edwards 1703–58
American theologian

14 Of all Insects no one is more wonderful than the spider especially with Respect to their sagacity and admirable way of working . . . I . . . once saw a very large spider to my surprise swimming in the air . . . and others have assured me that they often have seen spiders fly, the appearance is truly very pretty and pleasing.
  The Flying Spider—Observations by Jonathan Edwards when a boy 'Of Insects' in *Andover Review* vol. 13 (1890); see **Lowell** 494:13

15 The bodies of those that made such a noise and tumult when alive, when dead, lie as quietly

among the graves of their neighbours as any others.

Sermon on procrastination (*Miscellaneous Discourses*) in *Works* (1834) vol. 2

Oliver Edwards 1711–91

English lawyer

1 I have tried too in my time to be a philosopher; but, I don't know how, cheerfulness was always breaking in.

James Boswell *Life of Samuel Johnson* (1791) 17 April 1778

2 For my part now, I consider supper as a turnpike through which one must pass, in order to get to bed.

Boswell notes: '*I am not absolutely sure but this was my own suggestion, though it is truly in the character of Edwards*'

James Boswell *Life of Samuel Johnson* (1791) 17 April 1778

Richard Edwards c.1523–66

English poet and dramatist

3 The falling out of faithful friends, renewing is of love.

The Paradise of Dainty Devices (1576) 'Amantium Irae'; see **Proverbs** 630:1

Sarah Egerton 1670–1723

English poet

4 From the first dawn of life unto the grave, Poor womankind's in every state a slave.

'The Emulation' (1703)

5 We will our rights in learning's world maintain; Wit's empire now shall know a female reign.

'The Emulation' (1703)

Barbara Ehrenreich 1941–

American sociologist and writer

6 Exercise is the yuppie version of bulimia.

The Worst Years of Our Lives (1991) 'Food Worship'

Paul Ralph Ehrlich 1932–

American biologist

7 The first rule of intelligent tinkering is to save all the parts.

in *Saturday Review* 5 June 1971

John Ehrlichman 1925–99

*American Presidential assistant to Richard **Nixon***

8 I think we ought to let him hang there. Let him twist slowly, slowly in the wind.

*Richard **Nixon** had withdrawn his support for Patrick Gray, nominated as director of the FBI, although Gray himself had not been informed*

in a telephone conversation with John Dean; in *Washington Post* 27 July 1973

Max Ehrmann 1872–1945

American writer

9 Go placidly amid the noise and the haste, and remember what peace there may be in silence.

often wrongly dated to 1692, the date of foundation of a church in Baltimore whose vicar circulated the poem in 1956

'Desiderata' (1948)

Joseph von Eichendorff 1788–1857

German poet

10 *Wem Gott will rechte Gunst erweisen, Den schickt er in die weite Welt.*

Those whom God wishes to show true favour He sends out into the great wide world.

Der frohe Wandersmann (1826)

Einhard c.770–840

Frankish chronicler, friend and biographer of Charlemagne

11 He was large and strong and of lofty stature, though not disproportionately tall; the upper part of his head was round, his eyes very large and animated, nose a little long, hair fair, and face laughing and merry. Thus his appearance was always stately and dignified, whether he was standing or sitting; although his neck was somewhat short, and his belly rather prominent; but the symmetry of the rest of his body concealed these defects.

of Charlemagne

The Life of Charlemagne (ed. S. Painter, 1960)

Albert Einstein 1879–1955

German-born theoretical physicist; originator of the theory of relativity

*on Einstein: see **Anonymous** 16:16, **Squire** 753:15*

12 Science without religion is lame, religion without science is blind.

Science, Philosophy and Religion: a Symposium (1941) ch. 13

13 $E = mc^2$.

the usual form of Einstein's original statement: 'If a body releases the energy L in the form of radiation, its mass is decreased by L/V^2'

in *Annalen der Physik* 18 (1905)

14 God is subtle but he is not malicious.

remark made during a week at Princeton beginning 9 May 1921, later carved above the fireplace of the Common Room of Fine Hall (the Mathematical Institute), Princeton University; R. W. Clark *Einstein* (1973) ch. 14

15 I am convinced that *He* [God] does not play dice.

often quoted as: 'God does not play dice'

letter to Max Born, 4 December 1926; in *Einstein und Born Briefwechsel* (1969)

16 If my theory of relativity is proven correct, Germany will claim me as a German and France will declare that I am a citizen of the world. Should my theory prove untrue, France will say that I am a German and Germany will declare that I am a Jew.

address at the Sorbonne, Paris, possibly early December 1929, in *New York Times* 16 February 1930

1 I never think of the future. It comes soon enough.

in an interview, given on the *Belgenland*, December 1930

2 The eternal mystery of the world is its comprehensibility . . . The fact that it is comprehensible is a miracle.

usually quoted as 'The most incomprehensible fact about the universe is that it is comprehensible'

in *Franklin Institute Journal* March 1936 'Physics and Reality'

3 Some recent work by E. Fermi and L. Szilard, which has been communicated to me in manuscript, leads me to expect that the element uranium may be turned into a new and important source of energy in the immediate future. Certain aspects of the situation which has arisen seem to call for watchfulness and, if necessary, quick action on the part of the Administration.

warning of the possible development of an atomic bomb, and leading to the setting up of the Manhattan Project

letter to Franklin **Roosevelt**, 2 August 1939, drafted by Leo Szilard and signed by Einstein

4 The unleashed power of the atom has changed everything save our modes of thinking and we thus drift toward unparalleled catastrophe.

telegram to prominent Americans, 24 May 1946, in *New York Times* 25 May 1946

5 If *A* is a success in life, then *A* equals x plus y plus z. Work is x; y is play; and z is keeping your mouth shut.

in *Observer* 15 January 1950

6 Common sense is nothing more than a deposit of prejudices laid down in the mind before you reach eighteen.

Lincoln Barnett *The Universe and Dr Einstein* (1950 ed.)

7 The grand aim of all science [is] to cover the greatest number of empirical facts by logical deduction from the smallest possible number of hypotheses or axioms.

Lincoln Barnett *The Universe and Dr Einstein* (1950 ed.)

8 If I would be a young man again and had to decide how to make my living, I would not try to become a scientist or scholar or teacher. I would rather choose to be a plumber or a peddler in the hope to find that modest degree of independence still available under present circumstances.

in *Reporter* 18 November 1954

9 The distinction between past, present and future is only an illusion, however persistent.

letter to Michelangelo Besso, 21 March 1955

10 Nationalism is an infantile sickness. It is the measles of the human race.

Helen Dukas and Banesh Hoffman *Albert Einstein, the Human Side* (1979)

11 One must divide one's time between politics and equations. But our equations are much more important to me.

C. P. Snow 'Einstein' in M. Goldsmith et al. (eds.) *Einstein* (1980)

12 When I was young, I found out that the big toe always ends up making a hole in a sock. So I stopped wearing socks.

to Philippe Halsman; A. P. French *Einstein: A Centenary Volume* (1979)

Dwight D. Eisenhower 1890–1969

American Republican statesman; 34th President of the US 1953–61

13 This world in arms is not spending money alone. It is spending the sweat of its labourers, the genius of its scientists, the hopes of its children.

speech in Washington, 16 April 1953, in *Public Papers of Presidents 1953* (1960)

14 I just will not—I *refuse*—to get into the gutter with that guy.

explaining why he did not try to restrain Senator **McCarthy**

in 1953; in *American National Biography* (online edition) 'Joseph McCarthy'

15 You have broader considerations that might follow what you might call the 'falling domino' principle. You have a row of dominoes set up. You knock over the first one, and what will happen to the last one is that it will go over very quickly. So you have the beginning of a disintegration that would have the most profound influences.

speech at press conference, 7 April 1954, in *Public Papers of Presidents 1954* (1960)

16 I think that people want peace so much that one of these days governments had better get out of the way and let them have it.

broadcast discussion, 31 August 1959, in *Public Papers of Presidents 1959* (1960)

17 In preparing for battle I have always found that plans are useless, but planning is indispensable.

Richard Nixon *Six Crises* (1962); attributed

Alfred Eisenstaedt 1898–1995

German-born American photographer and photojournalist

18 It's more important to click with people than to click the shutter

in *Life* 24 August 1995 (electronic edition), obituary

Eleazar of Worms 1176–1238

Jewish rabbi

19 No crown carries such royalty with it as doth humility; no monument gives such glory as an unsullied name; no worldly gain can equal that which comes from observing God's laws.

Sefer Rokeah

20 The highest sacrifice is a broken and contrite heart; the highest wisdom is that which is found in the Torah; the noblest of all ornaments is modesty; and the most beautiful thing that man can do, is to forgive a wrong.

Sefer Rokeah; see **Book of Common Prayer** 137:13

21 If the means of thy support in life be measured out scantily to thee, remember that thou hast to be thankful and grateful even for the mere privilege to breathe, and that thou must look upon that

suffering as a test of thy piety and a preparation for better things.

Sefer Rokeah

Edward Elgar 1857–1934

English composer
on Elgar: see **Beecham** *62:11; see also* **Shelley** *731:16*

1 To my friends pictured within.

Enigma Variations (1899) dedication

2 *Bramo assai, poco spero, nulla chieggio.*

I essay much, I hope little, I ask nothing.

inscribed at the end of *Enigma Variations* (1899); see **Tasso** 773:8

3 There is music in the air.

R. J. Buckley *Sir Edward Elgar* (1905) ch. 4

George Eliot (Mary Ann Evans) 1819–80

English novelist
on Eliot: see **Gaskell** *340:21; see also* **Anonymous** *18:5*

4 Our deeds determine us, as much as we determine our deeds; and until we know what has been or will be the peculiar combination of outward with inward facts, which constitute a man's critical actions, it will be better not to think ourselves wise about his character.

Adam Bede (1859) ch. 29

5 He was like a cock who thought the sun had risen to hear him crow.

Adam Bede (1859) ch. 33

6 Deep, unspeakable suffering may well be called a baptism, a regeneration, the initiation into a new state.

Adam Bede (1859) ch. 42

7 We hand folks over to God's mercy, and show none ourselves.

Adam Bede (1859) ch. 42

8 The mother's yearning, that completest type of the life in another life which is the essence of real human love, feels the presence of the cherished child even in the debased, degraded man.

Adam Bede (1859) ch. 43

9 Vanity is as ill at ease under indifference as tenderness is under a love which it cannot return.

Daniel Deronda (1876) bk. 1 ch. 10

10 Gossip is a sort of smoke that comes from the dirty tobacco-pipes of those who diffuse it: it proves nothing but the bad taste of the smoker.

Daniel Deronda (1876) bk. 2, ch. 13

11 A difference of taste in jokes is a great strain on the affections.

Daniel Deronda (1876) bk. 2, ch. 15

12 There is a great deal of unmapped country within us which would have to be taken into account in an explanation of our gusts and storms.

Daniel Deronda (1876) bk. 3, ch. 24

13 Friendships begin with liking or gratitude—roots that can be pulled up.

Daniel Deronda (1876) bk. 4, ch. 32

14 Half the sorrows of women would be averted if they could repress the speech they know to be useless; nay, the speech they have resolved not to make.

Felix Holt (1866) ch. 2

15 There is no private life which has not been determined by a wider public life.

Felix Holt (1866) ch. 3

16 An election is coming. Universal peace is declared, and the foxes have a sincere interest in prolonging the lives of the poultry.

Felix Holt (1866) ch. 5

17 A little daily embroidery had been a constant element in Mrs Transome's life; that soothing occupation of taking stitches to produce what neither she nor any one else wanted, was then the resource of many a well-born and unhappy woman.

Felix Holt (1866) ch. 7

18 Speech is often barren; but silence also does not necessarily brood over a full nest. Your still fowl, blinking at you without remark, may all the while be sitting on one addled egg; and when it takes to cackling will have nothing to announce but that addled delusion.

Felix Holt (1866) ch. 15

19 A woman can hardly ever choose . . . she is dependent on what happens to her. She must take meaner things, because only meaner things are within her reach.

Felix Holt (1866) ch. 27

20 There's many a one who would be idle if hunger didn't pinch him; but the stomach sets us to work.

Felix Holt (1866) ch. 30

21 'Abroad', that large home of ruined reputations.

Felix Holt (1866) epilogue

22 Debasing the moral currency.

The Impressions of Theophrastus Such (1879) essay title

23 Many Theresas have been born who found for themselves no epic life wherein there was a constant unfolding of far-resonant action; perhaps only a life of mistakes, the offspring of a certain spiritual grandeur ill-matched with the meanness of opportunity; perhaps a tragic failure which found no sacred poet and sank unwept into oblivion.

Middlemarch (1871–2) Prelude

24 Pride helps us; and pride is not a bad thing when it only urges us to hide our own hurts, not to hurt others.

Middlemarch (1871–2) bk. 1, ch. 6

25 A woman dictates before marriage in order that she may have an appetite for submission afterwards.

Middlemarch (1871–2) bk. 1, ch. 9

26 He said he should prefer not to know the sources of the Nile, and that there should be some unknown regions preserved as hunting-grounds for the poetic imagination.

Middlemarch (1871–2) bk. 1, ch. 9

1 Among all forms of mistake, prophecy is the most gratuitous.
Middlemarch (1871–2) bk. 1, ch. 10

2 Plain women he regarded as he did the other severe facts of life, to be faced with philosophy and investigated by science.
Middlemarch (1871–2) bk. 1, ch. 11 (Lydgate)

3 Any one watching keenly the stealthy convergence of human lots, sees a slow preparation of effects from one life on another, which tells like a calculated irony on the indifference or the frozen stare with which we look at our unintroduced neighbour.
Middlemarch (1871–2) bk. 1, ch. 11

4 Fred's studies are not very deep . . . he is only reading a novel.
Middlemarch (1871–2) bk 1, ch. 11

5 If we had a keen vision and feeling of all ordinary human life, it would be like hearing the grass grow and the squirrel's heart beat, and we should die of that roar which lies on the other side of silence.
Middlemarch (1871–2) bk. 2, ch. 20

6 We do not expect people to be deeply moved by what is not unusual. That element of tragedy which lies in the very fact of frequency, has not yet wrought itself into the coarse emotion of mankind.
Middlemarch (1871–2) bk. 2, ch. 20

7 A woman, let her be as good as she may, has got to put up with the life her husband makes for her.
Middlemarch (1871–2) bk. 3, ch. 25

8 It is an uneasy lot at best, to be what we call highly taught and yet not to enjoy: to be present at this great spectacle of life and never to be liberated from a small hungry shivering self.
Middlemarch (1871–2) bk. 3, ch. 29

9 A man is seldom ashamed of feeling that he cannot love a woman so well when he sees a certain greatness in her: nature having intended greatness for men.
Middlemarch (1871–2) bk. 4, ch. 39

10 'I am going to London,' said Dorothea. 'How can you always live in a street? And you will be so poor.'
Middlemarch (1871–2) bk. 8, ch. 84

11 Anger and jealousy can no more bear to lose sight of their objects than love.
The Mill on the Floss (1860) bk. 1, ch. 10

12 Our instructed vagrancy, which has hardly time to linger by the hedgerows, but runs away early to the tropics, and is at home with palms and banyans—which is nourished on books of travel, and stretches the theatre of its imagination to the Zambesi.
The Mill on the Floss (1860) bk. 3, ch. 9

13 The dead level of provincial existence.
The Mill on the Floss (1860) bk. 5, ch. 3

14 The happiest women, like the happiest nations, have no history.
The Mill on the Floss (1860) bk. 6, ch. 3; see **Montesquieu** 545:11

15 I should like to know what is the proper function of women, if it is not to make reasons for husbands to stay at home, and still stronger reasons for bachelors to go out.
The Mill on the Floss (1860) bk. 6, ch. 6

16 'Character' says Novalis, in one of his questionable aphorisms—'character is destiny.'
The Mill on the Floss (1860) bk. 6, ch. 6; see **Heraclitus** 383:3, **Novalis** 565:18

17 In every parting there is an image of death.
Scenes of Clerical Life (1858) 'Amos Barton' ch. 10

18 Cruelty, like every other vice, requires no motive outside itself—it only requires opportunity.
Scenes of Clerical Life (1858) 'Janet's Repentance' ch. 13

19 Errors look so very ugly in persons of small means—one feels they are taking quite a liberty in going astray; whereas people of fortune may naturally indulge in a few delinquencies.
Scenes of Clerical Life (1858) 'Janet's Repentance' ch. 25

20 Oh may I join the choir invisible
Of those immortal dead who live again
In minds made better by their presence.
'Oh May I Join the Choir Invisible' (1867)

21 Life is too precious to be spent in this weaving and unweaving of false impressions, and it is better to live quietly under some degree of misrepresentation than to attempt to remove it by the uncertain process of letter-writing.
letter to Mrs Peter Taylor, 8 June 1856, in G. S. Haight (ed.) *The George Eliot Letters* vol. 2 (1954)

22 Whatever may be the success of my stories, I shall be resolute in preserving my incognito, having observed that a *nom de plume* secures all the advantages without the disagreeables of reputation.
letter to William Blackwood, 4 February 1857, in G. S. Haight (ed.) *The George Eliot Letters* vol. 3 (1954)

23 If art does not enlarge men's sympathies, it does nothing morally.
letter to Charles Bray, 5 July 1859, in G. S. Haight (ed.) *The George Eliot Letters* vol. 3 (1954)

24 Beginnings are always troublesome . . . Even Macaulay's few pages of introduction to his 'Introduction' in the English History are the worst bit of writing in the book.
letter to Sara Hennell, 15 August 1859, in G. S. Haight (ed.) *The George Eliot Letters* vol. 3 (1954)

25 The idea of God, so far as it has been a high spiritual influence, is the ideal of a goodness entirely human.
letter to the Hon. Mrs H. F. Ponsonby, 10 December 1874, in G. S. Haight (ed.) *The George Eliot Letters* vol. 6 (1956)

26 She, stirred somewhat beyond her wont, and taking as her text the three words which have been used so often as the inspiring trumpet-calls of men—the words *God, Immortality, Duty*—pronounced, with terrible earnestness, how

inconceivable was the *first*, how unbelievable the *second*, and yet how peremptory and absolute the third. Never, perhaps, have sterner accents affirmed the sovereignty of impersonal and unrecompensing Law.

F. W. H. Myers 'George Eliot', in *Century Magazine* November 1881

T. S. Eliot (Thomas Stearns Eliot) 1888–1965

American-born British poet, critic, and dramatist
on Eliot: see **Leavis** 478:5

1 Because I do not hope to turn again
Because I do not hope
Because I do not hope to turn.

Ash-Wednesday (1930) pt. 1

2 Teach us to care and not to care
Teach us to sit still.

Ash-Wednesday (1930) pt. 1

3 Lady, three white leopards sat under a juniper-tree
In the cool of the day.

Ash-Wednesday (1930) pt. 2

4 You've missed the point completely, Julia:
There *were* no tigers. *That* was the point.

The Cocktail Party (1950) act 1, sc. 1

5 What is hell?
Hell is oneself,
Hell is alone, the other figures in it
Merely projections. There is nothing to escape from
And nothing to escape to. One is always alone.

The Cocktail Party (1950) act 1, sc. 3; see **Sartre** 667:4

6 Over buttered scones and crumpets
Weeping, weeping multitudes
Droop in a hundred A.B.C.'s.

'Cooking Egg' (1920)

7 Success is relative:
It is what we can make of the mess we have made of things.

The Family Reunion (1939) pt. 2, sc. 3

8 Round and round the circle
Completing the charm
So the knot be unknotted
The cross be uncrossed
The crooked be made straight
And the curse be ended.

The Family Reunion (1939) pt. 2, sc. 3

9 Time present and time past
Are both perhaps present in time future,
And time future contained in time past.

Four Quartets 'Burnt Norton' (1936) pt. 1

10 Footfalls echo in the memory
Down the passage which we did not take
Towards the door we never opened
Into the rose-garden.

Four Quartets 'Burnt Norton' (1936) pt. 1

11 Human kind
Cannot bear very much reality.

Four Quartets 'Burnt Norton' (1936) pt. 1.

12 At the still point of the turning world.

Four Quartets 'Burnt Norton' (1936) pt. 2

13 Words strain,
Crack and sometimes break, under the burden,
Under the tension, slip, slide, perish,
Decay with imprecision, will not stay in place,
Will not stay still.

Four Quartets 'Burnt Norton' (1936) pt. 5

14 In my beginning is my end.

Four Quartets 'East Coker' (1940) pt. 1; see **Mary** 517:11

15 That was a way of putting it—not very satisfactory:
A periphrastic study in a worn-out poetical fashion,
Leaving one still with the intolerable wrestle
With words and meanings. The poetry does not matter.

Four Quartets 'East Coker' (1940) pt. 2

16 The houses are all gone under the sea.
The dancers are all gone under the hill.

Four Quartets 'East Coker' (1940) pt. 2

17 O dark dark dark. They all go into the dark,
The vacant interstellar spaces, the vacant into the vacant.

Four Quartets 'East Coker' (1940) pt. 3

18 The wounded surgeon plies the steel
That questions the distempered part;
Beneath the bleeding hands we feel
The sharp compassion of the healer's art
Resolving the enigma of the fever chart.

Four Quartets 'East Coker' (1940) pt. 4

19 Each venture
Is a new beginning, a raid on the inarticulate
With shabby equipment always deteriorating
In the general mess of imprecision of feeling.

Four Quartets 'East Coker' (1940) pt. 5

20 I think that the river
Is a strong brown god—sullen, untamed and intractable.

Four Quartets 'The Dry Salvages' (1941) pt. 1

21 The communication
Of the dead is tongued with fire beyond the language of the living.

Four Quartets 'Little Gidding' (1942) pt. 1

22 Ash on an old man's sleeve
Is all the ash the burnt roses leave.

Four Quartets 'Little Gidding' (1942) pt. 2

23 This is the death of air.

Four Quartets 'Little Gidding' (1942) pt. 2

24 Since our concern was speech, and speech impelled us
To purify the dialect of the tribe
And urge the mind to aftersight and foresight.

Four Quartets 'Little Gidding' (1942) pt. 2

25 We shall not cease from exploration
And the end of all our exploring
Will be to arrive where we started
And know the place for the first time.

Four Quartets 'Little Gidding' (1942) pt. 5

26 What we call the beginning is often the end
And to make an end is to make a beginning.

The end is where we start from.
Four Quartets 'Little Gidding' (1942) pt. 5

1   So, while the light fails
On a winter's afternoon, in a secluded chapel
History is now and England.
Four Quartets 'Little Gidding' (1942) pt. 5

2 And all shall be well and
All manner of thing shall be well
When the tongues of flame are in-folded
Into the crowned knot of fire
And the fire and the rose are one.
Four Quartets 'Little Gidding' (1942) pt. 5; see **Julian** 438:6

3 Here I am, an old man in a dry month
Being read to by a boy, waiting for rain.
'Gerontion' (1920)

4 After such knowledge, what forgiveness?
'Gerontion' (1920)

5 Tenants of the house,
Thoughts of a dry brain in a dry season.
'Gerontion' (1920)

6 We are the hollow men
We are the stuffed men
Leaning together
Headpiece filled with straw. Alas!
'The Hollow Men' (1925)

7 *Here we go round the prickly pear*
Prickly pear prickly pear
Here we go round the prickly pear
At five o'clock in the morning.
Between the idea
And the reality
Between the motion
And the act
Falls the Shadow.
'The Hollow Men' (1925)

8 This is the way the world ends
Not with a bang but a whimper.
'The Hollow Men' (1925)

9 A cold coming we had of it,
Just the worst time of the year
For a journey, and such a long journey:
The ways deep and the weather sharp,
The very dead of winter.
'Journey of the Magi' (1927); see **Andrewes** 14:12

10   I had seen birth and death
But had thought they were different.
'Journey of the Magi' (1927)

11 An alien people clutching their gods.
'Journey of the Magi' (1927)

12 Let us go then, you and I,
When the evening is spread out against the sky
Like a patient etherized upon a table.
'The Love Song of J. Alfred Prufrock' (1917); see **Lewis** 483:9

13 In the room the women come and go
Talking of Michelangelo.
'The Love Song of J. Alfred Prufrock' (1917)

14 The yellow fog that rubs its back upon the
window-panes.
'The Love Song of J. Alfred Prufrock' (1917)

15 I have measured out my life with coffee spoons.
'The Love Song of J. Alfred Prufrock' (1917)

16 I should have been a pair of ragged claws
Scuttling across the floors of silent seas.
'The Love Song of J. Alfred Prufrock' (1917)

17 I have seen the moment of my greatness flicker,
And I have seen the eternal Footman hold my
coat, and snicker,
And in short, I was afraid.
'The Love Song of J. Alfred Prufrock' (1917)

18 No! I am not Prince Hamlet, nor was meant to be;
Am an attendant lord, one that will do
To swell a progress, start a scene or two,
Advise the prince.
'The Love Song of J. Alfred Prufrock' (1917)

19 I grow old . . . I grow old . . .
I shall wear the bottoms of my trousers rolled.
'The Love Song of J. Alfred Prufrock' (1917)

20 Shall I part my hair behind? Do I dare to eat a
peach?
I shall wear white flannel trousers, and walk upon
the beach.
I have heard the mermaids singing, each to each.
I do not think that they will sing to me.
'The Love Song of J. Alfred Prufrock' (1917); see **Donne** 281:9

21 I am aware of the damp souls of housemaids
Sprouting despondently at area gates.
'Morning at the Window' (1917)

22 Polyphiloprogenitive
The sapient sutlers of the Lord.
'Mr Eliot's Sunday Morning Service' (1919)

23 Yet we have gone on living,
Living and partly living.
Murder in the Cathedral (1935) pt. 1

24 The last temptation is the greatest treason:
To do the right deed for the wrong reason.
Murder in the Cathedral (1935) pt. 1

25 Clear the air! clean the sky! wash the wind! take
the stone from stone, take the skin from the arm,
take the muscle from bone, and wash them.
Murder in the Cathedral (1935) pt. 2

26 The Naming of Cats is a difficult matter,
It isn't just one of your holiday games;
You may think at first I'm as mad as a hatter
when I tell you, a cat must have THREE DIFFERENT
NAMES.
Old Possum's Book of Practical Cats (1939) 'The Naming of Cats'

27 He always has an alibi, and one or two to spare:
At whatever time the deed took place—MACAVITY
WASN'T THERE!
Old Possum's Book of Practical Cats (1939) 'Macavity: the Mystery Cat'

28 The winter evening settles down
With smell of steaks in passageways.
Six o'clock.
The burnt-out ends of smoky days.
'Preludes' (1917)

1 Midnight shakes the memory
As a madman shakes a dead geranium.
'Rhapsody on a Windy Night' (1917)

2 Where is the wisdom we have lost in knowledge?
Where is the knowledge we have lost in
information?
The Rock (1934) pt. 1

3 And the wind shall say: 'Here were decent godless
people:
Their only monument the asphalt road
And a thousand lost golf balls.'
The Rock (1934) pt. 1

4 Birth, and copulation, and death.
That's all the facts when you come to brass tacks.
Sweeney Agonistes (1932) 'Fragment of an Agon'

5 I gotta use words when I talk to you.
Sweeney Agonistes (1932) 'Fragment of an Agon'

6 The nightingales are singing near
The Convent of the Sacred Heart,

And sang within the bloody wood
When Agamemnon cried aloud
And let their liquid siftings fall
To stain the stiff dishonoured shroud.
'Sweeney among the Nightingales' (1919)

7 April is the cruellest month, breeding
Lilacs out of the dead land.
The Waste Land (1922) pt. 1

8 I read, much of the night, and go south in the
winter.
The Waste Land (1922) pt. 1

9 I will show you fear in a handful of dust.
The Waste Land (1922) pt. 1; see **Conrad** 241:2

10 Madame Sosostris, famous clairvoyante,
Had a bad cold, nevertheless
Is known to be the wisest woman in Europe,
With a wicked pack of cards.
The Waste Land (1922) pt. 1

11 A crowd flowed over London Bridge, so many,
I had not thought death had undone so many.
The Waste Land (1922) pt. 1

12 The Chair she sat in, like a burnished throne,
Glowed on the marble.
The Waste Land (1922) pt. 2; see **Shakespeare** 679:3

13 And still she cried, and still the world pursues,
'Jug Jug' to dirty ears.
The Waste Land (1922) pt. 2; see **Lyly** 497:3

14 I think we are in rats' alley
Where the dead men lost their bones.
The Waste Land (1922) pt. 2

15 o o o o that Shakespeherian Rag—
It's so elegant
So intelligent.
The Waste Land (1922) pt. 2; see **Buck** 163:6

16 Hurry up please it's time.
The Waste Land (1922) pt. 2

17 But at my back from time to time I hear
The sound of horns and motors, which shall bring
Sweeney to Mrs Porter in the spring.

O the moon shone bright on Mrs Porter
And on her daughter
They wash their feet in soda water.
The Waste Land (1922) pt. 3; see **Marvell** 516:1

18 At the violet hour, when the eyes and back
Turn upward from the desk, when the human
engine waits
Like a taxi throbbing waiting.
The Waste Land (1922) pt. 3

19 I Tiresias, old man with wrinkled dugs.
The Waste Land (1922) pt. 3

20 One of the low on whom assurance sits
As a silk hat on a Bradford millionaire.
The Waste Land (1922) pt. 3

21 When lovely woman stoops to folly and
Paces about her room again, alone,
She smoothes her hair with automatic hand,
And puts a record on the gramophone.
The Waste Land (1922) pt. 3; see **Goldsmith** 355:33

22 Phlebas the Phoenician, a fortnight dead,
Forgot the cry of gulls, and the deep sea swell
And the profit and loss.
The Waste Land (1922) pt. 4

23 Who is the third who walks always beside you?
When I count, there are only you and I together
But when I look ahead up the white road
There is always another one walking beside you.
The Waste Land (1922) pt. 5

24 These fragments I have shored against my ruins.
The Waste Land (1922) pt. 5

25 Shantih, shantih, shantih.
The Waste Land (1922) closing words; see **Upanishads**
805:4

26 Webster was much possessed by death
And saw the skull beneath the skin.
'Whispers of Immortality' (1919)

27 The only way of expressing emotion in the form of
art is by finding an 'objective correlative'; in other
words, a set of objects, a situation, a chain of
events which shall be the formula of that *particular*
emotion; such that when the external facts, which
must terminate in sensory experience, are given,
the emotion is immediately evoked.
The Sacred Wood (1920) 'Hamlet and his Problems'

28 Immature poets imitate; mature poets steal.
The Sacred Wood (1920) 'Philip Massinger'

29 Someone said: 'The dead writers are remote from
us because we *know* so much more than they did.'
Precisely, and they are that which we know.
The Sacred Wood (1920) 'Tradition and Individual Talent'

30 In the seventeenth century a dissociation of
sensibility set in, from which we have never
recovered; and this dissociation, as is natural, was
due to the influence of the two most powerful
poets of the century, Milton and Dryden.
Selected Essays (1932) 'The Metaphysical Poets' (1921)

31 Poets in our civilization, as it exists at present,
must be *difficult*.
Selected Essays (1932) 'The Metaphysical Poets' (1921)

1 To me . . . [*The Waste Land*] was only the relief of a personal and wholly insignificant grouse against life; it is just a piece of rhythmical grumbling.

The Waste Land (ed. Valerie Eliot, 1971) epigraph

Elizabeth I 1533–1603

English monarch, Queen of England and Ireland from 1558
on Elizabeth: see **Bible** *75:1; see also* **Bacon** *46:22,* **Last words** *471:2,* **Mottoes** *552:17*

2 This judgement I have of you that you will not be corrupted by any manner of gift and that you will be faithful to the state; and that without respect of my private will you will give me that counsel which you think best.

to William **Cecil***, appointing him her Secretary of State in 1558*

Conyers Read *Mr Secretary Cecil and Queen Elizabeth* (1955)

3 The queen of Scots is this day leichter of a fair son, and I am but a barren stock.

to her ladies, June 1566, in Sir James Melville *Memoirs of His Own Life* (1827 ed.)

4 I am your anointed Queen. I will never be by violence constrained to do anything. I thank God that I am endued with such qualities that if I were turned out of the Realm in my petticoat, I were able to live in any place in Christome.

speech to Members of Parliament, 5 November 1566, in J. E. Neale *Elizabeth I and her Parliaments 1559–1581* (1953) pt. 3, ch. 1

5 I know what it is to be a subject, what to be a Sovereign, what to have good neighbours, and sometimes meet evil-willers.

speech to a Parliamentary deputation at Richmond, 12 November 1586, in Sir John Neale *Elizabeth I and her Parliaments 1584–1601* (1957, from a report 'which the Queen herself heavily amended in her own hand'; see **Misquotations** 538:2

6 I will make you shorter by the head.

to the leaders of her Council, who were opposing her course towards **Mary** *Queen of Scots*

F. Chamberlin *Sayings of Queen Elizabeth* (1923)

7 I know I have the body of a weak and feeble woman, but I have the heart and stomach of a king, and of a king of England too; and think foul scorn that Parma or Spain, or any prince of Europe, should dare to invade the borders of my realm.

speech to the troops at Tilbury on the approach of the Armada, 1588, in Lord Somers *A Third Collection of Scarce and Valuable Tracts* (1751)

8 The daughter of debate, that eke discord doth sow.

on **Mary** *Queen of Scots*

George Puttenham (ed.) *The Art of English Poesie* (1589) bk. 3, ch. 20

9 My lord, we make use of you, not for your bad legs, but for your good head.

to William **Cecil***, who suffered from gout*

F. Chamberlin *Sayings of Queen Elizabeth* (1923)

10 I do entreat heaven daily for your longer life, else will my people and myself stand in need of cordials

too. My comfort hath been in my people's happiness and their happiness in thy discretion.

to William **Cecil** *on his death-bed, 1598*

F. Chamberlin *Sayings of Queen Elizabeth* (1923)

11 Though God hath raised me high, yet this I count the glory of my crown: that I have reigned with your loves.

The Golden Speech, 1601, in *The Journals of All the Parliaments . . . Collected by Sir Simonds D'Ewes* (1682)

12 God may pardon you, but I never can.

to the dying Countess of Nottingham, February 1603, for her part in the death of the Earl of **Essex***; the story is almost certainly apocryphal*

David Hume *The History of England under the House of Tudor* (1759) vol. 2, ch. 7

13 Must! Is *must* a word to be addressed to princes? Little man, little man! thy father, if he had been alive, durst not have used that word.

to Robert **Cecil***, on his saying she must go to bed, shortly before her death*

J. R. Green *A Short History of the English People* (1874) ch. 7; *Dodd's Church History of England* vol. 3 (ed. M. A. Tierney, 1840) adds: 'but thou knowest I must die, and that maketh thee so presumptuous'

14 If thy heart fails thee, climb not at all.

lines after Sir Walter **Ralegh***, written on a window-pane*

Thomas Fuller *Worthies of England* vol. 1; see **Ralegh** 641:10

15 I think that, at the worst, God has not yet ordained that England shall perish.

F. Chamberlin *Sayings of Queen Elizabeth* (1923)

16 I would not open windows into men's souls.

oral tradition, in J. B. Black *Reign of Elizabeth 1558–1603* (1936); the words very possibly originating in a letter drafted by **Bacon**

17 Like strawberry wives, that laid two or three great strawberries at the mouth of their pot, and all the rest were little ones.

describing the tactics of the Commission of Sales, in their dealings with her

Francis Bacon *Apophthegms New and Old* (1625) no. 54

18 Madam I may not call you; mistress I am ashamed to call you; and so I know not what to call you; but howsoever, I thank you.

to the wife of the Archbishop of Canterbury, the Queen disapproving of marriage among the clergy

Sir John Harington *A Brief View of the State of the Church of England* (1653)

19 My Lord, I had forgot the fart.

to Edward de Vere, Earl of **Oxford***, on his return from seven years self-imposed exile, occasioned by the acute embarrassment to himself of breaking wind in the presence of the Queen*

John Aubrey *Brief Lives* 'Edward de Vere'

20 'Twas God the word that spake it,
He took the bread and brake it;
And what the word did make it;
That I believe, and take it.

answer on being asked her opinion of Christ's presence in the Sacrament

S. Clarke *The Marrow of Ecclesiastical History* (1675) pt. 2, bk. 1 'The Life of Queen Elizabeth'

Elizabeth II 1926–

British monarch, Queen of the United Kingdom from 1952; daughter of **George VI** *and Queen* **Elizabeth** *the Queen Mother, mother of Prince* **Charles**

1 I declare before you all that my whole life, whether it be long or short, shall be devoted to your service and the service of our great Imperial family to which we all belong.
   broadcast speech, as Princess Elizabeth, to the Commonwealth from Cape Town, 21 April 1947, in *The Times* 22 April 1947

2 I think everybody really will concede that on this, of all days, I should begin my speech with the words 'My husband and I'.
   speech at Guildhall, London, on her 25th wedding anniversary
   in *The Times* 21 November 1972

3 In the words of one of my more sympathetic correspondents, it has turned out to be an 'annus horribilis'.
   speech at Guildhall, London, 24 November 1992

4 I for one believe that there are lessons to be drawn from her life and from the extraordinary and moving reaction to her death.
   broadcast from Buckingham Palace on the evening before the funeral of **Diana**, *Princess of Wales, 5 September 1997*
   in *The Times* 6 September 1997

5 I thank you also from the bottom of my heart for the love you gave her during her life and the honour you now give her in death.
   on Queen **Elizabeth** *the Queen Mother*
   televised address to the nation, 8 April 2002, in *Daily Telegraph* 9 April 2002

Queen Elizabeth, the Queen Mother 1900–2002

British Queen Consort of **George VI**, *mother of* **Elizabeth II**

6 I'm glad we've been bombed. It makes me feel I can look the East End in the face.
   to a London policeman, 13 September 1940
   John Wheeler-Bennett *King George VI* (1958) pt. 3, ch. 6

7 The Princesses would never leave without me and I couldn't leave without the King, and the King will never leave.
   on the suggestion that the royal family be evacuated during the Blitz
   Penelope Mortimer *Queen Elizabeth* (1986) ch. 25

8 How small and selfish is sorrow. But it bangs one about until one is senseless.
   letter to Edith **Sitwell**, *shortly after the death of* **George VI**
   Victoria Glendinning *Edith Sitwell* (1983) ch. 25

Elizabeth, Countess von Arnim 1866–1941

Australian-born British writer

9 Guests can be, and often are, delightful, but they should never be allowed to get the upper hand.
   All the Dogs in My Life (1936)

Alf Ellerton

British songwriter

10 Belgium put the kibosh on the Kaiser.
   title of song (1914)

John Ellerton 1826–93

English clergyman

11 The day Thou gavest, Lord, is ended,
   The darkness falls at Thy behest.
   Hymn (1870), the first line borrowed from an earlier, anonymous hymn

Duke Ellington 1899–1974

American jazz pianist, composer, and band-leader
see also **Mills** 527:14

12 Playing 'Bop' is like scrabble with all the vowels missing.
   in *Look* 10 August 1954

Emily Elizabeth Steele Elliot 1836–97

English hymn-writer

13 O come to my heart, Lord Jesus!
   There is room in my heart for thee.
   'Thou didst leave thy throne and thy kingly crown' (1870 hymn)

Jane Elliot 1727–1805

Scottish poet

14 I've heard them lilting, at the ewe milking,
   Lasses a' lilting, before dawn of day;
   But now they are moaning, on ilka green loaning;
   The flowers of the forest are a' wede away.
   'The Flowers of the Forest' (1769), the most popular version of the traditional lament for the Battle of Flodden in 1513; see **Cockburn** 229:20

Charlotte Elliott 1789–1871

English hymn-writer

15 Just as I am, without one plea
   But that Thy blood was shed for me,
   And that Thou bidd'st me come to Thee,
   O Lamb of God, I come!
   Invalid's Hymn Book (1834) 'Just as I am'

16 'Christian! seek not yet repose,'
   Hear thy guardian angel say;
   Thou art in the midst of foes—
   'Watch and pray.'
   Morning and Evening Hymns (1836) 'Christian! seek not yet repose'; see **Bible** 99:6

Ebenezer Elliott 1781–1849

English poet known as the 'Corn Law Rhymer'

17 What is a communist? One who hath yearnings
   For equal division of unequal earnings.
   'Epigram' (1850)

18 When wilt thou save the people?
   Oh, God of Mercy! when?
   The people, Lord, the people!

Not thrones and crowns, but men!
'The People's Anthem' (1850)

George Ellis 1753–1815

English poet and journalist

1 Snowy, Flowy, Blowy,
Showery, Flowery, Bowery,
Hoppy, Croppy, Droppy,
Breezy, Sneezy, Freezy.
'The Twelve Months'

Havelock Ellis (Henry Havelock Ellis)
1859–1939

English sexologist

2 What we call 'progress' is the exchange of one
nuisance for another nuisance.
Impressions and Comments (1914) 31 July 1912

3 All civilization has from time to time become a
thin crust over a volcano of revolution.
Little Essays of Love and Virtue (1922) ch. 7

Thomas Edward Ellis 1859–99

British Liberal politician and Welsh nationalist

4 Over and above all, we shall work for a
Legislature, elected by the manhood and
womanhood of Wales.
speech at Bala, 1890

Friar Elstow

English Franciscan

5 With thanks to God we know the way to heaven,
to be as ready by water as by land, and therefore
we care not which way we go.
when threatened with drowning by **Henry VIII**
John Stow *The Annals of England* (1615); see **Gilbert** 347:1

Paul Éluard 1895–1952

French poet

6 *L'espoir ne fait pas de poussière.*
Hope raises no dust.
'Ailleurs, ici, partout' (1946)

7 *Adieu tristesse*
Bonjour tristesse
Tu es inscrite dans les lignes du plafond.
Farewell sadness
Good-day sadness
You are inscribed in the lines of the ceiling.
'À peine défigurée' (1932)

Buchi Emecheta 1944–

Nigerian writer

8 I am a woman and a woman of Africa. I am a
daughter of Nigeria and if she is in shame, I shall
stay and mourn with her in shame.
Destination Biafra (1982)

9 The whole world seemed so unequal, so unfair.
Some people were created with all the good things
ready-made for them, others were just created like
mistakes. God's mistakes.
Second-Class Citizen (1974) ch.9

Ralph Waldo Emerson 1803–82

American philosopher and poet
see also **Clough** 229:13

10 If the red slayer think he slays,
Or if the slain think he is slain,
They know not well the subtle ways
I keep, and pass, and turn again.
'Brahma' (1867); see **Lang** 466:10, **Upanishads** 805:6

11 I am the doubter and the doubt.
'Brahma' (1867)

12 By the rude bridge that arched the flood,
Their flag to April's breeze unfurled,
Here once the embattled farmers stood,
And fired the shot heard round the world.
'Concord Hymn' (1837)

13 Things are in the saddle,
And ride mankind.
'Ode' inscribed to W. H. Channing (1847)

14 He builded better than he knew;—
The conscious stone to beauty grew.
'The Problem' (1847)

15 The frolic architecture of the snow.
'The Snowstorm' (1847)

16 When Duty whispers low, *Thou must*,
The youth replies, *I can*.
'Voluntaries' no. 3 (1867)

17 Make yourself necessary to someone.
The Conduct of Life (1860) 'Considerations by the way'

18 All sensible people are selfish, and nature is
tugging at every contract to make the terms of it
fair.
The Conduct of Life (1860) 'Considerations by the way'

19 Art is a jealous mistress.
The Conduct of Life (1860) 'Wealth'

20 The louder he talked of his honour, the faster we
counted our spoons.
The Conduct of Life (1860) 'Worship'; see **Johnson** 428:10,
Shaw 726:12

21 I feel in regard to this aged England . . . that she
sees a little better on a cloudy day, and that, in
storm of battle and calamity, she has a secret
vigour and a pulse like a cannon.
speech at Manchester, November 1847 in *English Traits*
(1883 ed.)

22 Nothing great was ever achieved without
enthusiasm.
Essays (1841) 'Circles'

23 The only reward of virtue is virtue; the only way
to have a friend is to be one.
Essays (1841) 'Friendship'

24 We need books of this tart cathartic virtue, more
than books of political science or of private
economy.
on **Plutarch**'s Lives
Essays (1841) 'Heroism'

1 It was a high counsel that I once heard given to a young person, 'Always do what you are afraid to do.'
Essays (1841) 'Heroism'

2 There is properly no history; only biography.
Essays (1841) 'History'; see **Disraeli** 277:7

3 In skating over thin ice, our safety is in our speed.
Essays (1841) 'Prudence'

4 Whoso would be a man must be a nonconformist.
Essays (1841) 'Self-Reliance'

5 A foolish consistency is the hobgoblin of little minds, adored by little statesmen and philosophers and divines. With consistency a great soul has simply nothing to do.
Essays (1841) 'Self-Reliance'

6 Is it so bad, then, to be misunderstood? Pythagoras was misunderstood, and Socrates, and Jesus, and Luther, and Copernicus, and Galileo, and Newton, and every pure and wise spirit that ever took flesh. To be great is to be misunderstood.
Essays (1841) 'Self-Reliance'

7 To fill the hour—that is happiness.
Essays. Second Series (1844) 'Experience'

8 Every man is wanted, and no man is wanted much.
Essays. Second Series (1844) 'Nominalist and Realist'

9 Language is fossil poetry.
Essays. Second Series (1844) 'The Poet'

10 What is a weed? A plant whose virtues have not been discovered.
Fortune of the Republic (1878)

11 Every hero becomes a bore at last.
Representative Men (1850) 'Uses of Great Men'

12 Hitch your wagon to a star.
Society and Solitude (1870) 'Civilization'

13 We boil at different degrees.
Society and Solitude (1870) 'Eloquence'

14 America is a country of young men.
Society and Solitude (1870) 'Old Age'

15 There never was a child so lovely but his mother was glad to get asleep.
Journal 1836

16 I hate quotations. Tell me what you know.
Journals and Miscellaneous Notebooks (1961) May 1849

17 Glittering generalities! They are blazing ubiquities.
*on Rufus **Choate***
attributed; see **Choate** 218:6

18 If a man write a better book, preach a better sermon, or make a better mouse-trap than his neighbour, tho' he build his house in the woods, the world will make a beaten path to his door.
attributed to Emerson in Sarah S. B. Yule *Borrowings* (1889); Mrs Yule states in *The Docket* February 1912 that she copied this in her handbook from a lecture delivered by Emerson; the quotation was the occasion of a long controversy owing to Elbert **Hubbard**'s claim to its authorship

Robert Emmet 1778–1803
Irish nationalist

19 Let no man write my epitaph . . . When my country takes her place among the nations of the earth, *then*, and *not till then*, let my epitaph be written.
speech from the dock when condemned to death, 19 September 1803

William Empson 1906–84
English poet and literary critic

20 There is a Supreme God in the ethnological section;
A hollow toad shape, faced with a blank shield.
He needs his belly to include the Pantheon,
Which is inserted through a hole behind.
'Homage to the British Museum' (1935)

21 Waiting for the end, boys, waiting for the end.
'Just a smack at Auden' (1940)

22 You don't want madhouse and the whole thing there.
'Let it Go' (1955)

23 Slowly the poison the whole blood stream fills.
It is not the effort nor the failure tires.
The waste remains, the waste remains and kills.
'Missing Dates' (1935)

24 The central function of imaginative literature is to make you realize that other people act on moral convictions different from your own.
Milton's God (1981) ch. 7

25 Seven types of ambiguity.
title of book (1930)

26 Learning French is some trouble, but after that you have a clear and beautiful language; in English the undergrowth is part of the language.
in *Spectator* 14 June 1935

Friedrich Engels 1820–95
*German socialist; founder, with Karl **Marx**, of modern Communism*
*see also **Marx and Engels***

27 *Der Staat wird nicht 'abgeschafft', er stirbt ab.*
The State is not 'abolished', *it withers away.*
Anti-Dühring (1878) pt. 3, ch. 2

28 Naturally, the workers are perfectly free; the manufacturer does not force them to take his materials and his cards, but he says to them . . . 'If you don't like to be frizzled in my frying-pan, you can take a walk into the fire'.
The Condition of the Working Class in England in 1844 (1892) ch. 7

Thomas Dunn English 1819–1902
American physician, lawyer, and writer

29 Oh! don't you remember sweet Alice, Ben Bolt,
Sweet Alice, whose hair was so brown,
Who wept with delight when you gave her a smile,

And trembled with fear at your frown?
'Ben Bolt' (1885)

Ennius 239–169 BC

Roman writer
on Ennius: see Horace 403:8

1 *O Tite tute Tati tibi tanta tyranne tulisti!*

O tyrant Titus Tatius, what a lot you brought
upon yourself!
*Annals bk. 1 (l. 104 in O. Skutsch (ed.) Annals of Q. Ennius,
1985)*

2 *Moribus antiquis res stat Romana virisque.*

The Roman state survives by its ancient customs
and its manhood.
*Annals bk. 5 (l. 156 in O. Skutsch (ed.) Annals of Q. Ennius,
1985)*

3 *Unus homo nobis cunctando restituit rem.*

One man by delaying put the state to rights for us.
*referring to the Roman general Fabius Cunctator ('The
Delayer')*
*Annals bk. 12 (l. 363 in O. Skutsch (ed.) Annals of Q.
Ennius, 1985)*

4 *At tuba terribili sonitu taratantara dixit.*

And the trumpet in terrible tones went
taratantara.
*Annals (l. 451 in O. Skutsch (ed.) Annals of Q. Ennius,
1985)*

Ephelia

English 17th-century poet

5 And yet I love this false, this worthless man,
With all the passion that a woman can;
Dote on his imperfections, though I spy
Nothing to love; I love, and know not why.
*Female Poems (1679) 'To one that asked me why I loved
J.G.'*

Nora Ephron 1941–

American screenwriter and director
see also Film lines 319:17

6 The anecdote is a particularly dehumanising sort
of descriptive narrative.
Scribble, Scribble (1978)

Epictetus C.AD 50–120

Phrygian Stoic philosopher

7 Everything has two handles, by one of which it
ought to be carried and by the other not.
The Encheiridion sect. 43

Epicurus 341–271 BC

Greek philosopher

8 Death, therefore, the most awful of evils, is
nothing to us, seeing that, when we are death is
not come, and when death is come, we are not.
Diogenes Laertius Lives of Eminent Philosophers bk. 10

☐ Epitaphs

see box opposite
see also Cather 199:11, Spenser 751:21

Jacob Epstein 1880–1959

British sculptor
on Epstein: see Anonymous 16:3, Anonymous 16:16

9 Why don't they stick to murder and leave art to
us?
*on hearing that his statue of Lazarus in New College
chapel, Oxford, kept Khrushchev awake at night*
attributed

Olaudah Equiano c.1745–c.97

African writer and former slave

10 We are . . . a nation of dancers, singers and poets.
of the Ibo people
Narrative of the Life of Olaudah Equiano (1789) ch. 1

11 When I recovered a little I found some black
people about me . . . I asked them if we were not
to be eaten by those white men with horrible
looks, red faces, and loose hair.
Narrative of the Life of Olaudah Equiano (1789) ch. 3

Erasmus (Desiderius Erasmus) c.1469–1536

Dutch Christian humanist

12 *In regione caecorum rex est luscus.*
In the country of the blind the one-eyed man is
king.
Adages bk. 3, century 4, no. 96; see Proverbs 623:34

Ludwig Erhard 1897–1977

German statesman, Chancellor of West Germany (1963–6)

13 Without Britain Europe would remain only a
torso.
*remark on West German television, 27 May 1962; in The
Times 28 May 1962*

Susan Ertz 1894–1985

American writer

14 Millions long for immortality who don't know
what to do with themselves on a rainy Sunday
afternoon.
Anger in the Sky (1943)

Lord Esher 1913–

English architect and planner

15 When politicians and civil servants hear the word
'culture' they feel for their blue pencils.
speech, House of Lords, 2 March 1960; see Johst 434:1

Phil Esposito 1942–

Canadian ice-hockey player

16 This was more emotional than winning the
Stanley Cup. A Stanley Cup's for your team and
your city, but beating Russia is for your country.
*on Team Canada beating the USSR in ice hockey in
1972*
in Globe and Mail 2 October 1972

Epitaphs

1   The body of
Benjamin Franklin, printer,
(Like the cover of an old book,
Its contents worn out,
And stripped of its lettering and gilding)
Lies here, food for worms!
Yet the work itself shall not be lost,
For it will, as he believed, appear once more
In a new
And more beautiful edition,
Corrected and amended
By its Author!

> Benjamin **Franklin**'s epitaph for himself (1728); see
> **Turgot** 802:13

2 Commander Jacques-Yves Cousteau has rejoined
the world of silence.

> *announcement by the Cousteau Foundation, Paris,*
> *25 June 1997;* **Cousteau** *(1910–97) published* The
> Silent World *in 1953*
>
> in *Daily Telegraph* 26 June 1997

3 *Et in Arcadia ego.*

And I too in Arcadia.

> tomb inscription, of disputed meaning, often depicted in
> classical paintings, notably by **Poussin** in 1655; E.
> Panofsky 'Et in Arcadia ego' in R. K. Klibansky and H. J.
> Paton (eds.) *Philosophy and History: Essays Presented to E.*
> *Cassirer* (1936)

4 Excuse my dust.

> *Dorothy* **Parker** *(1893–1967); suggested epitaph*
> *for herself (1925)*
>
> Alexander Woollcott *While Rome Burns* (1934) 'Our Mrs
> Parker'

5 *Ex umbris et imaginibus in veritatem.*

From shadows and types to the reality.

> *John Henry* **Newman** *(1801–90)*
>
> motto on his memorial tablet, in Owen Chadwick
> *Newman* (1983)

6 Farewell, great painter of mankind!
Who reached the noblest point of art,
Whose pictured morals charm the mind
And through the eye correct the heart.

> *epitaph on William Hogarth (1697–1764)*
>
> monument in Chiswick churchyard (1772), by David
> **Garrick**

7 Free at last, free at last
Thank God almighty
We are free at last.

> *epitaph of Martin Luther* **King** *(1929–68), Atlanta,*
> *Georgia*
>
> anonymous spiritual, with which he ended his 'I have a
> dream' speech; see **King** 452:4

8 From Moses to Moses there was none like unto
Moses.

> later inscription on the tomb of the Jewish scholar Moses
> **Maimonides** (1135–1204)

9 God damn you all: I told you so.

> *H. G.* **Wells**' *suggestion for his own epitaph, in*
> *conversation with Ernest Barker, 1939*
>
> Ernest Barker *Age and Youth* (1953)

10 Good friend, for Jesu's sake forbear
To dig the dust enclosed here.
Blest be the man that spares these stones,
And curst be he that moves my bones.

> *William* **Shakespeare** *(1564–1616)*
>
> inscription on his grave, Stratford upon Avon, probably
> composed by himself

11 Go, tell the Spartans, thou who passest by,
That here obedient to their laws we lie.

> *epitaph for the 300 Spartans killed at Thermopylae,*
> *480 BC*
>
> attributed to **Simonides**; Herodotus *Histories* bk. 7, ch.
> 228

12 Hereabouts died a very gallant gentleman,
Captain L. E. G. Oates of the Inniskilling
Dragoons. In March 1912, returning from the
Pole, he walked willingly to his death in a
blizzard to try and save his comrades, beset by
hardships.

> *epitaph on cairn erected in the Antarctic, 15*
> *November 1912, by E. L. Atkinson (1882–1929)*
> *and Apsley Cherry-Garrard (1882–1959)*
>
> Apsley Cherry-Garrard *The Worst Journey in the World*
> (1922); see **Last words** 472:2

13 Here lie I, Martin Elginbrodde:
Hae mercy o' my soul, Lord God;
As I wad do, were I Lord God,
And ye were Martin Elginbrodde.

> George MacDonald *David Elginbrod* (1863) bk. 1, ch. 13

14 Here lies a great and mighty king
Whose promise none relies on;
He never said a foolish thing,
Nor ever did a wise one.

> *of* **Charles II** *(1630–85); an alternative first line*
> *reads: 'Here lies our sovereign lord the King'*
>
> John Wilmot, Earl of Rochester 'The King's Epitaph'; in
> C. E. Doble et al. *Thomas Hearne: Remarks and Collections*
> (1885–1921) 17 November 1706; see **Charles II** 209:11

15 Here lies a poor woman who always was tired,
For she lived in a place where help wasn't hired.
Her last words on earth were, Dear friends I am
going
Where washing ain't done nor sweeping nor
sewing,
And everything there is exact to my wishes,
For there they don't eat and there's no washing
of dishes . . .
Don't mourn for me now, don't mourn for me
never,
For I'm going to do nothing for ever and ever.

> epitaph in Bushey churchyard, before 1860; destroyed
> by 1916

▶

▶ Epitaphs *continued*

1 Here lies a valiant warrior
Who never drew a sword;
Here lies a noble courtier
Who never kept his word;
Here lies the Earl of Leicester
Who governed the estates
Whom the earth could never living love,
And the just heaven now hates.
of Robert Dudley, Earl of Leicester (c.1532–88)
> attributed to Ben **Jonson** in Silvester Tissington *A Collection of Epitaphs and Monumental Inscriptions* (1857)

2 Here lies Fred,
Who was alive and is dead:
Had it been his father,
I had much rather;
Had it been his brother,
Still better than another;
Had it been his sister,
No one would have missed her;
Had it been the whole generation,
Still better for the nation:
But since 'tis only Fred,
Who was alive and is dead,—
There's no more to be said.
*of Frederick Louis, Prince of Wales (1707–1751),
son of **George II** and **Caroline** of Ansbach*
> in Horace Walpole *Memoirs of George II* (1847) vol. 1

3 Here lies Groucho Marx—and lies and lies and lies. P.S. He never kissed an ugly girl.
his own suggestion for his epitaph
> B. Norman *The Movie Greats* (1981)

4 Here lies one whose name was writ in water.
*epitaph for himself by John **Keats** (1795–1821)*
> Richard Monckton Milnes *Life, Letters and Literary Remains of John Keats* (1848) vol. 2; see **Shakespeare** 695:20

5 Here lies that peerless paper peer Lord Peter,
Who broke the laws of God and man and metre.
*epitaph for Patrick ('Peter'), Lord Robertson
(1794–1855) by John Gibson **Lockhart***
> *The Journal of Sir Walter Scott* (1890) vol. 1

6 Here lies W. C. Fields. I would rather be living in Philadelphia.
> W. C. **Fields**' suggested epitaph for himself, in *Vanity Fair* June 1925

7 Here lies wise and valiant dust,
Huddled up, 'twixt fit and just:
Strafford, who was hurried hence
'Twixt treason and convenience.
He spent his time here in a mist,
A Papist, yet a Calvinist . . .
Riddles lie here, or in a word,
Here lies blood; and let it lie
Speechless still, and never cry.
> John **Cleveland** (1613–58) 'Epitaph on the Earl of Strafford' (1647)

8 Here Skugg
Lies snug
As a bug
In a rug.
letter to Georgiana Shipley on the death of her squirrel, 26 September 1772; skugg = squirrel
> Benjamin **Franklin**, in W. B. Willcox (ed.) *Papers of Benjamin Franklin* vol. 19 (1975)

9 He was an average guy who could carry a tune.
*Bing **Crosby**'s suggested epitaph for himself*
> in *Newsweek* 24 October 1977

10 His foe was folly and his weapon wit.
*W. S. **Gilbert** (1836–1911)*
> inscription by Anthony **Hope** on memorial on the Victoria Embankment, London, 1915

11 I will return. And I will be millions.
> inscription on the tomb of Eva **Perón** (1919–52), Buenos Aires

12 John Le Mesurier wishes it to be known that he conked out on November 15th. He sadly misses family and friends.
> obituary notice on the death of John Le Mesurier (1912–83), in *The Times* 16 November 1983

13 Life is a jest; and all things show it.
I thought so once; but now I know it.
*John **Gay** (1685–1732)*
> 'My Own Epitaph' (1720)

14 Long night succeeds thy little day
Oh blighted blossom! can it be,
That this grey stone and grassy clay
Have closed our anxious care of thee?
*Thomas Love **Peacock**'s epitaph on his daughter Margaret, who died at the age of three*
> H. Cole (ed.) *Works of Peacock* (1875)

15 Love made me poet,
And this I writ;
My heart did do it,
And not my wit.
> Elizabeth, Lady Tanfield (c.1565–1628); epitaph for her husband, in Burford Parish Church, Oxfordshire

16 My friend, judge not me,
Thou seest I judge not thee.
Betwixt the stirrup and the ground
Mercy I asked, mercy I found.
epitaph for 'A gentleman falling off his horse [who] brake his neck'
> William Camden *Remains Concerning Britain* (1605) 'Epitaphs'

17 My sledge and anvil lie declined
My bellows too have lost their wind
My fire's extinct, my forge decayed,
And in the dust my vice is laid
My coals are spent, my iron's gone

▶

▶ **Epitaphs** *continued*

My nails are drove, my work is done.
blacksmith's epitaph

in Nettlebed churchyard, commemorating William
Strange, d. 6 June 1746

1 *Olivarii Goldsmith,*
Poetae, Physici, Historici,
Qui nullum fere scribendi genus
Non tetigit,
Nullum quod tetigit non ornavit.

To Oliver Goldsmith, A Poet, Naturalist, and
Historian, who left scarcely any style of writing
untouched, and touched none that he did not
adorn.

epitaph on **Goldsmith** *(1728–74) by Samuel*
Johnson

James Boswell *Life of Samuel Johnson* (1791) 22 June
1776

2 O rare Ben Jonson.

inscription on the tomb of Ben **Jonson** in Westminster
Abbey

3 Poor G.K.C., his day is past—
Now God will know the truth at last.

mock epitaph for G. K. **Chesterton**, *by E. V. Lucas*
(1868–1938)

Dudley Barker *G. K. Chesterton* (1973)

4 Rest in peace. The mistake shall not be repeated.

inscription on the cenotaph at Hiroshima, Japan

5 She did it the hard way.

epitaph of Bette Davis (1908–89), chosen by herself

James Spada *More Than a Woman* (1993)

6 *Si monumentum requiris, circumspice.*

If you seek a monument, gaze around.

inscription in St Paul's Cathedral, London, attributed to
the son of Sir Christopher Wren (1632–1723), its
architect; see **Barham** 55:12

7 A soldier of the Great War known unto God.

standard epitaph for the unidentified dead of World
War One

adopted by the War Graves Commission

8 Their name liveth for evermore.

standard inscription on the Stone of Sacrifice in each
military cemetery of World War One, proposed by
Rudyard **Kipling** *as a member of the War Graves*
Commission

Charles Carrington *Rudyard Kipling* (rev. ed. 1978); see
Bible 93:34, **Sassoon** 667:23

9 Timothy has passed . . .

message on his Internet web page announcing the
death of Timothy **Leary**, 31 May 1996

in *Guardian* 1 June 1996

10 *Ubi saeva indignatio ulterius cor lacerare nequit.*

Where fierce indignation can no longer tear his
heart.

Jonathan **Swift** (1667–1745)

Shane Leslie *The Skull of Swift* (1928) ch. 15; see **Yeats**
855:22

11 Underneath this sable hearse
Lies the subject of all verse;
Sidney's sister, Pembroke's mother,
Death, ere thou hast slain another,
Fair and learn'd, and good as she,
Time shall throw a dart at thee.

William Browne (*c.*1590–1643) 'Epitaph on the
Countess Dowager of Pembroke' (1623)

12 Under this stone, Reader, survey
Dead Sir John Vanbrugh's house of clay.
Lie heavy on him, Earth! for he
Laid many heavy loads on thee!

Abel Evans (1679–1737) 'Epitaph on Sir John
Vanbrugh, Architect of Blenheim Palace'

13 We must know,
We will know.

David **Hilbert** (1862–1943)

epitaph on his tombstone, Göttingen; Constance Reid
Hilbert (1970) ch. 25

14 Were there but a few hearts and intellects like
hers this earth would already become the hoped-
for heaven.

epitaph (1859) inscribed by John Stuart **Mill** *on the*
tomb of his wife, Harriet (d. 1858), at the cemetery
of St Véran, near Avignon

M. St J. Packe *Life of John Stuart Mill* (1954) bk. 7, ch. 3

15 What Cato did, and Addison approved,
Cannot be wrong.

lines found on the desk of Eustace Budgell
(1686–1737), after he, too, had taken his own life

Colley Cibber *Lives of the Poets* (1753) vol. 5 'Life of
Eustace Budgell'

16 What wee gave, wee have;
What wee spent, wee had;
What wee kept, wee lost.

epitaph on Edward Courtenay, Earl of Devonshire
(d. 1419) and his wife

at Tiverton, in Thomas Westcote *A View of Devonshire in*
1630 (ed. G. Oliver and P. Jones, 1845); variants appear
in Tristram Risdon *Survey of the County of Devon* (1714)
and Edmund Spenser *The Shepherd's Calendar* (1579)

17 When you go home, tell them of us and say,
'For your tomorrow we gave our today.'

Kohima memorial to the Burma campaign of the Second
World War; in recent years used at Remembrance Day
parades in the UK; see **Binyon** 116:14

When you go home, tell them of us and say,
'For your tomorrows these gave their today.'

John Maxwell Edmonds (1875–1958) *Inscriptions*
Suggested for War Memorials (1919)

18 Without you, Heaven would be too dull to bear,
And Hell would not be Hell if you are there.

epitaph for Maurice **Bowra**

John **Sparrow**, in *Times Literary Supplement* 30 May 1975

Robert Devereux, Earl of Essex
1566–1601

English soldier and courtier, executed for treason

1 Reasons are not like garments, the worse for wearing.

> letter to Lord Willoughby, 4 January 1599, in *Notes and Queries* 10th Series, vol. 2 (1904)

Henri Estienne 1531–98

French printer and publisher

2 *Si jeunesse savait; si vieillesse pouvait.*

If youth knew; if age could.

> *Les Prémices* (1594) bk. 4, epigram 4

George Etherege c.1635–91

English dramatist

3 I walk within the purlieus of the Law.

> *Love in a Tub* (1664) act 1, sc. 3; see **Tennyson** 779:17

4 When love grows diseased, the best thing we can do is put it to a violent death; I cannot endure the torture of a lingering and consumptive passion.

> *The Man of Mode* (1676) act 2, sc. 2

5 Writing, Madam, 's a mechanic part of wit! A gentleman should never go beyond a song or a billet.

> *The Man of Mode* (1676) act 4, sc. 1

6 Fear not, though love and beauty fail,
My reason shall my heart direct:
Your kindness now will then prevail,
And passion turn into respect:
Chloris, at worst, you'll in the end
But change your Lover for a friend.

> *New Academy of Compliments* (1671) 'Chloris, 'tis not in your power'

Euclid fl. c.300 BC

Greek mathematician

7 *Quod erat demonstrandum.*

Which was to be proved.

often abbreviated to QED

> Latin translation from the Greek of *Elementa* bk. 1, proposition 5 and *passim*

8 A line is length without breadth.

> *Elementa* bk. 1, definition 2

9 There is no 'royal road' to geometry.

> addressed to Ptolemy I, in Proclus *Commentary on the First Book of Euclid's Elementa* prologue, pt. 2; see **Proverbs** 632:18

Infanta Eulalia of Spain 1864–1958

Spanish princess

10 We could not go anywhere without sending word ahead so that life might be put on parade for us.

> *Court Life from Within* (1915)

Euripides c.485–c.406 BC

Greek dramatist

*on Euripides: see **Aristotle** 25:24*

11 Never shall I say that marriage brings more joy than pain.

> *Alcestis* l. 238

12 Be happy, drink, think each day your own as you live it and leave the rest to fortune.

> *Alcestis* l. 788

13 Nothing have I found stronger than Necessity.

> *Alcestis* l. 965

14 Mere cleverness is not wisdom.

> *Bacchae* l. 395

15 The divine will manifests itself in many forms,
and the gods bring many things to pass against
    our expectations.
What we thought would happen remains
    unfulfilled,
while the god has found a way to accomplish the
    unexpected.
And that is what has happened here.

> *Bacchae* l. 1388; the same lines conclude Euripides' plays *Alcestis*, *Andromache*, and *Helen*

16 What we know and understand to be noble we fail to carry out, some from laziness, others because they give precedence to some other pleasure than honour.

> *Hippolytus* l. 380

17 My tongue swore, but my mind's unsworn.

> *Hippolytus lamenting his breaking of an oath*
> *Hippolytus* l. 612

18 Better a life of wretchedness than a noble death.

> *Iphigenia in Tauris* l. 1252

19 Men say of us that we live a life free from danger at home while they fight wars. How wrong they are! I would rather stand three times in the battle line than bear one child.

> *Medea* l. 247

20 When passions come upon men in strength beyond due measure their gift is neither one of glory nor of greatness.

> *Medea* l. 627

21 May temperance befriend me,
the gods' most lovely gift.

> *Medea* l. 636

22 The man is to be envied who has been fortunate in his children, and has avoided dire calamity.

> *Orestes* l. 542

23 You mention a slave's condition; not to say what one thinks.

> *The Phoenician Women* l. 392

24 Man's best possession is a sympathetic wife.

> fragment no. 164; Augustus Nauck *Tragicorum Graecorum Fragmenta*

John Evelyn 1620–1706
English diarist

1 This knight was indeed a valiant Gent: but not a
little given to romance, when he spake of himself.
E. S. de Beer (ed.) *Diary of John Evelyn* (1955) 6 September
1651

2 Mulberry Garden, now the only place of
refreshment about the town for persons of the best
quality to be exceedingly cheated at.
E. S. de Beer (ed.) *Diary of John Evelyn* (1955) 10 May 1654

3 That miracle of a youth, Mr Christopher Wren.
E. S. de Beer (ed.) *Diary of John Evelyn* (1955) 11 July 1654

4 I saw Hamlet Prince of Denmark played, but now
the old play began to disgust this refined age.
E. S. de Beer (ed.) *Diary of John Evelyn* (1955) 26 November
1661

Lord Eversley see Charles Shaw-Lefevre

Gavin Ewart 1916–95
British poet

5 So the last date slides into the bracket,
that will appear in all future anthologies—
And in quiet Cornwall and in London's ghastly
racket
We are now Betjemanless.
'In Memoriam, Sir John Betjeman (1906–84)' (1985)

6 The path of true love isn't smooth,
the ruffled feathers sex can soothe
ruffle again—for couples never
spend all their lives in bed together.
'24th March 1986' (1987)

7 Is it Colman's smile
That makes life worth while
Or Crawford's significant form?
Is it Lombard's lips
Or Mae West's hips
That carry you through the storm?
'Verse from an Opera' (1939)

William Norman Ewer 1885–1976
British writer

8 I gave my life for freedom—This I know:
For those who bade me fight had told me so.
'Five Souls' (1917)

9 How odd
Of God
To choose
The Jews.
Week-End Book (1924); see **Browne** 155:14

Winifred Ewing 1929–
Scottish Nationalist politician

10 The Scottish Parliament which adjourned on 25
March in the year 1707 is hereby reconvened.
*opening speech, as oldest member of the new
Parliament*
in *Scottish Parliament* 12 May 1999

Richard Eyre 1943–
English theatre director

11 We exercise the ultimate sanction of switching off
only in an extreme case, like a heroin addict
rejecting the needle in the face of death.
on television as an agent of cultural destruction
attributed, 1995

Frederick William Faber 1814–63
English priest

12 Faith of our Fathers! living still
In spite of dungeon, fire, and sword:
Oh, how our hearts beat fast with joy
Whene'er they hear that glorious word.
Faith of our Fathers! Holy Faith!
We will be true to thee till death.
'Faith of our Fathers'

13 Faith of our Fathers! Mary's prayers
Shall win our country back to thee
And by the truth that comes from God
England shall then indeed be free.
'Faith of our Fathers'

14 My God, how wonderful Thou art!
Thy Majesty how bright!
Oratory Hymns (1854) 'The Eternal Father'

15 The music of the Gospel leads us home.
Oratory Hymns (1854) 'The Pilgrims of the Night'

16 There's a wideness in God's mercy
Like the wideness of the sea.
Oratory Hymns (1854) 'Souls of men, why will ye scatter'

17 Dark night hath come down on us, Mother!
and we
Look out for thy shining, sweet Star of the Sea!
'O Purest of Creatures'

Quintus Fabius Maximus c.275–203 BC
Roman politician and general

18 To be turned from one's course by men's opinions,
by blame, and by misrepresentation shows a man
unfit to hold an office.
Plutarch *Parallel Lives* 'Fabius Maximus'

Robert Fabyan d. 1513
English chronicler

19 Finally he paid the debt of nature.
The New Chronicles of England and France (1516) vol. 1,
ch. 41

20 King Henry [I] being in Normandy, after some
writers, fell from or with his horse, whereof he
caught his death; but Ranulphe says he took a
surfeit by eating of a lamprey, and thereof died.
The New Chronicles of England and France (1516) vol. 1,
ch. 229

1 The Duke of Clarence . . . then being a prisoner in the Tower, was secretly put to death and drowned in a barrel of Malmesey wine within the said Tower.

> *The New Chronicles of England and France* (1516) vol. 2 '1478'; 'malvesye' for 'malmesey' in early editions

Clifton Fadiman 1904-

American critic

2 Milk's leap toward immortality.

> *of cheese*
> *Any Number Can Play* (1957)

3 The mama of dada.

> *of Gertrude* **Stein**
> *Party of One* (1955)

Émile Faguet 1847–1916

French writer and critic

4 It would be equally reasonable to say that sheep are born carnivorous, and everywhere nibble grass.

> *in response to Rousseau (see* **Rousseau** *657:4)*
> paraphrasing Joseph de Maistre; *Politiques et Moralistes du Dix-Neuvième Siècle* (1899)

Thomas Fairfax 1621–71

English Parliamentary general

5 Human probabilities are not sufficient grounds to make war upon a neighbour nation.

> *in 1650, refusing to lead an invasion of Scotland after the proclamation there of* **Charles II** *as king*
> in *Dictionary of National Biography* (1917–)

Marianne Faithfull 1946-

British singer

6 Maybe the most that you can expect from a relationship that goes bad is to come out of it with a few good songs.

> *Faithfull* (1994) 'Colston Hall'

Lucius Cary, Lord Falkland 1610–43

English royalist politician
on Falkland: see **Clarendon** *224:17,* **Clarendon** *224:18*

7 When it is not necessary to change, it is necessary not to change.

> *Discourses of Infallibility* (1660) 'A Speech concerning Episcopacy' delivered in 1641

Frantz Fanon 1925–61

French West Indian psychoanalyst and writer

8 Leave this Europe where they are never done talking of Man, yet murder men everywhere they find them.

> *The Wretched of the Earth* (1961)

9 The shape of Africa resembles a revolver, and Zaire is the trigger.

> attributed

Richard Fanshawe 1605–66

English diplomat and translator

10 Ten years the world upon him falsely smiled,
Sheathing in fawning looks the deadly knife
Long aimed at his head; that so beguiled
It more securely might bereave his life:
Then threw him to a scaffold from a throne.
Much doctrine lies under this little stone.

> *The Faithful Shepherd* (1648) 'The Fall'; translation of G. B. Guarini's *Il pastor fido,* 1589

11 White Peace (the beautiful'st of things)
Seems here her everlasting rest
To fix, and spreads her downy wings over the nest.

> *The Faithful Shepherd* (1648) 'An Ode, upon occasion of His Majesty's Proclamation in the Year 1630'

U. A. Fanthorpe 1929-

English poet

12 There is a kind of love called maintenance,
Which stores the WD40 and knows when to use it.

> 'Atlas' (1995)

13 Most of life's problems can be solved
By running fast and kicking something.

> 'Autumn Offer' (2000)

14 Now, children, the poet. He is less exciting.
All he brandishes is a ball-point,
Which he plays with on unastonishing paper.

> 'Painter and Poet' (1995)

Michael Faraday 1791–1867

English physicist and chemist

15 The most prominent requisite to a lecturer, though perhaps not really the most important, is a good delivery; for though to all true philosophers science and nature will have charms innumerable in every dress, yet I am sorry to say that the generality of mankind cannot accompany us one short hour unless the path is strewed with flowers.

> *Advice to a Lecturer* (1960); from his letters and notebook written at age 21

16 Nothing is too wonderful to be true, if it be consistent with the laws of nature, and in such things as these, experiment is the best test of such consistency.

> diary, 19 March 1849; *Faraday's Diary* (1934 ed.) vol. 5

17 Tyndall, I must remain plain Michael Faraday to the last; and let me now tell you, that if I accepted the honour which the Royal Society desires to confer upon me, I would not answer for the integrity of my intellect for a single year.

> *on being offered the Presidency of the Royal Society*
> J. Tyndall *Faraday as a Discoverer* (1868) 'Illustrations of Character'

18 Why sir, there is every possibility that you will soon be able to tax it!

> *to* **Gladstone**, *when asked about the usefulness of electricity*
> W. E. H. Lecky *Democracy and Liberty* (1899 ed.)

Wallace Fard c.1891–1934

American religious leader, founder of the Nation of Islam

1 The blue-eyed devil white man.
  Malcolm X with Alex Haley *The Autobiography of Malcolm X* (1965); see **Malcolm X** 508:9

Eleanor Farjeon 1881–1965

English writer for children

2 Morning has broken
  Like the first morning,
  Blackbird has spoken
  Like the first bird.
  Children's Bells (1957) 'A Morning Song (for the First Day of Spring)'

Herbert Farjeon 1887–1945

English writer and theatre critic

3 For I've danced with a man.
  I've danced with a man
  Who—well, you'll never guess.
  I've danced with a man who's danced with a girl
  Who's danced with the Prince of Wales!
  'I've danced with a man who's danced with a girl'; first written for Elsa Lanchester and sung at private parties; later sung on stage by Mimi Crawford (1928)

James Farley 1888–1976

American Democratic politician

4 As Maine goes, so goes Vermont.
  after predicting correctly that Franklin Roosevelt would carry all but two states in the election of 1936; see **Political slogans** 600:4
  statement to the press, 4 November 1936

Edward Farmer c.1809–76

English poet

5 I have no pain, dear mother, now;
  But oh! I am so dry:
  Just moisten poor Jim's lips once more;
  And, mother, do not cry!
  'The Collier's Dying Child'; see **Anonymous** 16:17

Farouk 1920–65

Egyptian monarch, King 1936–52

6 The whole world is in revolt. Soon there will be only five Kings left—the King of England, the King of Spades, the King of Clubs, the King of Hearts and the King of Diamonds.
  said to Lord Boyd-Orr at a conference in Cairo, 1948; *As I Recall* (1966) ch. 21

George Farquhar 1678–1707

Irish dramatist

7 I have fed purely upon ale; I have eat my ale, drank my ale, and I always sleep upon ale.
  The Beaux' Stratagem (1707) act 1, sc. 1

8 My Lady Bountiful.
  The Beaux' Stratagem (1707) act 1, sc. 1

9 There is no scandal like rags, nor any crime so shameful as poverty.
  The Beaux' Stratagem (1707) act 1, sc. 1

10 There's some diversion in a talking blockhead; and since a woman must wear chains, I would have the pleasure of hearing 'em rattle a little.
  The Beaux' Stratagem (1707) act 2, sc. 2

11 No woman can be a beauty without a fortune.
  The Beaux' Stratagem (1707) act 2, sc. 2

12 I believe they talked of me, for they laughed consumedly.
  The Beaux' Stratagem (1707) act 3, sc. 1

13 'Twas for the good of my country that I should be abroad.—Anything for the good of one's country—I'm a Roman for that.
  The Beaux' Stratagem (1707) act 3, sc. 2

14 AIMWELL: Then you understand Latin, Mr Bonniface?
  BONNIFACE: Not I, Sir, as the saying is, but he talks it so very fast that I'm sure it must be good.
  The Beaux' Stratagem (1707) act 3, sc. 2

15 Spare all I have, and take my life.
  The Beaux' Stratagem (1707) act 5, sc. 2

16 I hate all that don't love me, and slight all that do.
  The Constant Couple (1699) act 1, sc. 2

17 Grant me some wild expressions, Heavens, or I shall burst— . . . Words, words or I shall burst.
  The Constant Couple (1699) act 5, sc. 3

18 Charming women can true converts make,
  We love the precepts for the teacher's sake.
  The Constant Couple (1699) act 5, sc. 3; see **Defoe** 261:17

19 Crimes, like virtues, are their own rewards.
  The Inconstant (1702) act 4, sc. 2

20 Money is the sinews of love, as of war.
  Love and a Bottle (1698) act 2, sc. 1; see **Cicero** 223:20

21 Poetry's a mere drug, Sir.
  Love and a Bottle (1698) act 3, sc. 2; see **Lowell** 493:18

22 Hanging and marriage, you know, go by Destiny
  The Recruiting Officer (1706) act 3, sc. 2

23 I could be mighty foolish, and fancy my self mighty witty; Reason still keeps its throne, but it nods a little, that's all.
  The Recruiting Officer (1706) act 3, sc. 2

24 I'm privileged to be very impertinent, being an Oxonian.
  Sir Harry Wildair (1701) act 2, sc. 1

25 A lady, if undressed at Church, looks silly,
  One cannot be devout in dishabilly.
  The Stage Coach (1704) prologue

David Glasgow Farragut 1801–70

American admiral

26 Damn the torpedoes! Full speed ahead.
  at the battle of Mobile Bay, 5 August 1864 (torpedoes = mines)
  A. T. Mahan *Great Commanders: Admiral Farragut* (1892) ch. 10

William Faulkner 1897–1962

American novelist
see also **Film titles** 322:7

1 The past is never dead. It's not even past.
   Requiem for a Nun (1951) act 1

2 Maybe the only thing worse than having to give
   gratitude constantly all the time, is having to
   accept it.
   Requiem for a Nun (1951) act 2, sc. 1

3 He made the books and he died.
   his own 'sum and history of my life'
   letter to Malcolm Cowley, 11 February 1949

4 I believe man will not merely endure, he will
   prevail. He is immortal, not because he, alone
   among creatures, has an inexhaustible voice but
   because he has a soul, a spirit capable of
   compassion and sacrifice and endurance.
   Nobel Prize acceptance speech, Stockholm, 10 December
   1950

5 The writer's only responsibility is to his art. He
   will be completely ruthless if he is a good one. He
   has a dream. It anguishes him so much he must
   get rid of it. He has no peace until then.
   Everything goes by the board . . . If a writer has to
   rob his mother, he will not hesitate; the *Ode on a
   Grecian Urn* is worth any number of old ladies.
   in *Paris Review* Spring 1956

6 A man shouldn't fool with booze until he's fifty;
   then he's a damn fool if he doesn't.
   James M. Webb and A. Wigfall Green *William Faulkner of
   Oxford* (1965)

John Fawcett 1740–1817

English Baptist theologian

7 Blest be the tie that binds
   Our hearts in Jesu's love.
   'Blest be the tie that binds'

Guy Fawkes 1570–1606

English conspirator in the Gunpowder Plot, 1605

8 A desperate disease requires a dangerous remedy.
   6 November 1605, in *Dictionary of National Biography*
   (1917–); see **Proverbs** 617:30, **Shakespeare** 687:34

Dianne Feinstein 1933–

American Democratic politician

9 Toughness doesn't have to come in a pinstripe
   suit.
   in *Time* 4 June 1984

10 There was a time when you could say the least
   government was the best—but not in the nation's
   most populous state.
   campaign speech, 15 March 1990

James Fenton 1949–

English poet

11 It is not what they built. It is what they knocked
   down.

It is not the houses. It is the spaces between the
houses.
It is not the streets that exist. It is the streets that
no longer exist.
   German Requiem (1981)

12 'I didn't exist at Creation
   I didn't exist at the Flood,
   And I won't be around for Salvation
   To sort out the sheep from the cud—
   'Or whatever the phrase is. The fact is
   In soteriological terms
   I'm a crude existential malpractice
   And you are a diet of worms.'
   'God, A Poem' (1983)

13 Yes
   You have come upon the fabled lands where
   myths
   Go when they die.
   'The Pitt-Rivers Museum' (1983)

14 Windbags can be right. Aphorists can be wrong. It
   is a tough world.
   in *Times* 21 February 1985

Edna Ferber 1887–1968

American writer

15 Being an old maid is like death by drowning, a
   really delightful sensation after you cease to
   struggle.
   R. E. Drennan *Wit's End* (1973)

16 Roast Beef, Medium, is not only a food. It is a
   philosophy.
   foreword to *Roast Beef, Medium* (1911)

Samuel Ferguson 1810–86

Irish poet

17 I walked through Ballinderry in the springtime,
   When the bud was on the tree,
   And I said, in every fresh-ploughed field beholding
   The sowers striding free,
   Scattering broadcast forth the corn in golden
   plenty
   On the quick, seed-clasping soil
   Even such, this day, among the fresh-stirred
   hearts of Erin,
   Thomas Davis, is thy toil.
   'Lament for the Death of Thomas Davis'

18 As I heard the sweet lark sing
   In the clear air of the day.
   'The Lark in the Clear Air'

Robert Fergusson 1750–74

Scottish poet

19 For thof ye had as wise a snout on
   As Shakespeare or Sir Isaac Newton,
   Your judgement fouk woud hae a doubt on,
   I'll tak my aith,
   Till they could see ye wi' a suit on
   O' gude Braid Claith.
   'Braid Claith' (1773)

20 The Lawyers may revere that tree
   Where thieves so oft have swung,

Since, by the Law's most wise decree,
Her thieves are never hung.
'Epigram on a Lawyer's desiring one of the Tribe to look with respect to a Gibbet' (1779)

Pierre de Fermat 1601–65
French mathematician

1 *Cuius rei demonstrationem mirabilem sane detexi hanc marginis exiguitas non caperet.*

I have a truly marvellous demonstration of this proposition which this margin is too narrow to contain.
of 'Fermat's last theorem', written in the margin of his copy of Diophantus' Arithmetica, and subsequently published by his son in 1670 in an edition of the book containing Fermat's annotations
Simon Singh *Fermat's Last Theorem* (1997)

Enrico Fermi 1901–54
Italian-born American atomic physicist
on Fermi: see **Alvarez** 12:22

2 If I could remember the names of all these particles I'd be a botanist.
R. L. Weber *More Random Walks in Science* (1973)

3 Whatever Nature has in store for mankind, unpleasant as it may be, men must accept, for ignorance is never better than knowledge.
Laura Fermi *Atoms in the Family* (1955)

Ludwig Feuerbach 1804–72
German philosopher

4 *Der Mensch ist, was er isst.*

Man is what he eats.
Jacob Moleschott *Lehre der Nahrungsmittel: Für das Volk* (1850) 'Advertisement'; see **Brillat-Savarin** 151:15, **Proverbs** 635:23

Paul Feyerabend 1924–94
Austrian philosopher

5 The time is overdue for adding the separation of state and science to the by now customary separation of state and church. Science is only *one* of the many instruments man has invented to cope with his surroundings. It is not the only one, it is not infallible, and it has become too powerful, too pushy, and too dangerous to be left on its own.
Against Method (1975)

Richard Phillips Feynman 1918–88
American theoretical physicist

6 For a successful technology, reality must take precedence over public relations, for nature cannot be fooled.
appendix to the *Rogers Commission Report on the Space Shuttle Challenger Accident* 6 June 1986

7 What I cannot create, I do not understand.
attributed

Eugene Field 1850–95
American poet and journalist

8 But I, when I undress me
Each night, upon my knees,
Will ask the Lord to bless me,
With apple pie and cheese.
'Apple Pie and Cheese' (1889)

9 Wynken, Blynken, and Nod one night
Sailed off in a wooden shoe—
Sailed on a river of crystal light,
Into a sea of dew.
'Wynken, Blynken, and Nod' (1889)

10 He played the King as though under momentary apprehension that someone else was about to play the ace.
of Creston Clarke as King Lear
review attributed to Field, in the *Denver Tribune* c.1880

Frank Field 1942–
British Labour politician

11 The archbishop is usually to be found nailing his colours to the fence.
of Archbishop **Runcie**; *a similar comment has been recorded on A. J.* **Balfour**, *c.1904*
attributed in *Crockfords 1987/88* (1987)

Helen Fielding 1958–
British writer

12 I will not . . . sulk about having no boyfriend, but develop inner poise and authority and sense of self as woman of substance, complete *without* boyfriend, as best way to obtain boyfriend.
Bridget Jones's Diary (1996)

Henry Fielding 1707–54
English novelist and dramatist
on Fielding: see **Richardson** 647:17

13 It hath been often said, that it is not death, but dying, which is terrible.
Amelia (1751) bk. 3, ch. 4

14 One fool at least in every married couple.
Amelia (1751) bk. 9, ch. 4

15 The dusky night rides down the sky,
And ushers in the morn;
The hounds all join in glorious cry,
The huntsman winds his horn:
And a-hunting we will go.
Don Quixote in England (1733) act 2, sc. 5 'A-Hunting We Will Go'

16 Oh! The roast beef of England,
And old England's roast beef.
The Grub Street Opera (1731) act 3, sc. 3

17 He in a few minutes ravished this fair creature, or at least would have ravished her, if she had not, by a timely compliance, prevented him.
Jonathan Wild (1743) bk. 3, ch. 7

18 To whom nothing is given, of him can nothing be required.
Joseph Andrews (1742) bk. 2, ch. 8

1 I describe not men, but manners; not an individual, but a species.
Joseph Andrews (1742) bk. 3, ch. 1

2 Public schools are the nurseries of all vice and immorality.
Joseph Andrews (1742) bk. 3, ch. 5

3 A lottery is a taxation
Upon all the fools in creation
And Heaven be praised
It is easily rais'd,
Credulity's always in fashion.
The Lottery (1732) sc. 1

4 Love and scandal are the best sweeteners of tea.
Love in Several Masques (1728) act 4, sc. 11

5 Necessity is a bad recommendation to favours . . . which as seldom fall to those who really want them, as to those who really deserve them.
The Modern Husband (1732) act 2, sc. 5

6 Map me no maps, sir, my head is a map, a map of the whole world.
Rape upon Rape (1730) act 2, sc. 5

7 When I mention religion, I mean the Christian religion; and not only the Christian religion, but the Protestant religion; and not only the Protestant religion but the Church of England.
Tom Jones (1749) bk. 3, ch. 3

8 Thwackum was for doing justice, and leaving mercy to heaven.
Tom Jones (1749) bk. 3, ch. 10

9 What is commonly called love, namely the desire of satisfying a voracious appetite with a certain quantity of delicate white human flesh.
Tom Jones (1749) bk. 6, ch. 1

10 O! more than Gothic ignorance.
Tom Jones (1749) bk. 7, ch. 3

11 The only supernatural agents which can in any manner be allowed to us moderns, are ghosts; but of these I would advise an author to be extremely sparing. These are indeed like arsenic, and other dangerous drugs in physic, to be used with the utmost caution; nor would I advise the introduction of them at all in those works, or by those authors, to which or to whom a horse-laugh in the reader would be any great prejudice or mortification.
Tom Jones (1749) bk. 8, ch. 1

12 His designs were strictly honourable, as the phrase is; that is, to rob a lady of her fortune by way of marriage.
Tom Jones (1749) bk. 11, ch. 4

13 That monstrous animal, a husband and wife.
Tom Jones (1749) bk. 15, ch. 9

14 All Nature wears one universal grin.
Tom Thumb the Great (1731) act 1, sc. 1

15 When I'm not thanked at all, I'm thanked enough,
I've done my duty, and I've done no more.
Tom Thumb the Great (1731) act 1, sc. 3

Dorothy Fields 1905–74
American songwriter

16 A fine romance with no kisses.
A fine romance, my friend, this is.
'A Fine Romance' (1936 song)

17 Grab your coat, and get your hat,
Leave your worry on the doorstep,
Just direct your feet
To the sunny side of the street.
'On the Sunny Side of the Street' (1930 song)

W. C. Fields (William Claude Dukenfield) 1880–1946
American humorist
on Fields: see **Rosten** 656:17; see also **Epitaphs** 310:6

18 Never give a sucker an even break.
title of a W. C. Fields film (1941); the catchphrase (Fields's own) is said to have originated in the musical comedy *Poppy* (1923); see **Proverbs** 627:20

19 Some weasel took the cork out of my lunch.
You Can't Cheat an Honest Man (1939 film)

20 It ain't a fit night out for man or beast.
adopted by Fields but claimed by him not to be original; letter, 8 February 1944, in *W. C. Fields by Himself* (1974) pt. 2

21 Fish fuck in it.
on being asked why he never drank water
attributed

22 Hell, I never vote *for* anybody. I always vote *against*.
Robert Lewis Taylor *W. C. Fields* (1950); see **Adams** 2:6

23 Never cry over spilt milk, because it may have been poisoned.
Carlotta Monti with Cy Rice *W. C. Fields and Me* (1971)

Elizabeth Filkin 1940–
British academic and administrator, Parliamentary Commissioner for Standards, 1999–2001

24 I don't think you can investigate anything too rigorously, because you're not being fair to people unless you do that.
interview, in *Guardian* 16 February 2002

▫ Film lines
see box opposite
see also Woody **Allen**, W. C. **Fields**, Greta **Garbo**, Stan **Laurel**, Mae **West**

▫ Film titles
see box on page 322

Alain Finkielkraut
French philosopher

25 Civilized people must get off their high horse and learn with humble lucidity that they too are an indigenous variety.
describing **Lévi-Strauss**'s views
The Undoing of Thought (1988)

Continued

Film lines

1 Anyway, Ma, I made it . . . Top of the world!

White Heat (1949 film) written by Ivan Goff (1910–) and Ben Roberts (1916–84); last lines; spoken by James Cagney

2 Cancel the kitchen scraps for lepers and orphans. No more merciful beheadings. And call off Christmas!

Robin Hood, Prince of Thieves (1991 film) written by Pen Densham and John Watson; spoken by Alan Rickman

3 Don't let's ask for the moon! We have the stars!

Now, Voyager (1942 film), from the novel (1941) by Olive Higgins Prouty (1882–1974); spoken by Bette Davis

4 Either he's dead, or my watch has stopped.

A Day at the Races (1937 film) written by Robert Pirosh, George Seaton, and George Oppenheimer; spoken by Groucho **Marx**

5 E.T. phone home.

E.T. (1982 film) written by Melissa Mathison (1950–)

6 Fasten your seat-belts, it's going to be a bumpy night.

All About Eve (1950 film) written by Joseph L. Mankiewicz (1909–); spoken by Bette Davis

7 Frankly, my dear, I don't give a damn!

Gone with the Wind (1939 film) written by Sidney Howard; spoken by Clark Gable; see **Mitchell** 540:15

8 Go ahead, make my day.

Sudden Impact (1983 film) written by Joseph C. Stinson (1947–); spoken by Clint Eastwood

9 Greed—for lack of a better word—is good. Greed is right. Greed works.

Wall Street (1987 film) written by Stanley Weiser and Oliver Stone (1946–); see **Boesky** 125:5

10 Here's looking at you, kid.

Casablanca (1942 film) written by Julius J. Epstein (1909–2001), Philip G. Epstein (1909–52), and Howard Koch (1902–95); spoken by Humphrey Bogart to Ingrid Bergman

11 I could have had class. I could have been a contender.

On the Waterfront (1954 film) written by Budd **Schulberg**; spoken by Marlon Brando

12 I fear we have only awakened a sleeping giant, and his reaction will be terrible.

of the attack on Pearl Harbor

Tora! Tora! Tora! (1970 film) written by Larry Forrester, Hideo Oguni, and Ryuzo Kikushima; said by the Japanese admiral Isoruko **Yamamoto**, although there is no evidence that Yamamoto used these words; see **Yamamoto** 853:1

13 If she can stand it, I can. Play it!

usually quoted as 'Play it again, Sam'

Casablanca (1942 film) written by Julius J. Epstein (1909–2001), Philip G. Epstein (1909–52), and Howard Koch (1902–95); spoken by Humphrey Bogart; see **Misquotations** 538:13

14 If you can't leave in a taxi you can leave in a huff. If that's too soon, you can leave in a minute and a huff.

Duck Soup (1933 film) written by Bert Kalmar (1884–1947), Harry Ruby (1895–1974), Arthur Sheekman (1891–1978), and Nat Perrin; spoken by Groucho **Marx**

15 If you carry a oo number it means you're licensed to kill, not get killed.

Dr No (1962 film) written by Richard Maibaum, Johanna Harwood, and Berkely Mather, and based on the novel by Ian **Fleming**; spoken by Bernard Lee as 'M'; see **Fleming** 326:10

16 I'll be back.

The Terminator (1984 film) written by James Cameron (1954–) and Gale Anne Hurd; spoken by Arnold Schwarzenegger; see **Taglines for films** 771:4

17 I'll have what she's having.

woman to waiter, seeing Sally acting an orgasm

When Harry Met Sally (1989 film) written by Nora Ephron (1941–)

18 I love the smell of napalm in the morning. It smells like victory.

Apocalypse Now (1979 film) written by John Milius and Francis Ford Coppola (1939–); spoken by Robert Duvall

19 In Italy for thirty years under the Borgias they had warfare, terror, murder, bloodshed—they produced Michelangelo, Leonardo da Vinci and the Renaissance. In Switzerland they had brotherly love, five hundred years of democracy and peace and what did that produce . . . ? The cuckoo clock.

The Third Man (1949 film); words added by Orson **Welles** to Graham **Greene**'s screenplay

20 I see dead people.

The Sixth Sense (1999 film) written by Manoj Night Shyamalan; spoken by Haley Joel Osment

21 It's a funny old world—a man's lucky if he gets out of it alive.

You're Telling Me (1934 film) written by Walter de Leon and Paul M. Jones; spoken by W. C. **Fields**; see **Thatcher** 787:17

22 DRIFTWOOD (Groucho Marx): It's all right. That's—that's in every contract. That's—that's what they call a sanity clause.
FIORELLO (Chico Marx): You can't fool me. There ain't no Sanity Claus.

Night at the Opera (1935 film) written by George S. Kaufman (1889–1961) and Morrie Ryskind (1895–1985)

23 Let's get out of these wet clothes and into a dry Martini.

line coined in the 1920s by Robert **Benchley**'s press agent and adopted by Mae **West** in *Every Day's a Holiday* (1937 film)

▶

▶**Film lines** *continued*

1 Let's go to work.
Reservoir Dogs (1992 film) written and directed by Quentin Tarantino; spoken by Lawrence Tierney

2 Lunch? You gotta be kidding. Lunch is for wimps.
Wall Street (1987 film) written by Stanley Weiser and Oliver Stone (1946–)

3 Madness! Madness!
The Bridge on the River Kwai (1957 film of the novel by Pierre Boulle) written by Carl Foreman (1914–84), closing line

4 Major Strasser has been shot. Round up the usual suspects.
Casablanca (1942 film) written by Julius J. Epstein (1909–2001), Philip G. Epstein (1909–52), and Howard Koch (1902–95); spoken by Claude Rains

5 The man you love to hate.
anonymous billing for Erich von Stroheim in the film *The Heart of Humanity* (1918)

6 Man your ships, and may the force be with you.
Star Wars (1977 film) written by George Lucas (1944–)

7 Marriage isn't a word . . . it's a *sentence*!
The Crowd (1928 film) written by King Vidor (1895–1982)

8 Maybe just whistle. You know how to whistle, don't you, Steve? You just put your lips together and blow.
To Have and Have Not (1944 film) written by Jules Furthman (1888–1960) and William **Faulkner**; spoken by Lauren **Bacall**

9 EUNICE GRAYSON: Mr—?
SEAN CONNERY: Bond. James Bond.
Dr No (1962 film) written by Richard Maibaum, Johanna Harwood, and Berkely Mather, and based on the novel by Ian **Fleming**

10 Mr Kane was a man who got everything he wanted, and then lost it. Maybe Rosebud was something he couldn't get or something he lost. Anyway, it wouldn't have explained anything. I don't think any word can explain a man's life. No, I guess Rosebud is just a piece in a jigsaw puzzle, a missing piece.
Citizen Kane (1941 film) written by Herman J. Mankiewicz (1897–1953) and Orson **Welles**

11 My momma always said life was like a box of chocolates . . . you never know what you're gonna get.
Forrest Gump (1994 film) written by Eric Ross, based on the novel (1986) by Winston Groom; spoken by Tom Hanks

12 Nature, Mr Allnutt, is what we are put into this world to rise above.
The African Queen (1951 film) written by James Agee 1909–55; spoken by Katharine Hepburn; not in the novel by C. S. Forester

13 Of all the gin joints in all the towns in all the world, she walks into mine.
Casablanca (1942 film) written by Julius J. Epstein (1909–2001), Philip G. Epstein (1909–52), and Howard Koch (1902–95); spoken by Humphrey Bogart

14 Oh no, it wasn't the aeroplanes. It was Beauty killed the Beast.
King Kong (1933 film) written by James Creelman (1901–41) and Ruth Rose, final words

15 The pellet with the poison's in the vessel with the pestle. The chalice from the palace has the brew that is true.
The Court Jester (1955 film) written by Norman Panama (1914–) and Melvin Frank (1913–88); spoken by Danny Kaye

16 Remember, you're fighting for this woman's honour . . . which is probably more than she ever did.
Duck Soup (1933 film) written by Bert Kalmar (1884–1947), Harry Ruby (1895–1974), Arthur Sheekman (1891–1978), and Nat Perrin; spoken by Groucho **Marx**

17 The son of a bitch stole my watch!
The Front Page (1931 film), from the play (1928) by Charles MacArthur (1895–1956) and Ben **Hecht**

18 That was a little bit more information than I needed to know.
Pulp Fiction (1994 film) written by Quentin Tarantino (1963–); spoken by Uma Thurman

19 To infinity and beyond.
Toy Story (1995) written by Joel Cohen, et al.; spoken by Buzz Lightyear

20 Toto, I've a feeling we're not in Kansas any more.
The Wizard of Oz (1939 film) written by Noel Langley (1911–), Florence Ryerson, and Edgar Allan Wolfe; spoken by Judy Garland

21 GERRY: We can't get married at all . . . I'm a man.
OSGOOD: Well, nobody's perfect.
Some Like It Hot (1959 film) written by Billy **Wilder** and I. A. L. Diamond; closing words spoken by Jack Lemmon and Joe E. Brown

22 What a dump!
Beyond the Forest (1949 film) written by Lenore Coffee (?1897–1984); line spoken by Bette Davis, entering a room

23 What have the Romans ever done for us?
Monty Python's Life of Brian (1983 film) written by John Cleese, Graham Chapman, Eric Idle, Michael Palin, Terry Gilliam, and Terry Jones

24 When the legend becomes fact, print the legend.
The Man who Shot Liberty Valance (1962 film) written by Willis Goldbeck and James Warner Bellah; see **Johnson** 423:3

▶

▶ **Film lines** *continued*

1 Why, a four-year-old child could understand this report. Run out and find me a four-year-old child. I can't make head or tail of it.

Duck Soup (1933 film) written by Bert Kalmar (1884-1947), Harry Ruby (1895-1974), Arthur Sheekman (1891-1978), and Nat Perrin; spoken by Groucho **Marx**

2 NINOTCHKA: Why should you carry other people's bags?
PORTER: Well, that's my business, Madame.
NINOTCHKA: That's no business. That's social injustice.
PORTER: That depends on the tip.

Ninotchka (1939 film) written by Charles Brackett (1892-1969), Billy **Wilder**, and Walter Reisch (1903-1983)

3 You finally, really did it—you maniacs! You blew it up! Damn you! Damn you all to hell!

Planet of the Apes (1968 film) written by Michael Wilson and Rod Serling; spoken by Charlton Heston

4 You're going out a youngster but you've *got* to come back a star.

42nd Street (1933 film) written by James Seymour and Rian James

5 You're here to stay until the rustle in your dying throat relieves you!

Beau Hunks (1931 film; re-named *Beau Chumps* for British audiences) written by H. M. Walker; addressed to **Laurel** and Hardy

6 JOE GILLIS: You used to be in pictures. You used to be big.
NORMA DESMOND: I am big. It's the pictures that got small.

Sunset Boulevard (1950 film) written by Charles Brackett (1892-1969), Billy **Wilder**, and D. M. Marshman Jr

Alain Finkielkraut *continued*

7 In a world which has lost its transcendental significance, cultural identity serves to sanction those barbarous traditions which God is no longer in a position to endorse. Fanaticism is indefensible when it appeals to heaven, but beyond reproach when it is grounded in antiquity and cultural distinctiveness.

The Undoing of Thought (1988)

Carly Fiorina 1954-

American computer executive

8 Progress is not made by the cynics and the doubters, it is made by those who believe everything is possible.

speech, Las Vegas, 18 November 2002

Ronald Firbank 1886-1926

English novelist

9 'O! help me, heaven,' she prayed, 'to be decorative and to do right!'

The Flower Beneath the Foot (1923) ch. 2

10 There was a pause—just long enough for an angel to pass, flying slowly.

Vainglory (1915) ch. 6

11 The world is disgracefully managed, one hardly knows to whom to complain.

Vainglory (1915) ch. 10

L'Abbé Edgeworth de Firmont 1745-1807

*Irish-born priest, confessor to **Louis XVI***

12 *Fils de Saint Louis, montez au ciel.*
Son of Saint Louis, ascend to heaven.
*to **Louis XVI** as he mounted the steps of the guillotine, 1793*
attributed

Michael Fish 1944-

British weather forecaster

13 A woman rang to say she heard there was a hurricane on the way. Well don't worry, there isn't.

weather forecast on the night before serious gales in southern England
BBC TV, 15 October 1987

Carrie Fisher 1956-

American actress and writer

14 Here's how men think. Sex, work—and those are reversible, depending on age—sex, work, food, sports and lastly, begrudgingly, relationships. And here's how women think. Relationships, relationships, relationships, work, sex, shopping, weight, food.

Surrender the Pink (1990)

H. A. L. Fisher 1856-1940

English historian

15 Men wiser and more learned than I have discerned in history a plot, a rhythm, a predetermined pattern. These harmonies are concealed from me. I can see only one emergency following upon another as wave follows upon wave.

A History of Europe (1935)

16 Purity of race does not exist. Europe is a continent of energetic mongrels.

A History of Europe (1935) ch. 1

John Arbuthnot Fisher 1841-1920

British admiral

17 The best scale for an experiment is 12 inches to a foot.

Memories (1919)

Continued

Film titles

1 Back to the future.
  written by Robert Zemeckis and Bob Gale, 1985

2 Close encounters of the third kind.
  written by Steven Spielberg (1947–), 1977

3 The discreet charm of the bourgeoisie.
  written by Luis **Buñuel**, 1972

4 The Empire strikes back.
  written by George Lucas (1944–), 1980

5 Every which way but loose.
  written by Jeremy Joe Kronsberg, 1978; starring Clint
  Eastwood

6 The good, the bad, and the ugly.
  written by Age Scarpelli, Luciano Vincenzoni (1926–),
  and Sergio Leone (1921–), 1966

7 The long hot summer.
  based on stories by William **Faulkner**
  written by Irving Ravetch and Harriet Frank, 1958; 'The
  Long Summer' is the title of bk. 3 of Faulkner's *The
  Hamlet* (1940)

8 Naughty but nice.
  written by Jerry Wald (1911–62) and Richard Macaulay,
  1939

9 Never on Sunday.
  written by Jules Dassin (1911–), 1959

10 Rebel without a cause.
  written by R. M. Lindner (1914–56), 1959, based on his
  book (1944); starring James Dean

11 Sunday, bloody Sunday.
  written by Penelope Gilliatt (1933–), 1971

12 Suppose they gave a war and nobody came?
  written by Don McGuire and Hal Captain, 1969;
  'Suppose They Gave a War and No One Came?' was the
  title of a piece by Charlotte Keyes in *McCall's* October
  1966; see **Ginsberg** 349:14, **Sandburg** 666:1

13 Sweet smell of success.
  written by Ernest Lehman (1920–), 1957

John Arbuthnot Fisher *continued*

14 Sack the lot!
  on government overmanning and overspending
  letter to *The Times*, 2 September 1919

15 Never contradict
  Never explain
  Never apologize.
  letter to *The Times*, 5 September 1919; see **Disraeli** 278:4,
  Hubbard 406:10

16 Yours till Hell freezes.
  attributed to Fisher, but not original; see below

  Once an officer in India wrote to me and ended
  his letter 'Yours till Hell freezes'. I used this
  forcible expression in a letter to Fisher, and he
  adopted it.
  F. Ponsonby *Reflections of Three Reigns* (1951)

Marve Fisher

American songwriter

17 I like Chopin and Bizet, and the voice of Doris Day,
  Gershwin songs and old forgotten carols.
  But the music that excels is the sound of oil wells
  As they slurp, slurp, slurp into the barrels.
  'An Old-Fashioned Girl' (1954 song)

18 I want an old-fashioned house
  With an old-fashioned fence
  And an old-fashioned millionaire.
  'An Old-Fashioned Girl' (1954 song)

R. A. Fisher 1890–1962

English statistician and geneticist

19 The best causes tend to attract to their support the
  worst arguments.
  Statistical Methods and Scientific Inference (1956)

20 It was Darwin's chief contribution, not only to
  Biology but to the whole of natural science, to

have brought to light a process by which
contingencies *a priori* improbable are given, in the
process of time, an increasing probability, until it
is their non-occurrence, rather than their
occurence, which becomes highly probable.
*sometimes quoted as 'Natural selection is a
mechanism for generating an exceedingly high degree
of improbability'*
'Retrospect of the criticisms of the Theory of Natural
Selection' in Julian Huxley *Evolution as a Process* (1954)

Gerry Fitt 1926–

Northern Irish politician

21 People [in Northern Ireland] don't march as an
  alternative to jogging. They do it to assert their
  supremacy. It is pure tribalism, the cause of
  troubles all over the world.
  *referring to the 'marching season' in Northern
  Ireland, leading up to the anniversary of the Battle of
  the Boyne on 12 July, when parades by Orange
  communities traditionally take place*
  in *The Times* 5 August 1994

Albert H. Fitz

22 You are my honey, honeysuckle, I am the bee.
  'The Honeysuckle and the Bee' (1901 song)

Charles Fitzgeffrey c.1575–1638

English poet

23 And bold and hard adventures t' undertake,
  Leaving his country for his country's sake.
  Sir Francis Drake (1596) st. 213; see **Carter** 196:23

Edward Fitzgerald 1809–83

English scholar and poet

24 Awake! for Morning in the bowl of night
  Has flung the stone that puts the stars to flight:

And Lo! the Hunter of the East has caught
The Sultan's turret in a noose of light.
The Rubáiyát of Omar Khayyám (1859) st. 1

1 Each morn a thousand roses brings, you say;
Yes, but where leaves the rose of yesterday?
The Rubáiyát of Omar Khayyám (4th ed., 1879) st. 9

2 Here with a loaf of bread beneath the bough,
A flask of wine, a book of verse—and Thou
Beside me singing in the wilderness—
And wilderness is paradise enow.
The Rubáiyát of Omar Khayyám (1859) st. 11

A book of verses underneath the bough,
A jug of wine, a loaf of bread—and Thou
Beside me singing in the wilderness—
Oh, wilderness were paradise enow!
The Rubáiyát of Omar Khayyám (4th ed., 1879) st. 12

3 Ah, take the cash in hand and waive the rest;
Oh, the brave music of a *distant* drum!
The Rubáiyát of Omar Khayyám (1859) st. 12

Ah, take the cash and let the credit go,
Nor heed the rumble of a distant drum!
The Rubáiyát of Omar Khayyám (4th ed., 1879) st. 13

4 I sometimes think that never blows so red
The rose as where some buried Caesar bled.
The Rubáiyát of Omar Khayyám (1859) st. 18

5 Dust into dust, and under dust, to lie,
Sans wine, sans song, sans singer, and—sans End!
The Rubáiyát of Omar Khayyám (1859) st. 23

6 One thing is certain, and the rest is lies;
The flower that once hath blown for ever dies.
The Rubáiyát of Omar Khayyám (1859) st. 26

One thing is certain and the rest is lies;
The flower that once has blown for ever dies.
The Rubáiyát of Omar Khayyám (4th ed., 1879) st. 63

7 Ah, fill the cup:—what boots it to repeat
How time is slipping underneath our feet:
Unborn TOMORROW, and dead YESTERDAY,
Why fret about them if TODAY be sweet!
The Rubáiyát of Omar Khayyám (1859) st. 37

8 'Tis all a chequer-board of nights and days
Where Destiny with Men for pieces plays:
Hither and thither moves, and mates, and slays,
And one by one back in the closet lays.
The Rubáiyát of Omar Khayyám (1859) st. 49

But helpless pieces of the game he plays
Upon this chequerboard of nights and days;
Hither and thither moves, and checks, and slays,
And one by one back in the closet lays.
The Rubáiyát of Omar Khayyám (4th ed., 1879) st. 69

9 The ball no question makes of Ayes and Noes,
But here or there as strikes the player goes;
And he that tossed you down into the field,
He knows about it all—HE knows—HE knows!
The Rubáiyát of Omar Khayyám (4th ed., 1879) st. 70

10 The moving finger writes; and, having writ,
Moves on: nor all thy piety nor wit
Shall lure it back to cancel half a line,
Nor all thy tears wash out a word of it.
The Rubáiyát of Omar Khayyám (1859) st. 51; 'all your
tears' in 4th ed. (1879) st. 71

11 That inverted bowl we call The Sky.
The Rubáiyát of Omar Khayyám (1859) st. 52; 'they call the
Sky' in 4th ed. (1879) st. 72

12 They sneer at me for leaning all awry;
What! did the hand then of the potter shake?
The Rubáiyát of Omar Khayyám (4th ed., 1879) st. 86

13 Who *is* the potter, pray, and who the pot?
The Rubáiyát of Omar Khayyám (1859) st. 60

14 Then said another—'Surely not in vain
My substance from the common earth was ta'en,
That He who subtly wrought me into shape,
Should stamp me back to common earth again.'
The Rubáiyát of Omar Khayyám (1859) st. 61

15 Indeed the idols I have loved so long
Have done my credit in this world much wrong:
Have drowned my glory in a shallow cup
And sold my reputation for a song.
The Rubáiyát of Omar Khayyám (4th ed., 1879) st. 93

16 Alas, that spring should vanish with the rose!
That youth's sweet-scented manuscript should
close!
The Rubáiyát of Omar Khayyám (1859) st. 72

17 And when Thyself with shining foot shall pass
Among the guests star-scattered on the grass,
And in thy joyous errand reach the spot
Where I made one—turn down an empty glass!
The Rubáiyát of Omar Khayyám (1859) st. 75

And when like her, O Saki, you shall pass
Among the guests star-scattered on the grass,
And in your joyous errand reach the spot
Where I made one—turn down an empty glass!
The Rubáiyát of Omar Khayyám (4th ed., 1879) st. 101

18 Mrs Browning's death is rather a relief to me, I
must say: no more Aurora Leighs, thank God! A
woman of real genius, I know; but what is the
upshot of it all? She and her sex had better mind
the kitchen and their children; and perhaps the
poor: except in such things as little novels, they
only devote themselves to what men do much
better, leaving that which men do worse or not at
all.
letter to W. H. Thompson, 15 July 1861, in A. M. and A. B.
Terhune (eds.) *Letters of Edward Fitzgerald* (1980) vol. 2;
see **Browning** 161:30

19 Taste is the feminine of genius.
letter to J. R. Lowell, October 1877, in A. M. and A. B.
Terhune (eds.) *Letters of Edward Fitzgerald* (1980) vol. 4

F. Scott Fitzgerald 1896–1940
American novelist

20 Let me tell you about the very rich. They are
different from you and me.
to which Ernest **Hemingway** *replied, 'Yes, they have
more money' (in* Esquire *August 1936 'The Snows of
Kilimanjaro')*
All the Sad Young Men (1926) 'Rich Boy'

21 The beautiful and damned.
title of novel (1922)

1 At eighteen our convictions are hills from which we look; at forty-five they are caves in which we hide.
'Bernice Bobs her Hair' (1920)

2 No grand idea was ever born in a conference, but a lot of foolish ideas have died there.
Edmund Wilson (ed.) *The Crack-Up* (1945) 'Note-Books E'

3 Show me a hero and I will write you a tragedy.
Edmund Wilson (ed.) *The Crack-Up* (1945) 'Note-Books E'

4 I've been drunk for about a week now, and I thought it might sober me up to sit in a library.
The Great Gatsby (1925) ch. 3

5 Her voice is full of money.
The Great Gatsby (1925) ch. 7

6 They were careless people, Tom and Daisy—they smashed up things and creatures and then retreated back into their money or their vast carelessness, or whatever it was that kept them together, and let other people clean up the mess they had made.
The Great Gatsby (1925) ch. 9

7 In a real dark night of the soul it is always three o'clock in the morning.
'Handle with Care' in *Esquire* March 1936; see **Misquotations** 537:13

8 See that little stream—we could walk to it in two minutes. It took the British a month to walk it—a whole empire walking very slowly, dying in front and pushing forward behind. And another empire walked very slowly backward a few inches a day, leaving the dead like a million bloody rugs.
Tender is the Night (1934)

9 There are no second acts in American lives.
Edmund Wilson (ed.) *The Last Tycoon* (1941) 'Hollywood, etc.'

10 An author ought to write for the youth of his own generation, the critics of the next, and the schoolmasters of ever after.
letter to the Booksellers' Convention, April 1920; Andrew Turnbull (ed.) *Selected Letters of F. Scott Fitzgerald* (1963)

11 All good writing is *swimming under water* and holding your breath.
letter (undated) to his daughter, Frances Scott Fitzgerald; Andrew Turnbull (ed.) *Selected Letters of F. Scott Fitzgerald* (1963)

Penelope Fitzgerald 1916–2000
English novelist and biographer

12 Duty is what no-one else will do at the moment.
Offshore (1979) ch. 1

Robert Fitzsimmons 1862–1917
New Zealand boxer

13 The bigger they are, the further they have to fall.
prior to a fight
in *Brooklyn Daily Eagle* 11 August 1900; see **Proverbs** 615:39

Bud Flanagan 1896–1968
British comedian

14 Underneath the Arches,
I dream my dreams away,
Underneath the Arches,
On cobble-stones I lay.
'Underneath the Arches' (1932 song)

Michael Flanders 1922–75 and Donald Swann 1923–94
English songwriters

15 Have Some Madeira, M'dear.
title of song (*c.*1956)

16 Mud! Mud! Glorious mud!
Nothing quite like it for cooling the blood.
So, follow me, follow,
Down to the hollow,
And there let us wallow
In glorious mud.
'The Hippopotamus' (1952)

17 Ma's out, Pa's out—let's talk rude:
Pee, po, belly, bum, drawers.
'P**, P*, B****, B**, D******' (*c.*1956)

18 Eating people is wrong!
'The Reluctant Cannibal' (1956 song); adopted as the title of a novel (1959) by Malcolm Bradbury

19 That monarch of the road,
Observer of the Highway Code,
That big six-wheeler
Scarlet-painted
London Transport
Diesel-engined
Ninety-seven horse power
Omnibus!
'A Transport of Delight' (*c.*1956 song)

Thomas Flatman 1637–88
English poet

20 There's an experienced rebel, Time,
And in his squadrons Poverty;
There's Age that brings along with him
A terrible artillery:
And if against all these thou keep'st thy crown,
Th'usurper Death will make thee lay it down.
'The Defiance' (1686)

Gustave Flaubert 1821–80
French novelist

21 *Il la croyait heureuse; et elle lui en voulait de ce calme si bien assis, de cette pesanteur sereine, du bonheur même qu'elle lui donnait.*

He took it for granted that she was content; and she resented his settled calm, his serene dullness, the very happiness she herself brought him.
Madame Bovary (1857) pt. 1, ch. 7 (translated by F. Steegmuller)

22 *La parole humaine est comme un chaudron fêlé où nous battons des mélodies à faire danser les ours, quand on voudrait attendrir les étoiles.*

Human speech is like a cracked kettle on which we tap crude rhythms for bears to dance to, while we long to make music that will melt the stars.

Madame Bovary (1857) pt. 1, ch. 12 (translated by F. Steegmuller)

1 *Alors elle se rappela les héoïnes des livres qu'elle avait lus, et la légion lyrique de ces femmes adultères se mit à chanter dans sa mémoire avec des voix de soeurs qui la charmaient.*

She remembered the heroines of novels she had read, and the lyrical legion of those adulterous women began to sing in her memory with sisterly voices that enchanted her.

Madame Bovary (1857) pt. 2, ch. 9 (translated by F. Steegmuller)

2 *Emma ressemblait à toutes les maîtresses; et le charme de la noveauté, peu à peu tombant comme un vêtement, laissait voir à nu l'éternelle monotonie de la passion, qui a toujours les mêmes formes et la même langage.*

Emma was like all his other mistresses; and as the charm of novelty gradual slipped from her like a piece of her clothing, he saw revealed in all its nakedness the eternal monotony of passion, which always assumes the same forms and always speaks the same language.

Madame Bovary (1857) pt. 2, ch. 12 (translated by F. Steegmuller)

3 *Le dénigrement de ceux que nous aimons toujours nous en détache quelque peu. Il ne faut pas toucher aux idoles: la dorure en reste aux mains.*

Casting aspersions on those we love always does something to loosen our ties. We shouldn't maltreat our idols: the gilt comes off in our hands.

Madame Bovary (1857) pt. 3, ch. 6 (translated by F. Steegmuller)

4 *Une pareille aisance de manières, cette simplicité, qui est un raffinement, et où les naifs aperçoivent l'expression d'une sympathie instantée.*

Naturalness and ease of manner—a product of sophistication which the gullible interpret as a sign of instant affinity.

A Sentimental Education (1869) pt. 1, ch. 5 (translated by Douglas Parmée)

5 *Pour plaire aux femmes, il faut étaler une insouciance de bouffon ou des fureurs de tragédie! Elles se moquent de nous quand on leur dit qu'on les aime, simplement!*

To please women you either have to be carefree and play the fool or else be tragic and passionate. When you say to them quite simply that you love them, women laugh at you.

A Sentimental Education (1869) pt. 3, ch. 3 (translated by Douglas Parmée)

6 *Tous les deux ne trouvaient plus rien à se dire. Il y a un moment, dans les séparations, où la personne aimée n'est déja plus avec nous.*

Neither could find anything to say. There comes a moment during leave-taking when the loved one is no longer with us.

A Sentimental Education (1869) pt. 3, ch. 6 (translated by Douglas Parmée)

7 From time to time, in the towns, I open a newspaper. Things seem to be going at a dizzy rate. We are dancing not on a volcano, but on the rotten seat of a latrine.

letter to Louis Bouilhet, 14 November 1850, in M. Nadeau (ed.) *Correspondence 1846–51* (1964) (translated by F. Steegmuller)

8 What a heavy oar the pen is, and what a strong current ideas are to row in!

letter to Louise Colet, 23 October 1851, in *Letters of Gustave Flaubert* (1980) vol. 1 (translated by F. Steegmuller)

9 It is splendid to be a great writer, to put men into the frying pan of your words and make them pop like chestnuts.

letter to Louise Colet, 3 November 1851, in *Letters of Gustave Flaubert* (1980) vol. 1 (translated by F. Steegmuller)

10 Prose was born yesterday—this is what we must tell ourselves. Poetry is pre-eminently the medium of past literatures. All the metrical combinations have been tried but nothing like this can be said of prose.

letter to Louise Colet, 24 April 1852, in M. Nadeau (ed.) *Correspondence 1852* (1964)

11 You can calculate the worth of a man by the number of his enemies, and the importance of a work of art by the harm that is spoken of it.

letter to Louise Colet, 14 June 1853, in M. Nadeau (ed.) *Correspondence 1853–56* (1964)

12 Poetry is a subject as precise as geometry.

letter to Louise Colet, 14 August 1853, in M. Nadeau (ed.) *Correspondence 1853–56* (1964)

13 Style is life! It is the very life-blood of thought!

letter to Louise Colet, 7 September 1853, in M. Nadeau (ed.) *Correspondence 1853–56* (1964)

14 The artist must be in his work as God is in creation, invisible and all-powerful; one must sense him everywhere but never see him.

letter to Mademoiselle Leroyer de Chantepie, 18 March 1857, in M. Nadeau (ed.) *Correspondence 1857–64* (1965)

15 Books are made not like children but like pyramids . . . and they're just as useless! and they stay in the desert! . . . Jackals piss at their foot and the bourgeois climb up on them.

letter to Ernest Feydeau, November/December 1857, in M. Nadeau (ed.) *Correspondence 1857–64* (1965)

16 Human life is a sad show, undoubtedly: ugly, heavy and complex. Art has no other end, for people of feeling, than to conjure away the burden and bitterness.

letter to Amelie Bosquet, July 1864, in M. Nadeau (ed.) *Correspondence 1857–64* (1965)

17 *Madame Bovary, c'est moi.*
Madame Bovary is myself.

attributed

James Elroy Flecker 1884–1915

English poet

18 West of these out to seas colder than the Hebrides I must go
Where the fleet of stars is anchored and the young

Star captains glow.
'The Dying Patriot' (1913)

1 The dragon-green, the luminous, the dark, the
serpent-haunted sea.
'The Gates of Damascus' (1913)

2 We are the Pilgrims, master; we shall go
Always a little further.
The Golden Journey to Samarkand (1913) pt. 1, 'Epilogue'

3 For lust of knowing what should not be known,
We take the Golden Road to Samarkand.
The Golden Journey to Samarkand (1913) pt. 1, 'Epilogue'

4 I have seen old ships sail like swans asleep
Beyond the village which men still call Tyre,
With leaden age o'ercargoed, dipping deep
For Famagusta and the hidden sun
That rings black Cyprus with a lake of fire.
'Old Ships' (1915)

5 A ship, an isle, a sickle moon—
With few but with how splendid stars
The mirrors of the sea are strewn
Between their silver bars!
'A Ship, an Isle, and a Sickle Moon' (1913)

6 O friend unseen, unborn, unknown,
Student of our sweet English tongue,
Read out my words at night, alone:
I was a poet, I was young.
'To a Poet a Thousand Years Hence' (1910)

Richard Flecknoe d. c.1678

Irish poet

7 Still-born Silence! thou that art
Floodgate of the deeper heart.
'Invocation of Silence' (1653)

Ari Fleischer 1960–

*American government spokesman, White House Press
Secretary 2001–3*

8 The problem with guns that are hidden is you
can't see their smoke.
on BBC News Online, 10 January 2003; see **Blix** 123:11

Ian Fleming 1908–64

English thriller writer
see also **Film lines** 319:15, **Film lines** 320:9, **Misquotations**
538:6

9 A medium Vodka dry Martini—with a slice of
lemon peel. Shaken and not stirred.
Dr No (1958) ch. 14

10 The licence to kill for the Secret Service, the
double-o prefix, was a great honour.
Dr No (1958); see **Film lines** 319:15

Marjory Fleming 1803–11

English child writer

11 A direful death indeed they had
That would put any parent mad
But she was more than usual calm
She did not give a singel dam.
Journals, Letters and Verses (ed. A. Esdaile, 1934)

12 The most devilish thing is 8 times 8 and 7 times 7
it is what nature itselfe cant endure.
Journals, Letters and Verses (ed. A. Esdaile, 1934)

13 To-day I pronounced a word which should never
come out of a lady's lips it was that I called John a
Impudent Bitch.
Journals, Letters and Verses (ed. A. Esdaile, 1934)

14 I am going to turn over a new life and am going to
be a very good girl and be obedient to Isa Keith,
here there is planty of goosaberys which makes
my teath watter.
Journals, Letters and Verses (ed. A. Esdaile, 1934)

15 I hope I will be religious again but as for reganing
my charecter I despare for it.
Journals, Letters and Verses (ed. A. Esdaile, 1934)

16 An annibabtist is a thing I am not a member of.
Journals, Letters and Verses (ed. A. Esdaile, 1934)

17 Sentiment is what I am not acquainted with.
Journals, Letters and Verses (ed. A. Esdaile, 1934)

18 My dear Isa, I now sit down on my botom to
answer all your kind and beloved letters which
you was so good as to write to me.
Journals, Letters and Verses (ed. A. Esdaile, 1934) Letter to
Isabella

19 O lovely O most charming pug
Thy graceful air and heavenly mug . . .
His noses cast is of the roman
He is a very pretty weoman
I could not get a rhyme for roman
And was oblidged to call it weoman.
'Sonnet'

Robert, Marquis de Flers 1872–1927 and Arman de Caillavet 1869–1915

French dramatists

20 Democracy is the name we give the people
whenever we need them.
L'habit vert act 1, sc. 12, in *La petite Illustration série théâtre*
31 May 1913

Andrew Fletcher of Saltoun 1655–1716

Scottish patriot and anti-Unionist
see also **Last words** 473:1

21 If a man were permitted to make all the ballads,
he need not care who should make the laws of a
nation.
'An Account of a Conversation concerning a Right
Regulation of Government for the Good of Mankind. In a
Letter to the Marquis of Montrose' (1704) in *Political Works*
(1732) pt. 7

22 The Scots deserve no pity, if they voluntarily
surrender their united and separate interests to the
mercy of an united Parliament, where the English
have so vast a majority . . . their 45 Scots
members may dance round to all eternity, in this
trap of their own making.
*State of the Controversy betwixt United and Separate
Parliaments* (1706)

John Fletcher 1579–1625

English dramatist
*see also **Beaumont and Fletcher**, **Shakespeare** Henry VIII*

1 Best while you have it use your breath,
There is no drinking after death.
  The Bloody Brother, or Rollo Duke of Normandy (with Ben
  Jonson and others, performed *c.*1616) act 2, sc. 2 'Song'

2 And he that will go to bed sober,
Falls with the leaf still in October.
  The Bloody Brother act 2, sc. 2 'Song'

3 Three merry boys, and three merry boys,
And three merry boys are we,
As ever did sing in a hempen string
Under the Gallows-Tree.
  The Bloody Brother act 3, sc. 2

4 Death hath so many doors to let out life.
  The Custom of the Country (with Massinger) act 2, sc. 2; see
  Massinger 518:5, **Seneca** 677:2, **Webster** 825:25

5 Our acts our angels are, or good or ill,
Our fatal shadows that walk by us still.
  The Honest Man's Fortune epilogue

6 Nothing's so dainty sweet, as lovely melancholy.
  The Nice Valour (with Middleton) act 3, sc. 3, 'Song'

7 Are you at ease now? Is your heart at rest?
Now you have got a shadow, an umbrella
To keep the scorching world's opinion
From your fair credit.
  Rule a Wife and Have a Wife (performed 1624) act 3, sc. 1

8 Daisies smell-less, yet most quaint,
And sweet thyme true,
Primrose first born child of Ver,
Merry Springtime's Harbinger.
  Two Noble Kinsmen (with Shakespeare) act 1, sc. 1

9 Care-charming Sleep, thou easer of all woes,
Brother to Death.
  Valentinian (performed *c.*1610–14) act 5, sc. 7 'Song'; see
  Daniel 255:7, **Shelley** 731:11

10 Come sing now, sing; for I know ye sing well,
I see ye have a singing face.
  The Wild-Goose Chase (performed 1621) act 2, sc. 2

11 Whistle and she'll come to you.
  Wit Without Money act 4, sc. 4; see **Burns** 172:3

12 Charity and beating begins at home.
  Wit Without Money act 5, sc. 2; see **Proverbs** 616:33

Phineas Fletcher 1582–1650

English clergyman and poet

13 Drop, drop, slow tears,
And bathe those beauteous feet,
Which brought from Heaven
The news and Prince of Peace.
  Poetical Miscellanies (1633) 'An Hymn'

14 In your deep floods
Drown all my faults and fears;
Not let His eye
See sin, but through my tears.
  Poetical Miscellanies (1633) 'An Hymn'

15 Love's tongue is in the eyes.
  Piscatory Eclogues (1633) no. 5, st. 13

16 Poorly (poor man) he lived; poorly (poor man) he
died.
  The Purple Island (1633) canto 1, st. 19

17 His little son into his bosom creeps,
The lively picture of his father's face.
  The Purple Island (1633) canto 12, st. 6

18 Love is like linen often changed, the sweeter.
  Sicelides (performed 1614) act 3, sc. 5

19 The coward's weapon, poison.
  Sicelides (performed 1614) act 5, sc. 3

Jean-Pierre Claris de Florian 1755–94

French writer and poet

20 *Plaisir d'amour ne dure qu'un moment,*
Chagrin d'amour dure toute la vie.

Love's pleasure lasts but a moment;
Love's sorrow lasts all through life.
  Célestine (1784); see **Malory** 508:20

Dario Fo 1926–

Italian dramatist

21 *Non si paga, non si paga.*

We won't pay, we won't pay.
  title of play (1975; translated by Lino Pertile in 1978 as
  'We Can't Pay? We Won't Pay!' and performed in London
  in 1981 as '*Can't Pay? Won't Pay!*'); see **Political slogans**
  600:12

Ferdinand Foch 1851–1929

French Marshal

22 My centre is giving way, my right is retreating,
situation excellent, I am attacking.
  message during the first Battle of the Marne,
  September 1914
  R. Recouly *Foch* (1919) ch. 6

23 This is not a peace treaty, it is an armistice for
twenty years.
  at the signing of the Treaty of Versailles, 1919
  Paul Reynaud *Mémoires* (1963) vol. 2

J. Foley 1906–70

British songwriter

24 Old soldiers never die,
They simply fade away.
  'Old Soldiers Never Die' (1920 song); copyrighted by Foley
  but possibly a 'folk-song' from the First World War; see
  Proverbs 628:22

Jane Fonda 1937–

American actress

25 A man has every season, while a woman has only
the right to spring.
  in *Daily Mail* 13 September 1989

Michael Foot 1913–

British Labour politician

26 A speech from Ernest Bevin on a major occasion
had all the horrific fascination of a public

execution. If the mind was left immune, eyes and ears and emotions were riveted.

Aneurin Bevan (1962) vol. 1, ch. 13

1 Think of it! A second Chamber selected by the Whips. A seraglio of eunuchs.

speech in the House of Commons, 3 February 1969

2 It is not necessary that every time he rises he should give his famous imitation of a semi-house-trained polecat.

*of Norman **Tebbit***

speech in the House of Commons, 2 March 1978

Samuel Foote 1720–77

English actor and dramatist

3 Born in a cellar . . . and living in a garret.

The Author (1757) act 2

4 God's revenge against vanity.

*to David **Garrick**, who had asked him what he thought of a heavy shower of rain falling on the day of the **Shakespeare** Jubilee, organized by and chiefly starring Garrick himself*

W. Cooke *Memoirs of Samuel Foote* (1805) vol. 2

5 He is not only dull in himself, but the cause of dullness in others.

on a dull law lord

James Boswell *Life of Samuel Johnson* (1791) 1783; see **Shakespeare** 691:23

6 So she went into the garden to cut a cabbage-leaf to make an apple-pie; and at the same time a great she-bear coming up the street, pops its head into the shop. 'What! no soap?' So he died, and she very imprudently married the barber; and there were present the Picninnies, and the Joblillies, and the Garyulies, and the grand Panjandrum himself, with the little round button at top; and they all fell to playing the game of catch as catch can, till the gun powder ran out at the heels of their boots.

nonsense composed to test the vaunted memory of the actor Charles Macklin (1697?–1797)

Maria Edgeworth *Harry and Lucy* (1825) vol. 2

Miss C. F. Forbes 1817–1911

English writer

7 The sense of being well-dressed gives a feeling of inward tranquillity which religion is powerless to bestow.

R. W. Emerson *Letters and Social Aims* (1876)

Anna Ford 1943–

English journalist and broadcaster

8 Let's face it, there are no plain women on television.

in *Observer* 23 September 1979

Gerald Ford 1909–

American Republican statesman; 38th President of the US, 1974–7
*on Ford: see **Johnson** 423:17*

9 If the Government is big enough to give you everything you want, it is big enough to take away everything you have.

John F. Parker *If Elected* (1960)

10 I am a Ford, not a Lincoln.

on taking the vice-presidential oath, 6 December 1973
in *Washington Post* 7 December 1973

11 Our long national nightmare is over. Our Constitution works; our great Republic is a Government of laws and not of men.

on being sworn in as President, 9 August 1974
G. J. Lankevich *Gerald R. Ford* (1977); see **Adams** 2:20

Henry Ford 1863–1947

American car manufacturer and businessman

12 Any customer can have a car painted any colour that he wants so long as it is black.

on the Model T Ford, 1909
Henry Ford with Samuel Crowther *My Life and Work* (1922) ch. 2

13 History is more or less bunk.

in *Chicago Tribune* 25 May 1916 (interview with Charles N. Wheeler)

14 What we call evil is simply ignorance bumping its head in the dark.

in *Observer* 16 March 1930

John Ford 1586–after 1639

English dramatist

15 Tempt not the stars, young man, thou canst not play
With the severity of fate.

The Broken Heart (1633) act 1, sc. 3

16 I am . . . a mushroom
On whom the dew of heaven drops now and then.

The Broken Heart (1633) act 1, sc. 3

17 The joys of marriage are the heaven on earth,
Life's paradise, great princess, the soul's quiet,
Sinews of concord, earthly immortality,
Eternity of pleasures; no restoratives
Like to a constant woman.

The Broken Heart (1633) act 2, sc. 2

18   There's not a hair
Sticks on my head but, like a leaden plummet,
It sinks me to the grave: I must creep thither;
The journey is not long.

The Broken Heart (1633) act 4, sc. 2

19 He hath shook hands with time.

The Broken Heart (1633) act 5, sc. 2

20   Tell us, pray, what devil
This melancholy is, which can transform
Men into monsters.

The Lady's Trial (1639) act 3, sc. 1

1 Brother, even by our mother's dust, I charge you,
Do not betray me to your mirth or hate.
'Tis Pity She's a Whore (1633) act 1, sc. 2

2 View but her face, and in that little round,
You may observe a world of variety.
'Tis Pity She's a Whore (1633) act 2

3   Why, I hold fate
Clasped in my fist, and could command the course
Of time's eternal motion, hadst thou been
One thought more steady than an ebbing sea.
'Tis Pity She's a Whore (1633) act 5, sc. 4

Lena Guilbert Ford 1870–1916

English songwriter

4 Keep the Home-fires burning,
While your hearts are yearning,
Though your lads are far away
They dream of Home.
There's a silver lining
Through the dark cloud shining;
Turn the dark cloud inside out,
Till the boys come Home.
'Till the Boys Come Home!' (1914 song); music by Ivor
Novello; see **Proverbs** 619:4

Howell Forgy 1908–83

American naval chaplain

5 Praise the Lord and pass the ammunition.
*at Pearl Harbor, 7 December 1941, while Forgy
moved along a line of sailors passing ammunition by
hand to the deck*
in *New York Times* 1 November 1942; later the title of a
song by Frank Loesser, 1942

E. M. Forster 1879–1970

English novelist
*on Forster: see **Mansfield** 511:3*

6 American women shoot the hippopotamus with
eyebrows made of platinum.
Abinger Harvest (1936) 'Mickey and Minnie'; see **Belloc**
64:18

7 [Public schoolboys] go forth into a world that is
not entirely composed of public-school men or
even of Anglo-Saxons, but of men who are as
various as the sands of the sea; into a world of
whose richness and subtlety they have no
conception. They go forth into it with well-
developed bodies, fairly developed minds, and
undeveloped hearts.
Abinger Harvest (1936) 'Notes on English Character'

8 It is not that the Englishman can't feel—it is that
he is afraid to feel. He has been taught at his
public school that feeling is bad form. He must not
express great joy or sorrow, or even open his
mouth too wide when he talks—his pipe might fall
out if he did.
Abinger Harvest (1936) 'Notes on English Character'

9 Yes—oh dear yes—the novel tells a story.
Aspects of the Novel (1927) ch. 2

10 The test of a round character is whether it is
capable of surprising in a convincing way. If it

never surprises, it is flat. If it does not convince, it
is flat pretending to be round.
on fictional characters
Aspects of the Novel (1927) ch. 4

11 A dogged attempt to cover the universe with mud,
an inverted Victorianism, an attempt to make
crossness and dirt succeed where sweetness and
light failed.
*of James **Joyce**'s Ulysses*
Aspects of the Novel (1927) ch. 6; see **Arnold** 29:8, **Swift**
765:6

12 It is a period between two wars—the long weekend it has been called.
The Development of English Prose between 1918 and 1939
(1945)

13 Railway termini. They are our gates to the
glorious and the unknown. Through them we
pass out into adventure and sunshine, to them,
alas! we return.
Howards End (1910) ch. 2

14 To trust people is a luxury in which only the
wealthy can indulge; the poor cannot afford it.
Howards End (1910) ch. 5

15 Personal relations are the important thing for ever
and ever, and not this outer life of telegrams and
anger.
Howards End (1910) ch. 19

16 Only connect! . . . Only connect the prose and the
passion, and both will be exalted, and human love
will be seen at its height.
Howards End (1910) ch. 22

17 Of all means to regeneration Remorse is surely the
most wasteful. It cuts away healthy tissue with
the poisoned. It is a knife that probes far deeper
than the evil.
Howards End (1910) ch. 41

18 It's the worst thing that can ever happen to you in
all your life, and you've got to mind it . . . They'll
come saying, 'Bear up—trust to time.' No, no;
they're wrong. Mind it.
The Longest Journey (1907) ch. 5

19 The so-called white races are really pinko-grey.
A Passage to India (1924) ch. 7

20 Nothing in India is identifiable, the mere asking of
a question causes it to disappear or to merge in
something else.
A Passage to India (1924) ch. 8

21 Pathos, piety, courage—they exist, but are
identical, and so is filth. Everything exists, nothing
has value.
A Passage to India (1924) ch. 14

22 Where there is officialism every human
relationship suffers.
A Passage to India (1924) ch. 24

23 Like all gossip—it's merely one of those half-alive
things that try to crowd out real life.
A Passage to India (1924) ch. 31

24 God si [is] Love. Is this the final message of India?
A Passage to India (1924) ch. 33

1 If I had to choose between betraying my country and betraying my friend, I hope I should have the guts to betray my country.
Two Cheers for Democracy (1951) 'What I Believe'

2 So Two cheers for Democracy: one because it admits variety and two because it permits criticism. Two cheers are quite enough: there is no occasion to give three. Only Love the Beloved Republic deserves that.
Two Cheers for Democracy (1951) 'What I Believe'; see **Swinburne** 768:19

Venantius Fortunatus C.AD 530–c.610

Frankish poet and priest; Bishop of Poitiers from AD 599

3 *Pange, lingua, gloriosi*
Proelium certaminis.
Sing, my tongue, of the battle in the glorious struggle.
Passiontide hymn, most commonly sung as: 'Sing, my tongue, the glorious battle'
'Pange lingua gloriosi'; see **Thomas Aquinas** 788:15

4 *Vexilla regis prodeunt,*
Fulget crucis mysterium;
Qua vita mortem pertulit,
Et morte vitam protulit.
The banners of the king advance, the mystery of the cross shines bright; where his life went through with death, and from death brought forth life.
hymn, usually sung as 'The royal banners forward go'
'Vexilla Regis'

5 *Regnavit a ligno Deus.*
God reigned from the wood.
'Vexilla Regis'

Harry Emerson Fosdick 1878–1969

American Baptist minister

6 I renounce war for its consequences, for the lies it lives on and propagates, for the undying hatred it arouses, for the dictatorships it puts in the place of democracy, for the starvation that stalks after it.
Armistice Day Sermon in New York, 1933, in The Secret of Victorious Living (1934)

Charles Foster 1828–1904

American politician

7 Isn't this a billion dollar country?
responding to a Democratic gibe about a 'million dollar Congress'
at the 51st Congress; also attributed to Thomas B. Reed, who reported the exchange in *North American Review* March 1892, vol. 154

John Foster 1770–1843

English Baptist minister

8 But the two classes [the educated and the uneducated] so beheld in contrast, might they not seem to belong to two different nations?
Essay on the Evils of Popular Ignorance (1820); see **Disraeli** 277:23, **Disraeli** 277:25

9 They [the wealthy] are in a religious diving-bell; religion is not circumambient, but a little is conveyed down into the worldly depth, where they breathe by a sort of artificial inlet—a tube.
Journal Item 420 in Life and Correspondence (1846)

10 Is not the pleasure of feeling and exhibiting *power* over other beings, a principal part of the gratification of cruelty?
Journal Item 772 in Life and Correspondence (1846)

Stephen Collins Foster 1826–64

American songwriter

11 Beautiful dreamer, wake unto me,
Starlight and dewdrop are waiting for thee.
'Beautiful Dreamer' (1864 song)

12 Gwine to run all night!
Gwine to run all day!
I'll bet my money on de bobtail nag—
Somebody bet on de bay.
'De Camptown Races' (1850) chorus

13 I dream of Jeanie with the light brown hair,
Floating, like a vapour, on the soft summer air.
'Jeanie with the Light Brown Hair' (1854)

14 Way down upon the Swanee River,
Far, far, away,
There's where my heart is turning ever;
There's where the old folks stay.
'The Old Folks at Home' (1851)

15 All the world is sad and dreary
Everywhere I roam,
Oh! darkies, how my heart grows weary,
Far from the old folks at home.
'The Old Folks at Home' (1851) chorus

Charles Fourier 1772–1837

French social theorist

16 The extension of women's rights is the basic principle of all social progress.
Théorie des Quatre Mouvements (1808) vol. 2, ch. 4

H. W. Fowler 1858–1933

English lexicographer and grammarian

17 The English speaking world may be divided into (1) those who neither know nor care what a split infinitive is; (2) those who do not know, but care very much; (3) those who know and condemn; (4) those who know and approve; and (5) those who know and distinguish. Those who neither know nor care are the vast majority and are a happy folk, to be envied by most of the minority classes.
Modern English Usage (1926)

H. W. Fowler 1858–1933 and F. G. Fowler 1870–1918

English lexicographers and grammarians

18 Pretentious quotations being the surest road to tedium.
The King's English (1906)

Norman Fowler 1938–

British Conservative politician

1 I have a young family and for the next few years I should like to devote more time to them.
often quoted as 'spend more time with my family'
resignation letter to the Prime Minister, in *Guardian* 4 January 1990; see **Thatcher** 787:14

Caroline Fox d. 1774

*English wife of Henry Fox, Lord **Holland**, and mother of Charles James **Fox***

2 That little boy will be a thorn in Charles's side as long as he lives.
*seeing in the young William **Pitt** a prospective rival for her son Charles James **Fox***
attributed

Charles James Fox 1749–1806

English Whig politician
*on Fox: see **Shaw-Lefevre** 727:29; see also **Last words** 472:3*

3 He was uniformly of an opinion which, though not a popular one, he was ready to aver, that the right of governing was not property but a trust.
*on **Pitt** the Younger's scheme of Parliamentary Reform, 1785*
J. L. Hammond *Charles James Fox* (1903) ch. 4

4 How much the greatest event it is that ever happened in the world! and how much the best!
on the fall of the Bastille
letter to Richard Fitzpatrick, 30 July 1789, in Lord John Russell *Life and Times of C. J. Fox* vol. 2 (1859)

5 I will not close my politics in that foolish way.
in the last year of his life it had been suggested that he should accept a peerage
in *Dictionary of National Biography* (1917–)

George Fox 1624–91

English founder of the Society of Friends (Quakers)

6 I saw also that there was an ocean of darkness and death, but an infinite ocean of light and love, which flowed over the ocean of darkness.
Journal 1647

7 I told them I lived in the virtue of that life and power that took away the occasion of all wars.
on being offered a captaincy in the army of the Commonwealth, against the forces of the King
Journal 1651

8 I . . . espied three steeple-house spires, and they struck at my life.
on seeing the spires of Lichfield
Journal 1651

9 Walk cheerfully over the world, answering that of God in every one.
Journal 1656

10 Be still and cool in thy own mind and spirit from thy own thoughts, and then thou wilt feel the principle of God to turn thy mind to the Lord God.
Journal 1658

11 All bloody principles and practices, we, as to our own particulars, do utterly deny, with all outward wars and strife and fightings with outward weapons, for any end or under any pretence whatsoever. And this is our testimony to the whole world.
Journal 1661

Henry Fox see Lord Holland

Michael J. Fox 1961–

Canadian actor

12 When you're a short actor you stand on apple boxes, you walk on a ramp. When you're a short star everybody else walks in a ditch.
in *Toronto Star* 1 March 1991

13 It's all about losing your brain without losing your mind.
on his fight against Parkinson's disease
in *The Times* 16 September 2000

Terry Fox 1958–81

Canadian runner, whose right leg was amputated because of cancer

14 I'm not a dreamer . . . but I believe in miracles. I have to.
planning a fund-raising run across Canada; he completed two thirds of his 'Marathon of Hope'
letter to the Canadian Cancer Society, 15 October 1979

Janet Frame 1924–2004

New Zealand writer

15 For your own good is a persuasive argument that will eventually make a man agree to his own destruction.
Faces in the Water (1961) ch. 4

Anatole France (Jacques-Anatole-François Thibault) 1844–1924

French novelist and man of letters

16 Imitation lies at the root of most human actions. A respectable person is one who conforms to custom. People are called good when they do as others do.
Crainquebille (1923)

17 In every well-governed state, wealth is a sacred thing; in democracies it is the only sacred thing.
L'Île des pingouins (1908) pt. 6, ch. 2

18 Christianity has done a great deal for love by making a sin of it.
Le Jardin d'Épicure (1895)

19 They [the poor] have to labour in the face of the majestic equality of the law, which forbids the rich as well as the poor to sleep under bridges, to beg in the streets, and to steal bread.
Le Lys rouge (1894) ch. 7

20 Without lies humanity would perish of despair and boredom.
La Vie en fleur (1922)

1 The good critic is he who relates the adventures of his soul in the midst of masterpieces.
La Vie littéraire (1888) dedicatory letter

2 Make hatred hated!
to public school teachers
speech in Tours, August 1919; Carter Jefferson *Anatole France: The Politics of Scepticism.*

3 You think you are dying for your country; you die for the industrialists.
in *L'Humanité* 18 July 1922

Francis I 1494–1547
French monarch, King from 1515

4 *De toutes choses ne m'est demeuré que l'honneur et la vie qui est saulve.*
Of all I had, only honour and life have been spared.
letter to his mother following his defeat at Pavia,
1525; *see* **Misquotations** 537:1
in *Collection des Documents Inédits sur l'Histoire de France* (1847) vol. 1

St Francis of Assisi 1181–1226
Italian monk, founder of the Franciscan Order

5 Praised be You, my Lord, with all your creatures, especially Sir Brother Sun,
Who is the day and through whom You give us light.
'The Canticle of Brother Sun'

6 Lord, make me an instrument of Your peace!
Where there is hatred let me sow love;
Where there is injury, pardon;
Where there is doubt, faith;
Where there is despair, hope;
Where there is darkness, light;
Where there is sadness, joy.
O divine Master, grant that I may not so much seek
To be consoled as to console;
To be understood as to understand;
To be loved as to love.
'Prayer of St Francis' (attributed)

St Francis de Sales 1567–1622
French bishop of Geneva; leader of the Counter-Reformation

7 Big fires flare up in a wind, but little ones are blown out unless they are carried in under cover.
Introduction à la vie dévote (1609) pt. 3, ch. 34; *see* **Bussy-Rabutin** 175:8, **La Rochefoucauld** 469:18

8 *On a beau dire, mais le coeur parle au coeur, et la langue ne parle qu'aux oreilles.*
It has been said in vain, but heart speaks to heart, whereas language only speaks to the ears.
letter to the Archbishop of Bourges, 5 October 1604, in *Oeuvres de Saint François de Sales* (1834) vol. 3; *see* **Mottoes** 552:5

Anne Frank 1929–45
German-born Jewish diarist

9 I want to go on living even after death!
diary, 4 April 1944

Felix Frankfurter 1882–1965
American judge

10 It is a fair summary of history to say that the safeguards of liberty have been forged in controversies involving not very nice people.
dissenting opinion in *United States v. Rabinowitz* (1950)

Benjamin Franklin 1706–90
American politician, inventor, and scientist
on Franklin: *see* **Turgot** 802:13; *see also* **Anonymous** 20:9, **Epitaphs** 309:1, **Epitaphs** 310:8, **Toasts** 796:2

11 Remember that time is money.
Advice to a Young Tradesman (1748); *see* **Proverbs** 633:3

12 Some are weather-wise, some are otherwise.
Poor Richard's Almanac (1735) February

13 Necessity never made a good bargain.
Poor Richard's Almanac (1735) April

14 At twenty years of age, the will reigns; at thirty, the wit; and at forty, the judgement.
Poor Richard's Almanac (1741) June

15 He that lives upon hope will die fasting.
Poor Richard's Almanac (1758) preface

16 Fools need advice most, but wise men only are the better for it.
Poor Richard's Almanac (1758) January

17 We must indeed all hang together, or, most assuredly, we shall all hang separately.
at the signing of the Declaration of Independence, 4 July 1776 (possibly not original); P. M. Zall *Ben Franklin* (1980)

18 There never was a good war, or a bad peace.
letter to Josiah Quincy, 11 September 1783, in *Works* (1882) vol. 10

19 In this world nothing can be said to be certain, except death and taxes.
letter to Jean Baptiste Le Roy, 13 November 1789, in *Works of Benjamin Franklin* (1817) ch. 6.; *see* **Defoe** 261:6, **Proverbs** 628:8

20 Man is a tool-making animal.
James Boswell *Life of Samuel Johnson* (1791) 7 April 1778; *see* **Carlyle** 192:24

21 What is the use of a new-born child?
when asked what was the use of a new invention
J. Parton *Life and Times of Benjamin Franklin* (1864) pt. 4, ch. 17

Rosalind Franklin 1920–58
English physical chemist and molecular biologist

22 You look at science (or at least talk of it) as some sort of demoralizing invention of man, something apart from real life, and which must be cautiously guarded and kept separate from everyday existence. But science and everyday life cannot and should not be separated.
letter to her father, summer 1940; Brenda Maddox *Rosalind Franklin: the Dark Lady of DNA* (2002) ch. 4

Lord Franks 1905–92
British philosopher and administrator

1 The Pentagon, that immense monument to modern man's subservience to the desk.
  in Observer 30 November 1952

2 A secret in the Oxford sense: you may tell it to only one person at a time.
  in Sunday Telegraph 30 January 1977

Tommy Franks 1945–
American general

3 This will be a campaign unlike any other in history. A campaign characterized by shock, by surprise, by flexibility, by the employment of precise munitions on a scale never before seen, and by the application of overwhelming force.
  encapsulated in the phrase 'shock and awe', originally deriving from a Pentagon briefing document by Harlan Ullman and James P. Wade; see **Ullman** 804:7
  briefing in Qatar, 22 March 2003

Dawn Fraser 1937–
Australian swimmer

4 I hated the easy assumption that girls had to be slower than boys.
  attributed; Colin Jarman *Guinness Dictionary of Sports Quotations* (1990)

Malcolm Fraser 1930–
Australian Liberal statesman; Prime Minister 1975–83

5 Life is not meant to be easy.
  5th Alfred Deakin Lecture, 20 July 1971; see **Shaw** 724:18

Frederick the Great 1712–86
Prussian monarch, King from 1740
see also **Napoleon** 557:1

6 Rascals, would you live for ever?
  to hesitant Guards at Kolin, 18 June 1757
  attributed

7 Drive out prejudices through the door, and they will return through the window.
  letter to Voltaire, 19 March 1771, in *Oeuvres Complètes* (1790) vol. 12

8 My people and I have come to an agreement which satisfies us both. They are to say what they please, and I am to do what I please.
  his interpretation of benevolent despotism
  attributed

Cathy Freeman 1973–
Australian athlete

9 I was so angry because they were denying they had done anything wrong, denying that a whole generation was stolen.
  of official response to concerns about the 'stolen generation' of Aboriginal children forcibly removed from their families
  interview in *Daily Telegraph* 16 July 2000

E. A. Freeman 1823–92
English historian
on Freeman: see **Rogers** 652:15

10 History is past politics, and politics is present history.
  Methods of Historical Study (1886)

John Freeth c.1731–1808
English poet

11 The loss of America what can repay? New colonies seek for at Botany Bay.
  'Botany Bay' in *New London Magazine* (1786)

Marilyn French 1929–
American writer

12 The truth is that it is not the sins of the fathers that descend unto the third generation, but the sorrows of the mothers.
  Her Mother's Daughter (1987); see **Book of Common Prayer** 131:7

13 Whatever they may be in public life, whatever their relations with men, in their relations with women, all men are rapists, and that's all they are. They rape us with their eyes, their laws, and their codes.
  The Women's Room (1977)

14 'I hate discussions of feminism that end up with who does the dishes,' she said. So do I. But at the end, there are always the damned dishes.
  The Women's Room (1977)

Percy French 1854–1920
Irish songwriter

15 Come back, Paddy Reilly, to Ballyjamesduff; Come home, Paddy Reilly, to me.
  'Come Back, Paddy Reilly'

16 Oh Mary, this London's a wonderful sight, With the people all working by day and by night
  . . .
  But for all I found there, I might as well be Where the Mountains of Mourne sweep down to the sea.
  'The Mountains of Mourne'

John Hookham Frere 1769–1846
English poet

17 The feathered race with pinions skim the air— Not so the mackerel, and still less the bear!
  'The Progress of Man' (1798) canto 1, l. 34

18 Ah! who has seen the mailed lobster rise, Clap her broad wings, and soaring claim the skies.
  'The Progress of Man' (1798) canto 1, l. 44

Sigmund Freud 1856–1939
Austrian psychiatrist; originator of psychoanalysis
on Freud: see **Auden** 35:1, **Dodd** 278:19; *see also* **Riviere** 649:15

19 Anatomy is destiny.
  Collected Writings (1924) vol. 5

1 The interpretation of dreams is the royal road to a knowledge of the unconscious activities of the mind.
   The Interpretation of Dreams (2nd ed., 1909) ch. 7, sect. E; see **Misquotations** 537:10

2 Intolerance of groups is often, strangely enough, exhibited more strongly against small differences than against fundamental ones.
   Moses and Monotheism (1938)

3 Analogies decide nothing, that is true, but they can make one feel more at home.
   New Introductory Lectures on Psychoanalysis (1933)

4 'Itzig, where are you riding to?' 'Don't ask me, ask the horse.'
   letter to Wilhelm Fliess, 7 July 1898, in *Origins of Psychoanalysis* (1950)

5 The great question that has never been answered and which I have not yet been able to answer, despite my thirty years of research into the feminine soul, is 'What does a woman want?'
   letter to Marie Bonaparte, in Ernest Jones *Sigmund Freud: Life and Work* (1955) vol. 2, pt. 3, ch. 16

6 All that matters is love and work.
   attributed

7 Frozen anger.
   his definition of depression
   attributed

Nancy Friday 1937–
American writer

8 The older I get the more of my mother I see in myself.
   My Mother, My Self (1977) ch.1

9 It was the promise of men, that around each corner there was yet another man, more wonderful than the last, that sustained me. You see, I had men confused with life . . . You can't get what I wanted from a man, not in this life.
   My Mother, My Self (1977) ch.8

Betty Friedan 1921–
American feminist

10 The problem that has no name.
   being the fact that American women are kept from growing to their full human capacities
   The Feminine Mystique (1963) ch. 14

11 It is easier to live through someone else than to become complete yourself.
   The Feminine Mystique (1963) ch. 14

12 Today the problem that has no name is how to juggle work, love, home and children.
   The Second Stage (1987); see **Douglas** 283:13

Milton Friedman 1912–
*American economist and exponent of monetarism; policy adviser to President **Reagan** 1981–9*
see also **Sayings** 670:15

13 There is an invisible hand in politics that operates in the opposite direction to the invisible hand in the market. In politics, individuals who seek to promote only the public good are led by an invisible hand to promote special interests that it was no part of their intention to promote.
   Bright Promises, Dismal Performance: An Economist's Protest (1983)

14 Inflation is the one form of taxation that can be imposed without legislation.
   in *Observer* 22 September 1974

15 Thank heavens we do not get all of the government that we are made to pay for.
   attributed; quoted by Lord Harris of High Cross in the House of Lords, 24 November 1994

Brian Friel 1929–
Irish dramatist

16 Two such wonderful phrases—'I understand perfectly' and 'That is a lie'—a précis of life, aren't they?
   The Communication Cord (1983)

17 Do you want the whole countryside to be laughing at us?—women of our years?—mature women, *dancing*?
   Dancing at Lughnasa (1990)

Elisabeth Frink 1930–93
English sculptor and graphic artist
*on Frink: see **Pope-Hennessy** 606:27*

18 I feel that as religion is a vocation for many people—and nuns and monks are solitary people—so art is a comparable vocation for artists because of the solitariness of our work.
   Elisabeth Frink: Sculpture, Catalogue Raisonné (1984)

19 I have focused on the male because to me he is a subtle combination of sensuality and strength with vulnerability.
   Elisabeth Frink: Sculpture, Catalogue Raisonné (1984)

Max Frisch 1911–91
Swiss novelist and dramatist

20 *Jeder Bürger ist strafbar, genaugenommen, von einem gewissen Einkommen an.*
   Strictly speaking, every citizen above a certain level of income is guilty of some offence.
   The Fire Raisers (1953) sc. 3, translated by Michael Bullock

21 CHORFÜHRER: *Der, um zu wissen, was droht,*
   Zeitungen liest
   Täglich zum Frühstück entrüstet
   Über ein fernes Ereignis,
   Täglich beliefert mit Dautung,
   Die ihm das eigene Sinnen erspart,
   Täglich erfahrend, was gestern geschach,
   Schwerlich durchschaut er, was eben geschieht
   Unter dem eigenen Dach:—
   CHOR: *Unveröffentlichtes!*

   CHORUS LEADER: He who, in order to know
   What danger threatens, reads papers,
   Each day at breakfast indignant
   Over some distant disaster,
   Each day given explanations

That spare him the need to think,
Each day informed of what happened the day
  before,
He finds it hard to perceive what is happening
  now
Beneath his own roof—
CHORUS: Unpublished!
  The Fire Raisers (1953) sc. 3, translated by Michael Bullock

1 Technology . . . the knack of so arranging the
world that we need not experience it.
  Homo Faber (1957) pt. 2

Erich Fromm 1900–80
American philosopher and psychologist

2 Immature love says: 'I love you because I need
you.' Mature love says: 'I need you because I love
you.'
  The Art of Loving (1956) ch. 2

3 Love is often nothing but a favourable exchange
between two people who get the most out of what
they can expect, considering their value on the
personality market.
  The Sane Society (1955) ch. 5

4 In the nineteenth century the problem was that
God is dead; in the twentieth century the problem
is that *man is dead*. In the nineteenth century
inhumanity meant cruelty; in the twentieth
century it means schizoid self-alienation. The
danger of the past was that men became slaves.
The danger of the future is that men may become
robots.
  The Sane Society (1955) ch. 9

David Frost 1939–
English broadcaster and writer
*see also **Catchphrases** 200:25, **Catchphrases** 201:25*

5 Having one child makes you a parent; having two
you are a referee.
  in *Independent* 16 September 1989

Robert Frost 1874–1963
American poet

6 I have been one acquainted with the night.
  'Acquainted with the Night' (1928)

7 . . . Life is too much like a pathless wood
Where your face burns and tickles with the
  cobwebs
Broken across it, and one eye is weeping
From a twig's having lashed across it open.
  'Birches' (1916)

8 I'd like to get away from earth awhile
And then come back to it and begin over.
May no fate wilfully misunderstand me
And half grant what I wish and snatch me away
Not to return. Earth's the right place for love:
I don't know where it's likely to go better.
  'Birches' (1916)

9 Most of the change we think we see in life
Is due to truths being in and out of favour.
  'The Black Cottage' (1914)

10 Forgive, O Lord, my little jokes on Thee
And I'll forgive Thy great big one on me.
  'Cluster of Faith' (1962)

11 And nothing to look backward to with pride,
And nothing to look forward to with hope.
  'The Death of the Hired Man' (1914)

12 'Home is the place where, when you have to go
  there,
They have to take you in.'
'I should have called it
Something you somehow haven't to deserve.'
  'The Death of the Hired Man' (1914)

13 They cannot scare me with their empty spaces
Between stars—on stars where no human race is.
I have it in me so much nearer home
To scare myself with my own desert places.
  'Desert Places' (1936)

14 Some say the world will end in fire,
Some say in ice.
From what I've tasted of desire
I hold with those who favour fire.
But if it had to perish twice,
I think I know enough of hate
To say that for destruction ice
Is also great
And would suffice.
  'Fire and Ice' (1923)

15 The land was ours before we were the land's.
She was our land more than a hundred years
Before we were her people.
  'The Gift Outright' (1942)

16 Happiness makes up in height for what it lacks in
length.
  title of poem (1942)

17 And were an epitaph to be my story
I'd have a short one ready for my own.
I would have written of me on my stone:
I had a lover's quarrel with the world.
  'The Lesson for Today' (1942)

18 Something there is that doesn't love a wall,
That sends the frozen-ground-swell under it.
  'Mending Wall' (1914)

19 My apple trees will never get across
And eat the cones under his pines, I tell him.
He only says, 'Good fences make good
  neighbours.'
  'Mending Wall' (1914)

20 Before I built a wall I'd ask to know
What I was walling in or walling out,
And to whom I was like to give offence.
  'Mending Wall' (1914)

21 I never dared be radical when young
For fear it would make me conservative when old.
  'Precaution' (1936)

22 No memory of having starred
Atones for later disregard,
Or keeps the end from being hard.
  'Provide Provide' (1936)

23 Two roads diverged in a wood, and I—
I took the one less travelled by,

And that has made all the difference.
'The Road Not Taken' (1916)

1 We dance round in a ring and suppose,
But the Secret sits in the middle and knows.
'The Secret Sits' (1942)

2 I've broken Anne of gathering bouquets.
It's not fair to the child. It can't be helped though:
Pressed into service means pressed out of shape.
'The Self-Seeker' (1914)

3 The woods are lovely, dark and deep.
But I have promises to keep,
And miles to go before I sleep,
And miles to go before I sleep.
'Stopping by Woods on a Snowy Evening' (1923)

4 The figure a poem makes. It begins in delight and
ends in wisdom. The figure is the same as for love.
Collected Poems (1939) 'The Figure a Poem Makes'

5 No tears in the writer, no tears in the reader. No
surprise for the writer, no surprise for the reader.
Collected Poems (1939) 'The Figure a Poem Makes'

6 Like a piece of ice on a hot stove the poem must
ride on its own melting. A poem may be worked
over once it is in being, but may not be worried
into being.
Collected Poems (1939) 'The Figure a Poem Makes'

7 Poetry is a way of taking life by the throat.
Elizabeth S. Sergeant *Robert Frost* (1960) ch. 18

8 You can be a little ungrammatical if you come
from the right part of the country.
in *Atlantic Monthly* January 1962

9 I'd as soon write free verse as play tennis with the
net down.
Edward Lathem *Interviews with Robert Frost* (1966)

10 Poetry is what is lost in translation. It is also what
is lost in interpretation.
Louis Untermeyer *Robert Frost* (1964)

Christopher Fry 1907–

English dramatist

11 The dark is light enough.
title of play (1954)

12 The lady's not for burning.
title of play (1949); see **Thatcher** 787:3

13   What after all
Is a halo? It's only one more thing to keep clean.
The Lady's not for Burning (1949) act 1

14 Where in this small-talking world can I find
A longitude with no platitude?
The Lady's not for Burning (1949) act 3

15   The best
Thing we can do is to make wherever we're lost in
Look as much like home as we can.
The Lady's not for Burning (1949) act 3

Elizabeth Fry 1780–1845

English Quaker prison reformer

16 Does capital punishment tend to the security of
the people?

By no means. It hardens the hearts of men, and
makes the loss of life appear light to them; and it
renders life insecure, inasmuch as the law holds
out that property is of greater value than life.
note found among her papers; Rachel E. Cresswell and
Katharine Fry *Memoir of the Life of Elizabeth Fry* (1848)

17 Punishment is not for revenge, but to lessen crime
and reform the criminal.
note found among her papers; Rachel E. Cresswell and
Katharine Fry *Memoir of the Life of Elizabeth Fry* (1848)

Roger Fry 1866–1934

English art critic

18 Art is significant deformity.
Virginia Woolf *Roger Fry* (1940) ch. 8

19 Bach almost persuades me to be a Christian.
Virginia Woolf *Roger Fry* (1940) ch. 11

Carlos Fuentes 1928–

Mexican novelist and writer

20 New York: building itself up out of its own
disintegration, its inevitable destiny as the city for
everyone, energetic, tireless, brutal, murderous
city of the entire world, where we all recognize
ourselves and see our worst and our best.
The Crystal Frontier (1994) title story

21 In Eden the only wealth is nakedness and
unawareness.
The Orange Tree (1994) 'The Two Americas'

22 High on the agenda for the 21st century will be
the need to restore some kind of tragic
consciousness.
Rushworth M. Kidder *An Agenda for the 21st Century*
(1987)

Francis Fukuyama 1952–

American historian

23 What we may be witnessing is not just the end of
the Cold War but the end of history as such: that
is, the end point of man's ideological evolution
and the universalism of Western liberal
democracy.
in *Independent* 20 September 1989

J. William Fulbright 1905–95

American politician

24 The Soviet Union has indeed been our greatest
menace, not so much because of what it has done,
but because of the excuses it has provided us for
our failures.
in *Observer* 21 December 1958 'Sayings of the Year'

R. Buckminster Fuller 1895–1983

American designer and architect

25 Either war is obsolete or men are.
in *New Yorker* 8 January 1966

26 God, to me, it seems,
is a verb

not a noun,
proper or improper.

> *No More Secondhand God* (1963) (untitled poem written in 1940); see **Hugo** 407:15

1 Now there is one outstandingly important fact regarding Spaceship Earth, and that is that no instruction book came with it.

> *Operating Manual for Spaceship Earth* (1969) ch. 4

Sam Fuller

American film director

2 When you're in the battlefield, survival is all there is. Death is the only great emotion.

> in *Guardian* 26 February 1991

Thomas Fuller 1608–61

English preacher and historian

3 But our captain counts the Image of God nevertheless his image, cut in ebony as if done in ivory.

> *The Holy State and the Profane State* (1642) bk. 2 'The Good Sea-Captain'

4 Know most of the rooms of thy native country before thou goest over the threshold thereof.

> *The Holy State and the Profane State* (1642) bk. 3 'Of Travelling'

5 Anger is one of the sinews of the soul.

> *The Holy State and the Profane State* (1642) bk. 3 'Of Anger'

6 Light (God's eldest daughter) is a principal beauty in building.

> *The Holy State and the Profane State* (1642) bk. 3 'Of Building'

7 He was one of a lean body and visage, as if his eager soul, biting for anger at the clog of his body, desired to fret a passage through it.

> *The Holy State and the Profane State* (1642) bk. 5 'Life of the Duke of Alva'

Thomas Fuller 1654–1734

English writer and physician
*see also **Denning** 264:10*

8 He that plants trees loves others beside himself.

> *Gnomologia* (1732) no. 2247

9 We are all Adam's children but silk makes the difference.

> *Gnomologia* (1732) no. 5425

Alfred Funke b. 1869

German writer

10 *Gott strafe England!*
God punish England!

> *Schwert und Myrte* (1914)

Henry Fuseli (Johann Heinrich Füssli) 1741–1825

Swiss-born British painter and art critic

11 The Greeks were gods! The Greeks were gods!

> *on first seeing the Elgin marbles*
> J. Mordaunt Crook *The Greek Revival* (1995)

David Maxwell Fyfe see **Lord Kilmuir**

Rose Fyleman 1877–1957

English writer for children

12 There are fairies at the bottom of our garden!

> *Fairies and Chimneys* (1918) 'The Fairies' (first published in *Punch* 23 May 1917)

Clark Gable see **Film lines** 319:7

Thomas Gainsborough 1727–88

English painter
*see also **Last words** 474:11*

13 Damn gentlemen. There is not such a set of enemies to a real artist in the world as they are, if not kept at a proper distance.

> letter to the musician William Jackson, 2 September 1767; Mary Woodall (ed.) *The Letters of Thomas Gainsborough* (1961)

14 Recollect that painting and punctuality mix like oil and vinegar, and that genius and regularity are utter enemies, and must be to the end of time.

> speech to the Edward Stratford, 1 May 1772; Mary Woodall (ed.) *The Letters of Thomas Gainsborough* (1961)

Thomas Gaisford 1779–1855

English classicist; Dean of Christ Church, Oxford, from 1831

15 Nor can I do better, in conclusion, than impress upon you the study of Greek literature, which not only elevates above the vulgar herd, but leads not infrequently to positions of considerable emolument.

> Christmas Day Sermon in the Cathedral, Oxford, in W. Tuckwell *Reminiscences of Oxford* (2nd ed., 1907)

Hugh Gaitskell 1906–63

British Labour politician
*on Gaitskell: see **Bevan** 73:16*

16 The subtle terrorism of words.

> *in a warning given to his Party, c.1957*
> Harry Hopkins *The New Look* (1963); attributed

17 There are some of us . . . who will fight and fight and fight again to save the Party we love.

> speech at Labour Party Conference, 5 October 1960, in *Report of 59th Annual Conference*

18 It means the end of a thousand years of history.

> *on a European federation*
> speech at Labour Party Conference, 3 October 1962, in *Report of 61st Annual Conference*

Gaius (or Caius) c.AD 110–c.180

Roman jurist

19 *Damnosa hereditas.*
Ruinous inheritance.

> *The Institutes* bk. 2, ch. 163

J. K. Galbraith 1908–
Canadian-born American economist

1 The affluent society.
   title of book (1958)

2 These are the days when men of all social disciplines and all political faiths seek the comfortable and the accepted; when the man of controversy is looked upon as a disturbing influence; when originality is taken to be a mark of instability; and when, in minor modification of the scriptural parable, the bland lead the bland.
   The Affluent Society (1958) ch. 1, sect. 3

3 The greater the wealth, the thicker will be the dirt.
   The Affluent Society (1958) ch. 18, sect. 2

4 The salary of the chief executive of the large corporation is not a market reward for achievement. It is frequently in the nature of a warm personal gesture by the individual to himself.
   Annals of an Abiding Liberal (1979)

5 Trickle-down theory—the less than elegant metaphor that if one feeds the horse enough oats, some will pass through to the road for the sparrows.
   The Culture of Contentment (1992)

6 Meetings are held because men seek companionship or, at a minimum, wish to escape the tedium of solitary duties.
   The Great Crash 1929 (1954)

7 Politics is not the art of the possible. It consists in choosing between the disastrous and the unpalatable.
   speech to President Kennedy, 2 March 1962, in *Ambassador's Journal* (1969); see **Bismarck** 117:14

Galen AD 129–199
Greek physician

8 The chief merit of language is clearness, and we know that nothing detracts so much from this as do unfamiliar terms.
   On the Natural Faculties bk. 1, sect. 1

9 If anyone wishes to observe the works of nature, he should put his trust not in books of anatomy but in his own eyes.
   On the Usefulness of the Parts of the Body bk. 2 [1, 72] sect. 3

Galileo Galilei 1564–1642
Italian astronomer and physicist

10 Philosophy is written in that great book which ever lies before our eyes—I mean the universe . . . This book is written in mathematical language and its characters are triangles, circles and other geometrical figures, without whose help . . . one wanders in vain through a dark labyrinth.
   often quoted as 'The book of nature is written . . . '
   The Assayer (1623)

11 *Eppur si muove.*
   But it does move.
   after his recantation, that the earth moves around the sun, in 1632
   attributed; Baretti *Italian Library* (1757) is possibly the earliest appearance of the phrase

12 In disputes about natural phenomena one must begin not with the authority of Scriptural passage but with sensory experience and necessary demonstrations. For the Holy Scripture and nature derive equally from the Godhead, the former as the dictation of the Holy Spirit and the latter as the most obedient executrix of God's orders.
   letter to Christina Lotharinga, Arch-Duchess of Tuscany; P. MacHamer (ed.) *Cambridge Companion to Galileo* (1998)

John Galsworthy 1867–1933
English novelist

13 He was afflicted by the thought that where Beauty was, nothing ever ran quite straight, which, no doubt, was why so many people looked on it as immoral.
   In Chancery (1920) pt. 1, ch. 13

14 A man of action forced into a state of thought is unhappy until he can get out of it.
   Maid in Waiting (1931) ch. 3

John Galt 1779–1839
Scottish writer

15 From the lone shieling of the misty island
   Mountains divide us, and the waste of seas—
   Yet still the blood is strong, the heart is Highland,
   And we in dreams behold the Hebrides!
   'Canadian Boat Song' translated from the Gaelic in *Blackwoods Edinburgh Magazine* September 1829 'Noctes Ambrosianae' no. 46, and later attributed to Galt

Ray Galton 1930– and Alan Simpson 1929–
English scriptwriters

16 I came in here in all good faith to help my country. I don't mind giving a reasonable amount [of blood], but a pint . . . why that's very nearly an armful.
   Hancock's Half Hour 'The Blood Donor' (1961 BBC television programme); words spoken by Tony Hancock

17 It's red hot, mate. I hate to think of this sort of book getting into the wrong hands. As soon as I've finished this, I shall recommend they ban it.
   The Missing Page (1960 BBC television programme) words spoken by Tony Hancock

George Gamow 1904–68
Russian-born American physicist

18 We do not know why they [elementary particles] have the masses they do; we do not know why they transform into another the way they do; we do not know anything! The one concept that stands like the Rock of Gibraltar in our sea of confusion is the Pauli [exclusion] principle.

in *Scientific American* July 1959

1 With five free parameters, a theorist could fit the profile of an elephant.

attributed; in *Nature* 21 June 1990

Indira Gandhi 1917–84

Indian stateswoman; Prime Minister 1966–77 and 1980–4

2 We do not tilt on either side . . . we walk upright.

when asked by a reporter why India 'always tilted towards the Soviet Union'

in Washington, 1982; Inder Malhotra *Indira Gandhi* (1989)

3 I cannot understand how anyone can be an Indian and not be proud—the richness and infinite variety of our composite heritage, the magnificence of the people's spirit, equal to any disaster or burden, firm in their faith . . . even in poverty and hardship.

paper found after her death, *Remembered Moments* (1987)

4 I have lived a long life and I am proud that I spent the whole of my life in the service of my people. I am only proud of this and of nothing else. I shall continue to serve until my last breath and when I die, I can say, that every drop of my blood will invigorate India and strengthen it.

speech, Bhubaneshwar, 30 October 1984 (the night before she was assassinated); *Selected Speeches*(1986) vol. 5

Mahatma Gandhi (Mohandas Karamchand Gandhi) 1869–1948

Indian statesman

*on Gandhi: see **Naidhu** 556:1, **Nehru** 558:4; see also **Sayings** 669:17*

5 What difference does it make to the dead, the orphans and the homeless, whether the mad destruction is wrought under the name of totalitarianism or the holy name of liberty or democracy?

Non-Violence in Peace and War (1942) vol. 1, ch. 142

6 The moment the slave resolves that he will no longer be a slave, his fetters fall. He frees himself and shows the way to others. Freedom and slavery are mental states.

Non-Violence in Peace and War (1949) vol. 2, ch. 5

7 Non-violence is the first article of my faith. It is also the last article of my creed.

speech at Shahi Bag, 18 March 1922, on a charge of sedition, in *Young India* 23 March 1922

8 In my humble opinion, non-cooperation with evil is as much a duty as is cooperation with good.

speech in Ahmadabad, 23 March 1922

9 *on being asked what he thought of modern civilization:* That would be a good idea.

while visiting England in 1930

E. F. Schumacher *Good Work* (1979)

Greta Garbo (Greta Lovisa Gustafsson) 1905–90

Swedish film actress

*see also **Taglines for films** 771:3*

10 I want to be alone.

Grand Hotel (1932 film), the phrase already being associated with Garbo

Frederico García Lorca see Lorca

Gabriel García Márquez 1928–

Colombian novelist

11 Necessity has the face of a dog.

In Evil Hour (1968)

Richard Gardiner b. c.1533

English writer

12 Sowe Carrets in your Gardens, and humbly praise God for them, as for a singular and great blessing.

Profitable Instructions for the Manuring, Sowing and Planting of Kitchen Gardens (1599)

Ed Gardner 1901–63

American radio comedian

13 Opera is when a guy gets stabbed in the back and, instead of bleeding, he sings.

in *Duffy's Tavern* (US radio programme, 1940s)

James A. Garfield 1831–81

American Republican statesman; 20th President of the US 1881

*on Garfield: see **Thayer** 787:19*

14 Fellow-citizens: God reigns, and the Government at Washington lives!

speech on the assassination of President Lincoln, 17 April 1865; in *Death of President Garfield* (1881)

Giuseppe Garibaldi 1807–82

Italian patriot and military leader

15 Men, I'm getting out of Rome. Anyone who wants to carry on the war against the outsiders, come with me. I can offer you neither honours nor wages; I offer you hunger, thirst, forced marches, battles and death. Anyone who loves his country, follow me.

Giuseppe Guerzoni *Garibaldi* (1882) vol. 1 (not a verbatim record)

John Nance Garner 1868–1967

American Democratic politician; vice-president 1933–41

16 The vice-presidency isn't worth a pitcher of warm piss.

O. C. Fisher *Cactus Jack* (1978) ch. 11

David Garrick 1717–79

English actor-manager

on Garrick: see **Foote** *328:4,* **Goldsmith** *355:4,* **Goldsmith** *355:6,* **Goldsmith** *355:7,* **Johnson** *425:9; see also* **Colman and Garrick**, **Epitaphs** *309:6*

1 They smile with the simple, and feed with the poor.
   Florizel and Perdita (performed 1756) act 2, sc. 1; *see* **Johnson** 429:3

2 Heart of oak are our ships,
   Heart of oak are our men:
   We always are ready;
   Steady, boys, steady;
   We'll fight and we'll conquer again and again.
   Harlequin's Invasion (1759) 'Heart of Oak' (song)

3 Here lies Nolly Goldsmith, for shortness called Noll,
   Who wrote like an angel, but talked like poor Poll.
   'Impromptu Epitaph' (written 1773/4); *see* **Goldsmith** 355:4, **Johnson** 431:19

4 A fellow-feeling makes one wond'rous kind.
   'An Occasional Prologue on Quitting the Theatre' 10 June 1776

5 Are these the choice dishes the Doctor has sent us?
   Is this the great poet whose works so content us?
   This Goldsmith's fine feast, who has written fine books?
   Heaven sends us good meat, but the Devil sends cooks.
   'On Doctor Goldsmith's Characteristical Cookery' (1777)

6 Prologues precede the piece—in mournful verse;
   As undertakers—walk before the hearse.
   prologue to Arthur Murphy's *The Apprentice* (1756)

7 Kitty, a fair, but frozen maid,
   Kindled a flame I still deplore.
   'A Riddle' (1762)

William Lloyd Garrison 1805–79

American anti-slavery campaigner

8 I am in earnest—I will not equivocate—I will not excuse—I will not retreat a single inch—and I will be heard!
   in *The Liberator* 1 January 1831 'Salutatory Address'

9 Our country is the world—our countrymen are all mankind.
   The Liberator 15 December 1837 'Prospectus'

10 The compact which exists between the North and the South is 'a covenant with death and an agreement with hell'.
   resolution adopted by the Massachusetts Anti-Slavery Society, 27 January 1843, in Archibald H. Grimke *William Lloyd Garrison: The Abolitionist* (1891) ch. 16; *see* **Bible** 89:4

Samuel Garth 1661–1719

English poet and physician

11 Hard was their lodging, homely was their food;
   For all their luxury was doing good.
   'Claremont' (1715) l. 148

12 A barren superfluity of words.
   The Dispensary (1699) canto 2, l. 82

George Gascoigne c.1534–77

English soldier and poet

13 The common speech is, spend and God will send.
   But what sends he? a bottle and a bag,
   A staff, a wallet and a woeful end,
   For such as list in bravery so to brag.
   '*Magnum vectigal parsimonia* [Thrift makes a good income]' (1573)

14 The carrion crow, that loathsome beast,
   Which cries against the rain.
   'Gascoigne's Good Morrow' (1573)

15 As busy brains must beat on tickle toys,
   As rash invention breeds a raw device,
   So sudden falls do hinder hasty joys;
   And as swift baits do fleetest fish entice,
   So haste makes waste.
   'No haste but good' (1573)

Elizabeth Gaskell 1810–65

English novelist

16 A man . . . is *so* in the way in the house!
   Cranford (1853) ch. 1

17 Economy was always 'elegant', and money-spending always 'vulgar' and ostentatious— a sort of sour-grapeism, which made us very peaceful and satisfied.
   Cranford (1853) ch. 1

18 Bombazine would have shown a deeper sense of her loss.
   Cranford (1853) ch. 7

19 I'll not listen to reason . . . Reason always means what someone else has got to say.
   Cranford (1853) ch. 14

20 That kind of patriotism which consists in hating all other nations.
   Sylvia's Lovers (1863) ch. 1

21 It is a noble grand book, whoever wrote it—but Miss Evans' life taken at the best construction, does so jar against the beautiful book that one cannot help hoping against hope.
   on first hearing of the true identity of 'George **Eliot**', *author of* Adam Bede
   letter to George Smith, 4 August 1859; *The Letters of Mrs Gaskell* (1966)

22 I look at them as a child looks at a cake,—with glittering eyes and watering mouth, imagining the pleasure that awaits him!
   on the books she was planning to read
   letter to George Smith, 4 August 1859; *The Letters of Mrs Gaskell* (1966)

Paul Gauguin 1848–1903

French painter

23 A hint—don't paint too much direct from nature. Art is an abstraction! study nature then brood on it and treasure the creation which will result,

which is the only way to ascend towards God—to create like our Divine Master.

letter to Emile Schuffenecker, 14 August 1888; *Paul Gauguin: Letters to his wife and friends* (1946, ed. Maurice Malingue, trans. Henry J. Stenning)

Alan Gaunt 1935-

English hymn-writer

1 We pray for peace,
But not the easy peace
Built on complacency
And not the truth of God.
'We pray for peace' (hymn)

Théophile Gautier 1811-72

French poet, novelist, and critic

2 *Toute passe.—L'art robuste
Seul à l'éternité,
Le Buste
Survit à la cité.*

Everything passes. Robust art alone is eternal, the bust survives the city.
'L'Art' (1857); see **Dobson** 278:15

Gavarni (Guillaume Sulpice Chevalier) 1804-66

French lithographer

3 *Les enfants terribles.*
The little terrors.
title of a series of prints (1842)

John Gay 1685-1732

*English poet and dramatist
on Gay: see **Johnson** 425:4; see also **Epitaphs** 310:13*

4 O ruddier than the cherry,
O sweeter than the berry.
Acis and Galatea (performed 1718, published 1732) pt. 2

5 How, like a moth, the simple maid
Still plays about the flame!
The Beggar's Opera (1728) act 1, sc. 4, air 4

6 Our Polly is a sad slut! nor heeds what we have taught her.
I wonder any man alive will ever rear a daughter!
The Beggar's Opera (1728) act 1, sc. 8, air 7

7 Do you think your mother and I should have lived comfortably so long together, if ever we had been married?
The Beggar's Opera (1728) act 1, sc. 8

8 Can Love be controlled by advice?
The Beggar's Opera (1728) act 1, sc. 8, air 8

9 POLLY: Then all my sorrows are at an end.
MRS PEACHUM: A mighty likely speech, in troth, for a wench who is just married!
The Beggar's Opera (1728) act 1, sc. 8

10 Money, wife, is the true fuller's earth for reputations, there is not a spot or a stain but what it can take out.
The Beggar's Opera (1728) act 1, sc. 9

11 The comfortable estate of widowhood, is the only hope that keeps up a wife's spirits.
The Beggar's Opera (1728) act 1, sc. 10

12 If with me you'd fondly stray,
Over the hills and far away.
The Beggar's Opera (1728) act 1, sc. 13, air 16

13 Women and wine should life employ.
Is there ought else on earth desirous?
The Beggar's Opera (1728) act 2, sc. 1, air 19

14 If the heart of a man is deprest with cares,
The mist is dispelled when a woman appears.
The Beggar's Opera (1728) act 2, sc. 3, air 21

15 I must have women. There is nothing unbends the mind like them.
The Beggar's Opera (1728) act 2, sc. 3

16 Youth's the season made for joys;
Love is then our duty.
The Beggar's Opera (1728) act 2, sc. 4, air 22

17 To cheat a man is nothing; but the woman must have fine parts indeed who cheats a woman!
The Beggar's Opera (1728) act 2, sc. 4

18 I am ready, my dear Lucy, to give you satisfaction—if you think there is any in marriage?
The Beggar's Opera (1728) act 2, sc. 9

19 In one respect indeed, our employment may be reckoned dishonest, because, like great Statesmen, we encourage those who betray their friends.
The Beggar's Opera (1728) act 2, sc. 10

20 How happy could I be with either,
Were t'other dear charmer away!
The Beggar's Opera (1728) act 2, sc. 13, air 35

21 She who has never loved, has never lived.
The Captives (1724) act 2, sc. 2

22 She who trifles with all
Is less likely to fall
Than she who but trifles with one.
'The Coquet Mother and the Coquet Daughter' (1727)

23 He saw, he sighed, he loved, was scorned and died.
Dione (1720) act 1, sc. 1

24 A woman's friendship ever ends in love.
Dione (1720) act 4, sc. 6

25 Whence is thy learning? Hath thy toil
O'er books consumed the midnight oil?
Fables (1727) introduction, l. 15; see **Quarles** 638:20

26 Envy's a sharper spur than pay,
No author ever spared a brother,
Wits are gamecocks to one another.
Fables (1727) 'The Elephant and the Bookseller' l. 74

27 And when a lady's in the case,
You know, all other things give place.
Fables (1727) 'The Hare and Many Friends' l. 41

28 Those who in quarrels interpose,
Must often wipe a bloody nose.
Fables (1727) 'The Mastiffs' l. 1

29 An open foe may prove a curse,
But a pretended friend is worse.
Fables (1727) 'The Shepherd's Dog and the Wolf' l. 33

1 I know you lawyers can, with ease,
Twist words and meanings as you please;
That language, by your skill made pliant,
Will bend to favour ev'ry client.
Fables (1738) 'The Dog and the Fox' l. 1

2 Studious of elegance and ease,
Myself alone I seek to please.
Fables (1738) 'The Man, the Cat, the Dog, and the Fly' l.
127

3 That politician tops his part,
Who readily can lie with art.
Fables (1738) 'The Squire and his Cur' l. 27

4 Give me, kind heaven, a private station,
A mind serene for contemplation.
Fables (1738) 'The Vulture, the Sparrow, and Other Birds'
l. 69

5 Behold the bright original appear.
'A Letter to a Lady' (1714) l. 85

6 Praising all alike, is praising none.
'A Letter to a Lady' (1714) l. 114

7 Whether we can afford it or no, we must have
superfluities.
'Polly' (1729) act 1, sc. 1

8 No, sir, tho' I was born and bred in England, I can
dare to be poor, which is the only thing now-
a-days men are ashamed of.
'Polly' (1729) act 1, sc. 11

9 An inconstant woman, tho' she has no chance to
be very happy, can never be very unhappy.
'Polly' (1729) act 1, sc. 14

10 All in the Downs the fleet was moored,
The streamers waving in the wind,
When black-eyed Susan came aboard.
'Sweet William's Farewell to Black-Eyed Susan' (1720)

11 They'll tell thee, sailors, when away,
In ev'ry port a mistress find.
'Sweet William's Farewell to Black-Eyed Susan' (1720)

12 Adieu, she cries! and waved her lily hand.
'Sweet William's Farewell to Black-Eyed Susan' (1720)

13 A miss for pleasure, and a wife for breed.
'The Toilette' (1716)

Noel Gay (Richard Moxon Armitage)
1898–1954
British songwriter

14 I'm leaning on a lamp post at the corner of the
street,
In case a certain little lady comes by.
'Leaning on a Lamp Post' (1937); sung by George Formby
in the film *Father Knew Best*

Eric Geddes 1875–1937
British politician and administrator

15 The Germans, if this Government is returned, are
going to pay every penny; they are going to be
squeezed as a lemon is squeezed—until the pips
squeak.
speech at Cambridge, 10 December 1918, in *Cambridge
Daily News* 11 December 1918

Frank Gehry 1929–
Canadian-born American architect

16 People ask me if I'm an artist or an architect. But I
think they're the same.
in *Toronto Star* 4 September 1987

Bob Geldof 1954– and Midge Ure 1953–
Irish rock musician; Scottish rock musician

17 Do they know it's Christmas?
title of song (1984)

Martha Gellhorn 1908–98
American journalist

18 I believed that all one did about a war was go to it,
as a gesture of solidarity, and get killed, or survive
if lucky until the war was over . . . I had no idea
you could be what I became, an unscathed tourist
of wars.
The Face of War (1959)

19 *of the defeat of the Spanish Republic:*
I daresay we all became more competent press
tourists because of it, since we never again cared
so much. You can only love one war; afterward, I
suppose, you do your duty.
The Honeyed Peace (1953)

20 Never believe governments, not any of them, not a
word they say; keep an untrusting eye on all they
do.
in obituary, *Daily Telegraph* 17 February 1998

Jean Genet 1910–86
French novelist, poet, and dramatist

21 What we need is hatred. From it our ideas are
born.
The Blacks (1959); epigraph

22 Are you there . . . Africa of the millions of royal
slaves, deported Africa, drifting continent, are you
there? Slowly you vanish, you withdraw into the
past, into the tales of castaways, colonial
museums, the works of scholars.
The Blacks (1959)

23 Anyone who hasn't experienced the ecstasy of
betrayal knows nothing about ecstasy at all.
Prisoner of Love (1986)

Genghis Khan (Temujin) 1162–1227
*Mongol ruler, who took the name Genghis Khan ('ruler of
all') in 1206*

24 Happiness lies in conquering one's enemies, in
driving them in front of oneself, in taking their
property, in savouring their despair, in outraging
their wives and daughters.
Witold Rodzinski *The Walled Kingdom: A History of China*
(1979)

George I 1660–1727
*British monarch, King of Great Britain and Ireland from 1714
on George I: see* **Johnson** *430:3,* **Landor** *466:5*

25 I hate all Boets and Bainters.
John Campbell *Lives of the Chief Justices* (1849) 'Lord

Mansfield'; the remark 'I hate bainting and boetry too!' is attributed to **George II** in John Ireland *Hogarth Illustrated* (1791)

George II 1683–1760

British monarch, King of Great Britain and Ireland from 1727, husband of Caroline of Ansbach
on George II: see Landor 466:5; see also George I 342:25

1 We are come for your good, for all your goods.
   speech at Portsmouth, probably 1716, in Joseph Spence *Anecdotes* (ed. J. M. Osborn, 1966) no. 903

2 *Non, j'aurai des maîtresses.*
   No, I shall have mistresses.
   when Queen Caroline, on her deathbed in 1737, urged him to marry again; the Queen replied, 'Ah! mon dieu! cela n'empêche pas [Oh, my God! That won't make any difference]'
   John Hervey *Memoirs of the Reign of George II* (1848) vol. 2.

3 Mad, is he? Then I hope he will *bite* some of my other generals.
   replying to the Duke of Newcastle, who had complained that General Wolfe was a madman
   Henry Beckles Willson *Life and Letters of James Wolfe* (1909) ch. 17

George III 1738–1820

British monarch, King of Great Britain and Ireland from 1760
on George III: see Bagehot 48:13, Bentley 68:17, Byron 183:16, Landor 466:5, Shelley 731:20, Walpole 820:2; see also Edgeworth 296:4

4 Born and educated in this country, I glory in the name of Briton.
   The King's Speech on Opening the Session House of Lords, 18 November 1760

5 Was there ever such stuff as great part of Shakespeare? Only one must not say so! But what think you?—what?—Is there not sad stuff? what?—what?
   to Fanny Burney, in *Diary and Letters of Madame d'Arblay* vol. 2 (1842) diary, 19 December 1785

George IV 1762–1830

British monarch, King of Great Britain and Ireland from 1820
on George IV: see Brummell 162:6, Hunt 410:8, Landor 466:5; see also Toasts 796:6

6 Harris, I am not well; pray get me a glass of brandy.
   on first seeing Caroline of Brunswick, his future wife
   Earl of Malmesbury *Diaries and Correspondence* (1844) vol. 3, 5 April 1795

George V 1865–1936

British monarch, King of Great Britain and Ireland from 1910
on George V: see Betjeman 72:5, Dawson 259:19, Nicolson 563:13; see also Last words 471:5, Last words 471:18

7 Wake up, England.
   title of 1911 reprint of speech below

   I venture to allude to the impression which seemed generally to prevail among their brethren across the seas, that the Old Country must wake up if she intends to maintain her old position of pre-eminence in her Colonial trade against foreign competitors.
   speech at Guildhall, 5 December 1901, in Harold Nicolson *King George V* (1952)

8 I pray that my coming to Ireland today may prove to be the first step towards an end of strife among her people, whatever their race or creed. In that hope I appeal to all Irishmen to pause, to stretch out the hand of forbearance and conciliation, to forgive and forget, and to join with me in making for the land they love a new era of peace, contentment and goodwill.
   speech to the new Ulster Parliament at Stormont, 22 June 1921; Kenneth Rose *King George V* (1983)

9 I have many times asked myself whether there can be more potent advocates of peace upon earth through the years to come than this massed multitude of silent witnesses to the desolation of war.
   message read at Terlincthun Cemetery, Boulogne, 13 May 1922, in *The Times* 15 May 1922

10 After I am dead, the boy will ruin himself in twelve months.
   of his son, the future Edward VIII
   Keith Middlemas and John Barnes *Baldwin* (1969) ch. 34

11 Anything except that damned Mouse.
   on being asked what film he would like to see
   George Lyttelton, letter to Rupert Hart-Davis, 12 November 1959

12 *on H. G. Wells's comment on 'an alien and uninspiring court':*
   I may be uninspiring, but I'll be damned if I'm an alien!
   Sarah Bradford *George VI* (1989); attributed

13 My father was frightened of his mother; I was frightened of my father, and I am damned well going to see to it that my children are frightened of me.
   attributed in Randolph S. Churchill *Lord Derby* (1959), but said by Kenneth Rose in *George V* (1983) to be almost certainly apocryphal; see **Morshead** 550:17

George VI 1895–1952

British monarch, King of Great Britain and Northern Ireland from 1936
see also Haskins 375:2

14 Personally I feel happier now that we have no allies to be polite to and to pamper.
   to Queen Mary, 27 June 1940, in John Wheeler-Bennett *King George VI* (1958) pt. 3, ch. 6

15 Abroad is bloody.
   W. H. Auden *A Certain World* (1970) 'Royalty'; see **Mitford** 541:2

16 The family firm.
   description of the British monarchy
   attributed

Dan George 1899–1981
Canadian native chief and actor

1 When the white man came we had the land and they had the bibles; now they have the land and we have the bibles.
> Gerald Walsh *Indians in Transition: An Inquiry Approach* (1971)

Daniel George (Daniel George Bunting)
English writer

2 O Freedom, what liberties are taken in thy name!
> *The Perpetual Pessimist* (1963); see **Last words** 473:9

David Lloyd George see Lloyd George

Geronimo c.1829–1909
Apache chief

3 Once I moved about like the wind. Now I surrender to you and that is all.
> surrendering to General Crook, 25 March 1886; Dee Brown *Bury My Heart at Wounded Knee* (1970) ch. 17

Ira Gershwin 1896–1983
American songwriter
*see also **Heyward and Gershwin***

4 A foggy day in London Town
Had me low and had me down.
I viewed the morning with alarm,
The British Museum had lost its charm.
How long, I wondered, could this thing last?
But the age of miracles hadn't passed,
For, suddenly, I saw you there
And through foggy London town the sun was
    shining everywhere.
> 'A Foggy Day' (1937 song) in *Damsel in Distress*

5 I don't think I'll fall in love today.
> title of song (1928, from *Treasure Girl*); see **Chesterton** 215:20

6 I got rhythm.
> title of song (1930, from *Girl Crazy*)

7 In time the Rockies may crumble,
Gibraltar may tumble,
They're only made of clay,
But our love is here to stay.
> 'Love is Here to Stay' (1938 song) in *The Goldwyn Follies*

8 Holding hands at midnight
'Neath a starry sky,
Nice work if you can get it,
And you can get it if you try.
> 'Nice Work If You Can Get It' (1937 song) in *Damsel in Distress*

9 Ev'ry corner that you turn you meet a notable
With a statement that is eminently quotable!
> 'Of Thee I Sing' (title of song and show, 1931)

10 They all laughed at Christopher Columbus
When he said the world was round
They all laughed when Edison recorded sound
They all laughed at Wilbur and his brother
When they said that man could fly;

They told Marconi
Wireless was a phony—
It's the same old cry!
> 'They All Laughed' (1937 song)

11 A good lyric should be rhymed conversation.
> Philip Furia *Ira Gershwin* (1966)

12 I now belong, I see, to the rank of Brothers of the Great.
> *thanking a friend for clippings about his brother George's success*
> Philip Furia *Ira Gershwin* (1966)

13 The Show Must Go On—but not too long after eleven p.m.
> *on axing a skit and a song from a late running show*
> Philip Furia *Ira Gershwin* (1966)

Gervase of Canterbury c.1141–c.1210
English monastic chronicler

14 Him, therefore, they retained, on account of his lively genius and good reputation, and dismissed the others.
> *on the appointment of William of Sens as architect of the new work at Canterbury cathedral in 1174*
> Chronica Gervasii; F. Woodman *The Architectural History of Canterbury Cathedral* (1981)

J. Paul Getty 1892–1976
American industrialist

15 If you can actually count your money, then you are not really a rich man.
> in *Observer* 3 November 1957

16 If business always made the right decisions, business wouldn't be business.
> *How to be Rich* (1965)

Giuseppe Giacosa 1847–1906 and Luigi Illica 1857–1919
Italian librettists

17 *Che gelida manina.*
Your tiny hand is frozen.
Rodolfo to Mimi
> La Bohème (1896) act 1; music by Puccini

Edward Gibbon 1737–94
English historian
*on Gibbon: see **Byron** 179:1, **Colman** 236:4, **Gloucester** 351:15*

18 The various modes of worship, which prevailed in the Roman world, were all considered by the people as equally true; by the philosopher, as equally false; and by the magistrate, as equally useful. And thus toleration produced not only mutual indulgence, but even religious concord.
> The Decline and Fall of the Roman Empire (1776–88) ch. 2

19 In elective monarchies, the vacancy of the throne is a moment big with danger and mischief.
> The Declinè and Fall of the Roman Empire (1776–88) ch. 3

1 History . . . is, indeed, little more than the register of the crimes, follies, and misfortunes of mankind.
The Decline and Fall of the Roman Empire (1776–88) ch. 3; see **Voltaire** 816:5

2 In every age and country, the wiser, or at least the stronger, of the two sexes, has usurped the powers of the state, and confined the other to the cares and pleasures of domestic life.
The Decline and Fall of the Roman Empire (1776–88) ch. 6

3 Twenty-two acknowledged concubines, and a library of sixty-two thousand volumes, attested the variety of his inclinations, and from the productions which he left behind him, it appears that the former as well as the latter were designed for use rather than ostentation. [Footnote] By each of his concubines the younger Gordian left three or four children. His literary productions were by no means contemptible.
The Decline and Fall of the Roman Empire (1776–88) ch. 7

4 All taxes must, at last, fall upon agriculture.
quoting Artaxerxes, in *The Decline and Fall of the Roman Empire* (1776–88) ch. 8

5 Whenever the offence inspires less horror than the punishment, the rigour of penal law is obliged to give way to the common feelings of mankind.
The Decline and Fall of the Roman Empire (1776–88) ch. 14

6 Corruption, the most infallible symptom of constitutional liberty.
The Decline and Fall of the Roman Empire (1776–88) ch. 21

7 In every deed of mischief he had a heart to resolve, a head to contrive, and a hand to execute.
of Comnenus
The Decline and Fall of the Roman Empire (1776–88) ch. 48; see **Clarendon** 224:16

8 Our sympathy is cold to the relation of distant misery.
The Decline and Fall of the Roman Empire (1776–88) ch. 49

9 Persuasion is the resource of the feeble; and the feeble can seldom persuade.
The Decline and Fall of the Roman Empire (1776–88) ch. 68

10 All that is human must retrograde if it does not advance.
The Decline and Fall of the Roman Empire (1776–88) ch. 71

11 The satirist may laugh, the philosopher may preach, but Reason herself will respect the prejudices and habits which have been consecrated by the experience of mankind.
Memoirs of My Life (1796) ch. 1

12 To the University of Oxford I acknowledge no obligation; and she will as cheerfully renounce me for a son, as I am willing to disclaim her for a mother. I spent fourteen months at Magdalen College: they proved the fourteen months the most idle and unprofitable of my whole life.
Memoirs of My Life (1796) ch. 3

13 Their dull and deep potations excused the brisk intemperance of youth.
on the dons at Oxford
Memoirs of My Life (1796) ch. 3

14 Dr— well remembered that he had a salary to receive, and only forgot that he had a duty to perform.
Memoirs of My Life (1796) ch. 3

15 It was here that I suspended my religious inquiries (aged 17).
Memoirs of My Life (1796) ch. 4

16 I saw and loved.
Memoirs of My Life (1796) ch. 4

17 I sighed as a lover, I obeyed as a son.
Memoirs of My Life (1796) ch. 4 n.

18 Crowds without company, and dissipation without pleasure.
of London
Memoirs of My Life (1796) ch. 5

19 The captain of the Hampshire grenadiers . . . has not been useless to the historian of the Roman empire.
of his own army service
Memoirs of My Life (1796) ch. 5

20 It was at Rome, on the fifteenth of October, 1764, as I sat musing amidst the ruins of the Capitol, while the barefoot friars were singing vespers in the Temple of Jupiter, that the idea of writing the decline and fall of the city first started to my mind.
Memoirs of My Life (1796) ch. 6 n.

21 I will not dissemble the first emotions of joy on the recovery of my freedom, and, perhaps, the establishment of my fame. But my pride was soon humbled, and a sober melancholy was spread over my mind, by the idea that I had taken an everlasting leave of an old and agreeable companion, and that whatsoever might be the future date of my History, the life of the historian must be short and precarious.
on the completion of The Decline and Fall of the Roman Empire
Memoirs of My Life (1796) ch. 8

22 My English text is chaste, and all licentious passages are left in the obscurity of a learned language.
parodied as 'decent obscurity' in the Anti-Jacobin, *1797–8*
Memoirs of My Life (1796) ch. 8

23 The abbreviation of time, and the failure of hope, will always tinge with a browner shade the evening of life.
Memoirs of My Life (1796) ch. 8

Orlando Gibbons 1583–1625
English organist and composer

24 The silver swan, who, living had no note,
When death approached unlocked her silent throat.
The First Set of Madrigals and Motets of Five Parts (1612) 'The Silver Swan'

Stella Gibbons 1902–89
English novelist

1 When the sukebind hangs heavy from the wains.
Cold Comfort Farm (1932) ch. 5

2 Something nasty in the woodshed.
Cold Comfort Farm (1932) ch. 10

3 By god, D. H. Lawrence was right when he had
said there must be a dumb, dark, dull, bitter belly-
tension between a man and a woman, and how
else could this be achieved save in the long
monotony of marriage?
Cold Comfort Farm (1932) ch. 20

Wolcott Gibbs 1902–58
American critic

4 Backward ran sentences until reeled the mind.
satirizing the style of Time *magazine*
in *New Yorker* 28 November 1936 'Time . . . Fortune . . .
Life . . . Luce'

Kahlil Gibran 1883–1931
Syrian writer and painter

5 Are you a politician who says to himself: 'I will
use my country for my own benefit'? . . . Or are
you a devoted patriot, who whispers in the ear of
his inner self: 'I love to serve my country as a
faithful servant.'
The New Frontier (1931), translated by Anthony R. Ferris
in *The Voice of the Master* (1958); see **Kennedy** 449:2

6 Your children are not your children.
They are the sons and daughters of Life's longing
for itself.
They came through you but not from you
And though they are with you yet they belong not
to you.
You may give them your love but not your
thoughts,
For they have their own thoughts.
You may house their bodies but not their souls.
The Prophet (1923) 'On Children'

7 You shall be together when the white wings of
death scatter your days.
Ay, you shall be together even in the silent
memory of God.
But let there be spaces in your togetherness,
And let the winds of the heavens dance between
you.
The Prophet (1923) 'On Marriage'

8 Work is love made visible.
The Prophet (1923) 'On Work'

9 An exaggeration is a truth that has lost its temper.
Sand and Foam (1926)

Wilfrid Wilson Gibson 1878–1962
English poet

10 Nor feel the heart-break in the heart of things.
'Lament' (1918)

André Gide 1869–1951
French novelist and critic

11 *Dans le domaine des sentiments, le réel ne se distingue
pas de l'imaginaire.*
In the realm of the emotions, the real is
indistinguishable from the imaginary.
Les Faux Monnayeurs (1925) pt. 1, ch. 8

12 The whole effect of Christianity was to transfer the
drama onto the moral plane.
Les Faux Monnayeurs (1925) pt. 1, ch. 13 (translated by
Dorothy Bussy)

13 *Oh! si seulement nous pouvions, nous penchant sur
l'âme qu'on aime, voir en elle, comme en un miroir,
quelle image nous y posons!*
Oh, if only we could lean over the soul we love
and see as in a mirror the image we cast there!
La Porte Étroite (1909) pt. 2, translated by Dorothy Bussy

14 *Ah! que ce qu'on appelle bonheur est chose peu
étrangère à l'âme et que les éléments qui semblent le
composer du dehors importent peu!*
Ah, this, that we call happiness, how intimate a
part of the soul it is, and of what little importance
are the outside elements which seem to go to its
making!
La Porte Étroite (1909) pt. 5, translated by Dorothy Bussy

15 *Dans la vie, on se corrige, à ce qu'on dit, on
s'améliore; on ne peut corriger ce qu'on fait. C'est ce
droit de retouche qui fait de l'écriture une chose si
grise.*
In life one corrects *oneself*—one improves *oneself*—
so people say; but one can't correct what one *does*.
It's the power of revising that makes writing such
a colourless affair.
The Vatican Cellars (1914) bk. 2, ch. 6, translated by
Dorothy Bussy

16 The great secret of Stendhal, his great shrewdness,
consisted in writing *at once* . . . thought charged
with emotion.
Journal (1939) vol. 3, 3 September 1937 (translated by
Justin O'Brien)

17 Hugo—alas!
when asked who was the greatest 19th-century poet
Claude Martin *La Maturité d'André Gide* (1977)

Thomas Gilbart fl. c.1583
English poet

18 And when the fire did compass him
About on every side,
The people looked he then would speak,
And therefore loud they cried:
'Now call on Christ to save thy soul;
Now trust in Christ his death.'
But all in vain; no words he spake,
But thus yields up his breath.
Oh, woeful state, oh danger deep,
That he was drownèd in!
Oh grant us, God, for Christ his sake,
We fall not in such sin.
'A declaration of the death of John Lewes' (1583)

Humphrey Gilbert c.1537–83

English explorer

1 We are as near to heaven by sea as by land!
> Richard Hakluyt *Third and Last Volume of the Voyages . . . of the English Nation* (1600); see **Elstow** 306:5

W. S. Gilbert (Sir William Schwenck Gilbert)
1836–1911

English writer of comic and satirical verse
on Gilbert: see **Epitaphs** *310:10*

2 Then they began to sing
That extremely lovely thing,
'*Scherzando! ma non troppo ppp.*'
> The '*Bab*' *Ballads* (1869) 'Story of Prince Agib'

3 That celebrated,
Cultivated,
Underrated
Nobleman,
The Duke of Plaza Toro!
> *The Gondoliers* (1889) act 1

4 Of that there is no manner of doubt—
No probable, possible shadow of doubt—
No possible doubt whatever.
> *The Gondoliers* (1889) act 1

5 But the privilege and pleasure
That we treasure beyond measure
Is to run on little errands for the Ministers of State.
> *The Gondoliers* (1889) act 2

6 Take a pair of sparkling eyes,
Hidden, ever and anon,
In a merciful eclipse.
> *The Gondoliers* (1889) act 2

7 Ambassadors cropped up like hay,
Prime Ministers and such as they
Grew like asparagus in May,
And dukes were three a penny.
> *The Gondoliers* (1889) act 2

8 When every one is somebodee,
Then no one's anybody.
> *The Gondoliers* (1889) act 2

9 Bow, bow, ye lower middle classes!
Bow, bow, ye tradesmen, bow, ye masses.
> *Iolanthe* (1882) act 1

10 The Law is the true embodiment
Of everything that's excellent.
It has no kind of fault or flaw,
And I, my Lords, embody the Law.
> *Iolanthe* (1882) act 1

11 Hearts just as pure and fair
May beat in Belgrave Square
As in the lowly air
Of Seven Dials.
> *Iolanthe* (1882) act 1

12 I often think it's comical
How Nature always does contrive
That every boy and every gal,
That's born into the world alive,
Is either a little Liberal,
Or else a little Conservative!
> *Iolanthe* (1882) act 2

13 When in that House MPs divide,
If they've a brain and cerebellum too,
They have to leave that brain outside,
And vote just as their leaders tell 'em to.
> *Iolanthe* (1882) act 2

14 The prospect of a lot
Of dull MPs in close proximity,
All thinking for themselves is what
No man can face with equanimity.
> *Iolanthe* (1882) act 2

15 The House of Peers, throughout the war,
Did nothing in particular,
And did it very well.
> *Iolanthe* (1882) act 2

16 When you're lying awake with a dismal
  headache, and repose is taboo'd by anxiety,
I conceive you may use any language you choose
  to indulge in, without impropriety.
> *Iolanthe* (1882) act 2

17 For you dream you are crossing the Channel, and
  tossing about in a steamer from Harwich—
Which is something between a large bathing
  machine and a very small second class carriage.
> *Iolanthe* (1882) act 2

18 The shares are a penny, and ever so many are
  taken by Rothschild and Baring,
And just as a few are allotted to you, you awake
  with a shudder despairing.
> *Iolanthe* (1882) act 2

19 A wandering minstrel I—
A thing of shreds and patches.
Of ballads, songs and snatches,
And dreamy lullaby!
> *The Mikado* (1885) act 1; see **Shakespeare** 687:27

20 I can trace my ancestry back to a protoplasmal
primordial atomic globule. Consequently, my
family pride is something in-conceivable. I can't
help it. I was born sneering.
> *The Mikado* (1885) act 1

21 As some day it may happen that a victim must be
  found,
I've got a little list—I've got a little list
Of society offenders who might well be under
  ground
And who never would be missed—who never
  would be missed!
> *The Mikado* (1885) act 1

22 The idiot who praises, with enthusiastic tone,
All centuries but this, and every country but his
  own.
> *The Mikado* (1885) act 1; see **Canning** 189:5, **Disraeli** 276:16, **Overbury** 579:16

23 Three little maids from school are we,
Pert as a schoolgirl well can be,
Filled to the brim with girlish glee.
> *The Mikado* (1885) act 1

24 Three little maids who, all unwary,
Come from a ladies' seminary.
> *The Mikado* (1885) act 1

25 Modified rapture!
> *The Mikado* (1885) act 1

1 Awaiting the sensation of a short, sharp shock,
From a cheap and chippy chopper on a big black
block.
The Mikado (1885) act 1

2 Here's a how-de-doo!
The Mikado (1885) act 2

3 Here's a state of things!
The Mikado (1885) act 2

4 My object all sublime
I shall achieve in time—
To let the punishment fit the crime—
The punishment fit the crime.
The Mikado (1885) act 2

5 And there he plays extravagant matches
In fitless fingerstalls
On a cloth untrue
With a twisted cue
And elliptical billiard balls.
on the billiard sharp
The Mikado (1885) act 2

6 I have a left shoulder-blade that is a miracle of
loveliness. People come miles to see it. My right
elbow has a fascination that few can resist.
The Mikado (1885) act 2

7 Something lingering, with boiling oil in it, I fancy.
The Mikado (1885) act 2

8 Merely corroborative detail, intended to give
artistic verisimilitude to an otherwise bald and
unconvincing narrative.
The Mikado (1885) act 2

9 The flowers that bloom in the spring,
Tra la,
Have nothing to do with the case.
The Mikado (1885) act 2

10 On a tree by a river a little tom-tit
Sang 'Willow, titwillow, titwillow!'
And I said to him, 'Dicky-bird, why do you sit
Singing Willow, titwillow, titwillow?'
The Mikado (1885) act 2

11 There's a fascination frantic
In a ruin that's romantic;
Do you think you are sufficiently decayed?
The Mikado (1885) act 2

12 If you're anxious for to shine in the high aesthetic
line as a man of culture rare.
Patience (1881) act 1

13 The meaning doesn't matter if it's only idle chatter
of a transcendental kind.
Patience (1881) act 1

14 An attachment à la Plato for a bashful young
potato, or a not too French French bean!
Patience (1881) act 1

15 If you walk down Piccadilly with a poppy or a lily
in your medieval hand.
Patience (1881) act 1

16 Francesca di Rimini, miminy, piminy,
Je-ne-sais-quoi young man!
Patience (1881) act 2

17 A greenery-yallery, Grosvenor Gallery,
Foot-in-the-grave young man!
Patience (1881) act 2

18 I'm called Little Buttercup—dear Little Buttercup,
Though I could never tell why.
HMS Pinafore (1878) act 1

19 What, never?
No, never!
What, *never?*
Hardly ever!
HMS Pinafore (1878) act 1

20 Though 'Bother it' I may
Occasionally say,
I never use a big, big D—
HMS Pinafore (1878) act 1

21 And so do his sisters, and his cousins and his
aunts!
His sisters and his cousins,
Whom he reckons up by dozens,
And his aunts!
HMS Pinafore (1878) act 1

22 I cleaned the windows and I swept the floor,
And I polished up the handle of the big front door.
I polished up that handle so carefullee
That now I am the Ruler of the Queen's Navee!
HMS Pinafore (1878) act 1

23 I always voted at my party's call,
And I never thought of thinking for myself at all.
HMS Pinafore (1878) act 1

24 Stick close to your desks and never go to sea,
And you all may be Rulers of the Queen's Navee!
HMS Pinafore (1878) act 1

25 He is an Englishman!
For he himself has said it,
And it's greatly to his credit,
That he is an Englishman!
HMS Pinafore (1878) act 2

26 For he might have been a Roosian,
A French, or Turk, or Proosian,
Or perhaps Ital-ian!
But in spite of all temptations
To belong to other nations,
He remains an Englishman!
HMS Pinafore (1878) act 2

27 It is, it is a glorious thing
To be a Pirate King.
The Pirates of Penzance (1879) act 1

28 I'm very good at integral and differential calculus,
I know the scientific names of beings
animalculous;
In short, in matters vegetable, animal, and
mineral,
I am the very model of a modern Major-General.
The Pirates of Penzance (1879) act 1

29 About binomial theorem I'm teeming with a lot of
news,
With many cheerful facts about the square on the
hypotenuse.
The Pirates of Penzance (1879) act 1

1 When constabulary duty's to be done,
A policeman's lot is not a happy one.
  The Pirates of Penzance (1879) act 2

2 Man is Nature's sole mistake!
  Princess Ida (1884) act 2

3 He combines the manners of a Marquis with the morals of a Methodist.
  Ruddigore (1887) act 1

4 Some word that teems with hidden meaning—like Basingstoke.
  Ruddigore (1887) act 2

5 This particularly rapid, unintelligible patter
Isn't generally heard, and if it is it doesn't matter.
  Ruddigore (1887) act 2

6 I was a pale young curate then.
  The Sorcerer (1877) act 1

7 So I fell in love with a rich attorney's
Elderly ugly daughter.
  Trial by Jury (1875)

8 She may very well pass for forty-three
In the dusk with a light behind her!
  Trial by Jury (1875)

9 'Tis ever thus with simple folk—an accepted wit has but to say 'Pass the mustard', and they roar their ribs out!
  The Yeoman of the Guard (1888) act 2

Eric Gill 1882–1940
English sculptor, engraver, and typographer

10 That state is a state of slavery in which a man does what he likes to do in his spare time and in his working time that which is required of him.
  Art-nonsense and Other Essays (1929) 'Slavery and Freedom'; see **Collingwood** 235:1

Andrew Gilligan 1968–
British journalist

11 I have spoken to a British official who was involved in the preparation of the dossier, and he told me that until the week before it was published, the draft dossier produced by the intelligence services added little to what was already publicly known. He said: [Voiceover]: 'It was transformed in the week before it was published, to make it sexier'.
  BBC Radio 4 *Today* programme, 29 May 2003; in *Guardian* 27 June 2003

Charlotte Perkins Gilman 1860–1935
American writer and feminist

12 The labour of women in the house, certainly enables men to produce more wealth than they otherwise could; and in this way women are economic factors in society. But so are horses.
  Women and Economics (1898) ch. 1

13 There is no female mind. The brain is not an organ of sex. As well speak of a female liver.
  Women and Economics (1898) ch. 8

Allen Ginsberg 1926–97
American poet and novelist
see also **Last Words** 472:11

14 What if someone gave a war & Nobody came?
Life would ring the bells of Ecstasy and Forever be Itself again.
  'Graffiti' (1972); see **Film titles** 322:12, **Sandburg** 666:1

15 I saw the best minds of my generation destroyed
  by madness, starving hysterical naked,
dragging themselves through the negro streets at
  dawn looking for an angry fix,
angelheaded hipsters burning for the ancient
  heavenly connection to the starry dynamo in
  the machinery of the night.
  Howl (1956)

16 What thoughts I have of you tonight, Walt
  Whitman, for I walked
down the sidestreets under the trees with a
  headache self-
conscious looking at the full moon.
  'A Supermarket in California' (1956)

17 What peaches and what penumbras! Whole families shopping at night! Aisles full of husbands! Wives in the avocados, babies in the tomatoes!— and you, Garcia Lorca what were you doing down by the watermelons?
  'A Supermarket in California' (1956)

18 Ah, dear father, graybeard, lonely old courage-
  teacher, what
America did you have when Charon quit poling
  his ferry and you
got out on a smoking bank and stood watching
  the boat
disappear on the black waters of Lethe?
  on Walt **Whitman**
  'A Supermarket in California' (1956)

Nikki Giovanni 1943–
American poet

19 it's a sex object if you're pretty
and no love
or love and no sex if you're fat
  'Woman Poem' (1970)

George Gipp 1895–1920
American footballer

20 Tell them to go in there with all they've got and win just one for the Gipper.
  the catchphrase 'Win one for the Gipper' was later used by Ronald **Reagan**, *who played Gipp in the 1940 film* Knute Rockne, All American
  Knut Rockne 'Gipp the Great' in *Collier's* 22 November 1930

Giraldus Cambrensis (Gerald of Wales)
c.1146–c.1223

Welsh cleric and historian

1 The well of poisons brims over in the East.
The History and Topography of Ireland pt. 1, ch. 32

2 The Isle of Man . . . is equidistant from the north of Ireland and Britain. There was a great controversy in antiquity concerning the question, to which of the two countries should the island properly belong? . . . All agreed that since it allowed poisonous reptiles to live in it, it should belong to Britain.
The History and Topography of Ireland pt. 2, ch. 48

Jean Giraudoux 1882–1944
French dramatist

3 As soon as war is declared it will be impossible to hold the poets back. Rhyme is still the most effective drum.
La Guerre de Troie n'aura pas lieu (1935) act 2, sc. 4 (translated by Christopher Fry as *Tiger at the Gates*, 1955)

4 All of us here know there's no better way of exercising the imagination than the study of law. No poet ever interpreted nature as freely as a lawyer interprets the truth.
La Guerre de Troie n'aura pas lieu (1935) act 2, sc. 5

George Gissing 1857–1903
English novelist

5 Imagine the future historian writing in wonderment of the absurd reticence with which our novelists treat sexual subjects, and comparing this with their licence to describe in detail the most hideous of murders.
Commonplace Book (1962)

6 Mr Quarmby laughed in a peculiar way, which was the result of long years of mirth-subdual in the Reading-room.
New Grub Street (1891)

Rudolph Giuliani 1944–
American Republican politician, Mayor of New York 1993–2001

7 The number of casualties will be more than any of us can bear.
in the aftermath of the terrorist attacks which destroyed the World Trade Center in New York, and damaged the Pentagon, 11 September 2001
in *Times* 12 September 2001

Edna Gladney
American philanthropist

8 There are no illegitimate children, only illegitimate parents.
MGM paid her a large sum for the line for the 1941 film based on her life, 'Blossoms in the Dust'
A. Loos *Kiss Hollywood Good-Bye* (1978)

W. E. Gladstone 1809–98
British Liberal statesman; Prime Minister, 1868–74, 1880–5, 1886, 1892–4

on Gladstone: see **Anonymous** 16:9, **Churchill** 220:11, **Churchill** 220:12, **Churchill** 220:14, **Disraeli** 276:14, **Disraeli** 276:19, **Labouchere** 462:13, **Sellar and Yeatman** 676:25, **Victoria** 809:12, **Victoria** 809:14

9 Ireland, Ireland! that cloud in the west, that coming storm.
letter to his wife, 12 October 1845

10 This is the negation of God erected into a system of Government.
A Letter to the Earl of Aberdeen on the State Prosecutions of the Neapolitan Government (1851)

11 Finance is, as it were, the stomach of the country, from which all the other organs take their tone.
article on finance, 1858, in H. C. G. Matthew *Gladstone 1809–1874* (1986) ch. 5

12 I am come among you 'unmuzzled'.
speech in Manchester, 18 July 1865, after his parliamentary defeat at Oxford University
John Morley *Life of Gladstone* (1903) vol. 2

13 You cannot fight against the future. Time is on our side.
speech on the Reform Bill, in House of Commons, 27 April 1866

14 My mission is to pacify Ireland.
on receiving news that he was to form his first cabinet, 1st December 1868
H. C. G. Matthew *Gladstone 1809–1874* (1986) ch. 5

15 Swimming for his life, a man does not see much of the country through which the river winds.
diary, 31 December 1868 in M. R. D. Foot and H. C. G. Matthew (eds.) *The Gladstone Diaries* (1978) vol. 6

16 Let the Turks now carry away their abuses in the only possible manner, namely by carrying off themselves . . . one and all, bag and baggage, shall I hope clear out from the province they have desolated and profaned.
Bulgarian Horrors and the Question of the East (1876)

17 [An] Established Clergy will always be a Tory Corps d'Armée.
letter to Bishop Goodwin, 8 September 1881

18 It is perfectly true that these gentlemen wish to march through rapine to disintegration and dismemberment of the Empire, and, I am sorry to say, even to the placing of different parts of the Empire in direct hostility one with the other.
on the Irish Land League
speech at Knowsley, 27 October 1881, in *The Times*, 28 October 1881

19 There never was a Churchill from John of Marlborough down that had either morals or principles.
in conversation in 1882, recorded by Captain R. V. Briscoe; R. F. Foster *Lord Randolph Churchill* (1981)

20 Our first site in Egypt, be it by larceny or be it by emption, will be the almost certain egg of a North African Empire, that will grow and grow . . . till we finally join hands across the Equator with

Natal and Cape Town, to say nothing of the Transvaal and the Orange River on the south, or of Abyssinia or Zanzibar to be swallowed by way of *viaticum* on our journey.

Aggression on Egypt and Freedom in the East (1884)

1 Ideal perfection is not the true basis of English legislation. We look at the attainable; we look at the practical, and we have too much English sense to be drawn away by those sanguine delineations of what might possibly be attained in Utopia, from a path which promises to enable us to effect great good for the people of England.

speech on the Reform Bill, in House of Commons, 28 February 1884

2 I would tell them of my own intention to keep my counsel . . . and I will venture to recommend them, as an old Parliamentary hand, to do the same.

speech, House of Commons, 21 January 1886

3 This, if I understand it, is one of those golden moments of our history, one of those opportunities which may come and may go, but which rarely returns.

speech on the Second Reading of the Home Rule Bill, in House of Commons, 7 June 1886

4 I will venture to say, that upon the one great class of subjects, the largest and the most weighty of them all, where the leading and determining considerations that ought to lead to a conclusion are truth, justice, and humanity—upon these, gentlemen, all the world over, I will back the masses against the classes.

speech in Liverpool, 28 June 1886, in *The Times* 29 June 1886

5 One prayer absorbs all others: Ireland, Ireland, Ireland.

diary, 10 April 1887

6 The blubbering Cabinet.

of the colleagues who wept at his final Cabinet meeting
diary, 1 March 1894; note

7 What that Sicilian mule was to me, I have been to the Queen.

of a mule on which Gladstone rode, which he 'could neither love nor like', although it had rendered him 'much valuable service'
memorandum, 20 March 1894; H. C. G. Matthew *The Gladstone Diaries* vol. 8 (1994)

8 The God-fearing and God-sustaining University of Oxford. I served her, perhaps mistakenly, but to the best of my ability.

farewell message, just before his death, May 1898
Roy Jenkins *Gladstone* (1995)

9 I absorb the vapour and return it as a flood.

on public speaking
Lord Riddell *Some Things That Matter* (1927 ed.)

10 It is not a Life at all. It is a Reticence, in three volumes.

on J. W. Cross's Life of George Eliot
E. F. Benson *As We Were* (1930) ch. 6

11 [Money should] fructify in the pockets of the people.

H. G. C. Matthew *Gladstone 1809-1874* (1986)

12 We are bound to lose Ireland in consequence of years of cruelty, stupidity and misgovernment and I would rather lose her as a friend than as a foe.

Margot Asquith *More Memories* (1933) ch. 8

Thomas Glascock
American politician

13 No, sir! I am his adversary, and choose not to subject myself to his fascination.

*when Thomas Glascock of Georgia took his seat in the US Senate, a mutual friend expressed the wish to introduce him to Henry **Clay** of Virginia*
Robert V. Remini *Henry Clay* (1991) ch. 6

Hannah Glasse fl. 1747
English cook

14 Take your hare when it is cased.

cased = skinned
The Art of Cookery Made Plain and Easy (1747) ch. 1; see **Proverbs** 620:8

William Henry, Duke of Gloucester
1743–1805

15 Another damned, thick, square book! Always scribble, scribble, scribble! Eh! Mr Gibbon?

Henry Best *Personal and Literary Memorials* (1829); D. M. Low *Edward Gibbon* (1937) notes alternative attributions to the Duke of Cumberland and King George III

Jean-Luc Godard 1930–
French film director

16 Photography is truth. The cinema is truth 24 times per second.

Le Petit Soldat (1960 film)

17 *Ce n'est pas une image juste, c'est juste une image.*
This is not a just image, it is just an image.

Colin MacCabe *Godard: Images, Sounds, Politics* (1980)

18 GEORGES FRANJU: Movies should have a beginning, a middle and an end.
JEAN-LUC GODARD: Certainly, but not necessarily in that order.

in *Time* 14 September 1981; see **Aristotle** 25:21

A. D. Godley 1856–1925
English classicist

19 What is this that roareth thus?
Can it be a Motor Bus?
Yes, the smell and hideous hum
Indicat Motorem Bum!...
How shall wretches live like us
Cincti Bis Motoribus?
Domine, defende nos

Contra hos Motores Bos!

letter to C. R. L. Fletcher, 10 January 1914, in *Reliquiae* (1926) vol. 1

Sidney Godolphin 1610–43

English poet

1 Or love me less, or love me more
And play not with my liberty;
Either take all, or all restore,
Bind me at least, or set me free.
 'Song'

William Godwin 1756–1836

English philosopher and novelist; husband of Mary
Wollstonecraft** and father of Mary **Shelley

2 Perfectibility is one of the most unequivocal characteristics of the human species.
 An Enquiry concerning the Principles of Political Justice (1793) bk. 1, ch. 2

3 The illustrious bishop of Cambrai was of more worth than his chambermaid, and there are few of us that would hesitate to pronounce, if his palace were in flames, and the life of only one of them could be preserved, which of the two ought to be preferred.
 An Enquiry concerning the Principles of Political Justice (1793) bk. 2, ch. 2

4 Love of our country is another of those specious illusions, which have been invented by impostors in order to render the multitude the blind instruments of their crooked designs.
 An Enquiry concerning the Principles of Political Justice (1793) bk. 5, ch. 16

5 It is a most mistaken way of teaching men to feel they are brothers, by imbuing their mind with perpetual hatred.
 on the subject of war
 An Enquiry concerning the Principles of Political Justice (1793) bk. 5, ch. 18

6 What . . . can be more shameless than for society to make an example of those whom she has goaded to the breach of order, instead of amending her own institutions which, by straining order into tyranny, produced the mischief?
 on the penal laws
 An Enquiry concerning the Principles of Political Justice (1793) bk. 7, ch. 3

Joseph Goebbels 1897–1945

German Nazi leader

7 We can manage without butter but not, for example, without guns. If we are attacked we can only defend ourselves with guns not with butter.
 speech in Berlin, 17 January 1936, in *Deutsche Allgemeine Zeitung* 18 January 1936; see **Goering** 352:9

8 Making noise is an effective means of opposition.
 Ernest K. Bramsted *Goebbels and National Socialist Propaganda 1925–45* (1965)

Hermann Goering 1893–1946

German Nazi leader
*see also **Johst** 434:1*

9 We have no butter . . . but I ask you—would you rather have butter or guns? . . . preparedness makes us powerful. Butter merely makes us fat.
 speech at Hamburg, 1936, in W. Frischauer *Goering* (1951) ch. 10; see **Goebbels** 352:7

10 I herewith commission you to carry out all preparations with regard to . . . a *total solution* of the Jewish question in those territories of Europe which are under German influence.
 instructions to Heydrich, 31 July 1941, in W. L. Shirer *The Rise and Fall of the Third Reich* (1962) bk. 5, ch. 27; see **Heydrich** 387:14

Johann Wolfgang von Goethe 1749–1832

German poet, novelist, and dramatist
*see also **Last words** 473:5*

11 *Glücklich allein*
 Ist die Seele, die liebt.
 Only the soul that loves is happy.
 Egmont (1788) 'Clärchens Lied'

12 *Es irrt der Mensch, so lang er strebt.*
 Man will err while yet he strives.
 Faust pt. 1 (1808) 'Prolog im Himmel'

13 *Welch Schauspiel! Aber ach, ein Schauspiel nur!*
 What a show! But alas, only a show!
 Faust pt. 1 (1808) 'Nacht'

14 *Was du ererbt von deinen Vätern hast,*
 Erwirb es, um es zu besitzen.
 What you have inherited from your fathers
 Work on, that you may possess it.
 Faust pt. 1 (1808) 'Nacht'

15 *Zwei Seelen wohnen, ach! in meiner Brust.*
 Two souls dwell, alas! in my breast.
 Faust pt. 1 (1808) 'Vor dem Thor'

16 *Ich bin der Geist der stets verneint.*
 I am the spirit that always denies.
 Faust pt. 1 (1808) 'Studierzimmer'

17 *Entbehren sollst Du! sollst entbehren!*
 Das ist der ewige Gesang.
 Deny yourself! You must deny yourself!
 That is the song that never ends.
 Faust pt. 1 (1808) 'Studierzimmer'

18 *Grau, teurer Freund, ist alle Theorie*
 Und grün des Lebens goldner Baum.
 All theory, dear friend, is grey, but the golden tree of actual life springs ever green.
 Faust pt. 1 (1808) 'Studierzimmer'

19 *Sobald du' dir vertraust, sobald weisst du zu leben.*
 Just trust yourself and you'll learn the art of living.
 Faust pt. 1 (1808) 'Studierzimmer'

20 *Meine Ruh' ist hin,*
 Mein Herz ist schwer.
 My peace is gone,

My heart is heavy.
Faust pt. 1 (1808) 'Gretchen am Spinnrad'

1 *Das ist der Weisheit letzer Schluss:*
Nur der verdient sich Freiheit wie das Leben,
Der täglich sie erobern muss.

This is wisdom's final thought:
Freedom alone he earns as well as life
Who day by day must conquer them anew.
Faust pt. 2 (1832) act 5 'Grosser Vorhof des Palastes'

2 *Die Tat ist alles, nichts der Ruhm.*

The deed is all, the glory nothing.
Faust pt. 2 (1832) 'Hochgebirg'

3 *Das Ewig-Weibliche zieht uns hinan.*

Eternal Woman draws us upward.
Faust pt. 2 (1832) 'Hochgebirg' closing words

4 *Du musst herrschen und gewinnen,*
Oder dienen und verlieren,
Leiden oder triumphieren
Amboss oder Hammer sein.

You must be master and win, or serve and lose,
grieve or triumph, be the anvil or the hammer.
Der Gross-Cophta (1791) act 2

5 *Wenn es eine Freude ist das Gute zu geniessen, so ist*
es eine grössere das Bessere zu empfinden, und in der
Kunst ist das Beste gut genug.

Since it is a joy to have the benefit of what is good,
it is a greater one to experience what is better, and
in art the best is good enough.
Italienische Reise (1816-17) 3 March 1787

6 *Der Aberglaube ist die Poesie des Lebens.*

Superstition is the poetry of life.
Maximen und Reflexionen (1819) 'Literatur und Sprache'
no. 908

7 *Es bildet ein Talent sich in der Stille,*
Sich ein Charakter in dem Strom der Welt.

Talent develops in quiet places, character in the
full current of human life.
Torquato Tasso (1790) act 1, sc. 2

8 *Die Wahlverwandtschaften.*

Elective affinities.
title of novel (1809)

9 *Ach, ich bin des Treibens müde!*

Oh, how I am tired of the struggle!
Wandrers Nachtlied (1821)

10 *Über allen Gipfeln*
Ist Ruh'.

Over all the mountain tops is peace.
Wandrers Nachtlied (1821)

11 *Wer nie sein Brot mit Tränen ass,*
Wer nie die kummervollen Nächte
Auf seinem Bette weinend sass,
Der kennt euch nicht, ihr himmlischen Mächte.

Who never ate his bread in sorrow,
Who never spent the darksome hours
Weeping and watching for the morrow
He knows ye not, ye heavenly powers.
Wilhelm Meisters Lehrjahre (1795-6) bk. 2, ch. 13
(translated by Carlyle)

12 *Kennst du das Land, wo die Zitronen blühn?*
Im dunkeln Laub die Gold-Orangen glühn,
Ein sanfter Wind vom blauen Himmel weht,
Die Myrte still und hoch der Lorbeer steht—
Kennst du es wohl?
Dahin! Dahin
Möcht ich mit dir, o mein Geliebter, ziehn!

Know you the land where the lemon-trees bloom?
In the dark foliage the gold oranges glow; the
myrtle is still and the laurel stands tall—do you
know it well? There, there, I would go, O my
beloved, with thee!
Wilhelm Meisters Lehrjahre (1795-6) bk. 3, ch. 1

13 If I love you, what does that matter to you!
Wilhelm Meisters Lehrjahre (1795-6) bk. 4, ch. 9

14 *Nur, wer die Sehnsucht kennt,*
Weiss, was ich leide!

None but the lonely heart
Knows what I suffer!
Wilhelm Meisters Lehrjahre (1795-6) bk. 4, ch. 11
'Mignons Lied'

15 *Wenn wir, sagtest Du, die Menschen nur nehmen, wie*
sie sind, so machen wir sie schlecter; wenn wir sie
behandeln, als wären sie, was sie sein sollten so
bringen wir sie dahin, wohin sie zu bringen sind.

When we take people, thou wouldst say, merely as
they are, we make them worse; when we treat
them as if they were what they should be, we
improve them as far as they can be improved.
sometimes quoted as 'Treat a man as he is, and that is
what he remains. Treat a man as he can be, and that
is what he becomes'
Wilhelm Meisters Lehrjare (1795-6) bk. 8, ch. 4, translated
by Carlyle

16 *Ohne Hast, aber ohne Rast.*

Without haste, but without rest.
Zahme Xenien (with Schiller, 1796) sect. 2, no. 6, l. 281

17 For the rest of it, the last and greatest art is to
limit and isolate oneself.
J. P. Eckermann *Conversations with Goethe in the Last Years*
of his Life (1836-48) 20 April 1825

18 Classicism is health, romanticism is disease.
J. P. Eckermann *Conversations with Goethe in the Last Years*
of his Life (1836-48) 2 April 1829

19 I do not know myself, and God forbid that I
should.
J. P. Eckermann *Conversations with Goethe in the Last Years*
of his Life (1836-48) 10 April 1829; see **Proverbs** 624:44

Oliver St John Gogarty 1878-1957
Irish writer and surgeon

20 I said, 'It is most extraordinary weather for this
time of year!' He replied, 'Ah, it isn't this time of
year at all.'
It Isn't This Time of Year at All (1954)

21 Golden stockings you had on
In the meadow where you ran.
'Golden Stockings'

22 Only the Lion and the Cock;
As Galen says, withstand Love's shock.

So, dearest, do not think me rude
If I yield now to lassitude,
But sympathize with me. I know
You would not have me roar or crow.
'After Galen' (1957)

Nikolai Gogol 1809–52

Russian writer

1 As you pass from the tender years of youth into harsh and embittered manhood, make sure you take with you on your journey all the human emotions! Don't leave them on the road, for you will not pick them up afterwards!
Dead Souls (1842) pt. 1, ch. 6 (translated by David Magarshak)

2 A land that does not like doing things by halves.
of Russia
Dead Souls (1842) pt. 1, ch. 11 (translated by David Magarshak)

3 [Are not] you too, Russia, speeding along like a spirited *troika* that nothing can overtake? . . . Everything on earth is flying past, and looking askance, other nations and states draw aside and make way.
Dead Souls (1842) pt. 1, ch. 11 (translated by David Magarshak)

Isaac Goldberg 1887–1938

4 Diplomacy is to do and say
The nastiest thing in the nicest way.
in *The Reflex* October 1927

Whoopi Goldberg 1949–

American actress

5 I dislike this idea that if you're a black person in America then you must be called an African-American. I'm not an African. I'm an American. Just call me black, if you want to call me anything.
in *Irish Times* 25 April 1998 'Quotes of the Week'

William Golding 1911–93

English novelist

6 Nothing is so impenetrable as laughter in a language you don't understand.
An Egyptian Journal (1985)

7 Anyone who moved through those years without understanding that man produces evil as a bee produces honey, must have been blind or wrong in the head.
of the Second World War
The Hot Gates (1965) 'Fable'

Emma Goldman 1869–1940

American anarchist

8 Anarchism, then, really, stands for the liberation of the human mind from the dominion of religion; the liberation of the human body from the dominion of property; liberation from the shackles and restraints of government.
Anarchism and Other Essays (1910)

Oliver Goldsmith 1728–74

Irish writer, poet, and dramatist
on Goldsmith: see **Epitaphs** 311:1, **Garrick** 340:3, **Garrick** 340:5, **Johnson** 429:21

9 Sweet Auburn, loveliest village of the plain.
The Deserted Village (1770) l. 1

10 Ill fares the land, to hast'ning ills a prey,
Where wealth accumulates, and men decay;
Princes and lords may flourish, or may fade;
A breath can make them, as a breath has made;
But a bold peasantry, their country's pride,
When once destroyed, can never be supplied.
The Deserted Village (1770) l. 51

11 How happy he who crowns in shades like these,
A youth of labour with an age of ease.
The Deserted Village (1770) l. 99

12 The loud laugh that spoke the vacant mind.
The Deserted Village (1770) l. 122; see **Chesterfield** 215:7

13 A man he was to all the country dear,
And passing rich with forty pounds a year.
Remote from towns he ran his godly race,
Nor e'er had changed nor wished to change his place.
The Deserted Village (1770) l. 141

14 Truth from his lips prevailed with double sway,
And fools, who came to scoff, remained to pray.
The Deserted Village (1770) l. 179

15 A man severe he was, and stern to view;
I knew him well, and every truant knew;
Well had the boding tremblers learned to trace
The day's disasters in his morning face;
Full well they laughed with counterfeited glee,
At all his jokes, for many a joke had he.
The Deserted Village (1770) l. 197

16 The village all declared how much he knew;
'Twas certain he could write and cypher too.
The Deserted Village (1770) l. 207

17 In arguing too, the parson owned his skill,
For e'en though vanquished, he could argue still;
While words of learned length, and thund'ring sound
Amazed the gazing rustics ranged around,
And still they gazed, and still the wonder grew,
That one small head could carry all he knew.
The Deserted Village (1770) l. 211

18   How wide the limits stand
Between a splendid and a happy land.
The Deserted Village (1770) l. 267

19 In all the silent manliness of grief.
The Deserted Village (1770) l. 384

20 I see the rural virtues leave the land.
The Deserted Village (1770) l. 398

21 Thou source of all my bliss, and all my woe,
That found'st me poor at first, and keep'st me so.
of poetry
The Deserted Village (1770) l. 413

1 Man wants but little here below,
Nor wants that little long.
'Edwin and Angelina, or the Hermit' (1766); see **Holmes** 393:5, **Young** 857:17

2 The doctor found, when she was dead,—
Her last disorder mortal.
'Elegy on Mrs Mary Blaize' (1759)

3 The man recovered of the bite,
The dog it was that died.
'Elegy on the Death of a Mad Dog' (1766)

4 Our Garrick's a salad; for in him we see
Oil, vinegar, sugar, and saltness agree.
Retaliation (1774) l. 11; see **Garrick** 340:3

5 Too nice for a statesman, too proud for a wit.
*of Edmund **Burke***
Retaliation (1774) l. 32

6 An abridgement of all that was pleasant in man.
*of David **Garrick***
Retaliation (1774) l. 94

7 On the stage he was natural, simple, affecting;
'Twas only that when he was off he was acting.
*of David **Garrick***
Retaliation (1774) l. 101

8 Of praise a mere glutton, he swallowed what came,
And the puff of a dunce he mistook it for fame.
*of David **Garrick***
Retaliation (1774) l. 101

9 When they talked of their Raphaels, Correggios, and stuff,
He shifted his trumpet, and only took snuff.
*of Joshua **Reynolds***
Retaliation (1774) l. 145

10 Where'er I roam, whatever realms to see,
My heart untravelled fondly turns to thee;
Still to my brother turns with ceaseless pain,
And drags at each remove a lengthening chain.
The Traveller (1764) l. 7

11 Such is the patriot's boast, where'er we roam,
His first, best country ever is, at home.
The Traveller (1764) l. 73

12 And honour sinks where commerce long prevails.
The Traveller (1764) l. 92

13 Pride in their port, defiance in their eye,
I see the lords of human kind pass by.
The Traveller (1764) l. 327

14 Laws grind the poor, and rich men rule the law.
The Traveller (1764) l. 386

15 How small, of all that human hearts endure,
That part which laws or kings can cause or cure!
The Traveller (1764) l. 429; see **Johnson** 426:14

16 The true use of speech is not so much to express our wants as to conceal them.
The Bee no. 3 (20 October 1759) 'On the Use of Language'

17 Friendship is a disinterested commerce between equals; love, an abject intercourse between tyrants and slaves.
The Good-Natured Man (1768) act 1

18 Don't let us make imaginary evils, when you know we have so many real ones to encounter.
The Good-Natured Man (1768) act 1

19 Silence is become his mother tongue.
The Good-Natured Man (1768) act 2

20 Measures not men, have always been my mark.
The Good Natured Man (1768) act 2; see **Burke** 168:9, **Canning** 189:9

21 You, that are going to be married, think things can never be done too fast; but we, that are old, and know what we are about, must elope methodically, madam.
The Good-Natured Man (1768) act 2

22 Let schoolmasters puzzle their brain,
With grammar, and nonsense, and learning,
Good liquor, I stoutly maintain,
Gives genius a better discerning.
She Stoops to Conquer (1773) act 1, sc. 1 'Song'

23 The very pink of perfection.
She Stoops to Conquer (1773) act 1

24 I'll be with you in the squeezing of a lemon.
She Stoops to Conquer (1773) act 1

25 This is Liberty-Hall, gentlemen.
She Stoops to Conquer (1773) act 2

26 The first blow is half the battle.
She Stoops to Conquer (1773) act 2

27 A man who leaves home to mend himself and others is a philosopher; but he who goes from country to country, guided by a blind impulse of curiosity, is a vagabond.
The Citizen of the World (1762)

28 I was ever of opinion, that the honest man who married and brought up a large family, did more service than he who continued single and only talked of population.
The Vicar of Wakefield (1766) ch. 1

29 I . . . chose my wife, as she did her wedding gown, not for a fine glossy surface, but such qualities as would wear well.
The Vicar of Wakefield (1766) ch. 1

30 All our adventures were by the fire-side, and all our migrations from the blue bed to the brown.
The Vicar of Wakefield (1766) ch. 1

31 The virtue which requires to be ever guarded is scarce worth the sentinel.
The Vicar of Wakefield (1766) ch. 5

32 It seemed to me pretty plain, that they had more of love than matrimony in them.
The Vicar of Wakefield (1766) ch. 16

33 When lovely woman stoops to folly
And finds too late that men betray,
What charm can soothe her melancholy,
What art can wash her guilt away?
The Vicar of Wakefield (1766) ch. 29; see **Eliot** 303:21

34 There is no arguing with Johnson; for when his pistol misses fire, he knocks you down with the butt end of it.
James Boswell *Life of Samuel Johnson* (1791) 26 October 1769

1 As I take my shoes from the shoemaker, and my coat from the tailor, so I take my religion from the priest.

>   James Boswell *Life of Samuel Johnson* (1791) 9 April 1773

Barry Goldwater 1909–98
American Republican politician

2 I would remind you that extremism in the defence of liberty is no vice! And let me remind you also that moderation in the pursuit of justice is no virtue!

>   accepting the presidential nomination, 16 July 1964, in *New York Times* 17 July 1964

Sam Goldwyn (Samuel Goldfish) 1882–1974
American film producer
on Goldwyn: see **Hand** 370:14

3 Gentlemen, include me out.
resigning from the Motion Picture Producers and Distributors of America, October 1933

>   Michael Freedland *The Goldwyn Touch* (1986) ch. 10

4 That's the way with these directors, they're always biting the hand that lays the golden egg.

>   Alva Johnston *The Great Goldwyn* (1937) ch. 1

5 A verbal contract isn't worth the paper it is written on.

>   Alva Johnston *The Great Goldwyn* (1937) ch. 1

6 Any man who goes to a psychiatrist should have his head examined.

>   Norman Zierold *Moguls* (1969) ch. 3

7 Pictures are for entertainment, messages should be delivered by Western Union.

>   Arthur Marx *Goldwyn* (1976) ch. 15; see **Behan** 63:16

Ivan Goncharov 1812–91
Russian novelist

8 No devastating or redeeming fires have ever burnt in my life . . . My life began by flickering out.

>   *Oblomov* (1859) pt. 2, ch. 4 (translated by David Magarshak)

9 You lost your ability for doing things in childhood . . . It all began with your inability to put on your socks and ended by your inability to live.

>   *Oblomov* (1859) pt. 4, ch. 2 (translated by David Magarshak)

Maud Gonne (Maud Gonne MacBride) 1867–1953
Irish nationalist and actress

10 The Famine Queen.
*of Queen **Victoria***

>   in *L'Irlande libre* 1900

Amy Goodman 1957–
American journalist

11 Go to where the silence is and say something.
accepting an award from Columbia University for her coverage of the 1991 massacre in East Timor by Indonesian troops

>   in *Columbia Journalism Review* March/April 1994

Barnabe Googe 1540–94
English poet

12 Fair face show friends
When riches do abound:
Come time of proof,
Farewell, they must away.

>   'Of Money' (1563)

Thomas Goold 1766–1846
Irish lawyer and politician

13 The God of nature never intended that Ireland should be a province, and by God she never will.

>   speech opposing the Act of Union at a meeting of the Irish Bar, 9 December 1799

Mikhail Sergeevich Gorbachev 1931–
Soviet statesman; General Secretary of the Communist Party of the USSR 1985–91 and President 1988–91
on Gorbachev: see **Gromyko** 365:1, **Thatcher** 787:9, **Zhvanetsky** 858:8

14 The guilt of Stalin and his immediate entourage before the Party and the people for the mass repressions and lawlessness they committed is enormous and unforgivable.

>   speech on the seventieth anniversary of the Russian Revolution, 2 November 1987

15 The idea of restructuring [perestroika] . . . combines continuity and innovation, the historical experience of Bolshevism and the contemporaneity of socialism.

>   speech on the seventieth anniversary of the Russian Revolution, 2 November 1987

16 After leaving the Kremlin . . . my conscience was clear. The promise I gave to the people when I started the process of perestroika was kept: I gave them freedom.

>   *Memoirs* (1995)

Adam Lindsay Gordon 1833–70
Australian poet

17 Life is mostly froth and bubble,
Two things stand like stone,
Kindness in another's trouble,
Courage in your own.

>   *Ye Wearie Wayfarer* (1866) 'Fytte 8'

Mack Gordon 1904–59
American songwriter

18 Pardon me boy is that the Chattanooga Choo-choo,
Track twenty nine,
Boy you can gimme a shine.
I can afford to board a Chattanooga Choo-choo,
I've got my fare and just a trifle to spare.
You leave the Pennsylvania station 'bout a quarter to four,
Read a magazine and then you're in Baltimore,
Dinner in the diner nothing could be finer
Than to have your ham'n eggs in Carolina.

>   'Chattanooga Choo-choo' (1941 song)

Albert Gore Jr. 1948-

American Democratic politician, Vice-President 1993-2001;
presidential candidate in 2000

1 I am Al Gore, and I used to be the next president
of the United States of America.
addressing Bocconi University in Milan
in *Newsweek* 19 March 2001; see **Carter** 197:2

Eva Gore-Booth 1870-1926

Irish poet

2 The little waves of Breffny go stumbling through
my soul.
'The Waves of Breffny' (1920)

Maxim Gorky 1868-1936

Russian writer and revolutionary

3 The proletarian state must bring up thousands of
excellent 'mechanics of culture', 'engineers of the
soul'.
speech at the Writers' Congress 1934; see **Kennedy** 449:6,
Stalin 754:2

Stuart Gorrell 1902-63

American songwriter

4 Georgia, Georgia, no peace I find,
Just an old sweet song keeps Georgia on my mind.
'Georgia on my Mind' (1930 song)

George Joachim, Lord Goschen

1831-1907
British Liberal Unionist politician
on Goschen: see **Churchill** 220:15

5 I have the courage of my opinions, but I have not
the temerity to give a political blank cheque to
Lord Salisbury.
speech in the House of Commons, 19 February 1884

Edmund Gosse 1849-1928

English poet and man of letters

6 The theory, coarsely enough, and to my Father's
great indignation, was defined by a hasty press as
being this—that God hid the fossils in the rocks in
order to tempt geologists into infidelity.
on Philip Gosse's fundamentalist interpretation of
geology (in Omphalos, *1857), subsequently applied*
to evolution
Father and Son (1907) ch. 5

7 Man was the animal he studied less than any
other, understood most imperfectly, and, on the
whole, was least interested in.
of his father, the naturalist Philip Gosse
Life of P. H. Gosse (1890) ch. 12

8 A sheep in sheep's clothing.
of the 'woolly-bearded poet' Sturge **Moore**
F. Greenslet *Under the Bridge* (1943) ch. 10; see **Churchill**
222:23

Glenn Gould 1932-82

Canadian pianist and composer

9 The purpose of art is the lifelong construction of a
state of wonder.
commencement address, York University, Toronto, 6
November 1982

Stephen Jay Gould 1941-2002

American palaeontologist

10 A man does not attain the status of Galileo merely
because he is persecuted; he must also be right.
Ever since Darwin (1977)

11 Life is a copiously branching bush, continually
pruned by the grim reaper of extinction, not a
ladder of predictable progress.
Wonderful Life (1989) ch. 1

12 Science is an integral part of culture. It's not this
foreign thing, done by an arcane priesthood. It's
one of the glories of human intellectual tradition.
in *Independent* 24 January 1990

John Gower c.1330-1408

English poet

13 It hath and schal ben evermor
That love is maister wher he wile.
Confessio Amantis (1386-90) prologue, l. 34

Ernest Gowers 1880-1966

British public servant

14 It is not easy nowadays to remember anything so
contrary to all appearances as that officials are the
servants of the public; and the official must try not
to foster the illusion that it is the other way round.
Plain Words (1948) ch. 3

Goya (Francisco José de Goya y Lucientes)

1746-1828
Spanish painter

15 *No se puede mirar.*
One cannot look at this.
The Disasters of War (1863) title of etching, no. 26

16 *El sueño de la razón produce monstruos.*
The dream of reason produces monsters.
Los Caprichos (1799) plate 43 (title)

Baltasar Gracián 1601-58

Spanish philosopher

17 Never open the door to the least of evils, for many
other, greater ones lurk outside.
The Art of Worldly Wisdom (translated by Christopher
Maurer, 1994)

1 Renew your brilliance. It is the privilege of the Phoenix. Excellence grows old and so does fame. Custom wears down our admiration, and a mediocre novelty can conquer the greatest eminence in its old age. So be reborn in courage, in intellect, in happiness, and in all else. Dare to renew your brilliance, dawning many times, like the sun, only changing your surroundings. Withhold it and make people miss it; renew it and make them applaud.

   The Art of Worldly Wisdom (translated by Christopher Maurer, 1994)

2 Don't express your ideas too clearly. Most people think little of what they understand, and venerate what they do not.

   The Art of Worldly Wisdom (translated by Christopher Maurer, 1994)

Clementina Stirling Graham 1782–1877
Scottish writer

3 The best way to get the better of temptation is just to yield to it.

   Mystifications (1859) 'Soirée at Mrs Russel's'; see **Wilde** 836:5

D. M. Graham 1911–99
British broadcaster

4 That this House will in no circumstances fight for its King and Country.

   motion worded by Graham for a debate at the Oxford Union, of which he was Librarian, 9 February 1933 (passed by 275 votes to 153)

Harry Graham 1874–1936
British writer and journalist

5 Weep not for little Léonie
   Abducted by a French Marquis!
   Though loss of honour was a wrench
   Just think how it's improved her French.

   More Ruthless Rhymes for Heartless Homes (1930) 'Compensation'

6 O'er the rugged mountain's brow
   Clara threw the twins she nursed,
   And remarked, 'I wonder now
   Which will reach the bottom first?'

   Ruthless Rhymes for Heartless Homes (1899) 'Calculating Clara'

7 'There's been an accident,' they said,
   'Your servant's cut in half; he's dead!'
   'Indeed!' said Mr Jones, 'and please,
   Send me the half that's got my keys.'

   Ruthless Rhymes for Heartless Homes (1899) 'Mr Jones' (attributed to 'G.W.')

8 Billy, in one of his nice new sashes,
   Fell in the fire and was burnt to ashes;
   Now, although the room grows chilly,
   I haven't the heart to poke poor Billy.

   Ruthless Rhymes for Heartless Homes (1899) 'Tender-Heartedness'

James Graham see Marquess of Montrose

Martha Graham 1894–1991
American dancer, teacher, and choreographer

9 Dance is the hidden language of the soul.

   Blood Memory (1991)

Philip Graham 1915–63
American newspaper publisher

10 Let us today drudge on about our inescapably impossible task of providing every week a first rough draft of a history that will never be completed about a world we can never really understand.

   remarks to *Newsweek* correspondents, London, 29 April 1963

Kenneth Grahame 1859–1932
Scottish-born writer

11 The curate faced the laurels—hesitatingly. But Aunt Maria flung herself on him. 'O Mr Hodgitts!' I heard her cry, 'you are brave! for my sake do not be rash!' He was not rash.

   The Golden Age (1895) 'The Burglars'

12 There is *nothing*—absolutely nothing—half so much worth doing as simply messing about in boats.

   The Wind in the Willows (1908) ch. 1

13 The poetry of motion! The *real* way to travel! The *only* way to travel! Here today—in next week tomorrow! Villages skipped, towns and cities jumped—always somebody else's horizon!

   The Wind in the Willows (1908) ch. 2; see **Kaufman and Anthony** 442:2

14 O bliss! O poop-poop! O my!

   The Wind in the Willows (1908) ch. 2

15 The clever men at Oxford
   Know all that there is to be knowed.
   But they none of them know one half as much
   As intelligent Mr Toad!

   The Wind in the Willows (1908) ch. 10

James Grainger c.1721–66
English physician and man of letters

16 What is fame? an empty bubble;
   Gold? a transient, shining trouble.

   'Solitude' (1755) l. 96

17   Knock off the chains
   Of heart-debasing slavery; give to man,
   Of every colour and of every clime,
   Freedom, which stamps him image of his God.

   The Sugar Cane (1764) bk. 4

Phil Gramm 1942–
American Republican politician

18 I did not come to Washington to be loved, and I have not been disappointed.

   Michael Barone and Grant Ujifusa *The American Political Almanac* 1994

Bernie Grant 1944–2000
British Labour politician

1 The police were to blame for what happened on Sunday night and what they got was a bloody good hiding.
after a riot in which a policeman was killed
speech as leader of Haringey Council outside Tottenham Town Hall, 8 October 1985

George P. Grant 1918–88
Canadian social philosopher

2 What is so endearing about the young French Canadians revolting against their tradition is that they sometimes write as if Voltaire's *Candide* had come off the press last week instead of two hundred years ago.
Technology and Empire: Perspectives on North America (1969) 'Canadian Fate and Imperialism'

Robert Grant 1785–1838
British lawyer and politician

3 O worship the King, all-glorious above;
O gratefully sing his power and his love:
Our Shield and Defender, the Ancient of Days,
Pavilioned in splendour, and girded with praise.
'O worship the King, all glorious above' (1833 hymn)

Ulysses S. Grant 1822–85
American Unionist general and statesman; 18th President of the US 1869–77

4 No terms except unconditional and immediate surrender can be accepted. I propose to move immediately upon your works.
to Simon Bolivar Buckner, under siege at Fort Donelson, 16 February 1862; in P. C. Headley *The Life and Campaigns of General U. S. Grant* (1869) ch. 6

5 I purpose to fight it out on this line, if it takes all summer.
dispatch to Washington, from head-quarters in the field, 11 May 1864, in P. C. Headley *The Life and Campaigns of General U. S. Grant* (1869) ch. 23

6 The war is over—the rebels are our countrymen again.
*preventing his men from cheering after **Lee**'s surrender at Appomattox*
on 9 April, 1865

7 Let us have peace.
letter to General Joseph R. Hawkey, 29 May 1868, accepting the presidential nomination, in P. C. Headley *The Life and Campaigns of General U. S. Grant* (1869) ch. 29

8 I know no method to secure the repeal of bad or obnoxious laws so effective as their stringent execution.
inaugural address, 4 March 1869, in P. C. Headley *The Life and Campaigns of General U. S. Grant* (1869) ch. 29

9 Let no guilty man escape, if it can be avoided . . . No personal consideration should stand in the way of performing a public duty.
on the implication of his private secretary in a tax fraud
endorsement of a letter relating to the Whiskey Ring

received 29 July 1875, in E. P. Oberholtzer *History of the United States Since the Civil War* (1937) vol. 3, ch. 19

George Granville, Lord Lansdowne 1666–1735
English poet and dramatist

10 Bright as the day, and like the morning, fair,
Such Cloe is . . . and common as the air.
'Cloe' (1712)

11 Cowards in scarlet pass for men of war.
The She Gallants (1696) act 5

Günter Grass 1927–
German novelist, poet, and dramatist

12 The citizen's first duty is unrest.
The Citizen's First Duty address delivered 1967; in *Speak Out!* (1968)

13 I want to warn against this time-honoured means of dealing with the past; I prefer, myself, to keep the wound open.
Dokumente zur politischen Wirkung (1968)

14 *Was in jenen Zeiten, da man alles nur einigermassen gerade Gewachsene nach Verdun schickte, um es auf Frankreichs Boden in die ewige Waagrechte zu bringen.*

In those days, when every male who could stand half-way erect was being shipped to Verdun to undergo a radical change of posture from the vertical to the eternal horizontal.
The Tin Drum (1959) bk. 1 'Moth and Light Bulb', translated by Ralph Manheim

15 *Allein auf Rasputin wollte ich mich nicht verlassen, denn allzubald wurde mir klar, dass auf dieser Welt jedem Rasputin ein Goethe gegenübersteht, dass Rasputin Goethe oder der Goethe einen Rasputin nach sich zieht, sogar erschafft, wenn es sein muss, um ihn hinterher verurteilen zu können.*

Only too soon it became clear to me that in this world of ours every Rasputin has his Goethe, that every Rasputin draws a Goethe or if you prefer every Goethe a Rasputin in his wake, or even makes one if need be, in order to be able to condemn him later on.
The Tin Drum (1959) bk. 1 'Rasputin and the Alphabet', translated by Ralph Manheim

Henry Grattan 1746–1820
Irish nationalist leader

16 The thing he proposes to buy is what cannot be sold—liberty.
speech in the Irish Parliament against the proposed union, 16 January 1800
in *Dictionary of National Biography* (1917–)

17 He [Gladstone] quoted as I have heard him do before, a saying of Grattan about 'the Channel forbidding Union, the Ocean forbidding separation.'
as recalled by Lord Derby; R. F. Foster *Paddy and Mr Punch* (1993)

Arthur Percival Graves 1846–1931

Irish songwriter

1 Trottin' to the fair,
Me and Moll Maloney,
Seated, I declare
On a single pony.
  'Ridin' Double'

John Woodcock Graves 1795–1886

British huntsman and songwriter

2 D'ye ken John Peel with his coat so grey?
D'ye ken John Peel at the break of the day?
D'ye ken John Peel when he's far far away
With his hounds and his horn in the morning?
an alternative version 'coat so gay' is often sung
  'John Peel' (1820)

3 For Peel's view-hollo would waken the dead,
Or a fox from his lair in the morning.
  'John Peel' (1820)

4 Yes, I ken John Peel and Ruby too,
Ranter and Ringwood, Bellman and True;
From a find to a check, from a check to a view,
From a view to a death in the morning.
  'John Peel' (1820)

Robert Graves 1895–1985

English poet

5 Beware, madam, of the witty devil,
The arch intriguer who walks disguised
In a poet's cloak, his gay tongue oozing evil.
  'Beware, Madam!'

6 There's a cool web of language winds us in,
Retreat from too much joy or too much fear.
  'The Cool Web' (1927)

7 Truth-loving Persians do not dwell upon
The trivial skirmish fought near Marathon.
  'The Persian Version' (1945)

8 As you are woman, so be lovely:
As you are lovely, so be various,
Merciful as constant, constant as various,
So be mine, as I yours for ever.
  'Pygmalion to Galatea' (1927)

9 Love is a universal migraine.
A bright stain on the vision
Blotting out reason.
  'Symptoms of Love'

10 To evoke posterity
Is to weep on your own grave,
Ventriloquizing for the unborn.
  'To Evoke Posterity' (1938)

11 Goodbye to all that.
  title of autobiography (1929)

12 Imaginative readers rewrite books to suit their
own taste, omitting and mentally altering what
they read.
  The Reader over your Shoulder (1947)

13 The award of a pure gold medal for poetry would
flatter the recipient unduly: no poem ever attains
such carat purity.
  Address to the Oxford University Philological Society January
  1960

14 If there's no money in poetry, neither is there
poetry in money.
  speech at London School of Economics, 6 December 1963

15 Science has lost its virgin purity, has become
dogmatic instead of seeking for enlightenment and
has gradually fallen into the hands of the traders.
  Bruno Friedman *Flawed science, damaged human life* (1969)

16 LSD reminds me of the minks that escape from
mink-farms and breed in the forest and become
dangerous and destructive. It has escaped from the
drug factory and gets made in college laboratories.
  George Plimpton (ed.) *The Writer's Chapbook* (1989)

John Gray 1951–

17 Men are from Mars, women are from Venus.
  title of book (1992)

John Chipman Gray 1839–1915

American lawyer

18 Dirt is only matter out of place; and what is a blot
on the escutcheon of the Common Law may be a
jewel in the crown of the Social Republic.
  Restraints on the Alienation of Property (2nd ed., 1895)
  preface

Patrick, Lord Gray d. 1612

19 A dead woman bites not.
  *pressing for the execution of **Mary** Queen of Scots in
  1587*
    oral tradition; see below; see **Proverbs** 617:24

  Mortua non mordet.
  Being dead, she will bite no more.
    A. Darcy's 1625 translation of William Camden's *Annals of
    the Reign of Queen Elizabeth* (1615) vol. 1

Thomas Gray 1716–71

English poet
*on Gray: see **Johnson** 425:5, **Johnson** 429:27, **Johnson** 431:18,*
***Wolfe** 843:14*

20 Ruin seize thee, ruthless King!
Confusion on thy banners wait.
  The Bard (1757) l. 1

21 Loose his beard, and hoary hair
Streamed, like a meteor, to the troubled air.
  The Bard (1757) l. 19; see **Milton** 531:22

22 Weave the warp, and weave the woof,
The winding-sheet of Edward's race.
  The Bard (1757) l. 49

23 In gallant trim the gilded vessel goes;
Youth on the prow, and Pleasure at the helm.
  'The Bard' (1757) l. 73

24 The curfew tolls the knell of parting day,
The lowing herd wind slowly o'er the lea,

The ploughman homeward plods his weary way,
And leaves the world to darkness and to me.

Now fades the glimmering landscape on the sight,
And all the air a solemn stillness holds,
Save where the beetle wheels his droning flight,
And drowsy tinklings lull the distant folds.
Elegy Written in a Country Churchyard (1751) l. 1

1 Save that from yonder ivy-mantled tow'r,
The moping owl does to the moon complain.
Elegy Written in a Country Churchyard (1751) l. 9

2 Beneath those rugged elms, that yew-tree's shade,
Where heaves the turf in many a mouldering
heap,
Each in his narrow cell for ever laid,
The rude forefathers of the hamlet sleep.
Elegy Written in a Country Churchyard (1751) l. 13

3 Let not ambition mock their useful toil,
Their homely joys, and destiny obscure;
Nor grandeur hear with a disdainful smile,
The short and simple annals of the poor.

The boast of heraldry, the pomp of pow'r,
And all that beauty, all that wealth e'er gave,
Awaits alike th' inevitable hour,
The paths of glory lead but to the grave.
Elegy Written in a Country Churchyard (1751) l. 29

4 Can storied urn or animated bust
Back to its mansion call the fleeting breath?
Can honour's voice provoke the silent dust,
Or flatt'ry soothe the dull cold ear of death?
Elegy Written in a Country Churchyard (1751) l. 41

5 Full many a gem of purest ray serene,
The dark unfathomed caves of ocean bear:
Full many a flower is born to blush unseen,
And waste its sweetness on the desert air.

Some village-Hampden, that with dauntless breast
The little tyrant of his fields withstood;
Some mute inglorious Milton here may rest,
Some Cromwell guiltless of his country's blood.
Elegy Written in a Country Churchyard (1751) l. 53

6 Forbad to wade through slaughter to a throne,
And shut the gates of mercy on mankind.
Elegy Written in a Country Churchyard (1751) l. 67

7 Far from the madding crowd's ignoble strife,
Their sober wishes never learned to stray;
Along the cool sequestered vale of life
They kept the noiseless tenor of their way.
Elegy Written in a Country Churchyard (1751) l. 73

8 Here rests his head upon the lap of Earth
A youth to fortune and to fame unknown.
Fair Science frowned not on his humble birth,
And Melancholy marked him for her own.
Elegy Written in a Country Churchyard (1751) l. 117

9 Ye distant spires, ye antique towers,
That crown the wat'ry glade.
Ode on a Distant Prospect of Eton College (1747) l. 1

10 Alas, regardless of their doom,
The little victims play!
No sense have they of ills to come,
Nor care beyond to-day.
Ode on a Distant Prospect of Eton College (1747) l. 51

11 To each his suff'rings, all are men,
Condemned alike to groan;
The tender for another's pain,
Th' unfeeling for his own.
Ode on a Distant Prospect of Eton College (1747) l. 91

12 Thought would destroy their paradise.
No more; where ignorance is bliss,
'Tis folly to be wise.
Ode on a Distant Prospect of Eton College (1747) l. 98; see
Proverbs 634:39

13 Demurest of the tabby kind,
The pensive Selima reclined.
'Ode on the Death of a Favourite Cat' (1748)

14 What female heart can gold despise?
What cat's averse to fish?
'Ode on the Death of a Favourite Cat' (1748)

15 A favourite has no friend!
'Ode on the Death of a Favourite Cat' (1748)

16 Not all that tempts your wand'ring eyes
And heedless hearts, is lawful prize;
Nor all, that glisters, gold.
'Ode on the Death of a Favourite Cat' (1748)

17 The Attic warbler pours her throat,
Responsive to the cuckoo's note,
The untaught harmony of spring.
'Ode on the Spring' (1748) l. 5

18 In thy green lap was Nature's darling laid.
of **Shakespeare**
The Progress of Poesy (1757) l. 84

19 Nor second he, that rode sublime
Upon the seraph-wings of ecstasy,
The secrets of th' abyss to spy.
He passed the flaming bounds of place and time:
The living throne, the sapphire-blaze,
Where angels tremble, while they gaze,
He saw; but blasted with excess of light,
Closed his eyes in endless night.
of **Milton**
The Progress of Poesy (1757) l. 95

20 Thoughts, that breathe, and words, that burn.
The Progress of Poesy (1757) l. 110

21 Beyond the limits of a vulgar fate,
Beneath the good how far—but far above the
great.
The Progress of Poesy (1757) l. 122

22 Too poor for a bribe, and too proud to importune,
He had not the method of making a fortune.
'Sketch of his own Character' (written 1761)

23 The language of the age is never the language of
poetry, except among the French, whose verse,
where the thought or image does not support it,
differs in nothing from prose.
letter to Richard West, 8 April 1742, in H. W. Starr (ed.)
Correspondence of Thomas Gray (1971) vol. 1

24 It has been usual to catch a mouse or two (for
form's sake) in public once a year.
on refusing the Laureateship
letter to William Mason, 19 December 1757; in H. W.
Starr (ed.) *Correspondence of Thomas Gray* (1971) vol. 2

1 I shall be but a shrimp of an author.
> letter to Horace Walpole, 25 February 1768, in H. W. Starr
> (ed.) *Correspondence of Thomas Gray* (1971) vol. 3

2 Any fool may write a most valuable book by
chance, if he will only tell us what he heard and
saw with veracity.
> letter to Horace Walpole, 25 February 1768, in H. W. Starr
> (ed.) *Correspondence of Thomas Gray* (1971) vol. 3

Horace Greeley 1811–72
American founder and editor of the New York Tribune

3 Go West, young man, and grow up with the
country.
> *Hints toward Reforms* (1850); see **Newspaper headlines**
> 562:10

Matthew Green 1696–1737
English poet

4 They politics like ours profess,
The greater prey upon the less.
> *The Grotto* (1732) l. 69

5 To cure the mind's wrong bias, spleen,
Some recommend the bowling-green,
Some, hilly walks; all, exercise.
> *The Spleen* (1737) l. 89

6 Or to some coffee-house I stray
For news, the manna of a day.
> *The Spleen* (1737) l. 168

7 By happy alchemy of mind
They turn to pleasure all they find.
> *The Spleen* (1737) l. 610

Graham Greene 1904–91
English novelist

8 Catholics and Communists have committed great
crimes, but at least they have not stood aside, like
an established society, and been indifferent. I
would rather have blood on my hands than water
like Pilate.
> *The Comedians* (1966) pt. 3, ch. 4

9 He gave her a bright fake smile; so much of life
was a putting-off of unhappiness for another time.
Nothing was ever lost by delay.
> *The Heart of the Matter* (1948) bk. 1, pt. 1, ch. 1

10 Against the beautiful and the clever and the
successful, one can wage a pitiless war, but not
against the unattractive.
> *The Heart of the Matter* (1948) bk. 1, pt. 1, ch. 2

11 They had been corrupted by money, and he had
been corrupted by sentiment. Sentiment was the
more dangerous, because you couldn't name its
price. A man open to bribes was to be relied upon
below a certain figure, but sentiment might uncoil
in the heart at a name, a photograph, even a
smell remembered.
> *The Heart of the Matter* (1948) bk. 1, pt. 1, ch. 2

12 In human relations kindness and lies are worth a
thousand truths.
> *The Heart of the Matter* (1948) bk. 1, pt. 2, ch. 4

13 Point me out the happy man and I will point you
out either egotism, selfishness, evil—or else an
absolute ignorance.
> *The Heart of the Matter* (1948) bk. 2, pt. 1, ch. 1

14 He felt the loyalty we all feel to unhappiness—the
sense that that is where we really belong.
> *The Heart of the Matter* (1948) bk. 2, pt. 2, ch. 1

15 His hilarity was like a scream from a crevasse.
> *The Heart of the Matter* (1948) bk. 3, pt. 1, ch. 1

16 There is always one moment in childhood when
the door opens and lets the future in.
> *The Power and the Glory* (1940) pt. 1, ch. 1

17 Innocence always calls mutely for protection,
when we would be so much wiser to guard
ourselves against it: innocence is like a dumb leper
who has lost his bell, wandering the world
meaning no harm.
> *The Quiet American* (1955) pt. 1, ch. 3

18 I never knew a man who had better motives for all
the trouble he caused.
> *The Quiet American* (1955) pt. 1, ch. 4

19 People who like quotations love meaningless
generalizations.
> *Travels With My Aunt* (1969) ch. 13

Nancy Greene 1943–
Canadian alpine skier

20 You have to have a real love of your sport to carry
you through all the bad times, you still want to ski
even when things aren't working.
> in *Vancouver Sun* 23 November 1999

Robert Greene c.1560–92
English poet and dramatist

21 Hangs in the uncertain balance of proud time.
> *Friar Bacon and Friar Bungay* (1594) act 3, sc. 1

22 'Men, when they lust, can many fancies feign,'
Said Phillis. This not Coridon denied,
That lust had lies. 'But love,' quoth he, 'says
truth.'
> *Perimedes* (1588) 'Phillis kept sheep'

23 Ah! what is love! It is a pretty thing,
As sweet unto a shepherd as a king,
And sweeter too;
For kings have cares that wait upon a crown,
And cares can make the sweetest love to frown.
> 'The Shepherd's Wife's Song' (1590)

24 For there is an upstart crow, beautified with our
feathers, that with his tiger's heart wrapped in a
player's hide, supposes he is as well able to
bumbast out a blank verse as the best of you; and
being an absolute *Johannes fac totum*, is in his own
conceit the only Shake-scene in a country.
> *Groatsworth of Wit Bought with a Million of Repentance*
> (1592); see **Shakespeare** 694:25

Alan Greenspan 1926–

American economist

1 How do we know when irrational exuberance has unduly escalated asset values?
  speech in Washington, 5 December 1996

2 An infectious greed seemed to grip much of our business community.
  of the late 1990s
    in *New York Times* 17 July 2002 (online edition)

Germaine Greer 1939–

Australian feminist

3 The female eunuch.
  title of book (1970)

4 Women have very little idea of how much men hate them.
  The Female Eunuch (1970)

5 You can now see the Female Eunuch the world over . . . spreading herself wherever blue jeans and Coca-Cola may go. Wherever you see nail varnish, lipstick, brassieres, and high heels, the Eunuch has set up her camp.
  The Female Eunuch (20th anniversary ed., 1991) foreword

6 Human beings have an inalienable right to invent themselves; when that right is pre-empted it is called brain-washing.
  in *The Times* 1 February 1986

7 I didn't fight to get women out from behind the vacuum cleaner to get them onto the board of Hoover.
  in *Guardian* 27 October 1986

George Gregan 1973–

Zambian-born Australian rugby player

8 He's outstanding under pressure and he knocked over the one that mattered.
  *on Jonny **Wilkinson** in the Rugby World Cup final, Sydney, 22 November 2003*
    in *Weekend Australian* (online ed.) 23 November 2003

9 England . . . delivered when it counted but I'm so proud of my guys, they gutsed it out and clawed their way back into the game.
  on the Rugby World Cup final, Sydney, 22 November 2003
    in *Weekend Australian* (online ed.) 23 November 2003

Gregory the Great C.AD 540–604

Roman cleric, Pope from 590

10 *Non Angli sed Angeli.*
  Not Angles but Angels.
  on seeing English slaves in Rome
    oral tradition, based on

  Responsum est, quod Angli vocarentur. At ille: 'Bene,' inquit; 'nam et angelicam habent faciem, et tales angelorum in caelis decet esse coheredes'.
  They answered that they were called Angles. 'It is well,' he said, 'for they have the faces of angels, and such should be the co-heirs of the angels of heaven'.
    Bede *Historia Ecclesiastica* bk. 2, sect. 1

Stephen Grellet 1773–1855

French Quaker and missionary

11 I expect to pass through this world but once; any good thing therefore that I can do, or any kindness that I can show to any fellow-creature, let me do it now; let me not defer or neglect it, for I shall not pass this way again.
  attributed; some of the many other claimants to authorship are given in John o' London *Treasure Trove* (1925)

Joyce Grenfell 1910–79

English comedy actress and writer
*see also **Catchphrases** 200:19*

12 Stately as a galleon, I sail across the floor,
  Doing the Military Two-step, as in the days of yore
  . . .
  So gay the band,
  So giddy the sight,
  Full evening dress is a must,
  But the zest goes out of a beautiful waltz
  When you dance it bust to bust.
    'Stately as a Galleon' (1978 song)

Julian Grenfell 1888–1915

English soldier and poet

13 And Life is Colour and Warmth and Light
  And a striving evermore for these;
  And he is dead, who will not fight;
  And who dies fighting has increase.
    'Into Battle' in *The Times* 28 May 1915

George Grenville 1712–70

British Whig statesman; Prime Minister 1763–5

14 A wise government knows how to enforce with temper, or to conciliate with dignity.
  *speaking against the expulsion of John **Wilkes***
    in the House of Commons, 3 February 1769

Jean-Baptiste-Louis Gresset 1709–77

French poet and dramatist

15 *Les sots sont ici-bas pour nos menus plaisirs.*
  Fools are here below for our minor pleasures.
    Le Méchant (1747) act 2, sc. 1

Wayne Gretzky 1961–

Canadian ice-hockey player

16 I skate to where the puck is going to be, not where it's been.
  attributed, 1985; John Robert Colombo *Colombo's New Canadian Quotations* (1987)

Frances Greville (née Macartney) C.1724–89

Irish poet

17 Far as distress the soul can wound
  'Tis pain in each degree;

Bliss goes but to a certain bound,
Beyond is agony.
'A Prayer for Indifference' (1759)

Fulke Greville, Lord Brooke 1554–1628

English poet, writer, and politician
see also Dyer 293:12

1 Life is a top which whipping Sorrow driveth.
Caelica (1633) 'The earth with thunder torn, with fire blasted'

2 O wearisome condition of humanity!
Born under one law, to another bound;
Vainly begot, and yet forbidden vanity;
Created sick, commanded to be sound.
Mustapha (1609) act 5, sc. 4

Edward Grey, Lord Grey of Fallodon
1862–1933

British Liberal politician

3 The lamps are going out all over Europe; we shall not see them lit again in our lifetime.
on the eve of the First World War
25 Years (1925) vol. 2, ch. 18

Lady Jane Grey 1537–54

English monarch, niece of Henry VIII, queen of England 9–19 June 1553

4 One of the greatest benefits that God ever gave me is that he sent me so sharp and severe parents and so gentle a schoolmaster.
Roger Ascham *The Schoolmaster* (1570) bk. 1

Arthur Griffith 1871–1922

Irish statesman

5 The Irish leader who would connive in the name of Home Rule at the acceptance of any measure which alienated for a day—for an hour—for one moment of time—a square inch of the soil of Ireland would act the part of a traitor and would deserve a traitor's fate.
in *Sinn Féin* 21 February 1914

6 What I have signed I will stand by, in the belief that the end of the conflict of centuries is at hand.
statement to Dáil Éireann before the debate on the Treaty, December 1921

7 We have brought back the flag; we have brought back the evacuation of Ireland after 700 years by British troops and the formation of an Irish army. We have brought back to Ireland her full rights.
when moving acceptance of the Treaty in the Dáil, December 1921

Mervyn Griffith-Jones 1909–79

British lawyer

8 Is it a book you would even wish your wife or your servants to read?
of D. H. Lawrence's Lady Chatterley's Lover, while appearing for the prosecution at the Old Bailey, 20 October 1960
in *The Times* 21 October 1960

Philip Jones Griffiths

Welsh photojournalist

9 There are very few professions where even when you are at the top, a household name, you might still be standing on a draughty street corner with your feet getting wet and cold, waiting for something to happen.
of working as a photojournalist
Russell Miller *Magnum: Fifty Years at the Front Line of History* (1997)

John Grigg 1924–2001

British writer and journalist, who as Lord Altrincham disclaimed his hereditary title in 1963

10 The personality conveyed by the utterances which are put into her mouth is that of a priggish schoolgirl, captain of the hockey team, a prefect, and a recent candidate for confirmation. It is not thus that she will be able to come into her own as an independent and distinctive character.
of Queen Elizabeth II
in *National and English Review* August 1958

11 Autobiography is now as common as adultery and hardly less reprehensible.
in *Sunday Times* 28 February 1962

Nicholas Grimald 1519–62

English poet

12 Of all the heavenly gifts that mortal men commend,
What trusty treasure in the world can countervail a friend?
'Of Friendship' (1557)

Jacob Grimm 1785–1863 and Wilhelm Grimm 1786–1859

German philologists and folklorists

13 And so the little girl grew up: her skin was as white as snow, her cheeks as rosy as the blood, and her hair as black as ebony.
Kinder- und Hausmärchen [Fairytales and Household Stories] (1812–14) 'Snow White'

14 Mirror, mirror on the wall,
Who is the fairest of them all?
Kinder- und Hausmärchen [Fairytales and Household Stories] (1812–14) 'Snow White'

15 Rapunzel, Rapunzel, let down your hair.
Kinder- und Hausmärchen [Fairytales and Household Stories] (1812–14) 'Rapunzel'

Joseph ('Jo') Grimond 1913–93

British Liberal politician, Leader of the Liberal Party 1956–67

16 In bygone days, commanders were taught that when in doubt, they should march their troops towards the sound of gunfire. I intend to march my troops towards the sound of gunfire.
speech to the Liberal Party Assembly, 14 September 1963

Andrei Gromyko 1909–89
Soviet statesman; President of the USSR 1985–8

1 Comrades, this man has a nice smile, but he's got iron teeth.
of Mikhail **Gorbachev**
speech to Soviet Communist Party Central Committee, 11 March 1985

George Grossmith 1847–1912
English actor, singer, and writer

2 You should see me dance the Polka,
You should see me cover the ground,
You should see my coat-tails flying,
As I jump my partner round.
'See me Dance the Polka' (*c.*1887 song)

George Grossmith 1847–1912 and Weedon Grossmith 1854–1919
English writers

3 What's the good of a home if you are never in it?
The Diary of a Nobody (1894) ch. 1

4 I . . . recognized her as a woman who used to work years ago for my old aunt at Clapham. It only shows how small the world is.
The Diary of a Nobody (1894) ch. 2

5 He suggested we should play 'Cutlets', a game we never heard of. He sat on a chair, and asked Carrie to sit on his lap, an invitation which dear Carrie rightly declined.
The Diary of a Nobody (1894) ch. 7

6 I left the room with silent dignity, but caught my foot in the mat.
The Diary of a Nobody (1894) ch. 12

7 I am a poor man, but I would gladly give ten shillings to find out who sent me the insulting Christmas card I received this morning.
The Diary of a Nobody (1894) ch. 13

Andrew Grove 1936–
Hungarian-born American businessman

8 Only the paranoid survive.
dictum on which he has long run his company, the Intel Corporation
in *New York Times* 18 December 1994

Philip Guedalla 1889–1944
British historian and biographer

9 Any stigma, as the old saying is, will serve to beat a dogma.
Masters and Men (1923) 'Ministers of State'; see **Proverbs** 624:3

10 The little ships, the unforgotten Homeric catalogue of *Mary Jane* and *Peggy IV*, of *Folkestone Belle, Boy Billy,* and *Ethel Maud,* of *Lady Haig* and *Skylark* . . . the little ships of England brought the Army home.
on the evacuation of Dunkirk
Mr Churchill (1941) ch. 7

11 The cheerful clatter of Sir James Barrie's cans as he went round with the milk of human kindness.
Supers and Supermen (1920) 'Some Critics'

12 The work of Henry James has always seemed divisible by a simple dynastic arrangement into three reigns: James I, James II, and the Old Pretender.
Supers and Supermen (1920) 'Some Critics'

Edgar A. Guest 1881–1959
American writer, journalist, and poet

13 The best of all the preachers are the men who live their creeds.
'Sermons we See' (1926)

Ernesto ('Che') Guevara 1928–67
Argentinian revolutionary and guerrilla leader

14 The Revolution is made by man, but man must forge his revolutionary spirit from day to day.
Socialism and Man in Cuba (1968)

François Guizot 1787–1874
French historian and politician
see also **Sayings** 670:9

15 *L'humanité ne se passe pas longtemps de grandeur.*
Humanity cannot for long dispense with greatness.
in 1832; E. Percy *The Heresy of Democracy* (1954)

Nubar Gulbenkian 1896–1972
British industrialist and philanthropist

16 The best number for a dinner party is two—myself and a dam' good head waiter.
in *Daily Telegraph* 14 January 1965

Nikolai Gumilev 1886–1921
Russian poet

17 Our freedom is but a light that breaks through from another world.
'The Tram that Lost its Way' (1921) (translated by Dmitri Obolensky)

Thom Gunn 1929–
English poet

18 My thoughts are crowded with death
and it draws so oddly on the sexual
that I am confused
confused to be attracted
by, in effect, my own annihilation.
'In Time of Plague' (1992)

19 Their relationship consisted
In discussing if it existed.
'Jamesian' (1992)

Dorothy Frances Gurney 1858–1932
English poet

20 The kiss of the sun for pardon,
The song of the birds for mirth,

One is nearer God's Heart in a garden
Than anywhere else on earth.
'God's Garden' (1913)

Ivor Gurney 1890–1937

English poet

1 I paid the prices of life
Standing where Rome immortal heard October's
    strife,
A war poet whose right of honour cuts falsehood
    like a knife.
'Poem for End' (c.1922–5)

2 War told me truth: I have Severn's right of maker,
As of Cotswold: war told me: I was elect, I was
    born fit
To praise the three hundred feet depth of every
    acre
Between Tewkesbury and Stroudway, Side and
    Wales Gate.
'While I Write' (c.1922–5)

John Hampden Gurney 1802–62

English clergyman

3 Ye holy angels bright,
Who wait at God's right hand,
Or through the realms of light
Fly at your Lord's command,
Assist our song,
Or else the theme
Too high doth seem
For mortal tongue.
'Ye holy angels bright' (1838 hymn); based on a poem by
Richard Baxter (1615–91)

4 My soul, bear thou thy part,
Triumph in God above,
And with a well-tuned heart
Sing thou the songs of love.
'Ye holy angels bright' (1838 hymn)

Woody Guthrie (Woodrow Wilson Guthrie)
1912–67

American folksinger and songwriter

5 This land is your land, this land is my land,
From California to the New York Island.
From the redwood forest to the Gulf Stream waters
This land was made for you and me.
'This Land is Your Land' (1956 song)

Nell Gwyn 1650–87

English actress and courtesan

on Gwyn: see **Last words** 472:18, **Pepys** 592:8

6 Pray, good people, be civil. I am the Protestant
whore.
at Oxford, during the anti-Catholic ferment at the time of
the Popish Plot, 1681; in B. Bevan *Nell Gwyn* (1969)
ch.13

Peter John Gzowski 1934–2002

Canadian broadcaster

7 We need spring. We need it desperately and,
usually, we need it before God is willing to give it
to us.
Peter Gzowski's Spring Tonic (1979)

William Habington 1605–54

English poet

8 Direct your eyesight inward, and you'll find
A thousand regions in your mind
Yet undiscover'd. Travel them, and be
Expert in home cosmography.
'To my honoured friend Sir Ed. P. Knight', in *Castara*
(1634)

Alan Hackney

British novelist

9 Miles of cornfields, and ballet in the evening.
describing Russia
Private Life (1958) ch.11 (later filmed as *I'm All Right Jack*,
1959)

Hadrian AD 76–138

Roman emperor from 117

10 *Animula vagula blandula,*
Hospes comesque corporis,
Quae nunc abibis in loca
Pallidula rigida nudula,
Nec ut soles dabis iocos!

Ah! gentle, fleeting, wav'ring sprite,
Friend and associate of this clay!
To what unknown region borne,
Wilt thou now wing thy distant flight?
No more with wonted humour gay,
But pallid, cheerless, and forlorn.
J. W. Duff (ed.) *Minor Latin Poets* (1934); translated by
Byron as 'Adrian's Address to His Soul When Dying'; see
Pope 602:10

Ernst Haeckel 1834–1919

German biologist and philosopher

11 Ontogenesis, or the development of the individual,
is a short and quick recapitulation of phylogenesis,
or the development of the tribe to which it
belongs, determined by the laws of inheritance
and adaptation.
this discredited theory is often summarized as,
'ontogeny recapitulates phylogeny'
The History of Creation (1868)

Haggadah

the text recited at the Seder on the first two nights of the Jewish Passover

1 This is the bread of poverty which our fathers ate in the land of Egypt. Let all who are hungry come and eat; let all who are in need come to our Passover feast. Now we are here; next year may we be in the land of Israel! Now we are slaves; next year may we be free!
   The narration

2 It is this promise which has stood by our fathers and by us. For it is not simply a matter of one man rising up against us to destroy us. Rather, in every generation men have risen up against us to destroy us, but the Holy One, blessed be he, has saved us from their hands.
   In every generation

3 Rabban Gamaliel says: 'Whoever does not mention the following three things at Passover has not fulfilled his duty—the Passover sacrifice, unleavened bread, and bitter herbs.'
   The three essentials of the Seder

4 Therefore, we are duty-bound to thank, praise, laud, glorify, exalt, honour, bless, extol, and adore him who performed all these miracles for our fathers and for us. He has brought us out from slavery to freedom, from sorrow to joy, from mourning to holiday, from darkness to great light, and from bondage to redemption. Let us, then, sing before him a new song. Hallelujah!
   Praise to the Redeemer of Israel

5 Next year in Jerusalem!
   Accepted

H. Rider Haggard 1856–1925

English writer
on Haggard: see **Stephen** 756:1

6 Out of the dark we came, into the dark we go . . . Life is nothing. Life is all. It is the hand with which we hold off death. It is the glow-worm that shines in the night-time and is black in the morning; it is the white breath of the oxen in winter; it is the little shadow that runs across the grass and loses itself at sunset.
   King Solomon's Mines (1886) ch. 5; see **Crowfoot** 253:1

7 She who must be obeyed.
   She (1887) ch. 6 and *passim*

William Hague 1961–

British Conservative politician; Leader of the Conservative Party 1997–2001

8 Feather-bedding, pocket-lining, money-grabbing cronies.
   on the influence of lobbyists
   in the House of Commons, 8 July 1998

9 Let me take you on a journey to a foreign land—to Britain after a second term of Tony Blair.
   speech to Conservative Party spring conference, Harrogate, 4 March 2001

C. F. S. Hahnemann see Mottoes 552:19

Earl Haig 1861–1928

British general, Commander in France, 1915–18
on Haig: see **Beaverbrook** 60:15

10 A very weak-minded fellow I am afraid, and, like the feather pillow, bears the marks of the last person who has sat on him!
   describing the 17th Earl of Derby
   letter to Lady Haig, 14 January 1918; in R. Blake *Private Papers of Douglas Haig* (1952) ch. 16

11 Every position must be held to the last man: there must be no retirement. With our backs to the wall, and believing in the justice of our cause, each one of us must fight on to the end.
   order to British troops, 12 April 1918; A. Duff Cooper *Haig* (1936) vol. 2, ch. 23

Quintin Hogg, Lord Hailsham 1907–2001

British Conservative politician

12 Conservatives do not believe that the political struggle is the most important thing in life . . . The simplest of them prefer fox-hunting—the wisest religion.
   The Case for Conservatism (1947) pt. 1

13 A great party is not to be brought down because of a scandal by a woman of easy virtue and a proved liar.
   in a BBC television interview on the Profumo affair, in *The Times* 14 June 1963

14 The elective dictatorship.
   title of the Dimbleby Lecture, 19 October 1976

15 The English and, more latterly, the British, have the habit of acquiring their institutions by chance or inadvertence, and shedding them in a fit of absent-mindedness.
   'The Granada Guildhall Lecture 1987' 10 November 1987; see **Seeley** 675:16

Hakuin 1686–1769

Japanese monk, writer and artist; founder of modern Japanese Zen

16 If someone claps his hand a sound arises. Listen to the sound of the single hand!
   attributed

J. B. S. Haldane 1892–1964

Scottish mathematical biologist

17 Now, my own suspicion is that the universe is not only queerer than we suppose, but queerer than we *can* suppose . . . I suspect that there are more things in heaven and earth than are dreamed of, or can be dreamed of, in any philosophy.
   Possible Worlds and Other Essays (1927) 'Possible Worlds'; see **Shakespeare** 685:10

18 If my mental processes are determined wholly by the motions of atoms in my brain, I have no reason for supposing that my beliefs are true. They may be sound chemically, but that does not make

them sound logically. And hence I have no reason for supposing my brain to be composed of atoms.
Possible Worlds (1927) 'When I am Dead'

1 I wish I had the voice of Homer
To sing of rectal carcinoma,
Which kills a lot more chaps, in fact,
Than were bumped off when Troy was sacked.
'Cancer's a Funny Thing'; Ronald Clark *J. B. S.* (1968)

2 The Creator, if He exists, has a special preference for beetles.
on observing that there are 400,000 species of beetle on this planet, but only 8,000 species of mammals
report of lecture, 7 April 1951, in *Journal of the British Interplanetary Society* (1951) vol. 10

3 No-one could study mathematics intensively for more than five hours a day and remain sane.
in *Perspectives in Biology and Medicine* (1966) 'An Autobiography in Brief'

H. R. Haldeman 1929–93
*American Presidential assistant to Richard **Nixon***

4 Once the toothpaste is out of the tube, it is awfully hard to get it back in.
to John Dean on the Watergate affair, 8 April 1973, in *Hearings Before the Select Committee on Presidential Campaign Activities of US Senate: Watergate and Related Activities* (1973) vol. 4

Edward Everett Hale 1822–1909
American Unitarian clergyman; Senate chaplain for 1903

5 'Do you pray for the senators, Dr Hale?' 'No, I look at the senators and I pray for the country.'
Van Wyck Brooks *New England Indian Summer* (1940)

Matthew Hale 1609–76
English judge

6 Christianity is part of the laws of England.
William Blackstone's summary of Hale's words (Taylor's case, 1676) in *Commentaries* (1769) vol. 4; Holdsworth's *History of English Law* (1937 ed.) vol. 8 traces the origin of the expression to Sir John Prisot (d. 1460)

Nathan Hale 1755–76
American revolutionary
see also **Last Words** 472:13

7 Every kind of service necessary to the public good becomes honourable by being necessary.
letter to William Hull, 10 September 1776

Sarah Josepha Hale 1788–1879
American writer

8 Mary had a little lamb,
Its fleece was white as snow,
And everywhere that Mary went
The lamb was sure to go.
Poems for Our Children (1830) 'Mary's Little Lamb'

Judah Ha-Levi c.1075–1141
Jewish poet and philosopher, born in Spain

9 Israel amidst the nations is like the heart amidst the organs; it is the most sick and the most healthy of them all.
The Kuzari 2.36

10 I understand the difference between the God and the Lord and I see how great is the difference between the God of Abraham and the God of Aristotle.
The Kuzari 4.16

George Savile, Lord Halifax ('the Trimmer') 1633–95
English politician and essayist

11 Love is a passion that hath friends in the garrison.
Advice to a Daughter (1688) 'Behaviour and Conversation'

12 This innocent word *Trimmer* signifieth no more than this, that if men are together in a boat, and one part of the company would weigh it down on one side, another would make it lean as much to the contrary.
Character of a Trimmer (1685, printed 1688)

13 Men in business are in as much danger from those that work under them, as from those that work against them.
Political, Moral, and Miscellaneous Thoughts and Reflections (1750) 'Instruments of State: Ministers'

14 A known liar should be outlawed in a well-ordered government.
Political, Moral, and Miscellaneous Thoughts and Reflections (1750) 'Miscellaneous: Lying'

15 Anger is never without an argument, but seldom with a good one.
Political, Moral, and Miscellaneous Thoughts and Reflections (1750) 'Of Anger'

16 After a revolution, you see the same men in the drawing-room, and within a week the same flatterers.
Political, Moral, and Miscellaneous Thoughts and Reflections (1750) 'Of Courts'

17 Most men make little other use of their speech than to give evidence against their own understanding.
Political, Moral, and Miscellaneous Thoughts and Reflections (1750) 'Of Folly and Fools'

18 There is . . . no fundamental, but that *every supreme power must be arbitrary*.
Political, Moral, and Miscellaneous Thoughts and Reflections (1750) 'Of Fundamentals'

19 In corrupted governments the place is given for the sake of the man; in good ones the man is chosen for the sake of the place.
Political, Moral, and Miscellaneous Thoughts and Reflections (1750) 'Of Fundamentals'

20 It is in a disorderly government as in a river, the lightest things swim at the top.
Political, Moral, and Miscellaneous Thoughts and Reflections (1750) 'Of Government'

1 The best definition of the best government is, that it has no inconveniences but such as are supportable; but inconveniences there must be.
Political, Moral, and Miscellaneous Thoughts and Reflections (1750) 'Of Government'

2 Malice is of a low stature, but it hath very long arms.
Political, Moral, and Miscellaneous Thoughts and Reflections (1750) 'Of Malice and Envy'

3 The best party is but a kind of conspiracy against the rest of the nation.
Political, Moral, and Miscellaneous Thoughts and Reflections (1750) 'Of Parties'

4 When the people contend for their liberty, they seldom get anything by their victory but new masters.
Political, Moral, and Miscellaneous Thoughts and Reflections (1750) 'Of Prerogative, Power and Liberty'

5 Power is so apt to be insolent and Liberty to be saucy, that they are very seldom upon good terms.
Political, Moral, and Miscellaneous Thoughts and Reflections (1750) 'Of Prerogative, Power and Liberty'

6 Men are not hanged for stealing horses, but that horses may not be stolen.
Political, Moral, and Miscellaneous Thoughts and Reflections (1750) 'Of Punishment'

7 Wherever a knave is not punished, an honest man is laughed at.
Political, Moral, and Miscellaneous Thoughts and Reflections (1750) 'Of Punishment'

8 State business is a cruel trade; good nature is a bungler in it.
Political, Moral, and Miscellaneous Thoughts and Reflections (1750) 'Wicked Ministers'

9 To the question, What shall we do to be saved in this World? there is no other answer but this, Look to your Moat.
A Rough Draft of a New Model at Sea (1694)

10 Lord Rochester was made Lord president: which being a post superior in rank, but much inferior both in advantage and credit to that he held formerly, drew a jest from Lord Halifax . . . he had heard of many kicked down stairs, but never of any that was kicked up stairs before.
Gilbert Burnet *History of My Own Time* (written 1683–6) vol. 1 (1724)

Joseph Hall 1574–1656
English bishop

11 I first adventure, follow me who list And be the second English satirist.
Virgidemiae (1597) prologue

12 Perfection is the child of Time.
Works (1625)

Radclyffe Hall 1883–1943
English novelist

13 The well of loneliness
title of novel (1928)

14 You're neither unnatural, nor abominable, nor mad; you're as much a part of what people call nature as anyone else; only you're unexplained as yet—you've not got your niche in creation.
of lesbianism
The Well of Loneliness (1928) bk. 2, ch. 20, sect. 3

Fitz-Greene Halleck 1790–1867
American poet

15 They love their land because it is their own, And scorn to give aught other reason why; Would shake hands with a king upon his throne, And think it kindness to his Majesty.
'Connecticut' (1847)

16 Green be the turf above thee, Friend of my better days! None knew thee but to love thee, Nor named thee but to praise.
'On the Death of Joseph Rodman Drake' (1820)

Friedrich Halm see Closing lines 228:24

Margaret Halsey 1910–
American writer

17 The English never smash in a face. They merely refrain from asking it to dinner.
With Malice Toward Some (1938) pt. 3

W. F. ('Bull') Halsey 1882–1959
American admiral

18 The Third Fleet's sunken and damaged ships have been salvaged and are retiring at high speed toward the enemy.
on hearing claims that the Japanese had virtually annihilated the US fleet
report, 14 October 1944; E. B. Potter *Bull Halsey* (1985) ch. 17

Alexander Hamilton c.1755–1804
American politician

19 A national debt, if it is not excessive, will be to us a national blessing.
letter to Robert Morris, 30 April 1781, in John C. Hamilton (ed.) *Works of Alexander Hamilton* vol. 1 (1850)

William Hamilton 1788–1856
Scottish metaphysician

20 Truth, like a torch, the more it's shook it shines.
Discussions on Philosophy (1852) title page (epigram)

21 On earth there is nothing great but man; in man there is nothing great but mind.
Lectures on Metaphysics and Logic (ed. Mamsel and Veitch, 1859) vol. 1; attributed in a Latin form to Favorinus in Pico di Mirandola (1463–94) *Disputationes Adversus Astrologiam Divinatricem* (ed. E. Garin, 1946) bk. 3, ch. 27

Oscar Hammerstein II 1895–1960
American songwriter

22 Fish got to swim and birds got to fly I got to love one man till I die, Can't help lovin' dat man of mine.
'Can't Help Lovin' Dat Man of Mine' (1927 song) in *Showboat*

1 Climb ev'ry mountain, ford ev'ry stream
Follow ev'ry rainbow, till you find your dream.
'Climb Ev'ry Mountain' (1959 song) in *The Sound of Music*

2 I'm gonna wash that man right outa my hair.
title of song (1949) in *South Pacific*

3 June is bustin' out all over.
title of song (1945) in *Carousel*

4 The last time I saw Paris
Her heart was warm and gay,
I heard the laughter of her heart in ev'ry street
café.
'The Last Time I saw Paris' (1941 song) in *Lady Be Good*

5 The corn is as high as an elephant's eye,
An' it looks like it's climbin' clear up to the sky.
'Oh, What a Beautiful Mornin' ' (1943 song) in *Oklahoma!*

6 Ol' man river, dat ol' man river,
He must know sumpin', but don't say nothin',
He jus' keeps rollin',
He jus' keeps rollin' along.
'Ol' Man River' (1927 song) in *Showboat*

7 Some enchanted evening,
You may see a stranger,
You may see a stranger,
Across a crowded room.
'Some Enchanted Evening' (1949 song) in *South Pacific*

8 The hills are alive with the sound of music,
With songs they have sung for a thousand years.
The hills fill my heart with the sound of music,
My heart wants to sing ev'ry song it hears.
'The Sound of Music' (1959 title-song in show)

9 There is nothin' like a dame.
title of song (1949) in *South Pacific*

10 I'm as corny as Kansas in August,
High as a flag on the Fourth of July!
'A Wonderful Guy' (1949 song) in *South Pacific*

11 You'll never walk alone.
title of song (1945) in *Carousel*

12 You've got to be taught to be afraid
Of people whose eyes are oddly made,
Of people whose skin is a different shade.
You've got to be carefully taught.
'You've Got to be Carefully Taught' (1949 song) in *South Pacific*

Richard Hampden 1631–95

English politician

13 To tie a popish successor with laws for the
preservation of the Protestant religion was binding
Samson with withes.
*moving a bill to exclude the Duke of York by name
from the succession, 11 May 1679*
in *Dictionary of National Biography* (1917–)

Learned Hand 1872–1961

American judge

14 A self-made man may prefer a self-made name.
*on Samuel Goldfish's changing his name to Samuel
Goldwyn*
Bosley Crowther *Lion's Share* (1957) ch. 7

George Frederick Handel 1685–1759

*German-born composer and organist, resident in England
from 1712*

15 Whether I was in my body or out of my body as I
wrote it I know not. God knows.
of the 'Hallelujah Chorus' in his Messiah; *echoing St
Paul*
Romain Rolland *A Musical Tour Through the Land of the Past*
(1922); see **Bible** 108:23

Kate Hankey 1834–1911

English evangelist

16 Tell me the old, old story
Of unseen things above,
Of Jesus and his glory,
Of Jesus and his love.
'Tell me the old, old story' (1867 hymn)

Brian Hanrahan 1949–

British journalist

17 I counted them all out and I counted them all
back.
*on the number of British aeroplanes joining the raid
on Port Stanley in the Falkland Islands*
BBC broadcast report, 1 May 1982, in *Battle for the
Falklands* (1982)

Lorraine Hansberry 1930–65

American dramatist

18 Though it be a thrilling and marvellous thing to
be merely young and gifted in such times, it is
doubly so, doubly dynamic—to be young, gifted
and *black*.
*To be young, gifted and black: Lorraine Hansberry in her own
words* (1969) adapted by Robert Nemiroff; see **Irvine** 414:3

Rick Hansen 1957–

Canadian wheelchair athlete

19 My disability is that I cannot use my legs. My
handicap is your negative perception of that
disability, and thus of me.
Rick Hansen: Man in Motion (1987, with Jim Taylor)

Edmond Haraucourt 1856–1941

French poet

20 Partir c'est mourir un peu,
C'est mourir à ce qu'on aime:
On laisse un peu de soi-même
En toute heure et dans tout lieu.

To go away is to die a little, it is to die to that
which one loves: everywhere and always, one
leaves behind a part of oneself.
Seul (1891) 'Rondel de l'Adieu'

Otto Harbach 1873–1963

American songwriter

21 Now laughing friends deride tears I cannot hide,
So I smile and say 'When a lovely flame dies,

Smoke gets in your eyes.'
'Smoke Gets in your Eyes' (1933 song)

E. Y. ('Yip') Harburg 1898–1981
American songwriter

1 Brother can you spare a dime?
title of song (1932)

2 Say, it's only a paper moon,
Sailing over a cardboard sea.
'It's Only a Paper Moon' (1933 song, with Billy Rose)

3 Wanna cry, wanna croon.
Wanna laugh like a loon.
It's that Old Devil Moon in your eyes.
'Old Devil Moon' (1946 song) in *Finian's Rainbow*

4 Somewhere over the rainbow
Way up high,
There's a land that I heard of
Once in a lullaby.
'Over the Rainbow' (1939 song) in *The Wizard of Oz*

5 Follow the yellow brick road.
'We're Off to See the Wizard' (1939 song) in *The Wizard of Oz*; see **Baum** 59:6, **John** 422:15

William Harcourt 1827–1904
British Liberal politician

6 We are all socialists now.
during the passage of Lord **Goschen**'*s 1888 budget, noted for the reduction of the national debt*
attributed; Hubert Bland 'The Outlook' in G. B. Shaw (ed.) *Fabian Essays in Socialism* (1889)

Keir Hardie 1856–1915
Scottish Labour politician

7 From his childhood onward this boy will be surrounded by sycophants and flatterers by the score—[*Cries of* 'Oh, oh!']—and will be taught to believe himself as of a superior creation. [*Cries of* 'Oh, oh!'] A line will be drawn between him and the people whom he is to be called upon some day to reign over. In due course, following the precedent which has already been set, he will be sent on a tour round the world, and probably rumours of a morganatic alliance will follow—[*Loud cries of* 'Oh, oh!' *and* 'Order!']—and the end of it all will be that the country will be called upon to pay the bill. [*Cries of* Divide!]
of the future **Edward VIII**
speech in the House of Commons, 28 June 1894

8 Woman, even more than the working class, is the great unknown quantity of the race.
speech at Bradford, 11 April 1914

D. W. Harding 1906–
British psychologist and critic

9 Regulated hatred.
title of an article on the novels of Jane **Austen**
in *Scrutiny* March 1940

Warren G. Harding 1865–1923
American Republican statesman; 29th President of the US, 1921–3

10 America's present need is not heroics, but healing; not nostrums but normalcy; not revolution, but restoration.
speech at Boston, 14 May 1920, in Frederick E. Schortemeier *Rededicating America* (1920) ch. 17

Philip Yorke, Lord Hardwicke 1690–1764
English judge
on Hardwicke: see **Pulteney** 637:3

11 His doubts are better than most people's certainties.
of Lord Dirleton's Law Doubts (*1698*)
James Boswell *Life of Samuel Johnson* (1791)

Godfrey Harold Hardy 1877–1947
English mathematician

12 Beauty is the first test: there is no permanent place in the world for ugly mathematics.
A Mathematician's Apology (1940)

Thomas Hardy 1840–1928
English novelist and poet
see also **Borrowed titles** 146:6

13 A local thing called Christianity.
The Dynasts (1904) pt. 1, act 1, sc. 6

14 War makes rattling good history; but Peace is poor reading.
The Dynasts (1904) pt. 1, act 2, sc. 5

15 It is hard for a woman to define her feelings in language which is chiefly made by men to express theirs.
Far from the Madding Crowd (1874) ch. 81; see **Austen** 39:15

16 A lover without indiscretion is no lover at all.
The Hand of Ethelberta (1876) ch. 20

17 Done because we are too menny.
Jude the Obscure (1896) pt. 6, ch. 2

18 Some folk want their luck buttered.
The Mayor of Casterbridge (1886) ch. 13

19 Dialect words—those terrible marks of the beast to the truly genteel.
The Mayor of Casterbridge (1886) ch. 20

20 She whose youth had seemed to teach that happiness was but the occasional episode in a general drama of pain.
The Mayor of Casterbridge (1886) ch. 45, closing words

21 The regular resource of people who don't go enough into the world to live a novel is to write one.
A Pair of Blue Eyes (1873) ch. 12

22 It was at present a place perfectly accordant with man's nature—neither ghastly, hateful, nor ugly: neither commonplace, unmeaning, nor tame; but, like man, slighted and enduring; and withal

singularly colossal and mysterious in its swarthy monotony. As with some persons who have long lived a past, solitude seemed to look out of its countenance. It had a lonely face, suggesting tragical possibilities.

of Egdon Heath
  The Return of the Native (1878) bk. 1, ch. 1

1 Human beings, in their generous endeavour to construct a hypothesis that shall not degrade a First Cause, have always hesitated to conceive a dominant power of a lower moral quality than their own.
  The Return of the Native (1878) bk. 6, ch. 1

2 A novel is an impression, not an argument.
  Tess of the D'Urbervilles (5th ed., 1892) preface

3 Why it was that upon this beautiful feminine tissue, sensitive as gossamer, and practically blank as snow as yet, there should have been traced such a coarse pattern as it was doomed to receive; why so often the coarse appropriates the finer thus, the wrong man the woman, the wrong woman the man, many thousand years of analytical philosophy have failed to explain to our sense of order.
  Tess of the D'Urbervilles (1891) ch. 11

4 The two forces were at work here as everywhere, the inherent will to enjoy, and the circumstantial will against enjoyment.
  Tess of the D'Urbervilles (1891) ch. 43

5 'Justice' was done, and the President of the Immortals (in Aeschylean phrase) had ended his sport with Tess.
  Tess of the D'Urbervilles (1891) ch. 59

6 Good, but not religious-good.
  Under the Greenwood Tree (1872) ch. 2

7 It was one of those sequestered spots outside the gates of the world . . . where, from time to time, dramas of a grandeur and unity truly Sophoclean are enacted in the real, by virtue of the concentrated passions and closely knit interdependence of the lives therein.
  The Woodlanders (1887) ch. 1

8 The business of the poet and novelist is to show the sorriness underlying the grandest things, and the grandeur underlying the sorriest things.
  notebook entry for 19 April 1885, in Florence Hardy *The Early Life of Thomas Hardy 1840–91* (1928) ch. 13

9 When the Present has latched its postern behind my tremulous stay,
  And the May month flaps its glad green leaves like wings,
  Delicate-filmed as new-spun silk, will the neighbours say,
  'He was a man who used to notice such things'?
  'Afterwards' (1917)

10 The bower we shrined to Tennyson, Gentlemen,
  Is roof-wrecked; damps there drip upon
  Sagged seats, the creeper-nails are rust,
  The spider is sole denizen.
  'An Ancient to Ancients' (1922)

11 'Peace upon earth!' was said. We sing it,
  And pay a million priests to bring it.
  After two thousand years of mass
  We've got as far as poison-gas.
  'Christmas: 1924' (1928)

12 In a solitude of the sea
  Deep from human vanity,
  And the Pride of Life that planned her, stilly couches she.
  'Convergence of the Twain' (1914)

13 Over the mirrors meant
  To glass the opulent
  The sea-worm crawls—grotesque, slimed, dumb, indifferent.
  'Convergence of the Twain' (1914)

14 The Immanent Will that stirs and urges everything.
  'Convergence of the Twain' (1914)

15 An aged thrush, frail, gaunt, and small,
  In blast-beruffled plume.
  'The Darkling Thrush' (1902)

16 So little cause for carollings
  Of such ecstatic sound
  Was written on terrestrial things
  Afar or nigh around,
  That I could think there trembled through
  His happy good-night air
  Some blessed Hope, whereof he knew
  And I was unaware.
  'The Darkling Thrush' (1902)

17 If way to the Better there be, it exacts a full look at the worst.
  'De Profundis' (1902)

18 Well, World, you have kept faith with me,
  Kept faith with me;
  Upon the whole you have proved to be
  Much as you said you were.
  'He Never Expected Much' (1928)

19 I am the family face;
  Flesh perishes, I live on,
  Projecting trait and trace
  Through time to times anon,
  And leaping from place to place
  Over oblivion.
  'Heredity' (1917)

20 Only a man harrowing clods
  In a slow silent walk
  With an old horse that stumbles and nods
  Half asleep as they stalk.
  'In Time of "The Breaking of Nations" ' (1917)

21 Yonder a maid and her wight
  Come whispering by:
  War's annals will cloud into night
  Ere their story die.
  'In Time of "The Breaking of Nations" ' (1917)

22 Yes; quaint and curious war is!
  You shoot a fellow down
  You'd treat if met where any bar is,
  Or help to half-a-crown.
  'The Man he Killed' (1909)

1 What of the faith and fire within us
Men who march away
Ere the barn-cocks say
Night is growing grey,
To hazards whence no tears can win us;
What of the faith and fire within us
Men who march away?
'Men Who March Away' (1914)

2 In the third-class seat sat the journeying boy
And the roof-lamp's oily flame
Played down on his listless form and face,
Bewrapt past knowing to what he was going,
Or whence he came.
'Midnight on the Great Western' (1917)

3 Woman much missed, how you call to me, call to
me.
'The Voice' (1914)

4 This is the weather the cuckoo likes,
And so do I.
'Weathers' (1922)

5 And drops on gate-bars hang in a row,
And rooks in families homeward go,
And so do I.
'Weathers' (1922)

6 When I set out for Lyonnesse,
A hundred miles away,
The rime was on the spray,
And starlight lit my lonesomeness
When I set out for Lyonnesse
A hundred miles away.
'When I set out for Lyonnesse' (1914)

7 If this sort of thing continues no more novel-
writing for me. A man must be a fool to
deliberately stand up and be shot at.
of a hostile review of Tess of the D'Urbervilles, *1891*
Florence Hardy *The Early Life of Thomas Hardy* (1928)

David Hare 1947-
English actor and dramatist

8 What's courage? Failure of planning, that's all.
Bertolt Brecht *Mother Courage and her Children* (1995
version for the National Theatre)

Julius Hare 1795-1855 and Augustus Hare 1792-1834
English writers and clergymen

9 The ancients dreaded death: the Christian can
only fear dying.
Guesses at Truth (1827) Series 1

Maurice Evan Hare 1886-1967
English limerick writer

10 There once was an old man who said, 'Damn!
It is borne in upon me I am
An engine that moves
In determinate grooves,
I'm not even a bus, I'm a tram.'
'Limerick' (1905)

W. F. Hargreaves 1846-1919
British songwriter

11 I'm Burlington Bertie
I rise at ten thirty and saunter along like a toff,
I walk down the Strand with my gloves on my
hand,
Then I walk down again with them off.
'Burlington Bertie from Bow' (1915 song)

12 I acted so tragic the house rose like magic,
The audience yelled 'You're sublime.'
They made me a present of Mornington Crescent
They threw it a brick at a time.
'The Night I Appeared as Macbeth' (1922 song)

John Harington d. 1582
English poet

13 There was a battle fought of late,
Yet was the slaughter small;
The strife was, whether I should write,
Or send nothing at all.
Of one side were the captains' names
Short Time and Little Skill;
One fought alone against them both,
Whose name was Great Good-will.
'To his mother' (written 1540)

John Harington 1561-1612
English writer and courtier

14 When I make a feast,
I would my guests should praise it, not the cooks.
Epigrams (1618) bk. 1, no. 5

15 Treason doth never prosper, what's the reason?
For if it prosper, none dare call it treason.
Epigrams (1618) bk. 4, no. 5

David Ormsby Gore, Lord Harlech 1918-85
British diplomat; Ambassador to Washington, 1961-5

16 Britain will be honoured by historians more for
the way she disposed of an empire than for the
way in which she acquired it.
in *New York Times* 28 October 1962, sect. 4

Harold II c.1019-66
English monarch, King 1066

17 He will give him seven feet of English ground, or
as much more as he may be taller than other men.
his offer to Harald Hardrada of Norway, invading
England, before the battle of Stamford Bridge
King Harald's Saga sect. 91, in Snorri Sturluson
Heimskringla (c.1260, first translated by Samuel Laing as
History of the Norse Kings, 1844)

Jimmy Harper, Will E. Haines, and Tommy Connor

18 The biggest aspidistra in the world.
title of song (1938); popularized by Gracie Fields

Arthur Harris 1892–1984

British Air Force Marshal

1 I would not regard the whole of the remaining cities of Germany as worth the bones of one British Grenadier.

supporting the continued strategic bombing of German cities

letter to Norman Bottomley, deputy Chief of Air Staff, 29 March 1945; Max Hastings *Bomber Command* (1979); see **Bismarck** 117:17

Joel Chandler Harris 1848–1908

American writer

2 Hit look lak sparrer-grass, hit feel like sparrer-grass, hit tas'e lak sparrer-grass, en I bless ef 'taint sparrer-grass.
Nights with Uncle Remus (1883) ch. 27

3 All by my own-alone self.
Nights with Uncle Remus (1883) ch. 36

4 You know w'at de jay-bird say ter der squinch-owl! 'I'm sickly but sassy.'
Nights with Uncle Remus (1883) ch. 50

5 Bred en bawn in a brier-patch!
Uncle Remus and His Legends of the Old Plantation (1881) 'How Mr Rabbit was too Sharp for Mr Fox'

6 Lounjun 'roun' en suffer'n'.
Uncle Remus and His Legends of the Old Plantation (1881) 'Mr Wolf tackles Old Man Tarrypin'

7 Tar-baby ain't sayin' nuthin', en Brer Fox, he lay low.
Uncle Remus and His Legends of the Old Plantation (1881) 'The Wonderful Tar-Baby Story'

Tony Harrison 1953–

British poet

8 The ones we choose to love become our anchor when the hawser of the blood-tie's hacked, or frays.
v (1985)

Josephine Hart 1942–

Irish novelist

9 Damaged people are dangerous. They know they can survive.
Damage (1991) ch. 12

Lorenz Hart 1895–1943

American songwriter

10 I'm wild again
Beguiled again
A simpering, whimpering child again,
Bewitched, bothered, and bewildered am I.
'Bewitched' (1941 song) in *Pal Joey* (1941)

11 When love congeals
It soon reveals
The faint aroma of performing seals,
The double crossing of a pair of heels.
I wish I were in love again!
'I Wish I Were in Love Again' (1937 song) in *Babes in Arms*

12 I get too hungry for dinner at eight.
I like the theatre, but never come late.
I never bother with people I hate.
That's why the lady is a tramp.
'The Lady is a Tramp' (1937 song) in *Babes in Arms*

13 In a mountain greenery
Where God paints the scenery—
Just two crazy people together.
'Mountain Greenery' (1926 song)

14 Thou swell! Thou witty!
Thou sweet! Thou grand!
Wouldst kiss me pretty?
Wouldst hold my hand?
'Thou Swell' (1927 song)

Bret Harte 1836–1902

American poet

15 And on that grave where English oak and holly
And laurel wreaths entwine
Deem it not all a too presumptuous folly,—
This spray of Western pine!
'Dickens in Camp' (1870)

16 If, of all words of tongue and pen,
The saddest are, 'It might have been,'
More sad are these we daily see:
'It is, but hadn't ought to be!'
'Mrs Judge Jenkins' (1867); see **Whittier** 834:5

17 And he smiled a kind of sickly smile, and curled up on the floor,
And the subsequent proceedings interested him no more.
'The Society upon the Stanislaus' (1868) st. 7

18 All you know about it [luck] for certain is that it's bound to change.
'The Outcasts of Poker Flat' (1871) in *The Luck of the Roaring Camp and Other Stories* (1922)

L. P. Hartley 1895–1972

English novelist

19 The past is a foreign country: they do things differently there.
The Go-Between (1953) prologue; see **Morley** 549:3

F. W. Harvey b. 1888

English poet

20 From troubles of the world
I turn to ducks
Beautiful comical things.
'Ducks' (1919)

John Harvey-Jones 1924–

English businessman and writer

21 Business is becoming more and more akin to intellectual sumo wrestling.
All Together Now (1994)

Molly Haskell 1940–

American writer and film critic

1 Being alone and liking it is, for a woman, an act of treachery, an infidelity far more threatening than adultery.
Love and Other Infectious Diseases (1990)

Minnie Louise Haskins 1875–1957

English teacher and writer

2 And I said to the man who stood at the gate of the year: 'Give me a light that I may tread safely into the unknown.'
And he replied:
'Go out into the darkness and put your hand into the Hand of God. That shall be to you better than light and safer than a known way.'
quoted by **George VI** *in his Christmas broadcast, 1939*
Desert (1908) 'God Knows'

Edwin Hatch 1835–89

English clergyman and scholar

3 Breathe on me, Breath of God,
Fill me with life anew,
That I may love what thou dost love,
And do what thou wouldst do.
'Breathe on me, Breath of God' (1878 hymn)

Helen Hathaway 1893–1932

American writer

4 More tears have been shed over men's lack of manners than their lack of morals.
Manners for Men (1928)

Charles Haughey 1925–

Irish Fianna Fáil statesman; Taoiseach 1979–81, 1982, and 1987–92
on Haughey: see **O'Brien** *571:3*

5 It was a bizarre happening, an unprecedented situation, a grotesque situation, an almost unbelievable mischance.
on the series of events leading to the resignation of the Attorney General; the acronym GUBU *was subsequently coined by Conor Cruise* **O'Brien** *to describe Haughey's style of government*
at a press conference in 1982; T. Ryle Dwyer *Charlie: the Political Biography of Charles Haughey* (1987) ch. 12

Václav Havel 1936–

Czech dramatist and statesman; President of Czechoslovakia 1989–92 and of the Czech Republic 1993–2003

6 Truth is not merely what we are thinking, but also why, to whom and under what circumstances we say it.
Temptation (1985)

7 I really do inhabit a system in which words are capable of shaking the entire structure of government, where words can prove mightier than ten military divisions.
speech in Germany accepting a peace prize, October 1989, in *Independent* 9 December 1989

Stephen Hawes d. c.1523

English poet

8 After the day there cometh the dark night;
For though the day be never so long,
At last the bells ringeth to evensong.
The Pastime of Pleasure (1509) ch. 42, st. 10

R. S. Hawker 1803–75

English clergyman and poet

9 And have they fixed the where and when?
And shall Trelawny die?
Here's twenty thousand Cornish men
Will know the reason why!
the last three lines have been in existence since the imprisonment by James II, in 1688, of seven bishops, including Trelawny, Bishop of Bristol
'The Song of the Western Men'

Jacquetta Hawkes 1910–96

English archaeologist and writer

10 Every age has the Stonehenge it deserves—or desires.
in *Antiquity* no. 41, 1967

11 I was conscious of this vanished being and myself as part of an unbroken stream of consciousness . . . With an imaginative effort it is possible to see the eternal present in which all days, all the seasons of the plain, stand in enduring unity.
discovering a Neanderthal skeleton
in *New York Times Biographical Service* 21 March 1996

Stephen Hawking 1942–

English theoretical physicist

12 Each equation . . . in the book would halve the sales.
A Brief History of Time (1988)

13 In effect, we have redefined the task of science to be the discovery of laws that will enable us to predict events up to the limits set by the uncertainty principle.
A Brief History of Time (1988) ch. 11

14 What is it that breathes fire into the equations and makes a universe for them to describe . . . Why does the universe go to all the bother of existing?
A Brief History of Time (1988)

15 If we find the answer to that [why it is that we and the universe exist], it would be the ultimate triumph of human reason—for then we would know the mind of God.
A Brief History of Time (1988) ch. 11

Nathaniel Hawthorne 1804–64

American novelist

16 Dr Johnson's morality was as English an article as a beefsteak.
Our Old Home (1863) 'Lichfield and Uttoxeter'

17 The scarlet letter.
title of novel (1850)

1 America is now given over to a damned mob of
scribbling women.
> letter, 1855; Caroline Ticknor *Hawthorne and his Publisher*
> (1913)

Ian Hay (John Hay Beith) 1876–1952
Scottish novelist and dramatist

2 War is hell, and all that, but it has a good deal to
recommend it. It wipes out all the small nuisances
of peace-time.
> *The First Hundred Thousand* (1915)

3 What do you mean, funny? Funny-peculiar or
funny ha-ha?
> *The Housemaster* (1938) act 3

4 The dawn of legibility in his handwriting has
revealed his utter inability to spell.
> attributed; perhaps used in a dramatization of *The
> Housemaster* (1938)

Franz Joseph Haydn 1732–1809
Austrian composer

5 But all the world understands my language.
> *on being advised by* **Mozart**, *in 1790, not to visit
> England because he knew too little of the world and
> too few languages*
> Rosemary Hughes *Haydn* (1950) ch. 6

Alfred Hayes 1911–85
American songwriter

6 I dreamed I saw Joe Hill last night
Alive as you and me.
Says I, 'But Joe, you're ten years dead.'
'I never died,' says he.
> 'I Dreamed I Saw Joe Hill Last Night' (1936 song); see **Hill**
> 388:11

J. Milton Hayes 1884–1940
British writer

7 There's a one-eyed yellow idol to the north of
Khatmandu,
There's a little marble cross below the town,
There's a broken-hearted woman tends the grave
of Mad Carew,
And the Yellow God forever gazes down.
> *The Green Eye of the Yellow God* (1911)

Eliza Haywood c.1693–1756
English actress, dramatist, and novelist

8 One has no sooner left off one's bib and apron,
than people cry—'Miss will soon be married!'—
and this man, and that man, is presently picked
out for a husband. Mighty ridiculous! they want
to deprive us of all the pleasures of life, just when
one begins to have a relish for them.
> *The History of Miss Betty Thoughtless* (1751)

William Hazlitt 1778–1830
English essayist
see also **Last words** 474:13

9 His sayings are generally like women's letters; all
the pith is in the postscript.
of Charles **Lamb**
> *Conversations of James Northcote* (1826–7)

10 He talked on for ever; and you wished him to talk
on for ever.
of **Coleridge**
> *Lectures on the English Poets* (1818) 'On the Living Poets'

11 So have I loitered my life away, reading books,
looking at pictures, going to plays, hearing,
thinking, writing on what pleased me best. I have
wanted only one thing to make me happy, but
wanting that have wanted everything.
> *Literary Remains* (1836) 'My First Acquaintance with
> Poets'

12 The greatest test of courage I can conceive is to
speak the truth in the House of Commons.
> 'On the Difference between Writing and Speaking'; in
> *London Magazine* July 1820

13 The dupe of friendship, and the fool of love; have I
not reason to hate and to despise myself? Indeed I
do; and chiefly for not having hated and despised
the world enough.
> *The Plain Speaker* (1826) 'On the Pleasure of Hating'

14 The love of liberty is the love of others; the love of
power is the love of ourselves.
> *Political Essays* (1819) 'The Times Newspaper'

15 There is nothing good to be had in the country, or
if there is, they will not let you have it.
> *The Round Table* (1817) 'Observations on Mr Wordsworth's
> Poem *The Excursion*'

16 Comedy naturally wears itself out—destroys the
very food on which it lives; and by constantly and
successfully exposing the follies and weaknesses of
mankind to ridicule, in the end leaves itself
nothing worth laughing at.
> *The Round Table* (1817) 'On Modern Comedy'

17 The art of pleasing consists in being pleased.
> *The Round Table* (1817) 'On Manner'

18 A nickname is the heaviest stone that the devil
can throw at a man.
> *Sketches and Essays* (1839) 'Nicknames'

19 There is an unseemly exposure of the mind, as
well as of the body.
> *Sketches and Essays* (1839) 'On Disagreeable People'

20 Rules and models destroy genius and art.
> *Sketches and Essays* (1839) 'On Taste'

21 Death cancels everything but truth; and strips a
man of everything but genius and virtue. It is a
sort of natural canonization.
> *The Spirit of the Age* (1825) 'Lord Byron'

22 The present is an age of talkers, and not of doers;
and the reason is, that the world is growing old.
We are so far advanced in the Arts and Sciences,
that we live in retrospect, and dote on past
achievement.
> *The Spirit of the Age* (1825) 'Mr Coleridge'

1 He writes as fast as they can read, and he does not write himself down . . . His worst is better than any other person's best.
> *The Spirit of the Age* (1825) 'Sir Walter Scott'

2 His works (taken together) are almost like a new edition of human nature. This is indeed to be an author!
> *The Spirit of the Age* (1825) 'Sir Walter Scott'

3 Mr Wordsworth's genius is a pure emanation of the Spirit of the Age. Had he lived in any other period of the world, he would never have been heard of.
> *The Spirit of the Age* (1825) 'Mr Wordsworth'

4 You will hear more good things on the outside of a stagecoach from London to Oxford than if you were to pass a twelvemonth with the undergraduates, or heads of colleges, of that famous university.
> *Table Talk* vol. 1 (1821) 'The Ignorance of the Learned'

5 The English (it must be owned) are rather a foul-mouthed nation.
> *Table Talk* vol. 2 (1822) 'On Criticism'

6 We can scarcely hate any one that we know.
> *Table Talk* vol. 2 (1822) 'On Criticism'

7 Give me the clear blue sky over my head, and the green turf beneath my feet, a winding road before me, and a three hours' march to dinner—and then to thinking! It is hard if I cannot start some game on these lone heaths.
> *Table Talk* vol. 2 (1822) 'On Going a Journey'

Bessie Head 1937–86
South African-born writer

8 And if the white man thought that Asians were a low, filthy nation, Asians could still smile with relief—at least, they were not Africans. And if the white man thought that Africans were a low, filthy nation, Africans in southern Africa could still smile—at least, they were not bushmen. They all have their monsters.
> *Maru* (1971) pt. 1

9 Love is mutually feeding each other, not one living on another like a ghoul.
> *A Question of Power* (1973)

Denis Healey 1917–
*British Labour politician, husband of Edna **Healey***

10 I warn you there are going to be howls of anguish from the 80,000 people who are rich enough to pay over 75% [tax] on the last slice of their income.
> speech at Labour Party Conference, 1 October 1973

11 Like being savaged by a dead sheep.
> *on being criticized by Geoffrey **Howe** in the House of Commons*
> in the House of Commons, 14 June 1978

Edna Healey 1918–
*British writer, wife of Denis **Healey***

12 She has no hinterland; in particular she has no sense of history.
> *of Margaret **Thatcher***
> Denis Healey *The Time of My Life* (1989)

Timothy Michael Healy 1855–1931
Irish nationalist politician

13 REDMOND: Gladstone is now master of the Party! HEALY: Who is to be mistress of the Party?
> *at the meeting of the Irish Parliamentary Party on 6 December 1890, when the Party split over **Parnell**'s involvement in the O'Shea divorce; Healy's reference to Katherine O'Shea was particularly damaging to Parnell*
> Robert Kee *The Laurel and the Ivy* (1993)

14 The Sinns won in three years what we did not win in forty. You cannot make revolutions with rosewater, or omelettes without breaking eggs.
> letter to his brother; Frank Callanan *T. M. Healy* (1996)

Seamus Heaney 1939–
Irish poet

15 All agog at the plasterer on his ladder
Skimming our gable and writing our name there
With his trowel point, letter by strange letter.
> 'Alphabets' (1987)

16 And found myself thinking: if it were nowadays,
This is how Death would summon Everyman.
> 'A Call' (1996)

17 How culpable was he
That last night when he broke
Our tribe's complicity?
'Now you're supposed to be
An educated man,'
I hear him say. 'Puzzle me
The right answer to that one.'
> 'Casualty' (1979)

18 History says, *Don't hope
On this side of the grave.*
But then, once in a lifetime
The longed-for tidal wave
Of justice can rise up
And hope and history rhyme.
> *The Cure at Troy* (version of **Sophocles**' *Philoctetes*, 1990)

19 Between my finger and my thumb
The squat pen rests.
I'll dig with it.
> 'Digging' (1966)

20 Me waiting until I was nearly fifty
To credit marvels.
> 'Fosterling' (1991)

21 The annals say: when the monks of Clonmacnoise
Were all at prayers inside the oratory
A ship appeared above them in the air.
> 'Lightenings viii' (1991)

22 And then the ox would lurch against the gong
And deaden it and I would feel my tongue

Like the dropped gangplank of a cattle truck,
Trampled and rattled, running piss and muck.
'Mycenae Lookout' (1995); see **Aeschylus** 6:3

1 Don't be surprised
If I demur, for, be advised
My passport's green.
No glass of ours was ever raised
To toast *The Queen*.
rebuking the editors of The Penguin Book of
Contemporary British Poetry *for including him
among its authors*
Open Letter (Field Day pamphlet no. 2, 1983)

2 Who would connive
in civilised outrage
yet understand the exact
and tribal, intimate revenge.
'Punishment' (1975)

3 Until, on Vinegar Hill, the fatal conclave.
Terraced thousands died, shaking scythes at
cannon.
'Requiem for the Croppies' (1969)

4 My heart besieged by anger, my mind a gap of
danger,
I walked among their old haunts, the home
ground where they bled;
And in the dirt lay justice like an acorn in the
winter
Till its oak would sprout in Derry where the
thirteen men lay dead.
of Bloody Sunday, Londonderry, 30 January 1972
'The Road to Derry'

5   HERE IS THE NEWS,
Said the absolute speaker. Between him and us
A great gulf was fixed where pronunciation
Reigned tyrannically
'A Sofa in the Forties' (1996)

6   The famous
Northern reticence, the tight gag of place
And times: yes, yes. Of the 'wee six' I sing
Where to be saved you only must save face
And whatever you say, you say nothing.
'Whatever You Say Say Nothing' (1975)

7 If revolution is the kicking down of a rotten door,
evolution is more like pushing the stone from the
mouth of the tomb. There is an Easter energy
about it, a sense of arrival rather than wreckage.
in Observer 12 April 1998

8 No death outside my immediate family has left me
more bereft. No death in my lifetime has hurt
poets more.
funeral oration for Ted **Hughes**, 3 November 1998, in
Guardian 4 November 1998

William Randolph Hearst 1863–1951

American newspaper publisher and tycoon

9 The day when this nation ceases to shape its
foreign policy primarily for the safety and welfare
of the American people will be the day on which
its national doom is sealed—and its international
doom too.
in San Francisco Examiner 7 May 1924

10 You furnish the pictures and I'll furnish the war.
*message to the artist Frederic Remington in Havana,
Cuba, during the Spanish-American War of 1898*
attributed

Edward Heath 1916–

British Conservative statesman; Prime Minister, 1970–4

11 The unpleasant and unacceptable face of
capitalism.
on the Lonrho affair
in the House of Commons, 15 May 1973

12 Rejoice, rejoice, rejoice.
telephone call to his office on hearing of Margaret
Thatcher's *fall from power in 1990*
attributed; in *Daily Telegraph* 24 September 1998 (online
edition)

John Heath-Stubbs 1918–

English poet

13 Venerable Mother Toothache
Climb down from the white battlements,
Stop twisting in your yellow fingers
The fourfold rope of nerves;
And tomorrow I will give you a tot of whisky
To hold in your cupped hands,
A garland of anise flowers,
And three cloves like nails.
'A Charm Against the Toothache' (1954)

Reginald Heber 1783–1826

English clergyman; Bishop of Calcutta from 1823

14 Brightest and best of the sons of the morning,
Dawn on our darkness and lend us thine aid;
Star of the east, the horizon adorning,
Guide where our infant Redeemer is laid.
'Brightest and best of the sons of the morning' (1827
hymn)

15 From Greenland's icy mountains,
From India's coral strand,
Where Afric's sunny fountains
Roll down their golden sand.
'From Greenland's icy mountains' (1821 hymn)

16 What though the spicy breezes
Blow soft o'er Ceylon's isle;
Though every prospect pleases,
And only man is vile:
In vain with lavish kindness
The gifts of God are strown;
The heathen in his blindness
Bows down to wood and stone.
'From Greenland's icy mountains' (1821 hymn); Heber
later altered 'Ceylon's isle' to 'Java's isle'; see **Kipling**
453:21

17 Holy, Holy, Holy! Lord God Almighty!
Early in the morning our song shall rise to thee:
Holy, Holy, Holy! merciful and mighty!
God in Three Persons, blessèd Trinity!

Holy, Holy, Holy! all the saints adore thee,
Casting down their golden crowns around the
glassy sea,
Cherubim and Seraphim falling down before thee,

Which wert, and art, and evermore shalt be.
'Holy, Holy, Holy! Lord God Almighty!' (1826 hymn)

Ben Hecht 1894–1964

American screenwriter
*see also **Film lines** 320:17*

1 [Goldwyn] filled the room with wonderful panic and beat at your mind like a man in front of a slot machine, shaking it for a jackpot.
A. Scott Berg *Goldwyn* (1989) ch. 15

G. W. F. Hegel 1770–1831

German idealist philosopher
*see also **Marx** 516:16*

2 Gangrenous limbs cannot be cured with lavender water.
The German Constitution (1798–1802) pt. 9 'The growth of states in the rest of Europe', translated by M. Knox; see **Proverbs** 630:9

3 What experience and history teach is this—that nations and governments have never learned anything from history, or acted upon any lessons they might have drawn from it.
Lectures on the Philosophy of World History: Introduction (1830, translated by H. B. Nisbet, 1975) introduction

4 Only in the state does man have a rational existence . . . Man owes his entire existence to the state, and has his being within it alone. Whatever worth and spiritual reality he possesses are his solely by virtue of the state.
Lectures on the Philosophy of World History: Introduction (1830, translated by H. B. Nisbet, 1975)

5 It is a land of desire for all those who are weary of the historical arsenal of old Europe.
of America
Lectures on the Philosophy of World History: Introduction (1830, translated by H. B. Nisbet, 1975) introduction

6 In history, we are concerned with what has been and what is; in philosophy, however, we are concerned not with what belongs exclusively to the past or to the future, but with that which *is*, both now and eternally—in short, with reason.
Lectures on the Philosophy of World History: Introduction (1830, translated by H. B. Nisbet, 1975)

7 What is rational is actual and what is actual is rational.
Philosophy of Right (1821, translated by T. M. Knox, 1952)

8 When philosophy paints its grey on grey, then has a shape of life grown old. By philosophy's grey on grey it cannot be rejuvenated but only understood. The owl of Minerva spreads its wings only with the falling of the dusk.
Philosophy of Right (1821, translated by T. M. Knox, 1952)

9 Thus to be independent of public opinion is the first formal condition of achieving anything great or rational whether in life or in science. Great achievement is assured, however, of subsequent recognition and grateful acceptance by public opinion, which in due course will make it one of its own prejudices.
Philosophy of Right (1821, translated by T. M. Knox, 1952) sect. 318

Heikhalot Rabbati

Jewish mystical text of c.5th–6th century AD

10 I may tell them the mysteries that are hidden and concealed, the wonders of the weaving of the web on which depends the perfection and glory of the world . . . the wonders of the path of the celestial ladder, one end of which rests on earth and the other by the right foot of the Throne of Glory.
16:1

Christoph Hein 1944–

German writer

11 *Ich weiss ausserdem nicht, was ein persönliches Geschenk ist. Ich glaube, wenn ich wirklich jemandem ein persöliches Geschenk geben würde, er müsste erschrecken. Ich weiss nicht, wie ein persönliches Geschenk für mich aussehen könnte, aber ich bin überzeugt, wenn es wirklich persönlich wäre, ich würde anfangen zu heulen. Zumindest wüsste ich dann, was ich für eine Person bin.*

I don't know what a personal gift is. I think if I really gave someone a personal gift, it would scare him to death. I don't know what a personal gift for myself would be, either. But I'm sure that if it were really personal, I would burst into tears. At least I'd know then what sort of person I am.
The Distant Lover (1982) ch. 10, translated by Krishna Winston

Piet Hein 1905–

Danish poet and cartoonist

12 Problems worthy
of attack
prove their worth
by hitting back.
'Problems' (1969)

Heinrich Heine 1797–1856

German poet
*see also **Last words** 471:9*

13 *Dort, wo man Bücher*
Verbrennt, verbrennt man auch am Ende Menschen.
Wherever books will be burned, men also, in the end, are burned.
Almansor (1823) l. 245

14 *Auf Flügeln des Gesanges.*
On wings of song.
title of song (1823)

15 *Ich weiss nicht, was soll es bedeuten,*
Dass ich so traurig bin;
Ein Märchen aus alten Zeiten,
Das kommt mir nicht aus dem Sinn.
I know not why I am so sad; I cannot get out of my head a fairy-tale of olden times.
'Die Lorelei' (1826–31)

16 *Es ist eine alte Geschichte,*
Doch bleibt sie immer neu.
It is so old a story,

Yet somehow always new.

Lyrisches Intermezzo (1823) no. 39 (translated by Hal Draper)

1 Wild, dark times are rumbling towards us, and the prophet who wishes to write a new apocalypse will have to invent entirely new beasts, and beasts so terrible that the ancient animal symbols of Saint John will seem like cooing doves and cupids in comparison.

Lutezia (1855)

2 *Sie hatten sich beide so herzlich lieb,*
Spitzbübin war sie, er war ein Dieb.

They loved each other beyond belief—
She was a strumpet, he was a thief.

Neue Gedichte (1852) 'Ein Weib' (translated by Louis Untermeyer, 1938)

3 What then is music? . . . It exists between thought and phenomenon, like a twilight medium, it stands between spirit and matter, related to and yet different from both; it is spirit, but spirit governed by time; it is matter, but matter that can manage without space.

On the French Stage: Intimate letters to August Lewald (1857)

4 *Hört ihr das Glöckchen klingeln? Kniet nieder—Man bringt die Sakramente einem sterbenden Gotte.*

Do you hear the little bell tinkle? Kneel down. They are bringing the sacraments to a dying god.

Zur Geschichte der Religion und Philosophie in Deutschland (1834) bk. 2, closing words

5 Maximilien Robespierre was nothing but the hand of Jean Jacques Rousseau, the bloody hand that drew from the womb of time the body whose soul Rousseau had created.

Zur Geschichte der Religion und Philosophie in Deutschland (1834) bk. 3, para. 3

Werner Heisenberg 1901–76

German mathematical physicist

6 An expert is someone who knows some of the worst mistakes that can be made in his subject and who manages to avoid them.

Der Teil und das Ganze (1969) ch. 17 (translated by A. J. Pomerans as *Physics and Beyond*, 1971)

7 *on Felix Bloch's stating that space was the field of linear operations:*

Nonsense. Space is blue and birds fly through it.

Felix Bloch 'Heisenberg and the early days of quantum mechanics' in *Physics Today* December 1976

Joseph Heller 1923–99

American novelist

8 There was only one catch and that was Catch-22, which specified that a concern for one's own safety in the face of dangers that were real and immediate was the process of a rational mind . . . Orr would be crazy to fly more missions and sane if he didn't, but if he was sane he had to fly them. If he flew them he was crazy and didn't have to; but if he didn't want to he was sane and had to.

Catch-22 (1961) ch. 5

9 Some men are born mediocre, some men achieve mediocrity, and some men have mediocrity thrust upon them. With Major Major it had been all three.

Catch-22 (1961) ch. 9; see **Shakespeare** 720:32

10 When I read something saying I've not done anything as good as *Catch-22* I'm tempted to reply, 'Who has?'

in *The Times* 9 June 1993

Lillian Hellman 1905–84

American dramatist
on Hellman: see **McCarthy** *500:9*

11 Propaganda is a soft weapon: hold it in your hands too long, and it will move about like a snake, and strike the other way.

The Lark (1955), adapted from *L'Alouette* by Jean **Anouilh**

12 I cannot and will not cut my conscience to fit this year's fashions.

letter to John S. Wood, 19 May 1952, in *US Congress Committee Hearing on Un-American Activities* (1952) pt. 8

Leona Helmsley c.1920–

American hotelier

13 Only the little people pay taxes.

comment made to her housekeeper in 1983, and reported at her trial for tax evasion
in *New York Times* 12 July 1989

Héloïse c.1098–1164

French abbess, lover of **Abelard**

14 God knows I never sought anything in you except yourself; I wanted simply you, nothing of yours.

letter to Peter Abelard, c.1132; Betty Radice *The Letters of Abelard and Heloise* (1974)

15 My heart was not in me but with you, and now, even more, if it is not with you it is nowhere.

letter to Peter Abelard, c.1132; Betty Radice *The Letters of Abelard and Heloise* (1974)

Helvétius (Claude Arien Helvétius) 1715–71

French philosopher
on Helvétius: see **Misquotations** *538:1*

16 [We must] substitute the language of interest for the tone of injury. Do not complain, appeal to interest.

De l'esprit (1758) 'Discours 2' ch. 15

17 *L'éducation nous faisait ce que nous sommes.*

Education made us what we are.

De l'esprit (1758) 'Discours 3' ch. 30

18 When prejudice commands, reason is silent.

De l'homme (1773)

Felicia Hemans 1793–1835

English poet
on Hemans: see **Scott** *674:31*

19 The boy stood on the burning deck
Whence all but he had fled;
The flame that lit the battle's wreck
Shone round him o'er the dead.

'Casabianca' (1849)

1 The stately homes of England,
How beautiful they stand!
Amidst their tall ancestral trees,
O'er all the pleasant land.
'The Homes of England' (1849); see **Coward** 245:7

John Heming 1556–1630 and **Henry Condell** d. 1627

English joint editors of the First Folio

2 Well! it is now public, and you will stand for your privileges we know: to read, and censure. Do so, but buy it first. That doth best commend a book, the stationer says.
First Folio Shakespeare (1623) preface

3 Who, as he was a happy imitator of Nature, was a most gentle expresser of it. His mind and hand went together: And what he thought, he uttered with that easiness, that we have scarce received from him a blot.
First Folio Shakespeare (1623) preface; see **Jonson** 436:8, **Pope** 605:24

Ernest Hemingway 1899–1961

American novelist
see also **Borrowed titles** 146:1, **Borrowed titles** 146:7, **Fitzgerald** 323:20, **Stein** 755:10

4 Where do the noses go? I always wondered where the noses would go.
For Whom the Bell Tolls (1940) ch. 7

5 But did thee feel the earth move?
For Whom the Bell Tolls (1940) ch. 13

6 Paris is a movable feast.
A Movable Feast (1964) epigraph

7 The sun also rises.
title of novel (1926)

8 Grace under pressure.
when asked what he meant by 'guts' in an interview with Dorothy **Parker**
in *New Yorker* 30 November 1929

9 The most essential gift for a good writer is a built-in, shock-proof shit detector. This is the writer's radar, and all great writers have had it.
in *Paris Review* Spring 1958

Jimi Hendrix (James Marshall Hendrix) 1942–70

American rock musician

10 Purple haze is in my brain
Lately things don't seem the same.
'Purple Haze' (1967 song)

11 A musician, if he's a messenger, is like a child who hasn't been handled too many times by man, hasn't had too many fingerprints across his brain.
in *Life Magazine* (1969)

Arthur W. D. Henley

12 Nobody loves a fairy when she's forty.
title of song (1934)

W. E. Henley 1849–1903

English poet and dramatist
on Henley: see **Wilde** 837:9

13 A deal of Ariel, just a streak of Puck,
Much Antony, of Hamlet most of all,
And something of the Shorter-Catechist.
of Robert Louis **Stevenson**
'In Hospital' (1888)

14 Out of the night that covers me,
Black as the Pit from pole to pole,
I thank whatever gods may be
For my unconquerable soul.

In the fell clutch of circumstance,
I have not winced nor cried aloud:
Under the bludgeonings of chance
My head is bloody, but unbowed.
'Invictus. In Memoriam R.T.H.B.' (1888)

15 It matters not how strait the gate,
How charged with punishments the scroll,
I am the master of my fate:
I am the captain of my soul.
'Invictus. In Memoriam R.T.H.B.' (1888)

16 What have I done for you,
England, my England?
'Pro Rege Nostro' (1900); see **MacDonell** 501:12

17 Or ever the knightly years were gone
With the old world to the grave,
I was a King in Babylon
And you were a Christian slave.
'To W. A.' (1888)

Peter Hennessy 1947–

English historian

18 The model of a modern Prime Minister would be a kind of grotesque composite freak—someone with the dedication to duty of a Peel, the physical energy of a Gladstone, the detachment of a Salisbury, the brains of an Asquith, the balls of a Lloyd George, the word-power of a Churchill, the administrative gifts of an Attlee, the style of a Macmillan, the managerialism of a Heath, and the sleep requirements of a Thatcher. Human beings do not come like that.
The Hidden Wiring (1995); see **Gilbert** 348:28

Henri IV (of Navarre) 1553–1610

French monarch, King from 1589

19 I want there to be no peasant in my kingdom so poor that he is unable to have a chicken in his pot every Sunday.
Hardouin de Péréfixe *Histoire de Henry le Grand* (1681); see **Hoover** 395:23

20 Hang yourself, brave Crillon; we fought at Arques and you were not there.
traditional form given by Voltaire to a letter from Henri to Crillon, 20 September 1597; Henri's actual words were

My good man, Crillon, hang yourself for not having been at my side last Monday at the greatest event that's ever been seen and perhaps ever will be seen.

Lettres missives de Henri IV, Collection des documents inédits de l'histoire de France vol. 4 (1847)

1 *Paris vaut bien une messe.*

Paris is well worth a mass.

attributed to Henri IV; alternatively to his minister Sully, in conversation with Henri

2 The wisest fool in Christendom.

of James I of England

attributed both to Henri IV and Sully

Henry I 1068–1135

English monarch, King from 1100

3 An illiterate king is a crowned ass.

described as a proverbial usage on the part of Henry by William of Malmesbury in *De Gestis Regum Anglorum*, and probably first coined by Count Foulques II of Anjou, *c*.950

Henry II 1133–89

English monarch, King from 1154

4 Will no one rid me of this turbulent priest?

of Thomas Becket, Archbishop of Canterbury, murdered in Canterbury Cathedral, December 1170

oral tradition, conflating a number of variant forms, including G. Lyttelton *History of the Life of King Henry the Second* (1769) pt. 4: 'so many cowardly and ungrateful men in his court, none of whom would revenge him of the injuries he sustained from one turbulent priest'

Henry VIII 1491–1547

English monarch, King from 1509

*on Henry VIII: see **More** 548:9*

5 That man hath the sow by the right ear.

*of Thomas **Cranmer**, June 1529*

Acts and Monuments of John Foxe ['Foxe's Book of Martyrs'] (1570)

6 The King found her so different from her picture . . . that . . . he swore they had brought him a Flanders mare.

of Anne of Cleves

Tobias Smollett *A Complete History of England* (3rd ed., 1759) vol. 6

Henry of Huntingdon c.1084–1155

English chronicler

7 They beheaded priests at the very altar, and then cutting off the heads of the crucifixes on the roodbeams they put the priest's head on the trunk of the crucifix, and the head of the crucifix on the trunk of the priest.

description of atrocities occurring during the invasion of King David of Scotland in 1138

Historia Anglorum (ed. T. Arnold, Rolls series, 1879)

8 A new kind of monster, compounded of purity and corruption, a monk and a knight.

of Henry of Blois (1101–71), bishop of Winchester and brother of King Stephen

Historia Anglorum (ed. T. Arnold, Rolls series, 1879)

Matthew Henry 1662–1714

English divine

9 The better day, the worse deed.

An Exposition on the Old and New Testament (1710) Genesis ch. 3, v. 6, gloss 2

10 He rolls it under his tongue as a sweet morsel.

An Exposition on the Old and New Testament (1710) Psalm 36, v. 2, gloss 1

11 They that die by famine die by inches.

An Exposition on the Old and New Testament (1710) Psalm 59, v. 15, gloss 5 (referring incorrectly to v. 13)

O. Henry (William Sydney Porter) 1862–1910

American short-story writer
*see also **Last words** 474:8*

12 It was beautiful and simple as all truly great swindles are.

Gentle Grafter (1908) 'Octopus Marooned'

Patrick Henry 1736–99

American statesman

13 Caesar had his Brutus—Charles the First, his Cromwell—and George the Third—('Treason,' cried the Speaker) . . . *may profit by their example. If this* be treason, make the most of it.

speech in the Virginia assembly, May 1765, in William Wirt *Patrick Henry* (1818) sect. 2

14 I am not a Virginian, but an American.

in [John Adams's] Notes of Debates in the Continental Congress, Philadelphia, 6 September 1774; in L. H. Butterfield (ed.) *Diary and Autobiography of John Adams* (1961) vol. 2

15 I know not what course others may take; but as for me, give me liberty, or give me death!

speech in Virginia Convention, 23 March 1775, in William Wirt *Patrick Henry* (1818) sect. 4

Philip Henry 1631–96

English clergyman

16 All this, and heaven too!

in Matthew Henry *Life of Mr Philip Henry* (1698) ch. 5

Joseph Henshaw 1603–79

English divine; Bishop of Peterborough from 1663

17 One doth but breakfast here, another dines, he that liveth longest doth but sup; we must all go to bed in another world.

Horae Succisivae (1631) pt. 1

Barbara Hepworth 1903–75

English sculptor

18 I rarely draw what I see—I draw what I feel in my body.

Drawings from a Sculptor's Landscape (1966)

19 Carving is interrelated masses conveying an emotion: a perfect relationship between the mind and the colour, light and weight which is the stone, made by the hand which feels.

Herbert Read (ed.) *Unit One* (1934)

Heraclitus c.540–c.480 BC
Greek philosopher

1 Everything flows and nothing stays.
Plato *Cratylus* 402a

2 You can't step twice into the same river.
Plato *Cratylus* 402a

3 A man's character is his fate.
On the Universe fragment 121 (translated by W. H. S. Jones); see **Eliot** 300:16, **Novalis** 565:18

4 The road up and the road down are one and the same.
H. Diels and W. Kranz *Die Fragmente der Vorsokratiker* (7th ed., 1954) fragment 60

Lord Herbert of Cherbury 1583–1648
English philosopher and poet; brother of George **Herbert**

5 Now that the April of your youth adorns
The garden of your face.
'Ditty: Now that the April' (1665)

A. P. Herbert (Sir Alan Patrick Herbert) 1890–1971
English writer and humorist

6 Don't let's go to the dogs tonight,
For mother will be there.
'Don't Let's Go to the Dogs Tonight' (1926)

7 The Farmer will never be happy again;
He carries his heart in his boots;
For either the rain is destroying his grain
Or the drought is destroying his roots.
'The Farmer' (1922)

8 As my poor father used to say
In 1863,
Once people start on all this Art
Goodbye, moralitee!
'Lines for a Worthy Person' (1930)

9 This high official, all allow,
Is grossly overpaid;
There wasn't any Board, and now
There isn't any Trade.
'The President of the Board of Trade' (1922)

10 Nothing is wasted, nothing is in vain:
The seas roll over but the rocks remain.
Tough at the Top (operetta c.1949)

11 Holy deadlock.
title of novel (1934)

12 People must not do things for fun. We are not here for fun. There is no reference to fun in any Act of Parliament.
Uncommon Law (1935) 'Is it a Free Country?'

13 The critical period in matrimony is breakfast-time.
Uncommon Law (1935) 'Is Marriage Lawful?'

14 'Was the cow crossed?'
'No, your worship, it was an open cow.'
on an attempt to write a cheque on a cow
Uncommon Law (1935) 'The Negotiable Cow'

15 The Common Law of England has been laboriously built about a mythical figure—the figure of 'The Reasonable Man'.
Uncommon Law (1935) 'The Reasonable Man'

George Herbert 1593–1633
English poet and clergyman

16 Whereas my birth and spirit rather took
The way that takes the town;
Thou didst betray me to a lingering book,
And wrap me in a gown.
'Affliction (1)' (1633) l. 37

17 Now I am here, what thou wilt do with me
None of my books will show:
I read, and sigh, and wish I were a tree;
For then I should grow
To fruit or shade: at least some bird would trust
Her household to me, and I should be just.
'Affliction (1)' (1633) l. 55

18 Ah, my dear God! though I am clean forgot,
Let me not love Thee, if I love Thee not.
'Affliction (1)' (1633) l. 65

19 Love is that liquor sweet and most divine,
Which my God feels as blood; but I, as wine.
'The Agonie' (1633) l. 17

20 Let all the world in ev'ry corner sing
My God and King.
'Antiphon: Let all the world in ev'ry corner sing' (1633)

21 Hearken unto a Verser, who may chance
Rhyme thee to good, and make a bait of pleasure.
A verse may find him, who a sermon flies,
And turn delight into a sacrifice.
'The Church Porch' (1633) st. 1

22 Judge not the preacher, for he is thy Judge:
If thou mislike him, thou conceiv'st him not.
God calleth preaching folly. Do not grudge
To pick out treasures from an earthen pot.
The worst speaks something good: if all want sense,
God takes a text, and preacheth patience.
'The Church Porch' (1633) st. 72

23 I struck the board, and cried, 'No more.
I will abroad.'
What? shall I ever sigh and pine?
My lines and life are free; free as the road,
Loose as the wind, as large as store.
'The Collar' (1633)

24 Away; take heed:
I will abroad.
Call in thy death's-head there: tie up thy fears.
'The Collar' (1633)

25 But as I raved and grew more fierce and wild
At every word,
Methought I heard one calling, 'Child';
And I replied, 'My Lord.'
'The Collar' (1633)

26 O that thou shouldst give dust a tongue
To cry to thee,
And then not hear it crying!
'Denial' (1633) l. 16

1 Love is swift of foot;
Love's a man of war,
And can shoot,
And can hit from far.
'Discipline' (1633)

2 I got me flowers to strew Thy way;
I got me boughs off many a tree:
But Thou wast up by break of day,
And brought'st Thy sweets along with Thee.
'Easter' (1633)

3 Teach me, my God and King,
In all things Thee to see,
And what I do in any thing
To do it as for Thee.
'The Elixir' (1633)

4 A man that looks on glass,
On it may stay his eye;
Or if he pleaseth, through it pass,
And then the heaven espy.
'The Elixir' (1633)

5 A servant with this clause
Makes drudgery divine:
Who sweeps a room as for Thy laws
Makes that and th' action fine.
'The Elixir' (1633)

6 Oh that I were an orange-tree,
That busy plant!
Then I should ever laden be,
And never want
Some fruit for Him that dressed me.
'Employment: He that is weary, let him sit' (1633)

7 Who would have thought my shrivelled heart
Could have recovered greenness?
'The Flower' (1633)

8 And now in age I bud again,
After so many deaths I live and write;
I once more smell the dew and rain,
And relish versing.
'The Flower' (1633)

9 Lovely enchanting language, sugar-cane,
Honey of roses!
'The Forerunners' (1633)

10 Death is still working like a mole,
And digs my grave at each remove.
'Grace' (1633)

11 Who says that fictions only and false hair
Become a verse? Is there in truth no beauty?
Is all good structure in a winding stair?
'Jordan (I)' (1633)

12 I made a posy while the day ran by:
Here will I smell my remnant out, and tie
My life within this band.
But Time did beckon to the flowers, and they
By noon most cunningly did steal away,
And withered in my hand.
'Life' (1633)

13 Love bade me welcome: yet my soul drew back,
Guilty of dust and sin.
But quick-eyed Love, observing me grow slack
From my first entrance in,

Drew nearer to me, sweetly questioning,
If I lacked any thing.
'Love: Love bade me welcome' (1633)

14 'You must sit down,' says Love, 'and taste my
meat.'
So I did sit and eat.
'Love: Love bade me welcome' (1633)

15 For us the winds do blow,
The earth doth rest, heaven move, and fountains
flow.
Nothing we see, but means our good,
As our delight or as our treasure:
The whole is either our cupboard of food,
Or cabinet of pleasure.
'Man' (1633)

16 When boys go first to bed,
They step into their voluntary graves.
'Mortification' (1633)

17 Prayer: prayer the Church's banquet.
title of poem (1633)

18 Exalted manna, gladness of the best,
Heaven in ordinary, man well drest,
The Milky Way, the bird of Paradise,
Church-bells beyond the stars heard, the soul's
blood,
The land of spices; something understood.
'Prayer: Prayer the Church's banquet' (1633)

19 When God at first made man,
Having a glass of blessings standing by;
Let us (said he) pour on him all we can:
Let the world's riches, which dispersed lie,
Contract into a span.
'The Pulley' (1633)

20 He would adore my gifts instead of Me,
And rest in Nature, not the God of Nature:
So both should losers be.
'The Pulley' (1633)

21 Yet let him keep the rest,
But keep them with repining restlessness:
Let him be rich and weary, that at least,
If goodness lead him not, yet weariness
May toss him to My breast.
'The Pulley' (1633)

22 But who does hawk at eagles with a dove?
'The Sacrifice' (1633) l. 91

23 Man stole the fruit, but I must climb the tree.
'The Sacrifice' (1633) l. 202

24 Lord, with what care Thou hast begirt us round!
Parents first season us: then schoolmasters
Deliver us to laws; they send us bound
To rules of reason, holy messengers,
Pulpits and Sundays, sorrow dogging sin,
Afflictions sorted, anguish of all sizes,
Fine nets and stratagems to catch us in,
Bibles laid open, millions of surprises.
'Sin: Lord, with what care Thou hast begirt us round!'
(1633)

25 Yet all these fences and their whole array
One cunning bosom—sin blows quite away.
'Sin: Lord, with what care Thou hast begirt us round!'
(1633)

1 Grasp not at much, for fear thou losest all.
  'The Size' (1633)

2 The God of love my Shepherd is,
  And He that doth me feed:
  While He is mine, and I am His,
  What can I want or need?
  'The 23rd Psalm' (1633); see **Book of Common Prayer**
  135:3

3 My friend may spit upon my curious floor:
  Would he have gold? I lend it instantly;
  But let the poor,
  And Thou within them, starve at door.
  I cannot use a friend, as I use Thee.
  'Unkindness' (1633)

4 Sweet day, so cool, so calm, so bright,
  The bridal of the earth and sky,
  The dew shall weep thy fall to-night;
  For thou must die.

  Sweet rose, whose hue angry and brave
  Bids the rash gazer wipe his eye:
  Thy root is ever in its grave,
  And thou must die.

  Sweet spring, full of sweet days and roses,
  A box where sweets compacted lie;
  My music shows ye have your closes,
  And all must die.
  'Virtue' (1633)

5 Only a sweet and virtuous soul,
  Like seasoned timber, never gives;
  But though the whole world turn to coal,
  Then chiefly lives.
  'Virtue' (1633)

6 He that makes a good war makes a good peace.
  Outlandish Proverbs (1640) no. 420

7 He that lives in hope danceth without music.
  Outlandish Proverbs (1640) no. 1006; see **Proverbs** 621:50

Johann Gottfried von Herder 1744–1803

German critic and philosopher

8 I am not here to think, but to be, feel, live!
  Bernhard Suphan (ed.) J. G. Herder *Sämmtliche Werke*
  (1877–1913)

Hermetic Corpus

A collection of religious and philosophical writings of the mid-1st to late 3rd century AD, ascribed in the medieval period to Hermes Trismegistus

9 Because of man God changes and turns into the form of man.
  Jean-Pierre Mahé *The Way of Hermes* (1999) 'Fragmenta Hermetica 21'

Herodotus c.485–c.425 BC

Greek historian

10 No one is stupid enough to prefer war to peace; in peace sons bury their fathers and in war fathers bury their sons. However, I suppose the god must have wanted this to happen.
  Histories bk. 1 sect. 87

11 If one were to order all mankind to choose the best set of rules in the world, each group would, after due consideration, choose its own customs; each group regards its own as being by far the best.
  Histories bk. 3 sect. 38

12 Father, your visitor is going to corrupt you if you don't get up and leave.
  comment attributed to Gorgo, 8 or 9 year-old daughter of Cleomenes, King of Sparta, on Aristagoras' attempts to bribe her father
  Histories bk. 5 sect. 51

13 If the Persians hide the sun, the battle will be in shade rather than sunlight.
  comment attributed to Dianeces of Sparta, on being told that the Persians were so numerous that their arrows when shot hid the sun
  Histories bk. 7 sect. 226

14 The most hateful torment for men is to have knowledge of everything but power over nothing.
  Histories bk. 9 sect. 16

Robert Herrick 1591–1674

English poet and clergyman

15 Here a little child I stand,
  Heaving up my either hand;
  Cold as paddocks though they be,
  Here I lift them up to Thee,
  For a benison to fall
  On our meat, and on us all. Amen.
  'Another Grace for a Child' (1647)

16 I sing of brooks, of blossoms, birds, and bowers:
  Of April, May, of June, and July-flowers.
  I sing of May-poles, Hock-carts, wassails, wakes,
  Of bride-grooms, brides, and of their bridal-cakes.
  'The Argument of his Book' from *Hesperides* (1648)

17 And once more yet (ere I am laid out dead)
  Knock at a star with my exalted head.
  'The Bad Season Makes the Poet Sad' (1648)

18 Cherry-ripe, ripe, ripe, I cry,
  Full and fair ones; come and buy:
  If so be, you ask me where
  They do grow? I answer, there,
  Where my Julia's lips do smile;
  There's the land, or cherry-isle.
  'Cherry-Ripe' (1648)

19 Get up, sweet Slug-a-bed, and see
  The dew bespangling herb and tree.
  'Corinna's Going a-Maying' (1648)

20 Then while time serves, and we are but decaying;
  Come, my Corinna, come, let's go a-Maying.
  'Corinna's Going a-Maying' (1648)

21 A sweet disorder in the dress
  Kindles in clothes a wantonness:
  A lawn about the shoulders thrown
  Into a fine distraction . . .
  A careless shoe-string, in whose tie
  I see a wild civility:
  Do more bewitch me, than when Art
  Is too precise in every part.
  'Delight in Disorder' (1648)

22 It is the end that crowns us, not the fight.
  'The End' (1648)

1 When the artless doctor sees
No one hope, but of his fees,
And his skill runs on the lees;
Sweet Spirit, comfort me!

When his potion and his pill,
Has, or none, or little skill,
Meet for nothing, but to kill;
Sweet Spirit, comfort me!
'His Litany to the Holy Spirit' (1647)

2 Only a little more
I have to write,
Then I'll give o'er,
And bid the world Good-night.
'His Poetry his Pillar' (1648)

3 Love is a circle that doth restless move
In the same sweet eternity of love.
'Love What It Is' (1648)

4 Her eyes the glow-worm lend thee,
The shooting-stars attend thee;
And the elves also,
Whose little eyes glow,
Like the sparks of fire, befriend thee.
'The Night-Piece, to Julia' (1648)

5 Night makes no difference 'twixt the Priest and
Clerk;
Joan as my Lady is as good i' th' dark.
'No Difference i' th' Dark' (1648)

6 Made us nobly wild, not mad.
'An Ode for him [Ben Jonson]' (1648)

7 And yet each verse of thine
Out-did the meat, out-did the frolic wine.
'An Ode for him [Ben Jonson]' (1648)

8 Fain would I kiss my Julia's dainty leg,
Which is as white and hairless as an egg.
'On Julia's Legs' (1648)

9 Praise they that will times past, I joy to see
My self now live: this age best pleaseth me.
'The Present Time Best Pleaseth' (1648)

10 But, for Man's fault, then was the thorn,
Without the fragrant rose-bud, born;
But ne'er the rose without the thorn.
'The Rose' (1647)

11 A little saint best fits a little shrine,
A little prop best fits a little vine,
As my small cruse best fits my little wine.
'A Ternary of Littles, upon a Pipkin of Jelly sent to a Lady'
(1648)

12 For my Embalming (Sweetest) there will be
No Spices wanting, when I'm laid by thee.
'To Anthea: Now is the Time' (1648)

13 Bid me to live, and I will live
Thy Protestant to be:
Or bid me love, and I will give
A loving heart to thee.
'To Anthea, Who May Command Him Anything' (1648)

14 Bid me despair, and I'll despair,
Under that cypress tree:
Or bid me die, and I will dare
E'en Death, to die for thee.

Thou art my life, my love, my heart,
The very eyes of me:
And hast command of every part,
To live and die for thee.
'To Anthea, Who May Command Him Anything' (1648)

15 Fair daffodils, we weep to see
You haste away so soon.
'To Daffodils' (1648)

16 We have short time to stay, as you,
We have as short a Spring;
As quick a growth to meet decay,
As you or any thing.
'To Daffodils' (1648)

17 If any thing delight me for to print
My book, 'tis this; that Thou, my God, art in't.
'To God' (1647)

18 Gather ye rosebuds while ye may,
Old Time is still a-flying:
And this same flower that smiles to-day,
To-morrow will be dying.
'To the Virgins, to Make Much of Time' (1648)

19 Then be not coy, but use your time;
And while ye may, go marry:
For having lost but once your prime,
You may for ever tarry.
'To the Virgins, to Make Much of Time' (1648)

20 Whenas in silks my Julia goes,
Then, then (methinks) how sweetly flows
That liquefaction of her clothes.
Next, when I cast mine eyes and see
That brave vibration each way free;
O how that glittering taketh me!
'Upon Julia's Clothes' (1648)

21 So smooth, so sweet, so silvery is thy voice,
As, could they hear, the damned would make no
noise,
But listen to thee (walking in thy chamber)
Melting melodious words, to lutes of amber.
'Upon Julia's Voice' (1648)

22 To work a wonder, God would have her shown,
At once, a bud, and yet a rose full-blown.
'The Virgin Mary' (1647)

Lord Hervey 1696–1743
English politician and writer
*on Hervey: see **Montagu** 543:18, **Pope** 602:31*

23 Whoever would lie usefully should lie seldom.
Memoirs of the Reign of George II (ed. J. W. Croker, 1848)
vol. 1, ch. 19

24 I am fit for nothing but to carry candles and set
chairs all my life.
letter to Robert Walpole, 1737, in *Memoirs of the Reign of
George II* (ed. J. W. Croker, 1848) vol. 2, ch. 40

Alexander Herzen 1812–70
Russian writer and revolutionary

25 Art, and the summer lightning of individual
happiness: these are the only real goods we have.
Sobranie sochinenii v tridtsati tomakh (Moscow, 1954-66),
vol. 16, p. 135, translated by Isaiah Berlin

Theodor Herzl 1860–1904
Hungarian-born journalist, dramatist, and Zionist leader

1 At Basle I founded the Jewish state.
of the first Zionist congress, held in Basle in 1897
diary, 3 September 1897

Michael Heseltine 1933–
British Conservative politician

2 The fundamental question is is the Conservative Party leadable?
in the aftermath of disastrous electoral defeat
in *Daily Telegraph* 9 June 2001 (electronic edition)

Hesiod
Greek poet of c.700 BC

3 Then potter is potter's enemy, and
craftsman is craftsman's
rival; tramp is jealous of tramp
and singer of singer.
Works and Days l.25, translated by R. Lattimore

4 The half is greater than the whole.
Works and Days l. 40

5 Often a whole city is paid punishment
for one bad man.
Works and Days l. 240, translated by R. Lattimore

6 The man who does evil to another does evil
to himself,
and the evil counsel is most evil
for him who counsels it.
Works and Days l. 265, translated by R. Lattimore

7 Between us and excellence, the gods have placed
the sweat of our brows.
Works and Days l. 289

8 When the bottle has just been opened, and when
it's giving out, drink deep;
be sparing when it's half-full; but it's useless
to spare the fag end.
Works and Days l. 368, translated by R. Lattimore

Hermann Hesse 1877–1962
German novelist and poet

9 If you hate a person, you hate something in him
that is part of yourself. What isn't part of ourselves
doesn't disturb us.
Demian (1919) ch. 6

10 The bourgeois prefers comfort to pleasure,
convenience to liberty, and a pleasant temperature
to the deathly inner consuming fire.
Der Steppenwolf (1927) 'Tractat vom Steppenwolf',
translated by Basil Creighton

Gordon Hewart 1870–1943
British lawyer and politician

11 A long line of cases shows that it is not merely of
some importance, but is of fundamental
importance that justice should not only be done,
but should manifestly and undoubtedly be seen to
be done.
Rex v Sussex Justices, 9 November 1923, in *Law Reports
King's Bench Division* (1924) vol. 1

Foster William Hewitt see Catchphrases
200:28

John Hewitt 1907–87
Northern Irish poet

12 We would be strangers in the Capitol;
this is our country also, no-where else;
and we shall not be outcast on the world.
'The Colony' (1950)

13 I'm an Ulsterman, of planter stock. I was born in
the island of Ireland, so secondarily I'm an
Irishman. I was born in the British archipelago
and English is my native tongue, so I am British.
The British archipelago consists of offshore islands
to the continent of Europe, so I'm European. This
is my hierarchy of values and so far as I am
concerned, anyone who omits one step in that
sequence of values is falsifying the situation.
in *The Irish Times* 4 July 1974

Reinhard Heydrich 1904–42
German Nazi leader

14 Now the rough work has been done we begin the
period of finer work. We need to work in harmony
with the civil administration. We count on you
gentlemen as far as the final solution is concerned.
on the planned mass murder of all European Jews; see
Goering *352:10*
speech in Wannsee, 20 January 1942

Du Bose Heyward 1885–1940 and Ira Gershwin 1896–1983
American songwriters

15 It ain't necessarily so,
It ain't necessarily so,
De t'ings dat yo' li'ble
To read in de Bible
It ain't necessarily so.
'It ain't necessarily so' (1935 song) in *Porgy and Bess*

16 Summer time an' the livin' is easy,
Fish are jumpin' an' the cotton is high.
Oh, yo' daddy's rich, and yo' ma' is good-lookin',
So hush, little baby, don' yo' cry.
'Summertime' (1935 song) in *Porgy and Bess*

17 A woman is a sometime thing.
title of song (1935) in *Porgy and Bess*

John Heywood c.1497–c.1580
English dramatist

18 All a green willow, willow;
All a green willow is my garland.
'The Green Willow'; see **Shakespeare** 714:17

19 I never heard thy fire once spark,
I never heard thy dog once bark.
I never heard once in thy house
So much as one peep of one mouse.
I never heard thy cat once mew.
These praises are not small nor few.
'A quiet neighbour' (1556)

Thomas Heywood c.1574–1641

English dramatist

1 Seven cities warred for Homer, being dead,
Who, living, had no roof to shroud his head.
'The Hierarchy of the Blessed Angels' (1635); see
Anonymous 19:1

J. R. Hicks 1904–

British economist

2 The best of all monopoly profits is a quiet life.
Econometrica (1935) 'The Theory of Monopoly'

David Hilbert 1862–1943

German mathematician
see also **Epitaphs** 311:13

3 The importance of a scientific work can be
measured by the number of previous publications
it makes it superfluous to read.
attributed; Lewis Wolpert *The Unnatural Nature of Science*
(1993)

Hildegard of Bingen 1098–1179

German abbess, scholar, composer, and mystic

4 Listen now! a king sat on his throne, high pillars
before him splendidly adorned and set on
pediments of ivory . . . Then the king chose to lift a
small feather from the ground, and he
commanded it to fly just as the king himself
wished. But a feather does not fly of its own
accord, it is borne up by the air. So too I am not
imbued with human doctrine or strong powers . . .
Rather, I depend entirely on God's help.
*often summarized 'Thus am I a feather on the breath
of God'*
letter to Odo of Soissons, 1148, in *Selected Writings* (2001,
translated by M. Atherton)

5 I, a mere female and a fragile vessel, speak these
things not from me but from the serene Light.
letter to Elizabeth of Schönau, 1152–6, in *Selected Writings*
(2001, translated by M. Atherton)

Aaron Hill 1685–1750

English poet and dramatist

6 Tender-handed stroke a nettle,
And it stings you for your pains;
Grasp it like a man of mettle,
And it soft as silk remains.
'Verses Written on a Window in Scotland'

Christopher Hill 1912–

British historian

7 Only very slowly and late have men come to
realize that unless freedom is universal it is only
extended privilege.
Century of Revolution (1961)

Geoffrey Hill 1932–

English poet

8   Poetry
Unearths from among the speechless dead

Lazarus mystified, common man
Of death. The lily rears its gouged face
From the provided loam.
'History as Poetry' (1968)

9 She kept the siege. And every day
We watched her brooding over death
Like a strong bird above its prey.
The room filled with the kettle's breath.
'In Memory of Jane Fraser' (1959)

10 I love my work and my children. God
Is distant, difficult. Things happen.
Too near the ancient troughs of blood
Innocence is no earthly weapon.
'Ovid in the Third Reich' (1968)

Joe Hill (Joel Hägglund) 1879–1915

Swedish-born American labour leader and songwriter
on Hill: see **Hayes** 376:6; see also **Last words** 472:16

11 You will eat, bye and bye,
In that glorious land above the sky;
Work and pray, live on hay,
You'll get pie in the sky when you die.
'Preacher and the Slave' in *Songs of the Workers* (Industrial
Workers of the World, 1911)

Pattie S. Hill 1868–1946

American educationist

12 Happy birthday to you.
title of song (1935)

Rowland Hill 1744–1833

English clergyman

13 He did not see any reason why the devil should
have all the good tunes.
E. W. Broome *The Rev. Rowland Hill* (1881) ch. 7; see
Proverbs 635:9

Selima Hill 1945–

14 All we're allowed's anxiety like fishbones
lodged in our throats
as beauty parlours hum;
all we're allowed is having pretty faces
and cold and glittery hearts like water-ices . . .
Mine's more like a centrally-heated boiler-room,
evil and warm;
like kidneys on a plate.
'Do It Again' (1993)

Edmund Hillary 1919–

New Zealand mountaineer

15 Well, we knocked the bastard off!
on conquering Mount Everest, 1953
Nothing Venture, Nothing Win (1975) ch. 10; see **Mallory**
508:17

Fred Hillebrand 1893–1963

16 Home James, and don't spare the horses.
title of song (1934)

Hillel 'The Elder' c.60 BC–c.AD 9

Jewish scholar and teacher

1 What is hateful to you do not to your neighbour: that is the whole Torah.
   in *Talmud* Shabbat 31a

2 Be of the disciples of Aaron, loving peace and pursuing peace, loving mankind and bringing them nigh to the Law.
   in *Talmud* Mishnah 'Pirqei Avot' 1:12

3 A name made great is a name destroyed.
   in *Talmud* Mishnah 'Pirqei Avot' 1:13

4 If I am not for myself who is for me? and being for my own self what am I? If not now when?
   in *Talmud* Mishnah 'Pirqei Avot' 1:14

5 Keep not aloof from the congregation.
   in *Talmud* Mishnah 'Pirqei Avot' 2:5

6 Say not, When I have leisure I will study; perchance thou wilt never have leisure.
   in *Talmud* Mishnah 'Pirqei Avot' 2:5

James Hilton 1900–54

English novelist

7 Nothing really wrong with him—only anno domini, but that's the most fatal complaint of all, in the end.
   Goodbye, Mr Chips (1934) ch. 1

Hippocleides

Greek aristocrat of 6th century BC Athens

8 Hippocleides doesn't care.
   on being told that he had ruined his marriage chances with the daughter of a tyrant, concluding a dance by standing on his head and gesticulating with his legs
   Herodotus *Histories* bk. 6, sect. 129

Hippocrates c.460–357 BC

Greek physician

9 Life is short, the art long.
   often quoted as 'Ars longa, vita brevis', *after* **Seneca**'s *rendering in* De Brevitate Vitae *sect. 1*
   Aphorisms sect. 1, para. 1 (translated by W. H. S. Jones); see **Chaucer** 212:26, **Longfellow** 490:19, **Proverbs** 614:32

10 Extreme remedies are most appropriate for extreme diseases.
   Aphorisms sect. 1, para. 6 (translated by W. H. S. Jones); see **Proverbs** 617:30

11 I swear by Apollo the physician, by Asclepius, by Health, by Panacea and by all the gods and goddesses, making them my witnesses, that I will carry out, according to my ability and judgement, this oath and this indenture.
   The Hippocratic Oath (translated by W. H. S. Jones)

12 I will use treatment to help the sick according to my ability and judgement, but never with a view to injury or wrong-doing. Neither will I administer a poison to anybody when asked to do so, nor will I suggest such a course.
   The Hippocratic Oath (translated by W. H. S. Jones)

13 I will not use the knife, not even, verily, on sufferers from stone but I will give place to such as are craftsmen therein.
   The Hippocratic Oath (translated by W. H. S. Jones)

14 And whatsoever I shall see or hear in the course of my profession, as well as outside my profession in my intercourse with men, if it be what should not be published abroad, I will never divulge holding such things to be holy secrets.
   The Hippocratic Oath (translated by W. H. S. Jones)

15 Time is that wherein there is opportunity, and opportunity is that wherein there is no great time.
   Precepts ch. 1 (translated by W. H. S. Jones, 1923)

16 Healing is a matter of time, but it is sometimes also a matter of opportunity.
   Precepts ch. 1 (translated by W. H. S. Jones, 1923)

Emperor Hirohito 1901–89

Japanese monarch, Emperor from 1926

17 The war situation has developed not necessarily to Japan's advantage.
   announcing Japan's surrender, in a broadcast to his people after atom bombs had destroyed Hiroshima and Nagasaki
   on 15 August 1945

Damien Hirst 1965–

English artist

18 It's amazing what you can do with an E in A-level art, twisted imagination and a chainsaw.
   after winning the 1995 Turner Prize
   in *Observer* 3 December 1995 'Sayings of the Week'

Alfred Hitchcock 1899–1980

British-born film director

19 Actors are cattle.
   in *Saturday Evening Post* 22 May 1943

20 If I made Cinderella, the audience would immediately be looking for a body in the coach.
   in *Newsweek* 11 June 1956

21 Television has brought back murder into the home—where it belongs.
   in *Observer* 19 December 1965

22 There is no terror in a bang, only in the anticipation of it.
   Leslie Halliwell (ed.) *Halliwell's Filmgoer's Companion* (1984); attributed

Adolf Hitler 1889–1945

German dictator
on Hitler: see **Buchman** 163:1, **Chamberlain** 206:14

23 The broad mass of a nation . . . will more easily fall victim to a big lie than to a small one.
   Mein Kampf (1925) vol. 1, ch. 10

24 The night of the long knives.
   referring to the massacre of Ernst Roehm and his associates by Hitler on 29–30 June 1934

*(subsequently associated with Harold **Macmillan**'s Cabinet dismissals of 13 July 1962)*
S. H. Roberts *The House Hitler Built* (1937) pt. 2, ch. 3

1 I go the way that Providence dictates with the assurance of a sleepwalker.
speech in Munich, 15 March 1936, in Max Domarus (ed.) *Hitler: Reden und Proklamationen 1932–1945* (1962)

2 It is the last territorial claim which I have to make in Europe, but it is the claim from which I will not recede and which, God-willing, I will make good.
on the Sudetenland
speech at Berlin Sportpalast, 26 September 1938; in Max Domarus (ed.) *Hitler: Reden und Proklamationen 1932–1945* (1962)

3 With regard to the problem of the Sudeten Germans, my patience is now at an end!
speech at Berlin Sportpalast, 26 September 1938, in Max Domarus (ed.) *Hitler: Reden und Proklamationen 1932–1945* (1962)

4 Is Paris burning?
on 25 August 1944, in Larry Collins and Dominique Lapierre *Is Paris Burning?* (1965) ch. 5

Lady Ho fl. 300 BC

Chinese poet

5 When a pair of magpies fly together
They do not envy the pair of phoenixes.
'A Song of Magpies'; K. Rexroth and Chung (eds.) *The Orchid Boat: Women Poets of China* (1972)

Thomas Hobbes 1588–1679

English philosopher
on Hobbes: see **Aubrey** 33:16, **Swift** 767:10; see also **Last words** 471:19

6 Laughter is nothing else but sudden glory arising from some sudden conception of some eminency in ourselves, by comparison with the infirmity of others, or with our own formerly.
Human Nature (1650) ch. 9, sect. 13

7 By art is created that great Leviathan, called a commonwealth or state, (in Latin *civitas*) which is but an artificial man . . . and in which, the sovereignty is an artificial soul.
Leviathan (1651); introduction

8 True and False are attributes of speech, not of things. And where speech is not, there is neither Truth nor Falsehood.
Leviathan (1651) pt. 1, ch. 4

9 In Geometry (which is the only science that it hath pleased God hitherto to bestow on mankind) men begin at settling the significations of their words; which . . . they call Definitions.
Leviathan (1651) pt. 1, ch. 4

10 Words are wise men's counters, they do but reckon by them: but they are the money of fools, that value them by the authority of an Aristotle, a Cicero, or a Thomas, or any other doctor whatsoever, if but a man.
Leviathan (1651) pt. 1, ch. 4

11 The power of a man, to take it universally, is his present means, to obtain some future apparent good; and is either original or instrumental.
Leviathan (1651) pt. 1, ch. 10

12 I put for a general inclination of all mankind, a perpetual and restless desire of power after power, that ceaseth only in death.
Leviathan (1651) pt. 1, ch. 11

13 They that approve a private opinion, call it opinion; but they that mislike it, heresy: and yet heresy signifies no more than private opinion.
Leviathan (1651) pt. 1, ch. 11

14 During the time men live without a common power to keep them all in awe, they are in that condition which is called war; and such a war as is of every man against every man.
Leviathan (1651) pt. 1, ch. 13

15 For as the nature of foul weather, lieth not in a shower or two of rain; but in an inclination thereto of many days together: so the nature of war consisteth not in actual fighting, but in the known disposition thereto during all the time there is no assurance to the contrary.
Leviathan (1651) pt. 1, ch. 13

16 No arts; no letters; no society; and which is worst of all, continual fear and danger of violent death; and the life of man, solitary, poor, nasty, brutish, and short.
Leviathan (1651) pt. 1, ch. 13

17 Force, and fraud, are in war the two cardinal virtues.
Leviathan (1651) pt. 1, ch. 13

18 Liberties . . . depend on the silence of the law.
Leviathan (1651) pt. 2, ch. 16

19 I put down for one of the most effectual seeds of the death of any state, that the conquerors require not only a submission of men's actions to them for the future, but also an approbation of all their actions past.
Leviathan (1651) pt. 2, ch. 17

20 They that are discontented under *monarchy*, call it *tyranny*; and they that are displeased with *aristocracy*, call it *oligarchy*: so also, they which find themselves grieved under a *democracy*, call it *anarchy*, which signifies the want of government; and yet I think no man believes, that want of government, is any new kind of government.
Leviathan (1651) pt. 2, ch. 19

21 Whereas some have attributed the dominion [of the family] to the man only, as being of the more excellent sex; they misreckon in it. For there is not always that difference of strength, or prudence between the man and the woman, as that the right can be determined without war.
Leviathan (1651) pt. 2, ch. 20

22 For it is with the mysteries of our religion, as with wholesome pills for the sick, which swallowed whole, have the virtue to cure; but chewed, are for the most part cast up again without effect.
Leviathan (1651) pt. 3, ch. 32

1 The papacy is not other than the ghost of the deceased Roman Empire, sitting crowned upon the grave thereof.

> *Leviathan* (1651) pt. 4, ch. 47

2 The praise of ancient authors proceeds not from the reverence of the dead, but from the competition, and mutual envy of the living.

> *Leviathan* (1651) 'A Review and Conclusion'

John Cam Hobhouse, Lord Broughton
1786–1869
English politician

3 When I invented the phrase 'His Majesty's Opposition' [Canning] paid me a compliment on the fortunate hit.

> *Recollections of a Long Life* (1865) vol. 2, ch. 12; see below; see **Bagehot** 47:18

It is said to be very hard on his majesty's ministers to raise objections to this proposition. For my own part, I think it is more hard on his majesty's opposition (a laugh) to compel them to take this course.

> speech, House of Commons, 10 April 1826

Eric Hobsbawm 1917–
British historian

4 This was the kind of war which existed in order to produce victory parades.

> *of the Falklands War*
> in *Marxism Today* January 1983

Margaret Hoby 1571–1633
English diarist

5 This day I bestowed too much time in the garden, and thereby was worse able to perform spiritual duties.

> diary, 6 April 1605; Dorothy M. Meads (ed.) *Diary of Lady Margaret Hoby* (1930)

David Hockney 1937–
British artist

6 All painting, no matter what you're painting, is abstract in that it's got to be organized.

> *David Hockney* (1976)

7 Art has to move you and design does not, unless it's a good design for a bus.

> in *Guardian* 26 October 1988

Dorothy Hodgkin 1910–94
British chemist

8 I'm really an experimentalist. I used to say, I think with my hands. I just like manipulation. I began to like it as a child and it's continued to be a pleasure.

> Lewis Wolpert and Alison Richards *A Passion for Science* (1988) ch. 6

9 I was captured for life by chemistry and by crystals.

> Georgina Ferry *Dorothy Hodgkin* (1998) ch. 1

Ralph Hodgson 1871–1962
English poet

10 'Twould ring the bells of Heaven
The wildest peal for years,
If Parson lost his senses
And people came to theirs,
And he and they together
Knelt down with angry prayers
For tamed and shabby tigers
And dancing dogs and bears,
And wretched, blind, pit ponies,
And little hunted hares.

> 'Bells of Heaven' (1917)

11 Time, you old gipsy man,
Will you not stay,
Put up your caravan
Just for one day?

> 'Time, You Old Gipsy Man' (1917)

Al Hoffman 1902–60 and Dick Manning 1912–

12 Takes two to tango.

> title of song (1952); see **Proverbs** 624:28

August Heinrich Hoffman (Hoffman von Fallersleben) 1798–1874
German poet

13 *Deutschland über alles.*
Germany above all.

> title of poem (1841)

Heinrich Hoffmann 1809–94
German writer for children

14 Augustus was a chubby lad;
Fat ruddy cheeks Augustus had:
And everybody saw with joy
The plump and hearty, healthy boy.
He ate and drank as he was told,
And never let his soup get cold.
But one day, one cold winter's day,
He screamed out, 'Take the soup away!
O take the nasty soup away!
I won't have any soup today.'

> *Struwwelpeter* (1848) 'Augustus'

15 But fidgety Phil,
He won't sit still.

> *Struwwelpeter* (1848) 'Fidgety Philip'

16 Look at little Johnny there,
Little Johnny Head-In-Air!

> *Struwwelpeter* (1848) 'Johnny Head-In-Air'; see **Pudney** 636:17

17 The door flew open, in he ran,
The great, long, red-legged scissor-man.

> *Struwwelpeter* (1848) 'The Little Suck-a-Thumb'

18 Snip! Snap! Snip! They go so fast.
That both his thumbs are off at last.

> *Struwwelpeter* (1848) 'The Little Suck-a-Thumb'

19 The hare sits snug in leaves and grass,
And laughs to see the green man pass.

> *Struwwelpeter* (1848) 'The Man Who Went Out Shooting'

1 And now she's trying all she can,
To shoot the sleepy, green-coat man.
Struwwelpeter (1848) 'The Man Who Went Out Shooting'

2 The hare's own child, the little hare.
Struwwelpeter (1848) 'The Man Who Went Out Shooting'

3 Anything to me is sweeter
Than to see Shock-headed Peter.
Struwwelpeter (1848) 'Shock-Headed Peter' (title poem)

Gerard Hoffnung 1925–59
English humorist

4 Standing among savage scenery, the hotel offers
stupendous revelations. There is a French widow
in every bedroom, affording delightful prospects.
supposedly quoting a letter from a Tyrolean landlord
speech at the Oxford Union, 4 December 1958

Lancelot Hogben 1895–1975
English scientist

5 This is not the age of pamphleteers. It is the age of
the engineers. The spark-gap is mightier than the
pen. Democracy will not be salvaged by men who
talk fluently, debate forcefully and quote aptly.
Science for the Citizen (1938) epilogue; see **Proverbs** 629:19

James Hogg 1770–1835
Scottish poet
see also **Songs** 747:7

6 Where the pools are bright and deep
Where the gray trout lies asleep,
Up the river and o'er the lea
That's the way for Billy and me.
'A Boy's Song' (1838)

7 Cock up your beaver, and cock it fu' sprush;
We'll over the Border and gi'e them a brush;
There's somebody there we'll teach better
behaviour.
Hey, Johnnie lad, cock up your beaver!
'Cock Up Your Beaver' in *Jacobite Relics of Scotland* Second
Series (1821)

8 We'll o'er the water, we'll o'er the sea,
We'll o'er the water to Charlie;
Come weel, come wo, we'll gather and go,
And live or die wi' Charlie.
'O'er the Water to Charlie' in *Jacobite Relics of Scotland*
Second Series (1821)

9 Bird of the wilderness,
Blithesome and cumberless,
Sweet be thy matin o'er moorland and lea!
'The Skylark'

10 The private memoirs and confessions of a justified
sinner.
title of novel (1824)

Paul Henri, Baron d'Holbach 1723–89
French philosopher

11 Art is only Nature operating with the aid of the
instruments she has made.
Système de la Nature (1780 ed.) pt. 1, ch. 1

12 If ignorance of nature gave birth to the Gods,
knowledge of nature is destined to destroy them.
Système de la Nature (1770) pt. 2, ch. 1

Johann Christian Friedrich Hölderlin
1770–1843
German lyric poet

13 *So zu harren und was zu thun indess und zu sagen?*
Weiss ich nicht und wozu Dichter in durftiger Zeit?
Always waiting and what to do or to say in the
meantime
I don't know, and who wants poets at all in lean
years?
'Bread and Wine' (1800–01), translated by Michael
Hamburger in *Poems and Fragments* (1994)

14 *Alles Getrennte findet sich wieder.*
All that is divided will find itself again.
Hyperion

Billie Holiday (Eleanor Fagan) 1915–59
American singer
see also **Allen** 12:6, **Opening lines** 575:2

15 Mama may have, papa may have,
But God bless the child that's got his own!
That's got his own.
'God Bless the Child' (1941 song, with Arthur Herzog Jnr)

16 You can be up to your boobies in white satin, with
gardenias in your hair and no sugar cane for
miles, but you can still be working on a
plantation.
Lady Sings the Blues (1956, with William Duffy) ch. 11

17 In this country, don't forget, a habit is no damn
private hell. There's no solitary confinement
outside of jail. A habit is hell for those you love.
of a drug habit
Lady Sings the Blues (1956, with William Duffy) ch. 24

Henry Fox, Lord Holland 1705–74
English Whig politician
on Holland: see **Walpole** 819:21

18 If Mr Selwyn calls again, shew him up: if I am
alive I shall be delighted to see him; and if I am
dead he would like to see me.
during his last illness
J. H. Jesse *George Selwyn and his Contemporaries* (1844)
vol. 3

Henry Scott Holland 1847–1918
English theologian and preacher

19 Death is nothing at all; it does not count. I have
only slipped away into the next room.
sermon preached on Whitsunday 1910, in *Facts of the
Faith* (1919) 'The King of Terrors'

Stanley Holloway 1890–1982
English actor and singer

20 Sam, Sam, pick up tha' musket.
'Pick Up Tha' Musket' (1930 recorded monologue)

John H. Holmes 1879–1964
American Unitarian minister

1 This, now, is the judgement of our scientific age—
the third reaction of man upon the universe! This
universe is not hostile, nor yet is it friendly. It is
simply indifferent.
   The Sensible Man's View of Religion (1932) ch. 4

Oliver Wendell Holmes 1809–94
American physician, poet, and essayist

2 It is the province of knowledge to speak and it is
the privilege of wisdom to listen.
   The Poet at the Breakfast-Table (1872) ch. 10

3 Fate tried to conceal him by naming him Smith.
   of Samuel Francis **Smith**
   'The Boys' (1858)

4 Lean, hungry, savage anti-everythings.
   'A Modest Request' (1848)

5 Man wants but little drink below,
But wants that little strong.
   'A Song of other Days' (1848); see **Goldsmith** 355:1

6 Blank cheques of intellectual bankruptcy.
   definition of catchphrases
   attributed

Oliver Wendell Holmes Jr. 1841–1935
American lawyer

7 We pause to . . . recall what our country has done
for each of us and to ask ourselves what we can
do for our country in return.
   speech, Keene, New Hampshire, 30 May 1884; see
   Kennedy 449:2

8 It is better to be seventy years young than forty
years old!
   reply to invitation from Julia Ward **Howe** *to her*
   seventieth birthday party, 27 May 1889
   Laura Richards and Maud Howe Elliott *Julia Ward Howe*
   (1916) vol. 2

9 Certitude is not the test of certainty. We have been
cocksure of many things that were not so.
   'Natural Law' (1918)

10 The most stringent protection of free speech would
not protect a man falsely shouting fire in a theatre
and causing a panic . . . The question in every
case is whether the words used are used in such
circumstances and are of such a nature as to
create a clear and present danger that they will
bring about the substantive evils that Congress
has a right to prevent.
   sometimes quoted as, 'shouting fire in a crowded
   theatre'
   in *Schenck v. United States* (1919)

11 The minute a phrase becomes current it becomes
an apology for not thinking accurately to the end
of the sentence.
   letter to Harold Laski, 2 July 1917

12 But I have long thought that if you knew a
column of advertisements by heart, you could

achieve unexpected felicities with them. You can
get a happy quotation anywhere if you have the
eye.
   letter to Harold Laski, 31 May 1923

Miroslav Holub 1923–
Czech poet

13 But above all
we have
the ability
to sort peas,
to cup water in our hands,
to seek
the right screw
under the sofa
for hours.
   'Wings' (1967)

John Home 1722–1808
Scottish dramatist

14 My name is Norval; on the Grampian hills
My father feeds his flocks.
   Douglas (1756) act 2, sc. 1

15 Like Douglas conquer, or like Douglas die.
   Douglas (1756) act 5

Alec Douglas-Home, Lord Home
1903–95
British Conservative statesman; Prime Minister, 1963–4

16 As far as the fourteenth earl is concerned, I
suppose Mr Wilson, when you come to think of it,
is the fourteenth Mr Wilson.
   replying to Harold **Wilson***'s remark (on Home's*
   becoming leader of the Conservative party) that 'the
   whole [democratic] process has ground to a halt with
   a fourteenth Earl'
   in *Daily Telegraph* 22 October 1963

Homer
Greek poet of the 8th century BC
on Homer: see **Anonymous** *19:1,* **Arnold** *30:7,* **Horace** *398:15,*
Keats *445:20*

17 Achilles' cursed anger sing, O goddess, that son of
Peleus, which started a myriad sufferings for the
Achaeans.
   The Iliad bk. 1, l. 1; see **Pope** 605:14

18 In silence trailing away
by the shore of the tumbling clamorous
   whispering sea.
   The Iliad bk. 1, l. 34

19 Winged words.
   The Iliad bk. 1, l. 201

20 The son of Kronos [Zeus] spoke, and nodded with
his darkish brows, and immortal locks fell forward
from the lord's deathless head, and he made great
Olympus tremble.
   The Iliad bk. 1, l. 528

21 It is no cause for anger that the Trojans and the
well-greaved Achaeans have suffered for so long

over *such* a woman: she is wondrously like the immortal goddesses to look upon.

of Helen
The Iliad bk. 3, l. 156

1 Son of Atreus, what manner of speech has escaped the barrier of your teeth?
The Iliad bk. 4, l. 350

2   Very like leaves
upon this earth are the generations of men—
old leaves, cast on the ground by wind, young
  leaves
the greening forest bears when spring comes in.
The Iliad bk. 6, l. 146

3 Always to be best, and to be distinguished above the rest.
The Iliad bk. 6, l. 208

4 As he said this, Hector held out his arms
to take his baby. But the child squirmed round
on the nurse's bosom and begain to wail,
terrified by his father's great war helm.
The Iliad bk. 6, l. 466

5 Smiling through her tears.
The Iliad bk. 6, l. 484

6 Hateful to me as the gates of Hades is that man who hides one thing in his heart and speaks another.
The Iliad bk. 9, l. 312

7 This is the one best omen, to fight in defence of one's country.
The Iliad bk. 12, l. 243

8 He lay great and greatly fallen, forgetful of his horsemanship.
The Iliad bk. 16, l. 776

9 It lies in the lap of the gods.
The Iliad bk. 17, l. 514 and elsewhere

10 They ran, one fleeing, and one pursuing. In front a good man fled, but one mightier far pursued him swiftly; for it was not for beast of sacrifice or for bull's hide that they strove, such as are men's prizes for swiftness of foot, but it was for the life of horse-taming Hector that they ran.
Achilles and Hector
The Iliad bk. 22, l. 156

11 Great Priam entered in, and coming close to Achilles, clasped in his hands his knees, and kissed his hands, the terrible, man-slaying hands that had slain his many sons.
The Iliad bk. 24, l. 479

12   This is the way
the gods ordained the destiny of men,
to bear such burdens in our lives, while they
feel no affliction.
The Iliad bk. 24, l. 525

13 Tell me, Muse, of the man of many devices, who wandered far and wide after he had sacked Troy's sacred city, and saw the towns of many men and knew their mind.
of Odysseus
The Odyssey bk. 1, l. 1

14 Early-born rosy-fingered dawn.
The Odyssey bk. 2, l. 1 and *passim*

15 Athene sent them a following breeze, a strong west wind that whistled over the wine-dark sea.
The Odyssey bk. 2, l. 420

16 I would rather be tied to the soil as another man's serf, even a poor man's, who hadn't much to live on himself, than be King of all these the dead and destroyed.
The Odyssey bk. 11, l. 489

17 Come hither, renowned Odysseus, hither, you pride and glory of all Achaea! Pause with your ship; listen to our song. Never has any man passed this way in his dark vessel and left unheard the honey-sweet music from our lips; first he has taken his delight, then gone on his way a wiser man. We know of all the sorrows in the wide land of Troy that Argives and Trojans bore because the gods would needs have it so; we know of all things that come to pass on the fruitful earth.
the Sirens
The Odyssey bk. 12, l. 184

18 Have patience, heart. Once you endured worse than this.
The Odyssey bk. 12, l. 184

Arthur Honegger 1892–1955
Swiss composer

19 The first requirement for a composer is to be dead.
Je suis compositeur (1951)

Thomas Hood 1799–1845
English poet and humorist

20 Take her up tenderly,
Lift her with care;
Fashioned so slenderly,
Young, and so fair!
'The Bridge of Sighs' (1844)

21 Or was there a dearer one
Still, and a nearer one
Yet, than all other?
'The Bridge of Sighs' (1844)

22 The bleak wind of March
Made her tremble and shiver;
But not the dark arch,
Or the black flowing river.
'The Bridge of Sighs' (1844)

23 Mad from life's history,
Glad to death's mystery,
Swift to be hurled—
Anywhere, anywhere,
Out of the world!
'The Bridge of Sighs' (1844)

24 Two stern-faced men set out from Lynn,
Through the cold and heavy mist;
And Eugene Aram walked between,
With gyves upon his wrist.
'The Dream of Eugene Aram' (1829)

25 Ben Battle was a soldier bold,
And used to war's alarms:

But a cannon-ball took off his legs,
So he laid down his arms!
'Faithless Nelly Gray' (1826)

1 For here I leave my second leg,
And the Forty-second Foot!
'Faithless Nelly Gray' (1826)

2 They went and told the sexton, and
The sexton tolled the bell.
'Faithless Sally Brown' (1826)

3 I remember, I remember,
The house where I was born,
The little window where the sun
Came peeping in at morn.
'I Remember' (1826)

4 But evil is wrought by want of thought,
As well as want of heart!
'The Lady's Dream' (1844)

5 Home-made dishes that drive one from home.
Miss Kilmansegg and her Precious Leg (1841–3) 'Her Misery'

6 No sun—no moon!
No morn—no noon
No dawn—no dusk—no proper time of day.
'No!' (1844)

7 No warmth, no cheerfulness, no healthful ease,
No comfortable feel in any member—
No shade, no shine, no butterflies, no bees,
No fruits, no flowers, no leaves, no birds,—
November!
'No!' (1844)

8 I saw old Autumn in the misty morn
Stand shadowless like Silence, listening
To silence.
'Ode: Autumn' (1823)

9 Some minds improve by travel, others, rather
Resemble copper wire, or brass,
Which gets the narrower by going farther!
'Ode to Rae Wilson, Esq.'

10 She stood breast high amid the corn,
Clasped by the golden light of morn,
Like the sweetheart of the sun,
Who many a glowing kiss had won.
'Ruth' (1827); see **Keats** 445:1

11 With fingers weary and worn,
With eyelids heavy and red,
A woman sat, in unwomanly rags,
Plying her needle and thread—
Stitch! stitch! stitch!
In poverty, hunger, and dirt.
And still with a voice of dolorous pitch
She sang the 'Song of the Shirt'.
'The Song of the Shirt' (1843)

12 Oh! God! that bread should be so dear,
And flesh and blood so cheap!
'The Song of the Shirt' (1843)

13 What is a modern poet's fate?
To write his thoughts upon a slate;
The critic spits on what is done,
Gives it a wipe—and all is gone.
'To the Reviewers', dedication of *Whims and Oddities* (1826)

14 There are three things which the public will always clamour for, sooner or later: namely, novelty, novelty, novelty.
Announcement of Comic Annual for 1836, in 'Quote . . . Unquote' newsletter January 2001

15 The sedate, sober, silent, serious, sad-coloured sect.
of Quakers
Comic Annual (1839) 'The Doves and the Crows'

16 Holland . . . lies so low they're only saved by being dammed.
Up the Rhine (1840) 'Letter from Martha Penny to Rebecca Page'

Richard Hooker c.1554–1600
English theologian

17 He that goeth about to persuade a multitude, that they are not so well governed as they ought to be, shall never want attentive and favourable hearers.
Of the Laws of Ecclesiastical Polity (1593) bk. 1, ch. 1, sect. 1

18 Of Law there can be no less acknowledged, than that her seat is the bosom of God, her voice the harmony of the world: all things in heaven and earth do her homage, the very least as feeling her care, and the greatest as not exempted from her power.
Of the Laws of Ecclesiastical Polity (1593) bk. 1, ch. 16, sect. 8

19 Alteration though it be from worse to better hath in it inconveniences, and those weighty.
Of the Laws of Ecclesiastical Polity (1593) bk. 4, ch. 14, sect. 1; see **Johnson** 424:3

Ellen Sturgis Hooper 1816–41
American poet

20 I slept, and dreamed that life was beauty;
I woke, and found that life was duty.
'Beauty and Duty' (1840)

Herbert Hoover 1874–1964
American Republican statesman, 31st President of the US, 1929–33
on Hoover: see **Coolidge** 242:7

21 Our country has deliberately undertaken a great social and economic experiment, noble in motive and far-reaching in purpose.
on the Eighteenth Amendment enacting Prohibition
letter to Senator W. H. Borah, 23 February 1928; in Claudius O. Johnson *Borah of Idaho* (1936) ch. 21

22 The American system of rugged individualism.
speech in New York City, 22 October 1928, in *New Day* (1928) p. 154

23 The slogan of progress is changing from the full dinner pail to the full garage.
sometimes paraphrased as, 'a car in every garage and a chicken in every pot'
speech, 22 October 1928; see **Henri IV** 381:19

1 The grass will grow in the streets of a hundred cities, a thousand towns.

on proposals 'to reduce the protective tariff to a competitive tariff for revenue'

speech, 31 October 1932, in *State Papers of Herbert Hoover* (1934) vol. 2

2 Older men declare war. But it is youth who must fight and die.

speech at the Republican National Convention, Chicago, 27 June 1944, in *Addresses upon the American Road* (1946)

Anthony Hope (Anthony Hope Hawkins)
1863–1933
English novelist
see also **Epitaphs** 310:10

3 Economy is going without something you do want in case you should, some day, want something you probably won't want.

The Dolly Dialogues (1894) no. 12

4 'You oughtn't to yield to temptation.' 'Well, somebody must, or the thing becomes absurd,' said I.

The Dolly Dialogues (1894) no. 14

5 Oh, for an hour of Herod!

at the first night of J. M. Barrie's Peter Pan in 1904

Denis Mackail *The Story of JMB* (1941) ch. 17

Bob Hope 1903–2003
American comedian

6 A bank is a place that will lend you money if you can prove that you don't need it.

In Alan Harrington *Life in the Crystal Palace* (1959) 'The Tyranny of Farms'

Francis Hope 1938–74
British journalist and poet

7 And scribbled lines like fallen hopes
On backs of tattered envelopes.

'Instead of a Poet' (1965)

Laurence Hope (Adela Florence Nicolson)
1865–1904
English-born Indian poet

8 Pale hands I loved beside the Shalimar,
Where are you now? Who lies beneath your spell?

The Garden of Kama (1901) 'Kashmiri Song'

9 Less than the dust, beneath thy Chariot wheel,
Less than the rust, that never stained thy Sword
. . .
Less than the need thou hast in life of me.
Even less am I.

The Garden of Kama (1901) 'Less than the Dust'

Gerard Manley Hopkins 1844–89
English poet and priest

10 Not, I'll not, carrion comfort, Despair, not feast on thee;
Not untwist—slack they may be—these last strands of man

In me or, most weary, cry *I can no more*. I can;
Can something, hope, wish day come, not choose not to be.

'Carrion Comfort' (written 1885)

11 Towery city and branchy between towers;
Cuckoo-echoing, bell-swarmèd, lark-charmèd, rook-racked, river-rounded.

'Duns Scotus's Oxford' (written 1879)

12 The world is charged with the grandeur of God.
It will flame out like shining from shook foil . . .
Generations have trod, have trod, have trod;
And all is seared with trade; bleared, smeared with toil;
And wears man's smudge and shares man's smell: the soil
Is bare now, nor can foot feel, being shod.

'God's Grandeur' (written 1877)

13　　　　　Because the Holy Ghost over the bent
World broods with warm breast and with ah! bright wings.

'God's Grandeur' (written 1877)

14 Elected Silence, sing to me
And beat upon my whorlèd ear,
Pipe me to pastures still and be
The music that I care to hear.

'The Habit of Perfection' (written 1866)

15 Palate, the hutch of tasty lust,
Desire not to be rinsed with wine.

'The Habit of Perfection' (written 1866)

16 I have desired to go
Where springs not fail,
To fields where flies no sharp and sided hail
And a few lilies blow.

'Heaven-Haven' (written 1864)

17 What would the world be, once bereft
Of wet and wildness? Let them be left,
O let them be left, wildness and wet;
Long live the weeds and the wilderness yet.

'Inversnaid' (written 1881)

18 No worst, there is none. Pitched past pitch of grief,
More pangs will, schooled at forepangs, wilder wring.
Comforter, where, where is your comforting?

'No worst, there is none' (written 1885)

19 O the mind, mind has mountains; cliffs of fall
Frightful, sheer, no-man-fathomed. Hold them cheap
May who ne'er hung there.

'No worst, there is none' (written 1885)

20　　　　　All
Life death does end and each day dies with sleep.

'No worst, there is none' (written 1885)

21 Glory be to God for dappled things.

'Pied Beauty' (written 1877)

22 All things counter, original, spare, strange;
Whatever is fickle, freckled (who knows how?)
With swift, slow; sweet, sour; adazzle, dim;
He fathers-forth whose beauty is past change:
Praise him.

'Pied Beauty' (written 1877)

1 The glassy peartree leaves and blooms, they brush
The descending blue; that blue is all in a rush
With richness.
'Spring' (written 1877)

2 Márgarét, áre you grieving
Over Goldengrove unleaving?
'Spring and Fall: to a young child' (written 1880)

3 Áh! ás the heart grows older
It will come to such sights colder
By and by, nor spare a sigh
Though worlds of wanwood leafmeal lie;
And yet you *will* weep and know why.
'Spring and Fall: to a young child' (written 1880)

4 It ís the blight man was born for,
It is Margaret you mourn for.
'Spring and Fall: to a young child' (written 1880)

5 Look at the stars! look, look up at the skies!
O look at all the fire-folk sitting in the air!
The bright boroughs, the circle-citadels there!
'The Starlight Night' (written 1877)

6   This piece-bright paling shuts the
                   spouse
Christ home, Christ and his mother and all his
   hallows.
'The Starlight Night' (written 1877)

7 I am all at once what Christ is, since he was what
   I am, and
This Jack, joke, poor potsherd, patch, matchwood,
   immortal diamond,
Is immortal diamond.
'That Nature is a Heraclitean Fire' (written 1888)

8 Thou art indeed just, Lord, if I contend
With thee; but, sir, so what I plead is just.
Why do sinners' ways prosper? and why must
Disappointment all I endeavour end?
'Thou art indeed just, Lord' (written 1889)

9 Birds build—but not I build; no, but strain,
Time's eunuch, and not breed one work that
   wakes.
Mine, O thou lord of life, send my roots rain.
'Thou art indeed just, Lord' (written 1889); see **Hopkins**
397:17

10 I caught this morning morning's minion, kingdom
   of daylight's dauphin, dapple-dawn-drawn
   Falcon.
'The Windhover' (written 1877)

11   My heart in hiding
Stirred for a bird,—the achieve of, the mastery of
   the thing!
'The Windhover' (written 1877)

12   I did say yes
O at lightning and lashed rod;
Thou heardst me truer than tongue confess
Thy terror, O Christ, O God.
'The Wreck of the Deutschland' (written 1876) pt. 1

13 On Saturday sailed from Bremen,
American-outward-bound,
Take settler and seamen, tell men with women,
Two hundred souls in the round.
'The Wreck of the Deutschland' (written 1876) pt. 2

14 Time has three dimensions and one positive pitch
or direction. It is therefore not so much like any
river or any sea as like the Sea of Galilee, which
has the Jordan running through it and giving a
current to the whole.
'Creation and Redemption The Great Sacrifice' (written
1881), in Christopher Devlin (ed.) *The Sermons and
Devotional Writings of Gerard Manley Hopkins* (1959) ch. 8

15 To lift up the hands in prayer gives God glory, but
a man with a dungfork in his hand, a woman
with a slop-pail, give him glory too. He is so great
that all things give him glory if you mean they
should.
G. Roberts (ed.) *Gerard Manley Hopkins. Selected Prose*
(1980) 'The Principle or Foundation' (1882)

16 I am surprised you should say fancy and aesthetic
tastes have led me to my present state of mind;
these would be better satisfied in the Church of
England, for bad taste is always meeting one in
the accessories of Catholicism.
on his adoption of the Catholic faith
letter to his father, 16 October 1866; in G. Roberts (ed.)
Gerard Manley Hopkins. Selected Prose (1980)

17 The fine pleasure is not to do a thing but to feel
that you could . . . If I could but get on, if I could
but produce a work I should not mind its being
buried, silenced, and going no further; but it kills
me to be time's eunuch and never to beget.
letter to Robert Bridges, 1 September 1885, in C. C. Abbott
(ed.) *The Correspondence of Gerard Manley Hopkins and Robert
Bridges* (1935); see **Hopkins** 397:9

Joseph Hopkinson 1770–1842
American politician

18 Hail, Columbia! happy land!
Hail, ye heroes! heaven-born band!
'Hail, Columbia!' in *Porcupine's Gazette* 20 April 1798

Horace (Quintus Horatius Flaccus) 65–8 BC
Roman poet

19   *Ut turpiter atrum*
Desinat in piscem mulier formosa superne.
So that what is a beautiful woman on top ends in
a black and ugly fish.
Ars Poetica l. 3

20   '*Pictoribus atque poetis*
Quidlibet audendi semper fuit aequa potestas.'
*Scimus, et hanc veniam petimusque damusque
   vicissim.*
'Painters and poets alike have always had licence
to dare anything.' We know that, and we both
claim and permit others this indulgence.
Ars Poetica l. 9

21 *Inceptis gravibus plerumque et magna professis
Purpureus, late qui splendeat, unus et alter
Adsuitur pannus.*
Works of serious purpose and grand promises
often have a purple patch or two stitched on, to
shine far and wide.
Ars Poetica l. 14

22   *Brevis esse laboro,*
Obscurus fio.

I strive to be brief, and I become obscure.
Ars Poetica l. 25

1 *Dixeris egregie notum si callida verbum*
Reddiderit iunctura novum.

You will have written exceptionally well if, by
skilful arrangement of your words, you have made
an ordinary one seem original.
Ars Poetica l. 47

2   *Licuit semperque licebit*
Signatum praesente nota producere nomen.
Ut silvae foliis pronos mutantur in annos,
Prima cadunt: ita verborum vetus interit aetas,
Et iuvenum ritu florent modo nata vigentque.

It has ever been, and ever will be, permitted to
issue words stamped with the mint-mark of the
day. As forests change their leaves with each
year's decline, and the earliest drop off: so with
words, the old race dies, and like the young of
human kind, the new-born bloom and thrive.
Ars Poetica l. 58; see **Dillon** 274:8

3 *Multa renascentur quae iam cecidere, cadentque*
Quae nunc sunt in honore vocabula, si volet usus,
Quem penes arbitrium est et ius et norma loquendi.

Many terms which have now dropped out of
favour will be revived, and those that are at
present respectable will drop out, if usage so
choose, with whom lies the decision, the
judgement, and the rule of speech.
Ars Poetica l. 70

4 *Grammatici certant et adhuc sub iudice lis est.*

Scholars dispute, and the case is still before the
courts.
Ars Poetica l. 78

5 *Proicit ampullas et sesquipedalia verba.*

He throws aside his paint-pots and his words a
foot and a half long.
Ars Poetica l. 97; see **Wells** 828:8

6   *Si vis me flere, dolendum est*
Primum ipsi tibi.

If you want me to weep, you must first feel grief
yourself.
Ars Poetica l. 102

7 *Difficile est proprie communia dicere.*

It is hard to utter common notions in an
individual way.
Ars Poetica l. 128

8 *Parturient montes, nascetur ridiculus mus.*

Mountains will go into labour, and a silly little
mouse will be born.
Ars Poetica l. 139

9 *Non fumum ex fulgore, sed ex fumo dare lucem*
Cogitat.

His thinking does not produce smoke after the
flame, but light after smoke.
Ars Poetica l. 143

10 *Semper ad eventum festinat et in medias res*
Non secus ac notas auditorem rapit.

He always hurries to the main event and whisks

his audience into the middle of things as though
they knew already.
Ars Poetica l. 148

11 *Difficilis, querulus, laudator temporis acti*
Se puero, castigator censorque minorum.

Tiresome, complaining, a praiser of past times,
when he was a boy, a castigator and censor of the
young generation.
Ars Poetica l. 173

12   *Vos exemplaria Graeca*
Nocturna versate manu, versate diurnu.

You should turn the pages of your Greek models
by night and by day.
Ars Poetica l. 268

13 *Omne tulit punctum qui miscuit utile dulci,*
Lectorem delectando pariterque monendo.

He has gained every point who has mixed profit
with pleasure, by delighting the reader at the
same time as instructing him.
Ars Poetica l. 343

14 *Verum ubi plura nitent in carmine, non ego paucis*
Offendar maculis.

When many beauties grace a poem, I shall not
take offence at a few faults.
Ars Poetica l. 351

15 *Indignor quandoque bonus dormitat Homerus.*

I'm aggrieved when sometimes even excellent
Homer nods.
Ars Poetica l. 359; see **Byron** 181:10, **Proverbs** 622:26

16 *Ut pictura poesis.*

A poem is like a painting.
Ars Poetica l. 361

17   *Mediocribus esse poetis*
Non homines, non di, non concessere columnae.

Not gods, nor men, nor even booksellers have put
up with poets being second-rate.
Ars Poetica l. 372

18 *Nullius addictus iurare in verba magistri,*
Quo me cumque rapit tempestas, deferor hospes.

Not bound to swear allegiance to any master,
wherever the wind takes me I travel as a visitor.
Epistles bk. 1, no. 1, l. 14; see **Mottoes** 552:13

19 *Virtus est vitium fugere, et sapientia prima*
stultitia caruisse.

To flee vice is the beginning of virtue, and to have
got rid of folly is the beginning of wisdom.
Epistles bk. 1, no. 1, l. 41

20 *Condicio dulcis sine pulvere palmae.*

The happy state of winning the palm without the
dust of racing.
Epistles bk. 1, no. 1, l. 51

21 *O cives, cives, quarenda pecunia primum est;*
Virtus post nummos.

Citizens, citizens, the first thing to acquire is
money. Cash before conscience!
Epistles bk. 1, no. 1, l. 53

1 *Si possis recte, si non, quocumque modo rem.*

If possible honestly, if not, somehow, make money.

Epistles bk. 1, no. 1, l. 66; see **Pope** 605:17

2 *Olim quod vulpes aegroto cauta leoni*
Respondit referam: 'quia me vestigia terrent,
Omnia te adversum spectantia, nulla retrorsum.'

Let me remind you what the wary fox said once upon a time to the sick lion: 'Because those footprints scare me, all directed your way, none coming back.'
explaining why he did not follow popular opinion

Epistles bk. 1, no. 1, l. 73; see **Aesop** 6:16

3 *Quidquid delirant reges plectuntur Achivi.*

Whatever madness their kings commit, the Greeks take the beating.

Epistles bk. 1, no. 2, l. 14

4 *Nos numerus sumus et fruges consumere nati.*

We are just statistics, born to consume resources.

Epistles bk. 1, no. 2, l. 27

5 *Dimidium facti qui coepit habet: sapere aude.*

To have begun is half the job: dare to know.

Epistles bk. 1, no. 2, l. 40

6 *Ira furor brevis est.*

Anger is a short madness.

Epistles bk. 1, no. 2, l. 62

7 *Omnem crede diem tibi diluxisse supremum.*
Grata superveniet quae non sperabitur hora.
Me pinguem et nitidum bene curata cute vises
Cum ridere voles Epicuri de grege porcum.

Believe each day that has dawned is your last. Some hour to which you have not been looking forward will prove lovely. As for me, if you want a good laugh, you will come and find me fat and sleek, in excellent condition, one of Epicurus's herd of pigs.

Epistles bk. 1, no. 4, l. 13

8 *Nil admirari prope res est una, Numici,*
Solaque quae possit facere et servare beatum.

To marvel at nothing is just about the one and only thing, Numicius, that can make a man happy and keep him that way.

Epistles bk. 1, no. 6, l. 1; see **Pope** 605:18

9 *Naturam expelles furca, tamen usque recurret.*

You may drive out nature with a pitchfork, yet she'll be constantly running back.

Epistles bk. 1, no. 10, l. 24; see **Proverbs** 635:25

10 *Caelum non animum mutant qui trans mare currunt.*
Strenua nos exercet inertia: navibus atque
Quadrigis petimus bene vivere. Quod petis hic est,
Est Ulubris, animus si te non deficit aequus.

They change their clime, not their frame of mind, who rush across the sea. We strain at achieving nothing: we seek happiness in boats and carriage rides. What you seek is here, at Ulubrae, so long as peace of mind does not desert you.

Epistles bk. 1, no. 11, l. 27

11 *Concordia discors.*

Discordant harmony.

Epistles bk. 1, no. 12, l. 19

12 *Hae latebrae dulces et, iam si credis, amoenae*
Incolumem tibi me praestant septembribus horis.

This retreat, so sweet—yes, believe me, so bewitching—keeps me, my friend, in sound health in September's heat.

Epistles bk. 1, no. 16, l. 15

13 *Principibus placuisse viris non ultima laus est.*
Non cuivis homini contingit adire Corinthum.

It is not the least praise to have pleased leading men. Not everyone is lucky enough to get to Corinth.

Epistles bk. 1, no. 17, l. 35

14 *Et semel emissum volat irrevocabile verbum.*

And once sent out a word takes wing beyond recall.

Epistles bk. 1, no. 18, l. 71; see **Dillon** 274:9

15 *Nam tua res agitur, paries cum proximus ardet.*

For it is your business, when the wall next door catches fire.

Epistles bk. 1, no. 18, l. 84

16 *Fallentis semita vitae.*

The pathway of a life unnoticed.

Epistles bk. 1, no. 18, l. 103

17 *Nulla placere diu nec vivere carmina possunt*
Quae scribuntur aquae potoribus.

No verse can give pleasure for long, nor last, that is written by drinkers of water.

Epistles bk. 1, no. 19, l. 2

18 *O imitatores, servum pecus.*

O imitators, you slavish herd.

Epistles bk. 1, no. 19, l. 19

19 *Scribimus indocti doctique poemata passim.*

Skilled or unskilled, we all scribble poems.

Epistles bk. 2, no. 1, l. 117; see **Pope** 605:23

20 *Si foret in terris, rideret Democritus.*

If he were on earth, Democritus would laugh at the sight.

Epistles bk. 2, no. 1, l. 194

21 *Atque inter silvas Academi quaerere verum.*

And seek for truth in the groves of Academe.

Epistles bk. 2, no. 2, l. 45

22 *Caedimur et totidem plagis consumimus hostem*
Lento Samnites ad lumina prima duello.

We belabour each other, and with tit for tat use up our foe, like Samnites, in a long-drawn bout, till the first lamps are lighted.
of literary battles

Epistles bk. 2, no. 2, l. 97

23 *Multa fero, ut placem genus irritabile vatum.*

I have to put up with a lot, to please the touchy breed of poets.

Epistles bk. 2, no. 2, l. 102

24 *Quid te exempta iuvat spinis de pluribus una?*
Vivere si recte nescis, decede peritis.

Lusisti satis, edisti satis atque bibisti:
Tempus abire tibi est.

What pleasure does it give to be rid of one thorn
out of many? If you don't know how to live right,
give way to those who are expert at it. You have
had enough fun, eaten and drunk enough: it is
time for you to go.
> *Epistles* bk. 2, no. 2, l. 212

1 *Beatus ille, qui procul negotiis,*
Ut prisca gens mortalium,
Paterna rura bubus exercet suis,
Solutus omni faenore.

Happy the man who, far away from business, like
the race of men of old, tills his ancestral fields with
his own oxen, unbound by any interest to pay.
> *Epodes* epode 2, l. 1

2 *Quodsi me lyricis vatibus inseres,*
Sublimi feriam sidera vertice.

And if you include me among the lyric poets, I'll
hold my head so high it'll strike the stars.
> *Odes* bk. 1, no. 1, l. 35

3 *Animae dimidium meae.*

Half my own soul.
of **Virgil**
> *Odes* bk. 1, no. 3, l. 8

4 *Illi robur et aes triplex*
Circa pectus erat, qui fragilem truci
Commisit pelago ratem
Primus.

Oak was round his breast, and triple bronze, who
first launched his frail boat on the rough sea.
> *Odes* bk. 1, no. 3, l. 9

5 *Pallida Mors aequo pulsat pede pauperum tabernas*
Regumque turris.

Pale Death breaks into the cottages of the poor as
into the castles of kings.
> *Odes* bk. 1, no. 4, l. 13

6 *Vitae summa brevis spem nos vetat incohare longam.*

Life's short span forbids us to enter on far-
reaching hopes.
> *Odes* bk. 1, no. 4, l. 15

7 *Quis multa gracilis te puer in rosa*
Perfusus liquidis urget odoribus
Grato, Pyrrha, sub antro?
Cui flavam religas comam?

What slim youngster soaked in perfumes
is hugging you now, Pyrrha, on a bed of roses
deep in your lovely cave? For whom
are you tying up your blonde hair?
> *Odes* bk. 1, no. 5, l. 1

8 *Simplex munditiis.*

Plain in thy neatness.
> *Odes* bk. 1, no. 5, l. 5, translated by John **Milton**

9 *Nil desperandum.*

Never despair.
> *Odes* bk. 1, no. 7, l. 27

10 *Cras ingens iterabimus aequor.*

Tomorrow we shall sail again on the vast ocean.
> *Odes* bk. 1, no. 7, l. 32

11 *Quid sit futurum cras fuge quaerere et*
Quem Fors dierum cumque dabit lucro
Appone.

Drop the question what tomorrow may bring, and
count as profit every day that Fate allows you.
> *Odes* bk. 1, no. 9, l. 13

12 *Nunc et latentis proditor intumo*
Gratus puellae risus ab angulo
Pignusque dereptum lacertis
Aut digito male pertinaci.

Now is the time for the lovely laugh from the
secret corner
giving away the girl in her hiding-place,
and for the token snatched from her arm
or finger feebly resisting.
> *Odes* bk. 1, no. 9, l. 21

13 *Tu ne quaesieris, scire nefas, quem mihi, quem tibi*
Finem di dederint.

Do not try to find out—we're forbidden to know—
what end the gods may bestow on me or you.
> *Odes* bk. 1, no. 11, l. 1

14 *Dum loquimur, fugerit invida*
Aetas: carpe diem, quam minimum credula postero.

While we're talking, envious time is fleeing: seize
the day, put no trust in the future.
> *Odes* bk. 1, no. 11, l. 7

15 *Felices ter et amplius*
Quos irrupta tenet copula nec malis
Divulsus querimoniis
Suprema citius solvet amor die.

Thrice blessed (and more) are they whom an
unbroken bond holds and whose love, never
strained by nasty quarrels, will not slip until their
dying day.
written above the main entrance to Harvard Yard
> *Odes* bk. 1, no. 13, l. 17

16 *O matre pulchra filia pulchrior.*

Daughter lovelier than your lovely mother.
> *Odes* bk. 1, no. 16, l. 1

17 *Integer vitae scelerisque purus.*

Wholesome of life and free of crimes.
> *Odes* bk. 1, no. 22, l. 1

18 *Dulce ridentem Lalagen amabo,*
Dulce loquentem.

I will go on loving Lalage, who laughs so sweetly
and talks so sweetly.
> *Odes* bk. 1, no. 22, l. 23; see **Catullus** 202:20, **Sappho**
> 666:14

19 *Parcus deorum cultor et infrequens.*

A grudging and irregular worshipper of the gods.
> *Odes* bk. 1, no. 34, l. 1

20 *Nunc est bibendum, nunc pede libero*
Pulsanda tellus.

Now for drinking, now the Earth must shake
beneath a lively foot.
> *Odes* bk. 1, no. 37, l. 1

21 *Persicos odi, puer, apparatus.*

I hate all that Persian gear, boy.
> *Odes* bk. 1, no. 38, l. 1

1 *Mitte sectari rosa quo locorum*
Sera moretur.

Stop looking for the place where a late rose may yet linger.

> *Odes* bk. 1, no. 38, l. 3

2 *Aequam memento rebus in arduis*
Servare mentem.

When the going gets rough, remember to keep calm.

> *Odes* bk. 2, no. 3, l. 1

3 *Omnes eodem cogimur.*

We are all gathered to the same place.

> *Odes* bk. 2, no. 3, l. 25

4 *Auream quisquis mediocritatem*
Diligit.

Whoever loves the golden mean.

> *Odes* bk. 2, no. 10, l. 5

5   *Neque semper arcum*
Tendit Apollo.

Apollo does not always stretch his bow.

> *Odes* bk. 2, no. 10, l. 19

6 *Eheu fugaces, Postume, Postume,*
Labuntur anni.

Ah me, Postumus, Postumus, the fleeting years are slipping by.

> *Odes* bk. 2, no. 14, l. 1; see **Smart** 740:19

7   *Nihil est ab omni*
Parte beatum.

Nothing is an unmixed blessing.

> *Odes* bk. 2, no. 16, l. 27

8 *Credite posteri.*

Believe me, you who come after me!

> *Odes* bk. 2, no. 19, l. 2

9 *Odi profanum vulgus et arceo;*
Favete linguis; carmina non prius
Audita Musarum sacerdos
Virginibus puerisque canto.

I hate the common herd and keep them off. Hush your tongues; as a priest of the Muses, I sing songs never heard before to virgin girls and boys.

> *Odes* bk. 3, no. 1, l. 1; see **Callimachus** 186:2, **Cowley** 245:20

10   *Aequa lege Necessitas*
Sortitur insignis et imos;
Omne capax movet urna nomen.

Necessity with her impartial law picks out by lot both high and humble.
All names are shaken in that capacious urn.

> *Odes* bk. 3, no. 1, l. 14

11 *Post equitem sedet atra Cura.*

Black Care sits behind the horseman.

> *Odes* bk. 3, no. 1, l. 40

12 *Dulce et decorum est pro patria mori.*

Lovely and honourable it is to die for one's country.

> *Odes* bk. 3, no. 2, l. 13; see **Owen** 581:4, **Pound** 608:20

13 *Iustum et tenacem propositi virum*
Non civium ardor prava iubentium,

Non vultus instantis tyranni
Mente quatit solida.

The just man having a firm grasp of his intentions, neither the heated passions of his fellow men ordaining something awful, nor a tyrant staring him in the face, will shake in his convictions.

> *Odes* bk. 3, no. 3, l. 1

14 *Si fractus illabatur orbis,*
Impavidum ferient ruinae.

If the world should break and fall on him, its ruins would strike him unafraid.

> *Odes* bk. 3, no. 3, l. 7; see **Addison** 4:23, **Pope** 602:24

15 *Auditis an me ludit amabilis*
insania?

Do you hear? or does some seductive madness mock me?

> *Odes* bk. 3, no. 4, l. 5

16   *Opaco*
Pelion imposuisse Olympo.

To pile Pelion on top of shady Olympus.

> *Odes* bk. 3, no. 4, l. 52

17 *Vis consili expers mole ruit sua.*

Force, unaided by judgement, collapses through its own weight.

> *Odes* bk. 3, no. 4, l. 65

18 *Dis te minorem quod geris, imperas.*

You rule because you hold yourself inferior to the gods.

> *Odes* bk. 3, no. 6, l. 5

19 *Damnosa quid non imminuit dies?*
Aetas parentum peior avis tulit
Nos nequiores, mox daturos
Progeniem vitiosiorem.

What do the ravages of time not injure? Our parents' age (worse than our grandparents') has produced us, more worthless still, who will soon give rise to a yet more vicious generation.

> *Odes* bk. 3, no. 6, l. 45

20 *Splendide mendax et in omne virgo*
Nobilis aevum.

Gloriously deceitful and a virgin renowned for ever.

> *of the Danaid Hypermestra*
> *Odes* bk. 3, no. 11, l. 35

21 *O fons Bandusiae, splendidior vitro.*

O spring of Bandusia, brighter than glass.

> *Odes* bk. 3, no. 13, l. 1

22 *Magnas inter opes inops.*

A beggar amidst great riches.

> *Odes* bk. 3, no. 16, l. 28

23 *Vixi puellis nuper idoneus*
Et militavi non sine gloria;
Nunc arma defunctumque bello
barbiton hic paries habebit.

Till now I have lived my life without complaints from girls, and campaigned with my share of honours.
Now my armour and my lyre—its wars are over—

will hang on this wall.
Odes bk. 3, no. 26, l. 1

1 *Fumum et opes strepitumque Romae.*

The smoke and wealth and din of Rome.
Odes bk. 3, no. 29, l. 12

2 *Ille potens sui
Laetusque deget, cui licet in diem
Dixisse Vixi: cras vel atra
Nube polum pater occupato
Vel sole puro.*

That man shall live as his own master and in
happiness who can say each day 'I have lived':
tomorrow let the Father fill the sky with a black
cloud or clear sunshine.
Odes bk. 3, no. 29, l. 41; see **Dryden** 289:29

3 *Exegi monumentum aere perennius.*

I have erected a monument more lasting than
bronze.
Odes bk. 3, no. 30, l. 1

4 *Non omnis moriar.*

I shall not altogether die.
Odes bk. 3, no. 30, l. 6

5 *Usque ego postera
Crescam laude recens, dum Capitolium
Scandet cum tacita virgine pontifex.*

My fame will grow,
ever renewed in time to come, as long as
the priest climbs the Capitol with the silent Virgin.
Odes bk. 3, no. 30, l. 7

6 *Non sum qualis eram bonae
Sub regno Cinarae.*

I am not as I was when good Cinara was my
queen.
Odes bk. 4, no. 1, l. 3; see **Dowson** 284:6

7 *Sed cur heu, Ligurine, cur
Manat rara meas lacrima per genas?
Cur facunda parum decoro
Inter verba cadit lingua silentio?
Nocturnis ego somniis
Iam captum teneo iam volucrem sequor
Te per gramina Martii
Campi, te per aquas, dure, volubilis.*

But why, Ligurinus, oh why,
is that tear trickling down my cheek?
Why does my glib tongue
fall shamefully silent as I speak?
At night in my dreams sometimes I catch
and hold you, sometimes I pursue you as you run
over the grass of the Campus Martius
or swim, so hard of heart, the rolling waves.
Odes bk. 4, no. 1, l. 33

8 *Quod spiro et placeo, si placeo, tuum est.*

That I make poetry and give pleasure (if I give
pleasure) are because of you.
Odes bk. 4, no. 3, l. 24

9 *Merses profundo: pulchrior evenit.*

Plunge it in deep water: it comes up more
beautiful.
Odes bk. 4, no. 4, l. 65

10 *Occidit, occidit
Spes omnis et fortuna nostri
Nominis Hasdrubale interempto.*

All our hope is fallen, fallen, and the luck of our
name lost with Hasdrubal.
Odes bk. 4, no. 4, l. 70

11 *Diffugere nives, redeunt iam gramina campis
Arboribusque comae.*

The snows have fled, now grass returns to the
fields and leaves to the trees.
Odes bk. 4, no. 7, l. 1

12 *Immortalia ne speres, monet annus et almum
Quae rapit hora diem.*

The year and the hour which robs us of the fair
day warn us not to hope for things to last for ever.
Odes bk. 4, no. 7, l. 7

13 *Frigora mitescunt Zephyris, ver proterit aestas
Interitura, simul
Pomifer Autumnus fruges effuderit, et mox
Bruma recurrit iners.*

The cold melts in the Zephyrs, Summer tramples
  on the heels
of Spring, and will die the moment
Autumn laden with fruit pours out her crops, and
  soon
sluggish Winter comes running back.
Odes bk. 4, no. 7, l. 9

14 *Damna tamen celeres reparant caelestia lunae;
Nos ubi decidimus
Quo pius Aeneas, quo dives Tullus et Ancus,
Pulvis et umbra sumus.*

Swift moons make good their losses in the sky,
but when we go down to be
with pious Aeneas, wealthy Tullus, and Ancus,
we are dust and shadow.
Odes bk. 4, no. 7, l. 13

15 *Dignum laude virum Musa vetat mori.*

The man worthy of praise the Muse forbids to die.
Odes bk. 4, no. 8, l. 28

16 *Vixere fortes ante Agamemnona
Multi; sed omnes illacrimabiles
Urgentur ignotique longa
Nocte, carent quia vate sacro.*

Many brave men lived before Agamemnon's time;
but they are all, unmourned and unknown,
covered by the long night, because they lack their
sacred poet.
Odes bk. 4, no. 9, l. 25; see **Proverbs** 616:12

17 *Non possidentem multa vocaveris
Recte beatum: rectius occupat
Nomen beati, qui deorum
Muneribus sapienter uti
Duramque callet pauperiem pati
Peiusque leto flagitium timet.*

It is not he who has many possessions that you
should call blessed: he more rightly deserves that
name who knows how to use the gods' gifts wisely
and to endure harsh poverty, and who fears
dishonour more than death.
Odes bk. 4, no. 9, l. 45

1 *Misce stultitiam consiliis brevem:*
Dulce est desipere in loco.

Mix a little foolishness with your prudence: it's good to be silly at the right moment.

Odes bk. 4, no. 12, l. 27

2 *Qui fit, Maecenas, ut nemo, quam sibi sortem*
Seu ratio dederit seu fors obiecerit, illa
Contentus vivat, laudet diversa sequentis?

How is it, Maecenas, that no one lives contented with his lot, whether he has planned it for himself or fate has flung him into it, but yet he praises those who follow different paths?

Satires bk. 1, no. 1, l. 1

3 *Quamquam ridentem dicere verum*
Quid vetat?

Why should truth not be impress'd Beneath the cover of a jest.

Satires bk 1, no. 1, l. 24

4 *. . . Mutato nomine de te*
Fabula narratur.

Change the name and it's about you, that story.

Satires bk. 1, no. 1, l. 69

5 *Est modus in rebus.*

There is moderation in everything.

Satires bk. 1, no. 1, l. 106; see **Proverbs** 626:27, **Proverbs** 632:14

6 *Hoc genus omne.*

All that tribe.

Satires bk. 1, no. 2, l. 2

7 *. . . Ab ovo*
Usque ad mala.

From the egg right through to the apples.

from the start to the finish of a meal

Satires bk. 1, no. 3, l. 6

8 *Etiam disiecti membra poetae.*

Even though broken up, the limbs of a poet.

of **Ennius**

Satires bk. 1, no. 4, l. 62

9 *. . . Ad unguem*
Factus homo.

An accomplished man to his fingertips.

Satires bk. 1, no. 5, l. 32

10 *. . . Credat Iudaeus Apella,*
Non ego.

Let Apella the Jew believe it; I shan't.

Satires bk. 1, no. 5, l. 100

11 *In silvam . . . ligna feras insanius.*

It's insane to carry timber to the forest.

Satires bk. 1, no. 10, l. 34

12 *Solventur risu tabulae, tu missus abibis.*

The case will be dismissed with a laugh. You will get off scot-free.

Satires bk. 2, no. 1, l. 86 (translated by H. R. Fairclough)

13 *Par nobile fratrum.*

A noble pair of brothers.

Satires bk. 2, no. 3, l. 243 (i.e. notorious villains)

14 *Hoc erat in votis: modus agri non ita magnus,*
Hortus ubi et tecto vicinus iugis aquae fons

Et paulum silvae super his foret.

This was among my prayers: a piece of land not so very large, where a garden should be and a spring of ever-flowing water near the house, and a bit of woodland as well as these.

Satires bk. 2, no. 6, l. 1; see **Mallet** 508:16, **Swift** 766:31

15 *O noctes cenaeque deum!*

O nights and feasts divine!

Satires bk. 2, no. 6, l. 65

16 *Responsare cupidinibus, contemnere honores*
Fortis, et in se ipso totus, teres, atque rotundus.

Strong enough to answer back to desires, to despise honours, and a whole man in himself, polished and well-rounded.

Satires bk. 2, no. 7, l. 85

Nick Hornby 1957–

British writer

17 The natural state of the football fan is bitter disappointment, no matter what the score.

Fever Pitch (1992)

Samuel Horsley 1733–1806

English bishop

18 In this country . . . the individual subject . . . 'has nothing to do with the laws but to obey them.'

defending a maxim he had used earlier in committee

speech, House of Lords, 13 November 1795

A. E. Housman 1859–1936

English poet

19 Oh who is that young sinner with the handcuffs on his wrists?
And what has he been after that they groan and shake their fists?
And wherefore is he wearing such a conscience-stricken air?
Oh they're taking him to prison for the colour of his hair.

first drafted in summer 1895, following the trial and imprisonment of Oscar **Wilde**

Collected Poems (1939) 'Additional Poems' no. 18

20 Mud's sister, not himself, adorns my legs.

meaning dust

Fragment of a Greek Tragedy (Bromsgrovian vol. 2, no. 5, 1883)

21 The Grizzly Bear is huge and wild;
He has devoured the infant child.
The infant child is not aware
He has been eaten by the bear.

'Infant Innocence' (1938)

22 And how am I to face the odds
Of man's bedevilment and God's?
I, a stranger and afraid
In a world I never made.

Last Poems (1922) no. 12

23 The candles burn their sockets,
The blinds let through the day,
The young man feels his pockets

And wonders what's to pay.
Last Poems (1922) no. 21

1 These, in the day when heaven was falling,
The hour when earth's foundations fled,
Followed their mercenary calling
And took their wages and are dead.

Their shoulders held the sky suspended;
They stood, and earth's foundations stay;
What God abandoned, these defended,
And saved the sum of things for pay.
Last Poems (1922) no. 37 'Epitaph on an Army of
Mercenaries'

2 For nature, heartless, witless nature,
Will neither care nor know
What stranger's feet may find the meadow
And trespass there and go,
Nor ask amid the dews of morning
If they are mine or no.
Last Poems (1922) no. 40

3 The rainy Pleiads wester,
Orion plunges prone,
The stroke of midnight ceases,
And I lie down alone.
More Poems (1936) no. 11

4 Life, to be sure, is nothing much to lose;
But young men think it is, and we were young.
More Poems (1936) no. 36

5 Good-night. Ensured release
Imperishable peace,
Have these for yours,
While earth's foundations stand
And sky and sea and land
And heaven endures.
More Poems (1936) no. 48 'Alta Quies'

6 Loveliest of trees, the cherry now
Is hung with bloom along the bough,
And stands about the woodland ride
Wearing white for Eastertide.
A Shropshire Lad (1896) no. 2

7 And since to look at things in bloom
Fifty springs are little room,
About the woodlands I will go
To see the cherry hung with snow.
A Shropshire Lad (1896) no. 2

8 Clay lies still, but blood's a rover;
Breath's a ware that will not keep.
Up, lad: when the journey's over
There'll be time enough to sleep.
A Shropshire Lad (1896) no. 4

9 And naked to the hangman's noose
The morning clocks will ring
A neck God made for other use
Than strangling in a string.
A Shropshire Lad (1896) no. 9

10 When I was one-and-twenty
I heard a wise man say,
'Give crowns and pounds and guineas
But not your heart away;
Give pearls away and rubies,
But keep your fancy free.'
But I was one-and-twenty,

No use to talk to me.
A Shropshire Lad (1896) no. 13

11 In summertime on Bredon
The bells they sound so clear;
Round both the shires they ring them
In steeples far and near,
A happy noise to hear.

Here of a Sunday morning
My love and I would lie,
And see the coloured counties,
And hear the larks so high
About us in the sky.
A Shropshire Lad (1896) no. 21

12 The lads in their hundreds to Ludlow come in for
the fair,
There's men from the barn and the forge and the
mill and the fold,
The lads for the girls and the lads for the liquor are
there,
And there with the rest are the lads that will never
be old.
A Shropshire Lad (1896) no. 23

13 On Wenlock Edge the wood's in trouble;
His forest fleece the Wrekin heaves;
The wind it plies the saplings double,
And thick on Severn snow the leaves.
A Shropshire Lad (1896) no. 31

14 The gale, it plies the saplings double,
It blows so hard, 'twill soon be gone:
To-day the Roman and his trouble
Are ashes under Uricon.
A Shropshire Lad (1896) no. 31

15 From far, from eve and morning
And yon twelve-winded sky,
The stuff of life to knit me
Blew hither: here am I.
A Shropshire Lad (1896) no. 32

16 Into my heart an air that kills
From yon far country blows:
What are those blue remembered hills,
What spires, what farms are those?

That is the land of lost content,
I see it shining plain,
The happy highways where I went
And cannot come again.
A Shropshire Lad (1896) no. 40

17 And bound for the same bourn as I,
On every road I wandered by,
Trod beside me, close and dear,
The beautiful and death-struck year.
A Shropshire Lad (1896) no. 41

18 Shot? so quick, so clean an ending?
Oh that was right, lad, that was brave.
A Shropshire Lad (1896) no. 44

19 Oh soon, and better so than later
After long disgrace and scorn,
You shot dead the household traitor,
The soul that should not have been born.
A Shropshire Lad (1896) no. 44

20 Clunton and Clunbury,
Clungunford and Clun,

Are the quietest places
Under the sun.
A Shropshire Lad (1896) no. 50 (epigraph)

1 By brooks too broad for leaping
The lightfoot boys are laid;
The rose-lipt girls are sleeping
In fields where roses fade.
A Shropshire Lad (1896) no. 54

2 Say, for what were hop-yards meant,
Or why was Burton built on Trent?
Oh many a peer of England brews
Livelier liquor than the Muse,
And malt does more than Milton can
To justify God's ways to man.
Ale, man, ale's the stuff to drink
For fellows whom it hurts to think.
A Shropshire Lad (1896) no. 62; see **Milton** 531:6

3 I tell the tale that I heard told.
Mithridates, he died old.
A Shropshire Lad (1896) no. 62

4 Three minutes' thought would suffice to find this
out; but thought is irksome and three minutes is a
long time.
D. Iunii Iuvenalis Saturae (1905) preface

5 A year or two ago . . . I received from America a
request that I would define poetry. I replied that I
could no more define poetry than a terrier can
define a rat, but that I thought we both recognized
the object by the symptoms which it provokes in
us.
The Name and Nature of Poetry (1933)

6 Cambridge has seen many strange sights. It has
seen Wordsworth drunk and Porson sober. It is
now destined to see a better scholar than
Wordsworth and a better poet than Porson
betwixt and between.
speech at University College, London, 29 March 1911, in
R. W. Chambers *Man's Unconquerable Mind* (1939)

Samuel Houston 1793–1863
American politician and military leader

7 The North is determined to preserve this Union.
They are not a fiery, impulsive people as you are,
for they live in colder climates. But when they
begin to move in a given direction . . . they move
with the steady momentum and perseverance of a
mighty avalanche.
*in 1861, warning the people of Texas against
secession*
Geoffrey C. Ward *The Civil War* (1991) ch. 1

John Howard 1939–
Australian statesman; Prime Minister since 1996

8 I want people to reflect on the loss of life. I want
them to reflect on what it means in terms of the
loss of innocence . . . in relation to this country's
dealings with different parts of the world.
on the Bali bombing, 12 October 2002
interview on Australian television (Channel Ten News), 14
October 2002

9 I have said since September 11 last year that you
can't rule out the possibility of a terror attack of
this sort in Australia. Because of the nature of our
society, I believe it is less likely than in many other
parts of the world. But I cannot guarantee that it
won't happen. I can't.
in *The Age* (electronic edition) 19 October 2002

Michael Howard 1941–
British politician, Leader of the Conservative Party from 2003
*on Howard: see **Widdecombe** 834:12; see also **Paxman**
589:8*

10 I am happy to debate the past with the Prime
Minister any day he likes. I have a big dossier on
his past, and I did not even have to sex it up.
at Prime Minister's Questions in the House of Commons,
12 November 2003

Geoffrey Howe 1926–
British Conservative politician
*on Howe: see **Healey** 377:11*

11 It is rather like sending your opening batsmen to
the crease only for them to find the moment that
the first balls are bowled that their bats have been
broken before the game by the team captain.
*on the difficulties caused him as Foreign Secretary by
Margaret **Thatcher**'s anti-European views*
resignation speech as Deputy Prime Minister, in the House
of Commons, 13 November 1990

12 The time has come for others to consider their
own response to the tragic conflict of loyalties with
which I have myself wrestled for perhaps too long.
resignation speech
in the House of Commons, 13 November 1990

Gordie Howe 1928–
Canadian ice-hockey player

13 All pro athletes are bilingual. They speak English
and profanity.
in *Toronto Star* 27 May 1975

Joseph Howe 1804–73
Canadian journalist and politician

14 Yes, gentlemen, come what will, while I live,
Nova Scotia shall have the blessing of an open and
unshackled press.
*spoken at his trial in Halifax, Nova Scotia, for
publishing, in the* Novascotian *newspaper, a libellous
editorial on corruption in government*
'Address to the Jury' May 1835

Julia Ward Howe 1819–1910
American Unitarian lay preacher

15 Mine eyes have seen the glory of the coming of the
Lord:
He is trampling out the vintage where the grapes
of wrath are stored;
He hath loosed the fateful lightning of his terrible
swift sword:
His truth is marching on.
'Battle Hymn of the Republic' (1862)

James Howell c.1594–1666
Welsh-born English man of letters

1 Some hold translations not unlike to be
The wrong side of a Turkey tapestry.
Familiar Letters (1645–55) bk. 1, no. 6

2 One hair of a woman can draw more than a
hundred pair of oxen.
Familiar Letters (1645–55) bk. 2, no. 4; see **Proverbs** 615:3

3 The Netherlands have been for many years, as one
may say, the very cockpit of Christendom.
Instructions for Foreign Travel (1642)

Frankie Howerd (Francis Alex Howard)
1922–92
British comedian

4 Such cruel glasses.
of Robin **Day**
in *That Was The Week That Was* (BBC television series, from
1963)

Mary Howitt 1799–1888
English writer for children

5 Buttercups and daisies,
Oh, the pretty flowers;
Coming ere the springtime,
To tell of sunny hours.
'Buttercups and Daisies' (1838)

6 'Will you walk into my parlour?' said a spider to a
fly:
''Tis the prettiest little parlour that ever you did
spy.'
'The Spider and the Fly' (1834)

Edmond Hoyle 1672–1769
English writer on card-games

7 When in doubt, win the trick.
Hoyle's Games Improved (ed. Charles Jones, 1790) 'Twenty-
four Short Rules for Learners'; though attributed to Hoyle,
this may well have been an editorial addition by Jones,
since it is not found in earlier editions

Fred Hoyle 1915–2001
English astrophysicist

8 Space isn't remote at all. It's only an hour's drive
away if your car could go straight upwards.
in *Observer* 9 September 1979 'Sayings of the Week'

9 There is a coherent plan to the universe, though I
don't know what it's a plan for.
attributed

Elbert Hubbard 1859–1915
American writer
see also **Emerson** 307:18

10 Never explain—your friends do not need it and
your enemies will not believe you anyway.
The Motto Book (1907); see **Wodehouse** 843:2

11 Life is just one damned thing after another.
Philistine December 1909; often attributed to Frank Ward
O'Malley

12 Editor: a person employed by a newspaper, whose
business it is to separate the wheat from the chaff,
and to see that the chaff is printed.
The Roycroft Dictionary (1914)

Frank McKinney ('Kin') Hubbard
1868–1930
American humorist

13 Classic music is th'kind that we keep thinkin'll
turn into a tune.
Comments of Abe Martin and His Neighbors (1923)

14 It's no disgrace t'be poor, but it might as well be.
Short Furrows (1911)

Howard Hughes Jr. 1905–76
American industrialist, aviator, and film producer

15 That man's ears make him look like a taxi-cab
with both doors open.
of Clark Gable
Charles Higham and Joel Greenberg *Celluloid Muse* (1969)

Jimmy Hughes and Frank Lake

16 You'll get no promotion this side of the ocean,
So cheer up, my lads, Bless 'em all!
Bless 'em all! Bless 'em all! The long and the short
and the tall.
'Bless 'Em All' (1940 song)

Langston Hughes 1902–67
American writer and poet

17 I, too, sing America.
I am the darker brother.
They send me to eat in the kitchen
When company comes.
But I laugh,
And eat well,
And grow strong.
Tomorrow
I'll sit at the table
When company comes
Nobody'll dare
Say to me,
'Eat in the kitchen'
Then.
Besides, they'll see how
beautiful I am
And be ashamed,—
I, too, am America.
'I, Too' in *Survey Graphic* March 1925

18 I've known rivers:
I've known rivers ancient as the world and older
than the flow of human blood in human veins.
'The Negro Speaks of Rivers' (1921)

19 I bathed in the Euphrates when dawns were
young.
I built my hut near the Congo and it lulled me to
sleep.
I looked upon the Nile and raised the pyramids
above it.

I heard the singing of the Mississippi when Abe
  Lincoln went down to New Orleans, and I've
  seen its muddy bosom turn all golden in the
  sunset.
  'The Negro Speaks of Rivers' (1921)

1 'It's powerful,' he said.
  'What?'
  'That one drop of Negro blood—because just *one*
  drop of black blood makes a man coloured. *One*
  drop—you are a Negro!'
  Simple Takes a Wife (1953)

2 I got the Weary Blues
  And I can't be satisfied.
  'Weary Blues' (1926)

Robert Hughes 1938–
Australian writer

3 What the convict system bequeathed to later
  Australian generations was not the sturdy,
  skeptical independence . . . but an intense concern
  with social and political respectability. The idea of
  the 'convict stain', a moral blot soaked into our
  fabric, dominated all argument about Australian
  selfhood by the 1840s.
  The Fatal Shore (1987) introduction

Ted Hughes 1930–98
English poet
*on Hughes: see **Heaney** 378:8*

4 Daylong this tomcat lies stretched flat
  As an old rough mat, no mouth and no eyes,
  Continual wars and wives are what
  Have tattered his ears and battered his head.
  'Esther's Tomcat' (1960)

5 It took the whole of Creation
  To produce my foot, my each feather:
  Now I hold Creation in my foot.
  'Hawk Roosting' (1960)

6 Fourteen centuries have learned,
  From charred remains, that what took place
  When Alexandria's library burned
  Brain-damaged the human race.
  'Hear it Again' (1997)

7   I saw the horses:
  Huge in the dense grey—ten together—
  Megalith-still. They breathed, making no move,
  With draped manes and tilted hind-hooves,
  Making no sound.
  I passed: not one snorted or jerked its head.
  Grey silent fragments
  Of a grey silent world.
  'The Horses' (1957)

8 . . . With a sudden sharp hot stink of fox,
  It enters the dark hole of the head.
  'The Thought-Fox' (1957)

9 Ten years after your death
  I meet on a page of your journal, as never before,
  The shock of your joy.
  'Visit' (1998)

10 Grape is my mulatto mother
  In this frozen whited country.
  'Wino' (1967)

Thomas Hughes 1822–96
English lawyer, politician, and writer

11 Tom and his younger brothers as they grew up,
  went on playing with the village boys without the
  idea of equality or inequality (except in wrestling,
  running, and climbing) ever entering their heads,
  as it doesn't till it's put there by Jack Nastys or fine
  ladies' maids.
  Tom Brown's Schooldays (1857) pt. 1, ch. 3

12 'I don't care a straw for Greek particles, or the
  digamma, no more does his mother. What is he
  sent to school for? . . . If he'll only turn out a
  brave, helpful, truth-telling Englishman, and a
  gentleman, and a Christian, that's all I want,'
  thought the Squire.
  Tom Brown's Schooldays (1857) pt. 1, ch. 4

13 He never wants anything but what's right and
  fair; only when you come to settle what's right
  and fair, it's everything that he wants and
  nothing that you want. And that's his idea of a
  compromise. Give me the Brown compromise
  when I'm on his side.
  Tom Brown's Schooldays (1857) pt. 2, ch. 2

14 It's more than a game. It's an institution.
  of cricket
  Tom Brown's Schooldays (1857) pt. 2, ch. 7

Victor Hugo 1802–85
French poet, novelist, and dramatist
*on Hugo: see **Cocteau** 230:3, **Gide** 346:17*

15 *Le mot, c'est le Verbe, et le Verbe, c'est Dieu.*
  The word is the Verb, and the Verb is God.
  Contemplations (1856) bk. 1, no. 8

16 *Souffrons, mais souffrons sur les cimes.*
  If suffer we must, let's suffer on the heights.
  Contemplations (1856) bk. 5, no. 26 'Les Malheureux'

17 *On résiste à l'invasion des armées; on ne résiste pas à
  l'invasion des idées.*
  A stand can be made against invasion by an
  army; no stand can be made against invasion by
  an idea.
  Histoire d'un Crime (written 1851–2, published 1877) pt. 5,
  sect. 10; see **Sayings** 670:14

18 *La symétrie, c'est l'ennui, et l'ennui est le fond même
  du deuil. Le désespoir bâille.*
  Symmetry is tedious, and tedium is the very basis
  of mourning. Despair yawns.
  Les Misérables (1862) vol. 2, bk. 4, ch. 1

19 *Ôtez* Time is money, *que reste-t-il de l'Angleterre?
  ôtez* Cotton is king, *que reste-t-il d l'Amerique?*
  Take away *time is money*, and what is left of
  England? take away *cotton is king*, and what is left
  of America?
  Les Misérables (1862) 'Marius' bk. 4 ch. 4

1 Étourdir de grelots l'esprit qui veut penser.
  To daze with little bells the spirit that would think.
  Le Roi s'amuse (1833) act 2, sc. 2

2 Jésus a pleuré, Voltaire a souri; c'est de cette larme
  divine et de ce sourire humain qu'est faite la douceur
  de la civilisation actuelle. (Applaudissements
  prolongés.)
  Jesus wept; Voltaire smiled. Of that divine tear and
  of that human smile the sweetness of present
  civilisation is composed. (*Hearty applause.*)
  transcript of centenary oration on **Voltaire**, 30 May 1878,
  Centenaire de Voltaire (1878); see **Bible** 103:22

Hui-neng 638–713

Chinese philosopher, 6th Zen Patriarch
textual translations are those of Wong Mou-Lam, 1969

3 There is no Bodhi-tree,
  Nor stand of mirror bright.
  Since all is void,
  Where can the dust alight?
  Platform Scripture ch. 1

4 When you are thinking of neither good nor evil,
  what is at that particular moment, Venerable Sir,
  your real nature [original face]?
  Platform Scripture ch. 1

5 When a pennant was blown about by the wind,
  two Bhikkus [monks] entered into a dispute as to
  what it was that was in motion, the wind or the
  pennant. As they could not settle their difference I
  submitted to them that it was neither, and that
  what actually moved was their own mind.
  Platform Scripture ch. 1

6 Should we be so fortunate as to be followers of the
  Sudden School in this life,
  In a sudden we shall see the Bhagavat of our
  Essence of Mind.
  He who seeks the Buddha [from without] by
  practising certain doctrines
  Knows not where the real Buddha is to be found.
  He who is able to realize the Truth within his own
  mind
  Has sown the seed of Buddhahood.
  Platform Scripture ch. 1

Basil Hume 1923–99

English cardinal

7 It is harder for some people to believe that God
  loves them than to believe that he exists.
  in *Guardian* 18 June 1999

David Hume 1711–76

Scottish philosopher
on Hume: see **Smith** 743:10

8 Custom, then, is the great guide of human life.
  An Enquiry Concerning Human Understanding (1748) sect. 5,
  pt. 1

9 If we take in our hand any volume; of divinity or
  school metaphysics, for instance; let us ask, *Does it
  contain any abstract reasoning concerning quantity or
  number? No. Does it contain any experimental*

reasoning, concerning matter of fact and existence?
No. Commit it then to the flames: for it can
contain nothing but sophistry and illusion.
  An Enquiry Concerning Human Understanding (1748) sect.
  12, pt. 3

10 We soon learn that there is nothing mysterious or
  supernatural in the case, but that all proceeds
  from the usual propensity of mankind towards the
  marvellous, and that, though this inclination may
  at intervals receive a check from sense and
  learning, it can never be thoroughly extirpated
  from human nature.
  An Enquiry Concerning Human Understanding (1748) 'Of
  Miracles' pt. 2

11 The Christian religion not only was at first
  attended with miracles, but even at this day
  cannot be believed by any reasonable person
  without one. Mere reason is insufficient to
  convince us of its veracity: and whoever is moved
  by faith to assent to it, is conscious of a continued
  miracle in his own person, which subverts all the
  principles of his understanding, and gives him a
  determination to believe what is most contrary to
  custom and experience.
  An Enquiry Concerning Human Understanding (1748) 'Of
  Miracles' pt. 2

12 Avarice, the spur of industry, is so obstinate a
  passion, and works its way through so many real
  dangers and difficulties, that it is not likely to be
  scared by an imaginary danger, which is so small
  that it scarcely admits of calculation.
  Essays: Moral and Political (1741–2) 'Of Civil Liberty'

13 Money . . . is none of the wheels of trade: it is the
  oil which renders the motion of the wheels more
  smooth and easy.
  Essays: Moral and Political (1741–2) 'Of Money'

14 How many frivolous quarrels and disgusts are
  there, which people of common prudence
  endeavour to forget, when they lie under the
  necessity of passing their lives together; but which
  would soon inflame into the most deadly hatred,
  were they pursued to the utmost, under the
  prospect of an easy separation?
  Essays: Moral and Political (1741–2) 'Of Polygamy and
  Divorces'

15 A little miss, dressed in a new gown for a dancing-
  school ball, receives as complete enjoyment as the
  greatest orator, who triumphs in the splendour of
  his eloquence, while he governs the passions and
  resolutions of a numerous assembly.
  Essays: Moral and Political (1741–2) 'The Sceptic'

16 Should it be said, that, by living under the
  dominion of a prince, which one might leave,
  every individual has given a tacit assent to his
  authority . . . We may as well assert, that a man
  by remaining in a vessel, freely consents to the
  dominion of the master; though he was carried on
  board while asleep, and must leap into the ocean,
  and perish, the moment he leaves her.
  Essays, Moral, Political, and Literary (ed. T. H. Green and T.
  H. Grose, 1875) 'Of the Original Contract' (1748)

1 In all ages of the world, priests have been enemies of liberty.

> *Essays, Moral, Political, and Literary* (ed. T. H. Green and T. H. Grose, 1875) 'Of the Parties of Great Britain' (1741–2)

2 The heart of man is made to reconcile the most glaring contradictions.

> *Essays, Moral, Political, and Literary* (ed. T. H. Green and T. H. Grose, 1875) 'Of the Parties of Great Britain' (1741–2)

3 In all matters of opinion and science . . . the difference between men is . . . oftener found to lie in generals than in particulars; and to be less in reality than in appearance. An explanation of the terms commonly ends the controversy, and the disputants are surprised to find that they had been quarrelling, while at bottom they agreed in their judgement.

> *Essays, Moral, Political, and Literary* (ed. T. H. Green and T. H. Grose, 1875) 'Of the Standard of Taste' (1757)

4 Beauty is no quality in things themselves. It exists merely in the mind which contemplates them.

> *Essays, Moral, Political, and Literary* (ed. T. H. Green and T. H. Grose, 1875) 'Of the Standard of Taste' (1757)

5 Opposing one species of superstition to another, set them a quarrelling; while we ourselves, during their fury and contention, happily make our escape into the calm, though obscure, regions of philosophy.

> *Four Dissertations* (1757) 'The Natural History of Religion' sect. 15

6 Never literary attempt was more unfortunate than my Treatise of Human Nature. It fell *dead-born from the press.*

> *My Own Life* (1777) ch. 1

7 It is a just political maxim, that every man must be supposed a knave.

> *Political Discourses* (1751) essay 6

8 Poets . . . though liars by profession, always endeavour to give an air of truth to their fictions.

> *A Treatise upon Human Nature* (1739) bk. 1, pt. 3

9 Reason is, and ought only to be the slave of the passions, and can never pretend to any other office than to serve and obey them.

> *A Treatise upon Human Nature* (1739) bk. 2, pt. 3

10 It is not contrary to reason to prefer the destruction of the whole world to the scratching of my finger.

> *A Treatise upon Human Nature* (1739) bk. 2, pt. 3

11 In every system of morality, which I have hitherto met with, I have always remarked, that the author proceeds for some time in the ordinary way of reasoning, and establishes the being of a god, or makes observations concerning human affairs; when of a sudden I am surprized to find that instead of the usual copulations of proposition, *is* and *is not*, I meet with no proposition that is not connected with an *ought* or an *ought not*. This change is imperceptible; but it is, however, of the last consequence.

> *A Treatise upon Human Nature* (1739) bk. 3, pt. 1

Hubert Humphrey 1911–78
American Democratic politician

12 Here we are the way politics ought to be in America, the politics of happiness, the politics of purpose and the politics of joy.

> speech in Washington, 27 April 1968, in *New York Times* 28 April 1968

G. W. Hunt c.1829–1904
English composer of music-hall songs

13 We don't want to fight, but, by jingo if we do,
We've got the ships, we've got the men, we've got the money too.
We've fought the Bear before, and while Britons shall be true,
The Russians shall not have Constantinople.

> 'We Don't Want to Fight' (1878 music hall song)

Leigh Hunt 1784–1859
English poet and essayist
on Hunt: see **Shelley** 729:21

14 Abou Ben Adhem (may his tribe increase!)
Awoke one night from a deep dream of peace,
And saw, within the moonlight in his room,
Making it rich, and like a lily in bloom,
An angel writing in a book of gold:—
Exceeding peace had made Ben Adhem bold,
And to the presence in the room he said,
'What writest thou?'—The vision raised its head,
And with a look made of all sweet accord,
Answered, 'The names of those who love the Lord.'

> 'Abou Ben Adhem' (1838)

15 Write me as one that loves his fellow-men.

> 'Abou Ben Adhem' (1838)

16 You strange, astonished-looking, angle-faced,
Dreary-mouthed, gaping wretches of the sea.

> 'The Fish, the Man, and the Spirit' (1836)

17 The laughing queen that caught the world's great hands.

> *referring to Cleopatra*
> 'The Nile' (1818)

18 Jenny kissed me when we met,
Jumping from the chair she sat in;
Time, you thief, who love to get
Sweets into your list, put that in:
Say I'm weary, say I'm sad,
Say that health and wealth have missed me,
Say I'm growing old, but add,
Jenny kissed me.

> 'Rondeau' (1838)

19 Stolen sweets are always sweeter,
Stolen kisses much completer,
Stolen looks are nice in chapels,
Stolen, stolen, be your apples.

> 'Song of Fairies Robbing an Orchard' (1830)

20 The two divinest things this world has got,
A lovely woman in a rural spot!

> 'The Story of Rimini' (1816) canto 3, l. 257

1 His forehead was prodigious—a great piece of placid marble; and his fine eyes, in which all the activity of his mind seemed to concentrate, moved under it with a sprightly ease, as if it was pastime to them to carry all that thought.

of **Coleridge**

Autobiography (1850) ch. 16

2 It is the entire man that writes and thinks, and not merely the head. His leg has often as much to do with it as his head—the state of his calves, his vitals and his nerves.

Stories in Verse (1855) preface

3 Poetry, in the most comprehensive application of the term, I take to be the flower of any kind of experience, rooted in truth, and issuing forth into beauty.

The Story of Rimini (1832 ed.) preface

4 The pretension is nothing; the performance every thing. A good apple is better than an insipid peach.

The Story of Rimini (1832 ed.) preface

5 A mere gossiping entertainment: a few child's squalls, a few mumbled amens, and a few mumbled cakes, and a few smirks accompanied by a few fees.

on the christening of his godson

letter to Marianne Kent, February 1806; in T. L. Hunt *Correspondence of Leigh Hunt* (1862) vol. 1

6 Never lay yourself open to what is called conviction: you might as well open your waist-coat to receive a knock-down blow.

in *The Examiner* 6 March 1808 'Rules for the Conduct of Newspaper Editors'

7 A playful moderation in politics is just as absurd as a remonstrative whisper to a mob.

in *The Examiner* 6 March 1808 'Rules for the Conduct of Newspaper Editors'

8 This Adonis in loveliness was a corpulent man of fifty.

of the Prince Regent, later **George IV**

in *The Examiner* 22 March 1812

9 A pleasure so exquisite as almost to amount to pain.

on receiving 'a glorious batch of Examiners'

letter to Alexander Ireland, 2 June 1848, in T. L. Hunt *Correspondence of Leigh Hunt* (1862) vol. 2

Anne Hunter 1742–1821
Scottish poet

10 My mother bids me bind my hair
With bands of rosy hue,
Tie up my sleeves with ribbons rare,
And lace my bodice blue.

'A Pastoral Song' (1794)

Robert Hunter 1941–
Canadian writer

11 The word *Greenpeace* had a ring to it—it conjured images of Eden; it said ecology and antiwar in two syllables; it fit easily into even a one-column headline.

Warriors of the Rainbow (1979); see **Darnell** 256:18

William Hunter 1718–83
Scottish obstetrician

12 Some physiologists will have it that the stomach is a mill;—others, that it is a fermenting vat;—others again that it is a stew-pan;—but in my view of the matter, it is neither a mill, a fermenting vat, nor a stew-pan—but a *stomach,* gentlemen, a *stomach.*

MS note from his lectures, in J. A. Paris *A Treatise on Diet* (1824) epigraph

Herman Hupfeld 1894–1951
American songwriter

13 You must remember this, a kiss is still a kiss,
A sigh is just a sigh;
The fundamental things apply,
As time goes by.

'As Time Goes By' (1931 song); see **Misquotations** 538:13

Zora Neale Hurston c.1901–60
American writer

14 I do not weep at the world—I am too busy sharpening my oyster knife.

How It Feels to Be Colored Me (1928)

John Huss c.1372–1415
Bohemian preacher and reformer

15 *O sancta simplicitas!*
O holy simplicity!

at the stake, seeing an aged peasant bringing a bundle of twigs to throw on the pile

J. W. Zincgreff and J. L. Weidner *Apophthegmata* (Amsterdam, 1653) pt. 3; see **Jerome** 421:5

Saddam Hussein 1937–
Iraqi statesman; President 1979–2003

16 The mother of battles.

popular interpretation of his description of the approaching Gulf War; in The Times *7 January 1991 it was reported that he had no intention of relinquishing Kuwait and was ready for the 'mother of all wars'*

speech in Baghdad, 6 January 1991

17 Baghdad is determined to force the Mongols of our age to commit suicide at its gates.

in *Independent* 18 January 2003

Francis Hutcheson 1694–1746
Scottish philosopher

18 Wisdom denotes the pursuing of the best ends by the best means.

An Inquiry into the Original of our Ideas of Beauty and Virtue (1725) Treatise 1, sect. 5, subsect. 16

19 That action is best, which procures the greatest happiness for the greatest numbers.

An Inquiry into the Original of our Ideas of Beauty and Virtue (1725) Treatise 2, sect. 3, subsect. 8; see **Bentham** 68:5

Lord Hutton 1931-

British judge, Lord Chief Justice for Northern Ireland

1 I make it clear that it will be for me to decide as I think right within my terms of reference the matters which will be the subject of my investigation.

statement on the terms of the inquiry into the death of Dr David **Kelly**, 21 July 2003

Aldous Huxley 1894–1963

English novelist
see also **Borrowed titles** *146:2*

2 There are few who would not rather be taken in adultery than in provincialism.

Antic Hay (1923) ch. 10

3 Official dignity tends to increase in inverse ratio to the importance of the country in which the office is held.

Beyond the Mexique Bay (1934)

4 The proper study of mankind is books.

Crome Yellow (1921) ch. 28; see **Pope** 604:32

5 Too much consistency is as bad for the mind as it is for the body. Consistency is contrary to nature, contrary to life. The only completely consistent people are the dead.

Do What You Will (1929) 'Wordsworth in the Tropics'

6 The end cannot justify the means, for the simple and obvious reason that the means employed determine the nature of the ends produced.

Ends and Means (1937) ch. 1

7 So long as men worship the Caesars and Napoleons, Caesars and Napoleons will duly arise and make them miserable.

Ends and Means (1937) ch. 8

8 Chastity—the most unnatural of all the sexual perversions.

Eyeless in Gaza (1936) ch. 27

9 Several excuses are always less convincing than one.

Point Counter Point (1928) ch. 1

10 A million million spermatozoa,
All of them alive:
Out of their cataclysm but one poor Noah
Dare hope to survive.

And among that billion minus one
Might have chanced to be
Shakespeare, another Newton, a new Donne—
But the One was Me.

'Fifth Philosopher's Song' (1920)

11 Beauty for some provides escape,
Who gain a happiness in eyeing
The gorgeous buttocks of the ape
Or Autumn sunsets exquisitely dying.

'Ninth Philosopher's Song' (1920)

Julian Huxley 1887–1975

English biologist

12 Operationally, God is beginning to resemble not a ruler but the last fading smile of a cosmic Cheshire cat.

Religion without Revelation (1957 ed.) ch. 3; see **Carroll** 194:8

T. H. Huxley 1825–95

English biologist

13 Most of my colleagues [in the Metaphysical Society] were -*ists* of one sort or another; and, however kind and friendly they might be, I, the man without a rag of a label to cover himself with, could not fail to have some of the uneasy feelings which must have beset the historical fox when, after leaving the trap in which his tail remained, he presented himself to his normally elongated companions. So I took thought, and invented what I conceived to be the appropriate title of 'agnostic'.

Collected Essays (1893–4) 'Agnosticism'

14 The great tragedy of Science—the slaying of a beautiful hypothesis by an ugly fact.

Collected Essays (1893–4) 'Biogenesis and Abiogenesis'

15 Science is nothing but trained and organized common sense, differing from the latter only as a veteran may differ from a raw recruit: and its methods differ from those of common sense only as far as the guardsman's cut and thrust differ from the manner in which a savage wields his club.

Collected Essays (1893–4) 'The Method of Zadig'

16 If some great Power would agree to make me always think what is true and do what is right, on condition of being turned into a sort of clock and wound up every morning before I got out of bed, I should instantly close with the offer.

Collected Essays (1893–4) 'On Descartes' *Discourse on Method*' (written 1870)

17 If a little knowledge is dangerous, where is the man who has so much as to be out of danger?

Collected Essays vol. 3 (1895) 'On Elementary Instruction in Physiology' (written 1877)

18 The chessboard is the world; the pieces are the phenomena of the universe; the rules of the game are what we call the laws of Nature. The player on the other side is hidden from us. We know that his play is always fair, just, and patient. But also we know, to our cost, that he never overlooks a mistake, or makes the smallest allowance for ignorance.

Lay Sermons, Addresses, and Reviews (1870) 'A Liberal Education'

19 The necessity of making things plain to uninstructed people was one of the very best means of clearing up the obscure corners in one's own mind.

Man's Place in Nature (1894 ed.) preface

1 It is the customary fate of new truths to begin as heresies and to end as superstitions.

Science and Culture and Other Essays (1881) 'The Coming of Age of the Origin of Species'

2 Irrationally held truths may be more harmful than reasoned errors.

Science and Culture and Other Essays (1881) 'The Coming of Age of the Origin of Species'

3 Logical consequences are the scarecrows of fools and the beacons of wise men.

Science and Culture and Other Essays (1881) 'On the Hypothesis that Animals are Automata'

4 I asserted—and I repeat—that a man has no reason to be ashamed of having an ape for his grandfather. If there were an ancestor whom I should feel shame in recalling it would rather be a *man*—a man of restless and versatile intellect—who, not content with an equivocal success in his own sphere of activity, plunges into scientific questions with which he has no real acquaintance, only to obscure them by an aimless rhetoric, and distract the attention of his hearers from the real point at issue by eloquent digressions and skilled appeals to religious prejudice.

replying to Bishop Samuel **Wilberforce** *in the debate on* **Darwin**'s *theory of evolution; see* **Wilberforce** *835:1*

meeting of the British Association in Oxford, 30 June 1860; letter from J. R. Green to Professor Boyd Dawkins in Leonard Huxley (ed.) *Life and Letters of Thomas Henry Huxley* (1900)

5 I am too much of a sceptic to deny the possibility of anything.

letter to Herbert Spencer, 22 March 1886, in Leonard Huxley *Life and Letters of Thomas Henry Huxley* (1900) vol. 2, ch. 8

Edward Hyde see Earl of Clarendon

Lee Iacocca 1924–

American businessman

6 In times of stress and adversity, it's always best to keep busy, to plow your anger and your energy into something positive.

referring to financial crisis at Chrysler Corporation 1979

Iacocca: An Autobiography (with William Novak, 1986)

Dolores Ibarruri ('La Pasionaria') 1895–1989

Spanish Communist leader

7 *Il vaut mieux mourir debout que de vivre à genoux!*
It is better to die on your feet than to live on your knees.

also attributed to Emiliano **Zapata**

speech in Paris, 3 September 1936, in *L'Humanité* 4 September 1936

8 *No pasarán.*
They shall not pass.

radio broadcast, Madrid, 19 July 1936, in *Speeches and Articles 1936–38* (1938); see **Military sayings** 526:11

Henrik Ibsen 1828–1906

Norwegian dramatist

9 The worst enemy of truth and freedom in our society is the compact majority. Yes, the damned, compact, liberal majority.

An Enemy of the People (1882) act 4

10 The majority never has right on its side.

An Enemy of the People (1882) act 4; see **Dillon** 274:12

11 You should never have your best trousers on when you go out to fight for freedom and truth.

An Enemy of the People (1882) act 5

12 Mother, give me the sun.

Ghosts (1881) act 3

13 But good God, people don't do such things!

Hedda Gabler (1890) act 4

14 Castles in the air—they are so easy to take refuge in. And easy to build, too.

The Master Builder (1892) act 3

15 What ought a man to be? Well, my short answer is 'himself'.

Peer Gynt (1867) act 4

16 Take the life-lie away from the average man and straight away you take away his happiness.

The Wild Duck (1884) act 5

Ice-T 1958–

American rap musician

17 Passion makes the world go round. Love just makes it a safer place.

The Ice Opinion (as told to Heidi Sigmund, 1994) ch. 4

St Ignatius Loyola 1491–1556

Spanish theologian, founder of the Jesuits

18 Teach us, good Lord, to serve Thee as Thou deservest:
To give and not to count the cost;
To fight and not to heed the wounds;
To toil and not to seek for rest;
To labour and not to ask for any reward
Save that of knowing that we do Thy will.

'Prayer for Generosity' (1548)

I-Hsüan d. 867

Chinese monk and Zen master

19 Seekers of the Way. In Buddhism no effort is necessary. All one has to do is to do nothing except to move his bowels, urinate, put on his clothing, eat his meals, and lie down if he is tired. The stupid will laugh at him, but the wise will understand.

Recorded Conversations of Zen Master I-Hsüan v. 5

20 Kill anything that you happen on. Kill the Buddha if you happen to meet him . . . Kill your parents or

relatives if you happen to meet them. Only then can you be free, not bound by material things, and absolutely free and at ease.
Recorded Conversations of Zen Master I-Hsüan v. 6

Francis Iles see **Opening lines** 574:26

Ivan Illich 1926–
American sociologist

1 In a consumer society there are inevitably two kinds of slaves: the prisoners of addiction and the prisoners of envy.
Tools for Conviviality (1973) ch. 3

Mick Imlah 1956–
British poet

2 Oh, foolish boys!
The English elephant
Never lies!
'Tusking' (1988)

Charles Inge 1868–1957

3 This very remarkable man
Commends a most practical plan:
You can do what you want
If you don't think you can't,
So don't think you can't think you can.
'On Monsieur Coué' (1928); see **Coué** 244:10

William Ralph Inge 1860–1954
English writer; Dean of St. Paul's, 1911–34

4 The enemies of Freedom do not argue; they shout and they shoot.
End of an Age (1948) ch. 4

5 The effect of boredom on a large scale in history is underestimated. It is a main cause of revolutions, and would soon bring to an end all the static Utopias and the farmyard civilization of the Fabians.
End of an Age (1948) ch. 6

6 To become a popular religion, it is only necessary for a superstition to enslave a philosophy.
Idea of Progress (Romanes Lecture delivered at Oxford, 27 May 1920)

7 Many people believe that they are attracted by God, or by Nature, when they are only repelled by man.
More Lay Thoughts of a Dean (1931) pt. 4, ch. 1

8 It takes in reality only one to make a quarrel. It is useless for the sheep to pass resolutions in favour of vegetarianism, while the wolf remains of a different opinion.
Outspoken Essays: First Series (1919) 'Patriotism'

9 The nations which have put mankind and posterity most in their debt have been small states—Israel, Athens, Florence, Elizabethan England.
Outspoken Essays: Second Series (1922) 'State, visible and invisible'

10 A man may build himself a throne of bayonets, but he cannot sit on it.
*a similar image was used by Boris **Yeltsin** at the time of the failed military coup in Russia, August 1991*
Philosophy of Plotinus (1923) vol. 2, Lecture 22

Jean Ingelow 1820–97
English poet

11 Play uppe 'The Brides of Enderby'.
'The High Tide on the Coast of Lincolnshire, 1571' (1863)

12 'Cusha! Cusha! Cusha!' calling
E'er the early dews were falling,
Farre away I heard her song.
'The High Tide on the Coast of Lincolnshire, 1571' (1863)

13 But each will mourn his own (she saith)
And sweeter woman ne'er drew breath
Than my sonne's wife, Elizabeth.
'The High Tide on the Coast of Lincolnshire, 1571' (1863)

Robert G. Ingersoll 1833–99
American agnostic

14 An honest God is the noblest work of man.
The Gods (1876) pt. 1; see **Pope** 605:9

15 In nature there are neither rewards nor punishments—there are consequences.
Some Reasons Why (1881) pt. 8 'The New Testament'

Bernard Ingham 1932–
British journalist and public relations specialist

16 Blood sport is brought to its ultimate refinement in the gossip columns.
speech, 5 February 1986

John Kells Ingram 1823–1907
Irish social philosopher and songwriter

17 They rose in dark and evil days.
'The Memory of the Dead' (1843)

18 Who fears to speak of Ninety-Eight?
Who blushes at the name?
'The Memory of the Dead' (1843)

J. A. D. Ingres 1780–1867
French painter

19 *Le dessin est la probité de l'art.*
Drawing is the true test of art.
Pensées d'Ingres (1922)

20 Make copies, young man, many copies. You can only become a good artist by copying the masters.
to Degas; A. Vollard *Souvenirs d'un marchand de tableaux* (1937)

Eugène Ionesco 1912–94
French dramatist

21 *C'est une chose anormale de vivre.*
Living is abnormal.
Le Rhinocéros (1959) act 1

22 *Tu ne prévois les événements que lorsqu'ils sont déjà arrivés.*

You can only predict things after they have happened.
Le Rhinocéros (1959) act 3

1 *Un fonctionnaire ne plaisante pas.*
A civil servant doesn't make jokes.
Tueur sans gages (The Killer, 1958) act 1

St Irenaeus c.AD 130–c.200
Greek theologian

2 *Gloria Dei vivens homo.*
A living man is the glory of God.
Against the Heresies bk. 4, ch. 20

Weldon J. Irvine
American songwriter

3 Young, gifted and black.
title of song (1969); see **Hansberry** 370:18

Washington Irving 1783–1859
American writer

4 A sharp tongue is the only edged tool that grows keener with constant use.
The Sketch Book (1820) 'Rip Van Winkle'

5 There is a certain relief in change, even though it be from bad to worse . . . it is often a comfort to shift one's position and be bruised in a new place.
Tales of a Traveller (1824) 'To the Reader'

6 The almighty dollar, that great object of universal veneration throughout our land.
in *New Yorker* 12 November 1836 'The Creole Village'

Anne Ingram, Lady Irwin c.1696–1764
English poet

7 A female mind like a rude fallow lies;
No seed is sown, but weeds spontaneous rise.
As well might we expect, in winter, spring,
As land untilled a fruitful crop should bring.
'An Epistle to Mr Pope. Occasioned by his Characters of Women' in the *Gentleman's Magazine* (1736)

8 Untaught the noble end of glorious truth,
Bred to deceive even from their earliest youth.
'An Epistle to Mr Pope. Occasioned by his Characters of Women' in the *Gentleman's Magazine* (1736)

Christopher Isherwood 1904–86
English novelist
see also **Auden** 34:24

9 The common cormorant (or shag)
Lays eggs inside a paper bag,
You follow the idea, no doubt?
It's to keep the lightning out.
But what these unobservant birds
Have never thought of, is that herds
Of wandering bears might come with buns
And steal the bags to hold the crumbs.
'The Common Cormorant' (written c.1925)

10 I am a camera with its shutter open, quite passive, recording, not thinking.
Goodbye to Berlin (1939) 'Berlin Diary' Autumn 1930

St Isidore of Seville c.560–636
Spanish archbishop and Doctor of the Church

11 However Augustine surpassed the zeal of all these by his genius and wisdom. For he wrote so much that no one is able in the days and nights even to read his books, far less to write them.
Etymologies bk. 6, ch. 7, sect. 3

Alec Issigonis 1906–88
British engineer

12 A camel is a horse designed by a committee.
on his dislike of working in teams
in *Guardian* 14 January 1991 'Notes and Queries'; attributed

Charles Ives 1874–1954
American composer

13 Beauty in music is too often confused with something that lets the ears lie back in an easy chair.
Joseph Machlis *Introduction to Contemporary Music* (1963)

Alija Izetbegović 1925–2003
Bosnian statesman; President of Bosnia and Herzegovina 1990–2003

14 And to my people I say, this may not be a just peace, but it is more just than a continuation of war.
after signing the Dayton accord with representatives of Serbia and Croatia
in Dayton, Ohio, 21 November 1995

Eddie Izzard 1962–
British comedian

15 'Cake or death?' 'Cake, please.'
imagining how a Church of England Inquisition might have worked
Dress to Kill (stage show, San Francisco, 1998)

Andrew Jackson 1767–1845
American Democratic statesman; 7th President of the US, 1829–37

16 Our Federal Union: it must be preserved.
toast given on the Jefferson Birthday Celebration, 13 April 1830; in Thomas Hart Benton *Thirty Years' View* (1856) vol. 1

17 Each public officer who takes an oath to support the constitution swears that he will support it as he understands it, and not as it is understood by others.
vetoing the bill to re-charter the Bank of the United States
Presidential message, 10 July 1832, in H. S. Commager (ed.) *Documents of American History* vol. 1 (1963)

1 You are uneasy; you never sailed with *me* before, I see.

  James Parton *Life of Jackson* (1860) vol. 3, ch. 35

Glenda Jackson 1936–

British Labour politician and actress

2 I am very proud of my party; it is my Government of whom I am ashamed.

  in House of Commons, 12 February 2003, in *The Times* 13 February 2003

Holbrook Jackson 1874–1948

English writer and critic

3 Pedantry is the dotage of knowledge.

  Anatomy of Bibliomania (1930) vol. 1

Jesse Jackson 1941–

American Democratic politician and clergyman

4 When I look out at this convention, I see the face of America, red, yellow, brown, black, and white. We are all precious in God's sight—the real rainbow coalition.

  speech at Democratic National Convention, Atlanta, 19 July 1988

Mahalia Jackson 1911–72

American singer

5 It's easy to be independent when you've got money. But to be independent when you haven't got a thing—that's the Lord's test.

  Movin' On Up (with Evan McLoud Wylie 1966) ch.1

Michael Jackson 1958–

American pop singer

6 Before you judge me, try hard to love me, look
   within your heart
Then ask,—have you seen my childhood?

  'Childhood' (1995 song)

Robert H. Jackson 1892–1954

American lawyer and judge

7 That four great nations, flushed with victory and stung with injury, stay the hands of vengeance and voluntarily submit their captive enemies to the judgement of the law, is one of the most significant tributes that Power has ever paid to Reason.

  opening statement for the prosecution at Nuremberg
  before the International Military Tribunal in Nuremberg, 21 November 1945

Thomas Jonathan 'Stonewall' Jackson 1824–63

American Confederate general
*on Jackson: see **Bee** 62:9; see also **Last words** 472:20*

8 Always mystify, mislead, and surprise the enemy, if possible.

  his strategic motto during the Civil War
  M. Miner and H. Rawson *American Heritage Dictionary of American Quotations* (1997)

9 My duty is to obey orders.

  attributed

Joe Jacobs 1896–1940

American boxing manager

10 We was robbed!

  after Jack Sharkey beat Max Schmeling (of whom Jacobs was manager) in the heavyweight title fight, 21 June 1932
  Peter Heller *In This Corner* (1975)

11 I should of stood in bed.

  after leaving his sick-bed to attend the World Baseball Series in Detroit, 1935, and betting on the losers
  John Lardner *Strong Cigars* (1951)

Jacopone da Todi c.1230–1306

Italian Franciscan lay brother

12 *Stabat Mater dolorosa,*
Iuxta crucem lacrimosa,
Dum pendebat filius.

At the cross her station keeping,
Stood the mournful Mother weeping,
Where he hung, the dying Lord.

  'Stabat Mater dolorosa', ascribed also to Pope Innocent III and others (translation based on that of E. Caswall in *Lyra Catholica*, 1849)

Mick Jagger 1943– and Keith Richards 1943–

English rock musicians

13 Get off of my cloud.

  title of song (1966)

14 Mother needs something today to calm her down,
And though she's not really ill,
There's a little yellow pill:
She goes running for the shelter
Of a mother's little helper,
And it helps her on her way,
Gets her through her busy day.

  'Mother's Little Helper' (1966 song)

15 I can't get no satisfaction
I can't get no girl reaction.

  '(I Can't Get No) Satisfaction' (1965 song)

16 Ev'rywhere I hear the sound of marching,
   charging feet, boy,
'Cause summer's here and the time is right for
   fighting in the street, boy.
But what can a poor boy do
Except to sing for a rock 'n' roll band,
'Cause in sleepy London town
There's just no place for a street fighting man!

  'Street Fighting Man' (1968 song)

17 Please allow me to introduce myself
I'm a man of wealth and taste.

  'Sympathy for the Devil' (1968 song)

18 Pleased to meet you, hope you guess my name
But what's puzzling you
Is the nature of my game.

  'Sympathy for the Devil' (1968 song)

1 I shouted out 'Who killed the Kennedys?'
When after all, it was you and me.
'Sympathy for the Devil' (1968 song)

Richard Jago 1715–81

English poet

2 With leaden foot time creeps along
While Delia is away.
'Absence'

Jaina Sutras

Indian tradition, founded in the 6th century BC
textual translations are those of H. Jacobi, 1884

3 He believes in soul, believes in the world, believes
in reward, believes in action . . . these are all the
causes of sin, which must be comprehended and
renounced.
Ācārāṅga Sutra bk. 1, lecture 1, lesson 1, v. 5

4 There are some who, of a truth, know this
[causing injury] to be the bondage, the delusion,
the death, the hell.
Ācārāṅga Sutra bk. 1, lecture 1, lesson 2, v. 4

5 He who sees by himself, needs no instruction. But
the miserable, afflicted fool who delights in
pleasures and whose miseries do not cease, is
turned round in the whirl of pains.
Ācārāṅga Sutra bk. 1, lecture 2, lesson 3, v. 6

6 The world is greatly troubled by women.
Ācārāṅga Sutra bk. 1, lecture 2, lesson 4, v. 3

7 A wise man should avoid wrath, pride, deceit,
greed, love, hate, delusion, conception, birth,
death, hell, animal existence, and pain.
Ācārāṅga Sutra bk. 1, lecture 3, lesson 4, v. 4

8 All breathing, existing, living, sentient creatures
should not be slain, nor treated with violence, nor
abused, nor tormented, nor driven away.
This is the pure, unchangeable, eternal law.
Ācārāṅga Sutra bk. 1, lecture 4, lesson 1, v 1.

9 All the professors, conversant with pain, preach
renunciation.
Ācārāṅga Sutra bk. 1, lecture 4, lesson 3, v. 2

10 Four things of paramount value are difficult to
obtain here by a living being: human birth,
instruction in the Law, belief in it, and energy in
self-control.
Uttarādhyayana lecture 3, v. 1

11 These two ways of life ending with death have
been declared: death with one's will and death
against one's will.
Death against one's will is that of ignorant men
. . . death with one's will is that of wise men.
Uttarādhyayana lecture 5, v. 2

12 There are five causes which render wholesome
discipline impossible: egoism, delusion,
carelessness, illness, and idleness.
Uttarādhyayana lecture 11, v. 3

13 He who adopts the law in the intention to live as a
monk, should live in company, upright, and free
from desire; he should abandon his former
connections, and not longing for pleasures, he

should wander about as an unknown beggar;
then he is a true monk.
Uttarādhyayana lecture 15, v. 1

14 By the adoration of the twenty-four Jinas the soul
arrives at purity of faith.
Uttarādhyayana lecture 29, v. 9

15 By renouncing his body he acquires the pre-
eminent virtues of the Siddhas, by the possession
of which he goes to the highest region of the
universe, and becomes absolutely happy.
Uttarādhyayana lecture 29, v. 38

16 A monk destroys by austerities the bad karma
which he had acquired by love and hatred.
Uttarādhyayana lecture 30, v. 1

17 There are three ways of committing sins: by one's
own activity, by commission, by approval.
Sūtrakritāṅga bk. 1, lecture 1, ch. 3, v. 26

18 This is the quintessence of wisdom: not to kill
anything. Know this to be the legitimate
conclusion from the principle of the reciprocity
with regard to non-killing.
Sūtrakritāṅga bk. 1, lecture 1, ch. 4, v. 10

19 Exert and control yourself! For it is not easy to
walk on ways where there are minutely small
animals.
Sūtrakritāṅga bk. 1, lecture 2, ch. 1, v. 11

20 Know this to be thus as I [Mahāvīra] have told
you, because I am the Saviour.
Sūtrakritāṅga bk. 1, lecture 16, v. 6

21 This creed of the Nirgranthas [Jains] is true,
supreme, excellent, full of virtues, right, pure, it
removes doubts, it is the road to perfection,
liberation, Nirvana.
Sūtrakritāṅga bk. 2, lecture 7, v. 15

Jalal ad-Din ar-Rumi 1207–73

Persian poet and Sufi mystic

22 Each of us touches one place
and understands the whole in that way.
The palm and the fingers feeling in the dark are
how the senses explore the reality of the elephant.
If each of us held a candle there,
and if we went in together,
we could see it.
*on the inferences drawn by men touching different
parts of an elephant in the dark; see* **Sana'i** 665:12
Mathnawi bk. 3 (1259–69)

23 I go into the Muslim mosque and the Jewish
synagogue and the Christian church and I see one
altar.
Coleman Barks and John Moyne (eds.) *The Essential Rumi*
(1999)

James I (James VI of Scotland) 1566–1625

*British monarch, King of Scotland from 1567 and of England
from 1603*
on James: see **Henri IV** 382:2

24 A branch of the sin of drunkenness, which is the
root of all sins.
A Counterblast to Tobacco (1604)

1 A custom loathsome to the eye, hateful to the nose, harmful to the brain, dangerous to the lungs, and in the black, stinking fume thereof, nearest resembling the horrible Stygian smoke of the pit that is bottomless.
A Counterblast to Tobacco (1604)

2 No bishop, no King.
to a deputation of Presbyterians from the Church of Scotland, seeking religious tolerance in England
W. Barlow *Sum and Substance of the Conference* (1604)

3 The state of monarchy is the supremest thing upon earth; for kings are not only God's lieutenants upon earth, and sit upon God's throne, but even by God himself they are called gods.
speech to Parliament, 21 March 1610, in *Works* (1616)

4 The king is truly *parens patriae*, the politique father of his people.
speech to Parliament, 21 March 1610, in *Works* (1616)

5 I will govern according to the common weal, but not according to the common will.
December, 1621, in J. R. Green *History of the English People* vol. 3 (1879) bk. 7, ch. 4

6 Dr Donne's verses are like the peace of God; they pass all understanding.
remark recorded by Archdeacon Plume (1630–1704); see **Bible** 110:7

7 I made the carles lords, but who made the carlines ladies?
E. Grenville Murray *Embassies and Foreign Courts* (1855) ch. 14

8 You cannot name any example in any heathen author but I will better it in Scripture.
'Crumms Fal'n From King James's Table' no. 10, in E. F. Rimbault (ed.) *Miscellaneous Works of Sir Thomas Overbury* (1856)

James V 1512–42
Scottish monarch, King from 1513

9 It came with a lass, and it will pass with a lass.
of the crown of Scotland, on learning of the birth of **Mary Queen of Scots**, *December 1542*
Robert Lindsay of Pitscottie (c.1500–65) *History of Scotland* (1728)

Evan James
Welsh bard

10 The land of my fathers, how fair is thy fame.
'Land of My Fathers' (1856), translated by W. G. Rothery

11 Wales, Wales, sweet are thy hills and vales,
Thy speech, thy song,
To thee belong,
O may they live ever in Wales.
'Land of My Fathers' (1856)

Henry James 1843–1916
American novelist, brother of William **James**
on James: see **Guedalla** 365:12, **Maugham** 518:14, **Wells** 828:6

12 The ever-importunate murmur, 'Dramatize it, dramatize it!'
The Altar of the Dead (1909 ed.) preface

13 The Story is just the spoiled child of art.
The Ambassadors (1909 ed.) preface

14 Live all you can; it's a mistake not to. It doesn't so much matter what you do in particular, so long as you have your life. If you haven't had that, what *have* you had?
The Ambassadors (1903) bk. 5, ch. 11

15 The balloon of experience is in fact of course tied to the earth, and under that necessity we swing, thanks to a rope of remarkable length, in the more or less commodious car of the imagination; but it is by the rope we know where we are, and from the moment that cable is cut we are at large and unrelated.
The American (1909 ed.) preface

16 The historian, essentially, wants more documents than he can really use; the dramatist only wants more liberties than he can really take.
The Aspern Papers (1909 ed.) preface

17 Most English talk is a quadrille in a sentry-box.
The Awkward Age (1899) bk. 5, ch. 19

18 Vereker's secret, my dear man—the general intention of his books: the string the pearls were strung on, the buried treasure, the figure in the carpet.
The Figure in the Carpet (1896) ch. 11

19 One might enumerate the items of high civilization, as it exists in other countries, which are absent from the texture of American life, until it should become a wonder to know what was left. No State, in the European sense of the word, and indeed barely a specific national name. No sovereign, no court, no personal loyalty, no aristocracy, no church, no clergy, no army, no diplomatic service, no country gentlemen, no palaces, no castles, nor manors, nor old country houses, nor parsonages, nor thatched cottages, nor ivied ruins; no cathedrals nor abbeys, nor little Norman churches; no great universities nor public schools—no Oxford, nor Eton, nor Harrow; no literature, no novels, no museums, no pictures, no political society, no sporting class—no Epsom nor Ascot! . . . The natural remark in the almost lurid light of such an indictment, would be that if these things are left out, everything is left out.
Hawthorne (1879) ch. 2

20 He was worse than provincial—he was parochial.
of **Thoreau**
Hawthorne (1879) ch. 4

21 The black and merciless things that are behind the great possessions.
The Ivory Tower (1917) notes

22 Cats and monkeys—monkeys and cats—all human life is there!
The Madonna of the Future (1879) vol. 1; see **Advertising slogans** 7:3

23 We work in the dark—we do what we can—we give what we have. Our doubt is our passion and our passion is our task. The rest is the madness of art.
'The Middle Years' (short story, 1893)

1 Experience is never limited, and it is never complete; it is an immense sensibility, a kind of huge spider-web of the finest silken threads suspended in the chamber of consciousness, and catching every air-borne particle in its tissue.
Partial Portraits (1888) 'The Art of Fiction'

2 What is character but the determination of incident? What is incident but the illustration of character?
Partial Portraits (1888) 'The Art of Fiction'

3 The house of fiction has in short not one window, but a million . . . but they are, singly or together, as nothing without the posted presence of the watcher.
The Portrait of a Lady (1908 ed.) preface

4 The note I wanted; that of the strange and sinister embroidered on the very type of the normal and easy.
Prefaces (1909) 'The Altar of the Dead'

5 The fatal futility of Fact.
The Spoils of Poynton (1909 ed.) preface

6 The time-honoured bread-sauce of the happy ending.
Theatricals (1894) 2nd series

7 The turn of the screw.
title of novel (1898)

8 We were alone with the quiet day, and his little heart, dispossessed, had stopped.
The Turn of the Screw (1898)

9 There is no difficulty in beginning; the trouble is to leave off!
in 1891; Leon Edel (ed.) *The Diary of Alice James* (1965)

10 I could come back to America . . . to die—but never, never to live.
letter to Mrs William James, 1 April 1913, in Leon Edel (ed.) *Letters* vol. 4 (1984)

11 The war has used up words.
in *New York Times* 21 March 1915

12 Adjectives are the sugar of literature and adverbs the salt.
Theodora Bosanquet *Henry James at Work* (1924)

13 I should so much have loved to be popular!
Alfred Sutro *Celebrities and Simple Souls* (1933)

14 Of course, of course.
*on hearing that Rupert **Brooke** had died on a Greek island*
C. Hassall *Rupert Brooke* (1964) ch. 14

15 Summer afternoon—summer afternoon . . . the two most beautiful words in the English language.
Edith Wharton *A Backward Glance* (1934) ch. 10

16 So here it is at last, the distinguished thing!
on experiencing his first stroke
Edith Wharton *A Backward Glance* (1934) ch. 14

P. D. James 1920–
English writer of detective stories

17 What the detective story is about is not murder but the restoration of order.
in *Face* December 1986

18 I had an interest in death from an early age. It fascinated me. When I heard 'Humpty Dumpty sat on a wall,' I thought, 'Did he fall or was he pushed?'
in *Paris Review* 1995

William James 1842–1910
*American philosopher; brother of Henry **James***

19 There is no more miserable human being than one in whom nothing is habitual but indecision.
The Principles of Psychology (1890) vol. 1, ch. 4

20 The art of being wise is the art of knowing what to overlook.
The Principles of Psychology (1890) vol. 2, ch. 22

21 There is no worse lie than a truth misunderstood by those who hear it.
The Varieties of Religious Experience (1902)

22 Man, biologically considered, and whatever else he may be into the bargain, is simply the most formidable of all the beasts of prey, and, indeed, the only one that preys systematically on its own species.
in *Atlantic Monthly* December 1904

23 The moral flabbiness born of the exclusive worship of the bitch-goddess *success*.
letter to H. G. Wells, 11 September 1906, in *Letters* (1920) vol. 2

24 Hogamus, higamous
Man is polygamous
Higamus, hogamous
Woman monogamous.
in *Oxford Book of Marriage* (1990)

Randall Jarrell 1914–65
American poet

25 From my mother's sleep I fell into the State,
And I hunched in its belly till my wet fur froze.
Six miles from earth, loosed from its dream of life,
I woke to black flak and the nightmare fighters.
When I died they washed me out of the turret
with a hose.
'The Death of the Ball Turret Gunner' (1945)

26 As I look, the world contracts around you:
I see Brünnhilde had brown braids and glasses
She used for studying; Salome straight brown
bangs,
A calf's brown eyes, and sturdy light-brown limbs
Dusted with cinnamon, an apple-dumpling's . . .
'A Girl in a Library' (1951)

27 The firelight of a long, blind, dreaming story
Lingers upon your lips; and I have seen
Firm, fixed forever in your closing eyes,
The Corn King beckoning to his Spring Queen.
'A Girl in a Library' (1951)

28 In bombers named for girls, we burned
The cities we had learned about in school—
Till our lives wore out; our bodies lay among
The people we had killed and never seen.
When we lasted long enough they gave us
medals;

When we died they said, 'Our casualties were
   low.'
   'Losses' (1963)

1 To Americans, English manners are far more
frightening than none at all.
   Pictures from an Institution (1954) pt. 1, ch. 4

2 It is better to entertain an idea than to take it
home to live with you for the rest of your life.
   Pictures from an Institution (1954) pt. 1, ch. 4

Maria Jastrzebska 1953-

Polish-born British poet

3 I do
And then again
She does
And then sometimes
Neither of us
Wears any trousers at all.
   'Which of Us Wears the Trousers'

Douglas Jay 1907-96

British Labour politician
*see also **Political slogans** 600:15*

4 In the case of nutrition and health, just as in the
case of education, the gentleman in Whitehall
really does know better what is good for people
than the people know themselves.
   The Socialist Case (1939) ch. 30

Jean Paul see Johann Paul Friedrich Richter

James Jeans 1877-1946

English astronomer, physicist, and mathematician

5 Taking a very gloomy view of the future of the
human race, let us suppose that it can only expect
to survive for two thousand million years longer, a
period about equal to the past age of the earth.
Then, regarded as a being destined to live for
three-score years and ten, humanity, although it
has been born in a house seventy years old, is
itself only three days old.
   Eos (1928)

6 If we assume that the last breath of, say, Julius
Caesar has by now become thoroughly scattered
through the atmosphere, then the chances are
that each of us inhales one molecule of it with
every breath we take.
   now usually quoted as the 'dying breath of Socrates'
   An Introduction to the Kinetic Theory of Gases (1940)

7 Life exists in the universe only because the carbon
atom possesses certain exceptional properties.
   The Mysterious Universe (1930) ch. 1

8 From the intrinsic evidence of his creation, the
Great Architect of the Universe now begins to
appear as a pure mathematician.
   The Mysterious Universe (1930) ch. 5

Thomas Jefferson 1743-1826

*American Democratic Republican statesman; 3rd President of
the US, 1801-9*
*see also **Mottoes** 552:16*

9 When in the course of human events, it becomes
necessary for one people to dissolve the political
bonds which have connected them with another,
and to assume among the powers of the earth the
separate and equal station to which the laws of
nature and of Nature's God entitle them, a decent
respect to the opinions of mankind requires that
they should declare the causes which impel them
to the separation.
   American Declaration of Independence, 4 July 1776,
   preamble

10 We hold these truths to be sacred and undeniable;
that all men are created equal and independent,
that from that equal creation they derive rights
inherent and inalienable, among which are the
preservation of life, and liberty, and the pursuit of
happiness.
   'Rough Draft' of the American Declaration of
   Independence, in J. P. Boyd et al. *Papers of Thomas Jefferson*
   (1950) vol. 1; see **Anonymous** 19:17

11 Our liberty depends on freedom of the press, and
that cannot be limited without being lost.
   letter to James Currie, 28 January 1786, in *Papers of
   Thomas Jefferson* (1954) vol. 9

12 Experience declares that man is the only animal
which devours its own kind, for I can apply no
milder term to the governments of Europe, and to
the general prey of the rich on the poor.
   letter to Colonel Edward Carrington, 16 January 1787, in
   Papers of Thomas Jefferson (1955) vol. 11

13 A little rebellion now and then is a good thing.
   letter to James Madison, 30 January 1787, in *Papers of
   Thomas Jefferson* (1955) vol. 11

14 State a moral case to a ploughman and a
professor. The former will decide it as well, and
often better than the latter, because he has not
been led astray by artificial rules.
   letter to Peter Carr, 10 August 1787, in *Papers of Thomas
   Jefferson* (1955) vol. 12

15 The tree of liberty must be refreshed from time to
time with the blood of patriots and tyrants. It is its
natural manure.
   letter to W. S. Smith, 13 November 1787, in *Papers of
   Thomas Jefferson* (1955) vol. 12

16 I think our governments will remain virtuous for
many centuries; as long as they are chiefly
agricultural; and this will be as long as there shall
be vacant lands in any part of America. When
they get piled upon one another in large cities, as
in Europe, they will become corrupt as in Europe.
   letter to James Madison, 20 December 1787, in *Papers of
   Thomas Jefferson* (1955) vol. 12

17 Whenever a man has cast a longing eye on them
[official positions], a rottenness begins in his
conduct.
   letter to Tench Coxe, 21 May 1799, in P. L. Ford (ed.)
   Writings of Thomas Jefferson (1896) vol. 7

18 If the principle were to prevail, of a common law
[i.e. a single government] being in force in the U.S.

. . . it would become the most corrupt government on the earth.

> letter to Gideon Granger, 13 August 1800, in P. L. Ford (ed.) *Writings of Thomas Jefferson* (1896) vol. 7

1 Though the will of the majority is in all cases to prevail, that will to be rightful must be reasonable; . . . the minority possess their equal rights, which equal law must protect, and to violate would be oppression.

> first inaugural address, 4 March 1801

2 Would the honest patriot, in the full tide of successful experiment, abandon a government which has so far kept us free and firm?

> first inaugural address, 4 March 1801

3 Peace, commerce, and honest friendship with all nations—entangling alliances with none.

> first inaugural address, 4 March 1801

4 Freedom of religion; freedom of the press, and freedom of person under the protection of *habeas corpus*, and trial by juries impartially selected. These principles form the bright constellation which has gone before us, and guided our steps through an age of revolution and reformation.

> first inaugural address, 4 March 1801

5 I have learned to expect that it will rarely fall to the lot of imperfect man to retire from this station with the reputation and the favour which bring him into it.

> first inaugural address, 4 March 1801

6 If a due participation of office is a matter of right, how are vacancies to be obtained? Those by death are few; by resignation none.

> letter to E. Shipman and others, 12 July 1801, in P. L. Ford (ed.) *Writings of Thomas Jefferson* (1897) vol. 8; see **Misquotations** 537:14

7 When a man assumes a public trust, he should consider himself as public property.

> to Baron von Humboldt, 1807, in B. L. Rayner *Life of Jefferson* (1834)

8 Nothing can now be believed which is seen in a newspaper. Truth itself becomes suspicious by being put into that polluted vehicle.

> letter to John Norvell, 14 June 1807, in *The Portable Thomas Jefferson* (1977)

9 But though an old man, I am but a young gardener.

> letter to Charles Willson Peale, 20 August 1811, in *Thomas Jefferson's Garden Book* (1944)

10 I agree with you that there is a natural aristocracy among men. The grounds of this are virtue and talents.

> letter to John Adams, 28 October 1813, in P. L. Ford (ed.) *Writings of Thomas Jefferson* (1898) vol. 9

11 If a nation expects to be ignorant and free, in a state of civilization, it expects what never was and never will be.

> letter to Colonel Charles Yancey, 6 January 1816, in P. L. Ford (ed.) *Writings of Thomas Jefferson* (1899) vol. 10

12 We have the wolf by the ears; and we can neither hold him, nor safely let him go. Justice is in one scale, and self-preservation in the other.

> *on slavery*
> letter to John Holmes, 22 April 1820; in A. A. Lipscome and A. E. Berg (eds.) *Writings of Thomas Jefferson* (1903) vol. 15

13 I know no safe depository of the ultimate powers of the society but the people themselves; and if we think them not enlightened enough to exercise their control with a wholesome discretion, the remedy is not to take it from them, but to inform their discretion by education.

> letter to William Charles Jarvis, 28 September 1820, in P. L. Ford (ed.) *Writings of Thomas Jefferson* (1899) vol. 10

14 To attain all this [universal republicanism], however, rivers of blood must yet flow, and years of desolation pass over; yet the object is worth rivers of blood, and years of desolation.

> letter to John Adams, 4 September 1823, in P. L. Ford *Writings of Thomas Jefferson* (1899) vol. 10; see **Powell** 609:21, **Virgil** 812:8

15 The generation which commences a revolution can rarely complete it.

> letter to John Adams, 4 September 1823, in P. L. Ford *Writings of Thomas Jefferson* (1899) vol. 10

16 Millions of innocent men, women, and children, since the introduction of Christianity, have been burnt, tortured, fined, imprisoned; yet we have not advanced one inch towards uniformity [of opinion]. What has been the effect of coercion? To make one half the world fools, and the other half hypocrites.

> *Notes on the State of Virginia* (1781–5) Query 17

17 Indeed I tremble for my country when I reflect that God is just.

> *Notes on the State of Virginia* (1781–5) Query 18

18 No duty the Executive had to perform was so trying as to put the right man in the right place.

> J. B. MacMaster *History of the People of the United States* (1883–1913) vol. 2, ch. 13

Francis, Lord Jeffrey 1773–1850

Scottish critic

19 This will never do.

> *on* **Wordsworth**'s The Excursion (*1814*)
> in *Edinburgh Review* November 1814

David Jenkins 1925–

English theologian; Bishop of Durham 1984–94

20 I am not clear that God manoeuvres physical things . . . After all, a conjuring trick with bones only proves that it is as clever as a conjuring trick with bones.

> *on the Resurrection*
> in 'Poles Apart' (BBC radio, 4 October 1984)

Roy Jenkins 1920–2003

British politician; co-founder of the Social Democratic Party, 1981

21 The politics of the left and centre of this country are frozen in an out-of-date mould which is bad

for the political and economic health of Britain
and increasingly inhibiting for those who live
within the mould. Can it be broken?

speech to Parliamentary Press Gallery, 9 June 1980, in *The
Times* 10 June 1980

Elizabeth Jennings 1926–2001

English poet

1 I hate a word like 'pets': it sounds so much
Like something with no living of its own.

'My Animals' (1966)

Soame Jenyns 1704–87

English politician and writer

2 Those who profess outrageous zeal for the liberty
and prosperity of their country, and at the same
time infringe her laws, affront her religion and
debauch her people, are but despicable quacks.

A Free Enquiry into the Nature and Origin of Evil (1757)
Letter 5

3 Thousands are collected from the idle and the
extravagant for seeing dogs, horses, men and
monkeys perform feats of activity, and, in some
places, for the privilege only of seeing one another.

Works (1790) vol. 2 'Thoughts on the National Debt'

St Jerome c.AD 342–420

*Roman Christian monk and scholar; translator of the original
Bible texts into Latin (the Vulgate)*

4 *Aliorum vulnus nostra sit cautio.*

Let us take warning from another's wound.

letter 54, To Furia, AD 394

5 *Venerationi mihi semper fuit non verbosa rusticitas,
sed sancta simplicitas.*

I have revered always not crude verbosity, but
holy simplicity.

letter 57, To Pammachius; see **Huss** 410:15

6 *Romanus orbis ruit et tamen cervix nostra erecta non
flectitur.*

The Roman world is falling, yet we hold our heads
erect instead of bowing our necks.

letter 60, To Heliodorus, AD 396

7 *Cotidie morimur, cotidie commutamur, et tamen
aeternos esse nos credimus.*

Every day we die, every day we are changed, and
yet we believe ourselves to be eternal.

letter 60, To Heliodorus, AD 396

8 *Fiunt, non nascuntur Christiani.*

Christians are not born but made.

letter 107, To Laeta, AD 403

9 Holy writ is the scripture of peoples, for it is made,
that all peoples should know it.

attributed, in J. Forshall and F. Madden (eds.) *The Holy
Bible . . . in the Earliest English Versions* (1850) vol. 1 'The
Prologue' [probably by John Purvey, *c.*1353–*c.*1428]
ch. 15

Jerome K. Jerome 1859–1927

English writer

10 It is impossible to enjoy idling thoroughly unless
one has plenty of work to do.

Idle Thoughts of an Idle Fellow (1886) 'On Being Idle'

11 The passing of the third floor back.

title of story (1907) and play (1910)

12 I want a house that has got over all its troubles; I
don't want to spend the rest of my life bringing up
a young and inexperienced house.

They and I (1909) ch. 11

13 It is a most extraordinary thing, but I never read a
patent medicine advertisement without being
impelled to the conclusion that I am suffering from
the particular disease therein dealt with in its most
virulent form.

Three Men in a Boat (1889) ch. 1

14 I like work: it fascinates me. I can sit and look at it
for hours. I love to keep it by me: the idea of
getting rid of it nearly breaks my heart.

Three Men in a Boat (1889) ch. 15

William Jerome 1865–1932

American songwriter

15 Any old place I can hang my hat is home sweet
home to me.

title of song (1901)

Douglas Jerrold 1803–57

English dramatist and journalist

16 The best thing I know between France and
England is—the sea.

The Wit and Opinions of Douglas Jerrold (1859) 'The Anglo-
French Alliance'

17 Earth is here so kind, that just tickle her with a
hoe and she laughs with a harvest.

of Australia

The Wit and Opinions of Douglas Jerrold (1859) 'A Land of
Plenty'

18 Love's like the measles—all the worse when it
comes late in life.

The Wit and Opinions of Douglas Jerrold (1859) 'Love'

W. Stanley Jevons 1835–82

English economist

19 All classes of society are trades unionists at heart,
and differ chiefly in the boldness, ability, and
secrecy with which they pursue their respective
interests.

The State in Relation to Labour (1882)

John Jewel 1522–71

English bishop

20 In old time we had treen chalices and golden
priests, but now we have treen priests and golden
chalices.

Certain Sermons Preached Before the Queen's Majesty (1609)

Steve Jobs 1955–

American computer executive

1 The Web is exciting for two reasons: One, it's ubiquitous. There will be Web dial tone everywhere. And anything that's ubiquitous gets interesting.

in *Wired* February 1996

2 It turns out people want keyboards. When Apple first started out, people couldn't type. We realized: Death would eventually take care of this.

interview, 28 May 2003

John XXIII (Angelo Giuseppe Roncalli) 1881–1963

Italian cleric, Pope from 1958

3 If civil authorities legislate for or allow anything that is contrary to that order and therefore contrary to the will of God, neither the laws made or the authorizations granted can be binding on the consciences of the citizens, since God has more right to be obeyed than man.

Pacem in Terris (1963)

4 The social progress, order, security and peace of each country are necessarily connected with the social progress, order, security and peace of all other countries.

Pacem in Terris (1963)

5 [In the universal *Declaration of Human Rights* (December, 1948)] in most solemn form, the dignity of a person is acknowledged to all human beings; and as a consequence there is proclaimed, as a fundamental right, the right of free movement in search for truth and in the attainment of moral good and of justice, and also the right to a dignified life.

Pacem in Terris (1963)

6 I want to throw open the windows of the Church so that we can see out and the people can see in.

attributed

7 Signora, do you believe my blessing cannot pass through plastic?

to a pilgrim who asked him to bless again some medals and rosaries which he had blessed before she had time to remove them from her purse, 1959

Laureano López Rodó *Memorias* (1990)

John of Salisbury c.1115–80

English ecclesiastical scholar; supporter of Thomas Becket

8 The brevity of our life, the dullness of our senses, the torpor of our indifference, the futility of our occupation, suffer us to know but little: and that little is soon shaken and then torn from the mind by that traitor to learning, that hostile and faithless stepmother to memory, oblivion.

Prologue to the Policraticus (ed. C. C. I. Webb, 1909) vol. 1, translated by Helen Waddell

St John of the Cross 1542–91

Spanish mystic and poet
see also **Misquotations** 537:13

9 *Muero porque no muero.*
I die because I do not die.
the same words occur in St **Teresa** *of Ávila 'Versos nacidos del fuego del amor de Dios' (c.1571–3)*
'Coplas del alma que pena por ver a Dios' (c.1578)

10 *Con un no saber sabiendo.*
With a knowing ignorance.
'Coplas hechas sobre un éxtasis de alta contemplación'

Elton John 1947– and Bernie Taupin 1950–

English pop singer and songwriter; songwriter

11 It seems to me you lived your life
Like a candle in the wind.
Never knowing who to cling to
When the rain set in.
And I would have liked to have known you
But I was just a kid
The candle burned out long before
Your legend ever did.
Goodbye Norma Jean.
of Marilyn **Monroe**
'Candle in the Wind' (song, 1973); see **Meredith** 522:13

12 Even when you died
Oh the press still hounded you.
'Candle in the Wind' (song, 1973)

13 Goodbye England's rose;
May you ever grow in our hearts.
rewritten for and sung at the funeral of **Diana**, *Princess of Wales, 7 September 1997*
'Candle in the Wind' (song, revised version, 1997)

14 And it seems to me you lived your life
Like a candle in the wind:
Never fading with the sunset
When the rain set in.
And your footsteps will always fall here
On England's greenest hills;
Your candle's burned out long before
Your legend ever will.
'Candle in the Wind' (song, revised version, 1997)

15 Goodbye yellow brick road.
title of song (1973); see **Harburg** 371:5

John Paul II 1920–

Polish cleric, Pope since 1978

16 Love is never defeated, and I could add, the history of Ireland proves it.
speech in Galway, 30 September 1979

17 It would be simplistic to say that Divine Providence caused the fall of communism. It fell by itself as a consequence of its own mistakes and abuses. It fell by itself because of its own inherent weaknesses.
when asked if the fall of the USSR could be ascribed to God
Carl Bernstein and Marco Politi *His Holiness: John Paul II and the Hidden History of our Time* (1996)

Amryl Johnson 1944–2001

Trinidadian poet

1 for . . . I am
Black
And I am
Angry
My name is
Midnight
Without
Pity.
  'Midnight Without Pity' (1982)

Amy Johnson 1903–41

English aviator

2 Had I been a man I might have explored the Poles,
or climbed Mount Everest, but as it was, my spirit
found outlet in the air.
  Margot Asquith (ed.) *Myself When Young* (1938)

Dorothy Johnson 1905–84

3 If the myth gets bigger than the man, print the
myth.
  Indian Country (1953) 'The Man Who Shot Liberty
  Valance'; see **Film lines** 320:24

Hiram Johnson see Sayings 670:22

Linton Kwesi Johnson 1952–

Jamaican-born poet

4 Brothers and sisters rocking,
a dread beat pulsing fire, burning.
  'Dread Beat an Blood' (1975)

5 Cold lights hurting, breaking, hurting;
fire in the head and a dread beat bleeding, beating
  fire: dread.
  'Dread Beat an Blood' (1975)

Lyndon Baines Johnson 1908–73

*American Democratic statesman; 36th President of the US
1963–9*

6 *to a reporter who had queried his embracing Richard
Nixon on the vice-president's return from a
controversial tour of South America in :*
Son, in politics you've got to learn that overnight
chicken shit can turn to chicken salad.
  Fawn Brodie *Richard Nixon* (1983) ch. 25

7 I am a free man, an American, a United States
Senator, and a Democrat, in that order.
  in *Texas Quarterly* Winter 1958

8 I'll tell you what's at the bottom of it. If you can
convince the lowest white man that he's better
than the best coloured man, he won't notice
you're picking his pocket. Hell, give him someone
to look down on and he'll empty his pockets for
you.
  *during the 1960 Presidential campaign, to Bill
  Moyers*
  Robert Dallek *Lone Star Rising* (1991) ch. 16

9 All I have I would have given gladly not to be
standing here today.
  following the assassination of J. F. Kennedy
  first speech to Congress as President, 27 November 1963,
  in *Public Papers of . . . Lyndon B. Johnson 1963–64* vol. 1

10 We have talked long enough in this country about
equal rights. We have talked for a hundred years
or more. It is time now to write the next chapter,
and to write it in the books of law.
  speech to Congress, 27 November 1963, in *Public Papers of
  . . . Lyndon B. Johnson 1963–64* vol. 1

11 We hope that the world will not narrow into a
neighbourhood before it has broadened into a
brotherhood.
  speech at the lighting of the Nation's Christmas Tree, 22
  December 1963, in *Public Papers of . . . Lyndon B. Johnson
  1963–64* vol. 1

12 In your time we have the opportunity to move not
only toward the rich society and the powerful
society, but upward to the Great Society.
  speech at University of Michigan, 22 May 1964, in *Public
  Papers of . . . Lyndon B. Johnson 1963–64* vol. 1

13 We still seek no wider war.
  speech on radio and television, 4 August 1964, in *Public
  Papers of . . . Lyndon B. Johnson 1963–64* vol. 2

14 We are not about to send American boys 9 or
10,000 miles away from home to do what Asian
boys ought to be doing for themselves.
  speech at Akron University, 21 October 1964, in *Public
  Papers of . . . Lyndon B. Johnson 1963–64* vol. 2; see
  Roosevelt 653:18

15 I don't want loyalty. I want *loyalty*. I want him to
kiss my ass in Macy's window at high noon and
tell me it smells like roses. I want his pecker in my
pocket.
  discussing a prospective assistant
  David Halberstam *The Best and the Brightest* (1972) ch. 20

16 Better to have him inside the tent pissing out,
than outside pissing in.
  of J. Edgar Hoover
  David Halberstam *The Best and the Brightest* (1972) ch. 20

17 So dumb he can't fart and chew gum at the same
time.
  of Gerald Ford
  Richard Reeves *A Ford, not a Lincoln* (1975) ch. 2

Pauline Johnson (Tekahionwake) 1861–1913

Canadian poet

18 For soft is the song my paddle sings.
  'The Song My Paddle Sings'

Philander Chase Johnson 1866–1939

19 Cheer up! the worst is yet to come!
  in *Everybody's Magazine* May 1920

Philip Johnson 1906–

American architect

20 Architecture is the art of how to waste space.
  New York Times 27 December 1964

Samuel Johnson 1709–84

English poet, critic, and lexicographer

on Johnson: see **Brown** *155:6,* **Burney** *169:25,* **Churchill**
219:18, **Colman** *236:4,* **Cowper** *248:25,* **Goldsmith** *355:34,*
Hawthorne *375:16,* **Knowles** *458:5,* **Macaulay** *498:1,*
Pembroke *591:13,* **Smollett** *744:19,* **Walpole** *819:15; see also*
Epitaphs *311:1,* **Swift** *767:23*

1 In all pointed sentences, some degree of accuracy
must be sacrificed to conciseness.
'The Bravery of the English Common Soldier' in *The British
Magazine* January 1760

2 Liberty is, to the lowest rank of every nation, little
more than the choice of working or starving.
'The Bravery of the English Common Soldier' in *The British
Magazine* January 1760

3 Change is not made without inconvenience, even
from worse to better.
A Dictionary of the English Language (1755) preface; see
Hooker 395:19

4 I am not yet so lost in lexicography as to forget
that words are the daughters of earth, and that
things are the sons of heaven. Language is only
the instrument of science, and words are but the
signs of ideas: I wish, however, that the
instrument might be less apt to decay, and that
signs might be permanent, like the things which
they denote.
A Dictionary of the English Language (1755) preface; see
Madden 505:9

5 Every quotation contributes something to the
stability or enlargement of the language.
on citations of usage in a dictionary
A Dictionary of the English Language (1755) preface

6 But these were the dreams of a poet doomed at last
to wake a lexicographer.
A Dictionary of the English Language (1755) preface

7 If the changes we fear be thus irresistible, what
remains but to acquiesce with silence, as in the
other insurmountable distresses of humanity? It
remains that we retard what we cannot repel, that
we palliate what we cannot cure.
A Dictionary of the English Language (1755) preface

8 *Dull.* To make dictionaries is dull work.
A Dictionary of the English Language (1755) 'dull' (8th
definition)

9 *Excise.* A hateful tax levied upon commodities.
A Dictionary of the English Language (1755)

10 *Lexicographer.* A writer of dictionaries, a harmless
drudge.
A Dictionary of the English Language (1755)

11 *Network.* Anything reticulated or decussated at
equal distances, with interstices between the
intersections.
A Dictionary of the English Language (1755)

12 *Oats.* A grain, which in England is generally given
to horses, but in Scotland supports the people.
A Dictionary of the English Language (1755)

13 *Patron.* Commonly a wretch who supports with
insolence, and is paid with flattery.
A Dictionary of the English Language (1755)

14 *Pension.* Pay given to a state hireling for treason to
his country.
A Dictionary of the English Language (1755)

15 The only end of writing is to enable the readers
better to enjoy life, or better to endure it.
A Free Enquiry (1757, ed. D. Greene, 1984)

16 When two Englishmen meet, their first talk is of
the weather.
in *The Idler* no. 11 (24 June 1758)

17 Among the calamities of war may be jointly
numbered the diminution of the love of truth, by
the falsehoods which interest dictates and
credulity encourages.
in *The Idler* no. 30 (11 November 1758); see **Sayings**
670:22

18 Promise, large promise, is the soul of an
advertisement.
The Idler no. 40 (20 January 1759)

19 He whom nature has made weak, and idleness
keeps ignorant, may yet support his vanity by the
name of a critic.
in *The Idler* no. 61 9 June 1759

20 I directed them to bring a bundle [of hay] into the
room, and slept upon it in my riding coat. Mr
Boswell, being more delicate, laid himself sheets
with hay over and under him, and lay in linen like
a gentleman.
A Journey to the Western Islands of Scotland (1775) 'Glenelg'

21 A Scotchman must be a very sturdy moralist, who
does not love Scotland better than truth.
A Journey to the Western Islands of Scotland (1775) 'Ostig in
Sky'

22 At seventy-seven it is time to be in earnest.
A Journey to the Western Islands of Scotland (1775) 'Col'

23 A hardened and shameless tea-drinker, who has
for twenty years diluted his meals with only the
infusion of this fascinating plant; whose kettle has
scarcely time to cool; who with tea amuses the
evening, with tea solaces the midnight, and with
tea welcomes the morning.
review in the *Literary Magazine* vol. 2, no. 13 (1757)

24 About things on which the public thinks long it
commonly attains to think right.
Lives of the English Poets (1779–81) 'Addison'

25 Whoever wishes to attain an English style,
familiar but not coarse, and elegant but not
ostentatious, must give his days and nights to the
volumes of Addison.
Lives of the English Poets (1779–81) 'Addison'

26 The great source of pleasure is variety. Uniformity
must tire at last, though it be uniformity of
excellence. We love to expect; and, when
expectation is disappointed or gratified, we want
to be again expecting.
Lives of the English Poets (1779–81) 'Butler'

27 A man, doubtful of his dinner, or trembling at a
creditor, is not much disposed to abstracted
meditation, or remote enquiries.
Lives of the English Poets (1779–81) 'Collins'

1 The true genius is a mind of large general powers, accidentally determined to some particular direction.
   Lives of the English Poets (1779–81) 'Cowley'

2 Language is the dress of thought.
   Lives of the English Poets (1779–81) 'Cowley'; see **Pope** 604:6, **Wesley** 830:1

3 The father of English criticism.
   Lives of the English Poets (1779–81) 'Dryden'

4 This play . . . was first offered to Cibber and his brethren at Drury-Lane, and rejected; it being then carried to Rich had the effect, as was ludicrously said, of making Gay *rich*, and Rich *gay*.
   of **Gay***'s The Beggar's Opera*
   Lives of the English Poets (1779–81) 'John Gay'

5 In the character of his Elegy I rejoice to concur with the common reader; for by the common sense of readers uncorrupted with literary prejudices . . . must be finally decided all claim to poetical honours.
   Lives of the English Poets (1779–81) 'Gray'

6 An exotic and irrational entertainment, which has been always combated, and always has prevailed.
   of Italian opera
   Lives of the English Poets (1779–81) 'Hughes'

7 We are perpetually moralists, but we are geometricians only by chance. Our intercourse with intellectual nature is necessary; our speculations upon matter are voluntary and at leisure.
   Lives of the English Poets (1779–81) 'Milton'

8 An acrimonious and surly republican.
   Lives of the English Poets (1779–81) 'Milton'

9 I am disappointed by that stroke of death, which has eclipsed the gaiety of nations and impoverished the public stock of harmless pleasure.
   on the death of **Garrick**
   Lives of the English Poets (1779–81) 'Edmund Smith'

10 He washed himself with oriental scrupulosity.
   Lives of the English Poets (1779–81) 'Swift'

11 Friendship is not always the sequel of obligation.
   Lives of the English Poets (1779–81) 'James Thomson'

12 Nothing can please many, and please long, but just representations of general nature.
   Plays of William Shakespeare . . . (1765) preface

13 He that tries to recommend him by select quotations, will succeed like the pedant in Hierocles, who, when he offered his house to sale, carried a brick in his pocket as a specimen.
   of **Shakespeare**
   Plays of William Shakespeare . . . (1765) preface

14 Love is only one of many passions.
   Plays of William Shakespeare . . . (1765) preface

15 Shakespeare has united the powers of exciting laughter and sorrow not only in one mind but in one composition . . . That this is a practice contrary to the rules of criticism will be readily allowed; but there is always an appeal open from criticism to nature.
   Plays of William Shakespeare . . . (1765) preface

16 A quibble is to Shakespeare, what luminous vapours are to the traveller; he follows it at all adventures, it is sure to lead him out of his way and sure to engulf him in the mire.
   Plays of William Shakespeare . . . (1765) preface

17 We fix our eyes upon his graces, and turn them from his deformities, and endure in him what we should in another loathe or despise.
   of **Shakespeare**
   Plays of William Shakespeare . . . (1765) preface

18 I have always suspected that the reading is right, which requires many words to prove it wrong; and the emendation wrong, that cannot without so much labour appear to be right.
   Plays of William Shakespeare . . . (1765) preface

19 Notes are often necessary, but they are necessary evils.
   Plays of William Shakespeare . . . (1765) preface

20 It is better to suffer wrong than to do it, and happier to be sometimes cheated than not to trust.
   in Rambler no. 79 (18 December 1750)

21 There are minds so impatient of inferiority, that their gratitude is a species of revenge, and they return benefits, not because recompense is a pleasure, but because obligation is a pain.
   in The Rambler no. 87 (15 January 1751)

22 No place affords a more striking conviction of the vanity of human hopes, than a public library.
   in The Rambler no. 106 (23 March 1751)

23 I have laboured to refine our language to grammatical purity, and to clear it from colloquial barbarisms, licentious idioms, and irregular combinations.
   in The Rambler no. 208 (14 March 1752)

24 Ye who listen with credulity to the whispers of fancy, and pursue with eagerness the phantoms of hope; who expect that age will perform the promises of youth, and that the deficiencies of the present day will be supplied by the morrow; attend to the history of Rasselas prince of Abyssinia.
   Rasselas (1759) ch. 1

25 The business of a poet, said Imlac, is to examine, not the individual, but the species; to remark general properties and appearances: he does not number the streaks of the tulip, or describe the different shades in the verdure of the forest.
   Rasselas (1759) ch. 10

26 He [the poet] must write as the interpreter of nature, and the legislator of mankind, and consider himself as presiding over the thoughts and manners of future generations; as a being superior to time and place.
   Rasselas (1759) ch. 10; see **Shelley** 732:17

27 Human life is everywhere a state in which much is to be endured, and little to be enjoyed.
   Rasselas (1759) ch. 11

1 Marriage has many pains, but celibacy has no pleasures.
  Rasselas (1759) ch. 26

2 Example is always more efficacious than precept.
  Rasselas (1759) ch. 30

3 I consider this mighty structure as a monument of the insufficiency of human enjoyments.
  of the Pyramids
  Rasselas (1759) ch. 32

4 Integrity without knowledge is weak and useless, and knowledge without integrity is dangerous and dreadful.
  Rasselas (1759) ch. 41

5 There is perhaps no class of men, to whom the precept given by the Apostle to his converts against too great confidence in their understandings, may be more properly inculcated, than those who are dedicated to the profession of literature.
  Sermons (1788) no. 8

6 In this state of temporary honour, a proud man is too willing to exert his prerogative; and too ready to forget that he is dictating to those, who may one day dictate to him.
  on schoolmasters
  Sermons (1788) no. 8

7 He [God] will not leave his promises unfulfilled, nor his threats unexecuted . . . Neither can he want power to execute his purposes; he who spoke, and the world was made, can speak again, and it will perish.
  Sermons (1788) no. 10

8 How is it that we hear the loudest yelps for liberty among the drivers of negroes?
  Taxation No Tyranny (1775)

9 A generous and elevated mind is distinguished by nothing more certainly than an eminent degree of curiosity.
  dedication of his English translation of Fr. J. Lobo's *Voyage to Abyssinia* (1735), signed 'the editor' but attributed to Johnson in James Boswell *Life of Samuel Johnson* (1791) 1734

10 There Poetry shall tune her sacred voice, And wake from ignorance the Western World.
  Demetrius forecasting the Renaissance
  Irene (1749) act 4, sc. 1, l. 122

11 Here falling houses thunder on your head, And here a female atheist talks you dead.
  London (1738) l. 17

12 Of all the griefs that harrass the distressed, Sure the most bitter is a scornful jest;
  Fate never wounds more deep the gen'rous heart, Than when a blockhead's insult points the dart.
  London (1738) l. 166

13 The stage but echoes back the public voice.
  The drama's laws the drama's patrons give,
  For we that live to please, must please to live.
  'Prologue spoken at the Opening of the Theatre in Drury Lane' (1747)

14 How small of all that human hearts endure, That part which laws or kings can cause or cure.
  Still to ourselves in every place consigned,
  Our own felicity we make or find.
  lines added to Oliver Goldsmith's *The Traveller* (1764) l. 429; see **Goldsmith** 355:15

15 Let observation with extensive view, Survey mankind, from China to Peru.
  The Vanity of Human Wishes (1749) l. 1

16 There mark what ills the scholar's life assail, Toil, envy, want, the patron, and the jail.
  The Vanity of Human Wishes (1749) l. 159

17 A frame of adamant, a soul of fire, No dangers fright him, and no labours tire.
  of Charles XII of Sweden
  The Vanity of Human Wishes (1749) l. 193

18 His fall was destined to a barren strand, A petty fortress, and a dubious hand;
  He left the name, at which the world grew pale, To point a moral, or adorn a tale.
  of Charles XII of Sweden
  The Vanity of Human Wishes (1749) l. 219

19 Enlarge my life with multitude of days, In health, in sickness, thus the suppliant prays;
  Hides from himself his state, and shuns to know, That life protracted is protracted woe.
  Time hovers o'er, impatient to destroy, And shuts up all the passages of joy.
  The Vanity of Human Wishes (1749) l. 255

20 In life's last scene what prodigies surprise, Fears of the brave, and follies of the wise?
  From Marlb'rough's eyes the streams of dotage flow,
  And Swift expires a driv'ler and a show.
  The Vanity of Human Wishes (1749) l. 315

21 Must helpless man, in ignorance sedate, Roll darkling down the torrent of his fate?
  The Vanity of Human Wishes (1749) l. 345

22 Still raise for good the supplicating voice, But leave to heaven the measure and the choice.
  The Vanity of Human Wishes (1749) l. 351

23 A lawyer has no business with the justice or injustice of the cause which he undertakes, unless his client asks his opinion, and then he is bound to give it honestly. The justice or injustice of the cause is to be decided by the judge.
  James Boswell *Journal of a Tour to the Hebrides* (1785) 15 August 1773

24 Let him go abroad to a distant country; let him go to some place where he is *not* known. Don't let him go to the devil where he is known!
  Boswell having asked if someone should commit suicide to avoid certain disgrace
  James Boswell *Tour to the Hebrides* (1785) 18 August 1773

25 I have, all my life long, been lying till noon; yet I tell all young men, and tell them with great sincerity, that nobody who does not rise early will ever do any good.
  James Boswell *Tour to the Hebrides* (1785) 14 September 1773

1 I inherited a vile melancholy from my father, which has made me mad all my life, at least not sober.

James Boswell *Tour to the Hebrides* (1785) 16 September 1773; see **Johnson** 432:10

2 I am always sorry when any language is lost, because languages are the pedigree of nations.

James Boswell *Tour to the Hebrides* (1785) 18 September 1773

3 I do not much like to see a Whig in any dress; but I hate to see a Whig in a parson's gown.

James Boswell *Tour to the Hebrides* (1785) 24 September 1773

4 A cucumber should be well sliced, and dressed with pepper and vinegar, and then thrown out, as good for nothing.

James Boswell *Tour to the Hebrides* (1785) 5 October 1773

5 I am sorry I have not learned to play at cards. It is very useful in life: it generates kindness and consolidates society.

James Boswell *Tour to the Hebrides* (1785) 21 November 1773

6 JOHNSON: I had no notion that I was wrong or irreverent to my tutor.
BOSWELL: That, Sir, was great fortitude of mind.
JOHNSON: No, Sir; stark insensibility.

James Boswell *Life of Samuel Johnson* (1791) 31 October 1728

7 Sir, we are a nest of singing birds.
of Pembroke College, Oxford

James Boswell *Life of Samuel Johnson* (1791) 1730

8 He was a vicious man, but very kind to me. If you call a dog *Hervey*, I shall love him.
of his former patron Henry Hervey

James Boswell *Life of Samuel Johnson* (1791) 1737

9 My old friend, Mrs Carter, could make a pudding, as well as translate Epictetus.

James Boswell *Life of Samuel Johnson* (1791) Spring 1738

10 Tom Birch is as brisk as a bee in conversation; but no sooner does he take a pen in his hand, than it becomes a torpedo to him, and benumbs all his faculties.

James Boswell *Life of Samuel Johnson* (1791) 1743

11 I'll come no more behind your scenes, David; for the silk stockings and white bosoms of your actresses excite my amorous propensities.
*to **Garrick**; John **Wilkes** recalled the remark in the form: 'the silk stockings and white bosoms of your actresses do make my genitals to quiver'*

James Boswell *Life of Samuel Johnson* (1791) 1750

12 A man may write at any time, if he will set himself doggedly to it.

James Boswell *Life of Samuel Johnson* (1791) March 1750

13 A fly, Sir, may sting a stately horse and make him wince; but one is but an insect, and the other is a horse still.

James Boswell *Life of Samuel Johnson* (1791) 1754

14 This man I thought had been a Lord among wits; but, I find, he is only a wit among Lords.
*of Lord **Chesterfield***

James Boswell *Life of Samuel Johnson* (1791) 1754

15 They teach the morals of a whore, and the manners of a dancing master.
of the Letters *of Lord **Chesterfield***

James Boswell *Life of Samuel Johnson* (1791) 1754

16 I had done all that I could; and no man is well pleased to have his all neglected, be it ever so little.

James Boswell *Life of Samuel Johnson* (1791) letter to Lord Chesterfield, 7 February 1755

17 The shepherd in Virgil grew at last acquainted with Love, and found him a native of the rocks.

James Boswell *Life of Samuel Johnson* (1791) letter to Lord Chesterfield, 7 February 1755

18 Is not a Patron, my Lord, one who looks with unconcern on a man struggling for life in the water, and, when he has reached ground, encumbers him with help? The notice which you have been pleased to take of my labours, had it been early, had been kind; but it has been delayed till I am indifferent, and cannot enjoy it; till I am solitary, and cannot impart it; till I am known, and do not want it.

James Boswell *Life of Samuel Johnson* (1791) letter to Lord Chesterfield, 7 February 1755

19 There are two things which I am confident I can do very well: one is an introduction to any literary work, stating what it is to contain, and how it should be executed in the most perfect manner; the other is a conclusion, shewing from various causes why the execution has not been equal to what the author promised to himself and to the public.

James Boswell *Life of Samuel Johnson* (1791) 1755

20 Ignorance, madam, pure ignorance.
on being asked why he had defined pastern *as the 'knee' of a horse*

James Boswell *Life of Samuel Johnson* (1791) 1755

21 I have protracted my work till most of those whom I wished to please have sunk into the grave; and success and miscarriage are empty sounds.

James Boswell *Life of Samuel Johnson* (1791) 1755

22 If a man does not make new acquaintance as he advances through life, he will soon find himself left alone. A man, Sir, should keep his friendship in constant repair.

James Boswell *Life of Samuel Johnson* (1791) 1755

23 No man will be a sailor who has contrivance enough to get himself into a jail; for being in a ship is being in a jail, with the chance of being drowned . . . A man in a jail has more room, better food, and commonly better company.

James Boswell *Life of Samuel Johnson* (1791) 16 March 1759; see **Burton** 174:10

24 No, Sir, I am not a botanist; and (alluding, no doubt, to his near sightedness) should I wish to become a botanist, I must first turn myself into a reptile.

James Boswell *Life of Samuel Johnson* (1791) 20 July 1762

1 BOSWELL: I do indeed come from Scotland, but I cannot help it . . .
JOHNSON: That, Sir, I find, is what a very great many of your countrymen cannot help.
James Boswell *Life of Samuel Johnson* (1791) 16 May 1763

2 The notion of liberty amuses the people of England, and helps to keep off the *taedium vitae*. When a butcher tells you that *his heart bleeds for his country* he has, in fact, no uneasy feeling.
James Boswell *Life of Samuel Johnson* (1791) 16 May 1763

3 Yes, Sir, many men, many women, and many children.
on Dr Blair's asking whether any man of a modern age could have written Ossian
James Boswell *Life of Samuel Johnson* (1791) 24 May 1763

4 I did not think he ought to be shut up. His infirmities were not noxious to society. He insisted on people praying with him; and I'd as lief pray with Kit Smart as any one else. Another charge was, that he did not love clean linen; and I have no passion for it.
James Boswell *Life of Samuel Johnson* (1791) 24 May 1763

5 You *may* abuse a tragedy, though you cannot write one. You may scold a carpenter who has made you a bad table, though you cannot make a table. It is not your trade to make tables.
on literary criticism
James Boswell *Life of Samuel Johnson* (1791) 25 June 1763

6 I am afraid he has not been in the inside of a church for many years; but he never passes a church without pulling off his hat. This shows that he has good principles.
of Dr John Campbell
James Boswell *Life of Samuel Johnson* (1791) 1 July 1763

7 Great abilities are not requisite for an historian . . . imagination is not required in any high degree.
James Boswell *Life of Samuel Johnson* (1791) 6 July 1763

8 The noblest prospect which a Scotchman ever sees, is the high road that leads him to England!
James Boswell *Life of Samuel Johnson* (1791) 6 July 1763

9 A man ought to read just as inclination leads him; for what he reads as a task will do him little good.
James Boswell *Life of Samuel Johnson* (1791) 14 July 1763

10 But if he does really think that there is no distinction between virtue and vice, why, Sir, when he leaves our houses, let us count our spoons.
James Boswell *Life of Samuel Johnson* (1791) 14 July 1763;
see **Emerson** 306:20

11 All the arguments which are brought to represent poverty as no evil, show it to be evidently a great evil. You never find people labouring to convince you that you may live very happily upon a plentiful fortune.
James Boswell *Life of Samuel Johnson* (1791) 20 July 1763

12 Truth, Sir, is a cow, that will yield such people [sceptics] no more milk, and so they are gone to milk the bull.
James Boswell *Life of Samuel Johnson* (1791) 21 July 1763

13 Young men have more virtue than old men; they have more generous sentiments in every respect.
James Boswell *Life of Samuel Johnson* (1791) 21 July 1763

14 In my early years I read very hard. It is a sad reflection, but a true one, that I knew almost as much at eighteen as I do now.
James Boswell *Life of Samuel Johnson* (1791) 21 July 1763

15 Your levellers wish to level *down* as far as themselves; but they cannot bear levelling *up* to themselves.
James Boswell *Life of Samuel Johnson* (1791) 21 July 1763

16 It is no matter what you teach them [children] first, any more than what leg you shall put into your breeches first.
James Boswell *Life of Samuel Johnson* (1791) 26 July 1763

17 Why, Sir, Sherry is dull, naturally dull; but it must have taken him a great deal of pains to become what we now see him. Such an excess of stupidity, Sir, is not in Nature.
of Thomas Sheridan
James Boswell *Life of Samuel Johnson* (1791) 28 July 1763

18 It is burning a farthing candle at Dover, to shew light at Calais.
on Thomas Sheridan's influence on the English language
James Boswell *Life of Samuel Johnson* (1791) 28 July 1763;
see **Young** 857:7

19 A woman's preaching is like a dog's walking on his hinder legs. It is not done well; but you are surprised to find it done at all.
James Boswell *Life of Samuel Johnson* (1791) 31 July 1763

20 We could not have had a better dinner had there been a *Synod of Cooks*.
James Boswell *Life of Samuel Johnson* (1791) 5 August 1763

21 Don't, Sir, accustom yourself to use big words for little matters. It would *not* be *terrible*, though I *were* to be detained some time here.
when Boswell said it would be 'terrible' if Johnson should not be able to return speedily from Harwich
James Boswell *Life of Samuel Johnson* (1791) 6 August 1763

22 I refute it *thus*.
*on Boswell observing of Bishop **Berkeley**'s theory of the non-existence of matter that though they were satisfied it was not true, they were unable to refute it, Johnson struck his foot against a large stone, till he rebounded from it, with these words*
James Boswell *Life of Samuel Johnson* (1791) 6 August 1763

23 Sir John, Sir, is a very unclubbable man.
of Sir John Hawkins
James Boswell *Life of Samuel Johnson* (1791) Spring 1764

24 That all who are happy, are equally happy, is not true. A peasant and a philosopher may be equally *satisfied*, but not equally *happy*. Happiness consists in the multiplicity of agreeable consciousness.
James Boswell *Life of Samuel Johnson* (1791) February 1766

25 Our tastes greatly alter. The lad does not care for the child's rattle, and the old man does not care for the young man's whore.
James Boswell *Life of Samuel Johnson* (1791) Spring 1766

1 It was not for me to bandy civilities with my Sovereign.

James Boswell *Life of Samuel Johnson* (1791) February 1767

2 There was as great a difference between them as between a man who knew how a watch was made, and a man who could tell the hour by looking on the dial-plate.

James Boswell *Life of Samuel Johnson* (1791) Spring 1768

3 Let me smile with the wise, and feed with the rich.
responding to **Garrick**

James Boswell *Life of Samuel Johnson* (1791) 6 October 1769; see **Garrick** 340:1

4 We *know* our will is free, and *there's* an end on't.

James Boswell *Life of Samuel Johnson* (1791) 16 October 1769

5 In the description of night in Macbeth, the beetle and the bat detract from the general idea of darkness,—inspissated gloom.

James Boswell *Life of Samuel Johnson* (1791) 16 October 1769

6 Most schemes of political improvement are very laughable things.

James Boswell *Life of Samuel Johnson* (1791) 26 October 1769

7 It matters not how a man dies, but how he lives. The act of dying is not of importance, it lasts so short a time.

James Boswell *Life of Samuel Johnson* (1791) 26 October 1769

8 Burton's *Anatomy of Melancholy*, he said, was the only book that ever took him out of bed two hours sooner than he wished to rise.

James Boswell *Life of Samuel Johnson* (1791) 1770

9 Want of tenderness, he always alleged, was want of parts, and was no less a proof of stupidity than depravity.

James Boswell *Life of Samuel Johnson* (1791) 1770

10 That fellow seems to me to possess but one idea, and that is a wrong one.
of a chance-met acquaintance

James Boswell *Life of Samuel Johnson* (1791) 1770; see **Disraeli** 277:24

11 Johnson observed, that 'he did not care to speak ill of any man behind his back, but he believed the gentleman was an *attorney*.'

James Boswell *Life of Samuel Johnson* (1791) 1770

12 The triumph of hope over experience.
of a man who remarried immediately after the death of a wife with whom he had been unhappy

James Boswell *Life of Samuel Johnson* (1791) 1770

13 Every man has a lurking wish to appear considerable in his native place.

James Boswell *Life of Samuel Johnson* (1791) letter to Sir Joshua Reynolds, 17 July 1771

14 It is so far from being natural for a man and woman to live in a state of marriage, that we find all the motives which they have for remaining in that connection, and the restraints which civilized society imposes to prevent separation, are hardly sufficient to keep them together.

James Boswell *Life of Samuel Johnson* (1791) 31 March 1772

15 Nobody can write the life of a man, but those who have eat and drunk and lived in social intercourse with him.

James Boswell *Life of Samuel Johnson* (1791) 31 March 1772

16 I would not give half a guinea to live under one form of government rather than another. It is of no moment to the happiness of an individual.

James Boswell *Life of Samuel Johnson* (1791) 31 March 1772

17 If a sovereign oppresses his people to a great degree, they will rise and cut off his head. There is a remedy in human nature against tyranny, that will keep us safe under every form of government.

James Boswell *Life of Samuel Johnson* (1791) 31 March 1772

18 A man who is good enough to go to heaven, is good enough to be a clergyman.

James Boswell *Life of Samuel Johnson* (1791) 5 April 1772

19 Why, Sir, if you were to read Richardson for the story, your impatience would be so much fretted that you would hang yourself.

James Boswell *Life of Samuel Johnson* (1791) 6 April 1772

20 Grief is a species of idleness.

letter to Mrs Thrale, 17 March 1773, in R. W. Chapman (ed.) *Letters of Samuel Johnson* (1952) vol. I

21 He has, indeed, done it very well; but it is a foolish thing well done.
on **Goldsmith**'s *apology in the* London Chronicle *for physically assaulting Thomas Evans, who had published a damaging open letter to Goldsmith in the* London Packet 24 *March 1773*

James Boswell *Life of Samuel Johnson* (1791) 3 April 1773

22 All intellectual improvement arises from leisure.

James Boswell *Life of Samuel Johnson* (1791) 13 April 1773

23 ELPHINSTON: What, have you not read it through?
JOHNSON: No, Sir, do *you* read books *through*?

James Boswell *Life of Samuel Johnson* (1791) 19 April 1773

24 Read over your compositions, and where ever you meet with a passage which you think is particularly fine, strike it out.
quoting a college tutor

James Boswell *Life of Samuel Johnson* (1791) 30 April 1773

25 I hope I shall never be deterred from detecting what I think a cheat, by the menaces of a ruffian ['Ossian'].

James Boswell *Life of Samuel Johnson* (1791) letter to James Macpherson, 20 January 1775

26 There are few ways in which a man can be more innocently employed than in getting money.

James Boswell *Life of Samuel Johnson* (1791) 27 March 1775

27 He was dull in a new way, and that made many people think him *great*.
of Thomas **Gray**

James Boswell *Life of Samuel Johnson* (1791) 28 March 1775

1 I never think I have hit hard, unless it rebounds.
   James Boswell *Life of Samuel Johnson* (1791) 2 April 1775

2 Fleet-street has a very animated appearance; but I think the full tide of human existence is at Charing-Cross.
   James Boswell *Life of Samuel Johnson* (1791) 2 April 1775

3 George the First knew nothing, and desired to know nothing; did nothing, and desired to do nothing; and the only good thing that is told of him is, that he wished to restore the crown to its hereditary successor.
   James Boswell *Life of Samuel Johnson* (1791) 6 April 1775

4 It is wonderful, when a calculation is made, how little the mind is actually employed in the discharge of any profession.
   James Boswell *Life of Samuel Johnson* (1791) 6 April 1775

5 The greatest part of a writer's time is spent in reading, in order to write: a man will turn over half a library to make one book.
   James Boswell *Life of Samuel Johnson* (1791) 6 April 1775

6 Patriotism is the last refuge of a scoundrel.
   James Boswell *Life of Samuel Johnson* (1791) 7 April 1775

7 Knowledge is of two kinds. We know a subject ourselves, or we know where we can find information upon it.
   James Boswell *Life of Samuel Johnson* (1791) 18 April 1775

8 Politics are now nothing more than means of rising in the world.
   James Boswell *Life of Samuel Johnson* (1791) 18 April 1775

9 Players, Sir! I look upon them as no better than creatures set upon tables and joint-stools to make faces and produce laughter, like dancing dogs.
   James Boswell *Life of Samuel Johnson* (1791) 1775

10 In lapidary inscriptions a man is not upon oath.
   James Boswell *Life of Samuel Johnson* (1791) 1775

11 There is now less flogging in our great schools than formerly, but then less is learned there; so that what the boys get at one end they lose at the other.
   James Boswell *Life of Samuel Johnson* (1791) 1775

12 Nothing odd will do long. *Tristram Shandy* did not last.
   James Boswell *Life of Samuel Johnson* (1791) 20 March 1776

13 There is nothing which has yet been contrived by man, by which so much happiness is produced as by a good tavern or inn.
   James Boswell *Life of Samuel Johnson* (1791) 21 March 1776; see **Shenstone** 732:23

14 Marriages would in general be as happy, and often more so, if they were all made by the Lord Chancellor, upon a due consideration of characters and circumstances, without the parties having any choice in the matter.
   James Boswell *Life of Samuel Johnson* (1791) 22 March 1776

15 He is gone, and we are going.
   on the death of her son, Harry
   letter to Mrs Thrale, 25 March 1776, in R. W. Chapman (ed.) *Letters of Samuel Johnson* (1952) vol. 3

16 Questioning is not the mode of conversation among gentlemen. It is assuming a superiority.
   James Boswell *Life of Samuel Johnson* (1791) 25 March 1776

17 Fine clothes are good only as they supply the want of other means of procuring respect.
   James Boswell *Life of Samuel Johnson* (1791) 27 March 1776

18 If a madman were to come into this room with a stick in his hand, no doubt we should pity the state of his mind; but our primary consideration would be to take care of ourselves. We should knock him down first, and pity him afterwards.
   James Boswell *Life of Samuel Johnson* (1791) 3 April 1776

19 We would all be idle if we could.
   James Boswell *Life of Samuel Johnson* (1791) 1776

20 No man but a blockhead ever wrote, except for money.
   James Boswell *Life of Samuel Johnson* (1791) 5 April 1776

21 A man who has not been in Italy, is always conscious of an inferiority, from his not having seen what it is expected a man should see.
   James Boswell *Life of Samuel Johnson* (1791) 11 April 1776

22 BOSWELL: Sir, what is poetry?
   JOHNSON: Why Sir, it is much easier to say what it is not. We all *know* what light is; but it is not easy to *tell* what it is.
   James Boswell *Life of Samuel Johnson* (1791) 12 April 1776

23 Every man of any education would rather be called a rascal, than accused of deficiency in *the graces.*
   James Boswell *Life of Samuel Johnson* (1791) May 1776

24 Sir, you have but two topics, yourself and me. I am sick of both.
   James Boswell *Life of Samuel Johnson* (1791) May 1776

25 If I had no duties, and no reference to futurity, I would spend my life in driving briskly in a post-chaise with a pretty woman.
   James Boswell *Life of Samuel Johnson* (1791) 19 September 1777

26 Depend upon it, Sir, when a man knows he is to be hanged in a fortnight, it concentrates his mind wonderfully.
   on the execution of Dr Dodd for forgery, 27 June 1777
   James Boswell *Life of Samuel Johnson* (1791) 19 September 1777

27 When a man is tired of London, he is tired of life.
   James Boswell *Life of Samuel Johnson* (1791) 20 September 1777

28 All argument is against it; but all belief is for it.
   of the existence of ghosts
   James Boswell *Life of Samuel Johnson* (1791) 31 March 1778

29 John Wesley's conversation is good, but he is never at leisure. He is always obliged to go at a certain hour. This is very disagreeable to a man who loves to fold his legs and have out his talk, as I do.
   James Boswell *Life of Samuel Johnson* (1791) 31 March 1778

1 Though we cannot out-vote them we will out-argue them.
on the practical value of speeches in the House of Commons
James Boswell *Life of Samuel Johnson* (1791) 3 April 1778

2 Every man thinks meanly of himself for not having been a soldier, or not having been at sea.
James Boswell *Life of Samuel Johnson* (1791) 10 April 1778

3 Johnson had said that he could repeat a complete chapter of 'The Natural History of Iceland', from the Danish of Horrebow, the whole of which was exactly thus:—'CHAP. LXXII. *Concerning snakes.* There are no snakes to be met with throughout the whole island.'
James Boswell *Life of Samuel Johnson* (1791) 13 April 1778

4 The more contracted that power is, the more easily it is destroyed. A country governed by a despot is an inverted cone.
James Boswell *Life of Samuel Johnson* (1791) 14 April 1778

5 So it is in travelling; a man must carry knowledge with him, if he would bring home knowledge.
James Boswell *Life of Samuel Johnson* (1791) 17 April 1778

6 Sir, the insolence of wealth will creep out.
James Boswell *Life of Samuel Johnson* (1791) 18 April 1778

7 All censure of a man's self is oblique praise. It is in order to shew how much he can spare.
James Boswell *Life of Samuel Johnson* (1791) 25 April 1778

8 I have always said, the first Whig was the Devil.
James Boswell *Life of Samuel Johnson* (1791) 28 April 1778

9 Mutual cowardice keeps us in peace. Were one half of mankind brave and one half cowards, the brave would be always beating the cowards. Were all brave, they would lead a very uneasy life; all would be continually fighting: but being all cowards, we go on very well.
James Boswell *Life of Samuel Johnson* (1791) 28 April 1778

10 Were it not for imagination, Sir, a man would be as happy in the arms of a chambermaid as of a Duchess.
James Boswell *Life of Samuel Johnson* (1791) 9 May 1778

11 Madam, before you flatter a man so grossly to his face, you should consider whether or not your flattery is worth his having.
*remark to Hannah **More***
Charlotte Barrett (ed.) *Diary and Letters of Madame D'Arblay* [Fanny Burney] (1842) vol. 1, pt. 2, August 1778

12 Claret is the liquor for boys; port, for men; but he who aspires to be a hero (smiling) must drink brandy.
James Boswell *Life of Samuel Johnson* (1791) 7 April 1779

13 A man who exposes himself when he is intoxicated, has not the art of getting drunk.
James Boswell *Life of Samuel Johnson* (1791) 24 April 1779

14 Worth seeing, yes; but not worth going to see.
on the Giant's Causeway
James Boswell *Life of Samuel Johnson* (1791) 12 October 1779

15 If you are idle, be not solitary; if you are solitary, be not idle.
James Boswell *Life of Samuel Johnson* (1791) letter to Boswell, 27 October 1779; see **Closing lines** 228:6

16 Among the anfractuosities of the human mind, I know not if it may not be one, that there is a superstitious reluctance to sit for a picture.
James Boswell *Life of Samuel Johnson* (1791) 1780

17 Every man has a right to utter what he thinks truth, and every other man has a right to knock him down for it. Martyrdom is the test.
James Boswell *Life of Samuel Johnson* (1791) 1780

18 They are forced plants, raised in a hot-bed; and they are poor plants; they are but cucumbers after all.
of Thomas Gray's Odes
James Boswell *Life of Samuel Johnson* (1791) 1780

19 No man was more foolish when he had not a pen in his hand, or more wise when he had.
*of Oliver **Goldsmith***
James Boswell *Life of Samuel Johnson* (1791) 1780; see **Garrick** 340:3

20 If a man talks of his misfortunes there is something in them that is not disagreeable to him; for where there is nothing but pure misery, there never is any recourse to the mention of it.
James Boswell *Life of Samuel Johnson* (1791) 1780

21 I believe that is true. The dogs don't know how to write trifles with dignity.
to Fowke, who had observed that in writing biography Johnson infinitely exceeded his contemporaries
James Boswell *Life of Samuel Johnson* (1791) 1781

22 Mrs Montagu has dropt me. Now, Sir, there are people whom one should like very well to drop, but would not wish to be dropped by.
James Boswell *Life of Samuel Johnson* (1791) March 1781

23 This merriment of parsons is mighty offensive.
James Boswell *Life of Samuel Johnson* (1791) March 1781

24 We are not here to sell a parcel of boilers and vats, but the potentiality of growing rich, beyond the dreams of avarice.
at the sale of Thrale's brewery
James Boswell *Life of Samuel Johnson* (1791) 6 April 1781; see **Moore** 546:11

25 Classical quotation is the *parole* of literary men all over the world.
James Boswell *Life of Samuel Johnson* (1791) 8 May 1781

26 Why, that is, because, dearest, you're a dunce.
*to Miss Monckton, later Lady Corke, who said that **Sterne**'s writings affected her*
James Boswell *Life of Samuel Johnson* (1791) May 1781

27 Sir, I have two very cogent reasons for not printing any list of subscribers;—one, that I have lost all the names,—the other, that I have spent all the money.
James Boswell *Life of Samuel Johnson* (1791) May 1781

28 Always, Sir, set a high value on spontaneous kindness. He whose inclination prompts him to cultivate your friendship of his own accord, will love you more than one whom you have been at pains to attach to you.

James Boswell *Life of Samuel Johnson* (1791) May 1781

1 A wise Tory and a wise Whig, I believe, will agree. Their principles are the same, though their modes of thinking are different.

James Boswell *Life of Samuel Johnson* (1791) May 1781, written statement given to Boswell

2 I hate a fellow whom pride, or cowardice, or laziness drives into a corner, and who does nothing when he is there but sit and *growl*; let him come out as I do, and *bark*.

of Jeremiah Markland

James Boswell *Life of Samuel Johnson* (1791) 10 October 1782

3 Resolve not to be poor: whatever you have, spend less. Poverty is a great enemy to human happiness; it certainly destroys liberty, and it makes some virtues impracticable, and others extremely difficult.

James Boswell *Life of Samuel Johnson* (1791) letter to Boswell, 7 December 1782

4 How few of his friends' houses would a man choose to be at when he is sick.

James Boswell *Life of Samuel Johnson* (1791) 1783

5 There is a wicked inclination in most people to suppose an old man decayed in his intellects. If a young or middle-aged man, when leaving a company, does not recollect where he laid his hat, it is nothing; but if the same inattention is discovered in an old man, people will shrug up their shoulders, and say, 'His memory is going.'

James Boswell *Life of Samuel Johnson* (1791) 1783

6 A man might write such stuff for ever, if he would *abandon* his mind to it.

of Ossian

James Boswell *Life of Samuel Johnson* (1791) 1783

7 Sir, there is no settling the point of precedency between a louse and a flea.

on the relative merits of two minor poets

James Boswell *Life of Samuel Johnson* (1791) 1783

8 When I observed he was a fine cat, saying, 'Why yes, Sir, but I have had cats whom I liked better than this'; and then as if perceiving Hodge to be out of countenance, adding, 'but he is a very fine cat, a very fine cat indeed.'

James Boswell *Life of Samuel Johnson* (1791) 1783

9 Clear your mind of cant.

James Boswell *Life of Samuel Johnson* (1791) 15 May 1783

10 The black dog I hope always to resist, and in time to drive, though I am deprived of almost all those that used to help me . . . When I rise my breakfast is solitary, the black dog waits to share it, from breakfast to dinner he continues barking, except that Dr Brocklesby for a little keeps him at a distance . . . Night comes at last, and some hours of restlessness and confusion bring me again to a day of solitude. What shall exclude the black dog from a habitation like this?

on his attacks of melancholia; more recently associated with Winston **Churchill***, who used the phrase 'black dog' when alluding to his own periodic bouts of depression*

letter to Mrs Thrale, 28 June 1783, in R. W. Chapman (ed.) *Letters of Samuel Johnson* (1952) vol. 3

11 As I know more of mankind I expect less of them, and am ready now to call a man *a good man*, upon easier terms than I was formerly.

James Boswell *Life of Samuel Johnson* (1791) September 1783

12 If a man were to go by chance at the same time with Burke under a shed, to shun a shower, he would say—'this is an extraordinary man.'

on Edmund **Burke**

James Boswell *Life of Samuel Johnson* (1791) 15 May 1784

13 It is as bad as bad can be: it is ill-fed, ill-killed, ill-kept, and ill-drest.

on the roast mutton he had been served at an inn

James Boswell *Life of Samuel Johnson* (1791) 3 June 1784

14 JOHNSON: As I cannot be sure that I have fulfilled the conditions on which salvation is granted, I am afraid I may be one of those who shall be damned (looking dismally).
DR ADAMS: What do you mean by damned?
JOHNSON: (passionately and loudly) Sent to Hell, Sir, and punished everlastingly.

James Boswell *Life of Samuel Johnson* (1791) 12 June 1784

15 Milton, Madam, was a genius that could cut a Colossus from a rock; but could not carve heads upon cherry-stones.

to Hannah **More***, who had expressed a wonder that the poet who had written* Paradise Lost *should write such poor sonnets*

James Boswell *Life of Samuel Johnson* (1791) 13 June 1784

16 It might as well be said 'Who drives fat oxen should himself be fat.'

parodying Henry **Brooke**

James Boswell *Life of Samuel Johnson* (1791) June 1784; see **Brooke** 153:4

17 Sir, I have found you an argument; but I am not obliged to find you an understanding.

James Boswell *Life of Samuel Johnson* (1791) June 1784

18 No man is a hypocrite in his pleasures.

James Boswell *Life of Samuel Johnson* (1791) June 1784; see **Pope** 603:20

19 Talking of the Comedy of 'The Rehearsal,' he said, 'It has not wit enough to keep it sweet.' This was easy;—he therefore caught himself, and pronounced a more rounded sentence; 'It has not vitality enough to preserve it from putrefaction.'

James Boswell *Life of Samuel Johnson* (1791) June 1784

20 Who can run the race with Death?

James Boswell *Life of Samuel Johnson* (1791) letter to Dr Burney, 2 August 1784

21 Dictionaries are like watches, the worst is better than none, and the best cannot be expected to go quite true.

James Boswell *Life of Samuel Johnson* (1791) letter to Francesco Sastres, 21 August 1784

1 Sir, I look upon every day to be lost, in which I do not make a new acquaintance.
  James Boswell *Life of Samuel Johnson* (1791) November 1784

2 I will be conquered; I will not capitulate.
  on his illness
  James Boswell *Life of Samuel Johnson* (1791) November 1784

3 Long-expected one-and-twenty,
  Ling'ring year, at length is flown;
  Pride and pleasure, pomp and plenty,
  Great [Sir John], are now your own.
  James Boswell *Life of Samuel Johnson* (1791) December 1784

4 An odd thought strikes me:—we shall receive no letters in the grave.
  James Boswell *Life of Samuel Johnson* (1791) December 1784

5 Abstinence is as easy to me, as temperance would be difficult.
  William Roberts (ed.) *Memoirs of the Life and Correspondence of Mrs Hannah More* (1834) vol. 1

6 As with my hat upon my head
  I walked along the Strand,
  I there did meet another man
  With his hat in his hand.
  in *European Magazine* January 1785 'Anecdotes by George Steevens'

7 Corneille is to Shakespeare . . . as a clipped hedge is to a forest.
  Hester Lynch Piozzi *Anecdotes of . . . Johnson* (1786)

8 Difficult do you call it, Sir? I wish it were impossible.
  on the performance of a celebrated violinist
  William Seward *Supplement to the Anecdotes of Distinguished Persons* (1797)

9 Every man has, some time in his life, an ambition to be a wag.
  Joyce Hemlow (ed.) *Journals and Letters of Fanny Burney* vol. 1 (1972)

10 [Goldsmith] seeming to repine at the success of Beattie's Essay on Truth—'Here's such a stir (said he) about a fellow that has written one book, and I have written many.' Ah, Doctor (says his friend [Johnson]), there go two-and-forty sixpences you know to one guinea.
  Hester Lynch Piozzi *Anecdotes of . . . Johnson* (1786)

11 He hated a fool, and he hated a rogue, and he hated a whig; he was a very good hater.
  of Bathurst
  Hester Lynch Piozzi *Anecdotes of . . . Johnson* (1786)

12 I dogmatise and am contradicted, and in this conflict of opinions and sentiments I find delight.
  on his conversation in taverns
  John Hawkins *Life of Samuel Johnson* (1787) p. 87

13 *Iam moriturus.*
  I who am about to die.
  to Francesco Sastres, shortly before his death on 13 December 1784, in John Hawkins *Life of Samuel Johnson* (1787); see **Anonymous** 21:13

14 If the man who turnips cries,
  Cry not when his father dies,
  'Tis a proof that he had rather
  Have a turnip than his father.
  burlesque of Lope de Vega's lines 'si a quien los leones vence [He who can conquer a lion . . .]'
  Hester Lynch Piozzi *Anecdotes of . . . Johnson* (1786)

15 It is very strange, and very melancholy, that the paucity of human pleasures should persuade us ever to call hunting one of them.
  Hester Lynch Piozzi *Anecdotes of . . . Johnson* (1786)

16 Love is the wisdom of the fool and the folly of the wise.
  William Cooke *Life of Samuel Foote* (1805) vol. 2

17 A man is in general better pleased when he has a good dinner upon his table, than when his wife talks Greek.
  John Hawkins (ed.) *The Works of Samuel Johnson* (1787) 'Apophthegms, Sentiments, Opinions, etc.' vol. 11

18 Of music Dr Johnson used to say that it was the only sensual pleasure without vice.
  in *European Magazine* (1795)

19 One day at Streatham . . . a young gentleman called to him suddenly, and I suppose he thought disrespectfully, in these words: 'Mr Johnson, would you advise me to marry?' 'I would advise no man to marry, Sir,' returns for answer in a very angry tone Dr Johnson, 'who is not likely to propagate understanding.'
  Hester Lynch Piozzi *Anecdotes of . . . Johnson* (1786)

20 Was there ever yet anything written by mere man that was wished longer by its readers, excepting *Don Quixote, Robinson Crusoe,* and the *Pilgrim's Progress*?
  Hester Lynch Piozzi *Anecdotes of . . . Johnson* (1786)

21 What is written without effort is in general read without pleasure.
  William Seward *Biographia* (1799)

Samuel Johnson 1822–82

American nonconformist minister

22 City of God, how broad and far.
  title of hymn (1864)

Tom Johnston 1881–1965

Scottish Labour politician

23 I have become . . . uneasy lest we should get political power without our first having, or at least simultaneously having, an adequate economy to administer. What purport would there be in our getting a Scots parliament in Edinburgh if it has to administer an emigration system, a glorified Poor Law, and a graveyard!
  Memories (1952)

24 They have barred us by barbed wire fences from the bens and glens: the peasant has been ruthlessly swept aside to make room for the pheasant, and the mountain hare now brings forth her young on the hearthstone of the Gael!
  Our Scots Noble Families (1909)

Hanns Johst 1890–1978

German dramatist

1 Whenever I hear the word culture . . . I release the safety-catch of my Browning!

often attributed to Hermann **Goering**, *and quoted as 'Whenever I hear the word culture, I reach for my pistol!'*
Schlageter (1933) act 1, sc. 1

Jean de Joinville c.1224–1319

French historian, biographer of Louis IX of France

2 A *prudhomme* is so grand and good a thing that even to pronounce the word fills the mouth pleasantly.

prudhomme *'a man of valour and dignity'*
The Life of St Louis

3 Just like the writer who has finished his book and illuminates it with gold and azure, so the king illuminated his kingdom with the beautiful abbeys he made.

The Life of St Louis

Al Jolson (Asa Yoelson) 1886–1950

American singer
see also **Lewis** 483:19

4 You think that's noise—you ain't heard nuttin' yet!

in a café, competing with the din from a neighbouring building site, in 1906; *subsequently an aside in the* 1927 *film* The Jazz Singer

Martin Abramson *The Real Story of Al Jolson* (1950) (later the title of a Jolson song, 1919, in the form 'You Ain't Heard Nothing Yet')

Henry Arthur Jones 1851–1929 and Henry Herman 1832–94

English dramatists

5 O God! Put back Thy universe and give me yesterday.

The Silver King (1907) act 2, sc. 4

John Paul Jones 1747–92

American admiral

6 I have not yet begun to fight.

when asked whether he had lowered his flag, as his ship was sinking, 23 *September* 1779

Mrs Reginald De Koven *Life and Letters of John Paul Jones* (1914) vol. 1

LeRoi Jones see Imamu Amiri Baraka

Mary Harris 'Mother' Jones c.1837–1930

Irish-born American labour activist

7 Pray for the dead and fight like hell for the living!

The Autobiography of Mother Jones (1925)

Steve Jones 1944–

English geneticist

8 The Admiralty sent the *Beagle* to South America with Darwin on board not because they were interested in evolution but because they knew that the first step to understanding (and, with luck, controlling) the world was to make a map of it. The same is true of the genes.

The Language of the Genes (1993)

9 Sex and taxes are in many ways the same. Tax does to cash what males do to genes. It dispenses assets among the population as a whole. Sex, not death, is the great leveller.

speech to the Royal Society; in *Independent* 25 January 1997

William Jones 1746–94

English jurist

10 My opinion is, that power should always be distrusted, in whatever hands it is placed.

letter to Lord Althorpe, 5 October 1782, in Lord Teignmouth *Life of Sir W. Jones* (1835) vol. 1

11 Seven hours to law, to soothing slumber seven, Ten to the world allot, and *all* to Heaven.

lines in substitution for Sir Edward Coke's lines 'Six hours in sleep . . . ', in Lord Teignmouth *Life of Sir W. Jones* (1835) vol. 2; see **Coke** 230:19

Erica Jong 1942–

American novelist

12 The zipless fuck is absolutely pure. It is free of ulterior motives. There is no power game. The man is not 'taking' and the woman is not 'giving' . . . The zipless fuck is the purest thing there is. And it is rarer than the unicorn.

Fear of Flying (1973) ch. 1

13 Jealousy is all the fun you *think* they had.

How to Save Your Own Life (1977)

Ben Jonson c.1573–1637

English dramatist and poet
on Jonson: see **Dryden** 290:5, **Epitaphs** 311:2, **Milton** 529:27; *see also* **Epitaphs** 310:1

14 Fortune, that favours fools.

The Alchemist (1610) prologue

15   We will eat our mullets,
Soused in high-country wines, sup pheasants' eggs,
And have our cockles boiled in silver shells;
Our shrimps to swim again, as when they lived,
In a rare butter made of dolphins' milk,
Whose cream does look like opals.

The Alchemist (1610) act 4, sc. 1

16 The lungs of the tobacconist are rotted, the liver spotted, the brain smoked like the backside of the pig-woman's booth here, and the whole body within, black as her pan you saw e'en now without.

Bartholomew Fair (1614) act 2, sc. 1

17 Neither do thou lust after that tawney weed tobacco.

Bartholomew Fair (1614) act 2, sc. 6

18 PEOPLE: The Voice of Cato is the voice of Rome.
CATO: The voice of Rome is the consent of heaven!

Catiline his Conspiracy (1611) act 3, sc. 1

1   Where it concerns himself,
Who's angry at a slander makes it true.
Catiline his Conspiracy (1611) act 3, sc. 1

2 Queen and huntress, chaste and fair,
Now the sun is laid to sleep,
Seated in thy silver chair,
State in wonted manner keep:
Hesperus entreats thy light,
Goddess, excellently bright.
Cynthia's Revels (1600) act 5, sc. 3

3 This is Mab, the Mistress-Fairy
That doth nightly rob the dairy.
The Entertainment at Althorpe (1603)

4 Still to be neat, still to be drest,
As you were going to a feast;
Still to be powdered, still perfumed,
Lady, it is to be presumed,
Though art's hid causes are not found,
All is not sweet, all is not sound.
Epicene (1609) act 1, sc. 1

5 Such sweet neglect more taketh me,
Than all the adulteries of art;
They strike mine eyes, but not my heart.
Epicene (1609) act 1, sc. 1

6 I do utter as good things every hour, if they were
collected and observed, as either of 'em.
Epicene (1609) act 2, sc. 3

7   Blind Fortune still
Bestows her gifts on such as cannot use them.
Every Man out of His Humour (1599) act 2, sc. 2

8 Ramp up my genius, be not retrograde;
But boldly nominate a spade a spade.
The Poetaster (1601) act 5, sc. 1

9 Detraction is but baseness' varlet;
And apes are apes, though clothed in scarlet.
The Poetaster (1601) act 5, sc. 1; see **Proverbs** 614:25

10 'Twas only fear first in the world made gods.
Sejanus (1603) act 2, sc. 2

11 Riches, the dumb god that giv'st all men tongues,
That canst do nought, and yet mak'st men do all
      things;
The price of souls.
Volpone (1606) act 1, sc. 1

12   I glory
More in the cunning purchase of my wealth
Than in the glad possession.
Volpone (1606) act 1, sc. 1

13   Give 'em words;
Pour oil into their ears, and send them hence.
Volpone (1606) act 1, sc. 4

14   What a rare punishment
Is avarice to itself!
Volpone (1606) act 1, sc. 4

15 I have been at my book, and am now past the
craggy paths of study, and come to the flowery
plains of honour and reputation.
Volpone (1606) act 2, sc. 1

16 Calumnies are answered best with silence.
Volpone (1606) act 2, sc. 2

17   Almost
All the wise world is little else in nature
But parasites or sub-parasites.
Volpone (1606) act 3, sc. 1

18 Suns, that set, may rise again;
But if once we lose this light,
'Tis with us perpetual night.
Volpone (1606) act 3, sc. 5; see **Catullus** 202:13

19 Our drink shall be prepared gold and amber;
Which we will take, until my roof whirl around
With the *vertigo*: and my dwarf shall dance.
Volpone (1606) act 3, sc. 5

20 Come, my Celia, let us prove,
While we can, the sports of love.
Volpone (1606) act 3, sc. 5; see **Catullus** 202:13

21   Honour! tut, a breath,
There's no such thing in nature; a mere term
Invented to awe fools.
Volpone (1606) act 3, sc. 7

22 You have a gift, sir, (thank your education),
Will never let you want, while there are men,
And malice, to breed causes.
to a lawyer
Volpone (1606) act 5, sc. 1

23 Rest in soft peace, and, asked, say here doth lie
Ben Jonson his best piece of poetry.
'On My First Son' (1616)

24 This figure that thou here seest put,
It was for gentle Shakespeare cut,
Wherein the graver had a strife
With Nature, to out-do the life:
O could he but have drawn his wit
As well in brass, as he has hit
His face; the print would then surpass
All that was ever writ in brass:
But since he cannot, reader, look
Not on his picture, but his book.
*on the portrait of **Shakespeare***
First Folio Shakespeare (1623) 'To the Reader'

25 Follow a shadow, it still flies you;
Seem to fly it, it will pursue:
So court a mistress, she denies you;
Let her alone, she will court you.
Say, are not women truly then
Styled but the shadows of us men?
'That Women are but Men's Shadows' (1616)

26 Drink to me only with thine eyes,
And I will pledge with mine;
Or leave a kiss but in the cup,
And I'll not look for wine.
'To Celia' (1616)

27 In small proportions we just beauty see,
And in short measures life may perfect be.
'To the Immortal Memory . . . of . . . Sir Lucius Carey and
Sir H. Morison' (1640)

28   Soul of the Age!
The applause, delight, the wonder of our stage!
'To the Memory of My Beloved, the Author, Mr William
Shakespeare' (1623)

1   How far thou didst our Lyly outshine,
Or sporting Kyd, or Marlowe's mighty line.
'To the Memory of . . . Shakespeare' (1623)

2 Thou hadst small Latin, and less Greek.
'To the Memory of . . . Shakespeare' (1623)

3 He was not of an age, but for all time!
'To the Memory of . . . Shakespeare' (1623)

4 Sweet Swan of Avon! What a sight it were
To see thee in our waters yet appear,
And make those flights upon the banks of Thames
That so did take Eliza, and our James!
'To the Memory of . . . Shakespeare' (1623)

5 Thou art not, Penshurst, built to envious show
Of touch or marble, nor canst boast a row
Of polished pillars, or a roof of gold;
Thou hast no lantern whereof tales are told,
Or stair, or courts; but standst an ancient pile,
And these grudged at, art reverenced the while.
'To Penshurst' (1616) l. 1

6 The blushing apricot and woolly peach
Hang on thy walls, that every child may reach.
'To Penshurst' (1616) l. 43

7 Donne, for not keeping of accent, deserved
hanging . . . Shakespeare wanted art.
in *Conversations with William Drummond of Hawthornden* (written 1619) no. 3

8 The players have often mentioned it as an honour
to Shakespeare that in his writing, whatsoever he
penned, he never blotted out a line. My answer
hath been 'Would he had blotted a thousand' . . .
But he redeemed his vices with his virtues. There
was ever more in him to be praised than to be
pardoned.
Timber, or Discoveries made upon Men and Matter (1641) l.
658 'De Shakespeare Nostrati'; see **Heming** 381:3, **Pope**
605:24

9 The fear of every man that heard him was, lest he
should make an end.
on Francis **Bacon**
Timber, or Discoveries made upon Men and Matter (1641) l.
906 'Dominus Verulamius'

10 Talking and eloquence are not the same: to speak,
and to speak well, are two things.
Timber, or Discoveries made upon Men and Matter (1641) l.
1882 'Praecept[a] Element[aria]'

Janis Joplin 1943–70
American singer

11 Fourteen heart attacks and he had to die in my
week. In MY week.
when ex-President **Eisenhower**'s *death prevented her
photograph appearing on the cover of* Newsweek
in *New Musical Express* 12 April 1969

12 Onstage I make love to twenty-five thousand
people, then I go home alone.
in *New Yorker* 14 August 1971

Thomas Jordan c.1612–85
English poet and dramatist

13 They plucked communion tables down
And broke our painted glasses;

They threw our altars to the ground
And tumbled down the crosses.
They set up Cromwell and his heir—
The Lord and Lady Claypole—
Because they hated Common Prayer,
The organ and the maypole.
'How the War began' (1664)

Joseph II 1741–90
Austrian monarch, Holy Roman Emperor

14 Too beautiful for our ears, and much too many
notes, dear Mozart.
of The Abduction from the Seraglio (1782)
attributed; Franz Xaver Niemetschek *Life of Mozart* (1798)

Chief Joseph (Hinmaton-Yalaktit) c.1840–1904
Nez Percé chief

15 From where the sun now stands I will fight no
more forever.
speech at the end of the Nez Percé war in 1877; Dee Brown
Bury My Heart at Wounded Knee (1970) ch. 13

16 Good words do not last long unless they amount
to something. Words do not pay for my dead
people.
on a visit to Washington in 1879; Chester Anders Fee *Chief
Joseph* (1936)

Jenny Joseph 1932–
English poet

17 When I am an old woman I shall wear purple
With a red hat which doesn't go, and doesn't suit
me.
And I shall spend my pension on brandy and
summer gloves
And satin sandals, and say we've got no money
for butter.
'Warning' (1974)

Benjamin Jowett 1817–93
English classicist; Master of Balliol College, Oxford, from 1870
on Jowett: see **Beeching** 62:16

18 The lie in the soul is a true lie.
introduction to his translation (1871) of Plato's *Republic*
bk. 2

19 Nowhere probably is there more true feeling, and
nowhere worse taste, than in a churchyard.
Evelyn Abbott and Lewis Campbell (eds.) *Letters of Benjamin
Jowett* (1899) ch. 6

20 One man is as good as another until he has
written a book.
Evelyn Abbott and Lewis Campbell (eds.) *Life and Letters of
Benjamin Jowett* (1897) vol. 1

James Joyce 1882–1941
Irish novelist
on Joyce: see **Forster** 329:11, **Lawrence** 475:16, **Woolf** 845:11;
see also **Opening lines** 575:10, **Opening lines** 575:13

21 His soul swooned slowly as he heard the snow
falling faintly through the universe and faintly

falling, like the descent of their last end, upon all the living and the dead.
Dubliners (1914) 'The Dead'

1 Dear, dirty Dublin.
Dubliners (1914) 'A Little Cloud'

2 riverrun, past Eve and Adam's, from swerve of shore to bend of bay, brings us by a commodious vicus of recirculation back to Howth Castle and Environs.
Finnegans Wake (1939) pt. I

3 That ideal reader suffering from an ideal insomnia.
Finnegans Wake (1939) pt. I

4 The flushpots of Euston and the hanging garments of Marylebone.
Finnegans Wake (1939) pt. I

5 All moanday, tearsday, wailsday, thumpsday, frightday, shatterday till the fear of the Law.
Finnegans Wake (1939) pt. 2

6 Three quarks for Muster Mark!
Finnegans Wake (1939) pt. 2

7 A portrait of the artist as a young man.
title of book (1916)

8 Poor Parnell! he cried loudly. My dead king!
A Portrait of the Artist as a Young Man (1916) ch. I

9 When the soul of a man is born in this country, there are nets flung at it to hold it back from flight. You talk to me of nationality, language, religion. I shall try to fly by those nets.
A Portrait of the Artist as a Young Man (1916) ch. 5

10 Ireland is the old sow that eats her farrow.
A Portrait of the Artist as a Young Man (1916) ch. 5

11 The artist, like the God of the creation, remains within or behind or beyond or above his handiwork, invisible, refined out of existence, indifferent, paring his fingernails.
A Portrait of the Artist as a Young Man (1916) ch. 5

12 The only arms I allow myself to use, silence, exile, and cunning.
A Portrait of the Artist as a Young Man (1916) ch. 5

13 By an epiphany he meant a sudden spiritual manifestation, whether in vulgarity of speech or of gesture or in a memorable phase of the mind itself. He believed that it was for the man of letters to recover these epiphanies with extreme care, seeing that they themselves are the most delicate and evanescent of moments.
Stephen Hero (1944) ch. 25 (part of a first draft of *A Portrait of the Artist as a Young Man*)

14 The snotgreen sea. The scrotumtightening sea.
Ulysses (1922)

15 It is a symbol of Irish art. The cracked lookingglass of a servant.
Ulysses (1922)

16 I fear those big words, Stephen said, which make us so unhappy.
Ulysses (1922)

17 History, Stephen said, is a nightmare from which I am trying to awake.
Ulysses (1922)

18 Lawn Tennyson, gentleman poet.
Ulysses (1922)

19 Mr Leopold Bloom ate with relish the inner organs of beasts and fowls. He liked thick giblet soup, nutty gizzards, a stuffed roast heart, liverslices fried with crustcrumbs, fried hencod's roes. Most of all he liked grilled mutton kidneys which gave to his palate a fine tang of faintly scented urine.
Ulysses (1922)

20 He . . . saw the dark tangled curls of his bush floating, floating hair of the stream around the limp father of thousands, a languid floating flower.
Ulysses (1922)

21 Come forth, Lazarus! And he came fifth and lost the job.
Ulysses (1922)

22 Plenty to see and hear and feel yet. Feel live warm beings near you. They aren't going to get me this innings. Warm beds: warm full blooded life.
Ulysses (1922)

23 Greater love than this, he said, no man hath that a man lay down his wife for his friend. Go thou and do likewise. Thus, or words to that effect, saith Zarathustra, sometime regius professor of French letters to the university of Oxtail.
Ulysses (1922); see **Bible** 103:33

24 The heaventree of stars hung with humid nightblue fruit.
Ulysses (1922)

25 O, father forsaken,
Forgive your son!
'Ecce Puer'

26 Writing in English is the most ingenious torture ever devised for sins committed in previous lives. The English reading public explains the reason why.
letter, 5 September 1918; Richard Ellmann (ed.) *Selected Letters of James Joyce* (1975)

William Joyce (Lord Haw-Haw) 1906–46
American-born wartime broadcaster from Nazi Germany, executed for treason

27 Germany calling! Germany calling!
habitual introduction to propaganda broadcasts to Britain during the Second World War

Juan Carlos I 1938–
Spanish monarch, King from 1975

28 The Crown, the symbol of the permanence and unity of Spain, cannot tolerate any actions by people attempting to disrupt by force the democratic process.
on the occasion of the attempted coup in 1981
television broadcast at 1.15 a.m., 24 February 1981

29 I will neither abdicate the Crown nor leave Spain. Whoever rebels will provoke a new civil war and will be responsible.
on the occasion of the attempted coup in 1981
television broadcast at 1.15 a.m., 24 February 1981

Judah ben Samuel the Hasid d. 1217

Jewish mystic

1 In thy intercourse with non-Jews, be careful to be as wholly sincere as in that with Jews. In most places, Jews are not unlike Christians in their morals and usages.
  Sefer Hasidim

2 There are three [sorts of people] for whom we should sternly close our hearts: a cruel person who commits vile things; the fool who rushes into ruin in spite of warning; and the ingrate. Ingratitude is the blackest of faults.
  Sefer Hasidim

3 Sweet hymns shall be my chant and woven songs.
  For Thou art all for which my spirit longs—
  To be within the shadow of Thy hand
  And all Thy mystery to understand.

  The while Thy glory is upon my tongue,
  My inmost heart with love of Thee is wrung.
  'Hymn of Glory'

Jack Judge 1878–1938 and Harry Williams 1874–1924

British songwriters

4 It's a long way to Tipperary,
  It's a long way to go;
  It's a long way to Tipperary,
  To the sweetest girl I know!
  Goodbye, Piccadilly,
  Farewell, Leicester Square,
  It's a long, long way to Tipperary,
  But my heart's right there!
  'It's a Long Way to Tipperary' (1912 song)

Julian of Norwich 1343–after 1416

English anchoress

5 He showed me something small, no bigger than a hazelnut, lying in the palm of my hand, as it seemed to me, and it was as round as a ball. I looked at it with the eye of my understanding, and thought: What can this be? I was amazed that it could last, for I thought that because of its littleness it would suddenly have fallen into nothing. And I was answered in my understanding: It lasts and always will, because God loves it; and thus every thing has being through the love of God.
  Revelations of Divine Love (the long text) ch. 5

6 Sin is behovely, but all shall be well and all shall be well and all manner of thing shall be well.
  behovely = *expedient, necessary*
    Revelations of Divine Love (the long text) ch. 27, Revelation 13; see **Eliot** 302:2

7 Wouldest thou wit thy Lord's meaning in this thing? Wit it well: Love was his meaning. Who shewed it thee? Love. What shewed He thee? Love. Wherefore shewed it He? for Love . . . Thus was I learned that Love was our Lord's meaning.
    Revelations of Divine Love (the long text) ch. 86, Revelation 16

Julian the Apostate see Last words 474:10

Carl Gustav Jung 1875–1961

Swiss psychologist

8 A more or less superficial layer of the unconscious is undoubtedly personal. I call it the *personal unconscious*. But this personal unconscious rests upon a deeper layer, which does not derive from personal experience and is not a personal acquisition but is inborn. This deeper layer I call the *collective unconscious* . . . The contents of the personal unconscious are chiefly the *feeling-toned complexes* . . . The contents of the collective unconscious, on the other hand, are known as *archetypes*.
  Eranos Jahrbuch (1934)

9 A man who has not passed through the inferno of his passions has never overcome them.
  Memories, Dreams, Reflections (1962) ch. 9

10 As far as we can discern, the sole purpose of human existence is to kindle a light in the darkness of mere being.
  Memories, Dreams, Reflections (1962) ch. 11

11 Every form of addiction is bad, no matter whether the narcotic be alcohol or morphine or idealism.
  Memories, Dreams, Reflections (1962) ch. 12

12 The meeting of two personalities is like the contact of two chemical substances: if there is any reaction, both are transformed.
  Modern Man in Search of a Soul (1933)

13 The afternoon of human life must also have a significance of its own and cannot be merely a pitiful appendage to life's morning.
  The Stages of Life (1930)

14 If there is anything that we wish to change in the child, we should first examine it and see whether it is not something that could better be changed in ourselves.
  'Vom Werden der Persönlichkeit' (1932)

'Junius'

English 18th-century pseudonymous writer

15 The liberty of the press is the *Palladium* of all the civil, political, and religious rights of an Englishman.
  The Letters of Junius (1772 ed.) 'Dedication to the English Nation'

16 The right of election is the very essence of the constitution.
  in *Public Advertiser* 24 April 1769, letter 11

17 There is a holy mistaken zeal in politics as well as in religion. By persuading others, we convince ourselves.
  in *Public Advertiser* 19 December 1769, letter 35

18 The injustice done to an individual is sometimes of service to the public.
  in *Public Advertiser* 14 November 1770, letter 41

19 As for Mr Wedderburne, there is something about him, which even treachery cannot trust.
  in *Public Advertiser* 22 June 1771, letter 49

John Junor 1919–97
British journalist
see also **Catchphrases** 201:23

1 Such a graceful exit. And then he had to go and do this on the doorstep.
*on Harold **Wilson**'s 'Lavender List' (the honours list he drew up on resigning the British premiership in 1976)*
in *Observer* 23 January 1990

Donald Justice 1925–
American poet

2 Men at forty
Learn to close softly
The doors to rooms they will not be
Coming back to.
'Men at Forty' (1967)

Justinian AD 483–565
Roman emperor from AD 527

3 Justice is the constant and perpetual wish to render to every one his due.
Institutes bk. 1, ch. 1, para. 1

4 Solomon, I have vanquished thee.
at the dedication of Hagia Sophia in Constantinople, 27 December AD 537
attributed (according to a late tradition)

Claude Jutra 1930–86
Canadian film director

5 I can face death, but I cannot face watching myself disappear from within . . . I don't know who I am anymore.
from a conversation with the founder of The Right to Die Society about his Alzheimer's disease, a few months before his suicide
in *Homemaker's Magazine* November–December 1991

Juvenal C.AD 60–C.130
Roman satirist

6 *Semper ego auditor tantum?*
Must I always be a mere listener?
Satires no. 1, l. 1

7 *Difficile est saturam non scribere.*
It's hard not to write satire.
Satires no. 1, l. 30

8 *Probitas laudatur et alget.*
Honesty is praised and left to shiver.
Satires no. 1, l. 74 (translation by G. G. Ramsay)

9 *Si natura negat, facit indignatio versum.*
Even if nature says no, indignation makes me write verse.
Satires no. 1, l. 79

10 *Quidquid agunt homines, votum timor ira voluptas Gaudia discursus nostri farrago libelli est.*
Everything mankind does, their hope, fear, rage, pleasure, joys, business, are the hotch-potch of my little book.
Satires no. 1, l. 85

11 *Quis tulerit Gracchos de seditione querentes?*
Who would put up with the Gracchi complaining about subversion?
Satires no. 2, l. 24

12 *Dat veniam corvis, vexat censura columbis.*
Our censor's rule condemns the doves while acquitting the ravens.
Satires no. 2, l. 63 (translated by Niall Rudd)

13 *Nemo repente fuit turpissimus.*
No one ever suddenly became depraved.
Satires no. 2, l. 83

14 *Iam pridem Syrus in Tiberim defluxit Orontes Et linguam et mores.*
The Syrian Orontes has now for long been pouring into the Tiber, with its own language and ways of behaving.
Satires no. 3, l. 62

15 *Grammaticus, rhetor, geometres, pictor, aliptes, Augur, schoenobates, medicus, magus, omnia novit Graeculus esuriens: in caelum iusseris ibit.*
Scholar, public speaker, geometrician, painter, physical training instructor, diviner of the future, rope-dancer, doctor, magician, the hungry little Greek can do everything: send him to—heaven (and he'll go there).
Satires no. 3, l. 76

16 *Nil habet infelix paupertas durius in se Quam quod ridiculos homines facit.*
The misfortunes of poverty carry with them nothing harder to bear than that it makes men ridiculous.
Satires no. 3, l. 152

17 *Haud facile emergunt quorum virtutibus obstat Res angusta domi.*
They do not easily rise out of obscurity whose talents straitened circumstances obstruct at home.
Satires no. 3, l. 164

18 *. . . Omnia Romae Cum pretio.*
Everything in Rome has its price.
Satires no. 3, l. 183

19 *Rara avis in terris nigroque simillima cycno.*
A rare bird on this earth, like nothing so much as a black swan.
Satires no. 6, l. 165

20 *Hoc volo, sic iubeo, sit pro ratione voluntas.*
I will have this done, so I order it done; let my will replace reasoned judgement.
Satires no. 6, l. 223

21 *Nulla fere causa est, in qua non femina litem moverit.*
There's hardly a case that comes to court that is not inspired by a woman.
Satires no. 6, l. 242 (translated by Niall Rudd)

22 *'Pone seram, cohibe.' Sed quis custodiet ipsos Custodes? Cauta est et ab illis incipit uxor.*

'Bolt her in, keep her indoors.' But who is to
guard the guards themselves? Your wife is prudent
and begins with them.
Satires no. 6, l. 347

1   *Tenet insanabile multos*
Scribendi cacoethes et aegro in corde senescit.
Many suffer from the incurable disease of writing,
and it becomes chronic in their sick minds.
Satires no. 7, l. 51

2 *Occidit miseros crambe repetita magistros.*
Re-hashed cabbage wore out the wretched
teachers.
Satires no. 7, l. 154

3 *Nobilitas sola est atque unica virtus.*
Virtue is the one and only nobility.
Satires no, 8, l. 20

4 *Summum crede nefas animam praeferre pudori*
Et propter vitam vivendi perdere causas.
Count it the greatest sin to prefer mere existence
to honour, and for the sake of life to lose the
reasons for living.
Satires no. 8, l. 83 to honour

5 *Cantabit vacuus coram latrone viator.*
Travel light and you can sing in the robber's face.
Satires no. 10, l. 22

6 . . . *Verbosa et grandis epistula venit*
A Capreis.
A huge wordy letter came from Capri.
on the Emperor **Tiberius**'s *letter to the Senate, which*
caused the downfall of Sejanus in AD *31*
Satires no. 10, l. 71

7 . . . *Duas tantum res anxius optat,*
Panem et circenses.
Only two things does he [the modern citizen]
anxiously wish for—bread and circuses.
Satires no. 10, l. 80

8 *Expende Hannibalem: quot libras in duce summo*
Invenies?
Weigh Hannibal: how many pounds will you find
in that great general?
Satires no. 10, l. 147

9 . . . *I, demens, et saevas curre per Alpes*
Ut pueris placeas et declamatio fias.
Off you go, madman, and hurry across the
horrible Alps, duly to delight schoolboys and
become a subject for practising speech-making.
on Hannibal
Satires no. 10, l. 166

10   *Mors sola fatetur*
Quantula sint hominum corpuscula.
Death alone reveals how small are men's poor
bodies.
on Hannibal
Satires no. 10, l. 172

11 *Orandum est ut sit mens sana in corpore sano.*
One should pray for a sound mind in a sound
body.
Satires no. 10, l. 356

12 *Voluptates commendat rarior usus.*
The less we indulge our pleasures the more we
enjoy them.
Satires no. 11, l. 208 (translated by Niall Rudd)

13 . . . *Prima est haec ultio, quod se*
Iudice nemo nocens absolvitur.
This is the first of punishments, that no guilty
man is acquitted if judged by himself.
Satires no. 13, l. 2

14   *Quippe minuti*
Semper et infirmi est animi exiguique voluptas
Ultio.
Indeed, revenge is always the pleasure of a paltry,
feeble, tiny mind.
Satires no. 13, l. 189

15 *Maxima debetur puero reverentia, siquid*
Turpe paras, nec tu pueri contempseris annos.
A child is owed the greatest respect; if you ever
have something disgraceful in mind, don't ignore
your son's tender years.
Satires no. 14, l. 47

Pauline Kael 1919–
American film critic

16 The words 'Kiss Kiss Bang Bang' which I saw on
an Italian movie poster, are perhaps the briefest
statement imaginable of the basic appeal of
movies.
Kiss Kiss Bang Bang (1968) 'Note on the Title'

Franz Kafka 1883–1924
Czech novelist
see also **Opening lines** 575:19

17 There are two cardinal human sins from which all
others derive: impatience and indolence. Perhaps
there is only one cardinal sin: impatience. Because
of impatience we were driven out of Paradise;
because of impatience we cannot return.
Collected Aphorisms no. 3, in *Shorter Works* vol. 1 (1973)

18 When Gregor Samsa awoke one morning from
uneasy dreams he found himself transformed in
his bed into a gigantic insect.
The Metamorphosis (1915) ch. 1; see **Austin** 40:23

19 Was he an animal, that music could capture him
so completely? It seemed to him that he was being
shown the way to the longed for, unknown,
nourishment.
The Metamorphosis (1915) ch. 3

20 You may object that it is not a trial at all; you are
quite right, for it is only a trial if I recognize it as
such.
The Trial (1925) ch. 2

21 It's often better to be in chains than to be free.
The Trial (1925) ch. 8

1 'It is not necessary to accept everything as true, we must only accept it as necessary.'
'A melancholy conclusion . . . It turns lying into a universal principle.'
The Trial (1925) ch. 9

Frida Kahlo 1907–54

Mexican painter
see also Last words 472:8

2 I paint my own reality.
Hayden Herrera *Frida* (1983)

3 Feet, why do I need them if I have wings to fly?
after the amputation of her right leg due to gangrene
diary entry, 1953; Martha Zamora *Frida Kahlo: the Brush of Anguish* (1990)

Gus Kahn 1886–1941 and Raymond B. Egan 1890–1952

American songwriters

4 There's nothing surer,
The rich get rich and the poor get children.
In the meantime, in between time,
Ain't we got fun.
'Ain't We Got Fun' (1921 song)

Nicholas Kaldor 1908–86

British economist

5 There is no need for the economist to prove . . . that as a result of the adoption of a certain measure nobody is going to suffer. In order to establish his case, it is quite sufficient for him to show that even if all those who suffer as a result are fully compensated for their loss, the rest of the community will still be better off than before.
'Welfare Propositions of Economics' in *Economic Journal* September 1939

Immanuel Kant 1724–1804

German philosopher

6 Two things fill the mind with ever new and increasing wonder and awe, the more often and the more seriously reflection concentrates upon them: the starry heaven above me and the moral law within me.
Critique of Practical Reason (1788)

7 Nothing in the world—indeed nothing even beyond the world—can possibly be conceived which could be called good without qualification except a *good will*.
Foundation of the Metaphysics of Morals (1785) sect. 1

8 I am never to act otherwise than so that I could also will that my maxim should become a universal law.
Fundamental Principles of the Metaphysics of Ethics (1785) sect. 1 (translated by T. K. Abbott)

9 There is an imperative which commands a certain conduct immediately, without having as its condition any other purpose to be attained by it.

This imperative is Categorical . . . This imperative may be called that of Morality.
Fundamental Principles of the Metaphysics of Ethics (1785) sect. 2 (translated by T. K. Abbott)

10 Whoever wills the end, wills also (so far as reason decides his conduct) the means in his power which are indispensably necessary thereto.
Fundamental Principles of the Metaphysics of Ethics (1785) sect. 2 (translated by T. K. Abbott)

11 Happiness is not an ideal of reason but of imagination.
Fundamental Principles of the Metaphysics of Ethics (1785) sect. 2 (translated by T. K. Abbott)

12 So act as to treat humanity, whether in thine own person or in that of any other, in every case as an end withal, never as means only.
Fundamental Principles of the Metaphysics of Ethics (1785) sect. 2 (translated by T. K. Abbott)

13 Out of the crooked timber of humanity no straight thing can ever be made.
Idee zu einer allgemeinen Geschichte in weltbürgerlicher Absicht (1784) proposition 6

Rosabeth Moss Kanter 1943–

American management consultant and writer

14 Succeed, succeed, succeed — and raise terrific children.
referring to opportunities for women to balance work and family commitments
When Giants Learn to Dance (1989)

Donna Karan 1948–

American fashion designer and businesswoman

15 Sometimes fashion moves from the moment to the moment to the moment. But where is the integrity in design?
in *Detroit News* February 2000

Alphonse Karr 1808–90

French novelist and journalist

16 *Si l'on veut abolir la peine de mort en ce cas, que MM les assassins commencent.*
In that case, if we are to abolish the death penalty, let the murderers take the first step.
Les Guêpes January 1849 (6th series, 1859)

17 *Plus ça change, plus c'est la même chose.*
The more things change, the more they are the same.
Les Guêpes January 1849 (6th series, 1859)

George S. Kaufman 1889–1961

American dramatist

18 Satire is what closes Saturday night.
Scott Meredith *George S. Kaufman and his Friends* (1974) ch. 6

Gerald Kaufman 1930–

British Labour politician

1 The longest suicide note in history.
on the Labour Party manifesto New Hope for Britain
(*1983*)
   Denis Healey *The Time of My Life* (1989) ch. 23

Paul Kaufman and Mike Anthony

American songwriters

2 Poetry in motion.
   title of song (1960); see **Grahame** 358:13

Christoph Kaufmann 1753–95

German man of letters

3 *Sturm und Drang.*
   Storm and stress.
   title suggested by Kaufmann for a romantic drama of the
   American War of Independence by the German dramatist,
   F. M. Klinger (1775), and thereafter given to a period of
   literary ferment which prevailed in Germany during the
   latter part of the 18th century

Kenneth Kaunda 1924–

Zambian statesman, President 1964–91

4 Westerners have aggressive problem-solving
   minds; Africans experience people.
   attributed, 1990

Patrick Kavanagh 1904–67

Irish poet

5 Clay is the word and clay is the flesh
   Where the potato-gatherers like mechanized
      scarecrows move
   Along the side-fall of the hill—Maguire and his
      men.
   'The Great Hunger' (1947)

6   The weak, washy way of true
                  tragedy—
   A sick horse nosing around the meadow for a
      clean place to die.
   'The Great Hunger' (1947)

7 I hate what every poet hates in spite
   Of all the solemn talk of contemplation.
   Oh, Alexander Selkirk knew the plight
   Of being king and government and nation.
   A road, a mile of kingdom, I am king
   Of banks and stones and every blooming thing.
   'Inniskeen Road: July Evening' (1936); see **Cowper** 248:24

Danny Kaye see Film lines 320:15

Paul Keating 1944–

Australian Labor statesman; Prime Minister 1991–6

8 This is a recession that Australia had to have.
   speaking as Federal Treasurer, 29 November 1990

9 Even as it [Great Britain] walked out on you and
   joined the Common Market, you were still looking
   for your MBEs and your knighthoods, and all the
rest of the regalia that comes with it. You would
take Australia right back down the time tunnel to
the cultural cringe where you have always come
from.
*addressing Australian Conservative supporters of
Great Britain*
   speech, House of Representatives (Australia) 27 February
   1992; see **Phillips** 595:1

10 I'm a bastard. But I'm a bastard who gets the mail
   through. And they appreciate that.
   in 1994, to a senior colleague
   in *Sunday Telegraph* 20 November 1994

John Keats 1795–1821

English poet
on Keats: see **Bulwer-Lytton** *164:4,* **Byron** *181:27,* **Byron**
184:14, **Lockhart** *489:4,* **Yeats** *854:7; see also* **Epitaphs** *310:4*

11 Bright star, would I were steadfast as thou art.
   first line of sonnet (written 1819)

12 The imagination of a boy is healthy, and the
   mature imagination of a man is healthy; but there
   is a space of life between, in which the soul is in a
   ferment, the character undecided, the way of life
   uncertain, the ambition thick-sighted: thence
   proceeds mawkishness.
   Endymion (1818) preface

13 A thing of beauty is a joy for ever.
   Endymion (1818) bk. 1, l. 1; see **Rowland** 657:12

14 They alway must be with us, or we die.
   Endymion (1818) bk. 1, l. 33

15 St Agnes' Eve—Ah, bitter chill it was!
   The owl, for all his feathers, was a-cold;
   The hare limped trembling through the frozen
      grass,
   And silent was the flock in woolly fold.
   'The Eve of St Agnes' (1820) st. 1

16 The sculptured dead, on each side, seem to freeze,
   Emprisoned in black, purgatorial rails.
   'The Eve of St Agnes' (1820) st. 2

17 The silver, snarling trumpets 'gan to chide.
   'The Eve of St Agnes' (1820) st. 4

18 And soft adorings from their loves receive
   Upon the honeyed middle of the night.
   'The Eve of St Agnes' (1820) st. 6

19 Out went the taper as she hurried in;
   Its little smoke, in pallid moonshine, died.
   'The Eve of St Agnes' (1820) st. 23

20 A casement high and triple-arched there was,
   All garlanded with carven imag'ries
   Of fruits, and flowers, and bunches of knot-grass,
   And diamonded with panes of quaint device,
   Innumerable of stains and splendid dyes,
   As are the tiger-moth's deep-damasked wings.
   'The Eve of St Agnes' (1820) st. 24

21   By degrees
   Her rich attire creeps rustling to her knees.
   'The Eve of St Agnes' (1820) st. 26

22 Trembling in her soft and chilly nest.
   'The Eve of St Agnes' (1820) st. 27

1 As though a rose should shut, and be a bud again.
    'The Eve of St Agnes' (1820) st. 27

2 And still she slept an azure-lidded sleep,
    In blanchèd linen, smooth, and lavendered,
    While he from forth the closet brought a heap
    Of candied apple, quince, and plum, and gourd;
    With jellies soother than the creamy curd,
    And lucent syrops, tinct with cinnamon;
    Manna and dates, in argosy transferred
    From Fez; and spiced dainties, every one,
    From silken Samarcand to cedared Lebanon.
    'The Eve of St Agnes' (1820) st. 30

3 He played an ancient ditty, long since mute,
    In Provence called, 'La belle dame sans mercy.'
    'The Eve of St Agnes' (1820) st. 33

4 And they are gone: aye, ages long ago
    These lovers fled away into the storm.
    'The Eve of St Agnes' (1820) st. 42

5 Fanatics have their dreams, wherewith they
        weave
    A paradise for a sect.
    'The Fall of Hyperion' (written 1819) l. 1

6 The poet and the dreamer are distinct,
    Diverse, sheer opposite, antipodes.
    The one pours out a balm upon the world,
    The other vexes it.
    'The Fall of Hyperion' (written 1819) l. 199

7 Ever let the fancy roam,
    Pleasure never is at home.
    'Fancy' (1820) l. 1

8 O sweet Fancy! let her loose;
    Summer's joys are spoilt by use.
    'Fancy' (1820) l. 9

9 Deep in the shady sadness of a vale
    Far sunken from the healthy breath of morn,
    Far from the fiery noon, and eve's one star,
    Sat grey-haired Saturn, quiet as a stone.
    'Hyperion: A Fragment' (1820) bk. 1, l. 1

10   No stir of air was there,
    Not so much life as on a summer's day
    Robs not one light seed from the feathered grass,
    But where the dead leaf fell, there did it rest.
    'Hyperion: A Fragment' (1820) bk. 1, l. 7

11 That large utterance of the early gods!
    'Hyperion: A Fragment' (1820) bk. 1, l. 51

12 O aching time! O moments big as years!
    'Hyperion: A Fragment' (1820) bk. 1, l. 64

13 As when, upon a trancèd summer-night,
    Those green-robed senators of mighty woods,
    Tall oaks, branch-charmèd by the earnest stars,
    Dream, and so dream all night without a stir.
    'Hyperion: A Fragment' (1820) bk. 1, l. 72

14   Sometimes eagle's wings,
    Unseen before by gods or wondering men,
    Darkened the place.
    'Hyperion: A Fragment' (1820) bk. 1, l. 182

15 And still they were the same bright, patient stars.
    'Hyperion: A Fragment' (1820) bk. 1, l. 353

16 Knowledge enormous makes a god of me.
    'Hyperion: A Fragment' (1820) bk. 3, l. 113

17 I had a dove and the sweet dove died;
    And I have thought it died of grieving:
    O, what could it grieve for? Its feet were tied,
    With a silken thread of my own hand's weaving.
    'I had a dove and the sweet dove died' (written 1818)

18 So the two brothers and their murdered man
    Rode past fair Florence.
    'Isabella; or, The Pot of Basil' (1820) st. 27

19 And she forgot the stars, the moon, and sun,
    And she forgot the blue above the trees,
    And she forgot the dells where waters run,
    And she forgot the chilly autumn breeze;
    She had no knowledge when the day was done,
    And the new morn she saw not: but in peace
    Hung over her sweet Basil evermore,
    And moistened it with tears unto the core.
    'Isabella; or, The Pot of Basil' (1820) st. 53

20   'For cruel 'tis,' said she,
    'To steal my Basil-pot away from me.'
    'Isabella; or, The Pot of Basil' (1820) st. 62

21   And then there crept
    A little noiseless noise among the leaves,
    Born of the very sigh that silence heaves.
    'I stood tip-toe upon a little hill' (1817) l. 10

22 Here are sweet peas, on tip-toe for a flight.
    'I stood tip-toe upon a little hill' (1817) l. 57

23 Oh, what can ail thee knight at arms
    Alone and palely loitering?
    The sedge has withered from the lake
    And no birds sing!
    'La belle dame sans merci' (1820) st. 1

24 I see a lily on thy brow
    With anguish moist and fever dew,
    And on thy cheeks a fading rose
    Fast withereth too.
    'La belle dame sans merci' (1820) st. 3

25 I met a lady in the meads
    Full beautiful, a faery's child
    Her hair was long, her foot was light
    And her eyes were wild.
    'La belle dame sans merci' (1820) st. 4

26 She looked at me as she did love
    And made sweet moan.
    'La belle dame sans merci' (1820) st. 5

27 I set her on my pacing steed
    And nothing else saw all day long
    For sidelong would she bend and sing
    A faery's song.
    'La belle dame sans merci' (1820) st. 6

28 . . . La belle dame sans merci
    Thee hath in thrall.
    'La belle dame sans merci' (1820) st. 10

29 I saw their starved lips in the gloam
    With horrid warning gapèd wide
    And I awoke and found me here
    On the cold hill's side.
    'La belle dame sans merci' (1820) st. 11

30 She was a gordian shape of dazzling hue,
    Vermilion-spotted, golden, green, and blue;

Striped like a zebra, freckled like a pard,
Eyed like a peacock, and all crimson barred.
  'Lamia' (1820) pt. 1, l. 47

1 Love in a hut, with water and a crust,
Is—Love, forgive us!—cinders, ashes, dust;
Love in a palace is perhaps at last
More grievous torment than a hermit's fast.
  'Lamia' (1820) pt. 2, l. 1; see **Colman** 235:17

2 In pale contented sort of discontent.
  'Lamia' (1820) pt. 2, l. 135

3   Do not all charms fly
At the mere touch of cold philosophy?
  'Lamia' (1820) pt. 2, l. 229

4 Philosophy will clip an Angel's wings.
  'Lamia' (1820) pt. 2, l. 234

5 Souls of poets dead and gone,
What Elysium have ye known,
Happy field or mossy cavern,
Choicer than the Mermaid Tavern?
Have ye tippled drink more fine
Than mine host's Canary wine?
  'Lines on the Mermaid Tavern' (1820)

6 Thou still unravished bride of quietness,
Thou foster-child of silence and slow time.
  'Ode on a Grecian Urn' (1820) st. 1

7 What men or gods are these? What maidens loth?
What mad pursuit? What struggle to escape?
What pipes and timbrels? What wild ecstasy?
  'Ode on a Grecian Urn' (1820) st. 1

8 Heard melodies are sweet, but those unheard
Are sweeter.
  'Ode on a Grecian Urn' (1820) st. 2

9 For ever wilt thou love, and she be fair!
  'Ode on a Grecian Urn' (1820) st. 2

10 For ever piping songs for ever new.
  'Ode on a Grecian Urn' (1820) st. 3

11 For ever warm and still to be enjoyed,
For ever panting, and for ever young;
All breathing human passion far above,
That leaves a heart high-sorrowful and cloyed,
A burning forehead, and a parching tongue.
  'Ode on a Grecian Urn' (1820) st. 3

12 Who are these coming to the sacrifice?
To what green altar, O mysterious priest,
Lead'st thou that heifer lowing at the skies?
  'Ode on a Grecian Urn' (1820) st. 4

13 O Attic shape! Fair attitude!
  'Ode on a Grecian Urn' (1820) st. 5

14 Thou, silent form, dost tease us out of thought
As doth eternity: Cold Pastoral!
  'Ode on a Grecian Urn' (1820) st. 5

15 'Beauty is truth, truth beauty,'—that is all
Ye know on earth, and all ye need to know.
  'Ode on a Grecian Urn' (1820) st. 5

16 No, no, go not to Lethe, neither twist
Wolf's-bane, tight-rooted, for its poisonous wine.
  'Ode on Melancholy' (1820) st. 1

17 Nor let the beetle, nor the death-moth be
Your mournful Psyche.
  'Ode on Melancholy' (1820) st. 1

18 But when the melancholy fit shall fall
Sudden from heaven like a weeping cloud,
That fosters the droop-headed flowers all,
And hides the green hill in an April shroud;
Then glut thy sorrow on a morning rose,
Or on the rainbow of the salt sand-wave,
Or on the wealth of globèd peonies.
  'Ode on Melancholy' (1820) st. 2

19 She dwells with Beauty—Beauty that must die;
And Joy, whose hand is ever at his lips
Bidding adieu; and aching Pleasure nigh,
Turning to poison while the bee-mouth sips:
Ay, in the very temple of Delight
Veiled Melancholy has her sovran shrine,
Though seen of none save him whose strenuous
      tongue
Can burst Joy's grape against his palate fine;
His soul shall taste the sadness of her might,
And be among her cloudy trophies hung.
  'Ode on Melancholy' (1820) st. 3

20 My heart aches, and a drowsy numbness pains
My sense, as though of hemlock I had drunk,
Or emptied some dull opiate to the drains
One minute past, and Lethe-wards had sunk.
  'Ode to a Nightingale' (1820) st. 1

21 O, for a draught of vintage! that hath been
Cooled a long age in the deep-delvèd earth,
Tasting of Flora and the country green.
  'Ode to a Nightingale' (1820) st. 2

22 O for a beaker full of the warm South,
Full of the true, the blushful Hippocrene,
With beaded bubbles winking at the brim,
And purple-stainèd mouth;
That I might drink, and leave the world unseen,
And with thee fade away into the forest dim.
  'Ode to a Nightingale' (1820) st. 2

23 Fade far away, dissolve, and quite forget
What thou among the leaves hast never known,
The weariness, the fever, and the fret.
  'Ode to a Nightingale' (1820) st. 3

24 Where youth grows pale, and spectre-thin, and
      dies.
  'Ode to a Nightingale' (1820) st. 3

25 Away! away! for I will fly to thee,
Not charioted by Bacchus and his pards,
But on the viewless wings of Poesy,
Though the dull brain perplexes and retards:
Already with thee! tender is the night.
  'Ode to a Nightingale' (1820) st. 4

26 Fast fading violets covered up in leaves;
And mid-May's eldest child,
The coming musk-rose, full of dewy wine,
The murmurous haunt of flies on summer eves.
  'Ode to a Nightingale' (1820) st. 5

27 Darkling I listen; and, for many a time
I have been half in love with easeful Death,
Called him soft names in many a musèd rhyme,
To take into the air my quiet breath;

Now more than ever seems it rich to die,
To cease upon the midnight with no pain.
'Ode to a Nightingale' (1820) st. 6

1 Thou wast not born for death, immortal bird!
No hungry generations tread thee down;
The voice I hear this passing night was heard
In ancient days by emperor and clown:
Perhaps the self-same song that found a path
Through the sad heart of Ruth, when, sick for
home,
She stood in tears amid the alien corn;
The same that oft-times hath
Charmed magic casements, opening on the foam
Of perilous seas, in faery lands forlorn.
'Ode to a Nightingale' (1820) st. 7; see **Hood** 395:10

2 Forlorn! the very word is like a bell
To toll me back from thee to my sole self!
Adieu! the fancy cannot cheat so well
As she is famed to do, deceiving elf.
'Ode to a Nightingale' (1820) st. 8

3 Was it a vision, or a waking dream?
Fled is that music:—do I wake or sleep?
'Ode to a Nightingale' (1820) st. 8

4 'Mid hushed, cool-rooted flowers, fragrant-eyed,
Blue, silver-white, and budded Tyrian.
'Ode to Psyche' (1820) st. 1

5 Much have I travelled in the realms of gold,
And many goodly states and kingdoms seen.
'On First Looking into Chapman's Homer' (1817)

6 Then felt I like some watcher of the skies
When a new planet swims into his ken;
Or like stout Cortez when with eagle eyes
He stared at the Pacific—and all his men
Looked at each other with a wild surmise—
Silent, upon a peak in Darien.
'On First Looking into Chapman's Homer' (1817)

7   Mortality
Weighs heavily on me like unwilling sleep.
'On Seeing the Elgin Marbles' (1817)

8 The poetry of earth is never dead:
When all the birds are faint with the hot sun,
And hide in cooling trees, a voice will run
From hedge to hedge about the new-mown mead.
'On the Grasshopper and Cricket' (1817)

9 It keeps eternal whisperings around
Desolate shores,—and with its mighty swell
Gluts twice ten thousand Caverns.
'On the Sea' (1817)

10 O for ten years, that I may overwhelm
Myself in poesy; so I may do the deed
That my own soul has to itself decreed.
'Sleep and Poetry' (1817) l. 96

11 They swayed about upon a rocking horse,
And thought it Pegasus.
'Sleep and Poetry' (1817) l. 186

12 And they shall be accounted poet kings
Who simply tell the most heart-easing things.
'Sleep and Poetry' (1817) l. 267

13 Turn the key deftly in the oilèd wards,
And seal the hushèd casket of my soul.
'Sonnet to Sleep' (written 1819)

14 Season of mists and mellow fruitfulness,
Close bosom-friend of the maturing sun;
Conspiring with him how to load and bless
With fruit the vines that round the thatch-eaves
run.
'To Autumn' (1820) st. 1

15 Who hath not seen thee oft amid thy store?
Sometimes whoever seeks abroad may find
Thee sitting careless on a granary floor,
Thy hair soft-lifted by the winnowing wind;
Or on a half-reaped furrow sound asleep,
Drowsed with the fume of poppies while thy hook
Spares the next swath and all its twinèd flowers.
'To Autumn' (1820) st. 2

16 Where are the songs of Spring? Ay, where are
they?
Think not of them, thou hast thy music too.
'To Autumn' (1820) st. 3

17 Then in a wailful choir the small gnats mourn
Among the river sallows, borne aloft
Or sinking as the light wind lives or dies.
'To Autumn' (1820) st. 3

18 The red-breast whistles from a garden-croft;
And gathering swallows twitter in the skies.
'To Autumn' (1820) st. 3

19 How soon the film of death obscured that eye,
Whence genius wildly flashed.
'To Chatterton' (written 1815)

20 Aye on the shores of darkness there is light,
And precipices show untrodden green,
There is a budding morrow in midnight,
There is a triple sight in blindness keen.
'To Homer' (written 1818)

21   It is a flaw
In happiness, to see beyond our bourn.
'To J. H. Reynolds, Esq.' (written 1818)

22 To one who has been long in city pent,
'Tis very sweet to look into the fair
And open face of heaven.
'To one who has been long in city pent' (1817); see **Milton**
533:28

23 When I have fears that I may cease to be
Before my pen has gleaned my teeming brain.
'When I have fears that I may cease to be' (written 1818)

24 When I behold, upon the night's starred face
Huge cloudy symbols of a high romance.
'When I have fears that I may cease to be' (written 1818)

25   Then on the shore
Of the wide world I stand alone and think
Till love and fame to nothingness do sink.
'When I have fears that I may cease to be' (written 1818)

26 A long poem is a test of invention which I take to
be the polar star of poetry, as fancy is the sails,
and imagination the rudder.
letter to Benjamin Bailey, 8 October 1817, in H. E. Rollins
(ed.) *Letters of John Keats* (1958) vol. 1

1 I am certain of nothing but the holiness of the heart's affections and the truth of imagination—what the imagination seizes as beauty must be truth—whether it existed before or not.

letter to Benjamin Bailey, 22 November 1817, in H. E. Rollins (ed.) *Letters of John Keats* (1958) vol. 1; see **Keats** 444:15

2 O for a life of sensations rather than of thoughts!

letter to Benjamin Bailey, 22 November 1817, in H. E. Rollins (ed.) *Letters of John Keats* (1958) vol. 1

3 A man should have the fine point of his soul taken off to become fit for this world.

letter to J. H. Reynolds, 22 November 1817, in H. E. Rollins (ed.) *Letters of John Keats* (1958) vol. 1

4 Negative Capability, that is when man is capable of being in uncertainties, mysteries, doubts, without any irritable reaching after fact and reason—Coleridge, for instance, would let go by a fine isolated verisimilitude caught from the penetralium of mystery, from being incapable of remaining content with half knowledge.

letter to George and Thomas Keats, 21 December 1817, in H. E. Rollins (ed.) *Letters of John Keats* (1958) vol. 1

5 There is nothing stable in the world—uproar's your only music.

letter to George and Thomas Keats, 13 January 1818, in H. E. Rollins (ed.) *Letters of John Keats* (1958) vol. 1

6 For the sake of a few fine imaginative or domestic passages, are we to be bullied into a certain philosophy engendered in the whims of an egotist?
on the overbearing influence of **Wordsworth** *upon his contemporaries*

letter to J. H. Reynolds, 3 February 1818, in H. E. Rollins (ed.) *Letters of John Keats* (1958) vol. 1

7 We hate poetry that has a palpable design upon us—and if we do not agree, seems to put its hand in its breeches pocket. Poetry should be great and unobtrusive, a thing which enters into one's soul, and does not startle it or amaze it with itself, but with its subject.

letter to J. H. Reynolds, 3 February 1818, in H. E. Rollins (ed.) *Letters of John Keats* (1958) vol. 1

8 If poetry comes not as naturally as the leaves to a tree it had better not come at all.

letter to John Taylor, 27 February 1818, in H. E. Rollins (ed.) *Letters of John Keats* (1958) vol. 1

9 Scenery is fine—but human nature is finer.

letter to Benjamin Bailey, 13 March 1818, in H. E. Rollins (ed.) *Letters of John Keats* (1958) vol. 1

10 It is impossible to live in a country which is continually under hatches . . . Rain! Rain! Rain!

letter to J. H. Reynolds from Devon, 10 April 1818, in H. E. Rollins (ed.) *Letters of John Keats* (1958) vol. 1

11 I am in that temper that if I were under water I would scarcely kick to come to the top.

letter to Benjamin Bailey, 25 May 1818, in H. E. Rollins (ed.) *Letters of John Keats* (1958) vol. 1

12 O the flummery of a birth place! Cant! Cant! Cant! It is enough to give a spirit the guts-ache.

letter to John Hamilton Reynolds, 11 July 1818 in M. B. Forman (ed.) *Letters of John Keats* (1952)

13 I do think better of womankind than to suppose they care whether Mister John Keats five feet high likes them or not.

letter to Benjamin Bailey, 18 July 1818, in H. E. Rollins (ed.) *Letters of John Keats* (1958) vol. 1

14 There is an awful warmth about my heart like a load of immortality.

letter to J. H. Reynolds, 22 September 1818, in H. E. Rollins (ed.) *Letters of John Keats* (1958) vol. 1

15 In Endymion, I leaped headlong into the sea, and thereby have become better acquainted with the soundings, the quicksands, and the rocks, than if I had stayed upon the green shore, and piped a silly pipe, and took tea and comfortable advice.

letter to James Hessey, 8 October 1818, in H. E. Rollins (ed.) *Letters of John Keats* (1958) vol. 1

16 As to the poetical character itself, (I mean that sort of which, if I am any thing, I am a member; that sort distinguished from the Wordsworthian or egotistical sublime; which is a thing *per se* and stands alone) it is not itself—it has no self . . . It has as much delight in conceiving an Iago as an Imogen.

letter to Richard Woodhouse, 27 October 1818, in H. E. Rollins (ed.) *Letters of John Keats* (1958) vol. 1

17 The roaring of the wind is my wife and the stars through the window pane are my children.

letter to George and Georgiana Keats, 24 October 1818, in H. E. Rollins (ed.) *Letters of John Keats* (1958) vol. 1

18 I have come to this resolution—never to write for the sake of writing, or making a poem, but from running over with any little knowledge or experience which many years of reflection may perhaps give me—otherwise I shall be dumb.

letter to B. R. Haydon, 8 March 1819, in H. E. Rollins (ed.) *Letters of John Keats* (1958) vol. 2

19 I go among the fields and catch a glimpse of a stoat or a fieldmouse peeping out of the withered grass—The creature hath a purpose and its eyes are bright with it—I go amongst the buildings of a city and I see a man hurrying along—to what? The Creature has a purpose and his eyes are bright with it.

letter to George and Georgiana Keats, 19 March 1819, in H. E. Rollins (ed.) *Letters of John Keats* (1958) vol. 2

20 Call the world if you please 'The vale of soul-making'.

letter to George and Georgiana Keats, 21 April 1819, in H. E. Rollins (ed.) *Letters of John Keats* (1958) vol. 2

21 I have met with women whom I really think would like to be married to a poem and to be given away by a novel.

letter to Fanny Brawne, 8 July 1819, in H. E. Rollins (ed.) *Letters of John Keats* (1958) vol. 2

22 I have two luxuries to brood over in my walks, your loveliness and the hour of my death. O that I could have possession of them both in the same minute.

letter to Fanny Brawne, 25 July 1819, in H. E. Rollins (ed.) *Letters of John Keats* (1958) vol. 2

1 Fine writing is next to fine doing the top thing in the world.
> letter to J. H. Reynolds, 24 August 1819, in H. E. Rollins (ed.) *Letters of John Keats* (1958) vol. 2

2 All clean and comfortable I sit down to write.
> letter to George and Georgiana Keats, 17 September 1819, in H. E. Rollins (ed.) *Letters of John Keats* (1958) vol. 2

3 The only means of strengthening one's intellect is to make up one's mind about nothing—to let the mind be a thoroughfare for all thoughts. Not a select party.
> letter to George and Georgiana Keats, 24 September 1819, in H. E. Rollins (ed.) *Letters of John Keats* (1958) vol. 2

4 If you should have a boy do not christen him John . . . 'Tis a bad name and goes against a man. If my name had been Edmund I should have been more fortunate.
> letter to George and Georgiana Keats, 13 January 1820, in H. E. Rollins (ed.) *Letters of John Keats* (1958) vol. 2

5 'If I should die,' said I to myself, 'I have left no immortal work behind me—nothing to make my friends proud of my memory—but I have loved the principle of beauty in all things, and if I had had time I would have made myself remembered.'
> letter to Fanny Brawne, *c.*February 1820, in H. E. Rollins (ed.) *Letters of John Keats* (1958) vol. 2

6 I wish you could invent some means to make me at all happy without you. Every hour I am more and more concentrated in you; every thing else tastes like chaff in my mouth.
> letter to Fanny Brawne, August 1820, in H. E. Rollins (ed.) *Letters of John Keats* (1958) vol. 2

7 'Load every rift' of your subject with ore.
> letter to Shelley, August 1820, in H. E. Rollins (ed.) *Letters of John Keats* (1958) vol. 2; see **Spenser** 751:23

8 I shall soon be laid in the quiet grave—thank God for the quiet grave—O! I can feel the cold earth upon me—the daisies growing over me—O for this quiet—it will be my first.
> letter from Joseph Severn to John Taylor, 6 March 1821, in H. E. Rollins (ed.) *Letters of John Keats* (1958) vol. 2

9 In disease Medical Men guess: if they cannot ascertain a disease, they call it nervous.
> J. A. Gere and John Sparrow (eds.) *Geoffrey Madan's Notebooks* (1981); attributed

John Keats 1920–
American journalist

10 All this is so much hoopla, because our automobiles are so poorly designed as to be unsafe at *any* speed, and more speed simply increases the danger.
> *The Insolent Chariots* (1958) ch. 4

John Keble 1792–1866
English clergyman; leader of the Oxford Movement

11 Blessed are the pure in heart,
For they shall see our God,
The secret of the Lord is theirs,
Their soul is Christ's abode.
> *The Christian Year* (1827) 'Blessed are the pure in heart'

12 New every morning is the love
Our wakening and uprising prove;
Through sleep and darkness safely brought,
Restored to life, and power, and thought.
> *The Christian Year* (1827) 'Morning'

13 The trivial round, the common task,
Would furnish all we ought to ask.
> *The Christian Year* (1827) 'Morning'

14 There is a book, who runs may read,
Which heavenly truth imparts,
And all the lore its scholars need,
Pure eyes and Christian hearts.
> *The Christian Year* (1827) 'Septuagesima'

15 The voice that breathed o'er Eden,
That earliest wedding-day,
The primal marriage blessing,
It hath not passed away.
> 'Holy Matrimony' (1857 hymn)

16 If the Church of England were to fail, it would be found in my parish.
> D. Newsome *The Parting of Friends* (1966) ch. 8, pt. 3

Brian Keenan 1950–
Irish writer and teacher
see also **Borrowed titles** *146:5*

17 Politics can only be a small part of what we are. It's a *way* of seeing, it's not all-seeing in itself.
> *An Evil Cradling* (1992)

Helen Keller 1880–1968
American writer and social reformer, blind and deaf from the age of 19 months

18 The mystery of language was revealed to me. I knew then that 'w-a-t-e-r' meant the wonderful cool something that was flowing over my hand. That living word awakened my soul, gave it light, joy, set it free!
> *The Story of My Life* (1902) ch. 4

19 Everything has its wonders, even darkness and silence, and I learn, whatever state I may be in, therein to be content.
> *The Story of My Life* (1902) ch. 22

Frank B. Kellogg see Aristide Briand 151:2

David Kelly 1944–2003
British scientist

20 I will probably be found dead in the woods.
> *remark made in February 2003 on what would happen if Iraq was invaded*
> evidence from David Broucher to the Hutton Inquiry, 21 August 2003

Hugh Kelly 1739–77
Irish dramatist

21 Of all the stages in a woman's life, none is so dangerous as the period between her acknowledgment of a passion for a man, and the day set apart for her nuptials.
> *Memoirs of a Magdalen* (1767, ed. 1782)

1 Your people of refined sentiments are the most troublesome creatures in the world to deal with.
   False Delicacy (performed 1768) act 5, sc. 1

Ned Kelly see Last words 473:19

Thomas Kelly 1769–1855
Irish clergyman and hymn-writer

2 The head that once was crowned with thorns
   Is crowned with glory now.
   'The head that once was crowned with thorns' (1820 hymn)

Tom Kelly
British press officer

3 This is now a game of chicken with the Beeb.
   *on the argument between Downing Street and the BBC about the content of Andrew **Gilligan**'s Today report; see **Gilligan** 349:11*
   email of 10 July 2003; in *Guardian* 19 August 2003 (online edition)

Walt Kelly see Cartoon captions 198:9

Lord Kelvin 1824–1907
British scientist

4 When you can measure what you are speaking about, and express it in numbers, you know something about it; but when you cannot measure it, when you cannot express it in numbers, your knowledge is of a meagre and unsatisfactory kind: it may be the beginning of knowledge, but you have scarcely, in your thoughts, advanced to the stage of *science*, whatever the matter may be.
   often quoted as 'If you cannot measure it, then it is not science'
   Popular Lectures and Addresses vol. 1 (1889) 'Electrical Units of Measurement', delivered 3 May 1883

Thomas à Kempis see Thomas

Thomas Ken 1637–1711
*English divine; Bishop of Bath and Wells, 1684–91, and formerly chaplain to **Charles II***

5 Awake, my soul, and with the sun
   Thy daily stage of duty run.
   Shake off dull sloth, and joyful rise
   To pay thy morning sacrifice.
   'Morning Hymn' in Winchester College *Manual of Prayers* (1695) but already in use by 1674

6 Redeem thy mis-spent time that's past,
   And live this day as if thy last.
   'Morning Hymn' (1709 ed.) v. 2

7 All praise to thee, my God, this night,
   For all the blessings of the light;
   Keep me, O keep me, King of Kings,
   Beneath thy own almighty wings.
   the first line later changed to 'Glory to thee, my God this night'
   'Evening Hymn' in Winchester College *Manual of Prayers* (1695) but already in use by 1674

8 Teach me to live, that I may dread
   The grave as little as my bed.
   'Evening Hymn' (1695) v. 3

Jaan Kenbrovin and William Kellette

9 I'm forever blowing bubbles.
   title of song (1919)

Florynce Kennedy 1916–2000
American lawyer

10 If men could get pregnant, abortion would be a sacrament.
   in *Ms.* March 1973

11 When you want to get to the suites, start in the streets.
   her rule for political activism
   attributed; in *Los Angeles Times* 28 December 2000 (obituary)

Jimmy Kennedy and Michael Carr
British songwriters

12 We're gonna hang out the washing on the Siegfried Line.
   title of song (1939)

John F. Kennedy 1917–63
American Democratic statesman, 35th President of the US, 1961–3

13 Don't buy a single vote more than necessary. I'll be damned if I'm going to pay for a landslide.
   telegraphed message from his father, read at a Gridiron dinner in Washington, 15 March 1958, and almost certainly JFK's invention; J. F. Cutler *Honey Fitz* (1962)

14 We stand today on the edge of a new frontier.
   speech accepting the Democratic nomination in Los Angeles, 15 July 1960, in *Vital Speeches* 1 August 1960

15 Let the word go forth from this time and place, to friend and foe alike, that the torch has been passed to a new generation of Americans—born in this century, tempered by war, disciplined by a hard and bitter peace.
   inaugural address, 20 January 1961, in *Vital Speeches* 1 February 1961

16 Let every nation know, whether it wishes us well or ill, that we shall pay any price, bear any burden, meet any hardship, support any friend, oppose any foe to assure the survival and the success of liberty.
   inaugural address, 20 January 1961, in *Vital Speeches* 1 February 1961

17 If a free society cannot help the many who are poor, it cannot save the few who are rich.
   inaugural address, 20 January 1961, in *Vital Speeches* 1 February 1961

18 Let us never negotiate out of fear. But let us never fear to negotiate.
   inaugural address, 20 January 1961, in *Vital Speeches* 1 February 1961

1 All this will not be finished in the first 100 days.
Nor will it be finished in the first 1,000 days, nor
in the life of this Administration, nor even perhaps
in our lifetime on this planet. But let us begin.

> inaugural address, 20 January 1961, in *Vital Speeches* 1
> February 1961

2 And so, my fellow Americans: ask not what your
country can do for you—ask what you can do for
your country. My fellow citizens of the world: ask
not what America will do for you, but what
together we can do for the freedom of man.

> inaugural address, 20 January 1961, in *Vital Speeches* 1
> February 1961; see **Gibran** 346:5, **Holmes** 393:7

3 Mankind must put an end to war or war will put
an end to mankind.

> speech to United Nations General Assembly, 25 September
> 1961, in *New York Times* 26 September 1961

4 No one has been barred on account of his race
from fighting or dying for America—there are no
'white' or 'coloured' signs on the foxholes or
graveyards of battle.

> Message to Congress on proposed Civil Rights Bill, 19 June
> 1963, in *New York Times* 20 June 1963

5 *Ich bin ein Berliner.*

I am a Berliner.

> speech in West Berlin, 26 June 1963, in *New York Times*
> 27 June 1963; see **Cicero** 223:18

6 In free society art is not a weapon . . . Artists are
not engineers of the soul.

> speech at Amherst College, Mass., 26 October 1963, in
> *New York Times* 27 October 1963; see **Gorky** 357:3, **Stalin**
> 754:2

7 It was involuntary. They sank my boat.

on being asked how he became a war hero

> Arthur M. Schlesinger Jr. *A Thousand Days* (1965) ch. 4

Joseph P. Kennedy 1888–1969

American financier and diplomat; father of J. F. Kennedy

8 We're going to sell Jack like soapflakes.

when his son John made his bid for the Presidency

> John H. Davis *The Kennedy Clan* (1984) ch. 23

9 When the going gets tough, the tough get going.

also attributed to Knute Rockne

> J. H. Cutler *Honey Fitz* (1962); see **Proverbs** 634:30

Robert Kennedy 1925–68

*American Democratic politician, son of Joseph Kennedy and
Rose Kennedy, brother of John Fitzgerald Kennedy*

10 One-fifth of the people are against everything all
the time.

> speech, University of Pennsylvania, 6 May 1964; in
> *Philadelphia Inquirer* 7 May 1964

11 For every ten men who are willing to face the
guns of an enemy there is only one willing to
brave the disapproval of his fellow, the censure of
his colleagues, the wrath of his society. Moral

courage is a rarer commodity than bravery in
battle or great intelligence.

> speech in Cape Town, 7 June 1966

Rose Kennedy 1890–1995

*American wife of Joseph Kennedy, mother of John F. Kennedy
and Robert Kennedy*

12 It's our money, and we're free to spend it any way
we please . . . If you have money you spend it, and
win.

*in response to criticism of overlavish funding of her
son Robert's 1968 presidential campaign*

> in *Daily Telegraph* 24 January 1995 (obituary)

13 Now Teddy must run.

*to her daughter, on hearing of the assassination of
Robert Kennedy*

> in *The Times* 24 January 1995 (obituary); attributed,
> perhaps apocryphal

Kenojuak Ashevak 1927–

Canadian Inuit sculptor and artist

14 A piece of paper from the outside world is as thin
as the shell of a snowbird's egg.

> *Eskimo Artist: Kenojuak* (1962 film)

Jomo Kenyatta 1891–1978

*Kenyan statesman, Prime Minister of Kenya 1963 and
President 1964–78*

15 The African is conditioned, by the cultural and
social institutions of centuries, to a freedom of
which Europe has little conception, and it is not in
his nature to accept serfdom forever. He realizes
that he must fight unceasingly for his own
emancipation; for without this he is doomed to
remain the prey of rival imperialisms.

> *Facing Mount Kenya* (1938); conclusion

Lady Caroline Keppel b. 1735

English poet

16 What's this dull town to me?
Robin's not near.
He whom I wished to see,
Wished for to hear;
Where's all the joy and mirth
Made life a heaven on earth?
O! they're all fled with thee,
Robin Adair.

> 'Robin Adair' (c.1750)

Jack Kerouac 1922–69

American novelist

17 The beat generation.

> phrase coined in the course of a conversation; in *Playboy*
> June 1959

18 It is not my fault that certain so-called bohemian
elements have found in my writings something to
hang their peculiar beatnik theories on.

> in *New York Journal-American* 8 December 1960

Jean Kerr 1923–2003

American writer

1 As someone pointed out recently, if you can keep your head when all about you are losing theirs, it's just possible you haven't grasped the situation.

Please Don't Eat the Daisies (1957) introduction; see **Kipling** 454:12

2 I feel about airplanes the way I feel about diets. It seems to me that they are wonderful things for other people to go on.

The Snake Has All the Lines (1958)

3 I'm tired of all this nonsense about beauty being only skin-deep. That's deep enough. What do you want—an adorable pancreas?

The Snake has all the Lines (1958)

William Kethe d. 1594

Scottish Calvinist

4 All people that on earth do dwell,
Sing to the Lord with cheerful voice.

'All people that on earth do dwell' in *Fourscore and Seven Psalms of David* (Geneva, 1561; later known as the Geneva Psalter); usually sung to the tune 'Old Hundredth', and often known by that name

5 The Lord, ye know, is God indeed;
Without our aid he did us make;
We are his folk, he doth us feed,
And for his sheep he doth us take.

O enter then his gates with praise,
Approach with joy his courts unto;
Praise, laud, and bless his name always,
For it is seemly so to do.

'All people that on earth do dwell' in *Fourscore and Seven Psalms of David* (Geneva, 1561; later known as the Geneva Psalter)

Ralph Kettell 1563–1643

English scholar, President of Trinity College, Oxford, from 1599

6 Here is Hey for Garsington! and Hey for Cuddesdon! and Hey Hockley! but here's nobody cries, Hey for God Almighty!

sermon at Garsington Revel, in Oliver Lawson Dick (ed.) *Aubrey's Brief Lives* (1949) 'Ralph Kettell'

Thomas Kettle 1880–1916

Irish economist and poet

7 My only programme for Ireland consists, in equal parts, of Home Rule and the Ten Commandments. My only counsel to Ireland is, that in order to become deeply Irish, she must become European.

'Apology'

8 Ireland is a small but insuppressible island half an hour nearer the sunset than Great Britain.

'On Crossing the Irish Sea'

Francis Scott Key 1779–1843

American lawyer and verse-writer

9 'Tis the star-spangled banner; O long may it wave
O'er the land of the free, and the home of the brave!

'The Star-Spangled Banner' (1814)

John Maynard Keynes 1883–1946

English economist

10 I work for a Government I despise for ends I think criminal.

letter to Duncan Grant, 15 December 1917, in *British Library Add. MSS 57931* fo. 119

11 He felt about France what Pericles felt of Athens—unique value in her, nothing else mattering; but his theory of politics was Bismarck's. He had one illusion—France; and one disillusion—mankind, including Frenchmen, and his colleagues not least.

of Georges **Clemenceau**

The Economic Consequences of the Peace (1919) ch. 3

12 Like Odysseus, the President looked wiser when he was seated.

of Woodrow **Wilson**

The Economic Consequences of the Peace (1919) ch. 3

13 Lenin was right. There is no subtler, no surer means of overturning the existing basis of society than to debauch the currency. The process engages all the hidden forces of economic law on the side of destruction, and does it in a manner which not one man in a million is able to diagnose.

The Economic Consequences of the Peace (1919) ch. 6

14 I do not know which makes a man more conservative—to know nothing but the present, or nothing but the past.

The End of Laissez-Faire (1926) pt. 1

15 This extraordinary figure of our time, this syren, this goat-footed bard, this half-human visitor to our age from the hag-ridden magic and enchanted woods of Celtic antiquity.

Essays in Biography (1933) 'Mr Lloyd George'

16 If the Treasury were to fill old bottles with banknotes, bury them at suitable depths in disused coalmines which are then filled up to the surface with town rubbish, and leave it to private enterprise on well-tried principles of *laissez-faire* to dig the notes up again (the right to do so being obtained, of course, by tendering for leases of the note-bearing territory) there need be no more unemployment and, with the help of the repercussions, the real income of the community, and its capital wealth also, would probably become a good deal greater than it actually is.

General Theory (1936) bk. 3, ch. 10

17 Madmen in authority, who hear voices in the air, are distilling their frenzy from some academic scribbler of a few years back.

General Theory (1947 ed.) ch. 24

18 *In the long run* we are all dead.

A Tract on Monetary Reform (1923) ch. 3

19 We threw good housekeeping to the winds. But we saved ourselves and helped save the world.

of Britain in the Second World War

A. J. P. Taylor *English History, 1914–1945* (1965)

Ruhollah Khomeini 1900–89

Iranian Shiite Muslim leader

1 If laws are needed, Islam has established them all. There is no need . . . after establishing a government, to sit down and draw up laws.
    Islam and Revolution: Writings and Declarations of Imam Khomeini (1981) 'Islamic Government'

2 I would like to inform all the intrepid Muslims in the world that the author of the book entitled *The Satanic Verses*, which has been compiled, printed and published in opposition to Islam, the Prophet and the Qur'an, as well as those publishers who were aware of its contents, have been declared *madhur el dam* [those whose blood must be shed]. I call on all zealous Muslims to execute them quickly, wherever they find them, so that no-one will dare to insult Islam again. Whoever is killed in this path will be regarded as a martyr.
    fatwa against Salman **Rushdie**, issued 14 February 1989; Malise Ruthven *A Satanic Affair* (1990) ch. 5; see **Wesker** 828:20

Nikita Khrushchev 1894–1971

Soviet statesman; Premier, 1958–64
*see also **Epstein** 308:9*

3 If anyone believes that our smiles involve abandonment of the teaching of Marx, Engels and Lenin he deceives himself. Those who wait for that must wait until a shrimp learns to whistle.
    speech in Moscow, 17 September 1955, in *New York Times* 18 September 1955

4 Whether you like it or not, history is on our side. We will bury you.
    speech to Western diplomats at reception in Moscow for Polish leader Mr Gomulka, 18 November 1956, in *The Times* 19 November 1956

5 If one cannot catch the bird of paradise, better take a wet hen.
    in *Time* 6 January 1958

6 If you start throwing hedgehogs under me, I shall throw a couple of porcupines under you.
    in *New York Times* 7 November 1963

Kitty Kiernan d. 1945

*Irish fiancée of Michael **Collins***

7 I felt, if we were ever to part, it would be easier for us both, especially for me, to do it soon, because later it would be bitter for me. But I'd love you just the same.
    letter to Michael Collins, 1921; L. O'Broin (ed.) *The Letters of Michael Collins and Kitty Kiernan* (1983)

Joyce Kilmer 1886–1918

American poet

8 I think that I shall never see
A poem lovely as a tree.
    'Trees' (1914); see **Nash** 557:17

9 Poems are made by fools like me,
But only God can make a tree.
    'Trees' (1914)

David Maxwell Fyfe, Lord Kilmuir 1900–67

British Conservative politician and lawyer
*on Kilmuir: see **Anonymous** 17:22*

10 Loyalty is the Tory's secret weapon.
    Anthony Sampson *Anatomy of Britain* (1962) ch. 6

Francis Kilvert 1840–79

English clergyman and diarist

11 Of all noxious animals, too, the most noxious is a tourist. And of all tourists the most vulgar, ill-bred, offensive and loathsome is the British tourist.
    W. Plomer (ed.) *Selections from the Diary of the Rev. Francis Kilvert* (1938–40) 5 April 1870

12 It is a fine thing to be out on the hills alone. A man can hardly be a beast or a fool alone on a great mountain.
    W. Plomer (ed.) *Selections from the Diary . . .* 29 May 1871

Benjamin Franklin King 1857–94

American poet

13 Nothing to do but work,
Nothing to eat but food,
Nothing to wear but clothes
To keep one from going nude.
    'The Pessimist'

14 Nowhere to go but out,
Nowhere to come but back.
    'The Pessimist'

Henry King 1592–1669

English poet; Bishop of Chichester from 1642

15 Sleep on (my Love!) in thy cold bed
Never to be disquieted.
My last Good-night! Thou wilt not wake
Till I thy fate shall overtake:
Till age, or grief, or sickness must
Marry my body to that dust
It so much loves; and fill the room
My heart keeps empty in thy tomb.
Stay for me there: I will not fail
To meet thee in that hollow vale.
    'An Exequy' (1657) l. 81 (written for his wife Anne, d. 1624)

16 But hark! My pulse, like a soft drum
Beats my approach, tells thee I come.
    'An Exequy' (1657) l. 111

Martin Luther King 1929–68

American civil rights leader

17 I want to be the white man's brother, not his brother-in-law.
    in *New York Journal-American* 10 September 1962

18 Judicial decrees may not change the heart; but they can restrain the heartless.
    speech in Nashville, Tennessee, 27 December 1962, in James Melvin Washington (ed.) *A Testament of Hope: The Essential Writings of Martin Luther King, Jr.* (1986) ch. 22

1 Injustice anywhere is a threat to justice everywhere.

> letter from Birmingham Jail, Alabama, 16 April 1963, in *Atlantic Monthly* August 1963

2 The Negro's great stumbling block in the stride toward freedom is not the White Citizens Councillor or the Ku Klux Klanner but the white moderate who is more devoted to order than to justice; who prefers a negative peace which is the absence of tension to a positive peace which is the presence of justice.

> letter from Birmingham Jail, Alabama, 16 April 1963, in *Atlantic Monthly* August 1963

3 If a man hasn't discovered something he will die for, he isn't fit to live.

> speech in Detroit, 23 June 1963, in James Bishop *The Days of Martin Luther King* (1971) ch. 4

4 I have a dream that one day on the red hills of Georgia the sons of former slaves and the sons of former slave owners will be able to sit down together at the table of brotherhood . . .
I have a dream that my four little children will one day live in a nation where they will not be judged by the colour of their skin but by the content of their character.

> speech at Civil Rights March in Washington, 28 August 1963, in *New York Times* 29 August 1963

5 We must learn to live together as brothers or perish together as fools.

> speech at St Louis, 22 March 1964, in *St Louis Post-Dispatch* 23 March 1964

6 I just want to do God's will. And he's allowed me to go up to the mountain. And I've looked over, and I've seen the promised land . . . So I'm happy tonight. I'm not worried about anything. I'm not fearing any man.

on the day before his assassination

> speech in Memphis, 3 April 1968, in *New York Times* 4 April 1968

7 The means by which we live have outdistanced the ends for which we live. Our scientific power has outrun our spiritual power. We have guided missiles and misguided men.

> *Strength to Love* (1963) ch. 7

8 A riot is at bottom the language of the unheard.

> *Where Do We Go From Here?* (1967) ch. 4

Stephen King 1947–

American writer

9 Terror . . . often arises from a pervasive sense of disestablishment; that things are in the unmaking.

> *Danse Macabre* (1981)

Stoddard King 1889–1933

British songwriter

10 There's a long, long trail awinding
Into the land of my dreams.

> 'There's a Long, Long Trail' (1913 song)

William King 1650–1729

Irish cleric

11 The cry of the whole people is loud for bread; God knows what will be the consequence; many are starved, and I am afraid many more will be.

view of the Archbishop of Dublin in 1720

> Daniel Corkery *The Hidden Ireland* (1925)

William Lyon Mackenzie King 1874–1950

Canadian Liberal statesman, Prime Minister 1921–6, 1926–30, and 1935–48

12 If some countries have too much history, we have too much geography.

> speech, Canadian House of Commons, 18 June 1936

13 Not necessarily conscription, but conscription if necessary.

> speech, Canadian House of Commons, 7 July 1942

Charles Kingsley 1819–75

English writer and clergyman
on Kingsley: see **Stubbs** 762:19

14 Be good, sweet maid, and let who will be clever;
Do noble things, not dream them, all day long.

> 'A Farewell' (1858)

15 Do the work that's nearest,
Though it's dull at whiles,
Helping, when we meet them,
Lame dogs over stiles.

> 'The Invitation. To Tom Hughes' (1856)

16 Welcome, wild North-easter!
Shame it is to see
Odes to every zephyr;
Ne'er a verse to thee.

> 'Ode to the North-East Wind' (1858)

17 'Tis the hard grey weather
Breeds hard English men.

> 'Ode to the North-East Wind' (1858)

18 Come; and strong within us
Stir the Vikings' blood;
Bracing brain and sinew;
Blow, thou wind of God!

> 'Ode to the North-East Wind' (1858)

19 'O Mary, go and call the cattle home,
And call the cattle home,
And call the cattle home,
Across the sands of Dee.'
The western wind was wild and dank with foam,
And all alone went she.

> 'The Sands of Dee' (1858)

20 And never home came she.

> 'The Sands of Dee' (1858)

21 Three fishers went sailing away to the west,
Away to the west as the sun went down;
Each thought on the woman who loved him the best,
And the children stood watching them out of the town.

> 'The Three Fishers' (1858)

22 For men must work, and women must weep,
And there's little to earn, and many to keep,

Though the harbour bar be moaning.
'The Three Fishers' (1858)

1 When all the world is young, lad,
And all the trees are green;
And every goose a swan, lad,
And every lass a queen;
Then hey for boot and horse, lad,
And round the world away:
Young blood must have its course, lad,
And every dog his day.
'Young and Old' (from *The Water Babies*, 1863)

2 We have used the Bible as if it was a constable's
handbook—an opium-dose for keeping beasts of
burden patient while they are being overloaded.
Letters to the Chartists no. 2; see **Marx** 516:11

3 Eustace is a man no longer; he is become a thing,
a tool, a Jesuit.
Westward Ho! (1855) ch. 23

Hugh Kingsmill (Hugh Kingsmill Lunn)
1889–1949
English man of letters

4 What still alive at twenty-two,
A clean upstanding chap like you?
Sure, if your throat 'tis hard to slit,
Slit your girl's, and swing for it.
'Two Poems, after A. E. Housman' (1933) no. 1

5 But bacon's not the only thing
That's cured by hanging from a string.
'Two Poems, after A. E. Housman' (1933) no. 1

6 God's apology for relations.
of friends
Michael Holroyd *The Best of Hugh Kingsmill* (1970)
introduction

Neil Kinnock 1942–
British Labour politician

7 *during the Falklands War, replying to a heckler who
said that Mrs **Thatcher** 'showed guts'*
It's a pity others had to leave theirs on the ground
at Goose Green to prove it.
television interview, 6 June 1983

8 If Margaret Thatcher wins on Thursday, I warn
you not to be ordinary, I warn you not to be
young, I warn you not to fall ill, and I warn you
not to grow old.
on the prospect of a Conservative re-election
speech at Bridgend, 7 June 1983

9 Why am I the first Kinnock in a thousand
generations to be able to get to a university?
later plagiarized by the American politician Joe Biden
speech in party political broadcast, 21 May 1987

Alfred Kinsey 1894–1956
American zoologist and sex researcher

10 The only unnatural sex act is that which you
cannot perform.
in *Time* 21 January 1966

Rudyard Kipling 1865–1936
English writer and poet
*on Kipling: see **Stephen** 756:1; see also **Epitaphs** 311:8*

11 When you've shouted 'Rule Britannia', when
you've sung 'God save the Queen'—
When you've finished killing Kruger with your
mouth.
'The Absent-Minded Beggar' (1899) st. 1

12 He's an absent-minded beggar and his weaknesses
are great—
But we and Paul must take him as we find him—
He is out on active service, wiping something off a
slate—
And he's left a lot o' little things behind him!
'The Absent-Minded Beggar' (1899) st. 1

13 England's on the anvil—hear the hammers ring—
Clanging from the Severn to the Tyne!
Never was a blacksmith like our Norman King—
England's being hammered, hammered,
hammered into line!
'The Anvil' (1927)

14 Seek not to question other than
The books I leave behind.
'The Appeal' (1940)

15 Oh, East is East, and West is West, and never the
twain shall meet,
Till Earth and Sky stand presently at God's great
Judgement Seat;
But there is neither East nor West, Border, nor
Breed, nor Birth,
When two strong men stand face to face, tho' they
come from the ends of earth!
'The Ballad of East and West' (1892); see **Proverbs** 618:32

16 Four things greater than all things are,—
Women and Horses and Power and War.
'The Ballad of the King's Jest' (1892)

17 Foot—foot—foot—foot—sloggin' over Africa—
(Boots—boots—boots—boots—movin' up and
down again!)
'Boots' (1903)

18 If any question why we died,
Tell them, because our fathers lied.
'Common Form' (1919)

19 The Devil whoops, as he whooped of old: 'It's
clever, but is it Art?'
'The Conundrum of the Workshops' (1892)

20 For they're hangin' Danny Deever, you can hear
the Dead March play,
The regiment's in 'ollow square—they're hangin'
him to-day;
They've taken of his buttons off an' cut his stripes
away,
An' they're hangin' Danny Deever in the mornin'.
'Danny Deever' (1892)

21 The 'eathen in 'is blindness bows down to wood
an' stone;
'E don't obey no orders unless they is 'is own.
'The 'Eathen' (1896); see **Heber** 378:16

1 And what should they know of England who only
England know?
'The English Flag' (1892)

2 I could not dig: I dared not rob:
Therefore I lied to please the mob.
Now all my lies are proved untrue
And I must face the men I slew.
What tale shall serve me here among
Mine angry and defrauded young?
'Epitaphs of the War: A Dead Statesman' (1919)

3 My son was killed while laughing at some jest. I
would I knew
What it was, and it might serve me in a time
when jests are few.
'Epitaphs of the War: A Son' (1919)

4 The female of the species is more deadly than the
male.
'The Female of the Species' (1919); see **Proverbs** 619:48

5 So 'ere's *to* you, Fuzzy-Wuzzy, at your 'ome in the
Soudan;
You're a pore benighted 'eathen but a first-class
fightin' man.
'Fuzzy-Wuzzy' (1892)

6 We're poor little lambs who've lost our way,
Baa! Baa! Baa!
We're little black sheep who've gone astray,
Baa-aa-aa!
Gentlemen-rankers out on the spree,
Damned from here to Eternity,
God ha' mercy on such as we,
Baa! Yah! Bah!
'Gentlemen-Rankers' (1892)

7 We have done with Hope and Honour, we are lost
to Love and Truth,
We are dropping down the ladder rung by rung,
And the measure of our torment is the measure of
our youth.
God help us, for we knew the worst too young!
'Gentlemen-Rankers' (1892)

8 Our England is a garden, and such gardens are
not made
By singing:—'Oh, how beautiful!' and sitting in
the shade,
While better men than we go out and start their
working lives
At grubbing weeds from gravel paths with broken
dinner-knives.
'The Glory of the Garden' (1911)

9 As it will be in the future, it was at the birth of
Man—
There are only four things certain since Social
Progress began:—
That the Dog returns to his Vomit and the Sow
returns to her Mire,
And the burnt Fool's bandaged finger goes
wabbling back to the Fire.
'The Gods of the Copybook Headings' (1927)

10 Though I've belted you and flayed you,
By the livin' Gawd that made you,
You're a better man than I am, Gunga Din!
'Gunga Din' (1892)

11 What is a woman that you forsake her,
And the hearth-fire and the home-acre,
To go with the old grey Widow-maker?
'Harp Song of the Dane Women' (1906)

12 If you can keep your head when all about you
Are losing theirs and blaming it on you;
If you can trust yourself when all men doubt you,
But make allowance for their doubting too;
If you can wait and not be tired by waiting,
Or being lied about, don't deal in lies,
Or being hated, don't give way to hating,
And yet don't look too good, nor talk too wise;
If you can dream—and not make dreams your
master;
If you can think—and not make thoughts your
aim,
If you can meet with triumph and disaster
And treat those two impostors just the same...
'If—' (1910)

13 If you can talk with crowds and keep your virtue,
Or walk with Kings—nor lose the common touch,
If neither foes nor loving friends can hurt you,
If all men count with you, but none too much;
If you can fill the unforgiving minute
With sixty seconds' worth of distance run,
Yours is the Earth and everything that's in it,
And—which is more—you'll be a Man, my son!
'If—' (1910)

14 There are nine and sixty ways of constructing
tribal lays,
And—every—single—one—of—them—is—right!
'In the Neolithic Age' (1893)

15 Old days! the wild geese are flighting,
Head to the storm as they faced it before.
'The Irish Guards'

16 Then ye returned to your trinkets; then ye
contented your souls
With the flannelled fools at the wicket or the
muddied oafs at the goals.
'The Islanders' (1903)

17 I've taken my fun where I've found it,
An' now I must pay for my fun.
'The Ladies' (1896)

18 For the Colonel's Lady an' Judy O'Grady
Are sisters under their skins!
'The Ladies' (1896)

19 And Ye take mine honour from me if Ye take
away the sea!
'The Last Chantey' (1896)

20 Down to Gehenna or up to the Throne,
He travels the fastest who travels alone.
L'Envoi to *The Story of the Gadsbys* (1890), 'The Winners';
see **Proverbs** 622:5

21 By the old Moulmein Pagoda, lookin' eastward to
the sea,
There's a Burma girl a-settin', and I know she
thinks o' me;
For the wind is in the palm-trees, an' the temple-
bells they say:

'Come you back, you British soldier; come you
  back to Mandalay!'
  'Mandalay' (1892)

1 On the road to Mandalay,
  Where the flyin'-fishes play,
  An' the dawn comes up like thunder outer China
  'crost the Bay!
  'Mandalay' (1892)

2 Ship me somewheres east of Suez, where the best
  is like the worst,
  Where there aren't no Ten Commandments an' a
  man can raise a thirst.
  'Mandalay' (1892)

3 They shall not return to us, the resolute, the
  young,
  The eager and whole-hearted whom we gave:
  But the men who left them thriftly to die in their
  own dung,
  Shall they come with years and honour to the
  grave?
  'Mesopotamia' (1917)

4 Dawn off the Foreland—the young flood making
  Jumbled and short and steep—
  Black in the hollows and bright where it's
  breaking—
  Awkward water to sweep.
  'Mines reported in the fairway,
  'Warn all traffic and detain.
  ' 'Sent up *Unity*, *Claribel*, *Assyrian*, *Stormcock*, and
  Golden Gain.'
  'Mine Sweepers' (1915)

5 'Have you news of my boy Jack?'
  Not this tide.
  'When d'you think that he'll come back?'
  Not with this wind blowing, and this tide.
  'My Boy Jack' (1916)

6 And the end of the fight is a tombstone white,
  with the name of the late deceased,
  And the epitaph drear: 'A fool lies here who tried
  to hustle the East.'
  The Naulahka (1892) ch. 5

7 A Nation spoke to a Nation,
  A Throne sent word to a Throne:
  'Daughter am I in my mother's house,
  But mistress in my own.
  The gates are mine to open,
  As the gates are mine to close,
  And I abide by my Mother's House.'
  Said our Lady of the Snows.
  'Our Lady of the Snows' (1898)

8 The toad beneath the harrow knows
  Exactly where each tooth-point goes;
  The butterfly upon the road
  Preaches contentment to that toad.
  'Pagett, MP' (1886)

9 There is sorrow enough in the natural way
  From men and women to fill our day;
  But when we are certain of sorrow in store,
  Why do we always arrange for more?
  Brothers and Sisters, I bid you beware

Of giving your heart to a dog to tear.
  'The Power of the Dog' (1909)

10 The tumult and the shouting dies—
  The captains and the kings depart—
  Still stands Thine ancient Sacrifice,
  An humble and a contrite heart.
  Lord God of Hosts, be with us yet,
  Lest we forget—lest we forget!
  'Recessional' (1897)

11 Far-called our navies melt away—
  On dune and headland sinks the fire—
  Lo, all our pomp of yesterday
  Is one with Nineveh, and Tyre!
  'Recessional' (1897)

12 Such boasting as the Gentiles use,
  Or lesser breeds without the Law.
  'Recessional' (1897)

13 For frantic boast and foolish word—
  Thy mercy on Thy People, Lord.
  'Recessional' (1897)

14 How far is St. Helena from the field of Austerlitz?
  'A St. Helena Lullaby' (1910)

15 Who hath desired the Sea?—the sight of salt
  water unbounded—
  The heave and the halt and the hurl and the crash
  of the comber wind-hounded?
  'The Sea and the Hills' (1903)

16 Five and twenty ponies,
  Trotting through the dark—
  Brandy for the Parson,
  'Baccy for the Clerk;
  Laces for a lady, letters for a spy,
  Watch the wall, my darling, while the Gentlemen
  go by!
  'A Smuggler's Song' (1906)

17 Them that asks no questions isn't told a lie.
  Watch the wall, my darling, while the Gentlemen
  go by!
  'A Smuggler's Song' (1906)

18 If blood be the price of admiralty,
  Lord God, we ha' paid in full!
  'The Song of the Dead' (1896)

19 Or little, lost, Down churches praise
  The Lord who made the hills.
  'Sussex' (1903)

20 One man in a thousand, Solomon says,
  Will stick more close than a brother.
  'The Thousandth Man' (1910); see **Bible** 84:32

21 For the sin ye do by two and two ye must pay for
  one by one!
  'Tomlinson' (1892)

22 Then it's Tommy this, an' Tommy that, an'
  'Tommy 'ow's yer soul?'
  But it's 'Thin red line of 'eroes' when the drums
  begin to roll.
  'Tommy' (1892); see **Russell** 661:16

23 Of all the trees that grow so fair,
  Old England to adorn,
  Greater are none beneath the Sun,

Than Oak, and Ash, and Thorn.
'A Tree Song' (1906)

1 What answer from the North?
One Law, one Land, one Throne.
If England drive us forth,
We shall not fall alone.
'Ulster' (1912)

2 A fool there was and he made his prayer
(Even as you and I!)
To a rag and a bone and a hank of hair
(We called her the woman who did not care)
But the fool he called her his lady fair—
(Even as you and I!)
'The Vampire' (1897) st. 1

3 They shut the road through the woods
Seventy years ago.
Weather and rain have undone it again,
And now you would never know
There was once a road through the woods.
'The Way through the Woods' (1910)

4 It is always a temptation to a rich and lazy nation,
To puff and look important and to say:-
'Though we know we should defeat you, we have
not the time to meet you,
We will therefore pay you cash to go away.'

And that is called paying the Dane-geld;
But we've proved it again and again,
That if once you have paid him the Dane-geld
You never get rid of the Dane.
'What Dane-geld means' (1911)

5 And only the Master shall praise us, and only the
Master shall blame;
And no one shall work for money, and no one
shall work for fame,
But each for the joy of the working, and each, in
his separate star,
Shall draw the Thing as he sees It for the God of
Things as They are!
'When Earth's Last Picture is Painted' (1896)

6 When 'Omer smote 'is bloomin' lyre,
He'd 'eard men sing by land an' sea;
An' what he thought 'e might require,
'E went an' took—the same as me!
'When 'Omer smote 'is bloomin' lyre' (1896)

7 Take up the White Man's burden—
Send forth the best ye breed—
Go, bind your sons to exile
To serve your captives' need.
'The White Man's Burden' (1899)

8 When you're wounded and left on Afghanistan's
plains
And the women come out to cut up what remains
Just roll to your rifle and blow out your brains
An' go to your Gawd like a soldier.
'The Young British Soldier' (1892)

9 Lalun is a member of the most ancient profession
in the world.
In Black and White (1888) 'On the City Wall'; see **Reagan**
643:10

10 They settled things by making up a saying, 'What
the Bandar-log think now the Jungle will think
later': and that comforted them a great deal.
The Jungle Book (1894) 'Kaa's Hunting'

11 'We be of one blood, thou and I', Mowgli
answered.
The Jungle Book (1894) 'Kaa's Hunting'

12 The motto of all the mongoose family is, 'Run and
find out.'
The Jungle Book (1894) 'Rikki-Tikki-Tavi'

13 Brother, thy tail hangs down behind!
The Jungle Book (1894) 'Road Song of the Bandar-Log'

14 He walked by himself, and all places were alike to
him.
Just So Stories (1902) 'The Cat that Walked by Himself'

15 And he went back through the Wet Wild Woods,
waving his wild tail and walking by his wild lone.
But he never told anybody.
Just So Stories (1902) 'The Cat that Walked by Himself'

16 One Elephant—a new Elephant—an Elephant's
Child—who was full of 'satiable curtiosity.
Just So Stories (1902) 'The Elephant's Child'

17 The great grey-green, greasy, Limpopo River, all
set about with fever trees.
Just So Stories (1902) 'The Elephant's Child'

18 I keep six honest serving-men
(They taught me all I knew);
Their names are What and Why and When
And How and Where and Who.
Just So Stories (1902) 'The Elephant's Child'

19 You must *not* forget the suspenders, Best Beloved.
Just So Stories (1902) 'How the Whale got his Throat'

20 And the small 'Stute Fish said in a small 'stute
voice, 'Noble and generous Cetacean, have you
ever tasted Man?' 'No,' said the Whale. 'What is it
like?' 'Nice,' said the small 'Stute Fish. 'Nice but
nubbly.'
Just So Stories (1902) 'How the Whale got his Throat'

21 He had his Mummy's leave to paddle, or else he
would never have done it, because he was a man
of infinite-resource-and-sagacity.
Just So Stories (1902) 'How the Whale got his Throat'

22 Little Friend of all the World.
Kim's nickname
Kim (1901) ch. 1

23 The mad all are in God's keeping.
Kim (1901) ch. 2

24 He was the greatest, as he was the hugest, of the
war correspondents . . . and he always opened his
conversation with the news that there would be
trouble in the Balkans in the spring.
The Light that Failed (1891) ch. 4

25 The man who would be king.
title of short story (1888)

26 He swathed himself in quotations—as a beggar
would enfold himself in the purple of Emperors.
Many Inventions (1893) 'The Finest Story in the World'

1 Take my word for it, the silliest woman can manage a clever man; but it takes a very clever woman to manage a fool.
   Plain Tales from the Hills (1888) 'Three and—an Extra'

2 Now this is the Law of the Jungle—as old and as true as the sky;
   And the Wolf that shall keep it may prosper, but the Wolf that shall break it must die.
   The Second Jungle Book (1895) 'The Law of the Jungle'

3 One learns more from a good scholar in a rage than from a score of lucid and laborious drudges.
   Something of Myself (1937)

4 My Daemon was with me in the *Jungle Books, Kim*, and both Puck books, and good care I took to walk delicately lest he should withdraw. I know that he did not, because when these books were finished they said so themselves with, almost, the water-hammer click of a tap turned off.
   Something of Myself (1937)

5 I gloat!
   Stalky & Co. (1899)

6 A Flopshus Cad, an Outrageous Stinker, a Jelly-bellied Flag-flapper.
   Stalky & Co. (1899)

7 'Tisn't beauty, so to speak, nor good talk necessarily. It's just It. Some women'll stay in a man's memory if they once walked down a street.
   Traffics and Discoveries (1904) 'Mrs Bathurst'

8 Power without responsibility: the prerogative of the harlot throughout the ages.
   *summing up Lord **Beaverbrook**'s political standpoint vis-à-vis the Daily Express, and quoted by Stanley **Baldwin**, 18 March 1931*
   in *Kipling Journal* vol. 38, no. 180, December 1971; see **Dorfman** 282:15, **Stoppard** 761:8

Henry Kissinger 1923–
American politician

9 The management of a balance of power is a permanent undertaking, not an exertion that has a foreseeable end.
   White House Years (1979)

10 The conventional army loses if it does not win. The guerrilla wins if he does not lose.
   in *Foreign Affairs* January 1969

11 Power is the great aphrodisiac.
   in *New York Times* 19 January 1971

12 We are the President's men.
   M. and B. Kalb *Kissinger* (1974) ch. 7

13 For other nations, Utopia is a blessed past never to be recovered; for Americans it is just beyond the horizon.
   attributed

Lord Kitchener 1850–1916
British soldier and statesman
*on Kitchener: see **Asquith** 32:6*

14 You are ordered abroad as a soldier of the King to help our French comrades against the invasion of a common enemy . . . In this new experience you may find temptations both in wine and women. You must entirely resist both temptations, and, while treating all women with perfect courtesy, you should avoid any intimacy. Do your duty bravely. Fear God. Honour the King.
   message to soldiers of the British Expeditionary Force (1914), in *The Times* 19 August 1914

15 I don't mind your being killed, but I object to your being taken prisoner.
   to the Prince of Wales during the First World War
   in *Journals and Letters of Reginald Viscount Esher* (1938) vol. 3, 18 December 1914

Paul Klee 1879–1940
German-Swiss painter

16 Art does not reproduce the visible; rather, it makes visible.
   Inward Vision (1958) 'Creative Credo' (1920)

17 An active line on a walk, moving freely without a goal. A walk for walk's sake. The agent is a point that shifts position.
   Pedagogical Sketchbook (1925)

18 Colour has taken hold of me; no longer do I have to chase after it. I know that it has hold of me for ever. That is the significance of this blessed moment.
   on a visit to Tunis in 1914
   Herbert Read *A Concise History of Modern Painting* (1968)

Ralph Klein 1942–
Canadian Progressive Conservative politician

19 The critics say you can't run government like a business. I respond, well, we can't run government like a government any more.
   in *Globe and Mail* December 1994

Heinrich von Kleist 1777–1811
German dramatist

20 Man hat riel beissend abgefasste Schriften,
   Die, dass ein Gott sei, nicht gestehen wollen;
   Jedoch den Teufel hat, soviel ich weiss,
   Kein Atheist noch bündig wegbewiesen.

   We've had some very caustic writings
   Unwilling to concede that God exists.
   However, the devil, so far as I'm aware
   No atheist has yet quite proved away.
   The Broken Jug (1808) sc. 11, translated by David Constantine

21 Meinst Du, das Glück werd'immerdar, wie jüngst,
   Mit einem Kranz den Ungehorsam lohnen?
   Den Sieg nicht mag ich, der, ein Kind des Zufalls,
   Mir von der Bank fällt; das Gesetz will ich,
   Die Mutter meiner Krone, aufrecht halten,
   Die ein Geschlecht von Siegen mir erzeugt.

   Do you suppose that Fortune always will
   Crown disobedience with laurels, as lately?
   I do not want a victory that is
   The bastard child of chance. I want
   The law upheld which is the mother of my crown

To bear me a whole family of victories.
The Prince of Homburg (1821) act 5, sc. 5, translated by David Constantine

Friedrich Klopstock 1724–1803
German poet

1 God and I both knew what it meant once; now God alone knows.
on the meaning of a passage in one of his poems
C. Lombroso *The Man of Genius* (1891) pt. 1, ch. 2; see **Browning** 162:1

Charles Knight and Kenneth Lyle
British songwriters

2 When there's trouble brewing,
When there's something doing,
Are we downhearted?
No! Let 'em all come!
'Here we are! Here we are again!!' (1914 song)

Frank H. Knight 1885–1973
American economist

3 Costs merely register competing attractions.
Risk, Uncertainty and Profit (1921)

L. C. Knights 1906–97
English critic and academic

4 How many children had Lady Macbeth?
satirizing an over-realistic approach to criticism
title of essay (1933)

Mary Knowles 1733–1807
English Quaker

5 He gets at the substance of a book directly; he tears out the heart of it.
*on Samuel **Johnson***
James Boswell *The Life of Samuel Johnson* (1791) 15 April 1778

John Knox c.1505–72
Scottish Protestant reformer
*on Knox: see **Douglas** 283:15*

6 The first blast of the trumpet against the monstrous regiment of women.
regiment = *rule*
title of pamphlet (1558)

7 *Un homme avec Dieu est toujours dans la majorité.*
A man with God is always in the majority.
inscription on the Reformation Monument, Geneva

Ronald Knox 1888–1957
English writer and Roman Catholic priest

8 When suave politeness, tempering bigot zeal,
Corrected *I believe* to *One does feel.*
'Absolute and Abitofhell' (1913)

9 There once was a man who said, 'God
Must think it exceedingly odd

If he finds that this tree
Continues to be
When there's no one about in the Quad.'
Langford Reed *Complete Limerick Book* (1924), to which came the anonymous reply:

Dear Sir,
Your astonishment's odd:
I am always about in the Quad.
And that's why the tree
Will continue to be,
Since observed by
Yours faithfully,
God.

10 The baby doesn't understand English and the Devil knows Latin.
on being asked to perform a baptism in English
Evelyn Waugh *Ronald Knox* (1959) pt. 1, ch. 5

11 A loud noise at one end and no sense of responsibility at the other.
definition of a baby
attributed

Vicesimus Knox 1752–1821
English writer

12 All sensible people agree in thinking that large seminaries of young ladies, though managed with all the vigilance and caution which human abilities can exert, are in danger of great corruption.
Liberal Education (1780) sect. 27 'On the literary education of women'

13 Can anything be more absurd than keeping women in a state of ignorance, and yet so vehemently to insist on their resisting temptation?
Mary Wollstonecraft *A Vindication of the Rights of Woman* (1792) ch. 7

Ted Koehler
American songwriter

14 Stormy weather,
Since my man and I ain't together.
'Stormy Weather' (1933 song)

Arthur Koestler 1905–83
Hungarian-born writer

15 One may not regard the world as a sort of metaphysical brothel for emotions.
Darkness at Noon (1940) 'The Second Hearing' pt. 7

16 God seems to have left the receiver off the hook, and time is running out.
The Ghost in the Machine (1967) ch. 18

17 A writer's ambition should be . . . to trade a hundred contemporary readers for ten readers in ten years' time and for one reader in a hundred years.
in *New York Times Book Review* 1 April 1951

Helmut Kohl 1930–

German statesman, Chancellor of West Germany (1982–90) and first postwar Chancellor of united Germany (1990–8)

1 We Germans now have the historic chance to realize the unity of our fatherland.
on the reunification of Germany
in *Guardian* 15 February 1990

2 The policy of European integration is in reality a question of war and peace in the 21st century.
speech at Louvain University, 2 February 1996

Johann Georg Kohl 1808–78

German travel writer

3 We had now entered the notorious county of Tipperary, in which more murders and assaults are committed in one year than in the whole Kingdom of Saxony in five.
Ireland, Scotland and England (1844); see **Trollope** 799:14

Käthe Kollwitz 1867–1945

German sculptor and graphic artist

4 As you, the children of my body, have been my tasks, so too are my other works.
letter to her son Hans, 21 February 1915

5 I have never done any work cold . . . I have always worked with my blood, so to speak.
letter to her son Hans, 16 April 1917

The Koran

textual translations are those of A. J. Arberry, 1964

6 In the Name of God, the Merciful, the Compassionate.
sura 1

7 Praise belongs to God, the Lord of all Being, the All-merciful, the All-compassionate, the Master of the Day of Doom.
sura 1

8 Thee only we serve; to Thee alone we pray for succour.
Guide us in the straight path,
the path of those whom Thou hast blessed,
not of those against whom Thou art wrathful,
nor of those who are astray.
sura 1

9 That is the Book [the Koran], wherein is no doubt, a guidance to the godfearing
who believe in the Unseen.
sura 2

10 And if you are in doubt concerning that We have sent down on Our servant [Muhammad], then bring a sura
like it, and call your witnesses, apart from God, if you are truthful.
And if you do not—and you will not—then fear the Fire, whose fuel is men and stones, prepared for unbelievers.
sura 2

11 True piety is this:
to believe in God, and the Last Day,
the angels, the Book, and the Prophets,
to give of one's substance, however cherished, to kinsmen, and orphans,
the needy, the traveller, beggars,
and to ransom the slave,
to perform the prayer, to pay the alms.
sura 2

12 The month of Ramadan, wherein the Koran was sent down to be a guidance
to the people, and as clear signs
of the Guidance and the Salvation
So let those of you, who are present
at the month, fast it.
sura 2

13 And fight in the way of God with those who fight with you, but aggress not: God loves not the aggressors.
sura 2

14 No compulsion is there in religion.
sura 2

15 God is the protector of the believers;
He brings them forth from the shadows
into the light.
sura 2

16 God has
permitted trafficking, and forbidden usury.
sura 2

17 Say to the unbelievers: 'You shall be overthrown, and mustered into Gehenna— an evil cradling!'
sura 3

18 The true religion with God is Islam.
sura 3

19 Abraham in truth was not a Jew, neither a Christian; but he was a Muslim and one pure of faith; certainly he was never of the idolaters.
sura 3

20 Say: 'We believe in God, and that which has been sent
down on us, and sent down on Abraham and Ishmael,
Isaac and Jacob, and the Tribes, and in that which was
given to Moses and Jesus, and the Prophets of their
Lord; we make no division between any of them, and
to Him we surrender.'
sura 3

21 Whoso desires another religion than Islam, it shall not be accepted of him; in the next world he shall be among the losers.
sura 3

22 Every soul shall taste of death; you shall surely be paid in full your wages on the Day
of Resurrection.
sura 3

23 Men are the managers of the affairs of women.
sura 4

1 Righteous women are therefore obedient,
guarding the secret for God's guarding.
And those you fear may be rebellious
admonish; banish them to their couches,
and beat them.
sura 4

2 So let them fight in the way of God who
sell the present life for the world to come;
and whosoever fights in the way of God
and is slain, or conquers, We shall bring him
a mighty wage.
sura 4

3 How is it with you, that you do not fight
in the way of God, and for the men,
women, and children who, being abased,
say, 'Our Lord, bring us forth from this city
whose people are evildoers, and appoint to us
a protector from Thee, and appoint to us
from Thee a helper?'
sura 4

4 Whatever good visits thee, it is of God;
whatever evil visits thee is of thyself.
sura 4

5 What, do they not ponder the Koran?
If it had been from other than God
surely they would have found in it much
inconsistency.
sura 4

6 God—
there is no God but He.
He will surely gather you
to the Resurrection Day,
no doubt of it.
And who is truer in tidings than God?
sura 4

7 To God belongs all that is in the heavens
and in the earth, and God encompasses
everything.
sura 4

8 Souls are very
prone to avarice. If you do good
and are godfearing, surely God is aware of the
things you do.
sura 4;

Men's souls are naturally inclined to
covetousness; but if ye be kind towards women
and fear to wrong them, God is well acquainted
with what ye do.
in George Sale's translation, 1734

9 The Messiah, Jesus son of Mary,
was only the Messenger of God.
sura 4

10 Today I have perfected your religion
for you, and I have completed My blessing
upon you and I have approved Islam for
your religion.
sura 5

11 Whoso slays a soul not to retaliate for a soul slain,
nor for corruption done in the land, shall be as if
he had slain mankind altogether.
sura 5

12 And we have sent down to thee the Book
with the truth, confirming the Book
that was before it, and assuring it.
sura 5

13 He originates
creation, then He brings it back again
that He may recompense those who believe
and do deeds of righteousness, justly.
sura 10

14 Glory be to Him, who carried His servant by night
from the Holy Mosque to the Further Mosque
the precincts of which We have blessed,
that We might show him some of Our signs.
sura 17

15 Perform the prayer
at the sinking of the sun to the darkening of the
night
and the recital of dawn.
sura 17

16 Even so We have sent it down
as an Arabic Koran, and We
have turned about in it something
of threats, that haply they may be
godfearing, or it may arouse in
them remembrance.
sura 20

17 And do thou purify
My House [Kaaba] for those that shall go about it
and those that stand, for those that bow
and prostrate themselves;
and proclaim among men the Pilgrimage.
sura 22

18 He
named you Muslims
aforetime and in this, that the Messenger
might be a witness against you, and that
you might be witnesses against mankind.
sura 22

19 God is the Light of the heavens and the earth;
the likeness of His Light is as a niche
wherein is a lamp . . .
kindled from a Blessed Tree,
an olive that is neither of the East nor of the West
whose oil wellnigh would shine, even if no fire
touched it;
Light upon Light.
sura 24

20 Muhammad is not the father of any one
of your men, but the Messenger of God,
and the Seal of the Prophets
sura 33

21 God knows the Unseen in the heavens and the
earth;
He knows the thoughts within the breasts.
It is He who appointed you viceroys in the earth.
sura 35

22 The sending down of the Book is from God
the All-mighty, the All-wise.
We have sent down to thee the Book with the
truth;
so worship God, making thy religion

His sincerely.
sura 39

1 Not equal are the good deed and the evil deed.
Repel with that which is fairer
and behold, he between whom and thee
there is enmity shall be as if he were
a loyal friend.
sura 41;

Good and evil shall not be held equal. Turn
away evil with that which is better; and behold
the man between whom and thyself there was
enmity, shall become, as it were, thy warmest
friend.
in George Sale's translation, 1734

2 It belongs not to any mortal that
God should speak to him, except
by revelation, or from behind
a veil,
or that He should send a messenger
and he reveal whatsoever He will,
by His leave.
sura 42

3 Surely,
unto God all things come home.
sura 42

4 And those who are slain in the way of God, He
will not send their works astray,
He will guide them, and dispose their minds
aright,
and He will admit them to Paradise,
that He has made known to them.
sura 47

5 It is He who has sent his Messenger with
the guidance and the religion of truth, that
He may uplift it above every religion.
sura 48

6 Muhammed is the Messenger of God,
and those who are with him are hard
against the unbelievers, merciful
one to another.
sura 48

7 Thou seest them [believers]
bowing, prostrating, seeking bounty
from God and good pleasure. Their
mark is on their faces, the trace of
prostration. That is their likeness
in the Torah, and their likeness
in the Gospel.
sura 48

8 By the glorious Koran!
sura 50

9 We indeed created man; and We know
what his soul whispers within him,
and We are nearer to him than the
jugular vein.
sura 50

10 He [God] is the First and the Last, the Outward
and the Inward.
sura 57

11 He is God
the Creator, the Maker, the Shaper,

To Him belong the Names Most Beautiful.
sura 59

12 On that day [the Day of Judgement] you shall be
exposed, not one secret
of yours concealed.
Then as for him who is given his book in his right
hand,
he shall say, 'Here, take and read my book!
Certainly
I thought that I should encounter my reckoning.'
So he
shall be in a pleasing life
in a lofty Garden,
its clusters nigh to gather.
sura 69

13 Recite: In the Name of thy Lord who created
created Man of a blood-clot.
sura 96

Karl Kraus 1874–1936
Austrian satirist

14 How is the world ruled and how do wars start?
Diplomats tell lies to journalists and then believe
what they read.
Aphorisms and More Aphorisms (1909)

15 There is no unhappier creature on earth than a
fetishist who yearns to embrace a woman's shoe
and has to embrace the whole woman.
Aphorisms and More Aphorisms (1909)

16 What good is speed if the brain has oozed out on
the way?
in *Die Fackel* September 1909 'The Discovery of the North
Pole'

Jiddu Krishnamurti d. 1986
Indian spiritual philosopher

17 Religion is the frozen thought of men out of which
they build temples.
in *Observer* 22 April 1928 'Sayings of the Week'

18 Truth is a pathless land, and you cannot approach
it by any path whatsoever, by any religion, by any
sect.
speech in Holland, 3 August 1929

19 Happiness is a state of which you are unconscious,
of which you are not aware. The moment you are
aware that you are happy, you cease to be happy
. . . You want to be consciously happy; the
moment you are consciously happy, happiness is
gone.
Penguin Krishnamurti Reader (1970) 'Questions and
Answers'

Kris Kristofferson 1936–
American actor

20 Freedom's just another word for nothin' left to
lose,
Nothin' ain't worth nothin', but it's free.
'Me and Bobby McGee' (1969 song, with Fred Foster)

Leopold Kronecker 1823–91

German mathematician

1 God made the integers, all the rest is the work of man.

Jahrsberichte der Deutschen Mathematiker Vereinigung

Paul Kruger see Telegrams 776:3

Joseph Wood Krutch 1893–1970

American critic and naturalist

2 The most serious charge which can be brought against New England is not Puritanism but February.

The Twelve Seasons (1949) 'February'

Stanley Kubrick 1928–99

American film director

3 The great nations have always acted like gangsters, and the small nations like prostitutes.

in *Guardian* 5 June 1963

Satish Kumar 1937–

Indian writer

4 Lead me from death to life, from falsehood to truth.
Lead me from despair to hope, from fear to trust.
Lead me from hate to love, from war to peace.
Let peace fill our heart, our world, our universe.

'Prayer for Peace' (1981); adapted from the **Upanishads**; see **Upanishads** 805:4

Milan Kundera 1929–

Czech novelist

5 The struggle of man against power is the struggle of memory against forgetting.

The Book of Laughter and Forgetting (1979) pt. 1, ch. 2

6 The unbearable lightness of being.

title of novel (1984)

7 Mankind's true moral test, its fundamental test (which lies deeply buried from view) consists of its attitudes towards those who are at its mercy: animals.

The Unbearable Lightness of Being (1984)

Thomas Kyd 1558–94

English dramatist

8 Thus must we toil in other men's extremes,
That know not how to remedy our own.

The Spanish Tragedy (1592) act 3, sc. 6, l. 1

9 My son—and what's a son? A thing begot
Within a pair of minutes, thereabout,
A lump bred up in darkness.

The Spanish Tragedy (1592) act 3, sc. 11, The Third Addition (1602 ed.) l. 5

10 It grew a gallows and did bear our son,
It bore thy fruit and mine.

The Spanish Tragedy (1592) act 3, sc. 12, The Fourth Addition (1602 ed.) l. 70

11 For what's a play without a woman in it?

The Spanish Tragedy (1592) act 4, sc. 1, l. 97

12 Hieronimo is mad again.

alternative title given to *The Spanish Tragedy* in 1615

Henry Labouchere 1831–1912

British politician

13 He [Labouchere] did not object to the old man always having a card up his sleeve, but he did object to his insinuating that the Almighty had placed it there.

on **Gladstone**'s '*frequent appeals to a higher power*'
Earl Curzon *Modern Parliamentary Eloquence* (1913); another version is:

Who cannot refrain from perpetually bringing an ace down his sleeve, even when he has only to play fair to win the trick.

letter in A. L. Thorold *The Life of Henry Labouchere* (1913) ch. 15

Jean de la Bruyère 1645–96

French satiric moralist

14 *Il faut rire avant que d'être heureux, de peur de mourir sans avoir ri.*

We must laugh before we are happy, for fear of dying without having laughed at all.

Les Caractères ou les moeurs de ce siècle (1688) 'Du Coeur'

15 *Le commencement et le déclin de l'amour se font sentir par l'embarras où l'on est de se trouver seuls.*

The onset and the waning of love make themselves felt in the uneasiness experienced at being alone together.

Les Caractères ou les moeurs de ce siècle (1688) 'Du Coeur'

16 *Le peuple n'a guère d'esprit et les grands n'ont point d'âme . . . faut-il opter, je ne balance pas, ne veux être peuple.*

The people have little intelligence, the great no heart . . . if I had to choose I should have no hesitation: I would be of the people.

Les Caractères ou les moeurs de ce siècle (1688) 'Des Grands'

17 *Il n'y a pour l'homme que trois événements: naître, vivre et mourir. Il ne sent pas naître, il souffre à mourir, et il oublie de vivre.*

Man has but three events in his life: to be born, to live, and to die. He is not conscious of his birth, he suffers at his death and he forgets to live.

Les Caractères ou les moeurs de ce siècle (1688) 'De l'homme'

18 *Entre le bon sens et le bon goût il y a la différence de la cause et son effet.*

Between good sense and good taste there is the same difference as between cause and effect.

Les Caractères ou les moeurs de ce siècle (1688) 'Des Jugements'

19 *Tout est dit et l'on vient trop tard depuis plus de sept mille ans qu'il y a des hommes et qui pensent.*

Everything has been said, and we are more than seven thousand years of human thought too late.

Les Caractères ou les moeurs de ce siècle (1688) 'Des Ouvrages de l'esprit'

1 *C'est un métier que de faire un livre, comme de faire une pendule: il faut plus que de l'esprit pour être auteur.*

Making a book is a craft, as is making a clock; it takes more than wit to become an author.

Les Caractères ou les moeurs de ce siècle (1688) 'Des Ouvrages de l'esprit'

Nivelle de la Chaussée 1692–1754

French dramatist

2 *Quand tout le monde a tort, tout le monde a raison.*

When everyone is wrong, everyone is right.

La Gouvernante (1747) act 1, sc. 3

James Lackington 1746–1815

English bookseller

3 At last, by singing and repeating enthusiastic amorous hymns, and ignorantly applying particular texts of scripture, I got my imagination to the proper pitch, and thus was I born again in an instant.

Memoirs (1792 ed.) Letter 6

Pierre Choderlos de Laclos 1741–1803

French soldier and writer

4 *M. de Valmont, avec un beau nom, une grande fortune, beaucoup de qualités aimables, a reconnu de bonne heure que pour avoir l'empire dans la société, il suffisoit de manier, avec une égale adresse, la louange et la ridicule.*

Monsieur de Valmont, with an illustrious name, a large fortune, and many agreeable qualities, early realized that to achieve influence in society no more is required than to practise the arts of adulation and ridicule with equal skill.

Les Liaisons Dangereuses (1782) letter 32

5 *Voilà bien les hommes! tous également scélérats dans leurs projets, ce qu'ils mettent de faiblesse dans l'exécution, ils l'appellent probité.*

Our intentions make blackguards of us all; our weakness in carrying them out we call probity.

Les Liaisons Dangereuses (1782) letter 66

6 *Il me prise donc bien peu, s'il croit valoir assez pour me fixer!*

He cannot rate me very high if he thinks he is worth my fidelity!

Les Liaisons Dangereuses (1782) letter 113

7 *L'homme jouit du bonheur qu'il ressent, et la femme de celui qu'elle procure.*

A man enjoys the happiness he feels, a woman the happiness she gives.

Les Liaisons Dangereuses (1782) letter 130

8 *Si vous permettez à mon âge une réflexion qu'on ne fait guère au vôtre, c'est que, si on étoit éclairé sur son véritable bonheur, on ne le chercherait jamais hors des bornes prescrites par les loix et la religion.*

If you will allow me, at my age, a reflection that is scarcely ever made at yours, I must say that if one only knew where one's true happiness lay one would never look for it outside the limits prescribed by the law and by religion.

Les Liaisons Dangereuses (1782) letter 171

Christian Lacroix 1951–

French couturier

9 Haute Couture should be fun, foolish and almost unwearable.

in *Observer* 27 December 1987 'Sayings of the Year'

Madame de La Fayette 1634–93

French novelist

10 One reproaches a lover, but can one reproach a husband, when his only fault is that he no longer loves?

The Princess of Clèves (1678) pt. 4

Jean de la Fontaine 1621–95

French poet

11 *Je plie et ne romps pas.*

I bend and I break not.

Fables bk. 1 (1668) 'Le Chêne et le Roseau'

12 *C'est double plaisir de tromper le trompeur.*

It is doubly pleasing to trick the trickster.

Fables bk. 2 (1668) 'Le Coq et le Renard'

13 *Aide-toi, le ciel t'aidera.*

Help yourself, and heaven will help you.

Fables bk. 6 (1668) 'Le Chartier Embourbé'; see **Proverbs** 620:44

14 *Il connaît l'univers et ne se connaît pas.*

He knows the universe and does not know himself.

Fables bk. 8 (1678–9) 'Démocrite et les Abdéritains'

15 *La mort ne surprend point le sage,*
Il est toujours prêt à partir.

Death never takes the wise man by surprise; he is always ready to go.

Fables bk. 8 (1678–9) 'La Mort et le Mourant'; see **Montaigne** 544:1

16 *Certain renard voulut, dit-on, se faire loup. Hé! qui peut dire que pour le métier de mouton jamais aucun loup ne soupire?*

A certain fox, it is said, wanted to become a wolf. Ah! who can say why no wolf has ever craved the life of a sheep?

Fables Choisies (1693 ed.) bk. 7, no. 9

Jules Laforgue 1860–87

French poet

17 *Ah! que la vie est quotidienne.*

Oh, what a day-to-day business life is.

Complainte sur certains ennuis (1885)

Fiorello La Guardia 1882–1947
American politician

1 When I make a mistake, it's a beaut!
*on the appointment of Herbert O'Brien as a judge in
1936*
William Manners *Patience and Fortitude* (1976)

John Lahr 1941–
American critic

2 Criticism is a life without risk.
Light Fantastic (1996)

3 Society drives people crazy with lust and calls it
advertising.
in *Guardian* 2 August 1989

4 I know in an existential sense that life can change
on a dime . . . something has instantly and
inexorably changed in American life.
*in the aftermath of the terrorist attacks which
destroyed the World Trade Center in New York, and
damaged the Pentagon*
'Forever Changed', online correspondence with August
Wilson in *Slate*, posted 11 September 2001

R. D. Laing 1927–89
Scottish psychiatrist

5 The divided self.
title of book (1960) on schizophrenia

6 Madness need not be all breakdown. It may also
be break-through.
The Politics of Experience (1967) ch. 6

Alphonse de Lamartine 1790–1869
French poet

7 *Un être seul vous manque, et tout est dépeuplé.*
Only one being is wanting, and your whole world
is bereft of people.
'L'Isolement' (1820)

8 *Ô temps! suspend ton vol, et vous, heures propices!
Suspendez votre cours.*
O Time! arrest your flight, and you, propitious
hours, stay your course.
Le Lac (1820) st. 6

Lady Caroline Lamb 1785–1828
*English wife of William Lamb, Lord **Melbourne**
on Lamb: see **Byron** 183:3*

9 Mad, bad, and dangerous to know.
*of **Byron**, after their first meeting at a ball*
diary, March 1812; in Elizabeth Jenkins *Lady Caroline Lamb*
(1932) ch. 6

Charles Lamb 1775–1834
English writer
*on Lamb: see **Hazlitt** 376:9*

10 If the husband be a man with whom you have
lived on a friendly footing before marriage,—if you
did not come in on the wife's side,—if you did not

sneak into the house in her train, but were an old
friend in first habits of intimacy before their
courtship was so much as thought on,—look
about you . . . Every long friendship, every old
authentic intimacy, must be brought into their
office to be new stamped with their currency, as a
sovereign Prince calls in the good old money that
was coined in some reign before he was born or
thought of, to be new marked and minted with the
stamp of his authority, before he will let it pass
current in the world.
Essays of Elia (1823) 'A Bachelor's Complaint of the
Behaviour of Married People'

11 Ceremony is an invention to take off the uneasy
feeling which we derive from knowing ourselves to
be less the object of love and esteem with a fellow-
creature than some other person is. It endeavours
to make up, by superior attentions in little points,
for that invidious preference which it is forced to
deny in the greater.
Essays of Elia (1823) 'A Bachelor's Complaint of the
Behaviour of Married People'

12 Presents, I often say, endear Absents.
Essays of Elia (1823) 'A Dissertation upon Roast Pig'

13 The human species, according to the best theory I
can form of it, is composed of two distinct races,
the men who borrow, and *the men who lend*.
Essays of Elia (1823) 'The Two Races of Men'

14 Your *borrowers of books*—those mutilators of
collections, spoilers of the symmetry of shelves,
and creators of odd volumes.
Essays of Elia (1823) 'The Two Races of Men'

15 Not many sounds in life . . . exceed in interest a
knock at the door.
Essays of Elia (1823) 'Valentine's Day'

16 Books think for me.
Last Essays of Elia (1833) 'Detached Thoughts on Books
and Reading'

17 Things in books' clothing.
Last Essays of Elia (1833) 'Detached Thoughts on Books
and Reading'

18 [A pun] is a pistol let off at the ear; not a feather
to tickle the intellect.
Last Essays of Elia (1833) 'Popular Fallacies' no. 9

19 For thy sake, Tobacco, I
Would do any thing but die.
'A Farewell to Tobacco' l. 122

20 　　　　　　Gone before
To that unknown and silent shore.
'Hester' (1803) st. 7

21 I have had playmates, I have had companions,
In my days of childhood, in my joyful school-
days,—
All, all are gone, the old familiar faces.
'The Old Familiar Faces'

22 A child's a plaything for an hour.
'Parental Recollections' (1809); often attributed to Lamb's
sister Mary

1 I have something more to do than feel.
on the death of his mother, at his sister Mary's hands
letter to S. T. Coleridge, 27 September 1796, in E. W. Marrs (ed.) *Letters of Charles and Mary Lamb* (1975) vol. 1

2 Cultivate simplicity, Coleridge.
letter to S. T. Coleridge, 8 November 1796, in E. W. Marrs (ed.) *Letters of Charles and Mary Lamb* (1975) vol. 1

3 The man must have a rare recipe for melancholy, who can be dull in Fleet Street.
letter to Thomas Manning, 15 February 1802, in E. W. Marrs (ed.) *Letters of Charles and Mary Lamb* (1976) vol. 2

4 Nursed amid her noise, her crowds, her beloved smoke—what have I been doing all my life, if I have not lent out my heart with usury to such scenes?
of London
letter to Thomas Manning, 15 February 1802, in E. W. Marrs (ed.) *Letters of Charles and Mary Lamb* (1976) vol. 2

5 Nothing puzzles me more than time and space; and yet nothing troubles me less, as I never think about them.
letter to Thomas Manning, 2 January 1810, in E. W. Marrs (ed.) *Letters of Charles and Mary Lamb* (1978) vol. 3

6 This very night I am going to leave off tobacco! Surely there must be some other world in which this unconquerable purpose shall be realized.
letter to Thomas Manning, 26 December 1815, in E. W. Marrs (ed.) *Letters of Charles and Mary Lamb* (1978) vol. 3

7 An Archangel a little damaged.
*of **Coleridge***
letter to Wordsworth, 26 April 1816, in E. W. Marrs (ed.) *Letters of Charles and Mary Lamb* (1978) vol. 3

8 Fanny Kelly's divine plain face.
letter to Mary Wordsworth, 18 February 1818, in Henry H. Harper (ed.) *Letters of Charles Lamb* (1905) vol. 4

9   The ever-haunting importunity
Of business?
letter to Bernard Barton, 11 September 1822, in Henry H. Harper (ed.) *Letters of Charles Lamb* (1905) vol. 4

10 When my sonnet was rejected, I exclaimed, 'Damn the age; I will write for Antiquity!'
letter to B. W. Proctor, 22 January 1829, in *Works* (1912) vol. 6

11 The greatest pleasure I know, is to do a good action by stealth, and to have it found out by accident.
'Table Talk by the late Elia' in *The Athenaeum* 4 January 1834

12 I toiled after it, sir, as some men toil after virtue.
on being asked 'how he had acquired his power of smoking at such a rate'
Thomas Noon Talfourd *Memoirs of Charles Lamb* (1892)

Constant Lambert 1905–51
English composer

13 The whole trouble with a folk song is that once you have played it through there is nothing much you can do except play it over again and play it rather louder.
Music Ho! (1934) ch. 3

14 The average English critic is a don *manqué*, hopelessly parochial when not exaggeratedly teutonophile, over whose desk must surely hang the motto (presumably in Gothic lettering) 'Above all no enthusiasm'.
in *Opera* December 1950; see **Talleyrand** 771:16

John Lambert 1619–83
English soldier and Parliamentary supporter

15 The quarrel is now between light and darkness, not who shall rule, but whether we shall live or be preserved or no. Good words will not do with the cavaliers.
speech in the Parliament of 1656 supporting the rule of the major-generals
in *Dictionary of National Biography* (1917–)

John George Lambton see Lord Durham

George Lamming 1927–
Barbados-born novelist and poet

16 In the castle of my skin.
title of novel (1953)

Norman Lamont 1942–
British Conservative politician
see also **Misquotations** 537:17

17 Rising unemployment and the recession have been the price that we've had to pay to get inflation down. [Labour shouts] That is a price well worth paying.
speech in the House of Commons, 16 May 1991

18 We give the impression of being in office but not in power.
as a backbencher
speech in the House of Commons, 9 June 1993

Giuseppe di Lampedusa 1896–1957
Italian writer

19 If we want things to stay as they are, things will have to change.
The Leopard (1957)

20 Love. Of course, love. Flames for a year, ashes for thirty.
The Leopard (1957)

Osbert Lancaster 1908–86
English writer and cartoonist

21 Fan-vaulting . . . from an aesthetic standpoint frequently belongs to the 'Last-supper-carved-on-a-peach-stone' class of masterpiece.
Pillar to Post (1938) 'Perpendicular'

22 All over the country the latest and most scientific methods of mass-production are being utilized to turn out a stream of old oak beams, leaded window-panes and small discs of bottle-glass, all structural devices which our ancestors lost no time in abandoning as soon as an increase in wealth and knowledge enabled them to do so.
Pillar to Post (1938) 'Stockbroker's Tudor'

Letitia Elizabeth Landon (L. E. L.) 1802–38

English writer

1 Few, save the poor, feel for the poor.
'The Poor'

Walter Savage Landor 1775–1864

English poet

2 I strove with none; for none was worth my strife;
Nature I loved, and, next to Nature, Art.
'Dying Speech of an Old Philosopher' (1853)

3 Ireland never was contented . . .
Say you so? You are demented.
Ireland was contented when
All could use the sword and pen,
And when Tara rose so high
That her turrets split the sky.
'Ireland never was contented' (1853)

4 Ah, what avails the sceptred race!
Ah, what the form divine!
'Rose Aylmer' (1806)

5 George the First was always reckoned
Vile, but viler George the Second;
And what mortal ever heard
Any good of George the Third?
When from earth the Fourth descended
God be praised the Georges ended!
epigram in *The Atlas*, 28 April 1855; earlier versions are
discussed in *Notes and Queries* 3 May 1902

6 There are no fields of amaranth on this side of the
grave.
Imaginary Conversations 'Aesop and Rhodope' in *Works of
Walter Savage Landor* (1846) vol. 2

7 States, like men, have their growth, their
manhood, their decrepitude, their decay.
Imaginary Conversations 'Pollio and Calvus' in *Works of
Walter Savage Landor* (1876) vol. 2

8 I shall dine late; but the dining-room will be well-
lighted, the guests few and select. I neither am,
nor ever shall be, popular.
of the Edinburgh Review *on his* Hellenics
in April 1850, J. Forster *Walter Savage Landor: a Biography*
(1869)

Andrew Lang 1844–1912

Scottish man of letters

9 St Andrews by the Northern sea,
A haunted town it is to me!
'Almae Matres' (1884)

10 If the wild bowler thinks he bowls,
Or if the batsman thinks he's bowled,
They know not, poor misguided souls,
They too shall perish unconsoled.
I am the batsman and the bat,
I am the bowler and the ball.
'Brahma'; see **Emerson** 306:10

11 They hear like ocean on a western beach
The surge and thunder of the Odyssey.
'The Odyssey' (1881)

12 He uses statistics as a drunken man uses lamp
posts—for support rather than illumination.
Alan L. Mackay *Harvest of a Quiet Eye* (1977); attributed

Susanne Langer 1895–1985

American philosopher

13 Art is the objectification of feeling, and the
subjectification of nature.
Mind (1967) vol. 1

William Langland c.1330–c.1400

English poet

14 In a somer seson, whan softe was the sonne.
The Vision of Piers Plowman B text (ed. A. V. C. Schmidt,
1987) prologue l. 1

15 Ac on a May morwenynge on Malverne hilles
Me bifel a ferly, of Fairye me thoghte.
The Vision of Piers Plowman B text (ed. A. V. C. Schmidt,
1987) prologue l. 5

Ac on a May mornyng on Maluerne hulles
Me biful for to slepe, for werynesse of-walked.
The Vision of Piers Plowman C text (ed. D. Pearsall, 1978)
prologue l. 6

16 A faire feeld ful of folk fond I ther bitwene—
Of alle manere of men, the meene and the riche,
Werchynge and wandrynge as the world asketh.
The Vision of Piers Plowman B text (ed. A. V. C. Schmidt,
1987) prologue l. 17

17 Brewesters and baksters, bochiers and cokes—
For thise are men on this molde that moost harm
wercheth
To the povere peple.
The Vision of Piers Plowman B text (ed. A. V. C. Schmidt,
1987) Passus 3, l. 79

As bakeres and breweres, bocheres and cokes;
For thyse men don most harm to the mene peple.
The Vision of Piers Plowman C text (ed. D. Pearsall, 1978)
Passus 3, l. 80)

18 Suffraunce is a soverayn vertue, and a swift
vengeaunce.
Who suffreth moore than God?
The Vision of Piers Plowman B text (ed. A. V. C. Schmidt,
1987) Passus 11, l. 378

19 Grammer, the ground of al.
The Vision of Piers Plowman B text (ed. A. V. C. Schmidt,
1987) Passus 15, l. 370

20 Innocence is next God, and nyght and day it crieth
'Vengeaunce! Vengeaunce! Forgyve be it nevere
That shente us and shedde oure blood!'
The Vision of Piers Plowman B text (ed. A. V. C. Schmidt,
1987) Passus 17, l. 289

21 'After sharpest shoures,' quath Pees 'most shene is
the sonne;
Is no weder warmer than after watry cloudes.'
Pees = *Peace*
The Vision of Piers Plowman B text (ed. A. V. C. Schmidt,
1987) Passus 18, l. 411

Stephen Langton d. 1228

English cleric, Archbishop of Canterbury

22 *Veni, Sancte Spiritus,*
Et emitte coelitus

Lucis tuae radium.

Come, Holy Spirit, and send out from heaven the beam of your light.

> The 'Golden Sequence' for Whit Sunday (also attributed to several others, notably Pope Innocent III)

1 *Lava quod est sordidum,*
Riga quod est aridum,
Sana quod est saucium.
Flecte quod est rigidum,
Fove quod est frigidum,
Rege quod est devium.

Wash what is dirty, water what is dry, heal what is wounded. Bend what is stiff, warm what is cold, guide what goes off the road.

> The 'Golden Sequence' for Whit Sunday

Emilia Lanier 1569–1645

English-born poet

2 And since all arts at first from Nature came,
That goodly creature, mother of perfection,
Whom Jove's almighty hand at first did frame,
Taking both her and hers in his protection:
Why should not she now grace my barren muse,
And in a woman all defects excuse.

> 'The Dedications' (1611)

3 The walks put on their summer liveries,
And all things else did hold like similes:
The trees with leaves, with fruits, with flowers clad,
Embrac'd each other, seeming to be glad.

> 'The Description of Cookham' (1611)

Lao Tzu c.604–c.531 BC

Chinese philosopher; founder of Taoism
textual translations are those of Wing-Tsit Chan, 1963

4 The Tao [Way] that can be told of is not the eternal Tao;
The name that can be named is not the eternal name.
The Nameless is the origin of Heaven and Earth;
The Named is the mother of all things.

> *Tao-te Ching* ch. 1

5 Front and back follow each other.
Therefore the sage manages affairs without action
And spreads doctrines without words.

> *Tao-te Ching* ch. 2

6 Heaven and earth are not humane
They regard all things as straw dogs.
The sage is not humane.
He regards all people as straw dogs.

> *Tao-te Ching* ch. 5

7 Thirty spokes are united around the hub to make a wheel,
But it is on its non-being that the utility of the carriage depends.
Clay is moulded to form a utensil,
But it is on its non-being that the utility of the utensil depends.
Doors and windows are cut out to make a room,
But it is on its non-being that the utility of the room depends.

Therefore turn being into advantage, and non-being into utility.

> non-being *sometimes translated* hole
> *Tao-te-Ching* ch. 11

8 The best [rulers] are those whose existence is [merely] known by the people.
The next best are those who are loved and praised.
The next are those who are feared.
And the next are those who are reviled . . .
[The great rulers] accomplish their task; they complete their work.
Nevertheless their people say that they simply follow Nature.

> *Tao-te Ching* ch. 17

9 Let people hold on to these:
Manifest plainness,
Embrace simplicity,
Reduce selfishness,
Have few desires.

> *Tao-te Ching* ch. 19

10 The thing that is called Tao is eluding and vague.
Vague and eluding, there is in it the form.
Eluding and vague, in it are things.
Deep and obscure, in it is the essence.
The essence is very real; in it are evidences.

> *Tao-te Ching* ch. 21

11 I call it Tao.
If forced to give it a name, I shall call it Great.
Now being great means functioning everywhere.
Functioning everywhere means far-reaching.
Being far-reaching means returning to the original point.
Therefore Tao is great.

> *Tao-te Ching* ch. 25

12 The man of superior virtue is not [conscious of] his virtue,
And in this way he really possesses virtue.
The man of inferior virtue never loses [sight of] his virtue,
And in this way he loses his virtue.

> *Tao-te Ching* ch. 38

13 Reversion is the action of the Tao.
Weakness is the function of the Tao.
All things in the world come from being.
And being comes from non-being.

> *Tao-te Ching* ch. 40

14 Tao produced the One.
The One produced the two.
The two produced the three.
And the three produced the ten thousand things.
The ten thousand things carry the yin and embrace the yang,
and through the blending of the material force they achieve harmony.

> *Tao-te Ching* ch. 42

15 One may know the world without going out of doors.
One may see the Way of Heaven without looking through windows.
The further one goes, the less one knows.

> *Tao-te Ching* ch. 47

1 The pursuit of learning is to increase day after
    day.
  The pursuit of Tao is to decrease day after day.
  It is to decrease and further decrease until one
    reaches the point of taking no action.
  No action is undertaken, and yet nothing is left
    undone.
    Tao-te Ching ch. 48

2 He who knows does not speak.
  He who speaks does not know.
    Tao-te Ching ch. 56

3 The more laws and orders are made prominent,
  The more thieves and bandits there will be.
    Tao-te Ching ch. 57; see **Proverbs** 626:41

4 The female always overcomes the male by
    tranquillity,
  And by tranquillity she is underneath.
    Tao-te Ching ch. 61

5 A tower of nine storeys begins with a heap of
    earth.
  The journey of a thousand *li* starts from where
    one stands.
    Tao-te Ching ch. 64

6 Heaven's net is indeed vast.
  Though its meshes are wide, it misses nothing.
    Tao-te Ching ch. 73

7 There is nothing softer and weaker than water,
  And yet there is nothing better for attacking hard
    and strong things.
  For this reason there is no substitute for it.
  All the world knows that the weak overcomes the
    strong and the soft overcomes the hard.
  But none can practise it.
    Tao-te Ching ch. 78

8 The sage does not accumulate for himself.
  The more he uses for others, the more he has
    himself.
  The more he gives to others, the more he possesses
    of his own.
  The Way of Heaven is to benefit others and not to
    injure.
  The Way of the sage is to act but not to compete.
    Tao-te Ching ch. 81

Dionysius Lardner 1793–1859
Irish scientific writer

9 Men might as well project a voyage to the moon
  as attempt to employ steam navigation against the
  stormy North Atlantic Ocean.
    speech to the British Association for the Advancement of
    Science, 1838

Ring Lardner 1885–1933
American writer

10 Are you lost daddy I arsked tenderly.
   Shut up he explained.
    The Young Immigrunts (1920) ch. 10

James Larkin 1867–1947
Irish labour leader

11 Hell has no terror for me. I have lived there. Thirty
   six years of hunger and poverty have been my
   portion. They cannot terrify me with hell. Better to
   be in hell with Dante and Davitt than to be in
   heaven with Carson and Murphy.
    in 1913, during the 'Dublin lockout' labour dispute
    Ulick O'Connor *The Troubles* (rev. ed., 1996)

Philip Larkin 1922–85
English poet

12 Sexual intercourse began
   In nineteen sixty-three
   (Which was rather late for me) —
   Between the end of the *Chatterley* ban
   And the Beatles' first LP.
    'Annus Mirabilis' (1974)

13 Time has transfigured them into
   Untruth. The stone fidelity
   They hardly meant has come to be
   Their final blazon, and to prove
   Our almost-instinct almost true:
   What will survive of us is love.
    'An Arundel Tomb' (1964)

14 What are days for?
   Days are where we live.
    'Days' (1964)

15 Life is first boredom, then fear.
   Whether or not we use it, it goes.
    'Dockery & Son' (1964)

16 And that will be England gone,
   The shadows, the meadows, the lanes,
   The guildhalls, the carved choirs.
   There'll be books; it will linger on
   In galleries; but all that remains
   For us will be concrete and tyres.
    'Going, Going' (1974)

17 Rather than words comes the thought of high
     windows:
   The sun-comprehending glass,
   And beyond it, the deep blue air, that shows
   Nothing, and is nowhere, and is endless.
    'High Windows' (1974)

18 Nothing, like something, happens anywhere.
    'I Remember, I Remember' (1955)

19 Never such innocence,
   Never before or since,
   As changed itself to past
   Without a word—the men
   Leaving the gardens tidy,
   The thousands of marriages
   Lasting a little while longer:
   Never such innocence again.
    'MCMXIV' (1964)

20 I listen to money singing. It's like looking down
   From long french windows at a provincial town,
   The slums, the canal, the churches ornate and
     mad

In the evening sun. It is intensely sad.
'Money' (1974)

1 Perhaps being old is having lighted rooms
Inside your head, and people in them, acting.
People you know, yet can't quite name.
'The Old Fools' (1974)

2 They fuck you up, your mum and dad.
They may not mean to, but they do.
They fill you with the faults they had
And add some extra, just for you.
'This Be The Verse' (1974)

3 Man hands on misery to man.
It deepens like a coastal shelf.
Get out as early as you can,
And don't have any kids yourself.
'This Be The Verse' (1974)

4 Why should I let the toad *work*
Squat on my life?
Can't I use my wit as a pitchfork
And drive the brute off?
'Toads' (1955)

5 Give me your arm, old toad;
Help me down Cemetery Road.
'Toads Revisited' (1964)

6 I thought of London spread out in the sun,
Its postal districts packed like squares of wheat.
'The Whitsun Weddings' (1964)

7 A beginning, a muddle, and an end.
on the 'classic formula' for a novel
in *New Fiction* no. 15, January 1978; see **Aristotle** 25:21

8 Deprivation is for me what daffodils were for
Wordsworth.
Required Writing (1983); see **Wordsworth** 847:6

9 I am afraid the compulsion to write poems left me
about seven years ago, since when I have written
virtually nothing. Naturally this is a
disappointment, but I would sooner write no
poems than bad poems.
letter, 11 August 1984; Anthony Thwaite (ed.) *Selected Letters of Philip Larkin* (1992)

Duc de la Rochefoucauld 1613-80

French moralist

10 *Nous avons tous assez de force pour supporter les maux d'autrui.*
We are all strong enough to bear the misfortunes of others.
Maximes (1678) no. 19

11 *Il n'y a point de déguisement qui puisse longtemps cacher l'amour où il est, ni le feindre où il n'est pas.*
There is no disguise which can hide love for long where it exists, or feign it where it does not.
Maximes (1678) no. 70

12 *Il est plus honteux de se défier de ses amis que d'en être trompé.*
It is more shameful to doubt one's friends than to be duped by them.
Maximes (1678) no. 84

13 *Tout le monde se plaint de sa mémoire, et personne ne se plaint de son jugement.*

Everyone complains of his memory, and no one complains of his judgement.
Maximes (1678) no. 89

14 *Il y a de bons mariages, mais il n'y en a point de délicieux.*
There are good marriages, but no delightful ones.
Maximes (1678) no. 113

15 *L'hypocrisie est un hommage que le vice rend à la vertu.*
Hypocrisy is a tribute which vice pays to virtue.
Maximes (1678) no. 218

16 *C'est une grande habileté que de savoir cacher son habileté.*
The height of cleverness is to be able to conceal it.
Maximes (1678) no. 245

17 *Il n'y a guère d'homme assez habile pour connaître tout le mal qu'il fait.*
There is scarcely a single man sufficiently aware to know all the evil he does.
Maximes (1678) no. 269

18 *L'absence diminue les médiocres passions, et augmente les grandes, comme le vent éteint les bougies, et allume le feu.*
Absence diminishes commonplace passions and increases great ones, as the wind extinguishes candles and kindles fire.
Maximes (1678) no. 276; see **Bussy-Rabutin** 175:8, **Francis de Sales** 332:7

19 *La reconnaissance de la plupart des hommes n'est qu'une secrète envie de recevoir de plus grands bienfaits.*
In most of mankind gratitude is merely a secret hope for greater favours.
Maximes (1678) no. 298; see **Walpole** 820:9

20 *L'accent du pays où l'on est né demeure dans l'esprit et dans le coeur comme dans le langage.*
The accent of one's birthplace lingers in the mind and in the heart as it does in one's speech.
Maximes (1678) no. 342

21 *Dans l'adversité de nos meilleurs amis, nous trouvons toujours quelque chose qui ne nous déplaît pas.*
In the misfortune of our best friends, we always find something which is not displeasing to us.
Réflexions ou Maximes Morales (1665) maxim 99

22 *On n'est jamais si malheureux qu'on croit, ni si heureux qu'on espère.*
One is never as unhappy as one thinks, nor as happy as one hopes.
Sentences et Maximes de Morale (Dutch edition, 1664) maxim 128

Duc de la Rochefoucauld-Liancourt
1747-1827

French social reformer

23 LOUIS XVI: *C'est une grande révolte.*
LA ROCHEFOUCAULD-LIANCOURT: *Non, Sire, c'est une grande révolution.*
LOUIS XVI: It is a big revolt.

LA ROCHEFOUCAULD-LIANCOURT: No, Sir, it is a big revolution.

on a report reaching Versailles of the Fall of the Bastille, 1789

F. Dreyfus *La Rochefoucauld-Liancourt* (1903) ch. 2, sect. 3

Harold Laski 1893–1950

British Labour politician
see also **Crossman** 252:16, **Attlee** 33:2

1 That state of resentful coma that . . . dons dignify by the name of research.
letter to Oliver Wendell Holmes Jr., 10 October 1922

□ Last words

see page opposite
see also **Sappho** 666:16

Hugh Latimer c.1485–1555

English Protestant martyr
see also **Last words** 471:4

2 *Gutta cavat lapidem, non vi sed saepe cadendo.*
The drop of rain maketh a hole in the stone, not by violence, but by oft falling.
The Second Sermon preached before the King's Majesty (19 April 1549); see **Ovid** 580:7, **Proverbs** 617:10

William Laud 1573–1645

English churchman, Archbishop of Canterbury from 1633; executed for treason

3 Lord I am coming as fast as I can, I know I must pass through the shadow of death, before I can come to see thee; But it is but *Umbra Mortis*, a mere shadow of death, a little darkness upon nature; but thou by thy merits and passion, hast broke through the jaws of death; the Lord receive my soul, and have mercy upon me, and bless this kingdom with peace and plenty, and with brotherly love and charity, that there may not be this effusion of Christian blood amongst them, for Jesus Christ his sake, if it be thy will.
at the scaffold, in Peter Heylin *Cyprianus Anglicus* (1668)

Estée Lauder 1910–

American businesswoman

4 Let me teach you how to sell.
remark to employees more than 40 years after founding eponymous company
in *Time* April 1998

Harry Lauder (Hugh MacLennan) 1870–1950

Scottish music-hall entertainer
see also **Morrison** 550:10

5 Keep right on to the end of the road,
Keep right on to the end.
Tho' the way be long, let your heart be strong,
Keep right on round the bend.
'The End of the Road' (1924 song)

6 I love a lassie, a bonnie, bonnie lassie,
She's as pure as the lily in the dell.

She's as sweet as the heather, the bonnie bloomin' heather—
Mary, ma Scotch Bluebell.
'I Love a Lassie' (1905 song)

7 Roamin' in the gloamin',
On the bonnie banks o' Clyde.
'Roamin' in the Gloamin'' (1911 song)

Stan Laurel (Arthur Stanley Jefferson) 1890–1965

American film comedian, born in Britain

8 Another nice mess you've gotten me into.
often 'another fine mess'
Another Fine Mess (1930 film) and many other Laurel and Hardy films; spoken by Oliver Hardy

William L. Laurence 1888–1977

American journalist

9 At first it was a giant column that soon took the shape of a supramundane mushroom.
on the first atomic explosion in New Mexico, 16 July 1945
in *New York Times* 26 September 1945

Wilfrid Laurier 1841–1919

Canadian Liberal statesman, Prime Minister 1896–1911

10 Had I been born on the banks of the Saskatchewan, I would myself have shouldered a musket to fight against the neglect of governments and the shameless greed of speculators.
addressing meeting in the Champ de Mars, Montreal, 22 November 1885; O.D. Skelton *Life and Letters of Sir Wilfrid Laurier* (1921)

11 The nineteenth century was the century of the United States. I think we can claim that it is Canada that shall fill the twentieth century.
speech in Ottawa, 18 January 1904; see **Trudeau** 801:1

12 Quebec does not have opinions, only sentiments.
Mason Wade *The French Canadians:1760–1967* (1968)

Johann Kaspar Lavater 1741–1801

Swiss theologian

13 Trust not him with your secrets, who, when left alone in the room, turns over your papers.
Aphorisms on Man (c.1788)

14 The public seldom forgive twice.
Aphorisms on Man (c.1788)

Emily Lawless 1845–1913

Irish poet

15 She said, 'God knows they owe me nought,
I tossed them to the foaming sea,
I tossed them to the howling wastes,
Yet still their love comes home to me.'
'After Aughrim'

16 There's famine in the land, its grip is tightening still!
There's trouble, black and bitter, on every side I glance.
'An Exile's Mother'

Last words

1 *Adieu, mes amis. Je vais à la gloire.*
Farewell, my friends. I go to glory.
Isadora Duncan (1878-1927), before her scarf caught in a car wheel, breaking her neck
Mary Desti *Isadora Duncan's End* (1929) ch. 25

2 All my possessions for a moment of time.
Queen **Elizabeth I** (1533-1603)
attributed, but almost certainly apocryphal

3 All this buttoning and unbuttoning.
18th-century suicide note

4 Be of good comfort Master Ridley, and play the man. We shall this day light such a candle by God's grace in England, as (I trust) shall never be put out.
Hugh **Latimer** (c.1485-1555), *prior to being burned for heresy, 16 October 1555*
John Foxe *Actes and Monuments* (1570 ed.); see **Bible** 92:19

5 Bugger Bognor.
King **George V** (1865-1936) *on his deathbed in 1936, when someone remarked 'Cheer up, your Majesty, you will soon be at Bognor again.'; alternatively, a comment made in 1929, when it was proposed that the town be named Bognor Regis on account of the king's convalescence there after a serious illness*
probably apocryphal; Kenneth Rose *King George V* (1983) ch. 9; see **Last words** 471:18

6 Come closer, boys. It will be easier for you.
Erskine **Childers** (1870-1922) *to the firing squad at his execution*
Burke Wilkinson *The Zeal of the Convert* (1976) ch. 26

7 Crito, we owe a cock to Aesculapius; please pay it and don't forget it.
Socrates (469-399 BC)
Plato *Phaedo* 118

8 Die, my dear Doctor, that's the last thing I shall do!
Lord **Palmerston** (1784-1865)
E. Latham *Famous Sayings and their Authors* (1904)

9 *Dieu me pardonnera, c'est son métier.*
God will pardon me, it is His trade.
Heinrich **Heine** (1797-1856), *on his deathbed*
Alfred Meissner *Heinrich Heine. Erinnerungen* (1856) ch. 5; see **Catherine** 199:15

10 *Dilexi iustitiam et odi iniquitatem, propterea morior in exilio.*
I have loved justice and hated iniquity: therefore I die in exile.
Pope Gregory VII (c.1020-85) at Salerno, following his conflict with the Emperor Henry IV
J. W. Bowden *The Life and Pontificate of Gregory VII* (1840) vol. 2, bk. 3, ch. 20

11 Don't let the awkward squad fire over me.
said by Robert **Burns** (1759-96) *shortly before his death*
A. Cunningham *The Works of Robert Burns; with his Life* vol. 1 (1834)

12 An emperor ought to die standing.
Vespasian (AD 9-79)
Suetonius *Lives of the Caesars* 'Vespasian' sect. 24

13 For God's sake look after our people.
Robert Falcon **Scott** (1868-1912)
last diary entry, 29 March 1912, in *Scott's Last Expedition* (1913) vol. 1, ch. 20

14 For my name and memory, I leave it to men's charitable speeches, and to foreign nations, and the next ages.
will of Francis **Bacon** (1561-1626), *19 December 1625*
J. Spedding (ed.) *The Letters and Life of Francis Bacon* vol. 7 (1874)

15 Give Dayrolles a chair.
Lord **Chesterfield** (1694-1773) *to his godson Dayrolles*
W. H. Craig *Life of Lord Chesterfield* (1907)

16 God save Ireland!
called out from the dock by the Manchester Martyrs, William Allen (d. 1867), Michael Larkin (d. 1867), and William O'Brien (d. 1867)
Robert Kee *The Bold Fenian Men* (1989); see **Sullivan** 763:13

17 Greetings, we win!
dying words of Pheidippides (or Philippides) (d. 490 BC), having run back to Athens from Marathon with news of victory over the Persians
Lucian bk. 3, ch. 64 'Pro Lapsu inter salutandum' para. 3

18 How's the Empire?
said by King **George V** (1865-1936) *to his private secretary on the morning of his death*
letter from Lord Wigram, 31 January 1936, in J. E. Wrench *Geoffrey Dawson and Our Times* (1955) ch. 28; see **Last words** 471:5

19 I am about to take my last voyage, a great leap in the dark.
Thomas **Hobbes** (1588-1679)
attributed (see **Vanbrugh** 806:15), but with no authoritative source; a contemporary version is:
On his death bed he should say that he was 91 years finding out a hole to go out of this world, and at length found it.
Anthony Wood diary, 10 December 1679, in Andrew Clark (ed.) *The Life and Times of Anthony Wood* vol. 2 (1892)

▶

▶ Last words *continued*

1 *Je vais quérir un grand peut-être . . . Tirez le rideau,
la farce est jouée.*

I am going to seek a great perhaps . . . Bring
down the curtain, the farce is played out.
François **Rabelais** (*c.1494–c.1553*)

attributed, but probably apocryphal; Jean Fleury *Rabelais
et ses oeuvres* (1877) vol. 1, ch. 3, pt. 15

2 I am just going outside and may be some time.
Captain Lawrence Oates (*1880–1912*)

Robert Falcon **Scott** diary entry, 16–17 March 1912 in
Scott's Last Expedition (1913) ch. 20; see **Epitaphs**
309:12, **Mahon** 507:9

3 I die happy.
Charles James **Fox** (*1749–1806*)

Lord John Russell *Life and Times of C. J. Fox* vol. 3 (1860)
ch. 69

4 I find, then, I am but a bad anatomist.
Wolfe Tone (*1763–98*), *who in trying to cut his
throat in prison severed his windpipe instead of his
jugular, and lingered for several days*
Oliver Knox *Rebels and Informers* (1998)

5 If this is dying, then I don't think much of it.
Lytton **Strachey** (*1880–1932*), *on his deathbed*
Michael Holroyd *Lytton Strachey* vol. 2 (1968) pt. 2, ch. 6

6 I have a long journey to take, and must bid the
company farewell.
Walter **Ralegh** (*c.1552–1618*)
E. Thompson *Sir Walter Raleigh* (1935) ch. 26

7 I have lived as a philosopher and I die as a
Christian.
Giovanni Jacopo Casanova (*1725–98*), *Italian
adventurer*
The Memoirs of Casanova (1937) p. 492

8 I hope for a happy exit and I hope never to come
back.
Frida **Kahlo** (*1907–54*)

last diary entry; Martha Zamora *Frida Kahlo: the Brush of
Anguish* (1990)

9 I lived uncertain, I die doubtful: O thou Being of
beings, have mercy upon me!
Aristotle (*384–322* BC)

attributed, probably apocryphal; a Latin version was
current in the early 17th century

10 I love you, honey. I know we're all going to
die—but there's three of us who are going to do
something about it.
Thomas E. Burnett Jnr (*1963–2001*); *final phone
call to his wife from the hijacked Flight 93, which
crashed south of Pittsburgh, 11 September 2001*
in *Independent* 13 September 2001; see **McEwan** 501:15

11 I'm tired, and I have to go to sleep.
Allen **Ginsberg** (*1912–97*), *before lapsing into a
final coma*
in *Athens News* 9 April 1997

12 In this life there's nothing new in dying,
But nor, of course, is living any newer.
Sergei **Yesenin** (*1895–1925*); *his final poem,
written in his own blood the day before he hanged
himself in his Leningrad hotel room, 28 December
1925*
'Goodbye, my Friend, Goodbye' (translated by Gordon
McVay)

13 I only regret that I have but one life to lose for
my country.
Nathan **Hale** (*1755–76*), *prior to his execution by
the British for spying, 22 September 1776*
Henry Phelps Johnston *Nathan Hale, 1776* (1914) ch. 7;
see **Addison** 4:13

14 It is a bad cause which cannot bear the words of
a dying man.
Sir Henry Vane (*1613–62*) *as drums and trumpets
were ordered to sound at his execution to drown
anything he might say*
Charles Dickens *A Child's History of England* (1853)
ch. 35

15 It's been so long since I've had champagne.
Anton **Chekhov** (*1860–1904*), *after which, he
slowly drank the glass and died*
Henri Troyat *Chekhov* (1984)

16 I will die like a true-blue rebel. Don't waste any
time in mourning—organize.
Joe **Hill** (*1879–1915*) *before his death by firing
squad*
farewell telegram to Bill Haywood, 18 November 1915,
in *Salt Lake* (Utah) *Tribune* 19 November 1915

17 June 3, Cold Harbor. I was killed.
*the diary entry of a Unionist soldier, found in his
pocket after the failed attack on Cold Harbor, 3 June
1864*
attributed, perhaps apocryphal

18 Let not poor Nelly starve.
Charles II (*1630–85*), *referring to Nell* **Gwyn**, *his
mistress*
Bishop Gilbert Burnet *History of My Own Time* (1724) vol.
1, bk. 3

19 Let's roll.
Todd Beamer, 11 September 2001
heard by telephone operator as Beamer and other
passengers were planning to storm the cockpit of the
hijacked United Airlines Flight 93; the plane crashed in
Pennsylvania minutes later

20 Let us cross over the river and rest under the
shade of the trees.
Thomas Jonathan 'Stonewall' **Jackson** (*1824–63*)
M. Miner and H. Rawson *American Heritage Dictionary of
American Quotations* (1997)

▶

▶**Last Words** *continued*

1 Lord have mercy on my poor country that is so barbarously oppressed.
*Andrew **Fletcher** of Saltoun (1655–1716), Scottish patriot and anti-Unionist*
September 1716

2 Lord, open the King of England's eyes!
*William **Tyndale** (c.1494–1536), at the stake*
John Foxe *Actes and Monuments* (1570)

3 The love boat has crashed against the everyday. You and I, we are quits, and there is no point in listing mutual pains, sorrows, and hurts.
*from an unfinished poem found among **Mayakovsky**'s papers, a variant of which he quoted in his suicide letter*
Vladimir Mayakovsky (1893–1930) letter 12 April 1930

4 Love? What is it? Most natural painkiller. What there is . . . LOVE.
*final entry in the journal of William S. **Burroughs**, 1 August 1997, the day before he died*
in *New Yorker* 18 August 1997

5 *Mehr Licht!*
More light!
*Johann Wolfgang von **Goethe** (1749–1832); abbreviated version of* 'Macht doch den zweiten Fensterladen auch auf, damit mehr Licht hereinkomme [Open the second shutter, so that more light can come in]')
K. W. Müller *Goethes letze literarische Thätigkeit* (1832)

6 My design is to make what haste I can to be gone.
*Oliver **Cromwell** (1599–1658)*
John Morley *Oliver Cromwell* (1900) bk. 5, ch. 10

7 Now God be praised, I will die in peace.
*James **Wolfe** (1727–59)*
J. Knox *Historical Journal of the Campaigns in North America* (ed. A. G. Doughty, 1914) vol. 2

8 Now I'll have eine kleine Pause.
last words of Kathleen Ferrier (1912–53)
Gerald Moore *Am I Too Loud?* (1962)

9 Ô liberté! Ô liberté! que de crimes on commet en ton nom!
O liberty! O liberty! what crimes are committed in thy name!
*Mme **Roland** (1754–93), before being guillotined*
A. de Lamartine *Histoire des Girondins* (1847) bk. 51, ch. 8; see **George** 344:2

10 Oh, my country! how I leave my country!
*William **Pitt** (1759–1806); also variously reported as* 'How I love my country'; *and* 'My country! oh, my country!'
Earl Stanhope *Life of the Rt. Hon. William Pitt* vol. 3 (1879) ch. 43; Earl Stanhope *Life of the Rt. Hon. William Pitt* (1st ed.), vol. 4 (1862) ch. 43; and G. Rose *Diaries and Correspondence* (1860) vol. 2, 23 January 1806; oral tradition reports:
I think I could eat one of Bellamy's veal pies.
attributed

11 One of us must go.
*Oscar **Wilde** (1854–1900), of the wallpaper in the room where he was dying*
attributed, probably apocryphal

12 On, on, on.
*Tom Simpson (1937–67), British cyclist, after collapsing on Mont Ventoux in the Tour de France; see **Misquotations** 538:15*
William Fotheringham *Put Me Back on My Bike* (2002) ch. 2

13 On the contrary.
*Henrik **Ibsen** (1828–1906), after a nurse had said that he 'seemed to be a little better'*
Michael Meyer *Ibsen* (1967)

14 *Qualis artifex pereo!*
What an artist dies with me!
Nero (AD 37–68)
Suetonius *Lives of the Caesars* 'Nero' sect. 49

15 Remember—.
***Charles I** (1600–49), giving his George (insignia of the Order of the Garter) to Bishop Juxon*
speech on the scaffold, 30 January 1649

16 See in what peace a Christian can die.
*Joseph **Addison** (1672–1719), dying words to his stepson Lord Warwick*
Edward Young *Conjectures on Original Composition* (1759)

17 So little done, so much to do.
*Cecil **Rhodes** (1853–1902), on the day of his death*
Lewis Michell *Life of Rhodes* (1910) vol. 2, ch. 39; see **Tennyson** 779:11

18 Strike the tent.
*Robert E. **Lee** (1807–70), 12 October 1870*
attributed

19 Such is life.
Ned Kelly (1855–80) Australian outlaw, before being hanged, 11 November 1880
Frank Clune *The Kelly Hunters* (1955)

20 Tell them I've had a wonderful life.
*Ludwig **Wittgenstein** (1889–1951) to his doctor's wife, before losing consciousness, 28 April 1951*
Ray Monk *Ludwig Wittgenstein* (1990)

21 Tell them to stand up for Jesus.
*American evangelist, Dudley Atkins Tyng (d. 1858), to George **Duffield**, inspiring him to write the hymn; see **Duffield** 291:6*
Ian Bradley (ed.) *The Penguin Book of Hymns* (1989)

22 Thank God, I have done my duty.
*Horatio, Lord **Nelson** (1758–1805) at the battle of Trafalgar, 21 October 1805*
Robert Southey *Life of Nelson* (1813) ch. 9

▶

▶ **Last words** *continued*

1 That would really have been the last cigarette.
*Italo Svevo (1861–1928), when refused a cigarette as he lay dying after a car accident; see **Svevo** 765:2*
Livia Veneziani Svevo *Memoir of Italo Svevo* (1950)

2 They couldn't hit an elephant at this distance.
John Sedgwick (d. 1864), Union general, immediately prior to being killed by enemy fire at the battle of Spotsylvania in the American Civil War
Robert Denney *The Civil War Years* (1992)

3 This hath not offended the king.
*Thomas **More** (1478–1535), lifting his beard aside after laying his head on the block*
Francis Bacon *Apophthegms New and Old* (1625) no. 22

4 This *is* a beautiful country!
*John **Brown** (1800–59) as he rode to the gallows, seated on his coffin*
at his execution on 2 December 1859

5 This is the Fourth?
*Thomas **Jefferson** (1743–1826)*
on 4 July 1826

6 This, this is the end of earth. I am content.
*John Quincy **Adams** (1767–1848) on collapsing in the Senate, 21 February 1848 (he died two days later)*
William H. Seward *Eulogy of John Quincy Adams to Legislature of New York* 1848

7 Thomas—Jefferson—still surv—
***Jefferson** died on the same day*
John **Adams** (1735–1826), on 4 July 1826

8 Turn up the lights; I don't want to go home in the dark.
*O. **Henry** (1862–1910), quoting a song*
Charles Alphonso Smith *O. Henry Biography* (1916) ch. 9
I'm afraid to come home in the dark.
Harry Williams (1874–1924) title of song (1907)

9 Useless! Useless!
*John Wilkes **Booth** (1838–65)*
Philip van Doren Stern *The Man Who Killed Lincoln* (1939)

10 *Vicisti, Galilaee.*
You have won, Galilean.
supposed dying words of the Roman emperor Julian the Apostate (AD c.332–363)
a late embellishment of Theodoret *Ecclesiastical History* (AD c.450) bk. 3, ch. 25; see **Swinburne** 768:22

11 We are all going to Heaven, and Vandyke is of the company.
*Thomas **Gainsborough** (1727–88)*
attributed, in William B. Boulton *Thomas Gainsborough* (1905) ch. 9

12 We are putting passengers off in small boats . . . Engine room getting flooded . . . CQ.
CQD was the original SOS call for shipping
last signals sent from the *Titanic*, 15 April 1912

13 Well, I've had a happy life.
*William **Hazlitt** (1778–1830)*
W. C. Hazlitt *Memoirs of William Hazlitt* (1867)

14 'What *is* the answer?' No answer came. She laughed and said, 'In that case what is the question?'
*Gertrude **Stein** (1874–1946)*
Donald Sutherland *Gertrude Stein, A Biography of her Work* (1951)

15 Why fear death? It is the most beautiful adventure in life.
Charles Frohman (1860–1915), before drowning in the Lusitania, 7 May 1915
I. F. Marcosson and D. Frohman *Charles Frohman* (1916) ch. 19; see **Barrie** 57:4

16 Why not? Why not? Why not? Yeah.
*Timothy **Leary** (1920–96)*
in *Independent* 1 June 1996

17 Would to God this wound had been for Ireland.
Patrick Sarsfield (c.1655–93) on being mortally wounded at the battle of Landen, 19 August 1693, while fighting for France
attributed

D. H. Lawrence 1885–1930

English novelist and poet
*on Lawrence: see **Gibbons** 346:3, **Griffith-Jones** 364:8, **Robinson** 650:20*

18 To the Puritan all things are impure, as somebody says.
Etruscan Places (1932) 'Cerveteri'; see **Bible** 111:2

19 It was in 1915 the old world ended.
Kangaroo (1923)

20 John Thomas says good-night to Lady Jane, a little droopingly, but with a hopeful heart.
Lady Chatterley's Lover (1928) ch. 19

21 The English . . . are paralysed by fear. That is what thwarts and distorts the Anglo-Saxon existence . . . Nothing could be more lovely and fearless than Chaucer. But already Shakespeare is morbid with fear, fear of consequences. That is the strange phenomenon of the English Renaissance: this mystic terror of the consequences, the consequences of action.
Phoenix (1936) 'An Introduction to these Paintings'

22 Pornography is the attempt to insult sex, to do dirt on it.
Phoenix (1936) 'Pornography and Obscenity' ch. 3

23 Never trust the artist. Trust the tale. The proper function of a critic is to save the tale from the artist who created it.
Studies in Classic American Literature (1923) ch. 1

24 Be a good animal, true to your instincts.
The White Peacock (1911) pt. 2, ch. 2

25 Don't you find it a beautiful clean thought, a world empty of people, just uninterrupted grass, and a hare sitting up?
Women in Love (1920) ch. 11

1 Is it the secret of the long-nosed Etruscans?
The long-nosed, sensitive-footed, subtly-smiling
    Etruscans
Who made so little noise outside the cypress
    groves?
  'Cypresses' (1923)

2 How beastly the bourgeois is
Especially the male of the species.
  'How Beastly the Bourgeois Is' (1929)

3 While we have sex in the mind, we truly have
    none in the body.
  'Leave Sex Alone' (1929)

4 Men! The only animal in the world to fear!
  'Mountain Lion' (1923)

5 I never saw a wild thing
Sorry for itself.
  'Self-Pity' (1929)

6 Now it is autumn and the falling fruit
And the long journey towards oblivion . . .
Have you built your ship of death, O have you?
O build your ship of death, for you will need it.
  'Ship of Death' (1932)

7 A snake came to my water-trough
On a hot, hot day, and I in pyjamas for the heat,
To drink there.
  'Snake' (1923)

8 And so, I missed my chance with one of the lords
Of life.
And I have something to expiate:
A pettiness.
  'Snake' (1923)

9 Not I, not I, but the wind that blows through me!
  'Song of a Man who has Come Through' (1917)

10 When I read Shakespeare I am struck with
    wonder
That such trivial people should muse and thunder
In such lovely language.
  'When I Read Shakespeare' (1929)

11 Curse the blasted, jelly-boned swines, the slimy,
the belly-wriggling invertebrates, the miserable
sodding rotters, the flaming sods, the snivelling,
dribbling, dithering, palsied, pulse-less lot that
make up England today. They've got white of egg
in their veins, and their spunk is that watery it's a
marvel they can breed. They *can* nothing but frog-
spawn—the gibberers! God, how I hate them!
  letter to Edward Garnett, 3 July 1912, in H. T. Moore (ed.)
  Collected Letters of D. H. Lawrence (1962) vol. 1

12 Tragedy ought really to be a great kick at misery.
  letter to A. W. McLeod, 6 October 1912, in H. T. Moore
  (ed.) *Collected Letters of D. H. Lawrence* (1962) vol. 1

13 Australia has a marvellous sky and air and blue
clarity, and a hoary sort of land beneath it, like a
Sleeping Princess on whom the dust of ages has
settled.
  letter to Jan Juta, 20 May 1922; *Letters and Works* (1987)
  vol. 4

14 The dead don't die. They look on and help.
  letter to J. Middleton Murry, 2 February 1923, in H. T.
  Moore (ed.) *Collected Letters of D. H. Lawrence* (1962) vol. 2

15 I want to go south, where there is no autumn,
where the cold doesn't crouch over one like a
snow-leopard waiting to pounce. The heart of the
North is dead, and the fingers of cold are corpse
fingers.
  letter to J. Middleton Murry, 3 October 1924, in H. T.
  Moore (ed.) *Collected Letters of D. H. Lawrence* (1962) vol. 2

16 My God, what a clumsy *olla putrida* James Joyce is!
Nothing but old fags and cabbage-stumps of
quotations from the Bible and the rest, stewed in
the juice of deliberate, journalistic dirty-
mindedness.
  letter to Aldous and Maria Huxley, 15 August 1928, in H.
  T. Moore (ed.) *Collected Letters of D. H. Lawrence* (1962)
  vol. 2

T. E. Lawrence 1888–1935

English soldier and writer

on Lawrence: see **Berners** *71:6; see also* **Borrowed titles**
146:17

17 Many men would take the death-sentence without
a whimper to escape the life-sentence which fate
carries in her other hand.
  The Mint (1955) pt. 1, ch. 4

18 The trumpets came out brazenly with the last post
. . . A man hates to be moved to folly by a noise.
  The Mint (1955) pt. 3, ch. 9

19 I loved you, so I drew these tides of men into my
    hands and wrote my will across the sky in stars
To earn you freedom, the seven pillared worthy
    house, that your eyes might be shining for me
When we came.
  The Seven Pillars of Wisdom (1926) dedication

20 Surely the sex business isn't worth all this damned
fuss? I've met only a handful of people who cared
a biscuit for it.
  on reading Lady Chatterley's Lover
  Christopher Hassall *Edward Marsh* (1959)

Laws of Manu

*a code of Hindu religious law, dating in its present form from
the 1st century* BC

*textual translations are those of W. Doniger with B. K. Smith,
1991*

21 The very birth of a priest [brahmin] is the eternal
physical form of religion; for he is born for the
sake of religion and is fit to become one with
ultimate reality.
  ch. 1, v. 98

22 The man who gives him [the pupil] the benefit of
the revealed canon . . . should be known as his
guru.
  ch. 1, v. 149

23 Since people in the other three stages of life are
supported every day by the knowledge and the
food of the householder, therefore the householder
stage of life is the best.
  ch. 3, v. 78

24 You can never get meat without violence to
creatures with the breath of life, and the killing of

creatures with the breath of life does not get you to heaven; therefore you should not eat meat.
> ch. 5, v. 48

1 A girl, a young woman, or even an old woman should not do anything independently, even in [her own] house.
In childhood a woman should be under her father's control, in youth under her husband's, and when her husband is dead, under her sons'.
> ch. 5, v. 147

2 There is no difference at all between the goddesses of good fortune . . . who live in houses and women . . . who are the lamps of their houses, worthy of reverence and greatly blessed because of their progeny.
> ch. 9, v. 26

3 'Let there be mutual absence of infidelity until death'; this should be known as the supreme duty of a man and a woman, in a nutshell.
> ch. 9, v. 101

4 All of those castes who are excluded from the world of those who were born from the mouth, arms, thighs and feet (of the primordial Man) are traditionally regarded as aliens.
> ch. 10, v. 45

5 Manu has said that non-violence, truth, not stealing, purification, and the suppression of the sensory powers is the duty of the four classes, in a nutshell.
> ch. 10, v. 63

Nigel Lawson 1932–
British Conservative politician

6 It represented the tip of a singularly ill-concealed iceberg, with all the destructive potential that icebergs possess.
*of an article by Alan Walters, Margaret **Thatcher**'s economic adviser, criticizing the Exchange Rate Mechanism*
> in the House of Commons following his resignation as Chancellor, 31 October 1989

Kenneth L. Lay 1942–
American businessman, former CEO of Enron

7 I am deeply troubled about asserting these rights, because it may be perceived by some that I have something to hide.
invoking his Fifth Amendment protection and declining to answer Congress's questions on the Enron collapse
> in *Newsweek* 25 February 2002

Irving Layton 1912–
Canadian poet

8 An aphorism
should be
like a burr:
sting,
stick,
and leave

a little soreness
afterwards.
> *The Whole Bloody Bird* (1969) 'Aphs'

9 We love in another's soul
whatever of ourselves
we can deposit in it;
the greater the deposit,
the greater the love.
> *The Whole Bloody Bird* (1969) 'Aphs'

Emma Lazarus 1849–87
American poet

10 Give me your tired, your poor,
Your huddled masses yearning to breathe free,
The wretched refuse of your teeming shore,
Send these, the homeless, tempest-tossed, to me:
I lift my lamp beside the golden door.
inscription on the Statue of Liberty, New York
> 'The New Colossus' (1883)

Edmund Leach 1910–89
English anthropologist

11 Far from being the basis of the good society, the family, with its narrow privacy and tawdry secrets, is the source of all our discontents.
> BBC Reith Lectures, 1967, in *Listener* 30 November 1967

Stephen Leacock 1869–1944
Canadian humorist

12 The parent who could see his boy as he really is, would shake his head and say: 'Willie, is no good; I'll sell him.'
> *Essays and Literary Studies* (1916) 'Lot of a Schoolmaster'

13 Advertising may be described as the science of arresting human intelligence long enough to get money from it.
> *Garden of Folly* (1924) 'The Perfect Salesman'

14 I am what is called a *professor emeritus*—from the Latin *e*, 'out', and *meritus*, 'so he ought to be'.
> *Here are my Lectures* (1938) ch. 14

15 A sportsman is a man who, every now and then, simply has to get out and kill something. Not that he's cruel. He wouldn't hurt a fly. It's not big enough.
> *My Remarkable Uncle* (1942)

16 Lord Ronald said nothing; he flung himself from the room, flung himself upon his horse and rode madly off in all directions.
> *Nonsense Novels* (1911) 'Gertrude the Governess'

17 A decision of the courts decided that the game of golf may be played on Sunday, not being a game within the view of the law, but being a form of moral effort.
> *Over the Footlights* (1923) 'Why I Refuse to Play Golf'

Mary Leapor 1722–46
English poet

18 In spite of all romantic poets sing,
This gold, my dearest, is an useful thing.
> 'Mira to Octavia'

1 Woman, a pleasing but a short-lived flower,
Too soft for business and too weak for power:
A wife in bondage, or neglected maid:
Despised, if ugly; if she's fair, betrayed.
'An Essay on Woman'

Edward Lear 1812–88

English artist and writer of humorous verse

2 Who, or why, or which, or what,
Is the Akond of Swat?
'The Akond of Swat' (1888)

3 There was an Old Man with a beard,
Who said, 'It is just as I feared!—
Two Owls and a Hen,
Four Larks and a Wren,
Have all built their nests in my beard!'
A Book of Nonsense (1846)

4 On the coast of Coromandel
Where the early pumpkins blow,
In the middle of the woods,
Lived the Yonghy-Bonghy-Bó.
'The Courtship of the Yonghy-Bonghy-Bó' (1871)

5 The Dong with a luminous nose.
title of poem (1871)

6 When awful darkness and silence reign
Over the great Gromboolian plain.
'The Dong with a Luminous Nose' (1871)

7 When storm-clouds brood on the towering heights
Of the Hills of the Chankly Bore.
'The Dong with a Luminous Nose' (1871)

8 Far and few, far and few,
Are the lands where the Jumblies live;
Their heads are green, and their hands are blue,
And they went to sea in a Sieve.
'The Jumblies' (1871)

9 And they bought an Owl, and a useful Cart,
And a pound of Rice, and a Cranberry Tart,
And a hive of silvery Bees.
And they bought a Pig, and some green Jackdaws,
And a lovely Monkey with lollipop paws,
And forty bottles of Ring-Bo-Ree,
And no end of Stilton Cheese.
'The Jumblies' (1871)

10 Nasticreechia Krorluppia.
More Nonsense (1872) 'Nonsense Botany'

11 There was an old man of Thermopylae,
Who never did anything properly.
More Nonsense (1872) 'One Hundred Nonsense Pictures and Rhymes'

12 Till Mrs Discobbolos said
'Oh! W! X! Y! Z!
It has just come into my head—
Suppose we should happen to fall!!!!
Darling Mr Discobbolos?'
'Mr and Mrs Discobbolos' (1871)

13 'How pleasant to know Mr Lear!'
Who has written such volumes of stuff!
Some think him ill-tempered and queer,
But a few think him pleasant enough.
Nonsense Songs (1871) preface

14 Old Foss is the name of his cat:
His body is perfectly spherical,
He weareth a runcible hat.
Nonsense Songs (1871) preface

15 The Owl and the Pussy-Cat went to sea
In a beautiful pea-green boat.
They took some honey, and plenty of money,
Wrapped up in a five-pound note.
The Owl looked up to the Stars above
And sang to a small guitar,
'Oh lovely Pussy! O Pussy, my love,
What a beautiful Pussy you are.'
'The Owl and the Pussy-Cat' (1871)

16 Pussy said to the Owl, 'You elegant fowl!
How charmingly sweet you sing!
O let us be married! too long we have tarried:
But what shall we do for a ring?'
They sailed away for a year and a day,
To the land where the Bong-tree grows,
And there in a wood a Piggy-wig stood
With a ring at the end of his nose.
'The Owl and the Pussy-Cat' (1871)

17 'Dear Pig, are you willing to sell for one shilling
Your ring?' Said the Piggy, 'I will.'
'The Owl and the Pussy-Cat' (1871)

18 They dined on mince, and slices of quince,
Which they ate with a runcible spoon;
And hand in hand, on the edge of the sand,
They danced by the light of the moon.
'The Owl and the Pussy-Cat' (1871)

19 The Pobble who has no toes
Had once as many as we;
When they said, 'Some day you may lose them all';—
He replied,—'Fish fiddle de-dee!'
'The Pobble Who Has No Toes' (1871)

20 He has gone to fish, for his Aunt Jobiska's
Runcible Cat with crimson whiskers!
'The Pobble Who Has No Toes' (1871)

21 'But the longer I live on this Crumpetty Tree
The plainer than ever it seems to me
That very few people come this way
And that life on the whole is far from gay!'
Said the Quangle-Wangle Quee.
'The Quangle-Wangle's Hat' (1871)

Timothy Leary 1920–96

American psychologist
see also **Epitaphs** 311:9, **Last words** 474:16

22 If you take the game of life seriously, if you take
your nervous system seriously, if you take your
sense organs seriously, if you take the energy
process seriously, you must turn on, tune in and
drop out.
lecture, June 1966, in The Politics of Ecstasy (1968) ch. 21

23 The PC is the LSD of the '90s.
remark made in the early 1990s; in Guardian 1 June 1996

Mary Elizabeth Lease 1853–1933
American writer and lecturer

1 Kansas had better stop raising corn and begin raising hell.
   E. J. James et al. *Notable American Women 1607–1950* (1971) vol. 2

F. R. Leavis 1895–1978
English literary critic

2 The common pursuit.
   title of book (1952)

3 The few really great—the major novelists . . . are significant in terms of the human awareness they promote; awareness of the possibilities of life.
   The Great Tradition (1948) ch. 1

4 He energized the Garden-Suburb ethos with a certain original talent and the vigour of a prolonged adolescence . . . rather like Keats's vulgarity with a Public School accent.
   of Rupert **Brooke**
   New Bearings in English Poetry (1932) ch. 2

5 Self-contempt, well-grounded.
   on the foundation of T. S. **Eliot**'s *work*
   in *Times Literary Supplement* 21 October 1988 (quoted by Christopher Ricks in a BBC radio talk); see **Milton** 533:26

Fran Lebowitz 1946–
American writer

6 There is no such thing as inner peace. There is only nervousness or death.
   Metropolitan Life (1978)

7 The best fame is a writer's fame: it's enough to get a table at a good restaurant, but not enough that you get interrupted when you eat.
   in *Observer* 30 May 1993 'Sayings of the Week'

Stanislaw Lec 1909–66
Polish writer

8 Is it progress if a cannibal uses knife and fork?
   Unkempt Thoughts (1962)

John le Carré (David John Moore Cornwell) 1931–
English thriller writer

9 The spy who came in from the cold.
   title of novel (1963)

Le Corbusier (Charles-Édouard Jeanneret) 1887–1965
French architect

10 *Une maison est une machine-à-habiter.*
   A house is a machine for living in.
   Vers une architecture (1923); see **Tolstoy** 796:19

11 A hundred times I have thought: New York is a catastrophe, and fifty times: it is a beautiful catastrophe.
   When the Cathedrals were White (1947) 'The Fairy Catastrophe'

12 This frightful word [function] was born under other skies than those I have loved—those where the sun reigns supreme.
   Stephen Gardiner *Le Corbusier* (1974) introduction

Alexandre Auguste Ledru-Rollin 1807–74
French politician

13 Ah well! I am their leader, I really had to follow them!
   E. de Mirecourt *Les Contemporains* vol. 14 (1857) 'Ledru-Rollin'

Francis Ledwidge 1891–1917
Irish poet

14 He shall not hear the bittern cry
   In the wild sky where he is lain,
   Nor voices of the sweeter birds
   Above the wailing of the rain.
   'Lament for Thomas MacDonagh'

Gypsy Rose Lee (Rose Louise Hovick) 1914–70
American striptease artiste

15 God is love, but get it in writing.
   attributed

Harper Lee 1926–
American novelist

16 Shoot all the bluejays you want, if you can hit 'em, but remember it's a sin to kill a mockingbird.
   To Kill a Mockingbird (1960) ch. 10

Henry Lee ('Light-Horse Harry') 1756–1818
American soldier and politician

17 A citizen, first in war, first in peace, and first in the hearts of his countrymen.
   Funeral Oration on the death of General Washington (1800)

Laurie Lee 1914–97
English writer

18 I was set down from the carrier's cart at the age of three; and there with a sense of bewilderment and terror my life in the village began.
   Cider with Rosie (1959)

Nathaniel Lee c.1653–92
English dramatist

19 When the sun sets, shadows, that showed at noon But small, appear most long and terrible.
   Oedipus (with John Dryden, 1679) act 4, sc. 1

20 When Greeks joined Greeks, then was the tug of war!
   The Rival Queens (1677) act 4, sc. 2

21 Man, false man, smiling, destructive man.
   Theodosius (1680) act 3, sc. 2

1 They called me mad, and I called them mad, and damn them, they outvoted me.
> R. Porter *A Social History of Madness* (1987), introduction; attributed

Robert E. Lee 1807–70
American Confederate general
see also: **Last words** 473:18

2 It is well that war is so terrible. We should grow too fond of it.
> *after the battle of Fredericksburg, December 1862*
> attributed

3 I have fought against the people of the North because I believed they were seeking to wrest from the South its dearest rights. But I have never cherished toward them bitter or vindictive feelings, and I have never seen the day when I did not pray for them.
> Geoffrey C. Ward *The Civil War* (1991) ch. 5

4 *refusing an offer to write his memoirs:*
I should be trading on the blood of my men.
> attributed, perhaps apocryphal

Lynda Lee-Potter
British journalist

5 Powerful men often succeed through the help of their wives. Powerful women only succeed in spite of their husbands.
> in *Daily Mail* 16 May 1984

Richard Le Gallienne 1866–1947
English poet

6 The cry of the Little Peoples goes up to God in vain,
For the world is given over to the cruel sons of Cain.
> 'The Cry of the Little Peoples' (1899)

Ursula K. Le Guin 1929–
American writer

7 He had grown up in a country run by politicians who sent the pilots to man the bombers to kill the babies to make the world safer for children to grow up in.
> *The Lathe of Heaven* (1971) ch. 6

8 Love doesn't just sit there, like a stone, it has to be made, like bread; remade all the time, made new.
> *The Lathe of Heaven* (1971) ch. 10

Ernest Lehman *see* Film titles 322:13

Tom Lehrer 1928–
American humorist

9 Plagiarize! Let no one else's work evade your eyes,
Remember why the good Lord made your eyes.
> 'Lobachevski' (1953 song)

10 Poisoning pigeons in the park.
> song title, 1953

11 It is sobering to consider that when Mozart was my age he had already been dead for a year.
> N. Shapiro (ed.) *An Encyclopedia of Quotations about Music* (1978)

12 I hope to use the subjunctive until the end.
> attributed; in *The Times* 3 August 2000

Gottfried Wilhelm Leibniz 1646–1716
German philosopher

13 It is God who is the ultimate reason of things, and the knowledge of God is no less the beginning of science than his essence and will are the beginning of beings.
> *Letter on a General Principle Useful in Explaining the Laws of Nature* (1687)

14 It is the knowledge of necessary and eternal truths which distinguishes us from mere animals, and gives us *Reason* and the sciences, raising us to knowledge of ourselves and of God. It is this in us which we call the rational soul or *Mind*.
> *The Monadology* (1714) sect. 29 (translated by R. Latta)

15 *Nihil est sine ratione.*
There is nothing without a reason.
> *Studies in Physics and the Nature of Body* (1671)

16 *Eadem sunt quorum unum potest substitui alteri salva veritate.*
Two things are identical if one can be substituted for the other without affecting the truth.
> 'Table de définitions' (1704) in L. Coutourat (ed.) *Opuscules et fragments inédits de Leibniz* (1903)

17 We should like Nature to go no further; we should like it to be finite, like our mind; but this is to ignore the greatness and majesty of the Author of things.
> letter to S. Clarke, 1715, translated by M. Morris and G. H. R. Parkinson in *Leibniz: Philosophical Writings* (1973)

Fred W. Leigh d. 1924
British songwriter

18 Can't get away to marry you today,
My wife won't let me!
> 'Waiting at the Church (My Wife Won't Let Me)' (1906 song)

19 Why am I always the bridesmaid,
Never the blushing bride?
> 'Why Am I Always the Bridesmaid?' (1917 song, with Charles Collins and Lily Morris); see **Proverbs** 614:21

Vivien Leigh 1913–67
English actress

20 Shaw is like a train. One just speaks the words and sits in one's place. But Shakespeare is like bathing in the sea—one swims where one wants.
> letter from Harold Nicolson to Vita Sackville-West, 1 February 1956

Curtis E. LeMay 1906–90

American air-force officer

1 They've got to draw in their horns and stop their aggression, or we're going to bomb them back into the Stone Age.
on the North Vietnamese
   Mission with LeMay (1965)

Ninon de Lenclos 1620–1705

French courtesan

2 How often have I told you, that love seldom dies of hunger, but frequently of satiety?
   letter 41 to the Marquis de Sevigné, *The Memoirs of Ninon de L'Enclos* (1778)

Lenin (Vladimir Ilich Ulyanov) 1870–1924

Russian revolutionary
see also **Keynes** 450:13, **Misquotations** 537:6

3 Imperialism is the monopoly stage of capitalism.
   Imperialism as the Last Stage of Capitalism (1916) ch. 7
   'Briefest possible definition of imperialism'

4 No, Democracy is *not* identical with majority rule. Democracy is a *State* which recognizes the subjection of the minority to the majority, that is, an organization for the systematic use of *force* by one class against the other, by one part of the population against another.
   State and Revolution (1919) ch. 4

5 While the State exists, there can be no freedom. When there is freedom there will be no State.
   State and Revolution (1919) ch. 5

6 What is to be done?
   title of pamphlet (1902); originally the title of a novel (1863) by N. G. Chernyshevsky

7 Communism is Soviet power plus the electrification of the whole country.
   Report to 8th Congress, 1920, in *Collected Works* (ed. 5) vol. 42

8 Who? Whom? [i.e. Who masters whom?]
   definition of political science, meaning 'Who will outstrip whom?'
   in *Polnoe Sobranie Sochinenii* vol. 44 (1970) 17 October 1921 and elsewhere

9 A good man fallen among Fabians.
   of George Bernard **Shaw**
   Arthur Ransome *Six Weeks in Russia in 1919* (1919) 'Notes of Conversations with Lenin'

10 Liberty is precious—so precious that it must be rationed.
   Sidney and Beatrice Webb *Soviet Communism* (1936)

John Lennon 1940–80

English pop singer and songwriter
see also **Lennon and McCartney**

11 Happiness is a warm gun.
   title of song (1968); see **Advertising slogans** 7:27

12 Imagine there's no heaven,
   It's easy if you try,
   No hell below us,

Above us only sky.
   'Imagine' (1971 song)

13 Will the people in the cheaper seats clap your hands? All the rest of you, if you'll just rattle your jewellery.
   at the Royal Variety Performance, 4 November 1963, in R. Colman *John Winston Lennon* (1984) pt. 1, ch. 11

14 We're more popular than Jesus now; I don't know which will go first—rock 'n' roll or Christianity.
   of The Beatles
   interview in *Evening Standard* 4 March 1966

John Lennon 1940–80 and **Paul McCartney** 1942–

English pop singers and songwriters
see also **Lennon, McCartney**

15 Back in the USSR.
   title of song (1968)

16 For I don't care too much for money,
   For money can't buy me love.
   'Can't Buy Me Love' (1964 song)

17 Eleanor Rigby picks up the rice in the church where a wedding has been,
   Lives in a dream.
   Waits at the window, wearing the face that she keeps in a jar by the door,
   Who is it for?
   All the lonely people, where do they all come from?
   'Eleanor Rigby' (1966 song)

18 Give peace a chance.
   title of song (1969)

19 It's been a hard day's night,
   And I've been working like a dog.
   'A Hard Day's Night' (1964 song)

20 Strawberry fields forever.
   title of song (1967)

21 She's got a ticket to ride, but she don't care.
   'Ticket to Ride' (1965 song)

22 Will you still need me, will you still feed me,
   When I'm sixty four?
   'When I'm Sixty Four' (1967 song)

23 Oh I get by with a little help from my friends,
   Mm, I get high with a little help from my friends.
   'With a Little Help From My Friends' (1967 song)

Dan Leno (George Galvin) 1860–1904

English entertainer

24 Ah! what is man? Wherefore does he why? Whence did he whence? Whither is he withering?
   Dan Leno Hys Booke (1901) ch. 1

William Lenthall 1591–1662

English politician, Speaker of the House of Commons

25 I have neither eye to see, nor tongue to speak here, but as the House is pleased to direct me.
   to **Charles I**, *on being asked if he had seen any of the*

five MPs whom the King had ordered to be arrested, 4 January 1642

John Rushworth *Historical Collections. The Third Part* vol. 2 (1692); see **Lincoln** 485:13

Leonardo da Vinci 1452–1519

Italian painter and designer

1 Whoever in discussion adduces authority uses not intellect but rather memory.

Edward McCurdy (ed. and trans.) *Leonardo da Vinci's Notebooks* (1906) bk. 1

2 Life well spent is long.

Edward McCurdy (ed. and trans.) *Leonardo da Vinci's Notebooks* (1906) bk. 1

3 Iron rusts from disuse; stagnant water loses its purity and in cold weather becomes frozen; even so does inaction sap the vigour of the mind.

Edward McCurdy (ed. and trans.) *Leonardo da Vinci's Notebooks* (1906) bk. 1

4 Human subtlety . . . will never devise an invention more beautiful, more simple or more direct than does Nature, because in her inventions nothing is lacking, and nothing is superfluous.

Edward McCurdy (ed. and trans.) *Leonardo da Vinci's Notebooks* (1906) bk. 1

5 Perspective is the bridle and rudder of painting.

Irma Richter (ed.) *Selections from the Notebooks of Leonardo da Vinci* (World's Classics, 1952)

6 The span of a man's outspread arms is equal to his height.

Irma Richter (ed.) *Selections from the Notebooks of Leonardo da Vinci* (World's Classics, 1952)

7 Every man at three years old is half his height.

Irma A. Richter (ed.) *Selections from the Notebooks of Leonardo da Vinci* (World's Classics, 1952)

8 The poet ranks far below the painter in the representation of visible things, and far below the musician in that of invisible things.

Irma A. Richter (ed.) *Selections from the Notebooks of Leonardo da Vinci* (World's Classics, 1952)

Mikhail Lermontov 1814–41

Russian novelist and poet

9 The love of savages isn't much better than the love of noble ladies; ignorance and simple-heartedness can be as tiresome as coquetry.

A Hero of our Time (1840) 'Bella' (translated by Philip Longworth)

10 Of two close friends, one is always the slave of the other.

A Hero of our Time (1840) 'Princess Mary' (translated by Philip Longworth)

11 Ever since I lived and entered into action, fate has somehow led me to the climax of other people's dramas, as if no one could die, no one could despair without me. I have always been the essential character of the fifth act.

A Hero of our Time (1840) 'Princess Mary' (translated by Philip Longworth)

12 I am like a man yawning at a ball; the only reason he does not go home to bed is that his carriage has not arrived yet.

A Hero of our Time (1840) 'Princess Mary' (translated by Philip Longworth)

13 No, I'm not Byron, it's my role
To be an undiscovered wonder,
Like him, a persecuted wand'rer,
But furnished with a Russian soul.

'No, I'm not Byron' (1832) (translated by Alan Myers)

Alan Jay Lerner 1918–86

American songwriter

14 Don't let it be forgot
That once there was a spot
For one brief shining moment that was known
As Camelot.

now particularly associated with the White House of John F. Kennedy; see Onassis 573:7

'Camelot' (1960 song)

15 I'm getting married in the morning,
Ding! dong! the bells are gonna chime.
Pull out the stopper;
Let's have a whopper;
But get me to the church on time!

'Get me to the Church on Time' (1956 song) in *My Fair Lady*

16 Why can't a woman be more like a man?
Men are so honest, so thoroughly square;
Eternally noble, historically fair;
Who, when you win, will always give your back a pat.
Why can't a woman be like that?

'A Hymn to Him' (1956 song) in *My Fair Lady*

17 We met at nine.
We met at eight.
I was on time.
No, you were late.
Ah yes! I remember it well.

'I Remember it Well' (1958 song) in *Gigi*

18 I've grown accustomed to the trace
Of something in the air;
Accustomed to her face.

'I've Grown Accustomed to her Face' (1956 song) in *My Fair Lady*

19 The rain in Spain stays mainly in the plain.

'The Rain in Spain' (1956 song) in *My Fair Lady*

20 In Hertford, Hereford, and Hampshire,
Hurricanes hardly happen.

'The Rain in Spain' (1956 song) in *My Fair Lady*

21 Thank heaven for little girls!
For little girls get bigger every day.

'Thank Heaven for Little Girls' (1958 song) in *Gigi*

22 All I want is a room somewhere,
Far away from the cold night air,
With one enormous chair,
Oh, wouldn't it be loverly?

'Wouldn't it be Loverly' (1956 song) in *My Fair Lady*

23 Oozing charm from every pore,
He oiled his way around the floor.

'You Did It' (1956 song) in *My Fair Lady*

Doris Lessing 1919–

English writer

1 There's only one real sin, and that is to persuade oneself that the second-best is anything but the second-best.
   The Golden Notebook (1962)

2 When old settlers say 'One has to understand the country,' what they mean is, 'You have to get used to our ideas about the native.'
   The Grass is Singing (1950) ch. 1

3 What of October, that ambiguous month, the month of tension, the unendurable month?
   Martha Quest (1952) pt. 4, sect. 1

G. E. Lessing 1729–81

German dramatist and critic

4 *Gestern liebt' ich,*
   Heute leid' ich,
   Morgen sterb' ich:
   Dennoch denk' ich
   Heut und morgen
   Gern an gestern.

   Yesterday I loved, today I suffer, tomorrow I die: but I still think fondly, today and tomorrow, of yesterday.
   'Lied aus dem Spanischen' (1780)

5 *Ein einziger dankbarer Gedanke gen Himmel ist das vollkommenste Gebet.*

   One single grateful thought raised to heaven is the most perfect prayer.
   Minna von Barnhelm (1767) act 2, sc. 7

6 If God were to hold out enclosed in His right hand all Truth, and in His left hand just the active search for Truth, though with the condition that I should always err therein, and He should say to me: Choose! I should humbly take His left hand and say: Father! Give me this one; absolute Truth belongs to Thee alone.
   Eine Duplik (1778) pt. 1

Winifred Mary Letts 1882–1972

English writer

7 I saw the spires of Oxford
   As I was passing by,
   The grey spires of Oxford
   Against a pearl-grey sky;
   My heart was with the Oxford men
   Who went abroad to die.
   'The Spires of Oxford' (1916)

Lord Leverhulme 1851–1925

English industrialist and philanthropist

8 Half the money I spend on advertising is wasted, and the trouble is I don't know which half.
   David Ogilvy *Confessions of an Advertising Man* (1963)

Ada Leverson 1865–1936

English novelist

9 He seemed at ease and to have the look of the last gentleman in Europe.
   of Oscar **Wilde**
   Letters to the Sphinx (1930)

Denise Levertov 1923–

English-born American poet

10 Images
   split the truth
   in fractions.
   'A Sequence' (1961)

11 two by two in the ark of
   the ache of it.
   'The Ache of Marriage' (1964)

René Lévesque 1922–87

Canadian politician, founder of Parti Québecois

12 Outside Quebec, I don't find two great cultures. I feel like a foreigner. First and foremost, I am a Québecois, and second—with a rather growing sense of doubt—a Canadian.
   in *Toronto Star* 1 June 1963

Primo Levi 1919–87

Italian novelist and poet

13 Our language lacks words to express this offence, the demolition of a man.
   of a year spent in Auschwitz
   If This is a Man (1958)

Bernard Levin 1928–

British journalist

14 Whom the mad would destroy, they first make gods.
   of **Mao** *Zedong in* 1967
   Levin quoting himself in *The Times* 21 September 1987; see **Proverbs** 635:5

Duc de Lévis 1764–1830

French soldier and writer

15 *Noblesse oblige.*
   Nobility has its obligations.
   Maximes et Réflexions (1812 ed.) 'Morale: Maximes et Préceptes' no. 73

16 *Gouverner, c'est choisir.*
   To govern is to choose.
   Maximes et Réflexions (1812 ed.) 'Politique: Maximes de Politique' no. 19

Claude Lévi-Strauss 1908–

French social anthropologist

17 Language is a form of human reason, and has its reasons which are unknown to man.
   The Savage Mind (1962) ch. 9; see **Pascal** 587:12

18 The purpose of myth is to provide a logical model capable of overcoming a contradiction (an

impossible achievement if, as it happens, the contradiction is real).

Structural Anthropology (1968) ch. 11

G. H. Lewes 1817–78

English man of letters; common-law husband of George **Eliot**

1 Murder, like talent, seems occasionally to run in families.

The Physiology of Common Life (1859) ch. 12

2 The pen, in our age, weighs heavier in the social scale than the sword of a Norman Baron.

Ranthorpe (1847) epilogue

3 Many a genius has been slow of growth. Oaks that flourish for a thousand years do not spring up into beauty like a reed.

The Spanish Drama (1846) ch. 2

C. S. Lewis 1898–1963

English literary scholar

4 No one ever told me that grief felt so like fear.

A Grief Observed (1961)

5 Every one says forgiveness is a lovely idea, until they have something to forgive.

Mere Christianity (1952) bk. 3, ch. 7

6 We have trained them [men] to think of the Future as a promised land which favoured heroes attain—not as something which everyone reaches at the rate of sixty minutes an hour, whatever he does, whoever he is.

The Screwtape Letters (1942) no. 25

7 She's the sort of woman who lives for others—you can always tell the others by their hunted expression.

The Screwtape Letters (1942) no. 26

8 A young man who wishes to remain a sound atheist cannot be too careful of his reading.

Surprised by Joy (1955)

9 For twenty years I've stared my level best
To see if evening—any evening—would suggest
A patient etherized upon a table;
In vain. I simply wasn't able.

on contemporary poetry

'A Confession' (1964); see **Eliot** 302:12

10 Often when I pray I wonder if I am not posting letters to a non-existent address.

letter to Arthur Greeves, 24 December 1930

11 Courage is not simply *one* of the virtues but the form of every virtue at the testing point.

Cyril Connolly *The Unquiet Grave* (1944) ch. 3

12 He that but looketh on a plate of ham and eggs to lust after it, hath already committed breakfast with it in his heart.

letter, 10 March 1954

David Lewis 1909–81

Canadian politician

13 Louder voices: the corporate welfare bums.

title of book, 1972

14 Welfare is for the needy, not big and wealthy multinational corporations.

Louder Voices: the Corporate Welfare Bums (1972)

Esther Lewis (later Clark) fl. 1747–89

English poet

15 Are simple women only fit
To dress, to darn, to flower, or knit,
To mind the distaff, or the spit?
Why are the needle and the pen
Thought incompatible by men?

'A Mirror for Detractors' (1754) l. 146

George Cornewall Lewis 1806–63

British Liberal politician and writer

16 Life would be tolerable but for its amusements.

in *The Times* 18 September 1872; see **Surtees** 764:20

Robert Lewis

American pilot

17 It just seems impossible to comprehend. Just how many did we kill? I honestly have the feeling of groping for words to explain this or I might say 'my God, what have we done?' If I live a hundred years I'll never quite get those few minutes out of my mind.

on the bombing of Hiroshima

log book of the Enola Gay, 6 August 1945

Sam M. Lewis 1885–1959 and Joe Young 1889–1939

American songwriters

18 How 'ya gonna keep 'em down on the farm (after they've seen Paree)?

title of song (1919)

19 Mammy, Mammy, look at me. Don't you know me? I'm your little baby.

'My Mammy' (1918 song); sung by Al **Jolson**

Sinclair Lewis 1885–1951

American novelist

20 Our American professors like their literature clear and cold and pure and very dead.

The American Fear of Literature (Nobel Prize Address, 12 December 1930), in H. Frenz *Literature 1901–1967* (1969)

21 To George F. Babbitt, as to most prosperous citizens of Zenith, his motor car was poetry and tragedy, love and heroism. The office was his pirate ship but the car his perilous excursion ashore.

Babbitt (1922) ch. 3

22 She did her work with the thoroughness of a mind which reveres details and never quite understands them.

Babbitt (1922) ch. 18

23 It can't happen here.

title of novel (1935)

Willmott Lewis 1877–1950

British journalist

1 I think it well to remember that, when writing for the newspapers, we are writing for an elderly lady in Hastings who has two cats of which she is passionately fond. Unless our stuff can successfully compete for her interest with those cats, it is no good.

Claud Cockburn *In Time of Trouble* (1957)

Wyndham Lewis 1882–1957

English novelist, painter, and critic

2 Gertrude Stein's prose-song is a cold, black suet-pudding . . . Cut it at any point, it is the same thing . . . all fat, without nerve.

of Three Lives (*1909*)

Time and Western Man (1927)

3 Angels in jumpers.

describing the figures in Stanley **Spencer**'s *paintings*

attributed

Ludwig Lewisohn 1882–1955

German-born novelist

4 There are philosophies which are unendurable not because men are cowards, but because they are men.

The Modern Drama (1916)

George Leybourne d. 1884

English songwriter

5 He'd fly through the air with the greatest of ease, A daring young man on the flying trapeze.

'The Flying Trapeze' (1868 song)

Liberace (Wladziu Valentino Liberace) 1919–87

American showman

6 When the reviews are bad I tell my staff that they can join me as I cry all the way to the bank.

Autobiography (1973) ch. 2; originally:

He [Liberace] begins to belabour the critics announcing that *he* doesn't mind what they say but that poor George [his brother] 'cried all the way to the bank'.

in *Collier's* 17 September 1954

Libosus of Vaga

Roman Bishop present at Council of Carthage, 256 AD

7 The Lord says in the gospel; 'I am the Truth'. He does not say 'I am custom'. Therefore, when the truth is made manifest, custom must give way to truth.

St Augustine of Hippo *On Baptism* bk. 3, ch. 6, sect. 9; see **Bible** 103:29

Georg Christoph Lichtenberg 1742–99

German scientist and drama critic

8 The journalists have constructed for themselves a little wooden chapel, which they also call the Temple of Fame, in which they put up and take down portraits all day long and make such a hammering you can't hear yourself speak.

A. Leitzmann *Georg Christoph Lichtenberg Aphorismen* (1904)

9 There is a great deal of difference between *still* believing something, and *again* believing it.

Notebook E no. 8 1775–6 in *Aphorisms* (1990)

A. J. Liebling 1904–63

American writer

10 Freedom of the press is guaranteed only to those who own one.

'The Wayward Press: Do you belong in Journalism?' (1960)

Gordon Lightfoot 1938–

Canadian singer and songwriter

11 Does any one know where the love of God goes When the waves turn the minutes to hours?

'The Wreck of the Edmund Fitzgerald' (1976 song)

Charles-Joseph, Prince de Ligne 1735–1814

Belgian soldier

12 *Le congrès ne marche pas, il danse.*

The Congress makes no progress; it dances.

Auguste de la Garde-Chambonas *Souvenirs du Congrès de Vienne* (1820) ch. 1

Beatrice Lillie 1894–1989

British comedienne

13 Never darken my Dior again!

to a waiter who had spilled soup down her neck

in *Every Other Inch a Lady* (1973) ch. 14

George Lillo 1693–1739

Flemish-born dramatist

14 There's sure no passion in the human soul, But finds its food in music.

The Fatal Curiosity (1736) act 1, sc. 2

Abraham Lincoln 1809–65

American statesman, 16th President of the US

on Lincoln: see **Booth** 144:22, **Stanton** 754:8

15 To give victory to the right, not bloody bullets, but peaceful ballots only, are necessary.

speech, 18 May 1858, in R. P. Basler (ed.) *Collected Works of Abraham Lincoln* (1953) vol. 2; see **Misquotations** 537:3

16 'A house divided against itself cannot stand.' I believe this government cannot endure permanently, half slave and half free.

speech, 16 June 1858, in R. P. Basler (ed.) *Collected Works . . .* (1953) vol. 2; see **Bible** 99:17

17 What is conservatism? Is it not adherence to the old and tried, against the new and untried?

speech, 27 February 1860, in R. P. Basler (ed.) *Collected Works . . .* (1953) vol. 3

1 Let us have faith that right makes might, and in that faith, let us, to the end, dare to do our duty as we understand it.

  speech, 27 February 1860, in R. P. Basler (ed.) *Collected Works . . .* (1953) vol. 3

2 I take the official oath to-day with no mental reservations, and with no purpose to construe the Constitution or laws by any hypercritical rules.

  first inaugural address, 4 March 1861, in R. P. Basler (ed.) *Collected Works . . .* (1953) vol. 4

3 The mystic chords of memory, stretching from every battlefield and patriot grave to every living heart and heartstone all over this broad land, will yet swell the chorus of the Union when again touched, as surely they will be, by the better angels of our nature.

  first inaugural address, 4 March 1861

4 I think the necessity of being *ready* increases. Look to it.

  the whole of a letter to Governor Andrew Curtin of Pennsylvania, 8 April 1861, in R. P. Basler (ed.) *Collected Works . . .* (1953) vol. 4

5 My paramount object in this struggle is to save the Union . . . If I could save the Union without freeing any slave, I would do it; and if I could save it by freeing all the slaves, I would do it; and if I could save it by freeing some and leaving others alone, I would also do that . . . I have here stated my purpose according to my views of official duty and I intend no modification of my oft-expressed personal wish that all men everywhere could be free.

  letter to Horace Greeley, 22 August 1862, in R. P. Basler (ed.) *Collected Works . . .* (1953) vol. 5

6 In giving freedom to the slave, we assure freedom to the free—honourable alike in what we give and what we preserve. We shall nobly save, or meanly lose, the last, best hope of earth.

  Annual Message to Congress, 1 December 1862, in R. P. Basler (ed.) *Collected Works . . .* (1953) vol. 5

7 Fourscore and seven years ago our fathers brought forth upon this continent a new nation, conceived in liberty, and dedicated to the proposition that all men are created equal . . . In a larger sense we cannot dedicate, we cannot consecrate, we cannot hallow this ground. The brave men, living and these dead, who struggled here, have consecrated it far above our power to add or detract. The world will little note, nor long remember, what we say here, but it can never forget what they did here. It is for us, the living, rather to be dedicated here to the unfinished work which they who fought here have thus far so nobly advanced . . . we here highly resolve that the dead shall not have died in vain, that this nation, under God, shall have a new birth of freedom; and that government of the people, by the people, and for the people, shall not perish from the earth.

  the Lincoln Memorial inscription reads 'by the people, for the people'

  address at the dedication of the National Cemetery at Gettysburg, 19 November 1863, as reported the following day, in R. P. Basler (ed.) *Collected Works . . .* (1953) vol. 7; see **Webster** 825:11

8 The President tonight has a dream:—He was in a party of plain people, and, as it became known who he was, they began to comment on his appearance. One of them said:—'He is a very common-looking man.' The President replied:—'The Lord prefers common-looking people. That is the reason he makes so many of them.'

  John Hay *Letters of John Hay and Extracts from Diary* (1908) vol 1, 23 December 1863

9 I claim not to have controlled events, but confess plainly that events have controlled me.

  letter to A. G. Hodges, 4 April 1864, in R. P. Basler (ed.) *Collected Works . . .* (1953) vol. 7

10 It is not best to swap horses when crossing streams.

  reply to National Union League, 9 June 1864, in R. P. Basler (ed.) *Collected Works . . .* (1953) vol. 7; see **Proverbs** 618:7

11 Fondly do we hope, fervently do we pray, that this mighty scourge of war may speedily pass away. Yet, if God wills that it continue until all the wealth piled by the bond-man's two hundred and fifty years of unrequited toil shall be sunk, and until every drop of blood drawn with the lash shall be paid by another drawn with the sword, as was said three thousand years ago, so still it must be said, 'The judgements of the Lord are true and righteous altogether.'

  second inaugural address, 4 March 1865, in R. P. Basler (ed.) *Collected Works . . .* (1953) vol. 8; see **Book of Common Prayer** 134:22

12 With malice toward none; with charity for all; with firmness in the right, as God gives us to see the right, let us strive on to finish the work we are in: to bind up the nation's wounds; to care for him who shall have borne the battle, and for his widow and his orphan, to do all which may achieve and cherish a just and lasting peace among ourselves, and with all nations.

  second inaugural address, 4 March 1865, in R. P. Basler (ed.) *Collected Works . . .* (1953) vol. 8

13 As President, I have no eyes but constitutional eyes; I cannot see you.

  attributed reply to the South Carolina Commissioners; see **Lenthall** 480:25

14 People who like this sort of thing will find this the sort of thing they like.

  judgement of a book

  G. W. E. Russell *Collections and Recollections* (1898) ch. 30

15 So you're the little woman who wrote the book that made this great war!

  *on meeting Harriet Beecher **Stowe**, author of* Uncle Tom's Cabin

  Carl Sandburg *Abraham Lincoln: The War Years* (1936) vol. 2, ch. 39

16 You may fool all the people some of the time; you can even fool some of the people all the time; but you can't fool all of the people all the time.

  *also attributed to Phineas **Barnum***

  Alexander K. McClure *Lincoln's Yarns and Stories* (1904)

Charles Lindbergh 1902–74

American aviator

1 I was astonished at the effect my successful landing in France had on the nations of the world. To me, it was like a match lighting a bonfire.
Autobiography of Values (1978)

R. M. Lindner see Film titles 322:10

J. A. Lindon

2 Points
Have no parts or joints
How then can they combine
To form a line?
M. Gardner *Wheels, Life and Other Mathematical Amusements* (1983)

Vachel Lindsay 1879–1931

American poet

3 Then I saw the Congo, creeping through the black,
Cutting through the forest with a golden track.
'The Congo' pt. 1 (1914)

4 Booth led boldly with his big bass drum—
(Are you washed in the blood of the Lamb?)
'General William Booth Enters into Heaven' (1913); see **Bible** 113:19

5 Booth died blind and still by faith he trod,
Eyes still dazzled by the ways of God.
'General William Booth Enters into Heaven' (1913)

Graham Linehan and Arthur Mathews

Irish writers

6 It's great being a priest, isn't it, Ted?
'Good Luck, Father Ted' (1994), episode from *Father Ted* (Channel 4 TV, 1994–8)

Gary Lineker 1960–

English footballer

7 The nice aspect about football is that, if things go wrong, it's the manager who gets the blame.
remark before his first match as captain of England
in *Independent* 12 September 1990

Eric Linklater 1899–1974

Scottish novelist

8 'There won't be any revolution in America,' said Isadore. Nikitin agreed. 'The people are all too clean. They spend all their time changing their shirts and washing themselves. You can't feel fierce and revolutionary in a bathroom.'
Juan in America (1931) bk. 5, pt. 3

Art Linkletter 1912–

American broadcaster and humorist

9 The four stages of man are infancy, childhood, adolescence and obsolescence.
A Child's Garden of Misinformation (1965) ch. 8

George Linley 1798–1865

English songwriter

10 Among our ancient mountains,
And from our lovely vales,
Oh, let the prayer re-echo:
'God bless the Prince of Wales!'
'God Bless the Prince of Wales' (1862 song); translated from the Welsh original by J. C. Hughes (1837–87)

Lin Yutang 1895–1976

Chinese writer and philologist

11 A good traveller is one who does not know where he is going to, and a perfect traveller does not know where he came from.
The Importance of Living (1938) ch. 11

12 [The traveller can] get the greatest joy of travel even without going to the mountains, by staying at home and watching and going about the field to watch a sailing cloud, or a dog, or a hedge, or a lonely tree.
The Importance of Living (1938) ch. 11

Walter Lippmann 1889–1974

American journalist

13 Mr Coolidge's genius for inactivity is developed to a very high point. It is far from being an indolent activity. It is a grim, determined, alert inactivity which keeps Mr Coolidge occupied constantly. Nobody has ever worked harder at inactivity, with such force of character, with such unremitting attention to detail, with such conscientious devotion to the task.
Men of Destiny (1927)

14 The final test of a leader is that he leaves behind him in other men the conviction and the will to carry on.
in *New York Herald Tribune* 14 April 1945

Joseph Lister 1827–1912

English surgeon

15 There are people who do not object to eating a mutton chop—people who do not even object to shooting a pheasant . . . —and yet who consider it something monstrous to introduce under the skin of a guinea pig a little inoculation of some microbe to ascertain its action.
in *British Medical Journal* (1897) vol. 1, p. 317

Richard Littledale 1833–90

English clergyman

16 Come down, O Love divine,
Seek thou this soul of mine,
And visit it with thine own ardour glowing;
O Comforter, draw near,
Within my heart appear,
And kindle it, thy holy flame bestowing.

O let it freely burn,
Till earthly passion turn
To dust and ashes in its heat consuming.
'Come down, O Love divine' (1867 hymn); translation of 'Discendi, Amor santo' by Bianco da Siena (*c.*1350–1434)

1 Let holy charity
Mine outward vesture be,
And lowliness become mine inner clothing;
True lowliness of heart,
Which takes the humbler part,
And o'er its own shortcomings weeps with
  loathing.
'Come down, O Love divine' (1867 hymn)

Joan Littlewood 1914–2002 and Charles Chilton 1914–

2 Oh what a lovely war.
title of stage show (1963)

Maxim Litvinov 1876–1951
Soviet diplomat

3 Peace is indivisible.
note to the Allies, 25 February 1920; A. U. Pope *Maxim Litvinoff* (1943)

Penelope Lively 1933–
English novelist

4 Language tethers us to the world; without it we
spin like atoms.
Moon Tiger (1987)

5 We are walking lexicons. In a single sentence of
idle chatter we preserve Latin, Anglo-Saxon,
Norse; we carry a museum inside our heads, each
day we commemorate peoples of whom we have
never heard.
Moon Tiger (1987)

Ken Livingstone 1945–
British Labour politician

6 If voting changed anything, they'd abolish it.
title of book, 1987

Livy (Titus Livius) 59 BC–AD 17
Roman historian

7 *Vae victis.*
Down with the defeated!
*cry (already proverbial) of the Gallic King, Brennus,
on capturing Rome in 390 BC*
  Ab Urbe Condita bk. 5, ch. 48, sect. 9

8 *Pugna magna victi sumus.*
We were defeated in a great battle.
*announcement of disaster for the Romans in
Hannibal's ambush at Lake Trasimene in 217 BC*
  Ab Urbe Condita bk. 22, ch. 7, sect. 8

Richard Llewellyn (Richard Llewellyn Lloyd) 1907–83
Welsh novelist and dramatist

9 How green was my valley.
title of book (1939)

Robert Lloyd
English poet

10 Turn parson, Colman, that's the way to thrive;
Your parsons are the happiest men alive.
'The Law-Student' (1762)

11 Alone from Jargon born to rescue Law,
From precedent, grave hum, and formal saw!
To strip chicanery of its vain pretence,
And marry Common Law to Common Sense!
'The Law-Student' (1762); on Lord **Mansfield**, Lord Chief
Justice, 1756–88

12   All the art of Imitation,
Is pilf'ring from the first creation.
'Shakespeare' (1762)

David Lloyd George 1863–1945
British Liberal statesman; Prime Minister, 1916–22
*on Lloyd George: see **Asquith** 32:9, **Clemenceau** 226:13,
Keynes 450:15*

13 The leal and trusty mastiff which is to watch over
our interests, but which runs away at the first
snarl of the trade unions . . . A mastiff? It is the
right hon. Gentleman's poodle.
*on the House of Lords and A. J. **Balfour** respectively*
in the House of Commons, 26 June 1907

14 I have no nest-eggs. I am looking for someone
else's hen-roost to rob next year.
in 1908, as Chancellor
Frank Owen *Tempestuous Journey* (1954) ch. 10

15 A fully-equipped duke costs as much to keep up as
two Dreadnoughts; and dukes are just as great a
terror and they last longer.
speech at Newcastle, 9 October 1909, in *The Times* 11
October 1909

16 The great peaks of honour we had forgotten—
Duty, Patriotism, and—clad in glittering white—
the great pinnacle of Sacrifice, pointing like a
rugged finger to Heaven.
speech at Queen's Hall, London, 19 September 1914, in
The Times 20 September 1914

17 At eleven o'clock this morning came to an end the
cruellest and most terrible war that has ever
scourged mankind. I hope we may say that thus,
this fateful morning, came to an end all wars.
speech in the House of Commons, 11 November 1918; see
Wells 828:16

18 What is our task? To make Britain a fit country for
heroes to live in.
speech at Wolverhampton, 23 November 1918, in *The
Times* 25 November 1918

19 Unless I am mistaken, by the steps we have taken
[in Ireland] we have murder by the throat.
speech at the Mansion House, 9 November 1920; Frank
Owen *Tempestuous Journey* (1954) ch. 28

20 The world is becoming like a lunatic asylum run
by lunatics.
in *Observer* 8 January 1933; see **Rowland** 657:14

1 A politician was a person with whose politics you did not agree. When you did agree, he was a statesman.

speech at Central Hall, Westminster, 2 July 1935, in *The Times* 3 July 1935

2 Negotiating with de Valera . . . is like trying to pick up mercury with a fork.

to which **de Valera** *replied,* '*Why doesn't he use a spoon?*'

M. J. MacManus *Eamon de Valera* (1944) ch. 6

3 Sufficient conscience to bother him, but not sufficient to keep him straight.

of Ramsay **MacDonald**

A. J. Sylvester *Life with Lloyd George* (1975)

Liz Lochhead 1947–

British poet and dramatist

4 I wouldn't thank you for a Valentine
I won't wake up early wondering if the postman's been.
Should 10 red-padded satin hearts arrive with a sticky sickly saccharine
Sentiments in very vulgar verses I wouldn't wonder if you meant them.

'I Wouldn't Thank You for a Valentine' (1985)

John Locke 1632–1704

English philosopher

5 New opinions are always suspected, and usually opposed, without any other reason but because they are not already common.

An Essay concerning Human Understanding (1690) 'Dedicatory Epistle'

6 The commonwealth of learning is not at this time without master-builders, whose mighty designs, in advancing the sciences, will leave lasting monuments to the admiration of posterity . . . in an age that produces such masters as the great Huygenius and the incomparable Mr Newton . . . 'tis ambition enough to be employed as an under-labourer in clearing ground a little, and removing some of the rubbish that lies in the way of knowledge.

An Essay concerning Human Understanding (1690) 'Epistle to the Reader'

7 General propositions are seldom mentioned in the huts of Indians: much less are they to be found in the thoughts of children.

An Essay concerning Human Understanding (1690) bk. 1, ch. 2, sect. 11

8 Nature never makes excellent things for mean or no uses.

An Essay concerning Human Understanding (1690) bk. 2, ch. 1, sect. 15

9 No man's knowledge here can go beyond his experience.

An Essay concerning Human Understanding (1690) bk. 2, ch. 1, sect. 19

10 It is one thing to show a man that he is in error, and another to put him in possession of truth.

An Essay concerning Human Understanding (1690) bk. 4, ch. 7, sect. 11

11 There are very few lovers of truth, for truth-sake, even among those who persuade themselves that they are so. How a man may know, whether he be so, in earnest, is worth enquiry; and I think, there is this one unerring mark of it, viz. the not entertaining any proposition with greater assurance than the proofs it is built on will warrant. Whoever goes beyond this measure of assent, it is plain, receives not truth in the love of it, loves not truth for truth-sake, but for some other by-end.

An Essay concerning Human Understanding (1690) bk. 4, ch. 19, sect. 1

12 Reason is natural revelation, whereby the eternal Father of light, and fountain of all knowledge communicates to mankind that portion of truth which he has laid within the reach of their natural faculties.

An Essay concerning Human Understanding (1690) bk. 4, ch. 19, sect. 4

13 Crooked things may be as stiff and unflexible as straight: and men may be as positive in error as in truth.

An Essay concerning Human Understanding (1690) bk. 4, ch. 19, sect. 11

14 All men are liable to error; and most men are, in many points, by passion or interest, under temptation to it.

An Essay concerning Human Understanding (1690) bk. 4, ch. 20, sect. 17

15 Whatsoever . . . [man] removes out of the state that nature hath provided and left it in, he hath mixed his labour with, and joined to it something that is his own, and thereby makes it his property.

Second Treatise of Civil Government (1690) ch. 5, sect. 27

16 [That] ill deserves the name of confinement which hedges us in only from bogs and precipices. So that, however it may be mistaken, the end of law is, not to abolish or restrain, but to preserve and enlarge freedom.

Second Treatise of Civil Government (1690) ch. 6, sect. 57

17 Man . . . hath by nature a power . . . to preserve his property—that is, his life, liberty, and estate—against the injuries and attempts of other men.

Second Treatise of Civil Government (1690) ch. 7, sect. 87

18 Man being . . . by nature all free, equal, and independent, no one can be put out of this estate, and subjected to the political power of another, without his own consent.

Second Treatise of Civil Government (1690) ch. 8, sect. 95

19 The only way by which any one divests himself of his natural liberty and puts on the bonds of civil society is by agreeing with other men to join and unite into a community.

Second Treatise of Civil Government (1690) ch. 8, sect. 95

20 The great and chief end, therefore, of men's uniting into commonwealths, and putting themselves under government, is the preservation of their property.

Second Treatise of Civil Government (1690) ch. 9, sect. 124

21 This power to act according to discretion for the public good, without the prescription of the law,

and sometimes even against it, is that which is called prerogative.

Second Treatise of Civil Government (1690) ch. 14, sect. 160

1 The rod, which is the only instrument of government that tutors generally know, or ever think of, is the most unfit of any to be used in education.

Some Thoughts Concerning Education (5th ed., 1705) sect. 47

2 You would think him a very foolish fellow, that should not value a virtuous, or a wise man, infinitely before a great scholar.

Some Thoughts Concerning Education (5th ed., 1705) sect. 147

Frederick Locker-Lampson 1821–95

English writer of light verse

3 And many are afraid of God—
And more of Mrs Grundy.

'The Jester's Plea' (1868); see **Morton** 551:10

John Gibson Lockhart 1794–1854

Scottish writer and critic
*see also **Epitaphs** 310:5*

4 It is a better and a wiser thing to be a starved apothecary than a starved poet; so back to the shop Mr John, back to 'plasters, pills, and ointment boxes.'

reviewing Keats's Endymion
in *Blackwood's Edinburgh Magazine* August 1818

5 Barring drink and the girls, I ne'er heard of a sin:
Many worse, better few, than bright, broken
Maginn.

'Epitaph for William Maginn (1794–1842)', in William Maginn *Miscellanies* (1885) vol. 1, p. xviii

David Lodge 1935–

English novelist

6 Literature is mostly about having sex and not much about having children. Life is the other way round.

The British Museum is Falling Down (1965) ch. 4

7 Morris read through the letter. Was it a shade too fulsome? No, that was another law of academic life: *it is impossible to be excessive in flattery of one's peers.*

Small World (1984) pt. 3, ch. 1

Thomas Lodge 1558–1625

English man of letters

8 Love in my bosom like a bee
Doth suck his sweet;
Now with his wings he plays with me,
Now with his feet.
Within mine eyes he makes his nest,
His bed amidst my tender breast;
My kisses are his daily feast,
And yet he robs me of my rest.
Ah, wanton, will ye?

'Love in my bosom like a bee' (1590)

9 Love guards the roses of thy lips
And flies about them like a bee;

If I approach he forward skips,
And if I kiss he stingeth me.

'Love guards the roses of thy lips' (1593)

Frank Loesser 1910–69

American songwriter

10 See what the boys in the back room will have
And tell them I'm having the same.

'Boys in the Back Room' (1939 song)

11 Isn't it grand! Isn't it fine! Look at the cut, the style, the line!
The suit of clothes is altogether, but altogether it's altogether
The most remarkable suit of clothes that I have ever seen.

'The King's New Clothes' (1952 song); from the film *Hans Christian Andersen*

Christopher Logue 1926–

English poet

12 Come to the edge.
We might fall.
Come to the edge.
It's too high!
COME TO THE EDGE!
And they came
and he pushed
and they flew . . .

*on **Apollinaire***

'Come to the edge' (1969)

13 I, Christopher Logue, was baptized the year
Many thousands of Englishmen,
Fists clenched, their bellies empty,

Walked day and night on the capital city.

'The Song of Autobiography' (1996)

Jack London 1876–1916

American novelist

14 The call of the wild.

title of novel (1903)

Huey Long 1893–1935

American Democratic politician

15 For the present you can just call me the Kingfish.

Every Man a King (1933)

16 I can go Mr Wilson one better; I was born barefoot.

replying to the claim that an opponent had gone barefoot as a boy

T. Harry Williams *Huey Long* (1969)

17 Oh hell, say that I am *sui generis* and let it go at that.

to journalists attempting to analyse his political personality

T. Harry Williams *Huey Long* (1969)

Henry Wadsworth Longfellow 1807–82

American poet

1 I shot an arrow into the air,
It fell to earth, I knew not where.
'The Arrow and the Song' (1845)

2 Thou, too, sail on, O Ship of State!
Sail on, O Union, strong and great!
Humanity with all its fears,
With all the hopes of future years,
Is hanging breathless on thy fate!
'The Building of the Ship' (1849)

3 Between the dark and the daylight,
When the night is beginning to lower,
Comes a pause in the day's occupations,
That is known as the Children's Hour.
'The Children's Hour' (1859)

4 For thine own purpose, thou hast sent
The strife and the discouragement!
Christus: A Mystery (1872) pt. 2 'The Golden Legend' 'A
Village Church' l. 1077

5 The cares that infest the day
Shall fold their tents, like the Arabs,
And as silently steal away.
'The Day is Done' (1844)

6 If you would hit the mark, you must aim a little
above it;
Every arrow that flies feels the attraction of earth.
'Elegiac Verse' (1880)

7 This is the forest primeval.
Evangeline (1847) introduction

8 Sorrow and silence are strong, and patient
endurance is godlike.
Evangeline (1847) pt. 2, l. 60

9 The shades of night were falling fast,
As through an Alpine village passed
A youth, who bore, 'mid snow and ice,
A banner with the strange device,
Excelsior!
'Excelsior' (1841)

10   Giotto's tower,
The lily of Florence blossoming in stone.
'Giotto's Tower' (1866)

11 I like that ancient Saxon phrase, which calls
The burial-ground God's-Acre!
'God's-Acre' (1841)

12 The holiest of all holidays are those
Kept by ourselves in silence and apart;
The secret anniversaries of the heart.
'Holidays' (1877)

13 The heights by great men reached and kept
Were not attained by sudden flight,
But they, while their companions slept,
Were toiling upward in the night.
'The Ladder of Saint Augustine' (1850)

14 Standing, with reluctant feet,
Where the brook and river meet.
'Maidenhood' (1841)

15 A boy's will is the wind's will
And the thoughts of youth are long, long
thoughts.
'My Lost Youth' (1858)

16 *Emigravit* is the inscription on the tombstone
where he lies;
Dead he is not, but departed,—for the artist never
dies.
on Albrecht Dürer
'Nuremberg' (1844)

17 Not in the clamour of the crowded street,
Not in the shouts and plaudits of the throng,
But in ourselves, are triumph and defeat.
'The Poets' (1876)

18 Tell me not, in mournful numbers,
Life is but an empty dream!
For the soul is dead that slumbers,
And things are not what they seem.
Life is real! Life is earnest!
And the grave is not its goal;
Dust thou art, to dust returnest,
Was not spoken of the soul.
'A Psalm of Life' (1838); see **Bible** 75:27

19 Art is long, and Time is fleeting,
And our hearts, though stout and brave,
Still, like muffled drums, are beating
Funeral marches to the grave.
'A Psalm of Life' (1838); see **Hippocrates** 389:9

20 Trust no Future, howe'er pleasant!
Let the dead Past bury its dead!
Act,—act in the living Present!
Heart within, and God o'erhead!
'A Psalm of Life' (1838); see **Bible** 96:2

21 Lives of great men all remind us
We can make our lives sublime,
And, departing, leave behind us
Footprints on the sands of time.
'A Psalm of Life' (1838)

22 Let us, then, be up and doing,
With a heart for any fate;
Still achieving, still pursuing,
Learn to labour and to wait.
'A Psalm of Life' (1838)

23 Though the mills of God grind slowly, yet they
grind exceeding small;
Though with patience He stands waiting, with
exactness grinds He all.
'Retribution' (1870), translation of Friedrich von Logau
(1604–55) *Sinngedichte* (1654) no. 3224; see **Proverbs**
626:23

24 A Lady with a Lamp shall stand
In the great history of the land,
A noble type of good,
Heroic womanhood.
*on Florence **Nightingale***
'Santa Filomena' (1857)

25 The forests, with their myriad tongues,
Shouted of liberty;
And the Blast of the Desert cried aloud,
With a voice so wild and free,
That he started in his sleep and smiled

At their tempestuous glee.
  'The Slave's Dream' (1842)

1 By the shore of Gitche Gumee,
By the shining Big-Sea-Water,
Stood the wigwam of Nokomis,
Daughter of the Moon, Nokomis.
  The Song of Hiawatha (1855) 'Hiawatha's Childhood'

2 Dark behind it rose the forest,
Rose the black and gloomy pine-trees,
Rose the firs with cones upon them;
Bright before it beat the water,
Beat the clear and sunny water,
Beat the shining Big-Sea-Water.
  The Song of Hiawatha (1855) 'Hiawatha's Childhood'

3 From the waterfall he named her,
Minnehaha, Laughing Water.
  The Song of Hiawatha (1855) 'Hiawatha and Mudjekeewis'

4 Listen, my children, and you shall hear
Of the midnight ride of Paul Revere,
On the eighteenth of April in Seventy-five.
  Tales of a Wayside Inn pt. 1 (1863) 'The Landlord's Tale:
  Paul Revere's Ride'

5 One if by land and two if by sea;
And I on the opposite shore will be,
Ready to ride and sound the alarm.
  Tales of a Wayside Inn pt. 1 (1863) 'The Landlord's Tale:
  Paul Revere's Ride'; see **Revere** 645:14

6 The fate of a nation was riding that night.
  Tales of a Wayside Inn pt. 1 (1863) 'The Landlord's Tale:
  Paul Revere's Ride'

7 Ships that pass in the night, and speak each other
  in passing;
Only a signal shown and a distant voice in the
  darkness;
So on the ocean of life we pass and speak one
  another,
Only a look and a voice; then darkness again and
  a silence.
  Tales of a Wayside Inn pt. 3 (1874) 'The Theologian's Tale:
  Elizabeth' pt. 4

8 Under a spreading chestnut tree
The village smithy stands;
The smith, a mighty man is he,
With large and sinewy hands;
And the muscles of his brawny arms
Are strong as iron bands.
  'The Village Blacksmith' (1839)

9 Each morning sees some task begin,
Each evening sees it close;
Something attempted, something done,
Has earned a night's repose.
  'The Village Blacksmith' (1839)

10 It was the schooner Hesperus,
That sailed the wintry sea;
And the skipper had taken his little daughter,
To bear him company.
  'The Wreck of the Hesperus' (1839)

11 There was a little girl
Who had a little curl
Right in the middle of her forehead,
When she was good

She was very, very good,
But when she was bad she was horrid.
  *composed for, and sung to, his second daughter while
  a babe in arms, c.1850*
  B. R. Tucker-Macchetta *The Home Life of Henry W.
  Longfellow* (1882) ch. 5

12 The square root of half a number of bees, and also
eight-ninths of the whole, alighted on the
jasmines, and a female buzzed responsive to the
hum of the male inclosed at night in a water-lily.
O, beautiful damsel, tell me the number of bees.
  Kavanagh (1849) ch. 4

Longinus on the Sublime
Greek literary treatise of unknown authorship and date

13 Sublimity is the echo of a noble mind.
  sect. 9

Michael Longley 1939–
Irish poet

14 Astrologers or three wise men
Who may shortly be setting out
For a small house up the Shankill
Or the Falls, should pause on their way
To buy gifts at Jim Gibson's shop,
Dates and chestnuts and tambourines.
  'The Greengrocer' (1979)

15 I am travelling from one April to another.
It is the same train between the same
  embankments.
Gorse fires are smoking, but primroses burn
And celandines and white may and gorse flowers.
  'Gorse Fires' (1991)

Alice Roosevelt Longworth 1884–1980
*American daughter of Theodore **Roosevelt***

16 If you haven't got anything good to say about
anyone come and sit by me.
  maxim embroidered on a cushion in her home
  Michael Teague *Mrs L: Conversations with Alice Roosevelt
  Longworth* (1981)

Anita Loos 1893–1981
American writer

17 Gentlemen prefer blondes.
  title of book (1925)

18 So this gentleman said a girl with brains ought to
do something with them besides think.
  Gentlemen Prefer Blondes (1925) ch. 1

19 So I really think that American gentlemen are the
best after all, because kissing your hand may
make you feel very very good but a diamond and
safire bracelet lasts forever.
  Gentlemen Prefer Blondes (1925) ch. 4; see **Advertising
  slogans** 7:15, **Robin** 650:10

20 Fun is fun but no girl wants to laugh all of the
time.
  Gentlemen Prefer Blondes (1925) ch. 4

21 So then Dr Froyd said that all I needed was to
cultivate a few inhibitions and get some sleep.
  Gentlemen Prefer Blondes (1925) ch. 5

Federico García Lorca 1899–1936

Spanish poet and dramatist

1 *A las cinco de la tarde.*
Eran las cinco en punto de la tarde.
Un niño trajo la blanca sábana
a las cinco de la tarde.

At five in the afternoon.
It was exactly five in the afternoon.
A boy brought the white sheet
at five in the afternoon.
   Llanto por Ignacio Sánchez Mejías (1935) 'La Cogida y la
   muerte'

2 *Verde que te quiero verde.*
Verde viento. Verdes ramas.
El barco sobre la mar
y el caballo en la montaña.

Green how I want you green.
Green wind.
Green boughs.
The ship on the sea
and the horse on the mountain.
   Romance sonámbulo (1924–7)

Edward N. Lorenz 1917–

American meteorologist

3 Predictability: Does the flap of a butterfly's wings
in Brazil set off a tornado in Texas?
   title of paper given to the American Association for the
   Advancement of Science, Washington, 29 December 1979;
   James Gleick *Chaos* (1988)

Konrad Lorenz 1903–89

Austro-German zoologist

4 It is a good morning exercise for a research
scientist to discard a pet hypothesis every day
before breakfast. It keeps him young.
   Das Sogenannte Böse (1963; translated by Marjorie Latzke
   as On Aggression, 1966) ch. 2

Louis XIV (the 'Sun King') 1638–1715

French monarch, King from 1643

5 *L'État c'est moi.*
I am the State.
   before the Parlement de Paris, 13 April 1655
   probably apocryphal; J. A. Dulaure Histoire de Paris (1834)
   vol. 6

6 *J'ai failli attendre.*
I was nearly kept waiting.
   attribution queried, among others, by E. Fournier in
   L'Esprit dans l'Histoire (1857) ch. 48

7 *Toutes les fois que je donne une place vacante, je fais
cent mécontents et un ingrat.*
Every time I create an appointment, I create a
hundred malcontents and one ingrate.
   Voltaire Siècle de Louis XIV (1768 ed.) vol. 2, ch. 26

8 *Il n'y a plus de Pyrénées.*
The Pyrenees are no more.
   *on the accession of his grandson to the throne of
   Spain, 1700*
   attributed to Louis by Voltaire in Siècle de Louis XIV (1753)

ch. 26, but to the Spanish Ambassador to France in the
Mercure Galant (Paris) November 1700

9 It means I'm growing old when ladies declare war
on me.
   *following the accession of Queen Anne, Britain
   declared war on France*
   Gila Curtis The Life and Times of Queen Anne (1972);
   attributed

Louis XV 1710–74

French monarch, King from 1715

10 Are the streets being paved with gold over there? I
fully expect to awake one morning in Versailles to
see the walls of the fortress rising above the
horizon.
   *on the costs of fortifying Louisbourg on Cape Breton
   Island, Canada, c.1745*
   attributed

Louis XVI 1754–93

*French monarch, King from 1774; deposed in 1789 on the
outbreak of the French Revolution and executed in 1793*
*on Louis: see **Firmont** 321:12*

11 *diary entry for 14 July 1789, the day of the storming
of the Bastille:*
Rien.
Nothing.
   Simon Schama Citizens (1989) ch. 10

Louis XVIII 1755–1824

French monarch, King from 1814; titular king from 1795

12 *Rappelez-vous bien qu'il n'est aucun de vous qui n'ait
dans sa giberne le bâton de maréchal du duc de Reggio;
c'est à vous à l'en faire sortir.*
Remember that there is not one of you who does
not carry in his cartridge-pouch the marshal's
baton of the duke of Reggio; it is up to you to
bring it forth.
   speech to Saint-Cyr cadets, 9 August 1819, in Moniteur
   Universel 10 August 1819

13 *L'exactitude est la politesse des rois.*
Punctuality is the politeness of kings.
   attributed in Souvenirs de J. Lafitte (1844) bk. 1, ch. 3; see
   Proverbs 629:46

Joe Louis 1914–81

American boxer

14 He can run. But he can't hide.
   *of Billy Conn, his opponent, before a heavyweight title
   fight, 19 June 1946*
   Louis: My Life Story (1947)

Louis Philippe 1773–1850

French monarch, King 1830–48

15 Died, has he? Now I wonder what he meant by
that?
   *of **Talleyrand***
   attributed, perhaps apocryphal

Ada Lovelace 1815–52

*English mathematican, daughter of Lord **Byron***

1 The Analytical Engine weaves algebraic patterns just as the Jacquard loom weaves flowers and leaves.

   *of **Babbage**'s mechanical computer*

   Luigi Menabrea *Sketch of the Analytical Engine invented by Charles Babbage* (1843), translated and annotated by Ada Lovelace, Note A

Richard Lovelace 1618–58

English poet

2 Lucasta that bright northern star.
   'Amyntor from Beyond the Sea to Alexis' (1649)

3 Forbear, thou great good husband, little ant.
   'The Ant' (1660)

4 When Love with unconfinèd wings
   Hovers within my gates.
   'To Althea, From Prison' (1649)

5 When thirsty grief in wine we steep,
   When healths and draughts go free,
   Fishes, that tipple in the deep,
   Know no such liberty.
   'To Althea, From Prison' (1649)

6 Stone walls do not a prison make,
   Nor iron bars a cage;
   Minds innocent and quiet take
   That for an hermitage.
   If I have freedom in my love,
   And in my soul am free;
   Angels alone, that soar above,
   Enjoy such liberty.
   'To Althea, From Prison' (1649)

7 Tell me not, Sweet, I am unkind,
   That from the nunnery
   Of thy chaste breast, and quiet mind,
   To war and arms I fly.
   True; a new mistress now I chase,
   The first foe in the field;
   And with a stronger faith embrace
   A sword, a horse, a shield.
   'To Lucasta, Going to the Wars' (1649)

8 Yet this inconstancy is such,
   As you too shall adore;
   I could not love thee, Dear, so much,
   Loved I not honour more.
   'To Lucasta, Going to the Wars' (1649)

Bernard Lovell 1913–

British astronomer

9 The pursuit of the good and evil are now linked in astronomy as in almost all science . . . The fate of human civilization will depend on whether the rockets of the future carry the astronomer's telescope or a hydrogen bomb.
   The Individual and the Universe (1959)

10 Youth is vivid rather than happy, but memory always remembers the happy things.
   in *The Times* 20 August 1993

James Lovell 1928–

American astronaut

11 Houston, we've had a problem.
   on Apollo 13 space mission, 14 April 1970
   in *The Times* 15 April 1970

Samuel Lover 1797–1868

Irish writer

12 When once the itch of literature comes over a man, nothing can cure it but the scratching of a pen.
   Handy Andy (1842) ch. 36

13 Young Rory O'More courted Kathaleen bawn,
   He was bold as a hawk, and she soft as the dawn.
   'Rory O'More' (1837 song); see **Cartoon captions** 198:4

David Low 1891–1963

British political cartoonist

14 Colonel Blimp.
   cartoon creation, proponent of reactionary establishment opinions

15 I have never met anyone who wasn't against war. Even Hitler and Mussolini were, according to themselves.
   in *New York Times Magazine* 10 February 1946

Robert Lowe, Lord Sherbrooke 1811–92

British Liberal politician
*on Lowe: see **Bright** 151:12; see also **Misquotations** 538:22*

16 The Chancellor of the Exchequer is a man whose duties make him more or less of a taxing machine. He is intrusted with a certain amount of misery which it is his duty to distribute as fairly as he can.
   speech, House of Commons, 11 April 1870

Amy Lowell 1874–1925

American poet

17 And the softness of my body will be guarded by embrace
   By each button, hook, and lace.
   For the man who should loose me is dead,
   Fighting with the Duke in Flanders,
   In a pattern called a war.
   Christ! What are patterns for?
   'Patterns' (1916)

18 All books are either dreams or swords,
   You can cut, or you can drug, with words.
   'Sword Blades and Poppy Seed' (1914); see **Farquhar** 315:21

James Russell Lowell 1819–91

American poet

19 An' you've gut to git up airly
   Ef you want to take in God.
   The Biglow Papers (First Series, 1848) no. 1 'A Letter'

20 We've a war, an' a debt, an' a flag; an' ef this
   Ain't to be inderpendunt, why, wut on airth is?
   The Biglow Papers (Second Series, 1867) no. 4 'A Message of Jeff. Davis in Secret Session'

1 There comes Poe with his raven like Barnaby
    Rudge,
  Three-fifths of him genius, and two-fifths sheer
    fudge.
    'A Fable for Critics' (1848) l. 1215; see **Poe** 599:5

2 Blessèd are the horny hands of toil!
    'A Glance Behind the Curtain' (1844); see **Salisbury**
    664:11

3 Once to every man and nation comes the moment
    to decide,
  In the strife of Truth with Falsehood, for the good
    or evil side.
    'The Present Crisis' (1845)

4 Truth forever on the scaffold, Wrong forever on
    the throne,—
  Yet that scaffold sways the future, and, behind the
    dim unknown,
  Standeth God within the shadow, keeping watch
    above his own.
    'The Present Crisis' (1845)

5 May is a pious fraud of the almanac.
    'Under the Willows' (1869) l. 21

6 There is no good in arguing with the inevitable.
  The only argument available with an east wind is
  to put on your overcoat.
    Democracy and other Addresses (1887) 'Democracy'

Robert Lowell 1917-77
American poet

7 My eyes have seen what my hand did.
    'Dolphin' (1973)

8 Terrible that old life of decency
  without unseemly intimacy
  or quarrels, when the unemancipated woman
  still had her Freudian papa and maids!
    'During Fever' (1959)

9 The aquarium is gone. Everywhere,
  giant finned cars nose forward like fish;
  a savage servility
  slides by on grease.
    'For the Union Dead' (1964)

10 Their monument sticks like a fishbone
   in the city's throat.
    'For the Union Dead' (1964)

11 These are the tranquillized *Fifties*,
   and I am forty. Ought I to regret my seed-time?
    'Memories of West Street and Lepke' (1956)

12 At forty-five,
   What next, what next?
   At every corner,
   I meet my Father,
   my age, still alive.
    'Middle Age' (1964)

13 I saw the spiders marching through the air,
   Swimming from tree to tree that mildewed day
   In latter August when the hay
   Came creaking to the barn.
    'Mr Edwards and the Spider' (1950); see **Edwards** 296:14

14   This is death.
   To die and know it. This is the Black Widow,
     death.
    'Mr Edwards and the Spider' (1950)

15 The Lord survives the rainbow of His will.
    'The Quaker Graveyard in Nantucket' (1950)

16 If we see light at the end of the tunnel,
   It's the light of the oncoming train.
    'Since 1939' (1977); see **Dickson** 273:16

17 But I suppose even God was born
   too late to trust the old religion.
    'Tenth Muse' (1964)

18 None of the wilder subtleties
   of grace or art will sweeten these
   stiff quatrains shovelled out four-square.
    of hymns as contrasted with poetry and the Bible
    'Waking Early Sunday Morning' (1967)

19 Folly comes from something—
   the present, yes,
   we are in it,
   it's the infection
   of things gone.
    'We Took Our Paradise' (1977)

William Lowndes 1652-1724
English politician

20 Take care of the pence, and the pounds will take
   care of themselves.
    Lord Chesterfield *Letters to his Son* (1774) 5 February 1750
    ('*for the pounds* . . . ' in an earlier letter, 6 November
    1747); see **Carroll** 194:14, **Chesterfield** 215:3, **Proverbs**
    631:37

L. S. Lowry 1887-1976
English painter

21 I'm a simple man, and I use simple materials.
    Mervyn Levy *Paintings of L. S. Lowry* (1975)

Malcolm Lowry 1909-57
English novelist

22 How alike are the groans of love to those of the
   dying.
    Under the Volcano (1947) ch. 12

Mina Loy 1882-1966
English-born American poet and artist

23 [Be] *Brave* and deny at the outset—that pathetic
   clap-trap war cry *Woman is the equal of man* for
   She is NOT! . . . Leave off looking to men to find out
   what you are *not*—Seek within yourselves to find
   out what you *are*.
    'Feminist Manifesto' (1914, unpublished) in Virginia M.
    Kovidis *Mina Loy* (1980)

Lucan (Marcus Annaeus Lucanus) AD 39-65
Roman poet

24   *Quis iustius induit arma*
    Scire nefas, magno se iudice quisque tuetur:

Victrix causa deis placuit, sed victa Catoni.

It is not granted to know which man took up arms with more right on his side. Each pleads his cause before a great judge: the winning cause pleased the gods, but the losing one pleased Cato.

Pharsalia bk. 1, l. 128

1 *Stat magni nominis umbra.*

There stands the ghost of a great name.

of Pompey

Pharsalia bk. 1, l. 135

2 *Nil actum credens, dum quid superesset agendum.*

Thinking nothing done while anything remained to be done.

Pharsalia bk. 2, l. 657; see **Rogers** 652:10

3   *Coniunx*
Est mihi, sunt nati: dedimus tot pignora fatis.

I have a wife, I have sons: we have given so many hostages to the fates.

Pharsalia bk. 6, l. 661; see **Bacon** 44:30

4 *Jupiter est quodcumque vides, quocumque moveris.*

Jupiter is whatever you see, whichever way you move.

Pharsalia bk. 9, l. 580

George Lucas see **Film lines** 320:6, **Film titles** 322:4

Clare Booth Luce 1903–87

American diplomat, politician, and writer

5 Much of . . . his global thinking is, no matter how you slice it, still globaloney.

speech to the House of Representatives, February 1943

6 But if God had wanted us to think just with our wombs, why did He give us a brain?

in *Life* 16 October 1970

Lucilius (Gaius Lucilius) c.180–102 BC

Roman poet

7 *Maior erat natu; non omnia possumus omnes.*

He was greater in years; we cannot all do everything.

Macrobius *Saturnalia* bk. 6, ch. 1, sect. 35; see **Virgil** 814:8

Lucretius (Titus Lucretius Carus) c.94–55 BC

Roman poet
on Lucretius: see **Virgil** 814:17

8 *Aeneadum genetrix, divumque hominumque voluptas.*

Mother of Aeneas' race; pleasure of gods and mortals alike.

of Venus

De Rerum Natura bk. 1, l. 1

9 *Ergo vivida vis animi pervicit, et extra*
Processit longe flammantia moenia mundi
Atque omne immensum peragravit, mente animoque.

So the vital strength of his spirit won through, and he made his way far outside the flaming walls of the world and ranged over the measureless whole, both in mind and spirit.

on **Epicurus**

De Rerum Natura bk. 1, l. 72

10 *Tantum religio potuit suadere malorum.*

So much wrong could religion induce.

De Rerum Natura bk. 1, l. 101

11 *Lucida tela diei.*

Clear shafts of day.

De Rerum Natura bk. 1, l. 147

12 *. . . Nil posse creari*
De nilo.

Nothing can be created out of nothing.

De Rerum Natura bk. 1, l. 155

13 *Sed veluti pueris absinthia taetra medentes*
Cum dare conantur, prius oras pocula circum
Contingit mellis duci flavoque liquore.

For as with children, when the doctors try To give them loathsome wormwood, first they smear Sweet yellow honey on the goblet's rim.

De Rerum Natura bk. 1, l. 936

14 *Suave, mari magno turbantibus aequora ventis,*
E terra magnum alterius spectare laborem.
Non quia vexari quemquamst iucunda voluptas,
Sed quibus ipse malis careas quia cernere suave est.

Lovely it is, when the winds are churning up the waves on the great sea, to gaze out from the land on the great efforts of someone else; not because it's an enjoyable pleasure that somebody is in difficulties, but because it's lovely to realize what troubles you are yourself spared.

De Rerum Natura bk. 2, l. 1

15 *Augescunt aliae gentes, aliae minuuntur,*
Inque brevi spatio mutantur saecla animantum
Et quasi cursores vitai lampada tradunt.

Some races increase, others are reduced, and in a short while the generations of living creatures are changed and like runners relay the torch of life.

De Rerum Natura bk. 2, l. 8

16 *Nil igitur mors est ad nos neque pertinet hilum,*
Quandoquidem natura animi mortalis habetur.

Death therefore is nothing to us nor does it concern us a scrap, seeing that the nature of the spirit we possess is something mortal.

De Rerum Natura bk. 3, l. 830

17 *Vitaque mancipio, nulli datur, omnibus usu.*

And life is given to none freehold, but it is leasehold for all.

De Rerum Natura bk. 3, l. 971

18 *Scire licet nobis nil esse in morte timendum*
Nec miserum fieri qui non est posse neque hilum
Differre an nullo fuerit iam tempore natus,
Mortalem vitam mors cum immortalis ademit.

We can know there is nothing to be feared in death, that one who is not cannot be made unhappy, and that it matters not a scrap whether one might ever have been born at all, when death that is immortal has taken over one's mortal life.

De Rerum Natura bk. 3, l. 866

1 *Cur non ut plenus vitae conviva recedis*
Aequo animoque capis securam, stulte, quietem?

Why not, like a banqueter fed full of life, withdraw
with contentment and rest in peace, you fool?

De Rerum Natura bk. 3, l. 938

2　　　　　　*Medio de fonte leporum*
Surgit amari aliquid quod in ipsis floribus angat.

From the midst of the fountain of delights rises
something bitter that chokes them all amongst the
flowers.

De Rerum Natura bk. 4, l. 1133

Fray Luis de León c.1527–91

Spanish poet and religious writer

3 *Que descansada vida*
la del que huye el mundanal ruido,
y sigue la escondida
senda, por donde han ido
los pocos sabios que en el mundo han sido!

What a relaxed life is that which flees the worldly
clamour, and follows the hidden path down which
have gone the few wise men there have been in
the world!

'Vida Retirada'

4 *Dicebamus hesterno die . . .*

We were saying yesterday . . .

on resuming a lecture at Salamanca University in
1577, after five years' imprisonment

attributed, among others, by A. F. G. Bell in *Luis de León*
(1925) ch. 8

Luiz Inácio Lula da Silva 1945–

Brazilian statesman, President 2003–

5 A war can perhaps be won single-handedly. But
peace—lasting peace—cannot be secured without
the support of all.

speech, United Nations, 23 September 2003; in *Guardian*
(online edition) 24 September 2003

Alison Lurie 1926–

American novelist

6 There's a rule, I think. You get what you want in
life, but not your second choice too.

Real People (1969) 'July 5'

Martin Luther 1483–1546

German Protestant theologian
on Luther: see **Arnold** 30:6

7 *Esto peccator et pecca fortiter, sed fortius fide et gaude*
in Christo.

Be a sinner and sin strongly, but more strongly
have faith and rejoice in Christ.

letter to Melanchthon, 1521, in *Epistolae* (Jena, 1556) vol.
1, folio 345 verso

8 Here stand I. I can do no other. God help me.
Amen.

speech at the Diet of Worms, 18 April 1521; attributed

9 If I had heard that as many devils would set on me
in Worms as there are tiles on the roofs, I should
none the less have ridden there.

to the Princes of Saxony, 21 August 1524, in *Sämmtliche*
Schriften vol. 16 (1745) ch. 10, sect. 1, no. 763:15

10 For, where God built a church, there the devil
would also build a chapel . . . In such sort is the
devil always God's ape.

Colloquia Mensalia (1566) ch. 2 (translated by H. Bell as
Martin Luther's Divine Discourses, 1652); see **Proverbs**
634:38

11 *Eine feste Burg ist unser Gott,*
Ein gute Wehr und Waffen.

A safe stronghold our God is still,
A trusty shield and weapon.

'Eine feste Burg ist unser Gott' (1529); translated by
Thomas Carlyle

12 The confidence and faith of the heart alone make
both God and an idol.

Large Catechism (1529) 'The First Commandment'

13 Whatever your heart clings to and confides in,
that is really your God.

Large Catechism (1529) 'The First Commandment'

14 So our Lord God commonly gives riches to those
gross asses to whom He vouchsafes nothing else.

Tischreden oder Colloquia (collected by J. Aurifaber, 1566)
ch. 4

15 *Wer nicht liebt Wein, Weib und Gesang,*
Der bleibt ein Narr sein Leben lang.

Who loves not woman, wine, and song
Remains a fool his whole life long.

attributed (later inscribed in the Luther room in the
Wartburg, but with no proof of authorship)

Edwin Lutyens 1869–1944

English architect

16 There will never be great architects or great
architecture without great patrons.

in *Country Life* 8 May 1915

Rosa Luxemburg 1871–1919

German revolutionary

17 *Freiheit ist immer nur Freiheit des anders Denkenden.*

Freedom is always and exclusively freedom for the
one who thinks differently.

Die Russische Revolution (1918) sect. 4

John Lydgate c.1370–c.1451

English poet

18 Sithe off oure language he was the lodesterre.

of **Chaucer**

The Fall of Princes (1431–8) prologue l. 252

19 Comparisouns doon offte gret greuaunce.

The Fall of Princes (1431–8) bk. 3, l. 2188

20 Woord is but wynd; leff woord and tak the dede.

Secrets of Old Philosophers l. 1224

21 Love is mor than gold or gret richesse.

The Story of Thebes pt. 3, l. 2716

John Lyly c.1554–1606

English poet and dramatist

1 CAMPASPE: Were women never so fair, men would be false.
APELLES: Were women never so false, men would be fond.
Campaspe (1584) act 3, sc. 3

2 Cupid and my Campaspe played
At cards for kisses, Cupid paid.
Campaspe (1584) act 3, sc. 5

3 What bird so sings, yet so does wail?
O 'tis the ravished nightingale.
Jug, jug, jug, jug, tereu, she cries,
And still her woes at midnight rise.
Campaspe (1584) act 5, sc. 1; see **Eliot** 303:13

4 Night hath a thousand eyes.
The Maydes Metamorphosis (1600) act 3, sc. 1

5 If all the earth were paper white
And all the sea were ink
'Twere not enough for me to write
As my poor heart doth think.
'If all the earth were paper white'

Lord Lyndhurst 1772–1863

English politician and lawyer; three times Lord Chancellor

6 Campbell has added another terror to death.
on Lord Campbell's Lives of the Lord Chancellors being written without the consent of heirs or executors
E. Bowen-Rowlands *Seventy-Two Years At the Bar* (1924) ch. 10; see **Arbuthnot** 24:7, **Tree** 798:9, **Wetherell** 830:21

Jonathan Lynn 1943– and Antony Jay 1930–

English writers

7 I think it will be a clash between the political will and the administrative won't.
Yes Prime Minister (1987) vol. 2

Lysander d. 395 BC

Greek general

8 Deceive boys with toys, but men with oaths.
Plutarch *Parallel Lives* 'Lysander' ch. 8; see **Plutarch** 598:17

Henry Francis Lyte 1793–1847

English hymn-writer

9 Abide with me: fast falls the eventide;
The darkness deepens; Lord, with me abide.
'Abide with Me' (probably written in 1847); see **Bible** 102:11

10 Change and decay in all around I see;
O Thou, who changest not, abide with me.
'Abide with Me' (probably written in 1847)

11 Praise my soul, the King of heaven;
To his feet thy tribute bring.
Ransomed, healed, restored, forgiven,
Who like me his praise should sing?
'Praise, my soul, the King of heaven' (1834 hymn)

12 Father-like, he tends and spares us.
'Praise, my soul, the King of heaven' (1834 hymn)

George Lyttelton, Lord Lyttelton 1709–73

English politician and man of letters

13 Seek to be good, but aim not to be great;
A woman's noblest station is retreat.
'Advice to a Lady' (1773)

E. R. Bulwer, Lord Lytton see Owen Meredith

Mary McAleese 1951–

Irish stateswoman; President from 1997

14 Apart from the shamrock, the President should not wear emblems or symbols of any kind.
deciding not to wear a poppy at her inauguration on 11 November 1997
in *Guardian* 6 November 1997

Douglas MacArthur 1880–1964

American general
on MacArthur: see **Truman** 801:13

15 I came through and I shall return.
on reaching Australia, 20 March 1942, having broken through Japanese lines en route from Corregidor
in *New York Times* 21 March 1942

16 In war, indeed, there can be no substitute for victory.
in *Congressional Record* 19 April 1951, vol. 97, pt. 3

Rose Macaulay 1881–1958

English novelist
see also **Opening lines** 575:21

17 Love's a disease. But curable.
Crewe Train (1926)

Thomas Babington Macaulay 1800–59

English politician and historian
on Macaulay: see **Arnold** 29:19, **Carlyle** 193:3, **Smith** 743:25

18 In order that he might rob a neighbour whom he had promised to defend, black men fought on the coast of Coromandel, and red men scalped each other by the Great Lakes of North America.
Biographical Essays (1857) 'Frederic the Great'

19 The gallery in which the reporters sit has become a fourth estate of the realm.
Essays Contributed to the Edinburgh Review (1843) vol. 1 'Hallam'

20 He knew that the essence of war is violence, and that moderation in war is imbecility.
Essays Contributed to the Edinburgh Review (1843) vol. 1 'John Hampden'

1 The gigantic body, the huge massy face, seamed with the scars of disease, the brown coat, the black worsted stockings, the grey wig with the scorched foretop, the dirty hands, the nails bitten and pared to the quick.

Essays Contributed to the Edinburgh Review (1843) vol. 1 'Samuel Johnson'

2 Out of his surname they have coined an epithet for a knave, and out of his Christian name a synonym for the Devil.

Essays Contributed to the Edinburgh Review (1843) vol. 1 'Machiavelli'

3 As civilization advances, poetry almost necessarily declines.

Essays Contributed to the Edinburgh Review (1843) vol. 1 'Milton'

4 If men are to wait for liberty till they become wise and good in slavery, they may indeed wait for ever.

Essays Contributed to the Edinburgh Review (1843) vol. 1 'Milton'

5 They esteemed themselves rich in a more precious treasure, and eloquent in a more sublime language, nobles by the right of an earlier creation, and priests by the imposition of a mightier hand.

of the Puritans

Essays Contributed to the Edinburgh Review (1843) vol. 1 'Milton'

6 We know no spectacle so ridiculous as the British public in one of its periodical fits of morality.

Essays Contributed to the Edinburgh Review (1843) vol. 1 'Moore's *Life of Lord Byron*'

7 We have heard it said that five per cent is the natural interest of money.

Essays Contributed to the Edinburgh Review (1843) vol. 1 'Southey's Colloquies'

8 With the dead there is no rivalry. In the dead there is no change. Plato is never sullen. Cervantes is never petulant. Demosthenes never comes unseasonably. Dante never stays too long. No difference of political opinion can alienate Cicero. No heresy can excite the horror of Bossuet.

Essays Contributed to the Edinburgh Review (1843) vol. 2 'Lord Bacon'

9 An acre in Middlesex is better than a principality in Utopia.

Essays Contributed to the Edinburgh Review (1843) vol. 2 'Lord Bacon'

10 The highest intellects, like the tops of mountains, are the first to catch and to reflect the dawn.

Essays Contributed to the Edinburgh Review (1843) vol. 2 'Sir James Mackintosh'

11 The history of England is emphatically the history of progress.

Essays Contributed to the Edinburgh Review (1843) vol. 2 'Sir James Mackintosh'

12 Biographers, translators, editors, all, in short, who employ themselves in illustrating the lives or writings of others, are peculiarly exposed to the *Lues Boswelliana,* or disease of admiration.

Essays Contributed to the Edinburgh Review (1843) vol. 2 'William Pitt, Earl of Chatham'

13 On the day of the accession of George the Third, the ascendancy of the Whig party terminated; and on that day the purification of the Whig party began.

Essays Contributed to the Edinburgh Review (1843) vol. 2 'William Pitt, Earl of Chatham'

14 The conformation of his mind was such that whatever was little seemed to him great, and whatever was great seemed to him little.

Essays Contributed to the Edinburgh Review (1843) vol. 2 'Horace Walpole'

15 Every schoolboy knows who imprisoned Montezuma, and who strangled Atahualpa.

Essays Contributed to the Edinburgh Review (1843) vol. 3 'Lord Clive'; see **Taylor** 775:1

16 The Chief Justice was rich, quiet, and infamous.

Essays Contributed to the Edinburgh Review (1843) vol. 3 'Warren Hastings'

17 That temple of silence and reconciliation where the enmities of twenty generations lie buried.

of Westminster Abbey

Essays Contributed to the Edinburgh Review (1843) vol. 3 'Warren Hastings'

18 She [the Roman Catholic Church] may still exist in undiminished vigour when some traveller from New Zealand shall, in the midst of a vast solitude, take his stand on a broken arch of London Bridge to sketch the ruins of St Paul's.

Essays Contributed to the Edinburgh Review (1843) vol. 3 'Von Ranke'; see **Walpole** 819:9

19 She [the Church of Rome] thoroughly understands what no other church has ever understood, how to deal with enthusiasts.

Essays Contributed to the Edinburgh Review (1843) vol. 3 'Von Ranke'

20 Persecution produced its natural effect on them [Puritans and Calvinists]. It found them a sect; it made them a faction.

History of England vol. 1 (1849) ch. 1

21 It was a crime in a child to read by the bedside of a sick parent one of those beautiful collects which had soothed the griefs of forty generations of Christians.

History of England vol. 1 (1849) ch. 2

22 The Puritan hated bear-baiting, not because it gave pain to the bear, but because it gave pleasure to the spectators.

History of England vol. 1 (1849) ch. 2

23 The English Bible, a book which, if everything else in our language should perish, would alone suffice to show the whole extent of its beauty and power.

T. F. Ellis (ed.) *Miscellaneous Writings of Lord Macaulay* (1860) 'John Dryden' (1828)

24 His imagination resembled the wings of an ostrich. It enabled him to run, though not to soar.

T. F. Ellis (ed.) *Miscellaneous Writings of Lord Macaulay* (1860) 'John Dryden' (1828)

1 This province of literature is a debatable line. It lies on the confines of two distinct territories . . . It is sometimes fiction. It is sometimes theory.
of history
> T. F. Ellis (ed.) *Miscellaneous Writings of Lord Macaulay* (1860) vol. 1 'History' (1828)

2 History begins in novel and ends in essay.
> T. F. Ellis (ed.) *Miscellaneous Writings of Lord Macaulay* (1860) vol. 1 'History' (1828)

3 Till Skiddaw saw the fire that burned on Gaunt's embattled pile,
And the red glare on Skiddaw roused the burghers of Carlisle.
> 'The Armada' (1833)

4 Obadiah Bind-their-kings-in-chains-and-their-nobles-with-links-of-iron.
> 'The Battle of Naseby' (1824) fictitious author's name; see **Book of Common Prayer** 144:8

5 Oh, wherefore come ye forth in triumph from the north,
With your hands, and your feet, and your raiment all red?
> 'The Battle of Naseby' (1824)

6 And the Man of Blood was there, with his long essenced hair,
And Astley, and Sir Marmaduke, and Rupert of the Rhine.
> 'The Battle of Naseby' (1824)

7 By those white cliffs I never more must see,
By that dear language which I spake like thee,
Forget all feuds, and shed one English tear
O'er English dust. A broken heart lies here.
> 'A Jacobite's Epitaph' (1845)

8 Gay are the Martian Calends:
December's Nones are gay:
But the proud Ides, when the squadron rides,
Shall be Rome's whitest day!
> *Lays of Ancient Rome* (1842) 'The Battle of Lake Regillus' st. 1

9 Those trees in whose grim shadow
The ghastly priest doth reign,
The priest who slew the slayer,
And shall himself be slain.
> *Lays of Ancient Rome* (1842) 'The Battle of Lake Regillus' st. 10

10 Let no man stop to plunder,
But slay, and slay, and slay;
The Gods who live for ever
Are on our side to-day.
> *Lays of Ancient Rome* (1842) 'The Battle of Lake Regillus' st. 35

11 Lars Porsena of Clusium
By the nine gods he swore
That the great house of Tarquin
Should suffer wrong no more.
> *Lays of Ancient Rome* (1842) 'Horatius' st. 1

12 The harvests of Arretium,
This year, old men shall reap.
This year, young boys in Umbro
Shall plunge the struggling sheep;
And in the vats of Luna,

This year, the must shall foam
Round the white feet of laughing girls
Whose sires have marched to Rome.
> *Lays of Ancient Rome* (1842) 'Horatius' st. 8

13 And how can man die better
Than facing fearful odds,
For the ashes of his fathers,
And the temples of his Gods?
> *Lays of Ancient Rome* (1842) 'Horatius' st. 27

14 Now who will stand on either hand,
And keep the bridge with me?
> *Lays of Ancient Rome* (1842) 'Horatius' st. 29

15 Then none was for a party;
Then all were for the state;
Then the great man helped the poor,
And the poor man loved the great:
Then lands were fairly portioned;
Then spoils were fairly sold:
The Romans were like brothers
In the brave days of old.
> *Lays of Ancient Rome* (1842) 'Horatius' st. 32

16 But hark! the cry is Astur
And lo! the ranks divide,
And the great Lord of Luna
Comes with his stately stride.
> *Lays of Ancient Rome* (1842) 'Horatius' st. 42

17 Was none who would be foremost
To lead such dire attack;
But those behind cried 'Forward!'
And those before cried 'Back!'
> *Lays of Ancient Rome* (1842) 'Horatius' st. 50

18 Oh, Tiber! father Tiber
To whom the Romans pray,
A Roman's life, a Roman's arms,
Take thou in charge this day!
> *Lays of Ancient Rome* (1842) 'Horatius' st. 59

19 And even the ranks of Tuscany
Could scarce forbear to cheer.
> *Lays of Ancient Rome* (1842) 'Horatius' st. 60

20 With weeping and with laughter
Still is the story told,
How well Horatius kept the bridge
In the brave days of old.
> *Lays of Ancient Rome* (1842) 'Horatius' st. 70

21 On the left side goes Remus,
With wrists and fingers red,
And in his hand a boar-spear,
And on the point a head—
A wrinkled head and aged,
With silver beard and hair,
And holy fillets round it,
Such as the pontiffs wear—
The head of ancient Camers,
Who spoke the words of doom:
'The children to the Tiber,
The mother to the tomb.'
> *Lays of Ancient Rome* (1842) 'The Prophecy of Capys'

22 Thank you, madam, the agony is abated.
aged four, having had hot coffee spilt over his legs
> G. O. Trevelyan *Life and Letters of Lord Macaulay* (1876) ch. 1

1 We must at present do our best to form a class who may be interpreters between us and the millions whom we govern; a class of persons, Indian in blood and colour, but English in taste, in opinions, in morals, and in intellect.
minute, as Member of Supreme Council of India, 2 February 1835, in W. Nassan Lees *Indian Musalmâns* (1871)

2 How odd that people of sense should find any pleasure in being accompanied by a beast who is always spoiling conversation.
of dogs
G. O. Trevelyan *Life and Letters of Macaulay* (1876) ch. 14

Anthony McAuliffe 1898–1975
American general

3 Nuts!
replying to the German demand for surrender at Bastogne, Belgium, 22 December 1944
in *New York Times* 28 December 1944

Norman McCaig 1910–96
Scottish poet

4 Who owns this landscape?
The millionaire who bought it or
the poacher staggering downhill in the early
    morning
with a deer on his back?
'A Man in Assynt' (1969)

Joseph McCarthy 1908–57
American politician and anti-Communist agitator
*on McCarthy: see **Eisenhower** 298:14; **Welch** 827:3*

5 I have here in my hand a list of two hundred and five [people] that were known to the Secretary of State as being members of the Communist Party and who nevertheless are still working and shaping the policy of the State Department.
speech at Wheeling, West Virginia, 9 February 1950

6 McCarthyism is Americanism with its sleeves rolled.
speech in Wisconsin, 1952, in Richard Rovere *Senator Joe McCarthy* (1973)

Mary McCarthy 1912–89
American novelist

7 Europe is the unfinished negative of which America is the proof.
On the Contrary (1961) 'America the Beautiful'

8 If someone tells you he is going to make a 'realistic decision', you immediately understand that he has resolved to do something bad.
On the Contrary (1961) 'American Realist Playwrights'

9 Every word she writes is a lie, including 'and' and 'the'.
*on Lillian **Hellman***
in *New York Times* 16 February 1980

Paul McCartney 1942–
English pop singer and songwriter
*see also **Lennon and McCartney***

10 You cannot reheat a soufflé.
discounting rumours of a Beatles reunion
attributed; L. Botts *Loose Talk* (1980)

George B. McClellan 1826–85
American soldier and politician

11 All quiet along the Potomac.
said at the time of the American Civil War
attributed; see **Beers** 63:9

Ewen MacColl 1915–89
English folksinger and songwriter

12 Dirty old town.
title of song, 1950

13 And I used to sleep standing on my feet
As we hunted for the shoals of herring.
'The Shoals of Herring' (1960 song)

David McCord 1897–
14 By and by
God caught his eye.
'Remainders' (1935); epitaph for a waiter

P. D. McCormick c.1834–1916
Australian musician

15 In joyful strains then let us sing
Advance Australia fair.
the national anthem of Australia, from 1984
'Advance Australia Fair' (c.1878 song)

Horace McCoy 1897–1955
American novelist

16 They shoot horses don't they.
title of novel (1935)

John McCrae 1872–1918
Canadian poet and military physician

17 In Flanders fields the poppies blow
Between the crosses, row on row,
That mark our place; and in the sky
The larks, still bravely singing, fly
Scarce heard amid the guns below.
'In Flanders Fields' (1915)

18 To you from failing hands we throw
The torch; be yours to hold it high.
If ye break faith with us who die
We shall not sleep, though poppies grow.
In Flanders fields.
'In Flanders Fields' (1915)

Hugh MacDiarmid (Christopher Murray Grieve) 1892–1978
Scottish poet and nationalist

19 Scotland small? Our multiform, our infinite Scotland *small?*

Only as a patch of hillside may be a cliché corner
To a fool who cries 'Nothing but heather!' . . .
Direadh I (1974)

1 I'll ha'e nae hauf-way hoose, but aye be whaur
Extremes meet—it's the only way I ken
To dodge the curst conceit o' bein' richt
That damns the vast majority o' men.
A Drunk Man Looks at the Thistle (1926)

2 He's no a man ava',
And lacks a proper pride,
Gin less than a' the world
Can ser' him for a bride!
A Drunk Man Looks at the Thistle (1926)

3 Hold a glass of pure water to the eye of the sun!
. . . This is the nearest analogy to the essence of
human life
Which is even more difficult to see.
Dismiss anything you can see more easily;
It is not alive—it is not worth seeing.
'The Glass of Pure Water' (1962)

4 The rose of all the world is not for me.
I want for my part
Only the little white rose of Scotland
That smells sharp and sweet—and breaks the
heart.
'The Little White Rose' (1934)

Dwight Macdonald 1906–82
American writer and film critic

5 Götterdämmerung without the gods.
of the use of atomic bombs against the Japanese
in *Politics* September 1945 'The Bomb'

George MacDonald 1824–1905
Scottish writer and poet
see also **Epitaphs** 309:13

6 Where did you come from, baby dear?
Out of the everywhere into here.
At the Back of the North Wind (1871) ch. 33 'Song'

7 So, then, as darkness had no beginning, neither
will it ever have an end . . . Where the light
cannot come, there abideth the darkness. The
light doth but hollow a mine out of the infinite
extension of the darkness. And ever upon the steps
of the light treadeth the darkness; yea, springeth
in fountains and wells amidst it, from the secret
channels of its mighty sea.
Phantastes (1858) ch. 8

John A. Macdonald 1815–91
*Scottish-born Canadian Liberal-Conservative statesman,
Prime Minister 1867–73 and 1878–91*

8 When fortune empties her chamberpot on your
head, smile—and say 'we are going to have a
summer shower'.
spoken *c.*1875 when Leader of the Opposition

9 A British subject I was born, and a British subject
I will die.
speech, 17 February 1891, in Toronto *Empire* 18 February
1891

Ramsay MacDonald 1866–1937
British Labour statesman; Prime Minister, 1924, 1931–5
on MacDonald: see **Churchill** 220:23, **Lloyd George** 488:3,
Nicolson 563:11

10 We hear war called murder. It is not: it is suicide.
in *Observer* 4 May 1930

11 Tomorrow every Duchess in London will be
wanting to kiss me!
*after forming the National Government, 25 August
1931*
Viscount Snowden *An Autobiography* (1934) vol. 2

A. G. MacDonell 1889–1941
Scottish writer

12 England, their England.
title of novel (1933); see **Henley** 381:16

Neil McElroy
American businessman; pioneer of soap operas

13 The problem of improving literary taste is one for
the schools. Soap operas sell lots of soap.
attributed; Katie Hafner and Matthew Lyon *Where Wizards
Stay Up Late: the Origins of the Internet* (1996)

Ian McEwan 1948–
English novelist

14 Shakespeare would have grasped wave functions,
Donne would have understood complementarity
and relative time. They would have been excited.
What richness! They would have plundered this
new science for their imagery. And they would
have educated their audiences too. But you 'arts'
people, you're not only ignorant of these
magnificent things, you're rather proud of
knowing nothing.
The Child in Time (1987) ch. 2

15 I love you . . . That is what they were all saying
down their phones, from the hijacked planes and
the burning towers. There is only love, and then
oblivion. Love was all they had to set against the
hatred of their murderers.
*of the last messages received from those trapped by
terrorist attack in buildings and planes, 11 September
2001*
in *Guardian* 15 September 2001; see **Last words** 472:10

William McGonagall c.1825–1902
Scottish writer of doggerel

16 Beautiful Railway Bridge of the Silv'ry Tay!
Alas, I am very sorry to say
That ninety lives have been taken away
On the last Sabbath day of 1879,
Which will be remembered for a very long time.
'The Tay Bridge Disaster'

Patrick McGoohan 1928– , George Markstein, and David Tomblin

American actor; scriptwriters

1 I am not a number, I am a free man!
   Number Six, in *The Prisoner* (TV series 1967–68);
   additional title sequence from the second episode onwards

Roger McGough 1937–

English poet

2 You will put on a dress of guilt
   and shoes with broken high ideals.
   'Comeclose and Sleepnow' (1967)

3 Let me die a youngman's death
   Not a clean & in-between-
   The-sheets, holy-water death,
   Not a famous-last-words
   Peaceful out-of-breath death.
   'Let Me Die a Youngman's Death' (1967)

4 And though poets I admire have published poems
   Whose imperfections reflect our own decay,
   I could never begin a poem; 'When I am dead'
   In case it tempted Fate, and Fate gave way.
   'When I am Dead' (1982)

Jimmie McGregor 1932–

Scottish singer and songwriter

5 Oh, he's football crazy, he's football mad
   And the football it has robbed him o' the wee bit
     sense he had.
   And it would take a dozen skivvies, his clothes to
     wash and scrub,
   Since our Jock became a member of that terrible
     football club.
   'Football Crazy' (1960 song)

Martin McGuinness 1950–

Northern Irish politician

6 My war is over. My job as a political leader is to
   prevent war.
   in *Daily Telegraph* 30 October 2002

Niccolò Machiavelli 1469–1527

Italian political philosopher and Florentine statesman
on Machiavelli: see **Macaulay** *498:2*

7 If . . . sometimes you need to conceal a fact with
   words, do it in such a way that it does not become
   known, or, if it does become known, that you
   have a ready and quick defence.
   'Advice to Raffaello Girolami when he went as Ambassador
   to the Emperor' (October 1522) in *Machiavelli: The Chief
   Works and Others* (translated by Allan Gilbert, 1965)

8 It is necessary for him who lays out a state and
   arranges laws for it to presuppose that all men are
   evil and that they are always going to act
   according to the wickedness of their spirits
   whenever they have free scope.
   Discourse upon the First Ten Books of Livy (written 1513–17)
   bk. 1, ch. 3 (translated by Allan Gilbert)

9 Men should be either treated generously or
   destroyed, because they take revenge for slight
   injuries—for heavy ones they cannot.
   The Prince (written 1513) ch. 3 (translated by Allan
   Gilbert)

10 This leads to a debate: is it better to be loved than
   feared, or the reverse? The answer is that it is
   desirable to be both, but because it is difficult to
   join them together, it is much safer for a prince to
   be feared than loved, if he is to fail in one of the
   two.
   The Prince (written 1513) ch. 8 (translated by Allan
   Gilbert)

11 Let no one oppose this belief of mine with that
   well-worn proverb: 'He who builds on the people
   builds on mud.'
   The Prince (written 1513) ch. 9 (translated by Allan
   Gilbert)

12 Since, then, a prince is necessitated to play the
   animal well, he chooses among the beasts the fox
   and the lion, because the lion does not protect
   himself from traps; the fox does not protect himself
   from wolves. The prince must be a fox, therefore,
   to recognize the traps and a lion to frighten the
   wolves.
   The Prince (written 1513) ch. 18 (translated by Allan
   Gilbert)

13 So long as the great majority of men are not
   deprived of either property or honour, they are
   satisfied.
   The Prince (written 1513) ch. 19 (translated by Allan
   Gilbert)

14 There is no other way for securing yourself
   against flatteries except that men understand that
   they do not offend you by telling you the truth;
   but when everybody can tell you the truth, you
   fail to get respect.
   The Prince (written 1513) ch. 23 (translated by Allan
   Gilbert)

Jay McInerney 1955–

American writer

15 A party is like a marriage . . . making itself up
   while seeming to follow precedent, running on
   steel rails into uncharted wilderness while the
   promises shiver and wobble on the armrests like
   crystal stemware.
   Brightness Falls (1992) ch. 1

Claude McKay 1890–1948

American poet and novelist

16 If we must die, let it not be like hogs
   Hunted and penned in an inglorious spot,
   While round us bark the mad and hungry dogs,
   Making their mock at our accursed lot.
   'If We Must Die' (1953)

Compton Mackenzie 1883–1972

English novelist

17 Prostitution. Selling one's body to keep one's soul:
   this is the meaning of the sins that were forgiven

to the woman because she loved much: one might say of most marriages that they were selling one's soul to keep one's body.

The Adventures of Sylvia Scarlett (1918) bk. 2, ch. 5

1 Women do not find it difficult nowadays to behave like men, but they often find it extremely difficult to behave like gentlemen.

Literature in My Time (1933) ch. 22

2 You are offered a piece of bread and butter that feels like a damp handkerchief and sometimes, when cucumber is added to it, like a wet one.

Vestal Fire (1927) bk. 1, ch. 3

James Mackintosh 1765–1832

Scottish philosopher and historian

3 Men are never so good or so bad as their opinions.

Dissertation on the Progress of Ethical Philosophy (1830) sect. 6 'Jeremy Bentham'

4 The Commons, faithful to their system, remained in a wise and masterly inactivity.

Vindiciae Gallicae (1791) sect. 1

Alexander Maclaren 1826–1910

Scottish divine

5 'The Church is an anvil which has worn out many hammers', and the story of the first collision is, in essentials, the story of all.

Expositions of Holy Scripture: Acts of the Apostles (1907) ch. 4

Don McLean 1945–

American songwriter

6 Something touched me deep inside
The day the music died.

on the death of Buddy Holly

'American Pie' (1972 song)

7 So, bye, bye, Miss American Pie,
Drove my Chevy to the levee
But the levee was dry.
Them good old boys was drinkin' whiskey and rye
Singin' 'This'll be the day that I die.'

'American Pie' (1972 song)

Archibald MacLeish 1892–1982

American poet and public official

8 A Poem should be palpable and mute
As a globed fruit.

'Ars Poetica' (1926)

9 A poem should be wordless
As the flight of birds.

'Ars Poetica' (1926)

10 A poem should not mean
But be.

'Ars Poetica' (1926)

Murdoch McLennan fl. 1715

Scottish poet

11 There's some say that we wan, some say that they wan,

Some say that nane wan at a', man;
But one thing I'm sure, that at Sheriffmuir
A battle there was which I saw, man:
And we ran, and they ran, and they ran, and we ran,
And we ran; and they ran awa', man!

'Sheriffmuir' in J. Woodfall Ebsworth (ed.) *Roxburghe Ballads* vol. 6 (1889)

Iain Macleod 1913–70

British Conservative politician

on Macleod: see **Salisbury** 664:17

12 It is some measure of the tightness of the magic circle on this occasion that neither the Chancellor of the Exchequer nor the Leader of the House of Commons had any inkling of what was happening.

*of the 'evolvement' of Alec Douglas-**Home** as Conservative leader after the resignation of Harold **Macmillan***

in *The Spectator* 17 January 1964

13 The Conservative Party always in time forgives those who were wrong. Indeed often, in time, they forgive those who were right.

in *The Spectator* 21 February 1964

Marshall McLuhan 1911–80

Canadian communications scholar

14 The new electronic interdependence recreates the world in the image of a global village.

The Gutenberg Galaxy (1962)

15 The medium is the message.

Understanding Media (1964) ch. 1 (title)

16 Television brought the brutality of war into the comfort of the living room. Vietnam was lost in the living rooms of America—not the battlefields of Vietnam.

in *Montreal Gazette* 16 May 1975

17 Advertising is the greatest art form of the twentieth century.

in *Advertising Age* 3 September 1976

18 Gutenberg made everybody a reader. Xerox makes everybody a publisher.

in *Guardian Weekly* 12 June 1977

Comte de MacMahon 1808–93

French soldier and statesman; President of the Third Republic, 1873–9

19 *J'y suis, j'y reste.*

Here I am, and here I stay.

at the taking of the Malakoff fortress during the Crimean War, 8 September 1855

G. Hanotaux *Histoire de la France Contemporaine* (1903–8) vol. 2, ch. 1, sect. 1; MacMahon later denied that he had expressed himself in such 'lapidary form'

Harold Macmillan 1894–1986

British Conservative statesman; Prime Minister, 1957–63
*on Macmillan: see **Thorpe** 793:21; see also **Hitler** 389:24*

1 We . . . are Greeks in this American empire . . . We must run the Allied Forces HQ as the Greeks ran the operations of the Emperor Claudius.
*to Richard **Crossman** in 1944*
  in *Sunday Telegraph* 9 February 1964

2 There ain't gonna be no war.
  at a London press conference, 24 July 1955, following the Geneva summit; in *News Chronicle* 25 July 1955

3 Forever poised between a cliché and an indiscretion.
on the life of a Foreign Secretary
  in *Newsweek* 30 April 1956

4 Let us be frank about it: most of our people have never had it so good.
'You Never Had It So Good' was the Democratic Party slogan during the 1952 US election campaign
  speech at Bedford, 20 July 1957, in *The Times* 22 July 1957

5 I thought the best thing to do was to settle up these little local difficulties, and then turn to the wider vision of the Commonwealth.
on leaving for a Commonwealth tour, following the resignation of the Chancellor of the Exchequer and others
  statement at London airport, 7 January 1958; in *The Times* 8 January 1958

6 The wind of change is blowing through this continent, and, whether we like it or not, this growth of [African] national consciousness is a political fact.
  speech at Cape Town, 3 February 1960, in *Pointing the Way* (1972)

7 I was determined that no British government should be brought down by the action of two tarts.
comment on the Profumo affair, July 1963
  Anthony Sampson *Macmillan* (1967)

8 There are three bodies no sensible man directly challenges: the Roman Catholic Church, the Brigade of Guards and the National Union of Mineworkers.
  in *Observer* 22 February 1981; see **Baldwin** 51:1

9 First of all the Georgian silver goes, and then all that nice furniture that used to be in the saloon. Then the Canalettos go.
on privatization
  speech to the Tory Reform Group, 8 November 1985, in *The Times* 9 November 1985; see **Misquotations** 538:16

10 The opposition of events.
on his biggest problem; popularly quoted as, 'Events, dear boy. Events'
  David Dilks *The Office of Prime Minister in Twentieth Century Britain* (1993)

Robert McNamara 1916–

American Democratic politician, Secretary of Defense during the Vietnam War

11 I don't object to it's being called 'McNamara's War' . . . It is a very important war and I am pleased to be identified with it and do whatever I can to win it.
  in *New York Times* 25 April 1964

12 We . . . acted according to what we thought were the principles and traditions of this nation. We were wrong. We were terribly wrong.
*of the conduct of the Vietnam War by the **Kennedy** and **Johnson** administrations*
  speaking in Washington, just before the twentieth anniversary of the American withdrawal from Vietnam; in *Daily Telegraph* (electronic edition) 10 April 1995

13 Military force—especially when wielded by an outside power—cannot bring order in a country that cannot govern itself.
  in *Daily Telegraph* (electronic edition) 10 April 1995

Louis MacNeice 1907–63

British poet, born in Belfast

14 Better authentic mammon than a bogus god.
  Autumn Journal (1939)

15 It's no go the merrygoround, it's no go the
    rickshaw,
  All we want is a limousine and a ticket for the
    peepshow.
  'Bagpipe Music' (1938)

16 The glass is falling hour by hour, the glass will fall
    for ever,
  But if you break the bloody glass you won't hold
    up the weather.
  'Bagpipe Music' (1938)

17 So they were married—to be the more together—
  And found they were never again so much
    together,
  Divided by the morning tea,
  By the evening paper,
  By children and tradesmen's bills.
  'Les Sylphides' (1941)

18 Time was away and somewhere else,
  There were two glasses and two chairs
  And two people with the one pulse
  (Somebody stopped the moving stairs):
  Time was away and somewhere else.
  'Meeting Point' (1941)

19 I am not yet born; O fill me
  With strength against those who would freeze my
  humanity.
  'Prayer Before Birth' (1944)

20 Let them not make me a stone and let them not
    spill me,
  Otherwise kill me.
  'Prayer Before Birth' (1944)

21 Down the road someone is practising scales,
  The notes like little fishes vanish with a wink of
    tails,
  Man's heart expands to tinker with his car
  For this is Sunday morning, Fate's great bazaar.
  'Sunday Morning' (1935)

22 The sunlight on the garden
  Hardens and grows cold,
  We cannot cage the minute

Within its net of gold.
  'Sunlight on the Garden' (1938)

1 By a high star our course is set,
  Our end is Life. Put out to sea.
  'Thalassa' (1964)

2 I would have a poet able-bodied, fond of talking, a
  reader of the newspapers, capable of pity and
  laughter, informed in economics, appreciative of
  women, involved in personal relationships,
  actively interested in politics, susceptible to
  physical impressions.
  Modern Poetry (1938)

Robert MacNeil 1931-
Canadian writer

3 Parents can plant magic in a child's mind through
  certain words spoken with some thrilling quality
  of voice, some uplift of the heart and spirit.
  Wordstruck (1989)

William Macpherson of Cluny 1926-
Scottish lawyer

4 For the purposes of our Inquiry the concept of
  institutional racism which we apply consists of:
    The collective failure of an organisation to
  provide an appropriate and professional service to
  people because of their colour, culture, or ethnic
  origin. It can be seen or detected in processes,
  attitudes and behaviour which amount to
  discrimination through unwitting prejudice,
  ignorance, thoughtlessness and racist stereotyping
  with disadvantage minority ethnic people.
  The Stephen Lawrence Inquiry: Report (February 1999) ch. 6

Geoffrey Madan 1895-1947
English bibliophile

5 The great tragedy of the classical languages is to
  have been born twins.
  Geoffrey Madan's Notebooks (1981)

6 Conservative ideal of freedom and progress:
  everyone to have an unfettered opportunity of
  remaining exactly where they are.
  Geoffrey Madan's Notebooks (1981)

7 The dust of exploded beliefs may make a fine
  sunset.
  Livre sans nom: Twelve Reflections (privately printed 1934)
  no. 12

Salvador de Madariaga 1886-1978
Spanish writer and diplomat

8 Since, in the main, it is not armaments that cause
  wars but wars (or the fears thereof) that cause
  armaments, it follows that every nation will at
  every moment strive to keep its armament in an
  efficient state as required by its fear, otherwise
  styled security.
  Morning Without Noon (1974) pt. 1, ch. 9

Samuel Madden 1686-1765
Irish poet

9 Words are men's daughters, but God's sons are
  things.
  Boulter's Monument (1745) l. 377; see **Johnson** 424:4

Winnie Madikizela-Mandela 1934-
South African political activist; former wife of Nelson
Mandela

10 With that stick of matches, with our necklace, we
  shall liberate this country.
  speech in black townships, 14 April 1986, in *Guardian* 15
  April 1986

James Madison 1751-1836
*American Democratic Republican statesman; 4th President of
the US, 1809-17*

11 Liberty is to faction what air is to fire, an aliment
  without which it instantly expires. But it could not
  be less folly to abolish liberty, which is essential to
  political life, because it nourishes faction than it
  would be to wish the annihilation of air, which is
  essential to animal life, because it imparts to fire
  its destructive agency.
  The Federalist (1787) no. 10

12 The diversity in the faculties of men, from which
  the rights of property originate, is not less an
  insuperable obstacle to a uniformity of interests.
  The protection of these faculties is the first object
  of government. From the protection of different
  and unequal faculties of acquiring property, the
  possession of different degrees and kinds of
  property immediately results.
  The Federalist (1787) no. 10

Madonna 1958-
American pop singer and actress

13 Being blonde is definitely a different state of mind.
  I can't really put my finger on it, but the artifice of
  being blonde has some incredible sort of sexual
  connotation.
  in *Rolling Stone* 23 March 1989

Gaeus Cilnius Maecenas d. 8 BC
Roman statesman

14 Never allow any innovation in religion, because
  the peace of the state depends on it.
  attributed; M. F. Wiles *Archetypal Heresy* (1996)

Maurice Maeterlinck 1862-1949
Belgian poet, dramatist, and essayist

15 *Il n'y a pas de morts.*
  There are no dead.
  L'Oiseau bleu (1909) act 4

John Gillespie Magee 1922-41
American airman, member of the Royal Canadian Airforce

16 Oh! I have slipped the surly bonds of earth
  And danced the skies on laughter-silvered wings.
  'High Flight' (1943); see **Reagan** 643:16

1 And, while with silent lifting mind I've trod
The high, untrespassed sanctity of space,
Put out my hand and touched the face of God.
'High Flight' (1943); see **Reagan** 643:16

William Connor Magee 1821–91

English clergyman, Bishop of Peterborough and Archbishop of York

2 It would be better that England should be free
than that England should be compulsorily sober.
speech on the Intoxicating Liquor Bill, House of Lords, 2
May 1872

Magna Carta

Political charter signed by King John at Runnymede, 1215

3 *Quod Anglicana ecclesia libera sit.*
That the English Church shall be free.
Clause 1

4 *Nullius liber homo capiatur, vel imprisonetur, aut
dissaisiatur, aut utlagetur, aut exuletur, aut aliquo
modo destruatur, nec super eum ibimus, nec super
eum mittemus, nisi per legale judicium parium
suorum vel per legem terrae.*

No free man shall be taken or imprisoned or
dispossessed, or outlawed or exiled, or in any way
destroyed, nor will we go upon him, nor will we
send against him except by the lawful judgement
of his peers or by the law of the land.
Clause 39

5 *Nulli vendemus, nulli negabimus aut differemus,
rectum aut justitiam.*

To no man will we sell, or deny, or delay, right or
justice.
Clause 40; see **Sayings** 670:1

René Magritte 1898–1967

Belgian surrealist painter

6 The mind loves the unknown. It loves images
whose meaning is unknown, since the meaning of
the mind itself is unknown.
Suzy Gablik *Magritte* (1970) ch. 1

Mahāyāna Buddhist texts

a tradition which emerged in India around the 1st century AD,
which later spread to China, Japan, and elsewhere

7 Homage to thee, Perfect Wisdom,
Boundless and transcending thought!
All thy limbs are without blemish,
Faultless those who Thee discern.
'Hymn to Perfect Wisdom' by Rahulabhadra (*c.*150 AD)

8 This all-knowledge of the Tathagata has come
forth from the perfection of wisdom. The physical
personality of the Tathagata, on the other hand, is
the result of the skill in means of the perfection of
wisdom.
Perfect Wisdom in 8,000 Lines (*c.*100 BC–100 AD) ch. 3,
v. 58

9 Where there is no perception, appellation,
conception, or conventional expression, there one
speaks of 'perfect wisdom'.
Perfect Wisdom in 8,000 Lines (*c.*100 BC–100 AD) ch. 7, v.
177

10 A Bodhisattva who is full of pity and concerned
with the welfare of all beings, who dwells in
friendliness, compassion, sympathetic joy and
even mindedness.
Perfect Wisdom in 8,000 Lines (*c.*100 BC–100 AD) ch. 20, v.
373

11 A glow-worm, or some other luminous animal,
does not think that its light could illuminate the
Continent of Jambudvipa [India], or radiate over
it. Just so the Disciples and Pratyekabuddhas do
not think that they should, after winning full
enlightenment lead all beings to Nirvana. But the
sun, when it has arisen, radiates its light over the
whole of Jambudvipa. Just so a Bodhisattva, after
he has accomplished the practices which lead to
the full enlightenment of Buddhahood, leads
countless beings to Nirvana.
Large Sutra on Perfect Wisdom (in 25,000 lines) (*c.*50–200
AD) v. 41

12 Form is emptiness and the very emptiness is form;
emptiness does not differ from form, nor does form
differ from emptiness; whatever is form, that is
emptiness, whatever is emptiness, that is form.
Heart Sutra (4th century AD) v. 3

13 One should know the Prajnaparamita as the great
spell, the spell of great knowledge, the utmost
spell, the unequalled spell, allayer of all suffering,
in truth,—for what could go wrong? By the
Prajnaparamita has this spell been delivered. It
runs like this: gone, gone, gone beyond, gone
altogether beyond, O what an awakening, all hail!
Heart Sutra (4th century AD) v. 8

14 This saying has been taught by the Tathagata in a
hidden sense: 'Those who know the discourse on
dharma as a raft should forsake dharmas, and
how much more so non-dharmas.'
Diamond Sutra (4th century AD) v. 6

15 Those who by my form did see me,
And those who followed me by my voice,
Wrong are the efforts they engaged in,
Me those people will not see.
Diamond Sutra (4th century AD) v. 26a

16 As stars, a fault of vision, as a lamp,
A mock show, dew drops, or a bubble,
A dream, a lightning flash, or cloud,
So we should view what is conditioned.
Diamond Sutra (4th century AD) v. 32a

17 Foolish common people do not understand that
what is seen is merely their own mind.
Lankāvatāra Sutra (*c.*4th century AD) p. 90

18 The road to Buddhahood is open to all.
At all times have all living beings the Germ of
Buddhahood in them.
Ratnagotravibhāga (*c.*3th century AD) v. 28

19 When I rain down the rain of Dharma,
Then all this world is well refreshed . . .

And then, refreshed, just like the plants,
The world will burst forth into blossoms.
Lotus Sutra pt. 5, v. 36

1 In the world deluded by ignorance, the supreme
all-knowing one,
The Tathagata, the great physician, appears, full
of compassion.
Lotus Sutra pt. 5, v. 60

2 There is no triad of vehicles, but here there is only
one vehicle.
Lotus Sutra pt. 5, v. 82

3 [The Happy Land] which is the world system of
the Lord Amitabha [Buddha of Infinite Light], is
rich and prosperous, comfortable, fertile, delightful
and crowded with many gods and men.
Pure Land Sutra ch. 15

4 All beings are irreversible from the supreme
enlightenment if they hear the name of the Lord
Amitabha, and, on hearing it, with one single
thought only raise their hearts to him with a
resolve connected with serene faith.
Larger Pure Land Sutra ch. 26

5 Sons or daughters of good family, who may desire
to see that Tathagata Amitabha in this very life
. . . should dedicate their store of merit to being
reborn therein [Sukhāvatī].
Larger Pure Land Sutra ch. 27

6 Universally Good is present in all lands
Sitting on a jewelled lotus throne, beheld by all;
He manifests all psychic powers
And is able to enter infinite meditations.
Flower Garland Sutra (*c.*2nd century AD) bk. 3

Gustav Mahler 1860–1911
Austrian composer

7 Fortissimo at last!
on seeing Niagara Falls
K. Blaukopf *Gustav Mahler* (1973) ch. 8

8 The symphony must be like the world. It must
embrace everything.
remark to Sibelius, Helsinki, 1907; K. and H. Blaukopf
(eds.) *Mahler: his life, work and world* (1976)

Derek Mahon 1941–
Irish poet

9 'I am just going outside and may be some time.'
The others nod, pretending not to know.
At the heart of the ridiculous, the sublime.
Antarctica (1985) title poem; see **Last words** 472:2

10 Somewhere beyond the scorched gable end and
the burnt-out buses
there is a poet indulging
his wretched rage for order.
'Rage for Order' (1978)

Norman Mailer 1923–
American novelist and essayist

11 So we think of Marilyn who was every man's love
affair with America, Marilyn Monroe who was

blonde and beautiful and had a sweet little rinky-
dink of a voice and all the cleanliness of all the
clean American backyards.
Marilyn (1973)

12 Society is built on many people hurting many
people, it is just who does the hurting, which is
forever in dispute.
Miami and the Siege of Chicago (1968)

13 The world stood like a playing card on edge . . .
One looked at the buildings one passed and
wondered if one was to see them again.
looking back at the week of the Cuban Missile Crisis
The Presidential Papers (1964)

14 All the security around the American president is
just to make sure the man who shoots him gets
caught.
in *Sunday Telegraph* 4 March 1990

Maimonides (Moses ben Maimon) 1135–1204
Jewish philosopher and Rabbinic scholar, born in Spain
see also **Epitaphs** 309:8

15 The basic tenets of our Torah and its fundamental
principles are thirteen in number: *The first
fundamental principle* is the existence of the Creator.
There is a being who exists in the most perfect
mode of existence, and he is the cause of the
existence of all other beings.
Commentary on the Mishnah Sanhedrin 10 (Heleq)

16 When I find the road narrow, and can see no
other way of teaching a well established truth
except by pleasing one intelligent man and
displeasing ten thousand fools—I prefer to address
myself to the man.
The Guide for the Perplexed, introduction

17 Know that for the human mind there are certain
objects of perception which are within the scope of
its nature and capacity; on the other hand, there
are, amongst things which actually exist, certain
objects which the mind can in no way and by no
means grasp: the gates of perception are closed
against it.
The Guide for the Perplexed ch. 31

18 Man's love of God is identical with his knowledge
of Him.
The Guide for the Perplexed ch. 51

19 Astrology is a disease, not a science.
Laws of Repentance

Henry Maine 1822–88
English jurist

20 The movement of the progressive societies has
hitherto been a movement *from Status to Contract*.
Ancient Law (1861) ch. 5

21 So great is the ascendancy of the Law of Actions
in the infancy of Courts of Justice, that substantive
law has at first the look of being gradually secreted
in the interstices of procedure; and the early
lawyer can only see the law through the envelope
of its technical forms.
Dissertations on Early Law and Custom (1883) ch. 11

1 Except the blind forces of Nature, nothing moves in this world which is not Greek in its origin.
   Village Communities (3rd ed., 1876)

Joseph de Maistre 1753–1821
French writer and diplomat

2 *Toute nation a le gouvernement qu'elle mérite.*
   Every country has the government it deserves.
   Lettres et Opuscules Inédits (1851) vol. 1, letter 53 (15 August 1811)

John Major 1943–
British Conservative statesman; Prime Minister, 1990–7
on Major: see **Currie** 254:6

3 If the policy isn't hurting, it isn't working.
   on controlling inflation
   speech in Northampton, 27 October 1989; see **Political slogans** 601:18

4 Society needs to condemn a little more and understand a little less.
   interview with *Mail on Sunday* 21 February 1993

5 Fifty years on from now, Britain will still be the country of long shadows on county [cricket] grounds, warm beer, invincible green suburbs, dog lovers, and—as George Orwell said—old maids bicycling to Holy Communion through the morning mist.
   speech to the Conservative Group for Europe, 22 April 1993; see **Orwell** 577:11

6 It is time to get back to basics: to self-discipline and respect for the law, to consideration for others, to accepting responsibility for yourself and your family, and not shuffling it off on the state.
   speech to the Conservative Party Conference, 8 October 1993

Bernard Malamud 1914–86
American novelist and short-story writer

7 There's no such thing as an unpolitical man, especially a Jew.
   The Fixer (1966) ch. 9

8 Levin wanted friendship and got friendliness; he wanted steak and they offered spam.
   A New Life (1961)

Malcolm X 1925–65
American civil rights campaigner

9 The white man was *created* a devil, to bring chaos upon this earth.
   speech, *c.*1953; Malcolm X with Alex Haley *The Autobiography of Malcolm X* (1965); see **Fard** 315:1

10 If you're born in America with a black skin, you're born in prison.
   in an interview, June 1963

11 You can't separate peace from freedom because no one can be at peace unless he has his freedom.
   speech in New York, 7 January 1965, *Malcolm X Speaks* (1965)

12 We are not speaking of any *individual* white man. We are speaking of the *collective* white man's

historical record. We are speaking of the collective white man's cruelties, and evils, and greeds, that have seen him *act* like a devil toward the non-white man.
   Malcolm X with Alex Haley *The Autobiography of Malcolm X* (1965)

Stéphane Mallarmé 1842–98
French poet

13 *La chair est triste, hélas! et j'ai lu tous les livres.*
   The flesh, alas, is wearied; and I have read all the books there are.
   'Brise Marin' (1887)

14 *Prélude à l'après-midi d'un faune.*
   Prelude to the afternoon of a faun.
   title of poem (*c.*1865)

15 *Un coup de dés jamais n'abolira le hasard.*
   A throw of the dice will never eliminate chance.
   title of poem (1897)

David Mallet (or Malloch) c.1705–65
Scottish poet

16 O grant me, Heaven, a middle state,
   Neither too humble nor too great;
   More than enough, for nature's ends,
   With something left to treat my friends.
   'Imitation of Horace'; see **Horace** 403:14

George Leigh Mallory 1886–1924
British mountaineer

17 Because it's there.
   on being asked why he wanted to climb Mount Everest (*Mallory was lost on Everest in the following year*)
   in *New York Times* 18 March 1923

Thomas Malory d. 1471
English writer
see also **Caxton** 204:9

18 Whoso pulleth out this sword of this stone and anvil is rightwise King born of all England.
   Le Morte D'Arthur (finished 1470, printed by Caxton 1485) bk. 1, ch. 4

19 The questing beast . . . had in shape like a serpent's head and a body like a leopard, buttocked like a lion and footed like a hart. And in his body there was such a noise as it had been twenty couple of hounds questing, and such noise that beast made wheresomever he went.
   questing = yelping
   Le Morte D'Arthur (1485) bk. 9, ch. 12

20 God defend me, said Dinadan, for the joy of love is too short, and the sorrow thereof, and what cometh thereof, dureth over long.
   Le Morte D'Arthur (1485) bk. 10, ch. 56

21 Thus endeth the story of the Sangreal, that was briefly drawn out of French into English, the which is a story chronicled for one of the truest and the holiest that is in this world.
   Le Morte D'Arthur (1485) bk. 17, ch. 23

1 Therefore all ye that be lovers call unto your remembrance the month of May, like as did Queen Guenevere, for whom I make here a little mention, that while she lived she was a true lover, and therefore she had a good end.

Le Morte D'Arthur (1485) bk. 18, ch. 25

2 Wherefore, madam, I pray you kiss me and never no more. Nay, said the queen, that shall I never do, but abstain you from such works: and they departed. But there was never so hard an hearted man but he would have wept to see the dolour that they made.

Le Morte D'Arthur (1485) bk. 21, ch. 10

3 Thou wert never matched of earthly knight's hand; and thou wert the courteoust knight that ever bare shield; and thou wert the truest friend to thy lover that ever bestrad horse; and thou wert the truest lover of a sinful man that ever loved woman; and thou wert the kindest man that ever struck with sword; and thou wert the goodliest person that ever came among press of knights; and thou wert the meekest man and the gentlest that ever ate in hall among ladies; and thou wert the sternest knight to thy mortal foe that ever put spear in the rest.

to Sir Launcelot
Le Morte D'Arthur (1485) bk. 21, ch. 13

4 And many men say that there is written upon his tomb this verse: *Hic iacet Arthurus, rex quondam rexque futurus* [Here lies Arthur, the once and future king].

Le Morte d'Arthur (1485) bk. 31, ch. 7

André Malraux 1901-76

French novelist, essayist, and art critic

5 *La condition humaine.*
The human condition.
title of book (1933)

6 *Il n'y a pas cinquante manières de combattre, il n'y en a qu'une, c'est d'être vainqueur. Ni la révolution ni la guerre ne consistent à se plaire à soi-même.*
There are not fifty ways of fighting, there's only one, and that's to win. Neither revolution nor war consists in doing what one pleases.

L'Espoir (1937) pt. 2, sect. 2, ch. 12

7 *L'homme sait que le monde n'est pas à l'échelle humaine; et il voudrait qu'il le fût.*
Man knows that the world is not made on a human scale; and he wishes that it were.

Les Noyers d'Altenburg (1945) pt. 2, ch. 3

8 *L'art est un anti-destin.*
Art is a revolt against fate.

Les Voix du silence (1951) pt. 4, ch. 7

Thomas Robert Malthus 1766-1834

English political economist

9 Population, when unchecked, increases in a geometrical ratio. Subsistence only increases in an arithmetical ratio.

Essay on the Principle of Population (1798) ch. 1

10 The perpetual struggle for room and food.

Essay on the Principle of Population (1798) ch. 3

Lord Mancroft 1914-87

British Conservative politician

11 Cricket—a game which the English, not being a spiritual people, have invented in order to give themselves some conception of eternity.

Bees in Some Bonnets (1979)

W. R. Mandale

12 Up and down the City Road,
In and out the Eagle,
That's the way the money goes—
Pop goes the weasel!

'Pop Goes the Weasel' (1853 song); also attributed to Charles Twiggs

Nelson Mandela 1918-

South African statesman

13 I have dedicated my life to this struggle of the African people. I have fought against white domination, and I have fought against black domination. I have cherished the ideal of a democratic and free society in which all persons live together in harmony with equal opportunities. It is an ideal which I hope to live for, and to see realized. But my lord, if needs be, it is an ideal for which I am prepared to die.

speech in Pretoria, 20 April 1964, which he quoted on his release in Cape Town, 11 February 1990

14 I stand here before you not as a prophet but as a humble servant of you, the people. Your tireless and heroic sacrifices have made it possible for me to be here today. I therefore place the remaining years of my life in your hands.

speech in Cape Town, 11 February 1990

15 No one is born hating another person because of the colour of his skin, or his background, or his religion. People must learn to hate, and if they can learn to hate, they can be taught to love, for love comes more naturally to the human heart than its opposite.

Long Walk to Freedom (1994)

16 True reconciliation does not consist in merely forgetting the past.

speech, 7 January 1996

Peter Mandelson 1953-

British Labour politician

17 Before this campaign started, it was said that I was facing political oblivion, my career in tatters ... They underestimated me, because I am a fighter and not a quitter.

on winning back his Hartlepool seat in the General Election

speech, 8 June 2001

Osip Mandelstam 1892–1938

Russian poet

1 The age is rocking the wave
with human grief
to a golden beat, and an adder
is breathing in time with it in the grass.
'The Age' (1923) (translated by C. M. Bowra)

2 Cruel and feeble, you'll look back
with the smile of a half-wit:
an animal that could run once,
staring at its own tracks.
'The Age' (1923) (translated by C. M. Bowra)

3 Only in war our fate has consummation,
And divination too will perish then.
'Tristia' (1919) (translated by C. M. Bowra)

Manilius (Marcus Manilius)

Roman poet of the 1st century AD

4 *Eripuitque Jovi fulmen viresque tonandi,
et sonitum ventis concessit, nubibus ignem.*

And snatched from Jove the lightning shaft and
power to thunder, and attributed the noise to the
winds, the flame to the clouds.
of human intelligence
Astronomica bk. 1, l. 104; see **Turgot** 802:13

Mrs Manley 1663–1724

English novelist and dramatist

5 No time like the present.
The Lost Lover (1696) act 4, sc. 1

Horace Mann 1796–1859

American educationist

6 The object of punishment is, prevention from evil;
it never can be made impulsive to good.
Lectures and Reports on Education (1867 ed.) lecture 7

7 Lost, yesterday, somewhere between Sunrise and
Sunset, two golden hours, each set with sixty
diamond minutes. No reward is offered, for they
are gone forever.
'Lost, Two Golden Hours'

Thomas Mann 1875–1955

German novelist

8 *Unsere Fähigkeit zum Ekel ist, wie ich anmerken
möchte, desto grösser, je lebhafter unsere Begierde ist,
das heisst: je inbrünstiger wir eigentlich der Welt und
ihren Darbietungen anhangen.*

Our capacity for disgust, let me observe, is in
proportion to our desires; that is in proportion to
the intensity of our attachment to the things of
this world.
The Confessions of Felix Krull (1954) pt. 1, ch. 5 (translated
by Denver Lindley)

9 *Die Zeit hat in Wirklichkeit keine Einschnitte, es gibt
kein Gewitter oder Drommetengetön beim Beginn
eines neuen Monats oder Jahres, und selbst bei dem
eines neuen Säkulums sind es nur wir Menschen, die
schiessen und läuten.*

Time has no divisions to mark its passage, there is
never a thunderstorm or blare of trumpets to
announce the beginning of a new month or year.
Even when a new century begins it is only we
mortals who ring bells and fire off pistols.
The Magic Mountain (1924) ch. 4, sect. 4 (translated by H.
T. Lowe-Porter)

10 *Warten heisst: Voraneilen, heisst: Zeit und Gegenwart
nicht als Geschenk, sondern nur als Hindernis
empfinden, ihren Eigenwert verneinen und vernichten
und sie im Geist überspringen. Warten, sagt man, sei
langweilig. Es ist jedoch ebensowohl oder sogar
eigentlich kurzweilig, indem es Zeitmengen
verschlingt, ohne sie um ihrer selbst willen zu leben
und auszunutzen.*

And waiting means hurrying on ahead, it means
regarding time and the present moment not as a
boon, but an obstruction; it means making their
actual content null and void, by mentally
overleaping them. Waiting we say is long. We
might just as well—or more accurately—say it is
short, since it consumes whole spaces of time
without our living them or making any use of
them as such.
The Magic Mountain (1924) ch. 5, sect. 5 (translated by H.
T. Lowe-Porter)

11 *Die Sprach is Gesittung selbst . . . Das Wort, selbst
das widersprechendste, ist so verbindend . . . Aber die
Wortlosigkeit vereinsamt.*

Speech is civilisation itself. The word, even the
most contradictory word, preserves contact—it is
silence which isolates.
The Magic Mountain (1924) ch. 6 (translated by H. T. Lowe-
Porter)

12 *Wir kommen aus dem Dunkel und gehen ins Dunkel,
dazwischen liegen Erlebnisse; aber Anfang und Ende,
Geburt und Tod, werden von uns nicht erlebt, sie
haben keinen subjektiven Charakter, sie fallen als
Vorgänge ganz ins Gebiet des Objektiven, so ist es
damit.*

We come out of the dark and go into the dark
again, and in between lie the experiences of our
life. But the beginning and end, birth and death,
we do not experience; they have no subjective
character, they fall entirely in the category of
objective events, and that's that.
The Magic Mountain (1924) ch. 6, sect. 8 (translated by H.
T. Lowe-Porter)

13 *Unser Sterben ist mehr eine Angelegenheit der
Weiterlebenden als unserer selbst.*

A man's dying is more the survivors' affair than
his own.
The Magic Mountain (1924) ch. 6, sect. 8 (translated by H.
T. Lowe-Porter)

14 *Die Zeit ist das Element der Erzählung, wie sie das
Element des Lebens ist,—unlösbar damit verbunden,
wie mit den Körpern im Raum. Sie ist auch das
Element der Musik, als welche die Zeit misst und
gliedert, sie kurzweilig und kostbar auf einmal macht.*

For time is the medium of narration, as it is the
medium of life. Both are inextricably bound up
with it, as are bodies in space. Similarly, time is
the medium of music; music divides, measures,

articulates time, and can shorten it, yet enhance its value, both at once.
> *The Magic Mountain* (1924) ch. 7, sect. 1 (translated by H. T. Lowe-Porter)

1 *Das kühlt, das klärt, dem zuge der stunden hält eine bestimmte Gemütsverfassung nicht ungewandelt stand.*

Time cools, time clarifies; no mood can be maintained quite unaltered through the course of hours.
> *The Magic Mountain* (1924) ch. 7 (translated by H. T. Lowe-Porter)

John Manners, Duke of Rutland
1818–1906
English Tory politician and writer

2 Let wealth and commerce, laws and learning die, But leave us still our old nobility!
> *England's Trust* (1841) pt. 3, l. 227

Katherine Mansfield (Kathleen Mansfield Beauchamp) 1888–1923
New Zealand-born short-story writer

3 E. M. Forster never gets any further than warming the teapot. He's a rare fine hand at that. Feel this teapot. Is it not beautifully warm? Yes, but there ain't going to be no tea.
> *Journal* (1927) May 1917

4 I'm a writer first and a woman after.
> letter to John Middleton Murry, July 1917

5 Whenever I prepare for a journey I prepare as though for death. Should I never return, all is in order.
> *Journal* (1927) 29 January 1922

William Murray, Lord Mansfield
1705–93
Scottish lawyer and politician
on Mansfield: see Lloyd 487:11

6 The constitution does not allow reasons of state to influence our judgements: God forbid it should! We must not regard political consequences; however formidable soever they might be: if rebellion was the certain consequence, we are bound to say *'fiat justitia, ruat caelum'*.
> *Rex v. Wilkes*, 8 June 1768, in *The English Reports* (1909) vol. 98; see **Adams** 3:10, **Watson** 823:2

7 Consider what you think justice requires, and decide accordingly. But never give your reasons; for your judgement will probably be right, but your reasons will certainly be wrong.
> *advice to a newly appointed colonial governor ignorant in the law*
> John Lord Campbell *The Lives of the Chief Justices of England* (1849) vol. 2, ch. 40

Richard Mant 1776–1848
Irish divine and ecclesiastical historian

8 Bright the vision that delighted
Once the sight of Judah's seer;

Sweet the countless tongues united
To entrance the prophet's ear.
> 'Bright the vision that delighted' (1837 hymn)

Alessandro Manzoni 1785–1873
Italian novelist, dramatist, and poet

9 *Il primero svegliarsi, dopo una sciagura, e in impiccio, é un momento molto amaro. La mente, appena risentita ricorre all' idee abituali della vita tranquilla antecedente; ma il pensiero del nuovo stato di cose le si affacia subito sgarbatamente.*

The arousing from sleep, after a recent misfortune, is a bitter moment; the mind at first habitually recurs to its previous tranquillity, but is soon depressed by the thought of the contrast that awaits it.
> *The Betrothed* (1825–42) ch. 2

10 *La sposina ne fu l'idolo, il trastullo, la vittima.*

The young bride was the idol, the amusement, the victim of the evening.
> *The Betrothed* (1825–42) ch. 10

Mao Zedong 1893–1976
Chinese statesman; de facto leader of the Communist Party

11 Politics is war without bloodshed while war is politics with bloodshed.
> lecture, 1938, in *Selected Works* (1965) vol. 2

12 Every Communist must grasp the truth, 'Political power grows out of the barrel of a gun'.
> speech, 6 November 1938, in *Selected Works* (1965) vol. 2

13 The atom bomb is a paper tiger which the United States reactionaries use to scare people. It looks terrible, but in fact it isn't . . . All reactionaries are paper tigers.
> interview, 1946, in *Selected Works* (1961) vol. 4

14 Letting a hundred flowers blossom and a hundred schools of thought contend is the policy for promoting progress in the arts and the sciences and a flourishing socialist culture in our land.
> speech in Peking, 27 February 1957, in *Quotations of Chairman Mao* (1966)

Diego Maradona 1960–
Argentine football player

15 The goal was scored a little bit by the hand of God, another bit by head of Maradona.
> *on his controversial goal against England in the 1986 World Cup*
> in *Guardian* 1 July 1986

René Maran 1887–1960
French novelist, born in Martinique

16 Life is short. Work is for those who will never be able to understand life. Idleness cannot degrade a man. To the discriminating eye it differs from laziness.
> *Batouala* (1921) ch. 1, translated by Alvah C. Bessie

1 Ah, the whites! Their malignity and their omniscience—that was what made them terrifying!

Batouala (1921) ch. 2, translated by Alvah C. Bessie

William Learned Marcy 1786–1857

American politician

2 The politicians of New York . . . see nothing wrong in the rule, that to the victor belong the spoils of the enemy.

speech to the Senate, 25 January 1832, in James Parton *Life of Andrew Jackson* (1860) vol. 3, ch. 29

Princess Margaret 1930–2002

*British princess, sister of **Elizabeth II***

3 Mindful of the Church's teaching that Christian marriage is indissoluble, and conscious of my duty to the Commonwealth, I have resolved to put these considerations before any others.

announcing her decision not to marry a divorced man, Group Captain Peter Townsend

statement from Clarence House, 31 October 1955; in *The Times* 1 November 1955

Miriam Margolyes 1941–

English actress

4 Life, if you're fat, is a minefield—you have to pick your way, otherwise you blow up.

in *Observer* 9 June 1991

Marguerite of Angoulême 1492–1549

*French writer, sister of **Francis I** and Queen of Navarre*

5 Though jealousy be produced by love, as ashes are by fire, yet jealousy extinguishes love as ashes smother the flame.

Heptameron (1558) 'Novel 48, the Fifth Day'

Lynn Margulis 1938–

American biologist

6 Gaia is a tough bitch. People think the earth is going to die and they have to save it, that's ridiculous . . . There's no doubt that Gaia can compensate for our output of greenhouse gases, but the environment that's left will not be happy for any people.

in *New York Times Biographical Service* January 1996

Marie-Antoinette 1755–93

*French Queen consort of **Louis XVI***

7 *Qu'ils mangent de la brioche.*

Let them eat cake.

on being told that her people had no bread

attributed, but much older; in his *Confessions* (1740) Rousseau refers to a similar remark being a well-known saying; another version is:

Que ne mangent-ils de la croûte de pâté?

Why don't they eat pastry?

attributed to Marie-Thérèse (1638–83), wife of Louis XIV, in Louis XVIII *Relation d'un Voyage à Bruxelles et à Coblentz en 1791* (1823)

Edwin Markham 1852–1940

American poet

8 A thing that grieves not and that never hopes, Stolid and stunned, a brother to the ox?

'The Man with the Hoe' (1899)

Johnny Marks 1909–85

American songwriter

9 Rudolph, the Red-Nosed Reindeer Had a very shiny nose, And if you ever saw it, You would even say it glows.

'Rudolph, the Red-Nosed Reindeer' (1949 song)

Leo Marks 1920–2001

English cryptographer and screenwriter

10 The life that I have Is all that I have And the life that I have Is yours.

The love that I have Of the life that I have Is yours and yours and yours.

given to the British secret agent Violette Szabo (1921–45), for use with the Special Operations Executive

'The Life that I Have' (written 1943)

Sarah, Duchess of Marlborough 1660–1744

11 The Duke returned from the wars today and did pleasure me in his top-boots.

oral tradition, attributed in various forms; I. Butler *Rule of Three* (1967) ch. 7

12 If I were young and handsome as I was, instead of old and faded as I am, and you could lay the empire of the world at my feet, you should never share the heart and hand that once belonged to John, Duke of Marlborough.

refusing an offer of marriage from the Duke of Somerset

W. S. Churchill *Marlborough: His Life and Times* vol. 4 (1938) ch. 39

Bob Marley 1945–81

Jamaican reggae musician and songwriter

13 Get up, stand up Stand up for your rights Get up, stand up Never give up the fight.

'Get up, Stand up' (1973 song)

14 I shot the sheriff But I swear it was in self-defence I shot the sheriff And they say it is a capital offence.

'I Shot the Sheriff' (1974 song)

Christopher Marlowe 1564–93

English dramatist and poet
on Marlowe: see Drayton 286:3, Jonson 436:1; see also Anonymous 16:19

1 I'll have them fly to India for gold,
Ransack the ocean for orient pearl.
Doctor Faustus (1604) act 1, sc. 1

2 Why, this is hell, nor am I out of it.
Doctor Faustus (1604) act 1, sc. 3

3 Hell hath no limits nor is circumscribed
In one self place, where we are is Hell,
And to be short, when all the world dissolves,
And every creature shall be purified,
All places shall be hell that are not heaven.
Doctor Faustus (1604) act 2, sc. 1

4 Was this the face that launched a thousand ships,
And burnt the topless towers of Ilium?
Sweet Helen, make me immortal with a kiss!
Doctor Faustus (1604) act 5, sc. 1

5 Now hast thou but one bare hour to live,
And then thou must be damned perpetually.
Stand still, you ever-moving spheres of heaven,
That time may cease, and midnight never come.
Doctor Faustus (1604) act 5, sc. 2

6 *O lente lente currite noctis equi.*
The stars move still, time runs, the clock will
strike,
The devil will come, and Faustus must be damned.
O I'll leap up to my God: who pulls me down?
See, see, where Christ's blood streams in the
firmament.
One drop would save my soul, half a drop, ah my
Christ.
Doctor Faustus (1604) act 5, sc. 2; see **Ovid** 579:18

7 Cut is the branch that might have grown full
straight,
And burnèd is Apollo's laurel bough,
That sometime grew within this learned man.
Doctor Faustus (1604) epilogue

8 My men, like satyrs grazing on the lawns,
Shall with their goat feet dance an antic hay.
Edward II (1593) act 1, sc. 1

9 Tell Isabel the Queen, I looked not thus,
When for her sake I ran at tilt in France.
Edward II (1593) act 5, sc. 5

10 Base Fortune, now I see, that in thy wheel
There is a point, to which when men aspire,
They tumble headlong down.
Edward II (1593) act 5, sc. 6

11 Where both deliberate, the love is slight;
Who ever loved that loved not at first sight?
Hero and Leander (1598) First Sestiad, l. 175; see
Shakespeare 681:27

12 I count religion but a childish toy,
And hold there is no sin but ignorance.
The Jew of Malta (c.1592) prologue

13 Thus methinks should men of judgement frame
Their means of traffic from the vulgar trade,
And, as their wealth increaseth, so enclose

Infinite riches in a little room.
The Jew of Malta (c.1592) act 1, sc. 1

14 As for myself, I walk abroad o' nights
And kill sick people groaning under walls:
Sometimes I go about and poison wells.
The Jew of Malta (c.1592) act 2, sc. 3

15 BARNARDINE: Thou hast committed—
BARABAS: Fornication? But that was in another
country: and besides, the wench is dead.
The Jew of Malta (c.1592) act 4, sc. 1

16 Come live with me, and be my love,
And we will all the pleasures prove,
That valleys, groves, hills and fields,
Woods or steepy mountain yields.
'The Passionate Shepherd to his Love'; see **Donne** 280:15,
Ralegh 640:18

17 With milk-white harts upon an ivory sled
Thou shalt be drawn amidst the frozen pools,
And scale the icy mountains' lofty tops,
Which with thy beauty will be soon resolved.
Tamburlaine the Great (1590) pt. 1, act 1, sc. 2

18 Our swords shall play the orators for us.
Tamburlaine the Great (1590) pt. 1, act 1, sc. 2

19 Accurst be he that first invented war.
Tamburlaine the Great (1590) pt. 1, act 2, sc. 4

20 Is it not passing brave to be a king,
And ride in triumph through Persepolis?
Tamburlaine the Great (1590) pt. 1, act 2, sc. 5

21 The ripest fruit of all,
That perfect bliss and sole felicity,
The sweet fruition of an earthly crown.
Tamburlaine the Great (1590) pt. 1, act 2, sc. 7

22 Virtue is the fount whence honour springs.
Tamburlaine the Great (1590) pt. 1, act 4, sc. 4

23 Ah fair Zenocrate, divine Zenocrate,
Fair is too foul an epithet for thee.
Tamburlaine the Great (1590) pt. 1, act 5, sc. 5

24 Now walk the angels on the walls of heaven,
As sentinels to warn th' immortal souls,
To entertain divine Zenocrate.
Tamburlaine the Great (1590) pt. 2, act 2, sc. 4

25 More childish valorous than manly wise.
Tamburlaine the Great (1590) pt. 2, act 4, sc. 1

26 Holla, ye pampered jades of Asia!
What, can ye draw but twenty miles a day . . . ?
Tamburlaine the Great (1590) pt. 2, act 4, sc. 3; see
Shakespeare 692:1

Don Marquis 1878–1937

American poet and journalist

27 procrastination is the
art of keeping
up with yesterday.
archy and mehitabel (1927) 'certain maxims of archy'

28 an optimist is a guy
that has never had
much experience.
archy and mehitabel (1927) 'certain maxims of archy'

1 it s cheerio
my deario that
pulls a lady through.
archy and mehitabel (1927) 'cheerio, my deario'

2 I have got you out here
in the great open spaces
where cats are cats.
archy and mehitabel (1927) 'mehitabel has an adventure'

3 but wotthehell archy wotthehell
jamais triste archy jamais triste
that is my motto.
archy and mehitabel (1927) 'mehitabel sees paris'

4 did you ever
notice that when
a politician
does get an idea
he usually
gets it all wrong.
archys life of mehitabel (1933) 'archygrams'

5 Writing a book of poetry is like dropping a rose
petal down the Grand Canyon and waiting for the
echo.
E. Anthony *O Rare Don Marquis* (1962)

6 The art of newspaper paragraphing is to stroke a
platitude until it purrs like an epigram.
E. Anthony *O Rare Don Marquis* (1962)

John Marriot 1780–1825
English clergyman

7 Thou, whose eternal Word
Chaos and darkness heard,
And took their flight,
Hear us, we humbly pray,
And, where the Gospel-day
Sheds not its glorious ray,
Let there be light!
'almighty' substituted for 'eternal' from 1861
'Thou, whose eternal Word' (hymn written *c.*1813)

Frederick Marryat 1792–1848
English naval captain and novelist

8 As savage as a bear with a sore head.
The King's Own (1830) vol. 2, ch. 6

9 If you please, ma'am, it was a very little one.
the nurse, excusing her illegitimate baby
Mr Midshipman Easy (1836) ch. 3

10 All zeal . . . all zeal, Mr Easy.
Mr Midshipman Easy (1836) ch. 9

Arthur Marshall 1910–89
British journalist and former schoolmaster

11 What, knocked a tooth out? Never mind, dear,
laugh it off, laugh it off; it's all part of life's rich
pageant.
The Games Mistress (recorded monologue, 1937)

John Marshall 1755–1835
American jurist

12 The power to tax involves the power to destroy.
in *McCulloch v. Maryland* (1819)

13 The people made the Constitution, and the people
can unmake it. It is the creature of their own will,
and lives only by their will.
in *Cohens v. Virginia* (1821)

Thomas R. Marshall 1854–1925
American politician

14 What this country needs is a really good 5-cent
cigar.
in *New York Tribune* 4 January 1920, pt. 7

Thurgood Marshall 1908–93
American Supreme Court judge

15 We must never forget that the only real source of
power that we as judges can tap is the respect of
the people.
in *Chicago Tribune* 15 August 1981

Martial C.AD 40–C.104
Roman epigrammatist, born in Spain

16 *Non est, crede mihi, sapientis dicere 'Vivam':*
Sera nimis vita est crastina: vive hodie.
Believe me, wise men don't say 'I shall live to do
that', tomorrow's life's too late; live today.
Epigrammata bk. 1, no. 15

17 *Non amo te, Sabidi, nec possum dicere quare:*
Hoc tantum possum dicere, non amo te.
I don't love you, Sabidius, and I can't tell you
why; all I can tell you is this, that I don't love
you.
Epigrammata bk. 1, no. 32; see **Brown** 155:13, **Watkyns**
822:16

18 *Laudant illa sed ista legunt.*
They praise those works, but read these.
Epigrammata bk. 4, no. 49

19 *Bonosque*
Soles effugere atque abire sentit,
Qui nobis pereunt et imputantur.
Each of us feels the good days speed and depart,
and they're lost to us and counted against us.
Epigrammata bk. 5, no. 20

20 *Mollia non rigidus caespes tegat ossa; nec illi,*
Terra, gravis fueris: non fuit illa tibi.
Not hard be the turf that covers her soft bones, be
not heavy upon her, earth; she was not heavy
upon you.
on a dead child
Epigrammata bk. 5, no. 34, l. 9

21 *Thais habet nigros, niveos Laecania dentes.*
Quae ratio est? emptos haec habet, illa suos.
Thais' teeth are black, Laecania's snow-white. The
reason? The one has those she bought, the other
her own.
Epigrammata bk. 5, no. 43

1 *Non est vivere, sed valere vita est.*
Life's not just being alive, but being well.
Epigrammata bk. 6, no. 70

2 *Vitam quae faciant beatiorem,*
Iucundissime Martialis, haec sunt:
Res non parta labore sed relicta;
non ingratus ager, focus perennis.
The things that make life happier, most genial
Martial, are these: means not acquired by labour,
but bequeathed; fields not unkindly, an ever-
blazing hearth.
Epigrammata bk. 10, no. 47; see **Surrey** 764:4

3 *Difficilis facilis, iucundus acerbus es idem:*
Nec tecum possum vivere nec sine te.
Difficult or easy, pleasant or bitter, you are the
same you: I cannot live with you—or without
you.
Epigrammata bk. 12, no. 46(47); see **Addison** 4:25

4 *Rus in urbe.*
Country in the town.
Epigrammata bk. 12, no. 57

Harriet Martineau 1802–76
English writer

5 The sum and substance of female education in
America, as in England, is training women to
consider marriage as the sole object in life, and to
pretend that they do not think so.
Society in America (1837)

Andrew Marvell 1621–78
English poet

6 Where the remote Bermudas ride
In the ocean's bosom unespied.
'Bermudas' (c.1653)

7 He hangs in shades the orange bright,
Like golden lamps in a green night.
'Bermudas' (c.1653)

8 And makes the hollow seas, that roar,
Proclaim the ambergris on shore.
'Bermudas' (c.1653)

9 Echo beyond the Mexique Bay.
'Bermudas' (c.1653)

10 My love is of a birth as rare
As 'tis for object strange and high:
It was begotten by Despair
Upon Impossibility.

Magnanimous Despair alone
Could show me so divine a thing,
Where feeble Hope could ne'er have flown
But vainly flapped its tinsel wing.
'The Definition of Love' (1681)

11 As lines (so loves) oblique may well
Themselves in every angle greet:
But ours so truly parallel,
Though infinite, can never meet.

Therefore the love which us doth bind,
But Fate so enviously debars,

Is the conjunction of the mind,
And opposition of the stars.
'The Definition of Love' (1681)

12 So architects do square and hew,
Green trees that in the forest grew.
'A Dialogue between the Soul and the Body' (1681)

13 Choosing each stone, and poising every weight,
Trying the measures of the breadth and height;
Here pulling down, and there erecting new,
Founding a firm state by proportions true.
'The First Anniversary of the Government under His
Highness the Lord Protector, 1655' l. 245

14 How vainly men themselves amaze
To win the palm, the oak, or bays.
'The Garden' (1681) st. 1

15 The gods, that mortal beauty chase,
Still in a tree did end their race.
Apollo hunted Daphne so,
Only that she might laurel grow.
And Pan did after Syrinx speed,
Not as a nymph, but for a reed.
'The Garden' (1681) st. 4

16 What wondrous life is this I lead!
Ripe apples drop about my head;
The luscious clusters of the vine
Upon my mouth do crush their wine;
The nectarine, and curious peach,
Into my hands themselves do reach;
Stumbling on melons, as I pass,
Ensnared with flowers, I fall on grass.
'The Garden' (1681) st. 5

17 Annihilating all that's made
To a green thought in a green shade.
'The Garden' (1681) st. 6

18 *He* nothing common did or mean
Upon that memorable scene:
But with his keener eye
The axe's edge did try.
on the execution of **Charles I**
'An Horatian Ode upon Cromwell's Return from Ireland'
(written 1650) l. 57

19 So much one man can do,
That does both act and know.
'An Horatian Ode upon Cromwell's Return from Ireland'
(written 1650) l. 75

20 Ye country comets, that portend
No war, nor prince's funeral.
'The Mower to the Glow-worms' (1681)

21 Had it lived long, it would have been
Lilies without, roses within.
'The Nymph Complaining for the Death of her Fawn'
(1681) l. 91

22 Had we but world enough, and time,
This coyness, lady, were no crime.
'To His coy Mistress' (1681) l. 1

23   I would
Love you ten years before the flood:
And you should, if you please, refuse
Till the conversion of the Jews.
My vegetable love should grow

Vaster than empires, and more slow.
'To His coy Mistress' (1681) l. 7

1 But at my back I always hear
Time's wingèd chariot hurrying near:
And yonder all before us lie
Deserts of vast eternity.
'To His Coy Mistress' (1681) l. 21; see **Eliot** 303:17

2   Then worms shall try
That long preserved virginity:
And your quaint honour turn to dust;
And into ashes all my lust.
The grave's a fine and private place,
But none, I think, do there embrace.
'To His Coy Mistress' (1681) l. 27

3 Let us roll all our strength, and all
Our sweetness, up into one ball:
And tear our pleasures with rough strife,
Thorough the iron gates of life.
Thus, though we cannot make our sun
Stand still, yet we will make him run.
'To His Coy Mistress' (1681) l. 41

4 He is translation's thief that addeth more,
As much as he that taketh from the store
Of the first author.
'To His Worthy Friend Dr Witty' (1651)

5 Oh thou, that dear and happy isle
The garden of the world ere while,
Thou paradise of four seas,
Which heaven planted us to please,
But, to exclude the world, did guard
With watery if not flaming sword;
What luckless apple did we taste,
To make us mortal, and thee waste?
'Upon Appleton House' (1681) st. 41

6 But now the salmon-fishers moist
Their leathern boats begin to hoist;
And, like Antipodes in shoes,
Have shod their heads in their canoes.
How tortoise-like, but not so slow,
These rational amphibii go!
'Upon Appleton House' (1681) st. 97

Holt Marvell

English songwriter

7 A cigarette that bears a lipstick's traces,
An airline ticket to romantic places;
And still my heart has wings
These foolish things
Remind me of you.
'These Foolish Things Remind Me of You' (1935 song)

Chico Marx 1891–1961

American film comedian
see also **Film lines** 319:22

8 I wasn't kissing her, I was just whispering in her mouth.
on being discovered by his wife with a chorus girl
Groucho Marx and Richard J. Anobile *Marx Brothers Scrapbook* (1973) ch. 24

Groucho Marx 1895–1977

American film comedian
on Marx: see **Sayings** 740:6; see also **Epitaphs** 310:3, **Film lines** 319:4, **Film lines** 319:14, **Film lines** 319:22, **Film lines** 320:16, **Film lines** 321:1

9 PLEASE ACCEPT MY RESIGNATION. I DON'T WANT TO BELONG TO ANY CLUB THAT WILL ACCEPT ME AS A MEMBER.
Groucho and Me (1959) ch. 26

10 I never forget a face, but in your case I'll be glad to make an exception.
Leo Rosten *People I have Loved, Known or Admired* (1970) 'Groucho'

Karl Marx 1818–83

German political philosopher; founder of modern Communism
on Marx: see **Benn** 67:2, **Sayings** 740:6

11 Religion is the sigh of the oppressed creature, the heart of a heartless world . . . It is the opium of the people.
A Contribution to the Critique of Hegel's Philosophy of Right (1843–4) introduction; see **Kingsley** 453:2

12 Mankind always sets itself only such problems as it can solve; since, looking at the matter more closely, it will always be found that the task itself arises only when the material conditions for its solution already exist or are at least in the process of formation.
A Contribution to the Critique of Political Economy (1859) preface (translated by D. McLellan)

13 From each according to his abilities, to each according to his needs.
Critique of the Gotha Programme (written 1875, but of earlier origin); see **Blanc** 123:6, **Morelly** 549:1, and:

The formula of Communism, as propounded by Cabet, may be expressed thus:—'the duty of each is according to his faculties; his right according to his wants'.
in *North British Review* (1849) vol 10

14 And even when a society has got upon the right track for the discovery of the natural laws of its movement—and it is the ultimate aim of this work, to lay bare the economic law of motion of modern society—it can neither clear by bold leaps, nor remove by legal enactments, the obstacles offered by the successive phases of its normal development. But it can shorten and lessen the birth-pangs.
Das Kapital (1st German ed., 1867) preface (25 July 1865)

15 Centralization of the means of production, and socialization of labour at last reach a point where they become incompatible with their capitalist integument. This integument is burst asunder. The knell of capitalist private property sounds. The expropriators are expropriated.
Das Kapital (1867) ch. 32

16 Hegel says somewhere that all great events and personalities in world history reappear in one fashion or another. He forgot to add: the first time as tragedy, the second as farce.
The Eighteenth Brumaire of Louis Bonaparte (1852) sect. 1;

the origin of the Hegel reference is uncertain, but see **Hegel** 379:3

1 The philosophers have only interpreted the world in various ways; the point is to change it.

Theses on Feuerbach (written 1845, published 1888) no. 11

2 What I did that was new was to prove . . . that the class struggle necessarily leads to the dictatorship of the proletariat.

the phrase 'dictatorship of the proletariat' had been used earlier in the Constitution of the World Society of Revolutionary Communists (1850), signed by Marx and others

letter to Georg Weydemeyer 5 March 1852; Marx claimed that the phrase had been coined by Auguste Blanqui (1805–81), but it has not been found in this form in Blanqui's work

3 All I know is that I am not a Marxist.

attributed in a letter from Friedrich Engels to Conrad Schmidt, 5 August 1890; in Karl Marx and Friedrich Engels *Correspondence* (1934)

Karl Marx 1818–83 and Friedrich Engels 1820–95

German political philosopher and German socialist

4 A spectre is haunting Europe—the spectre of Communism.

The Communist Manifesto (1848) opening words

5 The history of all hitherto existing society is the history of class struggles.

The Communist Manifesto (1848) pt. 1

6 The proletarians have nothing to lose but their chains. They have a world to win. WORKING MEN OF ALL COUNTRIES, UNITE!

commonly rendered as 'Workers of the world, unite!'

The Communist Manifesto (1848) closing words (from the 1888 translation by Samuel Moore, edited by Engels)

Mary I (Mary Tudor) 1516–58

English monarch, Queen from 1553

7 When I am dead and opened, you shall find 'Calais' lying in my heart.

Holinshed's Chronicles vol. 4 (1808); see **Sellar and Yeatman** 676:20

Queen Mary 1867–1953

British princess, Queen Consort of George V

8 All *this* thrown away for *that*.

on returning home to Marlborough House, London after the abdication of her son, King Edward VIII, December 1936

David Duff *George and Elizabeth* (1983) ch. 10

9 I do not think you have ever realised the shock, which the attitude you took up caused your family and the whole nation. It seemed inconceivable to those who had made such sacrifices during the war that you, as their King, refused a lesser sacrifice.

letter to the Duke of Windsor (formerly **Edward VIII**), July 1938, in J. Pope-Hennessy *Queen Mary* (1959) ch. 7

Mary, Queen of Scots 1542–87

Scottish monarch, Queen 1542–67

*on Mary: see **Elizabeth I** 304:3, **Gray** 360:19, **James V** 417:9*

10 Look to your consciences and remember that the theatre of the world is wider than the realm of England.

to the commissioners appointed to try her at Fotheringhay, 13 October 1586

Antonia Fraser *Mary Queen of Scots* (1969) ch. 25

11 *En ma fin git mon commencement.*

In my end is my beginning.

motto embroidered with an emblem of her mother, Mary of Guise, and quoted in a letter from William Drummond of Hawthornden to Ben Jonson in 1619; see **Eliot** 301:14

John Masefield 1878–1967

English poet

12 Quinquireme of Nineveh from distant Ophir
Rowing home to haven in sunny Palestine,
With a cargo of ivory,
And apes and peacocks,
Sandalwood, cedarwood, and sweet white wine.

'Cargoes' (1903); see **Bible** 81:13

13 Dirty British coaster with a salt-caked smoke stack,
Butting through the Channel in the mad March days,
With a cargo of Tyne coal,
Road-rails, pig lead,
Firewood, ironware, and cheap tin trays.

'Cargoes' (1903)

14 O Christ, the plough, O Christ, the laughter
Of holy white birds flying after.

'The Everlasting Mercy' (1911)

15 I must go down to the seas again, to the lonely sea and the sky,
And all I ask is a tall ship and a star to steer her by,
And the wheel's kick and the wind's song and the white sail's shaking,
And a grey mist on the sea's face and a grey dawn breaking.

'Sea Fever' (1902)

16 I must go down to the sea again, for the call of the running tide
Is a wild call and a clear call that may not be denied.

'Sea Fever' (1902)

Donald Mason 1913–

American naval officer

17 Sighted sub, sank same.

on sinking a Japanese submarine in the Atlantic region (the first US naval success in the war)

radio message, 28 January 1942; in *New York Times* 27 February 1942

Philip Massinger 1583–1640

English dramatist

1 Ambition, in a private man a vice,
  Is in a prince the virtue.
  The Bashful Lover (licensed 1636, published 1655) act 1,
  sc. 2

2   Pray enter
  You are learned Europeans and we worse
  Than ignorant Americans.
  The City Madam (licensed 1632, published 1658) act 3,
  sc. 3

3   Greatness, with private men
  Esteemed a blessing, is to me a curse . . .
  Happy the golden mean!
  The Great Duke of Florence (licensed 1627, printed 1635) act
  1, sc. 1

4 Oh that thou hadst like others been all words,
  And no performance.
  The Parliament of Love (1624) act 4, sc. 2

5 Death has a thousand doors to let out life:
  I shall find one.
  A Very Woman (licensed 1634, published 1655) act 5, sc.
  4; see **Fletcher** 327:4, **Seneca** 677:2, **Webster** 825:25

Cotton Mather 1662–1728

American puritan preacher and divine, son of Increase
Mather

6 I write the wonders of the Christian religion, flying
  from the depravations of Europe, to the American
  strand: and, assisted by the Holy Author of that
  religion, I do, with all conscience of truth,
  required therein by Him, who is the Truth itself,
  report the wonderful displays of His infinite power,
  wisdom, goodness, and faithfulness, wherewith
  His Divine Providence hath irradiated an Indian
  wildnerness.
  introduction to *Magnalia Christi Americana* (1702), opening
  line

7 Every man will have his own style which will
  distinguish him as much as his gait.
  Manuductio ad Ministerium (1726) 'Of Style'

8 That there is a Devil is a thing doubted by none
  but such as are under the influences of the Devil.
  For any to deny the being of a Devil must be from
  an ignorance or profaneness worse than
  diabolical.
  The Wonders of the Invisible World (1693)

Increase Mather 1639–1723

American puritan divine and writer, father of Cotton **Mather**

9 Now as usually providence so ordereth that they
  who have been speaking all their lives long shall
  not say much when they come to die.
  The Life and Death of . . . Mr Richard Mather (1670)

10 Thunder is the voice of God, and, therefore, to be
  dreaded.
  Remarkable Providences (1684)

James Mathew 1830–1908

Irish judge

11 In England, justice is open to all—like the Ritz
  Hotel.
  R. E. Megarry *Miscellany-at-Law* (1955); see **Anonymous**
  16:4

Henri Matisse 1869–1954

French painter

12 What I dream of is an art of balance, of purity and
  serenity devoid of troubling or depressing subject
  matter . . . a soothing, calming influence on the
  mind, rather like a good armchair which provides
  relaxation from physical fatigue.
  Notes d'un peintre (1908)

Leonard Matlovich d. 1988

American Air Force Sergeant

13 When I was in the military, they gave me a medal
  for killing two men and a discharge for loving one.
  attributed

W. Somerset Maugham 1874–1965

English novelist

14 Poor Henry, he's spending eternity wandering
  round and round a stately park and the fence is
  just too high for him to peep over and they're
  having tea just too far away for him to hear what
  the countess is saying.
  of Henry **James**
  Cakes and Ale (1930) ch. 11

15 The most useful thing about a principle is that it
  can always be sacrificed to expediency.
  The Circle (1921) act 3

16 It is not true that suffering ennobles the character;
  happiness does that sometimes, but suffering, for
  the most part, makes men petty and vindictive.
  The Moon and Sixpence (1919) ch. 17

17 A woman can forgive a man for the harm he does
  her, but she can never forgive him for the
  sacrifices he makes on her account.
  The Moon and Sixpence (1919) ch. 41

18 Like all weak men he laid an exaggerated stress on
  not changing one's mind.
  Of Human Bondage (1915) ch. 39

19 People ask you for criticism, but they only want
  praise.
  Of Human Bondage (1915) ch. 50

20 Money is like a sixth sense without which you
  cannot make a complete use of the other five.
  Of Human Bondage (1915) ch. 51

21 I [Death] was astonished to see him in Baghdad,
  for I had an appointment with him tonight in
  Samarra.
  Sheppey (1933) act 3

22 Dying is a very dull, dreary affair. And my advice
  to you is to have nothing whatever to do with it.
  to his nephew Robin, in 1965
  Robin Maugham *Conversations with Willie* (1978)

Bill Mauldin 1921–

American cartoonist

1 I feel like a fugitive from th' law of averages.
  cartoon caption in *Up Front* (1945)

André Maurois 1885–1967

French writer

2 Growing old is no more than a bad habit which a busy man has no time to form.
  The Art of Living (1940) ch. 8

James Maxton 1885–1946

British Labour politician

3 All I say is, if you cannot ride two horses you have no right in the circus.
  opposing disaffiliation of the Scottish Independent Labour Party from the Labour Party; usually quoted as, ' . . . no right in the bloody circus'
  in *Daily Herald* 12 January 1931; see **Proverbs** 623:13

Glyn Maxwell 1962–

English poet

4 May his anorak grow big with jotters,
  Noting the numbers of trains he saw.
  'Curse on a Child' (1995)

James Clerk Maxwell 1831–79

Scottish physicist

5 Scientific truth should be presented in different forms, and should be regarded as equally scientific whether it appears in the robust form and the vivid colouring of a physical illustration, or in the tenuity and paleness of a symbolic expression.
  attributed; in *Physics Teacher* December 1969

Theresa May 1956–

British Conservative politician

6 You know what some people call us: the nasty party.
  speech to the Conservative Conference, 7 October 2002

Vladimir Mayakovsky 1893–1930

Russian poet
see also **Last words** 473:3

7 If you wish—
  . . . I'll be irreproachably tender;
  not a man, but—a cloud in trousers!
  'The Cloud in Trousers' (1915) (translated by Samuel Charteris)

8 Not a sound. The universe sleeps, resting a huge ear on its paw with mites of stars.
  'The Cloud in Trousers' (1915) (translated by Samuel Charteris)

9 In our language rhyme is a barrel. A barrel of dynamite. The line is a fuse. The line smoulders to the end and explodes; and the town is blown sky-high in a stanza.
  'Conversation with an Inspector of Taxes about Poetry' (1926) (translated by Dmitri Obolensky)

10 Oh for just
  one
  more conference
  regarding the eradication of all conferences!
  'In Re Conferences'; Herbert Marshall (ed.) *Mayakovsky* (1965)

11 To us love says humming that the heart's stalled motor has begun working again.
  'Letter from Paris to Comrade Kostorov on the Nature of Love' (1928) (translated by Samuel Charteris)

12 Ours is the land.
  The air—ours.
  Ours the diamond mines of stars.
  And we will never,
  never!
  Allow anyone,
  anyone!
  To ravage our land with shells,
  to tear our air with sharpened spear points.
  'Revolution: a Poet's Chronicle' (1917) (translated by C. M. Bowra)

Louis B. Mayer 1885–1957

Russian-born American film executive, head of MGM

13 We've got more stars than there are in the heavens, all of them except for that damned Mouse over at Disney.
  Sheridan Morley and Ruth Leon *Gene Kelly* (1996)

Jonathan Mayhew 1720–66

American divine

14 Rulers have no authority from God to do mischief.
  A Discourse Concerning Unlimited Submission and Non-Resistance to the Higher Powers (1750)

15 As soon as the prince sets himself up above the law, he loses the king in the tyrant; he does to all intents and purpose unking himself.
  A Discourse Concerning Unlimited Submission and Non-Resistance to the Higher Powers (1750)

Giuseppe Mazzini 1805–72

Italian nationalist leader

16 Insurrection—by means of guerrilla bands—is the true method of warfare for all nations desirous of emancipating themselves from a foreign yoke.
  General Instructions for the Members of Young Italy (1833) sect. 4

17 A nation is the universality of citizens speaking the same tongue.
  in *La Giovine Italia*, 1832

Margaret Mead 1901–78

American anthropologist

18 The knowledge that the personalities of the two sexes are socially produced is congenial to every programme that looks forward towards a planned order of society. It is a two-edged sword.

Sex and Temperament in Three Primitive Societies (1935) pt. 4 'Conclusion'

Shepherd Mead 1914–
American advertising executive

1 How to succeed in business without really trying.
title of book (1952)

Hughes Mearns 1875–1965
American writer

2 As I was walking up the stair
I met a man who wasn't there.
He wasn't there again today.
I wish, I wish he'd stay away.
lines written for *The Psycho-ed*, an amateur play, in Philadelphia, 1910 (set to music in 1939 as 'The Little Man Who Wasn't There')

Peter Medawar 1915–87
English immunologist and writer

3 A bishop wrote gravely to the *Times* inviting all nations to destroy 'the formula' of the atomic bomb. There is no simple remedy for ignorance so abysmal.
The Hope of Progress (1972)

4 If a scientist were to cut his ear off, no one would take it as evidence of a heightened sensibility.
'J. B. S.' (1968)

5 If politics is the art of the possible, research is surely the art of the soluble. Both are immensely practical-minded affairs.
in *New Statesman* 19 June 1964; see **Bismarck** 117:14

6 During the 1950s, the first great age of molecular biology, the English Schools of Oxford and particularly of Cambridge produced more than a score of graduates of quite outstanding ability— much more brilliant, inventive, articulate and dialectically skilful than most young scientists; right up in the Watson class. But Watson had one towering advantage over all of them: in addition to being extremely clever he had something important to be clever *about*.
review of James D. **Watson**'s *The Double Helix* in *New York Review of Books* 28 March 1968

Catherine de' Medici 1518–89
Italian-born queen consort of Henri II of France

7 A false report, if believed during three days, may be of great service to a government.
Isaac D'Israeli *Curiosities of Literature* 2nd series (1849) vol. 2; perhaps apocryphal

Cosimo de' Medici 1389–1464
Italian statesman and patron of the arts

8 We read that we ought to forgive our enemies; but we do not read that we ought to forgive our friends.
speaking of what **Bacon** *refers to as 'perfidious friends'*
Francis Bacon *Apophthegms* (1625) no. 206

Lorenzo de' Medici 1449–92
Italian statesman and poet

9 *Quanto è bella giovinezza*
Che si fugge tuttavia!
Chi vuol esser lieto sia:
Di doman non ci è certezza.

How beautiful is youth, that is always slipping away! Whoever wants to be happy, let him be so: of tomorrow there's no knowing.
'Trionfo di Bacco e di Arianna'

Golda Meir 1898–1978
Israeli stateswoman, Prime Minister 1969–74

10 Those that perished in Hitler's gas chambers were the last Jews to die without standing up to defend themselves.
speech to United Jewish Appeal Rally, New York, 11 June 1967

11 Pessimism is a luxury that a Jew can never allow himself.
in *Observer* 29 December 1974

Nellie Melba (Helen Porter Mitchell) 1861–1931
Australian operatic soprano

12 The first rule of opera is the first rule of life, a very simple and possibly unexciting rule, for which I shall receive no thanks. That is, see to everything yourself.
Melodies and Memories (1925) ch. 27

13 Art is not national. It is international. Music is not written in red, white and blue; it is written with the heart's blood of the composer.
Melodies and Memories (1925) ch. 28

14 Sing 'em muck! It's all they can understand!
advice to Dame Clara Butt, prior to her departure for Australia
W. H. Ponder *Clara Butt* (1928) ch. 12

William Lamb, Lord Melbourne 1779–1848
British Whig statesman, and husband of Lady Caroline **Lamb**; *Prime Minister 1834, 1835–41*
see also **Anonymous** 16:8

15 Universities never reform themselves; everyone knows that.
speech, House of Lords, 11 April 1837

16 Damn it! Another Bishop dead! I believe they die to vex me.
attributed; Lord David Cecil *Lord M* (1954) ch. 4

17 God help the Minister that meddles with art!
Lord David Cecil *Lord M* (1954) ch. 3

18 If left out he would be dangerous, but if taken in, he would be simply destructive.
when forming his second administration, Melbourne omitted the former Lord Chancellor, **Brougham**
Lord David Cecil *Lord M* (1954) ch. 4

1 I wish I was as cocksure of anything as Tom Macaulay is of everything.

   Lord Cowper's preface to *Lord Melbourne's Papers* (1889)

2 Now, is it to lower the price of corn, or isn't it? It is not much matter which we say, but mind, we must all say *the same.*

   attributed; Walter Bagehot *The English Constitution* (1867) ch. 1

3 Things have come to a pretty pass when religion is allowed to invade the sphere of private life.
   on hearing an evangelical sermon

   G. W. E. Russell *Collections and Recollections* (1898) ch. 6

4 What all the wise men promised has not happened, and what all the d—d fools said would happen has come to pass.
   of the Catholic Emancipation Act (1829)

   H. Dunckley *Lord Melbourne* (1890) ch. 9

5 What I like about the Order of the Garter is that there is no damned merit about it.

   Lord David Cecil *The Young Melbourne* (1939)

6 What I want is men who will support me when I am in the wrong.
   replying to a politician who said 'I will support you as long as you are in the right'

   Lord David Cecil *Lord M* (1954) ch. 4

7 When in doubt what should be done, do nothing.

   Lord David Cecil *Lord M* (1954) ch. 1

David Mellor 1949–

British Conservative politician and broadcaster

8 I do believe the popular press is drinking in the last chance saloon.

   interview on *Hard News* (Channel 4), 21 December 1989

Herman Melville 1819–91

American novelist and poet
see also **Opening lines** 574:9

9 That Calvinistic sense of innate depravity and original sin from whose visitations, in some shape or other, no deeply thinking mind is always and wholly free.

   Hawthorne and His Mosses (1850)

10 A whaleship was my Yale College and my Harvard.

   Moby Dick (1851) ch. 24

11 Towards thee I roll, thou all-destroying but unconquering whale . . . from hell's heart I stab at thee.

   Moby Dick (1851) ch. 135

Gilles Ménage 1613–92

French scholar

12 *Comme nous nous entretenions de ce qui pouvait rendre heureux, je lui dis; Sanitas sanitatum, et omnia sanitas.*
   While we were discussing what could make one happy, I said to him: *Sanitas sanitatum et omnia sanitas* [Health of healths and everything is health].

   from a conversation with Jean-Louis Guez de Balzac (1594–1654), in *Ménagiana* (1693); see **Bible** 115:7

Menander 342–c.292 BC

Greek comic dramatist

13 Whom the gods love dies young.

   Dis Exapaton fragment 4, in F. H. Sandbach (ed.) *Menandri Reliquiae Selectae* (1990); see **Byron** 181:14, **Proverbs** 635:2

14 We live, not as we wish to, but as we can.

   The Lady of Andros in *Menander: the Principal Fragments* (translated by F. G. Allinson, 1951)

Mencius see Meng-tzu

H. L. Mencken 1880–1956

American journalist and literary critic

15 Love is the delusion that one woman differs from another.

   Chrestomathy (1949) ch. 30; see **Shaw** 725:29

16 Puritanism. The haunting fear that someone, somewhere, may be happy.

   Chrestomathy (1949) ch. 30

17 Democracy is the theory that the common people know what they want, and deserve to get it good and hard.

   A Little Book in C major (1916)

18 Conscience: the inner voice which warns us that someone may be looking.

   A Little Book in C major (1916)

19 It is now quite lawful for a Catholic woman to avoid pregnancy by a resort to mathematics, though she is still forbidden to resort to physics and chemistry.

   Notebooks (1956) 'Minority Report'

20 There is always a well-known solution to every human problem—neat, plausible, and wrong.

   Prejudices 2nd series (1920)

Moses Mendelssohn 1729–86

German-born Jewish philosopher

21 To put it in one word: I believe that Judaism knows nothing of revealed religion, in the sense in which this is understood by Christians. The Israelites possess divine legislation.

   Jerusalem (1783) pt. 2

Meng-tzu (Mencius) 371–289 BC

Chinese philosopher

22 All men have the mind which cannot bear [to see the suffering of] others.

   The Book of Mencius bk. 2, pt. A, v. 6

1 It is useless to talk to those who do violence to their own nature, and it is useless to do anything with those who throw themselves away. To speak what is against propriety and righteousness is to do violence to oneself. To say that one cannot abide by humanity and follow righteousness is to throw oneself away.
The Book of Mencius bk. 4, pt. A, v. 10

2 The great man is the one who does not lose his [originally good] child's heart.
The Book of Mencius bk. 4, pt. B, v. 12

3 If you let people follow their feelings [original nature], they will be able to do good. This is what is meant by saying that human nature is good.
The Book of Mencius bk. 6, pt. A, v. 6

4 Moral principles please our minds as beef and mutton and pork please our mouths.
The Book of Mencius bk. 6, pt. A, v. 7

5 All things are already complete in oneself. There is no greater joy than to examine oneself and be sincere. When in ones' conduct one vigorously exercises altruism, humanity is not far to seek, but right by him.
The Book of Mencius bk. 7, pt. A, v. 4

Robert Gordon Menzies 1894–1978
Australian Liberal statesman, Prime Minister 1939–41 and 1949–66

6 What Great Britain calls the Far East is to us the near north.
in *Sydney Morning Herald* 27 April 1939

David Mercer 1928–80
English dramatist

7 A suitable case for treatment.
title of television play (1962); later filmed as *Morgan—A Suitable Case for Treatment* (1966)

Johnny Mercer 1909–76
American songwriter

8 You've got to ac-cent-tchu-ate the positive
Elim-my-nate the negative
Latch on to the affirmative
Don't mess with Mister In-between.
'Ac-cent-tchu-ate the Positive' (1944 song)

9 Jeepers Creepers—where you get them peepers?
'Jeepers Creepers' (1938 song)

10 Make it one for my baby
And one more for the road.
'One For My Baby' (1943 song)

11 That old black magic.
title of song (1942)

George Meredith 1828–1909
English novelist and poet
on Meredith: see **Wilde** 835:26, **Wilde** 836:4

12 'Tis Ireland gives England her soldiers, her generals too.
Diana of the Crossways (1885) ch. 2

13 The light of every soul burns upward. Of course, most of them are candles in the wind. Let us allow for atmospheric disturbance.
Diana of the Crossways (1885) ch. 39; see **John** 422:11

14 A dainty rogue in porcelain.
The Egoist (1879) ch. 5

15 Cynicism is intellectual dandyism without the coxcomb's feathers.
The Egoist (1879) ch. 7

16 Kissing don't last: cookery do!
The Ordeal of Richard Feverel (1859) ch. 28

17 Speech is the small change of silence.
The Ordeal of Richard Feverel (1859) ch. 34

18 The lark ascending.
title of poem (1881)

19 She whom I love is hard to catch and conquer,
Hard, but O the glory of the winning were she won!
'Love in the Valley' st. 2

20 On a starred night Prince Lucifer uprose.
Tired of his dark dominion swung the fiend . . .
He reached a middle height, and at the stars,
Which are the brain of heaven, he looked, and sank.
Around the ancient track marched, rank on rank,
The army of unalterable law.
'Lucifer in Starlight' (1883)

21 Not till the fire is dying in the grate,
Look we for any kinship with the stars.
Modern Love (1862) st. 4

22 Ah, what a dusty answer gets the soul
When hot for certainties in this our life!
Modern Love (1862) st. 50

23 Enter these enchanted woods,
You who dare.
'The Woods of Westermain' (1883)

Owen Meredith (Edward Robert Bulwer Lytton, Lord Lytton) 1831–91
English poet and statesman; Viceroy of India, 1876–80

24 Genius does what it must, and Talent does what it can.
'Last Words of a Sensitive Second-Rate Poet' (1868)

Bob Merrill 1921–98
American songwriter and composer

25 How much is that doggie in the window?
title of song (1953)

26 People who need people are the luckiest people in the world.
'People who Need People' (1964 song)

James Merrill 1926–95

American poet

1 Each thirteenth year he married. When he died
There were already several chilled wives
In sable orbit—rings, cars, permanent waves.
We'd felt him warming up for a green bride.
He could afford it. He was 'in his prime'
And three score ten. But money was not time.
'The Broken Home' (1966)

2 Always that same old story—
Father Time and Mother Earth,
a marriage on the rocks.
'The Broken Home' (1966)

Dixon Lanier Merritt 1879–1972

American editor

3 Oh, a wondrous bird is the pelican!
His bill will hold more than his belican.
He can take in his beak
Enough food for a week
But I'm damned if I see how the helican.
adapted from the original in *Nashville Banner* 22 April
1913

W. S. Merwin 1927–

American poet

4 Sometimes it is inconceivable that I should be the
age I am.
'The Child' (1968)

5 This is the black sea-brute bulling through wave-
wrack,
Ancient as ocean's shifting hills.
'Leviathan' (1956)

6 The sea curling
Star-climbed, wind-combed, cumbered with itself
still
As at first it was, is the hand not yet contented
Of the Creator. And he waits for the world to
begin.
'Leviathan' (1956)

Jean Meslier c.1664–1733

French priest

7 I remember, on this matter, the wish made once
by an ignorant, uneducated man . . . He said he
wished . . . that all the great men in the world and
all the nobility could be hanged, and strangled
with the guts of priests. For myself . . . I wish I
could have the strength of Hercules to purge the
world of all vice and sin, and to have the pleasure
of destroying all those monsters of error and sin
[priests] who make all the peoples of the world
groan so pitiably.
*often quoted as 'I should like . . . the last of the kings
to be strangled with the guts of the last priest'*
Testament (ed. R. Charles, 1864) vol. I, ch. 2; see **Diderot**
273:17

Methodist Service Book 1975

8 I am no longer my own, but yours. Put me to
what you will, rank me with whom you will; put
me to doing, put me to suffering; let me be
employed for you or laid aside for you, exalted for
you or brought low for you; let me be full, let me
be empty; let me have all things, let me have
nothing.
The Covenant Prayer (based on the words of Richard
Alleine in the First Covenant Service, 1782)

Prince Metternich 1773–1859

Austrian statesman

9 The greatest gift of any statesman rests not in
knowing what concessions to make, but
recognising when to make them.
Concessionen und Nichtconcessionen (1852)

10 The word 'freedom' means for me not a point of
departure but a genuine point of arrival. The point
of departure is defined by the word 'order'.
Freedom cannot exist without the concept of
order.
Mein Politisches Testament in *Aus Metternich's
Nachgelassenen Papieren* (ed. A. von Klinkowström, 1880)
vol. 7

11 Italy is a geographical expression.
discussing the Italian question with **Palmerston** *in
1847*
Mémoires, Documents, etc. de Metternich publiés par son fils
(1883) vol. 7

12 I feel obliged to call to the supporters of the social
uprising: Citizens of a dream-world, nothing is
altered. On 14 March 1848, there was merely one
man fewer.
of his own downfall
Aus Metternich's Nachgelassenen Papieren (ed. A. von
Klinkowström, 1880) vol. 8

13 The Emperor is everything, Vienna is nothing.
letter to Count Bombelles, 5 June 1848, in *Aus Metternich's
Nachgelassenen Papieren* (ed. A. von Klinkowström, 1880)
vol. 8

14 *L'erreur n'a jamais approché de mon esprit.*
Error has never approached my spirit.
addressed to Guizot in 1848, in François Pierre G. Guizot
Mémoires (1858–67) vol. 4

Charlotte Mew 1869–1928

English poet

15 She sleeps up in the attic there
Alone, poor maid. 'Tis but a stair
Betwixt us. Oh! my God! the down,
The soft young down of her, the brown,
The brown of her—her eyes, her hair, her hair!
'The Farmer's Bride' (1916)

Anthony Meyer 1920–

British Conservative politician

16 I question the right of that great Moloch, national
sovereignty, to burn its children to save its pride.
speaking against the Falklands War, 1982
in *Listener* 27 September 1990

Michelangelo 1475–1564
Italian sculptor, painter, architect, and poet

1 The marble not yet carved can hold the form
Of every thought the greatest artist has.
Sonnet 15, translated by Elizabeth Jennings

2 Love is a beautiful image
Imagined or seen within the heart,
The friend of virtue and gentility.
Sonnet 38, translated by Robert J. Clements

3 I've finished that chapel I was painting. The Pope
is quite satisfied.
on completing the ceiling of the Sistine chapel
letter to his father, October 1512; E. H. Ramsden (ed.) *The
Letters of Michelangelo* (1963)

4 Trifles make perfection, and perfection is no trifle.
attributed; Samuel Smiles *Self-Help* (1859) ch. 5

Jules Michelet 1798–1874
French historian

5 What is the first part of politics? Education. The
second? Education. And the third? Education.
Le Peuple (1846); see **Blair** 118:16

6 England is an empire, Germany is a nation, a race,
France is a person.
Histoire de France (1833–1867)

William Julius Mickle 1735–88
Scottish poet

7 For there's nae luck about the house,
There's nae luck at a',
There's little pleasure in the house
When our gudeman's awa.
'The Mariner's Wife' (1769)

Thomas Middleton c.1580–1627
English dramatist

8 Anything for a quiet life.
title of play (written *c.*1620, possibly with John Webster);
see **Dickens** 272:10

9 I could not get the ring without the finger.
The Changeling (with William Rowley, *c.*1622) act 3, sc. 4

10 My study's ornament, thou shell of death,
Once the bright face of my betrothèd lady.
The Revenger's Tragedy (1607) act 1, sc. 1 (previously
attributed to Cyril Tourneur, *c.*1575–1626)

11 Nine coaches waiting—hurry, hurry, hurry.
The Revenger's Tragedy (1607) act 2, sc. 1

12 Does the silk-worm expend her yellow labours
For thee? for thee does she undo herself?
The Revenger's Tragedy (1607) act 3, sc. 5

Bette Midler 1945–
American actress

13 When it's three o'clock in New York, it's still
1938 in London.
attributed

Midrash
*ancient commentary on the Hebrew scriptures, dating from
the 2nd century* AD

14 The Holy One, blessed be He, makes ladders by
which He makes one go up, and another go down.
Leviticus Rabbah 8:1

15 The Holy One, blessed be He, waits for the nations
of the world in the hope that they will repent, and
be brought beneath His wings.
Numbers Rabbah 10:1

16 Whatever you think of your friend, he thinks the
same of you.
Sifre Deuteronomy, piska 24

17 The words of Torah are likened to fire. Just as fire
was given from heaven, so were the words of
Torah given from heaven . . . just as fire lives
forever, so do the words of Torah live forever.
Sifre Deuteronomy, piska 343

18 Should a person tell you there is wisdom among
the nations, believe it . . . if he tells you that there
is Torah among the nations, do not believe it.
Lamentations Rabbah 2:13

19 When a person enters the world his hands are
clenched as though to say, 'The whole world is
mine, I shall inherit it'; but when he takes leave of
it his hands are spread open as though to say, 'I
have inherited nothing from the world.'
Ecclesiastes Rabbah 5:14

20 A man cannot say to the Angel of Death, 'Wait for
me until I make up my accounts.'
Ecclesiastes Rabbah 8:8

21 While God's face is above, His heart is below.
Song of Songs Rabbah 4:4

Ludwig Mies van der Rohe 1886–1969
German-born architect and designer
see also **Proverbs** 625:5

22 God is in the details.
in *New York Times* 19 August 1969; also attributed to Aby
Warburg (1866–1929)

George Mikes 1912–
Hungarian-born writer

23 On the Continent people have good food; in
England people have good table manners.
How to be an Alien (1946)

24 An Englishman, even if he is alone, forms an
orderly queue of one.
How to be an Alien (1946) p. 44

William Porcher Miles 1822–96

1 'Vote early and vote often,' the advice openly
displayed on the election banners in one of our
northern cities.
in the House of Representatives, 31 March 1858

☐ **Military sayings, slogans, and songs**
see box overleaf

John Stuart Mill 1806–73

English philosopher and economist
*on Mill: see Bentley 68:15; see also **Epitaphs** 311:14*

2 Ask yourself whether you are happy, and you
cease to be so.
Autobiography (1873) ch. 5

3 No great improvements in the lot of mankind are
possible, until a great change takes place in the
fundamental constitution of their modes of
thought.
Autobiography (1873) ch. 7

4 The Conservatives . . . being by the law of their
existence the stupidest party.
Considerations on Representative Government (1861) ch. 7 n.

5 I will call no being good, who is not what I mean
when I apply that epithet to my fellow-creatures;
and if such a being can sentence me to hell for not
so calling him, to hell I will go.
Examination of Sir William Hamilton's Philosophy (1865)
ch. 7

6 The only purpose for which power can be
rightfully exercised over any member of a civilized
community, against his will, is to prevent harm to
others. His own good, either physical or moral, is
not a sufficient warrant.
On Liberty (1859) ch. 1

7 If all mankind minus one were of one opinion, and
only one person were of the contrary opinion,
mankind would be no more justified in silencing
that one person, than he, if he had the power,
would be justified in silencing mankind.
On Liberty (1859) ch. 2

8 A party of order or stability, and a party of
progress or reform, are both necessary elements of
a healthy state of political life.
On Liberty (1859) ch. 2

9 The liberty of the individual must be thus far
limited; he must not make himself a nuisance to
other people.
On Liberty (1859) ch. 3

10 Liberty consists in doing what one desires.
On Liberty (1859) ch. 5

11 A State which dwarfs its men, in order that they
may be more docile instruments in its hands even
for beneficial purposes, will find that with small
men no great thing can really be accomplished.
On Liberty (1859) ch. 5

12 The principle which regulates the existing social
relations between the two sexes—the legal
subordination of one sex to the other—is wrong in
itself, and now one of the chief hindrances to
human improvement.
The Subjection of Women (1869) ch. 1

13 What is now called the nature of women is an
eminently artificial thing—the result of forced
repression in some directions, unnatural
stimulation in others.
The Subjection of Women (1869) ch. 1

14 No slave is a slave to the same lengths, and in so
full a sense of the word, as a wife is.
The Subjection of Women (1869) ch. 2

15 The laws of most countries are far worse than the
people who execute them, and many of them are
only able to remain laws by being seldom or never
carried into effect. If married life were all that it
might be expected to be, looking to the laws alone,
society would be a hell upon earth.
The Subjection of Women (1869) ch. 2

16 The true virtue of human beings is fitness to live
together as equals; claiming nothing for
themselves but what they as freely concede to
everyone else; regarding command of any kind as
an exceptional necessity, and in all cases a
temporary one.
The Subjection of Women (1869) ch. 2

17 It is better to be a human being dissatisfied than a
pig satisfied; better to be Socrates dissatisfied than
a fool satisfied.
Utilitarianism (1863) ch. 2

18 The most important thing women have to do is to
stir up the zeal of women themselves.
*letter to Alexander Bain, 14 July 1869, in Hugh S. R. Elliot
(ed.) Letters of John Stuart Mill vol. 2 (1910)*

Edna St Vincent Millay 1892–1950

American poet

19 Childhood is the kingdom where nobody dies.
Nobody that matters, that is.
'Childhood is the Kingdom where Nobody dies' (1934)

20 Down, down, down into the darkness of the grave
Gently they go, the beautiful, the tender, the kind;
Quietly they go, the intelligent, the witty, the
brave.
I know. But I do not approve. And I am not
resigned.
'Dirge Without Music' (1928)

21 My candle burns at both ends;
It will not last the night;
But ah, my foes, and oh, my friends—
It gives a lovely light.
A Few Figs From Thistles (1920) 'First Fig'

22 Euclid alone
Has looked on Beauty bare. Fortunate they
Who, though once only and then but far away,
Have heard her massive sandal set on stone.
The Harp-Weaver and Other Poems (1923) sonnet 22

23 Justice denied in Massachusetts.
*relating to the trial of Sacco and **Vanzetti** and their
execution on 22 August 1927*
title of poem (1928)

Continued

Military sayings, slogans, and songs

1 Action this day.
annotation as used by Winston Churchill at the
Admiralty in 1940

2 All present and correct.
King's Regulations (Army) Report of the Orderly Sergeant
to the Officer of the Day

3 Any officer who shall behave in a scandalous
manner, unbecoming the character of an officer
and a gentleman shall . . . be CASHIERED.
Articles of War (1872) 'Disgraceful Conduct' Article 79;
the Naval Discipline Act, 10 August 1860, Article 24,
uses the words 'conduct unbecoming the character of an
Officer'

4 Are we downhearted? No!
expression much taken up by British soldiers during the
First World War; see **Chamberlain** 206:9

5 Conduct . . . to the prejudice of good order and
military discipline.
Army Discipline and Regulation Act (1879) Section 40

6 The difficult we do immediately; the impossible
takes a little longer.
US Armed Forces' slogan; see **Calonne** 186:5, **Nansen**
556:5, **Proverbs** 617:40

7 Every person subject to military law who . . .
spreads reports calculated to create unnecessary
alarm or despondency . . . shall . . . be liable to
suffer penal servitude.
Army Act (1879); see **Peniakoff** 591:14

8 Fifty million Frenchmen can't be wrong.
saying popular with American servicemen during the
First World War; later associated with Mae **West** and
Texas Guinan (1884–1933), it was also the title of a
1927 song by Billy Rose and Willie Raskin

9 From the halls of Montezuma,
To the shores of Tripoli,
We fight our country's battles,
On the land as on the sea.
'The Marines' Hymn' (1847)

10 If it moves, salute it; if it doesn't move, pick it
up; and if you can't pick it up, paint it.
1940s saying, in Paul Dickson *The Official Rules* (1978)

11 *Ils ne passeront pas.*
They shall not pass.
slogan used by the French army at the defence of Verdun
in 1916; variously attributed to Marshal **Pétain** and to
General Robert Nivelle, and taken up by the Republicans
in the Spanish Civil War in the form *'No pasarán!'*; see
Ibarruri 412:8

12 Lions led by donkeys.
*associated with British soldiers during the First
World War*
attributed to Max Hoffman (1869–1927) in Alan Clark
The Donkeys (1961); this attribution has not been traced
elsewhere, and the phrase is of much earlier origin:
Unceasingly they had drummed into them the
utterance of *The Times*: 'You are lions led by
packasses.'
of French troops defeated by Prussians
Francisque Sarcey *Paris during the Siege* (1871)

13 Loose lips sink ships.
American Second World war security slogan

14 Mademoiselle from Armenteers,
Hasn't been kissed for forty years,
Hinky, dinky, parley-voo.
song of the First World War, variously attributed to
Edward Rowland and to Harry Carlton

15 O Death, where is thy sting-a-ling-a-ling,
O grave, thy victory?
The bells of Hell go ting-a-ling-a-ling
For you but not for me.
'For You But Not For Me', in S. Louis Guiraud (ed.) *Songs
That Won the War* (1930); see **Bible** 108:12

16 She was poor but she was honest
Victim of a rich man's game.
First he loved her, then he left her,
And she lost her maiden name . . .
It's the same the whole world over,
It's the poor wot gets the blame,
It's the rich wot gets the gravy.
Ain't it all a bleedin' shame?
'She was Poor but she was Honest' (sung by British
soldiers in the First World War)

17 We're here
Because
We're here.
sung to the tune of 'Auld Lang Syne', in John Brophy
and Eric Partridge *Songs and Slang of the British Soldier
1914–18* (1930)

18 What's the use of worrying?
It never was worth while,
So, pack up your troubles in your old kit-bag,
And smile, smile, smile.
'Pack up your Troubles' (1915 song), written by George
Asaf (1880–1951)

19 Your King and Country need you.
recruitment slogan for First World War, coined by Eric
Field, July 1914; *Advertising* (1959); see **Rubens** 658:3

Edna St Vincent Millay *continued*

20 The sun that warmed our stooping backs and
withered the weeds uprooted—
We shall not feel it again.
We shall die in darkness, and be buried in the
rain.
'Justice Denied in Massachusetts' (1928)

21 Death devours all lovely things;
Lesbia with her sparrow
Shares the darkness—presently
Every bed is narrow.
'Passer Mortuus Est' (1921); see **Catullus** 202:11

Alice Duer Miller 1874–1942

American writer

1 I am American bred,
I have seen much to hate here—much to forgive,
But in a world where England is finished and
  dead,
I do not wish to live.
  The White Cliffs (1940)

Arthur Miller 1915–

American dramatist
on Miller: see **Newspaper headlines** *562:6*

2 A suicide kills two people, Maggie, that's what it's
for!
  After the Fall (1964) act 2

3 Death of a salesman.
  title of play (1949)

4 The world is an oyster, but you don't crack it open
on a mattress.
  Death of a Salesman (1949) act 1

5 Willy Loman never made a lot of money. His name
was never in the paper. He's not the finest
character that ever lived. But he's a human being,
and a terrible thing is happening to him. So
attention must be paid.
  Death of a Salesman (1949) act 1

6 He's a man way out there in the blue, riding on a
smile and a shoeshine. And when they start not
smiling back—that's an earthquake . . . A
salesman is got to dream, boy. It comes with the
territory.
  Death of a Salesman (1949) 'Requiem'

7 The car, the furniture, the wife, the children—
everything has to be disposable. Because you see
the main thing today is—shopping.
  The Price (1968) act 1

8 This is Red Hook, not Sicily . . . This is the gullet of
New York swallowing the tonnage of the world.
  A View from the Bridge (1955) act 1

9 A good newspaper, I suppose, is a nation talking
to itself.
  in *Observer* 26 November 1961

Henry Miller 1891–1980

American novelist

10 Every man with a bellyful of the classics is an
enemy to the human race.
  Tropic of Cancer (1934)

Jonathan Miller 1934–

English writer and director

11 In fact, I'm not really a *Jew*. Just Jew-*ish*. Not the
whole hog, you know.
  Beyond the Fringe (1960 review) 'Real Class'

Spike Milligan (Terence Alan Milligan) 1918–2002

Irish comedian
see also **Catchphrases** *201:1,* **Catchphrases** *202:6,*
Catchphrases *202:8*

12 Money couldn't buy friends but you got a better
class of enemy.
  Puckoon (1963) ch. 6

A. J. Mills, Fred Godfrey, and Bennett Scott

British songwriters

13 Take me back to dear old Blighty.
  title of song (1916)

Irving Mills 1894–1985

14 It don't mean a thing
If it ain't got that swing.
  'It Don't Mean a Thing' (1932 song; music by Duke
  Ellington)

Henry Hart Milman 1791–1868

English clergyman

15 Ride on! ride on in majesty!
The wingèd squadrons of the sky
Look down with sad and wond'ring eyes
To see the approaching sacrifice.
  'Ride on! ride on in majesty!' (1827 hymn)

A. A. Milne 1882–1956

English writer for children

16 The more he looked inside the more Piglet wasn't
there.
  The House at Pooh Corner (1928) ch. 1

17 'I don't *want* him,' said Rabbit. 'But it's always
useful to know where a friend-and-relation *is*,
whether you want him or whether you don't.'
  The House at Pooh Corner (1928) ch. 3

18 He respects Owl, because you can't help respecting
anybody who can spell TUESDAY, even if he doesn't
spell it right; but spelling isn't everything. There
are days when spelling Tuesday simply doesn't
count.
  The House at Pooh Corner (1928) ch. 5

19 When you are a Bear of Very Little Brain, and you
Think of Things, you find sometimes that a Thing
which seemed very Thingish inside you is quite
different when it gets out into the open and has
other people looking at it.
  The House at Pooh Corner (1928) ch. 6

20 They're changing guard at Buckingham Palace—
Christopher Robin went down with Alice.
Alice is marrying one of the guard.
'A soldier's life is terrible hard,'
Says Alice.
  When We Were Very Young (1924) 'Buckingham Palace'

21 James James
Morrison Morrison

Weatherby George Dupree
Took great
Care of his Mother,
Though he was only three.
James James
Said to his Mother,
'Mother,' he said, said he;
'You must never go down to the end of the town,
   if you don't go down with me.'
   When We Were Very Young (1924) 'Disobedience'

1 There once was a Dormouse who lived in a bed
Of delphiniums (blue) and geraniums (red),
And all the day long he'd a wonderful view
Of geraniums (red) and delphiniums (blue).
   When We Were Very Young (1924) 'The Dormouse and the
   Doctor'

2 The King asked
The Queen, and
The Queen asked
The Dairymaid:
'Could we have some butter for
The Royal slice of bread?'
   When We Were Very Young (1924) 'The King's Breakfast'

3 And some of the bigger bears try to pretend
That they came round the corner to look for a
   friend;
And they try to pretend that nobody cares
Whether you walk on the lines or squares.
   When We Were Very Young (1924) 'Lines and Squares'

4 *What* is the matter with Mary Jane?
She's perfectly well and she hasn't a pain,
And it's lovely rice pudding for dinner again!
What *is* the matter with Mary Jane?
   When We Were Very Young (1924) 'Rice Pudding'

5 Little Boy kneels at the foot of the bed,
Droops on the little hands little gold head.
Hush! Hush! Whisper who dares!
Christopher Robin is saying his prayers.
   When We Were Very Young (1924) 'Vespers'; see **Morton**
   551:5

6 Isn't it funny
How a bear likes honey?
Buzz! Buzz! Buzz!
I wonder why he does?
   Winnie-the-Pooh (1926) ch. 1

7 How sweet to be a Cloud
Floating in the Blue!
It makes him very proud
To be a little cloud.
   Winnie-the-Pooh (1926) ch. 1

8 'Pathetic,' he [Eeyore] said. 'That's what it is.
Pathetic.'
   Winnie-the-Pooh (1926) ch. 6

9 Time for a little something.
   Winnie-the-Pooh (1926) ch. 6

10 My spelling is Wobbly. It's good spelling but it
Wobbles, and the letters get in the wrong places.
   Winnie-the-Pooh (1926) ch. 6

11 Owl hasn't exactly got Brain, but he Knows
Things.
   Winnie-the-Pooh (1926) ch. 9

12 Eeyore was saying to himself, 'This writing
business. Pencils and what-not. Over-rated, if you
ask me. Silly stuff. Nothing in it.'
   Winnie-the-Pooh (1926) ch. 10

Lord Milner 1854–1925
British colonial administrator

13 If we believe a thing to be bad, and if we have a
right to prevent it, it is our duty to try to prevent it
and to damn the consequences.
   speech in Glasgow, 26 November 1909, in *The Times* 27
   November 1909

John Milton 1608–74
English poet
on Milton: see **Aubrey** 33:19, **Aubrey** 33:20, **Aubrey** 33:21,
Blake 120:21, **Byron** 181:8, **Gray** 361:19, **Johnson** 425:8,
Johnson 432:15, **Tennyson** 782:10, **Wordsworth** 847:14

14 Such sweet compulsion doth in music lie.
   'Arcades' (1645) l. 68

15 Blest pair of Sirens, pledges of heaven's joy,
Sphere-born harmonious sisters, Voice, and Verse.
   'At a Solemn Music' (1645)

16 Where the bright seraphim in burning row
Their loud uplifted angel trumpets blow.
   'At a Solemn Music' (1645)

17 Above the smoke and stir of this dim spot,
Which men call earth.
   Comus (1637) l. 5

18 Yet some there be that by due steps aspire
To lay their just hands on that golden key
That opes the palace of eternity.
   Comus (1637) l. 12

19 An old and haughty nation proud in arms.
   Comus (1637) l. 33

20 And the gilded car of day
His glowing axle doth allay
In the steep Atlantic stream.
   Comus (1637) l. 95

21 What hath night to do with sleep?
   Comus (1637) l. 122

22 Come, knit hands, and beat the ground,
In a light fantastic round.
   Comus (1637) l. 143

23 Sweet Echo, sweetest nymph that liv'st unseen
Within thy airy shell
By slow Meander's margent green,
And in the violet-embroidered vale.
   Comus (1637) l. 230

24 Virtue could see to do what Virtue would
By her own radiant light, though sun and moon
Were in the flat sea sunk.
   Comus (1637) l. 373

25 Yet where an equal poise of hope and fear
Does arbitrate the event, my nature is
That I incline to hope, rather than fear,
And gladly banish squint suspicion.
   Comus (1637) l. 410

1 'Tis chastity, my brother, chastity:
  She that has that, is clad in complete steel.
  Comus (1637) l. 420

2 How charming is divine philosophy!
  Not harsh and crabbèd, as dull fools suppose,
  But musical as is Apollo's lute.
  Comus (1637) l. 475

3 Storied of old in high immortal verse
  Of dire chimeras and enchanted isles,
  And rifted rocks whose entrance leads to hell.
  Comus (1637) l. 516

4 And filled the air with barbarous dissonance.
  Comus (1637) l. 550

5   Against the threats
  Of malice or of sorcery, or that power
  Which erring men call chance, this I hold firm,
  Virtue may be assailed, but never hurt,
  Surprised by unjust force, but not enthralled.
  Comus (1637) l. 586

6 Those budge doctors of the Stoic fur.
  Comus (1637) l. 707

7 Sabrina fair,
  Listen where thou art sitting
  Under the glassy, cool, translucent wave,
  In twisted braids of lilies knitting
  The loose train of thy amber-dropping hair.
  Comus (1637) l. 859 'Song'

8 Thus I set my printless feet
  O'er the cowslip's velvet head,
  That bends not as I tread.
  Comus (1637) l. 897

9 Hence, vain deluding joys,
  The brood of folly without father bred.
  'Il Penseroso' (1645) l. 1

10 Come, pensive nun, devout and pure,
  Sober, steadfast, and demure.
  'Il Penseroso' (1645) l. 31

11 Sweet bird that shunn'st the noise of folly,
  Most musical, most melancholy!
  'Il Penseroso' (1645) l. 61

12 Where glowing embers through the room
  Teach light to counterfeit a gloom,
  Far from all resort of mirth,
  Save the cricket on the hearth.
  'Il Penseroso' (1645) l. 79

13 Or bid the soul of Orpheus sing
  Such notes as warbled to the string,
  Drew iron tears down Pluto's cheek.
  'Il Penseroso' (1645) l. 105

14 Where more is meant than meets the ear.
  'Il Penseroso' (1645) l. 120

15 Hide me from day's garish eye.
  'Il Penseroso' (1645) l. 141; see **Newman** 561:6

16 And storied windows richly dight,
  Casting a dim religious light.
  'Il Penseroso' (1645) l. 159

17 Hence, loathèd Melancholy,
  Of Cerberus, and blackest Midnight born,

In Stygian cave forlorn
  'Mongst horrid shapes, and shrieks, and sights
    unholy.
  'L'Allegro' (1645) l. 1

18 So buxom, blithe, and debonair.
  of Euphrosyne [Mirth], *one of the three Graces*
  'L'Allegro' (1645) l. 24

19 Nods, and becks, and wreathèd smiles.
  'L'Allegro' (1645) l. 28

20 Sport that wrinkled Care derides,
  And Laughter holding both his sides.
  Come, and trip it as ye go
  On the light fantastic toe.
  'L'Allegro' (1645) l. 31

21 Right against the eastern gate,
  Where the great sun begins his state.
  'L'Allegro' (1645) l. 59

22 And the milkmaid singeth blithe,
  And the mower whets his scythe,
  And every shepherd tells his tale
  Under the hawthorn in the dale.
  'L'Allegro' (1645) l. 65

23 Meadows trim with daisies pied,
  Shallow brooks, and rivers wide.
  'L'Allegro' (1645) l. 75

24 Where perhaps some beauty lies,
  The cynosure of neighbouring eyes.
  'L'Allegro' (1645) l. 79

25 Then to the spicy nut-brown ale.
  'L'Allegro' (1645) l. 100

26 Towered cities please us then,
  And the busy hum of men.
  'L'Allegro' (1645) l. 117

27 Such sights as youthful poets dream
  On summer eves by haunted stream.
  Then to the well-trod stage anon,
  If Jonson's learnèd sock be on,
  Or sweetest Shakespeare fancy's child,
  Warble his native wood-notes wild.
  'L'Allegro' (1645) l. 129

28 Let us with a gladsome mind
  Praise the Lord, for he is kind,
  For his mercies ay endure,
  Ever faithful, ever sure.
  'Let us with a gladsome mind' (1645); paraphrase of Psalm
  136; see **Book of Common Prayer** 143:11

29 Yet once more, O ye laurels, and once more
  Ye myrtles brown, with ivy never sere.
  'Lycidas' (1638) l. 1

30 Bitter constraint, and sad occasion dear,
  Compels me to disturb your season due;
  For Lycidas is dead, dead ere his prime,
  Young Lycidas, and hath not left his peer:
  Who would not sing for Lycidas?
  'Lycidas' (1638) l. 6

31 He must not float upon his watery bier
  Unwept, and welter to the parching wind,
  Without the meed of some melodious tear.
  'Lycidas' (1638) l. 12

1 For we were nursed upon the self-same hill.
  'Lycidas' (1638) l. 23

2 Were it not better done as others use,
  To sport with Amaryllis in the shade,
  Or with the tangles of Neaera's hair?
  Fame is the spur that the clear spirit doth raise
  (That last infirmity of noble mind)
  To scorn delights, and live laborious days.
  'Lycidas' (1638) l. 67

3 Comes the blind Fury with th' abhorrèd shears,
  And slits the thin-spun life.
  'Lycidas' (1638) l. 75

4 Fame is no plant that grows on mortal soil.
  'Lycidas' (1638) l. 78

5 Last came, and last did go,
  The pilot of the Galilean lake,
  Two massy keys he bore of metals twain
  (The golden opes, the iron shuts amain).
  'Lycidas' (1638) l. 108

6 Their lean and flashy songs
  Grate on their scrannel pipes of wretched straw,
  The hungry sheep look up, and are not fed.
  'Lycidas' (1638) l. 123

7 But that two-handed engine at the door
  Stands ready to smite once, and smite no more.
  'Lycidas' (1638) l. 130

8 Bring the rathe primrose that forsaken dies,
  The tufted crow-toe, and pale jessamine.
  'Lycidas' (1638) l. 142

9 Look homeward angel now, and melt with ruth.
  'Lycidas' (1638) l. 163

10 So sinks the day-star in the ocean bed,
  And yet anon repairs his drooping head,
  And tricks his beams, and with new spangled ore,
  Flames in the forehead of the morning sky.
  'Lycidas' (1638) l. 168

11 Through the dear might of Him that walked the
  waves.
  'Lycidas' (1638) l. 173

12 While the still morn went out with sandals grey.
  'Lycidas' (1638) l. 187

13 At last he rose, and twitched his mantle blue:
  Tomorrow to fresh woods, and pastures new.
  'Lycidas' (1638) l. 192

14 What needs my Shakespeare for his honoured
  bones,
  The labour of an age in pilèd stones.
  'On Shakespeare' (1632)

15 O fairest flower no sooner blown but blasted,
  Soft silken primrose fading timelessly.
  'On the Death of a Fair Infant Dying of a Cough' (1673)
  st. 1

16 For what can war, but endless war still breed?
  'On the Lord General Fairfax at the Siege of Colchester'
  (written 1648)

17 This is the month, and this the happy morn
  Wherein the son of heaven's eternal king,
  Of wedded maid, and virgin mother born,

Our great redemption from above did bring.
  'On the Morning of Christ's Nativity' (1645) st. 1

18 The star-led wizards haste with odours sweet.
  'On the Morning of Christ's Nativity' (1645) st. 4

19 It was the winter wild,
  While the heaven-born-child
  All meanly wrapped in the rude manger lies;
  Nature in awe to him
  Had doffed her gaudy trim,
  With her great master so to sympathize.
  'On the Morning of Christ's Nativity' (1645) 'The Hymn'
  st. 1

20 The helmèd cherubim
  And sworded seraphim
  Are seen in glittering ranks with wings displayed.
  'On the Morning of Christ's Nativity' (1645) 'The Hymn'
  st. 11

21 Ring out, ye crystal spheres,
  Once bless our human ears
  (If ye have power to touch our senses so),
  And let your silver chime
  Move in melodious time;
  And let the base of heaven's deep organ blow,
  And with your ninefold harmony
  Make up full consort to the angelic symphony.
  'On the Morning of Christ's Nativity' (1645) 'The Hymn'
  st. 13

22 Time will run back, and fetch the age of gold.
  'On the Morning of Christ's Nativity' (1645) 'The Hymn'
  st. 14

23 And hell itself will pass away,
  And leave her dolorous mansions to the peering
  day.
  'On the Morning of Christ's Nativity' (1645) 'The Hymn'
  st. 14

24 Swinges the scaly horror of his folded tail.
  'On the Morning of Christ's Nativity' (1645) 'The Hymn'
  st. 18

25 The oracles are dumb,
  No voice or hideous hum
  Runs through the archèd roof in words deceiving.
  Apollo from his shrine
  Can no more divine,
  With hollow shriek the steep of Delphos leaving.
  'On the Morning of Christ's Nativity' (1645) 'The Hymn'
  st. 19

26 So when the sun in bed,
  Curtained with cloudy red,
  Pillows his chin upon an orient wave.
  'On the Morning of Christ's Nativity' (1645) 'The Hymn'
  st. 26

27 Time is our tedious song should here have ending.
  'On the Morning of Christ's Nativity' (1645) 'The Hymn'
  st. 27

28 New *Presbyter* is but old *Priest* writ large.
  'On the New Forcers of Conscience under the Long
  Parliament' (1646)

29 Fly envious Time, till thou run out thy race,
  Call on the lazy leaden-stepping hours.
  'On Time' (1645)

1 If any ask for him, it shall be said,
Hobson has supped, and's newly gone to bed.
'On the University Carrier' (1645)

2 Rhyme being . . . but the invention of a barbarous
age, to set off wretched matter and lame metre.
Paradise Lost (1667) 'The Verse' (preface, added 1668)

3 The troublesome and modern bondage of
rhyming.
Paradise Lost (1667) 'The Verse' (preface, added 1668)

4 Of man's first disobedience, and the fruit
Of that forbidden tree, whose mortal taste
Brought death into the world, and all our woe,
With loss of Eden.
Paradise Lost (1667) bk. 1, l. 1

5 Things unattempted yet in prose or rhyme.
Paradise Lost (1667) bk. 1, l. 16

6 What in me is dark
Illumine, what is low raise and support;
That to the height of this great argument
I may assert eternal providence,
And justify the ways of God to men.
Paradise Lost (1667) bk. 1, l. 22; see **Housman** 405:2, **Pope**
604:18

7 The infernal serpent; he it was, whose guile
Stirred up with envy and revenge, deceived
The mother of mankind.
Paradise Lost (1667) bk. 1, l. 34

8 No light, but rather darkness visible
Served only to discover sights of woe.
Paradise Lost (1667) bk. 1, l. 63

9 What though the field be lost?
All is not lost; the unconquerable will,
And study of revenge, immortal hate,
And courage never to submit or yield.
Paradise Lost (1667) bk. 1, l. 105

10 To do aught good never will be our task,
But ever to do ill our sole delight.
Paradise Lost (1667) bk. 1, l. 159

11 And out of good still to find means of evil.
Paradise Lost (1667) bk. 1, l. 165

12 What reinforcement we may gain from hope;
If not, what resolution from despair.
Paradise Lost (1667) bk. 1, l. 190

13 The will
And high permission of all-ruling heaven
Left him at large to his own dark designs,
That with reiterated crimes he might
Heap on himself damnation.
Paradise Lost (1667) bk. 1, l. 211

14 The mind is its own place, and in itself
Can make a heaven of hell, a hell of heaven.
Paradise Lost (1667) bk. 1, l. 254

15 Better to reign in hell, than serve in heaven.
Paradise Lost (1667) bk. 1, l. 263

16 His spear, to equal which the tallest pine
Hewn on Norwegian hills, to be the mast
Of some great admiral, were but a wand,
He walked with to support uneasy steps
Over the burning marl.
Paradise Lost (1667) bk. 1, l. 292

17 Thick as autumnal leaves that strew the brooks
In Vallombrosa, where the Etrurian shades
High overarched imbower.
Paradise Lost (1667) bk. 1, l. 302

18 First Moloch, horrid king besmeared with blood
Of human sacrifice, and parents' tears.
Paradise Lost (1667) bk. 1, l. 392

19 Astarte, queen of heaven, with crescent horns.
Paradise Lost (1667) bk. 1, l. 439

20 Thammuz came next behind,
Whose annual wound in Lebanon allured
The Syrian damsels to lament his fate
In amorous ditties all a summer's day,
While smooth Adonis from his native rock
Ran purple to the sea.
Paradise Lost (1667) bk. 1, l. 446

21 And when night
Darkens the streets, then wander forth the sons
Of Belial, flown with insolence and wine.
Paradise Lost (1667) bk. 1, l. 500

22 The imperial ensign, which full high advanced
Shone like a meteor streaming to the wind.
Paradise Lost (1667) bk. 1, l. 536; see **Gray** 360:21

23 A shout that tore hell's concave, and beyond
Frighted the reign of Chaos and old Night.
Paradise Lost (1667) bk. 1, l. 542

24 Who overcomes
By force, hath overcome but half his foe.
Paradise Lost (1667) bk. 1, l. 648

25 Mammon led them on,
Mammon, the least erected spirit that fell
From heaven, for even in heaven his looks and
thoughts
Were always downward bent, admiring more
The riches of heaven's pavement, trodden gold,
Than aught divine or holy else enjoyed
In vision beatific.
Paradise Lost (1667) bk. 1, l. 678

26 Let none admire
That riches grow in hell; that soil may best
Deserve the precious bane.
Paradise Lost (1667) bk. 1, l. 690

27 From morn
To noon he fell, from noon to dewy eve,
A summer's day; and with the setting sun
Dropped from the zenith like a falling star.
Paradise Lost (1667) bk. 1, l. 742

28 Pandemonium, the high capital
Of Satan and his peers.
Paradise Lost (1667) bk. 1, l. 756

29 High on a throne of royal state, which far
Outshone the wealth of Ormuz and of Ind,
Or where the gorgeous East with richest hand
Showers on her kings barbaric pearl and gold,
Satan exalted sat, by merit raised
To that bad eminence.
Paradise Lost (1667) bk. 2, l. 1

30 Belial, in act more graceful and humane;
A fairer person lost not heaven; he seemed

For dignity composed and high exploit:
But all was false and hollow; though his tongue
Dropped manna, and could make the worse
  appear
The better reason.
  Paradise Lost (1667) bk. 2, l. 109; see **Aristophanes** 25:3

1 To perish rather, swallowed up and lost
In the wide womb of uncreated night,
Devoid of sense and motion?
  Paradise Lost (1667) bk. 2, l. 149

2 Thus Belial with words clothed in reason's garb
Counselled ignoble ease, and peaceful sloth,
Not peace.
  Paradise Lost (1667) bk. 2, l. 226

3 Our torments also may in length of time
Become our elements.
  Paradise Lost (1667) bk. 2, l. 274

4   With grave
Aspect he rose, and in his rising seemed
A pillar of state; deep on his front engraven
Deliberation sat and public care;
And princely counsel in his face yet shone,
Majestic though in ruin.
  Paradise Lost (1667) bk. 2, l. 300

5   To sit in darkness here
Hatching vain empires.
  Paradise Lost (1667) bk. 2, l. 377

6 And through the palpable obscure find out
His uncouth way.
  Paradise Lost (1667) bk. 2, l. 406

7   Long is the way
And hard, that out of hell leads up to light.
  Paradise Lost (1667) bk. 2, l. 432

8 For eloquence the soul, song charms the sense.
  Paradise Lost (1667) bk. 2, l. 556

9 Of good and evil much they argued then,
Of happiness and final misery,
Passion and apathy, and glory and shame,
Vain wisdom all, and false philosophy.
  Paradise Lost (1667) bk. 2, l. 562

10 O'er many a frozen, many a fiery alp,
Rocks, caves, lakes, fens, bogs, dens, and shades of
  death,
A universe of death, which God by curse
Created evil.
  Paradise Lost (1667) bk. 2, l. 620

11   Black it stood as night,
Fierce as ten Furies, terrible as hell,
And shook a dreadful dart.
  Paradise Lost (1667) bk. 2, l. 670

12 Incensed with indignation Satan stood
Unterrified, and like a comet burned
That fires the length of Ophiuchus huge
In the Arctic sky, and from his horrid hair
Shakes pestilence and war.
  Paradise Lost (1667) bk. 2, l. 707

13   Chaos umpire sits,
And by decision more embroils the fray
By which he reigns; next him high arbiter

Chance governs all.
  Paradise Lost (1667) bk. 2, l. 907

14 Sable-vested Night, eldest of things.
  Paradise Lost (1667) bk. 2, l. 962

15 With ruin upon ruin, rout on rout,
Confusion worse confounded.
  Paradise Lost (1667) bk. 2, l. 995

16 So he with difficulty and labour hard
Moved on, with difficulty and labour he.
  Paradise Lost (1667) bk. 2, l. 1021

17 Die he or justice must.
  Paradise Lost (1667) bk. 3, l. 210; see **Andrewes** 14:10

18 Dark with excessive bright.
  Paradise Lost (1667) bk. 3, l. 380

19 So on this windy sea of land, the fiend
Walked up and down alone bent on his prey.
  Paradise Lost (1667) bk. 3, l. 440

20 Into a limbo large and broad, since called
The Paradise of Fools, to few unknown.
  Paradise Lost (1667) bk. 3, l. 495

21 Hypocrisy, the only evil that walks
Invisible, except to God alone.
  Paradise Lost (1667) bk. 3, l. 683

22   At whose sight all the stars
Hide their diminished heads.
  Paradise Lost (1667) bk. 4, l. 34

23 Warring in heaven against heaven's matchless
  king.
  Paradise Lost (1667) bk. 4, l. 41

24 Me miserable! which way shall I fly
Infinite wrath, and infinite despair?
Which way I fly is hell; myself am hell.
  Paradise Lost (1667) bk. 4, l. 73

25 Farewell remorse! All good to me is lost;
Evil, be thou my good.
  Paradise Lost (1667) bk. 4, l. 109

26 Thence up he flew, and on the tree of life,
The middle tree and highest there that grew,
Sat like a cormorant.
  Paradise Lost (1667) bk. 4, l. 194

27 Groves whose rich trees wept odorous gums and
  balm,
Others whose fruit burnished with golden rind
Hung amiable, Hesperian fables true,
If true, here only.
  Paradise Lost (1667) bk. 4, l. 248

28 Flowers of all hue, and without thorn the rose.
  Paradise Lost (1667) bk. 4, l. 256

29   Not that fair field
Of Enna, where Proserpine gathering flowers
Herself a fairer flower by gloomy Dis
Was gathered, which cost Ceres all that pain.
  Paradise Lost (1667) bk. 4, l. 268

30 For contemplation he and valour formed,
For softness she and sweet attractive grace,
He for God only, she for God in him.
  Paradise Lost (1667) bk. 4, l. 297

1 Yielded with coy submission, modest pride,
And sweet reluctant amorous delay.
Paradise Lost (1667) bk. 4, l. 310

2 Adam, the goodliest man of men since born
His sons, the fairest of her daughters Eve.
Paradise Lost (1667) bk. 4, l. 323

3 These two
Emparadised in one another's arms
The happier Eden, shall enjoy their fill
Of bliss on bliss.
Paradise Lost (1667) bk. 4, l. 505

4 Now came still evening on, and twilight grey
Had in her sober livery all things clad.
Paradise Lost (1667) bk. 4, l. 598

5 Now glowed the firmament
With living sapphires: Hesperus that led
The starry host, rode brightest, till the moon
Rising in clouded majesty, at length
Apparent queen unveiled her peerless light,
And o'er the dark her silver mantle threw.
Paradise Lost (1667) bk. 4, l. 604

6 With thee conversing I forget all time.
Paradise Lost (1667) bk. 4, l. 639

7 Millions of spiritual creatures walk the earth
Unseen, both when we wake, and when we sleep.
Paradise Lost (1667) bk. 4, l. 677

8 Nor turned I ween
Adam from his fair spouse, nor Eve the rites
Mysterious of connubial love refused.
Paradise Lost (1667) bk. 4, l. 741

9 Sleep on
Blest pair; and O yet happiest if ye seek
No happier state, and know to know no more.
Paradise Lost (1667) bk. 4, l. 773

10 Him there they found
Squat like a toad, close at the ear of Eve.
Paradise Lost (1667) bk. 4, l. 799

11 But wherefore thou alone? Wherefore with thee
Came not all hell broke loose?
Paradise Lost (1667) bk. 4, l. 917

12 My fairest, my espoused, my latest found,
Heaven's last best gift, my ever new delight.
Paradise Lost (1667) bk. 5, l. 18

13 Best image of myself and dearer half.
Paradise Lost (1667) bk. 5, l. 95

14 Nor jealousy
Was understood, the injured lover's hell.
Paradise Lost (1667) bk. 5, l. 449

15 What if earth
Be but the shadow of heaven, and things therein
Each to other like, more than on earth is thought?
Paradise Lost (1667) bk. 5, l. 574

16 Hear all ye angels, progeny of light,
Thrones, dominations, princedoms, virtues,
powers.
Paradise Lost (1667) bk. 5, l. 600; see **Bible** 110:10

17 All seemed well pleased, all seemed, but were not
all.
Paradise Lost (1667) bk. 5, l. 617

18 Mystical dance, which yonder starry sphere
Of planets and of fixed in all her wheels
Resembles nearest, mazes intricate,
Eccentric intervolved, yet regular
Then most, when most irregular they seem,
And in their motions harmony divine
So smoothes her charming tones, that God's own
ear
Listens delighted.
Paradise Lost (1667) bk. 5, l. 620

19 Satan, so call him now, his former name
Is heard no more in heaven.
Paradise Lost (1667) bk. 5, l. 658

20 Servant of God, well done, well hast thou fought
The better fight, who single has maintained
Against revolted multitudes the cause
Of truth, in word mightier than they in arms.
Paradise Lost (1667) bk. 6, l. 29

21 Still govern thou my song,
Urania, and fit audience find, though few.
Paradise Lost (1667) bk. 7, l. 30

22 There Leviathan
Hugest of living creatures, on the deep
Stretched like a promontory sleeps or swims,
And seems a moving land, and at his gills
Draws in, and at his trunk spouts out a sea.
Paradise Lost (1667) bk. 7, l. 412

23 The planets in their stations listening stood,
While the bright pomp ascended jubilant.
Open, ye everlasting gates, they sung,
Open, ye heavens, your living doors; let in
The great creator from his work returned
Magnificent, his six days' work, a world.
Paradise Lost (1667) bk. 7, l. 563

24 In solitude
What happiness? who can enjoy alone,
Or all enjoying, what contentment find?
Paradise Lost (1667) bk. 8, l. 364

25 So absolute she seems
And in herself complete, so well to know
Her own, that what she wills to do or say
Seems wisest, virtuousest, discreetest, best.
Paradise Lost (1667) bk. 8, l. 547

26 Oft-times nothing profits more
Than self esteem, grounded on just and right
Well managed.
Paradise Lost (1667) bk. 8, l. 571; see **Leavis** 478:5

27 The serpent subtlest beast of all the field.
Paradise Lost (1667) bk. 9, l. 86

28 As one who long in populous city pent,
Where houses thick and sewers annoy the air,
Forth issuing on a summer's morn to breathe
Among the pleasant villages and farms
Adjoined, from each thing met conceives delight.
Paradise Lost (1667) bk. 9, l. 445; see **Keats** 445:22

29 She fair, divinely fair, fit love for gods.
Paradise Lost (1667) bk. 9, l. 489

30 God so commanded, and left that command
Sole daughter of his voice; the rest, we live

Law to our selves, our reason is our law.
Paradise Lost (1667) bk. 9, l. 652

1   Her rash hand in evil hour
Forth reaching to the fruit, she plucked, she ate:
Earth felt the wound, and Nature from her seat
Sighing through all her works gave signs of woe
That all was lost.
Paradise Lost (1667) bk. 9, l. 780

2 O fairest of creation, last and best
Of all God's works.
Paradise Lost (1667) bk. 9, l. 896

3   Flesh of flesh,
Bone of my bone thou art, and from thy state
Mine never shall be parted, bliss or woe.
Paradise Lost (1667) bk. 9, l. 914; see **Bible** 75:16

4   What thou art is mine;
Our state cannot be severed, we are one,
One flesh; to lose thee were to lose my self.
Paradise Lost (1667) bk. 9, l. 957

5 . . . Yet I shall temper so
Justice with mercy.
Paradise Lost (1667) bk. 10, l. 77

6   He hears
On all sides, from innumerable tongues
A dismal universal hiss, the sound
Of public scorn.
Paradise Lost (1667) bk. 10, l. 506

7 This novelty on earth, this fair defect
Of nature?
Paradise Lost (1667) bk. 10, l. 891

8 Demoniac frenzy, moping melancholy
And moon-struck madness.
Paradise Lost (1667) bk. 11, l. 485

9   The evening star,
Love's harbinger.
Paradise Lost (1667) bk. 11, l. 588

10   For now I see
Peace to corrupt no less than war to waste.
Paradise Lost (1667) bk. 11, l. 783

11 O goodness infinite, goodness immense!
That all this good of evil shall produce,
And evil turn to good; more wonderful
Than that which by creation first brought forth
Light out of darkness!
Paradise Lost (1667) bk. 12, l. 469

12   Then wilt thou not be loath
To leave this Paradise, but shalt possess
A paradise within thee, happier far.
Paradise Lost (1667) bk. 12, l. 585

13 In me is no delay; with thee to go,
Is to stay here; without thee here to stay,
Is to go hence unwilling; thou to me
Art all things under heaven, all places thou,
Who for my wilful crime art banished hence.
Paradise Lost (1667) bk. 12, l. 615

14 They looking back, all the eastern side beheld
Of Paradise, so late their happy seat.
Paradise Lost (1667) bk. 12, l. 641

15 The world was all before them, where to choose
Their place of rest, and Providence their guide:

They hand in hand, with wandering steps and
   slow,
Through Eden took their solitary way.
Paradise Lost (1667) bk. 12, l. 646

16 Of whom to be dispraised were no small praise.
Paradise Regained (1671) bk. 3, l. 56

17 But on occasion's forelock watchful wait.
Paradise Regained (1671) bk. 3, l. 173

18 He who seeking asses found a kingdom.
of Saul
Paradise Regained (1671) bk. 3, l. 242; see **Bible** 80:9

19   The childhood shows the man,
As morning shows the day.
Paradise Regained (1671) bk. 4, l. 220; see **Wordsworth**
847:16

20 Athens, the eye of Greece, mother of arts
And eloquence.
Paradise Regained (1671) bk. 4, l. 240

21 See there the olive grove of Academe,
Plato's retirement, where the Attic bird
Trills her thick-warbled notes the summer long.
Paradise Regained (1671) bk. 4, l. 244

22 The first and wisest of them all professed
To know this only, that he nothing knew.
Paradise Regained (1671) bk. 4, l. 293; see **Davies** 258:8,
Socrates 744:24

23 Deep-versed in books and shallow in himself.
Paradise Regained (1671) bk. 4, l. 327

24 But headlong joy is ever on the wing.
'The Passion' (1645) st. 1

25 Ask for this great deliverer now, and find him
Eyeless in Gaza at the mill with slaves.
Samson Agonistes (1671) l. 40

26 O dark, dark, dark, amid the blaze of noon,
Irrecoverably dark, total eclipse
Without all hope of day!
Samson Agonistes (1671) l. 80

27 The sun to me is dark
And silent as the moon,
When she deserts the night
Hid in her vacant interlunar cave.
Samson Agonistes (1671) l. 86

28 To live a life half dead, a living death.
Samson Agonistes (1671) l. 100

29 Just are the ways of God,
And justifiable to men;
Unless there be who think not God at all.
Samson Agonistes (1671) l. 293

30 What boots it at one gate to make defence,
And at another to let in the foe?
Samson Agonistes (1671) l. 560

31 Yet beauty, though injurious, hath strange power,
After offence returning, to regain
Love once possessed.
Samson Agonistes (1671) l. 1003

32 Like that self-begotten bird
In the Arabian woods embossed,
That no second knows nor third,

And lay erewhile a holocaust.
Samson Agonistes (1671) l. 1699

1 And though her body die, her fame survives,
A secular bird ages of lives.
Samson Agonistes (1671) l. 1706

2   Samson hath quit himself
Like Samson, and heroically hath finished
A life heroic.
Samson Agonistes (1671) l. 1709

3 Nothing is here for tears, nothing to wail.
Samson Agonistes (1671) l. 1721

4 And calm of mind, all passion spent.
Samson Agonistes (1671) l. 1758

5 Time the subtle thief of youth.
Sonnet 7 'How soon hath time' (1645)

6 Licence they mean when they cry liberty;
For who loves that, must first be wise and good.
Sonnet 12 'I did but prompt the age' (1673)

7 When I consider how my light is spent,
E're half my days, in this dark world and wide,
And that one talent which is death to hide
Lodged with me useless.
Sonnet 16 'When I consider how my light is spent' (1673)

8 Doth God exact day-labour, light denied,
I fondly ask; but patience to prevent
That murmur, soon replies, God doth not need
Either man's work or his own gifts, who best
Bear his mild yoke, they serve him best, his state
Is kingly. Thousands at his bidding speed
And post o'er land and ocean without rest:
They also serve who only stand and wait.
Sonnet 16 'When I consider how my light is spent' (1673)

9 Methought I saw my late espousèd saint
Brought to me like Alcestis from the grave.
Sonnet 19 'Methought I saw my late espousèd saint' (1673)

10 Cromwell, our chief of men.
'To the Lord General Cromwell' (written 1652)

11   Peace hath her victories
No less renowned than war.
'To the Lord General Cromwell' (written 1652)

12 He who would not be frustrate of his hope to write
well hereafter in laudable things, ought himself to
be a true poem.
An Apology for Smectymnuus (1642) introduction

13 For this is not the liberty which we can hope, that
no grievance ever should arise in the
Commonwealth, that let no man in this world
expect; but when complaints are freely heard,
deeply considered, and speedily reformed, then is
the utmost bound of civil liberty attained that wise
men look for.
Areopagitica (1644)

14 As good almost kill a man as kill a good book:
who kills a man kills a reasonable creature, God's
image; but he who destroys a good book, kills
reason itself, kills the image of God, as it were in
the eye.
Areopagitica (1644)

15 A good book is the precious life-blood of a master
spirit, embalmed and treasured up on purpose to a
life beyond life.
Areopagitica (1644)

16 I cannot praise a fugitive and cloistered virtue,
unexercised and unbreathed, that never sallies out
and sees her adversary, but slinks out of the race,
where that immortal garland is to be run for, not
without dust and heat . . . that which purifies us is
trial, and trial is by what is contrary.
Areopagitica (1644)

17 Here the great art lies, to discern in what the law
is to be to restraint and punishment, and in what
things persuasion only is to work.
Areopagitica (1644)

18 If we think to regulate printing, thereby to rectify
manners, we must regulate all recreations and
pastimes, all that is delightful to man . . . And who
shall silence all the airs and madrigals, that
whisper softness in chambers?
Areopagitica (1644)

19 From that time ever since, the sad friends of
Truth, such as durst appear, imitating the careful
search that Isis made for the mangled body of
Osiris, went up and down gathering up limb by
limb still as they could find them. We have not yet
found them all, Lords and Commons, nor ever
shall do, till her Master's second coming; He shall
bring together every joint and member, and shall
mould them into an immortal feature of loveliness
and perfection.
Areopagitica (1644)

20 To be still searching what we know not, by what
we know, still closing up truth to truth as we find
it (for all her body is homogeneal and
proportional), this is the golden rule in theology as
well as in arithmetic, and makes up the best
harmony in a church.
Areopagitica (1644)

21 God is decreeing to begin some new and great
period in his Church, even to the reforming of
Reformation itself. What does he then but reveal
Himself to his servants, and as his manner is, first
to his Englishmen?
Areopagitica (1644)

22 A city of refuge, the mansion-house of liberty.
of London
Areopagitica (1644)

23 Where there is much desire to learn, there of
necessity will be much arguing, much writing,
many opinions; for opinion in good men is but
knowledge in the making.
Areopagitica (1644) p. 31

24 Give me the liberty to know, to utter, and to argue
freely according to conscience, above all liberties.
Areopagitica (1644)

25 Though all the winds of doctrine were let loose to
play upon the earth, so Truth be in the field, we
do injuriously by licensing and prohibiting to
misdoubt her strength. Let her and Falsehood

grapple; who ever knew Truth put to the worse, in a free and open encounter?

Areopagitica (1644)

1 Let not England forget her precedence of teaching nations how to live.

The Doctrine and Discipline of Divorce (1643) 'To the Parliament of England'

2 What I have spoken, is the language of that which is not called amiss *The good old Cause.*

The Ready and Easy Way to Establish a Free Commonwealth (2nd ed., 1660); see **Wordsworth** 848:18

3 This manner of writing [prose] wherein knowing myself inferior to myself . . . I have the use, as I may account it, but of my left hand.

The Reason of Church Government (1642) bk. 2, introduction

4 The land had once enfranchised herself from this impertinent yoke of prelaty, under whose inquisitorious and tyrannical duncery no free and splendid wit can flourish.

The Reason of Church Government (1642) bk. 2, introduction

5 Beholding the bright countenance of truth in the quiet and still air of delightful studies.

The Reason of Church Government (1642) bk. 2, introduction

6 None can love freedom heartily, but good men; the rest love not freedom, but licence.

The Tenure of Kings and Magistrates (1649)

7 No man who knows aught, can be so stupid to deny that all men naturally were born free.

The Tenure of Kings and Magistrates (1649)

Comte de Mirabeau 1749–91

French revolutionary

8 War is the national industry of Prussia.

attributed to Mirabeau by Albert Sorel (1842–1906), based on Mirabeau's introduction to *De la monarchie prussienne sous Frédéric le Grand* (1788)

▢ Misquotations

see box opposite

The Missal

The Latin Eucharistic liturgy used by the Roman Catholic Church up to 1964

9 *Asperges me, Domine, hyssopo, et mundabor.*

Sprinkle me with hyssop, O Lord, and I shall be cleansed.

Anthem at Sprinkling the Holy Water; see **Book of Common Prayer** 137:12

10 *Dominus vobiscum.*
Et cum spiritu tuo.

The Lord be with you.
And with thy spirit.

The Ordinary of the Mass

11 *In Nomine Patris, et Filii, et Spiritus Sancti.*

In the Name of the Father, and of the Son, and of the Holy Ghost.

The Ordinary of the Mass

12 *Introibo ad altare Dei.*

I will go unto the altar of God.

The Ordinary of the Mass; see **Book of Common Prayer** 135:11

13 *Gloria Patri, et Filio, et Spiritui Sancto. Sicut erat in principio, et nunc, et semper, et in saecula saeculorum.*

Glory be to the Father, and to the Son, and to the Holy Ghost. As it was in the beginning, is now, and ever shall be, world without end.

The Ordinary of the Mass 'The Doxology'; see **Book of Common Prayer** 127:19

14 *Confiteor Deo omnipotenti . . . quia peccavi nimis cogitatione, verbo, et opere, mea culpa, mea culpa, mea maxima culpa.*

I confess to almighty God . . . that I have sinned exceedingly in thought, word, and deed, through my fault, through my fault, through my most grievous fault.

The Ordinary of the Mass

15 *Kyrie eleison . . . Christe eleison.*

Lord, have mercy upon us . . . Christ, have mercy upon us.

The Ordinary of the Mass

16 *Gloria in excelsis Deo, et in terra pax hominibus bonae voluntatis. Laudamus te, benedicimus te, adoramus te, glorificamus te.*

Glory be to God on high, and on earth peace to men of good will. We praise thee, we bless thee, we adore thee, we glorify thee.

The Ordinary of the Mass; see **Bible** 100:4

17 *Oremus.*

Let us pray.

The Ordinary of the Mass

18 *Deo gratias.*

Thanks be to God.

The Ordinary of the Mass

19 *Credo in unum Deum, Patrem omnipotentem, factorem coeli et terrae, visibilium omnium et invisibilium.*

I believe in one God, the Father almighty, maker of heaven and earth, and of all things visible and invisible.

The Ordinary of the Mass 'The Nicene Creed'; see **Book of Common Prayer** 128:10

20 *Deum de Deo, lumen de lumine, Deum verum de Deo vero.*

God of God, light of light; true God of true God.

The Ordinary of the Mass 'The Nicene Creed'

21 *Et incarnatus est de Spiritu Sancto, ex Maria Virgine;* ET HOMO FACTUS EST.

And became incarnate by the Holy Ghost, of the Virgin Mary; AND WAS MADE MAN.

The Ordinary of the Mass 'The Nicene Creed'

22 *Sursum corda.*

Lift up your hearts.

The Ordinary of the Mass; see **Book of Common Prayer** 131:20

23 *Dignum et justum est.*

It is right and fitting.

The Ordinary of the Mass; see **Book of Common Prayer** 131:22

Continued

Misquotations

1 All is lost save honour.

popular summary of the words of **Francis I** of France:

Of all I had, only honour and life have been spared.

letter to his mother following his defeat at Pavia, 1525; see **Francis I** 332:4

2 All rowed fast, but none so fast as stroke.

popular summary of the following passage:

His blade struck the water a full second before any other: the lad had started well. Nor did he flag as the race wore on . . . as the boats began to near the winning-post, his oar was dipping into the water nearly *twice* as often as any other.

Desmond Coke (1879–1931) *Sandford of Merton* (1903) ch. 12

3 The ballot is stronger than the bullet.

popular version of a speech by **Lincoln**, 18 May 1858; see **Lincoln** 484:15

4 Beam me up, Scotty.

supposedly the form in which Captain Kirk habitually requested to be returned from a planet to the Starship *Enterprise*; in fact the nearest equivalent found is

Beam us up, Mr Scott.

Gene Roddenberry *Star Trek* (1966 onwards) 'Gamesters of Triskelion'

5 The budget should be balanced, the treasury should be refilled, public debt should be reduced, the arrogance of officialdom should be tempered and controlled, assistance to foreign lands should be curtailed lest Rome should become bankrupt, the mobs should be forced to work and not depend on government for subsistence.

attributed to **Cicero** in *Congressional Record* 25 April 1968, but not traced in his works

6 The capitalists will sell us the rope with which to hang them.

attributed to **Lenin**, but not found in his published works; I. U. Annenkov, in 'Remembrances of Lenin' includes a manuscript note attributed to Lenin:

They [capitalists] will furnish credits which will serve us for the support of the Communist Party in their countries and, by supplying us materials and technical equipment which we lack, will restore our military industry necessary for our future attacks against our suppliers. To put it in other words, they will work on the preparation of their own suicide.

in *Novyi Zhurnal/New Review* September 1961

7 Come with me to the Casbah.

often attributed to Charles Boyer (1898–1978) in the film Algiers *(1938), but the line does not in fact occur*

L. Swindell *Charles Boyer* (1983)

8 Crisis? What Crisis?

Sun headline, 11 January 1979, summarizing James **Callaghan**'s remark

I don't think other people in the world would share the view there is mounting chaos.

interview at London Airport, 10 January 1979

9 Dark forces at work.

popular summary of comment attributed to Queen **Elizabeth II** by former royal butler Paul Burrell, reported in the *Daily Mirror* as:

There are powers at work in this country about which we have no knowledge.

in *The Times* 7 November 2002

10 Dreams are the royal road to the unconscious.

popular summary of **Freud**'s *The Interpretation of Dreams* (2nd ed., 1909); see **Freud** 334:1

11 Elementary, my dear Watson, elementary.

remark attributed to Sherlock Holmes, but not found in this form in any book by Arthur Conan **Doyle**, *first found in P.G.* **Wodehouse** Psmith Journalist *(1915)*

attributed; see **Doyle** 284:17

12 England and America are two countries divided by a common language.

attributed in this and other forms to George Bernard **Shaw**, but not found in Shaw's published writings; see **Wilde** 835:10

13 Faith, the dark night of the soul.

St **John** of the Cross *Complete Works* (1864), translated by David Lewis, vol. 1, bk. 1, ch. 3; the phrase appears in the translator's chapter heading for the poem:

Noche oscura.

Dark night.

title of poem, St John of the Cross (1542–91) *The Ascent of Mount Carmel* (1578–80)

14 Few die and none resign.

popular summary of a letter of Thomas **Jefferson**, 1801; see **Jefferson** 420:6

15 The good Christian should beware of mathematicians, and all those who make empty prophecies. The danger already exists that mathematicians have made a covenant with the Devil to darken the spirit and to confine man in the bonds of Hell.

mistranslation of St **Augustine**'s *De Genesi ad Litteram*; the Latin word 'mathematicus' means both 'mathematician' and 'astrologer'; see **Augustine** 37:12

16 A good day to bury bad news.

popular misquotation of Jo **Moore**'s email of 11 September 2001; see **Moore** 546:16

17 The green shoots of recovery.

popular misquotation of the Chancellor's upbeat assessment of the economic situation:

The green shoots of economic spring are appearing once again.

Norman **Lamont**, speech at Conservative Party Conference, 9 October 1991

▶

▶ **Misquotations** *continued*

1 I disapprove of what you say, but I will defend to the death your right to say it.
*to **Helvétius**, following the burning of De l'esprit in 1759*
attributed to **Voltaire**, but in fact a later summary of his attitude by S. G. Tallentyre in *The Friends of Voltaire* (1907); see **Voltaire** 816:20

2 In trust I have found treason.
traditional concluding words of a speech by **Elizabeth I** to a Parliamentary deputation at Richmond, 12 November 1586; see **Elizabeth I** 304:5

3 I paint with my prick.
attributed to Pierre Auguste **Renoir**; possibly an inversion of:
It's with my brush that I make love.
A. André *Renoir* (1919)

4 It is necessary only for the good man to do nothing for evil to triumph.
attributed (in a number of forms) to **Burke**, but not found in his writings; see **Burke** 168:8

5 It's life, Jim, but not as we know it.
late 20th century saying associated with the television series *Star Trek* (1966–), created by Gene **Roddenberry**; the saying does not occur in the series but derives from the 1987 song 'Star Trekkin' ' sung by The Firm

6 Licensed to kill.
popular description of the status of Secret Service agent James Bond, 007, in the novels of Ian **Fleming**
The licence to kill for the Secret Service, the double-o prefix, was a great honour.
Dr No (1958)

7 Man, if you gotta ask you'll never know.
alternative version of Louis **Armstrong**'s response when asked what jazz was; see **Armstrong** 26:14

8 Me Tarzan, you Jane.
Johnny Weissmuller (1904–84) summing up his role in Tarzan, the Ape Man *(1932 film)*
in *Photoplay Magazine* June 1932; the words do not occur in the film or in the original novel by Edgar Rice Burroughs

9 Mind has no sex.
summarizing the view of Mary **Wollstonecraft**; see **Wollstonecraft** 844:1

10 My lips are sealed.
popular version of **Baldwin**'s speech on the Abyssinian crisis, 10 December 1935; see **Baldwin** 50:17

11 No plan survives first contact with the enemy.
popular version of Helmuth von **Moltke**; see **Moltke** 542:16

12 Once aboard the lugger and the maid is mine.
popular version of the line:
I want you to assist me in forcing her on board the lugger; once there, I'll frighten her into marriage.
John Benn Johnstone (1803–91) *The Gipsy Farmer* (performed 1845)

13 Play it again, Sam.
in the film Casablanca, *written by Julius J. Epstein et al., Humphrey Bogart says, 'If she can stand it, I can. Play it!'; earlier in the film Ingrid Bergman says, 'Play it, Sam. Play As Time Goes By.'*
Casablanca (1942 film); see **Film lines** 319:13, **Hupfeld** 410:13

14 Praise from Sir Hubert is praise indeed.
popular version of 'Approbation from Sir Hubert Stanley . . .'; see **Morton** 551:9

15 Put me back on my bike.
*commonly quoted as the last words of Tom Simpson (1937–67), British cyclist, after collapsing on Mont Ventoux in the Tour de France; see **Last words** 473:12*
William Fotheringham *Put Me Back on My Bike* (2002) ch. 2

16 Selling off the family silver.
popular summary of Harold **Macmillan**'s attack on privatization, 8 November 1985; see **Macmillan** 504:9

17 The soft underbelly of Europe.
popular version of **Churchill**'s words in the House of Commons, 11 November 1942; see **Churchill** 221:16

18 Something must be done.
popular version of **Edward VIII**'s words at the derelict Dowlais Iron and Steel Works, 18 November 1936; see **Edward VIII** 296:11

19 Take away these baubles.
popular version of **Cromwell**'s words at the dismissal of the Rump Parliament, 20 April 1653; see **Cromwell** 252:3

20 Warts and all.
popular summary of **Cromwell**'s instructions to the court painter Lely:
Mr Lely, I desire you would use all your skill to paint my picture truly like me, and not flatter me at all; but remark all these roughnesses, pimples, warts, and everything as you see me; otherwise I will never pay a farthing for it.
Horace Walpole *Anecdotes of Painting in England* vol. 3 (1763) ch. 1

21 We are the masters now.
popular misquotation of Hartley **Shawcross**'s speech in the House of Commons, 2 April 1946; see **Shawcross** 727:28

22 We must educate our masters.
popular summary of Robert **Lowe**'s speech on the passing of the Reform Bill:
I believe it will be absolutely necessary that you should prevail on our future masters to learn their letters.
speech, House of Commons, 15 July 1867

▶

▶ **Misquotations** *continued*

1 We trained hard . . . but it seemed that every time we were beginning to form up into teams we would be reorganized. I was to learn later in life that we tend to meet any new situation by reorganizing; and a wonderful method it can be for creating the illusion of progress while producing confusion, inefficiency, and demoralization.

late 20th century saying, frequently attributed to **Petronius** Arbiter (d. AD 65), but not found in his works

2 *Was für plündern!*

What a place to plunder!

misquotation of the comment of **Blücher** on London, as seen from the Monument in June 1814; see **Blücher** 124:10

3 The white heat of technology.

popular version of Harold **Wilson**'s speech at the Labour Party Conference, 1 October 1963; see **Wilson** 840:6

4 Why don't you come up and see me sometime?

alteration of Mae **West**'s invitation in the film *She Done Him Wrong* (1933); see **West** 830:6

5 You dirty rat!

associated with James Cagney (1899–1986), but not used by him in any film; in a speech at the American Film Institute banquet, 13 March 1974, Cagney said, 'I never said "Mmm, you dirty rat!"'
Cagney by Cagney (1976)

The Missal *continued*

6 *Sanctus, sanctus, sanctus, Dominus Deus Sabaoth. Pleni sunt coeli et terra gloria tua. Hosanna in excelsis. Benedictus qui venit in nomine Domini.*

Holy, holy, holy, Lord God of Hosts. Heaven and earth are full of thy glory. Hosanna in the highest. Blessed is he that cometh in the name of the Lord.

The Ordinary of the Mass; see **Bible** 113:9, **Book of Common Prayer** 131:22

7 *Pater noster, qui es in coelis, sanctificetur nomen tuum; adveniat regnum tuum; fiat voluntas tua sicut in coelo, et in terra . . . sed libera nos a malo.*

Our Father, who art in heaven, hallowed be thy name; thy kingdom come; thy will be done on earth, as it is in heaven . . . but deliver us from evil.

The Ordinary of the Mass; see **Bible** 95:3

8 *Pax Domini sit semper vobiscum.*

The peace of the Lord be always with you.

The Ordinary of the Mass

9 *Agnus Dei, qui tollis peccata mundi, miserere nobis. Agnus Dei, qui tollis peccata mundi, dona nobis pacem.*

Lamb of God, who takest away the sins of the world, have mercy on us. Lamb of God, who takest away the sins of the world, give us peace.

The Ordinary of the Mass; see **Bible** 102:24

10 *Domine, non sum dignus ut intres sub tectum meum; sed tantum dic verbo, et sanabitur anima mea.*

Lord, I am not worthy that thou shouldst enter under my roof; but say only the word, and my soul shall be healed.

The Ordinary of the Mass; see **Bible** 95:27

11 *Ite missa est.*

Go, you are dismissed.

commonly interpreted as 'Go, the Mass is ended'
The Ordinary of the Mass

12 *In principio erat Verbum, et Verbum erat apud Deum, et Deus erat Verbum.*

In the beginning was the Word, and the Word was with God, and the Word was God.

The Ordinary of the Mass; see **Bible** 102:15

13 VERBUM CARO FACTUM EST.

THE WORD WAS MADE FLESH.

The Ordinary of the Mass; see **Bible** 102:21

14 *Requiem aeternam dona eis, Domine: et lux perpetua luceat eis.*

Grant them eternal rest, O Lord; and let perpetual light shine on them.

Order of Mass for the Dead

15 *Dies irae, dies illa,*
Solvet saeclum in favilla,
Teste David cum Sibylla.

That day, the day of wrath, will turn the universe to ashes, as David foretells (and the Sibyl too).

Order of Mass for the Dead 'Sequentia' l. 1; commonly known as *Dies Irae* and sometimes attributed to Thomas of Celano (c.1190–1260)

16 *Tuba mirum spargens sonum*
Per sepulcra regionum,
Coget omnes ante thronum.

Mors stupebit et natura,
Cum resurget creatura
Iudicanti responsura.

Liber scriptus proferetur,
In quo totum continetur
Unde mundus iudicetur.

The trumpet will fling out a wonderful sound through the tombs of all regions, it will drive everyone before the throne. Death will be aghast and so will nature, when creation rises again to make answer to the judge. The written book will be brought forth, in which everything is included whereby the world will be judged.

Order of Mass for the Dead 'Sequentia' l. 7

17 *Rex tremendae maiestatis,*
Qui salvandos salvas gratis,
Salva me, fons pietatis!

O King of tremendous majesty, who freely saves those who should be saved, save me, O source of pity!

Order of Mass for the Dead 'Sequentia' l. 22

1 *Inter oves locum praesta*
Et ab haedis me sequestra
Statuens in parte dextra.

Among the sheep set me a place and separate me from the goats, standing me on the right-hand side.

Order of Mass for the Dead 'Sequentia' l. 43

2 *Requiescant in pace.*

May they rest in peace.

Order of Mass for the Dead

3 *O felix culpa, quae talem ac tantum meruit habere Redemptorem.*

O happy fault, which has earned such a mighty Redeemer.

'Exsultet' on Holy Saturday

Mistinguette 1875–1956

French actress

4 A kiss can be a comma, a question mark or an exclamation point. That's basic spelling that every woman ought to know.

in *Theatre Arts* December 1955

Adrian Mitchell 1932–

English poet, novelist, and dramatist

5 Most people ignore most poetry
because
most poetry ignores most people.

Poems (1964)

Elma Mitchell 1919–2000

Scottish poet

6   Even the simplest poem
May destroy your immunity to human emotions.
All poems must carry a Government warning.
Words
Can seriously affect your heart.

'This Poem . . .' (1987)

7 Women reminded him of lilies and rose.
Me they remind rather of blood and soap,
Armed with a warm rag, assaulting noses,
Ears, neck and mouth and all the secret places.

'Thoughts After Ruskin' (1976)

George Mitchell 1933–

American politician, chairman of the Northern Ireland peace talks

8 I am pleased to announce that the two governments and the political parties in Northern Ireland have reached agreement.

announcing the Good Friday agreement

in *Times* 11 April 1998

John Mitchell 1785–1859

English soldier

9 The most important political question on which modern times have to decide is the policy that must now be pursued, in order to maintain the security of Western Europe against the overgrown power of Russia.

Thoughts on Tactics (1838)

Joni Mitchell (Roberta Joan Anderson) 1945–

Canadian singer and songwriter

10 They paved paradise
And put up a parking lot,
With a pink hotel,
A boutique, and a swinging hot spot.

'Big Yellow Taxi' (1970 song)

11 I've looked at life from both sides now,
From win and lose and still somehow
It's life's illusions I recall;
I really don't know life at all.

'Both Sides Now' (1967 song)

12 We are stardust,
We are golden,
And we got to get ourselves
Back to the garden.

'Woodstock' (1969 song)

Margaret Mitchell 1900–49

American novelist
*see also **Closing lines** 228:1*

13 Always providing you have enough courage—or money—you can do without a reputation.

Gone with the Wind (1936) ch. 9

14 Death and taxes and childbirth! There's never any convenient time for any of them.

Gone with the Wind (1936) ch. 38

15 I wish I could care what you do or where you go but I can't . . . My dear, I don't give a damn.

Gone with the Wind (1936) ch. 63; see **Film lines** 319:7

Mary Russell Mitford 1787–1855

English novelist and dramatist

16 Till *Pride and Prejudice* showed what a precious gem was hidden in that unbending case, she was no more regarded in society than a poker or a fire-screen, or any other thin upright piece of wood or iron that fills its corner in peace and quietness. The case is very different now; she is still a poker—but a poker of whom every one is afraid.

*of Jane **Austen***

letter to Sir William Elford, 3 April 1815, in R. Brimley Johnson (ed.) *The Letters of Mary Russell Mitford* (1925)

Nancy Mitford 1904–73

English writer

17 Love in a cold climate.

title of book (1949); see **Southey** 749:17

1 'Always be civil to the girls, you never know who they may marry' is an aphorism which has saved many an English spinster from being treated like an Indian widow.
> *Love in a Cold Climate* (1949) pt. 1, ch. 2; see **Ailesbury** 8:32

2 Frogs . . . are slightly better than Huns or Wops, but abroad is unutterably bloody and foreigners are fiends.
> *The Pursuit of Love* (1945) ch. 15; see **George VI** 343:15

François Mitterrand 1916–96
French socialist statesman; President of France 1981–95

3 She has the eyes of Caligula, but the mouth of Marilyn Monroe.
> *of Margaret Thatcher, briefing his new European Minister Roland Dumas*
> in *Observer* 25 November 1990

Wilson Mizner 1876–1933
American dramatist

4 Be nice to people on your way up because you'll meet 'em on your way down.
> Alva Johnston *The Legendary Mizners* (1953) ch. 4

5 If you steal from one author, it's plagiarism; if you steal from many, it's research.
> Alva Johnston *The Legendary Mizners* (1953) ch. 4

6 A trip through a sewer in a glass-bottomed boat.
> *of Hollywood; reworked by Mayor Jimmy Walker into 'A reformer is a guy who rides through a sewer in a glass-bottomed boat'*
> Alva Johnston *The Legendary Mizners* (1953) ch. 4

Ariane Mnouchkine 1934–
French theatre director

7 A cultural Chernobyl.
> *of Euro Disney*
> in *Harper's Magazine* July 1992; see **Ballard** 54:2

Emilio Mola 1887–1937
Spanish nationalist general

8 Fifth column.
> *an extra body of supporters claimed by General Mola in a broadcast as being within Madrid when he besieged the city with four columns of Nationalist forces*
> in *New York Times* 16 and 17 October 1936

Molière (Jean-Baptiste Poquelin) 1622–73
French comic dramatist

9 *Présentez toujours le devant au monde.*
Always present your front to the world.
> *L'Avare* (1669) act 3, sc. 1

10 *Il faut manger pour vivre et non pas vivre pour manger.*
One should eat to live, and not live to eat.
> *L'Avare* (1669) act 3, sc. 1

11 *Tout ce qui n'est point prose est vers; et tout ce qui n'est point vers est prose.*

All that is not prose is verse; and all that is not verse is prose.
> *Le Bourgeois Gentilhomme* (1671) act 2, sc. 4

12 M. JOURDAIN: *Quoi? quand je dis: 'Nicole, apportez-moi mes pantoufles, et me donnez mon bonnet de nuit', c'est de la prose?*
MAÎTRE DE PHILOSOPHIE: *Oui, Monsieur.*
M. JOURDAIN: *Par ma foi! il y a plus de quarante ans que je dis de la prose sans que j'en susse rien.*
M. JOURDAIN: What? when I say: 'Nicole, bring me my slippers, and give me my night-cap,' is that prose?
PHILOSOPHY TEACHER: Yes, Sir.
M. JOURDAIN: Good heavens! For more than forty years I have been speaking prose without knowing it.
> *Le Bourgeois Gentilhomme* (1671) act 2, sc. 4

13 *Ah, la belle chose que de savoir quelque chose.*
Ah, it's a lovely thing, to know a thing or two.
> *Le Bourgeois Gentilhomme* (1671) act 2, sc. 4

14 *C'est une étrange entreprise que celle de faire rire les honnêtes gens.*
It's an odd job, making decent people laugh.
> *La Critique de l'école des femmes* (1663) sc. 6

15 *Je voudrais bien savoir si la grande règle de toutes les règles n'est pas de plaire.*
I shouldn't be surprised if the greatest rule of all weren't to give pleasure.
> *La Critique de l'école des femmes* (1663) sc. 6

16 *On ne meurt qu'une fois, et c'est pour si longtemps!*
One dies only once, and it's for such a long time!
> *Le Dépit amoureux* (performed 1656, published 1662) act 5, sc. 3

17 *Qui vit sans tabac n'est pas digne de vivre.*
He who lives without tobacco is not worthy to live.
> *Don Juan* (performed 1665) act 1, sc. 1

18 *Je vis de bonne soupe et non de beau langage.*
It's good food and not fine words that keeps me alive.
> *Les Femmes savantes* (1672) act 2, sc. 7

19 *Guenille, si l'on veut: ma guenille m'est chère.*
Rags and tatters, if you like: I am fond of my rags and tatters.
> *Les Femmes savantes* (1672) act 2, sc. 7

20 *Un sot savant est sot plus qu'un sot ignorant.*
A knowledgeable fool is a greater fool than an ignorant fool.
> *Les Femmes savantes* (1672) act 4, sc. 3

21 *Les livres cadrent mal avec le mariage.*
Reading and marriage don't go well together.
> *Les Femmes savantes* (1672) act 5, sc. 3

22 *Que diable allait-il faire dans cette galère?*
What the devil was he doing in that galley?
> *Les Fourberies de Scapin* (1671) act 2, sc. 11

23 *Vous l'avez voulu, Georges Dandin, vous l'avez voulu.*
You've asked for it, Georges Dandin, you've asked for it.
> *Georges Dandin* (1668) act 1, sc. 9

1 GÉRONTE: *Il me semble que vous les placez autrement qu'ils ne sont: que le coeur est du côté gauche, et le foie du côté droit.*
SGANARELLE: *Oui, cela était autrefois ainsi, mais nous avons changé tout cela, et nous faisons maintenant la médecine d'une méthode toute nouvelle.*
GÉRONTE: It seems to me you are locating them wrongly: the heart is on the left and the liver is on the right.
SGANARELLE: Yes, in the old days that was so, but we have changed all that, and we now practise medicine by a completely new method.
Le Médecin malgré lui (1667) act 2, sc. 4

2 *Il faut, parmi le monde, une vertu traitable.*
What's needed in this world is an accommodating sort of virtue.
Le Misanthrope (1666) act 1, sc. 1

3 *Et c'est une folie à nulle autre seconde,*
De vouloir se mêler de corriger le monde.
Of all human follies there's none could be greater
Than trying to render our fellow-men better.
Le Misanthrope (1666) act 1, sc. 1

4 *On doit se regarder soi-même, un fort long temps,*
Avant que de songer à condamner les gens.
One should look long and carefully at oneself before one considers judging others.
Le Misanthrope (1666) act 3, sc. 4

5 *C'est un homme expéditif, qui aime à dépêcher ses malades; et quand on a à mourir, cela se fait avec lui le plus vite du monde.*
He's an expeditious man, who likes to hurry his patients along; and when you have to die, he sees to that quicker than anyone.
Monsieur de Pourceaugnac (1670) act 1, sc. 5

6 *Ils commencent ici par faire pendre un homme et puis ils lui font son procès.*
Here [in Paris] they hang a man first, and try him afterwards.
Monsieur de Pourceaugnac (1670) act 1, sc. 5

7 *Les gens de qualité savent tout sans avoir jamais rien appris.*
People of quality know everything without ever having been taught anything.
Les Précieuses ridicules (1660) sc. 9

8 *Assassiner c'est le plus court chemin.*
Assassination is the quickest way.
Le Sicilien (1668) sc. 12

9 *Ah, pour être dévot, je n'en suis pas moins homme.*
I am not the less human for being devout.
Le Tartuffe (performed 1664, published 1669) act 3, sc. 3

10 *On est aisement dupé par ce qu'on aime.*
One is easily fooled by that which one loves.
Le Tartuffe (1669) act 4, sc. 3

11 *Le ciel défend, de vrai, certains contentements,*
Mais on trouve avec lui des accommodements.
God, it is true, does some delights condemn,
But 'tis not hard to come to terms with Him.
Le Tartuffe (1669) act 4, sc. 5

12 *Le scandale du monde est ce qui fait l'offense,*
Et ce n'est pas pécher que pécher en silence.
It is public scandal that constitutes offence, and to sin in secret is not to sin at all.
Le Tartuffe (1669) act 4, sc. 5

13 *L'homme est, je vous l'avoue, un méchant animal.*
Man, I can assure you, is a nasty creature.
Le Tartuffe (1669) act 5, sc. 6

14 *Il m'est permis de reprendre mon bien où je le trouve.*
It is permitted me to take good fortune where I find it.
in J. L. Le Gallois *La Vie de Molière* (1704) p. 14

Mary Mollineux (née Southworth) 1651–95
English Quaker and poet

15 How sweet is harmless solitude!
What can its joys control?
Tumults and noise may not intrude,
To interrupt the soul.
'Solitude' (1670)

Helmuth von Moltke 1800–91
Prussian military commander
*on Moltke: see **Bagehot** 48:2*

16 No plan of operations reaches with any certainty beyond the first encounter with the enemy's main force.
Kriegsgechichtiche Einzelschriften (1880); see **Misquotations** 538:11

17 Everlasting peace is a dream, and not even a pleasant one; and war is a necessary part of God's arrangement of the world . . . Without war the world would deteriorate into materialism.
letter to Dr J. K. Bluntschli, 11 December 1880 (translated by Mary Herms), in *Helmuth von Moltke as a Correspondent* (1893)

Walter Mondale 1928–
American Democratic politician

18 When I hear your new ideas I'm reminded of that ad, 'Where's the beef?'
in a televised debate with Gary Hart, 11 March 1984; see **Advertising slogans** 8:24

Piet Mondrian 1872–1944
Dutch painter

19 The essence of painting has actually always been to make it [the universal] plastically perceptible through colour and line.
'Natural Reality and Abstract Reality' (written 1919)

20 In order to approach the spiritual in art, one employs reality as little as possible . . . This explains logically why primary forms are employed. Since these forms are abstract, an abstract art comes into being.
Sketchbook II (1914)

James, Duke of Monmouth 1649–85

*English illegitimate son of **Charles II**; leader of the failed Monmouth rebellion against James II*

1 Do not hack me as you did my Lord Russell.
to his executioner
> T. B. Macaulay *History of England* vol. 1 (1849) ch. 5

Jean Monnet 1888–1979

French economist and diplomat; founder of the European Community

2 Europe has never existed. It is not the addition of national sovereignties in a conclave which creates an entity. One must genuinely *create* Europe.
> Anthony Sampson *The New Europeans* (1968)

3 We should not create a nation Europe instead of a nation France.
> François Duchêne *Jean Monnet* (1994)

James Monroe 1758–1831

American Democratic Republican statesman, 5th President of the US 1817–25

4 We owe it . . . to the amicable relations existing between the United States and those [European] powers to declare that we should consider any attempt on their part to extend their system to any portion of this hemisphere as dangerous to our peace and safety.
principle that became known as the 'Monroe Doctrine'
> annual message to Congress, 2 December 1823

Marilyn Monroe 1926–62

American actress

*on Monroe: see **John** 422:11, **Mailer** 507:11, **Newspaper headlines** 562:6*

5 *when asked if she really had nothing on in a calendar photograph:*
I had the radio on.
> in *Time* 11 August 1952

6 *on being asked what she wore in bed:*
Chanel No. 5.
> Pete Martin *Marilyn Monroe* (1956)

John Samuel Bewley Monsell 1811–75

Irish-born clergyman

7 Fight the good fight with all thy might.
> 'The Fight for Faith' (1863 hymn); see **Bible** 110:27

8 O worship the Lord in the beauty of holiness,
Bow down before him, his glory proclaim;
With gold of obedience and incense of lowliness,
Kneel and adore him: the Lord is his name.
> 'O Worship the Lord' (1863 hymn)

Lady Mary Wortley Montagu 1689–1762

English writer

9 But the fruit that can fall without shaking,
Indeed is too mellow for me.
> 'Answered, for Lord William Hamilton' in J. Dodsley (ed.) *A Collection of Poems* vol. 6 (1758)

10 Let this great maxim be my virtue's guide:
In part she is to blame, who has been tried,
He comes too near, that comes to be denied.
> *The Plain Dealer* (27 April 1724) 'The Resolve'

11 And we meet with champagne and a chicken at last.
> *Six Town Eclogues* (1747) 'The Lover' l. 25

12 As Ovid has sweetly in parable told,
We harden like trees, and like rivers grow cold.
> *Six Town Eclogues* (1747) 'The Lover' l. 47

13 In chains and darkness, wherefore should I stay,
And mourn in prison, while I keep the key?
> 'Verses on Self-Murder' in *The London Magazine* (1749)

14 General notions are generally wrong.
> letter to her husband Edward Wortley Montagu, 28 March 1710, in Robert Halsband (ed.) *Complete Letters of Lady Mary Wortley Montagu* (1965) vol. 1

15 Men are vile inconstant toads.
> letter to Anne Justice, c.12 June 1710, in *Selected Letters* (1997)

16 Civility costs nothing and buys everything.
> letter to her daughter Lady Bute, 30 May 1756, in Robert Halsband (ed.) *Complete Letters of Lady Mary Wortley Montagu* (1967) vol. 3

17 I have too much indulged my sedentary humour and have been a rake in reading.
> letter to her daughter Lady Bute, 11 April 1759, in Robert Halsband (ed.) *Complete Letters of Lady Mary Wortley Montagu* (1967) vol. 3

18 This world consists of men, women, and Herveys.
*'Herveys' being a reference to Lord **Hervey***
> attributed by Lord Wharncliffe in *Letters and Works of Lady Mary Wortley Montagu* (1837) vol. 1

19 People wish their enemies dead—but I do not; I say give them the gout, give them the stone!
> W. S. Lewis et al. (eds.) *Horace Walpole's Correspondence* (1973) vol. 35

C. E. Montague 1867–1928

British writer

20 War hath no fury like a non-combatant.
> *Disenchantment* (1922) ch. 16

John Montague 1929–

Irish poet and writer

21   To grow
a second tongue, as
harsh a humiliation
as twice to be born.
> 'A Grafted Tongue' (1972)

22 Like dolmens round my childhood, the old people.
> 'Like Dolmens Round my Childhood' (1972)

Montaigne (Michel Eyquem de Montaigne) 1533–92

French moralist and essayist

23 *Pour juger des choses grandes et hautes, il faut une âme de même, autrement nous leur attribuons le vice qui est le nôtre.*

To make judgements about great and lofty things, a soul of the same stature is needed; otherwise we ascribe to them that vice which is our own.

Essais (1580, ed. M. Rat, 1958) bk. 1, ch. 14

1 *Il faut être toujours botté et prêt à partir.*

One should always have one's boots on, and be ready to leave.

Essais (1580, ed. M. Rat, 1958) bk. 1, ch. 20; see **La Fontaine** 463:15

2 *Je veux . . . que la mort me trouve plantant mes choux, mais nonchalant d'elle, et encore plus de mon jardin imparfait.*

I want death to find me planting my cabbages, but caring little for it, and even less about the imperfections of my garden.

Essais (1580, ed. M. Rat, 1958) bk. 1, ch. 20

3 *Le continuel ouvrage de votre vie, c'est bâtir la mort.*

The ceaseless labour of your life is to build the house of death.

Essais (1580, ed. M. Rat, 1958) bk. 1, ch. 20

4 *L'utilité du vivre n'est pas en l'espace, elle est en l'usage; tel a vécu longtemps qui a peu vécu . . . Il gît en votre volonté, non au nombre des ans, que vous ayez assez vécu.*

The value of life lies not in the length of days but in the use you make of them; he has lived for a long time who has little lived. Whether you have lived enough depends not on the number of your years but on your will.

Essais (1580, ed. M. Rat, 1958) bk. 1, ch. 20

5 *Il faut noter, que les jeux d'enfants ne sont pas jeux, et les faut juger en eux comme leurs plus sérieuses actions.*

It should be noted that children at play are not playing about; their games should be seen as their most serious-minded activity.

Essais (1580, ed. M. Rat, 1958) bk. 1, ch. 23

6 *Si on me presse de dire pourquoi je l'aimais, je sens que cela ne se peut s'exprimer, qu'en répondant: 'Parce que c'était lui; parce que c'était moi.'*
of his friend Étienne de la Boétie

If I am pressed to say why I loved him, I feel it can only be explained by replying: 'Because it was he; because it was me.'

Essais (1580, ed. M. Rat, 1958) bk. 1, ch. 28

7 *Chacun appelle barbarie ce qui n'est pas de son usage.*

Everyone calls barbarism what is not customary to him.

Essais (1580, ed. M. Rat, 1958) bk. 1, ch. 31

8 *Il n'y a guère moins de tourment au gouvernement d'une famille que d'un état entier . . . et, pour être les occupations domestiques moins importantes, elles n'en sont pas moins importunes.*

There is scarcely any less bother in the running of a family than in that of an entire state. And domestic business is no less importunate for being less important.

Essais (1580, ed. M. Rat, 1958) bk. 1, ch. 39

9 *Il se faut réserver une arrière boutique toute nôtre, toute franche, en laquelle nous établissons nôtre vraie liberté et principale retraite et solitude.*

A man should keep for himself a little back shop, all his own, quite unadulterated, in which he establishes his true freedom and chief place of seclusion and solitude.

Essais (1580, ed. M. Rat, 1958) bk. 1, ch. 39

10 *La plus grande chose du monde, c'est de savoir être à soi.*

The greatest thing in the world is to know how to be oneself.

Essais (1580, ed. M. Rat, 1958) bk. 1, ch. 39

11 *La gloire et le repos sont choses qui ne peuvent loger en même gîte.*

Fame and tranquillity can never be bedfellows.

Essais (1580, ed. M. Rat, 1958) bk. 1, ch. 39

12 *Mon métier et mon art c'est vivre.*

Living is my job and my art.

Essais (1580, ed. M. Rat, 1958) bk. 2, ch. 6

13 *La vertu refuse la facilité pour compagne . . . Elle demande un chemin âpre et épineux.*

Virtue shuns ease as a companion . . . It demands a rough and thorny path.

Essais (1580, ed. M. Rat, 1958) bk. 2, ch. 11

14 *Notre religion est faite pour extirper les vices; elle les couvre, les nourrit, les incite.*

Our religion is made so as to wipe out vices; it covers them up, nourishes them, incites them.

Essais (1580, ed. M. Rat, 1958) bk. 2, ch. 12

15 *Quand je me joue à ma chatte, qui sait si elle passe son temps de moi plus que je ne fais d'elle?*

When I play with my cat, who knows whether she isn't amusing herself with me more than I am with her?

Essais (1580, ed. M. Rat, 1958) bk. 2, ch. 12

16 *Que sais-je?*

What do I know?
on the position of the sceptic

Essais (1580, ed. M. Rat, 1958) bk. 2, ch. 12

17 *L'homme est bien insensé. Il ne saurait forger un ciron, et forge des dieux à douzaines.*

Man is quite insane. He wouldn't know how to create a maggot, and he creates gods by the dozen.

Essais (1580, ed. M. Rat, 1958) bk. 2, ch. 12

18 *Ceux qui ont apparié notre vie à un songe, ont eu de la raison, à l'aventure plus qu'ils ne pensaient . . . Nous veillons dormants, et veillants dormons.*

Those who have likened our life to a dream were more right, by chance, than they realised. We are awake while sleeping, and waking sleep.

Essais (1580, ed. M. Rat, 1958) bk. 2, ch. 12

19 *Pour chacun, son fumier sent bon!*

Every man's ordure well to his own sense doth smell.

Essais (1580, ed. M. Rat, 1958) bk. 3, ch. 8, Florio's translation of 1603

1 *Il n'est si homme de bien, qu'il mette à l'examen des lois toutes ses actions et pensées, qui ne soit pendable dix fois en sa vie.*

There is no man, good as he may be, who, if all his thoughts and actions were submitted to the scrutiny of the laws, would not deserve hanging ten times in his life.

Essais (1580, ed. M. Rat, 1958) bk. 3, ch. 9

2 *Quelqu'un pourrait dire de moi que j'ai seulement fait ici un amas de fleurs étrangères, n'y ayant fourni du mien que le filet à les lier.*

It could be said of me that in this book I have only made up a bunch of other men's flowers, providing of my own only the string that ties them together.

Essais (1580, ed. M. Rat, 1958) bk. 3, ch. 12

3 *Il y a plus affaire à interpréter les interprétations qu'à interpréter les choses, et plus de livres sur les livres que sur autre sujet: nous ne faisons que nous entregloser. Tout fourmille de commentaires; d'auteurs, il en est grand cherté.*

There is more business in interpreting interpretations than in interpreting things, and more books on books than on any other subject: all we do is gloss each other. All is a-swarm with commentaries: of authors there is a dearth.

Essais (1580, ed. M. Rat, 1958) bk. 3, ch. 13; see **Derrida** 265:7

Eugenio Montale 1896–1981
Italian poet

4 *Felicità raggiunta, si cammina
per te sul fil di lama.
Agli occhi sei barlume che vacilla
al piede, teso ghiaccio che s'incrina;
e dunque non ti tocchi chi piu t'ama.*

Happiness, for you we walk on a knife edge. To the eyes you are a flickering light, to the feet, thin ice that cracks; and so may no one touch you who loves you.

'Felicità raggiunta' (1925)

Montesquieu (Charles-Louis de Secondat) 1689–1755
French political philosopher

5 *Ce corps malade ne se soutient pas par un régime doux et tempéré, mais par des remèdes violents, qu'il épuisent et le minent sans cesse.*

That huge distempered body does not support itself by a mild and temperate regimen; but by violent remedies, which are incessantly corroding and exhausting its strength.

*of the Ottoman empire; see **Nicholas I** 563:7*

Lettres Persanes (1721) no. 19 (translated by J. Ozell, 1722)

6 *Il faut pleurer les hommes à leur naissance, et non pas à leur mort.*

Men should be bewailed at their birth, and not at their death.

Lettres Persanes (1721) no. 40 (translated by J. Ozell, 1722)

7 *Si les triangles faisoient un Dieu, ils lui donneroient trois côtés.*

If the triangles were to make a God they would give him three sides.

Lettres Persanes (1721) no. 59 (translated by J. Ozell, 1722)

8 *Le succès de la plupart des choses dépend de bien savoir combien il faut de temps pour réussir.*

In most things success depends on knowing how long it takes to succeed.

Pensées et fragments inédits . . . vol. 1 (1901) no. 630

9 *Les grands seigneurs ont des plaisirs, le peuple a de la joie.*

Great lords have their pleasures, but the people have fun.

Pensées et fragments inédits . . . vol. 2 (1901) no. 992

10 *Les Anglais sont occupés; ils n'ont pas le temps d'être polis.*

The English are busy; they don't have time to be polite.

Pensées et fragments inédits . . . vol. 2 (1901) no. 1428

11 Happy the people whose annals are blank in history-books!

attributed to Montesquieu by Thomas Carlyle in *History of Frederick the Great* (1858–65) bk. 16, ch. 1; see **Eliot** 300:14, **Proverbs** 621:31

Lord Montgomery of Alamein 1887–1976
British field marshal
*on Montgomery: see **Churchill** 222:6*

12 *Here* we will stand and fight; there will be no further withdrawal. I have ordered that all plans and instructions dealing with further withdrawal are to be burnt, and at once. We will stand and fight *here*. If we can't stay here alive, then let us stay here dead.

speech in Cairo, 13 August 1942

13 Rule 1, on page 1 of the book of war, is: 'Do not march on Moscow' . . . [Rule 2] is: 'Do not go fighting with your land armies in China.'

speech in the House of Lords, 30 May 1962

14 I have heard some say . . . [homosexual] practices are allowed in France and in other NATO countries. We are not French, and we are not other nationals. We are British, thank God!

on the 2nd reading of the Sexual Offences Bill
speech in the House of Lords, 24 May 1965

Robert Montgomery 1807–55
English clergyman and poet

15 The solitary monk who shook the world.

Luther: a Poem (1842) ch. 3 'Man's Need and God's Supply'

16 And thou, vast ocean! on whose awful face Time's iron feet can print no ruin-trace.

The Omnipresence of the Deity (1830 ed.) pt. 1, l. 105

Casimir, Comte de Montrond 1768–1843
French diplomat

17 Have no truck with first impulses for they are always generous ones.

attributed, in Comte J. d'Estourmel *Derniers Souvenirs* (1860), where the alternative attribution to Talleyrand is denied; see **Corneille** 243:6

1 If something pleasant happens to you, don't forget to tell it to your friends, to make them feel bad.
   attributed, in Comte J. d'Estourmel *Derniers Souvenirs* (1860) p. 319

James Graham, Marquess of Montrose
1612–50
Scottish royalist general and poet

2 Let them bestow on every airth a limb.
   'Lines written on the Window of his Jail the Night before his Execution'

3 He either fears his fate too much,
   Or his deserts are small,
   That puts it not unto the touch
   To win or lose it all.
   'My Dear and Only Love' (written *c.*1642)

4 But if thou wilt be constant then,
   And faithful of thy word,
   I'll make thee glorious by my pen,
   And famous by my sword.
   'My Dear and Only Love' (written *c.*1642)

Percy Montrose
American songwriter

5 In a cavern, in a canyon,
   Excavating for a mine,
   Dwelt a miner, Forty-niner,
   And his daughter, Clementine.
   Oh, my darling, oh my darling, oh my darling Clementine!
   Thou art lost and gone for ever, dreadful sorry, Clementine.
   'Clementine' (1884 song)

Monty Python's Flying Circus 1969–74
BBC TV programme, written by Graham Chapman (1941–89), John Cleese (1939–), Terry Gilliam (1940–), Eric Idle (1943–), Terry Jones (1942–), and Michael Palin (1943–)
see also **Catchphrases** 200:2, **Film lines** 320:23

6 Your wife interested in . . . *photographs?* Eh? Know what I mean—*photographs?* He asked him knowingly . . . nudge nudge, snap snap, grin grin, wink wink, say no more.
   Monty Python's Flying Circus (1969)

7 It's *not* pining—it's passed on! This parrot is no more! It has ceased to be! It's expired and gone to meet its maker! This is a late parrot! It's a stiff! Bereft of life it rests in peace—if you hadn't nailed it to the perch it would be pushing up the daisies! It's rung down the curtain and joined the choir invisible! THIS IS AN EX-PARROT!
   Monty Python's Flying Circus (1969)

8 Nobody expects the Spanish Inquisition!
   Monty Python's Flying Circus (1970)

Clement C. Moore 1779–1863
American writer

9 'Twas the night before Christmas, when all through the house
   Not a creature was stirring, not even a mouse;
   The stockings were hung by the chimney with care,
   In hopes that St Nicholas soon would be there.
   'A Visit from St Nicholas' (December 1823)

Edward Moore 1712–57
English dramatist

10 This is adding insult to injuries.
   The Foundling (1748) act 5, sc. 5

11 I am rich beyond the dreams of avarice.
   The Gamester (1753) act 2, sc. 2; see **Johnson** 431:24

George Moore 1852–1933
Irish novelist

12 All reformers are bachelors.
   The Bending of the Bough (1900) act 1

13 A man travels the world in search of what he needs and returns home to find it.
   The Brook Kerith (1916) ch. 11

Henry Moore 1898–1986
English sculptor and draughtsman

14 Sculpture in stone should look honestly like stone . . . to make it look like flesh and blood, hair and dimples is coming down to the level of the stage conjuror.
   in *Architectural Association Journal* May 1930

15 The first hole made through a piece of stone is a revelation.
   in *Listener* 18 August 1937

Jo Moore
British government adviser

16 It is now a very good day to get out anything we want to bury.
   email sent in the aftermath of the terrorist action in America, 11 September 2001
   in *Daily Telegraph* 10 October; see also **Misquotations** 537:16

Marianne Moore 1887–1972
American poet

17 She says 'Men are monopolists
   of "stars, garters, buttons
   and other shining baubles"—
   unfit to be the guardians
   of another person's happiness.'
   'Marriage' (1935); see below

   Men practically reserve for themselves stately funerals, splendid monuments, memorial statues, titles, honorary degrees, stars, garters, ribbons, buttons and other shining baubles, so valueless in themselves and yet so infinitely desirable because they are symbols of recognition by their fellow-craftsmen of difficult work well done.
   Miss M. Carey Thomas, Founder's address, Mount Holyoke, 1921

18   O to be a dragon,
   a symbol of the power of Heaven—of silkworm

size or immense; at times invisible.
Felicitous phenomenon!
'O To Be a Dragon' (1959)

1 I, too, dislike it: there are things that are
  important beyond all this fiddle.
  Reading it, however, with a perfect contempt for
  it, one discovers in it, after all, a place for the
  genuine.
  'Poetry' (1935)

2 Imaginary gardens with real toads in them.
  'Poetry' (1935)

3 My father used to say,
  'Superior people never make long visits,
  have to be shown Longfellow's grave
  or the glass flowers at Harvard.'
  'Silence' (1935)

4 Nor was he insincere in saying, 'Make my house
  your inn.'
  Inns are not residences.
  'Silence' (1935)

5 The passion for setting people right is in itself an
  afflictive disease.
  Distaste which takes no credit to itself is best.
  'Snakes, Mongooses. Snake-Charmers, and the Like'
  (1935)

6 I am troubled, I'm dissatisfied, I'm Irish.
  'Spenser's Ireland' (1941)

7   It is a privilege to see so
  much confusion.
  'The Steeple-Jack' (1935)

8 I never knew anyone who had a passion for words
  who had as much difficulty in saying things as I
  do. I very seldom say them in a manner I like. If I
  do it's because I don't know I'm trying.
  George Plimpton (ed.) *The Writer's Chapbook* (1989)

Sturge Moore 1870–1944

English poet and engraver
on Moore: see Gosse 357:8

9 Then, cleaving the grass, gazelles appear
  (The gentler dolphins of kindlier waves)
  With sensitive heads alert of ear;
  Frail crowds that a delicate hearing saves.
  'The Gazelles' (1904)

Thomas Moore 1779–1852

Irish musician and songwriter

10 Yet, who can help loving the land that has
  taught us
  Six hundred and eighty-five ways to dress eggs?
  The Fudge Family in Paris (1818) Letter 8, l. 64

11 Though an angel should write, still 'tis *devils* must
  print.
  The Fudges in England (1835) Letter 3, l. 65

12 Believe me, if all those endearing young charms,
  Which I gaze on so fondly today,
  Were to change by tomorrow, and fleet in my
  arms,

Like fairy gifts fading away!
  Irish Melodies (1807) 'Believe me, if all those endearing
  young charms'

13 'Twas from Kathleen's eyes he flew,
  Eyes of most unholy blue!
  Irish Melodies (1807) 'By that Lake'

14 You may break, you may shatter the vase, if you
  will,
  But the scent of the roses will hang round it still.
  Irish Melodies (1807) 'Farewell!—but whenever'

15 The harp that once through Tara's halls
  The soul of music shed,
  Now hangs as mute on Tara's walls
  As if that soul were fled.
  Irish Melodies (1807) 'The harp that once through Tara's
  halls'

16 No, there's nothing half so sweet in life
  As love's young dream.
  Irish Melodies (1807) 'Love's Young Dream'

17 The Minstrel Boy to the war is gone,
  In the ranks of death you'll find him;
  His father's sword he has girded on,
  And his wild harp slung behind him.
  Irish Melodies (1807) 'The Minstrel Boy'

18 Oh! breathe not his name, let it sleep in the shade,
  Where cold and unhonoured his relics are laid.
  Irish Melodies (1807) 'Oh! breathe not his name'

19 'Tis the last rose of summer
  Left blooming alone;
  All her lovely companions
  Are faded and gone.
  Irish Melodies (1807) ''Tis the last rose of summer'

20 I never nursed a dear gazelle,
  To glad me with its soft black eye,
  But when it came to know me well,
  And love me, it was sure to die!
  Lalla Rookh (1817) 'The Fire-Worshippers' pt. 1, l. 283; see
  Carroll 196:13, **Dickens** 271:7, **Payn** 589:10

21 Like Dead Sea fruits, that tempt the eye,
  But turn to ashes on the lips!
  Lalla Rookh (1817) 'The Fire-Worshippers' pt. 2, l. 484

22 Oft, in the stilly night,
  Ere Slumber's chain has bound me,
  Fond Memory brings the light
  Of other days around me.
  National Airs (1815) 'Oft in the Stilly Night'

Thomas Osbert Mordaunt 1730–1809

British soldier

23 One crowded hour of glorious life
  Is worth an age without a name.
  'A Poem, said to be written by Major Mordaunt during the
  last German War', in *The Bee, or Literary Weekly
  Intelligencer* 12 October 1791

Hannah More 1745–1833

English writer of tracts

24 For you'll ne'er mend your fortunes, nor help the
  just cause,

By breaking of windows, or breaking of laws.
'An Address to the Meeting in Spa Fields' (1817) in H. Thompson *Life of Hannah More* (1838) appendix, no. 7; see **Pankhurst** 585:9

1 He liked those literary cooks
Who skim the cream of others' books;
And ruin half an author's graces
By plucking bon-mots from their places.
Florio (1786) pt. 1, l. 123

2   Did not God
Sometimes withhold in mercy what we ask,
We should be ruined at our own request.
Moses in the Bulrushes (1782) pt. 1, l. 35

3 Whether we consider the manual industry of the poor, or the intellectual exertions of the superior classes, we shall find that diligent occupation, if not criminally perverted from its purposes, is at once the instrument of virtue and the secret of happiness. Man cannot be safely trusted with a life of leisure.
Christian Morals (1813) vol. 2, ch. 23

4 The prevailing manners of an age depend more than we are aware, or are willing to allow, on the conduct of the women; this is one of the principal hinges on which the great machine of human society turns.
Essays on Various Subjects . . . for Young Ladies (1777) 'On Dissipation'

5 How much it is to be regretted, that the British ladies should ever sit down contented to polish, when they are able to reform; to entertain, when they might instruct; and to dazzle for an hour, when they are candidates for eternity!
Essays on Various Subjects . . . for Young Ladies (1777) 'On Dissipation'

6 It is humbling to reflect, that in those countries in which the fondness for the mere persons of women is carried to the highest excess, they are slaves; and that their moral and intellectual degradation increases in direct proportion to the adoration which is paid to mere external charms.
Strictures on the Modern System of Female Education (1799) vol. 1, ch. 1

Thomas More 1478–1535

English scholar and saint; Lord Chancellor of England, 1529–32

on More: see **Whittington** 834:7; *see also* **Last words** 474:3

7 *Oves inquam vestrae, quae tam mites esse, tamque exiguo solent ali, nunc (uti fertur) tam edaces atque indomitae esse coeperunt ut homines devorent ipsos.*

Your sheep, that were wont to be so meek and tame, and so small eaters, now, as I hear say, be become so great devourers, and so wild, that they eat up and swallow down the very men themselves.
Utopia (1516) bk. 1

8 *Qui Magistratum ullum ambierit, ex spes omnium redditur.*

Anyone who campaigns for public office becomes disqualified for holding any office at all.
Utopia (1516) bk. 2

9 Son Roper, I may tell thee I have no cause to be proud thereof [the King having entertained him at Chelsea], for if my head could wish him a castle in France it should not fail to go.
of **Henry VIII**
William Roper *Life of Sir Thomas More*

10 We may not look at our pleasure to go to heaven in feather-beds; it is not the way.
William Roper *Life of Sir Thomas More*

11 If the parties will at my hands call for justice, then, all were it my father stood on the one side, and the Devil on the other, his cause being good, the Devil should have right.
William Roper *Life of Sir Thomas More*

12 In good faith, I rejoiced, son, that I had given the devil a foul fall, and that with those Lords I had gone so far, as without great shame I could never go back again.
William Roper *Life of Sir Thomas More*

13 'By god's body, master More, *Indignatio principis mors est* [The anger of the sovereign is death].' 'Is that all, my Lord?' quoth he [to the Duke of Norfolk]. 'Then in good faith is there no more difference between your grace and me, but that I shall die to-day, and you to-morrow.'
William Roper *Life of Sir Thomas More*

14 Son Roper, I thank our Lord the field is won.
William Roper *Life of Sir Thomas More*

15 Is not this house as nigh heaven as my own?
of the Tower of London
William Roper *Life of Sir Thomas More*

16 I cumber you good Margaret much, but I would be sorry, if it should be any longer than tomorrow, for it is S. Thomas even and the vtas of Saint Peter and therefore tomorrow long I to go to God, it were a day very meet and convenient for me. I never liked your manner toward me better than when you kissed me last for I love when daughterly love and dear charity hath no leisure to look to worldly courtesy. Fare well my dear child and pray for me, and I shall for you and all your friends that we may merrily meet in heaven.
vtas = *octave*
last letter to his daughter Margaret Roper, 5 July 1535, on the eve of his execution, in E. F. Rogers (ed.) *Correspondence of Sir Thomas More* (1947)

17 I pray you, master Lieutenant, see me safe up, and my coming down let me shift for my self.
of mounting the scaffold
William Roper *Life of Sir Thomas More*

18 Pluck up thy spirits, man, and be not afraid to do thine office; my neck is very short; take heed therefore thou strike not awry, for saving of thine honesty.
words addressed to the executioner; William Roper *Life of Sir Thomas More*

Thomas Morell 1703–84

English librettist

19 See, the conquering hero comes!
Sound the trumpets, beat the drums!
Judas Maccabeus (1747) 'A chorus of youths' and *Joshua* (1748) pt. 3 (to music by Handel)

Morelly fl. 1755

French writer

1 *Tout Citoyen contribuera pour sa part à l'utilité publique selon ses forces, ses talens et son âge; c'est sur cela que seront réglés ses devoirs, conformément aux loix distributives.*

Every citizen will make his own contribution to the activities of the community according to his strength, his talent, and his age: it is on this basis that his duties will be determined, conforming with the distributive laws.

Code de la Nature (1755) pt. 4; see **Blanc** 123:6, **Marx** 516:13

Robin Morgan 1941–

American feminist

2 Sisterhood is powerful.

title of book (1970)

Christopher Morley 1890–1957

American writer

3 Life is a foreign language: all men mispronounce it.

Thunder on the Left (1925) ch. 14; see **Hartley** 374:19

Lord Morley 1838–1923

British Liberal politician and writer

4 The golden Gospel of Silence is effectively compressed in thirty fine volumes.

on **Carlyle**'*s History of Frederick the Great (1858–65), Carlyle having written of his subject as 'that strong, silent man'*
Critical Miscellanies (1886) 'Carlyle'

5 You have not converted a man, because you have silenced him.

On Compromise (1874) ch. 5

Countess Morphy (Marcelle Azra Forbes) fl. 1930–50

6 The tragedy of English cooking is that 'plain' cooking cannot be entrusted to 'plain' cooks.

English Recipes (1935)

Charles Morris 1745–1838

English songwriter

7 But a house is much more to my mind than a tree, And for groves, O! a good grove of chimneys for me.

'Country and Town' (1840)

Desmond Morris 1928–

English anthropologist

8 The city is not a concrete jungle, it is a human zoo.

The Human Zoo (1969) introduction

9 There are one hundred and ninety-three living species of monkeys and apes. One hundred and ninety-two of them are covered with hair. The exception is a naked ape self-named *Homo sapiens.*

The Naked Ape (1967) introduction

Estelle Morris 1952–

British Labour politician

10 I am not good at dealing with the modern media . . . I have not felt I have been as effective as I should be, or as effective as you need me to be.

resignation letter to Tony Blair, 23 October 2002; in *Guardian* 24 October 2002 (electronic edition)

George Pope Morris 1802–64

American poet
see also **Political slogans** 600:22

11 Woodman, spare that tree!
Touch not a single bough!
In youth it sheltered me,
And I'll protect it now.

'Woodman, Spare That Tree' (1830); see **Campbell** 187:8

William Morris 1834–96

English writer, artist, and designer

12 What is this, the sound and rumour? What is this
  that all men hear,
Like the wind in hollow valleys when the storm is
  drawing near,
Like the rolling on of ocean in the eventide of fear?
'Tis the people marching on.

Chants for Socialists (1885) 'The March of the Workers'

13 The idle singer of an empty day.

The Earthly Paradise (1868–70) 'An Apology'

14 Dreamer of dreams, born out of my due time,
Why should I strive to set the crooked straight?

The Earthly Paradise (1868–70) 'An Apology'

15 Forget six counties overhung with smoke,
Forget the snorting steam and piston stroke,
Forget the spreading of the hideous town;
Think rather of the pack-horse on the down,
And dream of London, small and white and clean,
The clear Thames bordered by its gardens green.

The Earthly Paradise (1868–70) 'Prologue: The Wanderers' l. 1

16 Had she come all the way for this,
To part at last without a kiss?
Yea, had she borne the dirt and rain
That her own eyes might see him slain
Beside the haystack in the floods?

'The Haystack in the Floods' (1858) l. 1

17 And ever she sung from noon to noon,
'Two red roses across the moon.'

'Two Red Roses across the Moon' (1858)

18 Fellowship is heaven, and lack of fellowship is hell.

A Dream of John Ball (1888) ch. 4

19 Have nothing in your houses that you do not know to be useful, or believe to be beautiful.

Hopes and Fears for Art (1882) 'Making the Best of It'

20 The reward of labour is life.

News from Nowhere (1891) ch. 15

1 I spend my life ministering to the swinish luxury of the rich.
    reported by Sir Lowthian Bell to Alfred Powell, *c.*1877; W.R. Lethaby *Philip Webb* (1935)

Herbert Morrison 1888–1965

British Labour politician

2 Work is the call. Work at war speed. Good-night—and go to it.
    broadcast as Minister of Supply, 22 May 1940, in *Daily Herald* 23 May 1940

Herbert 'Herb' Morrison d. 1989

American radio announcer

3 It's bursting into flames . . . Oh, the humanity, and all the passengers!
    eyewitness account of the Hindenburg airship bursting into flames
    recorded broadcast, 6 May 1937

4 Listen folks, I'm going to have to stop for a minute, because I've lost my voice—This is the worst thing I've ever witnessed.
    eyewitness account of the Hindenburg disaster
    recorded broadcast, 6 May 1937

Jim Morrison 1943–71

American rock singer and songwriter

5 Five to one, baby, one in five,
No one here gets out alive . . .
They got the guns but we got the numbers
Gonna win, yeah, we're taking over.
    'Five to One' (1968 song)

6 C'mon, baby, light my fire.
    'Light My Fire' (1967 song, with Robby Krieger)

7 What have they done to the earth?
What have they done to our fair sister?
Ravaged and plundered and ripped her and did her,
Stuck her with knives in the side of the dawn,
And tied her with fences and dragged her down.
I hear a very gentle sound,
With your ear down to the ground:
WE WANT THE WORLD AND WE WANT IT NOW!
    'When the Music's Over' (1967 song)

8 I'm interested in anything about revolt, disorder, chaos, especially activity that appears to have no meaning. It seems to me to be the road toward freedom.
    in *Time* 24 January 1968

9 When you make your peace with authority, you become an authority.
    Andrew Doe and John Tobler *In Their Own Words: The Doors* (1988)

R. F. Morrison

10 Just a wee deoch-an-doris,
Just a wee yin, that's a'.
Just a wee deoch-an-doris,
Before we gang awa'.

There's a wee wifie waitin',
In a wee but-an-ben;
If you can say
'It's a braw bricht moonlicht nicht',
Ye're a' richt, ye ken.
    'Just a Wee Deoch-an-Doris' (1911 song); popularized by Harry **Lauder**

Toni Morrison 1931–

American novelist

11 Grab this land! Take it, hold it, my brothers, make it, my brothers, shake it, squeeze it, turn it, twist it, beat it, kick it, whip it, stomp it, dig it, plough it, seed it, reap it, rent it, buy it, sell it, own it, build it, multiply it, and pass it on—Can you hear me? Pass it on!
    Song of Solomon (1977) ch. 10

12 The unending problem of growing old was not how he changed, but how things did.
    Tar Baby (1981) ch. 5

Van Morrison 1945–

Irish singer, songwriter, and musician

13 Music is spiritual. The music business is not.
    in *The Times* 6 July 1990

Dwight Morrow 1873–1931

American lawyer, banker, and diplomat

14 The world is divided into people who do things and people who get the credit. Try, if you can, to belong to the first class. There's far less competition.
    letter to his son, in Harold Nicolson *Dwight Morrow* (1935) ch. 3

15 Any party which takes credit for the rain must not be surprised if its opponents blame it for the drought.
    attributed; William Safire *Safire's New Political Dictionary* (1993)

Wayne Lyman Morse 1900–74

American Democratic politician

16 I believe that history will record that we have made a great mistake.
    in the Senate debate on the Tonkin Gulf Resolution, which committed the United States to intervention in Vietnam; Morse was the only Senator to vote against the resolution
    in *Congressional Record* 6–7 August 1964

Owen Morshead 1893–1977

English librarian

17 The House of Hanover, like ducks, produce bad parents—they trample on their young.
    *as Royal Librarian, in conversation with Harold **Nicolson**, biographer of **George V***
    Harold Nicolson, letter to Vita Sackville-West, 7 January 1949

John Mortimer 1923–

English novelist, barrister, and dramatist

18 They do you a decent death on the hunting-field.
    Paradise Postponed (1985) ch. 18

1 At school I never minded the lessons. I just resented having to work terribly hard at playing.
A Voyage Round My Father (1971) act 1

2 No brilliance is needed in the law. Nothing but common sense, and relatively clean fingernails.
A Voyage Round My Father (1971) act 1

3 The worst fault of the working classes is telling their children they're not going to succeed, saying: 'There is life, but it's not for you.'
in *Daily Mail* 31 May 1988

J. B. Morton ('Beachcomber') 1893–1975
British journalist

4 One disadvantage of being a hog is that at any moment some blundering fool may try to make a silk purse out of your wife's ear.
By the Way (1931)

5 Hush, hush,
Nobody cares!
Christopher Robin
Has
Fallen
Down-
Stairs.
By the Way (1931); see **Milne** 528:5

6 Dr Strabismus (Whom God Preserve) of Utrecht has patented a new invention. It is an illuminated trouser-clip for bicyclists who are using main roads at night.
Morton's Folly (1933)

Jelly Roll Morton 1885–1941
American jazz pianist, composer, and bandleader

7 Jazz music is to be played sweet, soft, plenty rhythm.
Mister Jelly Roll (1950)

Rogers Morton 1914–79
American public relations officer

8 I'm not going to rearrange the furniture on the deck of the Titanic.
having lost five of the last six primaries as President **Ford**'s *campaign manager*
in *Washington Post* 16 May 1976

Thomas Morton c.1764–1838
English dramatist

9 Approbation from Sir Hubert Stanley is praise indeed.
A Cure for the Heartache (1797) act 5, sc. 2; see **Misquotations** 538:14

10 Always ding, dinging Dame Grundy into my ears—what will Mrs Grundy zay? What will Mrs Grundy think?
Speed the Plough (1798) act 1, sc. 1; see **Locker-Lampson** 489:3

Edwin Moses 1955–
American athlete

11 I don't really see the hurdles. I sense them like a memory.
attributed

Andrew Motion 1952–
English poet

12 Each sudden gust of light explains itself
as flames, but neither they, nor even
bombs redoubled on the hills tonight
can quite include me in their fear.
What does remains invisible, is lost
in curt societies whose deaths become
revenge by morning, and whose homes
are nothing more than all they pity most.
'Leaving Belfast' (1978)

13 Beside the river, swerving under ground.
your future tracked you, snapping at your heels:
Diana, breathless, hunted by your own quick
hounds.
'Mythology' (1997)

John Lothrop Motley 1814–77
American historian

14 As long as he lived, he was the guiding-star of a whole brave nation, and when he died the little children cried in the streets.
of William of Orange (1572–84)
The Rise of the Dutch Republic (1856) pt. 6, ch. 7; see **Auden** 34:26

15 Give us the luxuries of life, and we will dispense with its necessities.
Oliver Wendell Holmes *Autocrat of the Breakfast-Table* (1857–8) ch. 6

☐ Mottoes
see box overleaf

Lord Mountbatten 1900–79
British sailor, soldier, and statesman
on Mountbatten: see **Ziegler** 858:9

16 Right, now I understand people think you're the Forgotten Army on the Forgotten Front. I've come here to tell you you're quite wrong. You're not the Forgotten Army on the Forgotten Front. No, make no mistake about it. Nobody's ever *heard* of you.
encouragement to troops when taking over as Supreme Allied Commander South-East Asia in late 1943
R. Hough *Mountbatten* (1980)

Marjorie ('Mo') Mowlam 1949–
British Labour politician

17 It takes courage to push things forward.
on her decision to visit Loyalist prisoners in The Maze, when Secretary of State for Northern Ireland
in *Guardian* 8 January 1998

Daniel P. Moynihan 1927–
American Democratic politician

18 Welfare became a term of opprobrium—a contentious, often vindictive area of political conflict in which liberals and conservatives clashed and children were lost sight of.
in *The Washington Post* 25 November 1994

Mottoes

1 *Ad majorem Dei gloriam.*
To the greater glory of God.
motto of the Society of Jesus

2 *Aut Caesar, aut nihil.*
Caesar or nothing.
motto inscribed on the sword of Cesare Borgia
(1476–1507)

3 Be happy while y'er leevin,
For y'er a lang time deid.
Scottish motto for a house
in *Notes and Queries* 9th series, vol. 8, 7 December 1901

4 Be prepared.
*motto of the Scout Association, based on the ititials
of the founder, Lord Baden-Powell*
Robert Baden-Powell *Scouting for Boys* (1908) pt. 1

5 *Cor ad cor loquitur.*
Heart speaks to heart.
motto of John Henry **Newman**; see **Francis** 332:8

6 Defence, not defiance.
motto of the Volunteers Movement (1859)

7 *Dominus illuminatio mea.*
The Lord is my light.
motto of the University of Oxford; see **Bible** 114:26

8 *Fiat justitia et pereat mundus.*
Let justice be done, though the world perish.
motto of Ferdinand I (1503–64), Holy Roman Emperor;
Johannes Manlius *Locorum Communium Collectanea*
(1563) vol. 2 'De Lege: Octatum Praeceptum'; see
Watson 823:2

9 *Honi soit qui mal y pense.*
Evil be to him who evil thinks.
motto of the Order of the Garter, originated by **Edward III**,
probably on 23 April of 1348 or 1349; see **Sellar and
Yeatman** 676:18

10 *Laborare est orare.*
To work is to pray.
also found in the form 'Ora, lege, et labora [Pray,
read, and work]'
traditional motto of the Benedictine order

11 *Nemo me impune lacessit.*
No one provokes me with impunity.
motto of the Crown of Scotland and of all Scottish
regiments

12 *Nisi Dominus frustra.*
In vain without the Lord.
motto of the city of Edinburgh; see **Bible** 115:5

13 *Nullius in verba.*
In the word of none.
*emphasizing reliance on experiment rather than
authority*
motto of the Royal Society; see **Horace** 398:18

14 *Palmam qui meruit, ferat.*
Let him who has won it bear the palm.
adopted by Lord **Nelson** as his motto, from John Jortin
(1698–1770) *Lusus Poetici* (3rd ed., 1748) 'Ad Ventos'

15 *Per ardua ad astra.*
Through struggle to the stars.
motto of the Mulvany family, quoted and translated by
Rider **Haggard** in *The People of the Mist* (1894) ch. 1; still
in use as motto of the R.A.F., having been proposed by J.
S. Yule in 1912 and approved by King **George V** in 1913

16 Rebellion to tyrants is obedience to God.
motto of Thomas **Jefferson**, from John **Bradshaw**; see
Bradshaw 149:2

17 *Semper eadem.*
Ever the same.
motto of **Elizabeth I**

18 *Sic semper tyrannis.*
Thus always to tyrants.
motto of the State of Virginia; see **Booth** 144:22

19 *Similia similibus curantur.*
Like cures like.
motto of homeopathic medicine, although not found in
this form in the writings of C. F. S. Hahnemann
(1755–1843); the Latin appears as an anonymous side-
note in Paracelsus *Opera Omnia* (c.1490–1541, ed. 1658)
vol. 1

20 They always get their man.
unofficial motto of the Royal Canadian Mounted Police;
attributed to John J. Healy (1840–1908), American
newspaperman and whiskey trader, in 1877

21 They haif said: Quhat say they? Lat thame say.
motto of the Earls Marischal of Scotland, inscribed at
Marischal College, Aberdeen, 1593; a similarly defiant
motto in Greek has been found engraved in remains from
classical antiquity

22 Who dares wins.
motto of the British Special Air Service regiment, from
1942

Wolfgang Amadeus Mozart 1756–91

Austrian composer
on Mozart: see **Joseph II** 436:14, **Lehrer** 479:11, **Schnabel**
671:13

23 I am happier when I have something to compose,
for that, after all, is my sole delight and passion.
letter to his father Leopold, 11 October 1777; Emily
Anderson (ed.) *Letters of Mozart and his Family* (1966)
vol. 1

24 The happy medium—truth in all things—is no
longer either known or valued; to gain applause,
one must write things so inane that they may be
played on a barrel-organ, or so unintelligible that
no rational being can comprehend them, though
on that very account they are likely to please.
letter to his father Leopold, 28 December 1782; *The Letters*
(tr. Lady Wallace, 1865)

1 Melody is the essence of music. I compare a good
melodist to a fine racer, and counterpoints to hack
post-horses.
> remark to Michael Kelly, 1786; Michael Kelly
> *Reminiscences* (1826)

2 The whole, though it be long, stands almost
complete and finished in my mind, so that I can
survey it, like a fine picture or a beautiful statue,
at a glance. Nor do I hear in my imagination the
parts *successively*, but I hear them, as it were, all
at once. What a delight this is I cannot tell!
on his method of composition
> letter, Edward Holmes *The Life of Mozart* (1845)

Hosni Mubarak 1928-
Egyptian statesman, President since 1981

3 Instead of having one [Osama] bin Laden, we will
have 100 bin Ladens.
on the probable result of a western invasion of Iraq
> in *Newsweek* 14 April 2003

Robert Mugabe 1924-
*African statesman; Prime Minister of Zimbabwe, 1980-7,
President 1987-*

4 Cricket civilizes people and creates good
gentlemen. I want everyone to play cricket in
Zimbabwe; I want ours to be a nation of
gentlemen.
> in *Sunday Times* 26 February 1984

5 Our present state of mind is that you are now our
enemies.
to white farmers in Zimbabwe
> television broadcast, 18 April 2000

6 Blair, keep your England and let me keep my
Zimbabwe.
> at the Earth Summit in Johannesburg, 2 September 2002

Malcolm Muggeridge 1903-90
British journalist

7 Something beautiful for God.
> title of book (1971); see **Teresa** 785:11

8 The orgasm has replaced the Cross as the focus of
longing and the image of fulfilment.
> *Tread Softly* (1966)

9 He was not only a bore; he bored for England.
*of Anthony **Eden***
> *Tread Softly* (1966)

10 Good taste and humour . . . are a contradiction in
terms, like a chaste whore.
> in *Time* 14 September 1953

Edwin Muir 1887-1959
Scottish poet

11 And without fear the lawless roads
Ran wrong through all the land.
> 'Hölderlin's Journey' (1937)

12 Barely a twelvemonth after
The seven days war that put the world to sleep,
Late in the evening the strange horses came.
> 'The Horses' (1956)

Frank Muir 1920-98
English writer and broadcaster

13 The thinking man's crumpet.
of Joan Bakewell
> attributed

Jean Muir 1928-95
English fashion designer

14 Engineering with fabric.
her definition of dressmaking
> in *The Times* 30 May 1995, obituary

15 The clothes in themselves do not make a
statement. The woman makes the statement and
the dress helps.
> in *Vogue* August 1995

Paul Muldoon 1951-
Irish poet

16 I thought of you tonight, *a leanbh*, lying there in
your long barrow,
colder and dumber than a fish by Francisco de
Herrera.
> 'Incantata' (1994)

17 The Volkswagen parked in the gap,
But gently ticking over.
You wonder if it's lovers
And not men hurrying back
Across two fields and a river.
> 'Ireland' (1980)

Robert Muldoon 1921-92
New Zealand statesman, Prime Minister 1975-84

18 When New Zealanders emigrate to Australia, it
raises the average IQ of both countries.
> attributed

H. J. Muller 1890-1967
American geneticist

19 To say, for example, that a man is made up of
certain chemical elements is a satisfactory
description only for those who intend to use him
as a fertilizer.
> *Science and Criticism* (1943)

Herbert J. Muller 1905-80
American historian

20 Few have heard of Fra Luca Pacioli, the inventor
of double-entry bookkeeping; but he has probably
had much more influence on human life than has
Dante or Michelangelo.
> *Uses of the Past* (1957) ch. 8

Wilhelm Müller 1794-1827
German poet

21 *Vom Abendrot zum Morgenlicht*
Ward mancher Kopf zum Greise.

*Wer glaubt's? Und meiner ward es nicht
Auf dieser ganzen Reise.*

Between dusk and dawn many a head has turned
white. Who can believe it? And mine has not
changed on all this long journey.

Die Winterreise (1823) bk. 2 'Der greise Kopf'

Ethel Watts Mumford et al. 1878–1940
American writer and humorist

1 In the midst of life we are in debt.
Altogether New Cynic's Calendar (1907); see **Book of
Common Prayer** 133:17

Lewis Mumford 1895–1990
American sociologist

2 Every generation revolts against its fathers and
makes friends with its grandfathers.
The Brown Decades (1931)

3 Our national flower is the concrete cloverleaf.
in *Quote Magazine* 8 October 1961

Mumonkan c.1228
a Japanese Zen textbook

4 A monk once asked Jōshū, 'Has a dog the Buddha-
Nature?'
Jōshū answered, 'Mu!'
case 1

5 He [Buddha] held up a flower before the
congregation of monks. At this time all were silent
but the Venerable Kasyapa only smiled. The
World-Honoured One said . . .
'Without relying upon words and letters, beyond
all teaching as a special transmission, I pass this
all on to Mahakasyapa.'
case 6

6 A monk asked Tōzan, 'What is the Buddha?'
He replied 'Three pounds of flax.'
case 18

7 A monk asked Ummon, 'What is the Buddha?'
'It is a shit-wiping stick,' replied Ummon.
case 21

8 A monk asked Jōshū, 'What did Daruma
[Bodhidharma] come to China for?' Jōshū
answered, 'The oak tree in the [temple] front
garden.'
case 37

Edvard Munch 1863–1944
Norwegian painter and engraver

9 You should not paint the chair, but only what
someone has felt about it.
written c.1891; R. Heller *Munch* (1984) ch. 4

Murasaki Shikibu c.978–c.1031
Japanese writer and courtier

10 Anything whatsoever may become the subject of a
novel, provided only that it happens in this
mundane life and not in some fairyland beyond
our human ken.
The Tale of Genji

11 People who have become so precious that they go
out of their way to try and be sensitive in the most
unpromising situations, trying to capture every
moment of interest, are bound to look ridiculous
and superficial.
The Diary of Lady Murasaki (translated by Richard Bowring,
1996)

Iris Murdoch 1919–99
English novelist

12 Dora Greenfield left her husband because she was
afraid of him. She decided six months later to
return to him for the same reason.
The Bell (1958) ch. 1

13 All our failures are ultimately failures in love.
The Bell (1958) ch. 19

14 Those who are caught in mental cages can often
picture freedom, it just has no attractive power.
The Sea, The Sea (1978) ch. 6

15 One doesn't have to get anywhere in a marriage.
It's not a public conveyance.
A Severed Head (1961) ch. 3

16 Love is the extremely difficult realisation that
something other than oneself is real. Love, and so
art and morals, is the discovery of reality.
'The Sublime and the Good' in *Chicago Review* 13 (1959)

17 Anything that consoles is fake.
R. Harries *Prayer and the Pursuit of Happiness* (1985)

18 We live in a fantasy world, a world of illusion. The
great task in life is to find reality.
in *The Times* 15 April 1983 'Profile'

19 I'm just wandering, I think of things and then
they go away for ever.
*in September 1996 on her inability to write; the
following February it was announced that she was
suffering from Alzheimer's disease*
in *Times* 5 February 1997

Rupert Murdoch 1931–
Australian-born American publisher and media entrepreneur

20 *asked why he had allowed Page 3 to develop:*
I don't know. The editor did it when I was away.
in *Guardian* 25 February 1994

C. W. Murphy and Will Letters

21 Has anybody here seen Kelly?
Kelly from the Isle of Man?
'Has Anybody Here Seen Kelly?' (1909 song)

Fred Murray
American songwriter

22 Ginger, you're balmy!
title of song (1910)

James Augustus Henry Murray
1837–1915

Scottish lexicographer, first Editor of the Oxford English Dictionary

1 I feel that in many respects I and my assistants are simply pioneers, pushing our way experimentally through an untrodden forest, where no white man's axe has been before us.
'Report on the Philological Society's Dictionary' (1884) in *Transactions of the Philological Society* 1882–4

Les A. Murray 1938–
Australian poet

2   The trouble
with being best man is, you don't get a chance to prove it.
The Boys Who Stole the Funeral (1989)

3 Nothing's said till it's dreamed out in words
And nothing's true that figures in words only.
The Daylight Moon (1987) 'Poetry and Religion'

4 Men must have legends, else they will die of strangeness.
The Ilex Tree (1965) 'The Noonday Axeman'

Ed Murrow 1908–65
American broadcaster and journalist

5 No one can terrorize a whole nation, unless we are all his accomplices.
of Joseph **McCarthy**
'See It Now', broadcast, 7 March 1954

6 He mobilized the English language and sent it into battle to steady his fellow countrymen and hearten those Europeans upon whom the long dark night of tyranny had descended.
of Winston **Churchill**
broadcast, 30 November 1954, in *In Search of Light* (1967)

7 Anyone who isn't confused doesn't really understand the situation.
on the Vietnam War
Walter Bryan *The Improbable Irish* (1969) ch. 1

Alfred de Musset 1810–57
French poet and dramatist

8 *Je haïs comme la mort l'état de plagiaire;
Mon verre n'est pas grand mais je bois dans mon verre.*
I hate like death the situation of the plagiarist; the glass I drink from is not large, but at least it is my own.
La Coupe et les lèvres (1832)

9 *Malgré moi l'infini me tourmente.*
I can't help it, the idea of the infinite torments me.
'L'Espoir en Dieu' (1838)

10 *Le seul bien qui me reste au monde
Est d'avoir quelquefois pleuré.*
The only good thing left to me is that I have sometimes wept.
'Tristesse' (1841)

11 *Je suis venu trop tard dans un monde trop vieux.*
I have come too late into a world too old.
Rollo (1833)

Benito Mussolini 1883–1945
Italian Fascist dictator

12 We must leave exactly on time . . . From now on everything must function to perfection.
to a station-master
Giorgio Pini *Mussolini* (1939) vol. 2, ch. 6; an early report was:

The first benefit of Benito Mussolini's direction in Italy begins to be felt when one crosses the Italian Frontier and hears '*Il treno arriva all'orario* [The train is arriving on time]'.
Infanta Eulalia of Spain *Courts and Countries after the War* (1925)

A. J. Muste 1885–1967
American pacifist

13 If I can't love Hitler, I can't love at all.
at a Quaker meeting 1940; in *New York Times* 12 February 1967

14 There is no way to peace. Peace is the way.
in *New York Times* 16 November 1967

Nn

Vladimir Nabokov 1899–1977
Russian novelist
see also **Opening lines** 574:32

15 You can always count on a murderer for a fancy prose style.
Lolita (1955) ch. 1

16 Life is a great surprise. I do not see why death should not be an even greater one.
Pale Fire (1962)

17 The cradle rocks above an abyss, and common sense tells us that our existence is but a brief crack of light between two eternities of darkness.
Speak, Memory (1951) ch. 1

Ralph Nader 1934–
American consumer protectionist

18 Unsafe at any speed.
title of book (1965); see **Keats** 447:10

Nagarjuna c.2nd century AD
Indian philosopher

19 The doctrine of the Buddha is taught with reference to two truths—conventional truth and ultimate truth.
Those who do not understand the difference between these two truths do not understand the profound essence of the doctrine of the Buddha.
Root Verses of the Middle Way ch. 24, v. 8

Sarojini Naidu 1879–1949

Indian politician

1 If only Bapu knew the cost of setting him up in poverty!

of Mahatma Gandhi

A. Campbell-Johnson *Mission with Mountbatten* (1951) ch. 12

Shiva Naipaul 1945–85

Trinidadian writer

2 The Third World is an artificial construction of the West—an ideological empire on which the sun is always setting.

An Unfinished Journey (1986)

Ian Nairn 1930–

British architect

3 If what is called development is allowed to multiply at the present rate, then by the end of the century Great Britain will consist of isolated oases of preserved monuments in a desert of wire, concrete roads, cosy plots and bungalows . . . Upon this new Britain bestows a name in the hope that it will stick—SUBTOPIA.

in *Architectural Review* June 1955

Lewis Namier 1888–1960

Polish-born British historian

4 No number of atrocities however horrible can deprive a nation of its right to independence, nor justify its being put under the heel of its worst enemies and persecutors.

in 1919; Julia Namier *Lewis Namier* (1971)

Fridtjof Nansen 1861–1930

Norwegian polar explorer

5 Never stop because you are afraid—you are never so likely to be wrong. Never keep a line of retreat: it is a wretched invention. The difficult is what takes a little time; the impossible is what takes a little longer.

in *Listener* 14 December 1939; see **Calonne** 186:5, **Military sayings** 526:6

Napoleon I 1769–1821

French monarch, Emperor 1804–15

on Napoleon: see **Byron** 182:25, **Wellington** 827:16; *see also* **Dumouriez** 291:14

6 Think of it, soldiers; from the summit of these pyramids, forty centuries look down upon you.

speech to the Army of Egypt on 21 July 1798, before the Battle of the Pyramids

Gaspard Gourgaud *Mémoires* (1823) vol. 2 'Égypte—Bataille des Pyramides'

7 It [the Channel] is a mere ditch, and will be crossed as soon as someone has the courage to attempt it.

letter to Consul Cambacérès, 16 November 1803, in *Correspondance de Napoléon Ier* (1858–69) vol. 9

8 Let us be masters of the Channel for six hours, and we are masters of the world.

*c.*1803; J. R. Green *History of the English People* (1880) vol. 4, ch. 9

9 A prince who gets a reputation for good nature in the first year of his reign, is laughed at in the second.

letter to his brother Louis, King of Holland, 4 April 1807, in *Correspondance de Napoléon Ier* (1858–69) vol. 15

10 It is easier to put up with unpleasantness from a man of one's own way of thinking than from one who takes an entirely different point of view.

letter to J. Finckenstein, 14 April 1807, in *Mémoires et Correspondance politique et militaire du Roi Joseph* (1854) vol. 3

11 I want the whole of Europe to have one currency; it will make trading much easier.

letter to his brother Louis, 6 May 1807; Alistair Horne *How Far from Austerlitz?* (1996)

12 Religion is an all-important matter in a public school for girls. Whatever people say, it is the mother's safeguard, and the husband's. What we ask of education is not that girls should think, but that they should believe.

'Note sur L'Établissement D'Écouen' 15 May 1807, in *Correspondance de Napoléon Ier* (1858–69) vol. 15

13 In war, three-quarters turns on personal character and relations; the balance of manpower and materials counts only for the remaining quarter.

'Observations sur les affaires d'Espagne, Saint-Cloud, 27 août 1808' in *Correspondance de Napoléon Ier* (1858–69) vol. 17

14 It is a matter of great interest what sovereigns are doing; but as to what Grand Duchesses are doing—Who cares?

letter, 17 December 1811, in *Lettres inédits de Napoléon I* (1897) vol. 2

15 There is only one step from the sublime to the ridiculous.

to De Pradt, Polish ambassador, after the retreat from Moscow in 1812

D. G. De Pradt *Histoire de l'Ambassade dans le grand-duché de Varsovie en 1812* (1815); see **Paine** 582:5, **Proverbs** 620:32

16 *La France a plus besoin de moi que je n'ai besoin de la France.*

France has more need of me than I have need of France.

speech to the Corps Législatif, Paris, 31 December 1813

17 As to moral courage, I have very rarely met with two o'clock in the morning courage: I mean instantaneous courage.

E. A. de Las Cases *Mémorial de Ste-Hélène* (1823) vol. 1, pt. 2, 4–5 December 1815; see **Thoreau** 793:9

18 Nothing is more contrary to the organization of the mind, of the memory, and of the imagination . . . The new system of weights and measures will be a stumbling block and the source of difficulties for several generations . . . It's just tormenting the people with trivia!!!

on the introduction of the metric system

Mémoires . . . écrits à Ste-Hélène (1823–5) bk. 4, ch. 21, pt. 4

1 An army marches on its stomach.
  attributed, but probably condensed from a long passage in
  E. A. de Las Cases *Mémorial de Ste-Hélène* (1823) vol. 4, 14
  November 1816; also attributed to **Frederick the Great**, in
  Notes and Queries 10 March 1866; see **Proverbs** 614:31,
  Sellar and Yeatman 676:24

2 As though he had 200,000 men.
  when asked how to deal with the Pope
  J. M. Robinson *Cardinal Consalvi* (1987); see **Stalin** 754:3

3 *La carrière ouverte aux talents.*
  The career open to the talents.
  Barry E. O'Meara *Napoleon in Exile* (1822) vol. 1

4 England is a nation of shopkeepers.
  Barry E. O'Meara *Napoleon in Exile* (1822) vol. 2; see
  Adams 3:14, **Proverbs** 618:44, **Smith** 741:9

5 Not tonight, Josephine.
  attributed, but probably apocryphal; the phrase does not
  appear in contemporary sources, but was current by the
  early twentieth century

6 *of Talleyrand:*
  A pile of shit in a silk stocking.
  attributed

Ogden Nash 1902–71
American humorist

7 The turtle lives 'twixt plated decks
  Which practically conceal its sex.
  I think it clever of the turtle
  In such a fix to be so fertile.
  'Autres Bêtes, Autres Moeurs' (1931)

8 The camel has a single hump;
  The dromedary, two;
  Or else the other way around,
  I'm never sure. Are you?
  'The Camel' (1936)

9 The cow is of the bovine ilk;
  One end is moo, the other, milk.
  'The Cow' (1931)

10 One would be in less danger
  From the wiles of the stranger
  If one's own kin and kith
  Were more fun to be with.
  'Family Court' (1931)

11 Beneath this slab
  John Brown is stowed.
  He watched the ads,
  And not the road.
  'Lather as You Go' (1942)

12 Do you think my mind is maturing late,
  Or simply rotted early?
  'Lines on Facing Forty' (1942)

13 Good wine needs no bush,
  And perhaps products that people really want
    need no hard-sell or soft-sell TV push.
  Why not?
  Look at pot.
  'Most Doctors Recommend or yours For Fast, Fast, Fast
  Relief' (1972)

14 Any kiddie in school can love like a fool,
  But hating, my boy, is an art.
  'Plea for Less Malice Toward None' (1933)

15 Candy
  Is dandy
  But liquor
  Is quicker.
  'Reflections on Ice-breaking' (1931)

16 I test my bath before I sit,
  And I'm always moved to wonderment
  That what chills the finger not a bit
  Is so frigid upon the fundament.
  'Samson Agonistes' (1942)

17 I think that I shall never see
  A billboard lovely as a tree.
  Perhaps, unless the billboards fall,
  I'll never see a tree at all.
  'Song of the Open Road' (1933); see **Kilmer** 451:8

18 Sure, deck your lower limbs in pants;
  Yours are the limbs, my sweeting.
  You look divine as you advance—
  Have you seen yourself retreating?
  'What's the Use?' (1940)

Thomas Nashe 1567–1601
English pamphleteer and dramatist

19 O, tis a precious apothegmatical Pedant, who will
  find matter enough to dilate a whole day of the
  first invention of *Fy, fa, fum,* I smell the blood of
  an English-man.
  Have with you to Saffron-walden (1596); see **Anonymous**
  16:2, **Shakespeare** 701:2

20 Beauty is but a flower
  Which wrinkles will devour.
  Summer's Last Will and Testament (1600) l. 1588

21 Brightness falls from the air;
  Queens have died young and fair;
  Dust hath closed Helen's eye.
  I am sick, I must die.
  Lord have mercy on us.
  Summer's Last Will and Testament (1600) l. 1590

22 From winter, plague and pestilence, good lord,
    deliver us!
  Summer's Last Will and Testament (1600) l. 1878

James Ball Naylor 1860–1945

23 King David and King Solomon
  Led merry, merry lives,
  With many, many lady friends,
  And many, many wives;
  But when old age crept over them—
  With many, many qualms!—
  King Solomon wrote the Proverbs
  And King David wrote the Psalms.
  'King David and King Solomon' (1935)

John Mason Neale 1818–66
English clergyman

24 All glory, laud, and honour
  To thee, Redeemer, King,
  To whom the lips of children

Made sweet hosannas ring.

'All glory, laud, and honour' (1859 hymn); translated from the Latin traditionally attributed to St Theodulph of Orleans, c.820

1 Good King Wenceslas looked out,
On the feast of Stephen;
When the snow lay round about,
Deep and crisp and even.

'Good King Wenceslas'

2 Jerusalem the golden,
With milk and honey blessed.

'Jerusalem the golden' (1858 hymn); translated from the Latin of Bernard of Cluny (fl. 1140)

Jawaharlal Nehru 1889-1964

Indian statesman

3 At the stroke of the midnight hour, while the world sleeps, India will awake to life and freedom.

immediately prior to Independence

speech to the Indian Constituent Assembly, 14 August 1947

4 The light has gone out of our lives and there is darkness everywhere.

*following **Gandhi**'s assassination*

broadcast, 30 January 1948; Richard J. Walsh *Nehru on Gandhi* (1948) ch. 6

5 I may lose many things including my temper, but I do not lose my nerve.

at a press conference in Delhi, 4 June 1958

6 Democracy and socialism are means to an end, not the end itself.

'Basic Approach'; written for private circulation and reprinted in Vincent Shean *Nehru: the Years of Power* (1960)

7 There is no easy walk-over to freedom anywhere, and many of us will have to pass through the valley of the shadow again and again before we reach the mountain-tops of our desire.

'From Lucknow to Tripuri' (1939)

8 After every other Viceroy has been forgotten, Curzon will be remembered because he restored all that was beautiful in India.

in conversation with Lord Swinton

Kenneth Rose *Superior Person* (1969)

9 I shall be the last Englishman to rule in India.

J. K. Galbraith *A Life in Our Times* (1981)

A. S. Neill 1883-1973

Scottish teacher and educationist

10 If we have to have an exam at 11, let us make it one for humour, sincerity, imagination, character—and where is the examiner who could test such qualities.

letter to *Daily Telegraph* 1957; in *Daily Telegraph* 25 September 1973

Horatio, Lord Nelson 1758-1805

British admiral
*on Nelson: see **Southey** 749:16; see also **Last words** 473:22, **Mottoes** 552:14*

11 It is my turn now; and if I come back, it is yours.

exercising his privilege, as second lieutenant, to board a prize ship before the Master

Robert Southey *Life of Nelson* (1813) ch. 1

12 You must consider every man your enemy who speaks ill of your king: and . . . you must hate a Frenchman as you hate the devil.

Robert Southey *Life of Nelson* (1813) ch. 3

13 Before this time to-morrow I shall have gained a peerage, or Westminster Abbey.

before the battle of the Nile, 1798

Robert Southey *Life of Nelson* (1813) ch. 5

14 I have only one eye,—I have a right to be blind sometimes . . . I really do not see the signal!

at the battle of Copenhagen, 1801

Robert Southey *Life of Nelson* (1813) ch. 7

15 In honour I gained them, and in honour I will die with them.

when asked to cover the stars on his uniform

Robert Southey *Life of Nelson* (1813) ch. 9

16 I believe my arrival was most welcome, not only to the Commander of the Fleet but almost to every individual in it.

letter to Lady Hamilton, 1 October 1805, in Robert Southey *Life of Nelson* (1813) ch. 9

17 When I came to explain to them the '*Nelson* touch', it was like an electric shock. Some shed tears, all approved—'It was new—it was singular—it was simple!'

letter to Lady Hamilton, 1 October 1805, in Robert Southey *Life of Nelson* (1813) ch. 9

18 May the Great God, whom I worship, grant to my Country and for the benefit of Europe in general a great and glorious victory; and may no misconduct in anyone tarnish it; and may humanity after Victory be the predominant feature of the British Fleet. For myself, individually, I commit my life to Him who made me, and may His blessing light upon my endeavours for serving my Country faithfully. To Him I resign myself and the just cause which is entrusted to me to defend. Amen. Amen. Amen.

diary entry, on the eve of the battle of Trafalgar, 21 October 1805

Nicholas Harris Nicolas (ed.) *Dispatches and Letters of . . . Nelson* (1846) vol. 7, p. 139

19 England expects that every man will do his duty.

at the battle of Trafalgar, 21 October 1805

Robert Southey *Life of Nelson* (1813) ch. 9

20 This is too warm work, Hardy, to last long.

at the battle of Trafalgar, 21 October 1805

Robert Southey *Life of Nelson* (1813) ch. 9

21 Kiss me, Hardy.

at the battle of Trafalgar, 21 October 1805

Robert Southey *Life of Nelson* (1813) ch. 9

Howard Nemerov 1920–91

American poet and novelist

1 praise without end the go-ahead zeal
of whoever it was invented the wheel;
but never a word for the poor soul's sake
that thought ahead, and invented the brake.

'To the Congress of the United States, Entering Its Third
Century' 26 February 1989

Pablo Neruda 1904–73

Chilean poet

2 *Y pronto, entre la ropa y el humo, sobre la mesa
   handida,
como una barajada cantidad, queda el alma.*

Soon, caught between clothes and smoke, on the
sunken floor,
the soul's reduced to a shuffled pack,

'The Heights of Macchu Picchu' (1945) canto 2, translated
by Nathaniel Tarn

3 *Déjame olvidar hoy esta dicha, que es más ancha que
   el mar,
porque el hombre es más ancho que el mar y que sus
   islas,
y hay que caer en él como en un pozo para salir del
   fondo
con un ramo de agua secreta y de verdades
   sumergidas.*

Today let me forget this happiness, wider than all
the sea,
because man is wider than all the sea and her
necklace of islands
and we must fall into him as down a well to
clamber back with
branches of secret water, recondite truths.

'The Heights of Macchu Picchu' (1945) canto 11,
translated by Nathaniel Tarn

4 I have gone marking the blank atlas of your body
with crosses of fire.
My mouth went across: a spider, trying to hide.
In you, behind you, timid, driven by thirst.

'I Have Gone Marking' (1924), translated by W. S. Merwin

5 I did not come to solve anything.
I came here to sing
and for you to sing with me.

'Let the Rail Splitter Awake' (1950) translated by Waldeen

6 *Es tan corto el amor, y es tan largo el olvido.*

Love is so short, forgetting is so long.

'Tonight I Can Write' (1924)

Gérard de Nerval 1808–55

French poet

7 *Dieu est mort! le ciel est vide—
Pleurez! enfants, vous n'avez plus de père.*

God is dead! Heaven is empty—Weep, children,
you no longer have a father.

Les Chimères (1854) 'Le Christ aux Oliviers' epigraph
(summarizing a passage in Jean Paul's *Blumen-Frucht-und
Dornstücke* (1796–7) in which God's children are referred
to as 'orphans')

8 *Je suis le ténébreux,—le veuf,—l'inconsolé,
Le prince d'Aquitaine à la tour abolie:*

*Ma seule étoile est morte, et mon luth constellé
Porte le soleil noir de la mélancolie.*

I am the darkly shaded, the bereaved, the
inconsolate, the prince of Aquitaine, with the
blasted tower. My only *star* is dead, and my star-
strewn lute carries on it the black *sun* of
melancholy.

Les Chimères (1854) 'El Desdichado'

9 Why should a lobster be any more ridiculous than
a dog . . . or any other animal that one chooses to
take for a walk? I have a liking for lobsters. They
are peaceful, serious creatures. They know the
secrets of the sea, they don't bark, and they don't
gnaw upon one's monadic privacy like dogs do.
And Goethe had an aversion to dogs, and he
wasn't mad.

*justifying his walking a lobster on a lead in the
gardens of the Palais Royal*

T. Gautier *Portraits et Souvenirs Littéraires* (1875),
translated by Richard Holmes

Edith Nesbit 1858–1924

English writer

10 It is a curious thing that people only ask if you are
enjoying yourself when you aren't.

Five of Us, and Madeline (1925)

11 The affection you get back from children is
sixpence given as change for a sovereign.

Julia Briggs *A Woman of Passion* (1987)

John von Neumann 1903–57

*Hungarian-born American mathematician and computer
pioneer*

12 In mathematics you don't understand things. You
just get used to them.

Gary Zukav *The Dancing Wu Li Masters* (1979)

Otto Neurath 1882–1945

German philosopher

13 We are like sailors who must rebuild their ship on
the open sea, never able to dismantle it in dry-
dock and to reconstruct it there out of the best
materials.

'Protocol Sentences', in A. J. Ayer (ed.) *Logical Positivism*
(1959)

Allan Nevins 1890–1971

American historian

14 The former Allies had blundered in the past by
offering Germany too little, and offering even that
too late, until finally Nazi Germany had become a
menace to all mankind.

in *Current History* (New York) May 1935

Henry Newbolt 1862–1938

English lawyer, poet, and man of letters

1 'Take my drum to England, hang et by the shore,
   Strike et when your powder's runnin' low;
   If the Dons sight Devon, I'll quit the port o'
       Heaven,
   An' drum them up the Channel as we drummed
       them long ago.'
   'Drake's Drum' (1897)

2 Drake he's in his hammock till the great Armadas
       come.
   (Capten, art tha sleepin' there below?)
   Slung atween the round shot, listenin' for the
       drum,
   An' dreamin' arl the time o' Plymouth Hoe.
   'Drake's Drum' (1897)

3 Now the sunset breezes shiver,
   And she's fading down the river,
   But in England's song for ever
   She's the Fighting Téméraire.
   'The Fighting Téméraire' (1897)

4 'Qui procul hinc', the legend's writ,—
   The frontier-grave is far away—
   'Qui ante diem periit:
   Sed miles, sed pro patria.'
   The Island Race (1898) 'Clifton Chapel'

5 There's a breathless hush in the Close to-night—
   Ten to make and the match to win—
   A bumping pitch and a blinding light,
   An hour to play and the last man in.
   And it's not for the sake of a ribboned coat,
   Or the selfish hope of a season's fame,
   But his Captain's hand on his shoulder smote—
   'Play up! play up! and play the game!'
   'Vitaï Lampada' (1897)

Anthony Newley 1931–99 and **Leslie Bricusse** 1931–

6 Stop the world, I want to get off.
   title of musical (1961)

John Henry Newman 1801–90

English theologian and leader of the Oxford Movement; later Cardinal

see also **Epitaphs** 309:5, **Mottoes** 552:5, **Toasts** 796:4

7 It is very difficult to get up resentment towards
   persons whom one has never seen.
   Apologia pro Vita Sua (1864) 'Mr Kingsley's Method of
   Disputation'

8 There is such a thing as legitimate warfare: war
   has its laws; there are things which may fairly be
   done, and things which may not be done . . . He
   has attempted (as I may call it) to *poison the wells.*
   Apologia pro Vita Sua (1864) 'Mr Kingsley's Method of
   Disputation'

9 I will vanquish, not my Accuser, but my judges.
   Apologia pro Vita Sua (1864) 'True Mode of meeting Mr
   Kingsley'

10 Two and two only supreme and luminously self-
   evident beings, myself and my Creator.
   Apologia pro Vita Sua (1864) 'History of My Religious
   Opinions to the Year 1833'

11 It would be a gain to the country were it vastly
   more superstitious, more bigoted, more gloomy,
   more fierce in its religion than at present it shows
   itself to be.
   Apologia pro Vita Sua (1864) 'History of My Religious
   Opinions from 1833 to 1839'

12 From the age of fifteen, dogma has been the
   fundamental principle of my religion: I know no
   other religion; I cannot enter into the idea of any
   other sort of religion; religion, as a mere
   sentiment, is to me a dream and a mockery.
   Apologia pro Vita Sua (1864) 'History of My Religious
   Opinions from 1833 to 1839'

13 This is what the Church is said to want, not party
   men, but sensible, temperate, sober, well-judging
   persons, to guide it through the channel of
   no-meaning, between the Scylla and Charybdis of
   Aye and No.
   Apologia pro Vita Sua (1864) 'History of My Religious
   Opinions from 1833 to 1839'

14 Ten thousand difficulties do not make one doubt.
   Apologia pro Vita Sua (1864) 'Position of my Mind since
   1845'

15 The all-corroding, all-dissolving scepticism of the
   intellect in religious enquiries.
   Apologia pro Vita Sua (1864) 'Position of my Mind since
   1845'

16 It is almost a definition of a gentleman to say that
   he is one who never inflicts pain.
   The Idea of a University (1852) 'Knowledge and Religious
   Duty'

17 She [the Catholic Church] holds that it were better
   for sun and moon to drop from heaven, for the
   earth to fail, and for all the many millions who are
   upon it to die of starvation in extremest agony, as
   far as temporal affliction goes, than that one soul,
   I will not say, should be lost, but should commit
   one single venial sin, should tell one wilful
   untruth . . . or steal one poor farthing without
   excuse.
   Lectures on Anglican Difficulties (1852) Lecture 8

18 It is as absurd to argue men, as to torture them,
   into believing.
   'The Usurpations of Reason' (1831) in *Oxford University
   Sermons* (1843) no. 4

19 And this is all that is known, and more than all—
   yet nothing to what the angels know—of the life
   of a servant of God, who sinned and repented, and
   did penance and washed out his sins, and became
   a Saint, and reigns with Christ in heaven.
   Lives of the English Saints (1844–5) 'The Legend of Saint

Bettelin'; though attributed to Newman, 'and more than all' may have been added by J. A. Froude (1818–94)

1 When men understand what each other mean, they see, for the most part, that controversy is either superfluous or hopeless.

'Faith and Reason, contrasted as Habits of Mind' (Epiphany, 1839) in *Oxford University Sermons* (1843) no. 10

2 May He support us all the day long, till the shades lengthen, and the evening comes, and the busy world is hushed, and the fever of life is over, and our work is done! Then in His mercy may He give us a safe lodging, and a holy rest, and peace at the last.

'Wisdom and Innocence' (19 February 1843) in *Sermons Bearing on Subjects of the Day* (1843) no. 20

3 Firmly I believe and truly
God is Three, and God is One;
And I next acknowledge duly
Manhood taken by the Son.

The Dream of Gerontius (1865)

4 Praise to the Holiest in the height,
And in the depth be praise;
In all his words most wonderful,
Most sure in all His ways.

The Dream of Gerontius (1865)

5 Lead, kindly Light, amid the encircling gloom,
Lead thou me on;
The night is dark, and I am far from home,
Lead thou me on.
Keep Thou my feet; I do not ask to see
The distant scene; one step enough for me.

'Lead, kindly Light' (1834)

6 I loved the garish day, and spite of fears,
Pride ruled my will: remember not past years.

'Lead, kindly Light' (1834); see **Milton** 529:15

7 *We can believe what we choose.* We are answerable for what we choose to believe.

letter to Mrs William Froude, 27 June 1848, in C. S. Dessain (ed.) *Letters and Diaries of John Henry Newman* vol. 12 (1962)

□ **Newspaper headlines and leaders**

see box overleaf

Huey Newton 1942–

American political activist

8 I suggested [in 1966] that we use the panther as our symbol and call our political vehicle the Black Panther Party. The panther is a fierce animal, but he will not attack until he is backed into a corner; then he will strike out.

Revolutionary Suicide (1973) ch. 16; see **Political slogans** 601:6

Isaac Newton 1642–1727

English mathematician and physicist
on Newton: see **Auden** 35:17, **Blake** 120:17, **Brereton** 150:24, **Cowper** 248:2, **Pope** 603:27, **Thomson** 792:17, **Wordsworth** 849:11

9 Whence is it that Nature does nothing in vain: and whence arises all that order and beauty which we see in the world? . . . does it not appear from phenomena that there is a Being incorporeal, living, intelligent, omnipresent, who in infinite space, as it were in his Sensory, sees the things themselves intimately, and thoroughly perceives them, and comprehends them wholly.

Opticks (1730 ed.) bk. 3, pt. 1, question 28

10 The changing of bodies into light, and light into bodies, is very conformable to the course of Nature, which seems delighted with transmutations.

Opticks (1730 ed.) bk. 3, pt. 1, question 30

11 *Corpus omne perseverare in statu suo quiescendi vel movendi uniformiter in directum, nisi quatenus illud a viribus impressis cogitur statum suum mutare.*

Every body continues in its state of rest, or of uniform motion in a right line, unless it is compelled to change that state by forces impressed upon it.

Principia Mathematica (1687) Laws of Motion 1 (translated by Andrew Motte, 1729)

12 *Mutationem motus proportionalem esse vi motrici impressae et fieri secundum lineam rectam qua vis illa imprimitur.*

The alteration of motion is ever proportional to the motive force impressed; and is made in the direction of the right line in which that force is impressed.

Principia Mathematica (1687) Laws of Motion 2 (translated by Andrew Motte, 1729)

13 *Actioni contrarium semper et aequalem esse reactionem: sive corporum duorum actiones in se mutuo semper esse aequales et in partes contrarias dirigi.*

To every action there is always opposed an equal reaction: or, the mutual actions of two bodies upon each other are always equal, and directed to contrary parts.

Principia Mathematica (1687) Laws of Motion 3 (translated by Andrew Motte, 1729)

14 *Hypotheses non fingo.*
I do not feign hypotheses.

Principia Mathematica (1713 ed.) 'Scholium Generale'

15 If I have seen further it is by standing on the shoulders of giants.

letter to Robert Hooke, 5 February 1676, in H. W. Turnbull (ed.) *Correspondence of Isaac Newton* vol. 1 (1959); see **Bernard** 70:11, **Coleridge** 233:24

16 Philosophy is such an impertinently litigious lady that a man has as good be engaged in law suits as have to do with her.

letter to Edmond Halley, 20 June 1686, in H. W. Turnbull (ed.) *Correspondence of Isaac Newton* vol. 2 (1960)

Continued

Newspaper headlines and leaders

1 Believe it or not.
title of syndicated newspaper feature (from 1918), written by Robert L. Ripley (1893–1949)

2 Bush Wins It.
original headline in the Miami Herald for 8 November 2000; changed in final edition to 'It's Not Over Yet'
in *Daily Telegraph* 9 November 2000

3 Crisis? What crisis?
summarizing an interview with James **Callaghan**
headline in *Sun*, 11 January 1979; see **Misquotations** 537:8

4 Dewey defeats Truman.
anticipating the result of the Presidential election, which **Truman** *won against expectation*
in *Chicago Tribune* 3 November 1948

5 Downing Street's dodgy dossier of 'intelligence' about Iraq.
referring to a briefing document on Iraqi weaponry which was later withdrawn
leading article, *Observer* 9 February 2003

6 Egghead weds hourglass.
on the marriage of Arthur **Miller** *and Marilyn* **Monroe**
headline in *Variety* 1956; attributed

7 The filth and the fury.
following a notorious interview with the Sex Pistols broadcast live on Thames Television
headline in *Daily Mirror*, 2 December 1976

8 Freddie Starr ate my hamster.
headline in *Sun* 13 March 1986

9 GOTCHA!
on the sinking of the General Belgrano
headline in *Sun* 4 May 1982

10 Go West, young man, go West!
editorial in *Terre Haute* [Indiana] *Express* (1851), by John L. B. Soule (1815–91); see **Greeley** 362:3

11 In that case, it might be worthwhile for the Czechoslovak government to consider whether they should exclude altogether the project, which has found favour in some quarters, of making Czechoslovakia a more homogeneous State, by the secession of that fringe of alien populations who are contiguous to the nation with which they are united by race.
referring to the Sudeten Germans
leader in *The Times* 7 September 1938

12 Is THIS the most dangerous man in Britain?
headline beside a picture of Tony **Blair**, *attacking his perceived sympathy for the euro*
in *The Sun* 25 June 1998

13 It *is* a moral issue.
leader following the resignation of Profumo
in *The Times* 11 June 1963; see **Hailsham** 367:13, **Macmillan** 504:7

14 It's that man again . . . ! At the head of a cavalcade of seven black motor cars Hitler swept out of his Berlin Chancellery last night on a mystery journey.
headline in *Daily Express* 2 May 1939; the acronym ITMA became the title of a BBC radio show, from September 1939

15 It's The Sun wot won it.
following the 1992 general election
headline in *Sun* 11 April 1992

16 King's Moll Reno'd in Wolsey's home town.
US newspaper headline on the divorce proceedings of Wallis Simpson (later Duchess of **Windsor**) *in Ipswich*
Frances Donaldson *Edward VIII* (1974) ch. 7

17 Splendid isolation.
headline in *The Times* 22 January 1896, referring to
In these somewhat troublesome days when the great Mother Empire stands splendidly isolated in Europe.
speech by George Foster (1847–1931) 16 January 1896, in *Official Report of the Debates of the House of Commons of the Dominion of Canada* (1896) vol. 41

18 Sticks nix hick pix.
front-page headline on the lack of enthusiasm for farm dramas among rural populations
in *Variety* 17 July 1935

19 Unless the people—the people everywhere—come forward and petition, ay, thunder for reform.
leader on the Reform Bill, possibly written by Edward Sterling (1773–1847), resulting in the nickname 'The Thunderer'
in *The Times* 29 January 1831; the phrase 'we thundered out' had been used earlier, 11 February 1829

20 Wall St. lays an egg.
crash headline, *Variety* 30 October 1929

21 We shall not pretend that there is nothing in his long career which those who respect and admire him would wish otherwise.
on **Edward VII**'s *accession to the throne*
in *The Times* 23 January 1901, leading article

22 Who breaks a butterfly on a wheel?
defending Mick **Jagger** *after his arrest for cannabis possession*
leader in *The Times* 1 June 1967, written by William Rees-Mogg; see **Pope** 602:31

23 Whose finger do you want on the trigger?
referring to the atom bomb
headline in *Daily Mirror* 21 September 1951

24 Winter of discontent.
headline in *Sun* 30 April 1979; see **Callaghan** 185:17, **Shakespeare** 716:18

25 Yes, Virginia, there is a Santa Claus.
replying to a letter from eight-year-old Virginia O'Hanlon
editorial by Francis Pharcellus Church (1839–1906) in New York *Sun*, 21 September 1897

Isaac Newton *continued*

1 I don't know what I may seem to the world, but as to myself, I seem to have been only like a boy playing on the sea-shore and diverting myself in now and then finding a smoother pebble or a prettier shell than ordinary, whilst the great ocean of truth lay all undiscovered before me.

　　Joseph Spence *Anecdotes* (ed. J. Osborn, 1966) no. 1259

2 O Diamond! Diamond! thou little knowest the mischief done!

to a dog, who knocked over a candle which set fire to some papers and thereby 'destroyed the almost finished labours of some years'

　　Thomas Maude *Wensley-Dale . . . a Poem* (1772) st. 23 n.; probably apocryphal

3 By thinking on it continually.

on how he had discovered the law of gravity

　　attributed in Voltaire *Éléments de la philosophie de Newton* pt. 3, ch. 3 (Kehl ed. 1785–9); it did not appear in editions published during **Voltaire**'s lifetime

John Newton 1725–1807

English clergyman

4 Amazing grace! how sweet the sound
That saved a wretch like me!
I once was lost, but now am found,
Was blind, but now I see.

　　Olney Hymns (1779) 'Amazing grace'

5 Glorious things of thee are spoken,
Zion, city of our God!

　　Olney Hymns (1779) 'Glorious things of thee are spoken'

6 How sweet the name of Jesus sounds
In a believer's ear!
It soothes his sorrows, heals his wounds,
And drives away his fear.

　　Olney Hymns (1779) 'How sweet the name of Jesus sounds'

Nicholas I 1796–1855

Russian monarch, emperor from 1825

7 Turkey is a dying man. We may endeavour to keep him alive, but we shall not succeed. He will, he must die.

　　F. Max Müller (ed.) *Memoirs of Baron Stockmar* (translated by G. A. M. Müller, 1873) vol. 2; see **Montesquieu** 545:5

8 Russia has two generals in whom she can confide—Generals Janvier [January] and Février [February].

　　attributed; in *Punch* 10 March 1855

Nicias c.470–413 BC

Greek politician and Athenian general

9 For a city consists in men, and not in walls nor in ships empty of men.

speech to the defeated Athenian army at Syracuse, 413 BC

　　Thucydides *History of the Peloponnesian Wars* bk. 7, sect. 77

Harold Nicolson 1886–1968

English diplomat, politician, and writer; husband of Vita **Sackville-West**

10 Ponderous and uncertain is that relation between pressure and resistance which constitutes the balance of power. The arch of peace is morticed by no iron tendons . . . One night a handful of dust will patter from the vaulting: the bats will squeak and wheel in sudden panic: nor can the fragile fingers of man then stay the rush and rumble of destruction.

　　Public Faces (1932) ch. 6

11 I am haunted by mental decay such as I saw creeping over Ramsay MacDonald. A gradual dimming of the lights.

　　diary, 28 April 1947, in *Diaries and Letters 1945–62* (1968)

12 To be a good diarist one must have a little snouty, sneaky mind.

of Samuel **Pepys**

　　diary, 9 November 1947, in *Diaries and Letters 1945–62* (1968)

13 For seventeen years he did nothing at all but kill animals and stick in stamps.

of King **George V**

　　diary, 17 August 1949 in *Diaries and Letters 1945–62* (1968)

14 Suez—a smash and grab raid that was all smash and no grab.

　　in conversation with Antony Jay, November 1956; see also letter to Vita Sackville-West, 8 November 1956, 'Our smash-and-grab raid got stuck at the smash'

Reinhold Niebuhr 1892–1971

American theologian

15 Man's capacity for justice makes democracy possible, but man's inclination to injustice makes democracy necessary.

　　Children of Light and Children of Darkness (1944) foreword

16 Our gadget-filled paradise suspended in a hell of international insecurity.

　　Pious and Secular America (1957)

Martin Niemöller 1892–1984

German theologian

17 Ask the first man you meet what he means by defending freedom, and he'll tell you privately he means defending the standard of living.

　　address at Augsburg, January 1958; James Bentley *Martin Niemöller* (1984)

18 When Hitler attacked the Jews I was not a Jew, therefore, I was not concerned. And when Hitler attacked the Catholics, I was not a Catholic, and therefore, I was not concerned. And when Hitler attacked the unions and the industrialists, I was not a member of the unions and I was not concerned. Then, Hitler attacked me and the Protestant church—and there was nobody left to be concerned.

often quoted in the form 'In Germany they came first for the Communists, and I didn't speak up because I wasn't a Communist . . . ' and so on

in *Congressional Record* 14 October 1968

Friedrich Nietzsche 1844–1900

German philosopher and writer

1 *Ich lehre euch den Übermenschen. Der Mensch ist Etwas, das überwunden werden soll.*

I teach you the superman. Man is something to be surpassed.

Also Sprach Zarathustra (1883) prologue, sect. 3

2 You are going to women? Do not forget the whip!

Also Sprach Zarathustra (1883) bk. 1 'Von Alten und jungen Weiblein'

3 God's first blunder: Man didn't find the animals amusing,—he dominated them, and didn't even want to be an 'animal'.

Der Antichrist (1888) aphorism 48

4 Woman was God's second blunder.

Der Antichrist (1888) aphorism 48; see **Cowley** 246:3

5 What I understand by 'philosopher': a terrible explosive in the presence of which everything is in danger.

Ecce Homo (1908) 'Die Unzeitgemässen' sect. 3

6 God is dead: but considering the state the species Man is in, there will perhaps be caves, for ages yet, in which his shadow will be shown.

Die fröhliche Wissenschaft (1882) bk. 3, sect. 108; see **Plato** 597:15

7 Morality is the herd-instinct in the individual.

Die fröhliche Wissenschaft (1882) bk. 3, sect. 116

8 The secret of reaping the greatest fruitfulness and the greatest enjoyment from life is *to live dangerously*!

Die fröhliche Wissenschaft (1882) bk. 4, sect. 283

9 He who fights with monsters might take care lest he thereby become a monster. And if you gaze for long into an abyss, the abyss gazes also into you.

Jenseits von Gut und Böse (1886) ch. 4, no. 146

10 The thought of suicide is a great source of comfort: with it a calm passage is to be made across many a bad night.

Jenseits von Gut und Böse (1886) ch. 4, no. 157

11 Master-morality and slave-morality.

Jenseits von Gut und Böse (1886) ch. 9, no. 260

12 At the base of all these aristocratic races the predator is not to be mistaken, the splendorous *blond beast*, avidly rampant for plunder and victory.

Zur Genealogie der Moral (1887) 1st treatise, no. 11

Florence Nightingale 1820–1910

English nurse

on Nightingale: see **Longfellow** 490:24, **Strachey** 762:2

13 It may seem a strange principle to enunciate as the very first requirement in a Hospital that it should do the sick no harm.

Notes on Hospitals (1863 ed.) preface

14 I would earnestly ask my sisters to keep clear of both the jargons now current everywhere . . . of the jargon, namely about the 'rights' of women, which urges women to do all that men do . . . merely because men do it, and without regard to whether this is the best that women can do; and of the jargon which urges women to do nothing that men do, merely because they are women . . . Woman should bring the best she has, *whatever* that is . . . without attending to either of these cries.

Notes on Nursing (1860)

15 No *man*, not even a doctor, ever gives any other definition of what a nurse should be than this—'devoted and obedient.' This definition would do just as well for a porter. It might even do for a horse. It would not do for a policeman.

Notes on Nursing (1860)

16 Too kind, too kind.

on the Order of Merit being brought to her at her home, 5 December 1907

E. Cook *Life of Florence Nightingale* (1913) vol. 2, pt. 7, ch. 9

Anaïs Nin 1903–77

French-born American writer

17 The very touch of the letter was as if you had taken me all into your arms.

letter to Henry Miller, 6 August 1932

18 Anxiety is love's greatest killer. It creates the failures. It makes others feel as you might when a drowning man holds on to you. You want to save him, but you know he will strangle you with his panic.

diary, February 1947; *The Diary of Anaïs Nin* vol. 4 (1944–7)

Richard Milhous Nixon 1913–94

American Republican statesman, 37th President of the US

see also **Anonymous** 15:23

19 The great silent majority.

broadcast, 3 November 1969 in *New York Times* 4 November 1969

20 There can be no whitewash at the White House.

on Watergate

television speech, 30 April 1973, in *New York Times* 1 May 1973

21 I made my mistakes, but in all my years of public life, I have never profited, never profited from public service. I've earned every cent. And in all of my years in public life I have never obstructed justice . . . I welcome this kind of examination

because people have got to know whether or not their President is a crook. Well, I'm not a crook.

speech at press conference, 17 November 1973, in *New York Times* 18 November 1973

1 This country needs good farmers, good businessmen, good plumbers, good carpenters.

farewell address at White House, 9 August 1974, in *New York Times* 10 August 1974

2 When the President does it, that means that it is not illegal.

David Frost *I Gave Them a Sword* (1978) ch. 8

3 I brought myself down. I gave them a sword. And they stuck it in.

television interview, 19 May 1977, in David Frost *I Gave Them a Sword* (1978) ch. 10

Kwame Nkrumah 1900–72

Ghanaian statesman, Prime Minister 1957–60, President 1960–6

4 Freedom is not something that one people can bestow on another as a gift. They claim it as their own and none can keep it from them.

speech in Accra, 10 July 1953

5 We face neither East nor West: we face forward.

conference speech, Accra, 7 April 1960; *Axioms of Kwame Nkrumah* (1967)

Caroline Maria Noel 1817–77

English hymn-writer

6 At the name of Jesus
Every knee shall bow,
Every tongue confess him
King of glory now.

'At the name of Jesus' (1861 hymn); see **Bible** 109:25

Thomas Noel 1799–1861

English poet

7 Rattle his bones over the stones;
He's only a pauper, whom nobody owns!

'The Pauper's Drive' (1841)

Charles Howard, Duke of Norfolk 1746–1815

English peer

8 I cannot be a good Catholic; I cannot go to heaven; and if a man is to go to the devil, he may as well go thither from the House of Lords as from any other place on earth.

Henry Best *Personal and Literary Memorials* (1829) ch. 18

Christopher North (John Wilson) 1785–1854

Scottish literary critic

9 Minds like ours, my dear James, must always be above national prejudices, and in all companies it gives me true pleasure to declare, that, as a people, the English are very little indeed inferior to the Scotch.

Blackwood's Magazine (October 1826) 'Noctes Ambrosianae' no. 20

10 His Majesty's dominions, on which the sun never sets.

Blackwood's Magazine (April 1829) 'Noctes Ambrosianae' no. 42; see **Schiller** 670:26

11 Laws were made to be broken.

Blackwood's Magazine (May 1830) 'Noctes Ambrosianae' no. 49

12 I cannot sit still, James, and hear you abuse the shopocracy.

Blackwood's Magazine (February 1835) 'Noctes Ambrosianae' no. 71

Lord North 1732–92

British statesman, Prime Minister 1770–82

13 Oh God! It is all over!

on receiving the news of Cornwallis's surrender at Yorktown, 19 October 1781

in *Dictionary of National Biography* (1917–)

Alfred Harmsworth, Lord Northcliffe 1865–1922

British newspaper proprietor

*on Northcliffe: see **Anonymous** 16:7*

14 The power of the press is very great, but not so great as the power of suppress.

office message, *Daily Mail* 1918; Reginald Rose and Geoffrey Harmsworth *Northcliffe* (1959) ch. 22

15 When I want a peerage, I shall buy it like an honest man.

Tom Driberg *Swaff* (1974) ch. 2

Caroline Norton (née Sheridan) 1808–77

English poet and songwriter

16 And all our calm is in that balm—
Not lost but gone before.

'Not Lost but Gone Before'; see **Cyprian** 254:15, **Rogers** 652:11

Jack Norworth 1879–1959

American songwriter

17 Oh, shine on, shine on, harvest moon
Up in the sky.
I ain't had no lovin'
Since April, January, June, or July.

'Shine On, Harvest Moon' (1908 song)

Novalis (Friedrich von Hardenberg) 1772–1801

German poet and novelist

18 I often feel, and ever more deeply I realize, that Fate and character are the same conception.

often quoted as 'Character is destiny' or 'Character is fate'

Heinrich von Ofterdingen (1802) bk. 2; see **Eliot** 300:16, **Heraclitus** 383:3

19 Every Englishman is an island.

Fragmente (1929) no. 1496

20 A God-intoxicated man.

*of **Spinoza***

attributed

Alfred Noyes 1880–1958

English poet

1 Go down to Kew in lilac-time, in lilac-time, in
  lilac-time,
  Go down to Kew in lilac-time (it isn't far from
  London!).
  'The Barrel-Organ' (1904)

2 The wind was a torrent of darkness among the
  gusty trees,
  The moon was a ghostly galleon tossed upon
  cloudy seas,
  The road was a ribbon of moonlight over the
  purple moor,
  And the highwayman came riding—
  Riding—riding—
  The highwayman came riding, up to the old inn-
  door.
  'The Highwayman' (1907)

3 Look for me by moonlight;
  Watch for me by moonlight;
  I'll come to thee by moonlight, though hell should
  bar the way!
  'The Highwayman' (1907)

Lord Nuffield 1877–1963

British motor manufacturer and philanthropist

4 *on seeing the Morris Minor prototype in 1945:*
  It looks like a poached egg—we can't make that.
  attributed

Sam Nunn 1938–

American Democratic politician

5 Don't ask, don't tell.
  summary of the **Clinton** administration's compromise policy
  on homosexuals serving in the armed forces, in *New York
  Times* 12 May 1993

Nursery rhymes

*Citations given are generally for the first appearance of the rhyme.
For detailed bibliographical descriptions and variants, see* The
Oxford Dictionary of Nursery Rhymes

6 A was an apple-pie;
  B bit it;
  C cut it.
  John Eachard *Some Observations* (1671)

7 As I was going to St Ives
  I met a man with seven wives.
  Harley MS mid 18th century

8 Baa, baa, black sheep,
  Have you any wool?
  Yes, sir, yes, sir
  Three bags full:
  One for the master,
  And one for the dame,
  And one for the little boy
  Who lives down the lane.
  Tommy Thumb's Pretty Song Book (c.1744)

9 Boys and girls come out to play,
  The moon doth shine as bright as day.
  William King *Useful Transactions in Philosophy* (1708–9)

10 Bye, baby bunting,
  Daddy's gone a hunting,
  Gone to get a rabbit skin
  To wrap the baby bunting in.
  Gammer Gurton's Garland (1784)

11 The children in Holland take pleasure in making
  What the children in England take pleasure in
  breaking.
  traditional

12 Cock a doodle doo!
  My dame has lost her shoe,
  My master's lost his fiddlestick,
  And knows not what to do.
  *The Most Cruel and Bloody Murder Committed by an
  Innkeeper's Wife* (1606)

13 Cross-patch,
  Draw the latch,
  Sit by the fire and spin;
  Take a cup,
  And drink it up,
  Then call your neighbours in.
  Mother Goose's Melody (c.1765)

14 Curly locks, Curly locks,
  Wilt thou be mine?
  Thou shalt not wash dishes
  Nor yet feed the swine.
  But sit on a cushion
  And sew a fine seam,
  And feed upon strawberries,
  Sugar and cream.
  Infant Institutes (1797)

15 Dance to your daddy,
  My little babby,
  Dance to your daddy, my little lamb;
  You shall have a fishy
  In a little dishy,
  You shall have a fishy when the boat comes in.
  Vocal Harmony (c.1806)

16 Daffy-down-dilly is new come to town,
  With a yellow petticoat, and a green gown.
  Songs for the Nursery (1805)

17 Diddle, diddle, dumpling, my son John,
  Went to bed with his trousers on.
  Newest Christmas Box (c.1797)

18 Ding, dong, bell,
  Pussy's in the well.
  Mother Goose's Melody (c.1765)

19 Fiddle-de-dee, Fiddle-de-dee,
  The fly shall marry the humble-bee.
  'Fiddle-de-dee' (c.1803)

20 A frog he would a-wooing go,
  'Heigh-ho!' says Rowley . . .

  . . . while they were all a-merry-making,
  'Heigh-ho!' says Rowley,
  A cat and her kittens came tumbling in.
  Thomas Ravenscroft *Melismata* (1611)

21 Georgie Porgie, pudding and pie,
  Kissed the girls and made them cry;
  When the boys came out to play,
  Georgie Porgie ran away.
  J. O. Halliwell (ed.) *Nursery Rhymes* (1844)

1 Goosey, goosey gander,
Whither shall I wander?
Upstairs and downstairs,
And in my lady's chamber.
There I met an old man
Who would not say his prayers.
I took him by the left leg
And threw him down the stairs.
  Gammer Gurton's Garland (1784)

2 Grey goose and gander,
Waft your wings together,
And carry the good king's daughter
Over the one-strand river.
  J. O. Halliwell (ed.) *Nursery Rhymes* (1844)

3 Hark! Hark! The dogs do bark,
The beggars are coming to town.
Some in rags, some in jags,
And one in a velvet gown.
  Gammer Gurton's Garland (1784)

4 He began to bark,
And she began to cry,
Lawk a mercy on me,
This is none of I!
  'There was a little woman', Mansfield MS, *c.*1775; Iona
  and Peter Opie (eds.) *Oxford Dictionary of Nursery Rhymes*
  (new edn. 1997)

5 Here am I,
Little Jumping Joan;
When nobody's with me
I'm all alone.
  T. Hughes *Adventures of Jumping Joan* (advertised 1808)

6 Hey diddle diddle,
The cat and the fiddle,
The cow jumped over the moon;
The little dog laughed
To see such sport,
And the dish ran away with the spoon.
  Mother Goose's Melody (*c.*1765)

7 Hickety, pickety, my black hen,
She lays eggs for gentlemen.
  J. O. Halliwell (ed.) *Nursery Rhymes* (1853)

8 Hickory, dickory, dock,
The mouse ran up the clock.
The clock struck one,
The mouse ran down,
Hickory, dickory, dock.
  Tommy Thumb's Pretty Song Book (*c.*1744)

9 How many miles to Babylon?
Threescore miles and ten.
Can I get there by candle-light?
Yes, and back again.
  Songs for the Nursery (1805)

10 Humpty Dumpty sat on a wall,
Humpty Dumpty had a great fall;
All the king's horses,
And all the king's men,
Couldn't put Humpty together again.
  MS addition to a copy of *Mother Goose's Melody* (*c.*1803)

11 I had a little nut tree
Nothing would it bear
But a silver nutmeg
And a golden pear;
The King of Spain's daughter
Came to visit me,
And all for the sake
Of my little nut tree.
  Newest Christmas Box (*c.*1797)

12 I'll tell you a story
About Jack a Nory.
  Nurse Lovechild *Jacky Nory's Story Book for all Little Masters
  and Misses* (advertised December 1745)

13 I love little pussy,
Her coat is so warm,
And if I don't hurt her
She'll do me no harm.
  Hints for the Formation of Infant Schools (1829)

14 I'm the king of the castle,
Get down you dirty rascal.
  W. C. Hazlitt (ed.) *Brand's Popular Antiquities* (1870)

15 Jack and Jill went up the hill
To fetch a pail of water;
Jack fell down and broke his crown,
And Jill came tumbling after.
  Mother Goose's Melody (*c.*1765)

16 Jack be nimble,
Jack be quick,
Jack jump over
The candle stick.
  Douce MS, *c.*1815; J. O. Halliwell (ed.) *Nursery Rhymes*
  (1844)

17 Jack Sprat could eat no fat,
His wife could eat no lean,
And so between them both, you see,
They licked the platter clean.
  John Clarke *Paroemiologia Anglo-Latina* (1639)

18 Ladybird, ladybird,
Fly away home,
Your house is on fire
And your children all gone;

All except one
And that's little Ann
And she has crept under
The warming pan.
  Tommy Thumb's Pretty Song Book (*c.*1744)

19 Lavender's blue, diddle, diddle,
Lavender's green;
When I am king, diddle, diddle,
You shall be queen.
  J. Wright etc. *Diddle Diddle* (*c.*1680)

20 The lion and the unicorn
Were fighting for the crown;
The lion beat the unicorn
All round the town.

Some gave them white bread,
And some gave them brown;
Some gave them plum cake,
And sent them out of town.
  MS inscription (*c.*1691) beside a woodcut of the royal arms
  in a bible in the Opie Collection; William King *Useful
  Transactions in Philosophy* (1708–9)

21 Little Bo-Peep has lost her sheep,
And can't tell where to find them;

Leave them alone, and they'll come home,
And bring their tails behind them.

 Douce MS, *c.*1805; *Gammer Gurton's Garland* (1810)

1 Little Boy Blue,
Come blow your horn,
The sheep's in the meadow,
The cow's in the corn;
But where is the boy
Who looks after the sheep?
He's under a haycock,
Fast asleep.

 The Famous Tommy Thumb's Little Story Book (*c.*1760)

2 Little Jack Horner
Sat in the corner,
Eating a Christmas pie;
He put in his thumb,
And pulled out a plum,
And said, what a good boy am I!

 Henry Carey *Namby Pamby* (1725)

3 Little Miss Muffet
Sat on a tuffet
Eating her curds and whey;
There came a big spider,
Who sat down beside her
And frightened Miss Muffet away.

 Songs for the Nursery (1805)

4 Little Polly Flinders
Sat among the cinders,
Warming her pretty little toes;
Her mother came and caught her,
And whipped her little daughter
For spoiling her nice new clothes.

 J. Harris *Original Ditties for the Nursery* (*c.*1805)

5 Little Tommy Tucker
Sings for his supper;
What shall we give him?
White bread and butter.

 Tommy Thumb's Pretty Song Book (*c.*1744)

6 London Bridge is broken down
My fair lady.

 Henry Carey *Namby Pamby* (1725)

7 Lucy Locket lost her pocket
Kitty Fisher found it.

 J. O. Halliwell (ed.) *Nursery Rhymes* (1842)

8 A man in the wilderness asked me,
How many strawberries grow in the sea?
I answered him, as I thought good,
As many red herrings as grow in the wood.

 Bodleian MS; Iona and Peter Opie (eds.) *The Oxford Dictionary of Nursery Rhymes* (new edn., 1997)

9 Mary, Mary, quite contrary,
How does your garden grow?
With silver bells and cockle shells
And pretty maids all in a row.

 Tommy Thumb's Pretty Song Book (*c.*1744)

10 Monday's child is fair of face,
Tuesday's child is full of grace,
Wednesday's child is full of woe,
Thursday's child has far to go,
Friday's child is loving and giving,
Saturday's child works hard for his living,

And the child that is born of the Sabbath day,
Is bonny, and blithe, and good and gay.

 A. E. Bray *Traditions of Devonshire* (1838)

11 My mother said that I never should
Play with the gypsies in the wood.

 Robert Graves *Less Familiar Nursery Rhymes* (1927)

12 The north wind doth blow,
And we shall have snow,
And what will poor robin do then?
    Poor thing.
He'll sit in a barn,
To keep himself warm,
And hide his head under his wing.
    Poor thing.

 Songs for the Nursery (1805)

13 Old King Cole
Was a merry old soul,
And a merry old soul was he;
He called for his pipe,
And he called for his bowl,
And he called for his fiddlers three.

 William King *Useful Transactions in Philosophy* (1708–9)

14 Old Mother Hubbard
Went to the cupboard
To fetch her poor dog a bone;
But when she came there
The cupboard was bare
And so the poor dog had none.

 Sarah Catherine Martin *The Comic Adventures of Old Mother Hubbard* (1805), based on a traditional rhyme

15 Old Mother Slipper Slopper jumped out of bed,
And out of the window she popped her head:
Oh! John, John, John, the grey goose is gone,
And the fox is off to his den O! . . .

. . . And the little ones picked the bones O!

 'A fox jumped up one winter's night' in *Gammer Gurton's Garland* (1810)

16 One a penny, two a penny,
Hot cross buns!
If your daughters do not like them,
Give them to your sons.

 Christmas Box (1797)

17 One flew east and one flew west,
And one flew over the cuckoo's nest.

 traditional American version of counting-out rhyme 'Intry mintry cutry corn'; Roger D. Abrahams *Jump-Rope Rhymes* (1969)

18 One, two
Buckle my shoe;
Three, four,
Knock at the door;
Five, six,
Pick up sticks;
Seven, eight,
Lay them straight;
Nine, ten
A big fat hen.

 Songs for the Nursery (1805)

19 Oranges and lemons
Say the bells of St. Clements . . .

. . . When will you pay me?

Say the bells of Old Bailey.

When I grow rich,
Say the bells of Shoreditch . . .

. . . Here comes a candle to light you to bed,
Here comes a chopper to chop off your head.
> *Tommy Thumb's Pretty Song Book* (c.1744)

1 Pat-a-cake, pat-a-cake, baker's man,
Bake me a cake as fast as you can;
Pat it and prick it, and mark it with B,
Put it in the oven for baby and me.
> Tom D'Urfey *The Campaigners* (1698)

2 Pease porridge hot,
Pease porridge cold,
Pease porridge in the pot
Nine days old.
> *Newest Christmas Box* (c.1797)

3 Peter Piper picked a peck of pickled pepper.
> *Peter Piper's Practical Principles of Plain and Perfect Pronunciation* (1813)

4 Polly put the kettle on,
We'll all have tea.
> Charles Dickens *Barnaby Rudge* (1841)

5 Pussy cat, pussy cat, where have you been?
I've been to London to look at the queen.
> *Songs for the Nursery* (1805)

6 The Queen of Hearts
She made some tarts,
All on a summer's day;
The Knave of Hearts
He stole the tarts,
And took them clean away.
> 'The Hive, A Collection of Scraps' in *The European Magazine* April 1782

7 Rain, rain, go away,
Come again another day.
> James Howell *Proverbs* (1659)

8 Ride a cock-horse to Banbury Cross,
To see a fine lady upon a white horse;
Rings on her fingers and bells on her toes,
And she shall have music wherever she goes.
> *Gammer Gurton's Garland* (1784)

9 Ring-a-ring o'roses,
A pocket full of posies,
A-tishoo! A-tishoo!
We all fall down.
> Kate Greenaway *Mother Goose* (1881)

10 Round and round the garden
Like a teddy bear.
> orally collected, 1946–50; Iona and Peter Opie (eds.) *The Oxford Dictionary of Nursery Rhymes* (new edn., 1997)

11 Rub-a-dub-dub,
Three men in a tub
And how do you think they got there?
The butcher, the baker,
The candlestick-maker,
They all jumped out of a rotten potato
'Twas enough to make a man stare.
> *Christmas Box* vol. 2 (1798)

12 See-saw, Margery Daw,
Jacky shall have a new master;
Jacky shall have but a penny a day,
Because he can't work any faster.
> *Mother Goose's Melody* (c.1765)

13 Simple Simon met a pieman,
Going to the fair;
Says Simple Simon to the pieman,
Let me taste your ware.
> *Simple Simon*, chapbook advertisement, 1764

14 Sing a song of sixpence,
A pocket full of rye;
Four and twenty blackbirds,
Baked in a pie.

When the pie was opened,
The birds began to sing;
Was not that a dainty dish,
To set before the king?

The king was in his counting-house,
Counting out his money;
The queen was in the parlour,
Eating bread and honey.

The maid was in the garden,
Hanging out the clothes,
There came a little blackbird,
And snapped off her nose.
> *Tommy Thumb's Pretty Song Book* (c.1744)

15 Solomon Grundy,
Born on a Monday,
Christened on Tuesday,
Married on Wednesday,
Took ill on Thursday,
Worse on Friday,
Died on Saturday,
Buried on Sunday:
This is the end
Of Solomon Grundy.
> J. O. Halliwell *Nursery Rhymes* (1842)

16 Taffy was a Welshman, Taffy was a thief,
Taffy came to my house and stole a piece of beef.
> *Nancy Cock's Pretty Song Book* (c.1780)

17 Tell tale tit,
Your tongue shall be slit.
> *Mother Goose's Melody* (1780)

18 There was a crooked man, and he walked a crooked mile,
He found a crooked sixpence against a crooked stile;
He bought a crooked cat, which caught a crooked mouse,
And they all lived together in a little crooked house.
> J. O. Halliwell (ed.) *Nursery Rhymes* (1842)

19 There was a lady loved a swine,
Honey, quoth she,
Pig-hog wilt thou be mine?
Hoogh, quoth he.
> Bodley MS, c.1620; Iona and Peter Opie (eds.) *The Oxford Dictionary of Nursery Rhymes* (new edn, 1997)

20 There was a little man, and he had a little gun.
> *Tommy Thumb's Pretty Song Book* (c.1744)

1 There was an old woman who lived in a shoe,
She had so many children she didn't know what
  to do.
Gammer Gurton's Garland (1784)

2 This is the house that Jack built . . .

. . . This is the farmer sowing his corn,
That kept the cock that crowed in the morn,
That waked the priest all shaven and shorn,
That married the man all tattered and torn,
That kissed the maiden all forlorn,
That milked the cow with the crumpled horn,
That tossed the dog,
That worried the cat,
That killed the rat,
That ate the malt
That lay in the house that Jack built.
Nurse Truelove's New-Year's-Gift (1755)

3 This is the way the ladies ride.
Robert Chambers *The Popular Rhymes of Scotland* (1842)

4 This little pig went to market,
This little pig stayed at home,
This little pig had roast beef,
This little pig had none,
And this little pig cried, Wee-wee-wee-wee-wee, I
  can't find my way home.
The Famous Tommy Thumb's Little Story Book (c.1760)

5 Three blind mice, see how they run!
They all ran after the farmer's wife,
Who cut off their tails with a carving knife,
Did you ever see such a thing in your life,
As three blind mice?
Thomas Ravenscroft *Deuteromelia* (1609)

6 Three little kittens they lost their mittens.
Eliza Follen *New Nursery Songs* (1853)

7 Three wise men of Gotham
Went to sea in a bowl:
And if the bowl had been stronger,
My song would have been longer.
Mother Goose's Melody (c.1765)

8 Tinker,
Tailor,
Soldier,
Sailor,
Rich man,
Poor man,
Beggarman,
Thief.
traditional fortune-telling rhyme for counting out objects
such as cherry stones or daisy petals; Iona and Peter Opie
(eds.) *The Oxford Dictionary of Nursery Rhymes* (new edn,
1997)

9 To market, to market,
To buy a plum bun:
Home again, home again,
Market is done.
John Florio *Worlde of Wordes* (1611 edn.), *Songs for the
Nursery* (1805)

10 Tom he was a piper's son,
He learned to play when he was young,
But all the tune that he could play,
Was 'Over the hills and far away.'
Tom, the Piper's Son (chapbooks, from c.1795)

11 Tom, Tom, the piper's son,
Stole a pig and away he run;
The pig was eat
And Tom was beat
And Tom went howling down the street.
Tom, the Piper's Son (chapbooks, from c.1795)

12 Twist about, turn about, jump Jim Crow.
Humorous Adventures of Jump Jim Crow (c.1836)

13 Wee Willie Winkie runs through the town,
Upstairs and downstairs in his night-gown,
Rapping at the window, crying through the lock,
Are the children all in bed, for now it's eight
  o'clock.
Cries of Banbury and London (c.1840); this traditional
rhyme formed the basis for a longer poem by William Miller
(1810-72) in *Whistle-Binkie; A Collection of Songs for the
Social Circle* (1841)

14 What are little boys made of?
What are little boys made of?
Frogs and snails
And puppy-dogs' tails,
That's what little boys are made of.
What are little girls made of?
What are little girls made of?
Sugar and spice
And all that's nice,
That's what little girls are made of.
J. O. Halliwell *Nursery Rhymes* (1844)

15 Where are you going to, my pretty maid? . . .

. . . My face is my fortune, sir, she said.
Then I can't marry you, my pretty maid.
Nobody asked you, sir, she said.
William Pryce *Archaeologica Cornu-Britannica* (1790)

16 Who killed Cock Robin?
I, said the Sparrow,
With my bow and arrow,
I killed Cock Robin.
Who saw him die?
I, said the Fly,
With my little eye,
I saw him die . . .
. . . All the birds of the air
Fell a-sighing and a-sobbing,
When they heard the bell toll
For poor Cock Robin.
Tommy Thumb's Pretty Song Book (c.1744)

Bill Nye (Edgar Wilson Nye) 1850-96

American humorist

17 I have been told that Wagner's music is better
than it sounds.
Mark Twain *Autobiography* (1924) vol. 1

Julius Nyerere 1922-99

*Tanzanian statesman, President of Tanganyika 1962-4 and of
Tanzania 1964-85*

18 Should we really let our people starve so we can
pay our debts?
in *Guardian* 21 March 1985

19 We are a poor country and we opted for socialist
policies, but to build a socialist society you have to
have a developed society.
in *Observer* 28 July 1985 'Sayings of the Week'

Oo

Charles Edward Oakley 1832–65

English clergyman

1 Hills of the North, rejoice:
Rivers and mountain-spring,
Hark to the advent voice!
Valley and lowland, sing!
'Hills of the North, rejoice' (1870 hymn)

Lawrence Oates see Epitaphs 309:12, Last words 472:2

Conor Cruise O'Brien 1917–

Irish politician, writer, and journalist
*see also **Haughey** 375:5*

2 The strength of these men was that each of them
could look a Pearsean ghost in the eye . . . Each of
them, in their youth, had done the thing the ghost
asked them to do, in 1916 or 1919–21 or both.
That was it; from now on they would do what
seemed reasonable to themselves in the interests of
the actual people inhabiting the island of Ireland
and not of a personified abstraction, or of a
disembodied voice, or of a ghost.
*of Sean Lemass (1899–1971) and other senior Irish
politicians in the 1960s; see **Pearse** 590:8*
Ancestral Voices (1994)

3 If I saw Mr Haughey buried at midnight at a
crossroads, with a stake driven through his
heart—politically speaking—I should continue to
wear a clove of garlic round my neck, just in case.
in *Observer* 10 October 1982

Edna O'Brien 1932–

Irish novelist and short-story writer

4 August is a wicked month.
title of novel (1965)

Flann O'Brien (Brian O'Nolan or O Nuallain) 1911–66

Irish novelist and journalist

5 The conclusion of your syllogism, I said lightly, is
fallacious, being based upon licensed premises.
At Swim-Two-Birds (1939) ch. 1

6 A pint of plain is your only man.
At Swim-Two-Birds (1939) 'The Workman's Friend'

Sean O'Casey 1880–1964

Irish dramatist

7 I killin' meself workin', an' he sthruttin' about
from mornin' till night like a paycock!
Juno and the Paycock (1925) act 1

8 He's an oul' butty o' mine—oh, he's a darlin'
man, a daarlin' man.
Juno and the Paycock (1925) act 1

9 The whole worl's in a state o' chassis!
Juno and the Paycock (1925) act 1

10 English literature's performing flea.
*of P. G. **Wodehouse***
P. G. Wodehouse Performing Flea (1953)

William of Occam c.1285–1349

English Franciscan friar and philosopher

11 *Entia non sunt multiplicanda praeter necessitatem.*
No more things should be presumed to exist than
are absolutely necessary.
*'Occam's Razor', an ancient philosophical principle
often attributed to Occam but earlier in origin*
not found in this form in his writings, although he
frequently used similar expressions, such as:
Pluralitas non est ponenda sine necessitate.
Plurality should not be assumed unnecessarily.
Quodlibeta (c.1324) no. 5, question 1, art. 2

Daniel O'Connell 1775–1847

*Irish nationalist leader and social reformer, elected to
Parliament in 1828*

12 I have given my advice to my countrymen, and
whenever I feel it necessary I shall continue to do
so, careless whether it pleases or displeases this
House or any mad person out of it.
in *Dictionary of National Biography* (1917–)

Bernard O'Donoghue 1945–

Irish poet and academic

13 We were terribly lucky to catch
The Ceauşescus' execution, being
By sheer chance that Christmas Day
In the only house for twenty miles
With satellite TV. We sat,
Cradling brandies, by the fire
Watching those two small, cranky autocrats
Lying in snow against a blood-spattered wall,
Hardly able to believe our good fortune.
'Carolling' (1995)

□ Official advice

see box overleaf

David Ogilvy 1911–99

British-born advertising executive

14 The consumer isn't a moron; she is your wife.
Confessions of an Advertising Man (1963) ch. 5

James Ogilvy, Lord Seafield 1664–1730

Scottish lawyer, Lord Chancellor of Scotland

15 Now there's ane end of ane old song.
*as he signed the engrossed exemplification of the Act of
Union, 1706*
in *The Lockhart Papers* (1817) vol. 1

John O'Hara 1905–70

American writer

16 An artist is his own fault.
The Portable F. Scott Fitzgerald (1945) introduction

Official advice

1 Careless talk costs lives.
Second World War security slogan (popularly inverted as 'careless lives cost talk')

2 Clunk, click, every trip.
road safety campaign promoting the use of seat-belts, 1971

3 Coughs and sneezes spread diseases. Trap the germs in your handkerchief.
Second World War health slogan (1942)

4 Dig for Victory.
Second World War slogan; see below:

Let 'Dig for Victory' be the motto of every one with a garden and of every able-bodied man and woman capable of digging an allotment in their spare time.
Reginald Dorman-Smith (1899–1977) radio broadcast, 3 October 1939, in *The Times* 4 October 1939

5 Don't ask a man to drink and drive.
UK road safety slogan, from 1964

6 Don't die of ignorance.
Aids publicity campaign, 1987

7 Duck and cover.
US advice in the event of a missile attack, *c.*1950; associated particularly with children's cartoon character 'Bert the Turtle'

8 Is your journey *really* necessary?
slogan coined to discourage Civil Servants from going home for Christmas, 1939

9 Keep Britain tidy.
issued by the Central Office of Information, 1950s

10 Make do and mend.
wartime slogan, 1940s

11 Slip, slop, slap.
sun protection slogan, meaning slip *on a T-shirt,* slop *on some suncream,* slap *on a hat*
Australian health education programme, 1980s

12 Smoking can seriously damage your health.
government health warning now required by British law to be printed on cigarette packets
from early 1970s, in form 'Smoking can damage your health'

13 Stop-look-and-listen.
road safety slogan, current in the US from 1912

14 *Taisez-vous! Méfiez-vous! Les oreilles ennemies vous écoutent.*

Keep your mouth shut! Be on your guard! Enemy ears are listening to you.
official notice in France, 1915

15 Tradition dictates that we have a lawn—but do we really need one? Why not increase the size of your borders or replace lawned areas with paving stones or gravel?
Severn Trent Water 'The Gardener's Water Code' (1996)

Theodore O'Hara 1820–67
American poet

16 The bivouac of the dead.
title of poem (1847)

17 Sons of the dark and bloody ground.
popularized 'the dark and bloody ground' as a name for Kentucky
'The Bivouac of the Dead' (1847) st. 1

Georgia O'Keefe 1887–1986
American painter

18 Filling a space in a beautiful way. That's what art means to me.
in *Art News* December 1977

John O'Keeffe 1747–1833
Irish dramatist

19 Amo, amas, I love a lass,
As a cedar tall and slender;
Sweet cowslip's grace
Is her nom'native case,
And she's of the feminine gender.
The Agreeable Surprise (1781) act 2, sc. 2

20 Fat, fair and forty were all the toasts of the young men.
The Irish Mimic (1795) sc. 2

Dennis O'Kelly c.1720–87
Irish racehorse-owner

21 Eclipse first, the rest nowhere.
comment at Epsom on the occasion of the horse Eclipse's first race, 3 May 1769; the Dictionary of National Biography *gives the occasion as the Queen's Plate at Winchester, 1769*
in *Annals of Sporting* vol. 2 (1822)

Abraham Okpik d. 1997
Canadian Inuit spokesman

22 There are very few Eskimos, but millions of Whites, just like mosquitoes. It is something very special and wonderful to be an Eskimo—they are like the snow geese. If an Eskimo forgets his language and Eskimo ways, he will be nothing but just another mosquito.
attributed, 1966

Bruce Oldfield 1950–
English fashion designer

23 Fashion is more usually a gentle progression of revisited ideas.
in *Independent* 9 September 1989

William Oldys 1696–1761

English antiquary

1 Busy, curious, thirsty fly,
Gently drink, and drink as I;
Freely welcome to my cup.
'The Fly' (1732)

Frederick Scott Oliver 1864–1934

Scottish writer

2 A wise politician will never grudge a genuflexion
or a rapture if it is expected of him by prevalent
opinion.
The Endless Adventure (1930) vol. I, pt. I, ch. 20

Laurence Olivier 1907–89

English actor and director

3 The tragedy of a man who could not make up his
mind.
introduction to his 1948 screen adaptation of *Hamlet*

4 Shakespeare—the nearest thing in incarnation to
the eye of God.
in *Kenneth Harris Talking To* (1971) 'Sir Laurence Olivier'

5 Acting is a masochistic form of exhibitionism. It is
not quite the occupation of an adult.
in *Time* 3 July 1978

Frank Ward O'Malley see Hubbard 406:11

Omar c.581–644

Arab caliph, conqueror of Syria, Palestine, and Egypt

6 If these writings of the Greeks agree with the book
of God, they are useless and need not be
preserved; if they disagree, they are pernicious
and ought to be destroyed.
on burning the library of Alexandria, AD c.641
Edward Gibbon *The Decline and Fall of the Roman Empire*
(1776–88) ch. 51

Jacqueline Kennedy Onassis 1929–94

American wife of John F. Kennedy, First Lady of the US 1961–3

7 There'll be great Presidents again—and the
Johnsons are wonderful, they've been wonderful
to me—but there'll never be another Camelot
again.
in *Life* 6 December 1963; see **Lerner** 481:14

Eugene O'Neill 1888–1953

American dramatist

8 For de little stealin' dey gits you in jail soon or
late. For de big stealin' dey makes you Emperor
and puts you in de Hall o' Fame when you croaks.
The Emperor Jones (1921) sc. 1

9 The iceman cometh.
title of play (1946)

10 A long day's journey into night.
title of play (written 1940–1)

11 Life is perhaps most wisely regarded as a bad
dream between two awakenings, and every day is
a life in miniature.
Marco Millions (1928) act 2, sc. 2

12 Mourning becomes Electra.
title of play (1931)

13 The sea hates a coward!
Mourning becomes Electra (1931) pt. 2, act 4

14 The only living life is in the past and future . . . the
present is an interlude . . . strange interlude in
which we call on past and future to bear witness
we are living.
Strange Interlude (1928) pt. 2, act 8

Yoko Ono 1933–

Japanese poet and songwriter

15 Woman is the nigger of the world.
remark made in a 1968 interview for *Nova* magazine and
adopted by her husband John **Lennon** as the title of a song
(1972); J. Robertson *Art and Music of John Lennon* (1990)
ch. 11

Brian O'Nolan see Flann O'Brien

□ Opening lines

see box overleaf

John Opie 1761–1807

English painter

16 I mix them with my brains, sir.
on being asked with what he mixed his colours
Samuel Smiles *Self-Help* (1859) ch. 4

J. Robert Oppenheimer 1904–67

American physicist

17 I remembered the line from the Hindu scripture,
the *Bhagavad Gita* . . . 'I am become death, the
destroyer of worlds.'
*on the explosion of the first atomic bomb near
Alamogordo, New Mexico, 16 July 1945*
Len Giovannitti and Fred Freed *The Decision to Drop the
Bomb* (1965); see **Bhagavadgita** 74:15

18 The physicists have known sin; and this is a
knowledge which they cannot lose.
lecture at Massachusetts Institute of Technology, 25
November 1947, in *Open Mind* (1955) ch. 5

19 When you see something that is technically sweet,
you go ahead and do it and you argue about what
to do about it only after you have had your
technical success. That is the way it was with the
atomic bomb.
in *In the Matter of J. Robert Oppenheimer, USAEC Transcript
of Hearing Before Personnel Security Board* (1954)

Susie Orbach 1946–

American psychotherapist

20 Fat is a feminist issue.
title of book (1978)

Opening lines

1 Achilles' cursed anger sing, O goddess, that son of Peleus, which started a myriad sufferings for the Achaeans.
Homer *The Iliad*

2 Achilles' wrath, to Greece the direful spring
Of woes unnumbered, heavenly goddess, sing!
Alexander **Pope** translation of *The Iliad* (1715)

3 *Arma virumque cano.*
I sing of arms and the man.
Virgil *Aeneid*

4 Arms, and the man I sing, who, forced by fate,
And haughty Juno's unrelenting hate,
Expelled and exiled, left the Trojan shore.
John **Dryden** translation of Virgil *Aeneid* (*Aeneis*, 1697)

5 As I walked through the wilderness of this world.
John **Bunyan** *The Pilgrim's Progress* (1678) pt. 1

6 At the age of fifteen my grandmother became the concubine of a warlord general.
Jung Chang *Wild Swans* (1991)

7 *Aujourd'hui, maman est morte. Ou peut-être hier, je ne sais pas.*
Mother died today. Or perhaps it was yesterday, I don't know.
Albert **Camus** *L'Étranger* (1944)

8 The boy stood on the burning deck
Whence all but he had fled.
Felicia **Hemans** 'Casabianca' (1849)

9 Call me Ishmael.
Herman **Melville** *Moby Dick* (1851)

10 'Christmas won't be Christmas without any presents,' grumbled Jo, lying on the rug.
Louisa May **Alcott** *Little Women* (1868–9)

11 *Gallia est omnis divisa in partes tres.*
Gaul as a whole is divided into three parts.
Julius **Caesar** *De Bello Gallico*

12 Harry Potter was a highly unusual boy in many ways.
J. K. **Rowling** *Harry Potter and the Prisoner of Azkaban* (1999)

13 If I am out of my mind, it's all right with me, thought Moses Herzog.
Saul **Bellow** *Herzog* (1961)

14 If I should die, think only this of me:
That there's some corner of a foreign field
That is for ever England.
Rupert **Brooke** 'The Soldier' (1914)

15 If music be the food of love, play on.
William **Shakespeare** *Twelfth Night* (1601)

16 In a hole in the ground there lived a hobbit.
J. R. R. **Tolkien** *The Hobbit* (1937)

17 In my beginning is my end.
T. S. **Eliot** *Four Quartets* 'East Coker' (1940)

18 In the beginning God created the heaven and the earth. And the earth was without form, and void; and darkness was upon the face of the deep. And the Spirit of God moved upon the face of the waters.
And God said, Let there be light: and there was light.
Bible Genesis

19 In the beginning was the Word, and the Word was with God, and the Word was God.
Bible St John

20 I shall not say why and how I became, at the age of fifteen, the mistress of the Earl of Craven.
Harriette Wilson *Memoirs* (1825)

21 'Is there anybody there?' said the Traveller, Knocking on the moonlit door.
Walter **de la Mare** 'The Listener' (1912)

22 It is a truth universally acknowledged, that a single man in possession of a good fortune, must be in want of a wife.
Jane **Austen** *Pride and Prejudice* (1813)

23 It is Christmas Day in the Workhouse.
George R. Sims (1847–1922) 'In the Workhouse—Christmas Day' (1879)

24 It was a bright cold day in April, and the clocks were striking thirteen.
George **Orwell** *Nineteen Eighty-Four* (1949)

25 It was a dark and stormy night.
Edward George **Bulwer-Lytton** *Paul Clifford* (1830)

26 It was not until several weeks after he had decided to murder his wife that Dr Bickleigh took any active steps in the matter. Murder is a serious business.
Francis Iles *Malice Aforethought* (1931)

27 It was the afternoon of my eighty-first birthday, and I was in bed with my catamite when Ali announced that the archbishop had come to see me.
Anthony **Burgess** *Earthly Powers* (1980)

28 It was the best of times, it was the worst of times.
Charles **Dickens** *A Tale of Two Cities* (1859)

29 I write this sitting in the kitchen sink.
Dodie **Smith** *I Capture the Castle* (1948)

30 The king sits in Dunfermline town
Drinking the blude-red wine.
Ballads 'Sir Patrick Spens'

31 Last night I dreamt I went to Manderley again.
Daphne Du Maurier *Rebecca* (1938)

32 Lolita, light of my life, fire of my loins. My sin, my soul. Lo-lee-ta: the tip of the tongue taking a trip of three steps down the palate to tap, at three, on the teeth. Lo. Lee. Ta.
Vladimir **Nabokov** *Lolita* (1955)

▶

▶ Opening lines *continued*

1 Long ago in 1945 all the nice people in England were poor, allowing for exceptions.
Muriel **Spark** *The Girls of Slender Means* (1963)

2 Mom and Pop were just a couple of kids when they got married. He was eighteen, she was sixteen, and I was three.
Billie **Holiday** *Lady Sings the Blues* (1956)

3 Much have I travelled in the realms of gold, And many goodly states and kingdoms seen.
John **Keats** 'On First Looking into Chapman's Homer' (1817)

4 My heart aches, and a drowsy numbness pains My sense.
John **Keats** 'Ode to a Nightingale' (1820)

5 *Nel mezzo del cammin di nostra vita.*
Midway along the path of our life.
Dante *Divina Commedia* 'Inferno'

6 Of man's first disobedience, and the fruit Of that forbidden tree, whose mortal taste Brought death into the world, and all our woe, With loss of Eden.
John **Milton** *Paradise Lost* (1667)

7 O! for a Muse of fire, that would ascend The brightest heaven of invention.
William **Shakespeare** *Henry V* (1599)

8 Oh, what can ail thee knight at arms Alone and palely loitering?
John **Keats** 'La belle dame sans merci' (1820)

9 Once upon a time . . .
traditional opening to a story, especially a fairy story
Anonymous, recorded from 1595

10 Once upon a time and a very good time it was there was a moocow coming down along the road and this moocow that was down along the road met a nicens little boy named baby tuckoo.
James **Joyce** *A Portrait of the Artist as a Young Man* (1916)

11 The opening was barred by a black bank of clouds, and the tranquil waterway leading to the uttermost ends of the earth flowed sombre under an overcast sky—seemed to lead into the heart of an immense darkness.
Joseph **Conrad** *Heart of Darkness* (1902)

12 The past is a foreign country: they do things differently there.
L. P. **Hartley** *The Go-Between* (1953)

13 riverrun, past Eve and Adam's, from swerve of shore to bend of bay, brings us by a commodious vicus of recirculation back to Howth Castle and Environs.
James **Joyce** *Finnegans Wake* (1939)

14 St Agnes' Eve—Ah, bitter chill it was! The owl, for all his feathers, was a-cold.
John **Keats** 'The Eve of St Agnes' (1820)

15 Season of mists and mellow fruitfulness, Close bosom-friend of the maturing sun.
John **Keats** 'To Autumn' (1820)

16 Should auld acquaintance be forgot And never brought to mind?
Robert **Burns** 'Auld Lang Syne' (1796)

17 Sir Walter Elliot, of Kellynch-hall, in Somersetshire, was a man who, for his own amusement, never took up any book but the Baronetage; there he found occupation for an idle hour, and consolation in a distressed one.
Jane **Austen** *Persuasion* (1818)

18 The snow in the mountains was melting and Bunny had been dead for several weeks before we came to understand the gravity of our situation.
Donna Tartt *Secret History* (1992)

19 Someone must have traduced Joseph K., for without having done anything wrong he was arrested one fine morning.
Franz **Kafka** *The Trial* (1925)

20 Stately, plump Buck Mulligan came from the stairhead, bearing a bowl of lather on which a mirror and a razor lay crossed.
James **Joyce** *Ulysses* (1922)

21 'Take my camel, dear,' said my aunt Dot, as she climbed down from this animal on her return from High Mass.
Rose **Macaulay** *The Towers of Trebizond* (1956)

22 Tell me, Muse, of the man of many devices, who wandered far and wide after he had sacked Troy's sacred city, and saw the towns of many men and knew their mind.
Homer *The Odyssey*

23 There was no possibility of taking a walk that day.
Charlotte **Brontë** *Jane Eyre* (1847)

24 A thing of beauty is a joy for ever.
John **Keats** *Endymion* (1818)

25 Thou still unravished bride of quietness, Thou foster-child of silence and slow time.
John **Keats** 'Ode on a Grecian Urn' (1820)

26 To begin at the beginning: It is spring, moonless night in the small town, starless and bible-black.
Dylan **Thomas** *Under Milk Wood* (1954)

27 *Toute ma vie, je me suis fait une certaine idée de la France.*
All my life I have thought of France in a certain way.
Charles **de Gaulle** *War Memoirs* (1955) vol. 1

▶

▶ **Opening lines** *continued*

1 Whan that Aprill with his shoures soote
The droghte of March hath perced to the roote.
Geoffrey **Chaucer** *The Canterbury Tales* 'General Prologue'

2 When Gregor Samsa awoke one morning from
uneasy dreams he found himself transformed in
his bed into a gigantic insect.
Franz **Kafka** *The Metamorphosis* (1915)

3 When Mary Lennox was sent to Misselthwaite
Manor to live with her uncle, everybody said she
was the most disagreeable-looking child ever
seen.
Frances Hodgson Burnett *The Secret Garden* (1911)

4 Yet once more, O ye laurels, and once more
Ye myrtles brown, with ivy never sere.
John **Milton** 'Lycidas' (1638)

Roy Orbison 1936–88
American singer and songwriter and **Joe Melson**

5 Only the lonely (know the way I feel).
title of song (1960)

Orchoth Zadikkim
Jewish ethical work [The Ways of the Righteous] *of c.15th
century*

6 The thread on which the different good qualities of
human beings are strung as pearls, is the fear of
God. When the fastenings of this fear are
unloosed, the pearls roll in all directions, and are
lost one by one.
Orchoth Zaddikim

7 Be not blind, but open-eyed, to the great wonders
of Nature, familiar, everyday objects though they
be to thee. But men are more wont to be
astonished at the sun's eclipse than at his
unfailing rise.
Orchoth Zaddikim

8 Be grateful for, not blind to the many, many
sufferings which thou art spared; thou art no
better than those who have been searched out and
racked by them.
Orchoth Zaddikim

Baroness Orczy (Mrs Montague Barstow) 1865–1947
Hungarian-born novelist

9 We seek him here, we seek him there,
Those Frenchies seek him everywhere.
Is he in heaven?—Is he in hell?
That demmed, elusive Pimpernel?
The Scarlet Pimpernel (1905) ch. 12

Orderic Vitalis 1075–c.1142
English-born Norman monk and chronicler

10 For the mangled bodies that had been the flower of
the English nobility and youth covered the ground
as far as the eye could see.
*of the battlefield at Hastings after the Norman victory
in 1066*
Ecclesiastical History

11 For the fortifications called castles by the French
were scarcely known in the English provinces.
*explaining the weakness of the English resistance,
despite their fighting prowess*
Ecclesiastical History

Meta Orred
Scottish 19th-century writer and poet

12 In the gloaming, Oh my darling!
When the lights are dim and low,
And the quiet shadows falling
Softly come and softly go.
'In the Gloaming' (1877 song)

José Ortega y Gasset 1883–1955
Spanish writer and philosopher

13 *Yo soy yo y mi circunstancia, y si no la salvo a ella no
me salvo yo.*
I am I plus my surroundings, and if I do not
preserve the latter I do not preserve myself.
Meditaciones del Quijote (1914)

14 *La civilización no es otra cosa que el ensayo de reducir
la fuerza a ultima ratio.*
Civilization is nothing more than the effort to
reduce the use of force to the last resort.
La Rebelión de las Masas (1930)

Joe Orton 1933–67
English dramatist

15 I'd the upbringing a nun would envy . . . Until I
was fifteen I was more familiar with Africa than
my own body.
Entertaining Mr Sloane (1964) act 1

16 It's all any reasonable child can expect if the dad is
present at the conception.
Entertaining Mr Sloane (1964) act 3

17 Reading isn't an occupation we encourage among
police officers. We try to keep the paper work
down to a minimum.
Loot (1967) act 2

18 You were born with your legs apart. They'll send
you to the grave in a Y-shaped coffin.
What the Butler Saw (1969) act 1

George Orwell (Eric Blair) 1903–50
English novelist
see also **Opening lines** 574:24

19 Man is the only creature that consumes without
producing.
Animal Farm (1945) ch. 1

20 Four legs good, two legs bad.
Animal Farm (1945) ch. 3

1 All animals are equal but some animals are more equal than others.
   Animal Farm (1945) ch. 10

2 Good prose is like a window-pane.
   Collected Essays (1968) vol. 1 'Why I Write'

3 I'm fat, but I'm thin inside. Has it ever struck you that there's a thin man inside every fat man, just as they say there's a statue inside every block of stone?
   Coming up For Air (1939) pt. 1, ch. 3; see **Connolly** 240:5

4 Roast beef and Yorkshire, or roast pork and apple sauce, followed up by suet pudding and driven home, as it were, by a cup of mahogany-brown tea, have put you in just the right mood . . . In these blissful circumstances, what is it that you want to read about?
      Naturally, about a murder.
   Decline of the English Murder and other essays (1965) title essay, written 1946

5 Down and out in Paris and London.
   title of book (1933)

6 He was an embittered atheist (the sort of atheist who does not so much disbelieve in God as personally dislike Him), and took a sort of pleasure in thinking that human affairs would never improve.
   Down and Out in Paris and London (1933) ch. 30

7 Down here it was still the England I had known in my childhood: the railway cuttings smothered in wild flowers . . . the red buses, the blue policemen—all sleeping the deep, deep sleep of England, from which I sometimes fear that we shall never wake till we are jerked out of it by the roar of bombs.
   Homage to Catalonia (1938) ch. 14

8 Most revolutionaries are potential Tories, because they imagine that everything can be put right by altering the *shape* of society; once that change is effected, as it sometimes is, they see no need for any other.
   Inside the Whale (1940) 'Charles Dickens'

9 Keep the aspidistra flying.
   title of novel (1936)

10 England is not the jewelled isle of Shakespeare's much-quoted passage, nor is it the inferno depicted by Dr Goebbels. More than either it resembles a family, a rather stuffy Victorian family, with not many black sheep in it but with all its cupboards bursting with skeletons . . . A family with the wrong members in control.
   The Lion and the Unicorn (1941) pt. 1 'England Your England'

11 Old maids biking to Holy Communion through the mists of the autumn mornings . . . these are not only fragments, but *characteristic* fragments, of the English scene.
   The Lion and the Unicorn (1941) pt. 1 'England Your England'; see **Major** 508:5

12 Probably the battle of Waterloo *was* won on the playing-fields of Eton, but the opening battles of all subsequent wars have been lost there.
   The Lion and the Unicorn (1941) pt. 1 'England Your England'; see **Wellington** 828:1

13 BIG BROTHER IS WATCHING YOU.
   Nineteen Eighty-Four (1949) pt. 1, ch. 1

14 War is peace. Freedom is slavery. Ignorance is strength.
   Nineteen Eighty-Four (1949) pt. 1, ch. 1

15 Who controls the past controls the future: who controls the present controls the past.
   Nineteen Eighty-Four (1949) pt. 1, ch. 3

16 Don't you see that the whole aim of Newspeak is to narrow the range of thought? In the end we shall make thoughtcrime literally impossible, because there will be no words in which to express it.
   Nineteen Eighty-Four (1949) pt. 1, ch. 5

17 Freedom is the freedom to say that two plus two make four. If that is granted, all else follows.
   Nineteen Eighty-Four (1949) pt. 1, ch. 7

18 The Lottery, with its weekly pay-out of enormous prizes, was the one public event to which the proles paid serious attention . . . It was their delight, their folly, their anodyne, their intellectual stimulant . . . the prizes were largely imaginary. Only small sums were actually paid out, the winners of the big prizes being non-existent persons.
   Nineteen Eighty-Four (1949) pt. 1, ch. 8

19 Syme was not only dead, he was abolished, an un-person.
   Nineteen Eighty-Four (1949) pt. 2, ch. 5

20 *Doublethink* means the power of holding two contradictory beliefs in one's mind simultaneously, and accepting both of them.
   Nineteen Eighty-Four (1949) pt. 2, ch. 9

21 Power is not a means, it is an end. One does not establish a dictatorship in order to safeguard a revolution; one makes the revolution in order to establish the dictatorship.
   Nineteen Eighty-Four (1949) pt. 3, ch. 3

22 If you want a picture of the future, imagine a boot stamping on a human face—for ever.
   Nineteen Eighty-Four (1949) pt. 3, ch. 3

23 In a Lancashire cotton-town you could probably go for months on end without once hearing an 'educated' accent, whereas there can hardly be a town in the South of England where you could throw a brick without hitting the niece of a bishop.
   The Road to Wigan Pier (1937) ch. 7

24 To the ordinary working man, the sort you would meet in any pub on Saturday night, Socialism does not mean much more than better wages and shorter hours and nobody bossing you about.
   The Road to Wigan Pier (1937) ch. 11

25 The high-water mark, so to speak, of Socialist literature is W. H. Auden, a sort of gutless Kipling.
   The Road to Wigan Pier (1937) ch. 11

26 We of the sinking middle class . . . may sink without further struggles into the working class where we belong, and probably when we get there

it will not be so dreadful as we feared, for, after all, we have nothing to lose but our aitches.
The Road to Wigan Pier (1937) ch. 13

1 Serious sport has nothing to do with fair play. It is bound up with hatred, jealousy, boastfulness, disregard of all rules, and sadistic pleasure in witnessing violence: in other words it is war minus the shooting.
Shooting an Elephant (1950) 'I Write as I Please'

2 The great enemy of clear language is insincerity. When there is a gap between one's real and one's declared aims, one turns as it were instinctively to long words and exhausted idioms, like a cuttlefish squirting out ink.
Shooting an Elephant (1950) 'Politics and the English Language'

3 In our time, political speech and writing are largely the defence of the indefensible.
Shooting an Elephant (1950) 'Politics and the English Language'

4 Political language . . . is designed to make lies sound truthful and murder respectable, and to give an appearance of solidity to pure wind.
Shooting an Elephant (1950) 'Politics and the English Language'

5 Saints should always be judged guilty until they are proved innocent.
Shooting an Elephant (1950) 'Reflections on Gandhi'

6 Whatever is funny is subversive, every joke is ultimately a custard pie . . . A dirty joke is a sort of mental rebellion.
in *Horizon* September 1941 'The Art of Donald McGill'

7 The quickest way of ending a war is to lose it.
in *Polemic* May 1946 'Second Thoughts on James Burnham'

8 At 50, everyone has the face he deserves.
last words in his notebook, 17 April 1949, in *Collected Essays, Journalism and Letters . . .* (1968) vol. 4

9 Advertising is the rattling of a stick inside a swill bucket.
attributed

Dorothy Osborne 1627-95
English wife of William Temple from 1654

10 About six or seven o'clock, I walk out into a common that lies hard by the house, where a great many young wenches keep sheep and cows and sit in the shade singing of ballads . . . I talk to them, and find they want nothing to make them the happiest people in the world, but the knowledge that they are so.
Letters of Dorothy Osborne to William Temple (ed. G. C. Moore Smith, 1928) 2 June 1653

11 All letters, methinks, should be free and easy as one's discourse, not studied as an oration, nor made up of hard words like a charm.
letter to William Temple, September 1653

12 'Tis much easier sure to get a good fortune than a good husband, but whosoever marries without any consideration of fortune shall never be allowed to do it out of so reasonable an apprehension.
letter to William Temple, 4 February 1654

13 I do not see that it puts any value upon men when women marry them for love (as they term it); 'tis not their merit but our folly that is always presumed to cause it, and would it be any advantage to you to have your wife thought an indiscreet person?
letter to William Temple, 4 February 1654

14 Dr Taylor . . . says there is a great advantage to be gained in resigning up one's will to the command of another, because the same action which in itself is wholly indifferent if done upon our own choice, becomes an act of duty and religion if done in obedience to the command of any person whom nature, the laws, or our selves have given a power over us.
letter to William Temple, 19 February 1654

John Osborne 1929-94
English dramatist

15 Don't clap too hard—it's a very old building.
The Entertainer (1957) no. 7

16 But I have a go, lady, don't I? I 'ave a go. I do.
The Entertainer (1957) no. 7

17 Look back in anger.
title of play (1956); see **Paul** 589:2

18 Oh heavens, how I long for a little ordinary human enthusiasm. Just enthusiasm—that's all. I want to hear a warm, thrilling voice cry out Hallelujah! Hallelujah! I'm alive!
Look Back in Anger (1956) act 1

19 I don't think one 'comes down' from Jimmy's university. According to him, it's not even red brick, but white tile.
Look Back in Anger (1956) act 2, sc. 1

20 Reason and Progress, the old firm, is selling out! Everyone get out while the going's good. Those forgotten shares you had in the old traditions, the old beliefs are going up—up and up and up.
Look Back in Anger (1956) act 2, sc. 1

21 They spend their time mostly looking forward to the past.
Look Back in Anger (1956) act 2, sc. 1

22 There aren't any good, brave causes left. If the big bang does come, and we all get killed off, it won't be in aid of the old-fashioned, grand design. It'll just be for the Brave New-nothing-very-much-thank-you. About as pointless and inglorious as stepping in front of a bus.
Look Back in Anger (1956) act 3, sc. 1

23 Royalty is the gold filling in a mouthful of decay.
'They call it cricket' in T. Maschler (ed.) *Declaration* (1957)

24 This is a letter of hate. It is for you my countrymen, I mean those men of my country who have defiled it. The men with manic fingers leading the sightless, feeble, betrayed body of my country to its death . . . damn you England.
in *Tribune* 18 August 1961

Arthur O'Shaughnessy 1844–81

English poet

1 We are the music makers,
We are the dreamers of dreams . . .
We are the movers and shakers
Of the world for ever, it seems.
'Ode' (1874)

2 For each age is a dream that is dying,
Or one that is coming to birth.
'Ode' (1874)

William Osler 1849–1919

Canadian-born physician

3 That man can interrogate as well as observe
nature, was a lesson slowly learned in his
evolution.
Aphorisms from his Bedside Teachings (1961)

4 One finger in the throat and one in the rectum
makes a good diagnostician.
Aphorisms from his Bedside Teachings (1961)

5 The young physician starts life with twenty drugs
for each disease, and the old physician ends life
with one drug for twenty diseases.
Aphorisms from His Bedside Teachings and Writings (1950,
ed. William Bennett Bean)

6 The natural man has only two primal passions, to
get and beget.
Science and Immortality (1904) ch. 2

7 The desire to take medicine is perhaps the greatest
feature which distinguishes man from animals.
H. Cushing *Life of Sir William Osler* (1925) vol. 1, ch. 14

John L. O'Sullivan 1813–95

American journalist and diplomat

8 The best government is that which governs least.
in *United States Magazine and Democratic Review* (1837)
introduction; see **Thoreau** 792:23

9 A spirit of hostile interference against us . . .
checking the fulfilment of our manifest destiny to
overspread the continent allotted by Providence
for the free development of our yearly multiplying
millions.
on opposition to the annexation of Texas
in *United States Magazine and Democratic Review* (1845)
vol. 17

10 A torchlight procession marching down your
throat.
describing certain kinds of whisky
G. W. E. Russell *Collections and Recollections* (1898) ch. 19

James Otis 1725–83

American politician

11 Taxation without representation is tyranny.
associated with his attack on writs of assistance, 1761, and
later a watchword of the American Revolution, in
Dictionary of American Biography vol. 14; see **Camden**
186:15

Thomas Otway 1652–85

English dramatist

12 And for an apple damn'd mankind.
The Orphan (1680) act 3

13 No praying, it spoils business.
Venice Preserved (1682) act 2, sc. 1

14 Give but an Englishman his whore and ease,
Beef and a sea-coal fire, he's yours for ever.
Venice Preserved (1682) act 2, sc. 3

Peter Demianovich Ouspensky 1878–1947

Russian-born journalist and philosopher

15 Truths that become old become decrepit and
unreliable; sometimes they may be kept going
artificially for a certain time, but there is no life in
them.
A New Model of the Universe (2nd ed., 1934) preface

Thomas Overbury 1581–1613

English poet and courtier

16 He disdains all things above his reach, and
preferreth all countries before his own.
Miscellaneous Works (1632) 'An Affected Traveller'; see
Canning 189:5, **Disraeli** 276:16, **Gilbert** 347:22

Ovid (Publius Ovidius Naso) 43 BC–C.AD 17

Roman poet
on Ovid: see **Dryden** 288:28, **Quintilian** 639:14

17 *Et puer est et nudus Amor sine sordibus annos*
Et nullas vestes, ut sit apertus, habet.
Quid puerum Veneris pretio prostare iubetis?
Quo pretium condat non habet ille sinum.
Love is a child and naked; he has years that know
no meanness, and he has no clothes, so that he is
open in his ways. Why do you bid Venus' child
prostitute himself for a fee? He has no pockets in
which to store it.
Amores bk. 1, no. 10, l. 15

18 *Lente currite noctis equi.*
Run slowly, horses of the night.
Amores bk. 1, no. 13, l. 40; see **Marlowe** 513:6

19 *Procul omen abesto!*
Far be that fate from us!
Amores bk. 1, no. 14, l. 41

20 *Procul hinc, procul este, severae!*
Far hence, keep far from me, you grim women!
Amores bk. 2, no. 1, l. 3

21 *Spectatum veniunt, veniunt spectentur ut ipsae.*
The women come to see the show, they come to
make a show themselves.
Ars Amatoria bk. 1, l. 99

22 *Iuppiter ex alto periuria ridet amantum.*
Jupiter from on high laughs at lovers' perjuries.
Ars Amatoria bk. 1, l. 633; see **Dryden** 289:5, **Proverbs**
624:33

1 *Expedit esse deos, et, ut expedit, esse putemus.*
It is convenient that there be gods, and, as it is
convenient, let us believe that there are.
Ars Amatoria bk. 1, l. 637; see **Voltaire** 816:3

2 *Semibovemque virum semivirumque bovem.*
A man half-bull and a bull half-man.
of the minotaur
Ars Amatoria bk. 2, l. 24

3 *Forsitan et nostrum nomen miscebitur istis.*
Perhaps my name too will be linked with theirs.
on the names of famous poets
Ars Amatoria bk. 3, l. 339

4 *Nescioqua natale solum dulcedine cunctos*
Ducit et inmemores non sinit esse sui.
By what sweet charm I know not the native land
draws all men nor allows them to forget her.
Epistulae ex Ponto bk. 1, no. 3, l. 35

5 *Adde quod ingenuas didicisse fideliter artes*
Emollit mores nec sinit esse feros.
Add the fact that to have conscientiously studied
the liberal arts refines behaviour and does not
allow it to be savage.
Epistulae Ex Ponto bk. 2, no. 9, l. 47

6 *Ut desint vires, tamen est laudanda voluntas.*
Though the strength is lacking, yet the willingness
is commendable.
Epistulae Ex Ponto bk. 3, no. 4, l. 79

7 *Gutta cavat lapidem, consumitur anulus usu.*
Dripping water hollows out a stone, a ring is worn
away by use.
Epistulae Ex Ponto bk. 4, no. 10, l. 5; see **Latimer** 470:2,
Proverbs 617:10

8 *Chaos, rudis indigestaque moles.*
Chaos, a rough and unordered mass.
Metamorphoses bk. 1, l. 7

9 *Materiam superabat opus.*
The workmanship surpasses the material.
of the bronze doors made by Vulcan for the palace of
Apollo
Metamorphoses bk 2, l. 5

10 *Medio tutissimus ibis.*
You will go most safely by the middle way.
Metamorphoses bk. 2, l. 137

11 *Inopem me copia fecit.*
Plenty has made me poor.
Metamorphoses bk. 3, l. 466

12 *Ipse docet quid agam; fas est et ab hoste doceri.*
He himself teaches what I should do; it is right to
be taught by the enemy.
Metamorphoses bk. 4, l. 428

13 *Video meliora, proboque;*
Deteriora sequor.
I see the better things, and approve; I follow the
worse.
Metamorphoses bk. 7, l. 20; see **Bible** 106:15

14 *Tempus edax rerum.*
Time the devourer of everything.
Metamorphoses bk. 15, l. 234

15 *Iamque opus exegi, quod nec Iovis ira, nec ignis,*
Nec poterit ferrum, nec edax abolere vetustas.
And now I have finished the work, which neither
the wrath of Jove, nor fire, nor the sword, nor
devouring age shall be able to destroy.
Metamorphoses bk. 15, l. 871

16 *Principiis obsta; sero medicina paratur*
Cum mala per longas convaluere moras.
Stop it at the start, it's late for medicine to be
prepared when disease has grown strong through
long delays.
Remedia Amoris l. 91; see **Persius** 593:8

17 *Qui finem quaeris amoris,*
Cedet amor rebus; res age, tutus eris.
You who seek an end of love, love will yield to
business: be busy, and you will be safe.
Remedia Amoris l. 143

18 *Perdiderint cum me duo crimina, carmen et error.*
Although two crimes, a song and a mistake, have
done me in.
Tristia bk. 2, l. 207

19 *Teque, rebellatrix, tandem, Germania, magni*
Triste caput pedibus supposuisse ducis!
How you, rebellious Germany, laid your wretched
head beneath the feet of the great general.
Tristia bk. 3, no. 12, l. 47

20 *Sponte sua carmen numeros veniebat ad aptos,*
Et quod temptabam dicere versus erat.
Of its own accord my song would come in the
right rhythms, and what I was trying to say was
poetry.
Tristia bk. 4, no. 10, l. 25; see **Pope** 602:25

21 *Vergilium vidi tantum.*
I have only glimpsed Virgil.
Tristia bk. 4, no. 10, l. 51

John Owen c.1563–1622
Welsh epigrammatist

22 God and the doctor we alike adore
But only when in danger, not before;
The danger o'er, both are alike requited,
God is forgotten, and the Doctor slighted.
Epigrams; see **Quarles** 638:16

Robert Owen 1771–1858
Welsh-born socialist and philanthropist

23 All the world is queer save thee and me, and even
thou art a little queer.
to his partner W. Allen, on severing business relations
at New Lanark, 1828
attributed

Wilfred Owen 1893–1918
English poet

24 My subject is War, and the pity of War.
The Poetry is in the pity.
Preface (written 1918) in *Poems* (1963)

25 All a poet can do today is warn.
Preface (written 1918) in *Poems* (1963)

1 What passing-bells for these who die as cattle?
Only the monstrous anger of the guns.
  'Anthem for Doomed Youth' (written 1917)

2 The shrill, demented choirs of wailing shells;
And bugles calling for them from sad shires.
  'Anthem for Doomed Youth' (written 1917)

3 The pallor of girls' brows shall be their pall;
Their flowers the tenderness of patient minds,
And each slow dusk a drawing-down of blinds.
  'Anthem for Doomed Youth' (written 1917)

4 If you could hear, at every jolt, the blood
Come gargling from the froth-corrupted lungs,
Obscene as cancer, bitter as the cud
Of vile, incurable sores on innocent tongues,—
My friend, you would not tell with such high zest
To children ardent for some desperate glory,
The old Lie: Dulce et decorum est
Pro patria mori.
  'Dulce et Decorum Est' (1963 ed.); see **Horace** 401:12

5 Was it for this the clay grew tall?
  'Futility' (written 1918)

6 It seemed that out of battle I escaped
Down some profound dull tunnel, long since
  scooped
Through granites which titanic wars had groined.
  'Strange Meeting' (written 1918)

7 'Strange friend,' I said, 'here is no cause to
  mourn.'
'None,' said that other, 'save the undone years,
The hopelessness. Whatever hope is yours,
Was my life also.'
  'Strange Meeting' (written 1918)

8 I am the enemy you killed, my friend.
I knew you in this dark: for you so frowned
Yesterday through me as you jabbed and killed . . .
Let us sleep now.
  'Strange Meeting' (written 1918)

Count Oxenstierna 1583–1654
Swedish statesman

9 Dost thou not know, my son, with how little
wisdom the world is governed?
  letter to his son, 1648, in J. F. af Lundblad *Svensk Plutark* (1826) pt. 2; an alternative attribution quotes 'a certain Pope' (possibly Julius III, 1487–1555) saying:
  Thou little thinkest what *a little foolery governs the whole world!*
  John Selden *Table Talk* (1689) 'Pope' no. 2

Edward de Vere, Earl of Oxford
1550–1604
English poet
see also **Elizabeth I** 304:19

10 The labouring man, that tills the fertile soil,
And reaps the harvest fruit, hath not in deed
The gain, but pain; and if for all his toil
He gets the straw, the lord will have the seed.
  'The labouring man, that tills the fertile soil' (1573) st. 1

11 So he that takes the pain to pen the book
Reaps not the gifts of goodly golden Muse;

But those gain that who on the work shall look,
And from the sour the sweet by skill doth choose.
For he that beats the bush the bird not gets,
But who sits still and holdeth fast the nets.
  'The labouring man, that tills the fertile soil' (1573) st. 6

Pp

Vance Packard 1914–97
American writer and journalist

12 The hidden persuaders.
  title of a study of the advertising industry (1957)

John Page 1743–1808
American politician

13 We know the race is not to the swift nor the battle
to the strong. Do you think an angel rides in the
whirlwind and directs this storm.
  quoted by George W. **Bush** *in his first inaugural
address, 20 January 2001*
  letter to Thomas Jefferson, 20 July 1776; see **Addison** 4:6,
  Bible 86:16

William Tyler Page 1868–1942

14 I believe in the United States of America as a
government of the people, by the people, for the
people, whose just powers are derived from the
consent of the governed; a democracy in a
republic; a sovereign Nation of many sovereign
States; a perfect Union, one and inseparable,
established upon those principles of freedom,
equality, justice, and humanity for which
American patriots sacrificed their lives and
fortunes. I therefore believe it is my duty to my
country to love it, to support its Constitution, to
obey its laws, to respect its flag, and to defend it
against all enemies.
  American's Creed (prize-winning competition entry, 1918)
  in *Congressional Record* vol. 56; see **Lincoln** 485:7

Lord George Paget 1818–80
English soldier

15 As far as it engendered excitement the finest run
in Leicestershire could hardly bear comparison.
  *the second-in-command's view of the charge of the
Light Brigade*
  The Light Cavalry Brigade in the Crimea (1881) ch. 5

Camille Paglia 1947–
American writer and critic

16 Gay men may seek sex without emotion; lesbians
often end up in emotion without sex.
  in *Esquire* October 1991

17 All great art has come from mutilated egos.
  in *Vanity Fair* September 1992

Marcel Pagnol 1895–1974

French dramatist and film-maker

1 Honour is like a match, you can only use it once.
   Marius (1946) act 4, sc. 5

2 It's better to choose the culprits than to seek them
   out.
   Topaze (1930) act 1

Thomas Paine 1737–1809

English political theorist

3 It is necessary to the happiness of man that he be
   mentally faithful to himself. Infidelity does not
   consist in believing, or in disbelieving, it consists
   in professing to believe what one does not believe.
   The Age of Reason pt. 1 (1794)

4 Any system of religion that has any thing in it
   that shocks the mind of a child cannot be a true
   system.
   The Age of Reason pt. 1 (1794)

5 The sublime and the ridiculous are often so nearly
   related, that it is difficult to class them separately.
   One step above the sublime, makes the ridiculous;
   and one step above the ridiculous, makes the
   sublime again.
   The Age of Reason pt. 2 (1795); see **Napoleon** 556:15,
   Proverbs 620:32

6 Government, even in its best state, is but a
   necessary evil; in its worst state, an intolerable
   one. Government, like dress, is the badge of lost
   innocence; the palaces of kings are built upon the
   ruins of the bowers of paradise.
   Common Sense (1776) ch. 1

7 Though we have been wise enough to shut and
   lock a door against absolute Monarchy, we at the
   same time have been foolish enough to put the
   crown in possession of the key.
   Common Sense (1776) ch. 1

8 Monarchy and succession have laid . . . the world
   in blood and ashes.
   Common Sense (1776) ch. 2

9 Freedom hath been hunted round the globe. Asia
   and Africa have long expelled her. Europe regards
   her like a stranger, and England hath given her
   warning to depart. O! receive the fugitive, and
   prepare in time an asylum for mankind.
   to America
   Common Sense (1776) ch. 3

10 As to religion, I hold it to be the indispensable
   duty of government to protect all conscientious
   professors thereof, and I know of no other business
   which government hath to do therewith.
   Common Sense (1776) ch. 4

11 These are the times that try men's souls. The
   summer soldier and the sunshine patriot will, in
   this crisis, shrink from the service of their country;
   but he that stands it *now*, deserves the love and
   thanks of men and women.
   The Crisis (December 1776) introduction

12 Wisdom is not the purchase of a day.
   The Crisis (December 1776)

13 The religion of humanity.
   The Crisis (November 1778)

14 As he rose like a rocket, he fell like the stick.
   on Edmund **Burke**'s *losing the debate on the French
   Revolution to Charles James* **Fox**, *in the House of
   Commons*
   Letter to the Addressers on the late Proclamation (1792)

15 [He] is not affected by the reality of distress
   touching his heart, but by the showy resemblance
   of it striking his imagination. He pities the
   plumage, but forgets the dying bird.
   on Edmund **Burke**'s *Reflections on the Revolution in
   France, 1790*
   The Rights of Man (1791)

16 Lay then the axe to the root, and teach
   governments humanity. It is their sanguinary
   punishments which corrupt mankind.
   The Rights of Man (1791)

17 [In France] All that class of equivocal generation,
   which in some countries is called *aristocracy*, and
   in others *nobility*, is done away, and the peer is
   exalted into MAN.
   The Rights of Man (1791)

18 The idea of hereditary legislators is as inconsistent
   as that of hereditary judges, or hereditary juries;
   and as absurd as an hereditary mathematician, or
   an hereditary wise man; and as ridiculous as an
   hereditary poet laureate.
   The Rights of Man (1791)

19 Persecution is not an original feature of *any*
   religion; but it is always the strongly marked
   feature of all law-religions, or religions established
   by law.
   The Rights of Man (1791)

20 I compare it [monarchy] to something kept behind
   a curtain, about which there is a great deal of
   bustle and fuss, and a wonderful air of seeming
   solemnity; but when, by any accident, the curtain
   happens to be open, and the company see what it
   is, they burst into laughter.
   The Rights of Man pt. 2 (1792)

21 The Minister, whoever he at any time may be,
   touches it as with an opium wand, and it sleeps
   obedience.
   of Parliament
   The Rights of Man pt. 2 (1792)

22 When, in countries that are called civilized, we see
   age going to the workhouse and youth to the
   gallows, something must be wrong in the system
   of government.
   The Rights of Man pt. 2 (1792)

23 My country is the world, and my religion is to do
   good.
   The Rights of Man pt. 2 (1792)

24 I do not believe that any two men, on what are
   called doctrinal points, think alike who think at
   all. It is only those who have not thought that
   appear to agree.
   The Rights of Man pt. 2 (1792)

1 A share in two revolutions is living to some purpose.
Eric Foner *Tom Paine and Revolutionary America* (1976) ch. 7

Ian Paisley 1926-

Northern Irish politician and Presbyterian minister

2 The mother of all treachery.
on the Good Friday agreement
in *The Times* 16 April 1998

José de Palafox 1780–1847

Spanish general

3 *Guerra a cuchillo.*
War to the knife.
on 4 August 1808, at the siege of Saragossa, the French general Verdier sent a one-word suggestion: 'Capitulation'. Palafox replied 'Guerra y cuchillo [War and the knife]', *later reported as above; it subsequently appeared, at the behest of Palafox himself, on survivors' medals*
José Gòmez de Arteche y Moro *Guerra de la Independencia* (1875) vol. 2, ch. 4

William Paley 1743–1805

English theologian and philosopher

4 Suppose I had found a *watch* upon the ground, and it should be enquired how the watch happened to be in that place . . . the inference, we think, is inevitable; that the watch must have had a maker, that there must have existed, at some time and at some place or other, an artificer or artificers, who formed it for the purpose which we find it actually to answer; who comprehended its construction, and designed its use.
Natural Theology (1802) ch. 1; see **Dawkins** 259:13

5 Who can refute a sneer?
Principles of Moral and Political Philosophy (1785) bk. 5, ch. 9

Pali Tripitaka

the earliest collection of Buddhist sacred texts, c.2nd century BC

6 Is it fitting to consider what is impermanent, painful, and subject to change as, 'This is mine, this am I, this is my self'?
Vinaya, Mahāv. [Book of Discipline] 1, 6

7 I go, reverend one, to the Lord and to the doctrine and the Order of monks. May the Lord take me as a lay disciple from this day forth while life lasts, who have gone to him as a refuge.
He [Yasa] was the first layman in the world received by the triple utterance.
Vinaya, Mahāv. [Book of Discipline] 1, 7

8 1) Refraining from taking life. 2) Refraining from taking what is not given. 3) Refraining from incontinence. 4) Refraining from falsehood. 5) Refraining from strong drink, intoxicants, and liquor, which are occasions of carelessness.
The Five Precepts
Vinaya, Mahāv. [Book of Discipline] 1, 56

9 I [Buddha] directed my mind to the knowledge of the extinction of the outflows. I understood it as it really is: This is suffering, this its arising, this its stopping, this the course leading to its stopping.
Vinaya [Book of Discipline] 3, 6

10 Dhamma has been taught by me without making a distinction between esoteric and exoteric. For the Tathagata has not the closed fist of a teacher in respect of mental states.
Dīgha-nikāya [Longer Collection] pt. 2, p. 100

11 You [monks] should live as islands, unto yourselves, being your own refuge, with no one else as your refuge, with the Dhamma as an island, with the Dhamma as your refuge, with no other refuge.
some translations prefer 'lamps' to 'islands'
Dīgha-nikāya [Longer Collection] pt. 2, p. 100

12 'Now, monks, I declare to you: all conditioned things are of a nature to decay—strive on untiringly.' These were the Tathagata's last words.
Dīgha-nikāya [Longer Collection] pt. 2, p. 156

13 In regard to things that are past, future and present the Tathagata is a speaker at a suitable time, a speaker of fact, on what has bearing, of Dhamma, of Discipline. Therefore is he called Tathagata.
Dīgha-nikāya [Longer Collection] pt. 3, p. 135

14 Monks, I will teach you Dhamma—the Parable of the Raft—for crossing over, not for retaining.
Majjhima-nikāya [Medium Collection] pt. 1, p. 134

15 Precisely this do I teach, now as formerly: ill and the stopping of ill.
Majjhima-nikāya [Medium Collection] pt. 1, p. 140

16 Who sees Conditioned Genesis sees Dhamma; who sees Dhamma sees Conditioned Genesis.
Majjhima-nikāya [Medium Collection] pt. 1, p. 190; see **Pali Tripitaka** 584:1

17 It is called Nirvana because of the getting rid of craving.
Samyutta-nikāya [Kindred Sayings] pt. 1, p. 39

18 In the Sakyan clan there was born
A Buddha, peerless among men,
Conqueror of all, repelling Mara—
The Visioned One sees all.
Samyutta-nikāya [Kindred Sayings] pt. 1, p. 134

19 The instructed disciple of the Aryans well and wisely reflects on Conditioned Genesis itself: If this is that comes to be; from the arising of this that arises; if this is not that does not come to be; from the stopping of this that is stopped.
Samyutta-nikāya [Kindred Sayings] pt. 2, p. 64

20 If one does not behold any self or anything of the nature of self in the five groups of grasping (material shape, feeling, perception, the impulses, consciousness), one is an Arahant, the outflows extinguished.
Samyutta-nikāya [Kindred Sayings] pt. 3, p. 127

1 Whoso sees Dhamma sees me; whoso sees me sees Dhamma.
Samyutta-nikāya [Kindred Sayings] pt. 3, p. 120

2 To what extent is the world called 'empty' Lord? Because it is empty of self or what belongs to self, it is therefore said: 'The world is empty.'
Samyutta-nikāya [Kindred Sayings] pt. 4, p. 54

3 I teach Dhamma that is lovely at the beginning, lovely in the middle and lovely at the ending, with the spirit and the letter.
Samyutta-nikāya [Kindred Sayings] pt. 4, p. 315

4 Avoiding both these extremes, [indulgence of sense pleasures, devotion to self-mortification] the Tathagata has realized the Middle Path: it gives vision, it gives knowledge, and it leads to calm, to insight, to enlightenment, to Nirvana.
First Sermon of the Buddha
Samyutta-nikāya [Kindred Sayings] pt. 56, p. 11

5 The Noble Truth of Suffering is this: Birth is suffering, ageing is suffering; sickness is suffering; death is suffering; sorrow and lamentation, pain, grief and despair are suffering; association with the unpleasant is suffering; dissociation from the pleasant is suffering; not to get what one wants is suffering—in brief, the five aggregates of attachment are suffering.
First Sermon of the Buddha
Samyutta-nikāya [Kindred Sayings] pt. 56, p. 11

6 The Noble Truth of the Path leading to the Cessation of suffering is this: It is simply the Noble Eightfold Path, namely right view; right thought; right speech; right action; right livelihood; right effort; right mindfulness; right concentration.
First Sermon of the Buddha
Samyutta-nikāya [Kindred Sayings] pt. 56, p. 11

7 Bhikkhus [monks], all is burning.
Fire Sermon
Samyutta-nikāya [Kindred Sayings] pt. 35, p. 28

8 As the great ocean has but one taste, that of salt, so has this Dharma and Discipline but one taste, the taste of Freedom.
Anguttara-nikāya [Gradual Sayings] pt. 4, p. 203

9 What we are today comes from our thoughts of yesterday, and our present thoughts build our life of tomorrow: our life is the creation of our mind.
Dhammapada v. 1

10 For hate is not conquered by hate: hate is conquered by love. This is a law eternal.
Dhammapada v. 5

11 Even as rain breaks not through a well-thatched house, passions break not through a well-guarded mind.
Dhammapada v. 14

12 Who can trace the invisible path of the man who soars in the sky of liberation, the infinite Void without beginning, whose passions are peace and over whom pleasures have no power? His path is as difficult to trace as that of the birds in the air.
Dhammapada v. 93

13 If a man should conquer in battle a thousand and a thousand more, and another man should conquer himself, his would be the greater victory, because the greatest of victories is the victory over oneself.
Dhammapada v. 103

14 Because there is, monks, an unborn, not become, not made, uncompounded, therefore an escape can be shown for what is born, has become, is made, is compounded.
Udāna [Solemn Utterances] p. 81

15 I see no other single hindrance such as this hindrance of ignorance, obstructed by which mankind for a long long time runs on and circles on.
Itivuttaka [Thus Was Said] p. 8

16 The person who is searching for his own happiness should pull out the dart that he has stuck in himself, the arrow-head of grieving, of desiring, of despair.
Sutta-Nipāta [Woven Cadences] v. 592

17 Of all beings this one is perfect, this man is the pinnacle, the ultimate, the hero of creatures! This is the man who, from the forest of the Masters, will set the Wheel of Teaching turning—the roar of the lion, King of Beasts!
Sutta-Nipāta [Woven Cadences] v. 684

18 There are no waves in the depths of the sea: it is still, unbroken. It is the same with the monk. He is still, without any quiver of desire, without a remnant on which to build pride and desire.
Sutta-Nipāta [Woven Cadences] v. 920

Henry John Temple, Lord Palmerston
1784–1865
British statesman; Prime Minister, 1855–8, 1859–65
*on Palmerston: see **Disraeli** 278:6; see also **Last words** 471:8*

19 We have no eternal allies and we have no perpetual enemies. Our interests are eternal and perpetual, and those interests it is our duty to follow.
speech, House of Commons, 1 March 1848

20 I therefore fearlessly challenge the verdict which this House . . . is to give . . . whether, as the Roman, in days of old, held himself free from indignity, when he could say *Civis Romanus sum*; so also a British subject, in whatever land he may be, shall feel confident that the watchful eye and the strong arm of England will protect him against injustice and wrong.
in the debate on the protection afforded to the Greek trader David Pacifico (1784–1854) who had been born a British subject at Gibraltar
speech, House of Commons, 25 June 1850; see **Cicero** 223:18

21 You may call it combination, you may call it the accidental and fortuitous concurrence of atoms.
on a projected Palmerston–Disraeli coalition
speech, House of Commons, 5 March 1857

22 We do not want Egypt any more than any rational man with an estate in the north of England and a residence in the south, would have wished to possess the inns on the north road. All he could want would have been that the inns should be well kept, always accessible, and furnishing him, when he came, with mutton chops and post horses.

> letter to Earl Cowley, 25 November 1859, in Hon. Evelyn Ashley *Life of . . . Viscount Palmerston 1846–65* (1876) vol. 2, ch. 4

1 The function of a government is to calm, rather than to excite agitation.

> P. Guedalla *Gladstone and Palmerston* (1928)

2 How d'ye do, and how is the old complaint?
reputed to be his greeting to all those he did not know

> A. West *Recollections* (1899) vol. 1, ch. 2

3 Lord Palmerston, with characteristic levity had once said that only three men in Europe had ever understood [the Schleswig-Holstein question], and of these the Prince Consort was dead, a Danish statesman (unnamed) was in an asylum, and he himself had forgotten it.

> R. W. Seton-Watson *Britain in Europe 1789–1914* (1937) ch. 11

4 What is merit? The opinion one man entertains of another.

> T. Carlyle *Shooting Niagara: and After?* (1867) ch. 8

5 Yes we have. Humbug.
on being told there was no English word equivalent to sensibilité

> attributed

Christabel Pankhurst 1880–1958
English suffragette; daughter of Emmeline Pankhurst

6 Never lose your temper with the Press or the public is a major rule of political life.

> *Unshackled* (1959) ch. 5

7 We are here to claim our right as women, not only to be free, but to fight for freedom. That it is our right as well as our duty.

> in *Votes for Women* 31 March 1911

Emmeline Pankhurst 1858–1928
English suffragette leader; founder of the Women's Social and Political Union, 1903

8 There is something that Governments care far more for than human life, and that is the security of property, and so it is through property that we shall strike the enemy . . . I say to the Government: You have not dared to take the leaders of Ulster for their incitement to rebellion. Take me if you dare.

> speech at Albert Hall, 17 October 1912, in *My Own Story* (1914)

9 The argument of the broken window pane is the most valuable argument in modern politics.

> George Dangerfield *The Strange Death of Liberal England* (1936) pt. 2, ch. 3, sect. 4; see **More** 547:24

Laszlo Papp 1926–2003
Hungarian boxer

10 I fight for money, but I am not greedy. How many steaks can one man eat?

> attributed; in *Guardian* 18 October 2003, obituary

Paracelsus Theophrastus Phillipus Aureolus Bombastus von Hohenheim c.1493–1541
Swiss physician

11 There can be no surgeon who is not also a physician . . . Where the physician is not also a surgeon he is an idol that is nothing but a painted monkey.

> Walter Pagel *Paracelsus: An introduction to Philosophical Medicine in the Era of the Renaissance* (1958)

Mitchell Parish 1900–93
American songwriter

12 When the deep purple falls over sleepy garden walls,
And the stars begin to flicker in the sky,
Thru' the mist of a memory you wander back to me,
Breathing my name with a sigh.

> 'Deep Purple' (1939); words added to music (1934) by Peter de Rose

Charlie Parker 1920–55
American jazz saxophonist

13 Music is your own experience, your thoughts, your wisdom. If you don't live it, it won't come out of your horn.

> Nat Shapiro and Nat Hentoff *Hear Me Talkin' to Ya* (1955)

Dorothy Parker 1893–1967
American critic and humorist
*on Parker: see **Woollcott** 845:15; see also **Epitaphs** 309:4, **Telegrams** 776:5*

14 Oh, life is a glorious cycle of song,
A medley of extemporanea;
And love is a thing that can never go wrong;
And I am Marie of Roumania.

> 'Comment' (1937)

15 Four be the things I'd been better without:
Love, curiosity, freckles, and doubt.

> 'Inventory' (1937)

16 Men seldom make passes
At girls who wear glasses.

> 'News Item' (1937)

17 Why is it no one ever sent me yet
One perfect limousine, do you suppose?
Ah no, it's always just my luck to get
One perfect rose.

> 'One Perfect Rose' (1937)

18 If, with the literate, I am
Impelled to try an epigram,
I never seek to take the credit;
We all assume that Oscar said it.

> 'A Pig's-Eye View of Literature' (1937)

1 Guns aren't lawful;
Nooses give;
Gas smells awful;
You might as well live.
  'Résumé' (1937)

2 Where's the man could ease a heart like a satin gown?
  'The Satin Dress' (1937)

3 By the time you say you're his,
Shivering and sighing
And he vows his passion is
Infinite, undying—
Lady, make a note of this:
One of you is lying.
  'Unfortunate Coincidence' (1937)

4 Sorrow is tranquillity remembered in emotion.
  Here Lies (1939) 'Sentiment'; see **Wordsworth** 850:26

5 *House Beautiful* is play lousy.
  review in *New Yorker*, 1933, in Phyllis Hartnoll *Plays and Players* (1984)

6 She ran the whole gamut of the emotions from A to B.
  of Katharine Hepburn at a Broadway first night, 1933
  attributed

7 There's a hell of a distance between wise-cracking and wit. Wit has truth in it; wise-cracking is simply callisthenics with words.
  in *Paris Review* Summer 1956

8 How do they know?
  *on being told that Calvin **Coolidge** had died*
  Malcolm Cowley *Writers at Work* 1st Series (1958)

9 Hollywood money isn't money. It's congealed snow, melts in your hand, and there you are.
  Malcolm Cowley *Writers at Work* 1st Series (1958)

10 You can lead a horticulture, but you can't make her think.
  John Keats *You Might as well Live* (1970)

11 It serves me right for putting all my eggs in one bastard.
  on her abortion
  John Keats *You Might as well Live* (1970) pt. 2, ch. 3

Martin Parker d. c.1656
English balladmonger

12 You gentlemen of England
Who live at home at ease,
How little do you think
On the dangers of the seas.
  'The Valiant Sailors'; J. O. Halliwell (ed.) *Early Naval Ballads* (Percy Society, 1841)

13   The times will not mend
Till the King enjoys his own again.
  'Upon Defacing of Whitehall' (1671)

Ross Parker 1914–74 and Hugh Charles 1907–
British songwriters

14 There'll always be an England
While there's a country lane.
  'There'll always be an England' (1939 song)

Henry Parkes 1815–95
English-born Australian statesman

15 The crimson thread of kinship runs through us all.
  on Australian federation
  speech at banquet in Melbourne 6 February 1890; *The Federal Government of Australasia* (1890)

C. Northcote Parkinson 1909–93
English writer

16 Expenditure rises to meet income.
  The Law and the Profits (1960) ch. 1

17 Work expands so as to fill the time available for its completion.
  Parkinson's Law (1958) ch. 1

18 Time spent on any item of the agenda will be in inverse proportion to the sum involved.
  Parkinson's Law (1958) ch. 3

19 The man who is denied the opportunity of taking decisions of importance begins to regard as important the decisions he is allowed to take.
  Parkinson's Law (1958) ch. 10

Charles Stewart Parnell 1846–91
Irish nationalist leader
*on Parnell: see **Healy** 377:13*

20 Why should Ireland be treated as a geographical fragment of England . . . Ireland is not a geographical fragment, but a nation.
  in the House of Commons, 26 April 1875

21 No man has a right to fix the boundary of the march of a nation; no man has a right to say to his country—thus far shalt thou go and no further.
  speech at Cork, 21 January 1885, in *The Times* 22 January 1885

22 Get the advice of everybody whose advice is worth having—they are very few—and then do what you think best yourself.
  Conor Cruise O'Brien *Parnell* (1957)

Matthew Parris 1949–
British journalist and former politician

23 Being an MP feeds your vanity and starves your self-respect.
  in *The Times* 9 February 1994

Tony Parsons 1953–
English critic and writer

24 I never saw a beggar yet who would recognise guilt if it bit him on his unwashed ass.
  Dispatches from the Front Line of Popular Culture (1994)

Blaise Pascal 1623–62

French mathematician, physicist, and moralist

1 *Je n'ai fait celle-ci plus longue que parce que je n'ai pas eu le loisir de la faire plus courte.*

I have made this [letter] longer than usual, only because I have not had the time to make it shorter.

Lettres Provinciales (1657) no. 16; see **Thoreau** 792:27

2 *La dernière chose qu'on trouve en faisant un ouvrage, est de savoir celle qu'il faut mettre la première.*

The last thing one knows in constructing a work is what to put first.

Pensées (1670, ed. L. Brunschvicg, 1909) sect. 1, no. 19

3 *Quand on voit le style naturel, on est tout étonné et ravi, car on s'attendait de voir un auteur, et on trouve un homme.*

When we see a natural style, we are quite surprised and delighted, for we expected to see an author and we find a man.

Pensées (1670, ed. L. Brunschvicg, 1909) sect. 1, no. 29

4 *Car enfin, qu'est-ce que l'homme dans la nature? Un néant à l'égard de l'infini, un tout à l'égard du néant, un milieu entre rien et tout.*

For after all, what is man in nature? A nothing in respect of that which is infinite, an all in respect of nothing, a middle betwixt nothing and all.

Pensées (1670, ed. L. Brunschvicg, 1909) sect. 2, no. 72

5 *Quelle vanité que la peinture, qui attire l'admiration par la ressemblance des choses dont on n'admire point les originaux.*

How vain painting is, exciting admiration by its resemblance to things of which we do not admire the originals.

Pensées (1670, ed. L. Brunschvicg, 1909) sect. 2, no. 134

6 *Tout le malheur des hommes vient d'une seule chose, qui est de ne savoir pas demeurer en repos dans une chambre.*

All the misfortunes of men derive from one single thing, which is their inability to be at ease in a room.

Pensées (1670, ed. L. Brunschvicg, 1909) sect. 2, no. 139

7 *Le nez de Cléopâtre: s'il eût été plus court, toute la face de la terre aurait changé.*

Had Cleopatra's nose been shorter, the whole face of the world would have changed.

Pensées (1670, ed. L. Brunschvicg, 1909) sect. 2, no. 162

8 *Le silence éternel de ces espaces infinis m'effraie.*

The eternal silence of these infinite spaces [the heavens] terrifies me.

Pensées (1670, ed. L. Brunschvicg, 1909) sect. 2, no. 206

9 *Le dernier acte est sanglant, quelque belle que soit la comédie en tout le reste; on jette enfin de la terre sur la tête, et en voilà pour jamais.*

The last act is bloody, however charming the rest of the play may be; they throw earth over your head, and it is finished forever.

Pensées (1670, ed. L. Brunschvicg, 1909) sect. 3, no. 210

10 *On mourra seul.*

We shall die alone.

Pensées (1670, ed. L. Brunschvicg, 1909) sect. 3, no. 211

11 *'Dieu est, ou il n'est pas.' Mais de quel côté pencherons-nous? . . . Pesons le gain et la perte, en prenant croix que Dieu est. Estimons ces deux cas: si vous gagnez, vous gagnez tout; si vous perdez, vous ne perdez rien. Gagez donc qu'il est, sans hésiter.*

'God is or he is not.' But to which side shall we incline? . . . Let us weigh the gain and the loss in wagering that God is. Let us estimate the two chances. If you gain, you gain all; if you lose, you lose nothing. Wager then without hesitation that he is.

known as Pascal's wager

Pensées (1670, ed. L. Brunschvicg, 1909) sect. 3, no. 233

12 *Le coeur a ses raisons que la raison ne connaît point.*

The heart has its reasons which reason knows nothing of.

Pensées (1670, ed. L. Brunschvicg, 1909) sect. 4, no. 277

13 *L'homme n'est qu'un roseau, le plus faible de la nature; mais c'est un roseau pensant.*

Man is only a reed, the weakest thing in nature; but he is a thinking reed.

Pensées (1670, ed. L. Brunschvicg, 1909) sect. 6, no. 347

14 *L'éloquence continue ennuie.*

Continual eloquence is tedious.

Pensées (1670, ed. L. Brunschvicg, 1909) sect. 6, no. 355

15 *Le moi est haïssable.*

The self is hateful.

Pensées (1670, ed. L. Brunschvicg, 1909) sect. 7, no. 455

16 *Console-toi, tu ne me chercherais pas si tu ne m'avais trouvé.*

Comfort yourself, you would not seek me if you had not found me.

Pensées (1670, ed. L. Brunschvicg, 1909) sect. 7, no. 553

17 FEU. *Dieu d'Abraham, Dieu d'Isaac, Dieu de Jacob, non des philosophes et savants. Certitude. Certitude. Sentiment. Joie. Paix.*

FIRE. God of Abraham, God of Isaac, God of Jacob, not of the philosophers and scholars. Certainty. Certainty. Feeling. Joy. Peace.

on a paper, dated 23 November 1654, stitched into the lining of his coat and found after his death

Boris Pasternak 1890–1960

Russian novelist and poet

18 Man is born to live, not to prepare for life.

Doctor Zhivago (1958) pt. 2, ch. 9, sect. 14 (translated by Max Hayward and Manya Harari)

19 Most people experience love, without noticing that there is anything remarkable about it.

Doctor Zhivago (1958) pt. 2, ch. 13, sect. 10

20 I don't like people who have never fallen or stumbled. Their virtue is lifeless and it isn't of much value. Life hasn't revealed its beauty to them.

Doctor Zhivago (1958) pt. 2, ch. 13, sect. 12

1 Art always serves beauty, and beauty is the joy of possessing form, and form is the key to organic life since no living thing can exist without it.
   Doctor Zhivago (1958) pt. 2, ch. 14, sect. 14

2 One day Lara went out and did not come back . . . She died or vanished somewhere, forgotten as a nameless number on a list which was afterwards mislaid.
   Doctor Zhivago (1958) pt. 2, ch. 15, sect. 17

3 Yet the order of the acts is planned
   And the end of the way inescapable.
   I am alone; all drowns in the Pharisees' hypocrisy.
   To live your life is not as simple as to cross a field.
   Doctor Zhivago (1958) 'Zhivago's Poems: Hamlet'

4 As after a storm
   The surf floods over the reeds,
   So in his heart
   Her image is submerged.

   In the years of trial,
   When life was inconceivable,
   From the bottom of the sea the tide of destiny
   Washed her up to him.
   Doctor Zhivago (1958) 'Zhivago's Poems: Parting'

5 In time to come, I tell them, we'll be equal
   to any living now. If cripples, then
   no matter; we shall just have been run over
   by 'New Man' in the wagon of his 'Plan'.
   'When I Grow Weary' (1932) (translated by J. M. Cohen)

Louis Pasteur 1822-95
French chemist and bacteriologist

6 Where observation is concerned, chance favours only the prepared mind.
   address given on the inauguration of the Faculty of Science, University of Lille, 7 December 1854; in R. Vallery-Radot *La Vie de Pasteur* (1900) ch. 4

7 There are no such things as applied sciences, only applications of science.
   address, 11 September 1872, in *Comptes rendus des travaux du Congrès viticole et séricicole de Lyon, 9-14 septembre 1872*

8 Wine may well be considered the most healthful and most hygienic of beverages.
   Études sur le vin (1873) pt. 1, ch. 2

Walter Pater 1839-94
English essayist and critic

9 She is older than the rocks among which she sits; like the vampire, she has been dead many times, and learned the secrets of the grave.
   of the Mona Lisa
   Studies in the History of the Renaissance (1873) 'Leonardo da Vinci'

10 All art constantly aspires towards the condition of music.
   Studies in the History of the Renaissance (1873) 'The School of Giorgione'

11 To burn always with this hard, gemlike flame, to maintain this ecstasy, is success in life.
   Studies in the History of the Renaissance (1873) 'Conclusion'

'Banjo' Paterson (Andrew Barton Paterson) 1864-1941
Australian poet

12 Once a jolly swagman camped by a billabong,
   Under the shade of a coolibah tree;
   And he sang as he watched and waited till his 'Billy' boiled:
   'You'll come a-waltzing, Matilda, with me.'
   'Waltzing Matilda' (1903 song)

Sadashiv Kanoji Patil
Indian politician

13 The Prime Minister is like the great banyan tree. Thousands shelter beneath it, but nothing grows.
   *when asked in an interview who would be **Nehru**'s successor*
   J. K. Galbraith *A Life in Our Times* (1981)

Coventry Patmore 1823-96
English poet

14 The angel in the house.
   title of poem (1854-62)

15 'I saw you take his kiss!' ''Tis true.'
   'O modesty!' ''Twas strictly kept:
   He thought me asleep; at least, I knew
   He thought I thought he thought I slept.'
   The Angel in the House (1854-62) bk. 2, canto 8, 'The Kiss'

16 Some dish more sharply spiced than this
   Milk-soup men call domestic bliss.
   'Olympus' l. 15

17 He that but once too nearly hears
   The music of forfended spheres
   Is thenceforth lonely, and for all
   His days as one who treads the Wall
   Of China, and, on this hand, sees
   Cities and their civilities
   And, on the other, lions.
   The Victories of Love bk. 1 (1860) 'From Mrs Graham'

Alan Paton 1903-88
South African writer
*see also **Closing lines** 228:9*

18 Cry, the beloved country.
   title of novel (1948)

St Patrick fl. 5th cent.
Patron saint and Apostle of Ireland, of Romano-British parentage

19 Today I put on
   a terrible strength
   invoking the Trinity,
   confessing the Three
   with faith in the one
   as I face my Maker.
   'St Patrick's Breastplate', traditionally attributed to St Patrick; see **Alexander** 11:9

20 Christ beside me,
   Christ before me,

Christ behind me,
Christ within me,
Christ beneath me,
Christ above me.
'St Patrick's Breastplate'

Mark Pattison 1813–84

English educationist

1 In research the horizon recedes as we advance,
and is no nearer at sixty than it was at twenty. As
the power of endurance weakens with age, the
urgency of the pursuit grows more intense . . .
And research is always incomplete.
Isaac Casaubon (1875) ch. 10

Leslie Paul 1905–85

Irish writer

2 Angry young man.
the phrase was later associated with John **Osborne***'s
play* Look Back in Anger *(1956)*
title of book (1951)

Wolfgang Pauli 1900–58

*Austrian-born American physicist who worked chiefly in
Switzerland*
on Pauli: see **Weisskopf** 826:25

3 I don't mind your thinking slowly: I mind your
publishing faster than you think.
attributed

Tom Paulin 1949–

English-born Northern Irish poet and critic

4 Now dream
of that sweet
equal republic
where the juniper
talks to the oak,
the thistle,
the bandaged elm,
and the jolly jolly chestnut.
'The Book of Juniper' (1983)

5 The owl of Minerva in a hired car.
'Desertmartin' (1983)

6 That stretch of water, it's always
There for you to cross over
To the other shore, observing
The light of cities on blackness.
'States' (1977)

Cesare Pavese 1908–50

Italian novelist, poet, and critic

7 Waiting is still an occupation. It's having nothing
to wait for that is terrible.
Il Mestiere di Vivere (1952, translated as The Burning
Brand, 1961) 15 September 1946

Jeremy Paxman 1950–

British journalist and broadcaster
see also **Catchphrases** 200:8

8 Did you threaten to overrule him?
question asked 14 times of Michael **Howard***, referring
to the sacking of a prison governor by Derek Lewis,
Director of the Prison Service*
interview, BBC2 Newsnight 13 May 1997

9 No government in history has been as obsessed
with public relations as this one . . . Speaking for
myself, if there is a message I want to be off it.
*after criticism from Alastair Campbell of interviewing
tactics in* The World at One *and* Newsnight
in *Daily Telegraph* 3 July 1998

James Payn 1830–98

English writer

10 I had never had a piece of toast
Particularly long and wide,
But fell upon the sanded floor,
And always on the buttered side.
in *Chambers's Journal* 2 February 1884; see **Moore** 547:20

J. H. Payne 1791–1852

American actor, dramatist, and songwriter

11 Home, sweet home.
title of song, from *Clari, or, The Maid of Milan* (1823 opera)

12 Mid pleasures and palaces though we may roam,
Be it ever so humble, there's no place like home.
Clari, or, The Maid of Milan (1823 opera) 'Home, Sweet
Home'; see **Proverbs** 622:33

Thomas Love Peacock 1785–1866

English novelist and poet
on Peacock: see **Shelley** 729:23; *see also* **Epitaphs** 310:14

13 Ancient sculpture is the true school of modesty.
But where the Greeks had modesty, we have cant;
where they had poetry, we have cant; where they
had patriotism, we have cant; where they had
anything that exalts, delights, or adorns
humanity, we have nothing but cant, cant, cant.
Crotchet Castle (1831) ch. 7

14 The march of mind has marched in through my
back parlour shutters, and out again with my
silver spoons, in the dead of night . . . my house
has been broken open on the most scientific
principles.
Crotchet Castle (1831) ch. 17

15 'I distinguish the picturesque and the beautiful,
and I add to them, in the laying out of grounds, a
third and distinct character, which I call
unexpectedness.'
'Pray, sir,' said Mr Milestone, 'by what name do
you distinguish this character, when a person
walks round the grounds for the second time?'
Headlong Hall (1816) ch. 4

1 Marriage may often be a stormy lake, but celibacy is almost always a muddy horsepond.
Melincourt (1817) ch. 7

2 Not drunk is he, who from the floor
Can rise alone and still drink more;
But drunk is he, who prostrate lies,
Without the power to drink or rise.
The Misfortunes of Elphin (1829) pt.1 ch. 3

3 Laughter is pleasant, but the exertion is too much for me.
Nightmare Abbey (1818) ch. 5

4 Sir, I have quarrelled with my wife; and a man who has quarrelled with his wife is absolved from all duty to his country.
Nightmare Abbey (1818) ch. 11

5 The mountain sheep are sweeter,
But the valley sheep are fatter;
We therefore deemed it meeter
To carry off the latter.
'The War Song of Dinas Vawr' (1823)

Norman Vincent Peale 1898–1993
American religious broadcaster and writer

6 The power of positive thinking.
title of book (1952)

Patrick Pearse 1879–1916
Irish nationalist leader; executed after the Easter Rising
on Pearse: see **Yeats** 854:5

7 The fools, the fools, the fools, they have left us our Fenian dead, and while Ireland holds these graves Ireland unfree shall never be at peace.
oration over the grave of the Fenian Jeremiah O'Donovan Rossa, 1 August 1915

8 Here be ghosts that I have raised this Christmastide, ghosts of dead men that have bequeathed a trust to us living men. Ghosts are troublesome things in a house or in a family, as we knew even before Ibsen taught us. There is only one way to appease a ghost. You must do the thing it asks you. The ghosts of a nation sometimes ask very big things and they must be appeased, whatever the cost.
on Christmas Day, 1915; Conor Cruise O'Brien *Ancestral Voices* (1994); see **O'Brien** 571:2

Hesketh Pearson 1887–1964
English actor and biographer

9 Misquotation is, in fact, the pride and privilege of the learned. A widely-read man never quotes accurately, for the rather obvious reason that he has read too widely.
Common Misquotations (1934) introduction

10 There is no stronger craving in the world than that of the rich for titles, except perhaps that of the titled for riches.
The Pilgrim Daughters (1961) ch. 6

Lester Pearson 1897–1972
Canadian diplomat and Liberal statesman, Prime Minister 1963–8

11 The grim fact is that we prepare for war like precocious giants and for peace like retarded pygmies.
speech in Toronto, 14 March 1955

12 This is the flag of the future, but it does not dishonour the past.
on Canada obtaining a flag of its own, a project Pearson successfully achieved
speech in the House of Commons, Ottawa, 15 December 1964

Pedro I (Pedro IV of Portugal) 1798–1834
Portuguese monarch, first Emperor of Brazil, 1822–31

13 As it is for the good of all and the general happiness of the nation, I am ready and willing. Tell the people I'm staying.
in response to a popular delegation, and in defiance of a decree from Lisbon requiring his return; commonly rendered 'Fico [I'm staying]'
letter to D. João VI, 9 January 1822; R. J. Barman *Brazil* (1988)

Robert Peel 1788–1850
British Conservative statesman; Prime Minister, 1834–5, 1841–6
on Peel: see **Curran** 254:5, **Disraeli** 275:8

14 There is not a single law connected with my name which has not had as its object some mitigation of the severity of the criminal law; some prevention of abuse in the exercise of it; or some security for its impartial administration.
speech, House of Commons, 1 May 1827

15 As minister of the Crown . . . I reserve to myself, distinctly and unequivocally, the right of adapting my conduct to the exigency of the moment, and to the wants of the country.
in the House of Commons, 30 March 1829

16 All my experience in public life is in favour of the employment of what the world would call young men instead of old ones.
to Wellington in 1829; Norman Gash *Sir Robert Peel* (ed. 2, 1986)

17 The hasty inordinate demand for peace might be just as dangerous as the clamour for war.
in the House of Commons, 1832

18 I see no dignity in persevering in error.
in the House of Commons, 1833

19 Of all vulgar arts of government, that of solving every difficulty which might arise by thrusting the hand into the public purse is the most delusory and contemptible.
in the House of Commons, 1834

George Peele c.1556–96

English dramatist and poet
*see also **Closing lines** 228:13*

1   Love is a thing.
It is a prick, it is a sting,
It is a pretty, pretty thing;
It is a fire, it is a coal
Whose flame creeps in at every hole.
The Hunting of Cupid (c.1591)

2 When as the rye reach to the chin,
And chopcherry, chopcherry ripe within,
Strawberries swimming in the cream,
And schoolboys playing in the stream,
Then O, then O, then O, my true love said,
Till that time come again,
She could not live a maid.
The Old Wive's Tale (1595) l. 75 'Song'

3 His golden locks time hath to silver turned;
O time too swift, O swiftness never ceasing!
Polyhymnia (1590) 'Sonnet'

4 His helmet now shall make a hive for bees.
Polyhymnia (1590) 'Sonnet'

Charles Péguy 1873–1914

French poet and essayist

5 He who does not bellow the truth when he knows
the truth makes himself the accomplice of liars
and forgers.
Basic Verities (1943) 'Lettre du Provincial' 21 December
1899

6 Tyranny is always better organised than freedom.
Basic Verities (1943) 'War and Peace'; see **Baez** 47:9

7 The sinner is at the heart of Christianity . . . No
one is as competent as the sinner in matters of
Christianity. No one, except a saint.
Basic Verities (1943) 'Un Nouveau théologien . . . ' (1911)

Pelé 1940–

Brazilian footballer

8 Football? It's the beautiful game.
attributed

Mary Herbert, Countess of Pembroke

1561–1621

*English poet and translator, sister of Philip **Sidney***

9 Men drawn by worth a woman to obey.
'Even now that Care which on thy Crown attends' (poem
addressed to Queen Elizabeth)

10 Sing what God doth, and do what men may sing.
'Even now that Care which on thy Crown attends' (poem
addressed to Queen Elizabeth)

William Herbert, Lord Pembroke

c.1501–70

11 Out ye whores, to work, to work, ye whores, go
spin.
Andrew Clark (ed.) '*Brief Lives*' . . . *by John Aubrey* (1898)
vol. 1 'William Herbert, 1st Earl of Pembroke'; see **Scott**
674:26

Henry Herbert, Lord Pembroke

c.1534–1601

12 A parliament can do any thing but make a man a
woman, and a woman a man.
*quoted by his son, the 4th Earl, in a speech on 11
April 1648, proving himself Chancellor of Oxford*
in *Harleian Miscellany* (1745) vol. 5

Henry Herbert, Lord Pembroke 1734–94

13 Dr Johnson's sayings would not appear so
extraordinary, were it not for his bow-wow way.
James Boswell *Life of Samuel Johnson* (1791) 27 March
1775; see **Scott** 674:27

Vladimir Peniakoff 1897–1951

Belgian soldier and writer

14 A message came on the wireless for me. It said:
'SPREAD ALARM AND DESPONDENCY'. So the time had
come, I thought, Eighth Army was taking the
offensive. The date was, I think, May 18th, 1942.
Private Army (1950) pt. 2, ch. 5; see **Military sayings** 526:7

William Penn 1644–1718

English Quaker; founder of Pennsylvania

15 No pain, no palm; no thorns, no throne; no gall,
no glory; no cross, no crown.
No Cross, No Crown (1669 pamphlet); see **Proverbs** 627:36

16 It is a reproach to religion and government to
suffer so much poverty and excess.
Some Fruits of Solitude (1693) pt. 1, no. 52

17 Men are generally more careful of the breed of
their horses and dogs than of their children.
Some Fruits of Solitude (1693) pt. 1, no. 85

18 The taking of a bribe or gratuity, should be
punished with as severe penalties as the
defrauding of the State.
Some Fruits of Solitude (1693) pt. 1, no. 384

Roger Penrose 1931–

British mathematician and theoretical physicist

19 Consciousness . . . is the phenomenon whereby
the universe's very existence is made known.
The Emperor's New Mind (1989) ch. 10 'Conclusion'

Samuel Pepys 1633–1703

English diarist

20 And so to bed.
Diary 20 April 1660

21 I went out to Charing Cross, to see Major-general
Harrison hanged, drawn, and quartered; which
was done there, he looking as cheerful as any man
could do in that condition.
Diary 13 October 1660

22 A good honest and painful sermon.
Diary 17 March 1661

23 If ever I was foxed it was now.
Diary 23 April 1661

1 It lessened my esteem of a king, that he should not be able to command the rain.

Diary 19 July 1662

2 I see it is impossible for the King to have things done as cheap as other men.

Diary 21 July 1662

3 But Lord! to see the absurd nature of Englishmen, that cannot forbear laughing and jeering at everything that looks strange.

Diary 27 November 1662

4 My wife, who, poor wretch, is troubled with her lonely life.

Diary 19 December 1662

5 A woman sober, and no high flyer, as he calls it.

Diary 27 May 1663

6 Most of their discourse was about hunting, in a dialect I understand very little.

Diary 22 November 1663

7 While we were talking came by several poor creatures carried by, by constables, for being at a conventicle . . . I would to God they would either conform, or be more wise, and not be catched!

Diary 7 August 1664

8 Pretty witty Nell.

of Nell **Gwyn**

Diary 3 April 1665

9 I saw a dead corpse in a coffin lie in the close unburied—and a watch is constantly kept there, night and day, to keep the people in—the plague making us cruel as dogs one to another.

Diary 4 September 1665

10 Strange to see how a good dinner and feasting reconciles everybody.

Diary 9 November 1665

11 Strange to say what delight we married people have to see these poor fools decoyed into our condition.

Diary 25 December 1665

12 In the heighth of it [the plague] . . . bold people there were to go in sport to one another's burials. And in spite to well people, would breathe in the faces . . . of well people going by.

Diary 12 February 1666

13 Music and women I cannot but give way to, whatever my business is.

Diary 9 March 1666

14 But it is pretty to see what money will do.

Diary 21 March 1667

15 This day my wife made it appear to me that my late entertainment this week cost me above £12, an expense which I am almost ashamed of, though it is but once in a great while, and is the end for which, in the most part, we live, to have such a merry day once or twice in a man's life.

Diary 6 March 1669

16 And so I betake myself to that course, which is almost as much as to see myself go into my grave—for which, and all the discomforts that will accompany my being blind, the good God prepare me!

Diary 31 May 1669 closing lines

17 Memoirs are true and useful stars, whilst studied histories are those stars joined in constellations, according to the fancy of the poet.

J. R. Tanner (ed.) *Samuel Pepys's Naval Minutes* (1926)

S. J. Perelman 1904–79

American humorist

18 Crazy like a fox.

title of book (1944)

Shimon Peres 1923–

Israeli statesman

19 Television has made dictatorship impossible, but democracy unbearable.

at a Davos meeting, in *Financial Times* 31 January 1995

Pericles c.495–429 BC

Greek statesman and Athenian general

20 The spring has gone out of the year.

Funeral Oration, Athens, 439 BC; Aristotle *The Art of Rhetoric* bk. 1, 1365a 31–3

21 Our love of what is beautiful does not lead to extravagance; our love of the things of the mind does not make us soft.

Funeral Oration, Athens, 430 BC, in Thucydides *History of the Peloponnesian War* bk. 2, ch. 40, sect. 1 (translated by Rex Warner)

22 Taking everything together then, I declare that our city is an education to Greece.

of Athens

Thucydides *History of the Peloponnesian War* bk. 2 ch. 41

23 For famous men have the whole earth as their memorial.

Thucydides *History of the Peloponnesian War* bk. 2, ch. 43, sect. 3

24 Your great glory is not to be inferior to what God has made you, and the greatest glory of a woman is to be least talked about by men, whether they are praising you or criticizing you.

Thucydides *History of the Peloponnesian War* bk. 2, ch. 45, sect. 2

Eva Perón 1919–52

Argentinian wife of Juan Perón
on Perón: see **Epitaphs** *310:11*

25 Keeping books on charity is capitalist nonsense! I just use the money for the poor. I can't stop to count it.

Fleur Cowles *Bloody Precedent: the Peron Story* (1952)

Charles Perrault 1628–1703

French poet and critic

26 'Anne, sister Anne, do you see nothing coming?' And her sister Anne replied, 'I see nothing but the sun showing up the dust, and the grass looking green.'

Histoires et contes du temps passé [Stories and Tales of Past Times] (1697) 'Bluebeard'

1 'Oh Grandmother! What big ears you have!'
'All the better to hear you with.'
> *Histoires et contes du temps passé* [Stories and Tales of Past Times] (1697) 'Little Red Riding Hood'

2 It belongs to my lord the Marquis of Carabas.
> *Histoires et contes du temps passé* [Stories and Tales of Past Times] (1697) 'Puss in Boots'

Edward Perronet 1726–92
English clergyman

3 All hail the power of Jesus' Name;
Let Angels prostrate fall;
Bring forth the royal diadem
To crown Him Lord of all.
> 'All hail the power of Jesus' Name' (1780 hymn)

Jimmy Perry
British songwriter

4 Who do you think you are kidding, Mister Hitler?
If you think we're on the run?
We are the boys who will stop your little game
We are the boys who will make you think again.
> 'Who do you think you are kidding, Mister Hitler' (theme song of *Dad's Army*, BBC television, 1968–77)

Oliver Hazard Perry 1785–1819
American naval officer

5 We have met the enemy and they are ours.
> reporting his victory over the British in the battle of Lake Erie, 10 September 1813; see **Cartoon captions** 198:9

Persius (Aulus Persius Flaccus) AD 34–62
Roman poet

6 *Nec te quaesiveris extra.*
And don't consult anyone's opinions but your own.
> *Satires* no. 1, l. 7

7 *Virtutem videant intabescantque relicta.*
Let them recognize virtue and rot for having lost it.
> *Satires* no. 3, l. 38

8 *Venienti occurrite morbo.*
Confront disease at its onset.
> *Satires* no. 3, l. 64; see **Ovid** 580:16

9 *Tecum habita: noris quam sit tibi curta supellex.*
Live with yourself: get to know how poorly furnished you are.
> *Satires* no. 4, l. 52

Ted Persons

10 Things ain't what they used to be.
> title of song (1941)

Max Perutz 1914–
Austrian-born scientist

11 The priest persuades humble people to endure their hard lot; the politician urges them to rebel against it; and the scientist thinks of a method that does away with the hard lot altogether.
> *Is Science Necessary* (1989)

Henri Philippe Pétain 1856–1951
French soldier and statesman
*see also **Military sayings** 526:11*

12 To write one's memoirs is to speak ill of everybody except oneself.
> in *Observer* 26 May 1946

Laurence J. Peter 1919–90
Canadian writer

13 In a hierarchy every employee tends to rise to his level of incompetence.
> *The Peter Principle* (1969) ch. 1

Mike Peters 1943–
American cartoonist

14 When I go into the voting booth, do I vote for the person who is the best President? Or the slime bucket who will make my life as a cartoonist wonderful?
> in *Wall Street Journal* 20 January 1993

Petrarch (Francesco Petrarca) 1304–74
Italian poet
*on Petrarch: see **Byron** 180:28*

15 *Voi ch' ascoltate in rime sparse il suono*
di quei sospiri ond'io nudriva 'l core
in sul mio primo giovenile errore,
quand' era in parte altr' uom da quel ch' i' sono.
O you who hear within these scattered verses
the sound of sighs with which I fed my heart
in my first errant youthful days when I
in part was not the man I am today.
> *Canzoniere* no. 1 (*c.*1352) translated by Mark Musa

16 *E del mio vaneggiar vergogna è 'l frutto*
e 'l pentersi, e 'l conoscer chiaramente
che quanto piace al mondo è breve sogno.
And the fruit of my vanity is shame, and
repentance, and the clear knowledge that
whatever the world finds pleasing, is but a brief dream.
> *Canzoniere* no. 1 (*c.*1352)

17 *Italia mia, ben che 'l parlar sia indarno*
a le piaghe mortali
che nel bel corpo tuo sì spesse veggio.
Oh, my own Italy, though words be useless
to heal the mortal wounds
I see covering all your lovely body.
> *Canzoniere* no. 128 (*c.*1352) translated by Mark Musa

18 *Pace non trovo et non ò da far guerra,*
e temo et spero, et ardo et son un ghiaccio.
I find no peace, and I am not at war,
I fear and hope, and burn and I am ice.
> *Canzoniere* no. 134 (*c.*1352) translated by Mark Musa

19 *Altissimum regionis huius montem, quem non immerito Ventosum vocant, hodierno die, sola videndi insignem loco altitudinem cupiditate ductus, ascendi.*

Today I climbed the highest mountain in this region, which is not improperly called Ventosus (Windy). The only motive for my ascent was the wish to see what so great a height had to offer.

of Mont Ventoux in Provence, France

> letter to Dionisio da Borgo San Sepolcro *c.*1336; *Letters on Familiar Matters* bk. 4, no. 1 (translated by Mark Musa)

1 *Continue morimur, ego dum hec scribo, tu dum leges, alii dum audient, dumque non audient, ego quoque dum hec leges moriar, tu moreris dum hec scribo, ambo morimur, omnes morimur, semper morimur.*

We are continually dying; I while I am writing these words, you while you are reading them, others when they hear them or fail to hear them. I shall be dying when you read this, you die while I write, we both are dying, we all are dying, we are dying forever.

> letter to Philippe de Cabassoles *c.*1360; *Letters on Familiar Matters* bk. 24, no. 1 (translated by Morris Bishop)

Jamie Petrie and Peter Cunnah

British singers and songwriters

2 Things can only get better.

> title of song (1994); see **Political slogans and songs** 601:8

Petronius (Petronius Arbiter) d. 65

Roman satirist

on Petronius: see **Tacitus** 770:9; *see also* **Misquotations** 539:1

3 *Canis ingens, catena vinctus, in pariete erat pictus superque quadrata littera scriptum 'Cave canem.'*

A huge dog, tied by a chain, was painted on the wall and over it was written in capital letters 'Beware of the dog.'

> *Satyricon* 'Cena Trimalchionis' ch. 29, sect. 1

4 *Abiit ad plures.*

He's gone to join the majority.

meaning the dead

> *Satyricon* 'Cena Trimalchionis' ch. 42, sect. 5; see **Young** 857:22

5 *Nam Sibyllam quidem Cumis ego ipse oculis meis vidi in ampulla pendere, et cum illi pueri dicerent: Σίβυλλα, τί θέλεις; respondebat illa: ἀποθανεῖν θέλω.*

I myself with my own eyes saw the Sibyl at Cumae hanging in a flask; and when the boys cried at her: ' Sibyl, Sibyl, what do you want?' 'I would that I were dead,' she used to answer.

> *Satyricon* 'Cena Trimalchionis' ch. 48, sect. 8; see **Rossetti** 656:9

6 *Horatii curiosa felicitas.*

Horace's careful felicity.

> *Satyricon* ch. 118, sect. 5

7 *Foeda est in coitu et brevis voluptas Et taedet Veneris statim peractae.*

Delight of lust is gross and brief And weariness treads on desire.

> A. Baehrens *Poetae Latini Minores* (1882) vol. 4, no. 101 (translated by Helen Waddell)

Pheidippides see **Last words** 471:17

Edward John Phelps 1822–1900

American lawyer and diplomat

8 The man who makes no mistakes does not usually make anything.

> speech at the Mansion House, London, 24 January 1889; in *The Times* 25 January 1889; see **Proverbs** 623:15

Kim Philby (Harold Adrian Russell Philby) 1912–88

British intelligence officer and Soviet spy

9 To betray, you must first belong.

> in *Sunday Times* 17 December 1967

Philip, Duke of Edinburgh 1921–

*British prince, Greek-born husband of **Elizabeth II***

10 Gentlemen, I think it is about time we 'pulled our fingers out' . . . If we want to be more prosperous we've simply got to get down to it and work for it. The rest of the world does not owe us a living.

> speech in London, 17 October 1961

11 If you stay here much longer you'll all be slitty-eyed.

> remark to Edinburgh University students in Peking, 16 October 1986

12 Tolerance is the one essential ingredient . . . You can take it from me that the Queen has the quality of tolerance in abundance.

his recipe for a successful marriage, during celebrations for their golden wedding anniversary

> in *The Times* 20 November 1997

John Woodward ('Jack') Philip 1840–1900

American naval captain in the Spanish–American war

13 Don't cheer, men; those poor devils are dying.

at the Battle of Santiago, 4 July 1898

> in *Dictionary of American Biography* vol. 14 (1934) 'John Woodward Philip'

Ambrose Philips c.1675–1749

English poet

14 The flowers anew, returning seasons bring;
But beauty faded has no second spring.

> *The First Pastoral* (1708) 'Lobbin' l. 47

15 There solid billows of enormous size,
Alps of green ice, in wild disorder rise.

> 'A Winter-Piece' in *The Tatler* 7 May 1709

Katherine Philips 1632–64

English poet

16 I did but see him, and he disappeared,
I did but touch the rosebud, and it fell;
A sorrow unforeseen and scarcely feared,
So ill can mortals their afflictions spell.

> 'On the Death of my First and Dearest Child, Hector Philips' (1655)

Arthur Angell Phillips 1900–85

Australian critic and editor

1 Above our writers—and other artists—looms the intimidating mass of Anglo-Saxon culture. Such a situation almost inevitably produces the characteristic Australian Cultural Cringe— appearing either as the Cringe Direct, or as the Cringe Inverted, in the attitude of the Blatant Blatherskite, the God's-Own-Country and I'm-a-better-man-than-you-are Australian bore.

> *Meanjin* (1950) 'The Cultural Cringe'; see **Keating** 442:9

Morgan Phillips 1902–63

British Labour politician

2 The Labour Party owes more to Methodism than to Marxism.

> James Callaghan *Time and Chance* (1987) ch. 1

Pablo Picasso 1881–1973

Spanish painter

3 There is nothing more dangerous than justice in the hands of judges, and a paintbrush in the hands of a painter. Just think of the danger to society!

> conversation, 1935; Herschel B. Chipp *Theories of Modern Art* (1968)

4 No, painting is not made to decorate apartments. It's an offensive and defensive weapon against the enemy.

> interview with Simone Téry, 24 March 1945, in Alfred H. Barr *Picasso* (1946)

5 The artist is a receptacle for emotions that come from all over the place: from the sky, from the earth, from a scrap of paper, from a passing shape, from a spider's web.

> Alfred H. Barr Jr. *Picasso: Fifty Years of his Art* (1946)

6 When I was the age of these children I could draw like Raphael: it took me many years to learn how to draw like these children.

> to Herbert **Read**, *when visiting an exhibition of childen's drawings*
> quoted in letter from Read to *The Times* 27 October 1956

7 I paint objects as I think them, not as I see them.

> John Golding *Cubism* (1959)

8 God is really only another artist. He invented the giraffe, the elephant, and the cat. He has no real style. He just goes on trying other things.

> F. Gilot and C. Lake *Life With Picasso* (1964) pt. 1

9 Every positive value has its price in negative terms . . . The genius of Einstein leads to Hiroshima.

> F. Gilot and C. Lake *Life With Picasso* (1964) pt. 2

10 We all know that Art is not truth. Art is a lie that makes us realize truth.

> Dore Ashton *Picasso on Art* (1972) 'Two statements by Picasso'

Pindar 518–438 BC

Greek lyric poet

11 Water is best. But gold shines like fire blazing in the night, supreme of lordly wealth.

> *Olympian Odes* bk. 1, l. 1

12 I have many swift arrows in my quiver which speak to the wise, but for the crowd they need interpreters. The skilled poet is one who knows much through natural gift, but those who have learned their art chatter turbulently, like ravens, vainly, against the divine bird of Zeus.

> *Olympian Odes* bk. 2, l. 83

13 My soul, do not seek immortal life, but exhaust the realm of the possible.

> *Pythian Odes* bk. 3, l. 109

14 Creatures of a day, what is a man? What is he not? Mankind is a dream of a shadow. But when a god-given brightness comes, a radiant light rests on men, and a gentle life.

> *Pythian Odes* bk. 8, l. 135

Harold Pinter 1930–

English dramatist

15 If only I could get down to Sidcup! I've been waiting for the weather to break. He's got my papers, this man I left them with, it's got it all down there, I could prove everything.

> *The Caretaker* (1960) act 1

16 Apart from the known and the unknown, what else is there?

> *The Homecoming* (1965) act 2, sc. 1

17 The weasel under the cocktail cabinet.

> *on being asked what his plays were about*
> J. Russell Taylor *Anger and After* (1962)

Luigi Pirandello 1867–1936

Italian dramatist and novelist

18 *Sei personaggi in cerca d'autore.*
Six characters in search of an author.

> title of play (1921)

Robert M. Pirsig 1928–

American writer

19 Zen and the art of motorcycle maintenance.

> title of book (1974)

20 That's the classical mind at work, runs fine inside but looks dingy on the surface.

> *Zen and the Art of Motorcycle Maintenance* (1974) pt. 3, ch. 26

Walter B. Pitkin 1878–1953

21 Life begins at forty.

> title of book (1932); see **Proverbs** 625:13

William Pitt, Earl of Chatham 1708-78

British Whig statesman; Prime Minister, 1766-8
on Pitt: see **Walpole** *820:8*

1 The atrocious crime of being a young man . . . I shall neither attempt to palliate nor deny.
speech, House of Commons, 2 March 1741

2 The poorest man may in his cottage bid defiance to all the forces of the Crown. It may be frail—its roof may shake—the wind may blow through it—the storm may enter—the rain may enter—but the King of England cannot enter!
speech, *c.*March 1763, in Lord Brougham *Historical Sketches of Statesmen in the Time of George III* First Series (1845) vol. 1

3 Unlimited power is apt to corrupt the minds of those who possess it.
speech, House of Lords, 9 January 1770; see **Acton** 1:13

4 There is something behind the throne greater than the King himself.
speech, House of Lords, 2 March 1770

5 We have a Calvinistic creed, a Popish liturgy, and an Arminian clergy.
speech, House of Lords, 19 May 1772; Basil Williams *Life of William Pitt Earl of Chatham* (1913) vol. 2, ch. 24

6 You cannot conquer America.
speech, House of Lords, 18 November 1777

7 I invoke the genius of the Constitution!
speech, House of Lords, 18 November 1777

8 Our watchword is security.
attributed

9 The parks are the lungs of London.
quoted by William Windham in the House of Commons, 30 June 1808

William Pitt 1759-1806

British Tory statesman; Prime Minister, 1783-1801, 1804-6
on Pitt: see **Burke** *168:23,* **Canning** *189:8,* **Fox** *331:3; see also*
Last words *473:10*

10 Necessity is the plea for every infringement of human freedom: it is the argument of tyrants; it is the creed of slaves.
speech, House of Commons, 18 November 1783

11 We must anew commence the salvation of Europe.
in 1795; in *Dictionary of National Biography* (1917-)

12 We must recollect . . . what it is we have at stake, what it is we have to contend for. It is for our property, it is for our liberty, it is for our independence, nay, for our existence as a nation; it is for our character, it is for our very name as Englishmen, it is for everything dear and valuable to man on this side of the grave.
on the rupture of the Peace of Amiens and the resumption of war with Napoleon
speech, 22 July 1803, in *Speeches of the Rt. Hon. William Pitt* (1806) vol. 4

13 England has saved herself by her exertions, and will, as I trust, save Europe by her example.
replying to a toast in which he had been described as the saviour of his country in the wars with France
R. Coupland *War Speeches of William Pitt* (1915)

14 Roll up that map; it will not be wanted these ten years.
of a map of Europe, on hearing of Napoleon's victory at Austerlitz, December 1805
Earl Stanhope *Life of the Rt. Hon. William Pitt* vol. 4 (1862) ch. 43

Pius VII 1742-1823

Italian cleric, Pope from 1800

15 We are prepared to go to the gates of Hell—but no further.
attempting to reach an agreement with **Napoleon,** *c.1800-1*
J. M. Robinson *Cardinal Consalvi* (1987)

Pius XII 1876-1958

Italian cleric; Pope from 1939

16 One Galileo in two thousand years is enough.
on being asked to proscribe the works of **Teilhard de Chardin**
attributed; Stafford Beer *Platform for Change* (1975)

Max Planck 1858-1947

German physicist

17 A new scientific truth does not triumph by convincing its opponents and making them see the light, but rather because its opponents eventually die, and a new generation grows up that is familiar with it.
A Scientific Autobiography (1949, translated by F. Gaynor)

Sylvia Plath 1932-63

American poet

18 A living doll, everywhere you look.
It can sew, it can cook,
It can talk, talk, talk.
'The Applicant' (1966)

19 Is there no way out of the mind?
'Apprehensions' (1971)

20 I have always been scared of *you,*
With your Luftwaffe, your gobbledygoo.
And your neat moustache
And your Aryan eye, bright blue.
Panzer-man, panzer-man, O You—
'Daddy' (1963)

21 Every woman adores a Fascist,
The boot in the face, the brute
Brute heart of a brute like you.
'Daddy' (1963)

22 The woman is perfected
Her dead
Body wears the smile of accomplishment.
opening lines of her last poem, written a week before her suicide
'Edge'

23 I am the ghost of an infamous suicide,
My own blue razor rusting in my throat.
O pardon the one who knocks for pardon at
Your gate, father—your hound-bitch, daughter, friend.

It was my love that did us both to death.
'Electra on Azalea Path' (1959)

1 Dying,
Is an art, like everything else.
'Lady Lazarus' (1963)

2 Out of the ash
I rise with my red hair
And I eat men like air.
'Lady Lazarus' (1963)

3 Love set you going like a fat gold watch.
The midwife slapped your footsoles, and your bald cry
Took its place among the elements.
'Morning Song' (1965)

4 Widow. The word consumes itself.
'Widow' (1971)

Plato 429–347 BC

Greek philosopher
see also **Anonymous** 21:8

5 Socrates, he says, breaks the law by corrupting young men and not recognizing the gods that the city recognizes, but some other new deities.
Apologia 24b

6 Is that which is holy loved by the gods because it is holy, or is it holy because it is loved by the gods?
Euthyphro 10

7 It [rhetoric] doesn't involve expertise; all you need is a mind which is good at guessing, some courage, and a natural talent for interacting with people. The general term I use to refer to it is 'flattery'.
Gorgias 463b (translated by Robin Waterfield)

8 Searching and learning is a process of remembering . . . and I, believing this to be true, am ready to search with you what virtue is.
Meno 81d

9 Socrates, I shall not accuse you as I accuse others, of getting angry and cursing me when I tell them to drink the poison imposed by the authorities. I know you on the contrary in your time here to be the noblest and gentlest and best man of all who ever came here; and now I am sure you are not angry with me, for you know who are responsible, but with them.
spoken by Socrates' jailor
Phaedo 116c

10 This was the end, Echekrates, of our friend; a man of whom we may say that of all whom we met at that time he was the wisest and justest and best.
on the death of **Socrates**
Phaedo 118a

11 What I say is that 'just' or 'right' means nothing but what is in the interest of the stronger party.
spoken by Thrasymachus
The Republic bk. 1, 338c (translated by F. M. Cornford)

12 For our discussion is about no ordinary matter, but on the right way to conduct our lives.
The Republic bk. 1, 352d

13 Can we devise one of those lies—the kind which crop up as the occasion demands, which we were talking about not so long ago—so that with a single noble lie we can indocrinate the rulers themselves, preferably, but at least the rest of the community?
The Republic bk. 3, 414b (translated by Robin Waterfield)

14 And so with the objects of knowledge: these derive from the Good not only their power of being known, but their very being and reality; and Goodness is not the same thing as being, but even beyond being, surpassing it in dignity and power.
The Republic bk. 6, 509b (translated by F. M. Cornford)

15 Behold! human beings living in a underground den . . . Like ourselves . . . they see only their own shadows, or the shadows of one another, which the fire throws on the opposite wall of the cave.
The Republic bk. 7, 515b; see **Nietzsche** 564:6

16 The blame is his who chooses: God is blameless.
The Republic bk. 10, 617e

17 But if we are guided by me we shall believe that the soul is immortal and capable of enduring all extremes of good and evil, and so we shall hold ever to the upward way and pursue righteousness with wisdom always and ever, that we may be dear to ourselves and to the gods both during our sojourn here and when we receive our reward.
The Republic bk. 10, 621c

18 Evils, Theodorus, can never pass away, for there must always remain something which is antagonistic to good. Having no place among the gods in heaven, of necessity they hover around the mortal nature and this earthly sphere. Wherefore we ought to fly away from earth to heaven as quickly as we can; and to fly away is to become like God, as far as this is possible; and to become like him is to become holy, just, and wise.
Theaetetus 176a (translated by Benjamin Jowett)

19 God is always doing geometry.
Plutarch *Moralia*

Plautus c.250–184 BC

Roman comic dramatist

20 *Lupus est homo homini, non homo, quom qualis sit non novit.*
A man is a wolf rather than a man to another man, when he hasn't yet found out what he's like.
often quoted as 'Homo homini lupus [A man is a wolf to another man]'
Asinaria l. 495; see **Vanzetti** 807:4

21 *Dictum sapienti sat est.*
A sentence is enough for a sensible man.
proverbially: 'Verbum sapienti sat est [A word is enough for the wise]', *and abbreviated to* 'verb. sap.'
Persa l. 729; see **Proverbs** 635:19

22 LABRAX: *Immo edepol una littera plus sum quam medicus.*
GRIPUS: *Tum tu*
Mendicus es?
LABRAX: *Tetigisti acu.*

LABRAX: One letter more than a medical man,
that's what I am.
GRIPUS: Then you're a mendicant?
LABRAX: You've hit the point.
  Rudens l. 1305

Pliny the Elder AD 23-79

Roman statesman and scholar, uncle of **Pliny** *the Younger*

1 *Scito enim conferentum auctores me deprehendisse a iuratissimis et proximis veteres transcriptos ad verbum neque nominatos.*

  When collating authorities I have found that the most professedly reliable and modern writers have copied the old authors word for word, without acknowledgement.
  preface to *Historia Naturalis*

2 *Bruta fulmina.*
  Harmless thunderbolts.
  Historia Naturalis bk. 2, sect. 113

3 *Ut non sit satis aestimare, parens melior homini an tristior noverca fuerit.*

  So that it is far from easy to judge whether she has proved a kind parent to man or a harsh step-mother.
  on nature
  Historia Naturalis bk. 7, sect. 1

4 *Semper aliquid novi Africam adferre.*
  Africa always brings [us] something new.
  originally referring to hybridization of African animals
  Historia Naturalis bk. 8, sect. 42; see **Proverbs** 632:6

5 *Optimumque est, ut volgo dixere, aliena insania frui.*
  And the best plan is, as the popular saying was, to profit by the folly of others.
  Historia Naturalis bk. 18, sect. 31

6 *Addito salis grano.*
  With the addition of a grain of salt.
  commonly quoted as 'Cum grano salis [With a grain of salt]'
  Historia Naturalis bk. 23, sect. 149

7 *Dicere etiam solebat nullum esse librum tam malum ut non aliqua parte prodesset.*
  [Pliny] always said that there was no book so bad that some good could not be got out of it.
  Pliny the Younger *Letters* bk. 3, no. 5

Pliny the Younger c.AD 61-c.112

Roman senator and writer, nephew of **Pliny** *the Elder*

8 *Nihil est, inquis, quod scribam. At hoc ipsum scribe, nihil esse quod scribas, vel solum illud unde incipere priores solebant: 'Si vales, bene est; ego valeo.' Hoc mihi sufficit; est enim maximum.*

  You say you have nothing to write about. Well, you can at least write about *that*—or else simply the phrase our elders used to start a letter with: 'If you are well, well and good; I am well.' That will do for me—it is all that matters.
  letter to Fabius Justus, in *Letters* (Loeb ed., 1969) bk. 1, sect. 11

William Plomer 1903-73

British poet

9 Out of that bungled, unwise war
  An alp of unforgiveness grew.
  'The Boer War' (1960)

10 With first-rate sherry flowing into second-rate whores,
  And third-rate conversation without one single pause:
  Just like a young couple
  Between the wars.
  'Father and Son: 1939' (1945)

11 On a sofa upholstered in panther skin
  Mona did researches in original sin.
  'Mews Flat Mona' (1960)

12 A rose-red sissy half as old as time.
  'Playboy of the Demi-World: 1938' (1945); see **Burgon** 165:20

Plutarch c.AD 46-c.120

Greek philosopher and biographer

13 For the mind does not require filling like a bottle, but rather, like wood, it only requires kindling to create in it an impulse to think independently and an ardent desire for the truth.
  Moralia sect. 48c 'On Listening to Lectures'; see **Rabelais** 639:19

14 I am writing biography, not history, and the truth is that the most brilliant exploits often tell us nothing of the virtues or vices of the men who performed them, while on the other hand a chance remark or a joke may reveal far more of a man's character than the mere feat of winning battles in which thousands fall, or of marshalling great armies, or laying siege to cities.
  Parallel Lives 'Alexander' ch. 7

15 For we are told that when a certain man was accusing both of them to him, he [Caesar] said that he had no fear of those fat and long-haired fellows, but rather of those pale and thin ones.
  Parallel Lives 'Anthony' sect. 11; see **Shakespeare** 696:12

16 The man who is thought to have been the first to see beneath the surface of Caesar's public policy and to fear it, as one might fear the smiling surface of the sea.
  of **Cicero**
  Parallel Lives 'Julius Caesar' sect. 4

17 He who cheats with an oath acknowledges that he is afraid of his enemy, but that he thinks little of God.
  Parallel Lives 'Lysander' ch. 8; see **Lysander** 497:8

Edgar Allan Poe 1809-49

American writer
on Poe: see **Lowell** 494:1

18 I was a child and she was a child,
  In this kingdom by the sea;
  But we loved with a love which was more than love—

I and my Annabel Lee.
'Annabel Lee' (1849)

1 And so, all the night-tide, I lie down by the side
Of my darling, my darling, my life and my bride
In her sepulchre there by the sea,
In her tomb by the side of the sea.
'Annabel Lee' (1849)

2 Keeping time, time, time,
In a sort of Runic rhyme,
To the tintinnabulation that so musically wells
From the bells, bells, bells, bells.
'The Bells' (1849) st. 1

3 All that we see or seem
Is but a dream within a dream.
'A Dream within a Dream' (1849)

4 The fever called 'Living'
Is conquered at last.
'For Annie' (1849)

5 Once upon a midnight dreary, while I pondered,
weak and weary,
Over many a quaint and curious volume of
forgotten lore,
While I nodded, nearly napping, suddenly there
came a tapping,
As of some one gently rapping, rapping at my
chamber door.
'The Raven' (1845) st. 1

6 Eagerly I wished the morrow,—vainly had I
sought to borrow
From my books surcease of sorrow—sorrow for
the lost Lenore—
For the rare and radiant maiden whom the angels
name Lenore—
Nameless here for evermore.
'The Raven' (1845) st. 2

7 Ghastly, grim and ancient raven wandering from
the Nightly shore—
Tell me what thy lordly name is on the Night's
Plutonian shore!
'The Raven' (1845) st. 8

8 Take thy beak from out my heart, and take thy
form from off my door!
Quoth the Raven, 'Nevermore'.
'The Raven' (1845) st. 17

9 And his eyes have all the seeming of a demon's
that is dreaming.
'The Raven' (1845) st. 18

10   The glory that was Greece
And the grandeur that was Rome.
'To Helen' (1831)

Henri Poincaré 1854–1912
French mathematician and philosopher of science

11 Science is built up of facts, as a house is built of
stones; but an accumulation of facts is no more a
science than a heap of stones is a house.
Science and Hypothesis (1905) ch. 9

John C. Polanyi 1929–
German-born Canadian scientist

12 When . . . we fear science, we really fear ourselves.
Human dignity is better served by embracing
knowledge.
accepting the Nobel Prize for Chemistry, 10 December
1986

☐ Political slogans and songs
see box overleaf

see also **Connell** 239:25, **Marx and Engels** 517:6, **Pottier**
608:11

Jackson Pollock 1912–56
American painter

13 There was a reviewer a while back who wrote that
my pictures didn't have any beginning or any end.
He didn't mean it as a compliment, but it was. It
was a fine compliment.
Francis V. O'Connor *Jackson Pollock* (1967)

Polybius c.200–c.118 BC
Greek historian

14 Those who know how to win are much more
numerous than those who know how to make
proper use of their victories.
History bk. 10

John Pomfret 1667–1702
English clergyman

15 We live and learn, but not the wiser grow.
'Reason' (1700) l. 112

Madame de Pompadour (Antoinette Poisson, Marquise de Pompadour) 1721–64
French favourite of Louis XV of France

16 *Après nous le déluge.*
After us the deluge.
Madame du Hausset *Mémoires* (1824)

Pompey the Great 106–48 BC
Roman general and statesman

17 *Navigare necesse est, vivere non est.*
To sail is necessary; to live is not.
insisting on setting sail during a storm
Plutarch *Parallel Lives* 'Pompey' sect. 50

Georges Pompidou 1911–74
French statesman; President of France from 1969

18 A statesman is a politician who places himself at
the service of the nation. A politician is a
statesman who places the nation at his service.
in *Observer* 30 December 1973 'Sayings of the Year'

Political slogans and songs

1 All power to the Soviets.
workers in Petrograd, 1917

2 All the way with LBJ.
US Democratic Party campaign slogan, 1960

3 Are you now, or have you ever been, a member of the Communist Party?
from 1947, the question habitually put by the House Un-American Activities Committee (HUAC) to those appearing before it, now particularly associated with the McCarthy period of the 1950s

4 As Maine goes, so goes the nation.
American political saying, c.1840; see **Farley** 315:4

5 Ban the bomb.
US anti-nuclear slogan, adopted by the Campaign for Nuclear Disarmament, 1953 onwards

6 A bayonet is a weapon with a worker at each end.
British pacifist slogan (1940)

7 Better red than dead.
slogan of nuclear disarmament campaigners, late 1950s

8 A bigger bang for a buck.
Charles E. **Wilson**'s defence policy, in *Newsweek* 22 March 1954

9 The big tent.
slogan used by the American Republican Party to denote a policy of inclusiveness
recorded from 1990

10 Black is beautiful.
slogan of American civil rights campaigners, mid-1960s

11 Burn, baby, burn.
Black extremist slogan in use during the Los Angeles riots, August 1965

12 Can't pay, won't pay.
anti-Poll Tax slogan, c.1990; see **Fo** 327:21

13 Don't sell America short.
popular version of saying attributed, c.1890s, to John Pierpont Morgan (1837-1913)

14 *Ein Reich, ein Volk, ein Führer.*
One realm, one people, one leader.
Nazi Party slogan, early 1930s

15 Fair shares for all, is Labour's call.
*slogan for the North Battersea by-election, 1946, coined by Douglas **Jay***
Douglas Jay *Change and Fortune* (1980) ch. 7

16 Fifty-four forty, or fight!
slogan of expansionist Democrats in the US presidential campaign of 1844, in which the Oregon boundary definition was an issue (in 1846 the new Democratic president, James K. Polk, compromised on the 49th parallel with Great Britain)

17 Free by '93.
Scottish National Party, general election campaign, 1992

18 Give us back our eleven days.
protesting against the adoption of the Gregorian Calendar in 1752, and in this form associated with Hogarth's cartoon showing a rowdy Oxfordshire election of 1754
David Ewing Duncan *The Calendar* (1998)

19 Hey, hey, LBJ, how many kids did you kill today?
anti-Vietnam marching slogan, 1960s

20 I like Ike.
*used when General **Eisenhower** was first seen as a potential presidential nominee*
US button badge, 1947; coined by Henry D. Spalding (d. 1990)

21 I met wid Napper Tandy, and he took me by the hand,
And he said, 'How's poor ould Ireland, and how does she stand?'
She's the most disthressful country that iver yet was seen,
For they're hangin' men an' women for the wearin' o' the Green.
'The Wearin' o' the Green' (c.1795 ballad)

22 The iron-armed soldier, the true-hearted soldier,
The gallant old soldier of Tippecanoe.
*presidential campaign song for William Henry Harrison, 1840; see **Political slogans** 601:11 below*
attributed to George Pope Morris (1802-64)

23 It'll play in Peoria.
catchphrase of the **Nixon** administration (early 1970s) meaning 'it will be acceptable to middle America', but originating in a standard music hall joke of the 1930s

24 It's morning again in America.
slogan for Ronald **Reagan**'s election campaign, 1984; coined by Hal Riney (1932-); in *Newsweek* 6 August 1984

25 It's Scotland's oil.
Scottish National Party, 1972

26 It's the economy, stupid.
on a sign put up at the 1992 **Clinton** presidential campaign headquarters by campaign manager James Carville

27 *Kraft durch Freude.*
Strength through joy.
German Labour Front slogan, from 1933; coined by Robert Ley (1890-1945)

28 Labour isn't working.
on poster showing a long queue outside an unemployment office
Conservative Party slogan 1978-9

29 Labour's double whammy.
Conservative Party election slogan 1992

▶

▶ Political slogans and songs *continued*

1 *Liberté! Égalité! Fraternité!*

Freedom! Equality! Brotherhood!

motto of the French Revolution, but of earlier origin
the Club des Cordeliers passed a motion, 30 June 1793, 'that owners should be urged to paint on the front of their houses, in large letters, the words: Unity, indivisibility of the Republic, Liberty, Equality, Fraternity or death'; in *Journal de Paris* no. 182 (from 1795 the words 'or death' were dropped); see **Chamfort** 207:8

2 Life's better with the Conservatives. Don't let Labour ruin it.
Conservative Party election slogan, 1959

3 New Labour, new danger.
Conservative slogan, 1996

4 No surrender!
the defenders of the besieged city of Derry to the Jacobite army of James II, April 1689, adopted as a slogan of Protestant Ulster
Jonathan Bardon *A History of Ulster* (1992)

5 The personal is political.
1970s feminist slogan, attributed to Carol Hanisch (1945-)

6 Power to the people.
slogan of the Black Panther movement, from c.1968 onwards; see **Newton** 561:8

7 So on the Twelfth I proudly wear the sash my father wore.
'The Sash My Father Wore', traditional Orange song

8 Things can only get better.
Labour campaign slogan, 1997; see **Petrie** 594:2

9 Thirteen years of Tory misrule.
unofficial Labour party election slogan, also in the form 'Thirteen wasted years', 1964

10 Three acres and a cow.
regarded as the requirement for self-sufficiency; associated with the radical politician Jesse Collings (1831–1920) and his land reform campaign begun in 1885
Jesse Collings in the House of Commons, 26 January

1886, although used earlier by Joseph **Chamberlain** in a speech at Evesham (in *The Times* 17 November 1885), by which time it was already proverbial

11 Tippecanoe and Tyler, too.
presidential campaign song for William Henry Harrison, 1840
attributed to A. C. Ross (fl. 1840); see **Political slogans** 600:22 above

12 'Tis bad enough in man or woman
To steal a goose from off a common;
But surely he's without excuse
Who steals the common from the goose.
'On Inclosures'; in *The Oxford Book of Light Verse* (1938)

13 Votes for women.
*adopted when it proved impossible to use a banner with the longer slogan 'Will the Liberal Party Give Votes for Women?' made by Emmeline **Pankhurst** (1858–1928), Christabel **Pankhurst** (1880–1958), and Annie Kenney (1879–1953)*
slogan of the women's suffrage movement, from 13 October 1905; Emmeline Pankhurst *My Own Story* (1914)

14 War will cease when men refuse to fight.
pacifist slogan, from c.1936 (often quoted as, 'Wars will cease . . .')

15 We shall not be moved.
title of labour and civil rights song (1931) adapted from an earlier gospel hymn

16 We shall overcome.
title of song, originating from before the American Civil War, adapted as a Baptist hymn ('I'll Overcome Some Day', 1901) by C. Albert Tindley; revived in 1946 as a protest song by black tobacco workers, and in 1963 during the black Civil Rights Campaign

17 Would you buy a used car from this man?
campaign slogan directed against Richard **Nixon**, 1968

18 Yes it hurt, yes it worked.
Conservative Party slogan, 1996; see **Major** 508:3

19 Yesterday's men (they failed before!).
Labour Party slogan, referring to the Conservatives, 1970; coined by David Kingsley, Dennis Lyons, and Peter Lovell-Davis

Alexander Pope 1688–1744

English poet
on Pope: see **Arnold** 29:23, **Arnold** 30:7, **Bentley** 69:1, **Brereton** 150:24

20 Poetic Justice, with her lifted scale,
Where, in nice balance, truth with gold she weighs,
And solid pudding against empty praise.
The Dunciad (1742) bk. 1, l. 52

21 Or where the pictures for the page atone,
And Quarles is saved by beauties not his own.
The Dunciad (1742) bk. 1, l. 139

22 Gentle Dullness ever loves a joke.
The Dunciad (1742) bk. 2, l. 34

23 A brain of feathers, and a heart of lead.
The Dunciad (1742) bk. 2, l. 44

24 How little, mark! that portion of the ball,
Where, faint at best, the beams of science fall.
The Dunciad (1742) bk. 3, l. 83

25 All crowd, who foremost shall be damned to Fame.
The Dunciad (1742) bk. 3, l. 158

26 Flow Welsted, flow! like thine inspirer, Beer,
Tho' stale, not ripe; tho' thin, yet never clear;
So sweetly mawkish, and so smoothly dull;
Heady, not strong; o'erflowing tho' not full.
The Dunciad (1742) bk. 3, l. 169

27 'Till Isis' elders reel, their pupils' sport,
And Alma mater lie dissolved in port!
The Dunciad (1742) bk. 3, l. 337

28 A wit with dunces, and a dunce with wits.
The Dunciad (1742) bk. 4, l. 90

1 Whate'er the talents, or howe'er designed,
We hang one jingling padlock on the mind.
The Dunciad (1742) bk. 4, l. 161

2 The Right Divine of Kings to govern wrong.
The Dunciad (1742) bk. 4, l. 187

3 With the same cement, ever sure to bind,
We bring to one dead level ev'ry mind.
Then take him to develop, if you can,
And hew the block off, and get out the man.
The Dunciad (1742) bk. 4, l. 267

4 Isles of fragrance, lily-silver'd vales.
The Dunciad (1742) bk. 4, l. 303

5 Love-whisp'ring woods, and lute-resounding
waves.
The Dunciad (1742) bk. 4, l. 306

6 　　　　　She marked thee there,
Stretched on the rack of a too easy chair,
And heard thy everlasting yawn confess
The pains and penalties of idleness.
The Dunciad (1742) bk. 4, l. 342

7 Thy truffles, Perigord! thy hams, Bayonne!
The Dunciad (1742) bk. 4, l. 558

8 Religion blushing veils her sacred fires,
And unawares Morality expires.
The Dunciad (1742) bk. 4, l. 649

9 Lo! thy dread empire, Chaos! is restored;
Light dies before thy uncreating word:
Thy hand, great Anarch! lets the curtain fall;
And universal darkness buries all.
The Dunciad (1742) bk. 4, l. 653

10 Vital spark of heav'nly flame!
Quit, oh quit this mortal frame:
Trembling, hoping, ling'ring, flying,
Oh the pain, the bliss of dying!
'The Dying Christian to his Soul' (1730); see **Hadrian**
366:10

11 What beck'ning ghost, along the moonlight shade
Invites my step, and points to yonder glade?
'Elegy to the Memory of an Unfortunate Lady' (1717) l. 1

12 Is it, in heav'n, a crime to love too well?
'Elegy to the Memory of an Unfortunate Lady' (1717) l. 6

13 Is there no bright reversion in the sky,
For those who greatly think, or bravely die?
'Elegy to the Memory of an Unfortunate Lady' (1717) l. 9

14 Ambition first sprung from your blest abodes;
The glorious fault of angels and of gods.
'Elegy to the Memory of an Unfortunate Lady' (1717) l. 13

15 On all the line a sudden vengeance waits,
And frequent hearses shall besiege your gates.
'Elegy to the Memory of an Unfortunate Lady' (1717) l. 37

16 Oh happy state! when souls each other draw,
When love is liberty, and nature, law.
'Eloisa to Abelard' (1717) l. 91

17 Of all affliction taught a lover yet,
'Tis sure the hardest science to forget!
'Eloisa to Abelard' (1717) l. 189

18 How shall I lose the sin, yet keep the sense,
And love th'offender, yet detest th'offence?
'Eloisa to Abelard' (1717) l. 191; see **Augustine** 37:16

19 How happy is the blameless Vestal's lot!
The world forgetting, by the world forgot.
'Eloisa to Abelard' (1717) l. 207

20 You beat your pate, and fancy wit will come:
Knock as you please, there's nobody at home.
'Epigram: You beat your pate' (1732)

21 I am his Highness' dog at Kew;
Pray, tell me sir, whose dog are you?
'Epigram Engraved on the Collar of a Dog which I gave to
his Royal Highness' (1738)

22 Sir, I admit your gen'ral rule
That every poet is a fool:
But you yourself may serve to show it,
That every fool is not a poet.
'Epigram from the French' (1732)

23 Shut, shut the door, good John! fatigued I said,
Tie up the knocker, say I'm sick, I'm dead,
The dog-star rages!
'An Epistle to Dr Arbuthnot' (1735) l. 1

24 You think this cruel? take it for a rule,
No creature smarts so little as a fool.
Let peals of laughter, Codrus! round thee break,
Thou unconcerned canst hear the mighty crack.
Pit, box, and gall'ry in convulsions hurled,
Thou stand'st unshook amidst a bursting world.
'An Epistle to Dr Arbuthnot' (1735) l. 83; see **Addison**
4:23, **Horace** 401:14

25 As yet a child, nor yet a fool to fame,
I lisped in numbers, for the numbers came.
'An Epistle to Dr Arbuthnot' (1735) l. 127; see **Ovid**
580:20

26 The Muse but served to ease some friend, not wife,
To help me through this long disease, my life.
'An Epistle to Dr Arbuthnot' (1735) l. 131

27 Pretty! in amber to observe the forms
Of hairs, or straws, or dirt, or grubs, or worms;
The things, we know, are neither rich nor rare,
But wonder how the devil they got there?
'An Epistle to Dr Arbuthnot' (1735) l. 169

28 And he, whose fustian's so sublimely bad,
It is not poetry, but prose run mad.
'An Epistle to Dr Arbuthnot' (1735) l. 187

29 Damn with faint praise, assent with civil leer,
And without sneering, teach the rest to sneer;
Willing to wound, and yet afraid to strike,
Just hint a fault, and hesitate dislike.
of **Addison**
'An Epistle to Dr Arbuthnot' (1735) l. 201; see **Wycherley**
852:14

30 But still the great have kindness in reserve,
He helped to bury whom he helped to starve.
of a noble patron
'An Epistle to Dr Arbuthnot' (1735) l. 247

31 'Satire or sense, alas! can Sporus feel?
Who breaks a butterfly upon a wheel?'
Yet let me flap this bug with gilded wings,
This painted child of dirt that stinks and stings.
of Lord **Hervey**
'An Epistle to Dr Arbuthnot' (1735) l. 307; see **Newspaper
headlines** 562:22

1 Unlearn'd, he knew no schoolman's subtle art,
No language, but the language of the heart.
of his own father
'An Epistle to Dr Arbuthnot' (1735) l. 398

2 Virtue she finds too painful an endeavour,
Content to dwell in decencies for ever.
Epistles to Several Persons 'To a Lady' (1735) l. 163

3 A very heathen in the carnal part,
Yet still a sad, good Christian at her heart.
Epistles to Several Persons 'To a Lady' (1735) l. 67

4 Chaste to her husband, frank to all beside,
A teeming mistress, but a barren bride.
Epistles to Several Persons 'To a Lady' (1735) l. 71

5 Still round and round the ghosts of Beauty glide,
And haunt the places where their honour died.
See how the world its veterans rewards!
A youth of frolics, an old age of cards.
Epistles to Several Persons 'To a Lady' (1735) l. 241

6 And mistress of herself, though china fall.
Epistles to Several Persons 'To a Lady' (1735) l. 268

7 Woman's at best a contradiction still.
Epistles to Several Persons 'To a Lady' (1735) l. 270

8 Who shall decide, when doctors disagree?
Epistles to Several Persons 'To Lord Bathurst' (1733) l. 1

9 But thousands die, without or this or that,
Die, and endow a college, or a cat.
Epistles to Several Persons 'To Lord Bathurst' (1733) l. 97

10 The ruling passion, be it what it will,
The ruling passion conquers reason still.
Epistles to Several Persons 'To Lord Bathurst' (1733) l. 155;
see **Pope** 603:20

11 In the worst inn's worst room, with mat half-
hung,
The floors of plaister, and the walls of dung,
On once a flock-bed, but repaired with straw,
With tape-tied curtains, never meant to draw,
The George and Garter dangling from that bed
Where tawdry yellow strove with dirty red,
Great Villiers lies.
Epistles to Several Persons 'To Lord Bathurst' (1733) l. 299

12 Consult the genius of the place in all.
Epistles to Several Persons 'To Lord Burlington' (1731) l. 57;
see **Virgil** 812:18

13 To rest, the cushion and soft Dean invite,
Who never mentions Hell to ears polite.
Epistles to Several Persons 'To Lord Burlington' (1731) l.
149

14 Another age shall see the golden ear
Imbrown the slope, and nod on the parterre,
Deep harvests bury all his pride has planned,
And laughing Ceres re-assume the land.
Epistles to Several Persons 'To Lord Burlington' (1731) l.
173

15 'Tis use alone that sanctifies expense,
And splendour borrows all her rays from sense.
Epistles to Several Persons 'To Lord Burlington' (1731) l.
179

16 To observations which ourselves we make,
We grow more partial for th'observer's sake.
Epistles to Several Persons 'To Lord Cobham' (1734) l. 11

17 Like following life thro' creatures you dissect,
You lose it in the moment you detect.
Epistles to Several Persons 'To Lord Cobham' (1734) l. 39

18 'Tis from high life high characters are drawn;
A saint in crape is twice a saint in lawn.
Epistles to Several Persons 'To Lord Cobham' (1734) l. 87

19 'Tis education forms the common mind,
Just as the twig is bent, the tree's inclined.
Epistles to Several Persons 'To Lord Cobham' (1734) l. 101;
see **Proverbs** 614:36

20 Search then the Ruling Passion: There, alone,
The wild are constant, and the cunning known;
The fool consistent, and the false sincere.
Epistles to Several Persons 'To Lord Cobham' (1734) l. 174;
see **Pope** 603:10

21 Odious! in woollen! 'twould a saint provoke!
Epistles to Several Persons 'To Lord Cobham' (1734) l. 242

22 One would not, sure, be frightful when one's
dead—
And—Betty—give this cheek a little red.
Epistles to Several Persons 'To Lord Cobham' (1734) l. 246

23 Old politicians chew on wisdom past,
And totter on in business to the last.
Epistles to Several Persons 'To Lord Cobham' (1734) l. 248

24 Statesman, yet friend to Truth! of soul sincere,
In action faithful, and in honour clear;
Who broke no promise, served no private end,
Who gained no title, and who lost no friend.
Epistles to Several Persons 'To Mr Addison' (1720) l. 67

25 She went, to plain-work, and to purling brooks,
Old-fashioned halls, dull aunts, and croaking
rooks.
She went from op'ra, park, assembly, play,
To morning-walks, and prayers three hours a day.
'Epistle to Miss Blount, on her leaving the Town, after the
Coronation [of King George I, 1715]' (1717)

26 Or o'er cold coffee trifle with the spoon,
Court the slow clock, and dine exact at noon.
'Epistle to Miss Blount, on her leaving the Town, after the
Coronation [of King George I, 1715]' (1717)

27 Nature, and Nature's laws lay hid in night.
God said, *Let Newton be!* and all was light.
'Epitaph: Intended for Sir Isaac Newton' (1730); see **Squire**
753:15

28 Of manners gentle, of affections mild;
In wit, a man; simplicity, a child;
With native humour temp'ring virtuous rage,
Formed to delight at once and lash the age.
'Epitaph: On Mr Gay in Westminster Abbey' (1733)

29 Some are bewildered in the maze of schools,
And some made coxcombs Nature meant but
fools.
An Essay on Criticism (1711) l. 26

30 Some have at first for wits, then poets passed,
Turned critics next, and proved plain fools at last.
An Essay on Criticism (1711) l. 36

31 First follow Nature, and your judgement frame
By her just standard, which is still the same:
Unerring Nature, still divinely bright,
One clear, unchanged, and universal light,

Life, force and beauty must to all impart,
At once the source and end and test of art.
An Essay on Criticism (1711) l. 68

1 Great wits may sometimes gloriously offend,
And rise to faults true critics dare not mend.
From vulgar bounds with brave disorder part
And snatch a grace beyond the reach of art.
An Essay on Criticism (1711) l. 152; see **Addison** 5:13

2 A little learning is a dangerous thing;
Drink deep, or taste not the Pierian spring:
There shallow draughts intoxicate the brain,
And drinking largely sobers us again.
An Essay on Criticism (1711) l. 215; see **Drayton** 286:4,
Proverbs 625:26

3 Hills peep o'er hills, and Alps on Alps arise!
An Essay on Criticism (1711) l. 232

4 Whoever thinks a faultless piece to see,
Thinks what ne'er was, nor is, nor e'er shall be.
An Essay on Criticism (1711) l. 253

5 True wit is Nature to advantage dressed,
What oft was thought, but ne'er so well expressed.
An Essay on Criticism (1711) l. 297

6 Expression is the dress of thought.
An Essay on Criticism (1711) l. 318; see **Johnson** 425:2,
Wesley 830:1

7   As some to church repair,
Not for the doctrine, but the music there.
An Essay on Criticism (1711) l. 342

8 A needless Alexandrine ends the song,
That, like a wounded snake, drags its slow length
along.
An Essay on Criticism (1711) l. 356

9 True ease in writing comes from art, not chance,
As those move easiest who have learned to dance.
'Tis not enough no harshness gives offence,
The sound must seem an echo to the sense.
An Essay on Criticism (1711) l. 362

10 But when loud surges lash the sounding shore,
The hoarse, rough verse should like the torrent
roar.
When Ajax strives, some rock's vast weight to
throw,
The line too labours, and the words move slow.
An Essay on Criticism (1711) l. 368

11 What woeful stuff this madrigal would be,
In some starved hackney sonneteer, or me?
But let a Lord once own the happy lines,
How the wit brightens! how the style refines!
An Essay on Criticism (1711) l. 418

12 Some praise at morning what they blame at night;
But always think the last opinion right.
An Essay on Criticism (1711) l. 430

13 To err is human; to forgive, divine.
An Essay on Criticism (1711) l. 525; see **Proverbs** 633:9

14 All seems infected that th'infected spy,
As all looks yellow to the jaundiced eye.
An Essay on Criticism (1711) l. 558

15 Men must be taught as if you taught them not,
And things unknown proposed as things forgot.
An Essay on Criticism (1711) l. 574

16 The bookful blockhead, ignorantly read,
With loads of learned lumber in his head.
An Essay on Criticism (1711) l. 612

17 For fools rush in where angels fear to tread.
An Essay on Criticism (1711) l. 625; see **Proverbs** 620:23

18 Eye Nature's walks, shoot Folly as it flies,
And catch the Manners living as they rise.
Laugh where we must, be candid where we can;
But vindicate the ways of God to man.
An Essay on Man Epistle 1 (1733) l. 13; see **Milton** 531:6

19 Observe how system into system runs,
What other planets circle other suns.
An Essay on Man Epistle 1 (1733) l. 25

20 Pleased to the last, he crops the flowery food,
And licks the hand just raised to shed his blood.
An Essay on Man Epistle 1 (1733) l. 83

21 Who sees with equal eye, as God of all,
A hero perish, or a sparrow fall,
Atoms or systems into ruin hurled,
And now a bubble burst, and now a world.
An Essay on Man Epistle 1 (1733) l. 87

22 Hope springs eternal in the human breast:
Man never Is, but always To be blest.
An Essay on Man Epistle 1 (1733) l. 95; see **Proverbs** 622:32

23 Lo! the poor Indian, whose untutored mind
Sees God in clouds, or hears him in the wind.
An Essay on Man Epistle 1 (1733) l. 99; see **Crabbe** 249:2

24 But thinks, admitted to that equal sky,
His faithful dog shall bear him company.
An Essay on Man Epistle 1 (1733) l. 111

25 Pride still is aiming at the blest abodes,
Men would be angels, angels would be gods.
An Essay on Man Epistle 1 (1733) l. 125

26 Why has not man a microscopic eye?
For this plain reason, man is not a fly.
An Essay on Man Epistle 1 (1733) l. 193

27 Die of a rose in aromatic pain?
An Essay on Man Epistle 1 (1733) l. 200; see **Winchilsea** 841:9

28 The spider's touch, how exquisitely fine!
Feels at each thread, and lives along the line.
An Essay on Man Epistle 1 (1733) l. 217

29 All are but parts of one stupendous whole,
Whose body, Nature is, and God the soul.
An Essay on Man Epistle 1 (1733) l. 267

30 All nature is but art, unknown to thee;
All chance, direction, which thou canst not see;
All discord, harmony, not understood;
All partial evil, universal good.
An Essay on Man Epistle 1 (1733) l. 289

31 And, spite of Pride, in erring Reason's spite,
One truth is clear, 'Whatever IS, is RIGHT.'
An Essay on Man Epistle 1 (1733) l. 293

32 Know then thyself, presume not God to scan;
The proper study of mankind is man.
Placed on this isthmus of a middle state,
A being darkly wise, and rudely great.
An Essay on Man Epistle 2 (1733) l. 1; see **Charron** 209:17,
Huxley 411:4

1 Created half to rise, and half to fall;
Great lord of all things, yet a prey to all;
Sole judge of truth, in endless error hurled;
The glory, jest, and riddle of the world!
An Essay on Man Epistle 2 (1733) l. 15

2 Go, teach Eternal Wisdom how to rule—
Then drop into thyself, and be a fool!
An Essay on Man Epistle 2 (1733) l. 29

3 Vice is a monster of so frightful mien,
As, to be hated, needs but to be seen;
Yet seen too oft, familiar with her face,
We first endure, then pity, then embrace.
An Essay on Man Epistle 2 (1733) l. 217

4 The learn'd is happy nature to explore,
The fool is happy that he knows no more.
An Essay on Man Epistle 2 (1733) l. 263

5 Behold the child, by Nature's kindly law
Pleased with a rattle, tickled with a straw.
An Essay on Man Epistle 2 (1733) l. 275

6 For forms of government let fools contest;
Whate'er is best administered is best.
An Essay on Man Epistle 3 (1733) l. 303

7 Thus God and nature linked the gen'ral frame,
And bade self-love and social be the same.
An Essay on Man Epistle 3 (1733) l. 317; *An Essay on Man*
Epistle 4 (1734) l. 396 is similar

8 Oh Happiness! our being's end and aim!
Good, pleasure, ease, content! whate'er thy name:
That something still which prompts th' eternal
sigh,
For which we bear to live, or dare to die.
An Essay on Man Epistle 4 (1734) l. 1

9 An honest man's the noblest work of God.
An Essay on Man Epistle 4 (1734) l. 248; see **Burns** 170:23,
Ingersoll 413:14

10 And more true joy Marcellus exil'd feels
Than Caesar with a senate at his heels.
An Essay on Man Epistle 4 (1734) l. 258

11 See Cromwell, damned to everlasting fame!
An Essay on Man Epistle 4 (1734) l. 284

12 Slave to no sect, who takes no private road,
But looks thro' Nature, up to Nature's God.
An Essay on Man Epistle 4 (1734) l. 331

13 All our knowledge is, ourselves to know.
An Essay on Man Epistle 4 (1734) l. 398

14 Achilles' wrath, to Greece the direful spring
Of woes unnumbered, heavenly goddess, sing!
translation of *The Iliad* (1715) bk. 1, l. 1; see **Bentley** 69:1,
Homer 393:17

15 For I, who hold sage Homer's rule the best,
Welcome the coming, speed the going guest.
Imitations of Horace Horace bk. 2, Satire 2 (1734) l. 159;
'Speed the parting guest' in Pope's translation of *The
Odyssey* (1725–6) bk. 15, l. 84

16 Not to go back, is somewhat to advance,
And men must walk at least before they dance.
Imitations of Horace Horace bk. 1, Epistle 1 (1738) l. 53

17 Get place and wealth, if possible, with grace;
If not, by any means get wealth and place.
Imitations of Horace Horace bk. 1, Epistle 1 (1738) l. 103;
see **Horace** 399:1

18 Not to admire, is all the art I know,
To make men happy, and to keep them so.
Imitations of Horace Horace bk. 1, Epistle 6 (1738) l. 1; see
Horace 399:8

19 The worst of madmen is a saint run mad.
Imitations of Horace Horace bk. 1, Epistle 6 (1738) l. 27

20 Shakespeare (whom you and ev'ry play-house bill
Style the divine, the matchless, what you will)
For gain, not glory, winged his roving flight,
And grew immortal in his own despite.
Imitations of Horace Horace bk. 2, Epistle 1 (1737) l. 69

21 Who now reads Cowley? if he pleases yet,
His moral pleases, not his pointed wit.
Imitations of Horace Horace bk. 2, Epistle 1 (1737) l. 75

22   The people's voice is odd,
It is, and it is not, the voice of God.
Imitations of Horace Horace bk. 2, Epistle 1 (1737) l. 89; see
Alcuin 10:10

23 But those who cannot write, and those who can,
All rhyme, and scrawl, and scribble, to a man.
Imitations of Horace Horace bk. 2, Epistle 1 (1737) l. 187;
see **Horace** 399:19

24 Ev'n copious Dryden, wanted, or forgot,
The last and greatest art, the art to blot.
Imitations of Horace Horace bk. 2, Epistle 1 (1737) l. 280;
see **Heming** 381:3, **Jonson** 436:8

25 There still remains, to mortify a wit,
The many-headed monster of the pit.
Imitations of Horace Horace bk. 2, Epistle 1 (1737) l. 304

26 The feast of reason and the flow of soul.
Imitations of Horace Horace bk. 2, Satire 1, (1734) l. 128

27 Let humble Allen, with an awkward shame,
Do good by stealth, and blush to find it fame.
Imitations of Horace Epilogue to the Satires (1738) Dialogue
1, l. 135

28 Ask you what provocation I have had?
The strong antipathy of good to bad.
Imitations of Horace Epilogue to the Satires (1738) Dialogue
2, l. 197

29 Yes, I am proud; I must be proud to see
Men not afraid of God, afraid of me.
Imitations of Horace Epilogue to the Satires (1738) Dialogue
2, l. 208

30 Ye gods! annihilate but space and time,
And make two lovers happy.
Martinus Scriblerus . . . or The Art of Sinking in Poetry ch. 11
(Miscellanies, 1727); possibly quoting another poet

31 Happy the man, whose wish and care
A few paternal acres bound,
Content to breathe his native air,
In his own ground.
'Ode on Solitude' (written *c.*1700, aged about twelve)

32 Thus let me live, unseen, unknown;
Thus unlamented let me die;
Steal from the world, and not a stone

Tell where I lie.
'Ode on Solitude' (written *c*.1700)

1 Where'er you walk, cool gales shall fan the glade,
Trees, where you sit, shall crowd into a shade:
Where'er you tread, the blushing flow'rs shall rise,
And all things flourish where you turn your eyes.
Pastorals (1709) 'Summer' l. 73

2 To wake the soul by tender strokes of art,
To raise the genius, and to mend the heart;
To make mankind, in conscious virtue bold,
Live o'er each scene, and be what they behold:
For this the Tragic Muse first trod the stage.
Prologue to Addison's *Cato* (1713) l. 1

3 What dire offence from am'rous causes springs,
What mighty contests rise from trivial things.
The Rape of the Lock (1714) canto 1, l. 1

4 Now lap-dogs give themselves the rousing shake,
And sleepless lovers, just at twelve, awake.
The Rape of the Lock (1714) canto 1, l. 15

5 With varying vanities, from ev'ry part,
They shift the moving toyshop of their heart.
The Rape of the Lock (1714) canto 1, l. 100

6 Here files of pins extend their shining rows,
Puffs, powders, patches, bibles, billet-doux.
The Rape of the Lock (1714) canto 1, l. 137

7 Fair tresses man's imperial race insnare,
And beauty draws us with a single hair.
The Rape of the Lock (1714) canto 2, l. 27; see **Proverbs** 615:3

8 Belinda smiled, and all the world was gay.
The Rape of the Lock (1714) canto 2, l. 52

9 Whether the nymph shall break Diana's law,
Or some frail china jar receive a flaw,
Or stain her honour, or her new brocade,
Forget her pray'rs, or miss a masquerade.
The Rape of the Lock (1714) canto 2, l. 105

10 Here thou, great Anna! whom three realms obey,
Dost sometimes counsel take—and sometimes tea.
The Rape of the Lock (1714) canto 3, l. 7

11 At ev'ry word a reputation dies.
The Rape of the Lock (1714) canto 3, l. 16; see **Sheridan** 733:29

12 The hungry judges soon the sentence sign,
And wretches hang that jury-men may dine.
The Rape of the Lock (1714) canto 3, l. 21

13 Let spades be trumps! she said, and trumps they were.
The Rape of the Lock (1714) canto 3, l. 46

14 Coffee, (which makes the politician wise,
And see thro' all things with his half-shut eyes).
The Rape of the Lock (1714) canto 3, l. 117

15 Not louder shrieks to pitying heav'n are cast,
When husbands or when lapdogs breathe their last.
The Rape of the Lock (1714) canto 3, l. 157

16 Teach me to feel another's woe;
To hide the fault I see;

That mercy I to others show,
That mercy show to me.
'The Universal Prayer' (1738)

17 Here hills and vales, the woodland and the plain,
Here earth and water seem to strive again;
Not chaos-like together crushed and bruised,
But, as the world, harmoniously confused:
Where order in variety we see,
And where, though all things differ, all agree.
'Windsor Forest' (1711) l. 11

18 Party-spirit, which at best is but the madness of many for the gain of a few.
letter to Edward Blount, 27 August 1714, in G. Sherburn (ed.) *Correspondence of Alexander Pope* (1956) vol. 1

19 How often are we to die before we go quite off this stage? In every friend we lose a part of ourselves, and the best part.
letter to Jonathan Swift, 5 December 1732, in G. Sherburn (ed.) *Correspondence of Alexander Pope* (1956) vol. 3

20 To endeavour to work upon the vulgar with fine sense, is like attempting to hew blocks with a razor.
Miscellanies (1727) vol. 2 'Thoughts on Various Subjects'

21 A man should never be ashamed to own he has been in the wrong, which is but saying, in other words, that he is wiser to-day than he was yesterday.
Miscellanies (1727) vol. 2 'Thoughts on Various Subjects'

22 It is with narrow-souled people as with narrow-necked bottles: the less they have in them, the more noise they make in pouring it out.
Miscellanies (1727) vol. 2 'Thoughts on Various Subjects'

23 When men grow virtuous in their old age, they only make a sacrifice to God of the devil's leavings.
Miscellanies (1727) vol. 2 'Thoughts on Various Subjects'

24 The most positive men are the most credulous.
Miscellanies (1727) vol. 2 'Thoughts on Various Subjects'

25 All gardening is landscape-painting.
Joseph Spence *Anecdotes* (ed. J. Osborn, 1966) no. 606

26 Here am I, dying of a hundred good symptoms.
to George, Lord Lyttelton, 15 May 1744, in Joseph Spence *Anecdotes* (ed. J. Osborn, 1966) no. 637

John Pope-Hennessy 1913–94
British art historian

27 I still recall, with something of a shock the moment, at the end of the first sitting, when I looked at what had been a lump of clay, and found that a third person was in the room.
on sitting to Elizabeth **Frink**
Learning to Look (1991)

Karl Popper 1902–94
Austrian-born philosopher

28 I shall certainly admit a system as empirical or scientific only if it is capable of being *tested* by experience. These considerations suggest that not the *verifiability* but the *falsifiability* of a system is to be taken as a criterion of demarcation . . . *It must*

be possible for an empirical scientific system to be refuted by experience.
   The Logic of Scientific Discovery (1934) ch. 1, sect. 6

1 We may become the makers of our fate when we have ceased to pose as its prophets.
   The Open Society and its Enemies (1945) introduction

2 We should therefore claim, in the name of tolerance, the right not to tolerate the intolerant.
   The Open Society and Its Enemies (1945) ch. 7

3 We must plan for freedom, and not only for security, if for no other reason than that only freedom can make security secure.
   The Open Society and its Enemies (1945) vol. 2, ch. 21

4 There is no history of mankind, there are only many histories of all kinds of aspects of human life. And one of these is the history of political power. This is elevated into the history of the world.
   The Open Society and its Enemies (1945) vol. 2, ch. 25

5 Science must begin with myths, and with the criticism of myths.
   'The Philosophy of Science' in C. A. Mace (ed.) *British Philosophy in the Mid-Century* (1957)

6 On the pre-scientific level we hate the very idea that we may be mistaken. So we cling dogmatically to our conjectures, as long as possible. On the scientific level, we systematically search for our mistakes . . . Thus on the pre-scientific level, we are often ourselves destroyed, eliminated, with our false theories; we perish with our false theories. On the scientific level, we systematically try to eliminate our false theories— we try to let our false theories die in our stead.
   B. Magee (ed.) *Modern British Philosophy* (1971) 'Conversation with Karl Popper'

Cole Porter 1891–1964
American songwriter

7 But I'm always true to you, darlin', in my fashion. Yes I'm always true to you, darlin', in my way.
   'Always True to You in my Fashion' (1949 song)

8 In olden days a glimpse of stocking
Was looked on as something shocking
Now, heaven knows,
Anything goes.
   'Anything Goes' (1934 song)

9 When they begin the Beguine
It brings back the sound of music so tender,
It brings back a night of tropical splendour,
It brings back a memory ever green.
   'Begin the Beguine' (1935 song)

10 Oh, give me land, lots of land under starry skies above,
Don't fence me in.
Let me ride through the wide open country that I love,
Don't fence me in.
   'Don't Fence Me In' (1944 song)

11 But how strange the change from major to minor
Every time we say goodbye.
   'Every Time We Say Goodbye' (1944 song)

12 I get no kick from champagne,
Mere alcohol doesn't thrill me at all,
So tell me why should it be true
That I get a kick out of you?
   'I Get a Kick Out of You' (1934 song) in *Anything Goes*

13 It was great fun,
But it was just one of those things.
   'Just One of Those Things' (1935 song)

14 Birds do it, bees do it,
Even educated fleas do it.
Let's do it, let's fall in love.
   'Let's Do It' (1954 song; words added to the 1928 original)

15 Miss Otis regrets (she's unable to lunch today).
   title of song (1934)

16 My heart belongs to Daddy.
   title of song (1938)

17 Night and day, you are the one,
Only you beneath the moon and under the sun.
   'Night and Day' (1932 song) in *Gay Divorce*

18 Have you heard it's in the stars,
Next July we collide with Mars?
WELL, DID YOU EVAH! What a swell party this is.
   'Well, Did You Evah?' (1940 song; revived for the film *High Society*, 1956)

19 You're the top! You're the Coliseum,
You're the top! You're the Louvre Museum,
You're a melody
From a symphony by Strauss,
You're a Bendel bonnet,
A Shakespeare sonnet,
You're Mickey Mouse!
   'You're the Top' (1934 song) in *Anything Goes*

Beilby Porteus 1731–1808
English poet and prelate

20 . . . One murder made a villain,
Millions a hero.
   Death (1759) l. 154; see **Rostand** 656:16, **Young** 857:6

21 War its thousands slays, Peace its ten thousands.
   Death (1759) l. 179; see **Bible** 80:23

22   Teach him how to live,
And, oh! still harder lesson! how to die.
   Death (1759) l. 319

Michael Portillo 1953–
British Conservative politician

23 You don't look tall if you surround yourself by short grasses.
   on Iain Duncan **Smith**
   in *Independent* 22 February 2003

Francis Pott 1832–1909
English clergyman

24 The strife is o'er, the battle done;
Now is the Victor's triumph won;
O let the song of praise be sung:
Alleluia!
   'The strife is o'er, the battle done' (1861 hymn); translation of 'Finita iam sunt praelia' (c.1695)

Beatrix Potter 1866–1943
English writer for children

1 In the time of swords and periwigs and full-skirted coats with flowered lappets—when gentlemen wore ruffles, and gold-laced waistcoats of paduasoy and taffeta—there lived a tailor in Gloucester.
The Tailor of Gloucester (1903) p. 9

2 I am worn to a ravelling . . . I am undone and worn to a thread-paper, for I have NO MORE TWIST.
The Tailor of Gloucester (1903)

3 It is said that the effect of eating too much lettuce is 'soporific'.
The Tale of the Flopsy Bunnies (1909)

4 Don't go into Mr McGregor's garden: your father had an accident there, he was put into a pie by Mrs McGregor.
The Tale of Peter Rabbit (1902)

Dennis Potter 1935–94
English television dramatist

5 Below my window . . . the blossom is out in full now . . . I *see* it is the whitest, frothiest, blossomiest blossom that there ever could be, and I can see it. Things are both more trivial than they ever were, and more important than they ever were, and the difference between the trivial and the important doesn't seem to matter. But the nowness of everything is absolutely wondrous.
on his heightened awareness of things, in the face of his imminent death
interview with Melvyn Bragg on Channel 4, March 1994, in *Seeing the Blossom* (1994)

6 Religion to me has always been the wound, not the bandage.
interview with Melvyn Bragg on Channel 4, March 1994, in *Seeing the Blossom* (1994)

Stephen Potter 1900–69
British writer

7 A good general rule is to state that the bouquet is better than the taste, and vice versa.
on wine-tasting
One-Upmanship (1952) ch. 14

8 *How to be one up*—how to make the other man feel that something has gone wrong, however slightly.
Lifemanship (1950)

9 'Yes, but not in the South', with slight adjustments, will do for any argument about any place, if not about any person.
Lifemanship (1950) p. 43

10 The theory and practice of gamesmanship or The art of winning games without actually cheating.
title of book (1947)

Eugène Pottier 1816–87
French politician

11 *Debout! les damnés de la terre!*
Debout! les forçats de la faim!

La raison tonne en son cratère,
C'est l'éruption de la fin . . .
Nous ne sommes rien, soyons tout!
C'est la lutte finale
Groupons-nous, et, demain,
L'Internationale
Sera le genre humain.

On your feet, you damned souls of the earth! On your feet, inmates of hunger's prison! Reason is rumbling in its crater, and its final eruption is on its way . . . We are nothing, let us be everything! This is the final conflict: let us form up and, tomorrow, the International will encompass the human race.
'L'Internationale' (1871); in H. E. Piggot *Songs that made History* (1937) ch. 8

Ezra Pound 1885–1972
American poet

12 Winter is icummen in,
Lhude sing Goddamm,
Raineth drop and staineth slop,
And how the wind doth ramm!
Sing: Goddamm.
'Ancient Music' (1917); see **Anonymous** 19:6

13 With usura hath no man a house of good stone each block cut smooth and well fitting.
Cantos (1954) no. 45

14 Tching prayed on the mountain and wrote MAKE IT NEW on his bath tub.
Cantos (1954) no. 53; see **Bible** 114:17

15 Hang it all, Robert Browning,
There can be but the one 'Sordello'.
Draft of XXX Cantos (1930) no. 2

16 And even I can remember
A day when the historians left blanks in their
writings,
I mean for things they didn't know.
Draft of XXX Cantos (1930) no. 13

17 For three years, out of key with his time,
He strove to resuscitate the dead art
Of poetry; to maintain 'the sublime'
In the old sense. Wrong from the start.
Hugh Selwyn Mauberley (1920) 'E. P. Ode pour l'élection de son sépulcre' pt. 1

18 The age demanded an image
Of its accelerated grimace,
Something for the modern stage,
Not, at any rate, an Attic grace.
Hugh Selwyn Mauberley (1920) 'E. P. Ode . . .' pt. 2

19 Christ follows Dionysus,
Phallic and ambrosial
Made way for macerations;
Caliban casts out Ariel.
Hugh Selwyn Mauberley (1920) 'E. P. Ode . . .' pt. 3

20 Died some, pro patria,
non 'dulce' non 'et decor' . . .
walked eye-deep in hell

believing in old men's lies, the unbelieving
came home, home to a lie.

> *Hugh Selwyn Mauberley* (1920) 'E. P. *Ode* . . . ' pt. 4; see
> **Horace** 401:12

1 There died a myriad,
And of the best, among them,
For an old bitch gone in the teeth,
For a botched civilization.

> *Hugh Selwyn Mauberley* (1920) 'E. P. *Ode* . . . ' pt. 5

2 The apparition of these faces in the crowd;
Petals on a wet, black bough.

> 'In a Station of the Metro' (1916)

3 O woe, woe,
People are born and die,
We also shall be dead pretty soon
Therefore let us act as if we were dead already.

> *Mr Housman's Message* (1911)

4 The ant's a centaur in his dragon world.

> *Pisan Cantos* (1948) no. 81

5 Pull down thy VANITY
Thou art a beaten dog beneath the hail,
A swollen magpie in a fitful sun,
Half black half white
Nor knowst'ou wing from tail.

> *Pisan Cantos* (1948) no. 81

6 The leaves fall early this autumn, in wind.
The paired butterflies are already yellow with
    August
Over the grass in the West garden;
They hurt me. I grow older.
If you are coming down through the narrows of
    the river Kiang,
Please let me know beforehand,
And I will come out to meet you
As far as Cho-fu-Sa.

> 'The River Merchant's Wife' (1915); from the Chinese of
> Rihaku

7 He hath not heart for harping, nor in ring-having
Nor winsomeness to wife, nor world's delight
Nor any whit else save the wave's slash,
Yet longing comes upon him to fare forth on the
    water.
Bosque takes blossom, cometh beauty of berries.

> 'The Seafarer' (1912); from the Anglo-Saxon original

8 Music begins to atrophy when it departs too far
from the dance; that poetry begins to atrophy
when it gets too far from music.

> *The ABC of Reading* (1934) 'Warning'

9 Literature is news that STAYS news.

> *The ABC of Reading* (1934) ch. 2

10 Real education must ultimately be limited to one
who INSISTS on knowing, the rest is mere sheep-
herding.

> *The ABC of Reading* (1934) ch. 8

11 Poetry must be *as well written as prose*.

> letter to Harriet Monroe, January 1915, in D. D. Paige (ed.)
> *Selected Letters of Ezra Pound* (1950)

Nicolas Poussin 1594–1665

French painter
see also: **Epitaphs** 309:3

12 An imitation in lines and colours on any surface of
all that is to be found under the sun.

> *of painting*
>
> letter to M. de Chambray, 1665; C. Jouamy (ed.)
> *Correspondance de Nicolas Poussin* (1911)

Anthony Powell 1905–2000

English novelist

13 Books do furnish a room.

> title of novel (1971); see **Smith** 743:20

14 A dance to the music of time.

> title of novel sequence (1951–75), after
>
> *Le 4 stagioni che ballano al suono del tempo.*
>
> The four seasons dancing to the sound of time.
> title given by Giovanni Pietro Bellori to a painting by
> Nicolas **Poussin**

15 He's so wet you could shoot snipe off him.

> *A Question of Upbringing* (1951) ch. 1

16 Growing old is like being increasingly penalized for
a crime you haven't committed.

> *Temporary Kings* (1973) ch. 1

Colin Powell 1937–

American general and Republican politician

17 First, we are going to cut it off, and then, we are
going to kill it.

> *strategy for dealing with the Iraqi Army in the Gulf
> War*
>
> at a press conference, 23 January 1991

18 Nato is the bedrock of Europe. It is sacrosanct.

> in *Independent on Sunday* 21 January 2001

Dilys Powell 1902–95

English critic and writer

19 You come out of *Gone With the Wind* feeling that
history isn't so disturbing after all. One can always
make a dress out of a curtain.

> in *Independent on Sunday* 29 April 1990

Enoch Powell 1912–98

British Conservative politician

20 History is littered with the wars which everybody
knew would never happen.

> speech to the Conservative Party Conference, 19 October
> 1967, in *The Times* 20 October 1967

21 As I look ahead, I am filled with foreboding. Like
the Roman, I seem to see 'the River Tiber foaming
with much blood'.

> speech at the Annual Meeting of the West Midlands Area
> Conservative Political Centre, Birmingham, 20 April 1968,
> in *Observer* 21 April 1968; see **Virgil** 812:8

1 Judas was paid! I am sacrificing my whole political life.
response to a heckler's call of 'Judas', having advised Conservatives to vote Labour at the coming general election
speech at Bull Ring, Birmingham, 23 February 1974

2 To write a diary every day is like returning to one's own vomit.
interview in *Sunday Times* 6 November 1977

3 For a politician to complain about the press is like a ship's captain complaining about the sea.
in *Guardian* 3 December 1984

4 ANNE BROWN: How would you like to be remembered?
ENOCH POWELL: I should like to have been killed in the war.
in a radio interview, 13 April 1986

5 All political lives, unless they are cut off in midstream at a happy juncture, end in failure, because that is the nature of politics and of human affairs.
Joseph Chamberlain (1977)

John Powell 1645–1713
English judge

6 Nothing is law that is not reason.
Lord Raymond's *Reports* (1765) vol. 2

John O'Connor Power 1848–1919
Irish lawyer and politician

7 The mules of politics: without pride of ancestry, or hope of posterity.
of the Liberal Unionists
H. H. Asquith *Memories and Reflections* (1928) vol. 1, ch. 16; see **Disraeli** 277:3

Terry Pratchett 1948–
English science fiction writer

8 Personal isn't the same as important.
Men at Arms (1993)

9 Most modern fantasy just rearranges the furniture in Tolkien's attic.
Stan Nicholls (ed.) *Wordsmiths of Wonder* (1993)

□ **Prayers**
see box opposite

John Prescott 1938–
British Labour politician

10 People like me were branded, pigeon-holed, a ceiling put on our ambitions.
on failing his 11-plus
speech at Ruskin College, Oxford, 13 June 1996; in *Guardian* 14 June 1996

11 We did it! Let's wallow in our victory!
on Tony Blair's warning that the Labour Party should not be triumphalist in victory
speech to the Labour Party Conference, 29 September 1997

Keith Preston 1884–1927
American poet

12 Of all the literary scenes
Saddest this sight to me:
The graves of little magazines
Who died to make verse free.
'The Liberators'

Jacques Prévert 1900–77
French poet and screenwriter

13 *C'est tellement simple, l'amour.*
Love is so simple.
Les Enfants du Paradis (1945 film)

Anthony Price 1928–
English thriller writer and editor

14 The Devil himself had probably redesigned Hell in the light of information he had gained from observing airport layouts.
The Memory Trap (1989)

Richard Price 1723–91
English nonconformist minister

15 Now, methinks, I see the ardour for liberty catching and spreading; a general amendment beginning in human affairs; the dominion of kings changed for the dominion of laws, and the dominion of priests giving way to the dominion of reason and conscience.
A Discourse on the Love of our Country (1790)

Gerald Priestland 1927–91
English writer and journalist

16 Journalists belong in the gutter because that is where the ruling classes throw their guilty secrets.
on Radio London 19 May 1988; in *Observer* 22 May 1988

J. B. Priestley 1894–1984
English novelist, dramatist, and critic

17 I never read the life of any important person without discovering that he knew more and could do more than I could ever hope to know or to do in half a dozen lifetimes.
Apes and Angels (1928)

18 The first fall of snow is not only an event, but it is a magical event. You go to bed in one kind of world and wake up to find yourself in another quite different, and if this is not enchantment, then where is it to be found?
Apes and Angels (1928) 'First Snow'

19 To say that these men paid their shillings to watch twenty-two hirelings kick a ball is merely to say that a violin is wood and catgut, that *Hamlet* is so much paper and ink. For a shilling the Bruddersford United AFC offered you Conflict and Art.
Good Companions (1929) bk. 1, ch. 1

Continued

Prayers

1 *Ave Maria, gratia plena, Dominus tecum: Benedicta tu in mulieribus, et benedictus fructus ventris tui, Jesus.*

Hail Mary, full of grace, the Lord is with thee: Blessed art thou among women, and blessed is the fruit of thy womb, Jesus.

'Ave Maria' or 'Hail Mary', also known as 'The Angelic Salutation', dating from the 11th century; see **Bible** 99:30

2 From ghoulies and ghosties and long-leggety beasties
And things that go bump in the night,
Good Lord, deliver us!

'The Cornish or West Country Litany', in Francis T. Nettleinghame *Polperro Proverbs and Others* (1926) 'Pokerwork Panels'

3 God be in my head,
And in my understanding;
God be in my eyes,
And in my looking;
God be in my mouth,
And in my speaking;
God be in my heart,
And in my thinking;
God be at my end,
And at my departing.

Sarum Missal (11th century)

4 Matthew, Mark, Luke, and John,
The bed be blest that I lie on.
Four angels to my bed,
Four angels round my head,
One to watch, and one to pray,
And two to bear my soul away.

traditional (the first two lines in Thomas Ady *A Candle in the Dark*, 1656)

5 Now I lay me down to sleep;
I pray the Lord my soul to keep.

If I should die before I wake,
I pray the Lord my soul to take.

first printed in a late edition of the *New England Primer* (1781)

6 *Salve, regina, mater misericordiae,
Vita, dulcedo et spes nostra, salve!
Ad te clamamus exsules filii Evae,
Ad te suspiramus gementes et flentes
In hac lacrimarum valle.
Eia ergo, advocata nostra,
Illos tuos misericordes oculos ad nos converte.
Et Iesum, benedictum fructum ventris tui,
Nobis post hoc exsilium ostende,
O clemens, o pia,
O dulcis virgo Maria.*

Hail holy queen, mother of mercy, hail our life, our sweetness, and our hope! To thee do we cry, poor banished children of Eve; to thee do we send up our sighs, mourning and weeping in this vale of tears. Turn then, most gracious advocate, thine eyes of mercy towards us; and after this our exile show unto us the blessed fruit of thy womb, Jesus, O clement, O loving, O sweet virgin Mary.

attributed to various 11th century authors; *Analecta Hymnica* vol. 50 (1907) p. 318

7 *Te Deum laudamus: Te Dominum confitemur.*

We praise thee, God: we own thee Lord.

'Te Deum'; hymn traditionally attributed to St **Ambrose** and St **Augustine** in AD 387, though more recently to St Niceta (d. *c.*414); see **Book of Common Prayer** 127:20, **Prayers** 611:8

8 *In te Domine, speravi: non confundar in aeternum.*

Lord, I have set my hopes in thee, I shall not be destroyed for ever.

'Te Deum'; see **Book of Common Prayer** 128:2, **Prayers** 611:7

J. B. Priestley *continued*

9 I can't help feeling wary when I hear anything said about the masses. First you take their faces from 'em by calling 'em the masses and then you accuse 'em of not having any faces.

Saturn Over the Water (1961) ch. 2

10 This little steamer, like all her brave and battered sisters, is immortal. She'll go sailing proudly down the years in the epic of Dunkirk. And our great-grand-children, when they learn how we began this war by snatching glory out of defeat, and then swept on to victory, may also learn how the little holiday steamers made an excursion to hell and came back glorious.

radio broadcast, 5 June 1940, in *Listener* 13 June 1940

11 The weakness of American civilization, and perhaps the chief reason why it creates so much discontent, is that it is so curiously abstract. It is a bloodless extrapolation of a satisfying life . . . You

dine off the advertiser's 'sizzling' and not the meat of the steak.

in *New Statesman* 10 December 1971

12 *on being awarded the Order of Merit in 1977:*
I've only two things to say about it. First I deserve it. Second, they've been too long about giving me it. There'll be another vacancy very soon.

in a radio interview, October 1977; John Braine *J. B. Priestley* (1978)

Joseph Priestley 1733–1804

English nonconformist minister
see also **Bentham** 68:5

13 Every man, when he comes to be sensible of his natural rights, and to feel his own importance, will consider himself as fully equal to any other person whatever.

An Essay on the First Principles of Government (1768) pt. I

Matthew Prior 1664–1721

English poet

1 I court others in verse: but I love thee in prose:
And they have my whimsies, but thou hast my
heart.
'A Better Answer' (1718)

2 Be to her virtues very kind;
Be to her faults a little blind;
Let all her ways be unconfined;
And clap your padlock—on her mind.
'An English Padlock' (1705) l. 79

3 Nobles and heralds, by your leave,
Here lies what once was Matthew Prior,
The son of Adam and of Eve,
Can Stuart or Nassau go higher?
'Epitaph' (1702)

4 For the idiom of words very little she heeded,
Provided the matter she drove at succeeded,
She took and gave languages just as she needed.
'Jinny the Just' (after 1700)

5 The merchant, to secure his treasure,
Conveys it in a borrowed name:
Euphelia serves to grace my measure;
But Chloe is my real flame.
'An Ode' (1709)

6 He ranged his tropes, and preached up patience;
Backed his opinion with quotations.
'Paulo Purganti and his Wife' (1709) l. 138

7 Cured yesterday of my disease,
I died last night of my physician.
'The Remedy Worse than the Disease' (1727)

8 What is a King?—a man condemned to bear
The public burden of the nation's care.
Solomon (1718) bk. 3, l. 275

9 For, as our different ages move,
'Tis so ordained (would Fate but mend it!)
That I shall be past making love,
When she begins to comprehend it.
'To a Child of Quality of Five Years Old' (1704)

10 From ignorance our comfort flows,
The only wretched are the wise.
'To the Hon. Charles Montague' (1692) st. 9; see **Gray**
361:12

11 No, no; for my virginity,
When I lose that, says Rose, I'll die:
Behind the elms last night, cried Dick,
Rose, were you not extremely sick?
'A True Maid' (1718)

12 They never taste who always drink;
They always talk, who never think.
'Upon this Passage in Scaligerana' (1740)

V. S. Pritchett 1900–97

English writer and critic

13 The principle of procrastinated rape is said to be
the ruling one in all the great best-sellers.
The Living Novel (1946) 'Clarissa'

14 The detective novel is the art-for-art's-sake of our
yawning Philistinism, the classic example of a
specialized form of art removed from contact with
the life it pretends to build on.
in *New Statesman* 16 June 1951 'Books in General'

Procopius c.AD 499–565

Byzantine administrator and historian

15 So the church has become a spectacle of
marvellous beauty, overwhelming to those who
see it, but to those who know it by hearsay
altogether incredible. For it soars on high to match
the sky, and as if surging up from amongst the
other buildings it stands on high and looks down
on the remainder of the city.
*of the church of the Hagia Sophia; see **Justinian** 439:4*
Buildings

Adelaide Ann Procter 1825–64

English writer of popular verse

16 A lost chord.
title of poem (1858)

17 Seated one day at the organ,
I was weary and ill at ease,
And my fingers wandered idly
Over the noisy keys.
'A Lost Chord' (1858)

18 It may be that Death's bright Angel
Will speak in that chord again
It may be that only in Heaven
I shall hear that grand Amen.
'A Lost Chord' (1858)

Romano Prodi 1939–

*Italian statesman, President of the European Commission
since 1999*

19 I know very well that the stability pact is stupid,
like all decisions that are rigid.
on the rules underpinning the single currency
interview in *Le Monde* (electronic edition) 17 October 2002

Propertius c.50–after 16 BC

Roman poet

20 *Cynthia prima suis miserum me cepit ocellis,
Contactum nullis ante cupidinibus.*
Cynthia first, with her eyes, caught wretched me
Smitten before by no desires.
Elegies bk. 1, no. 1, l. 1

21 *Navita de ventis, de tauris narrat arator,
Enumerat miles vulnera, pastor oves.*
The seaman tells stories of winds, the ploughman
of bulls; the soldier details his wounds, the
shepherd his sheep.
Elegies bk. 2, no. 1, l. 43

22 *Quod si deficiant vires, audacia certe
Laus erit: in magnis et voluisse sat est.*
Even if strength fail, boldness at least will deserve
praise: in great endeavours even to have had the
will is enough.
Elegies bk. 2, no. 10, l. 5

23 *Cedite Romani scriptores, cedite Grai!
Nescioquid maius nascitur Iliade.*

Make way, you Roman writers, make way,
Greeks! Something greater than the Iliad is born.
*of **Virgil**'s Aeneid*
>Elegies bk. 2, no. 34, l. 65

Protagoras b. c.485 BC

Greek sophist

1 That man is the measure of all things.
>Plato *Theaetetus* 160d; see **Proverbs** 626:2

Pierre-Joseph Proudhon 1809–65

French social reformer

2 *La propriété c'est le vol.*
Property is theft.
>*Qu'est-ce que la propriété?* (1840) ch. 1

Marcel Proust 1871–1922

French novelist
*see also **Borrowed titles** 146:15*
Textual translations are those of C. K. Scott-Moncrieff and S.
Hudson, revised by T. Kilmartin, 1981

3 *Longtemps, je me suis couché de bonne heure.*
For a long time I used to go to bed early.
>*Du côté de chez Swann* (Swann's Way, 1913) vol. I, p. I

4 *Et tout d'un coup le souvenir m'est apparu. Ce goût*
c'était celui du petit morceau de madeleine que le
dimanche matin à Combray . . . ma tante Léonie
m'offrait après l'avoir trempé dans son infusion de thé
ou de tilleul.
And suddenly the memory revealed itself. The
taste was that of the little piece of madeleine
which on Sunday mornings at Combray . . . my
aunt Léonie used to give me, dipping it first in her
own cup of tea or tisane.
>*Du côté de chez Swann* (Swann's Way, 1913) vol. I

5 *Et il ne fut plus question de Swann chez les Verdurin.*
After which there was no more talk of Swann at
the Verdurins'.
>*Du côté de chez Swann* (Swann's Way, 1913) vol. 2

6 *Dire que j'ai gâché des années de ma vie, que j'ai voulu*
mourir, que j'ai eu mon plus grand amour, pour une
femme qui ne me plaisait pas, qui n'était pas mon
genre!
To think that I've wasted years of my life, that I've
longed to die, that I've experienced my greatest
love for a woman who didn't appeal to me, who
wasn't even my type!
>*Du côté de chez Swann* (Swann's Way, 1913) vol. 2

7 *On devient moral dès qu'on est malheureux.*
One becomes moral as soon as one is unhappy.
>*A l'ombre des jeunes filles en fleurs* (Within a Budding Grove,
>1918) vol. I

8 *Tout ce que nous connaissons de grand nous vient des*
nerveux. Ce sont eux et non pas d'autres qui ont fondé
les religions et composé les chefs-d'œuvre. Jamais le
monde ne saura tout ce qu'il leur doit et surtout ce
qu'eux ont souffert pour le lui donner.
Everything we think of as great has come to us
from neurotics. It is they and they alone who
found religions and create great works of art. The

world will never realise how much it owes to them
and what they have suffered in order to bestow
their gifts on it.
>*Le Côté de Guermantes* (Guermantes Way, 1921) vol. I

9 *Il n'y a rien comme le désir pour empêcher les choses*
qu'on dit d'avoir aucune ressemblance avec ce qu'on a
dans la pensée.
There is nothing like desire for preventing the
things one says from bearing any resemblance to
what one has in one's mind.
>*Le Côté de Guermantes* (Guermantes Way, 1921) vol. 2

10 *Un artiste n'a pas besoin d'exprimer directement sa*
pensée dans son ouvrage pour que celui-ci en reflète la
qualité; on a même pu dire que la louange la plus
haute de Dieu est dans la négation de l'athée qui
trouve la Création assez parfaite pour se passer d'un
créateur.
An artist has no need to express his thought
directly in his work for the latter to reflect its
quality; it has even been said that the highest
praise of God consists in the denial of Him by the
atheist who finds creation so perfect that it can
dispense with a creator.
>*Le Côté de Guermantes* (Guermantes Way, 1921) vol. 2

11 *J'ai horreur des couchers de soleil, c'est romantique,*
c'est opéra.
I have a horror of sunsets, they're so romantic, so
operatic.
>*Sodome et Gomorrhe* (Cities of the Plain, 1922) vol. I

12 *On ne guérit d'une souffrance qu'à condition de*
l'éprouver pleinement.
We are healed of a suffering only by experiencing
it to the full.
>*Albertine disparue* (The Sweet Cheat Gone, 1925) ch. I

13 *Une de ces dépêches dont M. de Guermantes avait*
spirituellement fixé le modèle: 'Impossible venir,
mensonge suit'.
One of those telegrams of which M. de
Guermantes had wittily fixed the formula: 'Cannot
come, lie follows'.
>*Le Temps retrouvé* (Time Regained, 1926) ch. I; see
>**Telegrams** 776:11

14 *Les vrais paradis sont les paradis qu'on a perdus.*
The true paradises are the paradises that we have
lost.
>*Le Temps retrouvé* (Time Regained, 1926) ch. 3

15 *Le bonheur seul est salutaire pour le corps, mais c'est*
le chagrin qui développe les forces de l'esprit.
For if unhappiness develops the forces of the mind,
happiness alone is salutary to the body.
>*Le Temps retrouvé* (Time Regained, 1926) ch. 3, p. 259

Proverbs

*see also **Sayings***
Dates given are generally for the first written appearance of a form
of the proverb in English; the proverb may well have been in
spoken use much earlier, and in many cases is cited as 'an old
saying' at that time. For more detailed information, see The
Concise Oxford Dictionary of Proverbs

16 Absence makes the heart grow fonder.
>mid 19th century; 1st century BC in Latin

1 Accidents will happen (in the best-regulated families).
mid 18th century; see **Dickens** 268:23

2 Actions speak louder than words.
early 17th century

3 Adventures are to the adventurous.
mid 19th century

4 Adversity makes strange bedfellows.
mid 19th century; see **Shakespeare** 718:31

5 After a storm comes a calm.
late 14th century

6 After dinner rest awhile, after supper walk a mile.
late 16th century

7 After the feast comes the reckoning.
early 17th century

8 The age of miracles is past.
late 16th century

9 All cats are grey in the dark.
mid 16th century

10 All good things must come to an end.
mid 15th century

11 All is fish that comes to the net.
early 16th century

12 All is grist that comes to the mill.
grist = *corn which is to be ground*
mid 17th century

13 All roads lead to Rome.
late 14th century; earlier in Latin

14 All's fair in love and war.
early 17th century

15 All's for the best in the best of all possible worlds.
early 20th century, from **Voltaire**; see **Voltaire** 815:8

16 All's well that ends well.
late 14th century

17 All that glitters is not gold.
early 13th century

18 All things are possible with God.
late 17th century; see **Bible** 97:28

19 All things come to those who wait.
early 16th century

20 All work and no play makes Jack a dull boy.
mid 17th century

21 Always a bridesmaid, never a bride.
early 20th century; see **Leigh** 479:19

22 Another day, another dollar.
late 19th century

23 Any port in a storm.
mid 18th century

24 Any publicity is good publicity.
early 20th century; see **Behan** 63:17

25 An ape's an ape, a varlet's a varlet, though they be clad in silk or scarlet.
mid 16th century; 2nd century AD in Greek

26 Appearances are deceptive.
mid 17th century

27 Appetite comes with eating.
mid 17th century, from **Rabelais**; see **Rabelais** 639:15

28 An apple a day keeps the doctor away.
mid 19th century

29 The apple never falls far from the tree.
mid 19th century

30 April showers bring forth May flowers.
mid 16th century

31 An army marches on its stomach.
mid 19th century, variously attributed to **Frederick** the Great and **Napoleon**; see **Napoleon** 557:1

32 Art is long and life is short.
late 14th century, from **Hippocrates**; see **Chaucer** 212:26, **Hippocrates** 389:9

33 As a tree falls, so shall it lie.
mid 16th century; see **Bible** 86:21

34 As good be an addled egg as an idle bird.
late 16th century

35 As the day lengthens, so the cold strengthens.
early 17th century

36 As the twig is bent, so is the tree inclined.
early 18th century, from **Pope**; see **Pope** 603:19

37 As you bake so shall you brew.
late 16th century

38 As you brew, so shall you bake.
late 16th century

39 As you make your bed, so you must lie upon it.
late 16th century, late 15th century in French

40 As you sow, so you reap.
late 15th century; see **Bible** 109:2

41 Ask a silly question and you get a silly answer.
early 14th century

42 Ask no questions and hear no lies.
late 18th century

43 Attack is the best form of defence.
late 18th century; see **Sayings** 669:3

44 A bad excuse is better than none.
mid 16th century

45 Bad money drives out good.
known as Gresham's Law, after Sir Thomas Gresham (c.1519–79), who formulated the principle, though not the proverb, in 1558
early 20th century

46 Bad news travels fast.
late 16th century

47 A bad penny always turns up.
mid 18th century

48 Bad things come in threes.
late 19th century

49 A bad workman blames his tools.
early 17th century; late 13th century in French

50 A barking dog never bites.
mid 16th century; 13th century in French

1 Barnaby bright, Barnaby bright, the longest day and the shortest night.
St Barnabas' Day, 11 June, in Old Style reckoned the longest day of the year
mid 17th century

2 Bear and forbear.
late 16th century

3 Beauty draws with a single hair.
late 16th century; see **Howell** 406:2, **Pope** 606:7

4 Beauty is in the eye of the beholder.
mid 18th century; 3rd century BC in Greek

5 Beauty is only skin deep.
early 17th century

6 Beggars can't be choosers.
mid 16th century

7 Be just before you're generous.
mid 18th century

8 Believe nothing of what you hear, and only half of what you see.
mid 19th century

9 A bellowing cow soon forgets her calf.
late 19th century

10 The best doctors are Dr Diet, Dr Quiet, and Dr Merryman.
mid 16th century

11 The best is the enemy of the good.
mid 19th century; see **Voltaire** 815:14

12 The best of friends must part.
early 17th century

13 The best of men are but men at best.
late 17th century

14 The best things come in small packages.
late 19th century

15 The best things in life are free.
early 20th century, from **De Sylva**; see **De Sylva** 265:16

16 The best-laid schemes of mice and men gang aft agley.
late 18th century, from **Burns**; see **Burns** 172:22

17 Be the day weary or be the day long, at last it ringeth to evensong.
early 16th century

18 Better a dinner of herbs than a stalled ox where hate is.
mid 16th century; see **Bible** 84:24

19 Better a good cow than a cow of a good kind.
early 20th century

20 Better are small fish than an empty dish.
late 17th century

21 Better be an old man's darling than a young man's slave.
mid 16th century

22 Better be envied than pitied.
mid 16th century; 5th century BC in Greek

23 Better be out of the world than out of the fashion.
mid 17th century

24 Better be safe than sorry.
mid 19th century

25 Better late than never.
early 14th century; 1st century BC in Greek

26 Better one house spoiled than two.
of two wicked or foolish people joined in marriage
late 16th century

27 The better the day, the better the deed.
early 17th century

28 Better the devil you know than the devil you don't know.
mid 19th century

29 Better to light one candle than to curse the darkness.
motto of the American Christopher Society, founded 1945
mid 20th century; see **Benenson** 66:10, **Stevenson** 758:18

30 Better to live one day as a tiger than a thousand years as a sheep.
early 19th century; see **Tipu** 794:18

31 Better to marry than to burn.
early 20th century; see **Bible** 107:13

32 Better to wear out than to rust out.
early 18th century; see **Cumberland** 253:4, **Shakespeare** 691:28

33 Better wed over the mixen than over the moor.
mixen = *midden; better to marry a neighbour than a stranger*
early 17th century

34 Between two stools one falls to the ground.
late 14th century

35 Beware of an oak, it draws the stroke; avoid an ash, it counts the flash; creep under the thorn, it can save you from harm.
on where to shelter from lightning
late 19th century

36 Be what you would seem to be.
late 14th century

37 Big fish eat little fish.
early 13th century

38 Big fleas have little fleas upon their backs to bite them, and little fleas have lesser fleas, and so *ad infinitum*.
early 18th century, from **Swift**; see **Swift** 767:11

39 The bigger they are, the harder they fall.
early 20th century; see **Fitzsimmons** 324:13

40 A bird in the hand is worth two in the bush.
mid 15th century; 13th century in Latin

41 A bird never flew on one wing.
early 18th century

42 Birds in their little nests agree.
early 18th century, from **Watts**; see **Watts** 823:11

43 Birds of a feather flock together.
mid 16th century

44 A bleating sheep loses a bite.
late 16th century

1 Blessed are the dead that the rain rains on.
early 17th century

2 Blessed is he who expects nothing, for he shall never be disappointed.
early 18th century

3 Blessings brighten as they take their flight.
mid 18th century

4 A blind man's wife needs no paint.
mid 17th century

5 Blood is thicker than water.
early 19th century

6 The blood of the martyrs is the seed of the Church.
mid 16th century; see **Tertullian** 786:1

7 Blood will have blood.
mid 15th century; see **Shakespeare** 706:8

8 Blood will tell.
mid 19th century

9 Blue are the hills that are far away.
late 19th century, northern in origin

10 Boys will be boys.
occasionally 'girls will be girls'
early 17th century

11 Brag is a good dog, but Holdfast is better.
early 18th century

12 Brave men lived before Agamemnon.
early 19th century; see **Horace** 402:16

13 The bread never falls but on its buttered side.
mid 19th century

14 Brevity is the soul of wit.
early 17th century, from **Shakespeare**; see **Shakespeare** 685:15

15 A bully is always a coward.
early 19th century

16 A burnt child dreads the fire.
mid 13th century

17 The busiest men have the most leisure.
late 19th century

18 Business before pleasure.
mid 19th century

19 The buyer has need of a hundred eyes, the seller of but one.
mid 17th century

20 Buy in the cheapest market and sell in the dearest.
late 16th century

21 Caesar's wife must be above suspicion.
late 18th century; see **Caesar** 185:3

22 Call no man happy till he dies.
mid 16th century; see **Solon** 745:13

23 Candlemas day, put beans in the clay; put candles and candlesticks away.
late 17th century

24 Care killed the cat.
late 16th century; see **Shakespeare** 712:32

25 A carpenter is known by his chips.
early 16th century

26 Catching's before hanging.
early 19th century

27 A cat in gloves catches no mice.
late 16th century; 14th century in French

28 A cat may look at a king.
mid 16th century

29 The cat would eat fish, but would not wet her feet.
early 13th century

30 A chain is no stronger than its weakest link.
mid 19th century

31 A change is as good as a rest.
late 19th century

32 Change the name and not the letter, change for the worse and not the better.
meaning that it is unlucky for a woman to marry a man whose surname begins with the same letter as her own
mid 19th century

33 Charity begins at home.
late 14th century

34 Charity covers a multitude of sins.
early 17th century; see **Bible** 112:14

35 Cheats never prosper.
early 19th century

36 A cherry year, a merry year; a plum year, a dumb year.
late 17th century

37 The child is the father of the man.
early 19th century, from **Wordsworth**; see **Wordsworth** 847:16

38 Children and fools tell the truth.
mid 16th century; late 14th century in French

39 Children are certain cares, but uncertain comforts.
mid 17th century

40 Children should be seen and not heard.
originally applied specifically to (young) women
early 15th century

41 The church is an anvil which has worn out many hammers.
early 20th century; see **Maclaren** 503:5

42 Circumstances alter cases.
late 17th century

43 Civility costs nothing.
early 18th century; late 15th century in French

44 A civil question deserves a civil answer.
mid 19th century

45 A clean conscience is a good pillow.
early 18th century

46 Cleanliness is next to godliness.
late 18th century; see **Wesley** 829:13

47 Clergymen's sons always turn out badly.
late 19th century

48 Clothes make the man.
early 15th century

49 The cobbler to his last and the gunner to his linstock.
mid 18th century

1 Cold hands, warm heart.
early 20th century

2 Come live with me and you'll know me.
early 20th century

3 Coming events cast their shadow before.
early 19th century

4 Common fame is seldom to blame.
mid 17th century

5 The company makes the feast.
mid 17th century

6 Comparisons are odious.
mid 15th century; see **Shakespeare** 712:25

7 Confess and be hanged.
late 16th century

8 Confession is good for the soul.
mid 17th century

9 Conscience makes cowards of us all.
early 17th century, from **Shakespeare**; see **Shakespeare** 686:12

10 Constant dropping wears away a stone.
mid 13th century, earlier in Greek; see **Latimer** 470:2

11 Corporations have neither bodies to be punished nor souls to be damned.
mid 17th century; see **Coke** 230:20, **Thurlow** 794:4

12 Councils of war never fight.
mid 19th century

13 The course of true love never did run smooth.
late 16th century, from **Shakespeare**; see **Shakespeare** 710:17

14 Cowards may die many times before their death.
late 16th century, from **Shakespeare**; see **Shakespeare** 697:4

15 The cowl does not make the monk.
late 14th century

16 A creaking door hangs longest.
late 18th century

17 Crime doesn't pay.
later associated with the US radio crime series The Shadow *and the cartoon detective Dick Tracy*
late 19th century

18 Crosses are ladders that lead to heaven.
early 17th century

19 Curiosity killed the cat.
early 20th century

20 Curses, like chickens, come home to roost.
late 14th century

21 The customer is always right.
early 20th century; see **Ritz** 649:13

22 Cut your coat according to your cloth.
mid 16th century

23 The darkest hour is just before dawn.
mid 17th century

24 Dead men don't bite.
mid 16th century; 1st century AD in Greek; see **Gray** 617:24

25 Dead men tell no tales.
mid 17th century

26 A deaf husband and a blind wife are always a happy couple.
late 16th century

27 Death is the great leveller.
early 18th century

28 Death pays all debts.
early 17th century; see **Shakespeare** 718:35

29 Delays are dangerous.
late 16th century

30 Desperate diseases must have desperate remedies.
mid 16th century; see **Fawkes** 316:8, **Hippocrates** 389:10, **Shakespeare** 687:34

31 The devil can quote Scripture for his own ends.
late 16th century

32 The devil finds work for idle hands to do.
early 18th century; see **Watts** 823:7

33 The devil is not so black as he is painted.
mid 16th century

34 The devil looks after his own.
early 18th century

35 The devil makes his Christmas pies of lawyers' tongues and clerks' fingers.
late 16th century

36 The devil's children have the devil's luck.
late 17th century

37 Devil take the hindmost.
early 17th century

38 The devil was sick, the Devil a saint would be; the Devil was well, the devil a saint was he.
'saint' is sometimes replaced by 'monk'
early 17th century, variant of a medieval Latin proverb

39 Diamond cuts diamond.
early 17th century

40 The difficult is done at once, the impossible takes a little longer.
late 19th century; see **Military sayings** 526:6

41 Diligence is the mother of good luck.
late 16th century

42 Dirty water will quench fire.
mid 16th century

43 Discretion is the better part of valour.
late 16th century, from **Shakespeare**; see **Shakespeare** 691:16

44 Distance lends enchantment to the view.
late 18th century, from **Campbell**; see **Campbell** 187:15

45 Divide and rule.
early 17th century

46 Do as I say, not as I do.
mid 16th century

47 Do as you would be done by.
late 16th century

48 Dog does not eat dog.
mid 16th century

49 The dog returns to its vomit.
late 14th century; see **Bible** 85:9

1 Dogs bark, but the caravan goes on.
late 19th century

2 A dog that will fetch a bone will carry a bone.
early 19th century

3 Do not meet troubles half-way.
late 19th century

4 Do not spoil the ship for a ha'porth of tar.
ship = *a dialectal pronunciation of sheep, and the original literal sense was 'do not allow sheep to die for the lack of a trifling amount of tar', tar being used to protect sores and wounds on sheep from flies*
early 17th century

5 Do not throw pearls to swine.
mid 14th century; see **Bible** 95:14

6 Don't care was made to care.
mid 20th century, from a traditional children's rhyme

7 Don't change horses in mid stream.
mid 19th century; see **Lincoln** 485:10

8 Don't count your chickens before they are hatched.
late 16th century

9 Don't cross the bridge till you come to it.
mid 19th century

10 Don't cry before you're hurt.
mid 16th century; early 14th century in French

11 Don't cut off your nose to spite your face.
mid 16th century; mid 14th century in French

12 Don't go near the water until you learn how to swim.
mid 19th century

13 Don't halloo till you are out of the wood.
late 18th century

14 Don't put all your eggs in one basket.
mid 17th century

15 Don't put the cart before the horse.
early 16th century

16 Don't sell the skin till you have caught the bear.
late 16th century

17 Don't teach your grandmother to suck eggs.
early 18th century

18 Don't throw out your dirty water until you get in fresh.
late 15th century

19 Don't throw the baby out with the bathwater.
mid 19th century; early 17th century in German

20 A door must be either shut or open.
mid 18th century

21 Do right and fear no man.
mid 15th century

22 Do unto others as you would they should do unto you.
late 15th century

23 Dream of a funeral and you hear of a marriage.
mid 17th century

24 Dreams go by contraries.
early 15th century

25 A dripping June sets all in tune.
mid 18th century

26 Drive gently over the stones.
early 18th century

27 A drowning man will clutch at a straw.
mid 16th century

28 Eagles don't catch flies.
mid 16th century

29 The early bird catches the worm.
mid 17th century; see **Sayings** 669:32

30 The early man never borrows from the late man.
mid 17th century

31 Early to bed and early to rise, makes a man healthy, wealthy, and wise.
late 15th century

32 East is east, and west is west.
late 19th century, from **Kipling**; see **Kipling** 453:15

33 East, west, home's best.
mid 19th century

34 Easy come, easy go.
mid 17th century

35 Easy does it.
mid 19th century

36 Eat, drink and be merry, for tomorrow we die.
late 19th century; a conflation of two biblical sayings: see **Bible** 86:12, **Bible** 88:26

37 Eat to live, not live to eat.
late 14th century; see **Socrates** 744:25

38 Empty sacks will never stand upright.
mid 17th century

39 Empty vessels make the most sound.
early 15th century

40 The end crowns the work.
early 16th century

41 The end justifies the means.
late 16th century

42 England is the paradise of women, the hell of horses, and the purgatory of servants.
late 16th century; a similar proverb in French is found applied to Paris in the mid 16th century

43 England's difficulty is Ireland's opportunity.
mid 19th century

44 The English are a nation of shopkeepers.
early 19th century; see **Napoleon** 557:4

45 An Englishman's home is his castle.
late 16th century; see **Coke** 230:18

46 An Englishman's word is his bond.
early 16th century

47 Enough is as good as a feast.
late 14th century

48 Enough is enough.
mid 16th century

49 Even a worm will turn.
mid 16th century

1 Everybody loves a lord.
late 19th century

2 Everybody's business is nobody's business.
early 17th century

3 Every bullet has its billet.
late 16th century; see **William III** 838:3

4 Every cloud has a silver lining.
mid 19th century; see **Coward** 245:8, **Ford** 329:4, **Weston** 830:20

5 Every cock will crow upon his own dunghill.
mid 13th century; 1st century AD in Latin

6 Every dog has his day.
mid 16th century

7 Every dog is allowed one bite.
based on the common law rule (dating at least from the 17th century) by which the keeper of a domestic animal was not liable for harm done by it unless he knew of its vicious propensities
early 20th century

8 Every elm has its man.
early 20th century

9 Every herring must hang by its own gill.
early 17th century

10 Every Jack has his Jill.
early 17th century

11 Every land has its own law.
early 17th century

12 Every little helps.
early 17th century

13 Every man for himself.
late 14th century

14 Every man for himself and God for us all.
mid 16th century

15 Every man for himself, and the Devil take the hindmost.
early 16th century

16 Every man has his price.
mid 18th century; see **Walpole** 820:6

17 Every man is the architect of his own fortune.
early 16th century; see **Claudius** 225:12

18 Every man to his taste.
late 16th century

19 Every man to his trade.
late 16th century

20 Everyone speaks well of the bridge which carries him over.
late 17th century

21 Everyone stretches his legs according to the length of his coverlet.
early 14th century

22 Every picture tells a story.
early 20th century; see **Advertising slogans** 7:22

23 Everything has an end.
late 14th century

24 Every tub must stand on its own bottom.
mid 16th century

25 Evil communications corrupt good manners.
early 15th century; see **Bible** 108:7

26 Evil doers are evil dreaders.
late 16th century

27 Example is better than precept.
early 15th century

28 The exception proves the rule.
mid 17th century

29 Experience is the best teacher.
late 16th century; see **Tacitus** 770:14

30 Experience is the father of wisdom.
mid 16th century

31 Experience keeps a dear school.
mid 18th century

32 Extremes meet.
mid 18th century; mid 17th century in French

33 The eye of a master does more work than both his hands.
mid 18th century

34 The eyes are the window of the soul.
mid 16th century

35 Fact is stranger than fiction.
mid 19th century

36 Facts are stubborn things.
early 18th century

37 Faint heart never won fair lady.
mid 16th century

38 Fair and softly goes far in a day.
mid 14th century

39 A fair exchange is no robbery.
mid 16th century

40 Fair play's a jewel.
early 19th century

41 Faith will move mountains.
late 19th century; see **Bible** 97:18

42 Familiarity breeds contempt.
late 14th century; 5th century AD in Latin

43 Far-fetched and dear-bought is good for ladies.
mid 14th century

44 A fault confessed is half redressed.
mid 16th century

45 Fear the Greeks bearing gifts.
late 19th century, from **Virgil**; see **Virgil** 811:11

46 February fill dyke, be it black or be it white.
mid 16th century

47 Feed a cold and starve a fever.
probably intended as two separate admonitions, but sometimes interpreted to mean that if you feed a cold you will have to starve a fever later
mid 19th century

48 The female of the species is more deadly than the male.
early 20th century, from **Kipling**; see **Kipling** 454:4

49 Fields have eyes and woods have ears.
early 13th century

1 Fight fire with fire.
mid 19th century

2 Finders keepers (losers weepers).
early 19th century

3 Findings keepings.
mid 19th century

4 Fine feathers make fine birds.
late 16th century

5 Fine words butter no parsnips.
mid 17th century

6 Fingers were made before forks.
the form 'God made hands before knives' is found in the mid 16th century
mid 18th century

7 Fire is a good servant but a bad master.
early 17th century

8 First catch your hare.
early 19th century, early 14th century in Latin; see **Glasse** 351:14

9 First come, first served.
late 14th century, late 13th century in French

10 The first duty of a soldier is obedience.
mid 19th century

11 First impressions are the most lasting.
early 18th century

12 First things first.
late 19th century

13 First thoughts are best.
early 20th century

14 The fish always stinks from the head downwards.
late 16th century

15 Fish and guests stink after three days.
late 16th century

16 A fool and his money are soon parted.
late 16th century

17 A fool at forty is a fool indeed.
early 18th century, from **Young**; see **Young** 857:4

18 A fool may give a wise man counsel.
mid 14th century

19 Fools and bairns should never see half-done work.
early 18th century

20 Fools ask questions that wise men cannot answer.
mid 17th century

21 Fools build houses and wise men live in them.
late 17th century

22 Fools for luck.
mid 19th century

23 Fools rush in where angels fear to tread.
from **Pope**, early 18th century; see **Pope** 604:17

24 For want of a nail the shoe was lost; for want of a shoe the horse was lost; and for want of a horse the man was lost.
early 17th century; late 15th century in French

25 Forewarned is forearmed.
early 16th century

26 Fortune favours fools.
mid 16th century

27 Fortune favours the brave.
late 14th century; see **Terence** 785:7, **Virgil** 813:8

28 Four eyes see more than two.
late 16th century

29 A friend in need is a friend indeed.
mid 11th century; 5th century BC in Greek

30 From clogs to clogs is only three generations.
late 19th century

31 From shirtsleeves to shirtsleeves in three generations.
early 20th century; often attributed to Andrew **Carnegie** but not found in his writings

32 From the sublime to the ridiculous is only one step.
late 19th century; see **Napoleon** 556:15, **Paine** 582:5

33 From the sweetest wine, the tartest vinegar.
late 16th century

34 Full cup, steady hand.
early 11th century

35 Genius is an infinite capacity for taking pains.
late 19th century; see **Carlyle** 192:4

36 Give a dog a bad name and hang him.
early 18th century

37 Give a man rope enough and he will hang himself.
mid 17th century

38 Give a thing, and take a thing, to wear the devil's gold ring.
late 16th century

39 Give and take is fair play.
late 18th century

40 Give credit where credit is due.
late 18th century

41 Give the Devil his due.
late 16th century

42 Go abroad and you'll hear news of home.
late 17th century

43 Go further and fare worse.
mid 16th century

44 God helps them that help themselves.
mid 16th century; early 15th century in French

45 God made the country and man made the town.
mid 17th century; see **Cowley** 245:19, **Cowper** 247:26

46 God makes the back to the burden.
early 19th century

47 God never sends mouths but He sends meat.
late 14th century

48 God's in his heaven; all's right with the world.
from early 16th century in the form 'God is where he was'; now largely replaced by **Browning**; see **Browning** 160:22

49 God sends meat, but the Devil sends cooks.
mid 16th century

50 The gods send nuts to those who have no teeth.
early 20th century

1 God tempers the wind to the shorn lamb.
mid 17th century

2 Gold may be bought too dear.
mid 16th century

3 A golden key can open any door.
late 16th century

4 Good Americans when they die go to Paris.
mid 19th century, from Thomas Gold **Appleton**; see
Appleton 23:14

5 A good beginning makes a good ending.
early 14th century

6 The good die young.
late 17th century

7 Good fences make good neighbours.
mid 17th century

8 A good horse cannot be of a bad colour.
early 17th century

9 The good is the enemy of the best.
early 20th century; see **Voltaire** 815:14

10 A good Jack makes a good Jill.
early 17th century

11 Good men are scarce.
early 17th century

12 Good seed makes a good crop.
late 16th century

13 Good wine needs no bush.
early 15th century

14 The grass is always greener on the other side of
the fence.
mid 20th century

15 A great book is a great evil.
early 17th century; see **Callimachus** 186:3

16 The greater the sinner, the greater the saint.
late 18th century

17 The greater the truth, the greater the libel.
late 18th century

18 Great minds think alike.
early 17th century

19 Great oaks from little acorns grow.
late 14th century

20 A green Yule makes a fat churchyard.
meaning a mild winter
mid 17th century

21 The grey mare is the better horse.
mid 16th century

22 A guilty conscience needs no accuser.
late 14th century; earlier in Latin

23 Half a loaf is better than no bread.
mid 16th century

24 The half is better than the whole.
mid 16th century

25 Half the truth is often a whole lie.
mid 18th century

26 Handsome is as handsome does.
late 16th century; see **Proverbs** 629:37

27 The hand that rocks the cradle rules the world.
mid 19th century, from **Wallace**; see **Wallace** 818:3

28 Hang a thief when he's young, and he'll no' steal
when he's old.
early 19th century

29 Hanging and wiving go by destiny.
mid 16th century

30 Happy is the bride that the sun shines on.
mid 17th century

31 Happy is the country which has no history.
early 19th century; see **Montesquieu** 545:11

32 Happy's the wooing that is not long a-doing.
late 16th century

33 Hard cases make bad law.
mid 19th century

34 Hard words break no bones.
late 17th century

35 Haste is from the Devil.
mid 17th century

36 Haste makes waste.
late 14th century

37 Hasty climbers have sudden falls.
mid 15th century

38 Hawks will not pick out hawks' eyes.
late 16th century

39 He gives twice who gives quickly.
mid 16th century; see **Publilius Syrus** 636:14

40 He is a good dog who goes to church.
early 19th century

41 He laughs best who laughs last.
early 17th century

42 He lives long who lives well.
mid 16th century

43 He that cannot obey cannot command.
early 16th century

44 He that cannot pay, let him pray.
early 17th century

45 He that complies against his will is of his own
opinion still.
late 17th century, from Samuel **Butler**; see **Butler** 176:17

46 He that drinks beer, thinks beer.
early 19th century

47 He that follows freits, freits will follow him.
freits = *omens*
early 18th century

48 He that goes a-borrowing, goes a-sorrowing.
late 15th century

49 He that has an ill name is half hanged.
early 15th century

50 He that lives in hope dances to an ill tune.
late 16th century

51 He that touches pitch shall be defiled.
early 14th century; see **Bible** 93:13

52 He that will not when he may, when he will he
shall have nay.
early 11th century

1 He that will thrive must first ask his wife.
early 16th century

2 He that will to Cupar maun to Cupar.
early 18th century

3 He that would eat the fruit must climb the tree.
early 18th century

4 He that would go to sea for pleasure would go to hell for a pastime.
late 19th century

5 He travels fastest who travels alone.
late 19th century; see **Kipling** 454:20

6 He who can does, he who cannot, teaches.
early 20th century, from **Shaw**; see **Shaw** 726:20

7 He who excuses, accuses himself.
early 17th century

8 He who fights and runs away, may live to fight another day.
mid 16th century

9 He who hesitates is lost.
early 18th century; see **Addison** 4:11

10 He who is absent is always in the wrong.
mid 17th century

11 He who laughs last, laughs longest.
early 20th century

12 He who lives by the sword dies by the sword.
mid 17th century; see **Bible** 99:8

13 He who pays the piper calls the tune.
late 19th century

14 He who rides a tiger is afraid to dismount.
late 19th century

15 He who sups with the Devil should have a long spoon.
late 14th century

16 He who wills the end, wills the means.
late 17th century

17 Hear all, see all, say nowt, tak'all, keep all, gie nowt, and if tha ever does owt for nowt do it for thysen.
early 15th century

18 Heaven protects children, sailors, and drunken men.
mid 19th century

19 Hell hath no fury like a woman scorned.
late 17th century, from **Congreve**; see **Congreve** 238:30

20 Help you to salt, help you to sorrow.
mid 17th century

21 The higher the monkey climbs the more he shows his tail.
late 14th century

22 History repeats itself.
mid 19th century

23 Home is home, as the Devil said when he found himself in the Court of Session.
early 19th century

24 Home is home though it's never so homely.
mid 16th century

25 Home is where the heart is.
late 19th century

26 Homer sometimes nods.
late 14th century, from **Horace**; see **Horace** 398:15

27 Honesty is the best policy.
early 17th century

28 Honey catches more flies than vinegar.
mid 17th century

29 Hope deferred makes the heart sick.
early 16th century; see **Bible** 84:15

30 Hope for the best and prepare for the worst.
mid 16th century

31 Hope is a good breakfast but a bad supper.
mid 17th century; see **Bacon** 46:21

32 Hope springs eternal.
early 18th century, from **Pope**; see **Pope** 604:22

33 Horses for courses.
late 19th century

34 A house divided cannot stand.
mid 11th century; see **Bible** 99:17

35 Hunger drives the wolf out of the wood.
late 15th century

36 Hunger is the best sauce.
early 16th century

37 A hungry man is an angry man.
mid 17th century

38 Hurry no man's cattle.
early 19th century

39 The husband is always the last to know.
early 17th century

40 An idle brain is the devil's workshop.
early 17th century

41 Idle people have the least leisure.
late 17th century

42 Idleness is the root of all evil.
early 15th century; see **Proverbs** 626:32

43 If anything can go wrong, it will.
commonly known as Murphy's Law
mid 20th century; said to have been invented by George Nichols in 1949, based on a remark by his colleague Captain E. Murphy

44 If a thing's worth doing, it's worth doing well.
mid 18th century

45 If at first you don't succeed, try, try, try again.
mid 19th century

46 If Candlemas day be sunny and bright, winter will have another flight; if Candlemas day be cloudy with rain, winter is gone and won't come again.
Candlemas Day = *2 February*
late 17th century

47 If every man would sweep his own door-step the city would soon be clean.
early 17th century

48 If ifs and ands were pots and pans, there'd be no work for tinkers' hands.
mid 19th century

1 If in February there be no rain, 'tis neither good for hay nor grain.
early 18th century

2 If it were not for hope, the heart would break.
mid 13th century

3 If Saint Paul's day be fair and clear, it will betide a happy year.
late 16th century

4 If the cap fits, wear it.
early 18th century

5 If the mountain will not come to Mahomet, Mahomet must go to the mountain.
early 17th century

6 If the shoe fits, wear it.
late 18th century

7 If the sky falls we shall catch larks.
mid 15th century

8 If there were no receivers, there would be no thieves.
late 14th century

9 If two ride on a horse, one must ride behind.
late 16th century

10 If wishes were horses, beggars would ride.
early 17th century

11 If you can't beat them, join them.
beat *is usually replaced by* lick *in the US*
mid 20th century saying

12 If you can't be good, be careful.
early 20th century; the Latin form *Si non caste tamen caute* is found from the mid 11th century

13 If you can't ride two horses at once, you shouldn't be in the circus.
early 20th century, from **Maxton**; see **Maxton** 519:3

14 If you don't like the heat, get out of the kitchen.
mid 20th century; see **Truman** 801:8

15 If you don't make mistakes you don't make anything.
late 19th century; see **Phelps** 594:8

16 If you don't speculate, you can't accumulate.
mid 20th century

17 If you don't work you shan't eat.
mid 16th century; see **Bible** 110:20

18 If you gently touch a nettle it'll sting you for your pains; grasp it like a lad of mettle, an' as soft as silk remains.
late 16th century; see **Hill** 388:6

19 If you lie down with dogs, you will get up with fleas.
late 16th century

20 If you pay peanuts, you get monkeys.
mid 20th century

21 If you play with fire you get burnt.
late 19th century

22 If you're born to be hanged then you'll never be drowned.
late 16th century

23 If you run after two hares you will catch neither.
early 16th century

24 If you want a thing done well, do it yourself.
mid 16th century

25 If you want peace, you must prepare for war.
mid 16th century; see **Vegetius** 808:9

26 If you want to live and thrive, let the spider run alive.
mid 19th century

27 If you would be happy for a week take a wife; if you would be happy for a month kill a pig; but if you would be happy all your life plant a garden.
mid 17th century; the saying exists in a variety of forms, but marriage is nearly always given as one of the ephemeral forms of happiness

28 If you would be well served, serve yourself.
mid 17th century

29 Ignorance of the law is no excuse for breaking it.
early 15th century; see **Selden** 676:4

30 Ill gotten goods never thrive.
early 16th century

31 Ill weeds grow apace.
late 15th century

32 Imitation is the sincerest form of flattery.
early 19th century

33 In for a penny, in for a pound.
late 17th century

34 In the country of the blind the one eyed man is king.
early 16th century; see **Erasmus** 308:12

35 In vain the net is spread in the sight of the bird.
late 14th century; see **Bible** 83:32

36 It is a long lane that has no turning.
early 17th century

37 It is a poor dog that's not worth whistling for.
mid 16th century

38 It is a poor heart that never rejoices.
mid 19th century

39 It is as cheap sitting as standing.
mid 17th century

40 It is a wise child that knows its own father.
late 16th century

41 It is best to be off with the old love before you are on with the new.
early 19th century

42 It is best to be on the safe side.
late 17th century

43 It is better to be born lucky than rich.
mid 17th century

44 It is better to give than to receive.
late 14th century; see **Bible** 105:24

45 It is better to travel hopefully than to arrive.
late 19th century, from **Stevenson**; see **Stevenson** 759:20

46 It is easier to pull down than to build up.
late 16th century

1 It is easier to raise the Devil than to lay him.
mid 17th century

2 It is easy to be wise after the event.
early 17th century

3 It is easy to find a stick to beat a dog.
mid 16th century

4 It is good to make a bridge of gold to a flying enemy.
late 16th century

5 It is idle to swallow the cow and choke on the tail.
mid 17th century

6 It is ill sitting at Rome and striving with the Pope.
early 17th century

7 It is merry in hall when beards wag all.
early 14th century

8 It is never too late to learn.
late 17th century

9 It is never too late to mend.
late 16th century

10 It is no use crying over spilt milk.
mid 17th century

11 It is not spring until you can plant your foot upon twelve daisies.
mid 19th century

12 It is not work that kills, but worry.
late 19th century

13 It is the first step that is difficult.
late 16th century; see **Du Deffand** 291:4

14 It is the last straw that breaks the camel's back.
mid 17th century

15 It is the pace that kills.
mid 19th century

16 It never rains but it pours.
early 18th century

17 It's an ill bird that fouls its own nest.
mid 13th century

18 It's an ill wind that blows nobody any good.
mid 16th century

19 It's a sin to steal a pin.
late 19th century

20 It's dogged as does it.
mid 19th century; see **Trollope** 799:19

21 It's ill speaking between a full man and a fasting.
mid 17th century

22 It's ill waiting for dead men's shoes.
early 16th century

23 It's too late to shut the stable-door after the horse has bolted.
mid 14th century

24 It takes all sorts to make a world.
early 17th century

25 It takes three generations to make a gentleman.
early 19th century

26 It takes two to make a bargain.
late 16th century

27 It takes two to make a quarrel.
early 18th century

28 It takes two to tango.
mid 20th century, from **Hoffman**; see **Hoffman** 391:12

29 Jack is as good as his master.
early 18th century

30 Jack of all trades and master of none.
early 18th century

31 Jam tomorrow and jam yesterday, but never jam today.
late 19th century, from **Carroll**; see **Carroll** 195:10

32 Jouk and let the jaw go by.
jouk = *stoop*, jaw = *a rush of water*
early 18th century

33 Jove but laughs at lovers' perjury.
mid 16th century; see **Dryden** 289:5, **Tibullus** 794:11

34 Judge not, that ye be not judged.
late 15th century; see **Bible** 95:12

35 Keep a thing seven years and you'll always find a use for it.
early 17th century

36 Keep no more cats than will catch mice.
late 17th century

37 Keep your own fish-guts for your own sea-maws.
early 18th century

38 Keep your shop and your shop will keep you.
early 17th century

39 Killing no murder.
mid 17th century, from **Sexby**; see **Sexby** 677:12

40 The king can do no wrong.
mid 17th century

41 A king's chaff is worth more than other men's corn.
early 17th century

42 Kings have long arms.
mid 16th century

43 Kissing goes by favour.
early 17th century

44 Know thyself.
inscribed on the temple of Apollo at Delphi, in the form γνῶθι σεαυτόν.; *Plato, in* Protagoras 343 b, *ascribes the saying to the Seven Wise Men*
late 14th century; see **Goethe** 353:19

45 Knowledge is power.
late 16th century; see **Bacon** 46:10

46 The labourer is worthy of his hire.
late 14th century; see **Bible** 100:19

47 The last drop makes the cup run over.
mid 17th century

48 Laugh and the world laughs with you, weep and you weep alone.
late 19th century, from **Wilcox**; see **Wilcox** 835:8

49 Lay-overs for meddlers.
late 18th century

50 Learning is better than house and land.
late 18th century

1 Least said, soonest mended.
mid 15th century

2 Lend your money and lose your friend.
late 15th century

3 Length begets loathing.
mid 18th century

4 The leopard does not change his spots.
mid 16th century; see **Bible** 91:1

5 Less is more.
mid 19th century, often associated with **Mies van der Rohe**

6 Let sleeping dogs lie.
late 14th century

7 Let the buyer beware.
early 16th century

8 Let the cobbler stick to his last
mid 16th century

9 Let the dead bury the dead.
early 19th century; see **Bible** 96:2

10 Let them laugh that win.
mid 16th century

11 Let well alone.
late 16th century

12 A liar ought to have a good memory.
mid 16th century; 1st century AD in Latin

13 Life begins at forty.
early 20th century, from **Pitkin**; see **Pitkin** 595:21

14 Life isn't all beer and skittles.
mid 19th century

15 Light come, light go.
late 14th century

16 Lightning never strikes the same place twice.
mid 19th century

17 Like breeds like.
mid 16th century

18 Like father, like son.
mid 14th century

19 Like master, like man.
early 16th century

20 Like mother, like daughter.
early 14th century; see **Bible** 91:12

21 Like people, like priest.
late 16th century; see **Bible** 91:27

22 Like will to like.
early 15th century

23 Listeners never hear any good of themselves.
mid 17th century

24 Little birds that can sing and won't sing must be made to sing.
late 17th century

25 Little fish are sweet.
early 19th century

26 A little knowledge is a dangerous thing.
from **Pope**, early 18th century; see **Pope** 604:2

27 Little leaks sink the ship.
early 17th century

28 Little pitchers have large ears.
mid 16th century

29 A little pot is soon hot.
mid 16th century

30 Little strokes fell great oaks.
early 15th century

31 Little thieves are hanged, but great ones escape.
mid 17th century

32 Little things please little minds.
late 16th century

33 Live and learn.
early 17th century

34 Live and let live.
early 17th century

35 A live dog is better than a dead lion.
late 14th century; see **Bible** 86:13

36 Long and lazy, little and loud; fat and fulsome, pretty and proud.
late 16th century

37 The longest way round is the shortest way home.
mid 17th century

38 Long foretold, long last; short notice, soon past.
mid 19th century

39 Look before you leap.
mid 14th century

40 Lookers-on see most of the game.
early 16th century

41 Love and a cough cannot be hid.
early 16th century

42 Love begets love.
mid 17th century

43 Love is blind.
late 14th century; see **Anonymous** 20:15

44 Love laughs at locksmiths.
early 19th century; see **Colman** 236:2

45 Love makes the world go round.
mid 19th century, from a traditional French song

46 Love me little, love me long.
early 16th century

47 Love me, love my dog.
early 16th century

48 Love will find a way.
early 17th century

49 Lucky at cards, unlucky in love.
mid 18th century

50 Make haste slowly.
late 16th century; see **Augustus** 37:21

51 Make hay while the sun shines.
mid 16th century

52 Man cannot live by bread alone.
late 19th century; see **Bible** 94:15

53 A man is as old as he feels, and a woman as old as she looks.
late 19th century

1 A man is known by the company he keeps.
mid 16th century

2 Man is the measure of all things.
mid 16th century; see **Protagoras** 613:1

3 Manners maketh man.
mid 14th century; motto of William of Wykeham (1324–1404)

4 Man proposes, God disposes.
mid 15th century; see **Thomas à Kempis** 788:6

5 Man's extremity is God's opportunity.
early 17th century

6 The man who is born in a stable is not a horse.
early 19th century

7 A man who is his own lawyer has a fool for his client.
early 19th century

8 Many a little makes a mickle.
mid 13th century

9 Many a mickle makes a muckle.
a popular corruption of 'Many a little makes a mickle'
late 18th century

10 Many are called but few are chosen.
late 19th century; see **Bible** 98:5

11 Many a true word is spoken in jest.
late 14th century

12 Many go out for wool and come home shorn.
late 16th century

13 Many hands make light work.
early 14th century

14 March comes in like a lion, and goes out like a lamb.
early 17th century

15 Marriage is a lottery.
mid 17th century

16 Marriages are made in heaven.
mid 16th century

17 Marry in haste and repent at leisure.
late 16th century; see **Congreve** 239:4

18 Marry in May, rue for aye.
late 17th century

19 May chickens come cheeping.
late 19th century

20 Meat and mass never hindered man.
early 17th century

21 Might is right.
early 14th century

22 The mill cannot grind with the water that is past.
early 17th century

23 The mills of God grind slowly, yet they grind exceeding small.
mid 17th century; translation of an anonymous verse in Sextus Empiricus *Adversus Mathematicos* bk. 1, sect. 287; see **Longfellow** 490:23

24 Misery loves company.
late 16th century

25 Misfortunes never come singly.
early 14th century

26 A miss is as good as a mile.
the syntax has been distorted by abridgement: the original form was 'an inch in a miss is as good as an ell'
early 17th century

27 Moderation in all things.
mid 19th century; see **Horace** 403:5

28 Monday's child is fair of face,
Tuesday's child is full of grace,
Wednesday's child is full of woe,
Thursday's child has far to go,
Friday's child is loving and giving,
Saturday's child works hard for its living,
And a child that's born on the Sabbath day
Is fair and wise and good and gay.
mid 19th century

29 Money can't buy happiness.
mid 19th century

30 Money has no smell.
early 20th century; see **Vespasian** 809:6

31 Money isn't everything.
early 20th century

32 Money is power.
mid 18th century

33 Money is the root of all evil.
mid 15th century; see **Bible** 110:26

34 A moneyless man goes fast through the market.
early 18th century; late 14th century in French

35 Money, like manure, does no good till it is spread.
early 19th century; see **Bacon** 45:13

36 Money makes a man.
early 16th century

37 Money makes money.
late 16th century

38 Money makes the mare to go.
early 16th century

39 Money talks.
mid 17th century

40 More haste, less speed.
mid 14th century

41 The more laws, the more thieves and bandits.
late 16th century; see **Lao Tzu** 468:3

42 More people know Tom Fool than Tom Fool knows.
mid 17th century

43 The more the merrier.
late 14th century

44 The more you get the more you want.
mid 14th century

45 The more you stir it the worse it stinks.
mid 16th century

46 Morning dreams come true.
mid 16th century

1 The mother of mischief is no bigger than a midge's wing.
early 17th century

2 A mouse may help a lion.
alluding to Aesop's fable of the lion and the rat
mid 16th century

3 Much cry and little wool.
late 15th century

4 Much would have more.
mid 14th century

5 Murder will out.
early 14th century; see **Chaucer** 212:1

6 My son is my son till he gets him a wife, but my daughter's my daughter all the days of her life.
late 17th century

7 Nature abhors a vacuum.
mid 16th century; see **Rabelais** 639:16

8 The nearer the bone, the sweeter the meat.
late 14th century

9 The nearer the church, the farther from God.
early 14th century

10 Near is my kirtle, but nearer is my smock.
mid 15th century

11 Near is my shirt, but nearer is my skin.
late 16th century

12 Necessity is the mother of invention.
mid 16th century

13 Necessity knows no law.
late 14th century; see **Publilius Syrus** 636:16

14 Needles and pins, needles and pins, when a man marries, his trouble begins.
mid 19th century

15 Needs must when the devil drives.
mid 15th century

16 Ne'er cast a clout till May be out.
early 18th century

17 Never bid the Devil good morrow until you meet him.
late 19th century

18 Never choose your women or linen by candlelight.
late 16th century

19 Never do evil that good may come of it.
late 16th century

20 Never give a sucker an even break.
early 20th century; see **Fields** 318:18

21 Never is a long time.
late 14th century

22 Never let the sun go down on your anger.
mid 17th century; see **Bible** 109:13

23 Never look a gift horse in the mouth.
early 16th century

24 Never marry for money, but marry where money is.
late 19th century; see **Tennyson** 782:13

25 Never mention rope in the house of a man who has been hanged.
late 16th century

26 Never put off till tomorrow what you can do today.
late 14th century

27 Never send a boy to do a man's job.
early 20th century

28 Never speak ill of the dead.
mid 16th century; 6th century BC in Greek

29 Never tell tales out of school.
early 16th century

30 Never too old to learn.
early 16th century

31 Never trouble trouble till trouble troubles you.
late 19th century

32 New brooms sweep clean.
mid 16th century

33 New lords, new laws.
mid 16th century

34 Night brings counsel.
late 16th century

35 Nine tailors make a man.
the literal meaning is that a gentleman must select his attire from various sources; it is now also associated with bell-ringing: tailors = tellers = strokes, the number of strokes on the passing bell indicating the sex of the deceased
early 17th century

36 No cross, no crown.
early 17th century; see **Penn** 591:15

37 No cure, no pay.
expression used on Lloyd's of London's Standard Form of Salvage Agreement
late 19th century

38 A nod's as good as a wink to a blind horse.
late 18th century

39 No foot, no horse.
in North America as 'no hoof, no horse'
mid 18th century

40 No man can serve two masters.
early 14th century; see **Bible** 95:6

41 No man is a hero to his valet.
mid 18th century; see **Cornuel** 243:15

42 No money, no Swiss.
the Swiss were particularly noted as mercenaries
late 16th century; see **Racine** 640:8

43 No moon, no man.
late 19th century

44 No names, no pack-drill.
early 20th century

45 No news is good news.
early 17th century

46 No one should be judge in his own cause.
mid 15th century

1 No pain, no gain.
late 16th century

2 No penny, no paternoster.
early 16th century

3 No smoke without fire.
late 14th century

4 No time like the present.
mid 16th century

5 None but the brave deserve the fair.
late 17th century, from **Dryden**; see **Dryden** 287:14

6 Nothing comes of nothing.
late 14th century

7 Nothing for nothing.
early 18th century

8 Nothing is certain but death and taxes.
early 18th century; see **Defoe** 261:6, **Franklin** 332:19

9 Nothing is certain but the unforeseen.
late 19th century

10 Nothing should be done in haste but gripping a flea.
mid 17th century

11 Nothing so bad but it might have been worse.
late 19th century

12 Nothing so bold as a blind mare.
early 17th century

13 Nothing succeeds like success.
mid 19th century

14 Nothing venture, nothing gain.
early 17th century

15 Nothing venture, nothing have.
late 14th century

16 Obey orders, if you break owners.
late 18th century

17 Of two evils choose the less.
late 14th century; similar sentiments are found in **Aristotle** and **Cicero**

18 Offenders never pardon.
mid 17th century

19 Old habits die hard.
mid 18th century

20 An old poacher makes the best gamekeeper.
late 14th century

21 Old sins cast long shadows.
early 20th century

22 Old soldiers never die.
early 20th century; see **Foley** 327:24

23 The only good Indian is a dead Indian.
mid 19th century; see **Sheridan** 733:4

24 On Saint Thomas the Divine kill all turkeys, geese and swine.
St Thomas the Apostle's feast is on 21 December
mid 18th century

25 On the first of March, the crows begin to search.
mid 19th century

26 Once a—, always a—
the formula is found from the early 17th century

27 Once a priest, always a priest.
mid 19th century

28 Once a whore, always a whore.
early 17th century

29 Once bitten, twice shy.
mid 19th century

30 One cannot love and be wise.
early 16th century

31 One does not wash one's dirty linen in public.
early 19th century

32 One Englishman can beat three Frenchmen.
late 16th century

33 One for sorrow; two for mirth; three for a wedding, four for a birth.
referring to the number of magpies seen
mid 19th century

34 One for the mouse, one for the crow, one to rot, one to grow.
referring to sowing seed
mid 19th century

35 One funeral makes many.
late 19th century

36 One good turn deserves another.
early 15th century

37 One half of the world does not know how the other half lives.
early 17th century

38 One hand for oneself and one for the ship.
late 18th century

39 One hand washes the other.
late 16th century

40 One hour's sleep before midnight is worth two after.
mid 17th century

41 One law for the rich and another for the poor.
early 19th century

42 One man may steal a horse, while another may not look over a hedge.
mid 16th century

43 One man's loss is another man's gain.
early 16th century

44 One man's meat is another man's poison.
late 16th century

45 One might as well be hanged for a sheep as a lamb.
late 17th century

46 One nail drives out another.
mid 13th century; also found in **Aristotle**

47 One picture is worth ten thousand words.
early 20th century; see **Barnard** 56:6

48 One size does not fit all.
early 17th century

49 One step at a time.
mid 19th century

1 One story is good till another is told.
late 16th century

2 One swallow does not make a summer.
mid 16th century

3 One volunteer is worth two pressed men.
early 18th century

4 One wedding brings another.
mid 17th century

5 One white foot, buy him; two white feet, try him; three white feet, look well about him; four white feet, go without him.
on horse-dealing
late 19th century

6 One year's seeding makes seven years weeding.
late 19th century

7 Opportunity makes a thief.
early 13th century

8 Opportunity never knocks twice at any man's door.
mid 16th century

9 Other times, other manners.
late 16th century

10 An ounce of practice is worth a pound of precept.
late 16th century

11 Out of debt, out of danger.
mid 17th century

12 Out of sight, out of mind.
mid 13th century; see **Thomas à Kempis** 788:9

13 Out of the fullness of the heart the mouth speaks.
late 14th century; see **Bible** 96:31

14 Out of the mouths of babes—.
late 19th century; see **Book of Common Prayer** 134:4

15 Parsley seed goes nine times to the Devil.
mid 17th century

16 Patience is a virtue.
late 14th century

17 Pay beforehand was never well served.
late 16th century

18 A peck of March dust is worth a king's ransom.
early 16th century

19 The pen is mightier than the sword.
late 16th century; see **Bulwer-Lytton** 164:5

20 A penny saved is a penny earned.
mid 17th century

21 Penny wise and pound foolish.
early 17th century

22 Physician, heal thyself.
early 15th century; see **Bible** 100:11

23 The pitcher will go to the well once too often.
mid 14th century

24 Pity is akin to love.
early 17th century

25 A place for everything, and everything in its place.
mid 17th century; often associated with Samuel **Smiles** and Mrs Beeton

26 Please your eye and plague your heart.
early 17th century

27 Politics makes strange bedfellows.
mid 19th century

28 Possession is nine points of the law.
early 17th century

29 A postern door makes a thief.
mid 15th century

30 The post of honour is the post of danger.
early 16th century

31 Poverty is no disgrace, but it's a great inconvenience.
late 16th century

32 Poverty is not a crime.
late 16th century

33 Power corrupts.
late 19th century, now commonly used in allusion to **Acton**; see **Acton** 1:13

34 Practice makes perfect.
mid 16th century

35 Practise what you preach.
late 14th century

36 Praise the child, and you make love to the mother.
early 19th century

37 Pretty is as pretty does.
mid 19th century, American equivalent of **Proverbs** 621:26

38 Prevention is better than cure.
early 17th century

39 Pride feels no pain.
early 17th century

40 Pride goes before a fall.
late 14th century; see **Bible** 84:26

41 Procrastination is the thief of time.
mid 18th century, from **Young**; see **Young** 857:12

42 Promises, like pie-crust, are made to be broken.
late 17th century

43 The proof of the pudding is in the eating.
early 14th century

44 A prophet is not without honour save in his own country.
late 15th century; see **Bible** 97:7

45 Providence is always on the side of the big battalions.
early 19th century; see **Bussy-Rabutin** 175:9, **Voltaire** 816:10

46 Punctuality is the politeness of princes.
mid 19th century; see **Louis XVIII** 492:13

47 Punctuality is the soul of business.
mid 19th century

48 Put a stout heart to a stey brae.
stey = *steep*
late 16th century

49 Put your trust in God, and keep your powder dry.
*attributed to Oliver **Cromwell***
mid 19th century; see **Blacker** 118:7

1 The quarrel of lovers is the renewal of love.
early 16th century; see **Edwards** 297:3

2 Quickly come, quickly go.
late 16th century

3 The race is not to the swift, nor the battle to the strong.
early 17th century; see **Bible** 86:16

4 Rain before seven, fine before eleven.
mid 19th century

5 Red sky at night, shepherd's delight; red sky in the morning, shepherd's warning.
late 14th century

6 A reed before the wind lives on, while mighty oaks do fall.
late 14th century

7 Revenge is a dish that can be eaten cold.
late 19th century

8 Revenge is sweet.
mid 16th century

9 Revolutions are not made with rose-water.
early 19th century; see **Hegel** 379:2

10 The rich man has his ice in the summer and the poor man gets his in the winter.
early 20th century

11 A rising tide lifts all boats.
principally known in the United States; associated with the Kennedy family
mid 20th century

12 The road to hell is paved with good intentions.
late 16th century

13 The robin and the wren are God's cock and hen; the martin and the swallow are God's mate and marrow.
late 18th century

14 Robin Hood could brave all weathers but a thaw wind.
mid 19th century

15 A rolling stone gathers no moss.
mid 14th century

16 Rome was not built in a day.
mid 16th century

17 The rotten apple injures its neighbour.
mid 14th century

18 Safe bind, safe find.
mid 16th century

19 Saint Swithun's day, if thou be fair, for forty days it will remain; Saint Swithun's day, if thou bring rain, for forty days it will remain.
Saint Swithun's day is 15 July
early 17th century

20 Save us from our friends.
late 15th century

21 Scratch a Russian and you find a Tartar.
early 19th century

22 The sea refuses no river.
early 17th century

23 Second thoughts are best.
late 16th century

24 See a pin and pick it up, all the day you'll have good luck; see a pin and let it lie, bad luck you'll have all day.
mid 19th century

25 Seeing is believing.
early 17th century

26 Seek and ye shall find.
early 16th century; see **Bible** 95:15

27 See no evil, hear no evil, speak no evil.
conventionally represented by the monkeys ('the three wise monkeys') covering their eyes, ears, and mouth respectively with their hands
early 20th century

28 Self-praise is no recommendation.
early 19th century

29 Self-preservation is the first law of nature.
early 17th century

30 September blow soft till the fruit's in the loft.
late 16th century

31 Set a beggar on horseback, and he'll ride to the Devil.
late 16th century

32 Set a thief to catch a thief.
mid 17th century

33 The sharper the storm, the sooner it's over.
late 19th century

34 The shoemaker's son always goes barefoot.
mid 16th century

35 A short horse is soon curried.
mid 14th century

36 Short reckonings make long friends.
early 16th century

37 Shrouds have no pockets.
mid 19th century

38 A shut mouth catches no flies.
late 16th century

39 Silence is a woman's best garment.
mid 16th century

40 Silence is golden.
mid 19th century

41 Silence means consent.
late 14th century

42 Sing before breakfast, cry before night.
early 17th century

43 Six hours sleep for a man, seven for a woman, and eight for a fool.
early 17th century

44 A slice off a cut loaf isn't missed.
late 16th century

45 Slow and steady wins the race.
mid 18th century

46 Slow but sure.
late 17th century

1 Small choice in rotten apples.
late 16th century

2 A soft answer turneth away wrath.
late 14th century; see **Bible** 84:22

3 Softly, softly, catchee monkey.
early 20th century

4 So many men, so many opinions.
late 14th century; see **Terence** 785:8

5 So many mists in March, so many frosts in May.
early 17th century

6 Something is better than nothing.
mid 16th century

7 The sooner begun, the sooner done.
late 16th century

8 Soon ripe, soon rotten.
late 14th century

9 Sow dry and set wet.
mid 17th century

10 A sow may whistle, though it has an ill mouth for it.
early 19th century

11 Spare at the spigot, and let out the bung-hole.
mid 17th century

12 Spare the rod and spoil the child.
early 11th century; see **Bible** 84:18, **Butler** 176:12

13 Spare well and have to spend.
mid 16th century

14 Speak as you find.
late 16th century

15 Speak not of my debts unless you mean to pay them.
mid 17th century

16 Speech is silver, but silence is golden.
mid 19th century

17 The squeaking wheel gets the grease.
mid 20th century

18 A stern chase is a long chase.
stern chase = *a chase in which the pursuing ship follows directly in the wake of the pursued*
early 19th century

19 Sticks and stones may break my bones, but words will never hurt me.
late 19th century

20 A still tongue makes a wise head.
mid 16th century

21 Still waters run deep.
early 15th century

22 A stitch in time saves nine.
early 18th century

23 Stolen fruit is sweet.
early 17th century

24 Stolen waters are sweet.
late 14th century; see **Bible** 84:7

25 Stone-dead hath no fellow.
mid 17th century

26 Straws tell which way the wind blows.
mid 17th century

27 A stream cannot rise above its source.
mid 17th century

28 Stretch your arm no further than your sleeve will reach.
mid 16th century

29 Strike while the iron is hot.
late 14th century

30 The style is the man.
early 20th century, from **Buffon**; see **Buffon** 163:13

31 Success has many fathers, while failure is an orphan.
mid 20th century; see **Ciano** 222:25

32 Sue a beggar and catch a louse.
mid 17th century

33 Sufficient unto the day is the evil thereof.
mid 18th century; see **Bible** 95:11

34 The sun loses nothing by shining into a puddle.
early 14th century, of Classical origin

35 Sussex won't be druv.
early 20th century

36 A swarm in May is worth a load of hay; a swarm in June is worth a silver spoon; but a swarm in July is not worth a fly.
beekeepers' saying
mid 17th century

37 Take care of the pence and the pounds will take care of themselves.
mid 18th century; see **Lowndes** 494:20

38 Take the goods the gods provide.
late 17th century

39 A tale never loses in the telling.
mid 16th century

40 Talk is cheap.
mid 19th century

41 Talk of the Devil, and he is bound to appear.
mid 17th century

42 Tastes differ.
early 19th century

43 Tell the truth and shame the Devil.
mid 16th century

44 There are as good fish in the sea as ever came out of it.
late 16th century

45 There are more ways of killing a cat than choking it with cream.
mid 19th century

46 There are more ways of killing a dog than choking it with butter.
mid 19th century

47 There are more ways of killing a dog than hanging it.
late 17th century

48 There are no birds in last year's nest.
early 17th century

1 There are tricks in every trade.
early 17th century

2 There are two sides to every question.
early 19th century

3 There goes more to marriage than four bare legs in a bed.
mid 16th century

4 There is always a first time.
late 18th century

5 There is always room at the top.
early 20th century; see **Webster** 825:18

6 There is always something new out of Africa.
mid 16th century, from **Pliny**; see **Pliny** 598:4

7 There is an exception to every rule.
late 16th century

8 There is a remedy for everything except death.
early 15th century

9 There is a time and place for everything.
early 16th century

10 There is a time for everything.
late 14th century; see **Bible** 85:32

11 There is honour among thieves.
early 19th century

12 There is luck in leisure.
late 17th century

13 There is luck in odd numbers.
late 16th century

14 There is measure in all things.
late 14th century; see **Horace** 403:5

15 There is more than one way to skin a cat.
mid 19th century

16 There is no accounting for tastes.
late 18th century

17 There is no little enemy.
mid 17th century

18 There is no royal road to learning.
early 19th century; see **Euclid** 312:9

19 There is nothing like leather.
late 17th century

20 There is nothing lost by civility.
late 19th century

21 There is nothing new under the sun.
late 16th century; see **Bible** 85:28

22 There is nothing so good for the inside of a man as the outside of a horse.
early 20th century

23 There is reason in the roasting of eggs.
mid 17th century

24 There is safety in numbers.
late 17th century

25 There is truth in wine.
mid 16th century

26 There's many a good cock come out of a tattered bag.
late 19th century

27 There's many a good tune played on an old fiddle.
early 20th century

28 There's many a slip 'twixt cup and lip.
mid 16th century

29 There's no fool like an old fool.
mid 16th century

30 There's no great loss without some gain.
mid 17th century

31 There's none so blind as those who will not see.
mid 16th century

32 There's none so deaf as those who will not hear.
mid 16th century

33 There's no place like home.
late 16th century; see **Payne** 589:12

34 There's nowt so queer as folk.
early 20th century

35 They that dance must pay the fiddler.
mid 17th century

36 They that live longest, see most.
early 17th century

37 They that sow the wind, shall reap the whirlwind.
late 16th century; see **Bible** 91:28

38 Things past cannot be recalled.
late 15th century

39 Think first and speak afterwards.
mid 16th century

40 Third time lucky.
mid 19th century

41 The third time pays for all.
late 16th century

42 Those who hide can find.
early 15th century

43 Those who live in glass houses shouldn't throw stones.
mid 17th century

44 Those who play at bowls must look out for rubbers.
mid 18th century

45 Thought is free.
late 14th century

46 Threatened men live long.
mid 16th century

47 Three may keep a secret, if two of them are dead.
mid 16th century

48 Three removals are as bad as a fire.
mid 18th century

49 Three things are not to be trusted; a cow's horn, a dog's tooth, and a horse's hoof.
late 14th century

50 Thrift is a great revenue.
mid 17th century

51 Throw dirt enough, and some will stick.
mid 17th century

52 Time and tide wait for no man.
late 14th century

1 Time flies.
late 14th century; see **Virgil** 815:1

2 Time is a great healer.
late 14th century

3 Time is money.
late 16th century

4 Time will tell.
mid 16th century

5 Time works wonders.
late 16th century

6 Times change and we with time.
attributed to the Emperor Lothar I (795–855) in the form 'Omnia mutantur, nos et mutamur in illis [All things change, and we change with them]'; *now sometimes quoted as* 'Tempora mutantur . . . '
late 16th century

7 'Tis better to have loved and lost, than never to have loved at all.
early 18th century; see **Congreve** 239:10, **Tennyson** 779:1

8 Today you; tomorrow me.
early 17th century

9 To err is human (to forgive divine).
late 16th century; see **Pope** 604:13

10 To know all is to forgive all.
mid 20th century; see **Staël** 753:16

11 Tomorrow is another day.
early 16th century; see **Closing lines** 228:1

12 Tomorrow never comes.
early 16th century

13 The tongue always returns to the sore tooth.
late 16th century

14 Too many cooks spoil the broth.
late 16th century

15 To the pure all things are pure.
mid 19th century; see **Bible** 111:2

16 Trade follows the flag.
late 19th century

17 Travel broadens the mind.
early 20th century

18 The tree is known by its fruit.
early 16th century; see **Bible** 96:30

19 A trouble shared is a trouble halved.
early 20th century

20 Truth is stranger than fiction.
early 19th century, from **Byron**; see **Byron** 182:1

21 Truth lies at the bottom of a well.
mid 16th century

22 Truth makes the Devil blush.
mid 20th century

23 Truth will out.
mid 15th century

24 Turkey, heresy, hops, and beer came into England all in one year.
late 16th century

25 Turn about is fair play.
mid 18th century

26 Two blacks don't make a white.
early 18th century

27 Two boys are half a boy, and three boys are no boy at all.
early 20th century

28 Two heads are better than one.
late 14th century

29 Two is company, but three is none.
often used with the alternative ending 'three's a crowd'
early 18th century

30 Two of a trade never agree.
early 17th century

31 Two wrongs don't make a right.
late 18th century

32 The unexpected always happens.
late 19th century

33 Union is strength.
mid 17th century

34 United we stand, divided we fall.
late 18th century, from **Dickinson**; see **Dickinson** 273:15

35 Variety is the spice of life.
late 18th century, from **Cowper**; see **Cowper** 247:30

36 Virtue is its own reward.
early 16th century

37 The voice of the people is the voice of God.
early 15th century; see **Alcuin** 10:10

38 Walls have ears.
late 16th century

39 Walnuts and pears you plant for your heirs.
mid 17th century

40 Wanton kittens make sober cats.
early 18th century

41 Waste not, want not.
late 18th century

42 A watched pot never boils.
mid 19th century

43 The way to a man's heart is through his stomach.
early 19th century

44 The weakest go to the wall.
early 16th century

45 Wedlock is a padlock.
late 17th century

46 Well begun is half done.
early 15th century

47 We must eat a peck of dirt before we die.
mid 18th century

48 We must learn to walk before we can run.
mid 14th century

49 What a neighbour gets is not lost.
mid 16th century

50 What can't be cured must be endured.
late 16th century

1 What can you expect from a pig but a grunt.
early 18th century

2 Whatever man has done, man may do.
mid 19th century

3 What everybody says must be true.
early 15th century

4 What goes up must come down.
early 20th century

5 What is got over the Devil's back is spent under his belly.
late 16th century

6 What is new cannot be true.
mid 17th century

7 What Manchester says today, the rest of England says tomorrow.
late 19th century

8 What must be, must be.
late 14th century

9 What's bred in the bone will come out in the flesh.
late 15th century

10 What's done cannot be undone.
mid 15th century

11 What's sauce for the goose is sauce for the gander.
late 17th century

12 What the eye doesn't see, the heart doesn't grieve over.
mid 16th century; earlier in Latin

13 What the soldier said isn't evidence.
mid 19th century; see **Dickens** 272:6

14 What you don't know can't hurt you.
late 16th century

15 What you have, hold.
mid 15th century

16 What you lose on the swings you gain on the roundabouts.
early 20th century

17 What you spend, you have.
early 14th century

18 What you've never had you never miss.
early 20th century

19 When Adam delved and Eve span, who was then the gentleman?
traditionally taken by John Ball as the text of his revolutionary sermon on the outbreak of the Peasants' Revolt, 1381
late 14th century; see **Rolle** 653:3

20 When all fruit fails, welcome haws.
early 18th century

21 When Greek meets Greek, then comes the tug of war.
late 17th century

22 When house and land are gone and spent, then learning is most excellent.
mid 18th century

23 When in doubt, do nowt.
late 19th century

24 When in Rome, do as the Romans do.
mid 16th century; see **Ambrose** 13:2

25 When one door shuts, another opens.
late 16th century

26 When poverty comes in at the door, love flies out of the window.
early 17th century

27 When the blind lead the blind, both shall fall into the ditch.
late 9th century; see **Bible** 97:12

28 When the cat's away, the mice will play.
early 17th century

29 When the furze is in bloom, my love's in tune.
mid 18th century

30 When the going gets tough, the tough get going.
mid 20th century; see **Kennedy** 449:9

31 When the gorse is out of bloom, kissing's out of fashion.
mid 19th century

32 When the oak is before the ash, then you will only get a splash; when the ash is before the oak, then you may expect a soak.
mid 19th century

33 When the wind is in the east, 'tis neither good for man nor beast.
early 17th century

34 When the wine is in, the wit is out.
late 14th century

35 When thieves fall out, honest men come by their own.
mid 16th century

36 When things are at the worst they begin to mend.
late 16th century

37 Where bees are, there is honey.
early 17th century

38 Where God builds a church, the Devil will build a chapel.
mid 16th century; see **Luther** 496:10

39 Where ignorance is bliss, 'tis folly to be wise.
mid 18th century, from **Gray**; see **Gray** 361:12

40 Where MacGregor sits at the head of the table.
mid 19th century

41 Where the carcase is, there shall the eagles be gathered together.
mid 16th century; see **Bible** 98:16

42 Where there's a will there's a way.
mid 17th century

43 Where there's muck there's brass.
late 17th century

44 While the grass grows, the steed starves.
mid 14th century

45 While there's life there's hope.
mid 16th century

46 While two dogs are fighting for a bone, a third runs away with it.
late 14th century

1 A whistling woman and a crowing hen are neither fit for God nor men.
early 18th century

2 Whom the Gods love die young.
mid 16th century; see **Menander** 521:13

3 Whom the gods would destroy, they first make mad.
early 17th century, earlier in Greek; see **Anonymous** 21:11

4 Who says A must say B.
mid 19th century, usually North American

5 Whosoever draws his sword against the prince must throw the scabbard away.
early 17th century

6 Who won't be ruled by the rudder must be ruled by the rock.
mid 17th century

7 Why buy a cow when milk is so cheap?
mid 17th century

8 Why keep a dog and bark yourself?
late 16th century

9 Why should the devil have all the best tunes?
mid 19th century; see **Hill** 388:13

10 A wilful man must have his way.
early 19th century

11 Wilful waste makes woeful want.
early 18th century

12 Winter never rots in the sky.
early 17th century

13 The wish is father to the thought.
late 16th century, from **Shakespeare**; see **Shakespeare** 692:17

14 A woman, a dog, and a walnut tree, the more you beat them the better they be.
late 16th century

15 A woman and a ship ever want mending.
late 16th century; 2nd century BC in Latin

16 A woman's place is in the home.
mid 19th century

17 A woman's work is never done.
late 16th century

18 Wonders will never cease.
late 18th century

19 A word to the wise is enough.
early 16th century; see **Plautus** 597:21

20 Work expands so as to fill the time available.
mid 20th century, from **Parkinson**; see **Parkinson** 586:17

21 The worth of a thing is what it will bring.
late 16th century

22 Yorkshire born and Yorkshire bred, strong in the arm and weak in the head.
the names of other (chiefly northern) English counties and towns are also used instead of Yorkshire
mid 19th century

23 You are what you eat.
mid 20th century; see **Feuerbach** 317:4

24 You buy land, you buy stones; you buy meat, you buy bones.
late 17th century

25 You can drive out nature with a pitchfork but she keeps on coming back.
mid 16th century; see **Horace** 399:9

26 You can have too much of a good thing.
late 15th century

27 You cannot catch old birds with chaff.
late 15th century

28 You cannot get a quart into a pint pot.
late 19th century

29 You cannot get blood from a stone.
mid 17th century

30 You cannot have your cake and eat it.
mid 16th century

31 You cannot lose what you never had.
late 16th century

32 You cannot make an omelette without breaking eggs.
mid 19th century

33 You cannot make bricks without straw.
mid 17th century

34 You cannot put an old head on young shoulders.
late 16th century

35 You cannot run with the hare and hunt with the hounds.
mid 15th century

36 You cannot serve God and Mammon.
early 16th century; see **Bible** 95:6

37 You cannot shift an old tree without it dying.
early 16th century

38 You can only die once.
mid 15th century

39 You can take a horse to the water, but you can't make him drink.
late 12th century

40 You can take the boy out of the country but you can't take the country out of the boy.
mid 20th century, usually North American

41 You can't make a silk purse out of a sow's ear.
early 16th century

42 You can't please everyone.
late 15th century

43 You can't put new wine in old bottles.
early 20th century; see **Bible** 96:8

44 You can't teach an old dog new tricks.
early 16th century

45 You can't tell a book by its cover.
early 20th century

46 You can't win them all.
mid 20th century

1 You don't get something for nothing.
late 19th century

2 You never know what you can do till you try.
early 19th century

3 You never miss the water till the well runs dry.
early 17th century

4 Young folks think old folks to be fools, but old folks know young folks to be fools.
late 16th century

5 A young man married is a young man marred.
late 16th century; see **Shakespeare** 678:10

6 Young men may die, but old men must die.
mid 16th century

7 Young saint, old devil.
early 15th century

8 You pays your money and you takes your choice.
mid 19th century

9 You should know a man seven years before you stir his fire.
early 19th century

10 Youth must be served.
early 19th century

11 You win a few, you lose a few.
mid 20th century

Pu Yi 1906–67
Chinese monarch, Emperor of China 1908–12; Japan's puppet emperor of Manchuria 1934–45

12 For the past 40 years I had never folded my own quilt, made my own bed, or poured out my own washing. I had never even washed my own feet or tied my shoes.
From *Emperor to Citizen* (1964)

Publilius Syrus
Roman freedman and writer of mimes of the 1st century BC

13 *Formosa facies muta commendatio est.*

A beautiful face is a mute recommendation.
Sententiae no. 199, in J. and A. Duff *Minor Latin Poets* (Loeb ed., 1934); translated by Thomas Tenison in *Baconiana* (1679) 'Ornamenta Rationalia' no. 12

14 *Inopi beneficium bis dat qui dat celeriter.*

He gives the poor man twice as much good who gives quickly.
proverbially 'Bis dat qui cito dat [He gives twice who gives soon]'
Sententiae no. 274, in J. and A. Duff *Minor Latin Poets*; see **Proverbs** 621:39

15 *Iudex damnatur ubi nocens absolvitur.*

The judge is condemned when the guilty party is acquitted.
Sententiae no. 296, in J. and A. Duff *Minor Latin Poets*

16 *Necessitas dat legem non ipsa accipit.*

Necessity gives the law without itself acknowledging one.
proverbially 'Necessitas non habet legem [Necessity has no law]'
Sententiae no. 444, in J. and A. Duff *Minor Latin Poets*; see **Cromwell** 252:5, **Proverbs** 627:13

John Pudney 1909–77
English poet and writer

17 Do not despair
For Johnny-head-in-air;
He sleeps as sound
As Johnny underground.
'For Johnny' (1942); see **Hoffmann** 391:16

18 And keep your tears
For him in after years.
Better by far
For Johnny-the-bright-star,
To keep your head,
And see his children fed.
'For Johnny' (1942)

Augustus Welby Pugin 1812–52
English architect and designer

19 The two great rules for design are these: *1st, that there should be no features about a building which are not necessary for convenience, construction or propriety; 2nd, that all ornament should consist of the essential construction of the building.* The neglect of these two rules is the cause of all the bad architecture of the present time.
True Principles (1841)

20 A man who remains any length of time in a modern Gothic room, and escapes without being wounded by some of its minutiae, may consider himself extremely fortunate.
True Principles (1841)

21 I seek *antiquity not novelty.* I strive to *revive* not *invent.*
letter to John Bloxam, 13 September 1840; *Collected Letters* (2001) vol. 1

22 There is nothing worth living for but Christian Architecture and a boat.
in *The Builder* 1852 vol. 10

23 How can you expect to convert England if you use a cope like that?
to an unidentified Catholic priest
Bernard England *The Sequel to Catholic Emancipation* (1915)

24 Nothing can be more dangerous than looking at prints of buildings, and trying to imitate bits of them. These architectural books are as bad as the Scriptures in the hands of the Protestants.
J. Mordaunt Crook *Dilemma of Style* (1987)

25 Yet notwithstanding the palpable impracticability of adapting Greek temples to our climate, habits and religion, we see the attempt and failure continuously made and repeated; post office, theatre, church, bath, reading-room, hotel, methodist chapel and turnpike gate, all the present the eternal sameness of a Grecian temple outraged in all its proportions and character.

J. Mordaunt Crook *The Greek Revival* (1995)

Joseph Pulitzer 1847–1911

Hungarian-born American newspaper proprietor and editor

1 Our Republic and its press will rise or fall together.
referring to the importance of media independence
in *North American Review* May 1904

2 A cynical, mercenary, demagogic, corrupt press will produce in time a people as base as itself.
inscribed on the gateway to the Columbia School of Journalism in New York
W. J. Granberg *The World of Joseph Pulitzer* (1965)

William Pulteney, Earl of Bath 1684–1764

English peer

3 For Sir Ph—p well knows
That innuendos
Will serve him no longer in verse or in prose,
Since twelve honest men have decided the cause,
And were judges of fact, tho' not judges of laws.
on the unsuccessful prosecution of The Craftsman, *1729 by Philip Yorke, later Lord* **Hardwicke**
'The Honest Jury' (1729) st. 3

Punch 1841–1992

English humorous weekly periodical

4 Advice to persons about to marry.—'Don't.'
4 January 1845; see **Bacon** 44:33

5 You pays your money and you takes your choice.
3 January 1846

6 The Half-Way House to Rome, Oxford.
27 January 1849

7 Never do to-day what you can put off till to-morrow.
22 December 1849

8 Who's 'im, Bill?
A stranger!
'Eave 'arf a brick at 'im.
25 February 1854

9 What is Matter?—Never mind.
What is Mind?—No matter.
14 July 1855

10 It ain't the 'unting as 'urts 'im, it's the 'ammer, 'ammer, 'ammer along the 'ard 'igh road.
31 May 1856

11 Mun, a had na' been the-erre abune two hours when—*bang*—went saxpence!!!
5 December 1868

12 Cats is 'dogs' and rabbits is 'dogs' and so's Parrots, but this 'ere 'Tortis' is a insect, so there ain't no charge for it.
6 March 1869

13 Nothink for nothink 'ere, and precious little for sixpence.
16 October 1869

14 Go directly—see what she's doing, and tell her she mustn't.
16 November 1872

15 There was one poor tiger that hadn't *got* a Christian.
3 April 1875

16 It's worse than wicked, my dear, it's vulgar.
Almanac (1876)

17 I never read books—I *write* them.
11 May 1878; see **Disraeli** 278:11

18 I am not hungry; but thank goodness, I am greedy.
28 December 1878

19 BISHOP: Who is it that sees and hears all we do, and before whom even I am but as a crushed worm?
PAGE: The Missus, my Lord.
14 August 1880

20 Ah whiles hae ma doobts aboot the meenister.
11 December 1880

21 WIFE OF TWO YEARS' STANDING: Oh yes! I'm sure he's not so fond of me as at first. He's away so much, neglects me dreadfully, and he's so cross when he comes home. What *shall* I do?
WIDOW: Feed the brute!
31 October 1885

22 Nearly all our best men are dead! Carlyle, Tennyson, Browning, George Eliot!—I'm not feeling very well myself.
6 May 1893

23 Botticelli isn't a wine, you Juggins! Botticelli's a *cheese*!
6 June 1894

24 I'm afraid you've got a bad egg, Mr Jones.
Oh no, my Lord, I assure you! Parts of it are excellent!
11 May 1895

25 Look here, Steward, if this is coffee, I want tea; but if this is tea, then I wish for coffee.
23 July 1902

26 Sometimes I sits and thinks, and then again I just sits.
24 October 1906

Al Purdy 1918–2000

Canadian poet and writer

27 Look here
You've never seen this country
it's not the way you thought it was
Look again.
of Canada
'The Country of the Young' (1976)

28 Looking into his eyes
it is possible to see the first hunters
(if you have your own vision)
after the last ice age.
'Inuit' (1967)

Alexander Pushkin 1799–1837
Russian poet

1 Storm-clouds whirl and storm-clouds scurry;
From behind them pale moonlight
Flickers where the snowflakes hurry.
Dark the sky and dark the night.
'Devils' (1830) (translated by C. M. Bowra)

2 From early youth his dedication
Was to a single occupation . . .
The science of the tender passion.
Eugene Onegin (1833) ch. 1, st. 8 (translated by Babette Deutsch)

3 A woman's love for us increases
The less we love her, sooth to say—
She stoops, she falls, her struggling ceases;
Caught fast, she cannot get away.
Eugene Onegin (1833) ch. 4, st. 1 (translated by Babette Deutsch)

4 A tedious season they await
Who hear November at the gate.
Eugene Onegin (1833) ch. 4, st. 40 (translated by Babette Deutsch)

5 Moscow: those syllables can start
A tumult in the Russian heart.
Eugene Onegin (1833) ch. 7, st. 36 (translated by Babette Deutsch)

6 A green oak grows by a curving shore;
And round that oak hangs a golden chain.
Ruslan and Lyudmila (1820) 'Prologue' (translated by Elisaveta Fen)

7 When trade and traffic and all the noise of town
Is dimmed, and on the streets and squares
The filmy curtain of the night sinks down
With sleep, the recompense of cares,
To me the darkness brings not sleep nor rest.
'Remembrances' (1828) (translated by R. M. Hewitt)

Vladimir Putin 1952–
Russian statesman, President of the Russian Federation since 2000

8 Please forgive us. We shall win this fight against international terrorism.
addressing the nation and apologising for failing to save all the hostages in the Moscow theatre siege
in *Sunday Telegraph* 27 October 2002

Israel Putnam 1718–90
American general

9 Men, you are all marksmen—don't one of you fire until you see the white of their eyes.
also attributed to William Prescott (1726–95)
at Bunker Hill, 1775, in R. Frothingham *History of the Siege of Boston* (1873) ch. 5

Mario Puzo 1920–99
American novelist

10 I'll make him an offer he can't refuse.
The Godfather (1969) ch. 1

11 A lawyer with his briefcase can steal more than a hundred men with guns.
The Godfather (1969) ch. 1

Barbara Pym 1913–80
English novelist

12 She experienced all the cosiness and irritation which can come from living with thoroughly nice people with whom one has nothing in common.
Less than Angels (1955) ch. 23

John Pym 1584–1643
English Parliamentary leader

13 To have granted liberties, and not to have liberties in truth and realities, is but to mock the kingdom.
*pointing out the illusory nature of **Charles I***'s promises*
in *Dictionary of National Biography* (1917–)

Pyrrhus 319–272 BC
Greek monarch, King of Epirus from 306 BC

14 One more such victory over the Romans and we are lost.
on defeating the Romans at Asculum, 279 BC
Plutarch *Parallel Lives* 'Pyrrhus' ch. 21, sect. 9

Qq

Mary Quant 1934–
English fashion designer

15 Being young is greatly overestimated . . . Any failure seems so total. Later on you realize you can have another go.
interview in *Observer* 5 May 1996

Francis Quarles 1592–1644
English poet

16 Our God and soldiers we alike adore
Ev'n at the brink of danger; not before:
After deliverance, both alike requited,
Our God's forgotten, and our soldiers slighted.
Divine Fancies (1632) 'Of Common Devotion'; see **Owen** 580:22

17 I wish thee as much pleasure in the reading, as I had in the writing.
Emblems (1635) 'To the Reader'

18 The heart is a small thing, but desireth great matters. It is not sufficient for a kite's dinner, yet the whole world is not sufficient for it.
Emblems (1635) bk. 1, no. 12 'Hugo de Anima'

19 My soul, sit thou a patient looker-on;
Judge not the play before the play is done:
Her plot hath many changes; every day
Speaks a new scene; the last act crowns the play.
Emblems (1635) bk. 1, no. 15 'Respice Finem'

20 We spend our midday sweat, our midnight oil;
We tire the night in thought, the day in toil.
Emblems (1635) bk. 2, no. 2, l. 33; see **Gay** 341:25

21 Be wisely worldly, be not worldly wise.
Emblems (1635) bk. 2, no. 2, l. 46

1 Thou art my way; I wander, if thou fly;
Thou art my light; if hid, how blind am I!
Thou art my life; if thou withdraw, I die.
  Emblems (1643) bk. 3, no. 7

2 He teaches to deny that faintly prays.
  A Feast for Worms (1620) sect. 7, Meditation 7, l. 2

3 Man is man's A.B.C. There is none that can
Read God aright, unless he first spell Man.
  Hieroglyphics of the Life of Man (1638) no. 1, l. 1

4 Physicians of all men are most happy; what good
success soever they have, the world proclaimeth,
and what faults they commit, the earth covereth.
  Hieroglyphics of the Life of Man (1638) no. 4; see **Wright**
  851:12

5 We'll cry both arts and learning down,
And hey! then up go we!
  The Shepherd's Oracles (1646) Eclogue 11 'Song of
  Anarchus'

François Quesnay 1694–1774
French political economist

6 *Vous ne connaissez qu'une seule règle du commerce;
c'est (pour me servir de vos propres termes) de laisser
passer et de laisser faire tous les acheteurs et tous les
vendeurs quelconques.*
You recognize but one rule of commerce; that is
(to avail myself of your own terms) to allow free
passage and freedom of action to all buyers and
sellers whoever they may be.
  letter from M. Alpha to Quesnay, 1767, in L. Salleron
  François Quesnay et la Physiocratie (1958) vol. 2; not found
  in Quesnay's own writings; see **Anonymous** 20:14,
  Argenson 24:19

Arthur Quiller-Couch ('Q') 1863–1944
English writer and critic

7 The best is the best, though a hundred judges
have declared it so.
  Oxford Book of English Verse (1900) preface

8 All the old statues of Victory have wings: but Grief
has no wings. She is the unwelcome lodger that
squats on the hearthstone between us and the fire
and will not move or be dislodged.
  Armistice Day anniversary sermon, Cambridge, November
  1923

Josiah Quincy 1772–1864
American Federalist politician

9 As it will be the right of all, so it will be the duty of
some, definitely to prepare for a separation,
amicably if they can, violently if they must.
  speech, 14 January 1811, in *Abridgement of Debates of
  Congress* vol. 4; see **Clay** 226:2

W. V. O. Quine 1908–2000
American philosopher

10 On the doctrinal side, I do not see that we are
farther along today than where [David] Hume left
us. The Humean predicament is the human
predicament.
  Ontological Relativity and Other Essays (1969) ch. 3

11 It is the tension between the scientist's laws and
his own attempted breaches of them that powers
the engines of science and makes it forge ahead.
  Quiddities (1987) p. 8 'Anomaly'

12 Students of the heavens are separable into
astronomers and astrologers as readily as are the
minor domestic ruminants into sheep and goats,
but the separation of philosophers into sages and
cranks seems to be more sensitive to frames of
reference.
  Theories and Things (1981) ch. 23

Quintilian c.AD 35–c.96
Roman rhetorician

13 *Satura quidem tota nostra est.*
Verse satire indeed is entirely our own.
  meaning Roman as opposed to Greek
  Institutio Oratoria bk. 10, ch. 1, sect. 93

14 *Ovidi Medea videtur mihi ostendere quantum ille vir
praestare potuerit si ingenio suo imperare quam
indulgere maluisset.*
The Medea of Ovid seems to me to show how
much that man could have excelled had he chosen
to rein in his cleverness rather than indulge it.
  Institutio Oratoria bk. 10, ch. 1, sect. 98

The Qur'an see The Koran

François Rabelais c.1494–c.1553
French humanist, satirist, and physician
*see also **Last words** 472:1*

15 *L'appétit vient en mangeant.*
The appetite grows by eating.
  Gargantua (1534) bk. 1, ch. 5; see **Proverbs** 614:27

16 *Natura vacuum abhorret.*
Nature abhors a vacuum.
  quoting, in Latin, an article of ancient wisdom
  Gargantua (1534) bk. 1, ch. 5; see **Proverbs** 627:7

17 *Fay ce que vouldras.*
Do what you like.
  Gargantua (1534) bk. 1, ch. 57; see **Crowley** 253:2

18 *Quaestio subtilissima, utrum chimera in vacuo
bombinans possit comedere secundas intentiones.*
A most subtle question: whether a chimera
buzzing in a vacuum can devour second
intentions.
  Pantagruel bk. 2, ch. 7

19 A child is not a vase to be filled, but a fire to be lit.
  attributed; see **Plutarch** 598:13

Yitzhak Rabin 1922–95
Israeli statesman and military leader, Prime Minister 1974–7 and 1992–5

1 We say to you today in a loud and a clear voice: enough of blood and tears. Enough.
to the Palestinians, at the signing of the Israel–Palestine Declaration
in Washington, 13 September 1993

Jean Racine 1639–99
French tragedian

2 *Je l'ai trop aimé pour ne le point haïr!*
I have loved him too much not to feel any hatred for him.
Andromaque (1667) act 2, sc. 1

3 *C'était pendant l'horreur d'une profonde nuit.*
It was during the horror of a deep night.
Athalie (1691) act 2, sc. 5

4 *Elle flotte, elle hésite; en un mot, elle est femme.*
She floats, she hesitates; in a word, she's a woman.
Athalie (1691) act 3, sc. 3

5 *Ce n'est plus une ardeur dans mes veines cachée: C'est Vénus tout entière à sa proie attachée.*
It's no longer a burning within my veins: it's Venus entire latched onto her prey.
Phèdre (1677) act 1, sc. 3

6 *Dans le fond des forêts votre image me suit.*
Deep in the forest glade your picture chases me.
Phèdre (1677) act 2, sc. 2

7 *Tous les jours se levaient clairs et sereins pour eux.*
Every day dawned clear and untroubled for them.
Phèdre (1677) act 4, sc. 6

8 *Point d'argent, point de Suisse, et ma porte était close.*
No money, no service, and my door stayed shut.
Les Plaideurs (1668) act 1, sc. 1; see **Proverbs** 627:42

9 *Sans argent l'honneur n'est qu'une maladie.*
Honour, without money, is just a disease.
Les Plaideurs (1668) act 1, sc. 1

Lord Radcliffe 1899–1977
British lawyer and public servant

10 Governments always tend to want not really a free press but a managed or well-conducted one.
in 1967; Peter Hennessy *What the Papers Never Said* (1985)

St Radegund 518–587
Frankish queen

11 If you shrink from consecrating me, and fear man more than God, the Shepherd will require His sheep's soul from your hand.
persuading Médard Bishop of Noyon to ordain her deaconess
Venantius Fortunatus *The Life of St Radegund*

James Rado 1939– and Gerome Ragni 1942–
American songwriters

12 When the moon is in the seventh house,
And Jupiter aligns with Mars,
Then peace will guide the planets,
And love will steer the stars;
This is the dawning of the age of Aquarius.
'Aquarius' (1967 song) in *Hair*

John Rae 1931–
English writer

13 War is, after all, the universal perversion . . . war stories, the pornography of war.
The Custard Boys (1960) ch. 13

Jean-Pierre Raffarin 1948–
French statesman, Prime Minister since 2002

14 We have a country which loves ideology, and we need pragmatism.
in *Independent* 11 May 2002

Thomas Rainborowe d. 1648
English soldier and parliamentarian

15 The poorest he that is in England hath a life to live as the greatest he.
during the Army debates at Putney, 29 October 1647, in C. H. Firth (ed.) *The Clarke Papers* vol. 1, Camden Society, New Series 49 (1891)

Craig Raine 1944–
English poet

16 In homes, a haunted apparatus sleeps,
that snores when you pick it up.
If the ghost cries, they carry it
to their lips and soothe it to sleep
with sounds. And yet, they wake it up
deliberately, but tickling it with a finger.
'A Martian sends a Postcard Home' (1979)

Kathleen Raine 1908–
British poet

17 He has married me with a ring, a ring of bright water
Whose ripples spread from the heart of the sea.
'The Marriage of Psyche' (1952)

Walter Ralegh c.1552–1618
English explorer and courtier
*see also **Last words** 472:6*

18 If all the world and love were young,
And truth in every shepherd's tongue,
These pretty pleasures might me move
To live with thee, and be thy love.
'Answer to Marlow'; see **Donne** 280:15, **Marlowe** 513:16

19 Now what is love? I pray thee, tell.
It is that fountain and that well,

Where pleasure and repentance dwell.
'A Description of Love'

1 A maze wherein affection finds no end,
A ranging cloud that runs before the wind,
A substance like the shadow of the sun,
A goal of grief for which the wisest run.
'Farewell false love' (1588)

2 Say to the court, it glows
And shines like rotten wood;
Say to the church, it shows
What's good, and doth no good:
If church and court reply,
Then give them both the lie.
'The Lie' (1608)

3 Tell zeal it wants devotion;
Tell love it is but lust;
Tell time it metes but motion;
Tell flesh it is but dust:
And wish them not reply,
For thou must give the lie.
'The Lie' (1608)

4 Only we die in earnest, that's no jest.
'On the Life of Man'

5 Give me my scallop-shell of quiet,
My staff of faith to walk upon,
My scrip of joy, immortal diet,
My bottle of salvation,
My gown of glory, hope's true gage,
And thus I'll take my pilgrimage.
'The Passionate Man's Pilgrimage' (1604)

6 Our passions are most like to floods and streams;
The shallow murmur, but the deep are dumb.
'Sir Walter Ralegh to the Queen' (1655)

7 Three things there be that prosper all apace,
And flourish while they are asunder far;
But on a day, they meet all in a place,
And when they meet, they one another mar.
And they be these: the Wood, the Weed, the Wag:
The Wood is that that makes the gallows tree;
The Weed is that that strings the hangman's bag;
The Wag, my pretty knave, betokens thee.
'Sir Walter Ralegh to his Son'

8 As you came from the holy land
Of Walsinghame,
Met you not with my true love
By the way as you came?

How shall I know your true love,
That have met many one
As I went to the holy land,
That have come, that have gone?
'Walsinghame'

9 But true love is a durable fire,
In the mind ever burning,
Never sick, never old, never dead,
From itself never turning.
'Walsinghame'

10 Fain would I climb, yet fear I to fall.
line written on a window-pane, in Thomas Fuller *History of the Worthies of England* (1662) 'Devonshire'; see **Elizabeth I** 304:14

11 Even such is Time, which takes in trust
Our youth, our joys, and all we have,
And pays us but with age and dust;
Who in the dark and silent grave,
When we have wandered all our ways,
Shuts up the story of our days:
And from which earth, and grave, and dust,
The Lord shall raise me up, I trust.
written the night before his death, and found in his Bible in the Gate-house at Westminster

12 [History] hath triumphed over time, which besides it, nothing but eternity hath triumphed over.
The History of the World (1614) preface

13 Whosoever, in writing a modern history, shall follow truth too near the heels, it may happily strike out his teeth.
The History of the World (1614) preface

14 O eloquent, just, and mighty Death! . . . thou hast drawn together all the farstretched greatness, all the pride, cruelty, and ambition of man, and covered it all over with these two narrow words, *Hic jacet* [Here lies].
The History of the World (1614) bk. 5, ch. 6

15 'Tis a sharp remedy, but a sure one for all ills.
on feeling the edge of the axe prior to his execution
D. Hume *History of Great Britain* (1754) vol. 1, ch. 4

16 So the heart be right, it is no matter which way the head lies.
at his execution, on being asked which way he preferred to lay his head
W. Stebbing *Sir Walter Raleigh* (1891) ch. 30

Walter Raleigh 1861–1922
English lecturer and critic

17 In examinations those who do not wish to know ask questions of those who cannot tell.
Laughter from a Cloud (1923) 'Some Thoughts on Examinations'

18 I wish I loved the Human Race;
I wish I loved its silly face;
I wish I liked the way it walks;
I wish I liked the way it talks;
And when I'm introduced to one
I wish I thought *What Jolly Fun!*
'Wishes of an Elderly Man' (1923)

19 An anthology is like all the plums and orange peel picked out of a cake.
letter to Mrs Robert Bridges, 15 January 1915

Srinivasa Ramanujan 1887–1920
Indian mathematician

20 *replying to G. H. **Hardy**'s suggestion that the number of a taxi-cab (1729) was 'dull':*
No, it is a very interesting number; it is the smallest number expressible as a sum of two cubes in two different ways.
the two ways being $1^3 + 12^3$ and $9^3 + 10^3$
in *Proceedings of the London Mathematical Society* 26 May 1921

Ayn Rand 1905–82

American writer

1 Civilization is the progress toward a society of privacy. The savage's noble existence is public, ruled by the laws of his tribe. Civilization is the process of setting man free from men.

The Fountainhead (1947)

John Randolph 1773–1833

American politician

2 God has given us Missouri, and the devil shall not take it from us.

in the debate in the US Senate in 1820 on the admission of Missouri to the Union as a slave state
Robert V. Remini *Henry Clay* (1991) ch. 11

3 Never were abilities so much below mediocrity so well rewarded; no, not when Caligula's horse was made Consul.

*on John Quincy **Adams**'s appointment of Richard Rush as Secretary of the Treasury*
speech, 1 February 1828

4 He is a man of splendid abilities but utterly corrupt. He shines and stinks like rotten mackerel by moonlight.

of Edward Livingston
W. Cabell Bruce *John Randolph of Roanoke* (1923) vol. 2

Ian Rankin 1960–

Scottish novelist

5 We can't really demolish it until they finish building it.

on the Scottish parliament building
in *Independent* 20 July 2002

John Crowe Ransom 1888–1974

American poet and critic

6 The lazy geese, like a snow cloud
Dripping their snow on the green grass,
Tricking and stopping, sleepy and proud,
Who cried in goose, alas.

'Bells for John Whiteside's Daughter' (1924)

7 Here lies a lady of beauty and high degree.
Of chills and fever she died, of fever and chills,
The delight of her husband, her aunts, an infant of three,
And of medicos marvelling sweetly on her ills.

'Here Lies a Lady' (1924)

8 Two evils, monstrous either one apart,
Possessed me, and were long and loath at going:
A cry of Absence, Absence, in the heart,
And in the wood the furious winter blowing.

'Winter Remembered' (1945)

Raoul Glabar c.985–c.1046

French Cluniac monk and chronicler

9 After the above-mentioned millennium which is now about three years past, there occurred throughout the whole world . . . a rebuilding of church basilicas . . . It was as if the whole earth, having cast off the old by shaking itself, were clothing itself everywhere in a white robe of churches.

of the rebuilding of churches in the 11th century
Histories bk 3, ch. 4

Frederic Raphael 1931–

British novelist and screenwriter
*see also **Borrowed titles** 146:8*

10 Your idea of fidelity is not having more than one man in bed at the same time.

Darling (1965) ch. 18

11 City of perspiring dreams.

of Cambridge
The Glittering Prizes (1976) ch. 3 ; see **Arnold** 28:24

Dan Rather 1931–

American journalist

12 I worry that patriotism run amok will trample the very values that the country seeks to defend.

in *Independent* 18 May 2002

Gerald Ratner 1949–

English businessman

13 We even sell a pair of earrings for under £1, which is cheaper than a prawn sandwich from Marks & Spencers. But I have to say the earrings probably won't last as long.

speech to the Institute of Directors, Albert Hall, 23 April 1991

Terence Rattigan 1911–77

English dramatist

14 Do you know what 'le vice Anglais'—the English vice—really is? Not flagellation, not pederasty—whatever the French believe it to be. It's our refusal to admit our emotions. We think they demean us, I suppose.

In Praise of Love (1973) act 2

15 You can be in the Horseguards and still be common, dear.

Separate Tables (1954) 'Table Number Seven' sc. 1

Gwen Raverat 1885–1957

English wood-engraver

16 Ladies were ladies in those days; they did not do things themselves.

Period Piece (1952) ch. 5

Derek Raymond 1931–94

English thriller writer

17 The psychopath is the furnace that gives no heat.

The Hidden Files (1992)

Herbert Read 1893–1968

English art historian

18 Do not judge this movement kindly. It is not just another amusing stunt. It is defiant—the desperate act of men too profoundly convinced of the rottenness of our civilization to want to save a shred of its respectability.

> International Surrealist Exhibition Catalogue, New Burlington Galleries, London, 11 June-4 July 1936, introduction

1 Images of flight, of ragged claws 'scuttling across the floors of silent seas', of excoriated flesh, frustrated sex, the geometry of fear.

on twentieth-century British sculpture

> introduction to catalogue of Venice Biennale, 1952; Richard Calvocoressi *British Sculpture in the Twentieth Century* (1981); see **Eliot** 302:16

2 Art is . . . pattern informed by sensibility.

> *The Meaning of Art* (1955) ch. 1

3 Lorca was killed, singing,
and Fox who was my friend.
The rhythm returns: the song
which has no end.

> 'The Heart Conscripted' (1938)

4 I saw him stab
And stab again
A well-killed Boche.

This is the happy warrior,
This is he . . .

> *Naked Warriors* (1919) 'The Scene of War, 4. The Happy Warrior'; see **Wordsworth** 846:5

Piers Paul Read 1941–

English novelist

5 Sins become more subtle as you grow older. You commit sins of despair rather than lust.

> in *Daily Telegraph* 3 October 1990

Charles Reade 1814–84

English novelist and dramatist

6 *Courage, mon ami, le diable est mort!*

Take courage, my friend, the devil is dead!

> *The Cloister and the Hearth* (1861) ch. 24, and *passim*

7 Sow an act, and you reap a habit. Sow a habit and you reap a character. Sow a character, and you reap a destiny.

> attributed; in *Notes and Queries* (9th Series) vol. 12, 17 October 1903

Nancy Reagan 1923–

American actress and wife of Ronald **Reagan***, First Lady of the US, 1981–9*

see also **Slogans** 740:7

8 A woman is like a teabag—only in hot water do you realize how strong she is.

> in *Observer* 29 March 1981

9 If the President has a bully pulpit, then the First Lady has a white glove pulpit . . . more refined, restricted, ceremonial, but it's a pulpit all the same.

> in *New York Times* 10 March 1988; see **Roosevelt** 654:11

Ronald Reagan 1911–

American Republican statesman; 40th President of the US, 1981–9

see also **Dempsey** 264:1, **Gipp** 349:20

10 Politics is supposed to be the second oldest profession. I have come to realize that it bears a very close resemblance to the first.

> at a conference in Los Angeles, 2 March 1977; in Bill Adler *Reagan Wit* (1981) ch. 5; see **Kipling** 456:9

11 I paid for this microphone.

> *in 1980, debating for the Republican nomination against George* **Bush***; the moderator had ordered Reagan's microphone turned off when he asked for the participation of other candidates, and the refusal to allow this was held to be very damaging to Bush*
>
> Lou Cannon *Ronald Reagan* (1982)

12 *President* **Carter** *had described a proposal for a national health insurance plan*

JIMMY CARTER: Governor Reagan, again, typically is against such a proposal.

RONALD REAGAN: There you go again!

> as Republican challenger debating with President Carter in the 1980 presidential campaign; in *Times* 30 October 1980

13 You can tell a lot about a fellow's character by his way of eating jellybeans.

> in *New York Times* 15 January 1981

14 An evil empire.

of the Soviet Union

> speech to the National Association of Evangelicals, 8 March 1983; in *New York Times* 9 March 1983

15 We are especially not going to tolerate these attacks from outlaw states run by the strangest collection of misfits, Looney Tunes, and squalid criminals since the advent of the Third Reich.

> speech following the hijack of a US plane, 8 July 1985, in *New York Times* 9 July 1985

16 We will never forget them, nor the last time we saw them this morning, as they prepared for the journey and waved goodbye and 'slipped the surly bonds of earth' to 'touch the face of God.'

after the loss of the space shuttle Challenger *with all its crew*

> broadcast from the Oval Office, 28 January 1986; see **Magee** 505:16

17 I now begin the journey that will lead me into the sunset of my life.

statement to the American people revealing that he had Alzheimer's disease

> in *Daily Telegraph* 5 January 1995

Erell Reaves

18 Lady of Spain, I adore you.
Right from the night I first saw you,
My heart has been yearning for you,
What else could any heart do?

> 'Lady of Spain' (1913 song)

Red Cloud (Mahpiua Luta) 1822–1909

Sioux chief

19 You have heard the sound of the white soldier's axe upon the Little Piney. His presence here is . . .

an insult to the spirits of our ancestors. Are we then to give up their sacred graves to be ploughed for corn? Dakotas, I am for war!

speech at council at Fort Laramie, 1866; Charles A. Eastman *Indian Heroes and Great Chieftains* (1918)

John Redmond 1856–1918

Irish politician and nationalist leader

1 *in the spring of 1914, having been asked if anything could now prevent Home Rule:*
A European war might do it.

in *Dictionary of National Biography* (1917–)

Henry Reed 1914–86

English poet and dramatist

2 As we get older we do not get any younger.
Seasons return, and today I am fifty-five,
And this time last year I was fifty-four,
And this time next year I shall be sixty-two.

'Chard Whitlow (Mr Eliot's Sunday Evening Postscript)' (1946)

3 Today we have naming of parts. Yesterday,
We had daily cleaning. And tomorrow morning,
We shall have what to do after firing. But today,
Today we have naming of parts. Japonica
Glistens like coral in all of the neighbour gardens,
And today we have naming of parts.

'Lessons of the War: 1, Naming of Parts' (1946)

4 They call it easing the Spring: it is perfectly easy
If you have any strength in your thumb: like the bolt,
And the breech, and the cocking-piece, and the point of balance,
Which in our case we have not got.

'Lessons of the War: 1, Naming of Parts' (1946)

5   And as for war, my wars
Were global from the start.

'Lessons of the War: 3, Unarmed Combat' (1946)

6 In a civil war, a general must know—and I'm afraid it's a thing rather of instinct than of practice—he must know exactly when to move over to the other side.

Not a Drum was Heard: The War Memoirs of General Gland (unpublished radio play, 1959)

7 And the sooner the tea's out of the way, the sooner we can get out the gin, eh?

Private Life of Hilda Tablet (1954 radio play) in *Hilda Tablet and Others* (1971)

8 Of course we've all *dreamed* of reviving the *castrati*; but it's needed Hilda to take the first practical steps towards making them a reality . . . She's drawn up a list of well-known singers who she thinks would benefit . . . It's only a question of getting them to agree.

Private Life of Hilda Tablet (1954 radio play) in *Hilda Tablet and Others* (1971)

9 Modest? My word, no . . . He was an all-the-lights-on man.

A Very Great Man Indeed (1953 radio play) in *Hilda Tablet and Others* (1971)

10 I have known her pass the whole evening without mentioning a single book, or *in fact anything unpleasant,* at all.

A Very Great Man Indeed (1953 radio play) in *Hilda Tablet and Others* (1971)

John Reed 1887–1920

American journalist and revolutionary

11 Ten days that shook the world.

title of book (1919)

Joseph Reed 1741–85

American Revolutionary politician

12 I am not worth purchasing, but such as I am, the King of Great Britain is not rich enough to do it.

replying to an offer from Governor George Johnstone of £10,000, and any office in the Colonies in the King's gift, if he were able successfully to promote a Union between the UK and the US

reply as recorded in a declaration of Congress, 11 August 1778; the earliest version is:

My influence is but small, but were it as great as Governor Johnstone would insinuate, the King of Great Britain has nothing within his gift that would tempt me.

reply to Mrs Elizabeth Ferguson, 21 June 1778; W. B. Read *Life and Correspondence of Joseph Reed* (1847) vol. 1, ch. 18

Christopher Reeve 1952–

American actor

13 To be able to feel the lightest touch is really a gift.

regaining some movement after being paralysed in a riding accident seven years before

in *Sunday Times* 15 September 2002

Max Reger 1873–1916

German composer

14 I am sitting in the smallest room of my house. I have your review before me. In a moment it will be behind me.

responding to a savage review by Rudolph Louis in Münchener Neueste Nachrichten, *7 February 1906*

Nicolas Slonimsky *Lexicon of Musical Invective* (1953)

Charles A. Reich 1928–

American jurist

15 The greening of America.

title of book (1970)

Keith Reid 1946–

English pop singer and songwriter

16 Her face, at first . . . just ghostly
Turned a whiter shade of pale.

'A Whiter Shade of Pale' (1967 song)

Lord Reith 1889–1971

British administrator and politician, first general manager (1922–7) and first director-general (1927–8) of the BBC

1 He who prides himself on giving what he thinks the public wants is often creating a fictitious demand for lower standards which he will then satisfy.
> memo to Crawford Committee 1926; Andrew Boyle *Only the Wind Will Listen* (1972)

2 By the time the civil service has finished drafting a document to give effect to a principle, there may be little of the principle left.
> *Into the Wind* (1949)

3 When people feel deeply, impartiality is bias.
> *Into the Wind* (1949)

Erich Maria Remarque 1898–1970

German novelist

4 All quiet on the western front.
> English title of *Im Westen nichts Neues* (1929 novel); see **Beers** 63:9, **McClellan** 500:12

Ernest Renan 1823–92

French philologist and historian

5 Before French culture, German culture, Italian culture, there is human culture.
> 'Qu'est-ce qu'une nation', address given in 1882

Jules Renard 1864–1910

French novelist and dramatist

6 *Les bourgeois, ce sont les autres.*
> The bourgeois are other people.
> diary, 28 January 1890, in *Oeuvres Complètes* (1925–7) vol. 5

Montague John Rendall 1862–1950

British member of the first BBC Board of Governors

7 Nation shall speak peace unto nation.
> motto of the BBC; see **Bible** 88:2

Jean Renoir 1894–1979

French film director

8 Is it possible to succeed without any act of betrayal?
> *My Life and My Films* (1974) 'Nana'

9 Don't think that this is a letter. It is only a small eruption of a disease called friendship.
> letter to Janine Bazin, 12 June 1974; D. Thompson and L. LoBianco (eds.) *Letters* (1994)

Pierre Auguste Renoir 1841–1919

French painter
see also **Misquotations** 538:3

10 *C'étaient des fous, mais ils avaient cette petite flamme qui ne s'éteint pas.*
> They were madmen; but they had in them that little flame which is not to be snuffed out.
> *on the men of the French Commune*
> Jean Renoir *Renoir, My Father* (translated by R. and D. Weaver, 1962) ch. 12

Jean-François Paul de Gondi, Cardinal de Retz 1613–79

French cardinal

11 *Il n'y a rien dans le monde qui n'ait son moment décisif, et le chef-d'oeuvre de la bonne conduite est de connaître et de prendre ce moment.*
> There is nothing in the world which does not have its decisive moment, and the masterpiece of good management is to recognize and grasp this moment.
> *Mémoires* (1717) bk. 2

12 *Un homme qui ne se fie pas à soi-même ne se fie jamais véritablement à personne.*
> A man who does not trust himself will never really trust anybody.
> *Mémoires* (1717) bk. 3

Walter Reuther 1907–70

American labour leader

13 If it looks like a duck, walks like a duck and quacks like a duck, then it just may be a duck.
> *as a test, during the* **McCarthy** *era, of Communist affiliations*
> attributed

Paul Revere 1735–1818

American patriot
on Revere: see **Longfellow** 491:4

14 [We agreed] that if the British went out by water, we would show two lanterns in the North Church steeple; and if by land, one as a signal; for we were apprehensive it would be difficult to cross the Charles River or get over Boston Neck.
> *signals to be used if the British troops moved out of Boston; see* **Longfellow** 491:5
> arrangements agreed with the Charlestown Committee of Safety on 16 April, 1775

Charles Revson 1906–75

American businessman

15 In the factory we make cosmetics; in the store we sell hope.
> A. Tobias *Fire and Ice* (1976)

Frederic Reynolds 1764–1841

English dramatist

16 It is better to have written a damned play, than no play at all—it snatches a man from obscurity.
> *The Dramatist* (1789) act 1, sc. 1

Joshua Reynolds 1723–92

English painter
on Reynolds: see **Goldsmith** 355:9, **Walpole** 819:16

17 Few have been taught to any purpose who have not been their own teachers.
> *Discourses on Art* (ed. R. Wark, 1975) no. 2 (11 December 1769)

1 If you have great talents, industry will improve them: if you have but moderate abilities, industry will supply their deficiency.
   Discourses on Art (ed. R. Wark, 1975) no. 2 (11 December 1769)

2 A mere copier of nature can never produce anything great.
   Discourses on Art (ed. R. Wark, 1975) no. 3 (14 December 1770)

3 Could we teach taste or genius by rules, they would be no longer taste and genius.
   Discourses on Art (ed. R. Wark, 1975) no. 3 (14 December 1770)

4 The value and rank of every art is in proportion to the mental labour employed in it, or the mental pleasure produced by it.
   Discourses on Art (ed. R. Wark, 1975) no. 4 (10 December 1771)

5 Genius . . . is the child of imitation.
   Discourses on Art (ed. R. Wark, 1975) no. 6 (10 December 1774)

6 The mind is but a barren soil; a soil which is soon exhausted, and will produce no crop, or only one, unless it be continually fertilized and enriched with foreign matter.
   Discourses on Art (ed. R. Wark, 1975) no. 6 (10 December 1774)

7 Art in its perfection is not ostentatious; it lies hid, and works its effect, itself unseen.
   Discourses on Art (ed. R. Wark, 1975) no. 6 (10 December 1774)

8 It is the very same taste which relishes a demonstration in geometry, that is pleased with the resemblance of a picture to an original, and touched with the harmony of music.
   Discourses on Art (ed. R. Wark, 1975) no. 7 (10 December 1776)

9 I should desire that the last words which I should pronounce in this Academy, and from this place, might be the name of—Michael Angelo.
   Discourses on Art (ed. R. Wark, 1975) no. 15 (10 December 1790)

Malvina Reynolds 1900–78

American songwriter

10 Little boxes on the hillside . . .
   And they're all made out of ticky-tacky
   And they all look just the same.
   on the tract houses in the hills to the south of San Francisco
   'Little Boxes' (1962 song)

Cecil Rhodes 1853–1902

South African statesman
see also **Last words** 473:17

11 Ask any man what nationality he would prefer to be, and ninety-nine out of a hundred will tell you that they would prefer to be Englishmen.
   Gordon Le Sueur *Cecil Rhodes* (1913)

Jean Rhys (Ella Gwendolen Rees Williams) c.1890–1979

British novelist and short-story writer

12 We can't all be happy, we can't all be rich, we can't all be lucky—and it would be so much less fun if we were . . . Some must cry so that others may be able to laugh the more heartily.
   Good Morning, Midnight (1939) pt. 1

13 The perpetual hunger to be beautiful and that thirst to be loved which is the real curse of Eve.
   The Left Bank (1927) 'Illusion'

14 Only the hopeless are starkly sincere and . . . only the unhappy can either give or take sympathy.
   The Left Bank (1927) 'In the Rue de l'Arrivée'

15 The feeling of Sunday is the same everywhere, heavy, melancholy, standing still. Like when they say 'As it was in the beginning, is now, and ever shall be, world without end.'
   Voyage in the Dark (1934) ch. 4, pt. 1

16 A doormat in a world of boots.
   describing herself
   in *Guardian* 6 December 1990

David Ricardo 1772–1823

British economist

17 Rent is that portion of the earth, which is paid to the landlord for the use of the original and indestructible powers of the soil.
   On the Principles of Political Economy and Taxation (1817) ch. 2

Alice Caldwell Rice 1870–1942

American humorist

18 Life is made up of desires that seem big and vital one minute and little and absurd the next. I guess we get what's best for us in the end.
   A Romance of Billy-Goat Hill (1912) ch. 2

Grantland Rice 1880–1954

American sports writer

19 For when the One Great Scorer comes to mark against your name,
   He writes—not that you won or lost—but how you played the Game.
   'Alumnus Football' (1941)

20 All wars are planned by old men
   In council rooms apart.
   'The Two Sides of War' (1955)

21 Outlined against a blue-grey October sky, the Four Horsemen rode again. In dramatic lore they were known as Famine, Pestilence, Destruction, and Death. These are only aliases. Their real names are Stuhldreher, Miller, Crowley, and Layden. They formed the crest of the South Bend cyclone before which another fighting Army football team was swept over the precipice.
   report of football match between US Military Academy at West Point NY and University of Notre Dame
   in *New York Tribune* 19 October 1924

Stephen Rice 1637–1715

Irish lawyer

1 I will drive a coach and six horses through the Act of Settlement.

> W. King *State of the Protestants of Ireland* (1672) ch. 3, sect. 8

Tim Rice 1944–

English songwriter

2 Prove to me that you're no fool
Walk across my swimming pool.

> *Jesus Christ Superstar* (1970) 'Herod's Song'; music by Andrew Lloyd Webber

Mandy Rice-Davies 1944–

English model and showgirl

3 He would, wouldn't he?

> *on hearing that Lord Astor denied her allegations, concerning himself and his house parties at Cliveden*
> at the trial of Stephen Ward, 29 June 1963; in *Guardian* 1 July 1963

Adrienne Rich 1923–

American poet and critic

4 The thing I came for:
the wreck and not the story of the wreck
the thing itself and not the myth.

> 'Diving into the Wreck' (1973)'

5 Memory says: Want to do right? Don't count on me.

> 'Eastern War Time' (1991)

6 I'm accused of child-death of drinking blood . . .
there is spit on my sleeve there are phonecalls in the night . . .

> 'Eastern War Time' (1991)

7 Our friends were not unearthly beautiful.
Nor spoke with tongues of gold; our lovers blundered
Now and again when most we sought perfection,
Or hid in cupboards when the heavens thundered.

> 'Ideal Landscape' (1955)

Ann Richards 1933–

American Democratic politician

8 Poor George, he can't help it—he was born with a silver foot in his mouth.

> *of George* **Bush**
> keynote speech at the Democratic convention, 1988; in *Independent* 20 July 1988

Frank Richards (Charles Hamilton) 1876–1961

English writer for boys

9 The fat greedy owl of the Remove.

> 'Billy Bunter' in the *Magnet* (1909) vol. 3, no. 72 'The Greyfriars Photographer'

I. A. Richards 1893–1979

English literary critic

10 It [poetry] is capable of saving us; it is a perfectly possible means of overcoming chaos.

> *Science and Poetry* (1926) ch. 7

Justin Richardson 1900–75

British poet

11 For years a secret shame destroyed my peace—
I'd not read Eliot, Auden or MacNeice.
But then I had a thought that brought me hope—
Neither had Chaucer, Shakespeare, Milton, Pope.

> 'Take Heart, Illiterates' (1966)

Samuel Richardson 1689–1761

English novelist
on Richardson: see **Diderot** 274:3, **Johnson** 429:19

12 I have known a bird actually starve itself, and die with grief, at its being caught and caged—But never did I meet with a lady who was so silly . . . And yet we must all own that it is more difficult to catch a bird than a lady.

> *Clarissa* (1747–8) vol. 3, letter 75

13 Mine is the most plotting heart in the world.

> *Clarissa* (1747–8) vol. 3, letter 76

14 The affair is over. Clarissa lives.

> *announcement by Lovelace of his successful seduction of Clarissa*
> *Clarissa* (1747–8) vol. 5, letter 22

15 What, my Lord, is ancestry? I live to my own heart.

> *History of Sir Charles Grandison* (1754) vol. 3, letter 26

16 A feeling heart is a blessing that no one, who has it, would be without; and it is a moral security of innocence; since the heart that is able to partake of the distress of another, cannot wilfully give it.

> *History of Sir Charles Grandison* (1754) vol. 3, letter 32

17 His spurious brat, Tom Jones.

> *of* **Fielding**
> letter to Thomas Edwards, 21 February 1752

18 Instruction, Madam, is the pill; amusement is the gilding.

> letter to Lady Echlin, 22 September 1755

Cardinal Richelieu 1585–1642

French cleric and statesman

19 If you give me six lines written by the hand of the most honest of men, I will find something in them which will hang him.

> attributed

Mordecai Richler 1931–2001

Canadian writer

20 I'm world famous, Dr Parks said, all over Canada.

> *The Incomparable Atuk* (1963)

21 Wherever I travel I'm too late. The orgy has moved elsewhere.

> *Shovelling Trouble* (1972) 'A Sense of the Ridiculous'

Hans Richter 1843–1916

German conductor

1 Up with your damned nonsense will I put twice, or
perhaps once, but sometimes always, by God,
never.
attributed

Johann Paul Friedrich Richter ('Jean Paul') 1763–1825

German novelist

2 Providence has given to the French the empire of
the land, to the English that of the sea, and to the
Germans that of—the air!
Thomas Carlyle 'Jean Paul Friedrich Richter' in *Edinburgh
Review* no. 91 (1827)

George Ridding 1828–1904

English Bishop of Southwell from 1884

3 I feel a feeling which I feel you all feel.
sermon in the London Mission, 1885; in G. W. E. Russell
Collections and Recollections (1898) ch. 29

Laura Riding 1901–91

American poet and novelist

4 Without dressmakers to connect
The good-will of the body
With the purpose of the head,
We should be two worlds
Instead of a world and its shadow
The flesh.
'Because of Clothes' (1938)

5 Art, whose honesty must work through artifice,
cannot avoid cheating truth.
Selected Poems: In Five Sets (1975) preface

Nicholas Ridley 1929–93

British Conservative politician

6 *of the European Community:*
This is all a German racket, designed to take over
the whole of Europe.
in *Spectator* 14 July 1990

Louis Riel 1844–85

Canadian Métis political leader

7 People say the native stands on the edge of a
chasm. It is not he who stands on the edge of a
chasm; his claims are not false. They are just . . .
Every step the Indian takes is based on a profound
step of fairness.
diary, 6 May 1885

8 I have been hunted as an elk for fifteen years.
speaking at the end of his trial, 1 August 1885; *The Queen
vs. Louis Riel* (1886)

9 Every day in which I have neglected to prepare
myself to die was a day of mental alienation.
interview published in the *Regina Leader* shortly before his
execution by hanging on 16 November 1885

Rig Veda

*a collection of hymns in early Sanskrit, composed in the 2nd
millenium BC*

10 We meditate on the lovely light of the god, Savitri:
May it stimulate our thoughts!
The Gāyatrī bk. 3, hymn 62, v. 10

11 Whence this creation has arisen—perhaps it
formed itself, or perhaps it did not—the one
who looks down on it, in the highest heaven,
only he knows—or perhaps he does not know.
Creation Hymn bk. 10, hymn 129, v. 7

12 When they divided the Man, into how many parts
did they apportion him? What did they call his
mouth, his two arms and thighs and feet?
His mouth became the Brahman; his arms were
made into the Warrior, his thighs the People,
and from his feet the Servants were born.
Hymn of Man bk. 10, hymn 190, v. 11

Rainer Maria Rilke 1875–1926

German poet

13 *Wer sass nicht bang vor seines Herzen Vorhang?*
Who has not sat nervously before the stage
curtain of his heart?
Duineser Elegien no. 4

14   *Alles
Ist nicht es selbst.*
Everything is not itself.
Duineser Elegien no. 4

15 *Wer hat uns also umgedreht, dass wir,
was wir auch tun, in jener Haltung sind
von einem, welcher fortgeht? Wie er auf
dem letzten Hügel, der ihm ganz sein Tal
noch einmal zeigt, sich wendet, anhält, weilt—,
So leben wir und nehmen immer Abschied.*
Who's turned us around like this, so that we
 always,
do what we may, retain the attitude
of someone who's departing? Just as he,
on the last hill, that shows him all his valley
for the last time, will turn and stop and linger,
We live our lives, for ever taking leave.
Duineser Elegien (translated by J. B. Leishman and Stephen
Spender, 1948) no. 8

16 *Wir haben, wo wir lieben, ja nur dies:
einander lassen; denn dass wir uns halten,
das fällt uns leicht und ist nicht erst zu lernen.*
We need in love to practise only this:
letting each other go. For holding on
comes easily; we do not need to learn it.
Requiem für eine Freundin ('Requiem for a Friend')

17 *Er ist einer der bleibenden Boten,
der noch weit in die Türen der Toten
Schalen mit rühmlichen Früchten halt.*
He is one of the staying messengers
Who still holds far into the doors of the dead
bowls of fruit worthy of praise.
'Sonnets to Orpheus', first part (*c.*1922)

18 Works of art are of an infinite solitariness, and
nothing is less likely to bring us near to them than

criticism. Only love can apprehend and hold them, and can be just towards them.

> *Letters to a Young Poet* (1929) 23 April 1903 (translated by Reginald Snell)

1 Love consists in this, that two solitudes protect and touch and greet each other.

> *Letters to a Young Poet* (1929) 14 May 1904 (translated by Hugh MacLennan)

2 People have already had to rethink so many concepts of motion, and they will also gradually come to realize that what we call fate does not come into us from the outside, but emerges from us.

> *Letters to a Young Poet* (1929) 12 August 1904 (translated by Stephen Mitchell)

3 I hold this to be the highest task for a bond between two people: that each protects the solitude of the other.

> letter to Paula Modersohn-Becker, 12 February 1902, in *Gesammelte Briefe* (1904) vol. 1

4 I don't think of work, only of gradually regaining my health through reading, rereading, reflecting.

> letter, c.1911; Donald Prater *A Ringing Glass* (1986)

Arthur Rimbaud 1854–91
French poet

5 *Plus douce qu'aux enfants la chair des pommes surettes,*
L'eau verte pénétra ma coque de sapin.

Sweeter than the flesh of tart apples to children, the green water penetrates my wooden hull.

> 'Le Bâteau ivre' (1883)

6 *. . . Je me suis baigné dans le Poème*
De la Mer, infusé d'astres, et lactescent,
Dévorant les azurs verts.

I have bathed in the Poem of the Sea, steeped in stars, and milky, devouring the green azures.

> 'Le Bâteau ivre' (1883)

7 *J'ai vu le soleil bas, taché d'horreurs mystiques*
Illuminant de longs figements violets,
Pareils à des acteurs de drames très-antiques.

I have seen the sun set, stained with mystic horrors, illuminating the long violet [blood-] clots, just like actors in very ancient plays.

> 'Le Bâteau ivre' (1883)

8 *Je regrette l'Europe aux anciens parapets!*

I pine for Europe of the ancient parapets!

> 'Le Bâteau ivre' (1883)

9 *Je m'en allais, les poings dans mes poches crevées;*
Mon paletot aussi devenait idéal.

I was walking along, hands in holey pockets; my overcoat also was entering the realms of the ideal.

> 'Ma Bohème' (1870)

10 *A l'aurore, armés d'une ardente patience, nous entrerons aux splendides villes.*

At dawn, armed with a burning patience, we shall enter the splendid cities.

> 'Une Saison en enfer' (1873)

11 *Ô saisons, ô châteaux!*
Quelle âme est sans défauts?

O saisons, ô châteaux,
J'ai fait la magique étude
Du bonheur, que nul n'élude.

O seasons, O castles! What soul is without fault? I have made the magic study of good fortune which not one eludes.

> 'Ô saisons, ô châteaux' (1872)

12 *A noir, E blanc, I rouge, U vert, O bleu: voyelles,*
Je dirais quelque jour vos naissances latentes . . .
I, pourpres, sang craché, rire des lèvres belles
Dans la colère ou les ivresses pénitentes.

A black, E white, I red, U green, O blue: vowels, some day I will tell of the births that may be yours. I, purples, coughed-up blood, laughter of beautiful lips in anger or penitent drunkennesses.

> 'Voyelles' (1870)

César Ritz 1850–1918
Swiss hotel proprietor

13 *Le client n'a jamais tort.*

The customer is never wrong.

> R. Nevill and C. E. Jerningham *Piccadilly to Pall Mall* (1908); see **Proverbs** 617:21

Antoine de Rivarol 1753–1801
French man of letters

14 *Ce qui n'est pas clair n'est pas français.*

What is not clear is not French.

> *Discours sur l'Universalité de la Langue Française* (1784)

Joan Riviere b. 1883

15 Civilization and its discontents.

> title given to her translation of Sigmund **Freud**'s *Das Unbehagen in der Kultur* (1930)

Alain Robbe-Grillet 1922–
French novelist

16 *De la commode à la table il y a six pas: trois pas jusqu'à la cheminée et trois autres ensuite. Il y a cinq pas de la table au coin du lit; quatre pas du lit à la commode. Le chemin qui va de la commode à la table n'est pas tout à fait rectiligne: il s'incurve légèrement pour passer plus près de la cheminée.*

From the chest of drawers to the table is six steps; three to the fireplace and three more after that. It is five steps from the table to the corner of the bed; four steps from the bed to the chest of drawers. The path from the chest of drawers to the table is not quite straight: it curves gently to pass nearer the fireplace.

> *In the Labyrinth* (1959) translated by Christine Brooke-Rose

Lord Robbins 1898–1984
British economist

17 Economics is the science which studies human behaviour as a relationship between ends and scarce means which have alternative uses.

> *Essay on the Nature and Significance of Economic Science* (1932) ch. 1, sect. 3

Robin Robertson 1955-

Scottish poet

1 then bite the tongue out by the root . . .
and chew, never swallow.
This is not sex, remember;
you are eating the sea.
'Oyster' (1997)

Maximilien Robespierre 1758-94

French revolutionary
on Robespierre: see **Carlyle** *192:8,* **Heine** *380:5*

2 I am no courtier, nor moderator, nor Tribune, nor
defender of the people: I am myself the people.
speech at the Jacobin Club, 27 April 1792; in G. Laurent
(ed.) *Le Defénseur de la Constitution* (1939)

3 *Citoyens, vouliez-vous une revolution sans revolution?*
Citizens, would you want a revolution without
revolution?
speech to the Convention, 5 November 1792

4 The general will rules in society as the private will
governs each separate individual.
Lettres à ses commettans (2nd series) 5 January 1793

5 Any law which violates the inalienable rights of
man is essentially unjust and tyrannical; it is not
a law at all.
Déclaration des droits de l'homme 24 April 1793, article 6;
this article, in slightly different form, is recorded as having
figured in Robespierre's *Projet* of 21 April 1793

6 Any institution which does not suppose the people
good, and the magistrate corruptible, is evil.
Déclaration des droits de l'homme 24 April 1793, article 25

7 Wickedness is the root of despotism as virtue is the
essence of the Republic.
in the Convention, 7 May 1794; in C. Vellay (ed.) *Discours
et Rapports de Robespierre* (1908)

8 One single will is necessary.
private note, in S. A. Berville and J. F. Barrière *Papiers
inédits trouvés chez Robespierre* vol. 2 (1828) no. 44

9 Intimidation without virtue is disastrous; virtue
without intimidation is powerless.
J. M. Thompson *The French Revolution* (1943); attributed

Leo Robin 1900-84

American songwriter

10 A kiss on the hand may be quite continental,
But diamonds are a girl's best friend.
'Diamonds are a Girl's Best Friend' (1949 song) from the
film *Gentlemen Prefer Blondes*; see **Loos** 491:19

11 Thanks for the memory.
title of song (with Ralph Rainger, 1937)

Elizabeth Robins 1862-1952

American writer

12 To say in print what she thinks is the last thing
the woman novelist or journalist is so rash as to
attempt . . . Her publishers are not women.
in 1908, as first president of the Women Writers' Suffrage
League

Edwin Arlington Robinson 1869-1935

American poet

13 I shall have more to say when I am dead.
'John Brown' (1920)

14 Go to the western gate, Luke Havergal,
There where the vines cling crimson on the wall,
And in the twilight wait for what will come.
'Luke Havergal' (1896)

15 So on we worked, and waited for the light,
And went without meat, and cursed the bread;
And Richard Cory, one calm summer night,
Went home and put a bullet through his head.
'Richard Cory' (1897)

16 The world is not a 'prison house', but a kind of
kindergarten, where millions of bewildered infants
are trying to spell God with the wrong blocks.
Literature in the Making (1917)

John Robinson ?1576-1625

English pastor to the Pilgrim Fathers

17 The Lord has more truth yet to break forth out of
his holy word.
alleged address to the departing pilgrims, 1620
in *Dictionary of National Biography* (1917-)

18 The Lutherans refuse to advance beyond what
Luther saw, while the Calvinists stick fast where
they were left by that great man of God, who saw
not all things.
*regretting the current state of the reformed churches,
in the alleged address to the departing pilgrims, 1620*
in *Dictionary of National Biography* (1917-)

John Robinson 1919-83

English theologian; Bishop of Woolwich, 1959-69

19 Honest to God.
title of book (1963)

20 I think Lawrence tried to portray this [sex] relation
as in a real sense an act of holy communion. For
him flesh was sacramental of the spirit.
*as defence witness in the case against Penguin Books
for publishing* Lady Chatterley's Lover
in *The Times* 28 October 1960

Mary Robinson 1758-1800

English poet

21 Pavement slippery, people sneezing,
Lords in ermine, beggars freezing;
Titled gluttons dainties carving,
Genius in a garret starving.
'January, 1795'

Mary Robinson 1944-

Irish Labour stateswoman; President 1990-97

22 Instead of rocking the cradle, they rocked the
system.
*in her victory speech, paying tribute to the women of
Ireland*
in *The Times* 10 November 1990; see **Wallace** 818:3

Boyle Roche 1743–1807

Irish politician

1 The best way to avoid danger is to meet it plump.

Jonah Barrington *Personal Sketches and Recollections of his own Times* (1827)

2 A disorderly set of people whom no king can govern and no God can please.

of the Ulster Protestants
attributed

3 Mr Speaker, I smell a rat; I see him forming in the air and darkening the sky; but I'll nip him in the bud.

attributed

John Wilmot, Lord Rochester 1647–80

English poet
see also **Epitaphs** 309:14

4 Tell me no more of constancy,
that frivolous pretence,
Of cold age, narrow jealousy,
disease and want of sense.

'Against Constancy' (1676)

5   'Is there then no more?'
She cries. 'All this to love and rapture's due;
Must we not pay a debt to pleasure too?'

'The Imperfect Enjoyment' (1680)

6 May'st thou ne'er piss, who didst refuse to spend
When all my joys did on false thee depend.

'The Imperfect Enjoyment' (1680)

7 Love . . .
That cordial drop heaven in our cup has thrown
To make the nauseous draught of life go down.

'A Letter from Artemisia in the Town to Chloe in the Country' (1679)

8 An age in her embraces passed
Would seem a winter's day,
Where life and light with envious haste
Are torn and snatched away.

'The Mistress: A Song' (1691)

9 Kind jealous doubts, tormenting fears,
And anxious cares, when past,
Prove our hearts' treasure fixed and dear,
And make us blest at last.

'The Mistress: A Song' (1691)

10   Natural freedoms are but just:
There's something generous in mere lust.

'A Ramble in St James' Park' (1680)

11 Reason, an *ignis fatuus* of the mind,
Which leaves the light of nature, sense, behind.

'A Satire against Mankind' (1679) l. 11

12 Then Old Age, and Experience, hand in hand,
Lead him to Death, and make him understand . . .
Huddled in dirt the reasoning engine lies,
Who was so proud, so witty and so wise.

'A Satire against Mankind' (1679) l. 25

13 For all men would be cowards if they durst.

'A Satire against Mankind' (1679) l. 158

14 A merry monarch, scandalous and poor.

'A Satire on King Charles II' (1697)

15 Love a woman? You're an ass!
'Tis a most insipid passion
To choose out for your happiness
The silliest part of God's creation.

'Song' (1680)

16 Ancient person, for whom I
All the flattering youth defy,
Long be it ere thou grow old,
Aching, shaking, crazy, cold;
But still continue as thou art,
Ancient person of my heart.

'A Song of a Young Lady to her Ancient Lover' (1691)

17 Ere time and place were, time and place were not;
Where primitive nothing something straight
begot;
Then all proceeded from the great united what.

'Upon Nothing' (1680)

18 Matter, the wickedest offspring of thy race,
By form assisted, flew from thy embrace,
And rebel light obscured thy reverend dusky face.

With form and matter, time and place did join;
Body, thy foe, with these did leagues combine,
To spoil thy peaceful realm, and ruin all thy line.

'Upon Nothing' (1680)

John D. Rockefeller 1839–1937

American industrialist and philanthropist

19 The growth of a large business is merely a survival of the fittest . . . The American beauty rose can be produced in the splendour and fragrance which bring cheer to its beholder only by sacrificing the early buds which grow up around it.

W. J. Ghent *Our Benevolent Feudalism* (1902); 'American Beauty Rose' became the title of a 1950 song by Hal David and others; see **Darwin** 257:9, **Spencer** 750:8

Gene Roddenberry 1921–91

American film producer
see also **Misquotations** 537:4, **Misquotations** 538:5

20 These are the voyages of the starship *Enterprise*. Its five-year mission . . . to boldly go where no man has gone before.

Star Trek (television series, from 1966)

Anita Roddick 1942–

English businesswoman

21 I think that business practices would improve immeasurably if they were guided by 'feminine' principles—qualities like love and care and intuition.

Body and Soul (1991)

22 Running a company on market research is like driving while looking in the rear view mirror.

in *Independent* 22 August 1997

Richard Rodgers 1902–79

American composer and songwriter

1 The sweetest sounds I'll ever hear
Are still inside my head.
The kindest words I'll ever know
Are waiting to be said.
The most entrancing sight of all
Is yet for me to see.
And the dearest love in all the world
Is waiting somewhere for me.
'The Sweetest Sounds' (1962 song) in *No Strings*

Almiro Rodrigues 1932–

Portuguese judge, presiding at the War Crimes Tribunal in The Hague

2 Individually you agreed to evil.
sentencing the Bosnian Serb General Radislav Krstic for his part in the massacre of Bosnian Muslims at Srebenica in July 1995
at The Hague, 2 August 2001

Theodore Roethke 1908–63

American poet

3 Thought does not crush to stone.
The great sledge drops in vain.
Truth never is undone;
Its shafts remain.
'The Adamant' (1941)

4 I have known the inexorable sadness of pencils,
Neat in their boxes, dolour of pad and paper-
weight,
All the misery of manilla folders and mucilage,
Desolation in immaculate public places.
'Dolour' (1948)

5 I remember the neckcurls, limp and damp, as
tendrils;
And her quick look, a sidelong pickerel smile;
And how, once startled into talk, the light
syllables leaped for her,
And she balanced in the delight of her thought.
'Elegy for Jane' (1953)

6 In a dark wood I saw—
I saw my several selves
Come running from the leaves,
Lewd, tiny, careless lives
That scuttled under stones,
Or broke, but would not go.
'The Exorcism' (1958)

7 The body and the soul know how to play
In that dark world where gods have lost thir way.
'Four for Sir John Davies' (1953) no. 2

8   O who can be
Both moth and flame? The weak moth blundering
by.
Whom do we love? I thought I knew the truth;
Of grief I died, but no one knew my death.
'The Sequel' (1964)

Richard Rogers 1933–

British architect

9 You should be able to read a building. It should be
what it does.
Walter Neurath Memorial lecture, London University,
March 1990

Samuel Rogers 1763–1855

English poet

10 Think nothing done while aught remains to do.
'Human Life' (1819) l. 49; see **Lucan** 495:2

11 But there are moments which he calls his own,
Then, never less alone than when alone,
Those whom he loved so long and sees no more,
Loved and still loves—not dead—but gone before,
He gathers round him.
'Human Life' (1819) l. 755; see **Cyprian** 254:15, **Norton**
565:16

12 By many a temple half as old as Time.
Italy (1838 ed.) epilogue; see **Burgon** 165:20

13 Go—you may call it madness, folly;
You shall not chase my gloom away.
There's such a charm in melancholy,
I would not, if I could, be gay.
'To —, 1814'

14 It doesn't much signify whom one marries, for one
is sure to find next morning that it was someone
else.
Alexander Dyce (ed.) *Table Talk of Samuel Rogers* (1860)

Thorold Rogers 1823–90

English economic historian

15 See, ladling butter from alternate tubs
Stubbs butters Freeman, Freeman butters Stubbs.
Stubbs and **Freeman** *both being historians*
W. H. Hutton (ed.) *Letters of William Stubbs* (1904)

Will Rogers 1879–1935

American actor and humorist

16 There is only one thing that can kill the movies,
and that is education.
Autobiography of Will Rogers (1949) ch. 6

17 Income Tax has made more Liars out of the
American people than Golf.
The Illiterate Digest (1924) 'Helping the Girls with their
Income Taxes'

18 Everything is funny as long as it is happening to
Somebody Else.
The Illiterate Digest (1924) 'Warning to Jokers: lay off the
prince'

19 Well, all I know is what I read in the papers.
in *New York Times* 30 September 1923

20 You can't say civilization don't advance, however,
for in every war they kill you in a new way.
in *New York Times* 23 December 1929

21 Half our life is spent trying to find something to do
with the time we have rushed through life trying
to save.
letter in *New York Times* 29 April 1930

Mme Roland (Marie-Jeanne Philipon)
1754–93
French revolutionary
see also **Last words** 473:9

1 The more I see of men, the more I like dogs.
attributed, in *Notes and Queries* 5 September 1908; see **Toussenel** 797:5

Frederick William Rolfe ('Baron Corvo')
1860–1913
English novelist

2 Pray for the repose of His soul. He was so tired.
Hadrian VII (1904) ch. 24

Richard Rolle de Hampole c.1290–1349
English mystic

3 When Adam dalfe and Eve spane
Go spire if thou may spede,
Where was than the pride of man
That now merres his mede?
G. G. Perry *Religious Pieces* (Early English Text Society, Original Series no. 26, revised ed. 1914); see **Proverbs** 634:19

Pierre de Ronsard 1524–85
French poet

4 *Mignonne, allons voir si la rose,*
Qui, ce matin, avait déclose
Sa robe de pourpre au soleil,
A point perdu, cette vêprée,
Les plis de sa robe pourprée
Et son teint au vôtre pareil.

See, Mignonne, hath not the rose
That this morning did unclose
Her purple mantle to the light,
Lost, before the day be dead,
The glory of her raiment red,
Her colour, bright as yours is bright?
Odes, à Cassandre (1555) bk. 1, no. 17 (translated by Andrew Lang)

5 *Quand vous serez bien vieille, au soir, à la chandelle,*
Assise auprès du feu, dévidant et filant,
Direz, chantant mes vers, en vous émerveillant,
Ronsard me célébrait du temps que j'étais belle.

When you are very old, and sit in the candle-light at evening spinning by the fire, you will say, as you murmur my verses, a wonder in your eyes, 'Ronsard sang of me in the days when I was fair.'
Sonnets pour Hélène (1578) bk. 2, no. 42

Eleanor Roosevelt 1884–1962
American humanitarian and diplomat
on Roosevelt: see **Stevenson** 758:18

6 The basis of all good human behaviour is kindness.
Book of Common Sense Etiquette (1962) introduction

7 Is there anything we can do for you? For you are the one in trouble now.
*to Harry **Truman**, who became President on the death of Franklin D. **Roosevelt***
in conversation, 12 April 1945

8 I cannot believe that war is the best solution. No one won the last war, and no one will win the next war.
letter to Harry Truman, 22 March 1948

9 No one can make you feel inferior without your consent.
in *Catholic Digest* August 1960

Franklin D. Roosevelt 1882–1945
American Democratic statesman, 32nd President of the US

10 These unhappy times call for the building of plans that . . . build from the bottom up and not from the top down, that put their faith once more in the forgotten man at the bottom of the economic pyramid.
radio address, 7 April 1932, in *Public Papers* (1938) vol. 1

11 I pledge you, I pledge myself, to a new deal for the American people.
speech to the Democratic Convention in Chicago, 2 July 1932, accepting the presidential nomination; in *Public Papers* (1938) vol. 1

12 The only thing we have to fear is fear itself.
inaugural address, 4 March 1933, in *Public Papers* (1938) vol. 2

13 In the field of world policy I would dedicate this Nation to the policy of the good neighbour.
inaugural address, 4 March 1933, in *Public Papers* (1938) vol. 2

14 We face the arduous days that lie before us in the warm courage of national unity.
inaugural address, 4 March 1933; see **Bush** 175:4

15 I have seen war . . . I hate war.
speech at Chautauqua, NY, 14 August 1936, in *Public Papers* (1938) vol. 5

16 I see one-third of a nation ill-housed, ill-clad, ill-nourished.
second inaugural address, 20 January 1937, in *Public Papers* (1941) vol. 6

17 We have always known that heedless self-interest was bad morals; we know now that it is bad economics.
second inaugural address, 20 January 1937

18 Your boys are not going to be sent into any foreign wars.
speech in Boston, 30 October 1940, in *Public Papers* (1941) vol. 9; see **Johnson** 423:14

19 We must be the great arsenal of democracy.
'Fireside Chat' radio broadcast, 29 December 1940, in *Public Papers* (1941) vol. 9

20 We look forward to a world founded upon four essential human freedoms. The first is freedom of speech and expression—everywhere in the world. The second is freedom of every person to worship God in his own way—everywhere in the world. The third is freedom from want . . . everywhere in

the world. The fourth is freedom from fear . . .
anywhere in the world.

message to Congress, 6 January 1941, in *Public Papers*
(1941) vol. 9

1 Yesterday, December 7, 1941—a date which will
live in infamy—the United States of America was
suddenly and deliberately attacked by naval and
air forces of the Empire of Japan.

address to Congress, 8 December 1941, in *Public Papers*
(1950) vol. 10

2 Books can not be killed by fire. People die, but
books never die. No man and no force can abolish
memory . . . In this war, we know, books are
weapons. And it is a part of your dedication
always to make them weapons for man's freedom.

'Message to the Booksellers of America' 6 May 1942, in
Publisher's Weekly 9 May 1942

3 Oh Lord, give us faith. Give us faith in Thee; faith
in our sons; faith in each other; faith in our united
crusade.

address to the nation, D-Day, 6 June 1944

4 The work, my friend, is peace. More than an end
of this war—an end to the beginnings of all wars.

undelivered address for Jefferson Day, 13 April 1945 (the
day after Roosevelt died) in *Public Papers* (1950) vol. 13

Theodore Roosevelt 1858–1919

*American Republican statesman, 26th President of the US
1901–9*

5 I wish to preach, not the doctrine of ignoble ease,
but the doctrine of the strenuous life.

speech to the Hamilton Club, Chicago, 10 April 1899, in
Works (Memorial edition, 1923–6) vol. 15

6 I am as strong as a bull moose and you can use
me to the limit.

*'Bull Moose' subsequently became the popular name
of the Progressive Party*

letter to Mark Hanna, 27 June 1900, in *Works* (Memorial
edition, 1923–6) vol. 23

7 There is a homely old adage which runs: 'Speak
softly and carry a big stick; you will go far.' If the
American nation will speak softly, and yet build
and keep at a pitch of the highest training a
thoroughly efficient navy, the Monroe Doctrine
will go far.

speech in Chicago, 3 April 1903, in *New York Times* 4 April
1903

8 A man who is good enough to shed his blood for
the country is good enough to be given a square
deal afterwards. More than that no man is entitled
to, and less than that no man shall have.

speech at the Lincoln Monument, Springfield, Illinois, 4
June 1903, in *Addresses and Presidential Messages 1902–4*
(1904)

9 You can no more make an agreement with those
leaders of Colombia than you can nail currant
jelly to the wall. And the failure to nail currant
jelly to the wall is not due to the nail. It's due to
the currant jelly.

at the time of the Panama revolution, 1903

attributed by Edmund Morris, John F. Kennedy Presidential
Historians Forum, 5 March 2002

10 The men with the muck-rakes are often
indispensable to the well-being of society; but only
if they know when to stop raking the muck.

speech in Washington, 14 April 1906, in *Works* (Memorial
edition, 1923–6) vol. 18; see **Bunyan** 165:1

11 I have got such a bully pulpit!

his personal view of the presidency

in *Outlook* (New York) 27 February 1909; see **Reagan**
643:9

12 It is not the critic who counts; not the man who
points out how the strong man stumbles, or where
the doer of deeds could have done better. The
credit belongs to the man who is actually in the
arena.

'Citizenship in a Republic', speech at the Sorbonne, Paris,
23 April 1910

13 We stand at Armageddon, and we battle for the
Lord.

speech at the Republican National Convention, 18 June
1912

14 There is no room in this country for hyphenated
Americanism . . . The one absolutely certain way
of bringing this nation to ruin, of preventing all
possibility of its continuing to be a nation at all,
would be to permit it to become a tangle of
squabbling nationalities.

speech in New York, 12 October 1915, in *Works* (Memorial
edition, 1923–6) vol. 20

15 One of our defects as a nation is a tendency to use
what have been called 'weasel words'. When a
weasel sucks eggs the meat is sucked out of the
egg. If you use a 'weasel word' after another,
there is nothing left of the other.

speech in St Louis, 31 May 1916

16 To announce that there must be no criticism of
the president, or that we are to stand by the
president, right or wrong, is not only unpatriotic
and servile, but is morally treasonable to the
American public.

in *Kansas City Star* 7 May 1918

Lord Rootes 1894–1964

English motor-car manufacturer

17 No other man-made device since the shields and
lances of ancient knights fulfils a man's ego like an
automobile.

attributed, 1958

Lord Rosebery 1847–1929

British Liberal statesman; Prime Minister, 1894–5

18 I have never known the sweets of place with
power, but of place without power, of place with
the minimum of power—that is a purgatory, and
if not a purgatory it is a hell.

in *Spectator* 6 July 1895

19 Imperialism, sane Imperialism, as distinguished
from what I may call wild-cat Imperialism, is
nothing but this—a larger patriotism.

speech, City of London Liberal Club, 5 May 1899, in *Daily
News* 6 May 1899

1 It is beginning to be hinted that we are a nation of amateurs.
> Rectorial Address at Glasgow University, 16 November 1900, in *The Times* 17 November 1900

2 I must plough my furrow alone.
> *on remaining outside the Liberal Party leadership*
> speech, 19 July 1901, in *The Times* 20 July 1901

3 There are two supreme pleasures in life. One is ideal, the other real. The ideal is when a man receives the seals of office from his Sovereign. The real pleasure comes when he hands them back.
> *Sir Robert Peel* (1899)

Ethel Rosenberg 1916–53 and **Julius Rosenberg** 1918–53

American husband and wife; convicted of spying for the Russians

4 We are innocent . . . To forsake this truth is to pay too high a price even for the priceless gift of life.
> petition for executive clemency, filed 9 January 1953, in Ethel Rosenberg *Death House Letters* (1953)

5 We are the first victims of American Fascism.
> letter from Julius to Emanuel Bloch before the Rosenbergs' execution, 19 June 1953; in *Testament of Ethel and Julius Rosenberg* (1954)

A. C. Ross see **Political slogans** 601:11

Christina Rossetti 1830–94

English poet; sister of Dante Gabriel **Rossetti**

6 My heart is like a singing bird
Whose nest is in a watered shoot.
> 'A Birthday' (1862)

7 Come to me in the silence of the night;
Come in the speaking silence of a dream;
Come with soft rounded cheeks and eyes as bright
As sunlight on a stream;
Come back in tears,
O memory, hope, love of finished years.
> 'Echo' (1862)

8 For there is no friend like a sister
In calm or stormy weather;
To cheer one on the tedious way,
To fetch one if one goes astray,
To lift one if one totters down,
To strengthen while one stands.
> 'Goblin Market' (1862)

9 In the bleak mid-winter
Frosty wind made moan,
Earth stood hard as iron,
Water like a stone;
Snow had fallen, snow on snow,
Snow on snow,
In the bleak mid-winter,
Long ago.
> 'Mid-Winter' (1875)

10 Oh roses for the flush of youth,
And laurel for the perfect prime;
But pluck an ivy branch for me
Grown old before my time.
> 'Oh roses for the flush of youth' (1862)

11 Remember me when I am gone away,
Gone far away into the silent land.
> 'Remember' (1862)

12 Better by far you should forget and smile
Than that you should remember and be sad.
> 'Remember' (1862)

13 O Earth, lie heavily upon her eyes;
Seal her sweet eyes weary of watching, Earth.
> 'Rest' (1862)

14 Silence more musical than any song.
> 'Rest' (1862)

15 Does the road wind up-hill all the way?
Yes, to the very end.
Will the day's journey take the whole long day?
From morn to night, my friend.
> 'Up-Hill' (1862)

16 When I am dead, my dearest,
Sing no sad songs for me;
Plant thou no roses at my head,
Nor shady cypress tree:
Be the green grass above me
With showers and dewdrops wet;
And if thou wilt, remember,
And if thou wilt, forget.
> 'When I am dead' (1862)

17 Our Indian Crown is in great measure the trapping of a splendid misery.
> letter to Amelia Heimann, 29 July 1880

Dante Gabriel Rossetti 1828–82

English poet and painter, brother of Christina **Rossetti**

18 Like the sweet apple which reddens upon the topmost bough,
A-top on the topmost twig,—which the pluckers forgot, somehow,—
Forgot it not, nay, but got it not, for none could get it till now.
> 'Beauty: A Combination from Sappho' (1861); see **Sappho** 666:15

19 The blessed damozel leaned out
From the gold bar of Heaven;
Her eyes were deeper than the depth
Of waters stilled at even;
She had three lilies in her hand,
And the stars in her hair were seven.
> 'The Blessed Damozel' (1870) st. 1

20 Her hair that lay along her back
Was yellow like ripe corn.
> 'The Blessed Damozel' (1870) st. 2

21 As low as where this earth
Spins like a fretful midge.
> 'The Blessed Damozel' (1870) st. 6

22 And the souls mounting up to God
Went by her like thin flames.
> 'The Blessed Damozel' (1870) st. 7

23 'We two,' she said, 'will seek the groves
Where the lady Mary is,
With her five handmaidens, whose names
Are five sweet symphonies,

Cecily, Gertrude, Magdalen,
Margaret and Rosalys.'
'The Blessed Damozel' (1870) st. 18

1 Oh! clasp we to our hearts, for deathless dower,
This close-companioned inarticulate hour
When twofold silence was the song of love.
The House of Life (1881) pt. 1 'Silent Noon'

2 They die not,—for their life was death,—but
cease;
And round their narrow lips the mould falls close.
The House of Life (1881) pt. 2 'The Choice' pt. 1

3 I do not see them here; but after death
God knows I know the faces I shall see,
Each one a murdered self, with low last breath.
'I am thyself,—what hast thou done to me?'
'And I—and I—thyself,' (lo! each one saith,)
'And thou thyself to all eternity!'
The House of Life (1881) pt. 2 'Lost Days'

4 Give honour unto Luke Evangelist;
For he it was (the aged legends say)
Who first taught Art to fold her hands and pray.
The House of Life (1881) pt. 2 'Old and New Art'

5 Look in my face; my name is Might-have-been;
I am also called No-more, Too-late, Farewell.
The House of Life (1881) pt. 2 'A Superscription'; see **Traill**
798:3

6 Sleepless with cold commemorative eyes.
The House of Life (1881) pt. 2 'A Superscription'

7 Unto the man of yearning thought
And aspiration, to do nought
Is in itself almost an act.
'Soothsay' (1881) st. 10

8 I have been here before,
But when or how I cannot tell:
I know the grass beyond the door,
The sweet keen smell,
The sighing sound, the lights around the shore.
'Sudden Light' (1870)

9 'I saw the Sibyl at Cumae'
(One said) 'with mine own eye.
She hung in a cage, and read her rune
To all the passers-by.
Said the boys, "What wouldst thou, Sibyl?"
She answered, "I would die." '
translation of Petronius *Satyricon* 'Cena Trimalchionis' ch.
48, sect. 8; see **Petronius** 594:5

Gioacchino Rossini 1792–1868
Italian composer

10 Wagner has lovely moments but awful quarters of
an hour.
to Emile Naumann, April 1867, in E. Naumann *Italienische
Tondichter* (1883) vol. 4

Edmond Rostand 1868–1918
French dramatist

11 . . . *Un grand nez est proprement l'indice
D'un homme affable, bon, courtois, spirituel,
Libéral, courageux, tel que je suis.*
A large nose is in fact the sign of an affable man,

good, courteous, witty, liberal, courageous, such
as I am.
Cyrano de Bergerac (1897) act 1, sc. 1

12 *Il y a malgré vous quelque chose
Que j'emporte, et ce soir, quand j'entrerai chez Dieu,
Mon salut balaiera largement le seuil bleu,
Quelque chose que sans un pli, sans une tache,
J'emporte malgré vous . . . et c'est . . . Mon panache!*
There is, in spite of you, something which I shall
take with me. And tonight, when I go into God's
house, my bow will make a wide sweep across the
blue threshold. Something which, with not a
crease, not a mark, I'm taking away in spite of
you . . . and it's . . . My panache!
Cyrano de Bergerac (1897) act 5, sc. 4

13 *Le seul rêve intéresse,
Vivre sans rêve, qu'est-ce?*
The dream, alone, is of interest. What is life,
without a dream?
La Princesse Lointaine (1895) act 1, sc. 4

Jean Rostand 1894–1977
French biologist

14 The biologist passes, the frog remains.
sometimes quoted as 'Theories pass. The frog remains'
Inquiétudes d'un biologiste (1967)

15 To be adult is to be alone.
Pensées d'un biologiste (1954)

16 Kill a man, and you are an assassin. Kill millions
of men, and you are a conqueror. Kill everyone,
and you are a god.
Pensées d'un biologiste (1939) p. 116; see **Porteus** 607:20,
Young 857:6

Leo Rosten 1908–97
American writer and social scientist

17 Any man who hates dogs and babies can't be all
bad.
*of W. C. **Fields**, and often attributed to him*
speech at Masquers' Club dinner, 16 February 1939; letter
in *Times Literary Supplement* 24 January 1975

Philip Roth 1933–
American novelist

18 A Jewish man with parents alive is a fifteen-year-
old boy, and will remain a fifteen-year-old boy
until *they die!*
Portnoy's Complaint (1967)

19 Doctor, my doctor, what do you say, LET'S PUT THE
ID BACK IN YID!
Portnoy's Complaint (1967)

Lord Rothschild 1910–90
British administrator and scientist

20 Politicians often believe that their world is the real
one. Officials sometimes take a different view.
in *The Times* 13 October 1974

21 The promises and panaceas that gleam like false
teeth in the party manifestoes.
Meditations of a Broomstick (1977)

Claude-Joseph Rouget de Lisle

1760–1836

French soldier

1 *Allons, enfants de la patrie,*
Le jour de gloire est arrivé . . .
Aux armes, citoyens!
Formez vos battaillons!
Come, children of our country, the day of glory
has arrived . . . To arms, citizens! Form your
battalions!
'La Marseillaise' (25 April 1792)

Charles Roupell

British lawyer

2 To play billiards well is a sign of an ill-spent youth.
attributed, in D. Duncan *Life of Herbert Spencer* (1908)
ch. 20

Jean-Jacques Rousseau 1712–78

French philosopher and novelist
*on Rousseau: see **Berlin** 70:6, **Blake** 121:16, **Heine** 380:5*

3 *Du contrat social.*
The social contract.
title of book, *Du contrat social* (1762)

4 *L'homme est né libre, et partout il est dans les fers.*
Man was born free, and everywhere he is in
chains.
Du Contrat social (1762) ch. I

5 *Laisse, mon ami, ces vains moralistes et rentre au fond*
de ton âme: c'est là que tu retrouveras toujours la
source de ce feu sacré qui nous embrasa tant de fois de
l'amour des sublimes vertus; c'est là que tu verras ce
simulacre éternel du vrai beau dont la contemplation
nous anime d'un saint enthousiasme.
Leave those vain moralists, my friend, and return
to the depth of your soul: that is where you will
always rediscover the source of the sacred fire
which so often inflamed us with love of the
sublime virtues; that is where you will see the
eternal image of true beauty, the contemplation of
which inspires us with a holy enthusiasm.
La Nouvelle Héloïse (1761, ed. M. Launay, 1967) pt. 2,
letter 11

Martin Joseph Routh 1755–1854

English classicist

6 You will find it a very good practice always to
verify your references, sir!
John William Burgon *Lives of Twelve Good Men* (1888 ed.)
vol. I

Matthew Rowbottom, Richard Stannard, and The Spice Girls (Melanie Brown, Victoria Adams, Geri Halliwell, Emma Bunton, and Melanie Chisholm)

English songwriters and English pop singers

7 Yo I'll tell you what I want, what I really really
want

so tell me what you want, what you really really
want.
'Wannabe' (1996 song)

Nicholas Rowe 1674–1718

English dramatist

8 Is this that haughty, gallant, gay Lothario?
The Fair Penitent (1703) act 5, sc. 1

9 Like Helen, in the night when Troy was sacked,
Spectatress of the mischief which she made.
The Fair Penitent (1703) act 5, sc. 1

10 Death is the privilege of human nature,
And life without it were not worth our taking.
The Fair Penitent (1703) act 5, sc. 1

Helen Rowland 1875–1950

American writer

11 A husband is what is left of a lover, after the nerve
has been extracted.
A Guide to Men (1922)

12 Somehow a bachelor never quite gets over the
idea that he is a thing of beauty and a boy forever.
A Guide to Men (1922); see **Keats** 442:13

13 The follies which a man regrets most, in his life,
are those which he didn't commit when he had
the opportunity.
A Guide to Men (1922)

Richard Rowland c.1881–1947

American film producer

14 The lunatics have taken charge of the asylum.
*on the take-over of United Artists by Charles **Chaplin***
and others
Terry Ramsaye *A Million and One Nights* (1926) vol. 2, ch.
79; see **Lloyd George** 487:20

J. K. Rowling 1965–

English novelist
*on Rowling: see **Byatt** 177:14; see also **Opening lines** 574:12*

15 Poverty is a lot like childbirth—you know it is
going to hurt before it happens, but you'll never
know how much until you experience it.
in *Mail on Sunday* 16 June 2002

Maude Royden 1876–1956

English religious writer

16 The Church should go forward along the path of
progress and be no longer satisfied only to
represent the Conservative Party at prayer.
address at Queen's Hall, London, 16 July 1917, in *The
Times* 17 July 1917

Naomi Royde-Smith c.1875–1964

English novelist and dramatist

17 I know two things about the horse
And one of them is rather coarse.
Weekend Book (1928)

Matthew Roydon fl. 1580–1622

English poet

1 A sweet attractive kind of grace,
  A full assurance given by looks,
  Continual comfort in a face,
  The lineaments of Gospel books;
  I trow that countenance cannot lie,
  Whose thoughts are legible in the eye.
  'An Elegy . . . for his Astrophill [Sir Philip Sidney]' (1593)
  st. 18

2 Was never eye, did see that face,
  Was never ear, did hear that tongue,
  Was never mind, did mind his grace,
  That ever thought the travel long—
  But eyes, and ears, and ev'ry thought,
  Were with his sweet perfections caught.
  'An Elegy . . . for his Astrophill' (1593) st. 19

Paul Alfred Rubens 1875–1917

English songwriter

3 Oh! we don't want to lose you but we think you
    ought to go
  For your King and your Country both need you so.
  'Your King and Country Want You' (1914 song); see
  Military sayings 526:19

Helena Rubinstein 1882–1965

Polish-born American beautician and businesswoman
see also **Advertising slogans** 7:9

4 With my product and her packaging we could
  have ruled the world.
  *of Elizabeth **Arden***
  Lindy Woodhead *War Paint* (2003) ch. 6

Richard Rumbold c.1622–85

English republican conspirator

5 I never could believe that Providence had sent a
  few men into the world, ready booted and spurred
  to ride, and millions ready saddled and bridled to
  be ridden.
  on the scaffold
  T. B. Macaulay *History of England* vol. 1 (1849) ch. 1

Carol Rumens 1944–

British poet

6 A slow psalm of two nations
  Mourning a common pain
  —Hebrew and Arabic mingling
  Their silver-rooted vine;
  Olives and roses falling
  To sweeten Palestine.
  'A New Song' (1993)

7 It's simple, isn't it?
  Never say the yes
  you don't mean, but the no
  you always meant, say that,
  even if it's too late,
  even if it kills you.
  'A Woman of a Certain Age' (1993)

Donald Rumsfeld 1932–

*American Republican politician and businessman, Defense
Secretary from 2001*

8 Learn to say, 'I don't know.' If used when
  appropriate, it will be often.
  'Rumsfeld's Rules'; interview in *Wall Street Journal* 29
  January 2001

9 If you are not criticized, you may not be doing
  much.
  'Rumsfeld's Rules'; interview in *Wall Street Journal* 29
  January 2001

10 When they are being moved from place to place,
  will they be restrained in a way so that they are
  less likely to be able to kill an American soldier?
  You bet. Is it inhumane to do that? No. Would it
  be stupid to do anything else? Yes.
  on al-Qaeda prisoners being held in Cuba
  in *The Times* 26 January 2002

11 You're thinking of Europe as Germany and
  France. I don't. I think that's old Europe. If you
  look at the entire Nato Europe today, the centre of
  gravity is shifting to the east.
  *to journalists who asked him about European hostility
  to a possible war, 22 January 2003*
  in *Independent* 21 February 2003

Robert Runcie 1921–2000

English Protestant clergyman; Archbishop of Canterbury
on Runcie: see **Field** 317:11

12 People are mourning on both sides of this conflict.
  In our prayers we shall quite rightly remember
  those who are bereaved in our own country and
  the relations of the young Argentinian soldiers
  who were killed. Common sorrow could do
  something to reunite those who were engaged in
  this struggle. A shared anguish can be a bridge of
  reconciliation. Our neighbours are indeed like us.
  service of thanksgiving at the end of the Falklands war, St.
  Paul's Cathedral, London, 26 July 1982

13 In the middle ages people were tourists because of
  their religion, whereas now they are tourists
  because tourism is their religion.
  speech in London, 6 December 1988

Damon Runyon 1884–1946

American writer

14 Guys and dolls.
  title of book (1931)

15 'My boy,' he says, 'always try to rub up against
  money, for if you rub up against money long
  enough, some of it may rub off on you.'
  in *Cosmopolitan* August 1929, 'A Very Honourable Guy'

16 I do see her in tough joints more than somewhat.
  in *Collier's* 22 May 1930, 'Social Error'

17 'You are snatching a hard guy when you snatch
  Bookie Bob. A very hard guy, indeed. In fact,' I
  say, 'I hear the softest thing about him is his front
  teeth.'
  in *Collier's* 26 September 1931, 'The Snatching of Bookie
  Bob'

1 I always claim the mission workers came out too early to catch any sinners on this part of Broadway. At such an hour the sinners are still in bed resting up from their sinning of the night before, so they will be in good shape for more sinning a little later on.

in *Collier's* 28 January 1933, 'The Idyll of Miss Sarah Brown'

2 I long ago come to the conclusion that all life is 6 to 5 against.

in *Collier's* 8 September 1934, 'A Nice Price'

3 You can keep the things of bronze and stone, and give me one man to remember me just once a year.

note to his friends shortly before he died
Ed Weiner *The Damon Runyon Story* (1948)

Salman Rushdie 1947-

Indian-born British novelist
on Rushdie: see **Khomeini** 451:2

4 Most of what matters in your life takes place in your absence.

Midnight's Children (1981) bk. 1

5 What is freedom of expression? Without the freedom to offend, it ceases to exist.

in *Weekend Guardian* 10 February 1990

Dean Rusk 1909-94

American politician; Secretary of State, 1961-9

6 We're eyeball to eyeball, and I think the other fellow just blinked.

on the Cuban missile crisis, 24 October 1962
in *Saturday Evening Post* 8 December 1962

John Ruskin 1819-1900

English art and social critic

7 You hear of me, among others, as a respectable architectural man-milliner; and you send for me, that I may tell you the leading fashion.

The Crown of Wild Olive (1866) Lecture 2 'Traffic'

8 Thackeray settled like a meat-fly on whatever one had got for dinner, and made one sick of it.

Fors Clavigera (1871-84) Letter 31, 1 July 1873

9 I have seen, and heard, much of Cockney impudence before now; but never expected to hear a coxcomb ask two hundred guineas for flinging a pot of paint in the public's face.

on **Whistler***'s Nocturne in Black and Gold*
Fors Clavigera (1871-84) Letter 79, 18 June 1877; see **Whistler** 831:21

10 No person who is not a great sculptor or painter can be an architect. If he is not a sculptor or painter, he can only be a *builder*.

Lectures on Architecture and Painting (1854) Lectures 1 and 2 (addenda)

11 Life without industry is guilt, and industry without art is brutality.

Lectures on Art (1870) Lecture 3 'The Relation of Art to Morals' sect. 95

12 What is poetry? . . . The suggestion, by the imagination, of noble grounds for the noble emotions.

Modern Painters (1856) vol. 3, pt. 4, ch. 1

13 All violent feelings . . . produce in us a falseness in all our impressions of external things, which I would generally characterize as the 'Pathetic Fallacy'.

Modern Painters (1856) vol. 3, pt. 4, ch. 12

14 To see clearly is poetry, prophecy, and religion—all in one.

Modern Painters (1856) vol. 3, pt. 4 'Of Modern Landscape'

15 Mountains are the beginning and the end of all natural scenery.

Modern Painters (1856) vol. 4, pt. 5, ch. 20

16 There was a rocky valley between Buxton and Bakewell . . . You enterprised a railroad . . . you blasted its rocks away . . . And now, every fool in Buxton can be at Bakewell in half-an-hour, and every fool in Bakewell at Buxton.

Praeterita vol. 3 (1889) 'Joanna's Cave'

17 All books are divisible into two classes, the books of the hour, and the books of all time.

Sesame and Lilies (1865) 'Of Kings' Treasuries'

18 Be sure that you go to the author to get at his meaning, not to find yours.

Sesame and Lilies (1865) 'Of Kings' Treasuries'

19 Which of us . . . is to do the hard and dirty work for the rest, and for what pay? Who is to do the pleasant and clean work, and for what pay?

Sesame and Lilies (1865) 'Of Kings' Treasuries'

20 How long most people would look at the best book before they would give the price of a large turbot for it.

Sesame and Lilies (1865) 'Of Kings' Treasuries'

21 We call ourselves a rich nation, and we are filthy and foolish enough to thumb each other's books out of circulating libraries!

Sesame and Lilies (1865) 'Of Kings' Treasuries'

22 I believe the right question to ask, respecting all ornament, is simply this: Was it done with enjoyment—was the carver happy while he was about it?

Seven Lamps of Architecture (1849) 'The Lamp of Life' sect. 24

23 Better the rudest work that tells a story or records a fact, than the richest without meaning.

Seven Lamps of Architecture (1849) 'The Lamp of Memory' sect. 7

24 When we build, let us think that we build for ever.

Seven Lamps of Architecture (1849) 'The Lamp of Memory' sect. 10

25 Remember that the most beautiful things in the world are the most useless; peacocks and lilies for instance.

Stones of Venice vol. 1 (1851) ch. 2, sect. 17

26 Labour without joy is base. Labour without sorrow is base. Sorrow without labour is base. Joy without labour is base.

Time and Tide (1867) Letter 5

1 Your honesty is *not* to be based either on religion or policy. Both your religion and policy must be based on *it*.
Time and Tide (1867) Letter 8

2 The first duty of a State is to see that every child born therein shall be well housed, clothed, fed and educated, till it attain years of discretion.
Time and Tide (1867) Letter 13

3 Fine art is that in which the hand, the head, and the heart of man go together.
The Two Paths (1859) Lecture 2

4 Not only is there but one way of *doing* things rightly, but there is only one way of *seeing* them, and that is, seeing the whole of them.
The Two Paths (1859) Lecture 2

5 Nobody cares much at heart about Titian; only there is a strange undercurrent of everlasting murmur about his name, which means the deep consent of all great men that he is greater than they.
The Two Paths (1859) Lecture 2

6 It ought to be quite as natural and straightforward a matter for a labourer to take his pension from his parish, because he has deserved well of his parish, as for a man in higher rank to take his pension from his country, because he has deserved well of his country.
Unto this Last (1862) preface, p. xviii

7 The force of the guinea you have in your pocket depends wholly on the default of a guinea in your neighbour's pocket. If he did not want it, it would be of no use to you.
Unto this Last (1862) Essay 2

8 Soldiers of the ploughshare as well as soldiers of the sword.
Unto this Last (1862) Essay 3, p. 102

9 Government and cooperation are in all things the laws of life; anarchy and competition the laws of death.
Unto this Last (1862) Essay 3, p. 102

10 Whereas it has long been known and declared that the poor have no right to the property of the rich, I wish it also to be known and declared that the rich have no right to the property of the poor.
Unto this Last (1862) Essay 3, p. 103

11 There is no wealth but life.
Unto this Last (1862) Essay 4, p. 156

12 The only letters it [his faith] can hold by at all are the old Evangelical formulae. If only the geologists would let me alone, I could do very well, but those dreadful hammers! I hear the clink of them at the end of every cadence of the Bible verses.
letter to Henry Acland, 24 May 1851

13 Remember that it is the glory of Gothic architecture that it can do *anything*.
J. Mordaunt Crook *Dilemma of Style* (1987)

Bertrand Russell 1872–1970
British philosopher and mathematician

14 Men who are unhappy, like men who sleep badly, are always proud of the fact.
The Conquest of Happiness (1930) ch. 1

15 Boredom is . . . a vital problem for the moralist, since half the sins of mankind are caused by the fear of it.
The Conquest of Happiness (1930) ch. 4

16 One of the symptoms of approaching nervous breakdown is the belief that one's work is terribly important, and that to take a holiday would bring all kinds of disaster.
The Conquest of Happiness (1930) ch. 5

17 One should as a rule respect public opinion in so far as is necessary to avoid starvation and to keep out of prison, but anything that goes beyond this is voluntary submission to an unnecessary tyranny.
The Conquest of Happiness (1930) ch. 9

18 A sense of duty is useful in work, but offensive in personal relations. People wish to be liked, not to be endured with patient resignation.
The Conquest of Happiness (1930) ch. 10

19 Of all forms of caution, caution in love is perhaps the most fatal to true happiness.
The Conquest of Happiness (1930) ch. 12

20 To be able to fill leisure intelligently is the last product of civilization.
The Conquest of Happiness (1930) ch. 14

21 Work is of two kinds: first, altering the position of matter at or near the earth's surface relatively to other such matter; second, telling other people to do so. The first kind is unpleasant and ill paid; the second is pleasant and highly paid.
In Praise of Idleness and Other Essays (1986) title essay (1932)

22 To fear love is to fear life, and those who fear life are already three parts dead.
Marriage and Morals (1929) ch. 19

23 Mathematics may be defined as the subject in which we never know what we are talking about, nor whether what we are saying is true.
Mysticism and Logic (1918) ch. 4

24 The law of causality, I believe, like much that passes muster among philosophers, is a relic of a bygone age, surviving, like the monarchy, only because it is erroneously supposed to do no harm.
Mysticism and Logic (1918) ch. 9

25 Only on the firm foundation of unyielding despair, can the soul's habitation henceforth be safely built.
Philosophical Essays (1910) no. 2

26 Mathematics, rightly viewed, possesses not only truth, but supreme beauty—a beauty cold and austere, like that of sculpture.
Philosophical Essays (1910) no. 4

27 The man who has fed the chicken every day throughout its life at last wrings its neck instead,

showing that a more refined view as to the uniformity of nature would have been useful to the chicken.

The Problems of Philosophy (1912)

1 The recrudescence of Puritanism.

title of essay, 1928

2 Every man, wherever he goes, is encompassed by a cloud of comforting convictions, which move with him like flies on a summer day.

Sceptical Essays (1928) 'Dreams and Facts'

3 The infliction of cruelty with a good conscience is a delight to moralists. That is why they invented Hell.

Sceptical Essays (1928) 'On the Value of Scepticism'

4 It is obvious that 'obscenity' is not a term capable of exact legal definition; in the practice of the Courts, it means 'anything that shocks the magistrate'.

Sceptical Essays (1928) 'The Recrudescence of Puritanism'

5 Next to enjoying ourselves, the next greatest pleasure consists in preventing others from enjoying themselves, or, more generally, in the acquisition of power.

Sceptical Essays (1928) 'The Recrudescence of Puritanism'

6 Man is a credulous animal, and must believe *something*; in the absence of good grounds for belief, he will be satisfied with bad ones.

Unpopular Essays (1950) 'An Outline of Intellectual Rubbish'

7 Fear is the main source of superstition, and one of the main sources of cruelty.

Unpopular Essays (1950) 'An Outline of Intellectual Rubbish'

8 'Change' is scientific, 'progress' is ethical; change is indubitable, whereas progress is a matter of controversy.

Unpopular Essays (1950) 'Philosophy and Politics'

Bob Russell and Bobby Scott 1937–90

American songwriters

9 He ain't heavy . . . he's my brother.

title of song (1969)

Dale Russell 1937–

Canadian palaeontologist

10 Dinosaurs are a touchstone that separates the mentality of children from that of adults.

An Odyssey in Time: the Dinosaurs of North America (1989)

Dora Russell 1894–1986

English feminist

11 We want better reasons for having children than not knowing how to prevent them.

Hypatia (1925) ch. 4

George William Russell see Æ

Lord John Russell 1792–1878

British Whig statesman; Prime Minister 1846–52, 1865–6
on Russell: see **Derby** 265:5

12 It is impossible that the whisper of a faction should prevail against the voice of a nation.

reply to an Address from a meeting of 150,000 persons at Birmingham on the defeat of the second Reform Bill, October 1831

S. Walpole *Life of Lord John Russell* (1889) vol. 1, ch. 7

13 If peace cannot be maintained with honour, it is no longer peace.

speech at Greenock, 19 September 1853, in *The Times* 21 September 1853; see **Chamberlain** 206:12, **Disraeli** 276:17

14 Among the defects of the Bill, which were numerous, one provision was conspicuous by its presence and another by its absence.

speech to the electors of the City of London, April 1859, in *The Times* 9 April 1859

15 A proverb is one man's wit and all men's wisdom.

R. J. Mackintosh *Sir James Mackintosh* (1835) vol. 2, ch. 7

William Howard Russell 1820–1907

British journalist; war correspondent of The Times

16 They dashed on towards that thin red line tipped with steel.

of the Russians charging the British at the battle of Balaclava, 1854

The British Expedition to the Crimea (1877); Russell's original dispatch read:

That thin red streak topped with a line of steel.

in *The Times* 14 November 1854; see **Kipling** 455:22

Ernest Rutherford 1871–1937

New Zealand physicist
on Rutherford: see **Bullard** 163:15

17 All science is either physics or stamp collecting.

J. B. Birks *Rutherford at Manchester* (1962)

18 If your experiment needs statistics, you ought to have done a better experiment.

Norman T. J. Bailey *The Mathematical Approach to Biology and Medicine* (1967)

19 It was quite the most incredible event that has ever happened to me in my life. It was almost as incredible as if you fired a 15-inch shell at a piece of tissue paper and it came back and hit you.

on the back-scattering effect of metal foil on alpha-particles

E. N. da C. Andrade *Rutherford and the Nature of the Atom* (1964)

20 We haven't got the money, so we've got to think!

in *Bulletin of the Institute of Physics* (1962) vol. 13 (as recalled by R. V. Jones)

Sue Ryder 1923–2000

British charity worker

1 I don't look for reward. Surely, according to God's judgement, our reward is when we die. We are all pilgrims on this earth.

after her peerage was awarded in 1979

in *Daily Telegraph* 3 November 2000; obituary

Gilbert Ryle 1900–76

English philosopher

2 A myth is, of course, not a fairy story. It is the presentation of facts belonging to one category in the idioms appropriate to another. To explode a myth is accordingly not to deny the facts but to re-allocate them.

The Concept of Mind (1949) introduction

3 Philosophy is the replacement of category-habits by category-disciplines.

The Concept of Mind (1949) introduction

4 The dogma of the Ghost in the Machine.

on the mental-conduct concepts of **Descartes**

The Concept of Mind (1949) ch. 1

Ss

Sa'adiah ben Joseph Gaon 882–942

Jewish philosopher

5 We enquire into and speculate on the teachings of our religion for two reasons: first, to find out for ourselves what we have learned as imparted knowledge from the prophets of God; and secondly, to be able to refute anyone who argues against us concerning anything to do with our religion.

The Book of Beliefs and Opinions introduction, sect. 6

6 Even women and children and those with no aptitude for speculation can attain to a complete religion, for all men are on an equal footing as far as knowledge derived from the senses is concerned. Praised be God who in his wisdom ordered things thus.

The Book of Beliefs and Opinions introduction, sect. 6

Rafael Sabatini 1875–1950

Italian novelist

7 He was born with a gift of laughter and a sense that the world was mad. And that was all his patrimony.

Scaramouche (1921) bk. 1, ch. 1

Jonathan Sacks 1948–

British Chief Rabbi

8 Modernity is the transition from fate to choice.

'The Persistence of Faith' (Reith Lecture, 1990)

Thomas Sackville, Lord Dorset

1536–1608

English poet and dramatist

9 And old Saturnus, with his frosty face,
With chilling cold had pierced the tender green . . .
All earthly things be born
To die the death, for nought long time may last;
The summer's beauty yields to winter's blast.

The Mirror for Magistrates (1563) st. 1

10 Crookbacked he was, tooth-shaken, and blear-eyed,
Went on three feet, and sometime crept on four,
With old lame bones that rattled by his side,
His scalp all pilled and he will eld forlore;
His withered fist still knocking at Death's door,
Fumbling and drivelling as he draws his breath;
For brief, the shape and messenger of Death.

of Old Age

The Mirror for Magistrates (1563) st. 48

Victoria ('Vita') Sackville-West

1892–1962

English writer and gardener; wife of Harold **Nicolson**

11 The greater cats with golden eyes
Stare out between the bars.
Deserts are there, and different skies,
And night with different stars.

The King's Daughter (1929) pt. 2, no. 1

12 The country habit has me by the heart,
For he's bewitched for ever who has seen,
Not with his eyes but with his vision, Spring
Flow down the woods and stipple leaves with sun.

The Land (1926) 'Winter'

Anwar al-Sadat 1918–81

Egyptian statesman, President 1970–81

13 Peace is much more precious than a piece of land.

speech in Cairo, 8 March 1978

Marquis de Sade 1740–1814

French writer and soldier

14 Do not breed. Nothing gives less pleasure than childbearing. Pregnancies are damaging to health, spoil the figure, wither the charms, and it's the cloud of uncertainty forever hanging over these events that darkens a husband's mood.

Juliette (1797) pt. 1

Sadi c.1213–91

Persian poet

15 I never complained at the vicissitudes of fortune, nor murmured at the ordinances of Heaven, excepting once, when my feet were bare, and I had not the means of procuring myself shoes. I entered the great mosque at Cufah with a heavy heart when I beheld a man who had no feet. I offered up praise and thanksgiving to God for his bounty, and bore with patience the want of shoes.

The Rose Garden (1258) ch. 3, Tale 19; see **Sayings** 669:24

1 Science is for the cultivation of religion, not for worldly enjoyment.
   The Rose Garden (1258)

Carl Sagan 1934–96
American scientist and writer

2 If you wish to make an apple pie from scratch, you must first invent the universe.
   Cosmos (1980) ch. 9

3 To me, it underscores our responsibility to deal more kindly with one another, and to preserve and cherish the pale blue dot, the only home we've ever known.
   of Earth as photographed by Voyager 1
   Pale Blue Dot (1995)

Françoise Sagan 1935–
French novelist

4 To jealousy, nothing is more frightful than laughter.
   La Chamade (1965) ch. 9

Mohammed al-Sahhaf
*Iraqi politician, Minister of Information in Saddam **Hussein**'s government*

5 Baghdad is safe, protected. There are no American infidels in Baghdad.
   press briefing during the war in Iraq
   in *Sunday Telegraph* 13 April 2003

6 I now inform you that you are too far from reality.
   final briefing to the press in Baghdad
   in *Sunday Telegraph* 13 April 2003

Charles-Augustin Sainte-Beuve 1804–69
French critic

7 *Et Vigny plus secret,*
   Comme en sa tour d'ivoire, avant midi rentrait.
   And Vigny more discreet, as if in his ivory tower, returned before noon.
   Les Pensées d'Août, à M. Villemain (1837)

Antoine de Saint-Exupéry 1900–44
French novelist

8 Grown-ups never understand anything for themselves, and it is tiresome for children to be always and forever explaining things to them.
   Le Petit Prince (1943) ch. 1

9 It is only with the heart that one can see rightly; what is essential is invisible to the eye.
   Le Petit Prince (1943) ch. 21

10 Experience shows us that love does not consist in gazing at each other but in looking together in the same direction.
   Terre des Hommes (translated as 'Wind, Sand and Stars', 1939) ch. 8

Andrei Sakharov 1921–89
Russian nuclear physicist

11 Every day I saw the huge material, intellectual and nervous resources of thousands of people being poured into the creation of a means of total destruction, something capable of annihilating all human civilization. I noticed that the control levers were in the hands of people who, though talented in their own ways, were cynical.
   Sakharov Speaks (1974)

Saki (Hector Hugh Munro) 1870–1916
Scottish writer

12 Waldo is one of those people who would be enormously improved by death.
   Beasts and Super-Beasts (1914) 'The Feast of Nemesis'

13 The people of Crete unfortunately make more history than they can consume locally.
   Chronicles of Clovis (1911) 'The Jesting of Arlington Stringham'

14 The cook was a good cook, as cooks go; and as cooks go, she went.
   Reginald (1904) 'Reginald on Besetting Sins'

15 Never be a pioneer. It's the Early Christian that gets the fattest lion.
   Reginald (1904) 'Reginald's Choir Treat'

16 I always say beauty is only sin deep.
   Reginald (1904) 'Reginald's Choir Treat'

17 Good gracious, you've got to educate him first. You can't expect a boy to be vicious till he's been to a good school.
   Reginald in Russia (1910) 'The Baker's Dozen'

18 A little inaccuracy sometimes saves tons of explanation.
   The Square Egg (1924) 'Clovis on the Alleged Romance of Business'

19 Children with Hyacinth's temperament don't know better as they grow older; they merely know more.
   Toys of Peace and Other Papers (1919) 'Hyacinth'

20 We all know that Prime Ministers are wedded to the truth, but like other married couples they sometimes live apart.
   The Unbearable Bassington (1912) ch. 13

J. D. Salinger 1919–
American novelist and short-story writer
*see also **Borrowed titles** 146:4*

21 Sex is something I really don't understand too hot. You never know *where* the hell you are. I keep making up these sex rules for myself, and then I break them right away.
   The Catcher in the Rye (1951) ch. 9

22 Take most people, they're crazy about cars. They worry if they get a little scratch on them, and they're always talking about how many miles they get to a gallon . . . I don't even like *old* cars. I mean they don't even interest me. I'd rather have

a goddam horse. A horse is at least *human*, for God's sake.

The Catcher in the Rye (1951) ch. 17

1 I keep picturing all these little kids playing some game in this big field of rye and all . . . I mean if they're running and they don't look where they're going I have to come out from somewhere and catch them. That's all I'd do all day. I'd just be the catcher in the rye.

The Catcher in the Rye (1951) ch. 22

Lord Salisbury (3rd Marquess of Salisbury)
1830–1903

British Conservative statesman; Prime Minister 1855–6, 1886–92, 1895–1902

on Salisbury: see **Bismarck** *118:3,* **Disraeli** *276:17*

2 Too clever by half.

of **Disraeli***'s amendment on Disestablishment*

speech, House of Commons, 30 March 1868; see **Salisbury** 664:17

3 English policy is to float lazily downstream, occasionally putting out a diplomatic boathook to avoid collisions.

letter to Lord Lytton, 9 March 1877; in Lady Gwendolen Cecil *Life of Robert, Marquis of Salisbury* (1921–32) vol. 2

4 A great deal of misapprehension arises from the popular use of maps on a small scale. As with such maps you are able to put a thumb on India and a finger on Russia, some persons at once think that the political situation is alarming and that India must be looked to. If the noble Lord would use a larger map—say one on the scale of the Ordnance Map of England—he would find that the distance between Russia and British India is not to be measured by the finger and thumb, but by a rule.

speech, House of Commons, 11 June 1877

5 No lesson seems to be so deeply inculcated by the experience of life as that you never should trust experts. If you believe the doctors, nothing is wholesome: if you believe the theologians, nothing is innocent: if you believe the soldiers, nothing is safe. They all require to have their strong wine diluted by a very large admixture of insipid common sense.

letter to Lord Lytton, 15 June 1877; in Lady Gwendolen Cecil *Life of Robert, Marquis of Salisbury* (1921–32) vol. 2

6 One of the nuisances of the ballot is that when the oracle has spoken you never know what it means.

after the Renfrew by-election of October 1877; Andrew Roberts *Salisbury: Victorian Titan* (1999)

7 The agonies of a man who has to finish a difficult negotiation, and at the same time to entertain four royalties at a country house can be better imagined than described.

letter to Lord Lyons, 5 June 1878

8 What with deafness, ignorance of French, and Bismarck's extraordinary mode of speech, Beaconsfield has the dimmest idea of what is going on—understands everything crossways—and imagines a perpetual conspiracy.

letter to Lady Salisbury from the Congress of Berlin, 23 June 1878

9 We are part of the community of Europe and we must do our duty as such.

speech at Caernarvon, 10 April 1888, in *The Times* 11 April 1888

10 Where property is in question I am guilty . . . of erecting individual liberty as an idol, and of resenting all attempts to destroy or fetter it; but when you pass from liberty to life, in no well-governed State, in no State governed according to the principles of common humanity, are the claims of mere liberty allowed to endanger the lives of the citizens.

speech in the House of Lords, 29 July 1897

11 Horny-handed sons of toil.

in *Quarterly Review* October 1873; later popularized in the US by Denis Kearney (1847–1907); see **Lowell** 494:2

12 If I had to do literary work of an absorbing character, Oxford is the last place in which I should attempt to do it.

letter to William Sanday, 30 May 1900; Brock and Curthoys (ed.) *History of the University of Oxford* (2000) vol. 7, pt. 2, ch. 25

13 By office boys for office boys.

of the Daily Mail

H. Hamilton Fyfe *Northcliffe, an Intimate Biography* (1930) ch. 4

14 If these gentlemen had their way, they would soon be asking me to defend the moon against a possible attack from Mars.

of his senior military advisers, and their tendency to see threats which did not exist

Robert Taylor *Lord Salisbury* (1975)

15 I rank myself no higher in the scheme of things than a policeman—whose utility would disappear if there were no criminals.

comparing his role in the Conservative Party with that of **Gladstone**

Lady Gwendolen Cecil *Biographical Studies . . . of Robert, Third Marquess of Salisbury* (1962)

16 To defend a bad policy as an 'error of judgement' does not excuse it—the right functioning of a man's judgement is his most fundamental responsibility.

Lady Gwendolen Cecil *Life of Robert, Marquis of Salisbury* (1921–32) vol. 3

Lord Salisbury (5th Marquess of Salisbury)
1893–1972

British Conservative politician

17 Too clever by half.

of Iain Macleod, Colonial Secretary 'in his relationship to the white communities of Africa'

in the House of Lords, 7 March 1961; see **Salisbury** 664:2

Sallust (Gaius Sallustius Crispus) 86–35 BC
Roman historian

1 *Alieni appetens, sui profusus.*
Greedy for the property of others, extravagant
with his own.
Catiline ch. 5

2 *Nam idem velle atque idem nolle, ea demum firma amicitia est.*
To like and dislike the same things, that is indeed
true friendship.
Catiline ch. 20

3 *Quieta movere magna merces videbatur.*
To stir up undisputed matters seemed a great
reward in itself.
Catiline ch. 21

4 *Esse quam videri bonus malebat.*
He preferred to be rather than to seem good.
of Cato
Catiline ch. 54

5 *Urbem venalem et mature perituram, si emptorem invenerit.*
A venal city ripe to perish, if a buyer can be found.
of Rome
Jugurtha ch. 35

6 *Punica fide.*
With Carthaginian trustworthiness.
meaning treachery
Jugurtha ch. 108, sect. 3

Alex Salmond 1954–
Scottish Nationalist politician

7 Nobody ever celebrated Devolution Day.
asserting his belief in full independence
in *Independent* 2 April 1992

8 The Scottish parliament is our passport to
independence.
*outgoing speech as party leader to the Scottish
Nationalist Party Conference*
in *Guardian* 23 September 2000

Sambandar (Tirunanacampantar)
Tamil poet and saint of the 6th–7th century

9 Let us praise the tender feet
worshipped by the gods,
the feet of our Lord.
hymn to Shiva, from the Tevaram

Lord Samuel 1870–1963
British Liberal politician

10 A library is thought in cold storage.
A Book of Quotations (1947)

Paul A. Samuelson 1915–
American economist

11 The consumer, so it is said, is the king ... each is
a voter who uses his money as votes to get the
things done that he wants done.
Economics (8th ed., 1970)

Sana'i d. c.1131
Persian poet

12 Each had but known one part, and no man all;
Hence into deadly error each did fall.
No way to know the All man's heart can find:
Can knowledge e'er accompany the blind?
*on blind men's conclusions on touching different parts
of an elephant*
'The Blind Men and the Elephant'; see **Jalal** 416:22

George Sand (Amandine-Aurore Lucille Dupin, Baronne Dudevant) 1804–76
French novelist

13 *Nous ne pouvons arracher une seule page de notre vie,
mais nous pouvons jeter le livre au feu.*
We cannot tear out a single page of our life, but
we can throw the book in the fire.
Mauprat (1837)

14 There is only one happiness in life, to love and be
loved.
letter to Lina Calamatta, 31 March 1862

15 Faith is an excitement and an enthusiasm; it is a
condition of intellectual magnificence to which we
must cling as to a treasure, and not squander on
our way through life in the small coin of empty
words, or in exact and priggish argument.
letter to Des Planches, 25 May 1866

16 Art for art's sake is an empty phrase. Art for the
sake of the true, art for the sake of the good and
the beautiful, that is the faith I am searching for.
letter to Alexandre Saint-Jean, 1872

Carl Sandburg 1878–1967
American poet

17 Hog Butcher for the World,
Tool Maker, Stacker of Wheat,
Player with Railroads and the Nation's Freight
Handler;
Stormy, husky, brawling,
City of the Big Shoulders.
'Chicago' (1916)

18 When Abraham Lincoln was shovelled into the
tombs,
he forgot the copperheads and the assassin ...
in the dust, in the cool tombs.
'Cool Tombs' (1918)

19 The fog comes
on little cat feet.
It sits looking
over harbour and city
on silent haunches
and then moves on.
'Fog' (1916)

20 Pile the bodies high at Austerlitz and Waterloo.
Shovel them under and let me work—
I am the grass; I cover all.
'Grass' (1918)

21 I tell you the past is a bucket of ashes.
'Prairie' (1918)

1 Little girl . . . Sometime they'll give a war and nobody will come.
The People, Yes (1936); see **Film titles** 322:12, **Ginsberg** 349:14

2 Poetry is the achievement of the synthesis of hyacinths and biscuits.
in *Atlantic Monthly* March 1923 'Poetry Considered'

3 Slang is a language that rolls up its sleeves, spits on its hands and goes to work.
in *New York Times* 13 February 1959

Henry 'Red' Sanders 1905–58
American football coach

4 Sure, winning isn't everything. It's the only thing.
in *Sports Illustrated* 26 December 1955; often attributed to Vince Lombardi

Lord Sandwich 1718–92
British politician and diplomat; First Lord of the Admiralty

5 If any man will draw up his case, and put his name at the foot of the first page, I will give him an immediate reply. Where he compels me to turn over the sheet, he must wait my leisure.
N. W. Wraxall *Memoirs* (1884) vol. 1

Martha Sansom 1690–1736
English poet

6 Foolish eyes, thy streams give over,
Wine, not water, binds the lover:
At the table then be shining,
Gay coquette, and all designing.
'Song' (written *c.*1726)

George Santayana 1863–1952
Spanish-born philosopher and critic

7 Fanaticism consists in redoubling your effort when you have forgotten your aim.
The Life of Reason (1905) vol. 1, introduction

8 Those who cannot remember the past are condemned to repeat it.
The Life of Reason (1905) vol. 1, ch. 12

9 It takes patience to appreciate domestic bliss; volatile spirits prefer unhappiness.
The Life of Reason (1905) vol. 2, ch. 2

10 Music is essentially useless, as life is: but both have an ideal extension which lends utility to its conditions.
The Life of Reason (1905) vol. 4, ch. 4

11 There is no cure for birth and death save to enjoy the interval.
Soliloquies in England (1922) 'War Shrines'

Sappho
Greek lyric poet of the late 7th century BC
on Sappho: see **Byron** 178:10

12 Some say an army of cavalry or of infantry or a fleet of ships is the most beautiful thing on the black earth. But I say it is whatever one loves.
D. L. Page (ed.) *Lyrica Graeca Selecta* (1968) no. 16

13 I want neither the honey nor the bee.
D. L. Page (ed.) *Lyrica Graeca Selecta* (1968) no. 146

14 That man seems to me on a par with the gods who sits in your company and listens to you so close to him speaking sweetly and laughing sexily, such a thing makes my heart flutter in my breast, for when I see you even for a moment, then power to speak another word fails me, instead my tongue freezes into silence, and at once a gentle fire has caught throughout my flesh, and I see nothing with my eyes, and there's a drumming in my ears, and sweat pours down me, and trembling seizes all of me, and I become paler than grass, and I seem to fail almost to the point of death in my very self.
D. L. Page (ed.) *Lyrica Graeca Selecta* (1968) no. 199; see **Catullus** 202:20

15 Just as the sweet-apple reddens on the high branch, high on the highest, and the apple-pickers missed it, or rather did not miss it out, but could not reach it.
describing a girl before her marriage
D. L. Page (ed.) *Lyrica Graeca Selecta* (1968) no. 224; see **Rossetti** 655:18

16 For in a house that serves the Muses there must be no lamentation: such a thing does not befit it.
sometimes described as her dying words
A. Weighall *Sappho of Lesbos* (1932)

John Singer Sargent 1856–1925
American painter
on Sargent: see **Anonymous** 17:3

17 Every time I paint a portrait I lose a friend.
attributed; N. Bentley and E. Esar *Treasury of Humorous Quotations* (1951)

Leslie Sarony 1897–1985
British songwriter

18 Ain't it grand to be blooming well dead?
title of song (1932)

Nathalie Sarraute 1902–99
French novelist

19 Radio and television . . . have succeeded in lifting the manufacture of banality out of the sphere of handicraft and placed it in that of a major industry.
in *Times Literary Supplement* 10 June 1960

Jean-Paul Sartre 1905–80
French philosopher, novelist, dramatist, and critic
on Sartre: see **de Gaulle** 262:14

20 *Quand les riches se font la guerre ce sont les pauvres qui meurent.*
When the rich wage war it's the poor who die.
Le Diable et le bon Dieu (1951) act 1, tableau 1

21 Nothingness haunts being.
L'Être et le néant (1943)

1 *L'existence précède et commande l'essence.*

Existence precedes and rules essence.

L'Être et le néant (1943) pt. 4, ch. 1

2 *Je suis condamné à être libre.*

I am condemned to be free.

L'Être et le néant (1943) pt. 4, ch. 1

3 *L'homme est une passion inutile.*

Man is a useless passion.

L'Être et le néant (1943) pt. 4, ch. 2

4 *Alors, c'est ça l'Enfer. Je n'aurais jamais cru . . . Vous vous rappelez: le soufre, le bûcher, le gril . . . Ah! quelle plaisanterie. Pas besoin de gril, L'Enfer, c'est les Autres.*

So that's what Hell is: I'd never have believed it . . . Do you remember, brimstone, the stake, the gridiron? . . . What a joke! No need of a gridiron, Hell is other people.

Huis Clos (1944) sc. 5; see **Eliot** 301:5

5 *Comme tous les songe-creux, je confondis le désenchantement avec la vérité.*

Like all dreamers, I mistook disenchantment for truth.

Les Mots (1964) 'Écrire'

6 *Je confondis les choses avec leurs noms: c'est croire.*

I confused things with their names: that is belief.

Les Mots (1964) 'Écrire'

7 *Il n'y a pas de bon père, c'est la règle; qu'on n'en tienne pas grief aux hommes mais au lien de paternité qui est pourri. Faire des enfants, rien de mieux; en avoir, quelle iniquité!*

There is no good father, that's the rule. Don't lay the blame on men but on the bond of paternity, which is rotten. To beget children, nothing better; to *have* them, what iniquity!

Les Mots (1964) 'Lire'

8 *Les bons pauvres ne savent pas que leur office est d'exercer notre générosité.*

The poor don't know that their function in life is to exercise our generosity.

Les Mots (1964) 'Lire'

9 *Elle ne croyait à rien; seul, son scepticisme l'empêchait d'être athée.*

She believed in nothing; only her scepticism kept her from being an atheist.

Les Mots (1964) 'Lire'

10 *La vie humaine commence de l'autre côté du désespoir.*

Human life begins on the far side of despair.

Les Mouches (1943) act 3, sc. 2

11 *Ma pensée, c'est moi: voilà pourquoi je ne peux pas m'arrêter. J'existe par ce que je pense . . . et je ne peux pas m'empêcher de penser.*

My thought is *me*: that's why I can't stop. I exist by what I think . . . and I can't prevent myself from thinking.

La Nausée (1938) 'Lundi'

12 *Je me méfie des incommunicables, c'est la source de toute violence.*

I distrust the incommunicable: it is the source of all violence.

'Qu'est-ce que la littérature?' in *Les Temps Modernes* July 1947, p. 106

13 *Je déteste les victimes quand elles respectent leurs bourreaux.*

I hate victims who respect their executioners.

Les Séquestrés d'Altona (1960) act 1, sc. 1

14 *L'écrivain doit donc refuser de se laisser transformer en institution.*

A writer must refuse, therefore, to allow himself to be transformed into an institution.

refusing the Nobel Prize at Stockholm, 22 October 1964; in M. Contat and M. Rybalka (eds.) *Les Écrits de Sartre* (1970)

Siegfried Sassoon 1886–1967
English poet

15 If I were fierce, and bald, and short of breath,
I'd live with scarlet Majors at the Base,
And speed glum heroes up the line to death.
'Base Details' (1918)

16 I'd like to see a Tank come down the stalls,
Lurching to rag-time tunes, or 'Home, sweet Home',—
And there'd be no more jokes in Music-halls
To mock the riddled corpses round Bapaume.
'Blighters' (1917)

17 Does it matter?—losing your sight? . . .
There's such splendid work for the blind;
And people will always be kind,
As you sit on the terrace remembering
And turning your face to the light.
'Does it Matter?' (1918)

18 Soldiers are citizens of death's grey land,
Drawing no dividend from time's tomorrows.
'Dreamers' (1918)

19 You are too young to fall asleep for ever;
And when you sleep you remind me of the dead.
'The Dug-Out' (1919)

20 Everyone suddenly burst out singing;
And I was filled with such delight
As prisoned birds must find in freedom.
'Everyone Sang' (1919)

21 The song was wordless; the singing will never be done.
'Everyone Sang' (1919)

22 'Good-morning; good morning!' the General said
When we met him last week on our way to the line.
Now the soldiers he smiled at are most of 'em dead,
And we're cursing his staff for incompetent swine.
'He's a cheery old card,' grunted Harry to Jack
As they slogged up to Arras with rifle and pack.
But he did for them both by his plan of attack.
'The General' (1918)

23 Here was the world's worst wound. And here with pride
'Their name liveth for ever' the Gateway claims.

Was ever an immolation so belied
As these intolerably nameless names?
'On Passing the New Menin Gate' (1928); see **Epitaphs**
311:8

Cicely Saunders 1916–
English founder of St Christopher's Hospice, London

1 Deception is not as creative as truth. We do best in
life if we look at it with clear eyes, and I think that
applies to coming up to death as well.
of the Hospice movement
in *Time* 5 September 1988

Ferdinand de Saussure 1857–1913
Swiss linguistics scholar

2 In language there are only differences.
Course in General Linguistics (1916)

3 Language can . . . be compared with a sheet of
paper: thought is the front and sound the back;
one cannot cut the front without cutting the back
at the same time.
Course in General Linguistics (1916)

George Savile see Lord Halifax

Dorothy L. Sayers 1893–1957
English writer of detective fiction

4 A society in which consumption has to be
artificially stimulated in order to keep production
going is a society founded on trash and waste, and
such a society is a house built upon sand.
Creed or Chaos? (1947) ch. 6

5 I admit it is better fun to punt than to be punted,
and that a desire to have all the fun is nine-tenths
of the law of chivalry.
Gaudy Night (1935) ch. 14

6 I always have a quotation for everything—it saves
original thinking.
Have His Carcase (1932)

7 Perhaps it is no wonder that the women were first
at the Cradle and last at the Cross. They had never
known a man like this Man—there has never
been such another . . . who never made arch jokes
about them, never treated them either as 'The
women, God help us', or 'The ladies, God bless
them!'
Unpopular Opinions (1946) 'The Human-Not-Quite-Human'

☐ Sayings
see box opposite

Gerald Scarfe 1936–
English caricaturist

8 I find a particular delight in taking the caricature
as far as I can. It satisfies me to stretch the human
frame about and recreate it and yet keep a
likeness.
Scarfe by Scarfe (1986)

Arthur Scargill 1938–
British trades-union leader

9 Parliament itself would not exist in its present
form had people not defied the law.
evidence to House of Commons Select Committee on
Employment, 2 April 1980, in *House of Commons Paper no.
462 of Session 1979–80*

Lord Scarman 1911–
British judge

10 The people as a source of sovereign power are in
truth only occasional partners in the
constitutional minuet danced for most of the time
by Parliament and the political party in power.
The Shape of Things to Come (1989) ch. 1

11 A government above the law is a menace to be
defeated.
Why Britain Needs a Written Constitution (1992)

Friedrich von Schelling 1775–1854
German philosopher

12 Architecture in general is frozen music.
Philosophie der Kunst (1809)

Elsa Schiaparelli 1896–1973
Italian-born French fashion designer

13 If I have become what I am, I owe it to two
distinct things—poverty and Paris. Poverty forced
me to work, and Paris gave me a liking for it and
courage.
in *Constellation* March 1954

14 The daring is gone. No one can dream any more.
on fashions after her last collection in 1954
Palmer White *Elsa Schiaparelli: Empress of Paris Fashion*
(1986) ch. 22

Ferdinand von Schill 1776–1809
Prussian soldier

15 *Leiber ein Ende mit Schrecken als ein Schrecken ohne
Ende.*
Better a terrible end than terror without end.
to his troops before attacking the kingdom of Westphalia,
1809; Heinrich von Treitschke *History of Germany in the
Nineteenth Century* (1915) vol. 1, p. 403

Friedrich von Schiller 1759–1805
German dramatist and poet

16 *Freude, schöner Götterfunken,
Tochter aus Elysium,
Wir betreten feuertrunken,
Himmlische, dein Heiligtum.
Deine Zauber binden wieder,
Was die Mode streng geteilt.*

Joy, beautiful radiance of the gods, daughter of
Elysium, we set foot in your heavenly shrine
dazzled by your brilliance. Your charms re-unite
what common use has harshly divided.
'An die Freude' (1785)

Continued

Sayings

1 And this, too, shall pass away.

traditional saying said to be true for all times and situations; see below:

The Sultan asked for a signet motto, that should hold good for Adversity or Prosperity. Solomon gave him—'This also shall pass away'.

Edward Fitzgerald *Polonius* (1852)

2 Been there, done that, got the T-shirt.

'been there, done that' recorded from 1980s, expanded form from 1990s

3 The best defence is a good offence.

late 20th century American saying; see **Proverbs** 614:43

4 Business is like a car: it will not run by itself except downhill.

American saying

5 Children: one is one, two is fun, three is a houseful.

American

6 Christ has no body now on earth but yours, no hands but yours, no feet but yours, yours are the eyes through which he looks compassion on this world, yours are the feet with which he is to go about doing good.

modern saying, often attributed to St **Teresa** of Ávila (1512–82), but not found in her writings

7 Close your eyes and think of England.

said to derive from a 1912 entry in the journal of Lady Hillingdon (1857–1940), but the journal has never been traced

8 A committee is a group of the unwilling, chosen from the unfit, to do the unnecessary.

various attributions (origin unknown)

9 *Corruptio optimi pessima.*

Corruption of the best becomes the worst.

Latin saying, found in English from the early 17th century

10 Daddy, what did you do in the Great War?

daughter to father in First World War recruiting poster

11 [Death is] nature's way of telling you to slow down.

life insurance proverb; in *Newsweek* 25 April 1960

12 The Devil is in the details.

late 20th century saying

13 Different strokes for different folks.

strokes = *comforting gestures of approval or congratulation*

of US origin, late 20th century saying

14 Do not fold, spindle or mutilate.

instruction on punched cards (1950s, and in differing forms from the 1930s)

15 Don't get mad, get even.

late 20th century saying

16 The enemy of my enemy is my friend.

late 20th century, said to be 'an old Arab proverb'

17 An eye for an eye makes the whole world blind.

modern saying, often attributed to Mahatma **Gandhi**

18 The family that prays together stays together.

motto devised by Al Scalpone for the Roman Catholic Family Rosary Crusade, 1947

19 Garbage in, garbage out.

in computing, incorrect or faulty input will always cause poor output; origin of the acronym GIGO

20 Give a man a fish, and you feed him for a day; show him how to catch fish, and you feed him for a lifetime.

mid 20th century saying, perhaps deriving from the Chinese proverb 'Who teaches me for a day is my father for a lifetime'

21 Give me a child for the first seven years, and you may do what you like with him afterwards.

attributed as a Jesuit maxim, in *Lean's Collectanea* vol. 3 (1903); see **Spark** 749:26

22 Go to jail. Go directly to jail. Do not pass go. Do not collect £200.

instructions on 'Community Chest' card in the game 'Monopoly'; invented by Charles Brace Darrow (1889–1967) in 1931

23 Grief is the price we pay for love.

late 20th century saying

24 I cried because I had no shoes, until I met a man who had no feet.

modern saying, deriving from a Persian original; see **Sadi** 662:15

25 If it ain't broke, don't fix it.

Bert Lance (1931–) in *Nation's Business* May 1977

26 If life hands you lemons, make lemonade.

late 20th century saying

27 If you're not part of the solution, you're part of the problem.

late 20th century saying; see **Cleaver** 226:8

28 *Il ne faut pas être plus royaliste que le roi.*

You mustn't be more of a royalist than the king.

saying from the time of Louis XVI; François René, Vicomte de Chateaubriand *De la monarchie selon la charte* (1816) ch. 81

29 I married my husband for life, not for lunch.

origin unknown

30 It's not a bug, it's a feature.

bug = *an error in a computer program or system*

late 20th century saying

31 It's not what you know, it's who you know.

late 20th century saying

32 It's the second mouse that gets the cheese.

modern addition to the proverb 'The early bird . . . '; see **Proverbs** 618:29

▶

▶ **Sayings** continued

1 Justice delayed is justice denied.
late 20th century saying; see **Magna Carta** 506:5

2 Laughter is the best medicine.
late 20th century saying

3 Let's run it up the flagpole and see if anyone salutes it.
Reginald Rose *Twelve Angry Men* (1955); recorded as an established advertising expression in the 1960s

4 Life is a sexually transmitted disease.
graffito found on the London Underground, in D. J. Enright (ed.) *The Faber Book of Fevers and Frets* (1989)

5 Members [of civil service orders] rise from CMG (known sometimes in Whitehall as 'Call Me God') to the KCMG ('Kindly Call Me God') to—for a select few governors and super-ambassadors—the GCMG ('God Calls Me God').
Anthony Sampson *Anatomy of Britain* (1962) ch. 18

6 *Nil carborundum illegitimi.*
Don't let the bastards grind you down.
cod Latin saying in circulation during the Second World War, though possibly of earlier origin; often quoted as 'nil carborundum' or 'illegitimi non carborundum'

7 Nostalgia isn't what it used to be.
graffito; taken as title of book by Simone Signoret, 1978

8 Nothing is for ever.
late 20th century saying

9 Not to be a republican at twenty is proof of want of heart; to be one at thirty is proof of want of head.
often used in the form 'Not to be a socialist . . . '
adopted by **Clemenceau**, and attributed by him to **Guizot**

10 The opera ain't over 'til the fat lady sings.
Dan Cook, in *Washington Post* 3 June 1978

11 *Post coitum omne animal triste.*
After coition every animal is sad.
post-classical saying

12 Sell in May and go away (come back on St Leger day).
relating to the cycle of activity on the London Stock Exchange: trading was slack in the summer. The St Leger horse race is in early September
late 20th century saying

13 *Se non è vero, è molto ben trovato.*
If it is not true, it is a happy invention.
common saying from the 16th century

14 There is one thing stronger than all the armies in the world; and that is an idea whose time has come.
in *Nation* 15 April 1943; see **Hugo** 407:17

15 There's no such thing as a free lunch.
colloquial axiom in US economics from the 1960s, much associated with Milton **Friedman**; recorded in form 'there ain't no such thing as a free lunch' from 1938, which gave rise to the acronym TANSTAAFL in Robert Heinlein's *The Moon is a Harsh Mistress* (1966) ch. 11

16 Thirty days hath September,
April, June, and November;
All the rest have thirty-one,
Excepting February alone,
And that has twenty-eight days clear
And twenty-nine in each leap year.
Stevins MS (*c*.1555)

17 To err is human but to really foul things up requires a computer.
Farmers' Almanac for 1978 'Capsules of Wisdom'; see **Pope** 604:13

18 What goes around comes around.
late 20th century saying

19 What matters is what works.
late 20th century saying

20 What you see is what you get.
a computing expression, from which the acronym wysiwyg *derives*
late 20th century saying

21 When all you have is a hammer, everything looks like a nail.
late 20th century saying, mainly North American

22 When war is declared, Truth is the first casualty.
attributed to Hiram Johnson, speaking in the US Senate, 1918, but not recorded in his speech; the first recorded use is as epigraph to Arthur Ponsonby's *Falsehood in Wartime* (1928); see **Johnson** 424:17

23 A woman without a man is like a fish without a bicycle.
late 20th century saying, sometimes attributed to Gloria **Steinem**

Friedrich von Schiller continued

24 *Alle Menschen werden Brüder*
Wo dein sanfter Flügel weilt.
All men become brothers under your tender wing.
'An die Freude' (1785)

25 *Ein Augenblick, gelebt im Paradiese,*
Wird nicht zu teuer mit dem Tod gebüsst.
One moment spent in Paradise
Is not too dearly paid for with one's life.
Don Carlos (1787) act 1, sc. 5

26 *Die Sonne geht in meinem Staat nicht unter.*
The sun does not set in my dominions.
Philip II
Don Carlos (1787) act 1, sc. 6; see **North** 565:10

27 *Dreiundzwanzig Jahre,*
Und nichts für die Unsterblichkeit getan!
Twenty-three years old,
and I've done nothing for my immortality!
Don Carlos (1787) act 2, sc. 2

28 *Nur durch das Morgenthor des Schönen*
Drangst du in der Erkenntnis Land.
Only through beauty's gate, can you penetrate the land of knowledge.
'Die Künstler' (1789)

29 *Mit der Dummheit kämpfen Götter selbst vergebens.*
With stupidity the gods themselves struggle in vain.
The Maid of Orleans (1801) act 3, sc. 6

1 *Was ist der langen Rede kurzer Sinn?*
What is the brief meaning of the lengthy speech?
Die Piccolomini (1800) act 1, sc. 2

2 *Ich bein mein Himmel und meine Hölle.*
I am my heaven and my hell.
Die Räuber (1781)

3 *Die Weltgeschichte ist das Weltgericht.*
The world's history is the world's judgement.
'Resignation' (1786) st. 19

4 *Der Mohr hat seine Arbeit getan, der Mohr kann gehen.*
The Moor has done his work, the Moor can go.
usually misquoted as 'Der Mohr hat seine Schuldigkeit getan ['The Moor has done his duty]'
Die Verschwörung des Fiesco (1782) act 3, sc. 4

5 *Anklagen ist meine Amt und meine Sendung.*
To accuse is my duty and my mission.
Wallenstein (1800)

6 *Wir wollen sein ein einzig Volk von Brüdem*
In keiner Not uns trennen und Gefahr.
We would be a single nation of brothers
Standing together in any hour of need or danger.
Wilhelm Tell (1804) act 2, sc. 2

7 If man is ever to solve that problem of politics in practice he will have to approach it through the problem of the aesthetic, because it is only through Beauty that man makes his way to Freedom.
On the Aesthetic Education of Man (1795) letter 2, para. 5

Arthur M. Schlesinger Jr. 1917–
American historian

8 The answer to the runaway Presidency is not the messenger-boy Presidency. The American democracy must discover a middle way between making the President a czar and making him a puppet.
The Imperial Presidency (1973) preface

Moritz Schlick 1882–1936
German philosopher

9 The meaning of a proposition is the method of its verification.
Philosophical Review (1936) vol. 45

Heinrich Schliemann 1822–90
German archaeologist

10 I have gazed upon the face of Agamemnon.
on discovering a gold mask at Mycenae, 1876; traditional version of his telegram to the minister at Athens: 'This one is very like the picture which my imagination formed of Agamemnon long ago'
W. M. Calder and D. A. Traill *Myth, Scandal, and History* (1986)

Artur Schnabel 1882–1951
Austrian-born pianist

11 I know two kinds of audiences only—one coughing, and one not coughing.
My Life and Music (1961) pt. 2, ch. 10

12 The notes I handle no better than many pianists. But the pauses between the notes—ah, that is where the art resides!
in *Chicago Daily News* 11 June 1958

13 Too easy for children, and too difficult for artists.
of Mozart's sonatas
Nat Shapiro (ed.) *Encyclopaedia of Quotations about Music* (1978); see below:

Children are given Mozart because of the small *quantity* of the notes; grown-ups avoid Mozart because of the great *quality* of the notes.
My Life and Music (1961)

Arnold Schoenberg 1874–1951
Austrian-born American composer and musical theorist

14 If it is art, it is not for the masses. 'If it is for the masses it is not art' is a topic which is rather similar to a word of yourself.
letter to W. S. Schlamm, 1 July 1945

15 I am delighted to add another unplayable work to the repertoire. I want the Concerto to be difficult and I want the little finger to become longer. I can wait.
of his Violin Concerto
Joseph Machlis *Introduction to Contemporary Music* (1963)

Arthur Schopenhauer 1788–1860
German philosopher

16 The ordinary man has no sense for general truths . . . the genius on the contrary, overlooks and neglects what is individual.
Parerga and Paralipomena (1851)

Patricia Schroeder 1940–
American Democratic politician

17 Ronald Reagan . . . is attempting a great breakthrough in political technology—he has been perfecting the Teflon-coated Presidency. He sees to it that nothing sticks to him.
speech in the US House of Representatives, 2 August 1983

Budd Schulberg 1914–
American writer
see also **Film lines** *319:11*

18 What makes Sammy run?
title of book (1941)

E. F. Schumacher 1911–77
German-born economist

19 It was not the power of the Spaniards that destroyed the Aztec Empire but the disbelief of the Aztecs in themselves.
Roots of Economic Growth (1962)

20 Small is beautiful. A study of economics as if people mattered.
title of book (1973)

21 Call a thing immoral or ugly, soul-destroying or a degradation of man, a peril to the peace of the world or to the well-being of future generations: as long as you have not shown it to be 'uneconomic' you have not really questioned its right to exist, grow, and prosper.

Small is Beautiful (1973) pt. 1, ch. 3

1 The most striking thing about modern industry is that it requires so much and accomplishes so little. Modern industry seems to be inefficient to a degree that surpasses one's ordinary powers of imagination. Its inefficiency therefore remains unnoticed.

Small is Beautiful (1973) pt. 2, ch. 3

2 It is of little use trying to suppress terrorism if the production of deadly devices continues to be deemed a legitimate employment of man's creative powers.

Small is Beautiful (1973) epilogue

Robert Schumann 1810–56

German composer

3 Hats off, gentlemen—a genius!
of Chopin
'An Opus 2' (1831); H. Pleasants (ed.) *Schumann on Music* (1965)

J. A. Schumpeter 1883–1950

American economist

4 The cold metal of economic theory is in Marx's pages immersed in such a wealth of steaming phrases as to acquire a temperature not naturally its own.

Capitalism, Socialism and Democracy (1942)

5 One servant is worth a thousand gadgets.
J. K. Galbraith *A Life in our Times* (1981) ch. 6

Carl Schurz 1829–1906

American soldier and politician

6 My country, right or wrong; if right, to be kept right; and if wrong, to be set right!
speech, US Senate, 29 February 1872, in *Congressional Globe* vol. 45; see **Decatur** 261:1

Delmore Schwartz 1913–66

American poet

7 Dogs are Shakespearean, children are strangers. Let Freud and Wordsworth discuss the child, Angels and Platonists shall judge the dog.
'Dogs are Shakespearean, Children are Strangers' (1938)

8 The heavy bear who goes with me,
A manifold honey to smear his face,
Clumsy and lumbering here and there,
The central ton of every place,
The hungry beating brutish one
In love with candy, anger, and sleep,
Crazy factotum, dishevelling all,
Climbs the building, kicks the football,
Boxes his brother in the hate-ridden city.
'The Heavy Bear Who Goes With Me' (1958)

Albert Schweitzer 1875–1965

Franco-German missionary

9 Late on the third day, at the very moment when, at sunset, we were making our way through a herd of hippopotamuses, there flashed upon my mind, unforeseen and unsought, the phrase, 'Reverence for Life'.

Aus meinem Leben und Denken (1933) ch. 13

10 Truth has no special time of its own. Its hour is now—always, and indeed then most truly when it seems most unsuitable to actual circumstances.

Zwischen Wasser und Urwald (On the Edge of the Primeval Forest, 1922) ch. 11

Kurt Schwitters 1887–1948

German painter

11 I am a painter and I nail my pictures together.
R. Hausmann *Am Anfang war Dada* (1972)

Scipio Africanus Publius Cornelius Scipio Africanus Major 236–c.184 BC

Roman general and politician

12 *Numquam se minus otiosum esse quam cum otiosus, nec minus solum quam cum solus esset.*
Never less idle than when wholly idle, nor less alone than when wholly alone.
Cicero *De Officiis* bk. 3, ch. 1

Alexander Scott c.1525–c.84

Scottish poet

13 Love is ane fervent fire,
Kindled without desire,
Short pleasure, long displeasure;
Repentance is the hire;
And pure treasure without measure.
Love is ane fervent fire.
'Lo, What it is to Love' (c.1568)

C. P. Scott 1846–1932

British journalist; editor of the Manchester Guardian, *1872–1929*

14 Comment is free, but facts are sacred.
in *Manchester Guardian* 5 May 1921; see **Stoppard** 761:11

15 *Television?* The word is half Greek, half Latin. No good can come of it.
Asa Briggs *The BBC: the First Fifty Years* (1985)

Robert Falcon Scott 1868–1912

English polar explorer
see also **Last words** 471:13

16 Great God! this is an awful place.
of the South Pole
diary, 17 January 1912, in *Scott's Last Expedition* (1913) vol. 1, ch. 18

17 Make the boy interested in natural history if you can; it is better than games.
last letter to his wife, in *Scott's Last Expedition* (1913) vol. 1, ch. 20

1 Had we lived, I should have had a tale to tell of the hardihood, endurance, and courage of my companions which would have stirred the heart of every Englishman. These rough notes and our dead bodies must tell the tale.

'Message to the Public' in late editions of *The Times* 11 February 1913, and those of the following day; in *Scott's Last Expedition* (1913) vol. 1, ch. 20

Sir Walter Scott 1771–1832

Scottish novelist and poet
on Scott: see **Anonymous** 18:7, **Hazlitt** 377:1

2 The valiant Knight of Triermain
Rung forth his challenge-blast again,
But answer came there none.

The Bridal of Triermain (1813) canto 3, st. 10; see **Carroll** 195:8

3 Come fill up my cup, come fill up my can,
Come saddle your horses, and call up your men;
Come open the West Port, and let me gang free,
And it's room for the bonnets of Bonny Dundee!'

The Doom of Devorgoil (1830) act 2, sc. 2 'Bonny Dundee';
see **Scott** 674:21

4 Yet seemed that tone, and gesture bland,
Less used to sue than to command.

The Lady of the Lake (1810) canto 1, st. 21; see **Shakespeare** 715:6

5 He is gone on the mountain,
He is lost to the forest,
Like a summer-dried fountain,
When our need was the sorest.

The Lady of the Lake (1810) canto 3, st. 16

6 Respect was mingled with surprise,
And the stern joy which warriors feel
In foemen worthy of their steel.

The Lady of the Lake (1810) canto 5, st. 10

7 Vengeance, deep-brooding o'er the slain,
Had locked the source of softer woe;
And burning pride and high disdain
Forbade the rising tear to flow.

The Lay of the Last Minstrel (1805) canto 1, st. 9

8 If thou would'st view fair Melrose aright,
Go visit it by the pale moonlight;
For the gay beams of lightsome day
Gild, but to flout, the ruins grey.

The Lay of the Last Minstrel (1805) canto 2, st. 1

9   For ne'er
Was flattery lost on poet's ear:
A simple race! they waste their toil
For the vain tribute of a smile.

The Lay of the Last Minstrel (1805) canto 4, closing words

10 It is the secret sympathy,
The silver link, the silken tie,
Which heart to heart, and mind to mind,
In body and in soul can bind.

The Lay of the Last Minstrel (1805) canto 5, st. 13

11 Breathes there the man, with soul so dead,
Who never to himself hath said,
This is my own, my native land!

The Lay of the Last Minstrel (1805) canto 6, st. 1

12 Despite those titles, power, and pelf,
The wretch, concentred all in self,

Living, shall forfeit fair renown,
And, doubly dying, shall go down
To the vile dust, from whence he sprung,
Unwept, unhonoured, and unsung.

The Lay of the Last Minstrel (1805) canto 6, st. 1

13 O Caledonia! stern and wild,
Meet nurse for a poetic child!
Land of brown heath and shaggy wood,
Land of the mountain and the flood,
Land of my sires! what mortal hand
Can e'er untie the filial band
That knits me to thy rugged strand!

The Lay of the Last Minstrel (1805) canto 6, st. 2

14 O! many a shaft, at random sent,
Finds mark the archer little meant!
And many a word, at random spoken,
May soothe or wound a heart that's broken.

The Lord of the Isles (1813) canto 5, st. 18

15 Had'st thou but lived, though stripped of power,
A watchman on the lonely tower.

Marmion (1808) introduction to canto 1, st. 8

16 Now is the stately column broke,
The beacon-light is quenched in smoke,
The trumpet's silver sound is still,
The warder silent on the hill!

Marmion (1808) introduction to canto 1, st. 8

17 And come he slow, or come he fast,
It is but Death who comes at last.

Marmion (1808) canto 2, st. 30

18 O, young Lochinvar is come out of the west,
Through all the wide Border his steed was the best.

Marmion (1808) canto 5, st. 12 ('Lochinvar' st. 1)

19 So faithful in love, and so dauntless in war,
There never was knight like the young Lochinvar.

Marmion (1808) canto 5, st. 12 ('Lochinvar' st. 1)

20 For a laggard in love, and a dastard in war,
Was to wed the fair Ellen of brave Lochinvar.

Marmion (1808) canto 5, st. 12 ('Lochinvar' st. 2)

21 O come ye in peace here, or come ye in war,
Or to dance at our bridal, young Lord Lochinvar?

Marmion (1808) canto 5, st. 12 ('Lochinvar' st. 3)

22 And now I am come, with this lost love of mine,
To lead but one measure, drink one cup of wine.

Marmion (1808) canto 5, st. 12 ('Lochinvar' st. 4)

23 O what a tangled web we weave,
When first we practise to deceive!

Marmion (1808) canto 6, st. 17

24 O Woman! in our hours of ease,
Uncertain, coy, and hard to please,
And variable as the shade
By the light quivering aspen made;
When pain and anguish wring the brow,
A ministering angel thou!

Marmion (1808) canto 6, st. 30; see **Shakespeare** 689:1

25 The stubborn spear-men still made good
Their dark impenetrable wood,
Each stepping where his comrade stood,
The instant that he fell.

Marmion (1808) canto 6, st. 34

1 Still from the sire the son shall hear
Of the stern strife, and carnage drear,
Of Flodden's fatal field,
Where shivered was fair Scotland's spear,
And broken was her shield!
Marmion (1808) canto 6, st. 34

2 O, Brignal banks are wild and fair,
And Greta woods are green,
And you may gather garlands there
Would grace a summer queen.
Rokeby (1813) canto 3, st. 16

3 It's no fish ye're buying—it's men's lives.
The Antiquary (1816) ch. 11

4 Widowed wife, and married maid,
Betrothed, betrayer, and betrayed!
The Betrothed (1825) ch. 15

5 Vacant heart and hand, and eye,—
Easy live and quiet die.
The Bride of Lammermoor (1819) ch. 2

6 I live by twa trades . . . fiddle, sir, and spade; filling
the world, and emptying of it.
The Bride of Lammermoor (1819) ch. 24

7 Touch not the cat but a glove.
but = *without*
The Fair Maid of Perth (1828) ch. 34

8 It's ill taking the breeks aff a wild Highlandman.
The Fortunes of Nigel (1822) ch. 5

9 For three wild lads were we, brave boys,
And three wild lads were we;
Thou on the land, and I on the sand,
And Jack on the gallows-tree!
Guy Mannering (1815) ch. 34

10 The hour is come, but not the man.
The Heart of Midlothian (1818) ch. 4, title

11 The passive resistance of the Tolbooth-gate.
The Heart of Midlothian (1818) ch. 6

12 Proud Maisie is in the wood,
Walking so early,
Sweet Robin sits in the bush,
Singing so rarely.
The Heart of Midlothian (1818) ch. 40

13 'Pax vobiscum [Peace be with you]' will answer
all queries.
Ivanhoe (1819) ch. 26

14 His morning walk was beneath the elms in the
churchyard; 'for death,' he said, 'had been his
next-door neighbour for so many years, that he
had no apology for dropping the acquaintance.'
A Legend of Montrose (1819) introduction

15 March, march, Ettrick and Teviotdale,
Why the deil dinna ye march forward in order?
March, march, Eskdale and Liddesdale,
All the Blue Bonnets are bound for the Border.
The Monastery (1820) ch. 25

16 It is fortunate for tale-tellers that they are not tied
down like theatrical writers to the unities of time
and place.
'Old Mortality' (*Tales of My Landlord* 1st series, 1816)

17 Ah! County Guy, the hour is nigh,
The sun has left the lea,
The orange flower perfumes the bower,
The breeze is on the sea.
Quentin Durward (1823) ch. 4

18 And it's ill speaking between a fou man and a
fasting.
Redgauntlet (1824) letter 11 'Wandering Willie's Tale'

19 The ae half of the warld thinks the tither daft.
Redgauntlet (1824) 'Journal of Darsie Latimer' ch. 7

20 But with the morning cool repentance came.
Rob Roy (1817) ch. 12

21 Come fill up my cup, come fill up my cann,
Come saddle my horses, and call up my man;
Come open your gates, and let me gae free,
I daurna stay langer in bonny Dundee.
Rob Roy (1817) ch. 23; see **Scott** 673:3

22 There's a gude time coming.
Rob Roy (1817) ch. 32

23 The play-bill, which is said to have announced the
tragedy of Hamlet, the character of the Prince of
Denmark being left out.
commonly alluded to as 'Hamlet without the Prince'
The Talisman (1825) introduction; W. J. Parke *Musical
Memories* (1830) vol. 1 gives a similar anecdote from 1787

24 Rouse the lion from his lair.
The Talisman (1825) ch. 6

25 Turner's palm is as itchy as his fingers are
ingenious.
letter to James Skene, 30 April 1823; *Letters* (1934)

26 But I must say to the Muse of fiction, as the Earl of
Pembroke said to the ejected nun of Wilton, 'Go
spin, you jade, go spin'.
diary, 9 February 1826; see **Pembroke** 591:11

27 The Big Bow-Wow strain I can do myself like any
now going; but the exquisite touch, which renders
ordinary commonplace things and characters
interesting, from the truth of the description and
the sentiment, is denied to me.
on Jane **Austen**
W. E. K. Anderson (ed.) *Journals of Sir Walter Scott* (1972)
14 March 1826; see **Pembroke** 591:13

28 I would like to be there, were it but to see how the
cat jumps.
W. E. K. Anderson (ed.) *Journals of Sir Walter Scott* (1972) 7
October 1826

29 The blockheads talk of my being like
Shakespeare—not fit to tie his brogues.
W. E. K. Anderson (ed.) *Journals of Sir Walter Scott* (1972)
11 December 1826

30 Were I my own man . . . I would refuse this offer
(with all gratitude); but as I am situated, L.300 or
L.400 a-year is not to be sneezed at.
on being offered the Laureateship
letter to James Ballantyne, 24 August 1813; John Gibson
Lockhart *Memoirs of the Life of Sir Walter Scott* (1837–8)

31 Too many flowers . . . too little fruit.
describing the work of Felicia **Hemans**
letter to Joanna Baillie, 18 July 1823, in *Letters* (Centenary
ed.) vol. 8

1 We shall never learn to feel and respect our real calling and destiny, unless we have taught ourselves to consider every thing as moonshine, compared with the education of the heart.

> to J. G. Lockhart, August 1825, in Lockhart's *Life of Sir Walter Scott* vol. 6 (1837) ch. 2

2 Their factions have been so long envenomed and having so little ground to fight their battle in that they [the Irish] are like people fighting with daggers in a hogshead.

> letter to Joanna Baillie, 12 October 1825, in H. J. C. Grierson (ed.) *Letters of Sir Walter Scott* vol. 9 (1935)

3 All men who have turned out worth anything have had the chief hand in their own education.

> letter to J. G. Lockhart, *c.*16 June 1830, in H. J. C. Grierson (ed.) *Letters of Sir Walter Scott* vol. 11 (1936)

Scottish Metrical Psalms 1650

4 The Lord's my shepherd, I'll not want.
He makes me down to lie
In pastures green: he leadeth me
the quiet waters by.
My soul he doth restore again;
and me to walk doth make
Within the paths of righteousness,
ev'n for his own name's sake.

Yea, though I walk in death's dark vale,
yet will I fear none ill:
For thou art with me; and thy rod
and staff me comfort still.
My table thou hast furnished
in presence of my foes;
My head thou dost with oil anoint,
and my cup overflows.

> Psalm 23, v. 1; see **Book of Common Prayer** 135:3

5 How lovely is thy dwelling-place,
O Lord of hosts, to me!
The tabernacles of thy grace
how pleasant, Lord, they be!

> Psalm 84, v. 1; see **Book of Common Prayer** 139:15

6 I to the hills will lift mine eyes
from whence doth come mine aid.
My safety cometh from the Lord,
who heav'n and earth hath made.

> Psalm 121, v. 1; see **Book of Common Prayer** 142:16

7 The race that long in darkness pined
have seen a glorious light.

> Paraphrase 19; see **Bible** 88:17

Edmund Hamilton Sears 1810–76
American minister

8 It came upon the midnight clear,
That glorious song of old,
From Angels bending near the earth
To touch their harps of gold;
'Peace on the earth, good will to man
From Heaven's all gracious King.'
The world in solemn stillness lay
To hear the angels sing.

> *The Christian Register* (1850) 'That Glorious Song of Old'

Charles Sedley c.1639–1701
English dramatist and poet

9 Ah, Chloris! that I now could sit
As unconcerned as when
Your infant beauty could beget
No pleasure, nor no pain!

> 'Child and Maiden' (1668)

10 Love still has something of the sea
From whence his mother rose.

> 'Love still has something'

11 Phyllis, without frown or smile,
Sat and knotted all the while.

> 'Phyllis Knotting' (1694)

12 Phyllis is my only joy,
Faithless as the winds or seas;
Sometimes coming, sometimes coy,
Yet she never fails to please.

> 'Song'

Alan Seeger 1888–1916
American poet

13 I have a rendezvous with Death
At some disputed barricade.

> 'I Have a Rendezvous with Death' (1916)

Pete Seeger 1919–
American folk singer and songwriter

14 Where have all the flowers gone?

> title of song (1961)

15 Education is when you read the fine print; experience is what you get when you don't.

> L. Botts *Loose Talk* (1980)

John Seeley 1834–95
English historian

16 We [the English] seem, as it were, to have conquered and peopled half the world in a fit of absence of mind.

> *The Expansion of England* (1883) Lecture 1

Sefer Yezirah
Hebrew esoteric text on cosmology, 3rd–6th century AD

17 Thirty-two wondrous paths were engraved by Yah, the Lord of hosts, the God of Israel, the living God, God Almighty . . . who . . . created his world by three principles: by limit, by letter and by number.
There are ten primordial numbers and twenty-two fundamental letters.

> 1:1

Erich Segal see **Taglines for films** 771:8

Sei Shōnagon c.966–c.1013
Japanese diarist and writer

18 There is nothing in the whole world so painful as feeling that one is not liked. It always seems to me that people who hate me must be suffering from some strange form of lunacy.

The Pillow Book of Sei Shōnagōn

1 If writing did not exist, what terrible depressions we should suffer from.

The Pillow Book of Sei Shōnagōn

John Selden 1584–1654

English historian and antiquary

2 *Scrutamini scripturas* [Let us look at the scriptures]. These two words have undone the world.

Table Talk (1689) 'Bible Scripture'; see **Bible** 102:38

3 Old friends are best. King James used to call for his old shoes; they were easiest for his feet.

Table Talk (1689) 'Friends'

4 Ignorance of the law excuses no man; not that all men know the law, but because 'tis an excuse every man will plead, and no man can tell how to confute him.

Table Talk (1689) 'Law'; see **Proverbs** 623:29

5 Take a straw and throw it up into the air, you shall see by that which way the wind is.

Table Talk (1689) 'Libels'

6 Marriage is nothing but a civil contract.

Table Talk (1689) 'Marriage'

7 A king is a thing men have made for their own sakes, for quietness' sake. Just as in a family one man is appointed to buy the meat.

Table Talk (1689) 'Of a King'

8 There never was a merry world since the fairies left off dancing, and the Parson left conjuring.

Table Talk (1689) 'Parson'

9 There is not anything in the world so much abused as this sentence, *Salus populi suprema lex esto.*

Table Talk (1689) 'People'; see **Cicero** 223:9

10 Pleasure is nothing else but the intermission of pain.

Table Talk (1689) 'Pleasure'

11 Syllables govern the world.

Table Talk (1689) 'Power: State'

12 Preachers say, Do as I say, not as I do.

Table Talk (1689) 'Preaching'

Arthur Seldon 1916–

British economist

13 Government of the busy by the bossy for the bully.

on over-government

Capitalism (1990)

W. C. Sellar 1898–1951 and R. J. Yeatman 1898–1968

British writers

14 For every person who wants to teach there are approximately thirty who don't want to learn—much.

And Now All This (1932) introduction

15 1066 and all That

title of book (1930)

16 History is not what you thought. *It is what you can remember.*

1066 and All That (1930) 'Compulsory Preface'

17 The Roman Conquest was, however, a *Good Thing*, since the Britons were only natives at the time.

1066 and All That (1930) ch. 1

18 Edward III had very good manners . . . and made the memorable epitaph: 'Honi soie qui mal y pense' ('Honey, your silk stocking's hanging down').

1066 and All That (1930) ch. 24; see **Mottoes** 552:9

19 Are you Edmund Mortimer? If not, have you got him?

1066 and All That (1930) ch. 28

20 The cruel Queen died and a post-mortem examination revealed the word 'CALLOUS' engraved on her heart.

1066 and All That (1930) ch. 32; see **Mary** 517:7

21 The Cavaliers (Wrong but Wromantic) and the Roundheads (Right but Repulsive).

1066 and All That (1930) ch. 35

22 Charles II was always very merry and was therefore not so much a king as a Monarch.

1066 and All That (1930) ch. 36; see **Rochester** 651:14

23 The National Debt is a very Good Thing and it would be dangerous to pay it off, for fear of Political Economy.

1066 and All That (1930) ch. 38

24 Napoleon's armies always used to march on their stomachs shouting: 'Vive l'Intérieur!'

1066 and All That (1930) ch. 48; see **Napoleon** 557:1

25 Gladstone . . . spent his declining years trying to guess the answer to the Irish Question; unfortunately whenever he was getting warm, the Irish secretly changed the Question.

1066 and All That (1930) ch. 57

26 AMERICA was thus clearly top nation, and History came to a .

1066 and All That (1930) ch. 62

Seneca ('the Younger') c.4 BC–AD 65

Roman philosopher and poet

27 *Ignoranti, quem portum petat, nullus suus ventus est.*

If one does not know to which port one is sailing, no wind is favourable.

Epistulae ad Lucilium no. 71, sect. 3

28 *Homines dum docent discunt.*

Even while they teach, men learn.

Epistulae Morales no. 7, sect. 8

29 *Non habemus illos hostes, sed facimus.*

They are not enemies when we acquire them; we make them so.

on slaves

Epistulae Morales no. 47, sect. 5

30 *Nil melius aeterna lex fecit, quam quod unum introitum nobis ad vitam dedit, exitus multos.*

Eternal law has arranged nothing better than this, that it has given us one way in to life, but many ways out.
> *Epistulae Morales* no. 70, sect. 14

1 *Curae leves locuntur, ingentes stupent.*
Small sorrows speak; great ones are silent.
> *Hippolytus* l. 607

2 *Eripere vitam nemo non homini potest,*
At nemo mortem; mille ad hanc aditus patent.
Anyone can stop a man's life, but no one his death; a thousand doors open on to it.
> *Phoenissae* l. 152; see **Massinger** 327:4, **Webster** 825:25

3 *Illi mors gravis incubat*
Qui notus nimis omnibus
Ignotus moritur sibi.
On him does death lie heavily who, but too well known to all, dies to himself unknown.
> *Thyestes* chorus 2 (translated by F. J. Miller)

Gitta Sereny 1923-
Hungarian-born British writer and journalist

4 *to Albert Speer, who having always denied knowledge of the Holocaust had said that he was at fault in having 'looked away':*
You cannot look away from something you don't know. If you looked away, then you knew.
> recalled on BBC2 *Reputations*, 2 May 1996

Nicholas Serota 1946-
British art expert, Director of the Tate Gallery

5 This is a plea for patience. Your scepticism will gradually diminish and your fear will turn to love ... All art was modern once.
> *to critics of modern art*
> in *Independent* 26 November 2000

Robert W. Service 1874-1958
Canadian poet

6 A promise made is a debt unpaid, and the trail has its own stern code.
> 'The Cremation of Sam McGee' (1907)

7 Ah! the clock is always slow;
It is later than you think.
> 'It Is Later Than You Think' (1921)

8 This is the law of the Yukon, that only the Strong shall thrive;
That surely the Weak shall perish, and only the Fit survive.
> 'The Law of the Yukon' (1907)

9 When we, the Workers, all demand: 'What are WE fighting for?' ...
Then, then we'll end that stupid crime, that devil's madness—War.
> 'Michael' (1921)

10 Back of the bar, in a solo game, sat Dangerous Dan McGrew,
And watching his luck was his light-o'-love, the lady that's known as Lou.
> 'The Shooting of Dan McGrew' (1907)

William Seward 1801-72
American politician

11 I know, and all the world knows, that revolutions never go backward.
> speech at Rochester, 25 October 1858, in *The Irrepressible Conflict* (1858)

Edward Sexby d. 1658
English conspirator

12 Killing no murder briefly discourst in three questions.
> *an apology for tyrannicide*
> title of pamphlet (1657)

Anne Sexton 1928-74
American poet

13 I was tired of being a woman,
tired of the spoons and the pots,
tired of my mouth and my breasts
tired of the cosmetics and silks ...
I was tired of the gender of things.
> 'Consorting with angels' (1967)

14 God owns heaven
but He craves the earth.
> 'The Earth' (1975)

15 My sleeping pill is white.
It is a splendid pearl;
it floats me out of myself,
my stung skin as alien
as a loose bolt of cloth.
> 'Lullaby' (1960)

16 In a dream you are never eighty.
> 'Old' (1962)

17 But suicides have a special language.
Like carpenters they want to know *which tools*.
They never ask *why build*.
> 'Wanting to Die' (1966)

Ernest Shackleton 1874-1922
British explorer

18 Ship and stores have gone—so now we'll go home.
> *to his men on the loss of the* Endurance, *27 October 1915*
> *South* (1991 ed.)

19 Superhuman effort isn't worth a damn unless it achieves results.
> to his navigator Frank Worsley, 1916; F. P. Worsley *Endurance* (1931)

Thomas Shadwell c.1642-92
English dramatist
on Shadwell: see **Dryden** 288:31

20 Words may be false and full of art,
Sighs are the natural language of the heart.
> *Psyche* (1675) act 3

21 And wit's the noblest frailty of the mind.
> *A True Widow* (1679) act 2, sc. 1; see **Dryden** 288:22

1 Every man loves what he is good at.
  A True Widow (1679) act 5, sc. 1

Peter Shaffer 1926–

English dramatist

2 All my wife has ever taken from the
  Mediterranean—from that whole vast intuitive
  culture—are four bottles of Chianti to make into
  lamps.
  Equus (1973) act 1, sc. 18

Anthony Ashley Cooper, 1st Earl of Shaftesbury 1621–83

English statesman

3 Admit lords, and you admit all.
  refusing the claims of Cromwell's House of Lords
    in *Dictionary of National Biography* (1917–)

4 'People differ in their discourse and profession
  about these matters, but men of sense are really
  but of one religion.' . . . 'Pray, my lord, what
  religion is that which men of sense agree in?'
  'Madam,' says the earl immediately, 'men of sense
  never tell it.'
    Bishop Gilbert Burnet *History of My Own Time* vol. 1 (1724)
    bk. 2, ch. 1 n.; see **Disraeli** 277:12

Anthony Ashley Cooper, 3rd Earl of Shaftesbury 1671–1713

English statesman and philosopher

5 How comes it to pass, then, that we appear such
  cowards in reasoning, and are so afraid to stand
  the test of ridicule?
    A Letter Concerning Enthusiasm (1708) sect. 2

6 Truth, 'tis supposed, may bear all lights: and one
  of those in which things are to be viewed, in order
  to [attain] a thorough recognition is that by which
  we discern whatever is liable to ridicule in any
  subject.
    Sensus Communis: an essay on the freedom of wit and humour
    (1709) pt. 1, sect. 1; see **Chesterfield** 215:12

William Shakespeare 1564–1616

English dramatist

on Shakespeare: see **Arnold** 28:12, **Aubrey** 34:2, **Basse** 58:7,
Browning 159:21, **Coleridge** 233:23, **Dryden** 290:4, **Dryden**
290:7, **George III** 343:5, **Gray** 361:18, **Greene** 362:24,
Johnson 425:13, **Johnson** 425:15, **Johnson** 425:16, **Johnson**
425:17, **Jonson** 435:24, **Jonson** 435:28, **Jonson** 436:2, **Jonson**
436:3, **Jonson** 436:4, **Lawrence** 474:21, **Milton** 529:12, **Milton**
530:14, **Olivier** 573:4, **Pope** 605:20, **Scott** 674:29,
Walpole 819:1, **Wordsworth** 849:26; *see also* **Epitaphs**
309:10, **Fletcher** 327:8

*The line number is given without brackets where the scene is all
verse up to the quotation and the line number is certain, and in
square brackets where prose makes it variable. All references are
to the Oxford Standard Authors edition in one volume*

ALL'S WELL THAT ENDS WELL

7   It were all one
  That I should love a bright particular star
  And think to wed it, he is so above me.
    All's Well that Ends Well (1603–4) act 1, sc. 1, l. [97]

8 Our remedies oft in ourselves do lie
  Which we ascribe to heaven.
    All's Well that Ends Well (1603–4) act 1, sc. 1, l. [232]

9 It is like a barber's chair that fits all buttocks.
    All's Well that Ends Well (1603–4) act 2, sc. 2, l. [18]

10 A young man married is a man that's marred.
    All's Well that Ends Well (1603–4) act 2, sc. 3, l. [315]; see
    Proverbs 636:5

11 The flowery way that leads to the broad gate and
   the great fire.
    All's Well that Ends Well (1603–4) act 4, sc. 5, l. [58]; see
    Shakespeare 705:6

ANTONY AND CLEOPATRA

12 The triple pillar of the world transformed
   Into a strumpet's fool.
    Antony and Cleopatra (1606–7) act 1, sc. 1, l. 12

13 CLEOPATRA: If it be love indeed, tell me how much.
   ANTONY: There's beggary in the love that can be
     reckoned.
   CLEOPATRA: I'll set a bourn how far to be beloved.
   ANTONY: Then must thou needs find out new
     heaven, new earth.
    Antony and Cleopatra (1606–7) act 1, sc. 1, l. 14

14 Let Rome in Tiber melt, and the wide arch
   Of the ranged empire fall. Here is my space.
   Kingdoms are clay.
    Antony and Cleopatra (1606–7) act 1, sc. 1, l. 33

15 I love long life better than figs.
    Antony and Cleopatra (1606–7) act 1, sc. 2, l. [34]

16   On the sudden
   A Roman thought hath struck him.
    Antony and Cleopatra (1606–7) act 1, sc. 2, l. [90]

17 The nature of bad news infects the teller.
    Antony and Cleopatra (1606–7) act 1, sc. 2, l. [103]

18 Indeed the tears live in an onion that should water
   this sorrow.
    Antony and Cleopatra (1606–7) act 1, sc. 2, l. [181]

19 CHARMIAN: In each thing give him way, cross him
     in nothing.
   CLEOPATRA: Thou teachest like a fool; the way to
     lose him.
    Antony and Cleopatra (1606–7) act 1, sc. 3, l. 9

20 In time we hate that which we often fear.
    Antony and Cleopatra (1606–7) act 1, sc. 3, l. 12

21 Eternity was in our lips and eyes,
   Bliss in our brows bent.
    Antony and Cleopatra (1606–7) act 1, sc. 3, l. 35

22 O! my oblivion is a very Antony,
   And I am all forgotten.
    Antony and Cleopatra (1606–7) act 1, sc. 3, l. 90

23 Give me to drink mandragora . . .
   That I might sleep out this great gap of time
   My Antony is away.
    Antony and Cleopatra (1606–7) act 1, sc. 5, l. 4

24 O happy horse, to bear the weight of Antony!
    Antony and Cleopatra (1606–7) act 1, sc. 5, l. 21

25   He's speaking now,
   Or murmuring, 'Where's my serpent of old Nile?'
    Antony and Cleopatra (1606–7) act 1, sc. 5, l. 24

1 My salad days,
When I was green in judgment, cold in blood,
To say as I said then!
Antony and Cleopatra (1606–7) act 1, sc. 5, l. 73

2 I do not much dislike the matter, but
The manner of his speech.
Antony and Cleopatra (1606–7) act 2, sc. 2, l. 117

3 The barge she sat in, like a burnished throne,
Burned on the water; the poop was beaten gold,
Purple the sails, and so perfumed, that
The winds were love-sick with them, the oars
 were silver,
Which to the tune of flutes kept stroke, and made
The water which they beat to follow faster,
As amorous of their strokes. For her own person,
It beggared all description.
Antony and Cleopatra (1606–7) act 2, sc. 2, l. [199]; see
 Eliot 303:12

4 Her gentlewomen, like the Nereides,
So many mermaids, tended her i' the eyes,
And made their bends adornings.
Antony and Cleopatra (1606–7) act 2, sc. 2, l. [214]

5 Antony,
Enthroned i' the market-place, did sit alone,
Whistling to the air; which, but for vacancy,
Had gone to gaze on Cleopatra too
And made a gap in nature.
Antony and Cleopatra (1606–7) act 2, sc. 2, l. [222]

6 I saw her once
Hop forty paces through the public street;
And having lost her breath, she spoke, and panted
That she did make defect perfection,
And, breathless, power breathe forth.
Antony and Cleopatra (1606–7) act 2, sc. 2, l. [236]

7 Age cannot wither her, nor custom stale
Her infinite variety; other women cloy
The appetites they feed, but she makes hungry
Where most she satisfies; for vilest things
Become themselves in her, that the holy priests
Bless her when she is riggish.
Antony and Cleopatra (1606–7) act 2, sc. 2, l. [243]

8 I have not kept the square, but that to come
Shall all be done by the rule.
Antony and Cleopatra (1606–7) act 2, sc. 3, l. 6

9 I' the east my pleasure lies.
Antony and Cleopatra (1606–7) act 2, sc. 3, l. 40

10 Give me some music—music, moody food
Of us that trade in love.
Antony and Cleopatra (1606–7) act 2, sc. 5, l. 1

11 Give me mine angle; we'll to the river: there—
My music playing far off—I will betray
Tawny-finned fishes; my bended hook shall pierce
Their slimy jaws; and, as I draw them up,
I'll think them every one an Antony,
And say, 'Ah, ha!' you're caught.
Antony and Cleopatra (1606–7) act 2, sc. 5, l. 10

12 I laughed him out of patience; and that night
I laughed him into patience: and next morn,
Ere the ninth hour, I drunk him to his bed.
Antony and Cleopatra (1606–7) act 2, sc. 5, l. 19

13 LEPIDUS: What manner o' thing is your crocodile?
ANTONY: It is shaped, sir, like itself, and it is as
 broad as it hath breadth; it is just so high as it
 is, and moves with its own organs; it lives by
 that which nourisheth it; and the elements once
 out of it, it transmigrates.
Antony and Cleopatra (1606–7) act 2, sc. 7, l. [47]

14 Egypt, thou knew'st too well
My heart was to thy rudder tied by th' strings,
And thou shouldst tow me after.
Antony and Cleopatra (1606–7) act 3, sc. 9, l. 56

15 He wears the rose
Of youth upon him.
Antony and Cleopatra (1606–7) act 3, sc. 11, l. 20

16 I found you as a morsel, cold upon
Dead Caesar's trencher.
Antony and Cleopatra (1606–7) act 3, sc. 11, l. 116

17 Let's have one other gaudy night: call to me
All my sad captains; fill our bowls once more;
Let's mock the midnight bell.
Antony and Cleopatra (1606–7) act 3, sc. 11, l. 182

18 O! my fortunes have
Corrupted honest men.
Antony and Cleopatra (1606–7) act 4, sc. 5, l. 16

19 O infinite virtue! com'st thou smiling from
The world's great snare uncaught?
Antony and Cleopatra (1606–7) act 4, sc. 8, l. 17

20 The hearts
That spanieled me at heels, to whom I gave
Their wishes, do discandy, melt their sweets
On blossoming Caesar.
Antony and Cleopatra (1606–7) act 4, sc. 10, l. 33

21 The soul and body rive not more in parting
Than greatness going off.
Antony and Cleopatra (1606–7) act 4, sc. 11, l. 5

22 Sometimes we see a cloud that's dragonish;
A vapour sometime like a bear or lion,
A towered citadel, a pendant rock,
A forked mountain, or blue promontory
With trees upon 't, that nod unto the world
And mock our eyes with air.
Antony and Cleopatra (1606–7) act 4, sc. 12, l. 2

23 Unarm, Eros; the long day's task is done,
And we must sleep.
Antony and Cleopatra (1606–7) act 4, sc. 12, l. 35

24 Stay for me:
Where souls do couch on flowers, we'll hand in
 hand,
And with our sprightly port make the ghosts gaze;
Dido and her Aeneas shall want troops,
And all the haunt be ours.
Antony and Cleopatra (1606–7) act 4, sc. 12, l. 50

25 I will be
A bridegroom in my death, and run into 't
As to a lover's bed.
Antony and Cleopatra (1606–7) act 4, sc. 12, l. 99

26 None but Antony
Should conquer Antony.
Antony and Cleopatra (1606–7) act 4, sc. 13, l. 16

1 I am dying, Egypt, dying.
Antony and Cleopatra (1606–7) act 4, sc. 13, l. 18

2   A Roman by a Roman
Valiantly vanquished.
Antony and Cleopatra (1606–7) act 4, sc. 13, l. 57

3 O! withered is the garland of the war,
The soldier's pole is fall'n; young boys and girls
Are level now with men; the odds is gone,
And there is nothing left remarkable
Beneath the visiting moon.
Antony and Cleopatra (1606–7) act 4, sc. 13, l. 64

4   What's brave, what's noble,
Let's do it after the high Roman fashion,
And make death proud to take us.
Antony and Cleopatra (1606–7) act 4, sc. 13, l. 86

5 My desolation does begin to make
A better life. 'Tis paltry to be Caesar;
Not being Fortune, he's but Fortune's knave,
A minister of her will; and it is great
To do that thing that ends all other deeds,
Which shackles accidents, and bolts up change,
Which sleeps, and never palates more the dug,
The beggar's nurse and Caesar's.
Antony and Cleopatra (1606–7) act 5, sc. 2, l. 1

6 He words me, girls, he words me, that I should not
Be noble to myself.
Antony and Cleopatra (1606–7) act 5, sc. 2, l. 190

7 Finish, good lady; the bright day is done,
And we are for the dark.
Antony and Cleopatra (1606–7) act 5, sc. 2, l. 192

8   Antony
Shall be brought drunken forth, and I shall see
Some squeaking Cleopatra boy my greatness
I' the posture of a whore.
Antony and Cleopatra (1606–7) act 5, sc. 2, l. 217

9 My resolution's placed, and I have nothing
Of woman in me; now from head to foot
I am marble-constant, now the fleeting moon
No planet is of mine.
Antony and Cleopatra (1606–7) act 5, sc. 2, l. 237

10 His biting is immortal; those that do die of it do
seldom or never recover.
Antony and Cleopatra (1606–7) act 5, sc. 2, l. [246]

11 I wish you all joy of the worm.
Antony and Cleopatra (1606–7) act 5, sc. 2, l. [260]

12 Give me my robe, put on my crown; I have
Immortal longings in me.
Antony and Cleopatra (1606–7) act 5, sc. 2, l. [282]

13 I am fire and air; my other elements
I give to baser life.
Antony and Cleopatra (1606–7) act 5, sc. 2, l. [291]

14   Come, thou mortal wretch,
With thy sharp teeth this knot intrinsicate
Of life at once untie; poor venomous fool,
Be angry, and dispatch. O! couldst thou speak,
That I might hear thee call great Caesar ass
Unpolicied.
Antony and Cleopatra (1606–7) act 5, sc. 2, l. [305]

15 CHARMIAN: O eastern star!
CLEOPATRA: Peace! peace!

Dost thou not see my baby at my breast,
That sucks the nurse asleep?
Antony and Cleopatra (1606–7) act 5, sc. 2, l. [309]

16 Now boast thee, death, in thy possession lies
A lass unparalleled.
Antony and Cleopatra (1606–7) act 5, sc. 2, l. [317]

17   She looks like sleep,
As she would catch a second Antony
In her strong toil of grace.
Antony and Cleopatra (1606–7) act 5, sc. 2, l. [347]

18 She hath pursued conclusions infinite
Of easy ways to die.
Antony and Cleopatra (1606–7) act 5, sc. 2, l. [356]

AS YOU LIKE IT

19 Fleet the time carelessly, as they did in the golden
world.
As You Like It (1599) act 1, sc. 1, l. [126]

20 Let us sit and mock the good housewife Fortune
from her wheel, that her gifts may henceforth be
bestowed equally.
As You Like It (1599) act 1, sc. 2, l. [35]

21 Hereafter, in a better world than this,
I shall desire more love and knowledge of you.
As You Like It (1599) act 1, sc. 2, l. [301]

22 Thus must I from the smoke into the smother;
From tyrant duke unto a tyrant brother.
As You Like It (1599) act 1, sc. 2, l. [304]

23 O, how full of briers is this working-day world!
As You Like It (1599) act 1, sc. 3, l. [12]

24 We'll have a swashing and a martial outside,
As many other mannish cowards have
That do outface it with their semblances.
As You Like It (1599) act 1, sc. 3, l. [123]

25   Are not these woods
More free from peril than the envious court?
Here feel we but the penalty of Adam,
The seasons' difference; as, the icy fang
And churlish chiding of the winter's wind,
Which, when it bites and blows upon my body,
Even till I shrink with cold, I smile and say,
'This is no flattery.'
As You Like It (1599) act 2, sc. 1, l. 3

26 Sweet are the uses of adversity,
Which like the toad, ugly and venomous,
Wears yet a precious jewel in his head;
And this our life, exempt from public haunt,
Finds tongues in trees, books in the running
   brooks,
Sermons in stones, and good in everything.
As You Like It (1599) act 2, sc. 1, l. 12; see **Bernard** 70:12

27 Unregarded age in corners thrown.
As You Like It (1599) act 2, sc. 3, l. 42

28 Therefore my age is as a lusty winter,
Frosty, but kindly.
As You Like It (1599) act 2, sc. 3, l. 52

29 O good old man! how well in thee appears
The constant service of the antique world,
When service sweat for duty, not for meed!
Thou art not for the fashion of these times,

Where none will sweat but for promotion.
As You Like It (1599) act 2, sc. 3, l. 56

1 Ay, now am I in Arden; the more fool I. When I was at home I was in a better place; but travellers must be content.
As You Like It (1599) act 2, sc. 4, l. [16]

2 In thy youth thou wast as true a lover
As ever sighed upon a midnight pillow.
As You Like It (1599) act 2, sc. 4, l. [26]

3 Under the greenwood tree
Who loves to lie with me,
And turn his merry note
Unto the sweet bird's throat,
Come hither, come hither, come hither:
Here shall he see
No enemy
But winter and rough weather.
As You Like It (1599) act 2, sc. 5, l. 1

4 I can suck melancholy out of a song as a weasel sucks eggs.
As You Like It (1599) act 2, sc. 5, l. [12]

5 Who doth ambition shun
And loves to live i' the sun,
Seeking the food he eats,
And pleased with what he gets.
As You Like It (1599) act 2, sc. 5, l. [38]

6 I met a fool i' the forest.
As You Like It (1599) act 2, sc. 7, l. 12

7 And so, from hour to hour, we ripe and ripe,
And then from hour to hour, we rot and rot:
And thereby hangs a tale.
As You Like It (1599) act 2, sc. 7, l. 26

8 A worthy fool! Motley's the only wear.
As You Like It (1599) act 2, sc. 7, l. 34

9 All the world's a stage,
And all the men and women merely players:
They have their exits and their entrances;
And one man in his time plays many parts,
His acts being seven ages.
As You Like It (1599) act 2, sc. 7, l. 139

10 At first the infant,
Mewling and puking in the nurse's arms.
And then the whining schoolboy, with his satchel,
And shining morning face, creeping like snail
Unwillingly to school.
As You Like It (1599) act 2, sc. 7, l. 143

11 Then a soldier,
Full of strange oaths, and bearded like the pard,
Jealous in honour, sudden and quick in quarrel,
Seeking the bubble reputation
Even in the cannon's mouth. And then the justice,
In fair round belly with good capon lined.
As You Like It (1599) act 2, sc. 7, l. 149

12 The sixth age shifts
Into the lean and slippered pantaloon,
With spectacles on nose and pouch on side,
His youthful hose well saved a world too wide
For his shrunk shank.
As You Like It (1599) act 2, sc. 7, l. 157

13 Last scene of all,
That ends this strange eventful history,
Is second childishness, and mere oblivion,
Sans teeth, sans eyes, sans taste, sans everything.
As You Like It (1599) act 2, sc. 7, l. 163

14 Blow, blow, thou winter wind,
Thou art not so unkind
As man's ingratitude.
As You Like It (1599) act 2, sc. 7, l. 174

15 Heigh-ho! sing, heigh-ho! unto the green holly:
Most friendship is feigning, most loving mere folly.
Then heigh-ho! the holly!
This life is most jolly.
As You Like It (1599) act 2, sc. 7, l. 180

16 Run, run, Orlando: carve on every tree
The fair, the chaste, and unexpressive she.
As You Like It (1599) act 3, sc. 2, l. 9

17 From the east to western Ind,
No jewel is like Rosalind.
As You Like It (1599) act 3, sc. 2, l. [94]

18 Let us make an honourable retreat; though not with bag and baggage, yet with scrip and scrippage.
As You Like It (1599) act 3, sc. 2, l. [170]

19 O wonderful, wonderful, and most wonderful wonderful! and yet again wonderful, and after that, out of all whooping!
As You Like It (1599) act 3, sc. 2, l. [202]

20 Do you not know I am a woman? when I think, I must speak.
As You Like It (1599) act 3, sc. 2, l. [265]

21 I do desire we may be better strangers.
As You Like It (1599) act 3, sc. 2, l. [276]

22 JAQUES: I do not like her name.
ORLANDO: There was no thought of pleasing you when she was christened.
As You Like It (1599) act 3, sc. 2, l. [283]

23 Time travels in divers paces with divers persons. I'll tell you who Time ambles withal, who Time trots withal, who Time gallops withal, and who Time stands still withal.
As You Like It (1599) act 3, sc. 2, l. [328]

24 I am not a slut, though I thank the gods I am foul.
As You Like It (1599) act 3, sc. 3, l. [40]

25 Down on your knees,
And thank heaven, fasting, for a good man's love.
As You Like It (1599) act 3, sc. 5, l. 57

26 I pray you, do not fall in love with me,
For I am falser than vows made in wine.
As You Like It (1599) act 3, sc. 5, l. [72]

27 Dead shepherd, now I find thy saw of might:
'Who ever loved that loved not at first sight?'
As You Like It (1599) act 3, sc. 5, l. [81]; see **Marlowe** 513:11

28 Come, woo me, woo me; for now I am in a holiday humour, and like enough to consent.
As You Like It (1599) act 4, sc. 1, l. [70]

1 You were better speak first, and when you were gravelled for lack of matter, you might take occasion to kiss.
As You Like It (1599) act 4, sc. 1, l. [75]

2 Men are April when they woo, December when they wed: maids are May when they are maids, but the sky changes when they are wives.
As You Like It (1599) act 4, sc. 1, l. [153]

3 The horn, the horn, the lusty horn
Is not a thing to laugh to scorn.
As You Like It (1599) act 4, sc. 2, l. [17]

4 Oh! how bitter a thing it is to look into happiness through another man's eyes.
As You Like It (1599) act 5, sc. 2, l. [48]

5 'Tis like the howling of Irish wolves against the moon.
As You Like It (1599) act 5, sc. 2, l. [120]

6 It was a lover and his lass,
With a hey, and a ho, and a hey nonino,
That o'er the green cornfield did pass,
In the spring time, the only pretty ring time,
When birds do sing, hey ding a ding, ding;
Sweet lovers love the spring.
As You Like It (1599) act 5, sc. 3, l. [18]

7 A poor virgin, sir, an ill-favoured thing, sir, but mine own.
As You Like It (1599) act 5, sc. 4, l. [60]

8 The retort courteous . . . the quip modest . . . the reply churlish . . . the reproof valiant . . . the countercheck quarrelsome . . . the lie circumstantial . . . the lie direct.
of the degrees of a lie
As You Like It (1599) act 5, sc. 4, l. [96]

9 Your 'if' is the only peace-maker; much virtue in 'if'.
As You Like It (1599) act 5, sc. 4, l. [108]

10 He uses his folly like a stalking-horse, and under the presentation of that he shoots his wit.
As You Like It (1599) act 5, sc. 4, l. [112]

11 If it be true that 'good wine needs no bush', 'tis true that a good play needs no epilogue.
As You Like It (1599) act 5, sc. 4, epilogue l. [3]; see
Proverbs 621:13

CORIOLANUS

12 He's a very dog to the commonalty.
Coriolanus (1608) act 1, sc. 1, l. [29]

13 What's the matter, you dissentious rogues,
That, rubbing the poor itch of your opinion,
Make yourselves scabs?
Coriolanus (1608) act 1, sc. 1, l. [170]

14 He that depends
Upon your favours swims with fins of lead,
And hews down oaks with rushes.
Coriolanus (1608) act 1, sc. 1, l. 179

15 My gracious silence, hail!
Coriolanus (1608) act 2, sc. 1, l. [194]

16 Hear you this Triton of the minnows? mark you His absolute 'shall'?
Coriolanus (1608) act 3, sc. 1, l. 88

17 What is the city but the people?
Coriolanus (1608) act 3, sc. 1, l. 198

18 You common cry of curs! whose breath I hate
As reek o' the rotten fens, whose loves I prize
As the dead carcases of unburied men
That do corrupt my air,—I banish you.
Coriolanus (1608) act 3, sc. 3, l. 118

19 Despising,
For you, the city, thus I turn my back:
There is a world elsewhere.
Coriolanus (1608) act 3, sc. 3, l. 131

20 The beast
With many heads butts me away.
Coriolanus (1608) act 4, sc. 1, l. 1

21 Let me have war, say I; it exceeds peace as far as day does night; it's spritely, waking, audible, and full of vent. Peace is a very apoplexy, lethargy: mulled, deaf, sleepy, insensible; a getter of more bastard children than war's a destroyer of men.
Coriolanus (1608) act 4, sc. 5, l. [237]

22 I think he'll be to Rome
As is the osprey to the fish, who takes it
By sovereignty of nature.
Coriolanus (1608) act 4, sc. 7, l. 33

23 Like a dull actor now,
I have forgot my part, and I am out,
Even to a full disgrace.
Coriolanus (1608) act 5, sc. 3, l. 40

24 O! a kiss
Long as my exile, sweet as my revenge!
Now, by the jealous queen of heaven, that kiss
I carried from thee, dear, and my true lip
Hath virgined it e'er since.
Coriolanus (1608) act 5, sc. 3, l. 44

25 Chaste as the icicle
That's curdied by the frost from purest snow,
And hangs on Dian's temple.
Coriolanus (1608) act 5, sc. 3, l. 65

26 O mother, mother!
What have you done? Behold, the heavens do ope,
The gods look down, and this unnatural scene
They laugh at.
Coriolanus (1608) act 5, sc. 3, l. 182

27 If you have writ your annals true, 'tis there,
That, like an eagle in a dove-cote, I
Fluttered your Volscians in Corioli:
Alone I did it.
Coriolanus (1608) act 5, sc. 5, l. 114

CYMBELINE

28 If she be furnished with a mind so rare,
She is alone the Arabian bird, and I
Have lost the wager. Boldness be my friend!
Arm me, audacity.
Cymbeline (1609–10) act 1, sc. 6, l. 16

29 On her left breast
A mole cinque-spotted, like the crimson drops
I' the bottom of a cowslip.
Cymbeline (1609–10) act 2, sc. 2, l. 37

30 Hark! hark! the lark at heaven's gate sings,
And Phoebus 'gins arise,

His steeds to water at those springs
On chaliced flowers that lies;
And winking Mary-buds begin
To ope their golden eyes:
With everything that pretty is,
My lady sweet, arise!
Cymbeline (1609-10) act 2, sc. 3, l. [22]

1   I thought her
As chaste as unsunned snow.
Cymbeline (1609-10) act 2, sc. 5, l. 12

2 The natural bravery of your isle, which stands
As Neptune's park, ribbed and paled in
With rocks unscalable, and roaring waters.
Cymbeline (1609-10) act 3, sc. 1, l. 18

3 O, for a horse with wings!
Cymbeline (1609-10) act 3, sc. 2, l. [49]

4 How hard it is to hide the sparks of nature!
Cymbeline (1609-10) act 3, sc. 3, l. 79

5 Hath Britain all the sun that shines?
Cymbeline (1609-10) act 3, sc. 4, l. [139]

6 Great griefs, I see, medicine the less.
Cymbeline (1609-10) act 4, sc. 2, l. 243

7 Thersites' body is as good as Ajax'
When neither are alive.
Cymbeline (1609-10) act 4, sc. 2, l. 252

8 Fear no more the heat o' the sun,
Nor the furious winter's rages;
Thou thy worldly task hast done,
Home art gone and ta'en thy wages:
Golden lads and girls all must,
As chimney-sweepers, come to dust.
Cymbeline (1609-10) act 4, sc. 2, l. 258

9 No exorciser harm thee!
Nor no witchcraft charm thee!
Ghost unlaid forbear thee!
Nothing ill come near thee!
Quiet consummation have:
And renowned be thy grave!
Cymbeline (1609-10) act 4, sc. 2, l. 276

10   Hang there like fruit, my soul,
Till the tree die.
Cymbeline (1609-10) act 5, sc. 5, l. 263

HAMLET

11 You come most carefully upon your hour.
Hamlet (1601) act 1, sc. 1, l. 6

12 For this relief much thanks; 'tis bitter cold
And I am sick at heart.
Hamlet (1601) act 1, sc. 1, l. 8

13 Not a mouse stirring.
Hamlet (1601) act 1, sc. 1, l. 10

14 Look, where it comes again!
Hamlet (1601) act 1, sc. 1, l. 40

15 This bodes some strange eruption to our state.
Hamlet (1601) act 1, sc. 1, l. 69

16 In the most high and palmy state of Rome,
A little ere the mightiest Julius fell,
The graves stood tenantless and the sheeted dead
Did squeak and gibber in the Roman streets.
Hamlet (1601) act 1, sc. 1, l. 113

17 And then it started like a guilty thing
Upon a fearful summons.
Hamlet (1601) act 1, sc. 1, l. 148

18 It faded on the crowing of the cock.
Some say that ever 'gainst that season comes
Wherein our Saviour's birth is celebrated,
The bird of dawning singeth all night long;
And then, they say, no spirit can walk abroad.
The nights are wholesome; then no planets strike,
No fairy takes, nor witch hath power to charm,
So hallowed and so gracious is the time.
Hamlet (1601) act 1, sc. 1, l. 157

19 But, look, the morn, in russet mantle clad,
Walks o'er the dew of yon high eastern hill.
Hamlet (1601) act 1, sc. 1, l. 166

20 Though yet of Hamlet our dear brother's death
The memory be green.
Hamlet (1601) act 1, sc. 2, l. 1

21 Therefore our sometime sister, now our queen . . .
Have we, as 'twere with a defeated joy,
With one auspicious and one dropping eye,
With mirth in funeral and with dirge in marriage,
In equal scale weighing delight and dole,
Taken to wife.
Hamlet (1601) act 1, sc. 2, l. 8

22 The head is not more native to the heart,
The hand more instrumental to the brain,
Than is the throne of Denmark to thy father.
Hamlet (1601) act 1, sc. 2, l. 47

23 A little more than kin, and less than kind.
Hamlet (1601) act 1, sc. 2, l. 65

24 Not so, my lord; I am too much i' the sun.
Hamlet (1601) act 1, sc. 2, l. 67

25 Good Hamlet, cast thy nighted colour off,
And let thine eye look like a friend on Denmark.
Hamlet (1601) act 1, sc. 2, l. 68

26 QUEEN: Thou know'st 'tis common; all that live
     must die,
Passing through nature to eternity.
HAMLET: Ay, madam, it is common.
Hamlet (1601) act 1, sc. 2, l. 72

27 Seems, madam! Nay, it is; I know not 'seems'.
'Tis not alone my inky cloak, good mother,
Nor customary suits of solemn black,
Nor windy suspiration of forced breath,
No, nor the fruitful river in the eye,
Nor the dejected 'haviour of the visage,
Together with all forms, modes, shows of grief,
That can denote me truly.
Hamlet (1601) act 1, sc. 2, l. 76

28 But I have that within which passeth show;
These but the trappings and the suits of woe.
Hamlet (1601) act 1, sc. 2, l. 85

29 O! that this too too solid flesh would melt,
Thaw, and resolve itself into a dew;
Or that the Everlasting had not fixed
His canon 'gainst self-slaughter!
Hamlet (1601) act 1, sc. 2, l. 129

1 How weary, stale, flat, and unprofitable
Seem to me all the uses of this world.
Hamlet (1601) act 1, sc. 2, l. 133

2   Things rank and gross in nature
Possess it merely. That it should come to this!
Hamlet (1601) act 1, sc. 2, l. 136

3 So excellent a king; that was, to this,
Hyperion to a satyr: so loving to my mother,
That he might not beteem the winds of heaven
Visit her face too roughly.
Hamlet (1601) act 1, sc. 2, l. 139

4   Frailty, thy name is woman!
A little month; or ere those shoes were old
With which she followed my poor father's body,
Like Niobe, all tears; why she, even she,—
O God! a beast, that wants discourse of reason,
Would have mourned longer.
Hamlet (1601) act 1, sc. 2, l. 146

5 My father's brother, but no more like my father
Than I to Hercules.
Hamlet (1601) act 1, sc. 2, l. 152

6 It is not, nor it cannot come to good;
But break, my heart, for I must hold my tongue!
Hamlet (1601) act 1, sc. 2, l. 158

7 A truant disposition, good my lord.
Hamlet (1601) act 1, sc. 2, l. 169

8 Thrift, thrift, Horatio! the funeral baked meats
Did coldly furnish forth the marriage tables.
Hamlet (1601) act 1, sc. 2, l. 180

9 In my mind's eye, Horatio.
Hamlet (1601) act 1, sc. 2, l. 185

10 He was a man, take him for all in all,
I shall not look upon his like again.
Hamlet (1601) act 1, sc. 2, l. 187

11 But answer made it none.
Hamlet (1601) act 1, sc. 2, l. 215

12 A countenance more in sorrow than in anger.
Hamlet (1601) act 1, sc. 2, l. 231

13   All is not well;
I doubt some foul play.
Hamlet (1601) act 1, sc. 2, l. 254

14   Foul deeds will rise,
Though all the earth o'erwhelm them, to men's
    eyes.
Hamlet (1601) act 1, sc. 2, l. 256

15 And keep you in the rear of your affection,
Out of the shot and danger of desire.
The chariest maid is prodigal enough
If she unmask her beauty to the moon.
Hamlet (1601) act 1, sc. 3, l. 34

16 Do not, as some ungracious pastors do,
Show me the steep and thorny way to heaven,
Whiles, like a puffed and reckless libertine,
Himself the primrose path of dalliance treads,
And recks not his own rede.
Hamlet (1601) act 1, sc. 3, l. 47

17 The friends thou hast, and their adoption tried,
Grapple them to thy soul with hoops of steel.
Hamlet (1601) act 1, sc. 3, l. 62

18 Costly thy habit as thy purse can buy,
But not expressed in fancy; rich, not gaudy;
For the apparel oft proclaims the man.
Hamlet (1601) act 1, sc. 3, l. 70

19 Neither a borrower, nor a lender be;
For loan oft loses both itself and friend.
Hamlet (1601) act 1, sc. 3, l. 75

20 This above all: to thine own self be true,
And it must follow, as the night the day,
Thou canst not then be false to any man.
Hamlet (1601) act 1, sc. 3, l. 78; see **Bacon** 46:1

21   You speak like a green girl,
Unsifted in such perilous circumstance.
Hamlet (1601) act 1, sc. 3, l. 101

22 Ay, springes to catch woodcocks.
Hamlet (1601) act 1, sc. 3, l. 115

23 It is a nipping and an eager air.
Hamlet (1601) act 1, sc. 4, l. 2

24 But to my mind,—though I am native here,
And to the manner born,—it is a custom
More honoured in the breach than the
    observance.
Hamlet (1601) act 1, sc. 4, l. 14

25 Angels and ministers of grace defend us!
Be thou a spirit of health or goblin damned,
Bring with thee airs from heaven or blasts from
    hell,
Be thy intents wicked or charitable,
Thou com'st in such a questionable shape
That I will speak to thee: I'll call thee Hamlet,
King, father; royal Dane, O! answer me.
Hamlet (1601) act 1, sc. 4, l. 39

26   What may this mean,
That thou, dead corse again in complete steel
Revisit'st thus the glimpses of the moon,
Making night hideous,
Hamlet (1601) act 1, sc. 4, l. 51

27 I do not set my life at a pin's fee;
And for my soul, what can it do to that,
Being a thing immortal as itself?
Hamlet (1601) act 1, sc. 4, l. 65

28   Unhand me, gentlemen,
By heaven! I'll make a ghost of him that lets me.
Hamlet (1601) act 1, sc. 4, l. 84

29 Something is rotten in the state of Denmark.
Hamlet (1601) act 1, sc. 4, l. 90

30 I am thy father's spirit;
Doomed for a certain term to walk the night.
Hamlet (1601) act 1, sc. 5, l. 9

31 List, list, O, list!
Hamlet (1601) act 1, sc. 5, l. 13

32 I could a tale unfold whose lightest word
Would harrow up thy soul, freeze thy young
    blood,
Make thy two eyes, like stars, start from their
    spheres,
Thy knotted and combinèd locks to part,
And each particular hair to stand on end,
Like quills upon the fretful porpentine.
Hamlet (1601) act 1, sc. 5, l. 15

1 Revenge his foul and most unnatural murder.
Hamlet (1601) act 1, sc. 5, l. 25

2 Murder most foul, as in the best it is;
But this most foul, strange, and unnatural.
Hamlet (1601) act 1, sc. 5, l. 27

3   O my prophetic soul!
My uncle!
Hamlet (1601) act 1, sc. 5, l. 40

4 But, soft! methinks I scent the morning air.
Hamlet (1601) act 1, sc. 5, l. 58

5 Thus was I, sleeping, by a brother's hand,
Of life, of crown, of queen, at once dispatched;
Cut off even in the blossoms of my sin,
Unhouseled, disappointed, unaneled,
No reckoning made, but sent to my account
With all my imperfections on my head:
O, horrible! O, horrible! most horrible!
Hamlet (1601) act 1, sc. 5, l. 74

6   Remember thee!
Ay, thou poor ghost, while memory holds a seat
In this distracted globe.
Hamlet (1601) act 1, sc. 5, l. 95

7 O most pernicious woman!
O villain, villain, smiling, damnèd villain!
My tables,—meet it is I set it down,
That one may smile, and smile, and be a villain;
At least I'm sure it may be so in Denmark.
Hamlet (1601) act 1, sc. 5, l. 105

8 These are but wild and whirling words, my lord.
Hamlet (1601) act 1, sc. 5, l. 133

9 Well said, old mole! canst work i' the earth so
fast?
Hamlet (1601) act 1, sc. 5, l. 162

10 There are more things in heaven and earth,
Horatio,
Than are dreamt of in your philosophy.
Hamlet (1601) act 1, sc. 5, l. 166; see **Haldane** 367:17

11 To put an antic disposition on.
Hamlet (1601) act 1, sc. 5, l. 172

12 Rest, rest, perturbèd spirit.
Hamlet (1601) act 1, sc. 5, l. 182

13 The time is out of joint; O cursèd spite,
That ever I was born to set it right!
Hamlet (1601) act 1, sc. 5, l. 188

14 By indirections find directions out.
Hamlet (1601) act 2, sc. 1, l. 66

15 Brevity is the soul of wit.
Hamlet (1601) act 2, sc. 2, l. 90; see **Proverbs** 616:14

16   To define true madness,
What is't but to be nothing else but mad?
Hamlet (1601) act 2, sc. 2, l. 93

17 More matter with less art.
Hamlet (1601) act 2, sc. 2, l. 95

18 POLONIUS: What do you read, my lord?
HAMLET: Words, words, words.
Hamlet (1601) act 2, sc. 2, l. [195]

19 Though this be madness, yet there is method in't.
Hamlet (1601) act 2, sc. 2, l. [211]

20 POLONIUS: My honourable lord, I will most humbly
take my leave of you.
HAMLET: You cannot, sir, take from me any thing
that I will more willingly part withal; except my
life, except my life, except my life.
Hamlet (1601) act 2, sc. 2, l. [221]

21 HAMLET: Then you live about her waist, or in the
middle of her favours?
GUILDENSTERN: Faith, her privates, we.
HAMLET: In the secret parts of Fortune? O! most
true; she is a strumpet.
Hamlet (1601) act 2, sc. 2, l. [240]

22 There is nothing either good or bad, but thinking
makes it so.
Hamlet (1601) act 2, sc. 2, l. [259]

23 O God! I could be bounded in a nut-shell, and
count myself a king of infinite space, were it not
that I have bad dreams.
Hamlet (1601) act 2, sc. 2, l. [263]

24 It goes so heavily with my disposition that this
goodly frame, the earth, seems to me a sterile
promontory; this most excellent canopy, the air,
look you, this brave o'erhanging firmament, this
majestical roof fretted with golden fire, why, it
appears no other thing to me but a foul and
pestilent congregation of vapours. What a piece of
work is a man! How noble in reason! how infinite
in faculty! in form, in moving, how express and
admirable! in action how like an angel! in
apprehension how like a god! the beauty of the
world! the paragon of animals! And yet, to me,
what is this quintessence of dust? man delights
not me; no, nor woman neither, though, by your
smiling, you seem to say so.
Hamlet (1601) act 2, sc. 2, l. [316]

25 He that plays the king shall be welcome; his
majesty shall have tribute of me.
Hamlet (1601) act 2, sc. 2, l. [341]

26 There is something in this more than natural, if
philosophy could find it out.
Hamlet (1601) act 2, sc. 2, l. [392]

27 I am but mad north-north-west; when the wind is
southerly, I know a hawk from a handsaw.
Hamlet (1601) act 2, sc. 2, l. [405]

28 The best actors in the world, either for tragedy,
comedy, history, pastoral, pastoral-comical,
historical-pastoral, tragical-historical, tragical-
comical-historical-pastoral, scene individable, or
poem unlimited.
Hamlet (1601) act 2, sc. 2, l. [424]

29 The play, I remember, pleased not the million;
'twas caviare to the general.
Hamlet (1601) act 2, sc. 2, l. [465]

30 Good my lord, will you see the players well
bestowed? Do you hear, let them be well used; for
they are the abstracts and brief chronicles of the
time: after your death you were better have a bad
epitaph than their ill report while you live.
Hamlet (1601) act 2, sc. 2, l. [553]

1 Use every man after his desert, and who should
  'scape whipping?
  Hamlet (1601) act 2, sc. 2, l. [561]

2 O, what a rogue and peasant slave am I.
  Hamlet (1601) act 2, sc. 2, l. [584]

3 For Hecuba!
  What's Hecuba to him or he to Hecuba
  That he should weep for her?
  Hamlet (1601) act 2, sc. 2, l. [592]

4   He would drown the stage with tears,
  And cleave the general ear with horrid speech,
  Make mad the guilty, and appal the free,
  Confound the ignorant, and amaze, indeed,
  The very faculties of eyes and ears.
  Hamlet (1601) act 2, sc. 2, l. [596]

5 But I am pigeon-livered, and lack gall
  To make oppression bitter.
  Hamlet (1601) act 2, sc. 2, l. [613]

6   Bloody, bawdy villain!
  Remorseless, treacherous, lecherous, kindless
    villain!
  Hamlet (1601) act 2, sc. 2, l. [616]

7   I have heard,
  That guilty creatures sitting at a play
  Have by the very cunning of the scene
  Been struck so to the soul that presently
  They have proclaimed their malefactions;
  For murder, though it have no tongue, will speak
  With most miraculous organ.
  Hamlet (1601) act 2, sc. 2, l. [625]

8   The play's the thing
  Wherein I'll catch the conscience of the king.
  Hamlet (1601) act 2, sc. 2, l. [641]

9 To be, or not to be: that is the question:
  Whether 'tis nobler in the mind to suffer
  The slings and arrows of outrageous fortune,
  Or to take arms against a sea of troubles,
  And by opposing end them? To die: to sleep;
  No more; and, by a sleep to say we end
  The heart-ache and the thousand natural shocks
  That flesh is heir to, 'tis a consummation
  Devoutly to be wished. To die, to sleep;
  To sleep: perchance to dream: ay, there's the rub;
  For in that sleep of death what dreams may come
  When we have shuffled off this mortal coil,
  Must give us pause.
  Hamlet (1601) act 3, sc. 1, l. 56

10 For who would bear the whips and scorns of time,
  The oppressor's wrong, the proud man's
    contumely,
  The pangs of disprized love, the law's delay,
  The insolence of office, and the spurns
  That patient merit of the unworthy takes,
  When he himself might his quietus make
  With a bare bodkin?
  And makes us rather bear those ills we have,
  Than fly to others that we know not of?
  Hamlet (1601) act 3, sc. 1, l. 70

11 The undiscovered country from whose bourn
  No traveller returns.
  Hamlet (1601) act 3, sc. 1, l. 79

12 Thus conscience doth make cowards of us all;
  And thus the native hue of resolution
  Is sicklied o'er with the pale cast of thought,
  And enterprises of great pith and moment
  With this regard their currents turn awry,
  And lose the name of action.
  Hamlet (1601) act 3, sc. 1, l. 83; see **Proverbs** 617:9

13   Nymph, in thy orisons
  Be all my sins remembered.
  Hamlet (1601) act 3, sc. 1, l. 89

14 Get thee to a nunnery: why wouldst thou be a
  breeder of sinners?
  Hamlet (1601) act 3, sc. 1, l. [124]

15 Be thou as chaste as ice, as pure as snow, thou
  shalt not escape calumny. Get thee to a nunnery,
  go; farewell.
  Hamlet (1601) act 3, sc. 1, l. [142]

16 I have heard of your paintings too, well enough.
  God hath given you one face and you make
  yourselves another.
  Hamlet (1601) act 3, sc. 1, l. [150]

17 I say, we will have no more marriages.
  Hamlet (1601) act 3, sc. 1, l. [156]

18 O! what a noble mind is here o'erthrown:
  The courtier's, soldier's, scholar's, eye, tongue,
    sword;
  The expectancy and rose of the fair state,
  The glass of fashion, and the mould of form,
  The observèd of all observers, quite, quite, down!
  Hamlet (1601) act 3, sc. 1, l. [159]

19 Now see that noble and most sovereign reason,
  Like sweet bells jangled, out of tune and harsh.
  Hamlet (1601) act 3, sc. 1, l. [166]

20   O! woe is me,
  To have seen what I have seen, see what I see!
  Hamlet (1601) act 3, sc. 1, l. [169]

21 Speak the speech, I pray you, as I pronounced it to
  you, trippingly on the tongue; but if you mouth it,
  as many of your players do, I had as lief the town-
  crier spoke my lines. Nor do not saw the air too
  much with your hand, thus; but use all gently.
  Hamlet (1601) act 3, sc. 2, l. 1

22 I would have such a fellow whipped for o'erdoing
  Termagant; it out-herods Herod.
  Hamlet (1601) act 3, sc. 2, l. 14

23 Suit the action to the word, the word to the
  action.
  Hamlet (1601) act 3, sc. 2, l. [20]

24 To hold, as 'twere, the mirror up to nature.
  Hamlet (1601) act 3, sc. 2, l. [25]

25 I have thought some of nature's journeymen had
  made men and not made them well, they imitated
  humanity so abominably.
  Hamlet (1601) act 3, sc. 2, l. [38]

26   Give me that man
  That is not passion's slave, and I will wear him
  In my heart's core, ay, in my heart of heart,
  As I do thee.
  Hamlet (1601) act 3, sc. 2, l. [76]

1 The chameleon's dish: I eat the air, promise-
crammed; you cannot feed capons so.
   Hamlet (1601) act 3, sc. 2, l. [98]

2 Here's metal more attractive.
   Hamlet (1601) act 3, sc. 2, l. [117]

3 For, O! for, O! the hobby-horse is forgot.
   Hamlet (1601) act 3, sc. 2, l. [145]

4 Marry, this is miching mallecho; it means
mischief.
   Hamlet (1601) act 3, sc. 2, l. [148]

5 The lady doth protest too much, methinks.
   Hamlet (1601) act 3, sc. 2, l. [242]

6 HAMLET: No, no, they do but jest, poison in jest;
   no offence i' the world.
   KING: What do you call the play?
   HAMLET: The Mouse-trap.
   Hamlet (1601) act 3, sc. 2, l. [247]

7 Let the galled jade wince, our withers are
unwrung.
   Hamlet (1601) act 3, sc. 2, l. [256]

8 What! frighted with false fire?
   Hamlet (1601) act 3, sc. 2, l. [282]

9 Why, let the stricken deer go weep,
   The hart ungallèd play;
   For some must watch, while some must sleep:
   So runs the world away.
   Hamlet (1601) act 3, sc. 2, l. [287]; see **Cowper** 247:31

10 You would play upon me; you would seem to
know my stops; you would pluck out the heart of
my mystery; you would sound me from my lowest
note to the top of my compass.
   Hamlet (1601) act 3, sc. 2, l. [387]

11 Very like a whale.
   Hamlet (1601) act 3, sc. 2, l. [406]

12 They fool me to the top of my bent.
   Hamlet (1601) act 3, sc. 2, l. [408]

13 'Tis now the very witching time of night,
   When churchyards yawn and hell itself breathes
   out
   Contagion to this world: now could I drink hot
   blood,
   And do such bitter business as the day
   Would quake to look on.
   Hamlet (1601) act 3, sc. 2, l. [413]

14 Let me be cruel, not unnatural;
   I will speak daggers to her, but use none.
   Hamlet (1601) act 3, sc. 2, l. [420]

15 O! my offence is rank, it smells to heaven.
   Hamlet (1601) act 3, sc. 3, l. 36

16 Now might I do it pat, now he is praying.
   Hamlet (1601) act 3, sc. 3, l. 73

17 He took my father grossly, full of bread,
   With all his crimes broad blown, as flush as May;
   And how his audit stands who knows save
   heaven?
   Hamlet (1601) act 3, sc. 3, l. 80

18 My words fly up, my thoughts remain below:
   Words without thoughts never to heaven go.
   Hamlet (1601) act 3, sc. 3, l. 97

19 You go not, till I set you up a glass
   Where you may see the inmost part of you.
   Hamlet (1601) act 3, sc. 4, l. 19

20 How now! a rat? Dead, for a ducat, dead!
   Hamlet (1601) act 3, sc. 4, l. 23

21 A bloody deed! almost as bad, good mother,
   As kill a king, and marry with his brother.
   Hamlet (1601) act 3, sc. 4, l. 28

22 Thou wretched, rash, intruding fool, farewell!
   I took thee for thy better.
   Hamlet (1601) act 3, sc. 4, l. 31

23 You cannot call it love, for at your age
   The hey-day in the blood is tame, it's humble,
   And waits upon the judgment.
   Hamlet (1601) act 3, sc. 4, l. 68

24   Speak no more;
   Thou turn'st mine eyes into my very soul.
   Hamlet (1601) act 3, sc. 4, l. 88

25   Nay, but to live
   In the rank sweat of an enseamèd bed,
   Stewed in corruption, honeying and making love
   Over the nasty sty.
   Hamlet (1601) act 3, sc. 4, l. 91

26 A cut-purse of the empire and the rule,
   That from a shelf the precious diadem stole,
   And put it in his pocket!
   Hamlet (1601) act 3, sc. 4, l. 99

27 A king of shreds and patches.
   Hamlet (1601) act 3, sc. 4, l. 102; see **Gilbert** 347:19

28   Mother, for love of grace,
   Lay not that flattering unction to your soul.
   Hamlet (1601) act 3, sc. 4, l. 142

29 For in the fatness of these pursy times,
   Virtue itself of vice must pardon beg.
   Hamlet (1601) act 3, sc. 4, l. 153

30 Assume a virtue, if you have it not.
   That monster, custom, who all sense doth eat,
   Of habits devil, is angel yet in this.
   Hamlet (1601) act 3, sc. 4, l. 160

31 I must be cruel only to be kind.
   Hamlet (1601) act 3, sc. 4, l. 178

32 For 'tis the sport to have the enginer
   Hoist with his own petar.
   Hamlet (1601) act 3, sc. 4, l. 206

33 I'll lug the guts into the neighbour room.
   Hamlet (1601) act 3, sc. 4, l. 212

34   Diseases desperate grown,
   By desperate appliances are relieved,
   Or not at all.
   Hamlet (1601) act 4, sc. 2, l. 9; see **Fawkes** 316:8, **Proverbs**
   617:30

35 A certain convocation of politic worms are e'en at
   him. Your worm is your only emperor for diet.
   Hamlet (1601) act 4, sc. 2, l. [21]

36 A man may fish with the worm that hath eat of a
   king, and eat of the fish that hath fed of that
   worm.
   Hamlet (1601) act 4, sc. 2, l. [29]

1 We go to gain a little patch of ground,
That hath in it no profit but the name.
Hamlet (1601) act 4, sc. 4, l. 18

2 How all occasions do inform against me,
And spur my dull revenge!
Hamlet (1601) act 4, sc. 4, l. 32

3   Some craven scruple
Of thinking too precisely on the event.
Hamlet (1601) act 4, sc. 4, l. 40

4   Rightly to be great
Is not to stir without great argument,
But greatly to find quarrel in a straw
When honour's at the stake.
Hamlet (1601) act 4, sc. 4, l. 53

5 How should I your true love know
From another one?
By his cockle hat and staff,
And his sandal shoon.
Hamlet (1601) act 4, sc. 5, l. [23]

6 He is dead and gone, lady,
He is dead and gone,
At his head a grass-green turf;
At his heels a stone.
Hamlet (1601) act 4, sc. 5, l. [29]

7 Lord! we know what we are, but know not what
we may be.
Hamlet (1601) act 4, sc. 5, l. [43]

8 Come, my coach! Good-night, ladies; good-night,
sweet ladies; good-night, good-night.
Hamlet (1601) act 4, sc. 5, l. [72]

9 When sorrows come, they come not single spies,
But in battalions.
Hamlet (1601) act 4, sc. 5, l. [78]

10   We have done but greenly
In hugger-mugger to inter him.
Hamlet (1601) act 4, sc. 5, l. [83]

11 There's such divinity doth hedge a king,
That treason can but peep to what it would.
Hamlet (1601) act 4, sc. 5, l. [123]

12 There's rosemary, that's for remembrance; pray,
love, remember: and there is pansies, that's for
thoughts.
Hamlet (1601) act 4, sc. 5, l. [174]

13 There's fennel for you, and columbines; there's
rue for you; and here's some for me; we may call
it herb of grace o' Sundays. O! you must wear
your rue with a difference. There's a daisy; I
would give you some violets, but they withered all
when my father died. They say he made a good
end,— For bonny sweet Robin is all my joy.
Hamlet (1601) act 4, sc. 5, l. [179]

14 His means of death, his obscure burial,
No trophy, sword, nor hatchment o'er his bones,
No noble rite nor formal ostentation.
Hamlet (1601) act 4, sc. 5, l. [213]

15 And where the offence is let the great axe fall.
Hamlet (1601) act 4, sc. 5, l. [218]

16 A very riband in the cap of youth.
Hamlet (1601) act 4, sc. 7, l. 77

17 There is a willow grows aslant a brook,
That shows his hoar leaves in the glassy stream.
Hamlet (1601) act 4, sc. 7, l. 167

18 There with fantastic garlands did she come,
Of crow-flowers, nettles, daisies, and long purples,
That liberal shepherds give a grosser name,
But our cold maids do dead men's fingers call
them.
Hamlet (1601) act 4, sc. 7, l. 169

19 There, on the pendent boughs her coronet weeds
Clambering to hang, an envious sliver broke,
When down her weedy trophies and herself
Fell in the weeping brook. Her clothes spread
wide,
And, mermaid-like, awhile they bore her up;
Which time she chanted snatches of old tunes,
As one incapable of her own distress.
Hamlet (1601) act 4, sc. 7, l. 173

20 Too much of water hast thou, poor Ophelia,
And therefore I forbid my tears; but yet
It is our trick, nature her custom holds,
Let shame say what it will.
Hamlet (1601) act 4, sc. 7, l. 186

21 Is she to be buried in Christian burial that wilfully
seeks her own salvation?
Hamlet (1601) act 5, sc. 1, l. 1

22 There is no ancient gentlemen but gardeners,
ditchers and grave-makers; they hold up Adam's
profession.
Hamlet (1601) act 5, sc. 1, l. [32]

23 FIRST CLOWN: What is he that builds stronger than
either the mason, the shipwright, or the
carpenter?
SECOND CLOWN: The gallows-maker; for that frame
outlives a thousand tenants.
Hamlet (1601) act 5, sc. 1, l. [44]

24 Cudgel thy brains no more about it, for your dull
ass will not mend his pace with beating.
Hamlet (1601) act 5, sc. 1, l. [61]

25 But age, with his stealing steps
Hath clawed me in his clutch,
And hath shipped me intil the land,
As if I had never been such.
Hamlet (1601) act 5, sc. 1, l. [77]; see **Vaux** 808:5

26 This might be the pate of a politician . . . one that
would circumvent God, might it not?
Hamlet (1601) act 5, sc. 1, l. [84]

27 The age is grown so picked that the toe of the
peasant comes so near the heel of the courtier, he
galls his kibe.
Hamlet (1601) act 5, sc. 1, l. [150]

28 Alas, poor Yorick. I knew him, Horatio; a fellow of
infinite jest, of most excellent fancy.
Hamlet (1601) act 5, sc. 1, l. [201]

29 To what base uses we may return, Horatio!
Hamlet (1601) act 5, sc. 1, l. [222]

30 Imperious Caesar, dead, and turned to clay,
Might stop a hole to keep the wind away.
Hamlet (1601) act 5, sc. 1, l. [235]

1   Lay her i' the earth;
And from her fair and unpolluted flesh
May violets spring! I tell thee, churlish priest,
A ministering angel shall my sister be,
When thou liest howling.
Hamlet (1601) act 5, sc. 1, l. [260]; see **Scott** 673:24

2 Sweets to the sweet: farewell!
Hamlet (1601) act 5, sc. 1, l. [265]

3 I thought thy bride-bed to have decked, sweet
maid,
And not have strewed thy grave.
Hamlet (1601) act 5, sc. 1, l. [267]

4 I loved Ophelia: forty thousand brothers
Could not, with all their quantity of love,
Make up my sum.
Hamlet (1601) act 5, sc. 1, l. [291]

5 There's a divinity that shapes our ends,
Rough-hew them how we will.
Hamlet (1601) act 5, sc. 2, l. 10

6 I once did hold it, as our statists do,
A baseness to write fair, and laboured much
How to forget that learning; but, sir, now
It did me yeoman's service.
Hamlet (1601) act 5, sc. 2, l. 33

7 Not a whit, we defy augury; there's a special
providence in the fall of a sparrow. If it be now,
'tis not to come; if it be not to come, it will be
now; if it be not now, yet it will come: the
readiness is all.
Hamlet (1601) act 5, sc. 2, l. [232]

8 I have shot mine arrow o'er the house,
And hurt my brother.
Hamlet (1601) act 5, sc. 2, l. [257]

9 A hit, a very palpable hit.
Hamlet (1601) act 5, sc. 2, l. [295]

10 Why, as a woodcock to mine own springe, Osric;
I am justly killed with my own treachery.
Hamlet (1601) act 5, sc. 2, l. [320]

11   This fell sergeant, death,
Is swift in his arrest.
Hamlet (1601) act 5, sc. 2, l. [350]

12   Report me and my cause aright
To the unsatisfied.
Hamlet (1601) act 5, sc. 2, l. [353]

13 I am more an antique Roman than a Dane.
Hamlet (1601) act 5, sc. 2, l. [355]

14 If thou didst ever hold me in thy heart,
Absent thee from felicity awhile,
And in this harsh world draw thy breath in pain,
To tell my story.
Hamlet (1601) act 5, sc. 2, l. [360]

15 The rest is silence.
Hamlet (1601) act 5, sc. 2, l. [372]

16 Now cracks a noble heart. Good-night, sweet
prince,
And flights of angels sing thee to thy rest!
Hamlet (1601) act 5, sc. 2, l. [373]

17 That Rosencrantz and Guildenstern are dead.
Hamlet (1601) act 5, sc. 2, l. [385]

18   Let four captains
Bear Hamlet, like a soldier, to the stage;
For he was likely, had he been put on,
To have proved most royally.
Hamlet (1601) act 5, sc. 2, l. [409]

HENRY IV, PART 1

19 Let us be Diana's foresters, gentlemen of the
shade, minions of the moon.
Henry IV, Part 1 (1597) act 1, sc. 2, l. [28]

20 FALSTAFF: And is not my hostess of the tavern a
most sweet wench?
PRINCE: As the honey of Hybla, my old lad of the
castle.
Henry IV, Part 1 (1597) act 1, sc. 2, l. [44]

21 What, in thy quips and thy quiddities?
Henry IV, Part 1 (1597) act 1, sc. 2, l. [50]

22 Shall there be gallows standing in England when
thou art king, and resolution thus fobbed as it is
with the rusty curb of old father antick, the law.
Henry IV, Part 1 (1597) act 1, sc. 2, l. [66]

23 O! thou hast damnable iteration, and art, indeed,
able to corrupt a saint.
Henry IV, Part 1 (1597) act 1, sc. 2, l. [101]

24 Why, Hal, 'tis my vocation, Hal; 'tis no sin for a
man to labour in his vocation.
referring to stealing
Henry IV, Part 1 (1597) act 1, sc. 2, l. [116]

25 If all the year were playing holidays,
To sport would be as tedious as to work;
But when they seldom come, they wished for
come.
Henry IV, Part 1 (1597) act 1, sc. 2, l. [226]

26 So pestered with a popinjay.
Henry IV, Part 1 (1597) act 1, sc. 3, l. 50

27 To put down Richard, that sweet lovely rose,
And plant this thorn, this canker, Bolingbroke.
Henry IV, Part 1 (1597) act 1, sc. 3, l. 175

28   O! the blood more stirs
To rouse a lion than to start a hare.
Henry IV, Part 1 (1597) act 1, sc. 3, l. 197

29 By heaven methinks it were an easy leap
To pluck bright honour from the pale-faced moon,
Or dive into the bottom of the deep,
Where fathom-line could never touch the ground,
And pluck up drownèd honour by the locks.
Henry IV, Part 1 (1597) act 1, sc. 3, l. 201

30 Why, what a candy deal of courtesy
This fawning greyhound then did proffer me!
Henry IV, Part 1 (1597) act 1, sc. 3, l. 251

31 I know a trick worth two of that.
Henry IV, Part 1 (1597) act 2, sc. 1, l. [40]

32 We have the receipt of fern-seed, we walk
invisible.
Henry IV, Part 1 (1597) act 2, sc. 1, l. [95]

33 Go hang thyself in thine own heir-apparent
garters!
Henry IV, Part 1 (1597) act 2, sc. 2, l. [49]

34 On, bacons, on!
Henry IV, Part 1 (1597) act 2, sc. 2, l. [99]

1 It would be argument for a week, laughter for a month, and a good jest for ever.
   Henry IV, Part 1 (1597) act 2, sc. 2, l. [104]

2   Falstaff sweats to death
And lards the lean earth as he walks along.
   Henry IV, Part 1 (1597) act 2, sc. 2, l. [119]

3 Out of this nettle, danger, we pluck this flower, safety.
   Henry IV, Part 1 (1597) act 2, sc. 3, l. [11]

4 Away, you trifler! Love! I love thee not,
I care not for thee, Kate: this is no world
To play with mammets and to tilt with lips:
We must have bloody noses and cracked crowns.
   Henry IV, Part 1 (1597) act 2, sc. 3, l. [95]

5 I am not yet of Percy's mind, the Hotspur of the North; he that kills me some six or seven dozen of Scots at a breakfast, washes his hands, and says to his wife, 'Fie upon this quiet life! I want work.'
   Henry IV, Part 1 (1597) act 2, sc. 4, l. [116]

6 There live not three good men unhanged in England, and one of them is fat and grows old.
   Henry IV, Part 1 (1597) act 2, sc. 4, l. [146]

7 Call you that backing of your friends? A plague upon such backing! give me them that will face me.
   Henry IV, Part 1 (1597) act 2, sc. 4, l. [168]

8 Nay that's past praying for: I have peppered two of them: two I am sure I have paid, two rogues in buckram suits. I tell thee what, Hal, if I tell thee a lie, spit in my face, call me horse. Thou knowest my old ward; here I lay, and thus I bore my point. Four rogues in buckram let drive at me,—
   Henry IV, Part 1 (1597) act 2, sc. 4, l. [214]

9 O monstrous! eleven buckram men grown out of two.
   Henry IV, Part 1 (1597) act 2, sc. 4, l. [247]

10 These lies are like the father that begets them; gross as a mountain, open, palpable.
   Henry IV, Part 1 (1597) act 2, sc. 4, l. [253]

11 Give you a reason on compulsion! if reasons were as plentiful as blackberries I would give no man a reason upon compulsion, I.
   Henry IV, Part 1 (1597) act 2, sc. 4, l. [267]

12 Mark now, how a plain tale shall put you down.
   Henry IV, Part 1 (1597) act 2, sc. 4, l. [285]

13 Instinct is a great matter, I was a coward on instinct.
   Henry IV, Part 1 (1597) act 2, sc. 4, l. [304]

14 I will do it in King Cambyses' vein.
   Henry IV, Part 1 (1597) act 2, sc. 4, l. [430]

15 Shall the blessed sun of heaven prove a micher and eat blackberries? a question not to be asked.
   Henry IV, Part 1 (1597) act 2, sc. 4, l. [454]

16 There is a devil haunts thee in the likeness of a fat old man; a tun of man is thy companion.
   Henry IV, Part 1 (1597) act 2, sc. 4, l. [498]

17 That roasted Manningtree ox with the pudding in his belly, that reverend vice, that grey iniquity, that father ruffian, that vanity in years.
   Henry IV, Part 1 (1597) act 2, sc. 4, l. [504]

18 If sack and sugar be a fault, God help the wicked!
   Henry IV, Part 1 (1597) act 2, sc. 4, l. [524]

19 No, my good lord; banish Peto, banish Bardolph, banish Poins; but for sweet Jack Falstaff, kind Jack Falstaff, true Jack Falstaff, valiant Jack Falstaff, and therefore more valiant, being, as he is, old Jack Falstaff, banish not him thy Harry's company, banish not him thy Harry's company: banish plump Jack and banish all the world.
   Henry IV, Part 1 (1597) act 2, sc. 4, l. [528]

20 O monstrous! but one half-pennyworth of bread to this intolerable deal of sack!
   Henry IV, Part 1 (1597) act 2, sc. 4, l. [598]

21 GLENDOWER: At my nativity
The front of heaven was full of fiery shapes,
Of burning cressets; and at my birth
The frame and huge foundation of the earth
Shaked like a coward.
HOTSPUR: Why, so it would have done at the same
   season, if your mother's cat had but kittened.
   Henry IV, Part 1 (1597) act 3, sc. 1, l. 13

22 GLENDOWER: I can call spirits from the vasty deep.
HOTSPUR: Why, so can I, or so can any man;
But will they come when you do call for them?
   Henry IV, Part 1 (1597) act 3, sc. 1, l. [53]

23 I had rather be a kitten and cry mew
Than one of these same metre ballad-mongers.
   Henry IV, Part 1 (1597) act 3, sc. 1, l. [128]

24 That would set my teeth nothing on edge,
Nothing so much as mincing poetry:
'Tis like the forced gait of a shuffling nag.
   Henry IV, Part 1 (1597) act 3, sc. 1, l. [132]

25 Now I perceive the devil understands Welsh.
   Henry IV, Part 1 (1597) act 3, sc. 1, l. [233]

26 You swear like a comfit-maker's wife.
   Henry IV, Part 1 (1597) act 3, sc. 1, l. [252]

27 Swear me, Kate, like a lady as thou art,
A good mouth-filling oath.
   Henry IV, Part 1 (1597) act 3, sc. 1, l. [257]

28 He was but as the cuckoo is in June,
Heard, not regarded.
   Henry IV, Part 1 (1597) act 3, sc. 2, l. 75

29 My near'st and dearest enemy.
   Henry IV, Part 1 (1597) act 3, sc. 2, l. 123

30 Company, villanous company, hath been the spoil of me.
   Henry IV, Part 1 (1597) act 3, sc. 3, l. [10]

31 Thou knowest in the state of innocency Adam fell; and what should poor Jack Falstaff do in the days of villainy. Thou seest I have more flesh than another man, and therefore more frailty.
   Henry IV, Part 1 (1597) act 3, sc. 3, l. [184]

32 I saw young Harry, with his beaver on,
His cushes on his thighs, gallantly armed,

Rise from the ground like feathered Mercury,
And vaulted with such ease into his seat,
As if an angel dropped down from the clouds,
To turn and wind a fiery Pegasus,
And witch the world with noble horsemanship.
Henry IV, Part 1 (1597) act 4, sc. 1, l. 104

1 Doomsday is near; die all, die merrily.
Henry IV, Part 1 (1597) act 4, sc. 1, l. 134

2 Tut, tut; good enough to toss; food for powder,
food for powder; they'll fill a pit as well as better:
tush, man, mortal men, mortal men.
Henry IV, Part 1 (1597) act 4, sc. 2, l. [72]

3 Greatness knows itself.
Henry IV, Part 1 (1597) act 4, sc. 3, l. 74

4   I could be well content
To entertain the lag-end of my life
With quiet hours.
Henry IV, Part 1 (1597) act 5, sc. 1, l. 23

5 Rebellion lay in his way, and he found it.
Henry IV, Part 1 (1597) act 5, sc. 1, l. 28

6 I would it were bed-time, Hal, and all well.
Henry IV, Part 1 (1597) act 5, sc. 1, l. [125]

7 Thou owest God a death.
Henry IV, Part 1 (1597) act 5, sc. 1, l. [126]; see
Shakespeare 692:9

8 Honour pricks me on. Yea, but how if honour
prick me off when I come on? how then?
Henry IV, Part 1 (1597) act 5, sc. 1, l. [131]

9 What is honour? A word. What is that word,
honour? Air. A trim reckoning! Who hath it? He
that died o' Wednesday.
Henry IV, Part 1 (1597) act 5, sc. 1, l. [136]

10 Now, *Esperance!* Percy! and set on.
Henry IV, Part 1 (1597) act 5, sc. 2, l. 96

11 Two stars keep not their motion in one sphere.
Henry IV, Part 1 (1597) act 5, sc. 4, l. 65

12 But thought's the slave of life, and life time's fool;
And time, that takes survey of all the world,
Must have a stop.
Henry IV, Part 1 (1597) act 5, sc. 4, l. [81]

13 When that this body did contain a spirit,
A kingdom for it was too small a bound;
But now two paces of the vilest earth
Is room enough: this earth, that bears thee dead,
Bears not alive so stout a gentleman.
Henry IV, Part 1 (1597) act 5, sc. 4, l. [89]

14 Thy ignominy sleep with thee in the grave,
But not remembered in thy epitaph!
Henry IV, Part 1 (1597) act 5, sc. 4, l. [100]

15   Poor Jack, farewell!
I could have better spared a better man.
Henry IV, Part 1 (1597) act 5, sc. 4, l. [103]

16 The better part of valour is discretion; in the
which better part, I have saved my life.
Henry IV, Part 1 (1597) act 5, sc. 4, l. [121]; see **Proverbs**
617:43

17 Lord, Lord, how this world is given to lying! I
grant you I was down and out of breath; and so

was he; but we rose both at an instant, and
fought a long hour by Shrewsbury clock.
Henry IV, Part 1 (1597) act 5, sc. 4, l. [148]

18 For my part, if a lie may do thee grace,
I'll gild it with the happiest terms I have.
Henry IV, Part 1 (1597) act 5, sc. 4, l. [161]

19 I'll purge, and leave sack, and live cleanly, as a
nobleman should do.
Henry IV, Part 1 (1597) act 5, sc. 4, l. [168]

HENRY IV, PART 2

20 Enter Rumour, painted full of tongues.
Henry IV, Part 2 (1597) act 1, sc. 1, stage direction

21   Rumour is a pipe
Blown by surmises, jealousies, conjectures,
And of so easy and so plain a stop
That the blunt monster with uncounted heads,
The still-discordant wavering multitude,
Can play upon it.
Henry IV, Part 2 (1597) induction, l. 15

22 Yet the first bringer of unwelcome news
Hath but a losing office, and his tongue
Sounds ever after as a sullen bell,
Remembered knolling a departed friend.
Henry IV, Part 2 (1597) act 1, sc. 1, l. 100

23 I am not only witty in myself, but the cause that
wit is in other men.
Henry IV, Part 2 (1597) act 1, sc. 2, l. [10]; see **Foote**
328:5

24 It is the disease of not listening, the malady of not
marking, that I am troubled withal.
Henry IV, Part 2 (1597) act 1, sc. 2, l. [139]

25 I am as poor as Job, my lord, but not so patient.
Henry IV, Part 2 (1597) act 1, sc. 2, l. [145]

26 CHIEF JUSTICE: God send the prince a better
          companion!
FALSTAFF: God send the companion a better
          prince! I cannot rid my hands of him.
Henry IV, Part 2 (1597) act 1, sc. 2, l. [227]

27 It was always yet the trick of our English nation, if
they have a good thing, to make it too common.
Henry IV, Part 2 (1597) act 1, sc. 2, l. [244]

28 I would to God my name were not so terrible to
the enemy as it is: I were better to be eaten to
death with rust than to be scoured to nothing
with perpetual motion.
Henry IV, Part 2 (1597) act 1, sc. 2, l. [247]; see **Proverbs**
615:32

29 I can get no remedy against this consumption of
the purse: borrowing only lingers and lingers it
out, but the disease is incurable.
Henry IV, Part 2 (1597) act 1, sc. 2, l. [268]

30 Away, you scullion! you rampallion! you
fustilarian! I'll tickle your catastrophe.
Henry IV, Part 2 (1597) act 2, sc. 1, l. [67]

31 Doth it not show vilely in me to desire small beer?
Henry IV, Part 2 (1597) act 2, sc. 2, l. [7]

32   He was indeed the glass
Wherein the noble youth did dress themselves.
Henry IV, Part 2 (1597) act 2, sc. 3, l. 21

1   Shall pack-horses,
And hollow pampered jades of Asia,
Which cannot go but thirty miles a day,
Compare with Caesars, and with Cannibals,
And Trojan Greeks?
  Henry IV, Part 2 (1597) act 2, sc. 4, l. [176]; see **Marlowe**
  513:26

2 Thou whoreson little tidy Bartholomew boar-pig.
  Henry IV, Part 2 (1597) act 2, sc. 4, l. [249]

3 Is it not strange that desire should so many years
outlive performance?
  Henry IV, Part 2 (1597) act 2, sc. 4, l. [283]

4 Uneasy lies the head that wears a crown.
  Henry IV, Part 2 (1597) act 3, sc. 1, l. 31

5 There is a history in all men's lives,
Figuring the nature of the times deceased,
The which observed, a man may prophesy,
With a near aim, of the main chance of things
As yet not come to life, which in their seeds
And weak beginnings lie intreasurèd.
  Henry IV, Part 2 (1597) act 3, sc. 1, l. 80

6 A soldier is better accommodated than with a wife.
  Henry IV, Part 2 (1597) act 3, sc. 2, l. [73]

7 Most forcible Feeble.
  Henry IV, Part 2 (1597) act 3, sc. 2, l. [181]

8 We have heard the chimes at midnight.
  Henry IV, Part 2 (1597) act 3, sc. 2, l. [231]

9 I care not; a man can die but once; we owe God a
death.
  Henry IV, Part 2 (1597) act 3, sc. 2, l. [253]; see
  Shakespeare 691:7

10 He that dies this year is quit for the next.
  Henry IV, Part 2 (1597) act 3, sc. 2, l. [257]

11 When a' was naked, he was, for all the world, like
a forked radish, with a head fantastically carved
upon it with a knife.
  Henry IV, Part 2 (1597) act 3, sc. 2, l. [335]

12 Against ill chances men are ever merry,
But heaviness foreruns the good event.
  Henry IV, Part 2 (1597) act 4, sc. 2, l. 81

13 That I may justly say with the hook-nosed fellow
of Rome, 'I came, saw, and overcame.'
  Henry IV, Part 2 (1597) act 4, sc. 3, l. [44]; see **Caesar**
  185:7

14 A man cannot make him laugh; but that's no
marvel; he drinks no wine.
  Henry IV, Part 2 (1597) act 4, sc. 3, l. [95]

15 O polished perturbation! golden care!
  Henry IV, Part 2 (1597) act 4, sc. 5, l. 22

16 This sleep is sound indeed; this is a sleep
That from this golden rigol hath divorced
So many English kings.
  Henry IV, Part 2 (1597) act 4, sc. 5, l. 34

17 Thy wish was father, Harry, to that thought.
  Henry IV, Part 2 (1597) act 4, sc. 5, l. 91; see **Proverbs**
  635:13

18   Commit
The oldest sins the newest kind of ways.
  Henry IV, Part 2 (1597) act 4, sc. 5, l. 124

19 It hath been prophesied to me many years
I should not die but in Jerusalem,
Which vainly I supposed the Holy Land.
But bear me to that chamber; there I'll lie:
In that Jerusalem shall Harry die.
  Henry IV, Part 2 (1597) act 4, sc. 5, l. 235

20 This is the English, not the Turkish court;
Not Amurath an Amurath succeeds,
But Harry, Harry.
  Henry IV, Part 2 (1597) act 5, sc. 2, l. 47

21 My father is gone wild into his grave.
  Henry IV, Part 2 (1597) act 5, sc. 2, l. 123

22 I speak of Africa and golden joys.
  Henry IV, Part 2 (1597) act 5, sc. 3, l. [101]

23 I know thee not, old man: fall to thy prayers;
How ill white hairs become a fool and jester!
  Henry IV, Part 2 (1597) act 5, sc. 5, l. [52]

24 Presume not that I am the thing I was.
  Henry IV, Part 2 (1597) act 5, sc. 5, l. [61]

25 Falstaff shall die of a sweat, unless already a' be
killed with your hard opinions.
  Henry IV, Part 2 (1597) act 5, sc. 5, epilogue, l. [32]

HENRY V

26 O! for a Muse of fire, that would ascend
The brightest heaven of invention;
A kingdom for a stage, princes to act
And monarchs to behold the swelling scene.
  Henry V (1599) chorus, l. 1

27   Can this cockpit hold
The vasty fields of France? or may we cram
Within this wooden O the very casques
That did affright the air at Agincourt?
  Henry V (1599) chorus, l. 11

28 Consideration like an angel came,
And whipped the offending Adam out of him.
  Henry V (1599) act 1, sc. 1, l. 28

29   For so work the honey-bees,
Creatures that by a rule in nature teach
The act of order to a peopled kingdom.
They have a king and officers of sorts;
Where some, like magistrates, correct at home,
Others, like merchants, venture trade abroad,
Others, like soldiers, armèd in their stings,
Make boot upon the summer's velvet buds;
Which pillage they with merry march bring home
To the tent-royal of their emperor:
Who, busied in his majesty, surveys
The singing masons building roofs of gold.
  Henry V (1599) act 1, sc. 2, l. 187

30 When we have matched our rackets to these balls,
We will in France, by God's grace, play a set
Shall strike his father's crown into the hazard.
  Henry V (1599) act 1, sc. 2, l. 261

31 Now all the youth of England are on fire,
And silken dalliance in the wardrobe lies.
  Henry V (1599) act 2, chorus, l. 1

32 For now sits Expectation in the air
And hides a sword from hilts unto the point
With crowns imperial, crowns and coronets,

Promised to Harry and his followers.
Henry V (1599) act 2, chorus, l. 8

1 He's in Arthur's bosom, if ever man went to
Arthur's bosom.
Henry V (1599) act 2, sc. 3, l. [9]

2 His nose was as sharp as a pen, and a' babbled of
green fields.
Henry V (1599) act 2, sc. 3, l. [17]

3   Trust none;
For oaths are straws, men's faiths are wafer-cakes,
And hold-fast is the only dog, my duck.
Henry V (1599) act 2, sc. 3, l. [53]

4 Once more unto the breach, dear friends, once
     more;
Or close the wall up with our English dead!
In peace there's nothing so becomes a man
As modest stillness and humility:
But when the blast of war blows in our ears,
Then imitate the action of the tiger;
Stiffen the sinews, summon up the blood,
Disguise fair nature with hard-favoured rage;
Then lend the eye a terrible aspect.
Henry V (1599) act 3, sc. 1, l. 1

5 I see you stand like greyhounds in the slips,
Straining upon the start. The game's afoot:
Follow your spirit; and, upon this charge
Cry 'God for Harry! England and Saint George!'
Henry V (1599) act 3, sc. 1, l. 31

6 Give them great meals of beef and iron and steel,
they will eat like wolves and fight like devils.
Henry V (1599) act 3, sc. 7, l. [166]

7 Now entertain conjecture of a time
When creeping murmur and the poring dark
Fills the wide vessel of the universe.
Henry V (1599) act 4, chorus, l. 1

8 The royal captain of this ruined band.
Henry V (1599) act 4, chorus, l. 29

9 A little touch of Harry in the night.
Henry V (1599) act 4, chorus, l. 47

10 Thus may we gather honey from the weed,
And make a moral of the devil himself.
Henry V (1599) act 4, sc. 1, l. 11

11 The king's a bawcock, and a heart of gold,
A lad of life, an imp of fame,
Of parents good, of fist most valiant:
I kiss his dirty shoe, and from my heart-string
I love the lovely bully.
Henry V (1599) act 4, sc. 1, l. 44

12 If you would take the pains but to examine the
wars of Pompey the Great, you shall find, I
warrant you, that there is no tiddle-taddle nor
pibble-pabble in Pompey's camp.
Henry V (1599) act 4, sc. 1, l. [69]

13 Though it appear a little out of fashion,
There is much care and valour in this Welshman.
Henry V (1599) act 4, sc. 1, l. [86]

14 I think the king is but a man, as I am: the violet
smells to him as it doth to me.
Henry V (1599) act 4, sc. 1, l. [106]

15 I am afeard there are few die well that die in a
battle; for how can they charitably dispose of any
thing when blood is their argument?
Henry V (1599) act 4, sc. 1, l. [149]

16 Every subject's duty is the king's; but every
subject's soul is his own.
Henry V (1599) act 4, sc. 1, l. [189]

17 Upon the king! let us our lives, our souls,
Our debts, our careful wives,
Our children, and our sins lay on the king!
Henry V (1599) act 4, sc. 1, l. [250]

18   What infinite heart's ease
Must kings neglect, that private men enjoy!
And what have kings that privates have not too,
Save ceremony, save general ceremony?
Henry V (1599) act 4, sc. 1, l. [256]

19 'Tis not the balm, the sceptre and the ball,
The sword, the mace, the crown imperial,
The intertissued robe of gold and pearl,
The farcèd title running 'fore the king,
The throne he sits on, nor the tide of pomp
That beats upon the high shore of this world,
No, not all these, thrice-gorgeous ceremony,
Not all these, laid in bed majestical,
Can sleep so soundly as the wretched slave,
Who with a body filled and vacant mind
Gets him to rest, crammed with distressful bread.
Henry V (1599) act 4, sc. 1, l. [280]

20 O God of battles! steel my soldiers' hearts;
Possess them not with fear; take from them now
The sense of reckoning, if the opposèd numbers
Pluck their hearts from them.
Henry V (1599) act 4, sc. 1, l. [309]

21 If we are marked to die, we are enow
To do our country loss; and if to live,
The fewer men, the greater share of honour.
Henry V (1599) act 4, sc. 3, l. 20

22 He which hath no stomach to this fight,
Let him depart; his passport shall be made,
And crowns for convoy put into his purse:
We would not die in that man's company
That fears his fellowship to die with us.
This day is called the feast of Crispian:
He that outlives this day and comes safe home,
Will stand a tip-toe when this day is named,
And rouse him at the name of Crispian.
Henry V (1599) act 4, sc. 3, l. 35

23 Then will he strip his sleeve and show his scars,
And say, 'These wounds I had on Crispin's day.'
Old men forget: yet all shall be forgot,
But he'll remember with advantages
What feats he did that day.
Henry V (1599) act 4, sc. 3, l. 47

24 And Crispin Crispian shall ne'er go by,
From this day to the ending of the world,
But we in it shall be rememberèd;
We few, we happy few, we band of brothers;
For he to-day that sheds his blood with me
Shall be my brother; be he ne'er so vile
This day shall gentle his condition:
And gentlemen in England, now a-bed

Shall think themselves accursed they were not here,
And hold their manhoods cheap whiles any speaks
That fought with us upon Saint Crispin's day.
Henry V (1599) act 4, sc. 3, l. 57

1   But now behold,
In the quick forge and working-house of thought,
How London doth pour out her citizens.
Henry V (1599) act 5, chorus, l. 22

2 Not for Cadwallader and all his goats.
Henry V (1599) act 5, sc. 1, l. [29]

3 By this leek, I will most horribly revenge.
Henry V (1599) act 5, sc. 1, l. [49]

4   The naked, poor, and manglèd Peace,
Dear nurse of arts, plenties, and joyful births.
Henry V (1599) act 5, sc. 2, l. 34

5 For these fellows of infinite tongue, that can
rhyme themselves into ladies' favours, they do
always reason themselves out again.
Henry V (1599) act 5, sc. 2, l. [162]

HENRY VI, PART 1

6 Hung be the heavens with black, yield day to
night!
Henry VI, Part 1 (1592) act 1, sc. 1, l. 1

7 Expect Saint Martin's summer, halcyon days.
Henry VI, Part 1 (1592) act 1, sc. 2, l. 131

8   Unbidden guests
Are often welcomest when they are gone.
Henry VI, Part 1 (1592) act 2, sc. 2, l. 55

9 But in these nice sharp quillets of the law,
Good faith, I am no wiser than a daw.
Henry VI, Part 1 (1592) act 2, sc. 4, l. 17

10 From off this brier pluck a white rose with me.
Plantagenet
Henry VI, Part 1 (1592) act 2, sc. 4, l. 30

11 Pluck a red rose from off this thorn with me.
Somerset
Henry VI, Part 1 (1592) act 2, sc. 4, l. 33

12 I owe him little duty and less love.
Henry VI, Part 1 (1592) act 4, sc. 4, l. 34

13 She's beautiful and therefore to be wooed;
She is a woman, therefore to be won.
Henry VI, Part 1 (1592) act 5, sc. 3, l. 78; see **Shakespeare**
719:14

HENRY VI, PART 2

14 Put forth thy hand, reach at the glorious gold.
Henry VI, Part 2 (1592) act 1, sc. 2, l. 11

15 Is this the government of Britain's isle,
And this the royalty of Albion's king?
Henry VI, Part 2 (1592) act 1, sc. 3, l. [47]

16 Thrice is he armed that hath his quarrel just.
Henry VI, Part 2 (1592) act 3, sc. 2, l. 233

17 The gaudy, blabbing, and remorseful day
Is crept into the bosom of the sea.
Henry VI, Part 2 (1592) act 4, sc. 1, l. 1

18 More can I bear than you dare execute.
Henry VI, Part 2 (1592) act 4, sc. 1, l. 130

19 I say it was never merry world in England since
gentlemen came up.
Henry VI, Part 2 (1592) act 4, sc. 2, l. [10]

20 CADE: There shall be in England seven halfpenny
loaves sold for a penny; the three-hooped pot
shall have ten hoops; and I will make it felony
to drink small beer. All the realm shall be in
common, and in Cheapside shall my palfrey go
to grass. And when I am king,—as king I will
be,— . . . there shall be no money; all shall eat
and drink on my score; and I will apparel them
all in one livery, that they may agree like
brothers, and worship me their lord.
DICK: The first thing we do, let's kill all the
lawyers.
Henry VI, Part 2 (1592) act 4, sc. 2, l. [73]

21 Is not this a lamentable thing, that of the skin of
an innocent lamb should be made parchment?
that parchment, being scribbled o'er, should undo
a man?
Henry VI, Part 2 (1592) act 4, sc. 2, l. [88]

22 And Adam was a gardener.
Henry VI, Part 2 (1592) act 4, sc. 2, l. [146]

23 Thou hast most traitorously corrupted the youth
of the realm in erecting a grammar school: and
whereas, before, our forefathers had no other
books but the score and the tally, thou hast
caused printing to be used; and, contrary to the
king, his crown and dignity, thou hast built a
paper-mill.
Henry VI, Part 2 (1592) act 4, sc. 7, l. [35]

24 Away with him! away with him! he speaks Latin.
Henry VI, Part 2 (1592) act 4, sc. 7, l. [62]

HENRY VI, PART 3

25 O tiger's heart wrapped in a woman's hide!
Henry VI, Part 3 (1592) act 1, sc. 4, l. 137

26 This battle fares like to the morning's war,
When dying clouds contend with growing light,
What time the shepherd, blowing of his nails,
Can neither call it perfect day nor night.
Henry VI, Part 3 (1592) act 2, sc. 5, l. 1

27 Gives not the hawthorn bush a sweeter shade
To shepherds, looking on their silly sheep,
Than doth a rich embroidered canopy
To kings that fear their subjects' treachery?
Henry VI, Part 3 (1592) act 2, sc. 5, l. 42

28 Why, I can smile, and murder whiles I smile.
Henry VI, Part 3 (1592) act 3, sc. 2, l. 182

29 I'll drown more sailors than the mermaid shall;
I'll slay more gazers than the basilisk;
I'll play the orator as well as Nestor,
Deceive more slyly than Ulysses could,
And, like a Sinon, take another Troy.
I can add colours to the chameleon,
Change shapes with Proteus for advantages,
And set the murderous Machiavel to school.
Can I do this, and cannot get a crown?
Tut, were it farther off, I'll pluck it down.
Henry VI, Part 3 (1592) act 3, sc. 2, l. 186

1 Peace! impudent and shameless Warwick, peace;
Proud setter up and puller down of kings.
Henry VI, Part 3 (1592) act 3, sc. 3, l. 156

2 A little fire is quickly trodden out,
Which, being suffered, rivers cannot quench.
Henry VI, Part 3 (1592) act 4, sc. 8, l. 7

3 Suspicion always haunts the guilty mind;
The thief doth fear each bush an officer.
Henry VI, Part 3 (1592) act 5, sc. 6, l. 11

4 Down, down to hell; and say I sent thee thither.
Henry VI, Part 3 (1592) act 5, sc. 6, l. 67

HENRY VIII

5 Heat not a furnace for your foe so hot
That it do singe yourself.
Henry VIII (1613) act 1, sc. 1, l. 140; play written with
John **Fletcher**

6 Go with me, like good angels, to my end;
And, as the long divorce of steel falls on me,
Make of your prayers one sweet sacrifice,
And lift my soul to heaven.
Henry VIII (1613) act 2, sc. 1, l. 75

7 Heaven will one day open
The king's eyes, that so long have slept upon
This bold bad man.
Henry VIII (1613) act 2, sc. 2, l. [42]; see **Spenser** 751:14

8 Orpheus with his lute made trees,
And the mountain-tops that freeze,
Bow themselves when he did sing.
Henry VIII (1613) act 3, sc. 1, l. 3

9 In sweet music is such art,
Killing care and grief of heart
Fall asleep, or hearing die.
Henry VIII (1613) act 3, sc. 1, l. 12

10 I shall fall
Like a bright exhalation in the evening,
And no man see me more.
Henry VIII (1613) act 3, sc. 2, l. 226

11 Farewell! a long farewell, to all my greatness!
This is the state of man: to-day he puts forth
The tender leaves of hope; to-morrow blossoms,
And bears his blushing honours thick upon him;
The third day comes a frost, a killing frost;
And, when he thinks, good easy man, full surely
His greatness is a-ripening, nips his root,
And then he falls, as I do. I have ventured,
Like little wanton boys that swim on bladders,
This many summers in a sea of glory,
But far beyond my depth.
Henry VIII (1613) act 3, sc. 2, l. 352

12 O how wretched
Is that poor man that hangs on princes' favours!
There is, betwixt that smile we would aspire to,
That sweet aspect of princes, and their ruin,
More pangs and fears than wars or women have;
And when he falls, he falls like Lucifer,
Never to hope again.
Henry VIII (1613) act 3, sc. 2, l. 367

13 A peace above all earthly dignities,
A still and quiet conscience.
Henry VIII (1613) act 3, sc. 2, l. 380

14 Cromwell, I charge thee, fling away ambition:
By that sin fell the angels.
Henry VIII (1613) act 3, sc. 2, l. 441

15 Love thyself last: cherish those hearts that hate
thee;
Corruption wins not more than honesty.
Henry VIII (1613) act 3, sc. 2, l. 444

16 Had I but served my God with half the zeal
I served my king, he would not in mine age
Have left me naked to mine enemies.
Henry VIII (1613) act 3, sc. 2, l. 456; see **Wolsey** 844:12

17 An old man, broken with the storms of state
Is come to lay his weary bones among ye;
Give him a little earth for charity.
Henry VIII (1613) act 4, sc. 2, l. 21; see **Wolsey** 844:11

18 So may he rest; his faults lie gently on him!
Henry VIII (1613) act 4, sc. 2, l. 31

19 His promises were, as he then was, mighty;
But his performance, as he is now, nothing.
Henry VIII (1613) act 4, sc. 2, l. 41

20 Men's evil manners live in brass; their virtues
We write in water.
Henry VIII (1613) act 4, sc. 2, l. 45; see **Epitaphs** 310:4

21 He was a scholar, and a ripe and good one;
Exceeding wise, fair-spoken, and persuading:
Lofty and sour to them that loved him not;
But, to those men that sought him, sweet as
summer.
Henry VIII (1613) act 4, sc. 2, l. 51

22 Those twins of learning that he raised in you,
Ipswich and Oxford!
Henry VIII (1613) act 4, sc. 2, l. 58

23 'Tis a cruelty
To load a falling man.
Henry VIII (1613) act 5, sc. 3, l. 76

24 In her days every man shall eat in safety
Under his own vine what he plants; and sing
The merry songs of peace to all his neighbours.
Henry VIII (1613) act 5, sc. 5, l. 34

25 Nor shall this peace sleep with her; but as when
The bird of wonder dies, the maiden phoenix,
Her ashes new-create another heir
As great in admiration as herself.
Henry VIII (1613) act 5, sc. 5, l. 40

26 Some come to take their ease
And sleep an act or two.
Henry VIII (1613) act 5, epilogue, l. 2

JULIUS CAESAR

27 Hence! home, you idle creatures, get you home:
Is this a holiday?
Julius Caesar (1599) act 1, sc. 1, l. 1

28 You blocks, you stones, you worse than senseless
things!
O you hard hearts, you cruel men of Rome,
Knew you not Pompey?
Julius Caesar (1599) act 1, sc. 1, l. [39]

29 CAESAR: Who is it in the press that calls on me?
I hear a tongue, shriller than all the music,

Cry 'Caesar'. Speak; Caesar is turned to hear.
SOOTHSAYER: Beware the ides of March.
Julius Caesar (1599) act 1, sc. 2, l. 15

1   I do lack some part
Of that quick spirit that is in Antony.
Julius Caesar (1599) act 1, sc. 2, l. 28

2 Brutus, I do observe you now of late:
I have not from your eyes that gentleness
And show of love as I was wont to have:
You bear too stubborn and too strange a hand
Over your friend that loves you.
Julius Caesar (1599) act 1, sc. 2, l. 32

3   Poor Brutus, with himself at war,
Forgets the shows of love to other men.
Julius Caesar (1599) act 1, sc. 2, l. 46

4 Set honour in one eye and death i' the other,
And I will look on both indifferently.
Julius Caesar (1599) act 1, sc. 2, l. 86

5 Well, honour is the subject of my story.
I cannot tell what you and other men
Think of this life: but, for my single self,
I had as lief not be as live to be
In awe of such a thing as I myself.
Julius Caesar (1599) act 1, sc. 2, l. 92

6 I was born free as Caesar; so were you:
We both have fed as well, and we can both
Endure the winter's cold as well as he.
Julius Caesar (1599) act 1, sc. 2, l. 97

7 He had a fever when he was in Spain,
And when the fit was on him, I did mark
How he did shake; 'tis true, this god did shake.
Julius Caesar (1599) act 1, sc. 2, l. 119

8   Ye gods, it doth amaze me,
A man of such a feeble temper should
So get the start of the majestic world,
And bear the palm alone.
Julius Caesar (1599) act 1, sc. 2, l. 128

9 Why, man, he doth bestride the narrow world
Like a Colossus; and we petty men
Walk under his huge legs, and peep about
To find ourselves dishonourable graves.
Men at some time are masters of their fates:
The fault, dear Brutus, is not in our stars,
But in ourselves, that we are underlings.
Julius Caesar (1599) act 1, sc. 2, l. 134

10 'Brutus' will start a spirit as soon as 'Caesar'.
Now in the names of all the gods at once,
Upon what meat doth this our Caesar feed,
That he is grown so great?
Julius Caesar (1599) act 1, sc. 2, l. 146

11 When could they say, till now, that talked of Rome,
That her wide walls encompassed but one man?
Now is it Rome indeed and room enough,
When there is in it but one only man.
Julius Caesar (1599) act 1, sc. 2, l. 153

12 Let me have men about me that are fat;
Sleek-headed men and such as sleep o' nights;
Yond' Cassius has a lean and hungry look;

He thinks too much: such men are dangerous.
Julius Caesar (1599) act 1, sc. 2, l. 191; see **Plutarch** 598:15

13 Would he were fatter! but I fear him not:
Yet if my name were liable to fear,
I do not know the man I should avoid
So soon as that spare Cassius. He reads much;
He is a great observer.
Julius Caesar (1599) act 1, sc. 2, l. 197

14   He loves no plays,
As thou dost, Antony.
Julius Caesar (1599) act 1, sc. 2, l. 202

15 Such men as he be never at heart's ease,
Whiles they behold a greater than themselves,
And therefore are they very dangerous.
I rather tell thee what is to be feared
Than what I fear, for always I am Caesar.
Julius Caesar (1599) act 1, sc. 2, l. 207

16 'Tis very like: he hath the falling sickness.
Julius Caesar (1599) act 1, sc. 2, l. [255]

17 CASSIUS: Did Cicero say any thing?
CASCA: Ay, he spoke Greek.
CASSIUS: To what effect?
CASCA: Nay, an I tell you that, I'll ne'er look you i'
the face again; but those that understood him
smiled at one another and shook their heads;
but, for mine own part, it was Greek to me.
Julius Caesar (1599) act 1, sc. 2, l. [288]

18   Yesterday the bird of night did sit,
Even at noon-day, upon the market-place,
Hooting and shrieking.
Julius Caesar (1599) act 1, sc. 3, l. 26

19 Cassius from bondage will deliver Cassius.
Julius Caesar (1599) act 1, sc. 3, l. 90

20 Nor stony tower, nor walls of beaten brass,
Nor airless dungeon, nor strong links of iron,
Can be retentive to the strength of spirit;
But life, being weary of these worldly bars,
Never lacks power to dismiss itself.
Julius Caesar (1599) act 1, sc. 3, l. 93

21 It is the bright day that brings forth the adder;
And that craves wary walking.
Julius Caesar (1599) act 2, sc. 1, l. 14

22 Between the acting of a dreadful thing
And the first motion, all the interim is
Like a phantasma, or a hideous dream.
Julius Caesar (1599) act 2, sc. 1, l. 63

23 Let us be sacrificers, but not butchers, Caius.
Julius Caesar (1599) act 2, sc. 1, l. 166

24 Let's carve him as a dish fit for the gods,
Not hew him as a carcass fit for hounds.
Julius Caesar (1599) act 2, sc. 1, l. 173

25 For he is superstitious grown of late,
Quite from the main opinion he held once
Of fantasy, of dreams, and ceremonies.
Julius Caesar (1599) act 2, sc. 1, l. 195

26 But when I tell him he hates flatterers,
He says he does, being then most flattered.
Julius Caesar (1599) act 2, sc. 1, l. 207

27   What! is Brutus sick,
And will he steal out of his wholesome bed

To dare the vile contagion of the night?
Julius Caesar (1599) act 2, sc. 1, l. 263

1 PORTIA: Dwell I but in the suburbs
Of your good pleasure? If it be no more,
Portia is Brutus' harlot, not his wife.
BRUTUS: You are my true and honourable wife,
As dear to me as are the ruddy drops
That visit my sad heart.
Julius Caesar (1599) act 2, sc. 1, l. 285

2 I grant I am a woman, but, withal,
A woman that Lord Brutus took to wife;
I grant I am a woman, but, withal,
A woman well-reputed, Cato's daughter.
Think you I am no stronger than my sex,
Being so fathered and so husbanded?
Julius Caesar (1599) act 2, sc. 1, l. 292

3 When beggars die, there are no comets seen;
The heavens themselves blaze forth the death of
   princes.
Julius Caesar (1599) act 2, sc. 2, l. 30

4 Cowards die many times before their deaths;
The valiant never taste of death but once.
Of all the wonders that I yet have heard,
It seems to me most strange that men should fear;
Seeing that death, a necessary end,
Will come when it will come.
Julius Caesar (1599) act 2, sc. 2, l. 32

5   Danger knows full well
That Caesar is more dangerous than he:
We are two lions littered in one day,
And I the elder and more terrible.
Julius Caesar (1599) act 2, sc. 2, l. 44

6 The cause is in my will: I will not come.
Julius Caesar (1599) act 2, sc. 2, l. 71

7 See! Antony, that revels long o' nights,
Is notwithstanding up.
Julius Caesar (1599) act 2, sc. 2, l. 116

8 CAESAR: The ides of March are come.
SOOTHSAYER: Ay, Caesar; but not gone.
Julius Caesar (1599) act 3, sc. 1, l. 1

9 But I am constant as the northern star,
Of whose true-fixed and resting quality
There is no fellow in the firmament.
Julius Caesar (1599) act 3, sc. 1, l. 60

10 *Et tu, Brute?* Then fall, Caesar!
Julius Caesar (1599) act 3, sc. 1, l. 77; see **Caesar** 185:8

11 Ambition's debt is paid.
Julius Caesar (1599) act 3, sc. 1, l. 83

12   How many ages hence
Shall this our lofty scene be acted o'er,
In states unborn, and accents yet unknown!
Julius Caesar (1599) act 3, sc. 1, l. 111

13 O mighty Caesar! dost thou lie so low?
Are all thy conquests, glories, triumphs, spoils,
Shrunk to this little measure?
Julius Caesar (1599) act 3, sc. 1, l. 148

14   Live a thousand years,
I shall not find myself so apt to die:
No place will please me so, no mean of death,

As here by Caesar, and by you cut off,
The choice and master spirits of this age.
Julius Caesar (1599) act 3, sc. 1, l. 159

15 O! pardon me, thou bleeding piece of earth,
That I am meek and gentle with these butchers;
Thou art the ruins of the noblest man
That ever livèd in the tide of times.
Julius Caesar (1599) act 3, sc. 1, l. 254

16   Caesar's spirit, ranging for revenge,
With Ate by his side, come hot from hell,
Shall in these confines, with a monarch's voice
Cry, 'Havoc!' and let slip the dogs of war.
Julius Caesar (1599) act 3, sc. 1, l. 270

17 Passion, I see, is catching.
Julius Caesar (1599) act 3, sc. 1, l. 283

18 Not that I loved Caesar less, but that I loved Rome
more.
Julius Caesar (1599) act 3, sc. 2, l. [22]

19 As he was valiant, I honour him: but, as he was
ambitious, I slew him.
Julius Caesar (1599) act 3, sc. 2, l. [27]

20 Who is here so base that would be a bondman? If
any, speak; for him have I offended. Who is here
so rude that would not be a Roman? If any, speak;
for him have I offended. Who is here so vile that
will not love his country? If any, speak; for him
have I offended. I pause for a reply.
Julius Caesar (1599) act 3, sc. 2, l. [31]

21 Friends, Romans, countrymen, lend me your ears;
I come to bury Caesar, not to praise him.
The evil that men do lives after them,
The good is oft interrèd with their bones.
Julius Caesar (1599) act 3, sc. 2, l. [79]

22   The noble Brutus
Hath told you Caesar was ambitious;
If it were so, it was a grievous fault;
And grievously hath Caesar answered it.
Julius Caesar (1599) act 3, sc. 2, l. [83]

23 For Brutus is an honourable man;
So are they all, all honourable men.
Julius Caesar (1599) act 3, sc. 2, l. [88]

24 He was my friend, faithful and just to me:
But Brutus says he was ambitious;
And Brutus is an honourable man.
Julius Caesar (1599) act 3, sc. 2, l. [91]

25 When that the poor have cried, Caesar hath wept;
Ambition should be made of sterner stuff.
Julius Caesar (1599) act 3, sc. 2, l. [97]

26   On the Lupercal
I thrice presented him a kingly crown
Which he did thrice refuse: was this ambition?
Julius Caesar (1599) act 3, sc. 2, l. [101]

27 You all did love him once, not without cause.
Julius Caesar (1599) act 3, sc. 2, l. [108]

28 But yesterday the word of Caesar might
Have stood against the world; now lies he there,
And none so poor to do him reverence.
Julius Caesar (1599) act 3, sc. 2, l. [124]

29 You are not wood, you are not stones, but men;
And, being men, hearing the will of Caesar,

It will inflame you, it will make you mad.
Julius Caesar (1599) act 3, sc. 2, l. [148]

1 If you have tears, prepare to shed them now.
Julius Caesar (1599) act 3, sc. 2, l. [174]

2 This was the most unkindest cut of all.
Julius Caesar (1599) act 3, sc. 2, l. [188]

3 O! what a fall was there, my countrymen;
Then I, and you, and all of us fell down,
Whilst bloody treason flourished over us.
Julius Caesar (1599) act 3, sc. 2, l. [195]

4 I am no orator, as Brutus is;
But, as you know me all, a plain, blunt man,
That love my friend.
Julius Caesar (1599) act 3, sc. 2, l. [221]

5 For I have neither wit, nor words, nor worth,
Action, nor utterance, nor power of speech,
To stir men's blood; I only speak right on;
I tell you that which you yourselves do know.
Julius Caesar (1599) act 3, sc. 2, l. [225]

6 　　　　　But were I Brutus,
And Brutus Antony, there were an Antony
Would ruffle up your spirits, and put a tongue
In every wound of Caesar, that should move
The stones of Rome to rise and mutiny.
Julius Caesar (1599) act 3, sc. 2, l. [230]

7 　　　　　He hath left you all his walks,
His private arbours, and new-planted orchards,
On this side Tiber; he hath left them you,
And to your heirs for ever; common pleasures,
To walk abroad, and recreate yourselves.
Julius Caesar (1599) act 3, sc. 2, l. [252]

8 Here was a Caesar! when comes such another?
Julius Caesar (1599) act 3, sc. 2, l. [257]

9 Now let it work; mischief, thou art afoot,
Take thou what course thou wilt!
Julius Caesar (1599) act 3, sc. 2, l. [265]

10 Tear him for his bad verses, tear him for his bad verses.
Julius Caesar (1599) act 3, sc. 3, l. [34]

11 He shall not live; look, with a spot I damn him.
Julius Caesar (1599) act 4, sc. 1, l. 6

12 This is a slight unmeritable man,
Meet to be sent on errands.
Julius Caesar (1599) act 4, sc. 1, l. 12

13 Let me tell you, Cassius, you yourself
Are much condemned to have an itching palm.
Julius Caesar (1599) act 4, sc. 3, l. 7

14 I had rather be a dog, and bay the moon,
Than such a Roman.
Julius Caesar (1599) act 4, sc. 3, l. 27

15 Do not presume too much upon my love;
I may do that I shall be sorry for.
Julius Caesar (1599) act 4, sc. 3, l. 63

16 There is no terror, Cassius, in your threats;
For I am armed so strong in honesty
That they pass by me as the idle wind,
Which I respect not.
Julius Caesar (1599) act 4, sc. 3, l. 66

17 A friend should bear his friend's infirmities,
But Brutus makes mine greater than they are.
Julius Caesar (1599) act 4, sc. 3, l. 85

18 Cassius is aweary of the world;
Hated by one he loves; braved by his brother.
Julius Caesar (1599) act 4, sc. 3, l. 94

19 O Cassius! you are yokèd with a lamb
That carries anger as the flint bears fire;
Who, much enforcèd, shows a hasty spark,
And straight is cold again.
Julius Caesar (1599) act 4, sc. 3, l. 109

20 Good reasons must, of force, give place to better.
Julius Caesar (1599) act 4, sc. 3, l. 202

21 There is a tide in the affairs of men,
Which, taken at the flood, leads on to fortune;
Omitted, all the voyage of their life
Is bound in shallows and in miseries.
Julius Caesar (1599) act 4, sc. 3, l. 217; see **Byron** 181:20

22 But for your words, they rob the Hybla bees,
And leave them honeyless.
Julius Caesar (1599) act 5, sc. 1, l. 34

23 Forever, and forever, farewell, Cassius!
If we do meet again, why, we shall smile!
If not, why then, this parting was well made.
Julius Caesar (1599) act 5, sc. 1, l. 118

24 　　　　　O! that a man might know
The end of this day's business, ere it come;
But it sufficeth that the day will end,
And then the end is known.
Julius Caesar (1599) act 5, sc. 1, l. 123

25 O hateful error, melancholy's child!
Why dost thou show, to the apt thoughts of men,
The things that are not?
Julius Caesar (1599) act 5, sc. 3, l. 67

26 O Julius Caesar! thou art mighty yet!
Thy spirit walks abroad, and turns our swords
In our own proper entrails.
Julius Caesar (1599) act 5, sc. 3, l. 94

27 Thou seest the world, Volumnius, how it goes;
Our enemies have beat us to the pit:
It is more worthy to leap in ourselves,
Than tarry till they push us.
Julius Caesar (1599) act 5, sc. 5, l. 22

28 Thy life hath had some smatch of honour in it.
Julius Caesar (1599) act 5, sc. 5, l. 46

29 This was the noblest Roman of them all;
All the conspirators save only he
Did that they did in envy of great Caesar;
He only in a general honest thought
And common good to all, made one of them.
His life was gentle, and the elements
So mixed in him that Nature might stand up
And say to all the world, 'This was a man!'
Julius Caesar (1599) act 5, sc. 5, l. 68

KING JOHN

30 　　　　　Hadst thou rather be a Faulconbridge
And like thy brother, to enjoy thy land,
Or the reputed son of Coeur-de-Lion,
Lord of thy presence and no land beside.
King John (1591-8) act 1, sc. 1, l. 134

1 And if his name be George, I'll call him Peter;
For new-made honour doth forget men's names.
King John (1591–8) act 1, sc. 1, l. 186

2 Mad world! mad kings! mad composition!
King John (1591–8) act 2, sc. 1, l. 561

3 Well, whiles I am a beggar, I will rail,
And say there is no sin, but to be rich;
And, being rich, my virtue then shall be,
To say there is no vice, but beggary.
King John (1591–8) act 2, sc. 1, l. 593

4 Old Time the clock-setter, that bald sexton, Time.
King John (1591–8) act 3, sc. 1, l. 324

5 Bell, book, and candle shall not drive me back,
When gold and silver becks me to come on.
King John (1591–8) act 3, sc. 3, l. 12

6 Grief fills the room up of my absent child,
Lies in his bed, walks up and down with me,
Puts on his pretty looks, repeats his words,
Remembers me of all his gracious parts,
Stuffs out his vacant garments with his form:
Then have I reason to be fond of grief.
King John (1591–8) act 3, sc. 4, l. 93

7 Life is as tedious as a twice-told tale,
Vexing the dull ear of a drowsy man.
King John (1591–8) act 3, sc. 4, l. 108

8 Heat me these irons hot.
King John (1591–8) act 4, sc. 1, l. 1

9   Will you put out mine eyes?
These eyes that never did nor never shall
So much as frown on you?
King John (1591–8) act 4, sc. 1, l. 56

10 To gild refinèd gold, to paint the lily,
To throw a perfume on the violet,
To smooth the ice, or add another hue
Unto the rainbow, or with taper light
To seek the beauteous eye of heaven to garnish,
Is wasteful and ridiculous excess.
King John (1591–8) act 4, sc. 2, l. 11; see **Byron** 181:3

11 Another lean unwashed artificer
Cuts off his tale and talks of Arthur's death.
King John (1591–8) act 4, sc. 2, l. 201

12 How oft the sight of means to do ill deeds
Makes ill deeds done!
King John (1591–8) act 4, sc. 2, l. 219

13 Heaven take my soul, and England keep my
bones!
King John (1591–8) act 4, sc. 3, l. 10

14 Whate'er you think, good words, I think, were
best.
King John (1591–8) act 4, sc. 3, l. 28

15   I do not ask you much:
I beg cold comfort.
King John (1591–8) act 5, sc. 7, l. 41

16 This England never did, nor never shall,
Lie at the proud foot of a conqueror,
But when it first did help to wound itself.
Now these her princes are come home again,
Come the three corners of the world in arms,

And we shall shock them: nought shall make us
rue,
If England to itself do rest but true.
King John (1591–8) act 5, sc. 7, l. 112

KING LEAR

17 Nothing will come of nothing: speak again.
King Lear (1605–6) act 1, sc. 1, l. [92]

18 LEAR: So young, and so untender?
CORDELIA: So young, my lord, and true.
LEAR: Let it be so; thy truth then be thy dower:
For, by the sacred radiance of the sun,
The mysteries of Hecate and the night,
By all the operation of the orbs
From whom we do exist and cease to be,
Here I disclaim all my paternal care,
Propinquity and property of blood,
And as a stranger to my heart and me
Hold thee from this for ever.
King Lear (1605–6) act 1, sc. 1, l. [108]

19 Come not between the dragon and his wrath.
King Lear (1605–6) act 1, sc. 1, l. [124]

20   I want that glib and oily art
To speak and purpose not; since what I well
intend,
I'll do't before I speak.
King Lear (1605–6) act 1, sc. 1, l. [227]

21 It is no vicious blot nor other foulness,
No unchaste action, or dishonoured step,
That hath deprived me of your grace and favour,
But even for want of that for which I am richer,
A still-soliciting eye, and such a tongue
That I am glad I have not, though not to have it
Hath lost me in your liking.
King Lear (1605–6) act 1, sc. 1, l. [230]

22   Love is not love
When it is minglèd with regards that stand
Aloof from the entire point.
King Lear (1605–6) act 1, sc. 1, l. [241]

23 'Tis the infirmity of his age; yet he hath ever but
slenderly known himself.
King Lear (1605–6) act 1, sc. 1, l. 293

24   Why bastard? wherefore base?
When my dimensions are as well compact,
My mind as generous, and my shape as true,
As honest madam's issue?
King Lear (1605–6) act 1, sc. 2, l. 6

25 I grow, I prosper;
Now, gods, stand up for bastards!
King Lear (1605–6) act 1, sc. 2, l. 21

26 This is the excellent foppery of the world, that,
when we are sick in fortune,—often the surfeit of
our own behaviour,— we make guilty of our own
disasters the sun, the moon, and the stars; as if we
were villains by necessity, fools by heavenly
compulsion, knaves, thieves, and treachers by
spherical predominance, drunkards, liars, and
adulterers by an enforced obedience of planetary
influence.
King Lear (1605–6) act 1, sc. 2, l. [132]

27 My father compounded with my mother under the
dragon's tail, and my nativity was under *ursa*

major; so that it follows I am rough and lecherous. 'Sfoot! I should have been that I am had the maidenliest star in the firmament twinkled on my bastardizing.
King Lear (1605–6) act 1, sc. 2, l. [144]

1 My cue is villanous melancholy, with a sigh like Tom o' Bedlam.
King Lear (1605–6) act 1, sc. 2, l. [151]

2 LEAR: Dost thou call me fool, boy?
FOOL: All thy other titles thou hast given away; that thou wast born with.
King Lear (1605–6) act 1, sc. 4, l. [163]

3 Who is it that can tell me who I am?
King Lear (1605–6) act 1, sc. 4, l. 230

4 Ingratitude, thou marble-hearted fiend,
More hideous, when thou show'st thee in a child,
Than the sea-monster.
King Lear (1605–6) act 1, sc. 4, l. [283]

5 How sharper than a serpent's tooth it is
To have a thankless child!
King Lear (1605–6) act 1, sc. 4, l. [312]

6 O! let me not be mad, not mad, sweet heaven;
Keep me in temper; I would not be mad!
King Lear (1605–6) act 1, sc. 5, l. [51]

7 Thou whoreson zed! thou unnecessary letter!
King Lear (1605–6) act 2, sc. 2, l. [68]

8 Goose, if I had you upon Sarum plain,
I'd drive ye cackling home to Camelot.
King Lear (1605–6) act 2, sc. 2, l. [88]

9 Down, thou climbing sorrow!
Thy element's below.
King Lear (1605–6) act 2, sc. 4, l. [57]

10 O, sir! you are old;
Nature in you stands on the very verge
Of her confine.
King Lear (1605–6) act 2, sc. 4, l. [148]

11 O reason not the need! Our basest beggars
Are in the poorest thing superfluous.
Allow not nature more than nature needs,
Man's life is cheap as beast's.
King Lear (1605–6) act 2, sc. 4, l. 264

12 I will do such things,—
What they are yet I know not,—but they shall be
The terrors of the earth.
King Lear (1605–6) act 2, sc. 4, l. [283]

13 No, I'll not weep:
I have full cause of weeping, but this heart
Shall break into a hundred thousand flaws
Or ere I'll weep. O fool! I shall go mad.
King Lear (1605–6) act 2, sc. 4, l. [286]

14 Contending with the fretful elements;
Bids the wind blow the earth into the sea,
Or swell the curlèd waters 'bove the main,
That things might change or cease.
King Lear (1605–6) act 3, sc. 1, l. 4

15 Blow, winds, and crack your cheeks! rage! blow!
You cataracts and hurricanoes, spout
Till you have drenched our steeples, drowned the cocks!

You sulphurous and thought-executing fires,
Vaunt-couriers to oak-cleaving thunderbolts,
Singe my white head! And thou, all-shaking thunder,
Strike flat the thick rotundity o' the world!
Crack nature's moulds, all germens spill at once
That make ingrateful man!
King Lear (1605–6) act 3, sc. 2, l. 1

16 Rumble thy bellyful! Spit, fire! Spout, rain!
Nor rain, wind, thunder, fire, are my daughters:
I tax not you, you elements, with unkindness.
King Lear (1605–6) act 3, sc. 2, l. 14

17 There was never yet fair woman but she made mouths in a glass.
King Lear (1605–6) act 3, sc. 2, l. [35]

18 No, I will be the pattern of all patience; I will say nothing.
King Lear (1605–6) act 3, sc. 2, l. [37]

19 I am a man
More sinned against than sinning.
King Lear (1605–6) act 3, sc. 2, l. [59]; see **Bowra** 148:14

20 He that has and a little tiny wit,
With hey, ho, the wind and the rain,
Must make content with his fortunes fit,
Though the rain it raineth every day.
King Lear (1605–6) act 3, sc. 2, l. [74]

21 O! that way madness lies; let me shun that.
King Lear (1605–6) act 3, sc. 4, l. 21

22 Poor naked wretches, wheresoe'er you are,
That bide the pelting of this pitiless storm,
How shall your houseless heads and unfed sides,
Your loopèd and windowed raggedness, defend you
From seasons such as these?
King Lear (1605–6) act 3, sc. 4, l. 28

23 Take physic, pomp;
Expose thyself to feel what wretches feel.
King Lear (1605–6) act 3, sc. 4, l. 33

24 Pillicock sat on Pillicock-hill:
Halloo, halloo, loo, loo!
King Lear (1605–6) act 3, sc. 4, l. [75]

25 Keep thy foot out of brothels, thy hand out of plackets, thy pen from lenders' books, and defy the foul fiend.
King Lear (1605–6) act 3, sc. 4, l. [96]

26 Thou art the thing itself; unaccommodated man is no more but such a poor, bare, forked animal as thou art. Off, off, you lendings! Come; unbutton here.
King Lear (1605–6) act 3, sc. 4, l. [109]

27 This is the foul fiend Flibbertigibbet: he begins at curfew, and walks till the first cock; he gives the web and the pin, squints the eye, and makes the harelip; mildews the white wheat, and hurts the poor creatures of earth.
King Lear (1605–6) act 3, sc. 4, l. [118]

28 The green mantle of the standing pool.
King Lear (1605–6) act 3, sc. 4, l. [136]

29 The prince of darkness is a gentleman.
King Lear (1605–6) act 3, sc. 4, l. [148]

1 Poor Tom's a-cold.
   King Lear (1605–6) act 3, sc. 4, l. [151]

2 Child Roland to the dark tower came,
   His word was still, Fie, foh, and fum,
   I smell the blood of a British man.
   King Lear (1605–6) act 3, sc. 4, l. [185]; see **Browning**
   159:2, **Nashe** 557:19

3   The little dogs and all,
   Tray, Blanch, and Sweet-heart, see, they bark at
   me.
   King Lear (1605–6) act 3, sc. 6, l. [65]

4 I am tied to the stake, and I must stand the course.
   King Lear (1605–6) act 3, sc. 7, l. [54]

5   Out, vile jelly!
   Where is thy lustre now?
   King Lear (1605–6) act 3, sc. 7, l. [83]

6 The lowest and most dejected thing of fortune,
   Stands still in esperance, lives not in fear:
   The lamentable change is from the best;
   The worst returns to laughter.
   King Lear (1605–6) act 4, sc. 1, l. 3

7   The worst is not,
   So long as we can say, 'This is the worst.'
   King Lear (1605–6) act 4, sc. 1, l. 27

8 As flies to wanton boys, are we to the gods;
   They kill us for their sport.
   King Lear (1605–6) act 4, sc. 1, l. 36

9 You are not worth the dust which the rude wind
   Blows in your face.
   King Lear (1605–6) act 4, sc. 2, l. 30

10   It is the stars,
   The stars above us, govern our conditions.
   King Lear (1605–6) act 4, sc. 3, l. [34]

11 Crowned with rank fumitor and furrow weeds,
   With burdocks, hemlock, nettles, cuckoo-flowers,
   Darnel, and all the idle weeds that grow
   In our sustaining corn.
   King Lear (1605–6) act 4, sc. 4, l. 3

12   How fearful
   And dizzy 'tis to cast one's eyes so low!
   The crows and choughs that wing the midway air
   Show scarce so gross as beetles; half-way down
   Hangs one that gathers samphire, dreadful trade!
   Methinks he seems no bigger than his head.
   The fishermen that walk upon the beach
   Appear like mice.
   King Lear (1605–6) act 4, sc. 6, l. 12

13 GLOUCESTER: Is't not the king?
   LEAR: Ay, every inch a king.
   King Lear (1605–6) act 4, sc. 6, l. [110]

14   Die: die for adultery! No:
   The wren goes to't, and the small gilded fly
   Does lecher in my sight.
   Let copulation thrive.
   King Lear (1605–6) act 4, sc. 6, l. [115]

15 LEAR: But to the girdle do the Gods inherit,
   Beneath is all the fiends':
   There's hell, there's darkness, there is the
   sulphurous pit,

Burning, scalding, stench, consumption; fie, fie,
fie! pah, pah! Give me an ounce of civet, good
apothecary, to sweeten my imagination; there's
money for thee.
GLOUCESTER: O! let me kiss that hand!
LEAR: Let me wipe it first; it smells of mortality.
GLOUCESTER: O ruined piece of nature! This great
world
Should so wear out to nought.
   King Lear (1605–6) act 4, sc. 6, l. [129]

16 A man may see how this world goes with no eyes.
   Look with thine ears: see how yond justice rails
   upon yond simple thief. Hark, in thine ear: change
   places; and, handy-dandy, which is the justice,
   which is the thief?
   King Lear (1605–6) act 4, sc. 6, l. [154]

17 Thou rascal beadle, hold thy bloody hand!
   Why dost thou lash that whore? Strip thine own
   back;
   Thou hotly lust'st to use her in that kind
   For which thou whipp'st her.
   King Lear (1605–6) act 4, sc. 6, l. 158

18   Get thee glass eyes;
   And, like a scurvy politician, seem
   To see the things thou dost not.
   King Lear (1605–6) act 4, sc. 6, l. [175]

19 When we are born we cry that we are come
   To this great stage of fools.
   King Lear (1605–6) act 4, sc. 6, l. [187]

20   Mine enemy's dog,
   Though he had bit me, should have stood that
   night
   Against my fire.
   King Lear (1605–6) act 4, sc. 7, l. 36

21 Thou art a soul in bliss; but I am bound
   Upon a wheel of fire.
   King Lear (1605–6) act 4, sc. 7, l. 46

22 I am a very foolish, fond old man,
   Fourscore and upward, not an hour more or less;
   And, to deal plainly,
   I fear I am not in my perfect mind.
   King Lear (1605–6) act 4, sc. 7, l. 60

23   Men must endure
   Their going hence, even as their coming hither:
   Ripeness is all.
   King Lear (1605–6) act 5, sc. 2, l. 9

24   Come, let's away to prison;
   We two alone will sing like birds i' the cage:
   When thou dost ask me blessing, I'll kneel down,
   And ask of thee forgiveness: and we'll live
   And pray, and sing, and tell old tales, and laugh
   At gilded butterflies.
   King Lear (1605–6) act 5, sc. 3, l. 8; see **Webster** 826:11

25 Talk of court news; and we'll talk with them too,
   Who loses, and who wins; who's in, who's out;
   And take upon 's the mystery of things,
   As if we were God's spies; and we'll wear out,
   In a walled prison, packs and sets of great ones
   That ebb and flow by the moon.
   King Lear (1605–6) act 5, sc. 3, l. 14

1 Upon such sacrifices, my Cordelia,
The gods themselves throw incense.
King Lear (1605–6) act 5, sc. 3, l. 20

2 The gods are just, and of our pleasant vices
Make instruments to plague us.
King Lear (1605–6) act 5, sc. 3, l. [172]

3 The wheel is come full circle.
King Lear (1605–6) act 5, sc. 3, l. [176]

4 Howl, howl, howl, howl! O! you are men of
stones:
Had I your tongue and eyes, I'd use them so
That heaven's vaults should crack. She's gone for
ever!
King Lear (1605–6) act 5, sc. 3, l. [259]

5 KENT: Is this the promised end?
EDGAR: Or image of that horror?
ALBANY: Fall and cease?
King Lear (1605–6) act 5, sc. 3, l. [265]

6   Her voice was ever soft,
Gentle and low, an excellent thing in woman.
King Lear (1605–6) act 5, sc. 3, l. [274]

7 And my poor fool is hanged! No, no, no life!
Why should a dog, a horse, a rat, have life,
And thou no breath at all? Thou'lt come no more,
Never, never, never, never, never!
Pray you, undo this button.
King Lear (1605–6) act 5, sc. 3, l. [307]

8 Vex not his ghost: O! let him pass; he hates him
That would upon the rack of this tough world
Stretch him out longer.
King Lear (1605–6) act 5, sc. 3, l. [314]

9 The oldest hath borne most: we that are young,
Shall never see so much, nor live so long.
King Lear (1605–6) act 5, sc. 3, l. [327]

LOVE'S LABOUR'S LOST

10 Cormorant devouring Time.
Love's Labour's Lost (1595) act 1, sc. 1, l. 4

11 At Christmas I no more desire a rose
Than wish a snow in May's new-fangled mirth;
But like of each thing that in season grows.
Love's Labour's Lost (1595) act 1, sc. 1, l. 105

12 Assist me some extemporal god of rime, for I am
sure I shall turn sonneter. Devise, wit; write, pen;
for I am for whole volumes in folio.
Love's Labour's Lost (1595) act 1, sc. 2, l. [192]

13 Warble, child; make passionate my sense of
hearing.
Love's Labour's Lost (1595) act 3, sc. 1, l. 1

14 This wimpled, whining, purblind, wayward boy,
This senior-junior, giant-dwarf, Dan Cupid.
Love's Labour's Lost (1595) act 3, sc. 1, l. [189]

15 A wightly wanton with a velvet brow,
With two pitch balls stuck in her face for eyes.
Love's Labour's Lost (1595) act 3, sc. 1, l. [206]

16 He hath not fed of the dainties that are bred in a
book; he hath not eat paper, as it were; he hath
not drunk ink.
Love's Labour's Lost (1595) act 4, sc. 2, l. [25]

17 Old Mantuan! old Mantuan! Who understandeth
thee not, loves thee not.
Love's Labour's Lost (1595) act 4, sc. 2, l. [102]

18 From women's eyes this doctrine I derive:
They are the ground, the books, the academes,
From whence doth spring the true Promethean
fire.
Love's Labour's Lost (1595) act 4, sc. 3, l. [302]; see
Shakespeare 702:20

19 For valour, is not love a Hercules,
Still climbing trees in the Hesperides?
Love's Labour's Lost (1595) act 4, sc. 3, l. [340]

20 From women's eyes this doctrine I derive:
They sparkle still the right Promethean fire;
They are the books, the arts, the academes,
That show, contain, and nourish all the world.
Love's Labour's Lost (1595) act 4, sc. 3, l. [350]; see
Shakespeare 702:18

21 They have been at a great feast of languages, and
stolen the scraps.
Love's Labour's Lost (1595) act 5, sc. 1, l. [39]

22 Taffeta phrases, silken terms precise.
Love's Labour's Lost (1595) act 5, sc. 2, l. 407

23 Henceforth my wooing mind shall be expressed
In russet yeas and honest kersey noes.
Love's Labour's Lost (1595) act 5, sc. 2, l. 413

24 A jest's prosperity lies in the ear
Of him that hears it, never in the tongue
Of him that makes it.
Love's Labour's Lost (1595) act 5, sc. 2, l. [869]

25 When daisies pied and violets blue
And lady-smocks all silver-white
And cuckoo-buds of yellow hue
Do paint the meadows with delight,
The cuckoo then, on every tree,
Mocks married men.
Love's Labour's Lost (1595) act 5, sc. 2, l. [902]

26 When icicles hang by the wall,
And Dick the shepherd, blows his nail,
And Tom bears logs into the hall,
And milk comes frozen home in pail,
When blood is nipped and ways be foul,
Then nightly sings the staring owl,
Tu-who;
Tu-whit, tu-who—a merry note,
While greasy Joan doth keel the pot.
Love's Labour's Lost (1595) act 5, sc. 2, l. [920]

27 The words of Mercury are harsh after the songs of
Apollo. You, that way: we, this way.
Love's Labour's Lost (1595) act 5, sc. 2, l. [938]

MACBETH

28 FIRST WITCH: When shall we three meet again
In thunder, lightning, or in rain?
SECOND WITCH: When the hurly-burly's done,
When the battle's lost and won.
THIRD WITCH: That will be ere the set of sun.
FIRST WITCH: Where the place?
SECOND WITCH: Upon the heath.
THIRD WITCH: There to meet with Macbeth.
FIRST WITCH: I come, Graymalkin!

SECOND WITCH: Paddock calls.
THIRD WITCH: Anon!
Macbeth (1606) act 1, sc. 1, l. 1

1 Fair is foul, and foul is fair:
Hover through the fog and filthy air.
Macbeth (1606) act 1, sc. 1, l. 11

2 What bloody man is that?
Macbeth (1606) act 1, sc. 2, l. 1

3 Till he unseamed him from the nave to the chaps,
And fixed his head upon our battlements.
Macbeth (1606) act 1, sc. 2, l. 22

4 Bellona's bridegroom, lapped in proof,
Confronted him with self-comparisons,
Point against point, rebellious arm 'gainst arm,
Curbing his lavish spirit.
Macbeth (1606) act 1, sc. 2, l. 55

5 A sailor's wife had chestnuts in her lap,
And munched, and munched, and munched:
'Give me,' quoth I:
'Aroint thee, witch!' the rump-fed ronyon cries.
Her husband's to Aleppo gone, master o' the
Tiger:
But in a sieve I'll thither sail,
And, like a rat without a tail,
I'll do, I'll do, and I'll do.
Macbeth (1606) act 1, sc. 3, l. 4

6 Sleep shall neither night nor day
Hang upon his pent-house lid.
He shall live a man forbid.
Weary se'nnights nine times nine
Shall he dwindle, peak, and pine:
Though his bark cannot be lost,
Yet it shall be tempest-tost.
Macbeth (1606) act 1, sc. 3, l. 19

7 The weird sisters, hand in hand,
Posters of the sea and land,
Thus do go about, about.
Macbeth (1606) act 1, sc. 3, l. 32

8 So foul and fair a day I have not seen.
Macbeth (1606) act 1, sc. 3, l. 38

9 What are these,
So withered, and so wild in their attire,
That look not like th' inhabitants o' the earth,
And yet are on 't?
Macbeth (1606) act 1, sc. 3, l. 39

10 If you can look into the seeds of time,
And say which grain will grow and which will
not,
Speak then to me, who neither beg nor fear
Your favours nor your hate.
Macbeth (1606) act 1, sc. 3, l. 58

11 Say, from whence
You owe this strange intelligence? or why
Upon this blasted heath you stop our way
With such prophetic greeting?
Macbeth (1606) act 1, sc. 3, l. 72

12 Or have we eaten on the insane root
That takes the reason prisoner?
Macbeth (1606) act 1, sc. 3, l. 84

13 What! can the devil speak true?
Macbeth (1606) act 1, sc. 3, l. 107

14 Two truths are told,
As happy prologues to the swelling act
Of the imperial theme.
Macbeth (1606) act 1, sc. 3, l. 127

15 Present fears
Are less than horrible imaginings;
My thought, whose murder yet is but fantastical,
Shakes so my single state of man that function
Is smothered in surmise, and nothing is
But what is not.
Macbeth (1606) act 1, sc. 3, l. 137

16 Come what come may,
Time and the hour runs through the roughest
day.
Macbeth (1606) act 1, sc. 3, l. 146

17 MALCOLM: Nothing in his life
Became him like the leaving it: he died
As one that had been studied in his death
To throw away the dearest thing he owed
As 'twere a careless trifle.
DUNCAN: There's no art
To find the mind's construction in the face;
He was a gentleman on whom I built
An absolute trust.
Macbeth (1606) act 1, sc. 4, l. 7

18 Glamis thou art, and Cawdor; and shalt be
What thou art promised. Yet I do fear thy nature;
It is too full o' the milk of human kindness
To catch the nearest way; thou wouldst be great,
Art not without ambition; but without
The illness should attend it; what thou wouldst
highly,
That thou wouldst holily; wouldst not play false,
And yet wouldst wrongly win.
Macbeth (1606) act 1, sc. 5, l. [16]

19 The raven himself is hoarse
That croaks the fatal entrance of Duncan
Under my battlements. Come, you spirits
That tend on mortal thoughts! unsex me here,
And fill me from the crown to the toe top full
Of direst cruelty; make thick my blood,
Stop up the access and passage to remorse,
That no compunctious visitings of nature
Shake my fell purpose.
Macbeth (1606) act 1, sc. 5, l. [38]

20 Come to my woman's breasts,
And take my milk for gall, you murdering
ministers.
Macbeth (1606) act 1, sc. 5, l. [47]

21 Come, thick night,
And pall thee in the dunnest smoke of hell,
That my keen knife see not the wound it makes,
Nor heaven peep through the blanket of the dark,
To cry 'Hold, hold!'
Macbeth (1606) act 1, sc. 5, l. [50]

22 Your face, my thane, is as a book where men
May read strange matters. To beguile the time,
Look like the time; bear welcome in your eye,
Your hand, your tongue: look like the innocent
flower,

But be the serpent under't.
Macbeth (1606) act 1, sc. 5, l. [63]

1 This castle hath a pleasant seat; the air
Nimbly and sweetly recommends itself
Unto our gentle senses.
Macbeth (1606) act 1, sc. 6, l. 1

2   This guest of summer,
The temple-haunting martlet, does approve
By his loved mansionry that the heaven's breath
Smells wooingly here: no jutty, frieze,
Buttress, nor coign of vantage, but this bird
Hath made his pendent bed and procreant cradle.
Macbeth (1606) act 1, sc. 6, l. 3

3 If it were done when 'tis done, then 'twere well
It were done quickly: if the assassination
Could trammel up the consequence, and catch
With his surcease success; that but this blow
Might be the be-all and the end-all here,
But here, upon this bank and shoal of time,
We'd jump the life to come.
Macbeth (1606) act 1, sc. 7, l. 1

4   We but teach
Bloody instructions, which, being taught, return,
To plague the inventor.
Macbeth (1606) act 1, sc. 7, l. 8

5   Besides, this Duncan
Hath borne his faculties so meek, hath been
So clear in his great office, that his virtues
Will plead like angels trumpet-tongued, against
The deep damnation of his taking-off.
Macbeth (1606) act 1, sc. 7, l. 16

6 And pity, like a naked new-born babe,
Striding the blast, or heaven's cherubim, horsed
Upon the sightless couriers of the air,
Shall blow the horrid deed in every eye,
That tears shall drown the wind.
Macbeth (1606) act 1, sc. 7, l. 21

7   I have no spur
To prick the sides of my intent, but only
Vaulting ambition, which o'erleaps itself,
And falls on the other.
Macbeth (1606) act 1, sc. 7, l. 25

8 We will proceed no further in this business:
He hath honoured me of late; and I have bought
Golden opinions from all sorts of people.
Macbeth (1606) act 1, sc. 7, l. 31

9   Was the hope drunk,
Wherein you dressed yourself? hath it slept since,
And wakes it now, to look so green and pale
At what it did so freely? From this time
Such I account thy love.
Macbeth (1606) act 1, sc. 7, l. 35

10 Letting 'I dare not' wait upon 'I would,'
Like the poor cat i' the adage?
Macbeth (1606) act 1, sc. 7, l. 44

11 I dare do all that may become a man;
Who dares do more is none.
Macbeth (1606) act 1, sc. 7, l. 46

12 LADY MACBETH: I have given suck, and know
How tender 'tis to love the babe that milks me:

I would, while it was smiling in my face,
Have plucked my nipple from his boneless gums,
And dash'd the brains out, had I so sworn as you
Have done to this.
MACBETH: If we should fail,—
LADY MACBETH: We fail!
But screw your courage to the sticking-place,
And we'll not fail.
Macbeth (1606) act 1, sc. 7, l. 54

13   Bring forth men-children only;
For thy undaunted mettle should compose
Nothing but males.
Macbeth (1606) act 1, sc. 7, l. 72

14 False face must hide what the false heart doth
know.
Macbeth (1606) act 1, sc. 7, l. 82

15   There's husbandry in heaven;
Their candles are all out.
Macbeth (1606) act 2, sc. 1, l. 4

16 Is this a dagger which I see before me,
The handle toward my hand? Come, let me clutch
thee:
I have thee not, and yet I see thee still.
Art thou not, fatal vision, sensible
To feeling as to sight? or art thou but
A dagger of the mind, a false creation,
Proceeding from the heat-oppressed brain?
Macbeth (1606) act 2, sc. 1, l. 33

17   Witchcraft celebrates
Pale Hecate's offerings; and withered murder,
Alarumed by his sentinel, the wolf,
Whose howl's his watch, thus with his stealthy
pace,
With Tarquin's ravishing strides, toward his
design
Moves like a ghost.
Macbeth (1606) act 2, sc. 1, l. 49

18   The bell invites me.
Hear it not, Duncan; for it is a knell
That summons thee to heaven or to hell.
Macbeth (1606) act 2, sc. 1, l. 62

19 That which hath made them drunk hath made me
bold,
What hath quenched them hath given me fire.
Macbeth (1606) act 2, sc. 2, l. 1

20 It was the owl that shrieked, the fatal bellman,
Which gives the stern'st good-night.
Macbeth (1606) act 2, sc. 2, l. 4

21   The attempt and not the deed,
Confounds us.
Macbeth (1606) act 2, sc. 2, l. 12

22   Had he not resembled
My father as he slept I had done't.
Macbeth (1606) act 2, sc. 2, l. 14

23 . . . Wherefore could not I pronounce 'Amen'?
I had most need of blessing, and 'Amen'
Stuck in my throat.
Macbeth (1606) act 2, sc. 2, l. 32

24 Methought I heard a voice cry, 'Sleep no more!
Macbeth does murder sleep,' the innocent sleep,

Sleep that knits up the ravelled sleave of care,
The death of each day's life, sore labour's bath,
Balm of hurt minds, great nature's second course,
Chief nourisher in life's feast.
  Macbeth (1606) act 2, sc. 2, l. 36

1 Glamis hath murdered sleep, and therefore
    Cawdor
Shall sleep no more, Macbeth shall sleep no more!
  Macbeth (1606) act 2, sc. 2, l. 43

2 MACBETH: I am afraid to think what I have done;
Look on't again I dare not.
LADY MACBETH: Infirm of purpose!
Give me the daggers. The sleeping and the dead
Are but as pictures; 'tis the eye of childhood
That fears a painted devil.
If he do bleed
I'll gild the faces of the grooms withal;
For it must seem their guilt.
  Macbeth (1606) act 2, sc. 2, l. 53

3 Will all great Neptune's ocean wash this blood
Clean from my hand? No, this my hand will rather
The multitudinous seas incarnadine,
Making the green one red.
  Macbeth (1606) act 2, sc. 2, l. 61

4 A little water clears us of this deed.
  Macbeth (1606) act 2, sc. 2, l. 68

5 Here's a knocking, indeed! If a man were porter of
hell-gate he should have old turning the key.
Knock, knock, knock! Who's there i' the name of
Beelzebub? Here's a farmer that hanged himself on
the expectation of plenty.
  Macbeth (1606) act 2, sc. 3, l. 1

6 This place is too cold for hell. I'll devil-porter it no
further: I had thought to have let in some of all
professions, that go the primrose way to the
everlasting bonfire.
  Macbeth (1606) act 2, sc. 3, l. [19]; see **Shakespeare**
  678:11

7 PORTER: Drink, sir, is a great provoker of three
    things.
MACDUFF: What three things does drink especially
    provoke?
PORTER: Marry, sir, nose-painting, sleep, and
    urine. Lechery, sir, it provokes, and
    unprovokes; it provokes the desire, but it takes
    away the performance.
  Macbeth (1606) act 2, sc. 3, l. [28]

8 The labour we delight in physics pain.
  Macbeth (1606) act 2, sc. 3, l. [56]

9 The night has been unruly: where we lay
Our chimneys were blown down; and, as they
    say,
Lamentings heard i' the air; strange screams of
    death,
And prophesying with accents terrible
Of dire combustion and confused events
New-hatched to the woeful time. The obscure bird
Clamoured the live-long night: some say the earth
Was feverous and did shake.
  Macbeth (1606) act 2, sc. 3, l. [60]

10 Confusion now hath made his masterpiece!
Most sacrilegious murder hath broke ope

The Lord's anointed temple, and stole thence
The life o' the building!
  Macbeth (1606) act 2, sc. 3, l. [72]

11 Shake off this downy sleep, death's counterfeit,
And look on death itself! up, up, and see
The great doom's image!
  Macbeth (1606) act 2, sc. 3, l. [83]

12 MACDUFF: Our royal master's murdered!
LADY MACBETH: Woe, alas!
What! in our house?
  Macbeth (1606) act 2, sc. 3, l. [95]

13 Had I but died an hour before this chance,
I had lived a blessed time.
  Macbeth (1606) act 2, sc. 3, l. [98]

14   Where we are,
There's daggers in men's smiles: the near in blood,
The nearer bloody.
  Macbeth (1606) act 2, sc. 3, l. [146]

15 A falcon, towering in her pride of place,
Was by a mousing owl hawked at and killed.
  Macbeth (1606) act 2, sc. 4, l. 12

16 Thou hast it now: King, Cawdor, Glamis, all,
As the weird women promised; and, I fear,
Thou play'dst most foully for't.
  Macbeth (1606) act 3, sc. 1, l. 1

17 BANQUO: Go not my horse the better,
I must become a borrower of the night
For a dark hour or twain.
MACBETH: Fail not our feast.
  Macbeth (1606) act 3, sc. 1, l. 26

18 FIRST MURDERER: We are men, my liege.
MACBETH: Ay, in the catalogue ye go for men,
As hounds and greyhounds, mongrels, spaniels,
    curs,
Shoughs, water-rugs, and demi-wolves are clipt
All by the name of dogs.
  Macbeth (1606) act 3, sc. 1, l. 90

19 Leave no rubs nor botches in the work.
  Macbeth (1606) act 3, sc. 1, l. 134

20 LADY MACBETH: Things without all remedy
Should be without regard: what's done is done.
MACBETH: We have scotched the snake, not killed
    it:
She'll close and be herself, whilst our poor malice
Remains in danger of her former tooth.
  Macbeth (1606) act 3, sc. 2, l. 11

21   Duncan is in his grave;
After life's fitful fever he sleeps well;
Treason has done his worst: nor steel, nor poison,
Malice domestic, foreign levy, nothing,
Can touch him further.
  Macbeth (1606) act 3, sc. 2, l. 22

22   Ere the bat hath flown
His cloistered flight, ere, to black Hecate's
    summons
The shard-borne beetle with his drowsy hums
Hath rung night's yawning peal, there shall be
    done
A deed of dreadful note.
  Macbeth (1606) act 3, sc. 2, l. 40

1   Come, seeling night,
Scarf up the tender eye of pitiful day,
And with thy bloody and invisible hand,
Cancel and tear to pieces that great bond
Which keeps me pale! Light thickens, and the
     crow
Makes wing to the rooky wood;
Good things of day begin to droop and drowse,
Whiles night's black agents to their preys do
     rouse.
Macbeth (1606) act 3, sc. 2, l. 46

2 The west yet glimmers with some streaks of day:
Now spurs the lated traveller apace
To gain the timely inn.
Macbeth (1606) act 3, sc. 3, l. 5

3 But now I am cabined, cribbed, confined, bound in
To saucy doubts and fears.
Macbeth (1606) act 3, sc. 4, l. 24

4 Now good digestion wait on appetite,
And health on both!
Macbeth (1606) act 3, sc. 4, l. 38

5 Thou canst not say I did it: never shake
Thy gory locks at me.
Macbeth (1606) act 3, sc. 4, l. 50

6 What man dare, I dare;
Approach thou like the rugged Russian bear,
The armed rhinoceros or the Hyrcan tiger,
Take any shape but that, and my firm nerves
Shall never tremble.
Macbeth (1606) act 3, sc. 4, l. 99

7 Stand not upon the order of your going.
Macbeth (1606) act 3, sc. 4, l. 119

8 It will have blood, they say; blood will have blood:
Stones have been known to move and trees to
     speak;
Augurs and understood relations have
By maggot-pies and choughs and rooks brought
     forth
The secret'st man of blood.
Macbeth (1606) act 3, sc. 4, l. 122; see **Proverbs** 616:7

9   I am in blood
Stepped in so far that, should I wade no more,
Returning were as tedious as go o'er.
Macbeth (1606) act 3, sc. 4, l. 136

10 You lack the season of all natures, sleep.
Macbeth (1606) act 3, sc. 4, l. 141

11 Round about the cauldron go;
In the poisoned entrails throw.
Toad, that under cold stone
Days and nights hast thirty-one
Sweltered venom sleeping got,
Boil thou first i' the charmèd pot.
Double, double toil and trouble;
Fire burn and cauldron bubble.
Macbeth (1606) act 4, sc. 1, l. 4

12 Eye of newt, and toe of frog,
Wool of bat, and tongue of dog,
Adder's fork, and blind-worm's sting,
Lizard's leg, and howlet's wing,
For a charm of powerful trouble,

Like a hell-broth boil and bubble.
Macbeth (1606) act 4, sc. 1, l. 14

13 Liver of blaspheming Jew,
Gall of goat, and slips of yew
Slivered in the moon's eclipse,
Nose of Turk, and Tartar's lips,
Finger of birth-strangled babe
Ditch-delivered by a drab,
Make the gruel thick and slab.
Macbeth (1606) act 4, sc. 1, l. 26

14   By the pricking of my thumbs,
Something wicked this way comes.
Macbeth (1606) act 4, sc. 1, l. 44

15 MACBETH: How now, you secret, black, and
     midnight hags!
What is't you do?
WITCHES: A deed without a name.
Macbeth (1606) act 4, sc. 1, l. 48

16 Be bloody, bold, and resolute; laugh to scorn
The power of man, for none of woman born
Shall harm Macbeth.
Macbeth (1606) act 4, sc. 1, l. 79

17 But yet, I'll make assurance double sure,
And take a bond of fate.
Macbeth (1606) act 4, sc. 1, l. 83

18 Macbeth shall never vanquished be until
Great Birnam wood to high Dunsinane hill
Shall come against him.
Macbeth (1606) act 4, sc. 1, l. 92

19 His flight was madness: when our actions do not,
Our fears do make us traitors.
Macbeth (1606) act 4, sc. 2, l. 3

20   He loves us not;
He wants the natural touch.
Macbeth (1606) act 4, sc. 2, l. 8

21 SON: And must they all be hanged that swear and
     lie?
LADY MACDUFF: Every one.
SON: Who must hang them?
LADY MACDUFF: Why, the honest men.
SON: Then the liars and swearers are fools, for
     there are liars and swearers enow to beat the
     honest men and hang up them.
Macbeth (1606) act 4, sc. 2, l. [51]

22 Stands Scotland where it did?
Macbeth (1606) act 4, sc. 3, l. 164

23 Give sorrow words: the grief that does not speak
Whispers the o'er-fraught heart, and bids it break.
Macbeth (1606) act 4, sc. 3, l. 209

24 He has no children. All my pretty ones?
Did you say all? O hell-kite! All?
What! all my pretty chickens and their dam,
At one fell swoop?
Macbeth (1606) act 4, sc. 3, l. 216

25 Out, damned spot! out, I say! One; two: why
then, 'tis time to do't. Hell is murky! Fie, my lord,
fie! a soldier, and afeard? What need we fear who
knows it, when none can call our power to

account? Yet who would have thought the old
man to have had so much blood in him?
Macbeth (1606) act 5, sc. 1, l. [38]

1 The Thane of Fife had a wife: where is she now?
Macbeth (1606) act 5, sc. 1, l. [46]

2 All the perfumes of Arabia will not sweeten this
little hand.
Macbeth (1606) act 5, sc. 1, l. [56]

3 What's done cannot be undone.
Macbeth (1606) act 5, sc. 1, l. [74]

4 More needs she the divine than the physician.
Macbeth (1606) act 5, sc. 1, l. [81]

5   Now does he feel his title
Hang loose about him, like a giant's robe
Upon a dwarfish thief.
Macbeth (1606) act 5, sc. 2, l. 20

6 Bring me no more reports; let them fly all:
Till Birnam wood remove to Dunsinane
I cannot taint with fear.
Macbeth (1606) act 5, sc. 3, l. 1

7 The devil damn thee black, thou cream-faced
loon!
Where gott'st thou that goose look?
Macbeth (1606) act 5, sc. 3, l. 11

8 I have lived long enough: my way of life
Is fall'n into the sear, the yellow leaf;
And that which should accompany old age,
As honour, love, obedience, troops of friends,
I must not look to have.
Macbeth (1606) act 5, sc. 3, l. 22; see **Byron** 181:12, **Byron**
183:1

9 Canst thou not minister to a mind diseased?
Pluck from the memory a rooted sorrow,
Raze out the written troubles of the brain,
And with some sweet oblivious antidote
Cleanse the stuffed bosom of that perilous stuff
Which weighs upon the heart?
Macbeth (1606) act 5, sc. 3, l. 37

10 Throw physic to the dogs; I'll none of it.
Macbeth (1606) act 5, sc. 3, l. 47

11 The cry is still, 'They come'.
Macbeth (1606) act 5, sc. 5, l. 2

12 I have almost forgot the taste of fears.
Macbeth (1606) act 5, sc. 5, l. 9

13 I have supped full with horrors.
Macbeth (1606) act 5, sc. 5, l. 13

14 She should have died hereafter;
There would have been a time for such a word,
To-morrow, and to-morrow, and to-morrow,
Creeps in this petty pace from day to day,
To the last syllable of recorded time;
And all our yesterdays have lighted fools
The way to dusty death. Out, out, brief candle!
Life's but a walking shadow, a poor player,
That struts and frets his hour upon the stage,
And then is heard no more; it is a tale
Told by an idiot, full of sound and fury,
Signifying nothing.
Macbeth (1606) act 5, sc. 5, l. 16

15 I 'gin to be aweary of the sun,
And wish the estate o' the world were now
undone.
Ring the alarum-bell! Blow, wind! come, wrack!
At least we'll die with harness on our back.
Macbeth (1606) act 5, sc. 5, l. 49

16 I bear a charmèd life, which must not yield
To one of woman born.
Macbeth (1606) act 5, sc. 7, l. 41

17   Macduff was from his mother's womb
Untimely ripped.
Macbeth (1606) act 5, sc. 7, l. 44

18   Lay on, Macduff;
And damned be him that first cries, 'Hold,
enough!'
Macbeth (1606) act 5, sc. 7, l. 62

MEASURE FOR MEASURE

19   Now, as fond fathers,
Having bound up the threat'ning twigs of birch,
Only to stick it in their children's sight
For terror, not to use, in time the rod
Becomes more mocked than feared; so our
decrees,
Dead to infliction, to themselves are dead,
And liberty plucks justice by the nose;
The baby beats the nurse, and quite athwart
Goes all decorum.
Measure for Measure (1604) act 1, sc. 3, l. 23

20 I hold you as a thing enskyed and sainted;
By your renouncement an immortal spirit,
And to be talked with in sincerity,
As with a saint.
Measure for Measure (1604) act 1, sc. 4, l. 34

21   A man whose blood
Is very snow-broth; one who never feels
The wanton stings and motions of the sense.
Measure for Measure (1604) act 1, sc. 4, l. 57

22 We must not make a scarecrow of the law,
Setting it up to fear the birds of prey,
And let it keep one shape, till custom make it
Their perch and not their terror.
Measure for Measure (1604) act 2, sc. 1, l. 1

23 'Tis one thing to be tempted, Escalus,
Another thing to fall.
Measure for Measure (1604) act 2, sc. 1, l. 17

24 This will last out a night in Russia,
When nights are longest there.
Measure for Measure (1604) act 2, sc. 1, l. [144]

25 Condemn the fault and not the actor of it?
Measure for Measure (1604) act 2, sc. 2, l. 37

26 No ceremony that to great ones 'longs,
Not the king's crown, nor the deputed sword,
The marshal's truncheon, nor the judge's robe,
Become them with one half so good a grace
As mercy does.
Measure for Measure (1604) act 2, sc. 2, l. 59

27   O! it is excellent
To have a giant's strength, but it is tyrannous
To use it like a giant.
Measure for Measure (1604) act 2, sc. 2, l. 107

1   Man, proud man,
Drest in a little brief authority,
Most ignorant of what he's most assured,
His glassy essence, like an angry ape,
Plays such fantastic tricks before high heaven,
As make the angels weep.
Measure for Measure (1604) act 2, sc. 2, l. 117

2 That in the captain's but a choleric word,
Which in the soldier is flat blasphemy.
Measure for Measure (1604) act 2, sc. 2, l. 130

3   Is this her fault or mine?
The tempter or the tempted, who sins most?
Measure for Measure (1604) act 2, sc. 2, l. 162

4 O cunning enemy, that, to catch a saint,
With saints dost bait thy hook!
Measure for Measure (1604) act 2, sc. 2, l. 186

5   Ever till now
When men were fond, I smiled and wondered
      how.
Measure for Measure (1604) act 2, sc. 2, l. 192

6 Might there not be a charity in sin
To save this brother's life?
Measure for Measure (1604) act 2, sc. 4, l. 64

7 The miserable have no other medicine
But only hope.
Measure for Measure (1604) act 3, sc. 1, l. 2

8 Be absolute for death; either death or life
Shall thereby be the sweeter. Reason thus with
      life:
If I do lose thee, I do lose a thing
That none but fools would keep: a breath thou art.
Measure for Measure (1604) act 3, sc. 1, l. 5

9   If I must die,
I will encounter darkness as a bride,
And hug it in mine arms.
Measure for Measure (1604) act 3, sc. 1, l. 81

10 CLAUDIO: Death is a fearful thing.
ISABELLA: And shamed life a hateful.
CLAUDIO: Ay, but to die, and go we know not
      where;
To lie in cold obstruction and to rot;
This sensible warm motion to become
A kneaded clod; and the delighted spirit
To bathe in fiery floods or to reside
In thrilling region of thick-ribbèd ice.
Measure for Measure (1604) act 3, sc. 1, l. 114

11 There, at the moated grange, resides this dejected
Mariana.
Measure for Measure (1604) act 3, sc. 1, l. [279]; see
Tennyson 781:14

12 When he makes water his urine is congealed ice.
Measure for Measure (1604) act 3, sc. 2, l. [119]

13 Take, O take those lips away,
That so sweetly were forsworn;
And those eyes, the break of day,
Lights that do mislead the morn.
Measure for Measure (1604) act 4, sc. 1, l. 1

14   Music oft hath such a charm
To make bad good, and good provoke to harm.
Measure for Measure (1604) act 4, sc. 1, l. 16

15 The old fantastical Duke of dark corners.
Measure for Measure (1604) act 4, sc. 3, l. 156

16 I am a kind of burr; I shall stick.
Measure for Measure (1604) act 4, sc. 3, l. [193]

17 Haste still pays haste, and leisure answers leisure;
Like doth quit like, and Measure still for Measure.
Measure for Measure (1604) act 5, sc. 1, l. [411]

18 They say best men are moulded out of faults,
And, for the most, become much more the better
For being a little bad: so may my husband.
Measure for Measure (1604) act 5, sc. 1, l. [440]

THE MERCHANT OF VENICE

19 In sooth I know not why I am so sad:
It wearies me; you say it wearies you.
The Merchant of Venice (1596–8) act 1, sc. 1, l. 1

20 I hold the world but as the world, Gratiano;
A stage where every man must play a part,
And mine a sad one.
The Merchant of Venice (1596–8) act 1, sc. 1, l. 77

21   I am Sir Oracle,
And when I ope my lips let no dog bark!
The Merchant of Venice (1596–8) act 1, sc. 1, l. 93

22   Fish not, with this melancholy bait,
For this fool gudgeon, this opinion.
The Merchant of Venice (1596–8) act 1, sc. 1, l. 101

23 In Belmont is a lady richly left,
And she is fair, and fairer than the word,
Of wondrous virtues.
The Merchant of Venice (1596–8) act 1, sc. 1, l. [162]

24 They are as sick that surfeit with too much, as
they that starve with nothing.
The Merchant of Venice (1596–8) act 1, sc. 2, l. [5]

25 If to do were as easy as to know what were good
to do, chapels had been churches, and poor men's
cottages princes' palaces. It is a good divine that
follows his own instructions; I can easier teach
twenty what were good to be done, than be one of
the twenty to follow mine own teaching.
The Merchant of Venice (1596–8) act 1, sc. 2, l. [13]

26 God made him, and therefore let him pass for a
man.
The Merchant of Venice (1596–8) act 1, sc. 2, l. [59]

27 I think he bought his doublet in Italy, his round
hose in France, his bonnet in Germany, and his
behaviour everywhere.
The Merchant of Venice (1596–8) act 1, sc. 2, l. [78]

28 Ships are but boards, sailors but men; there be
land-rats and water-rats, land-thieves and water-
thieves.
The Merchant of Venice (1596–8) act 1, sc. 3, l. [22]

29 I will buy with you, sell with you, talk with you,
walk with you, and so following; but I will not eat
with you, drink with you, nor pray with you.
What news on the Rialto?
The Merchant of Venice (1596–8) act 1, sc. 3, l. [36]

30 He hates our sacred nation, and he rails,
Even there where merchants most do congregate,
On me, my bargains, and my well-won thrift,

Which he calls interest.
The Merchant of Venice (1596–8) act 1, sc. 3, l. [49]

1 The devil can cite Scripture for his purpose.
The Merchant of Venice (1596–8) act 1, sc. 3, l. [99]

2 Still have I borne it with a patient shrug,
For sufferance is the badge of all our tribe.
You call me misbeliever, cut-throat dog,
And spit upon my Jewish gabardine,
And all for use of that which is mine own.
The Merchant of Venice (1596–8) act 1, sc. 3, l. [110]

3 Mislike me not for my complexion,
The shadowed livery of the burnished sun,
To whom I am a neighbour and near bred.
The Merchant of Venice (1596–8) act 2, sc. 1, l. 1

4 My conscience says, 'Launcelot, budge not.'
'Budge,' says the fiend. 'Budge not,' says my
conscience. 'Conscience,' say I, 'you counsel well;'
'fiend,' say I, 'you counsel well.'
The Merchant of Venice (1596–8) act 2, sc. 2, l. [19]

5 It is a wise father that knows his own child.
The Merchant of Venice (1596–8) act 2, sc. 2, l. [83]; see
Proverbs 623:39

6 Truth will come to light; murder cannot be hid
long.
The Merchant of Venice (1596–8) act 2, sc. 2, l. [86]

7 My daughter! O my ducats! O my daughter!
The Merchant of Venice (1596–8) act 2, sc. 8, l. 15

8   Like the martlet,
Builds in the weather on the outward wall,
Even in the force and road of casualty.
The Merchant of Venice (1596–8) act 2, sc. 9, l. 28

9 The portrait of a blinking idiot.
The Merchant of Venice (1596–8) act 2, sc. 9, l. 54

10 Thus hath the candle singed the moth.
O, these deliberate fools!
The Merchant of Venice (1596–8) act 2, sc. 9, l. 79

11 The Goodwins, I think they call the place; a very
dangerous flat, and fatal, where the carcasses of
many a tall ship lie buried, as they say, if my
gossip Report be an honest woman of her word.
The Merchant of Venice (1596–8) act 3, sc. 1, l. [4]

12 Let him look to his bond.
The Merchant of Venice (1596–8) act 3, sc. 1, l. [51]

13 Hath not a Jew eyes? hath not a Jew hands,
organs, dimensions, senses, affections, passions?
The Merchant of Venice (1596–8) act 3, sc. 1, l. [63]

14 If you prick us, do we not bleed? if you tickle us,
do we not laugh? if you poison us, do we not die?
and if you wrong us, shall we not revenge?
The Merchant of Venice (1596–8) act 3, sc. 1, l. [69]

15 The villainy you teach me I will execute, and it
shall go hard but I will better the instruction.
The Merchant of Venice (1596–8) act 3, sc. 1, l. [76]

16   He makes a swan-like end,
Fading in music.
The Merchant of Venice (1596–8) act 3, sc. 2, l. 44

17 Tell me where is fancy bred.
Or in the heart or in the head?
The Merchant of Venice (1596–8) act 3, sc. 2, l. 63

18 So may the outward shows be least themselves:
The world is still deceived with ornament.
The Merchant of Venice (1596–8) act 3, sc. 2, l. 73

19 . . . An unlessoned girl, unschooled, unpractised;
Happy in this, she is not yet so old
But she may learn; happier than this,
She is not bred so dull but she can learn.
The Merchant of Venice (1596–8) act 3, sc. 2, l. 160

20 I will have my bond.
The Merchant of Venice (1596–8) act 3, sc. 3, l. 17

21 I pray thee, understand a plain man in his plain
meaning.
The Merchant of Venice (1596–8) act 3, sc. 5, l. [63]

22 I am not bound to please thee with my answer.
The Merchant of Venice (1596–8) act 4, sc. 1, l. 65

23 I am a tainted wether of the flock,
Meetest for death: the weakest kind of fruit
Drops earliest to the ground.
The Merchant of Venice (1596–8) act 4, sc. 1, l. 114

24 I never knew so young a body with so old a head.
The Merchant of Venice (1596–8) act 4, sc. 1, l. [163]

25 The quality of mercy is not strained,
It droppeth as the gentle rain from heaven
Upon the place beneath: it is twice blessed;
It blesseth him that gives and him that takes:
'Tis mightiest in the mightiest: it becomes
The thronèd monarch better than his crown.
The Merchant of Venice (1596–8) act 4, sc. 1, l. [182]

26 Though justice be thy plea, consider this,
That in the course of justice none of us
Should see salvation: we do pray for mercy,
And that same prayer doth teach us all to render
The deeds of mercy.
The Merchant of Venice (1596–8) act 4, sc. 1, l. [197]

27 My deeds upon my head! I crave the law.
The Merchant of Venice (1596–8) act 4, sc. 1, l. [206]

28 Wrest once the law to your authority:
To do a great right, do a little wrong.
The Merchant of Venice (1596–8) act 4, sc. 1, l. [215]

29 A Daniel come to judgement! yea, a Daniel!
The Merchant of Venice (1596–8) act 4, sc. 1, l. [223]

30 Now, infidel, I have you on the hip.
The Merchant of Venice (1596–8) act 4, sc. 1, l. [229]

31 The court awards it, and the law doth give it.
The Merchant of Venice (1596–8) act 4, sc. 1, l. [301]

32 Nay, take my life and all; pardon not that:
You take my house when you do take the prop
That doth sustain my house; you take my life
When you do take the means whereby I live.
The Merchant of Venice (1596–8) act 4, sc. 1, l. [375]

33 He is well paid that is well satisfied.
The Merchant of Venice (1596–8) act 4, sc. 1, l. [416]

34 You taught me first to beg, and now methinks
You teach me how a beggar should be answered.
The Merchant of Venice (1596–8) act 4, sc. 1, l. [440]

35 The moon shines bright: in such a night as this
. . .

Troilus methinks mounted the Troyan walls,
And sighed his soul toward the Grecian tents,
Where Cressid lay that night.
The Merchant of Venice (1596–8) act 5, sc. 1, l. 1

1   In such a night
Stood Dido with a willow in her hand
Upon the wild sea-banks, and waft her love
To come again to Carthage.
The Merchant of Venice (1596–8) act 5, sc. 1, l. 9

2 How sweet the moonlight sleeps upon this bank!
Here will we sit, and let the sounds of music
Creep in our ears; soft stillness and the night
Become the touches of sweet harmony.
The Merchant of Venice (1596–8) act 5, sc. 1, l. 54

3   Look, how the floor of heaven
Is thick inlaid with patines of bright gold.
The Merchant of Venice (1596–8) act 5, sc. 1, l. 58

4 I am never merry when I hear sweet music.
The Merchant of Venice (1596–8) act 5, sc. 1, l. 69

5 The man that hath no music in himself,
Nor is not moved with concord of sweet sounds,
Is fit for treasons, stratagems, and spoils.
The Merchant of Venice (1596–8) act 5, sc. 1, l. 79

6 How far that little candle throws his beams!
So shines a good deed in a naughty world.
The Merchant of Venice (1596–8) act 5, sc. 1, l. 90

7 The nightingale, if she should sing by day,
When every goose is cackling, would be thought
No better a musician than the wren.
How many things by season seasoned are
To their right praise and true perfection!
The Merchant of Venice (1596–8) act 5, sc. 1, l. 104

8 These blessed candles of the night.
The Merchant of Venice (1596–8) act 5, sc. 1, l. 220

THE MERRY WIVES OF WINDSOR

9 I will make a Star-Chamber matter of it.
The Merry Wives of Windsor (1597) act 1, sc. 1, l. 1

10 She has brown hair, and speaks small like a
woman.
The Merry Wives of Windsor (1597) act 1, sc. 1, l. [48]

11 Here will be an old abusing of God's patience, and
the king's English.
The Merry Wives of Windsor (1597) act 1, sc. 4, l. [5]

12 We burn daylight.
The Merry Wives of Windsor (1597) act 2, sc. 1, l. [54]

13 Why, then the world's mine oyster,
Which I with sword will open.
The Merry Wives of Windsor (1597) act 2, sc. 2, l. 2

14 There is divinity in odd numbers, either in
nativity, chance or death.
The Merry Wives of Windsor (1597) act 5, sc. 1, l. 3

A MIDSUMMER NIGHT'S DREAM

15 To live a barren sister all your life,
Chanting faint hymns to the cold fruitless moon.
A Midsummer Night's Dream (1595–6) act 1, sc. 1, l. 72

16 But earthlier happy is the rose distilled,
Than that which withering on the virgin thorn

Grows, lives, and dies, in single blessedness.
A Midsummer Night's Dream (1595–6) act 1, sc. 1, l. 76

17 The course of true love never did run smooth.
A Midsummer Night's Dream (1595–6) act 1, sc. 1, l. 134

18 So quick bright things come to confusion.
A Midsummer Night's Dream (1595–6) act 1, sc. 1, l. 149

19 Love looks not with the eyes, but with the mind,
And therefore is winged Cupid painted blind.
A Midsummer Night's Dream (1595–6) act 1, sc. 1, l. 234

20 The most lamentable comedy, and most cruel
death of Pyramus and Thisby.
A Midsummer Night's Dream (1595–6) act 1, sc. 2, l. [11]

21 I could play Ercles rarely, or a part to tear a cat in,
to make all split.
A Midsummer Night's Dream (1595–6) act 1, sc. 2, l. [31]

22 This is Ercles' vein, a tyrant's vein.
A Midsummer Night's Dream (1595–6) act 1, sc. 2, l. [43]

23 Nay, faith, let me not play a woman; I have a
beard coming.
A Midsummer Night's Dream (1595–6) act 1, sc. 2, l. [50]

24 I will roar you as gently as any sucking dove; I
will roar you as 'twere any nightingale.
A Midsummer Night's Dream (1595–6) act 1, sc. 2, l. [85]

25 Pyramus is a sweet-faced man; a proper man, as
one shall see in a summer's day.
A Midsummer Night's Dream (1595–6) act 1, sc. 2, l. [89]

26 Hold, or cut bow-strings.
A Midsummer Night's Dream (1595–6) act 1, sc. 2, l. [115]

27 PUCK: How now, spirit! whither wander you?
FAIRY: Over hill, over dale,
Thorough bush, thorough brier,
Over park, over pale,
Thorough flood, thorough fire,
I do wander everywhere,
Swifter than the moone's sphere;
And I serve the fairy queen.
A Midsummer Night's Dream (1595–6) act 2, sc. 1, l. 1

28 The cowslips tall her pensioners be;
In their gold coats spots you see;
Those be rubies, fairy favours,
In those freckles live their savours:
I must go seek some dew-drops here,
And hang a pearl in every cowslip's ear.
A Midsummer Night's Dream (1595–6) act 2, sc. 1, l. 10

29 The wisest aunt, telling the saddest tale.
A Midsummer Night's Dream (1595–6) act 2, sc. 1, l. 51

30 Ill met by moonlight, proud Titania.
A Midsummer Night's Dream (1595–6) act 2, sc. 1, l. 60

31 The fold stands empty in the drownèd field,
And crows are fatted with the murrion flock;
The nine men's morris is filled up with mud.
A Midsummer Night's Dream (1595–6) act 2, sc. 1, l. 96

32 Therefore the moon, the governess of floods,
Pale in her anger, washes all the air,
That rheumatic diseases do abound:
And thorough this distemperature we see
The seasons alter: hoary-headed frosts
Fall in the fresh lap of the crimson rose.
A Midsummer Night's Dream (1595–6) act 2, sc. 1, l. 103

1 Since once I sat upon a promontory,
And heard a mermaid on a dolphin's back
Uttering such dulcet and harmonious breath,
That the rude sea grew civil at her song,
And certain stars shot madly from their spheres,
To hear the sea-maid's music.
A Midsummer Night's Dream (1595–6) act 2, sc. 1, l. 149

2 And the imperial votaress passed on,
In maiden meditation, fancy-free.
Yet marked I where the bolt of Cupid fell:
It fell upon a little western flower,
Before milk-white, now purple with love's wound,
And maidens call it, Love-in-idleness.
A Midsummer Night's Dream (1595–6) act 2, sc. 1, l. 163

3 I'll put a girdle round about the earth
In forty minutes.
A Midsummer Night's Dream (1595–6) act 2, sc. 1, l. 175

4 I know a bank whereon the wild thyme blows,
Where oxlips and the nodding violet grows
Quite over-canopied with luscious woodbine,
With sweet musk-roses, and with eglantine.
A Midsummer Night's Dream (1595–6) act 2, sc. 1, l. 249

5 And there the snake throws her enamelled skin,
Weed wide enough to wrap a fairy in.
A Midsummer Night's Dream (1595–6) act 2, sc. 1, l. 255

6 You spotted snakes with double tongue,
Thorny hedge-hogs, be not seen;
Newts, and blind-worms, do no wrong;
Come not near our fairy queen.
A Midsummer Night's Dream (1595–6) act 2, sc. 2, l. 9

7 Weaving spiders come not here;
Hence you long-legged spinners, hence!
Beetles black, approach not near;
Worm nor snail, do no offence.
A Midsummer Night's Dream (1595–6) act 2, sc. 2, l. 20

8 God shield us!—a lion among ladies, is a most
dreadful thing; for there is not a more fearful wild-
fowl than your lion living.
A Midsummer Night's Dream (1595–6) act 3, sc. 1, l. [32]

9 Look in the almanack; find out moonshine, find
out moonshine.
A Midsummer Night's Dream (1595–6) act 3, sc. 1, l. [55]

10 What hempen home-spuns have we swaggering
here,
So near the cradle of the fairy queen?
A Midsummer Night's Dream (1595–6) act 3, sc. 1, l. [82]

11 Bless thee, Bottom! bless thee! thou art translated.
A Midsummer Night's Dream (1595–6) act 3, sc. 1, l. [124]

12 What angel wakes me from my flowery bed?
A Midsummer Night's Dream (1595–6) act 3, sc. 1, l. [135]

13 Out of this wood do not desire to go.
A Midsummer Night's Dream (1595–6) act 3, sc. 1, l. [159]

14 Lord, what fools these mortals be!
A Midsummer Night's Dream (1595–6) act 3, sc. 2, l. 115

15 Two lovely berries moulded on one stem;
So, with two seeming bodies, but one heart.
A Midsummer Night's Dream (1595–6) act 3, sc. 2, l. 211

16 O! when she's angry she is keen and shrewd.
She was a vixen when she went to school:

And though she be but little, she is fierce.
A Midsummer Night's Dream (1595–6) act 3, sc. 2, l. 323

17 . . . Night's swift dragons cut the clouds full fast,
And yonder shines Aurora's harbinger;
At whose approach, ghosts, wandering here and
there,
Troop home to churchyards.
A Midsummer Night's Dream (1595–6) act 3, sc. 2, l. 379

18 Cupid is a knavish lad,
Thus to make poor females mad.
A Midsummer Night's Dream (1595–6) act 3, sc. 2, l. 440

19 Jack shall have Jill;
Nought shall go ill;
The man shall have his mare again,
And all shall be well.
A Midsummer Night's Dream (1595–6) act 3, sc. 2, l. 461

20 Let us have the tongs and the bones.
A Midsummer Night's Dream (1595–6) act 4, sc. 1, l. [33]

21 Methinks I have a great desire to a bottle of hay:
good hay, sweet hay, hath no fellow.
A Midsummer Night's Dream (1595–6) act 4, sc. 1, l. [37]

22 I have an exposition of sleep come upon me.
A Midsummer Night's Dream (1595–6) act 4, sc. 1, l. [43]

23 My Oberon! what visions have I seen!
Methought I was enamoured of an ass.
A Midsummer Night's Dream (1595–6) act 4, sc. 1, l. [82]

24 I was with Hercules and Cadmus once,
When in a wood of Crete they bayed the bear
With hounds of Sparta: never did I hear . . .
So musical a discord, such sweet thunder.
A Midsummer Night's Dream (1595–6) act 4, sc. 1, l. [118]

25 I have had a dream, past the wit of man to say
what dream it was.
A Midsummer Night's Dream (1595–6) act 4, sc. 1, l. [211]

26 The eye of man hath not heard, the ear of man
hath not seen, man's hand is not able to taste, his
tongue to conceive, nor his heart to report, what
my dream was.
A Midsummer Night's Dream (1595–6) act 4, sc. 1, l. [218]

27 The lunatic, the lover, and the poet,
Are of imagination all compact.
A Midsummer Night's Dream (1595–6) act 5, sc. 1, l. 7

28   The lover, all as frantic,
Sees Helen's beauty in a brow of Egypt:
The poet's eye, in a fine frenzy rolling,
Doth glance from heaven to earth, from earth to
heaven;
And, as imagination bodies forth
The forms of things unknown, the poet's pen
Turns them to shapes, and gives to airy nothing
A local habitation and a name.
A Midsummer Night's Dream (1595–6) act 5, sc. 1, l. 10

29 Or in the night, imagining some fear,
How easy is a bush supposed a bear!
A Midsummer Night's Dream (1595–6) act 5, sc. 1, l. 21

30 Merry and tragical! tedious and brief!
That is, hot ice and wondrous strange snow.
A Midsummer Night's Dream (1595–6) act 5, sc. 1, l. 58

1   To show our simple skill,
That is the true beginning of our end.
   A Midsummer Night's Dream (1595–6) act 5, sc. 1, l. [110]

2 Whereat, with blade, with bloody blameful blade,
He bravely broached his boiling bloody breast.
   A Midsummer Night's Dream (1595–6) act 5, sc. 1, l. [148]

3 I see a voice: now will I to the chink,
To spy an I can hear my Thisby's face.
   A Midsummer Night's Dream (1595–6) act 5, sc. 1, l. [195]

4 The best in this kind are but shadows, and the
worst are no worse, if imagination amend them.
   A Midsummer Night's Dream (1595–6) act 5, sc. 1, l. [215]

5 The iron tongue of midnight hath told twelve;
Lovers, to bed; 'tis almost fairy time.
   A Midsummer Night's Dream (1595–6) act 5, sc. 1, l. [372]

6 Now the hungry lion roars,
And the wolf behowls the moon;
Whilst the heavy ploughman snores,
All with weary task fordone.
   A Midsummer Night's Dream (1595–6) act 5, sc. 2, l. 1

7   Not a mouse
Shall disturb this hallowed house:
I am sent with broom before,
To sweep the dust behind the door.
   A Midsummer Night's Dream (1595–6) act 5, sc. 2, l. 17

8 If we shadows have offended,
Think but this, and all is mended,
That you have but slumbered here
While these visions did appear.
   A Midsummer Night's Dream (1595–6) act 5, sc. 2, l. 54

MUCH ADO ABOUT NOTHING

9 He hath indeed better bettered expectation than
you must expect of me to tell you how.
   Much Ado About Nothing (1598–9) act 1, sc. 1, l. [15]

10 He is a very valiant trencher-man.
   Much Ado About Nothing (1598–9) act 1, sc. 1, l. [52]

11 I see, lady, the gentleman is not in your books.
   Much Ado About Nothing (1598–9) act 1, sc. 1, l. [79]

12 BEATRICE: I wonder that you will still be talking,
   Signior Benedick: nobody marks you.
   BENEDICK: What! my dear Lady Disdain, are you
   yet living?
   Much Ado About Nothing (1598–9) act 1, sc. 1, l. [121]

13 Lord! I could not endure a husband with a beard
on his face: I had rather lie in the woollen.
   Much Ado About Nothing (1598–9) act 2, sc. 1, l. [31]

14 Speak low, if you speak love.
   Much Ado About Nothing (1598–9) act 2, sc. 1, l. [104]

15 Friendship is constant in all other things
Save in the office and affairs of love.
   Much Ado About Nothing (1598–9) act 2, sc. 1, l. [184]

16 There was a star danced, and under that was I
born.
   Much Ado About Nothing (1598–9) act 2, sc. 1, l. [351]

17 Is it not strange, that sheeps' guts should hale
souls out of men's bodies?
   Much Ado About Nothing (1598–9) act 2, sc. 3, l. [62]

18 Sigh no more, ladies, sigh no more,
Men were deceivers ever;

One foot in sea, and one on shore,
To one thing constant never.
   Much Ado About Nothing (1598–9) act 2, sc. 3, l. [65]

19 Sits the wind in that corner?
   Much Ado About Nothing (1598–9) act 2, sc. 3, l. [108]

20 For look where Beatrice, like a lapwing, runs
Close by the ground, to hear our counsel.
   Much Ado About Nothing (1598–9) act 3, sc. 1, l. 24

21 Disdain and scorn ride sparkling in her eyes.
   Much Ado About Nothing (1598–9) act 3, sc. 1, l. 51

22 Contempt, farewell! and maiden pride, adieu!
No glory lives behind the back of such.
And, Benedick, love on; I will requite thee,
Taming my wild heart to thy loving hand.
   Much Ado About Nothing (1598–9) act 3, sc. 1, l. 109

23 He hath a heart as sound as a bell, and his tongue
is the clapper; for what his heart thinks his tongue
speaks.
   Much Ado About Nothing (1598–9) act 3, sc. 2, l. [12]

24 Well, every one can master a grief but he that has
it.
   Much Ado About Nothing (1598–9) act 3, sc. 2, l. [28]

25 Comparisons are odorous.
   Much Ado About Nothing (1598–9) act 3, sc. 5, l. [18]; see
   Proverbs 617:6

26 A good old man, sir; he will be talking: as they
say, 'when the age is in, the wit is out.'
   Much Ado About Nothing (1598–9) act 3, sc. 5, l. [36]

27 O! what men dare do! what men may do! what
men daily do, not knowing what they do!
   Much Ado About Nothing (1598–9) act 4, sc. 1, l. [19]

28 You have stayed me in a happy hour.
   Much Ado About Nothing (1598–9) act 4, sc. 1, l. [283]

29 O God, that I were a man! I would eat his heart in
the market-place.
   Much Ado About Nothing (1598–9) act 4, sc. 1, l. [311]

30 Patch grief with proverbs.
   Much Ado About Nothing (1598–9) act 5, sc. 1, l. 17

31   There was never yet philosopher
That could endure the toothache patiently.
   Much Ado About Nothing (1598–9) act 5, sc. 1, l. 35

32 What though care killed a cat, thou hast mettle
enough in thee to kill care.
   Much Ado About Nothing (1598–9) act 5, sc. 1, l. [135]; see
   Proverbs 616:24

33 No, I was not born under a rhyming planet.
   Much Ado About Nothing (1598–9) act 5, sc. 2, l. [40]

34   Look, the gentle day,
Before the wheels of Phoebus, round about
Dapples the drowsy east with spots of grey.
   Much Ado About Nothing (1598–9) act 5, sc. 3, l. 25

OTHELLO

35 But I will wear my heart upon my sleeve
For daws to peck at: I am not what I am.
   Othello (1602–4) act 1, sc. 1, l. 64

36 Even now, now, very now, an old black ram
Is tupping your white ewe.
   Othello (1602–4) act 1, sc. 1, l. 88

1 Your daughter and the Moor are now making the
beast with two backs.
Othello (1602–4) act 1, sc. 1, l. [117]

2 Though I do hate him as I do hell-pains,
Yet, for necessity of present life,
I must show out a flag and sign of love,
Which is indeed but sign.
Othello (1602–4) act 1, sc. 1, l. [155]

3 Though in the trade of war I have slain men,
Yet do I hold it very stuff o' the conscience
To do no contrived murder: I lack iniquity
Sometimes to do me service.
Othello (1602–4) act 1, sc. 2, l. 1

4 Keep up your bright swords, for the dew will rust
them.
Othello (1602–4) act 1, sc. 2, l. 59

5 The wealthy curlèd darlings of our nation.
Othello (1602–4) act 1, sc. 2, l. 67

6 Rude am I in my speech,
And little blessed with the soft phrase of peace.
Othello (1602–4) act 1, sc. 3, l. 81

7 I will a round unvarnished tale deliver
Of my whole course of love; what drugs, what
charms,
What conjuration, and what mighty magic,
For such proceeding I am charged withal,
I won his daughter.
Othello (1602–4) act 1, sc. 3, l. 90

8 Wherein I spake of most disastrous chances,
Of moving accidents by flood and field.
Othello (1602–4) act 1, sc. 3, l. 134

9 And of the Cannibals that each other eat,
The Anthropophagi, and men whose heads
Do grow beneath their shoulders.
Othello (1602–4) act 1, sc. 3, l. 143

10 My story being done,
She gave me for my pains a world of sighs:
She swore, in faith, 'twas strange, 'twas passing
strange;
'Twas pitiful, 'twas wondrous pitiful.
Othello (1602–4) act 1, sc. 3, l. 158

11 She loved me for the dangers I had passed,
And I loved her that she did pity them.
Othello (1602–4) act 1, sc. 3, l. 167

12 I do perceive here a divided duty.
Othello (1602–4) act 1, sc. 3, l. 181

13 The robbed that smiles steals something from the
thief.
Othello (1602–4) act 1, sc. 3, l. 208

14 But words are words; I never yet did hear
That the bruised heart was piercèd through the
ear.
Othello (1602–4) act 1, sc. 3, l. 218

15 The tyrant custom, most grave senators,
Hath made the flinty and steel couch of war
My thrice-driven bed of down.
Othello (1602–4) act 1, sc. 3, l. [230]

16 Hell and night
Must bring this monstrous birth to the world's
light.
Othello (1602–4) act 1, sc. 3, l. [409]

17 Our great captain's captain.
Othello (1602–4) act 2, sc. 1, l. 74

18 To suckle fools and chronicle small beer.
Othello (1602–4) act 2, sc. 1, l. 163

19 If it were now to die,
'Twere now to be most happy.
Othello (1602–4) act 2, sc. 1, l. [192]

20 A slipper and subtle knave.
Othello (1602–4) act 2, sc. 1, l. [247]

21 Make the Moor thank me, love me, and
reward me
For making him egregiously an ass
And practising upon his peace and quiet
Even to madness.
Othello (1602–4) act 2, sc. 1, l. [320]

22 Silence that dreadful bell! it frights the isle
From her propriety.
Othello (1602–4) act 2, sc. 3, l. [177]

23 O! I have lost my reputation. I have lost the
immortal part of myself, and what remains is
bestial.
Othello (1602–4) act 2, sc. 3, l. [264]

24 O! thereby hangs a tail.
Othello (1602–4) act 3, sc. 1, l. [8]

25 Excellent wretch! Perdition catch my soul
But I do love thee! and when I love thee not,
Chaos is come again.
Othello (1602–4) act 3, sc. 3, l. 90

26 Who steals my purse steals trash; 'tis something,
nothing;
'Twas mine, 'tis his, and has been slave to
thousands;
But he that filches from me my good name
Robs me of that which not enriches him,
And makes me poor indeed.
Othello (1602–4) act 3, sc. 3, l. 157

27 O! beware, my lord, of jealousy;
It is the green-eyed monster which doth mock
The meat it feeds on.
Othello (1602–4) act 3, sc. 3, l. 165

28 If I do prove her haggard,
Though that her jesses were my dear heart-
strings,
I'd whistle her off and let her down the wind,
To prey at fortune.
Othello (1602–4) act 3, sc. 3, l. 260

29 I had rather be a toad,
And live upon the vapour of a dungeon,
Than keep a corner in the thing I love
For others' uses.
Othello (1602–4) act 3, sc. 3, l. 270

30 If she be false, O! then heaven mocks itself.
I'll not believe it.
Othello (1602–4) act 3, sc. 3, l. 278

31 Trifles light as air
Are to the jealous confirmations strong

As proofs of holy writ.
Othello (1602–4) act 3, sc. 3, l. 323

1   Not poppy, nor mandragora,
Nor all the drowsy syrups of the world,
Shall ever medicine thee to that sweet sleep
Which thou owedst yesterday.
Othello (1602–4) act 3, sc. 3, l. 331

2 Farewell the tranquil mind; farewell content!
Farewell the plumèd troop and the big wars
That make ambition virtue!
Othello (1602–4) act 3, sc. 3, l. 349

3 Pride, pomp, and circumstance of glorious war!
Othello (1602–4) act 3, sc. 3, l. 355

4 Othello's occupation's gone!
Othello (1602–4) act 3, sc. 3, l. 358

5 This denoted a foregone conclusion.
Othello (1602–4) act 3, sc. 3, l. 429

6   Like to the Pontick sea,
Whose icy current and compulsive course
Ne'er feels retiring ebb, but keeps due on
To the Propontic and the Hellespont,
Even so my bloody thoughts, with violent pace,
Shall ne'er look back.
Othello (1602–4) act 3, sc. 3, l. 454

7 That handkerchief
Did an Egyptian to my mother give.
Othello (1602–4) act 3, sc. 4, l. 56

8 A sibyl, that had numbered in the world
The sun to course two hundred compasses,
In her prophetic fury sewed the work;
The worms were hallowed that did breed the silk,
And it was dyed in mummy which the skilful
Conserved of maidens' hearts.
Othello (1602–4) act 3, sc. 4, l. 71

9   O! it comes o'er my memory,
As doth the raven o'er the infected house,
Boding to all.
Othello (1602–4) act 4, sc. 1, l. 20

10 But yet the pity of it, Iago! O! Iago, the pity of it,
Iago!
Othello (1602–4) act 4, sc. 1, l. [205]

11 O well-painted passion!
Othello (1602–4) act 4, sc. 1, l. [268]

12   Is this the noble nature
Whom passion could not shake?
Othello (1602–4) act 4, sc. 1, l. [277]

13 Your mystery, your mystery; nay, dispatch.
Othello (1602–4) act 4, sc. 2, l. 29

14 Those that do teach young babes
Do it with gentle means and easy tasks;
He might have chid me so; for, in good faith,
I am a child to chiding.
Othello (1602–4) act 4, sc. 2, l. 111

15   Unkindness may do much;
And his unkindness may defeat my life,
But never taint my love.
Othello (1602–4) act 4, sc. 2, l. 159

16 The poor soul sat sighing by a sycamore tree,
Sing all a green willow;

Her hand on her bosom, her head on her knee,
Sing willow, willow, willow.
Othello (1602–4) act 4, sc. 3, l. [41]

17 Sing all a green willow must be my garland.
Othello (1602–4) act 4, sc. 3, l. [49]; see **Heywood** 387:18

18   This is the night
That either makes me or fordoes me quite.
Othello (1602–4) act 5, sc. 1, l. 128

19 It is the cause, it is the cause, my soul;
Let me not name it to you, you chaste stars!
It is the cause.
Othello (1602–4) act 5, sc. 2, l. 1

20 Put out the light, and then put out the light.
Othello (1602–4) act 5, sc. 2, l. 7

21 Kill me to-morrow; let me live to-night!
Othello (1602–4) act 5, sc. 2, l. 80

22 It is the very error of the moon;
She comes more near the earth than she was
      wont,
And makes men mad.
Othello (1602–4) act 5, sc. 2, l. 107

23   Murder's out of tune,
And sweet revenge grows harsh.
Othello (1602–4) act 5, sc. 2, l. 113

24 OTHELLO: She's like a liar gone to burning hell;
'Twas I that killed her.
EMILIA: O! the more angel she,
And you the blacker devil.
Othello (1602–4) act 5, sc. 2, l. 127

25   I will play the swan,
And die in music.
Othello (1602–4) act 5, sc. 2, l. 245

26 Here is my journey's end, here is my butt,
And very sea-mark of my utmost sail.
Othello (1602–4) act 5, sc. 2, l. 266

27   O ill-starred wench!
Pale as thy smock! when we shall meet at compt,
This look of thine will hurl my soul from heaven,
And fiends will snatch at it. Cold, cold, my girl!
Even like thy chastity.
Othello (1602–4) act 5, sc. 2, l. 271

28 Blow me about in winds! roast me in sulphur!
Wash me in steep-down gulfs of liquid fire!
O Desdemona! Desdemona! dead!
Othello (1602–4) act 5, sc. 2, l. 278

29 An honourable murderer, if you will;
For nought did I in hate, but all in honour.
Othello (1602–4) act 5, sc. 2, l. 293

30 I have done the state some service, and they know
      't;
No more of that. I pray you, in your letters,
When you shall these unlucky deeds relate,
Speak of me as I am; nothing extenuate,
Nor set down aught in malice: then, must you
      speak
Of one that loved not wisely but too well;
Of one not easily jealous, but, being wrought,
Perplexed in the extreme; of one whose hand,
Like the base Indian, threw a pearl away

Richer than all his tribe.
Othello (1602–4) act 5, sc. 2, l. 338

1 And say besides, that in Aleppo once,
Where a malignant and a turbaned Turk
Beat a Venetian and traduced the state,
I took by the throat the circumcised dog,
And smote him thus.
Othello (1602–4) act 5, sc. 2, l. 351

2 I kissed thee ere I killed thee, no way but this,
Killing myself to die upon a kiss.
Othello (1602–4) act 5, sc. 2, l. 357

PERICLES

3 THIRD FISHERMAN: Master, I marvel how the fishes
live in the sea.
FIRST FISHERMAN: Why, as men do a-land: the
great ones eat up the little ones.
Pericles (1606–8) act 2, sc. 1, l. 26; see **Sidney** 735:16

RICHARD II

4 Old John of Gaunt, time-honoured Lancaster.
Richard II (1595) act 1, sc. 1, l. 1

5 The purest treasure mortal times afford
Is spotless reputation; that away,
Men are but gilded loam or painted clay.
Richard II (1595) act 1, sc. 1, l. 177

6 We were not born to sue, but to command.
Richard II (1595) act 1, sc. 1, l. 196; see **Scott** 673:4

7 The language I have learned these forty years,
My native English, now I must forego;
And now my tongue's use is to me no more
Than an unstringèd viol or a harp.
Richard II (1595) act 1, sc. 3, l. 159

8 How long a time lies in one little word!
Four lagging winters and four wanton springs
End in a word; such is the breath of kings.
Richard II (1595) act 1, sc. 3, l. 213

9 Things sweet to taste prove in digestion sour.
Richard II (1595) act 1, sc. 3, l. 236

10 All places that the eye of heaven visits
Are to a wise man ports and happy havens.
Teach thy necessity to reason thus;
There is no virtue like necessity.
Richard II (1595) act 1, sc. 3, l. 275

11 O! who can hold a fire in his hand
By thinking on the frosty Caucasus?
Or cloy the hungry edge of appetite,
By bare imagination of a feast?
Or wallow naked in December snow
By thinking on fantastic summer's heat?
Richard II (1595) act 1, sc. 3, l. 294

12 More are men's ends marked than their lives
before:
The setting sun, and music at the close,
As the last taste of sweets, is sweetest last,
Writ in remembrance more than things long past.
Richard II (1595) act 2, sc. 1, l. 11

13 This royal throne of kings, this sceptered isle,
This earth of majesty, this seat of Mars,
This other Eden, demi-paradise,
This fortress built by Nature for herself

Against infection and the hand of war,
This happy breed of men, this little world,
This precious stone set in the silver sea.
Richard II (1595) act 2, sc. 1, l. 40

14 This blessèd plot, this earth, this realm, this
England,
This nurse, this teeming womb of royal kings,
Feared by their breed and famous by their birth,
Renownèd for their deeds as far from home,—
For Christian service and true chivalry,—
As is the sepulchre in stubborn Jewry
Of the world's ransom, blessèd Mary's Son.
Richard II (1595) act 2, sc. 1, l. 50

15 Grace me no grace, nor uncle me no uncle.
Richard II (1595) act 2, sc. 3, l. 87

16 The caterpillars of the commonwealth.
Richard II (1595) act 2, sc. 3, l. 166

17 Things past redress are now with me past care.
Richard II (1595) act 2, sc. 3, l. 171

18 Eating the bitter bread of banishment.
Richard II (1595) act 3, sc. 1, l. 21

19 Not all the water in the rough rude sea
Can wash the balm from an anointed king;
The breath of worldly men cannot depose
The deputy elected by the Lord.
For every man that Bolingbroke hath pressed
To lift shrewd steel against our golden crown,
God for his Richard hath in heavenly pay
A glorious angel; then, if angels fight,
Weak men must fall, for heaven still guards the
right.
Richard II (1595) act 3, sc. 2, l. 54

20 O! call back yesterday, bid time return.
Richard II (1595) act 3, sc. 2, l. 69

21 The worst is death, and death will have his day.
Richard II (1595) act 3, sc. 2, l. 103

22 Let's talk of graves, of worms, and epitaphs;
Make dust our paper, and with rainy eyes
Write sorrow on the bosom of the earth.
Let's choose executors, and talk of wills.
Richard II (1595) act 3, sc. 2, l. 145

23 For God's sake, let us sit upon the ground
And tell sad stories of the death of kings:
How some have been deposed, some slain in war,
Some haunted by the ghosts they have deposed,
Some poisoned by their wives, some sleeping
killed;
All murdered.
Richard II (1595) act 3, sc. 2, l. 155

24   Within the hollow crown
That rounds the mortal temples of a king
Keeps Death his court, and there the antick sits,
Scoffing his state and grinning at his pomp;
Richard II (1595) act 3, sc. 2, l. 160

25 Comes at the last, and with a little pin
Bores through his castle wall, and farewell king!
Richard II (1595) act 3, sc. 2, l. 169

26 What must the king do now? Must he submit?
The king shall do it: must he be deposed?

The king shall be contented.
Richard II (1595) act 3, sc. 3, l. 143

1 I'll give my jewels for a set of beads,
My gorgeous palace for a hermitage,
My gay apparel for an almsman's gown.
Richard II (1595) act 3, sc. 3, l. 147

2 And my large kingdom for a little grave,
A little little grave, an obscure grave.
Richard II (1595) act 3, sc. 3, l. 153

3 Go, bind thou up yon dangling apricocks.
Richard II (1595) act 3, sc. 4, l. 29

4 Old Adam's likeness, set to dress this garden.
Richard II (1595) act 3, sc. 4, l. 73

5 Here did she fall a tear; here, in this place,
I'll set a bank of rue, sour herb of grace;
Rue, even for ruth, here shortly shall be seen,
In the remembrance of a weeping queen.
Richard II (1595) act 3, sc. 4, l. 104

6 Disorder, horror, fear and mutiny
Shall here inhabit, and this land be called
The field of Golgotha and dead men's skulls.
Richard II (1595) act 4, sc. 1, l. 142

7 God save the king! Will no man say, amen?
Am I both priest and clerk? Well then, amen.
Richard II (1595) act 4, sc. 1, l. 172

8 You may my glories and my state depose,
But not my griefs; still am I king of those.
Richard II (1595) act 4, sc. 1, l. 192

9 With mine own tears I wash away my balm,
With mine own hands I give away my crown.
Richard II (1595) act 4, sc. 1, l. 207

10   This is the way
To Julius Caesar's ill-erected tower.
Richard II (1595) act 5, sc. 1, l. 1

11   I am sworn brother, sweet,
To grim Necessity, and he and I
Will keep a league till death.
Richard II (1595) act 5, sc. 1, l. 20

12 That were some love but little policy.
Richard II (1595) act 5, sc. 1, l. 84

13   Who are the violets now
That strew the green lap of the new come spring?
Richard II (1595) act 5, sc. 2, l. 46

14 I have been studying how I may compare
This prison where I live unto the world.
Richard II (1595) act 5, sc. 5, l. 1

15   How sour sweet music is,
When time is broke, and no proportion kept!
So is it in the music of men's lives.
Richard II (1595) act 5, sc. 5, l. 42

16 I wasted time, and now doth time waste me.
Richard II (1595) act 5, sc. 5, l. 49

17 Mount, mount, my soul! thy seat is up on high,
Whilst my gross flesh sinks downwards here to
die.
Richard II (1595) act 5, sc. 5, l. 112

RICHARD III

18 Now is the winter of our discontent
Made glorious summer by this sun of York.
Richard III (1591) act 1, sc. 1, l. 1; see **Newspaper
headlines** 562:24

19 Grim-visaged war hath smoothed his wrinkled
front;
And now, instead of mounting barbèd steeds,
To fright the souls of fearful adversaries,—
He capers nimbly in a lady's chamber
To the lascivious pleasing of a lute.
Richard III (1591) act 1, sc. 1, l. 9

20 But I, that am not shaped for sportive tricks,
Nor made to court an amorous looking-glass;
I, that am rudely stamped, and want love's
majesty
To strut before a wanton ambling nymph;
I, that am curtailed of this fair proportion,
Cheated of feature by dissembling nature,
Deformed, unfinished, sent before my time
Into this breathing world, scarce half made up,
And that so lamely and unfashionable
That dogs bark at me, as I halt by them.
Richard III (1591) act 1, sc. 1, l. 14

21 This weak piping time of peace.
Richard III (1591) act 1, sc. 1, l. 24

22 And therefore, since I cannot prove a lover,
To entertain these fair well-spoken days,
I am determinèd to prove a villain,
And hate the idle pleasures of these days.
Richard III (1591) act 1, sc. 1, l. 28

23 No beast so fierce but knows some touch of pity.
Richard III (1591) act 1, sc. 2, l. 71

24 Was ever woman in this humour wooed?
Was ever woman in this humour won?
I'll have her, but I will not keep her long.
Richard III (1591) act 1, sc. 2, l. 229

25 Cannot a plain man live and think no harm,
But that his simple truth must be abused
By silken, sly, insinuating Jacks?
Richard III (1591) act 1, sc. 3, l. 51

26 Since every Jack became a gentleman
There's many a gentle person made a Jack.
Richard III (1591) act 1, sc. 3, l. 72

27 And thus I clothe my naked villainy
With odd old ends stol'n forth of holy writ,
And seem a saint when most I play the devil.
Richard III (1591) act 1, sc. 3, l. 336

28 Clarence is come,—false, fleeting, perjured
Clarence.
Richard III (1591) act 1, sc. 4, l. 55

29 Woe to the land that's governed by a child!
Richard III (1591) act 2, sc. 3, l. 11; see **Bible** 86:18

30 So wise so young, they say, do never live long.
Richard III (1591) act 3, sc. 1, l. 79

31 Talk'st thou to me of 'ifs'? Thou art a traitor:
Off with his head!
Richard III (1591) act 3, sc. 4, l. 74; see **Cibber** 223:2

32 I am not in the giving vein to-day.
Richard III (1591) act 4, sc. 2, l. 115

1 The sons of Edward sleep in Abraham's bosom.
Richard III (1591) act 4, sc. 3, l. 38

2 Thou cam'st on earth to make the earth my hell.
Richard III (1591) act 4, sc. 4, l. 167

3 Harp not on that string.
Richard III (1591) act 4, sc. 4, l. 365

4 True hope is swift, and flies with swallow's wings;
Kings it makes gods, and meaner creatures kings.
Richard III (1591) act 5, sc. 2, l. 23

5 The king's name is a tower of strength.
Richard III (1591) act 5, sc. 3, l. 12

6 Give me another horse! bind up my wounds!
Have mercy, Jesu! Soft! I did but dream.
O coward conscience, how dost thou afflict me!
Richard III (1591) act 5, sc. 3, l. 178

7 I shall despair. There is no creature loves me;
And if I die, no soul will pity me:
Nay, wherefore should they, since that I myself
Find in myself no pity to myself?
Richard III (1591) act 5, sc. 3, l. 201

8 By the apostle Paul, shadows to-night
Have struck more terror to the soul of Richard
Than can the substance of ten thousand soldiers.
Richard III (1591) act 5, sc. 3, l. 217

9 Conscience is but a word that cowards use,
Devised at first to keep the strong in awe.
Richard III (1591) act 5, sc. 3, l. 310

10 A horse! a horse! my kingdom for a horse!
Richard III (1591) act 5, sc. 4, l. 7

11 Slave! I have set my life upon a cast,
And I will stand the hazard of the die.
Richard III (1591) act 5, sc. 4, l. 9

ROMEO AND JULIET

12 A pair of star-crossed lovers.
Romeo and Juliet (1595) prologue

13 The two hours' traffick of our stage.
Romeo and Juliet (1595) prologue

14 Younger than she are happy mothers made.
Romeo and Juliet (1595) act 1, sc. 2, l. 12

15 O! then, I see, Queen Mab hath been with you . . .
She is the fairies' midwife, and she comes
In shape no bigger than an agate-stone.
Romeo and Juliet (1595) act 1, sc. 4, l. 53

16 You and I are past our dancing days.
Romeo and Juliet (1595) act 1, sc. 5, l. [35]

17 O! she doth teach the torches to burn bright.
It seems she hangs upon the cheek of night
Like a rich jewel in an Ethiop's ear;
Beauty too rich for use, for earth too dear.
Romeo and Juliet (1595) act 1, sc. 5, l. [48]

18 My only love sprung from my only hate!
Too early seen unknown, and known too late!
Romeo and Juliet (1595) act 1, sc. 5, l. [142]

19 He jests at scars, that never felt a wound.
But, soft! what light through yonder window
breaks?
It is the east, and Juliet is the sun.
Romeo and Juliet (1595) act 2, sc. 2, l. 1

20 See! how she leans her cheek upon her hand:
O! that I were a glove upon that hand,
That I might touch that cheek.
Romeo and Juliet (1595) act 2, sc. 2, l. 23

21 O Romeo, Romeo! wherefore art thou Romeo?
Romeo and Juliet (1595) act 2, sc. 2, l. 33

22 What's in a name? that which we call a rose
By any other name would smell as sweet.
Romeo and Juliet (1595) act 2, sc. 2, l. 43

23 For stony limits cannot hold love out,
And what love can do that dares love attempt.
Romeo and Juliet (1595) act 2, sc. 2, l. 67

24 O! swear not by the moon, the inconstant moon,
That monthly changes in her circled orb,
Lest that thy love prove likewise variable.
Romeo and Juliet (1595) act 2, sc. 2, l. 109

25 It is too rash, too unadvised, too sudden.
Romeo and Juliet (1595) act 2, sc. 2, l. 118

26 Love goes toward love, as schoolboys from their
books;
But love from love, toward school with heavy
looks.
Romeo and Juliet (1595) act 2, sc. 2, l. 156

27 O! for a falconer's voice,
To lure this tassel-gentle back again.
Romeo and Juliet (1595) act 2, sc. 2, l. 158

28 How silver-sweet sound lovers' tongues by night,
Like softest music to attending ears!
Romeo and Juliet (1595) act 2, sc. 2, l. 165

29 Good-night, good-night! parting is such sweet
sorrow
That I shall say good-night till it be morrow.
Romeo and Juliet (1595) act 2, sc. 2, l. 184

30 O flesh, flesh, how art thou fishified!
Romeo and Juliet (1595) act 2, sc. 4, l. [41]

31 I am the very pink of courtesy.
Romeo and Juliet (1595) act 2, sc. 4, l. [63]

32 No, 'tis not so deep as a well, nor so wide as a
church door; but 'tis enough, 'twill serve.
Romeo and Juliet (1595) act 3, sc. 1, l. [100]

33 A plague o' both your houses!
Romeo and Juliet (1595) act 3, sc. 1, l. [112]

34 O! I am Fortune's fool.
Romeo and Juliet (1595) act 3, sc. 1, l. [142]

35 Gallop apace, you fiery-footed steeds,
Towards Phoebus' lodging.
Romeo and Juliet (1595) act 3, sc. 2, l. 1

36   Come, civil night,
Thou sober-suited matron, all in black.
Romeo and Juliet (1595) act 3, sc. 2, l. 10

37 Give me my Romeo: and, when he shall die,
Take him and cut him out in little stars,
And he will make the face of heaven so fine
That all the world will be in love with night,
And pay no worship to the garish sun.
Romeo and Juliet (1595) act 3, sc. 2, l. 21

38 Adversity's sweet milk, philosophy.
Romeo and Juliet (1595) act 3, sc. 3, l. 54

1 Wilt thou be gone? it is not yet near day:
It was the nightingale, and not the lark,
That pierced the fearful hollow of thine ear.
Romeo and Juliet (1595) act 3, sc. 5, l. 1

2 Night's candles are burnt out, and jocund day
Stands tiptoe on the misty mountain tops.
Romeo and Juliet (1595) act 3, sc. 5, l. 9

3 I have more care to stay than will to go.
Romeo and Juliet (1595) act 3, sc. 5, l. 23

4 Thank me no thankings, nor proud me no prouds.
Romeo and Juliet (1595) act 3, sc. 5, l. 153

5 Romeo's a dishclout to him.
Romeo and Juliet (1595) act 3, sc. 5, l. 221

6 Death lies on her like an untimely frost
Upon the sweetest flower of all the field.
Romeo and Juliet (1595) act 4, sc. 5, l. 28

7 Tempt not a desperate man.
Romeo and Juliet (1595) act 5, sc. 3, l. 59

8 How oft when men are at the point of death
Have they been merry! which their keepers call
A lightning before death.
Romeo and Juliet (1595) act 5, sc. 3, l. 88

9 Beauty's ensign yet
Is crimson in thy lips and in thy cheeks,
And death's pale flag is not advancèd there.
Romeo and Juliet (1595) act 5, sc. 3, l. 94

10 Seal with a righteous kiss
A dateless bargain to engrossing death!
Romeo and Juliet (1595) act 5, sc. 3, l. 114

THE TAMING OF THE SHREW

11 I must dance bare-foot on her wedding day,
And, for your love to her, lead apes in hell.
The Taming of the Shrew (1592) act 2, sc. 1, l. 33

12 You are called plain Kate,
And bonny Kate, and sometimes Kate the curst;
But, Kate, the prettiest Kate in Christendom;
Kate of Kate-Hall, my super-dainty Kate,
For dainties are all cates: and therefore, Kate,
Take this of me, Kate of my consolation.
The Taming of the Shrew (1592) act 2, sc. 1, l. 186

13 Kiss me Kate, we will be married o' Sunday.
The Taming of the Shrew (1592) act 2, sc. 1, l. 318

14 This is the way to kill a wife with kindness.
The Taming of the Shrew (1592) act 4, sc. 1, l. [211]

15 A woman moved is like a fountain troubled,
Muddy, ill-seeming, thick, bereft of beauty.
The Taming of the Shrew (1592) act 5, sc. 2, l. 143

16 Such duty as the subject owes the prince,
Even such a woman oweth to her husband.
The Taming of the Shrew (1592) act 5, sc. 2, l. 156

17 I am ashamed that women are so simple
To offer war where they should kneel for peace.
The Taming of the Shrew (1592) act 5, sc. 2, l. 162

THE TEMPEST

18 He hath no drowning mark upon him; his
complexion is perfect gallows.
The Tempest (1611) act 1, sc. 1, l. [33]; see **Proverbs**
623:22

19 Now would I give a thousand furlongs of sea for
an acre of barren ground.
The Tempest (1611) act 1, sc. 1, l. [70]

20 What seest thou else
In the dark backward and abysm of time?
The Tempest (1611) act 1, sc. 2, l. 49

21 My library
Was dukedom large enough.
The Tempest (1611) act 1, sc. 2, l. 109

22 The still-vexed Bermoothes.
The Tempest (1611) act 1, sc. 2, l. 229

23 As wicked dew as e'er my mother brushed
With raven's feather from unwholesome fen
Drop on you both! A southwest blow on ye,
And blister you all o'er!
The Tempest (1611) act 1, sc. 2, l. 321

24 You taught me language; and my profit on't
Is, I know how to curse: the red plague rid you,
For learning me your language!
The Tempest (1611) act 1, sc. 2, l. 363

25 I must obey; his art is of such power,
It would control my dam's god, Setebos,
And make a vassal of him.
The Tempest (1611) act 1, sc. 2, l. 372

26 Come unto these yellow sands,
And then take hands.
The Tempest (1611) act 1, sc. 2, l. 375

27 Full fathom five thy father lies;
Of his bones are coral made:
Those are pearls that were his eyes:
Nothing of him that doth fade,
But doth suffer a sea-change
Into something rich and strange.
The Tempest (1611) act 1, sc. 2, l. 394

28 He receives comfort like cold porridge.
The Tempest (1611) act 2, sc. 1, l. 10

29 What's past is prologue.
The Tempest (1611) act 2, sc. 1, l. [261]

30 A very ancient and fish-like smell.
The Tempest (1611) act 2, sc. 2, l. [27]

31 Misery acquaints a man with strange bedfellows.
The Tempest (1611) act 2, sc. 2, l. [42]

32 'Ban, 'Ban, Ca-Caliban,
Has a new master—Get a new man.
The Tempest (1611) act 2, sc. 2, l. [197]

33 Thou deboshed fish thou.
The Tempest (1611) act 3, sc. 2, l. [30]

34 Flout 'em, and scout 'em; and scout 'em, and flout
'em;
Thought is free.
The Tempest (1611) act 3, sc. 2, l. [133]

35 He that dies pays all debts.
The Tempest (1611) act 3, sc. 2, l. [143]; see **Proverbs**
617:28

36 Be not afeard: the isle is full of noises,
Sounds and sweet airs, that give delight, and hurt
not.
The Tempest (1611) act 3, sc. 2, l. [147]

1 Our revels now are ended. These our actors,
As I foretold you, were all spirits and
Are melted into air, into thin air:
And, like the baseless fabric of this vision,
The cloud-capped towers, the gorgeous palaces,
The solemn temples, the great globe itself,
Yea, all which it inherit, shall dissolve
And, like this insubstantial pageant faded,
Leave not a rack behind. We are such stuff
As dreams are made on, and our little life
Is rounded with a sleep.
The Tempest (1611) act 4, sc. 1, l. 148

2 I do begin to have bloody thoughts.
The Tempest (1611) act 4, sc. 1, l. [221]

3   To the dread rattling thunder
Have I given fire, and rifted Jove's stout oak
With his own bolt.
The Tempest (1611) act 5, sc. 1, l. 44

4   Graves at my command
Have waked their sleepers, oped, and let 'em forth
By my so potent art. But this rough magic
I here abjure.
The Tempest (1611) act 5, sc. 1, l. 48

5   I'll break my staff,
Bury it certain fathoms in the earth,
And, deeper than did ever plummet sound,
I'll drown my book.
The Tempest (1611) act 5, sc. 1, l. 54

6 Where the bee sucks, there suck I
In a cowslip's bell I lie;
There I couch when owls do cry.
On the bat's back I do fly
After summer merrily:
Merrily, merrily shall I live now
Under the blossom that hangs on the bough.
The Tempest (1611) act 5, sc. 1, l. 88

7 How beauteous mankind is! O brave new world,
That has such people in't.
The Tempest (1611) act 5, sc. 1, l. 183

TIMON OF ATHENS

8 'Tis not enough to help the feeble up,
But to support him after.
Timon of Athens (c.1607) act 1, sc. 1, l. 108

9 Men shut their doors against a setting sun.
Timon of Athens (c.1607) act 1, sc. 2, l. [152]

10 We have seen better days.
Timon of Athens (c.1607) act 4, sc. 2, l. 27

11 O! the fierce wretchedness that glory brings us.
Timon of Athens (c.1607) act 4, sc. 2, l. 30

12   The moon's an arrant thief,
And her pale fire she snatches from the sun.
Timon of Athens (c.1607) act 4, sc. 3, l. 437

13 Timon hath made his everlasting mansion
Upon the beachèd verge of the salt flood;
Who once a day with his embossèd froth
The turbulent surge shall cover.
Timon of Athens (c.1607) act 5, sc. 1, l. [220]

TITUS ANDRONICUS

14 She is a woman, therefore may be wooed;
She is a woman, therefore may be won;

She is Lavinia, therefore must be loved.
Titus Andronicus (1590) act 2, sc. 1, l. 82; see **Shakespeare** 694:13

15 Come, and take choice of all my library,
And so beguile thy sorrow.
Titus Andronicus (1590) act 4, sc. 1, l. 34

16   Both bakèd in this pie
Whereof their mother daintily hath fed,
Eating the flesh that she herself hath bred.
Titus Andronicus (1590) act 5, sc. 3, l. 59

TROILUS AND CRESSIDA

17 Things won are done; joy's soul lies in the doing.
Troilus and Cressida (1602) act 1, sc. 2, l. [311]

18 Take but degree away, untune that string,
And, hark! what discord follows.
Troilus and Cressida (1602) act 1, sc. 3, l. 109

19   We are soldiers;
And may that soldier a mere recreant prove,
That means not, hath not, or is not in love!
Troilus and Cressida (1602) act 1, sc. 3, l. 286

20 I am giddy, expectation whirls me round.
The imaginary relish is so sweet
That it enchants my sense.
Troilus and Cressida (1602) act 3, sc. 2, l. [17]

21   To be wise, and love,
Exceeds man's might.
Troilus and Cressida (1602) act 3, sc. 2, l. [163]

22 Time hath, my lord, a wallet at his back,
Wherein he puts alms for oblivion,
A great-sized monster of ingratitudes:
Those scraps are good deeds past; which are
  devoured
As fast as they are made, forgot as soon
As done.
Troilus and Cressida (1602) act 3, sc. 3, l. 145

23   Perseverance, dear my lord,
Keeps honour bright.
Troilus and Cressida (1602) act 3, sc. 3, l. 150

24 One touch of nature makes the whole world kin.
Troilus and Cressida (1602) act 3, sc. 3, l. 175

25 A plague of opinion! a man may wear it on both
sides, like a leather jerkin.
Troilus and Cressida (1602) act 3, sc. 3, l. [267]

26 What a pair of spectacles is here!
Pandarus, of the lovers
Troilus and Cressida (1602) act 4, sc. 4, l. [13]

27   Fie, fie upon her!
There's language in her eye, her cheek, her lip,
Nay, her foot speaks; her wanton spirits look out
At every joint and motive of her body.
Troilus and Cressida (1602) act 4, sc. 5, l. 54

28   The end crowns all,
And that old common arbitrator, Time,
Will one day end it.
Troilus and Cressida (1602) act 4, sc. 5, l. 223

29 Lechery, lechery; still, wars and lechery: nothing
else holds fashion.
Troilus and Cressida (1602) act 5, sc. 2, l. 192

1 Words, words, mere words, no matter from the heart.
  Troilus and Cressida (1602) act 5, sc. 3, l. [109]

2 Hector is dead; there is no more to say.
  Troilus and Cressida (1602) act 5, sc. 10, l. 22

TWELFTH NIGHT

3 If music be the food of love, play on.
  Twelfth Night (1601) act 1, sc. 1, l. 1

4 That strain again! it had a dying fall.
  Twelfth Night (1601) act 1, sc. 1, l. 4

5   Enough! no more:
  'Tis not so sweet now as it was before.
  Twelfth Night (1601) act 1, sc. 1, l. 7

6 O! when mine eyes did see Olivia first,
  Methought she purged the air of pestilence.
  Twelfth Night (1601) act 1, sc. 1, l. 19

7 And what should I do in Illyria?
  My brother he is in Elysium.
  Twelfth Night (1601) act 1, sc. 2, l. 2

8 I am a great eater of beef, and I believe that does harm to my wit.
  Twelfth Night (1601) act 1, sc. 3, l. [92]

9 I would I had bestowed that time in the tongues that I have in fencing, dancing, and bear-baiting. O! had I but followed the arts!
  Twelfth Night (1601) act 1, sc. 3, l. [99]

10 Many a good hanging prevents a bad marriage.
  Twelfth Night (1601) act 1, sc. 5, l. [20]

11 A plague o' these pickle herring!
  Twelfth Night (1601) act 1, sc. 5, l. [127]

12 He is very well-favoured, and he speaks very shrewishly: one would think his mother's milk were scarce out of him.
  Twelfth Night (1601) act 1, sc. 5, l. [170]

13 Make me a willow cabin at your gate,
  And call upon my soul within the house;
  Write loyal cantons of contemnèd love,
  And sing them loud even in the dead of night;
  Halloo your name to the reverberate hills,
  And make the babbling gossip of the air
  Cry out, 'Olivia!'
  Twelfth Night (1601) act 1, sc. 5, l. [289]

14 Not to be a-bed after midnight is to be up betimes.
  Twelfth Night (1601) act 2, sc. 3, l. 1

15 O mistress mine! where are you roaming?
  O! stay and hear; your true love's coming,
  That can sing both high and low.
  Trip no further, pretty sweeting;
  Journeys end in lovers meeting,
  Every wise man's son doth know.
  Twelfth Night (1601) act 2, sc. 3, l. [42]

16 What is love? 'tis not hereafter;
  Present mirth hath present laughter;
  What's to come is still unsure:
  In delay there lies no plenty;
  Then come kiss me, sweet and twenty,
  Youth's a stuff will not endure.
  Twelfth Night (1601) act 2, sc. 3, l. [50]

17 Am not I consanguineous? am I not of her blood?
  Twelfth Night (1601) act 2, sc. 3, l. [85]

18 He does it with a better grace, but I do it more natural.
  Twelfth Night (1601) act 2, sc. 3, l. [91]

19 Dost thou think, because thou art virtuous, there shall be no more cakes and ale?
  Twelfth Night (1601) act 2, sc. 3, l. [124]

20 My purpose is, indeed, a horse of that colour.
  Twelfth Night (1601) act 2, sc. 3, l. [184]

21 I was adored once too.
  Twelfth Night (1601) act 2, sc. 3, l. [200]

22 Now, good Cesario, but that piece of song,
  That old and antique song we heard last night.
  Twelfth Night (1601) act 2, sc. 4, l. 2

23   Let still the woman take
  An elder than herself, so wears she to him,
  So sways she level in her husband's heart.
  Twelfth Night (1601) act 2, sc. 4, l. 29

24 Then let thy love be younger than thyself,
  Or thy affection cannot hold the bent.
  Twelfth Night (1601) act 2, sc. 4, l. 36

25 The spinsters and the knitters in the sun.
  Twelfth Night (1601) act 2, sc. 4, l. 44

26 Come away, come away, death,
  And in sad cypress let me be laid;
  Fly away, fly away, breath:
  I am slain by a fair cruel maid.
  Twelfth Night (1601) act 2, sc. 4, l. 51

27 Now, the melancholy god protect thee, and the tailor make thy doublet of changeable taffeta, for thy mind is a very opal.
  Twelfth Night (1601) act 2, sc. 4, l. [74]

28 My father had a daughter loved a man,
  As it might be, perhaps, were I a woman,
  I should your lordship.
  Twelfth Night (1601) act 2, sc. 4, l. [108]

29 DUKE: And what's her history?
  VIOLA: A blank, my lord. She never told her love,
  But let concealment, like a worm i' the bud,
  Feed on her damask cheek: she pined in thought;
  And with a green and yellow melancholy,
  She sat like patience on a monument,
  Smiling at grief. Was not this love indeed?
  Twelfth Night (1601) act 2, sc. 4, l. [111]

30 I am all the daughters of my father's house,
  And all the brothers too.
  Twelfth Night (1601) act 2, sc. 4, l. [122]

31 Now is the woodcock near the gin.
  Twelfth Night (1601) act 2, sc. 5, l. [93]

32 But be not afraid of greatness: some men are born great, some achieve greatness, and some have greatness thrust upon them.
  Twelfth Night (1601) act 2, sc. 5, l. [158]; see **Heller** 380:9

33 Remember who commended thy yellow stockings, and wished to see thee ever cross-gartered.
  Twelfth Night (1601) act 2, sc. 5, l. [168]

1 Jove and my stars be praised! Here is yet a postscript.
Twelfth Night (1601) act 2, sc. 5, l. [190]

2 O! what a deal of scorn looks beautiful
In the contempt and anger of his lip.
Twelfth Night (1601) act 3, sc. 1, l. [159]

3 Love sought is good, but giv'n unsought is better.
Twelfth Night (1601) act 3, sc. 1, l. [170]

4 You are now sailed into the north of my lady's opinion; where you will hang like an icicle on a Dutchman's beard.
Twelfth Night (1601) act 3, sc. 2, l. [29]

5 As many lies as will lie in thy sheet of paper, although the sheet were big enough for the bed of Ware in England, set 'em down.
Twelfth Night (1601) act 3, sc. 2, l. [51]

6 Look, where the youngest wren of nine comes.
Twelfth Night (1601) act 3, sc. 2, l. [73]

7 He does smile his face into more lines than are in the new map with the augmentation of the Indies.
Twelfth Night (1601) act 3, sc. 2, l. [85]

8 In the south suburbs, at the Elephant,
Is best to lodge.
Twelfth Night (1601) act 3, sc. 3, l. 39

9 I think we do know the sweet Roman hand.
Twelfth Night (1601) act 3, sc. 4, l. [31]

10 Why, this is very midsummer madness.
Twelfth Night (1601) act 3, sc. 4, l. [62]

11 If this were played upon a stage now, I could condemn it as an improbable fiction.
Twelfth Night (1601) act 3, sc. 4, l. [142]

12 More matter for a May morning.
Twelfth Night (1601) act 3, sc. 4, l. [158]

13 Still you keep o' the windy side of the law.
Twelfth Night (1601) act 3, sc. 4, l. [183]

14 Nay, let me alone for swearing.
Twelfth Night (1601) act 3, sc. 4, l. [204]

15 In nature there's no blemish but the mind;
None can be called deformed but the unkind.
Twelfth Night (1601) act 3, sc. 4, l. [403]

16 Thus the whirligig of time brings in his revenges.
Twelfth Night (1601) act 5, sc. 1, l. [388]

17 I'll be revenged on the whole pack of you.
Twelfth Night (1601) act 5, sc. 1, l. [390]

18 When that I was and a little tiny boy,
With hey, ho, the wind and the rain;
A foolish thing was but a toy,
For the rain it raineth every day.
Twelfth Night (1601) act 5, sc. 1, l. [401]

THE TWO GENTLEMEN OF VERONA

19 I have no other but a woman's reason:
I think him so, because I think him so.
The Two Gentlemen of Verona (1592–3) act 1, sc. 2, l. 23

20 Fie, fie! how wayward is this foolish love
That, like a testy babe, will scratch the nurse
And presently all humbled kiss the rod!
The Two Gentlemen of Verona (1592–3) act 1, sc. 2, l. 55

21 O! how this spring of love resembleth
The uncertain glory of an April day.
The Two Gentlemen of Verona (1592–3) act 1, sc. 3, l. 84

22 Who is Silvia? what is she,
That all our swains commend her?
Holy, fair, and wise is she;
The heaven such grace did lend her.
The Two Gentlemen of Verona (1592–3) act 4, sc. 2, l. 40

23 Is she kind as she is fair?
For beauty lives with kindness.
The Two Gentlemen of Verona (1592–3) act 4, sc. 2, l. 45

THE WINTER'S TALE

24 Two lads that thought there was no more behind
But such a day to-morrow as to-day,
And to be boy eternal.
The Winter's Tale (1610–11) act 1, sc. 2, l. 63

25 But to be paddling palms and pinching fingers,
As now they are, and making practised smiles,
As in a looking-glass.
The Winter's Tale (1610–11) act 1, sc. 2, l. 116

26 A sad tale's best for winter.
I have one of sprites and goblins.
The Winter's Tale (1610–11) act 2, sc. 1, l. 24

27   There may be in the cup
A spider steeped, and one may drink, depart,
And yet partake no venom, for his knowledge
Is not infected; but if one present
Th' abhorred ingredient to his eye, make known
How he hath drunk, he cracks his gorge, his sides,
With violent hefts. I have drunk, and seen the spider.
The Winter's Tale (1610–11) act 2, sc. 1, l. 39

28 It is a heretic that makes the fire,
Not she which burns in 't.
The Winter's Tale (1610–11) act 2, sc. 3, l. 114

29 I am a feather for each wind that blows.
The Winter's Tale (1610–11) act 2, sc. 3, l. 153

30 What's gone and what's past help
Should be past grief.
The Winter's Tale (1610–11) act 3, sc. 2, l. [223]

31 Exit, pursued by a bear.
stage direction
The Winter's Tale (1610–11) act 3, sc. 3

32 When daffodils begin to peer,
With heigh! the doxy, over the dale,
Why, then comes in the sweet o' the year.
The Winter's Tale (1610–11) act 4, sc. 2, l. 1

33 While we lie tumbling in the hay.
The Winter's Tale (1610–11) act 4, sc. 2, l. 12

34 My father named me Autolycus; who being, as I am, littered under Mercury, was likewise a snapper-up of unconsidered trifles.
The Winter's Tale (1610–11) act 4, sc. 2, l. [24]

35 Jog on, jog on the foot-path way,
And merrily hent the stile-a:
A merry heart goes all the day,
Your sad tires in a mile-a.
The Winter's Tale (1610–11) act 4, sc. 2, l. [133]

1 For you there's rosemary and rue; these keep
Seeming and savour all the winter long.
The Winter's Tale (1610–11) act 4, sc. 3, l. 74

2   The fairest flowers o' the season
Are our carnations and streaked gillyvors,
Which some call nature's bastards.
The Winter's Tale (1610–11) act 4, sc. 3, l. 81

3   I'll not put
The dibble in earth to set one slip of them.
The Winter's Tale (1610–11) act 4, sc. 3, l. 99

4   Here's flowers for you;
Hot lavender, mints, savory, marjoram;
The marigold, that goes to bed wi' the sun,
And with him rises weeping.
The Winter's Tale (1610–11) act 4, sc. 3, l. 103

5   O Proserpina!
For the flowers now that frighted thou let'st fall
From Dis's waggon! daffodils,
That come before the swallow dares, and take
The winds of March with beauty.
The Winter's Tale (1610–11) act 4, sc. 3, l. 118

6   Pale prime-roses,
That die unmarried, ere they can behold
Bright Phoebus in his strength,—a malady
Most incident to maids; bold oxlips and
The crown imperial; lilies of all kinds,
The flower-de-luce being one.
The Winter's Tale (1610–11) act 4, sc. 3, l. 122

7   Each your doing,
So singular in each particular,
Crowns what you are doing in the present deed,
That all your acts are queens.
The Winter's Tale (1610–11) act 4, sc. 3, l. 144

8 The queen of curds and cream.
The Winter's Tale (1610–11) act 4, sc. 3, l. 161

9 I love a ballad in print, a-life, for then we are sure
they are true.
The Winter's Tale (1610–11) act 4, sc. 3, l. [262]

10 The self-same sun that shines upon his court
Hides not his visage from our cottage, but
Looks on alike.
The Winter's Tale (1610–11) act 4, sc. 3, l. [457]

11 Being now awake, I'll queen it no inch further,
But milk my ewes and weep.
The Winter's Tale (1610–11) act 4, sc. 3, l. [463]

12 Though I am not naturally honest, I am so
sometimes by chance.
The Winter's Tale (1610–11) act 4, sc. 3, l. [734]

13   Stars, stars!
And all eyes else dead coals.
The Winter's Tale (1610–11) act 5, sc. 1, l. 67

14   O! she's warm.
If this be magic, let it be an art
Lawful as eating.
The Winter's Tale (1610–11) act 5, sc. 3, l. 109

THE PASSIONATE PILGRIM (ATTRIBUTION DOUBTFUL)

15 Crabbed age and youth cannot live together:
Youth is full of pleasance, age is full of care.
The Passionate Pilgrim (1599) no. 12

16 Age, I do abhor thee, youth, I do adore thee.
The Passionate Pilgrim (1599) no. 12

THE RAPE OF LUCRECE

17 Beauty itself doth of itself persuade
The eyes of men without an orator.
The Rape of Lucrece (1594) l. 29

18 Time's glory is to calm contending kings,
To unmask falsehood, and bring truth to light.
The Rape of Lucrece (1594) l. 939

19 And now this pale swan in her watery nest
Begins the sad dirge of her certain ending.
The Rape of Lucrece (1594) l. 1611

SONNETS

20 To the onlie begetter of these insuing sonnets, Mr.
W. H.
also attributed to Thomas Thorpe, the publisher
Sonnets (1609) dedication

21 From fairest creatures we desire increase,
That thereby beauty's rose might never die.
Sonnet 1

22 When forty winters shall besiege thy brow,
And dig deep trenches in thy beauty's field.
Sonnet 2

23 Thou art thy mother's glass, and she in thee
Calls back the lovely April of her prime.
Sonnet 3

24 Shall I compare thee to a summer's day?
Thou art more lovely and more temperate:
Rough winds do shake the darling buds of May,
And summer's lease hath all too short a date.
Sonnet 18

25 But thy eternal summer shall not fade,
Nor lose possession of that fair thou ow'st,
Nor shall death brag thou wander'st in his shade,
When in eternal lines to time thou grow'st;
So long as men can breathe, or eyes can see,
So long lives this, and this gives life to thee.
Sonnet 18

26 As an unperfect actor on the stage,
Who with his fear is put beside his part,
Or some fierce thing replete with too much rage,
Whose strength's abundance weakens his own
heart.
Sonnet 23

27 O! let my books be then the eloquence
And dumb presagers of my speaking breast.
Sonnet 23

28 When in disgrace with fortune and men's eyes
I all alone beweep my outcast state.
Sonnet 29

29 Desiring this man's art, and that man's scope,
With what I most enjoy contented least.
Sonnet 29

30 Haply I think on thee,—and then my state,
Like to the lark at break of day arising
From sullen earth, sings hymns at heaven's gate.
Sonnet 29

1 When to the sessions of sweet silent thought
I summon up remembrance of things past.
Sonnet 30; see **Borrowed titles** 146:15

2 Full many a glorious morning have I seen
Flatter the mountain-tops with sovereign eye,
Kissing with golden face the meadows green,
Gilding pale streams with heavenly alchemy.
Sonnet 33

3 Roses have thorns, and silver fountains mud;
Clouds and eclipses stain both moon and sun,
And loathsome canker lives in sweetest bud.
Sonnet 35

4 What is your substance, whereof are you made,
That millions of strange shadows on you tend?
Sonnet 53

5 Not marble, nor the gilded monuments
Of princes, shall outlive this powerful rhyme.
Sonnet 55

6 Like as the waves make towards the pebbled
shore,
So do our minutes hasten to their end.
Sonnet 60

7 When I have seen the hungry ocean gain
Advantage on the kingdom of the shore.
Sonnet 64

8 Since brass, nor stone, nor earth, nor boundless
sea,
But sad mortality o'ersways their power,
How with this rage shall beauty hold a plea,
Whose action is no stronger than a flower?
Sonnet 65

9 No longer mourn for me when I am dead
Than you shall hear the surly sullen bell
Give warning to the world that I am fled
From this vile world, with vilest worms to dwell.
Sonnet 71

10 Bare ruined choirs, where late the sweet birds
sang.
Sonnet 73

11 So all my best is dressing old words new,
Spending again what is already spent.
Sonnet 76

12 Time's thievish progress to eternity.
Sonnet 77

13 Farewell! thou art too dear for my possessing.
Sonnet 87

14 Thus have I had thee, as a dream doth flatter,
In sleep a king, but, waking, no such matter.
Sonnet 87

15 For sweetest things turn sourest by their deeds;
Lilies that fester smell far worse than weeds.
Sonnet 94

16 When in the chronicle of wasted time
I see descriptions of the fairest wights,
And beauty making beautiful old rime,
In praise of ladies dead and lovely knights.
Sonnet 106

17 For we, which now behold these present days,
Have eyes to wonder, but lack tongues to praise.
Sonnet 106

18 Not mine own fears, nor the prophetic soul
Of the wide world dreaming on things to come.
Sonnet 107

19 And thou in this shalt find thy monument,
When tyrants' crests and tombs of brass are spent.
Sonnet 107

20 Alas! 'tis true I have gone here and there,
And made myself a motley to the view.
Sonnet 110

21 My nature is subdued
To what it works in, like the dyer's hand.
Sonnet 111

22 Let me not to the marriage of true minds
Admit impediments. Love is not love
Which alters when it alteration finds,
Or bends with the remover to remove:
O, no! it is an ever-fixèd mark,
That looks on tempests and is never shaken.
Sonnet 116

23 Love's not Time's fool.
Sonnet 116

24 Love alters not with his brief hours and weeks,
But bears it out even to the edge of doom.
If this be error, and upon me proved,
I never writ, nor no man ever loved.
Sonnet 116

25 The expense of spirit in a waste of shame
Is lust in action; and till action, lust
Is perjured, murderous, bloody, full of blame,
Savage, extreme, rude, cruel, not to trust;
Enjoyed no sooner but despisèd straight.
Sonnet 129

26 My mistress' eyes are nothing like the sun;
Coral is far more red than her lips' red:
If snow be white, why then her breasts are dun;
If hairs be wires, black wires grow on her head.
Sonnet 130

27 And yet, by heaven, I think my love as rare
As any she belied with false compare.
Sonnet 130

28 Whoever hath her wish, thou hast thy *Will*,
And *Will* to boot, and *Will* in over-plus.
Sonnet 135

29 When my love swears that she is made of truth,
I do believe her, though I know she lies.
Sonnet 138

30 Two loves I have of comfort and despair,
Which like two spirits do suggest me still:
The better angel is a man right fair,
The worser spirit a woman, coloured ill.
Sonnet 144

31 So shalt thou feed on Death, that feeds on men,
And Death once dead, there's no more dying then.
Sonnet 146

32 For I have sworn thee fair, and thought thee
bright,

Who art as black as hell, as dark as night.
Sonnet 147

VENUS AND ADONIS

1 If the first heir of my invention prove deformed, I shall be sorry it had so noble a godfather.
Venus and Adonis (1593) dedication

2 Love is a spirit all compact of fire,
Not gross to sink, but light, and will aspire.
Venus and Adonis (1593) l. 145

3 Love comforteth like sunshine after rain.
Venus and Adonis (1593) l. 799

4 For he being dead, with him is beauty slain,
And, beauty dead, black chaos comes again.
Venus and Adonis (1593) l. 1019

5 Item, I give unto my wife my second best bed, with the furniture.
will, 1616; E. K. Chambers *William Shakespeare* (1930) vol. 2

Shammai c.1st century BC–1st century AD

Jewish scholar and teacher

6 Say little and do much. Receive all men with a cheerful countenance.
in *Talmud* Mishnah 'Pirqei Avot' 1:15

Bill Shankly 1914–81

Scottish footballer

7 Some people think football is a matter of life and death . . . I can assure them it is much more serious than that.
in *Sunday Times* 4 October 1981

Shantideva c.685–763

Indian scholar, monk, and poet

8 May I allay all the suffering of every living being. I am the medicine for the sick. May I be both the doctor and their nurse, until the sickness does not recur.
Bodhicaryāvatāra ch. 3, v. 6

9 Whoever longs to rescue quickly both himself and others should practise the supreme mystery: exchange of self and other.
Bodhicaryāvatāra ch. 8, v. 120

10 All those who suffer in the world do so because of their desire for their own happiness. All those happy in the world are so because of their desire for the happiness of others.
Bodhicaryāvatāra ch. 8, v. 129

11 Whatever suffering is in store for the world, may it all ripen in me. May the world find happiness through all the pure deeds of the Bodhisattvas.
Bodhicaryāvatāra ch. 10, v. 56

Ariel Sharon 1928–

Israeli Likud statesman, Prime Minister from 2001

12 I'm not going to make any compromise whatsoever.
on relations with the Palestinians
in *Sunday Times* 12 August 2001

George Bernard Shaw 1856–1950

Irish dramatist
on Shaw: see **Lenin** 480:9, **Wilde** 837:10; see also
Misquotations 537:12

13 All great truths begin as blasphemies.
Annajanska (1919)

14 One man that has a mind and knows it can always beat ten men who haven't and don't.
The Apple Cart (1930) act 1

15 You can always tell an old soldier by the inside of his holsters and cartridge boxes. The young ones carry pistols and cartridges; the old ones, grub.
Arms and the Man (1898) act 1

16 Oh, you are a very poor soldier—a chocolate cream soldier!
Arms and the Man (1898) act 1

17 I enjoy convalescence. It is the part that makes illness worth while.
Back to Methuselah (1921) pt. 2

18 Life is not meant to be easy, my child; but take courage: it can be delightful.
Back to Methuselah (rev. ed., 1930); see also **Fraser** 333:5

19 He [the Briton] is a barbarian, and thinks that the customs of his tribe and island are the laws of nature.
Caesar and Cleopatra (1901) act 2

20 When a stupid man is doing something he is ashamed of, he always declares that it is his duty.
Caesar and Cleopatra (1901) act 3

21 A man of great common sense and good taste, meaning thereby a man without originality or moral courage.
Notes to Caesar and Cleopatra (1901) 'Julius Caesar'

22 We have no more right to consume happiness without producing it than to consume wealth without producing it.
Candida (1898) act 1

23 Do you think that the things people make fools of themselves about are any less real and true than the things they behave sensibly about? They are more true: they are the only things that are true.
Candida (1898) act 1

24 It is easy—terribly easy— to shake a man's faith in himself. To take advantage of that to break a man's spirit is devil's work.
Candida (1898) act 1

25 I'm only a beer teetotaller, not a champagne teetotaller.
Candida (1898) act 3

26 The worst sin towards our fellow creatures is not to hate them, but to be indifferent to them: that's the essence of inhumanity.
The Devil's Disciple (1901) act 2

27 Martyrdom . . . the only way in which a man can become famous without ability.
The Devil's Disciple (1901) act 3

28 I never expect a soldier to think.
The Devil's Disciple (1901) act 3

1 SWINDON: What will history say?
BURGOYNE: History, sir, will tell lies as usual.
   The Devil's Disciple (1901) act 3

2 The British soldier can stand up to anything
except the British War Office.
   The Devil's Disciple (1901) act 3

3 There is at bottom only one genuinely scientific
treatment for all diseases, and that is to stimulate
the phagocytes.
   The Doctor's Dilemma (1911) act 1

4 All professions are conspiracies against the laity.
   The Doctor's Dilemma (1911) act 1

5 A government which robs Peter to pay Paul can
always depend on the support of Paul.
   Everybody's Political What's What? (1944) ch. 30

6 It's all that the young can do for the old, to shock
them and keep them up to date.
   Fanny's First Play (1914) 'Induction'

7 Home life as we understand it is no more natural
to us than a cage is natural to a cockatoo.
   Getting Married (1911) preface 'Hearth and Home'

8 The one point on which all women are in furious
secret rebellion against the existing law is the
saddling of the right to a child with the obligation
to become the servant of a man.
   Getting Married (1911) preface 'The Right to Motherhood'

9 Physically there is nothing to distinguish human
society from the farm-yard except that children
are more troublesome and costly than chickens
and calves, and that men and women are not so
completely enslaved as farm stock.
   Getting Married (1911) preface 'The Personal Sentimental
   Basis of Monogamy'

10 What God hath joined together no man ever shall
put asunder: God will take care of that.
   Getting Married (1911) p. 216; see **Book of Common Prayer**
   133:11

11 I am a woman of the world, Hector; and I can
assure you that if you will only take the trouble
always to do the perfectly correct thing, and to say
the perfectly correct thing, you can do just what
you like.
   Heartbreak House (1919) act 1

12 Go anywhere in England where there are natural,
wholesome, contented, and really nice English
people; and what do you always find? That the
stables are the real centre of the household.
   Heartbreak House (1919) act 3

13 The captain is in his bunk, drinking bottled ditch-
water; and the crew is gambling in the forecastle.
She will strike and sink and split. Do you think the
laws of God will be suspended in favour of England
because you were born in it?
   Heartbreak House (1919) act 3

14 You have to choose (as a voter) between trusting
to the natural stability of gold and the natural
stability of the honesty and intelligence of the
members of the Government. And, with due

respect for these gentlemen, I advise you, as long
as the Capitalist system lasts, to vote for gold.
   The Intelligent Woman's Guide to Socialism and Capitalism
   (1928) ch. 55

15 Money is indeed the most important thing in the
world; and all sound and successful personal and
national morality should have this fact for its
basis.
   The Irrational Knot (1905) preface

16 A man who has no office to go to—I don't care
who he is—is a trial of which you can have no
conception.
   The Irrational Knot (1905) ch. 18

17 John Bull's other island.
   title of play (1907)

18 An Irishman's heart is nothing but his
imagination.
   John Bull's Other Island (1907) act 1

19 What really flatters a man is that you think him
worth flattering.
   John Bull's Other Island (1907) act 4

20 There are only two qualities in the world:
efficiency and inefficiency, and only two sorts of
people: the efficient and the inefficient.
   John Bull's Other Island (1907) act 4

21 The greatest of evils and the worst of crimes is
poverty . . . our first duty—a duty to which every
other consideration should be sacrificed—is not to
be poor.
   Major Barbara (1907) preface

22 Nobody can say a word against Greek: it stamps a
man at once as an educated gentleman.
   Major Barbara (1907) act 1

23 I am a Millionaire. That is my religion.
   Major Barbara (1907) act 2

24 I can't talk religion to a man with bodily hunger
in his eyes.
   Major Barbara (1907) act 2

25 Wot prawce Selvytion nah?
   Major Barbara (1907) act 2

26 Alcohol is a very necessary article . . . It enables
Parliament to do things at eleven at night that no
sane person would do at eleven in the morning.
   Major Barbara (1907) act 2

27 He knows nothing; and he thinks he knows
everything. That points clearly to a political
career.
   Major Barbara (1907) act 3

28 Nothing is ever done in this world until men are
prepared to kill one another if it is not done.
   Major Barbara (1907) act 3

29 Like all young men, you greatly exaggerate the
difference between one young woman and
another.
   Major Barbara (1907) act 3; see **Mencken** 521:15

30 But a lifetime of happiness! No man alive could
bear it: it would be hell on earth.
   Man and Superman (1903) act 1

1 The more things a man is ashamed of, the more respectable he is.
   Man and Superman (1903) act 1

2 Vitality in a woman is a blind fury of creation.
   Man and Superman (1903) act 1

3 Of all human struggles there is none so treacherous and remorseless as the struggle between the artist man and the mother woman.
   Man and Superman (1903) act 1

4 You think that you are Ann's suitor; that you are the pursuer and she the pursued . . . Fool: it is you who are the pursued, the marked down quarry, the destined prey.
   Man and Superman (1903) act 2

5 MENDOZA: I am a brigand: I live by robbing the rich.
   TANNER: I am a gentleman: I live by robbing the poor.
   Man and Superman (1903) act 3

6 Hell is full of musical amateurs: music is the brandy of the damned.
   Man and Superman (1903) act 3

7 Englishmen never will be slaves: they are free to do whatever the Government and public opinion allow them to do.
   Man and Superman (1903) act 3

8 An Englishman thinks he is moral when he is only uncomfortable.
   Man and Superman (1903) act 3

9 In the arts of life man invents nothing; but in the arts of death he outdoes Nature herself, and produces by chemistry and machinery all the slaughter of plague, pestilence and famine.
   Man and Superman (1903) act 3

10 In the arts of peace Man is a bungler.
   Man and Superman (1903) act 3

11 As an old soldier I admit the cowardice: it's as universal as sea sickness, and matters just as little.
   Man and Superman (1903) act 3

12 When the military man approaches, the world locks up its spoons and packs off its womankind.
   Man and Superman (1903) act 3; see **Emerson** 306:20

13 What is virtue but the Trade Unionism of the married?
   Man and Superman (1903) act 3

14 Those who talk most about the blessings of marriage and the constancy of its vows are the very people who declare that if the chain were broken and the prisoners were left free to choose, the whole social fabric would fly asunder. You can't have the argument both ways. If the prisoner is happy, why lock him in? If he is not, why pretend that he is?
   Man and Superman (1903) act 3

15 Beauty is all very well at first sight; but who ever looks at it when it has been in the house three days?
   Man and Superman (1903) act 4

16 Revolutions have never lightened the burden of tyranny: they have only shifted it to another shoulder.
   Man and Superman (1903) 'The Revolutionist's Handbook' foreword

17 The art of government is the organization of idolatry.
   Man and Superman (1903) 'Maxims: Idolatry'

18 Democracy substitutes election by the incompetent many for appointment by the corrupt few.
   Man and Superman (1903) 'Maxims: Democracy'

19 Liberty means responsibility. That is why most men dread it.
   Man and Superman (1903) 'Maxims: Liberty and Equality'

20 He who can, does. He who cannot, teaches.
   Man and Superman (1903) 'Maxims: Education'

21 Marriage is popular because it combines the maximum of temptation with the maximum of opportunity.
   Man and Superman (1903) 'Maxims: Marriage'

22 Titles distinguish the mediocre, embarrass the superior, and are disgraced by the inferior.
   Man and Superman (1903) 'Maxims: Titles'

23 If you strike a child take care that you strike it in anger, even at the risk of maiming it for life. A blow in cold blood neither can nor should be forgiven.
   Man and Superman (1903) 'Maxims: How to Beat Children'

24 Beware of the man whose god is in the skies.
   Man and Superman (1903) 'Maxims: Religion'

25 Self-denial is not a virtue: it is only the effect of prudence on rascality.
   Man and Superman (1903) 'Maxims: Virtues and Vice'

26 The reasonable man adapts himself to the world: the unreasonable one persists in trying to adapt the world to himself. Therefore all progress depends on the unreasonable man.
   Man and Superman (1903) 'Maxims: Reason'

27 The man who listens to Reason is lost: Reason enslaves all whose minds are not strong enough to master her.
   Man and Superman (1903) 'Maxims: Reason'

28 Decency is Indecency's conspiracy of silence.
   Man and Superman (1903) 'Maxims: Decency'

29 Life levels all men: death reveals the eminent.
   Man and Superman (1903) 'Maxims: Fame'

30 Home is the girl's prison and the woman's workhouse.
   Man and Superman (1903) 'Maxims: Women in the Home'

31 Every man over forty is a scoundrel.
   Man and Superman (1903) 'Maxims: Stray Sayings'

32 Youth, which is forgiven everything, forgives itself nothing: age, which forgives itself everything, is forgiven nothing.
   Man and Superman (1903) 'Maxims: Stray Sayings'

33 Take care to get what you like or you will be forced to like what you get.
   Man and Superman (1903) 'Maxims: Stray Sayings'

1 Beware of the man who does not return your blow: he neither forgives you nor allows you to forgive yourself.
Man and Superman (1903) 'Maxims: Stray Sayings'

2 Self-sacrifice enables us to sacrifice other people without blushing.
Man and Superman (1903) 'Maxims: Self-Sacrifice'

3 There is nothing so bad or so good that you will not find Englishmen doing it; but you will never find an Englishman in the wrong. He does everything on principle. He fights you on patriotic principles; he robs you on business principles; he enslaves you on imperial principles; he bullies you on manly principles; he supports his king on loyal principles and cuts off his king's head on republican principles.
The Man of Destiny (1898)

4 Anarchism is a game at which the police can beat you.
Misalliance (1914)

5 The only way for a woman to provide for herself decently is for her to be good to some man that can afford to be good to her.
Mrs Warren's Profession (1898) act 2

6 A great devotee of the Gospel of Getting On.
Mrs Warren's Profession (1898) act 4

7 You'll never have a quiet world till you knock the patriotism out of the human race.
O'Flaherty V.C. (1919)

8 The secret of being miserable is to have leisure to bother about whether you are happy or not. The cure for it is occupation.
Parents and Children (1914) 'Children's Happiness'

9 A perpetual holiday is a good working definition of hell.
Parents and Children (1914) 'Children's Happiness'

10 There is only one religion, though there are a hundred versions of it.
Plays Pleasant and Unpleasant (1898) vol. 2, preface

11 It is impossible for an Englishman to open his mouth without making some other Englishman hate or despise him.
Pygmalion (1916) preface

12 I don't want to talk grammar, I want to talk like a lady.
Pygmalion (1916) act 2

13 PICKERING: Have you no morals, man?
DOOLITTLE: Can't afford them, Governor.
Pygmalion (1916) act 2

14 I'm one of the undeserving poor . . . up agen middle-class morality all the time . . . What is middle-class morality? Just an excuse for never giving me anything.
Pygmalion (1916) act 2

15 Gin was mother's milk to her.
Pygmalion (1916) act 3

16 Walk! Not bloody likely.
Pygmalion (1916) act 3

17 No Englishman is ever fairly beaten.
Saint Joan (1924) sc. 4

18 How can what an Englishman believes be heresy? It is a contradiction in terms.
Saint Joan (1924) sc. 4

19 Must then a Christ perish in torment in every age to save those that have no imagination?
Saint Joan (1924) epilogue

20 Assassination is the extreme form of censorship.
The Showing-Up of Blanco Posnet (1911) 'Limits to Toleration'

21 'Do you know what a pessimist is?' 'A man who thinks everybody is as nasty as himself, and hates them for it.'
An Unsocial Socialist (1887) ch. 5

22 You never can tell.
title of play (1898)

23 The great advantage of a hotel is that it's a refuge from home life.
You Never Can Tell (1898) act 2

24 The younger generation is knocking at the door, and as I open it there steps spritely in the incomparable Max.
on handing over the theatre review column to Max **Beerbohm**
in *Saturday Review* 21 May 1898 'Valedictory'

25 The photographer is like the cod which produces a million eggs in order that one may reach maturity.
introduction to the catalogue for Alvin Langdon Coburn's exhibition at the Royal Photographic Society, 1906; Bill Jay and Margaret Moore *Bernard Shaw and Photography* (1989)

26 The trouble, Mr Goldwyn, is that you are only interested in art and I am only interested in money.
telegraphed version of the outcome of a conversation between Shaw and Sam **Goldwyn**
Alva Johnson *The Great Goldwyn* (1937) ch. 3

27 [Dancing is] a perpendicular expression of a horizontal desire.
in *New Statesman* 23 March 1962

Hartley Shawcross 1902–2003
British Labour politician

28 'But,' said Alice, 'the question is whether you can make a word mean different things.' 'Not so,' said Humpty-Dumpty, 'the question is which is to be the master. That's all.' We are the masters at the moment, and not only at the moment, but for a very long time to come.
speech in the House of Commons, 2 April 1946; see **Carroll** 195:16, **Misquotations** 538:21

Charles Shaw-Lefevre, Lord Eversley
1794–1888

29 What is that fat gentleman in such a passion about?
as a child, on hearing Charles James **Fox** *speak in Parliament*
G. W. E. Russell *Collections and Recollections* (1898) ch. 11

Patrick Shaw-Stewart 1888–1917

1 I saw a man this morning
Who did not wish to die;
I ask and cannot answer
If otherwise wish I.
    poem (1916); M. Baring *Have You Anything to Declare?*
    (1936)

2 Stand in the trench, Achilles,
Flame-capped, and shout for me.
    poem (1916); M. Baring *Have You Anything to Declare?*
    (1936)

3 Nowadays we who are alive have the sense of
being old, old survivors.
    letter from Gallipoli, where he was killed; Brian Gardner
    (ed.) *Up the Line to Death* (rev. ed., 1976)

Lord Shelburne 1737–1805

British Whig politician; Prime Minister

4 The country will neither be united at home nor
respected abroad, till the reins of government are
lodged with men who have some little pretensions
to common sense and common honesty.
    in the House of Lords, 22 November 1770

5 The sun of Great Britain will set whenever she
acknowledges the independence of America . . .
the independence of America would end in the
ruin of England.
    in the House of Lords, October 1782

Mary Shelley (née Godwin) 1797–1851

*English novelist; daughter of William **Godwin** and Mary*
Wollstonecraft**, wife of Percy Bysshe **Shelley

6 'We will each write a ghost story,' said Lord
Byron; and his proposition was acceded to. There
were four of us . . . *Have you thought of a story?* I
was asked each morning, and each morning I was
forced to reply with a mortifying negative . . . On
the morrow I announced that I had *thought of a
story* . . . At first I thought but of a few pages—of a
short tale; but Shelley urged me to develop the
idea at greater length.
on beginning Frankenstein
    introduction to *Frankenstein* (ed. 3, 1831)

7 You seek for knowledge and wisdom as I once did;
and I ardently hope that the gratification of your
wishes may not be a serpent to sting you, as mine
has been.
    Frankenstein (1818) Letter 4

8 I beheld the wretch—the miserable monster
whom I had created.
    Frankenstein (1818) ch. 5

9 All men hate the wretched; how, then, must I be
hated, who am miserable beyond all living things!
Yet you, my creator, detest and spurn me, thy
creature, to whom thou art bound by ties only
dissoluble by the annihilation of one of us.
    Frankenstein (1818) ch. 10

10 Everywhere I see bliss, from which I alone am
irrevocably excluded.
    Frankenstein (1818) ch. 10

11 Teach him to think for himself? Oh, my God, teach
him rather to think like other people!
on her son's education
    Matthew Arnold *Essays in Criticism* Second Series (1888)
    'Shelley'

Percy Bysshe Shelley 1792–1822

*English poet; husband of Mary **Shelley***
*on Shelley: see **Arnold** 29:21, **Browning** 160:8*

12 The cemetery is an open space among the ruins,
covered in winter with violets and daisies. It might
make one in love with death, to think that one
should be buried in so sweet a place.
    Adonais (1821) preface

13 I weep for Adonais—he is dead!
O, weep for Adonais! though our tears
Thaw not the frost which binds so dear a head!
    Adonais (1821) st. 1

14   He died,
Who was the Sire of an immortal strain,
Blind, old and lonely.
    Adonais (1821) st. 4

15   The quick Dreams,
The passion-wingèd Ministers of thought.
    Adonais (1821) st. 9

16 She faded, like a cloud which had outwept its rain.
    Adonais (1821) st. 10

17   Winter is come and gone,
But grief returns with the revolving year.
    Adonais (1821) st. 18

18 From the great morning of the world when first
God dawned on Chaos.
    Adonais (1821) st. 19

19 Alas! that all we loved of him should be,
But for our grief, as if it had not been,
And grief itself be mortal!
    Adonais (1821) st. 21

20 A pardlike Spirit, beautiful and swift—
A Love in desolation masked.
    Adonais (1821) st. 32

21 He wakes or sleeps with the enduring dead;
Thou canst not soar where he is sitting now—
Dust to the dust! but the pure spirit shall flow
Back to the burning fountain whence it came,
A portion of the Eternal.
    Adonais (1821) st. 38

22 He hath awakened from the dream of life.
    Adonais (1821) st. 39

23 He has out-soared the shadow of our night;
Envy and calumny and hate and pain,
And that unrest which men miscall delight,
Can touch him not and torture not again;
From the contagion of the world's slow stain
He is secure, and now can never mourn
A heart grown cold, a head grown grey in vain.
    Adonais (1821) st. 40

24 He lives, he wakes,—'tis Death is dead, not he.
    Adonais (1821) st. 41

1 He is a portion of the loveliness
Which once he made more lovely.
Adonais (1821) st. 43

2 The One remains, the many change and pass;
Heaven's light forever shines, Earth's shadows fly;
Life, like a dome of many-coloured glass,
Stains the white radiance of Eternity.
Adonais (1821) st. 52

3 A widow bird sat mourning for her love
Upon a wintry bough.
Charles the First (1822) sc. 5, l. 9

4 That orbèd maiden, with white fire laden,
Whom mortals call the Moon.
'The Cloud' (1819)

5 I am the daughter of Earth and Water,
And the nursling of the Sky.
I pass through the pores of the ocean and shores;
I change, but I cannot die.
'The Cloud' (1819)

6 I silently laugh at my own cenotaph,
And out of the caverns of rain,
Like a child from the womb, like a ghost from the
tomb,
I arise and unbuild it again.
'The Cloud' (1819)

7 I never was attached to that great sect,
Whose doctrine is that each one should select
Out of the crowd a mistress or a friend,
And all the rest, though fair and wise, commend
To cold oblivion.
'Epipsychidion' (1821) l. 149

8 The beaten road
Which those poor slaves with weary footsteps
tread,
Who travel to their home among the dead
By the broad highway of the world, and so
With one chained friend, perhaps a jealous foe,
The dreariest and the longest journey go.
'Epipsychidion' (1821) l. 154

9 Chameleons feed on light and air:
Poets' food is love and fame.
'An Exhortation' (1820)

10 Let there be light! said Liberty,
And like sunrise from the sea,
Athens arose!
Hellas (1822) l. 682

11 The world's great age begins anew,
The golden years return,
The earth doth like a snake renew
Her winter weeds outworn.
Hellas (1822) l. 1060

12 O cease! must hate and death return?
Cease! must men kill and die?
Hellas (1822) l. 1096

13 I pursued a maiden and clasped a reed.
Gods and men, we are all deluded thus!
It breaks in our bosom and then we bleed.
'Hymn of Pan' (1824)

14 The awful shadow of some unseen Power
Floats though unseen among us,—visiting

This various world with as inconstant wing
As summer winds that creep from flower to flower.
'Hymn to Intellectual Beauty' (1816)

15 The day becomes more solemn and serene
When noon is past—there is a harmony
In autumn, and a lustre in its sky,
Which through the summer is not heard or seen,
As if it could not be, as if it had not been!
'Hymn to Intellectual Beauty' (1816)

16 Thou Paradise of exiles, Italy!
'Julian and Maddalo' (1818) l. 57

17 *Me*—who am as a nerve o'er which do creep
The else unfelt oppressions of this earth.
'Julian and Maddalo' (1818) l. 449

18 Most wretched men
Are cradled into poetry by wrong:
They learn in suffering what they teach in song.
'Julian and Maddalo' (1818) l. 544

19 . . . London, that great sea, whose ebb and flow
At once is deaf and loud, and on the shore
Vomits its wrecks, and still howls on for more.
'Letter to Maria Gisborne' (1820) l. 193

20 You will see Coleridge—he who sits obscure
In the exceeding lustre and the pure
Intense irradiation of a mind,
Which, with its own internal lightning blind,
Flags wearily through darkness and despair—
A cloud-encircled meteor of the air,
A hooded eagle among blinking owls.
of Samuel Taylor **Coleridge**
'Letter to Maria Gisborne' (1820) l. 202

21 You will see Hunt—one of those happy souls
Which are the salt of the earth, and without
whom
This world would smell like what it is—a tomb.
of Leigh **Hunt**
'Letter to Maria Gisborne' (1820) l. 209

22 Have you not heard
When a man marries, dies, or turns Hindoo,
His best friends hear no more of him?
'Letter to Maria Gisborne' (1820) l. 235

23 His fine wit
Makes such a wound, the knife is lost in it.
of Thomas Love **Peacock**
'Letter to Maria Gisborne' (1820) l. 240

24 When the lamp is shattered
The light in the dust lies dead—
When the cloud is scattered
The rainbow's glory is shed.
When the lute is broken,
Sweet tones are remembered not;
When the lips have spoken,
Loved accents are soon forgot.
'Lines: When the lamp' (1824)

25 Beneath is spread like a green sea
The waveless plain of Lombardy.
'Lines written amongst the Euganean Hills' (1818) l. 90

26 Underneath Day's azure eyes
Ocean's nursling, Venice lies,

A peopled labyrinth of walls,
Amphitrite's destined halls.
'Lines written amongst the Euganean Hills' (1818) l. 94

1 Sun-girt city, thou hast been
Ocean's child, and then his queen;
Now is come a darker day,
And thou soon must be his prey.
of Venice
'Lines written amongst the Euganean Hills' (1818) l. 115

2 The fountains mingle with the river,
And the rivers with the ocean;
The winds of heaven mix for ever
With a sweet emotion;
Nothing in the world is single;
All things, by a law divine,
In one spirit meet and mingle.
Why not I with thine?
'Love's Philosophy' (written 1819)

3 I met Murder on the way—
He had a mask like Castlereagh—
Very smooth he looked, yet grim,
Seven bloodhounds followed him.
'The Mask of Anarchy' (1819) st. 2

4 His big tears, for he wept well,
Turned to mill-stones as they fell.

And the little children, who
Round his feet played to and fro,
Thinking every tear a gem,
Had their brains knocked out by them.
of 'Fraud' [Lord Eldon]
'The Mask of Anarchy' (1819) st. 4

5 Nought may endure but Mutability.
'Mutability' (1816)

6 I stood within the City disinterred;
And heard the autumnal leaves like light footfalls
Of spirits passing through the streets; and heard
The Mountain's slumberous voice at intervals
Thrill through those roofless halls.
'Ode to Naples' (1820) l. 1

7 O wild West Wind, thou breath of Autumn's
being,
Thou, from whose unseen presence the leaves
dead
Are driven, like ghosts from an enchanter fleeing,
Yellow, and black, and pale, and hectic red,
Pestilence-stricken multitudes: O thou,
Who chariotest to their dark wintry bed
The wingèd seeds, where they lie cold and low,
Each like a corpse within its grave, until
Thine azure sister of the spring shall blow
Her clarion o'er the dreaming earth, and fill
(Driving sweet buds like flocks to feed in air)
With living hues and odours plain and hill:
Wild Spirit, which art moving everywhere;
Destroyer and preserver; hear, oh, hear!
'Ode to the West Wind' (1819) l. 1

8   There are spread
On the blue surface of thine aëry surge,
Like the bright hair uplifted from the head

Of some fierce Maenad.
'Ode to the West Wind' (1819) l. 18

9 Thou who didst waken from his summer dreams
The blue Mediterranean, where he lay,
Lulled by the coil of his crystàlline streams

Beside a pumice isle in Baiae's bay,
And saw in sleep old palaces and towers
Quivering within the wave's intenser day.
'Ode to the West Wind' (1819) l. 29

10 The sea-blooms and the oozy woods which wear
The sapless foliage of the ocean.
'Ode to the West Wind' (1819) l. 39

11 Oh, lift me as a wave, a leaf, a cloud!
I fall upon the thorns of life! I bleed!
'Ode to the West Wind' (1819) l. 53

12 Make me thy lyre, even as the forest is:
What if my leaves are falling like its own!
'Ode to the West Wind' (1819) l. 57

13 And, by the incantation of this verse,
Scatter, as from an unextinguished hearth
Ashes and sparks, my words among mankind!
'Ode to the West Wind' (1819) l. 65

14   O, Wind,
If Winter comes, can Spring be far behind?
'Ode to the West Wind' (1819) l. 69

15 Its horror and its beauty are divine.
'On the Medusa of Leonardo da Vinci' (1824)

16 I met a traveller from an antique land
Who said: Two vast and trunkless legs of stone
Stand in the desert.
'Ozymandias' (1819)

17 The hand that mocked them and the heart that
fed.
'Ozymandias' (1819)

18 'My name is Ozymandias, king of kings:
Look on my works, ye Mighty, and despair!'
Nothing beside remains. Round the decay
Of that colossal wreck, boundless and bare
The lone and level sands stretch far away.
'Ozymandias' (1819)

19 Hell is a city much like London—
A populous and smoky city.
'Peter Bell the Third' (1819) pt. 3, st. 1

20 But from the first 'twas Peter's drift
To be a kind of moral eunuch,
He touched the hem of Nature's shift,
Felt faint—and never dared uplift
The closest, all-concealing tunic.
'Peter Bell the Third' (1819) pt. 4, st. 11

21   Ere Babylon was dust,
The Magus Zoroaster, my dead child,
Met his own image walking in the garden,
That apparition, sole of men, he saw.
Prometheus Unbound (1819) act 1, l. 191

22 Cruel he looks, but calm and strong,
Like one who does, not suffers wrong.
Prometheus Unbound (1819) act 1, l. 238

23 Grief for awhile is blind, and so was mine.
Prometheus Unbound (1820) act 1, l. 304

1 Kingly conclaves stern and cold
Where blood with guilt is bought and sold.
Prometheus Unbound (1820) act 1, l. 530

2 The good want power, but to weep barren tears.
The powerful goodness want: worse need for
them.
The wise want love; and those who love want
wisdom.
Prometheus Unbound (1820) act 1, l. 625

3   Peace is in the grave.
The grave hides all things beautiful and good:
I am a God and cannot find it there.
Prometheus Unbound (1820) act 1, l. 638

4 The dust of creeds outworn.
Prometheus Unbound (1820) act 1, l. 697

5   To be
Omnipotent but friendless is to reign.
Prometheus Unbound (1820) act 2, sc. 4, l. 47

6 He gave man speech, and speech created thought,
Which is the measure of the universe.
Prometheus Unbound (1820) act 2, sc. 4, l. 72

7 My soul is an enchanted boat,
Which, like a sleeping swan, doth float
Upon the silver waves of thy sweet singing.
Prometheus Unbound (1820) act 2, sc. 5, l. 72

8 The loathsome mask has fallen, the man remains
Sceptreless, free, uncircumscribed, but man
Equal, unclassed, tribeless, and nationless,
Exempt from awe, worship, degree, the king
Over himself; just, gentle, wise: but man
Passionless?—no, yet free from guilt or pain,
Which were, for his will made or suffered them,
Nor yet exempt, though ruling them like slaves,
From chance, and death, and mutability,
The clogs of that which else might oversoar
The loftiest star of unascended heaven,
Pinnacled dim in the intense inane.
Prometheus Unbound (1820) act 3, sc. 4, l. 193

9 A traveller from the cradle to the grave
Through the dim night of this immortal day.
Prometheus Unbound (1820) act 4, l. 551

10 To suffer woes which Hope thinks infinite;
To forgive wrongs darker than death or night;
To defy Power, which seems omnipotent;
To love, and bear; to hope till Hope creates
From its own wreck the thing it contemplates;
Neither to change, nor falter, nor repent;
This, like thy glory, Titan, is to be
Good, great and joyous, beautiful and free;
This is alone Life, Joy, Empire and Victory.
Prometheus Unbound (1820) act 4, l. 570

11 How wonderful is Death,
Death and his brother Sleep!
Queen Mab (1813) canto 1, l. 1; see **Daniel** 255:7, **Fletcher**
327:9

12 I dreamed that, as I wandered by the way,
Bare Winter suddenly was changed to Spring.
'The Question' (1822)

13 Daisies, those pearled Arcturi of the earth,
The constellated flower that never sets.
'The Question' (1822)

14 A Sensitive Plant in a garden grew.
'The Sensitive Plant' (1820) pt. 1, l. 1

15 And the jessamine faint, and the sweet tuberose,
The sweetest flower for scent that blows.
'The Sensitive Plant' (1820) pt. 1, l. 37

16 Rarely, rarely, comest thou,
Spirit of Delight!
'Song' (1824); epigraph to **Elgar**'s Second Symphony

17 Men of England, wherefore plough
For the lords who lay ye low?
'Song to the Men of England' (written 1819)

18 The seed ye sow, another reaps;
The wealth ye find, another keeps;
The robes ye weave, another wears;
The arms ye forge, another bears.
'Song to the Men of England' (written 1819)

19 Lift not the painted veil which those who live
Call Life.
'Sonnet' (1824)

20 An old, mad, blind, despised, and dying king.
of **George III**
'Sonnet: England in 1819' (written 1819)

21 I see the waves upon the shore,
Like light dissolved in star-showers, thrown.
'Stanzas Written in Dejection, near Naples' (1818)

22 Alas! I have nor hope nor health,
Nor peace within nor calm around,
Nor that content surpassing wealth
The sage in meditation found.
'Stanzas Written in Dejection, near Naples' (1818)

23 Music, when soft voices die,
Vibrates in the memory—
Odours, when sweet violets sicken,
Live within the sense they quicken.
'To—: Music, when soft voices die' (1824)

24 The desire of the moth for the star,
Of the night for the morrow,
The devotion to something afar
From the sphere of our sorrow.
'To—: One word is too often profaned' (1824)

25 Hail to thee, blithe Spirit!
Bird thou never wert,
That from Heaven, or near it,
Pourest thy full heart
In profuse strains of unpremeditated art.
'To a Skylark' (1819)

26 And singing still dost soar, and soaring ever
singest.
'To a Skylark' (1819)

27 Thou art unseen, but yet I hear thy shrill delight.
'To a Skylark' (1819)

28 Like a Poet hidden
In the light of thought,
Singing hymns unbidden,
Till the world is wrought
To sympathy with hopes and fears it heeded not.
'To a Skylark' (1819)

29 We look before and after,
And pine for what is not:

Our sincerest laughter
With some pain is fraught;
Our sweetest songs are those that tell of saddest
thought.
'To a Skylark' (1819)

1 Teach me half the gladness
That thy brain must know,
Such harmonious madness
From my lips would flow
The world should listen then—as I am listening
now.
'To a Skylark' (1819)

2 Less oft is peace in Shelley's mind,
Than calm in waters, seen.
'To Jane: The Recollection' (written 1822)

3 Swiftly walk o'er the western wave,
Spirit of Night!
'To Night' (1824)

4 Death will come when thou art dead,
Soon, too soon.
'To Night' (1824)

5 Art thou pale for weariness
Of climbing heaven, and gazing on the earth,
Wandering companionless
Among the stars that have a different birth,—
And ever changing, like a joyless eye
That finds no object worth its constancy?
'To the Moon' (1824)

6 In honoured poverty thy voice did weave
Songs consecrate to truth and liberty,—
Deserting these, thou leavest me to grieve,
Thus having been, that thou shouldst cease to be.
'To Wordsworth' (1816)

7 And like a dying lady, lean and pale,
Who totters forth, wrapped in a gauzy veil.
'The Waning Moon' (1824)

8 A lovely lady, garmented in light
From her own beauty.
'The Witch of Atlas' (written 1820) st. 5

9 For she was beautiful—her beauty made
The bright world dim, and everything beside
Seemed like the fleeting image of a shade.
'The Witch of Atlas' (written 1820) st. 12

10 The discussion of any subject is a right that you
have brought into the world with your heart and
tongue. Resign your heart's blood before you part
with this inestimable privilege of man.
An Address to the Irish People (1812)

11 The accident of her birth neither made her life
more virtuous nor her death more worthy of grief.
An Address to the People on the Death of the Princess Charlotte
(1817)

12 Titles are tinsel, power a corrupter, glory a bubble,
and excessive wealth a libel on its possessor.
Declaration of Rights (1812) article 27

13 The vanity of translation; it were as wise to cast a
violet into a crucible that you might discover the
formal principle of its colour and odour, as seek to
transfuse from one language to another the

creations of a poet. The plant must spring again
from its seed, or it will bear no flower.
A Defence of Poetry (written 1821)

14 The great instrument of moral good is the
imagination; and poetry administers to the effect
by acting on the cause.
A Defence of Poetry (written 1821)

15 A single word even may be a spark of
inextinguishable thought.
A Defence of Poetry (written 1821)

16 Poetry is the record of the best and happiest
moments of the happiest and best minds.
A Defence of Poetry (written 1821)

17 Poets are the hierophants of an unapprehended
inspiration; the mirrors of the gigantic shadows
which futurity casts upon the present; the words
which express what they understand not; the
trumpets which sing to battle, and feel not what
they inspire; the influence which is moved not,
but moves. Poets are the unacknowledged
legislators of the world.
A Defence of Poetry (written 1821); see **Johnson** 425:26

18 What is Love? It is that powerful attraction
towards all that we conceive, or fear, or hope
beyond ourselves.
'On Love' (notebook essay, *c.*1815), in D. L. Clark (ed.)
Shelley's Prose (1966)

19 Tyranny entrenches itself within the existing
interests of the most refined citizens of a nation
and says 'If you dare trample upon these, be free.'
A Philosophical View of Reform (written 1819–20) ch. 1

20 Monarchy is only the string that ties the robber's
bundle.
A Philosophical View of Reform (written 1819–20) ch. 2

21 Thought can with difficulty visit the intricate and
winding chambers which it inhabits. It is like a
river whose rapid and perpetual stream flows
outwards—like one in dread who speeds through
the recesses of some haunted pile and dares not
look behind.
'Speculations on Metaphysics [On the Science of Mind]'
(written 1815), in D. L. Clark (ed.) *Shelley's Prose* (1966)

William Shenstone 1714–63

English poet and essayist

22 The charm dissolves; th' aerial music's past;
The banquet ceases, and the vision flies.
'Elegy 11. He complains how soon the pleasing novelty of
life is over' (1764)

23 Whoe'er has travelled life's dull round,
Where'er his stages may have been,
May sigh to think he still has found
The warmest welcome, at an inn.
'Written at an Inn at Henley' (1758); see **Johnson** 430:13

24 Laws are generally found to be nets of such a
texture, as the little creep through, the great break
through, and the middle-sized are alone entangled
in.
Works in Verse and Prose (1764) vol. 2 'On Politics'; see
Anacharsis 13:18

1 The world may be divided into people that read, people that write, people that think, and fox-hunters.
Works . . . (1764) vol. 2 'On Writing and Books'

2 Every good poet includes a critic; the reverse will not hold.
Works . . . (1764) vol. 2 'On Writing and Books'

3 To endeavour, all one's days, to fortify our minds with learning and philosophy, is to spend so much in armour that one has nothing left to defend.
Works . . . (1764) vol. 2 'On Writing and Books'

Philip Henry Sheridan 1831–88

American Union cavalry commander in the Civil War

4 The only good Indians I ever saw were dead.
in response to the Comanche chief Toch-a-way, who described himself as a 'good Indian'
at Fort Cobb, January 1869; attributed but denied by Sheridan; a similar remark had been made by J. M. Cavanaugh in Congress on 28 May 1868; see **Proverbs** 628:23

Richard Brinsley Sheridan 1751–1816

Irish dramatist and Whig politician
on Sheridan: see **Anonymous** 16:5, **Byron** 184:11, **Walpole** 819:17

5 The newspapers! Sir, they are the most villainous—licentious—abominable—infernal—Not that I ever read them—No—I make it a rule never to look into a newspaper.
The Critic (1779) act 1, sc. 1

6 If it is abuse,—why one is always sure to hear of it from one damned goodnatured friend or another!
The Critic (1779) act 1, sc. 1

7 Egad I think the interpreter is the hardest to be understood of the two!
The Critic (1779) act 1, sc. 2

8 I wish sir, you would practise this without me. I can't stay dying here all night.
The Critic (1779) act 3, sc. 1

9 O Lord, Sir—when a heroine goes mad she always goes into white satin.
The Critic (1779) act 3, sc. 1

10 Enter Tilburina stark mad in white satin, and her confidante stark mad in white linen.
The Critic (1779) act 3, sc. 1

11 An oyster may be crossed in love!
The Critic (1779) act 3, sc. 1

12 Conscience has no more to do with gallantry than it has with politics.
The Duenna (1775) act 2, sc. 4

13 The throne *we* honour is the *people's choice*.
Pizarro (1799) act 2, sc. 2

14 Illiterate him, I say, quite from your memory.
The Rivals (1775) act 1, sc. 2

15 'Tis safest in matrimony to begin with a little aversion.
The Rivals (1775) act 1, sc. 2

16 Madam, a circulating library in a town is as an evergreen tree of diabolical knowledge; it blossoms throughout the year. And depend on it . . . that they who are so fond of handling the leaves, will long for the fruit at last.
The Rivals (1775) act 1, sc. 2

17 He is the very pineapple of politeness!
The Rivals (1775) act 3, sc. 3

18 An aspersion upon my parts of speech!
The Rivals (1775) act 3, sc. 3

19 If I reprehend any thing in this world, it is the use of my oracular tongue, and a nice derangement of epitaphs!
The Rivals (1775) act 3, sc. 3

20 She's as headstrong as an allegory on the banks of the Nile.
The Rivals (1775) act 3, sc. 3

21 Our ancestors are very good kind of folks; but they are the last people I should choose to have a visiting acquaintance with.
The Rivals (1775) act 4, sc. 1

22 No caparisons, Miss, if you please!—Caparisons don't become a young woman.
The Rivals (1775) act 4, sc. 2

23 You are not like Cerberus, three gentlemen at once, are you?
The Rivals (1775) act 4, sc. 2

24 The quarrel is a very pretty quarrel as it stands—we should only spoil it by trying to explain it.
The Rivals (1775) act 4, sc. 3

25 My valour is certainly going!—it is sneaking off!—I feel it oozing out as it were at the palms of my hands!
The Rivals (1775) act 5, sc. 3

26 You shall see them on a beautiful quarto page where a neat rivulet of text shall meander through a meadow of margin.
The School for Scandal (1777) act 1, sc. 1

27 You had no taste when you married me.
The School for Scandal (1777) act 2, sc. 1

28 MRS CANDOUR: I'll swear her colour is natural—I have seen it come and go—
LADY TEAZLE: I dare swear you have, ma'am; it goes of a night and comes again in the morning.
The School for Scandal (1777) act 2, sc. 2

29 Here is the whole set! a character dead at every word.
The School for Scandal (1777) act 2, sc. 2; see **Pope** 606:11

30 I'm called away by particular business—but I leave my character behind me.
The School for Scandal (1777) act 2, sc. 2

31 Here's to the maiden of bashful fifteen
Here's to the widow of fifty
Here's to the flaunting, extravagant quean;
And here's to the housewife that's thrifty.
Let the toast pass—
Drink to the lass—
I'll warrant she'll prove an excuse for the glass!
The School for Scandal (1777) act 3, sc. 3

1 An unforgiving eye, and a damned disinheriting countenance!

The School for Scandal (1777) act 4, sc. 1

2 ROWLEY: I believe there is no sentiment he has more faith in as that 'Charity begins at home'.

SIR OLIVER SURFACE: And his I presume is of that domestic sort which never stirs abroad at all.

The School for Scandal (1777) act 5, sc. 1

3 There is no trusting appearances.

The School for Scandal (1777) act 5, sc. 2

4 You write with ease, to show your breeding,
But easy writing's vile hard reading.

'Clio's Protest' (written 1771, published 1819)

5 A man may surely be allowed to take a glass of wine by his own fireside.

on being encountered drinking a glass of wine in the street, while watching his theatre, the Drury Lane, burn down

T. Moore *Life of Sheridan* (1825) vol. 2

6 The Right Honourable gentleman is indebted to his memory for his jests, and to his imagination for his facts.

speech in reply to Mr Dundas, in T. Moore *Life of Sheridan* (1825) vol. 2

7 They talk of avarice, lust, ambition, as great passions. It is a mistake; they are little passions. Vanity is the great commanding passion of all.

to Lord Holland

Thomas Moore *Journal* (1984) 5 August 1824

8 To her! To that magnificent and appalling creature! I should as soon have thought of making love to the Archbishop of Canterbury!

responding to Samuel Rogers's suggestion that Sheridan might 'make open love' to Mrs Siddons

Henry Colborn (ed.) *Sheridaniana* (1826)

9 Won't you come into the garden? I would like my roses to see you.

to a young lady; attributed

Hugh Sherlock 1905–

10 Lord, thy church on earth is seeking
Thy renewal from above;
Teach us all the art of speaking
With the accent of thy love.

'Lord, thy church on earth is seeking' (hymn)

Sidney Sherman 1805–73

American soldier

11 Remember the Alamo!

battle cry at San Jacinto, 21 April 1836, traditionally attributed to General Sherman

William Tecumsah Sherman 1820–91

American Union general

12 I will never again command an army in America if we must carry along paid spies. I will banish myself to some foreign country first.

a reference to war correspondents

letter to his wife, February 1863

13 *Vox populi, vox humbug.*

letter to his wife Jane, 2 June 1863; see **Alcuin** 10:10, **Proverbs** 633:37

14 Hold out. Relief is coming.

usually quoted as 'Hold the fort! I am coming!'

flag signal from Kennesaw Mountain to General John Murray Corse at Allatoona Pass, 5 October 1864; see **Bliss** 123:10

15 [Grant] stood by me when I was crazy, and I stood by him when he was drunk; and now we stand by each other always.

*of his relationship with his fellow Union commander, Ulysses S. **Grant***

in 1864; Geoffrey C. Ward *The Civil War* (1991)

16 War is the remedy our *enemies* have chosen, and I say let us give them all they want.

in 1864; Geoffrey C. Ward *The Civil War* (1991)

17 There is many a boy here to-day who looks on war as all glory, but, boys, it is all hell.

speech at Columbus, Ohio, 11 August 1880, in Lloyd Lewis *Sherman, Fighting Prophet* (1932)

18 I will not accept if nominated, and will not serve if elected.

telegram to General Henderson, on being urged to stand as Republican candidate in the 1884 US presidential election

Memoirs (4th ed., 1891) ch. 27

Carol Shields 1935–2003

American-born Canadian novelist and poet

19 To be like everyone else. Isn't that what we all want in the end?

Larry's Party (1997) ch. 9

20 Canada is . . . a country always dressed in its Sunday go-to-meeting clothes. A country you wouldn't ask to dance a second waltz. Clean. Christian. Dull. Quiescent. But growing.

The Stone Diaries (1993)

Emanuel Shinwell 1884–1986

British Labour politician

21 We know that the organised workers of the country are our friends. As for the rest, they don't matter a tinker's cuss.

speech to the Electrical Trades Union conference at Margate, 7 May 1947; in *Manchester Guardian* 8 May 1947

Arthur Shipley 1861–1927

English zoologist

22 When we were a soft amoeba, in ages past and gone,
Ere you were Queen of Sheba, or I King Solomon,
Alone and undivided, we lived a life of sloth,
Whatever you did, I did; one dinner served for both.
Anon came separation, by fission and divorce,
A lonely pseudopodium I wandered on my course.

Life (1923) ch. 13 'Ere you were Queen of Sheba'

Jonathan Shipley 1714-88

English clergyman, Bishop of St Asaph

1 I look upon North America as the only great nursery of freemen left on the face of the earth.

in 1774, after voting against the alteration of the constitution of Massachusetts, proposed as a punishment for the tea-ship riots at Boston

in *Dictionary of National Biography* (1917-)

William Shippen 1673-1743

English Jacobite politician

2 Robin and I are two honest men: he is for King George and I for King James, but those men in long cravats [Sandys, Rushout, Pulteney, and their following] only desire places under one or the other.

*view of his relationship with his political opponent Robert **Walpole***

in *Dictionary of National Biography* (1917-)

James Shirley 1596-1666

English dramatist

3 The glories of our blood and state
Are shadows, not substantial things;
There is no armour against fate;
Death lays his icy hand on kings.

The Contention of Ajax and Ulysses (1659) act 1, sc. 3

4 Only the actions of the just
Smell sweet, and blossom in their dust.

The Contention of Ajax and Ulysses (1659) act 1, sc. 3

5 I presume you're mortal, and may err.

The Lady of Pleasure (1637) act 2, sc. 2

6   How little room
Do we take up in death, that, living know
No bounds?

The Wedding (1629) act 4, sc. 4

Mikhail Sholokhov 1905-84

Russian novelist

7 And quiet flows the Don.

title of novel (1934)

Clare Short 1946-

British Labour politician

8 Reckless with our government; reckless with his own future, position and place in history. It's extraordinarily reckless.

*when asked if she thought that Tony **Blair** was acting recklessly on Iraq*

in an interview on *Westminster Hour* (BBC Radio 4), 9 March 2003

The Shorter Catechism (1647)

9 'What is the chief end of man?'
'To glorify God and to enjoy him for ever'.

Nevil Shute 1899-1960

British novelist

10 It has been said that an engineer is a man who can do for ten shillings what any fool can do for a pound.

Slide Rule (1954) ch. 3

Walter Sickert 1860-1942

English painter

11 Nothing knits man to man, the Manchester School wisely taught, like the frequent passage from hand to hand of cash.

'The Language of Art' in *New Age* 28 July 1910

The Siddur

Jewish prayer book

12 Hear, O Israel: the Lord our God, the Lord is One.

The Shema; see **Bible** 78:26

13 Blessed are you, O Lord our God and God of our fathers, God of Abraham, God of Isaac, God of Jacob, the great, mighty, and revered God, God most high, generous and kind, owner of all things. You remember the pious deeds of the patriarchs, and in love will bring a redeemer to their children's children, for your name's sake, O King, Helper, Saviour and Shield. Blessed are you, O Lord, the Shield of Abraham.

The Amidah Benediction 1

14 Blessed are you, O Lord our God, King of the universe, who has made a distinction between the holy and the profane, between light and darkness, between Israel and the nations, between the seventh day and the six working days.

The Havdalah

Algernon Sidney 1622-83

English conspirator, executed for his alleged part in the Rye House Plot, 1683

15 Liars ought to have good memories.

Discourses concerning Government (1698) ch. 2, sect. 15

16 Men lived like fishes; the great ones devoured the small.

Discourses concerning Government (1698) ch. 2, sect. 18; see **Shakespeare** 715:3

17 'Tis not necessary to light a candle to the sun.

Discourses concerning Government (1698) ch. 2, sect. 23; see **Burton** 174:13, **Young** 857:7

18 The law is established, which no passion can disturb. 'Tis void of desire and fear, lust and anger . . . 'Tis deaf, inexorable, inflexible.

Discourses concerning Government (1698) ch. 3, sect. 15

Philip Sidney 1554-86

English soldier, poet, and courtier
*on Sidney: see **Browning** 161:14, **Carew** 190:10, **Cokayne** 230:13, **Dyer** 293:12*

19 Shallow brooks murmur most, deep silent slide away.

Arcadia ('Old Arcadia', completed 1581) bk. 1 'First Eclogues: Lalus and Dorus'

1 Who shoots at the mid-day sun, though he be sure
he shall never hit the mark; yet as sure he is he
shall shoot higher than who aims but at a bush.
Arcadia ('New Arcadia', 1590) bk. 2

2 My true love hath my heart and I have his,
By just exchange one for the other giv'n.
Arcadia ('Old Arcadia', completed 1581) bk. 3

3 Biting my truant pen, beating myself for spite,
'Fool,' said my Muse to me; 'look in thy heart and
write.'
Astrophil and Stella (1591) sonnet 1

4 With how sad steps, O Moon, thou climb'st the
skies;
How silently, and with how wan a face.
What, may it be that even in heavenly place
That busy archer his sharp arrows tries?
Astrophil and Stella (1591) sonnet 31

5   O moon, tell me,
Is constant love deemed there but want of wit?
Are beauties there as proud as here they be?
Do they above love to be loved, and yet
These lovers scorn whom that love doth possess?
Do they call virtue there ungratefulness?
Astrophil and Stella (1591) sonnet 31

6 That sweet enemy, France.
Astrophil and Stella (1591) sonnet 41

7 Dumb swans, not chattering pies, do lovers prove;
They love indeed who quake to say they love.
Astrophil and Stella (1591) sonnet 54

8 I never drank of Aganippe well,
Nor ever did in shade of Tempe sit.
Astrophil and Stella (1591) sonnet 74

9 I am no pick-purse of another's wit.
Astrophil and Stella (1591) sonnet 74

10 Highway, since you my chief Parnassus be.
Astrophil and Stella (1591) sonnet 84

11 Stella, think not that I by verse seek fame;
Who seek, who hope, who love, who live, but
thee:
Thine eyes my pride, thy lips my history;
If thou praise not, all other praise is shame.
Astrophil and Stella (1591) sonnet 90

12 Leave me, O Love which reachest but to dust,
And thou, my mind, aspire to higher things;
Grow rich in that which never taketh rust;
Whatever fades, but fading pleasure brings.
Certain Sonnets (written 1577–81) no. 32

13 O fair! O sweet! When I do look on thee,
In whom all joys so well agree,
Heart and soul do sing in me,
Just accord all music makes.
'To the Tune of a Spanish Song' (written *c.*1581)

14 Nature never set forth the earth in so rich tapestry
as diverse poets have done . . . her world is brazen,
the poets only deliver a golden.
The Defence of Poetry (1595)

15 Poetry therefore, is an art of *imitation* . . . that is to
say, a representing, counterfeiting, or figuring

forth to speak metaphorically. A speaking picture,
with this end: to teach and delight.
The Defence of Poetry (1595)

16 With a tale forsooth he [the poet] cometh unto
you, with a tale which holdeth children from play,
and old men from the chimney corner.
The Defence of Poetry (1595)

17 Comedy is an imitation of the common errors of
our life.
The Defence of Poetry (1595)

18 Certainly I must confess mine own barbarousness,
I never heard the old song of Percy and Douglas,
that I found not my heart moved more than with
a trumpet.
The Defence of Poetry (1595)

19 Laughter almost ever cometh of things most
disproportioned to our selves, and nature. Delight
hath a joy in it either permanent or present.
Laughter hath only a scornful tickling.
The Defence of Poetry (1595)

20 Thy necessity is yet greater than mine.
*on giving his water-bottle to a dying soldier on the
battle-field of Zutphen, 1586; commonly quoted as
'thy need is greater than mine'*
Fulke Greville *Life of Sir Philip Sidney* (1652) ch. 12

Emmanuel Joseph Sieyès 1748–1836
French abbot and statesman

21 *La mort, sans phrases.*
Death, without rhetoric.
*on voting in the French Convention for the death of
Louis XVI, 16 January 1793*
    attributed to Sieyès, but afterwards repudiated by him; *Le
    Moniteur* 20 January 1793 records his vote as 'La mort'

22 *J'ai vécu.*
I survived.
*when asked what he had done during the French
Revolution*
    F. A. M. Mignet *Notice historique sur la vie et les travaux de
    M. le Comte de Sieyès* (1836)

Maurice Sigler 1901–61 and Al Hoffman 1902–60
American songwriters

23 Little man, you've had a busy day.
title of song (1934)

Simone Signoret 1921–85
French actress

24 Chains do not hold a marriage together. It is
threads, hundreds of tiny threads which sew
people together through the years. That is what
makes a marriage last—more than passion or
even sex!
in *Daily Mail* 4 July 1978

Sikh Scriptures

a monotheistic religion founded in the Punjab in the 15th century by Guru Nanak

translated by W. H. McLeod, 1984

1 There is one Supreme Being, the Eternal Reality. He is the Creator, without fear and devoid of enmity. He is immortal, never incarnated, self-existent, known by grace through the Guru.

Adi Granth: Guru Nanak Japji mul mantra

2 If as the lord of powerful armies, if as a king enthroned,
Though my commands bring prompt obedience, yet would my strength be vain.
Grant that your name remain, O Master, in my thoughts and in my heart.

Adi Granth: Guru Nanak Siri Raga I

3 When the Guru comes, O mother, joyous bliss is mine;
Boundless blessing, mystic rapture, rise within my soul.
Surging music, strains of glory, fill my heart with joy;
Breaking forth in songs of gladness, praise to God within.
Comes the Guru, I have found him; joyous bliss is mine.

Adi Granth: Guru Amar Das Ramkali Anand

4 The Name of God is sweet ambrosia, source of all inner peace and joy.
The Name of God brings blissful peace to the hearts of the truly devout.

Adi Granth: Guru Arjan Sukhmani

5 Better by far than any other way is the act of repeating the perfect Name of God.
Better by far than any other rite is the cleansing of one's heart in the company of the devout.
Better by far than any other skill is endlessly to utter the wondrous Name of God.
Better by far than any sacred text is hearing and repeating the praises of the Lord.
Better by far than any other place is the heart wherein abides that most precious Name of God.

Adi Granth: Guru Arjan Sukhmani

6 Grant me protection, merciful Lord, prostrate here at your door;
Guard me and keep me, Friend of the humble, weary from wandering far.
You love the devout and recover the sinful; to you alone I address this prayer:
Take me and hold me, merciful Lord, carry me safely to joy.

Adi Granth: Guru Arjan Var Jaitasari

7 Strengthen me, O Lord, that I shrink not from righteous deeds,
That freed from the fear of my enemies I may fight with faith and win.
The wisdom which I crave is the grace to sing your praises.
When this life's allotted course has run may I meet my death in battle.

Dasam Granth: Guru Gobind Singh Chandi Charitra

8 Around us lies God's dwelling place, his joyous presence on every side.
Self-existent and supremely beautiful, he dwells as a presence immanent in all creation.
Birth and death are abolished by his power, by the grace made manifest in his being.
Eternally present within all humanity he reigns in glory for ever.

Dasam Granth: Guru Gobind Singh Jap

9 Some worship stones, borne on their heads; some hang lingams from their necks.
Some claim that God dwells in the south, whilst others bow to the West.
Some worship idols, foolishly ignorant; others put trust in the tombs of the dead.
All are astray, seduced by false ritual; none knows the secret of God.

Dasam Granth: Guru Gobind Singh Ten Savayyas

10 A Sikh should rise as night draws near to dawn and begin each day with an early-morning bathe.
Devoutly reading the Guru's words he goes to the dharamsala to hear eternal truth.
Joining the sangat there assembled he hears with deepest reverence the Guru's sacred songs.

Bhai Gurdas (d. 1633) var 40, v. 11

11 The light which shone from each of the ten Masters shines now from the sacred pages of the Guru Granth Sahib. Turn your thoughts to its message and call on God, saying, *Vahiguru!*

Ardas

12 Grant to your Sikhs a true knowledge of their faith, the blessing of uncut hair, guidance in conduct, spiritual perception, patient trust, abiding faith, and the supreme gift of the divine Name.

Ardas

13 You must always wear the Five Ks. These are uncut hair [*kes*], a sword or dagger [*kirpan*], a pair of shorts [*kachh*], a comb [*kangha*], and a steel bangle [*kara*].

Sikh Rahit Maryada

14 After three days and three nights had passed he [Guru Nanak] emerged from the stream, and having done so he declared: 'There is neither Hindu nor Muslim'

Mahima Prakas Varatak

15 The Guru [Ram Das] then pronounced his blessing on the sacred pool [Amritsar]. 'He who bathes here with a heart filled with devotion to God shall thereby receive the deliverance which I confer. This will assuredly happen. Even a bird which flies over this pool shall attain to the same sure deliverance without any effort on its part. They who obtain this salvation will find blissful peace in mystical union with God.'

Mahima Prakas Kavita

Alan Sillitoe 1928–

English writer

16 The loneliness of the long-distance runner.

title of novel (1959)

Georges Simenon 1903–89

Belgian novelist

1 Writing is not a profession but a vocation of unhappiness.

  interview in *Paris Review* Summer 1955

Paul Simon 1942–

American singer and songwriter

2 Like a bridge over troubled water
I will lay me down.

  'Bridge over Troubled Water' (1970 song)

3 And here's to you, Mrs Robinson
Jesus loves you more than you will know.

  'Mrs Robinson' (1967 song, from the film *The Graduate*)

4 People talking without speaking
People hearing without listening . . .
'Fools,' said I, 'You do not know
Silence like a cancer grows.'

  'Sound of Silence' (1964 song)

5 Still crazy after all these years.

  title of song (1975)

6 Improvisation is too good to leave to chance.

  in *International Herald Tribune* 12 October 1990

Simonides c.556–468 BC

Greek poet
see also **Epitaphs** 309:11

7 Painting is silent poetry, poetry is eloquent painting.

  Plutarch *Moralia* 'De Gloria Atheniensium' sect. 3

Konstantin Simonov 1915–79

Russian poet

8 Wait for me and I'll return . . .
Only you and I know how I survived.
It's because you waited as no one else did.

  'Wait for Me' (1942)

Harold Simpson

9 Down in the forest something stirred:
It was only the note of a bird.

  'Down in the Forest' (1906 song)

Kirke Simpson 1881–1972

American journalist

10 [Warren] Harding of Ohio was chosen by a group of men in a smoke-filled room early today as Republican candidate for President.

  often attributed to Harry Daugherty, one of Harding's supporters, who appears merely to have concurred with this version of events, when pressed for comment by Simpson

  news report, filed 12 June 1920; William Safire *New Language of Politics* (1968)

Tom Simpson see Last words 473:12, Misquotations 538:15

George R. Sims see Opening lines 574:23

C. H. Sisson 1914–2003

English poet

11 Here lies a civil servant. He was civil
To everyone, and servant to the devil.

  The London Zoo (1961)

Sitting Bull (Tatanka Iyotake) c.1831–90

Sioux chief

12 What law have I broken? Is it wrong for me to love my own? Is it wicked for me because my skin is red, because I am Sioux, because I was born where my fathers lived, because I would die for my people and my country?

  to Major Brotherton, recorded July 1881; Gary C. Anderson *Sitting Bull* (1996)

13 The Black Hills belong to me. If the whites try to take them, I will fight.

  Dee Brown *Bury My Heart at Wounded Knee* (1970) ch. 12

Edith Sitwell 1887–1964

English poet and critic
on Sitwell: see **Bowen** 148:6

14 Jane, Jane,
Tall as a crane,
The morning light creaks down again.

  Façade (1923) 'Aubade'

15 The fire was furry as a bear.

  Façade (1923) 'Dark Song'

16 Still falls the Rain—
Dark as the world of man, black as our loss—
Blind as the nineteen hundred and forty nails
Upon the Cross.

  'Still Falls the Rain' (1942)

17 I feel as if all my blood had been sucked, and my brains eaten by clothes moths. What I would give to be able to work uninterrupted!

  letter to Allen Tanner, 15 August 1933, in Richard Green (ed.) *Selected Letters of Edith Sitwell* (1997)

18 Calling a spade a spade never made the spade interesting yet. Take my advice, leave spades alone.

  letter to Charles Henri Ford, 23 August 1933, in Richard Green (ed.) *Selected Letters of Edith Sitwell* (1997)

19 I enjoyed talking to her, but thought *nothing* of her writing. I considered her 'a beautiful little knitter'.

  of Virginia **Woolf**

  letter to Geoffrey Singleton, 11 July 1955, in John Lehmann and Derek Palmer (eds.) *Selected Letters* (1970)

Osbert Sitwell 1892–1969

English writer

20 The British Bourgeoise
Is not born,

And does not die,
But, if it is ill,
It has a frightened look in its eyes.
At the House of Mrs Kinfoot (1921) p. 8

1 In reality, killing time
Is only the name for another of the multifarious
ways
By which Time kills us.
'Milordo Inglese' (1958); see **Boucicault** 147:4

2 On the coast of Coromandel
Dance they to the tunes of Handel.
'On the Coast of Coromandel' (1943)

Antonio Skarmeta 1940-

Chilean novelist

3 All men who first touch with words go much
further afterwards with their hands.
Burning Patience (1985) translated by Katherine Silver

4 Poetry belongs to those who use it, not those who
write it!
Burning Patience (1985) translated by Katherine Silver

John Skelton c.1460–1529

English poet

5 The sovereign'st thing that any man may have
Is little to say, and much to hear and see.
The Bouge of Court (1499) l. 211

6 Far may be sought
Erst that ye can find
So courteous, so kind,
As Merry Margaret,
This midsummer flower,
Gentle as falcon
Or hawk of the tower.
The Garland of Laurel (1523) 'To Mistress Margaret Hussey'

7 With margerain gentle,
The flower of goodlihead,
Embroidered the mantle
Is of your maidenhead.
The Garland of Laurel (1523) 'To Mistress Margery
Wentworth'

8 So many vagabonds, so many beggars bold;
So much decay of monasteries and of religious
places;
So hot hatred against the Church, and charity so
cold;
So much of 'my Lord's Grace,' and in him no
grace is;
So much hollow hearts, and so double faces;
So much sanctuary-breaking, and privilege-
barred—
Since Deucalion's flood was never seen nor lered.
'Speak, Parrot' (written *c.*1520) l. 498

Noel Skelton 1880–1935

British Conservative politician

9 To state as clearly as may be what means lie ready
to develop a property-owning democracy, to bring
the industrial and economic status of the wage-
earner abreast of his political and educational, to
make democracy stable and four-square.
in *The Spectator* 19 May 1923

B. F. Skinner 1904–90

American psychologist

10 The real question is not whether machines think
but whether men do.
Contingencies of Reinforcement (1969) ch. 9

11 Education is what survives when what has been
learned has been forgotten.
New Scientist 21 May 1964

☐ Slogans

see box overleaf

Joseph Roberts Smallwood 1900–91

*Canadian journalist and politician, Premier of Newfoundland
1949–70*

12 I am king of my own little island, and that's all
I've ever wanted to be.
Richard Gwyn *Smallwood: The Unlikely Revolutionary*
(1968)

Christopher Smart 1722–71

English poet
on Smart: see **Johnson** 428:4

13 Nature's decorations glisten
Far above their usual trim;
Birds on box and laurels listen,
As so near the cherubs hymn.
Hymns and Spiritual Songs (1765) 'The Nativity of Our Lord
and Saviour Jesus Christ'

14 God all-bounteous, all-creative,
Whom no ills from good dissuade,
Is incarnate, and a native
Of the very world he made.
Hymns and Spiritual Songs (1765) 'The Nativity of Our Lord
and Saviour Jesus Christ'

15 For in my nature I quested for beauty, but God,
God hath sent me to sea for pearls.
Jubilate Agno (*c.*1758–63) Fragment B, l. 30

16 For Charity is cold in the multitude of possessions,
and the rich are covetous of their crumbs.
Jubilate Agno (*c.*1758–63) Fragment B, l. 154

17 For I will consider my Cat Jeoffry.
For he is the servant of the Living God duly and
daily serving him.
For at the first glance of the glory of God in the
East he worships in his way.
For this is done by wreathing his body seven times
round with elegant quickness.
Jubilate Agno (*c.*1758–63) Fragment B, l. 695

18 For when his day's work is done his business more
properly begins.
For he keeps the Lord's watch in the night against
the adversary.

Continued

Slogans

1 Burn your bra.
feminist slogan, 1970s

2 A dog is for life, not just for Christmas.
slogan of the National Canine Defence League, from 1978

3 Guns don't kill people; people kill people.
National Rifle Association slogan

4 I'm backing Britain.
slogan coined by workers at the Colt factory, Surbiton, Surrey and subsequently used in a national campaign, in *The Times* 1 January 1968

5 It takes 40 dumb animals to make a fur coat, but only one to wear it.
slogan of an anti-fur campaign poster, 1980s; sometimes attributed to David **Bailey**

6 *Je suis Marxiste—tendance Groucho.*
I am a Marxist—of the Groucho tendency.
slogan used at Nanterre in Paris, 1968

7 Just say no.
slogan of the Nancy **Reagan** Drug Abuse Fund, founded 1985

8 Lousy but loyal.
London East End slogan at George V's Jubilee (1935)

9 Make love not war.
student slogan, 1960s

10 Pile it high, sell it cheap.
slogan coined by John Cohen (1898–1979), founder of Tesco

11 Save the whale.
environmental slogan associated with alarm over the rapidly declining whale population which led in 1985 to a moratorium on commercial whaling

12 Think globally, act locally.
Friends of the Earth slogan, *c.*1985

Christopher Smart *continued*
For he counteracts the powers of darkness by his electrical skin and glaring eyes.
For he counteracts the Devil, who is death, by brisking about the life.
Jubilate Agno (*c.*1758–63) Fragment B, l. 719

13 Ye beauties! O how great the sum
Of sweetness that ye bring;
On what a charity ye come
To bless the latter spring!
How kind the visit that ye pay,
Like strangers on a rainy day.
'On a Bed of Guernsey Lilies' (1764)

14 Yet still the philosophic mind
Consolatory food can find,
And hope her anchorage maintain:
We never are deserted quite;
'Tis by succession of delight
That love supports his reign.
'On a Bed of Guernsey Lilies' (1764)

15 Strong is the lion—like a coal
His eye-ball—like a bastion's mole
His chest against his foes.
Strong, the gier-eagle on his sail,
Strong against tide, th' enormous whale
Emerges as he goes.
A Song to David (1763) st. 76

16 But stronger still, in earth and air,
And in the sea, the man of pray'r;
And far beneath the tide;
And in the seat to faith assigned,
Where ask is have, where seek is find,
Where knock is open wide.
A Song to David (1763) st. 77

17 Beauteous the garden's umbrage mild,
Walk, water, meditated wild,
And all the bloomy beds.
A Song to David (1763) st. 78

18 Glorious the northern lights astream;
Glorious the song, when God's the theme;
Glorious the thunder's roar:
Glorious hosanna from the den;
Glorious the catholic amen;
Glorious the martyr's gore.

Glorious—more glorious is the crown
Of Him that brought salvation down
By meekness, called thy Son;
Thou that stupendous truth believed,
And now the matchless deed's achieved,
Determined, dared, and done.
A Song to David (1763) st. 85

19 Ah! Posthumus, the years, the years
Glide swiftly on, nor can our tears
Or piety the wrinkled age forefend,
Or for one hour retard th' inevitable end.
translation of Horace *Odes* bk. 2, no. 14; see **Horace** 401:6

Samuel Smiles 1812–1904
English writer

20 We each day dig our graves with our teeth.
Duty (1880) ch. 16

21 This extraordinary metal, the soul of every manufacture, and the mainspring perhaps of civilised society.
of iron
Men of Invention and Industry (1884) ch. 4

22 The spirit of self-help is the root of all genuine growth in the individual.
Self-Help (1859) ch. 1

23 The shortest way to do many things is to do only one thing at once.
Self-Help (1859) ch. 9

24 Middle class people are apt to live up to their incomes, if not beyond them.
Self-Help (1859) ch. 9

1 Cheerfulness gives elasticity to the spirit. Spectres fly before it.

Self-Help (1859) ch. 12

Adam Smith 1723–90

Scottish philosopher and economist

2 Wonder . . . and not any expectation of advantage from its discoveries, is the first principle which prompts mankind to the study of Philosophy, of that science which pretends to lay open the concealed connections that unite the various appearances of nature.

Essays on Philosophical Subjects (1795) 'The History of Astronomy' sect. 3, para. 3

3 And thus, *Place*, that great object which divides the wives of aldermen, is the end of half the labours of human life; and is the cause of all the tumult and bustle, all the rapine and injustice, which avarice and ambition have introduced into this world.

Theory of Moral Sentiments (1759) pt. 1, sect. 3, ch. 2

4 Though our brother is on the rack, as long as we ourselves are at our ease, our senses will never inform us of what he suffers . . . It is by imagination that we can form any conception of what are his sensations.

Theory of Moral Sentiments (2nd ed., 1762) p. 2

5 It is not from the benevolence of the butcher, the brewer, or the baker, that we expect our dinner, but from their regard to their own interest. We address ourselves not to their humanity but their self love.

Wealth of Nations (1776) bk. 1, ch. 2

6 People of the same trade seldom meet together, even for merriment and diversion, but the conversation ends in a conspiracy against the public, or in some contrivance to raise prices.

Wealth of Nations (1776) bk. 1, ch. 10, pt. 2

7 The chief enjoyment of riches consists in the parade of riches.

Wealth of Nations (1776) bk. 1, ch. 11

8 Every individual necessarily labours to render the annual revenue of society as great as he can. He generally neither intends to promote the public interest, nor knows how much he is promoting it. He intends only his own gain, and he is, in this, as in many other cases, led by an invisible hand to promote an end which was no part of his intention.

Wealth of Nations (1776) bk. 4, ch. 3

9 To found a great empire for the sole purpose of raising up a people of customers, may at first sight appear a project fit only for a nation of shopkeepers. It is, however, a project altogether unfit for a nation of shopkeepers; but extremely fit for a nation whose government is influenced by shopkeepers.

Wealth of Nations (1776) bk. 4, ch. 7, pt. 3; see **Adams** 3:14, **Napoleon** 557:4

10 Consumption is the sole end and purpose of production; and the interest of the producer ought to be attended to only so far as it may be necessary for promoting that of the consumer.

Wealth of Nations (1776) bk. 4, ch. 8

11 The discipline of colleges and universities is in general contrived, not for the benefit of the students, but for the interest, or more properly speaking, for the ease of the masters.

Wealth of Nations (1776) bk. 5, ch. 1, pt. 3

12 There is no art which one government sooner learns of another than that of draining money from the pockets of the people.

Wealth of Nations (1776) bk. 5, ch. 2

13 If any of the provinces of the British empire cannot be made to contribute towards the support of the whole empire, it is surely time that Great Britain should free herself from the expense of defending those provinces in time of war, and of supporting any part of their civil or military establishments in time of peace, and endeavour to accommodate her future views and designs to the real mediocrity of her circumstances.

Wealth of Nations (1776) bk. 5, ch. 3

Alfred Emanuel Smith 1873–1944

American politician

14 All the ills of democracy can be cured by more democracy.

speech in Albany, 27 June 1933, in *New York Times* 28 June 1933; see **Addams** 3:19

Delia Smith

English cook

15 A hen's egg is, quite simply, a work of art, a masterpiece of design and construction with, it has to be said, brilliant packaging.

How To Cook (1998)

Dodie Smith 1896–1990

English novelist and dramatist

see also **Opening lines** 574:29

16 The family—that dear octopus from whose tentacles we never quite escape.

Dear Octopus (1938)

17 Must talk, want to talk, got to talk, going to talk.

said as a very small child

Valerie Grove *Dear Dodie* (1996) ch. 1

Edgar Smith 1857–1938

American songwriter

18 You may tempt the upper classes
With your villainous demi-tasses,
But; Heaven will protect a working-girl!

'Heaven Will Protect the Working-Girl' (1909 song)

F. E. Smith, Lord Birkenhead 1872–1930

British Conservative politician and lawyer
on Smith: see **Asquith** *32:8,* **Chesterton** *215:18*

1 The world continues to offer glittering prizes to
those who have stout hearts and sharp swords.
rectorial address, Glasgow University, 7 November 1923,
in *The Times* 8 November 1923; see **Borrowed titles** 146:8

2 We have the highest authority for believing that
the meek shall inherit the earth; though I have
never found any particular corroboration of this
aphorism in the records of Somerset House.
Contemporary Personalities (1924) 'Marquess Curzon'; see
Bible 94:20

3 Nature has no cure for this sort of madness,
though I have known a legacy from a rich relative
work wonders.
of Bolshevism
Law, Life and Letters (1927) vol. 2, ch. 19

4 JUDGE DARLING: And who is George Robey?
SMITH: Mr George Robey is the Darling of the
music halls, m'lud.
A. E. Wilson *The Prime Minister of Mirth* (1956) ch. 1

5 JUDGE: What do you suppose I am on the Bench
for, Mr Smith?
SMITH: It is not for me, Your Honour, to attempt to
fathom the inscrutable workings of Providence.
2nd Earl of Birkenhead *F. E.* (1959 ed.) ch. 9

6 JUDGE: You are extremely offensive, young man.
SMITH: As a matter of fact, we both are, and the
only difference between us is that I am trying to
be, and you can't help it.
2nd Earl of Birkenhead *Earl of Birkenhead* (1933) vol. 1,
ch. 9

Godfrey Smith 1926–

English journalist and columnist

7 In a world full of audio visual marvels, may words
matter to you and be full of magic.
letter to a new grandchild, in *Sunday Times* 5 July 1987

Iain Duncan Smith 1954–

British Conservative politician, Leader of the Conservative
Party 2001–3
on Smith: see **Portillo** *607:23*

8 Do not underestimate the determination of a quiet
man.
speech to the Conservative Party Conference, 10 October
2002

Ian Smith 1919–

Rhodesian statesman; Prime Minister of Rhodesia (now
Zimbabwe), 1964–79

9 I don't believe in black majority rule in
Rhodesia—not in a thousand years.
broadcast speech, 20 March 1976, in *Sunday Times* 21
March 1976

John Smith 1938–94

Scottish-born Labour politician, Leader of the Labour Party
from 1992

10 The settled will of the Scottish people.
of the creation of a Scottish parliament
speech at the Scottish Labour Conference, 11 March 1994

Langdon Smith 1858–1908

11 When you were a tadpole, and I was a fish,
In the Palaeozoic time,
And side by side in the ebbing tide
We sprawled through the ooze and slime.
'A Toast to a Lady' in *The Scrap-Book* April 1906

Logan Pearsall Smith 1865–1946

American-born man of letters

12 There is more felicity on the far side of baldness
than young men can possibly imagine.
Afterthoughts (1931) 'Age and Death'

13 The test of a vocation is the love of the drudgery it
involves.
Afterthoughts (1931) 'Art and Letters'

14 A best-seller is the gilded tomb of a mediocre
talent.
Afterthoughts (1931) 'Art and Letters'

15 People say that life is the thing, but I prefer
reading.
Afterthoughts (1931) 'Myself'

16 Thank heavens, the sun has gone in, and I don't
have to go out and enjoy it.
Afterthoughts (1931) 'Myself'

17 What I like in a good author is not what he says,
but what he whispers.
All Trivia (1933) 'Afterthoughts' pt. 5

Samuel Francis Smith 1808–95

American poet and divine
on Smith: see **Holmes** *393:3*

18 My country, 'tis of thee,
Sweet land of liberty,
Of thee I sing:
Land where my fathers died,
Land of the pilgrims' pride,
From every mountain-side
Let freedom ring.
'America' (1831)

Stevie Smith (Florence Margaret Smith)
1902–71

English poet and novelist

19 Oh I am a cat that likes to
Gallop about doing good.
'The Galloping Cat' (1972)

20 A good time was had by all.
title of book (1937)

21 Why does my Muse only speak when she is
unhappy?

She does not, I only listen when I am unhappy.
'My Muse' (1964)

1 I was much too far out all my life
And not waving but drowning.
'Not Waving but Drowning' (1957)

2 People who are always praising the past
And especially the times of faith as best
Ought to go and live in the Middle Ages
And be burnt at the stake as witches and sages.
'The Past' (1957)

3 Private Means is dead
God rest his soul, officers and fellow-rankers said.
'Private Means is Dead' (1962)

4 This Englishwoman is so refined
She has no bosom and no behind.
'This Englishwoman' (1937)

5 I long for the Person from Porlock
To bring my thoughts to an end,
I am growing impatient to see him
I think of him as a friend.
'Thoughts about the "Person from Porlock" ' (1962); see
Coleridge 232:2

6 If you cannot have your dear husband for a
comfort and a delight, for a breadwinner and a
crosspatch, for a sofa, chair or a hot-water bottle,
one can use him as a Cross to be Borne.
Novel on Yellow Paper (1936) p. 24

7 If there wasn't death, I think you couldn't go on.
in *Observer* 9 November 1969

Sydney Smith 1771–1845
English clergyman and essayist

8 The moment the very name of Ireland is
mentioned, the English seem to bid adieu to
common feeling, common prudence, and common
sense, and to act with the barbarity of tyrants,
and the fatuity of idiots.
Letters of Peter Plymley (1807) letter 2

9 A Curate—there is something which excites
compassion in the very name of a Curate!!!
'Persecuting Bishops' in *Edinburgh Review* (1822)

10 Bishop Berkeley destroyed this world in one
volume octavo; and nothing remained, after his
time, but mind; which experienced a similar fate
from the hand of Mr Hume in 1739.
Sketches of Moral Philosophy (1849) introduction

11 We shall generally find that the triangular person
has got into the square hole, the oblong into the
triangular, and a square person has squeezed
himself into the round hole. The officer and the
office, the doer and the thing done, seldom fit so
exactly that we can say they were almost made for
each other.
Sketches of Moral Philosophy (1849) Lecture 9

12 I look upon Switzerland as an inferior sort of
Scotland.
letter to Lord Holland, 1815, in N. C. Smith (ed.) *Letters of
Sydney Smith* (1953)

13 Tory and Whig in turns shall be my host,
I taste no politics in boiled and roast.
letter to John Murray, November 1834, in *Letters of Sidney
Smith* (1953)

14 I have no relish for the country; it is a kind of
healthy grave.
letter to Miss G. Harcourt, 1838, in *Letters of Sidney Smith*
(1953)

15 If there is a pure and elevated pleasure in this
world it is a roast pheasant with bread sauce.
Barn-door fowls for dissenters, but for the real
Churchman, the thiry-nine-times articled clerk—
the pheasant, the pheasant.
letter to R. H. Barham, 15 November 1841, in *Letters of
Sidney Smith* (1953)

16 I have seen nobody since I saw you, but persons in
orders. My only varieties are vicars, rectors,
curates, and every now and then (by way of
turbot) an archdeacon.
letter to Miss Berry, 28 January 1843, in *Letters of Sidney
Smith* (1953)

17 It requires a surgical operation to get a joke well
into a Scotch understanding. Their only idea of
wit . . . is laughing immoderately at stated
intervals.
Lady Holland *Memoir* (1855) vol. 1, ch. 2

18 That knuckle-end of England—that land of Calvin,
oat-cakes, and sulphur.
of Scotland
Lady Holland *Memoir* (1855) vol. 1, ch. 2

19 Take short views, hope for the best, and trust in
God.
Lady Holland *Memoir* (1855) vol. 1, ch. 6

20 No furniture so charming as books.
Lady Holland *Memoir* (1855) vol. 1, ch. 9; see **Powell**
609:13

21 How can a bishop marry? How can he flirt? The
most he can say is, 'I will see you in the vestry
after service.'
Lady Holland *Memoir* (1855) vol. 1, ch. 9

22 As the French say, there are three sexes—men,
women, and clergymen.
Lady Holland *Memoir* (1855) vol. 1, ch. 9

23 Daniel Webster struck me much like a steam-
engine in trousers.
Lady Holland *Memoir* (1855) vol. 1, ch. 9

24 My definition of marriage . . . it resembles a pair of
shears, so joined that they cannot be separated;
often moving in opposite directions, yet always
punishing anyone who comes between them.
Lady Holland *Memoir* (1855) vol. 1, ch. 11

25 He has occasional flashes of silence, that make his
conversation perfectly delightful.
*of **Macaulay***
Lady Holland *Memoir* (1855) vol. 1, ch. 11

26 Let onion atoms lurk within the bowl,
And, scarce-suspected, animate the whole.
Lady Holland *Memoir* (1855) vol. 1, ch. 11 'Receipt for a
Salad'

1 Serenely full, the epicure would say,
Fate cannot harm me, I have dined to-day.
Lady Holland *Memoir* (1855) vol. 1, ch. 11 'Receipt for a Salad'; see **Dryden** 289:29

2 Deserves to be preached to death by wild curates.
Lady Holland *Memoir* (1855) vol. 1, ch. 11

3 Brighton Pavilion looks as if St Paul's had slipped down to Brighton and pupped.
attributed; Alan Bell (ed.) *The Sayings of Sydney Smith* (1993)

4 Death must be distinguished from dying, with which it is often confused.
H. Pearson *The Smith of Smiths* (1934) ch. 11

5 I am just going to pray for you at St Paul's, but with no very lively hope of success.
H. Pearson *The Smith of Smiths* (1934) ch. 13

6 I never read a book before reviewing it; it prejudices a man so.
H. Pearson *The Smith of Smiths* (1934) ch. 3

7 Minorities . . . are almost always in the right.
H. Pearson *The Smith of Smiths* (1934) ch. 9

8 My idea of heaven is, eating *pâté de foie gras* to the sound of trumpets.
view ascribed by Smith to his friend Henry Luttrell
H. Pearson *The Smith of Smiths* (1934) ch. 10; see **Disraeli** 277:34

9 Science is his forte, and omniscience his foible.
on **Whewell**
Isaac Todhunter *William Whewell* (1876) vol. 1

10 What a pity it is that we have no amusements in England but vice and religion!
H. Pearson *The Smith of Smiths* (1934) ch. 10

11 What two ideas are more inseparable than Beer and Britannia?
H. Pearson *The Smith of Smiths* (1934) ch. 11

Walter Chalmers Smith 1824–1908
Scottish clergyman

12 Immortal, invisible, God only wise.
'God, All in All' (1867 hymn)

13 Unresting, unhasting, and silent as light,
Nor wanting, nor wasting, thou rulest in might.
'God, All in All' (1867 hymn)

14 We blossom and flourish as leaves on the tree,
And wither and perish; but naught changeth thee.
'God, All in All' (1867 hymn)

Tobias Smollett 1721–71
Scottish novelist

15 I think for my part one half of the nation is mad—and the other not very sound.
The Adventures of Sir Launcelot Greaves (1762) ch. 6

16 The capital [London] is become an overgrown monster; which, like a dropsical head, will in time leave the body and extremities without nourishment and support.
Humphry Clinker (1771) vol. 1 (letter from Matthew Bramble, 29 May)

17 'Begging your honour's pardon, (replied Clinker) may not the new light of God's grace shine upon the poor and the ignorant in their humility, as well as upon the wealthy, and the philosopher in all his pride of human learning?' What you imagine to be the new light of grace, (said his master) I take to be a deceitful vapour, glimmering through a crack in your upper storey.
Humphry Clinker (1771) vol. 2 (letter from Jery Melford, 10 June)

18 Mourn, hapless Caledonia, mourn
Thy banished peace, thy laurels torn.
'The Tears of Scotland' (1746)

19 That great Cham of literature, Samuel Johnson.
letter to John Wilkes, 16 March 1759, in James Boswell *Life of Samuel Johnson* (1934 ed.) vol. 1

Jan Christiaan Smuts 1870–1950
South African soldier and statesman, Prime Minister 1919–24 and 1939–48

20 Mankind is once more on the move. The very foundations have been shaken and loosened, and things are again fluid. The tents have been struck, and the great caravan of humanity is once more on the march.
on the setting up of the League of Nations, in the wake of the First World War
W. K. Hancock *Smuts* (1968)

C. P. Snow 1905–80
English novelist and scientist

21 The official world, the corridors of power.
Homecomings (1956) ch. 22

22 The two cultures and the scientific revolution.
title of The Rede Lecture (1959)

Socrates 469–399 BC
Greek philosopher
on Socrates: see **Plato** 597:10; *see also* **Burton** 174:6, **Last words** 471:7

23 How many things I can do without!
on looking at a multitude of goods exposed for sale
Diogenes Laertius *Lives of the Philosophers* bk. 2, ch. 25

24 I know nothing except the fact of my ignorance.
Diogenes Laertius *Lives of the Philosophers* bk. 2, sect. 32; see **Davies** 258:8, **Milton** 534:22

25 The rest of the world lives to eat, while I eat to live.
Diogenes Laertius *Lives of the Philosophers* bk. 2, sect. 34; see **Proverbs** 618:37

26 Most excellent man, are you who are a citizen of Athens, the greatest of cities and the most famous for wisdom and power, not ashamed to care for the acquisition of wealth and for reputation and honour, when you neither care nor take thought for wisdom and truth and the perfection of your soul?
Plato *Apology* 29d

1 Virtue does not come from money, but from virtue comes money and all other good things to man, both to the individual and to the state.

Plato *Apology* 30b

2 Then I, however, showed again, by action, not in word only, that I did not care a whit for death … but that I did care with all my might not to do anything unjust or unholy.

on being ordered by the Thirty Commissioners to take part in the liquidation of Leon of Salamis

Plato *Apology* 32d

3 The unexamined life is not worth living.

Plato *Apology* 38a

4 It [death] is, you see, one or other of two things: either to be dead is to be non-existent, as it were, and a dead person has no awareness of anything at all; or else, as we are told, the soul undergoes some sort of transformation, or exchanging of this present world for another.

Plato *Apology* 41c (translated by David Gallop)

5 But already it is time to depart, for me to die, for you to go on living; which of us takes the better course, is not known to anyone except God.

Plato *Apology* 42a

6 It is never right to do wrong or to requite wrong with wrong, or when we suffer evil to defend ourselves by doing evil in return.

Plato *Crito* 49d

7 It is perfectly certain that the soul is immortal and imperishable, and our souls will actually exist in another world.

Plato *Phaedo* 107a

8 A man should feel confident concerning his soul, who has renounced those pleasures and fineries that go with the body, as being alien to him, and considering them to result more in harm than in good, but has pursued the pleasures that go with learning and made the soul fine with no alien but rather its own proper refinements, moderation and justice and courage and freedom and truth; thus he is ready for the journey to the world below, ready to go when Fate calls him.

Plato *Phaedo* 114d

9 'What do you say about pouring a libation to some god from this cup? Is it allowed or not?' 'We only prepare just the right amount to drink, Socrates,' he [the jailer] said. 'I understand,' he went on; 'but it is allowed and necessary to pray to the gods, that my moving from hence to there may be blessed; thus I pray, and so be it.'

Plato *Phaedo* 117b

10 But, my dearest Agathon, it is truth which you cannot contradict; you can without any difficulty contradict Socrates.

Plato *Symposium* 201d

11 I am not Athenian or Greek but a citizen of the world.

Plutarch *Moralia* bk. 7 'On Exile'

Solon c.640–after 556 BC
Greek poet and Athenian statesman

12 I grow old ever learning many things.

Theodor Bergk (ed.) *Poetae Lyrici Graeci* (1843) no. 18

13 Call no man happy before he dies, he is at best but fortunate.

Herodotus *Histories* bk. 1, ch. 32; see **Bible** 93:12, **Proverbs** 616:22

Alexander Solzhenitsyn 1918–
Russian novelist

14 You only have power over people as long as you don't take *everything* away from them. But when you've robbed a man of *everything* he's no longer in your power — he's free again.

The First Circle (1968) ch. 17

15 The Gulag archipelago.

title of book (1973–5)

16 How can you expect a man who's warm to understand one who's cold?

One Day in the Life of Ivan Denisovich (1962) p. 22 (translated by Ralph Parker)

17 The thoughts of a prisoner—they're not free either. They keep returning to the same things.

One Day in the Life of Ivan Denisovich (1962) p. 34 (translated by Ralph Parker)

18 After the suffering of decades of violence and oppression, the human soul longs for higher things, warmer and purer than those offered by today's mass living habits, introduced as by a calling card by the revolting invasion of commercial advertising, by TV stupor and by intolerable music.

speech in Cambridge, Massachusetts, 8 June 1978

19 The clock of communism has stopped striking. But its concrete building has not yet come crashing down. For that reason, instead of freeing ourselves, we must try to save ourselves being crushed by the rubble.

in *Komsomolskaya Pravda* 18 September 1990

20 The Iron Curtain did not reach the ground and under it flowed liquid manure from the West.

speaking at Far Eastern Technical University, Vladivostok, 30 May 1994; see **Churchill** 221:20

William Somerville 1675–1742
English country gentleman

21   My hoarse-sounding horn
Invites thee to the chase, the sport of kings;
Image of war, without its guilt.

The Chase (1735) bk. 1, l. 13; see **D'Avenant** 257:22, **Surtees** 764:12

22 Hail, happy Britain! highly favoured isle,
And Heaven's peculiar care!

The Chase (1735) bk. 1, l. 84

Anastasio Somoza 1925–80

Nicaraguan dictator
on Somoza: see **Cardenal** *190:8*

1 You won the elections, but I won the count.
replying to an accusation of ballot-rigging
in *Guardian* 17 June 1977; see **Stoppard** 761:7

Stephen Sondheim 1930–

American songwriter

2 I like to be in America!
O.K. by me in America!
Ev'rything free in America
For a small fee in America!
'America' (1957 song) in *West Side Story*

3 Every day a little death
title of song (1973) in *A Little Night Music*

4 Ev'ry day a little death
On the lips and in the eyes,
In the murmurs, in the pauses,
In the gestures, in the sighs.
Ev'ry day a little dies.
'Every Day a Little Death' (1973 song) in *A Little Night Music*

5 Everything's coming up roses.
title of song (1959) in *Gypsy*

6 Isn't it rich?
Are we a pair?
Me here at last on the ground, you in mid-air.
'Send in the Clowns' (1973 song) in *A Little Night Music*

7 Where are the clowns?
Send in the clowns.
'Send in the Clowns' (1973 song) in *A Little Night Music*

☐ Songs, spirituals, and shanties

see box opposite
see also **Ballads**, **Political slogans and songs**

Susan Sontag 1933–

American writer

8 Societies need to have one illness which becomes identified with evil, and attaches blame to its 'victims'.
AIDS and its Metaphors (1989)

9 What pornography is really about, ultimately, isn't sex but death.
in *Partisan Review* Spring 1967

10 The white race *is* the cancer of human history, it is the white race, and it alone—its ideologies and inventions—which eradicates autonomous civilizations wherever it spreads, which has upset the ecological balance of the planet, which now threatens the very existence of life itself.
in *Partisan Review* Winter 1967

Donald Soper 1903–98

British Methodist minister

11 It is, I think, good evidence of life after death.
on the quality of debate in the House of Lords
in *Listener* 17 August 1978

Sophocles c.496–406 BC

Greek dramatist
on Sophocles: see **Aristophanes** *25:5*, **Aristotle** *25:24*, **Arnold** *28:29; see also* **Anonymous** *21:11*, **Heaney** *377:18*

12 My son, may you be happier than your father.
Ajax l. 550

13 Enemies' gifts are no gifts and do no good.
Ajax l. 665

14 His death concerns the gods, not those men, no!
of Ajax's enemies, the Greek leaders
Ajax l. 970

15 There are many wonderful things, and nothing is more wonderful than man.
Antigone l. 333

16 Nor could I think that a decree of yours—
A man—could override the laws of Heaven
Unwritten and unchanging. Not of today
Or yesterday is their authority;
They are eternal; no man saw their birth.
Antigone l. 454

17 Not to be born is, past all prizing, best.
Oedipus Coloneus l. 1225 (translation by R. C. Jebb); see **Auden** 34:23, **Yeats** 854:9

18 You are blind in your ears and mind, as well as your eyes.
Oedipus to Tiresias
Oedipus Tyrannus l. 370

19 I think I heard you say that Laius
Was murdered at a place where three ways meet?
Oedipus Tyrannus l. 729 (translated by H. D. F. Kitto)

20 So do not fear this marriage with your mother;
Many a man has suffered this before—
But only in his dreams.
Oedipus Tyrannus l. 977 (translated by H. D. F. Kitto)

21 Someone asked Sophocles, 'How is your sex-life now? Are you still able to have a woman?' He replied, 'Hush, man; most gladly indeed am I rid of it all, as though I had escaped from a mad and savage master.'
Plato *Republic* bk. 1, 329b

Charles Hamilton Sorley 1895–1915

English poet

22 We swing ungirded hips,
And lightened are our eyes,
The rain is on our lips,
We do not run for prize.
'Song of the Ungirt Runners' (1916)

23 When you see millions of the mouthless dead
Across your dreams in pale battalions go,
Say not soft things as other men have said,
That you'll remember. For you need not so.
Give them not praise. For, deaf, how should they know
It is not curses heaped on each gashed head?
'A Sonnet' (1916)

Continued

Songs, spirituals, and shanties

1 A-roving! A-roving!
Since roving's been my ru-i-n
I'll go no more a-roving
With you fair maid.
'A-roving' (traditional song)

2 Come, landlord, fill the flowing bowl
Until it doth run over . . .
For to-night we'll merry be,
To-morrow we'll be sober.
'Come, Landlord, Fill the Flowing Bowl' (traditional song)

3 Come lasses and lads, get leave of your dads,
And away to the Maypole hie,
For every he has got him a she,
And the fiddler's standing by.
For Willie shall dance with Jane,
And Johnny has got his Joan,
To trip it, trip it, trip it, trip it, trip it up and
down.
'Come Lasses and Lads' (traditional song, c.1670)

4 Early one morning, just as the sun was rising,
I heard a maid sing in the valley below:
'Oh, don't deceive me; Oh, never leave me!
How could you use a poor maiden so?'
'Early One Morning' (traditional song)

5 Frankie and Albert were lovers, O Lordy, how
they could love.
Swore to be true to each other, true as the stars
above;
He was her man, but he done her wrong.
'Frankie and Albert', in John Huston *Frankie and Johnny*
(1930) (St Louis ballad later better known as 'Frankie
and Johnny')

6 God gave Noah the rainbow sign,
No more water, the fire next time.
Home in that Rock (Negro spiritual)

7 God save our gracious king!
Long live our noble king!
God save the king!
Send him victorious,
Happy, and glorious,
Long to reign over us:
God save the king!
'God save the King', attributed to various authors of the
mid eighteenth century, including Henry **Carey**; Jacobite
variants, such as James Hogg 'The King's Anthem' in
Jacobite Relics of Scotland Second Series (1821) also exist

8 Confound their politics,
Frustrate their knavish tricks.
'God save the King'

9 Greensleeves was all my joy,
Greensleeves was my delight,
Greensleeves was my heart of gold,
And who but Lady Greensleeves?
'A new Courtly Sonnet of the Lady Greensleeves, to the
new tune of "Greensleeves" ', in *A Handful of Pleasant
Delights* (1584)

10 The holly and the ivy,
When they are both full grown,

Of all the trees that are in the wood,
The holly bears the crown:
The rising of the sun
And the running of the deer,
The playing of the merry organ,
Sweet singing in the choir.
'The Holly and the Ivy' (traditional carol)

11 I'll sing you twelve O.
Green grow the rushes O.
What is your twelve O?
Twelve for the twelve apostles,
Eleven for the eleven who went to heaven,
Ten for the ten commandments,
Nine for the nine bright shiners,
Eight for the eight bold rangers,
Seven for the seven stars in the sky,
Six for the six proud walkers,
Five for the symbol at your door,
Four for the Gospel makers,
Three for the rivals,
Two, two, the lily-white boys,
Clothed all in green O,
One is one and all alone
And ever more shall be so.
'The Dilly Song', in G. Grigson (ed.) *The Faber Book of
Popular Verse* (1971); see **Burns** 171:6

12 In good King Charles's golden days,
When loyalty no harm meant;
A furious High-Churchman I was,
And so I gained preferment.
Unto my flock I daily preached,
Kings are by God appointed,
And damned are those who dare resist,
Or touch the Lord's Anointed.
And this is law, I will maintain,
Unto my dying day, Sir,
That whatsoever King shall reign,
I will be the Vicar of Bray, sir!
'The Vicar of Bray' in *British Musical Miscellany* (1734)
vol. I

13 John Brown's body lies a mould'ring in the
grave,
His soul is marching on.
inspired by the execution of the abolitionist John
Brown*, after the raid on Harper's Ferry, on 2*
December 1859
song (1861), variously attributed to Charles Sprague
Hall, Henry Howard Brownell, and Thomas Brigham
Bishop

14 Like a fine old English gentleman,
All of the olden time.
'The Fine Old English Gentleman' (traditional song)

15 Maxwelton braes are bonnie
Where early fa's the dew.
William Douglas of Fingland (fl. 1700) 'Annie Laurie'

▶

▸ Songs, spirituals, and shanties *continued*

1 And for bonnie Annie Laurie
I'd lay me doun and dee.
  William Douglas of Fingland (fl. 1700) 'Annie Laurie'

2 One Friday morn when we set sail,
And our ship not far from land,
We there did espy a fair pretty maid,
With a comb and a glass in her hand.
While the raging seas did roar,
And the stormy winds did blow,
And we jolly sailor-boys were all up aloft
And the land-lubbers lying down below.
  'The Mermaid' (traditional song)

3 O ye'll tak' the high road, and I'll tak' the low
road,
And I'll be in Scotland afore ye,
But me and my true love will never meet again,
On the bonnie, bonnie banks o' Loch Lomon'.
  'The Bonnie Banks of Loch Lomon'' (traditional song)

4 A ship I have got in the North Country
And she goes by the name of the *Golden Vanity*,
O I fear she will be taken by a Spanish Ga-la-lee,
As she sails by the Low-lands low.
  'The Golden Vanity' (traditional song)

5 Some talk of Alexander, and some of Hercules;
Of Hector and Lysander, and such great names
as these;
But of all the world's brave heroes, there's none
that can compare
With a tow, row, row, row, row, row, for the
British Grenadier.
  'The British Grenadiers' (traditional song)

6 Swing low, sweet chariot—
Comin' for to carry me home;
I looked over Jordan and what did I see?
A band of angels comin' after me—
Comin' for to carry me home.
  Negro spiritual (*c.*1850)

7 There is a tavern in the town,
And there my dear love sits him down,
And drinks his wine 'mid laughter free,
And never, never thinks of me.
Fare thee well, for I must leave thee,
Do not let this parting grieve thee,
And remember that the best of friends must part.
Adieu, adieu, kind friends, adieu, adieu, adieu,
I can no longer stay with you,
I'll hang my harp on a weeping willow-tree,
And may the world go well with thee.
  'There is a Tavern in the Town' (traditional song)

8 This lass so neat, with smiles so sweet,
Has won my right good-will,
I'd crowns resign to call thee mine,
Sweet lass of Richmond Hill.
  Leonard MacNally (1752–1820) 'The Lass of Richmond
  Hill'; also attributed to W. Upton in *The Oxford Song Book*
  (1916), and to W. Hudson in S. Baring-Gould *English
  Minstrelsie* (1895) vol. 3

9 Were you there when they crucified my Lord?
  title of Negro spiritual (1865)

10 When Israel was in Egypt land,
Let my people go,
Oppressed so hard they could not stand,
Let my people go.
Go down, Moses,
Way-down in Egypt land,
Tell old Pharaoh
To let my people go.
  'Go Down, Moses' (Negro spiritual); see **Bible** 77:26

11 Yankee Doodle came to town
Riding on a pony;
Stuck a feather in his cap
And called it Macaroni.
  'Yankee Doodle' (song, 1755 or earlier); Nicholas Smith
  Stories of Great National Songs (1899) ch. 2; see **Cohan**
  230:8

Charles Hamilton Sorley *continued*

12 If Goethe really died saying 'more light', it was
very silly of him: what *he* wanted was more
warmth.
  letter, July 1914; *The Letters of Charles Sorley* (1919); see
  Last words 473:5

13 I do wish people would not deceive themselves by
talk of a just war. There is no such thing as a just
war. What we are doing is casting out Satan by
Satan.
  letter to his mother from Aldershot, March 1915; *The
  Letters of Charles Sorley* (1919); see **Bible** 99:16

Robert South 1634–1716

English court preacher

14 An Aristotle was but the rubbish of an Adam, and
Athens but the rudiments of Paradise.
  Twelve Sermons . . . (1692) vol. 1, no. 2

Thomas Southerne 1660–1746

Irish dramatist

15   When we're worn,
Hacked hewn with constant service, thrown aside
To rust in peace, or rot in hospitals.
  The Loyal Brother (1682) act 1

16 For love is but discovery:
When that is made, the pleasure's done.
  Sir Anthony Love (1690) act 2 'Song'

Robert Southey 1774–1843

English poet and writer

17 It was a summer evening,
Old Kaspar's work was done,
And he before his cottage door
Was sitting in the sun,
And by him sported on the green
His little grandchild Wilhelmine.
  'The Battle of Blenheim' (1800)

1 Now tell us all about the war,
And what they fought each other for.
'The Battle of Blenheim' (1800)

2 'And everybody praised the Duke,
Who this great fight did win.'
'But what good came of it at last?'
Quoth little Peterkin.
'Why that I cannot tell,' said he,
'But 'twas a famous victory.'
'The Battle of Blenheim' (1800)

3 Curses are like young chickens, they always come
home to roost.
The Curse of Kehama (1810) motto

4 No stir in the air, no stir in the sea,
The ship was still as she could be.
'The Inchcape Rock' (1802)

5 And then they knew the perilous rock,
And blessed the Abbot of Aberbrothock.
'The Inchcape Rock' (1802)

6 Oh Christ! It is the Inchcape Rock!
'The Inchcape Rock' (1802)

7 My name is Death: the last best friend am I.
'The Lay of the Laureate' (1816) st. 87

8 Blue, darkly, deeply, beautifully blue.
Madoc (1805) pt. 1, canto 5 'Lincoya' l. 102

9 You are old, Father William, the young man cried,
The few locks which are left you are grey;
You are hale, Father William, a hearty old man,
Now tell me the reason, I pray.
'The Old Man's Comforts' (1799); see **Carroll** 194:4

10 The arts babblative and scribblative.
Colloquies on the Progress and Prospects of Society (1829) no.
10, pt. 2

11 The march of intellect.
Colloquies on the Progress and Prospects of Society (1829)
no. 14

12 Your true lover of literature is never fastidious.
The Doctor (1812) ch. 17

13 Show me a man who cares no more for one place
than another, and I will show you in that same
person one who loves nothing but himself. Beware
of those who are homeless by choice.
The Doctor (1812) ch. 34

14 Live as long as you may, the first twenty years are
the longest half of your life.
The Doctor (1812) ch. 130

15 Somebody has been sitting in my chair!
The Doctor vol. 4 (1837) 'The Story of the Three Bears'

16 Men started at the intelligence, and turned pale,
as if they had heard of the loss of a dear friend.
*on the death of **Nelson***
The Life of Nelson (1813) ch. 9

17 She has made me in love with a cold climate, and
frost and snow, with a northern moonlight.
*on Mary **Wollstonecraft**'s letters from Sweden and
Norway*
letter to his brother Thomas, 28 April 1797, in Charles
Southey *Life and Correspondence of Robert Southey* vol. 1
(1849); see **Mitford** 540:17

18 Literature cannot be the business of a woman's
life: and it ought not to be.
letter to Charlotte Brontë, 12 March 1837, in Margaret
Smith (ed.) *The Letters of Charlotte Brontë* (1995)

Robert Southwell c.1561–95
English poet and Roman Catholic martyr

19 As I in hoary winter night stood shivering in the
snow,
Surprised was I with sudden heat which made my
heart to glow;
And lifting up a fearful eye to view what fire was
near
A pretty Babe all burning bright did in the air
appear.
'The Burning Babe' (c.1590)

20 My faultless breast the furnace is,
The fuel wounding thorns;
Love is the fire, and sighs the smoke,
The ashes, shame and scorns;
The fuel Justice layeth on,
And Mercy blows the coals;
The metal in this furnace wrought
Are men's defiled souls.
'The Burning Babe' (c.1590)

21 To rise by other's fall
I deem a losing gain;
All states with others' ruins built
To ruin run amain.
'Content and Rich' (1595)

22 Times go by turns, and chances change by course,
From foul to fair, from better hap to worse.
'Times go by Turns' (1595)

23 Before my face the picture hangs,
That daily should put me in mind
Of those cold qualms, and bitter pangs,
That shortly I am like to find:
But yet alas full little I
Do think hereon that I must die.
'Upon the Image of Death' (attributed)

Muriel Spark 1918–
British novelist
*see also **Opening lines** 575:1*

24 I am a hoarder of two things: documents and
trusted friends.
Curriculum Vitae (1992)

25 I am putting old heads on your young shoulders
. . . all my pupils are the crème de la crème.
The Prime of Miss Jean Brodie (1961) ch. 1

26 Give me a girl at an impressionable age, and she is
mine for life.
The Prime of Miss Jean Brodie (1961) ch. 1; see **Sayings**
669:21

27 One's prime is elusive. You little girls, when you
grow up, must be on the alert to recognise your
prime at whatever time of your life it may occur.
The Prime of Miss Jean Brodie (1961) ch. 1

28 To me education is a leading out of what is
already there in the pupil's soul. To Miss Mackay

it is a putting in of something that is not there, and that is not what I call education, I call it intrusion.

The Prime of Miss Jean Brodie (1961) ch. 2

1 If you're going to do a thing, you should do it thoroughly. If you're going to be a Christian, you may as well be a Catholic.

in *Independent* 2 August 1989

John Sparrow 1906–92

English academic, Warden of All Souls College, Oxford, 1952–77
see also Epitaphs 311:18

2 That indefatigable and unsavoury engine of pollution, the dog.

letter to *The Times* 30 September 1975

Rachel Speght fl. 1621

English poet

3 God's image man doth bear
Without it he is but a human shape,
Worse than the Devil.

'Mortality's Memorandum' (1621)

Herbert Spencer 1820–1903

English philosopher

4 Science is organized knowledge.

Education (1861) ch. 2

5 People are beginning to see that the first requisite to success in life is to be a good animal.

Education (1861) ch. 2

6 Absolute morality is the regulation of conduct in such a way that pain shall not be inflicted.

Essays (1891) vol. 3 'Prison Ethics'

7 Evolution . . . is—a change from an indefinite, incoherent homogeneity, to a definite coherent heterogeneity.

First Principles (1862) ch. 16

8 This survival of the fittest which I have here sought to express in mechanical terms, is that which Mr Darwin has called 'natural selection, or the preservation of favoured races in the struggle for life'.

Principles of Biology (1865) pt. 3, ch. 12; see **Darwin** 257:9

9 How often misused words generate misleading thoughts.

Principles of Ethics (1879) bk. 1, pt. 2, ch. 8, sect. 152

10 Progress, therefore, is not an accident, but a necessity . . . It is a part of nature.

Social Statics (1850) pt. 1, ch. 2, sect. 4

11 A clever theft was praiseworthy amongst the Spartans; and it is equally so amongst Christians, provided it be on a sufficiently large scale.

Social Statics (1850) pt. 2, ch. 16, sect. 3

12 Hero-worship is strongest where there is least regard for human freedom.

Social Statics (1850) pt. 4, ch. 30, sect. 6

13 No one can be perfectly free till all are free; no one can be perfectly moral till all are moral; no one can be perfectly happy till all are happy.

Social Statics (1850) pt. 4, ch. 30, sect. 16

Lord Spencer 1964–

English peer

14 She needed no royal title to continue to generate her particular brand of magic.

*tribute at the funeral of his sister, **Diana**, Princess of Wales, 7 September 1997*
in *Guardian* 8 September 1997

15 We, your blood family, will do all we can to continue the imaginative way in which you were steering these two exceptional young men so that their souls are not simply immersed by duty and tradition but can sing openly as you planned.

referring to his nephews, Prince William and Prince Harry; funeral tribute, 7 September 1997
in *Guardian* 8 September 1997

Raine, Countess Spencer 1929–

16 Alas, for our towns and cities. Monstrous carbuncles of concrete have erupted in gentle Georgian Squares.

The Spencers on Spas (1983) p. 14; see **Charles** 209:15

Stanley Spencer 1891–1959

English painter
*on Spencer: see **Lewis** 484:3*

17 Painting is saying 'Ta' to God.

letter from Spencer's daughter Shirin, in *Observer* 7 February 1988

Stephen Spender 1909–95

English poet
*on Spender: see **Waugh** 824:18*

18 After the first powerful plain manifesto
The black statement of pistons, without more fuss
But gliding like a queen, she leaves the station.

'The Express' (1933)

19 I think continually of those who were truly great.

title of poem (1933)

20 Born of the sun they travelled a short while
    towards the sun,
And left the vivid air signed with their honour.

'I think continually of those who were truly great' (1933)

21   Their collected
Hearts wound up with love, like little watch
    springs.

'The Past Values' (1939)

22 Pylons, those pillars
Bare like nude, giant girls that have no secret.

'The Pylons' (1933)

23 What I had not foreseen
Was the gradual day
Weakening the will
Leaking the brightness away.

'What I expected, was' (1933)

1 Who live under the shadow of a war,
What can I do that matters?
  'Who live under the shadow of a war' (1933)

Edmund Spenser c.1552–99

English poet
on Spenser: see **Cecil** 204:15

2 The merry cuckoo, messenger of Spring,
His trumpet shrill hath thrice already sounded.
  Amoretti (1595) sonnet 19

3 Most glorious Lord of life, that on this day
Didst make thy triumph over death and sin:
And, having harrowed hell, didst bring away
Captivity thence captive, us to win.
  Amoretti (1595) sonnet 68

4 One day I wrote her name upon the strand,
But came the waves and washèd it away:
Again I wrote it with a second hand,
But came the tide, and made my pains his prey.
Vain man, said she, that dost in vain assay,
A mortal thing so to immortalize.
  Amoretti (1595) sonnet 75

5 So love is Lord of all the world by right.
  Colin Clout's Come Home Again (1595) l. 883

6 So you great Lord, that with your counsel sway
The burden of this kingdom mightily,
With like delights sometimes may eke delay,
The rugged brow of careful Policy.
  'Dedicatory Sonnet to Sir Christopher Hatton' (1590)

7 Hark how the cheerful birds do chant their lays
And carol of love's praise.
The merry lark her matins sings aloft,
The thrush replies, the mavis descant plays,
The ouzel shrills, the ruddock warbles soft,
So goodly all agree with sweet consent,
To this day's merriment.
  'Epithalamion' (1595) l. 74

8 Open the temple gates unto my love,
Open them wide that she may enter in.
  'Epithalamion' (1595) l. 204

9 Ah! when will this long weary day have end,
And lend me leave to come unto my love?
How slowly do the hours their numbers spend!
How slowly does sad Time his feathers move!
  'Epithalamion' (1595) l. 278

10 Song made in lieu of many ornaments,
With which my love should duly have been
  decked.
  'Epithalamion' (1595) l. 427

11 The general end therefore of all the book is to
fashion a gentleman or noble person in virtuous
and gentle discipline.
  The Faerie Queene (1596) preface

12 A gentle knight was pricking on the plain.
  The Faerie Queene (1596) bk. 1, canto 1, st. 1

13 But on his breast a bloody cross he bore,
The dear remembrance of his dying Lord.
  The Faerie Queene (1596) bk. 1, canto 1, st. 2

14 A bold bad man, that dared to call by name
Great Gorgon, Prince of darkness and dead night.
  The Faerie Queene (1596) bk. 1, canto 1, st. 37; see
  Shakespeare 695:7

15 　　　　Her angel's face
As the great eye of heaven shinèd bright,
And made a sunshine in the shady place;
Did never mortal eye behold such heavenly grace.
  The Faerie Queene (1596) bk. 1, canto 3, st. 4

16 And all the hinder parts, that few could spy,
Were ruinous and old, but painted cunningly.
  The Faerie Queene (1596) bk. 1, canto 4, st. 5

17 The noble heart, that harbours virtuous thought,
And is with child of glorious great intent,
Can never rest, until it forth have brought
Th' eternal brood of glory excellent.
  The Faerie Queene (1596) bk. 1, canto 5, st. 1

18 　　　　A cruel crafty crocodile,
Which in false grief hiding his harmful guile,
Doth weep full sore, and sheddeth tender tears.
  The Faerie Queene (1596) bk. 1, canto 5, st. 18

19 Still as he fled, his eye was backward cast,
As if his fear still followed him behind.
  The Faerie Queene (1596) bk. 1, canto 9, st. 21

20 That darksome cave they enter, where they find
That cursèd man, low sitting on the ground,
Musing full sadly in his sullen mind.
  The Faerie Queene (1596) bk. 1, canto 9, st. 35

21 Sleep after toil, port after stormy seas,
Ease after war, death after life does greatly please.
  written on Joseph **Conrad**'s *gravestone*
  The Faerie Queene (1596) bk. 1, canto 9, st. 40

22 Upon her eyelids many Graces sate,
Under the shadow of her even brows.
  The Faerie Queene (1596) bk. 2, canto 3, st. 25

23 And with rich metal loaded every rift.
  The Faerie Queene (1596) bk. 2, canto 7, st. 28; see **Keats**
  447:7

24 And all for love, and nothing for reward.
  The Faerie Queene (1596) bk. 2, canto 8, st. 2

25 So passeth, in the passing of a day,
Of mortal life the leaf, the bud, the flower,
No more doth flourish after first decay,
That erst was sought to deck both bed and bower.
  The Faerie Queene (1596) bk. 2, canto 12, st. 75

26 Gather therefore the rose, whilst yet is prime,
For soon comes age, that will her pride deflower:
Gather the rose of love, whilst yet is time,
Whilst loving thou mayst lovèd be with equal
  crime.
  The Faerie Queene (1596) bk. 2, canto 12, st. 75

27 　　　　The dunghill kind
Delights in filth and foul incontinence:
Let Grill be Grill, and have his hoggish mind.
  The Faerie Queene (1596) bk. 2, canto 12, st. 87

28 　　　　Whether it divine tobacco were,
Or panachaea, or polygony.
  The Faerie Queene (1596) bk. 3, canto 5, st. 32

29 And painful pleasure turns to pleasing pain.
  The Faerie Queene (1596) bk. 3, canto 10, st. 60

1 And as she looked about, she did behold,
How over that same door was likewise writ,
Be bold, be bold, and everywhere Be bold . . .
At last she spied at that room's upper end
Another iron door, on which was writ
Be not too bold.
The Faerie Queene (1596) bk. 3, canto 11, st. 54

2 Dan Chaucer, well of English undefiled,
On Fame's eternal beadroll worthy to be filed.
The Faerie Queene (1596) bk. 4, canto 2, st. 32

3 For all that nature by her mother wit
Could frame in earth.
The Faerie Queene (1596) bk. 4, canto 10, st. 21

4 Ill can he rule the great, that cannot reach the
small.
The Faerie Queene (1596) bk. 5, canto 2, st. 43

5 O sacred hunger of ambitious minds.
The Faerie Queene (1596) bk. 5, canto 12, st. 1

6 A monster, which the Blatant beast men call,
A dreadful fiend of gods and men ydrad.
The Faerie Queene (1596) bk. 5, canto 12, st. 37

7 The gentle mind by gentle deeds is known.
For a man by nothing is so well bewrayed,
As by his manners.
The Faerie Queene (1596) bk. 6, canto 3, st. 1

8 What man that sees the ever-whirling wheel
Of Change, the which all mortal things doth sway,
But that thereby doth find, and plainly feel,
How Mutability in them doth play
Her cruel sports, to many men's decay?
The Faerie Queene (1596) bk. 7, canto 6, st. 1

9 For all that moveth doth in Change delight:
But thenceforth all shall rest eternally
With Him that is the God of Sabbaoth hight:
O that great Sabbaoth God, grant me that
Sabbaoth's sight.
The Faerie Queene (1596) bk. 7, canto 8, st. 2

10 That beauty is not, as fond men misdeem,
An outward show of things, that only seem.
'An Hymn in Honour of Beauty' (1596) l. 90

11 For of the soul the body form doth take;
For soul is form, and doth the body make.
'An Hymn in Honour of Beauty' (1596) l. 132

12 What more felicity can fall to creature,
Than to enjoy delight with liberty.
'Muiopotmos' (1591) l. 209

13 Of such deep learning little had he need,
Ne yet of Latin, ne of Greek that breed
Doubts 'mongst Divines, and difference of texts,
From whence arise diversity of sects,
And hateful heresies.
'Prosopopoia or Mother Hubberd's Tale' (1591) l. 385

14 Calm was the day, and through the trembling air,
Sweet breathing Zephyrus did softly play.
Prothalamion (1596) l. 1

15 With that, I saw two swans of goodly hue,
Come softly swimming down along the Lee.
Prothalamion (1596) l. 37

16 So purely white they were,
That even the gentle stream, the which them
bare,
Seemed foul to them, and bade his billows spare
To wet their silken feathers, lest they might
Soil their fair plumes with water not so fair
And mar their beauties bright,
That shone as Heaven's light,
Against their bridal day, which was not long:
Sweet Thames, run softly, till I end my song.
Prothalamion (1596) l. 46

17 To be wise and eke to love,
Is granted scarce to God above.
The Shepherd's Calendar (1579) 'March. Willy's Emblem'

18 Bring hither the pink and purple columbine,
With gillyflowers:
Bring coronation, and sops in wine,
Worn of paramours.
Strew me the ground with daffadowndillies,
And cowslips, and kingcups, and loved lilies.
The Shepherd's Calendar (1579) 'April' l. 136

19 And he that strives to touch the stars,
Oft stumbles at a straw.
The Shepherd's Calendar (1579) 'July' l. 99

20 Uncouth unkist, said the old famous poet Chaucer.
The Shepherd's Calendar (1579) 'Letter to Gabriel Harvey'

21 So now they have made our English tongue a
gallimaufry or hodgepodge of all other speeches.
The Shepherd's Calendar (1579) 'Letter to Gabriel Harvey'

22 Out of every corner of the woods and glens they
came creeping forth upon their hands, for their
legs could not bear them; they looked like
anatomies of death, they spake like ghosts crying
out of their graves; they did eat the dead carrions
. . . insomuch as the very carcases they spared not
to scrape out of their graves; and, if they found a
plot of watercresses or shamrocks, there they
flocked as to a feast.
A View of the Present State of Ireland (1596)

Baruch Spinoza 1632–77

Dutch philosopher
*on Spinoza: see **Novalis** 565:20*

23 *Deus, sive Natura.*
God, or in other words, Nature.
Ethics (1677) pt. 1, para. 6

24 There is no hope without fear, and no fear
without hope.
Ethics (1677) pt. 2, para. 178

25 I have striven not to laugh at human actions, not
to weep at them, nor to hate them, but to
understand them.
Tractatus Politicus (1677) ch. 1, sect. 4

Benjamin Spock 1903–98

American paediatrician

26 You know more than you think you do.
Common Sense Book of Baby and Child Care (1946) [later
Baby and Child Care], opening words

1 To win in Vietnam, we will have to exterminate a nation.
Dr Spock on Vietnam (1968) ch. 7

William Archibald Spooner 1844–1930
English clergyman; Warden of New College, Oxford, 1903–24

2 You will find as you grow older that the weight of rages will press harder and harder upon the employer.
William Hayter *Spooner* (1977) ch. 6

3 Her late husband, you know, a very sad death— eaten by missionaries—poor soul!
William Hayter *Spooner* (1977) ch. 6

Thomas Sprat 1635–1713
English clergyman and writer

4 A most venomous thing in the making of sciences; for whoever has fixed on his cause, before he has experimented, can hardly avoid fitting his experiment to his own cause ... rather than the cause to the truth of the experiment itself.
on 'Aristotelian experiments, intended to illustrate a preconceived truth and convince people of its validity'
History of the Royal Society (1667)

Cecil Spring-Rice 1859–1918
British diplomat; Ambassador to Washington from 1912

5 I vow to thee, my country—all earthly things above—
Entire and whole and perfect, the service of my love,
The love that asks no question: the love that stands the test,
That lays upon the altar the dearest and the best:
The love that never falters, the love that pays the price,
The love that makes undaunted the final sacrifice.
'I Vow to Thee, My Country' (written on the eve of his departure from Washington, 12 January 1918)

6 And there's another country, I've heard of long ago—
Most dear to them that love her, most great to them that know.
'I Vow to Thee, My Country' (written 1918)

7 Her ways are ways of gentleness and all her paths are Peace.
'I Vow to Thee, My Country' (written 1918); see **Bible** 83:35

8 I am the Dean of Christ Church, Sir:
There's my wife; look well at her.
She's the Broad and I'm the High;
We are the University.
The Masque of Balliol (composed by and current among members of Balliol College, Oxford, in the 1870s) in W. G. Hiscock (ed.) *The Balliol Rhymes* (1939); the first couplet was unofficially altered to:

I am the Dean, and this is Mrs Liddell;
She the first, and I the second fiddle.
see **Anonymous** 17:20, **Beeching** 62:16

Bruce Springsteen 1949–
American rock singer and songwriter

9 Born in the USA.
title of song (1984)

10 Born down in a dead man's town
The first kick I took was when I hit the ground.
'Born in the USA' (1984 song)

11 We gotta get out while we're young,
'Cause tramps like us, baby, we were born to run.
'Born to Run' (1974 song)

12 Is a dream a lie if it don't come true,
Or is it something worse?
'The River' (1980 song)

C. H. Spurgeon 1834–92
English nonconformist preacher

13 If you want truth to go round the world you must hire an express train to pull it; but if you want a lie to go round the world, it will fly: it is as light as a feather, and a breath will carry it. It is well said in the old proverb, 'a lie will go round the world while truth is pulling its boots on'.
Gems from Spurgeon (1859)

J. C. Squire 1884–1958
English man of letters

14 But I'm not so think as you drunk I am.
'Ballade of Soporific Absorption' (1931)

15 It did not last: the Devil howling 'Ho!
Let Einstein be!' restored the status quo.
'In continuation of Pope on Newton' (1926); see **Pope** 603:27

Mme de Staël (Anne-Louise-Germaine Necker) 1766–1817
French writer

16 *Tout comprendre rend très indulgent.*
To be totally understanding makes one very indulgent.
Corinne (1807) bk. 18, ch. 5; see **Proverbs** 633:10

17 *Un homme peut braver l'opinion; une femme doit s'y soumettre.*
A man can brave opinion, a woman must submit to it.
Delphine (1802) epigraph

18 Speech happens not to be his language.
on being asked what she found to talk about with her new lover, a hussar
attributed

Lord Stair 1648–1707
Scottish politician

19 It's a great work of charity to be exact in rooting out that damnable sept, the worst in all the Highlands.
*on hearing that Alasdair MacIan, chief of the Glencoe MacDonalds, had been too late in taking the required oath of loyalty to **William III***
letter to Thomas Livingston, 11 January 1692

Joseph Stalin (Iosif Vissarionovich Dzhugashvili) 1879–1953
Soviet dictator

1 The State is an instrument in the hands of the ruling class, used to break the resistance of the adversaries of that class.
  Foundations of Leninism (1924) section 4/6

2 There are various forms of production: artillery, automobiles, lorries. You also produce 'commodities', 'works', 'products'. Such things are highly necessary. Engineering things. For people's souls. 'Products' are highly necessary too. 'Products' are very important for people's souls. You are engineers of human souls.
  speech to writers at **Gorky**'s house, 26 October 1932; A. Kemp-Welch *Stalin and the Literary Intelligentsia, 1928–39* (1991); see **Gorky** 357:3

3 The Pope! How many divisions has *he* got?
  on being asked to encourage Catholicism in Russia by way of conciliating the Pope, 13 May 1935
  W. S. Churchill *The Gathering Storm* (1948) ch. 8; see **Napoleon** 557:2

4 There is one eternally true legend—that of Judas.
  at the trial of Radek in 1937
  Robert Payne *The Rise and Fall of Stalin* (1966)

5 One death is a tragedy, a million deaths a statistic.
  attributed

Henry Morton Stanley 1841–1904
British explorer

6 Dr Livingstone, I presume?
  How I found Livingstone (1872) ch. 11

Charles E. Stanton 1859–1933
American soldier

7 *Lafayette, nous voilà!*
  Lafayette, we are here.
  at the tomb of Lafayette in Paris, 4 July 1917; in *New York Tribune* 6 September 1917

Edwin Mcmasters Stanton 1814–69
American lawyer

8 Now he belongs to the ages.
  *of Abraham **Lincoln**, following his assassination, 15 April 1865*
  I. M. Tarbell *Life of Abraham Lincoln* (1900) vol. 2

Elizabeth Cady Stanton 1815–1902
American suffragist

9 The Bible teaches that woman brought sin and death into the world, that she precipitated the fall of the race . . . marriage for her was to be a condition of bondage, maternity a period of suffering and anguish, and in silence and subjection, she was to play the role of a dependant on man's bounty for all her material wants.
  The Woman's Bible (1895) pt. 1, introduction

10 Woman's degradation is in man's idea of his sexual rights. Our religion, laws, customs, are all founded on the belief that woman was made for man.
  letter to Susan B. Anthony, 14 June 1860, in T. Stanton and H. Stanton Blatch (eds.) *Elizabeth Cady Stanton* (1922) vol. 2

Frank L. Stanton 1857–1927
American journalist and poet

11 Sweetes' li'l' feller,
  Everybody knows;
  Dunno what to call him,
  But he's mighty lak' a rose!
  'Mighty Lak' a Rose' (1901 song)

John Stark 1728–1822
American Revolutionary officer

12 We beat them to-day or Molly Stark's a widow.
  before the Battle of Bennington, 16 August 1777, in *Cyclopaedia of American Biography* vol. 5

Christina Stead 1902–83
Australian novelist

13 A self-made man is one who believes in luck and sends his son to Oxford.
  House of All Nations (1938) 'Credo'

David Steel 1938–
British Liberal politician; Leader of the Liberal Party 1976–88

14 I have the good fortune to be the first Liberal leader for over half a century who is able to say to you at the end of our annual assembly: go back to your constituencies and prepare for government.
  speech to the Liberal Party Assembly, 18 September 1981

15 It is the settled will of the majority of people in Scotland that they want not just the symbol, but the substance of the return of democratic control over internal affairs.
  on the announcement that the Stone of Destiny would be returned to Scotland
  in *Scotsman* 4 July 1996

Richard Steele 1672–1729
Irish-born essayist and dramatist

16 The insupportable labour of doing nothing.
  in *The Spectator* no. 54 (2 May 1711)

17 A woman seldom writes her mind but in her postscript.
  in *The Spectator* no. 79 (31 May 1711); see **Bacon** 43:30

18 We were in some little time fixed in our seats, and sat with that dislike which people not too good-natured usually conceive of each other at first sight.
  in *The Spectator* no. 132 (1 August 1711)

19 There are so few who can grow old with a good grace.
  in *The Spectator* no. 263 (1 January 1712)

20 It is to be noted that when any part of this paper appears dull there is a design in it.
  in *The Tatler* no. 38 (7 July 1709)

1 To love her is a liberal education.
of Lady Elizabeth Hastings
in *The Tatler* no. 49 (2 August 1709)

2 Reading is to the mind what exercise is to the body.
in *The Tatler* no. 147 (18 March 1710)

3 It was very prettily said, that we may learn the little value of fortune by the persons on whom heaven is pleased to bestow it.
in *The Tatler* no. 203 (27 July 1710); see **Luther** 496:14, **Swift** 766:4

Lincoln Steffens 1866–1936
American journalist

4 I have seen the future; and it works.
following a visit to the Soviet Union in 1919
letter to Marie Howe, 3 April 1919, in *Letters* (1938) vol. 1; in J. M. Thompson *Russia, Bolshevism and the Versailles Treaty* (1954) it is recalled that Steffens had composed the expression before he had even arrived in Russia

Edward Steichen 1879–1973
Luxembourg-born American photographer

5 The mission of photography is to explain man to man and each man to himself.
Cornell Capa (ed.) *The Concerned Photographer* (1972)

Gertrude Stein 1874–1946
American writer
on Stein: see **Anonymous** 16:16, **Fadiman** 314:3, **Lewis** 484:2; see also **Last words** 474:14

6 Remarks are not literature.
Autobiography of Alice B. Toklas (1933) ch. 7

7 Pigeons on the grass alas.
Four Saints in Three Acts (1934) act 3, sc. 2

8 In the United States there is more space where nobody is than where anybody is. That is what makes America what it is.
The Geographical History of America (1936)

9 Rose is a rose is a rose, is a rose.
Sacred Emily (1913)

10 You are all a lost generation.
of the young who served in the First World War
the phrase having been borrowed (in translation) from a French garage mechanic, whom Stein heard address it disparagingly to an incompetent apprentice; Ernest **Hemingway** subsequently took it as his epigraph to *The Sun Also Rises* (1926)

John Steinbeck 1902–68
American novelist
see also **Borrowed titles** 146:10

11 Man, unlike any other thing organic or inorganic in the universe, grows beyond his work, walks up the stairs of his concepts, emerges ahead of his accomplishments.
The Grapes of Wrath (1939) ch. 14

12 Okie use' ta mean you was from Oklahoma. Now it means you're a dirty son-of-a-bitch. Okie means you're scum. Don't mean nothing itself, it's the way they say it.
The Grapes of Wrath (1939) ch. 18

Gloria Steinem 1934–
American journalist
see also **Sayings** 670:23

13 We are becoming the men we wanted to marry.
in *Ms* July/August 1982

14 Outrageous acts and everyday rebellions.
title of book (1983)

Peter Steiner see **Cartoon captions** 198:7

Stendhal (Henri Beyle) 1783–1842
French novelist
on Stendhal: see **Gide** 346:16

15 For those who have tasted the profound activity of writing, reading is no more than a secondary pleasure.
De l'Amour (1822)

16 *Un roman est un miroir qui se promène sur une grande route. Tantôt il reflète à vos yeux l'azur des cieux, tantôt la fange des bourbiers de la route.*
A novel is a mirror which passes over a highway. Sometimes it reflects to your eyes the blue of the skies, at others the churned-up mud of the road.
Le Rouge et le noir (1830) bk. 2, ch. 19

17 *La politique au milieu des intérêts d'imagination, c'est un coup de pistolet au milieu d'un concert.*
Politics in the middle of things that concern the imagination are like a pistol-shot in the middle of a concert.
Le Rouge et le noir (1830) bk. 2, ch. 22

18 *J'aimais, et j'aime encore, les mathématiques pour elles-mêmes comme n'admettant pas l'hypocrisie et le vague, mes deux bêtes d'aversion.*
I used to love mathematics for its own sake, and I still do, because it allows for no hypocrisy and no vagueness, my two *bêtes noires*.
La Vie d'Henri Brulard (1890) ch. 10

19 I know of only one rule: style cannot be too *clear*, too *simple*.
letter to Balzac, 30 October 1840

J. K. Stephen 1859–92
English journalist and writer of light verse

20 Ah! Matt.: old age has brought to me
Thy wisdom, less thy certainty:
The world's a jest, and joy's a trinket:
I knew that once: but now—I think it.
'Senex to Matt. Prior' (1891); see **Epitaphs** 310:13

21 Two voices are there: one is of the deep;
It learns the storm-cloud's thunderous melody,
Now roars, now murmurs with the changing sea,
Now bird-like pipes, now closes soft in sleep:
And one is of an old half-witted sheep
Which bleats articulate monotony,

And indicates that two and one are three,
That grass is green, lakes damp, and mountains
   steep
And, Wordsworth, both are thine.
   'A Sonnet' (1891); see **Wordsworth** 850:14

1 When the Rudyards cease from kipling
And the Haggards ride no more.
   'To R.K.' (1891)

Leslie Stephen 1832–1904

English scholar and philosopher, first editor of the Dictionary of National Biography

2 The editor of such a work must, by the necessity of the case, be autocratic. He will do his best to be a considerate autocrat.
   of the compilation of a dictionary of national biography
   in *Athenaeum* 23 December 1882

James Stephens 1882–1950

Irish poet and nationalist

3 Finality is death. Perfection is finality.
Nothing is perfect. There are lumps in it.
   The Crock of Gold (1912) bk. 1, ch. 4

4 I hear a sudden cry of pain!
There is a rabbit in a snare:
Now I hear the cry again,
But I cannot tell from where . . .
Little one! Oh, little one!
I am searching everywhere.
   'The Snare' (1915)

5 People say: 'Of course, they will be beaten.' The statement is almost a query, and they continue, 'but they are putting up a decent fight.' For being beaten does not matter greatly in Ireland, but not fighting does matter.
   The Insurrection in Dublin (1916)

6 In my definition they were good men—men, that is, who willed no evil. No person living is the worse off for having known Thomas MacDonagh.
   The Insurrection in Dublin (1916)

Laurence Sterne 1713–68

English novelist
on Sterne: see **Johnson** 431:26

7 They order, said I, this matter better in France.
   A Sentimental Journey (1768) opening words

8 I pity the man who can travel from Dan to Beersheba, and cry, 'tis all barren.
   A Sentimental Journey (1768) 'In the Street. Calais'

9 If ever I do a mean action, it must be in some interval betwixt one passion and another.
   A Sentimental Journey (1768) 'Montriul'

10 Vive l'amour! et vive la bagatelle!
   A Sentimental Journey (1768) 'The letter'

11 There are worse occupations in this world than feeling a woman's pulse.
   A Sentimental Journey (1768) 'The Pulse. Paris'

12 God tempers the wind, said Maria, to the shorn lamb.
   derived from a French proverb, but familiar in this form of words
   A Sentimental Journey (1768) 'Maria'

13 Dear sensibility! source inexhausted of all that's precious in our joys, or costly in our sorrows!
   A Sentimental Journey (1768) 'The Bourbonnois'

14 I wish either my father or my mother, or indeed both of them, as they were in duty both equally bound to it, had minded what they were about when they begot me.
   Tristram Shandy (1759–67) bk. 1, ch. 1

15 'Pray, my dear,' quoth my mother, 'have you not forgot to wind up the clock?'—'Good G—!' cried my father, making an exclamation, but taking care to moderate his voice at the same time,—'Did ever woman, since the creation of the world, interrupt a man with such a silly question?'
   Tristram Shandy (1759–67) bk. 1, ch. 1

16 As we jog on, either laugh with me, or at me, or in short do anything,—only keep your temper.
   Tristram Shandy (1759–67) bk. 1, ch. 6

17 So long as a man rides his Hobby-Horse peaceably and quietly along the King's highway, and neither compels you or me to get up behind him,—pray, Sir, what have either you or I to do with it?
   Tristram Shandy (1759–67) bk. 1, ch. 7

18 He was in a few hours of giving his enemies the slip for ever.
   Tristram Shandy (1759–67) bk. 1, ch. 12

19 'Tis known by the name of perseverance in a good cause,—and of obstinacy in a bad one.
   Tristram Shandy (1759–67) bk. 1, ch. 17

20 My uncle Toby would never offer to answer this by any other kind of argument, than that of whistling half a dozen bars of Lillabullero.
   Tristram Shandy (1759–67) bk. 1, ch. 21; see **Wharton** 831:4

21 Digressions, incontestably, are the sunshine;—they are the life, the soul of reading;—take them out of this book for instance,—you might as well take the book along with them.
   Tristram Shandy (1759–67) bk. 1, ch. 22

22 I should have no objection to this method, but that I think it must smell too strong of the lamp.
   Tristram Shandy (1759–67) bk. 1, ch. 23

23 Writing, when properly managed (as you may be sure I think mine is) is but a different name for conversation.
   Tristram Shandy (1759–67) bk. 2, ch. 11

24 'I'll not hurt thee,' says my uncle Toby, rising from his chair, and going across the room, with the fly in his hand,—'I'll not hurt a hair of thy head:—Go,' says he, lifting up the sash, and opening his hand as he spoke, to let it escape;—'go, poor devil, get thee gone, why should I hurt thee?—This world surely is wide enough to hold both thee and me.'
   Tristram Shandy (1759–67) bk. 2, ch. 12

1 Whenever a man talks loudly against religion,—always suspect that it is not his reason, but his passions which have got the better of his creed.
Tristram Shandy (1759–67) bk. 2, ch. 17

2 It is the nature of an hypothesis, when once a man has conceived it, that it assimilates every thing to itself, as proper nourishment; and, from the first moment of your begetting it, it generally grows the stronger by every thing you see, hear, read, or understand.
Tristram Shandy (1759–67) bk. 2, ch. 19

3 'Our armies swore terribly in Flanders,' cried my uncle Toby,—'but nothing to this.'
Tristram Shandy (1759–67) bk. 3, ch. 11

4 The corregiescity of Corregio.
Tristram Shandy (1759–67) bk. 3, ch. 12

5 Of all the cants which are canted in this canting world,—though the cant of hypocrites may be the worst,—the cant of criticism is the most tormenting!
Tristram Shandy (1759–67) bk. 3, ch. 12

6 True *Shandeism*, think what you will against it, opens the heart and lungs, and like all those affections which partake of its nature, it forces the blood and other vital fluids of the body to run freely through its channels, and makes the wheel of life run long and cheerfully round.
Tristram Shandy (1759–67) bk. 4, ch. 32

7 'There is no terror, brother Toby, in its [death's] looks, but what it borrows from groans and convulsions—and the blowing of noses, and the wiping away of tears with the bottoms of curtains, in a dying man's room—Strip it of these, what is it?'—''Tis better in battle than in bed', said my uncle Toby.
Tristram Shandy (1759–67) bk. 5, ch. 3

8 There is a North-west passage to the intellectual World.
Tristram Shandy (1759–67) bk. 5, ch. 42

9 'The poor soul will die:—' 'He shall not die, by G—', cried my uncle Toby.—The Accusing Spirit, which flew up to heaven's chancery with the oath, blushed as he gave it in;—and the Recording Angel, as he wrote it down, dropped a tear upon the word, and blotted it out for ever.
Tristram Shandy (1759–67) bk. 6, ch. 8

10 To say a man is fallen in love,—or that he is deeply in love,—or up to the ears in love,—and sometimes even over head and ears in it,—carries an idiomatical kind of implication, that love is a thing below a man:—this is recurring again to Plato's opinion, which, with all his divinityship,—I hold to be damnable and heretical:—and so much for that.
 Let love therefore be what it will,—my uncle Toby fell into it.
Tristram Shandy (1759–67) bk. 6, ch. 37

11 My brother Toby, quoth she, is going to be married to Mrs Wadman.

Then he will never, quoth my father, lie *diagonally* in his bed again as long as he lives.
Tristram Shandy (1759–67) bk. 6, ch. 39

12 Now hang it! quoth I, as I look'd towards the French coast—A man should know something of his own country too, before he goes abroad.
Tristram Shandy (1759–67) bk. 7, ch. 2

13 And who are you? said he.—Don't puzzle me, said I.
Tristram Shandy (1759–67) bk. 7, ch. 33

14 'A soldier,' cried my Uncle Toby, interrupting the corporal, 'is no more exempt from saying a foolish thing, Trim, than a man of letters.'—'But not so often, an' please your honour,' replied the corporal.
Tristram Shandy (1759–67) bk. 8, ch. 19

15 Everything presses on—whilst thou art twisting that lock,—see! it grows grey; and every time I kiss thy hand to bid adieu, and every absence which follows it, are preludes to that eternal separation which we are shortly to make.
Tristram Shandy (1759–67) bk. 9, ch. 10

16 —d! said my mother, 'what is all this story about?'— 'A Cock and a Bull,' said Yorick.
Tristram Shandy (1759–67) bk. 9, ch. 33

17 This sad vicissitude of things.
Sermons (1767) no. 16 'The character of Shimei'

Brooks Stevens 1911–
American industrial designer

18 Our whole economy is based on planned obsolescence.
Vance Packard *The Waste Makers* (1960) ch. 6

Wallace Stevens 1879–1955
American poet

19 The poet is the priest of the invisible.
'Adagia' (1957)

20 Chieftain Iffucan of Azcan in caftan
Of tan with henna hackles, halt!
'Bantams in Pine Woods' (1923)

21 Call the roller of big cigars,
The muscular one, and bid him whip
In kitchen cups concupiscent curds.
'The Emperor of Ice-Cream' (1923)

22 Let be be finale of seem.
The only emperor is the emperor of ice-cream.
'The Emperor of Ice-Cream' (1923)

23 Frogs Eat Butterflies. Snakes Eat Frogs. Hogs Eat Snakes. Men Eat Hogs.
title of poem (1923)

24 Poetry is the supreme fiction, madame.
'A High-Toned old Christian Woman' (1923)

25 They said, 'You have a blue guitar,
You do not play things as they are.'
The man replied, 'Things as they are
Are changed upon the blue guitar.'
'The Man with the Blue Guitar' (1937)

1 They will get it straight one day at the Sorbonne.
We shall return at twilight from the lecture
Pleased that the irrational is rational.
Notes Toward a Supreme Fiction (1947) 'It Must Give
Pleasure' no. 10

2 The palm at the end of the mind,
Beyond the last thought, rises . . .
A gold-feathered bird
Sings in the palm.
'Of Mere Being' (1957)

3 Music is feeling, then, not sound.
'Peter Quince at the Clavier' (1923) pt. 1

4 Beauty is momentary in the mind—
The fitful tracing of a portal;
But in the flesh it is immortal.
The body dies; the body's beauty lives.
'Peter Quince at the Clavier' (1923) pt. 4

5 Susanna's music touched the bawdy strings
Of those white elders.
'Peter Quince at the Clavier' (1923) pt. 4

6 One must have a mind of winter
To regard the frost and the boughs
Of the pine trees crusted with snow;
And have been cold a long time
To behold the junipers shagged with ice,
The spruces rough in the distant glitter
Of the January sun; and not to think
Of any misery in the sound of the wind.
'The Snow Man' (1921)

7 For the listener, who listens in the snow,
And, nothing himself, beholds
Nothing that is not there and the nothing that is.
'The Snow Man' (1921)

8 Complacencies of the peignoir, and late
Coffee and oranges in a sunny chair,
And the green freedom of a cockatoo
Upon a rug mingle to dissipate
The holy hush of ancient sacrifice.
'Sunday Morning' (1923) st. 1

9 Deer walk upon our mountains, and the quail
Whistle about us their spontaneous cries;
Sweet berries ripen in the wilderness;
And, in the isolation of the sky,
At evening, casual flocks of pigeons make
Ambiguous undulations as they sink,
Downward to darkness, on extended wings.
'Sunday Morning' (1923) st. 8

10 I do not know which to prefer,
The beauty of inflections
Or the beauty of innuendoes,
The blackbird whistling
Or just after.
'Thirteen Ways of Looking at a Blackbird' (1923)

Adlai Stevenson 1900–65

American Democratic politician
see also Anonymous 14:18

11 I suppose flattery hurts no one, that is, if he
doesn't inhale.
television broadcast, 30 March 1952, in N. F. Busch *Adlai
E. Stevenson* (1952) ch. 5

12 If they [the Republicans] will stop telling lies about
the Democrats, we will stop telling the truth about
them.
speech during 1952 Presidential campaign; in J. B. Martin
Adlai Stevenson and Illinois (1976) ch. 8

13 Let's talk sense to the American people. Let's tell
them the truth, that there are no gains without
pains.
speech of acceptance at the Democratic National
Convention, Chicago, Illinois, 26 July 1952; in *Speeches*
(1952)

14 In America any boy may become President and I
suppose it's just one of the risks he takes!
speech in Indianapolis, 26 September 1952; in *Major
Campaign Speeches . . . 1952* (1953)

15 A free society is a society where it is safe to be
unpopular.
speech in Detroit, 7 October 1952; in *Major Campaign
Speeches . . . 1952* (1953)

16 The young man who asks you to set him one
heart-beat from the Presidency of the United
States.
*of Richard **Nixon** as Vice-Presidential nominee*
speech at Cleveland, Ohio, 23 October 1952, in *New York
Times* 24 October 1952

17 We hear the Secretary of State boasting of his
brinkmanship—the art of bringing us to the edge
of the abyss.
speech in Hartford, Connecticut, 25 February 1956; in
New York Times 26 February 1956; see **Dulles** 291:10

18 She would rather light a candle than curse the
darkness, and her glow has warmed the world.
*of Eleanor **Roosevelt***
in *New York Times* 8 November 1962; see **Proverbs** 615:29

Anne Stevenson 1933–

English poet

19 Blackbirds are the cellos of the deep farms.
'Green Mountain, Black Mountain' (1982)

20 At fifty, menopausal, nervous, thin,
She joined a women's group and studied Zen.
Her latest book, *The Happy Lesbian*,
Is recommended reading for gay men.
'A Quest' (1993)

Robert Louis Stevenson 1850–94

Scottish novelist

21 Every one lives by selling something.
Across the Plains (1892) 'Beggars' pt. 3

22 The harmless art of knucklebones has seen the fall
of the Roman empire and the rise of the United
States.
Across the Plains (1892) 'The Lantern-Bearers' pt. 1

23 The bright face of danger.
Across the Plains (1892) 'The Lantern-Bearers' pt. 4

24 Here lies one who meant well, tried a little, failed
much:—surely that may be his epitaph, of which
he need not be ashamed.
Across the Plains (1892) 'A Christmas Sermon' pt. 4

25 The web, then, or the pattern; a web at once
sensuous and logical, an elegant and pregnant

texture: that is style, that is the foundation of the art of literature.
The Art of Writing (1905) 'On some technical Elements of Style in Literature' (written 1885)

1 Politics is perhaps the only profession for which no preparation is thought necessary.
Familiar Studies of Men and Books (1882) 'Yoshida-Torajiro'

2 Am I no a bonny fighter?
Kidnapped (1886) ch. 10

3 I've a grand memory for forgetting, David.
Kidnapped (1886) ch. 18

4 I have thus played the sedulous ape to Hazlitt, to Lamb, to Wordsworth, to Sir Thomas Browne, to Defoe, to Hawthorne, to Montaigne, to Baudelaire and to Obermann.
Memories and Portraits (1887) ch. 4 'A College Magazine'

5 These are my politics: to change what we can; to better what we can; but still to bear in mind that man is but a devil weakly fettered by some generous beliefs and impositions; and for no word however sounding, and no cause however just and pious, to relax the stricture of these bonds.
More New Arabian Nights: The Dynamiter (1885) 'Epilogue of the Cigar Divan'

6 He who was prepared to help the escaping murderer or to embrace the impenitent thief, found, to the overthrow of all his logic, that he objected to the use of dynamite.
More New Arabian Nights: The Dynamiter (1885) 'The Superfluous Mansion'

7 I regard you with an indifference closely bordering on aversion.
New Arabian Nights (1882) 'The Rajah's Diamond: Story of the Bandbox'

8 The strange case of Dr Jekyll and Mr Hyde.
title of novel, 1886

9 With every day, and from both sides of my intelligence, the moral and the intellectual, I thus drew steadily nearer to that truth, by whose partial discovery I have been doomed to such a dreadful shipwreck: that man is not truly one, but truly two.
The Strange Case of Dr Jekyll and Mr Hyde (1886)

10 A faddling hedonist.
Travels with a Donkey (1879) 'The Boarders'

11 For my part, I travel not to go anywhere, but to go. I travel for travel's sake. The great affair is to move.
Travels with a Donkey (1879) 'Cheylard and Luc'

12 I own I like definite form in what my eyes are to rest upon; and if landscapes were sold, like the sheets of characters of my boyhood, one penny plain and twopence coloured, I should go the length of twopence every day of my life.
Travels with a Donkey (1879) 'Father Apollinaris'

13 Fifteen men on the dead man's chest
Yo-ho-ho, and a bottle of rum!
Drink and the devil had done for the rest—
Yo-ho-ho, and a bottle of rum!
Treasure Island (1883) ch. 1

14 Tip me the black spot.
Treasure Island (1883) ch. 3

15 Pieces of eight, pieces of eight, pieces of eight!
Treasure Island (1883) ch. 10

16 Many's the long night I've dreamed of cheese—toasted, mostly.
Treasure Island (1883) ch. 15

17 Even if the doctor does not give you a year, even if he hesitates about a month, make one brave push and see what can be accomplished in a week.
Virginibus Puerisque (1881) 'Aes Triplex'

18 There is no duty we so much underrate as the duty of being happy.
Virginibus Puerisque (1881) 'An Apology for Idlers'

19 Old and young, we are all on our last cruise.
Virginibus Puerisque (1881) 'Crabbed Age and Youth'

20 To travel hopefully is a better thing than to arrive, and the true success is to labour.
Virginibus Puerisque (1881) 'El Dorado'; see **Proverbs** 623:45

21 In marriage, a man becomes slack and selfish, and undergoes a fatty degeneration of his moral being.
Virginibus Puerisque (1881) title essay, pt. 1

22 Even if we take matrimony at its lowest, even if we regard it as no more than a sort of friendship recognised by the police.
Virginibus Puerisque (1881) title essay, pt. 1

23 A little amateur painting in water-colour shows the innocent and quiet mind.
Virginibus Puerisque (1881) title essay, pt. 1

24 Marriage is like life in this—that it is a field of battle, and not a bed of roses.
Virginibus Puerisque (1881) title essay, pt. 1

25 To marry is to domesticate the Recording Angel. Once you are married, there is nothing left for you, not even suicide, but to be good.
Virginibus Puerisque (1881) title essay, pt. 2

26 Man is a creature who lives not upon bread alone, but principally by catchwords.
Virginibus Puerisque (1881) title essay, pt. 2

27 The cruellest lies are often told in silence.
Virginibus Puerisque (1881) title essay, pt. 4

28 What hangs people . . . is the unfortunate circumstance of guilt.
The Wrong Box (with Lloyd Osbourne, 1889) ch. 7

29 Nothing like a little judicious levity.
The Wrong Box (with Lloyd Osbourne, 1889) ch. 7

30 Between the possibility of being hanged in all innocence, and the certainty of a public and merited disgrace, no gentleman of spirit could long hesitate.
The Wrong Box (with Lloyd Osbourne, 1889) ch. 10

31 If you are going to make a book end badly, it must end badly from the beginning.
letter to J. M. Barrie, November 1892, in Sidney Colvin (ed.) *Letters of Robert Louis Stevenson* (1911) vol. 4

32 I am an Epick writer with a k to it, but without the necessary genius.
letter to Henry James, 5 December 1892, in Sidney Colvin (ed.) *Letters of Robert Louis Stevenson* (1911) vol. 4

1 I believe in an ultimate decency of things.
  letter to Sidney Colvin, 23 August 1893, in Sidney Colvin
  (ed.) *Letters of Robert Louis Stevenson* (1911) vol. 4

2 In winter I get up at night
  And dress by yellow candle-light.
  In summer, quite the other way,—
  I have to go to bed by day.
  A Child's Garden of Verses (1885) 'Bed in Summer'

3 The world is so full of a number of things,
  I'm sure we should all be as happy as kings.
  A Child's Garden of Verses (1885) 'Happy Thought'

4 I was the giant great and still
  That sits upon the pillow-hill,
  And sees before him, dale and plain,
  The pleasant land of counterpane.
  A Child's Garden of Verses (1885) 'The Land of
  Counterpane'

5 I have a little shadow that goes in and out with
    me,
  And what can be the use of him is more than I
    can see.
  He is very, very like me from the heels up to the
    head;
  And I see him jump before me, when I jump into
    my bed.
  A Child's Garden of Verses (1885) 'My Shadow'

6 Let us arise and go like men,
  And face with an undaunted tread
  The long black passage up to bed.
  A Child's Garden of Verses (1885) 'North-West Passage.
  Good-Night'

7 A child should always say what's true,
  And speak when he is spoken to,
  And behave mannerly at table:
  At least as far as he is able.
  A Child's Garden of Verses (1885) 'Whole Duty of Children'

8 Whenever the moon and stars are set,
  Whenever the wind is high,
  All night long in the dark and wet,
  A man goes riding by.
  Late in the night when the fires are out,
  Why does he gallop and gallop about?
  A Child's Garden of Verses (1885) 'Windy Nights'

9 But all that I could think of, in the darkness and
    the cold,
  Was that I was leaving home and my folks were
    growing old.
  'Christmas at Sea' (1890)

10 In the highlands, in the country places,
   Where the old plain men have rosy faces,
   And the young fair maidens
   Quiet eyes.
   Songs of Travel (1896) 'In the highlands, in the country
   places'

11 I will make you brooches and toys for your delight
   Of bird-song at morning and star-shine at night.
   Songs of Travel (1896) 'I will make you brooches and toys
   for your delight'

12 I will make my kitchen, and you shall keep your
     room,
   Where white flows the river and bright blows the
     broom,

And you shall wash your linen and keep your
    body white
In rainfall at morning and dewfall at night.
  Songs of Travel (1896) 'I will make you brooches and toys
  for your delight'

13 Trusty, dusky, vivid, true,
   With eyes of gold and bramble-dew,
   Steel-true and blade-straight,
   The great artificer
   Made my mate.
   Songs of Travel (1896) 'My Wife'

14 Sing me a song of a lad that is gone,
   Say, could that lad be I?
   Merry of soul he sailed on a day
   Over the sea to Skye.
   Songs of Travel (1896) 'Sing me a song of a lad that is gone'

15 Be it granted to me to behold you again in dying,
   Hills of home! and to hear again the call;
   Hear about the graves of the martyrs the peewees
     crying,
   And hear no more at all.
   Songs of Travel (1896) 'To S. R. Crockett'

16 Give to me the life I love,
   Let the lave go by me,
   Give the jolly heaven above
   And the byway nigh me.
   Bed in the bush with stars to see,
   Bread I dip in the river—
   There's the life for a man like me,
   There's the life for ever.
   Songs of Travel (1896) 'The Vagabond'

17 Let the blow fall soon or late,
   Let what will be o'er me;
   Give the face of earth around
   And the road before me.
   Wealth I seek not, hope nor love,
   Nor a friend to know me;
   All I seek, the heaven above
   And the road below me.
   Songs of Travel (1896) 'The Vagabond'

18 Of all my verse, like not a single line;
   But like my title, for it is not mine.
   That title from a better man I stole;
   Ah, how much better, had I stol'n the whole!
   Underwoods (1887) foreword

19 Go, little book, and wish to all
   Flowers in the garden, meat in the hall,
   A bin of wine, a spice of wit,
   A house with lawns enclosing it,
   A living river by the door,
   A nightingale in the sycamore!
   Underwoods (1887) 'Envoy'; see **Chaucer** 213:14

20 Under the wide and starry sky
   Dig the grave and let me lie.
   Glad did I live and gladly die,
   And I laid me down with a will.
   This be the verse you grave for me:
   'Here he lies where he longed to be;
   Home is the sailor, home from sea,
   And the hunter home from the hill.'
   Underwoods (1887) 'Requiem'

1 And what should Master Gauger play
But 'Over the hills and far away'?
Underwoods (1887) 'A Song of the Road'

Ian Stewart 1945–

British mathematician

2 Genes are not like engineering blueprints; they are more like recipes in a cookbook. They tell us what ingredients to use, in what quantities, and in what order—but they do not provide a complete, accurate plan of the final result.
Life's Other Secret (1998) preface

Sting (Gordon Sumner) 1951–

English rock singer, songwriter, and actor

3 If I were a Brazilian without land or money or the means to feed my children, I would be burning the rain forest too.
in *International Herald Tribune* 14 April 1989

Caskie Stinnett 1911–

American writer

4 A diplomat . . . is a person who can tell you to go to hell in such a way that you actually look forward to the trip.
Out of the Red (1960) ch. 4

Samuel John Stone 1839–1900

English clergyman

5 The Church's one foundation
Is Jesus Christ, her Lord;
She is his new creation
By water and the word:
From heaven he came and sought her
To be his holy bride,
With his own blood he bought her,
And for her life he died.
Lyra Fidelium (1866) 'The Church's one foundation'

Marie Stopes 1880–1958

Scottish pioneer of birth-control clinics

6 An impersonal and scientific knowledge of the structure of our bodies is the surest safeguard against prurient curiosity and lascivious gloating.
Married Love (1918) ch. 5

Tom Stoppard 1937–

British dramatist

7 It's not the voting that's democracy, it's the counting.
Jumpers (1972) act 1; see **Somoza** 746:1

8 The House of Lords, an illusion to which I have never been able to subscribe—responsibility without power, the prerogative of the eunuch throughout the ages.
Lord Malquist and Mr Moon (1966) pt. 6; see **Dorfman** 282:15**Kipling** 457:8

9 The media. It sounds like a convention of spiritualists.
Night and Day (1978) act 1

10 I'm with you on the free press. It's the newspapers I can't stand.
Night and Day (1978) act 1

11 Comment is free but facts are on expenses.
Night and Day (1978) act 2; see **Scott** 672:14

12 You're familiar with the tragedies of antiquity, are you? The great homicidal classics?
Rosencrantz and Guildenstern are Dead (1967) act 1

13 I can do you blood and love without the rhetoric, and I can do you blood and rhetoric without the love, and I can do you all three concurrent or consecutive, but I can't do you love and rhetoric without the blood. Blood is compulsory—they're all blood, you see.
Rosencrantz and Guildenstern are Dead (1967) act 1

14 Eternity's a terrible thought. I mean, where's it all going to end?
Rosencrantz and Guildenstern are Dead (1967) act 2

15 The bad end unhappily, the good unluckily. That is what tragedy means.
Rosencrantz and Guildenstern are Dead (1967) act 2; see **Wilde** 835:19

16 Life is a gamble at terrible odds—if it was a bet, you wouldn't take it.
Rosencrantz and Guildenstern are Dead (1967) act 3

17 War is capitalism with the gloves off and many who go to war know it but they go to war because they don't want to be a hero.
Travesties (1975) act 1

William Stoughton 1631–1701

American clergyman

18 God hath sifted a nation that he might send choice grain into this wilderness.
sermon in Boston, 29 April 1669

Harriet Beecher Stowe 1811–96

American novelist
on Stowe: see **Lincoln** 485:15

19 I s'pect I growed. Don't think nobody never made me.
Topsy
Uncle Tom's Cabin (1852) ch. 20

William Scott, Lord Stowell 1745–1836

English jurist

20 The elegant simplicity of the three per cents.
Lord Campbell *Lives of the Lord Chancellors* (1857) vol. 10, ch. 212; see **Disraeli** 277:13

21 A precedent embalms a principle.
an opinion, while Advocate-General, 1788, quoted by Disraeli in House of Commons, 22 February 1848

Lytton Strachey 1880–1932

English biographer
see also: **Last words** 472:5

22 Francis Bacon has been described more than once with the crude vigour of antithesis . . . He was no striped frieze; he was shot silk.
Elizabeth and Essex (1928) ch. 5

1 The time was out of joint, and he was only too delighted to have been born to set it right.
of Hurrell Froude
Eminent Victorians (1918) 'Cardinal Manning' pt. 2; see **Shakespeare** 685:13

2 Her conception of God was certainly not orthodox. She felt towards Him as she might have felt towards a glorified sanitary engineer; and in some of her speculations she seems hardly to distinguish between the Deity and the Drains.
Eminent Victorians (1918) 'Florence Nightingale' pt. 4

3 CHAIRMAN OF MILITARY TRIBUNAL: What would you do if you saw a German soldier trying to violate your sister?
STRACHEY: I would try to get between them.
otherwise rendered as, 'I should interpose my body'
Robert Graves Good-bye to All That (1929) ch. 23

4 Discretion is not the better part of biography.
Michael Holroyd Lytton Strachey vol. 1 (1967) preface

Thomas Wentworth, Lord Strafford
1593–1641
English statesman

5 The authority of a King is the keystone which closeth up the arch of order and government which, once shaken, all the frame falls together in a confused heap of foundation and battlement.
Hugh Trevor-Roper Historical Essays (1952) 'The Outbreak of the Great Rebellion'

William L. Strauss and A. J. E. Cave

6 Notwithstanding, if he could be reincarnated and placed in a New York subway—provided that he were bathed, shaved, and dressed in modern clothing—it is doubtful whether he would attract any more attention than some of its other denizens.
of Neanderthal man
in Quarterly Review of Biology Winter 1957

Igor Stravinsky 1882–1971
Russian composer

7 Tradition is entirely different from habit, even from an excellent habit, since habit is by definition an unconscious acquisition and tends to become mechanical, whereas tradition results from a conscious and deliberate acceptance . . . Tradition presupposes the reality of what endures.
Poetics of Music (1947) ch. 3 (translated by A. Knodel and I. Dahl)

8 Conductors' careers are made for the most part with 'romantic' music. 'Classic' music eliminates the conductor; we do not remember him in it.
Robert Craft Conversations with Stravinsky (1958) ch. 4

9 My music is best understood by children and animals.
in Observer 8 October 1961

10 Academism results when the reasons for the rule change, but not the rule.
attributed

John Whitaker ('Jack') Straw 1946–
British Labour politician

11 The divide in the modern world is not the so-called 'clash of civilizations' between Islam and the West. The divide is between order and chaos.
in Newsweek 20 January 2003

12 There is no list, and Syria isn't on it.
on the US description of Syria as a rogue state
speech, Qatar; in Guardian 15 April 2003 (online edition)

August Strindberg 1849–1912
Swedish dramatist and novelist

13 Family! . . . the home of all social evil, a charitable institution for comfortable women, an anchorage for house-fathers, and a hell for children.
The Son of a Servant (1886)

Randall E. Stross
American business historian

14 American anti-intellectualism will never again be the same because of Bill Gates. Gates embodies what was supposed to be impossible—the practical intellectual.
The Microsoft Way (1996)

Jan Struther (Joyce Anstruther) 1901–53
English-born novelist and poet

15 Lord of all hopefulness, Lord of all joy,
Whose trust, ever childlike, no cares could
destroy,
Be there at our waking, and give us, we pray,
Your bliss in our hearts, Lord, at the break of the
day.
'All Day Hymn' (1931 hymn)

16 Hard words will break no bones,
But more than bones are broken
By the inescapable stones
Of fond words left unspoken.
'Variation on an Old Proverb' (1937)

17 When a knight won his spurs, in the stories of old,
He was gentle and brave, he was gallant and bold.
'When a Knight Won His Spurs' (1936)

18 Giving a party is very like having a baby: its conception is more fun than its completion, and once you have begun it is almost impossible to stop.
Ysenda Maxtone Graham The Real Mrs Miniver (2001) ch. 3

William Stubbs 1825–1901
English historian and prelate
on Stubbs: see **Rogers** 652:15

19 Froude informs the Scottish youth
That parsons do not care for truth.
The Reverend Canon Kingsley cries
History is a pack of lies.
What cause for judgements so malign?
A brief reflection solves the mystery—

Froude believes Kingsley a divine,
And Kingsley goes to Froude for history.
> letter to J. R. Green, 17 December 1871, in *Letters* (1904)

G. A. Studdert Kennedy 1883–1929
British poet

1 Waste of Blood, and waste of Tears,
Waste of youth's most precious years,
Waste of ways the saints have trod,
Waste of Glory, waste of God,
War!
> *More Rough Rhymes of a Padre* by 'Woodbine Willie' (1919)
> 'Waste'

2 When Jesus came to Birmingham they simply
passed Him by,
They never hurt a hair of Him, they only let Him
die.
> *Peace Rhymes of a Padre* (1921) 'Indifference'

John Suckling 1609–42
English poet and dramatist

3 Women enjoyed (whatsoe'er before they've been)
Are like romances read, or sights once seen.
> 'Against Fruition' (1646)

4 Why so pale and wan, fond lover?
Prithee, why so pale?
Will, when looking well can't move her,
Looking ill prevail?
Prithee, why so pale?
> *Aglaura* (1637) act 4, sc. 1 'Song'

5 Her feet beneath her petticoat,
Like little mice, stole in and out.
> 'A Ballad upon a Wedding' (1646) st. 8

6 Love is the fart
Of every heart:
It pains a man when 'tis kept close,
And others doth offend, when 'tis let loose.
> 'Love's Offence' (1646)

7 Out upon it, I have loved
Three whole days together;
And am like to love three more,
If it prove fair weather.
> 'A Poem with the Answer' (1659)

Suger 1081–1151
*French monk and statesman, abbot of Saint-Denis, and
regent of France during the Second Crusade*

8 Thus, when—out of my delight in the beauty of
the house of God—the loveliness of the many-
coloured gems has called me away from external
cares, and worthy meditation has induced me to
reflect, transferring that which is material to that
which is immaterial, on the diversity of the sacred
virtues; then it seems to me that I see myself
dwelling, as it were, in some strange region of the
universe which neither exists entirely in the slime
of the earth nor entirely in the purity of Heaven;
and that, by the grace of God, I can be transported
from this inferior to that higher world in an
anagogical manner.
> *De Consecratione*

9 No one among the countless thousands of people
because of their very density could move a foot;
that no one, because of their very congestion
could do anything but stand like a marble statue,
stay benumbed or, as a last resort, scream.
> *description of the church of St-Denis on a feast day*
> *De Consecratione*

Annie Sullivan 1866–1936
*American educator; tutor of Helen **Keller***

10 Language grows out of life, out of its needs and
experiences . . . *Language* and *knowledge* are
indissolubly connected; they are interdependent.
Good work in language presupposes and depends
on a real knowledge of things
> speech to the American Association to Promote the
> Teaching of Speech to the Deaf, July 1894; Helen Keller
> *The Story of My Life* (1902)

Louis Henri Sullivan 1856–1924
American architect

11 Form follows function.
> *The Tall Office Building Artistically Considered* (1896)

Terry Sullivan
*see also **Bedford and Sullivan***

12 She sells sea-shells on the sea-shore,
The shells she sells are sea-shells, I'm sure,
For if she sells sea-shells on the sea-shore,
Then I'm sure she sells sea-shore shells.
> 'She Sells Sea-Shells' (1908 song)

Timothy Daniel Sullivan 1827–1914
Irish writer and politician

13 'God save Ireland!' said the heroes;
'God save Ireland', say they all:
Whether on the scaffold high
Or the battlefield we die,
Oh, what matter when for Erin dear we fall.
> 'God Save Ireland' (1867); see **Last words** 471:16

Maximilien de Béthune, Duc de Sully
1559–1641
French statesman
*see also **Henri IV** 382:2*

14 Tilling and grazing are the two breasts by which
France is fed.
> *Mémoires* (1638) pt. 1, ch. 15

15 The English take their pleasures sadly after the
fashion of their country.
> attributed

Arthur Hays Sulzberger 1891–1968
American newspaper proprietor

16 We tell the public which way the cat is jumping.
The public will take care of the cat.
> *on journalism*
> in *Time* 8 May 1950

Edith Summerskill 1901–80

British Labour politician

1 Nagging is the repetition of unpalatable truths.

speech to the Married Women's Association, House of Commons, 14 July 1960; in *The Times* 15 July 1960

Charles Sumner 1811–74

American politician and orator

2 Where Slavery is, there Liberty cannot be; and where Liberty is, there Slavery cannot be.

'Slavery and the Rebellion'; speech at Cooper Institute 5 November 1864

3 There is the national flag. He must be cold, indeed, who can look upon its folds rippling in the breeze without pride of country.

Are We a Nation? 19 November 1867

Henry Howard, Earl of Surrey c.1517–47

English poet

4 Martial, the things for to attain
The happy life be these, I find:
The riches left, not got with pain;
The fruitful ground, the quiet mind.

'The Happy Life' (1547); translation of Martial *Epigrams* bk. 10, no. 47; see **Martial** 515:2

5 Love, that doth reign and live within my thought,
And built his seat within my captive breast,
Clad in the arms wherein with me he fought,
Oft in my face he doth his banner rest.

'Love, that doth reign' (1557)

6 Set me whereas the sun doth parch the green,
Or where his beams may not dissolve the ice,
In temperate heat, where he is felt and seen,
With proud people, in presence sad and wise;
Set me in base, or yet in high degree,
In the long night, or in the shortest day,
In clear weather, or where mists thickest be,
In lusty youth, or when my hairs be grey . . .
Yours will I be, and with that only thought
Comfort myself when that my hap is nought.

'Set me whereas the sun doth parch the green' (1557)

7 So cruel prison how could betide, alas,
As proud Windsor? Where I in lust and joy
With a king's son my childish years did pass
In greater feast than Priam's sons of Troy.

'So cruel prison' (1557)

8 Wyatt resteth here, that quick could never rest;
Whose heavenly gifts increased by disdain,
And virtue sank the deeper in his breast;
Such profit he of envy could obtain.

'Wyatt resteth here' (1557)

R. S. Surtees 1805–64

English sporting journalist and novelist

9 More people are flattered into virtue than bullied out of vice.

The Analysis of the Hunting Field (1846) ch. 1

10 The only infallible rule we know is, that the man who is always talking about being a gentleman never is one.

Ask Mamma (1858) ch. 1

11 Major Yammerton was rather a peculiar man, inasmuch as he was an ass, without being a fool.

Ask Mamma (1858) ch. 25

12 'Unting is all that's worth living for—all time is lost wot is not spent in 'unting—it is like the hair we breathe—if we have it not we die—it's the sport of kings, the image of war without its guilt, and only five-and-twenty per cent of its danger.

Handley Cross (1843) ch. 7; see **D'Avenant** 257:22, **Somerville** 745:21

13 Many a good run I have in my sleep. Many a dig in the ribs I gives Mrs J when I think they're running into the warmint . . . No man is fit to be called a sportsman wot doesn't kick his wife out of bed on a haverage once in three weeks!

Handley Cross (1843) ch. 11

14 I'll fill hup the chinks wi' cheese.

Handley Cross (1843) ch. 15

15 It ar'n't that I loves the fox less, but that I loves the 'ound more.

Handley Cross (1843) ch. 16

16 Three things I never lends—my 'oss, my wife, and my name.

Hillingdon Hall (1845) ch. 33

17 Champagne certainly gives one werry gentlemanly ideas, but for a continuance, I don't know but I should prefer mild hale.

Jorrocks's Jaunts and Jollities (1838) 'Mr Jorrocks in Paris'

18 Jorrocks, who is not afraid of 'the pace' so long as there is no leaping.

Jorrocks's Jaunts and Jollities (1838) 'Swell and the Surrey'

19 Better be killed than frightened to death.

Mr Facey Romford's Hounds (1865) ch. 32

20 Life would be very pleasant if it were not for its enjoyments.

Mr Facey Romford's Hounds (1865) ch. 32; see **Lewis** 483:16

21 Everyone knows that the real business of a ball is either to look out for a wife, to look after a wife, or to look after somebody else's wife.

Mr Facey Romford's Hounds (1865) ch. 56

22 The young ladies entered the drawing-room in the full fervour of sisterly animosity.

Mr Sponge's Sporting Tour (1853) ch. 17

23 Women never look so well as when one comes in wet and dirty from hunting.

Mr Sponge's Sporting Tour (1853) ch. 21

24 He was a gentleman who was generally spoken of as having nothing a-year, paid quarterly.

Mr Sponge's Sporting Tour (1853) ch. 24

25 There is no secret so close as that between a rider and his horse.

Mr Sponge's Sporting Tour (1853) ch. 31

David Sutton 1944-

English poet

1 Sorrow in all lands, and grievous omens.
Great anger in the dragon of the hills,
And silent now the earth's green oracles
That will not speak again of innocence.
'Geomancies' (1991)

Italo Svevo 1861–1928

Italian novelist and businessman
see also **Last words** 474:1

2 Last cigarette!!
Zeno's Conscience (1923) ch. 1 and elsewhere

Hannen Swaffer 1879–1962

British journalist

3 Freedom of the press in Britain means freedom to
print such of the proprietor's prejudices as the
advertisers don't object to.
Tom Driberg *Swaff* (1974) ch. 2

Jonathan Swift 1667–1745

Irish poet and satirist
on Swift: see **Coleridge** 234:6, **Dryden** 290:15, **Johnson**
425:10; see also **Epitaphs** 311:10

4 I conceive some scattered notions about a superior
power to be of singular use for the common
people, as furnishing excellent materials to keep
children quiet when they grow peevish, and
providing topics of amusement in a tedious winter-
night.
An Argument Against Abolishing Christianity (1708)

5 Satire is a sort of glass, wherein beholders do
generally discover everybody's face but their own.
The Battle of the Books (1704) preface

6 Instead of dirt and poison we have rather chosen
to fill our hives with honey and wax; thus
furnishing mankind with the two noblest of
things, which are sweetness and light.
The Battle of the Books (1704); see **Arnold** 29:8, **Forster**
329:11

7 It is the folly of too many, to mistake the echo of a
London coffee-house for the voice of the kingdom.
The Conduct of the Allies (1711)

8 I have heard of a man who had a mind to sell his
house, and therefore carried a piece of brick in his
pocket, which he shewed as a pattern to
encourage purchasers.
The Drapier's Letters (1724) no. 2

9 He [the emperor] is taller by almost the breadth of
my nail than any of his court, which alone is
enough to strike an awe into the beholders.
Gulliver's Travels (1726) 'A Voyage to Lilliput' ch. 2

10 He put this engine to our ears, which made an
incessant noise like that of a water-mill; and we
conjecture it is either some unknown animal, or
the god that he worships; but we are more
inclined to the latter opinion.
a watch
Gulliver's Travels (1726) 'A Voyage to Lilliput' ch. 2

11 It is alleged indeed, that the high heels are most
agreeable to our ancient constitution: but
however this be, his Majesty hath determined to
make use of only low heels in the administration
of the government.
Gulliver's Travels (1726) 'A Voyage to Lilliput' ch. 4

12 It is computed, that eleven thousand persons
have, at several times, suffered death, rather than
submit to break their eggs at the smaller end.
Many large volumes have been published upon
this controversy: but the books of the Big-Endians
have been long forbidden, and the whole party
rendered incapable by law of holding
employments.
Gulliver's Travels (1726) 'A Voyage to Lilliput' ch. 4

13 And he gave it for his opinion, that whoever could
make two ears of corn or two blades of grass to
grow upon a spot of ground where only one grew
before, would deserve better of mankind, and do
more essential service to his country than the
whole race of politicians put together.
Gulliver's Travels (1726) 'A Voyage to Brobdingnag' ch. 7

14 He had been eight years upon a project for
extracting sun-beams out of cucumbers, which
were to be put into vials hermetically sealed, and
let out to warm the air in raw inclement summers.
Gulliver's Travels (1726) 'A Voyage to Laputa, etc.' ch. 5

15 These unhappy people were proposing schemes for
persuading monarchs to choose favourites upon
the score of their wisdom, capacity and virtue; of
teaching ministers to consult the public good; of
rewarding merit, great abilities and eminent
services; of instructing princes to know their true
interest by placing it on the same foundation with
that of their people: of choosing for employment
persons qualified to exercise them; with many
other wild impossible chimeras, that never entered
before into the heart of man to conceive, and
confirmed in me the old observation, that there is
nothing so extravagant and irrational which some
philosophers have not maintained for truth.
Gulliver's Travels (1726) 'A Voyage to Laputa, etc.' ch. 6;
see **Cicero** 223:7

16 He replied that I must needs be mistaken, or that I
said the thing which was not. (For they have no
word in their language to express lying or
falsehood.)
Gulliver's Travels (1726) 'A Voyage to the Houyhnhnms'
ch. 3

17 I told him . . . that we ate when we were not
hungry, and drank without the provocation of
thirst.
Gulliver's Travels (1726) 'A Voyage to the Houyhnhnms'
ch. 6

18 We are so fond of one another, because our
ailments are the same.
Journal to Stella (in *Works*, 1768) 1 February 1711

19 Will she pass in a crowd? Will she make a figure
in a country church?
Journal to Stella (in *Works*, 1768) 9 February 1711

1 I value not your bill of fare, give me your bill of company.
Journal to Stella (in *Works*, 1768) 2 September 1711

2 We were to do more business after dinner; but after dinner is after dinner—an old saying and a true, 'much drinking, little thinking'.
Journal to Stella (in *Works*, 1768) 26 February 1712

3 Proper words in proper places, make the true definition of a style.
Letter to a Young Gentleman lately entered into Holy Orders (9 January 1720)

4 If Heaven had looked upon riches to be a valuable thing, it would not have given them to such a scoundrel.
letter to Miss Vanhomrigh, 12–13 August 1720, in H. Williams (ed.) *Correspondence of Jonathan Swift* (1963) vol. 2; see **Steele** 755:3

5 I have ever hated all nations, professions and communities, and all my love is towards individuals . . . But principally I hate and detest that animal called man; although I heartily love John, Peter, Thomas, and so forth.
letter to Pope, 29 September 1725, in H. Williams (ed.) *Correspondence of Jonathan Swift* (1963) vol. 3

6 Not die here in a rage, like a poisoned rat in a hole.
letter to Bolingbroke, 21 March 1730, in H. Williams (ed.) *Correspondence of Jonathan Swift* (1963) vol. 3

7 Surely mortal man is a broomstick!
A Meditation upon a Broomstick (1710)

8 I have been assured by a very knowing American of my acquaintance in London, that a young healthy child well nursed is at a year old a most delicious, nourishing, and wholesome food, whether stewed, roasted, baked, or boiled, and I make no doubt that it will equally serve in a fricassee, or a ragout.
A Modest Proposal for Preventing the Children of Ireland from being a Burden to their Parents or Country (1729)

9 I mean, you lie—under a mistake.
Polite Conversation (1738) Dialogue 1

10 She wears her clothes, as if they were thrown on her with a pitchfork.
Polite Conversation (1738) Dialogue 1

11 He was a bold man that first eat an oyster.
Polite Conversation (1738) Dialogue 2

12 Faith, that's as well said, as if I had said it myself.
Polite Conversation (1738) Dialogue 2

13 I always love to begin a journey on Sundays, because I shall have the prayers of the church, to preserve all that travel by land, or by water.
Polite Conversation (1738) Dialogue 2; see **Book of Common Prayer** 129:12

14 Books, like men their authors, have no more than one way of coming into the world, but there are ten thousand to go out of it, and return no more.
A Tale of a Tub (1704) 'Epistle Dedicatory'; see **Seneca** 677:2

15 Satire, being levelled at all, is never resented for an offence by any.
A Tale of a Tub (1704) 'Author's Preface'

16 What though his head be empty, provided his commonplace book be full.
A Tale of a Tub (1704) ch. 7 'Digression in Praise of Digressions'

17 Last week I saw a woman flayed, and you will hardly believe, how much it altered her person for the worse.
A Tale of a Tub (1704) ch. 9

18 I never saw, heard, nor read, that the clergy were beloved in any nation where Christianity was the religion of the country. Nothing can render them popular, but some degree of persecution.
Thoughts on Religion (1765)

19 We have just enough religion to make us hate, but not enough to make us love one another.
Thoughts on Various Subjects (1711)

20 When a true genius appears in the world, you may know him by this sign, that the dunces are all in confederacy against him.
Thoughts on Various Subjects (1711)

21 What they do in heaven we are ignorant of; what they do *not* we are told expressly, that they neither marry, nor are given in marriage.
Thoughts on Various Subjects (1711); see **Bible** 98:7

22 The stoical scheme of supplying our wants, by lopping off our desires, is like cutting off our feet when we want shoes.
Thoughts on Various Subjects (1711)

23 The reasons why so few marriages are happy, is, because young ladies spend their time in making nets, not in making cages.
Thoughts on Various Subjects (1711)

24 Few are qualified to shine in company; but it is in most men's power to be agreeable.
Thoughts on Various Subjects (1727 ed.)

25 Every man desires to live long; but no man would be old.
Thoughts on Various Subjects (1727 ed.)

26 Old men and comets have been reverenced for the same reason; their long beards, and pretences to foretell events.
Thoughts on Various Subjects (1727 ed.)

27 Laws are like cobwebs, which may catch small flies, but let wasps and hornets break through.
A Tritical Essay upon the Faculties of the Mind (1709); see **Anacharsis** 13:18

28 There is nothing in this world constant, but inconstancy.
A Tritical Essay upon the Faculties of the Mind (1709)

29 A coming shower your shooting corns presage.
'A Description of a City Shower' (1710) l. 9

30 They never would hear,
But turn the deaf ear,
As a matter they had no concern in.
'Dingley and Brent' (written 1724)

31 I often wished that I had clear,
For life, six hundred pounds a-year,
A handsome house to lodge a friend,
A river at my garden's end,

A terrace walk, and half a rood
Of land, set out to plant a wood.
'Imitation of Horace' (written 1714); see **Horace** 403:14

1 How haughtily he lifts his nose,
To tell what every schoolboy knows.
'The Journal' (1727) l. 81

2 Nor do they trust their tongue alone,
But speak a language of their own;
Can read a nod, a shrug, a look,
Far better than a printed book;
Convey a libel in a frown,
And wink a reputation down.
'The Journal of a Modern Lady' (1729) l. 188

3 Hail, fellow, well met,
All dirty and wet:
Find out, if you can,
Who's master, who's man.
'My Lady's Lamentation' (written 1728) l. 165

4 Th' artillery of words.
'Ode to Dr William Sancroft' (written 1692)

5 Philosophy! the lumber of the schools.
'Ode to Sir W. Temple' (written 1692)

6 Say, Britain, could you ever boast,—
Three poets in an age at most?
Our chilling climate hardly bears
A sprig of bays in fifty years.
'On Poetry' (1733) l. 5

7 Then, rising with Aurora's light,
The Muse invoked, sit down to write;
Blot out, correct, insert, refine,
Enlarge, diminish, interline.
'On Poetry' (1733) l. 85

8 As learned commentators view
In Homer more than Homer knew.
'On Poetry' (1733) l. 103

9 So geographers, in Afric-maps,
With savage-pictures fill their gaps;
And o'er unhabitable downs
Place elephants for want of towns.
'On Poetry' (1733) l. 177

10 Hobbes clearly proves, that every creature
Lives in a state of war by nature.
'On Poetry' (1733) l. 319

11 So, naturalists observe, a flea
Hath smaller fleas that on him prey;
And these have smaller fleas to bite 'em,
And so proceed *ad infinitum*.
Thus every poet, in his kind,
Is bit by him that comes behind.
'On Poetry' (1733) l. 337; see **Proverbs** 615:38

12 Walls have tongues, and hedges ears.
'A Pastoral Dialogue between Richmond Lodge and Marble
Hill' (written 1727) l. 8

13 Humour is odd, grotesque, and wild,
Only by affectation spoiled;
'Tis never by invention got,
Men have it when they know it not.
'To Mr Delany' (written 1718) l. 25

14 Hated by fools, and fools to hate,
Be that my motto and my fate.
'To Mr Delany' (written 1718) l. 171

15 In all distresses of our friends,
We first consult our private ends;
While nature, kindly bent to ease us,
Points out some circumstance to please us.
'Verses on the Death of Dr Swift' (1731) l. 7

16 Poor Pope will grieve a month, and Gay
A week, and Arbuthnot a day.
St John himself will scarce forbear
To bite his pen, and drop a tear.
The rest will give a shrug, and cry,
'I'm sorry—but we all must die!'
'Verses on the Death of Dr Swift' (1731) l. 207

17 Yet malice never was his aim;
He lashed the vice, but spared the name;
No individual could resent,
Where thousands equally were meant.
'Verses on the Death of Dr Swift' (1731) l. 512

18 He gave the little wealth he had
To build a house for fools and mad;
And showed, by one satiric touch,
No nation wanted it so much.
'Verses on the Death of Dr Swift' (1731) l. 538

19 In Church your grandsire cut his throat;
To do the job too long he tarried,
He should have had my hearty vote,
To cut his throat before he married.
'Verses on the Upright Judge' (written 1724)

20 'Libertas et natale solum':
Fine words! I wonder where you stole 'em.
Libertas . . . = *Freedom and my native skies*
'Whitshed's Motto on his Coach' (written 1724)

21 Good God! what a genius I had when I wrote that
book.
of A Tale of a Tub
Sir Walter Scott (ed.) *Works of Swift* (1814) vol. 1

22 I shall be like that tree, I shall die at the top.
Sir Walter Scott (ed.) *Works of Swift* (1814) vol. 1

23 A stick and a string, with a fly at one end and a
fool at the other.
*description of angling; the remark has also been
attributed to Samuel* **Johnson**, *in the form 'Fly fishing
may be a very pleasant amusement; but angling or
float fishing I can only compare to a stick and a string,
with a worm at one end and a fool at the other'*
in *The Indicator* 27 October 1819

Algernon Charles Swinburne 1837–1909
English poet

24 Maiden, and mistress of the months and stars
Now folded in the flowerless fields of heaven.
Atalanta in Calydon (1865) l. 1

25 When the hounds of spring are on winter's traces,
The mother of months in meadow or plain
Fills the shadows and windy places
With lisp of leaves and ripple of rain;
And the brown bright nightingale amorous

Is half assuaged for Itylus,
For the Thracian ships and the foreign faces,
The tongueless vigil and all the pain.

Atalanta in Calydon (1865) chorus 'When the hounds of spring'

1 For winter's rains and ruins are over,
And all the season of snows and sins;
The days dividing lover and lover,
The light that loses, the night that wins;
And time remembered is grief forgotten,
And frosts are slain and flowers begotten,
And in green underwood and cover
Blossom by blossom the spring begins.

Atalanta in Calydon (1865) chorus 'When the hounds of spring'

2 And soft as lips that laugh and hide
The laughing leaves of the tree divide,
And screen from seeing and leave in sight
The god pursuing, the maiden hid.

Atalanta in Calydon (1865) chorus 'When the hounds of spring'

3 Before the beginning of years
There came to the making of man
Time with a gift of tears,
Grief with a glass that ran.

Atalanta in Calydon (1865) chorus 'Before the beginning of years'

4 Strength without hands to smite,
Love that endures for a breath;
Night, the shadow of light,
And Life, the shadow of death.

Atalanta in Calydon (1865) chorus 'Before the beginning of years'

5 For words divide and rend;
But silence is most noble till the end.

Atalanta in Calydon (1865) chorus 'Who hath given man speech'

6 Sleep; and if life was bitter to thee, pardon,
If sweet, give thanks; thou hast no more to live;
And to give thanks is good, and to forgive.

'Ave atque Vale' (1878) st. 17

7 Villon, our sad bad glad mad brother's name.

'Ballad of François Villon' (1878)

8 O slain and spent and sacrificed
People, the grey-grown speechless Christ.

'Before a Crucifix' (1871)

9 We shift and bedeck and bedrape us,
Thou art noble and nude and antique.

'Dolores' (1866) st. 7

10   Change in a trice
The lilies and languors of virtue
For the raptures and roses of vice.

'Dolores' (1866) st. 9

11 O splendid and sterile Dolores,
Our Lady of Pain.

'Dolores' (1866) st. 9

12 No thorns go as deep as a rose's,
And love is more cruel than lust.

'Dolores' (1866) st. 20

13 In a coign of the cliff between lowland and highland,

At the sea-down's edge between windward and lee,
Walled round with rocks as an inland island,
The ghost of a garden fronts the sea.

'A Forsaken Garden' (1878)

14 As a god self-slain on his own strange altar,
Death lies dead.

'A Forsaken Garden' (1878)

15 Pale, beyond porch and portal,
Crowned with calm leaves, she stands
Who gathers all things mortal
With cold immortal hands.

'The Garden of Proserpine' (1866)

16 We are not sure of sorrow,
And joy was never sure.

'The Garden of Proserpine' (1866)

17 From too much love of living,
From hope and fear set free,
We thank with brief thanksgiving
Whatever gods may be
That no man lives forever,
That dead men rise up never;
That even the weariest river
Winds somewhere safe to sea.

'The Garden of Proserpine' (1866)

18 Fiddle, we know, is diddle: and diddle, we take it,
is dee.

The Heptalogia (1880) 'The Higher Pantheism in a Nutshell'; see **Tennyson** 777:12

19 Even love, the beloved Republic, that feeds upon
freedom lives.

'Hertha' (1871); see **Forster** 330:2

20 Glory to Man in the highest! for Man is the master
of things.

'Hymn of Man' (1871); see **Bible** 100:4

21 Yea, is not even Apollo, with hair and harpstring
of gold,
A bitter God to follow, a beautiful God to behold?

'Hymn to Proserpine' (1866)

22 Thou hast conquered, O pale Galilean; the world
has grown grey from Thy breath;
We have drunken of things Lethean, and fed on
the fullness of death.

'Hymn to Proserpine' (1866); see **Last words** 474:10

23 Though these that were Gods are dead, and thou
being dead art a God,
Though before thee the throned Cytherean be
fallen, and hidden her head,
Yet thy kingdom shall pass, Galilean, thy dead
shall go down to thee dead.

'Hymn to Proserpine' (1866)

24 And the best and the worst of this is
That neither is most to blame,
If you have forgotten my kisses
And I have forgotten your name.

'An Interlude' (1866)

25 Swallow, my sister, O sister swallow,
How can thine heart be full of the spring?
A thousand summers are over and dead.
What hast thou found in the spring to follow?

What hast thou found in thine heart to sing?
What wilt thou do when the summer is shed?
'Itylus' (1864)

1 Till life forget and death remember,
Till thou remember and I forget.
'Itylus' (1864)

2 The small slain body, the flowerlike face,
Can I remember if thou forget?

O sister, sister, thy first-begotten!
The hands that cling and the feet that follow,
The voice of the child's blood crying yet
Who hath remembered me? Who hath forgotten?
Thou hast forgotten, O summer swallow,
But the world shall end when I forget.
'Itylus' (1864)

3 Apples of gold for the king's daughter.
'The King's Daughter'

4 Ah, yet would God this flesh of mine might be
Where air might wash and long leaves cover me;
Where tides of grass break into foam of flowers,
Or where the wind's feet shine along the sea.
'Laus Veneris' (1866)

5 I am the queen Aholibah
My lips kissed dumb the word of *Ah*.
'The Masque of Queen Bersabe' (1866)

6 If love were what the rose is,
And I were like the leaf,
Our lives would grow together
In sad or singing weather,
Blown fields or flowerful closes,
Green pleasure or grey grief.
'A Match' (1866)

7 There was a poor poet named Clough,
Whom his friends all united to puff,
But the public, though dull,
Had not such a skull
As belonged to believers in Clough.
'Matthew Arnold' (1875)

8 I will go back to the great sweet mother,
Mother and lover of men, the sea.
I will go down to her, I and no other,
Close with her, kiss her and mix her with me.
'The Triumph of Time' (1866)

9 I shall sleep, and move with the moving ships,
Change as the winds change, veer in the tide.
'The Triumph of Time' (1866)

Thomas Sydenham 1624–89

English physician

10 Almighty God hath not bestowed on mankind a
remedy of so universal an extent and so efficacious
in curing divers maladies as opiates.
manuscript version of published text, *Observationes Medicae*
(1676, G. G. Meynell (ed.) 1991)

John Millington Synge 1871–1909

Irish dramatist

11 'A man who is not afraid of the sea will soon be
drownded,' he said 'for he will be going out on a

day he shouldn't. But we do be afraid of the sea,
and we do only be drownded now and again.'
The Aran Islands (1907) pt. 2

12 'A translation is no translation,' he said, 'unless it
will give you the music of a poem along with the
words of it.'
The Aran Islands (1907) pt. 3

13 Oh my grief, I've lost him surely. I've lost the only
Playboy of the Western World.
The Playboy of the Western World (1907) act 3

Thomas Szasz 1920–

Hungarian-born psychiatrist

14 A teacher should have maximal authority and
minimal power.
The Second Sin (1973) 'Education'

15 Happiness is an imaginary condition, formerly
often attributed by the living to the dead, now
usually attributed by adults to children, and by
children to adults.
The Second Sin (1973) 'Emotions'

16 The stupid neither forgive nor forget; the naïve
forgive and forget; the wise forgive but do not
forget.
The Second Sin (1973) 'Personal Conduct'

17 If you talk to God, you are praying; if God talks to
you, you have schizophrenia. If the dead talk to
you, you are a spiritualist; if God talks to you, you
are a schizophrenic.
The Second Sin (1973) 'Schizophrenia'

18 Formerly, when religion was strong and science
weak, men mistook magic for medicine; now,
when science is strong and religion weak, men
mistake medicine for magic.
The Second Sin (1973) 'Science and Scientism'

19 Two wrongs don't make a right, but they make a
good excuse.
The Second Sin (1973) 'Social Relations'

Albert von Szent-Györgyi 1893–1986

Hungarian-born biochemist

20 Discovery consists of seeing what everybody has
seen and thinking what nobody has thought.
Irving Good (ed.) *The Scientist Speculates* (1962)

Tt

Tacitus (Cornelius Tacitus) c.AD 56–after 117

Roman senator and historian

21 *Res olim dissociabiles miscuerit, principatum ac
libertatem.*
He [Nerva] has united things long incompatible,
the principate and liberty.
Agricola ch. 3; see **Disraeli** 276:21

1 *Haud semper errat fama.*

Rumour is not always wrong.

Agricola ch. 9

2 *Nunc terminus Britanniae patet, atque omne ignotum pro magnifico est.*

Now the boundary of Britain is revealed, and everything unknown is held to be glorious.

reporting the speech of a British leader, Calgacus

Agricola ch. 30

3 *Solitudinem faciunt pacem appellant.*

They make a wilderness and call it peace.

Agricola ch. 30

4 *Proprium humani ingenii est odisse quem laeseris.*

It is part of human nature to hate the man you have hurt.

Agricola ch. 42

5 *Sciant, quibus moris est inlicita mirari, posse etiam sub malis principibus magnos viros esse, obsequiumque ac modestiam, si industria ac vigor adsint, eo laudis excedere, quo plerique per abrupta, sed in nullum rei publicae usum, ambitiosa morte inclaruerunt.*

Those whose habit it is to admire what is forbidden ought to know that there can be great men even under bad emperors, and that duty and discretion, if coupled with energy and a career of action, will bring a man to no less glorious summits than are attained by perilous paths and ostentatious deaths that do not benefit the Commonwealth.

Agricola ch. 42 (translated by A. R. Birling)

6 *Tu vero felix, Agricola, non vitae tantum claritate, sed etiam opportunitate mortis.*

You were indeed fortunate, Agricola, not only in the distinction of your life, but also in the lucky timing of your death.

Agricola ch. 45

7 *Sine ira et studio.*

With neither anger nor partiality.

Annals bk. 1, ch. 1

8 *Corruptissima re publica plurimae leges.*

The more corrupt the state, the more numerous the laws.

Annals bk. 3, ch. 27

9 *Elegantiae arbiter.*

The arbiter of taste.

*of **Petronius***

Annals bk. 16, ch. 18

10 *Rara temporum felicitate ubi sentire quae velis et quae sentias dicere licet.*

These times having the rare good fortune that you may think what you like and say what you think.

Histories bk. 1, ch. 1

11 *Maior privato visus dum privatus fuit, et omnium consensu capax imperii nisi imperasset.*

He seemed much greater than a private citizen while he still was a private citizen, and by

everyone's consent capable of reigning if only he had not reigned.

of the Emperor Galba

Histories bk. 1, ch. 49

12 *Cupido gloriae novissima exuitur.*

Love of fame is the last thing to be given up.

Histories bk. 4, ch. 6

13 *Deos fortioribus adesse.*

The gods are on the side of the stronger.

*Histories bk. 4, ch. 17; see **Bussy-Rabutin** 175:9, **Proverbs** 629:45*

14 *Experientia docuit.*

Experience has taught.

commonly quoted as 'Experientia docet [experience teaches]'

*The Histories bk. 5, ch. 6; see **Dickens** 268:12, **Proverbs** 619:29*

William Howard Taft 1857–1930

American Republican statesman, 27th President of the US, 1909–13

15 Next to the right of liberty, the right of property is the most important individual right guaranteed by the Constitution and the one which, united with that of personal liberty, has contributed more to the growth of civilization than any other institution established by the human race.

Popular Government (1913) ch. 3

☐ Taglines for films

see box opposite

Rabindranath Tagore 1861–1941

Bengali poet and philosopher

16 Bigotry tries to keep truth safe in its hand With a grip that kills it.

Fireflies (1928)

17 Touch my life with the magic of thy fire.

*sung at the funeral of Mother **Teresa** in Calcutta, 13 September 1997*

'The Magic of thy Fire'

18 Man goes into the noisy crowd to drown his own clamour of silence.

'Stray Birds' (1916)

Nellie Talbot

19 Jesus wants me for a sunbeam.

title of hymn (1921) in CSSM Choruses No. 1

Charles-Maurice de Talleyrand

1754–1838

French statesman

*on Talleyrand: see **Louis Philippe** 492:15*

20 *Voilà le commencement de la fin.*

This is the beginning of the end.

on the announcement of Napoleon's Pyrrhic victory at Borodino, 1812

attributed; Sainte-Beuve M. de Talleyrand (1870) ch. 3

Continued

Taglines for films

1 Be afraid. Be very afraid.
The Fly (1986 film)

2 Being the adventures of a young man whose principal interests are rape, ultra-violence and Beethoven.
A Clockwork Orange (1972 film)

3 Garbo talks.
Anna Christie (1930 film), her first talkie

4 He said 'I'll be back!' . . . and he meant it!
Terminator 2: Judgment Day (1991 film); see **Film lines** 319:16

5 In space no one can hear you scream.
Alien (1979 film)

6 Just when you thought it was safe to go back in the water.
Jaws 2 (1978)

7 A long time ago in a galaxy far, far away . . .
Star Wars (1977)

8 Love means never having to say you're sorry.
Love Story (1970 film); from the novel (1970) by Erich Segal (1937–)

9 Mean, Moody and Magnificent!
The Outlaw (1946 film) starring Jane Russell

10 Please don't tell the ending. It's the only one we have.
Psycho (1960 film)

11 Somewhere in the universe, there must be something better than Man.
Planet of the Apes (1968 film)

12 They're young . . . they're in love . . . and they kill people.
Bonnie and Clyde (1967 film)

13 We are not alone.
Close Encounters of the Third Kind (1977 film)

14 Where were you in '62?
American Graffiti (1973 film)

Charles-Maurice de Talleyrand *continued*

15 It is not an event, it is an item of news.
*on hearing of the death of **Napoleon** in 1821*

Philip Henry Stanhope *Notes of Conversations with the Duke of Wellington* (1888) 1 November 1831

16 *Surtout, Messieurs, point de zèle.*

Above all, gentlemen, not the slightest zeal.

to young diplomats; P. Chasles *Voyages d'un critique à travers la vie et les livres* (1868) vol. 2; see **Lambert** 465:14

17 *Qui n'a pas vécu dans les années voisines de 1789 ne sait pas ce que c'est que le plaisir de vivre.*

He who has not lived during the years around 1789 can not know what is meant by the pleasure of life.

M. Guizot *Mémoires pour servir à l'histoire de mon temps* (1858) vol. 1, ch. 6

18 *Ils n'ont rien appris, ni rien oublié.*

They have learnt nothing, and forgotten nothing.

of the Bourbons in exile

oral tradition, attributed to Talleyrand by the Chevalier de Panat, see below; see **Dumouriez** 291:14

Personne n'est corrigé, personne n'a su ni rien oublier ni rien apprendre.

Nobody has improved, nobody has known how to forget or to learn.

letter from the Chevalier de Panat to Mallet du Pan, January 1796); A. Sayons (ed.) *Mémoires et correspondance de Mallet du Pan* (1851) vol. 2

19 That, Sire, is a question of dates.
often quoted as, 'treason is a matter of dates'; replying to the Tsar's criticism of those who 'betrayed the cause of Europe'

Duff Cooper *Talleyrand* (1932)

20 *Quelle triste vieillesse vous vous préparez.*

What a sad old age you are preparing for yourself.
to a young diplomat who boasted of his ignorance of whist

J. Amédée Pichot *Souvenirs Intimes sur M. de Talleyrand* (1870) 'Le Pour et le Contre'

The Talmud

compilation of Jewish civil and ceremonial law and legend, dating from the 5th century AD, and comprising the Mishnah and the Gemara. There are two versions of the Talmud, the Babylonian Talmud and the earlier Palestinian or Jerusalem Talmud

*see also **Hillel**, **Shammai***

MISHNAH

21 A single man was created in the world, to teach that if any man caused a single soul to perish from Israel, Scripture imputes it to him as though he had caused a whole world to perish; and if any man saves alive a single soul from Israel Scripture imputes it to him as though he had saved alive a whole world.
Mishnah Sanhedrin 4:5

22 Moses received the Law from Sinai and committed it to Joshua, and Joshua to the elders, and the elders to the Prophets; and the Prophets committed it to the men of the Great Synagogue. They said three things: Be deliberate in judgement, raise up many disciples, and make a fence around the Law.
Mishnah Pirqei Avot 1:1

23 By three things is the world sustained: by the Law, by the [Temple-]service, and by deeds of loving-kindness.
Mishnah Pirqei Avot 1:2

24 Love labour and hate mastery and seek not acquaintance with the ruling power.
Mishnah Pirqei Avot 1:10

1 By three things is the world sustained: by truth, by judgement, and by peace.
Mishnah Pirqei Avot 1:18

2 Let the property of thy fellow be dear to thee as thine own.
Mishnah Pirqei Avot 2:12

3 The day is short and the task is great and the labourers are idle and the wage is abundant and the master of the house is urgent.
Mishnah Pirqei Avot 2:15

4 The tradition is a fence around the Law.
Mishnah Pirqei Avot 3:14

5 Beloved is man, for he was created in the image [of God]; still greater was the love in that it was made known to him that he was created in the image of God.
Mishnah Pirqei Avot 3:15

6 All is foreseen, but freedom of choice is given; and the world is judged by grace, yet all is according to the excess of works [that be good or evil].
Mishnah Pirqei Avot 3:16

7 He that neglects the Law in wealth shall in the end neglect it in poverty.
Mishnah Pirqei Avot 4:9

8 He that performs one precept gets for himself one advocate . . . Repentance and good works are as a shield against retribution.
Mishnah Pirqei Avot 4:11

9 Turn it [Torah] and turn it again, for everything is in it.
Mishnah Pirqei Avot 5:22

GEMARA

10 Let thy tongue acquire the habit of saying, 'I know not', lest thou be led to falsehoods.
Babylonian Talmud Berakhot 4a

11 The seal of the Holy One, blessed be He, is *emeth* [truth].
Babylonian Talmud Shabbat 55a

12 If circumcision . . . supersedes the Sabbath, the saving of life, *a minori*, must supersede the Sabbath.
Babylonian Talmud Shabbat 132a

13 As to every man who becomes angry, if he is a sage, his wisdom departs from him; if he is a prophet, his prophecy departs from him.
Babylonian Talmud Pesahim 66b

14 Even an iron partition cannot interpose between Israel and their Father in Heaven.
Babylonian Talmud Pesahim 85b

15 *He shall live by them* [the laws of the Torah], but he shall not die because of them.
Babylonian Talmud Yoma 85b; see **Bible** 78:13

16 Repentance is so great that premeditated sins are accounted as though they were merits.
Babylonian Talmud Yoma 86b

17 The talk of the child in the market-place is either that of his father or of his mother.
Babylonian Talmud Sukkah 56b

18 A man's prayer is only answered if he takes his heart into his hand.
Babylonian Talmud Taanit 8a

19 A man . . . loves his wife as himself . . . honours her more than himself.
Babylonian Talmud Yevamot 62b

20 This nation [Israel] is distinguished by three characteristics; They are merciful, bashful, and benevolent.
Babylonian Talmud Yevamot 79a

21 Great is labour, for it honours the worker.
Babylonian Talmud Nedarim 49b

22 Whoever eats bread without previously washing the hands is as though he had intercourse with a harlot.
Babylonian Talmud Sotah 1.46

23 Unfaithfulness in the house is like a worm in a sesame plant.
Babylonian Talmud Sotah 3b

24 As to someone who started to do something which someone else came along and finished, Scripture regards the one who completed the task as if he had done [the whole of it].
Babylonian Talmud Sotah 13b

25 The father loves the son, and the son loves his sons.
Babylonian Talmud Sotah 49a

26 If a man divorces his first wife, even the altar sheds tears.
Babylonian Talmud Gittin 90b

27 He who does not teach his son a craft, teaches him brigandage.
Babylonian Talmud Qiddushin 29a

28 A man who gives charity in secret is greater than Moses.
Babylonian Talmud Bava Bathra 9b

29 It is the penalty of a liar, that should he even tell the truth, he is not listened to.
Babylonian Talmud Sanhedrin 89b

30 One is allowed to follow the road he wishes to pursue.
Babylonian Talmud Makkot 10b

31 If the soft [water] can wear away the hard [stone], how much more can the words of the Torah, which are hard like iron, carve a way into my heart which is of flesh and blood!
Babylonian Talmud Avot de Rabbi Nathan 20b

32 All that the Holy One, blessed be He, created in the world, He also created in man.
Babylonian Talmud Avot de Rabbi Nathan 29a

33 No man bruises his finger here on earth unless it was so decreed against him in heaven.
Babylonian Talmud Hullin 7b

34 Why [does Yohanan say that one may pray all day long]? Because prayer never loses its value.
Jerusalem Talmud Berakhot 1:1

35 One should not [recite one's prayers] as if he were reading a letter.
Jerusalem Talmud Berakhot 4:4

1 The Holy Spirit rests only on someone whose heart is happy.
Jerusalem Talmud Sukkah 5:1

2 [If] a man keeps himself from transgression one time, then a second and a third time, the Holy One, blessed be He, keeps him from transgressing further.
Jerusalem Talmud Qiddushin 1:9

Tantric Buddhist texts
ritualist form of Buddhism, dating from the 7th century or earlier

3 Just as water that has entered the ear may be removed by water and just as a thorn may be removed by a thorn, so those who know how, remove passion by means of passion itself.
Just as a washerman removes the grime from a garment by means of grime, so the wise man renders himself free of impurity by means of impurity itself.
Citta Vishuddhiprakarana v. 37

4 By the enjoyment of all desires, to which one devotes oneself just as one pleases, it is by such practice as this that one may speedily gain Buddhahood.
With the enjoyment of all desires, to which one devotes oneself just as one pleases, in union with one's chosen divinity, one worships oneself, the Supreme One.
Guhyasamāja Tantra v. 7

5 Mantras and tantras, meditation and concentration
They are all a cause of self-deception.
Do not defile in contemplation thought that is pure in its own nature,
But abide in the bliss of yourself and cease those torments.
Saraha *Dohākosha* (*c.*9th century) v. 23

6 Enjoying the world of sense, one is undefiled by the world of sense,
One plucks the lotus without touching the water.
So the yogi who has gone to the root of things,
Is not enslaved by the senses although he enjoys them.
Saraha *Dohākosha* (*c.*9th century) v. 64

Booth Tarkington 1869–1946
American novelist

7 There are two things that will be believed of any man whatsoever, and one of them is that he has taken to drink.
Penrod (1914) ch. 10

Donna Tartt see Opening lines 575:18

Torquato Tasso 1544–95
Italian poet and writer

8 *Brama assai, poco spera, e nulla chiede.*
Much wished, hoped little, and demanded nought.
Jerusalem Delivered (1580) bk. 2, stanza 16; see **Elgar** 299:2

Allen Tate 1899–1979
American poet

9 Alice grown lazy, mammoth but not fat,
Declines upon her lost and twilight age;
Above in the dozing leaves the grinning cat
Quivers forever with his abstract rage.
'Last Days of Alice' (1932)

10 Row after row with strict impunity
The headstones yield their names to the element,
The wind whirrs without recollection;
In the riven troughs the splayed leaves
Pile up, of nature the casual sacrament
To the seasonal eternity of death.
'Ode to the Confederate Dead' (1928)

11 The shut gate and the decomposing wall:
The gentle serpent, green in the mulberry bush,
Riots with his tongue through the hush—
Sentinel of the grave who counts us all!
'Ode to the Confederate Dead' (1928)

Nahum Tate 1652–1715
English dramatist

12 As pants the hart for cooling streams
When heated in the chase.
New Version of the Psalms (1696) Psalm 42 (with Nicholas Brady); see **Book of Common Prayer** 136:11

13 Through all the changing scenes of life,
In trouble and in joy,
The praises of my God shall still
My heart and tongue employ.
New Version of the Psalms (1696) Psalm 34 (with Nicholas Brady)

14 While shepherds watched their flocks by night,
All seated on the ground,
The angel of the Lord came down,
And glory shone around.
Supplement to the New Version of the Psalms (1700) 'While Shepherds Watched'

Wilbert Joseph ('Billy') Tauzin 1943–
American Republican politician

15 In many respects, this case appears to be eerily similar to the accounting hocus-pocus that occurred at Enron.
on the WorldCom collapse
in *BBC News* 28 June 2002 (electronic edition)

R. H. Tawney 1880–1962
British economic historian

16 Militarism . . . is fetish worship. It is the prostration of men's souls and the laceration of their bodies to appease an idol.
The Acquisitive Society (1921) ch. 4

17 That seductive border region where politics grease the wheels of business and polite society smiles hopefully on both.
Business and Politics under James I (1958)

1 Those who dread a dead-level of income or wealth . . . do not dread, it seems, a dead-level of law and order, and of security for life and property.
  Equality (4th ed., 1931) ch. 3, sect. 3

2 Freedom for the pike is death for the minnows.
  Equality (ed. 4, rev. ed., 1938) ch. 5, sect. 2

3 Private property is a necessary institution, at least in a fallen world; men work more and dispute less when goods are private than when they are common. But it is to be tolerated as a concession to human frailty, not applauded as desirable in itself.
  Religion and the Rise of Capitalism (1926) ch. 1, sect. 1

4 To take usury is contrary to Scripture; it is contrary to Aristotle; it is contrary to nature, for it is to live without labour; it is to sell time, which belongs to God, for the advantage of wicked men; it is to rob those who use the money lent, and to whom, since they make it profitable, the profits should belong.
  Religion and the Rise of Capitalism (1926) ch. 1, sect. 2

5 Both the existing economic order, and too many of the projects advanced for reconstructing it, break down through their neglect of the truism that, since even quite common men have souls, no increase in material wealth will compensate them for arrangements which insult their self-respect and impair their freedom . . . unless industry is to be paralysed by recurrent revolts on the part of outraged human nature, it must satisfy criteria which are not purely economic.
  Religion and the Rise of Capitalism (1926) conclusion

6 What harm have I ever done to the Labour Party?
  declining the offer of a peerage
  in *Evening Standard* 18 January 1962

A. J. P. Taylor 1906–90
British historian

7 German history reached its turning-point and failed to turn. This was the fateful essence of 1848.
  The Course of German History (1945) ch. 4

8 He aroused every feeling except trust.
  of Lloyd George
  English History 1914–1945 (1965) ch. 5

9 History gets thicker as it approaches recent times.
  English History 1914–45 (1965); bibliography

10 The First World War had begun—imposed on the statesmen of Europe by railway timetables. It was an unexpected climax to the railway age.
  The First World War (1963) ch. 1

11 Human blunders, usually, do more to shape history than human wickedness.
  The Origins of the Second World War (1961) ch. 10

12 Crimea: The war that would not boil.
  Rumours of Wars (1952) ch. 6; originally the title of an essay in *History Today* 2 February 1951

13 Bismarck was a political genius of the highest rank, but he lacked one essential quality of the constructive statesman: he had no faith in the future.
  in *Encyclopedia Britannica* (1954)

Ann Taylor 1782–1866 and Jane Taylor 1783–1824
English writers of books for children

14 I thank the goodness and the grace
  Which on my birth have smiled,
  And made me, in these Christian days,
  A happy English child.
  Hymns for Infant Minds (1810) 'A Child's Hymn of Praise'

15 Who ran to help me when I fell,
  And would some pretty story tell,
  Or kiss the place to make it well?
  My Mother.
  Original Poems for Infant Minds (1804) 'My Mother'

16 Twinkle, twinkle, little star,
  How I wonder what you are!
  Up above the world so high,
  Like a diamond in the sky!
  Rhymes for the Nursery (1806) 'The Star'; see **Carroll** 194:10

17 How pleasant it is, at the end of the day,
  No follies to have to repent;
  But reflect on the past, and be able to say,
  That my time has been properly spent.
  Rhymes for the Nursery (1806) 'The Way to be Happy'

Bayard Taylor 1825–78
American traveller and writer

18 Till the sun grows cold,
  And the stars are old,
  And the leaves of the Judgement Book unfold.
  'Bedouin Song'

Edward Taylor ?1645–1729
American puritan divine and poet

19 Who laced and filleted the earth so fine
  With rivers like green ribbons smaragdine?
  Who made the seas its selvage, and its locks
  Like a quilt ball within a silver box?
  Who spread its canopy? Or curtains spun?
  Who in this bowling alley bowled the sun?
  'God's Determination Touching His Elect'; Perry Miller *The American Puritans* (1956)

Henry Taylor 1800–86
British writer

20 Good nature and kindness towards those with whom they come in personal contact, at the expense of public interests, that is of those whom they never see, is the besetting sin of public men.
  The Statesman (1836)

Jeremy Taylor 1613–67

English divine

1 This thing . . . that can be understood and not expressed, may take a neuter gender;—and every schoolboy knows it.
The Real Presence . . . (1654) sect. 5, subsect. 1; see **Macaulay** 498:15

2 As our life is very short, so it is very miserable, and therefore it is well it is short.
The Rule and Exercise of Holy Dying (1651) ch. 1, sect. 4

3 How many people there are that weep with want, or are mad with oppression, or are desperate by too quick a sense of a constant infelicity.
The Rule and Exercise of Holy Dying (1651) ch. 1, sect. 5

4 The union of hands and hearts.
XXV Sermons Preached at Golden Grove (1653) 'The Marriage Ring' pt. 1

Tom Taylor 1817–80

English dramatist; editor of Punch from 1874

5 Hawkshaw, the detective.
usually quoted as 'I am Hawkshaw, the detective'
The Ticket-of-leave Man (1863) act 4, sc. 1

Norman Tebbit 1931–

British Conservative politician
*on Tebbit: see **Foot** 328:2*

6 I grew up in the Thirties with our unemployed father. He did not riot, he got on his bike and looked for work.
speech at Conservative Party Conference, 15 October 1981, in *Daily Telegraph* 16 October 1981

7 The cricket test—which side do they cheer for? . . . Are you still looking back to where you came from or where you are?
on the loyalties of Britain's immigrant population
interview in *Los Angeles Times*, reported in *Daily Telegraph* 20 April 1990

Tecumseh 1768–1813

Shawnee chief

8 Where today are the Pequot? Where are the Narragansett, the Mohican, the Pokanoket, and many other once powerful tribes of our people? They have vanished before the avarice and oppression of the white man, as snow before the summer sun.
Dee Brown *Bury My Heart at Wounded Knee* (1970) ch. 1

Pierre Teilhard de Chardin 1881–1955

French Jesuit philosopher and palaeontologist
*on Teilhard de Chardin: see **Pius XII** 596:16*

9 The history of the living world can be summarised as the elaboration of ever more perfect eyes within a cosmos in which there is always something more to be seen.
The Phenomenon of Man (1959)

□ Telegrams

see box overleaf

William Temple 1628–99

English diplomat and essayist

10 When all is done, human life is, at the greatest and the best, but like a froward child, that must be played with and humoured a little to keep it quiet till it falls asleep, and then the care is over.
Miscellanea. The Second Part (1690) 'Of Poetry'

William Temple 1881–1944

English theologian; Archbishop of Canterbury from 1942

11 Human status ought not to depend upon the changing demands of the economic process.
in *The Life of the Church and the Order of Society* (Malvern, 1941) p. 221

12 It is a mistake to suppose that God is only, or even chiefly, concerned with religion.
R. V. C. Bodley *In Search of Serenity* (1955) ch. 12

13 Personally, I have always looked on cricket as organized loafing.
attributed

John Tenniel 1820–1914

English draughtsman

14 Dropping the pilot.
*on **Bismarck**'s departure from office*
cartoon caption, and title of poem, in *Punch* 29 March 1890

Alfred, Lord Tennyson 1809–92

English poet
*on Tennyson: see **Bagehot** 49:11, **Bulwer-Lytton** 164:4, **Chesterton** 217:10; see also **Closing lines** 228:5*

15 Cleave ever to the sunnier side of doubt.
'The Ancient Sage' (1885) l. 68

16 Break, break, break,
On thy cold grey stones, O Sea!
And I would that my tongue could utter
The thoughts that arise in me.
'Break, Break, Break' (1842)

17 And the stately ships go on
To their haven under the hill;
But O for the touch of a vanished hand,
And the sound of a voice that is still!
'Break, Break, Break' (1842)

18 I come from haunts of coot and hern,
I make a sudden sally
And sparkle out among the fern,
To bicker down a valley.
'The Brook' (1855) l. 23

19 For men may come and men may go,
But I go on for ever.
'The Brook' (1855) l. 33

Continued

Telegrams

1 AM IN MARKET HARBOROUGH. WHERE OUGHT I TO BE?

*sent by G. K. **Chesterton** to his wife in London*

G. K. Chesterton *Autobiography* (1936)

2 BETTER DROWNED THAN DUFFERS IF NOT DUFFERS WONT DROWN.

Arthur Ransome *Swallows and Amazons* (1930) ch. 1

3 A bill of indemnity . . . for raid by Dr Jameson and the British South Africa Company's troops. The amount falls under two heads—first, material damage, total of claim, £677,938 3s. 3d.—second, moral or intellectual damage, total of claim, £1,000,000.

from Paul Kruger (1825–1904) representing the South African Republic

communicated to the House of Commons by Joseph Chamberlain, 18 February 1897

4 DEEPLY REGRET INFORM YOUR GRACE LAST NIGHT TWO BLACK OWLS CAME AND PERCHED ON BATTLEMENTS REMAINED THERE THROUGH NIGHT HOOTING AT DAWN FLEW AWAY NONE KNOWS WHITHER AWAITING INSTRUCTIONS JELLINGS.

Max Beerbohm *Zuleika Dobson* (1911) ch. 14; see **Telegrams** 776:9

5 GOOD WORK, MARY. WE ALL KNEW YOU HAD IT IN YOU.

*from Dorothy **Parker** to Mrs Sherwood on the arrival of her baby*

Alexander Woollcott *While Rome Burns* (1934) 'Our Mrs Parker'

6 HOW DARE YOU BECOME PRIME MINISTER WHEN I'M AWAY GREAT LOVE CONSTANT THOUGHT VIOLET.

*from Violet Bonham Carter (1887–1969) to her father, H. H. **Asquith**, 7 April 1908*

Mark Bonham Carter and Mark Pottle (eds.) *Lantern Slides* (1996)

7 QUESTION: HOW OLD CARY GRANT?
ANSWER: OLD CARY GRANT FINE. HOW YOU?

from Cary Grant (1904–86)

R. Schickel *Cary Grant* (1983)

8 PLEASE FENCE ME IN BABY THE WORLD'S TOO BIG OUT HERE AND I DON'T LIKE IT WITHOUT YOU.

*from Humphrey Bogart (1899–1957) to Lauren **Bacall***

Lauren Bacall *By Myself* (1978)

9 PREPARE VAULT FOR FUNERAL MONDAY DORSET.

Max Beerbohm *Zuleika Dobson* (1911) ch. 14; see **Telegrams** 776:4

10 STREETS FLOODED. PLEASE ADVISE.

*message sent by Robert **Benchley** on arriving in Venice*

R. E. Drennan (ed.) *Wits End* (1973) 'Robert Benchley'

11 VERY SORRY CAN'T COME. LIE FOLLOWS BY POST.

message from Lord Charles Beresford (1846–1919) to the Prince of Wales, on being summoned to dine at the eleventh hour

Ralph Nevill *The World of Fashion 1837-1922* (1923) ch. 5; see **Proust** 613:13

12 What hath God wrought.

Samuel Morse, in the first electric telegraph message, 24 May 1844; see **Bible** 78:21

Alfred, Lord Tennyson *continued*

13 Half a league, half a league,
Half a league onward,
All in the valley of Death
Rode the six hundred.

'The Charge of the Light Brigade' (1854)

14 'Forward, the Light Brigade!'
Was there a man dismayed?
Not though the soldier knew
Some one had blundered:
Their's not to make reply,
Their's not to reason why,
Their's but to do and die:
Into the valley of Death
Rode the six hundred.

Cannon to right of them,
Cannon to left of them,
Cannon in front of them
Volleyed and thundered.

'The Charge of the Light Brigade' (1854)

15 Into the jaws of Death,
Into the mouth of Hell.

'The Charge of the Light Brigade' (1854)

16 Sunset and evening star,
And one clear call for me!
And may there be no moaning of the bar,
When I put out to sea.

'Crossing the Bar' (1889)

17 For though from out our bourne of time and place
The flood may bear me far,
I hope to see my pilot face to face
When I have crossed the bar.

'Crossing the Bar' (1889)

18 A dream of fair women.

title of poem (1832)

19 A daughter of the gods, divinely tall,
And most divinely fair.

'A Dream of Fair Women' (1832) l. 87

20 He clasps the crag with crookèd hands;
Close to the sun in lonely lands,
Ringed with the azure world, he stands.

The wrinkled sea beneath him crawls;
He watches from his mountain walls,
And like a thunderbolt he falls.

'The Eagle' (1851)

21 The mellow lin-lan-lone of evening bells.

'Far-Far-Away' (1889)

22 O Love, O fire! once he drew
With one long kiss my whole soul through
My lips, as sunlight drinketh dew.

'Fatima' (1832) st. 3

1 There beneath the Roman ruin where the purple
    flowers grow,
    Came that 'Ave atque Vale' of the Poet's hopeless
    woe,
    Tenderest of Roman poets nineteen-hundred years
    ago,
    'Frater Ave atque Vale'—as we wander'd to and
    fro
    Gazing at the Lydian laughter of the Garda Lake
    below
    Sweet Catullus's all-but-island, olive-silvery
    Sirmio!
    'Frater Ave atque Vale' (1885); see **Catullus** 202:16,
    Catullus 203:10

2 More black than ashbuds in the front of March.
    'The Gardener's Daughter' (1842) l. 28

3 A sight to make an old man young.
    'The Gardener's Daughter' (1842) l. 140

4 I waited for the train at Coventry.
    'Godiva' (1842) l. 1

5 Then she rode forth, clothed on with chastity.
    'Godiva' (1842) l. 53

6 With twelve great shocks of sound, the shameless
    noon
    Was clashed and hammered from a hundred
    towers.
    'Godiva' (1842) l. 74

7   Ah! when shall all men's good
    Be each man's rule, and universal peace
    Lie like a shaft of light across the land?
    'The Golden Year' (1846) l. 47

8 Through all the circle of the golden year.
    'The Golden Year' (1846) l. 51

9 That a lie which is all a lie may be met and fought
    with outright,
    But a lie which is part a truth is a harder matter to
    fight.
    'The Grandmother' (1859) st. 8

10 That man's the true Conservative
    Who lops the mouldered branch away.
    'Hands all Round' (1882) l. 7

11 Gigantic daughter of the West,
    We drink to thee across the flood,
    We know thee most, we love thee best,
    For art thou not of British blood?
    'Hands all Round' (1852) st. 4

12 Speak to Him thou for He hears, and Spirit with
    Spirit can meet—
    Closer is He than breathing, and nearer than
    hands and feet.
    'The Higher Pantheism' (1869); see **Swinburne** 768:18

13 Wearing the white flower of a blameless life,
    Before a thousand peering littlenesses,
    In that fierce light which beats upon a throne,
    And blackens every blot.
    of Prince **Albert**
    Idylls of the King (1862 ed.) dedication l. 24

14 Man's word is God in man.
    Idylls of the King 'The Coming of Arthur' (1869) l. 132

15 Clothed in white samite, mystic, wonderful.
    Idylls of the King 'The Coming of Arthur' (1869) l. 284;
    'The Passing of Arthur' (1869) l. 199

16 From the great deep to the great deep he goes.
    Idylls of the King 'The Coming of Arthur' (1869) l. 410

17 Blow trumpet, for the world is white with May.
    Idylls of the King 'The Coming of Arthur' (1869) l. 481

18 Live pure, speak true, right wrong, follow the
    King—
    Else, wherefore born?
    Idylls of the King 'Gareth and Lynette' (1872) l. 117

19   The city is built
    To music, therefore never built at all,
    And therefore built for ever.
    Idylls of the King 'Gareth and Lynette' (1872) l. 272

20 To reverence the King, as if he were
    Their conscience, and their conscience as their
    King,
    To break the heathen and uphold the Christ,
    To ride abroad redressing human wrongs,
    To speak no slander, no, nor listen to it,
    To honour his own word as if his God's.
    Idylls of the King 'Guinevere' (1859) l. 465

21 To love one maiden only, cleave to her,
    And worship her by years of noble deeds,
    Until they won her; for indeed I knew
    Of no more subtle master under heaven
    Than is the maiden passion for a maid.
    Idylls of the King 'Guinevere' (1859) l. 472

22 I thought I could not breathe in that fine air
    That pure severity of perfect light—
    I yearned for warmth and colour which I found
    In Lancelot.
    Idylls of the King 'Guinevere' (1859) l. 640

23 We needs must love the highest when we see it.
    Idylls of the King 'Guinevere' (1859) l. 655

24 For good ye are and bad, and like to coins,
    Some true, some light, but every one of you
    Stamped with the image of the King.
    Idylls of the King 'The Holy Grail' (1869) l. 25

25 I will be deafer than the blue-eyed cat,
    And thrice as blind as any noonday owl,
    To holy virgins in their ecstasies,
    Henceforward.
    Idylls of the King 'The Holy Grail' (1869) l. 862

26 Elaine the fair, Elaine the loveable,
    Elaine, the lily maid of Astolat.
    Idylls of the King 'Lancelot and Elaine' (1859) l. 1

27 He is all fault who hath no fault at all:
    For who loves me must have a touch of earth.
    Idylls of the King 'Lancelot and Elaine' (1859) l. 132

28   In me there dwells
    No greatness, save it be some far-off touch
    Of greatness to know well I am not great.
    Idylls of the King 'Lancelot and Elaine' (1859) l. 447

29 I know not if I know what true love is,
    But if I know, then, if I love not him,
    I know there is none other I can love.
    Idylls of the King 'Lancelot and Elaine' (1859) l. 672

1 His honour rooted in dishonour stood,
And faith unfaithful kept him falsely true.
Idylls of the King 'Lancelot and Elaine' (1859) l. 871

2 He makes no friend who never made a foe.
Idylls of the King 'Lancelot and Elaine' (1859) l. 1082

3 The greater man, the greater courtesy.
Idylls of the King 'The Last Tournament' (1871) l. 628

4 For man is man and master of his fate.
Idylls of the King 'The Marriage of Geraint' (1859) l. 355

5 It is the little rift within the lute,
That by and by will make the music mute,
And ever widening slowly silence all.
Idylls of the King 'Merlin and Vivien' (1859) l. 388

6 And trust me not at all or all in all.
Idylls of the King 'Merlin and Vivien' (1859) l. 396

7 Man dreams of fame while woman wakes to love.
Idylls of the King 'Merlin and Vivien' (1859) l. 458

8 But every page having an ample marge,
And every marge enclosing in the midst
A square of text that looks a little blot.
Idylls of the King 'Merlin and Vivien' (1859) l. 667

9 And none can read the text, not even I;
And none can read the comment but myself.
Idylls of the King 'Merlin and Vivien' (1859) l. 679

10 I found Him in the shining of the stars,
I marked Him in the flowering of His fields,
But in His ways with men I find Him not.
Idylls of the King 'The Passing of Arthur' (1869) l. 9

11 So all day long the noise of battle rolled
Among the mountains by the winter sea.
Idylls of the King 'The Passing of Arthur' (1869) l. 170

12 On one side lay the Ocean, and on one
Lay a great water, and the moon was full.
Idylls of the King 'The Passing of Arthur' (1869) l. 179

13 Authority forgets a dying king.
Idylls of the King 'The Passing of Arthur' (1869) l. 289

14 Clothed with his breath, and looking, as he
    walked,
Larger than human on the frozen hills.
He heard the deep behind him, and a cry
Before.
Idylls of the King 'The Passing of Arthur' (1869) l. 350

15 And the days darken round me, and the years,
Among new men, strange faces, other minds.
Idylls of the King 'The Passing of Arthur' (1869) l. 405

16 The old order changeth, yielding place to new,
And God fulfils himself in many ways,
Lest one good custom should corrupt the world.
Idylls of the King 'The Passing of Arthur' (1869) l. 408

17 If thou shouldst never see my face again,
Pray for my soul. More things are wrought by
    prayer
Than this world dreams of.
Idylls of the King 'The Passing of Arthur' (1869) l. 414

18 I am going a long way . . .
To the island-valley of Avilion;
Where falls not hail, or rain, or any snow,

Nor ever wind blows loudly; but it lies
Deep-meadowed, happy, fair with orchard lawns
And bowery hollows crowned with summer sea,
Where I will heal me of my grievous wound.
Idylls of the King 'The Passing of Arthur' (1869) l. 424

19 Like some full-breasted swan
That, fluting a wild carol ere her death,
Ruffles her pure cold plume, and takes the flood
With swarthy webs.
Idylls of the King 'The Passing of Arthur' (1869) l. 434

20 Our little systems have their day;
They have their day and cease to be:
They are but broken lights of thee,
And thou, O Lord, art more than they.
In Memoriam A. H. H. (1850) Prologue

21 Let knowledge grow from more to more,
But more of reverence in us dwell;
That mind and soul, according well,
May make one music as before.
In Memoriam A. H. H. (1850) Prologue

22 I held it truth, with him who sings
To one clear harp in divers tones,
That men may rise on stepping-stones
Of their dead selves to higher things.
In Memoriam A. H. H. (1850) canto 1

23 For words, like Nature, half reveal
And half conceal the Soul within.
In Memoriam A. H. H. (1850) canto 5

24 But, for the unquiet heart and brain,
A use in measured language lies;
The sad mechanic exercise,
Like dull narcotics, numbing pain.
In Memoriam A. H. H. (1850) canto 5

25 Never morning wore
To evening, but some heart did break.
In Memoriam A. H. H. (1850) canto 6

26 Dark house, by which once more I stand
Here in the long unlovely street,
Doors, where my heart was used to beat
So quickly, waiting for a hand.
In Memoriam A. H. H. (1850) canto 7

27 And ghastly through the drizzling rain
On the bald street breaks the blank day.
In Memoriam A. H. H. (1850) canto 7

28 The last red leaf is whirled away,
The rooks are blown about the skies.
In Memoriam A. H. H. (1850) canto 15

29 There twice a day the Severn fills;
The salt sea-water passes by,
And hushes half the babbling Wye,
And makes a silence in the hills.
In Memoriam A. H. H. (1850) canto 19

30 The Shadow cloaked from head to foot,
Who keeps the keys of all the creeds.
In Memoriam A. H. H. (1850) canto 23

31 I envy not in any moods
The captive void of noble rage,
The linnet born within the cage,
That never knew the summer woods.
In Memoriam A. H. H. (1850) canto 27

1 'Tis better to have loved and lost
Than never to have loved at all.
> *In Memoriam A. H. H.* (1850) canto 27; see **Butler** 176:26,
> **Clough** 229:9, **Congreve** 239:10, **Proverbs** 633:7

2 A solemn gladness even crowned
The purple brows of Olivet.
> *In Memoriam A. H. H.* (1850) canto 31

3 Short swallow-flights of song, that dip
Their wings in tears, and skim away.
> *In Memoriam A. H. H.* (1850) canto 48

4 Be near me when my light is low,
When the blood creeps, and the nerves prick
And tingle; and the heart is sick,
And all the wheels of Being slow.

Be near me when the sensuous frame
Is racked with pains that conquer trust;
And Time, a maniac scattering dust,
And Life, a Fury slinging flame.
> *In Memoriam A. H. H.* (1850) canto 50

5 Oh yet we trust that somehow good
Will be the final goal of ill.
> *In Memoriam A. H. H.* (1850) canto 54

6 That nothing walks with aimless feet;
That not one life shall be destroyed,
Or cast as rubbish to the void,
When God hath made the pile complete.
> *In Memoriam A. H. H.* (1850) canto 54

7   But what am I?
An infant crying in the night:
An infant crying for the light:
And with no language but a cry.
> *In Memoriam A. H. H.* (1850) canto 54

8 So careful of the type she seems,
So careless of the single life.
of Nature
> *In Memoriam A. H. H.* (1850) canto 55

9   The great world's altar-stairs
That slope through darkness up to God.
> *In Memoriam A. H. H.* (1850) canto 55

10 Man . . .
Who trusted God was love indeed
And love Creation's final law—
Though Nature, red in tooth and claw
With ravine, shrieked against his creed.
> *In Memoriam A. H. H.* (1850) canto 56

11 So many worlds, so much to do,
So little done, such things to be.
> *In Memoriam A. H. H.* (1850) canto 73; see **Last words**
> 473:17

12 Death has made
His darkness beautiful with thee.
> *In Memoriam A. H. H.* (1850) canto 74

13 And round thee with the breeze of song
To stir a little dust of praise.
> *In Memoriam A. H. H.* (1850) canto 75

14 O last regret, regret can die!
> *In Memoriam A. H. H.* (1850) canto 78

15 Laburnums, dropping-wells of fire.
> *In Memoriam A. H. H.* (1850) canto 83

16 God's finger touched him, and he slept.
> *In Memoriam A. H. H.* (1850) canto 85

17   Fresh from brawling courts
And dusty purlieus of the law.
> *In Memoriam A. H. H.* (1850) canto 89; see **Etherege** 312:3

18 You tell me, doubt is Devil-born.
> *In Memoriam A. H. H.* (1850) canto 96

19 There lives more faith in honest doubt,
Believe me, than in half the creeds.
> *In Memoriam A. H. H.* (1850) canto 96

20 Their meetings made December June,
Their every parting was to die.
> *In Memoriam A. H. H.* (1850) canto 97

21 He seems so near and yet so far.
> *In Memoriam A. H. H.* (1850) canto 97

22 Ring out, wild bells, to the wild sky,
The flying cloud, the frosty light:
The year is dying in the night;
Ring out, wild bells, and let him die.

Ring out the old, ring in the new,
Ring, happy bells, across the snow:
The year is going, let him go;
Ring out the false, ring in the true.
> *In Memoriam A. H. H.* (1850) canto 106

23 Ring out the want, the care, the sin,
The faithless coldness of the times;
Ring out, ring out my mournful rhymes,
But ring the fuller minstrel in.
> *In Memoriam A. H. H.* (1850) canto 106

24 Ring out the thousand wars of old,
Ring in the thousand years of peace.

Ring in the valiant man and free,
The larger heart, the kindlier hand;
Ring out the darkness of the land;
Ring in the Christ that is to be.
> *In Memoriam A. H. H.* (1850) canto 106

25   Not the schoolboy heat,
The blind hysterics of the Celt.
> *In Memoriam A. H. H.* (1850) canto 109

26 Now fades the last long streak of snow,
Now burgeons every maze of quick
About the flowering squares, and thick
By ashen roots the violets blow.
> *In Memoriam A. H. H.* (1850) canto 115

27 And drowned in yonder living blue
The lark becomes a sightless song.
> *In Memoriam A. H. H.* (1850) canto 115

28 There, where the long street roars, hath been
The stillness of the central sea.
> *In Memoriam A. H. H.* (1850) canto 123

29   Wearing all that weight
Of learning lightly like a flower.
> *In Memoriam A. H. H.* (1850) canto 131

30 One God, one law, one element,
And one far-off divine event,
To which the whole creation moves.
> *In Memoriam A. H. H.* (1850) canto 131

31 The voice of the dead was a living voice to me.
> 'In the Valley of Cauteretz' (1864)

1 Below the thunders of the upper deep;
Far, far beneath in the abysmal sea,
His ancient, dreamless, uninvaded sleep
The Kraken sleepeth.
'The Kraken' (1830)

2 There hath he lain for ages and will lie
Battening upon huge seaworms in his sleep,
Until the latter fire shall heat the deep.
'The Kraken' (1830)

3 The daughter of a hundred Earls,
You are not one to be desired.
'Lady Clara Vere de Vere' (1842) st. 1

4 Kind hearts are more than coronets,
And simple faith than Norman blood.
'Lady Clara Vere de Vere' (1842) st. 7

5 On either side the river lie
Long fields of barley and of rye,
That clothe the wold and meet the sky;
And through the field the road runs by
To many-towered Camelot.
'The Lady of Shalott' (1832, revised 1842) pt. 1

6 Willows whiten, aspens quiver,
Little breezes dusk and shiver.
'The Lady of Shalott' (1832, revised 1842) pt. 1

7 Only reapers, reaping early
In among the bearded barley,
Hear a song that echoes cheerly
From the river winding clearly,
Down to towered Camelot.
'The Lady of Shalott' (1832, revised 1842) pt. 1

8 Or when the moon was overhead,
Came two young lovers lately wed;
'I am half sick of shadows,' said
The Lady of Shalott.
'The Lady of Shalott' (1832, revised 1842) pt. 2

9 A bow-shot from her bower-eaves,
He rode between the barley-sheaves,
The sun came dazzling through the leaves,
And flamed upon the brazen greaves
Of bold Sir Lancelot.
A red-cross knight for ever kneeled
To a lady in his shield,
That sparkled on the yellow field,
Beside remote Shalott.
'The Lady of Shalott' (1832, revised 1842) pt. 3

10 All in the blue unclouded weather
Thick-jewelled shone the saddle-leather,
The helmet and the helmet-feather
Burned like one burning flame together,
As he rode down to Camelot.
'The Lady of Shalott' (1832, revised 1842) pt. 3

11 'Tirra lirra,' by the river
Sang Sir Lancelot.
'The Lady of Shalott' (1832, revised 1842) pt. 3

12 She left the web, she left the loom,
She made three paces through the room,
She saw the water-lily bloom,
She saw the helmet and the plume,
She looked down to Camelot.
Out flew the web and floated wide;

The mirror cracked from side to side;
'The curse is come upon me,' cried
The Lady of Shalott.
'The Lady of Shalott' (1832, revised 1842) pt. 3

13 But Lancelot mused a little space;
He said 'She has a lovely face;
God in his mercy lend her grace,
The Lady of Shalott.'
'The Lady of Shalott' (1832, revised 1842) pt. 4

14 Airy, fairy Lilian.
'Lilian' (1830)

15 In the spring a livelier iris changes on the
burnished dove;
In the spring a young man's fancy lightly turns to
thoughts of love.
'Locksley Hall' (1842) l. 19

16 He will hold thee, when his passion shall have
spent its novel force,
Something better than his dog, a little dearer than
his horse.
'Locksley Hall' (1842) l. 49

17 This is truth the poet sings,
That a sorrow's crown of sorrow is remembering
happier things.
'Locksley Hall' (1842) l. 75; see **Boethius** 125:6, **Dante**
255:18

18 But the jingling of the guinea helps the hurt that
Honour feels.
'Locksley Hall' (1842) l. 105

19 Men, my brothers, men the workers, ever reaping
something new:
That which they have done but earnest of the
things that they shall do:
'Locksley Hall' (1842) l. 117

20 For I dipped into the future, far as human eye
could see,
Saw the vision of the world, and all the wonder
that would be;
Saw the heavens fill with commerce, argosies of
magic sails,
Pilots of the purple twilight, dropping down with
costly bales;
Heard the heavens fill with shouting, and there
rained a ghastly dew
From the nations' airy navies grappling in the
central blue;
Far along the world-wide whisper of the south-
wind rushing warm,
With the standards of the peoples plunging
through the thunder-storm;
Till the war-drum throbbed no longer, and the
battle-flags were furled
In the Parliament of man, the Federation of the
world.
'Locksley Hall' (1842) l. 119

21 Science moves, but slowly slowly, creeping on
from point to point.
'Locksley Hall' (1842) l. 134

22 Yet I doubt not through the ages one increasing
purpose runs,

And the thoughts of men are widened with the
process of the suns.
'Locksley Hall' (1842) l. 137

1 Knowledge comes, but wisdom lingers.
'Locksley Hall' (1842) l. 141

2 I will take some savage woman, she shall rear my
dusky race.
'Locksley Hall' (1842) l. 168

3 I the heir of all the ages, in the foremost files of
time.
'Locksley Hall' (1842) l. 178

4   Forward, forward let us range,
Let the great world spin for ever down the ringing
grooves of change.
'Locksley Hall' (1842) l. 181

5 Better fifty years of Europe than a cycle of Cathay.
'Locksley Hall' (1842) l. 184

6 Music that gentlier on the spirit lies,
Than tired eyelids upon tired eyes.
'The Lotos-Eaters' (1832) Choric Song, st. 1

7 There is no joy but calm!
'The Lotos-Eaters' (1832) Choric Song, st. 2

8 Death is the end of life; ah, why
Should life all labour be?
'The Lotos-Eaters' (1832) Choric Song, st. 4

9   Live and lie reclined
On the hills like Gods together, careless of
mankind.
For they lie beside their nectar, and the bolts are
hurled
Far below them in the valleys, and the clouds are
lightly curled
Round their golden houses, girdled with the
gleaming world.
'The Lotos-Eaters' (1832) Choric Song, st. 8 (1842
revision)

10 Surely, surely, slumber is more sweet than toil,
the shore
Than labour in the deep mid-ocean, wind and
wave and oar;
Oh rest ye, brother mariners, we will not wander
more.
'The Lotos-Eaters' (1832) Choric Song, st. 8

11   I saw the flaring atom-streams
And torrents of her myriad universe,
Ruining along the illimitable inane.
'Lucretius' (1868) l. 38

12   Nor at all can tell
Whether I mean this day to end myself,
Or lend an ear to Plato where he says,
That men like soldiers may not quit the post
Allotted by the Gods.
'Lucretius' (1868) l. 145

13 Passionless bride, divine Tranquillity,
Yearned after by the wisest of the wise,
Who fail to find thee, being as thou art
Without one pleasure and without one pain.
'Lucretius' (1868) l. 265

14 Weeded and worn the ancient thatch
Upon the lonely moated grange.

She only said, 'My life is dreary,
He cometh not,' she said;
She said, 'I am aweary, aweary,
I would that I were dead!'
'Mariana' (1830) st. 1; see **Shakespeare** 708:11

15 I hate that dreadful hollow behind the little wood.
Maud (1855) pt. 1, sect. 1

16 Faultily faultless, icily regular, splendidly null,
Dead perfection, no more.
Maud (1855) pt. 1, sect. 2

17 And most of all would I flee from the cruel
madness of love,
The honey of poison-flowers and all the
measureless ill.
Maud (1855) pt. 1, sect. 4, st. 10

18 That jewelled mass of millinery,
That oiled and curled Assyrian Bull.
Maud (1855) pt. 1, sect. 6, st. 6

19 She came to the village church,
And sat by a pillar alone;
An angel watching an urn
Wept over her, carved in stone.
Maud (1855) pt. 1, sect. 8

20 I kissed her slender hand,
She took the kiss sedately;
Maud is not seventeen,
But she is tall and stately.
Maud (1855) pt. 1, sect. 12, st. 4

21 Gorgonised me from head to foot
With a stony British stare.
Maud (1855) pt. 1, sect. 13, st. 2

22 A livelier emerald twinkles in the grass,
A purer sapphire melts into the sea.
Maud (1855) pt. 1, sect. 18, st. 6

23 Come into the garden, Maud,
For the black bat, night, has flown,
Come into the garden, Maud,
I am here at the gate alone.
And the woodbine spices are wafted abroad,
And the musk of the rose is blown.

For a breeze of morning moves,
And the planet of Love is on high,
Beginning to faint in the light that she loves
On a bed of daffodil sky.
Maud (1855) pt. 1, sect. 22, st. 1

24 All night has the casement jessamine stirred
To the dancers dancing in tune;
Till a silence fell with the waking bird,
And a hush with the setting moon.
Maud (1855) pt. 1, sect. 22, st. 3

25 Queen rose of the rosebud garden of girls.
Maud (1855) pt. 1, sect. 22, st. 9

26 There has fallen a splendid tear
From the passion-flower at the gate.
She is coming, my dove, my dear;
She is coming, my life, my fate;
The red rose cries, 'She is near, she is near;'
And the white rose weeps, 'She is late.'
The larkspur listens, 'I hear, I hear;'

And the lily whispers, 'I wait.'
Maud (1855) pt. 1, sect. 22, st. 10

1 She is coming, my own, my sweet;
Were it ever so airy a tread,
My heart would hear her and beat,
Were it earth in an earthy bed;
My dust would hear her and beat;
Had I lain for a century dead;
Would start and tremble under her feet,
And blossom in purple and red.
Maud (1855) pt. 1, sect. 22, st. 11

2 O that 'twere possible
After long grief and pain
To find the arms of my true love
Round me once again!
Maud (1855) pt. 2, sect. 4, st. 1

3 But the churchmen fain would kill their church,
As the churches have killed their Christ.
Maud (1855) pt. 2, sect. 5, st. 2

4 O me, why have they not buried me deep enough?
Is it kind to have made me a grave so rough,
Me, that was never a quiet sleeper?
Maud (1855) pt. 2, sect. 5, st. 11

5 My life has crept so long on a broken wing
Through cells of madness, haunts of horror and fear,
That I come to be grateful at last for a little thing.
Maud (1855) pt. 3, sect. 6, st. 1

6 The blood-red blossom of war with a heart of fire.
Maud (1855) pt. 3, sect. 6, st. 4

7 It is better to fight for the good, than to rail at the ill;
I have felt with my native land, I am one with my kind,
I embrace the purpose of God, and the doom assigned.
Maud (1855) pt. 3, sect. 6, st. 5

8 You must wake and call me early, call me early, mother dear;
Tomorrow 'ill be the happiest time of all the glad New-year;
Of all the glad New-year, mother, the maddest merriest day;
For I'm to be Queen o' the May, mother, I'm to be Queen o' the May.
'The May Queen' (1832)

9 *I* am Merlin
Who follow the Gleam
'Merlin and The Gleam' (1889) st. 1

10 O mighty-mouthed inventor of harmonies,
O skilled to sing of time or eternity,
God-gifted organ-voice of England,
Milton, a name to resound for ages.
'Milton: Alcaics' (1863)

11   All that bowery loneliness,
The brooks of Eden mazily murmuring.
'Milton: Alcaics' (1863)

12 O you chorus of indolent reviewers.
'Milton: Hendecasyllabics' (1863)

13 Doänt thou marry for munny, but goä wheer munny is!
'Northern Farmer. New Style' (1869) st. 5; see **Proverbs** 627:24

14 The last great Englishman is low.
'Ode on the Death of the Duke of Wellington' (1852) st. 3

15 O good grey head which all men knew!
'Ode on the Death of the Duke of Wellington' (1852) st. 4

16 O fall'n at length that tower of strength
Which stood four-square to all the winds that blew!
'Ode on the Death of the Duke of Wellington' (1852) st. 4

17 That world-earthquake, Waterloo!
'Ode on the Death of the Duke of Wellington' (1852) st. 6

18 Who never sold the truth to serve the hour,
Nor paltered with Eternal God for power.
'Ode on the Death of the Duke of Wellington' (1852) st. 7

19 And at their feet the crocus brake like fire,
Violet, amaracus, and asphodel,
Lotos and lilies.
'Oenone' (1832, revised 1842) l. 94

20 Still as, while Saturn whirls, his steadfast shade
Sleeps on his luminous ring.
'The Palace of Art' (1832) st. 4

21 An English home—grey twilight poured
On dewy pasture, dewy trees,
Softer than sleep—all things in order stored,
A haunt of ancient Peace.
'The Palace of Art' (1832) st. 22

22 Vex not thou the poet's mind
With thy shallow wit:
Vex not thou the poet's mind;
For thou canst not fathom it.
'The Poet's Mind' (1830)

23 With prudes for proctors, dowagers for deans,
And sweet girl-graduates in their golden hair.
The Princess (1847) 'Prologue' l. 141

24 And blessings on the falling out
That all the more endears,
When we fall out with those we love
And kiss again with tears!
The Princess (1847) pt. 2, song (added 1850)

25 And quoted odes, and jewels five-words-long,
That on the stretched forefinger of all Time
Sparkle for ever.
The Princess (1847) pt. 2, l. 355

26 Sweet and low, sweet and low,
Wind of the western sea,
Low, low, breathe and blow,
Wind of the western sea!
Over the rolling waters go,
Come from the dying moon, and blow,
Blow him again to me;
While my little one, while my pretty one, sleeps.
The Princess (1847) pt. 3, song (added 1850)

27 The splendour falls on castle walls
And snowy summits old in story:
The long light shakes across the lakes,
And the wild cataract leaps in glory.

Blow, bugle, blow, set the wild echoes flying,
Blow, bugle; answer, echoes, dying, dying, dying.
The Princess (1847) pt. 4, song (added 1850)

1 O sweet and far from cliff and scar
The horns of Elfland faintly blowing!
The Princess (1847) pt. 4, song (added 1850)

2 O love, they die in yon rich sky,
They faint on hill or field or river:
Our echoes roll from soul to soul,
And grow for ever and for ever.
The Princess (1847) pt. 4, song (added 1850)

3 Tears, idle tears, I know not what they mean,
Tears from the depth of some divine despair
Rise in the heart, and gather to the eyes,
In looking on the happy autumn-fields,
And thinking of the days that are no more.
The Princess (1847) pt. 4, l. 21, song (added 1850)

4 So sad, so fresh, the days that are no more.
The Princess (1847) pt. 4, l. 30, song (added 1850)

5 Ah, sad and strange as in dark summer dawns
The earliest pipe of half-awakened birds
To dying ears, when unto dying eyes
The casement slowly grows a glimmering square;
So sad, so strange, the days that are no more.

Dear as remembered kisses after death,
And sweet as those by hopeless fancy feigned
On lips that are for others; deep as love,
Deep as first love, and wild with all regret;
O Death in Life, the days that are no more.
The Princess (1847) pt. 4, l. 31, song (added 1850)

6 O Swallow, Swallow, flying, flying South,
Fly to her, and fall upon her gilded eaves,
And tell her, tell her, what I tell to thee.

O tell her, Swallow, thou that knowest each,
That bright and fierce and fickle is the South,
And dark and true and tender is the North.
The Princess (1847) pt. 4, l. 75, song (added 1850)

7 O tell her, Swallow, that thy brood is flown:
Say to her, I do but wanton in the South,
But in the North long since my nest is made.
The Princess (1847) pt. 4, l. 90, song (added 1850)

8 Man is the hunter; woman is his game:
The sleek and shining creatures of the chase,
We hunt them for the beauty of their skins;
They love us for it, and we ride them down.
The Princess (1847) pt. 5, l. 147

9 Home they brought her warrior dead.
She nor swooned, nor uttered cry:
All her maidens, watching said,
'She must weep or she will die.'
The Princess (1847) pt. 6, song (added 1850)

10 Rose a nurse of ninety years,
Set his child upon her knee—
Like summer tempest came her tears—
'Sweet my child, I live for thee.'
The Princess (1847) pt. 6, song (added 1850)

11 The woman is so hard
Upon the woman.
The Princess (1847) pt. 6, l. 205

12 Now sleeps the crimson petal, now the white;
Nor waves the cypress in the palace walk;
Nor winks the gold fin in the porphyry font:
The fire-fly wakens: waken thou with me.
The Princess (1847) pt. 7, l. 161, song (added 1850)

13 Now lies the Earth all Danaë to the stars,
And all thy heart lies open unto me.
The Princess (1847) pt. 7, l. 167, song (added 1850)

14 Now folds the lily all her sweetness up,
And slips into the bosom of the lake:
So fold thyself, my dearest, thou, and slip
Into my bosom and be lost in me.
The Princess (1847) pt. 7, l. 171, song (added 1850)

15 Come down, O maid, from yonder mountain
height:
What pleasure lives in height?
The Princess (1847) pt. 7, l. 177, song (added 1850)

16 For Love is of the valley, come thou down
And find him; by the happy threshold, he,
Or hand in hand with Plenty in the maize,
Or red with spirted purple of the vats,
Or foxlike in the vine.
The Princess (1847) pt. 7, l. 184, song (added 1850)

17 Sweet is every sound,
Sweeter thy voice, but every sound is sweet;
Myriads of rivulets hurrying through the lawn,
The moan of doves in immemorial elms,
And murmuring of innumerable bees.
The Princess (1847) pt. 7, l. 203, song (added 1850)

18 No little lily-handed baronet he,
A great broad-shouldered genial Englishman.
The Princess (1847) 'Conclusion' l. 84

19 At Flores in the Azores Sir Richard Grenville lay,
And a pinnace, like a fluttered bird, came flying
from far away:
'Spanish ships of war at sea! we have sighted fifty-
three!'
Then sware Lord Thomas Howard: ''Fore God I
am no coward;
But I cannot meet them here, for my ships are out
of gear,
And the half my men are sick. I must fly, but
follow quick.
We are six ships of the line; can we fight with
fifty-three?'
Then spake Sir Richard Grenville: 'I know you are
no coward;
You fly them for a moment to fight with them
again.
But I've ninety men and more that are lying sick
ashore.
I should count myself the coward if I left them, my
Lord Howard,
To these Inquisition dogs and the devildoms of
Spain.'
'The Revenge' (1878) st. 1

20 And Sir Richard said again: 'We be all good
English men.
Let us bang these dogs of Seville, the children of
the devil,

For I never turned my back upon Don or devil
yet.'
'The Revenge' (1878) st. 4

1 And the sun went down, and the stars came out
far over the summer sea,
But never a moment ceased the fight of the one
and the fifty-three.
'The Revenge' (1878) st. 9

2 Sink me the ship, Master Gunner—sink her, split
her in twain!
Fall into the hands of God, not into the hands of
Spain!
'The Revenge' (1878) st. 11

3 And they praised him to his face with their courtly
foreign grace;
But he rose upon their decks, and he cried:
'I have fought for Queen and Faith like a valiant
man and true;
I have only done my duty as a man is bound to
do:
With a joyful spirit I Sir Richard Grenville die!'
And he fell upon their decks, and he died.
'The Revenge' (1878) st. 13

4 And the little Revenge herself went down by the
island crags
To be lost evermore in the main.
'The Revenge' (1878) st. 14

5 My strength is as the strength of ten,
Because my heart is pure.
'Sir Galahad' (1842)

6 Alone and warming his five wits,
The white owl in the belfry sits.
'Song—The Owl' (1830)

7 The woods decay, the woods decay and fall,
The vapours weep their burthen to the ground,
Man comes and tills the field and lies beneath,
And after many a summer dies the swan.
Me only cruel immortality
Consumes: I wither slowly in thine arms,
Here at the quiet limit of the world.
'Tithonus' (1860, revised 1864) l. 1

8 The gods themselves cannot recall their gifts.
'Tithonus' (1860, revised 1864) l. 52

9 Of happy men that have the power to die,
And grassy barrows of the happier dead.
'Tithonus' (1860, revised 1864) l. 70

10 All the charm of all the Muses
often flowering in a lonely word.
'To Virgil' (1882) st. 3

11 I salute thee, Mantovano,
I that loved thee since my day began,
Wielder of the stateliest measure
Ever moulded by the lips of man.
'To Virgil' (1882) st. 10

12 No life that breathes with human breath
Has ever truly longed for death.
'The Two Voices' (1842) st. 132

13 It little profits that an idle king,
By this still hearth, among these barren crags,

Matched with an agèd wife, I mete and dole
Unequal laws unto a savage race.
'Ulysses' (1842) l. 1

14 I am become a name;
For always roaming with a hungry heart
Much have I seen and known; cities of men
And manners, climates, councils, governments,
Myself not least, but honoured of them all;
And drunk delight of battle with my peers,
Far on the ringing plains of windy Troy.
'Ulysses' (1842) l. 16

15 I am a part of all that I have met;
Yet all experience is an arch wherethrough
Gleams that untravelled world, whose margin
fades
For ever and for ever when I move.
How dull it is to pause, to make an end,
To rust unburnished, not to shine in use!
As though to breathe were life.
'Ulysses' (1842) l. 23; see **Adams** 2:10

16 This grey spirit yearning in desire
To follow knowledge like a sinking star,
Beyond the utmost bound of human thought.
'Ulysses' (1842) l. 30

17 This is my son, mine own Telemachus.
'Ulysses' (1842) l. 33

18 Old age hath yet his honour and his toil;
Death closes all: but something ere the end,
Some work of noble note, may yet be done,
Not unbecoming men that strove with gods.
'Ulysses' (1842) l. 51

19 For my purpose holds
To sail beyond the sunset, and the baths
Of all the western stars, until I die.
It may be that the gulfs will wash us down:
It may be we shall touch the Happy Isles,
And see the great Achilles, whom we knew.
Though much is taken, much abides.
'Ulysses' (1842) l. 66

20 That which we are, we are;
One equal temper of heroic hearts,
Made weak by time and fate, but strong in will
To strive, to seek, to find, and not to yield.
'Ulysses' (1842) l. 74

21 Every moment dies a man,
Every moment one is born.
'The Vision of Sin' (1842) pt. 4, st. 9; see **Babbage** 42:2

22 I grow in worth, and wit, and sense,
Unboding critic-pen,
Or that eternal want of pence,
Which vexes public men.
'Will Waterproof's Lyrical Monologue' (1842) st. 6

23 A land of settled government,
A land of just and old renown,
Where Freedom slowly broadens down
From precedent to precedent.
'You ask me, why, though ill at ease' (1842) st. 3

24 In the end I accepted the honour, because during
dinner Venables told me, that, if I became Poet

Laureate, I should always when I dined out be offered the liver-wing of a fowl.
on being made Poet Laureate in 1850
in *Alfred Lord Tennyson: A Memoir by his Son* (1897) vol. 1

1 I see land! Mr Kendal is just going to be confirmed.
in Charlotte Yonge's novel The Young Stepmother, *the happiness of the Kendal family depends on their being full members of the Anglican church*
Alethea Hayter *Charlotte Yonge* (1996)

2 It is the height of luxury to sit in a hot bath and read about little birds.
having had running hot water installed in his new house at Aldworth
Hallam Tennyson *Tennyson and his Friends* (1911)

3 A louse in the locks of literature.
of Churton Collins
Evan Charteris *Life and Letters of Sir Edmund Gosse* (1931) ch. 14

Terence (Publius Terentius Afer) c.190–159 BC
Roman comic dramatist

4 *Hinc illae lacrimae.*
Hence those tears.
Andria l. 126

5 *Nullumst iam dictum quod non dictum sit prius.*
Nothing has yet been said that's not been said before.
Eunuchus prologue l. 41

6 *Homo sum; humani nil a me alienum puto.*
I am a man, I count nothing human foreign to me.
Heauton Timorumenos l. 77

7 *Fortis fortuna adiuvat.*
Fortune assists the brave.
Phormio l. 203; see **Proverbs** 620:27, **Virgil** 813:8

8 *Quot homines tot sententiae: suus cuique mos.*
There are as many opinions as there are people: each has his own correct way.
Phormio l. 454; see **Proverbs** 631:4

Terentianus Maurus
Roman writer of the late 2nd century AD

9 *Pro captu lectoris habent sua fata libelli.*
The reader's fancy makes the fate of books.
De Syllabis et Metris

Mother Teresa 1910–97
Roman Catholic nun and missionary, born in what is now Macedonia of Albanian parentage

10 We ourselves feel that what we are doing is just a drop in the ocean. But if that drop was not in the ocean, I think the ocean would be less because of that missing drop. I do not agree with the big way of doing things.
A Gift for God (1975)

11 Now let us do something beautiful for God.
letter to Malcolm Muggeridge before making a BBC TV programme about the Missionaries of Charity, 1971; see **Muggeridge** 553:7

12 The biggest disease today is not leprosy or tuberculosis, but rather the feeling of being unwanted, uncared for and deserted by everybody.
in *The Observer* 3 October 1971

13 I see God in every human being. When I wash the leper's wounds I feel I am nursing the Lord himself.
in 1977; in obituary, *Guardian* 6 September 1997

14 By blood and origin I am Albanian. My citizenship is Indian. I am a Catholic nun. As to my calling, I belong to the whole world. As to my heart, I belong entirely to the heart of Jesus.
in *Independent* 6 September 1997; obituary

St Teresa of Ávila 1512–82
Spanish Carmelite nun and mystic
see also **John** *422:9,* **Sayings** *669:6*

15 Our goodness derives not from our capacity to think but to love.
Book of the Foundations (1610)

16 The important thing is not to think much but to love much.
The Interior Castle (1588) Mansion 4, ch. 1, para. 7

17 Alas, O Lord, to what a state dost Thou bring those who love Thee!
Interior Castle Mansion 6, ch. 11, para. 6 (translated by the Benedictines of Stanbrook, 1921)

18 Let nothing trouble you, nothing frighten you. All things are passing; God never changes. Patient endurance attains all things. Whoever possesses God lacks nothing: God alone suffices.
'St Teresa's Bookmark'; found in her breviary after her death

St Teresa of Lisieux 1873–97
French Carmelite nun

19 I will spend my heaven doing good on earth.
T. N. Taylor (ed.) *Soeur Thérèse of Lisieux* (1912) epilogue

20 After my death I will let fall a shower of roses.
T. N. Taylor (ed.) *Soeur Thérèse of Lisieux* (1912) epilogue

Tertullian (Quintus Septimius Florens Tertullianus) c.AD 160–c.225
Roman theologian and Church Father from Carthage

21 *O testimonium animae naturaliter Christianae.*
O evidence of a naturally Christian soul!
Apologeticus ch. 17, sect. 6

22 *'Vide', inquiunt, 'ut invicem se diligant'—ipsi enim invicem oderunt—'et ut pro alteruto mori sint parati'; ipsi enim od occidendum alterutrum paratiores erunt.*
'Look,' they say, 'how they [Christians] love one another' (for they themselves hate one another); 'and how they are ready to die for each other' (for they themselves are readier to kill each other).
usually quoted as, 'See how these Christians love one another'
Apologeticus ch. 39, sect. 7

1 *Plures efficimus quoties metimur a vobis, semen est sanguis Christianorum.*

As often as we are mown down by you, the more we grow in numbers; the blood of Christians is the seed.

traditionally 'The blood of the martyrs is the seed of the Church'

Apologeticus ch. 50, sect. 13; see **Proverbs** 616:6

2 *Certum est quia impossibile est.*

It is certain because it is impossible.

often quoted as 'Credo quia impossibile'

De Carne Christi ch. 5

A. S. J. Tessimond 1902–62

3 Cats, no less liquid than their shadows,
Offer no angles to the wind.
They slip, diminished, neat, through loopholes
Less than themselves.

Cats (1934) p. 20

William Makepeace Thackeray 1811–63

English novelist
on Thackeray: see **Ruskin** 659:8

4 He who meanly admires mean things is a Snob.

The Book of Snobs (1848) ch. 2

5 'Tis not the dying for a faith that's so hard, Master Harry—every man of every nation has done that—'tis the living up to it that is difficult.

The History of Henry Esmond (1852) bk. 1, ch. 6

6 'Tis strange what a man may do, and a woman yet think him an angel.

The History of Henry Esmond (1852) bk. 1, ch. 7

7 What money is better bestowed than that of a school-boy's tip?

The Newcomes (1853–5) vol. 1, ch. 16

8 Yes, I am a fatal man, Madame Fribsbi. To inspire hopeless passion is my destiny.

Mirobolant

Pendennis (1848–50) ch. 23

9 For a slashing article, sir, there's nobody like the Capting.

Mr Bungay

Pendennis (1848–50) ch. 32

10 The *Pall Mall Gazette* is written by gentlemen for gentlemen.

Pendennis (1848–50) ch. 32

11 Business first; pleasure afterwards.

The Rose and the Ring (1855) ch. 1

12 A woman with fair opportunities and without a positive hump, may marry whom she likes.

Vanity Fair (1847–8) ch. 4

13 Whenever he met a great man he grovelled before him, and my-lorded him as only a free-born Briton can do.

Vanity Fair (1847–8) ch. 13

14 If a man's character is to be abused, say what you will, there's nobody like a relation to do the business.

Vanity Fair (1847–8) ch. 19

15 Them's my sentiments!

Fred Bullock

Vanity Fair (1847–8) ch. 21

16 Darkness came down on the field and city: and Amelia was praying for George, who was lying on his face, dead, with a bullet through his heart.

Vanity Fair (1847–8) ch. 32

17 Nothing like blood, sir, in hosses, dawgs, and men.

James Crawley

Vanity Fair (1847–8) ch. 35

18 How to live well on nothing a year.

Vanity Fair (1847–8) ch. 36 (title)

19 I think I could be a good woman if I had five thousand a year.

Vanity Fair (1847–8) ch. 36

20 As she had never thought or done anything mortally guilty herself, she had not that abhorrence for wickedness which distinguishes moralists much more knowing.

Vanity Fair (1847–8) ch. 65

21 Ah! *Vanitas Vanitatum!* Which of us is happy in this world? Which of us has his desire? or, having it, is satisfied?—Come, children, let us shut up the box and the puppets, for our play is played out.

Vanity Fair (1847–8) ch. 67

22 Werther had a love for Charlotte
Such as words could never utter;
Would you know how first he met her?
She was cutting bread and butter.

'Sorrows of Werther' (1855)

23 Charlotte, having seen his body
Borne before her on a shutter,
Like a well-conducted person
Went on cutting bread and butter.

'Sorrows of Werther' (1855)

24 Mind, no biography!

injunction to his daughters

John Sutherland *Is Heathcliff a Murderer?* (1996)

Margaret Thatcher 1925–

British Conservative stateswoman; Prime Minister, 1979–90
on Thatcher: see **Callaghan** 185:19, **Healey** 377:12, **Kinnock** 453:8, **Mitterrand** 541:3

25 No woman in my time will be Prime Minister or Chancellor or Foreign Secretary—not the top jobs. Anyway I wouldn't want to be Prime Minister. You have to give yourself 100%.

on her appointment as Shadow Education Spokesman

in *Sunday Telegraph* 26 October 1969

26 In politics if you want anything said, ask a man. If you want anything done, ask a woman.

in *People* (New York) 15 September 1975

27 I stand before you tonight in my red chiffon evening gown, my face softly made up, my fair hair gently waved . . . the Iron Lady of the Western World! Me? A cold war warrior? Well, yes—if that is how they wish to interpret my defence of values and freedoms fundamental to our way of life.

> speech at Finchley, 31 January 1976; see below:

The iron lady.

name given to Thatcher by the Soviet defence ministry newspaper Red Star, *which accused her of trying to revive the cold war*

> in *Sunday Times* 25 January 1976

1 Pennies don't fall from heaven. They have to be earned on earth.

> in *Observer* 18 November 1979 'Sayings of the Week'; see **Burke** 169:13

2 No one would remember the Good Samaritan if he'd only had good intentions. He had money as well.

> television interview, 6 January 1980, in *The Times* 12 January 1980

3 To those waiting with bated breath for that favourite media catchphrase, the U-turn, I have only this to say. 'You turn if you want; the lady's not for turning.'

> speech at Conservative Party Conference in Brighton, 10 October 1980; see **Fry** 336:12

4 Just rejoice at that news and congratulate our armed forces and the Marines. Rejoice!

> *on the recapture of South Georgia, usually quoted as, 'Rejoice, rejoice!'*
>
> to newsmen outside 10 Downing Street, 25 April 1982

5 It is exciting to have a real crisis on your hands, when you have spent half your political life dealing with humdrum issues like the environment.

> *on the Falklands campaign, 1982*
>
> speech to Scottish Conservative Party conference, 14 May 1982, in Hugo Young *One of Us* (1990) ch. 13

6 We have to see that the spirit of the South Atlantic—the real spirit of Britain—is kindled not only by war but can now be fired by peace. We have the first prerequisite. We know that we can do it—we haven't lost the ability. That is the Falklands Factor.

> speech in Cheltenham, 3 July 1982

7 I was asked whether I was trying to restore Victorian values. I said straight out I was. And I am.

> speech to the British Jewish Community, 21 July 1983, referring to an interview with Brian Walden on 17 January 1983

8 Now it must be business as usual.

> *on the steps of Brighton police station a few hours after the bombing of the Grand Hotel, Brighton; often quoted as 'We shall carry on as usual'*
>
> in *The Times* 13 October 1984

9 We can do business together.

> *of Mikhail* **Gorbachev**
>
> in *The Times* 18 December 1984

10 We must try to find ways to starve the terrorist and the hijacker of the oxygen of publicity on which they depend.

> speech to American Bar Association in London, 15 July 1985, in *The Times* 16 July 1985

11 There is no such thing as Society. There are individual men and women, and there are families.

> in *Woman's Own* 31 October 1987

12 We have become a grandmother.

> in *The Times* 4 March 1989

13 Advisers advise and ministers decide.

> *on the respective roles of her personal economic adviser, Alan Walters, and her Chancellor, Nigel* **Lawson** *(who resigned the following day)*
>
> in the House of Commons, 26 October 1989

14 I am naturally very sorry to see you go, but understand . . . your wish to be able to spend more time with your family.

> *reply to Norman* **Fowler**'s *resignation letter*
>
> in *Guardian* 4 January 1990; see **Fowler** 331:1

15 No! No! No!

> *making clear her opposition to a single European currency, and more centralized controls from Brussels*
>
> in the House of Commons, 30 October 1990

16 I fight on, I fight to win.

> *having failed to win outright in the first ballot for party leader*
>
> comment, 21 November 1990

17 It's a funny old world.

> *on withdrawing from the contest for leadership of the Conservative party*
>
> comment, 22 November 1990; see **Film lines** 319:21

18 Home is where you come to when you have nothing better to do.

> in *Vanity Fair* May 1991

William Roscoe Thayer 1859–1923

American biographer and historian

19 Log-cabin to White House.

> title of biography (1910) of James **Garfield**

Themistocles c.528–c.462 BC

Greek historian and Athenian statesman

20 The wooden wall is your ships.

> *interpreting the words of the Delphic oracle to the Athenians, before the battle of Salamis in 480 BC*
>
> Plutarch *Parallel Lives* 'Themistocles' bk. 2, ch. 1; see below
>
> Yet Zeus the all-seeing grants to Athene's prayer That the wooden wall only shall not fall, but help you and your children.
>
> words of the prophetess at Delphi; Herodotus *Histories* bk. 7, sect. 141

Theocritus c.300–260 BC

Greek poet, born in Sicily

21 Something sweet is the whisper of the pine, O goatherd, that makes her music by yonder springs.

> *Idylls* no. 1

Louis Adolphe Thiers 1797–1877

French statesman and historian

1 [Le roi] *règne et le peuple se gouverne.*

The king reigns, and the people govern themselves.

unsigned article in *Le National*, 20 January 1830; see below:

Le roi n'administre pas, ne gouverne pas, il règne.

The king neither administers nor governs, he reigns.

signed article in *Le National*, 4 February 1830

Thomas à Kempis c.1380–1471

German ascetical writer

2 *Opto magis sentire compunctionem: quam scire eius definitionem.*

I would far rather feel remorse than know how to define it.

De Imitatione Christi bk. 1, ch. 1, sect. 3

3 *O quam cito transit gloria mundi.*

Oh how quickly the glory of the world passes away!

De Imitatione Christi bk. 1, ch. 3, sect. 6; see **Anonymous** 22:4

4 *Non quaeras quis hoc dixerit: sed, quid diciatur attende.*

Seek not to know who said this or that, but take note of what has been said.

De Imitatione Christi bk. 1, ch. 5, sect. 1

5 *Multo tutius est stare in subiectione: quam in praelatura.*

It is much safer to be in a subordinate position than in authority.

De Imitatione Christi bk. 1, ch. 9, sect. 1

6 *Nam homo proponit, sed Deus disponit.*

For man proposes, but God disposes.

De Imitatione Christi bk. 1, ch. 19, sect. 2; see **Proverbs** 626:4

7 *Numquam sis ex toto otiosus, sed aut legens, aut scribens, aut orans, aut meditans, aut aliquid utilitatis pro communi laborans.*

Never be completely idle, but either reading, or writing, or praying, or meditating, or at some useful work for the common good.

De Imitatione Christi bk. 1, ch. 19, sect. 4

8 *Nemo secure praecipit, nisi qui bene obedire didicit.*

Nobody rules safely but he who has learned well how to obey.

De Imitatione Christi bk. 1, ch. 20, sect. 2

9 *Hodie homo est: et cras non comparet. Cum autem sublatus fuerit ab oculis: etiam cito transit a mente.*

Today the man is here; tomorrow he is gone. And when he is 'out of sight', quickly also is he out of mind.

De Imitatione Christi bk. 1, ch. 23, sect. 1; see **Proverbs** 629:12

10 *Utinam per unam diem bene essemus conversati in hoc mundo.*

Would that we had spent one whole day well in this world!

De Imitatione Christi bk. 1, ch. 23, sect. 2

11 *Multi annos computant conversionis: sed saepe parvus et fructus emendationis. Si formidolosum est mori: forsitan periculosius erit diutius vivere. Beatus qui horam mortis suae semper ante oculos habet: et ad moriendum cotidiae se disponsit.*

Many count the years since their conversion, but their lives often show little sign of improvement. If it is dreadful to die, it is perhaps more dangerous to live long. Happy is the man who keeps the hour of death always in mind, and daily prepares himself to die.

De Imitatione Christi bk. 1, ch. 23, sect. 2

12 *Passione interdum movemur: et zelum putamus.*

We are sometimes stirred by emotion and take it for zeal.

De Imitatione Christi bk. 2, ch. 5, sect. 1

13 *Si libenter crucem portas portabit te.*

If you bear the cross gladly, it will bear you.

De Imitatione Christi bk. 2, ch. 12, sect. 5

14 *De duobus malis minus est semper eligendum.*

Of the two evils the lesser is always to be chosen.

De Imitatione Christi bk. 3, ch. 12, sect. 2

St Thomas Aquinas c.1225–74

Italian Dominican friar and Doctor of the Church

15 *Pange, lingua, gloriosi*
Corporis mysterium,
Sanguinisque pretiosi,
Quem in mundi pretium
Fructus ventris generosi
Rex effudit gentium.

Now, my tongue, the mystery telling
Of the glorious Body sing,
And the Blood, all price excelling,
Which the Gentiles' Lord and King,
In a Virgin's womb once dwelling,
Shed for this world's ransoming.

'Pange Lingua Gloriosi' (Corpus Christi hymn, translated by J. M. Neale, E. Caswall, and others); see **Fortunatus** 330:3

16 *Tantum ergo sacramentum*
Veneremur cernui;
Et antiquum documentum
Novo cedat ritui.

Therefore we, before him bending,
This great Sacrament revere;
Types and shadows have their ending,
For the newer rite is here.

'Pange Lingua Gloriosi' (Corpus Christi hymn, translated by J. M. Neale, E. Caswall, and others)

17 *Multo ergo magis ad moralem pertinet considerare de amicitia quam de justitia.*

Moral science is better occupied when treating of friendship than of justice.

Exposition of Aristotle's Ethics (c.1271) bk. 8, lecture 1

18 *Finis autem nostri desiderii Deus est; unde actus quo ei primo coniungimur, est originaliter et*

substantialiter nostra beatitudo. Primo autem Deo coniungimur per actum intellectus; *et ideo ipsa Dei visio, quae est actus intellectus, est substantialiter et originaliter nostra beatitudo.*

Now, the end of our desires is God; hence, the act whereby we are primarily joined to Him is basically and substantially our happiness. But we are primarily united with God by an act of understanding; and therefore, the very seeing of God, which is an act of the intellect, is substantially and basically our happiness.

> *Quodlibetal Questions* (c.1256) vol. 8, bk. 9, pt. 19 (translated by Bourke)

1 *Ergo necesse est devenire ad aliquod primum movens, quod a nullo movetur; et hoc omnes intelligunt Deum.*

Therefore it is necessary to arrive at a prime mover, put in motion by no other; and this everyone understands to be God.

> *Summa Theologicae* (c.1265) pt. 1, qu. 2, art. 3 (translated by English Dominican Fathers)

2 *Si enim omnia mala impedirentur, multa bona deessent universo: non enim esset vita lionis, si non esset occisio animalium; nec esset patientia martyrum, si non esset persecutio tyrannorum.*

If all evil were prevented, much good would be absent from the universe. A lion would cease to live, if there were no slaying of animals; and there would be no patience of martyrs if there were no tyrannical persecution.

> *Summa Theologicae* (c.1265) pt. 1, qu. 22, art. 2 (translated by English Dominican Fathers)

3 *Et tamen minimum quod potest haberi de cognitione rerum altissimum desiderabilius est quam certissima cognitio quae habetur de minimis rebus, ut dicitur in De Animal.*

As Aristotle also points out, the slenderest acquaintance we can form with heavenly things is more desirable than a thorough grasp of mundane matters.

> *Summa Theologiae* (c.1265) pt. 1a, qu. 1, art. 5; see **Aristotle** 25:19

4 Everything I have written seems like straw by comparison with what I have seen and what has been revealed to me.

> *following a mystical experience, after which he did no more teaching or writing*
> on 6 December 1273

Brandon Thomas 1856–1914

English dramatist

5 I'm Charley's aunt from Brazil—where the nuts come from.

> *Charley's Aunt* (1892) act 1

Dylan Thomas 1914–53

Welsh poet
see also **Opening lines** 575:26

6 Though lovers be lost love shall not;
And death shall have no dominion.

> 'And death shall have no dominion' (1936); see **Bible** 106:12

7 Do not go gentle into that good night,
Old age should burn and rave at close of day;
Rage, rage against the dying of the light.

> 'Do Not Go Gentle into that Good Night' (1952)

8 Oh as I was young and easy in the mercy of his means,
Time held me green and dying
Though I sang in my chains like the sea.

> 'Fern Hill' (1946)

9 The force that through the green fuse drives the flower
Drives my green age; that blasts the roots of trees
Is my destroyer.
And I am dumb to tell the crooked rose
My youth is bent by the same wintry fever.

> 'The force that through the green fuse drives the flower' (1934)

10 And I am dumb to tell the lover's tomb
How at my sheet goes the same crooked worm.

> 'The force that through the green fuse drives the flower' (1934)

11 The hand that signed the paper felled a city;
Five sovereign fingers taxed the breath,
Doubled the globe of dead and halved a country;
These five kings did a king to death.

> 'The hand that signed the paper felled a city' (1936)

12 The hand that signed the treaty bred a fever,
And famine grew, and locusts came;
Great is the hand that holds dominion over
Man by a scribbled name.

> 'The hand that signed the paper felled a city' (1936)

13 Light breaks where no sun shines;
Where no sea runs, the waters of the heart
Push in their tides.

> 'Light breaks where no sun shines' (1934)

14 It was my thirtieth year to heaven
Woke to my hearing from harbour and neighbour wood
And the mussel pooled and the heron
Priested shore
The morning beckon.

> 'Poem in October' (1946)

15 Pale rain over the dwindling harbour
And over the sea wet church the size of a snail
With its horns through mist and the castle
Brown as owls
But all the gardens
Of spring and summer were blooming in the tall vales
Beyond the border and under the lark full cloud.
There could I marvel
My birthday
Away but the weather turned around.

> 'Poem in October' (1946)

16 Deep with the first dead lies London's daughter,
Robed in the long friends,
The grains beyond age, the dark veins of her mother,
Secret by the unmourning water
Of the riding Thames.

After the first death, there is no other.
'A Refusal to Mourn the Death, by Fire, of a Child in London' (1946)

1 I can never remember whether it snowed for six days and six nights when I was twelve or whether it snowed for twelve days and twelve nights when I was six.
A Child's Christmas in Wales (1954)

2 Books that told me everything about the wasp, except why.
A Child's Christmas in Wales (1954)

3 There is only one position for an artist anywhere: and that is, upright.
on the position of the artists of Wales
Quite Early One Morning (1954) pt. 2 'Wales and the Artist'

4 Chasing the naughty couples down the grassgreen gooseberried double bed of the wood.
Under Milk Wood (1954)

5 Before you let the sun in, mind it wipes its shoes.
Under Milk Wood (1954)

6 Oh, isn't life a terrible thing, thank God?
Under Milk Wood (1954) p. 30

7 I want, above all, to work like a fiend, a *good* fiend.
letter to Edith **Sitwell**, 11 April 1947; *Collected Letters* (1987)

8 The land of my fathers. My fathers can have it.
of Wales
in *Adam* December 1953; see **James** 417:10

9 A man you don't like who drinks as much as you do.
definition of an alcoholic
Constantine Fitzgibbon *Life of Dylan Thomas* (1965) ch. 6

10 Poetry is not the most important thing in life . . . I'd much rather lie in a hot bath reading Agatha Christie and sucking sweets.
Joan Wyndham *Love is Blue* (1986) 6 July 1943

Edward Thomas 1878–1917
English poet

11 Yes; I remember Adlestrop—
The name, because one afternoon
Of heat the express-train drew up there
Unwontedly. It was late June.
'Adlestrop' (1917)

12 The past is the only dead thing that smells sweet.
'Early one morning in May I set out' (1917)

13 If I should ever by chance grow rich
I'll buy Codham, Cockridden, and Childerditch,
Roses, Pyrgo, and Lapwater,
And let them all to my elder daughter.
'Household Poems: Bronwen' (1917)

14 I have come to the borders of sleep,
The unfathomable deep
Forest where all must lose
Their way.
'Lights Out' (1917)

15 ⁣ ⁣ I see and hear nothing;
Yet seem, too, to be listening, lying in wait

For what I should, yet never can, remember.
'Old Man' (1917)

16 Out in the dark over the snow
The fallow fawns invisible go
With the fallow doe;
And the winds blow
Fast as the stars are slow.
'Out in the dark' (1917)

17 As well as any bloom upon a flower
I like the dust on the nettles, never lost
Except to prove the sweetness of a shower.
'Tall Nettles' (1917)

Elizabeth Thomas 1675–1731
English poet

18 From marrying in haste, and repenting at leisure;
Not liking the person, yet liking his treasure:
Libera nos.
'A New Litany, occasioned by an invitation to a wedding' (1722); see **Proverbs** 626:17

Gwyn Thomas 1913–81
Welsh novelist and dramatist

19 I wanted a play that would paint the full face of sensuality, rebellion and revivalism. In South Wales these three phenomena have played second fiddle only to Rugby Union which is a distillation of all three.
introduction to *Jackie the Jumper* (1962)

20 There are still parts of Wales where the only concession to gaiety is a striped shroud.
in *Punch* 18 June 1958

Irene Thomas 1919–2001
British writer and broadcaster

21 Protestant women may take the pill. Roman Catholic women must keep taking The Tablet.
in *Guardian* 28 December 1990

R. S. Thomas 1913–2000
Welsh poet and clergyman

22 The ousel singing in the woods of Cilgwri,
Tirelessly as a stream over the mossed stones,
Is not so old as the toad of Cors Fochno
Who feels the cold skin sagging round his bones.
'The Ancients of the World' (1952)

23 Or the dry whisper of unseen wings,
Bats not angels, in the high roof.
'In a Country Church' (1955)

24 ⁣ ⁣ Doctors in verse
Being scarce now, most poets
Are their own patients, compelled to treat
Themselves first, their complaint being
Peculiar always.
'The Cure' (1958)

25 There is no love
For such, only a willed
gentleness.
'They' (1968)

1 Hate takes a long time
To grow in, and mine
Has increased from birth;
Not for the brute earth . . .
. . . I find
This hate's for my own kind . . .
'Those Others' (1961)

2   God is that great absence
In our lives, the empty silence
Within, the place where we go
Seeking, not in hope to
Arrive or find.
'Via Negativa' (1972)

3 There is no present in Wales,
And no future;
There is only the past,
Brittle with relics . . .
And an impotent people,
Sick with inbreeding,
Worrying the carcase of an old song.
'Welsh Landscape' (1955)

Francis Thompson 1859–1907

English poet

4 As the run-stealers flicker to and fro,
To and fro:—
O my Hornby and my Barlow long ago!
'At Lord's' (1913)

5 The fairest things have fleetest end,
Their scent survives their close:
But the rose's scent is bitterness
To him that loved the rose!
'Daisy' (1913)

6 Nothing begins, and nothing ends,
That is not paid with moan;
For we are born in other's pain,
And perish in our own.
'Daisy' (1913)

7 I fled Him, down the nights and down the days;
I fled Him, down the arches of the years;
I fled Him, down the labyrinthine ways
Of my own mind; and in the mist of tears
I hid from Him, and under running laughter.
'The Hound of Heaven' (1913) pt. 1

8 But with unhurrying chase,
And unperturbèd pace,
Deliberate speed, majestic instancy,
They beat—and a Voice beat
More instant than the Feet—
All things betray thee, who betrayest Me.
'The Hound of Heaven' (1913) pt. 1

9 I said to Dawn: Be sudden—to Eve:
Be soon.
'The Hound of Heaven' (1913) pt. 2

10 Such is: what is to be?
The pulp so bitter, how shall taste the rind?
'The Hound of Heaven' (1913) pt. 4

11 Yet ever and anon a trumpet sounds
From the hid battlements of Eternity;
Those shaken mists a space unsettle, then

Round the half-glimpsèd turrets slowly wash
again.
'The Hound of Heaven' (1913) pt. 4

12 Lo, all things fly thee, for thou fliest Me!
'The Hound of Heaven' (1913) pt. 5

13 There is no expeditious road
To pack and label men for God,
And save them by the barrel-load.
Some may perchance, with strange surprise,
Have blundered into Paradise.
'A Judgement in Heaven' (1913) epilogue

14 O world invisible, we view thee,
O world intangible, we touch thee,
O world unknowable, we know thee,
Inapprehensible, we clutch thee!
'The Kingdom of God' (1913)

15 The angels keep their ancient places;—
Turn but a stone, and start a wing!
'Tis ye, 'tis your estrangèd faces,
That miss the many-splendoured thing.
'The Kingdom of God' (1913)

16   Upon thy so sore loss
Shall shine the traffic of Jacob's ladder
Pitched betwixt Heaven and Charing Cross.
'The Kingdom of God' (1913)

17 And lo, Christ walking on the water
Not of Gennesareth, but Thames!
'The Kingdom of God' (1913)

18 Look for me in the nurseries of heaven.
'To My Godchild Francis M.W.M.' (1913)

19 Insculped and embossed,
With His hammer of wind,
And His graver of frost.
'To a Snowflake' (1913)

Julian Thompson 1934–

British soldier, second-in-command of the land forces during the Falklands campaign.

20 You don't mind dying for Queen and country, but
you certainly don't want to die for politicians.
'The Falklands War—the Untold Story' (Yorkshire
Television) 1 April 1987; see **France** 332:3, **Graham** 358:4

Robert Norman Thompson 1914–97

American-born Canadian mission worker, politician and academic

21 The Americans are our best friends whether we
like it or not.
Peter C. Newman *Home Country: People, Places, and Power
Politics* (1973)

William Hepworth Thompson 1810–86

English classicist; Master of Trinity College, Cambridge, from 1866

22 What time he can spare from the adornment of his
person he devotes to the neglect of his duties.
*of Sir Richard Jebb, later Professor of Greek at
Cambridge University*
M. R. Bobbit *With Dearest Love to All* (1960) ch. 7

James Thomson 1700–48
Scottish poet

1 When Britain first, at heaven's command,
Arose from out the azure main,
This was the charter of the land,
And guardian angels sung this strain:
'Rule, Britannia, rule the waves;
Britons never will be slaves.'
*when Thomas Arne set this to music the last two lines
became 'Rule, Britannia! Britannia rule the waves!
Britons never never never shall be slaves'*
Alfred: a Masque (1740) act 2;

2 Soft quilts on quilts, on carpets carpets spread,
And couches stretch around in seemly band;
And endless pillows rise to prop the head.
The Castle of Indolence (1748) canto 1, st. 33

3 A bard here dwelt, more fat than bard beseems.
The Castle of Indolence (1748) canto 1, st. 68 (of himself)

4 A little round, fat, oily man of God,
Was one I chiefly marked among the fry:
He had a roguish twinkle in his eye.
The Castle of Indolence (1748) canto 1, st. 69

5 Here lies a man who never lived,
Yet still from death was flying;
Who, if not sick, was never well;
And died—for fear of dying!
'Epitaph on Solomon Mendez' (published 1782)

6 But now those white unblemished minutes, whence
The fabling poets took their golden age,
Are found no more amid these iron times,
These dregs of life!
The Seasons (1746) 'Spring' l. 272

7 The daisy, primrose, violet, darkly blue,
And polyanthus of unnumbered dyes;
The yellow wall-flower, stained with iron brown;
And lavish stock that scents the garden round.
The Seasons (1746) 'Spring' l. 531

8 Delightful task! to rear the tender thought,
To teach the young idea how to shoot.
The Seasons (1746) 'Spring' l. 1152

9 An elegant sufficiency, content,
Retirement, rural quiet, friendship, books.
The Seasons (1746) 'Spring' l. 1161

10 Ships, dim-discovered, dropping from the clouds.
The Seasons (1746) 'Summer' l. 946

11 Sighed and looked unutterable things.
The Seasons (1746) 'Summer' l. 1188

12 While listening senates hang upon thy tongue.
The Seasons (1746) 'Autumn' l. 15

13 Find other lands beneath another sun.
The Seasons (1746) 'Autumn' l. 1286

14 See, Winter comes to rule the varied year,
Sullen and sad.
The Seasons (1746) 'Winter' l. 1

15 Welcome, kindred glooms!
Congenial horrors, hail!
The Seasons (1746) 'Winter' l. 5

16 For ever, Fortune, wilt thou prove
An unrelenting foe to Love;
And, when we meet a mutual heart,
Come in between and bid us part?
'Song' (1732)

17 Even Light itself, which every thing displays,
Shone undiscovered, till his brighter mind
Untwisted all the shining robe of day.
*on **Newton**'s Opticks*
'To the Memory of Sir Isaac Newton' (1727) l. 96

18 Did ever poet image aught so fair,
Dreaming in whispering groves, by the hoarse brook!
Or prophet, to whose rapture heaven descends!
*on **Newton**'s explanation of the rainbow in terms of refraction*
'To the Memory of Sir Isaac Newton' (1727) l. 96

James Thomson 1834–82
Scottish poet

19 The city of dreadful night.
title of poem, written 1870–3

20 As we rush, as we rush in the train,
The trees and the houses go wheeling back,
But the starry heavens above that plain
Come flying on our track.
'Sunday at Hampstead' (written 1863–5) st. 10

21 Give a man a horse he can ride,
Give a man a boat he can sail.
'Sunday up the River' (written 1865) st. 15

Roy Thomson 1894–1976
Canadian-born British newspaper proprietor

22 Like having your own licence to print money.
on the profitability of commercial television in Britain
R. Braddon *Roy Thomson* (1965) ch. 32

Henry David Thoreau 1817–62
American writer
*on Thoreau: see **James** 417:20*

23 I heartily accept the motto, 'That government is
best which governs least' . . . Carried out, it finally
amounts to this, which I also believe,— 'That
government is best which governs not at all.'
*Civil Disobedience (1849); see **O'Sullivan** 579:8*

24 Under a government which imprisons any
unjustly, the true place for a just man is also a
prison.
Civil Disobedience (1849)

25 What does education often do? It makes a
straight-cut ditch of a free, meandering brook.
Journal c.November 1850

26 Some circumstantial evidence is very strong, as
when you find a trout in the milk.
Journal 11 November 1850

27 Not that the story need be long, but it will take a
long while to make it short.
*letter to Harrison Blake, 16 November 1857, in Writings
(1906 ed.) vol. 6; see **Pascal** 587:1*

1 By avarice and selfishness, and a grovelling habit, from which none of us is free, of regarding the soil as property . . . the landscape is deformed.
   Walden (1854) 'The Bean Field'

2 I have travelled a good deal in Concord.
   Walden (1854) 'Economy'

3 As if you could kill time without injuring eternity.
   Walden (1854) 'Economy'

4 The mass of men lead lives of quiet desperation.
   Walden (1854) 'Economy'; in *Histoire de ma vie* vol. 4 (1854), George Sand described Chopin as being in a state of '*désespérance tranquille*'

5 In any weather, at any hour of the day or night, I have been anxious to improve the nick of time, and notch it on my stick too; to stand on the meeting of two eternities, the past and the future, which is precisely the present moment; to toe that line.
   Walden (1854) 'Economy'

6 Beware of all enterprises that require new clothes.
   Walden (1854) 'Economy'

7 For more than five years I maintained myself thus solely by the labour of my hands, and I found, that by working about six weeks in a year, I could meet all the expenses of living.
   Walden (1854) 'Economy'

8 As for Doing-good, that is one of the professions which are full.
   Walden (1854) 'Economy'

9 The three-o'-clock in the morning courage, which Bonaparte thought was the rarest.
   Walden (1854) 'Sounds'; see **Napoleon** 556:17

10 Wherever a man goes, men will pursue him and paw him with their dirty institutions, and, if they can, constrain him to belong to their desperate oddfellow society.
   Walden (1854) 'The Village'

11 I had three chairs in my house; one for solitude, two for friendship, three for society.
   Walden (1854) 'Visitors'

12 I wanted to live deep and suck out all the marrow of life . . . to drive life into a corner, and reduce it to its lowest terms, and, if it proved to be mean, why then to get the whole and genuine meanness of it, and publish its meanness to the world; or if it were sublime, to know it by experience.
   Walden (1854) 'Where I lived, and what I lived for'

13 Our life is frittered away by detail . . . Simplify, simplify.
   Walden (1854) 'Where I lived, and what I lived for'

14 I once had a sparrow alight upon my shoulder for a moment while I was hoeing in a village garden, and I felt that I was more distinguished by that circumstance than I should have been by any epaulette I could have worn.
   Walden (1854) 'Winter Animals'

15 It is not worthwhile to go around the world to count the cats in Zanzibar.
   Walden (1854) 'Conclusion'

16 If a man does not keep pace with his companions, perhaps it is because he hears a different drummer. Let him step to the music which he hears, however measured or far away.
   Walden (1854) 'Conclusion'

17 The government of the world I live in was not framed, like that of Britain, in after-dinner conversations over the wine.
   Walden (1854) 'Conclusion'

18 It takes two to speak the truth,—one to speak, and another to hear.
   A Week on the Concord and Merrimack Rivers (1849) 'Wednesday'

19 It were treason to our love
   And a sin to God above
   One iota to abate
   Of a pure impartial hate.
   'Indeed, Indeed I Cannot Tell' (1852)

Robert Thorne d. 1527
English merchant and geographical writer

20 There is no land unhabitable nor sea innavigable.
   Richard Hakluyt *The Principal Navigations, Voyages, and Discoveries of the English Nation* (1589)

Jeremy Thorpe 1929–
British Liberal politician

21 Greater love hath no man than this, that he lay down his friends for his life.
   on Harold **Macmillan**'s sacking seven of his Cabinet on 13 July 1962
   D. E. Butler and Anthony King *The General Election of 1964* (1965) ch. 1; see **Bible** 103:33

Thucydides c.455–c.400 BC
Greek historian

22 I have written my work, not as an essay which is to win the applause of the moment, but as a possession for all time.
   History of the Peloponnesian War bk. 1, ch. 22, sect. 18 (translated by Richard Crawley, 1874)

23 Happiness depends on being free, and freedom depends on being courageous.
   History of the Peloponnesian War bk. 2, ch. 43, sect. 4 (translated by Rex Warner)

24 Of the gods we believe, and of men we know, that by a necessary law of their nature they rule wherever they can.
   History of the Peloponnesian War bk. 5, ch. 105

James Thurber 1894–1961
American humorist
see also **Cartoon captions** 198:2, **Cartoon captions** 198:4, **Cartoon captions** 198:10

25 Her own mother lived the latter years of her life in the horrible suspicion that electricity was dripping invisibly all over the house.
   My Life and Hard Times (1933) ch. 2

26 You might as well fall flat on your face as lean over too far backward.
   'The Bear Who Let It Alone' in *New Yorker* 29 April 1939

1 The war between men and women.
cartoon series title in *New Yorker* 20 January–28 April
1934

2 Early to rise and early to bed makes a male
healthy and wealthy and dead.
'The Shrike and the Chipmunks' in *New Yorker* 18
February 1939; see **Proverbs** 618:31

3 Humour is emotional chaos remembered in
tranquillity.
in *New York Post* 29 February 1960; see **Wordsworth**
850:26

Edward, Lord Thurlow 1731–1806

English jurist; Lord Chancellor, 1778–83, 1783–92

4 Corporations have neither bodies to be punished,
nor souls to be condemned, they therefore do as
they like.
*usually quoted as 'Did you ever expect a corporation
to have a conscience, when it has no soul to be
damned, and no body to be kicked?'*
John Poynder *Literary Extracts* (1844) vol. 1; see **Coke**
230:20, **Proverbs** 617:11

Edward, Lord Thurlow 1781–1829

English poet

5 Nature is always wise in every part.
'To a Bird, that haunted the Waters of Lacken, in the
Winter'

Anthony Thwaite 1930–

English writer

6 The name is history.
        The thick Miljacka flows
Under its bridges through a canyon's breadth
Fretted with minarets and plump with domes,
Cupped in its mountains, caught on a drawn
    breath.
'Sarajevo: I' (1973)

Tiberius 42 BC–AD 37

Roman emperor from AD 14

7 It is the part of the good shepherd to shear his
flock, not skin it.
to governors who recommended burdensome taxes
Suetonius *Lives of the Caesars* 'Tiberius'

The Tibetan Book of the Dead

*A Tibetan Buddhist text recited during funerary rites, dating
from the 8th century AD*

8 When the consciousness-principle getteth outside
[the body it sayeth to itself] 'Am I dead or am I not
dead?' It cannot determine. It seeth its relatives
and connections as it had been used to seeing
them before. It even heareth the wailings.
bk. 1, pt. 1

Tibullus (Albius Tibullus) c.50–19 BC

Roman poet

9 *Te spectem, suprema mihi cum venerit hora,*
Et teneam moriens deficiente manu.
May I be looking at you when my last hour has
come, and dying may I hold you with my
weakening hand.
Elegies bk. 1, no. 1, l. 59

10 *Te propter nullos tellus tua postulat imbres,*
Arida nec pluvio supplicat herba Iovi.
Because of you your land never pleads for
showers, nor does its parched grass pray to Jupiter
the Rain-giver.
of the River Nile in Egypt
Elegies bk. 1, no. 7, l. 25

11 *Periuria ridet amantum Iuppiter.*
Jupiter laughs at lovers' perjuries.
Elegies bk. 3, no. 6, l. 49; see **Proverbs** 624:33

Chidiock Tichborne c.1558–86

English Roman Catholic conspirator

12 My prime of youth is but a frost of cares;
My feast of joy is but a dish of pain;
My crop of corn is but a field of tares;
And all my good is but vain hope of gain.
The day is past, and yet I saw no sun;
And now I live, and now my life is done.
'Elegy' (composed in the Tower of London prior to his
execution)

Thomas Tickell 1686–1740

English poet

13 There taught us how to live; and (oh! too high
The price for knowledge) taught us how to die.
'To the Earl of Warwick. On the Death of Mr Addison'
(1721) l. 76

Lionel Tiger 1937–

American anthropologist

14 Male bonding.
Men in Groups (1969)

Paul Tillich 1886–1965

German-born Protestant theologian

15 Neurosis is the way of avoiding non-being by
avoiding being.
The Courage To Be (1952) pt. 2, ch. 3

16 Faith is the state of being ultimately concerned.
Dynamics of Faith (1957) ch. 1

Kahn Tineta-Horn 1940–

*American-born Canadian political activist, fashion model and
civil servant*

17 Why don't you all go back to where you came
from? We own this land; we're your landlords.
And the rent is due.
*on white Canadians occupying land belonging to
Native Canadians*
Myrna Kostash *Long Way From Home* (1980)

Tipu Sultan c.1750–99

18 In this world I would rather live two days like a
tiger, than two hundred years like a sheep.
Alexander Beatson *A View of the Origin and Conduct of the
War with Tippoo Sultan* (1800) ch. 10; see **Proverbs** 615:30

Titus (Titus Flavius Vespasianus) AD 39–81

Roman emperor from AD 79

1 *Amici, diem perdidi.*

Friends, I have lost a day.

*on reflecting that he had done nothing to help anybody
all day*

Suetonius *Lives of the Caesars* 'Titus' ch. 8, sect. 1

☐ Toasts

see box overleaf

see also **Bossidy** 145:15, **Decatur** 261:1, **Jackson** 414:16

Alexis de Tocqueville 1805–59

French historian and politician

2 Freedom alone substitutes from time to time for
the love of material comfort more powerful and
more lofty passions; it alone supplies ambition
with greater objectives than the acquisition of
riches, and creates the light that makes it possible
to see and to judge the vices and virtues of
mankind.

L'Ancien régime (1856, ed. J. P. Mayer, 1951; translated by
M. W. Patterson, 1933)

3 Where is the man of soul so base that he would
prefer to depend on the caprices of one of his
fellow men rather than obey the laws which he
has himself contributed to establish?

L'Ancien régime (1856)

4 Despots themselves do not deny that freedom is
excellent; only they desire it for themselves alone,
and they maintain that everyone else is altogether
unworthy of it.

L'Ancien régime (1856)

5 The French Revolution operated in reference to
this world in exactly the same manner as religious
revolutions acted in view of the other world. It
considered the citizen as an abstract proposition
apart from any particular society, in the same way
as religions considered man as man, independent
of country and time.

L'Ancien régime (1856)

6 History is a gallery of pictures in which there are
few originals and many copies.

L'Ancien régime (1856)

7 He who desires in liberty anything other than
itself is born to be a servant.

L'Ancien régime (1856)

8 It is not always by going from bad to worse that a
society falls into revolution . . . The social order
destroyed by a revolution is almost always better
than that which immediately preceded it, and
experience shows that the most dangerous
moment for a bad government is generally that in
which it sets about reform.

L'Ancien régime (1856)

9 Providence has not created mankind entirely
independent or entirely free. It is true that around

every man a fatal circle is traced, beyond which
he cannot pass; but within the wide verge of that
circle he is powerful and free.

De la Démocratie en Amérique (1835–40, translated by H.
Reeve, 1841, ed. J. P. Mayer, 1951) vol. 1

10 Of all nations, those submit to civilization with the
most difficulty which habitually live by the chase.

De la Démocratie en Amérique (1835–40) vol. 1

11 What is understood by republican government in
the United States is the slow and quiet action of
society upon itself.

De la Démocratie en Amérique (1835–40) vol. 1

12 There are, at the present time, two great nations
in the world, which seem to tend towards the
same end, although they started from different
points; I allude to the Russians and the Americans
. . . Their starting point is different, and their
courses are not the same; yet each of them seems
to be marked out by the will of Heaven to sway
the destinies of half the globe.

De la Démocratie en Amérique (1835–40) vol. 1

13 Unable to judge at once of the social position of
those he meets, an Englishman prudently avoids
all contact with them. Men are afraid less some
slight service rendered should draw them into an
unsuitable acquaintance; they dread civilities, and
they avoid the obtrusive gratitude of a stranger
quite as much as his hatred.

De la Démocratie en Amérique (1835–40)

14 The French want no-one to be their *superior*. The
English want *inferiors*. The Frenchman constantly
raises his eyes above him with anxiety. The
Englishman lowers his beneath him with
satisfaction. On either side it is pride, but
understood in a different way.

Voyage en Angleterre et en Irlande de 1835 (ed. J. P. Mayer,
1958) 8 May 1835

15 It is from the midst of this putrid sewer that the
greatest river of human industry springs up and
carries fertility to the whole world. From this foul
drain pure gold flows forth. Here it is that
humanity achieves for itself both perfection and
brutalization, that civilization produces its
wonders, and that civilized man becomes again
almost a savage.

of Manchester

Voyage en Angleterre et en Irlande de 1835 (ed. J. P. Mayer,
1958) 2 July 1835

Alvin Toffler 1928–

American writer

16 Culture shock is relatively mild in comparison
with a much more serious malady that might be
called 'future shock'. Future shock is the dizzying
disorientation brought on by the premature
arrival of the future.

in *Horizon* Summer 1965; the book *Future Shock* was
published 1970

Toasts

1 A bloody war and a sickly season.

*naval toast in the time of **Nelson***

> W. N. T. Beckett *A Few Naval Customs, Expressions,
> Traditions, and Superstitions* (1931) 'Customs'

2 George Washington, Commander of the
American Armies, who, like Joshua of old,
commanded the sun and the moon to stand still,
and they obeyed him.

*proposed by Benjamin **Franklin** (1706–90) at a
dinner at Versailles, supposedly after the British
minister had proposed a toast to **George III**, likening
him to the sun, and the French minister had likened
Louis XVI to the moon*

> attributed, perhaps apocryphal

3 Here's tae us; wha's like us?
Gey few, and they're a' deid.

> Scottish toast, probably of 19th-century origin; the first
> line appears in T. W. H. Crosland *The Unspeakable Scot*
> (1902), and various versions of the second line are
> current

4 If I am obliged to bring religion into after-dinner
toasts (which indeed does not seem quite the
thing) I shall drink—to the Pope, if you please—
still, to Conscience first, and to the Pope
afterwards.

> John Henry Newman *A Letter Addressed to the Duke of
> Norfolk . . .* (1875) sect. 5

5 The King over the Water.

> Jacobite toast (18th-century)

6 PRINCE OF WALES: True blue and Mrs Crewe.
MRS CREWE: Buff and blue and all of you.

*toast proposed by **George IV** when Prince of Wales to
Mrs Crewe, in honour of her support for the Whigs
and Charles James **Fox** in the Westminster election
of 1784 (buff and blue were the Whig colours)*

> at a dinner at Carlton House, May 1784; Amanda
> Foreman *Georgiana Duchess of Devonshire* (1998)

7 A willing foe and sea room.

*naval toast in the time of **Nelson***

> W. N. T. Beckett *A Few Naval Customs, Expressions,
> Traditions, and Superstitions* (1931) 'Customs'

J. R. R. Tolkien 1892–1973

*British philologist and writer
on Tolkien: see **Pratchett** 610:9; see also **Opening lines**
574:16*

8 What has it got in its pocketses?
Gollum trying to solve Bilbo's riddle
> *The Hobbit* (1937) ch. 5

9 Never laugh at live dragons.
> *The Hobbit* (1937) ch. 12

10 One Ring to rule them all, One Ring to find them
One Ring to bring them all and in the darkness
bind them.
> *The Fellowship of the Ring* (1954) epigraph

11 Do not meddle in the affairs of Wizards, for they
are subtle and quick to anger.
> *The Lord of the Rings* pt. 1 *The Fellowship of the Ring* (1954)
> bk. 1, ch. 3

12 Precious . . . My Precious!
Gollum, referring to the Ring
> *The Lord of the Rings* pt. 3 *The Return of the King* (1955) bk.
> 6, ch. 3

Leo Tolstoy 1828–1910

Russian novelist

13 All happy families resemble one another, but each
unhappy family is unhappy in its own way.
> *Anna Karenina* (1875–7) pt. 1, ch. 1 (translated by A. and
> L. Maude)

14 There are no conditions of life to which a man
cannot get accustomed, especially if he sees them
accepted by everyone about him.
> *Anna Karenina* (1875–7) pt. 7, ch. 13 (translated by
> Rosemary Edmonds)

15 The candle by which she had been reading the
book filled with trouble and deceit, sorrow and
evil, flared up with a brighter light, illuminating
for her everything that before had been
enshrouded in darkness, flickered, grew dim, and
went out for ever.
> *Anna Karenina* (1875–7) pt. 7, ch. 31 (translated by
> Rosemary Edmonds)

16 The hero of my tale—whom I love with all the
power of my soul, whom I have tried to portray in
all his beauty, who has been, is, and will be
beautiful—is Truth.
> *Sevastopol in May* (1855) ch. 16 (translated by A. and L.
> Maude)

17 In historical events great men—so-called—are but
labels serving to give a name to the event, and like
labels they have the least possible connexion with
the event itself.
> *War and Peace* (1868–9) bk. 3, pt. 1, ch. 1 (translated by
> Rosemary Edmonds)

18 The cudgel of the people's war was lifted with all
its menacing and majestic might, and caring
nothing for good taste and procedure, with dull-
witted simplicity but sound judgement it rose and
fell, making no distinctions.
> *War and Peace* (1868–9) bk. 4, pt. 3, ch. 1 (translated by
> Rosemary Edmonds)

19 Our body is a machine for living. It is organized for
that, it is its nature. Let life go on in it unhindered
and let it defend itself, it will do more than if you
paralyse it by encumbering it with remedies.
> *War and Peace* (1865–9) bk. 10, ch. 29 (translated by A.
> and L. Maude); see **Le Corbusier** 478:10

20 I sit on a man's back, choking him and making
him carry me, and yet assure myself and others
that I am very sorry for him and wish to ease his

lot by all possible means—except by getting off his back.

What Then Must We Do? (1886) ch. 16 (translated by A. Maude)

1 All newspaper and journalistic activity is an intellectual brothel from which there is no retreat.

letter to Prince V. P. Meshchersky, 22 August 1871, in *Letters* (ed. R. F. Christian, 1978) vol. 1

Augustus Montague Toplady 1740–78

English clergyman

2 Rock of Ages, cleft for me,
Let me hide myself in Thee.
Let the water and the blood,
From Thy riven side which flowed,
Be of sin the double cure,
Cleanse me from its guilt and power.

'Rock of Ages, cleft for me' (1776 hymn)

Michael Torke 1961–

American composer

3 Why waste money on psychotherapy when you can listen to the B Minor Mass?

in *Observer* 23 September 1990 'Sayings of the Week'

Robert Torrens 1780–1864

British economist

4 In the first stone which he [the savage] flings at the wild animals he pursues, in the first stick that he seizes to strike down the fruit which hangs above his reach, we see the appropriation of one article for the purpose of aiding in the acquisition of another, and thus discover the origin of capital.

An Essay on the Production of Wealth (1821) ch. 2

Cyril Tourneur see Middleton 524:10

A. Toussenel 1803–85

French writer

5 *Plus on apprend à connaître l'homme, plus on apprend à estimer le chien.*

The more one gets to know of men, the more one values dogs.

L'Esprit des bêtes (1847) ch. 3; see **Roland** 653:1

Pete Townshend 1945–

British rock musician and songwriter

6 Hope I die before I get old.

'My Generation' (1965 song)

Arnold Toynbee 1889–1975

English historian

7 Civilization is a movement and not a condition, a voyage and not a harbour.

in *Readers Digest* October 1958

8 The twentieth century will be remembered chiefly, not as an age of political conflicts and technical inventions, but as an age in which human society dared to think of the health of the whole human race as a practical objective.

attributed

Polly Toynbee 1946–

English journalist

9 Feminism is the most revolutionary idea there has ever been. Equality for women demands a change in the human psyche more profound than anything Marx dreamed of. It means valuing parenthood as much as we value banking.

in *Guardian* 19 January 1987

Thomas Traherne c.1637–74

English mystic

10 An empty book is like an infant's soul, in which anything may be written. It is capable of all things, but containeth nothing.

Centuries of Meditations 'First Century' opening line

11 You never enjoy the world aright, till the sea itself floweth in your veins, till you are clothed with the heavens, and crowned with the stars: and perceive yourself to be the sole heir of the whole world.

Centuries of Meditations 'First Century' sect. 29

12 All appeared new, and strange at first, inexpressibly rare and delightful and beautiful. I was a little stranger, which at my entrance into the world was saluted and surrounded with innumerable joys. My knowledge was divine.

Centuries of Meditations 'Third Century' sect. 2

13 All things were spotless and pure and glorious . . . I knew not that there were any sins or complaints or laws. I dreamed not of poverties, contentions or vices. All tears and quarrels were hidden from my eyes. Everything was at rest, free and immortal.

Centuries of Meditations 'Third Century' sect. 2

14 The corn was orient and immortal wheat, which never should be reaped, nor was ever sown. I thought it had stood from everlasting to everlasting.

Centuries of Meditations 'Third Century' sect. 3

15 The green trees when I saw them first . . . transported and ravished me, their sweetness and unusual beauty made my heart to leap and almost mad with ecstasy, they were such strange and wonderful things.

Centuries of Meditations 'Third Century' sect. 3

16 O what venerable creatures did the aged seem! Immortal cherubims! And young men glittering and sparkling angels, and maids strange seraphic pieces of life and beauty! Boys and girls tumbling in the street, and playing, were moving jewels. I knew not that they were born or should die; but all things abided eternally.

Centuries of Meditations 'Third Century' sect. 3

17 The hands are a sort of feet, which serve us in our passage towards Heaven, curiously distinguished into joints and fingers, and fit to be applied to any thing which reason can imagine or desire.

Meditations on the Six Days of Creation (1717) 'Sixth Day'

1 Contentment is a sleepy thing
If it in death alone must die;
A quiet mind is worse than poverty,
Unless it from enjoyment spring!
That's blessedness alone that makes a King!
'Of Contentment'

2 I within did flow
With seas of life, like wine.
I nothing in this world did know,
But 'twas divine!
'Wonder'

Henry Duff Traill 1842–1900
British journalist

3 Look in my face. My name is Used-to-was;
I am also called Played-out and Done-to-death,
And It-will-wash-no-more.
'After Dilettante Concetti' (i.e. Dante Gabriel Rossetti) st. 8;
see **Rossetti** 656:5

Joseph Trapp 1679–1747
English poet and pamphleteer

4 The King, observing with judicious eyes
The state of both his universities,
To Oxford sent a troop of horse, and why?
That learned body wanted loyalty;
To Cambridge books, as very well discerning
How much that loyal body wanted learning.
*lines written on **George I**'s donation of the Bishop of
Ely's Library to Cambridge University*
John Nichols *Literary Anecdotes* (1812–16) vol. 3; see
Browne 157:14

Merle Travis 1917–83
American country singer

5 Sixteen tons, what do you get?
Another day older and deeper in debt.
Say brother, don't you call me 'cause I can't go
I owe my soul to the company store.
'Sixteen Tons' (1947 song)

Herbert Beerbohm Tree 1852–1917
English actor-manager

6 He is an old bore. Even the grave yawns for him.
*of Israel **Zangwill***
Max Beerbohm *Herbert Beerbohm Tree* (1920) appendix 4

7 Ladies, just a little more virginity, if you don't
mind.
*to a motley collection of females, assembled to play
ladies-in-waiting to a queen*
Alexander Woollcott *Shouts and Murmurs* (1923) 'Capsule
Criticism'

8 My poor fellow, why not carry a watch?
to a man in the street, carrying a grandfather clock
Hesketh Pearson *Beerbohm Tree* (1956) ch. 12

9 Sirs, I have tested your machine. It adds a new
terror to life and makes death a long-felt want.
*when pressed by a gramophone company for a written
testimonial*
Hesketh Pearson *Beerbohm Tree* (1956) ch. 19; see
Wetherell 830:21

G. M. Trevelyan 1876–1962
English historian

10 Disinterested intellectual curiosity is the life-blood
of real civilization.
English Social History (1942) introduction

11 If the French noblesse had been capable of playing
cricket with their peasants, their chateaux would
never have been burnt.
English Social History (1942) ch. 8

12 [Education] has produced a vast population able to
read but unable to distinguish what is worth
reading, an easy prey to sensations and cheap
appeals.
English Social History (1942) ch. 18

13 In a world of voluble hates, he plotted to make
men like, or at least tolerate one another.
*of Stanley **Baldwin***
in *Dictionary of National Biography 1941–50* (1959)

William Trevor (William Trevor Cox) 1928–
Irish novelist and short story writer

14 Marriage was all defeat and victory, and worked
better when women were the defeated ones since
men apparently could not bear to be and had no
philosophy for that condition.
The Children of Dynmouth (1976) ch. 3

15 When you looked at the map Ireland and England
seemed like lovers . . . 'Does the map remind you
curiously of an embrace? A most extraordinary
embrace to throw up all this.'
Fools of Fortune (1983)

Calvin Trillin 1935–
American journalist and writer

16 The shelf life of the modern hardback writer is
somewhere between the milk and the yoghurt.
in *Sunday Times* 9 June 1991; attributed

David Trimble 1944–
Northern Irish politician, leader of the Ulster Unionists

17 The fundamental Act of Union is there, intact.
of the Northern Ireland settlement
in *Daily Telegraph* 11 April 1998

18 Once we are agreed our only weapons will be our
words, then there is nothing that cannot be said,
there is nothing that cannot be achieved.
in *Guardian* 4 September 1998

Tommy Trinder 1909–89
British comedian

19 Overpaid, overfed, oversexed, and over here.
*of American troops in Britain during the Second
World War*
associated with Trinder, but probably not his invention

Anthony Trollope 1815–82
English novelist

20 He must have known me had he seen me as he
was wont to see me, for he was in the habit of

flogging me constantly. Perhaps he did not recognize me by my face.
Autobiography (1883) ch. 1

1 Take away from English authors their copyrights, and you would very soon take away from England her authors.
Autobiography (1883) ch. 6

2 A novel can hardly be made interesting or successful without love . . . It is necessary because the passion is one which interests or has interested all. Everyone feels it, has felt it, or expects to feel it.
Autobiography (1883) ch. 12

3 Three hours a day will produce as much as a man ought to write.
Autobiography (1883) ch. 15

4 A man who entertains in his mind any political doctrine, except as a means of improving the condition of his fellows, I regard as a political intriguer, a charlatan, and a conjuror.
Autobiography (1883) ch. 16

5 I think that Plantagenet Palliser, Duke of Omnium, is a perfect gentleman. If he be not, then I am unable to describe a gentleman.
Autobiography (1883) ch. 20

6 A man's mind will very generally refuse to make itself up until it be driven and compelled by emergency.
Ayala's Angel (1881) ch. 41

7 She was rich in apparel, but not bedizened with finery . . . she well knew the great architectural secret of decorating her constructions, and never descended to construct a decoration.
Barchester Towers (1857) ch. 9

8 The end of a novel, like the end of a children's dinner-party, must be made up of sweetmeats and sugar-plums.
Barchester Towers (1857) ch. 53

9 When taken in the refreshing waters of office any . . . pill can be swallowed.
The Bertrams (1859) ch. 16

10 Those who have courage to love should have courage to suffer.
The Bertrams (1859) ch. 27

11 Mr Palliser was one of those politicians in possessing whom England has perhaps more reason to be proud than of any other of her resources, and who, as a body, give to her that requisite combination of conservatism and progress which is her present strength and best security for the future.
Can You Forgive Her? (1864) ch. 24

12 There is no road to wealth so easy and respectable as that of matrimony.
Doctor Thorne (1858) ch. 16

13 Let no man boast himself that he has got through the perils of winter till at least the seventh of May.
Doctor Thorne (1858) ch. 47

14 'It's in Tipperary—not at all a desirable country to live in.'

'Oh, dear, no! Don't they murder the people?'
The Eustace Diamonds (1872) ch. 8; see **Kohl** 459:3

15 We cannot have heroes to dine with us. There are none. And were those heroes to be had, we should not like them . . . the persons whom you cannot care for in a novel, because they are so bad, are the very same that you so dearly love in your life, because they are so good.
The Eustace Diamonds (1873) ch. 35

16 For the most of us, if we do not talk of ourselves, or at any rate of the individual circles of which we are the centres, we can talk of nothing. I cannot hold with those who wish to put down the insignificant chatter of the world.
Framley Parsonage (1860) ch. 10

17 They who do not understand that a man may be brought to hope that which of all things is the most grievous to him, have not observed with sufficient closeness the perversity of the human mind.
He Knew He Was Right (1869) ch. 38

18 She understood how much louder a cock can crow in its own farmyard than elsewhere.
The Last Chronicle of Barset (1867) ch. 17

19 It's dogged as does it. It ain't thinking about it.
Giles Hoggett
The Last Chronicle of Barset (1867) ch. 61

20 With many women I doubt whether there be any more effectual way of touching their hearts than ill-using them and then confessing it. If you wish to get the sweetest fragrance from the herb at your feet, tread on it and bruise it.
Miss Mackenzie (1865) ch. 10

21 There is nothing more tyrannical than a strong popular feeling among a democratic people.
North America (1862) vol. 1, ch. 11

22 I have sometimes thought that there is no being so venomous, so bloodthirsty as a professed philanthropist.
North America (1862) vol. 1, ch. 16

23 We cannot bring ourselves to believe it possible that a foreigner should in any respect be wiser than ourselves. If any such point out to us our follies, we at once claim those follies as the special evidences of our wisdom.
Orley Farm (1862) ch. 18

24 It is because we put up with bad things that hotel-keepers continue to give them to us.
Orley Farm (1862) ch. 18

25 A fainéant government is not the worst government that England can have. It has been the great fault of our politicians that they have all wanted to do something.
Phineas Finn (1869) ch. 13

26 The first necessity for good speaking is a large audience.
Phineas Finn (1869) ch. 18

1 Mr Turnbull had predicted evil consequences . . . and was now doing the best in his power to bring about the verification of his own prophecies.
   Phineas Finn (1869) ch. 25

2 A man destined to sit conspicuously on our Treasury Bench, or on the seat opposite to it, should ask the Gods for a thick skin as a first gift.
   Phineas Finn (1869) ch. 33

3 She knew how to allure by denying, and to make the gift rich by delaying it.
   Phineas Finn (1869) ch. 57

4 What man thinks of changing himself so as to suit his wife? And yet men expect that women shall put on altogether new characters when they are married, and girls think that they can do so.
   Phineas Redux (1874) ch. 3

5 It is the necessary nature of a political party in this country to avoid, as long as it can be avoided, the consideration of any question which involves a great change . . . The best carriage horses are those which can most steadily hold back against the coach as it trundles down the hill.
   Phineas Redux (1874) ch. 4

6 Newspaper editors sport daily with the names of men of whom they do not hesitate to publish almost the severest words that can be uttered; but let an editor be himself attacked, even without his name, and he thinks that the thunderbolt of heaven should fall upon the offender.
   Phineas Redux (1874) ch. 27

7 Equality would be a heaven, if we could attain it.
   The Prime Minister (1876) ch. 68

8 To think of one's absent love is very sweet; but it becomes monotonous . . . I doubt whether any girl would be satisfied with her lover's mind if she knew the whole of it.
   The Small House at Allington (1864) ch. 4

9 Why is it that girls so constantly do this,—so frequently ask men who have loved them to be present at their marriages with other men? There is no triumph in it. It is done in sheer kindness and affection. They intend to offer something which shall soften and not aggravate the sorrow that they have caused . . . I fully appreciate the intention, but in honest truth, I doubt the eligibility of the proffered entertainment.
   The Small House at Allington (1864) ch. 9

10 It may almost be a question whether such wisdom as many of us have in our mature years has not come from the dying out of the power of temptation, rather than as the results of thought and resolution.
   The Small House at Allington (1864) ch. 14

11 Never think that you're not good enough yourself. A man should never think that. My belief is that in life people will take you very much at your own reckoning.
   The Small House at Allington (1864) ch. 32

12 The tenth Muse, who now governs the periodical press.
   The Warden (1855) ch. 14

13 Is it not singular how some men continue to obtain the reputation of popular authorship without adding a word to the literature of their country worthy of note? . . . To puff and to get one's self puffed have become different branches of a new profession.
   The Way We Live Now (1875) ch. 1

14 Nothing perhaps is so efficacious in preventing men from marrying as the tone in which married women speak of the struggles made in that direction by their unmarried friends.
   The Way We Live Now (1875) ch. 32

15 Love is like any other luxury. You have no right to it unless you can afford it.
   The Way We Live Now (1875) ch. 84

Frances Trollope 1780–1863
English writer, mother of Anthony Trollope

16 I draw from life—but I always pulp my acquaintance before serving them up. You would never recognize a pig in a sausage.
   remark, c.1848; S. Baring-Gould *Early Reminiscences 1834-1864* (1923)

Leon Trotsky (Lev Davidovich Bronstein) 1879–1940
Russian revolutionary

17 Old age is the most unexpected of all things that happen to a man.
   Diary in Exile (1959) 8 May 1935

18 Civilization has made the peasantry its pack animal. The bourgeoisie in the long run only changed the form of the pack.
   History of the Russian Revolution (1933) vol. 3, ch. 1

19 You [the Mensheviks] are pitiful isolated individuals; you are bankrupts; your role is played out. Go where you belong from now on — into the dustbin of history!
   History of the Russian Revolution (1933) vol. 3, ch. 10; see **Birrell** 117:1

20 It was the supreme expression of the mediocrity of the apparatus that Stalin himself rose to his position.
   My Life (1930) ch. 40

21 Where force is necessary, there it must be applied boldly, decisively and completely. But one must know the limitations of force; one must know when to blend force with a manoeuvre, a blow with an agreement.
   What Next? (1932) ch. 14

22 Not believing in force is the same thing as not believing in gravitation.
   G. Maximov *The Guillotine at Work* (1940)

Pierre Trudeau 1919–2000
Canadian Liberal statesman, Prime Minister, 1968–79 and 1980–4

23 The state has no place in the nation's bedrooms.
   interview, Ottawa, 22 December 1967

1 The twentieth century really belongs to those who will build it. The future can be promised to no one.
in 1968; see **Laurier** 470:11

2 Living next to you is in some ways like sleeping with an elephant. No matter how friendly and even-tempered the beast, one is affected by every twitch and grunt.
on relations between Canada and the US
speech at National Press Club, Washington D. C., 25 March 1969

François Truffaut 1932–84
French film director

3 Airing one's dirty linen never makes for a masterpiece.
Bed and Board (1972)

4 I've always had the impression that real militants are like cleaning women, doing a thankless, daily but necessary job.
letter to Jean-Luc Godard, May-June 1973

Harry S. Truman 1884–1972
American Democratic statesman, 33rd President of the US 1945–53
on Truman: see **Roosevelt** 653:7; *see also* **Newspaper headlines** 562:4

5 *to reporters the day after his accession to the Presidency on the death of Franklin D. Roosevelt:*
When they told me yesterday what had happened, I felt like the moon, the stars and all the planets had fallen on me.
on 13 April 1945

6 All the President is, is a glorified public relations man who spends his time flattering, kissing and kicking people to get them to do what they are supposed to do anyway.
letter to his sister, 14 November 1947, in *Off the Record* (1980)

7 What we are doing in Korea is this: we are trying to prevent a third world war.
after the recall of **MacArthur**
address to the nation, 16 April 1951

8 If you can't stand the heat, get out of the kitchen.
associated with Truman, but attributed by him to Harry Vaughan, his 'military jester'; in *Time* 28 April 1952; see **Proverbs** 623:14

9 I never give them [the public] hell. I just tell the truth, and they think it is hell.
in *Look* 3 April 1956

10 A politician is a man who understands government, and it takes a politician to run a government. A statesman is a politician who's been dead 10 or 15 years.
in *New York World Telegram and Sun* 12 April 1958

11 It's a recession when your neighbour loses his job; it's a depression when you lose yours.
in *Observer* 13 April 1958

12 Wherever you have an efficient government you have a dictatorship.
lecture at Columbia University, 28 April 1959, in *Truman Speaks* (1960)

13 I didn't fire him [General MacArthur] because he was a dumb son of a bitch, although he was, but that's not against the law for generals. If it was, half to three-quarters of them would be in jail.
Merle Miller *Plain Speaking* (1974) ch. 24

14 Always be sincere, even if you don't mean it.
attributed

15 The buck stops here.
unattributed motto on Truman's desk

Donald Trump 1946–
American businessman

16 Deals are my art form. Other people paint beautifully on canvas or write wonderful poetry. I like making deals, preferably big deals. That's how I get my kicks.
Donald Trump and Tony Schwartz *The Art of the Deal* (1987)

Sojourner Truth c.1797–1883
American evangelist and reformer

17 That man . . . says that women need to be helped into carriages, and lifted over ditches, and to have the best place everywhere. Nobody ever helps me into carriages, or over mud puddles, or gives me any best place, and aren't I a woman? . . . I have ploughed, and planted, and gathered into barns, and no man could head me—and aren't I a woman? I could work as much and eat as much as a man (when I could get it), and bear the lash as well—and aren't I a woman? I have borne thirteen children and seen them most all sold off into slavery, and when I cried out with a mother's grief, none but Jesus heard—and aren't I a woman?
speech at Women's Rights Convention, Akron, Ohio, 1851

18 That little man . . . he says women can't have as much rights as men, cause Christ wasn't a woman. Where did your Christ come from? From God and a woman. Man had nothing to do with Him.
speech at Women's Rights Convention, Akron, Ohio, 1851

19 There is a great stir about coloured men getting their rights, but not a word about the coloured women; and if coloured men get their rights, and not coloured women theirs, you see the coloured men will be masters over the women, and it will be just as bad as it was before. So I am for keeping the thing going while things are stirring; because if we wait till it is still, it will take a great while to get it going again.
speech, Equal Rights Convention, New York, 9 May 1867

Barbara W. Tuchman 1912–89
American writer

20 Dead battles, like dead generals, hold the military mind in their dead grip and Germans, no less than other peoples, prepare for the last war.
August 1914 (1962) ch. 2

1 For one August in its history Paris was French—and silent.

  August 1914 (1962) ch. 20

Sophie Tucker (Sophia Abuza) 1884–1966

Russian-born American vaudeville artiste

2 From birth to 18 a girl needs good parents. From 18 to 35, she needs good looks. From 35 to 55, good personality. From 55 on, she needs good cash.

  Michael Freedland *Sophie* (1978)

Martin Tupper 1810–89

English writer

3 A good book is the best of friends, the same to-day and for ever.

  Proverbial Philosophy Series I (1838) 'Of Reading'

Ivan Turgenev 1818–83

Russian novelist

4 Superfluous, superfluous . . . A supernumerary—that's all. Nature, obviously, hadn't counted on my showing up and consequently treated me as an unexpected and uninvited guest.

  Diary of a Superfluous Man (1850) 23 March (translated by Franklin Reeve)

5 Nature is not a temple, but a workshop, and man's the workman in it.

  Fathers and Sons (1862) ch. 9 (translated by Rosemary Edmonds)

6 I share no one's ideas. I have my own.

  Fathers and Sons (1862) ch. 13 (translated by Rosemary Edmonds)

7 Your sort, the gentry, can never go farther than well-bred resignation or well-bred indignation.

  Fathers and Sons (1862) ch. 26 (translated by Rosemary Edmonds)

8 Just try and set death aside. It sets you aside, and that's the end of it!

  Fathers and Sons (1862) ch. 27 (translated by Rosemary Edmonds)

9 No matter how often you knock at nature's door, she won't answer in words you can understand—for Nature is dumb. She'll vibrate and moan like a violin, but you mustn't expect a song.

  On the Eve (1860) ch. 1 (translated by Gilbert Gardiner)

10 Death is like a fisherman, who, having caught a fish in his net, leaves it in the water for a time; the fish continues to swim about, but all the while the net is round it, and the fisherman will snatch it out in his own good time.

  On the Eve (1860) ch. 35 (translated by Gilbert Gardiner)

11 Whatever a man prays for, he prays for a miracle. Every prayer reduces itself to this: Great God, grant that twice two be not four.

  Poems in Prose (1881) 'Prayer'

12 The only people who remain misunderstood are those who either do not know what they want or are not worth understanding.

  Rudin (1856) ch. 5 (translated by Richard Freeborn)

A. R. J. Turgot 1727–81

French economist and statesman

13 *Eripuit coelo fulmen, sceptrumque tyrannis.*

  He snatched the lightning shaft from heaven, and the sceptre from tyrants.

  inscription for a bust of Benjamin **Franklin**, inventor of the lightning conductor; see **Manilius** 510:4

Alan Turing 1912–54

English mathematician and codebreaker

14 We are not interested in the fact that the brain has the consistency of cold porridge.

  A. P. Hodges *Alan Turing: the Enigma* (1983)

Charles Tennyson Turner 1808–79

English poet

15 Bright over Europe fell her golden hair.

  'Letty's Globe' (1880)

J. M. W. Turner 1775–1851

English landscape painter

on Turner: see **Scott** 674:25

16 He *sees* more in my pictures than I ever painted!

  of John **Ruskin**

  Mary Lloyd *Sunny Memories* (1879) vol. 1

17 If I could find anything blacker than black, I'd use it.

  when a friend complained of the blackness of the sails in 'Peace—Burial at Sea' (1844)

  in *Dictionary of National Biography* (1917–)

18 I did not expect to escape, but I felt bound to record it if I did.

  of watching a storm at sea, while on board a Margate steamer

  in *Dictionary of National Biography* (1917–)

Thomas Turner 1729–93

English diarist

19 Our diversion was dancing (or jumping about) without a violin or any music, singing of foolish and bawdy healths and more such-like stupidity, and drinking all the time as fast as could be poured down; and the parson of the parish was one amongst the mixed multitude, all the time.

  Diary (ed. D. Vaisey, 1984) 22 February 1758

Walter James Redfern Turner 1889–1946

British writer and critic

20 When I was but thirteen or so
I went into a golden land,
Chimborazo, Cotopaxi
Took me by the hand.

  'Romance' (1916)

John Tusa 1936–

British broadcaster and radio journalist

1 Management that wants to change an institution must first show it loves that institution.
   in *Observer* 27 February 1994 'Sayings of the Week'; see **Arnold** 30:17

Desmond Tutu 1931–

South African Anglican clergyman, Archbishop of Cape Town

2 I have struggled against tyranny. I didn't do that in order to substitute one tyranny with another.
   on the attempt by the African National Congress to prevent publication of the Truth Commission report
   in *Irish Times* 31 October 1998 'This Week They Said'

Mark Twain (Samuel Langhorne Clemens) 1835–1910

American writer
see also **Anonymous** 15:19

3 There was things which he stretched, but mainly he told the truth.
   The Adventures of Huckleberry Finn (1884) ch. 1

4 'Pilgrim's Progress', about a man that left his family it didn't say why . . . The statements was interesting, but tough.
   The Adventures of Huckleberry Finn (1884) ch. 17

5 All kings is mostly rapscallions.
   The Adventures of Huckleberry Finn (1884) ch. 23

6 Hain't we got all the fools in town on our side? and ain't that a big enough majority in any town?
   The Adventures of Huckleberry Finn (1884) ch. 26

7 Soap and education are not as sudden as a massacre, but they are more deadly in the long run.
   A Curious Dream (1872) 'Facts concerning the Recent Resignation'

8 Truth is the most valuable thing we have. Let us economize it.
   Following the Equator (1897) ch. 7; see **Armstrong** 26:18

9 It is by the goodness of God that in our country we have those three unspeakably precious things: freedom of speech, freedom of conscience, and the prudence never to practise either of them.
   Following the Equator (1897) ch. 20

10 Man is the Only Animal that Blushes. Or needs to.
   Following the Equator (1897) ch. 27

11 There are several good protections against temptations, but the surest is cowardice.
   Following the Equator (1897) ch. 36

12 It takes your enemy and your friend, working together, to hurt you to the heart: the one to slander you and the other to get the news to you.
   Following the Equator (1897) ch. 45

13 The innocents abroad.
   title of book (1869)

14 They spell it Vinci and pronounce it Vinchy; foreigners always spell better than they pronounce.
   The Innocents Abroad (1869) ch. 19

15 Lump the whole thing! say that the Creator made Italy from designs by Michael Angelo!
   The Innocents Abroad (1869) ch. 27

16 If you've got a nice *fresh* corpse, fetch him out!
   The Innocents Abroad (1869) ch. 27

17 There are laws to protect the freedom of the press's speech, but none that are worth anything to protect the people from the press.
   'License of the Press' (1873)

18 What a good thing Adam had. When he said a good thing he knew nobody had said it before.
   Notebooks (1935)

19 Familiarity breeds contempt—and children.
   Notebooks (1935)

20 Good breeding consists in concealing how much we think of ourselves and how little we think of the other person.
   Notebooks (1935)

21 Adam was but human—this explains it all. He did not want the apple for the apple's sake; he wanted it only because it was forbidden.
   Pudd'nhead Wilson (1894) ch. 2

22 Whoever has lived long enough to find out what life is, knows how deep a debt of gratitude we owe to Adam, the first great benefactor of our race. He brought death into the world.
   Pudd'nhead Wilson (1894) ch. 3

23 Cauliflower is nothing but cabbage with a college education.
   Pudd'nhead Wilson (1894) ch. 5

24 When angry, count four; when very angry, swear.
   Pudd'nhead Wilson (1894) ch. 10

25 As to the Adjective: when in doubt, strike it out.
   Pudd'nhead Wilson (1894) ch. 11

26 Few things are harder to put up with than the annoyance of a good example.
   Pudd'nhead Wilson (1894) ch. 19

27 There is a sumptuous variety about the New England weather that compels the stranger's admiration—and regret. The weather is always doing something there; always attending strictly to business; always getting up new designs and trying them on the people to see how they will go.
   speech to New England Society, 22 December 1876, in *Speeches* (1910)

28 All you need in this life is ignorance and confidence; then success is sure.
   letter to Mrs Foote, 2 December 1887, in B. DeCasseres *When Huck Finn Went Highbrow* (1934)

29 The report of my death was an exaggeration.
   usually quoted as 'Reports of my death have been greatly exaggerated'
   in *New York Journal* 2 June 1897

30 At bottom he was probably fond of them [Americans], but he was always able to conceal it.
   of Thomas **Carlyle**
   in *New York World* 10 December 1899 'Mark Twain's Christmas Book'

1 Get your facts first, and then you can distort them as much as you please.

Rudyard Kipling *From Sea to Sea* (1899) letter 37

Kenneth Tynan 1927–80

English theatre critic

2 A good drama critic is one who perceives what is happening in the theatre of his time. A great drama critic also perceives what is *not* happening.

Tynan Right and Left (1967)

3 Oh, I think so, certainly. I doubt if there are very many rational people in this world to whom the word 'fuck' is particularly diabolical or revolting or totally forbidden.

on 13 November 1965 on a late-night programme called BBC-3

Kathleen Tynan (ed.) *Kenneth Tynan: Letters* (1994)

4 A critic is a man who knows the way but can't drive the car.

in *New York Times Magazine* 9 January 1966

5 A neurosis is a secret you don't know you're keeping.

Kathleen Tynan *Life of Kenneth Tynan* (1987) ch. 19

William Tyndale c.1494–1536

*English translator of the **Bible** and Protestant martyr*
*see also **Last words** 473:2*

6 If God spare my life, ere many years I will cause a boy that driveth the plough shall know more of the scripture than thou doest!

to an opponent

in *Dictionary of National Biography* (1917–)

Harlan K. Ullman and James P. Wade

American strategic analysts

7 The basis for rapid dominance rests in the ability to affect the will, perception, and understanding of the adversary through imposing sufficient Shock and Awe to achieve the necessary political, strategic, and operational goals of the conflict or crisis that led to the use of force.

Shock and Awe: Achieving Rapid Dominance (1996) ch. 2

Ulpian (Domitius Ulpianus) d. 228

Roman jurist

8 *Nulla iniuria est, quae in volentem fiat.*

No injustice is done to someone who wants that thing done.

usually quoted as 'Volenti non fit iniuria'

Corpus Iuris Civilis Digests bk. 47, ch. 10, sect. 1, subsect. 5 (usually quoted as '*Volenti non fit iniuria*')

Miguel de Unamuno 1864–1937

Spanish philosopher and writer

9 *La vida es duda,*
y la fe sin la duda es sólo muerte.

Life is doubt,
And faith without doubt is nothing but death.

Poesías (1907) 'Salmo II'

10 An idea does not pass from one language to another without change.

The Tragic Sense of Life (1913)

11 Cure yourself of the condition of bothering about how you look to other people. Concern yourself only with how you appear to God, with the idea that God has of you.

Vida de Don Quixote y Sancho (1905) pt. 1

The Upanishads

Hindu sacred treatises written in Sanskrit c.800–200 BC

12 From delusion lead me to Truth.
From darkness lead me to Light.
from death lead me to immortality.

Brihadāranyaka Upanishad ch. 1, pt. 3, v. 28; see **Kumar** 462:4

13 Even as airy threads come from a spider, or small sparks come from a fire, so from Atman, the Spirit in man, come all the powers of life, all the worlds, all the gods: all beings. To know the Atman is to know the mystery of the *Upanishads*: the Truth of truth.

Brihadāranyaka Upanishad ch. 2, pt. 1, v. 20

14 Then spoke Yajñavalkya:
In truth it is not for the love of a husband that a husband is dear; but for the love of Soul in the husband that a husband is dear.
It is not for love of a wife that a wife is dear; but for the love of the Soul in the wife that a wife is dear.

to his wife Maitreyi

Brihadāranyaka Upanishad ch. 2, pt. 4, v. 5

15 How can the Knower be known?

Brihadāranyaka Upanishad ch. 2, pt. 4, v. 14

16 He who, dwelling in all things, yet is other than all things, whom all things do not know, whose body all things are, who controls all things from within—He is your Soul, the Inner Controller, the Immortal.

Brihadāranyaka Upanishad ch. 3, pt. 7, v. 15

17 Even as a caterpillar, when coming to the end of a blade of grass, reaches out to another blade of grass and draws itself over to it, in the same way the Soul, leaving the body and unwisdom behind, reaches out to another body and draws itself over to it.

Brihadāranyaka Upanishad ch. 4, pt. 4, v. 3

18 That Soul [*Atman*] is not this, it is not that [*neti, neti*]. It is unseizable, for it cannot be seized; it is indestructible, for it cannot be destroyed; unattached, for it does not attach itself; is unbound, does not tremble, is not injured.

Brihadāranyaka Upanishad ch. 4, pt. 5, v. 15

1 This same thing does the divine voice hear, thunder, repeat: *Da! Da! Da!* that is, restrain yourselves, give, be compassionate. One should practise this same triad: self-restraint, giving, compassion.

Brihadāranyaka Upanishad ch. 5, pt. 2, v. 3

2 We should consider that in the inner world Brahman is consciousness; and we should consider that in the outer world Brahman is space. These are the two meditations.

Chāndogya Upanishad ch. 3, pt. 18, v. 1

3 This invisible and subtle essence is the Spirit of the whole universe. That is Reality. That is Truth.
THOU ART THAT.

Chāndogya Upanishad ch. 6, pt. 14

4 *Shantih, shantih, shantih.*
Peace! Peace! Peace!

Taittirīya Upanishad ch. 1, pt. 1, mantra; see **Eliot** 303:25

5 Abiding in the midst of ignorance, thinking themselves wise and learned, fools go aimlessly hither and thither, like blind led by the blind.

Katha Upanishad ch. 2, v. 5; see **Bible** 97:12

6 If any man thinks he slays, and if another thinks he is slain, neither knows the ways of truth. The Eternal in man cannot kill: the Eternal in man cannot die.

Katha Upanishad ch. 2, v. 19; see **Bhagavadgita** 74:9, **Emerson** 306:10

7 Concealed in the hearts of all beings is the Atman, the Spirit, the Self; smaller than the smallest atom, greater than the vast spaces.

Katha Upanishad ch. 2, v. 20

8 Know the Atman as Lord of a chariot; and the body as the chariot itself. Know that reason is the charioteer; and the mind indeed is the reins. The horses they say are the senses; and their paths are the objects of sense.

Katha Upanishad ch. 3, v. 3

9 Sages say the path is narrow and difficult to tread, narrow as the edge of a razor.

Katha Upanishad ch. 3, v. 15

10 The Tree of Eternity has its roots in heaven above and its branches reach down to earth. It is Brahman, pure Spirit, who in truth is called the Immortal.

Katha Upanishad ch. 6, v. 1

11 There is ONE in whose hands is the net of Maya, who rules with his power, who rules all the worlds with his power. He is the same at the time of creation and at the time of dissolution.

Shvetāshvatara Upanishad ch. 3, v. 1

12 Two birds, close-linked companions,
Cling to the selfsame tree:
Of these the one eats of the sweet fruit,
The other, eating nothing, looks on intent.

Mundaka Upanishad ch. 3, pt. 2, v. 1

13 Whoever really knows that all-highest Brahman, really becomes Brahman.

Mundaka Upanishad ch. 3, pt. 2, v. 9

14 Let the spirit of life surrender itself into what is called *turya*, the fourth condition of consciousness. For it has been said:
There is something beyond our mind which abides in silence within our mind. It is the supreme mystery beyond thought.

Maitri Upanishad ch. 6, v. 19

15 The sound of Brahman is OM. At the end of OM is silence. It is a silence of joy.

Maitri Upanishad ch. 6, v. 23

John Updike 1932–
American novelist and short-story writer

16 A soggy little island huffing and puffing to keep up with Western Europe.

of England

Picked Up Pieces (1976) 'London Life' (written 1969)

17 America is a land whose centre is nowhere; England one whose centre is everywhere.

Picked Up Pieces (1976) 'London Life' (written 1969)

18 America is a vast conspiracy to make you happy.

Problems (1980) 'How to love America and Leave it at the Same Time'

19 You shouldn't sit in judgment of your parents. We did the best we could while being people too.

Rabbit at Rest (1990) pt. 2

20 Without the cold war, what's the point of being an American?

Rabbit at Rest (1990) pt. 3

21 Celebrity is a mask that eats into the face.

Self-Consciousness: Memoirs (1989)

22 Neutrinos, they are very small
They have no charge and have no mass
And do not interact at all.

'Cosmic Gall ' (1964)

23 The artist brings something into the world that didn't exist before, and . . . he does it without destroying something else.

George Plimpton (ed.) *Writers at Work* (4th series, 1977) ch. 16

24 Some sense of religious mission is part of being American.

interview in *New York Review of Books* 29 February 1996

Urban II (Odo of Lagery) c.1035–99
French cleric, Pope from 1088

25 Let such as are going to fight for Christianity put the form of the cross upon their garments, that they might outwardly demonstrate their devotion to their inward faith.

launching the First Crusade

at the Council of Clermont in 1095; William of Malmesbury *De Gestis Regum Anglorum*

26 Let no attachment to your native soil be an impediment, because . . . all the world is exile to the Christian, and all the world his country: thus exile is his country, and his country exile.

launching the First Crusade

at the Council of Clermont in 1095; William of Malmesbury *De Gestis Regum Anglorum*

James Ussher 1581–1656
Irish prelate and scholar

1 Which beginning of time according to our Chronology, fell upon the entrance of the night preceding the twenty third day of *Octob.* in the year of the Julian Calendar, 710.
giving the date of the Creation as 4004 BC
The Annals of the World (1658)

Peter Ustinov 1921–
Russian-born actor, director, and writer

2 Laughter . . . the most civilized music in the world.
Dear Me (1977) ch. 3

3 I do not believe that friends are necessarily the people you like best, they are merely the people who got there first.
Dear Me (1977) ch. 5; see **Adams** 2:8

4 I sometimes wished he would realize that he was poor instead of being that most nerve-racking of phenomena, a rich man without money.
Dear Me (1977) ch. 6

5 At the age of four with paper hats and wooden swords we're all Generals. Only some of us never grow out of it.
Romanoff and Juliet (1956) act 1

6 Laughter would be bereaved if snobbery died.
in *Observer* 13 March 1955

Paul Valéry 1871–1945
French poet, critic, and man of letters

7 *Le rire est un refus de penser.*
Laughter is a refusal to think.
Mon Faust (1946) 'Lust' act 1, sc. 1

8 Science means simply the aggregate of all the recipes that are always successful. The rest is literature.
Moralités (1932) p. 41; see **Verlaine** 808:15

9 God created man and, finding him not sufficiently alone, gave him a companion to make him feel his solitude more keenly.
Tel Quel 1 (1941) 'Moralités'

10 Politics is the art of preventing people from taking part in affairs which properly concern them.
Tel Quel 2 (1943) 'Rhumbs'

11 *Il faut entrer en soi-même armé jusqu'aux dents.*
To enter into your own mind you need to be armed to the teeth.
Oeuvres (1960) vol. 2 'Quelques pensées de Monsieur Teste'

John Vanbrugh 1664–1726
English architect and dramatist
on Vanbrugh: see **Epitaphs** 311:12

12 Much of a muchness.
The Provoked Husband (1728) act 1, sc. 1

13 BELINDA: Ay, but you know we must return good for evil.
LADY BRUTE: That may be a mistake in the translation.
The Provoked Wife (1697) act 1, sc. 1

14 LADY BRUTE: 'Tis a hard fate I should not be believed.
SIR JOHN: 'Tis a damned atheistical age, wife.
The Provoked Wife (1697) act 5, sc. 2

15 So, now I am in for Hobbes's voyage, a great leap in the dark.
'Heartfree' on marriage
The Provoked Wife (1697) act 5, sc. 5; see **Last words** 471:19

16 When once a woman has given you her heart, you can never get rid of the rest of her body.
The Relapse (1696) act 3, sc. 1

17 In matters of love men's eyes are always bigger than their bellies. They have violent appetites, 'tis true; but they have soon dined.
The Relapse (1696) act 5, sc. 2

Vivian van Damm c.1889–1960
British theatre manager

18 We never closed.
of the Windmill Theatre, London, during the Second World War
Tonight and Every Night (1952) ch. 18

William Henry Vanderbilt 1821–85
American railway magnate

19 The public be damned!
on whether the public should be consulted about luxury trains
letter from A. W. Cole to *New York Times* 25 August 1918

Laurens van der Post 1906–96
South African explorer and writer

20 Human beings are perhaps never more frightening than when they are convinced beyond doubt that they are right.
Lost World of the Kalahari (1958)

Henry Van Dyke 1852–1933
American Presbyterian minister and writer

21 Time is
Too slow for those who wait,
Too swift for those who fear,
Too long for those who grieve,
Too short for those who rejoice;
But for those who love,
Time is eternity.
'Time is too slow for those who wait' (1905), read at the

funeral of **Diana**, Princess of Wales; Nigel Rees in 'Quote
. . . Unquote' October 1997 notes that the original form of
the last line is 'Time is not'

Henry Vane see Last words 472:14

Raoul Vaneigem 1934–
Belgian philosopher

1 Work to survive, survive by consuming, survive to
consume: the hellish cycle is complete.
> *The Revolution of Everyday Life* (1967)

Vincent Van Gogh 1853–90
Dutch painter

2 I cannot help it that my pictures do not sell.
Nevertheless the time will come when people will
see that they are worth more than the price of the
paint.
> letter to his brother Theo, 20 October 1888; *Further Letters
> of Vincent Van Gogh to his Brother* (1929)

William Cornelius Van Horne 1843–1915
*American-born Canadian railway official, general manager
and president of the Canadian Pacific Railway*

3 Building that railroad would have made a
Canadian out of the German Emperor.
> *on the construction of the Canadian Pacific Railway
> across Canada*
>> in *Canadian Encyclopedia* (1988) vol. 1

Bartolomeo Vanzetti 1888–1927
American anarchist, born in Italy

4 Sacco's name will live in the hearts of the people
and in their gratitude when Katzmann's and
yours bones will be dispersed by time, when your
name, his name, your laws, institutions, and your
false god are but a deem rememoring of a cursed
past in which man was wolf to the man.
> *statement disallowed at his trial, with Nicola Sacco,
> for murder and robbery; both were sentenced to death
> on 9 April 1927, and executed on 23 August 1927*
>> M. D. Frankfurter and G. Jackson *Letters of Sacco and
>> Vanzetti* (1928); see **Plautus** 597:20

5 If it had not been for these thing, I might have live
out my life talking at street corners to scorning
men. I might have die, unmarked, unknown, a
failure. Now we are not a failure. This is our
career and our triumph. Never in our full life
could we hope to do such work for tolerance, for
joostice, for man's onderstanding of man as now
we do by accident.
> statement after being sentenced to death, in M. D.
> Frankfurter and G. Jackson *Letters of Sacco and Vanzetti*
> (1928) preface

Michel Vaucaire
French songwriter

6 *Non! rien de rien,*
Non! je ne regrette rien,
Ni le bien, qu'on m'a fait,

Ni le mal—tout ça m'est bien égal!
No, no regrets,
No, we will have no regrets,
As you leave, I can say—
Love was king, tho' for only a day.
> '*Non, je ne regrette rien*' (1960 song); sung by Edith Piaf

Henry Vaughan 1622–95
English poet

7 Man is the shuttle, to whose winding quest
And passage through these looms
God ordered motion, but ordained no rest.
> *Silex Scintillans* (1650–5) 'Man'

8 Wise Nicodemus saw such light
As made him know his God by night.
> *Silex Scintillans* (1650–5) 'The Night'

9 Most blest believer he!
Who in that land of darkness and blind eyes
Thy long expected healing wings could see
When Thou didst rise!
> *Silex Scintillans* (1650–5) 'The Night'

10 Dear Night! this world's defeat;
The stop to busy fools; care's check and curb.
> *Silex Scintillans* (1650–5) 'The Night'

11 My soul, there is a country
Far beyond the stars,
Where stands a wingèd sentry
All skilful in the wars.
> *Silex Scintillans* (1650–5) 'Peace'

12 Happy those early days, when I
Shined in my angel-infancy.
Before I understood this place
Appointed for my second race,
Or taught my soul to fancy aught
But a white, celestial thought.
> *Silex Scintillans* (1650–5) 'The Retreat'

13 And in those weaker glories spy
Some shadows of eternity.
> *Silex Scintillans* (1650–5) 'The Retreat'

14 But felt through all this fleshly dress
Bright shoots of everlastingness.
> *Silex Scintillans* (1650–5) 'The Retreat'

15 Some men a forward motion love,
But I by backward steps would move,
And when this dust falls to the urn,
In that state I came, return.
> *Silex Scintillans* (1650–5) 'The Retreat'

16 They are all gone into the world of light,
And I alone sit lingering here.
> *Silex Scintillans* (1650–5) 'They are all gone'

17 I see them walking in an air of glory,
Whose light doth trample on my days:
My days, which are at best but dull and hoary,
Mere glimmering and decays.
> *Silex Scintillans* (1650–5) 'They are all gone'

18 Dear, beauteous death! the jewel of the just,
Shining nowhere but in the dark.
> *Silex Scintillans* (1650–5) 'They are all gone'

1 And yet, as angels in some brighter dreams
Call to the soul when man doth sleep,
So some strange thoughts transcend our wonted themes,
And into glory peep.
  Silex Scintillans (1650–5) 'They are all gone'

2 If a star were confined into a tomb
Her captive flames must needs burn there;
But when the hand that locked her up gives room,
She'll shine through all the sphere.
  Silex Scintillans (1650–5) 'They are all gone'

3 I saw Eternity the other night,
Like a great ring of pure and endless light,
All calm, as it was bright;
And round beneath it, Time in hours, days, years,
Driv'n by the spheres.
  Silex Scintillans (1650–5) 'The World'

Janet-Maria Vaughan 1899–1993
English scientist

4 I am here—trying to do science in hell.
  working as a doctor in Belsen at the end of the war
  letter to a friend, 12 May 1945; P. A. Adams (ed.) *Janet-Maria Vaughan* (1993)

Thomas, Lord Vaux 1510–56
English writer and courtier

5 For age with stealing steps
Hath clawed me with his clutch,
And lusty life away she leaps,
As there had been none such.
  'The Aged Lover Renounceth Love' (1557); a garbled version is sung by the gravedigger in *Hamlet*; see **Shakespeare** 688:25

6 When all is done and said, in the end thus shall you find,
He most of all doth bathe in bliss that hath a quiet mind;
And, clear from worldly cares, to deem can be content
The sweetest time in all his life in thinking to be spent.
  'The Pleasures of Thinking' (1576)

Thorstein Veblen 1857–1929
American economist and social scientist

7 Conspicuous consumption of valuable goods is a means of reputability to the gentleman of leisure.
  Theory of the Leisure Class (1899) ch. 4

8 From the foregoing survey of conspicuous leisure and consumption, it appears that the utility of both alike for the purposes of reputability lies in the element of waste that is common to both. In the one case it is a waste of time and effort, in the other it is a waste of goods.
  Theory of the Leisure Class (1899) ch. 4

Vegetius (Flavius Vegetius Renatus) fl. AD 379–95
Roman military writer

9 *Qui desiderat pacem, praeparet bellum.*
  Let him who desires peace, prepare for war.
  usually quoted as 'Si vis pacem, para bellum [If you want peace, prepare for war]'
  Epitoma Rei Militaris bk. 3, prologue; see **Aristotle** 25:17, **Proverbs** 623:25

Robert Venturi 1925–
American architect

10 Less is a bore.
  Complexity and Contradiction in Architecture (1966) ch. 2; see **Proverbs** 625:5

Giovanni Verga 1840–1922
Italian novelist, dramatist, and short-story writer

11 *Le vicine avevano fatto come le lumache quando piove, e lungo la straduccio non si udiva che un continuo chiacchierio da un uscio all' altro.*
  The neighbours had come out like snails after a rainstorm, and all down the road you heard the continuous murmur of people talking from doorway to doorway.
  I Malavoglia (The House by the Medlar Tree, 1881) ch. 2, translated by Raymond Rosenthal

12 *Il cuore si stanca anche lui, vedi; e se ne va a pezzo a pezzo, come le robe vecchie si disfanno nel bucato.*
  The heart gets tired too; and it falls apart bit by bit, like an old cloth wears out in the wash.
  I Malavoglia (The House by the Medlar Tree, 1881) ch. 11, translated by Raymond Rosenthal

13 *Il peggio . . . è spatriare dal proprio paese, dove fino i sassi vi conoscono, e dev' essere una cosa da rompere il cuore il lasciarseli dietro per la strada.*
  The worst thing . . . is to leave your own town, where even the stones know you, and it must break your heart to leave them behind on the road.
  I Malavoglia (The House by the Medlar Tree, 1881) ch. 11, translated by Raymond Rosenthal

Pierre Vergniaud 1753–93
French revolutionary; executed with other Girondists

14 There was reason to fear that the Revolution, like Saturn, might devour in turn each one of her children.
  Alphonse de Lamartine *Histoire des Girondins* (1847) bk. 38, ch. 20

Paul Verlaine 1844–96
French poet

15 *Et tout le reste est littérature.*
  All the rest is mere fine writing.
  'Art poétique' (1882); see **Valéry** 806:8

16 *Les sanglots longs
Des violons
De l'automne*

Blessent mon cœur
D'une langueur
Monotone.

The drawn-out sobs of autumn's violins wound my heart with a monotonous languor.

'Chanson d'Automne' (1866)

1 *Prends l'éloquence et tords-lui le cou.*

Take eloquence and break its neck.

Jadis et naguère (1884)

2 *Et, Ô ces voix d'enfants chantants dans la coupole!*

And oh those children's voices, singing beneath the dome!

'Parsifal' A Jules Tellier (1886)

3 *Il pleure dans mon coeur*
Comme il pleut sur la ville.

Tears are shed in my heart like the rain on the town.

Romances sans paroles (1874) 'Ariettes oubliées' no. 3

René Aubert, Abbé de Vertot 1655-1735

French historian

4 *Mon siège est fait.*

My siege is over.

on receiving long-awaited documents for his history of the siege of Rhodes when it had already been completed

J. Le Rond d'Alembert *Œuvres* (1821 ed.) vol. 2, pt. 1

Hendrik Frensch Verwoerd 1901-66

South African statesman; Prime Minister from 1958

5 Up till now he [the Bantu] has been subjected to a school system which drew him away from his own community and practically misled him by showing him the green pastures of the European but still did not allow him to graze there . . . It is abundantly clear that unplanned education creates many problems, disrupts the communal life of the Bantu and endangers the communal life of the European.

speech in South African Senate, 7 June 1954

Vespasian (Titus Flavius Vespasianus) AD 9-79

Roman emperor from AD 69
*see also **Last words** 471:12*

6 *Pecunia non olet.*

Money has no smell.

*upon **Titus**'s objecting to his tax on public lavatories, Vespasian held a coin to Titus's nose; on being told it didn't smell, he replied, 'Atque e lotio est [Yes, that's made from urine]'*

traditional summary of Suetonius *Lives of the Caesars* 'Vespasian' sect. 23, subsect. 3; see **Proverbs** 626:30

7 *Vae, puto deus fio.*

Woe is me, I think I am becoming a god.

when fatally ill

Suetonius *Lives of the Caesars* 'Vespasian' sect. 23, subsect. 4

Queen Victoria 1819-1901

British monarch, Queen of the United Kingdom from 1837
*on Victoria: see **Disraeli** 276:24*

8 I will be good.

on being shown a chart of the line of succession, 11 March 1830

Theodore Martin *The Prince Consort* (1875) vol. 1, ch. 2

9 It was with some emotion . . . that I beheld Albert—who is beautiful.

*of her first meeting with the adult Prince **Albert**, c.1838*

attributed; Stanley Weintraub *Albert: Uncrowned King* (1997)

10 What you say of the pride of giving life to an immortal soul is very fine, dear, but I own I can not enter into that; I think much more of our being like a cow or a dog at such moments; when our poor nature becomes so very animal and unecstatic.

letter to the Princess Royal, 15 June 1858; Roger Fulford *Dearest Child* (1964)

11 Dirty, dark, and undevotional.

of St Paul's Cathedral, where a service of Thanksgiving had been held, following the recovery of the Prince of Wales from typhoid fever

attributed in this form, but recorded in her Journal, 27 February 1872, as 'so cold, dreary and dingy. It so badly lacks decoration and colour.'; G. E. Buckle (ed.) *Letters of Queen Victoria: 2nd Series* vol. 2 (1870-78)

12 The danger to the country, to Europe, to her vast Empire, which is involved in having all these great interests entrusted to the shaking hand of an old, wild, and incomprehensible man of 82, is very great!

*on **Gladstone**'s last appointment as Prime Minister*

letter to Lord Lansdowne, 12 August 1892, in T. Wodehouse Legh *Lord Lansdowne* (1929)

13 The future Vice Roy must . . . not be guided by the *snobbish* and vulgar, over-bearing and offensive behaviour of our Civil and Political Agents, if we are to go on peaceably and happily in India . . . not trying to trample on the people and continuously reminding them and making them feel they are a conquered people.

letter to Lord Salisbury, 27 May 1898, in Kenneth Rose *Superior Person* (1969) ch. 23

14 He speaks to Me as if I was a public meeting.

*of **Gladstone***

G. W. E. Russell *Collections and Recollections* (1898) ch. 14

15 We are not interested in the possibilities of defeat; they do not exist.

on the Boer War during 'Black Week', December 1899

Lady Gwendolen Cecil *Life of Robert, Marquis of Salisbury* (1931) vol. 3, ch. 6

16 We are not amused.

attributed, in Caroline Holland *Notebooks of a Spinster Lady* (1919) ch. 21, 2 January 1900

Gore Vidal 1925-

American novelist and critic

1 Whenever a friend succeeds, a little something in me dies.

in *Sunday Times Magazine* 16 September 1973

2 *of Truman Capote's death:*
Good career move.

attributed, 1984

3 He will lie even when it is inconvenient: the sign of the true artist.

attributed

José Antonio Viera Gallo 1943-

Chilean politician

4 Socialism can only arrive by bicycle.

Ivan Illich *Energy and Equity* (1974) epigraph

Gilles Vigneault 1928-

Canadian singer, songwriter and poet

5 *Mon pays ce n'est pas un pays, c'est l'hiver.*
My country is not a country, it is winter.

'Mon Pays' (1964)

Alfred de Vigny 1797–1863

French poet

6 *J'aime le son du cor, le soir, au fond des bois.*
I love the sound of the horn, at night, in the depth of the woods.

'Le Cor' (1826)

7 *J'aime la majesté des souffrances humaines.*
I love the majesty of human suffering.

La Maison du Berger (1844)

8 *Seul le silence est grand; tout le reste est faiblesse . . .*
Puis, après, comme moi, souffre et meurs sans parler.
Silence alone is great; all else is feebleness . . . then as do I, say naught, but suffer and die.

'La mort du loup' (1843) pt. 3

Matteo Villani d. c.1363

Italian chronicler, of Florence

9 My mind is stupefied as it approaches the task of recording the sentence that divine justice mercifully delivered upon men, who deserve, because they have been corrupted by sin, a last judgement.

of the outbreak of the Black Death in the mid 14th century

Chronicle of Matteo Villani bk 1; M. Meiss *Painting in Florence and Siena after the Black Death* (1951)

Philippe-Auguste Villiers de L'Isle-Adam 1838–89

French writer

10 *Vivre? les serviteurs feront cela pour nous.*
Living? The servants will do that for us.

Axël (1890) pt. 4, sect. 2

François Villon c.1431–after 63

French poet
on Villon: see **Swinburne** 768:7

11 *Frères humains qui après nous vivez,*
N'ayez les cœurs contre nous endurcis,
Car, si pitié de nous pauvres avez,
Dieu en aura plus tôt de vous mercis . . .
Mais priez Dieu que tous nous veuille absoudre!
Brothers in humanity who live after us, let not your hearts be hardened against us, for, if you take pity on us poor ones, God will be more likely to have mercy on you. But pray God that he may be willing to absolve us all.

'Ballade des pendus'

12 *Mais où sont les neiges d'antan?*
But where are the snows of yesteryear?

Le Grand Testament (1461) 'Ballade des dames du temps jadis' (translated by D. G. Rossetti)

13 *En cette foi je veux vivre et mourir.*
In this faith I wish to live and to die.

Le Grand Testament (1461) 'Ballade pour prier Nostre Dame'

St Vincent of Lerins d. c.450

14 *Quod ubique, quod semper, quod ab omnibus creditum est.*
What is everywhere, what is always, what is by all people believed.

Commonitorium Primum sect. 2

Virgil (Publius Vergilius Maro) 70–19 BC

Roman poet
on Virgil: see **Arnold** 30:7, **Horace** 400:3, **Propertius** 612:23, **Tennyson** 784:11; see also **Anonymous** 22:2, **Borrowed titles** 146:9

15 *Arma virumque cano, Troiae qui primus ab oris*
Italiam fato profugus Laviniaque venit
Litora, multum ille et terris iactatus et alto
Vi superum, saevae memorem Iunonis ob iram.
I sing of arms and the man who first from the shores of Troy came destined an exile to Italy and the Lavinian beaches, a man much buffeted on land and on the deep by force of the gods because of fierce Juno's never-forgetting anger.

Aeneid bk. 1, l. 1; see **Dryden** 289:34

16 *Tantaene animis caelestibus irae?*
Why such great anger in those heavenly minds?

Aeneid bk. 1, l. 11

17 *Tantae molis erat Romanam condere gentem.*
So massive was the effort to found the Roman nation.

Aeneid bk. 1, l. 33

18 *Apparent rari nantes in gurgite vasto.*
A few figures swimming were glimpsed in the waste of waters.

Aeneid bk. 1, l. 118

19 *Furor arma ministrat.*
Anger supplies the arms.

Aeneid bk. 1, l.150

1 *Constitit hic arcumque manu celerisque sagittas*
Corripuit fidus quae tela gerebat Achates.

Hereupon he stopped and snatched up in his hand
a bow and swift arrows, the weapons that trusty
Achates carried.

Aeneid bk. 1, l. 187

2 *O passi graviora, dabit deus his quoque finem.*

O you who have borne even heavier things, God
will grant an end to these too.

Aeneid bk. 1, l. 199

3 *Forsan et haec olim meminisse iuvabit.*

Maybe one day it will be cheering to remember
even these things.

Aeneid bk. 1, l. 203

4 *Dux femina facti.*

The leader of the enterprise a woman.

Aeneid bk. 1, l. 364

5 *Dixit et avertens rosea cervice refulsit,*
Ambrosiaeque comae divinum vertice odorem
Spiravere; pedes vestis defluxit ad imos,
Et vera incessu patuit dea.

Thus she spoke and turned away with a flash of
her rosy neck, and her ambrosial hair exhaled a
divine fragrance; her dress flowed right down to
her feet and her true godhead was evident from
her walk.

Aeneid bk. 1, l. 405

6 *Sunt lacrimae rerum et mentem mortalia tangunt.*

There are tears shed for things even here and
mortality touches the heart.

Aeneid bk. 1, l. 463

7 *Di tibi, si qua pios respectant numina, si quid*
Usquam iustitia est et mens sibi conscia recti,
Praemia digna ferant.

If the divine powers take note of the dutiful in any
way, if there is any justice anywhere and a mind
recognizing in itself what is right, may the gods
bring you your earned rewards.

Aeneid bk. 1, l. 603

8 *Non ignara mali miseris succurrere disco.*

No stranger to trouble myself I am learning to care
for the unhappy.

Aeneid bk. 1, l. 630

9 *Infandum, regina, iubes renovare dolorem.*

A grief too much to be told, O queen, you bid me
renew.

Aeneid bk. 2, l. 3

10 *Quaeque ipse miserrima vidi*
Et quorum pars magna fui.

And the most miserable things which I myself saw
and of which I was a major part.

Aeneid bk. 2, l. 5

11 *Equo ne credite, Teucri.*
Quidquid id est, timeo Danaos et dona ferentes.

Do not trust the horse, Trojans. Whatever it is, I
fear the Greeks even when they bring gifts.

Aeneid bk. 2, l. 48; see **Proverbs** 619:45

12 *. . . Crimine ab uno*
Disce omnis.

From the one crime recognize them all as culprits.

Aeneid bk. 2, l. 65

13 *Horresco referens.*

I shudder as I recall it.

Aeneid bk. 2, l. 205

14 *Tacitae per amica silentia lunae.*

Through the friendly silence of the soundless
moonlight.

Aeneid bk. 2, l. 255

15 *Tempus erat quo prima quies mortalibus aegris*
Incipit et dono divum gratissima serpit.

It was the time when first sleep begins for weary
mortals and by the gift of the gods creeps over
them most welcomely.

Aeneid bk. 2, l. 268

16 *Quantum mutatus ab illo*
Hectore qui redit exuvias indutus Achilli.

How greatly changed from that Hector who came
back arrayed in the armour of Achilles!

Aeneid bk. 2, l. 274

17 *Iam proximus ardet*
Ucalegon.

Ucalegon burns very near.

Aeneid bk. 2, l. 311

18 *Fuimus Troes, fuit Ilium et ingens*
Gloria Teucrorum.

We Trojans are at an end, Ilium has ended and
the vast glory of the Trojans.

Aeneid bk. 2, l. 325

19 *Moriamur et in media arma ruamus.*
Una salus victis nullam sperare salutem.

Let us die even as we rush into the midst of the
battle. The only safe course for the defeated is to
expect no safety.

Aeneid bk. 2, l. 354

20 *Dis aliter visum.*

The gods thought otherwise.

Aeneid bk. 2, l. 428

21 *Non tali auxilio nec defensoribus istis*
Tempus eget.

Neither the hour requires such help, nor those
defenders.

Aeneid bk. 2, l. 521

22 *Quid non mortalia pectora cogis,*
Auri sacra fames!

To what do you not drive human hearts, cursed
craving for gold!

Aeneid bk. 3, l. 56

23 *Cum procul obscuros collis humileque videmus*
Italiam. Italiam primus conclamat Achates,
Italiam laeto socii clamore salutant.

We sighted, far away, dim hills and a low coast-
line,
Italy. Achates was the first to hail, 'Italy!'
'Italy!' my comrades echoed in cheerful greeting.

Aeneid bk. 3, l. 522 (translated by C. Day Lewis)

24 *Monstrum horrendum, informe, ingens, cui lumen*
ademptum.

A monster horrendous, hideous and vast, deprived of sight.
Aeneid bk. 3, l. 658

1 *Agnosco veteris vestigia flammae.*

I feel again a spark of that ancient flame.
Aeneid bk. 4, l. 23; see **Dante** 256:9

2 *Quis fallere possit amantem?*

Who could deceive a lover?
Aeneid bk. 4, l. 296

3   *Nec me meminisse pigebit Elissae*
Dum memor ipse mei, dum spiritus hos regit artus.

Nor will it ever upset me to remember Elissa so long as I can remember who I am, so long as the breath of life controls these limbs.
Aeneid bk. 4, l. 335

4 *Italiam non sponte sequor.*

Not of my own free will do I pursue Italy.
Aeneid bk. 4, l. 361

5   *Varium et mutabile semper*
Femina.

A fickle and changeable thing always is woman.
Aeneid bk. 4, l. 569; see below

    A windfane changabil huf puffe
    Always is a woomman.
Richard Stanyhurst's translation, 1582

6 *Exoriare aliquis nostris ex ossibus ultor.*

Rise up from my dead bones, avenger!
Aeneid bk. 4, l. 625 (translated by C. Day-Lewis)

7 *Hos successus alit: possunt, quia posse videntur.*

These success encourages: they can because they think they can.
Aeneid bk. 5, l. 231

8   *Bella, horrida bella,*
Et Thybrim multo spumantem sanguine cerno.

I see wars, horrible wars, and the Tiber foaming with much blood.
Aeneid bk. 6, l. 86; see **Powell** 609:21

9   *Facilis descensus Averno:*
Noctes atque dies patet atri ianua Ditis;
Sed revocare gradum superasque evadere ad auras,
Hoc opus, hic labor est.

Easy is the way down to the Underworld: by night and by day dark Hades' door stands open; but to retrace one's steps and to make a way out to the upper air, that's the task, that is the labour.
Aeneid bk. 6, l. 126

10 *Procul, o procul este, profani.*

Far off, Oh keep far off, you uninitiated ones.
Aeneid bk. 6, l. 258

11 *Ibant obscuri sola sub nocte per umbram*
Perque domos Ditis vacuas et inania regna.

Darkling they went under the lonely night through the shadow and through the empty dwellings and unsubstantial realms of Hades.
Aeneid bk. 6, l. 268

12 *Vestibulum ante ipsum primisque in faucibus Orci*
Luctus et ultrices posuere cubilia Curae,

Pallentesque habitant Morbi tristisque Senectus,
Et Metus et malesuada Fames ac turpis Egestas,
Terribiles visu formae, Letumque Labosque.

Before the very forecourt and in the opening of the jaws of hell Grief and avenging Cares have placed their beds, and wan Diseases and sad Old Age live there, and Fear and Hunger that urges to wrongdoing, and shaming Destitution, figures terrible to see, and Death and Toil.
Aeneid bk. 6, l. 273

13 *Stabant orantes primi transmittere cursum*
Tendebantque manus ripae ulterioris amore.

They stood begging to be the first to make the voyage over and they reached out their hands in longing for the further shore.
Aeneid bk. 6, l. 313

14 *Spiritus intus alit, totamque infusa per artus*
Mens agitat molem et magno se corpore miscet.

The spirit within nourishes, and mind instilled throughout the living parts activates the whole mass and mingles with the vast frame.
Aeneid bk. 6, l. 726

15 *Excudent alii spirantia mollius aera*
(Credo equidem), vivos ducent de marmore vultus,
Orabunt causas melius, caelique meatus
Describent radio et surgentia sidera dicent:
Tu regere imperio populos, Romane, memento
(Hae tibi erunt artes), pacique imponere morem,
Parcere subiectis et debellare superbos.

Others shall shape bronzes more smoothly so that they seem alive (yes, I believe it), shall mould from marble living faces, shall better plead their cases in court, and shall demonstrate with a pointer the motions of the heavenly bodies and tell the stars as they rise: you, Roman, make your task to rule nations by your government (these shall be your skills), to impose ordered ways upon a state of peace, to spare those who have submitted and to subdue the arrogant.
Aeneid bk. 6, l. 847

16 *Heu, miserande puer, si qua fata aspera rumpas,*
Tu Marcellus eris. Manibus date lilia plenis.

Alas, pitiable boy—if only you might break your cruel fate!—you are to be Marcellus. [People,] give me lilies in armfuls.
Aeneid bk. 6, l. 883

17 *Sunt geminae Somni portae, quarum altera fertur*
Cornea, qua veris facilis datur exitus umbris,
Altera candenti perfecta nitens elephanto,
Sed falsa ad caelum mittunt insomnia Manes.

There are two gates of Sleep, one of which it is held is made of horn and by it easy egress is given to real ghosts; the other shining, fashioned of gleaming white ivory, but the shades send deceptive visions that way to the light.
Aeneid bk. 6, l. 893

18   *Geniumque loci primamque deorum*
Tellurem Nymphasque et adhuc ignota precatur
Flumina.

He prays to the spirit of the place and to Earth, the

first of the gods, and to the Nymphs and as yet unknown rivers.

> *Aeneid* bk. 7, l. 136; see **Pope** 603:12

1 *Flectere si nequeo superos, Acheronta movebo.*

If I am unable to make the gods above relent, I shall move Hell.

> *Aeneid* bk. 7, l. 312

2 *Pedibus timor addidit alas.*

Fear gave wings to his feet.

> *Aeneid* bk. 8, l. 224

3 *Nox ruit et fuscit tellurem amplectitur alis.*

Night came down, and enfolded the earth in her dusky wings.

> *Aeneid* bk. 8, l. 369

4 *O mihi praeteritos referat si Iuppiter annos.*

Oh if only Jupiter would give me back my past years.

> *Aeneid* bk. 8, l. 560

5 *Quadripedante putrem sonitu quatit ungula campum.*

The hoof with a galloping sound is shaking the powdery plain.

> *Aeneid* bk. 8, l. 596

6 *Me, me, adsumqui feci, in me convertite ferrum.*

Here I am! Here I am! I am the one who did it! Aim your weapons at me!

> *Aeneid* bk. 9, l. 427 (translated by David West)

7 *Macte nova virtute, puer, sic itur ad astra.*

Blessings on your young courage, boy; that's the way to the stars.

> *Aeneid* bk. 9, l. 641

8 *Audentis Fortuna iuvat.*

Fortune assists the bold.

> *often quoted as 'Fortune favours the brave'*
> *Aeneid* bk. 10, l. 284; see **Proverbs** 620:27, **Terence** 785:7

9 *Et dulcis moriens reminiscitur Argos.*

And dying remembers his sweet Argos.

> *Aeneid* bk. 10, l. 782

10 *Experto credite.*

Trust one who has gone through it.

> *Aeneid* bk. 11, l. 283

11 *Ac velut in somnis, oculos ubi languida pressit*
Nocte Quies, nequiquam avidos extendere cursus
Velle videmur et in mediis conatibus aegri
Succidimus; non lingua valet, non corpore notae
Sufficiunt vires nec vox aut verba sequuntur:
Sic Turno.

But, as it is in a nightmare, when sleep's narcotic hand
Is leaden on our eyes, we seem to be desperately trying
To run and run, but we cannot—for all our efforts, we sink down
Nerveless, our usual strength is just not there, and our tongue
Won't work at all—we can't utter a word or produce one sound:
So with Turnus.

> *Aeneid* bk. 12, l. 908 (translated by C. Day Lewis)

12 *Tityre, tu patulae recubans sub tegmine fagi*
Silvestrem tenui Musam meditaris avena.

Tityrus, you who lie under cover of the spreading beech-tree, you are practising your pastoral music on a thin stalk.

> *Eclogues* no. 1, l. 1

13 *O Meliboee, deus nobis haec otia fecit.*

O Meliboeus, it is a god that has made this peaceful life for us.

> *Eclogues* no. 1, l. 6

14 *Non equidem invideo, miror magis.*

Indeed I am not envious, rather I am amazed.

> *Eclogues* no. 1, l. 11

15 *At nos hinc alii sitientis ibimus Afros,*
Pars Scythiam et rapidum cretae veniemus Oaxen
Et penitus toto divisos orbe Britannos.

But we from here are to go some to the parched Africans, another group to Scythia and others of us shall come to the Oaxes swirling with clay, and amongst the Britons who are kept far away from the whole world.

> *Eclogues* no. 1, l. 64

16 *Et iam summa procul villarum culmina fumant,*
Maioresque cadunt altis de montibus umbrae.

Look over there—smoke rises already from the rooftops
And longer fall the shadows cast by the mountain heights.

> *Eclogues* no. 1, l. 82 (translated by C. Day Lewis)

17 *Formosum pastor Corydon ardebat Alexin,*
Delicias domini, nec quid speraret habebat.

The Shepherd, Corydon, burned with love for handsome Alexis, his master's favourite, but he was not getting what he hoped for.

> *Eclogues* no. 2, l. 1

18 *O formose puer, nimium ne crede colori.*

Don't bank too much on your complexion, lovely boy.

> *Eclogues* no. 2, l. 17

19 *Quem fugis, a! demens? Habitarunt di quoque silvas.*

Who are you running from, you crazy man? . . . Even gods have lived in the woods like me.

> *Eclogues* no. 2, l. 60

20 *Trahit sua quemque voluptas.*

Everyone is dragged on by their favourite pleasure.

> *Eclogues* no. 2, l. 65

21 *Malo me Galatea petit, lasciva puella,*
Et fugit ad salices et se cupit ante videri.

Galatea aims at me with an apple, sexy girl, and runs away into the willows and wants to have been spotted.

> *Eclogues* no. 3, l. 64

22 *Latet anguis in herba.*

There's a snake hidden in the grass.

> *Eclogues* no. 3, l. 93

23 *Non nostrum inter vos tantas componere lites.*

It's not in my power to decide such a great dispute between you.

> *Eclogues* no. 3, l. 108

1 *Claudite iam rivos, pueri; sat prata biberunt.*

Close the sluices now, lads; the fields have drunk enough.

Eclogues no. 3, l. 111

2 *Sicelides Musae, paulo maiora canamus!*
Non omnis arbusta iuvant humilesque myricae;
Si canimus silvas, silvae sint consule dignae.
Ultima Cumaei venit iam carminis aetas;
Magnus ab integro saeclorum nascitur ordo.
Iam redit et virgo, redeunt Saturnia regna,
Iam nova progenies caelo demittitur alto.

Sicilian Muses, let us sing of rather greater things. Bushes and low tamarisks do not please everyone; if we sing of the woods, let them be woods of consular dignity. Now has come the last age according to the oracle at Cumae; the great series of lifetimes starts anew. Now too the virgin goddess returns, the golden days of Saturn's reign return, now a new race is sent down from high heaven.

Eclogues no. 4, l. 1

3 *Incipe, parve puer, risu cognoscere matrem.*

Begin, baby boy, to recognize your mother with a smile.

Eclogues no. 4, l. 60

4 *Incipe, parve puer: qui non risere parenti,*
Nec deus hunc mensa, dea nec dignata cubili est.

Begin, baby boy: if you haven't had a smile for your parent, then neither will a god think you worth inviting to dinner, nor a goddess to bed.

Eclogues no. 4, l. 62

5 *Ambo florentes aetatibus, Arcades ambo,*
Et cantare pares et respondere parati.

Both in the flower of their youth, Arcadians both, and matched and ready alike to start a song and to respond.

Eclogues no. 7, l. 4

6 *Saepibus in nostris parvam te roscida mala*
(Dux ego vester eram) vidi cum matre legentem.
Alter ab undecimo tum me iam acceperat annus,
Iam fragilis poteram a terra contingere ramos:
Ut vidi, ut perii, ut me malus abstulit error!

In our orchard I saw you as a child picking dewy apples with your mother (I was showing you the way). I had just turned twelve years old, I could reach the brittle branches even from the ground: as I saw you, how I perished [for love of you]! how an awful madness swept me away!

Eclogues no. 8, l. 37

7 *Nunc scio quid sit Amor.*

Now I know what Love is.

Eclogues no. 8, l. 43

8 *Non omnia possumus omnes.*

We can't all do everything.

Eclogues no. 8, l. 63; see **Lucilius** 495:7

9 *Et me fecere poetam*
Pierides, sunt et mihi carmina, me quoque dicunt
Vatem pastores; sed non ego credulus illis.
Nam neque adhuc Vario videor nec dicere Cinna
Digna, sed argutos inter strepere anser olores.

Me too the Muses made write verse. I have songs of my own, the shepherds call me also a poet; but I'm not inclined to trust them. For I don't seem yet to write things as good either as Varius or as Cinna, but to be a goose honking amongst tuneful swans.

Eclogues no. 9, l. 32

10 *Omnia vincit Amor: et nos cedamus Amori.*

Love conquers all things: let us too give in to Love.

Eclogues no. 10, l. 69; see **Chaucer** 210:13

11 *Ite domum saturae, venit Hesperus, ite capellae.*

Go on home, you have fed full, the evening star is coming, go on, my she-goats.

Eclogues no. 10, l. 77

12 *Ultima Thule.*

Farthest Thule.

Georgics no. 1, l. 30

13 *Labor omnia vincit*
Improbus et duris urgens in rebus egestas.

Unremitting labour
And harsh necessity's hand will master anything.

Georgics no. 1, l. 145 (translated by C. Day Lewis)

14 *Nosque ubi primus equis Oriens adflavit anhelis*
Illic sera rubens accendit lumina Vesper.

And when the rising sun has first breathed on us with his panting horses, over there the red evening-star is lighting his late lamps.

Georgics no. 1, l. 250

15 *Ter sunt conati imponere Pelio Ossam*
Scilicet atque Ossae frondosum involvere Olympum;
Ter pater exstructos disiecit fulmine montis.

Three times they endeavoured to pile Ossa on Pelion, no less, and to roll leafy Olympus on top of Ossa; three times our Father broke up the towering mountains with a thunderbolt.

Georgics no. 1, l. 281

16 *O fortunatos nimium, sua si bona norint,*
Agricolas!

O farmers excessively fortunate if only they recognized their blessings!

Georgics no. 2, l. 458

17 *Felix qui potuit rerum cognoscere causas.*

Lucky is he who has been able to understand the causes of things.

of **Lucretius**

Georgics no. 2, l. 490

18 *Fortunatus et ille deos qui novit agrestis.*

Fortunate too is the man who has come to know the gods of the countryside.

Georgics no. 2, l. 493

19 *Optima quaeque dies miseris mortalibus aevi*
Prima fugit; subeunt morbi tristisque senectus
Et labor, et durae rapit inclementia mortis.

All the best days of life slip away from us poor mortals first; illnesses and dreary old age and pain sneak up, and the fierceness of harsh death snatches away.

Georgics no. 3, l. 66

1 *Sed fugit interea, fugit inreparabile tempus.*

But meanwhile it is flying, irretrievable time is flying.

usually quoted as 'tempus fugit [time flies]'

Georgics no. 3, l. 284; see **Proverbs** 633:1

2 *Litoraque alcyonen resonant, acalanthida dumi.*

And the shore echoes the song of the kingfisher, and the woods echo the song of the goldfinch.

Georgics bk. 3, l. 338

3 *Hi motus animorum atque haec certamina tanta Pulveris exigui iactu compressa quiescent.*

These movements of souls and these contests, however great, having been contained by the throwing of a little dust, will be quiet.

Georgics no. 4, l. 86 (of the battle of the bees)

4 *Non aliter, si parva licet componere magnis, Cecropias innatus apes amor urget habendi Munere quamque suo.*

Just so, if one may compare small things with great, an innate love of getting drives these Attic bees each with his own function.

Georgics no. 4, l. 176

5 *At genus immortale manet, multosque per annos Stat fortuna domus, et avi numberantur avorum.*

But the race remains immortal, the fortune of the house stands firm for many years, and the grandfathers' grandfathers are numbered in the roll.

of a community of bees

Georgics no. 4, l. 208

6 *Septem illum totos perhibent ex ordine menses Rupe sub aëria deserti ad Strymonis undam Flesse sibi et gelidis haec evolvisse sub antris Mulcentem tigres et agentem carmine quercus; Qualis populea maerens philomela sub umbra Amissos queritur fetus.*

Month after month, they say, for seven months alone
He wept beneath a crag high up by the lonely waters
Of Strymon, and under the ice-cold stars poured out his dirge
That charmed the tigers and made the oak-trees follow him.
As a nightingale he sang that sorrowing under a poplar's
Shade laments the young she has lost.

Georgics no. 4, l. 507, translated by C. Day Lewis

7 *Sic vos non vobis mellificatis apes.
Sic vos non vobis nidificatis aves.
Sic vos non vobis vellera fertis oves.*

Thus you bees make honey not for yourselves.
Thus you birds build nests not for yourselves.
Thus you sheep bear fleeces not for yourselves.

on Bathyllus claiming authorship of certain lines by Virgil

attributed

Voltaire (François-Marie Arouet) 1694–1778

French writer and philosopher

on Voltaire: see **Blake** 121:16, **Hugo** 408:2, **Wordsworth** 846:15; *see also* **Misquotations** 538:1

8 *Dans ce meilleur des mondes possibles . . . tout est au mieux.*

In this best of possible worlds . . . all is for the best.

usually quoted as 'All is for the best in the best of all possible worlds'

Candide (1759) ch. 1; see **Proverbs** 614:15

9 *Si nous ne trouvons pas des choses agréables, nous trouverons du moins des choses nouvelles.*

If we do not find anything pleasant, at least we shall find something new.

Candide (1759) ch. 17

10 *Vous savez que ces deux nations sont en guerre pour quelques arpens de neiges vers le Canada, et qu'elles dépensent pour cette belle guerre beaucoup plus que tout le Canada ne vaut.*

These two nations have been at war over a few acres of snow near Canada, and . . . they are spending on this fine struggle more than Canada itself is worth.

of the struggle between the French and the British for the control of colonial north Canada

Candide (1759) ch. 23

11 *Dans ce pays-ci il est bon de tuer de temps en temps un amiral pour encourager les autres.*

In this country [England] it is thought well to kill an admiral from time to time to encourage the others.

referring to the contentious execution of Admiral Byng (1704–57) for neglect of duty in failing to relieve Minorca

Candide (1759) ch. 23; see **Walpole** 819:22

12 *Il faut cultiver notre jardin.*

We must cultivate our garden.

Candide (1759) ch. 30

13 *Ils ne se servent de la pensée que pour autoriser leurs injustices, et n'emploient les paroles que pour déguiser leurs pensées.*

[Men] use thought only to justify their injustices, and speech only to conceal their thoughts.

Dialogues (1763) 'Le Chapon et la poularde'

14 *Le mieux est l'ennemi du bien.*

The best is the enemy of the good.

Contes (1772) 'La Begueule' l. 2; though often attributed to Voltaire, the notion in fact derives from an Italian proverb quoted in his Dictionnaire philosophique (1770 ed.) 'Art Dramatique': 'Le meglio è l'inimico del bene'; see **Proverbs** 615:11

15 *Le sens commun est fort rare.*

Common sense is not so common.

Dictionnaire philosophique (1765) 'Sens Commun'

16 *La superstition met le monde entier en flammes; la philosophie les éteint.*

Superstition sets the whole world in flames; philosophy quenches them.

Dictionnaire philosophique (1764) 'Superstition'

1 *Le secret d'ennuyer est . . . de tout dire.*

The secret of being a bore . . . is to tell everything.

Discours en vers sur l'homme (1737) 'De la nature de l'homme' l. 172

2 *Tous les genres sont bons hors le genre ennuyeux.*

All styles are good except the tiresome kind.

L'Enfant prodigue (1736) preface

3 *Si Dieu n'existait pas, il faudrait l'inventer.*

If God did not exist, it would be necessary to invent him.

Épîtres no. 96 'A l'Auteur du livre des trois imposteurs'; see **Ovid** 580:1

4 *Ce corps qui s'appelait et qui s'appelle encore le saint empire romain n'était en aucune manière ni saint, ni romain, ni empire.*

This agglomeration which was called and which still calls itself the Holy Roman Empire was neither holy, nor Roman, nor an empire.

Essai sur l'histoire générale et sur les moeurs et l'esprit des nations (1756) ch. 70

5 *En effet, l'histoire n'est que le tableau des crimes et des malheurs.*

Indeed, history is nothing more than a tableau of crimes and misfortunes.

L'Ingénu (1767) ch. 10; see **Gibbon** 345:1

6 *C'est une des superstitions de l'esprit humain d'avoir imaginé que la virginité pouvait être une vertu.*

It is one of the superstitions of the human mind to have imagined that virginity could be a virtue.

'The Leningrad Notebooks' (*c.*1735–50) in T. Besterman (ed.) *Voltaire's Notebooks* (2nd ed., 1968) vol. 2, p. 455

7 *Le superflu, chose très nécessaire.*

The superfluous, a very necessary thing.

Le Mondain (1736) l. 22

8 *Il faut qu'il y ait des moments tranquilles dans les grands ouvrages, comme dans la vie après les instants de passions, mais non pas des moments de dégoût.*

There ought to be moments of tranquillity in great works, as in life after the experience of passions, but not moments of disgust.

'The Piccini Notebooks' (*c.*1735–50) in T. Besterman (ed.) *Voltaire's Notebooks* (2nd ed., 1968) vol. 2

9 *Il faut, dans le gouvernement, des bergers et des bouchers.*

Governments need both shepherds and butchers.

'The Piccini Notebooks' (*c.*1735–50) in T. Besterman (ed.) *Voltaire's Notebooks* (2nd ed., 1968) vol. 2

10 *Dieu n'est pas pour les gros bataillons, mais pour ceux qui tirent le mieux.*

God is on the side not of the heavy battalions, but of the best shots.

'The Piccini Notebooks' (*c.*1735–50) in T. Besterman (ed.) *Voltaire's Notebooks* (2nd ed., 1968) vol. 2; see **Anouilh** 22:15, **Bussy-Rabutin** 175:9, **Proverbs** 629:45

11 *On doit des égards aux vivants; on ne doit aux morts que la vérité.*

We owe respect to the living; to the dead we owe only truth.

'Première Lettre sur Oedipe' in *Oeuvres* (1785) vol. 1

12 *Quoi que vous fassiez, écrasez l'infâme, et aimez qui vous aime.*

Whatever you do, stamp out abuses [superstition], and love those who love you.

letter to M. d'Alembert, 28 November 1762, in Voltaire Foundation (ed.) *Complete Works* vol. 25 (1973)

13 *Il est plaisant qu'on fait une vertu du vice de chasteté; et voilà encore une drôle de chasteté que celle qui mène tout droit les hommes au péché d'Onan, et les filles aux pâles couleurs!*

It is amusing that a virtue is made of the vice of chastity; and it's a pretty odd sort of chastity at that, which leads men straight into the sin of Onan, and girls to the waning of their colour.

letter to M. Mariott, 28 March 1766, in Voltaire Foundation (ed.) *Complete Works* vol. 30 (1973)

14 *Quand la populace se mêle de raisonner, tout est perdu.*

When the masses get involved in reasoning, everything is lost.

letter to Etienne Noël Darnilaville, 1 April 1766; Theodore Besterman et al. (eds.) *The Complete Works of Voltaire* (1973) vol. 114

15 *Je ne suis pas comme une dame de la cour de Versailles, qui disait: c'est bien dommage que l'aventure de la tour de Babel ait produit la confusion des langues; sans cela tout le monde aurait toujours parlé français.*

I am not like a lady at the court of Versailles, who said: 'What a dreadful pity that the bother at the tower of Babel should have got language all mixed up; but for that, everyone would always have spoken French.'

letter to Catherine the Great, 26 May 1767, in Voltaire Foundation (ed.) *Complete Works* vol. 32 (1974)

16 The art of government is to make two-thirds of a nation pay all it possibly can pay for the benefit of the other third.

attributed; Walter Bagehot *The English Constitution* (1867) ch. 5

17 The composition of a tragedy requires *testicles.*

on being asked why no woman had ever written 'a tolerable tragedy'

letter from Byron to John Murray, 2 April 1817, in L. A. Marchand (ed.) *Byron's Letters and Journals* vol. 5 (1976)

18 The English plays are like their English puddings: nobody has any taste for them but themselves.

Joseph Spence *Anecdotes* (ed. J. M. Osborn, 1966) no. 1033

19 *Habacuc était capable de tout.*

Habakkuk was capable of anything.

attributed; in *Notes and Queries* 26 July 1941

20 What a fuss about an omelette!

what Voltaire apparently said on the burning of De l'esprit

James Parton *Life of Voltaire* (1881) vol. 2, ch. 25; see **Misquotations** 538:1

21 This is no time for making new enemies.

on being asked to renounce the Devil, on his deathbed

attributed

Andrei Voznesensky 1933-

Russian poet

1 I am Goya
of the bare field, by the enemy's beak gouged
till the craters of my eyes gape,
I am grief,
I am the tongue
of war, the embers of cities
on the snows of the year 1941
I am hunger.
'Goya' (published 1960) (translated by Stanley Kunitz)

Peter Vyazemsky 1792–1878

Russian poet

2 God of frostbite, God of famine,
beggars, cripples by the yard,
farms with no crops to examine—
that's him, that's your Russian God.
'The Russian God' (1828) (translated by Alan Myers)

Richard Wagner 1813–83

German composer

3 *Frisch weht der Wind*
der Heimat zu:—
mein irisch Kind,
wo weilest du?
Freshly blows the wind homewards: my Irish
child, where are you dwelling?
Tristan und Isolde (1865) act 1, sc. 1

Derek Walcott 1930-

West Indian poet and dramatist

4 I who have cursed
The drunken officer of British rule, how choose
Between this Africa and the English tongue I love?
'A Far Cry From Africa' (1962)

5 Famine sighs like scythe
across the field of statistics and the desert
is a moving mouth.
'The Fortunate Traveller' (1981)

6 I come from a backward place: your duty is
supplied by life around you. One guy plants
bananas; another plants cocoa; I'm a writer, I
plant lines. There's the same clarity of occupation,
and the sense of devotion.
in *Guardian* 12 July 1997

Lech Wałęsa 1943-

Polish trade unionist and statesman, President since 1990

7 You have riches and freedom here but I feel no
sense of faith or direction. You have so many
computers, why don't you use them in the search
for love?
in Paris, on his first journey outside the Soviet area, in
Daily Telegraph 14 December 1988

Alice Walker 1944-

American poet

8 Did this happen to your mother? Did your sister
throw up a lot?
title of poem (1979)

9 I thought love would adapt itself
to my needs.
But needs grow too fast;
they come up like weeds.
Through cracks in the conversation.
Through silences in the dark.
Through everything you thought was concrete.
'Did This Happen to Your Mother? Did Your Sister Throw
Up a Lot?' (1979)

10 Expect nothing. Live frugally
on surprise.
'Expect nothing' (1973)

11 The quietly pacifist peaceful
always die
to make room for men
who shout. Who tell lies to
children, and crush the corners
off of old men's dreams.
'The QPP' (1973)

12 We have a beautiful
mother
Her green lap
immense
Her brown embrace
eternal
Her blue body
everything
we know.
'We Have a Beautiful Mother' (1991)

13 I think it pisses God off if you walk by the colour
purple in a field somewhere and don't notice it.
The Colour Purple (1982)

Felix Walker fl. 1820

American politician

14 I'm talking to Buncombe ['bunkum'].
excusing a long, dull, irrelevant speech in the House of
Representatives, c.1820 (Buncombe being his
constituency)
W. Safire *New Language of Politics* (2nd ed., 1972); see
Carlyle 192:17

Edgar Wallace 1875–1932

English thriller writer

15 Dreamin' of thee! Dreamin' of thee!
'T. A. in Love' (1900); popularized by Cyril Fletcher in
1930s radio shows

George Wallace 1919–98

American Democratic politician

16 Segregation now, segregation tomorrow and
segregation forever!
inaugural speech as Governor of Alabama, January 1963,
in *Birmingham World* 19 January 1963

Henry Wallace 1888–1965

American Democratic politician

1 The century on which we are entering—the century which will come out of this war—can be and must be the century of the common man.
  speech, 8 May 1942, in *Vital Speeches* (1942) vol. 8

William Wallace

American general

2 The enemy we're fighting is a bit different than the one we war-gamed against.
  of the campaign in Iraq
  in *New York Times* 28 March 2003

William Ross Wallace d. 1881

American poet

3 For the hand that rocks the cradle
  Is the hand that rules the world.
  'What rules the world' (1865); see **Proverbs** 621:27,
  Robinson 650:22

Graham Wallas 1858–1932

British politicial scientist

4 The little girl had the making of a poet in her who, being told to be sure of her meaning before she spoke, said, 'How can I know what I think till I see what I say?'
  The Art of Thought (1926) ch. 4

Edmund Waller 1606–87

English poet

5 So was the huntsman by the bear oppressed,
  Whose hide he sold—before he caught the beast!
  'The Battle of the Summer Islands' (1645) canto 2

6 Go, lovely rose!
  Tell her, that wastes her time and me,
  That now she knows,
  When I resemble her to thee,
  How sweet and fair she seems to be.
  'Go, lovely rose!' (1645)

7 Others may use the ocean as their road,
  Only the English make it their abode.
  'Of a War with Spain' (1658) l. 25

8 Poets that lasting marble seek
  Must carve in Latin or in Greek.
  'Of English Verse' (1645)

9 The soul's dark cottage, battered and decayed
  Lets in new light through chinks that time has made.
  'Of the Last Verses in the Book' (1685) l. 18

10 Rome, though her eagle through the world had flown,
  Could never make this island all her own.
  'Panegyric to My Lord Protector' (1655) st. 17

11 Illustrious acts high raptures do infuse,
  And every conqueror creates a Muse.
  'Panegyric to My Lord Protector' (1655) st. 46

12 It is not that I love you less
  Than when before your feet I lay:

But, to prevent the sad increase
  Of hopeless love, I keep away.

In vain, alas! for every thing
  Which I have known belong to you,
  Your form does to my fancy bring
  And makes my old wounds bleed anew.
  'The Self-Banished' (1645)

13 Why came I so untimely forth
  Into a world which, wanting thee,
  Could entertain us with no worth,
  Or shadow of felicity?
  'To My Young Lady Lucy Sidney' (1645)

14 So all we know
  Of what they do above,
  Is that they happy are, and that they love.
  'Upon the Death of My Lady Rich' (1645) l. 75

15 Under the tropic is our language spoke,
  And part of Flanders hath received our yoke.
  'Upon the Late Storm, and of the Death of His Highness Ensuing the Same' (1659) l. 21

William Waller 1598–1668

English Parliamentary general

16 With what a perfect hatred I detest this war without an enemy.
  letter to the Royalist Ralph Hopton, 16 June 1643; Samuel R. Gardiner *History of the Great Civil War* (1894)

Horace Walpole, Lord Orford 1717–97

English writer and connoisseur
on Walpole: see **Macaulay** 498:14

17 Our supreme governors, the mob.
  letter to Horace Mann, 7 September 1743, in *Correspondence* (Yale ed. 1937–83) vol. 18

18 [Lovat] was beheaded yesterday, and died extremely well, without passion, affectation, buffoonery or timidity: his behaviour was natural and intrepid.
  letter to Horace Mann, 10 April 1747, in *Correspondence* (Yale ed.) vol. 19

19 [Strawberry Hill] is a little plaything-house that I got out of Mrs Chenevix's shop, and is the prettiest bauble you ever saw. It is set in enamelled meadows, with filigree hedges.
  letter to Hon. Henry Conway, 8 June 1747, in *Correspondence* (Yale ed.) vol. 37

20 But, thank God! the Thames is between me and the Duchess of Queensberry.
  letter to Hon. Henry Conway, 8 June 1747, in *Correspondence* (Yale ed.) vol. 37

21 Every drop of ink in my pen ran cold.
  letter to George Montagu, 30 July 1752, in *Correspondence* (Yale ed.) vol. 9

22 At present, nothing is talked of, nothing admired, but what I cannot help calling a very insipid and tedious performance: it is a kind of novel, called *The Life and Opinions of Tristram Shandy*; the great humour of which consists in the whole narration always going backwards.
  letter to David Dalrymple, 4 April 1760, in *Correspondence* (Yale ed.) vol. 15

1 One of the greatest geniuses that ever existed, Shakespeare, undoubtedly wanted taste.

> letter to Christopher Wren, 9 August 1764, in *Correspondence* (Yale ed.) vol. 40

2 What has one to do, when one grows tired of the world, as we both do, but to draw nearer and nearer, and gently waste the remains of life with friends with whom one began it?

> letter to George Montagu, 21 November 1765, in *Correspondence* (Yale ed.) vol. 10

3 It is charming to totter into vogue.

> letter to George Selwyn, 2 December 1765, in *Correspondence* (Yale ed.) vol. 30

4 The best sun we have is made of Newcastle coal.

> letter to George Montagu, 15 June 1768, in *Correspondence* (Yale ed.) vol. 10

5 Everybody talks of the constitution, but all sides forget that the constitution is extremely well, and would do very well, if they would but let it alone.

> letter to Horace Mann, 18–19 January 1770, in *Correspondence* (Yale ed.) vol. 23

6 One's mind suffers only when one is young and while one is ignorant of the world. When one has lived for some time, one learns that the young think too little and the old too much, and one grows careless about both.

> letter to Horace Mann, 14 January 1772, in *Correspondence* (Yale ed.) vol. 23

7 It was easier to conquer it [the East] than to know what to do with it.

> letter to Horace Mann, 27 March 1772, in *Correspondence* (Yale ed.) vol. 23

8 The way to ensure summer in England is to have it framed and glazed in a comfortable room.

> letter to Revd William Cole, 28 May 1774, in *Correspondence* (Yale ed.) vol. 1

9 The next Augustan age will dawn on the other side of the Atlantic. There will, perhaps, be a Thucydides at Boston, a Xenophon at New York, and, in time, a Virgil at Mexico, and a Newton at Peru. At last, some curious traveller from Lima will visit England and give a description of the ruins of St Paul's, like the editions of Balbec and Palmyra.

> letter to Horace Mann, 24 November 1774, in *Correspondence* (Yale ed.) vol. 24; see **Macaulay** 498:18

10 By the waters of Babylon we sit down and weep, when we think of thee, O America!

> letter to Revd William Mason, 12 June 1775, in *Correspondence* (Yale ed.) vol. 28; see **Book of Common Prayer** 143:12

11 This world is a comedy to those that think, a tragedy to those that feel.

> letter to Anne, Countess of Upper Ossory, 16 August 1776, in *Correspondence* (Yale ed.) vol. 32

12 When will the world know that peace and propagation are the two most delightful things in it?

> letter to Horace Mann, 7 July 1778, in *Correspondence* (Yale ed.) vol. 24

13 When men write for profit, they are not very delicate.

> letter to Revd William Cole, 1 September 1778, in *Correspondence* (Yale ed.) vol. 2

14 When people will not weed their own minds, they are apt to be overrun with nettles.

> letter to Caroline, Countess of Ailesbury, 10 July 1779, in *Correspondence* (Yale ed.) vol. 39

15 It is the story of a mountebank and his zany.

> *of* **Boswell***'s* Tour of the Hebrides
> letter to Hon. Henry Conway, 6 October 1785, in *Correspondence* (Yale ed.) vol. 39

16 All his own geese are swans, as the swans of others are geese.

> *of Joshua* **Reynolds**
> letter to Anne, Countess of Upper Ossory, 1 December 1786, in *Correspondence* (Yale ed.) vol. 33

17 How should such a fellow as Sheridan, who has no diamonds to bestow, fascinate all the world?— yet witchcraft, no doubt there has been, for when did simple eloquence ever convince a majority?

> letter to Lady Ossory, 9 February 1787, in *Correspondence* (Yale ed.) vol. 33

18 That hyena in petticoats, Mrs Wollstonecraft.

> letter to Hannah More, 26 January 1795, in *Correspondence* (Yale ed.) vol. 31

19 His speeches were fine, but as much laboured as his extempore sayings.

> *of Lord* **Chesterfield**
> *Memoirs of the Reign of King George II* (ed. Lord Holland, 1846) vol. 1, 1751

20 Whoever knows the interior of affairs, must be sensible to how many more events the faults of statesmen give birth, than are produced by their good intentions.

> *Memoirs of the Reign of King George II* (ed. Lord Holland, 1846) vol. 1, 1754

21 The keenness of his sabre was blunted by the difficulty with which he drew it from the scabbard; I mean, the hesitation and ungracefulness of his delivery took off from the force of his arguments.

> *of Henry Fox, Lord* **Holland**
> *Memoirs of the Reign of King George II* (ed. Lord Holland, 1846) vol. 2, 1755

22 While he felt like a victim, he acted like a hero.

> *of Admiral Byng, on the day of his execution*
> *Memoirs of the Reign of King George II* (ed. Lord Holland, 1846) vol. 2, 1757; see **Voltaire** 815:11

23 Perhaps those, who, trembling most, maintain a dignity in their fate, are the bravest: resolution on reflection is real courage.

> *Memoirs of the Reign of King George II* (ed. Lord Holland, 1846) vol. 2, 1757

24 They seem to know no medium between a mitre and a crown of martyrdom. If the clergy are not called to the latter, they never deviate from the pursuit of the former. One would think their motto was, *Canterbury or Smithfield*.

> *Memoirs of the Reign of King George II* (ed. Lord Holland, 1846) vol. 3, 1758

1 All his passions were expressed by one livid smile.
of George Grenville
Memoirs of the Reign of King George III (ed. D. Le Marchant, 1845) vol. 1, 1763

2 He lost his dominions in America, his authority over Ireland, and all influence in Europe, by aiming at despotism in England; and exposed himself to more mortifications and humiliations than can happen to a quiet Doge of Venice.
of King **George III**
Memoirs of the Reign of King George III (ed. D. Le Marchant, 1845) vol. 4, 1770

3 Pieces of land and sea so natural that one steps back for fear of being splashed.
of two landscapes by Thomas **Gainsborough**, *exhibited in 1781*
in Dictionary of National Biography (1917-)

4 Virtue knows to a farthing what it has lost by not having been vice.
L. Kronenberger The Extraordinary Mr Wilkes (1974) pt. 3, ch. 2

Robert Walpole, Lord Orford 1676–1745

English Whig statesman; first British Prime Minister, 1721–42

5 They now *ring* the bells, but they will soon *wring* their hands.
on the declaration of war with Spain, 1739
W. Coxe Memoirs of Sir Robert Walpole (1798) vol. 1

6 All those men have their price.
of fellow parliamentarians
W. Coxe Memoirs of Sir Robert Walpole (1798) vol. 1; see **Proverbs** 619:16

7 Madam, there are fifty thousand men slain this year in Europe, and not one Englishman.
to Queen **Caroline**, *1734, on the war of the Polish succession, in which the English had refused to participate*
John Hervey Memoirs (written 1734–43, published 1848) vol. 1

8 We must muzzle this terrible young cornet of horse.
of the elder William **Pitt**, *who had held a cornetcy before his election to Parliament, c.1736*
in Dictionary of National Biography (1917-)

9 [Gratitude of place-expectants] is a lively sense of future favours.
W. Hazlitt Lectures on the English Comic Writers (1819) 'On Wit and Humour'; see **La Rochefoucauld** 469:19

10 You can read. It is a great happiness. I totally neglected it while I was in business, which has been the whole of my life, and to such a degree that I cannot now read a page—a warning to all Ministers.
on seeing Henry Fox (Lord **Holland**) *reading in the library at Houghton*
Edmund Fitzmaurice Life of Shelburne (1875) vol. 1

William Walsh 1663–1708

English poet

11 A lover forsaken
A new love may get,

But a neck when once broken
Can never be set.
'The Despairing Lover' l. 17

12 By partners, in each other kind,
Afflictions easier grow;
In love alone we hate to find
Companions of our woe.
'Song: Of All the Torments'

13 I can endure my own despair,
But not another's hope.
'Song: Of All the Torments'

Izaak Walton 1593–1683

English writer

14 Angling may be said to be so like the mathematics, that it can never be fully learnt.
The Compleat Angler (1653) 'Epistle to the Reader'

15 And for winter fly-fishing it is as useful as an almanac out of date.
The Compleat Angler (1653) 'Epistle to the Reader'

16 As no man is born an artist, so no man is born an angler.
The Compleat Angler (1653) 'Epistle to the Reader'

17 I shall stay him no longer than to wish him a rainy evening to read this following discourse; and that if he be an honest angler, the east wind may never blow when he goes a-fishing.
The Compleat Angler (1653) 'Epistle to the Reader'

18 I am, Sir, a Brother of the Angle.
The Compleat Angler (1653) pt. 1, ch. 1

19 Sir Henry Wotton . . . was also a most dear lover, and a frequent practiser of the art of angling; of which he would say, 'it was an employment for his idle time, which was then not idly spent . . . a rest to his mind, a cheerer of his spirits, a diverter of sadness, a calmer of unquiet thoughts, a moderator of passions, a procurer of contentedness; and that it begat habits of peace and patience in those that professed and practised it.'
The Compleat Angler (1653) pt. 1, ch. 1

20 Good company and good discourse are the very sinews of virtue.
The Compleat Angler (1653) pt. 1, ch. 2

21 An excellent angler, and now with God.
The Compleat Angler (1653) pt. 1, ch. 4

22 I love such mirth as does not make friends ashamed to look upon one another next morning.
The Compleat Angler (1653) pt. 1, ch. 5

23 A good, honest, wholesome, hungry breakfast.
The Compleat Angler (1653) pt. 1, ch. 5

24 No man can lose what he never had.
The Compleat Angler (1653) pt. 1, ch. 5

25 In so doing, use him as though you loved him.
on baiting a hook with a live frog
The Compleat Angler (1653) pt. 1, ch. 8

26 This dish of meat is too good for any but anglers, or very honest men.
The Compleat Angler (1653) pt. 1, ch. 8

1 I love any discourse of rivers, and fish and fishing.
  The Compleat Angler (1653) pt. 1, ch. 18

2 Look to your health; and if you have it, praise
  God, and value it next to a good conscience; for
  health is the second blessing that we mortals are
  capable of; a blessing that money cannot buy.
  The Compleat Angler (1653) pt. 1, ch. 21

3 Let the blessing of St Peter's Master be . . . upon all
  that are lovers of virtue; and dare trust in His
  providence; and be quiet; and go a-Angling.
  The Compleat Angler (1653) pt. 1, ch. 21

4 But God, who is able to prevail, wrestled with him,
  as the Angel did with Jacob, and marked him;
  marked him for his own.
  Life of Donne (1670 ed.)

5 The great Secretary of Nature and all learning, Sir
  Francis Bacon.
  Life of Herbert (1670 ed.)

6 Of this blest man, let his just praise be given,
  Heaven was in him, before he was in heaven.
  written in a copy of Dr Richard Sibbes's *The Returning
  Backslider*, now preserved in Salisbury Cathedral Library.

Sam Walton 1919–92
American businessman

7 There is only one boss. The customer. And he can
  fire everybody in the company from the chairman
  on down, simply by spending his money
  somewhere else.
  Sam Walton: Made in America, My Story, with J. Huey
  (1990)

William Warburton 1698–1779
English theologian; Bishop of Gloucester from 1759

8 Orthodoxy is my doxy; heterodoxy is another
  man's doxy.
  to Lord Sandwich, in Joseph Priestley *Memoirs* (1807) vol.
  1; see **Carlyle** 192:7

Artemus Ward (Charles Farrar Browne) 1834–67
American humorist

9 It is a pity that Chawcer, who had geneyus, was
  so unedicated. He's the wuss speller I know of.
  Artemus Ward in London (1867) ch. 4

10 Let us all be happy, and live within our means,
   even if we have to borrer the money to do it with.
   Artemus Ward in London (1867) ch. 7

11 I am happiest when I am idle. I could live for
   months without performing any kind of labour,
   and at the expiration of that time I should feel
   fresh and vigorous enough to go right on in the
   same way for numerous more months.
   Artemus Ward in London (1867) ch. 9

12 He is dreadfully married. He's the most married
   man I ever saw in my life.
   Artemus Ward's Lecture (1869) 'Brigham Young's Palace'

13 Why is this thus? What is the reason of this
   thusness?
   Artemus Ward's Lecture (1869) 'Heber C. Kimball's Harem'

Barbara Ward 1914–81
British writer and educator

14 We cannot cheat on DNA. We cannot get round
   photosynthesis. We cannot say I am not going to
   give a damn about phytoplankton. All these tiny
   mechanisms provide the preconditions of our
   planetary life. To say we do not care is to say in
   the most literal sense that 'we choose death'.
   Only One Earth (1972)

Nathaniel Ward 1578–1652
English clergyman

15 The world is full of care, much like unto a bubble;
   Woman and care, and care and women, and
      women and care and trouble.
   epigram, attributed by Ward to a lady at the Court of the
   Queen of Bohemia, in *The Simple Cobbler of Aggawam in
   America* (1647)

Andy Warhol 1927–87
American artist

16 In the future everybody will be world famous for
   fifteen minutes.
   Andy Warhol (1968) (volume released to mark his
   exhibition in Stockholm, February–March, 1968)

17 Being good in business is the most fascinating kind
   of art.
   Philosophy of Andy Warhol (From A to B and Back Again)
   (1975)

18 An artist is someone who produces things that
   people don't need to have but that he—for *some
   reason*—thinks it would be a good idea to give
   them.
   Philosophy of Andy Warhol (From A to B and Back Again)
   (1975)

19 The things I want to show are mechanical.
   Machines have less problems.
   Mike Wrenn *Andy Warhol: In His Own Words* (1991)

Sylvia Townsend Warner 1893–1978
English writer

20 One need not write in a diary what one is to
   remember for ever.
   diary, 22 October 1930

21 One cannot overestimate the power of a good
   rancorous hatred on the part of the *stupid*. The
   stupid have so much more industry and energy to
   expend on hating. They build it up like coral
   insects.
   diary, 26 September 1954

22 Total grief is like a minefield. No knowing when
   one will touch the tripwire.
   diary, 11 December 1969

Earl Warren 1891–1974
American Chief Justice

23 In civilized life, law floats in a sea of ethics.
   in *New York Times* 12 November 1962

Robert Penn Warren 1905–89

American poet, novelist, and critic

1 Long ago in Kentucky, I, a boy, stood
By a dirt road, in first dark, and heard
The great geese hoot northward.
Audubon (1969) 'Tell Me a Story'

2 Ages to our construction went,
Dim architecture, hour by hour:
And violence, forgot now, lent
The present stillness all its power.
'Bearded Oaks' (1942)

3 They were human, they suffered, wore long black
coat and gold watch chain.
They stare from daguerrotype with severe
reprehension,
Or from genuine oil, and you'd never guess any
pain
In those merciless eyes that now remark our own
time's sad declension.
'Promises' (1957)

Booker T. Washington 1856–1915

American educationist and emancipated slave

4 No race can prosper till it learns that there is as
much dignity in tilling a field as in writing a poem.
Up from Slavery (1901)

5 You can't hold a man down without staying down
with him.
attributed

George Washington 1732–99

American statesman, 1st President of the US
on Washington: see **Byron** 182:27, **Lee** 478:17

6 The time is now near at hand which must
probably determine whether Americans are to be
freemen or slaves; whether they are to have any
property they can call their own . . . The fate of
unborn millions will now depend, under God, on
the courage and conduct of this army. Our cruel
and unrelenting enemy leaves us only the choice
of brave resistance, or the most abject submission.
We have, therefore, to resolve to conquer or die.
General orders, 2 July 1776, in J. C. Fitzpatrick (ed.)
Writings of George Washington vol. 5 (1932)

7 Few men have virtue to withstand the highest
bidder.
letter, 17 August 1779

8 'Tis our true policy to steer clear of permanent
alliances, with any portion of the foreign world.
President's Address . . . retiring from Public Life 17 September
1796

9 Let me . . . warn you in the most solemn manner
against the baneful effects of the spirit of party.
President's Address . . . 17 September 1796

10 The nation which indulges toward another an
habitual hatred or an habitual fondness is in some
degree a slave. It is a slave to its animosity or to its
affection, either of which is sufficient to lead it
astray from its duty and its interest.
President's Address . . . 17 September 1796

11 I can't tell a lie, Pa; you know I can't tell a lie. I
did cut it with my hatchet.
M. L. Weems *Life of George Washington* (10th ed., 1810)
ch. 2

12 Liberty, when it begins to take root, is a plant of
rapid growth.
attributed

Ned Washington 1901–76

American songwriter

13 Hi diddle dee dee (an actor's life for me).
title of song (1940) from the film *Pinocchio*

14 The night is like a lovely tune,
Beware my foolish heart!
How white the ever-constant moon,
Take care, my foolish heart!
'My Foolish Heart' (1949 song)

Edward Waterfield

15 Two men wrote a lexicon, Liddell and Scott;
Some parts were clever, but some parts were not.
Hear, all ye learned, and read me this riddle,
How the wrong part wrote Scott, and the right
part wrote Liddell.
of Henry Liddell (1811–98) and Robert Scott
(1811–87) co-authors of the Greek Lexicon *(1843),*
Liddell being in the habit of ascribing to his co-author
usages which he criticised in his pupils, and which
they said that they had culled from the Lexicon
L. E. Tanner *Westminster School: A History* (1934) ch. 9

Rowland Watkyns c.1616–64

16 I love him not, but show no reason can
Wherefore, but this, *I do not love* the man.
'Antipathy'; see **Brown** 155:13, **Martial** 514:17

17 For every marriage then is best in tune,
When that the wife is May, the husband June.
'To the most Courteous and Fair Gentlewoman, Mrs Elinor
Williams'

James Dewey Watson 1928–

American biologist
on Watson: see **Medawar** 520:6; *see also* **Crick and Watson**
251:7

18 No *good* model ever accounted for *all* the facts,
since some data was bound to be misleading if not
plain wrong.
Francis Crick *Some Mad Pursuit* (1988)

19 Some day a child is going to sue its parents for
being born. They will say, my life is so awful with
these terrible genetic defects and you just callously
didn't find out.
on the question of genetic screening of foetuses
interview in *Sunday Telegraph* 16 February 1997

Thomas Watson Snr. 1874–1956

American businessman; Chairman of IBM 1914–52

20 Clothes don't make the man . . . but they go a
long way toward making a businessman.
Robert Sobel *IBM: Colossus in Transition* (1981)

1 You cannot be a success in any business without believing that it is the greatest business in the world . . . You have to put your heart in the business and the business in your heart.

> Robert Sobel *IBM: Colossus in Transition* (1981)

William Watson c.1559–1603

English Roman Catholic conspirator

2 *Fiat justitia et ruant coeli.*

Let justice be done though the heavens fall.

> *A Decacordon of Ten Quodlibeticall Questions Concerning Religion and State* (1602), being the first citation in an English work of a famous maxim; see **Mansfield** 511:6, **Mottoes** 552:8

William Watson 1858–1936

English poet

3 April, April,
Laugh thy girlish laughter.
Then, the moment after,
Weep thy girlish tears!

> 'April'

4 His friends he loved. His direst earthly foes—
Cats—I believe he did but feign to hate.
My hand will miss the insinuated nose,
Mine eyes the tail that wagged contempt at Fate.

> 'An Epitaph'

Isaac Watts 1674–1748

English hymn-writer

5 One sickly sheep infects the flock,
And poisons all the rest.

> *Divine Songs for Children* (1715) 'Against Evil Company'

6 How doth the little busy bee
Improve each shining hour,
And gather honey all the day
From every opening flower!

> *Divine Songs for Children* (1715) 'Against Idleness and Mischief'; see **Carroll** 193:19

7 For Satan finds some mischief still
For idle hands to do.

> *Divine Songs for Children* (1715) 'Against Idleness and Mischief'; see **Proverbs** 617:32

8 Let me be dressed fine as I will,
Flies, worms, and flowers, exceed me still.

> *Divine Songs for Children* (1715) 'Against Pride in Clothes'

9 Let dogs delight to bark and bite,
For God hath made them so.

> *Divine Songs for Children* (1715) 'Against Quarrelling'

10 But, children, you should never let
Such angry passions rise;
Your little hands were never made
To tear each other's eyes.

> *Divine Songs for Children* (1715) 'Against Quarrelling'

11 Birds in their little nests agree
And 'tis a shameful sight,
When children of one family
Fall out, and chide, and fight.

> *Divine Songs for Children* (1715) 'Love between Brothers and Sisters'; see **Proverbs** 615:42

12 'Tis the voice of the sluggard; I heard him complain,
'You have waked me too soon, I must slumber again'.
As the door on its hinges, so he on his bed,
Turns his sides and his shoulders and his heavy head.

> *Divine Songs for Children* (1715) 'The Sluggard'; see **Carroll** 194:19

13 Come, let us join our cheerful songs
With angels round the throne;
Ten thousand thousand are their tongues,
But all their joys are one.

'Worthy the Lamb that died,' they cry,
'To be exalted thus;'
'Worthy the Lamb,' our lips reply,
'For he was slain for us.'

> *Hymns and Spiritual Songs* (1707) 'Come, let us join our cheerful songs'

14 We are a garden walled around,
Chosen and made peculiar ground;
A little spot enclosed by grace,
Out of the world's wide wilderness.

> *Hymns and Spiritual Songs* (1707) 'The Church the Garden of Christ'

15 When I survey the wondrous cross
On which the prince of glory died,
My richest gain I count but loss,
And pour contempt on all my pride.

> *Hymns and Spiritual Songs* (1707) 'Crucifixion to the World, by the Cross of Christ'

16 Hark! from the tombs a doleful sound.

> *Hymns and Spiritual Songs* (1707) 'Hark! from the Tombs'

17 There is a land of pure delight,
Where saints immortal reign.

> *Hymns and Spiritual Songs* (1707) 'A Prospect of Heaven makes Death easy'

18 Death like a narrow sea divides
This heavenly land from ours.

> *Hymns and Spiritual Songs* (1707) 'A Prospect of Heaven makes Death easy'

19 Jesus shall reign where'er the sun
Does his successive journeys run;
His kingdom stretch from shore to shore,
Till moons shall wax and wane no more.

> *The Psalms of David Imitated* (1719) Psalm 72

20 Our God, our help in ages past
Our hope for years to come,
Our shelter from the stormy blast,
And our eternal home.

Beneath the shadow of Thy Throne
Thy saints have dwelt secure;
Sufficient is Thine Arm alone,
And our defence is sure.

Before the hills in order stood,
Or earth received her frame,
From everlasting Thou art God,
To endless years the same.

A thousand ages in Thy sight
Are like an evening gone;
Short as the watch that ends the night
Before the rising sun.

Time, like an ever-rolling stream,
Bears all its sons away;
They fly forgotten, as a dream
Dies at the opening day.
'Our God' altered to 'O God' by John **Wesley**, *1738*
The Psalms of David Imitated (1719) Psalm 90

1 Alexander the Great . . . when he had conquered what was called the Eastern World . . . wept for want of more Worlds to conquer.
The Improvement of the Mind (1741); see **Alexander** 11:4

Evelyn Waugh 1903–66
English novelist

2 I am not I: thou art not he or she: they are not they.
Brideshead Revisited (1945) 'Author's Note'

3 Charm is the great English blight. It does not exist outside these damp islands. It spots and kills anything it touches. It kills love, it kills art.
Brideshead Revisited (1945) bk. 3, ch. 2

4 Any who have heard that sound will shrink at the recollection of it; it is the sound of English county families baying for broken glass.
Decline and Fall (1928) 'Prelude'; see **Belloc** 65:17

5 I expect you'll be becoming a schoolmaster, sir. That's what most of the gentlemen does, sir, that gets sent down for indecent behaviour.
Decline and Fall (1928) 'Prelude'

6 Any one who has been to an English public school will always feel comparatively at home in prison. It is the people brought up in the gay intimacy of the slums, Paul learned, who find prison so soul-destroying.
Decline and Fall (1928) pt. 3, ch. 4

7 Only when one has lost all curiosity about the future has one reached the age to write an autobiography.
A Little Learning (1964)

8 You never find an Englishman among the under-dogs—except in England, of course.
The Loved One (1948) ch. 1

9 His strongest tastes were negative. He abhorred plastics, Picasso, sunbathing and jazz—everything in fact that had happened in his own lifetime.
The Ordeal of Gilbert Pinfold (1957) ch. 1

10 *The Beast* stands for strong mutually antagonistic governments everywhere . . . Self-sufficiency at home, self-assertion abroad.
Scoop (1938) bk. 1, ch. 1

11 Up to a point, Lord Copper.
Scoop (1938) bk. 1, ch. 1

12 'Feather-footed through the plashy fen passes the questing vole' . . . 'Yes,' said the Managing Editor. 'That must be good style.'
Scoop (1938) bk. 1, ch. 1

13 Remember that the Patriots are in the right and are going to win . . . But they must win quickly. The British public has no interest in a war that drags on indecisively. A few sharp victories, some

conspicuous acts of personal bravery on the Patriot side and a colourful entry into the capital. That is *The Beast* Policy for the war.
Scoop (1938) bk. 1, ch. 3

14 News is what a chap who doesn't care much about anything wants to read. And it's only news until he's read it. After that it's dead.
Scoop (1938) bk. 1, ch. 5

15 Other nations use 'force'; we Britons alone use 'Might'.
Scoop (1938) bk. 2, ch. 5

16 Is there any place that is free from evil? It is too simple to say that only the Nazis wanted war . . . Even good men thought that their private honour would be satisfied by war. They could assert their manhood by killing and being killed. They would accept hardship in recompense for having been selfish and lazy. Danger justified privilege.
Unconditional Surrender (1961) bk. 3, sect. 4

17 All this fuss about sleeping together. For physical pleasure I'd sooner go to my dentist any day.
Vile Bodies (1930) ch. 6

18 To see him fumbling with our rich and delicate language is to experience all the horror of seeing a Sèvres vase in the hands of a chimpanzee.
of Stephen **Spender**
in *The Tablet* 5 May 1951

19 Punctuality is the virtue of the bored.
Michael Davie (ed.) *Diaries of Evelyn Waugh* (1976) 'Irregular Notes 1960–65', 26 March 1962

20 A typical triumph of modern science to find the only part of Randolph that was not malignant and remove it.
on hearing that Randolph Churchill's lung, when removed, proved non-malignant
Michael Davie (ed.) *Diaries of Evelyn Waugh* (1976) 'Irregular Notes 1960–65', March 1964

21 I drink for it.
when asked, while at Oxford, what he did for his college
attributed

Frederick Weatherly 1848–1929
English songwriter

22 Where are the boys of the old Brigade,
Who fought with us side by side?
'The Old Brigade' (1886 song)

23 Roses are flowering in Picardy,
But there's never a rose like you.
'Roses of Picardy' (1916 song)

Beatrice Webb 1858–1943
English socialist

24 I never visualised labour as separate men and women of different sorts and kinds . . . labour was an abstraction, which seemed to denote an arithmetically calculable mass of human beings, each individual a repetition of the other.
My Apprenticeship (1926) ch. 1

Sidney Webb 1859–1947

English socialist

1 The inevitability of gradualness.

Presidential address to the annual conference of the Labour Party, 26 June 1923, in *The Labour Party on the Threshold* (Fabian Tract no. 207, 1923)

2 Marriage is the waste-paper basket of the emotions.

Bertrand Russell *Autobiography* (1967) vol. 1, ch. 4

Max Weber 1864–1920

German sociologist

3 The protestant ethic and the spirit of capitalism.

Archiv für Sozialwissenschaft Sozialpolitik vol. 20 (1904–5) (title of article)

4 In Baxter's view the care for external goods should only lie on the shoulders of the saint like 'a light cloak, which can be thrown aside at any moment.' But fate decreed that the cloak should become an iron cage.

Gesammelte Aufsätze zur Religionssoziologie (1920) vol. 1 (translated by T. Parsons, 1930)

5 The State is a relation of men dominating men, a relation supported by means of legitimate (i.e. considered to be legitimate) violence.

'Politik als Beruf' (1919) (translated by H. Gerth and C. Wright Mills, 1948)

6 The authority of the 'eternal yesterday'.

'Politik als Beruf' (1919)

7 The experience of the irrationality of the world has been the driving force of all religious revolution.

'Politik als Beruf' (1919)

8 The concept of the 'official secret' is its [bureaucracy's] specific invention.

'Politik als Beruf' (1919)

Daniel Webster 1782–1852

American politician
on Webster: see **Smith** *743:23*

9 It is, Sir, as I have said, a small college. And yet *there are those who love it!*

argument in the case of the Trustees of Dartmouth College v. Woodward, 10 March 1818

10 The past, at least, is secure.

second speech in the Senate on Foote's Resolution, 26 January 1830; *Writings and Speeches* (1903) vol. 6

11 The people's government, made for the people, made by the people, and answerable to the people.

second speech in the Senate on Foote's Resolution, 26 January 1830; *Writings and Speeches* (1903) vol. 6; see **Lincoln** 485:7

12 Liberty *and* Union, now and forever, one and inseparable!

second speech in the Senate on Foote's Resolution, 26 January 1830; *Writings and Speeches* (1903) vol. 6

13 On this question of principle, while actual suffering was yet afar off, they [the Colonies] raised their flag against a power, to which, for purposes of foreign conquest and subjugation,

Rome, in the height of her glory, is not to be compared; a power which has dotted over the surface of the whole globe with her possessions and military posts, whose morning drum-beat, following the sun, and keeping company with the hours, circles the earth with one continuous and unbroken strain of the martial airs of England.

speech in the Senate on the President's Protest, 7 May 1834; *Writings and Speeches* (1903) vol. 7

14 Whatever government is not a government of laws, is a despotism, let it be called what it may.

at a reception in Bangor, Maine, 25 August 1835; *Writings and Speeches* (1903) vol. 2

15 Thank God, I—I also—am an American!

speech on the completion of Bunker Hill Monument, 17 June 1843; *Writings and Speeches* (1903) vol. 1

16 The Law: It has honoured us, may we honour it.

speech at the Charleston Bar Dinner, 10 May 1847; *Writings and Speeches* (1903) vol. 4

17 I was born an American; I will live an American; I shall die an American.

speech in the Senate on 'The Compromise Bill', 17 July 1850; *Writings and Speeches* (1903) vol. 10

18 There is always room at the top.

on being advised against joining the overcrowded legal profession

attributed; see **Proverbs** 632:5

John Webster c.1580–c.1625

English dramatist
on Webster: see **Eliot** *303:26*

19 Vain the ambition of kings
Who seek by trophies and dead things,
To leave a living name behind,
And weave but nets to catch the wind.

The Devil's Law-Case (1623) act 5, sc. 4

20   Why should only I . . .
Be cased up, like a holy relic? I have youth
And a little beauty.

The Duchess of Malfi (1623) act 3, sc. 2

21 Raised by that curious engine, your white hand.

The Duchess of Malfi (1623) act 3, sc. 2

22   O, that it were possible,
We might but hold some two days' conference
With the dead!

The Duchess of Malfi (1623) act 4, sc. 2

23 I am Duchess of Malfi still.

The Duchess of Malfi (1623) act 4, sc. 2

24 Glories, like glow-worms, afar off shine bright,
But looked to near, have neither heat nor light.

The Duchess of Malfi (1623) act 4, sc. 2

25 I know death hath ten thousand several doors
For men to take their exits.

The Duchess of Malfi (1623) act 4, sc. 2; see **Fletcher** 327:4, **Massinger** 518:5, **Seneca** 677:2

26 Cover her face; mine eyes dazzle: she died young.

The Duchess of Malfi (1623) act 4, sc. 2

27 Physicians are like kings,—they brook no contradiction.

The Duchess of Malfi (1623) act 5, sc. 2

1 Strangling is a very quiet death.
The Duchess of Malfi (1623) act 5, sc. 4

2 We are merely the stars' tennis-balls, struck and
bandied
Which way please them.
The Duchess of Malfi (1623) act 5, sc. 4

3 Is not old wine wholesomest, old pippins
toothsomest, old wood burn brightest, old linen
wash whitest? Old soldiers, sweethearts, are
surest, and old lovers are soundest.
Westward Hoe (1607) act 2, sc. 2

4 ⁣⁣⁣⁣⁣⁣⁣⁣⁣⁣⁣⁣⁣⁣⁣⁣Fortune's a right whore:
If she give aught, she deals it in small parcels,
That she may take away all at one swoop.
The White Devil (1612) act 1, sc. 1

5 'Tis just like a summer birdcage in a garden; the
birds that are without despair to get in, and the
birds that are within despair, and are in a
consumption, for fear they shall never get out.
The White Devil (1612) act 1, sc. 2

6 A mere tale of a tub, my words are idle.
The White Devil (1612) act 2, sc. 1

7 Cowardly dogs bark loudest.
The White Devil (1612) act 3, sc. 2

8 A rape! a rape! . . .
Yes, you have ravished justice;
Forced her to do your pleasure.
The White Devil (1612) act 3, sc. 2

9 Call for the robin-red-breast and the wren,
Since o'er shady groves they hover,
And with leaves and flowers do cover
The friendless bodies of unburied men.
The White Devil (1612) act 5, sc. 4

10 But keep the wolf far thence that's foe to men,
For with his nails he'll dig them up again.
The White Devil (1612) act 5, sc. 4

11 We think caged birds sing, when indeed they cry.
The White Devil (1612) act 5, sc. 4; see **Dunbar** 291:15,
Shakespeare 701:24

12 And of all axioms this shall win the prize,—
'Tis better to be fortunate than wise.
The White Devil (1612) act 5, sc. 6

13 There's nothing of so infinite vexation
As man's own thoughts.
The White Devil (1612) act 5, sc. 6

14 My soul, like to a ship in a black storm,
Is driven, I know not whither.
The White Devil (1612) act 5, sc. 6

15 Prosperity doth bewitch men, seeming clear;
But seas do laugh, show white, when rocks are
near.
The White Devil (1612) act 5, sc. 6

16 ⁣⁣⁣⁣⁣⁣⁣⁣⁣⁣⁣⁣⁣⁣⁣⁣I have caught
An everlasting cold; I have lost my voice
Most irrecoverably.
The White Devil (1612) act 5, sc. 6

Josiah Wedgwood 1730–95
English potter

17 Am I not a man and a brother.
*legend on Wedgwood cameo, depicting a kneeling
Negro slave in chains*
reproduced in facsimile in E. Darwin *The Botanic Garden* pt.
1 (1791)

Simone Weil 1909–43
French essayist and philosopher

18 I would suggest that barbarism be considered as a
permanent and universal human characteristic
which becomes more or less pronounced
according to the play of circumstances.
Écrits Historiques et politiques (1960) 'Réflexions sur la
barbarie' (written *c*.1939)

19 An obligation which goes unrecognized by
anybody loses none of the full force of its
existence. A right which goes unrecognized by
anybody is not worth very much.
L'Enracinement (1949) 'Les Besoins de l'âme' (translated by
A. F. Wills)

20 All sins are attempts to fill voids.
La Pesanteur et la grâce (1948)

21 The authentic and pure values—truth, beauty,
and goodness—in the activity of a human being
are the result of one and the same act, a certain
application of the full attention to the object.
La Pesanteur et la grâce (1948)

22 What a country calls its vital economic interests
are not the things which enable its citizens to live,
but the things which enable it to make war.
W. H. Auden *A Certain World* (1971)

Max Weinreich 1894–1969
American Yiddish scholar

23 A language is a dialect with an army and a navy.
in *Yivo Bleter* January–February 1945

Arabella Weir see Catchphrases 200:11

Robert Stanley Weir 1856–1926
Canadian lawyer

24 *O Canada! Terre de nos aïeux,
Ton front est ceint de fleurons glorieux!
Car ton bras sait porter l'épée,
Il sait porter la croix!*
O Canada! Our home and native land!
True patriot love in all thy sons command.
With glowing hearts we see thee rise,
The True North strong and free!
'O Canada' (1908 song); French words written in 1880 by
Adolphe-Basile Routhier (1839–1920)

Victor Weisskopf 1908–2002
American physicist

25 It was absolutely marvellous working for Pauli.
You could ask him anything. There was no worry

that he would think a particular question was stupid, since he thought *all* questions were stupid.
in American Journal of Physics 1977

Johnny Weissmuller *see* Misquotations 538:8

Chaim Weizmann 1874–1952
Russian-born Israeli statesman, President 1949–52

1 Something had been done for us which, after two thousand years of hope and yearning, would at last give us a resting-place in this terrible world.
of the Balfour declaration
speech in Jerusalem, 25 November 1936; see **Balfour** 51:5

Thomas Earle Welby 1881–1933
British writer

2 'Turbot, Sir,' said the waiter, placing before me two fishbones, two eyeballs, and a bit of black mackintosh.
The Dinner Knell (1932) 'Birmingham or Crewe?'

Joseph Welch 1890–1960
American lawyer

3 Until this moment, Senator, I think I never really gauged your cruelty or your recklessness . . . Have you no sense of decency, sir? At long last, have you left no sense of decency?
*to Joseph **McCarthy**, 9 June 1954, defending the US Army against allegations of harbouring subversive activities; the televised confrontation was deeply damaging to McCarthy*
in *American National Biography* (online edition) 'Joseph McCarthy'

Fay Weldon 1931–
British novelist and scriptwriter
*see also **Advertising slogans** 7:25*

4 There seems to be a general overall pattern in most lives, that nothing happens, and nothing happens, and then all of a sudden everything happens.
Auto da Fay (2002)

5 She was the kind of wife who looks out of her front door in the morning and, if it's raining, apologizes.
Heart of the Country (1987)

6 The life and loves of a she-devil.
title of novel (1984)

7 Every time you open your wardrobe, you look at your clothes and you wonder what you are going to wear. What you are really saying is 'Who am I going to be today?'
in New Yorker 26 June 1995

Orson Welles 1915–85
American actor and film director
*see also **Film lines** 319:19, **Film lines** 320:10*

8 This is the biggest electric train a boy ever had!
of the RKO studios
Roy Fowler *Orson Welles* (1946) ch. 6

9 I hate television. I hate it as much as peanuts. But I can't stop eating peanuts.
in New York Herald Tribune 12 October 1956

10 There are only two emotions in a plane: boredom and terror.
interview to celebrate his 70th birthday, in *The Times* 6 May 1985

Duke of Wellington 1769–1852
British soldier and statesman
*on Wellington: see **Bagehot** 48:2, **Byron** 177:20, **Tennyson** 782:14*

11 As Lord Chesterfield said of the generals of his day, 'I only hope that when the enemy reads the list of their names, he trembles as I do.'
usually quoted as, 'I don't know what effect these men will have upon the enemy, but, by God, they frighten me'
letter, 29 August 1810, in *Supplementary Despatches . . .* (1860) vol. 6

12 Up Guards and at them!
letter from an officer in the Guards, 22 June 1815, in *The Battle of Waterloo* by a Near Observer [J. Booth] (1815); later denied by Wellington

13 Hard pounding this, gentlemen; let's see who will pound longest.
at the Battle of Waterloo, 1815
Sir Walter Scott *Paul's Letters* (1816) Letter 8

14 Next to a battle lost, the greatest misery is a battle gained.
in *Diary of Frances, Lady Shelley 1787–1817* (ed. R. Edgcumbe, 1912) vol. 1, ch. 9; Wellington made a similar remark many times

15 Publish and be damned.
*replying to a blackmail threat prior to the publication of Harriette **Wilson**'s Memoirs (1825); see **Opening lines** 574:20*
attributed; Elizabeth Longford *Wellington: The Years of the Sword* (1969) ch. 10

16 I used to say of him that his presence on the field made the difference of forty thousand men.
*of **Napoleon***
Philip Henry Stanhope *Notes of Conversations with the Duke of Wellington* (1888) 2 November 1831

17 Ours is composed of the scum of the earth—the mere scum of the earth.
of the army
Philip Henry Stanhope *Notes of Conversations with the Duke of Wellington* (1888) 4 November 1831

18 I never saw so many shocking bad hats in my life.
on seeing the first Reformed Parliament, 1832
William Fraser *Words on Wellington* (1889)

19 All the business of war, and indeed all the business of life, is to endeavour to find out what you don't

know by what you do; that's what I called
'guessing what was at the other side of the hill'.
in *The Croker Papers* (1885) vol. 3 ch. 28

1 The battle of Waterloo was won on the playing
fields of Eton.
oral tradition, but probably apocryphal; the earliest
reference is a remark said to have been made when
revisiting Eton, below; see **Orwell** 577:12

It is here that the battle of Waterloo was won!
C. F. R. Montalembert *De l'avenir politique de l'Angleterre*
(1856) ch. 10

2 A conquerer, like a cannonball, must go on; if he
rebounds, his career is over.
attributed; Alistair Horne *How Far from Austerlitz?* (1996)

3 An extraordinary affair. I gave them their orders
and they wanted to stay and discuss them.
of his first Cabinet meeting as Prime Minister
attributed; Peter Hennessy *Whitehall* (1990)

4 If you believe that, you'll believe anything.
*to a gentleman who had accosted him in the street
saying, 'Mr Jones, I believe?'; George Jones RA
(1786–1869), painter of military subjects, bore a
striking resemblance to Wellington*
Elizabeth Longford *Pillar of State* (1972) ch. 10

5 You must build your House of Parliament upon
the river . . . the populace cannot exact their
demands by sitting down round you.
William Fraser *Words on Wellington* (1889)

H. G. Wells 1866–1946
English novelist
see also **Epitaphs** 309:9

6 It is leviathan retrieving pebbles. It is a
magnificent but painful hippopotamus resolved at
any cost, even at the cost of its dignity, upon
picking up a pea which has got into a corner of its
den.
of Henry James
Boon (1915) ch. 4

7 He had read Shakespeare and found him weak in
chemistry.
Complete Short Stories (1927) 'Lord of the Dynamos'

8 'Sesquippledan,' he would say. 'Sesquippledan
verboojuice.'
The History of Mr Polly (1909) ch. 1, pt. 5; see **Horace**
398:5

9 A drink that tasted, she thought, like weak
vinegar mixed with a packet of pins.
of champagne
Joan and Peter (1918) ch. 12

10 'I'm a Norfan, both sides,' he would explain, with
the air of one who had seen trouble.
Kipps (1905) bk. 1, ch. 6, pt. 1

11 I was thinking jest what a Rum Go everything is.
Kipps (1905) bk. 3, ch. 3, pt. 8

12 The Social Contract is nothing more or less than a
vast conspiracy of human beings to lie to and
humbug themselves and one another for the

general Good. Lies are the mortar that bind the
savage individual man into the social masonry.
Love and Mr Lewisham (1900) ch. 23

13 Human history becomes more and more a race
between education and catastrophe.
The Outline of History (1920) vol. 2, ch. 41, pt. 4

14 Bah! the thing is not a nose at all, but a bit of
primordial chaos clapped on to my face.
Select Conversations with an Uncle (1895) 'The Man with a
Nose'

15 The shape of things to come.
title of book (1933)

16 The war that will end war.
title of book (1914); see **Lloyd George** 487:17

17 We fight not to destroy a nation, but a nest of evil
ideas . . . Our business is to kill ideas. The ultimate
purpose of this war is propaganda, the destruction
of certain beliefs, and the creation of others.
The War That Will End War (1914) ch. 11

18 Moral indignation is jealousy with a halo.
The Wife of Sir Isaac Harman (1914) ch. 9, sect. 2

Arnold Wesker 1932–
English dramatist

19 Chips with every damn thing. You breed babies
and you eat chips with everything.
Chips with Everything (1962) act 1, sc. 2

20 The Khomeini cry for the execution of Rushdie is
an infantile cry. From the beginning of time we
have seen that. To murder the thinker does not
murder the thought.
in *Weekend Guardian* 3 June 1989; see **Khomeini** 451:2

Charles Wesley 1707–88
English Methodist preacher and hymn-writer

21 Amazing love! How can it be
That thou, my God, shouldst die for me?
'And can it be' (1738 hymn)

22 My chains fell off, my heart was free,
I rose, went forth, and followed thee.
'And can it be' (1738 hymn)

23 Hark! how all the welkin rings,
Glory to the King of kings.
Peace on earth and mercy mild,
God and sinners reconciled.
Hymns and Sacred Poems (1739) 'Hymn for Christmas'; the
first two lines altered to:

Hark! the herald-angels sing
Glory to the new born king.
George Whitefield *Hymns for Social Worship* (1753)

24 Hail, the heaven-born Prince of Peace!
Hail, the Sun of Righteousness!
Hymns and Sacred Poems (1739) 'Hymn for Christmas'; see
Bible 92:14

25 O for a thousand tongues to sing.
Hymns and Sacred Poems (1740) 'For the Anniversary Day
of one's Conversion'

26 Jesu, lover of my soul,
Let me to thy bosom fly.
Hymns and Sacred Poems (1740) 'In Temptation'

1 Gentle Jesus, meek and mild,
Look upon a little child;
Pity my simplicity,
Suffer me to come to thee.
  Hymns and Sacred Poems (1742) 'Gentle Jesus, Meek and Mild'

2 Come, O thou Traveller unknown,
Whom still I hold, but cannot see.
  Hymns and Sacred Poems (1742) 'Wrestling Jacob'

3 Wrestling, I will not let thee go,
Till I thy name, thy nature know.
  Hymns and Sacred Poems (1742) 'Wrestling Jacob'

4 Forth in thy name, O Lord, I go,
My daily labour to pursue;
Thee, only thee, resolved to know,
In all I think or speak or do.
  Hymns and Sacred Poems (1749) 'Forth in thy name, O Lord, I go'

5 Soldiers of Christ, arise,
And put your armour on.
  Hymns and Sacred Poems (1749) 'The Whole Armour of God'

6 God is gone up on high
With a triumphant noise.
  Hymns for our Lord's Resurrection (1746) 'God is gone up'

7 Rejoice, the Lord is King!
Your Lord and King adore;
Mortals, give thanks and sing,
And triumph evermore:
Lift up your heart, lift up your voice;
Rejoice, again, I say rejoice.
  Hymns for our Lord's Resurrection (1746) 'Rejoice, the Lord is King!'

8 Love divine, all loves excelling,
Joy of heav'n, to earth come down,
Fix in us thy humble dwelling,
All thy faithful mercies crown.
Jesu, thou art all compassion,
Pure unbounded love thou art;
Visit us with thy salvation,
Enter every trembling heart.
  Hymns for those that seek . . . Redemption (1747) 'Love divine', based on Dryden; see **Dryden** 288:27

9 Lo! He comes with clouds descending,
Once for favoured sinners slain;
Thousand thousand Saints attending
Swell the triumph of His train.
  Hymns of Intercession for all Mankind (1758) 'Lo! He comes'

John Wesley 1703–91

English preacher; founder of Methodism
on Wesley: see **Johnson** *430:29*

10 Thou hidden love of God, whose height,
Whose depth unfathomed no man knows,
I see from far thy beauteous light,
Inly I sigh for thy repose.
  A Collection of Psalms and Hymns (1738) 'Divine Love' (a translation of G. Tersteegen's 'Verborgen Gottesliebe du', 1729)

11 The Gospel of Christ knows of no religion but social; no holiness but social holiness.
  Hymns and Sacred Poems (1739) Preface

12 I design plain truth for plain people.
  Sermons on Several Occasions (1746)

13 Slovenliness is no part of religion; that neither this, nor any text of Scripture, condemns neatness of apparel. Certainly this is a duty, not a sin. 'Cleanliness is, indeed, next to godliness.'
  Sermons on Several Occasions (1788) Sermon 88; see **Proverbs** 616:46

14 No circumstances can make it necessary for a man to burst in sunder all the ties of humanity.
  Thoughts upon Slavery (1774) in *Works* (Centenary ed.) vol. 11, p. 72

15 I went to America to convert the Indians; but oh, who shall convert me?
  Journal (ed. N. Curnock) 24 January 1738

16 I felt my heart strangely warmed. I felt I did trust in Christ, Christ alone for salvation; and an assurance was given me that He had taken away *my* sins, even *mine*, and saved *me* from the law of sin and death.
  on his conversion
  Journal (ed. N. Curnock) 24 May 1738

17 I look upon all the world as my parish.
  Journal (ed. N. Curnock) 11 June 1739

18 Either I or you mistake the whole meaning of Christianity from the beginning to the end.
  letter to John Taylor, who rejected the accepted orthodoxy on the subject of original sin
  Journal (ed. N. Curnock) 3 July 1759

19 I let you loose, George, on the great continent of America. Publish your message in the open face of the sun, and do all the good you can.
  letter to a preacher, George Shadford, March 1773 in *Letters* (ed. J. Telford, 1931) vol. 6

20 Though I am always in haste, I am never in a hurry.
  letter to Miss March, 10 December 1777, in *Letters* (ed. J. Telford, 1931) vol. 6

21 I have this day lived fourscore years . . . God grant that I may never live to be useless!
  Journal (ed. N. Curnock) 28 June 1783

22 Time has shaken me by the hand and death is not far behind.
  letter to Ezekiel Cooper, 1 February 1791, in *Letters* (ed. J. Telford, 1931) vol. 8

23 Men may call me a knave or a fool, a rascal, a scoundrel, and I am content; but they shall never by my consent call me a Bishop!
  Betty M. Jarboe *Wesley Quotations* (1990)

Mary Wesley 1912–2002

English novelist

24 When people discussed tonics, pick-me-ups after a severe illness, she kept to herself the prescription of a quick dip in bed with someone you liked but were not in love with. A shock of sexual astonishment which could make you feel astonishingly well and high spirited.
  Not That Sort of Girl (1987)

Samuel Wesley 1662–1735
English clergyman and poet

1 Style is the dress of thought; a modest dress,
Neat, but not gaudy, will true critics please.
'An Epistle to a Friend concerning Poetry' (1700); see
Johnson 425:2, **Pope** 604:6

Mae West 1892–1980
American film actress
see also **Film lines** 319:23

2 I always say, keep a diary and some day it'll keep
you.
Every Day's a Holiday (1937 film)

3 Beulah, peel me a grape.
I'm No Angel (1933 film)

4 It's not the men in my life that counts—it's the life
in my men.
I'm No Angel (1933 film)

5 'Goodness, what beautiful diamonds!'
'Goodness had nothing to do with it.'
Night After Night (1932 film)

6 Why don't you come up sometime, and see me?
She Done Him Wrong (1933 film); see **Misquotations** 539:4

7 Is that a gun in your pocket, or are you just glad
to see me?
usually quoted as 'Is that a pistol in your pocket . . . '
Joseph Weintraub *Peel Me a Grape* (1975)

8 I used to be Snow White . . . but I drifted.
Joseph Weintraub *Peel Me a Grape* (1975)

Rebecca West (Cicily Isabel Fairfield)
1892–1983
English novelist and journalist

9 Were I to . . . take a [Yugoslav] peasant by the
shoulders and whisper to him, 'In your lifetime,
have you known peace?' wait for his answer,
shake his shoulders and transform him into his
father, and ask him the same question, and
transform him in turn into his father, I would
never hear the word 'yes' if I carried my
questioning of the dead back for a thousand years.
Black Lamb and Grey Falcon (1940)

10 Having watched the form of our traitors for a
number of years, I cannot think that espionage
can be recommended as a technique for building
an impressive civilization. It's a lout's game.
The Meaning of Treason (1982 ed.), introduction

11 She was not so much a person as an implication of
dreary poverty, like an open door in a mean house
that lets out the smell of cooking cabbage and the
screams of children.
The Return of the Soldier (1918)

12 The point is that nobody likes having salt rubbed
into their wounds, even if it is the salt of the earth.
The Salt of the Earth (1935) ch. 2

13 There is no such thing as conversation. It is an
illusion. There are intersecting monologues, that is
all.
There is No Conversation (1935) 'The Harsh Voice' sect. 1

14 I myself have never been able to find out precisely
what feminism is: I only know that people call me
a feminist whenever I express sentiments that
differentiate me from a doormat or a prostitute.
in *The Clarion* 14 November 1913

15 Journalism—an ability to meet the challenge of
filling the space.
in *New York Herald Tribune* 22 April 1956

16 Whatever happens, never forget that people would
rather be led to *perdition* by a man, than to *victory*
by a woman.
in conversation in 1979, just before Margaret
Thatcher's first election victory
in *Sunday Telegraph* 17 January 1988

17 Every other inch a gentleman.
*of Michael Arlen; the phrase is also attributed to
Arlen himself*
Victoria Glendinning *Rebecca West* (1987) pt. 3, ch. 5

William C. Westmoreland 1914–
American general

18 Vietnam was the first war ever fought without
censorship. Without censorship, things can get
terribly confused in the public mind.
attributed, 1982

John Fane, Lord Westmorland 1759–1841

19 *Merit*, indeed! . . . We are come to a pretty pass if
they talk of *merit* for a bishopric.
noted in Lady Salisbury's diary, 9 December 1835; C.
Oman *The Gascoyne Heiress* (1968) pt. 5

R. P. Weston 1878–1936 and Bert Lee
1880–1947
British songwriters

20 Good-bye-ee!—Good-bye-ee!
Wipe the tear, baby dear, from your eye-ee.
Tho' it's hard to part, I know,
I'll be tickled to death to go.
Don't cry-ee—don't sigh-ee!
There's a silver lining in the sky-ee!
Bonsoir, old thing! cheerio! chin-chin!
Nahpoo! Toodle-oo! Good-bye-ee!
'Good-bye-ee!' (*c.*1915 song)

Charles Wetherell 1770–1846
English lawyer and politician

21 Then there is my noble and biographical friend
who has added a new terror to death.
of Lord Campbell
Lord St Leonards *Misrepresentations in Campbell's Lives of
Lyndhurst and Brougham* (1869); see **Arbuthnot** 24:7,
Lyndhurst 497:6

Adelheid Wette 1858–1916
German librettist; sister of Engelbert Humperdinck

22 When at night I go to sleep,
Fourteen angels watch do keep.
Two stand here beside me,

Two stand there to guide me . . .
Two more light the path to heaven!
> *Hansel and Gretel* (1893); music by Engelbert Humperdinck

Edith Wharton 1862–1937
American novelist

1 An unalterable and unquestioned law of the
musical world required that the German text of
French operas sung by Swedish artists should be
translated into Italian for the clearer
understanding of English-speaking audiences.
> *The Age of Innocence* (1920) bk. 1, ch. 1

2 My last page is always latent in my first; but the
intervening windings of the way become clear
only as I write.
> *A Backward Glance* (1934)

3 Mrs Ballinger is one of the ladies who pursue
Culture in bands, as though it were dangerous to
meet it alone.
> *Xingu and Other Stories* (1916) 'Xingu'

Thomas, Lord Wharton 1648–1715

4 Ho, Brother Teague, dost hear de decree?
Lilli burlero bullen a la.
Dat we shall have a new Debity,
Lilli burlero bullen a la.
> debity = *deputy; the refrain parodies the Irish
> language*
> 'A New Song' (written 1687), in *Poems on Affairs of State*
> (1704) vol. 3

5 Ara! but why does King James stay behind?
Lilli burlero bullen a la
Ho! by my shoul 'tis a Protestant wind.
> 'A New Song' (written 1687)

6 I sang a king out of three kingdoms.
> *said to have been Wharton's boast after 'A New Song'
> became a propaganda weapon against James II*
> in *Dictionary of National Biography* (1917–)

Richard Whately 1787–1863
*English philosopher and theologian; Archbishop of Dublin
from 1831*

7 Preach not because you have to say something,
but because you have something to say.
> *Apophthegms* (1854)

8 Happiness is no laughing matter.
> *Apophthegms* (1854)

9 It is a folly to expect men to do all that they may
reasonably be expected to do.
> *Apophthegms* (1854)

10 Honesty is the best policy; but he who is governed
by that maxim is not an honest man.
> *Apophthegms* (1854)

11 It is not that pearls fetch a high price *because* men
have dived for them; but on the contrary, men
dive for them because they fetch a high price.
> *Introductory Lectures on Political Economy* (1832) p. 253

12 'Never forget, gentlemen,' he [Whateley] said, to
his astonished hearers, as he held up a copy of the
'Authorized Version' of the Bible, 'never forget
that this is *not* the Bible,' then, after a moment's
pause, he continued, 'This, gentlemen, is only a
translation of the Bible.'
> *to a meeting of his diocesan clergy, in H. Solly* These Eighty
> Years *(1893) vol. 2, ch. 2*

William Whewell 1794–1866
English philosopher and scientist
on Whewell: see **Smith** 744:9

13 Nature, so far as it is the object of scientific
research, is a collection of facts governed by *laws:*
our knowledge of nature is our knowledge of laws.
> *Astronomy and General Physics considered with reference to
> Natural Theology* (1834) ch. 1

14 Hence no force however great can stretch a cord
however fine into an horizontal line which is
accurately straight: there will always be a bending
downwards.
> *often cited as an example of accidental metre and
> rhyme, and changed in later editions*
> *Elementary Treatise on Mechanics* (1819) ch. 4, problem 2

15 Man is the interpreter of nature, science the right
interpretation.
> *Philosophy of the Inductive Sciences* (1840) Aphorism 17

James McNeill Whistler 1834–1903
American-born painter
on Whistler: see **Ruskin** 659:9

16 I am not arguing with you—I am telling you.
> *The Gentle Art of Making Enemies* (1890)

17 Art is upon the Town!
> *Mr Whistler's 'Ten O'Clock'* (1885) p. 7

18 Listen! There never was an artistic period. There
never was an Art-loving nation.
> *Mr Whistler's 'Ten O'Clock'* (1885)

19 Nature is usually wrong.
> *Mr Whistler's 'Ten O'Clock'* (1885)

20 I maintain that two and two would continue to
make four, in spite of the whine of the amateur for
three, or the cry of the critic for five.
> *Whistler v. Ruskin. Art and Art Critics* (1878)

21 No, I ask it for the knowledge of a lifetime.
> *in his case against* **Ruskin***, replying to the question:
> 'For two days' labour, you ask two hundred guineas?'*
> D. C. Seitz *Whistler Stories* (1913)

22 OSCAR WILDE: How I wish I had said that.
WHISTLER: You will, Oscar, you will.
> R. Ellman *Oscar Wilde* (1987) pt. 2, ch. 5

23 Yes madam, Nature is creeping up.
> *to a lady who had been reminded of his work by an
> 'exquisite haze in the atmosphere'*
> D. C. Seitz *Whistler Stories* (1913)

E. B. White 1899–1985
American humorist
see also **Cartoon captions** 198:3

24 Commuter—one who spends his life
In riding to and from his wife;

A man who shaves and takes a train,
And then rides back to shave again.
'The Commuter' (1982)

1 Democracy is the recurrent suspicion that more
than half of the people are right more than half of
the time.
in *New Yorker* 3 July 1944

H. Kirke White 1785–1806

English poet

2 Oft in danger, oft in woe,
Onward, Christians, onward go.
'Oft in danger, oft in woe' (1812 hymn)

Patrick White 1912–90

Australian novelist
see also **Closing lines** 228:22

3 Conversation is imperative if gaps are to be filled,
and old age, it is the last gap but one.
The Tree of Man (1955) ch. 22

4 In all directions stretched the great Australian
Emptiness, in which the mind is the least of
possessions.
The Vital Decade (1968) 'The Prodigal Son'

T. H. White 1906–64

English novelist

5 Everything not forbidden is compulsory.
The Sword in the Stone (1938) ch. 13

Theodore H. White 1915–86

American writer and journalist

6 America is a nation created by all the hopeful
wanderers of Europe, not out of geography and
genetics, but out of purpose.
The Making of the President (1960)

7 The flood of money that gushes into politics today
is a pollution of democracy.
in *Time* 19 November 1984

Alfred North Whitehead 1861–1947

English philosopher and mathematician

8 Life is an offensive, directed against the repetitious
mechanism of the Universe.
Adventures of Ideas (1933) pt. 1, ch. 5

9 It is more important that a proposition be
interesting than that it be true. This statement is
almost a tautology. For the energy of operation of
a proposition in an occasion of experience is its
interest, and is its importance. But of course a true
proposition is more apt to be interesting than a
false one.
Adventures of Ideas (1933) pt. 4, ch. 16

10 There are no whole truths; all truths are half-
truths. It is trying to treat them as whole truths
that plays the devil.
Dialogues (1954) prologue

11 *Ideas won't keep.* Something must be done about
them.
Dialogues (1954) 28 April 1938

12 Intelligence is quickness to apprehend as distinct
from ability, which is capacity to act wisely on the
thing apprehended.
Dialogues (1954) 15 December 1939

13 What is morality in any given time or place? It is
what the majority then and there happen to like,
and immorality is what they dislike.
Dialogues (1954) 30 August 1941

14 Art is the imposing of a pattern on experience, and
our aesthetic enjoyment is recognition of the
pattern.
Dialogues (1954) 10 June 1943

15 Civilization advances by extending the number of
important operations which we can perform
without thinking about them.
Introduction to Mathematics (1911) ch. 5

16 The safest general characterization of the
European philosophical tradition is that it consists
of a series of footnotes to Plato.
Process and Reality (1929) pt. 2, ch. 1

17 Since a babe was born in a manger, it may be
doubted whether so great a thing has happened
with so little stir.
on the scientific revolution in the sixteenth century
Science and the Modern World (1925) ch. 1

Katharine Whitehorn 1928–

English journalist

18 An office party is not, as is sometimes supposed,
the Managing Director's chance to kiss the tea-
girl. It is the tea-girl's chance to kiss the Managing
Director.
Roundabout (1962) 'The Office Party'

19 I wouldn't say when you've seen one Western
you've seen the lot; but when you've seen the lot
you get the feeling you've seen one.
Sunday Best (1976) 'Decoding the West'

George Whiting

American songwriter

20 My blue heaven.
title of song (1927)

21 When you're all dressed up and have no place to
go.
title of song (1912)

William Whiting 1825–78

*English teacher; master of the Quiristers of Winchester
College from 1842*

22 Eternal Father, strong to save,
Whose arm doth bind the restless wave,
Who bidd'st the mighty ocean deep
Its own appointed limits keep:
O hear us when we cry to thee,
For those in peril on the sea.
'Eternal Father, Strong to Save' (1869 hymn)

Gough Whitlam 1916–

Australian Labor statesman, Prime Minister 1972–5

1 *the Governor-General, Sir John Kerr, had dismissed the Labor government headed by Gough Whitlam in November 1975:*
Well may he say 'God Save the Queen'. But after this nothing will save the Governor-General . . .
Maintain your rage and your enthusiasm through the campaign for the election now to be held and until polling day.

speech in Canberra, 11 November 1975

Walt Whitman 1819–92

American poet
on Whitman: see **Ginsberg** *349:18*

2 I dreamed in a dream I saw a city invincible to the attacks of the whole of the rest of the earth,
I dreamed that was the new city of Friends.
'I dreamed in a dream' (1867)

3 I sing the body electric.
title of poem (1855)

4 O Captain! my Captain! our fearful trip is done,
The ship has weathered every rack, the prize we sought is won,
The port is near, the bells I hear, the people all exulting.
'O Captain! My Captain!' (1871)

5 The ship is anchored safe and sound, its voyage closed and done.
From fearful trip the victor ship comes in with object won;
Exult O shores, and ring O bells! But I with mournful tread
Walk the deck my Captain lies, Fallen cold and dead.
'O Captain! My Captain!' (1871)

6 Out of the cradle endlessly rocking,
Out of the mocking-bird's throat, the musical shuttle . . .
A reminiscence sing.
'Out of the cradle endlessly rocking' (1881)

7 Have you your pistols? have you your sharp-edged axes?
Pioneers! O pioneers!
'Pioneers! O Pioneers!' (1881)

8 Camerado, this is no book,
Who touches this touches a man.
'So Long!' (1881)

9 I celebrate myself, and sing myself.
'Song of Myself' (written 1855) pt. 1

10 Urge and urge and urge,
Always the procreant urge of the world.
'Song of Myself' (written 1855) pt. 3

11 Has any one supposed it lucky to be born?
I hasten to inform him or her, it is just as lucky to die and I know it.
'Song of Myself' (written 1855) pt. 7

12 I believe a leaf of grass is no less than the journey-work of the stars,

And the pismire is equally perfect, and a grain of sand, and the egg of the wren,
And the tree toad is a chef-d'oeuvre for the highest,
And the running blackberry would adorn the parlours of heaven.
'Song of Myself' (written 1855) pt. 31

13 I think I could turn and live with animals, they are so placid and self-contained,
I stand and look at them long and long.
They do not sweat and whine about their condition,
They do not lie awake in the dark and weep for their sins,
They do not make me sick discussing their duty to God,
Not one is dissatisfied, not one is demented with the mania of owning things,
Not one kneels to another, nor to his kind that lived thousands of years ago,
Not one is respectable or unhappy over the whole earth.
'Song of Myself' (written 1855) pt. 32

14 Behold, I do not give lectures or a little charity,
When I give I give myself.
'Song of Myself' (written 1855) pt. 40

15 My rendezvous is appointed, it is certain,
The Lord will be there and wait till I come on perfect terms.
'Song of Myself' (written 1855) pt. 45

16 Do I contradict myself?
Very well then I contradict myself,
(I am large, I contain multitudes.)
'Song of Myself' (written 1855) pt. 51

17 I sound my barbaric yawp over the roofs of the world.
'Song of Myself' (written 1855) pt. 52

18 Where the populace rise at once against the never-ending audacity of elected persons.
'Song of the Broad Axe' (1881) pt. 5, l. 12

19 Afoot and light-hearted I take to the open road,
Healthy, free, the world before me,
The long brown path before me leading wherever I choose.
'Song of the Open Road' (1871) pt. 1, l. 1

20 The earth does not argue,
Is not pathetic, has no arrangements.
'A Song of the Rolling Earth' (1881) pt. 1

21 This dust was once the man,
Gentle, plain, just and resolute, under whose cautious hand,
Against the foulest crime in history known in any land or age,
Was saved the Union of these States.
'This dust was once the man' (1881)

22 When lilacs last in the dooryard bloomed,
And the great star early drooped in the western sky in the night,
I mourned, and yet shall mourn with ever-returning spring.
'When lilacs last in the dooryard bloomed' (1881) st. 1

1 The United States themselves are essentially the greatest poem.

Leaves of Grass (1855) preface

Isabella Whitney fl. 1573

English poet

2 Had I a husband or a house, and all that longs
   thereto
Myself could frame about to rouse as other women
   do,
But til some household cares me tie
My books and pen I will apply.

A Sweet Nosegay (1573)

John Greenleaf Whittier 1807–92

American poet

3 'Shoot, if you must, this old grey head,
But spare your country's flag,' she said.

'Barbara Frietchie' (1863)

4 Dear Lord and Father of mankind,
Forgive our foolish ways!
Re-clothe us in our rightful mind,
In purer lives thy service find,
In deeper reverence praise.

'The Brewing of Soma' (1872)

5 For of all sad words of tongue or pen,
The saddest are these: 'It might have been!'

'Maud Muller' (1854); see **Harte** 374:16

6 O brother man! fold to thy heart thy brother.

'Worship' (1848)

Robert Whittington

English grammarian

7 As time requireth, a man of marvellous mirth and pastimes, and sometime of as sad gravity, as who say: a man for all seasons.

of Sir Thomas **More**

Vulgaria (1521) pt. 2 'De constructione nominum';
Erasmus had applied the idea earlier, saying that More
played

Omnium horarum hominem.

A man of all hours.

Erasmus *In Praise of Folly* (1509) prefatory letter

Charlotte Whitton 1896–1975

Canadian writer and politician

8 Whatever women do they must do twice as well as men to be thought half as good.

in *Canada Month* June 1963

Cornelius Whur

9 On firmer ties his joys depend
Who has a polished female friend . . .

While lasting joys the man attend
Who has a faithful female friend.

'The Female Friend' (1837)

William H. Whyte 1917–

American writer

10 This book is about the organization man . . . I can think of no other way to describe the people I am talking about. They are not the workers, nor are they the white-collar people in the usual, clerk sense of the word. These people only work for the Organization. The ones I am talking about *belong* to it as well.

The Organization Man (1956) ch. 1

George John Whyte-Melville 1821–78

Scottish-born novelist, killed in the hunting-field

11 But I freely admit that the best of my fun
I owe it to horse and hound.

'The Good Grey Mare' (1933)

Ann Widdecombe 1947–

British Conservative politician

12 He has something of the night in him.

of Michael **Howard** *as a contender for the Conservative leadership in 1997*

in *Sunday Times* 11 May 1997 (electronic edition)

Elie Wiesel 1928–

Romanian-born American writer and Nobel Prize winner; Auschwitz survivor

13 The opposite of love is not hate, it's indifference. The opposite of art is not ugliness, it's indifference. The opposite of faith is not heresy, it's indifference. And the opposite of life is not death, it's indifference.

in *U.S. News and World Report* 27 October 1986

14 Take sides. Neutrality helps the oppressor, never the victim. Silence encourages the tormentor, never the tormented.

accepting the Nobel Peace Prize

in *New York Times* 11 December 1986

15 God of forgiveness, do not forgive those murderers of Jewish children here.

at Auschwitz

in *The Times* 27 January 1995

Michael Wigglesworth 1631–1705

English-born American puritan preacher and writer

16 By the power of eloquence old truth receives a new habit; though its essence be the same, yet its visage is so altered that it may currently pass and be accepted as a novelty.

oration, 1650; Perry Miller *The American Puritans* (1956)

Samuel Wilberforce 1805–73

English prelate
on Wilberforce: see **Huxley** 412:4

17 If I were a cassowary
On the plains of Timbuctoo,
I would eat a missionary,
Cassock, band, and hymn-book too.

impromptu verse (attributed)

1 Was it through his grandfather or his grandmother that he claimed his descent from a monkey?

> addressed to T. H. Huxley at a meeting of the British Association for the Advancement of Science, Oxford, June 1860; in *Macmillan's Magazine* vol. 78 (October 1898); see **Huxley** 412:4

Richard Wilbur 1921–

American poet

2 Spare us all word of the weapons, their force and range,
The long numbers that rocket the mind.
> 'Advice to a Prophet' (1961)

3 There is a poignancy in all things clear,
In the stare of the deer, in the ring of a hammer in the morning.
> 'Clearness' (1950)

4 We milk the cow of the world, and as we do
We whisper in her ear, 'You are not true.'
> 'Epistemology' (1950)

5 Mind in its purest play is like some bat
That beats about in caverns all alone,
Contriving by a kind of senseless wit
Not to conclude against a wall of stone.
> 'Mind' (1956)

6 The good grey guardians of art
Patrol the halls on spongy shoes,
Impartially protective, though
Perhaps suspicious of Toulouse.
> 'Museum Piece' (1950)

7 Love is the greatest mercy,
A volley of the sun
That lashes all with shade,
That the first day be mended.
> 'Someone Talking to Himself' (1961)

Ella Wheeler Wilcox 1855–1919

American poet

8 Laugh and the world laughs with you;
Weep, and you weep alone;
For the sad old earth must borrow its mirth,
But has trouble enough of its own.
> 'Solitude'

9 So many gods, so many creeds,
So many paths that wind and wind,
While just the art of being kind
Is all the sad world needs.
> 'The World's Need'

Oscar Wilde 1854–1900

Irish dramatist and poet
on Wilde: see **Betjeman** 72:2, **Housman** 403:19, **Leverson** 482:9, **Parker** 585:18, **Whistler** 831:22

10 We have really everything in common with America nowadays except, of course, language.
> *The Canterville Ghost* (1887); see **Misquotations** 537:12

11 Really, if the lower orders don't set us a good example, what on earth is the use of them?
> *The Importance of Being Earnest* (1895) act 1

12 The truth is rarely pure, and never simple.
> *The Importance of Being Earnest* (1895) act 1

13 I have invented an invaluable permanent invalid called Bunbury, in order that I may be able to go down into the country whenever I choose.
> *The Importance of Being Earnest* (1899) act 1

14 In married life three is company and two none.
> *The Importance of Being Earnest* (1895) act 1

15 Ignorance is like a delicate exotic fruit; touch it and the bloom is gone. The whole theory of modern education is radically unsound. Fortunately, in England, at any rate, education produces no effect whatsoever.
> *The Importance of Being Earnest* (1895) act 1

16 To lose one parent, Mr Worthing, may be regarded as a misfortune; to lose both looks like carelessness.
> *The Importance of Being Earnest* (1895) act 1

17 LADY BRACKNELL: A handbag?
> *The Importance of Being Earnest* (1895) act 1

18 All women become like their mothers. That is their tragedy. No man does. That's his.
> *The Importance of Being Earnest* (1895) act 1; the same words occur in dialogue form in *A Woman of No Importance* (1893) act 2

19 The good ended happily, and the bad unhappily. That is what fiction means.
> *The Importance of Being Earnest* (1895) act 2; see **Stoppard** 761:15

20 I hope you have not been leading a double life, pretending to be wicked and being really good all the time. That would be hypocrisy.
> *The Importance of Being Earnest* (1895) act 2

21 Charity, dear Miss Prism, charity! None of us are perfect. I myself am peculiarly susceptible to draughts.
> *The Importance of Being Earnest* (1895) act 2

22 I never travel without my diary. One should always have something sensational to read in the train.
> *The Importance of Being Earnest* (1895) act 2

23 CECILY: When I see a spade I call it a spade.
GWENDOLEN: I am glad to say that I have never seen a spade.
> *The Importance of Being Earnest* (1895) act 3

24 Thirty-five is a very attractive age. London society is full of women of the very highest birth who have, of their own free choice, remained thirty-five for years.
> *The Importance of Being Earnest* (1895) act 3

25 Every great man nowadays has his disciples, and it is always Judas who writes the biography.
> *Intentions* (1891) 'The Critic as Artist' pt. 1

26 Meredith's a prose Browning, and so is Browning.
> *Intentions* (1891) 'The Critic as Artist' pt. 1

27 The one duty we owe to history is to rewrite it.
> *Intentions* (1891) 'The Critic as Artist' pt. 1

28 It is through Art, and through Art only, that we can realise our perfection; through Art, and

through Art only, that we can shield ourselves from the sordid perils of actual existence.
Intentions (1891) 'The Critic as Artist' pt. 2

1 All art is immoral.
Intentions (1891) 'The Critic as Artist' pt. 2

2 A little sincerity is a dangerous thing, and a great deal of it is absolutely fatal.
Intentions (1891) 'The Critic as Artist' pt. 2

3 Life imitates Art far more than Art imitates Life.
Intentions (1891) 'The Decay of Lying'

4 Meredith! Who can define him? His style is chaos illuminated by flashes of lightning.
Intentions (1891) 'The Decay of Lying'; Ada Leverson *Letters to the Sphinx* (1930) attributes to Wilde a similar remark about **Browning**

5 I can resist everything except temptation.
Lady Windermere's Fan (1892) act 1; see **Graham** 358:4

6 Many a woman has a past, but I am told that she has at least a dozen, and that they all fit.
Lady Windermere's Fan (1892) act 1

7 We are all in the gutter, but some of us are looking at the stars.
Lady Windermere's Fan (1892) act 3

8 There is nothing in the whole world so unbecoming to a woman as a Nonconformist conscience.
Lady Windermere's Fan (1892) act 3

9 A man who knows the price of everything and the value of nothing.
definition of a cynic
Lady Windermere's Fan (1892) act 3

10 Experience is the name every one gives to their mistakes.
Lady Windermere's Fan (1892) act 3

11 There is no such thing as a moral or an immoral book. Books are well written, or badly written.
The Picture of Dorian Gray (1891) preface

12 The nineteenth century dislike of Realism is the rage of Caliban seeing his own face in the glass.
The Picture of Dorian Gray (1891) preface

13 The moral life of man forms part of the subject matter of the artist, but the morality of art consists in the perfect use of an imperfect medium.
The Picture of Dorian Gray (1891) preface

14 There is only one thing in the world worse than being talked about, and that is not being talked about.
The Picture of Dorian Gray (1891) ch. 1

15 A man cannot be too careful in the choice of his enemies.
The Picture of Dorian Gray (1891) ch. 1

16 A cigarette is the perfect type of a perfect pleasure. It is exquisite, and it leaves one unsatisfied.
The Picture of Dorian Gray (1891) ch. 6

17 It is better to be beautiful than to be good. But . . . it is better to be good than to be ugly.
The Picture of Dorian Gray (1891) ch. 17

18 Anybody can be good in the country.
The Picture of Dorian Gray (1891) ch. 19

19 A thing is not necessarily true because a man dies for it.
The Portrait of Mr W. H. (1901)

20 MRS ALLONBY: They say, Lady Hunstanton, that when good Americans die they go to Paris.
LADY HUNSTANTON: Indeed? And when bad Americans die, where do they go to?
LORD ILLINGWORTH: Oh, they go to America.
A Woman of No Importance (1893) act 1; see **Appleton** 23:15

21 The English country gentleman galloping after a fox—the unspeakable in full pursuit of the uneatable.
A Woman of No Importance (1893) act 1

22 One should never trust a woman who tells one her real age. A woman who would tell one that, would tell one anything.
A Woman of No Importance (1893) act 1

23 LORD ILLINGWORTH: The Book of Life begins with a man and a woman in a garden.
MRS ALLONBY: It ends with Revelations.
A Woman of No Importance (1893) act 1

24 Children begin by loving their parents; after a time they judge them; rarely, if ever, do they forgive them.
A Woman of No Importance (1893) act 2

25 GERALD: I suppose society is wonderfully delightful!
LORD ILLINGWORTH: To be in it is merely a bore. But to be out of it simply a tragedy.
A Woman of No Importance (1893) act 3

26 You should study the Peerage, Gerald . . . It is the best thing in fiction the English have ever done.
A Woman of No Importance (1893) act 3

27 He did not wear his scarlet coat,
For blood and wine are red,
And blood and wine were on his hands
When they found him with the dead.
The Ballad of Reading Gaol (1898) pt. 1, st. 1

28 I never saw a man who looked
With such a wistful eye
Upon that little tent of blue
Which prisoners call the sky.
The Ballad of Reading Gaol (1898) pt. 1, st. 3

29 Yet each man kills the thing he loves,
By each let this be heard,
Some do it with a bitter look,
Some with a flattering word.
The coward does it with a kiss,
The brave man with a sword!
The Ballad of Reading Gaol (1898) pt. 1, st. 7

30 The Governor was strong upon
The Regulations Act:
The Doctor said that Death was but
A scientific fact:
And twice a day the Chaplain called,
And left a little tract.
The Ballad of Reading Gaol (1898) pt. 3, st. 3

31 Something was dead in each of us,
And what was dead was Hope.
The Ballad of Reading Gaol (1898) pt. 3, st. 31

1 And the wild regrets, and the bloody sweats,
None knew so well as I:
For he who lives more lives than one
More deaths than one must die.
    The Ballad of Reading Gaol (1898) pt. 3, st. 37

2 And alien tears will fill for him
Pity's long-broken urn,
For his mourners will be outcast men,
And outcasts always mourn.
    inscribed on Wilde's tomb in Père Lachaise cemetery
    The Ballad of Reading Gaol (1898) pt. 4, st. 23

3 How else but through a broken heart
May Lord Christ enter in?
    The Ballad of Reading Gaol (1898) pt. 5, st. 14

4 All her bright golden hair
Tarnished with rust,
She that was young and fair
Fallen to dust.
    'Requiescat' (1881)

5 Democracy means simply the bludgeoning of the
people by the people for the people.
    in *Fortnightly Review* February 1891 'The Soul of Man
    under Socialism'; see **Lincoln** 485:7

6 When I ask for a watercress sandwich, I do not
mean a loaf with a field in the middle of it.
    to a waiter
    Max Beerbohm, letter to Reggie Turner, 15 April 1893

7 Ah, well, then, I suppose that I shall have to die
beyond my means.
    at the mention of a huge fee for a surgical operation
    R. H. Sherard *Life of Oscar Wilde* (1906) ch. 18

8 Do you want to know the great drama of my life?
It's that I have put my genius into my life; all I've
put into my works is my talent.
    André Gide *Oscar Wilde* (1910) 'In Memoriam'

9 He has fought a good fight and has had to face
every difficulty except popularity.
    *of W. E. **Henley***
    unpublished character sketch, written for Rothenstein's
    English Portraits; W. Rothenstein *Men and Memories* vol. 1
    (1931) ch. 25

10 Shaw has not an enemy in the world; and none of
his friends like him.
    letter from Bernard Shaw to Archibald Henderson, 22
    February 1911; Bernard Shaw *Collected Letters*,
    1911–1925 (1985)

11 I have nothing to declare except my genius.
at the New York Custom House
    Frank Harris *Oscar Wilde* (1918)

12 Work is the curse of the drinking classes.
    H. Pearson *Life of Oscar Wilde* (1946) ch. 12

Billy Wilder (Samuel Wilder) 1906–2002
American screenwriter and director
see also: **Film lines** *320:21*, **Film lines** *321:2*, **Film lines** *321:6*

13 Hindsight is always twenty-twenty.
    J. R. Columbo *Wit and Wisdom of the Moviemakers* (1979)
    ch. 7

Thornton Wilder 1897–1975
American novelist and dramatist

14 Even memory is not necessary for love. There is a
land of the living and a land of the dead and the
bridge is love, the only survival, the only
meaning.
    The Bridge of San Luis Rey (1927), closing words

15 Marriage is a bribe to make a housekeeper think
she's a householder.
    The Merchant of Yonkers (1939) act 1

16 Literature is the orchestration of platitudes.
    in *Time* 12 January 1953

Robert Wilensky 1951–
American academic

17 We've all heard that a million monkeys banging
on a million typewriters will eventually reproduce
the entire works of Shakespeare. Now, thanks to
the Internet, we know this is not true.
    in *Mail on Sunday* 16 February 1997 'Quotes of the Week';
    see **Eddington** 295:3

Wilhelm II ('Kaiser Bill') 1859–1941
German monarch, emperor 1888–1918

18 We have . . . fought for our place in the sun and
have won it. It will be my business to see that we
retain this place in the sun unchallenged, so that
the rays of that sun may exert a fructifying
influence upon our foreign trade and traffic.
    speech in Hamburg, 18 June 1901; in *The Times* 20 June
    1901; see **Bülow** 164:1

John Wilkes 1727–97
English parliamentary reformer

19 EARL OF SANDWICH: 'Pon my soul, Wilkes, I don't
know whether you'll die upon the gallows or of
the pox.
WILKES: That depends, my Lord, whether I first
embrace your Lordship's principles, or your
Lordship's mistresses.
    Charles Petrie *The Four Georges* (1935); probably
    apocryphal

Jonny Wilkinson 1979–
English rugby player

20 It was probably the easiest attempt I had all day.
*on his winning drop goal in the Rugby World Cup
final, Sydney, 22 November 2003*
    in *Weekend Australian* (online ed.) 23 November 2003

Emma Hart Willard 1787–1870
American pioneer of women's education

21 Rocked in the cradle of the deep.
    title of song (1840), inspired by a prospect of the Bristol
    Channel

William I (William the Conqueror) 1027–87

Norman-born English monarch, Duke of Normandy and from 1066 King of England

1 If the Normans are disciplined under a just and firm rule they are men of great valour, who . . . fight resolutely to overcome all enemies. But without such rule they tear each other to pieces and destroy themselves, for they hanker after rebellion, cherish sedition, and are ready for any treachery.
attributed deathbed speech
Orderic Vitalis *Ecclesiastical History*

William III (William of Orange) 1650–1702

British monarch, King of Great Britain and Ireland from 1688

2 'Do you not see your country is lost?' asked the Duke of Buckingham. 'There is one way never to see it lost' replied William, 'and that is to die in the last ditch.'
Bishop Gilbert Burnet *History of My Own Time* (1838 ed.)

3 Every bullet has its billet.
John Wesley *Journal* (1827) 6 June 1765; see **Proverbs** 619:3

William le Breton fl. 13th century

French priest, chaplain to King Philip Augustus of France

4 You could well ask whether the king loved his people more than the people their king. It was as if each tried to outdo the other in their love.
Philippide; G. Duby *France in the Middle Ages* (1991)

William of Malmesbury c.1090–c.1143

English monastic chronicler

5 The English at that time wore short garments, reaching to the mid-knee; they had their hair cropped, their beards shaven, their arms laden with golden bracelets, their skin adorned with punctured designs; they were accustomed to eat until they became surfeited, and to drink till they were sick. These latter qualities they imparted to their conquerors.
De Gestis Regum Anglorum (A History of the Norman Kings)

6 The Normans are a race inured to war, and can hardly live without it, fierce in rushing against the enemy, and, where force fails of success, ready to use stratagem, or corrupt by bribery.
De Gestis Regum Anglorum (A History of the Norman Kings)

Heathcote Williams 1941–

British dramatist and poet

7 Whales play, in an amniotic paradise.
Their light minds shaped by buoyancy,
    unrestricted by gravity,
Somersaulting.
Like angels, or birds;
Like our own lives, in the womb.
Whale Nation (1988)

Isaac Williams 1802–65

English clergyman

8 Be thou my Guardian and my Guide.
title of hymn (1842)

Peter Williams

9 Guide me, O thou great Jehovah,
Pilgrim through this barren land;
I am weak, but thou art mighty;
Hold me with thy powerful hand;
Bread of heaven, bread of heaven,
Feed me till I want no more.
first line frequently in the form 'O thou great Redeemer'
'Praying for Strength' (1771); translation of 'Arglwydd, arwain trwy'r anialwch' (1745) by William Williams (1717–91)

10 When I tread the verge of Jordan,
Bid my anxious fears subside.
'Praying for Strength' (1771)

R. J. P. Williams 1926–

British chemist

11 Biology is the search for the chemistry that works.
lecture in Oxford, June 1996

Rowan Williams 1950–

British Anglican clergyman, Archbishop of Canterbury from 2002

12 I can only ask your prayers as, like Augustine shivering in his shoes on the French coast at the prospect of dealing with the savage English, I stand on the shore wondering what lies ahead.
in *The Times* 28 September 2002

13 We have to learn to be human alongside all sorts of others, the ones whose company we don't greatly like.
in *Independent* 1 March 2003

Sarah Williams 1814–68

British writer

14 Though my soul may set in darkness, it will rise in
    perfect light;
I have loved the stars too truly to be fearful of the
    night.
'The Old Astronomer to His Pupil' (1920)

Serena Williams 1981–

American tennis player

15 If you can keep playing tennis when somebody is shooting a gun down the street, that's concentration. I didn't grow up playing at the country club.
in *Sunday Times* 2 June 2002

Shirley Williams 1930–

British Labour and Social Democrat politician

1 No test tube can breed love and affection. No
frozen packet of semen ever read a story to a
sleepy child.
in Daily Mirror 2 March 1978

2 The Catholic Church has never really come to
terms with women. What I object to is being
treated either as Madonnas or Mary Magdalenes.
in Observer 22 March 1981

Tennessee Williams (Thomas Lanier Williams) 1911–83

American dramatist

3 We have to distrust each other. It's our only
defence against betrayal.
Camino Real (1953) block 10

4 We're all of us guinea pigs in the laboratory of
God. Humanity is just a work in progress.
Camino Real (1953) block 12

5 What is the victory of a cat on a hot tin roof?—I
wish I knew . . . Just staying on it, I guess, as long
as she can.
Cat on a Hot Tin Roof (1955) act 1

6 BRICK: Well, they say nature hates a vacuum, Big
Daddy.
BIG DADDY: That's what they say, but sometimes I
think that a vacuum is a hell of a lot better than
some of the stuff that nature replaces it with.
Cat on a Hot Tin Roof (1955) act 2

7 I didn't go to the moon, I went much further—for
time is the longest distance between two places.
The Glass Menagerie (1945)

8 We're all of us sentenced to solitary confinement
inside our own skins, for life!
Orpheus Descending (1958) act 2, sc. 1

9 Turn that off! I won't be looked at in this merciless
glare!
A Streetcar Named Desire (1947) sc. 1

10 BLANCHE: I don't want realism.
MITCH: Naw, I guess not.
BLANCHE: I'll tell you what I want. Magic!
A Streetcar Named Desire (1947) sc. 9

11 I have always depended on the kindness of
strangers.
A Streetcar Named Desire (1947) sc. 11

William Carlos Williams 1883–1963

American poet

12 Minds like beds always made up,
(more stony than a shore)
unwilling or unable.
Paterson (1946) bk. 1, preface

13 so much depends
upon
a red wheel
barrow
glazed with rain
water
beside the white
chickens.
'The Red Wheelbarrow' (1923)

14 Is it any better in Heaven, my friend Ford,
Than you found it in Provence?
'To Ford Madox Ford in Heaven' (1944)

Marianne Williamson 1953–

American writer and philanthropist

15 Our deepest fear is not that we are inadequate.
Our deepest fear is that we are powerful beyond
measure. It is our light, not our darkness, that
most frightens us.
A Return to Love (1992) ch. 7

Roy Williamson 1936–90

Scottish folksinger and musician

16 O flower of Scotland, when will we see your like
again,
that fought and died for your bit hill and glen
and stood against him, proud Edward's army,
and sent him homeward tae think again.
unofficial Scottish Nationalist anthem
'O Flower of Scotland' (1968)

Love Maria Willis (née Whitcomb) 1824–1908

American doctor's wife

17 Father, hear the prayer we offer:
Not for ease that prayer shall be,
But for strength that we may ever
Live our lives courageously.

Not for ever in green pastures
Do we ask our way to be,
But the steep and rugged pathway
May we tread rejoicingly.
'Father, hear the prayer we offer' (1864 hymn)

Wendell Willkie 1892–1944

American lawyer and politician

18 The constitution does not provide for first and
second class citizens.
An American Programme (1944) ch. 2

19 Freedom is an indivisible word. If we want to
enjoy it, and fight for it, we must be prepared to
extend it to everyone, whether they are rich or
poor, whether they agree with us or not, no
matter what their race or the colour of their skin.
One World (1943) ch. 13

Angus Wilson 1913–91

English novelist and short-story writer

20 Once a Catholic always a Catholic.
The Wrong Set (1949) p. 168

Charles E. Wilson 1890–1961

American industrialist; President of General Motors, 1941–53
see also **Political slogans** 600:8

1 For years I thought what was good for our
country was good for General Motors and vice
versa. The difference did not exist. Our company is
too big. It goes with the welfare of the country.
  testimony to the Senate Armed Services Committee on his
  proposed nomination for Secretary of Defence, 15 January
  1953, in *New York Times* 24 February 1953

Edward O. Wilson 1929–

American sociobiologist

2 Every human brain is born not as a blank tablet (a
tabula rasa) waiting to be filled in by experience
but as 'an exposed negative waiting to be slipped
into developer fluid'.
  on the nature v. nurture debate
  attributed; Tom Wolfe in *Independent on Sunday* 2 February
  1997

Harold Wilson 1916–95

British Labour statesman; Prime Minister, 1964–70, 1974–6
on Wilson: see **Home** 393:16, **Junor** 439:1

3 All these financiers, all the little gnomes in Zurich.
  speech in the House of Commons 12 November 1956

4 This party is a moral crusade or it is nothing.
  speech at the Labour Party Conference, 1 October 1962; in
  The Times 2 October 1962

5 The university of the air.
  an early term for the Open University
  in *Glasgow Herald* 9 September 1963

6 The Britain that is going to be forged in the white
heat of this revolution will be no place for
restrictive practices or for outdated methods on
either side of industry.
  speech at the Labour Party Conference, 1 October 1963;
  see **Misquotations** 539:3

7 A week is a long time in politics.
  probably first said at the time of the 1964 sterling
  crisis
  Nigel Rees *Sayings of the Century* (1984) ; see **Chamberlain**
  206:6

8 [Labour is] the natural party of government.
  in 1965; Anthony Sampson *The Changing Anatomy of*
  Britain (1982)

9 From now the pound abroad is worth 14 per cent
or so less in terms of other currencies. It does not
mean, of course, that the pound here in Britain, in
your pocket or purse or in your bank, has been
devalued.
  often quoted as 'the pound in your pocket'
  ministerial broadcast, 19 November 1967, in *The Times* 20
  November 1967

10 Get your tanks off my lawn, Hughie.
  to the trade union leader Hugh Scanlon, at Chequers
  in June 1969
  Peter Jenkins *The Battle of Downing Street* (1970)

11 If I had the choice between smoked salmon and
tinned salmon, I'd have it tinned. With vinegar.
  in *Observer* 11 November 1962

12 Whichever party is in office, the Treasury is in
power.
  while in opposition, c.1974
  Anthony Sampson *The Changing Anatomy of Britain* (1982)

13 The Monarchy is a labour-intensive industry.
  in *Observer* 13 February 1977

Harriette Wilson see Opening lines 574:20

John Wilson see Christopher North

Sandy Wilson 1924–

English songwriter

14 We've got to have
We plot to have
For it's so dreary not to have
That certain thing called the Boy Friend.
  The Boyfriend (1954) title song

Woodrow Wilson 1856–1924

American Democratic statesman, 28th President of the US
on Wilson: see **Clemenceau** 226:13, **Keynes** 450:12

15 The future is not for parties 'playing politics', but
for measures conceived in the largest spirit,
pushed by parties whose leaders are statesmen,
not demagogues, who love, not their offices, but
their duty and their opportunity for service
  speech at Trenton, New Jersey, 5 September 1910

16 It is like writing history with lightning. And my
only regret is that it is all so terribly true.
  on seeing D. W. Griffith's film The Birth of a Nation
  at the White House, 18 February 1915

17 No nation is fit to sit in judgement upon any other
nation.
  speech in New York, 20 April 1915; in *Selected Addresses*
  (1918)

18 There is such a thing as a man being too proud to
fight.
  speech in Philadelphia, 10 May 1915; in *Selected Addresses*
  (1918) p. 88

19 We have stood apart, studiously neutral.
  speech to Congress, 7 December 1915, in *New York Times* 8
  December 1915

20 It must be a peace without victory . . . Only a
peace between equals can last.
  speech to US Senate, 22 January 1917, in *Messages and*
  Papers (1924) vol. I

21 Armed neutrality is ineffectual enough at best.
  speech to Congress, 2 April 1917, in *Selected Addresses*
  (1918)

22 The world must be made safe for democracy.
  speech to Congress, 2 April 1917, in *Selected Addresses*
  (1918); see **Wolfe** 843:17

23 Once lead this people into war and they will forget
there ever was such a thing as tolerance.
  John Dos Passos *Mr Wilson's War* (1917) pt. 3, ch. 12

1 Open covenants of peace, openly arrived at.
the first of the 'Fourteen Points'
   speech to Congress, 8 January 1918, in *Selected Addresses*
   (1918)

2 America is the only idealistic nation in the world.
   speech at Sioux Falls, South Dakota, 8 September 1919; in
   Messages and Papers (1924) vol. 2

Walter Winchell 1897–1972
American journalist

3 Good evening, Mr and Mrs North America and all
the ships at sea. Let's go to press! Flash!
   habitual introduction to network radio spot, 1931–56

Anne Finch, Lady Winchilsea 1661–1720
English poet

4 Thirst of wealth no quiet knows,
But near the death-bed fiercer grows.
   'Enquiry after Peace' (1713) l. 30

5 Poetry's the feverish fit,
Th' o'erflowing of unbounded wit.
   'Enquiry after Peace' (1713) l. 40

6 Alas! a woman that attempts the pen
Such an intruder on the rights of men,
Such presumptuous creature is esteemed
The fault can by no virtue be redeemed.
   'The Introduction' (1713) l. 9

7 How are we fallen! Fallen by mistaken rules,
And education's, more than nature's, fools;
Debarred from all improvements of the mind,
And to be dull, expected and designed.
   'The Introduction' (1713) l. 51

8 Give me yet before I die
A sweet, yet absolute retreat,
'Mongst paths so lost and trees so high
That the world may ne'er invade
Through such windings and such shade.
   'The Petition for an Absolute Retreat' (1713) l. 2

9 Now the jonquil o'ercomes the feeble brain;
We faint beneath the aromatic pain.
   'The Spleen' (1701); see **Pope** 604:27

10 My hand delights to trace unusual things,
And deviates from the known and common way;
Nor will in fading silks compose
Faintly the inimitable rose.
   'The Spleen' (1701) l. 82

William Windham 1750–1810
English politician

11 No one would select the hurricane season in
which to begin repairing his house.
   speech opposing Flood's reform bill in 1790; *Dictionary of
   National Biography* (1917–)

12 Those entrusted with arms . . . should be persons
of some substance and stake in the country.
   speech in the House of Commons, 22 July 1807

Duchess of Windsor (Wallis Simpson)
1896–1986
American-born wife of the former **Edward VIII**
on Windsor: see **Newspaper headlines** 562:16

13 You can never be too rich or too thin.
   attributed

Duke of Windsor see Edward VIII

Catherine Winkworth 1827–78
English translator of German hymns

14 Now thank we all our God,
With heart and hands and voices,
Who wondrous things hath done,
In whom his world rejoices;
Who from our mother's arms
Hath blessed us on our way
With countless gifts of love,
And still is ours to-day.
   Lyra Germanica (1858) 'Now thank we all our God'
   (translation of Martin Rinkart's 'Nun danket alle Gott',
   *c.*1636)

15 Praise to the Lord! the Almighty, the King of
creation!
   title of hymn (1863); translated from the German of
   Joachim Neander (1650–80)

16 Hast thou not seen?
All that is needful hath been
Granted in what he ordaineth.
   'Praise to the Lord! the Almighty . . . ' (1863 hymn)

17 Ponder anew
What the Almighty can do
If with his love he befriend thee.
   'Praise to the Lord! the Almighty . . . ' (1863 hymn)

18 *Peccavi*—I have Sindh.
*of Sir Charles Napier's conquest of Sindh, 1843,
supposedly sent by Napier to Lord Ellenborough;
peccavi = I have sinned*
   in *Punch* 18 May 1844; attributed in *Notes and Queries* May
   1954

Yvor Winters 1900–68
American poet and critic

19 The young are quick of speech.
Grown middle-aged, I teach
Corrosion and distrust,
Exacting what I must.
   'On Teaching the Young' (1934)

John Winthrop 1588–1649
American settler

20 We must consider that we shall be a city upon a
hill, the eyes of all people are on us; so that if we
shall deal falsely with our God in this work we
have undertaken, and so cause Him to withdraw
His present help from us, we shall be made a story
and a byword through the world.
   Christian Charity, A Model Hereof (sermon, 1630) in
   Massachusetts Historical Society *Winthrop Papers*
   (1929–47) vol. 2

Robert Charles Winthrop 1809–94
American politician

1 A Star for every State, and a State for every Star.
   speech on Boston Common, 27 August 1862, in *Addresses
   and Speeches* vol. 2 (1867)

Nicholas Wiseman 1802–65
English Catholic priest, Cardinal-archbishop of Westminster

2 Full in the panting heart of Rome,
   Beneath the apostle's crowning dome,
   From pilgrims' lips that kiss the ground,
   Breathes in all tongues one only sound:
   God bless our Pope, the great, the good.
   'Full in the panting heart of Rome'

Owen Wister 1860–1938
American novelist

3 When you call me that, *smile!*
   '*that*' being '*you son-of-a—*'
   The Virginian (1902) ch. 2

George Wither 1588–1667
English poet and pamphleteer

4 When I behold the havoc and the spoil
   Which, even within the compass of my days,
   Is made through every quarter of this isle,
   In woods and groves, which were this kingdom's
      praise.
   A Collection of Emblems (1635) bk. 1, no. 35

5 We seek the present gain in everything,
   Not caring (so our lust we may possess)
   What damage to posterity we bring . . .
   What our forefathers planted, we destroy:
   A Collection of Emblems (1635) bk. 1, no. 35

6 I loved a lass, a fair one,
   As fair as e'er was seen;
   She was indeed a rare one,
   Another Sheba queen.
   A Description of Love (1620) 'I loved a lass, a fair one'

Ludwig Wittgenstein 1889–1951
Austrian-born philosopher
*see also **Last words** 473:20*

7 Philosophy is a battle against the bewitchment of
   our intelligence by means of language.
   Philosophische Untersuchungen (1953) pt. 1, sect. 109

8 The philosopher's treatment of a question is like
   the treatment of an illness.
   Philosophische Untersuchungen (1953) pt. 1, sect. 255

9 What is your aim in philosophy?—To show the fly
   the way out of the fly-bottle.
   Philosophische Untersuchungen (1953) pt. 1, sect. 309

10 What can be said at all can be said clearly; and
   whereof one cannot speak thereof one must be
   silent.
   Tractatus Logico-Philosophicus (1922) preface

11 The world is everything that is the case.
   Tractatus Logico-Philosophicus (1922)

12 Death is not an event in life: we do not live to
   experience death.
   Tractatus Logico-Philosophicus (1922)

13 The limits of my language mean the limits of my
   world.
   Tractatus Logico-Philosophicus (1922)

14 The world of the happy is quite different from that
   of the unhappy.
   Tractatus Logico-Philosophicus (1922)

P. G. Wodehouse 1881–1975
English writer; an American citizen from 1955
*on Wodehouse: see **O'Casey** 571:10; see also **Misquotations**
537:11*

15 Chumps always make the best husbands . . . All
   the unhappy marriages come from the husbands
   having brains.
   The Adventures of Sally (1920) ch. 10

16 It is never difficult to distinguish between a
   Scotsman with a grievance and a ray of sunshine.
   Blandings Castle and Elsewhere (1935) 'The Custody of the
   Pumpkin'

17 There was another ring at the front door. Jeeves
   shimmered out and came back with a telegram.
   Carry On, Jeeves! (1925) 'Jeeves Takes Charge'

18 He spoke with a certain what-is-it in his voice, and
   I could see that, if not actually disgruntled, he was
   far from being gruntled.
   The Code of the Woosters (1938) ch. 1

19 Slice him where you like, a hellhound is always a
   hellhound.
   The Code of the Woosters (1938) ch. 1

20 It is no use telling me that there are bad aunts and
   good aunts. At the core, they are all alike. Sooner
   or later, out pops the cloven hoof.
   The Code of the Woosters (1938) ch. 2

21 Roderick Spode? Big chap with a small moustache
   and the sort of eye that can open an oyster at sixty
   paces?
   The Code of the Woosters (1938) ch. 2

22 To my daughter Leonora without whose never-
   failing sympathy and encouragement this book
   would have been finished in half the time.
   The Heart of a Goof (1926) dedication

23 I turned to Aunt Agatha, whose demeanour was
   now rather like that of one who, picking daisies on
   the railway, has just caught the down express in
   the small of the back.
   The Inimitable Jeeves (1923) ch. 4

24 Sir Roderick Glossop . . . is always called a nerve
   specialist, because it sounds better, but everybody
   knows that he's really a sort of janitor to the
   looney-bin.
   The Inimitable Jeeves (1923) ch. 7

25 When Aunt is calling to Aunt like mastodons
   bellowing across primeval swamps.
   The Inimitable Jeeves (1923) ch. 16

1 It was my Uncle George who discovered that alcohol was a food well in advance of medical thought.
   The Inimitable Jeeves (1923) ch. 16

2 It is a good rule in life never to apologize. The right sort of people do not want apologies, and the wrong sort take a mean advantage of them.
   The Man Upstairs (1914) title story; see **Hubbard** 406:10

3 She fitted into my biggest armchair as if it had been built round her by someone who knew they were wearing armchairs tight about the hips that season.
   My Man Jeeves (1919) 'Jeeves and the Unbidden Guest'

4 What with excellent browsing and sluicing and cheery conversation and what-not, the afternoon passed quite happily.
   My Man Jeeves (1919) 'Jeeves and the Unbidden Guest'

5 Ice formed on the butler's upper slopes.
   Pigs Have Wings (1952) ch. 5

6 The Right Hon. was a tubby little chap who looked as if he had been poured into his clothes and had forgotten to say 'When!'
   Very Good, Jeeves (1930) 'Jeeves and the Impending Doom'

Terry Wogan 1938–
Irish broadcaster

7 Television contracts the imagination and radio expands it.
   in *Observer* 30 December 1984 'Sayings of the Year'

Christa Wolf 1929–
German writer

8 *Auf dieser Fähigkeit, Unerträgliches zu ertragen und weiterzuleben, weiter zu tun, was zu tun man gewöhnt ist, auf dieser unheimlichen Fähigkeit beruht der Bestand des Menschengeschechts.*
   It is this ability to bear what is unbearable and to go on living, to go on doing what one is used to doing—it is this uncanny ability that the existence of the human species is based on.
   Medea (1996) ch. 10, translated by John Cullen

Naomi Wolf 1962–
American writer

9 To ask women to become unnaturally thin is to ask them to relinquish their sexuality.
   The Beauty Myth (1990)

Charles Wolfe 1791–1823
Irish poet

10 Not a drum was heard, not a funeral note,
   As his corse to the rampart we hurried.
   'The Burial of Sir John Moore at Corunna' (1817)

11 We buried him darkly at dead of night,
   The sods with our bayonets turning.
   'The Burial of Sir John Moore at Corunna' (1817)

12 We carved not a line, and we raised not a stone—
   But we left him alone with his glory.
   'The Burial of Sir John Moore at Corunna' (1817)

Humbert Wolfe 1886–1940
British poet

13 You cannot hope
   to bribe or twist,
   thank God! the
   British journalist.

   But, seeing what
   the man will do
   unbribed, there's
   no occasion to.
   'Over the Fire' (1930)

James Wolfe 1727–59
British general; captor of Quebec
on Wolfe: see **George II** 343:3; see also **Last words** 473:7

14 The General . . . repeated nearly the whole of Gray's Elegy . . . adding, as he concluded, that he would prefer being the author of that poem to the glory of beating the French to-morrow.
   J. Playfair *Biographical Account of J. Robinson* in *Transactions of the Royal Society of Edinburgh* vol. 7 (1815)

Thomas Wolfe 1900–38
American novelist

15 Which of us has not remained forever prison-pent? Which of us is not forever a stranger and alone?
   foreword to *Look Homeward, Angel* (1929)

16 Most of the time we think we're sick, it's all in the mind.
   Look Homeward, Angel (1929) pt. 1, ch. 1

17 'Where they got you stationed now, Luke?' said Harry Tugman peering up snoutily from a mug of coffee. 'At the p-p-p-present time in Norfolk at the Navy base,' Luke answered, 'm-m-making the world safe for hypocrisy.'
   Look Homeward, Angel (1929) pt. 3, ch. 36; see **Wilson** 840:22

18 You can't go home again.
   title of book, 1940

Tom Wolfe 1931–
American writer

19 The bonfire of the vanities.
   title of novel (1987); deriving from Savonarola's 'burning of the vanities' in Florence, 1497

20 A liberal is a conservative who has been arrested.
   The Bonfire of the Vanities (1987) ch. 24

21 Electric Kool-Aid Acid test.
   title of novel on hippy culture (1968)

22 We are now in the Me Decade.
   Mauve Gloves and Madmen (1976) 'The Me Decade'

23 Radical Chic . . . is only radical in Style; in its heart it is part of Society and its tradition—Politics, like Rock, Pop, and Camp, has its uses.
   in *New York* 8 June 1970

Mary Wollstonecraft 1759–97

English feminist; mother of Mary Shelley
on Wollstonecraft: see Southey 749:17, Walpole 819:18

1 To give a sex to mind was not very consistent with the principles of a man [Rousseau] who argued so warmly, and so well, for the immortality of the soul.
A Vindication of the Rights of Woman (1792) ch. 3; see **Misquotations** 538:9

2 The mind will ever be unstable that has only prejudices to rest on, and the current will run with destructive fury when there are no barriers to break its force.
A Vindication of the Rights of Woman (1792) ch. 4

3 She [woman] was created to be the toy of man, his rattle, and it must jingle in his ears whenever, dismissing reason, he chooses to be amused.
A Vindication of the Rights of Woman (1792) ch. 4

4 I do not wish them [women] to have power over men; but over themselves.
A Vindication of the Rights of Woman (1792) ch. 4

5 When a man seduces a woman, it should, I think, be termed a *left-handed* marriage.
A Vindication of the Rights of Woman (1792) ch. 4

6 Taught from infancy that beauty is woman's sceptre, the mind shapes itself to the body, and roaming round its gilt cage, only seeks to adorn its prison.
A Vindication of the Rights of Woman (1792) ch. 5

7 The pure animal spirits which make both mind and body shoot out, and unfold the tender blossoms of hope, are turned sour and vented in vain wishes, or pert repinings, that contract the faculties and spoil the temper; else they mount to the brain, and sharpening the understanding before it gains proportional strength, produce that pitiful cunning which disgracefully characterizes the female mind and I fear will characterize it whilst women remain the slaves of power.
A Vindication of the Rights of Woman (1792) ch. 9

8 A slavish bondage to parents cramps every faculty of the mind.
A Vindication of the Rights of Woman (1792) ch. 11

9 Was not the world a vast prison, and women born slaves?
The Wrongs of Woman: or, Maria (1798)

10 Minute attention to propriety stops the growth of virtue.
Collected Letters (ed. R. Wardle, 1979) p. 141

Thomas Wolsey c.1475–1530

English cardinal; Lord Chancellor, 1515–29

11 Father Abbot, I am come to lay my bones amongst you.
George Cavendish *Negotiations of Thomas Wolsey* (1641); see **Shakespeare** 695:17

12 Had I but served God as diligently as I have served the King, he would not have given me over in my grey hairs.
George Cavendish *Negotiations of Thomas Wolsey* (1641); see **Shakespeare** 695:16

Kenneth Wolstenholme

English sports commentator

13 They think it's all over—it is now.
television commentary in closing moments of the World Cup Final, 30 July 1966

Mrs Henry Wood (née Ellen Price) 1814–87

English novelist

14 Dead! and . . . never called me mother.
East Lynne (dramatized by T. A. Palmer, 1874, the words do not occur in the novel of 1861)

Woodbine Willie see G. A. Studdert Kennedy

George Woodcock 1912–95

Canadian writer

15 Canadians do not like heroes, and so they do not have them.
Canada and the Canadians (1970)

Marion Woodman 1928–

Canadian Jungian analyst and writer

16 It takes great courage to break with one's past history and stand alone.
Addiction to Perfection: The Still Unravished Bride (1982)

Thomas Woodrooffe 1899–1978

British naval officer

17 At the present moment, the whole Fleet's lit up. When I say 'lit up', I mean lit up by fairy lamps.
live outside broadcast, Spithead Review, 20 May 1937
Asa Briggs *History of Broadcasting in the UK* (1965) vol. 2

Harry Woods

18 Oh we ain't got a barrel of money,
Maybe we're ragged and funny,
But we'll travel along
Singin' a song,
Side by side.
'Side by Side' (1927 song)

Clive Woodward 1956–

English rugby coach

19 The whole team was fantastic, Dad's Army kept going in extra time.
on the England team (labelled 'Dad's Army' because of its average age) in the Rugby World Cup final, Sydney, 22 November 2003
in *Weekend Australian* (online ed.) 23 November 2003

Virginia Woolf 1882–1941

English novelist
on Woolf: see **Sitwell** 738:19

1 Trivial personalities decomposing in the eternity of print.
The Common Reader (1925) 'The Modern Essay'

2 Examine for a moment an ordinary mind on an ordinary day.
The Common Reader (1925) 'Modern Fiction'

3 Life is not a series of gig lamps symmetrically arranged; life is a luminous halo, a semi-transparent envelope surrounding us from the beginning of consciousness to the end.
The Common Reader (1925) 'Modern Fiction'

4 Let us record the atoms as they fall upon the mind in the order in which they fall, let us trace the pattern, however disconnected and incoherent in appearance, which each sight or incident scores upon the consciousness. Let us not take it for granted that life exists more fully in what is commonly thought big than in what is commonly thought small.
The Common Reader (1925) 'Modern Fiction'

5 On or about December 1910 human nature changed . . . All human relations have shifted—those between masters and servants, husbands and wives, parents and children. And when human relations change there is at the same time a change in religion, conduct, politics, and literature.
'Mr Bennett and Mrs Brown' (1924)

6 A woman must have money and a room of her own if she is to write fiction.
A Room of One's Own (1929) ch. 1

7 Women have served all these centuries as looking-glasses possessing the magic and delicious power of reflecting the figure of a man at twice its natural size.
A Room of One's Own (1929) ch. 2

8 This is an important book, the critic assumes, because it deals with war. This is an insignificant book because it deals with the feelings of women in a drawing-room.
A Room of One's Own (1929) ch. 4

9 So that is marriage, Lily thought, a man and a woman looking at a girl throwing a ball.
To the Lighthouse (1927) pt. 1, ch. 13

10 Things have dropped from me. I have outlived certain desires; I have lost friends, some by death . . . others through sheer inability to cross the street.
The Waves (1931)

11 The scratching of pimples on the body of the bootboy at Claridges.
of James **Joyce**'s *Ulysses*
letter to Lytton Strachey, 24 April 1922, in *Letters* (ed. N. Nicolson and J. Trautmann, 1976) vol. 2

12 I read the book of Job last night. I don't think God comes well out of it.
letter to Lady Robert Cecil, 12 November 1922, in *Letters* (ed. N. Nicolson and J. Trautmann, 1976) vol. 2

13 As an experience, madness is terrific . . . and in its lava I still find most of the things I write about.
letter to Ethel Smyth, 22 June 1930, in *Letters* (ed. N. Nicolson and J. Trautmann, 1976) vol. 2

Alexander Woollcott 1887–1943

American writer

14 She was like a sinking ship firing on the rescuers.
of Mrs Patrick **Campbell**
While Rome Burns (1944) 'The First Mrs Tanqueray'

15 She is so odd a blend of Little Nell and Lady Macbeth. It is not so much the familiar phenomenon of a hand of steel in a velvet glove as a lacy sleeve with a bottle of vitriol concealed in its folds.
of Dorothy **Parker**
While Rome Burns (1934) 'Our Mrs Parker'

16 All the things I really like to do are either illegal, immoral, or fattening.
R. E. Drennan *Wit's End* (1973)

Dorothy Wordsworth 1771–1855

English writer; sister of William **Wordsworth**

17 One only leaf upon the top of a tree—the sole remaining leaf—danced round and round like a rag blown by the wind.
'Alfoxden Journal' 7 March 1798, in *Journals* (ed. E. de Selincourt, 1941)

18 Coleridge dined with us. He brought his ballad [*The Ancient Mariner*] finished. A beautiful evening, very starry, the horned moon.
'Alfoxden Journal' 23 March 1798, in *Journals* (ed. E. de Selincourt, 1941); see **Coleridge** 232:23

19 We saw a raven very high above us. It called out, and the dome of the sky seemed to echo the sound. It called again and again as it flew onwards, and the mountains gave back the sound, seeming as if from their centre; a musical bell-like answering to the bird's hoarse voice.
'Grasmere Journal' 27 July 1800, in *Journals* (ed. E. de Selincourt, 1941)

20 I never saw daffodils so beautiful. They grew among the mossy stones about and about them; some rested their heads upon these stones as on a pillow for weariness; and the rest tossed and reeled and danced, and seemed as if they verily laughed with the wind that blew upon them over the lake.
'Grasmere Journal' 15 April 1802, in *Journals* (ed. E. de Selincourt, 1941); see **Wordsworth** 847:5

21 We walked up to the house and stood some minutes watching the swallows that flew about restlessly, and flung their shadows upon the sunbright walls of the old building; the shadows glanced and twinkled, interchanged and crossed

each other, expanded and shrunk up, appeared
and disappeared every instant.

'Recollections of a Tour made in Scotland' 16 August
1803, in *Journals* (ed. E. de Selincourt, 1941)

Elizabeth Wordsworth 1840–1932

*English educationist; first Principal of Lady Margaret Hall,
Oxford*

1 If all the good people were clever,
And all clever people were good,
The world would be nicer than ever
We thought that it possibly could.
But somehow, 'tis seldom or never
The two hit it off as they should;
The good are so harsh to the clever,
The clever so rude to the good!

'Good and Clever'

William Wordsworth 1770–1850

English poet; brother of Dorothy **Wordsworth**
on Wordsworth: see **Arnold** *27:16,* **Arnold** *29:25,* **Bagehot**
49:11, **Browning** *160:2,* **Bulwer-Lytton** *164:4,* **Byron** *181:9,*
Byron *181:10,* **Byron** *182:11,* **Byron** *182:15,* **Byron** *184:8,*
Hazlitt *377:3,* **Jeffrey** *420:19,* **Keats** *446:6,* **Shelley** *732:6,*
Stephen *755:21; see also* **Arnold** *30:7*

2 My apprehensions come in crowds;
I dread the rustling of the grass;
The very shadows of the clouds
Have power to shake me as they pass.

'The Affliction of Margaret —' (1807)

3 And five times did I say to him
'Why, Edward, tell me why?'

'Anecdote for Fathers' (1798)

4 Suffering is permanent, obscure and dark,
And shares the nature of infinity.

The Borderers (1842) act 3, l. 1542

5 Who is the happy Warrior? Who is he
Whom every man in arms should wish to be?

'Character of the Happy Warrior' (1807); see **Read** 643:4

6 Earth has not anything to show more fair:
Dull would he be of soul who could pass by
A sight so touching in its majesty:
This City now doth like a garment wear
The beauty of the morning; silent, bare,
Ships, towers, domes, theatres, and temples lie
Open unto the fields, and to the sky;
All bright and glittering in the smokeless air.

'Composed upon Westminster Bridge' (1807)

7 Dear God! the very houses seem asleep;
And all that mighty heart is lying still!

'Composed upon Westminster Bridge' (1807)

8 The light that never was, on sea or land,
The consecration, and the Poet's dream.
on a picture of Peele Castle in a storm

'Elegiac Stanzas' (1807)

9 Not in the lucid intervals of life
That come but as a curse to party-strife . . .
Is Nature felt, or can be.

'Evening Voluntaries' (1835) no. 4

10 By grace divine,
Not otherwise, O Nature! we are thine.

'Evening Voluntaries' (1835) no. 4

11 The Mind of Man—
My haunt, and the main region of my song.

The Excursion (1814) Preface, l. 40

12 Oh! many are the Poets that are sown
By Nature; men endowed with highest gifts,
The vision and the faculty divine;
Yet wanting the accomplishment of verse.

The Excursion (1814) bk. 1, l. 77

13 What soul was his, when from the naked top
Of some bold headland, he beheld the sun
Rise up, and bathe the world in light!

The Excursion (1827 ed.) bk. 1, l. 198

14 The good die first,
And they whose hearts are dry as summer dust
Burn to the socket.

The Excursion (1814) bk. 1, l. 500

15 This dull product of a scoffer's pen.
of **Voltaire***'s* Candide

The Excursion (1814) bk. 2, l. 484

16 Society became my glittering bride,
And airy hopes my children.

The Excursion (1814) bk. 3, l. 735

17 'Tis a thing impossible, to frame
Conceptions equal to the soul's desires;
And the most difficult of tasks to keep
Heights which the soul is competent to gain.

The Excursion (1814) bk. 4, l. 136

18 'To every Form of being is assigned,'
Thus calmly spoke the venerable Sage,
'An *active* Principle.'

The Excursion (1814) bk. 9, l. 1

19 How fast has brother followed brother,
From sunshine to the sunless land!

'Extempore Effusion upon the Death of James Hogg' (1835)

20 Bliss was it in that dawn to be alive,
But to be young was very heaven!

'The French Revolution, as it Appeared to Enthusiasts'
(1809); also *The Prelude* (1850) bk. 9, l. 108

21 A genial hearth, a hospitable board,
And a refined rusticity.

'A genial hearth, a hospitable board' (1822)

22 Not choice
But habit rules the unreflecting herd.

'Grant that by this unsparing hurricane' (1822)

23 The moving accident is not my trade;
To freeze the blood I have no ready arts:
'Tis my delight, alone in summer shade,
To pipe a simple song for thinking hearts.

'Hart-Leap Well' (1800) pt. 2, l. 1

24 All shod with steel
We hissed along the polished ice, in games
Confederate.

'Influence of Natural Objects' (1809); also *The Prelude*
(1850) bk. 1, l. 414

25 Leaving the tumultuous throng,
To cut across the reflex of a star;

Image, that, flying still before me, gleamed
Upon the glassy plain.
'Influence of Natural Objects' (1809)

1 Yet still the solitary cliffs
Wheeled by me—even as if the earth had rolled
With visible motion her diurnal round!
'Influence of Natural Objects' (1809); also *The Prelude*
(1850) bk. 1, l. 458

2 It is a beauteous evening, calm and free;
The holy time is quiet as a nun
Breathless with adoration.
'It is a beauteous evening, calm and free' (1807)

3 We must be free or die, who speak the tongue
That Shakespeare spake; the faith and morals hold
Which Milton held.
'It is not to be thought of that the Flood' (1807)

4 I travelled among unknown men,
In lands beyond the sea;
Nor England! did I know till then
What love I bore to thee.
'I travelled among unknown men' (1807)

5 I wandered lonely as a cloud
That floats on high o'er vales and hills,
When all at once I saw a crowd,
A host, of golden daffodils;
Beside the lake, beneath the trees,
Fluttering and dancing in the breeze.
'I wandered lonely as a cloud' (1815 ed.); see **Wordsworth**
845:20

6 For oft, when on my couch I lie
In vacant or in pensive mood,
They flash upon that inward eye
Which is the bliss of solitude;
And then my heart with pleasure fills,
And dances with the daffodils.
'I wandered lonely as a cloud' (1815 ed.)

7 I have owed to them
In hours of weariness, sensations sweet,
Felt in the blood, and felt along the heart;
And passing even into my purer mind,
With tranquil restoration:—feelings too
Of unremembered pleasure: such, perhaps,
As may have had no trivial influence
On that best portion of a good man's life,
His little, nameless, unremembered, acts
Of kindness and of love.
'Lines composed a few miles above Tintern Abbey' (1798)
l. 33

8 That blessed mood
In which the burthen of the mystery,
In which the heavy and the weary weight
Of all this unintelligible world,
Is lightened.
'Lines composed . . . above Tintern Abbey' (1798) l. 37

9 The sounding cataract
Haunted me like a passion: the tall rock,
The mountain, and the deep and gloomy wood,
Their colours and their forms, were then to me
An appetite.
'Lines composed . . . above Tintern Abbey' (1798) l. 72

10 I have learned
To look on nature, not as in the hour

Of thoughtless youth; but hearing oftentimes
The still, sad music of humanity.
'Lines composed . . . above Tintern Abbey' (1798) l. 88

11 And I have felt
A presence that disturbs me with the joy
Of elevated thoughts; a sense sublime
Of something far more deeply interfused,
Whose dwelling is the light of setting suns,
And the round ocean and the living air,
And the blue sky, and in the mind of man.
'Lines composed . . . above Tintern Abbey' (1798) l. 93

12 All the mighty world
Of eye and ear, both what they half-create,
And what perceive.
'Lines composed . . . above Tintern Abbey' (1798) l. 106;
see **Young** 857:16

13 And much it grieved my heart to think
What man has made of man.
'Lines Written in Early Spring' (1798)

14 Milton! thou shouldst be living at this hour:
England hath need of thee: she is a fen
Of stagnant waters: altar, sword, and pen,
Fireside, the heroic wealth of hall and bower,
Have forfeited their ancient English dower
Of inward happiness.
'Milton! thou shouldst be living at this hour' (1807)

15 Some happy tone
Of meditation, slipping in between
The beauty coming and the beauty gone.
'Most sweet it is' (1835)

16 My heart leaps up when I behold
A rainbow in the sky:
So was it when my life began;
So is it now I am a man;
So be it when I shall grow old,
Or let me die!
The Child is father of the Man;
And I could wish my days to be
Bound each to each by natural piety.
'My heart leaps up when I behold' (1807); see **Milton**
534:19, **Proverbs** 616:37

17 Nuns fret not at their convent's narrow room;
And hermits are contented with their cells.
'Nuns fret not at their convent's narrow room' (1807)

18 Bound
Within the Sonnet's scanty plot of ground.
'Nuns fret not at their convent's narrow room' (1807)

19 With gentle hand
Touch—for there is a spirit in the woods.
'Nutting' (1800)

20 There was a time when meadow, grove, and
stream,
The earth, and every common sight,
To me did seem
Apparelled in celestial light,
The glory and the freshness of a dream.
'Ode. Intimations of Immortality' (1807) st. 1

21 The rainbow comes and goes,
And lovely is the rose,
The moon doth with delight
Look round her when the heavens are bare;

Waters on a starry night
Are beautiful and fair;
The sunshine is a glorious birth;
But yet I know, where'er I go,
That there hath passed away a glory from the
    earth.
'Ode. Intimations of Immortality' (1807) st. 2

1 A timely utterance gave that thought relief,
And I again am strong.
'Ode. Intimations of Immortality' (1807) st. 3

2 The winds come to me from the fields of sleep.
'Ode. Intimations of Immortality' (1807) st. 3

3 Shout round me, let me hear thy shouts, thou
    happy Shepherd Boy!
'Ode. Intimations of Immortality' (1807) st. 3

4 Both of them speak of something that is gone:
The pansy at my feet
Doth the same tale repeat:
Whither is fled the visionary gleam?
Where is it now, the glory and the dream?
'Ode. Intimations of Immortality' (1807) st. 4

5 Our birth is but a sleep and a forgetting:
The Soul that rises with us, our life's Star,
Hath had elsewhere its setting,
And cometh from afar:
Not in entire forgetfulness,
And not in utter nakedness,
But trailing clouds of glory do we come
From God, who is our home:
Heaven lies about us in our infancy!
Shades of the prison-house begin to close
Upon the growing boy.
'Ode. Intimations of Immortality' (1807) st. 5

6 And by the vision splendid
Is on his way attended;
At length the man perceives it die away,
And fade into the light of common day.
'Ode. Intimations of Immortality' (1807) st. 5

7 As if his whole vocation
Were endless imitation.
'Ode. Intimations of Immortality' (1807) st. 7

8   Thou Eye among the blind,
That, deaf and silent, read'st the eternal deep,
Haunted for ever by the eternal mind.
'Ode. Intimations of Immortality' (1807) st. 8

9 Full soon thy Soul shall have her earthly freight,
And custom lie upon thee with a weight,
Heavy as frost, and deep almost as life!
'Ode. Intimations of Immortality' (1807) st. 8

10 O joy! that in our embers
Is something that doth live,
That nature yet remembers
What was so fugitive!
The thought of our past years in me doth breed
Perpetual benediction.
'Ode. Intimations of Immortality' (1832 ed.) st. 9

11 Not for these I raise
The song of thanks and praise;
But for those obstinate questionings
Of sense and outward things,

Fallings from us, vanishings;
Blank misgivings of a creature
Moving about in worlds not realised,
High instincts before which our mortal nature
Did tremble like a guilty thing surprised.
'Ode. Intimations of Immortality' (1807) st. 9

12 Our noisy years seem moments in the being
Of the eternal Silence: truths that wake,
To perish never.
'Ode. Intimations of Immortality' (1807) st. 9

13 Hence, in a season of calm weather,
Though inland far we be,
Our souls have sight of that immortal sea
Which brought us hither,
Can in a moment travel thither,
And see the children sport upon the shore,
And hear the mighty waters rolling evermore.
'Ode. Intimations of Immortality' (1807) st. 9

14 Though nothing can bring back the hour
Of splendour in the grass, of glory in the flower;
We will grieve not, rather find
Strength in what remains behind . . .
In the faith that looks through death,
In years that bring the philosophic mind.
'Ode. Intimations of Immortality' (1807) st. 10

15 Another race hath been, and other palms are
    won.
Thanks to the human heart by which we live,
Thanks to its tenderness, its joys, and fears,
To me the meanest flower that blows can give
Thoughts that do often lie too deep for tears.
'Ode. Intimations of Immortality' (1807) st. 11

16 But Thy most dreaded instrument,
In working out a pure intent,
Is man—arrayed for mutual slaughter,
—Yea, Carnage is thy daughter!
'Ode 1815' (1845); substituted for the original 1816
version which had caused widespread offence

17 Stern daughter of the voice of God!
O Duty! if that name thou love
Who art a light to guide, a rod
To check the erring, and reprove.
'Ode to Duty' (1807)

18 Plain living and high thinking are no more:
The homely beauty of the good old cause
Is gone.
'O friend! I know not which way I must look' (1807); see
Milton 536:2

19 Once did she hold the gorgeous East in fee,
And was the safeguard of the West.
'On the Extinction of the Venetian Republic' (1807)

20 There's something in a flying horse,
There's something in a huge balloon;
But through the clouds I'll never float
Until I have a little Boat,
Shaped like the crescent-moon.
Peter Bell (1819) prologue, l. 1

21 Is it some party in a parlour,
Crammed just as they on earth were crammed—
Some sipping punch, some sipping tea,
But as you by their faces see

All silent, and all damned?
Peter Bell pt. 1, l. 541 in 1819 MS (subsequently deleted so as 'not to offend the pious')

1 Physician art thou?—one, all eyes,
Philosopher!—a fingering slave,
One that would peep and botanize
Upon his mother's grave?
'A Poet's Epitaph' (1800)

2 A reasoning, self-sufficing thing,
An intellectual All-in-all!
'A Poet's Epitaph' (1800)

3 In common things that round us lie
Some random truths he can impart,—
The harvest of a quiet eye
That broods and sleeps on his own heart.
'A Poet's Epitaph' (1800)

4   Escaped
From the vast city, where I long had pined
A discontented sojourner.
The Prelude (1850) bk. 1, l. 6

5   I recoil and droop, and seek repose
In listlessness from vain perplexity;
Unprofitably travelling toward the grave.
The Prelude (1850) bk. 1, l. 267

6 Made one long bathing of a summer's day.
The Prelude (1850) bk. 1, l. 290

7 Fair seed-time had my soul, and I grew up
Fostered alike by beauty and by fear.
The Prelude (1850) bk. 1, l. 301

8 Dust as we are, the immortal spirit grows
Like harmony in music; there is a dark
Inscrutable workmanship that reconciles
Discordant elements, makes them cling together
In one society.
The Prelude (1850) bk. 1, l. 340

9 And I was taught to feel, perhaps too much,
The self-sufficing power of Solitude.
The Prelude (1850) bk. 2, l. 76

10   To thee
Science appears but what in truth she is,
Not as our glory and our absolute boast,
But as a succedaneum, and a prop
To our infirmity.
The Prelude (1850) bk. 2, l. 211

11   The statue stood
Of Newton, with his prism, and silent face:
The marble index of a mind for ever
Voyaging through strange seas of Thought, alone.
The Prelude (1850) bk. 3, l. 60

12   Spirits overwrought
Were making night do penance for a day
Spent in a round of strenuous idleness.
The Prelude (1850) bk. 4, l. 376

13 And, through the turnings intricate of verse,
Present themselves as objects recognised,
In flashes, and with glory not their own.
The Prelude (1850) bk. 5, l. 605

14   We were brothers all
In honour, as in one community,

Scholars and gentlemen.
The Prelude (1850) bk. 9, l. 227

15   All things have second birth;
The earthquake is not satisfied at once.
The Prelude (1850) bk. 10, l. 83

16 Not in Utopia,—subterranean fields,—
Or some secreted island, Heaven knows where!
But in the very world, which is the world
Of all of us,—the place where in the end
We find our happiness, or not at all!
The Prelude (1850) bk. 11, l. 140

17   There is
One great society alone on earth,
The noble Living, and the noble Dead.
The Prelude (1850) bk. 11, l. 393

18   I shook the habit off
Entirely and for ever, and again
In Nature's presence stood, as now I stand,
A sensitive being, a *creative* soul.
The Prelude (1850) bk. 12, l. 204

19   Imagination, which in truth,
Is but another name for absolute power
And clearest insight, amplitude of mind,
And Reason, in her most exalted mood.
The Prelude (1850) bk. 14, l. 190

20 I thought of Chatterton, the marvellous boy,
The sleepless soul that perished in its pride.
'Resolution and Independence' (1807) st. 7

21 We poets in our youth begin in gladness;
But thereof comes in the end despondency and
madness.
'Resolution and Independence' (1807) st. 7

22 Cold, pain, and labour, and all fleshly ills;
And mighty Poets in their misery dead.
'Resolution and Independence' (1820 ed.) st. 17

23 Still glides the Stream, and shall for ever glide;
The Form remains, the Function never dies.
'The River Duddon' (1820) no. 34 'After-Thought'

24 Enough, if something from our hands have power
To live, and act, and serve the future hour;
And if, as toward the silent tomb we go,
Through love, through hope, and faith's
transcendent dower,
We feel that we are greater than we know.
'The River Duddon' (1820) no. 34 'After-Thought'

25   The good old rule
Sufficeth them, the simple plan,
That they should take who have the power,
And they should keep who can.
'Rob Roy's Grave' (1807) l. 37

26 Scorn not the Sonnet; Critic, you have frowned,
Mindless of its just honours; with this key
Shakespeare unlocked his heart.
'Scorn not the Sonnet' (1827); see **Browning** 159:21

27 She dwelt among the untrodden ways
Beside the springs of Dove,
A maid whom there were none to praise
And very few to love.
'She dwelt among the untrodden ways' (1800)

1 A violet by a mossy stone
Half hidden from the eye!
'She dwelt among the untrodden ways' (1800)

2 She lived unknown, and few could know
When Lucy ceased to be;
But she is in her grave, and, oh,
The difference to me!
'She dwelt among the untrodden ways' (1800)

3 She was a phantom of delight.
title of poem (1807)

4 And now I see with eye serene
The very pulse of the machine;
A being breathing thoughtful breath;
A traveller betwixt life and death.
'She was a phantom of delight' (1807)

5 A perfect woman; nobly planned,
To warn, to comfort, and command.
'She was a phantom of delight' (1807)

6 A slumber did my spirit seal;
I had no human fears:
She seemed a thing that could not feel
The touch of earthly years.
'A slumber did my spirit seal' (1800)

7 O Man! that from thy fair and shining youth
Age might but take the things Youth needed not!
'The Small Celandine' (1807)

8 Behold her, single in the field,
Yon solitary Highland lass!
'The Solitary Reaper' (1807)

9 Will no one tell me what she sings?
Perhaps the plaintive numbers flow
For old, unhappy, far-off things,
And battles long ago.
'The Solitary Reaper' (1807)

10 What, you are stepping westward?
'Stepping Westward' (1807)

11 Surprised by joy—impatient as the wind
I wished to share the transport—Oh! with whom
But thee, long buried in the silent tomb.
'Surprised by joy—impatient as the wind' (1815)

12 One impulse from a vernal wood
May teach you more of man,
Of moral evil and of good,
Than all the sages can.
'The Tables Turned' (1798); see **Bernard** 70:12

13 Our meddling intellect
Mis-shapes the beauteous forms of things:—
We murder to dissect.

Enough of science and of art;
Close up these barren leaves.
'The Tables Turned' (1798)

14 Two Voices are there; one is of the sea,
One of the mountains; each a mighty Voice:
In both from age to age thou didst rejoice,
They were thy chosen music, Liberty!
'Thought of a Briton on the Subjugation of Switzerland'
(1807); see **Stephen** 755:21

15 O blithe new-comer! I have heard,
I hear thee and rejoice:

O Cuckoo! Shall I call thee bird,
Or but a wandering voice?
'To the Cuckoo' (1807)

16 Oft on the dappled turf at ease
I sit, and play with similes,
Loose types of things through all degrees.
'To the Daisy' ('With little here to do or see', 1820 ed.)

17 Type of the wise who soar, but never roam;
True to the kindred points of heaven and home!
'To a Skylark' ('Ethereal minstrel! pilgrim of the sky',
1827)

18 Though fallen thyself, never to rise again,
Live, and take comfort. Thou hast left behind
Powers that will work for thee; air, earth, and
    skies;
There's not a breathing of the common wind
That will forget thee; thou hast great allies;
Thy friends are exultations, agonies,
And love, and man's unconquerable mind.
'To Toussaint L'Ouverture' (1807)

19 We are seven.
title of poem (1798)

20 A simple child, dear brother Jim,
That lightly draws its breath,
And feels its life in every limb,
What should it know of death?
'We are Seven' (1798)

21 The world is too much with us; late and soon,
Getting and spending, we lay waste our powers.
'The world is too much with us' (1807)

22   Great God! I'd rather be
A Pagan suckled in a creed outworn;
So might I, standing on this pleasant lea,
Have glimpses that would make me less forlorn;
Have sight of Proteus rising from the sea;
Or hear old Triton blow his wreathèd horn.
'The world is too much with us' (1807)

23 I propose to myself to imitate, and as far as
possible, to adopt the very language of men . . . I
wish to keep my reader in the company of flesh
and blood.
Lyrical Ballads (1800) preface

24 It may be safely affirmed, that there neither is, nor
can be, any *essential* difference between the
language of prose and metrical composition.
Lyrical Ballads (1800) preface

25 The Poet writes under one restriction only,
namely, the necessity of giving immediate
pleasure to a human Being possessed of that
information which may be expected from him, not
as a lawyer, a physician, a mariner, an
astronomer or a natural philosopher, but as a
Man.
Lyrical Ballads (2nd ed., 1802) preface

26 Poetry is the spontaneous overflow of powerful
feelings: it takes its origin from emotion recollected
in tranquillity.
Lyrical Ballads (2nd ed., 1802) preface; see **Parker** 586:4,
Thurber 794:3

1 Poetry is the breath and finer spirit of all knowledge; it is the impassioned expression which is in the countenance of all science.

Lyrical Ballads (2nd ed., 1802) Preface

2 Never forget what I believe was observed to you by Coleridge, that every great and original writer, in proportion as he is great and original, must himself create the taste by which he is to be relished.

letter to Lady Beaumont, 21 May 1807, in E. de Selincourt (ed.) *Letters of William and Dorothy Wordsworth* vol. 2 (revised by M. Moorman, 1969)

Henry Wotton 1568–1639
English poet and diplomat
see also **Walton** 820:19

3 This man is freed from servile bands,
Of hope to rise, or fear to fall:—
Lord of himself, though not of lands,
And having nothing, yet hath all.

'The Character of a Happy Life' (1614)

4 You meaner beauties of the night,
That poorly satisfy our eyes,
More by your number, than your light;
You common people of the skies,
What are you when the moon shall rise?

'On His Mistress, the Queen of Bohemia' (1624)

5 He first deceased; she for a little tried
To live without him: liked it not, and died.

'Upon the Death of Sir Albertus Moreton's Wife' (1651)

6 Dazzled thus with height of place,
Whilst our hopes our wits beguile,
No man marks the narrow space
'Twixt a prison and a smile.

'Upon the sudden restraint of the Earl of Somerset' (1651)

7 In architecture as in all other operative arts, the end must direct the operation. The end is to build well. Well building hath three conditions. Commodity, firmness, and delight.

Elements of Architecture (1624) pt. 1

8 An ambassador is an honest man sent to lie abroad for the good of his country.

written in the album of Christopher Fleckmore in 1604; Izaak Walton *Reliquiae Wottonianae* (1651) 'The Life of Sir Henry Wotton'

9 Critics are like brushers of noblemen's clothes.

Francis Bacon *Apophthegms New and Old* (1625) no. 64

10 Take heed of thinking, *The farther you go from the church of Rome, the nearer you are to God.*

Izaak Walton *Reliquiae Wottonianae* (1651) 'The Life of Sir Henry Wotton'

Frank Lloyd Wright 1867–1959
American architect

11 The necessities were going by default to save the luxuries until I hardly knew which were necessities and which luxuries.

Autobiography (1945) bk. 2

12 The physician can bury his mistakes, but the architect can only advise his client to plant vines—so they should go as far as possible from home to build their first buildings.

in *New York Times* 4 October 1953, sect. 6; see **Quarles** 639:4

13 The modern city is a place for banking and prostitution and very little else.

Robert C. Twombly *Frank Lloyd Wright* (1973) ch. 9

James Wright 1927–80
American poet

14 Suddenly I realize
That if I stepped out of my body I would break
Into blossom.

'A Blessing' (1963)

15 Between two cold white shadows,
But I dreamed they would rise
Together,
My black Ohioan swan.

'Three Sentences for a Dead Swan' (1968)

Mehetabel ('Hetty') Wright (née Wesley) 1697–1750
English poet

16 Transient lustre, beauteous clay,
Smiling wonder of a day.

'To an Infant Expiring the Second Day of its Birth' (1733)

17 Thou tyrant whom I will not name,
Whom heaven and hell alike disclaim;
Abhorred and shunned, for different ends,
By angels, Jesuits, beasts and fiends!
What terms to curse thee shall I find,
Thou plague peculiar to mankind? . . .
That wretch, if such a wretch there be,
Who hopes for happiness from thee,
May search successfully as well
For truth in whores and ease in hell.

'Wedlock' (*c.*1730)

Lady Mary Wroth c.1586–c.1652
English poet

18 Love, a child, is ever crying:
Please him and he straight is flying,
Give him, he the more is craving,
Never satisfied with having.

'Love, a child, is ever crying' (1621)

St Wulfstan c.1009–95
English monk and prelate, bishop of Worcester from 1062

19 We miserable people have destroyed the work of saints, that we may provide praise for ourselves. The age of that most happy man did not know how to build pompous buildings, but knew how to offer themselves to God under any sort of roof, and to attract to their example subordinates. We on the contrary strive that, neglecting our souls, we may pile up stones.

on the demolition of St Oswald's Anglo-Saxon cathedral at Worcester, the new Romanesque choir having been recently completed

William of Malmesbury *Gesta Pontificum* (Rolls series) (1870) vol. 52)

Thomas Wyatt c.1503-42

English poet

1 Farewell, Love, and all thy laws forever.
Thy baited hooks shall tangle me no more.
'Farewell, Love' (1557)

2 For hitherto though I have lost all my time,
Me lusteth no longer rotten boughs to climb.
'Farewell, Love' (1557)

3 With serving still
This have I won:
For my good will
To be undone.

And for redress
Of all my pain
Disdainfulness
I have again.
'With serving still'

4 They flee from me, that sometime did me seek
With naked foot, stalking in my chamber.
'They flee from me' (1557)

5 When her loose gown from her shoulders did fall,
And she me caught in her arms long and small;
Therewith all sweetly did me kiss,
And softly said, 'Dear heart, how like you this?'
'They flee from me' (1557)

6 It was no dream: I lay broad waking.
'They flee from me' (1557)

7 Throughout the world, if it were sought,
Fair words enough a man shall find.
They be good cheap; they cost right naught;
Their substance is but only wind.
But well to say and so to mean—
That sweet accord is seldom seen.
'Throughout the world, if it were sought' (1557)

8 There is written her fair neck round about:
'Noli me tangere for Caesar's I am,
And wild for to hold though I seem tame.'
'Whoso list to hunt, I know where is an hind' (1557)

William Wycherley c.1640-1716

English dramatist

9 A mistress should be like a little country retreat
near the town, not to dwell in constantly, but only
for a night and away.
The Country Wife (1675) act 1, sc. 1

10 Go to your business, I say, pleasure, whilst I go to
my pleasure, business.
The Country Wife (1675) act 2

11 Women and fortune are truest still to those that
trust 'em.
The Country Wife (1675) act 5, sc. 4

12 Nay, you had both felt his desperate deadly
daunting dagger:—there are your d's for you!
The Gentleman Dancing-Master (1672) act 5

13 Fy! madam, do you think me so ill bred as to love
a husband?
Love in a Wood (1672) act 3, sc. 4

14 You who scribble, yet hate all who write . . .
And with faint praises one another damn.
of drama critics
The Plain Dealer (1677) prologue; see **Pope** 602:29

15 A man without money needs no more fear a
crowd of lawyers than a crowd of pickpockets.
The Plain Dealer (1677) act 3, sc. 1

Tammy Wynette 1942-98 and Billy Sherrill c.1938-

16 Stand by your man.
title of song (1968)

Andrew of Wyntoun c.1350-c.1420

Scottish churchman

17 Quhen Alysander oure kyng wes dede,
That Scotland led in luve and le,
Away wes sons of ale and brede,
Of wyne and wax, of gamyn and gle;
Oure gold wes changyd into lede,
Cryst, borne into virgynyte,
Succour Scotland, and remede,
That stad is in perplexyte.
The Orygynale Cronykil (1795 ed.) vol. 1, bk. 7, ch. 10, l.
527

Xx

Xenophon c.428-c.354 BC

Greek historian

18 θάλαττα θάλαττα

The sea! the sea!
Anabasis bk. 4, ch. 7, sect. 24

Xerxes I c.519-465 BC

Persian monarch, King from 486 BC

19 My men have turned into women and my women
into men.
on the exploits of Artemisia at Salamis, 480 BC
Herodotus *Histories* bk. 8, sect. 88

Augustin, Marquis de Ximénèz

1726-1817
French poet

20 *Attaquons dans ses eaux*
La perfide Albion!

Let us attack in her own waters perfidious Albion!
'L'Ère des Français' (October 1793) in *Poésies
Révolutionnaires et contre-révolutionnaires* (1821) vol. 1; see
Bossuet 145:16

Yy

Isoroku Yamamoto 1884–1943

Japanese admiral, Commander-in-Chief responsible for planning the Japanese attack on Pearl Harbor

1 A military man can scarcely pride himself on having 'smitten a sleeping enemy'; in fact, to have it pointed out is more a matter of shame.
   letter, 9 January 1942; Hirosuki Asawa *The Reluctant Admiral* (1979, tr. John Bester); see **Film lines** 319:12

Minoru Yamasaki 1912–88

American architect, designer of the World Trade Center (1973; destroyed by terrorist attack in September 2001)

2 The World Trade Center should, because of its importance, become a living representation of man's belief in humanity, his need for individual dignity, his belief in the co-operation of men, and through this co-operation his ability to find greatness.
   Paul Heyer *Architects on Architecture* (1967)

William Yancey 1814–63

American Confederate politician

3 The man and the hour have met.
   of Jefferson **Davis**, *President-elect of the Confederacy, in 1861*
   Shelby Foote *The Civil War: Fort Sumter to Perryville* (1991)

Thomas Russell Ybarra b. 1880

4 A Christian is a man who feels
   Repentance on a Sunday
   For what he did on Saturday
   And is going to do on Monday.
   'The Christian' (1909)

W. F. Yeames 1835–1918

British painter

5 And when did you last see your father?
   a Roundhead officer addressing the child of a Cavalier family
   title of painting (1878), now in the Walker Art Gallery, Liverpool

W. B. Yeats 1865–1939

Irish poet
on Yeats: see **Auden** 35:3, **Auden** 35:5

6 O body swayed to music, O brightening glance,
   How can we know the dancer from the dance?
   'Among School Children' (1928)

7 A young man when the old men are done talking
   Will say to an old man, 'Tell me of that lady
   The poet stubborn with his passion sang us
   When age might well have chilled his blood.'
   'Broken Dreams' (1914)

8 The unpurged images of day recede;
   The Emperor's drunken soldiery are abed.
   'Byzantium' (1933)

9 A starlit or a moonlit dome disdains
   All that man is,
   All mere complexities,
   The fury and the mire of human veins.
   'Byzantium' (1933)

10 Those images that yet
   Fresh images beget,
   That dolphin-torn, that gong-tormented sea.
   'Byzantium' (1933)

11 The intellect of man is forced to choose
   Perfection of the life, or of the work,
   And if it take the second must refuse
   A heavenly mansion, raging in the dark.
   'The Choice' (1933)

12 Now that my ladder's gone
   I must lie down where all the ladders start,
   In the foul rag-and-bone shop of the heart.
   'The Circus Animals' Desertion' (1939) pt. 3

13 I made my song a coat
   Covered with embroideries
   Out of old mythologies
   From heel to throat;
   But the fools caught it,
   Wore it in the world's eye
   As though they'd wrought it.
   Song, let them take it,
   For there's more enterprise
   In walking naked.
   'A Coat' (1914)

14 We were the last romantics — chose for theme
   Traditional sanctity and loveliness.
   'Coole Park and Ballylee, 1931' (1933)

15 The years like great black oxen tread the world,
   And God the herdsman goads them on behind,
   And I am broken by their passing feet.
   The Countess Cathleen (1895) act 4

16 A woman can be proud and stiff
   When on love intent;
   But Love has pitched his mansion in
   The place of excrement;
   For nothing can be sole or whole
   That has not been rent.
   'Crazy Jane Talks with the Bishop' (1932)

17 Nor dread nor hope attend
   A dying animal;
   A man awaits his end
   Dreading and hoping all.
   'Death' (1933)

18 He knows death to the bone—
   Man has created death.
   'Death' (1933)

19 Down by the salley gardens my love and I did meet;
   She passed the salley gardens with little snow-white feet.
   She bid me take love easy, as the leaves grow on the tree;
   But I, being young and foolish, with her would not agree.
   'Down by the Salley Gardens' (1889)

1 She bid me take life easy, as the grass grows on
    the weirs;
But I was young and foolish, and now am full of
    tears.
    'Down by the Salley Gardens' (1889)

2 I have met them at close of day
Coming with vivid faces
From counter or desk among grey
Eighteenth-century houses.
I have passed with a nod of the head
Or polite meaningless words.
    'Easter, 1916' (1921)

3 All changed, changed utterly:
A terrible beauty is born.
    'Easter, 1916' (1921)

4 Too long a sacrifice
Can make a stone of the heart.
O when may it suffice?
    'Easter, 1916' (1921)

5 I write it out in a verse—
MacDonagh and MacBride
And Connolly and Pearse
Now and in time to be,
Wherever green is worn,
Are changed, changed utterly:
A terrible beauty is born.
    'Easter, 1916' (1921)

6 The rhetorician would deceive his neighbours,
The sentimentalist himself; while art
Is but a vision of reality.
    'Ego Dominus Tuus' (1917)

7 I see a schoolboy when I think of him
With face and nose pressed to a sweet-shop
    window.
    of **Keats**
    'Ego Dominus Tuus' (1917)

8 The fascination of what's difficult
Has dried the sap of my veins, and rent
Spontaneous joy and natural content
Out of my heart.
    'The Fascination of What's Difficult' (1910)

9 Never to have lived is best, ancient writers say;
Never to have drawn the breath of life, never to
    have looked into the eye of day;
The second best's a gay goodnight and quickly
    turn away.
    'From *Oedipus at Colonus*' (1928); see **Sophocles** 746:17

10 The ghost of Roger Casement
Is beating on the door.
    'The Ghost of Roger Casement' (1939)

11 Had I the heavens' embroidered cloths,
Enwrought with golden and silver light,
The blue and the dim and the dark cloths
Of night and light and the half-light,
I would spread the cloths under your feet:
But I, being poor, have only my dreams;
I have spread my dreams under your feet;
Tread softly because you tread on my dreams.
    'He Wishes for the Cloths of Heaven' (1899)

12 The light of evening, Lissadell,
Great windows open to the south,

Two girls in silk kimonos, both
Beautiful, one a gazelle.
    'In Memory of Eva Gore Booth and Con Markiewicz' (1933)

13 The innocent and the beautiful
Have no enemy but time.
    'In Memory of Eva Gore Booth and Con Markiewicz' (1933)

14 Soldier, scholar, horseman, he,
As 'twere all life's epitome.
What made us dream that he could comb grey
    hair?
    'In Memory of Major Robert Gregory' (1919)

15 My country is Kiltartan Cross;
My countrymen Kiltartan's poor.
    'An Irish Airman Foresees his Death' (1919)

16 Nor law, nor duty bade me fight,
Nor public men, nor cheering crowds,
A lonely impulse of delight
Drove to this tumult in the clouds;
I balanced all, brought all to mind,
The years to come seemed waste of breath,
A waste of breath the years behind
In balance with this life, this death.
    'An Irish Airman Foresees his Death' (1919)

17 I will arise and go now, and go to Innisfree,
And a small cabin build there, of clay and wattles
    made;
Nine bean rows will I have there, a hive for the
    honey-bee,
And live alone in the bee-loud glade.
    'The Lake Isle of Innisfree' (1893)

18 I hear lake water lapping with low sounds by the
    shore . . .
I hear it in the deep heart's core.
    'The Lake Isle of Innisfree' (1893)

19 Land of Heart's Desire,
Where beauty has no ebb, decay no flood,
But joy is wisdom, Time an endless song.
    The Land of Heart's Desire (1894) p. 36

20 A sudden blow: the great wings beating still
Above the staggering girl, her thighs caressed
By the dark webs, her nape caught in his bill,
He holds her helpless breast upon his breast.

How can those terrified vague fingers push
The feathered glory from her loosening thighs?
    'Leda and the Swan' (1928)

21 A shudder in the loins engenders there
The broken wall, the burning roof and tower
And Agamemnon dead.
    'Leda and the Swan' (1928)

22 Like a long-legged fly upon the stream
His mind moves upon silence.
    'Long-Legged Fly' (1939)

23 Did that play of mine send out
Certain men the English shot?
    'The Man and the Echo' (1939)

24 We had fed the heart on fantasies,
The heart's grown brutal from the fare;
More substance in our enmities
Than in our love; O, honey-bees

Come build in the empty house of the stare.
'Meditations in Time of Civil War' no. 6 'The Stare's Nest by my Window' (1928)

1 Think where man's glory most begins and ends,
And say my glory was I had such friends.
'The Municipal Gallery Re-visited' (1939)

2 Why, what could she have done, being what she is?
Was there another Troy for her to burn?
'No Second Troy' (1910)

3 I think it better that at times like these
A poet's mouth be silent, for in truth
We have no gift to set a statesman right;
He has had enough of meddling who can please
A young girl in the indolence of her youth
Or an old man upon a winter's night.
'On being asked for a War Poem' (1919)

4 Where, where but here have Pride and Truth,
That long to give themselves for wage,
To shake their wicked sides at youth
Restraining reckless middle-age?
'On hearing that the Students of our New University have joined the Agitation against Immoral Literature' (1910)

5 A pity beyond all telling,
Is hid in the heart of love.
'The Pity of Love' (1893)

6 How but in custom and in ceremony
Are innocence and beauty born?
Ceremony's a name for the rich horn,
And custom for the spreading laurel tree.
'A Prayer for My Daughter' (1921)

7 Out of Ireland have we come.
Great hatred, little room,
Maimed us at the start.
I carry from my mother's womb
A fanatic heart.
'Remorse for Intemperate Speech' (1933)

8 That is no country for old men. The young
In one another's arms, birds in the trees
—Those dying generations—at their song,
The salmon-falls, the mackerel-crowded seas.
'Sailing to Byzantium' (1928)

9 An aged man is but a paltry thing,
A tattered coat upon a stick, unless
Soul clap its hands and sing, and louder sing
For every tatter in its mortal dress.
'Sailing to Byzantium' (1928)

10 And therefore I have sailed the seas and come
To the holy city of Byzantium.
'Sailing to Byzantium' (1928)

11 All shuffle there; all cough in ink;
All wear the carpet with their shoes;
All think what other people think;
All know the man their neighbour knows.
Lord, what would they say
Did their Catullus walk that way?
'The Scholars' (1919)

12 Turning and turning in the widening gyre
The falcon cannot hear the falconer;
Things fall apart; the centre cannot hold;

Mere anarchy is loosed upon the world,
The blood-dimmed tide is loosed, and everywhere
The ceremony of innocence is drowned;
The best lack all conviction, while the worst
Are full of passionate intensity.
'The Second Coming' (1921)

13 The darkness drops again; but now I know
That twenty centuries of stony sleep
Were vexed to nightmare by a rocking cradle,
And what rough beast, its hour come round at last,
Slouches towards Bethlehem to be born?
'The Second Coming' (1921)

14 Far-off, most secret and inviolate Rose.
'The Secret Rose' (1899)

15 A woman of so shining loveliness
That men threshed corn at midnight by a tress,
A little stolen tress.
'The Secret Rose' (1899)

16 Romantic Ireland's dead and gone,
It's with O'Leary in the grave.
'September, 1913' (1914)

17 O, who could have foretold
That the heart grows old?
'A Song' (1919)

18 The woods of Arcady are dead,
And over is their antique joy;
Of old the world on dreaming fed;
Grey Truth is now her painted toy.
'The Song of the Happy Shepherd' (1889)

19 And pluck till time and times are done
The silver apples of the moon,
The golden apples of the sun.
'Song of Wandering Aengus' (1899)

20 You think it horrible that lust and rage
Should dance attendance upon my old age;
They were not such a plague when I was young;
What else have I to spur me into song?
'The Spur' (1939)

21 We Irish, born into that ancient sect
But thrown upon this filthy modern tide
And by its formless spawning fury wrecked,
Climb to our proper dark, that we may trace
The lineaments of a plummet-measured face.
'The Statues' (1939)

22 Swift has sailed into his rest;
Savage indignation there
Cannot lacerate his breast.
Imitate him if you dare,
World-besotted traveller; he
Served human liberty.
'Swift's Epitaph' (1933); see **Epitaphs** 311:10

23 But was there ever dog that praised his fleas?
'To a Poet, Who would have Me Praise certain bad Poets, Imitators of His and of Mine' (1910)

24 Red Rose, proud Rose, sad Rose of all my days!
Come near me, while I sing the ancient ways.
'To the Rose upon the Rood of Time' (1893)

1 What shall I do with this absurdity—
O heart, O troubled heart—this caricature,
Decrepit age that has been tied to me
As to a dog's tail?
'The Tower' (1928) pt. 1

2 Michael Angelo left a proof
On the Sistine Chapel roof,
Where but half-awakened Adam
Can disturb globe-trotting Madam.
'Under Ben Bulben' (1939) pt. 4

3 Irish poets, learn your trade,
Sing whatever is well made.
'Under Ben Bulben' (1939) pt. 5

4 Cast your mind on other days
That we in coming days may be
Still the indomitable Irishry.
'Under Ben Bulben' (1939) pt. 5

5 On limestone quarried near the spot
By his command these words are cut:
Cast a cold eye
On life, on death.
Horseman, pass by!
'Under Ben Bulben' (1939) pt. 6

6 When you are old and grey and full of sleep,
And nodding by the fire, take down this book,
And slowly read, and dream of the soft look
Your eyes had once, and of their shadows deep.
'When You Are Old' (1893)

7 Unwearied still, lover by lover,
They paddle in the cold
Companionable streams or climb the air;
Their hearts have not grown old.
'The Wild Swans at Coole' (1919)

8 We make out of the quarrel with others, rhetoric,
but of the quarrel with ourselves, poetry.
Essays (1924) 'Anima Hominis' sect. 5

9 Even when the poet seems most himself . . . he is
never the bundle of accident and incoherence that
sits down to breakfast; he has been reborn as an
idea, something intended, complete.
Essays and Introductions (1961) 'A General Introduction for
my Work'

10 In dreams begins responsibility.
Responsibilities (1914) epigraph

11 *of the Anglo-Irish:*
We . . . are no petty people. We are one of the
great stocks of Europe. We are the people of
Burke; we are the people of Swift, the people of
Emmet, the people of Parnell. We have created
most of the modern literature of this country. We
have created the best of its political intelligence.
speech in the Irish Senate, 11 June 1925

12 Think like a wise man but express yourself like the
common people.
Letters on Poetry from W. B. Yeats to Dorothy Wellesley
(1940) 21 December 1935; see **Ascham** 31:9

Boris Yeltsin 1931–

*Russian statesman, President of the Russian Federation since
1991*

13 You can make a throne of bayonets, but you can't
sit on it for long.
*from the top of a tank, during the attempted military
coup against* **Gorbachev**
in *Independent* 24 August 1991; see **Inge** 413:10

14 Today is the last day of an era past.
*at a Berlin ceremony to end the Soviet military
presence*
in *Guardian* 1 September 1994

15 Europe is in danger of plunging into a cold peace.
*at the summit meeting of the Conference on Security
and Co-operation in Europe*
in *Newsweek* 19 December 1994; see **Baruch** 57:16

Sergei Yesenin 1895–1925

Russian poet
see also **Last words** 472:12

16 The poet's gift is to soothe and harass,
He bears the stamp of fate.
On earth I wanted to marry
A white rose to a pitch-black toad.
'I Have One Remaining Pastime' (1923) (translated by
Gordon McVay)

17 It's always the good feel rotten.
Pleasure's for those who are bad.
'Pleasure's for the Bad' (1923) (translated by Gordon
McVay)

Yevgeny Yevtushenko 1933–

Russian poet

18 Over Babiy Yar
There are no memorials.
The steep hillside like a rough inscription.
'Babiy Yar' (1961) (translated by Robin Milner-Gulland)

19 So on and on
we walked without thinking of rest
passing craters, passing fire,
under the rocking sky of '41
tottering crazy on its smoking columns.
'The Companion' (1954) (translated by Robin Milner-
Gulland)

20 No people are uninteresting.
Their fate is like the chronicle of planets.
Nothing in them is not particular,
and planet is dissimilar from planet.
'No People are Uninteresting' (1961) (translated by Robin
Milner-Gulland)

21 Life is a rainbow which also includes black.
in *Guardian* 11 August 1987

Shoichi Yokoi 1915–97

Japanese soldier

22 It is a terrible shame for me—I came back, still
alive, without having won the war.
on returning to Japan after surviving for 28 years in

the jungles of Guam before surrendering to the Americans in 1972
in *Independent* 26 September 1997

Andrew Young 1932–
American clergyman and diplomat

1 Nothing is illegal if one hundred well-placed business men decide to do it.
Morris K. Udall *Too Funny to be President* (1988)

Edward Young 1683–1765
English poet and dramatist

2 Some for renown on scraps of learning dote,
And think they grow immortal as they quote.
The Love of Fame (1725–8) Satire 1, l. 89

3 None think the great unhappy, but the great.
The Love of Fame (1725–8) Satire 1, l. 238

4 Be wise with speed;
A fool at forty is a fool indeed.
The Love of Fame (1725–8) Satire 2, l. 282; see **Proverbs** 620:17

5 Hot, envious, noisy, proud, the scribbling fry
Burn, hiss, and bounce, waste paper, stink, and die.
The Love of Fame (1725–8) Satire 3, l. 65

6 One to destroy, is murder by the law;
And gibbets keep the lifted hand in awe;
To murder thousands, takes a specious name,
'War's glorious art', and gives immortal fame.
The Love of Fame (1725–8) Satire 7, l. 55; see **Porteous** 607:20, **Rostand** 656:16

7 How science dwindles, and how volumes swell,
How commentators each dark passage shun,
And hold their farthing candle to the sun.
The Love of Fame (1725–8) Satire 7, l. 96; see **Burton** 174:13, **Johnson** 428:18, **Sidney** 735:17

8 Tired Nature's sweet restorer, balmy sleep!
Night Thoughts (1742–5) 'Night 1' l. 1

9 We take no note of Time
But from its loss.
Night Thoughts (1742–5) 'Night 1' l. 55

10 Death! Great proprietor of all! 'Tis thine
To tread out empire, and to quench the stars.
Night Thoughts (1742–5) 'Night 1' l. 204

11 Be wise to-day; 'tis madness to defer.
Night Thoughts (1742–5) 'Night 1' l. 390

12 Procrastination is the thief of time.
Night Thoughts (1742–5) 'Night 1' l. 393; see **Proverbs** 629:41

13 At thirty a man suspects himself a fool;
Knows it at forty, and reforms his plan;
At fifty chides his infamous delay,
Pushes his prudent purpose to resolve;
In all the magnanimity of thought
Resolves; and re-resolves; then dies the same.
Night Thoughts (1742–5) 'Night 1' l. 417

14 All men think all men mortal, but themselves.
Night Thoughts (1742–5) 'Night 1' l. 424

15 By night an atheist half believes a God.
Night Thoughts (1742–5) 'Night 5' l. 176

16 [The senses] Take in at once the landscape of the world,
At a small inlet, which a grain might close,
And half create the wondrous world they see.
Night Thoughts (1742–5) 'Night 6' l. 425; see **Wordsworth** 847:12

17 To know the world, not love her, is thy point,
She gives but little, nor that little, long.
Night Thoughts (1742–5) 'Night 8' l. 1276; see **Goldsmith** 355:1

18 To know ourselves diseased, is half our cure.
Night Thoughts (1742–5) 'Night 9' l. 38

19 Devotion! daughter of astronomy!
An undevout astronomer is mad.
Night Thoughts (1742–5) 'Night 9' l. 769

20 How glorious, then, appears the mind of man,
When in it all the stars, and planets, roll.
And what it seems, it is: great objects make
Great minds.
Night Thoughts (1742–5) 'Night 9' l. 1062

21 The course of Nature is the art of God.
Night Thoughts (1742–5) 'Night 9' l. 1267

22 Life is the desert, life the solitude;
Death joins us to the great majority.
The Revenge (1721) act 4; see **Petronius** 594:4

George W. Young 1846–1919

23 The lips that touch liquor must never touch mine.
title of poem (*c.*.1870); also attributed, in a different form, to Harriet A. Glazebrook, 1874

Neil Young 1945– and **Jeff Blackburn**
Canadian singer and songwriter

24 It's better to burn out
Than to fade away.
quoted by Kurt **Cobain** *in his suicide note, 8 April 1994*
'My My, Hey Hey (Out of the Blue)' (1978 song)

Zz

Yevgeny Zamyatin 1884–1937
Russian writer

25 Heretics are the only bitter remedy against the entropy of human thought.
'Literature, Revolution and Entropy' quoted in *The Dragon and other Stories* (1967, translated by M. Ginsberg) introduction

1 Yesterday there was a tsar and there were slaves; today there is no tsar, but the slaves remain; tomorrow there will be only tsars . . . We have lived through the epoch of suppression of the masses; we are living in an epoch of suppression of the individual in the name of the masses; tomorrow will bring the liberation of the individual—in the name of man.
'Tomorrow' (1919) in *A Soviet Heretic* (1970)

Israel Zangwill 1864–1926
Jewish spokesman and writer

2 Scratch the Christian and you find the pagan—spoiled.
Children of the Ghetto (1892) bk. 2, ch. 6

3 America is God's Crucible, the great Melting-Pot where all the races of Europe are melting and re-forming!
The Melting Pot (1908) act 1

Emiliano Zapata 1879–1919
Mexican revolutionary
see also Ibarruri 412:7

4 Many of them, so as to curry favour with tyrants, for a fistful of coins, or through bribery or corruption, are shedding the blood of their brothers.
on the maderistas *who, in Zapata's view, had betrayed the revolutionary cause*
Plan de Ayala 28 November 1911, para. 10

Frank Zappa 1940–93
American rock musician and songwriter

5 A drug is neither moral or immoral—it's a chemical compound. The compound itself is not a menace to society until a human being treats it as if consumption bestowed a temporary licence to act like an asshole.
The Real Frank Zappa Book (1989)

6 Rock journalism is people who can't write interviewing people who can't talk for people who can't read.
Linda Botts *Loose Talk* (1980); see **Capp** 190:1

Zeno of Citium c.335–c.263 BC
Greek philosopher, founder of Stoicism

7 The reason why we have two ears and only one mouth is that we may listen the more and talk the less.
to a youth who was talking nonsense
Diogenes Laertius *Lives of the Philosophers* 'Zeno' ch. 7

Zhuangzi see Chuang Tzu

Mikhail Zhvanetsky 1934–
Russian writer

8 We enjoyed . . . his slyness. He mastered the art of walking backward into the future. He would say

'After me'. And some people went ahead, and some went behind, and he would go backward.
of Mikhail **Gorbachev**
in *Time* 12 September 1994; attributed

Philip Ziegler 1929–
British historian

9 Remember. In Spite of Everything, He Was A Great Man.
notice kept on his desk while working on his biography of **Mountbatten** (*published* 1985)
Andrew Roberts *Eminent Churchillians* (1994)

Ronald L. Ziegler 1939–
American government spokesman

10 [Mr Nixon's latest statement] is the Operative White House Position . . . and all previous statements are inoperative.
in *Boston Globe* 18 April 1973

Grigori Zinoviev 1883–1936
Soviet politician

11 Armed warfare must be preceded by a struggle against the inclinations to compromise which are embedded among the majority of British workmen, against the ideas of evolution and peaceful extermination of capitalism. Only then will it be possible to count upon complete success of an armed insurrection.
letter to the British Communist Party, 15 September 1924, in *The Times* 25 October 1924; the 'Zinoviev Letter', said by some to be a forgery

Hiller B. Zobel
American judge

12 Asking the ignorant to use the incomprehensible to decide the unknowable.
'The Jury on Trial' in *American Heritage* July–August 1995

13 Judges must follow their oaths and do their duty, heedless of editorials, letters, telegrams, threats, petitions, panellists and talk shows.
judicial ruling reducing the conviction of Louise Woodward from murder to manslaughter, 10 November 1997

Zohar
chief text of the Jewish Kabbalah, dating from the 13th century, presented as an allegorical or mystical interpretation of the Pentateuch

14 The Holy One, blessed be He, said to the world, when he had made it, and created man: O world, world, you and your laws can be sustained only through the Torah. That is why I created man [to live] in you, so that he might study it. But if he does not do so, I will return you to chaos.
bk. 1, 134b

1 Come and see . . . whatever is in the earth has its parallel in the world above. There is not a single thing, however small, in the world that does not depend on something that is higher . . . for everything is interdependent.

bk. 1, 156b

2 He made this world to match the world above, and whatever exists above has its counterpart below . . . and all is one.

bk. 2, 20a

3 We have taught that every man who talks of the Exodus from Egypt and rejoices fully in its narration will eventually rejoice in the *Shekinah* in the world to come, and this is the greatest joy of all.

bk. 2, 40b

4 After he had fashioned the image of the Chariot of Supernal Man, he descended into it and was known under the image of YHVH, so that man might apprehend him through his attributes, through each of them severally, and he was called El, Elohim, Shaddai, Zeva'ot, and YHVH, so that man might apprehend him through each of his attributes and perceive how the world is governed by kindness and by justice in accordance with men's deeds.

bk. 2, 42b

5 The narratives of the Torah are the garments of the Torah. If a man thinks that the garment is the actual Torah itself, and not something quite other, may his spirit depart, and may he have no portion in the world to come.

bk. 3, 152a

Émile Zola 1840–1902

French novelist

6 Don't go on looking at me like that, because you'll wear your eyes out.

La Bête humaine (1889–90) ch. 5

7 One forges one's style on the terrible anvil of daily deadlines.

Le Figaro 1881

8 Smut detected in it by moral men is theirs rather than mine. Scientific truth was my touchstone for every scene, even the most febrile.

Thérèse Raquin, preface to 2nd edition (1868)

9 *La vérité est en marche, et rien ne l'arrêtera.*

Truth is on the march, and nothing will stop it.

on the Dreyfus affair

in *Le Figaro* 25 November 1897

10 *J'accuse.*

I accuse.

title of an open letter to the President of the French Republic, in connection with the Dreyfus affair

in *L'Aurore* 13 January 1898

Zoroastrian Scriptures

a religion of ancient Persia founded by Zoroaster in the 6th century BC; texts compiled in the 4th century

translations by M. Boyce, 1984

11 We worship Mithra of wide pastures, possessing a thousand ears, possessing ten thousand eyes, the divinity worshipped with spoken name.

The Yashts yasht 10: Avestan Hymn to Mithra, v.1

12 Never break a covenant, whether you make it with a false man or a just man of good conscience. The covenant holds for both, the false and the just.

The Yashts yasht 10: Avestan Hymn to Mithra, v. 2

13 O Green One [Haoma], I call down your intoxication, your strength, victory, health, healing, furtherance, increase, power for the whole body, ecstasy of all kinds.

The Gathas yasna 9, v. 17

14 I profess myself a Mazda-worshipper, a follower of Zarathustra, opposing the Daevas, accepting the Ahuric doctrine; one who praises the Amesha Spentas, who worships the Amesha Spentas.

The Gathas The Creed (Fravarane) yasna 12, v. 1

15 This one, Zarathustra Spitama, has been found here by me, who alone has hearkened to our teachings. He wishes, O Mazda, to chant hymns of praise for Us and for Truth. So let us give him sweetness of utterance.

The Gathas yasna 29, v. 8

16 Truly there are two primal Spirits, twins renowned to be in conflict. In thought and word, in act they are two: the better and the bad. And those who act well have chosen rightly between these two, not so the evildoers.

The Gathas yasna 30, v. 3

17 I am Zarathustra, Were I able, I should be a true foe to the Deceiver, but a strong support to the Just One.

The Gathas yasna 43, v. 8

18 May truth be embodied, strong with life.

The Gathas yasna 43, v. 16

19 This I ask Thee, tell me truly, Lord. Who in the beginning, at creation, was Father of Order [Asha]? Who established the course of sun and stars? Through whom does the moon wax, then wane? This and yet more, O Mazda, I seek to know.

The Gathas yasna 44, v. 3

20 Him shall I seek to glorify for us with sacrifices of devotion, Him who is known in the soul as Lord Mazda; for he has promised by his truth and good purpose that there shall be wholeness and immortality within His kingdom, strength and perpetuity within His house.

The Gathas yasna 45, v. 10

21 They truly shall be 'saoshyants' [saviours] of the lands who follow knowledge of Thy teaching, Mazda, with good purpose, with acts inspired by truth. They indeed have been appointed opponents of Fury.

The Gathas yasna 48, v. 12

1 But the wicked, of bad power, bad act, bad word, bad Inner Self, bad purpose . . . they shall be rightful guests in the House of the Lie.

The Gathas yasna 49, v. 11

2 As the Master, so is the Judge to be chosen in accord with truth. Establish the power of acts arising from a life lived with good purpose, for Mazda and for the lord whom they made pastor for the poor.

The Gathas 'Ahuna Vairyo'

3 It is thus revealed in the Good Religion that Ohrmazd was on high in omniscience and goodness. For boundless time He was ever in the light. That light is the space and place of Ohrmazd. Some call it Endless Light . . . Ahriman was abased in slowness of knowledge and the lust to smite. The lust to smite was his sheath and darkness his place. Some call it Endless Darkness. And between them was emptiness.

Greater Bundahishn ch. 1

4 For the sake of freedom in the end from the enmity of the Adversary, and restoration, whole and immortal, in the future body for ever and ever, they [the *fravahrs* or souls of men] agreed to go into the world.

Greater Bundahishn ch. 3

5 He [the Evil Spirit] defiled the whole creation . . . So the things of the material world appeared in duality, turning, opposites, fights, up and down, and mixture.

Greater Bundahishn ch. 4

access (cont.):
not be difficult of a. · ADDA 4:3
accident A. counts for much · ADAM 2:8
a. of her birth · SHEL 732:11
chance and a. · BACO 47:4
found out by a. · LAMB 465:11
like witnessing a car a. · CANN 189:12
moving a. is not my trade · WORD 846:23
never the bundle of a. · YEAT 856:9
There's been an a. · GRAH 358:7
accidents A. will happen · PROV 614:1
A. will occur · DICK 268:23
chapter of a. · CHES 215:14
Of moving a. · SHAK 713:8
shackles a. · SHAK 680:5
accommodating a. sort of virtue · MOLI 542:2
accompany a. me with a pure heart · BOOK 127:14
accomplice a. of liars · PÉGU 591:5
accomplices we are all his a. · MURR 555:5
accomplished a. in a week · STEV 759:17
a. man · HORA 403:9
desire a. · BIBL 84:17
accomplishments a. give lustre · CHES 215:13
emerges ahead of his a. · STEI 755:11
accord a. all music makes · SIDN 736:13
sweet a. is seldom seen · WYAT 852:7
with one a. · BOOK 128:18
according a. to his abilities · MARX 516:13
a. to his strength · MORE 549:1
account give a. thereof · BIBL 96:32
sent to my a. · SHAK 685:5
accountable To whom are you a. · BENN 67:4
accounting a. for the moral sense · CARL 191:23
a. hocus-pocus · TAUZ 773:15
accounts make up my a. · MIDR 524:20
accumulate you can't a. · PROV 623:16
accuracy a. must be sacrificed · JOHN 424:1
accurately not thinking a. · HOLM 393:11
accursed think themselves a. · SHAK 693:24
accuse J'a. · ZOLA 859:10
To a. is my duty · SCHI 671:5
accused a. of child death · RICH 647:6
a. of deficiency · JOHN 430:23
before you be a. · CHAR 208:22
accuser conscience needs no a. · PROV 621:22
not my A. · NEWM 560:9
accuses excuses, a. himself · PROV 622:7
accusing a. the rest of the human race · CAMU 188:10
accustomed A. to her face · LERN 481:18
cannot get a. · TOLS 796:14
ace about to play the a. · FIEL 317:10
a. caff with a nice museum · ADVE 7:2
a. down his sleeve · LABO 462:13
Achaeans sufferings for the A. · HOME 393:17
sufferings for the A. · OPEN 574:1
well-greaved A. have suffered · HOME 393:21
Achates fidus quae tela gerebat A. · VIRG 811:1
ache ark of the a. · LEVE 482:11
Acheronta A. movebo · VIRG 813:1
achieve a. of, the mastery of · HOPK 397:11
I shall a. in time · GILB 348:4
some a. greatness · SHAK 720:32
achieved a. without enthusiasm · EMER 306:22
that cannot be a. · TRIM 798:14
achievement Great a. is assured · HEGE 379:9
achieving Still a. · LONG 490:22
Achilles A.' cursed anger · OPEN 574:1
A.' cursed anger sing · HOME 393:17
A. his armour · BROW 156:2
A.'s wrath · OPEN 574:2
A.' wrath · POPE 605:14
armour of A. · VIRG 811:6
in the trench, A. · SHAW 728:2
I've stood upon A.' tomb · BYRO 181:15
name A. assumed · BROW 156:12
see the great A. · TENN 784:19
aching A., shaking, crazy · ROCH 651:16
O a. time · KEAT 443:12
Achitophel false A. was first · DRYD 286:19
Achivi plectuntur A. · HORA 399:3

acid Electric Kool-Aid A. test · WOLF 843:21
acknowledge a. my faults · BOOK 137:10
a. thee to be the Lord · BOOK 127:20
acknowledgement a. passes for current payment · BURN 169:20
acorns oaks from little a. · PROV 621:19
acquaintance A. I would have · COWL 245:22
apology for dropping the a. · SCOT 674:14
auld a. be forgot · BURN 170:8
auld a. be forgot · OPEN 575:16
make a new a. · JOHN 433:1
make new a. · JOHN 427:22
visiting a. · SHER 733:21
acquainted a. with grief · BIBL 90:2
a. with the night · FROS 335:6
what I am not a. with · FLEM 326:17
acquisition not a personal a. · JUNG 438:8
acquitted guilty party is a. · PUBL 636:15
acre a. in Middlesex · MACA 498:9
a. of barren ground · SHAK 718:19
acres a. o' charms · BURN 171:8
few a. of snow · VOLT 815:10
few paternal a. · POPE 605:31
Three a. and a cow · POLI 601:10
Two wise a. and a cow · COWA 245:16
acrimonious a. and surly republican · JOHN 425:8
acrostic province in A. Land · DRYD 288:32
act a. but not to compete · LAO 468:8
a. of dying · JOHN 429:7
A. of Union is there · TRIM 798:17
Between the motion And the a. · ELIO 302:7
both a. and know · MARV 515:19
character of the fifth a. · LERM 481:11
easier to a. than to think · AREN 24:17
If in the first a. · CHEK 214:15
in any A. of Parliament · HERB 383:12
in itself almost an a. · ROSS 656:7
sleep an a. or two · SHAK 695:26
swelling a. · SHAK 703:14
To see him a. · COLE 234:2
wants to get inta the a. · CATC 200:17
within the meaning of the A. · ANON 18:9
acted I a. so tragic · HARG 373:12
lofty scene be a. o'er · SHAK 697:12
acting A. a masochistic form · OLIV 573:5
a. of a dreadful thing · SHAK 696:22
when he was off he was a. · GOLD 355:7
action a. Is a most dangerous thing · CLOU 227:14
A. is consolatory · CONR 240:21
a. of the tiger · SHAK 693:4
a.'s dizzying eddy · ARNO 27:26
A. this day · MILI 526:1
a. to the word · SHAK 686:23
affairs without a. · LAO 467:5
again third, 'a.' · DEMO 263:19
end of man is an a. · CARL 192:27
honourable a. · AGES 8:28
in a. how like an angel · SHAK 685:24
lose the name of a. · SHAK 686:12
lust in a. · SHAK 723:25
Makes that and th' a. fine · HERB 384:5
man of a. · GALS 338:14
Place, and A. · DRYD 290:2
point of taking no a. · LAO 468:1
single completed a. · BOIL 125:14
talents of a. · BYRO 184:5
Thought is the child of A. · DISR 277:32
world only grasped by a. · BRON 152:5
actions a. are what they are · BUTL 175:13
a. of the just · SHIR 735:4
a. of two bodies · NEWT 561:13
A. receive their tincture · DEFO 261:19
a. speak louder than words · PROV 614:2
Great a. are not always · BUTL 176:8
laugh at human a. · SPIN 752:25
my a. are my ministers' · CHAR 209:11
active a. line on a walk · KLEE 457:17
a. Principle · WORD 846:18
to seem a. · BONA 127:2
activity just a new a. · DYSO 294:19
actor a.'s life for me · WASH 822:13

Like a dull a. · SHAK 682:23
unperfect a. on the stage · SHAK 722:26
When you're a short a. · FOX 331:12
actors A. are cattle · HITC 389:19
best a. in the world · SHAK 685:28
actress a. to be a success · BARR 57:11
acts a. being seven ages · SHAK 681:9
all your a. are queens · SHAK 722:7
desires but a. not · BLAK 120:24
first four a. · BERK 69:15
no second a. in American lives · FITZ 324:9
Our a. our angels are · FLET 327:5
actual for the a. object · BOCC 125:2
What is rational is a. · HEGE 379:7
actualité economical with the a. · CLAR 224:22
actum Nil a. credens · LUCA 495:2
ad great a. campaign · BERN 71:3
reminded of that a. · MOND 542:18
adage poor cat i' the a. · SHAK 704:10
Adam A. from his fair spouse · MILT 533:8
A. Had 'em · ANON 14:19
A., the goodliest man · MILT 533:2
A. was a gardener · SHAK 694:22
A. was born hungry · BRIL 151:17
A. was but human · TWAI 803:21
good thing A. had · TWAI 803:18
gratitude we owe to A. · TWAI 803:22
half-awakened A. · YEAT 856:2
hold up A.'s profession · SHAK 688:22
in A. all die · BIBL 108:4
old A. in this Child · BOOK 132:10
Old A.'s likeness · SHAK 716:4
penalty of A. · SHAK 680:25
riverrun, past Eve and A.'s · JOYC 437:2
riverrun, past Eve and A.'s · OPEN 575:13
rubbish of an A. · SOUT 748:14
sleep to fall upon A. · BIBL 75:15
When A. dalfe · ROLL 653:3
When A. delved and Eve span · PROV 634:19
Whilst A. slept · ANON 20:2
whipped the offending A. · SHAK 692:28
adamant a. for drift · CHUR 221:1
frame of a. · JOHN 426:17
adapting right of a. my conduct · PEEL 590:15
adazzle sweet, sour; a., dim · HOPK 396:22
added all these things shall be a. · BIBL 95:10
adder a. is breathing in time with it · MAND 510:1
A.'s fork · SHAK 706:12
brings forth the a. · SHAK 696:21
deaf as an a. · ADAM 2:18
like the deaf a. · BOOK 137:24
lion and a. · BOOK 140:4
stingeth like an a. · BIBL 85:1
addeth that a. more · MARV 516:4
addicted a. to prayers · ASHF 31:13
addiction a. is bad · JUNG 438:11
prisoners of a. · ILLI 413:1
addictive sin tends to be a. · AUDE 36:14
Addison Cato did, and A. approved · EPIT 311:15
addled a. delusion · ELIO 299:18
address non-existent a. · LEWI 483:10
adeste A., fideles · ANON 21:12
adieu A., she cries · GAY 342:12
Bidding a. · KEAT 444:19
ad infinitum proceed a. · SWIF 767:11
adire a. Corinthum · HORA 399:13
adjective As to the A. · TWAI 803:25
adjectives a. are the sugar · JAME 418:12
Adlestrop Yes; I remember A. · THOM 790:11
administered Whate'er is best a. · POPE 605:6
administration a. of the government · SWIF 765:11
criticism of a. · BAGE 47:18
administrative a. won't · LYNN 497:7
admiral kill an a. from time to time · VOLT 815:11
mast Of some great a. · MILT 531:16
admirals A. extolled · COWP 247:20
admiralty price of a. · KIPL 455:18
admirari Nil a. · HORA 399:8
admiration disease of a. · MACA 498:12

against (*cont.*):
those that work a. them HALI 368:13
vote a. somebody ADAM 2:6
who can be a. us BIBL 106:22
Agamemnon And A. dead YEAT 854:21
face of A. SCHL 671:10
lived before A. PROV 616:12
When A. cried aloud ELIO 303:6
Agamemnona *ante* A. HORA 402:16
agate bigger than an a.-stone SHAK 717:15
age A. cannot wither her SHAK 679:7
a. demanded an image POUN 608:18
a., Disease, or sorrows CLOU 229:3
a. fatal to Revolutionists DESM 265:14
a. going to the workhouse PAIN 582:22
A., I do abhor thee SHAK 722:16
a. in her embraces ROCH 651:8
a. is a dream that is dying O'SH 579:2
A. is deformed BAST 58:8
a. is in, the wit is out SHAK 712:26
a. is rocking the wave MAND 510:1
A. might but take the things WORD 850:7
a. might well have chilled YEAT 853:7
a. of chivalry BURK 167:14
a. of ease GOLD 354:11
A. of Machinery CARL 191:24
a. shall not weary them BINY 116:14
a. we live in BURK 168:3
a., which forgives itself SHAW 726:32
A. will not be defied BACO 45:7
a., with his stealing steps SHAK 688:25
a. with stealing steps VAUX 808:5
be the a. I am MERW 523:4
caricature, Decrepit a. YEAT 856:1
cold a., narrow jealousy ROCH 651:4
commendation of old a. BACO 43:4
Crabbed a. and youth SHAK 722:15
dawning of the a. of Aquarius RADO 640:12
days of our a. BOOK 139:23
died in a good old a. BIBL 82:19
die in the flower of their a. BIBL 80:3
Diseases and sad Old A. VIRG 812:12
dreary old a. VIRG 814:19
Every a. DRYD 290:1
fetch the a. of gold MILT 530:22
for at your a. SHAK 687:23
good old a. BIBL 76:16
harsh a. changed my course AKHM 9:7
He was not of an a. JONS 436:3
if a. could ESTI 312:2
I meet my Father, my a. LOWE 494:12
infirmity of his a. SHAK 699:23
in the time of a. BOOK 138:21
invention of a barbarous a. MILT 531:2
labour of an a. MILT 530:14
language of the a. GRAY 361:23
my a. is as a lusty winter SHAK 680:28
nor devouring as OVID 580:15
now in a. I bud again HERB 384:8
of a. BIBL 103:14
old a. always fifteen years older BARU 57:17
Old A., and Experience ROCH 651:12
Old-a., a second child CHUR 219:21
Old a. hath yet his honour TENN 784:18
Old a. is the most unexpected TROT 800:17
Old a. should burn THOM 789:7
serene, That men call a. BROO 153:5
son of his old a. BIBL 76:37
soon comes a. SPEN 751:26
Soul of the A. JONS 435:28
Spirit of the A. HAZL 377:3
tells her real a. WILD 836:22
Their a., not Charlemagne's BROW 157:18
this a. best pleaseth me HERR 386:9
To youth and a. in common ARNO 29:6
very attractive WILD 835:24
virtuous in their old a. POPE 606:23
wealth a well-spent a. CAMP 188:3
well an old a. is out DRYD 289:15
well stricken in a. BIBL 76:18
when Mozart was my a. LEHR 479:11
with a. and dust RALE 641:11
With leaden a. o'ercargoed FLEC 326:4

worth an a. without a name MORD 547:23
wrinkled a. forefend SMAR 740:19
aged a. man is but a paltry thing YEAT 855:9
a. thrush HARD 372:15
allow this a. man his right CLOS 228:13
did the a. seem TRAH 797:16
I saw an a., aged man CARR 195:26
learn how to be a. BLYT 124:15
means Certainly a. BYRO 181:21
agenda any item of the a. PARK 586:18
agendum *quid superessit* a. LUCA 495:2
agents Civil and Political A. VICT 809:13
night's black a. SHAK 706:1
ages acts being seven a. SHAK 681:9
a. of imagination BLAK 121:12
A. to our construction went WARR 822:2
belongs to the a. STAN 754:8
different a. move PRIO 612:9
God, our help in a. past WATT 823:20
heir of all the a. TENN 781:3
Rock of A. TOPL 797:2
aggressors God loves not the a. KORA 459:13
Agincourt affright the air at A. SHAK 692:27
agitation hope and a. BARA 55:3
than to excite a. PALM 585:1
Agnes St A.' Eve KEAT 442:15
St A.' Eve OPEN 575:14
agnostic title of 'a.' HUXL 411:13
agnosticism all a. means DARR 256:19
agnus A. *Dei* MISS 539:9
agog All a. at the plasterer HEAN 377:15
agonies exultations, a. WORD 850:18
agony a. is abated MACA 499:22
am in a. CATU 203:9
Beyond is a. GREV 363:17
By thine A. BOOK 129:8
intense the a. BRON 152:19
it was a., Ivy CATC 200:15
most extreme a. BETT 73:7
My soul in a. COLE 232:25
agree a. in the truth BOOK 131:13
a. with the book of God OMAR 573:6
all things differ, all a. POPE 606:17
appear to a. PAIN 582:24
both a. is wrong CECI 204:11
colours will a. BACO 45:33
how a. the kettle BIBL 93:14
in which they a. BAGE 49:3
Two of a trade never a. PROV 633:30
agreeable power to be a. SWIF 766:24
agreed except they be a. BIBL 92:5
you a. to evil RODR 652:2
agreement a. between two men CECI 204:11
a. with hell GARR 340:10
blow with an a. TROT 800:21
have reached a. MITC 540:8
Too much a. kills CLEA 226:7
with hell are we at a. BIBL 89:4
agrestis *ille deos qui novit* a. VIRG 814:18
agri *modus* a. HORA 403:14
agriculture taxes must fall upon a.
GIBB 345:4
well-bred man than a. CICE 223:12
Ahab ran before A. BIBL 81:25
ahead get a., get a hat ADVE 7:32
Aholibah I am the queen A. SWIN 769:5
Ahriman A. was abased ZORO 860:3
a-hunting a. we will go FIEL 317:15
We daren't go a. ALLI 12:18
ail Oh, what can a. thee KEAT 443:23
what can a. thee OPEN 575:8
ailes a. de géant BAUD 58:11
ailments our a. are the same SWIF 765:18
aim a. a little above it LONG 490:6
That at which all things a. ARIS 25:13
when you have forgotten your a.
SANT 666:7
aimez a. *qui vous aime* VOLT 816:12
aiming a. at a million BROW 159:15
aimless nothing walks with a. feet
TENN 779:6
aims divided a. ARNO 28:9
ain hame to my a. countree CUNN 253:18

ain't a. necessarily so HEYW 387:15
Say it a. so ANON 18:19
air A. and angels DONN 280:11
a. a solemn stillness holds GRAY 360:24
a. broke into a mist BROW 160:18
a. Nimbly and sweetly SHAK 704:1
a. of delightful studies MILT 536:5
a. that kills HOUS 404:16
along the dusky a. COLE 233:14
conscience-stricken a. HOUS 403:19
death of a. ELIO 301:23
deep blue a. LARK 468:17
do only pierce the a. BUNY 164:12
England was too pure an A. ANON 18:6
excellent canopy, the a. SHAK 685:24
fly through the a. LEYB 484:5
fowl of the a. BIBL 75:8
fowls of the a. BIBL 95:7
I am fire and a. SHAK 680:13
In the clear a. FERG 316:18
into thin a. SHAK 719:1
lands hatless from the a. BETJ 72:6
music in the a. ELGA 299:3
nipping and an eager a. SHAK 684:23
Now a. is hushed COLL 235:11
Of a.-balloons BYRO 180:10
one that beateth the a. BIBL 107:20
or climb the a. YEAT 856:7
outlet in the a. JOHN 423:2
speak into the a. BIBL 107:27
that word, honour? A. SHAK 691:9
through the trembling a. SPEN 752:14
to the Germans that of—the a. RICH 648:2
'twixt a. and angels' purity DONN 280:13
university of the a. WILS 840:5
Where a. might wash SWIN 769:4
with pinions skim the a. FRER 333:17
airconditioning respectability and a.
BARA 55:2
airline a. ticket to romantic places
MARV 516:7
airplanes feel about a. KERR 450:2
airport observing a. layouts PRIC 610:14
airs a. and madrigals MILT 535:18
don't give yourself a. CARR 194:5
Sounds and sweet a. SHAK 718:36
airy A., fairy Lilian TENN 780:14
A. nothing, as they deemed COLE 231:4
cuts the a. way BLAK 121:11
nations' a. navies TENN 780:20
aitches nothing to lose but our a.
ORWE 577:26
Ajalon Moon, in the valley of A. BIBL 79:13
Ajax A. strives POPE 604:10
as good as A.' SHAK 683:7
Akond A. of Swat LEAR 477:2
alabaster a. box BIBL 98:27
Alamo Remember the A. SHER 734:11
alarm little a. now and then BURN 169:15
SPREAD A. AND DESPONDENCY
unnecessary a. and despondency MILI 526:7
viewed the morning with a. GERS 344:4
alarms a. of struggle and flight ARNO 27:5
alas A. but cannot pardon AUDE 36:10
A., poor Yorick SHAK 688:28
Hugo—a. GIDE 346:17
on the grass a. STEI 755:7
albatross I shot the A. COLE 232:16
Albert A. is beautiful VICT 809:9
message to A. DISR 276:24
Went there with young A. EDGA 295:13
Albion perfidious A. XIMÉ 852:20
alchemy happy a. of mind GREE 362:7
with heavenly a. SHAK 723:2
alcohol A. a very necessary article
SHAW 725:26
a. doesn't thrill me PORT 607:12
a. or morphine JUNG 438:11
a. was a food WODE 843:1
taken more out of a. CHUR 222:5
aldermen divides the wives of a. SMIT 741:3
Aldershot burnish'd by A. sun BETJ 73:1
ale a.'s the stuff to drink HOUS 405:2

bliss in a. CRAB 249:2
fed purely upon a. FARQ 315:7
good a. enough ANON 15:5
no more cakes and a. SHAK 720:19
prefer mild a. SURT 764:17
spicy nut-brown a. MILT 529:25
Aleppo husband's to A. gone SHAK 703:5
in A. once SHAK 715:1
Alexander A. oure kyng wes dede
WYNT 852:17
gane, like A. BURN 170:16
not A. ALEX 11:3
Some talk of A. SONG 748:5
Alexandria A.'s library burned HUGH 407:6
Alexandrine needless A. POPE 604:8
Alexin *pastor Corydon ardebat A.* VIRG 813:17
algebraic weaves a. patterns LOVE 493:1
alget *Probitas laudatur et a.* JUVE 439:8
alibi always has an a. ELIO 302:27
Alice A. grown lazy TATE 773:9
Christopher Robin went down with A.
MILN 527:20
Pass the sick bag, A. CATC 201:23
remember sweet A. ENGL 307:29
alien a. people clutching their gods
ELIO 302:11
a. tears will fill for him WILD 837:2
amid the a. corn KEAT 445:1
blame the a. AESC 6:10
damned if I'm an a. GEOR 343:12
fringe of a. populations NEWS 562:11
alienated any measure which a. GRIF 364:5
alienation day of mental a. RIEL 648:9
alieni *A. appetens* SALL 665:1
alienum *humani nil a me a.* TERE 785:6
alike all places were a. to him KIPL 456:14
By nature men are a. CONF 238:9
aliter *Dis a. visum* VIRG 811:20
alive a. and well ANON 17:4
a. I shall be delighted HOLL 392:18
all be made a. BIBL 108:4
Bears not a. SHAK 691:13
came back, still a. YOKO 856:22
gets out of it a. MORR 550:5
gets out a. FILM 319:21
Half dead and half a. BETJ 72:4
hallelujah! I'm a. OSBO 578:18
I am a. for evermore BIBL 112:30
If we can't stay here a. MONT 545:12
main thing, to be a. BYAT 177:11
noise and tumult when a. EDWA 296:15
no longer a. BENT 68:13
not just being a. MART 515:1
Not while I'm a. BEVI 74:7
Officiously to keep a. CLOU 229:5
show that one's a. BURN 169:24
still a. at twenty-two KING 453:4
was dead, and is a. BIBL 101:18
ways of being a. DAWK 259:14
what keeps you a. CAST 198:17
all 1066 and a. that SELL 676:15
A. by my own-alone HARR 374:3
a. for love SPEN 751:24
A. for one, one for all DUMA 291:12
a. gone out of the way BOOK 134:11
a. hell broke loose MILT 533:11
a. in respect of nothing PASC 587:4
a. men are evil MACH 502:8
A.-merciful KORA 459:7
a. must have prizes CARR 194:2
A. my pretty ones SHAK 706:24
a. our yesterdays SHAK 707:14
a. shall be well ELIO 302:2
a. shall be well JULI 438:6
A. that a man hath BIBL 82:28
A. that I am I give BOOK 133:10
a. the silent manliness GOLD 354:19
a. the world is young KING 453:1
A. things are lawful for me BIBL 107:21
a. things to all men ANON 17:7
a. things to all men BIBL 107:18
A. things were made by him BIBL 102:16
a. this for a song CECI 204:15

a. to Heaven JONE 434:11
Christ is a. BIBL 110:12
Evening, a. CATC 200:16
Fair shares for a. POLI 600:15
given Her a. on earth BYRO 179:27
have a. in all CARE 190:10
have his a. neglected JOHN 427:16
Hear a., see all PROV 622:17
it's a. right DYLA 294:6
Jack — I'm a. right BONE 127:6
Lord upholdeth a. BOOK 143:24
man for a. seasons WHIT 834:7
or a. in all TENN 778:6
we should at a. times BOOK 131:22
you were a. to me BROW 161:25
allegiance a. to the flag BELL 64:15
religious a. BAGE 47:13
to which you have pledged a. BALD 50:10
allegory headstrong as an a. SHER 733:20
things are an a. BIBL 108:27
Alleluia A.! sing to Jesus DIX 278:13
Allen love of Barbara A. BALL 51:12
alley lives in our a. CARE 191:8
rats' a. ELIO 303:14
alleys vilest a. in London DOYL 284:10
alleyways in the a. CATU 203:1
alliance A., *n.* In international politics
BIER 116:1
morganatic a. HARD 371:7
alliances clear of permanent a. WASH 822:8
entangling a. with none JEFF 420:3
allies no a. to be polite to GEOR 343:14
no eternal a. PALM 584:19
alliteration A.'s artful aid CHUR 220:4
allons *A., enfants de la patrie* ROUG 657:1
allow Government and public opinion a.
SHAW 726:7
Allsopp Guinness, A., Bass CALV 186:7
allure a. by denying TROL 800:3
alluring more a. than a levee CONG 239:15
Almack go to Carlisle's, and to A.'s too
ANST 23:3
alma mater A. lie dissolved in port
POPE 601:27
almanac as an a. out of date WALT 820:15
pious fraud of the a. LOWE 494:5
almanack Look in the a. SHAK 711:9
almighty a. dollar IRVI 414:6
A. had placed it there LABO 462:13
A.'s orders to perform ADDI 4:6
A., the King of Creation WINK 841:15
almond a. tree shall flourish BIBL 86:25
almost A. thou persuadest me BIBL 105:32
alms and oblations BOOK 131:13
a. may be in secret BIBL 95:1
puts a. for oblivion SHAK 719:22
alone adult is to be a. ROST 656:15
all a. went she KING 452:19
a. against smiling enemies BOWE 148:3
A., alone, all, all alone COLE 232:25
a. and completely unsuspecting
DANT 255:19
A. and palely loitering KEAT 443:23
A. and palely loitering OPEN 575:8
A. I did it SHAK 682:27
A., poor maid MEW 523:15
a. upon the house-top BOOK 140:18
be a. on earth BYRO 178:13
Being a. and liking it HASK 375:1
being a. together LA B 462:15
dangerous to meet it a. WHAR 831:3
go home a. JOPL 436:12
I'm all a. NURS 567:5
I want to be a. GARB 339:10
Let me a. BIBL 83:2
Let well a. PROV 625:11
live a. and smash his mirror ANON 20:16
live, as we dream — a. CONR 240:14
Lives not a. BLAK 119:18
more a. while living CARR 193:14
never a. with a Strand ADVE 3:7
never less a. ROGE 652:11
never walk a. HAMM 370:11

not sufficiently a. VALÉ 806:9
One is always a. ELIO 301:5
One is one and all a. SONG 747:11
past history and stand a. WOOD 844:16
plough my furrow a. ROSE 655:2
stranger and a. WOLF 843:15
that the man should be a. BIBL 75:14
travels a. PROV 622:5
We are not a. TAGL 771:13
We were a. JAME 418:8
when wholly a. SCIP 672:12
who travels a. KIPL 454:20
would but let it a. WALP 819:5
along All a., down along BALL 53:20
aloof a. from the congregation HILL 389:5
regards that stand A. SHAK 699:22
aloud Angels cry a. BOOK 127:20
Prayed a. AUBR 33:23
alp a. of unforgiveness PLOM 598:9
many a fiery a. MILT 532:10
Alpes *saevas curre per A.* JUVE 440:9
Alph A., the sacred river, ran COLE 232:3
Alpha A. and Omega BIBL 112:25
alpine through an A. village LONG 490:9
alps a. and archipelagoes ALDR 11:1
A. of green ice PHIL 594:15
A. on Alps arise POPE 604:3
O'er the white A. DONN 279:11
passages through the A. COLM 236:4
altar a. of God BOOK 136:16
a. with this inscription BIBL 105:18
even the a. sheds tears TALM 772:26
great world's a.-stairs TENN 779:9
high a. on the move BOWE 148:6
lays upon the a. SPRI 753:5
on his own strange a. SWIN 768:14
so will I go to thine a. BOOK 135:11
To what green a. KEAT 444:12
altars a. to the ground JORD 436:13
thy a., O Lord BOOK 139:15
alter tastes greatly a. JOHN 428:25
alteram *Audi partem a.* AUGU 37:11
alteration A. though it be HOOK 395:19
alters when it a. finds SHAK 723:22
altered a. her person for the worse
SWIF 766:17
alternative Considering the a. CHEV 217:17
alternatives a. that are not their own
BONH 127:9
exhausted all other a. EBAN 294:24
ignorance of a. ANGE 14:14
altitudo to an O a. BROW 156:24
altogether A. elsewhere, vast herds
AUDE 34:27
righteous a. BOOK 134:22
altruism conscientiousness and a.
CONF 237:15
vigorously exercises a. MENG 522:5
alway a. must be with us KEAT 442:14
I am with you a. BIBL 99:14
always a. be an England PARK 586:14
a. get their man MOTT 552:20
a. in the majority KNOX 458:7
not a. be chiding BOOK 141:2
Once a—, a. a— PROV 628:26
sometimes a. RICH 648:1
Alzheimer about his A.'s disease JUTR 439:5
from A.'s disease BAYL 59:8
he had A.'s disease REAG 643:17
on A.'s disease MURD 554:19
am a.—yet what I am CLAR 224:11
I A. THAT I AM BIBL 77:20
I think, therefore I a. DESC 265:11
Ama *A. et fac quod vis* AUGU 37:13
amantem *Quis fallere possit a.* VIRG 812:2
amaranth no fields of a. LAND 466:6
amare *amans a.* AUGU 36:25
amari *Surgit a.* LUCR 496:2
Amaryllis sport with A. MILT 530:2
amateur a. is a man who can't AGAT 6:23
a. sport DOYL 284:22
whine of the a. for three WHIS 831:20
amateurs Hell full of musical a. SHAW 726:6

a. of the Lord came upon them | BIBL 100:2
a. rides in the whirlwind | PAGE 581:13
a. should write | MOOR 547:11
a. watching an urn | TENN 781:19
ape or an a. | DISR 276:1
as the A. did with Jacob | WALT 821:4
beautiful and ineffectual a. | ARNO 29:21
better a. is a man | SHAK 723:30
clip an A.'s wings | KEAT 444:4
Death's bright a. | PROC 612:18
domesticate the Recording A. | STEV 759:25
drew an a. down | DRYD 287:20
for an a. to pass | FIRB 321:10
Her a.'s face | SPEN 751:15
in action how like an a. | SHAK 685:24
Like a.-visits, few | CAMP 187:18
Look homeward a. | MILT 530:9
mighty a. took up a stone | BIBL 114:10
ministering a. | SHAK 689:1
ministering a. thou | SCOT 673.24
O! the more a. she | SHAK 714:24
Recording A., as he wrote it down | STER 757:9
say to the A. of Death | MIDR 524:20
Shined in my a.-infancy | VAUG 807:12
What a. wakes me | SHAK 711:12
White as an a. | BLAK 122:6
woman think him an a. | THAC 786:6
wrote like an a. | GARR 340:3
angelheaded a. hipsters burning | GINS 349:15
angeli Non Angli sed A. | GREG 363:10
angels Air and a. | DONN 280:11
all the a. stood | BIBL 113:17
A. affect us | DONN 280:12
a. all were singing | BYRO 183:15
A. and Archangels | BOOK 131:22
A. and ministers of grace | SHAK 684:25
A. bending near the earth | SEAR 675:8
A. came and ministered | BIBL 94:18
A. cry aloud | BOOK 127:20
a. fear to tread | POPE 604:17
a. fear to tread | PROV 620:23
A. in jumpers | LEWI 484:3
a. in some brighter dreams | VAUG 808:1
a. keep their ancient places | THOM 791:15
a., nor principalities | BIBL 106:23
a. on the walls | MARL 513:24
a. would be gods | POPE 604:25
band of a. comin' after me | SONG 748:6
behold the a. of God | BIBL 76:30
better a. of our nature | LINC 485:3
By that sin fell the a. | SHAK 695:14
entertained a. unawares | BIBL 111:14
flights of a. | SHAK 689:16
Four a. round my head | PRAY 611:4
Fourteen a. watch | WETT 830:22
give his a. charge over thee | BOOK 140:4
glorious fault of a. | POPE 602:14
God and a. | BACO 42:21
Hear all ye a. | MILT 533:16
if a. fight | SHAK 715:19
lower than the a. | BOOK 134:5
make the a. weep | SHAK 708:1
maketh his a. spirits | BOOK 141:5
man did eat a.' food | BOOK 139:10
Michael and his a. | BIBL 113:28
neglect God and his A. | DONN 282:8
Not Angles but A. | GREG 363:10
Our acts our a. are | FLET 327:5
plead like a. | SHAK 704:5
saw a treefull of a. | BENÉ 66:15
sparkling a. | TRAH 797:16
tongues of men and of a. | BIBL 107:25
tree filled with a. | BLAK 123:3
'twixt air and a.' purity | DONN 280:13
what the a. know | NEWM 560:19
Where a. tremble | GRAY 361:19
With a. round the throne | WATT 823:13
women are a. | BYRO 183:13
Ye holy a. bright | GURN 366:3
anger Achilles' cursed a. | OPEN 574:1
Achilles' cursed a. sing | HOME 393:17
A. and jealousy | ELIO 300:11

A. is a short madness | HORA 399:6
A. is never without an argument | HALI 368:15
a. is not turned away | BIBL 88:9
A. is one of the sinews | FULL 337:5
A. makes dull men | BACO 46:22
a. of his lip | SHAK 721:2
a. of men who have no opinions | CHES 216:23
a. of the sovereign | MORE 548:13
A. supplies the arms | VIRG 810:19
Frozen a. | FREU 334:7
Great a. in the dragon | SUTT 765:1
Juno's never-forgetting a. | VIRG 810:15
lamb That carries a. | SHAK 698:19
life of telegrams and a. | FORS 329:15
Look back in a. | OSBO 578:17
monstrous a. of the guns | OWEN 581:1
more in sorrow than in a. | SHAK 684:12
neither a. nor partiality | TACI 770:7
neither keepeth he his a. | BOOK 141:2
slow to a. | BIBL 84:27
strike it in a. | SHAW 726:23
such great a. | VIRG 810:16
sun go down on your a. | PROV 627:22
your a. and your energy | IACO 412:6
angle a.-faced, Dreary mouthed | HUNT 409:16
Brother of the A. | WALT 820:18
Give me mine a. | SHAK 679:11
in every a. greet | MARV 515:11
angler excellent a. | WALT 820:21
if he be an honest a. | WALT 820:17
no man is born an a. | WALT 820:16
anglers too good for any but a. | WALT 820:26
angles Bats not a. | THOM 790:23
Not A. but Angels | GREG 363:16
Offer no a. | TESS 786:3
Angli Non A. sed Angeli | GREG 363:10
angling A. may be said to be | WALT 820:14
be quiet and go a-A. | WALT 821:3
Anglo-Irishman He was an A. | BEHA 63:12
Anglo-Saxon A. attitudes | CARR 195:20
idol of the A. | BAGE 48:4
angry a. at a slander | JONS 435:1
a. nearly every day | ALCO 10:9
a. with my friend | BLAK 122:16
A. young man | PAUL 589:2
Be ye a. | BIBL 109:13
hungry man is an a. man | PROV 622:37
man who becomes a. | TALM 772:13
O! when she's a. | SHAK 711:16
When he was a. | BECK 61:29
when very a., swear | TWAI 803:24
anguis Latet a. in herba | VIRG 813:22
anguish howls of a. | HEAL 377:10
With a. moist | KEAT 443:24
angusta Res a. domi | JUVE 439:17
anima Swift was a. Rabelaisii | COLE 234:6
animae A. dimidium meae | HORA 400:3
animal a. he studied less | GOSS 357:7
attend a dying a. | YEAT 853:17
Be a good a. | LAWR 474:24
be a good a. | SPEN 750:5
every a. is sad | SAYI 670:11
Man is a noble a. | BROW 156:18
Man is the Only A. | TWAI 803:10
only a. in the world to fear | LAWR 475:4
political a. | ARIS 25:25
pure a. spirits | WOLL 844:7
religious a. | BURK 167:20
so very a. and unecstatic | VICT 809:10
vegetable, a., and mineral | GILB 348:28
Was he an a. | KAFK 440:19
animalculous beings a. | GILB 348:28
animals All a. are equal | ORWE 577:1
a. are divided | BORG 145:5
A., whom we have | DARW 257:13
at its mercy: a. | KUND 462:7
distinguishes us from mere a. | LEIB 479:14
distinguish us from other a. | BEAU 60:2
find the a. amusing | NIET 564:3
man from a. | OSLE 579:7
mind of the lower a. | DARW 257:15

minutely small a. | JAIN 416:19
not over-fond of a. | ATTE 32:21
production of the higher a. | DARW 257:10
soft little a. pottering | CASS 198:16
takes 40 dumb a. | SLOG 740:5
turn and live with a. | WHIT 833:13
animam Liberavi a. meam | BERN 70:14
animate a. the whole | SMIT 743:26
animated all a. nature | COLE 231:14
animation too old for a. | DISN 275:2
animi natura a. | LUCR 495:16
vivida vis a. | LUCR 495:9
animosity sisterly a. | SURT 764:22
animula A. vagula blandula | HADR 366:10
animum Caelum non a. mutant | HORA 399:10
Anjou sweetness of A. | DU B 290:19
Ann that's little A. | NURS 567:18
Anna Here thou, great A. | POPE 606:10
Annabel Lee I and my A. | POE 598:18
annals a. are blank | MONT 545:11
a. of the poor | GRAY 361:3
War's a. will cloud | HARD 372:21
Anne of A. of Cleves | HENR 382:6
sister A., do you see nothing | PERR 592:26
Annie bonnie A. Laurie | SONG 748:1
annihilate a. but space and time | POPE 605:30
annihilated illimitable a. was a. | DISR 275:18
annihilating a. all civilization | SAKH 663:11
A. all that's made | MARV 515:17
annihilation a. of one of us | SHEL 728:9
my own a. | GUNN 365:18
anniversaries secret a. | LONG 490:12
Anno Domini only a. | HILT 389:7
annoy a. with what you write | AMIS 13:17
only does it to a. | CARR 194:7
annoyance a. of a good example | TWAI 803:26
source of a. | BAED 47:7
annuity a. is a very serious business | AUST 40:6
annus a. horribilis | ELIZ 305:3
motet a. et almum | HORA 402:12
anointed a. my head with oil | BOOK 135:4
balm from an a. king | SHAK 715:19
anointing Thou the a. Spirit art | BOOK 144:13
anorak a. grow big with jotters | MAXW 519:4
another always a. one walking | ELIO 303:23
a. fine mess | LAUR 470:8
a. shall gird thee | BIBL 104:22
in a. country | MARL 513:15
members one of a. | BIBL 109:12
not a. thing | BUTL 175:12
when comes such a. | SHAK 698:8
anser inter strepere a. olores | VIRG 814:9
answer A. a fool | BIBL 85:8
a. came there none | CARR 195:8
a. came there none | SCOT 673:2
a. is blowin' in the wind | DYLA 294:3
a. is 'himself' | IBSE 412:15
a. made it none | SHAK 684:11
a. the phone | CART 198:10
a. to 'Hi!' | CARR 196:6
a. to the Irish Question | SELL 676:25
on the way to a pertinent a. | BRON 152:6
please thee with my a. | SHAK 709:22
sent an a. back to me | CARR 195:19
soft a. | BIBL 84:22
soft a. turneth | PROV 631:2
stay for an a. | BACO 45:29
what a dusty a. | MERE 522:22
What is the a. | LAST 474:14
wise men cannot a. | PROV 620:20
wisest man can a. | COLT 236:9
answerable a. for what we choose | NEWM 561:7
answerably a. to your Christian calling | BOOK 132:11
answered hath Caesar a. it | SHAK 697:22
no one a. | DE L 263:3
prayer is only a. | TALM 772:18
answering a. that of God | FOX 331:9
bell-like a. | WORD 845:19
answers Kind are her a. | CAMP 188:6
Science offers best a. | DAWK 259:17

experience is an a. ADAM 2:10
like a triumphal a. DUNN 292:12
triumphant a. COMM 236:15
archangel A. a little damaged LAMB 465:7
archangels Angels and A. BOOK 131:22
archbishop a. had come to see me OPEN 574:27
love to the A. SHER 734:8
My Lord A. BULL 163:17
archdeacon (by way of turbot) an a. SMIT 743:16
archer a. his sharp arrows SIDN 736:4
mark the A. little meant SCOT 673:14
arches down the a. of the years THOM 791:7
Underneath the A. FLAN 324:14
archetypes known as a. JUNG 438:8
archipelago Gulag a. SOLZ 745:15
archipelagoes alps and a. ALDR 11:1
architect a. can only advise WRIG 851:12
a. of own fortune PROV 619:17
A. of the Universe JEAN 419:8
artist or an a. GEHR 342:16
can be an a. RUSK 659:10
consent to be the a. DOST 283:4
architects great a. LUTY 496:16
So a. do square and hew MARV 515:12
architectural a. books PUGI 636:24
a. man-milliner RUSK 659:7
great a. secret TROL 799:7
architecture A. acts the most slowly DIMN 274:14
A. at the head BLOM 124:1
A. in general SCHE 668:12
A. is the art JOHN 423:20
a., the ancients CHAM 206:17
Christian A. PUGI 636:22
Dim a. WARR 822:2
frolic a. of the snow EMER 306:15
Gothic a. RUSK 660:13
great a. LUTY 496:16
In a. as in all other WOTT 851:7
rise and fall of English a. BETJ 73:6
archwives Ye a., stondeth CHAU 211:5
Arcturi Daisies, those pearled A. SHEL 731:13
Arden Ay, now am I in A. SHAK 681:1
ardet paries cum proximus a. HORA 399:15
ardeur a. dans mes veines RACI 640:5
ardua a. ad astra MOTT 552:15
arduis rebus in a. HORA 401:2
are A. you now POLI 600:3
be as they a. CLEM 226:14
we know what we a. SHAK 688:7
arena actually in the a. ROOS 654:12
Argentinian young A. soldiers RUNC 658:12
Argos remembers his sweet A. VIRG 813:9
argosies a. of magic sails TENN 780:20
argue absurd to a. men NEWM 560:18
a. freely MILT 535:24
cannot a. with AUCT 34:5
earth does not a. WHIT 833:20
arguing no good in a. LOWE 494:6
not a. with you WHIS 831:16
will be much a. MILT 535:23
argument All a. is against it JOHN 430:28
a. for a week SHAK 690:1
a. of the broken window PANK 585:9
a. of tyrants PITT 596:10
exact and priggish a. SAND 665:15
height of this great a. MILT 531:6
I have found you an a. JOHN 432:17
impression, not an a. HARD 372:2
never without an a. HALI 368:15
nice knock-down a. CARR 195:15
no a. but force BROW 157:14
no force but a. BROW 157:14
rotten a. ANON 19:12
stir without great a. SHAK 688:4
argumentative then talky, then a. BYRO 184:7
arguments attract the worst a. FISH 322:19

force of his a. WALP 819:21
argutos a. inter strepere VIRG 814:9
Ariel Caliban casts out A. POUN 608:19
deal of A. HENL 381:13
aright sought the Lord a. BURN 170:20
arise a. and go like men STEV 760:6
a. and unbuild it again SHEL 729:6
A., shine BIBL 90:17
My lady sweet, a. SHAK 682:30
will a. and go now YEAT 854:17
arising from the a. of this PALI 583:19
aristocracy a. means government by CHES 217:15
a. of Great Britain BRIG 151:8
A. of the moneybag CARL 192:10
called a. PAIN 582:17
displeased with a. HOBB 390:20
natural a. among men JEFF 420:10
aristocratic a. class ARNO 29:10
Aristotle A. and his philosophie CHAU 210:17
A. was but the rubbish SOUT 748:14
God of A. HA-L 368:10
arithmetic theology as in a. MILT 535:20
arithmetical a. ratio MALT 509:9
ark a. of bulrushes BIBL 77:13
entered into the a. BIBL 98:18
into the A. BIBL 76:6
two by two in the a. LEVE 482:11
arm a. of the Lord BIBL 90:1
auld moon in her a. BALL 53:5
by a stretched out a. BIBL 78:25
crowns my a. DONN 280:25
did not put your a. around it BLAC 118:6
long a. of coincidence CHAM 206:15
pearls upon an Ethiop's a. DYER 293:17
strength with his a. BIBL 99:32
Stretch your a. no further PROV 631:28
with his holy a. BOOK 140:13
arma A. virumque cano OPEN 574:3
A. virumque cano VIRG 810:15
Cedant a. togae CICE 223:13
leges inter a. CICE 223:21
Moriamur et in media a. ruamus VIRG 811:19
armadas till the great A. come NEWB 560:2
Armageddon called in the Hebrew tongue A. BIBL 114:7
Lincoln County Road or A. DYLA 294:14
We stand at A. ROOS 654:13
armaments not a. that cause wars MADA 505:8
armchair like a good a. MATI 518:12
armchairs a. tight about the hips WODE 843:3
armed a. conflict EDEN 295:10
A. neutrality is ineffectual WILS 840:21
a. so strong in honesty SHAK 698:16
A. warfare must be preceded ZINO 858:11
a. with more than complete steel ANON 16:19
own mind you need to be a. VALÉ 806:11
Armenteers Mademoiselle from A. MILI 526:14
armes Aux a., citoyens ROUG 657:1
armful very nearly an a. GALT 338:16
armies a. clash by night ARNO 27:5
a. swore terribly STER 757:3
commander of three a. CONF 238:1
disbanding hired a. CARL 192:23
Kings with their a. BOOK 138:12
money and large a. ANOU 22:15
stronger than all the a. SAYI 670:14
Arminian A. clergy PITT 596:5
armistice It is an a. for twenty years FOCH 327:23
armour Achilles his a. BROW 156:2
a. of Achilles VIRG 811:16
a. of God BIBL 109:20
a. of light BIBL 106:32
a. of light BOOK 129:22
put your a. on WESL 829:5

spend so much in a. SHEN 733:3
armoured a. cars of dreams BISH 117:7
arms Anger supplies the a. VIRG 810:19
a. against a sea of troubles SHAK 686:9
a. and the man OPEN 574:3
a. and the man VIRG 810:15
A., and the man I sing DRYD 289:34
A. and the man I sing OPEN 574:4
a. do flourish BACO 45:35
a. of a chambermaid JOHN 431:10
a. were made the Warrior RIG 648:12
a. ye forge SHEL 731:18
caught in her a. WYAT 852:5
Emparadised in one another's a. MILT 533:3
everlasting a. BIBL 79:5
he laid down his a. HOOD 394:25
if my love were in my a. ANON 19:19
in my a. BALL 52:6
it hath very long a. HALI 369:2
keep and bear a. CONS 241:14
Kings have long a. PROV 624:42
man's outspread a. LEON 481:6
mightier than they in a. MILT 533:20
proud in a. MILT 528:19
This world in a. EISE 298:13
Those entrusted with a. WIND 841:12
To war and a. LOVE 493:7
world in a. SHAK 699:16
army a. marches on its stomach NAPO 557:1
a. marches on its stomach PROV 614:31
a. of Martyrs BOOK 127:20
a. of unalterable law MERE 522:20
a. would be a base rabble BURK 166:31
command an a. SHER 734:12
contemptible little a. ANON 15:24
Dad's A. kept going WOOD 844:19
dialect with an a. WEIN 826:23
Forgotten A. MOUN 551:16
formation of an Irish a. GRIF 364:7
invasion by an a. HUGO 407:17
little ships brought the A. home GUED 365:10
terrible as an a. BIBL 87:17
Your poor a. CROM 252:6
aroint A. thee, witch SHAK 703:5
aroma a. of performing seals HART 374:11
rose in a. pain WINC 841:9
aromatic beneath the a. pain POPE 604:27
arose a. and followed him BIBL 96:4
around goes a. comes around SAYI 670:18
aroused a. every feeling TAYL 774:8
a-roving go no more a. SONG 747:1
arrange French a. CATH 199:8
arrangements has no a. WHIT 833:20
arrears pay glad life's a. BROW 161:2
arrest a. all beauty CAME 186:16
swift in his a. SHAK 689:11
arrested a. one fine morning OPEN 575:19
conservative been a. WOLF 843:20
arrival a. was most welcome NELS 558:16
arrive A. or find THOM 791:2
a. where I am BUNY 165:9
a. where we started ELIO 301:25
barbarians are to a. CAVA 203:17
better thing than to a. STEV 759:20
arrived a. and to prove it CATC 201:11
arrogant subdue the a. VIRG 812:15
arrow a. from the Almighty's bow BLAK 120:11
a.-head of grieving PALI 584:16
a. that flieth by day BOOK 140:3
Every a. that flies LONG 490:6
shot an a. LONG 490:1
shot mine a. SHAK 689:8
time's a. EDDI 295:2
arrows archer his sharp a. SIDN 736:4
a. of desire BLAK 121:5
Like as the a. BOOK 143:2
mine a. upon them BIBL 79:4
slings and a. SHAK 686:9
swift a. in my quiver PIND 595:12

ars *A. longa, vita brevis* — HIPP 389:9
arse politician is an a. upon — CUMM 253:9
arsenal a. of old Europe — HEGE 379:5
  great a. of democracy — ROOS 653:19
arsenic like a. — FIEL 318:11
art adulteries of a. — JONS 435:5
  Advertising is the greatest a. form — MCLU 503:17
  All a. was modern once — SERO 677:5
  All great a. has come from — PAGL 581:17
  all the rules of a. — ADDI 5:13
  almost lost in a. — COLL 235:16
  A. alone Enduring stays — DOBS 278:15
  A. always serves beauty — PAST 588:1
  A. and Religion are two roads — BELL 66:4
  A., and the summer lightning — HERZ 386:25
  A. a revolt against fate — MALR 509:8
  a. can wash her guilt away — GOLD 355:33
  A. constantly aspires — PATE 588:10
  A. does not reproduce the visible — KLEE 457:16
  A. for art's sake — CONS 241:10
  a. for art's sake — COUS 244:12
  A. for art's sake — DIET 274:7
  a. for the sake — SAND 665:16
  a. has no other end — FLAU 325:16
  A. has something to do — BELL 66:2
  A. has to move you — HOCK 391:7
  A. in its perfection — REYN 646:7
  a. is a comparable vocation — FRIN 334:18
  A. is a jealous mistress — EMER 306:19
  A. is an abstraction — GAUG 340:23
  A. is born of humiliation — AUDE 36:18
  a. is but a vision of reality — YEAT 854:6
  a. is immoral — WILD 836:1
  A. is long — LONG 490:19
  A. is long — PROV 614:32
  A. is meant to disturb — BRAQ 149:17
  A. is not a *brassière* — BARN 56:8
  A. is not a weapon — KENN 449:6
  a. is not truth — PICA 595:10
  A. is only Nature — HOLB 392:11
  A. is pattern informed by sensibility — READ 643:2
  A. is significant deformity — FRY 336:18
  A. is the imposing of a pattern — WHIT 832:14
  A. is the objectification — LANG 466:13
  A. is upon the Town — WHIS 831:17
  A. is vice — DEGA 261:29
  A. most cherishes — BROW 160:12
  a. of balance — MATI 518:12
  a. of being wise — JAME 418:20
  a. of getting drunk — JOHN 431:13
  a. of the possible — BISM 117:14
  a. of the possible — GALB 338:7
  a. of the soluble — MEDA 520:5
  a.'s hid causes — JONS 435:4
  a. which one government sooner — SMIT 741:12
  A., whose honesty must work — RIDI 648:5
  beyond the reach of a. — POPE 604:1
  clever, but is it A. — KIPL 453:19
  dead a. Of poetry — POUN 608:17
  Deals are my a. form — TRUM 801:16
  Desiring this man's a. — SHAK 722:29
  detective novel is a.-for-art's-sake — PRIT 612:14
  Dying is an a. — PLAT 597:1
  E in A-level a. — HIRS 389:18
  end and test of a. — POPE 603:31
  enemy of good a. — CONN 240:3
  example of modern a. — CHUR 222:21
  fascinating kind of a. — WARH 821:17
  Fine a. is that — RUSK 660:3
  first taught A. — ROSS 656:4
  from a., not chance — POPE 604:9
  genius and a. — HAZL 376:20
  glib and oily a. — SHAK 699:20
  good grey guardians of a. — WILB 835:6
  great design of a. — DENN 264:14
  great religious a. of the world — CLAR 225:1
  have learned their a. — PIND 595:12
  Here the great a. lies — MILT 535:17

history of a. — BUTL 176:29
If a. does not enlarge — ELIO 300:23
In a. the best is good enough — GOET 353:5
industry without a. — RUSK 659:11
in Jonson, A. — DENH 264:6
is the a. of God — YOUN 857:21
it is not a. — SCHO 671:14
last and greatest a. — GOET 353:17
last and greatest a. — POPE 605:24
Life imitates A. — WILD 836:3
Life is short, the a. long — HIPP 389:9
madness of a. — JAME 417:23
Minister that meddles with a. — MELB 520:17
morality of a. — WILD 836:13
More matter with less a. — SHAK 685:17
my job and my a. — MONT 544:12
nature is the a. of God — BROW 156:28
nature's handmaid is a. — DRYD 287:25
Nature that is above all a. — DANI 255:4
necessary a. — DULL 291:10
never was an A.-loving nation — WHIS 831:18
next to Nature, A. — LAND 466:2
noblest point of a. — EPIT 309:6
offered you Conflict and A. — PRIE 610:19
only interested in a. — SHAW 727:26
people start on all this A. — HERB 383:8
practical form of a. — COOP 242:13
probité de l'a. — INGR 413:19
purpose of a. — GOUL 357:9
rank of every a. — REYN 646:4
responsibility is to his a. — FAUL 316:5
Robust a. alone is eternal — GAUT 341:2
Shakespeare wanted a. — JONS 436:7
stick to murder and leave a. — EPST 308:9
Story the spoiled child of a. — JAME 417:13
supreme master of a. — CONR 240:24
symbol of Irish a. — JOYC 437:15
through A., and through Art only — WILD 835:28
true test of a. — INGR 413:19
War's glorious a. — YOUN 857:6
what a. means to me — O'KE 572:18
what great a. removes — BOLA 126:2
when A. Is too precise — HERR 385:21
where the a. resides — SCHN 671:12
work of a. — SMIT 741:15
works of a. — ALBE 10:6
Works of a. — RILK 648:18
artful a. Dodger — DICK 271:10
Arthur in A.'s bosom — SHAK 693:1
  talks of A.'s death — SHAK 699:11
article excellent a. — BAGE 49:8
  first a. of my faith — GAND 339:7
  snuffed out by an a. — BYRO 181:27
articles These a. subscribed — CONG 239:17
articulate made a. all that I saw — BROW 154:19
artifact Death's a. — ABSE 1:5
artificer great a. Made my mate — STEV 760:13
  lean unwashed a. — SHAK 699:11
artificial All things are a. — BROW 156:28
  but an a. man — HOBB 390:7
  said it was a. respiration — BURG 165:16
  sort of a. inlet — FOST 330:9
artillery a. of words — SWIF 767:4
  love's great a. — CRAS 250:14
  terrible a. — FLAT 324:20
artisan employment to the a. — BELL 65:16
artist a. is a receptacle — PICA 595:5
  a. brings something into — UPDI 805:23
  a. has a way of working — ATWO 33:10
  a. has no need to express — PROU 613:10
  a. is his own fault — O'HA 571:16
  a. is someone who — WARH 821:18
  a. man and the mother woman — SHAW 726:3
  a. must be in his work — FLAU 325:14
  a. never dies — LONG 490:16
  a. or an architect — GEHR 342:16
  a. remains within or behind — JOYC 437:11
  a. will be judged — CONN 240:8
  become a good a. by copying — INGR 413:20
  enemies to a real a. — GAIN 337:13
  God only another a. — PICA 595:8

Industry, Which dignifies the a. — DYER 293:15
Never trust the a. — LAWR 474:23
No a. should ever marry — DELI 263:11
no man is born an a. — WALT 820:16
one position for an a. — THOM 790:3
portrait of the a. — JOYC 437:7
sign of a true a. — VIDA 810:3
task of the a. — BECK 61:11
What an a. dies — LAST 473:14
artistic a. verisimilitude — GILB 348:8
  never was an a. period — WHIS 831:18
artists A. not engineers of the soul — KENN 449:6
arts a. at first from Nature came — LANI 467:2
  a. babblative and scribblative — SOUT 749:10
  cry both a. and learning — QUAR 639:5
  Dear nurse of a. — SHAK 694:4
  followed the a. — SHAK 720:9
  France, famed in all great a. — ARNO 29:1
  France, mother of a. — DU B 290:17
  head of the a. — BLOM 124:1
  interested in the a. — AYCK 41:4
  In the a. of life — SHAW 726:9
  mother of a. — MILT 534:20
  No a.; no letters — HOBB 390:16
  one of the fine a. — DE Q 265:1
  recreation in the a. — CONF 237:21
  studied the liberal a. — OVID 580:5
  virtues were his a. — BURK 169:11
  you 'a.' people — MCEW 501:14
artus *totamque infusa per a.* — VIRG 812:14
Aryan your A. eye — PLAT 596:20
ascend that would a. — OPEN 575:7
ascendancy a. of the Whig party — MACA 498:13
ascended a. into heaven — BOOK 128:10
ascendeth a. up for ever and ever — BIBL 114:3
ascending angels of God a. — BIBL 76:30
  lark a. — MERE 522:18
ascribe A. unto the Lord — BOOK 140:11
ash a. on an old man's sleeve — ELIO 301:22
  avoid an a. — PROV 615:35
  empty a. can — CRAN 249:25
  Oak, and A., and Thorn — KIPL 455:23
  oak is before the a. — PROV 634:32
  Out of the a. — PLAT 597:2
ashamed a. and confounded — BOOK 138:19
  a. thereof — BROW 157:1
  a. to look upon one another — WALT 820:22
  feel a. of home — DICK 269:16
  Government of whom I am a. — JACK 415:2
  men are a. of — GAY 342:8
  more things a man is a. of — SHAW 726:1
  something he is a. of — SHAW 724:20
ashbuds a. in the front of March — TENN 777:2
ashen in oure a. olde — CHAU 212:7
  Your a. hair Shulamith — CELA 205:1
ashes a. for thirty — LAMP 465:20
  a. new-create — SHAK 695:25
  a. of an Oak — DONN 282:5
  a. of his fathers — MACA 499:13
  a. on the lips — MOOR 547:21
  a. taken to Australia — ANON 16:20
  a. to ashes — BOOK 133:18
  a. to the taste — BYRO 178:22
  a. under Uricon — HOUS 404:14
  beauty for a. — BIBL 90:19
  burnt to a. — GRAH 358:8
  Dust and a. — BROW 161:22
  I am a. — BYRO 183:12
  into a. all my lust — MARV 516:2
  past is a bucket of a. — SAND 665:21
  sour grapes and a. — ASHF 31:16
  universe to a. — MISS 539:15
Asia churches which are in A. — BIBL 112:24
  churches which are in A. — BIBL 112:27
  not in A. — ARDR 24:13
  pampered jades of A. — MARL 513:26
  Will end up in A. — BLY 124:11
Asian A. boys ought to be — JOHN 423:14
Asians A. could still smile — HEAD 377:8
aside set death a. — TURG 802:8
ask all that we do a. — BIBL 109:9

a. and cannot answer SHAW 728:1
A., and it shall be given BIBL 95:15
a. faithfully BOOK 130:20
a. if you are enjoying NESB 559:10
a. is have SMAR 740:16
A. me no more CARE 191:1
a. nothing ELGA 299:2
a. not what your country KENN 449:2
could a. him anything WEIS 826:25
Don't a., don't tell NUNN 566:5
Don't a. me, ask the horse FREU 334:4
Don't let's a. for the moon FILM 319:3
for our blindness we cannot a. BOOK 132:8
if you gotta a. ARMS 26:14
if you gotta a. MISQ 538:7
To a. the hard question AUDE 36:11
Would this man a. why AUDE 34:25
askance looking a., other nations
GOGO 354:3
asked Nobody a. you NURS 570:15
You've a. for it MOLI 541:23
asketh Every one that a. receiveth BIBL 95:16
asking a. too much CANN 189:4
mere a. of a question FORS 329:20
time of a. BOOK 133:3
aslant grows a. a brook SHAK 688:17
asleep Fall a., or hearing die SHAK 695:9
Half a. as they stalk HARD 372:20
men were all a. BRID 151:6
mother was glad to get a. EMER 307:15
sucks the nurse a. SHAK 680:15
till it falls a. TEMP 775:10
very houses seem a. WORD 846:7
asp hole of the a. BIBL 88:22
asparagus Grew like a. in May GILB 347:7
aspens Willows whiten, a. quiver
TENN 780:6
asperges A. me, Domine MISS 536:9
A. me hyssopo BIBL 114:27
aspersion a. upon my parts of speech
SHER 733:18
aspersions Casting a. on those FLAU 325:3
aspes as an a. leef CHAU 213:6
asphalt only monument the a. road
ELIO 303:3
aspidistra biggest a. in the world
HARP 373:18
Keep the a. flying ORWE 577:9
aspiration a., to do nought ROSS 656:7
aspire by due steps a. MILT 528:18
gaze, and there a. ARNO 28:19
light, and will a. SHAK 724:2
when men a. MARL 513:10
aspirin a. for a brain tumour CHAN 207:14
ass a., without being a fool SURT 764:11
call great Caesar a. SHAK 680:14
crowned a. HENR 382:3
dull a. will not mend SHAK 688:24
enamoured of an a. SHAK 711:23
firstborn the greatest a. CARO 193:12
kiss my a. in Macy's window JOHN 423:15
law is a a. DICK 271:15
law is such an a. CHAP 208:16
making him egregiously an a. SHAK 713:21
not covet his a. BIBL 78:5
on his unwashed a. PARS 586:24
with the jaw of an a. BIBL 79:32
You're an a. ROCH 651:15
assailed A., fight, taken DONN 279:11
assassin copperheads and the a. SAND 665:18
you are an a. ROST 656:16
assassination absolutism moderated by a.
ANON 15:21
a. Could trammel up SHAK 704:3
A. has never changed DISR 276:2
A. is the extreme form SHAW 727:20
A. is the quickest MOLI 542:8
assault a. and hurt the soul BOOK 130:5
assaults a. of our enemies BOOK 128:12
a. of the devil BOOK 129:4
assay a. so hard CHAU 212:26
asserted boldly a. BURR 173:10
asserting a. these rights LAY 476:7

asses Death hath a.' ears BEDD 62:4
go seek the a. BIBL 80:9
seeking a. found MILT 534:18
to those great a. LUTH 496:14
assigned doom a. TENN 782:7
assume A. a virtue SHAK 687:30
assurance a. given by looks ROYD 658:1
a. of incorruption BIBL 92:29
low on whom a. sits ELIO 303:20
make a. double sure SHAK 706:17
Assyrian A. came down BYRO 180:1
curled A. Bull TENN 781:18
Astarte A., queen of heaven MILT 531:19
Astolat lily maid of A. TENN 777:26
astonish A. me DIAG 266:14
a. Paris with an apple CÉZA 206:2
a. the bourgeois BAUD 59:8
astonished a. at eclipse ORCH 576:7
a. at my own moderation CLIV 227:11
rightly a. by events BART 57:13
astonishment Your a.'s odd KNOX 458:9
astounded a. by them ATTE 32:21
astra ardua ad a. MOTT 552:15
sic itur ad a. VIRG 813:7
astray as sheep going a. BIBL 112:9
like sheep have gone a. BIBL 90:3
not send their works a. KORA 461:4
astrologer a. came the astronomer
DOYL 285:7
astrologers A. or three wise men
LONG 491:14
astronomers and a. QUIN 639:12
Christian must avoid a. AUGU 37:12
astrology A. is a disease MAIM 507:19
astronomer astrologer came the a.
DOYL 285:7
undevout a. is mad YOUN 857:19
astronomers a. and astrologers QUIN 639:12
astronomy daughter of a. YOUN 857:19
linked in a. LOVE 493:9
Astur cry is A. MACA 499:16
asunder bones are smitten a. BOOK 136:14
let no man put a. BOOK 133:11
let not man put a. BIBL 97:24
asylum lunatic a. run by lunatics
LLOY 487:20
taken charge of the a. ROWL 657:14
was in an a. PALM 583:3
ate a. when we were not hungry
SWIF 765:17
Freddie Starr a. my hamster NEWS 562:8
With A. by his side SHAK 697:16
atheism inclineth man's mind to a.
BACO 43:17
owlet A. COLE 231:17
atheist a. half believes a God YOUN 857:15
a. is a man BUCH 162:20
a.-laugh's a poor exchange BURN 171:1
denial of Him by the a. PROU 613:10
female a. JOHN 426:11
from being an a. SART 667:9
I am still an a. BUÑU 164:11
remain a sound a. LEWI 483:8
sort of a. ORWE 577:6
superstitious a. BROW 158:16
village a. brooding CHES 217:9
was no a. CHAR 209:5
atheistical damned a. age VANB 806:14
atheists far from a. CUDW 253:3
no a. in the foxholes CUMM 253:16
Athenian not A. or Greek SOCR 745:11
Athenians A. and strangers BIBL 105:17
Athens A. arose SHEL 729:10
A., the eye of Greece MILT 534:20
citizen of A. SOCR 744:26
Ye men of A. BIBL 105:18
athirst give unto him that is a. BIBL 114:18
athletes All pro a. are bilingual HOWE 405:13
Atlanta A. is gone CHES 214:16
Atlantic if I flew the A. EARH 294:23
steep A. stream MILT 528:20
stormy North A. Ocean LARD 468:9
Atlas A. of the state COWP 247:16

atlas blank a. of your body NERU 559:4
atman A., the Spirit in man UPAN 804:13
A., the Spirit, the Self UPAN 805:7
That [A.] is not this UPAN 804:18
atmosphere shove against an a. EDDI 295:5
atom a. has changed everything EINS 298:4
carbon a. JEAN 419:7
defence against the a. bomb ANON 15:7
flaring a.-streams TENN 781:15
grasped the mystery of the a. BRAD 148:22
leads through the a. EDDI 295:6
atomic primordial a. globule GILB 347:20
win an a. war BRAD 148:21
atoms a. and space DEMO 263:14
a. of Democritus BLAK 121:17
A. or systems POPE 604:21
concurrence of a. PALM 584:21
motions of a. in my brain HALD 367:18
record the a. WOOL 845:4
atone a. for our past CHEK 213:23
atrocities a. however horrible NAMI 556:4
attach wish to a. AUST 39:8
attachment free from a. BHAG 74:16
attack a. from Mars SALI 664:14
A. is best form of defence PROV 614:43
by his plan of a. SASS 667:22
lead such dire a. MACA 499:17
Problems worthy of a. HEIN 379:12
terror a. HOWA 405:9
attacked when a. it defends itself
ANON 20:10
attacking I am a. FOCH 327:22
attain I cannot a. unto it BOOK 143:15
attainable We look at the a. GLAD 351:1
attempt a. and not the deed SHAK 704:21
that dares love a. SHAK 717:23
attempted Something a. LONG 491:9
attendant a. lord, one that will do
ELIO 302:18
attention a. must be paid MILL 527:5
a. to the object WEIL 826:21
attentive a. and favourable hearers
HOOK 395:17
attic A. grace POUN 608:18
Beauty crieth in an a. BUTL 177:8
brain a. stocked DOYL 284:11
furniture in Tolkien's a. PRAT 610:9
glory of the A. stage ARNO 28:29
O A. shape KEAT 444:13
sleeps up in the a. there MEW 525:15
Where the A. bird MILT 534:21
attire bride forget her a. BIBL 90:23
Her rich a. KEAT 442:21
attitude Fair a. KEAT 444:13
attitudes Anglo-Saxon a. CARR 195:20
attorney a.'s Elderly ugly daughter
GILB 349:7
gentleman was an a. JOHN 429:11
attracted a. by God INGE 413:7
attraction A. and repulsion BLAK 120:19
feels the a. of earth LONG 490:6
put a. on BEHN 63:21
that powerful a. SHEL 732:18
attractions Costs register competing a.
KNIG 458:3
attributes through each of his a. ZOHA 859:4
auburn Sweet A., loveliest village
GOLD 354:9
audace toujours de l'a. DANT 256:14
audacity Arm me, a. SHAK 682:28
a. of elected persons WHIT 833:18
tactful in a. COCT 230:4
aude sapere a. HORA 399:5
audendi a. semper fuit aequa potestas
HORA 397:20
audi A. partem alteram AUGU 37:11
audience fit a. find MILT 533:21
is a large a. TROL 799:26
whisks his a. HORA 398:10
audiences English-speaking a. WHAR 831:1
two kinds of a. SCHN 671:11
audio-visual full of a. marvels SMIT 742:7
audit how his a. stands SHAK 687:17

auditorem *notas a. rapit* — HORA 398:10
augmentation a. of the Indies — SHAK 721:7
augury we defy a. — SHAK 689:7
august A. for the people — AUDE 34:22
  A. is a wicked month — O'BR 571:4
  corny as Kansas in A. — HAMM 370:10
  recommence in A. — BYRO 181:32
Augustan next A. age — WALP 819:9
Augustus A. was a chubby lad — HOFF 391:14
auld do wi' an a. man — BURN 173:7
  For a. lang syne — BURN 170:9
aunt A. is calling to Aunt — WODE 842:25
  Charley's a. from Brazil — THOM 789:5
aunts bad a. and good aunts — WODE 842:20
  dull a., and croaking rooks — POPE 603:25
  his cousins and his a. — GILB 348:21
auream *A. quisquis mediocritatem* — HORA 401:4
auri *A. sacra fames* — VIRG 811:22
Auschwitz saved one Jew from A. — AUDE 36:21
  write a poem after A. — ADOR 6:1
  year spent in A. — LEVI 482:13
austere beauty cold and a. — RUSS 660:26
austerities monk destroys by a. — JAIN 416:16
Austerlitz A. and Waterloo — SAND 665:20
  field of A. — KIPL 455:14
Australia Advance A. fair — MCCO 500:15
  A. has a marvellous sky — LAWR 475:13
  A. looks to America — CURT 254:7
  emigrate to A. — MULD 553:18
  recession that A. had to have — KEAT 442:8
  take A. right back — KEAT 442:9
Australian A. selfhood — HUGH 407:3
  great A. Emptiness — WHIT 832:4
Australians A. wouldn't give — ADVE 7:7
Austria Don John of A. is going — CHES 216:7
author amended By its A. — EPIT 309:1
  a. and finisher of our faith — BIBL 111:10
  a. and giver — BOOK 130:15
  a. of his own disgrace — COWP 246:16
  a. of peace — BOOK 128:12
  a. ought to write — FITZ 324:10
  a. who speaks — DISR 276:11
  Choose an a. — DILL 274:10
  expected to see an a. — PASC 587:3
  go to the a. — RUSK 659:18
  half an a.'s graces — MORE 548:1
  in search of an a. — PIRA 595:18
  like in a good a. — SMIT 742:17
  majesty of the A. of things — LEIB 479:17
  more than wit to become an a. — LA B 463:1
  No a. ever spared a brother — GAY 341:26
  shrimp of an a. — GRAY 362:1
  store Of the first a. — MARV 516:4
  to be an a. — HAZL 377:2
authoress dared to be an a. — AUST 40:17
authorities imposed by the a. — PLAT 597:9
authority adduces a. — LEON 481:1
  A. forgets a dying king — TENN 778:13
  a. of the eternal yesterday — WEBE 825:6
  A. without wisdom — BRAD 149:7
  Experience, though noon a. — CHAU 212:13
  in a. under her — BOOK 131:14
  little brief a. — SHAK 708:1
  make your peace with a. — MORR 550:9
  man under a. — BIBL 95:28
  maximal a. and minimal power — SZAS 769:14
  no a. from God to do mischief — MAYH 519:14
  taught them as one having a. — BIBL 95:26
  than in a. — THOM 788:5
authorized copy of the A. Version — WHAT 831:12
authors a. their copyrights — TROL 799:1
  damn those a. — CHUR 219:11
  great a. have their due — BACO 42:12
  invades a. like a monarch — DRYD 290:5
  praise of ancient a. — HOBB 391:2
  'Till a. hear at length — COWP 247:19
  women-a. — COOP 242:12
authorship popular a. — TROL 800:13
autobiography age to write an a. — WAUG 824:7
  a. is an obituary — CRIS 251:9

A. is now as common — GRIG 364:11
autocrat a.: that's my trade — CATH 199:15
  considerate a. — STEP 756:2
automatic smoothes her hair with a. hand — ELIO 303:21
automobile fix up his a. — CLAR 225:8
  like an a. — ROOT 654:17
autres *encourager les a.* — VOLT 815:11
autumn a. arrives — BOWE 147:17
  a. evening — ARNO 28:1
  cloudy days of a. — CLAR 224:14
  Early a. — BASH 57:21
  happy a. fields — TENN 783:3
  harmony In a. — SHEL 729:15
  I saw old A. — HOOD 395:8
  mists of the a. mornings — ORWE 577:11
  Now it is a. — LAWR 475:6
autumnal one a. face — DONN 279:7
availeth all this a. me nothing — BIBL 82:22
  struggle naught a. — CLOU 229:10
avalanche perseverance of a mighty a. — HOUS 405:7
avarice a. begin — AUST 40:1
  a., lust, ambition — SHER 734:7
  a. seems to grow — AUGU 37:10
  A., the spur — HUME 408:12
  By a. and selfishness — THOR 793:1
  dreams of a. — JOHN 431:24
  dreams of a. — MOOR 546:11
  must take up with a. — BYRO 180:18
  punishment Is a. — JONS 435:14
  very prone to a. — KORA 460:8
ave *a. atque vale* — CATU 203:10
  A. Maria — PRAY 611:1
  A. verum corpus — ANON 21:14
  songs were A. Marys — CORB 243:2
avenge a. even a look — BURK 167:13
avenger from my dead bones, a. — VIRG 812:6
  Time, the a. — BYRO 179:10
average a. guy who could carry — EPIT 310:9
averages fugitive from th' law of a. — MAUL 519:1
Averno *Facilis descensus A.* — VIRG 812:9
aversion begin with a little a. — SHER 733:15
  bordering on a. — STEV 759:7
  manner which is my a. — BYRO 181:9
avertant *si omen a.* — CICE 223:19
Avilion island-valley of A. — TENN 778:18
avis *Rara a.* — JUVE 439:19
avocados Wives in the a. — GINS 349:17
Avogadro bigness of A.'s number — BENT 68:2
avoid wise man should a. wrath — JAIN 416:7
avoiding a. being — TILL 794:15
  a. superstition — BACO 42:2
Avon Sweet Swan of A. — JONS 436:4
awake A., my soul — KEN 448:5
  A., O north wind — BIBL 87:13
  a. right early — BOOK 137:23
  a. while sleeping — MONT 544:18
  Being now a. — SHAK 722:11
  England! a. — BLAK 120:14
  West's a. — DAVI 259:9
  When you're lying a. — GILB 347:16
awaked must be a. — BIBL 81:22
  So the Lord a. — BOOK 139:11
awakened a. a sleeping giant — FILM 319:12
awakenings dream between two a. — O'NE 573:11
aware a. of all the evil — LA R 469:17
  a. that you are happy — KRIS 461:19
  insignificant and is a. of it — BECK 60:19
  surely God is a. — KORA 460:8
away a.! for I will fly — KEAT 444:25
  A. from me — BOOK 134:3
  go a. for ever — MURD 554:19
  Over the hills and far a. — STEV 761:1
  Rain, rain, go a. — NURS 569:7
  When I'M A. — TELE 776:6
awe a. into the beholders — SWIF 765:9
  In a. of such a thing — SHAK 696:5
  keep the strong in a. — SHAK 717:9
  Shock and A. — ANON 18:10
  Shock and A. — ULLM 804:7

Stand in a., and sin not — BOOK 133:23
  wonder and a. — KANT 441:6
aweary a. of the sun — SHAK 707:15
  Cassius is a. — SHAK 698:18
  I am a., aweary — TENN 781:14
awful this is an a. place — SCOT 672:16
awfully a. big adventure — BARR 57:4
awkward a. squad fire over me — LAST 471:11
awoke a. one morning — BYRO 184:15
  a. one morning — OPEN 576:2
  So I a., and behold — BUNY 164:26
  When Gregor Samsa a. one morning — KAFK 440:18
awry leaning all a. — FITZ 323:12
axe a. is laid unto the root — BIBL 94:13
  a.'s edge did try — MARV 515:18
  a. to the root — PAIN 582:16
  heavy a. without an edge — BRAD 149:7
  let the great a. fall — SHAK 688:15
  Lizzie Borden took an a. — ANON 17:9
axes have you your sharp-edged a. — WHIT 833:7
  no a. being ground — BROU 154:17
axis a. of evil — BUSH 175:6
  sword the a. of the world — DE G 262:12
axle fly sat upon the a.-tree — BACO 45:34
Azores Flores in the A. — TENN 783:19
Aztec destroyed the A. Empire — SCHU 671:19
azure a. sister of the spring — SHEL 730:7
  a., white, and red — DRUM 286:12
  out of the a. main — THOM 792:1
  slept an a.-lidded sleep — KEAT 443:2

baa B., baa, black sheep — NURS 566:8
babblative b. and scribblative — SOUT 749:10
babble Coffee house b. — DISR 276:15
babbled b. of green fields — SHAK 693:2
babbler this b. — BIBL 105:16
babe b. was born in a manger — WHIT 832:17
  birth-strangled b. — SHAK 706:13
  Come little b. — BRET 151:1
  love the b. — SHAK 704:12
  naked new-born b. — SHAK 704:6
  pretty B. all burning — SOUT 749:19
  young b. were born — BALL 53:19
Babel bother at the tower of B. — VOLT 816:15
  stir Of the great B. — COWP 248:7
babes As newborn b. — BIBL 112:4
  b. and sucklings — BOOK 134:4
  mouths of b. — PROV 629:14
babies b. in the tomatoes — GINS 349:17
  hates dogs and d. — ROST 656:17
  putting milk into b. — CHUR 221:18
Babiy Yar Over B. there are no memorials — YEVT 856:14
Bab-lock-hithe Thames at B. — ARNO 28:5
baboon he who understands b. — DARW 257:14
baby arms to take his b. — HOME 394:4
  b. beats the nurse — SHAK 707:19
  b. doesn't understand English — KNOX 458:10
  B. in an ox's stall — BETJ 72:3
  b. out with the bathwater — PROV 618:19
  Begin, b. boy — VIRG 814:3
  Burn, b., burn — POLI 600:11
  come from, b. dear — MACD 501:6
  first b. laughed — BARR 57:2
  I'm your little b. — LEWI 483:19
  my b. at my breast — SHAK 680:15
  one for my b. — MERC 522:10
  Who loves ya, b. — CATC 201:34
Babylon B. be thrown down — BIBL 114:10
  B. in all its desolation — DAVI 258:17
  B. is fallen — BIBL 114:2
  By the waters of B. — BOOK 143:12
  By the waters of B. — WALP 819:10
  Ere B. was dust — SHEL 730:21
  How many miles to B. — NURS 567:9
  King in B. — HENL 381:17
  modern b. — DISR 277:30
  MYSTERY, B. THE GREAT — BIBL 114:9
Bacchus charioted by B. — KEAT 444:25

banquet b. ceases   SHEN 732:22
Church's b.   HERB 384:17
banqueter b. fed full   LUCR 496:1
banqueting b. upon borrowing   BIBL 93:17
banter how does fortune b. us   BOLI 126:10
Bantu [B.] has been subjected   VERW 809:5
banyan like the great b. tree   PATI 588:13
baptism B., and the Supper   BOOK 132:19
b., a regeneration   ELIO 299:6
B. be administered   BOOK 132:9
in my B.   BOOK 132:12
baptize I b. with water   BIBL 102:23
bar no moaning of the b.   TENN 776:16
treat if met where any b. is   HARD 372:22
When I have crossed the b.   TENN 776:17
Barabbas B. was a publisher   CAMP 187:22
B. was a robber   BIBL 104:2
crowd will always save B.   COCT 230:5
Barbara love of B. Allen   BALL 51:12
barbarian as a b. boxes   DEMO 263:16
He is a b.   SHAW 724:19
barbarians b. are to arrive   CAVA 203:17
B., Philistines, and Populace   ARNO 29:7
Greeks, and to the B.   BIBL 105:35
in my own mind the B.   ARNO 29:10
without the b.   CAVA 203:18
young b. all at play   BYRO 179:12
barbaric sound my b. yawp   WHIT 833:17
barbarism b. be considered   WEIL 826:18
Everyone calls b.   MONT 544:7
barbarisms colloquial b.   JOHN 425:23
barbarity b. of tyrants   SMIT 743:8
barbarous b. ages   BAGE 49:1
b. dissonance   MILT 529:4
b., savage   DIDE 273:18
b. to write a poem   ADOR 6:1
invention of a b. age   MILT 531:2
barbarousness confess mine own b.   SIDN 736:18
barber like a b.'s chair   SHAK 678:9
bard goat-footed b.   KEYN 450:15
more fat than b. beseems   THOM 792:3
voice of the B.   BLAK 122:9
bards as b. will not   CRAB 249:18
worst of b. confessed   CATU 202:19
bare Back and side go b.   ANON 15:5
B. like nude, giant girls   SPEN 750:22
b. mountain tops   ARNO 29:25
B. ruined choirs   SHAK 723:10
barefoot always goes b.   PROV 630:34
b. friars   GIBB 345:20
I was born b.   LONG 489:16
bargain dateless b.   SHAK 718:10
made a good b.   FRAN 332:13
two to make a b.   PROV 624:26
bargains rule for b.   DICK 270:2
barge b. she sat in   SHAK 679:3
Baring Rothschild and B.   GILB 347:18
bark come out, and b.   JOHN 432:2
dogs b. at me   SHAK 716:20
He began to b.   NURS 567:4
his b. cannot be lost   SHAK 703:8
keep a dog and b. yourself   PROV 635:8
see, they b. at me   SHAK 701:3
barking b. dog never bites   PROV 614:50
Barkis B. is willin'   DICK 268:10
barley among the bearded b.   TENN 780:7
Corn rigs, an' b. rigs   BURN 171:14
fields of b. and of rye   TENN 780:5
barleycorn bold John B.   BURN 172:13
Barlow Hornby and my B.   THOM 791:4
barn b. and the forge   HOUS 404:12
b.-cocks say Night is growing   HARD 373:1
Barnaby B. bright   PROV 615:1
like B. Rudge   LOWE 494:1
Barney Give him the money, B.   CATC 200:20
barns nor gather into b.   BIBL 95:7
baronet No little lily-handed b.   TENN 783:18
baronetage any book but the B.   AUST 39:11
any book but the B.   OPEN 575:17
barrel ain't got a b. of money   WOOD 844:18
drowned in a b. of Malmesey   FABY 314:1
grows out of the b. of a gun   MAO 511:12

meal in a b.   BIBL 81:20
barrel-organ played on a b.   MOZA 552:24
barren b. and dry land   BOOK 138:3
b. strand   JOHN 426:18
b. superfluity of words   GART 340:12
b. woman to keep house   BOOK 142:1
cry, 'tis all b.   STER 756:8
I am but a b. stock   ELIZ 304:3
live a b. sister   SHAK 710:15
none is b.   BIBL 87:10
barricade some disputed b.   SEEG 675:13
barrier b. of your teeth   HOME 394:1
barriers b. of our prison   EDGE 296:2
there are no b.   WOLL 844:2
barrow there in your long b.   MULD 553:16
barrows grassy b. of the happier dead   TENN 784:9
bars weary of these worldly b.   SHAK 696:20
Basan fat bulls of B.   BOOK 134:28
Og the king of B.   BOOK 143:10
base Labour without joy is b.   RUSK 659:26
man of soul so b.   TOCQ 795:3
people as b. as itself   PULI 637:2
To what b. uses may we   SHAK 688:29
Why bastard? wherefore b.   SHAK 699:24
baseless b. fabric   SHAK 719:1
baseness b.' varlet   JONS 435:9
baser fellows of the b. sort   BIBL 105:14
bashfulness particular b.   ADDI 5:6
basia Da mi b. mille   CATU 202:14
basics time to get back to b.   MAJO 508:6
basil Hung over her sweet B.   KEAT 443:19
steal my B.-pot   KEAT 443:20
Basingstoke hidden meaning—like B.   GILB 349:4
basket come from the same b.   CONR 240:23
eggs in one b.   PROV 618:14
Basle At B. I founded   HERZ 387:1
Basques say of the B.   CHAM 207:5
Bass Guinness, Allsopp, B.   CALV 186:7
bassoon heard the loud b.   COLE 232:14
bastard all my eggs in one b.   PARK 586:11
b. who gets the mail   KEAT 442:10
God . . . the b.   BECK 61:5
more b. children   SHAK 682:21
we knocked the b. off   HILL 388:15
Why b.? wherefore base   SHAK 699:24
bastardizing twinkled on my b.   SHAK 699:27
bastards Don't let the b.   SAYI 670:6
some call nature's b.   SHAK 722:2
stand up for b.   SHAK 699:25
Bastille Voltaire in the B.   DE G 262:14
bat b. that beats about in caverns   WILB 835:5
beetle and the b.   JOHN 429:5
black b., night, has flown   TENN 781:23
couldn't b. for the time   COMP 236:16
Ere the b. hath flown   SHAK 705:22
On the b.'s back   SHAK 719:6
Twinkle, twinkle, little b.   CARR 194:10
weak-eyed b.   COLL 235:11
Wool of b.   SHAK 706:12
bath rather lie in a hot b.   THOM 790:10
sit in a hot b.   TENN 785:2
sore labour's b.   SHAK 704:24
test my b. before I sit   NASH 557:16
tired of B.   AUST 39:7
bathe b. in his tears   DONN 281:25
b. those beauteous feet   FLET 327:13
early-morning b.   SIKH 737:10
bathes He who b. here   SIKH 737:15
bathing caught the Whigs b.   DISR 275:8
large b. machine   GILB 347:17
one long b. of a summer's day   WORD 849:6
bathroom can't feel revolutionary in a b.   LINK 486:8
baths Two walking b.   CRAS 250:16
bathwater baby out with the b.   PROV 618:19
baton marshal's b.   LOUI 492:12
bâton dans sa giberne le b.   LOUI 492:12
bats b. amongst birds   BACO 45:24
b. have been broken   HOWE 405:11
B. not angels   THOM 790:23
b. will squeak and wheel   NICO 563:10

batsman I am the b.   LANG 466:10
batsmen opening b. to the crease   HOWE 405:11
battalions big b.   PROV 629:45
in pale b. go   SORL 746:23
not of the heavy b.   VOLT 816:10
battening B. upon huge seaworms   TENN 780:2
batter B. my heart   DONN 279:21
battle at Sheriffmuir A b.   MCLE 503:11
b. and murder   BOOK 129:7
b. done   POTT 607:24
b. flags were furled   TENN 780:20
b. fought of late   HARI 373:13
b., n. A method   BIER 116:3
b.'s lost and won   SHAK 702:28
b. to the strong   BIBL 86:16
b. to the strong   DAVI 258:5
b. to the strong   PROV 630:3
b. will be in the shade   HERO 385:13
better in b. than in bed   STER 757:7
defeated in a great b.   LIVY 487:8
die in a b.   SHAK 693:15
die in the b.   CLOU 227:15
forefront of the hottest b.   BIBL 80:31
foremost in b.   BALL 52:14
France has lost a b.   DE G 262:1
glorious b.   FORT 330:3
half the b.   GOLD 355:26
happen to one in a b.   CARR 195:9
into the midst of the b.   VIRG 811:19
Ireland's b.   CONN 240:10
it is a field of b.   STEV 759:24
Lord mighty in b.   BOOK 135:6
make them ready to b.   BOOK 142:15
meet my death in b.   SIKH 737:7
Next to a b. lost   WELL 827:14
noise of b. rolled   TENN 778:11
out of b. I escaped   OWEN 581:6
prepare himself to the b.   BIBL 107:26
See the front o' b.   BURN 172:5
smelleth the b. afar off   BIBL 83:25
stand three times in the b.   EURI 312:19
This b. fares   SHAK 694:26
we b. for the Lord   ROOS 654:13
battledore B. and shuttlecock   DICK 271:29
battlefield b. is the heart   DOST 283:1
battlements down from the white b.   HEAT 378:13
his head upon our b.   SHAK 703:3
PERCHED ON B.   TELE 776:4
battles b. long ago   WORD 850:9
Dead b., like dead generals   TUCH 801:20
forced marches, b. and death   GARI 339:15
mother of all b.   HUSS 410:16
O God of b.   SHAK 693:20
opening b. of subsequent wars   ORWE 577:12
baubles Take away these b.   MISQ 538:19
Baum Lebens goldner B.   GOET 352:18
bawcock king's a b.   SHAK 693:11
bawdy Bloody, b. villain   SHAK 686:6
touched the b. strings   STEV 758:5
bay b. the moon   SHAK 698:14
flourishing like a green b.-tree   BOOK 136:2
bayonet b. is a weapon   POLI 600:6
bayonets throne of b.   INGE 413:10
throne of b.   YELT 856:13
with our b. turning   WOLF 843:11
Bayonne hams, B.   POPE 602:7
bays oak, or b.   MARV 515:14
sprig of b. in fifty years   SWIF 767:6
bazaar Fate's great b.   MACN 504:21
be b.-all and the end-all   SHAK 704:3
b. as they are   CLEM 226:14
better to b.   AUCT 34:8
B. what you would seem   PROV 615:36
How less what we may b.   BYRO 182:5
Let b. be finale of seem   STEV 757:22
poem should not mean but b.   MACL 503:10
that which shall b.   BIBL 85:28
To b., or not to be   SHAK 686:9
beach On the b.   CHES 216:24
beachèd Upon the b. verge   SHAK 719:13

beaches fight on the b.	CHUR 221:8	No b. so fierce	SHAK 716:23	b. upon the mountains	BIBL 89:28
beacon b.-light is quenched	SCOT 673:16	number of the b.	BIBL 113:31	believe to be b.	MORR 549:19
beacons b. of wise men	HUXL 412:3	questing b.	MALO 508:19	better to be b.	WILD 836:17
beaded With b. bubbles	KEAT 444:22	serpent subtlest b.	MILT 533:27	Black is b.	POLI 600:10
beadsman be your b.	CLOS 228:13	whan a b. is deed	CHAU 211:12	comes up more b.	HORA 402:9
beak b. from out my heart	POE 599:8	What rough b.	YEAT 855:13	how b. they are	COLE 231:8
in his b. Food enough	MERR 523:3	Who is like unto the b.	BIBL 113:29	hunger to be b.	RHYS 646:13
beaker O for a b. full	KEAT 444:22	who worship the b.	BIBL 114:3	in a b. way	O'KE 572:18
Beale Miss Buss and Miss B.	ANON 17:17	**beastie** cow'rin', tim'rous b.	BURN 172:20	innocent and the b.	YEAT 854:19
beam B. me up, Scotty	MISQ 537:4	**beasties** long-leggety b.	PRAY 611:2	Love is a b. image	MICH 524:2
b. that is in thine own eye	BIBL 95:13	**beastly** b. the bourgeois is	LAWR 477:3	love of what is b.	PERI 592:21
beamish But oh, b. nephew	CARR 196:10	b. to the Germans	COWA 244:16	most b. thing	SAPP 666:12
my b. boy	CARR 194:26	**beasts** b. at Ephesus	BIBL 108:6	most b. things	RUSK 659:25
beams b. of his chambers	BOOK 141:5	b. of the earth	BIBL 105:6	Names Most B.	KORA 461:11
bean b. and the cod	BOSS 145:15	b. of the field	BOOK 141:6	scorn looks b.	SHAK 721:2
Nine b. rows	YEAT 854:17	b. of the forest	BOOK 137:8	She's b.	SHAK 694:13
not too French French b.	GILB 348:14	b. of the forest	BOOK 137:7	singing:—'Oh, how b.!'	KIPL 454:8
beans B. meanz Heinz	ADVE 7:8	compared unto the b.	BOOK 137:7	slaying of a b. hypothesis	HUXL 411:14
put b. in the clay	PROV 616:23	elders and the four b.	BIBL 113:17	Small is b.	SCHU 671:20
bear any of us can b.	GIUL 350:7	four b.	BIBL 113:12	Something b. for God	MUGG 553:7
B. and forbear	PROV 615:2	four b. full of eyes	BIBL 113:8	something b. for God	TERE 785:11
B. of Very Little Brain	MILN 527:19	invent new b.	HEIN 380:1	When a woman isn't b.	CHEK 214:7
b. thee in their hands	BOOK 140:4	kin to the b.	BACO 43:18	**beauty** all that b., all that wealth	GRAY 361:3
b. the yoke in his youth	BIBL 91:9	like brute b.	BOOK 133:5	American b. rose	ROCK 651:16
B. up—trust to time	FORS 329:18	**beat** b. down Satan	BOOK 129:11	arrest all b.	CAME 186:16
b. very much reality	ELIO 301:11	b. generation	KERO 449:17	b. all very well at first sight	SHAW 726:15
b. with a sore head	MARR 514:8	b. him when he sneezes	CARR 194:7	b. being only skin-deep	KERR 450:3
bush supposed a b.	SHAK 711:29	b. their swords	BIBL 88:2	b. coming and the beauty gone	
cannot b. them	BIBL 103:36	can't b. them, join them	PROV 623:11		WORD 847:15
Exit, pursued by a b.	SHAK 721:31	dread b.	JOHN 423:4	B. crieth in an attic	BUTL 177:8
fire was furry as a b.	SITW 738:15	enemies have b. us	SHAK 698:27	b. draws us	POPE 606:7
fitted by nature to b.	AURE 38:6	he b. them all	BYRO 184:11	B. draws with single	PROV 615:3
Grizzly B. is huge and wild	HOUS 403:21	We b. them today	STAR 754:12	b. faded	PHIL 594:14
heavy b. who goes with me	SCHW 672:8	**beaten** b. path to his door	EMER 307:18	b. for ashes	BIBL 90:19
How a b. likes honey	MILN 528:6	b. road	SHEL 729:8	B. for some provides escape	HUXL 411:11
huntsman by the b. oppressed	WALL 818:5	being b. does not matter	STEP 756:5	b. in music	IVES 414:13
More can I b.	SHAK 694:18	No Englishman is ever fairly b.	SHAW 727:17	b. in one's equations	DIRA 275:1
No dancing b. was so genteel	COWP 246:22	Thrice was I b.	BIBL 108:21	B. is but a flower	NASH 557:20
Puritan hated b.-baiting	MACA 498:22	**beateth** one that b. the air	BIBL 107:20	B. is in the eye	PROV 615:4
rugged Russian b.	SHAK 706:6	**beating** b. Russia is for your country		B. is momentary in the mind	STEV 758:4
so b. ourselves that	CHUR 221:9		ESPO 308:16	B. is mysterious	DOST 283:1
still less the b.	FRER 333:17	Charity and b.	FLET 327:12	B. is no quality	HUME 409:4
till you have caught the b.	PROV 618:16	driven by b.	ASCH 31:1	b. is not, as fond men misdeem	SPEN 752:10
who can b.	BIBL 84:31	glory of b. the French	WOLF 843:14	b. is only skin deep	SAKI 663:16
beard By thy long grey b.	COLE 232:11	Greeks take the b.	HORA 399:3	b. is past change	HOPK 396:22
husband with a b.	SHAK 712:13	hearts b.	BROW 160:7	B. is power	ADVE 7:9
I have a b. coming	SHAK 710:23	mend his pace with b.	SHAK 688:24	B. is the first test	HARD 371:12
King of Spain's B.	DRAK 285:16	**beatings** dread of b.	BETJ 73:4	B. is the lover's gift	CONG 239:13
Loose his b.	GRAY 360:21	**Beatles** B.' first LP	LARK 468:12	B. is truth	KEAT 444:15
Old Man with a b.	LEAR 477:3	**beatnik** peculiar b. theories	KERO 449:18	b. is woman's sceptre	WOLL 844:6
on a Dutchman's b.	SHAK 721:4	**beats** b. as it sweeps	ADVE 7:35	B. itself doth of itself	SHAK 722:17
womman hath no b.	CHAU 211:23	**Beattock** Pulling up B.	AUDE 35:15	B. killed the Beast	FILM 320:14
bearded all scroungy and b.	CORS 243:18	**beatum** *ab omni Parte b.*	HORA 401:7	b. lives with kindness	SHAK 721:23
b. like the pard	SHAK 681:11	*vocaveris Recte b.*	HORA 402:17	b. made The bright world dim	SHEL 732:9
beards long b., and pretences	SWIF 766:26	**beatus** B. *ille, qui procul negotiis*	HORA 400:1	b. making beautiful old rime	SHAK 723:16
when b. wag all	PROV 624:7	*B. vir qui timet Dominum*	BIBL 115:2	b. of a rare kind	DIMN 274:13
beareth B. all things	BIBL 107:25	**beaut** it's a b.	LA G 464:1	b. of holiness	BOOK 140:11
b. up things light	BACO 45:6	**beauteous** b. and sublime	AKEN 9:4	b. of holiness	MONS 543:8
bears b. might come with buns	ISHE 414:9	B. the garden's umbrage	SMAR 740:7	b. of inflections	STEV 758:10
b. the marks of the last person	HAIG 367:10	How b. mankind is	SHAK 719:7	b. of Israel	BIBL 80:27
bigger b. try to pretend	MILN 528:3	It is a b. evening	WORD 847:2	b. of the house of God	SUGE 763:8
dancing dogs and b.	HODG 391:10	**beauties** b.! O how great the sum		B. only skin deep	PROV 615:5
rhythms for b. to dance	FLAU 324:22		SMAR 740:13	B.'s ensign	SHAK 718:9
Teddy B. have their Picnic	BRAT 149:20	many b. grace a poem	HORA 398:14	B. so ancient	AUGU 37:5
beast above a b.	BIBL 86:1	meaner b. of the night	WOTT 851:4	b.'s rose	SHAK 722:21
b. hath devoured him	BIBL 77:2	pale, unripened b.	ADDI 4:10	b.'s self she is	ANON 17:23
b. or a fool	KILV 451:12	saved by b. not his own	POPE 601:21	b.'s Silent music	CAMP 188:5
b. or a god	ARIS 25:26	**beautiful** b. with his presence	BOOK 133:5	B. that must die	KEAT 444:19
b., or a god	BACO 44:13	**beautiful** Albert is b.	VICT 809:9	b. the joy of possessing form	PAST 588:1
b. who is always spoiling	MACA 500:2	All things bright and b.	ALEX 11:6	b., though injurious	MILT 534:31
B. With many heads	SHAK 682:20	b. and damned	FITZ 323:21	B. too rich for use	SHAK 717:17
b. with two backs	SHAK 713:1	b. and death-struck year	HOUS 404:17	b. unadorned	BEHN 64:5
Beauty killed the B.	FILM 320:14	b. and ineffectual angel	ARNO 29:21	B. vanishes	DE L 262:23
before he caught the b.	WALL 818:5	b. and simple	HENR 382:12	b. will be soon resolved	MARL 513:17
Blatant b. men call	SPEN 752:6	b. and the clever	GREE 362:10	b. without vanity	BYRO 183:24
blond b.	NIET 564:12	b. are thy feet	BIBL 87:19	befriended us with b.	CAVE 204:4
but a just b.	ANON 15:6	b. cannot be the way	COUS 244:12	body's b. lives	STEV 758:4
fit night out for man or b.	FIEL 318:20	b. catastrophe	LE C 478:11	do not spring into b.	LEWE 483:3
life of his b.	BIBL 84:13	b. country	LAST 474:4	dreamed that life was b.	HOOP 395:20
Man's life is cheap as b.'s	SHAK 700:11	B. dreamer	FOST 330:11	England, home and b.	ARNO 30:12
mark, or the name of the b.	BIBL 113:30	b. face is a mute	PUBL 636:13	Exuberance is b.	BLAK 121:8
marks of the b.	HARD 371:19	b. game	PELÉ 591:8	fatal gift of b.	BYRO 179:24
more subtil than any b.	BIBL 75:18	b. God to behold	SWIN 768:21	Fostered alike by b.	WORD 849:7

benefacta *recordanti b. priora* — CATU 203:5
benefactor become the b. of someone — DOST 283:7
b. of our race — TWAI 803:22
benefit Every human b. — BURK 166:26
benefits forget not all his b. — BOOK 141:1
benevolence b. of mankind — BAGE 48:25
b. of the butcher — SMIT 741:5
enticed by b. — BAGE 47:12
benevolent bashful, and b. — TALM 772:20
B. Knowledge — BORG 145:5
benighted poor b. 'eathen — KIPL 454:5
benison For a b. to fall — HERR 385:15
Benjamin of the tribe of B. — BIBL 110:2
bent top of my b. — SHAK 687:12
bereaved b. if snobbery died — USTI 806:6
bereft b. Of wet — HOPK 396:17
Berliner *Ich bin ein B.* — KENN 449:5
Bermoothes still-vexed B. — SHAK 718:22
Bermudas remote B. ride — MARV 515:6
berries Sweet b. ripen — STEV 758:9
Two lovely b. — SHAK 711:15
berry made a better b. — BUTL 177:9
sweeter than the b. — GAY 341:4
Bertie Burlington B. — HARG 373:11
beryl rings set with the b. — BIBL 87:16
beseech pray and b. you — BOOK 127:14
beside b. thyself — BIBL 105:30
Christ b. me — PATR 588:20
fall b. thee — BOOK 140:3
besiege b. thy brow — SHAK 722:2
best All's for the b. — PROV 614:15
all the great b.-sellers — PRIT 612:13
Always to be b. — HOME 394:3
any other person's b. — HAZL 377:1
bad in the b. of us — ANON 19:9
being b. man is — MURR 555:2
b. and the worst of this — SWIN 768:24
b. chosen language — AUST 39:6
b. days of life — VIRG 814:19
b. in this kind — SHAK 712:4
b. is enemy of good — PROV 615:11
b. is like the worst — KIPL 455:2
b. is the best — QUIL 639:7
b. is the enemy of the good — VOLT 815:14
b. is yet to be — BROW 161:3
b. lack all conviction — YEAT 855:12
b.-laid schemes — PROV 615:16
b. men are dead — PUNC 637:22
b. of all possible worlds — BRAD 148:19
b. of all possible worlds — CABE 184:17
b. of all possible worlds — PROV 614:15
b. of all possible worlds — VOLT 815:8
b. of men — PROV 615:13
b. of times — OPEN 574:28
b. Prime Minister we have — BUTL 175:16
b. rulers — LAO 467:8
b.-seller is the gilded tomb — SMIT 742:14
b. thing God invents — BROW 159:10
b. things in life — PROV 615:15
b. things in life are free — DE S 265:16
b. years are gone — BECK 61:6
Corruption of the b. — SAYI 669:9
did the b. we could — UPDI 805:19
discreetest, b. — MILT 533:25
enemy of the b. — PROV 621:9
get what's b. for us — RICE 646:18
In art the b. is good enough — GOET 353:5
It was the b. of times — DICK 272:13
justest and b. — PLAT 597:10
past all prizing, b. — SOPH 746:17
poetry = the *b.* words — COLE 234:3
propagate the b. that is known — ARNO 29:17
pursuing of the b. ends — HUTC 410:18
record of the b. — SHEL 732:16
Send forth the b. — KIPL 456:7
that is the b. — AUST 39:14
we two, one another's b. — DONN 280:20
Whate'er is b. administered — POPE 605:6
Beste *das B. gut genug* — GOET 353:5
bestow b. on every airth a limb — MONT 546:2
bestride b. the narrow world — SHAK 696:9
bet You b. your sweet bippy — CATC 202:3

betake b. myself to that course — PEPY 592:16
Bethel O God of B. — DODD 278:21
Bethlehem But thou, B. — BIBL 92:8
little town of B. — BROO 154:8
Slouches towards B. — YEAT 855:13
Betjemanless We are now B. — EWAR 313:5
betray All things b. thee — THOM 791:8
b. me to a lingering book — HERB 383:16
b. me to your mirth or hate — FORD 329:1
guts to b. my country — FORS 330:1
those who b. their friends — GAY 341:19
To b., you must first belong — PHIL 594:9
betrayal any act of b. — RENO 645:8
ecstasy of b. — GENE 342:23
only defence against b. — WILL 839:3
betrayed betrayer, and b. — SCOT 674:4
by ourselves, b. — CONG 238:33
If she's fair, b. — LEAP 477:1
night that he was b. — BOOK 132:2
one of them b. me — BEAV 60:17
betrayer b., and betrayed — SCOT 674:4
betrayeth he that b. thee — BIBL 104:23
betrothed B., betrayer — SCOT 674:4
of my b. lady — MIDD 524:10
better All the b. to hear you with — PERR 593:1
appear the b. reason — MILT 531:30
b. angels of our nature — LINC 485:3
B. by far than any — SIKH 737:5
B. by far you should forget — ROSS 655:12
b. day, the worse deed — HENR 382:9
b. hap to worse — SOUT 749:22
B. is the end — BIBL 86:7
b. man than I am — KIPL 454:10
B. red than dead — POLI 600:7
better spared a b. man — SHAK 691:15
B. than a play — CHAR 209:4
b. than a thousand — BOOK 139:17
b. than it sounds — NYE 570:17
b. than Man — TAGL 771:11
b. than ourselves — CAMU 188:11
b. the day — PROV 615:27
b. the instruction — SHAK 709:15
b. to be — AUCT 34:8
b. to have fought and lost — CLOU 229:9
b. to have loved and lost — TENN 779:1
b. what we can — STEV 759:5
can only get b. — PETR 594:2
can only get b. — POLI 601:8
desires what is b. — AUCT 34:10
don't know b. — SAKI 663:19
Every day, I am getting b. — COUÉ 244:10
Fail b. — BECK 61:25
far, far b. thing — DICK 272:19
for b. for worse — BOOK 133:9
from worse to b. — HOOK 395:19
from worse to b. — JOHN 424:3
Gad! she'd b. — CARL 193:2
give place to b. — SHAK 698:20
go b. with Coke — ADVE 8:18
go the b. things — CATH 199:10
He is not b. — ANON 15:2
Hereafter, in a b. world — SHAK 680:21
If way to the B. there be — HARD 372:17
I took thee for thy b. — SHAK 687:22
I was in a b. place — SHAK 681:1
made b. by their presence — ELIO 300:20
make a b. mouse-trap — EMER 307:18
much b. than likely — BRON 153:1
nae b. than he shou'd be — BURN 170:25
nothing *b.* — CARR 195:22
nothing b. to do — THAT 787:18
see b. days — BEHN 64:1
seemed a little b. — LAST 473:13
see the b. things — OVID 580:13
takes the b. course — SOCR 745:5
We have seen b. days — SHAK 719:10
bettered b. expectation — SHAK 712:9
between B. the idea And the reality — ELIO 302:7
'ouses in b. — BATE 58:9
try to get b. them — STRA 762:3
betwixt B. the stirrup and the ground — EPIT 310:16

bewailed b. at their birth — MONT 545:6
beware B., lest in the worm — BARB 55:5
B., madam — GRAV 360:5
B. my foolish heart — WASH 822:14
B. of desperate steps — COWP 246:21
B. of rudely crossing it — AUDE 35:22
b. of the dog — BLIX 123:12
B. of the dog — PETR 594:3
B. the ides of March — SHAK 695:29
bid you b. — KIPL 455:9
cry, B.! Beware — COLE 232:8
beweep b. my outcast state — SHAK 722:28
bewildered Bewitched, bothered, and b. — HART 374:10
to the utterly b. — CAPP 190:1
bewitch Do more b. me — HERR 385:21
bewitched B., bothered, and bewildered — HART 374:10
bewrapt B. past knowing — HARD 373:2
bewrayeth speech b. thee — BIBL 99:9
beyond But is there anything b. — BROO 153:7
loved each other b. belief — HEIN 380:2
bias impartiality is b. — REIT 645:3
mind's wrong b. — GREE 362:5
biases critic is a bundle of b. — BALL 54:3
bibendum *Nunc est b.* — HORA 400:20
bibisti *edisti satis atque b.* — HORA 399:24
Bible B. and the Bible only — CHIL 217:22
B.-Society . . . is found — CARL 192:1
B. teaches that woman — STAN 754:9
big ha'-B. — BURN 170:22
Both read the B. — BLAK 119:20
cadence of the B. verses — RUSK 660:12
English B. — MACA 498:23
have used the B. — KING 453:2
knows even his B. — ARNO 29:13
read in de B. — HEYW 387:15
starless and b.-black — OPEN 575:26
that book is the B. — ARNO 30:9
translation of the B. — WHAT 831:12
Bibles B. laid open — HERB 384:24
bibles they had the b. — GEOR 344:1
bicker b. down a valley — TENN 775:18
bicycle arrive by b. — VIER 810:4
b.-pump the human heart — AMIS 13:12
fish without a b. — SAYI 670:23
so is a b. repair kit — CONN 239:27
bicycling old maids b. — MAJO 508:5
bicyclists illuminated trouser-clip for b. — MORT 551:6

bid b. the Devil good morrow — PROV 627:17
bidder withstand the highest b. — WASH 822:7
bien *mieux est l'ennemi du b.* — VOLT 815:14
bier upon his watery b. — MILT 529:31
big b. enough to take away everything — FORD 328:9
B. fish eat little fish — PROV 615:37
B. fleas have little fleas — PROV 615:38
b. squadrons against the small — BUSS 175:9
b. tent — POLI 600:9
b. way of doing things — TERE 785:10
b. words for little matters — JOHN 428:21
books of the B.-Endians — SWIF 765:12
commonly thought b. — WOOL 845:4
Does my bum look b. — CATC 200:11
fall victim to a b. lie — HITL 389:23
I am b. — FILM 321:6
shining B.-Sea-Water — LONG 491:1
What b. ears you have — PERR 593:1
bigamy B. is having — ANON 15:8
bigger b. bang for a buck — POLI 600:8
b. they are — FITZ 324:13
b. they are — PROV 615:39
biggest b. aspidistra in the world — HARP 373:18
b. electric train — WELL 827:8
bigness b. of Avogadro's number — BENT 68:2
bigoted more superstitious, more b. — NEWM 560:11
bigotry B. the anger of men who — CHES 216:23
B. tries to keep truth — TAGO 770:16
bike got on his b. — TEBB 775:6

Mind my b. CATC 201:18
Put me back on my b. MISQ 538:15
Bilbo B.'s the word CONG 238:34
bilingual All pro athletes are b. HOWE 405:13
bill b. of my divorce DONN 279:26
called upon to pay the b. HARD 371:7
give me your b. of company SWIF 766:1
nape caught in his b. YEAT 854:20
billabong swagman camped by a b.
PATE 588:12
billboard b. lovely as a tree NASH 557:17
billet bullet has its b. PROV 619:3
bullet has its b. WILL 838:3
billets-doux bibles, b. POPE 606:6
billiard elliptical b. balls GILB 348:5
billiards play b. well ROUP 657:2
billion b. dollar country FOST 330:7
billow Fierce was the wild b. ANAT 13:19
billows b. of enormous size PHIL 594:15
bills By children and tradesmen's b.
MACN 504:17
inflammation of his weekly b. BYRO 181:1
Receipted b. AUDE 35:16
billy B., in one of his sashes GRAH 358:8
That's the way for B. HOGG 392:6
till his 'B.' boiled PATE 588:12
bind B. me, or set me free GODO 352:1
b. my hair HUNT 410:10
b. their kings in chains BOOK 144:8
b. the sweet influences BIBL 83:24
b. unto myself today ALEX 11:9
b. your sons to exile KIPL 456:7
Obadiah B.-their-kings MACA 499:4
Safe b., safe find PROV 630:18
binds b. to himself a joy BLAK 121:22
Blest be the tie that b. FAWC 316:7
bin Laden having one b. MUBA 553:3
Binnorie B., O Binnorie BALL 51:15
binomial b. theorem GILB 348:29
biographers B., translators MACA 498:12
Grubstreet b. ADDI 4:19
muck-raking b. BENN 67:16
picklocks of b. BENÉ 66:13
biographical noble and b. friend
WETH 830:21
biographies essence of innumerable b.
CARL 191:17
biography better part of b. STRA 762:4
B. is about Chaps BENT 68:12
Judas who writes the b. WILD 835:25
no b. THAC 786:24
no history; only b. EMER 307:2
nothing but b. DISR 277:7
biologist b. passes ROST 656:14
biology B. is the search for WILL 838:11
bippy You bet your sweet b. CATC 202:3
bird addled egg as an idle b. PROV 614:34
b.-haunted English lawn ARNO 27:19
b. in the hand PROV 615:40
b. never flew on one PROV 615:41
b. not gets OXFO 581:11
b. of dawning SHAK 683:18
b. of night SHAK 696:18
b. of Paradise HERB 384:18
B. of the wilderness HOGG 392:9
b. of wonder dies SHAK 695:25
b. on the wing BOUL 147:7
b.'s battling in its own home AESC 6:8
b. that cuts the airy way BLAK 121:11
B. thou never wert SHEL 731:25
Both man and b. COLE 233:10
cannot catch the b. of paradise KHRU 451:5
catch a b. RICH 647:12
divine b. of Zeus PIND 595:12
early b. catches worm PROV 618:29
escaped even as a b. BOOK 142:21
forgets the dying b. PAIN 587:5
gold-feathered b. STEV 758:2
household b. DONN 279:15
immortal b. KEAT 445:1
It's a b. ANON 15:25
like a singing b. ROSS 655:6
obscure b. clamoured SHAK 705:9

only the note of a b. SIMP 738:9
rare b. on this earth JUVE 439:19
secular b. MILT 535:1
self-begotten b. MILT 534:32
Shall I call thee b. WORD 850:15
sight of any b. BIBL 83:32
sight of the b. PROV 623:35
silence fell with the waking b. TENN 781:24
some b. would trust HERB 383:17
Stirred for a b. HOPK 397:11
sweet b.'s throat SHAK 681:3
Sweet b. that shunn'st MILT 529:11
What b. so sings LYLY 497:3
why the caged b. sings DUNB 291:15
birdcage And a b., sir DICK 272:8
like a summer b. WEBS 826:5
birds All the b. of the air NURS 570:16
As the flight of b. MACL 503:9
b., and Prime Ministers BALD 50:14
b. are faint KEAT 445:8
b. are flown CHAR 208:23
B. build HOPK 397:9
b. build nests VIRG 815:7
b. do chant their lays SPEN 751:7
b. fly through it HEIS 380:7
b. got to fly HAMM 369:22
B. in their little nests PROV 615:42
B. in their little nests agree WATT 823:11
B. of a feather PROV 615:43
b. of the air BIBL 97:5
b. of the air have nests BIBL 96:1
B. on box and laurels SMAR 739:13
b. that are without despair WEBS 826:5
b. trying to communicate AUDE 36:19
catch old b. with chaff PROV 635:27
half-awakened b. TENN 783:5
holy white b. flying after MASE 517:14
If b. confabulate or no COWP 247:7
late the sweet b. sang SHAK 723:10
like small b. DISR 276:14
Little b. that can sing PROV 625:24
nest of singing b. JOHN 427:7
no b. sing KEAT 443:23
prisoned b. must find SASS 667:20
read about little b. TENN 785:2
singing of b. BIBL 87:6
sing like b. i' the cage SHAK 701:24
these unobservant b. ISHE 414:9
think caged b. sing WEBS 826:11
Two b., close-linked UPAN 805:12
voices of the sweeter b. LEDW 478:14
birdsong b. at morning STEV 760:11
Birmingham B. by way of Beachy Head
CHES 216:10
B. Six released DENN 264:12
no great hopes from B. AUST 38:22
When Jesus came to B. STUD 763:2
Birnam Great B. wood SHAK 706:18
Till B. wood remove SHAK 707:6
birth accident of her b. SHEL 732:11
bewailed at their b. MONT 545:6
B., and copulation, and death ELIO 303:4
b. is but a sleep WORD 848:5
b.-strangled babe SHAK 706:13
disqualified by the accident of b. CHES 217:4
flummery of a b. place KEAT 446:12
give b. astride of a grave BECK 61:23
grace, new b. ARNO 30:2
Invisible before b. BHAG 74:11
lessen the b.-pangs MARX 516:14
my b. and spirit HERB 383:16
Nobility of b. BACO 45:3
no cure for b. and death SANT 666:11
not conscious of his b. LA B 462:17
one that is coming to b. O'SH 579:2
on my b. have smiled TAYL 774:14
present at the b. ORTO 576:16
Rainbow gave thee b. DAVI 258:20
Saviour's b. is celebrated SHAK 683:18
seen b. and death ELIO 302:10
this monstrous b. SHAK 713:16
birthday eighty-first b. OPEN 574:27
Happy b. to you HILL 388:12

marvel my b. away THOM 789:15
birthplace accent of one's b. LA R 469:20
birthright Esau selleth his b. BIBL 76:24
sold his b. BIBL 76:26
births b. of time BACO 44:26
plenties, and joyful b. SHAK 694:4
tell of the b. RIMB 649:12
bis B. dat qui cito dat
biscuit b., or confectionary plum COWP 247:5
cared a b. for it LAWR 475:20
biscuits hyacinths and b. SAND 666:2
bisexuality b. doubles your chances
ALLE 12:15
bishop Another B. dead MELB 520:16
b. must be blameless BIBL 110:22
B. of Rome BOOK 144:18
B. of your souls BIBL 112:9
call me a B. WESL 829:23
hitting the niece of a b. ORWE 577:21
How can a b. marry SMIT 743:21
illustrious b. of Cambrai GODW 352:3
make a b. kick a hole CHAN 207:11
No b., no King JAME 417:2
There lies the B. AUBR 33:14
bishopric merit for a b. WEST 830:19
bishops B., and Curates BOOK 128:17
B. and Curates BOOK 131:15
B., Priests, and Deacons BOOK 129:10
much against the B. AUBR 33:23
bit b. by him that comes behind SWIF 767:11
b. the babies BROW 160:20
for requital b. CHIL 217:23
Though he had b. me SHAK 701:20
bitch b.-goddess success JAME 418:23
called John a Impudent B. FLEM 326:13
Gaia is a tough b. MARG 512:6
old b. gone in the teeth POUN 609:1
bite b. his pen SWIF 767:16
b. some of my other generals GEOR 343:3
b. the hand that fed them BURK 168:2
bleating sheep loses b. PROV 615:44
Dead men don't b. PROV 617:24
dog is allowed one b. PROV 619:7
man recovered of the b. GOLD 355:3
bites barking dog never b. PROV 614:50
dead woman b. not GRAY 360:19
biteth b. like a serpent BIBL 85:1
biting b. is immortal SHAK 680:10
b. the hand that lays GOLD 356:4
bitten Once b., twice shy PROV 628:29
bitter be not b. against them BIBL 110:13
b. as wormwood BIBL 83:38
b. bread of banishment SHAK 715:18
b. God to follow SWIN 768:21
b. herbs BIBL 77:29
b. tears to shed CORY 244:3
life unto the b. in soul BIBL 82:34
make oppression b. SHAK 686:5
my belly was b. BIBL 113:26
rises something b. LUCR 496:2
sweet water and b. BIBL 111:28
bittern hear the b. cry LEDW 478:14
bitterness b. of his soul BIBL 93:7
b. of life CARR 196:14
b. of my soul BIBL 89:14
rose's scent is b. THOM 791:5
bivouac b. of the dead O'HA 572:16
bizarre b. happening HAUG 375:15
Bizet Chopin and B. FISH 322:17
blabbing b., and remorseful day SHAK 694:17
black art as b. as hell SHAK 723:20
Baa, baa, b. sheep NURS 566:8
b. against may BUNT 164:10
b. and merciless things JAME 417:21
b. as he is painted PROV 617:33
b. as if bereaved of light BLAK 122:6
b. as our loss SITW 738:16
b. as they might be BALL 53:13
b. black oxen YEAT 853:15
b., but comely BIBL 87:3
b. chaos comes again SHAK 724:2
b. dog JOHN 432:10
blacker than b. TURN 802:17

black (*cont.*):
B. Hills belong to me — SITT 738:13
B. is beautiful — POLI 600:10
B. it stood as night — MILT 532:11
b. majority rule — SMIT 742:9
b. man or a fair man — ADDI 4:24
b. men fought — MACA 497:18
B. Panther Party — NEWT 561:8
B. Power — CARM 193:7
b., purgatorial rails — KEAT 442:16
B.'s not so black — CANN 189:6
b. water beetle — BLY 124:12
B. Widow, death — LOWE 494:14
bread is b. — BARC 55:11
devil damn thee b. — SHAK 707:7
drop of b. blood — HUGH 407:1
during the B. Death — BOCC 124:16
growth of b. consciousness — BIKO 116:11
Hung be the heavens with b. — SHAK 694:6
I am B. — JOHN 423:1
I found some b. people — EQUI 308:11
Just call me b. — GOLD 354:5
little b. sheep — KIPL 454:6
looking for a b. hat — BOWE 148:8
matron, all in b. — SHAK 717:36
More b. than ashbuds — TENN 777:2
neutralize the b. — BROW 161:11
night's b. agents — SHAK 706:1
not b. and white — BOY 148:15
old b. magic — MERC 522:11
old b. ram — SHAK 712:36
rainbow which includes b. — YEVT 856:21
sad, b. isle — BAUD 58:15
so long as it is b. — FORD 328:12
Thais' teeth are b. — MART 514:21
thou read'st b. — BLAK 119:20
Tip me the b. spot — STEV 759:14
wearing a b. gown — CHES 214:22
Why do you wear b. — CHEK 213:24
with a b. skin — MALC 508:10
young, gifted and b. — HANS 370:18
Young, gifted and b. — IRVI 414:3
blackberries as plentiful as b. — SHAK 690:11
micher and eat b. — SHAK 690:15
blackbird B. has spoken — FARJ 315:2
b. whistling — STEV 758:10
blackbirds B. are the cellos — STEV 758:19
Four and twenty b. — NURS 569:14
blackens b. all the water — ADDI 5:10
blacker b. than black — TURN 802:17
blackguard Sesquipedalian b. — CLOU 227:16
blackguards intentions make b. — LACL 463:5
Blackpool famous seaside place called B. — EDGA 295:13
blacks poor are Europe's b. — CHAM 207:7
Two b. don't make a white — PROV 633:26
blacksmith Never was a b. — KIPL 453:13
bladders boys that swim on b. — SHAK 695:11
blade bloody blameful b. — SHAK 712:2
Steel-true and b.-straight — STEV 760:13
trenchant b. — BUTL 176:6
vorpal b. went snicker-snack — CARR 194:26
Blair Atholl B.'s mine — BALL 52:7
blame Bad women never take the b. — BROO 153:17
b. at night — POPE 604:12
b. is his who chooses — PLAT 597:16
b. Marx for what was done — BENN 67:2
b. the alien — AESC 6:10
grief as is the b. — AYTO 41:12
manager who gets the b. — LINE 486:7
neither is most to b. — SWIN 768:24
poor wot gets the b. — MILI 526:16
she is to b. — MONT 543:10
blamed never had been b. — D'AV 257:21
blameless bishop must be b. — BIBL 110:22
Fearless, b. knight — ANON 20:11
flower of a b. life — TENN 777:13
blames bad workman b. his tools — PROV 614:49
blaming b. it on you — KIPL 454:12
b. on his boots — BECK 61:14

blanch B., and Sweet-heart — SHAK 701:3
when counsellors b. — BACO 43:27
bland bland lead the b. — GALB 338:2
composed and b. — ARNO 27:22
liquid lines mellifluously b. — BYRO 181:16
blandula *Animula vagula b.* — HADR 366:10
blank B. cheques — HOLM 393:6
b., my lord — SHAK 720:29
political b. cheque — GOSC 357:5
blanket b. of the dark — SHAK 703:21
blankets rough male kiss of b. — BROO 153:6
blasphemies truths begin as b. — SHAW 724:13
blaspheming Liver of b. Jew — SHAK 706:13
blasphemous b. fables — BOOK 144:17
blasphemy b. against the Holy Ghost — BIBL 96:29
flat b. — SHAK 708:2
blast b.-beruffled plume — HARD 372:15
B. from the Desert — LONG 490:25
b. of vain doctrine — BOOK 131:1
b. of war — SHAK 693:4
blasted b. with excess — GRAY 361:19
Kindled he was, and b. — BYRO 178:26
no sooner blown but b. — MILT 530:15
Upon this b. heath — SHAK 703:11
blatant B. beast men call — SPEN 752:6
blatherskite Blatant B. — PHIL 595:1
blaze b. of living light — BYRO 179:29
heavens themselves b. forth — SHAK 697:3
bleak In the b. mid-winter — ROSS 655:9
bleating b. sheep loses bite — PROV 615:44
bleed b. a while — BALL 53:2
b., fall, and die — DONN 279:11
do we not b. — SHAK 709:14
old wounds b. anew — WALL 818:12
thorns of life! I b. — SHEL 730:11
bleeding Ain't it all a b. shame — MILI 526:16
b., beating fire — JOHN 423:5
b. piece of earth — SHAK 697:15
instead of b., he sings — GARD 339:13
pageant of his b. heart — ARNO 28:21
bleeds 'til it b. daylight — COCK 229:22
blemish lamb shall be without b. — BIBL 77:28
no b. but the mind — SHAK 721:15
Blenheim still fighting B. — BEVA 73:11
bless B. 'em all — HUGH 406:16
b. me, With apple pie — FIEL 317:8
B. relaxes — BLAK 121:7
B. the Lord — BIBL 115:9
b. ye the Lord — BOOK 128:3
dying, b. the hand — DRYD 289:22
except thou b. me — BIBL 76:35
God b. us every one — DICK 268:5
holy priests B. her — SHAK 679:7
load and b. With fruit — KEAT 445:14
blessed B. are the dead — BIBL 114:4
B. are the eyes — BIBL 100:21
B. are the poor — BIBL 94:20
B. are the pure in heart — KEBL 447:11
B. are you, O Lord — SIDD 735:13
b. art thou among women — BIBL 99:30
B. art thou among women — PRAY 611:1
B. be that cometh — BOOK 142:11
b. be the name of the Lord — BIBL 82:27
b. damozel — ROSS 655:19
b. is the man — BOOK 135:23
B. is the man — BOOK 139:16
b. them unaware — COLE 233:2
blessest is b. — BIBL 78:19
from hence to there may be b. — SOCR 745:9
generations shall call me b. — BIBL 99:31
Judge none b. — BIBL 93:12
Lord b. the latter end — BIBL 83:31
more b. to give — BIBL 105:24
That b. mood — WORD 847:8
This b. plot — SHAK 715:14
thou hast b. them — BIBL 78:22
you should call b. — HORA 402:17
blessedness b. alone that makes a King — TRAH 798:1
dies, in single b. — SHAK 710:16

blesseth b. him that gives — SHAK 709:25
blessing b. cannot pass through — JOHN 422:7
b. of a rainbow — ABSE 1:5
b. of God Almighty — BOOK 132:5
b. that money cannot buy — WALT 821:2
b. to the country — BISM 117:12
boon and a b. — ADVE 8:17
continual dew of thy b. — BOOK 128:17
contrariwise b. — BIBL 112:12
give us his b. — BOOK 138:9
national b. — HAMI 369:19
Prosperity is the b. — BACO 43:13
taken away thy b. — BIBL 76:29
unmixed b. — HORA 401:7
When thou dost ask me b. — SHAK 701:24
Yet possessing every b. — EDME 296:7
blessings B. brighten — PROV 616:3
b. of the light — KEN 448:7
b. on the falling out — TENN 782:24
b. on your head — COWP 246:24
glass of b. — HERB 384:19
blest always to be b. — ARMS 26:12
always To be b. — POPE 604:22
B. be the tie that binds — FAWC 316:7
B. pair of Sirens — MILT 528:15
b. that I lie on — PRAY 611:4
Kings may be b. — BURN 172:10
make us b. at last — ROCH 651:9
Of this b. man — WALT 821:6
O Mother b. — ALPH 12:19
promotion to the b. — DRYD 289:26
blew You b. it up — FILM 321:3
blight b. man was born for — HOPK 397:4
great English b. — WAUG 824:3
Blighty back to dear old B. — MILL 527:13
blimp Colonel B. — LOW 493:14
blind accompany my being b. — PEPY 592:16
b. as any noonday owl — TENN 777:25
b., but now I see — NEWT 563:4
b. guides — BIBL 98:10
b. in your ears and mind — SOPH 746:18
b. lead the blind — BIBL 97:12
b. led by the blind — UPAN 805:5
b. man in a dark room — BOWE 148:8
b. man's wife needs — PROV 616:4
B., old and lonely — SHEL 728:14
b. side of the heart — CHES 215:23
b. watchmaker — DAWK 259:13
b. wife — PROV 617:26
bold as a b. mare — PROV 628:12
Booth died b. — LIND 486:5
country of the b. — ERAS 308:12
country of the b. — PROV 623:34
Cupid painted b. — SHAK 710:19
darkness and b. eyes — VAUG 807:9
Eye among the b. — WORD 848:8
eyes to the b. — BIBL 83:16
giveth sight to the b. — BOOK 144:1
Grief for awhile is b. — SHEL 730:23
halt, and the b. — BIBL 101:8
I was b., now I see — BIBL 103:15
Justice, though she's painted b. — BUTL 176:18
knowledge e'er accompany the b. — SANA 665:12
Love is b. — ANON 20:15
Love is b. — PROV 625:43
my being b. — CLOS 228:3
none so b. as those — PROV 632:31
O b. entencioun — CHAU 212:28
old, mad, b. — SHEL 731:20
religion without science is b. — EINS 297:12
right to be b. sometimes — NELS 558:14
splendid work for the b. — SASS 667:17
though she be b. — BACO 44:12
Three b. mice — NURS 570:5
When the b. lead the blind — PROV 634:27
whole world b. — SAYI 669:17
blindness 'eathen in 'is b. — KIPL 453:21
for our b. we cannot ask — BOOK 132:8
heathen in his b. — HEBE 378:15
Love comes from b. — BUSS 175:7
triple sight in b. — KEAT 445:20
blinds drawing-down of b. — OWEN 581:3

Truth, like the light, b. CAMU 188:20
blindworm b.'s sting SHAK 706:12
blindworms Newts, and b. SHAK 711:6
blinked other fellow just b. RUSK 659:6
blinking portrait of a b. idiot SHAK 709:9
bliss appreciate domestic b. SANT 666:9
B. goes but to a certain bound GREV 363:17
b. in ale CRAB 249:2
B. in our brows bent SHAK 678:21
b. or woe MILT 534:3
B. was it in that dawn WORD 846:20
doth bathe in b. VAUX 808:6
Everywhere I see b. SHEL 728:10
joyous b. is mine SIKH 737:3
men call domestic b. PATM 588:16
Of b. on bliss MILT 533:3
soul in b. SHAK 701:21
source of all my b. GOLD 354:21
Where ignorance is b. GRAY 361:12
wingèd hours of b. CAMP 187:18
blissful b. old times BLAM 123:5
blister b. you all o'er SHAK 718:23
blithe b. Spirit SHEL 731:25
buxom, b., and debonair MILT 529:18
blithesome B. and cumberless HOGG 392:9
blitz b. of a boy is Timothy Winters
CAUS 203:13
blizzard walked to his death in a b.
EPIT 309:12
block each b. cut smooth POUN 608:13
hew the b. off POPE 602:3
old b. itself BURK 168:23
blockhead b.'s insult JOHN 426:12
bookful b. POPE 604:16
diversion in a talking b. FARQ 315:10
No man but a b. JOHN 430:20
very great b. CHAR 209:7
blocks hew b. with a razor POPE 606:20
You b., you stones SHAK 695:28
blond b. beast NIET 564:12
B. comme un soleil BANV 54:19
blonde Being b. is definitely MADO 505:13
b. to make a bishop kick CHAN 207:11
blondes Gentlemen prefer b. LOOS 491:17
blood am I not of her b. SHAK 720:17
ancient troughs of b. HILL 388:10
b. and ashes PAIN 582:8
b. and iron BISM 117:20
b. and love without STOP 761:13
b. and wine WILD 836:27
b. be the price KIPL 455:18
b. come gargling OWEN 581:4
b.-dimmed tide is loosed YEAT 855:12
b. drawn with the lash LINC 485:11
b. his blood YEAT 853:7
b. is their argument SHAK 693:15
b. Is very snow-broth SHAK 707:21
b. more stirs SHAK 689:28
b. of an Englishman ANON 16:2
b. of Christians is the seed TERT 786:1
b. Of human sacrifice MILT 531:18
b. of patriots JEFF 419:15
b. of the martyrs PROV 616:6
b.-red flag BLOK 123:16
b.'s a rover HOUS 404:8
B. sport brought INGH 413:16
B., sweat, and tear-wrung BYRO 177:22
B. thicker than water PROV 616:5
b., toil, tears and sweat CHUR 221:5
B. will have blood PROV 616:7
b. will have blood SHAK 706:8
B. will tell PROV 616:8
b. with guilt is bought SHEL 731:1
but with b. BROW 155:8
by b. Albanian TERE 785:14
cheeks as rosy as the b. GRIM 364:13
Christ's b. streams MARL 513:6
coughed-up b. RIMB 649:12
created Man of a b.-clot KORA 461:13
Deliver me from b.-guiltiness BOOK 137:14
Dread Beat an B. JOHN 423:4
drink the b. of goats BOOK 137:9

drop of Negro b. HUGH 407:1
effusion of Christian b. LAUD 470:3
enough of b. and tears RABI 640:1
flesh and b. BIBL 109:21
flesh and b. so cheap HOOD 395:12
flow of human b. HUGH 406:18
foaming with much b. POWE 609:21
for cooling the b. FLAN 324:16
fountain filled with b. COWP 246:27
get b. from a stone PROV 635:29
give me B. DICK 268:21
glories of our b. and state SHIR 735:3
guiltless of his country's b. GRAY 361:5
hawser of the b.-tie HARR 374:8
heart within b.-tinctured BROW 157:26
Here lies b. EPIT 310:7
His b. be on us BIBL 99:11
in b. Stepped in SHAK 706:9
innocent of the b. BIBL 99:10
I smell the b, NASH 557:19
I smell the b. SHAK 701:2
is this b., then, formed BYRO 181:17
Let there be b. BYRO 181:22
make thick my b. SHAK 703:19
Man of B. was there MACA 499:6
mingle my b. BROW 155:7
my b. will invigorate India GAND 339:4
my God feels as b. HERB 383:19
near in b. SHAK 705:14
Nothing like b., sir THAC 786:17
of b. and soap MITC 540:7
one glorious b.-red BROW 159:19
on the b. of my men LEE 479:4
pay the b. price BLAI 119:1
Propinquity and property of b. SHAK 699:18
pure and eloquent b. DONN 280:5
raised to shed his b. POPE 604:20
rather have b. on my hands GREE 362:8
redeemed us by his b. DIX 278:13
rivers of b. JEFF 420:14
seas of b. COBB 229:15
shall his b. be shed BIBL 76:11
shedde oure b. LANG 466:20
shed innocent b. BIBL 90:16
sheds his b. with me SHAK 693:24
show business with b. BRUN 162:10
so much b. in him SHAK 706:25
summon up the b. SHAK 693:4
thicks man's b. with cold COLE 232:21
this is my B. BOOK 132:2
Thy b. was shed for me ELLI 305:15
Tiber foaming with much b. VIRG 812:8
tincture in the b. DEFO 261:18
voice of the child's b. SWIN 769:2
voice of thy brother's b. BIBL 75:29
waded thro' red b. BALL 53:12
washed in the b. of the Lamb LIND 486:4
wash this b. Clean SHAK 705:3
We be of one b. KIPL 456:11
We, your b. family SPEN 750:15
When b. is nipped SHAK 702:26
When the b. creeps TENN 779:4
white in the b. of the Lamb BIBL 113:19
With his own b. he bought her STON 761:5
Without shedding of b. BIBL 111:4
worked with my b. KOLL 459:5
Young b. must have its course KING 453:1
bloodhounds Seven b. followed SHEL 730:3
bloodless b. lay the untrodden snow
CAMP 187:11
bloodshed war without b. MAO 511:11
bloodthirsty so venomous, so b. TROL 799:22
bloody Abroad is b. GEOR 343:15
b. blameful blade SHAK 712:2
b., bold, and resolute SHAK 706:16
b., but unbowed HENL 381:14
b. cross he bore SPEN 751:13
b. noses and cracked crowns SHAK 690:4
B., pale, and wan CLAU 225:14
b. principles and practices FOX 331:11
b. war and a sickly season TOAS 796:1
come out, thou b. man BIBL 81:4
dark and b. ground O'HA 572:17

have b. thoughts SHAK 719:2
last act is b. PASC 587:9
my b. thoughts SHAK 714:6
no right in the b. circus MAXT 519:3
Not b. likely SHAW 727:16
sang within the b. wood ELIO 303:6
Sunday, b. Sunday FILM 322:11
teach B. instructions SHAK 704:4
What b. man SHAK 703:2
wipe a b. nose GAY 341:28
Woe to the b. city BIBL 92:10
bloom b. in the spring GILB 348:9
b. is gone WILD 835:15
How can ye b. sae fresh BURN 170:13
hung with b. HOUS 404:6
Leopold B. ate with relish JOYC 437:19
lilac is in b. BROO 153:8
look at things in b. HOUS 404:7
sort of b. on a woman BARR 57:7
with the b. go I ARNO 28:25
blooming grand to be b. well dead
SARO 666:18
bloomy all the b. beds SMAR 740:17
blossom blood-red b. of war TENN 782:6
b. about me BOSW 146:20
b. and flourish SMIT 744:14
b. as the rose BIBL 89:9
B. by blossom SWIN 768:1
b. in purple and red TENN 782:1
b. in the dust SHIR 735:4
b. into a Duchess AILE 8:32
b. on the tomb CRAB 248:28
b. soup BASH 58:3
b. that hangs on the bough SHAK 719:6
break Into b. WRIG 851:14
frothiest, blossomiest b. POTT 608:5
hundred flowers b. MAO 511:14
blossoms b., birds, and bowers HERR 385:16
to-morrow b. SHAK 695:11
blot art to b. POPE 605:24
b. on the escutcheon GRAY 360:18
B. out, correct SWIF 767:7
b. out his name BIBL 113:3
looks a little b. TENN 778:8
scarce received from him a b. HEMI 381:3
This world's no b. BROW 159:11
blotted b. a thousand JONS 436:8
b. from life's page BYRO 178:13
b. it out for ever STER 757:9
blow Blow, b., thou winter wind
SHAK 681:14
B., bugle, blow TENN 782:27
b. fall soon or late STEV 760:17
B. him again to me TENN 782:26
B. out, you bugles BROO 153:5
B., thou wind of God KING 452:18
b. upon my garden BIBL 87:13
B. up the trumpet BOOK 139:13
B., winds, and crack SHAK 700:15
b. with an agreement TROT 800:21
first b. is half GOLD 355:26
great winds shorewards b. ARNO 27:11
hand that gave the b. DRYD 289:22
knock-down b. HUNT 410:6
not return your b. SHAW 727:1
strike the b. BYRO 178:12
sudden b.: the great wings YEAT 854:20
when will thou b. ANON 19:19
bloweth wind b. where it listeth BIBL 102:31
blowing answer is b. in the wind DYLA 294:3
I'm forever b. bubbles KENB 448:9
blown flower that once hath b. FITZ 323:6
no sooner b. but blasted MILT 530:15
pipe B. by surmises SHAK 691:21
rooks are b. TENN 778:28
blows b. so red The rose FITZ 323:4
It b. so hard HOUS 404:14
blubbering b. Cabinet GLAD 351:6
bludgeoning b. of the people WILD 837:5
bludgeonings b. of chance HENL 381:14
blue across the b. threshold ROST 656:12
b. above the trees KEAT 443:19

blue (cont.):
B. are the hills — PROV 616:9
b. bed to the brown — GOLD 355:30
B. Bonnets are bound — SCOT 674:15
b.-eyed devil white man — FARD 315:1
b. guitar — STEV 757:25
b. is all in a rush — HOPK 397:1
b. of the night — CROS 252:9
b. remembered hills — HOUS 404:16
B., silver-white — KEAT 445:4
cherish the pale b. dot — SAGA 663:3
deeply, beautifully b. — SOUT 749:8
Eyes of most unholy b. — MOOR 547:13
floating in the B. — MILN 528:7
Her b. body — WALK 817:12
Lavender's b. — NURS 567:19
Little Boy B. — NURS 568:1
little tent of b. — WILD 836:28
My b. heaven — WHIT 832:20
Space is b. — HEIS 380:7
True b. and Mrs Crewe — TOAS 796:6
yonder living b. — TENN 779:27
bluebell Mary, ma Scotch B. — LAUD 470:6
bluebirds b. over the white cliffs — BURT 173:16
blueprints Genes not like b. — STEW 761:2
blues got the Weary B. — HUGH 407:2
blunder frae mony a b. free us — BURN 172:19
God's first b. — NIET 564:3
it is a b. — BOUL 147:5
so grotesque a b. — BENT 68:17
Youth is a b. — DISR 277:2
blundered b. on some virtue unawares — CHUR 220:7
Some one had b. — TENN 776:14
blunders Human b. — TAYL 774:11
Nature's agreeable b. — COWL 246:3
blunt plain, b. man — SHAK 698:4
blush b. into the cheek — DICK 271:20
born to b. unseen — GRAY 361:5
Truth makes the Devil b. — PROV 633:22
blushed saw its God, and b. — CRAS 250:7
blushes Only Animal that B. — TWAI 803:10
blushful b. Hippocrene — KEAT 444:22
blushing bears his b. honours — SHAK 695:1
b. apricot — JONS 436:6
b. either for a sign — CONG 239:9
other people without b. — SHAW 727:2
boar tidy Bartholomew b.-pig — SHAK 692:2
board carried on b. — HUME 408:16
hospitable b. — WORD 846:21
I struck the b. — HERB 383:23
There wasn't any B. — HERB 383:9
boards Ships are but b. — SHAK 708:28
boast B. not thyself of to morrow — BIBL 85:12
b. of heraldry — GRAY 361:3
do falsely b. — BOOK 144:20
For frantic b. — KIPL 455:13
Such is the patriot's b. — GOLD 355:11
boasteth then he b. — BIBL 84:37
boat Architecture and a b. — PUGI 636:22
b. he can sail — THOM 792:21
first launched his frail b. — HORA 400:4
if men are together in a b. — HALI 368:12
love b. has crashed — LAST 473:3
sank my b. — KENN 449:7
sewer in a glass-bottomed b. — MIZN 541:6
soul is an enchanted b. — SHEL 731:7
Speed, bonnie b. — BOUL 147:7
Until I have a little b. — WORD 848:20
When the b. comes in — NURS 566:15
boathook diplomatic b. — SALI 664:3
boating Jolly b. weather — CORY 244:1
boatman B., do not tarry — CAMP 187:13
boats leathern b. — MARV 516:6
messing about in b. — GRAH 358:12
passengers off in small b. — LAST 474:12
seek happiness in b. — HORA 399:10
bobtail money on de b. nag — FOST 330:12
Boche well-killed B. — READ 643:4
bodes b. some strange eruption — SHAK 683:15

Bodhidharma [B.] come to China — MUMO 554:8
Bodhisattva B. who is full of pity — MAHĀ 506:10
Bodhisattvas pure deeds of the B. — SHAN 724:11
bodice lace my b. blue — HUNT 410:10
bodies b. are buried in peace — BIBL 93:34
b. but not their souls — GIBR 346:6
b. into light — NEWT 561:10
B. never lie — DE M 263:13
b. of those — EDWA 296:15
b. of unburied men — WEBS 826:9
contact of two b. — CHAM 207:4
men's poor b. — JUVE 440:10
One soul inhabiting two b. — ARIS 26:7
Our b. why do we forbear — DONN 280:21
our dead b. — SCOT 673:1
outwardly in our b. — BOOK 130:5
Pile the b. high — SAND 665:20
present your b. — BIBL 106:25
scorn their b. — BAST 58:8
souls out of men's b. — SHAK 712:17
structure of our b. — STOP 761:6
well-developed b. — FORS 329:7
with two seeming b. — SHAK 711:15
bodkin With a bare b. — SHAK 686:10
body Absent in b. — BIBL 107:9
Africa than my own b. — ORTO 576:15
b. and the soul know — ROET 652:7
b. as the chariot — UPAN 805:8
b. between your knees — CORY 244:1
b. Borne before her — THAC 786:23
b. continues in its state of rest — NEWT 561:11
b. did contain a spirit — SHAK 691:13
b. form doth take — SPEN 752:11
b. is a machine — TOLS 796:19
b. is the temple — BIBL 107:12
b., Nature is — POPE 604:29
b. of a weak and feeble woman — ELIZ 304:7
b. of Benjamin Franklin — EPIT 309:1
b. of this death — BIBL 106:16
b., of thought — CARL 192:26
B., remember not only — CAVA 203:14
b.'s beauty lives — STEV 758:4
b. swayed to music — YEAT 853:6
b. than raiment — BIBL 95:7
change our vile b. — BOOK 133:18
commit his b. to the deep — BOOK 144:12
commit his b. to the ground — BOOK 133:18
draw what I feel in my b. — HEPW 382:18
every interstice of my b. — EDDI 295:5
exercise is to the b. — STEE 755:2
Fretted the pigmy b. — DRYD 286:19
future b. for ever — ZORO 860:4
getteth outside [the b.] — TIBE 794:8
gigantic b. — MACA 498:1
Gin a body meet a b. — BURN 170:17
give my b. to be burned — BIBL 107:25
good-will of the b. — RIDI 648:4
her b. thought — DONN 280:5
huge distempered b. — MONT 545:5
I keep under my b. — BIBL 107:20
i like my b. — CUMM 253:14
in a sound b. — JUVE 440:11
in mind, b., or estate — BOOK 129:19
interpose my b. — STRA 762:3
in the midst of my b. — BOOK 135:1
John Brown's b. — SONG 747:13
keep your b. white — STEV 760:12
liberation of the human b. — GOLD 354:8
looking for a b. in the coach — HITC 389:20
Marry my b. to that dust — KING 451:15
my useless b. — BROW 154:19
no b. now on earth — SAYI 669:6
no b. to be kicked — THUR 794:4
none in the b. — LAWR 475:3
Of the glorious B. sing — THOM 788:15
out of my b. — HAND 370:15
out of the b. — BIBL 108:23
renouncing his b. — JAIN 416:15
Resurrection of the b. — BOOK 128:10
rid of the rest of her b. — VANB 806:16

salutary to the b. — PROU 613:15
shapes itself to the b. — WOLL 844:6
sing the b. electric — WHIT 833:3
Soul, leaving the b. — UPAN 804:17
so young a b. — SHAK 709:24
spirit leaves his mortal b. — BHAG 74:10
stepped out of my b. — WRIG 851:14
Thersites' b. — SHAK 683:7
this is my b. — BIBL 99:1
though her b. die — MILT 535:1
to keep one's b. — MACK 502:17
use of my b. — BECK 61:8
wanders on to a new b. — BHAG 74:8
with my b. I thee worship — BOOK 133:10
woman watches her b. uneasily — COHE 230:11
wreathing his b. — SMAR 739:17
Boets hate all B. and Bainters — GEOR 342:25
bog b.-standard comprehensive — CAMP 186:18
recognize the term b.-standard — BLUN 124:7
Bognor Bugger B. — LAST 471:5
bogs from b. and precipices — LOCK 488:16
bogus than a b. god — MACN 504:14
bohemian so-called b. elements — KERO 449:18
boil b. at different degrees — EMER 307:13
war that would not b. — TAYL 774:12
boiled in b. and roast — SMIT 743:13
boiler centrally-heated b.-room — HILL 388:14
boilers b. and vats — JOHN 431:24
boiling b. bloody breast — SHAK 712:2
boils watched pot never b. — PROV 633:42
bois au fond des b. — VIGN 810:6
Nous n'irons plus aux b. — ANON 20:18
bold Be b., be bold — SPEN 752:1
b. as a blind mare — PROV 628:12
b. as a hawk — CART 198:4
b. as a hawk — LOVE 493:13
b. as a lion — BIBL 85:16
b. bad man — SPEN 751:14
b. man that first — SWIF 766:11
Fortune assists the b. — VIRG 813:8
let our minds be b. — BRAN 149:11
made me b. — SHAK 704:19
This b. bad man — SHAK 695:7
boldest b. held his breath — CAMP 187:6
boldly to b. go — RODD 651:20
boldness B., and again boldness — DANT 256:14
b. at least will deserve — PROP 612:22
B. be my friend — SHAK 682:28
B. is an ill keeper — BACO 43:23
what first? b. — BACO 43:22
Bolingbroke this canker, B. — SHAK 689:27
bolt b., and the breech — REED 644:4
b. is shot back somewhere — ARNO 27:2
bolts b. are hurled — TENN 781:9
bomb atom b. is a paper tiger — MAO 511:13
Ban the b. — POLI 600:5
b. them back into the Stone Age — LEMA 480:1
defence against the atom b. — ANON 15:7
'formula' of the atomic b. — MEDA 520:3
ones we intended to b. — BLY 124:11
bombazine B. would have shown — GASK 340:18
bombed glad we've been b. — ELIZ 305:6
protect him from being b. — BALD 50:15
bomber b. will always get through — BALD 50:15
bombers b. named for girls — JARR 418:28
bombinans chimera in vacuo b. — RABE 639:18
bombs b. redoubled on the hills — MOTI 551:12
Come, friendly b. — BETJ 72:17
bond b. between two people — RILK 649:3
B. James Bond. — FILM 320:9
b. nor free — BIBL 110:12
break that sole b. — BURK 166:30
great b. — SHAK 706:1
I will have my b. — SHAK 709:20
look to his b. — SHAK 709:12
take a b. of fate — SHAK 706:17
word is his b. — PROV 618:46

bondage b. of fear — CLOS 228:9
b. of rhyming — MILT 531:3
b. to parents — WOLL 844:8
Cassius from b. will deliver — SHAK 696:19
condition of b. — STAN 754:9
house of b. — BIBL 77:37
spirit of b. — BIBL 106:18
bonding male b. — TIGE 794:14
bondman b.'s two hundred and fifty years — LINC 485:11
so base that would be a b. — SHAK 697:20
bonds b. of civil society — LOCK 488:19
except these b. — BIBL 105:33
surly b. of earth — MAGE 505:16
surly b. of earth — REAG 643:16
bondsmen Hereditary b. — BYRO 178:12
bondwoman of the b. — BIBL 108:27
bone B. of my bone — MILT 534:3
b. of my bones — BIBL 75:16
commend the b. — DICK 273:12
dog that will fetch a b. — PROV 618:2
fighting for a b. — PROV 634:46
hair about the b. — DONN 281:8
knows death to the b. — YEAT 853:18
nearer the b. — PROV 627:8
poor dog a b. — NURS 568:14
rag and a b. — KIPL 456:2
What's bred in the b. — PROV 634:9
boneless b. wonder — CHUR 220:23
bones b. are out of joint — BOOK 135:1
b. are smitten asunder — BOOK 136:14
b. of a single Pomeranian — BISM 117:17
b. of one British Grenadier — HARR 374:1
b. which thou hast broken — BOOK 137:12
Can these b. live — BIBL 91:17
come to lay his weary b. — SHAK 695:17
conjuring trick with b. — JENK 420:20
dead men lost their b. — ELIO 303:14
dead men's b. — BIBL 98:11
England keep my b. — SHAK 699:13
for his honoured b. — MILT 530:14
from my dead b., avenger — VIRG 812:6
grind his b. — ANON 16:2
hadde pigges b. — CHAU 211:2
Hard words break no b. — PROV 621:34
hatchment o'er his b. — SHAK 688:14
he that moves my b. — EPIT 309:10
his b. are coral — SHAK 718:27
I may tell all my b. — BOOK 135:2
lay my b. amongst you — WOLS 844:11
little ones picked the b. O! — NURS 568:15
my b. consumed away — BOOK 135:20
O ye dry b. — BIBL 91:18
Rattle his b. — NOEL 565:7
subsist in b. — BROW 156:13
tongs and the b. — SHAK 711:20
turf that covers her soft b. — MART 514:20
valley full of b. — BIBL 91:16
you buy meat, you buy b. — PROV 635:24
bonfire of the vanities — WOLF 843:19
match lighting a b. — LIND 486:1
to the everlasting b. — SHAK 705:6
Bong-tree where the B. grows — LEAR 477:16
bonheur b. seul est salutaire — PROU 613:15
bonhomie natural b. — BENT 68:15
bonjour B. tristesse — ÉLUA 306:7
bon-mots b. from their places — MORE 548:1
bonnets Blue B. are bound — SCOT 674:15
b. of Bonny Dundee — SCOT 673:3
bonnie b. Annie Laurie — SONG 748:1
Maxwelton braes are b. — SONG 747:15
bonny Am I no a b. fighter — STEV 759:2
Belbroughton Road is b. — BETJ 72:12
bonnets of B. Dundee — SCOT 673:3
b., bonnie banks — SONG 748:3
longer in b. Dundee — SCOT 674:21
saw ye b. Lesley — BURN 170:16
bono Cui b. — CICE 223:22
bonum Summum b. — CICE 223:11
bonus b. homo — AUCT 34:11
videri b. malebat — SALL 665:4

Boojum Snark was a B. — CARR 196:12
book agree with the b. of God — OMAR 573:6
any b. but the Baronetage — AUST 39:11
any b. but the Baronetage — OPEN 575:17
Bell, b., and candle — SHAK 699:5
b. a devil's chaplain — DARW 257:12
B., and the Prophets — KORA 459:11
b. cannot take the place — ANON 19:11
b. is the precious life-blood — MILT 535:15
b. is the purest essence — CARL 193:1
b. of life — BIBL 113:3
B. of Life begins — WILD 836:23
b. of nature — GALI 338:10
b. of the living — BOOK 138:18
b. of verse—and Thou — FITZ 323:2
b. that ever took him out of bed — JOHN 429:8
B. wherein is no doubt — KORA 459:9
b., who runs may read — KEBL 447:14
b. would have been finished — WODE 842:22
bred in a b. — SHAK 702:16
but his b. — JONS 435:24
Camerado, this is no b. — WHIT 833:8
damned, thick, square b. — GLOU 351:15
destroys a good b. — MILT 535:14
doth best commend a b. — HEMI 381:2
Each country B.-club — BYRO 182:10
empty b. is like an infant's — TRAH 797:10
Farewell my b. — CHAU 212:22
Galeotto was the b. — DANT 255:20
Go, litel b. — CHAU 213:14
Go, little b. — STEV 760:19
good b. is the best of friends — TUPP 802:3
great b. — CALL 186:3
great b. is a great evil — PROV 621:15
had been reading the b. — TOLS 796:15
I'll drown my b. — SHAK 719:5
insignificant b. because — WOOL 845:8
In the volume of the b. — BOOK 136:7
Kiss the b.'s outside — COWP 246:11
knows this out of the b. — DICK 270:18
leaves of the Judgement B. unfold — TAYL 774:18
little volume, but large b. — CRAS 250:13
look at the best b. — RUSK 659:20
make one b. — JOHN 430:5
Making a b. is a craft — LA B 463:1
my little b. — JUVE 439:10
nice new little b. — CATU 199:22
noble aspect b. — GASK 340:21
no b. so bad that — PLIN 598:7
no Frigate like a B. — DICK 273:2
non-reading a b. — BYRO 184:13
noted in thy b. — BOOK 137:19
oldest rule in the b. — CARR 194:22
pain to pen the b. — OXFO 581:11
peruses a b. — ADDI 4:24
print My b. — HERR 386:17
read a b. before reviewing it — SMIT 744:6
sending down of the B. — KORA 460:22
sent down to thee the B. — KORA 460:12
substance of a b. directly — KNOW 458:5
take the b. along — STER 756:21
tell a b. by its cover — PROV 635:45
this b. I directe To the — CHAU 213:18
throw b. in the fire — SAND 665:13
throw this b. about — BELL 64:17
to every b. its copy — COLU 236:12
use of a b. — CARR 193:17
valuable b. by chance — GRAY 362:2
when I wrote that b. — SWIF 767:21
where's the b. — CHUR 219:18
without mentioning a single b. — REED 644:10
worthy to open the b. — BIBL 113:11
write in a b. — BIBL 112:27
writing a b. — BRON 153:1
written a b. — JOWE 436:20
written b. — MISS 539:16
wrote the b. — LINC 485:15
Your face, my thane, is as a b. — SHAK 703:22
bookful b. blockhead — POPE 604:16
bookkeeping inventor of double-entry b. — MULL 553:20
books b. are divisible — RUSK 659:17

b. are either dreams or swords — LOWE 493:18
B. are made — FLAU 325:15
b. are to be tasted — BACO 45:20
b. are weapons — ROOS 654:2
B. are well written — WILD 836:11
b. be then the eloquence — SHAK 722:27
b., clad in blak or reed — CHAU 210:17
B. do furnish a room — POWE 609:13
B. from Boots' and country lanes — BETJ 72:10
b. I leave behind — KIPL 453:14
b. in the running brooks — SHAK 680:26
B., like men their authors — SWIF 766:14
B. must follow sciences — BACO 46:19
b. of law — JOHN 423:10
b. of travel — ELIO 300:12
B. say: she did this because — BARN 56:9
b., the academes — SHAK 702:18
B. think for me — LAMB 464:16
b. to gather facts from — CARL 192:31
b. undeservedly forgotten — AUDE 36:17
b. were opened — BIBL 91:24
B. will speak plain — BACO 43:27
borrowers of b. — LAMB 464:14
collection of b. — CARL 192:14
cream of others' b. — MORE 548:1
Deep-versed in b. — MILT 534:23
even to read his b. — ISID 414:11
fate of b. — TERE 785:9
gentleman is not in your b. — SHAK 712:11
God has written all the b. — BUTL 176:30
his b. were read — BELL 65:21
If my b. had been any worse — CHAN 207:16
in b.' clothing — LAMB 464:17
In b. lies the soul — CARL 192:13
I never read b. — PUNC 637:17
Keeping b. on charity — PERÓ 592:25
lard their lean b. — BURT 173:20
learn men from b. — DISR 277:32
made the b. and he died — FAUL 316:3
making many b. — BIBL 86:26
more b. on books — MONT 545:3
more in woods than b. — BERN 70:12
new French b. — BROW 158:6
proper study of mankind is b. — HUXL 411:4
quiet, friendship, b. — THOM 792:9
read all the b. — MALL 508:13
read any good b. lately — CATC 200:24
read b. through — JOHN 429:23
reading of good b. — DESC 265:8
so charming as b. — SMIT 743:20
speaks about his own b. — DISR 276:11
spectacles of b. — DRYD 290:4
studied b. than men — BACO 46:7
thumb each other's b. — RUSK 659:21
thy toil O'er b. — GAY 341:25
to Cambridge b. he sent — BROW 157:14
Wherever b. will be burned — HEIN 379:13
booksellers nor men, nor even b. — HORA 398:17
boon b. and a blessing — ADVE 8:17
boot b. in the face — PLAT 596:21
B., saddle, to horse — BROW 158:22
b. stamping on a human face — ORWE 577:22
bootboy body of the b. at Claridges — WOOL 845:11
booted b. and spurred — RUMB 658:5
boots b. blaming on his b. — BECK 61:14
Books from B.' and country lanes — BETJ 72:10
boots—b.—movin' — KIPL 453:17
doormat in a world of b. — RHYS 646:16
have one's b. on — MONT 544:1
in his top-b. — MARL 512:11
truth is pulling its b. on — SPUR 753:13
when I take my b. off — DICK 269:11
booze fool with b. — FAUL 316:6
boozes tell a man who "b." — BURT 173:14
bop Playing 'B.' — ELLI 305:12
Bo-Peep Little B. — NURS 567:21
Borden Lizzie B. took an axe — ANON 17:9
border B., nor Breed — KIPL 453:15
bound for the B. — SCOT 674:15
crossing the B. — AUDE 35:15
gaed o'er the b. — BURN 170:16

bread (cont.):
our daily b.   BIBL 95:3
ravens brought him b.   BIBL 81:19
Royal slice of b.   MILN 528:2
shalt thou eat b.   BIBL 75:26
taste of another man's b.   DANT 256:12
that which is not b.   BIBL 90:6
took B.   BOOK 132:2
took b., and blessed it   BIBL 99:1
took the b. and brake it   ELIZ 304:20
unleavened b.   BIBL 77:29
unleavened b. of sincerity   BIBL 107:11
we did eat b.   BIBL 77:36
Whoever eats b. without   TALM 772:22
breadth length and b.   BALL 52:2
break at the b. of the day   STRU 762:15
bend and I b. not   LA F 463:11
b. a man's spirit   SHAW 724:24
B., break, break   TENN 775:16
b. every yoke   BIBL 90:14
b. Into blossom   WRIG 851:14
b. the ice   BACO 43:29
b. them at pleasure   EDGE 296:3
But b., my heart   SHAK 684:6
Have a b.   ADVE 7:28
if you b. the bloody glass   MACN 504:16
I'll b. my staff   SHAK 719:5
lark at b. of day   SHAK 722:30
Never give a sucker an even b.   FIEL 318:18
shall he not b.   BIBL 89:22
sucker an even b.   PROV 627:20
thyself must b. at last   ARNO 27:14
breakdown approaching nervous b.
   RUSS 660:16
Madness need not be all b.   LAIN 464:6
breaketh b. the bow   BOOK 136:26
b. the cedar-trees   BOOK 135:16
breakfast committed b. with it   LEWI 483:12
critical period is b.-time   HERB 383:13
embarrassment and b.   BARN 56:7
Hope is a good b.   BACO 46:21
Hope is a good b.   PROV 622:31
impossible things before b.   CARR 195:12
One doth but b. here   HENS 382:17
our b. take   BALL 53:13
Sing before b.   PROV 630:42
that sits down to b.   YEAT 856:9
wholesome, hungry b.   WALT 820:23
breakfasted b. with you   BRUC 162:4
breaking b. of bread   BIBL 102:13
b. of windows   MORE 547:24
take pleasure in b.   NURS 566:11
without b. eggs   PROV 635:32
breast boiling bloody b.   SHAK 712:2
b. high amid the corn   HOOD 395:10
broods with warm b.   HOPK 396:13
dwell, alas! in my b.   GOET 352:15
faultless b. the furnace is   SOUT 749:20
leaned on his b. at supper   BIBL 104:23
Oak was round his b.   HORA 400:4
parts of the b.   BYRD 177:15
sooth a savage b.   CONG 238:29
weariness May toss him to My b.
   HERB 384:21
with dauntless b.   GRAY 361:5
breastie panic's in thy b.   BURN 172:20
breastplate b. of faith   BIBL 110:17
b. of judgement   BIBL 78:7
b. of righteousness   BIBL 109:21
breasts betwixt my b.   BIBL 87:4
b. are like two young roes   BIBL 87:10
b. by which France is fed   SULL 763:14
her b. are dun   SHAK 723:26
Sestos and Abydos of her b.   DONN 279:9
breath boldest held his b.   CAMP 187:6
b. can make them   GOLD 354:10
Breathe on me, B. of God   HATC 375:3
breathes with human b.   TENN 784:12
breathing thoughtful b.   WORD 850:4
b. of life   BIBL 75:11
b. of worldly men   SHAK 715:19
B.'s a ware   HOUS 404:8
b. thou art   SHAK 708:8

call the fleeting b.   GRAY 361:4
Clothed with his b.   TENN 778:14
down and out of b.   SHAK 691:17
drawn the b. of life   YEAT 854:9
draw thy b. in pain   SHAK 689:14
every thing that hath b.   BOOK 144:9
feather on the b. of God   HILD 388:4
fly away, b.   SHAK 720:26
having lost her b., she spoke   SHAK 679:6
healthy b. of morn   KEAT 443:9
last b. of Julius Caesar   JEAN 419:6
lighter than b.   BERR 71:14
lightly draws its b.   WORD 850:20
love thee with the b.   BROW 158:4
sweeter woman ne'er drew b.   INGE 413:13
taxed the b.   THOM 789:11
thou no b. at all   SHAK 702:7
toil of b.   COLE 231:16
waste of b.   YEAT 854:16
while you have it use your b.   FLET 327:1
breathe As though to b. were life
   TENN 784:15
b. by a sort of artificial inlet   FOST 330:9
b. in that fine air   TENN 777:22
b. in the faces   PEPY 592:12
b. not his name   MOOR 547:18
B. on me, Breath of God   HATC 375:3
b. when I expire   BYRO 179:11
privilege to b.   ELEA 298:21
So long as men can b.   SHAK 722:25
summer's morn to b.   MILT 533:28
yearning to b. free   LAZA 476:10
breathes B. there the man   SCOT 673:11
breathing Closer is He than b.   TENN 777:12
breathless b. hush in the Close   NEWB 560:5
b. on thy fate   LONG 490:2
B. with adoration   WORD 847:2
bred B. en bawn in a brier-patch   HARR 374:5
What's b. in the bone   PROV 634:9
Bredon In summertime on B.   HOUS 404:11
bree little abune her b.   BALL 53:8
breeches boys with b.   BARB 55:7
breed Border, nor B.   KIPL 453:15
b. of their horses   PENN 591:17
b. one work that wakes   HOPK 397:9
Feared by their b.   SHAK 715:14
happy b. of men   SHAK 715:13
wife for b.   GAY 342:13
breeding b. consists in concealing
   TWAI 803:20
show your b.   SHER 734:4
without any b.   CART 198:2
breeks b. aff a wild Highlandman   SCOT 674:8
breeze b. from foggy mount   BYRO 179:31
b. is on the sea   SCOT 674:17
b. of morning moves   TENN 781:23
dancing in the b.   WORD 847:5
wander like a b.   COLE 231:21
with the b. of song   TENN 779:11
breezes b. dusk and shiver   TENN 780:6
breezy B., Sneezy, Freezy   ELLI 306:1
Breffny little waves of B.   GORE 357:2
brekekekex B. koax koax   ARIS 25:6
brethren b., to dwell together   BOOK 143:9
Dearly beloved b.   BOOK 127:13
least of these my b.   BIBL 98:26
my mother and my b.   BIBL 97:2
we be b.   BIBL 76:14
brevis Ars longa, vita b.   HIPP 389:9
B. esse laboro   HORA 397:22
Vitae summa b.   HORA 400:6
brevity B. is the sister   CHEK 214:10
B. is the soul of wit   PROV 616:14
B. is the soul of wit   SHAK 685:15
Its body b.   COLE 231:15
brew bake so shall you b.   PROV 614:37
b., so shall you bake   PROV 614:38
b. that is true   FILM 320:15
brewers bakeres and b.   LANG 466:17
brewery take me to a b.   ANON 16:17
bribe b. or gratuity   PENN 591:18
cannot hope to b. or twist   WOLF 843:13
done without a b.   CENT 205:7

Marriage is a b.   WILD 837:15
Too poor for a b.   GRAY 361:22
bribery corrupt by b.   WILL 838:6
bribes open to b.   GREE 362:11
bricht braw b. moonlicht   MORR 550:10
brick b. in his pocket   JOHN 425:13
carried a piece of b.   SWIF 765:8
'Eave arf a b. at 'im   PUNC 637:8
Follow the yellow b. road   HARB 371:5
Goodbye yellow b. road   JOHN 422:15
hardly throw a b.   ORWE 577:23
inherited it b.   AUGU 37:22
paved with yellow b.   BAUM 59:6
threw it a b. at a time   HARG 373:12
bricks b. to Lewley   BETJ 72:16
make b. without straw   PROV 635:33
bridal Against their b. day   SPEN 752:16
b. of the earth and sky   HERB 385:4
dance at our b.   SCOT 673:21
bride as a b. adorned for her husband
   BIBL 114:16
barren b.   POPE 603:4
became my glittering b.   WORD 846:16
b. forget her attire   BIBL 90:23
b. of a ducal coronet   DICK 270:12
b. of quietness   OPEN 575:25
b. that sun shines on   PROV 621:30
encounter darkness as a b.   SHAK 708:9
jealousy to the b.   BARR 57:6
mourning b.   DRYD 289:9
my life and my b.   POE 599:1
never a b.   PROV 614:21
Never the blushing b.   LEIG 479:19
Passionless b.   TENN 781:13
ser' him for a b.   MACD 501:2
thy b.-bed to have decked   SHAK 689:3
To be his holy b.   STON 761:5
unravished b. of quietness   KEAT 444:6
virgin, yet a b.   CARE 190:16
young b. was the idol   MANZ 511:10
bridegroom Bellona's b.   SHAK 703:4
b. in my death   SHAK 679:25
cometh forth as a b.   BOOK 134:20
Like a b.   AYTO 41:13
bridegrooms Of b., brides   HERR 385:16
brides B. of Enderby   INGE 413:11
Of bride-grooms, b.   HERR 385:16
bridesmaid Always a b.   PROV 614:21
always the b.   LEIG 479:19
bridge Beautiful Railway B.   MCGO 501:16
b. is love   WILD 837:14
b. of gold   PROV 624:4
b. over troubled water   SIMO 738:2
cross the b.   PROV 618:9
going a b. too far   BROW 158:6
Horatius kept the b.   MACA 499:20
keep the b. with me   MACA 499:14
London B. is broken down   NURS 568:6
man on the bridge   BALD 50:19
On the B. of Toome   CARB 190:5
speaks well of the b.   PROV 619:20
Women, and Champagne, and B.
   BELL 65:19
brief little b. authority   SHAK 708:1
strive to be b.   HORA 397:22
tedious and b.   SHAK 711:30
brier bawn in a b.-patch   HARR 374:5
instead of the b.   BIBL 90:9
Thorough bush, thorough b.   SHAK 710:27
briers O, how full of b.   SHAK 680:23
brig From B. o' Dread   BALL 52:12
brigade boys of the old B.   WEAT 824:22
brigand I am a b.   SHAW 726:5
brigandage teaches him b.   TALM 772:27
bright All things b. and beautiful   ALEX 11:6
Behold the b. original   GAY 342:5
b. and fierce and fickle   TENN 783:4
B. as the day   GRAN 359:10
b. day is done   SHAK 680:7
b. day that brings forth   SHAK 696:21
b. face of danger   STEV 758:23
b. northern star   LOVE 493:2
b. particular star   SHAK 678:7

B. the vision MANT 511:8
dark and b. BYRO 183:4
Death's b. angel PROC 612:18
excessive b. MILT 532:18
eyes are b. KEAT 446:19
future's b. ADVE 7:24
Goddess, excellently b. JONS 435:2
Keep up your b. swords SHAK 713:4
look, the land is b. CLOU 229:12
obscurely b. BYRO 179:29
quick b. things SHAK 710:18
thought thee b. SHAK 723:32
torches to burn b. SHAK 717:17
Tyger, burning b. BLAK 122:19
young lady named B. BULL 163:16
brighten Blessings b. PROV 616:3
brightest B. and best HEBE 38:14
brightness B. falls from the air NASH 557:21
b. of his presence BOOK 134:17
his Darkness and his B. BYRO 183:19
leaking the b. away SPEN 750:23
Brighton B. Pavilion looks as if SMIT 744:3
Brignal B. banks are wild SCOT 674:2
brilliance Renew your b. GRAC 358:1
brilliant dullard's envy of b. men BEER 63:5
brillig 'Twas b. CARR 194:25
brim sparkles near the b. BYRO 178:16
winking at the b. KEAT 444:22
brimstone fire and b. BOOK 134:8
smouldering b. ALAB 9:12
bring b. home knowledge JOHN 431:5
B. me my arrows of desire BLAK 121:15
B. out number BLAK 121:2
day may b. forth BIBL 85:12
what it will b. PROV 635:21
bringer b. of unwelcome news SHAK 691:22
bringing b. me up by hand DICK 269:15
brink walked to the b. DULL 291:10
brinkmanship boasting of his b. STEV 758:17
brioche *mangent de la b.* MARI 512:7
brisk b. as a bee JOHN 427:10
b. little somebody BROW 158:13
brisking b. about the life SMAR 739:18
Britain boundary of B. TACI 770:2
B. a fit country LLOY 487:18
B., could you ever boast SWIF 767:6
B.'s stand alone DE V 266:4
B. will be honoured by historians HARL 373:16
B. will still be MAJO 508:5
dangerous man in B. NEWS 562:12
government of B.'s isle SHAK 694:15
hail, happy B. SOME 745:22
Hath B. all the sun SHAK 683:5
I'm backing B. SLOG 740:4
Keep B. tidy OFFI 572:9
should belong to B. GIRA 350:2
speak for B. BOOT 145:2
When B. first THOM 792:1
Without B., Europe ERHA 308:13
Britannia Beer and B. SMIT 744:11
Rule, B. THOM 792:1
shouted 'Rule B.' KIPL 453:11
British as the B. public MACA 498:6
blood of a B. man SHAK 701:2
bones of one B. Grenadier HARR 374:1
B. Grenadier SONG 748:5
B. Museum had lost its charm GERS 344:4
B. Nation ADDI 5:3
B. subject I was born MACD 501:9
Come you back, you B. soldier KIPL 454:21
destinies of the B. Empire DISR 275:19
drunken officer of B. rule WALC 817:4
less known by the B. BORR 145:9
of B. blood TENN 777:11
removed By B. hands BYRO 178:8
so also a B. subject PALM 584:20
stony B. stare TENN 781:21
thank God! the B. journalist WOLF 843:13
We are B., thank God MONT 545:14
west from the B. coast BOWE 148:4
Briton free-born B. can THAC 786:13
glory in the name of B. GEOR 343:4

No good man is a B. AUSO 38:14
Britons B. alone use 'Might' WAUG 824:15
B. never will be slaves THOM 792:1
B. who are kept far away VIRG 813:15
broad b. is the way BIBL 95:19
B. of Church BETJ 73:5
how b. and far JOHN 433:22
She's the B. SPRI 753:8
too b. for leaping HOUS 405:1
broadens travel b. the mind; but CHES 217:7
broadminded superior man is b. CONF 237:13
Broadway sinners on this part of B. RUNY 659:1
broccoli b., dear CART 198:3
eat any more b. BUSH 174:24
brogues not fit to tie his b. SCOT 674:29
broke If it ain't b. SAYI 669:25
broken bats have been b. HOWE 405:11
bones which thou hast b. BOOK 137:12
b. and contrite heart BOOK 137:15
b. Anne of gathering bouquets FROS 336:2
b. by their passing feet YEAT 853:15
b.-hearted woman HAYE 376:7
b. the lock AUDE 35:21
Can it be b. JENK 420:21
healeth those that are b. BOOK 144:3
house has been b. open PEAC 589:14
London Bridge is b. down NURS 568:6
made to be b. NORT 565:11
made to be b. PROV 629:42
Morning has b. FARJ 315:2
neck once b. WALS 820:11
not quickly b. BIBL 86:3
old man, b. SHAK 695:17
taken up the b. blade DE G 262:3
through a b. heart WILD 837:3
brokenhearted bind up the b. BIBL 90:18
broker honest b. BISM 117:19
bronze b. and stone RUNY 659:3
monument more lasting than b. HORA 402:3
noontide was b. CHUR 222:8
bronzes Others shall shape b. VIRG 812:15
brooches b. and toys STEV 760:11
brood b. of folly MILT 529:9
b. of glory SPEN 751:17
thy b. is flown TENN 783:7
broods b. with warm breast HOPK 396:13
brook b. and river meet LONG 490:14
dwelt by the b. Cherith BIBL 81:19
free, meandering b. THOR 792:25
grows aslant a b. SHAK 688:17
noise like a hidden b. COLE 233:6
salad from the b. COWP 248:16
willows of the b. BIBL 83:28
brooks b. of Eden TENN 782:11
By b. too broad HOUS 405:1
broom sent with b. before SHAK 712:7
brooms New b. sweep clean PROV 627:32
broomstick mortal man is a b. SWIF 766:7
broth spoil the b. PROV 633:14
brothel intellectual b. TOLS 797:1
metaphysical b. for the emotions KOES 458:15
brothels b. with bricks of religion BLAK 121:4
Keep thy foot out of b. SHAK 700:25
brother Be my b. CHAM 207:8
BIG B. IS WATCHING YOU ORWE 577:13
b. came with subtilty BIBL 76:29
B. can you spare a dime HARB 371:1
b. followed brother WORD 846:19
b., hail, and farewell CATU 203:10
b. he is in Elysium SHAK 720:7
b. in God BELL 65:10
b. is born for adversity BIBL 84:29
b. is on the rack SMIT 741:4
B. of the Angle WALT 820:18
b. sin against me BIBL 97:23
b.'s soul BARB 55:5
B., thy tail hangs down KIPL 456:13
B. to Death DANI 255:7
b. to dragons BIBL 83:18
closer than a b. BIBL 84:32

dear b. here departed BOOK 133:18
Death and his b. SHEL 731:11
especially Sir B. Sun FRAN 332:5
every man's b. BIBL 76:10
fold to thy heart thy b. WHIT 834:6
glad mad b.'s name SWIN 768:7
Had it been his b. EPIT 310:2
hateth his b. BIBL 112:22
he's my b. RUSS 661:9
hurt my b. SHAK 689:8
lo'ed him like a vera b. BURN 172:9
man and a b. WEDG 826:17
marry with his b. SHAK 687:21
my b. is a hairy man BIBL 76:27
my b. Jonathan BIBL 80:29
my b.'s keeper BIBL 75:28
my likeness—my b. BAUD 58:12
O b. man WHIT 834:6
stick more close than a b. KIPL 455:20
to my b. turns GOLD 355:10
unto a tyrant b. SHAK 680:22
voice of thy b.'s blood BIBL 75:29
want to be the white man's b. KING 451:17
what my b. will do CHAR 209:9
brotherhood broadened into a b. JOHN 423:11
crown thy good with b. BATE 58:10
Love the b. BIBL 112:7
sit down at the table of b. KING 452:4
brotherly b. love continue BIBL 111:13
brothers All men become b. SCHI 670:24
all the b. too SHAK 720:30
B. and sisters rocking JOHN 423:4
B. in humanity VILL 810:11
B. of the Great GERS 344:12
feel they are b. GODW 352:5
forty thousand b. SHAK 689:4
live together as b. KING 452:5
noble pair of b. HORA 403:13
single nation of b. SCHI 671:6
So the two b. KEAT 443:18
we band of b. SHAK 693:24
We were b. all WORD 849:14
brought b. forth her firstborn son BIBL 100:2
safely b. KEBL 447:12
brow b. of Egypt SHAK 711:28
b. of labour BRYA 162:12
rugged b. of careful Policy SPEN 751:6
with a velvet b. SHAK 702:15
Your bonny b. was brent BURN 171:15
brown b. coat MACA 498:1
b. of her MEW 523:15
b. study CONG 238:19
Brünnhilde had b. braids JARR 418:26
falling on the city b. BRID 151:6
Her b. embrace WALK 817:12
Jeanie with the light b. hair FOST 330:13
John B.'s body SONG 747:13
river Is a strong b. god ELIO 301:20
She has b. hair SHAK 710:10
browner tinge with a b. shade GIBB 345:23
Browning God and Robert B. BROW 162:1
Hang it all, Robert B. POUN 608:15
safety-catch of my B. JOHS 434:1
brows Bliss in our b. bent SHAK 678:21
nodded with his darkish b. HOME 393:20
pallor of girls' b. OWEN 581:3
shadow of her even b. SPEN 751:22
browsing b. and sluicing WODE 843:4
bruise b. them with a rod of iron BOOK 133:21
It shall b. thy head BIBL 75:24
tread on it and b. it TROL 799:20
bruised b. for our iniquities BIBL 90:3
b. in a new place IRVI 414:5
b. reed BIBL 82:17
b. reed BIBL 89:22
bruisers b. of England BORR 145:11
bruises No man b. his finger TALM 772:33
Brünnhilde B. had brown braids JARR 418:26
brunt Bear the b. BROW 161:2
brush so fine a b. AUST 40:18
with my b. I make love MISQ 538:3

brushers b. of noblemen's clothes
WOTT 851:9
Brust *in meiner B.* GOET 352:15
bruta *B. fulmina* PLIN 598:2
brutal heart's grown b. from the fare
YEAT 854:24
brutality without art is b. RUSK 659:11
brute b. vote BAGE 48:3
Et tu, B.? SHAK 697:10
Feed the b. PUNC 637:21
heart of a b. like you PLAT 596:21
like b. beasts BOOK 133:5
brutes Exterminate all the b. CONR 240:15
made to live as b. DANT 256:3
brutish hungry beating b. one SCHW 672:8
nasty, b., and short HOBB 390:16
Brutus B. is an honourable man SHAK 697:23
B. makes mine greater SHAK 698:17
B. took to wife SHAK 697:2
'B.' will start a spirit SHAK 696:10
is B. sick SHAK 696:27
noble B. Hath told you SHAK 697:22
Portia is B.' harlot SHAK 697:1
You too, B. CAES 185:8
bubble dew drops, or a b. MAHĀ 506:16
empty b. GRAI 358:16
Honour but an empty b. DRYD 287:17
light-blown b. BOLT 126:17
like unto a b. WARD 821:15
mostly froth and b. GORD 356:17
now a b. burst POPE 604:21
Seeking the b. reputation SHAK 681:11
world's a b. BACO 46:23
bubbles frill of b. DUNM 292:7
I'm forever blowing b. KENB 448:9
With beaded b. KEAT 444:22
bubus *b. exercet suis* HORA 400:1
Bücher *wo man B. Verbrennt* HEIN 379:13
buck bigger bang for a b. POLI 600:8
b. stops here TRUM 801:15
bucket as a drop of a b. BIBL 89:19
past is a b. of ashes SAND 665:21
stick inside a swill b. ORWE 578:9
buckets b. into empty wells COWP 248:1
Buckingham so much for B. CIBB 223:2
Buckingham Palace changing guard at B.
MILN 527:20
buckle B. my shoe NURS 568:18
b. which fastens BAGE 47:17
buckram eleven b. men SHAK 690:9
Four rogues in b. SHAK 690:8
bud be a b. again KEAT 443:1
b., and yet a rose HERR 386:22
leaf, the b., the flower SPEN 751:25
nip him in the b. ROCH 651:3
now in age I b. again HERB 384:8
Buddha B., peerless among men PALI 583:18
Has a dog the B.-Nature MUMO 554:4
Kill the B. I-HS 412:20
real B. is to be found HUI- 408:6
What is the B. MUMO 554:6
What is the B. MUMO 554:7
Buddhahood Germ of B. MAHĀ 506:18
speedily gain B. TANT 773:4
budding b. morrow in midnight KEAT 445:20
budge b. doctors of the Stoic fur MILT 529:6
'B.,' says the fiend SHAK 709:4
budget b. should be balanced MISQ 537:5
buds darling b. of May SHAK 722:24
sweet b. like flocks SHEL 730:7
buffalo breath of a b. CROW 253:1
buffeted b. for your faults BIBL 112:8
bug b. with gilded wings POPE 602:31
not a b., it's a feature SAYI 669:30
snug As a b. In a rug EPIT 310:8
bugger B. Bognor LAST 471:5
bugle Blow, b., blow TENN 782:27
bugles Blow out, you b. BROO 153:5
b. calling from sad shires OWEN 581:2
build Birds b. HOPK 397:9
b. a tower BIBL 101:10
b. the house of death MONT 544:3
easy to b. IBSE 412:14

end is to b. well WOTT 851:7
Lord b. the house BOOK 143:1
never ask *why* b. SEXT 677:17
than to b. up PROV 623:46
think we b. for ever RUSK 659:24
those who will b. it TRUD 801:1
builded b. better than he knew EMER 306:14
builder can only be a *b.* RUSK 659:10
maker and b. is God BIBL 111:7
builders stone which the b. refused
BOOK 142:10
building be able to read a b. ROGE 652:9
finish b. it RANK 642:5
principal beauty in b. FULL 337:6
very old b. OSBO 578:15
buildings pompous b. WULF 851:19
builds b. on mud MACH 502:11
he that b. stronger SHAK 688:23
Office b. up a man BENN 67:1
built All we have b. ARNO 27:18
b. in a day PROV 630:16
not what they b. FENT 316:11
therefore b. for ever TENN 777:19
Till we have b. Jerusalem BLAK 121:15
Who b. Thebes BREC 150:16
bulimia yuppie version of b. EHRE 297:6
bull b. half-man OVID 580:2
Cock and a B. STER 757:16
curled Assyrian B. TENN 781:18
Dance tiptoe, b. BUNT 164:10
milk the b. JOHN 428:12
strong as a b. moose ROOS 654:6
bullet b. has its billet PROV 619:3
b. has its billet WILL 838:3
b. through his head ROBI 650:15
b. through his heart THAC 786:16
Faster than a speeding b. ANON 15:25
stronger than the b. MISQ 537:3
bullets bloody b. LINC 484:15
b. made of platinum BELL 64:18
bullfighters b. of Spain BORR 145:11
bullied b. into a certain philosophy
KEAT 446:6
b. out of vice SURT 764:9
bulling b. through wave-wrack MERW 523:5
bullocks talk is of b. BIBL 93:29
bulls eat b.' flesh BOOK 137:9
fat b. of Basan BOOK 134:28
bully b. is always a coward PROV 616:15
by the bossy for the b. SELD 676:13
love the lovely b. SHAK 693:11
such a b. pulpit ROOS 654:11
bulrushes ark of b. BIBL 77:13
bulwark floating b. of the island BLAC 118:10
bulwarks Mark well her b. BOOK 137:6
bum Does my b. look big CATC 200:11
Indicat Motorem B. GODL 351:19
Pee, po, belly, b., drawers FLAN 324:17
bump go b. in the night PRAY 611:2
bumpy going to be a b. night FILM 319:6
bums corporate welfare b. LEWI 483:13
Bunbury invalid called B. WILD 835:13
Buncombe talking to B. WALK 817:14
through reporters to B. CARL 192:17
bundle never the b. of accident YEAT 856:9
bungler good nature is a b. HALI 369:8
Man is a b. SHAW 726:10
bunk History more or less b. FORD 328:13
bunny B. had been dead OPEN 575:18
buns bears might come with b. ISHE 414:9
hot cross b. NURS 568:16
bunting Bye, baby b. NURS 566:10
burbled b. as it came CARR 194:26
burd b. Helen dropt BALL 52:6
burden bear any b. KENN 448:16
bear the b. and the heat ARNO 27:18
borne the b. BIBL 98:2
b. of them is intolerable BOOK 131:18
b. of the nation's care PRIO 612:8
impossible to carry the heavy b.
EDWA 296:12
makes back to the b. PROV 620:46
my b. is light BIBL 96:27

White Man's B. KIPL 456:7
burdens bear such b. in our lives
HOME 394:12
undo the heavy b. BIBL 90:14
bureaucracy [b.'s] specific invention
WEBE 825:8
bureaucrats b. will care more BAGE 48:19
Guidelines for b. BORE 145:3
Burg *Eine feste B.* LUTH 496:11
burghers b. of Carlisle MACA 499:3
burgundy naive domestic B. CART 198:2
burial b.-ground God's-Acre LONG 490:11
buried in Christian b. SHAK 688:21
his obscure b. SHAK 688:14
thought they had only one b. BOCC 124:16
buried all b. here BRON 152:16
bodies are b. in peace BIBL 93:34
b. at midnight O'BR 571:3
b. him darkly WOLF 843:11
b. in a good old age BIBL 76:16
b. in so sweet a place SHEL 728:12
b. in the rain MILL 526:20
This living b. man DONN 280:8
when they b. him CLOS 228:5
where some b. Caesar bled FITZ 323:4
why have they not b. me deep TENN 782:4
burlesque once romantic to b. BYRO 181:12
Burlington B. Bertie HARG 373:11
Burma B. girl a-settin' KIPL 454:21
burn another Troy for her to b. YEAT 855:2
better to b. out YOUN 857:24
better to marry than to b. BIBL 107:13
Better to marry than to b. PROV 615:31
b. always with this hard, gemlike
PATE 588:11
b. and I am ice PETR 593:18
B., baby, burn POLI 600:11
b. inwardly BRON 152:10
b. its children to save MEYE 523:16
B. to the socket WORD 846:14
B. your bra SLOG 740:1
b. your letters ADAM 2:22
Did not our heart b. BIBL 102:12
let it freely b. LITT 486:16
Old age should b. THOM 789:7
sun shall not b. thee BOOK 142:16
We b. daylight SHAK 710:12
burned Alexandria's library b. HUGH 407:6
B. on the water SHAK 679:3
b. women BRAN 149:12
bush b. with fire BIBL 77:16
clothes not be b. BIBL 84:3
give my body to be b. BIBL 107:25
men also, in the end, are b. HEIN 379:13
burning all is b. PALI 584:7
boy stood on the b. deck HEMA 380:19
b. and a shining light BIBL 102:37
b. fiery furnace BIBL 91:19
B. for burning BIBL 78:6
b. of the leaves BINY 116:15
b. patience RIMB 649:10
b. roof and tower YEAT 854:21
b. the rain forest STIN 761:3
by b. him CEAU 204:10
Is Paris b. HITL 390:4
Keep the Home-fires b. FORD 329:4
lady's not for b. FRY 336:12
out of the b. BIBL 92:7
pretty Babe all b. SOUT 749:19
smell of b. BELL 65:18
stood on the b. deck OPEN 574:8
Tyger, b. bright BLAK 122:19
burnished Furnish'd and b. BETJ 73:1
like a b. throne ELIO 303:12
burns B., Shelley, were with us BROW 160:3
candle b. at both ends MILL 525:21
Not she which b. in 't SHAK 721:28
Ucalegon b. very near VIRG 811:17
burnt b. at the stake as witches SMIT 743:2
b. child dreads the fire PROV 616:16
b. each other BYRO 180:9
b.-out ends of smoky days ELIO 302:28
b., tortured, fined JEFF 420:16

delightest not in b.-offerings BOOK 137:15
burps History just b. BARN 56:11
burr aphorism should be like a b. LAYT 476:8
I am a kind of b. SHAK 708:16
Burren Stony outcrop of the B. BETJ 72:11
burst Words, words or I shall b. FARQ 315:17
burthen b. of the mystery WORD 847:8
Burton B. built on Trent HOUS 405:2
bury anything we want to b. MOOR 546:16
B. it certain fathoms SHAK 719:5
B. my heart at Wounded Knee BENÉ 66:12
dead b. the dead PROV 625:9
dead b. their dead BIBL 96:2
give them a finger to b. DORF 282:16
good day to b. bad news MISQ 537:16
helped to b. POPE 602:30
I come to b. Caesar SHAK 697:21
in war fathers b. their sons HERO 385:10
physician can b. his mistakes WRIG 851:1
We will b. you KHRU 451:4
bus Can it be a Motor B. GODL 351:19
good design for a b. HOCK 391:7
missed the b. CHAM 206:14
not even a b., I'm a tram HARE 373:10
stepping in front of a b. OSBO 578:22
bush beats the b. OXFO 581:11
Behold, the b. burned BIBL 77:16
b. afire with God BROW 157:21
b. supposed a bear SHAK 711:29
B. wins it NEWS 562:2
copiousy branching b. GOUL 357:11
fear each b. an officer SHAK 695:3
Good wine needs no b. PROV 621:13
Thorough b., thorough brier SHAK 710:27
worth two in the b. PROV 615:40
bushel neither under a b. BIBL 100:29
bushes B. and low tamarisks VIRG 814:2
bushmen they were not b. HEAD 377:8
busier semed b. than he was CHAU 210:19
busiest b. have most leisure PROV 616:17
business about my Father's b. BIBL 100:9
attended b. college ADE 5:17
Being good in b. WARH 821:17
b. as usual THAT 787:8
B. before pleasure PROV 616:18
B. carried on as usual CHUR 220:19
B. first THAC 786:11
B. is becoming more and more HARV 374:21
B. is like a car SAYI 669:4
b. like show business BERL 69:22
b. of consequence BARH 56:3
b. of the day DRYD 288:6
b. practices improve RODD 651:21
B. was his aversion EDGE 296:1
conduct of b. CORN 243:13
do b. together THAT 787:9
do your own b. BIBL 110:16
Everybody's b. PROV 619:2
far away from b. HORA 400:1
go to my pleasure, b. WYCH 852:10
growth of a large b. ROCK 651:19
heart in the b. WATS 823:4
How to succeed in b. MEAD 520:1
If b. always made the right decisions
GETT 344:16
importunity Of b. LAMB 465:9
In civil b. BACO 43:22
it is your b. HORA 399:15
it spoils b. OTWA 579:13
Liberty is unfinished b. ANON 17:6
little b. BIBL 93:28
make b. for itself DICK 267:23
minded their own b. CARR 194:6
Murder is a serious b. OPEN 574:26
music b. is not MORR 550:13
occupy their b. BOOK 141:18
of the American people is b. COOL 242:6
principal b. of life BUTL 176:23
requisite in b. ADDI 4:18
run government like a b. KLEI 457:19
serious b. AUST 40:6
servants of b. BACO 44:21
settled b. BACO 46:4

soul of b. PROV 629:47
spring of b. BAGE 47:16
That's no b. FILM 321:2
thief to b. DEFO 261:3
Too soft for b. LEAP 477:1
totter on in b. POPE 603:23
true b. precept DICK 270:2
wheels of b. TAWN 773:17
businessman toward making a b.
WATS 822:20
businessmen well-placed b. decide
YOUN 857:1
Buss Miss B. and Miss Beale ANON 17:17
bust animated b. GRAY 361:4
b. survives the city GAUT 341:2
dance it b. to bust GREN 363:12
buste Le B. Survit à la cité GAUT 341:2
busting June is b. out HAMM 370:3
bustle B. in a House DICK 273:3
busy be b. OVID 580:17
B., curious OLDY 573:1
b. man has no time MAUR 519:2
B. old fool DONN 281:12
Government of the b. SELD 676:13
had a b. day SIGL 736:23
how b. I must be ASTL 32:17
Nowher so b. a man CHAU 210:19
butcher benevolence of the b. SMIT 741:5
b., the baker NURS 569:11
Hog B. for the World SAND 665:17
Prime Minister has to be a b. BUTL 175:17
right have they to b. me DICK 271:16
When a b. tells you JOHN 428:2
butchered B. to make a Roman holiday
BYRO 179:12
butchers gentle with these b. SHAK 697:15
sacrificers, but not b. SHAK 696:23
shepherds and b. VOLT 816:9
butler b. did it CATC 200:5
b.'s upper slopes WODE 843:5
butt here is my b. SHAK 714:26
knocks you down with the b. GOLD 355:34
butter B. and eggs CALV 186:6
B. and honey BIBL 88:15
b. for the Royal slice of bread MILN 528:2
b. from alternate tubs ROGE 652:15
b. made of dolphins' milk JONS 434:15
b. no parsnips PROV 620:5
choking it with b. PROV 631:46
cutting bread and b. THAC 786:22
manage without b. GOEB 352:7
no money for b. JOSE 436:17
rather have b. or guns GOER 352:9
she brought forth b. BIBL 79:19
softer than b. BOOK 137:18
Stork from b. ADVE 7:13
buttercup I'm called Little B. GILB 348:18
buttercups B. and daisies HOWI 406:5
buttered always on the b. side PAYN 589:10
on its b. side PROV 616:13
want their luck b. HARD 371:18
butterflies b. of vertigo BECK 61:3
Frogs eat B. STEV 757:23
I look for b. CARR 195:27
butterfly breaks a b. POPE 602:31
breaks a b. on a wheel NEWS 562:22
b. dreaming that CHUA 219:2
b. upon the road KIPL 455:8
flap of a b.'s wings LORE 492:3
Float like a b. ALI 12:2
You, the b. BASH 58:4
butting B. through the Channel MASE 517:13
buttock boiling his b. AUBR 33:22
buttocks chair that fits all b. SHAK 678:9
gorgeous b. of the ape HUXL 411:11
button each b., hook, and lace LOWE 493:17
job of sewing on a b. BROU 154:15
little round b. at top FOOT 328:6
undo this b. SHAK 702:7
You press the b. ADVE 8:26
buttoning b. and unbuttoning LAST 471:3
buttons soul above b. COLM 236:3
stars, garters, b. MOOR 546:17

buttresses [the Church's] b. ANON 16:8
butts b. me away SHAK 682:20
butty oul' b. o' mine O'CA 571:8
buxom b., blithe, and debonair MILT 529:18
Buxton every fool in B. RUSK 659:16
buy b. a used car POLI 601:17
b. Codham, Cockridden THOM 790:13
B. in the cheapest market PROV 616:20
b. it first HEMI 381:2
b. it like an honest man NORT 565:15
b. wine and milk BIBL 90:6
client will beg to b. BURR 173:11
Don't b. a single vote more KENN 448:13
I will b. with you SHAK 708:29
money can't b. me love LENN 480:16
no man might b. or sell BIBL 113:30
Stop me and b. one ADVE 8:15
where none come to b. BLAK 120:6
You b. land, you buy stones PROV 635:24
buyer b. can be found SALL 665:15
b. needs hundred eyes PROV 616:19
Let the b. beware PROV 625:7
naught, saith the b. BIBL 84:37
buying b. and selling of people CARD 190:6
no fish ye're b. SCOT 674:3
buys b. everything MONT 543:16
buzz B.! Buzz! Buzz! MILN 528:6
stings, The crowd, and b. COWL 245:26
stumbling B. DICK 273:1
by B. and by MCCO 500:14
bymatter been a b. BACO 43:30
Byron I'm not B. LERM 481:13
Byronic think all poets were B. COPE 242:16
bystander never be a b. BAUE 59:5
byway And the b. nigh me STEV 760:16
his own b. to heaven DEFO 261:22
byword b. among all people BIBL 81:10
story and a b. WINT 841:20
Byzantium holy city of B. YEAT 855:10
Soldan of B. CHES 216:4

C C Major BROW 158:8
ça Ç. ira ANON 20:9
cabbage c.-leaf to make an apple-pie
FOOT 328:6
c. with a college education TWAI 803:23
Re-hashed c. wore out JUVE 440:2
smell of cooking c. WEST 830:11
cabbages Of c.—and kings CARR 195:7
planting my c. MONT 544:2
cabin c. left still standing DUFF 291:5
Make me a willow c. SHAK 720:13
cabined c. ample Spirit ARNO 27:23
c., cribbed, confined SHAK 706:3
cabinet another to mislead the C. ASQU 32:5
blubbering C. GLAD 351:6
c. is a combining BAGE 47:17
c. of pleasure HERB 384:15
group of C. Ministers CURZ 254:9
cable little c. cars climb CROS 252:14
No cord nor c. BURT 174:14
Cabots Lowells talk to the C. BOSS 145:15
cacoethes Scribendi c. JUVE 440:1
cad Cocoa is a c. and coward CHES 216:16
Flopshus C. KIPL 457:6
cadence dans les vers une juste c. BOIL 125:12
harsh c. of a rugged line DRYD 289:25
Cadiz reeking into C. Bay BROW 159:19
Cadwallader C. and all his goats SHAK 694:2
caelum C. non animum mutant HORA 399:10
Caesar always I am C. SHAK 696:15
appeal unto C. BIBL 105:28
Aut C., aut nihil MOTT 552:2
Ave C., morituri te salutant ANON 21:13
blossoming C. SHAK 679:20
C. and his fortune CAES 185:5
C. hath wept SHAK 697:25
C. is more dangerous SHAK 697:5
C.'s laurel crown BLAK 119:12
C.'s public policy PLUT 598:16

Caesar (*cont.*):
C.'s self is God's · CRAS 250:17
C.'s wife · CAES 185:3
C.'s wife · PROV 616:21
C. with the senate · POPE 605:10
call great C. ass · SHAK 680:14
decree from C. Augustus · BIBL 100:1
decrees of C. · BIBL 105:15
doth this our C. feed · SHAK 696:10
for C.'s I am · WYAT 852:8
Hail C. · ANON 21:13
Here was a C. · SHAK 698:8
I come to bury C. · SHAK 697:21
Imperious C., dead · SHAK 688:30
in envy of great C. · SHAK 698:29
Like C.'s wife · ANON 17:7
loved C. less · SHAK 697:18
O mighty C. · SHAK 697:13
Render unto C. · BIBL 98:6
that C. might be great · CAMP 187:17
Then fall, C. · SHAK 697:10
unto C. shalt thou go · BIBL 105:29
upon Dead C.'s trencher · SHAK 679:16
where some buried C. bled · FITZ 323:4
word of C. · SHAK 697:28
your boy, your C. · DRYD 287:23
Caesars C. and Napoleons · HUXL 411:7
Compare with C. · SHAK 692:1
cafe in ev'ry street c. · HAMM 370:4
caff ace c. with a nice museum · ADVE 7:2
caftan Iffucan of Azcan in c. · STEV 757:20
cage become an iron c. · WEBE 825:4
born within the c. · TENN 778:31
c. upon the wall · BISH 117:8
cannot c. the minute · MACN 504:22
lady in a c. · CHES 216:15
no more natural to us than a c. · SHAW 725:7
Nor iron bars a c. · LOVE 493:6
red breast in a c. · BLAK 119:6
roaming round its gilt c. · WOLL 844:6
sing like birds i' the c. · SHAK 701:24
caged think c. birds sing · WEBS 826:11
why the c. bird sings · DUNB 291:15
cages mental c. · MURD 554:14
not in making c. · SWIF 766:23
Cain cruel sons of C. · LE G 479:6
first city C. · COWL 245:19
Had C. been Scot · CLEV 227:1
land God gave to C. · CART 197:7
mark upon C. · BIBL 76:1
cake Bake me a c. · NURS 569:1
C. or death · IZZA 414:15
child looks at a c. · GASK 340:22
have your c. and eat it · PROV 635:30
Let them eat c. · MARI 512:7
picked out of a c. · RALE 641:19
cakes no more c. and ale · SHAK 720:19
Calais 'C.' lying in my heart · MARY 517:7
shew light at C. · JOHN 428:18
calamities C. are of two kinds · BIER 116:4
perturbations and c. · BACO 46:6
calamity Oh, c. · CATC 201:20
power of no c. · BROW 157:3
calamus *quam sit c. saevior ense* · BURT 174:5
calculating desiccated c. machine · BEVA 73:16
calculation c. shining out · DICK 269:26
calculus integral and differential c.
· GILB 334:17
Caledonia Mourn, hapless C. · SMOL 744:18
O C.! stern and wild · SCOT 673:13
calends Gay are the Martian C. · MACA 499:8
calf c. and the young lion · BIBL 88:21
fatted c. · BIBL 101:17
golden–c. of self-love · CARL 191:13
skip like a c. · BOOK 135:16
Caliban C. casts out Ariel · POUN 608:19
C., Has a new master · SHAK 718:32
rage of C. · WILD 836:12
calico c. millennium · CARL 193:4
California C. to the New York Island
· GUTH 366:5
Caligula C.'s horse was made Consul
· RAND 642:3

eyes of C. · MITT 541:3
call c. it a day · COMD 236:14
c. me early, mother dear · TENN 782:8
C. me Ishmael · OPEN 574:9
c. of the running tide · MASE 517:16
c. of the wild · LOND 489:14
c. the cattle home · KING 452:19
c. themselves Christians · BOOK 129:18
c. ye upon him · BIBL 90:7
come when you do c. · SHAK 690:22
Go, for they c. you · ARNO 28:2
how you c. to me · HARD 373:3
Labour's c. · POLI 600:15
May I c. you 338 · COWA 245:13
Now c. on Christ · GILB 346:18
O! c. back yesterday · SHAK 715:20
one clear c. for me · TENN 776:16
please God to c. me · BOOK 132:18
When you c. me that · WIST 842:3
called c. unto thee, O Lord · BOOK 143:6
many are c. · BIBL 98:5
Many are c. · PROV 626:10
calleth c. them all by their names
· BOOK 144:3
One deep c. another · BOOK 136:13
calling answerably to your Christian c.
· BOOK 132:11
dignity of this high c. · BURK 167:2
Germany c. · JOYC 437:27
heard my c. · BOOK 136:6
callisthenics c. with words · PARK 586:7
callous 'c.' engraved · SELL 676:20
calls If anybody c. · BENT 68:16
calm After a storm comes a c. · PROV 614:5
c., as it was bright · VAUG 808:3
c., rather than to excite · PALM 585:1
C. soul of all things · ARNO 27:15
c. the troubled mind · CONG 239:20
C. was the day · SPEN 752:14
famous c. and dead · BROW 159:12
hopelessness and c. · BARA 55:3
more than usual c. · FLEM 326:11
no joy but c. · TENN 781:7
remember to keep c. · HORA 401:2
season of c. weather · WORD 848:13
still c. of life · ADAM 1:16
Than c. in waters · SHEL 732:2
calumnies C. are answered best · JONS 435:16
calumny thou shalt not escape c.
· SHAK 686:15
Calvinism C. [in Switzerland] · BANC 54:13
Calvinist Papist, yet a C. · EPIT 310:7
Calvinistic C. creed · PITT 596:5
C. sense of innate depravity · MELV 521:9
Calvinists C. stick fast · ROBI 650:18
Cambridge C. ladies in furnished souls
· CUMM 253:15
C. people rarely smile · BROO 153:12
fields of C. · COWL 245:29
more attractive than C. · BAED 47:6
To C. books · TRAP 798:4
to C. books he sent · BROW 157:14
Cambyses in King C.' vein · SHAK 690:14
came c. first for the Communists · NIEM 563:18
c. unto his own · BIBL 102:20
I c., I saw, I conquered · CAES 185:7
I c., saw, and overcame · SHAK 692:13
I c. through · MACA 497:15
nobody c. · FILM 322:12
Tell them I c. · DE L 263:3
camel breaks the c.'s back · PROV 624:14
c. has a single hump · NASH 557:8
c. is a horse · ISSI 414:12
easier for a c. · BIBL 97:27
raiment of c.'s hair · BIBL 94:11
swallow a c. · BIBL 98:10
Take my c., dear · OPEN 575:21
Camelot cackling home to C. · SHAK 700:8
C. to minstrels seemed · BROW 157:19
known as C. · LERN 481:4
many-towered C. · TENN 780:5
never be another C. · ONAS 573:7
rode down to C. · TENN 780:10

camera I am a c. · ISHE 414:10
camerado C., this is no book · WHIT 833:8
cammin c. *del nostra vita* · OPEN 575:5
c. *di nostra vita* · DANT 255:12
campaign c. in poetry · CUOM 254:1
campaigns c. for public office · MORE 548:8
camps Courts and c. · CHES 214:25
can but as we c. · MENA 521:14
C. something, hope · HOPK 396:10
He who c. does · PROV 622:6
He who c., does · SHAW 726:20
know a man who c. · ADVE 7:12
they c. because they think they can
· VIRG 812:7
They c. nothing but frog-spawn
· LAWR 475:11
think you c. · INGE 413:3
youth replies, I c. · EMER 306:16
Canada all over C. · RICH 647:20
C. could have enjoyed · COLO 236:7
C. . . . is a country · SHIE 734:20
C. is not a real country · BOUC 147:3
C. that shall fill · LAUR 470:11
dedication to C.'s future · DIEF 274:6
I see C. · DAVI 258:15
more than C. itself is worth · VOLT 815:10
O C.! Our home · WEIR 826:24
that city, like C. itself · COHE 230:10
Canadian C. did a *Moby Dick* · ATWO 33:11
C. out of the German Emperor · VAN 807:3
definition of a C. · BERT 71:20
no C. patriotism · BOUR 147:9
sense of doubt—a C. · LÉVE 482:12
Canadians C. do not like heroes
· WOOD 844:15
young French C. · GRAN 359:2
canary mine host's C. wine · KEAT 444:5
cancel back to c. half a line · FITZ 323:10
C. and tear to pieces · SHAK 706:1
cancer c. close to the Presidency · DEAN 260:7
Obscene as c. · OWEN 581:4
Silence like a c. grows · SIMO 738:4
white race *is* the c. · SONT 746:10
candelabrum c. of gold · BERN 70:17
candid be c. where we can · POPE 604:18
c. friend · CANN 189:7
candied c. apple, quince · KEAT 443:2
candle Bell, book, and c. · SHAK 699:5
better to light a c. · BENE 66:10
Better to light one c. · PROV 615:20
blew out the c. · ALAI 9:14
called him 'C.-ends' · CARR 196:7
c. burns at both ends · MILL 525:21
c. by which she · TOLS 796:15
c. in that great turnip · CHUR 222:2
c. in the wind · JOHN 422:11
c. in the wind · JOHN 422:14
c. of understanding · BIBL 92:19
c. singed the moth · SHAK 709:10
c. to the sun · SIDN 735:17
c. to the sun · YOUN 857:7
farthing c. at Dover · JOHN 428:18
Fire and fleet and c.-lighte · BALL 52:11
lighted a c. · BIBL 100:29
light such a c. · LAST 471:4
little c. throws his beams · SHAK 710:6
Out, out, brief c. · SHAK 707:14
rather light a c. · STEV 758:18
scarcely fit to hold a c. · BYRO 177:18
set a c. in the sun · BURT 174:13
candlelight Colours seen by c. · BROW 158:1
dress by yellow c. · STEV 760:2
get there by c. · NURS 567:9
linen by c. · PROV 627:18
Candlemas C. day be sunny and bright
· PROV 622:46
C. day, put beans · PROV 616:23
candles c. are all out · SHAK 704:15
c. burn their sockets · HOUS 403:23
c. in the wind · MERE 522:13
carry c. and set chairs · HERV 386:24
Night's c. · SHAK 718:2
These blessed c. · SHAK 710:8

wind extinguishes c.   LA R 469:18
candlestick baker, The c.-maker   NURS 569:11
wrote over against the c.   BIBL 91:21
candlesticks seven golden c.   BIBL 112:28
candour combines force with c.   CHUR 222:21
candy C. is dandy   NASH 557:15
canem *Cave c.*   PETR 594:3
canisters steel c. hurtling about   CASS 198:16
canker loathsome c. lives   SHAK 723:3
this c., Bolingbroke   SHAK 689:27
cankerworm c., and the caterpillar   BIBL 92:2
cannibal c. uses knife and fork   LEC 478:8
cannibals Caesars, and with C.   SHAK 692:1
C. that each other eat   SHAK 713:9
cannon C. to right of them   TENN 776:14
in the c.'s mouth   SHAK 681:11
pulse like a c.   EMER 306:21
shaking scythes at c.   HEAN 378:3
cannonball c. took off his legs   HOOD 394:25
like a c.   WFII 828:2
cano *Arma virumque c.*   VIRG 810:15
canoe coffin clapt in a c.   BYRO 177:23
make love in a c.   BERT 71:20
canoes heads in their c.   MARV 516:6
canonization sort of natural c.   HAZL 376:21
canopy excellent c., the air   SHAK 685:24
rich embroidered c.   SHAK 694:27
Canossa not go to C.   BISM 117:16
can't c. go on   BECK 61:12
something c. be done   DELL 263:12
cant c. about DECORUM   BURN 171:19
c. of criticism   STER 757:5
c. of *Not men*   BURK 168:9
Clear your mind of c.   JOHN 432:9
we have nothing but c.   PEAC 589:13
cantate *C. Domino canticum novum*
   BIBL 114:28
Canterbury C. or Smithfield   WALP 819:24
to the Archbishop of C.   SHER 734:8
canting in this c. world   STER 757:5
cantons Write loyal c.   SHAK 720:13
cantos c. of unvanquished space
   CRAN 249:23
Cantuar how full of C.   BULL 163:17
canvasses c. and factions   BACO 43:28
cap If the c. fits, wear it   PROV 623:4
riband in her c.   SHAK 688:16
capability Negative C.   KEAT 446:4
capable *c. de tout*   VOLT 816:19
c. of all things   TRAH 797:10
c. of reigning   TACI 770:11
caparisons No c., Miss   SHER 733:22
cape Nobly, nobly C. Saint Vincent
   BROW 159:19
Round the c.   BROW 160:16
capers He c. nimbly   SHAK 716:19
Cape Town Natal and C.   GLAD 350:20
capital C. must be propelled   BAGE 47:12
Does c. punishment tend   FRY 336:16
high c. Of Satan   MILT 531:28
origin of c.   TORR 797:4
capitalism C. is using its money   CAST 199:2
c. with the gloves off   STOP 761:17
extermination of c.   ZINO 858:11
monopoly stage of c.   LENI 480:3
spirit of c.   WEBE 825:3
unacceptable face of c.   HEAT 378:11
What is c. but buying   CARD 190:6
capitalist slave of the c. society   CONN 240:9
capitalists c. will sell us   MISQ 537:6
Capitol strangers in the C.   HEWI 387:12
capitulate I will not c.   JOHN 433:2
capons cannot feed c. so   SHAK 687:1
Capri letter came from C.   JUVE 440:6
caprices depend on the c.   TOCQ 795:3
caps C. tilted   BLOK 123:15
captain broken by the team c.   HOWE 405:11
c. is in his bunk   SHAW 725:13
c. of my soul   HENL 381:15
c. of the Hampshire grenadiers   GIBB 345:19
c. of twenty-four soldiers   ANON 20:13
Fighting in the c.'s tower   DYLA 294:5
my C. lies, Fallen   WHIT 833:5

nobody like the C.   THAC 786:9
O C.! my Captain   WHIT 833:4
Our great captain's c.   SHAK 713:17
plain russet-coated c.   CROM 251:13
royal c. of this ruined   SHAK 693:8
ship's c. complaining   POWE 610:3
spruce sea-c.   BARN 56:10
tall and dandy c.   ARCH 24:8
That in the c.   SHAK 708:2
train-band c. eke was he   COWP 246:18
captains All my sad c.   SHAK 679:17
c. and the kings   KIPL 455:10
c. courageous   BALL 52:14
C. of industry   CARL 192:22
Star c. glow   FLEC 325:18
thunder of the c.   BIBL 83:25
captive led captivity c.   BOOK 138:14
within my c. breast   SURR 764:5
captives all prisoners and c.   BOOK 129:12
proclaim liberty to the c.   BIBL 90:18
captivity c. of Sion   BOOK 142:23
prisoners out of c.   BOOK 138:11
Turn our c., O Lord   BOOK 142:24
car Business is like a c.   SAYI 669:4
buy a used c.   POLI 601:17
can't drive the c.   TYNA 804:4
c. could go straight upwards   HOYL 406:8
c. crash as a sexual event   BALL 54:1
c. in every garage   HOOV 395:23
commodious c.   JAME 417:15
gilded c. of day   MILT 528:20
motor c. was poetry and tragedy
   LEWI 483:21
owl of Minerva in a hired c.   PAUL 589:5
to tinker with his c.   MACN 504:21
Carabas my lord the Marquis of C.
   PERR 593:2
caravan c. goes on   PROV 618:1
great c. of humanity   SMUT 744:20
Put up your c.   HODG 391:11
carbon c. atom   JEAN 419:7
carborundum *Nil c.*   SAYI 670:6
carbuncle monstrous c.   CHAR 209:15
carbuncles Monstrous c.   SPEN 750:16
carcase c. of an old song   THOM 791:3
Wheresoever the c. is   BIBL 98:16
Where the c. is   PROV 634:41
carcases c. of unburied men   SHAK 682:18
carcass hew him as a c.   SHAK 696:24
carcinoma sing of rectal c.   HALD 368:1
card c. up his sleeve   LABO 462:13
memories are c.-indexes   CONN 240:6
Orange c.   CHUR 220:12
stood like a playing c.   MAIL 507:13
cardboard C. Iron. Their hardships
   BOLA 126:1
over a c. sea   HARB 371:2
cardinal on the C.'s chair   BARH 55:14
cards buy a pack of c.   COLE 234:15
c. with a man called Doc   ALGR 11:15
learned to play at c.   JOHN 427:5
Lucky at c.   PROV 625:49
old age of c.   POPE 603:5
pack the c.   BACO 43:28
played At c. for kisses   LYLY 497:2
shuffle the c.   CERV 205:14
wicked pack of c.   ELIO 303:10
care age is full of c.   SHAK 722:15
better c. of myself   BLAK 119:2
Black C. sits behind   HORA 401:11
c. for nobody   BICK 115:22
c. for the unhappy   VIRG 811:8
C. killed the cat   PROV 616:24
c. of all the churches   BIBL 108:21
c.'s check and curb   VAUG 807:10
c. whether Mr John Keats   KEAT 446:13
closed our anxious c.   EPIT 310:14
disclaim all my paternal c.   SHAK 699:18
don't c. too much for money   LENN 480:16
Don't c. was made to care   PROV 618:6
feeling her c.   HOOK 395:18
Heaven's peculiar c.   SOME 745:22
Hippocleides doesn't c.   HIPP 389:8

if, full of c.   DAVI 259:1
kill c.   SHAK 712:32
Killing c.   SHAK 695:9
more c. to stay   SHAK 718:3
much c. and valour   SHAK 693:13
Nor c. beyond to-day   GRAY 361:10
ravelled sleave of c.   SHAK 704:24
she don't c.   LENN 480:21
Sorrow and C.   BURN 170:18
take c. of minutes   CHES 215:3
Teach us to c.   ELIO 301:2
Took great C. of his Mother   MILN 527:21
To say we do not c.   WARD 821:14
wish I could c. what you do   MITC 540:15
with artful c. Affecting   CONG 239:19
with me past c.   SHAK 715:17
women and c. and trouble   WARD 821:15
wrinkled C. derides   MILT 529:20
career c. in tatters   MAND 509:17
c. ls over   WELL 828:2
C. open to the talents   CARL 191:21
c. open to the talents   NAPO 557:3
East is a c.   DISR 277:29
Good c. move   VIDA 810:2
loyal to his own c.   DALT 255:1
nothing in his long c.   NEWS 562:21
our c. and our triumph   VANZ 807:5
careful be c. out there   CATC 201:16
cannot be too c.   WILD 836:15
can't be good, be c.   PROV 623:12
c. felicity   PETR 594:6
c. of the type   TENN 779:8
carefully got to be c. taught   HAMM 370:12
You come most c.   SHAK 683:11
careless c. of the single life   TENN 779:8
C. she is with artful care   CONG 239:19
C. talk costs lives   OFFI 572:1
c. trifle   SHAK 703:17
first fine c. rapture   BROW 159:18
impudently c.   CENT 205:5
They were c. people   FITZ 324:6
carelessness both looks like c.   WILD 835:16
carefullest c.   BETJ 73:2
cares anxious c., when past   ROCH 651:9
c. and pleasures   GIBB 345:2
c. can make the sweetest love   GREE 362:23
c. that infest the day   LONG 490:5
Children are certain c.   PROV 616:39
Grief and avenging C.   VIRG 812:12
Nobody c.   MORT 551:5
none c. or knows   CLAR 224:11
one c. for none of them   AUST 40:14
Carew grave of Mad C.   HAYE 376:7
carf c. biforn his fader   CHAU 210:9
caricature c. as far as I can   SCAR 668:8
c., Decrepit age   YEAT 863:1
carlines made the c. ladies   JAME 417:7
Carlisle burghers of C.   MACA 499:3
carmina *Nulla placere diu c. possunt*
   HORA 399:17
sunt et mihi c.   VIRG 814:9
carmine *Verum ubi plura nitent in c.*
   HORA 398:14
carnage C. is thy daughter   WORD 848:16
strife, and c. drear   SCOT 674:1
carnal c. lusts and appetites   BOOK 133:5
heathen in the c. part   POPE 603:3
pearl for c. swine   BUTL 176:14
carnally to be c. minded is death   BIBL 106:17
carnations c. and streaked gillyvors
   SHAK 722:2
morn Of bright c.   DRUM 286:13
carnivorous sheep born c.   FAGU 314:4
caro *VERBUM C. FACTUM EST*   MISS 539:13
carol fluting a wild c.   TENN 778:19
carollings little cause for c.   HARD 372:16
carpe *c. diem*   HORA 400:14
carpenter c. known by his chips   PROV 616:25
I said to the c.   CART 197:4
Walrus and the C.   CARR 195:6
You may scold a c.   JOHN 428:5
carpenters special language like c.
   SEXT 677:17

carpet figure in the c.   JAME 417:18
wear the c. with their shoes   YEAT 855:11
carping each c. tongue   BRAD 149:4
carriage C. held but just Ourselves
   DICK 272:22
small second class c.   GILB 347:17
carried ought to be c.   EPIC 308:7
carrier down from the c.'s cart   LEE 478:18
carrion c. comfort, Despair   HOPK 396:10
graced his c. with   BROW 158:19
carrots Sowe C. in your Gardens
   GARD 339:12
carry c. a big stick   ROOS 654:7
c. knowledge with him   JOHN 431:5
c. nothing out   BIBL 110:25
c. them in his bosom   BIBL 89:18
making him c. me   TOLS 796:20
cars c. the great Gothic cathedrals
   BART 57:15
crazy about c.   SALI 663:22
cart and a useful C.   LEAR 477:9
c. before the horse   PROV 618:15
Carthage C. must be destroyed   CATO 199:16
Carthaginian C. trustworthiness   SALL 665:6
cartoonist life as a c. wonderful   PETE 593:14
carve c. heads upon cherry-stones
   JOHN 432:15
c. my epitaph   BROW 158:20
c. on every tree   SHAK 681:16
Let's c. him   SHAK 696:24
must c. in Latin   WALL 818:8
carved c. not a line   WOLF 843:12
marble not yet c.   MICH 524:1
carver was the c. happy   RUSK 659:22
carving C. is interrelated   HEPW 382:19
tails with a c. knife   NURS 570:5
casbah Come with me to the C.   MISQ 537:7
case c. is concluded   AUGU 37:17
corpse in the c.   BARH 55:19
everything that is the c.   WITT 842:11
in our c. we have not got   REED 644:4
lady's in the c.   GAY 341:27
nothing to do with the c.   GILB 348:9
this c. is that case   ARAB 23:18
would have passed in any c.   BECK 61:20
cased c. up, like a holy relic   WEBS 825:20
casements magic c.   KEAT 445:1
cases Circumstances alter c.   PROV 616:42
Hard c. make bad law   PROV 621:33
plead their c. in court   VIRG 812:15
cash c. before conscience   HORA 398:21
c. payment   CARL 191:12
from hand to hand of c.   SICK 735:11
needfu' c.   BURN 172:24
needs good c.   TUCK 802:2
pay you c. to go away   KIPL 456:4
takes your c.   CHUR 219:18
take the c. in hand   FITZ 323:3
casket seal the hushèd c.   KEAT 445:13
Cassius C. from bondage will deliver
   SHAK 696:19
C. is aweary   SHAK 698:18
cassock C., band, and hymn-book
   WILB 834:17
cassocked c. huntsman   COWP 247:9
cassowary If I were a c.   WILB 834:17
cast C. a cold eye   YEAT 856:5
c. me in the teeth   BOOK 136:14
C. me not away   BOOK 137:13
c. off the works of darkness   BIBL 106:32
C. thy bread   BIBL 86:20
C. your mind on other days   YEAT 856:4
die is c.   CAES 185:6
for the most part c. up   HOBB 390:22
in no wise c. out   BIBL 103:5
let him first c. a stone   BIBL 103:9
more he c. away   BUNY 165:5
my life upon a c.   SHAK 717:11
Ne'er c. a clout   PROV 627:16
never be c. down   BOOK 134:7
Satan c. out Satan   BIBL 99:16
suddenly c. down   BOOK 137:4
castaway c. wine-pots   CLOU 227:13

I myself should be a c.   BIBL 107:20
castaways tales of c., colonial museums
   GENE 342:22
castes c. who are excluded   LAWS 476:4
casteth c. out devils   BIBL 96:11
Castilian old C. Poor noble   BYRO 183:20
castle c. hath a pleasant seat   SHAK 704:1
c. in France   MORE 548:9
c. of my skin   LAMM 465:16
Doubting C.   BUNY 164:21
falls on c. walls   TENN 782:27
home is his c.   PROV 618:45
house is his c.   COKE 230:18
king of the c.   NURS 567:14
old lad of the c.   SHAK 689:20
owre the C. Downe   BALL 51:17
rich man in his c.   ALEX 11:7
Castlereagh had a mask like C.   SHEL 730:3
intellectual eunuch C.   BYRO 180:4
castles C. in the air   IBSE 412:14
fortifications called c.   ORDE 576:11
Thou shalt make c.   CHAU 212:27
castrati reviving the c.   REED 644:8
casualties c. were low   JARR 418:28
number of c.   GIUL 350:7
casualty is the first c.   SAYI 670:22
road of c.   SHAK 709:8
cat Care killed the c.   PROV 616:24
c. and her kittens   NURS 566:20
c. and the fiddle   NURS 567:6
c. in gloves   PROV 616:27
c. may look at a king   PROV 616:28
c. on a hot tin roof   WILL 839:5
c. that likes to gallop   SMIT 742:19
C. that Walked by Himself   KIPL 456:14
C., the Rat, and Lovell   COLL 234:21
C. with crimson whiskers   LEAR 477:20
c. would eat fish   PROV 616:29
consider my C. Jeoffrey   SMAR 739:17
cosmic Cheshire c.   HUXL 411:12
Curiosity killed the c.   PROV 617:19
endow a college, or a c.   POPE 603:9
Foss is the name of his c.   LEAR 477:14
grinning c. Quivers   TATE 773:9
Had Tiberius been a c.   ARNO 27:22
Hanging of his c.   BRAT 149:19
if a c. is black or white   DENG 264:3
killed the c.   NURS 570:2
Lat take a c.   CHAU 211:19
Like a powerful graceful c.   CHUR 222:7
part to tear a c. in   SHAK 710:21
play with my c.   MONT 544:15
poor c. i' the adage   SHAK 704:10
see how the c. jumps   SCOT 674:28
Touch not the c.   SCOT 674:7
very fine c.   JOHN 432:8
want to swing a c.   DICK 268:26
ways of killing a c.   PROV 631:45
way to skin a c.   PROV 632:15
What c.'s averse to fish   GRAY 361:14
When the c.'s away   PROV 634:28
which way the c. is jumping   SULZ 763:16
catalogue c. of human crime   CHUR 221:6
in the c. ye go for men   SHAK 705:18
catalyst c. that sparks the revolution
   DURY 293:10
catamite in bed with my c.   OPEN 574:27
cataract sounding c. Haunted me
   WORD 847:9
wild c. leaps   TENN 782:27
cataracts You c. and hurricanoes
   SHAK 700:15
catastrophe between education and c.
   WELL 828:13
drift toward unparalleled c.   EINS 298:4
New York is a c.   LE C 478:11
tickle your c.   SHAK 691:30
catch catch as c. can   FOOT 328:6
First c. your hare   PROV 620:8
hard to c. and conquer   MERE 522:19
If I can c. him once   SHAK 708:30
show him how to c. fish   SAYI 669:20
thief to c. a thief   PROV 630:32

Catch-22 anything as good as C.   HELL 380:10
only one catch and that was C.   HELL 380:8
catched and not be c.   PEPY 592:7
catcher c. in the rye   BORR 146:4
c. in the rye   SALI 664:1
catches c. no mice   PROV 616:27
catching C.'s before hanging   PROV 616:26
Passion, I see, is c.   SHAK 697:17
poverty's c.   BEHN 64:3
catchwords principally by c.   STEV 759:26
catechist Shorter-C.   HENL 381:13
categorical imperative is C.   KANT 441:9
category replacement of c.-habits   RYLE 662:3
caterpillar cankerworm, and the c.   BIBL 92:2
c. on the leaf   BLAK 119:9
c., when coming to   UPAN 804:17
caterpillars c. of the commonwealth
   SHAK 715:16
cates dainties are all c.   SHAK 718:12
Cathay cycle of C.   TENN 781:5
cathedral C. time   ANON 15:9
Heft Of C. Tunes   DICK 273:8
cathedrals cars the great Gothic c.
   BART 57:15
Catherine child of Karl Marx and C.
   ATTL 33:4
catholic cannot be a good C.   NORF 565:8
C. and Apostolick Church   BOOK 131:11
C. Church has never come   WILL 839:2
C. Faith   BOOK 128:21
Gentlemen, I am a C.   BELL 65:30
holy C. Church   BOOK 128:10
lawful for a C. woman   MENC 521:19
may as well be a C.   SPAR 750:1
Once a C.   WILS 839:20
Roman C. Church   MACM 504:8
Roman C. women must   THOM 790:21
She [the C. Church]   NEWM 560:17
was C.   AMIS 13:11
Catholicism accessories of C.   HOPK 397:16
Catholics C. and Communists   GREE 362:8
When Hitler attacked the C.   NIEM 563:18
Catiline our patience, C.   CICE 223:15
Cato C.'s daughter   SHAK 697:2
losing one pleased C.   LUCA 494:24
Voice of C.   JONS 434:18
What C. did   EPIT 311:15
cats All c. are grey in the dark   PROV 614:9
C. and monkeys   JAME 417:22
c. are cats   MARQ 514:2
c. is 'dogs'   PUNC 637:12
C. look down on us   CHUR 222:19
C., no less liquid   TESS 786:3
count the c. in Zanzibar   THOR 793:15
direst earthly foes—c.   WATS 823:4
elderly lady who has two c.   LEWI 484:1
greater c. with golden eyes   SACK 662:11
Keep no more c.   PROV 624:36
killed the c.   BROW 160:20
make sober c.   PROV 633:40
Naming of c.   ELIO 302:26
cattle Actors are c.   HITC 389:19
call the c. home   KING 452:19
C. die   ANON 22:12
c. upon a thousand hills   BOOK 137:8
dominion over the c.   BIBL 75:8
gangplank of a c. truck   HEAN 377:22
grass for the c.   BOOK 141:7
Hurry no man's c.   PROV 622:38
thousands of great c.   BURK 167:19
Catullus Did their C. walk that way
   YEAT 855:11
Poor C.   CATU 202:15
caught man who shoots him gets c.
   MAIL 507:14
cauldron Fire burn and c. bubble
   SHAK 706:11
cauliflower C. is nothing but cabbage
   TWAI 803:23
causality law of c.   RUSS 660:24
causas *rerum cognoscere c.*   VIRG 814:17
vitam vivende perdere c.   JUVE 440:4

chance (cont.):

c., and death	SHEL 731:8
c. favours only the prepared	PAST 588:6
C. governs all	MILT 532:13
C. has appointed her	BUNT 164:9
C. herself	DAVI 258:12
erring men call c.	MILT 529:5
Give peace a c.	LENN 480:18
I missed my c.	LAWR 475:8
in the last c. saloon	MELL 521:8
it was by c.	BRAD 149:4
law, c., hath slain	DONN 279:18
never eliminate c.	MALL 508:15
no gifts from c.	ARNO 27:25
too good to leave to c.	SIMO 738:6

Chancellor C. of the Exchequer — LOWE 493:16

chances c. change — SOUT 749:22

changes and c.	BOOK 132:6

Chanel C. No. 5 — MONR 543:6

change bolts up c. — SHAK 680:5

C. and decay	LYTE 497:10
C. as the winds change	SWIN 769:9
c., but I cannot die	SHEL 729:5
c. from Jane to Elizabeth	AUST 39:21
c. his spots	PROV 625:4
c. horses in mid stream	PROV 618:7
c. is as good as a rest	PROV 616:31
C. is constant	DISR 276:4
'C.' is scientific	RUSS 661:8
c. our vile body	BOOK 133:18
c. partners	BERL 69:16
C. the name	HORA 403:4
C. the name	PROV 616:32
c. the past	AGAT 6:24
c. the people who teach	BYAT 177:12
c. we think we see	FROS 335:9
c. what we can	STEV 759:5
C. without inconvenience	JOHN 424:3
c. your mind	AURE 38:10
compelled to c. that state	NEWT 561:11
doth in C. delight	SPEN 752:9
in all c.	BAUD 59:1
involves a great c.	TROL 800:5
it's bound to c.	HART 374:18
lamentable c.	SHAK 701:6
life can c. on a dime	LAHR 464:4
Management that wants to c.	TUSA 803:1
means of some c.	BURK 167:7
more things c.	KARR 441:17
most stupid do not c.	CONF 238:10
necessary not to c.	FALK 314:7
Neither to c., nor falter	SHEL 731:10
point is to c. it	MARX 517:1
relief in c.	IRVI 414:5
religion, knavery, and c.	BEHN 64:1
see c. in the things	ARIS 25:16
shalt thou c. them	BOOK 140:19
subject to c.	PALI 583:6
things will have to c.	LAMP 465:19
Times c.	PROV 633:6
torrent of c.	CHES 217:5
try to c. things	BOLD 126:5
wheel Of C.	SPEN 752:8
wind of c. is blowing	MACM 504:6
wish to c. in the child	JUNG 438:14
without c.	UNAM 804:10

changeable fickle and c. thing — VIRG 812:5

changed all things are c. — BACO 43:5

changed, c. utterly	YEAT 854:3
changed, c. utterly	YEAT 854:5
c. from that Hector	VIRG 811:16
c. upon the blue guitar	STEV 757:25
human nature c.	WOOL 845:5
If voting c. anything	LIVI 487:6
its name c.	DANT 256:8
not how he c.	MORR 550:12
we shall all be c.	BIBL 108:11

changes c. and chances — BOOK 132:6

c. we fear be thus irresistible	JOHN 424:7
sundry and manifold c.	BOOK 130:8

changing c. countries — BREC 150:19

c. scenes of life	TATE 773:13
ever c., like a joyless eye	SHEL 732:5

everything within them was c.	DIDE 273:20
fixed point in a c. age	DOYL 284:16
stress on not c. one's mind	MAUG 518:18
thinks of c. himself	TROL 800:4
times they are a-c.	DYLA 294:16

Chankly Hills of the C. Bore — LEAR 477:7

channel C. forbidding Union — GRAT 359:17

[C.] is a mere ditch	NAPO 556:7
crossing the C.	GILB 347:17
Fog in C.	CART 198:1
in a different c.	AKHM 9:7
masters of the C.	NAPO 556:8

chanting C. faint hymns — SHAK 710:15

chaos bit of primordial c. — WELL 828:14

black c. comes again	SHAK 724:4
C. and darkness	MARR 514:7
C. and old Night	MILT 531:23
c. illuminated by lightning	WILD 836:4
C. is come again	SHAK 713:25
C. often breeds life	ADAM 2:13
C., rough and unordered mass	OVID 580:8
C. umpire sits	MILT 532:13
dread empire, C.	POPE 602:9
God dawned on C.	SHEL 728:18
Humour is emotional c.	THUR 794:3
means of overcoming c.	RICH 647:10
Not c.-like together crushed	POPE 606:17
return you to c.	ZOHA 858:14
stillness in the midst of c.	BELL 66:2

chapel also build a c. — LUTH 496:10

c. I was painting	MICH 524:3
Devil will build a c.	PROV 634:38

chapels nice in c. — HUNT 409:19

chaplain twice a day the C. called — WILD 836:30

chaps Biography is about C. — BENT 68:12

kills a lot more c.	HALD 368:1
nave to the c.	SHAK 703:3

chapter c. of accidents — CHES 215:14

repeat a complete c.	JOHN 431:3
write the next c.	JOHN 423:10

character about a fellow's c. — REAG 643:13

by the content of their c.	KING 452:4
c. dead at every word	SHER 733:29
c. in the full current	GOET 353:7
c. is destiny	ELIO 300:16
c. is his fate	HERA 383:3
c. is to be abused	THAC 786:14
c. of the fifth act	LERM 481:11
discover their real c.	EDGE 295:16
elucidation of c.	CREI 250:23
Fate and c.	NOVA 565:18
incrustations of national c.	BULW 164:2
leave my c. behind me	SHER 733:30
reap a c.	READ 643:7
reganing my c.	FLEM 326:15
reveal more of a man's c.	PLUT 598:14
Sports do not build c.	BROU 154:14
turns on personal c.	NAPO 556:13
What is c.	JAME 418:2
wise about his c.	ELIO 299:4

characteristics c. of the human species — GODW 352:2

characters c. and conduct of their rulers — ADAM 3:5

c. to lose	BURN 171:19
high c. are drawn	POPE 603:18
Six c. in search	PIRA 595:18

charge c. of the clattering train — BEAV 60:18

give his angels c. over thee	BOOK 140:4
I'm in c.	CATC 201:6
Take thou in c.	MACA 499:18

charged c. the troops — BROW 156:21

thought c. with emotion	GIDE 346:16

charges die to save c. — BURT 174:3

warily to begin c.	BACO 44:9

charging marching, c. feet — JAGG 415:16

chariest c. maid is prodigal — SHAK 684:15

Charing Cross existence is at C. — JOHN 430:2

Heaven and C.	THOM 791:16

chariot axle-tree of the c.-wheel — BACO 45:34

body as the c.	UPAN 805:8
c. of fire	BLAK 121:15

C. of Supernal Man	ZOHA 859:4
clouds his c.	BOOK 141:5
Swing low, sweet c.	SONG 748:6
Time's wingèd c.	MARV 516:1

charioted c. by Bacchus — KEAT 444:25

chariots burneth the c. — BOOK 136:26

trust in c.	BOOK 134:24
wheels of his c.	BIBL 79:21

charitably c. dispose of any thing — SHAK 693:15

charities cold c. — CRAB 249:20

Defer not c.	BACO 45:10

charity C. and beating — FLET 327:12

C. and Mercy	DICK 270:1
C. begins at home	PROV 616:33
C. begins at home	SHER 734:2
C. covers a multitude	PROV 616:34
C., dear Miss Prism	WILD 835:21
c. edifieth	BIBL 107:16
c. for all	LINC 485:12
c. in sin	SHAK 708:6
c. is cold	SMAR 739:16
C. never faileth	BIBL 107:25
c. shall cover	BIBL 112:14
c. so cold	SKEL 739:8
C. suffereth long	BIBL 107:25
c. will hardly water	BACO 44:31
gives c. in secret	TALM 772:28
give with c. a stone	BLAK 119:22
have not c.	BIBL 107:25
in love and c.	BOOK 131:17
Keeping books on c.	PERÓ 592:8
lectures or a little c.	WHIT 833:14
Let holy c.	LITT 487:1
little earth for c.	SHAK 695:17
living need c.	ARNO 26:22
love and dear c.	MORE 548:16
On what a c. ye come	SMAR 740:13

charlatan c., and a conjuror — TROL 799:4

Charles C. II was always very merry — SELL 676:22

gentle-hearted C.	COLE 233:15
keep King C. the First out	DICK 268:15
King C.'s golden days	SONG 747:12
King C.'s head	DICK 268:16

Charley C.'s aunt from Brazil — THOM 789:5

Charlie o'er the water to C. — HOGG 392:8

Charlotte C. has been writing — BRON 153:1

charm British Museum had lost its c. — GERS 344:4

By what sweet c.	OVID 580:4
C. a sort of bloom on a woman	BARR 57:7
c. dissolves	SHEN 732:22
c. he never so wisely	BOOK 137:24
c. in melancholy	ROGE 652:13
c. of all the Muses	TENN 784:10
c. of powerful trouble	SHAK 706:12
C. the great English blight	WAUG 824:3
Completing the c.	ELIO 301:8
discreet c. of the bourgeoisie	FILM 322:3
double c.	DYER 293:17
hard words like a c.	OSBO 578:11
Oozing c. from every pore	LERN 481:23
What c. can soothe	GOLD 355:33
what c. is	CAMU 188:9

charmed c. it with smiles — CARR 196:11

I bear a c. life	SHAK 707:16

charmer voice of the c. — BOOK 137:24

Were t'other dear c. away	GAY 341:20

charms acres o' c. — BURN 171:8

Do not all c. fly	KEAT 444:3
endearing young c.	MOOR 547:12
fields and flocks have c.	CRAB 249:17
hath a thousand c.	COWP 247:21
mere external c.	MORE 548:6
Music has c.	CONG 238:29
nameless c. unmarked	BYRO 178:3

Charon C. quit poling — GINS 349:18

charter c. of the land — THOM 792:1

chase have to c. after it — KLEE 457:18

live by the c.	TOCQ 795:10
stern c. a long chase	PROV 631:18
with unhurrying c.	THOM 791:8

chases your picture c. me RACI 640:6
chassis worl's in a state o' c. O'CA 571:9
chaste as c. as ice SHAK 686:15
  c. and fair JONS 435:2
  C. as the icicle SHAK 682:25
  c. as unsunned snow SHAK 683:1
  c. polygamy CARE 190:16
  C. to her husband POPE 603:4
  Married, charming, c. BYRO 180:7
  My English text is c. GIBB 345:22
  Nor ever c. DONN 279:22
  Was Jesus c. BLAK 120:1
chasteneth he c. BIBL 111:11
chastised c. you with whips BIBL 81:16
chastisement c. of our peace BIBL 90:3
chastity c. and continency AUGU 37:2
  C.—the most unnatural HUXL 411:8
  clothed on with c. TENN 777:5
  Even like thy c. SHAK 714:27
  'Tis c., my brother MILT 529:1
  vice of c. VOLT 816:13
chat agreement kills a c. CLEA 226:7
chateaux ô c. RIMB 649:11
Chatham Great C. ANON 16:6
chats spoiled the women's c. BROW 160:20
Chattanooga C. Choo-choo GORD 356:18
chatter c. of the world TROL 799:16
  hare-brained c. DISR 276:20
  only idle c. GILB 348:13
chattering not c. pies SIDN 736:7
Chatterley Between the end of the C. ban LARK 468:12
Chatterton C., the marvellous boy WORD 849:20
cheap c. but wholesome salad COWP 248:16
  c. sitting as standing PROV 623:39
  done as c. as other men PEPY 592:2
  flesh and blood so c. HOOD 395:12
  hold their manhoods c. SHAK 693:24
  how potent c. music is COWA 245:11
  maketh himself c. BACO 43:26
  Man's life is c. as beast's SHAK 700:11
  milk is so c. PROV 635:7
  sell it c. SLOG 740:10
  Talk is c. PROV 631:40
  They be good c. WYAT 852:7
  Words are c. CHAP 208:6
cheaper c. than a prawn sandwich RATN 642:13
  c. to do this BUTL 177:2
  in the c. seats LENN 480:13
cheapest Buy in the c. market PROV 616:20
cheat cannot c. on DNA WARD 821:14
  c. at cards genteelly BOSW 146:26
  detecting what I think a c. JOHN 429:25
  so lucrative to c. CLOU 229:7
  To c. a man is nothing GAY 341:17
cheated be exceedingly c. EVEL 313:2
  c. than not to trust JOHN 425:20
  Of being c. BUTL 176:15
  Old men who never c. BETJ 72:6
cheating c. of our friends CHUR 219:18
  period of c. BIER 116:7
cheats C. never prosper PROV 616:35
  c. with an oath PLUT 598:17
cheek blush into the c. DICK 271:20
  c. of night SHAK 717:17
  dancing c.-to-cheek BERL 69:17
  Feed on her damask c. SHAK 720:29
  giveth his c. BIBL 91:10
  give this c. a little red POPE 603:22
  how she leans her c. SHAK 717:20
  iron tears down C.'s cheek MILT 529:13
  iron tears down Pluto's c. MILT 529:13
  loves a rosy cheek CARE 190:11
  smite thee on thy right c. BIBL 94:29
cheeks blood Spoke in her c. DONN 280:5
  crack your c.! rage! blow SHAK 700:15
  on thy c. KEAT 443:24
  ruddy c. Augustus had HOFF 391:14
cheer Be ay of c. CHAU 211:6
  Be of good c. BIBL 97:9
  be of good c. BIBL 103:38

c. but not inebriate BERK 69:10
c. but not inebriate COWP 248:6
Don't c., men PHIL 594:13
let thy heart c. thee BIBL 86:24
scarce forbear to c. MACA 499:19
So c. up, my lads HUGH 406:16
which side do they c. for TEBB 775:7
with a c. BROW 158:12
cheerer c. of his spirits WALT 820:19
cheerful as c. as any man could PEPY 591:21
  c. countenance BIBL 84:23
  c. countenance BOOK 141:7
  c. giver BIBL 108:18
  It's being so c. CATC 201:10
  join our c. songs WATT 823:13
  make a c. noise BOOK 139:13
  with a c. countenance SHAM 724:6
cheerfulness C. gives elasticity SMIL 741:1
  c. keeps up ADDI 5:2
  c. was always breaking in EDWA 297:1
cheeriness Chintzy, Chintzy c. BETJ 72:4
cheering c. us all up BENN 67:18
cheerio c. my deario MARQ 514:1
cheers Two c. for Democracy FORS 330:2
cheese apple pie and c. FIEL 317:8
  Botticelli's a c. PUNC 637:23
  chinks wi' c. SURT 764:14
  I've dreamed of c. STEV 759:16
  like some valley c. AUDE 36:7
  of c. FADI 314:2
  pound of c. CALV 186:6
  second mouse that gets the c. SAYI 669:32
  varieties of c. DE G 262:8
chemical made up of c. elements MULL 553:19
  two c. substances JUNG 438:12
chemically They may be sound c. HALD 367:18
chemist as objective as a c. CHEK 214:8
  c., fiddler, statesman DRYD 287:6
chemistry captured for life by c. HODG 391:9
  c. that works WILL 838:11
  found him weak in c. WELL 828:7
  produces by c. SHAW 726:9
cheque political blank c. GOSC 357:5
chequerboard c. of nights and days FITZ 323:8
cheques Blank c. HOLM 393:6
cherchez C. la femme DUMA 291:11
cherish c. those hearts SHAK 695:15
  love, c., and to obey BOOK 133:9
cherished lay aside long-c. love CATU 203:6
Chernobyl cultural C. MNOU 541:7
cherries apples, c., hops DICK 271:26
  Life is just a bowl of c. BROW 155:10
cherry American as c. pie BROW 155:4
  carve heads upon c.-stones JOHN 432:15
  c. hung with snow HOUS 404:7
  c. now HOUS 404:6
  C. ripe CAMP 188:4
  C.-ripe, ripe, ripe HERR 385:18
  c. year, a merry year PROV 616:36
  ruddier than the c. GAY 341:4
  Under the c. BASH 58:3
cherubim C. and Seraphim HEBE 378:17
  c. does cease to sing BLAK 119:7
  helmèd c. MILT 530:20
cherubims Immortal c. TRAH 797:16
  rode upon the c. BOOK 134:16
  sitteth between the c. BOOK 140:16
cherubin C., and Seraphin BOOK 127:20
cherubs so near the c. hymn SMAR 739:13
Cheshire cosmic C. cat HUXL 411:12
chess First of the c. CHAU 210:3
chessboard c. is the world HUXL 411:18
chest on the dead man's c. STEV 759:13
Chesterton dared attack my C. BELL 65:11
chestnut spreading c. tree LONG 491:8
chestnuts pop like c. FLAU 325:9
chevalier *c. sans peur et sans reproche* ANON 20:11
Chevy Drove my C. to the levee MCLE 503:7
chew can't c. and c. gum JOHN 423:17

chewed c., are cast up HOBB 390:22
cheweth c. not the cud BIBL 78:11
chewing gum c. for the eyes ANON 19:5
Chianti bottles of C. SHAF 678:2
chic Radical C. . . . only radical in Style WOLF 843:23
chicken champagne and a c. MONT 543:11
  c. in every pot HOOV 395:23
  c. in his pot HENR 381:19
  c. shit JOHN 423:6
  fed the c. every day RUSS 660:25
  game of c. with the Beeb KELL 448:3
  Some c.! Some neck CHUR 221:13
chickens all my pretty c. SHAK 706:24
  as a hen gathereth her c. BIBL 98:12
  beside the white c. WILL 839:13
  costly than c. SHAW 725:9
  count your c. PROV 618:8
  Curses are like young c. SOUT 749:3
  Curses, like c. PROV 617:20
  May c. come cheeping PROV 626:19
chiding c. of the winter's wind SHAK 680:25
  I am a child to c. SHAK 714:14
  not alway be c. BOOK 141:2
chief c. end of man SHOR 735:9
  C. Justice was rich MACA 498:16
  c. of the ways BIBL 83:27
  Cromwell, our c. of men MILT 535:10
  Sinners; of whom I am c. BIBL 110:21
chieftain C. Iffucan of Azcan STEV 757:20
  c. o' the puddin'-race BURN 172:18
child accused of c. death RICH 647:6
  As yet a c. POPE 602:25
  battle line than bear one c. EURI 312:19
  cherished c. ELIO 299:8
  C.! do not throw BELL 64:17
  c. for the first seven SAYI 669:21
  c. imposes on the man DRYD 288:19
  c. in a forest BART 57:13
  C. is father WORD 847:16
  c. is father of the man PROV 616:37
  c. is known by his doings BIBL 84:35
  c. is not a vase RABE 639:19
  c. is owed the greatest JUVE 440:15
  c. looks at a cake GASK 340:22
  c. of God BOOK 132:12
  c. of law BENT 68:3
  c. of Time HALL 369:12
  c. ought to be of the party AUST 40:7
  c.'s a plaything LAMB 464:22
  c. shall lead them BIBL 88:21
  c. should always say what's true STEV 760:7
  c.'s rattle JOHN 428:25
  devoured the infant c. HOUS 403:21
  disagreeable-looking c. OPEN 576:3
  English c. BLAK 122:6
  every c. born therein RUSK 660:2
  every c. may reach JONS 436:6
  Get with c. a mandrake DONN 281:9
  God bless the c. HOLI 392:15
  governed by a c. SHAK 716:29
  happy English c. TAYL 774:14
  hare's own c. HOFF 392:2
  have a thankless c. SHAK 700:5
  healthy c. well nursed SWIF 766:8
  I am a c. to chiding SHAK 714:14
  I am to have his c. BURG 165:16
  If you strike a c. SHAW 726:23
  I heard one calling, 'C.' HERB 383:25
  Is it well with the c. BIBL 82:4
  I was a c. POE 598:18
  knows his own c. SHAK 709:5
  leave a c. alone BROW 161:8
  like a froward c. TEMP 775:10
  little c., a limber elf COLE 231:7
  little c. I stand HERR 385:15
  lose his c.'s heart MENG 522:2
  Love, a c. WROT 851:18
  Magus Zoroaster, my dead c. SHEL 730:21
  man c. conceived BIBL 82:31
  mid-May's eldest c. KEAT 444:9
  Monday's c. is fair PROV 626:28
  mother for the c. COLE 233:12

child (cont.):

my absent c.	SHAK 699:6
never was a c. so lovely	EMER 307:15
not fair to the c.	FROS 336:2
On a cloud I saw a c.	BLAK 121:26
one c. makes you a parent	FROS 335:5
Praise the c.	PROV 629:36
receive one such little c.	BIBL 97:20
right to a c.	SHAW 725:8
shocks the mind of a c.	PAIN 582:4
show'st thee in a c.	SHAK 700:4
simple c., dear brother	WORD 850:20
spare the rod, and spoil the c.	BUTL 176:12
sucking c. shall play	BIBL 88:22
talk of the c.	TALM 772:17
this thy C.	BOOK 133:2
thy king is a c.	BIBL 86:18
Train up a c.	BIBL 84:40
unto us a c. is born	BIBL 88:18
use of a new-born c.	FRAN 332:21
voice of the c.'s blood	SWIN 769:2
When I was a c.	BIBL 107:25
While the c. was yet alive	BIBL 81:2
wise c. that knows its own	PROV 623:40
wish to change in the c.	JUNG 438:14
with c. of glorious great intent	SPEN 751:17
woman forget her sucking c.	BIBL 89:27

childbirth Death and taxes and c.

	MITC 540:14
Poverty is a lot like c.	ROWL 657:15

childhood C. is the kingdom

	MILL 525:19
c. shows the man	MILT 534:19
dolmens round my c.	MONT 543:22
eye of c.	SHAK 705:2
From his c. onward	HARD 371:7
have you seen my c.	JACK 415:6
lost your ability in c.	GONC 356:9
moment in c.	GREE 362:16
wove a web in c.	BRON 152:15

childish c. pleasures

	ALAI 9:14
c. valorous	MARL 513:25
chime his c. verse	BYRO 182:15
put away c. things	BIBL 107:25

childishness second c.

	SHAK 681:13

children airy hopes my c.

	WORD 846:16
as c. fear	BACO 44:1
become as little c.	BIBL 97:19
bring forth c.	BIBL 75:25
burn its c. to save	MEYE 523:16
By c. and tradesmen's bills	MACN 504:17
by c. to adults	SZAS 769:15
c. all gone	NURS 567:18
C. and fools tell	PROV 616:38
C. are certain cares	PROV 616:39
C. are given Mozart	SCHN 671:13
c. are more troublesome	SHAW 725:9
c. are not your children	GIBR 346:6
c. are strangers	SCHW 672:7
c. at play	MONT 544:5
C. begin by loving	WILD 836:24
c. died in the streets	AUDE 34:26
C. have never been very good	BALD 50:6
c. in Holland	NURS 566:11
c. in whom is no faith	BIBL 79:3
c. like the olive-branches	BOOK 143:3
c. love their parents	AUCT 34:14
c. of a larger growth	CHES 215:8
c. of a larger growth	DRYD 287:24
c. of God	BIBL 94:20
c. of God	BIBL 106:19
c. of light	BIBL 101:19
c. of light	BOOK 132:11
C. of my body	KOLL 459:4
C. of the future age	BLAK 122:15
C.: one is one	SAYI 669:5
c. only scream	BYRO 184:2
c. produce adults	DE V 266:8
c., sailors, and drunken men	PROV 622:18
c.'s birthplace taken	DUFF 291:5
C. should be seen	PROV 616:40
c. sooner allured by love	ASCH 31:1
c. sport upon the shore	WORD 848:13
C.'s talent to endure	ANGE 14:14

c. stood watching	KING 452:21
c. sweeten labours	BACO 45:5
c. were lost sight of	MOYN 551:18
c., when then doctors	LUCR 495:13
C. with Hyacinth's temperament	
	SAKI 663:19
c. with their play	COWP 246:15
c., you should never let	WATT 823:10
Come, dear c.	ARNO 27:10
committed by c. on children	BOWE 148:1
contempt—and c.	TWAI 803:19
draw like these c.	PICA 595:6
each one of her c.	VERG 808:14
efforts to shield c.	ADDA 4:2
first class, and with c.	BENC 66:7
fortunate in his c.	EURI 312:22
get back from c.	NESB 559:11
Goodnight, c.	CATC 200:23
had so many c.	NURS 570:1
hear the c. weeping	BROW 157:23
He has no c.	SHAK 706:24
hell for c.	STRI 762:13
holdeth c. from play	SIDN 736:16
How many c.	KNIG 458:4
idea that all c.	ANNE 14:17
in the hands of young c.	DYLA 294:7
in the thoughts of c.	LOCK 488:7
keep c. quiet	SWIF 765:4
kept from c. and from fools	DRYD 289:16
kitchen and their c.	FITZ 323:18
known as the C.'s Hour	LONG 490:3
little c. cried	MOTL 551:14
made c. laugh	AWDR 41:2
many women, and many c.	JOHN 428:3
mentality of c.	RUSS 661:10
more than all his c.	BIBL 76:37
music understood by c.	STRA 762:9
my c. are frightened of me	GEOR 343:13
Myself and c. three	COWP 246:19
my work and my c.	HILL 388:10
not much about having c.	LODG 489:6
Nourish thy c.	BIBL 92:17
oh those c.'s voices	VERL 809:2
old men and c.	BOOK 144:7
on us, and on our c.	BIBL 99:11
parents obey their c.	EDWA 296:13
pitieth his own c.	BOOK 141:3
poor get c.	KAHN 441:4
procreation of c.	BOOK 133:6
provoke not your c. to wrath	BIBL 109:18
raise terrific c.	KANT 441:11
reasons for having c.	RUSS 661:11
remember the c. you got	BROO 154:5
screams of c.	WEST 830:11
see his c. fed	PUDN 636:18
sleepless c.'s hearts are glad	BETJ 72:3
so are the young c.	BOOK 143:2
some c., in some schools	BLUN 124:7
stars are my c.	KEAT 446:17
Suffer the little c.	BIBL 99:25
teach them [c.] first	JOHN 428:16
than of their c.	PENN 591:17
their unborn c.	DURC 293:1
They were privileged c.	BROO 154:2
thou shalt have c.	BOOK 136:23
tiresome for c.	SAIN 663:8
To beget c.	SART 667:7
upon the c.	BIBL 78:1
voices of c.	BLAK 122:7
Weep, c.	NERV 559:7
weeping for her c.	BIBL 94:8
wife and c.	BACO 44:30
world safer for c.	LE G 479:7

child-wife only my c.

	DICK 269:1

Chile Small earthquake in C.

	COCK 229:23

chill bitter c. it was

	KEAT 442:15
bitter c. it was	OPEN 575:14

chills Of c. and fever

	RANS 642:7

chilly c. and grown old

	BROW 161:24
our c. women	BYRO 177:26
room grows c.	GRAH 358:8

chimaera c. of my age

	BERN 70:13

Chimborazo C., Cotopaxi

	TURN 802:20

chime let your silver c.

	MILT 530:21

chimera c. buzzing in a vacuum

	RABE 639:18
c. in my brains	DONN 282:9

chimeras dire c. and enchanted isles

	MILT 529:3
wild impossible c.	SWIF 765:15

chimes c. at midnight

	SHAK 692:8

chimney c.-sweepers, come to dust

	SHAK 683:8
old men from the c. corner	SIDN 736:16

chimneys c. were blown down

	SHAK 705:9
grove of c.	MORR 549:7
your c. I sweep	BLAK 122:1

chimpanzee vase in the hands of a c.

	WAUG 824:18

china C. to Peru

	JOHN 426:15
frail c. jar	POPE 606:9
land armies in C.	MONT 545:13
outer C. 'crost the Bay	KIPL 455:1
though c. fall	POPE 603:6
Till C. and Africa meet	AUDE 34:19
wall of C. was finished	BREC 150:16

chinks c. wi' cheese

	SURT 764:14

chintzy Chintzy, C. cheeriness

	BETJ 72:4

chip c. of the old 'block'

	BURK 168:23

chips carpenter known by his c.

	PROV 616:25
c. with everything	WESK 828:19

chivalry age of c.

	BURK 167:14
age of c. is past	DISR 277:35
Christian service and true c.	SHAK 715:14
He loved c.	CHAU 210:6
nine-tenths of the law of c.	SAYE 668:5
noble acts of c.	CAXT 204:9
smiled Spain's c. away	BYRO 181:31

Chloris C.! that I now could sit

	SEDL 675:9

chocolate c. cream soldier

	SHAW 724:16

chocolates life like a box of c.

	FILM 320:11

choice c. and master spirits

	SHAK 697:14
c. in rotten apples	PROV 631:1
c. of all my library	SHAK 719:15
c. of working or starving	JOHN 424:2
freedom of c. is given	TALM 772:6
from fate to c.	SACK 662:8
is the *people's* c.	SHER 733:13
just the terrible c.	BROW 161:11
measure and the c.	JOHN 426:22
Not c. But habit	WORD 846:22
not your second c. too	LURI 496:6
parties having any c.	JOHN 430:14
perpetual potential c.	BAGE 48:5
simply *independent* c.	DOST 283:12
these the c. dishes	GARR 340:5
when c. was any more	DIDI 274:4
you takes your c.	PROV 636:8
you takes your c.	PUNC 637:5

choir in a waliful c.

	KEAT 445:17
join the c. invisible	ELIO 300:20
singing in the c.	SONG 747:10

choirs Bare ruined c.

	SHAK 723:10
C. and Places	BOOK 128:14
c. of wailing shells	OWEN 581:2

choisir *Gouverner, c'est c.*

	LÉVI 482:16

choke c. on the tail

	PROV 624:5
c. the word	BIBL 97:4

choked sprang up and c. them

	BIBL 97:3

choking on a man's back, c. him

	TOLS 796:20

choleric but a c. word

	SHAK 708:2

choo-choo Chattanooga C.

	GORD 356:18

choose *believe what we c.*

	NEWM 561:7
better to c. the culprits	PAGN 582:2
cannot c. but hear	COLE 232:13
C. an author	DILL 274:10
c. time	BACO 44:7
c. your women or linen	PROV 627:18
He should say to me: 'C.'	LESS 482:6
intellect of man is forced to c.	YEAT 853:11
Let's c. executors	SHAK 715:22
not c. not to be	HOPK 396:10
Of two evils c.	PROV 628:17
ones we c. to love	HARR 374:8
therefore c. life	BIBL 79:1
to govern is to c.	LÉVI 482:16

woman can hardly ever c. ELIO 299:19
choosers Beggars can't be c. PROV 615:6
choosing C. each stone MARV 515:13
just c. so BROW 159:1
chopcherry c. ripe within PEEL 591:2
Chopin C. and Bizet FISH 322:17
chopper cheap and chippy c. GILB 348:1
Here comes a c. NURS 568:19
chord common c. again BROW 158:8
lost c. PROC 612:16
chords c. in the human mind DICK 267:20
chortled c. in his joy CARR 194:26
chorus c.-ending from Euripides
BROW 158:14
c. of indolent reviewers TENN 782:12
chose c. him five smooth stones BIBL 80:21
chosen best c. language AUST 39:6
c. generation BIBL 112:5
few c. BIBL 98:5
few are c. PROV 626:10
I have c. thee BIBL 89:24
Mary hath c. BIBL 100:27
Ye have not c. me BIBL 103:34
choughs crows and c. that wing SHAK 701:12
Christ all at once what C. is HOPK 397:7
all things through C. BIBL 110:9
C. adorned and beautified BOOK 133:5
C. and his mother HOPK 397:6
C. and His saints ANON 22:11
C. being raised from the dead BIBL 106:12
C. beside me PATR 588:20
[C.] came and preached peace BIBL 109:5
C. cannot find ANON 20:6
C. follows Dionysus POUN 608:19
C. has no body now SAYI 669:6
C. is all BIBL 110:12
C. our passover BIBL 107:11
C. perish in torment SHAW 727:19
C. risen from the dead BIBL 108:4
C. sailing to me BLOK 123:13
C.'s blood streams MARL 513:6
C.'s particular love's sake BROW 161:8
C. that is to be TENN 779:24
C. walking on the water THOM 791:17
C. wasn't a woman TRUT 801:18
churches have killed their C. TENN 782:3
counted loss for C. BIBL 110:3
hope in C. BIBL 108:3
I did trust in C. WESL 829:16
If Jesus C. were to come CARL 193:5
in C. Church hall ARNO 28:7
in C. shall all be made alive BIBL 108:4
Jesus C. BIBL 111:15
Jesus C. his only Son BOOK 128:10
joint-heirs with C. BIBL 106:19
lady of C.'s College AUBR 33:20
Lord C. enter in WILD 837:3
love of C. BIBL 109:8
ministers of C. BIBL 108:20
Now call on C. GILB 346:18
Priest did offer C. BOOK 144:17
rejoice in C. LUTH 496:7
speechless C. SWIN 768:8
to live is C. BIBL 109:22
uphold the C. TENN 777:20
Vision of C. BLAK 119:19
We preach C. crucified BIBL 107:4
Christabel softly tread, said C. COLE 231:5
Christe C. *eleison* MISS 536:15
C. receive thy saule BALL 52:11
christened when she was c. SHAK 681:22
Christian buried in C. burial SHAK 688:21
C. Architecture PUGI 636:22
C. boys ARNO 30:13
C. can die LAST 473:16
C. can only fear dying HARE 373:9
C. ideal has not been tried CHES 217:11
C. is a man who feels YBAR 853:4
C. marriage MARG 512:3
C. religion HUME 408:11
C. service and true chivalry SHAK 715:14
die as C. CHAR 209:2
Early C. that gets the fattest SAKI 663:15

effusion of C. blood LAUD 470:3
exile to the C. URBA 805:26
forgive them as a C. AUST 40:4
gentleman, and a C. HUGH 407:12
going to be a C. SPAR 750:1
hadn't *got* a C. PUNC 637:15
I die as a C. LAST 472:7
I mean the C. religion FIEL 318:7
Jewish synagogue and the C. church
JALA 416:23
made me, in these C. days TAYL 774:14
naturally C. soul TERT 785:21
Onward, C. soldiers BARI 56:4
persuades me to be a C. FRY 336:19
persuadest me to be a C. BIBL 105:32
reconstruction of C. life BONH 127:7
sad, good C. POPE 603:3
Scratch the C. ZANG 858:2
wonders of the c. religion MATH 518:6
you were a C. slave HENL 381:17
Christianity at the heart of C. PÉGU 591:7
C. better than Truth COLE 233:17
C. has done a great deal for love
FRAN 331:18
C. is not so much BUTL 175:10
C. is part of the laws HALE 368:6
C., of course BALF 51:8
C. was the religion SWIF 766:18
Disneyfication of C. CUPI 254:2
Evidences of C. COLE 233:18
fight for C. URBA 805:25
His C. was muscular DISR 277:9
local thing called C. HARD 371:13
meaning of C. WESL 829:18
rock 'n' roll or C. LENN 480:14
whole effect of C. GIDE 346:12
Christians blood of C. is the seed TERT 786:1
call themselves C. BOOK 129:18
C. are not born JERO 421:8
C., awake BYRO 177:17
C. have burnt each other BYRO 180:9
generations of C. MACA 498:21
how C. love one another TERT 785:22
Jews are not unlike C. JUDA 438:1
Christmas At C. I no more desire
SHAK 702:11
call off C. FILM 319:2
child on C. Eve BART 57:13
C. Day in the Workhouse OPEN 574:23
C. is the Disneyfication CUPI 254:2
C.-morning bells say 'Come!' BETJ 72:3
C. stories tortured BYRO 182:11
C. won't be Christmas OPEN 574:10
Do they know it's C. GELD 342:17
Ghost of C. Past DICK 268:4
insulting C. card GROS 365:7
night before C. MOOR 546:9
not just for C. SLOG 740:2
Out of the C. flame CAUS 203:12
turkeys vote for C. CALL 185:18
well that C. should fall ADDI 4:28
white C. BERL 69:23
Christopher Robin C. has fallen MORT 551:5
C. is saying his prayers MILN 528:5
chronicle c. of the planets YEVT 856:20
c. of wasted time SHAK 723:16
c. small beer SHAK 713:18
chronicles abstracts and brief c. SHAK 685:30
Chuang Tzu C.'s dreaming heart BASH 58:4
chuck C. it, Smith CHES 215:19
chuckles c. of the waves AESC 6:9
chumps C. make the best husbands
WODE 842:15
church beset the C. of England CECI 204:13
best harmony in a c. MILT 535:20
Broad of C. BETJ 73:5
came to the village c. TENN 781:19
Catholick and Apostolick C. BOOK 131:11
Catholick C. BOOK 129:18
Christ's C. militant BOOK 131:12
c. for his mother CYPR 254:14
c. furniture at best COWP 248:20
c. has become a spectacle PROC 612:15

c. he currently did not attend AMIS 13:11
C. is an anvil MACL 503:5
c. is an anvil PROV 616:41
C. is 'one generation' CARE 191:5
C. is said to want NEWM 560:13
C. of England CHAR 209:2
C. of [England] should ROYD 657:16
C. of England were to fail KEBL 447:16
[C. of Rome] thoroughly MACA 498:19
C.'s banquet HERB 384:17
C. shall be free MAGN 506:3
C.'s one foundation STON 761:5
C.'s Restoration BETJ 72:9
except in the C. CYPR 254:16
free c. CAVO 204:6
Get me to the church LERN 481:15
glory in the c. BIBL 109:9
God built a c. LUTH 496:10
good dog goes to c. PROV 621:40
hatred against the C. SKEL 739:8
Housbondes and to c. dore CHAU 210:21
household and the c. BOOK 130:19
in a country c. SWIF 765:19
I will build my c. BIBL 97:16
nearer the c. PROV 627:9
never passes a c. JOHN 428:6
no salvation outside the c. AUGU 37:9
open the windows of the C. JOHN 422:6
publick Prayer in the C. BOOK 144:16
religion the C. of England FIEL 318:7
satisfied in C. of England HOPK 397:4
Say to the c., it shows RALE 641:2
seed of the C. PROV 616:6
She [the Catholic C.] NEWM 560:17
some to c. repair POPE 604:7
Stands the C. clock BROO 153:13
[the c.'s] buttresses ANON 16:8
there must be the C. AMBR 13:1
thy c. on earth is seeking SHER 734:10
What is a c. CRAB 248:27
Where God builds a c. PROV 634:38
wisdom of the C. of England BOOK 127:11
churches care of all the c. BIBL 108:21
C. built to please BURN 171:18
c. have killed their Christ TENN 782:3
c. which are in Asia BIBL 112:27
John to the seven c. BIBL 112:24
little, lost, Down c. KIPL 455:19
white robe of c. RAOU 642:9
Churchill never was a C. GLAD 350:19
churchman for the real C. SMIT 743:15
churchmen c. fain would kill TENN 782:3
doth well with c. BACO 44:31
churchyard dust of the C. DONN 282:6
lone c. at night BLAI 118:14
makes a fat c. PROV 621:20
worse taste, than in a c. JOWE 436:19
churchyards Troop home to c. SHAK 711:17
When c. yawn SHAK 687:13
ciel *montez au c.* FIRM 321:12
cigar c. called Hamlet ADVE 7:27
really good 5-cent c. MARS 514:14
cigarette c. is the perfect type WILD 836:16
c. that bears a lipstick's traces MARV 516:7
have been the last c. LAST 474:1
Last c. SVEV 765:2
cigars roller of big c. STEV 757:21
Cinara C. was my queen HORA 402:6
Cinarae *bonae Sub regno C.* HORA 402:6
Cincinnatus C. of the West BYRO 182:27
cinco c. *en punto de la tarde* LORC 492:1
Cinderella If I made C. HITC 389:20
cinders c., ashes, dust KEAT 444:1
Sat among the c. NURS 568:4
cinema c. is truth 24 times per second
GODA 351:16
cinnamon tinct with c. KEAT 443:2
circenses *Panem et c.* JUVE 440:7
circle c. of the golden year TENN 777:8
fatal c. is traced TOCQ 795:9
God is a c. ANON 17:21
Love is a c. HERR 386:3

circle (cont.):
makes by c. just — DONN 281:18
Round and round the c. — ELIO 301:8
tightness of the magic c. — MACL 503:12
Weave a c. round him — COLE 232:8
wheel is come full c. — SHAK 702:3
circles individual c. — TROL 799:16
circling sharks are c. — ANON 17:5
circumcised c. dog — SHAK 715:1
circumcision c. nor uncircumcision
— BIBL 110:12
circumference c. is nowhere — ANON 17:21
circumlocution C. Office — DICK 269:21
circumnavigation c. of our globe — DISR 275:18
circumspectly walk c. — BIBL 109:16
circumspice *Si monumentum requiris, c.*
— EPIT 311:6
circumstance fell clutch of c. — HENL 381:14
force of c. — DIDE 273:19
Pride, pomp, and c. — SHAK 714:3
circumstances C. alter cases — PROV 616:42
C. beyond my control — DICK 269:2
play of c. — WEIL 826:18
circumstantial c. evidence — THOR 792:26
lie c. — SHAK 682:8
circumvent c. God — SHAK 688:26
circunstancia *Yo soy yo y mi c.* — ORTE 576:13
circus no right in the c. — MAXT 519:3
shouldn't be in the c. — PROV 623:13
circuses bread and c. — JUVE 440:7
citadels circle-c. there — HOPK 397:5
cities C. and their civilities — PATM 588:17
c. we had learned about — JARR 418:28
flower of c. — ANON 17:12
hell to c. — AESC 6:5
hum Of human c. — BYRO 178:25
lousy skin scabbed by c. — BUNT 164:9
not look in great c. — AUST 39:2
Seven c. warred — HEYW 388:1
splendid C. — RIMB 649:10
streets of a hundred c. — HOOV 396:1
Towered c. please us — MILT 529:26
citizen c. as an abstract proposition
— TOCQ 795:5
c., first in war — LEE 478:17
c. in this world — AURE 38:13
c. of no mean city — BIBL 105:25
c. of the world — BACO 44:19
c. of the world — BOSW 146:21
c. of the world — SOCR 745:11
c. or the police — AUDE 36:4
c.'s first duty — GRAS 359:12
Every c. will make — MORE 549:1
good man and a good c. — AUCT 34:11
greater than a private c. — TACI 770:11
I am a Roman c. — CICE 223:18
John Gilpin was a c. — COWP 246:18
zealous c. — BURK 167:28
citizens c. of death's grey land — SASS 667:18
first and second class c. — WILL 839:18
refined c. — SHEL 732:19
citizenship c. Indian — TERE 785:14
cito *Bis dat qui c. dat* — PUBL 636:14
città C. DOLENTE — DANT 255:13
city abstract and premeditated c.
— DOST 283:10
as of a c. — BROW 156:22
big hard-boiled c. — CHAN 207:12
bring us forth from this c. — KORA 460:3
buildings of a c. — KEAT 446:19
citizen of no mean c. — BIBL 105:25
c. consists in men — NICI 563:9
c. for everyone — FUEN 336:20
c. is built — TENN 777:19
c. is not a concrete jungle — MORR 549:8
C. now doth like a garment wear
— WORD 846:6
c. of dreadful night — THOM 792:19
c. of God — AURE 38:3
c. of God — BOOK 139:20
C. of God — JOHN 433:22
c. of perspiring dreams — RAPH 642:11
c. of refuge — MILT 535:22

C. of the Big Shoulders — SAND 665:17
c. that is set on an hill — BIBL 94:22
c. upon a hill — WINT 841:20
c., where I long had pined — WORD 849:4
c. which hath foundations — BIBL 111:7
c. will follow you — CAVA 203:19
Despising, For you, the c. — SHAK 682:19
down the C. Road — MAND 509:12
evil in a c. — BIBL 92:6
feel, amid the c.'s jar — ARNO 27:15
first c. Cain — COWL 245:19
Hell is a c. — SHEL 730:19
holy c., new Jerusalem — BIBL 114:16
How doth the c. sit solitary — BIBL 91:6
in populous c. pent — MILT 533:28
In the great c., pent — COLE 231:21
Jerusalem is built as a c. — BOOK 142:18
live in a c. — COLT 236:10
long in c. pent — KEAT 445:22
Lord keep the c. — BOOK 143:1
modern c. is a place — WRIG 851:13
nation, not a c. — DISR 277:19
new c. of Friends — WHIT 833:2
no continuing c. — BIBL 111:16
oppressing c. — BIBL 92:12
paper felled a c. — THOM 789:11
people went up into the c. — BIBL 79:11
rose-red c. — BURG 165:20
set all the c. on an uproar — BIBL 105:14
stood within the C. disinterred — SHEL 730:6
street of the c. was gold — BIBL 114:19
streets and lanes of the c. — BIBL 101:8
Sun-girt c. — SHEL 730:1
that great c. — BIBL 114:2
this great hive, the c. — COWL 245:26
What is the c. but the people — SHAK 682:17
whole c. is paid — HESI 387:5
Without a c. wall — ALEX 11:10
Woe to the bloody c. — BIBL 92:10
civet Give me an ounce of c. — SHAK 701:15
civil Always be c. to the girls — MITF 541:1
c. discord — CLOS 228:11
c. question deserves — PROV 616:44
c. to everyone — SISS 738:11
In a c. war — REED 644:6
In c. business — BACO 43:22
never lost our c. war — BIRN 116:18
nothing but a c. contract — SELD 676:6
Pray, good people, be c. — GWYN 366:6
rude sea grew c. — SHAK 711:1
utmost bound of c. liberty — MILT 535:13
civilian mushroom rich c. — BYRO 183:20
civilities bandy c. — JOHN 429:1
dread c. — TOCQ 795:13
civility C. costs nothing — MONT 543:16
C. costs nothing — PROV 616:43
c. of my knee — BROW 156:20
I see a wild c. — HERR 385:21
nothing lost by c. — PROV 632:20
civilization annihilating all c. — SAKH 663:11
can't say c. don't advance — ROGE 652:20
c. advances — MACA 498:3
C. advances by extending — WHIT 832:15
C. a movement — TOYN 797:7
C. and its discontents — RIVI 649:15
C. and profits — COOL 242:5
c. has from time to time — ELLI 306:3
C. has made the peasantry — TROT 800:18
C. nothing more than — ORTE 576:14
c. of the Fabians — INGE 413:5
c. started from the day — CARN 193:9
C. the progress — RAND 642:1
elements of modern c. — CARL 192:3
For a botched c. — POUN 609:1
in a state of c. — JEFF 420:11
items of high c. — JAME 417:19
last product of c. — RUSS 660:20
life-blood of real c. — TREV 798:10
rottenness of our c. — READ 642:18
Speech is c. itself — MANN 510:11
submit to c. — TOCQ 795:10
sweetness of present c. — HUGO 408:2
thought of modern c. — GAND 339:9

civilized c. circumstances — BAGE 49:1
C. people must get off — FINK 318:25
c. suffice — CASS 198:15
of c. society — SMIL 740:21
that are called c. — PAIN 582:22
civilizers two c. of man — DISR 276:9
civilizes Cricket c. people — MUGA 553:4
civil servant c. doesn't make jokes
— IONE 414:1
Here lies a c. — SISS 738:11
civil servants of c. — BRID 151:4
Civil Service business of the C. — ARMS 26:19
c. has finished — REIT 645:2
C. is deferential — CROS 252:17
civis *C. Romanus sum* — CICE 223:18
C. Romanus sum — PALM 584:20
claes some upo' their c. — BURN 171:9
claim last territorial c. — HITL 390:2
claims c. are not false — RIEL 648:7
clair *n'est pas c.* — RIVA 649:14
clairvoyante famous c. — ELIO 303:10
clamorous c. whispering sea — HOME 393:18
clamour c. for war — PEEL 590:17
c. of silence — TAGO 770:18
c. of the crowded street — LONG 490:17
clap C. her broad wings — FRER 333:18
Don't c. too hard — OSBO 578:15
If you believe, c. your hands — BARR 57:5
in the cheaper seats c. your hands
— LENN 480:13
O c. your hands together — BOOK 137:1
Clapham man on the C. omnibus
— BOWE 148:7
clapped-out c., post-imperial — DRAB 285:13
claps If someone c. his hand — HAKU 367:16
Clarence perjured C. — SHAK 716:28
claret c. is the liquor for boys — JOHN 431:12
Claridges body of the bootboy at C.
— WOOL 845:11
clarion c. o'er the dreaming earth — SHEL 730:7
Clarissa C. lives — RICH 647:14
clash c. of civilizations — STRA 762:11
clasped C. by the golden light — HOOD 395:10
clasps c. the crag — TENN 776:20
class c. struggle — MARX 517:2
first and second c. citizens — WILL 839:18
hands of the ruling c. — STAL 754:1
history of c. struggles — MARX 517:5
I could have had c. — FILM 319:11
In education no c. distinction — CONF 238:8
solvent of c. distinction — BENN 67:8
use of *force* by one c. — LENI 480:4
whatever his c. — CHEK 214:3
While there is a lower c. — DEBS 260:18
classes All c. of society — JEVO 421:19
But the two c. — FOST 330:8
lower c. had such white — CURZ 254:11
masses against the c. — GLAD 351:4
two c. of travel — BENC 66:7
While c. exist no one is free — CARD 190:6
classic 'c.' music eliminates — STRA 762:8
C. music is th'kind — HUBB 406:13
tread on c. ground — ADDI 4:20
classical c. mind at work — PIRS 595:20
C. quotation — JOHN 431:25
tragedy of the c. languages — MADA 505:5
classicism C. is health — GOET 353:18
classics bellyful of the c. — MILL 527:10
classify Germans c. — CATH 199:8
clattering charge of the c. train — BEAV 60:18
Claudel pardon Paul C. — AUDE 35:7
claudite *C. iam rivos* — VIRG 814:1
Claus ain't no Sanity C. — FILM 319:22
claw red in tooth and c. — TENN 779:10
clawed c. me with his clutch — VAUX 808:5
c. their way back — GREG 363:9
claws neatly spreads his c. — CARR 194:1
pair of ragged c. — ELIO 302:16
clay associate of this c. — HADR 366:10
beauteous c. — WRIG 851:16
C. is moulded — LAO 467:7
C. is the word — KAVA 442:5

C. lies still	HOUS 404:8	
for this the c. grew tall	OWEN 581:5	
grey stone and grassy c.	EPIT 310:14	
had been a lump of c.	POPE 606:27	
Kingdoms are c.	SHAK 678:14	
mire and c.	BOOK 136:6	
potter and c. endure	BROW 161:5	
potter power over the c.	BIBL 106:24	
Shall the c. say	BIBL 89:23	
clean All c. and comfortable	KEAT 447:2	
c. American backyards	MAIL 507:11	
c. place to die	KAVA 442:6	
c. the sky	ELIO 302:25	
c., verb active	DICK 270:18	
did not love c. linen	JOHN 428:4	
I shall be c.	BOOK 137:12	
let other people c. up	FITZ 324:6	
Make me a c. heart	BOOK 137:13	
New brooms sweep c.	PROV 627:32	
nice c. faces	BARH 55:15	
Not a c. & in-between-the-sheets		
	MCGO 502:3	
so quick, so c. an ending	HOUS 404:18	
thing to keep c.	FRY 336:13	
tragedy is c.	ANOU 22:17	
cleaned I c. the windows	GILB 348:22	
cleaning militants like c. women	TRUF 801:4	
cleanliness C. is, indeed, next	WESL 829:13	
C. is next to	PROV 616:46	
of late for c.	CORB 243:1	
cleanness swimmers into c. leaping		
	BROO 153:14	
cleans sweeps as it c.	ADVE 7:35	
cleanse c. me from my sin	BOOK 137:10	
C. the thoughts of our hearts	BOOK 131:6	
cleansed doors of perception were c.		
	BLAK 121:13	
What God hath c.	BIBL 105:7	
clear c. and present danger	HOLM 393:10	
c. in his great office	SHAK 704:5	
C. shafts of day	LUCR 495:11	
C. your mind of cant	JOHN 432:9	
In the c. air	FERG 316:18	
poignancy in all things c.	WILB 835:3	
too c., too simple	STEN 755:19	
What is not c.	RIVA 649:14	
clearing c. up the obscure corners		
	HUXL 411:19	
clearing-house c. of the world	CHAM 206:7	
clearly ideas too c.	GRAC 358:2	
clearness merit of language is c.	GALE 338:8	
clears little water c. us	SHAK 705:4	
cleave c. the general ear	SHAK 686:4	
c. the wood	ANON 18:18	
c. unto his wife	BIBL 75:17	
cleaveth spirit c. not stedfastly	BOOK 139:8	
cleaving to the grass	MOOR 547:9	
cleft c. for me	TOPL 797:2	
clementine his daughter, C.	MONT 546:5	
clenched hands are c.	MIDR 524:19	
Cleopatra C.'s nose been shorter	PASC 587:7	
gone to gaze on C. too	SHAK 679:5	
in the bed of C.	BROW 156:5	
squeaking C.	SHAK 680:8	
with less than C.	DRYD 287:23	
clercs trahison des c.	BEND 66:9	
clergy Arminian c.	PITT 596:5	
benefit o' the C.	CONG 238:21	
c. are not called	WALP 819:24	
c. were beloved	SWIF 766:18	
Established C.	GLAD 350:17	
clergyman good enough to be a c.		
	JOHN 429:18	
clergymen C.'s sons always	PROV 616:47	
men, women, and c.	SMIT 743:22	
cleric C. before, and Lay behind	BUTL 176:9	
neither c. nor layman	BERN 70:13	
clerk C. there was of Oxenford	CHAU 210:16	
'twixt the Priest and C.	HERR 386:5	
clerks gretteste c. been noght wisest		
	CHAU 212:8	
statesmen or of c.	DISR 276:27	
treason of all c.	AUDE 34:21	

clever beautiful and the c.	GREE 362:10	
c., but is it Art	KIPL 453:19	
c. enough to get all that	CHES 217:13	
c. men at Oxford	GRAH 358:15	
c. theft was praiseworthy	SPEN 750:11	
c. to a fault	BROW 158:17	
good people were c.	WORD 846:1	
important to be c. *about*	MEDA 520:6	
let who will be c.	KING 452:14	
manage a c. man	KIPL 457:1	
Too c. by half	SALI 664:2	
Too c. by half	SALI 664:17	
cleverness height of c.	LA R 469:16	
Mere c. is not wisdom	EURI 312:14	
rein in his c.	QUIN 639:14	
cliché c. and an indiscretion	MACM 504:3	
click c. with people	EISE 298:18	
Clunk, c., every trip	OFFI 572:2	
client bend to favour ev'ry c.	GAY 342:1	
c. n'a jamais tort	RITZ 649:13	
c. will crawl through	BURR 173:11	
fool for his c.	PROV 626:7	
cliff coign of the c.	SWIN 768:13	
cliffs bluebirds over the white c.	BURT 173:16	
chalk c. of Dover	BALD 50:16	
c. of fall	HOPK 396:19	
glittering c. on cliffs	BEAT 59:11	
still the solitary c.	WORD 847:1	
white c. I never more must see	MACA 499:7	
climate adapting to our c.	PUGI 636:25	
chilling c. hardly bears	SWIF 767:6	
c.'s ruined	CHEK 214:6	
in love with a cold c.	SOUT 749:17	
lived in a warm, sunny c.	COWA 245:9	
Love in a cold c.	MITF 540:17	
Our cloudy c.	BYRO 177:26	
whole c. of opinion	AUDE 35:1	
climax c. of all human ills	BYRO 181:1	
climb ev'ry mountain	HAMM 370:1	
c. not at all	ELIZ 304:14	
c. up into the heaven	BOOK 143:16	
Fain would I c.	RALE 641:10	
climbed c. the highest mountain	PETR 593:19	
climbers Hasty c.	PROV 621:37	
climbing c. clear up to the sky	HAMM 370:5	
c., shakes his dewy wings	D'AV 257:23	
clime mottie, misty c.	BURN 173:6	
They change their c.	HORA 399:10	
clinging c. to life	ARNO 29:14	
c. to their crosses	CHES 215:18	
cloak c. become an iron cage	WEBE 825:4	
knyf under the c.	CHAU 211:15	
clock as is making a c.	LA B 463:1	
by Shrewsbury c.	SHAK 691:17	
c. is always slow	SERV 677:7	
c. of communism has stopped	SOLZ 745:19	
c. will strike	MARL 513:6	
Court the slow c.	POPE 603:26	
forgot to wind up the c.	STER 756:15	
mouse ran up the c.	NURS 567:6	
Old Time the c.-setter	SHAK 699:4	
Stands the Church c.	BROO 153:13	
turned into a sort of c.	HUXL 411:16	
clocks c. were striking thirteen	OPEN 574:24	
morning c. will ring	HOUS 404:9	
Stop all the c.	AUDE 34:28	
clockwork c. orange	BURG 165:15	
clods harrowing c.	HARD 372:20	
clog c. of his body	FULL 337:7	
clogs From c. to clogs	PROV 620:30	
cloistered fugitive and c. virtue	MILT 535:16	
Clonmacnoise monks at C.	HEAN 377:21	
close breathless hush in the C.	NEWB 560:5	
C. encounters	FILM 322:2	
c. the wall up	SHAK 693:4	
c. your eyes before	AYCK 41:3	
Doth c. behind him tread	COLE 233:7	
hasten to a c.	COWP 246:7	
not c. enough	CAPA 189:16	
peacefully towards its c.	DAWS 259:19	
closed We never c.	VAN 806:18	
closer C. is He than breathing	TENN 777:12	
c. walk with God	COWP 246:28	

Come c., boys	LAST 471:6	
friend that sticketh c.	BIBL 84:32	
closest c. friends won't tell you	ADVE 7:21	
closet back in the c. lays	FITZ 323:8	
from forth the c.	KEAT 443:2	
not in a c.	CHES 214:23	
put me in the c.	DICK 273:9	
closing c. time in the gardens	CONN 240:8	
cloth according to your c.	PROV 617:22	
fair white linen c.	BOOK 131:5	
On a c. untrue	GILB 348:5	
trick of wearing a c. coat	BALM 54:5	
clothe c. my naked villainy	SHAK 716:27	
clothed c., fed, and educated	RUSK 660:2	
C. in white samite	TENN 777:15	
c. on with chastity	TENN 777:5	
C. with his breath	TENN 778:14	
man c. in soft raiment	BIBL 96:24	
Naked, and ye c. me	BIBL 98:25	
woman c. with the sun	BIBL 113:27	
clothes between c. and smoke	NERU 559:2	
brushers of noblemen's c.	WOTT 851:9	
c. do not make a statement	MUIR 553:15	
C. don't make the man	WATS 822:20	
c. make the man	PROV 616:48	
c. not be burned	BIBL 84:3	
Emperor's new c.	ANDE 14:1	
Fine c. are good	JOHN 430:17	
in c. a wantonness	HERR 385:21	
liquefaction of her c.	HERR 386:20	
poured into his c.	WODE 843:6	
remarkable suit of c.	LOES 489:11	
require new c.	THOR 793:6	
wears her c.	SWIF 766:10	
Who touched my c.	BIBL 99:21	
witnesses laid down their c.	BIBL 104:32	
clothing c. is of wrought gold	BOOK 136:22	
c. itself in a robe	RAOU 642:9	
go in long c.	BIBL 99:26	
in books' c.	LAMB 464:17	
in sheep's c.	BIBL 95:21	
sheep in sheep's c.	CHUR 222:23	
sheep in sheep's c.	GOSS 357:8	
Strength and honour are her c.	BIBL 85:24	
cloths heavens' embroidered c.	YEAT 854:11	
clotted lump of c. nonsense	DRYD 290:12	
cloud c.-continents	ALDR 11:1	
c. has a silver lining	PROV 619:4	
c. in the west	GLAD 350:9	
c. in trousers	MAYA 519:7	
c. of comforting convictions	RUSS 661:2	
c. of unknowing	ANON 15:10	
c. of witnesses	BIBL 111:10	
c. that runs before the wind	RALE 641:1	
c. that's dragonish	SHAK 679:22	
each c. contains pennies	BURK 169:13	
faded, like a c.	SHEL 728:16	
fair luminous c.	COLE 231:10	
fiend hid in a c.	BLAK 122:14	
Get off my c.	JAGG 415:13	
lonely as a c.	WORD 847:5	
On a c. I saw a child	BLAK 121:26	
pillar of c.	BIBL 77:34	
set my bow in the c.	BIBL 76:12	
sweet to be a C.	MILN 528:7	
There ariseth a little c.	BIBL 81:24	
watch a sailing c.	LIN 486:12	
wat'ry c.	AKEN 9:5	
cloudcuckooland How about 'C.'	ARIS 25:2	
clouded upon our c. hills	BLAK 121:15	
clouds C. and eclipses	SHAK 723:3	
c. and wind without rain	BIBL 85:4	
c. his chariot	BOOK 141:5	
c. rain down righteousness	BIBL 115:8	
c. return after the rain	BIBL 86:25	
c. would break	BROW 158:11	
c. ye so much dread	COWP 246:24	
comes with c. descending	WESL 829:9	
cometh with c.	BIBL 112:25	
dropping from the c.	THOM 792:10	
dying c. contend	SHAK 694:26	
his c. removed	BOOK 134:17	
O c., unfold!	BLAK 121:15	

clouds (*cont.*):

prince of the c. BAUD 58:11

through the c. I'll never float WORD 848:20

thy c. drop fatness BOOK 138:7

trailing c. of glory WORD 848:5

clout Ne'er cast a c. PROV 627:16

clouts stones and c. make martyrs
BROW 156:9

cloven out pops the c. hoof WODE 842:20

though he be c.-footed BIBL 78:11

cloverleaf concrete c. MUMF 554:3

clowns Send in the c. SOND 746:7

club best c. in London DICK 271:21

don't want to belong to any c. MARX 516:9

savage wields his c. HUXL 411:15

that terrible football c. MCGR 502:5

clue almost invariably a c. DOYL 284:9

Clun Clungunford and C. HOUS 404:20

Clunbury Clunton and C. HOUS 404:20

Clungunford C. and Clun HOUS 404:20

clunk C., click, every trip OFFI 572:2

Clunton C. and Clunbury HOUS 404:20

clutch clawed me with his c. VAUX 808:5

fell c. of circumstance HENL 381:14

clutching alien people c. their gods
ELIO 302:11

c. the inviolable shade ARNO 28:10

Clyde poems should be C.-built DUNN 292:9

CMG C. (Call Me God) SAYI 670:5

coach c. and six horses RICE 647:1

indifference and a c. and six COLM 235:17

looking for a body in the c. HITC 389:20

rattling of a c. DONN 282:8

coaches Nine c. waiting MIDD 524:11

coal island made mainly of c. BEVA 73:8

like a c. His eye-ball SMAR 740:15

live in his hand BIBL 88:12

made of Newcastle c. WALP 819:4

coalition rainbow c. JACK 415:4

coalitions England does not love c.
DISR 275:16

coals all eyes else dead c. SHAK 722:13

c. of fire BIBL 85:6

c. of fire BOOK 134:17

My c. are spent EPIT 310:17

sleep on the c. DICK 268:11

coarse one of them is rather c. ROYD 657:17

coast c. of Coromandel SITW 739:2

dim hills and a low c.-line VIRG 811:23

On the c. of Coromandel LEAR 477:4

coaster Dirty British c. MASE 517:13

coat c. is so warm NURS 567:13

c. of many colours BIBL 76:37

Cut your c. PROV 617:22

eternal Footman hold my c. ELIO 302:17

long black c. WARR 822:3

made my song a c. YEAT 853:13

stick in his c. BROW 160:2

tattered c. upon a stick YEAT 855:9

cobble On c.-stones I lay FLAN 324:14

Cobbleigh Uncle Tom C. BALL 53:20

cobbler c. stick to his last PROV 625:8

c. to his last PROV 616:49

Cobden C. is an inspired bagman CARL 193:4

cobweb c. of the brain BUTL 176:10

cobwebs Laws are like c. SWIF 766:27

tickles with the c. FROS 335:7

Coca-Cola blue jeans and C. GREE 363:5

cocaine C. habit-forming BANK 54:14

cock before the c. crow BIBL 99:2

C. a doodle doo! NURS 566:12

C. and a Bull STER 757:16

c. crowing on its own dunghill ALDI 10:11

c. had in his governaunce CHAU 211:27

C. up your beaver HOGG 392:7

c. who thought the sun ELIO 299:5

crowing of the c. SHAK 683:18

Every c. will crow PROV 619:5

good c. come out of PROV 632:26

immediately the c. crew BIBL 99:9

Lion and the C. GOGA 353:22

louder a c. can crow TROL 799:18

Our c. won't fight BEAV 60:16

owe a c. to Aesculapius LAST 471:7

Ride a c.-horse NURS 569:8

walks till the first c. SHAK 700:27

Who killed C. Robin NURS 570:16

cockatoo cage is natural to a c. SHAW 725:7

green freedom of a c. STEV 758:8

cockatrice hand on the c.' den BIBL 88:22

cockle c. hat and staff SHAK 688:5

cockles c. boiled in silver shells JONS 434:15

cockleshells silver bells and c. NURS 568:9

Cockney C. impudence RUSK 659:9

cockpit Can this c. hold SHAK 692:27

c. of Christendom HOWE 406:3

cocks drowned the c. SHAK 700:15

cocksure c. of anything MELB 521:1

c. of many things HOLM 393:9

cocktail weasel under the c. cabinet
PINT 595:17

cocoa c. for Kingsley Amis COPE 242:15

C. is a cad and coward CHES 216:16

cod bean and the c. BOSS 145:15

O stynkyng c. CHAU 212:5

photographer is like the c. SHAW 727:25

code trail has its own stern c. SERV 677:6

Codlin C.'s the friend DICK 271:6

coeli *Rorate, c.* BIBL 115:8

coercion effect of c. JEFF 420:16

coeur *Il pleure dans mon c.* VERL 809:3

Coeur-de-Lion reputed son of C. SHAK 698:30

coffee C. and oranges STEV 758:8

c. and other slop-kettle COBB 229:16

c.-house SWIF 765:7

C. house babble DISR 276:15

C., (which makes the politician wise)
POPE 606:14

if this is c. PUNC 637:25

measured out my life with c. spoons
ELIO 302:15

o'er cold c. POPE 603:26

put poison in your c. CHUR 222:20

to some c.-house I stray GREE 362:6

coffin c. clapt in a canoe BYRO 177:23

in a Y-shaped c. ORTO 576:18

silver plate on a c. CURR 254:5

cogimur *Omnes eodem c.* HORA 401:5

cogito C., *ergo sum* DESC 265:11

cognoscere *rerum c. causas* VIRG 814:17

cohorts his c. were gleaming BYRO 180:1

coign c. of the cliff SWIN 768:13

coil Lulled by the c. SHEL 730:9

coin C., Tiberius DOBS 278:15

coincidence long arm of c. CHAM 206:15

coiner c. of sweet words ARNO 28:14

coins for a fistful of c. ZAPA 858:4

like to c. TENN 777:24

coition way of c. BROW 157:6

coitu *Foeda est in c.* PETR 594:7

coitum *Post c.* SAYI 670:11

coke go better with C. ADVE 8:18

cold can be eaten c. PROV 630:7

Cast a c. eye YEAT 856:5

caught An everlasting c. WEBS 826:16

chilling c. had pierced SACK 662:9

c. a long time STEV 758:6

c. charities CRAB 249:20

Cold, c., my girl SHAK 714:27

c. coming they had of it ANDR 14:12

c. coming we had of it ELIO 302:9

c. grave BALL 53:16

C. hands, warm heart PROV 617:1

c. in blood SHAK 679:1

C. in the earth BRON 152:20

C. lights hurting JOHN 423:5

c. metal of economic theory SCHU 672:4

C. Pastoral KEAT 444:14

c. relation BURK 167:28

c. war BARU 57:16

c. war warrior THAT 786:27

come with your c. music BROW 161:21

Fallen c. and dead WHIT 833:5

Feed a c. PROV 619:47

fingers of c. are corpse fingers LAWR 475:15

I beg c. comfort SHAK 699:15

ink in my pen ran c. WALP 818:21

in love with a c. climate SOUT 749:17

in the darkness and the c. STEV 760:9

i' the c. o' the moon BROW 158:26

lie in c. obstruction SHAK 708:10

like c. porridge SHAK 718:28

like rivers grow c. MONT 543:12

Love in a c. climate MITF 540:17

neither c. nor hot BIBL 113:5

offspring of c. hearts BURK 167:15

O ye Frost and C. BOOK 128:6

past the common c. AYRE 41:11

plunging into a c. peace YELT 856:15

Poor Tom's a-c. SHAK 701:1

so the c. strengthens PROV 614:35

spy who came in from the c. LE C 478:9

straight is c. again SHAK 698:19

till I shrink with c. SHAK 680:25

'tis bitter c. SHAK 683:12

To c. oblivion SHEL 729:7

too c. for hell SHAK 705:6

understand one who's c. SOLZ 745:16

waxeth c. BALL 53:18

Without the c. war UPDI 805:20

colder c. and dumber than a fish
MULD 553:16

coldly C., sadly descends ARNO 28:1

Cole Old King C. NURS 568:13

Coliseum While stands the C. BYRO 179:14

You're the C. PORT 607:19

collapse c. in deepest humiliation EDDI 295:4

C. of Stout Party ANON 15:11

collar braw brass c. BURN 173:8

collateral c. security CHES 215:11

collected if they were c. JONS 435:6

collections mutilators of c. LAMB 464:14

collective c. unconscious JUNG 438:8

collects beautiful c. MACA 498:21

college cabbage with a c. education
TWAI 803:23

endow a c. POPE 603:9

Master of this c. BEEC 62:16

small c. WEBS 825:9

colleges discipline of c. SMIT 741:11

Collins marry Mr C. AUST 39:23

collision avoid foreign c. CLAY 226:1

colonel C. Blimp LOW 493:14

C.'s Lady KIPL 454:18

colonial tales of castaways, c. museums
GENE 342:22

colonies commerce with our c. BURK 166:19

New c. seek FREE 333:11

These wretched c. DISR 275:14

colonnade sound of the cool c. COWP 247:8

Colonus Singer of sweet C. ARNO 28:29

colori *nimium ne crede c.* VIRG 813:18

colossus C. from a rock JOHN 432:15

Like a C. SHAK 696:9

colour any c. that he wants FORD 328:12

By convention there is c. DEMO 263:14

by the c. of their skin KING 452:4

cannot be of a bad c. PROV 621:8

cast thy nighted c. off SHAK 683:25

c., culture or ethnic origin MACP 505:4

C. has taken hold of me KLEE 457:18

c. of his hair HOUS 403:19

c. purple WALK 817:13

C. seems to radiate CLIF 227:2

Her c. comes and goes DOBS 278:17

her c. is natural SHER 733:28

horse of that c. SHAK 720:20

I know the c. rose ABSE 1:4

Life is C. GREN 363:13

or the c. of their skin WILL 839:19

perceptible through c. MOND 542:19

problem of the c. line DU B 290:21

sense of c. BLUN 124:9

waning of their c. VOLT 816:13

yearned for warmth and c. TENN 777:22

coloured about the c. women TRUT 801:19

best c. man JOHN 423:8

makes a man c. HUGH 407:1

no 'white' or 'c.' signs KENN 449:4

penny plain and twopence c. STEV 759:12
see the c. counties HOUS 404:11
colourless C. green ideas CHOM 218:8
colours add c. to the chameleon SHAK 694:29
coat of many c. BIBL 76:37
c. and their forms WORD 847:9
c. laid so thick DRYD 288:7
C. seen by candle-light BROW 158:1
c. will agree BACO 45:33
lines and c. POUS 609:12
map-makers' c. BISH 117:6
nailing his c. FIEL 317:11
Who put the c. BOOT 144:23
Columbia Hail, C.! happy land HOPK 397:18
columbine pink and purple c. SPEN 752:18
Columbus laughed at C. GERS 344:10
column Fifth c. MOLA 541:8
like a black c. BABE 42:6
stately c. broke SCOT 673:16
columnae *non concessere c.* HORA 398:17
columns crazy on its smoking c. YEVT 856:19
coma state of resentful c. LASK 470:1
comae *Arboribusque c.* HORA 402:11
comb c. and a glass in her hand SONG 748:2
c. was redder than the fyn coral
 CHAU 211:27
siller c. BALL 52:9
two bald men over a c. BORG 145:8
combat c. may be glorious COWP 248:5
comber crash of the c. KIPL 455:15
combination call it c. PALM 584:21
combinations irregular c. JOHN 425:23
metrical c. FLAU 325:10
combine When bad men c. BURK 168:8
combining c. committee BAGE 47:17
come All things c. to those who wait
 PROV 614:19
behold, I c. quickly BIBL 114:23
believe in the life to c. BECK 61:4
better not C. at all KEAT 446:8
But will they c. SHAK 690:22
cannot c. again HOUS 404:16
c. all the way for this MORR 549:16
C., and he cometh BIBL 95:28
C. away, come away, death SHAK 720:26
C., come, dear Night CHAP 208:13
C., dear children ARNO 27:10
C. down, O Love divine LITT 486:16
c. for your good GEOR 343:1
C., Holy Spirit LANG 466:22
C. in the speaking silence ROSS 655:7
C. into the garden TENN 781:23
C., let us join our cheerful songs
 WATT 823:13
c., let us sing BOOK 140:9
c., Lord Jesus BIBL 114:25
C. mothers and fathers DYLA 294:17
C., my Celia JONS 435:20
C. not between the dragon SHAK 699:19
C. on CATC 200:8
c. out, thou bloody man BIBL 81:4
C. over into Macedonia BIBL 105:12
C. to me in my dreams ARNO 27:9
c. to my father AUBR 34:1
c. to my heart ELLI 305:13
C. to the edge LOGU 489:12
C. unto me BIBL 96:27
c. unto my love SPEN 751:9
C. unto these yellow sands SHAK 718:26
C. what come may SHAK 703:16
c. without warning DAVI 259:8
don't want to c. out BERR 71:9
dreaming on things to c. SHAK 723:18
Easy c., easy go PROV 618:34
First c. PROV 620:9
he that should c. BIBL 96:23
I go—I c. back CATC 201:3
it needn't c. to that CARR 195:18
I will not c. SHAK 697:6
jump the life to c. SHAK 704:3
King of glory shall c. in BOOK 135:6
let him c. out JOHN 432:2
Light c., light go PROV 625:15

men may c. TENN 775:19
mine hour is not yet c. BIBL 102:27
Mr Watson, c. here BELL 64:8
nobody will c. SAND 666:1
O c., all ye faithful ANON 21:12
One to c., and one to go CARR 195:21
Quickly c., quickly go PROV 630:2
shape of things to c. WELL 828:15
Sumer is c. in ANON 19:6
That it should c. to this SHAK 684:2
therefore I cannot c. BIBL 101:7
'tis not to c. SHAK 689:7
What's to c. is still unsure SHAK 720:16
wheel is c. full circle SHAK 702:3
when death is c., we are not EPIC 308:8
where do they all c. from LENN 480:17
wherefore art thou c. BIBL 99:7
which is to c. BIBL 112:24
whistle, an' I'll c. BURN 172:3
Why don't you c. up WEST 830:6
comeback c. kid CLIN 227:7
comedies All c. are ended BYRO 180:29
comedy All I need to make a c. CHAP 208:5
C. is an imitation SIDN 736:17
C. is tragedy that happens CART 196:21
c. to those that think WALP 819:11
C. wears itself out HAZL 376:16
most lamentable c. SHAK 710:20
tragedy, c., history SHAK 685:28
comely black, but c. BIBL 87:3
comes c. again in the morning SHER 733:28
conquering hero c. MORE 548:19
Look, where it c. again SHAK 683:14
nobody c. BECK 61:17
Tomorrow never c. PROV 633:12
comest c. into thy kingdom BIBL 102:5
cometh Blessed be he that c. BOOK 142:11
c. unto the Father BIBL 103:29
c. with clouds BIBL 112:25
He c. not TENN 781:14
Him that c. to me BIBL 103:5
master of the house c. BIBL 99:28
comets country c. MARV 515:20
no c. seen SHAK 697:3
Old men and c. SWIF 766:26
comfit like a c.-maker's wife SHAK 690:26
comfort a' the c. we're to get BURN 173:2
bourgeois prefers c. HESS 387:10
carrion c., Despair HOPK 396:10
c. all that mourn BIBL 90:18
c. and despair SHAK 723:30
c. and help the weak-hearted BOOK 129:11
c. and relieve them BOOK 129:19
c. cruel men CHES 216:3
c. in my people's happiness ELIZ 304:10
c. of feeling safe ANON 18:5
c. of thy help BOOK 137:13
C.'s a cripple DRAY 285:20
c. ye my people BIBL 89:15
found I any to c. me BOOK 138:16
good c., Master Ridley LAST 471:4
great source of c. NIET 564:10
I beg cold c. SHAK 699:15
love her, c. her BOOK 133:8
love of material c. TOCQ 795:2
naught for your c. CHES 215:21
our c. flows PRIO 612:10
receives c. SHAK 718:28
Sacrament to your c. BOOK 131:17
take c. a little BIBL 83:2
to c., and command WORD 850:5
waters of c. BOOK 135:3
What a c. CARR 194:24
comfortable All clean and c. KEAT 447:2
c. and the accepted GALB 338:2
c. estate of widowhood GAY 341:11
c. words BOOK 131:19
comfortably lived c. so long together
 GAY 341:7
sitting c. CATC 200:4
Speak ye c. BIBL 89:15
comforted c. his people BIBL 89:29
they shall be c. BIBL 94:20

would not be c. BIBL 94:8
comforter C. will not come BIBL 103:35
Guide, a C. AUBE 33:13
O C., draw near LITT 486:16
comforters Miserable c. BIBL 83:9
comforting cloud of c. convictions
 RUSS 661:2
where is your c. HOPK 396:18
comfortless leave us not c. BOOK 103:30
comforts recapture the c. BRYS 162:14
uncertain c. PROV 616:39
comic business of a c. poet CONG 238:13
comical Beautiful c. things HARV 374:20
I often think it's c. GILB 347:12
coming cold c. we had of it ELIO 302:9
c. as fast as I can LAUD 470:3
C. events cast PROV 617:3
c. events cast their shadows CAMP 187:12
c. for us that night BALD 50:11
C. in on a wing and a pray'r ADAM 3:17
c. of the King of Heaven ANON 20:6
c. of the Son of Man BIBL 98:18
C. thro' the rye BURN 170:17
c. to that holy room DONN 280:1
Everything's c. up roses SOND 746:5
good time c. SCOT 674:22
He is c. AYTO 41:13
my c. down MORE 548:1
She is c., my dove TENN 781:26
their c. hither SHAK 701:23
Yanks are c. COHA 230:7
comma c.-hunting CORN 243:13
kiss can be a c. MIST 540:4
command cannot obey cannot c.
 PROV 621:43
c. of any kind as an exceptional MILL 525:16
c. success ADDI 4:8
c. the rain PEPY 592:1
give what you c. AUGU 37:6
left that c. MILT 533:30
not born to sue, but to c. SHAK 715:6
sue than to c. SCOT 673:4
to comfort, and c. WORD 850:5
to the c. of another OSBO 578:14
commander c. of three armies CONF 238:1
commandest thing which thou c.
 BOOK 130:8
commandment c. of the Lord BOOK 134:21
first and great c. BIBL 98:8
commandments gave the ten c. to the
world BAUE 59:5
hearkened to my c. BIBL 89:25
keep his c. BIBL 87:1
learn by these C. BOOK 132:14
Ten for the ten c. SONG 747:11
commencement c. de la fin TALL 770:20
commend c. my spirit BIBL 102:7
c. my spirit BOOK 135:19
c. the bone DICK 273:12
virtue to c. CONG 239:22
virtue to c. CONG 239:23
commendatio Formosafacies muta c.
 PUBL 636:13
commendeth obliquely c. himself
 BROW 155:15
comment C. is free SCOT 672:14
C. is free STOP 761:11
couldn't possibly c. CATC 202:4
none can read the c. TENN 778:9
commentaries a-swarm with c. MONT 545:3
commentators c. each dark passage
 YOUN 857:7
learned c. view SWIF 767:8
commerce c. between equals GOLD 355:17
c. with our colonies BURK 166:19
In matters of c. CANN 189:4
Peace, c. JEFF 420:3
where c. long prevails GOLD 355:12
commercial put to c. use EDIS 296:6
commissary Destiny the c. of God
 DONN 280:7
commit c. his body to the deep BOOK 144:12
c. his body to the ground BOOK 133:18

No c. in religion   KORA 459:14
reason on c.   SHAK 690:11
Such sweet c.   MILT 528:14
compulsive c. course   SHAK 714:6
compulsory forbidden is c.   WHIT 832:5
compunctious c. visitings of nature
  SHAK 703:19
computer modern c. hovers   BREN 150:23
requires a c.   SAYI 670:17
work of an eyeless c.   BETJ 72:14
computers C. are anti-Faraday   CORN 243:7
so many c.   WALE 817:7
conceal able to c. it   LA R 469:16
able to c. it   TWAI 803:30
c. a fact with words   MACH 502:7
c. our wants   GOLD 355:16
Fate tried to c. him   HOLM 393:3
should c. it   AUST 39:8
concealing hazard of c.   BURN 170:28
concealment c., like a worm   SHAK 720:29
conceit curst c. o' bein' richt   MACD 501:1
folly and c.   AUST 39:22
man wise in his own c.   BIBL 85:10
never forgive any c.   DRYD 290:11
wise in his own c.   BIBL 85:8
wiser in his own c.   BIBL 85:11
conceits accepted for c.   BACO 42:19
c. do prove the greatest liars   DRAY 285:22
wise in your own c.   BIBL 106:27
conceive virgin shall c.   BIBL 88:15
conceived c. by the Holy Ghost   BOOK 128:10
man child c.   BIBL 82:31
my mother c. me   BOOK 137:11
concentrated c. in you   KEAT 447:6
concentrates c. his mind   JOHN 430:26
conception c. is more fun   STRU 762:18
present at the c.   ORTO 576:16
conceptions C. equal to the soul's
  WORD 846:17
concepts walks up the stairs of his c.
  STEI 755:11
concern had no c. in   SWIF 766:30
concerned being ultimately c.   TILL 794:16
nobody left to be c.   NIEM 563:18
concert middle of a c.   STEN 755:17
concerto C. to be difficult   SCHO 671:15
concessions c. of the weak   BURK 166:18
what c. to make   METT 523:9
conciseness sacrificed to c.   JOHN 424:1
conclaves Kingly c. stern   SHEL 731:1
concluded case is c.   AUGU 37:17
conclusion c., shewing from various
  causes   JOHN 427:19
denoted a foregone c.   SHAK 714:5
conclusions pursued c. infinite   SHAK 680:18
concord c. of sweet sounds   SHAK 710:5
lover of c.   BOOK 128:12
travelled a good deal in C.   THOR 793:2
truth, unity, and c.   BOOK 131:13
concordia C. discors   HORA 399:11
concrete city is not a c. jungle   MORR 549:8
c. and tyres   LARK 468:16
c. cloverleaf   MUMF 554:3
everything you thought was c.   WALK 817:9
concubine c. of a warlord   OPEN 574:6
concupiscent c. curds   STEV 757:21
concupiscite sine dolo lac c.   BIBL 115:18
condamner c. les gens   MOLI 542:4
condemn c. a little more   MAJO 508:4
C. the fault   SHAK 707:25
Neither do I c. thee   BIBL 103:10
some delights c.   MOLI 542:11
condemned c. to be free   SART 667:2
you yourself Are much c.   SHAK 698:13
condemns c. the doves   JUVE 439:12
c. whatever he disapproves   BURN 169:25
condition c. upon which God   CURR 254:2
could do in that c.   PEPY 591:21
wearisome c. of humanity   GREV 364:2
conditioned all c. things   PALI 583:12
C. Genesis   PALI 583:16
conditions c. of men   BOOK 129:17
govern our c.   SHAK 701:10

no c. of life   TOLS 796:14
conduct C. is three-fourths   ARNO 30:4
c. of a losing party   BURK 166:2
c. of their rulers   ADAM 3:5
c. of the women   MORE 548:4
C. . . . to the prejudice   MILI 526:5
c. unbecoming   MILI 526:3
regulation of c.   SPEN 750:6
rottenness begins in his c.   JEFF 419:17
conductor music eliminates the c.
  STRA 762:8
conductors third-rate foreign c.   BEEC 62:14
cone inverted c.   JOHN 431:4
sphere, the c.   CÉZA 206:1
cones eat the c. under his pines   FROS 335:19
confabulate If birds c. or no   COWP 247:7
confederacy dunces are all in c.   SWIF 766:20
if the C. fails   DAVI 259:4
confederate in games C.   WORD 846:24
conference c. a ready man   BACO 45:21
ever born in a c.   FITZ 324:2
hold some two days' c.   WEBS 825:22
naked into the c. chamber   BEVA 73:15
conferences eradication of c.   MAYA 519:10
confess C. and be hanged   PROV 617:7
c. them   BOOK 127:13
c. to almighty God   MISS 536:14
Never c.! Never, never   CONR 240:12
confessed fault c.   PROV 619:44
confessing then c. it   TROL 799:20
confession be there at the C.   DONN 282:3
C. good for soul   PROV 617:8
make your humble c.   BOOK 131:17
confessions c. of a justified sinner
  HOGG 392:10
confidante c. stark mad   SHER 733:10
confide seldom c.   CAMU 188:11
confidence c. of the people   CONF 238:4
ignorance and c.   TWAI 803:28
to inspire c.   CARR 196:16
too great c.   JOHN 426:5
confident c. in each other   ARIS 26:4
glad c. morning   BROW 160:4
confine verge Of her c.   SHAK 700:10
confined cabined, cribbed, c.   SHAK 706:3
c. him home   CLEV 227:1
confinement ill deserves the name of c.
  LOCK 488:16
solitary c. inside our own skins   WILL 839:8
confirmed to be c.   TENN 785:1
confiscation legalized c.   DISR 276:6
Confiteor C. Deo omnipotenti   MISS 536:14
conflict armed c.   EDEN 295:10
end of the c. of centuries   GRIF 364:6
Never in the field of human c.   CHUR 221:10
offered you C. and Art   PRIE 610:19
tragic c. of loyalties   HOWE 405:12
conflicts all disputes or c.   BRIA 151:2
conform c., or be more wise   PEPY 592:7
conforms man c.   ANON 18:21
confound C. their politics   SONG 747:8
c. the wise   BIBL 107:5
confounded Confusion worse c.   MILT 532:15
let me never be c.   BOOK 128:2
confounding c. the Persons   BOOK 128:22
confundar non c. in aeternum   PRAY 611:8
confused anyone who isn't c.   MURR 555:7
casts aside whatever is c.   CHUA 219:1
confusion come to c.   SHAK 710:18
C. now hath made   SHAK 705:10
C. on thy banners wait   GRAY 360:20
C. worse confounded   MILT 532:15
couch in some c.   CONG 239:15
in our sea of c.   GAMO 338:18
see so much c.   MOOR 547:7
confute tell how to c. him   SELD 676:4
congeals When love c.   HART 374:11
Congo C., creeping through the black
  LIND 486:3
congratulatory c. regrets   DISR 276:18
congregation aloof from the c.   HILL 389:5
c. of the poor   BOOK 139:3
c. of vapours   SHAK 685:24

face of this c.   BOOK 133:4
largest c.   DEFO 261:21
praise the Lord in the c.   BOOK 135:12
whole c.   ADDI 4:26
congregations all c.   BOOK 128:17
congress C. makes no progress   LIGN 484:12
conies rocks for the c.   BOOK 141:8
coniunx C. Est mihi   LUCA 495:3
conjecture not beyond all c.   BROW 156:12
Now entertain c.   SHAK 693:7
conjectures dogmatically to our c.
  POPP 607:6
conjuring c. trick with bones   JENK 420:20
Parson left off c.   SELD 676:8
conjuror charlatan, and a c.   TROL 799:4
level of the stage c.   MOOR 546:14
conked c. out on November 15th   EPIT 310:12
connaît ne se c. pas   LA F 463:14
Connaught Hell or C.   CROM 252:8
connect Only c.   FORS 329:16
connection without c.   BYRO 184:11
connections concealed c.   SMIT 741:2
connive c. in civilised outrage   HEAN 378:2
connubial c. of c. love   MILT 533:8
conquer c. Antony   SHAK 679:26
c. or die   WASH 822:6
c. without risk   CORN 243:4
easier to c. it   WALP 819:7
hard to catch and c.   MERE 522:19
Like Douglas c.   HOME 393:15
man should c. himself   PALI 584:13
must c. them anew   GOET 353:1
shalt thou c.   CONS 241:11
want of more Worlds to c.   WATT 824:1
we will c.   BEE 62:9
conquered c. and peopled   SEEL 675:16
I came, I saw, I c.   CAES 185:7
I will be c.   JOHN 433:2
perpetually to be c.   BURK 166:20
they are a c. people   VICT 809:13
They c. continents   DUNN 292:10
Thou hast c.   SWIN 768:22
conquering c. hero comes   MORE 548:19
C. kings   CHAN 207:10
c. one's enemies   GENG 342:24
He went forth c.   BIBL 113:13
conqueror c. must go on   WELL 828:2
every c. creates a Muse   WALL 818:11
Every other c.   BURK 168:24
proud foot of a c.   SHAK 699:16
you are a c.   ROST 656:16
conquerors to their c.   WILL 838:5
conquest c. and subjugation   WEBS 825:13
c. of the earth   CONR 240:13
urge for c.   ADLE 5:20
conquests c., glories, triumphs   SHAK 697:13
spread her c.   BURN 170:16
consanguineous Am I not c.   SHAK 720:17
conscience according to c.   MILT 535:24
Cash before c.   HORA 398:21
clean c. is a good pillow   PROV 616:45
c. as their King   TENN 777:20
C. avaunt   CIBB 223:4
c. doth make cowards   SHAK 686:12
C. has no more to do   SHER 733:12
c. is afraid   BOOK 130:16
C. is but a word   SHAK 717:9
C. is thoroughly well-bred   BUTL 177:6
C. makes cowards   PROV 617:9
c. of the king   SHAK 686:8
c. says, 'Launcelot, budge not.'   SHAK 709:4
c.-stricken air   HOUS 403:19
C.: the inner voice   MENC 521:18
c. void of offence   BIBL 105:27
corporation to have a c.   THUR 794:4
cruelty with a good c.   RUSS 661:3
cut my c.   HELL 380:12
ease your c.   ALAI 10:1
freedom of c.   TWAI 803:9
guilty c. needs   PROV 621:22
no c. in intrusion   AUST 40:8
Nonconformist c.   WILD 836:8
O coward c.   SHAK 717:6

contraception oral c. ALLE 12:12
contract C. into a span HERB 384:19
nothing but a civil c. SELD 676:6
social c. ROUS 657:3
Social C. is nothing more WELL 828:12
Society is indeed a c. BURK 167:22
to C. MAIN 507:20
tugging at every c. EMER 306:18
verbal c. isn't worth GOLD 356:5
contradict Do I c. myself WHIT 833:16
I never c. DISR 278:3
Never c. FISH 322:15
Read not to c. BACO 45:19
truth which you cannot c. SOCR 745:10
contradicted c. by observation EDDI 295:4
dogmatise and am c. JOHN 433:12
contradiction c. in terms SHAW 727:18
c. is real LÉVI 482:18
they brook no c. WEBS 825:27
Woman's at best a c. POPE 603:7
contradictions bundle of c. COLT 236:11
chain of c. CLAR 224:4
glaring c. HUME 409:2
contraries c. there is no progression BLAK 120:19
Dreams go by c. PROV 618:24
contrariwise 'C.,' continued Tweedledee CARR 195:5
contrary directed to c. parts NEWT 561:13
everythink goes c. with me DICK 268:7
Mary, quite c. NURS 568:9
most c. to custom HUME 408:11
On the c. LAST 473:13
trial is by what is c. MILT 535:16
contrast c. that awaits it MANZ 511:9
contribution make his own c. MORE 549:1
contrite broken and c. heart BOOK 137:15
broken and c. heart ELEA 298:20
sighing of a c. heart GRIN 429:15
contrive How Nature always does c. GILB 347:12
control Circumstances beyond my c. DICK 269:2
Ground c. to Major Tom BOWI 148:10
ought to c. our thoughts DARW 257:3
woman under her father's c. LAWS 476:1
wrong members in c. ORWE 577:10
controller Soul, the Inner C. UPAN 804:16
controlling (with luck, c.) the world JONE 434:8
controls Who c. the past ORWE 577:15
controversies forged in c. FRAN 332:10
controversy c. is either superfluous NEWM 561:1
man of c. GALB 338:2
contumely proud man's c. SHAK 686:10
convalescence enjoy c. SHAW 724:17
convenience prefers c. to liberty HESS 387:10
'Twixt treason and c. EPIT 310:7
convenient c. that there be gods OVID 580:1
food c. for me BIBL 85:20
convent C. of the Sacred Heart ELIO 303:6
c.'s narrow room WORD 847:17
convention By c. there is colour DEMO 263:14
Lords of C. SCOT 673:3
conventional c. truth NAGA 555:19
merely c. signs CARR 196:8
conventionality C. is not morality BRON 152:9
conversation always spoiling c. MACA 500:2
bee in c. JOHN 427:10
careless c. EDGE 295:14
c. among gentlemen JOHN 430:16
C. is imperative WHIT 832:3
c. perfectly delightful SMIT 743:25
c.-scraps, Kitchen-cabals CRAB 248:29
c. with the best men DESC 265:8
different name for c. STER 756:23
no such thing as c. WEST 830:13
rhymed c. GERS 344:11
subject of c. CHES 214:20
third-rate c. PLOM 598:10

use metaphors in c. ARIS 25:10
conversations after-dinner c. THOR 793:17
without pictures or c. CARR 193:17
conversing With thee c. MILT 533:6
conversion c. of the Jews MARV 515:23
convert to c. England PUGI 636:23
who shall c. me WESL 829:15
converted Except ye be c. BIBL 97:19
have not c. a man MORL 549:5
converts can true c. make FARQ 315:18
convict c. stain HUGH 407:3
conviction best lack all c. YEAT 855:12
what is called c. HUNT 410:6
convictions cloud of comforting c. RUSS 661:2
c. are hills FITZ 324:1
convince we c. ourselves JUNI 438:17
convinces man who c. the world DARW 257:18
convincing less c. than one HUXL 411:9
Oh! too c. BYRO 179:26
conviva plenus vitae c. LUCR 496:1
convoy crowns for c. SHAK 693:22
convulsions gall'ry in c. POPE 602:24
cookery c. do MERE 522:16
cookies baked c. and had teas CLIN 227:4
cooking C. is the most ancient BRIL 151:17
c. of the Mediterranean DAVI 258:2
'plain' c. cannot be entrusted MORP 549:6
cooks as c. go SAKI 663:14
Devil sends c. GARR 340:5
Devil sends c. PROV 620:49
literary c. MORE 548:1
praise it, not the c. HARI 373:14
Synod of C. JOHN 428:20
Too many c. PROV 633:14
cool Be still and c. FOX 331:10
c. as a mountain stream ADVE 7:14
c. web of language GRAV 360:6
in the c. of the day BIBL 75:20
rather be dead than c. COBA 229:14
Sweet day, so c. HERB 384:4
cooled C. a long age KEAT 444:21
cooling for c. the blood FLAN 324:16
cools Time c. MANN 511:1
cooperation Government and c. RUSK 660:9
partnership and c. ANON 15:13
co-operation belief in c. YAMA 853:2
coot haunts of c. and hern TENN 775:18
cope use a c. like that PUGI 636:23
copied c. the old authors PLIN 598:1
copier mere c. of nature REYN 646:2
copies few originals and many c. TOCQ 795:6
Make c. INGR 413:20
copperheads c. and the assassin SAND 665:18
coppers like the old time 'c.' COLL 235:3
cops C. are like a doctor CHAN 207:14
copulating skeletons c. BEEC 62:10
copulation Birth, and c., and death ELIO 303:4
Let c. thrive SHAK 701:14
copy to every book its c. COLU 236:12
copyrights authors their c. TROL 799:1
coque pénétra ma c. RIMB 649:5
coquetry tiresome as c. LERM 481:9
coquette Gay c. SANS 666:6
cor C. ad cor loquitur MOTT 552:5
J'aime le son du c. VIGN 810:6
coral C. is far more red SHAK 723:26
c. lip admires CARE 190:11
his bones are c. SHAK 718:27
India's c. strand HEBE 378:15
like c. insects WARN 821:21
redder than the fyn c. CHAU 211:27
corbies twa c. BALL 53:15
cord silver c. be loosed BIBL 86:25
stretch a c. however fine WHEW 831:14
threefold c. BIBL 86:3
triple c. BURK 166:6

corda Sursum c. MISS 536:22
Cordelia such sacrifices, my C. SHAK 702:1
cordial Love . . . That c. drop ROCH 651:7
cords scourge of small c. BIBL 102:29
core c. of a world's culture BOLD 126:3
deep heart's c. YEAT 854:18
Corinth lucky enough to get to C. HORA 399:13
Corinthian C. capital BURK 167:23
Corinthum adire C. HORA 399:13
cork c. out of my lunch FIEL 318:19
corkscrew tumbler, and a c. DICK 271:2
corkscrews crooked as c. AUDE 34:23
cormorant common c. (or shag) ISHE 414:9
C. devouring Time SHAK 702:10
Sat like a c. MILT 532:26
corn amid the alien c. KEAT 445:1
breast high amid the c. HOOD 395:10
c. as high as an elephant's eye HAMM 370:5
C. King beckoning JARR 418:27
C. rigs, an' barley rigs BURN 171:14
c. was orient TRAH 797:14
lower the price of c. MELB 521:2
My crop of c. TICH 794:12
our sustaining c. SHAK 701:11
raise the price of c. BYRO 177:21
stop raising c. LEAS 478:1
there was c. in Egypt BIBL 77:6
thick with c. BOOK 138:7
threshed c. at midnight YEAT 855:15
two ears of c. SWIF 765:13
yellow like ripe c. ROSS 655:20
cornea C., qua veris facilis VIRG 812:17
corner At every c., I meet my Father LOWE 494:12
came round the c. MILN 528:3
c. in the thing I love SHAK 713:29
c. of a foreign field BROO 153:15
c. of a foreign field OPEN 574:14
draughty street c. GRIF 364:9
drive life into a c. THOR 793:12
head-stone in the c. BOOK 142:10
in a c., some untidy spot AUDE 35:13
just around the c. COWA 245:8
not done in a c. BIBL 105:31
round the c. of nonsense COLE 234:9
Sat in the c. NURS 568:2
wind in that c. SHAK 712:19
corners age in c. thrown SHAK 680:27
clearing up the obscure c. HUXL 411:19
c. of the earth BOOK 140:10
Duke of dark c. SHAK 708:15
polished c. of the temple BOOK 143:23
round earth's imagined c. DONN 279:17
sheet knit at the four c. BIBL 105:6
three c. of the world SHAK 699:16
cornet young c. of horse WALP 820:8
cornfield o'er the green c. SHAK 682:6
cornfields Miles of c. HACK 366:9
Cornish twenty thousand C. men HAWK 375:9
corns shooting c. presage SWIF 766:29
corny c. as Kansas in August HAMM 370:10
Coromandel coast of C. SITW 739:2
On the coast of C. LEAR 477:4
coronation c., and sops in wine SPEN 752:18
coronet bride of a ducal c. DICK 270:12
coronets more than c. TENN 780:4
corporate c. welfare bams LEWI 483:13
corporation c. to have a conscience THUR 794:2
corporations [c.] cannot commit treason COKE 230:20
C. have neither bodies PROV 617:11
wealthy multinational c. LEWI 483:14
corpore Mens sana in c. sano JUVE 440:11
corpse carry one's father's c. APOL 23:12
c. in a coffin PEPY 592:9
c. in the case BARH 55:19
good wishes to the c. BARR 57:6

my c. 'tis of centuries | CUMM 253:6
My c., 'tis of thee | SMIT 742:18
My soul, there is a c. | VAUG 807:11
no c. for old men | YEAT 855:8
no relish for the c. | SMIT 743:14
Our c. is the world | GARR 340:9
our c., right or wrong | DECA 261:1
past is a foreign c. | HART 374:19
past is a foreign c. | OPEN 575:12
peace of each c. | JOHN 422:4
playing at the c. club | WILL 838:15
quarrel in a far away c. | CHAM 206:11
Queen and c. | THOM 791:20
right part of the c. | FROS 336:8
see much of the c. | GLAD 350:15
serve our c. | ADDI 4:13
service of their c. | PAIN 582:11
she is my c. still | CHUR 219:13
sucked on c. pleasures | DONN 280:26
there's another c. | SPRI 753:6
This was my c. | BLUN 124:6
to all the c. dear | GOLD 354:13
to be had in the c. | HAZL 376:15
too long in c. towns | CATH 199:12
tremble for my c. | JEFF 420:17
understand the c. | LESS 482:2
undone his c. | ADDI 4:12
unmapped c. | ELIO 299:12
vow to thee, my c. | SPRI 753:5
we can do for our c. | HOLM 393:7
what was good for our c. | WILS 840:1
While there's a c. lane | PARK 586:14
win our c. back | FABE 313:13
your King and your C. | RUBE 658:3
You've never seen this c. | PURD 637:27
countryman c. must have praise | BLYT 124:14
countrymen advice to my c. | O'CO 571:12
c. are all mankind | GARR 340:9
Friends, Romans, c. | SHAK 697:21
hearts of his c. | LEE 478:17
rebels are our c. | GRAN 359:6
countryside gods of the c. | VIRG 814:18
smiling and beautiful c. | DOYL 284:10
county C. Guy, the hour is nigh | SCOT 674:17
English c. families | WAUG 824:4
countymen fellow-c. won't kill me | COLL 235:7
coup c. de dés | MALL 508:15
couple young c. between the wars | PLOM 598:10
courage Be strong and of a good c. | BIBL 79:8
c. and skill | BUNY 165:9
C. in your own | GORD 356:17
C. is the price that Life | EARH 294:21
C., mon ami | READ 643:6
c. never to submit | MILT 531:9
C. not simply one of the virtues | LEWI 483:11
c. the greater | ANON 22:6
c. to suffer | TROL 799:10
c. without ferocity | BYRO 183:24
endurance and c. | SCOT 673:1
enough c.—or money | MITC 540:13
fresh c. take | COWP 246:24
have the c. to dare | DOST 283:6
in the morning c. | THOR 793:9
It takes c. | MOWL 551:17
Moral c. is a rarer commodity | KENN 449:11
on reflection is real c. | WALP 819:23
Pathos, piety, c. | FORS 329:21
red badge of c. | CRAN 250:4
screw your c. | SHAK 704:12
test of c. | HAZL 376:12
two o'clock in the morning c. | NAPO 556:17
warm c. | BUSH 175:4
warm c. | ROOS 653:14
with a good c. | BOOK 135:22
without originality or moral c. | SHAW 724:21
courageous captains c. | BALL 52:14
freedom depends on being c. | THUC 793:23
couriers Vaunt-c. | SHAK 700:15
cours Suspendez votre c. | LAMA 464:8
course c. of human events | JEFF 419:9
c. of true love | SHAK 710:17

finished my c. | BIBL 111:1
I must stand the c. | SHAK 701:4
myself to that c. | PEPY 592:16
Of c., of course | JAME 418:14
run his c. | BOOK 134:20
what c. thou wilt | SHAK 698:9
courses Horses for c. | PROV 622:33
court bright lustre of a c. | CECI 204:14
case that comes to c. | JUVE 439:21
c. awards it | SHAK 709:31
c. for owls | BIBL 89:8
C. of Session | PROV 622:23
c. others in verse | PRIO 612:1
envious c. | SHAK 680:25
four ways in c. | ASCH 31:4
not having a C. | BAGE 48:14
Say to the c., it glows | RALE 641:2
she will c. you | JONS 435:25
shines upon his c. | SHAK 722:10
Talk of c. news | SHAK 701:25
courteous C. he was, lowely | CHAU 210:9
c. to strangers | BACO 44:19
Courtesy Grace of God is in C. | BELL 65:6
courtesy candy deal of c. | SHAK 689:30
greater man, the greater c. | TENN 778:3
mirour of alle c. | CHAU 211:18
very pink of c. | SHAK 717:31
women with perfect c. | KITC 457:14
courtier heel of the c. | SHAK 688:27
Here lies a noble c. | EPIT 310:1
courtmartialled c. in my absence | BEHA 63:14
courts Approach with joy his c. | KETH 450:5
case is still before the c. | HORA 398:4
C. and camps | CHES 214:25
C. for cowards were erected | BURN 171:18
c. of the Lord | BOOK 139:15
c. of the sun | CHES 216:4
Fresh from brawling c. | TENN 779:17
one day in thy c. | BOOK 139:17
courtship C. to marriage | CONG 239:5
cousins C. and his aunts | GILB 348:21
couture Haute C. should be fun | LACR 463:9
covenant c. with death | BIBL 89:4
c. with death | GARR 340:10
Never break a c. | ZORO 859:12
token of a c. | BIBL 76:12
covenanted c. with him | BIBL 98:29
covenants Open c. of peace | WILS 841:1
Coventry for the train at C. | TENN 777:4
cover C. her face | WEBS 825:26
c. of a jest | HORA 403:3
Duck and c. | OFFI 572:7
I c. all | SAND 665:20
tell a book by its c. | PROV 635:45
covered c. his face | BIBL 88:10
coverlet length of his c. | PROV 619:21
covers c. a multitude of sins | PROV 616:34
covet Thou shalt not c. | BIBL 78:5
Thou shalt not c. | CLOU 229:8
covetous not c. | BIBL 110:22
covetousness inclined to c. | KORA 460:8
uncleanness, or c. | BIBL 109:14
cow bellowing c. soon forgets | PROV 615:9
Better a good c. | PROV 615:19
c. is of the bovine ilk | NASH 557:9
c. jumped over | NURS 567:6
c.'s horn | PROV 632:49
c.'s in the corn | NURS 568:1
c. with the crumpled horn | NURS 570:2
grass to graze a c. | BETJ 72:17
keep a c. | BUTL 177:2
like a c. or a dog | VICT 809:10
milk the c. of the world | WILB 835:4
never saw a Purple C. | BURG 165:18
swallow the c. | PROV 624:5
three acres and a c. | POLI 601:10
To every c. her calf | COLU 236:12
Truth, Sir, is a c. | JOHN 428:12
Two wise acres and a c. | COWA 245:16
Was the c. crossed | HERB 383:14
Why buy a c. when | PROV 635:7
coward bully is always a c. | PROV 616:15
c. does it with a kiss | WILD 836:29

c. on instinct | SHAK 690:13
c. shame | BURN 171:22
c.'s weapon, poison | FLET 327:19
No c. soul is mine | BRON 152:18
sea hates a c. | O'NE 573:13
cowardice c. keeps us in peace | JOHN 431:9
I admit the c. | SHAW 726:11
surest is c. | TWAI 803:11
cowardly C. dogs bark loudest | WEBS 826:7
cowards all men would be c. | ROCH 651:13
being all c. | JOHN 431:9
Conscience makes c. | PROV 617:9
C. die many times | SHAK 697:4
c. in reasoning | SHAF 678:5
C. in scarlet | GRAN 359:11
C. may die many times | PROV 617:14
make c. of us all | SHAK 686:12
many other mannish c. | SHAK 680:24
not because men are c. | LEWI 484:4
word that c. use | SHAK 717:9
cowl c. does not make monk | PROV 617:15
cows contented—that's for the c. | CHAN 208:1
C. are my passion | DICK 269:10
cowslip C. and shad-blow | CRAN 249:24
In a c.'s bell | SHAK 719:6
I' the bottom of a c. | SHAK 682:29
O'er the c.'s velvet head | MILT 529:8
cowslips c. tall her pensioners be | SHAK 710:28
coxcombs some made c. | POPE 603:29
coy sometimes c. | SEDL 675:12
Then be not c. | HERR 386:19
coyness This c., lady | MARV 515:22
cozenage greatest c. | CROM 252:5
crabbed C. age and youth | SHAK 722:15
crabs like wet c. in a basket | DURR 293:7
sidelong c. had scrawled | CRAB 248:31
crack C. and sometimes break | ELIO 301:13
c. in the tea-cup opens | AUDE 34:20
c. in your upper storey | SMOL 744:17
heaven's vaults should c. | SHAK 702:4
cracked bloody noses and c. crowns | SHAK 690:4
c. from side to side | TENN 780:12
crackling c. of thorns | BIBL 86:6
cracks c. in the conversation | WALK 817:9
Now c. a noble heart | SHAK 689:16
cradle c. and the grave | DYER 293:16
c. endlessly rocking | WHIT 833:6
c. of an infant | BURK 166:10
c. of the deep | WILL 837:21
c. of the fairy queen | SHAK 711:10
c. rocks above an abyss | NABO 555:17
c. to the grave | SHEL 731:9
from the c. to the grave | CHUR 221:17
hand that rocks the c. | PROV 621:27
hand that rocks the c. | WALL 818:3
rocking the c. | ROBI 650:22
cradles babies in the c. | BROW 160:20
cradling evil c. | BORR 146:5
evil c. | KORA 459:17
craft c. and credulity | BURK 166:8
c. so long to lerne | CHAU 212:26
not teach his son a c. | TALM 772:27
craftier c. to pley she was | CHAU 210:3
crafts c. and assaults | BOOK 129:4
crag c. with crookèd hands | TENN 776:20
craggy c. paths of study | JONS 435:15
cramped won't lie too c. | CELA 205:1
cranberry And a C. Tart | LEAR 477:9
crane tall as a c. | SITW 738:14
cranks into sages and c. | QUIN 639:12
crankum crinkum c. | AUBR 33:18
cras C. ingens iterabimus aequor | HORA 400:20
crash car c. as a sexual event | BALL 54:1
c. will come twenty years after | BISM 118:1
whether it would c. | BERN 71:7
crastina Pereat, qui c. curat | ANON 22:2
Sera nimis vita est c. | MART 514:16
craters passing c., passing fire | YEVT 856:19
crave my mind forbids to c. | DYER 293:13
craving full as c. too | DRYD 287:24

craving (cont.):
getting rid of c. · PALI 583:17
he the more is c. · WROT 851:18
crawls sea-worm c.—grotesque · HARD 372:13
crazed c. with the spell of far Arabia · DE L 262:22
crazy C. like a fox · PERE 592:18
c. to fly more missions · HELL 380:8
he's football c. · MCGR 502:5
Still c. after all · SIMO 738:5
stood by me when I was c. · SHER 734:15
two c. people together · HART 374:13
creaking c. door hangs longest · PROV 617:16
c. to the barn · LOWE 494:13
creaks morning light c. down again · SITW 738:14
cream choking it with c. · PROV 631:45
c.-faced loon · SHAK 707:7
queen of curds and c. · SHAK 722:8
crease with not a c. · ROST 656:12
create c. the taste · WORD 851:2
c. the wondrous world · YOUN 857:16
genuinely c. Europe · MONN 543:2
must c. a system · BLAK 120:7
new-c. another heir · SHAK 695:25
transmit but do not c. · CONF 237:20
What I cannot c. · FEYN 317:7
what they half-c. · WORD 847:12
created all men are c. equal · ANON 19:17
c. all things · BIBL 113:10
c. him in his own image · DOST 283:2
c. in the image · TALM 772:5
c. Man of a blood-clot · KORA 461:13
C. sick · GREV 364:2
He also c. in man · TALM 772:32
just c. like mistakes · EMEC 306:9
men are c. equal · JEFF 419:10
monster whom I had c. · SHEL 728:8
Nothing can be c. · LUCR 495:12
why I c. man · ZOHA 858:14
creation bless thee for our c. · BOOK 129:20
blind fury of c. · SHAW 726:2
C. has become so broad · BÜCH 163:5
c. rises again · MISS 539:16
eternal act of c. · COLE 233:21
finds c. so perfect · PROU 613:10
from the first c. · LLOY 487:12
I hold C. in my foot · HUGH 407:5
immanent in all c. · SIKH 737:8
love C.'s final law · TENN 779:10
originates c. · KORA 460:13
present at the C. · ALFO 11:12
this c. has arisen · RIG 648:11
whole c. groaneth · BIBL 106:20
whole c. moves · TENN 779:30
your niche in c. · HALL 369:14
creative c. hate · CATH 199:14
c. soul · WORD 849:18
c. urge · BAKU 50:4
Deception is not as c. · SAUN 668:1
man's c. powers · SCHU 672:2
creator abide with my C. God · CLAR 224:12
can dispense with a c. · PROU 613:10
C., if He exists · HALD 368:2
C. made Italy · TWAI 803:15
C., without fear · SIKH 737:1
creature more than the C. · BIBL 105:37
existence of the C. · MAIM 507:15
feel at times like the C. · BELL 64:14
glory of the C. · BACO 42:14
great c. from his work · MILT 533:23
image of the C. · BONA 127:4
myself and my C. · NEWM 560:10
Of the C. · MERW 523:6
Remember now thy C. · BIBL 86:25
creature c. hath a purpose · KEAT 446:19
c. more than the Creator · BIBL 105:37
God's first C. · BACO 46:12
lone lorn c. · DICK 268:7
no lyves c. Withouten love · CHAU 213:3
one tiny c. · DOST 283:4
creatures c. great and small · ALEX 11:6
c. set upon tables · JOHN 430:9

living, sentient c. · JAIN 416:8
credat C. Iudaeus Apella · HORA 403:10
credence no c. to his word · BOOK 141:14
credit citizen Of c. and renown · COWP 246:18
c. where credit is due · PROV 620:40
greatly to his c. · GILB 348:25
In science the c. goes · DARW 257:18
let the c. go · FITZ 323:3
my c. in this world · FITZ 323:15
people who get the c. · MORR 550:14
To c. marvels · HEAN 377:20
credite Experto c. · VIRG 813:10
creditor trembling at a c. · JOHN 424:27
credo C. in unum Deum · MISS 536:19
C. quia impossibile · TERT 786:2
credulity craft and c. · BURK 166:8
craving c. · DISR 275:21
soften into a c. · BURK 168:6
credulous are the most c. · POPE 606:24
Man is a c. animal · RUSS 661:6
creed Calvinistic c. · PITT 596:5
c. of slaves · PITT 596:10
got the better of his c. · STER 757:1
last article of my c. · GAND 339:7
my political c. · ADAM 3:4
Sapping a solemn c. · BYRO 179:1
suckled in a c. outworn · WORD 850:22
This c. of the Nirgranthas · JAIN 416:21
creeds dust of c. outworn · SHEL 731:4
keys of all the c. · TENN 778:30
Light half-believers in our casual c. · ARNO 28:8
live their c. · GUES 365:13
so many c. · WILC 835:9
than in half the c. · TENN 779:19
creep Ambition can c. · BURK 168:1
bade me c. past · BROW 161:2
c. again, leap again · DE L 262:25
C. into thy narrow bed · ARNO 27:14
make your flesh c. · DICK 271:27
music c. in our ears · SHAK 710:2
creeping c. things · BIBL 105:6
every c. thing · BIBL 75:8
creeps C. in this petty pace · SHAK 707:14
c. rustling to her knees · KEAT 442:21
crème c. de la crème · SPAR 749:25
crescent with c. horns · MILT 531:19
Crete people of C. · SAKI 663:13
Cretes C. and Arabians · BIBL 104:27
crevasse like a scream from a c. · GREE 362:15
crew We were a ghastly c. · COLE 233:5
Crewe True blue and Mrs C. · TOAS 796:6
crib shadow of the c. · BISH 117:8
cribbed cabined, c., confined · SHAK 706:3
cricket C.—a game which the English · MANC 509:11
c. as organized loafing · TEMP 775:13
C. civilizes people · MUGA 553:4
c. on the hearth · MILT 529:12
c. test · TEBB 775:7
c. with their peasants · TREV 798:11
everything lost but c. · CARD 190:9
When you play Test c. · BRAD 149:1
cried little children c. · MOTL 551:14
pig c., Wee-wee-wee · NURS 570:4
poor have c. · SHAK 697:25
when he c. · AUDE 34:26
cries on me she c. · BALL 52:6
crieth c. in the wilderness · BIBL 89:16
Crillon Hang yourself, brave C. · HENR 381:20
crime catalogue of human c. · CHUR 221:6
commonplace a c. · DOYL 284:9
C. doesn't pay · PROV 617:17
c. of being a young man · PITT 596:1
c. so shameful as poverty · FARQ 315:9
c. to love too well · POPE 602:12
c. you haven't committed · POWE 609:16
foulest in history · WHIT 833:21
From the one c. · VIRG 811:12
lovèd be with equal c. · SPEN 751:26
my wilful c. · MILT 534:13
Napoleon of c. · DOYL 284:18
never a c. · CORN 243:6

No c.'s so great · CHUR 219:12
Poverty is not a c. · PROV 629:32
punishment fit the c. · GILB 348:4
Tough on c. · BLAI 118:15
was thought a c. · BLAK 122:15
worse than a c. · BOUL 147:5
worse than a c. · BRAD 148:16
crimes all his c. broad blown · SHAK 687:17
c. are committed in thy name · LAST 473:9
c., follies, and misfortunes · GIBB 345:1
C., like virtues · FARQ 315:19
c. of this guilty land · BROW 155:8
one virtue, and a thousand c. · BYRO 179:28
Successful c. alone · DRYD 289:2
virtues made or c. · DEFO 261:19
with reiterated c. · MILT 531:13
worst of c. · SHAW 725:21
criminal crime and the c. · AREN 24:15
ends I think c. · KEYN 450:10
severity of the c. law · PEEL 590:14
while there is a c. element · DEBS 260:18
criminals if there were no c. · SALI 664:15
Looney Tunes, and squalid c. · REAG 643:15
crimine C. ab uno · VIRG 811:12
crimson Cat with c. whiskers · LEAR 477:20
c. in thy lips · SHAK 718:9
c. thread of kinship · PARK 586:15
Now sleeps the c. petal · TENN 783:12
cringe Australian Cultural C. · PHIL 595:1
to the cultural c. · KEAT 442:9
crinkum c. crankum · AUBR 33:18
cripples If c., then no matter · PAST 588:5
crisis C.? What Crisis? · MISQ 537:8
C.? What crisis · NEWS 562:3
drama out of a c. · ADVE 8:23
fit for a great c. · BAGE 47:20
Moments of c. produce in man · CHAT 210:2
real c. on your hands · THAT 787:5
crisp Deep and c. and even · NEAL 558:1
Crispian feast of C. · SHAK 693:22
Crispin C. Crispian shall ne'er go by · SHAK 693:24
crisps like eating c. · BOY 148:15
criterion infallible c. of wisdom · BURK 166:2
critic average English c. · LAMB 465:14
C. and whippersnapper · BROW 158:13
c. is a bundle of biases · BALL 54:3
c. is a man who knows the way · TYNA 804:4
c. spits on what is done · HOOD 395:13
C., you have frowned · WORD 849:26
cry of the c. for five · WHIS 831:20
function of the c. · BELL 64:10
good c. is he who relates · FRAN 332:1
great drama c. · TYNA 804:2
important book, the c. assumes · WOOL 845:8
knew the c.'s part · COLL 235:16
not the c. who counts · ROOS 654:12
poet includes a c. · SHEN 733:2
true c. ought · ADDI 4:29
Unboding c.-pen · TENN 784:22
criticism cant of c. · STER 757:5
C. is a life without risk · LAHR 464:2
c. of life · ARNO 29:24
father of English c. · JOHN 425:3
from c. to nature · JOHN 425:15
my own definition of c. · ARNO 29:17
near to them than c. · RILK 648:18
no c. of the president · ROOS 654:16
People ask you for c. · MAUG 518:19
wreathed the rod of c. · D'IS 278:12
criticize c. What you can't understand · DYLA 294:17
criticized If you are not c. · RUMS 658:9
to be c. is not always · EDEN 295:11
critics c. all are ready made · BYRO 182:9
C. are like brushers · WOTT 851:9
c. of the next · FITZ 324:10
know who the c. are · DISR 277:22
therefore they turn c. · COLE 233:27
Turned c. next · POPE 603:30
croaks c. the fatal entrance · SHAK 703:19
crocodile cruel crafty c. · SPEN 751:18
How doth the little c. · CARR 193:19

manner o' thing is your c.   SHAK 679:13
these c.'s tears   BURT 174:15
crocodiles wisdom of the c.   BACO 46:3
crocus c. brake like fire   TENN 782:19
Cromwell C., I charge thee   SHAK 695:14
ruin that C. knocked about   BEDF 62:8
Some C. guiltless   GRAY 361:5
cronies money-grabbing c.   HAGU 367:8
crony rusty, drouthy c.   BURN 172:9
crook President is a c.   NIXO 564:21
crookbacked C. he was   SACK 662:10
crooked crag with c. hands   TENN 776:20
c. as corkscrews   AUDE 34:23
c. be made straight   ELIO 301:8
c. shall be made straight   BIBL 89:16
C. things may be as stiff   LOCK 488:13
c. timber of humanity   KANT 441:13
set the c. straight   MORR 549:14
There was a c. man   NURS 569:18
croon Wanna cry, wanna c.   HARB 371:3
crop c.-headed Parliament   BROW 160:5
fruitful c. should bring   IRWI 414:7
Good seed makes good c.   PROV 621:12
croppy Hoppy, C., Droppy   ELLI 306:1
crops c. the flowery food   POPE 604:20
cross bear the c. gladly   THOM 788:13
bloody c. he bore   SPEN 751:13
by thy C. and Passion   BOOK 129:8
c. him in nothing   SHAK 678:19
c. of gold   BRYA 162:12
c. of Jesus   BARI 56:4
c. the bridge   PROV 618:9
c. upon their garments   URBA 805:25
death upon the c.   BOOK 132:1
first at Cradle and the C.   SAYE 668:7
hangs upon the C.   DONN 281:25
mystery of the c.   FORT 330:4
no c., no crown   PENN 591:15
No c., no crown   PROV 627:36
old rugged c.   BENN 67:7
orgasm has replaced the C.   MUGG 553:8
see thee ever c.-gartered   SHAK 720:33
survey the wondrous c.   WATT 823:15
There for you to c.   PAUL 589:6
use him as a C.   SMIT 743:6
crossbow With my c. I shot   COLE 232:16
crossed may be c. in love   SHER 733:11
Was the cow c.   HERB 383:14
crosses Between the c., row on row   MCCR 500:17
clinging to their c.   CHES 215:18
C. are ladders   PROV 617:18
tumbled down the c.   JORD 436:13
with c. of fire   NERU 559:4
crossing double c. of a pair of heels   HART 374:11
crossness make c. and dirt succeed   FORS 329:11
crosspatch C., Draw the latch   NURS 566:13
crossways understands everything c.   SALI 664:8
crow before the cock c.   BIBL 99:2
carrion c., that loathsome beast   GASC 340:14
c. in its own farmyard   TROL 799:18
c. Makes wing   SHAK 706:1
c. upon his own dunghill   PROV 619:5
jump Jim C.   NURS 570:12
one for the c.   PROV 628:34
risen to hear him c.   ELIO 299:5
thenk upon the c.   CHAU 211:20
upstart c.   GREE 362:24
crowd c. flowed over London Bridge   ELIO 303:11
c. is not company   BACO 44:14
c. will always save Barabbas   COCT 230:5
Far from the madding c.'s   GRAY 361:7
not feel the c.   COWP 248:7
pass in a c.   SWIF 765:19
try to c. out real life   FORS 329:23
crowded Across a c. room   HAMM 370:7
c. hour of glorious life   MORD 547:23
crowds C. without company   GIBB 345:18

her noise, her c.   LAMB 465:4
nor cheering c.   YEAT 854:16
talk with c.   KIPL 454:13
crowing whistling woman and a c. hen   PROV 635:1
crown abdicate the C.   JUAN 437:29
better than his c.   SHAK 709:25
both divide the c.   DRYD 287:20
broke his c.   NURS 567:15
Caesar's laurel c.   BLAK 119:12
cannot get a c.   SHAK 694:29
corruptible c.   BIBL 107:20
c. in possession   PAIN 582:7
C. is, according to the saying   BAGE 47:16
c. of life   BIBL 111:19
c. of life   BIBL 113:2
c. of snowflake pearls   BLOK 123:16
c. of thorns   BEVA 73:13
C. of Thorns   BRON 152:9
c. of thorns   BRYA 162:12
c. of twelve stars   BIBL 113:27
c. ourselves with rosebuds   BIBL 92:21
c. the just   ANON 22:1
C., the symbol of permanence   JUAN 437:28
c. thy good with brotherhood   BATE 58:10
c. to her husband   BIBL 84:12
fighting for the c.   NURS 567:20
glory of my c.   ELIZ 304:11
head that wears a c.   SHAK 692:4
I give away my c.   SHAK 716:9
Indian c.   ROSS 655:17
influence of the C.   DUNN 292:14
king's c.   SHAK 707:26
mace, the c. imperial   SHAK 693:19
no cross, no c.   PENN 591:15
No cross, no c.   PROV 627:36
of an earthly c.   MARL 513:21
of c., of queen   SHAK 685:5
power of the c.   BURK 168:5
presented him a kingly c.   SHAK 697:26
put on my c.   SHAK 680:12
sorrow's c. of sorrow   TENN 780:17
strike his father's c.   SHAK 692:30
to an incorruptible c.   CHAR 209:3
wished to restore the c.   JOHN 430:3
Within the hollow c.   SHAK 715:24
worn the c.   BIBL 93:11
crowned C. with rank fumitor   SHAK 701:11
c. with thorns   KELL 448:2
sitting c. upon the grave   HOBB 391:1
crowner C.'s Quest   BARH 55:19
crownest Thou c. the year   BOOK 138:7
crowning c. mercy   CROM 252:1
crowns Casting down their golden c.   HEBE 378:17
c. and coronets, Promised   SHAK 692:32
c. are empty things   DEFO 261:28
c. for convoy   SHAK 693:22
c. resign to call thee mine   SONG 748:8
end c. the work   PROV 618:40
end that c. us   HERR 385:22
crows c. and choughs that wing   SHAK 701:12
c. begin to search   PROV 628:25
Til c. feet be growe   CHAU 213:1
crucible America is God's C.   ZANG 858:3
violet into a c.   SHEL 732:13
crucified c., dead, and buried   BOOK 128:10
when they c. my Lord   SONG 748:9
crucifix on the trunk of the c.   HENR 382:7
crucify c. mankind   BRYA 162:12
God they ought to c.   CART 197:4
not even c. him   CARL 193:5
cruel comfort c. men   CHES 216:3
c. and unusual punishment   CONS 241:15
C., but composed   ARNO 27:2
C. he looks, but calm   SHEL 730:22
c. men of Rome   SHAK 695:28
C. necessity   CROM 251:14
c., not unnatural   SHAK 687:14
c. only to be kind   SHAK 687:31
c. person who commits   JUDA 438:2
c. to be kind   COMP 236:18
c. works of nature   DARW 257:12

jealousy is c. as the grave   BIBL 87:22
State business is a c. trade   HALI 369:8
Such c. glasses   HOWE 406:4
cruellest April is the c. month   ELIO 303:7
c. lies are often told   STEV 759:27
cruelty C. has a human heart   BLAK 122:22
C., like every other vice   ELIO 300:18
c. To load a falling man   SHAK 695:23
full Of direst c.   SHAK 703:19
gratification of c.   FOST 330:10
infliction of c.   RUSS 661:3
main sources of c.   RUSS 661:7
never really gauged your c.   WELC 827:3
years of c.   GLAD 351:12
cruise on our last c.   STEV 759:7
crumbling c. to dust   DIDE 273:20
crumbs bags to hold the c.   ISHE 414:9
covetous of their c.   SMAR 739:16
dogs eat of the c.   BIBL 97:13
fed with the c.   BIBL 101:22
learning's c.   BROW 159:8
crumpet Muffin and C.   DICK 270:13
thinking man's c.   MUIR 553:13
crumpled cow with the c. horn   NURS 570:2
crunch munch on, c. on   BROW 160:21
crusade faith in our united c.   ROOS 654:3
party is a moral c.   WILS 840:4
this 'c.', this war   BUSH 175:5
crusaders C. have multiplied   BERN 70:16
cruse my small c.   HERR 386:11
oil in a c.   BIBL 81:20
crush c. people to the earth   CHIL 217:19
c., to annihilate a man   DOST 283:9
cry and a c. Before   TENN 778:14
behold a c.   BIBL 88:6
bubbling c.   BYRO 180:20
continually do c.   BOOK 127:20
c. all the way to the bank   LIBE 484:6
c. before night   PROV 630:42
c. before you're hurt   PROV 618:10
c. come unto thee   BOOK 133:1
c. in the day-time   BOOK 134:26
c. is still   SHAK 707:11
C. not when his father dies   JOHN 433:14
c. of gulls   ELIO 303:22
c. of the Little Peoples   LE G 479:6
c. of the whole people   KING 452:11
c. over me, There, there   BOOK 138:19
C., the beloved country   PATO 588:18
cuckoo's parting c.   ARNO 28:25
great c. in Egypt   BIBL 77:32
his little son should c.   CORN 243:9
hush, little baby, don' yo' c.   HEYW 387:16
indeed they c.   WEBS 826:11
Much c. and little wool   PROV 627:3
Never c. over spilt milk   FIEL 318:23
no language but a c.   TENN 779:7
she began to c.   NURS 567:4
Some must c.   RHYS 646:12
Speechless still, and never c.   EPIT 310:7
stones would c. out   BIBL 101:30
Truth is the c.   BERK 69:11
we c. that we are come   SHAK 701:19
we still should c.   BACO 47:1
crying child is ever c.   WROT 851:18
c. in the wilderness   BIBL 94:10
c. over spilt milk   PROV 624:10
except those c.   ABSE 1:3
not hear it c.   HERB 383:26
crystal clear as c.   BIBL 114:21
like unto c.   BIBL 113:8
crystals by chemistry and by c.   HODG 391:9
instants become c.   BLY 124:11
cubes sum of two c.   RAMA 641:20
cubit add one c.   BIBL 95:8
cuckoo as the c. is in June   SHAK 690:28
c.-buds of yellow hue   SHAK 702:25
c. clock   FILM 319:19
C.-echoing, bell-swarmèd   HOPK 396:11
C.! Shall I call thee bird   WORD 850:15
c.'s parting cry   ARNO 28:25
c. then, on every tree   SHAK 702:25

cuckoo (cont.):
hear the pleasant c. — DAVI 258:18
Lhude sing c. — ANON 19:6
merry c. — SPEN 751:2
over the c.'s nest — NURS 568:17
rainbow and a c.'s song — DAVI 258:19
to the c.'s note — GRAY 361:17
weather the c. likes — HARD 373:4
cucumber c. should be well sliced — JOHN 427:4
when c. is added to it — MACK 503:2
cucumbers but c. after all — JOHN 431:18
garden of c. — BIBL 87:25
sun-beams out of c. — SWIF 765:14
cud cheweth not the c. — BIBL 78:11
Cuddesdon Hey for C. — KETT 450:6
cuddled c. by a complete stranger — ANNE 14:17
cudgel c. of the people's war — TOLS 796:18
cue With a twisted c. — GILB 348:5
cui C. bono — CICE 223:22
cully Woman's c. made — CONG 238:33
culpa mea c. — MISS 536:14
O felix c. — MISS 540:3
culpable How c. was he — HEAN 377:17
culprits better to choose the c. — PAGN 582:2
recognize them all as c. — VIRG 811:12
cult What's a c. — ALTM 12:21
cultivate c. our garden — VOLT 815:12
C. simplicity — LAMB 465:2
c. your friendship — JOHN 431:28
cultiver Il faut c. notre jardin — VOLT 815:12
cultural Australian C. Cringe — PHIL 595:1
c. Chernobyl — MNOU 541:7
c. identity serves — FINK 321:7
c. Stalingrad — BALL 54:2
culture Before French c. — RENA 645:5
core of a world's c. — BOLD 126:3
hear the word 'c.' — ESHE 308:15
hear the word c. — JOHS 434:1
integral part of c. — GOUL 357:12
man of c. rare — GILB 348:12
men of c. — ARNO 29:9
pursue C. in bands — WHAR 831:3
stage in moral c. — DARW 257:3
vast intuitive c. — SHAF 678:2
cultures two c. — SNOW 744:22
two great c. — LÉVE 482:12
Cumae saw the Sibyl at C. — ROSS 656:9
Cumaei Ultima C. — VIRG 814:2
cumber c. you good Margaret — MORE 548:16
cumbered c. about much serving — BIBL 100:26
cumberless Blithesome and c. — HOGG 392:9
cumin tithes of mint and c. — BIBL 98:9
cunctando c. restituit rem — ENNI 308:3
cunning C. is the dark sanctuary — CHES 214:21
c. men pass for wise — BACO 43:31
c. plan — CATC 201:4
produce that pitiful c. — WOLL 844:7
right hand forget her c. — BOOK 143:13
silence, exile, and c. — JOYC 437:12
cunningly little world made c. — DONN 279:23
cup after supper he took the C. — BOOK 132:2
Ah, fill the c. — FITZ 323:7
death in the c. — BURN 171:12
fill up my c. — SCOT 674:21
glory in a shallow c. — FITZ 323:15
let this c. pass — BIBL 99:4
my c. overflows — SCOT 675:4
my c. shall be full — BOOK 135:4
tak a c. o' kindness yet — BURN 170:9
'twixt c. and lip — PROV 632:28
welcome to my c. — OLDY 573:1
Cupar will to C. maun to Cupar — PROV 622:2
cupboard c. of food — HERB 384:15
c. was bare — NURS 568:14
Cupid C. and my Campaspe — LYLY 497:2
C. is a knavish lad — SHAK 711:18
C. painted blind — SHAK 710:19
C.'s darts do not feel — ANON 17:17
giant-dwarf, Dan C. — SHAK 702:14
Cupidinesque Veneres C. — CATU 202:11

cupidinibus Responsare c. — HORA 403:16
cupidons all the little c. — BURN 169:21
cups c., That cheer — COWP 248:6
cur half lurcher and half c. — COWP 248:11
cura sedet atra C. — HORA 401:11
curable disease. But c. — MACA 497:17
curantur Similia similibus c. — MOTT 552:19
curate c. faced the laurels — GRAH 358:11
like a shabby c. — AUDE 36:16
name of a C. — SMIT 743:9
pale young c. — GILB 349:6
curates abundant shower of c. — BRON 152:12
Bishops, and C. — BOOK 128:17
Bishops, and C. — BOOK 131:15
C., long dust — BROO 153:10
preached to death by wild c. — SMIT 744:2
curb rusty c. — SHAK 689:22
use the snaffle and the c. — CAMP 187:5
curds queen of c. and cream — SHAK 722:8
cure better than c. — PROV 629:38
c. for admiring — BAGE 48:7
c. for the ills of Democracy — ADDA 3:19
c. of all diseases — BROW 157:8
c. of a romantic first flame — BURN 169:19
C. the disease — BACO 44:16
c. thine heart — BEDD 62:2
half our c. — YOUN 857:18
malady without a c. — DRYD 289:4
no c. for birth and death — SANT 666:11
no C. for this Disease — BELL 64:21
No c., no pay — PROV 627:37
palliate what we cannot c. — JOHN 424:7
cured can't be c. must be endured — PROV 633:50
c. by hanging from a string — KING 453:5
c. by more democracy — SMIT 741:14
C. yesterday of my disease — PRIO 612:7
cures c. are suggested — CHEK 213:21
Like c. like — MOTT 552:19
curfew begins at c. — SHAK 700:27
c. tolls the knell — GRAY 360:24
curiosa c. felicitas — PETR 594:6
curiosities c. would be quite forgot — AUBR 33:15
curiosity c. about the future — WAUG 824:7
c., freckles, and doubt — PARK 585:15
C. killed the cat — PROV 617:19
c. of individuals — ARTS 30:20
Disinterested intellectual c. — TREV 798:10
curious c. in unnecessary matters — BIBL 93:4
Raised by that c. engine — WEBS 825:21
curiouser C. and curiouser — CARR 193:18
curl had a little c. — LONG 491:11
curled C. minion — ARNO 28:14
curlèd wealthy c. darlings — SHAK 713:5
curls Frocks and C. — DICK 273:11
curly C. locks, Wilt thou — NURS 566:14
currency c. that buys all — CERV 205:16
Debasing the moral c. — ELIO 299:22
debauch the moral c. — KEYN 450:13
one c. — NAPO 556:11
current c. to the whole — HOPK 397:14
c. will run with fury — WOLL 844:2
icy c. — SHAK 714:6
what a strong c. ideas are — FLAU 325:8
currents their c. turn awry — SHAK 686:12
curried short horse soon c. — PROV 630:35
curs You common cry of c. — SHAK 682:18
curse c. be ended — ELIO 301:8
C. God, and die — BIBL 82:30
c. is come upon me — TENN 780:12
c. mine enemies — BIBL 78:22
c. of the drinking classes — WILD 837:12
C. on his virtues — ADDI 4:12
C. the blasted, jelly-boned swines — LAWR 475:11
c. thine own inconstancy — CARE 191:4
c. with their heart — BOOK 137:27
I know how to c. — SHAK 718:24
is to me a c. — MASS 518:3
open foe may prove a c. — GAY 341:29
real c. of Eve — RHYS 646:13
terrible c. — BARH 55:17

than to c. the darkness — PROV 615:29
What terms to c. thee — WRIG 851:17
cursed C. be the heart — BALL 52:6
c. him in sleeping — BARH 55:16
cursest is c. — BIBL 78:19
That c. man — SPEN 751:20
curses C. are like young chickens — SOUT 749:3
c. from pole to pole — BLAK 120:2
C., like chickens — PROV 617:20
not c. heaped — SORL 746:23
cursing blessing and c. — BIBL 79:1
curst c. be he that moves my bones — EPIT 309:10
to all succeeding ages c. — DRYD 286:19
curtain Bring down the c. — LAST 472:1
c. of the night — PUSH 638:7
iron c. — CHUR 221:20
Iron C. did not reach — SOLZ 745:20
kept behind a c. — PAIN 582:20
lets the c. fall — POPE 602:9
make a dress out of a c. — POWE 609:9
putteth aside the c. — BIBL 75:3
stage c. of his heart — RILK 648:13
Up with the c. — BROW 159:13
curtained C. with cloudy red — MILT 530:26
curtiosity full of 'satiable c. — KIPL 456:16
curtsey C. while you're thinking — CARR 195:1
curveship of the c. lend a myth — CRAN 250:2
Cusha Cusha! Cusha! C. — INGE 413:12
cushion c. and soft Dean — POPE 603:13
cuss don't matter a tinker's c. — SHIN 734:21
custodes quis custodiet ipsos C. — JUVE 439:22
custodiet quis c. ipsos Custodes — JUVE 439:22
custody Wragg is in c. — ARNO 29:16
custom c. and experience — HUME 408:11
C. is the great guide — HUME 408:8
c. lie upon thee — WORD 848:9
c. loathsome to the eye — JAME 417:1
c. must give way to truth — LIBO 484:7
c. reconciles us — BURK 167:4
c. stale Her infinite variety — SHAK 679:7
C. that is before all law — DANI 255:4
C., that unwritten law — D'AV 257:19
follow the c. — AMBR 13:2
in c. and in ceremony — YEAT 855:6
Lest one good c. — TENN 778:16
receipt of c. — BIBL 96:4
That monster, c. — SHAK 687:30
unwritten c. supported — CATT 199:20
customary what is not c. to him — MONT 544:7
customer c. is always right — PROV 617:21
c. is never wrong — RITZ 649:13
only one boss. The c. — WALT 821:7
customers people of c. — SMIT 741:9
customs ancient c. and its manhood — ENNI 308:2
choose its own c. — HERO 385:11
c. of his tribe — SHAW 724:19
cut c. him out in little stars — SHAK 717:37
c. his ear off — MEDA 520:4
c. his throat before — SWIF 767:19
c. my conscience to fit — HELL 380:12
c. off — BIBL 90:4
c. off my head — CHAR 208:24
C. your coat — PROV 617:22
etiquette to c. any one — CARR 196:3
guardsman's c. and thrust — HUXL 411:15
in the evening it is c. down — BOOK 139:22
Look at the c. — LOES 489:11
man who c. his country's — BYRO 182:19
most unkindest c. of all — SHAK 698:2
shall not be c. off — BIBL 90:10
we are going to c. it off — POWE 609:17
will I c. off Israel — BIBL 81:10
cutpurse c. of the empire — SHAK 687:26
cuts c. from Homer — AESC 6:11
cutting hand the c. edge of the mind — BRON 152:5
cuttlefish like a c. — ORWE 578:2
Cutty-sark Weel done, C. — BURN 172:15
cycle c. of Cathay — TENN 781:5
cyclone crest of the South Bend c. — RICE 646:21

Cyclops c. with one eye   COLE 233:26
cylinder in terms of the c.   CÉZA 206:1
cymbal talk but a tinkling c.   BACO 44:14
   tinkling c.   BIBL 107:25
cymbals well-tuned c.   BOOK 144:9
Cynara faithful to thee, C.   DOWS 284:6
cynic definition of a c.   WILD 836:9
cynicism C. is intellectual dandyism
   MERE 522:15
cynics c. and the doubters   FIOR 321:8
cynosure c. of neighbouring eyes   MILT 529:24
Cynthia C. first, with her eyes   PROP 612:20
cypress in sad c.   SHAK 720:26
   outside the c. groves   LAWR 475:9
Cyprus rings black C.   FLEC 326:4
Cyrene Libya about C.   BIBL 104:27
Cyril Nice one, C.   ADVE 8:7
Cythera C., so they say   BAUD 58:15
Cytherean throned C. be fallen   SWIN 768:23
Czechoslovak C. government   NEWS 562:11

D never use a big, big D   GILB 348:20
   there are your d's for you   WYCH 852:12
da D.! Da! Da   UPAN 805:1
dad D.'s Army kept going   WOOD 844:19
   girls in slacks remember D.   BETJ 72:3
   if the d. is present   ORTO 576:16
   They fuck you up, your mum and d.
   LARK 469:2
   To meet their D.   BURN 170:19
dada mama of d.   FADI 314:3
daddy D.'s gone a-hunting   NURS 566:10
   D., what did you do   SAYI 669:10
   Dance to your d.   NURS 566:15
   heart belongs to d.   PORT 607:16
   Oh, yo' d.'s rich   HEYW 387:16
daemon D. was with me   KIPL 457:4
daemonum call poesy *vinum d.*   BACO 43:1
daffadowndillies d., And cowslips
   SPEN 752:18
daffodil bed of d. sky   TENN 781:23
daffodils d., That come before   SHAK 722:5
   dances with the d.   WORD 847:6
   Fair d., we weep   HERR 386:15
   host, of golden d.   WORD 847:5
   never saw d. so beautiful   WORD 845:20
   what d. were for Wordsworth   LARK 469:8
   When d. begin to peer   SHAK 721:32
daffy D.-down-dilly   NURS 566:16
daft thinks the tither d.   SCOT 674:19
dagger d. of the mind   SHAK 704:14
   deadly daunting d.   WYCH 852:12
   Is this a d.   SHAK 704:16
daggers d. in a hogshead   SCOT 675:2
   d. in men's smiles   SHAK 705:14
   Give me the d.   SHAK 705:2
   speak d. to her   SHAK 687:14
daguerrotype stare from d.   WARR 822:3
daily d. complaining   BOOK 135:20
   d. increase in thy holy Spirit   BOOK 133:2
   d. Labour to pursue   WESL 829:4
   our d. bread   BIBL 95:3
dainties d. are all cates   SHAK 718:12
   fed of the d.   SHAK 702:16
   spiced d.   KEAT 443:2
daintily I must have things d. served
   BETJ 72:7
dainty d. rogue in porcelain   MERE 522:14
   d. that is in that hous   CHAU 211:19
   Nothing's so d. sweet   FLET 327:6
dairy doth nightly rob the d.   JONS 435:3
dairymaid Queen asked the D.   MILN 528:2
daisies Buttercups and d.   HOWI 406:5
   d. growing over me   KEAT 447:8
   d. pied and violets blue   SHAK 702:25
   D., those pearled Arcturi   SHEL 731:13
   foot upon twelve d.   PROV 624:19
   Meadows trim with d. pied   MILT 529:23
   Swiche as men callen d.   CHAU 212:23
daisy 'd.,' or elles the 'ye of day'
   CHAU 212:24
   d., primrose, violet   THOM 792:7

Dakotas D., I am for war   RED 643:19
dalliance d. in the wardrobe lies   SHAK 692:31
   primrose path of d.   SHAK 684:16
dam pretty chickens and their d.
   SHAK 706:24
damage d. to the earth   COUS 244:13
   I can pay for the d.   CLOU 227:20
   MORAL OR INTELLECTUAL D.   TELE 776:3
   seriously d. your health   OFFI 572:12
damaged Archangel a little d.   LAMB 465:7
   D. people are dangerous   HART 374:9
damages d. his mind   ANON 21:11
Damascus rivers of D.   BIBL 82:7
damasked deep-d. wings   KEAT 442:20
dame belle d. sans merci   KEAT 443:28
   belle d. sans mercy   KEAT 443:3
   My d. has lost her shoe   NURS 566:12
   nothin' like a d.   HAMM 370:9
dammed saved by being d.   HOOD 395:16
damn D. braces   BLAK 121:7
   D. the age   LAMB 465:10
   D. the consequences   MILN 528:13
   D. the torpedoes   FARR 315:26
   d. those authors   CHUR 219:11
   D. with faint praise   POPE 602:29
   D. you all to hell   FILM 321:3
   d. you England   OSBO 578:24
   don't give a d.   MITC 540:15
   give a singel d.   FLEM 326:11
   I care not a d.   CLOU 227:20
   I don't give a d.   FILM 319:7
   old man who said, 'D.!'   HARE 373:10
   one another d.   WYCH 852:14
   with a spot I d. him   SHAK 698:11
damnation d. of his taking-off   SHAK 704:5
   everlasting d.   BOOK 129:4
   From sleep and from d.   CHES 216:3
   Heap on himself d.   MILT 531:13
damnations Twenty-nine distinct d.
   BROW 161:13
damned All silent, and all d.   WORD 848:21
   beautiful and d.   FITZ 323:21
   brandy of the d.   SHAW 726:6
   D. below Judas   COWP 246:13
   D. from here to Eternity   KIPL 454:6
   d. if you don't   DOW 284:5
   d. (looking dismally)   JOHN 432:14
   d. to everlasting fame   POPE 605:11
   d. to Fame   POPE 601:25
   d. would make no noise   HERR 386:21
   Faustus must be d.   MARL 513:6
   for an apple d. mankind   OTWA 579:12
   lies, d. lies and statistics   DISR 278:9
   public be d.   VAND 806:19
   Publish and be d.   WELL 827:15
   souls to be d.   PROV 617:11
   written a d. play   REYN 645:16
damnedest doing one's d. with one's mind
   BRID 151:3
damning d. those they have no mind to
   BUTL 176:5
damnosa D. hereditas   GAIU 337:19
   D. quid non imminuit dies   HORA 401:19
damozel blessed d.   ROSS 655:19
damp d. souls of housemaids   ELIO 302:21
damsel d. with a dulcimer   COLE 232:7
Dan D. even to Beer-sheba   BIBL 79:38
   Dangerous D. McGrew   SERV 677:10
Danaë all D. to the stars   TENN 783:13
Danaos timeo D. et dona ferentes   VIRG 811:11
dance ae best d. e'er cam   BURN 170:26
   at least before they d.   POPE 605:16
   d. at our bridal   SCOT 673:21
   D., dance, dance, little lady   COWA 244:15
   d. is a measured pace   BACO 42:20
   D. is the hidden language   GRAH 358:9
   d. it bust to bust   GREN 363:12
   d. round in a ring   FROS 336:1
   D. tiptoe, bull   BUNT 164:10
   d. to the music of time   POWE 609:14
   D. to your daddy   NURS 566:15
   d. with me   BERL 69:16
   d. wyt me, in irlaunde   ANON 16:14

   know the dancer from the d.   YEAT 853:6
   Learn them to d.   DAVI 258:13
   Let's face the music and d.   BERL 69:19
   Lord of the D.   CART 197:5
   Love makes them d.   DAVI 258:11
   Mystical d.   MILT 533:18
   On with the d.   BYRO 178:20
   see me d. the Polka   GROS 365:2
   They that d. must pay   PROV 632:35
   too far from the d.   POUN 609:8
   will you join the d.   CARR 194:18
danced d. by the light of the moon
   LEAR 477:18
   d. his did   CUMM 253:5
   d. in the morning   CART 197:5
   d. with the Prince of Wales   FARJ 315:3
   David d. before the Lord   BIBL 80:30
   reeled and d.   WORD 845:20
   remaining leaf—d.   WORD 845:17
   There was a star d.   SHAK 712:16
   ye have not d.   BIBL 96:25
dancer know the d. from the dance
   YEAT 853:6
   minion, d.   ARNO 28:14
dancers Breaks time, as d.   CAMP 188:6
   d. are all gone under the hill   ELIO 301:16
   d. dancing in tune   TENN 781:24
   nation of d.   EQUI 308:10
dances d. to an ill tune   PROV 621:50
   d. were procession   CORB 243:2
   d. with the daffodils   WORD 847:6
   it d.   LIGN 484:12
   truest expression in its d.   DE M 263:13
danceth d. without music   HERB 385:7
dancing [D.] a perpendicular expression
   SHAW 727:27
   d. cheek-to-cheek   BERL 69:17
   d. dogs and bears   HODG 391:10
   D., double-talking   CAUS 203:12
   d. is love's proper exercise   DAVI 258:10
   d. not on a volcano   FLAU 325:7
   diversion was d.   TURN 802:19
   Fluttering and d.   WORD 847:5
   like a Mask d.   ACHE 1:8
   manners of a d. master   JOHN 427:15
   mature women, d.   FRIE 334:17
   past our d. days   SHAK 717:16
dandy Yankee Doodle D.   COHA 230:8
dandyism intellectual d.   MERE 522:15
Dane paying the D.-geld   KIPL 456:4
   Roman than a D.   SHAK 689:13
danger avoid d.   ROCH 651:1
   big with d. and mischief   GIBB 344:19
   bright face of d.   STEV 758:23
   clear and present d.   HOLM 393:10
   d. from all men   ADAM 2:19
   d. from those that work   HALI 368:13
   D. justified privilege   WAUG 824:16
   D. knows full well   SHAK 697:5
   d. of her former tooth   SHAK 705:20
   d. of the past   FROM 335:4
   D., the spur   CHAP 208:19
   d. to the country   VICT 809:12
   everything is in d.   NIET 564:5
   in d. of hell fire   BIBL 94:26
   less d. from the wiles   NASH 557:10
   life free from d.   EURI 312:19
   New Labour, new d.   POLI 601:3
   no d. to a man   CHAP 208:12
   Oft in d.   WHIT 832:2
   only when in d.   OWEN 580:22
   out of d.   PROV 629:11
   out of d. sit   ASTE 32:11
   Out of this nettle, d.   SHAK 690:3
   post of d.   PROV 629:20
   run into any kind of d.   BOOK 128:13
   so much as to be out of d.   HUXL 411:17
   What d. threatens   FRIS 334:21
dangerous Damaged people are d.
   HART 374:9
   d. deceits   BOOK 144:17
   d. edge of things   BROW 158:16
   d. to know   LAMB 464:9

dangerous (*cont.*):
d. to meet it alone — WHAR 831:3
delays are d. in war — DRYD 289:28
generalizations d. — DUMA 291:13
knowledge is d. — HUXL 411:17
left out he would be d. — MELB 520:18
little knowledge is d. — PROV 625:26
many a d. thing — BISH 117:7
more d. than an idea — ALAI 9:13
more d. than justice — PICA 595:3
most d. man — NEWS 562:12
most d. moment — TOCQ 795:8
such men are d. — SHAK 696:12
dangers D. by being despised — BURK 169:6
d. of the seas — PARK 586:12
d. of this night — BOOK 128:20
d. thou canst make us scorn — BURN 172:13
No d. fright him — JOHN 426:17
She loved me for the d. — SHAK 713:11
so many great d. — BOOK 130:4
tomorrow's d. — DONN 282:9
dangling d. apricocks — SHAK 716:3
Daniel D. come to judgement — SHAK 709:29
Danish fame of D. kings — ANON 22:7
Danny hangin' D. Deever — KIPL 453:20
dapper You look d. — COLL 235:2
dapple d.-dawn-drawn Falcon — HOPK 397:10
dappled d. things — HOPK 396:21
dapples D. the drowsy east — SHAK 712:34
dare d. to be poor — GAY 342:8
d. to know — HORA 399:5
for our unworthiness we d. not — BOOK 132:8
have the courage to d. — DOST 283:6
I d. not — SHAK 704:10
licence to d. anything — HORA 397:20
none d. call it treason — HARI 373:15
O! what men d. do — SHAK 712:27
Take me if you d. — PANK 585:8
What man d., I dare — SHAK 706:6
You who d. — MERE 522:23
dared d., and done — SMAR 740:18
dares that d. love attempt — SHAK 717:23
Who d. do more is none — SHAK 704:11
Who d. wins — MOTT 552:22
Darien peak in D. — CLOS 228:21
Silent, upon a peak in D. — KEAT 445:6
daring d. is gone — SCHI 668:14
d. pilot in extremity — DRYD 289:6
d. young man — LEYB 484:5
dark agree in the d. — BACO 45:33
All cats are grey in the d. — PROV 624:9
as good i' th' d. — HERR 386:5
blanket of the d. — SHAK 703:21
blind man in a d. room — BOWE 148:8
come out of the d. — MANN 510:12
comes the d. — COLE 232:22
d. and bloody ground — O'HA 572:17
d. and bright — BYRO 183:4
d. and evil days — INGR 413:17
d. and stormy night — OPEN 574:25
d. and true and tender — TENN 783:6
d. as night — SHAK 723:32
D. as the world of man — SITW 738:16
D. behind it rose the forest — LONG 491:2
d. cold day — AUDE 35:2
d., dark, dark — MILT 534:26
D. forces — MISQ 537:9
d. into the life — BERR 71:14
d. is light enough — FRY 336:11
d. night of the soul — FITZ 324:7
d. night of the soul — MISQ 537:13
d. Satanic mills — BLAK 121:15
d. summer dawns — TENN 783:5
D. the sky — PUSH 638:1
D. with excessive bright — MILT 532:18
d. world of sin — BICK 115:23
d. world where gods — ROET 652:7
Duke of d. corners — SHAK 708:15
fear to go in the d. — BACO 44:1
feeling in the d. — JALA 416:22
go home in the d. — LAST 474:8
great leap in the d. — VANB 806:15
I knew you in the d. — OWEN 581:8

In a d. wood I saw — ROET 652:6
In the d. backward — SHAK 718:20
In the nightmare of the d. — AUDE 35:6
in thy d. streets — BROO 154:8
leap in the d. — LAST 471:19
leap into the d. — BROW 155:12
O d. dark dark — ELIO 301:17
Out in the d. — THOM 790:16
poring d. — SHAK 693:7
raging in the d. — YEAT 853:11
Tired of his d. dominion — MERE 522:20
we are for the d. — SHAK 680:7
We work in the d. — JAME 417:23
What in me is d. — MILT 531:6
within a d. wood — DANT 255:12
darken Never d. my Dior again — LILL 484:13
darkeneth d. counsel — BIBL 83:20
darker I am the d. brother — HUGH 406:17
darkest d. day — COWP 246:21
d. hour — PROV 617:23
darkies Oh! d., how my heart — FOST 330:15
darkling D. I listen — KEAT 444:27
d. plain — ARNO 27:5
darkly through a glass, d. — BIBL 107:25
darkness cast off the works of d. — BIBL 106:32
chains and d. — MONT 543:13
Chaos and d. — MARR 514:7
counteracts the powers of d. — SMAR 739:18
curse the d. — STEV 758:18
d. and silence — LEAR 477:6
d. brings not sleep — PUSH 638:7
d. comprehended it not — BIBL 102:17
d. falls at Thy behest — ELLE 305:11
d. had no beginning — MACD 501:7
d. of mere being — JUNG 438:10
d. of the land — TENN 779:24
d. visible — MILT 531:8
d. was upon the face — BIBL 75:4
d. which may be felt — BIBL 77:27
Dawn on our d. — HEBE 378:14
Downward to d. — STEV 758:9
encounter d. as a bride — SHAK 708:9
even d. and silence — KELL 447:19
Go out into the d. — HASK 375:2
Gorgon, Prince of d. — SPEN 751:14
Got to kick at the d. — COCK 229:22
heart of an immense d. — OPEN 575:11
his D. and his Brightness — BYRO 183:19
horror of great d. — BIBL 76:15
In me d. — BONH 127:8
in the d. and the cold — STEV 760:9
in the d. bind them — TOLK 796:10
into outer d. — BIBL 95:30
land of d. — BIBL 83:2
leaves the world to d. — GRAY 360:24
Lighten our d. — BOOK 128:20
light excelleth d. — BIBL 85:31
light is as d. — BIBL 83:3
light to them that sit in d. — BIBL 99:33
little d. — LAUD 470:3
long in d. pined — SCOT 675:7
lump bred up in d. — KYD 462:9
made His d. beautiful — TENN 779:12
make d. more visible — EDGE 296:2
Men loved d. — BIBL 102:33
ocean of d. — FOX 331:6
on the shores of d. — KEAT 445:20
people that walked in d. — BIBL 88:17
pestilence that walketh in d. — BOOK 140:3
prince of d. — SHAK 700:29
rulers of the d. — BIBL 109:21
sit in d. — BOOK 141:16
sit in d. here — MILT 532:5
soul may set in d. — WILL 838:14
struggling with the d. — COLE 232:1
than curse the d. — BENE 66:10
than to curse the d. — PROV 615:29
there is d. everywhere — NEHR 558:4
Thou makest d. — BOOK 141:9
through d. up to God — TENN 779:9
time of d. — BREC 150:18
two eternities of d. — NABO 555:17
universal d. buries all — POPE 602:9

works of d. — BOOK 129:22
darksome d. road — CATU 202:12
spent the d. hours — GOET 353:11
darling call you d. after sex — BARN 56:12
d. buds of May — SHAK 722:24
d. in an urn — CARE 190:18
d. man, a daarlin' man — O'CA 571:8
D. of the music halls — SMIT 742:4
my d. from the lions — BOOK 135:27
Nature's d. — GRAY 361:18
Of my d., my darling — POE 599:1
old man's d. — PROV 615:21
darlings wealthy curlèd d. — SHAK 713:5
dart shook a dreadful d. — MILT 532:11
Time shall throw a d. — EPIT 311:11
darts fiery d. of the wicked — BIBL 109:21
dastard d. in war — SCOT 673:20
data some d. was bound to be — WATS 822:18
d. which will live in infamy — ROOS 654:1
doubles your chances for a d. — ALLE 12:15
keep them up to d. — SHAW 725:6
last d. slides — EWAR 313:5
Standards are always out of d. — BENN 67:12
dateless d. bargain — SHAK 718:10
dates Manna and d. — KEAT 443:2
matter of d. — TALL 771:19
daubed d. it with slime — BIBL 77:13
daughter attorney's Elderly ugly d.
— GILB 349:7
bailiff's d. — BALL 51:11
Carnage is thy d. — WORD 848:16
Cato's d. — SHAK 697:2
D. am I in my mother's house — KIPL 455:7
D. lovelier than — HORA 400:16
d. of a hundred earls — TENN 780:3
d. of debate — ELIZ 304:8
d. of Earth and Water — SHEL 729:5
d. of the gods — TENN 776:19
d. of the West — TENN 777:11
d. of Zion — BIBL 87:25
d.'s my daughter — PROV 627:6
d. went through the river — BUNY 165:8
Don't put your d. on the stage — COWA 245:4
ever rear a d. — GAY 341:6
farmer's d. — CALV 186:6
father had a d. — SHAK 720:28
for the d.'s daughter — SWIN 769:3
King's d. — BOOK 136:22
lies London's d. — THOM 789:16
Like mother, like d. — PROV 625:20
Lord Ullin's d. — CAMP 187:14
O my ducats! O my d. — SHAK 709:7
so is her d. — BIBL 91:12
Sole d. of his voice — MILT 533:30
taken his little d. — LONG 491:10
to my elder d. — THOM 790:13
virgin-d. of the skies — DRYD 289:26
wish his d. to see — ANON 16:3
daughterly d. love — MORE 548:16
daughters d. of men — BIBL 76:5
d. of my father's house — SHAK 720:30
d. of the Philistines — BIBL 80:27
Kings' d. — BOOK 136:21
that our d. may be — BOOK 143:23
thunder, fire, are my d. — SHAK 700:16
Words are men's d. — MADD 505:9
words are the d. — JOHN 424:4
dauntless D. the slug-horn — BROW 159:2
so d. in war — SCOT 673:19
with d. breast — GRAY 361:5
dauphin kingdom of daylight's d.
— HOPK 397:10
David D. his ten thousands — BIBL 80:23
D. wrote the Psalms — NAYL 557:23
royal D.'s city — ALEX 11:8
Davis Thomas D., is thy toil — FERG 316:17
Davy Sir Humphrey D. — BENT 68:14
daw no wiser than a d. — SHAK 694:9
See-saw, Margery D. — NURS 569:12
Dawley Webb from D. — BETJ 72:16
dawn Between dusk and d. — MÜLL 553:21
d. comes up like thunder — KIPL 455:1
D. on our darkness — HEBE 378:14

dead (cont.):

He is d. and gone, lady	SHAK 688:6
he is d., who will not fight	GREN 363:13
home among the d.	SHEL 729:8
	HOMER 20.1
if the d. rise not	BIBL 108:6
If the d. talk to you	SZAS 769:17
if two of them are d.	PROV 632:47
immortal. who live again	ELIO 300:20
In praise of ladies d.	SHAK 723:16
I see d. people	FILM 319:20
judge the quick and the d.	BOOK 128:10
King of all these the d.	HOME 394:16
know that thou wert d.	CONS 241:5
lain for a century d.	TENN 782:1
land of the d.	WILD 837:14
lang time d.	MOTT 552:3
Lilacs out of the d. land	ELIO 303:7
Lycidas is d.	MILT 529:30
mansions of the d.	CRAB 249:3
millions of the mouthless d.	SORL 746:23
Mistah Kurtz—he d.	CONR 240:17
more than the d.	ARNO 26:22
more to say when I am d.	ROBI 650:13
My d. king	JOYC 437:8
No one wept for the d.	AGNO 8:31
not d.—but gone	ROGE 652:11
not d., but sleepeth	BIBL 96:10
Not many d.	COCK 229:23
Of their d. selves	TENN 778:22
only the d. smiled	AKHM 9:8
on the d. man's chest	STEV 759:13
oure kyng wes d.	WYNT 852:17
our English d.	SHAK 693:4
past is the only d. thing	THOM 790:12
past never d.	FAUL 316:1
pay for my d. people	JOSE 436:16
quick, and the d.	DEWA 266:12
quite for ever d.	CONG 238:31
rather be d. than cool	COBA 229:14
remind me of the d.	SASS 667:19
resurrection of the d.	BIBL 108:9
saying 'Lord Jones D.'	CHES 217:14
sculptured d.	KEAT 442:16
sea gave up the d.	BIBL 114:15
Sea shall give up her d.	BOOK 144:12
sheeted d. Did squeak	SHAK 683:16
She, she is d.	DONN 279:5
simplify me when I'm d.	DOUG 283:17
sleeping and the d.	SHAK 705:2
speak ill of the d.	PROV 627:28
Stone-d. hath no fellow	PROV 631:25
Strike them all d.	DICK 271:16
talks you d.	JOHN 426:11
There are no d.	MAET 505:15
they're a' d.	TOAS 796:3
thirteen men lay d.	HEAN 378:4
those who are d.	BURK 167:22
told me you were d.	CORY 244:3
to the d. we owe only truth	VOLT 816:11
very d. of Winter	ANDR 14:12
very d. of winter	ELIO 302:9
voice of the d.	TENN 779:31
waken the d.	GRAV 360:3
was alive and is d.	EPIT 310:2
was d., and is alive	BIBL 101:18
water—fire live—and we d.	BYRO 181:17
ways of being d.	DAWK 259:14
we are all d.	KEYN 450:18
Weep me not d.	DONN 281:19
wench is d.	MARL 513:15
we, that are d. to sin	BIBL 106:10
what was d. was Hope	WILD 836:31
When I am d.	MCGO 502:4
When I am d.	ROSS 655:16
Where d. men meet	BUTL 177:7
where there was not one d.	BIBL 77:32
wife, or himself must be d.	AUST 40:13
without works is d.	BIBL 111:25
with the enduring d.	SHEL 728:21
would that I were d.	TENN 781:14
you're ten years d.	HAYE 376:6
deaded told you I'd be d.	CATC 202:6

deadener Habit is a great d.	BECK 61:24
deadlines daily d.	ZOLA 859:7
deadlock Holy d.	HERB 383:11
deadly more d. in the long run	TWAI 803:7
more d. than the male	KIPL 454:4
more d. than the male	PROV 619:48
Dead Sea apples on the D.'s shore	BYRO 178:22
Like D. fruits	MOOR 547:21
deaf d. as an adder	ADAM 2:18
d., how should they know	SORL 746:23
d. husband	PROV 617:26
d., inexorable	SIDN 735:18
none so d. as those	PROV 632:32
prove me d. and blind	BROW 161:18
turn the d. ear	SWIF 766:30
deafer d. the blue-eyed cat	TENN 777:25
deal new d. for the American people	ROOS 653:11
square d. afterwards	ROOS 654:8
dealing d. with the modern media	MORR 549:10
deals D. are my art form	TRUM 801:16
dean cushion and soft D.	POPE 603:13
I am the D.	SPRI 753:8
no dogma, no D.	DISR 278:7
sly shade of a Rural D.	BROO 153:10
deans dowagers for d.	TENN 782:23
dear bread should be so d.	HOOD 395:12
dangerously d.	BYRO 179:26
D. 338171	COWA 245:13
D. dead women	BROW 161:24
D., dirty Dublin	JOYC 437:1
d. in the sight	BOOK 142:8
d. to them that love her	SPRI 753:6
Far-fetched and d.-bought	PROV 619:43
fault, d. Brutus	SHAK 696:9
Plato is d. to me	ARIS 26:6
too d. for my possessing	SHAK 723:13
dearer D. than self	BYRO 178:9
d. unto me	BOOK 142:12
d. was the mother	COLE 233:12
Or was there a d. one	HOOD 394:21
dearest d. thing he owed	SHAK 703:17
d., you're a dunce	JOHN 431:26
near'st and d. enemy	SHAK 690:29
she's the d. girl	DICK 268:22
dearie For thinking on my d.	BURN 170:12
deario cheerio my d.	MARQ 514:1
dearly D. beloved	BOOK 133:4
D. beloved brethren	BOOK 127:13
dearth in a year of d.	BLAK 121:2
death abolish the d. penalty	KARR 441:16
accused of child d.	RICH 647:6
afraid of d.	BROW 157:1
After the first d.	THOM 789:16
All Life d. does end	HOPK 396:20
anatomies of d.	SPEN 752:22
ancients dreaded d.	HARE 373:9
angel of d.	BRIG 151:7
Angel of D.	BYRO 180:2
another terror to d.	LYND 497:6
any man's d. diminishes me	DONN 282:2
at the point of d.	SHAK 718:8
bargain to engrossing d.	SHAK 718:10
Be absolute for d.	SHAK 708:8
beautiful and d.-struck year	HOUS 404:17
before his d.	BIBL 93:12
betwixt life and d.	WORD 850:4
Birth, and copulation, and d.	ELIO 303:4
black d.'s wing	AKHM 9:6
Black Widow, d.	LOWE 494:14
body of this d.	BIBL 106:16
born for d.	KEAT 445:1
bridegroom in my d.	SHAK 679:25
brooding over d.	HILL 388:9
brother of d.	BROW 157:12
Brother to D.	DANI 255:7
Brother to D.	FLET 327:9
Brought d. into the world	MILT 531:4
brought d. into the world	TWAI 803:22
brought sin and d.	STAN 754:9
build the house of d.	MONT 544:3

build your ship of d.	LAWR 475:6
by man came d.	BIBL 108:4
Cake or d.	IZZA 414:15
Call in thy d.'s-head there	HERB 383:24
came d. into the world	BIBL 92:22
caught his d.	FABY 313:20
chance, and d.	SHEL 731:8
citizens of d.'s grey land	SASS 667:18
Come away, come away, d.	SHAK 720:26
Comes d.	BARN 56:18
coming up to d.	SAUN 668:1
consenting unto his d.	BIBL 104:33
could not stop for D.	DICK 272:22
covenant with d.	BIBL 89:4
covenant with d.	GARR 340:10
day of his d.	AUDE 35:2
day of our Jubilee is d.	BROW 157:2
dead which he slew at his d.	BIBL 79:36
Dear, beauteous d.	VAUG 807:18
d. after life	SPEN 751:21
D. alone reveals	JUVE 440:10
D. a long-felt want	TREE 798:9
D. and his brother	SHEL 731:11
d. and taxes	DEFO 261:6
d. and taxes	FRAN 332:19
d. and taxes	PROV 628:8
D. and taxes and childbirth	MITC 540:11
D. and Toil	VIRG 812:12
d. bandaged my eyes	BROW 161:2
D. be not proud	DONN 279:19
D. cancels everything	HAZL 376:21
D. closes all	TENN 784:18
[D.] comes equally	DONN 282:5
d. concerns the gods	SOPH 746:14
d. could not daunt	BALL 52:14
D. devours all lovely things	MILL 526:21
d., ere thou hast slain another	EPIT 311:11
d. ever life devouring	ALAB 9:12
D.! Great proprietor	YOUN 857:10
d. . . . had been his next-door neighbour	SCOT 674:14
d. had undone so many	ELIO 303:11
D. has a thousand doors	MASS 518:5
D. has got something	AMIS 13:15
D. has made His darkness	TENN 779:12
D. hath asses' ears	BEDD 62:4
d. hath no more dominion	BIBL 106:12
D. hath so many doors	FLET 327:4
d. hath ten thousand	WEBS 825:25
D., in itself, is nothing	DRYD 287:27
d. in life	ANON 17:22
D. in Life	TENN 783:5
d. in the cup	BURN 171:12
d. in the pot	BIBL 82:5
D. is a fearful thing	SHAK 708:10
D. is a master from Germany	CELA 205:3
d. is but a groom	DONN 280:4
D. is dead, not he	SHEL 728:24
d. is in our own	BROW 157:3
D. is like a fisherman	TURG 802:10
[D. is] nature's way	ANON 15:16
[D. is] nature's way	SAYI 669:11
D. is not an event in life	WITT 842:12
d. is not far behind	WESL 829:22
D. is nothing at all	HOLL 392:19
D. is still working	HERB 384:10
d. is the cure	BROW 157:8
d. is the end of life	TENN 781:8
D. is the great leveller	PROV 617:27
D. is the only great emotion	FULL 337:2
D. is the privilege	ROWE 657:10
d. i' the other	SHAK 696:4
D. joins us to	YOUN 857:22
D. lays his icy hand	SHIR 735:3
D. lies dead	SWIN 768:14
D. lies on her	SHAK 718:6
D. like a narrow sea	WATT 823:18
D. must be distinguished	SMIT 744:4
D. never takes the wise man	LA F 463:15
d., nor life	BIBL 106:23
d. of a great man	ADDI 4:19
d. of air	ELIO 301:23
d. of a political economist	BAGE 48:21

D. of a salesman MILL 527:3
d. of each day's life SHAK 704:24
d. of his saints BOOK 142:8
d. of kings SHAK 715:23
d. of princes SHAK 697:3
d. on the hunting-field MORT 550:18
D. . . . openeth the gate BACO 44:4
d. or Santa Claus BERN 71:5
d. part thee and me BIBL 80:2
D. pays all debts PROV 617:28
d. reveals the eminent SHAW 726:29
D.'s artifact ABSE 1:5
D.'s bright angel PROC 612:18
d. shall have no dominion THOM 789:6
d.-shot glowing BYRO 178:6
d.'s pale flag SHAK 718:9
D. stepped tacitly BROW 161:20
d. that is immortal LUCR 495:18
d., the grand physician CLAR 224:7
d. the journey's end DRYD 289:8
D., the most awful of evils EPIC 308:8
D. therefore is nothing LUCR 495:16
D. thou shalt die DONN 279:20
d.-tick is audible CURZ 254:9
D. was but a scientific fact WILD 836:30
d., where is thy sting BIBL 108:12
D., where is thy sting-a-ling MILI 526:15
D. who comes at last SCOT 673:17
d., who had the soldier singled DOUG 283:18
D. will be aghast MISS 539:16
D. will come SHEL 732:4
d. will have his day SHAK 719:21
d. will provide the meaning ALAI 10:2
d. with one's will JAIN 416:11
D., without rhetoric SIEY 736:21
D. would eventually take care JOBS 422:2
D. would summon Everyman HEAN 377:16
Defer not charities till d. BACO 45:10
did not care a whit for d. SOCR 745:2
direful d. indeed FLEM 326:11
disqualified by the accident of d. CHES 217:4
doth d. lie heavily SENE 677:3
Do we take up in d. SHIR 735:6
dull cold ear of d. GRAY 361:4
easeful D. KEAT 444:27
eaten to d. with rust SHAK 691:28
ere her d. TENN 778:19
Even d. is unreliable BECK 61:28
everyone expected d. AGNO 8:31
everything except d. PROV 632:8
evidence of life after d. SOPE 746:11
Ev'ry day a little d. SOND 746:4
faithful unto d. BIBL 113:2
faith that looks through d. WORD 848:14
Fear d. BROW 161:1
fed on the fullness of d. SWIN 768:22
feed on D. SHAK 723:31
feet go down to d. BIBL 83:38
fierceness of harsh d. VIRG 814:19
film of d. KEAT 445:19
Finality is d. STEP 756:3
finished by a d. BYRO 180:29
forced marches, battles and d. GARI 339:15
Found d. in life COLE 231:16
From a view to a d. GRAV 360:4
from d. lead me to UPAN 804:12
Glad to d.'s mystery HOOD 394:23
go on living even after d. FRAN 332:9
hard at d.'s door BOOK 141:17
her own d.-warrant BAGE 48:15
His means of d. SHAK 688:14
his name that sat on him was d. BIBL 113:14
hour of d. BOOK 129:9
hour of my d. KEAT 446:22
I am become d. OPPE 573:17
I can face d. JUTR 439:5
If there wasn't d. SMIT 743:7
image of d. ELIO 300:17
improved by d. SAKI 663:12
in d.'s dark vale SCOT 673:12
interest in d. JAME 418:18
in that sleep of d. SHAK 686:9
in their d. not divided BIBL 80:28

in the shadow of d. BIBL 99:33
in the valley of D. TENN 776:11
Into the jaws of D. TENN 776:15
I signed my d. warrant COLL 235:5
isn't sex but d. SONT 746:9
just, and mighty D. RALE 641:14
keep a league till d. SHAK 716:11
Keeps D. his court SHAK 715:24
keys of hell and of d. BIBL 112:30
laws of d. RUSK 660:9
Lead me from d. to life KUMA 462:4
liberty, or give me d. HENR 382:15
life forget and d. remember SWIN 769:1
Life, the shadow of d. SWIN 768:4
life went through with d. FORT 330:4
living d. MILT 534:28
love is strong as d. BIBL 87:22
love thee better after d. BROW 158:4
make d. proud SHAK 680:4
make one in love with d. SHEL 728:12
man after his d. CHAU 211:12
Man has created d. YEAT 853:18
matter of life and d. SHAN 724:7
Men fear d. BACO 44:1
messenger of D. SACK 662:10
Morning after D. DICK 273:3
much possessed by d. ELIO 303:26
must hate and d. return SHEL 729:12
My name is D. SOUT 749:7
new terrors of d. ARBU 24:7
new terror to d. WETH 830:21
no cure for birth and d. SANT 666:11
No d. in my lifetime HEAN 378:8
no drinking after d. FLET 327:1
no mean of d. SHAK 697:14
no one his d. SENE 677:2
no one knew my d. ROET 652:8
not at their d. MONT 545:6
not d., but dying FIEL 317:13
nothing but d. AUST 40:22
nothing but d. UNAM 804:9
Now boast thee, d. SHAK 680:16
now give her in d. ELIZ 305:5
O D. BURN 171:25
of the sovereign is d. MORE 548:13
one fear, D.'s shadow BLUN 124:3
one life and one d. BROW 159:24
only nervousness or d. LEBO 478:6
owe God a d. SHAK 692:9
owest God a d. SHAK 691:7
Pale D. breaks HORA 400:5
preached to d. by wild curates SMIT 744:2
prepare as though for d. MANS 511:5
put it to a violent d. ETHE 312:4
reaction to her d. ELIZ 305:4
remedy is d. CHAM 207:1
removes Hazard and d. BOLA 126:2
rendezvous with D. SEEG 675:13
Reports of my d. TWAI 803:29
Revenge triumphs over d. BACO 44:2
run the race with D. JOHN 432:20
say to the Angel of D. MIDR 524:20
seasonal eternity of d. TATE 773:10
seeds of the d. of any state HOBB 390:19
seen birth and d. ELIO 302:10
set d. aside TURG 802:8
shadow of d. BIBL 83:2
shadow of d. BIBL 88:17
shadow of d. BOOK 141:16
shadow of d. BROW 156:1
shall be destroyed is d. BIBL 108:5
shall men seek d. BIBL 113:24
sharpness of d. BOOK 128:1
sin, d., and Hell BUNY 165:4
sleep, d.'s counterfeit SHAK 705:11
snares of d. BOOK 142:5
so cheap a d. DONN 280:23
some one's d. BROW 158:14
soul shall taste of d. KORA 459:22
still from d. was flying THOM 792:5
stroke of d. JOHN 425:9
studied in his d. SHAK 703:17
sudden d. BOOK 129:7

suffers at his d. LA B 462:17
suicide 25 years after his d. BEAV 60:15
swallow up d. in victory BIBL 89:2
Swarm over, D. BETJ 72:17
talks of Arthur's d. SHAK 699:11
Ten years after your d. HUGH 407:9
than a noble d. EURI 312:18
than frightened to d. SURT 764:19
there shall be no more d. BIBL 114:17
This fell sergeant, d. SHAK 689:11
Those by d. are few JEFF 420:6
thoughts so crowded with d. GUNN 365:18
thou shell of d. MIDD 524:10
thou wilt bring me to d. BIBL 83:17
till d. us do part BOOK 133:9
timing of your d. TACI 770:6
to be carnally minded is d. BIBL 106:17
triumph over d. and sin SPEN 751:3
true to thee till d. FABE 313:12
truly longed for d. TENN 784:12
universe of d. MILT 532:10
up the line to d. SASS 667:15
valley of the shadow of d. BOOK 133:9
vasty hall of d. ARNO 27:23
very quiet d. WEBS 826:1
wages of sin is d. BIBL 106:13
way to dusty d. SHAK 707:14
we are in d. BOOK 133:9
week of d. DONN 281:24
What life and d. is CHAP 208:12
What should it know of d. WORD 850:20
When d. approached GIBB 345:24
While there is d. CROS 252:16
Why fear d. LAST 474:15
yet afraid of d. CHUR 219:21
deathbed near the d. fiercer grows
WINC 841:4
deaths After so many d. I live HERB 384:8
by feigned d. to die DONN 281:11
million d. a statistic STAL 754:5
More d. than one must die WILD 837:1
death sentence take the d. without a
whimper LAWR 475:17
debasing D. the moral currency ELIO 299:22
debatable d. line MACA 499:1
debate daughter of d. ELIZ 304:8
Rupert of D. BULW 164:3
debonair blithe, and d. MILT 529:18
deboshed Thou d. fish SHAK 718:33
debout D.! les damnés POTT 608:11
debt Ambition's d. is paid SHAK 697:11
d. by disputation BUTL 175:20
d. of nature FABY 313:19
deeper in d. TRAV 798:5
in love, and in d. BROM 152:3
national d. HAMI 369:19
National D. is a very Good Thing
SELL 676:23
Out of d. PROV 629:11
pay a d. to pleasure ROCH 651:5
promise made is a d. unpaid SERV 677:6
public d. should be reduced MISQ 537:5
war, an' a' d. LOWE 493:20
we are in d. MUMF 554:1
debtor d. to his profession BACO 43:10
I am d. BIBL 105:35
debts Death pays all d. PROV 617:28
forgive us our d. BIBL 95:3
pays all d. SHAK 718:35
so we can pay our d. NYER 570:18
Speak not of my d. PROV 631:17
decade now in the Me D. WOLF 843:22
decay Change and d. LYTE 497:10
D. with imprecision ELIO 301:13
decrepitude, their d. LAND 466:7
flourish after first d. SPEN 751:25
found its d. COCK 229:20
human things are subject to d. DRYD 288:30
of a nature to d. PALI 583:12
our love hath no d. DONN 280:14
to many men's d. SPEN 752:8
decayed sufficiently d. GILB 348:11
decays Mere glimmering and d. VAUG 807:17

delectable D. Mountains BUNY 164:23
delectando d. pariterque monendo
  HORA 398:13
delegate When in trouble, d. BORE 145:3
delenda D. est Carthago CATO 199:16
deleted Expletive d. ANON 15:23
Delia While D. is away JAGO 416:2
deliberate O, these d. fools SHAK 709:10
  Where both d. MARL 513:11
deliberates woman who d. ADDI 4:11
deliberation D. sat and public care
  MILT 532:4
delicate not very d. WALP 819:13
delicias D. domini VIRG 813:17
delicious Afloat. We move: D. CLOU 227:19
delight begins in d. FROS 336:4
  born to sweet d. BLAK 119:15
  by succession of d. SMAR 740:14
  D. hath a joy SIDN 736:19
  d. in conceiving KEAT 446:16
  D. in lust PETR 594:7
  d. is in lies BOOK 137:27
  d. with liberty SPEN 752:12
  do ill our sole d. MILT 531:10
  Energy is Eternal D. BLAK 120:20
  ever new d. MILT 533:12
  firmness, and d. WOTT 851:7
  Formed to d. POPE 603:28
  give d., and hurt not SHAK 718:36
  hear thy shrill d. SHEL 731:27
  immense world of d. BLAK 121:11
  labour we d. in SHAK 705:8
  land of pure d. WATT 823:17
  Let dogs d. WATT 823:9
  men miscall d. SHEL 728:23
  phantom of d. WORD 850:3
  Spirit of D. SHEL 731:16
  still my d. BURN 171:16
  Studies serve for d. BACO 45:16
  temple of D. KEAT 444:19
  thing met conceives d. MILT 533:28
  turn d. into a sacrifice HERB 383:21
delighteth king d. to honour BIBL 82:24
  neither d. he BOOK 144:4
delightful it can be d. SHAW 724:18
  no d. ones LA R 469:14
delighting d. the reader HORA 398:13
delights king of intimate d. COWP 248:8
  man d. not me SHAK 685:24
  some d. condemn MOLI 542:11
delinquencies indulge in a few d.
  ELIO 300:19
delinquent condemns a less d. BUTL 176:21
delirant Quidquid d. reges HORA 399:8
delitabill Storys to rede ar d. BARB 55:9
deliver D. Israel, O God BOOK 135:9
  d. us from evil BIBL 95:3
  d. us from evil MISS 539:7
  d. us, good Lord CHES 216:3
  let him d. him BOOK 134:27
  Lord, d. us BOOK 129:4
  O d. me from the deceitful BOOK 136:15
  O d. my soul BOOK 135:27
  who shall d. me BIBL 106:16
deliverance d. from chains DOUG 284:3
delivered d. my soul BOOK 142:6
  d. them BIBL 79:15
  God hath d. him BIBL 80:25
delivereth he d. them BOOK 141:19
delivery ungracefulness of his d.
  WALP 819:21
delphiniums d. (blue) and geraniums (red)
  MILN 528:1
Delphos steep of D. leaving MILT 530:25
deluding dear d. woman BURN 172:25
deluge Après nous le d. POMP 599:16
delusion d., a mockery DENM 264:8
  under some d. BURK 169:1
delusive d. seduction BURN 169:26
demanded d. nought TASS 773:8
demands cannot exact their d. WELL 828:5
demens Quem fugis, a! d. VIRG 813:19
demi-paradise other Eden, d. SHAK 715:13

demitasses villainous d. SMIT 741:18
democracies d. against despots DEMO 263:18
  in d. it is the only sacred FRAN 331:17
democracy conception of D. ADDA 3:18
  cured by more d. SMIT 741:14
  cure for the ills of D. ADDA 3:19
  D. and socialism are means NEHR 558:6
  D. is the current suspicion WHIT 832:1
  D. is the name we give FLER 326:20
  D. is the theory MENC 521:17
  D. is the worst form CHUR 221:21
  d. means government ATTL 33:5
  D. means government by CHES 217:15
  D. means simply WILD 837:5
  D. not identical with majority rule
  LENI 480:4
  d. of the dead CHES 217:3
  d. or absolute oligarchy ARIS 26:3
  D. resumed her reign BELL 65:19
  D. substitutes election SHAW 726:18
  d. unbearable PERE 592:19
  d. was renewed DEWA 266:10
  five hundred years of d. FILM 319:19
  great arsenal of d. ROOS 653:19
  grieved under a d. HOBB 390:20
  justice makes d. possible NIEB 563:15
  less d. to save ATKI 32:20
  made safe for d. WILS 840:22
  no d. can afford BEVE 73:21
  no d. in physics ALVA 12:22
  not the voting that's d. STOP 761:7
  perfect d. BURK 167:21
  pollution of d. WHIT 832:7
  property-owning d. SKEL 739:9
  risk more d. BRAN 149:14
  Russia an empire or d. BRZE 162:15
  Two cheers for D. FORS 330:2
democrat Senator, and a D. JOHN 423:7
democratic among a d. people TROL 799:21
  disrupt the d. process JUAN 437:28
democrats D. object to men being
  disqualified CHES 217:4
Democritus D. would laugh HORA 399:20
demolish can't really d. it RANK 642:5
demolition d. of a man LEVI 482:13
demon d.'s that is dreaming POE 599:9
  wailing for her d.-lover COLE 232:4
demonstrandum Quod erat d. EUCL 312:7
den d. of thieves BIBL 98:4
denial d. of Him by the atheist PROU 613:10
denied comes to be d. MONT 543:10
  Justice d. MILL 525:23
  justice d. SAYI 670:1
denies spirit that always d. GOET 352:16
deniges Who d. of it DICK 270:9
denizen spider is sole d. HARD 372:10
Denmark in the state of D. SHAK 684:29
  it may be so in D. SHAK 685:7
  throne of D. SHAK 683:22
dens d. o' Yarrow BALL 52:3
  hid themselves in the d. BIBL 113:15
dentist sooner go to my d. WAUG 824:17
deny d. a God BACO 43:18
  d. me thrice BIBL 99:2
  d., or delay MAGN 506:5
  d. the being of a devil MATH 518:8
  He teaches to d. QUAR 639:2
  I never d. DISR 278:3
  will I not d. thee BIBL 99:3
  You must d. yourself GOET 352:17
denying allure by d. TROL 800:3
  they were d. FREE 333:9
Deo D. gratias MISS 536:18
  Jubilate D., omnis terra BIBL 115:1
deoch-an-doris Just a wee d. MORR 550:10
deorum Parcus d. cultor HORA 400:19
depart already time to d. SOCR 745:5
  desire to d. BIBL 100:23
  servant d. in peace BIBL 100:6
  will not d. BIBL 84:40
departed Dead he is not, but d. LONG 490:16
  dear brother here d. BOOK 133:18
  d., he withdrew CICE 223:17

  d. into their own country BIBL 94:7
  D., never to return BURN 170:15
  d. this life BOOK 131:16
  glory is d. BIBL 80:8
  glory is d. BROW 161:28
  Lord was d. BIBL 79:34
departing and at my d. PRAY 611:3
departure point of d. METT 523:10
dépêches Une de ces d. PROU 613:13
depend did on false thee d. ROCH 651:6
dependant d. on man's bounty STAN 754:9
depends d. on the tip FILM 321:2
  d. upon a red wheel barrow WILL 839:13
  d. what you mean by CATC 201:8
dépeuplé tout est d. LAMA 464:7
deportment adapt her methods and d.
  CRAN 249:27
  for his D. DICK 267:18
depose my state d. SHAK 716:8
deposit greater the d. LAYT 476:9
depraved suddenly became d. JUVE 439:13
depravity sense of innate d. MELV 521:9
  stupidity than d. JOHN 429:9
depression d. when you lose yours
  TRUM 801:11
depressions terrible d. SEI 676:1
deprivation D. is for me LARK 469:8
depth d. and breadth and height BROW 158:3
  d. of every acre GURN 366:2
  far beyond my d. SHAK 695:11
deputy d. elected by the Lord SHAK 715:19
  we shall have a new D. WHAR 831:4
derangement nice d. of epitaphs SHER 733:19
Derry oak would sprout in D. HEAN 378:4
descansada Que d. vida LUIS 496:3
descending comes with clouds d. WESL 829:9
descensus Facilis d. Averno VIRG 812:9
descent d. from a monkey WILB 835:1
description beggared all d. SHAK 679:3
descriptions d. of the fairest wights
  SHAK 723:16
Desdemona D.! dead SHAK 714:28
desert Blast from the D. LONG 490:25
  d. is a moving mouth WALC 817:5
  d. shall rejoice BIBL 89:9
  d. sighs in the bed AUDE 34:20
  d. were my dwelling-place BYRO 179:16
  in a d. land BIBL 79:2
  Life is the d. YOUN 857:22
  make straight in the d. BIBL 89:16
  Nothing went unrewarded, but d.
  DRYD 287:7
  on the d. air GRAY 361:5
  out into the d. CLOU 229:13
  owl that is in the d. BOOK 140:18
  scare myself with my own d. FROS 335:13
  Stand in the d. SHEL 730:16
  Use every man after his d. SHAK 686:1
  water but the d. BYRO 179:8
deserted D. in his utmost need DRYD 287:16
  towns are d. BERN 70:16
deserts d. of the heart AUDE 35:8
  D. of vast eternity MARV 516:1
  his d. are small MONT 546:3
  she d. the night MILT 534:27
deserve and d. to get it MENC 521:17
  d. any thanks CATU 203:4
  d. success ADDI 4:8
  I d. it PRIE 611:12
  only d. it CHUR 221:11
  those who really d. them FIEL 318:5
  you somehow haven't to d. FROS 335:12
deserves Everyone gets what he d.
  BOLD 126:3
  gets what he d. ANON 21:6
  Stonehenge it d. HAWK 375:10
desiccated d. calculating machine
  BEVA 73:16
design good d. for a bus HOCK 391:7
  integrity in d. KARA 441:15
  there is a d. in it STEE 754:20
  two rules for d. PUGI 636:19

designs at large to his own dark d.

d. were strictly honourable FIEL 318:12
instruments of their crooked d. GODW 352:4
Official d. BETJ 72:14
desinat D. in piscem HORA 397:19
desipere Dulce est d. HORA 403:1
desire by nature d. knowledge ARIS 25:11
d. accomplished BIBL 84:17
d. and longing BOOK 139:15
d. for their own happiness SHAN 724:10
d. of power HOBB 390:12
d. of the moth SHEL 731:24
d. other men's goods BOOK 132:18
d. shall fail BIBL 86:25
d. should so many years SHAK 692:3
fond d. ADDI 4:15
gratified d. BLAK 121:23
her d.,— Shining suspension CRAN 249:26
land of d. HEGE 379:5
Land of Heart's D. YEAT 854:19
man's d. is for the woman COLE 234:4
nothing like d. PROU 613:9
provokes the d. SHAK 705:7
shot and danger of d. SHAK 684:15
weariness treads on d. PETR 594:7
what I've tasted of d. FROS 335:14
when the d. cometh BIBL 84:15
Which of us has his d. THAC 786:21
without any quiver of d. PALI 584:18
desired chiefly to be d. CICE 223:23
I have d. to go HOPK 396:16
More to be d. BOOK 134:22
not one to be d. TENN 780:3
You who d. so much— CRAN 250:3
desires all d. known BOOK 131:6
all holy d. BOOK 128:19
answer back to d. HORA 403:16
d. and petitions BOOK 128:18
d. but acts not BLAK 120:24
d. of our own hearts BOOK 127:15
d. of the heart AUDE 34:23
d. of the mind BACO 42:16
d. that seem big RICE 646:18
d. which thereof did ensue DONN 279:10
doing what one d. MILL 525:10
end of our d. THOM 788:18
enjoyment of all d. TANT 773:4
fondly flatter our d. DRAY 285:22
lopping off our d. SWIF 766:22
nurse unacted d. BLAK 121:9
proportion to our d. MANN 510:8
desirest d. no sacrifice BOOK 137:15
desireth as the hart d. BOOK 136:11
desiring D. this man's art SHAK 722:29
desirous ought else on earth d. GAY 341:13
desk but a d. to write upon BUTL 176:11
modern man's subservience to the d.
FRAN 333:1
Turn upward from the d. ELIO 303:18
desks Stick close to your d. GILB 348:24
desolate d. and oppressed BOOK 129:13
d. places BIBL 82:32
sold in the d. market BLAK 120:6
vast d. night BYRO 178:4
desolated province they have d. GLAD 350:16
desolation abomination of d. BIBL 98:15
D. in immaculate public places ROET 652:4
Love in D. SHEL 728:20
Magnificent d. ALDR 11:2
years of d. JEFF 420:14
despair begotten by D. MARV 515:16
Bid me d. HERR 386:14
black d. CONG 238:19
carrion comfort, D. HOPK 396:10
comfort and d. SHAK 723:30
D. a smilingness assume BYRO 178:18
D. had a wife BUNY 164:22
D. yawns HUGO 407:18
Do not d. PUDN 636:17
endure my own d. WALS 820:13
far side of d. SART 667:10
Giant D. BUNY 164:21

Heaven in Hell's d. BLAK 122:11
I d. for it FLEM 326:15
In d. there are DOST 283:11
I shall d. SHAK 717:7
needst not then d. ARNO 27:8
perpetual d. CARL 192:21
sins of d. READ 643:5
some divine d. TENN 783:3
unyielding d. RUSS 660:25
what resolution from d. MILT 531:12
ye Mighty, and d. SHEL 730:18
despairer Too quick d. ARNO 28:26
desperandum Nil d. HORA 400:9
desperate Beware of d. steps COWP 246:21
D. diseases PROV 617:30
Diseases d. grown SHAK 687:34
Tempt not a d. man SHAK 718:7
desperation lives of quiet d. THOR 793:4
despise and d. him DICK 270:22
ere you d. the other DRYD 290:7
shalt thou not d. BOOK 137:15
work for a Government I d. KEYN 450:10
despised Dangers by being d. BURK 169:6
d. and rejected BIBL 90:2
d. Mr Tattle CONG 238:28
d. the world HAZL 376:13
despite Hell in Heaven's d. BLAK 122:12
despond slough was D. BUNY 164:13
despondency d. and madness WORD 849:21
last words of Mr D. BUNY 165:8
SPREAD ALARM AND D. PENI 591:14
unnecessary alarm and d. MILI 526:7
despot country governed by a d. JOHN 431:4
despotism D. accomplishes great things
BALZ 54:10
d. in England WALP 820:2
d., let it be called WEBS 825:14
d., or unlimited sovereignty ADAM 3:4
d. tempered by epigrams CARL 192:9
d. will come ARIS 26:3
root of d. ROBE 650:7
despots against d.—suspicion DEMO 263:18
D. themselves do not deny TOCQ 795:4
dessin d. est la probité INGR 413:19
destinies d. of half the globe TOCQ 795:12
destiny Anatomy is d. FREU 333:19
character is d. ELIO 300:16
d. obscure GRAY 361:3
D. the commissary of God DONN 280:7
D. with Men for pieces FITZ 323:8
fabric of human d. DOST 283:4
gods ordained the d. of men HOME 394:12
manifest d. O'SU 579:9
tide of d. PAST 588:4
wiving go by d. PROV 621:29
destitution shaming D. VIRG 812:12
destroy against us to d. us HAGG 367:2
d. the town to save it ANON 17:2
gods wish to d. CONN 240:2
in search of monsters to d. ADAM 3:11
man determined to d. himself CUMM 253:13
not to d., but to fulfil BIBL 94:24
One to d. YOUN 857:6
planted, we d. WITH 842:5
power to d. MARS 514:12
shall be able to d. OVID 580:15
shall not hurt nor d. BIBL 88:22
Whom the gods would d. PROV 635:3
Whom the mad would d. LEVI 482:14
winged life d. BLAK 121:22
worms d. this body BIBL 83:12
destroyed Carthage must be d. CATO 199:16
enemy that shall be d. BIBL 108:5
name d. HILL 389:3
not one life shall be d. TENN 779:6
ought to be d. OMAR 573:6
treated generously or d. MACH 502:9
destroyer D. and preserver SHEL 730:7
d. of worlds OPPE 573:17
destroyeth d. in the noon-day BOOK 140:3
destroying without d. something
UPDI 805:23
destroys d. a good book MILT 535:14

Time which d. all things BHAG 74:15
destruction d. of the poor BIBL 84:9
d. of the whole world HUME 409:10
for d. ice Is also great FROS 335:14
leadeth to d. BIBL 95:19
means of total d. SAKH 663:11
Pride goeth before d. BIBL 84:26
to his own d. FRAM 331:15
to their d. draw DONN 280:14
urge for d. BAKU 50:4
whether the mad d. is wrought GAND 339:5
destructive smiling, d. man LEE 478:21
To the d. element CONR 240:19
would be simply destructive MELB 520:18
detached except he be d. BAHA 49:14
detail corroborative d. GILB 348:8
frittered away by d. THOR 793:13
occupied in trivial d. BAGE 48:2
details Devil is in the d. SAYI 669:12
God is in the d. MIES 524:22
mind which reveres d. LEWI 483:22
detect lose it in the moment you d.
POPE 603:17
detection D. is an exact science DOYL 284:23
detective d. novel is art-for-art's-sake
PRIT 612:14
d. story is about JAME 418:17
Hawkshaw, the d. TAYL 775:5
deteriora D. sequor OVID 580:13
determination d. of a quiet man SMIT 742:8
d. of incident JAME 418:2
determine we d. our deeds ELIO 299:4
determined D., dared, and done
SMAR 740:18
determinèd d. to prove a villain SHAK 716:22
detest d. at leisure BYRO 181:30
I hate and d. SWIF 766:5
detraction D. is but baseness' varlet
JONS 435:9
Deum D. de Deo MISS 536:20
deus d. nobis haec otia fecit VIRG 813:13
puto d. fio VESP 809:7
Deutschland D. über alles HOFF 391:13
devastating d. or redeeming fires
GONC 356:8
developed fairly d. minds FORS 329:7
have a d. society NYER 570:19
developer slipped into d. WILS 840:2
development what is called d. NAIR 556:3
De Vere name and dignity of D. CREW 251:3
deviates d. into sense DRYD 288:31
deviation Without hesitation, d. CATC 202:1
device imagined such a d. BOOK 134:25
with the strange d. LONG 490:9
devices d. and desires BOOK 127:15
man of many d. HOME 394:13
man of many d. OPEN 575:22
devil act like a d. MALC 508:12
apology for the D. BUTL 176:30
assaults of the d. BOOK 129:4
Better the d. you know PROV 615:28
bid the D. good morrow PROV 627:17
blue-eyed d. white man FARD 315:1
can the d. speak true SHAK 703:13
cleft the D.'s foot DONN 281:9
counteracts the D. SMAR 739:18
covenant with the D. MISQ 537:15
D. always builds a chapel DEFO 261:21
d. and all his works BOOK 132:13
d. can cite Scripture SHAK 709:1
d. can quote Scripture PROV 617:31
d. damn thee black SHAK 707:7
d. doesn't exist DOST 283:2
d. finds work PROV 617:32
d. have all the best tunes PROV 635:9
D. howling 'Ho' SQUI 753:15
d. is dead READ 643:6
D. is in the details SAYI 669:12
d. is not so black PROV 617:33
D. knows Latin KNOX 458:10
d. looks after his own PROV 617:34
d. makes his Christmas pies PROV 617:35

D. Moon in your eyes | HARB 371:3
d. more wicked | BALL 52:19
d.-porter it no further | SHAK 705:6
D. said when he found himself | PROV 622:23
d.'s awa wi' th'Exciseman | BURN 170:26
D. sends cooks | GARR 340:5
D. sends cooks | PROV 620:49
d. shall not take it from us | RAND 642:2
d. should have all | HILL 388:13
D. should have right | MORE 548:11
d.'s leavings | POPE 606:23
d.'s luck | PROV 617:36
d.'s madness—War | SERV 677:9
d.'s most devilish | BROW 157:20
d., so far as I'm aware | KLEI 457:20
d.'s walking parody | CHES 215:24
D. take the hindmost | PROV 617:37
D. take the hindmost | PROV 619:15
d. taketh him up | BIBL 94:17
d., taking him up | BIBL 100:10
d. understands Welsh | SHAK 690:25
d. was sick | PROV 617:38
d. weakly fettered | STEV 759:5
D. whoops | KIPL 453:19
D. will build a chapel | PROV 634:38
d. will come | MARL 513:6
d. would also build | LUTH 496:10
doubt is D.-born | TENN 779:18
dreamed of the d. | ANST 23:2
dream of the d. | BARH 55:16
Drink and the d. | STEV 759:13
easier to raise the D. | PROV 624:1
envy of the d. | BIBL 92:22
face the d. | BURN 172:13
fears a painted d. | SHAK 705:2
first Whig was the D. | JOHN 431:8
flesh, and the d. | BOOK 129:6
given the d. a foul fall | MORE 548:12
Give the d. his due | PROV 620:41
God and d. | DOST 283:1
go to the d. | JOHN 426:24
go to the d. | NORF 565:8
got over the D.'s back | PROV 634:5
Haste is from the D. | PROV 621:35
idle brain is d.'s workshop | PROV 622:40
laughing d. | BYRO 179:23
moral of the d. | SHAK 693:10
my back upon Don or d. | TENN 783:20
of the D.'s party | BLAK 120:21
of the witty d. | GRAV 360:5
of your father the d. | BIBL 103:12
Poetry is d.'s wine | AUGU 37:7
puzzle the d. | BURN 172:7
reference to the d. | CHUR 222:15
serpent, which is the D. | BIBL 114:13
shame the D. | PROV 631:43
sups with the D. | PROV 622:15
synonym for the D. | MACA 498:2
Talk of the D. | PROV 631:41
there is a D. | MATH 518:8
Truth makes the D. blush | PROV 633:22
wedlock's the d. | BYRO 183:13
What the d. was he doing | MOLI 541:22
when most I play the d. | SHAK 716:27
when the d. drives | PROV 627:15
white man was *created* a d. | MALC 508:9
Young saint, old d. | PROV 636:7
your adversary the d. | BIBL 112:15
you the blacker d. | SHAK 714:24
devilish most d. thing | FLEM 326:12
Tough, and d. sly | DICK 269:4
devils casteth out devils | BIBL 96:11
d. in life and condition | ASCH 31:7
d. must print | MOOR 547:11
d. would set on me | LUTH 496:9
fight like d. | SHAK 693:6
devised so well a d. | BOOK 127:12
devolution D. Day | SALM 665:7
d. takes longer | CART 198:6
Devon glorious D. | BOUL 147:6
If the Dons sight D. | NEWB 560:1
devote d. themselves to what men do | FITZ 323:18

devotion D.! daughter of astronomy | YOUN 857:19
my bok and my d. | CHAU 212:22
Tell zeal it wants d. | RALE 641:3
devour d. in turn each one | VERG 808:14
seeking whom he may d. | BIBL 112:15
when they would d. | BACO 46:3
devoured beast hath d. him | BIBL 77:2
devourer Time the d. | OVID 580:14
devourers become so great d. | MORE 548:7
devout d. in dishabilly | FARQ 315:25
for being d. | MOLI 542:9
dew as sunlight drinketh d. | TENN 776:22
begotten the d. | BIBL 83:23
continual d. of thy blessing | BOOK 128:17
d. bespangling herb | HERR 385:19
d. shall weep thy fall | HERB 385:4
d. will rust them | SHAK 713:4
drenched with d. | DE L 263:6
Drop down d., heavens | BIBL 115:8
early fa's the d. | SONG 747:15
fades awa' like morning d. | BALL 53:18
let there be no d. | BIBL 80:27
morning d. | ARNO 28:28
On whom the d. of heaven drops | FORD 328:16
resolve itself into a d. | SHAK 683:29
Showers, and D. | BOOK 128:5
smell the d. and rain | HERB 384:8
soft falls the d. | BEER 83:9
Walks o'er the d. | SHAK 683:19
wicked d. | SHAK 718:23
dewdrop Starlight and d. | FOST 330:11
dewdrops seek some d. here | SHAK 710:28
dewfall d. at night | STEV 760:12
dews early d. were falling | INGE 413:12
dewy d. pasture, dewy trees | TENN 782:21
shakes his d. wings | D'AV 257:23
dhamma D. has been taught | PALI 583:10
sees D. sees me | PALI 584:1
teach you D. | PALI 583:14
dharamsala goes to the d. | SIKH 737:10
dharma discourse on d. as a raft | MAHĀ 506:14
rain of D. | MAHĀ 506:19
di d. omen avertant | CICE 223:19
diable d. est mort | READ 643:6
diabolical tree of d. knowledge | SHER 733:16
diadem d. of frost | BLOK 123:16
precious d. stole | SHAK 687:26
diagnostician makes a good d. | OSLE 579:4
diagonally lie d. in his bed | STER 757:11
dialect Babylonish d. | BUTL 175:22
d. I understand very little | PEPY 592:6
d. with an army | WEIN 826:23
D. words | HARD 371:19
purify the d. of the tribe | ELIO 301:24
dial-plate looking on the d. | JOHN 429:2
diamond d. and safire bracelet | LOOS 491:19
D. cuts diamond | PROV 617:39
d. in the sky | TAYL 774:16
d. is forever | ADVE 7:15
like a rough d. | DEFO 261:4
matchwood, immortal d. | HOPK 397:7
O D.! Diamond | NEWT 563:2
polished d. | CHES 215:9
diamonds d. a girl's best friend | ROBI 650:10
has no d. | WALP 819:17
what beautiful d. | WEST 830:5
Dian hangs on D.'s temple | SHAK 682:25
Diana D., breathless, hunted | MOTI 551:13
D.'s foresters | SHAK 689:19
Great is D. | BIBL 105:22
diapason d. closing full | DRYD 289:17
diarist To be a good d. | NICO 563:12
diary discreet d. | CHAN 208:3
keep a d. and some day | WEST 830:2
never travel without my d. | WILD 835:22
write a d. every day | POWE 610:2
write in a d. | WARN 821:20
diaspora for the new d. | DUNN 292:13
dibble put The d. in earth | SHAK 722:3
dic *sed tantum d. verbo* | MISS 539:10

dice God does not play d. | EINS 297:15
throw of the d. | MALL 508:15
Dick D. the shepherd | SHAK 702:26
Mr. D. had been for upwards of ten years | DICK 268:15
dicky D.-bird, why do you sit | GILB 348:10
dictate one day d. to him | JOHN 426:6
suggest, never to d. | BRON 152:17
dictates still d. to us | ALLI 12:17
woman d. | ELIO 299:25
dictation told at d. speed | AMIS 13:9
dictator d. of Nicaragua | CARD 190:8
Every d. uses religion | BHUT 74:19
dictators D. ride to and fro upon tigers | CHUR 221:2
weed d. may cultivate | BEVE 73:21
dictatorship d. impossible | PERE 592:19
d. of the proletariat | MARX 517:2
elective d. | HAIL 367:14
establish a d. | ORWE 577:21
have a d. | TRUM 801:12
dictionaries D. are like watches | JOHN 432:21
d. is dull work | JOHN 424:8
Lexicographer. A writer of d. | JOHN 424:10
dictionary but a walking d. | CHAP 208:20
D. is | CARR 194:24
dictum D. *sapienti* | PLAU 597:21
non d. sit prius | TERE 785:5
did danced his d. | CUMM 253:5
d. for them both | SASS 667:22
I d. it my way | ANKA 14:16
diddle D., diddle, dumpling | NURS 566:17
d., we take it, is dee | SWIN 768:18
Hey d. diddle | NURS 567:6
Dido Stood D. with a willow | SHAK 710:1
die Americans when they d. | PROV 621:4
and gladly d. | STEV 760:20
And shall Trelawny d. | HAWK 375:9
apt to d. | SHAK 697:14
as if you were to d. tomorrow | EDMU 296:8
Ay, but to d., and go | SHAK 708:10
being born, to d. | BACO 47:1
better to d. on your feet | IBAR 412:7
bid me d. | HERR 386:14
bleed, fall, and d. | DONN 279:11
bravely d. | POPE 602:13
Christian can d. | LAST 473:16
clean place to d. | KAVA 442:6
conquer or d. | WASH 822:6
Cowards d. many times | SHAK 697:4
Cowards may d. many times | PROV 617:14
Curse God, and d. | BIBL 82:30
day that I d. | MCLE 503:7
Death thou shalt d. | DONN 279:20
determine to d. here | BEE 62:9
did not wish to d. | SHAW 728:1
d. a Christian | CHAR 209:2
d. all, die merrily | SHAK 691:1
D., and endow a college | POPE 603:9
d. before I wake | PRAY 611:5
d. beyond my means | WILD 837:2
d. but do not surrender | CAMB 186:14
d.—but never to live | JAME 418:10
d. but once | ADDI 4:13
die, dear, once | BEDD 62:2
d. eating ortolans | DISR 277:34
d. for adultery | SHAK 701:14
d. for him to-morrow | BALL 51:13
d. for one's country | HORA 401:12
d. for politicians | THOM 791:20
d. for the industrialists | FRAN 332:3
d. for the people | BIBL 103:23
D. he or justice must | MILT 532:17
d. here in a rage | SWIF 766:6
d. in music | SHAK 714:25
d. in my week | JOPL 436:11
d. in peace | LAST 473:7
d. in that man's company | SHAK 693:22
d. in the flower of their age | BIBL 80:3
d. in the last ditch | WILL 838:2
d. is cast | CAES 185:6
d. like a true-blue rebel | LAST 472:16
d. like men | BOOK 139:14

die (cont.):

D., my dear Doctor	LAST 471:8
d. of that roar	ELIO 300:5
d. to save charges	BURT 174:3
d. to vex me	MELB 520:16
d. upon a kiss	SHAK 715:2
d. when the body dies	BHAG 74:9
d. when the trees were green	CLAR 224:3
d. with harness	SHAK 707:15
d. with thee	BIBL 99:3
Don't d. of ignorance	OFFI 572:6
do we not d.	SHAK 709:14
Easy live and quiet d.	SCOT 674:5
easy ways to d.	SHAK 680:18
Every day we d.	JERO 421:7
faith is something you d. for	BENN 67:3
Fall asleep, or hearing d.	SHAK 695:9
Few d. and none resign	MISQ 537:14
few d. well	SHAK 693:15
for me to d.	SOCR 745:5
for tomorrow we d.	PROV 618:36
frogs don't d. for 'fun'	BION 116:16
Gods love d. young	PROV 635:2
Good Americans, when they d.	APPL 23:14
good d. early	DEFO 261:16
good d. young	PROV 621:6
have the power to d.	TENN 784:9
hazard of that roar	SHAK 717:11
he can d. who complains	BROW 157:3
he must d.	NICH 563:7
He shall not d.	STER 757:9
Hope I d. before	TOWN 797:6
how can man d. better	MACA 499:13
how to d.	PORT 607:22
I did not d.	ANON 15:18
I die because I do not d.	JOHN 422:9
I d. happy	LAST 472:3
I d., if he die not	ANDR 14:10
if he d., I die too	ANDR 14:10
If I should d.	BROO 153:15
If I should d.	KEAT 447:5
If I should d.	OPEN 574:6
If it were now to d.	SHAK 713:19
If we must d.	MCKA 502:16
I'll d. young	BRUC 162:3
I must d.	SOUT 749:23
in Adam all d.	BIBL 108:4
I shall d. at the top	SWIF 767:22
I shall d. today	MORE 548:13
I shall not altogether d.	HORA 402:4
I Sir Richard Grenville d.	TENN 784:3
it was sure to d.	MOOR 547:20
I who am about to d.	JOHN 433:13
I will d. with them	NELS 558:15
I would d.	ROSS 656:9
just as lucky to d.	WHIT 833:11
last Jews to d.	MEIR 520:4
lay me doun and d.	SONG 748:1
Let me d. a youngman's death	MCGO 502:3
Let us d.	VIRG 811:19
Let us do—or d.	BURN 172:6
let us do or d.	CAMP 187:9
like Douglas d.	HOME 393:15
longed to d.	PROU 613:6
love her till I d.	ANON 19:8
love one another or d.	AUDE 36:4
make a malefactor d. sweetly	DRYD 290:14
man can d. but once	SHAK 692:9
marked to d.	SHAK 693:21
Muse forbids to d.	HORA 402:15
natural to d.	BACO 44:3
not d. because of them	TALM 772:15
not so difficult to d.	BYRO 182:23
not that I'm afraid to d.	ALLE 12:13
often are we to d.	POPE 606:19
Old soldiers never d.	FOLE 327:24
Old soldiers never d.	PROV 628:22
O love, they d.	TENN 783:2
only let Him d.	STUD 763:2
Only we d. in earnest	RALE 641:4
or dare to d.	POPE 605:8
ought to d. standing	LAST 471:12
People can't d.	DICK 268:25

prepare myself to d.	RIEL 648:9
seemed to d.	BIBL 92:23
seems it rich to d.	KEAT 444:27
shall Harry d.	SHAK 692:19
something he will d. for	KING 452:3
taught us how to d.	TICK 794:13
Their's but to do and d.	TENN 776:14
these who d. as cattle	OWEN 581:1
They d. not	ROSS 656:2
They that d. by famine	HENR 382:11
those who are about to d.	ANON 21:13
thou must d.	HERB 385:4
thou shalt surely d.	BIBL 75:13
time to d.	BIBL 85:32
To d. and know it	LOWE 494:14
To d. in wisdom	CERV 205:17
to d. is gain	BIBL 109:22
To d. will be an awfully big	BARR 57:4
To go away is to d.	HARA 370:20
to live and to d.	VILL 810:13
tomorrow we d.	BIBL 108:6
to morrow we shall d.	BIBL 88:26
unlamented let me d.	POPE 605:32
we all must d.	SWIF 767:16
weep or she will d.	TENN 783:9
we needs must d.	BIBL 81:3
went abroad to d.	LETT 482:7
We shall d. alone	PASC 587:10
What 'tis to d.	BEAU 60:8
When beggars d.	SHAK 697:3
when they come to d.	MATH 518:9
when you d.	HILL 388:11
when you have to d.	MOLI 542:5
where myths Go when they d.	FENT 316:13
Who saw him d.	NURS 570:16
who would wish to d.	BORR 145:10
will d. of strangeness	MURR 555:4
wisdom shall d. with you	BIBL 83:5
with us, or we d.	KEAT 442:14
wretch that dares not d.	BURN 171:22
You and I ought not to d.	ADAM 3:3
You can only d. once	PROV 635:38
Young men may d.	PROV 636:6
Dieb er war ein D.	HEIN 380:2
died could have d. contented	DICK 269:7
d. an hour before	SHAK 705:13
d. extremely well	WALP 818:18
d.—for fear of dying	THOM 792:5
D., has he	LOUI 492:15
d. hereafter	SHAK 707:14
d. in a good old age	BIBL 82:19
d. in faith	BIBL 111:8
d. last night of my physician	PRIO 612:7
d. of grieving	KEAT 443:17
D. some, pro patria	POUN 608:20
d. to save their country	CHES 216:1
d. unto sin once	BIBL 106:12
dog it was that d.	GOLD 355:3
He that d. o' Wednesday	SHAK 691:9
'I never d.,' says he	HAYE 376:6
liked it not, and d.	WOTT 851:5
made the books and he d.	FAUL 316:3
Mithridates, he d. old	HOUS 405:3
Mother d. today	OPEN 574:7
question why we d.	KIPL 453:18
she d. young	WEBS 825:26
think of the ones who d.	CARD 190:7
What millions d.	CAMP 187:17
would God I had d. for thee	BIBL 81:5
Would to God we had d.	BIBL 77:36
diem carpe d.	HORA 400:14
d. perdidi	TITU 795:1
d. tibi diluxisse supremum	HORA 399:7
dienen d. und verlieren	GOET 353:4
dies because a man d. for it	WILD 836:19
before he d.	SOLO 745:13
d. from lack of sex	ATWO 33:9
D. irae	MISS 539:15
d. only once	MOLI 541:16
d., or turns Hindoo	SHEL 729:22
d. to himself unknown	SENE 677:3
d. young	MENA 521:13
Every moment d. a man	BABB 42:2

He that d.	SHAK 718:35
He that d. this year	SHAK 692:10
kingdom where nobody d.	MILL 525:19
king never d.	BLAC 118:9
love seldom d. of hunger	LENC 480:2
man who d. . . . rich	CARN 193:8
matters not how a man d.	JOHN 429:7
moment d. a man	TENN 784:21
no man happy till he d.	PROV 616:22
once hath blown for ever d.	FITZ 323:6
Optima quaeque d. miseris	VIRG 814:19
something in me d.	VIDA 810:1
then d. the same	YOUN 857:13
diesel London Transport d.-engined	FLAN 324:19
diest Where thou d., will I die	BIBL 80:2
diet best doctors are Dr D.	PROV 615:10
d. unparalleled	DICK 270:14
dietetics first law of d.	ASIM 31:19
diets feel about d.	KERR 450:2
Dieu D. est mort	NERV 559:7
Si D. n'existait pas	VOLT 816:3
differ all things d.	POPE 606:17
d. from others	BAGE 49:3
difference d. of forty thousand	WELL 827:16
exaggerate the d.	SHAW 725:29
made all the d.	FROS 335:23
oh, The d. to me	WORD 850:2
wear your rue with a d.	SHAK 688:13
What d. does it make	GAND 339:5
differences against small d.	FREU 334:2
in language there are only d.	SAUS 668:2
different boil at d. degrees	EMER 307:13
convictions d. from your own	EMPS 307:24
D. strokes	SAYI 669:13
follow d. paths	HORA 403:2
hears a d. drummer	THOR 793:16
How d. from us	ANON 17:17
how very d.	ANON 16:13
other naturs thinks d.	DICK 270:4
rich are d. from you and me	FITZ 323:20
something completely d.	CATC 200:2
thought they were d.	ELIO 302:10
differential integral and d. calculus	GILB 348:28
differently do things d. there	HART 374:19
do things d. there	OPEN 575:12
freedom for the one who thinks d.	LUXE 496:17
difficile D. est	JUVE 439:7
D. est longum	CATU 203:6
difficult d.; and left untried	CHES 217:11
D. do you call it, Sir	JOHN 433:8
d. is done at once	PROV 617:40
d. takes a little time	NANS 556:5
d. to be a father	BUSC 174:19
d. to speak	BURK 169:3
d. we do immediately	MILI 526:6
fascination of what's d.	YEAT 854:8
first step that is d.	DU D 291:4
first step that is d.	PROV 624:13
not so d. to die	BYRO 182:23
Poets must be d.	ELIO 303:31
too d. for artists	SCHN 671:13
difficulties d. do not make one doubt	NEWM 560:14
d. for several generations	NAPO 556:18
little local d.	MACM 504:5
somebody is in d.	LUCR 495:14
difficulty d. in saying things	MOOR 547:8
England's d.	PROV 618:43
every d. except popularity	WILD 837:9
no d. in beginning	JAME 418:9
solving every d.	PEEL 590:19
with d. and labour	MILT 532:16
with great d. I am got hither	BUNY 165:9
diffidence her name was D.	BUNY 164:22
diffugere D. nives	HORA 402:11
dig D. for victory	OFFI 572:4
he'll d. them up again	WEBS 826:10
I could not d.	KIPL 454:2
I'll d. with it	HEAN 377:19
digest learn, and inwardly d.	BOOK 130:1

digestion good d. wait on appetite
SHAK 706:4
  in d. sour
SHAK 715:9
diggeth He that d. a pit
BIBL 86:17
dignified d. parts
BAGE 47:14
dignitate Cum d. otium
CICE 223:23
dignities by indignities men come to d.
BACO 44:23
dignity conciliate with d.
GREN 363:14
  d. in tilling a field
WASH 822:4
  d. of history
BOLI 126:7
  d. of this high calling
BURK 167:2
  d. which His Majesty
BALD 50:18
  individual d.
YAMA 853:2
  maintain a d. in their fate
WALP 819:23
  no d. in persevering in error
PEEL 590:18
  Official d.
HUXL 411:3
  with silent d.
GROS 365:6
  write trifles with d.
JOHN 431:21
dignum D. et justum
MISS 536:23
  D. laude virum Musa vetat mori
HORA 402:15
dignus non sum d.
MISS 539:10
digression began a lang d.
BURN 173:4
digressions D. are the sunshine
STER 756:21
  eloquent d.
HUXL 412:4
digs d. my grave
HERB 384:10
Dijon young man of D.
ANON 20:12
dilige D. et quod vis fac
AUGU 37:13
diligence D. is the mother
CERV 205:15
  D. is the mother
PROV 617:41
dillied But I d. and dallied
COLL 235:3
dilly-dally Don't d. on the way
COLL 235:3
dim d. religious light
MILT 529:16
  flickered, grew d.
TOLS 796:15
  made The bright world d.
SHEL 732:9
  Nor d. nor red
COLE 232:17
dime Brother can you spare a d.
HARB 371:1
  life can change on a d.
LAHR 464:4
dimensions my d. are as well compact
SHAK 699:24
  Time has three d.
HOPK 397:14
dimidium Animae d. meae
HORA 400:3
diminished ought to be d.
DUNN 292:14
dimittis Nunc d.
BIBL 115:12
dimming d. of the lights
NICO 563:11
dine d. exact at noon
POPE 603:26
  gang and d.
BALL 53:15
  heroes to d. with us
TROL 799:15
dined I have d. today
SMIT 744:1
  more d. against
BOWR 148:14
ding D., dong, bell
NURS 566:18
dining-room d. will be well-lighted
LAND 466:8
dinner after d. is after dinner
SWIF 766:2
  After d. rest awhile
PROV 614:6
  ask him to d.
CARL 193:5
  best number for a d. party
GULB 365:16
  d. bell
BYRO 181:18
  D. in the diner
GORD 356:18
  d. of herbs
BIBL 84:24
  d. of herbs
PROV 615:18
  doubtful of his d.
JOHN 424:27
  good d. and feasting
PEPY 592:10
  good d. upon his table
JOHN 433:17
  have had a better d.
JOHN 428:20
  hungry for d. at eight
HART 374:4
  refrain from asking it to d.
HALS 369:17
  three hours' march to d.
HAZL 377:7
  we expect our d.
SMIT 741:5
  with broken d.-knives
KIPL 454:8
  worth inviting to d.
VIRG 814:4
dinners Homer's mighty d.
AESC 6:11
dinosaurs D. are a touchstone
RUSS 661:10
diocese All the air is thy D.
DONN 279:14
Diogenes would be D.
ALEX 11:3
Dior Never darken my D. again
LILL 484:13
diplomacy D. is to do and say
GOLD 354:4
diplomat d. . . . is a person
STIN 761:4
diplomatic d. boathook
SALI 664:3
diplomats D. tell lies
KRAU 461:14
direct d. and rule our hearts
BOOK 130:17
  lie d.
SHAK 682:8
directed all d. your way
HORA 399:2

direction d., which thou canst not see
POPE 604:30
  move in a given d.
HOUS 405:7
  pitch or d.
HOPK 397:14
  some particular d.
JOHN 425:1
directions By indirections find d. out
SHAK 685:14
  rode madly off in all d.
LEAC 476:16
directors way with these d.
GOLD 356:4
direful d. death indeed
FLEM 326:11
  d. in the sound
AUST 38:22
  to Greece the d. spring
POPE 605:14
dirge Begins the sad d.
SHAK 722:19
  their d. is sung
COLL 235:13
dirt d. doesn't get any worse
CRIS 251:8
  D. is only matter
GRAY 360:18
  eat a peck of d.
PROV 633:47
  in d. the reasoning engine
ROCH 651:12
  In poverty, hunger, and d.
HOOD 395:11
  in the d. lay justice
HEAN 378:4
  make crossness and d. succeed
FORS 329:11
  painted child of d.
POPE 602:31
  thicker will be the d.
GALB 338:3
  Throw d. enough
PROV 632:51
dirty Airing one's d. linen
TRUF 801:3
  Dear, d. Dublin
JOYC 437:1
  D., dark, and undevotional
VICT 809:11
  d. old town
MACC 500:12
  D. water will quench
PROV 617:42
  hard and d. work
RUSK 659:19
  Is sex d.
ALLE 12:9
  journalistic d.-mindedness
LAWR 475:16
  'Jug Jug' to d. ears
ELIO 303:13
  throw out your d. water
PROV 618:18
  too d. for the light
CLAR 224:6
  wash one's d. linen
PROV 628:31
  You d. rat
MISQ 539:5
dis D. aliter visum
VIRG 811:20
disability My d. is that I cannot
HANS 370:19
disagree if they d.
OMAR 573:6
  when doctors d.
POPE 603:8
disagreeable d.-looking child
OPEN 576:3
disappear d. from within
JUTR 439:5
disappointed d. by that stroke
JOHN 425:9
  d. in human nature
DONL 279:2
  never be d.
PROV 616:2
  you have d. us
BELL 65:1
disappointeth d. him not
BOOK 134:13
disappointing least d.
BARU 57:18
disappointment D. all I endeavour end
HOPK 397:8
  d., no matter what
HORN 403:17
disappointments most mortifying d.
BURK 169:12
disapproval moral d.
AYER 41:7
disapprove d. of what you say
MISQ 538:1
disapproves condemns whatever he d.
BURN 169:25
disarm d. a military capacity
COOK 242:3
disaster 'Gainst all d.
DEAR 260:10
  triumph and d.
KIPL 454:12
disasters d. in his morning face
GOLD 354:15
  guilty of our own d.
SHAK 699:26
disastrous d. and the unpalatable
GALB 338:7
  win a war is as d.
CHRI 218:14
disbelief willing suspension of d.
COLE 233:22
discandy d., melt their sweets
SHAK 679:20
disce D. omnis
VIRG 811:12
discern do we d.
ARNO 27:18
discerning genius a better d.
GOLD 355:22
discharge d. for loving one
MATL 518:13
  no d. in that war
BIBL 86:11
disciple d. did outrun Peter
BIBL 104:10
  d. is not above his master
BIBL 96:17
  d. whom Jesus loved
BIBL 104:23
  in the name of a d.
BIBL 96:22
disciples great man has his d.
WILD 835:25
discipline D. must be maintained
DICK 267:22
  d. of colleges
SMIT 741:11
  gentle d.
SPEN 751:11
  of Dhamma, of D.
PALI 583:13

  order and military d.
MILI 526:5
  wholesome d. impossible
JAIN 416:12
disciplines by category-d.
RYLE 662:3
disclaim d. her for a mother
GIBB 345:12
disco mali miseris succurrere d.
VIRG 811:8
Discobbolos Darling Mr D.
LEAR 477:12
discomfort great d. of my soul
BOOK 135:26
discomforts all the d.
CLOS 228:3
discommendeth He who d. others
BROW 155:15
discontent in common—d.
ARNO 29:6
  pale contented sort of d.
KEAT 444:2
  winter of d.
CALL 185:17
  Winter of d.
NEWS 562:24
  winter of our d.
SHAK 716:18
discontented every one that was d.
BIBL 80:24
discontents Civilization and its d.
RIVI 649:15
  source of all our d.
LEAC 476:11
discord civil d.
CLOS 228:11
  d. doth sow
ELIZ 304:8
  hark! what d. follows
SHAK 719:18
discordant D. elements
WORD 849:8
  still-d. wavering multitude
SHAK 691:21
discors Concordia d.
HORA 399:11
discouragement strife and the d.
LONG 490:4
  There's no d.
BUNY 165:7
discourse company and good d.
WALT 820:20
  d. of rivers
WALT 821:1
  Miss not the d.
BIBL 93:8
discover another can d.
DOYL 284:20
discoverers ill d.
BACO 42:18
discovery D. consists of seeing
SZEN 769:20
  d. of a new dish
BRIL 151:16
  love is but d.
SOUT 748:16
  Medicinal d.
AYRE 41:11
discreet d. charm of the bourgeoisie
FILM 322:3
  d. diary
CHAN 208:3
discretion d. end
AUST 40:1
  D. is better part
PROV 617:43
  D. is not the better part
STRA 762:4
  fair woman without d.
BIBL 84:11
  guide his words with d.
BOOK 141:23
  inform their d.
JEFF 420:13
  part of valour is d.
SHAK 691:16
  surety to subsequent d.
BURN 169:19
  their happiness in thy d.
ELIZ 304:10
discount dum docent d.
SENE 676:28
discuss stay and d. them
WELL 828:3
discussing d. if it existed
GUIN 365:19
discussion compliance with my wishes after reasonable d.
CHUR 222:16
  d. of any subject
SHEL 732:10
  government by d.
ATTL 33:5
disdain D. and scorn
SHAK 712:21
  little d. is not amiss
CONG 239:14
  my dear Lady D.
SHAK 712:12
  pride and high d.
SCOT 673:7
disdained If now I be d.
ANON 19:2
disdainfulness D. I have again
WYAT 852:3
disdains d. all things
OVER 579:16
disease afflictive d.
MOOR 547:5
  age, D., or sorrows
CLOU 229:3
  Astrology is a d.
MAIM 507:19
  biggest d. today
TERE 785:12
  cannot ascertain a d.
KEAT 447:9
  Cured yesterday of my d.
PRIO 612:7
  Cure the d.
BACO 44:16
  desperate d.
FAWK 316:8
  d. at its onset
PERS 593:8
  d. called friendship
RENO 645:9
  d. has grown strong
OVID 580:10
  D., Ignorance, and Idleness
BEVE 73:22
  D. is an experience
EDDY 295:9
  d. is incurable
CHEK 213:21
  d. is incurable
SHAK 691:29
  d. of admiration
MACA 498:12
  d. of modern life
ARNO 28:9
  d. of not listening
SHAK 691:24
  incurable d. of writing
JUVE 440:1
  Life is an incurable d.
COWL 245:30
  Love's a d.
MACA 497:17

disease (cont.):
no Cure for this D.	BELL 64:21
Progress is a comfortable d.	CUMM 253:11
remedy is worse than the d.	BACO 45:14
sexually transmitted d.	SAYI 670:4
suffering from the particular d.	JERO 421:13
this long d., my life	POPE 602:26
twenty drugs for each d.	OSLE 579:5

diseased mind d. | BYRO 179:9
| minister to a mind d. | SHAK 707:9 |
| To know ourselves d. | YOUN 857:18 |

diseases cure of all d. | BROW 157:8
Desperate d.	PROV 617:30
D. and sad Old Age	VIRG 812:12
D. desperate grown	SHAK 687:34
extreme d.	HIPP 389:10
spread d.	OFFI 572:3

disenchantment mistook d. for truth | SART 667:5

disentangle cannot d. | ANON 19:2

disestablishment sense of d. | KING 452:9

disgrace author of his own d. | COWP 246:16
Even to a full d.	SHAK 682:23
in d. with fortune	SHAK 722:28
Intellectual d. Stares	AUDE 35:6
no d. t'be poor	HUBB 406:14
passing d.	DIDE 273:19
Poverty is no d.	PROV 629:31
private life is a d.	ANON 18:17
public and merited d.	STEV 759:30

disgraced dies . . . rich dies d. | CARN 193:8

disgraceful something d. in mind | JUVE 440:15

disgruntled if not actually d. | WODE 842:18

disguise better go in d. | BRAT 149:20
D. fair nature	SHAK 693:4
d. which can hide love	LA R 469:11
men in d.	ABSE 1:3
naked is the best d.	CONG 238:18
this identical d.	BROO 154:4

disguised England is a d. republic | BAGE 48:9

disgust capacity for d. | MANN 510:8
| not moments of d. | VOLT 816:8 |
| play began to d. | EVEL 313:4 |

dish discovery of a new d. | BRIL 151:16
d. fit for the gods	SHAK 696:24
d. ran away	NURS 567:6
in a lordly d.	BIBL 79:19
than an empty d.	PROV 615:20

dishabilly devout in d. | FARQ 315:25

dishclout Romeo's a d. | SHAK 718:5

dishcover d. the riddle | CARR 196:4

dishes these the choice d. | GARR 340:5
these were the d.	AUGU 37:1
washing of d.	EPIT 309:15
who does the d.	FREN 333:14

dishonour another unto d. | BIBL 106:24
| rooted in d. | TENN 778:1 |

dishonourable d. graves | SHAK 696:9

disiecti *Etiam d. membra poetae* | HORA 403:8

disinheriting d. countenance | SHER 734:1

disintegration d. and dismemberment | GLAD 350:18
| out of its own d. | FUEN 336:20 |

disinterested d. endeavour | ARNO 29:17
| D. intellectual curiosity | TREV 798:10 |

dislike d. every thing | CENT 205:8
d. the matter	SHAK 679:2
hesitate d.	POPE 602:29
I, too, d. it	MOOR 547:1
like and d. the same	SALL 665:2
sat with that d.	STEE 754:18

dismal beset him round With d. stories | BUNY 165:7
| D. Science | CARL 192:18 |

dismayed neither be thou d. | BIBL 79:8
| Was there a man d. | TENN 776:14 |

dismemberment d. of the Empire | GLAD 350:18

dismiss Lord, d. us | BUCK 163:11

Disney Mouse over at Disney | MAYE 519:15
| of Euro D. | BALL 54:2 |
| *of Euro D.* | MNOU 541:7 |

Disneyfication D. of Christianity | CUPI 254:2

disobedience children of d. | BIBL 109:15
crown d. with laurels	KLEI 457:21
man's first d.	MILT 531:4
man's first d.	OPEN 575:6

disorder D., horror, fear | SHAK 716:6
d. in its geometry	DE B 260:15
sweet d. in the dress	HERR 385:21
with brave d. part	POPE 604:1

dispatch in business than d. | ADDI 4:18

displeasing not d. to us | LA R 469:21

dispoged when I am so d. | DICK 270:3

disposable everything has to be d. | MILL 527:7

dispose d. of all things | ANON 22:1
| d. the way of thy servants | BOOK 132:6 |

disposes God d. | THOM 788:6

disposition antic d. | SHAK 685:11
| truant d. | SHAK 684:7 |

dispossessed imprisoned or d. | MAGN 506:4

dispraised Of whom to be d. | MILT 534:16

disputants d. put me in mind | ADDI 5:10

disputations Doubtful d. | BIBL 106:34

dispute great d. between you | VIRG 813:23

disqualified d. for holding any office | MORE 548:8

disquieted d. within me | BOOK 136:12

disquieteth d. himself in vain | BOOK 136:5

disregard Atones for later d. | FROS 335:22

dissatisfied human being d. | MILL 525:17
| I'm d. | MOOR 547:6 |
| Not one is d. | WHIT 833:13 |

dissect creatures you d. | POPE 603:17
| murder to d. | WORD 850:13 |

dissemble d. sometimes your knowledge | BACO 44:5

dissent dissidence of d. | BURK 166:22

dissenters Barn-door fowls for d. | SMIT 743:15

dissentious you d. rogues | SHAK 682:13

dissimulation one word—d. | DISR 277:8

dissipation d. without pleasure | GIBB 345:18

dissolution lingering d. | BECK 61:1

dissolve d., and quite forget | KEAT 444:23
| d. the people | BREC 150:17 |

dissolved d. into something | CATH 199:11
| tabernacle were d. | BIBL 108:15 |

dissonance barbarous d. | MILT 529:4

distaff mind the d. | LEWI 483:15

distance d. is nothing | DU D 291:4
d. lends enchantment	CAMP 187:15
D. lends enchantment	PROV 617:44
longest d. between two places	WILL 839:7
scale of the d.	SALI 664:4

distant d. from Heaven | BURT 174:11
music of a d. drum	FITZ 323:3
prospect of a d. good	DRYD 288:18
relation of d. misery	GIBB 345:8

distempered questions the d. part | ELIO 301:18

distillation d. of rumour | CARL 192:6

distinction make no d. | BUSH 175:3
| think that there is no d. | JOHN 428:10 |

distinctive man's d. mark | BROW 159:5

distinguish style which will d. | MATH 518:7

distinguished d. above the rest | HOME 394:3
| d. by that circumstance | THOR 793:14 |
| d. thing | JAME 418:16 |

distort then you can d. them | TWAI 804:1

distracted this d. globe | SHAK 685:6

distraction thrown Into a fine d. | HERR 385:21

distress d. of another | RICH 647:16
every one that was in d.	BIBL 80:24
Far as d.	GREV 363:17
out of their d.	BOOK 141:19
pray in their d.	BLAK 122:2

distressed afflicted, or d. | BOOK 129:19
| I am d. for thee | BIBL 80:29 |

distresses d. of our friends | SWIF 767:15

distressful most d. country | POLI 600:21

distribute d. as fairly as he can | LOWE 493:16

distrust have to d. each other | WILL 839:3

ditch [Channel] is a mere d. | NAPO 556:7
| die in the last d. | WILL 838:2 |

D.-delivered. by a drab | SHAK 706:13
dull as d. water	DICK 271:23
environed with a great d.	CROM 252:7
fall into the d.	BIBL 97:12
makes a straight-cut d.	THOR 792:25

ditchers gardeners, d. | SHAK 688:22

ditches of Dutchmen and of d. | BYRO 181:24

ditties amorous d. | MILT 531:20

ditty played an ancient d. | KEAT 443:3

diurnal her d. round | WORD 847:1

dive must d. below | DRYD 287:21

diver Don't forget the d. | CATC 200:12

diversa *laudet d. sequentis* | HORA 403:2

diversity d. of sects | SPEN 752:13
| some d. | BARC 55:11 |

divide D. and rule | PROV 617:45
| d. the spoil | BIBL 88:17 |
| though he d. the hoof | BIBL 78:11 |

divided All that is d. | HÖLD 392:14
d. aims	ARNO 28:9
d. by a common language	MISQ 537:12
D. by the morning tea	MACN 504:17
d. duty	SHAK 713:12
d. into three parts	CAES 185:1
d. into three parts	OPEN 574:11
d. self	LAIN 464:5
d. the spoil	BOOK 138:12
d. we fall	PROV 633:34
has harshly d.	SCHI 668:16
He d. the sea	BOOK 139:9
house d. cannot stand	PROV 622:34
If a house be d.	BIBL 99:17
in their death not d.	BIBL 80:28

dividend no d. from time's tomorrow | SASS 667:18

dividing by d. we fall | DICK 273:15

divination d. too will perish | MAND 510:3

divine believes Kingsley a d. | STUB 762:19
Come down, O Love d.	LITT 486:16
d. Majority	DICK 273:6
d. plain face	LAMB 465:8
d. powers take note	VIRG 811:7
d. Zenocrate	MARL 513:23
faculty d.	WORD 846:12
good d. that follows his own	SHAK 708:25
hand that made us is d.	ADDI 5:8
heavy, but no less d.	BYRO 181:8
horror and its beauty are d.	SHEL 730:15
human form d.	BLAK 122:3
knowledge was d.	TRAH 797:12
More needs she the d.	SHAK 707:4
one far-off d. event	TENN 779:30
possess d. legislation	MEND 521:21
Right D. of Kings	POPE 602:2
say that D. providence	JOHN 422:17
some d. despair	TENN 783:3
To forgive, d.	POPE 604:13
to forgive d.	PROV 633:9
what the form d.	LAND 466:4

divinely most d. fair | TENN 776:19

divineness participation of d. | BACO 42:16

divines Doubts 'mongst D. | SPEN 752:13

divinest two d. things | HUNT 409:20

diving-bell religious d. | FOST 330:9

divinity d. doth hedge a king | SHAK 688:11
d. in odd numbers	SHAK 710:14
d. that shapes our ends	SHAK 689:5
mysteries in d.	BROW 156:23
piece of d. in us	BROW 157:10

division D. is as bad | ANON 17:19
| we make no d. between any | KORA 459:20 |

divisions How many d. has he got | STAL 754:3

divisos *penitus toto d. orbe* | VIRG 813:15

divorce bill of my d. | DONN 279:26
| long d. of steel | SHAK 695:6 |

divorces d. his first wife | TALM 772:26

dixeris D. *egregie notum* | HORA 398:1

dixit *Ipse d.* | CICE 223:10

dizzy d. 'tis to cast one's eyes | SHAK 701:12

DNA cannot cheat on D. | WARD 821:14

do All one has to d. is | I-HS 412:19
| Can I d. you now, sir | CATC 200:6 |
| can't all d. everything | VIRG 814:8 |

damned if you d.   DOW 284:5
did not d. things themselves   RAVE 642:16
D. as I say   PROV 617:46
D. as I say   SELD 676:12
D. as you would be done by   CHES 215:2
D. as you would be done by   PROV 617:47
D. IT YOURSELF   BARH 56:3
Do not d. to others what   CONF 238:6
d. not to your neighbour   HILL 389:1
don't d. it at all   BISH 117:10
d. only one thing   SMIL 740:23
D. other men   DICK 270:2
D. unto others as you would   PROV 618:22
d. what I please   FRED 333:8
d. what is right   HUXL 411:16
D. what thou wilt   CROW 253:2
d. what thou wouldst do   HATC 375:3
d. ye even so to them   BIBL 95:18
fine pleasure is not to d.   HOPK 397:17
George—don't d. that   CATC 200:19
HOW NOT TO D. IT   DICK 269:21
I can d. no other   LUTH 496:8
If to d. were as easy   SHAK 708:25
I'll do, I'll do, and I'll d.   SHAK 703:5
I'll d.'t before I speak   SHAK 699:20
know not what they d.   BIBL 102:4
Let's d. it   PORT 607:14
Let us d.—or die   BURN 172:6
let us d. or die   CAMP 187:9
Love and d. what you will   AUGU 37:13
never know what you can d.   PROV 636:2
not knowing what they d.   SHAK 712:27
people who d. things   MORR 550:14
Say little and d. much   SHAM 724:6
so much to d.   LAST 473:17
supposed to d. anyway   TRUM 801:6
to my servant, D. this   BIBL 95:28
We cannot d. it, Sir   CARR 195:19
what I d. in any thing   HERB 384:3
What must I d. to be saved   BIBL 105:13
what you are afraid to d.   EMER 307:1
would they should d. unto me   BOOK 132:15
doc cards with a man called D.   ALGR 11:15
What's up, D.   CATC 201:33
docent dum d. discunt   SENE 676:28
doctor any other d. whatsoever   HOBB 390:10
artless d. sees   HERR 386:1
d. does not give you a year   STEV 759:17
d. found, when she was dead   GOLD 355:2
d. full of phrase   ARNO 29:5
fee the d.   DRYD 288:8
God and the d.   OWEN 580:22
keeps the d. away   PROV 614:28
doctors believe the d.   SALI 664:5
best d. are Dr Diet   PROV 615:10
budge d. of the stoic fur   MILT 529:9
D. in verse   THOM 790:24
d. know a hopeless case   CUMM 253:12
might be medical d.   DICK 272:18
when d. disagree   POPE 603:8
when the d. try   LUCR 495:13
doctrinal On the d. side   QUIN 639:10
doctrine all the winds of d.   MILT 535:25
blast of vain d.   BOOK 131:1
d. of ignoble ease   ROOS 654:5
d. of the enclitic De   BROW 159:16
d. something you kill for   BENN 67:3
every wind of d.   BIBL 109:11
life and d.   BOOK 131:15
loved the d.   DEFO 261:17
Much d. lies under   FANS 314:10
not for the d.   POPE 604:7
doctrines d. without words   LAO 467:5
makes all d. plain   BUTL 176:16
documents d. and friends   SPAR 749:24
dodger artful D.   DICK 271:10
dodgy d. dossier   NEWS 562:5
doers be ye d. of the word   BIBL 111:22
Evil d. evil dreaders   PROV 619:26
does d., not suffers wrong   SHEL 730:22
D. she or doesn't she   ADVE 7:16
He who can d.   PROV 622:6
doest That thou d., do quickly   BIBL 103:26

dog Am I a d.   BIBL 80:22
barking d. never bites   PROV 614:50
beaten d. beneath the hail   POUN 609:5
better than his d.   TENN 780:16
beware of the d.   BLIX 123:12
Beware of the d.   PETR 594:3
black d.   JOHN 432:10
call a d. Hervey   JOHN 427:8
cut-throat d.   SHAK 709:2
D. does not eat dog   PROV 617:48
d. in the night-time   DOYL 284:19
d. is allowed one bite   PROV 619:7
d. is for life   SLOG 740:2
d. is turned to his own vomit   BIBL 112:17
d. it was that died   GOLD 355:3
d. returneth to his vomit   BIBL 85:9
D. returns to his Vomit   KIPL 454:9
d. returns to its vomit   PROV 617:49
d. shall bear him company   POPE 604:24
d.-star rages   POPE 602:23
d. starved at his master's gate   BLAK 119:7
d.'s tooth   PROV 632:49
d.'s walking on his hinder legs   JOHN 428:19
d. that will fetch a bone   PROV 618:2
D., the Meat and the Reflection   AESO 6:13
d. with eyes as big as   ANDE 14:6
engine of pollution, the d.   SPAR 750:2
Every d. has his day   PROV 619:6
every d. his day   KING 453:1
face of a d.   GARC 339:11
Give a d. a bad name   PROV 620:36
good d. goes to church   PROV 621:40
Has a d. the Buddha-Nature   MUMO 554:4
heart to a d. to tear   KIPL 455:9
I had rather be a d.   SHAK 698:14
I never heard thy d.   HEYW 387:19
Is thy servant a d.   BIBL 82:10
keep a d. and bark yourself   PROV 635:8
lame d. over a stile   CHIL 217:23
let no d. bark   SHAK 708:21
limps the hungry d.   BLOK 123:16
live d. is better   PROV 625:35
living d.   BIBL 86:13
lost d. somewhere   ANOU 23:1
Lovell our d.   COLL 234:21
Love me, love my d.   PROV 625:47
man bites a d.   BOGA 125:8
Mine enemy's d.   SHAK 701:20
more ridiculous than a d.   NERV 559:9
My d.! what remedy remains   COWP 247:1
nobody knows you're a d.   CART 198:7
over the lazy d.   ANON 18:16
poor d. had none   NURS 568:14
poor d. that's not worth   PROV 623:37
poor d. Tray   CAMP 187:10
stick to beat a d.   PROV 624:3
teach an old d. new tricks   PROV 635:44
to a d.'s tail   YEAT 856:1
tongue of d.   SHAK 706:12
very d. to the commonalty   SHAK 682:12
was there ever d.   YEAT 855:23
ways of killing a d.   PROV 631:46
ways of killing a d.   PROV 631:47
whose d. are you   POPE 602:21
woman, d., and walnut tree   PROV 635:14
working like a d.   LENN 480:19
Doge quiet D. of Venice   WALP 820:2
dogged d. as does it   PROV 624:20
d. as does it   TROL 799:19
doggie How much is that d.   MERR 522:25
dogma Any stigma to beat a d.   GUED 365:9
d. has been the fundamental principle   NEWM 560:12
no d., no Dean   DISR 278:7
dogmatize d. and am contradicted   JOHN 433:12
dogs all things as straw d.   LAO 467:6
Cowardly d. bark loudest   WEBS 826:7
cruel as d. one to another   PEPY 592:9
d. and apes   BROW 159:14
D. are Shakespearean   SCHW 672:7
d. bark at me   SHAK 716:20
D. bark, but the caravan   PROV 618:1

d. do bark   NURS 567:3
d. eat of the crumbs   BIBL 97:13
d. go on with their doggy life   AUDE 35:13
d., horses   JENY 421:3
d. licked his sores   BIBL 101:22
D. look up to us   CHUR 222:19
d. of Europe bark   AUDE 35:6
fought the d.   BROW 160:20
gaze of d.   CALV 186:11
go to the d. tonight   HERB 383:6
hates d. and babies   ROST 656:17
Lame d. over stiles   KING 452:15
Let d. delight   WATT 823:9
Let sleeping d. lie   PROV 625:6
let slip the d. of war   SHAK 697:16
lie down with d.   PROV 623:19
like dancing d.   JOHN 430:9
little d. and all   SHAK 701:3
mad and hungry d.   MCKA 502:16
Mad d. and Englishmen   COWA 245:3
more I like d.   ROLA 653:1
more one values d.   TOUS 797:5
na men, but d.   BURN 173:5
Throw physic to the d.   SHAK 707:10
two d. are fighting   PROV 634:46
without are d.   BIBL 114:24
doileys soiling the d.   BETJ 72:8
doing As for D.-good   THOR 793:8
continuance in well d.   BIBL 106:1
d. in that galley   MOLI 541:22
joy's soul lies in the d.   SHAK 719:17
may not be d. much   RUMS 658:9
not be weary in well d.   BIBL 109:3
one way of d.   RUSK 660:4
put me to d.   METH 523:8
see what she's d.   PUNC 637:14
still be d.   BUTL 176:4
This is the Lord's d.   BOOK 142:10
doings child is known by his d.   BIBL 84:35
doleful Knight of the D. Countenance   CERV 205:9
dolendum d. est Primum ipsi tibi   HORA 398:6
dolente CITTÀ D.   DANT 255:13
doll d. in the doll's house   DICK 271:24
living d., everywhere you look   PLAT 596:18
dollar almighty d.   IRVI 414:6
Another day, another d.   PROV 614:22
billion d. country   FOST 330:7
costs only a d.   ARDE 24:12
dolmens d. round my childhood   MONT 543:22
dolore Nessun maggior d.   DANT 255:18
dolorem iubes renovare d.   VIRG 811:9
Dolores splendid and sterile D.   SWIN 768:11
dolorous d. mansions   MILT 530:23
dolour d. of pad and paper-weight   ROET 652:4
d. that they made   MALO 509:2
dolphin d.-torn, that gong-tormented   YEAT 853:10
mermaid on a d.'s back   SHAK 711:1
dolphins butter made of d.' milk   JONS 434:15
gentler d.   MOOR 547:9
dome d. of many-coloured glass   SHEL 729:2
d. of the sky   WORD 845:19
singing beneath the d.   VERL 809:2
starlit or a moonlit d.   YEAT 853:9
domes plump with d.   THWA 794:6
domestic appreciate d. bliss   SANT 666:9
d. business   MONT 544:8
d. sort which never stirs   SHER 734:2
Malice d.   SHAK 705:21
men call d. bliss   PATM 588:16
pleasures of d. life   GIBB 345:2
respectable d. establishment   BENN 67:10
domesticate d. the Recording Angel   STEV 759:25
domi Res angusta d.   JUVE 439:17
dominant Hark, the d.'s persistence   BROW 161:19
domination against white d.   MAND 509:13
dominations Thrones, d.   MILT 533:16
domine D., defende nos   GODL 351:19

dominion death hath no more d.   BIBL 106:12
death shall have no d.   THOM 789:6
d. of kings changed   PRIC 610:15
d. of the English   ANON 19:4
d. of the master   HUME 408:16
hand that holds d.   THOM 789:12
His d. shall be also   BOOK 138:23
let them have d.   BIBL 75:8
Man's d.   BURN 172:21
dominions His Majesty's d.   NORT 565:10
not set in my d.   SCHI 670:26
domino 'falling d.' principle   EISE 298:15
dominus D. illuminatio mea   BIBL 114:26
D. illuminatio mea   MOTT 552:7
D. vobiscum   MISS 536:10
Nisi D.   BIBL 115:5
domum Ite d. saturae   VIRG 814:11
domus Stat fortuna d.   VIRG 815:5
don D. John of Austria is going   CHES 216:7
d. manqué   LAMB 465:14
my back upon D. or devil   TENN 783:20
quiet flows the D.   SHOL 735:7
Remote and ineffectual D.   BELL 65:11
dona d. nobis pacem   MISS 539:9
Requiem aeternam d. eis   MISS 539:14
timeo Danaos et d. ferentes   VIRG 811:11
done Been there, d. that   SAYI 669:2
decide that nothing can be d.   ALLE 12:5
Do as you would be d. by   CHES 215:2
Do as you would be d. by   PROV 617:47
D. because we are too menny   HARD 371:17
d. the state some service   SHAK 714:30
d. very well out of the war   BALD 50:12
d. when 'tis done   SHAK 704:3
ever d. for us   FILM 320:23
he d. her wrong   SONG 747:5
If you want anything d.   THAT 786:26
Inasmuch as ye have d.   BIBL 98:26
Nay, I have d.   DRAY 285:23
not a genius, I'm done for   BALZ 54:11
not d. in a corner   BIBL 105:31
Nothing to be d.   BECK 61:13
remained to be d.   LUCA 495:2
something d.   LONG 491:9
Something must be d.   WHIT 832:11
surprised to find it d.   JOHN 428:19
that which is d.   BIBL 85:28
Things won are d.   SHAK 719:17
this that thou hast d.   BIBL 75:22
thou hast not d.   DONN 280:2
want a thing d. well   PROV 623:24
we have d. those things   BOOK 127:16
What could she have d.   YEAT 855:2
Whatever man has d.   PROV 634:2
What is to be d.   LENI 480:6
What's d. cannot be undone   PROV 634:10
What's d. cannot be undone   SHAK 707:3
what's d. is done   SHAK 705:20
what should be d.   MELB 521:7
dong D. with a luminous nose   LEAR 477:5
donkey dead d.   DICK 272:11
donkeys Lions led by d.   MILI 526:12
Donne another Newton, a new D.   HUXL 411:10
John D., Anne Donne   DONN 282:14
donné Si le Roi m'avait d.   ANON 21:2
Don Quixote D., Robinson Crusoe   JOHN 433:20
dons If the D. sight Devon   NEWB 560:1
don't about to marry.—'d.'   PUNC 637:4
damned if you d.   DOW 284:5
D. ask me, ask the horse   FREU 334:4
D. think twice   DYLA 294:6
doodle Cock a d. doo!   NURS 566:12
Yankee D.   SONG 748:11
doom changed his d.   CLEV 227:1
d. assigned   TENN 782:7
great d.'s image   SHAK 703:7
Master of the Day of D.   KORA 459:7
national d. is sealed   HEAR 378:9
regardless of their d.   GRAY 361:10
scaffold and the d.   AYTO 41:13
to the edge of d.   SHAK 723:24

doomed D. for a certain term   SHAK 684:30
d. to death   DRYD 288:11
Doomsday D. is near   SHAK 691:1
Doon braes o' bonny D.   BURN 170:13
door angel from your d.   BLAK 122:4
beating on the d.   YEAT 854:10
coming in at one d.   BEDE 62:7
creaking d. hangs longest   PROV 617:16
Death's darkness at the d.   BLUN 124:3
d. flew open   HOFF 391:17
d. must be either shut   PROV 618:20
d. we never opened   ELIO 301:10
handle of the big front d.   GILB 348:22
hard at death's d.   BOOK 141:17
I am the d.   BIBL 103:16
knock at the d.   LAMB 464:15
knocking at Preferment's d.   ARNO 28:4
knocking at the d.   SHAW 727:24
make a d. and bar   BIBL 93:21
my d. stayed shut   RACI 640:8
Never open the d.   GRAC 357:17
prejudices through the d.   FRED 333:7
rapping at my chamber d.   POE 599:5
splintered the d.   AUDE 35:21
stand at the d., and knock   BIBL 113:6
Then—shuts the D.   DICK 273:6
through the d. with a gun   CHAN 207:18
When one d. shuts   PROV 634:25
when the d. opens   GREE 362:16
whining of a d.   DONN 282:8
wide as a church d.   SHAK 717:32
wrong side of the d.   CHES 215:23
doorkeeper d. in the house of my God   BOOK 139:17
doormat d. in a world of boots   RHYS 646:16
d. or a prostitute   WEST 830:14
doors close softly the d.   JUST 439:2
Death has a thousand d.   MASS 518:5
Death hath so many d.   FLET 327:4
d. of perception   BLAK 121:13
D., where my heart was   TENN 778:26
Men shut their d.   SHAK 719:9
slamming D.   BELL 65:4
ten thousand several d.   WEBS 825:25
thousand d. open on to it   SENE 677:2
with both d. open   HUGH 406:15
ye everlasting d.   BOOK 135:6
your living d.   MILT 539:17
doorstep do this on the d.   JUNO 439:1
sweep his own d.   PROV 622:47
doorway from d. to doorway   VERG 808:11
dooryard last in the d. bloomed   WHIT 833:22
Dorcas D.: this woman   BIBL 105:5
dormitat bonus d. Homerus   HORA 398:15
Dorset FUNERAL MONDAY D.   TELE 776:9
dossier dodgy d.   NEWS 562:5
d. on his past   HOWA 405:10
draft d. produced   GILL 349:11
dot cherish the pale blue d.   SAGA 663:3
dotage Pedantry is the d.   JACK 415:3
streams of d. flow   JOHN 426:20
dote D. on his imperfections   EPHE 308:5
Dotheboys D. Hall   DICK 270:14
dots damned d. meant   CHUR 220:16
double Double, d. toil and trouble   SHAK 706:11
Labour's d. whammy   POLI 600:29
leading a d. life   WILD 835:20
peace of the d.-bed   CAMP 187:2
doubles d. your chances for a date   ALLE 12:15
doublet bought his d. in Italy   SHAK 708:27
tailor make thy d.   SHAK 720:27
doublethink D. means the power   ORWE 577:20
doubt Book wherein is no d.   KORA 459:9
curiosity, freckles, and d.   PARK 585:15
do not make one d.   NEWM 560:14
d. and sorrow   BARI 56:5
d. is Devil-born   TENN 779:18
Humility is the only d.   BLAK 119:23
in d., strike it out   TWAI 803:25
in d. what should be done   MELB 521:7

let us never, never d.   BELL 65:15
Life is d.   UNAM 804:9
more faith in honest d.   TENN 779:19
No possible. d. whatever   GILB 347:4
Our d. is our passion   JAME 417:23
philosophy calls all in d.   DONN 279:4
shameful to d. one's friends   LA R 469:12
sunnier side of d.   TENN 775:15
time will d. of Rome   BYRO 181:15
When in d., do nowt   PROV 634:23
wherefore didst thou d.   BIBL 97:10
doubter d. and the doubt   EMER 306:11
doubters cynics and the d.   FIOR 321:8
doubtful D. disputations   BIBL 106:34
I die d.   LAST 472:9
doubting D. Castle   BUNY 164:21
doubtless d. come again with joy   BOOK 142:24
doubts Ah whiles hae ma d.   PUNC 637:20
D. 'mongst Divines   SPEN 752:13
end in d.   BACO 42:13
His d. are better   HARD 371:11
Kind jealous d.   ROCH 651:9
my d. are done   DRYD 288:14
saucy d. and fears   SHAK 706:3
Douglas doughty D.   BALL 51:14
Like D. conquer   HOME 393:15
dove all the d.   CRAS 250:9
at eagles with a d.   HERB 384:22
d. found no rest   BIBL 76:7
on the burnished d.   TENN 780:15
sweet d. died   KEAT 443:17
wings like a d.   BOOK 137:16
wings of a d.   BOOK 138:12
dovecote eagle in a d.   SHAK 682:27
Dover farthing candle at D.   JOHN 428:18
milestones on the D. Road   DICK 269:22
white cliffs of D.   BURT 173:16
doves condemns the d.   JUVE 439:12
d.' eyes   BIBL 87:10
harmless as d.   BIBL 96:16
moan of d.   TENN 783:17
dovetailedness universal d.   DICK 270:25
dowagers d. for deans   TENN 782:23
dower faith's transcendent d.   WORD 849:24
truth then be thy d.   SHAK 699:18
dowie d. dens   BALL 52:3
down born with D.'s syndrome   DE G 262:13
D. among the dead   DYER 294:2
D. and out in Paris   ORWE 577:5
d. and out of breath   SHAK 691:17
d. express in the small of the back   WODE 842:23
D. in the forest   SIMP 738:9
d. into the darkness   MILL 525:20
D. to Gehenna   KIPL 454:20
Easy is the way d.   VIRG 812:9
fled Him, d. the nights   THOM 791:7
go d. to the sea   BOOK 141:18
Had me low and had me d.   GERS 344:4
He that is d.   BUNY 165:3
kicked d. stairs   HALI 369:10
knowest my d.-sitting   BOOK 143:14
little, lost, D. churches   KIPL 455:19
meet 'em on your way d.   MIZN 541:4
quite, quite, d.   SHAK 686:18
soft young d. of her   MEW 523:15
staying d. with him   WASH 822:5
What goes up must come d.   PROV 634:4
downfall regress is either a d.   BACO 44:23
downhearted Are we d.   KNIG 458:2
Are we d.   MILI 526:4
We are not d.   CHAM 206:9
downhill run by itself except d.   SAYI 669:4
downs in the D. the fleet was moored   GAY 342:10
downstairs kick me d.   BICK 115:20
downwards gross flesh sinks d.   SHAK 716:17
look no way but d.   BUNY 165:1
doxy Heterodoxy or Thy-d.   CARL 192:7
dozens Whom he reckons up by d.   GILB 348:21
drab Ditch-delivered by a d.   SHAK 706:13

drinking (cont.):

in a tavern, d.	ANON 21:18
merry, dancing, d.	DRYD 289:13
much d., little thinking	SWIF 766:2
no d. after death	FLET 327:1
Now for d.	HORA 400:20
drinks d. as much as you do	THOM 790:9
d. beer, thinks beer	PROV 621:46
get at the d. and food	CORS 243:18
dripping d. June sets all	PROV 618:25
D. water hollows out	OVID 580:7
electricity was d.	THUR 793:25
drive can't d. the car	TYNA 804:4
difficult to d.	BROU 154:13
drink and d.	OFFI 572:5
D. gently over the stones	PROV 618:26
I d. through the street	CLOU 227:20
driver in the d.'s seat	BEAV 60:12
drives Who d. fat oxen	JOHN 432:16
driveth d. furiously	BIBL 82:12
driving d. briskly in a post-chaise	
	JOHN 430:25
d. while looking	RODD 651:22
like the d. of Jehu	BIBL 82:12
drizzly every d. brain	BYRO 179:31
Drogheda endeavours at D.	CROM 251:15
drollery fatal d.	DISR 277:27
dromedary d., two	NASH 557:8
muse on d. trots	COLE 232:10
droning beetle wheels his d. flight	
	GRAY 360:24
droon d. twa	ANON 18:20
droop D. in a hundred A.B.C.'s	ELIO 301:6
silkworms d.	BASH 58:2
droopingly d., but with a hopeful heart	
	LAWR 474:20
drop as a d. of a bucket	BIBL 89:19
Drop, d., slow tears	FLET 327:13
d. in the ocean	TERE 785:10
d. into thyself	POPE 605:2
d. of Negro blood	HUGH 407:1
last d. makes the cup	PROV 624:47
like very well to d.	JOHN 431:22
Nor any d. to drink	COLE 232:20
thy clouds d. fatness	BOOK 138:3
turn on, tune in and d. out	LEAR 477:22
dropped heavens d.	BOOK 138:11
Things have d. from me	WOOL 845:10
wish to be d. by	JOHN 431:22
dropping Constant d. wears away	
	PROV 617:10
continual d.	BIBL 85:15
d. down the ladder	KIPL 454:7
D. the pilot	TENN 775:14
drops D. earliest to the ground	SHAK 709:23
d. on gate-bars hang	HARD 373:5
Little d. of water	CARN 193:11
ruddy d.	SHAK 697:1
drought blame it for the d.	MORR 550:15
d. is destroying his roots	HERB 383:7
d. of March	CHAU 210:4
d. of March	OPEN 576:1
drove d. them all out of the temple	
	BIBL 102:29
drown D. all my faults	FLET 327:14
I'll d. my book	SHAK 719:5
drownded d. now and again	SYNG 769:11
drowned BETTER D. THAN DUFFERS	TELE 776:2
d. in the depth of the sea	BIBL 97:20
d. in yonder living blue	TENN 779:27
d. my glory	FITZ 323:15
he was d. in	GILB 346:18
never be d.	PROV 623:22
drowning d. man will clutch	PROV 618:27
d. their speaking	BROW 160:09
like death by d.	FERB 316:15
no d. mark	SHAK 718:18
not waving but d.	SMIT 743:1
drowns d. things weighty	BACO 45:6
drowsy Dapples the d. east	SHAK 712:34
d. numbness	OPEN 575:4
d. numbness pains	KEAT 444:20
d. syrups of the world	SHAK 714:1

ear of a d. man	SHAK 699:7
drudge Lexicographer. A harmless d.	
	JOHN 424:10
drudgery love of the d.	SMIT 742:13
Makes d. divine	HERB 384:5
drudges laborious d.	KIPL 457:3
drug consciousness-expanding d.	CLAR 225:5
d. neither moral nor immoral	ZAPP 858:5
literature is a d.	BORR 145:12
Poetry's a mere d.	FARQ 315:21
you can d., with words	LOWE 493:18
drugs Sex and d. and rock and roll	
	DURY 293:9
twenty d. for each disease	OSLE 579:5
what d., what charms	SHAK 713:7
drum big bass d.	LIND 486:4
morning d.-beat	WEBS 825:13
music of a *distant* d.	FITZ 323:3
My pulse, like a soft d.	KING 451:16
Not a d. was heard	WOLF 843:10
Rhyme still the most effective d.	GIRA 350:3
Take my d. to England	NEWB 560:1
drummer hears a different d.	THOR 793:16
drumming d. in my ears	SAPP 666:14
in the valley d.	AUDE 35:20
drums d. begin to roll	KIPL 455:22
like muffled d.	LONG 490:19
drunk art of getting d.	JOHN 431:13
be not d. with wine	BIBL 109:17
drink and no be d.	BURN 172:17
d. for about a week	FITZ 324:4
d. him to his bed	SHAK 679:12
d. moderately	BIBL 93:24
d. old wine	BIBL 100:13
eaten and d. enough	HORA 399:24
fields have d. enough	VIRG 814:1
from Philip d.	ANON 15:4
genteel when he gets d.	BOSW 146:26
hasten to be d.	DRYD 288:6
I have d.	SHAK 721:27
inarticulate, and then d.	BYRO 184:7
made them d.	SHAK 704:19
must get d.	BYRO 180:22
Not d. is he	PEAC 590:2
not so think as you d.	SQUI 753:14
partly she was d.	BURN 171:17
stood by him when he was d.	SHER 734:15
this d. is drunk	DICK 272:4
Was the hope d.	SHAK 704:9
when men have well d.	BIBL 102:28
Wordsworth d. and Porson sober	
	HOUS 405:6
drunken brought d. forth	SHAK 680:8
children, sailors, and d. men	PROV 622:18
d. in my dreams	COLE 233:4
d. man uses lampposts	LANG 466:12
stagger like a d. man	BOOK 141:19
drunkenness sin of d.	JAME 416:24
druv Sussex won't be d.	PROV 631:35
dry barren and d. land	BOOK 138:3
But oh! I am so d.	FARM 315:5
done in the d.	BIBL 102:3
d. as summer dust	WORD 846:14
d. brain in a dry season	ELIO 302:5
dwelling in a d. place	COLE 234:6
in a d. place	BIBL 89:7
keep your powder d.	BLAC 118:7
keep your powder d.	PROV 629:49
oh, I am so d.	ANON 16:1
old man in a d. month	ELIO 302:3
on d. ground	BIBL 79:10
or being d.	ALDR 10:13
O ye d. bones	BIBL 91:18
refresh it when it was d.	BOOK 129:21
Sow d. and set wet	PROV 631:9
duality world appeared in d.	ZORO 860:5
dubious d. hand	JOHN 426:18
Dublin Dear, dirty D.	JOYC 437:1
ducat Dead, for a d.	SHAK 687:20
ducats O my d.! O my daughter	SHAK 709:7
duce in d. summo	JUVE 440:8
duchess blossom into a D.	AILE 8:32
chambermaid as of a D.	JOHN 431:10

every D. in London	MACD 501:11
I am D. of Malfi still	WEBS 825:23
That's my last D.	BROW 160:9
duck D. and cover	OFFI 572:7
just forgot to d.	DEMP 264:1
looks like a d.	REUT 645:13
duckling when I was the ugly d.	ANDE 14:5
ducks d., produce bad parents	MORS 550:17
I turn to d.	HARV 374:20
stealing d.	ARAB 23:19
due Give the Devil his d.	PROV 620:41
in d. time	BOOK 129:14
to every one his d.	JUST 439:3
dues Render to all their d.	BIBL 106:31
duffers BETTER DROWNED THAN D.	TELE 776:2
dugs old man with wrinkled d.	ELIO 303:19
duke D. of Plaza Toro	GILB 347:3
everybody praised the D.	SOUT 749:2
From tyrant d.	SHAK 680:22
fully-equipped d.	LLOY 487:15
knows enough who knows a d.	
	COWP 248:19
dukedom d. large enough	SHAK 718:21
dukes drawing room full of d.	AUDE 36:16
d. were three a penny	GILB 347:7
dulce D. est desipere	HORA 403:1
D. et decorum est	HORA 401:12
D. et decorum est	OWEN 581:4
D. ridentem	HORA 400:18
dulcet d. and harmonious breath	SHAK 711:1
dulci qui miscuit utile d.	HORA 398:13
dulcimer damsel with a d.	COLE 232:7
psaltery, d.	BIBL 91:19
dull at best but d. and hoary	VAUG 807:17
Clean. Christian. D.	SHIE 734:20
dictionaries is d. work	JOHN 424:8
d. and deep potations	GIBB 345:13
d. as ditch water	DICK 271:23
d. in a new way	JOHN 429:27
d. in himself	FOOT 328:5
d. it is to pause	TENN 784:15
D. 'mongst the dullest	CHUR 220:6
d. product of a scoffer's pen	WORD 846:15
D. would he be of soul	WORD 846:6
makes Jack a d. boy	PROV 614:20
not bred so d.	SHAK 709:19
paper appears d.	STEE 754:20
Sherry is d.	JOHN 428:17
smoothly d.	POPE 601:26
some d. opiate	KEAT 444:20
venerably d.	CHUR 220:8
very d., dreary affair	MAUG 518:22
What's this d. town to me	KEPP 449:16
who can be d. in Fleet Street	LAMB 465:3
dullard d.'s envy of brilliant men	BEER 63:5
dullness cause of d. in others	FOOT 328:5
d. and stupidity	ASTE 32:12
Gentle D.	POPE 601:22
his serene d.	FLAU 324:21
dumb as a sheep is d.	BIBL 90:3
d. presagers	SHAK 722:27
d. son of a bitch	TRUM 801:13
d. to tell	THOM 789:10
My lips kissed d.	SWIN 769:5
Nature is d.	TURG 802:9
otherwise I shall be d.	KEAT 446:18
So d. he can't fart	JOHN 423:17
takes 40 d. animals	SLOG 740:5
tongue of the d.	BIBL 89:11
dump What a d.	FILM 320:22
dumpling Diddle, diddle, d.	NURS 566:17
dun her breasts are d.	SHAK 723:26
Duncan fatal entrance of D.	SHAK 703:19
dunce dearest, you're a d.	JOHN 431:26
d. that has been sent	COWP 247:13
d. with wits	POPE 601:28
Satan, thou art but a d.	BLAK 120:5
duncery tyrannical d.	MILT 536:4
dunces d. are all in confederacy	SWIF 766:20
Dundee bonnets of Bonny D.	SCOT 673:3
longer in D.	SCOT 674:21
Dunfermline D. town	BALL 53:3
D. town	OPEN 574:30

dung die in their own d.   KIPL 455:3
d.-heaps   CHEK 214:8
Fulfilled of d.   CHAU 212:5
dungeons Brightest in d., Liberty   BYRO 183:7
dungfork man with a d.   HOPK 397:15
dunghill cock crowing on its own d.
    ALDI 10:11
crow upon his own d.   PROV 619:5
d. kind Delights in filth   SPEN 751:20
Dunkirk D. to Belgrade   DAVI 259:6
dunnest d. smoke of hell   SHAK 703:21
Dunsinane high D. hill   SHAK 706:18
remove to D.   SHAK 707:6
duodecimos humbler band of d.   CRAB 249:4
dupe d. of friendship   HAZL 376:13
duped be d. by them   LA R 469:12
dupes If hopes were d.   CLOU 229:11
durable true love is a d. fire   RALE 641:9
duration fallacy in d.   BROW 156:13
dure *Pourvu que ça d.*   BONA 126:19
dusk Between d. and dawn   MÜLL 553:21
each slow d.   OWEN 581:3
falling of the d.   HEGE 379:8
forty-three In the d.   GILB 349:8
dusky along the d. air   COLE 233:14
D. like night   BYRO 182:17
rear my d. race   TENN 781:2
dust blossom in the d.   SHIR 735:4
by our mother's d.   FORD 329:1
chimney-sweepers, come to d.   SHAK 683:8
D. and ashes   BROW 161:22
D. as we are   WORD 849:8
d. falls to the urn   VAUG 807:15
D. hath closed Helen's eye   NASH 557:21
d. of creeds outworn   SHEL 731:4
d. of exploded beliefs   MADA 505:7
d. of the Churchyard   DONN 282:6
d. on the nettles   THOM 790:17
d. return to the earth   BIBL 86:25
d. thou art   BIBL 75:27
D. thou art   LONG 490:18
d. to dust   BOOK 133:18
D. to the dust   SHEL 728:21
d. upon the paper eye   DOUG 283:18
d. was once the man   WHIT 833:21
d. would hear her and beat   TENN 782:1
enemies shall lick the d.   BOOK 138:23
Excuse my d.   EPIT 309:4
Fallen to d.   WILD 837:4
fear in a handful of d.   ELIO 303:9
forbear To dig the d.   EPIT 309:10
give d. a tongue   HERB 383:26
Grind them into the d.   BRAD 149:1
Half d., half deity   BYRO 182:21
handful of d.   CONR 241:2
honour turn to d.   MARV 516:2
Hope raises no d.   ÉLUA 306:6
in the d., in the cool tombs   SAND 665:18
in the d. my vice is laid   EPIT 310:17
Less than the d.   HOPE 396:9
little d. of praise   TENN 779:13
lovers o'er the d.   BYRO 178:8
Marry my body to that d.   KING 451:15
much learned d.   COWP 247:32
not without d. and heat   MILT 535:16
not worth the d.   SHAK 701:9
O'er English d.   MACA 499:7
of the d. of the ground   BIBL 75:11
peck of March d.   PROV 629:18
provoke the silent d.   GRAY 361:4
quintessence of d.   SHAK 685:24
raised a d.   BERK 69:13
rich earth a richer d.   BROO 153:15
shake off the d.   BIBL 96:15
small d. of the balance   BIBL 89:19
sweep the d.   SHAK 712:7
Tell flesh it is but d.   RALE 641:3
This quiet D.   DICK 273:11
throwing of a little d.   VIRG 815:3
To d. and ashes   LITT 486:16
we are d. and shadow   HORA 402:14
what a d. do I raise   BACO 45:34
Where can the d. alight   HUI- 408:3

with age and d.   RALE 641:11
without the d. of racing   HORA 398:20
writes in d.   BACO 46:24
dustbin d. of history   TROT 800:19
dustheap d. called 'history'   BIRR 117:1
dusty what a d. answer   MERE 522:22
Dutch fault of the D.   CANN 189:4
Dutchman on a D.'s beard   SHAK 721:4
Dutchmen water-land of D.   BYRO 181:24
duties d. as well as its rights   DRUM 286:11
d. of the heart   BAHY 49:15
d. will be determined   MORE 549:1
If I had no d.   JOHN 430:25
neglect of his d.   THOM 791:22
spiritual d.   HOBY 391:5
dutiful take note of the d.   VIRG 811:7
duty act of d. and religion   OSBO 578:14
as much a d. as cooperation   GAND 339:8
bounden d. and service   BOOK 132:3
citizen's first d.   GRAS 359:12
daily stage of d.   KEN 448:5
dare to do our d.   LINC 485:1
declares it is his d.   SHAW 724:20
die in one's d. is life   BHAG 74:14
divided d.   SHAK 713:12
do our d. as such   SALI 664:9
Do your d.   CORN 243:5
d. is to obey orders   JACK 415:9
D. is what no-one else will do   FITZ 324:12
d. of an Opposition   DERB 265:4
d. of government   PAIN 582:10
d. of the four classes   LAWS 476:5
d. towards God   BOOK 132:14
d. we owe to history   WILD 835:27
d. we so much underrate   STEV 759:18
every man's d.   COBB 229:17
every man will do his d.   NELS 558:19
Every subject's d.   SHAK 693:16
first d. of a State   RUSK 660:2
forgot that he had a d.   GIBB 345:14
God, Immortality, D.   ELIO 300:26
I have done my d.   LAST 473:22
I've done my d.   FIEL 318:15
life was d.   HOOP 395:20
little d. and less love   SHAK 694:12
Love is then our d.   GAY 341:16
Moor has done his d.   SCHI 671:4
Nor law, nor d.   YEAT 854:16
of the voice of God! O D.   WORD 848:17
only done my d.   TENN 784:3
owe a d.   BEHN 63:22
performing a public d.   GRAN 359:9
picket's off d. forever   BEER 63:9
sense of d. useful   RUSS 660:18
Such d. as the subject owes   SHAK 718:16
supreme d. of a man   LAWS 476:3
terrible notions of d.   CLOU 227:14
To accuse is my d.   SCHI 671:5
When D. whispers low   EMER 306:16
whole d. of man   BIBL 87:1
dux D. *femina facti*   VIRG 811:4
dwarf d. sees farther   COLE 233:24
my d. shall dance   JONS 435:19
dwarfish d. whole   COLE 231:15
dwarfs d. on the shoulders   BERN 70:11
State which d. its men   MILL 525:11
dwell all that d. in it   BOOK 133:13
constrained to d. with Mesech   BOOK 142:14
d. in a corner   BIBL 84:38
d. in realms of day   BLAK 119:16
d. in the house of the Lord   BOOK 135:4
d. in their tents   BOOK 138:17
d. in the land   BIBL 88:17
d. in thy tabernacle   BOOK 134:12
d. with sothfastnesse   CHAU 213:19
people that on earth do d.   KETH 450:4
dwelleth d. not in temples   BIBL 105:19
dwelling desert were my d.-place
    BYRO 179:16
d. in all things   UPAN 804:16
d. is the light   WORD 847:11
God's d. place   SIKH 737:8
lovely is thy d.-place   SCOT 675:5

dwellings amiable are thy d.   BOOK 139:15
dwells She d. with Beauty   KEAT 444:19
dwelt d. among the untrodden ways
    WORD 849:27
d. among us   BIBL 102:21
d. by the brook Cherith   BIBL 81:19
dwindle d. into a wife   CONG 239:17
dyer like the d.'s hand   SHAK 723:21
dyes stains and splendid d.   KEAT 442:20
dying achieve it through not d.   ALLE 12:16
attend a d. animal   YEAT 853:17
Autumn sunsets exquisitely d.   HUXL 411:11
behold you again in d.   STEV 760:15
bliss of d.   POPE 602:10
can't stay d. here all night   SHER 733:8
Christian can only fear d.   HARE 373:9
continually d.   PETR 594:1
distinguished from d.   SMIT 744:4
D. and living   ROOK 132:4
D. a very dull, dreary   MAUG 518:22
d., bless the hand   DRYD 289:22
d. breath of Socrates   JEAN 419:6
d. deer   AYTO 41:14
d. for a faith   THAC 786:5
d., has made us gifts   BROO 153:5
d. in the last dyke   BURK 169:4
D. is an art   PLAT 597:1
d. is nothing   ANOU 22:20
d. man's room   STER 757:7
d. may I hold you   TIBU 794:9
d. of a hundred good symptoms   POPE 606:26
d. of the light   THOM 789:7
d. remembers   VIRG 813:9
d. without having laughed   LA B 462:14
feel that he is d.   CALI 185:14
groans of love to those of the d.
    LOWR 494:22
he hung, the d. Lord   JACO 415:12
I am d., Egypt   SHAK 680:1
If this is d.   LAST 472:5
indisposeth us for d.   BROW 156:11
like a d. lady   SHEL 732:7
lips of d. men   ARNO 28:16
man's d. is more the survivors' affair
    MANN 510:13
mouth of the d. day   AUDE 35:2
My d. sight   BLOK 123:13
no more d. then   SHAK 723:31
not death, but d.   FIEL 317:13
nothing new in d.   LAST 472:12
poor devils are d.   PHIL 594:13
sacraments to a d. god   HEIN 380:4
Those d. generations   YEAT 855:8
to a d. god   CLOS 228:15
To d. ears   TENN 783:5
Turkey is a d. man   NICH 563:7
unconscionable time d.   CHAR 209:12
words of a d. man   LAST 472:14
dyke auld fail d.   BALL 53:15
February fill d.   PROV 619:46
last d. of prevarication   BURK 169:4
dynamite barrel of d.   MAYA 519:9
objected to the use of d.   STEV 759:6
dynamo starry d.   GINS 349:15
E E = mc²   EINS 297:13
each beating each to e.   BROW 160:7
eagle all the e. in thee   CRAS 250:9
e. among blinking owls   SHEL 729:20
E. has landed   ARMS 26:16
e. in a dove-cote   SHAK 682:27
e. in the air   BIBL 85:21
e. know what is in the pit   BLAK 119:17
e.'s wings, Unseen   KEAT 443:14
e. through the world had flown   WALL 818:10
Fate is not an e.   BOWE 148:2
In and out the E.   MAND 509:12
with e. eyes   KEAT 445:6
eagles e. be gathered   BIBL 98:16
e. be gathered together   PROV 634:41
E. don't catch flies   PROV 618:28
hawk at e.   HERB 384:22
swifter than e.   BIBL 80:28
with wings as e.   BIBL 89:21

wind's in the e.	DICK 267:16	
wise men from the e.	BIBL 94:5	
Easter E. energy about it	HEAN 378:7	
eastern against the e. gate	MILT 529:21	
E. promise	ADVE 7:23	
Eastertide Wearing white for E.	HOUS 404:6	
eastward garden e. in Eden	BIBL 75:11	
easy E. come, easy go	PROV 618:34	
E. does it	PROV 618:35	
E. is the way down	VIRG 812:9	
E. live and quiet die	SCOT 674:5	
e. to take refuge in	IBSE 412:14	
e. ways to die	SHAK 680:18	
e. writing's vile hard reading	SHER 734:4	
If to do were as e.	SHAK 708:25	
Life is not meant to be e.	FRAS 333:5	
Life is not meant to be e.	SHAW 724:18	
normal and e.	JAME 418:4	
rack of a too e. chair	POPE 602:6	
should be free and e.	OSBO 578:11	
Summer time an' the livin' is e.		
	HEYW 387:16	
Too e. for children	SCHN 671:13	
woman of e. virtue	HAIL 367:13	
Words e. to be understood	BUNY 164:12	
eat Big fish e. little fish	PROV 615:37	
Dog does not e. dog	PROV 617:48	
don't work shan't e.	PROV 623:17	
e. and drunk and lived	JOHN 429:15	
e. a peck of dirt	PROV 633:47	
e. at a place called Mom's	ALGR 11:15	
e. bulls' flesh	BOOK 137:9	
e., drink, and be merry	BIBL 100:32	
E., drink and be merry	PROV 618:36	
E. my shorts	CATC 200:14	
e. one of Bellamy's veal pies	LAST 473:10	
e. the fat of the land	BIBL 77:9	
e. to live	MOLI 541:10	
E. to live	PROV 618:37	
e. up and swallow down	MORE 548:7	
great ones e. up	SHAK 715:3	
have meat and cannot e.	BURN 171:20	
have your cake and e. it	PROV 635:30	
I did e.	BIBL 75:21	
I would e. his heart	SHAK 712:29	
Let them e. cake	MARI 512:7	
Let us e. and drink	BIBL 88:26	
let us e. and drink	BIBL 108:6	
lives to e.	SOCR 744:25	
neither should he e.	BIBL 110:20	
see what I e.	CARR 194:9	
shalt thou e. bread	BIBL 75:26	
Take, e.	BIBL 99:1	
Take, e., this is my Body	BOOK 132:2	
Tell me what you e.	BRIL 151:15	
thou shalt not e. of it	BIBL 75:13	
to e., and to drink	BIBL 86:12	
ye e. but ye have not enough	BIBL 92:13	
Ye shall e. it in haste	BIBL 77:30	
You are what you e.	PROV 635:23	
eaten e. and drunk enough	HORA 399:24	
e. by missionaries	SPOO 753:3	
e. by the bear	HOUS 403:21	
e. of worms	BIBL 105:9	
e. to death with rust	SHAK 691:28	
God made and e.	BROW 158:21	
They'd e. every one	CARR 195:8	
we've already e.	BENN 66:18	
eater great e. of beef	SHAK 720:8	
Out of the e.	BIBL 79:29	
eateth e. grass as an ox	BIBL 83:26	
Why e. your Master	BIBL 96:5	
eating Appetite comes with e.	PROV 614:27	
appetite grows by e.	RABE 639:15	
E. people is wrong	FLAN 324:18	
e. the sea	ROBE 650:1	
eats e. of the sweet fruit	UPAN 805:12	
Man is what he e.	FEUE 317:4	
eau L'e. verte pénétra	RIMB 649:5	
eave e.-drops fall	COLE 231:23	
ebbing e. sea	FORD 329:3	
Ebenezer Pale E. thought it wrong		
	BELL 65:22	

ebony hair as black as e.	GRIM 364:13	
his image, cut in e.	FULL 337:3	
ecce E. homo	BIBL 115:15	
eccentric E. intervolved	MILT 533:18	
ecclesia Ubi Petrus, ibi ergo e.	AMBR 13:1	
ecclesiam Salus extra e.	AUGU 37:9	
Ecclesiastes Vanitas vanitatum, dixit E.		
	BIBL 115:7	
ecclesiastic E. tyranny	DEFO 261:27	
ecclesiologist keen e.	BETJ 73:5	
echo E. beyond the Mexique Bay	MARV 515:9	
e. of a noble mind	LONG 491:13	
e. of a pistol-shot	DURR 293:8	
e. of a platitude	BIER 116:2	
E., sweetest nymph	MILT 528:23	
Footfalls in the memory	ELIO 301:10	
sound must seem an e.	POPE 604:9	
waiting for the e.	MARQ 514:5	
echoes Our e. roll	TENN 783:2	
stage but e. back	JOHN 426:13	
wild e. flying	TENN 782:27	
echoing e. straits between us	ARNO 29:2	
eclipse astonished at e.	ORCH 576:7	
at least an e.	BACO 44:23	
E. first	O'KE 572:21	
in the moon's e.	SHAK 706:13	
merciful e.	GILB 347:6	
total e.	MILT 534:26	
eclipsed e. the gaiety	JOHN 425:9	
eclipses Clouds and e.	SHAK 723:3	
ecology e. and antiwar	HUNT 410:11	
economic because of the e. position		
	ADDA 4:3	
cold metal of e. theory	SCHU 672:4	
demands of the e. process	TEMP 775:11	
e. law of motion	MARX 516:14	
not purely e.	TAWN 774:5	
vital e. interests	WEIL 826:22	
economical e. with the *actualité*	CLAR 224:22	
e. with the truth	ARMS 26:18	
economics E. is the science	ROBB 649:17	
it is bad e.	ROOS 653:17	
study of e.	SCHU 671:20	
economist e. to prove	KALD 441:5	
political e.	BAGE 48:21	
economists e., and calculators	BURK 167:14	
economize Let us e. it	TWAI 803:8	
economy E. is going without	HOPE 396:3	
e. of truth	BURK 168:14	
E. was always 'elegant'	GASK 340:17	
fear of Political E.	SELL 676:23	
It's the e., stupid	POLI 600:26	
Principles of Political E.	BENT 68:15	
There can be no e.	DISR 276:5	
ecstasies virgins in their e.	TENN 777:25	
ecstasy e. of being ever	BROW 156:19	
e. of betrayal	GENE 342:23	
mad with e.	TRAH 797:15	
ring the bells of E.	GINS 349:14	
seraph-wings of e.	GRAY 361:19	
What wild e.	KEAT 444:7	
ecstatic such e. sound	HARD 372:16	
eddy dizzying e.	ARNO 27:26	
Eden brooks of E.	TENN 782:11	
E.'s dread probationary tree	COWP 247:14	
garden eastward in E.	BIBL 75:11	
happier E.	MILT 533:3	
In E. the only wealth	FUEN 336:21	
loss of E.	MILT 531:4	
loss of E.	OPEN 575:6	
on the east of E.	BIBL 76:2	
other E.	SHAK 715:13	
Through E. took	CLOS 228:23	
Through E. took	MILT 534:15	
voice that breathed o'er E.	KEBL 447:15	
walls of E.	BYRO 178:4	
edge Come to the e.	LOGU 489:12	
dangerous e. of things	BROW 158:16	
hungry e. of appetite	SHAK 715:11	
teeth are set on e.	BIBL 91:13	
teeth nothing on e.	SHAK 690:24	
edged Science is an e. tool	EDDI 295:7	
edifice found that e.	DOST 283:4	

edifieth charity e.	BIBL 107:16	
Edinburgh travels north to E.	BEAV 60:11	
edisti e. satis atque bibisti	HORA 399:24	
edition new And more beautiful e.		
	EPIT 309:1	
editions e. of Balbec and Palmyra		
	WALP 819:9	
editor E.: a person employed	HUBB 406:12	
e. did it when I was away	MURD 554:20	
e. himself be attacked	TROL 800:6	
e. of such a work	STEP 756:2	
Edom over E. will I cast out	BOOK 137:26	
wisdom in E.	MIDR 524:18	
educate e. our masters	MISQ 538:22	
e. our party	DISR 276:3	
educated as an e. gentleman	SHAW 725:22	
clothed, fed, and e.	RUSK 660:2	
e. and the uneducated	FOST 330:8	
government by the badly e.	CHES 217:15	
women are not e.	CAVE 204:5	
education ask of e.	NAPO 556:12	
between e. and catastrophe	WELL 828:13	
By e. most have been misled	DRYD 288:19	
cabbage with a college e.	TWAI 803:23	
difference of e.	ADAM 1:15	
discretion by e.	JEFF 420:13	
e., education, and education	BLAI 118:16	
e. forms the common mind	POPE 603:19	
E. has been theirs	AUST 39:15	
[E.] has produced	TREV 798:12	
e. is a little too	CONG 238:27	
E. is what survives	SKIN 739:11	
E. is when you read	SEEG 675:15	
E. made us what we are	HELV 380:17	
E. makes a people	BROU 154:13	
e. of the heart	SCOT 675:1	
e. of the people	DISR 276:12	
e. produces no effect	WILD 835:15	
e. serves as a rattle	ARIS 26:5	
e.'s, more than nature's	WINC 841:7	
e. to Greece	PERI 592:22	
first part of politics? E.	MICH 524:5	
I do not call it e.	SPAR 749:28	
In e. no class distinction	CONF 238:8	
in their own e.	SCOT 675:3	
is a liberal e.	STEE 755:1	
liberal e.	BANK 54:16	
part of e.	BACO 45:28	
poor e. I have received	BOTT 147:2	
Real e. ultimately limited	POUN 609:10	
Soap and e.	TWAI 803:7	
Standards of e.	DAY 261:1	
substance of female e.	MART 515:5	
thank your e.	JONS 435:22	
that is e.	ROGE 652:16	
unfit of any to be used in e.	LOCK 489:1	
unplanned e. creates	VERW 809:5	
What does e. often do	THOR 792:25	
educe e. the man	BROW 159:25	
eels e. boil'd in broo	BALL 52:10	
effect found in the e.	BERG 69:6	
little e. after much labour	AUST 40:18	
name for an e.	COWP 248:15	
effective as e. as I should be	MORR 549:10	
effectually obtain e.	BOOK 130:20	
efficiency where there is no e.	DISR 276:5	
efficient and the inefficient	SHAW 725:20	
e. parts	BAGE 47:14	
have an e. government	TRUM 801:12	
effort e. be too great	ANON 17:18	
no e. is necessary	I-HS 412:19	
not the e. nor the failure tires	EMPS 307:23	
redoubling your e.	SANT 666:7	
Superhuman e. isn't worth	SHAC 677:19	
when you're making some e.	AESO 6:17	
written without e.	JOHN 433:21	
effugere Soles e. atque abire sentit		
	MART 514:19	
effugies non e.	CATU 203:11	
Égalité É.! Fraternité	POLI 601:1	
egg addled e. as an idle bird	PROV 614:34	
eating a demnition e.	DICK 270:23	
e. boiled very soft	AUST 38:16	

egg (cont.):
e. by pleasure laid — COWP 247:11
e. is, quite simply — SMIT 741:15
e. of a North African Empire — GLAD 350:20
e. of the wren — WHIT 833:12
e. on our face — BROK 152:2
From the e. — HORA 403:7
got a bad e. — PUNC 637:24
Go to work on an e. — ADVE 7:25
hairless as an e. — HERR 386:8
hatched from a swan's e. — ANDE 14:4
lays an e. — NEWS 562:20
looks like a poached e. — NUFF 566:4
one addled e. — ELIO 299:18
radish and an e. — COWP 248:9
See this e. — DIDE 274:2
shell of a snowbird's e. — KENO 449:14
egghead E. weds hourglass — NEWS 562:6
eggs all my e. in one bastard — PARK 586:11
as a weasel sucks e. — SHAK 681:4
e. at the smaller end — SWIF 765:12
e. for gentlemen — NURS 567:7
e. in one basket — PROV 618:14
grandmother to suck e. — PROV 618:17
Lays e. inside a paper bag — ISHE 414:9
partridge sitteth on e. — BIBL 91:4
roasting of e. — PROV 632:23
roast their e. — BACO 46:2
ways to dress e. — MOOR 547:10
eglantine with e. — SHAK 711:4
ego Et in Arcadia e. — EPIT 309:3
fulfils a man's e. — ROOT 654:17
egos from mutilated e. — PAGL 581:17
egotism e., selfishness, evil — GREE 362:13
egotist whims of an e. — KEAT 446:6
egotistical e. sublime — KEAT 446:16
egregiously making him e. an ass — SHAK 713:21
Egypt brow of E. — SHAK 711:28
E.'s might — COLE 231:4
firstborn in the land of E. — BIBL 77:31
first site in E. — GLAD 350:20
great cry in E. — BIBL 77:32
Israel came out of E. — BOOK 142:2
out of the land of E. — BIBL 77:37
there was corn in E. — BIBL 77:9
We do not want E. — PALM 584:22
wonders in the land of E. — BIBL 77:24
Egyptian E. to my mother — SHAK 714:7
Egyptians spoiled the E. — BIBL 77:33
eheu E. fugaces Labuntur anni — HORA 401:6
eight Pieces of e. — STEV 759:15
We want e. — ANON 19:18
eighteen before you reach e. — EINS 298:6
e.-forty-eight — TAYL 774:7
eightfold E. Path — PALI 584:6
eighty In a dream you are never e. — SEXT 677:16
rottenness of e. years — BYRO 183:16
Einstein Let E. be — SQUI 753:15
either e. to other — BOOK 133:12
happy could I be with e. — GAY 341:20
Elaine E., the lily maid — TENN 777:26
élan é. vital — BERG 69:7
elasticity Cheerfulness gives e. — SMIL 741:1
elbow e. has a fascination — GILB 348:6
elder but five days e. — BROW 156:25
e. man not at all — BACO 44:33
I the e. — SHAK 697:5
take An e. than herself — SHAK 720:23
elderly e. man of 42 — ASHF 31:11
elders discourse of the e. — BIBL 93:8
e. and the four beasts — BIBL 113:17
four and twenty e. — BIBL 113:12
Of those white e. — STEV 758:5
Eldorado E. of all the old fools — BAUD 58:15
elect dissolve the people and e. — BREC 150:17
I was e., I was born fit — GURN 366:2
knit together thine e. — BOOK 131:2
elected audacity of e. persons — WHIT 833:18
e. by the manhood — ELLI 306:4
will not serve if e. — SHER 734:18

election e. by the incompetent many — SHAW 726:18
e. is coming — ELIO 299:16
right of e. — JUNI 438:16
When you have won the e. — CARD 190:7
elections e. are won — ADAM 2:6
You won the e. — SOMO 746:1
elective E. affinities — GOET 353:8
e. dictatorship — HAIL 367:14
Electra Mourning becomes E. — O'NE 573:12
electric biggest e. train — WELL 827:8
E. Kool-Aid Acid test — WOLF 843:21
sing the body e. — WHIT 833:3
tried to mend the E. Light — BELL 65:16
electrical e. skin and glaring eyes — SMAR 739:18
electrician E. is no longer there — BELL 65:18
electricity e. was dripping — THUR 793:25
usefulness of e. — FARA 314:18
electrification e. of the whole country — LENI 480:7
electronic new e. interdependence — MCLU 503:14
elegance e. and ease — GAY 342:2
elegant Economy was always 'e.' — GASK 340:17
e. and pregnant texture — STEV 758:25
e. but not ostentatious — JOHN 424:25
e. simplicity — STOW 761:20
e. sufficiency — THOM 792:9
Most intelligent, very e. — BUCK 163:6
so e. — ELIO 303:15
with e. quickness — SMAR 739:17
You e. fowl — LEAR 477:16
elegy character of his e. — JOHN 425:5
whole of Gray's E. — WOLF 843:14
eleison Kyrie e. — MISS 536:15
element Thy e.'s below — SHAK 700:9
To the destructive e. — CONR 240:19
elementary E., my dear Watson — MISQ 537:11
'E.,' said he — DOYL 284:17
elements Become our e. — MILT 532:3
conflict of its e. — BYRO 182:21
element our e. mar — BYRO 181:17
e. So mixed in him — SHAK 698:29
formation of heavier e. — EDDI 295:1
I tax not you, you e. — SHAK 700:16
made cunningly Of e. — DONN 279:23
with the fretful e. — SHAK 700:14
elephant Appears a monstrous e. — COTT 244:6
at the E. — SHAK 721:8
can say is 'e.' — CHAP 208:6
corn as high as an e.'s eye — HAMM 370:5
couldn't hit an e. — LAST 474:2
E.'s Child — KIPL 456:16
English e. Never lies — IMLA 413:2
fit the profile of an e. — GAMO 339:1
herd of e. pacing — DINE 274:5
masterpiece, an e. — DONN 280:9
reality of the e. — JALA 416:22
sleeping with an e. — TRUD 801:2
thought he saw an E. — CARR 196:14
elephanto candenti perfecta nitens e. — VIRG 812:17
elephants e. for want of towns — SWIF 767:9
elevated generous and e. mind — JOHN 426:9
elevates e. above the vulgar herd — GAIS 337:15
eleven e. buckram men — SHAK 690:9
failing his e.-plus — PRES 610:10
fine before e. — PROV 630:4
our e. days — POLI 600:18
too long after e. — GERS 344:13
elf deceiving e. — KEAT 445:2
little child, a limber e. — COLE 231:7
elfland horns of E. — TENN 783:1
Elginbrodde Martin E. — EPIT 309:13
Eli Eli, E., lama sabachthani — BIBL 99:13
Elijah as E. did Elisha — BURN 173:9
E. passed by him — BIBL 81:28
E. went up by a whirlwind — BIBL 82:1
spirit of E. — BIBL 82:2
eliminated e. the impossible — DOYL 285:1

Elisha rest on E. — BIBL 82:2
Elizabeth my sonne's wife, E. — INGE 413:13
elk hunted as an e. — RIEL 648:8
Ellen fair E. of brave Lochinvar — SCOT 673:20
elliptical e. billiard balls — GILB 348:5
elm Every e. has its man — PROV 619:8
Round the e.-tree bole — BROW 159:17
signal-e. — ARNO 28:23
vine about the e. — DAVI 258:11
elms Behind the e. last night — PRIO 612:11
Beneath those rugged e. — GRAY 361:2
e., Fade into dimness — ARNO 28:1
in immemorial e. — TENN 783:17
elope e. methodically — GOLD 355:21
elopement love-story or an e. — DOYL 284:23
eloquence books be then the e. — SHAK 722:27
e. is tedious — PASC 587:14
e. the soul — MILT 532:8
ornate e. in our English — CAXT 204:7
parliamentary e. — CARL 192:19
power of e. — WIGG 834:16
simple e. ever convince — WALP 819:17
Take E. and break — VERL 809:1
Talking and e. — JONS 436:10
eloquent e. in a more sublime language — MACA 498:5
else happening to Somebody E. — ROGE 652:18
elsewhere Altogether e., vast herds — AUDE 34:27
There is a world e. — SHAK 682:19
Elsinore stormy steep, E. — CAMP 187:7
elves criticizing e. — CHUR 220:9
e. also, Whose little eyes glow — HERR 386:4
Elysian in the E. fields — DISR 278:1
Elysium brother he is in E. — SHAK 720:7
Keep alive our lost E. — BETJ 72:13
What E. have ye known — KEAT 444:5
embalming For my E. (Sweetest) — HERR 386:12
embarras e. des richesses — ALLA 12:4
embarrassment annoyance and e. — BAED 47:7
e. and breakfast — BARN 56:7
e. of riches — ALLA 12:4
keeps us in our place is e. — BENN 67:8
embers glowing e. through the room — MILT 529:12
joy! that in our e. — WORD 848:10
emblem e. of mortality — DISR 276:23
embrace do there e. — MARV 516:2
e. your Lordship's principles — WILK 837:19
most extraordinary e. — TREV 798:15
pity, then e. — POPE 605:3
embraces age in her e. — ROCH 651:8
embraceth mercy e. him — BOOK 135:21
embracing e. knowledge — POLA 599:12
embroidered heavens' e. cloths — YEAT 854:11
embroideries Covered with e. — YEAT 853:13
embroidery little daily e. — ELIO 299:17
Emelye up roos E. — CHAU 211:16
emendation e. wrong — JOHN 425:18
emerald green as e. — COLE 232:15
like unto an e. — BIBL 113:7
livelier e. twinkles — TENN 781:22
men, of the E. Isle — DREN 286:7
emergency compelled by e. — TROL 799:6
one e. following upon another — FISH 321:15
emeritus called a professor e. — LEAC 476:14
emigration doubt but that our e. — CART 196:23
e. system — JOHN 433:23
emigravit E. is the inscription — LONG 490:16
Emily E., hear — CRAN 250:3
eminence raised To that bad e. — MILT 531:29
eminency some e. in ourselves — HOBB 390:6
eminent death reveals the e. — SHAW 726:29
Emmanuel from E.'s veins — COWP 246:27
emolument positions of considerable e. — GAIS 337:15
emotion degree of my aesthetic e. — BELL 64:10
dependable international e. — ALSO 12:20
e. recollected in tranquillity — WORD 850:26
masses conveying an e. — HEPW 382:19

morality touched by e.   ARNO 30:3
sex without e.   PAGL 581:16
stirred by e.   THOM 788:12
thought charged with e.   GIDE 346:16
tranquillity remembered in e.   PARK 586:4
emotional e. agitation   ADLE 5:20
Gluttony an e. escape   DE V 266:6
emotions all the human e.   GOGO 354:1
e. were riveted   FOOT 327:26
for the noble e.   RUSK 659:12
gamut of the e.   PARK 586:6
metaphysical brothel for the e.   KOES 458:15
only two e. in a plane   WELL 827:10
realm of the e.   GIDE 346:11
receptacle for e.   PICA 595:5
refusal to admit our e.   RATT 642:14
Television strikes at e.   DAY 259:20
waste-paper basket of the e.   WEBB 825:2
world of the e.   COLE 234:13
emparadised E. in one another's arms
  MILT 533:3
emperice e. and flour   CHAU 212:24
emperor belong to the E.   BORG 145:5
Canadian out of the German E.   VAN 807:3
dey makes you E.   O'NE 573:8
E. has nothing on   ANDE 14:2
e. holds the key   CUST 254:13
E. is everything   METT 523:13
e. of ice-cream   STEV 757:22
E.'s drunken soldiery   YEAT 853:8
e. to die standing   LAST 471:12
sacred E.   BRAM 149:9
emperors E. can do nothing   BREC 150:9
great men even under bad e.   TACI 770:5
empire All e. is no more   DRYD 287:3
arch Of the ranged e.   SHAK 678:14
course of the e.   BERK 69:15
cut-purse of the e.   SHAK 687:26
destinies of the British E.   DISR 275:16
dismemberment of the E.   GLAD 350:18
E. splendidly isolated   NEWS 562:17
E. strikes back   FILM 322:4
e., vast as it is   CUST 254:13
e. walking very slowly   FITZ 324:8
evil e.   REAG 643:14
found a great e.   SMIT 741:9
glorious e.   BURK 167:2
great e. and little minds   BURK 167:1
Greeks in this American e.   MACM 504:1
How's the E.   LAST 471:18
ideological e.   NAIP 556:2
idlers of the E.   DOYL 285:4
Life, Joy, E.   SHEL 731:10
lost an e.   ACHE 1:10
meaning of E. Day   CHES 216:17
metropolis of the e.   COBB 229:19
nor Roman, nor an e.   VOLT 816:4
provinces of the British e.   SMIT 741:13
Russia an e. or democracy   BRZE 162:15
tread out e.   YOUN 857:10
unity of the e.   BURK 166:30
way she disposed of an e.   HARL 373:16
empires day of E.   CHAM 206:8
e. of the future   CHUR 221:19
Hatching vain e.   MILT 532:5
Vaster than e.   MARV 515:23
empirical e. scientific system   POPP 606:28
empiricist e. view   CHOM 218:9
employed innocently e.   JOHN 429:26
employee In a hierarchy every e.
  PETE 593:13
employer harder upon the e.   SPOO 753:2
employment e. for his idle time   WALT 820:19
e. may be reckoned dishonest   GAY 341:19
e. to the artisan   BELL 65:16
seek gainful e.   ACHE 1:9
emporium Celestial E.   BORG 145:5
emprisoned E. in black   KEAT 442:16
emptiness Form is e.   MAHĀ 506:12
great Australian E.   WHIT 832:4
empty Bring on the e. horses   CURT 254:8
E. sacks will never   PROV 618:38
e. spaces Between stars   FROS 335:13

e., swept, and garnished   BIBL 96:35
E. vessels make   PROV 618:39
fold stands e.   SHAK 710:31
house would e. be   BOOT 145:1
let me be e.   METH 523:8
rich he hath sent e. away   BIBL 99:32
singer of an e. day   MORR 549:13
turn down an e. glass   FITZ 323:17
very e. heads   BACO 46:20
world is e.   PALI 584:2
enamelled e. meadows   WALP 818:19
throws her e. skin   SHAK 711:5
enamoured So e. on peace   CLAR 224:18
enchanted e. isles   MILT 529:3
Enter these e. woods   MERE 522:23
holy and e.   COLE 232:4
Some e. evening   HAMM 370:7
enchantment distance lends e.   CAMP 187:15
Distance lends e.   PROV 617:44
enchantments e. of the Middle Age
  ARNO 29:15
e. of the Middle Age   BEER 63:4
enchants e. my sense   SHAK 719:20
encircling amid the e. gloom   NEWM 561:5
encompassed e. but one man   SHAK 696:11
encompasses God e. everything   KORA 460:7
encounter beyond the first e.   MOLT 542:16
e. darkness as a bride   SHAK 708:9
encounters Close e.   FILM 322:2
encourage e. those who betray   GAY 341:19
right to e.   BAGE 48:17
to e. the others   VOLT 815:11
encourager e. les autres   VOLT 815:11
end ane e. of an old song   OGIL 571:15
any beginning or any e.   POLL 599:13
appointment at the e. of the world
  DINE 274:15
at the e. of the day   TAYL 774:17
be-all and the e.-all   SHAK 704:3
beginning of the e.   TALL 770:20
Better is the e.   BIBL 86:7
came to an e. all wars   LLOY 487:17
commit adultery at one e.   CARY 197:13
continuing unto the e.   DRAK 285:15
draw to our e.   BIBL 92:27
eggs at the smaller e.   SWIF 765:12
e. badly   STEV 759:31
e. cannot justify the means   HUXL 411:6
e. crowns all   SHAK 719:28
e. crowns the work   PROV 618:40
e. in doubts   BACO 42:13
e. is bitter as wormwood   BIBL 83:38
e. is not yet   BIBL 98:13
e. is where we start from   ELIO 301:26
e. justifies the means   BUSE 174:20
e. justifies the means   PROV 618:41
e., never as means   KANT 441:12
e. of all things   BIBL 112:13
e. of a novel   TROL 799:8
e. of a thousand years of history   GAIT 337:18
e. of earth   LAST 474:6
e. of history   FUKU 336:23
e. of man is an action   CARL 192:27
e. of Solomon Grundy   NURS 569:15
e. of the beginning   CHUR 221:15
e. of these men   BOOK 139:2
e. of the way inescapable   PAST 588:3
e. of this day's business   SHAK 698:24
e. that crowns us   HERR 385:22
e. the gods may bestow   HORA 400:13
e. to be without honour   BIBL 92:26
e. to the beginnings of all wars   ROOS 654:4
e. to the old Britain   BROW 155:2
e. where I began   DONN 281:18
Everything has an e.   PROV 619:23
flood unto the world's e.   BOOK 138:23
God be at my e.   PRAY 611:3
God will grant an e.   VIRG 811:2
good things must come to an e.   PROV 614:10
highest political e.   ACTO 1:12
In my beginning is my e.   ELIO 301:14
In my beginning is my e.   OPEN 574:17
In my e. is my beginning   MARY 517:11

Is this the promised e.   SHAK 702:5
let me know mine e.   BOOK 136:4
look to the e.   ANON 22:3
Lord blessed the latter e.   BIBL 83:31
made a good e.   SHAK 688:13
make an e.   JONS 436:9
make an e. the sooner   BACO 44:6
middle, and an e.   ARIS 25:21
muddle, and an e.   LARK 469:7
on to the e. of the road   LAUD 470:5
Our e. is Life   MACN 505:1
reserved for some e.   CLIV 227:12
retard th'inevitable e.   SMAR 740:19
right true e. of love   DONN 279:8
sans singer, and—sans E.   FITZ 323:5
she had a good e.   MALO 509:1
terror without e.   SCHI 668:15
there's an e. on't   ANON 20:1
there's an e. on't   JOHN 429:4
there was no e.   CLOS 228:22
this day to e. myself   TENN 781:12
This was the e.   PLAT 597:10
till you come to the e.   CARR 194:21
unto the e. of the world   BIBL 99:14
Waiting for the e.   EMPS 307:21
war that will e. war   WELL 828:16
where's it all going to e.   STOP 761:14
Whoever wills the e.   KANT 441:10
wills the e.   PROV 622:16
world may e. tonight   BROW 159:29
world will e. in fire   FROS 335:14
world without e.   BOOK 127:19
endearing e. young charms   MOOR 547:12
endeavours e. are unlucky explorers
  DOUG 283:16
ended continued, and e. in thee   BOOK 132:7
Georges e.   LAND 466:5
Ilium has e.   VIRG 811:18
in 1915 the old world e.   LAWR 474:19
Mass is e.   MISS 539:11
Enderby Brides of E.   INGE 413:11
ending bread-sauce of the happy e.
  JAME 418:6
Don't tell the e.   TAGL 771:10
her certain e.   SHAK 722:19
makes a good e.   PROV 621:5
so quick, so clean an e.   HOUS 404:18
way of e. a war   ORWE 578:7
endless born to e. night   BLAK 119:15
E. Light   ZORO 860:3
in e. night   GRAY 361:19
is e. nothing   LARK 468:17
endogenous neoclassical e. growth
  BROW 155:1
endow I thee e.   BOOK 133:10
ends All's well that e. well   PROV 614:16
between e. and scarce means   ROBB 649:17
divinity that shapes our e.   SHAK 689:5
e. all other deeds   SHAK 680:5
e. by our beginnings know   DENH 264:5
e. of the earth   BOOK 138:6
e. of the world   BOOK 134:20
More are men's e. marked   SHAK 715:12
pursuing of the best e.   HUTC 410:18
endue E. her plenteously   BOOK 128:15
endurance e. and courage   SCOT 673:1
e. is godlike   LONG 490:8
endure Children's talent to e.   ANGE 14:14
e. for a night   BOOK 135:18
e. my own despair   WALS 820:13
e. Their going hence   SHAK 701:23
e. them   AURE 38:11
e., then pity   POPE 605:3
e. the toothache   SHAK 712:31
E. the winter's cold   SHAK 696:6
human hearts e.   JOHN 426:14
man will not merely e.   FAUL 316:4
nature itselfe cant e.   FLEM 326:12
potter and clay e.   BROW 161:5
stuff will not e.   SHAK 720:16
thou shalt e.   BOOK 140:19
endured can't be cured must be e.
  PROV 633:50

endured (cont.):
e. with patient resignation	RUSS 660:18
Once you e. worse	HOME 394:18
state to be e.	JOHN 425:27

endureth e. all things · BIBL 107:25
e. for ever	BOOK 141:22
mercy e. for ever	BOOK 143:11

Endymion In E., I leaped · KEAT 446:15
enemies alone against smiling e. · BOWE 148:3
assaults of our e.	BOOK 128:12
choice of his e.	WILD 836:15
conquering one's e.	GENG 342:24
curse mine e.	BIBL 78:22
e. be scattered	BOOK 138:10
E.' gifts are no gifts	SOPH 746:13
e. of Freedom do not argue	INGE 413:4
e. of liberty	HUME 409:1
e. of truth	BROW 156:21
e. shall lick the dust	BOOK 138:23
e. to a real artist	GAIN 337:13
e. to laws	BURK 168:19
e. will not believe	HUBB 406:10
forgive e.	BLAK 121:19
giving his e.	STER 756:18
left me naked to mine e.	SHAK 695:16
Love your e.	BIBL 100:15
making new e.	VOLT 816:21
no perpetual e.	PALM 584:19
not e. when we acquire them	SENE 676:29
number of his e.	FLAU 325:11
Our e. have beat us	BOOK 143:2
speak with their e.	BOOK 141:20
thine e. thy footstool	BOOK 141:20
we make our e.	CHES 216:22
wish their e. dead	MONT 543:19
you are now our e.	MUGA 553:5

enemy afraid of his e. · PLUT 598:10
better class of e.	MILL 527:12
bridge to a flying e.	PROV 624:4
E. ears are listening	OFFI 572:11
e. of good art	CONN 240:3
e. of my enemy	SAYI 669:16
e. of the best	PROV 621:9
e. oppresseth me	BOOK 136:14
e.'s main force	MOLT 542:16
e. that shall be destroyed	BIBL 108:5
e. that will run me through	BURN 169:16
e. to the human race	MILL 527:10
e. we're fighting	WALL 818:4
every man your e.	NELS 558:12
first contact with the e.	MISQ 538:11
greatest is inclination	BAHY 49:16
high speed toward the e.	HALS 369:18
Hush! Here comes the e.	COND 237:6
I am the e. you killed	OWEN 581:8
If thine e. be hungry	BIBL 85:6
last e.	BORR 146:12
life, its e.	ANOU 22:18
met the e.	CART 198:9
met the e.	PERR 593:5
Mine e.'s dog	SHAK 701:20
near'st and dearest e.	SHAK 690:29
no e. but time	YEAT 854:13
no little e.	PROV 632:17
not an e. in the world	WILD 837:10
O mine e.	BIBL 81:31
one e.	ALI 11:16
Our friends, the e.	BÉRA 69:4
potter is potter's e.	HESI 387:3
quieten your e. by talking	CEAU 204:10
see No e. But winter	SHAK 681:3
smitten a sleeping e.	YAMA 853:1
sometimes his own worst e.	BEVI 74:7
spoils of the e.	MARC 512:2
sweet e., France	SIDN 736:6
taught by the e.	OVID 580:12
vision's greatest e.	BLAK 119:19
war without an e.	WALL 818:16
will have upon the e.	WELL 827:11
your e. and your friend	TWAI 803:12

energy E. is Eternal Delight · BLAK 120:20
important source of e.	EINS 298:3
Symbol or e.	ADAM 2:16

enfants e. de la patrie · ROUG 657:1
Les e. terribles · GAVA 341:3
enfin E. Malherbe vint · BOIL 125:12
enfolded e. the earth · VIRG 813:3
engine be a Really Useful E. · AWDR 41:1
e. of pollution, the dog	SPAR 750:2
e.-room was never installed	BARN 56:10
He put this e. to our ears	SWIF 765:10
human e. waits	ELIO 303:18
I am An e.	HARE 373:10
in dirt reasoning e.	ROCH 651:12
Raised by that curious e.	WEBS 825:21
two-handed e.	MILT 530:7

engineer e. is a man who can do · SHUT 735:10

engineering E. with fabric · MUIR 553:14
engineers age of the e. · HOGB 392:5
e. of human souls	STAL 754:2
e. of the soul	GORK 357:3
not e. of the soul	KENN 449:6

enginer have the e. Hoist · SHAK 687:32
engines e. to play a little · BURK 167:6
England ah, faithless E. · BOSS 145:16
always be an E.	PARK 586:14
apple falling towards E.	AUDE 35:17
Be E. what she will	CHUR 219:13
between France and E.	JERR 421:16
bored for E.	MUGG 553:9
born and bred in E.	GAY 342:8
children in E.	NURS 566:11
Church of E.	CHAR 209:2
damn you E.	OSBO 578:24
deep sleep of E.	ORWE 577:7
end in the ruin of E.	SHEL 728:5
E.—a happy land	CHUR 219:15
E. and America divided	MISQ 537:12
E. and Ireland	BOWE 147:15
E. and Saint George	SHAK 693:5
E.! awake	BLAK 120:14
E. cannot afford to go on	BALF 51:4
E. expects	NELS 558:19
E. has saved herself	PITT 596:13
E. hath need of thee	WORD 847:14
E., home and beauty	ARNO 30:12
E. invented the phrase	BAGE 47:18
E. is a disguised republic	BAGE 48:9
E. is a garden	KIPL 454:8
E. is a nation of shopkeepers	NAPO 557:4
E. is an empire	MICH 524:6
E. is the paradise of women	PROV 618:42
E. keep my bones	SHAK 699:13
E., my England	HENL 381:16
E. not the jewelled isle	ORWE 577:10
E. one whose centre	UPDI 805:17
E.'s difficulty	PROV 618:43
E.'s green and pleasant	BLAK 120:15
E.'s green and pleasant land	BLAK 121:15
E. shall perish	ELIZ 304:15
E. should be free	MAGE 506:2
E.'s not a bad country	DRAB 285:13
E.'s on the anvil	KIPL 453:13
E.'s the one land	BROO 153:11
E.'s winding sheet	BLAK 119:14
E., their England	MACD 501:12
E. then indeed be free	FABE 313:13
E. to be the workshop	DISR 275:5
E. was too pure an Air	ANON 18:6
E. will have her neck wrung	CHUR 221:13
E., with all thy faults	COWP 247:28
ensure summer in E.	WALP 819:8
for ever E.	OPEN 574:14
gentlemen of E.	PARK 586:12
gives E. her soldiers	MERE 522:12
God punish E.	FUNK 337:10
Goodbye, E.'s rose	JOHN 422:13
Gott strafe E.	FUNK 337:10
Heart of E.	DRAY 286:1
here did E. help me	BROW 159:20
History is now and E.	ELIO 302:1
history of E.	MACA 498:11
in E. a particular bashfulness	ADDI 5:6
in E. people have	MIKE 524:23
in E.'s song for ever	NEWB 560:3

in regard to this aged E.	EMER 306:21
Ireland and E. seemed like lovers	
	TREV 798:15
keep your E.	MUGA 553:6
landscape of E.	AUST 38:24
leads him to E.	JOHN 428:8
Let not E. forget	MILT 536:1
lot that make up E. today	LAWR 475:11
no amusements in E.	SMIT 744:10
Nor E.! did I know till then	WORD 847:4
Oh, to be in E.	BROW 159:17
roast beef of old E.	BURK 168:7
Rule all E.	COLL 234:21
Slaves cannot breathe in E.	COWP 247:27
Speak for E.	AMER 13:4
stately homes of E.	HEMA 381:1
strong arm of E.	PALM 584:20
Such is E. herself	CANN 189:11
suspended in favour of E.	SHAW 725:13
That is for ever E.	BROO 153:15
that will be E. gone	LARK 468:16
think of E.	SAYI 669:7
think of the defence of E.	BALD 50:16
This E. never did	SHAK 699:16
this Realm of E.	BOOK 144:18
this realm, this E.	SHAK 715:14
to convert E.	PUGI 636:23
Wake up, E.	GEOR 343:7
we are the people of E.	CHES 216:12
who only E. know	KIPL 454:1
world where E. is finished	MILL 527:1
Ye Mariners of E.	CAMP 187:20
youth of E.	SHAK 692:31

Englanders Little E. · ANON 17:8
English as E. as a beefsteak · HAWT 375:16
attain an E. style	JOHN 424:25
baby doesn't understand E.	KNOX 458:10
bird-haunted E. lawn	ARNO 27:19
can't think of the E.	CARR 195:3
Certain men the E. shot	YEAT 854:23
Cricket—a game which the E.	MANC 509:11
diversity In E.	CHAU 213:14
dominion of the E.	ANON 19:4
E. a nation of	PROV 618:44
E. are busy	MONT 545:10
E. are foul-mouthed	HAZL 377:5
E. . . . are paralysed by fear	LAWR 474:21
E. are very little indeed inferior	NORT 565:9
E. at that time	WILL 838:5
E. Bible	MACA 498:23
E. child	BLAK 122:6
E. Church shall be free	MAGN 506:3
E. elephant *Never* lies	IMLA 413:2
E. home	TENN 782:21
E. in taste	MACA 500:1
E. is the language	BAGE 49:7
E. kept history in mind	BOWE 148:5
E. know-how	COLO 236:7
E. make it their abode	WALL 818:7
E. manners more frightening	JARR 419:1
E. never smash in a face	HALS 369:17
E., not the Turkish court	SHAK 692:20
E. plays are like	VOLT 816:18
E. subject's sole prerogative	DRYD 289:24
E. sweete upon his tonge	CHAU 210:15
E. take their pleasures	SULL 763:15
E. tongue I love	WALC 817:4
E. unofficial rose	BROO 153:9
E. up with which I will not put	CHUR 221:22
E. want *inferiors*	TOCQ 795:14
expression in E.	ARNO 29:18
fine old E. gentleman	SONG 747:14
flower of E. nobility	ORDE 576:10
fragments of the E. scene	ORWE 577:11
God does not love the E.	CARD 190:8
great E. blight	WAUG 824:3
happy E. child	TAYL 774:14
hard E. men	KING 452:17
in E. the undergrowth	EMPS 307:26
in the E. language	JAME 418:15
king's E.	SHAK 710:11
made our E. tongue	SPEN 752:21
mobilized the E. language	MURR 555:6

Most E. talk	JAME 417:17
My native E.	SHAK 715:7
our sweet E. tongue	FLEC 326:6
raped and speaks E.	ANON 15:3
really nice E. people	SHAW 725:12
rolling E. road	CHES 216:9
Saxon-Danish-Norman E.	DEFO 261:24
scarcely known in E. provinces	ORDE 576:11
second E. satirist	HALL 369:11
seven feet of E. ground	HARO 373:17
shed one E. tear	MACA 499:7
talent of our E. nation	DRYD 289:10
to the E. that of the sea	RICH 648:2
trick of our E. nation	SHAK 691:27
We be all good E. men	TENN 783:20
we E. will long maintain	CARL 192:12
We French, we E.	BIRN 116:18
well of E. undefiled	SPEN 752:2
writing in E.	JOYC 437:26
Englishman blood of an E.	ANON 16:2
blood of an E.	NASH 557:19
broad-shouldered genial E.	TENN 783:18
E. among the under-dogs	WAUG 824:8
E., Being flattered	CHAP 208:8
E. can't feel	FORS 329:8
E., even if he is alone	MIKE 524:24
E. in the wrong	SHAW 727:3
E. of the strongest type	DAVI 259:12
E. prudently avoids	TOCQ 795:13
E.'s consitution	AUST 39:4
E.'s home	PROV 618:45
E.'s word	PROV 618:46
E. thinks he is moral	SHAW 726:8
E. to open his mouth	SHAW 727:11
E. to rule in India	NEHR 558:9
Every E. is an island	NOVA 565:19
for E. or Jew	BLAK 120:3
Give but an E.	OTWA 579:14
He is an E.	GILB 348:25
He remains an E.	GILB 348:26
last great E.	TENN 782:14
No E. is ever fairly beaten	SHAW 727:17
not one E.	WALP 820:7
One E. can beat	PROV 628:32
one E. could beat	ADDI 5:3
rights of an E.	JUNI 438:15
There is in the E.	DICK 271:20
thing, an E.	DEFO 261:23
truth-telling E.	HUGH 407:12
what an E. believes	SHAW 727:18
Englishmen absurd nature of E.	PEPY 592:3
don't give E. an inch	BRAD 149:1
E. never will be slaves	SHAW 726:7
first to his E.	MILT 535:21
Mad dogs and E.	COWA 245:3
prefer to be E.	RHOD 646:11
very name as E.	PITT 596:12
When two E. meet	JOHN 424:16
Englishness all the eternal E.	CARD 190:9
Englishwoman E. is so refined	SMIT 743:4
Princess leave the E.	BISM 117:12
engrafted in E. word	BIBL 111:21
enigma e. of the fever chart	ELIO 301:18
mystery inside an e.	CHUR 221:4
enjoy business of life is to e.	BUTL 176:23
e. both operations at once	CARY 197:13
e. convalescence	SHAW 724:17
e. her while she's kind	DRYD 289:31
e. him for ever	SHOR 735:9
e. Paradise	BECK 61:30
E. yourself	BÜCH 163:3
have to go out and e. it	SMIT 742:16
inherent will to e.	HARD 372:4
we may e. them	BOOK 129:14
what I most e.	SHAK 722:29
who can e. alone	MILT 533:24
yet not to be	ELIO 300:8
enjoyed little to be e.	JOHN 425:27
still to be e.	KEAT 444:11
enjoying from e. themselves	RUSS 661:5
if you are e.	NESB 559:10
oh think, it worth e.	DRYD 287:17
enjoyment chief e. of riches	SMIT 741:7

complete e.	HUME 408:15
e. of all desires	TANT 773:4
from e. spring	TRAH 798:1
not for worldly e.	SADI 663:1
stock of intellectual e.	ADDA 4:3
was it done with e.	RUSK 659:22
enjoyments Fire-side e.	COWP 248:8
if it were not for its e.	SURT 764:20
insufficiency of human e.	JOHN 426:3
most intense e.	DOST 283:11
enlarge E., diminish	SWIF 767:7
enlargement stability or e.	JOHN 424:5
enlightenment leads to e.	PALI 584:4
supreme e.	MAHÃ 507:4
winning full e.	MAHÃ 506:11
enmities e. of twenty generations	
	MACA 498:17
enmity no e. among seekers	AUCT 34:13
there was e.	KORA 461:1
ennuie L'éloquence continue e.	PASC 587:14
ennuyer secret d'e.	VOLT 816:1
ennuyeux hors le genre e.	VOLT 816:2
Enoch E. walked with God	BIBL 76:3
enough eaten and drunk e.	HORA 399:24
E. as good as a feast	PROV 618:47
e. for everyone's need	BUCH 163:2
E. is enough	PROV 618:48
E.! no more	SHAK 720:5
e. of blood and tears	RABI 640:1
E. that he heard it	BROW 158:7
Give a man rope e.	PROV 620:37
Hold, e.	SHAK 707:18
not to go far e.	CONF 238:3
Patriotism is not e.	CAVE 204:1
'tis e., 'twill serve	SHAK 717:32
two thousand years is e.	PIUS 596:16
When thou hast e.	BIBL 93:16
ye eat but ye have not e.	BIBL 92:13
enquiries remote e.	JOHN 424:27
ense quam sit calamus saevior e.	BURT 174:5
ensign imperial e.	MILT 531:22
enskyed thing e. and sainted	SHAK 707:20
enslave impossible to e.	BROU 154:13
enslaved should have been more e.	
	CAVE 204:4
ensue seek peace, and e. it	BOOK 135:25
entangled middle-sized are alone e.	
	SHEN 732:24
Entbehren E. sollst Du	GOET 352:17
enter about to e. a room	EDDI 295:5
e. into the kingdom of heaven	BIBL 94:25
E. not into judgement	BOOK 143:22
King of England cannot e.	PITT 596:2
Let no one e.	ANON 21:8
rich man to e.	BIBL 97:27
shall not e.	BIBL 97:19
she may e. in	SPEN 751:8
you who e.	DANT 255:13
entered iron e. into his soul	BOOK 141:12
enterprise leave it to private e.	KEYN 450:16
more e. In walking naked	YEAT 853:13
voyages of the starship E.	RODD 651:20
enterprised not by any to be e.	BOOK 133:5
enterprises e. of great pith and moment	
	SHAK 686:12
entertain better to e. an idea	JARR 419:2
e. divine Zenocrate	MARL 513:24
e. four royalties	SALI 664:7
e. the lag-end of my life	SHAK 691:4
e. this starry stranger	CRAS 250:11
E., when they might instruct	MORE 548:5
Tickle and e. us	COWP 247:19
entertained e. angels unawares	BIBL 111:14
entertainment e. this week	PEPY 592:15
irrational e.	JOHN 425:6
mere gossiping e.	HUNT 410:5
proffered e.	TROL 800:9
enthral Except you e. me	DONN 279:22
enthralled but not e.	MILT 529:5
enthusiasm achieved without e.	EMER 306:22
no e.	LAMB 465:14
ordinary human e.	OSBO 578:18
with a holy e.	ROUS 657:5

enthusiasts few e. can be trusted	BALF 51:2
how to deal with e.	MACA 498:19
entia E. non sunt multiplicanda	OCCA 571:11
entice e. thee secretly	BIBL 78:28
enticing with her e. parts	ANON 17:1
entire E. and whole and perfect	SPRI 753:5
e. surrender	BELH 64:7
entrails golden e.	DRAY 286:2
swords In our own proper e.	SHAK 698:26
entrance give back my e. ticket	DOST 283:3
entrances exits and their e.	SHAK 681:9
entreat heaven daily	ELIZ 304:10
entropy e. of human thought	ZAMY 857:25
entrusted Those e. with arms	WIND 841:12
envelope e. of its technical forms	
	MAIN 507:21
semi-transparent e.	WOOL 845:3
envelopes backs of tattered e.	HOPE 396:7
envied Better e. than pitied	PROV 615:22
envious e. sliver broke	SHAK 688:19
Hot, e., noisy	YOUN 857:9
I am not e.	VIRG 813:14
environed e. with a great ditch	CROM 252:7
environment humdrum issues like the e.	
	THAT 787:5
environmental any e. group	BRUN 162:9
envy competition, and mutual e.	HOBB 391:2
E. and wrath	BIBL 93:22
e., hatred, and malice	BOOK 129:5
e. not in any moods	TENN 778:31
e. of the devil	BIBL 92:22
E.'s a sharper spur	GAY 341:26
E.'s greener	BALL 52:19
e. the pair of phoenixes	HO 390:5
extinguisheth e.	BACO 44:4
in e. of great Caesar	SHAK 698:29
moved with e.	BIBL 105:14
prisoners of e.	ILLI 413:1
Toil, e., want	JOHN 426:16
Too low for e.	COWL 245:21
with e. and revenge	MILT 531:7
épater é. le bourgeois	BAUD 59:3
epaulette been by any e.	THOR 793:14
Ephesians Diana of the E.	BIBL 105:22
Ephesus beasts at E.	BIBL 108:6
Ephraim grapes of E.	BIBL 79:25
epic E. writer with a k	STEV 759:32
name of E.'s no misnomer	BYRO 180:16
epicure Serenely full, the e.	SMIT 744:1
Epicurus E.' herd of pigs	HORA 399:7
E. owene sone	CHAU 210:20
epigram Impelled to try an e.	PARK 585:18
purrs like an e.	MARQ 514:6
What is an E.	COLE 231:15
epigrams despotism tempered by e.	
	CARL 192:9
epilogue good play needs no e.	SHAK 682:11
epiphany e. a sudden spiritual	JOYC 437:13
episcopal e. hat	AUBR 33:14
episode but the occasional e.	HARD 371:20
epistula Verbosa et grandis e.	JUVE 446:1
epitaph better have a bad e.	SHAK 685:30
carve my e.	BROW 158:20
e. to be my story	FROS 335:17
no man write my e.	EMME 307:19
not remembered in thy e.	SHAK 691:14
that may be his e.	STEV 758:24
epitaphs nice derangement of e.	SHER 733:19
of worms, and e.	SHAK 715:22
epithet e. for thee	MARL 513:23
epitome all life's e.	YEAT 854:14
all mankind's e.	DRYD 287:6
eppur E. si muove	GALI 338:11
equal all men are created e.	LINC 485:7
consider our e.	DARW 257:13
e. division of unequal earnings	ELLI 305:17
e. in dignity and rights	ANON 15:1
E. Pay	ANTH 23:5
e. to any other person	PRIE 611:13
e. with God	BIBL 109:24
faith shines in e.	BRON 152:18
law has made him e.	DARR 257:1

equal (*cont.*):

men are created e.	JEFF 419:10
more e. than others	ORWE 577:1
one e. eternity	DONN 282:13
separate and e. station	JEFF 419:9
talked about e. rights	JOHN 423:10
to that e. sky	POPE 604:24
we'll be e.	PAST 588:5
Woman is the e. of man	LOY 494:23

equality apostles of e. ARNO 29:9
E. for women demands TOYN 797:9
e. in the servants' hall BARR 57:1
e. or inequality HUGH 407:11
E. would be heaven TROL 800:7
liberty and e. ARIS 26:2
majestic e. of the law FRAN 331:19
not e. or fairness BERL 70:4
we value e. ADAM 3:12
equalization natural e. CHUA 218:20
equalize never e. BURK 167:10
equally [Death] comes e. DONN 282:5
equals commerce between e. GOLD 355:17
least of all between e. BACO 44:10
live together as e. MILL 525:16
peace between e. WILS 840:20
Pigs treat us as e. CHUR 222:19
equanimity face with e. GILB 347:14
equation each e. would halve the sales HAWK 375:12
equations beauty in one's e. DIRA 275:1
fire into the e. HAWK 375:14
in disagreement with Maxwell's e. EDDI 295:4
politics and e. EINS 298:11
equator join hands across the E. GLAD 350:20
equators North Poles and E. CARR 196:8
equi *currite noctis e.* MARL 513:6
currite noctis e. OVID 579:18
equinox when was the e. BROW 156:17
equity people with e. BOOK 140:15
equivocate I will not e. GARR 340:8
equo *E. ne credite* VIRG 811:11
eradication e. of conferences MAYA 519:10
erected least e. spirit MILT 531:25
eremite patient, sleepless E. KEAT 442:11
Erin for E. dear we fall SULL 763:13
fresh-stirred hearts in E. FERG 316:17
eripuit *E. coelo fulmen* TURG 802:13
eripuitque *E. Jovi* MANI 510:4
err e. is human SAYI 670:17
Man will e. GOET 352:12
mortal, and may e. SHIR 735:5
most may e. DRYD 287:9
prefer To e. ANON 20:5
To e. is human POPE 604:13
To e. is human PROV 633:9
errand thy joyous e. FITZ 323:17
errands Meet to be sent on e. SHAK 698:12
run on little e. GILB 347:5
erred e., and strayed from thy ways BOOK 127:15
e. exceedingly BIBL 80:26
erreur *L'e. n'a jamais approché* METT 523:14
error as an 'e. of judgement' SALI 664:16
E. has never approached METT 523:14
e. is immense BOLI 126:9
he is in e. LOCK 488:10
Hence into deadly e. SANA 665:12
leading his soul into e. AUGU 37:12
limit to infinite e. BREC 150:5
made the e. double CLAR 224:5
men are liable to e. LOCK 488:14
no dignity in persevering in e. PEEL 590:18
O hateful e. SHAK 698:25
positive in e. as in truth LOCK 488:13
stalking-horse to e. BOLI 126:6
troops of e. BROW 156:21
ut me malus abstulit e. VIRG 811:16
very e. of the moon SHAK 714:22
errors common e. of our life SIDN 736:17
e. and absurdities BURN 169:17
E., like straws DRYD 287:21
E. look so very ugly ELIO 300:19

e. of a wise man BLAK 121:20
reasoned e. HUXL 412:2
ersatz e. magic from the real BYAT 177:13
erupit *evasit, e.* CICE 223:17
eruption bodes some strange e. SHAK 683:15
Esau E. my brother BIBL 76:27
E. selleth his birthright BIBL 76:24
E. was a cunning hunter BIBL 76:25
hands are the hands of E. BIBL 76:28
escalier *esprit de l'e.* DIDE 274:1
escape Beauty for some provides e. HUXL 411:11
can be no e. from it CHUA 219:3
did not expect to e. TURN 802:18
e. can be shown PALI 584:14
e. my iambics CATU 203:11
Gluttony an emotional e. DE V 266:6
great ones e. PROV 625:31
let me ever e. BOOK 143:21
Let no guilty man e. GRAN 359:9
many deaths do they e. BYRO 181:14
nothing to e. to ELIO 301:5
What struggle to e. KEAT 444:7
escaped e. with the skin of my teeth BIBL 83:11
Our soul is e. BOOK 142:21
through language and e. BROW 161:4
eschew E. evil BOOK 135:25
escutcheon blot on the e. GRAY 360:18
Eskdale E. and Liddesdale SCOT 674:15
Eskimo E. forgets his language OKPI 572:22
esperance Now, E.! Percy SHAK 691:10
stands still in e. SHAK 701:6
espionage e. can be recommended WEST 830:10
espoused My fairest, my e. MILT 533:12
my late e. saint MILT 535:9
esprit *e. de l'escalier* DIDE 274:1
n'a jamais approché de mon e. METT 523:14
essay ends in e. MACA 499:2
e. much ELGA 299:2
esse *E. quam videri bonus* SALL 665:4
essence e. is very real LAO 467:10
e. of a human soul CARL 193:1
e. of human life MACD 501:3
e. of innumerable biographies CARL 191:17
e. of the true sublime BYRO 182:11
precedes and rules e. SART 667:1
essenced long e. hair MACA 499:6
essential e. ingredient PHIL 594:12
what is e. SAIN 663:9
established so sure e. BOOK 127:12
estate e. of the Catholick Church BOOK 129:18
e. o' the world SHAK 707:15
fourth e. of the realm MACA 497:19
holy e. BOOK 133:5
in mind, body, or e. BOOK 129:19
low e. of his handmaiden BIBL 99:31
ordered their e. ALEX 11:7
esteemed e. him not BIBL 90:2
estranging unplumbed, salt, e. sea ARNO 29:4
esuriens *Graeculus e.* JUVE 439:15
esurientes *E. implevit bonis* BIBL 115:11
état *L'É. c'est moi* LOUI 492:5
éteint *qui ne s'é.* RENO 645:10
eternal authority of the e. yesterday WEBE 825:6
boy e. SHAK 721:24
by the e. mind WORD 848:8
contact with e. beings ARIS 25:19
E. Father, strong to save WHIT 832:22
e. Footman hold my coat ELIO 302:17
E. in man cannot kill BHAG 74:9
E. in man cannot kill UPAN 805:6
E. Passion ARNO 27:21
e. rocks beneath BRON 152:21
e. silence PASC 587:8
e. triangle ANON 15:20
Grant them e. rest MISS 539:14
Hope springs e. POPE 604:22
Hope springs e. PROV 622:32

lose not the things e. BOOK 130:12
our e. home WATT 823:20
ourselves to be e. JERO 421:7
portion of the E. SHEL 728:21
Promised from e. years CASW 199:5
Robust art alone is e. GAUT 341:2
thy e. summer SHAK 722:25
way to e. suffering DANT 255:13
whose e. Word MARR 514:7
eternally things abided e. TRAH 797:16
eternities meeting of two e. THOR 793:5
eternity battlements of E. THOM 791:11
candidates for e. MORE 548:5
day joins the past e. BYRO 179:5
Deserts of vast e. MARV 516:1
e. hath triumphed RALE 641:12
e. in an hour BLAK 119:5
E. is in love BLAK 121:1
e. of print WOOL 845:1
E.'s a terrible thought STOP 761:14
E. shut in a span CRAS 250:12
E.'s sunrise BLAK 121:22
E.'s too short ADDI 5:5
E.! thou pleasing, dreadful thought ADDI 4:16
E. was in our lips and eyes SHAK 678:21
E. was in that moment CONG 239:2
Heads Were toward E. DICK 272:23
image of e. BYRO 179:20
one equal e. DONN 282:13
palace of e. MILT 528:18
pinprick of e. AURE 38:8
progress to e. SHAK 723:12
same sweet e. HERR 386:3
saw E. the other night VAUG 808:3
shadows of e. VAUG 807:13
Silence is deep as E. CARL 191:20
some conception of e. MANC 509:11
speak of e. BROW 156:25
speculations of e. ADDI 5:4
teacher affects e. ADAM 2:14
through nature to e. SHAK 683:26
travellers of e. BASH 58:5
Tree of E. UPAN 805:10
white radiance of E. SHEL 729:2
who love, time is e. VAN 806:21
without injuring e. THOR 793:3
etherized patient e. upon a table ELIO 302:12
patient e. upon a table LEWI 483:9
ethic protestant e. WEBE 825:3
ethical e. dimension COOK 242:2
nuclear giants and e. infants BRAD 148:23
ethics law floats in a sea of e. WARR 821:23
Ethiop E.'s ear SHAK 717:17
Ethiopian E. change his skin BIBL 91:1
ethnological in the e. section EMPS 307:20
etiquette It isn't e. CARR 196:3
Eton playing-fields of E. ORWE 577:12
playing fields of E. WELL 828:1
étonne *É.-moi* DIAG 266:14
étrange *é. entreprise* MOLI 541:14
Etrurian where the E. shades MILT 531:17
Etruscans long-nosed E. LAWR 475:1
Euclid E. alone has looked MILL 525:22
fifth proposition of E. DOYL 284:23
Eugene Aram E., though a thief CALV 186:10
eunuch female e. GREE 363:3
Female E. GREE 363:5
intellectual e. Castlereagh BYRO 180:4
kills me to be time's e. HOPK 397:17
kind of moral e. SHEL 730:20
prerogative of the e. STOP 761:8
strain, Time's e. HOPK 397:9
eunuchs seraglio of e. FOOT 328:1
euphemism e. for the fading power BLIS 123:9
euphoric In an e. dream AUDE 36:3
Euphrates bathed in the E. HUGH 406:19
Eureka E.! [I've got it!] ARCH 24:10
Euripides chorus-ending from E. BROW 158:14
Europe another war in E. BISM 118:2
arsenal of old E. HEGE 379:5

e. which I am almost ashamed of
                                    PEPY 592:15
sanctifies e.   POPE 603:15
trouble and e.   BELL 64:19
expenses e. run on   CATO 199:18
facts are on e.   STOP 761:11
meet all the e.   THOR 793:7
expensive how e. it is to be poor   BALD 50:7
experience all e. is an arch   TENN 784:15
balloon of e.   JAME 417:15
but recorded e.   CARL 191:16
can go beyond his e.   LOCK 488:9
custom and e.   HUME 408:11
e. and good sense   DU B 290:18
E. father of wisdom   PROV 619:30
E. has taught   TACI 770:14
e. has taught me   EDEN 295:11
e. is an arch   ADAM 2:10
E. is best teacher   PROV 619:29
E. is never limited   JAME 418:1
E. is the child of Thought   DISR 277:32
E. is the name   WILD 836:10
e. is what you get   SEEG 675:15
E. keeps dear school   PROV 619:31
e. one thing   BAGE 48:23
E., though noon auctoritee   CHAU 212:13
flower of any kind of e.   HUNT 410:3
founded upon my e.   DOYL 284:10
I have e.   CONG 239:8
know by e.   ASCH 31:6
know it from e.   ARAB 24:1
light which e. gives   COLE 234:8
man of no e.   CURZ 254:10
never had much e.   MARQ 513:28
Old Age, and E.   ROCH 651:12
one year's e. 30 times   CARR 193:16
part of e.   BACO 45:28
perfected by e.   BACO 45:28
refuted by e.   POPP 606:28
than e. in twenty   ASCH 31:5
to be filled in by e.   WILS 840:2
triumph of hope over e.   JOHN 429:12
trying every e. once   ANON 20:7
we need not e. it   FRIS 335:1
experiences lie the e. of our life   MANN 510:12
experiencing only by e. it   PROU 613:12
experientia E. does it   DICK 268:12
experiment best scale for an e.   FISH 321:17
e. is the best test   FARA 314:16
e. needs statistics   RUTH 661:18
e. to his own cause   SPRA 753:4
have them fit e.   DIRA 275:1
never tried an e.   DARW 257:16
social and economic e.   HOOV 395:21
tide of successful e.   JEFF 420:2
experimental e. reasoning   HUME 408:9
experimentalist really an e.   HODG 391:8
experimentalists e. do bungle things
                                    EDDI 295:4
experimentation e. an active science
                                    BERN 71:1
expers *Vis consili e. mole*   HORA 401:17
expert e. is one who knows more and
  more   BUTL 175:15
e. is someone who knows   HEIS 380:6
experto E. credite   VIRG 813:10
experts never trust e.   SALI 664:5
expiate something to e.   LAWR 475:8
explain e. his explanation   BYRO 180:3
e. man to man   STEI 755:5
e. why it didn't happen   CHUR 222:18
Never complain and never e.   DISR 278:4
Never e.   FISH 322:15
Never e.   HUBB 406:10
trying to e. it   SHER 733:24
explained e. ourselves to each other
                                    ADAM 3:3
Shut up he e.   LARD 468:10
when being e.   BALF 51:10
explaining forever e. things   SAIN 663:8
explanation saves tons of e.   SAKI 663:18
explanations Each day given e.   FRIS 334:21
expletive E. deleted   ANON 15:23

explodes line smoulders and e.   MAYA 519:9
exploits most brilliant e.   PLUT 598:14
explore E. farthest Spain   CLAU 225:11
explorers endeavours are unlucky e.
                                    DOUG 283:16
exploring end of all our e.   ELIO 301:25
explosive terrible e.   NIET 564:5
exposes man who e. himself   JOHN 431:13
exposition e. of sleep   SHAK 711:22
exposure unseemly e. of the mind
                                    HAZL 376:19
express down e. in the small of the back
                                    WODE 842:23
e. our wants   GOLD 355:16
e. yourself like   YEAT 856:12
Never e. yourself more   BOHR 125:10
expressed ne'er so well e.   POPE 604:5
expressing worth e. in music   DELI 263:10
expression conventional e.   MAHÄ 506:9
E. is the dress   POPE 604:6
impassioned e.   WORD 851:1
expropriated expropriators e.   MARX 516:15
expropriators e. expropriated   MARX 516:15
exquisite e. touch   SCOT 674:27
pleasure so e.   HUNT 410:9
extant pyramidally e.   BROW 156:13
extempore as his e. sayings   WALP 819:19
extend attempt to e. their system
                                    MONR 543:4
extension both have an ideal e.   SANT 666:10
extenuate nothing e.   SHAK 714:30
exterminate E. all the brutes   CONR 240:15
e. a nation   SPOC 753:1
extermination e. of capitalism   ZINO 858:11
extinct wild life's become e.   CHEK 214:6
extinction one generation from e.
                                    CARE 191:5
extinguished outflows e.   PALI 583:20
extra add some e., just for you   LARK 469:2
extraordinary e. man   JOHN 432:12
extras No e., no vacations   DICK 270:14
extravagance does not lead to e.   PERI 592:21
if there is e.   CATO 199:17
extravagant e. with his own   SALL 665:1
extreme e. part is most irritated   BAGE 49:5
If thou, Lord, wilt be e.   BOOK 143:6
extremes E. meet   MACD 501:1
E. meet   PROV 619:32
lean to wild e.   DURY 293:10
mean between the two e.   BOOK 127:11
other men's e.   KYD 462:8
two e.   CHEK 214:12
extremism e. in the defence of liberty
                                    GOLD 356:2
extremity daring pilot in e.   DRYD 286:20
Man's e.   PROV 626:5
exuberance E. is beauty   BLAK 121:8
irrational e.   GREE 363:1
exultations e., agonies   WORD 850:18
exulting people all e.   WHIT 833:4
exuvias *redit e. indutus Achilli*
                                    VIRG 811:16
eye apple of his e.   BIBL 79:2
beam that is in thine own e.   BIBL 95:13
bright e. of peninsulas   CATU 202:16
Cast a cold e.   YEAT 856:5
cast a longing e.   JEFF 419:17
close one e.   DOUG 283:19
custom loathsome to the e.   JAME 417:1
day's garish e.   MILT 529:15
every e. shall see him   BIBL 112:25
E. among the blind   WORD 848:8
e. begins to see   BRON 152:19
e., did see that face   ROYD 658:2
e. for an eye   SAYI 669:17
e. for eye   BIBL 78:6
e. in the back of the head   COLE 233:26
e. is not satisfied   BIBL 85:27
e. of a master   PROV 619:33
e. of a needle   BIBL 97:27
e. of heaven   SHAK 699:10
e. of man hath not heard   SHAK 711:26
e. of the beholder   PROV 615:4
e. sinks inward   ARNO 27:2

e. that can open an oyster   WODE 842:21
e. to the main chance   CECI 204:12
e. was backward cast   SPEN 751:19
great e. of heaven   SPEN 751:15
Green E.   HAYE 376:7
had but one e.   DICK 270:15
harvest of a quiet e.   WORD 849:3
he that made the e.   BOOK 140:8
If thine e. offend thee   BIBL 97:21
if you have the e.   HOLM 393:12
In my mind's e.   SHAK 684:9
in the twinkling of an e.   BIBL 108:11
language in her e.   SHAK 719:27
like a joyless e.   SHEL 732:5
looked into the e. of day   YEAT 854:9
man a microscopic e.   POPE 604:26
mild and magnificent e.   BROW 160:3
mine e. seeth thee   BIBL 83:30
Monet is only an e.   CÉZA 206:3
My tiny watching e.   DE L 263:8
neither e. to see   LENT 480:25
obscured that e.   KEAT 445:19
Of e. and ear   WORD 847:12
one e. is weeping   FROS 335:7
On it may stay his e.   HERB 384:4
Please your e.   PROV 629:26
see e. to eye   BIBL 89:29
seeing e.   BIBL 84:36
soft black e.   MOOR 547:20
still-soliciting e.   SHAK 699:21
through the e.   EPIT 309:6
to the e. of God   OLIV 573:4
unforgiving e.   SHER 734:1
untrusting e. on all they do   GELL 342:20
What the e. doesn't see   PROV 634:12
'with his e. on the object'   ARNO 30:7
with his glittering e.   COLE 232:12
With my little e.   NURS 570:16
with, not through, the e.   BLAK 119:23
eyeball e. to eyeball   RUSK 659:6
like a coal His e.   SMAR 740:15
eyebrows e. made of platinum   FORS 329:6
eyed one e. man is king   PROV 623:34
eyeless E. in Gaza   MILT 534:25
work of an e. computer   BETJ 72:14
eyelids e. heavy and red   HOOD 395:11
tired e. upon tired eyes   TENN 781:6
Upon her e. many Graces   SPEN 751:22
eyes all e. else dead coals   SHAK 722:13
And her e. were wild   KEAT 443:25
bodily hunger in his e.   SHAW 725:24
buyer needs hundred e.   PROV 616:19
chewing gum for the e.   ANON 19:5
Closed his e.   GRAY 361:19
Close your e.   SAYI 669:7
close your e. before   AYCK 41:3
close your e. with holy dread   COLE 232:8
cocking their medical e.   DICK 272:18
cold commemorative e.   ROSS 656:6
constitutional e.   LINC 485:13
cynosure of neighbouring e.   MILT 529:24
Cynthia first, with her e.   PROP 612:20
dark e. darting light   BYRO 180:23
death bandaged my e.   BROW 161:2
Donna Julia's e.   BYRO 180:10
doves' e.   BIBL 87:10
drew his e. along   AUGU 37:3
electrical skin and glaring e.   SMAR 739:18
Eternity was in our lips and e.   SHAK 678:21
ever more perfect e.   TEIL 775:9
e. are bright   KEAT 446:19
e. are oddly made   HAMM 370:12
e. are window of soul   PROV 619:34
e. as big as millstones   ANDE 14:6
e. as wide as a football-pool   CAUS 203:13
e. became so terrible   BECK 61:29
e. did see Olivia   SHAK 720:6
e. have all the seeming   POE 599:9
e. have seen   LOWE 494:7
e. have they, and see not   BOOK 142:4
e. like lead   BROW 159:13
e. like the fishpools   BIBL 87:21
e. of Caligula   MITT 541:3

failing from f. hands — MCCR 500:18
fails One sure, if another f. — BROW 161:13
failure Any f. seems so total — QUAN 638:15
  f. is an orphan — PROV 631:31
  f. of hope — GIBB 345:23
  F. of planning — HARE 373:8
  f.'s no success at all — DYLA 294:11
  not the effort nor the f. tires — EMPS 307:23
  Now we are not a f. — VANZ 807:5
  political lives end in f. — POWE 610:5
  tragic f. — ELIO 299:23
  Women can't forgive f. — CHEK 214:1
failures f. in love — MURD 554:13
fain F. would I climb — RALE 641:10
faint eating hay when you're f. — CARR 195:22
  f. heart ne'er wan A lady — BURN 172:23
  F. heart never won — PROV 619:37
  f. on hill — TENN 783:2
  F., yet pursuing — BIBL 79:26
  pray, and not to f. — DIDL 101:26
  reap, if we f. not — BIBL 109:3
  walk, and not f. — BIBL 89:21
  with f. praises — WYCH 852:14
fainted f. Alternately — AUST 38:25
  should utterly have f. — BOOK 135:15
fair All's f. in love and war — PROV 614:14
  anything to show more f. — WORD 846:6
  brave deserve the f. — PROV 628:5
  British f. play — AITK 9:3
  chaste and f. — JONS 435:2
  child is f. of face — PROV 626:28
  deserves the f. — DRYD 287:14
  dream of f. women — TENN 776:18
  F. and softly — PROV 619:38
  f. as an Italian sun — BANV 54:19
  f. as the rose — CHAU 212:25
  f. as the moon — BIBL 87:17
  f. defect of nature — MILT 534:7
  f. exchange no robbery — PROV 619:39
  F. is foul — SHAK 703:1
  F. is too foul — MARL 513:23
  F. play's a jewel — PROV 619:40
  F. shares for all — POLI 600:15
  F. stood the wind — DRAY 286:6
  f. white linen cloth — BOOK 131:5
  Fat, f. and forty — O'KE 572:20
  Give and take f. play — PROV 620:39
  If Saint Paul's day be f. — PROV 623:3
  I have sworn thee f. — SHAK 723:32
  kind as she is f. — SHAK 721:23
  make so f. — BERN 70:15
  never won f. lady — PROV 619:37
  not being f. — FILK 318:24
  not f. to outward view — COLE 231:3
  not f. to the child — FROS 336:2
  Outward be f. — CHUR 219:22
  Sabrina f. — MILT 529:7
  see them all so excellently f. — COLE 231:8
  set f. — BENN 67:17
  she be f. — KEAT 444:9
  She f., divinely fair — MILT 533:29
  so f. that they called him — AUBR 33:20
  So foul and f. a day — SHAK 703:8
  sweet and f. she seems — WALL 818:6
  Thou art all f. — BIBL 87:11
  thou art f., my love — BIBL 87:10
  Trottin' to the f. — GRAV 360:1
  Turn about is f. play — PROV 633:25
  what's right and f. — HUGH 407:13
  With you f. maid — SONG 747:1
  woman true and f. — DONN 281:10
fairer f. way is not much about — BACO 43:3
fairest F. Isle — DRYD 288:27
  f. of creation — MILT 534:2
  f. things have fleetest end — THOM 791:5
  From f. creatures — SHAK 722:21
  Who is the f. of them all — GRIM 364:14
fairies beginning of f. — BARR 57:2
  don't believe in f. — BARR 57:3
  Do you believe in f. — BARR 57:3
  f. at the bottom of our garden — FYLE 337:12
  f. left off dancing — SELD 676:8
  f.' midwife — SHAK 717:15

F. Were of the old profession — CORB 243:2
  rewards and F. — CORB 242:18
fairy believes it was a f. — AUBR 34:3
  By f. hands — COLL 235:13
  cradle of the f. queen — SHAK 711:10
  f. kind of writing — DRYD 288:25
  f. when she's forty — HENL 381:12
  Like f. gifts fading — MOOR 547:12
  myth not a f. story — RYLE 662:2
  near our f. queen — SHAK 711:6
  No f. takes — SHAK 683:18
  'tis almost f. time — SHAK 712:5
fairy-tale f. of olden times — HEIN 379:15
fait un seul f. accompli — BOIL 125:14
faith author and finisher of our f. — BIBL 111:10
  breastplate of f. — BIBL 110:17
  Catholic F. — BOOK 128:21
  children in whom is no f. — BIBL 79:3
  connected with serene f. — MAHA 507:4
  died in f. — BIBL 111:8
  do very little with f. — BUTL 177:3
  Draw near with f. — BOOK 131:7
  dying for a f. — THAC 786:5
  f. and morals hold — WORD 847:3
  f. as a grain of mustard seed — BIBL 97:18
  f. hath made thee whole — BIBL 96:9
  f., hope, charity, these three — BIBL 107:25
  f. I am searching for — SAND 665:16
  f. in a nation of sectaries — DISR 277:4
  f. in our united crusade — ROOS 654:3
  f. in the people — DICK 272:20
  F. is an excitement — SAND 665:15
  F. is defying — BARN 56:17
  f. is something you die for — BENN 67:3
  f. is the state — TILL 794:16
  F. is the substance — BIBL 111:6
  F. of our Fathers — FABE 313:12
  f. of the heart — LUTH 496:12
  f. shall be my shield — ASKE 31:20
  f. shall wax — DANI 255:6
  f. shines equal — BRON 152:18
  f.'s transcendent dower — WORD 849:24
  f. that looks through death — WORD 848:14
  f. unfaithful — TENN 778:1
  F. will move mountains — PROV 619:41
  F. without doubt — UNAM 804:9
  F. without works — BIBL 111:25
  fight with f. and win — SIKH 737:7
  first article of my f. — GAND 339:7
  fought for Queen and F. — TENN 784:3
  good fight of f. — BIBL 110:27
  have f. — LUTH 496:7
  if ye break f. — MCCR 500:18
  In this f. I wish to live — VILL 810:13
  in thy f. and fear — BOOK 131:16
  just shall live by f. — BIBL 105:36
  kept the f. — BIBL 111:1
  left to f. — BYRO 180:29
  Let us have f. — LINC 485:1
  more f. in honest doubt — TENN 779:19
  of the f. — AMIS 13:11
  O thou of little f. — BIBL 97:10
  scientific f.'s absurd — BROW 159:7
  Sea of F. — ARNO 27:3
  seat to f. assigned — SMAR 740:16
  shake a man's f. in himself — SHAW 724:24
  shield of f. — BIBL 109:21
  so great f. — BIBL 95:29
  sudden explosions of f. — BREN 150:21
  test of f. — ADDA 3:18
  though I have all f. — BIBL 107:25
  unity of the f. — BIBL 109:11
  What more could fright my f. — DRYD 288:14
  What of the f. — HARD 373:1
  whoever is moved by f. — HUME 408:11
  work of f. — BIBL 110:15
  World, you have kept f. — HARD 372:18
faithful company of all f. people — BOOK 132:4
  Ever f., ever sure — MILT 529:28
  f. and just to me — SHAK 697:24
  F. and True — BIBL 114:11
  F. are the wounds — BIBL 85:14
  f. female friend — WHUR 834:9

  f. in that which is least — BIBL 101:21
  f. to thee, Cynara — DOWS 284:6
  f. unto death — BIBL 113:2
  good and f. servant — BIBL 98:21
  mentally f. to himself — PAIN 582:3
  O come, all ye f. — ANON 21:12
  So f. in love — SCOT 673:19
faithfully ask f. — BOOK 130:20
faithfulness Great is thy f. — CHIS 218:5
faithless Be not f. — BIBL 104:15
  f. and stubborn generation — BOOK 130:9
  F. as the winds — SEDL 675:12
  f. coldness of the times — TENN 779:23
  Human on my f. arm — AUDE 35:11
faiths men's f. are wafer-cakes — SHAK 693:3
fake Anything that consoles is f. — MURD 554:17
falcon dapple-dawn-drawn F. — HOPK 397:10
  f., towering in her pride — SHAK 705:15
  Gentle as f. — SKEL 739:6
falconer O! for a f.'s voice — SHAK 717:27
Falklands F. Factor — THAT 787:6
  F. thing was a fight — BORG 145:8
fall all such as f. — BOOK 134:6
  and half to f. — POPE 605:1
  Another thing to f. — SHAK 707:23
  before a f. — BIBL 84:26
  by dividing we f. — DICK 273:15
  dew shall weep thy f. — HERB 385:4
  did he f. — JAME 418:18
  F. and cease — SHAK 702:5
  f. by little and little — BIBL 93:18
  f. flat on your face — THUR 793:26
  f. in love today — GERS 344:5
  f. into it — BIBL 86:17
  f. into the hands — BIBL 111:5
  f. into the hands of God — TENN 784:2
  f. into the hands of the Lord — BIBL 93:3
  f. like rain — AUDE 36:13
  f. not out among yourselves — ASTL 32:18
  f. not out by the way — BIBL 77:10
  F. on us — BIBL 113:15
  f. out with those we love — TENN 782:24
  f. to rise — BROW 158:11
  f. without shaking — MONT 543:9
  fear no f. — BUNY 165:3
  further they have to f. — FITZ 324:13
  great was the f. — BIBL 95:25
  harder they f. — PROV 615:39
  hard rain's a gonna f. — DYLA 294:7
  His f. was destined — JOHN 426:18
  Humpty Dumpty had a great f. — NURS 567:10
  it had a dying f. — SHAK 720:4
  less likely to f. — GAY 341:22
  Life is a horizontal f. — COCT 230:2
  never f. — BOOK 134:13
  O! what a f. was there — SHAK 698:3
  Pride goes before a f. — PROV 629:40
  raise up them that f. — BOOK 129:11
  rise by other's f. — SOUT 749:21
  Then f., Caesar — SHAK 697:10
  Things f. apart — YEAT 855:12
  thousand shall f. — BOOK 140:3
  to human nature by the f. — DENN 264:14
  Weak men must f. — SHAK 715:19
  We all f. down — NURS 569:9
  we should happen to f. — LEAR 477:12
  worship and f. down — BOOK 140:10
  yet I fear to f. — RALE 641:10
fallacy Pathetic F. — RUSK 659:13
fallen Babylon is f. — BIBL 114:2
  Christopher Robin has f. — MORT 551:5
  F. by mistaken rules — WINC 841:7
  f. by the edge of the sword — BIBL 93:20
  F. cold and dead — WHIT 833:5
  f. from grace — BIBL 108:28
  f. from heaven — BIBL 88:24
  f. into the midst of it — BOOK 137:22
  good man f. among Fabians — LENI 480:9
  how are the mighty f. — BIBL 80:27
  lay great and greatly f. — HOME 394:8
  lot is f. unto me — BOOK 134:14
  people who have never f. — PAST 587:20

fallen (*cont.*):
planets had f. on me — TRUM 801:5
say a man is f. in love — STER 757:10
Though f. thyself — WORD 850:18
throned Cytherean be f. — SWIN 768:23
fallere *Quis f. possit amantem* — VIRG 812:2
falleth where the tree f. — BIBL 86:21
falling amidst a f. world — ADDI 4:23
apple f. towards England — AUDE 35:17
catch a f. star — DONN 281:9
'f. domino' principle — EISE 298:15
f. from stair to stair — BAYL 59:8
f. sickness — SHAK 696:16
load a f. man — SHAK 695:23
my feet from f. — BOOK 142:6
fallings F. from us, vanishings — WORD 848:11
fallow like a rude f. lies — IRWI 414:7
falls f. far from tree — PROV 614:29
F. the Shadow — ELIO 302:7
F. with the leaf — FLET 327:2
sudden f. — PROV 621:37
false all was f. and hollow — MILT 531:30
bear f. witness — BIBL 78:5
Beware of f. prophets — BIBL 95:21
f. creation — SHAK 704:16
f. face must hide — SHAK 704:14
f., fleeting, perjured — SHAK 716:28
f. gift — BIBL 85:4
f. report, if believed — MEDI 520:7
f. sincere — POPE 603:20
f. to any man — SHAK 684:20
f. to others — BACO 46:1
Followed f. lights — DRYD 288:13
If she be f. — SHAK 713:30
in f. grief hiding — SPEN 751:18
in perils among f. brethren — BIBL 108:22
Man, f. man — LEE 478:21
one f. step — AUST 40:2
perish with our f. theories — POPP 607:6
philosopher, as equally f. — GIBB 344:18
Ring out the f. — TENN 779:22
Thou f. to him — BYRO 183:3
unweaving of f. impressions — ELIO 300:21
women never so f. — LYLY 497:1
wouldst not play f. — SHAK 703:18
falsehood cuts f. like a knife — GURN 366:1
express lying or f. — SWIF 765:16
F. has a perennial spring — BURK 166:15
Let her and F. grapple — MILT 535:25
neither Truth nor F. — HOBB 390:4
strife of Truth with F. — LOWE 494:3
To unmask f. — SHAK 722:18
falsehoods f. which interest dictates — JOHN 424:17
led to f. — TALM 772:10
falsely do f. boast — BOOK 144:20
prophets prophesy f. — BIBL 90:25
falseness pleasure in proving their f. — DARW 257:4
produce in us a f. — RUSK 659:13
falser f. than vows made in wine — SHAK 681:26
falsifiability f. of a system — POPP 606:28
Falstaff F. shall die — SHAK 692:25
F. sweats to death — SHAK 690:2
sweet Jack F. — SHAK 690:19
falter not the time to f. — BLAI 119:2
falters f. that never f. — SPRI 753:5
Famagusta F. and the hidden sun — FLEC 326:4
fame best f. is a writer's fame — LEBO 478:7
blush to find it f. — POPE 605:27
call the Temple of F. — LICH 484:8
came here for f. — DISR 278:10
Common f. is seldom — PROV 617:4
damned to everlasting f. — POPE 605:11
damned to F. — POPE 601:25
establishment of my f. — GIBB 345:21
F. and tranquillity — MONT 544:11
F. is a food — DOBS 278:16
F. is like a river — BACO 45:6
F. is no plant — MILT 530:4
F. is the spur — MILT 530:2
food is love and f. — SHEL 729:9

for his f. — BARN 56:16
gate to good f. — BACO 44:4
gives immortal f. — YOUN 857:6
her f. survives — MILT 535:1
love and f. — KEAT 445:25
Love of f. is the last thing — TACI 770:12
Man dreams of f. — TENN 778:7
mistook it for f. — GOLD 355:8
My f. will grow — HORA 402:5
no one shall work for f. — KIPL 456:5
nor yet a fool to f. — POPE 602:25
Oh my f. Live — CHAP 208:11
Physicians of the Utmost F. — BELL 64:21
purchase f. In keen iambics — DRYD 288:32
servants of f. — BACO 44:21
to f. unknown — GRAY 361:8
What is f. — GRAI 358:16
famed France, f. in all great arts — ARNO 29:1
fames *Aura sacra f.* — VIRG 811:22
Metus et malesuada F. — VIRG 812:12
familiar f. friend — BOOK 136:10
mine own f. friend — BOOK 137:17
old f. faces — LAMB 464:21
familiarity F. breeds contempt — PROV 619:42
F. breeds contempt — TWAI 803:19
families American f. more like — BUSH 175:2
antediluvian f. — CONG 238:26
best-regulated f. — DICK 268:23
best-regulated f. — PROV 614:1
f. fatal to the Commonwealth — DRUM 286:14
f. in a country village — AUST 40:16
f. last not three oaks — BROW 156:14
f. shopping at night — GINS 349:17
Great f. of yesterday — DEFO 261:26
happy f. resemble — TOLS 796:13
mothers of large f. — BELL 64:19
rooks in f. homeward go — HARD 373:5
there are f. — THAT 787:11
to run in f. — LEWE 483:1
worst f. are those — BAGE 48:20
family brought up a large f. — GOLD 355:28
dominion [of the f.] — HOBB 390:21
f. firm — GEOR 343:16
f.—that dear octopus — SMIT 741:16
f. that prays together — SAYI 669:18
F.! . . . the home of all — STRI 762:13
f., with its narrow privacy — LEAC 476:11
f. with the wrong members — ORWE 577:10
have a young f. — FOWL 331:1
I am the f. face — HARD 372:19
man that left his f. — TWAI 803:4
running of a f. — MONT 544:8
Selling off the f. silver — MISQ 538:16
spend more time with f. — THAT 787:14
We, your blood f. — SPEN 750:15
famine f. in his face — CHUR 220:6
f. in the land — LAWL 470:16
F. Queen — GONN 356:10
F. sighs like scythe — WALC 817:5
feed her f. fat — BYRO 181:23
God of f. — VYAZ 817:2
They that die by f. — HENR 382:11
famous by that time I was too f. — BENC 66:8
f. by my sword — MONT 546:4
f. by their birth — SHAK 715:14
f. calm and dead — BROW 159:12
f. for fifteen minutes — WARH 821:16
f. men have the whole earth — PERI 592:23
f. without ability — SHAW 724:27
found myself f. — BYRO 184:15
praise f. men — BIBL 93:30
'twas a f. victory — SOUT 749:2
world f. — RICH 647:20
fan f. spread and streamers out — CONG 239:11
F.-vaulting . . . from an aesthetic — LANC 465:21
state of the football f. — HORN 403:17
fanatic f. is a great leader — BROU 154:18
fanaticism f. consists in — SANT 666:7
F. is indefensible — FINK 321:7
fanatics F. have their dreams — KEAT 443:5
fancies drop your silly f. — CATU 202:15
F. that broke — BROW 161:4

heart of furious f. — ANON 20:4
many f. reign — GREE 362:22
fancy F. a thousand wondrous — BEAT 59:11
f. is the sails — KEAT 445:26
form does to my f. bring — WALL 818:4
keep your f. free — HOUS 404:10
let the f. roam — KEAT 443:7
maiden meditation, f.-free — SHAK 711:2
most excellent f. — SHAK 688:28
Now my sere f. — BYRO 181:12
where is f. bred — SHAK 709:17
whispers of f. — JOHN 425:24
young man's f. — TENN 780:15
fans f. into their hand — BALL 53:6
fantasies fed the heart on f. — YEAT 854:24
fantastic f. summer's heat — SHAK 715:11
light f. round — MILT 528:22
light f. toe — MILT 529:20
fantastical joys are but f. — DONN 280:19
fantasy live in a f. world — MURD 554:18
Most modern f. — PRAT 610:9
much too strong for f. — DONN 280:18
Of f., of dreams — SHAK 696:25
far f. above the great — GRAY 361:21
F. and few — LEAR 477:8
F. be that fate from us — OVID 579:19
f., far better thing — DICK 272:19
F.-fetched and dear-bought — PROV 619:43
F. from the madding — BORR 146:6
F. from the madding crowd's — GRAY 361:7
f. side of despair — SART 667:10
f. to go — PROV 626:28
galaxy f., far away — TAGL 771:7
going a bridge too f. — BROW 158:6
good news from a f. country — BIBL 85:7
hills and f. away — GAY 341:12
How f. is — KIPL 455:14
how f. one can go too far — COCT 230:4
keep f. from me — OVID 579:20
Mexico, so f. from God — DIAZ 267:4
much too f. out all my life — SMIT 743:1
Oh keep f. off — VIRG 812:10
Over the hills and f. away — NURS 570:10
quarrel in a f. away country — CHAM 206:11
so near and yet so f. — TENN 779:21
To go too f. — CONF 238:3
unhappy, f.-off things — WORD 850:9
Faraday anti-F. machines — CORN 243:7
farce f. is played out — LAST 472:1
second as f. — MARX 516:16
second time as f. — BARN 56:11
fare value not your bill of f. — SWIF 766:1
farewell Ae f., and then for ever — BURN 170:6
bid the company f. — LAST 472:6
F.! a long farewell — SHAK 695:11
f. content — SHAK 714:2
f., great painter — EPIT 309:6
f., he is gon — CHAU 211:7
f. king — SHAK 715:25
F., Leicester Square — JUDG 438:4
F., Love — WYAT 852:1
F. my bok — CHAU 212:22
F., my friends — LAST 471:1
F. night — BUNY 165:8
F., rewards — CORB 242:18
f. to the shade — COWP 247:8
forever, f., Cassius — SHAK 698:23
hail, and f. — CATU 203:10
So f. then — CATC 201:27
Too-late, F. — ROSS 656:5
farm down on the f. — LEWI 483:18
f. is like a man — CATO 199:17
farmer after the f.'s wife — NURS 570:5
F. will never be happy again — HERB 383:7
Here's a f. — SHAK 705:5
farmers embattled f. stood — EMER 306:12
f. excessively fortunate — VIRG 814:16
Our f. round — CRAB 249:9
farms cellos of the deep f. — STEV 758:19
for him that f. — CRAB 249:17
lass wi' the weel-stockit f. — BURN 171:8
What spires, what f. — HOUS 404:16
farmyard crow in its own f. — TROL 799:18

fathers (cont.):
Victory has a hundred f. — CIAN 222:25
years ago our f. brought forth — LINC 485:7
your f. tempted me — BOOK 140:10
Father William You are old, F. — SOUT 749:9
fathom f.-line could never touch — SHAK 689:29
f. the inscrutable workings — SMIT 742:5
Full f. five — SHAK 718:27
many a f. deep — CAMP 187:7
thou canst not f. it — TENN 782:22
fathoms fifty f. deep — BALL 53:7
fatling lion and the f. — BIBL 88:21
fatness thy clouds drop f. — BOOK 138:7
fatted f. calf — BIBL 101:17
fattening illegal, immoral, or f. — WOOL 845:16
fatter Would he were f. — SHAK 696:13
fatty f. degeneration — STEV 759:21
faucibus in f. Orci — VIRG 812:12
Faulconbridge rather be a F. — SHAK 698:30
fault all f. who hath no fault — TENN 777:27
artist is his own f. — O'HA 571:16
clever to a f. — BROW 158:17
Condemn the f. — SHAK 707:25
f. confessed — PROV 619:44
f., dear Brutus — SHAK 696:9
glorious f. of angels — POPE 602:14
hide the f. I see — POPE 606:16
it was a grievous f. — SHAK 697:22
Just hint a f. — POPE 602:29
most grievous f. — MISS 536:14
Nature's f. alone — CHUR 220:10
no kind of f. or flaw — GILB 347:10
O happy f. — MISS 540:3
soul is without f. — RIMB 649:11
sting to thee is a little f. — DANT 256:5
think it is their f. — BROO 153:17
faultless Faultily f. — TENN 781:16
f. piece to see — POPE 604:4
F. to a fault — BROW 161:10
faults acknowledge my f. — BOOK 137:10
acknowledge our f. — BURN 169:20
all, their f. confessing — BUCK 163:11
buffeted for your f. — BIBL 112:8
Drown all my f. — FLET 327:14
England, with all thy f. — COWP 247:28
f. a little blind — PRIO 612:2
f. of his feet — BECK 61:14
f. of statesmen — WALP 819:20
fill you with the f. they had — LARK 469:2
his f. lie gently — SHAK 695:18
Jesus! with all thy f. — BUTL 177:5
moulded out of f. — SHAK 708:18
rise to f. — POPE 604:1
what f. they commit — QUAR 639:4
With all her f. — CHUR 219:13
faune après-midi d'un f. — MALL 508:14
favilla Solvet saeclum in f. — MISS 539:15
favour bend to f. ev'ry client — GAY 342:1
Fools out of f. — DEFO 261:20
in f. of the people — BURK 168:4
truths being in and out of f. — FROS 335:9
favourable O be f. and gracious — BOOK 137:15
favoured Hail, thou that art highly f.
— BIBL 99:30
favourite f. has no friend — GRAY 361:15
second f. organ — ALLE 12:11
favourites monarchs to choose f.
— SWIF 765:15
favours depends Upon your f. — SHAK 682:14
felt all its f. — COCK 229:20
hope for greater f. — LA R 469:19
in the middle of her f. — SHAK 685:21
recommendation to f. — FIEL 318:5
sense of future f. — WALP 820:9
fawns fallow f. invisible — THOM 790:16
fay F. ce que vouldras — RABE 639:17
fear begins in f. — COLE 234:7
bondage of f. — CLOS 228:9
by beauty and by f. — WORD 849:7
by means of pity and f. — ARIS 25:20
cannot taint with f. — SHAK 707:6
Causing f. is what constitutes — DURA 292:16
concessions of f. — BURK 166:18

Do right and f. no man — PROV 618:21
drives away his f. — NEWT 563:6
English . . . are paralysed by f. — LAWR 474:21
eventide of f. — MORR 549:12
F. and Hunger — VIRG 812:12
f. and trembling — BIBL 110:1
f. casteth out love — CONN 240:7
F. gave wings to his feet — VIRG 813:2
F. God — BIBL 87:1
F. God — BIBL 112:7
F. God — BORR 145:13
F. God. Honour the King — KITC 457:14
f. in a handful of dust — ELIO 303:9
F. is the foundation — ADAM 3:8
F. is the main source — RUSS 661:7
f. made manifest — EDDY 295:9
f. man more than God — RADE 640:11
f. my name — BIBL 92:14
f. no evil — BOOK 135:4
f. no fall — BUNY 165:3
F. no more the heat — SHAK 683:8
f. of the Law — JOYC 437:5
f. of the Lord — BIBL 88:20
f. of the Lord — BOOK 141:22
f. science — POLA 599:12
f. still followed him — SPEN 751:19
f. thee, ancient Mariner — COLE 232:24
f. those big words — JOYC 437:16
f., To be we know not what — DRYD 287:27
f. to negotiate — KENN 448:18
f. will turn to love — SERO 677:5
Fly hence, our contact f. — ARNO 28:9
For f. of finding something worse — BELL 64:22
fourth is freedom from f. — ROOS 653:20
From hope and f. set free — SWIN 768:17
geometry of f. — READ 643:1
grief felt so like f. — LEWI 483:4
hate that which we often f. — SHAK 678:20
in thy faith and f. — BOOK 131:16
keepet by thy f. — BURN 171:11
let him be your f. — BIBL 88:16
Life is first boredom, then f. — LARK 468:15
Men f. death — BACO 44:1
never had a f. — COWP 248:22
no hope without f. — SPIN 752:24
not wholly banish f. — AESC 6:7
No tyrant need f. till — ARIS 26:4
one f., Death's shadow — BLUN 124:3
only thing we have to f. — ROOS 653:12
Our deepest f. is not — WILL 839:15
out of f. — DONN 281:1
pearls, is the f. of God — ORCH 576:6
Possess them not with f. — SHAK 693:20
robs the mind as f. — BURK 167:3
Severity breedeth f. — BACO 44:24
so long as they f. — ACCI 1:6
spirit of f. — BIBL 110:28
There is no f. in love — BIBL 112:21
those who f. life — RUSS 660:22
too much joy or too much f. — GRAV 360:6
travel in the direction of our f. — BERR 71:16
trembled with f. — ENGL 307:29
try to have no f. — CHES 214:16
'Twas only f. — JONS 435:10
whom then shall I f. — BOOK 135:13
without f. the lawless roads — MUIR 553:11
feared neither f. nor flattered — DOUG 283:15
prince to be f. — MACH 502:10
fearful f. of the night — WILL 838:14
f. symmetry — BLAK 122:19
f. thing — BIBL 111:5
f. trip is done — WHIT 833:4
fearfully f. and wonderfully made
— BOOK 143:17
fearless F., blameless knight — ANON 20:11
fears anxious f. subside — WILL 838:10
f. dishonour more than death — HORA 402:17
f. do make us traitors — SHAK 706:19
f. his fate too much — MONT 546:3
f. his fellowship — SHAK 693:22
f. it heeded not — SHEL 731:28
f. may be liars — CLOU 229:11
F. of the brave — JOHN 426:20

f. that I may cease to be — KEAT 445:23
f. to speak of Ninety-Eight — INGR 413:18
forgot the taste of f. — SHAK 707:12
from sudden f. — BYRO 183:2
griefs and f. — BACO 45:4
hopes and f. — BROO 154:8
man who f. the Lord — BIBL 115:2
Not mine own f. — SHAK 723:18
Present f. — SHAK 703:15
saucy doubts and f. — SHAK 706:3
tie up thy f. — HERB 383:24
tormenting f. — ROCH 651:9
feast After the f. comes — PROV 614:7
bare imagination of a f. — SHAK 715:11
Chief nourisher in life's f. — SHAK 704:24
company makes the f. — PROV 617:5
compared to a f. — BARN 56:18
Enough as good as a f. — PROV 618:47
f. at ease — DUCK 291:2
f. of fat things — BIBL 89:1
f. of languages — SHAK 702:21
f. of reason — POPE 605:26
going to a f. — JONS 435:4
Paris is a movable f. — HEMI 381:6
upon our solemn f.-day — BOOK 139:13
When I make a f. — HARI 373:14
feasting dinner and f. — PEPY 592:10
feasts nights and f. divine — HORA 403:15
feather Birds of a f. — PROV 615:43
f.-footed through the plashy fen
— WAUG 824:12
f. for each wind — SHAK 721:29
f. in his cap — SONG 748:11
f. on the breath of God — HILD 388:4
f. to tickle — LAMB 464:18
go to heaven in f.-beds — MORE 548:10
my each f. — HUGH 407:5
feathered f. glory — YEAT 854:20
f. race — FRER 333:17
feathers f. like gold — BOOK 138:12
Fine f. — PROV 620:4
largest possible amount of f. — COLB 230:23
feats What f. he did that day — SHAK 693:23
feature every f. works — AUST 38:18
not a bug, it's a f. — SAYI 669:30
February F. fill dyke — PROV 619:46
F. there be no rain — PROV 623:1
not Puritanism but F. — KRUT 462:2
fed both have f. as well — SHAK 696:6
clothed, f., and educated — RUSK 660:2
f. of the dainties — SHAK 702:16
f. the chicken every day — RUSS 660:27
you have f. full — VIRG 814:11
federal Our F. Union — JACK 414:16
federation F. of the world — TENN 780:20
fee For a small f. in America — SOND 746:2
gorgeous East in f. — WORD 848:19
feeble confirm the f. knees — BIBL 89:10
f. can seldom persuade — GIBB 345:9
help the f. up — SHAK 719:8
man of such a f. temper — SHAK 696:8
Most forcible F. — SHAK 692:7
o'ercomes the f. brain — WINC 841:9
feebleness all else is f. — VIGN 810:8
feed doth this our Caesar f. — SHAK 696:10
F. a cold — PROV 619:47
f. his flock — BIBL 89:18
f. me in a green pasture — BOOK 135:3
F. my lambs — BIBL 104:19
F. my sheep — BIBL 104:20
f. on Death — SHAK 723:31
F. the brute — PUNC 637:21
f. with the rich — JOHN 429:3
will you still f. me — LENN 480:22
you f. him for a day — SAYI 669:20
feeding Love is mutually f. — HEAD 377:9
feel be, f., live — HERD 385:8
draw what I f. in my body — HEPW 382:18
Englishman can't f. — FORS 329:8
f. it happen — CATU 203:9
f. that he is dying — CALI 185:14
f. that you could — HOPK 397:17
f. the heart-break — GIBS 346:10

fiction (*cont.*):
stranger than f. — PROV 633:20
That is what f. means — WILD 835:19
fictions f. only and false hair — HERB 384:11
truth to their f. — HUME 409:8
fiddle cat and the f. — NURS 567:6
F.-de-dee — NURS 566:19
f., sir, and spade — SCOT 674:6
F., we know, is diddle — SWIN 768:18
important beyond all this f. — MOOR 547:1
I the second f. — SPRI 753:8
played on an old f. — PROV 632:27
fiddler must pay the f. — PROV 632:35
fiddlers his f. three — NURS 568:13
fide f. et gaude in Christo — LUTH 496:7
Punica f. — SALL 665:6
Fidele fair F.'s grassy tomb — COLL 235:10
fideles Adeste, f. — ANON 21:12
fidelity stone f. they hardly meant
LARK 468:13
thinks he is worth my f. — LACL 463:6
Your idea of f. — RAPH 642:10
fidgety f. Phil — HOFF 391:15
fidus f. quae tela gerebat Achates — VIRG 811:1
field comes and tills the f. — TENN 784:7
corner of a foreign f. — BROO 153:15
corner of a foreign f. — OPEN 574:14
fair f. full of folk — LANG 466:16
f. is won — MORE 548:14
f. of Golgotha — SHAK 716:6
F. Strewn — ARNO 28:1
lay f. to field — BIBL 88:7
lilies of the f. — BIBL 95:9
man of the f. — BIBL 76:25
not as simple as to cross a f. — PAST 588:3
Not that fair f. Of Enna — MILT 532:29
only inhabitants of the f. — BURK 167:19
presence on the f. — WELL 827:16
single in the f. — WORD 850:8
What though the f. be lost — MILT 531:9
fields babbled of green f. — SHAK 693:2
f. and flocks have charms — CRAB 249:17
f. from Islington — BLAK 120:9
f. have eyes — PROV 619:49
f. of Cambridge — COWL 245:29
f. where roses fade — HOUS 405:1
flowerless f. of heaven — SWIN 767:24
from the f. of sleep — WORD 848:2
I go among the f. — KEAT 446:19
In Flanders f. — MCCR 500:18
Open unto the f. — WORD 846:6
plough the f. — CAMP 187:1
tills his ancestral f. — HORA 400:1
fiend defy the foul f. — SHAK 700:25
dreadful f. — SPEN 752:6
f. Flibbertigibbet — SHAK 700:27
f. hid in a cloud — BLAK 122:14
f. Walked up and down — MILT 532:19
foul F. — BUNY 164:16
frightful f. — COLE 233:7
swung the f. — MERE 522:20
thou f. to me — BYRO 183:3
work like a f. — THOM 790:7
fiends Beneath is all the f.' — SHAK 701:15
fierce as I raved and grew more f.
HERB 383:25
but little, she is f. — SHAK 711:16
F. as ten Furies — MILT 532:11
f. light which beats — TENN 777:13
F. was the wild billow — ANAT 13:19
fiery burning f. furnace — BIBL 91:19
f. darts of the wicked — BIBL 109:21
full of f. shapes — SHAK 690:21
throne was like the f. flame — BIBL 91:24
fife practised on a f. — CARR 196:14
Thane of F. had a wife — SHAK 707:1
fifteen At the age of f. — OPEN 574:16
at the age of f. — OPEN 574:20
famous for f. minutes — WARH 821:16
F. men on the dead man's chest — STEV 759:13
f. wild Decembers — BRON 152:20
old age always f. years older — BARU 57:17
fifth came f. and lost — JOYC 437:21

F. column — MOLA 541:8
fifties tranquillized F. — LOWE 494:11
fifty At f. chides his infamous delay
YOUN 857:13
At f., everyone — ORWE 578:8
At f., menopausal — STEV 758:20
corpulent man of f. — HUNT 410:8
F.-four forty — POLI 600:16
until he's f. — FAUL 316:6
until I was nearly f. — HEAN 377:20
fig f. for those by law protected — BURN 171:18
sewed f. leaves together — BIBL 75:20
figements f. violets — RIMB 649:7
fight begun to f. — JONE 434:6
better to f. for the good — TENN 782:7
Councils of war never f. — PROV 617:12
don't want to f. — HUNT 409:13
end of the f. is a tombstone — KIPL 455:6
Fifty-four forty, or f. — POLI 600:16
f. against the future — GLAD 350:13
f. and fight again — GAIT 337:17
f. and no be slain — BURN 172:17
f. and not to heed the wounds — IGNA 412:18
F. fire with fire — PROV 620:1
f. for freedom — PANK 585:7
f. for freedom and truth — IBSE 412:11
f. for its King and Country — GRAH 358:4
f. for the living — JONE 434:7
f. for what I believe in — CAST 198:17
f. in defence — HOME 394:7
f. in the way of God — KORA 459:13
f. in the way of God — KORA 460:2
f. in the way of God — KORA 460:3
f. it out on this line — GRAN 359:5
f. no more — JOSE 436:15
F. on, my men — BALL 53:2
f. on the beaches — CHUR 221:8
f. on to the end — HAIG 367:11
f. our country's battles — MILI 526:9
F. the good fight — BIBL 110:27
F. the good fight — MONS 543:7
f. with faith and win — SIKH 737:7
f. with them again — TENN 783:19
fought a good f. — BIBL 111:1
fought a good f. — WILD 837:9
fought The better f. — MILT 533:20
give the f. up — BROW 160:15
go f. tomorrow — BALL 52:3
Good at a f. — ANON 16:5
he is dead, who will not f. — GREN 363:13
I f. on — THAT 787:16
I will f. — SITT 738:13
like men, and f. — BIBL 80:7
never a moment ceased the f. — TENN 784:1
Never give up the f. — MARL 512:13
nor duty bade me f. — YEAT 854:16
no stomach to this f. — SHAK 693:22
not the f. — HERR 385:22
refuse to f. — POLI 601:14
rise and f. againe — BALL 53:2
those who bade me f. — EWER 313:8
thought it wrong to f. — BELL 65:22
too proud to f. — WILS 840:18
Ulster will f. — CHUR 220:13
We shall win this f. — PUTI 638:8
When badgers f. — CLAR 224:2
fighter Am I no a bonny f. — STEV 759:2
f. not a quitter — MAND 509:17
I was ever a f. — BROW 161:2
fighting enemy we're f. — WALL 818:2
f. for this woman's honour — FILM 320:16
F. in the captain's tower — DYLA 294:5
F. still — DRYD 287:17
f. with daggers — SCOT 675:2
first-class f. man — KIPL 454:5
foremost f., fell — BYRO 178:21
In f. to the death — DAYA 260:2
not fifty ways of f. — MALR 505:2
not f. does matter — STEP 756:5
still f. at Blenheim — BEVA 73:11
street f. man — JAGG 415:16
two dogs are f. — PROV 634:46
What are WE f. for — SERV 677:9

who dies f. has increase — GREN 363:13
fights f. and runs away — PROV 622:8
figs f. of thistles — BIBL 95:22
love long life better than f. — SHAK 678:15
figurative f., a metaphorical God
DONN 281:26
figure f. a poem makes — FROS 336:4
f. in the carpet — JAME 417:18
f. that thou here seest — JONS 435:24
losing her f. or her face — CART 197:10
make a f. — SWIF 765:19
figures f. in words only — MURR 555:3
prove anything by f. — CARL 191:10
filches f. from me my good name
SHAK 713:26
files foremost f. of time — TENN 781:3
filia f. pulchrior — HORA 400:16
filial may be called f. — CONF 237:9
filigree f. hedges — WALP 818:19
fill Ah, f. the cup — FITZ 323:7
F. me with life anew — HATC 375:3
f. the hour — EMER 307:7
O f. me — MACN 504:19
space you f. — COOP 242:14
take our f. of love — BIBL 84:4
trying to f. them — CIOR 223:28
fillest f. all things living — BOOK 143:25
filling f. the space — WEST 830:15
mind does not require f. — PLUT 598:13
film f. of death — KEAT 445:19
f., which fluttered — COLE 231:20
films seldom go to f. — BERR 71:18
fils F. de Saint Louis — FIRM 321:12
filth Delights in f. — SPEN 751:27
f. and the fury — NEWS 562:7
identical, and so is f. — FORS 329:21
filthy are as f. rags — BIBL 90:20
f. and polluted — BIBL 92:12
greedy of f. lucre — BIBL 110:22
fin commencement de la f. — TALL 770:20
final f. solution — HEYD 387:14
finale Let be be f. of seem — STEV 757:22
finality F. is death — STEP 756:3
F. is not the language — DISR 275:17
finance F. is the stomach — GLAD 350:11
find do not f. anything pleasant — VOLT 815:9
f. it after many days — BIBL 86:20
f. itself again. — HÖLD 392:14
f. out God — BIBL 83:4
New places you will not f. — CAVA 203:19
returns home to f. it — MOOR 546:13
Run and f. out — KIPL 456:12
Safe bind, safe f. — PROV 630:18
Seek and ye shall f. — PROV 630:26
Someday I'll f. you — COWA 245:6
Speak as you f. — PROV 631:14
strive, to seek, to f. — TENN 784:20
Those who hide can f. — PROV 632:42
thou shalt f. me — ANON 18:18
where I f. it — MOLI 542:14
finders F. keepers — PROV 620:2
findeth f. his life — BIBL 96:21
he that seeketh f. — BIBL 95:16
findings F. keepings — PROV 620:3
finds he Who f. himself — ARNO 28:11
fine bring in f. things — BUCK 163:9
F. art is that — RUSK 660:3
F. clothes are good — JOHN 430:17
F. feathers — PROV 620:4
f. point of his soul — KEAT 446:3
f. romance with no kisses — FIEL 318:16
F. words — PROV 620:5
F. writing — KEAT 447:1
passage which is particularly f. — JOHN 429:24
very f. cat — JOHN 432:8
fine arts one of the f. — STEI 755:5
finem F. di dederint — HORA 400:13
respice f. — ANON 22:3
finer nothing could be f. — GORD 356:18
finery not bedizened with f. — TROL 799:7
finest f. hour — CHUR 221:9
finger bruises his f. here on earth
TALM 772:33

fishers Blest f. — BASS 58:6
f. of men — BIBL 94:19
f. went sailing away — KING 452:21
fishes f. flew and forests walked — CHES 215:24
F., that tipple — LOVE 493:5
how the f. live in the sea — SHAK 715:3
little f. of the sea — CARR 195:19
Men lived like f. — SIDN 735:16
notes like little f. — MACN 504:21
Tawny-finned f. — SHAK 679:11
two small f. — BIBL 103:1
welcomes little f. in — CARR 194:1
fishified how art thou f. — SHAK 717:30
fishing I go a f. — BIBL 104:18
when he goes a-f. — WALT 820:17
fishlike ancient and f. smell — SHAK 718:30
fishpond great f. (the sea) — DEKK 262:15
fishpools eyes like the f. — BIBL 87:21
fishy You shall have a f. — NURS 566:15
fist closed f. of a teacher — PALI 583:10
of f. most valiant — SHAK 693:11
fistful for a f. of coins — ZAPA 858:4
fists F. clenched — LOGU 489:13
groan and shake their f. — HOUS 403:19
fit f. audience find — MILT 533:21
f. for this world — KEAT 446:3
I am f. for nothing — HERV 386:24
only the F. survive — SERV 677:8
fitful life's f. fever — SHAK 705:21
fitly word f. spoken — BIBL 85:3
fits If the cap f., wear it — PROV 623:4
If the shoe f. — PROV 623:6
fittest Survival of the F. — DARW 257:9
survival of the f. — SPEN 750:8
fitting right and f. — MISS 536:23
five At f. in the afternoon — LORC 492:1
f. minutes too late — COWL 246:1
f. per cent — MACA 498:7
F. to one — MORR 550:5
Full fathom f. — SHAK 718:27
had f. thousand a year — THAC 786:19
I have wedded f. — CHAU 212:14
in a f.-pound note — LEAR 477:15
she hadde f. — CHAU 210:21
warming his f. wits — TENN 784:6
fix don't f. it — SAYI 669:25
f. up his automobile — CLAR 225:8
looking for an angry f. — GINS 349:15
fixed f. point in a changing age — DOYL 284:16
great gulf f. — BIBL 101:23
flag allegiance to the f. — BELL 64:15
blood-red f. — BLOK 123:16
brought back the f. — GRIF 364:7
death's pale f. — SHAK 718:9
f. and sign of love — SHAK 713:2
f. of the future — PEAR 590:12
f. to which you have pledged — BALD 50:10
High as a f. — HAMM 370:10
Jelly-bellied F.-flapper — KIPL 457:6
keep the red f. flying — CONN 239:26
national f. — SUMN 764:3
people's f. is deepest red — CONN 239:25
raised their f. — WEBS 825:13
shall not f. or fail — CHUR 221:8
spare your country's f. — WHIT 834:3
Trade follows the f. — PROV 633:16
flagellation Not f., not pederasty — RATT 642:14
flagitium f. timet — HORA 402:17
flagpole run it up the f. — SAYI 670:3
flame Both moth and f. — ROET 652:8
Chloe is my real f. — PRIO 612:5
eyes were as a f. — BIBL 112:29
feed his sacred f. — COLE 232:9
F.-capped, and shout — SHAW 728:2
f. I still deplore — GARR 340:7
f. out like shining — HOPK 396:12
full of subtil f. — BEAU 60:5
hard, gemlike f. — PATE 588:11
in a shapeless f. — DONN 280:12
plays about the f. — GAY 341:5
romantic first f. — BURN 169:9
signals of the ancient f. — DANT 256:9
spark of that ancient f. — VIRG 812:1

that little f. — RENO 645:10
thin blue f. — COLE 231:20
throne was like the fiery f. — BIBL 91:24
thy holy f. bestowing — LITT 486:16
tongues of f. are in-folded — ELIO 302:2
tongues of living f. — AUBE 33:13
When a lovely f. dies — HARB 370:21
flames bursting into f. — MORR 550:3
by her like thin f. — ROSS 655:22
Commit it then to the f. — HUME 408:9
f. in the forehead — MILT 530:10
f. must waste away — CARE 190:11
love. F. for a year — LAMP 465:20
rich f. and hired tears — BROW 156:8
flaming f. bounds of place and time — GRAY 361:19
ministers a f. fire — BOOK 141:5
flammae *veteris vestigia f.* — VIRG 812:1
flamme *cette petite f.* — RENO 645:10
Flanders brought him a F. mare — HENR 382:6
In F. fields the poppies blow — MCCR 500:17
part of F. — WALL 818:15
flashes f. of silence — SMIT 743:25
In f., and with glory — WORD 849:13
flashing His f. eyes — COLE 232:8
flask f. of wine — FITZ 323:2
flat debt, an' a f. — LOWE 493:20
F. and flexible truths — BROW 156:2
half so f. as Walter Scott — ANON 18:7
never surprises, it is f. — FORS 329:10
very dangerous f. — SHAK 709:11
Very f., Norfolk — COWA 245:10
flats sharps and f. — BROW 160:20
flatten hide is sure to f. 'em — BELL 64:18
flatter before you f. a man — JOHN 431:11
F. the mountain-tops — SHAK 723:2
fondly f. our desires — DRAY 285:22
lie, an' f. — ASCH 31:4
flattered being then most f. — SHAK 696:26
Englishman, Being f. — CHAP 208:8
f. into virtue — SURT 764:9
f. its rank breath — BYRO 179:2
neither feared nor f. — DOUG 283:15
flatterer hypocrite and f. — BLAK 120:12
flatterers petty f. — BACO 44:29
sycophants and f. — HARD 371:7
tell him he hates f. — SHAK 696:26
within a week the same f. — HALI 368:16
flatteries against f. — MACH 502:14
flattering f., kissing and kicking — TRUM 801:6
f. unction — SHAK 687:28
think him worth f. — SHAW 725:19
flattery Everyone likes f. — DISR 277:37
f. hurts no one — STEV 758:11
f. is worth his having — JOHN 431:11
f. lost on poet's ear — SCOT 673:9
f. of one's peers — LODG 489:7
f. soothe the dull cold ear — GRAY 361:4
ne'er was f. lost — CLOS 228:10
paid with f. — JOHN 424:13
refer to it is 'f.' — PLAT 597:7
sincerest form of f. — PROV 623:32
This is no f. — SHAK 680:25
flaunting f., extravagant quean — SHER 733:31
flavour high celestial f. — BYRO 180:27
flaw no kind of fault or f. — GILB 347:10
flaws hundred thousand f. — SHAK 700:13
Psychological f. — ANON 18:14
flax smoking f. — BIBL 89:22
Three pounds of f. — MUMO 554:6
flayed saw a woman f. — SWIF 766:17
flea gripping a f. — PROV 628:10
literature's performing f. — O'CA 571:10
louse and a f. — JOHN 432:7
naturalists observe, a f. — SWIF 767:11
fleas Big f. have little fleas — PROV 615:38
educated f. do it — PORT 607:14
f. that tease in the High Pyrenees — BELL 65:26
get up with f. — PROV 623:19
praised his f. — YEAT 855:23
flectere F. si nequeo superos — VIRG 813:1
fled f. far, far away — COCK 229:20
f. From this vile world — SHAK 723:9

F. is that music — KEAT 445:3
I f. Him — THOM 791:7
sea saw that, and f. — BOOK 142:2
Still as he f. — SPEN 751:19
flee death shall f. from them — BIBL 113:24
f., and were discomfited — BOOK 138:12
f. away, and be at rest — BOOK 137:16
f. from the wrath to come — BIBL 94:12
F. fro the press — CHAU 213:19
f. when no man pursueth — BIBL 85:16
f. from me — WYAT 852:4
fleece f. was white as snow — HALE 368:8
His forest f. — HOUS 404:13
won the F. and then came home — DU B 290:18
fleeces sheep bear f. — VIRG 815:7
fleet care of our f. — ADDI 5:3
Fire and f. — BALL 52:11
F. in which we serve — BOOK 144:10
F. the time carelessly — SHAK 680:19
in the Downs the f. was moored — GAY 342:10
whole F.'s lit up — WOOD 844:17
fleetest have f. end — THOM 791:5
fleeth My soul f. — BOOK 143:7
fleets Ten thousand f. — BYRO 179:18
Fleet Street F. to our poets — BROW 157:19
who can be dull in F. — LAMB 465:3
flere *Si vis me f.* — HORA 398:6
flesh All f. is grass — BIBL 89:17
all f. shall see it — BIBL 89:16
born after the f. — BIBL 108:27
bread and f. — BIBL 81:19
delicate white human f. — FIEL 318:9
east wind made f. — APPL 23:15
eat bulls' f. — BOOK 137:9
Eating the f. — SHAK 719:16
fair and unpolluted f. — SHAK 689:1
flattered any f. — DOUG 283:15
f., alas, is wearied — MALL 508:13
f. and blood — BIBL 109:21
f. and blood so cheap — HOOD 395:12
f., and the devil — BOOK 129:6
f. is as grass — BIBL 112:3
f. is weak — BIBL 99:6
F. of flesh — MILT 534:3
f. of my flesh — BIBL 75:16
F. perishes. I live on — HARD 372:19
f. to feel the chain — BRON 152:19
f. was sacramental — ROBI 650:20
gross f. sinks downwards — SHAK 716:17
heart o' f. — BALL 53:9
human f. subsisting — BOOK 129:2
in my f. shall I see God — BIBL 83:12
lusts of the f. — BOOK 132:13
makes man and wife one f. — CONG 238:16
make your f. creep — DICK 271:27
more f. than another man — SHAK 690:31
my heart and my f. — BOOK 139:15
My Lord should take Frail f. — CROS 252:18
O flesh, f. — SHAK 717:30
outlive all f. — BYRO 182:7
provision for the f. — BIBL 106:33
shall all f. come — BOOK 138:5
Tell f. it is but dust — RALE 641:3
these our f. upright — DONN 279:12
they shall be one f. — BIBL 75:17
things of the f. — BIBL 106:17
this too too solid f. — SHAK 683:29
thorn in the f. — BIBL 108:24
trust in the f. — BIBL 110:2
we are one, One f. — MILT 534:4
Word was made f. — BIBL 102:21
WORD WAS MADE F. — MISS 539:13
world and its shadow, The f. — RIDI 648:4
would God this f. — SWIN 769:4
fleshly all this f. dress — VAUG 807:14
flesh pots we sat by the f. — BIBL 77:36
flew and they f. — LOGU 489:32
f. between me and the sun — BLUN 124:6
f. over the cuckoo's nest — NURS 568:17
if I f. the Atlantic — EARH 294:23
flexible Flat and f. truths — BROW 156:2
your f. friend — ADVE 7:1

Flibbertigibbet fiend F. SHAK 700:27
flicker moment of my greatness f.
  ELIO 302:17
flies As f. to wanton boys SHAK 701:8
  catch small f. SWIF 766:27
  Eagles don't catch f. PROV 618:28
  F., worms, and flowers WATT 823:8
  full fast he f. BLAI 118:14
  Honey catches more f. PROV 622:28
  joy as it f. BLAK 121:22
  murmurous haunt of f. KEAT 444:26
  shut mouth catches no f. PROV 630:38
  swart f. move DOUG 283:18
  Time f. PROV 633:1
fliest for thou f. Me THOM 791:12
flight His cloistered f. SHAK 705:22
  His f. was madness SHAK 706:19
  not attained by sudden f. LONG 490:13
  puts the stars to f. FITZ 322:24
flights f. upon the banks JONS 436:4
flinders Little Polly F. NURS 568:4
fling f. the ringleaders ARNO 30:15
flint as the f. bears fire SHAK 698:19
flirtation innocent f. BYRO 181:29
flittings tellest my f. BOOK 137:19
float f. lazily downstream SALI 664:3
  F. like a butterfly ALI 12:2
  f. upon his watery bier MILT 529:31
floating f. bulwark of the island BLAC 118:10
  his f. hair COLE 232:8
floats She f., she hesitates RACI 640:4
flock feed his f. BIBL 89:18
  keeping watch over their f. BIBL 100:2
  tainted wether of the f. SHAK 709:23
flocks My father feeds his f. HOME 393:14
  My f. feed not BARN 56:17
  shepherds watched their f. TATE 773:14
  sweet buds like f. SHEL 730:7
flog f. the rank and file ARNO 30:15
flogging in the habit of f. me TROL 798:20
  less f. in our great schools JOHN 430:11
flood days before the f. BIBL 98:18
  f. could not wash away CONG 238:26
  f. unto the world's end BOOK 138:23
  just cause reaches its f.-tide CATT 199:21
  return it as a f. GLAD 351:9
  Since Deucalion's f. SKEL 739:8
  swam the brackish f. DRAY 286:2
  taken at the f. SHAK 698:21
  ten years before the f. MARV 515:23
  Thorough f., thorough fire SHAK 710:27
  Thunder like a mighty f. DIX 278:13
  verge of the salt f. SHAK 719:13
flooded STREETS F. TELE 776:10
floodgate F. of the deeper heart FLEC 326:7
floods f. are risen BOOK 140:7
  f. drown it BIBL 87:23
  haystack in the f. MORR 549:16
  most like to f. RALE 641:6
  quells the f. below CAMP 187:21
floor fell upon the sanded f. PAYN 589:10
  f. of heaven SHAK 710:3
floors Scuttling across the f. of silent seas
  ELIO 302:16
flopping go f. yourself down DICK 272:16
flopshus F. Cad KIPL 457:6
Flora Tasting of F. KEAT 444:21
floraisons mois des f. ARAG 24:3
Florence lily of F. LONG 490:10
  Rode past fair F. KEAT 443:18
Flores F. in the Azores TENN 783:19
flos Ut f. in saeptis CATU 203:2
flourish f. after first decay SPEN 751:25
  f. and complain CRAB 249:9
  Princes and lords may f. GOLD 354:10
  things f. where you turn POPE 606:1
  Truth shall f. BOOK 139:19
flourisheth f. as a flower BOOK 141:4
flourishing f. like a green bay-tree
  BOOK 136:2
flout scout 'em, and f. 'em SHAK 718:24
flow blood must yet f. JEFF 420:14
  F. gently, sweet Afton BURN 170:7

I within did f. TRAH 798:2
What need you f. so fast ANON 19:16
flower as the f. of the field BIBL 89:17
  [Buddha] held up a f. MUMO 554:5
  Chaucer, of makaris f. DUNB 292:3
  cometh forth like a f. BIBL 83:8
  constellated f. SHEL 731:13
  cracks into furious f. BROO 154:6
  die in the f. of their age BIBL 80:3
  drives the f. THOM 789:9
  every opening f. WATT 823:6
  fairest f., no sooner blown MILT 530:15
  flourisheth as a f. BOOK 141:4
  f. fadeth BIBL 89:17
  f. grows concealed CATU 203:2
  f. in his hand COLE 233:19
  f. of all the field SHAK 718:6
  f. of any kind of experience HUNT 410:3
  f. of English nobility ORDE 576:10
  f. of floures alle CHAU 212:74
  f. of goodlihead SKEL 739:7
  f. of roses BIBL 94:1
  f. of Scotland WILL 839:16
  f. that once hath blown FITZ 323:6
  f. thereof falleth BIBL 112:3
  Full many a f. is born GRAY 361:5
  heaven in a wild f. BLAK 119:5
  her f., her glory pass DANI 255:5
  Herself a fairer f. MILT 532:29
  it will bear no f. SHEL 732:13
  leaf, the bud, the f. SPEN 751:25
  lightly like a f. TENN 779:29
  like the innocent f. SHAK 703:22
  little western f. SHAK 711:2
  London, thou art the f. ANON 17:12
  meanest f. that blows WORD 848:15
  no stronger than a f. SHAK 723:8
  pluck this f., safety SHAK 690:3
  seize the f. BURN 172:11
  short-lived f. LEAP 477:1
  sweetest f. for scent SHEL 731:29
  this same f. that smiles HERR 386:18
  white f. of a blameless TENN 777:13
flowering About the f. squares TENN 779:26
  f. of His fields TENN 778:10
flowerlike f. face SWIN 769:2
flowerpots your damned f. BROW 161:12
flowers among the f. LUCR 496:2
  beckon to the f. HERB 384:12
  bring forth May f. PROV 614:30
  but as a bed of f. DONN 282:7
  cool-rooted f. KEAT 445:4
  droop-headed f. KEAT 444:18
  Ensnared with f. MARV 515:16
  fairest f. o' the season SHAK 722:2
  fishermen hold f. DYLA 294:5
  Flies, worms, and f. WATT 823:8
  f. and fruits of love BYRO 183:1
  f. appear on the earth BIBL 87:6
  F. in the garden STEV 760:19
  f. in the mede CHAU 212:23
  F. of all hue MILT 532:28
  f. of the forest COCK 229:21
  f. of the forest ELLI 305:14
  f. that bloom in the spring GILB 348:9
  f. the tenderness of patient minds
  OWEN 581:3
  foam of f. SWIN 769:4
  hundred f. blossom MAO 511:14
  I got me f. to strew HERB 384:2
  No f., by request AING 9:1
  other men's f. MONT 545:2
  path is strewed with f. FARA 314:15
  Say it with f. ADVE 8:12
  souls do couch on f. SHAK 679:24
  speckled gigantic f. DINE 274:16
  Too many f. SCOT 674:31
  Where have all the f. gone SEEG 675:14
  wild f., and Prime Ministers BALD 50:14
  won't let f. AUDE 36:13
flowery crops the f. food POPE 604:20
  f. lap of earth ARNO 27:16
  f. plains of honour JONS 435:15

f. way SHAK 678:11
flowing f. sea CUNN 253:17
  f. with milk and honey BIBL 77:19
flown birds are f. CHAR 208:23
flows Everything f. HERA 383:1
fluidity solid for f. CHUR 221:1
flummery f. of a birth place KEAT 446:12
flung f. himself from the room LEAC 476:16
flush for the f. of youth ROSS 655:10
flushpots f. of Euston JOYC 437:4
flute f. and hautboys COLM 236:4
  f., harp, sackbut BIBL 91:19
  soft complaining f. DRYD 289:19
flutter F. and bear him up BETJ 72:5
fluttering F. and dancing WORD 847:5
fly all things F. thee THOM 791:12
  f. at one end SWIF 767:23
  F. at your Lord's command GURN 366:3
  F. away home NURS 567:18
  F. envious Time MILT 530:29
  f. from BYRO 178:24
  F. hence, our contact fear ARNO 28:9
  f. in his hand STER 756:24
  f. like thee BLAK 122:13
  f. sat upon the axletree BACO 45:34
  f. shall marry NURS 566:19
  f., Sir, may sting JOHN 427:13
  f. them for a moment TENN 783:19
  f. through the air LEYB 484:5
  f. to India MARL 513:1
  for I will f. to thee KEAT 444:25
  if I have wings to f. KAHL 441:3
  I, said the F. NURS 570:16
  long-legged f. upon the stream YEAT 854:22
  man is not a f. POPE 604:26
  noise of a f. DONN 282:8
  said a spider to a f. HOWI 406:6
  seen spiders f. EDWA 296:14
  settled like a meat-f. RUSK 659:8
  show the f. the way out WITT 842:9
  small gilded f. Does lecher SHAK 701:14
  There interposed a F. DICK 273:1
  They f. forgotten WATT 823:20
  thirsty f. OLDY 573:1
  To f. is safe COWP 248:5
  try to f. by those nets JOYC 437:9
  which way shall I f. MILT 532:24
  wings to f. away CLAR 224:6
  wouldn't hurt a f. LEAC 476:15
fly-fishing for winter f. WALT 820:15
flying f. is the most wonderful BISH 117:3
  f. upon the wings BOOK 134:16
  on the f. trapeze LEYB 484:5
  time is f. VIRG 815:1
flying-fishes f. play KIPL 455:1
Flying Scotsman F. is no less splendid
  BEAV 60:11
foam f. Of perilous seas KEAT 445:1
  To Noroway o'er the f. BALL 53:4
  wild and dank with f. KING 452:19
foaming f. with much blood POWE 609:21
foe angry with my f. BLAK 122:16
  as a friend than as a f. GLAD 351:12
  erect and manly f. CANN 189:7
  everyone's a f. CLAR 224:2
  f. outstretched BLAK 122:17
  furnace for your f. SHAK 695:5
  His f. was folly EPIT 310:10
  never made a f. TENN 778:2
  open f. may prove a curse GAY 341:29
  that's f. to men WEBS 826:10
  unrelenting f. THOM 792:16
  use up our f. HORA 399:22
  Where breathes the f. DRAK 285:19
  willing f. and sea room TOAS 796:7
  wish my deadly f. BRET 150:26
foeda F. est in coitu PETR 594:7
foes man's f. BIBL 96:20
fog a little f. SHAK 703:1
  f. comes on little cat feet SAND 665:10
  F. in Channel CART 198:1
  f. in my throat BROW 161:1

fog (cont.):
f. that rubs its back — ELIO 302:14
London particular . . . A f. — DICK 267:14
foggy f. day in London Town — GERS 344:4
fogs f. prevail upon the day — DRYD 288:1
insular country, subject to f. — DISR 277:10
foi En cette f. je veux vivre — VILL 810:13
foible omniscience his f. — SMIT 744:9
foil shining from shook f. — HOPK 396:12
fold Do not f. — ANON 15:17
f., spindle or mutilate — SAYI 669:14
f. stands empty — SHAK 710:31
f. to thy heart thy brother — WHIT 834:6
like the wolf on the f. — BYRO 180:1
not of this f. — BIBL 103:19
folded sweetest leaves yet f. — BYRO 182:3
undo the f. lie — AUDE 36:4
folding f. of the hands — BIBL 84:2
folds f. rippling — SUMN 764:3
f. shall be full of sheep — BOOK 138:7
tinklings lull the distant f. — GRAY 360:24
folie belle f. — BANV 54:19
f. à nulle autre seconde — MOLI 542:3
folio whole volumes in f. — SHAK 702:12
folios mighty f. first — CRAB 249:4
folk all music is f. music — ARMS 26:15
incest and f.-dancing — ANON 20:7
nowt so queer as f. — PROV 632:34
trouble with a f. song — LAMB 465:13
folks for different f. — SAYI 669:13
my f. were growing old — STEV 760:9
O yonge, fresshe f. — CHAU 213:16
where the old f. stay — FOST 330:14
follies crimes, f., and misfortunes — GIBB 345:1
f. a man regrets most — ROWL 657:13
f. naturally grow — CHUR 219:15
f. of the wise — JOHN 426:20
No f. to have to repent — TAYL 774:17
Of all human f. — MOLI 542:3
point out to us our f. — TROL 799:23
vices and f. of human kind — CONG 238:13
follow allowed to f. the road — TALM 772:30
F. me — BIBL 94:19
f. mine own teaching — SHAK 708:25
f. the Gleam — TENN 782:9
F. the van — COLL 235:3
f. the worse — OVID 580:13
f. your Saint — CAMP 188:2
F. your spirit — SHAK 693:5
I really had to f. them — LEDR 478:13
Pay, pack, and f. — BURT 173:17
So, f. me, follow — FLAN 324:16
their works do f. them — BIBL 114:4
followed arose and f. him — BIBL 96:4
first he f. it hymselve — CHAU 210:24
follows f. freits — PROV 621:47
lie f. — PROU 613:13
folly according to his f. — BIBL 85:8
brood of f. — MILT 529:9
by the f. of others — PLIN 598:5
Fashion, though F.'s child — CRAB 249:5
f. and conceit — AUST 39:22
f. of people's not staying — AUST 38:19
f. of the wise — JOHN 433:16
F.'s at full length — BRER 150:24
f. to be wise — PROV 634:39
fool returneth to his f. — BIBL 85:9
having lived in f. — CERV 205:17
His foe was f. — EPIT 310:10
lovely woman stoops to f. — ELIO 303:21
lovely woman stoops to f. — GOLD 355:33
most loving mere f. — SHAK 681:15
not their merit but our f. — OSBO 578:13
persist in his f. — BLAK 121:3
public f. feeds — COWP 248:18
shoot F. as it flies — POPE 604:18
shunn'st the noise of f. — MILT 529:11
'Tis f. to be wise — GRAY 361:12
to have got rid of f. — HORA 398:19
too presumptuous f. — HART 374:15
uses his f. — SHAK 682:10
usually ends in f. — COLE 234:7
Wisdom excelleth f. — BIBL 85:31

fond au f. des bois — VIGN 810:6
f. of grief — SHAK 699:6
grow too f. of it — LEE 479:2
men would be f. — LYLY 497:1
over-f. of resisting — BECK 61:31
probably f. of them — TWAI 803:30
so f. of one another — SWIF 765:18
When men were f. — SHAK 708:5
fondly F. do we hope — LINC 485:11
fondness habitual f. — WASH 822:10
fons aquae f. — HORA 403:14
f. Bandusiae — HORA 401:21
f. pietatis — MISS 539:17
food alcohol was a f. — WODE 843:1
chief of Scotia's f. — BURN 170:21
Continent have good f. — MIKE 524:23
finds its f. in music — LILL 484:14
F. comes first — BREC 150:14
f. convenient for me — BIBL 85:20
F. enough for a week — MERR 523:3
f. for powder — SHAK 691:2
f. from heaven — BOOK 139:10
f. of love — OPEN 574:15
f. out of the earth — BOOK 141:7
f. that dead men eat — DOBS 278:16
give f. to the poor — CAMA 186:13
good f. and not fine words — MOLI 541:18
Good f. is always a trouble — DAVI 258:1
homely was their f. — GART 340:11
music be the f. of love — SHAK 720:3
problem is f. — DONL 279:3
room and f. — MALT 509:10
wholesome f. — SWIF 766:8
fool and be a f. — POPE 605:2
Answer a f. — BIBL 85:8
Any f. may write — GRAY 362:2
ass, without being a f. — SURT 764:11
beast or a f. — KILV 451:12
become the golden f. — BLAK 121:18
burnt F.'s bandaged finger — KIPL 454:9
Busy old f. — DONN 281:12
carefree and play the f. — FLAU 325:5
Dost thou call me f. — SHAK 700:2
every f. in Buxton — RUSK 659:16
every f. is not a poet — POPE 602:22
f. all the people — LINC 485:16
f. and his money — PROV 620:16
f. at forty — PROV 620:17
f. at forty — YOUN 857:4
f. at the other — SWIF 767:23
f. bolts pleasure — ANTR 23:7
f. consistent — POPE 603:20
f. for his client — PROV 626:7
F. had stuck himself up — BENT 68:6
f. hath said in his heart — BOOK 134:10
f. his whole life long — LUTH 496:15
f. . . . is a man who never tried — DARW 257:16
f. is happy — POPE 605:4
f. i' the forest — SHAK 681:6
f. lies here — KIPL 455:6
f. may give wise man — PROV 620:18
f. returneth to his folly — BIBL 85:9
'F.,' said my Muse — SIDN 736:3
f.'s bauble, the mace — CROM 252:3
f. sees not the same tree — BLAK 120:25
f. there was — KIPL 456:2
f. uttereth all his mind — BIBL 85:18
f. will be meddling — BIBL 84:34
f. with booze — FAUL 316:6
f. would persist — BLAK 121:3
greater f. to admire him — BOIL 125:13
greatest f. may ask — COLT 236:9
He hated a f. — JOHN 433:11
Into a strumpet's f. — SHAK 678:12
knowledgeable f. — MOLI 541:20
laughter of a f. — BIBL 86:6
life time's f. — SHAK 691:12
Love's not Time's f. — SHAK 723:23
make a man appear a f. — DRYD 290:13
more f. am I — ANON 19:20
more hope of a f. — BIBL 85:10
More people know Tom F. — PROV 626:42
muddle-headed f. — CERV 205:12

no fool like an old f. — PROV 632:29
One f. at least — FIEL 317:14
patriot yet, but was a f. — DRYD 287:10
perfections of a f. — BLAK 121:20
played the f. — BIBL 80:26
Prove to me that you're no f. — RICE 647:2
say, Thou f. — BIBL 94:26
smarts so little as a f. — POPE 602:24
stupendous genius! damned f. — BYRO 184:8
suspects himself a f. — YOUN 857:13
They f. me — SHAK 687:12
Thou f. — BIBL 101:1
to manage a f. — KIPL 457:1
wise man or a f. — BLAK 120:16
wisest f. in Christendom — HENR 382:2
fooled f. by that which one loves — MOLI 542:10
foolery little f. — OXEN 581:9
foolish Beware my f. heart — WASH 822:14
could be mighty f. — FARQ 315:23
f., fond old man — SHAK 701:22
f. son — BIBL 84:8
f. thing — BIBL 94:3
f. things of the world — BIBL 107:5
f. thing was but a toy — SHAK 721:18
f. thing well done — JOHN 429:21
Forgive our f. ways — WHIT 834:4
frantic boast and f. word — KIPL 455:13
never said a f. thing — EPIT 309:14
No man was more f. — JOHN 431:19
pound f. — PROV 629:21
saying a f. thing — STER 757:14
These f. things — MARV 516:7
young and f. — YEAT 853:19
foolishest f. act a wise man commits — BROW 157:6
foolishness Mix a little f. — HORA 403:1
unto the Greeks f. — BIBL 107:4
fools all the f. in town — TWAI 803:6
Children and f. tell — PROV 616:38
flannelled f. at the wicket — KIPL 454:16
F. and bairns — PROV 620:19
F. and knaves — BUCK 163:8
F. are my theme — BYRO 182:8
F. ask questions — PROV 620:20
f. build houses — PROV 620:21
f. by heavenly compulsion — SHAK 699:26
F.! For I also had my hour — CHES 215:25
f. for luck — PROV 620:22
f. go aimlessly — UPAN 805:5
F. here below for minor pleasures — GRES 363:15
F. need advice most — FRAN 332:16
f. out of favour — DEFO 261:20
f. rush in — POPE 604:17
F. rush in — PROV 620:23
f. said would happen — MELB 521:4
f., the fools, the fools — PEAR 590:7
f., who came to scoff — GOLD 354:14
For f. to sing — BURN 173:6
Fortune favours f. — PROV 620:26
Hated by f. — SWIF 767:14
house for f. and mad — SWIF 767:18
I am two f. — DONN 281:15
kept from children and from f. — DRYD 289:16
leaves 'em still two f. — CONG 238:16
let f. contest — POPE 605:6
lighted f. The way — SHAK 707:14
make f. of themselves about — SHAW 724:23
millions mostly f. — CARL 192:17
money of f. — HOBB 390:10
Nature meant but f. — POPE 603:29
one half the world f. — JEFF 420:16
O, these deliberate f. — SHAK 709:10
Paradise of F. — MILT 532:20
perish together as f. — KING 452:5
plain f. at last — POPE 603:30
poor f. decoyed — PEPY 592:11
scarecrows of f. — HUXL 412:3
shoal of f. — CONG 239:11
suffer f. gladly — BIBL 108:19
term Invented to awe f. — JONS 435:21
this great stage of f. — SHAK 701:19

forgive (cont.):
would f. you | ALAI 10:1
forgiven f. everything | SHAW 726:32
Her sins are f. | BIBL 100:17
restored, f. | LYTE 497:11
forgiveness After such knowledge, what f. | ELIO 302:4
ask of thee f. | SHAK 701:24
f. is a lovely idea | LEWI 483:5
F. of each vice | BLAK 120:4
F. of sins | BOOK 128:10
F. to the injured | DRYD 288:1
forgiveth f. sins | BIBL 93:2
forgot auld acquaintance be f. | BURN 170:8
auld acquaintance be f. | OPEN 575:16
by the world f. | POPE 602:19
curiosities would be quite f. | AUBR 33:15
F. it not | ROSS 655:18
f. the fart | ELIZ 304:19
f. the taste of fears | SHAK 707:12
I have f. my part | SHAK 682:23
just f. to duck | DEMP 264:1
names ignoble, born to be f. | COWP 247:4
Napoleon f. Blücher | CHUR 220:15
proposed as things f. | POPE 604:15
she f. the stars | KEAT 443:19
forgotten always a f. thing | CHES 215:23
been learned has been f. | SKIN 739:11
books undeservedly f. | AUDE 36:17
F. Army | MOUN 551:16
f. as a nameless number | PAST 588:2
f. even by God | BROW 160:15
f. man at the bottom | ROOS 653:10
f. nothing and learnt nothing | DUMO 291:14
he himself had f. it | PALM 585:3
I am all f. | SHAK 678:22
injury is much sooner f. | CHES 214:24
learnt nothing and f. nothing | TALL 771:18
not one of them is f. | BIBL 100:31
ruins of f. times | BROW 156:7
things one has f. | CANE 189:3
Thou hast f. | SWIN 769:2
fork pick up mercury with a f. | LLOY 488:2
forked poor, bare, f. animal | SHAK 700:26
forks made before f. | PROV 620:6
pursued it with f. | CARR 196:11
forlorn faery lands f. | KEAT 445:1
F.! the very word | KEAT 445:2
maiden all f. | NURS 570:2
wait f. | ARNO 28:20
form earth was without f. | BIBL 75:4
find a f. | BECK 61:11
F. follows function | SULL 763:11
f. from off my door | POE 599:8
F. is emptiness | MAHĀ 506:12
f. of a servant | BIBL 109:24
f. of sound words | BIBL 110:29
F. remains | WORD 849:23
f. the key to organic life | PAST 588:1
human f. divine | BLAK 122:22
lick it into f. | BURT 173:22
mould of f. | SHAK 686:18
no action or physical f. | CHUA 219:4
Thou, silent f. | KEAT 444:14
To every F. of being | WORD 846:18
formal every f. visit | AUST 40:7
f. feeling comes | DICK 272:21
formalistic more f. than conservatives | CALV 186:12
formed him that f. it | BIBL 106:24
perhaps it f. itself | RIG 648:11
small, but perfectly f. | COOP 242:11
former f. and the latter | BOOK 129:21
f. days were better | BIBL 86:8
f. things are passed away | BIBL 114:17
formerly not what we were f. told | BLUN 124:5
formosa F. *facies muta commendatio* | PUBL 636:13
forms By f. unseen | COLL 235:13
f. of government | POPE 605:6
f. of things unknown | SHAK 711:28
give A breath to f. | BYRO 182:7

I like definite f. | STEV 759:12
manifests itself in many f. | EURI 312:15
formula 'f.' of the atomic bomb | MEDA 520:3
fornication F., and all uncleanness | BIBL 109:14
fors F. *dierum cumque dabit* | HORA 400:11
forsake f. me not | BOOK 138:21
F. not an old friend | BIBL 93:10
nor f. thee | BIBL 79:7
forsaken never the righteous f. | BOOK 136:1
O, father f. | JOYC 437:25
primrose that f. dies | MILT 530:8
utterly f. | BETT 73:7
why hast thou f. me | BIBL 99:13
why hast thou f. me | BOOK 134:26
forsaking f. all other | BOOK 133:8
forsworn so sweetly were f. | SHAK 708:13
fort Hold the f. | BLIS 123:10
Hold the f. | SHER 734:14
fortes *Vixere f.* | HORA 402:16
forth F. in thy name | WESL 829:4
F., pilgrim | CHAU 213:20
fortifications f. called castles | ORDE 576:11
fortissimo F. at last | MAHL 507:7
fortiter *pecca f.* | LUTH 496:7
fortitude f. the Soul contains | DICK 272:24
fortnight beyond the next f. | CHAM 206:6
f. dead | ELIO 303:22
fortress f. built by Nature | SHAK 715:13
f. rising above the horizon | LOUI 492:10
petty f. | JOHN 426:18
fortresses brambles in the f. | BIBL 89:8
fortuna *Audentis F. iuvat* | VIRG 813:8
Stat f. domus | VIRG 815:5
fortunate at best but f. | SOLO 745:13
better to be f. | WEBS 826:12
farmers excessively f. | VIRG 814:16
fortunatus *F. et ille deos qui novit* | VIRG 814:18
fortune architect of own f. | PROV 619:17
Base F. | MARL 513:10
beauty without a f. | FARQ 315:11
Blind F. still Bestows | JONS 435:7
Caesar and his f. | CAES 185:5
do F. what she can | DRAY 285:21
face is my f. | NURS 570:15
F. assists the brave | TERE 785:7
f. empties her chamberpot | MACD 501:8
F. favours fools | PROV 620:26
F. favours the brave | PROV 620:27
F. list to flee | CHAU 211:24
F.'s a right whore | WEBS 826:4
f.s sharpe adversitee | CHAU 213:8
F., that favours fools | JONS 434:14
F., wilt thou prove | THOM 792:16
good f. than a good husband | OSBO 578:12
good f. to others | BIER 116:4
good housewife F. | SHAK 680:20
great, ere f. made him so | DRYD 288:10
he shall see F. | BACO 44:12
hostages to f. | BACO 44:30
how does f. banter us | BOLI 126:10
I am F.'s fool | SHAK 717:34
leads on to f. | SHAK 698:21
leave the rest to f. | EURI 312:12
little value of f. | STEE 755:3
method of making a f. | GRAY 361:22
mother of good f. | CERV 205:15
mould of a man's f. | BACO 44:11
outrageous f. | SHAK 686:9
people of f. | ELIO 300:19
possession of a good f. | AUST 39:18
possession of a good f. | OPEN 574:22
rob a lady of her f. | FIEL 318:12
secret parts of F. | SHAK 685:21
sick in f. | SHAK 699:26
smiling of F. | COCK 229:20
smith of his own f. | CLAU 225:12
take good f. | MOLI 542:14
to f. and to fame unknown | GRAY 361:8
upon a plentiful f. | JOHN 428:11
vicissitudes of f. | SADI 662:15
with f. and men's eyes | SHAK 722:28
Women and f. | WYCH 852:11

fortunes content with his f. fit | SHAK 700:20
my f. have | SHAK 679:18
forty at f., the judgement | FRAN 332:14
Every man over f. | SHAW 726:31
fairy when she's f. | HENL 381:12
Fat, fair and f. | O'KE 572:20
fool at f. | PROV 620:17
fool at f. | YOUN 857:4
f. days it will remain | PROV 630:19
f. stripes save one | BIBL 108:21
F. years long | BOOK 140:10
F. years on | BOWE 147:14
In f. minutes | SHAK 711:3
Knows it at f. | YOUN 857:13
Life begins at f. | PITK 595:21
Life begins at f. | PROV 625:13
look young till f. | DRYD 288:33
Men at f. | JUST 439:2
miner, F.-niner | MONT 546:5
When f. winters shall besiege | SHAK 722:22
forty-five At f., what next | LOWE 494:12
forty-three pass for f. | GILB 349:8
forward F., forward let us range | TENN 781:4
f. motion love | VAUG 807:15
from this day f. | BOOK 133:9
look f. to posterity | BURK 167:9
looking f. to the past | OSBO 578:21
marched breast f. | BROW 158:11
nothing to look f. to | FROS 335:11
those behind cried 'F.!' | MACA 499:17
to push things f. | MOWL 551:17
Foss F. is the name of his cat | LEAR 477:14
fossil Language is f. poetry | EMER 307:9
fossils God hid the f. | GOSS 357:6
foster f.-child of silence | KEAT 444:6
f.-child of silence | OPEN 575:25
fostered F. alike by beauty | WORD 849:7
fou f. for weeks thegither | BURN 172:9
f. man and a fasting | SCOT 674:18
f. o' brandy | BURN 171:10
I wasna f. | BURN 170:24
fought better to have f. and lost | CLOU 229:9
f. against me | BOOK 143:4
f. against Sisera | BIBL 79:18
f. a good fight | BIBL 111:1
f. a long hour | SHAK 691:17
f. each other for | SOUT 749:1
f. the dogs | BROW 160:20
to have f. well | COUB 244:9
we f. at Arques | HENR 381:20
foul F. as their soil | BYRO 179:31
F. deeds will rise | SHAK 684:14
f. Fiend | BUNY 164:16
f. is fair | SHAK 703:1
f.-mouthed nation | HAZL 377:5
however f. within | CHUR 219:22
Murder most f. | SHAK 685:2
really f. things up | SAYI 670:17
So f. and fair a day | SHAK 703:8
some f. play | SHAK 684:13
soon be made so f. | BERN 70:15
thank the gods I am f. | SHAK 681:24
too f. an epithet | MARL 513:23
ways be f. | SHAK 702:26
foulest commonly the f. | BACO 43:3
foully play'dst most f. for't | SHAK 705:16
fouls f. its own nest | PROV 624:17
found awoke and f. me here | KEAT 443:29
f. a kingdom | MILT 534:18
F. him in the shining | TENN 778:10
f. my sheep which was lost | BIBL 101:12
f. no more of her | BIBL 82:16
f. the Roman nation | VIRG 810:17
Hast thou f. me | BIBL 81:31
man who has f. himself out | BARR 57:9
was lost, and is f. | BIBL 101:18
When f., make a note | DICK 269:8
foundation Church's one f. | STON 761:5
f. of all good things | BURK 167:29
f. of most governments | ADAM 3:8
f. of the earth | BOOK 140:19
f. of unyielding despair | RUSS 660:25
foundations city which hath f. | BIBL 111:7

earth's f. fled — HOUS 404:1
f. of the earth — BIBL 83:21
f. of the earth — BOOK 141:5
founded f. the Jewish state — HERZ 387:1
founder f. and embellisher — CAXT 204:7
founding f. a bank — BREC 150:15
fount f. whence honour springs — MARL 513:22
fountain Back to the burning f. — SHEL 728:21
Doth a f. send forth — BIBL 111:28
f. filled with blood — COWP 246:27
f. momently was forced — COLE 232:4
f. of all goodness — BOOK 128:16
f. of delights — LUCR 496:2
f. of good sense — DRYD 290:10
f. of honour — BACO 43:12
f. of the water of life — BIBL 114:18
f. sealed — BIBL 87:12
healing f. — AUDE 35:8
It is that f. — RALE 640:19
like a f. troubled — SHAK 718:15
Like a summer-dried f. — SCOT 673:5
fountains Afric's sunny f. — HEBE 378:15
f. mingle with the river — SHEL 730:2
living f. — AKEN 9:4
sad f. — ANON 19:16
silver f. mud — SHAK 723:3
founts White f. falling — CHES 216:4
four all f.-footed things — CHES 215:24
At the age of f. — USTI 806:5
fiery f.-in-hand — COLE 234:9
f. beasts full of eyes — BIBL 113:8
F. eyes see more — PROV 620:28
f.-footed beasts — BIBL 105:6
f. for a birth — PROV 628:33
F. lagging winters — SHAK 715:8
f.-legged friend — BROO 154:7
F. legs good — ORWE 576:20
f.-year-old child could — FILM 321:1
say that two plus two make f. — ORWE 577:17
twice two be not f. — TURG 802:11
fourscore come to f. years — BOOK 139:23
fourteenth f. Mr Wilson — HOME 393:16
fourth f. estate of the realm — MACA 497:19
This is the F. — LAST 474:5
fous C'étaient des f. — RENO 645:10
fowl f. of the air — BIBL 75:8
liver-wing of a f. — TENN 784:24
fowler snare of the f. — BOOK 142:21
fowls all small f. singis — DOUG 283:14
Barn-door f. for dissenters — SMIT 743:15
f. of the air — BIBL 95:7
f. of the air — BIBL 105:6
f. of the air — BOOK 141:6
smale f. maken melodye — CHAU 210:5
fox beset the historical f. — HUXL 411:13
certain f. wanted — LA F 463:16
Crazy like a f. — PERE 592:18
f. from his lair in the morning — GRAV 360:3
f.-hunting—the wisest religion — HAIL 367:12
f. is off to his den — NURS 568:15
f. knows many things — ARCH 24:9
F. who was my friend — READ 643:3
galloping after a f. — WILD 836:21
loves the f. less — SURT 764:15
people that think, and f.-hunters — SHEN 733:1
prince must be a f. — MACH 502:12
quick brown f. — ANON 18:16
sharp hot stink of f. — HUGH 407:8
They've shot our f. — BIRC 116:17
what the wary f. said — HORA 399:2
foxed If ever I was f. — PEPY 591:23
foxes f. have a sincere interest — ELIO 299:16
f. have holes — BIBL 96:1
f., that spoil the vines — BIBL 87:7
portion for f. — BOOK 138:4
second to the f. — BERL 70:3
foxholes no atheists in the f. — CUMM 253:16
signs on the f. — KENN 449:4
foxlike f. in the vine — TENN 783:16
frabjous O f. day — CARR 194:26
fraction wretched f. — CARL 191:15
fragment not a geographical f. — PARN 586:20

fragments f. that remain — BIBL 103:2
These f. I have shored — ELIO 303:24
fragrance Isles of f. — POPE 602:4
frail F. crowds — MOOR 547:9
frailty concession to human f. — TAWN 774:3
f. of our nature — BOOK 130:4
f. of the mind — SHAD 677:21
F., thy name is woman — SHAK 684:4
love's the noblest f. — DRYD 288:22
therefore more f. — SHAK 690:31
frame f. in the earth — SPEN 752:3
f. of adamant — JOHN 426:17
f. of nature — ADDI 4:23
f. of the world — BERK 69:14
my f. perish — BYRO 179:11
universal f. — BACO 43:16
framed f. and glazed — WALP 819:8
français n'est pas f. — RIVA 649:14
France better in F. — STER 756:7
between F. and England — JERR 421:16
by which F. is fed — SULL 763:14
F., famed in all great arts — ARNO 29:1
F. has lost a battle — DE G 262:1
F. has more need of me — NAPO 556:16
F. in a certain way — OPEN 575:27
F. is a person — MICH 524:6
F., mother of arts — DU B 290:17
F. wants you to take part — CHIR 218:1
F. was long a despotism — CARL 192:9
F. will say that I am a German — EINS 297:16
I now speak for F. — DE G 262:2
not love the English in F. — CARD 190:8
one illusion—F. — KEYN 450:11
Political thought, in F. — ARON 30:18
round hose in F. — SHAK 708:27
stood the wind for F. — DRAY 286:6
sweet enemy, F. — SIDN 736:6
vasty fields of F. — SHAK 692:27
wield the sword of F. — DE G 262:3
Francesca di Rimini F., miminy — GILB 348:16
Frankie F. and Albert — SONG 747:5
frankincense f., and myrrh — BIBL 94:6
frankly F., my dear — FILM 319:7
frantic fascination f. — GILB 348:11
frater f., ave atque vale — CATU 203:10
Fraternité Égalité F. — POLI 601:1
fraternize beckon you to f. — AUDE 35:22
fratrum Par nobile f. — HORA 403:13
fraud Force, and f. — HOBB 390:17
May is a pious f. — LOWE 494:5
frauds all great men are f. — BONA 127:3
freak grotesque composite f. — HENN 381:18
freckled f. like a pard — KEAT 443:30
Whatever is fickle, f. — HOPK 396:22
freckles curiosity, f., and doubt — PARK 585:15
In those f. — SHAK 710:28
Fred Here lies F. — EPIT 310:2
Frederick death of F. the Great — BISM 118:1
free as any spirit f. — CHAU 211:7
as soon write f. verse — FROS 336:9
be f. — SHEL 732:19
be perfectly f. — SPEN 750:13
best things are f. — PROV 615:15
best things in life are f. — DE S 265:16
Bind me, or set me f. — GODO 352:1
bond nor f. — BIBL 110:12
born f. — ANON 15:1
born f. as Caesar — SHAK 696:6
but it's f. — KRIS 461:20
Church shall be f. — MAGN 506:3
Comment is f. — SCOT 672:14
condemned to be f. — SART 667:2
England should be f. — MAGE 506:2
Ev'rything f. in America — SOND 746:2
favours f. speech — BROU 154:17
f. again — SOLZ 745:14
f. agent — AURE 38:10
f. and immortal — TRAH 797:13
f. as nature first made man — DRYD 287:30
F. at last — EPIT 309:7
F. by '93 — POLI 600:17
f. church — CAVO 204:6
freedom to the f. — LINC 485:6

f. man, an American — JOHN 423:7
f. society is a society where — STEV 758:15
F. women are not women — COLE 234:16
Greece might still be f. — BYRO 181:5
half f. — LINC 484:16
I am a f. man — MCGO 502:1
I am not f. — DEBS 260:18
ignorant and f. — JEFF 420:11
in a f. country — BURK 166:28
in chains than to be f. — KAFK 440:21
I was f. born — BIBL 105:26
know our will is f. — JOHN 429:4
land of the f. — KEY 450:9
let him go f. — BOOK 141:13
Man was born f. — ROUS 657:4
men everywhere could be f. — LINC 485:5
Mother of the F. — BENS 67:25
naturally were born f. — MILT 536:7
No f. man shall be taken — MAGN 506:4
no such thing as a f. lunch — SAYI 670:15
not a f. press but a managed — RADC 640:10
not f. either — SOLZ 745:17
Not of my own f. will — VIRG 812:4
not only to be f. — PANK 585:7
protection of f. speech — HOLM 393:10
set f. in our remembering — BERR 71:1
should themselves be f. — BROO 153:4
so far kept us f. — JEFF 420:2
Teach the f. man — AUDE 35:8
that moment they are f. — COWP 247:27
Thou art f. — ARNO 28:12
Thought is f. — PROV 632:45
Thought is f. — SHAK 718:34
truth makes men f. — AGAR 6:20
truth shall make you f. — BIBL 103:11
Was he f. — AUDE 36:12
We must be f. or die — WORD 847:3
wholly slaves or wholly f. — DRYD 288:16
Who would be f. — BYRO 178:17
free-born f. mouse — BARB 55:4
freed f. my soul — BERN 70:14
freedom abridging the f. of speech — CONS 241:13
apprenticeship for f. — BARA 55:1
better organised than f. — PÉGU 591:6
But what is F. — COLE 231:2
can often picture f. — MURD 554:14
cause of f. — BOWL 148:13
conditioned to a f. — KENY 449:15
Conservative ideal of f. — MADA 505:6
depends on f. of the press — JEFF 419:11
destroy the f. — ADAM 3:6
enemies of f. do not argue — INGE 413:4
fight for f. and truth — IBSE 412:11
first is f. of speech — ROOS 653:20
for f. freedom — SPEN 750:12
For the sake of f. — ZORO 860:4
F. alone he earns — GOET 353:1
F. alone substitutes — TOCQ 795:2
f. alone that we fight — ANON 19:4
F. and not servitude — BURK 166:25
F. and slavery are mental states — GAND 339:6
F. and Whisky — BURN 170:11
F. an English subject's — DRYD 289:24
F. cannot exist — METT 523:10
f. depends on being courageous — THUC 793:23
f. for the one who thinks differently — LUXE 496:17
f. for the pike — TAWN 774:2
F. has a thousand charms — COWP 247:21
F. hunted — PAIN 582:9
F. is an indivisible word — WILL 839:19
f. is a noble thing — BARB 55:10
f. is but a light — GUMI 365:17
F. is excellent — TOCQ 795:4
F. is not a gift — NKRU 565:4
F. is slavery — ORWE 577:14
f. is something — BALD 50:8
F. is the freedom to say — ORWE 577:17
f. of person — JEFF 420:4
f. of speech — TWAI 803:9
F. of the press guaranteed — LIEB 484:10
F. of the press in Britain — SWAF 765:3

freedom (*cont.*):
f. of the press's speech   TWAI 803:17
F.'s banner   DRAK 285:19
F. shrieked—as Kosciuszko fell   CAMP 187:16
F.'s just another word   KRIS 461:20
F. slowly broadens down   TENN 784:23
f. to offend   RUSH 659:5
f. to the slave   LINC 485:6
from slavery to f.   HAGG 367:4
gave my life for f.   EWER 313:8
give to man F.   GRAI 358:17
green f. of a cockatoo   STEV 758:8
I gave them f.   GORB 356:16
Let f. ring   SMIT 742:18
love not f., but licence   MILT 536:6
man makes his way to F.   SCHI 671:7
means by defending f.   NIEM 563:17
no easy walk-over to f.   NEHR 558:7
obtained I this f.   BIBL 105:26
O F., what liberties are taken   GEOR 344:2
own true f.   MONT 544:9
participation of f.   BURK 166:30
peace from f.   MALC 508:11
Perfect f. is reserved   COLL 235:1
plan for f.   POPP 607:3
preserve and enlarge f.   LOCK 488:16
riches and f.   WALĘ 817:7
road toward f.   MORR 550:8
service is perfect f.   BOOK 128:12
taste of F.   PALI 584:8
there can be no f.   LENI 480:5
they treasure f.   ADAM 3:12
unless f. is universal   HILL 388:7
freedoms four essential human f.
    ROOS 653:20
F. you'll not to me allow   BEHN 63:23
freehold given to none f.   LUCR 495:17
freeing f. some   LINC 485:5
freely F. ye have received   BIBL 96:14
Freeman F. butters Stubbs   ROGE 652:15
freemasonry bitter f.   BEER 63:6
freemen Americans are to be f.   WASH 822:6
great nursery of f.   SHIP 735:1
rule o'er f.   BROO 153:4
freewoman he of the f.   BIBL 108:27
freeze f. my humanity   MACN 504:19
f. thy young blood   SHAK 684:32
freezes Yours till Hell f.   FISH 322:16
frei Arbeit macht f.   ANON 21:5
freight shall have her earthly f.   WORD 848:9
Freiheit F. is immer nur   LUXE 496:17
freits follows f.   PROV 621:47
French always have spoken F.   VOLT 816:15
Before F. culture   RENA 645:5
drawn out of F.   MALO 508:21
F. are wiser   BACO 45:15
F. are with equal advantage   CANN 189:4
F. arrange   CATH 199:8
F. government   COLO 236:7
F. is the *patois*   BAGE 49:7
F. of Parys   CHAU 210:11
F., or Turk   GILB 348:26
F. Revolution operated   TOCQ 795:5
F. want no-one to be   TOCQ 795:14
F. widow in every bedroom   HOFF 392:4
glory of beating the F.   WOLF 843:14
how it's improved her F.   GRAH 358:5
If the F. noblesse   TREV 798:11
Learning F. is some trouble   EMPS 307:26
new F. books   BROW 158:16
no more F.   ANON 18:2
not clear is not F.   RIVA 649:14
not too French F. bean   GILB 348:14
Paris was F.—and silent   TUCH 802:1
professor of F. letters   JOYC 437:23
Speak in F.   CARR 195:3
to men F.   CHAR 209:13
to the F. the empire of the land   RICH 648:2
We are not F.   MONT 545:14
We F., we English   BIRN 116:18
Frenchman must hate a F.   NELS 558:12
Frenchmen beat three F.   ADDI 5:3
beat three F.   PROV 628:32

Fifty million F.   MILI 526:8
frenzy Demoniac f.   MILT 534:8
poet's eye, in a fine f.   SHAK 711:28
What is life? a f.   CALD 185:12
frequency very fact of f.   ELIO 300:6
frequent f. hearses   POPE 602:15
frère Sois mon f.   CHAM 207:8
frères f. humains après nous   VILL 810:11
fresh ancient and so f.   AUGU 37:5
f. air and fun   EDGA 295:13
f. as is the month of May   CHAU 210:8
F. as the Angel   BYRO 178:1
f. lap of the crimson rose   SHAK 710:32
F. shalt thou see in me   DANI 255:6
It's tingling f.   ADVE 7:39
nice f. corpse   TWAI 803:16
O yonge, f. folkes   CHAU 213:16
So sad, so f.   TENN 783:4
fret fever, and the f.   KEAT 444:23
f. a passage through   FULL 337:7
F. not thyself   BOOK 135:28
frets struts and f. his hour   SHAK 707:14
fretted F. the pigmy body   DRYD 286:19
Freud trouble with F.   DODD 278:19
Freude F., schöner Götterfunken   SCHI 668:16
Freudian still had her F. papa   LOWE 494:8
friars cannot all be f.   CERV 205:11
f. were singing vespers   GIBB 345:20
fricassee f., or a ragout   SWIF 766:8
friction f. which no man can imagine
    CLAU 225:15
Friday F.'s child   NURS 568:10
My man F.   DEFO 261:12
on a F. fil al this meschaunce   CHAU 212:3
one F. morn   SONG 748:2
friend angry with my f.   BLAK 122:16
as you choose a f.   DILL 274:10
betraying my f.   FORS 330:1
Boldness be my f.   SHAK 682:28
candid f.   CANN 189:7
Codlin's the f.   DICK 271:6
countervail a f.   GRIM 364:12
damned goodnatured f.   SHER 733:6
diamonds a girl's best f.   ROBI 650:10
ease some f.   POPE 602:26
enemy is my f.   SAYI 669:16
faithful f.   BIBL 93:6
familiar f.   BOOK 136:10
fat f.   BRUM 162:6
favourite has no f.   GRAY 361:15
forgave a f.   BLAK 121:19
Forsake not an old f.   BIBL 93:10
four-legged f.   BROO 154:7
F. and associate of this clay   HADR 366:10
f.-and-relation   MILN 527:17
F., go up higher   BIBL 101:4
f. in need   PROV 620:29
f. in power   ADAM 2:11
f. loveth at all times   BIBL 84:29
f. of every country   CANN 189:5
F. of my better days   HALL 369:16
F. of the humble   SIKH 737:6
f. should bear   SHAK 698:17
f. sincere enough   BULW 164:7
f. that sticketh closer   BIBL 84:32
f. that will go to jail   BURN 169:16
F., wherefore   BIBL 99:7
He was my f.   SHAK 697:24
homes without a f.   CLAR 224:9
house to lodge a f.   SWIF 766:31
I finds a f.   DIBD 267:7
I lose a f.   SARG 666:17
In every f. we lose a part   POPE 606:19
Is such a f.   COWP 246:12
last best f. am I   SOUT 749:7
lay down his wife for his f.   JOYC 437:23
Little F. of all the World   KIPL 456:22
look like a f.   SHAK 683:25
lose her as a f.   GLAD 351:12
lose your f.   PROV 625:2
loss of a dear f.   SOUT 749:16
lost no f.   POPE 603:24
Lover for a f.   ETHE 312:6

makes not f.   TENN 778:2
man, That love my f.   SHAK 698:4
mine own familiar f.   BOOK 137:17
mistress or a f.   SHEL 729:7
My f. may spit   HERB 385:3
no f. like a sister   ROSS 655:8
Nor a f. to know me   STEV 760:17
not a f. to close his eyes   DRYD 287:16
O f. unseen   FLEC 326:6
only way to have a f.   EMER 306:23
Phone a f.   CATC 201:24
polished female f.   WHUR 834:9
poor man's dearest f.   BURN 171:25
pretended f. is worse   GAY 341:29
'Strange f.,' I said   OWEN 581:7
think of him as a f.   SMIT 743:5
To find a f.   DOUG 283:19
want a f. in need   DICK 269:8
Whatever you think of your f.   MIDR 524:16
What is a f.   ARIS 26:7
Whenever a f. succeeds   VIDA 810:1
wounds of a f.   BIBL 85:14
your enemy and your f.   TWAI 803:12
your f. that loves you   SHAK 696:2
friendless f. bodies of unburied men
    WEBS 826:9
    SHEL 731:5
Omnipotent but f.   SHEL 731:5
friendliness friendship and f.   MALA 508:8
friends All her family and her f.   CORS 243:18
Americans are our best f.   THOM 791:21
best f. hear no more   SHEL 729:22
best of f.   TUPP 802:3
best of f. must part   SONG 748:7
by their unmarried f.   TROL 800:14
Champagne for my real f.   BACO 47:3
choice of f.   COWL 245:22
closest f. won't tell you   ADVE 7:21
comes to meet one's f.   BURN 169:24
distresses of our f.   SWIF 767:15
documents and f.   SPAR 749:24
doubt one's f.   LA R 469:12
Fair face show f.   GOOG 356:12
falling out of faithful f.   EDWA 297:3
forgive our f.   MEDI 520:8
f. are necessarily   USTI 806:3
f. do not need it   HUBB 406:10
f.' houses   JOHN 432:4
f. in the garrison   HALI 368:11
f. must part   PROV 615:12
f. of every country   DISR 276:16
F. part forever   BASH 57:22
F., Romans, countrymen   SHAK 697:21
f. thou hast   SHAK 684:31
f. were not unearthly beautiful   RICH 647:7
His f. he loved   WATS 823:4
his only f.   CAMP 188:3
I had such f.   YEAT 855:1
I have lost f.   WOOL 845:10
in the house of God as f.   BOOK 137:17
I wish thee f.   CORB 243:3
lay down his f. for his life   THOR 793:21
life for his f.   BIBL 103:33
love of f.   BELL 65:28
Make to yourselves f.   BIBL 101:20
misfortune of our best f.   LA R 469:21
Money couldn't buy f.   MILL 527:12
my f. pictured within   ELGA 299:1
my list of f.   COWP 248:17
nearly deceiving your f.   CORN 243:14
new city of F.   WHIT 833:2
none of his f. like him   WILD 837:10
no true f. in politics   CLAR 224:21
Old f. are best   SELD 676:3
old f. to trust   BACO 43:4
Our f., the enemy   BÉRA 69:4
Save us from our f.   PROV 630:20
separateth very f.   BIBL 84:28
Some of my best f. are white   DURE 293:2
tavern for his f.   DOUG 283:21
tell it to your f.   MONT 546:1
thousand f.   ALI 11:16
to all thy f.   BIBL 91:5
treat my f.   MALL 508:16

furnished (*cont.*):
F. and burnish'd — BETJ 73:1
how poorly f. you are — PERS 593:9
furniture church f. at best — COWP 248:20
don't trip over the f. — COWA 245:14
f. on the deck of the Titanic — MORT 551:8
No f. so charming — SMIT 743:20
rearranges the f. — PRAT 610:9
stocked with all the f. — DOYL 284:11
furor *Ira f. brevis est* — HORA 399:6
furrow on a half-reaped f. — KEAT 445:15
plough my f. alone — ROSE 655:2
furrows made long f. — BOOK 143:5
furry fire was f. as a bear — SITW 738:15
further Always a little f. — FLEC 326:2
but no f. — PIUS 596:15
f. one goes — LAO 467:15
f. they have to fall — FITZ 324:13
f. us — BOOK 132:7
Go f. and fare worse — PROV 620:43
fury blind f. of creation — SHAW 726:2
Comes the blind F. — MILT 530:3
filth and the f. — NEWS 562:7
f. and the mire of human veins — YEAT 853:9
f., like a woman scorned — CONG 238:30
f. of a patient man — DRYD 287:11
Hell hath no f. — PROV 622:19
In her prophetic f. — SHAK 714:8
opponents of F. — ZORO 859:21
sound and f. — SHAK 707:14
War hath no f. — MONT 543:20
furze When the f. is in bloom — PROV 634:29
fuse line is a f. — MAYA 519:9
through the green f. — THOM 789:9
fuss f. about an omelette — VOLT 816:20
fustian f.'s so sublimely bad — POPE 602:28
futility fatal f. of fact — JAME 418:5
future Back to the f. — FILM 322:1
call on past and f. — O'NE 573:14
Children of the f. age — BLAK 122:15
controls the f. — ORWE 577:15
curiosity about the f. — WAUG 824:7
danger of the f. — FROM 335:4
dedication to Canada's f. — DIEF 274:6
dipped into the f. — TENN 780:20
empires of the f. — CHUR 221:19
fight against the f. — GLAD 350:13
flag of the f. — PEAR 590:12
f. ain't what it used to be — BERR 71:8
f. and the past — BOLA 124:9
F. as a promised land — LEWI 483:6
f. can be promised to no one — TRUD 801:1
F. not for parties — WILS 840:15
f. of the human race — JEAN 419:5
f.'s bright — ADVE 7:24
F. shock — TOFF 795:16
f. states of both — BYRO 180:29
hopes of the f. — BURK 168:3
lets the f. in — GREE 362:16
never think of the f. — EINS 298:1
no faith in the f. — TAYL 774:13
no preparation for the f. — DISR 276:28
no trust in the f. — HORA 400:14
once and f. king — MALO 509:4
past, present and f. — EINS 298:9
perhaps present in time f. — ELIO 301:9
picture of the f. — ORWE 577:22
plan the f. by the past — BURK 166:5
scaffold sways the f. — LOWE 494:4
seen the f. and it works — STEF 755:4
sense of f. favours — WALP 820:9
serve the f. hour — WORD 849:24
Trust no F. — LONG 490:20
walking backward into f. — ZHVA 858:8
futurum *Quid sit f.* — HORA 400:11
fuzzy-wuzzy 'ere's *to* you, F. — KIPL 454:5
Fyfe David Patrick Maxwell F. — ANON 17:22
fyr is f. yreke — CHAU 212:7

gabardine my Jewish g. — SHAK 709:2
gable Skimming our g. — HEAN 377:16
gadget g.-filled paradise — NIEB 563:16

gadgets One servant worth a thousand g. — SCHU 672:5
Gael hearthstone of the G. — JOHN 433:24
Gaels great G. of Ireland — CHES 215:22
gag tight g. of place — HEAN 378:6
Gaia G. is a tough bitch — MARG 512:6
gaiety eclipsed the g. — JOHN 425:9
only concession to g. — THOM 790:20
Our own g. — BLY 124:11
gaily G. into Ruislip gardens — BETJ 72:13
gain another man's g. — PROV 628:43
deem a losing g. — SOUT 749:21
g., not glory — POPE 605:20
g., not pain — OXFO 581:10
g. of a few — POPE 606:18
g. the whole world — BIBL 99:23
g. to me — BIBL 110:3
loss without some g. — PROV 632:30
No pain, no g. — PROV 628:1
So might I g. — BROW 159:30
to die is g. — BIBL 109:22
gained misery is a battle g. — WELL 827:14
gainful seek g. employment — ACHE 1:9
gains Light g. make heavy purses — BACO 43:25
no g. without pains — STEV 758:13
gait as much as his g. — MATH 518:7
gaiters gas and g. — DICK 271:3
Galatea *Malo me G. petit* — VIRG 813:21
Galatians great text in G. — BROW 161:13
galaxy g. far, far away — TAGL 771:7
gale g., it plies the saplings — HOUS 404:14
Galen as G. says — GOGA 353:22
Galeotto G. was the book — DANT 255:20
galère *dans cette g.* — MOLI 541:22
gales cool g. shall fan the glade — POPE 606:1
Galilean O pale G. — SWIN 768:22
pilot of the G. lake — MILT 530:5
You have won, G. — LAST 474:10
Galilee nightly on deep G. — BYRO 180:1
Galileo G. in two thousand years — PIUS 596:16
status of G. — GOUL 357:10
gall gave me g. to eat — BOOK 138:16
take my milk for g. — SHAK 703:20
wormwood and the g. — BIBL 91:8
gallant braw g. — BALL 51:17
died a very g. gentleman — EPIT 309:12
gallantry no more to do with g. — SHER 733:12
What men call g. — BYRO 180:8
galleon Stately as a g. — GREN 363:12
gallery g. of pictures — BACO 44:14
galley doing in that g. — MOLI 541:22
Gallia *G. est omnis divisa* — CAES 185:1
G. est omnis divisa — OPEN 574:11
gallimaufry g. or hodgepodge — SPEN 752:21
gallop G. about doing good — SMIT 742:19
G. apace — SHAK 717:35
Why does he g. — STEV 760:8
galloped we g. all three — BROW 159:23
galloping hoof with a g. sound — VIRG 813:5
gallops who Time g. withal — SHAK 681:23
gallow grew a g. — KYD 462:10
gallows die upon the g. — WILK 837:19
g. in every one — CARL 192:31
g. in my garden — CHES 215:20
g.-maker; for that frame — SHAK 688:23
g. that he had prepared — BIBL 82:23
Jack on the g.-tree — SCOT 674:9
nothing but the g. — BURK 167:16
perfect g. — SHAK 718:18
Under the G.-Tree — FLET 327:3
galumphing went g. back — CARR 194:26
gamble Life is a g. — STOP 761:16
gambler whore and the g. — BLAK 119:14
game Anarchism is a g. — SHAW 727:4
beautiful g. — PELÉ 591:8
don't like this g. — CATC 201:1
g. at which two can play — BEER 63:7
g. is about glory — BLAN 123:8
g. of the few — BERK 69:11
g. on these lone heaths — HAZL 377:7
g.'s afoot — SHAK 693:5
giving over of a g. — BEAU 60:8

how you played the G. — RICE 646:19
nature of my g. — JAGG 415:18
not being a g. — LEAC 476:17
play the g. — NEWB 560:5
see most of the g. — PROV 625:40
'The g.,' said he — CRAB 249:13
time to win this g. — DRAK 285:18
war's a g. — COWP 248:12
woman is his g. — TENN 783:8
gamecocks Wits are g. — GAY 341:26
gamekeeper life of an English g. — ANON 19:11
makes the best g. — PROV 628:20
games better than g. — SCOT 672:17
dread of g. — BETJ 73:4
G. people play — BERN 71:4
g. should be seen — MONT 544:5
gamesmanship theory and practice of g. — POTT 608:10
gammon world of g. and spinnage — DICK 268:20
gamut g. of the emotions — PARK 586:6
gander goosey g. — NURS 567:1
Grey goose and g. — NURS 567:2
sauce for the g. — PROV 634:11
gangrenous G. limbs cannot be — HEGE 379:2
gangsters great nations acted like g. — KUBR 462:3
gaol world's thy g. — DONN 281:21
gap last g. but one — WHIT 832:3
made a g. in nature — SHAK 679:5
this great g. of time — SHAK 678:23
gaping g. wretches — HUNT 409:16
gaps God lived in g. — DRUM 286:10
garage to the full g. — HOOV 395:23
garbage G. in, garbage out — SAYI 669:19
Garbo G. talks — TAGL 771:3
Garcia Lorca —and you, G. — GINS 349:17
Garde *La G. meurt* — CAMB 186:14
garden all your life plant a g. — PROV 623:27
as a lodge in a g. — BIBL 87:25
Back to the g. — MITC 540:12
blow upon my g. — BIBL 87:13
Come into the g. — TENN 781:23
enclosed g. — CATU 203:2
England is a g. — KIPL 454:8
fairies at the bottom of our g. — FYLE 337:12
gallows in my g. — CHES 215:20
g. eastward in Eden — BIBL 75:11
g. inclosed — BIBL 87:12
g. in her face — CAMP 188:4
g. is a lovesome thing — BROW 155:11
g. of bright images — BRAM 149:8
g. of the world — MARV 516:5
g. of your face — HERB 383:5
g.'s umbrage mild — SMAR 740:17
g. with pedantic weeds — CARE 190:12
ghost of a g. — SWIN 768:13
God the first g. made — COWL 245:19
imperfections of my g. — MONT 544:2
in a lofty G. — KORA 461:12
Lord God walking in the g. — BIBL 75:20
man and a woman in a g. — WILD 836:23
nearer God's Heart in a g. — GURN 365:20
planted a g. — BACO 44:17
rosebud g. of girls — TENN 781:25
Round and round the g. — NURS 569:10
set to dress this g. — SHAK 716:4
sunlight on the g. — MACN 504:22
too much time in the g. — HOBY 391:5
We are a g. walled around — WATT 823:14
where a g. should be — HORA 403:14
Gārdena *Hwæt! wē G.* — ANON 22:7
gardener Adam was a g. — SHAK 694:32
I am but a young g. — JEFF 420:9
supposing him to be the g. — BIBL 104:12
gardeners g., ditchers — SHAK 688:22
gardenias g. in your hair — HOLI 392:16
gardening g. is but landscape-painting — POPE 606:25
gardens Sowe Carrets in your G. — GARD 339:12
sweetest delight of g. — BROW 156:5
garish day's g. eye — MILT 529:15

loved the g. day NEWM 561:6
no worship to the g. sun SHAK 717:37
garland green willow is my g. HEYW 387:18
O! withered is the g. SHAK 680:3
willow must be my g. SHAK 714:17
garlands may gather g. SCOT 674:2
they are g. BENN 67:11
garlic clove of g. round my neck O'BR 571:3
Wel loved he g. CHAU 210:27
garment g. of thought CARL 192:26
g. was white as snow BIBL 91:24
grasp the hem of his g. BISM 118:5
leaves an old g. BHAG 74:10
left his g. in her hand BIBL 77:3
like as with a g. BOOK 141:5
not know the g. from the man BLAK 120:5
wax old as doth a g. BOOK 140:19
garmented g. in light SHEL 732:8
garments cross upon their g. URBA 805:25
g. of the Torah ZOHA 859:5
part my g. BOOK 135:2
Reasons are not like g. ESSE 312:1
Stuffs out his vacant g. SHAK 699:6
garnished empty, swept, and g. BIBL 96:35
garret Born in the g. BYRO 183:6
Genius in a g. ROBI 650:21
living in a g. FOOT 328:3
garrison friends in the g. HALI 368:11
Garsington Hey for G. KETT 450:6
garter knight of the g. ATTL 33:3
like about the Order of the G. MELB 521:5
garters own heir-apparent g. SHAK 689:33
gas g. and gaiters DICK 271:3
G. smells awful PARK 586:1
g. was on BETJ 72:16
got as far as poison-g. HARD 372:11
gash be it g. or gold BROO 154:4
gasp last g. BIBL 94:4
gate A-sitting on a g. CARR 195:26
at one g. to make defence MILT 534:30
cabin at your g. SHAK 720:13
Death . . . openeth the g. BACO 44:4
drops on g.-bars hang HARD 373:5
enemies in the g. BOOK 143:2
g. of glory BOOK 134:2
g. of heaven BIBL 76:32
how strait the g. HENL 381:15
laid at his g. BIBL 101:22
leads to the broad g. SHAK 678:11
lead you to Heaven's g. BLAK 120:13
man at the g. of the year HASK 375:2
November at the g. PUSH 638:4
Only through beauty's g. SCHI 670:28
out of the ivory g. BROW 157:13
watchful at his g. DODD 278:20
Wide is the g. BIBL 95:19
gates besiege your g. POPE 602:15
enter then his g. KETH 450:5
g. are mind to open KIPL 455:7
g. of hell BIBL 97:16
g. of it shall not be shut BIBL 114:20
g. of perception MAIM 507:17
g. to the glorious and unknown FORS 329:13
Open the temple g. SPEN 751:8
O ye g. BOOK 135:6
Sprouting despondently at area g.
ELIO 302:21
stand in thy g. BOOK 142:18
suicide at its g. HUSS 410:17
to the g. of Hell PIUS 596:15
two g. of Sleep VIRG 812:17
Gath Tell it not in G. BIBL 80:27
gather G. ye rosebuds HERR 386:18
He will surely g. you KORA 460:6
who shall g. them BOOK 136:5
gathered cannot be g. up again BIBL 81:3
eagles be g. together PROV 634:41
g. together in my name BIBL 97:22
two or three are g. BOOK 128:18
gathering g. where thou hast not strawed
BIBL 98:22
gat-toothed G. I was CHAU 212:18
gaude g. in Christo LUTH 496:7

gaudeamus G. igitur, Juvenes dum sumus
ANON 21:17
gaudia ira voluptas G. JUVE 439:10
gaudy g., blabbing, and remorseful day
SHAK 694:17
Neat, but not g. WESL 830:1
one other g. night SHAK 679:17
rich, not g. SHAK 684:18
gauger what should Master G. play
STEV 761:1
Gaul G. as a whole OPEN 574:11
G. as a whole is divided CAES 185:1
Gaunt G.'s embattled pile MACA 499:3
Old John of G. SHAK 715:4
gauze shoot her through g. BANK 54:17
gauzy wrapped in a g. veil SHEL 732:7
gave Lord g., and the Lord BIBL 82:27
she g. me of the tree BIBL 75:21
What wee g., wee have EPIT 311:16
gay g. deceiver COLM 236:2
g. Lothario ROWE 657:8
G. men may seek sex PAGL 581:16
good and g. PROV 626:28
heart was warm and g. HAMM 370:4
if I could, be g. ROGE 652:13
impiously g. CRAB 249:6
making Gay rich, and Rich g. JOHN 425:4
reading for g. men STEV 758:20
second best's a g. goodnight YEAT 854:9
So g. the band GREN 363:12
without feeling g. CHUR 220:2
Gaza Eyeless in G. MILT 534:25
gaze bade me g. ARNO 28:19
gazelle never loved a dear G. CARR 196:13
nursed a dear G. DICK 271:7
nursed a dear G. MOOR 547:20
one a g. YEAT 854:12
gazelles g. appear MOOR 547:9
gazer g. wipe his eye HERB 385:4
gazette Pall Mall G. is written THAC 786:10
gazing g. at each other SAIN 663:10
g. up into heaven BIBL 104:25
géant ailes de g. BAUD 58:11
geese G. are swans ARNO 27:14
g., like a snow cloud RANS 642:6
great g. honk northward WARR 822:1
kill all turkeys, g. PROV 628:24
Like g. about the sky AUDE 34:19
swans of others are g. WALP 819:16
wild g. are flighting KIPL 454:15
wild g. lost BASH 57:22
Gehazi Whence comest thou, G. BIBL 82:9
Gehenna Down to G. KIPL 454:20
Geist Ich bin der G. GOET 352:16
gem g. of purest ray serene GRAY 361:5
precious g. was hidden MITF 540:16
Thinking every tear a g. SHEL 730:4
geminae g. Somni portae VIRG 812:17
gemlike hard, g. flame PATE 588:11
gender of the feminine g. O'KE 572:19
tired of the g. SEXT 677:13
general caviare to the g. SHAK 685:29
feet of the great g. OVID 580:19
find in that great g. JUVE 440:8
G. notions MONT 543:14
good g. because he has CHAM 207:6
generalities glittering and sounding g.
CHOA 218:6
Glittering g. EMER 307:17
generalizations g. dangerous DUMA 291:13
love meaningless g. GREE 362:19
generally g. necessary to salvation
BOOK 132:19
talk of g. held ideas BAUD 58:17
General Motors good for G. WILS 840:1
generals against the law for g. TRUM 801:13
bite some of my other g. GEOR 343:3
Dead battles, like dead g. TUCH 801:20
g. than in particulars HUME 409:3
Russia has two g. NICH 563:8
we're all G. USTI 806:5
generation beat g. KERO 449:17
best minds of my g. GINS 349:15

chosen g. BIBL 112:5
Every g. revolts MUMF 554:2
evil and adulterous g. BIBL 96:33
faithless and stubborn g. BOOK 139:8
froward g. BIBL 79:3
g. passeth away BIBL 85:25
g. was stolen FREE 333:9
g. which commences JEFF 420:15
G. X COUP 244:11
grieved with this g. BOOK 140:10
Had it been the whole g. EPIT 310:2
in their g. wiser BIBL 101:19
lost g. STEI 755:10
O g. of vipers BIBL 94:12
one g. from extinction CARE 191:5
third and fourth g. BIBL 78:1
generations g. have trod HOPK 396:12
g. of men HOME 394:2
G. pass BROW 156:14
g. shall call me blessed BIBL 99:31
hungry g. KEAT 445:1
in three g. PROV 620:31
manners of future g. JOHN 425:26
only three g. PROV 620:30
Those dying g. YEAT 855:8
three g. to make PROV 624:25
generosity exercise our g. SART 667:8
generous always g. ones MONT 545:17
g. and elevated mind JOHN 426:9
g. and honest feeling BURK 168:10
just before you're g. PROV 615:7
more g. sentiments JOHN 428:13
My mind as g. SHAK 699:24
generously treated g. or destroyed
MACH 502:9
genes G. not like blueprints STEW 761:2
go by the name of g. DAWK 259:16
true of the g. JONE 434:8
what males do to g. JONE 434:9
Genesis Conditioned G. PALI 583:16
genetic mechanism for g. material
CRIC 251:7
terrible g. defects WATS 822:19
genetics geography and g. WHIT 832:6
Geneva grim G. ministers AYTO 41:14
genitals make my g. to quiver JOHN 427:11
geniumque G. loci VIRG 812:18
genius except my g. WILD 837:11
feminine of g. FITZ 323:19
g. a better discerning GOLD 355:22
g. and art HAZL 376:20
g. and regularity GAIN 337:14
g. and virtue HAZL 376:21
G. capacity for taking pains PROV 620:35
G. does what it must MERE 522:24
G. from the throne BYRO 182:10
g. has been slow of growth LEWE 483:3
G. in a garret ROBI 650:21
g. in religion ARNO 30:6
g. into my life WILD 837:8
G. is one per cent inspiration EDIS 296:5
G. is only a greater aptitude BUFF 163:14
G. is the child REYN 646:5
g. of Einstein leads to Hiroshima PICA 595:9
g. of its scientists EISE 298:13
g. of the Constitution PITT 596:7
g. of the place POPE 603:12
g. overlooks individual SCHO 671:16
'G.' which means CARL 192:4
g. would wish to live ADAM 1:16
gentlemen—a g. SCHU 672:3
great g. BEAU 60:3
If I'm not a g. BALZ 54:11
kind of universal g. DRYD 290:1
lively g. GERV 344:14
Milton, Madam, was a g. JOHN 432:15
Mr Wordsworth's g. HAZL 377:3
Poetic G. of my country BURN 173:9
Ramp up my g. JONS 435:8
singular g. DIDE 274:3
stupendous g.! damned fool BYRO 184:8
talent instantly recognizes g. DOYL 285:9

genius (*cont.*):
taste or g. REYN 646:3
Three-fifths of him g. LOWE 494:1
true g. JOHN 425:1
true g. appears SWIF 766:20
what a g. I had SWIF 767:21
Whence g. wildly flashed KEAT 445:19
works of a great g. ADDI 5:13
geniuses One of the greatest g. WALP 819:1
genres *Tous les g. sont bons* VOLT 816:2
gent indeed a valiant G. EVEL 313:1
genteel g. when he gets drunk BOSW 146:26
No dancing bear was so g. COWP 246:22
to the truly g. HARD 371:19
gentes *Laudate Dominum, omnes g.* BIBL 115:4
gentil verray, parfit g. knyght CHAU 210:7
Gentiles boasting as the G. use KIPL 455:12
light to lighten the G. BIBL 100:7
preach among the G. BIBL 109:6
gentility marks of g. BLAK 119:21
gentle Do not go g. THOM 789:7
G. as falcon SKEL 739:6
G. Child of gentle Mother DEAR 260:11
g.-hearted Charles COLE 233:15
g. his condition SHAK 693:24
G. Jesus WESL 829:1
g. mind by gentle deeds SPEN 752:7
g. rain from heaven SHAK 709:25
His life was g. SHAK 698:29
gentleman as an educated g. SHAW 725:22
cannot make a g. BURK 169:10
definition of a g. NEWM 560:16
describe a g. TROL 799:5
died a very gallant g. EPIT 309:12
Every other inch a g. WEST 830:17
fashion a g. SPEN 751:11
fine old English g. SONG 747:14
first true g. DEKK 262:16
g. and scholar BURN 173:3
g. in Whitehall JAY 419:4
g. is not in your books SHAK 712:11
g. should never go beyond ETHE 312:5
g.'s park CONS 241:7
g. who was generally spoken SURT 764:24
God send every g. BALL 53:14
I am a g. SHAW 726:5
in linen like a g. JOHN 424:20
Jack became a g. SHAK 716:26
last g. in Europe LEVE 482:9
make a g. PROV 624:25
mariner with the g. DRAK 285:17
not quite a g. ASHF 31:12
officer and a g. MILI 526:3
Once a g. DICK 269:25
prince of darkness is a g. SHAK 700:29
so stout a g. SHAK 691:13
talking about being a g. SURT 764:10
too pedantic for a g. CONG 238:27
what a g. should be DEFO 261:2
who was then the g. PROV 634:19
gentlemanly g. conduct ARNO 30:14
werry g. ideas SURT 764:17
gentlemen Damn g. GAIN 337:13
difficult to behave like g. MACK 503:1
eggs for g. NURS 567:7
forget we are g. BURK 168:11
G. and Ladies DICK 273:11
g. both CARL 192:30
G. do not take soup at luncheon
CURZ 254:12
G. go by KIPL 455:16
g. in England SHAK 693:24
g. of England PARK 586:12
G. prefer blondes LOOS 491:17
G.-rankers KIPL 454:6
Great-hearted g. BROW 160:6
nation of g. MUGA 553:4
religion for g. CHAR 209:6
Scholars and g. WORD 849:14
since g. came up SHAK 694:19
Three jolly g. DE L 263:1
written by gentlemen for g. THAC 786:10
gentleness g. And show of love SHAK 696:2

only a willed g. THOM 790:25
ways are ways of g. SPRI 753:7
gently his faults lie g. SHAK 695:18
roar you as g. SHAK 710:24
genuflexion never grudge a g. OLIV 573:2
genuine g. poetry is conceived ARNO 29:23
place for the g. MOOR 547:1
genus *Hoc g. omne* HORA 403:6
geographers g., in Afric-maps SWIF 767:9
geographical g. concept BISM 117:18
g. expression METT 523:11
not a g. fragment PARN 586:20
geography g. and genetics WHIT 832:6
G. is about Maps BENT 68:12
too much g. KING 452:12
geologists g. into infidelity GOSS 357:6
g. would let me alone RUSK 660:12
geometrical g. ratio MALT 509:5
geometricians g. only by chance JOHN 425:7
geometry always doing g. PLAT 597:19
as precise as g. FLAU 325:12
demonstration in g. REYN 646:3
disorder in its g. DE B 260:15
does not know g. ANON 21:8
g. of fear READ 643:1
G. (which is the only science HOBB 390:9
'royal road' to g. EUCL 312:9
George accession of G. the Third
MACA 498:13
England and Saint G. SHAK 693:5
G.—don't do that CATC 200:19
if his name be G. SHAK 699:1
Georges G. ended LAND 466:5
Georgia G. on my mind GORR 357:4
red hills of G. KING 452:4
Georgie G. Porgie, pudding and pie
NURS 566:21
geranium madman shakes a dead g.
ELIO 303:1
geraniums delphiniums (blue) and g. (red)
MILN 528:1
germ G. of Buddhahood MAHĀ 506:18
German all a G. racket RIDL 648:6
G. history reached TAYL 774:7
G. *Reich* is made BISM 117:21
language of poems is G. CELA 205:4
to my horse—G. CHAR 209:13
Germans beastly to the G. COWA 244:16
G. . . . are going to be squeezed GEDD 342:15
G. classify CATH 199:8
G. have historic chance KOHL 459:1
to the G. that of—the air RICH 648:2
Germany at war with G. CHAM 206:13
bonnet in G. SHAK 708:27
Christian life in G. BONH 127:7
Death is a master from G. CELA 205:3
G. above all HOFF 391:13
G. calling JOYC 437:27
G. in the saddle BISM 117:15
G. is a nation MICH 524:6
G. will declare that I am a Jew EINS 297:16
offering G. too little NEVI 559:14
rebellious G. OVID 580:19
remaining cities of G. HARR 374:1
germs Kills all known g. ADVE 7:42
Gershwin G. songs FISH 322:17
Gesang *Das ist der ewige G.* GOET 352:17
Weib und G. LUTH 496:15
Gestern *G. liebt' ich* LESS 482:4
gestures In the g. SOND 746:4
get G. me to the church LERN 481:15
G. out as early as you can LARK 469:3
g. out of these wet clothes FILM 319:23
G. thee behind me, Satan BIBL 97:17
g. up airly LOWE 493:19
g. what you like SHAW 726:33
g. where I am today without CATC 200:29
What you see is what you g. SAYI 670:20
getting G. and spending WORD 850:21
Gospel of G. On SHAW 727:6
gewgaw This g. world DRYD 287:23
ghastly G. good taste BETJ 73:6
G., grim and ancient POE 599:7

g. through the drizzling rain TENN 778:27
We were a g. crew COLE 233:5
ghost but a kind of g. DONN 280:16
each frustrate g. BROW 161:17
each write a g. story SHEL 728:6
gave up the g. BIBL 105:9
g. asked them to do O'BR 571:2
G. in the Machine RYLE 662:4
g. of a garden SWIN 768:13
g. of a great name LUCA 495:1
g. of a rose BROW 156:5
g. of Roger Casement YEAT 854:10
g. of the deceased HOBB 391:1
G. unlaid forbear thee SHAK 683:9
I am the g. PLAT 596:23
If the g. cries RAIN 640:16
I'll make a g. of him SHAK 684:28
Moves like a g. SHAK 704:17
some old lover's g. DONN 281:5
Vex not his g. SHAK 702:8
What beck'ning g. POPE 602:11
ghosties ghoulies and g. PRAY 611:2
ghosts allowed to us moderns, are g.
FIEL 318:11
egress is given to real g. VIRG 812:17
g. from an old enchanter SHEL 730:7
g. of a nation PEAR 590:8
g. of Beauty glide POPE 603:5
g. of departed quantities BERK 69:9
g. of the slaughtered CLAU 225:14
g. outnumber us DUNN 292:8
G., wandering here and there SHAK 711:17
lack of g. BIRN 116:18
make the g. gaze SHAK 679:24
ghoul dug them up like a g. DICK 269:6
living on another like a g. HEAD 377:9
ghoulies g. and ghosties PRAY 611:2
giant awakened a sleeping g. FILM 319:12
G. Despair BUNY 164:21
G. Despair BUNY 164:22
g. great and still STEV 760:4
G. on the mountain stands BYRO 178:6
g.'s strength SHAK 707:27
g.'s wings BAUD 58:11
hand of the g. BOOK 143:2
like a g. BOOK 139:11
like a g.'s robe SHAK 707:5
rejoiceth as a g. BOOK 134:20
sees farther than the g. COLE 233:24
giants for war like precocious g. PEAR 590:11
g. in the earth BIBL 76:5
nuclear g. and ethical infants BRAD 148:23
on the shoulders of g. NEWT 561:15
shoulders of g. BERN 70:11
there we saw the g. BIBL 78:17
Want one only of five g. BEVE 73:22
we ought to be g. CHEK 213:22
gibber squeak and g. SHAK 683:16
gibbets cells and g. COOK 241:17
g. keep the lifted hand in awe YOUN 857:6
Gibbon Eh! Mr G. GLOU 351:15
Gibeon stand thou still upon G. BIBL 79:13
giberne *dans sa g. le bâton* LOUI 492:1
gibes great master of g. DISR 276:13
giblet liked thick g. soup JOYC 437:19
Gibraltar G. may tumble GERS 344:7
giddy I am g. SHAK 719:20
So g. the sight GREN 363:12
Gideon Lord came upon G. BIBL 79:23
gift Beauty is the lover's g. CONG 239:13
every perfect gift BIBL 111:20
Freedom is not a g. NKRU 565:4
g. horse in the mouth PROV 627:23
g. of God BIBL 105:1
g. of the divine Name SIKH 737:12
gods' most lovely g. EURI 312:21
last best g. MILT 533:12
love is the g. of oneself ANOU 22:19
make the g. rich TROL 800:3
really is a g. REEV 644:13
what a personal g. is HEIN 379:11
You have a g. JONS 435:22
your g. survived it all AUDE 35:3

gifted vividly g. in love   DUFF 291:7
young, g. and black   HANS 370:18
Young, g. and black   IRVI 414:3
giftie g. gie us   BURN 172:19
gifts Bestows her g.   JONS 435:7
bring g.   BOOK 138:23
buy g. at Jim Gibson's   LONG 491:14
cannot recall their g.   TENN 784:8
countless g. of love   WINK 841:14
diversities of g.   BIBL 107:24
Enemies' g. are no gifts   SOPH 746:13
even when they bring g.   VIRG 811:11
g. of God are strown   HEBE 378:16
Greeks bearing g.   PROV 619:45
He would adore my g.   HERB 384:20
no g. from chance   ARNO 27:25
Of all the heavenly g.   GRIM 364:12
presented unto him g.   BIBL 94:6
received g. for men   BOOK 138:14
gigantic g. body   MACA 498:1
gild g. refinèd gold   BYRO 181:3
g. refinèd gold   SHAK 699:10
I'll g. it   SHAK 691:18
gilded g. car of day   MILT 528:20
g. loam   SHAK 715:5
gilding amusement is the g.   RICH 647:18
G. pale streams   SHAK 723:2
Gilead G. is mine   BOOK 137:25
no balm in G.   BIBL 90:28
gill hang by its own g.   PROV 619:9
Gilpin John G. was a citizen   COWP 246:18
gilt g. comes off in our hands   FLAU 325:3
gin get out the g.   REED 644:7
g. and vermouth   DE V 266:5
G. was mother's milk   SHAW 727:15
Of all the g. joints   FILM 320:13
woodcock near the g.   SHAK 720:31
ginger G., you're balmy   MURR 554:22
ginless wicked as a g. tonic   COPE 242:16
Gioconda one isn't the real G.   CRAN 249:27
Giotto G. has the palm   DANT 256:7
G.'s tower   LONG 490:10
giovinezza Quanto è bella g.   MEDI 520:9
Gipfeln Über allen G. Ist Ruh'   GOET 353:10
Gipper Win just one for the G.   GIPP 349:20
gipsy Time, you old g. man   HODG 391:11
giraffe g., in their gracefulness   DINE 274:16
giraffes G.!—a People Who live   CAMP 187:4
girded g. himself with strength   BOOK 140:6
g. up his loins   BIBL 81:25
g. with praise   GRAN 359:3
girdle bright g. furled   ARNO 27:3
g. round about the earth   SHAK 711:3
to the g.   SHAK 701:15
girdled g. with the gleaming world   TENN 781:9
girl Above the staggering g.   YEAT 854:20
can't get no g. reaction   JAGG 415:15
danced with a g.   FARJ 315:3
diamonds a g.'s best friend   ROBI 650:10
g. at an impressionable age   SPAR 749:26
g. in the indolence of youth   YEAT 855:3
g. needs good parents   TUCK 802:2
g. throwing a ball   WOOL 845:9
g. with brains ought to   LOOS 491:18
no g. wants to laugh   LOOS 491:20
Poor little rich g.   COWA 245:5
pretty g. is like a melody   BERL 69:20
speak like a green g.   SHAK 684:21
sweetest g. I know   JUDG 438:4
unlessoned g.   SHAK 709:19
was a little g.   LONG 491:11
girlish g. glee   GILB 347:23
Laugh thy g. laughter   WATS 823:3
girls abhors In Little G.   BELL 65:4
Always be civil to the g.   MITF 541:1
assumption that g.   FRAS 333:4
bombers named for g.   JARR 418:28
Boys and g.   NURS 566:9
G. aren't like that   AMIS 13:12
g. in slacks remember Dad   BETJ 72:3
g. that are so smart   CARE 191:8
g. who wear glasses   PARK 585:16

lads for the g.   HOUS 404:12
little g. made of   NURS 570:14
not that g. should think   NAPO 556:12
nude, giant g.   SPEN 750:22
rosebud garden of g.   TENN 781:25
rose-lipt g. are sleeping   HOUS 405:1
Secrets with g.   CRAB 249:15
Thank heaven for little g.   LERN 481:21
Treaties like g. and roses   DE G 262:10
white feet of laughing g.   MACA 499:12
without complaints from g.   HORA 401:23
Gitche Gumee By the shore of G.   LONG 491:1
give All that I am I g.   BOOK 133:10
better to g. than to receive   PROV 623:44
freely g.   BIBL 96:14
G., and it shall be given   BIBL 100:16
g. and not to count   IGNA 412:18
G. and take fair play   PROV 620:39
g. a singel dam   FLEM 326:11
G. a thing   PROV 620:38
G. crowns and pounds   HOUS 404:10
g. me back my legions   AUGU 37:20
G. me my Romeo   SHAK 717:37
G. me yet before I die   WINC 841:8
G. to me the life I love   STEV 760:16
g. to the poor   BIBL 97:25
G. us back   POLI 600:18
g. what you command   AUGU 37:6
more blessed to g.   BIBL 105:24
not as the world giveth, g. I   BIBL 103:32
peace which the world cannot g.   BOOK 128:19
receive but what we g.   COLE 231:9
such as I have g. I thee   BIBL 104:29
given g. away by a novel   KEAT 446:21
I would have g. gladly   JOHN 423:9
shall be g.   BIBL 98:23
taking what is not g.   PALI 583:8
To whom nothing is g.   FIEL 317:18
giver author and g.   BOOK 130:15
cheerful g.   BIBL 108:18
Lord and g. of life   BOOK 131:11
gives g. twice who gives quickly   PROV 621:39
happiness she g.   LACL 463:7
who g. soon   PUBL 636:14
giving g. and receiving of a Ring   BOOK 133:12
Godlike in g.   ANON 16:5
not in the g. vein   SHAK 716:32
glacier g. knocks in the cupboard   AUDE 34:20
glad g. confident morning   BROW 160:4
G. did I live   STEV 760:20
g. father   BIBL 84:8
g. when they said unto me   BOOK 142:18
just g. to see me   WEST 830:7
maketh g. the heart   BOOK 141:7
rejoice and be g.   BOOK 142:10
shew ourselves g. in him   BOOK 140:9
too soon made g.   BROW 160:10
glade bee-loud g.   YEAT 854:17
crown the wat'ry g.   GRAY 361:9
gladiators g. of Rome   BORR 145:11
gladly bear the cross g.   THOM 788:13
g. wolde he lerne   CHAU 210:18
I would have given g.   JOHN 423:9
gladness As with g. men of old   DIX 278:14
obtain joy and g.   BIBL 89:12
oil of g.   BOOK 136:20
serve the Lord with g.   BOOK 140:17
solemn g. even crowned   TENN 779:2
Teach me half the g.   SHEL 732:1
gladsome g. light   COKE 230:17
g. light of jurisprudence   CLOS 228:12
Let us with a g. mind   MILT 529:28
Glamis G. hath murdered sleep   SHAK 705:1
G. thou art, and Cawdor   SHAK 703:18
glance g. from heaven to earth   SHAK 711:28
O brightening g.   YEAT 853:6
glare looked in at this merciless g.   WILL 839:9
red g. on Skiddaw   MACA 499:3

Glasgow G. Empire on a Saturday night   DODD 278:19
glass baying for broken g.   WAUG 824:4
brighter than g.   HORA 401:21
comb and a g. in her hand   SONG 748:2
dome of many-coloured g.   SHEL 729:2
excuse for the g.   SHER 733:31
face in a g.   BIBL 111:21
Get thee g. eyes   SHAK 701:18
g. I drink from   MUSS 555:8
g. of blessings   HERB 384:19
g. o' the invariable   DICK 272:3
g. the opulent   HARD 372:13
Grief with a g.   SWIN 768:3
He was indeed the g.   SHAK 691:32
if you break the bloody g.   MACN 504:16
liked the Sound of Broken G.   BELL 65:17
live in g. houses   PROV 632:43
made mouths in a g.   SHAK 700:15
man that looks on g.   HERB 384:4
No g. of ours was raised   HEAN 378:1
own face in the g.   WILD 836:12
Satire is a sort of g.   SWIF 765:5
sea of g.   BIBL 113:8
sea of g.   BIBL 114:5
set you up a g.   SHAK 687:19
sun-comprehending g.   LARK 468:17
take a g. of wine   SHER 734:5
through a g., darkly   BIBL 107:25
turn down an empty g.   FITZ 323:17
glasses broke our painted g.   JORD 436:13
brown braids and g.   JARR 418:26
Fill all the g. there   COWL 245:18
girls who wear g.   PARK 585:16
ladder and some g.   BATE 58:9
Such cruel g.   HOWE 406:4
glassy around the g. sea   HEBE 378:17
g., cool, translucent   MILT 529:7
in the g. stream   SHAK 688:17
Upon the g. plain   WORD 846:25
gleam follow the G.   TENN 782:9
gleaning g. of the grapes   BIBL 79:25
glee At their tempestuous g.   LONG 490:16
girlish g.   GILB 347:23
glen Down the rushy g.   ALLI 12:18
glib g. and oily art   SHAK 699:20
gliding g. like a queen   SPEN 750:18
glimmering fades the g. landscape   GRAY 360:24
Mere g. and decays   VAUG 807:17
glimpses g. of the moon   SHAK 684:26
g. that would make me   WORD 850:22
glittering g. and sounding generalities   CHOA 218:6
g. in the smokeless air   WORD 846:6
g. prizes   BORR 146:8
g. prizes   SMIT 742:1
how that g. taketh me   HERR 386:20
with his g. eye   COLE 232:12
glitters All that is not gold   PROV 614:17
medal g.   CHUR 221:14
gloaming In the g.   ORRE 576:12
Roamin' in the g.   LAUD 470:7
gloat I g.   KIPL 457:5
global g. thinking   LUCE 495:5
image of a g. village   MCLU 503:14
my wars Were g.   REED 644:5
globally Think g.   SLOG 740:12
globaloney still g.   LUCE 495:5
globe g.-trotting Madam   YEAT 856:2
great g. itself   SHAK 719:1
hunted round the g.   PAIN 582:9
rattle of a g.   DRYD 287:23
this distracted g.   SHAK 685:6
globèd wealth of g. peonies   KEAT 444:18
globule primordial atomic g.   GILB 347:20
Glöckchen das G. klingeln   HEIN 380:4
G. klingeln   CLOS 228:15
gloire g. et le repos   MONT 544:11
gloom counterfeit a g.   MILT 529:12
inspissated g.   JOHN 429:5
glooms kindred g.   THOM 792:15
gloomy by g. Dis Was gathered   MILT 532:29

good (*cont.*):

g. unluckily	STOP 761:15
g. want power	SHEL 731:2
g. when they do as others do	FRAN 331:16
g. Will be the final goal	TENN 779:5
g. will never be our task	MILT 531:10
g. will toward men	BIBL 100:4
G. wine needs no bush	PROV 621:13
g. without qualification	KANT 441:7
G. women always think	BROO 153:17
G. words do not last long	JOSE 436:16
g. words, I think, were best	SHAK 699:14
g. works are not wasted	CALD 185:11
g. ye are and bad	TENN 777:24
Greed is g.	FILM 319:9
Guinness is g. for you	ADVE 7:26
had been g. for that man	BIBL 98:30
Hanging is too g. for him	BUNY 164:18
have a g. thing	SHAK 691:27
heaven doing g. on earth	TERE 785:19
He wos wery g. to me	DICK 267:17
highest g.	CICE 223:11
His own g.	MILL 525:6
hold fast that which is g.	BIBL 110:19
human nature is g.	MENG 522:3
impulsive to g.	MANN 510:6
In art the best is g. enough	GOET 353:5
it cannot come to g.	SHAK 684:6
It's a g. thing	CATC 201:9
I will be g.	VICT 809:8
kept the g. wine	BIBL 102:28
knowing g. and evil	BIBL 75:19
leave assured g.	DRAY 286:2
like a *g.* fiend	THOM 790:7
loves what he is g. at	SHAD 678:1
luxury of doing g.	CRAB 249:12
luxury was doing g.	GART 340:11
making people feel g.	CHRÉ 218:12
Men have never been g.	BART 57:12
much g. would be absent	THOM 789:2
neither g. nor bad	BALZ 54:6
never had it so g.	MACM 504:14
never so g. or so bad	MACK 503:3
No g. man is a Briton	AUSO 38:14
no ills from g. dissuade	SMAR 739:14
none that doeth g.	BOOK 134:10
not enough to have a g. mind	DESC 265:10
not g. company	AUST 39:14
nothing g. to be had	HAZL 376:15
obscurely g.	ADDI 4:14
Of g. and evil much they argued	MILT 532:9
of g. report	BIBL 110:8
One g. turn deserves	PROV 628:36
only g. Indian	PROV 628:23
only g. Indians	SHER 733:4
only g. thing left	MUSS 555:10
on the evil and on the g.	BIBL 94:31
or be thought half as g.	WHIT 834:8
out of g. still to find	MILT 531:11
overcome evil with g.	BIBL 106:29
policy of the g. neighbour	ROOS 653:13
prospect of a distant g.	DRYD 288:18
records g. things of good men	BEDE 62:6
rejected what was g.	AESO 6:18
return g. for evil	VANB 806:13
rewarded me evil for g.	BOOK 135:26
Roman Conquest was a *G. Thing*	SELL 676:17
said a g. thing	TWAI 803:18
Seek to be g.	LYTT 497:13
So shines a g. deed	SHAK 710:6
temptation to be g.	BREC 150:3
than to seem g.	SALL 665:4
that you're not g. enough	TROL 800:11
they were g. men	STEP 756:6
thy g. with brotherhood	BATE 58:10
too much of a g. thing	PROV 635:26
truly great who are truly g.	CHAP 208:17
universal licence to be g.	COLE 231:2
Universally G.	MAHĀ 507:6
utter as g. things	JONS 435:6
very g. day	MOOR 546:10
Whatever g. visits thee	KORA 460:4
what g. came of it	SOUT 749:2

what was g. for our country	WILS 840:1
when shall all men's g.	TENN 777:7
When she was g.	LONG 491:11
woman was full of g. works	BIBL 105:5
work together for g.	BIBL 106:21
would be a g. idea	GAND 339:9
would do g. to another	BLAK 120:12
your g. works	BIBL 94:23
goodbye Every time we say g.	PORT 607:11
G.!—Good-bye-ee	WEST 830:20
G., moralitee	HERB 383:8
G., Piccadilly	JUDG 438:4
G. to all that	GRAV 360:11
goodlihead flower of g.	SKEL 739:7
goodly g. to look to	BIBL 80:17
I have a g. heritage	BOOK 134:14
goodman our g.'s awa	MICK 524:7
goodness fountain of all g.	BOOK 128:16
g. derives not from	TERE 785:15
g. entirely human	ELIO 300:25
g. faileth never	BAKE 50:2
G. had nothing to do with it	WEST 830:5
g. infinite	MILT 534:11
G. is not the same thing	PLAT 597:14
g. of the Lord	BOOK 135:15
If g. lead him not	HERB 384:21
inclination to g.	BACO 44:20
long-suffering, and of great g.	BOOK 141:2
My G., My Guinness	ADVE 8:5
goodnight bid the world G.	HERR 386:2
gives the stern'st g.	SHAK 704:20
G., children	CATC 200:23
G.. Ensured release	HOUS 404:5
g., sweet ladies	SHAK 688:8
G., sweet prince	SHAK 689:16
I shall say g.	SHAK 717:29
John Thomas says g.	LAWR 474:20
My last G.	KING 451:15
second best's a gay g.	YEAT 854:9
goods all my worldly g.	BOOK 133:10
care for external g.	WEBE 825:4
desire other men's g.	BOOK 132:18
for your good, for all your g.	GEOR 343:1
g. are in peace	BIBL 100:28
g. the gods provide	PROV 631:38
Ill gotten g. never thrive	PROV 623:30
Riches and G.	BOOK 144:20
when g. are private	TAWN 774:3
goodwill In peace; g.	CHUR 222:13
name was Great G.	HARI 373:13
goose cried in g., alas	RANS 642:6
every g. a swan	KING 453:1
g. honking amongst tuneful swans	
	VIRG 814:9
G., if I had you	SHAK 700:8
Grey g. and gander	NURS 567:2
grey g. is gone	NURS 568:15
on the ground at G. Green	KINN 453:7
sauce for the g.	PROV 634:11
steal a g.	POLI 601:12
steals a g.	ANON 16:1
that g. look	SHAK 707:7
gooseberried g. double bed	THOM 790:4
gooseberries planty of g.	FLEM 326:14
goosey G., goosey gander	NURS 567:1
gordian She was a g. shape	KEAT 443:30
gore hope it mayn't be human g.	
	DICK 267:11
gored you tossed and g.	BOSW 146:25
gorgeous g. East in fee	WORD 848:19
g. East with richest hand	MILT 531:29
gorgon G., Prince of darkness	SPEN 751:14
gorgonized G. me from head to foot	
	TENN 781:21
gormed I'm G.—and I can't say	DICK 269:3
gorse G. fires are smoking	LONG 491:15
g. is out of bloom	PROV 634:31
gory never shake Thy g. locks	SHAK 706:5
Welcome to your g. bed	BURN 172:5
Goschen forgot G.	CHUR 220:15
gosh by gee by g. by gum	CUMM 253:6
goshawk gay g.	BALL 52:4
gospel Four for the G. makers	SONG 747:11

G. of Christ	WESL 829:11
G. of Getting On	SHAW 727:6
likeness in the G.	KORA 461:7
music of the G.	FABE 313:15
preach the g.	BIBL 99:29
truth of thy holy G.	BOOK 131:1
gossip babbling g. of the air	SHAK 720:13
g. from all the nations	AUDE 35:16
G. is a sort of smoke	ELIO 299:10
I admit there is g.	DISR 276:20
in the g. columns	INGH 413:16
Like all g.	FORS 329:23
my g. Report	SHAK 709:11
got If not, have you g. him	SELL 676:19
I g. rhythm	GERS 344:6
in our case we have not g.	REED 644:4
gotcha G.	NEWS 562:9
Gotham Three wise men of G.	NURS 570:7
Gothic cars the great G. cathedrals	
	BART 57:15
glory of G.	RUSK 660:13
modern G. room	PUGI 636:20
more than G. ignorance	FIEL 318:10
Gott *ist unser G.*	LUTH 496:11
gotta g. use words when I talk to you	
	ELIO 303:5
Gotte *einem sterbenden G.*	HEIN 380:4
gotten g. himself the victory	BOOK 140:13
Götterdämmerung G. without the gods	
	MACD 501:5
gout give them the g.	MONT 543:19
gouverner G. *c'est choisir*	LÉVI 482:16
govern cannot g. itself	MCNA 504:13
easy to g.	BROU 154:13
g. according to the common	JAME 417:5
g. in prose	CUOM 254:1
g. New South Wales	BELL 65:1
g. our conditions	SHAK 701:10
of Kings to g. wrong	POPE 602:2
people g. themselves	THIE 788:1
to g. is to choose	LÉVI 482:16
With words we g. men	DISR 277:6
governance by thy g.	BOOK 130:13
governed faith in The People g.	DICK 272:20
g. by thy good Spirit	BOOK 129:18
nation is not g.	BURK 166:20
not so well g.	HOOK 395:17
governer G. was strong upon	WILD 836:30
governess Be a g.	BRON 152:13
governing incapable of g.	CHES 215:15
right of g.	FOX 331:3
government abandon a g.	JEFF 420:2
administration of the g.	SWIF 765:11
art of g.	VOLT 816:16
art of g. is	SHAW 726:17
asks you to form a G.	ATTL 33:7
at g. expense	ARTS 30:20
become the most corrupt g.	JEFF 419:18
best g. is that which	O'SU 579:8
definition of the best g.	HALI 369:1
duty of g.	PAIN 582:10
end of g.	ADAM 3:7
every form of g.	JOHN 429:17
for a bad g.	TOCQ 795:8
forms of g.	POPE 605:6
function of a g.	PALM 585:1
g. above the law	SCAR 668:11
G. and co-operation	RUSK 660:9
G. and public opinion	SHAW 726:7
g. as an adversary	BRUN 162:9
G. at Washington lives	GARF 339:14
g. by discussion	ATTL 33:5
g. by the uneducated	CHES 217:15
G., even in its best state	PAIN 582:6
G. is a contrivance	BURK 167:12
g. is best	THOR 792:23
g. is influenced by	SMIT 741:9
g. it deserves	MAIS 508:2
g. of Britain's isle	SHAK 694:15
g. of laws	ADAM 2:20
G. of laws and not of men	FORD 328:11
g. of statesmen	DISR 276:27
G. of the busy	SELD 676:13

g. of the people | LINC 485:7
g. of the people | PAGE 581:14
g. of the world | DISR 276:20
g. of the world | THOR 793:17
G. of whom I am ashamed | JACK 415:2
g. shall be upon his shoulder | BIBL 88:18
g. which imprisons | THOR 792:24
g. which robs Peter | SHAW 725:5
g. without a king | BANC 54:13
great service to a g. | MEDI 520:7
have an efficient g. | TRUM 801:12
If the G. is big enough | FORD 328:9
in a disorderly g. | HALI 368:20
increase of his g. | BIBL 88:18
land of settled g. | TENN 784:23
least g. was the best | FEIN 316:10
members of the G. | SHAW 725:14
natural party of g. | WILS 840:8
no British g. should be brought down | MACM 504:7
No G. can be long secure | DISR 276:26
not a g. of laws | WEBS 825:14
not depend on g. | MISQ 537:5
not get all of the g. | FRIE 334:15
not set by g. | DAY 260:1
not the worst g. | TROL 799:25
one form of g. | JOHN 429:16
one g. sooner learns | SMIT 741:12
only instrument of g. | LOCK 489:1
Parliamentary g. is impossible | DISR 276:7
Peace, order, and good g. | ANON 18:8
people's g. | WEBS 825:11
pillars of g. | BACO 45:11
prepare for g. | STEE 754:14
reins of g. are lodged | SHEL 728:4
representative g. | DISR 277:27
restraints of g. | GOLD 354:8
rule nations by your g. | VIRG 812:15
run g. like a business | KLEI 457:19
signifies the want of g. | HOBB 390:20
sister is given to g. | DICK 269:12
structure of g. | HAVE 375:7
support their g. | CLEV 226:17
system of G. | GLAD 350:10
to run a g. | TRUM 801:10
understood by republican g. | TOCQ 795:11
virtue of paper g. | BURK 166:17
vulgar arts of g. | PEEL 590:19
wee pretendy g. | CONN 240:1
well-ordered g. | HALI 368:14
work for a G. I despise | KEYN 450:10
worst form of G. | CHUR 221:21
governments corrupted g. | HALI 368:19
foundation of most g. | ADAM 3:8
G. always want | RADC 640:10
g. had better get out of the way | EISE 298:16
g. need both shepherds | VOLT 816:9
g. of Europe | JEFF 419:12
Never believe a g. | GELL 342:20
that the two g. | MITC 540:8
governor save the G.-General | WHIT 833:1
governors g., teachers | BOOK 132:16
supreme g., the mob | WALP 818:17
governs g. his state by virtue | CONF 237:10
g. the passions | HUME 408:15
that which g. least | O'SU 579:8
which g. not at all | THOR 792:23
gowd man's the g. | BURN 171:4
Gower O moral G. | CHAU 213:18
gown wearing a black g. | CHES 214:22
wrap me in a g. | HERB 383:16
Goya I am G. | VOZN 817:1
grab all smash and no g. | NICO 563:14
G. this land | MORR 550:11
Gracchos Quis tulerit G. | JUVE 439:11
grace Amazing g. | NEWT 563:4
Angels and ministers of g. | SHAK 684:25
attractive kind of g. | ROYD 658:1
But for the g. of God | BRAD 148:17
by special g. | BOOK 130:6
by the g. of God | BIBL 108:1
courtly foreign g. | TENN 784:3
fallen from g. | BIBL 108:28

full of g. | PRAY 611:1
full of g. | PROV 626:28
G. be unto you | BIBL 112:24
g. did much more abound | BIBL 106:9
G. is given of God | CLOU 227:18
G. me no grace | SHAK 715:15
g., new birth | ARNO 30:2
g. of a boy | BETJ 73:2
G. of God is in Courtesy | BELL 65:6
g. of God which was with me | BIBL 108:2
g.-proud faces | BURN 173:1
G. under pressure | HEMI 381:8
grow old with a good g. | STEE 754:19
inward and spiritual g. | BOOK 132:19
lend her g. | TENN 780:13
means of g. | BOOK 129:20
new light of g. | SMOL 744:17
REGRET INFORM YOUR G. | TELE 776:4
snatch a g. | POPE 604:1
speech be alway with g. | BIBL 110:14
strong toil of g. | SHAK 680:17
such g. did lend her | SHAK 721:22
such heavenly g. | SPEN 751:15
sweet attractive g. | MILT 532:30
that g. may abound | BIBL 106:10
throne of the heavenly g. | BOOK 127:14
with a better g. | SHAK 720:18
wordy o' a g. | BURN 172:18
world is judged by g. | TALM 772:6
graceful g. air and heavenly mug | FLEM 326:19
Such a g. exit | JUNO 439:1
graces deficiency in the g. | JOHN 430:23
G. do not seem to be natives | CHES 215:9
g. slighted | CRAB 248:28
sacrifice to the g. | BURK 167:30
Upon her eyelids many G. | SPEN 751:22
gracing either other Sweetly g. | CAMP 188:5
gracious all his g. parts | SHAK 699:6
he is g. | BOOK 143:11
how g. the Lord is | BOOK 135:23
Lord is g. | BIBL 112:4
O be favourable and g. | BOOK 137:15
So hallowed and so g. | SHAK 683:18
gradient g.'s against her | AUDE 35:15
gradual g. day weakening | SPEN 750:23
gradualness inevitability of g. | WEBB 825:1
graduates sweet girl-g. | TENN 782:23
Graeculus G. esuriens | JUVE 439:15
graft G. in our hearts | BOOK 130:15
grail g. of laughter | CRAN 249:25
grain choice g. | STOU 761:18
g. of salt | PLIN 598:6
rain is destroying his g. | HERB 383:7
world in a g. of sand | BLAK 119:5
gramina g. campis | HORA 402:11
grammar attention to g. | CHAM 206:5
destroy every g. school | CROS 252:11
don't want to talk g. | SHAW 727:12
erecting a g. school | SHAK 694:23
g., and nonsense | GOLD 355:22
G., the ground of al | LANG 466:19
Heedless of g. | BARH 55:18
talking bad g. | DISR 276:25
grammatical g. purity | JOHN 425:23
grammatici G. certant | HORA 398:4
grammaticus G., rhetor, geometres | JUVE 439:15
gramophone g. company | TREE 798:9
puts a record on the g. | ELIO 303:21
granary on a g. floor | KEAT 445:15
grand down the G. Canyon | MARQ 514:5
G. Duchesses are doing | NAPO 556:14
g. Perhaps | BROW 158:15
g. style | ARNO 30:10
g. to be blooming well dead | SARO 666:18
grandeur certain spiritual g. | ELIO 299:23
charged with the g. | HOPK 396:12
g. hear with a disdainful smile | GRAY 361:3
g. in this view | DARW 257:11
g. that was Rome | POE 599:10
g. underlying the sorriest things | HARD 372:8
old Scotia's g. | BURN 170:23

grandfather ape for his g. | HUXL 412:4
carrying a g. clock | TREE 798:8
g. or his grandmother | WILB 835:1
grandfathers g.'s grandfathers | VIRG 815:5
makes friends with its g. | MUMF 554:2
grandmother grandfather or his g. | WILB 835:1
teach your g. | PROV 618:17
We have become a g. | THAT 787:12
grandsire g. cut his throat | SWIF 767:19
grange at the moated g. | SHAK 708:11
lonely moated g. | TENN 781:14
granites Through g. which titanic wars | OWEN 581:6
grant g. me this in return | CATU 203:8
half g. what I wish | FROS 335:8
OLD CARY G. FINE | TELE 776:7
granted g. scarce to God | SPEN 752:17
Granth Guru G. Sahib | SIKH 737:11
grape burst Joy's g. | KEAT 444:19
G. is my mulatto mother | HUGH 407:10
peel me a g. | WEST 830:3
grapes brought forth wild g. | BIBL 88:5
gleaning of the g. | BIBL 79:25
g. of thorns | BIBL 95:22
g. of wrath | BORR 146:10
g. of wrath | HOWE 405:15
need any sour g. | AESO 6:14
sour g. | BIBL 91:13
sour g. and ashes | ASHF 31:16
grapeshot whiff of g. | CARL 192:5
grapple G. them to thy soul | SHAK 684:17
grasp exceed his g. | BROW 158:9
G. it like a man of mettle | HILL 388:6
G. not at much | HERB 385:1
grasped haven't g. the situation | KERR 450:1
grass All flesh is g. | BIBL 89:17
bringeth forth g. | BOOK 141:7
but as g. | BOOK 141:4
eateth g. as an ox | BIBL 83:26
everywhere nibble g. | FAGU 314:4
flesh is as g. | BIBL 112:3
g. below | CLAR 224:12
g. beyond the door | ROSS 656:8
g. cannot dissolve | BLY 124:11
g. grows on the weirs | YEAT 854:1
g. is always greener | PROV 621:14
g. looking green | PERR 592:26
g. returns to the fields | HORA 402:11
g. to graze a cow | BETJ 72:17
g. will grow in the streets | HOOV 396:1
greener than the g. | BALL 52:19
green g. growing over me | BALL 53:19
green g. shorn | BACO 44:18
hearing the g. grow | ELIO 300:5
I am the g. | SAND 665:20
I fall on g. | MARV 515:16
leaf of g. is no less | WHIT 833:12
like the g. | BOOK 139:22
parched g. pray | TIBU 794:10
Pigeons on the g. | STEI 755:7
snake hidden in the g. | VIRG 813:22
splendour in the g. | WORD 848:14
star-scattered on the g. | FITZ 323:17
tides of g. | SWIN 769:4
twinkles in the g. | TENN 781:22
two blades of g. | SWIF 765:13
While the g. grows | PROV 634:44
grasses by short g. | PORT 607:23
grasshopper g. shall be a burden | BIBL 86:25
grasshoppers half a dozen g. | BURK 167:19
we were as g. | BIBL 78:17
grassy fair Fidele's g. tomb | COLL 235:10
grate fire is dying in the g. | MERE 522:21
fluttered on the g. | COLE 231:20
grateful anybody can be g. | CATU 203:4
single g. thought | LESS 482:5
gratefully O g. sing | GRAN 359:3
gratias Deo g. | MISS 536:18
gratification g. of cruelty | FOST 330:10
gratified g. desire | BLAK 121:23
gratissima g. serpit | VIRG 811:15

gratitude g. is a species of revenge
JOHN 425:21
g. is merely a secret hope LA R 469:19
G., like love ALSO 12:20
g. of a stranger TOCQ 795:13
g. we owe to Adam TWAI 803:22
having to give g. FAUL 316:2
liking or g. ELIO 299:13
gratuity bribe or g. PENN 591:18
grau G. ist alle Theorie GOET 352:18
grave And on that g. HART 374:15
at her g. BALL 53:16
bed is the cold g. BALL 51:18
cold g. BALL 53:16
come to seek a g. DONN 281:23
cradle and the g. DYER 293:16
cradle to the g. SHEL 731:9
digs my g. HERB 384:10
Dig the g. and let me lie STEV 760:20
ditchers and g.-makers SHAK 688:22
dread The g. as little KEN 448:8
Even the g. yawns TREE 798:6
from the cradle to the g. CHUR 221:17
frontier-g. is far away NEWB 560:4
Funeral marches to the g. LONG 490:19
give birth astride of a g. BECK 61:23
go into my g. CLOS 228:3
go into my g. PEPY 592:16
gone wild into his g. SHAK 692:21
g., and not taunting BACO 44:24
g. hides all things SHEL 731:3
g. is not its goal LONG 490:18
g. of a dead Fenian COLL 235:4
g. of Mad Carew HAYE 376:7
g.'s a fine and private MARV 516:2
g., where is thy victory BIBL 108:12
g., whither thou goest BIBL 86:15
G. without thought CHUR 220:2
In every g. make room D'AV 251:23
in peace in his g. DONN 281:25
into the darkness of the g. MILL 525:20
Is that ayont the g. BURN 173:2
jealousy is cruel as the g. BIBL 87:22
kind of healthy g. SMIT 743:14
kingdom for a little g. SHAK 716:2
lead but to the g. GRAY 361:3
letters in the g. JOHN 433:4
made me a g. so rough TENN 778:2
Marriage is the g. CAVE 204:3
now in his colde g. CHAU 211:17
pompous in the g. BROW 156:18
renowned be thy g. SHAK 683:9
requires g. statesmen DISR 277:10
root is ever in its g. HERB 385:4
send you to the g. ORTO 576:18
Sentinel of the g. TATE 773:11
she is in her g. WORD 850:2
shovel a g. in the air CELA 205:1
shown Longfellow's g. MOOR 547:3
sinks me to the g. FORD 328:18
sitting crowned upon the g. HOBB 391:1
stand at my g. and cry ANON 15:18
thank God for the quiet g. KEAT 440:6
this side of the g. LAND 466:6
travelling toward the g. WORD 849:5
When my g. is broke up DONN 281:8
Without a g. BYRO 179:19
with sorrow to the g. BIBL 77:8
years and honour to the g. KIPL 455:3
graved G. inside of it BROW 159:6
gravelled g. for lack of matter SHAK 682:1
graven g. image BIBL 77:37
graves dig our g. with our teeth SMIL 740:20
dishonourable g. SHAK 696:9
g. of deceased languages DICK 269:6
g. of little magazines PRES 610:12
g. of their neighbours EDWA 296:15
g. of the martyrs STEV 760:15
g. stood tenantless SHAK 683:16
Let's talk of g. SHAK 715:22
voluntary g. HERB 384:16
watch from their g. BROW 160:3
with us in our g. DONN 282:4

graveyard for each g. BOCC 125:1
Poor Law, and a g. JOHN 433:23
gravitation not believing in g. TROT 800:22
gravy Abominated g. BENT 68:14
grazing Tilling and g. SULL 763:14
grease gets the g. PROV 631:17
slides by on g. LOWE 494:9
greasy grey-green, g., Limpopo KIPL 456:17
top of the g. pole DISR 278:2
great aim not to be g. LYTT 497:13
all g. men are frauds BONA 127:3
between the small and g. COWP 248:21
both g. and small COLE 233:10
Brothers of the G. GERS 344:12
desireth g. matters QUAR 638:18
far above the g. GRAY 361:21
From the g. deep TENN 777:16
g. and lofty things MONT 543:23
g. book CALL 186:3
g. book is a great evil PROV 621:15
g. break through SHEN 732:24
g., ere fortune made him so DRYD 288:10
g. gulf fixed BIBL 101:23
g. have kindness POPE 602:30
g. have no heart LA B 462:16
G.-hearted gentlemen BROW 160:6
g. illusion ANGE 14:13
G. is Diana BIBL 105:22
G. is the hand THOM 789:12
g. is truth BROO 154:9
g. life if you don't weaken BUCH 162:18
g. man has his disciples WILD 835:25
g. man helped the poor MACA 499:15
G. men BIBL 83:19
g. men contending BURT 174:8
g. men even under bad emperors TACI 770:5
g. men make mistakes CHUR 220:15
g. men—so-called TOLS 796:17
G. minds think alike PROV 621:18
g. objects make Great minds YOUN 857:20
g. ones devoured the small SIDN 735:16
g. regions of the mind BROC 151:20
g. seemed to him little MACA 498:14
G. Society JOHN 423:12
g.—the major novelists LEAV 478:3
g. things from the valley CHES 217:1
g. To do that thing SHAK 680:5
g. to them that know SPRI 753:6
g. was the fall BIBL 95:25
grown so g. SHAK 696:10
he is always g. DRYD 290:4
He Was A G. Man ZIEG 858:9
How g. a matter BIBL 111:26
Ill can he rule the g. SPEN 752:4
know well I am not g. TENN 777:28
lay g. and greatly fallen HOME 394:8
Lives of g. men LONG 490:21
make the Way g. CONF 238:7
many people think him g. JOHN 429:27
name made g. HILL 389:3
nothing g. but man HAMI 369:21
Nothing g. was ever achieved EMER 306:22
only truly g. DISR 277:5
Rightly to be g. SHAK 688:4
small things with g. VIRG 815:4
so g. a thing happened WHIT 832:17
some men are born g. SHAK 720:32
think the g. unhappy YOUN 857:3
those who were truly g. SPEN 750:19
though fallen, g. BYRO 178:11
thou wouldst be g. SHAK 703:18
To be g. is to be misunderstood EMER 307:6
truly g. who are truly good CHAP 208:17
with small men no g. thing MILL 525:11
Great Britain G. has lost an empire
ACHE 1:10
G. should free herself SMIT 741:13
natives of G. CHES 215:9
greater G. love hath no man BIBL 103:33
g. man, the greater courtesy TENN 778:3
g. prey upon the less GREE 362:4
g. than a private citizen TACI 770:11
g. than Solomon BIBL 96:34

g. than the whole HESI 387:4
g. than vast spaces UPAN 805:7
g. than we know WORD 849:24
g. the sinner PROV 621:16
he is g. than they RUSK 660:5
they behold a g. SHAK 696:15
thy need is g. SIDN 736:20
greatest firstborn the g. ass CARO 193:12
g. event it is FOX 331:4
g. happiness HUTC 410:19
g. thing in the world MONT 544:10
happiness of the g. number BENT 68:5
I'm the g. ALI 12:1
life to live as the g. he RAIN 640:15
greatly g. to his credit GILB 348:25
would g. win BYRO 182:24
greatness dispense with g. GUIZ 365:15
farewell, to all my g. SHAK 695:15
g. going off SHAK 679:21
G. knows itself SHAK 691:3
g. of the Lord BIBL 99:31
g., save it be some far-off TENN 777:28
g. thrust upon them SHAK 720:32
G., with private men MASS 518:3
intended g. for men ELIO 300:9
moment of my g. flicker ELIO 302:17
nature of all g. BURK 166:14
Greece Athens, the eye of G. MILT 534:20
Cold is the heart, fair G. BYRO 178:8
education to G. PERI 592:22
Fair G.! sad relic BYRO 178:11
for G. a tear BYRO 181:6
glory that was G. POE 599:10
G. is fallen and Troy COLE 231:4
G. might still be free BYRO 181:5
isles of G. BYRO 181:4
To Gaul, to G. COWP 247:18
to G. the direful spring OPEN 574:2
greed G. is all right BOES 125:5
G. is good FILM 319:9
g. of speculators LAUR 470:10
infectious g. GREE 363:2
not enough for everyone's g. BUCH 163:2
greedy G. for the property SALL 665:1
I am g. PUNC 637:18
I am not g. PAPP 585:10
Greek adapting G. temples PUGI 636:25
G. can do everything JUVE 439:15
G. in its origin MAIN 508:1
G. particles HUGH 407:12
half G., half Latin SCOT 672:15
in Latin or in G. WALL 818:8
it was G. to me SHAK 696:17
loving, natural, and G. BYRO 180:24
neither G. nor Jew BIBL 110:12
pages of your G. models HORA 398:12
pay at the G. Kalends AUGU 37:23
questioned him in G. CARR 196:15
say a word against G. SHAW 725:22
small Latin, and less G. JONS 436:2
study of G. literature GAIS 337:15
When G. meets Greek PROV 634:21
wife talks G. JOHN 433:17
Greeks For G. a blush BYRO 181:6
G., and to the Barbarians BIBL 105:35
G. bearing gifts PROV 619:45
G. had a word AKIN 9:11
G. had modesty PEAC 589:13
G. in this American empire MACM 504:1
G. joined Greeks LEE 478:20
G. seek after wisdom BIBL 107:3
G. take the beating HORA 399:3
G. were gods FUSE 337:11
I fear the G. VIRG 811:11
Let G. be Greeks BRAD 149:5
make way, G. PROP 612:23
unto the G. foolishness BIBL 107:4
writings of G. OMAR 573:6
green and a g. gown NURS 566:16
bordered by its gardens g. MORR 549:15
Colourless g. ideas CHOM 218:8
die when the trees were g. CLAR 224:3
drives my g. age THOM 789:9

feed me in a g. pasture · BOOK 135:3
Flora and the country g. · KEAT 444:21
g. and pleasant bowers · BLAK 120:15
g. and pleasant land · BLAK 121:15
g. as emerald · COLE 232:15
g. banks of Shannon · CAMP 187:10
G. Eye · HAYE 376:7
g.-eyed monster · SHAK 713:27
g. grass shorn · BACO 44:18
G. grow the rashes, O · BURN 171:6
G. grow the rushes O · SONG 747:11
g. herb · BOOK 141:7
g. hill far away · ALEX 11:10
G. how I want you · LORC 492:2
g. in judgment · SHAK 679:1
g. pastures of the European · VERW 809:5
G. pleasure or grey grief · SWIN 769:6
g. shoots of recovery · MISQ 537:17
g. trees when I saw them · TRAH 797:15
g. Yule makes · PROV 621:20
heard of the g. · BLAK 122:7
Her g. lap · WALK 817:12
How g. was my valley · LLEW 487:9
in a g. tree · BIBL 102:3
in g. pastures · WILL 839:17
In the morning it is g. · BOOK 139:22
In thy g. lap · GRAY 361:18
laid him on the g. · BALL 51:16
lamps in a g. night · MARV 515:7
laughs to see the g. man · HOFF 391:19
life springs ever g. · GOET 352:18
Make it a g. peace · DARN 256:18
Making the g. one red · SHAK 705:3
memory be g. · SHAK 683:20
My passport's g. · HEAN 378:1
O all ye G. Things · BOOK 128:8
O G. One [Haoma] · ZORO 859:13
one g. · BASH 57:21
Praise the g. earth · BUNT 164:9
shoot the sleepy, g.-coat man · HOFF 392:1
strew the g. lap · SHAK 716:13
sun doth parch the g. · SURR 764:6
To a g. thought · MARV 515:17
wearin' o' the G. · POLI 600:21
Wherever g. is worn · YEAT 854:5
greener grass is always g. · PROV 621:14
g. than the grass · BALL 52:19
greenery g. of the trees · DANT 256:7
In a mountain g. · HART 374:13
greenery-yallery g., Grosvenor Gallery
· GILB 348:17
greenfly weren't any g. · AYCK 41:5
greenhouse g. gases · MARG 512:6
greening g. of America · REIC 644:15
Greenland From G.'s icy mountains
· HEBE 378:15
greenly We have done but g. · SHAK 688:10
greenness recovered g. · HERB 384:7
Greenpeace G. had a ring to it · HUNT 410:11
greens healing g. · ABSE 1:4
Greensleeves G. was all my joy · SONG 747:9
greenwood to the g. go · BALL 52:16
Under the g. tree · SHAK 681:3
greet G. the unseen · BROW 158:12
How should I g. thee · BYRO 183:23
Greise Kopf zum G. · MÜLL 553:21
grenadier British G. · SONG 748:5
Pomeranian g. · BISM 117:17
Grenville Richard G. lay · TENN 783:19
grey All cats are g. in the dark · PROV 614:9
bring down my g. hairs · BIBL 77:8
could comb g. hair · YEAT 854:14
good g. head · TENN 782:15
Green pleasure or g. grief · SWIN 769:6
g.-green, greasy, Limpopo · KIPL 456:17
G. silent fragments · HUGH 407:7
hair is g. · BYRO 183:2
in my g. hairs · WOLS 844:12
lend me your g. mare · BALL 53:20
little g. cells · CHRI 218:15
philosophy paints its g. · HEGE 379:8
this old g. head · WHIT 834:3
world has grown g. · SWIN 768:22

you are old and g. · YEAT 856:6
greyhound This fawning g. · SHAK 689:30
greyhounds g. in the slips · SHAK 693:5
grief acquainted with g. · BIBL 90:2
But g. returns · SHEL 728:17
first feel g. yourself · HORA 398:6
forethought of g. · BERR 71:12
goal of g. · RALE 641:1
Green pleasure or grey g. · SWIN 769:6
G. and avenging Cares · VIRG 812:12
g. felt so like fear · LEWI 483:4
G. fills the room up · SHAK 699:6
g. flieth to it · BACO 44:2
G. for awhile is blind · SHEL 730:23
g. forgotten · SWIN 768:1
G. has no wings · QUIL 639:8
g. I did sustain · CONS 241:5
G. is a species of idleness · JOHN 429:20
G. is itself a med'cine · COWP 246:5
g. is like a minefield · WARN 821:22
G. is the price · SAYI 669:23
g. itself be mortall · SHEL 728:19
g. just collected · DEAN 260:9
g. of heart · SHAK 695:9
g. that does not speak · SHAK 706:23
g. too much to be told · VIRG 811:9
G. with a glass · SWIN 768:3
hopeless g. is passionless · BROW 157:25
I am g. · VOZN 817:1
in false g. hiding · SPEN 751:18
long g. and pain · TENN 782:2
master a g. · SHAK 712:24
more worthy of g. · SHEL 732:11
Of g. I died · ROET 652:8
pain and g. · BOOK 136:3
Patch g. with proverbs · SHAK 712:30
pitch of g. · HOPK 396:18
see another's g. · BLAK 122:8
Should be past g. · SHAK 721:30
shows of g. · SHAK 683:27
Silence augmenteth g. · DYER 293:12
silent manliness of g. · GOLD 354:19
Smiling at g. · SHAK 720:29
Thine be the g. · AYTO 41:12
thirsty g. in wine we steep · LOVE 493:5
griefs borne our g. · BIBL 90:2
But not my g. · SHAK 716:8
cutteth g. in halves · BACO 44:15
Great g. · SHAK 683:6
g. and fears · BACO 45:4
g. that harrass · JOHN 426:12
soothed the g. · MACA 498:21
grievance doon offte gret g. · LYDG 496:19
Scotsman with a g. · WODE 842:16
grieve g. or triumph · GOET 353:4
heart doesn't g. over · PROV 634:12
Pope will g. a day · SWIF 767:16
what could it g. for · KEAT 443:17
grieved g. my heart to think · WORD 847:13
g. with this generation · BOOK 140:10
grieves thing that g. not · MARK 512:8
grieving áre you g. · HOPK 397:2
grievous most g. fault · MISS 536:14
most g. to him · TROL 799:17
remembrance of them is g. · BOOK 131:18
grill Let G. be Grill · SPEN 751:27
grim g. for me, grim for TB · CAMP 186:19
g. grew his countenance · BALL 51:19
grimace accelerated g. · POUN 608:18
grin cheerfully he seems to g. · CARR 194:1
ending with the g. · CARR 194:8
one universal g. · FIEL 318:14
Relaxed into a universal g. · COWP 248:10
grind bastards g. you down · SAYI 670:6
g. in the prison house · BIBL 79:35
g. the faces of the poor · BIBL 88:3
Laws g. the poor · GOLD 355:14
mill cannot g. with · PROV 626:22
mills of God g. slowly · LONG 490:23
mills of God g. slowly · PROV 626:23
one demd horrid g. · DICK 271:4
grinders g. cease · BIBL 86:25
incisors and g. · BAGE 48:22

Grisilde G. is deed · CHAU 211:4
grist g. that comes to the mill · PROV 614:12
groan Condemned alike to g. · GRAY 361:11
g. and shake their fists · HOUS 403:19
groaneth whole creation g. · BIBL 106:20
groaning g. under walls · MARL 513:14
weary of my g. · BOOK 134:2
groans g. of love to those of the dying
· LOWR 494:22
grocer made the wicked G. · CHES 216:14
groined titanic wars had g. · OWEN 581:6
Gromboolian G. plain · LEAR 477:6
groom death is but a g. · DONN 280:4
grooves moves In determinate g.
· HARE 373:10
ringing g. of time · TENN 781:4
groping g. for words · LEWI 483:17
gross g. as a mountain · SHAK 690:10
Not g. to sink · SHAK 724:2
Things rank and g. · SHAK 684:2
grosser g. name · SHAK 688:18
Grosvenor Gallery greenery-yallery, G.
· GILB 348:17
grotesque g. situation · HAUG 375:5
ornate, and g. · BAGE 49:11
Groucho of the G. tendency · SLOG 740:6
ground acre of barren g. · SHAK 718:19
as water spilt on the g. · BIBL 81:3
Chosen and made peculiar g. · WATT 823:14
commit his body to the g. · BOOK 133:18
crieth from the g. · BIBL 75:29
fell into good g. · BIBL 97:3
gain a little patch of g. · SHAK 688:1
Grammar, the g. of al · LANG 466:9
G. control to Major Tom · BOWI 148:10
g. of my heart · BOOK 143:19
g. won to-day · ARNO 28:8
here at last on the g. · SOND 746:6
holy g. · BIBL 77:17
in a fair g. · BOOK 134:14
In his own g. · POPE 605:31
let us sit upon the g. · SHAK 715:23
see me cover the g. · GROS 365:2
seven feet of English g. · HARO 373:17
stirrup and the g. · EPIT 310:16
They are the g. · SHAK 702:18
tread on classic g. · ADDI 4:20
upon the g. I se thee stare · CHAU 212:10
when I hit the g. · SPRI 753:10
grounds laying out of g. · PEAC 589:15
grove g. of chimneys · MORR 549:7
olive g. of Academe · MILT 534:21
windings of the g. · BEAT 59:12
grovelled g. before him · THAC 786:13
groves g. of Academe · HORA 399:21
g. of their academy · BURK 167:16
G. whose rich trees · MILT 532:27
whispering the g. · THOM 792:16
grow g. in worth · TENN 784:22
g. To fruit or shade · HERB 383:17
g. up with the country · GREE 362:3
one to g. · PROV 628:34
Please help me g. God · BLUM 124:2
They shall g. not old · BINY 116:14
growed I s'pect I g. · STOW 761:19
growl sit and g. · JOHN 432:2
growth children of a larger g. · CHES 215:8
children of a larger g. · DRYD 287:24
neoclassical endogenous g. · BROW 155:1
new g. in the plant · ADDA 4:1
root of all genuine g. · SMIL 740:22
States, like men, have their g. · LAND 466:7
grub old ones, g. · SHAW 724:15
Grubstreet G. biographers · ADDI 4:19
grudge ancient g. I bear him · SHAK 708:30
gruel g. thick and slab · SHAK 706:13
grumbling rhythmical g. · ELIO 304:1
Grundy need of Mrs G. · LOCK 489:3
Solomon G. · NURS 569:15
What will Mrs G. think · MORT 551:10
grunt expect from a pig but a g. · PROV 634:1
gruntled far from being g. · WODE 842:14
guarantee cannot g. it won't · HOWA 405:9

guarantees g. all others	CHUR 222:9
guard Be on your g.	OFFI 572:14
G. us, guide us	EDME 296:7
guarded requires to be ever g.	GOLD 355:31
well-g. mind	PALI 584:11
guardian G. and my Guide	WILL 838:8
guardians good grey g. of art	WILB 835:6
guards Brigade of G.	MACM 504:8
G. die	CAMB 186:14
Up G. and at them	WELL 827:12
who is to guard the g.	JUVE 439:22
guardsman g.'s cut and thrust	HUXL 411:15
gubu acronym G.	HAUG 375:5
gude g. time coming	SCOT 674:22
gudgeon this fool g.	SHAK 708:22
gué au g.	ANON 21:2
guenille ma g. m'est chère	MOLI 541:19
guerre ce n'est pas la g.	BOSQ 145:14
guerrilla by means of g. bands	MAZZ 519:16
g. wins if he does not	KISS 457:10
guess Medical Men g.	KEAT 447:9
guessing G. so much	CHES 216:2
g. what was at the other side	WELL 827:19
mind which is good at g.	PLAT 597:7
guest be your g. tomorrow night	ANON 20:6
Earth, receive an honoured g.	AUDE 35:5
g. that tarrieth but a day	BIBL 92:28
second g. to entertain	DONN 281:8
speed the going g.	POPE 605:15
Speed the parting g.	POPE 605:15
uninvited g.	TURG 802:4
Wedding-G. here beat	COLE 232:14
guests Fish and g. stink	PROV 620:15
G. can be delightful	ELIZ 305:9
g. should praise it	HARI 373:14
g. star-scattered	FITZ 323:17
hosts and g.	BEER 63:1
Unbidden g.	SHAK 694:8
guidance Messenger with the g.	KORA 461:5
sent down to be a g.	KORA 459:12
guide God to be his g.	BUNY 165:3
Guardian and my G.	WILL 838:8
G., a Comforter	AUBE 33:13
g. by the light of reason	BRAN 149:11
G. me, O thou great Jehovah	WILL 838:9
g. our feet	BIBL 99:33
g. what goes off the road	LANG 467:1
G. where our infant Redeemer	HEBE 378:14
ruler and g.	BOOK 130:12
very g. of life	BUTL 175:11
guided g. missiles	KING 452:7
guides blind g.	BIBL 98:10
guiding g.-star of a whole brave nation	
	MOTL 551:14
Guildenstern Rosencrantz and G.	
	SHAK 689:17
guile hiding his harmful g.	SPEN 751:18
in whom is no g.	BIBL 102:26
lips, that they speak no g.	BOOK 135:25
there is no g.	BOOK 135:20
urban, squat, and packed with g.	
	BROO 153:12
guilt assumption of g.	CROS 252:13
beggar would recognise g.	PARS 586:24
blood with g. is bought	SHEL 731:1
dwell on g.	AUST 39:5
for a sign of g.	CONG 239:9
free from g. or pain	SHEL 731:8
G. in his heart	CHUR 220:6
g. of Stalin	GORB 356:14
Life without industry is g.	RUSK 659:11
no wish to carry the g.	CLAU 225:13
put on a dress of g.	MCGO 502:2
unfortunate circumstance of g.	STEV 759:28
war without its g.	SURT 764:12
wash her g. away	GOLD 355:33
without its g.	SOME 745:21
guilty crimes of this g. land	BROW 155:8
g. conscience needs	PROV 621:22
g. man is acquitted	JUVE 440:13
G. of dust and sin	HERB 384:13
g. of our own disasters	SHAK 699:26
g. of some offence	FRIS 334:20

g. party is acquitted	PUBL 636:15
g. thing surprised	WORD 848:11
haunts the g. mind	SHAK 695:3
Let no g. man escape	GRAN 359:9
Make mad the g.	SHAK 686:4
Saints should be judged g.	ORWE 578:5
started like a g. thing	SHAK 683:17
ten g. persons escape	BLAC 118:12
guinea but the g.'s stamp	BURN 171:4
disc of fire like a g.	BLAK 123:2
g. pigs in the laboratory of God	WILL 839:4
g. you have in your pocket	RUSK 660:7
jingling of the g.	TENN 780:18
to one g.	JOHN 433:10
Worth a g. a box	ADVE 8:25
guinea pig skin of a g.	LIST 486:15
Guinness G., Allsopp, Bass	CALV 186:7
G. is good for you	ADVE 7:26
My Goodness, My G.	ADVE 8:5
guitar blue g.	STEV 757:25
sang to a small g.	LEAR 477:15
gulag G. archipelago	SOLZ 745:15
gulf great g. fixed	BIBL 101:23
redwood forest to the G. Stream	GUTH 366:5
gulfs g. of liquid fire	SHAK 714:28
g. will wash us down	TENN 784:19
whelmed in deeper g.	COWP 246:4
gullet g. of New York	MILL 527:8
gullible g. interpret as a sign	FLAU 325:4
gulls cry of g.	ELIO 303:22
gum can't fart and chew g.	JOHN 423:17
gums Don't forget the fruit g.	ADVE 7:18
wept odorous g.	MILT 532:27
gun Fire your little g.	DE L 262:25
grows out of the barrel of a g.	MAO 511:12
had a little g.	NURS 569:20
Happiness is a warm g.	LENN 480:11
Maxim G.	BELL 65:12
no g., but I can spit	AUDE 35:22
through the door with a g.	CHAN 207:18
gunboat send a g.	BEVA 73:11
gunfire towards the sound of g.	GRIM 364:16
Gunga Din than I am, G.	KIPL 454:10
gunner g. to his linstock	PROV 616:49
Sink me the ship, Master G.	TENN 784:8
gunpowder G., Printing	CARL 192:3
g. ran out	FOOT 328:6
G. Treason and Plot	ANON 18:12
Printing, g.	BACO 46:17
guns g. and sharp swords	DYLA 294:7
G. aren't lawful	PARK 586:1
G. don't kill people	SLOG 740:3
g. that are hidden	FLEI 326:8
hundred men with g.	PUZO 638:11
loaded g. with boys	CRAB 249:15
monstrous anger of the g.	OWEN 581:1
not found any smoking g.	BLIX 123:11
rather have butter or g.	GOER 352:9
They got the g.	MORR 550:5
with g. not with butter	GOEB 352:7
gunslinger Hip young g.	ANON 16:12
gurgite rari nantes in g. vasto	VIRG 810:18
gurly G. grew the sea	BALL 51:19
guru by grace through the G.	SIKH 737:1
G. Granth Sahib	SIKH 737:11
known as his g.	LAWS 475:22
reading the G.'s words	SIKH 737:10
When the G. comes	SIKH 737:3
gusts our g. and storms	ELIO 299:12
Gutenberg G. made everybody	MCLU 503:18
gutless sort of g. Kipling	ORWE 577:25
guts full of g.	ARCH 24:8
g. of the last priest	DIDE 273:17
lug the g.	SHAK 687:33
Mrs Thatcher 'showed g.'	KINN 453:7
sheeps' g.	SHAK 712:17
Spill your g. at Wimbledon	CONN 240:11
strangled with the g.	MESL 523:7
gutsed they g. it out	GREG 363:9
gutta G. cavat lapidem	OVID 580:7
gutter in the g. with that guy	EISE 298:14
Journalists belong in g.	PRIE 610:16
We are all in the g.	WILD 836:7

guys G. and dolls	RUNY 658:14
Nice g. finish last	DURO 293:6
gypsies play with the g.	NURS 568:11
gyre Did g. and gimble	CARR 194:25
gyves With g. upon his wrist	HOOD 394:24
ha H., ha	BIBL 83:25
habeas corpus protection of h.	JEFF 420:4
habit Cocaine h.-forming	BANK 54:14
entirely different from h.	STRA 762:7
Growing old a bad h.	MAUR 519:2
H. is a great deadener	BECK 61:24
h. is hell	HOLI 392:17
H. is second nature	AUCT 34:4
H. with him was all	CRAB 248:30
long h. of living	BROW 156:11
Not choice But h.	WORD 846:22
order breeds h.	ADAM 2:13
shook the h. off	WORD 849:18
Sow a h.	READ 643:7
habitarunt H. di quoque silvas	VIRG 813:19
habitation God in his holy h.	BOOK 138:11
h. among the tents of Kedar	BOOK 142:14
h. be void	BOOK 138:17
h. of dragons	BIBL 89:8
local h. and a name	SHAK 711:28
soul's h. henceforth	RUSS 660:25
habitations everlasting h.	BIBL 101:20
habits Old h. die hard	PROV 628:19
prejudices and h.	GIBB 345:11
habitual h. hatred	WASH 822:10
nothing is h. but indecision	JAME 418:19
hack Do not h. me	MONM 543:1
hacked H. with constant service	SOUT 748:15
Hackney Marshes You could see to H.	
	BATE 58:9
had What I ne'er h.	ASTE 32:11
Hades dark H.' door	VIRG 812:9
gates of H.	HOME 394:6
unsubstantial realms of H.	VIRG 812:11
haedis ab h. me sequestra	MISS 540:1
hag h. obscene	BEAT 59:12
haggard prove her h.	SHAK 713:28
Haggards H. ride no more	STEP 756:1
hags black, and midnight h.	SHAK 706:15
Haig ask for H.	ADVE 7:17
hail beaten dog beneath the h.	POUN 609:5
Fire and h.	BOOK 144:6
h., and farewell	CATU 203:10
H., fellow, well met	SWIF 767:3
H. holy queen	PRAY 611:6
H. Mary	PRAY 611:1
h. the power	PERR 593:3
H., thou that art highly favoured	BIBL 99:30
H. to thee, blithe Spirit	SHEL 731:25
sharp and sided h.	HOPK 396:16
hair All her h.	BROW 160:25
amber-dropping h.	MILT 529:7
bind my h.	HUNT 410:10
bracelet of bright h.	DONN 281:8
braided her yellow h.	BALL 53:8
bright golden h.	WILD 837:4
colour of his h.	HOUS 403:19
draws with a single h.	PROV 615:3
fell her golden h.	TURN 802:15
h. has become very white	CARR 194:4
h. is as a flock of goats	BIBL 87:10
h. is grey	BYRO 180:2
h. of a woman	HOWE 406:2
h. of his head	BIBL 91:24
h. of my flesh stood up	BIBL 82:35
h. that lay upon her back	ROSS 655:20
h. to stand on end	SHAK 684:32
h. turns white	BERR 71:13
her eyes, her h.	MEW 523:15
Her h. was long	KEAT 443:25
if a woman have long h.	BIBL 107:23
Like the bright h. uplifted	SHEL 730:8
long essenced h.	MACA 499:6
part my h. behind	ELIO 302:20
pin up my h. with prose	CONG 239:12
raiment of camel's h.	BIBL 94:11

hands (*cont.*):

temples made with h.	BIBL 105:19
terrible, man-slaying h.	HOME 394:11
think with my h.	HODG 391:8
union of h. and hearts	TAYL 775:4
washed his h.	BIBL 99:10
wash my h. in innocency	BOOK 135:11
With mine own h.	SHAK 716:9
with one of his h.	BIBL 82:20
world's great h.	HUNT 409:17
your face in your h.	ANON 17:3

handsaw know a hawk from a h.

	SHAK 685:27

handsome H. is as handsome does

	PROV 621:26

handwriting legibility in his h. HAY 376:4

hang all h. together FRAN 332:17

Go h. thyself	SHAK 689:33
h. a man first	MOLI 542:6
h. a pearl	SHAK 710:28
H. a thief when he's young	PROV 621:28
H. it all, Robert Browning	POUN 608:15
h. my hat	JERO 421:15
h. the man over again	BARH 55:13
h. upon him	DONN 281:25
H. yourself, brave Crillon	HENR 381:20
in them which will h. him	RICH 647:19
let him h. there	EHRL 297:8
neither go nor h.	BIGO 116:10
will not h. myself today	CHES 215:20
with which to h. them	MISQ 537:6
wretches h.	POPE 606:12
you would h. yourself	JOHN 429:19

hanged born to be h. PROV 623:22

Confess and be h.	PROV 617:7
farmer that h. himself	SHAK 705:5
h., drawn, and quartered	PEPY 591:21
h. for a sheep	PROV 628:45
h. for stealing horses	HALI 369:6
h. in a fortnight	JOHN 430:26
h. in all innocence	STEV 759:30
if they'd been h.	DENN 264:12
ill name is half h.	PROV 621:49
Little thieves are h.	PROV 625:31
man who has been h.	PROV 627:25
must they all be h.	SHAK 706:21
my poor fool is h.	SHAK 702:7
our harps, we h. them up	BOOK 143:12
see him h.	BELL 65:7
So they h. Haman	BIBL 82:23

hanging bare h. DRYD 290:14

Catching's before h.	PROV 616:26
cured by h. from a string	KING 453:5
deserve h.	MONT 545:1
dog than h. it	PROV 631:47
H. and marriage	FARQ 315:22
H. and wiving	PROV 621:29
h. Danny Deever	KIPL 453:20
h. garments of Marylebone	JOYC 437:4
H. is too good for him	BUNY 164:18
h.-look to me	CONG 238:21
h. men an' women	POLI 600:21
H. of his cat	BRAT 149:19
Many a good h.	SHAK 720:10
postcards of the h.	DYLA 294:4

hangman h.'s thrusting The final nail

	BLOK 123:13
naked to the h.'s noose	HOUS 404:9

hangs H. in the uncertain balance

	GREE 362:21
thereby h. a tale	SHAK 681:7
What h. people	STEV 759:28

hank bone and a h. of hair KIPL 456:2

Hannibalem *Expende* H. JUVE 440:8

hante *h. la tempête* BAUD 58:11

Haoma O Green One [H.] ZORO 859:13

happen can't h. here LEWI 483:23

fools said would h.	MELB 521:4
h. to your mother	WALK 817:8
know it's about to h.	CANN 189:12
no evil h. unto thee	BOOK 140:4
poetry makes nothing h.	AUDE 35:4

happened after they have h. IONE 413:22

happening believe what isn't h. COLE 231:1

what is *not* h.	TYNA 804:2

happens be there when it h. ALLE 12:13

Nothing h.	BECK 61:17
nothing h.	WELD 827:4
Nothing, like something, h. anywhere	
	LARK 468:18
what h. to her	ELIO 299:19

happier h. than your father SOPH 746:12

make life h.	MART 515:2
remembering h. things	TENN 780:17
seek No h. state	MILT 533:9

happiest h. and best minds SHEL 732:16

h. men alive	LLOY 487:10
h. people in the world	OSBO 578:10
h. women	ELIO 300:14

happily h. ever after CLOS 228:4

happiness another person's h. MOOR 546:17

basically our h.	THOM 788:18
brief period of h.	ARIS 25:15
consume h. without producing	SHAW 724:22
desire for their own h.	SHAN 724:10
enemy to human h.	JOHN 432:3
fatal to true h.	RUSS 660:19
flaw In h.	KEAT 445:21
greatest h.	HUTC 410:19
H. a cigar	ADVE 7:27
h. alone is salutary	PROU 613:15
h. and final misery	MILT 532:9
H. depends on being free	THUC 793:23
H., for you	MONT 545:4
h. he feels	LACL 463:7
H. is an imaginary	SZAS 769:15
H. is a warm gun	LENN 480:11
H. is no laughing matter	WHAT 831:8
H. is not an ideal	KANT 441:11
h. is produced	JOHN 430:13
H. lies in conquering	GENG 342:24
h. makes up in height	FROS 335:16
h. mankind can gain	DRYD 288:24
h. of an individual	JOHN 429:16
h. of society	ADAM 3:7
h. of the greatest number	BENT 68:5
h. of the human race	BURK 167:2
h. of the next world	BROW 156:10
H.! our being's end	POPE 605:8
h. she herself brought	FLAU 324:21
h. that went on	CHEK 214:11
h. was but the occasional	HARD 371:20
H. washes away many things	BÖLL 126:14
home-born h.	COWP 248:8
hopes for h. from thee	WRIG 851:17
In solitude What h.	MILT 533:24
let me forget this h.	NERU 559:3
lifetime of h.	SHAW 725:30
lightning of individual h.	HERZ 386:25
look into h.	SHAK 682:4
Money can't buy h.	PROV 626:29
more for human h.	BRIL 151:16
my people's h.	ELIZ 304:10
no greatest h. principle	CARL 191:23
one's true h.	LACL 463:8
only one h. in life	SAND 665:14
only thing for h.	EDGE 295:17
or justice or human h.	BERL 70:4
politics of h.	HUMP 409:14
prayer to h.	ALAI 10:4
pursuit of h.	ANON 19:17
pursuit of h.	JEFF 419:10
recipe for h.	AUST 39:3
result h.	DICK 268:14
ruin of all h.	BURN 169:22
searching for his own h.	PALI 584:16
secret of h.	MORE 548:3
seek h. in boats	HORA 399:10
short-lived h.	BEHN 63:21
suited to human h.	DEFO 261:9
take away his h.	IBSE 412:16
that is h.	CATH 199:11
that is h.	EMER 307:7
that we call h.	GIDE 346:14
two combined make H.	BUCH 162:17

We find our h.	WORD 849:16

happy all be as h. as kings STEV 760:3

all who are h.	JOHN 428:24
ask if they were h.	CHAN 208:1
attain The h. life	SURR 764:4
aware that you are h.	KRIS 461:19
bread-sauce of the h. ending	JAME 418:6
Call no man h.	SOLO 745:13
conspiracy to make you h.	UPDI 805:18
duty of being h.	STEV 759:18
earthlier h.	SHAK 710:16
had a h. life	LAST 474:13
h. as one hopes	LA R 469:22
H. birthday to you	HILL 388:12
h. breed of men	SHAK 715:13
h. could I be with either	GAY 341:20
h. families resemble	TOLS 796:13
H. field or mossy cavern	KEAT 444:5
h. for a week	PROV 623:27
h. he who crowns in shades	GOLD 354:11
H. he who like Ulysses	DU B 290:18
h. highways where I went	HOUS 404:16
H. in this	SHAK 709:19
h. issue	BOOK 129:19
H. is the country	PROV 621:31
H. is the man	BOOK 143:2
H. is the man who fears	BIBL 115:2
H. Land	MAHÀ 507:3
h. men that have the power	TENN 784:9
h. noise to hear	HOUS 404:11
h. Rome, born when I	CICE 223:25
H. the hare at morning	AUDE 34:24
H. the man	DRYD 289:29
H. the man	HORA 400:1
H. the man	POPE 605:31
H. the people	MONT 545:11
H. those early days	VAUG 807:12
h. while y'er leevin	MOTT 552:3
hope for a h. exit	LAST 472:8
I die h.	LAST 472:3
in general be as h.	JOHN 430:14
make a man h.	HORA 399:8
make men h.	POPE 605:18
man would be as h.	JOHN 431:10
must laugh before we are h.	LA B 462:14
no man h. till he dies	PROV 616:22
object of making men h.	DOST 283:4
one of those h. souls	SHEL 729:21
one thing to make me h.	HAZL 376:11
one who has been h.	BOET 125:6
Point me out the h. man	GREE 362:13
policeman's lot is not a h. one	GILB 349:1
prevent from being h.	ANOU 23:1
remember a h. time	DANT 255:18
remembers the h. things	LOVE 493:10
so late their h. seat	MILT 534:14
someone, somewhere, may be h.	
	MENC 521:16
soul that loves is h.	GOET 352:11
splendid and a h. land	GOLD 354:18
stayed me in a h. hour	SHAK 712:28
that they h. are	WALL 818:14
This is the h. warrior	READ 643:4
till all are h.	SPEN 750:13
touch the H. Isles	TENN 784:19
'Twere now to be most h.	SHAK 713:19
Was he h.	AUDE 36:12
was the carver h.	RUSK 659:22
whether you are h.	MILL 525:2
whether you are h.	SHAW 727:8
Whoever wants to be h.	MEDI 520:9
Who is the h. Warrior	WORD 846:5
whose heart is h.	TALM 773:1
world of the h.	WITT 842:14

harbinger Love's h. MILT 534:9

harbour h. bar be moaning KING 452:22

those who h. them	BUSH 175:3
voyage not a h.	TOYN 797:7

hard h. day's night LENN 480:19

h. English men	KING 452:17
h.-faced men	BALD 50:6
h. rain's a gonna fall	DYLA 294:7
h.-sell or soft-sell TV push	NASH 557:13

h. sentences of old — BOOK 139:7
H. was their lodging — GART 340:11
Long is the way, And h. — MILT 532:7
made up of h. words — OSBO 578:11
never think I have hit h. — JOHN 430:1
She did it the h. way — EPIT 311:5
soft can wear away the h. — TALM 772:31
thine own h. case — CARE 190:18
thou art an h. man — BIBL 98:22
To ask the h. question — AUDE 36:11
too h. for me — BOOK 139:2
very h. guy indeed — RUNY 658:17
woman is so h. — TENN 783:11
harden h. not your hearts — BOOK 140:10
h. Pharaoh's heart — BIBL 77:24
harder h. they fall — PROV 615:39
hardly Johnny, I h. knew ye — BALL 52:8
hardships h. parcelled within them — BOLA 126:1
Hardy Kiss me, H. — NELS 558.21
hare First catch your h. — PROV 620:8
Happy the h. at morning — AUDE 34:24
h. limped trembling — KEAT 442:15
h. sits snug in leaves — HOFF 391:19
h. sitting up — LAWR 474:25
h.'s own child — HOFF 392:2
h. when it is cased — GLAS 351:14
Hound that Caught the Pubic H. — BEHA 63:13
outcry of the hunted h. — BLAK 119:7
run with the h. — PROV 635:35
than to start a h. — SHAK 689:28
thou woldest fynde an h. — CHAU 212:10
hares little hunted h. — HODG 391:10
run after two h. — PROV 623:23
hark H., my soul — COWP 246:26
H.! The dogs do bark — NURS 567:3
H., the dominant's persistence — BROW 161:19
H.! the herald-angels — WESL 828:23
harlot Every h. was a virgin once — BLAK 120:5
h.'s cry — BLAK 119:14
hollow-cheeked h. — BYRO 184:6
Portia is Brutus' h. — SHAK 697:1
prerogative of the h. — KIPL 457:8
harlotries synne and h. — CHAU 210:25
harlots MOTHER OF H. — BIBL 114:9
Harlow silent, as in H. — ASQU 32:7
harm does h. to my wit — SHAK 720:8
does most good or h. — BAGE 48:25
do so much h. — CREI 251:1
do the sick no h. — NIGH 564:13
False news do little h. — DARW 257:4
fear we'll come to h. — BALL 53:5
h. Macbeth — SHAK 706:16
h. that is spoken of it — FLAU 325:11
meaning no h. — GREE 362:17
men don most h. — LANG 466:17
no h. come to the state — ANON 21:15
supposed to do no h. — RUSS 660:24
to prevent h. — MILL 525:6
What h. have I ever done — TAWN 774:6
harmless h. as doves — BIBL 96:16
only h. great thing — DONN 280:9
harmonical h. and ingenious soul — AUBR 33:19
harmonies inventor of h. — TENN 782:10
harmonious dulcet and h. breath — SHAK 711:1
h. madness — SHEL 732:1
harmonizes sage h. the right — CHUA 218:20
harmony All discord, h. — POPE 604:30
best h. in a church — MILT 535:20
Discordant h. — HORA 399:11
from heavenly h. — DRYD 289:17
h. In autumn — SHEL 729:15
h. of music — REYN 646:8
h. of spring — GRAY 361:17
h. of the world — HOOK 395:18
h., order or proportion — BROW 157:7
herkenyng h. — CHAU 213:15
immortal god of h. — BEET 63:11
in their motions h. divine — MILT 533:18
ninefold h. — MILT 530:21
price is asked for h. — DOST 283:3
touches of sweet h. — SHAK 710:2

harness h. on our back — SHAK 707:15
joints of the h. — BIBL 81:34
Harold King H. was killed — ANON 22:9
harp flute, h., sackbut — BIBL 91:19
H. not on that string — SHAK 717:3
h. that once through Tara's halls — MOOR 547:15
h. with the lute — BOOK 139:13
lute and h. — BOOK 137:23
No h. like my own — CAMP 187:10
sing to the h. — BOOK 140:14
sweet h., the story — BAKE 50:3
upon the h. — BOOK 136:16
wild h. slung behind him — MOOR 547:17
harping hath not heart for h. — POUN 607:9
harps Be but organic h. — COLE 231:14
h., and golden vials — BIBL 113:12
our h., we hanged them up — BOOK 143:12
touch their h. of gold — SEAR 675:8
harpsichord describing the h. — BEEC 62:10
harrass h. the distressed — JOHN 426:12
harrow H. the house of the dead — AUDE 36:8
h. up thy soul — SHAK 684:32
toad beneath the h. — KIPL 455:8
harrowing h. clods — HARD 372:20
Harry God for H. — SHAK 693:5
little touch of H. — SHAK 693:9
Promised to H. — SHAK 692:32
shall H. die — SHAK 692:19
thy H.'s company — SHAK 690:19
harsh h. and embittered manhood — GOGO 354:1
so h. to the clever — WORD 846:1
hart As pants the h. — TATE 773:12
as the h. desireth — BOOK 136:11
footed like a h. — MALO 508:10
h. ungallèd — SHAK 687:9
leap as an h. — BIBL 89:11
young h. — BIBL 87:24
harts milk-white h. — MARL 513:17
Harvard glass flowers at H. — MOOR 547:3
Yale College and my H. — MELV 521:10
harvest h. is past — BIBL 90:27
h. of a quiet eye — WORD 849:3
h. truly is plenteous — BIBL 96:12
joy in h. — BIBL 88:17
laughs with a h. — JERR 421:17
seedtime and h. — BIBL 76:9
shine on, h. moon — NORW 565:17
harvests Deep h. bury all — POPE 603:14
h. of Arretium — MACA 499:12
Harwich steamer from H. — GILB 347:17
Hasdrubale Nominis H. interempto — HORA 402:10
Hast Ohne H., aber ohne Rast — GOET 353:16
haste always in h. — WESL 829:20
done in h. — PROV 628:10
H. is from the Devil — PROV 621:35
H. makes waste — PROV 621:36
H. still pays haste — SHAK 708:17
Make h. slowly — AUGU 37:21
Make h. slowly — PROV 625:50
maketh h. to be rich — BIBL 85:17
Marry in h. — PROV 626:17
Men love in h. — BYRO 181:30
More h., less speed — PROV 626:40
repent in h. — CONG 239:4
said in my h. — BOOK 142:7
what h. I can to be gone — LAST 473:6
Without h., but without rest — GOET 353:16
Ye shall eat it in h. — BIBL 77:30
hasten minutes h. to their end — SHAK 723:6
hasty H. climbers — PROV 621:37
hat get ahead, get a h. — ADVE 7:32
hang my h. — JERO 421:15
h. upon my head — JOHN 433:6
looking for a black h. — BOWE 148:8
my knee, my h., and hand — BROW 156:20
pulling off his h. — JOHN 428:6
think without his h. — BECK 61:18
hatched h. from a swan's egg — ANDE 14:4
hatches continually under h. — KEAT 446:10
hatchet cut it with my h. — WASH 822:11

hatcheth h. them not — BIBL 91:4
hatching H. vain empires — MILT 532:5
hate betray me to your mirth or h. — FORD 329:1
creative h. — CATH 199:14
h. a fellow whom pride — JOHN 432:2
h. all Boets and Bainters — GEOR 342:25
h. all that don't love me — FARQ 315:16
h. a song that has sold — BERL 70:1
h. is conquered by love — PALI 584:10
h., mankind — BYRO 178:24
H. takes a long time — THOM 791:1
h. that which we often fear — SHAK 678:20
h. the idle pleasures — SHAK 716:22
h. the man you have hurt — TACI 770:4
h. ye all — COWL 245:20
hearts that h. thee — SHAK 695:15
how much men h. them — GREE 363:4
If h. killed men — BROW 161:12
I h. and detest — SWIF 766:5
I h. and I love — CATU 203:9
I h. the common herd — HORA 401:9
I h. war — ROOS 653:15
immortal h. — MILT 531:9
know enough of h. — FROS 335:14
letter of h. — OSBO 578:24
Let them h. — ACCI 1:6
make us h. — SWIF 766:19
man you love to h. — ADVE 8:2
man you love to h. — FILM 320:5
must h. a Frenchman — NELS 558:12
must h. and death return — SHEL 729:12
never bother with people I h. — HART 374:12
not to h. them — SHAW 724:26
nought did I in h. — SHAK 714:29
of love is not h. — WIES 834:13
People must learn to h. — MAND 509:15
people who h. me — SEI 675:18
pure impartial h. — THOR 793:19
roughness breedeth h. — BACO 44:24
seen much to h. here — MILL 527:1
sprung from my only h. — SHAK 717:18
supernatural h. — BYRO 183:18
them also that h. him — BOOK 138:10
them which h. you — BIBL 100:15
time to h. — BIBL 85:32
We can scarcely h. — HAZL 377:6
Yet I do h. him — SHAK 713:2
you h. something in him — HESS 387:9
hated H. by fools — SWIF 767:14
h. the ruling few — BENT 68:10
how, then, must I be h. — SHEL 728:9
loved well because he h. — BROW 160:13
Make hatred i — FRAN 332:2
She might have h. — BROW 159:30
hateful shamed life a h. — SHAK 708:10
What is h. to you — HILL 389:1
hater very good h. — JOHN 433:11
hates h. dogs and babies — ROST 656:17
h. them for it — SHAW 727:21
just heaven now h. — EPIT 310:1
marry a man who h. his mother — BENN 67:24
world of voluble h. — TREV 798:13
hateth h. his brother — BIBL 112:22
hath Unto every one that h. — BIBL 98:23
hating By h. vices too much — BURK 167:27
h. all other nations — GASK 340:20
h., my boy, is an art — NASH 557:14
hatless lands h. from the air — BETJ 72:6
hatred common h. for something — CHEK 214:14
envy, h., and malice — BOOK 129:5
good rancorous h. — WARN 821:21
Great h., little room — YEAT 855:7
habitual h. — WASH 822:10
h. against the Church — SKEL 739:8
H. is a tonic — BALZ 54:9
h. is by far the longest — BYRO 181:30
h. therewith — BIBL 84:24
love to h. turned — CONG 238:30
Make h. hated — FRAN 332:2
most deadly h. — HUME 408:14
perpetual h. — GODW 352:5

hatred (cont.):
public h. CLAY 226:3
Regulated h. HARD 371:9
set against the h. MCEW 501:15
What we need is h. GENE 342:21
With what a perfect h. WALL 818:16
hatreds organization of h. ADAM 2:7
hats H. off, gentlemen SCHU 672:3
inside men's Sunday h. BROW 160:20
shocking bad h. WELL 827:18
Haughey H. buried at midnight O'BR 571:3
haughty h. spirit BIBL 84:26
haunted h. town it is to me LANG 466:9
haunts h. of coot and hern TENN 775:18
hause-bane white h. BALL 53:15
have h.-his-carcase, next to the perpetual DICK 272:9
h. it when they know it not SWIF 767:13
haves and the h.-nots CERV 205:13
h. to take you in FROS 335:12
I h. thee not SHAK 704:16
I'll h. her SHAK 716:24
to h. and to hold BOOK 133:9
What you h., hold PROV 634:15
What you spend, you h. PROV 634:17
will not let you h. it HAZL 376:15
haven h. under the hill TENN 775:17
havens ports and happy h. SHAK 715:10
Havergal Luke H. ROBI 650:14
haves h. and the have-nots CERV 205:13
having have what she's h. FILM 319:17
Never satisfied with h. WROT 851:18
havoc Cry, 'H.!' and let slip SHAK 697:16
hawk h. at eagles HERB 384:22
h. is in the air DISR 276:14
h. of the tower SKEL 739:6
his h., his hound BALL 53:15
know a h. from a handsaw SHAK 685:27
hawking h. his conscience round BEVI 74:2
hawks pick out h.' eyes PROV 621:38
Such hounds, such h. BALL 53:14
Hawkshaw H., the detective TAYL 775:5
haws fruit fails, welcome h. PROV 634:20
hawthorn h. bush SHAK 694:27
h. in the dale MILT 529:22
hay bottle of h. SHAK 711:21
eating h. when you're faint CARR 195:22
lie tumbling in the h. SHAK 721:33
live on h. HILL 388:11
Make h. PROV 625:51
sheets with h. over JOHN 424:20
When the h. came creaking LOWE 494:13
haycock under a h. NURS 568:1
haystack h. in the floods MORR 549:16
hazard h. of the die SHAK 717:11
hazards h. whence no tears HARD 373:1
haze Purple h. is in my brain HEND 381:10
hazelnut no bigger than a h. JULI 438:5
he Art thou h. BIBL 96:23
H. would, wouldn't he RICE 647:3
While H. is mine, and I am His HERB 385:2
head at the h. of the table PROV 634:40
bear with a sore h. MARR 514:8
brains go to his h. ASQU 32:8
cut off his h. JOHN 429:17
dark hole of the h. HUGH 407:8
eye in the back of the h. COLE 233:26
feet than their h. CAVE 204:5
from the h. downwards PROV 620:14
get one's h. cut off CARR 195:9
God be in my h. PRAY 611:3
good grey h. TENN 782:15
Go up, thou bald h. BIBL 82:3
hairs of your h. BIBL 96:18
hand, the h. RUSK 660:3
hat upon my h. JOHN 433:6
h. beneath the feet OVID 580:19
h. could wish him MORE 548:9
h. grown grey SHEL 728:23
h. is not more native SHAK 683:22
h. on her knee SHAK 714:16
h. on his knee BARH 56:1
h. that once was crowned KELL 448:2

h. that wears a crown SHAK 692:4
h. to contrive CLAR 224:16
h. to contrive GIBB 345:7
his h. with his legs BIBL 77:29
hold my h. so high HORA 400:2
ideas of its "h." DISR 275:10
if S-E-X rears its h. AYCK 41:3
if you can keep your h. KERR 450:1
If you can keep your h. KIPL 454:12
imperfections on my h. SHAK 685:5
It shall bruise thy h. BIBL 75:24
jerked its h. HUGH 407:7
Johnny-h.-in-air PUDN 636:17
keep your h. PUDN 636:18
King Charles's h. DICK 268:16
learned lumber in his h. POPE 604:16
Many a h. has turned white MÜLL 553:21
maugree his h. CHAU 212:19
My deeds upon my h. SHAK 709:27
my h. is a map FIEL 318:6
My h. is bloody, but unbowed HENL 381:14
Off with her h. CARR 194:12
Off with his h. CIBB 223:2
old h. on young shoulders PROV 635:34
on each gashed h. SORL 746:23
one small h. could carry GOLD 354:17
Or in the heart or in the h. SHAK 709:17
proof of want of h. SAYI 670:9
purpose of the h. RIDI 648:4
room at your h. BALL 51:18
shorter by the h. ELIZ 304:6
should have his h. examined GOLD 356:6
show my h. to the people DANT 256:15
so old a h. SHAK 709:24
stand on your h. CARR 194:4
takes my laily h. BALL 52:9
under my h. BALL 52:2
What though his h. be empty SWIF 766:16
where to lay his h. BIBL 96:1
which way the h. lies RALE 641:16
your good h. ELIZ 304:9
headache with a dismal h. GILB 347:16
heading do you know where we're h. DYLA 294:14
headland Be like a h. AURE 38:5
some bold h. WORD 846:13
headmasters H. have powers CHUR 222:10
headpiece H. filled with straw ELIO 302:6
heads h. Do grow beneath SHAK 713:9
h. replete with thoughts COWP 248:13
H. Were toward Eternity DICK 272:23
Hide their diminished h. MILT 532:22
hold our h. erect JERO 421:6
Lift up your h. BOOK 135:6
Two h. are better than one PROV 633:28
very empty h. BACO 46:20
headstone h. in the corner BOOK 142:10
headstones h. yield their names TATE 773:10
headstrong h. as an allegory SHER 733:20
heady H., not strong POPE 601:26
heal h. me of my grievous wound TENN 778:18
h. what is wounded LANG 467:1
Physician, h. thyself BIBL 100:11
Physician, h. thyself PROV 629:22
time to h. BIBL 85:32
healed h. also the hurt BIBL 90:26
h. of a suffering PROU 613:12
my soul shall be h. MISS 539:10
ransomed, h. LYTE 497:11
with his stripes we are h. BIBL 90:3
healer sharp compassion of the h.'s art ELIO 301:18
Time is a great h. PROV 633:2
Time not a great h. COMP 236:17
healeth h. those that are broken BOOK 144:3
healing h. fountain AUDE 35:8
h. in his wings BIBL 92:14
H. is a matter of time HIPP 389:16
h. of the nations BIBL 114:22
h. wings could see VAUG 807:9
not heroics, but h. HARD 371:10
health best thing is h. ANON 21:10

damaging to h. SADE 662:14
everything is h. MÉNA 521:12
h. and wealth HUNT 409:18
h. of the whole human race TOYN 797:8
h. shall spring forth BIBL 90:15
h. unbought DRYD 288:8
in h. and wealth BOOK 128:15
in sickness and in h. BOOK 133:9
in sound h. in September's heat HORA 399:12
Look to your h. WALT 821:2
no h. in us BOOK 127:16
regaining my h. RILK 649:4
seriously damage your h. OFFI 572:12
so far from my h. BOOK 134:26
thy saving h. BOOK 138:8
When you have both, it's h. DONL 279:3
healthful h. Spirit of thy grace BOOK 128:17
most h. of beverages PAST 588:8
healths h. and draughts go free LOVE 493:5
healthy cuts away h. tissue FORS 329:17
h. and wealthy and dead THUR 794:2
h. bones of a single Pomeranian BISM 117:17
h. state of political life MILL 525:8
h., wealthy, and wise PROV 618:31
heap waters to stand on an h. BOOK 139:9
heapeth h. up riches BOOK 136:5
hear All the better to h. you with PERR 593:1
another to h. THOR 793:16
Believe nothing of what you h. PROV 615:8
Be swift to h. BIBL 111:21
cannot choose but h. COLE 232:13
Can you h. me, mother CATC 200:7
do not wish to h. BUTL 177:6
hath ears to h. BIBL 99:18
H. all, see all PROV 622:17
h. a smile CROS 252:15
h. in my imagination MOZA 553:2
h. more good things HAZL 377:4
H. my law BOOK 139:7
h. my Thisby's face SHAK 712:3
h. no evil PROV 630:27
h. no more at all STEV 760:15
h., oh, hear SHEL 730:7
H., O Israel BIBL 78:26
h. our prayers BOOK 133:1
h. the larks HOUS 404:11
H. the other side AUGU 37:11
h. the word of the Lord BIBL 91:18
h. thy shrill delight SHEL 731:9
in such wise h. them BOOK 130:1
let me h. thee speaking BODE 125:4
Listeners never h. any good PROV 625:23
make you h. CONR 240:20
never would h. SWIF 766:30
Plenty to see and h. JOYC 437:22
prefer not to h. AGAR 6:20
shall he not h. BOOK 140:8
shall not h. the bittern LEDW 478:14
those who will not h. PROV 632:32
we shall h. it by-and-by BROW 158:7
you will h. me DISR 275:4
heard have not h. them BIBL 100:21
have ye not h. BIBL 89:20
h. and known BOOK 139:7
h. for their much speaking BIBL 95:2
h. it's in the stars PORT 607:18
H., not regarded SHAK 690:28
I have h. of thee BIBL 83:30
I never h. thy fire HEYW 387:19
I will be h. GARR 340:8
Oon ere it h. CHAU 213:9
seen and not h. PROV 616:40
then is h. no more SHAK 707:14
twice I have also h. BOOK 138:2
You ain't h. nuttin' yet JOLS 434:4
hearers attentive and favourable h. HOOK 395:17
not h. only BIBL 111:22
heareth thy servant h. BIBL 80:5
hearing delicate h. saves MOOR 547:9
Fall asleep, or h. die SHAK 695:9

my sense of h. SHAK 702:13
People h. without listening SIMO 738:4
hearken to h. than the fat BIBL 80:14
hearkened h. not unto the voice
BOOK 141:14
h. to my commandments BIBL 89:25
hearsay formerly lived by h. BUNY 165:11
hearse Underneath this sable h. EPIT 311:11
walk before the h. GARR 340:6
hearses frequent h. POPE 602:15
heart Absence makes h. grow fonder
PROV 613:16
abundance of the h. BIBL 96:31
accompany me with a pure h. BOOK 127:14
Ancient person of my h. ROCH 651:16
And I am sick at h. SHAK 683:12
anniversaries of the h. LONG 490:12
As my poor h. doth think LYLY 497:5
ás the h. grows older HOPK 397:3
Batter my h. DONN 279:21
beak form out my h. POE 599:8
Beware my foolish h. WASH 822:14
bicycle-pump the human h. AMIS 13:12
blind side of the h. CHES 215:23
broken h. lies here MACA 499:7
bruised h. was piercèd SHAK 713:14
Bury my h. at Wounded Knee BENÉ 66:12
But break, my h. SHAK 684:6
Chuang Tzu's dreaming h. BASH 58:4
Cold hands, warm h. PROV 617:1
committed adultery in my h. CART 197:3
correct the h. EPIT 309:6
corrupt the h. BYRO 182:14
curse with their h. BOOK 137:27
deceiveth his own h. BIBL 111:23
deep h.'s core YEAT 854:18
deserts of the h. AUDE 35:8
desires of the h. AUDE 34:23
Did not our h. burn BIBL 102:12
duties of the h. BAHY 49:15
ease a h. like a satin gown PARK 586:2
ease thine h. BEDD 62:1
education of the h. SCOT 675:1
engraved on her h. SELL 676:20
examine my own h. DE V 266:1
eyes, but not my h. JONS 435:5
faint h. ne'er wan A lady BURN 172:23
faith of the h. LUTH 496:12
fed my h. PETR 593:15
fed the h. on fantasies YEAT 854:24
feeling h. is a blessing RICH 647:16
found not my h. moved more SIDN 736:18
Fourteen h. attacks JOPL 436:11
from hell's h. MELV 521:11
from the h. of joy BEEC 62:15
fullness of the h. PROV 629:13
gentil h. CHAU 211:14
give A loving h. to thee HERR 386:13
given you her h. VANB 806:16
God be in my h. PRAY 611:3
God dwells in thy h. BHAG 74:17
great have no h. LA B 462:16
grieved my h. to think WORD 847:13
harden Pharaoh's h. BIBL 77:24
hath not h. for harping POUN 609:7
Have patience, h. HOME 394:18
h. amidst the organs HA-L 368:9
h. and hands and voices WINK 841:14
H. and soul do sing SIDN 736:13
h. and stomach of a king ELIZ 304:7
h. and tongue employ TATE 773:13
h. as sound as a bell SHAK 712:23
h. belongs to Daddy PORT 607:16
h. be troubled BIBL 103:27
h. bleeds for his country JOHN 428:2
heart-break in the h. of things GIBS 346:10
h. clings to LUTH 496:9
h. doesn't grieve over PROV 634:12
h. for any fate LONG 490:22
h. gets tired too VERG 808:12
h. grown cold SHEL 728:23
h. grows old YEAT 855:17

h. had never known ye ANON 19:2
h. has its reasons PASC 587:12
h.—how shall I say? BROW 160:10
h. in the business WATS 823:1
h. into his hand TALM 772:18
h. is a lonely hunter BORR 146:11
h. is a small thing QUAR 638:18
h. is deceitful BIBL 91:3
h. is Highland GALT 338:15
h. is inditing BOOK 136:19
h. is like a singing bird ROSS 655:6
h. is on the left MOLI 542:1
h. is restless AUGU 36:24
h. is sick TENN 779:4
h. is sorrowful BIBL 84:19
h. leaps up WORD 847:16
h. less bounding ARNO 28:28
h. likes a little disorder DE B 260:15
h. of a man GAY 341:14
h. of an immense darkness OPEN 575:11
H. of England DRAY 286:1
h. of furious fancies ANON 20:4
h. of kings BIBL 85:2
h. of lead POPE 601:23
h. o' flesh BALL 53:9
h. of man DOST 283:1
h. of man HUME 409:12
H. of oak GARR 340:2
h. responsive swells BYRO 179:24
h. speaks to heart FRAN 332:8
H. speaks to heart MOTT 552:5
H.'s renying BARN 56:17
h.'s stalled motor MAYA 519:11
h. strangely warmed WESL 829:16
h. that fed SHEL 730:17
h. the keener ANON 22:6
h. to a dog to tear KIPL 455:9
h. to heart SCOT 673:10
h. to poke poor Billy GRAH 358:8
h. to report SHAK 711:26
h. to resolve GIBB 345:7
h. upon my sleeve SHAK 712:35
h. was not in me HÉLO 380:15
h. was to thy rudder tied SHAK 679:14
h. was warm and gay HAMM 370:4
h. was with the Oxford men LETT 482:7
h. within blood-tinctured BROW 157:26
h. would hear her and beat TENN 782:1
h. you first beguiled BALL 52:8
hides one thing in his h. HOME 394:6
His h. is below MIDR 524:21
his little h. JAME 418:8
holiness of the h.'s affections KEAT 446:1
Home is where the h. is PROV 622:25
human h. is strong BAGE 48:12
If thy h. fails thee ELIZ 304:14
imagination of man's h. BIBL 76:8
In my h.'s core SHAK 686:26
Into my h. an air HOUS 404:16
Irishman's h. SHAW 725:18
I sleep, but my h. waketh BIBL 87:14
Is your h. at rest FLET 327:7
I would eat his h. SHAK 712:29
key of my h. CLAY 226:5
Land of H.'s Desire YEAT 854:19
language of the h. POPE 603:1
language of the h. SHAD 677:20
left my h. in San Francisco CROS 252:14
lent out my h. LAMB 465:4
let thy h. cheer thee BIBL 86:24
let your h. be strong LAUD 470:5
Lift up your h. WESL 829:7
live to my own h. RICH 647:15
locked my h. BALL 53:19
look in thy h. and write SIDN 736:3
loosed our h. in tears ARNO 27:16
lose his child's h. MENG 522:2
lying in my h. MARY 517:7
make a stone of the h. YEAT 854:4
Make me a clean h. BOOK 137:13
maketh glad the h. BOOK 141:7
maketh the h. sick BIBL 84:15
man after his own h. BIBL 80:12

Man's h. expands MACN 504:21
may not change the h. KING 451:18
Mercy has a human h. BLAK 122:3
merry h. BIBL 84:23
merry h. doeth good BIBL 84:30
more native to the h. SHAK 683:22
most h.-easing things KEAT 445:12
most plotting h. RICH 647:13
My h. aches KEAT 444:20
My h. aches OPEN 575:4
my h. also BOOK 135:1
my h. and my flesh BOOK 139:15
my h. beats BERL 69:17
My h. did do it EPIT 310:15
My h. in hiding HOPK 397:11
my h. is heavy GOET 352:20
my h. is pure TENN 784:5
My h.'s in the Highlands BURN 172:17
my h.'s right there JUDG 438:4
My h. untravelled GOLD 355:10
my h. was free WESL 828:22
my reins and my h. BOOK 135:10
my shrivelled h. HERB 384:7
naked thinking h. DONN 280:16
never share the h. MARL 512:12
no longer tear his h. EPIT 311:10
no man layeth it to h. BIBL 90:12
no man's h. fail BIBL 80:19
no matter from the h. SHAK 720:1
None but the h. GOET 353:14
not for hope, h. would break PROV 623:2
not your h. away HOUS 404:10
of the deeper h. FLEC 326:7
of thine h. BIBL 80:18
only with the h. SAIN 663:9
Open my h. BROW 159:6
Open not thine h. BIBL 93:9
opens the h. and lungs STER 757:6
Or in the h. or in the head SHAK 709:17
O tiger's h. SHAK 694:25
panting h. of Rome WISE 842:2
plague your h. PROV 629:26
pondered them in her h. BIBL 100:5
poor h. that never rejoices PROV 623:38
proof of want of h. SAYI 670:8
rag-and-bone shop of the h. YEAT 853:12
rebellious h. BIBL 90:24
rebuke hath broken my h. BOOK 138:16
room in my h. for thee ELLI 305:13
seal upon thine h. BIBL 87:22
seen within the h. MICH 524:2
Shakespeare unlocked his h. BROW 159:21
sighing of a contrite h. BOOK 129:15
softer pillow than my h. BYRO 184:16
some h. did break TENN 778:25
So the h. be right RALE 641:16
squirrel's h. beat ELIO 300:5
stage curtain of his h. RILK 648:13
sunshine of the h. CONS 241:8
Sweeping up the H. DICK 273:3
Taming my wild h. SHAK 712:22
tears out the h. of it KNOW 458:5
there will your h. be BIBL 95:5
this h. Shall break SHAK 700:13
thou hast my h. PRIO 612:1
time by h.-throbs BAIL 49:18
true love hath my h. SIDN 736:2
visit my sad h. SHAK 697:1
want of h. HOOD 395:4
war in his h. BOOK 137:18
warmth about my h. KEAT 446:14
waters of the h. THOM 789:13
way to a man's h. PROV 633:43
weakens his own h. SHAK 722:26
where my h. is turning ever FOST 330:14
Whispers the o'er-fraught h. SHAK 706:23
whose h. is happy TALM 773:1
with all thy h. BIBL 98:8
with a well-tuned h. Sing GURN 366:4
wounding h. CRAS 250:8
heartache say we end The h. SHAK 686:9
heartbeat h. from the Presidency
STEV 758:16

heartbreak h. in the heart of things
　　　　　　　　　　　　　　GIBS 346:10
hearth By this still h.　　　TENN 784:13
cricket on the h.　　　　　MILT 529:12
from an unextinguished h.　SHEL 730:13
genial h.　　　　　　　　WORD 846:21
h.-fire and the home-acre　KIPL 454:11
hearthstone squats on the h.　QUIL 639:8
heartily let us h. rejoice　BOOK 140:6
heartless h., witless nature　HOUS 404:2
restrain the h.　　　　　　KING 451:18
hearts all h. be open　　　BOOK 131:16
all that human h. endure　GOLD 355:15
arise in your h.　　　　　BIBL 112:16
cold and glittery h.　　　HILL 388:14
harden not your h.　　　BOOK 140:10
h. and house-keepings　DICK 271:13
h. and intellects　　　　EPIT 311:14
h. and minds　　　　　BIBL 110:7
h. are dry　　　　　　　WORD 846:14
h. are in the right place　DISR 277:16
h. beating　　　　　　　BROW 160:7
h. have not grown old　YEAT 856:7
H. just as pure　　　　GILB 347:11
h. of his countrymen　　LEE 478:17
h. That spanieled me　SHAK 679:20
H. wound up with love　SPEN 750:21
heedless h.　　　　　　GRAY 361:11
imagination of their h.　BIBL 99:32
improvident, indecent h.　BROW 157:17
Incline our h.　　　　　BOOK 131:8
Kind h. are more than coronets　TENN 780:4
let not your h. be hardened　VILL 810:11
Lift up your h.　　　　BOOK 131:20
men with Splendid H.　BROO 153:11
offspring of cold h.　　BURK 167:15
O you hard h.　　　　SHAK 695:28
Pluck their h. from them　SHAK 693:20
Pure eyes and Christian h.　KEBL 447:14
queen in people's h.　DIAN 267:1
Queen of H. she made　NURS 569:6
Two h. that beat as one　CLOS 228:24
undeveloped h.　　　FORS 329:7
union of hands and h.　TAYL 775:4
heartstrings jesses were my dear h.
　　　　　　　　　　　　　SHAK 713:28
heat bear the burden and the h.　ARNO 27:18
can't stand the h.　　　TRUM 801:8
don't like the h.　　　PROV 623:14
furnace that gives no h.　RAYM 642:17
H. me these irons　　SHAK 694:8
H. not a furnace　　　SHAK 695:5
h. of the day　　　　BIBL 98:2
h.-oppressed. brain　SHAK 704:16
h. o' the sun　　　　SHAK 683:8
neither h. nor light　WEBS 825:24
not without dust and h.　MILT 535:16
one h., all know　　CHAP 208:15
sound health in September's h.　HORA 399:12
white h. of revolution　WILS 840:6
white h. of technology　MISQ 539:3
heath Upon this blasted h.　SHAK 703:11
heathen any h. author　JAME 417:8
as the h. do　　　　BIBL 95:2
be avenged of the h.　BOOK 144:8
break the h.　　　　TENN 777:20
converting the H.　CARL 192:1
exalted among the h.　BOOK 136:26
h. in his blindness　HEBE 378:16
h. in 'is blindness　KIPL 453:21
h. in the carnal part　POPE 603:3
h. make much ado　BOOK 136:25
h. so furiously rage　BOOK 133:20
heather bonnie bloomin' h.　LAUD 470:6
cries 'Nothing but h.'　MACD 500:19
heaths game on these lone h.　HAZL 377:7
heave h. and the halt　KIPL 455:15
H. arf a brick at 'im.　PUNC 637:8
heaven all going the H.　LAST 474:11
All this, and h. too　HENR 382:16
all to H.　　　　JONE 434:10
all we know of h.　DICK 273:5
any better in H.　WILL 839:14

ascend to h.　　　FIRM 321:12
become the hoped-for h.　EPIT 311:14
Bread of h.　　　WILL 838:9
by a whirlwind into h.　BIBL 82:1
cannot go to h.　NORF 565:8
climbing h., and gazing　SHEL 732:5
climb up into the h.　BOOK 143:16
consent of h.　　JONS 434:18
day when h. was falling　HOUS 404:1
decreed against him in h.　TALM 772:33
distant from H.　BURT 174:11
Does H. say anything　CONF 238:11
Earth's crammed with h.　BROW 157:21
eleven who went to h.　SONG 747:11
enter into the kingdom of h.　BIBL 94:25
Equality would be h.　TROL 800:7
eye of h.　　　SHAK 699:10
face of h. so fine　SHAK 717:37
fallen from h.　BIBL 88:24
Fellowship is h.　MORR 549:18
floor of h.　　SHAK 710:3
flowerless fields of h.　SWIN 767:24
food from h.　BOOK 139:10
from earth to h.　PLAT 597:18
gate of h.　　BIBL 76:32
gazing up into h.　BIBL 104:25
given from h.　MIDR 524:17
Give the jolly h. above　STEV 760:16
God owns h.　SEXT 677:14
God's in his h.　BROW 160:22
God's in his h.　PROV 620:48
gold bar of H.　ROSS 655:19
go to h. in feather-beds　MORE 548:10
great wonder in h.　BIBL 113:27
hand toward h.　BIBL 77:27
H. and Charing Cross　THOM 791:16
h. and earth shall pass　BIBL 98:17
h. and the earth　BIBL 75:4
h. and the earth　OPEN 574:18
h. descends　　THOM 792:18
h. doing good on earth　TERE 785:19
h. endures　　HOUS 404:5
h. expands　　BROW 158:24
H. has no rage　CONG 238:30
H.—I'm in Heaven　BERL 69:17
H. in a rage　BLAK 119:6
h. in a wild flower　BLAK 119:5
H. in Hell's despair　BLAK 122:11
H. in ordinary　HERB 384:18
H. lies about us　WORD 848:5
h. mocks itself　SHAK 713:30
h. peep　　SHAK 703:21
h. planted us to please　MARV 516:5
H. sends us good meat　GARR 340:5
H.'s great lamps　CAMP 187:23
h.'s matchless king　MILT 532:23
H.'s peculiar care　SOME 745:22
h. still guards the right　SHAK 715:19
h.'s vaults should crack　SHAK 702:4
H. take my soul　SHAK 699:13
H. was in him　WALT 821:6
H. what I cannot　DICK 273:4
h. will help you　LA F 463:13
H. will protect　SMIT 741:18
h. with their tears　BLAK 122:21
H. would be too dull　EPIT 311:18
Hell in H.'s despite　BLAK 122:12
hills o' H.　BALL 52:1
his own by-way to h.　DEFO 261:22
hope for h. thereby　CASW 199:4
house as nigh h.　MORE 548:15
how high the h. is　BOOK 141:3
hurl my soul from h.　SHAK 714:27
hymns at h.'s gate　SHAK 722:30
I am my h. and my hell　SCHI 671:2
idea of h.　SMIT 744:8
Imagine there's no h.　LENN 480:12
inheritor of the kingdom of h.　BOOK 132:12
into the kingdom of h.　BIBL 97:19
I saw h. opened　BIBL 114:11
jealous queen of h.　SHAK 682:24
just h. now hates　EPIT 310:1
kingdom of h.　BIBL 94:20

kingdom of h.　BIBL 97:5
kingdom of h. is at hand　BIBL 94:9
King of h.　LYTE 497:11
lead you to H.'s gate　BLAK 120:13
leave to h. the measure　JOHN 426:22
leaving mercy to h.　FIEL 318:8
lightning fall from h.　BIBL 100:20
looketh this way to H.　CECI 204:14
made h. and earth　BOOK 132:20
made h. and earth　BOOK 142:21
make a h. of hell　MILT 531:14
Mandate of H.　CONF 237:11
Marriages are made in h.　PROV 626:16
merrily meet in h.　MORE 548:16
more than all in h.　BYRO 179:27
more things in h. and earth　HALD 367:17
My blue h.　WHIT 832:20
near to h. by sea　GILB 347:1
neither by h.　BIBL 94:28
new h. and a new earth　BIBL 114:16
new h., new earth　SHAK 678:13
Not H. itself　DRYD 289:30
nurseries of h.　THOM 791:18
of h. we have below　ADDI 4:22
One h., one hell　BROW 159:24
On whom the dew of h. drops　FORD 328:16
open face of h.　KEAT 445:22
open the Kingdom of H.　BOOK 128:1
override the laws of h.　SOPH 746:16
passage toward H.　TRAH 797:17
Pennies don't fall from h.　THAT 787:1
pennies from h.　BURK 169:13
permission of all-ruling h.　MILT 531:13
points of h. and home　WORD 850:17
quincunx of h.　BROW 156:3
riches of h.'s pavement　MILT 531:25
ring the bells of H.　HODG 391:10
Road to H.　BALL 53:11
saw h. opened　BIBL 105:6
send him to—h.　JUVE 439:15
silence in h.　BIBL 113:22
sinned against h.　BIBL 101:16
spark from h.　ARNO 28:6
starry h. above me　KANT 441:6
strayed into H.　ALAI 10:3
summons thee to h.　SHAK 704:18
Thank h. for little girls　LERN 481:21
that are not h.　MARL 513:3
that serve in h.　MILT 531:15
then the h. espy　HERB 384:4
things are the sons of h.　JOHN 424:4
things in h. and earth　SHAK 685:10
third h.　BIBL 108:23
thirtieth year to h.　THOM 789:14
thorny way to h.　SHAK 684:16
top of it reached to h.　BIBL 76:30
unextinguishable laugh in h.　BROW 155:16
voice from h.　BIBL 114:1
waitest for the spark from h.　ARNO 28:8
war in h.　BIBL 113:28
we know the way to h.　ELST 306:5
what's a h. for　BROW 158:9
What they do in h.　SWIF 766:21
which art in h.　BIBL 95:3
Which we ascribe to h.　SHAK 678:8
young was very h.　WORD 846:20
heavenly ancient h. connection　GINS 349:15
fools by h. compulsion　SHAK 699:26
form with h. things　THOM 789:3
h. mansion, raging in the dark　YEAT 853:11
in those h. minds　VIRG 810:16
with h. alchemy　SHAK 723:2
heavens behold, I create new h.　BIBL 90:22
H., and all the Powers therein　BOOK 127:20
h. are the work of thy hands　BOOK 140:19
h. declare the glory　BOOK 134:19
h. dropped　BOOK 138:11
h.' embroidered cloths　YEAT 854:11
h. fill with commerce　TENN 780:20
h. my wide roof-tree　AYTO 41:16
h. themselves blaze forth　SHAK 697:3
rideth upon the h.　BOOK 138:11
starry h. above　THOM 792:20

herbs (*cont.*):

for a garden of h.	BIBL 81:30

Hercules is not love a H. | SHAK 702:19
I to H. | SHAK 684:5
some of H. | SONG 748:5
herd elevates above the vulgar h. | |
| | GAIS 337:15 |
h. wind slowly o'er the lea | GRAY 360:24
Morality is the h.-instinct | NIET 564:7
unreflecting h. | WORD 846:22
herdsman God the h. goads | YEAT 853:15
here Are *you* h. | DANT 256:1
can't happen h. | LEWI 483:23
he answered, H. am I | BIBL 80:4
H. am I | BIBL 88:19
h. because we're queer | BEHA 63:15
h. for the beer | ADVE 7:34
H. I am | MACM 503:19
H.'s a how-de-doo | GILB 348:2
H.'s looking at you | FILM 319:10
H.'s tae us | TOAS 796:3
H.'s to thee, Corbet | AUBR 33:14
h.'s to you, Mrs Robinson | SIMO 738:3
H. today—in next week tomorrow | |
| | GRAH 358:13 |
H. were decent godless people | ELIO 303:3
If we can't stay h. alive | MONT 545:12
I have been h. before | ROSS 656:8
Mr Watson, come h. | BELL 64:8
We're h. | MILI 526:17
What you seek is h. | HORA 399:10
hereafter died h. | SHAK 707:14
h. for ever | BOOK 133:7
world may talk of h. | COLL 234:22
hereditary H. bondsmen | BYRO 178:12
h. monarch was insane | BAGE 48:1
idea of h. legislators | PAIN 582:18
hereditas *Damnosa h.* | GAIU 337:19
Hereford H., and Hampshire | LERN 481:20
heresies begin as h. | HUXL 412:1
hateful h. | SPEN 752:13
kept alive by h. | BREN 150:21
heresy believes be h. | SHAW 727:18
h. signifies no more | HOBB 390:13
Turkey, h., hops | PROV 633:24
heretic h. which makes the fire | SHAK 721:28
oppressor or a h. | CAMU 188:18
heretics H. the only bitter remedy | |
| | ZAMY 857:25 |
heritage h. unto Israel | BOOK 143:10
I have a goodly h. | BOOK 134:14
Hermes H. in the wax | ARIS 26:8
hermit h.'s fast | KEAT 444:1
hermitage for an h. | LOVE 493:6
palace for a h. | SHAK 716:1
hermits h. are contented | WORD 847:17
hern haunts of coot and h. | TENN 775:18
hero acted like a h. | WALP 819:22
aspires to be a h. | JOHN 431:12
conquering h. comes | MORE 548:19
don't want to be a h. | STOP 761:17
h. becomes a bore | EMER 307:11
h. from his prison | AYTO 41:13
h. of my tale | TOLS 796:16
h. perish | POPE 604:21
h. to his valet | CORN 243:15
h. to his valet | PROV 627:41
H.-worship strongest | SPEN 750:12
Millions a h. | PORT 607:20
seemed a h. | BYRO 177:24
Show me a h. | FITZ 324:3
Herod for an hour of H. | HOPE 396:5
H. is his name | CAUS 203:12
out-herods H. | SHAK 686:22
heroes Canadians do not like h. | |
| | WOOD 844:15 |
feats worked by those h. | ANON 22:7
fit country for h. | LLOY 487:18
greatest h. | COLL 234:20
h. of old | BROW 161:2
h. to dine with us | TROL 799:15
of all the worlds brave h. | SONG 748:5
speed glum h. | SASS 667:15

Thin red line of h.	KIPL 455:22
Unhappy the land that needs h.	BREC 150:6
heroic finished A life h.	MILT 535:2
h. for earth too hard	BROW 158:7
h. poem of its sort	CARL 191:19
H. womanhood	LONG 490:24
heroically h. mad	DRYD 287:12
heroics not h., but healing	HARD 371:10
heroine take a h.	AUST 40:21
when a h. goes mad	SHER 733:9
heroines h. of novels	FLAU 325:1
herring Every h. must hang	PROV 619:9
plague o' these pickle h.	SHAK 720:11
roast thee like a h.	BURN 172:16
shoals of h.	MACC 500:13
herrings As many red h.	NURS 568:8
herrschen h. *und gewinnen*	GOET 353:4
Hertford H., Hereford, and Hampshire	
	LERN 481:20
Hervey call a dog H.	JOHN 427:8
Herveys men, women, and H.	MONT 543:18
Herz *Mein H. ist schwer*	GOET 352:20
hesitate could long h.	STEV 759:30
hesitates h. is lost	PROV 622:9
She floats, she h.	RACI 640:4
hesitating H. doesn't matter	BREC 150:4
hesitation Without h., deviation	CATC 202:1
Hesperides climbing trees in the H.	
	SHAK 702:19
Hesperus H. entreats thy light	JONS 435:2
It was the schooner H.	LONG 491:10
venit H.	VIRG 814:11
heterodoxy h. is another man's doxy	
	WARB 821:8
H. or Thy-doxy	CARL 192:7
heterogeneity coherent h.	SPEN 750:7
heterosexual h. love no solution	
	DURA 292:18
heu H., *miserande puer* | VIRG 812:16
heures h. *propices* | LAMA 464:8
Heute H. *leid'* ich | LESS 482:4
hew h. him as a carcass | SHAK 696:24
hewers h. of wood | BIBL 79:12
hewn h. out her seven pillars | BIBL 84:6
hey h. for boot and horse | KING 453:1
H. for God Almighty | KETT 450:6
'H.-ho!' says Rowley | NURS 566:20
heyday h. in the blood | SHAK 687:23
hi answer to 'H.!' | CARR 196:6
hic H. *jacet* | RALE 641:14
Quod petis h. est | HORA 399:10
hick Sticks nix h. pix | NEWS 562:18
hickety H., pickety | NURS 567:7
hickory H., dickory, dock | NURS 567:8
hid cannot be h. | BIBL 94:22
h. as it were our faces | BIBL 90:2
h. from thine eyes | BIBL 101:31
h. themselves in the dens | BIBL 113:15
I h. from Him | THOM 791:7
Which is, to keep that h. | DONN 281:16
hidden follows the h. path | LUIS 496:3
guns that are h. | FLEI 326:8
h. from the eye | WORD 850:1
h. love of God | WESL 829:10
h. persuaders | PACK 581:12
teems with h. meaning | GILB 349:4
hide chose from man to h. | CRAB 248:31
disguise which can h. love | LA R 469:11
he can't h. | LOUI 492:14
h. in cooling trees | KEAT 445:8
h. is sure to flatten 'em | BELL 64:18
h. of a rhinoceros | BARR 57:11
h. our own hurts | ELIO 299:24
h. thy face from me | BOOK 134:9
h. us from the face | BIBL 113:15
in a woman's h. | SHAK 694:25
Let me h. myself | TOPL 797:2
something to h. | LAY 476:7
Those who h. can find | PROV 632:42
Whose h. he sold | WALL 818:5
wise man h. a pebble | CHES 216:4
wrapped in a player's h. | GREE 362:24
hideous Making night h. | SHAK 684:26

hides H. from himself his state	JOHN 426:19
h. one thing in his heart	HOME 394:6
hiding bloody good h.	GRAN 359:1
girl in her h.-place	HORA 400:12
My heart in h.	HOPK 397:11
Hieronimo H. is mad again	KYD 462:12
Hierusalem H., my happy home	ANON 16:11
high Be ye never so h.	DENN 264:10
cannot rate me very h.	LACL 463:6
corn as h. as an elephant's eye	HAMM 370:5
from h. life	POPE 603:18
get h. with a little help	LENN 480:23
h. heels are most agreeable	SWIF 765:11
h.-minded. descendants	CATU 203:1
h. road	JOHN 428:8
h. that proved too high	BROW 158:7
h.-water mark of Socialist literature	
	ORWE 577:25
house of defence very h.	BOOK 140:4
how h. the heaven is	BOOK 141:3
I'm the H.	SPRI 753:8
Lord, I am not h.-minded	BOOK 143:8
Lord most H.	BOOK 131:22
no h. flier	PEPY 592:5
Pile it h.	SLOG 740:10
slain upon thy h. places	BIBL 80:27
This h. man	BROW 159:15
too h. for me	BOOK 143:8
upon the h. horse	BROW 155:6
wickedness in h. places	BIBL 109:21
ye'll tak' the h. road	SONG 748:3
higher Friend, go up h.	BIBL 101:4
he shall shoot h.	SIDN 736:1
h. the monkey climbs	PROV 622:21
production of the h. animals	DARW 257:10
Stuart or Nassau go h.	PRIO 612:3
subject unto the h. powers	BIBL 106:30
highest children of the most H.	BOOK 139:14
h. good	CICE 223:11
in the h. room	BIBL 101:3
needs must love the h.	TENN 777:23
Highland heart is H.	GALT 338:15
solitary H. lass!	WORD 850:8
Highlandman breeks aff a wild H.	SCOT 674:8
highlands H. and ye Lawlands	BALL 51:6
In the h.	STEV 760:10
My heart's in the H.	BURN 171:27
worst in all the H.	STAI 753:19
highly what thou wouldst h.	SHAK 703:18
highness his H.' dog at Kew	POPE 602:21
highway broad h. of the world	SHEL 729:8
each and ev'ry h.	ANKA 14:16
h. for our God	BIBL 89:16
H., since you my chief	SIDN 736:10
passes over a h.	STEN 755:16
highwayman h. came riding	NOYE 566:2
highways happy h. where I went	
	HOUS 404:16
into the h. and hedges	BIBL 101:9
hilarity h. like a scream	GREE 362:15
hill city that is set on an h.	BIBL 94:22
city upon a h.	WINT 841:20
dancers are all gone under the h.	
	ELIO 301:16
green h. far away | ALEX 11:10
haven under the h. | TENN 775:17
heard on the h. | BLAK 122:7
hides the green h. | KEAT 444:18
h. that holds his peace | BERR 71:14
hunter home from h. | STEV 760:20
light on the h. | CHIF 217:18
mountain and h. | BIBL 89:16
On a huge h. | DONN 280:10
On the cold h.'s side | KEAT 443:29
rest upon thy holy h. | BOOK 134:12
self-same h. | MILT 530:1
unto thy holy h. | BOOK 136:16
hills and the little h. | BOOK 138:22
Black H. belong to me | SITT 738:13
Blue are the h. | PROV 616:9
blue remembered h. | HOUS 404:16
cattle upon a thousand h. | BOOK 137:8
convictions are h. | FITZ 324:1

dim h. and a low coast-line | VIRG 811:23
h. are alive | HAMM 370:8
h. are a refuge | BOOK 141:8
h. be carried | BOOK 136:24
h. in order stood | WATT 823:20
h. like young sheep | BOOK 142:2
H. of home | STEV 760:15
H. of the Chankly Bore | LEAR 477:7
H. of the North | OAKL 571:1
h. of the South Country | BELL 65:23
h. of the South Country | BELL 65:24
h. o' Heaven | BALL 52:1
H. peep o'er hills | POPE 604:3
h. shall rejoice | BOOK 138:7
h. stand about Jerusalem | BOOK 142:22
I to the h. will lift | SCOT 675:6
Lord who made the h. | KIPL 455:19
mine eyes unto the h. | BOOK 142:16
On the h. like Gods | TENN 781:9
out on the h. alone | KILV 451:12
Over the h. | GAY 341:12
Over the h. and far away | NURS 570:10
Over the h. and far away | STEV 761:1
red h. of Georgia | KING 452:4
strength of the h. | BOOK 140:10
to the reverberate h. | SHAK 720:13
touch the h. | BOOK 141:11
ye high h. | BOOK 138:13
hillside h.'s dew-pearled | BROW 160:22
him cried, 'That's h.!' | BARH 55:18
himself answer is 'h.' | IBSE 412:15
Each man for h. | CHAU 211:11
Every man for h. | PROV 619:13
He h. said | CICE 223:10
speak for h. | BIBL 103:14
subdue all things to h. | BOOK 133:18
with h. at war | SHAK 696:3
hinan Ewig-Weibliche zieht uns h. | GOET 353:3
zieht uns h. | CLOS 228:8
hinder all the h. parts | SPEN 751:16
hindered let and h. | BOOK 130:2
hinders wickedness that h. loving | BROW 160:13
hindmost Devil take the h. | PROV 617:37
hindrance to his own h. | BOOK 134:13
hindsight H. is always twenty-twenty | WILD 837:13
Hindu dies, or turns H. | SHEL 729:22
neither H. nor Muslim | SIKH 737:14
hinky H., dinky, parley-voo | MILI 526:14
hinterland She has no h. | HEAL 377:12
hip H. young gunslinger | ANON 16:12
I have you on the h. | SHAK 709:30
once upon the h. | SHAK 708:30
smote them h. and thigh | BIBL 79:31
Hippocrene blushful H. | KEAT 444:22
hippopotamus h. resolved at any cost | WELL 828:6
shoot the H. | BELL 64:18
shoot the h. | FORS 329:6
hips armchairs tight about the h. | WODE 843:3
Or Mae West's h. | EWAR 313:7
swing out ungirded h. | SORL 746:22
hipsters angelheaded h. burning | GINS 349:15
hire labourer is worthy of his h. | BIBL 100:19
labourer worthy of h. | PROV 624:46
hired rich flames and h. tears | BROW 156:8
They h. the money | COOL 242:9
hireling h. fleeth | BIBL 103:18
Pay given to a state h. | JOHN 424:14
Hiroshima After H. | BOLD 126:5
genius of Einstein leads to H. | PICA 595:9
his we are h. people | BOOK 140:17
hiss dismal universal h. | MILT 534:6
fright and a h. | DEAN 260:8
hissed h. along the polished ice | WORD 846:24
hissing smallest possible amount of h. | COLB 230:23
historian h. of the Roman empire | GIBB 345:19

h.'s first task | CREI 250:23
h. wants more documents | JAME 417:16
life of the h. must be short | GIBB 345:21
requisite for an h. | JOHN 428:7
historians alter the past, h. can | BUTL 176:22
h. left blanks in their writings | POUN 608:16
h. repeat one another | BROO 153:16
historical any h. romance | CLAR 225:9
histories H. make men wise | BACO 45:22
studied H. | PEPY 592:17
history Antiquities are h. defaced | BACO 42:15
blank in h.-books | MONT 545:11
break with one's past h. | WOOD 844:16
by writing h. | BREN 150:22
country which has no h. | PROV 621:31
dignity of h. | BOLI 126:7
discerned in h. a plot | FISH 321:15
Does h. repeat itself | BARN 56:11
dustbin of h. | TROT 800:19
dust-heap called 'h.' | BIRR 117:1
duty we owe to h. | WILD 835:27
end of h. | FUKU 336:23
fair summary of h. | FRAN 332:10
happiest nations, have no h. | ELIO 300:14
H. a distillation | CARL 192:6
H. begins in novel | MACA 499:2
H. came to a . | SELL 676:26
H. gets thicker | TAYL 774:9
[H.] hath triumphed | RALE 641:12
h. in all men's lives | SHAK 692:5
H. is a combination | COCT 230:1
H. is a gallery of pictures | TOCQ 795:6
H. is a nightmare | JOYC 437:17
H. is a pack of lies | STUB 762:19
H. . . . is, indeed, little more | GIBB 345:1
h. is nothing more | VOLT 816:5
H. is not what you thought | SELL 676:16
h. is now and England | ELIO 302:1
h. is on our side | KHRU 451:4
H. is past politics | FREE 333:10
H. is philosophy | DION 274:21
H. is the essence | CARL 191:17
H. littered with the wars | POWE 609:20
h.-making creature | AUDE 36:15
H. more or less bunk | FORD 328:13
H., n. An account | BIER 116:6
h. of art | BUTL 176:29
h. of class struggles | MARX 517:5
h. of progress | MACA 498:11
h. of the world | DISR 276:2
h. records good things | BEDE 62:6
H. repeats itself | BROO 153:16
H. repeats itself | PROV 622:22
H. teaches us | EBAN 294:24
H. to the defeated | AUDE 36:10
H. will absolve me | CAST 199:1
h. will record | MORS 550:16
hope and h. rhyme | HEAN 377:18
Human h. becomes more | WELL 828:13
In h., we are concerned | HEGE 379:6
kept h. in mind more | BOWE 148:5
learned anything from h. | HEGE 379:3
lips my h. | SIDN 736:11
make more h. | SAKI 663:13
men could learn from h. | COLE 234:8
more to shape h. | TAYL 774:11
more worthy than h. | ARIS 25:22
name is h. | THWA 794:6
No h. much | DURR 293:8
no h. of mankind | POPP 607:4
no h.; only biography | EMER 307:2
product of h. | CARL 191:16
Read no h. | DISR 277:7
rough draft of a h. | GRAH 358:10
Thames is liquid h. | BURN 170:2
thousand years of h. | GAIT 337:18
too much h. | KING 452:12
tragedy, comedy, h. | SHAK 685:28
War makes good h. | HARD 371:14
what's her h. | SHAK 720:29
What will h. say | SHAW 725:1
world's h. | SCHI 671:3
writing a modern h. | RALE 641:13

writing h. with lightning | WILS 840:16
hit can h. from far | HERB 384:1
never think I have h. hard | JOHN 430:1
very palpable h. | SHAK 689:9
hitch H. your wagon to a star | EMER 307:12
hither come hither, come h. | SHAK 681:3
Hitler H. swept out | NEWS 562:14
H. thought he might | CHAM 206:14
If H. invaded hell | CHUR 222:15
If I can't love H. | MUST 555:13
kidding, Mister H. | PERR 593:4
When H. attacked the Jews | NIEM 563:18
hitting prove their worth by h. back | HEIN 379:12
without h. below it | ASQU 32:9
hive h. for the honey-bee | YEAT 854:17
make a h. for bees | PEEL 591:4
murmurings Of this great h. | COWL 245:26
hoar shows his h. leaves | SHAK 688:17
hoarder h. of two things | SPAR 749:24
hoarfrost scattereth the h. | BOOK 144:5
hoarse bird's h. voice | WORD 845:19
raven himself is h. | SHAK 703:19
hoary h. sort of land | LAWR 475:13
Hobbes in for H.'s voyage | VANB 806:15
hobbit there lived a h. | OPEN 574:16
hobby h.-horse is forgot | SHAK 687:3
rides his H. horse | STER 756:17
hobgoblin h. of little minds | EMER 307:5
Hobson H. has supped | MILT 531:1
hoc H. erat in votis | HORA 403:14
hock weak h. and seltzer | BETJ 72:2
Hockley Hey for H. | KETT 450:6
hocus accounting h.-pocus | TAUZ 773:15
hodgepodge gallimaufry or h. | SPEN 752:21
Hodgitts 'O Mr H.!' I heard her cry | GRAH 358:11
hoe tickle her with a h. | JERR 421:17
hog all England under a h. | COLL 234:21
disadvantage of being a h. | MORT 551:4
Not the whole h. | MILL 527:11
hogamus H., higamous | JAME 418:24
Hogarth epitaph on William H. | EPIT 309:6
hoggish have his h. mind | SPEN 751:27
hogs let it not be like h. | MCKA 502:16
Men eat H. | STEV 757:23
hogshead daggers in a h. | SCOT 675:2
hoi polloi multitude, the h. | DRYD 290:6
hoist H. with his own petar | SHAK 687:32
hold can neither h. him | JEFF 420:12
can't h. a man down | WASH 822:5
cry 'H., hold!' | SHAK 703:21
gat h. upon me | BOOK 142:5
h., but cannot see | WESL 829:2
H., enough | SHAK 707:18
h. fast that which is good | BIBL 110:19
H., or cut bow-strings | SHAK 710:26
H. the fort | BLIS 123:10
H. the fort | SHER 734:14
to have and to h. | BOOK 133:9
What you have, h. | PROV 634:15
holdfast H. is better | PROV 616:11
h. is the only dog | SHAK 693:3
holding h. on comes easily | RILK 648:16
hole dark h. of the head | HUGH 407:8
first h. made through | MOOR 546:15
h. in a sock | EINS 298:12
h. to go out of this world | LAST 471:19
if you knows of a better h. | CART 198:11
In a h. in the ground | OPEN 574:16
maketh a h. in the stone | LATI 470:2
mint with the h. | ADVE 8:4
poisoned rat in a h. | SWIF 766:6
holes bag with h. | BIBL 92:13
foxes have h. | BIBL 96:1
holiday Butchered to make a Roman h. | BYRO 179:12
I am in a h. humour | SHAK 681:28
Is this a h. | SHAK 695:27

holiday (*cont.*):
perpetual h.   SHAW 727:9
to take a h.   RUSS 660:16
holidays holiest of all h.   LONG 490:12
playing h.   SHAK 689:25
holier h. than thou   BIBL 90:21
holiest Praise to the H.   NEWM 561:4
holiness beauty of h.   BOOK 140:11
beauty of h.   MONS 543:8
h. becometh thine house   BOOK 140:7
holiness but social h.   WESL 829:11
h. of the heart's affections   KEAT 446:1
put off h.   BLAK 120:16
Holland children in H.   NURS 566:11
H. . . . lies so low   HOOD 395:16
hollow Down to the h.   FLAN 324:16
hate the dreadful h.   TENN 781:15
regiment's in h. square   KIPL 453:20
We are the h. men   ELIO 302:6
Within the h. crown   SHAK 715:24
holly English oak and h.   HART 374:15
heigh-ho! the h.   SHAK 681:15
h. and the ivy   SONG 747:10
Hollywood H. money isn't money
   PARK 586:9
not have been invited to H.   CHAN 207:16
holocaust erewhile a h.   MILT 534:32
Holy and to the H. Ghost   BOOK 127:19
holy coming to that h. room   DONN 280:1
from the h. land   RALE 641:8
h. and the profane   SIDD 735:14
h. city, new Jerusalem   BIBL 114:16
H. deadlock   HERB 383:11
H., fair, and wise   SHAK 721:22
h. ground   BIBL 77:17
H., Holy, Holy   HEBE 378:17
H., holy, holy, Lord   BIBL 113:9
H., holy, holy, Lord   BOOK 131:22
Holy, H., Holy: Lord God   BOOK 127:20
h., is the Lord of hosts   BIBL 88:10
h. kiss   BIBL 107:1
h. nation   BIBL 112:5
h. simplicity   JERO 421:5
H. Spirit rests only   TALM 773:1
h.-water death   MCGO 502:3
h. white birds flying after   MASE 517:14
h. writ   SHAK 716:27
in h. wedlock   BOOK 133:12
light of thy H. Spirit   BOOK 130:10
neither h., nor Roman   VOLT 816:4
nothing is h.   BOOK 130:12
sabbath day, keep it h.   BIBL 78:3
stand in the h. place   BIBL 98:15
suffer thy H. One   BOOK 134:15
that which is h.   PLAT 597:6
unto thy h. hill   BOOK 136:16
Holy Ghost be any H.   BIBL 105:21
blasphemy against the h.   BIBL 96:29
Come, H.   BOOK 144:13
gifts of the H.   BUTL 175:14
H. over the bent World   HOPK 396:13
H. which is given   BIBL 106:8
pencil of the h.   BACO 43:14
temple of the H.   BIBL 107:12
homage do her h.   HOOK 395:18
h. of a tear   BYRO 178:9
home all the comforts of h.   BRYS 162:14
all the h. I have   AYTO 41:16
at h. while they fight wars   EURI 312:19
battling in its own h.   AESC 6:8
beating begins at h.   FLET 327:12
by staying at h.   LIN 486:12
can't find your way h.   COLL 235:3
can't go h. again   WOLF 843:18
Charity begins at h.   PROV 616:33
come h. Bill Bailey   CANN 189:13
comes safe h.   SHAK 693:22
comfortably at h.   AUST 38:19
drive one from h.   HOOD 395:5
East, west, h.'s best   PROV 618:43
England, h. and beauty   ARNO 30:12
Englishman's h.   PROV 618:45

E.T. phone h.   FILM 319:5
feel ashamed of h.   DICK 269:16
for to carry me h.   SONG 748:6
go back h.   BLUN 124:8
go h. in the dark   LAST 474:8
goodman is not at h.   BIBL 84:4
Go on h.   VIRG 814:11
hear news of h.   PROV 620:42
hearth-fire and the h.-acre   KIPL 454:11
Hierusalem, my happy h.   ANON 16:11
H. again, home again   NURS 570:9
H. art gone   SHAK 683:8
H. is home   PROV 622:24
H. is home, as the Devil said   PROV 622:23
H. is the girl's prison   SHAW 726:30
H. is the place   FROS 335:12
H. is the sailor   STEV 760:20
h. is the Sule Skerry   BALL 52:5
H. is where the heart is   PROV 622:25
H. is where you come to   THAT 787:18
H. James   HILL 388:16
H. life as we understand it   SHAW 725:7
h. life of our own dear Queen   ANON 16:13
H. of lost causes   ARNO 29:15
h. of the brave   KEY 450:9
h., rejoicing, brought me   BAKE 50:2
h. sweet home   JERO 421:15
H., sweet home   PAYN 589:11
H. they brought her warrior   TENN 783:9
h., you idle creatures   SHAK 695:27
house is not a h.   ADLE 5:21
hunter h. from hill   STEV 760:20
in h. cosmography   HABI 366:8
I was leaving h.   STEV 760:9
Keep the H.-fires burning   FORD 329:4
kept at h.   COWP 247:13
leaves h. to mend himself   GOLD 355:27
Look as much like h.   FRY 336:15
man goeth to his long h.   BIBL 86:25
murder into the h.   HITC 389:21
never h. came she   KING 452:20
never is at h.   COWP 246:10
no place like h.   PAYN 589:12
no place like h.   PROV 632:33
O, h., hame   CUNN 253:18
points of heaven and h.   WORD 850:17
princes are come h. again   SHAK 699:16
refuge from h. life   SHAW 727:23
shortest way h.   PROV 625:37
so now we'll go h.   SHAC 677:18
Sweet Stay-at-h.   DAVI 259:3
there's nobody at h.   POPE 602:20
thinks to found a h.   DOUG 283:21
Till the boys come h.   FORD 329:4
unto God all things come h.   KORA 461:3
what is it to be at h.   BECK 61:1
What's the good of a h.   GROS 365:3
woman's place in the h.   PROV 635:16
won't go h. till morning   BUCK 163:12
won the Fleece and then came h.
   DU B 290:18
homeland loved my h.   BELL 66:4
homeless h. by choice   SOUT 749:13
h., tempest-tossed   LAZA 476:10
homely h. was their food   GART 340:11
never so h.   PROV 622:24
home-made H. dishes   HOOD 395:5
Homer excellent H. nods   HORA 398:15
Gladstone read H. for fun   CHUR 222:11
had the voice of H.   HALD 368:1
H. dead   ANON 19:1
H.'s mighty dinners   AESC 6:11
H. smote 'is bloomin' lyre   KIPL 456:6
H. sometimes nods   PROV 622:26
H. sometimes sleeps   BYRO 181:10
more than H. knew   SWIF 767:8
must not call it H.   BENT 69:1
warred for H., being dead   HEYW 388:1
Home Rule morning H. passes   CARS 196:18
separation as well as H.   BALF 51:4
homes h. without a friend   CLAR 224:9
In h., a haunted apparatus   RAIN 640:16
Stately H. of England   COWA 245:7

stately h. of England   HEMA 381:1
homespuns What hempen h.   SHAK 711:10
homeward h. take your way   COLL 234:18
Look h. angel   MILT 530:9
ploughman h. plods   GRAY 360:24
homicidal h. classics   STOP 761:12
homo *Ecce h.*   BIBL 115:15
ET H. FACTUS EST   MISS 536:21
homogeneity incoherent h.   SPEN 750:7
homogeneous more h. State   NEWS 562:11
homosexual composer and *not* h.
   DIAG 266:15
h. sex you know exactly   BURR 173:13
honest beat the h. men   SHAK 706:21
buy it like an h. man   NORT 565:15
Corrupted h. men   SHAK 679:18
few h. men   CROM 251:12
general h. thought   SHAK 698:29
h. broker   BISM 117:19
h. God   INGE 413:14
h. madam's issue   SHAK 699:24
h. man is laughed at   HALI 369:7
h. man's the noblest work   BURN 170:23
h. man's the noblest work   POPE 605:9
h. men come by their own   PROV 634:35
h., sonsie face   BURN 172:18
H. to God   ROBI 650:19
h. woman of her word   SHAK 709:11
I am not naturally h.   SHAK 722:12
is not an h. man   WHAT 831:10
least h. with themselves   AUST 39:1
looking for an h. man   DIOG 274:19
most h. of men   RICH 647:19
poor but she was h.   MILI 526:16
Robin and I are two h. men   SHIP 735:2
third h. wealth   ANON 21:10
whatsoever things are h.   BIBL 110:8
while the nation is h.   DOUG 284:4
honestly If possible h.   HORA 399:1
honesty armed so strong in h.   SHAK 698:16
common sense and common h.   SHEL 728:4
h. is *not* to be based   RUSK 660:1
H. is praised   JUVE 439:8
H. is the best policy   PROV 622:27
H. is the best policy   WHAT 831:10
h. must work through artifice   RIDI 648:5
saving of thine h.   MORE 548:18
honey bee produces h.   GOLD 354:7
bees make h.   VIRG 815:7
Eating bread and h.   NURS 569:14
flowing with milk and h.   BIBL 77:19
gather h. all the day   WATT 823:6
hive for the h.-bee   YEAT 854:17
hives with h. and wax   SWIF 765:6
H. catches more flies   PROV 622:28
h. from the weed   SHAK 693:10
h. of Hybla   SHAK 689:20
h. of poison-flowers   TENN 781:17
H. of roses   HERB 384:9
h. on the goblet's rim   LUCR 495:13
H., quoth she   NURS 569:19
h. shall he eat   BIBL 88:15
h. still for tea   BROO 153:13
h. to smear his face   SCHW 672:8
H., your silk stocking   SELL 676:18
How a bear likes h.   MILN 528:6
I did but taste a little h.   BIBL 80:13
in my mouth sweet as h.   BIBL 113:26
locusts and wild h.   BIBL 94:11
neither the h. nor the bee   SAPP 666:13
sweeter also than h.   BOOK 134:22
there is h.   PROV 634:37
took some h.   LEAR 477:15
With milk and h. blessed   NEAL 558:2
honeycomb drop as an h.   BIBL 83:38
honey, and the h.   BOOK 134:22
of an h.   BIBL 102:14
honeydew he on h. hath fed   COLE 232:8
honeyed h. middle of the night   KEAT 442:18
honeysuckle You are my honey, h.
   FITZ 322:22
honi H. soie qui mal y pense   SELL 676:18

H. soit qui mal y pense MOTT 552:9
honking goose h. amongst tuneful swans
VIRG 814:9

honores *contemnere* h.
HORA 403:16
honour abide in h. BOOK 137:7
all in h. SHAK 714:29
All is lost save h. MISQ 537:1
As he was valiant, I h. him SHAK 697:19
cannot be maintained with h. RUSS 661:13
existence to h. JUVE 440:4
Fear God. H. the King KITC 457:14
flowery plains of h. JONS 435:15
for this woman's h. FILM 320:16
fountain of h. BACO 43:12
greater share of h. SHAK 693:21
great peaks of h. LLOY 487:16
H. all men BIBL 112:7
h. among thieves PROV 632:11
h., and keep her BOOK 133:8
h. and life FRAN 332:4
h. and renown ye ANON 19:2
H. a physician BIBL 93:26
h. aspireth to it BACO 44:2
H. but an empty bubble DRYD 287:17
h. due unto his Name BOOK 140:11
h. in one eye SHAK 696:4
H. is like a match PAGN 582:1
h. is the subject SHAK 696:5
H. pricks me on SHAK 691:8
h. rooted in dishonour TENN 778:1
h. sinks where commerce GOLD 355:12
h.'s voice GRAY 361:4
H. the greatest poet DANT 255:16
h. therof EDWA 296:9
h. those whom they have slain DOST 283:5
H. thy father and thy mother BIBL 78:5
h. turn to dust MARV 516:2
H.! tut, a breath JONS 435:21
h. unto Luke Evangelist ROSS 656:4
h. unto the wife BIBL 112:11
H., without money RACI 640:9
h. you now give her ELIZ 305:5
hurt that H. feels TENN 780:18
in h. clear POPE 603:24
In h. I gained them NELS 558:15
Keeps h. bright SHAK 719:23
king delighteth to h. BIBL 82:24
Leisure with h. CICE 223:23
loss of h. was a wrench GRAH 358:5
louder he talked of his h. EMER 306:20
Loved I not h. more LOVE 493:8
may we h. it WEBS 825:16
new-made h. doth forget SHAK 699:1
one vessel unto h. BIBL 106:24
peace I hope with h. DISR 276:17
peace with h. CHAM 206:12
pluck bright h. SHAK 689:29
pluck up drownèd h. SHAK 689:29
post of h. ADDI 4:14
post of h. PROV 629:30
property or h. MACH 502:13
prophet is not without h. BIBL 97:7
prophet not without h. PROV 629:44
ready her to h. BEST 71:21
reputation and h. SOCR 744:26
riches and h. BIBL 83:34
right of h. GURN 366:1
roll of h. CLEV 226:16
safety, h., and welfare CHAR 209:10
signed with their h. SPEN 750:20
some smatch of h. SHAK 698:28
stain in thine h. BIBL 93:25
state of temporary h. JOHN 426:6
take mine h. from me KIPL 454:19
throne we h. SHER 733:13
Trouthe and h. CHAU 210:6
What is h. SHAK 691:9
whence h. springs MARL 513:22
When h.'s at the stake SHAK 688:4
where their h. died POPE 603:5
without h. BIBL 92:26
years and h. to the grave KIPL 455:3
honourable Brutus is an h. man SHAK 697:23

designs were strictly h. FIEL 318:12
h. alike in what we give LINC 485:6
h. among all men BOOK 133:5
h. by being necessary HALE 368:7
humble as h. CHUA 219:1
make an h. retreat SHAK 681:18
more h. man BIBL 101:3
only h. provision AUST 39:24
thy h. women BOOK 136:21
honoured h. me of late SHAK 704:8
More h. in the breach SHAK 684:24
honours bears his blushing h. SHAK 695:11
despise h. HORA 403:16
good card to play for H. BENN 67:23
h. her more than himself TALM 772:19
h. the worker TALM 772:21
neither h. nor wages GARI 339:15
hood bold Robin H. BALL 52:2
hoof No h., no horse PROV 627:39
though he divide the h. BIBL 78:11
hoof-marks many h. going in AESO 6:16
hoofs h. of a swinish multitude BURK 167:18
plunging h. were gone DE L 263:4
hook bended h. shall pierce SHAK 679:11
h.-nosed fellow of Rome SHAK 692:13
That nose, the h. BYRO 177:20
thy h. Spares the next swath KEAT 445:15
with an h. BIBL 83:29
hooks Thy baited h. WYAT 852:1
hooter because the h. hoots CHES 216:8
hooting H. and shrieking SHAK 696:18
h. at the glorious sun COLE 231:17
Hoover onto the board of H. GREE 363:7
hop for what were h.-yards meant
HOUS 405:2
H. forty paces SHAK 679:6
Why h. ye so BOOK 138:13
hope Abandon all h. DANT 255:13
All my h. on God BRID 151:5
All our h. is fallen HORA 402:10
believed in h. BIBL 106:7
Can something, h. HOPK 396:10
Evelyn H. is dead BROW 159:9
failure of h. GIBB 345:23
From h. and fear set free SWIN 768:17
God is our h. BOOK 136:24
have not h. nor health SHEL 731:22
He has no h. COWP 248:22
heirs through h. BOOK 132:4
He that lives in h. HERB 385:7
He that lives upon h. FRAN 332:15
h. and agitation BARA 55:3
h. and history rhyme HEAN 377:18
h. beyond ourselves SHEL 732:18
H. deferred BIBL 84:15
H. deferred PROV 622:29
h., fear, rage, pleasure JUVE 439:10
H., for a season CAMP 187:16
H. for the best PROV 622:30
h. for the best SMIT 743:19
H. for years to come WATT 823:20
h. grew ground me COLE 231:11
h. in Christ BIBL 108:3
H. is a good breakfast BACO 46:21
H. is a good breakfast PROV 622:31
h. is gone AUST 39:16
h. is perished BIBL 91:8
h. I will be religious again FLEM 326:15
Hopeless h. hopes on CLAR 224:9
h. little ELGA 299:2
H. maketh not ashamed BIBL 106:8
h. of all the ends BOOK 138:6
h. of glory BOOK 129:20
h. of the ungodly BIBL 92:28
h. once crushed ARNO 28:28
H. raises no dust ÉLUA 306:6
H. springs eternal POPE 604:22
H. springs eternal PROV 622:32
h. till Hope creates SHEL 731:10
I can give you no h. EDDI 295:4
I fear and h. PETR 593:18
in the store we sell h. REVS 645:15
Land of H. and Glory BENS 67:25

last best h. LINC 485:6
life there's h. PROV 634:45
lives in h. PROV 621:50
look forward to with h. FROS 335:11
more h. of a fool BIBL 85:10
Never to h. again SHAK 695:12
no h. without fear SPIN 752:24
Nor dread nor h. attend YEAT 853:17
not another's h. WALS 820:13
not for h., heart would break PROV 623:2
nursing the unconquerable h. ARNO 28:10
only h. that keeps up GAY 341:11
phantoms of h. JOHN 425:24
pleasing h. ADDI 4:15
poise of h. and fear MILT 528:25
Some blessed H. HARD 372:16
sure and certain h. BOOK 133:18
tender leaves of h. SHAK 695:11
there is h. CROS 252:16
There is no h. CHES 214:16
Through love, through h. WORD 849:24
triumph of h. over experience JOHN 429:12
True h. is swift SHAK 717:4
two thousand years of h. WEIZ 827:1
warns us not to h. HORA 402:12
Was the h. drunk SHAK 704:9
we may gain from h. MILT 531:12
Whatever h. is yours OWEN 581:7
What is h. BYRO 184:6
what was dead was H. WILD 836:31
Where there is despair, h. FRAN 332:6
Work without h. COLE 233:16
Youth and H. COLE 234:11
hoped Much wished, h. little TASS 773:8
things h. for BIBL 111:6
hoped-for become the h. heaven EPIT 311:14
hopeful droopingly, but with a h. heart
LAWR 474:20
hopefully travel h. PROV 623:45
travel h. is a better thing STEV 759:20
hopefulness Lord of all h. STRU 762:15
hopeless doctors know a h. case
CUMM 253:12
h. are starkly sincere RHYS 646:14
h. grief is passionless BROW 157:25
H. hope hopes on CLAR 224:9
inspire h. passion THAC 786:8
perennially h. DICK 267:13
hopelessness h. and calm BARA 55:3
h. of one's position DOST 283:11
hopes airy h. my children WORD 846:16
enter on far-reaching h. HORA 400:6
happy as one h. LA R 469:22
h. and fears BROO 154:8
h. and fears it heeded not SHEL 731:28
h. of its children EISE 298:13
h. our wits beguile WOTT 851:6
If h. were dupes CLOU 229:11
no great h. from Birmingham AUST 38:22
no h. but from power BURK 168:19
scribbled lines like fallen h. HOPE 396:7
set my h. in thee PRAY 611:8
vanity of human h. JOHN 425:22
wholly h. to be BROW 159:5
hopeth h. all things BIBL 107:25
hoping Dreading and h. all YEAT 853:17
hops apples, cherries, h. DICK 271:26
heresy, h., and beer PROV 633:24
Horatius H. kept the bridge MACA 499:20
horizon always somebody else's h.
GRAH 358:13
fortress rising above the h. LOUI 492:10
h. adorning HEBE 378:14
In research the h. recedes PATT 589:1
just beyond the h. KISS 457:13
horizons immense fields, wide h.
CHEK 213:22
horizontal h. desire SHAW 727:27
Life is a h. fall COCT 230:2
vertical to the eternal h. GRAS 359:14
horn blow his wreathèd h. WORD 850:22
h. of the hunter CRAW 250:20
horn, the lusty h. SHAK 682:3

horn (cont.):
one of which is made of h. VIRG 812:17
sound of the h. VIGN 810:6
through the mellow h. COLL 235:14
won't come out of your h. PARK 585:13
Hornby H. and my Barlow THOM 791:4
horned h. moon WORD 845:18
Horner Little Jack H. NURS 568:2
Hornie Auld H., Satan BURN 170:3
hornpipes h. and strathspeys BURN 170:26
horns h. of Elfland TENN 783:1
memories are hunting h. APOL 23:9
horny H.-handed sons of toil SALI 664:11
h. hands of toil LOWE 494:2
horresco H. referens VIRG 811:13
horribilis annus h. ELIZ 305:3
horrible h. imaginings SHAK 703:15
O, horrible! O, h. SHAK 685:5
out of the h. pit BOOK 136:6
horrid she was h. LONG 491:11
very h. thing BUTL 175:14
With h. warning KEAT 443:29
horror haunts of h. and fear TENN 782:5
h. its beauty SHEL 730:15
h. of a deep night RACI 640:3
h. of great darkness BIBL 76:15
h. of sunsets PROU 613:11
h.! The horror CONR 240:16
image of that h. SHAK 702:5
scaly h. of his folded tail MILT 530:24
there is no h. DOYL 285:6
horrors Congenial h. THOM 792:15
stained with ancient h. RIMB 649:7
supped full with h. SHAK 707:13
horse behold a pale h. BIBL 113:14
behold a white h. BIBL 114:11
Boot, saddle, to h. BROW 158:22
cart before the h. PROV 618:5
dearer than his h. TENN 780:16
Do not trust the h. VIRG 811:11
Don't ask me, ask the h. FREU 334:4
feeds the h. enough oats GALB 338:5
gift h. in the mouth PROV 627:23
good h. cannot be PROV 621:8
h. designed by a committee ISSI 414:12
h. has bolted PROV 624:23
h. he can ride THOM 792:21
h. is at least *human* SALI 663:22
h.-laugh in the reader FIEL 318:11
h. misused upon the road BLAK 119:7
h. of air ANON 20:4
h. of that colour SHAK 720:20
h. on the mountain LORC 492:2
h.'s cry ARNO 28:15
h.'s hoof PROV 632:49
h. was made Consul RAND 642:3
mare is the better h. PROV 621:21
might even do for a h. NIGH 564:15
my h., my wife, and my name SURT 764:16
my kingdom for a h. SHAK 717:10
never heard no h. sing ARMS 26:15
Ninety-seven h. power FLAN 324:19
No foot, no h. PROV 627:39
not a h. PROV 626:6
O, for a h. with wings SHAK 683:3
O happy h. SHAK 678:24
old h. that stumbles HARD 372:20
One man may steal a h. PROV 628:42
outside of a h. PROV 632:22
owe it to h. and hound WHYT 834:11
rider and his h. SURT 764:25
short h. soon curried PROV 630:35
sick h. nosing around KAVA 442:6
something in a flying h. WORD 848:20
sting a stately h. JOHN 427:13
strength of an h. BOOK 144:4
take a h. to the water PROV 635:39
to my h.—German CHAR 209:13
torturer's h. scratches AUDE 35:13
two ride on a h. PROV 623:9
two things about the h. ROYD 657:17
upon the high h. BROW 155:6
want of a h. PROV 620:24

where's the bloody h. CAMP 187:5
young cornet of h. WALP 820:8
horseback beggar on h. PROV 630:31
ride On h. COWP 246:19
Horseguards be in the H. RATT 642:15
horseman H., *pass by* YEAT 856:5
sits behind the h. HORA 401:11
horsemanship forgetful of his h. HOME 394:8
horsemen Four H. rode again RICE 646:21
horses All the king's h. NURS 567:10
breed of their h. PENN 591:17
Bring on the empty h. CURT 254:8
change h. in mid stream PROV 618:7
dogs, h. JENY 421:3
don't spare the h. HILL 388:16
frighten the h. CAMP 187:3
generally given to h. JOHN 424:12
hell of h. PROV 618:42
h. are the senses UPAN 805:8
H. for courses PROV 622:33
h. of instruction BLAK 121:6
h. of the night OVID 579:18
If wishes were h. PROV 623:10
if you cannot ride two h. MAXT 519:3
in h., dawgs, and men THAC 786:17
I saw the h. HUGH 407:7
ride two h. at once PROV 623:13
Rode their h. Up to bed DE L 263:1
some in h. BOOK 134:24
surmised the H. Heads DICK 272:23
swap h. when crossing LINC 485:10
that h. may not be stolen HALI 369:6
They shoot h. don't they MCCO 500:16
watered our h. in Helicon CHAP 208:14
wild white h. play ARNO 27:11
with his panting h. VIRG 814:14
Women and H. KIPL 453:16
horse-taming life of h. Hector HOME 394:10
horticulture lead a h. PARK 586:10
hortis nascitur h. CATU 203:2
hortus H. ubi et tecto vicinus iugis
  HORA 403:14
hosanna Glorious h. SMAR 740:18
H. in excelsis MISS 539:6
hosannas sweet h. ring NEAL 557:24
hose out of the turret with a h. JARR 418:25
youthful h. well saved SHAK 681:12
hospes deferor h. HORA 398:18
hospital first requirement in a H.
  NIGH 564:13
not an inn, but an h. BROW 157:9
hospitals rot in h. SOUT 748:15
host find such a h. ANST 23:3
h., of golden daffodils WORD 847:5
h. of Midian BIBL 79:24
hostages h. to fortune BACO 44:30
h. to the fates LUCA 495:3
hostile universe is not h. HOLM 393:1
hosts h. and guests BEER 63:1
Lord God of h. BOOK 131:22
Lord of h. BOOK 135:7
Lord of h. is with us BOOK 136:25
hot beat the iron while it is h. DRYD 289:35
h. cross buns NURS 568:16
h. for certainties MERE 522:22
It's red h., mate GALT 338:17
little pot is soon h. PROV 625:29
long h. summer FILM 322:7
only in h. water BIBL 113:5
On a h., hot day LAWR 475:7
only in h. water REAG 643:8
stars are not h. enough EDDI 295:1
That is, h. ice SHAK 711:30
while the iron is h. PROV 631:29
hotel great advantage of a h. SHAW 727:23
h.-keepers continue TROL 799:24
hoti settled H.'s business BROW 159:16
Hotspur H. of the North SHAK 690:5
Houlihan Kathaleen Ni H. CARB 190:4
hound his hawk, his h. BALL 53:15
H. that Caught the Pubic Hare BEHA 61:9
loves to h. more SURT 764:15
owe it to horse and h. WHYT 834:11

slepyng h. to wake CHAU 213:4
hounds by your own quick h. MOTI 551:13
carcass fit for h. SHAK 696:24
h. all join in glorious cry FIEL 317:15
h. and his horn in the morning GRAV 360:2
h. of Sparta SHAK 711:24
h. of spring SWIN 767:25
smale h. hadde she CHAU 210:12
Such h., such hawks BALL 53:14
hour accompany us one short h. FARA 314:15
Awaits alike th' inevitable h. GRAY 361:3
books of the h. RUSK 659:17
close-companioned inarticulate h.
  ROSS 656:1
darkest h. PROV 617:23
Ere the parting h. go by ARNO 27:17
fill the h. EMER 307:7
finest h. CHUR 221:9
for an h. of Herod HOPE 396:5
for one h. retard SMAR 740:19
h. is come SCOT 674:10
h. of death BOOK 129:9
h. of glorious life MORD 547:23
h. requires such help VIRG 811:21
I also had my h. CHES 215:25
I have had my h. DRYD 289:30
Improve each shining h. WATT 823:6
its h. come round at last YEAT 855:13
Its h. is now SCHW 672:10
known as the Children's H. LONG 490:3
know not what h. BIBL 98:20
man and the h. YANC 853:3
matched us with His h. BROO 153:14
mine h. is not yet come BIBL 102:27
most carefully upon your h. SHAK 683:11
now's the h. BURN 172:5
stayed me in a happy h. SHAK 712:28
struts and frets his h. SHAK 707:14
tell the h. JOHN 429:2
Time and the h. SHAK 703:16
'tis the h. of prayer BYRO 181:11
to serve the h. TENN 782:18
watch with me one hour BIBL 99:5
hourglass Egghead weds h. NEWS 562:6
hours better wages and shorter h.
  ORWE 577:24
h. will take care of themselves CHES 215:3
leaden-stepping h. MILT 530:29
more than five h. a day HALD 368:3
see the h. pass CIOR 223:28
Seven h. to law JONE 434:11
Six h. in sleep COKE 230:19
Six h. sleep for a man PROV 630:43
two golden h. MANN 510:7
two h.' traffick SHAK 717:13
house angel in the h. PATM 588:14
another man's h. AUST 38:19
barren woman to keep h. BOOK 142:1
beat upon that h. BIBL 95:24
Better one h. spoiled PROV 615:26
build a h. for fools SWIF 767:18
Carrying his own h. DONN 281:21
Dark h., by which I once more TENN 778:26
displeases this H. O'CO 571:12
doll in the doll's h. DICK 271:24
dwell in the h. of the Lord BOOK 136:3
fortune of the h. stands VIRG 815:5
Harrow the h. of the dead AUDE 36:8
heap of stones is a h. POIN 599:11
h. and land are gone PROV 634:22
h. appointed for all living BIBL 83:17
h. as nigh heaven MORE 548:15
H. Beautiful is play lousy PARK 586:5
h. built upon sand SAYE 668:4
h. divided LINC 484:16
h. divided cannot stand PROV 622:34
h. is a machine for living in LE C 478:10
h. is his castle COKE 230:18
h. is much more MORR 549:7
h. is not a home ADLE 5:21
h. not made with hands BIBL 108:15
h. not made with hands BROW 158:24
h. of defence BOOK 140:4

hung (*cont.*):
h. with bloom · HOUS 404:6
hunger bodily h. in his eyes · SHAW 725:24
Fear and H. · VIRG 812:12
H. allows no choice · AUDE 36:4
h. and poverty · LARK 468:11
h. and thirst · BIBL 94:20
H. drives the wolf · PROV 622:35
H. is the best sauce · PROV 622:36
h. to be beautiful · RHYS 646:13
I am h. · VOZN 817:1
In poverty, h., and dirt · HOOD 395:11
lack, and suffer h. · BOOK 135:24
love seldom dies of h. · LENC 480:2
offer you h., thirst · GARI 339:15
sacred h. · SPEN 752:5
shall h. no more · BIBL 113:20
shall never h. · BIBL 103:4
time of h. · BIBL 93:16
where mass h. reigns · BRAN 149:15
hungered h., and ye gave me meat
· BIBL 98:25
hungry Adam was born h. · BRIL 151:17
ate when we were not h. · SWIF 765:17
filled the h. · BIBL 99:32
filled the h. · BIBL 115:11
h. for dinner at eight · HART 374:12
h. man is an angry man · PROV 622:37
h. sheep look up · MILT 530:4
I am not h. · PUNC 637:18
If thine enemy be h. · BIBL 85:6
lean and h. look · SHAK 696:12
Let all who are h. · HAGG 367:1
makes h. Where most she satisfies
· SHAK 679:7
roaming with a h. heart · TENN 784:14
seen the h. ocean · SHAK 723:7
Huns H. or Wops · MITF 541:2
hunt Better to h. in fields · DRYD 288:8
h. with the hounds · PROV 635:35
hunted H. and penned · MCKA 502:16
h. as an elk · RIEL 648:8
h. round the globe · PAIN 582:9
hunter Esau was a cunning h. · BIBL 76:25
heart is a lonely h. · BORR 146:11
h. home from hill · STEV 760:20
H. of the East · FITZ 322:24
h.'s javelin · ARNO 28:15
H.'s waking thoughts · AUDE 34:24
Man is the h. · TENN 783:8
Nimrod the mighty h. · BIBL 76:13
snare of the h. · BOOK 140:2
Hunter Dunn Miss J. H. · BETJ 73:1
hunters h. ben nat hooly men · CHAU 210:14
see the first h. · PURD 637:28
hunting ain't the h. · PUNC 637:10
call h. one of them · JOHN 433:15
Daddy's gone a-h. · NURS 566:10
death on the h.-field · MORT 550:18
discourse was about h. · PEPY 592:6
handsome h. man · DE L 262:25
H. is all that's worth · SURT 764:12
h. the wild boar · BENJ 66:16
passion for h. · DICK 271:11
preserved as h.-grounds · ELIO 299:26
weary wi' h. · BALL 52:10
wet and dirty from h. · SURT 764:23
Huntingtower bower, and H. · BALL 52:7
huntress Queen and h. · JONS 435:2
huntsman cassocked h. · COWP 247:9
h. by the bear oppressed · WALL 818:5
huntsmen h. are up in America · BROW 156:6
hurdles don't really see the h. · MOSE 551:11
hurl h. my soul from heaven · SHAK 714:27
hurled Swift to be h. · HOOD 394:23
hurly-burly When the h.'s done · SHAK 702:28
hurricane h. on the way · FISH 321:13
select the h. season · WIND 841:11
hurricanes H. hardly happen · LERN 481:20
hurricanoes You cataracts and h.
· SHAK 700:15
hurry h., hurry, hurry · MIDD 524:11
H. no man's cattle · PROV 622:38

H. up please it's time · ELIO 303:16
never in a h. · WESL 829:20
old man in a h. · CHUR 220:14
sick h. · ARNO 28:9
hurrying waiting means h. on · MANN 510:10
hurt assault and h. the soul · BOOK 130:5
cry before you're h. · PROV 618:10
don't know can't h. you · PROV 634:14
hate the man you have h. · TACI 770:4
healed also the h. · BIBL 90:26
h. but I am not slain · BALL 53:2
h. not thy foot · BOOK 140:4
h. of my soul · BOOK 138:4
h. you to the heart · TWAI 803:12
if I don't h. her · NURS 567:13
I'll not h. thee · STER 756:24
it is going to h. · ROWL 657:15
never h. a hair · STUD 763:2
no one was to be h. · BROO 153:18
power to h. us · BEAU 60:7
shall not h. nor destroy · BIBL 88:22
wish to h. · BRON 152:7
words will never h. me · PROV 631:19
Yes it h. · POLI 601:18
hurting Cold lights h. · JOHN 423:5
If the policy isn't h. · MAJO 508:3
people h. people · MAIL 507:12
hurts hide our own h. · ELIO 299:24
h. to think · HOUS 405:2
husband as a bride adorned for her h.
· BIBL 114:16
as to love a h. · WYCH 852:13
Chaste to her h. · POPE 603:4
crown to her h. · BIBL 84:12
darkens a h.'s mood · SADE 662:14
deaf h. · PROV 617:26
good fortune than a good h. · OSBO 578:12
great good h. · LOVE 493:3
his being my h. · CONG 238:28
h. and wife · FIEL 318:13
h. be a man with whom you have lived
· LAMB 464:10
h. is always the last · PROV 622:39
h. is a whole-time job · BENN 67:21
h. is fro the world ygon · CHAU 212:14
h. June · WATK 822:17
h. of one wife · BIBL 110:22
h. or a house · WHIT 834:2
h.'s first praise · BARB 55:8
h. what is left of a lover · ROWL 657:11
h. with a beard · SHAK 712:13
in her h.'s heart · SHAK 720:23
left her h. because · MURD 554:12
life her h. makes for her · ELIO 300:7
love of Soul in the h. · UPAN 804:14
married my h. for life · SAYI 669:29
My h. and I · ELIZ 305:2
one h. too many · ANON 15:8
over hir h. as hir love · CHAU 212:20
picked out for a h. · HAYW 376:8
quarrels with one's h. · BONA 126:18
reproach a h. · LA F 463:10
safeguard, and the h.'s · NAPO 556:12
splendid h. · CHEK 214:11
unbelieving h. · BIBL 107:14
woman oweth to her h. · SHAK 718:16
your dear h. for a comfort · SMIT 743:6
husbanded so fathered and so h. · SHAK 697:2
husbandry h. in heaven · SHAK 704:15
husbands Aisles full of h. · GINS 349:17
Chumps make the best h. · WODE 842:15
hands of the h. · ADAM 1:14
H. at chirche dore · CHAU 210:21
H., love your wives · BIBL 110:13
h. to stay at home · ELIO 300:15
in spite of their h. · LEE- 479:5
When h. or when lapdogs · POPE 606:15
hush breathless h. in the Close · NEWB 560:5
holy h. of ancient sacrifice · STEV 758:8
H., hush · MORT 551:5
H.! Hush! Whisper who dares · MILN 528:5
h., little baby, don' yo' cry · HEYW 387:16
h. with the setting moon · TENN 781:24

hushing H. the latest traffic · BRID 151:6
husks h. that the swine did eat · BIBL 101:15
hustle tried to h. the East · KIPL 455:6
hut Love in a h. · KEAT 444:1
huts in the h. of Indians · LOCK 488:17
Hwæt *H.! wē Gārdena* · ANON 22:7
hyacinths h. and biscuits · SAND 666:2
rob the H. bees · SHAK 698:22
Hybla rob the H. bees · SHAK 698:22
Hyde Dr Jekyll and Mr H. · STEV 759:8
hydrogen telescope or h. bomb · LOVE 493:9
hydroptic h. earth hath drunk · DONN 281:7
hyena h. in petticoats · WALP 819:18
hygienic most h. of beverages · PAST 588:8
hymns Chanting learn h. · SHAK 710:15
enthusiastic amorous h. · LACK 463:3
h. at heaven's gate · SHAK 722:30
Singing h. unbidden · SHEL 731:28
Sweet h. shall be my chant · JUDA 438:3
hyperbole perpetual h. · BACO 44:28
hypercritical by any h. rules · LINC 485:2
Hyperion H. to a satyr · SHAK 684:3
hyphen *h.* which joins · BAGE 47:17
hyphenated h. Americanism · ROOS 654:14
hypocrisy allows for no h. · STEN 755:18
H. is a tribute · LA R 469:15
H., the only evil · MILT 532:21
organized h. · DISR 275:10
That would be h. · WILD 835:20
world safe for h. · WOLF 843:17
hypocrite h. and flatterer · BLAK 120:12
h. in his pleasures · JOHN 432:18
h. is really rotten · AREN 24:15
H. lecteur,—mon semblable · BAUD 58:12
hypocrites cant of h. · STER 757:5
other half h. · JEFF 420:16
scribes and Pharisees, h. · BIBL 98:9
hypotenuse square on the h. · GILB 348:29
hypotheses do not feign h. · NEWT 561:14
smallest number of h. · EINS 298:7
hypothesis construct a h. · HARD 372:1
discard a pet h. · LORE 492:4
nature of an h. · STER 757:2
slaying of a beautiful h. · HUXL 411:14
hyssop purge me with h. · BOOK 137:12
Sprinkle me with h. · MISS 536:9
hysteria thin whine of h. · DIDI 274:5
hysterical starving h. naked · GINS 349:15
hysterics h. of the Celt · TENN 779:25

I I am a camera · ISHE 414:10
I am not I · WAUG 824:2
I AM THAT I AM · BIBL 77:20
I am the one who did it · VIRG 813:6
I am the State · LOUI 492:5
in the infinite I AM · COLE 233:21
I plus my surroundings · ORTE 576:13
I shall never be · BOOK 134:7
My husband and I · ELIZ 305:2
person becomes I · BUBE 162:16
such as I am · BIBL 105:33
tell me who I am · SHAK 700:3
Through which we go Is I · DE L 263:5
Iago I. as an Imogen · KEAT 446:16
I.'s soliloquy · COLE 233:25
iambics escape my i. · CATU 203:11
purchase fame In keen i. · DRYD 288:32
ibant *I. obscuri sola sub nocte* · VIRG 812:11
ibit *in caelum iusseris i.* · JUVE 439:15
IBM for buying I. · ADVE 8:8
ice after the last i. age · PURD 637:28
along the polished i. · WORD 846:24
Alps of green i. · PHIL 594:15
break the i. · BACO 43:29
burn and I am i. · PETR 593:18
caves of i. · COLE 232:5
emperor of i.-cream · STEV 757:22
I. and Snow · BOOK 128:6
i.-cream out of the container · BRYS 162:13
I. formed · WODE 843:5
i. in the summer · PROV 630:10
i. like morsels · BOOK 144:5
i., mast-high · COLE 232:15

It's fresh as i.	ADVE 7:39
Like a piece of i. on a hot stove	FROS 336:6
region of thick-ribbèd i.	SHAK 708:10
skating over thin i.	EMER 307:3
smooth the i.	SHAK 699:10
Some say in i.	FROS 335:14
That is, hot i.	SHAK 711:30
thin i. that cracks	MONT 545:4
urine is congealed i.	SHAK 708:12
iceberg i. cuts its facets	BISH 117:5
ill-concealed i.	LAWS 476:6
iced three parts i. over	ARNO 30:1
Iceland Natural History of I.	JOHN 431:3
iceman i. cometh	O'NE 573:9
Ichabod I., Ichabod	BROW 161:28
named the child I.	BIBL 80:8
icicle Chaste as the i.	SHAK 682:25
hang like an i.	SHAK 721:4
icicles hang them up in silent i.	COLE 231:23
When i. hang by the wall	SHAK 702:26
icy lays his i. hand on kings	SHIR 735:3
id PUT THE I. BACK IN YID	ROTH 656:19
idea After the i., plenty of time	DYSO 294:20
better to entertain an i.	JARR 419:2
Between the i. And the reality	ELIO 302:7
does get an i.	MARQ 514:4
endowed with the i. of God	DESC 265:12
forgiveness is a lovely i.	LEWI 483:5
good i.—son	CATC 200:21
i. does not pass	UNAM 804:10
i. first occurs	DARW 257:18
i. whose time has come	SAYI 670:14
invasion by an i.	HUGO 407:17
landed with an i.	BIRT 117:2
more dangerous than an i.	ALAI 9:13
no grand i. was ever born	FITZ 324:2
only one i.	DISR 277:24
pain of a new i.	BAGE 48:24
possess but one i.	JOHN 429:10
teach the young i.	THOM 792:8
wilderness of i.	BUTL 176:31
would be a good i.	GAND 339:9
ideal i. for which I am prepared	MAND 509:13
i. of reason	KANT 441:11
i. reader suffering from	JOYC 437:3
idealism morphine or i.	JUNG 438:11
idealistic only i. nation	WILS 841:2
ideals i. of a nation	DOUG 283:20
men without i.	CAMU 188:8
shoes with broken high i.	MCGO 502:2
ideas because he has plenty of i.	CHAM 207:6
business is to kill i.	WELL 828:17
Colourless green i.	CHOM 218:8
express your i.	GRAC 358:2
From it our i. are born	GENE 342:21
genuine i., Bright Ideas	BENT 68:18
i. to literature	BOUR 147:12
i. which least belong to us	BERG 69:8
I. won't keep	WHIT 832:11
share no one's i.	TURG 802:6
signs of i.	JOHN 424:4
talk of generally held i.	BAUD 58:17
identical they exist, but are i.	FORS 329:21
Two things are i.	LEIB 479:16
ideological i. empire	NAIP 556:2
ideology country which loves i.	RAFF 640:14
ides Beware the i. of March	SHAK 695:29
i. of March are come	SHAK 697:8
proud I., when the squadron rides	MACA 499:8
idiom i. of words	PRIO 612:4
idioms i. appropriate to another	RYLE 662:2
licentious i.	JOHN 425:23
idiot i. who praises	GILB 347:22
portrait of a blinking i.	SHAK 709:9
tale Told by an i.	SHAK 707:14
idiots fatuity of i.	SMIT 743:8
idle addled egg as an i. bird	PROV 614:34
be not i.	CLOS 228:6
employment for his i. time	WALT 820:19
Every i. word	BIBL 96:32
For i. hands to do	WATT 823:7
happiest when I am i.	WARD 821:11
home, you i. creatures	SHAK 695:27
i. as a painted ship	COLE 232:19
i. brain is devil's workshop	PROV 622:40
i. have the least leisure	PROV 622:41
i. if hunger didn't pinch	ELIO 299:20
i., shivering creatures	AUST 38:19
i. singer of an empty day	MORR 549:13
i. smoke of praise	DANI 255:8
i. tales	BIBL 102:10
little profits that an i. king	TENN 784:13
most i. and unprofitable	GIBB 345:12
Never be completely i.	THOM 788:7
occupation for an i. hour	AUST 39:11
occupation for an i. hour	OPEN 575:17
only i. chatter	GILB 348:13
solitary, be not i.	JOHN 431:15
Tears, i. tears	TENN 783:3
vivacity of an i. man	BAGE 49:4
We would all be i.	JOHN 430:19
when wholly i.	SCIP 672:12
work for i. hands	PROV 617:32
idleness Grief is a species of i.	JOHN 429:20
I. cannot degrade a man	MARA 511:16
I. is only the refuge	CHES 215:10
I. is root of all evil	PROV 622:42
i. keeps ignorant	JOHN 424:19
in I. alone	CARL 192:21
penalties of i.	POPE 602:6
round of strenuous i.	WORD 849:12
idlers i. and Belgians	BAUD 59:2
i. of the Empire	DOYL 285:4
idling impossible to enjoy i.	JERO 421:10
idol God and an i.	LUTH 496:12
i. of its own	BYRO 182:10
i. of the Anglo-Saxon	BAGE 48:4
i. that is nothing	PARA 585:11
one-eyed yellow i.	HAYE 376:7
young bride was the i.	MANZ 511:10
idolaters murderers, and i.	BIBL 114:24
never of the i.	KORA 459:19
idolatries bowed To its i.	BYRO 179:2
idolatry ancients without i.	CHES 215:6
god of our i.	COWP 247:14
organization of i.	SHAW 726:17
idols i. I have loved	FITZ 323:15
maltreat our i.	FLAU 325:3
if I. it moves, salute it	MILI 526:10
i. you can keep your head	KERR 450:1
I. you can keep your head	KIPL 454:12
much virtue in 'i.'	SHAK 682:9
ifs If i. and ands were pots and pans	PROV 622:48
Talk'st thou to me of 'i.'	SHAK 716:31
ignara Non i. mali	VIRG 811:8
ignis fatuus Reason, an i.	ROCH 651:11
ignoble i. ease	ROOS 654:5
names i., born to be forgot	COWP 247:4
ignominy i. sleep with thee	SHAK 691:14
ignorance Disease, I., and Idleness	BEVE 73:22
Don't die of i.	OFF! 572:6
else an absolute i.	GREE 362:13
evil is simply i.	FORD 328:14
fact of my i.	SOCR 744:24
From i. our comfort flows	PRIO 612:10
from i. the Western World	JOHN 426:10
hindrance of i.	PALI 584:15
i. and confidence	TWAI 803:28
i. and simple-heartedness	LERM 482:8
I. excuses from sin	AUCT 34:7
I. is an evil weed	BEVE 73:21
i. is bliss	PROV 634:39
I. is like a delicate	WILD 835:15
i. is never better	FERM 317:3
I. is not innocence	BROW 159:27
I. is strength	ORWE 577:14
i. of nature	HOLB 392:12
I. of the law	PROV 623:29
I. of the law	SELD 676:4
i. or profaneness	MATH 518:8
i. so abysmal	MEDA 520:3
in i. sedate	JOHN 426:21
more than Gothic i.	FIEL 318:10
no sin but i.	MARL 513:12
pity his i.	DICK 270:22
pure i.	JOHN 427:20
smallest allowance for i.	HUXL 411:18
some i. or other	BALZ 54:7
understand a writer's i.	COLE 233:20
Where i. is bliss	GRAY 361:12
With a knowing i.	JOHN 422:10
women in a state of i.	KNOX 458:13
ignorant always be i.	AUST 39:8
Asking the i.	ZOBE 858:12
Be not i. of any thing	BIBL 93:5
Confound the i.	SHAK 686:4
idleness keeps i.	JOHN 424:19
i. and free	JEFF 420:11
i. armies clash	ARNO 27:5
i. of these magnificent things	MCEW 501:14
In language, the i.	DUPP 292:15
judgements of the i.	BURK 169:12
many i. men are sure	DARR 256:19
right of the i. man	CARL 191:11
ignorantly i. worship	BIBL 105:18
ignores most poetry i. most people	MITC 540:5
Ignotus I. moritur sibi	SENE 677:3
Ike I like I.	POLI 600:20
Iliad greater than the I.	PROP 612:23
Ilium fuit I.	VIRG 811:18
topless towers of I.	MARL 513:4
ill Against i. chances	SHAK 692:12
ever to do i.	MILT 531:10
final goal of i.	TENN 779:5
For certain i.	DRAY 286:2
i. and the stopping of ill	PALI 583:15
ill-clad, i.-nourished	ROOS 653:16
I. fares the land	GOLD 354:10
i.-favoured thing, sir	SHAK 682:7
i.-fed, ill-killed	JOHN 432:13
I. gotten goods never thrive	PROV 623:30
i. he cannot cure	ARNO 29:5
I. met by moonlight	SHAK 710:30
I. news hath wings	DRAY 285:20
i. wind that blows	PROV 624:18
Looking i. prevail	SUCK 763:4
means to do i. deeds	SHAK 699:12
Nothing i. come near thee	SHAK 683:9
one-third of a nation i.-housed	ROOS 653:16
or of i. breeding	CONG 239:9
she's not really i.	JAGG 415:14
so illiberal and so i.-bred	CHES 215:7
Some think him i.-tempered	LEAR 477:13
speak i. of the dead	PROV 627:28
suppressed i.-feeling	BAGE 48:20
think me so i. bred	WYCH 852:13
vain, i.-natured	DEFO 261:23
warn you not to fall i.	KINN 453:8
illacrimabiles omnes i.	HORA 402:16
illegal i., immoral, or fattening	WOOL 845:16
means that it is not i.	NIXO 565:2
Nothing is i. if	YOUN 857:1
illegally accomplishes great things i.	BALZ 54:10
illegitimate i. child of Karl Marx	ATTL 33:4
no i. children	GLAD 350:8
illegitimi Nil carborundum i.	SAYI 670:6
illiberal so i. and so ill-bred	CHES 215:7
illimitable i. was annihilated	DISR 275:18
illiterate I. him, I say	SHER 733:14
i. king	HENR 382:3
illness i. identified with evil	SONT 746:8
i. should attend it	SHAK 703:18
Living is an i.	CHAM 207:1
makes i. worthwhile	SHAW 724:17
treatment of an i.	WITT 842:8
ills climax of all human i.	BYRO 181:1
cure for the i. of Democracy	ADDA 3:19
i. of democracy	SMIT 741:14
i. to come	GRAY 361:10
mark what i.	JOHN 426:16
O'er a' the i. o' life	BURN 172:10
illuminated i. his kingdom	JOIN 434:3
i. trouser-clip for bicyclists	MORT 551:6

illuminating i. for her everything

	TOLS 796:15

illuminatio *Dominus i. mea* BIBL 114:26
Dominus i. mea MOTT 552:7
illumine What in me is dark, I. MILT 531:6
illusion great i. ANGE 14:13
one i.—France KEYN 450:1
only an i. EINS 298:9
sophistry and i. HUME 408:9
universe was an i. BORG 145:7
illusions friend of flattering i. CONR 240:21
life's i. I recall MITC 540:11
specious i. GODW 352:4
illustration i. of character JAME 418:2
illustrious I. acts high raptures WALL 818:11
Illyria what should I do in I. SHAK 720:7
ilnesses i. and dreary old age VIRG 814:19
image age demanded an i. POUN 608:18
Best i. of myself MILT 533:13
created him in his own i. DOST 283:2
God's i. man doth bear SPEG 750:3
graven i. BIBL 77:37
his i., cut in ebony FULL 337:3
his Maker's i. DRYD 286:16
i. of a shade SHEL 732:9
i. of death ELIO 300:17
i. of eternity BYRO 179:20
i. of God TALM 772:5
i. of his God GRAI 358:17
i. of his person BIBL 111:3
i. of passion BART 57:14
i. of the Creator BONA 127:4
I., that, flying WORD 846:25
just an i. GODA 351:17
kills the i. of God MILT 535:14
kindly paternal i. DANT 256:2
make man in our i. BIBL 75:8
Met his own i. SHEL 730:21
Stamped with the i. TENN 777:24
votre i. me suit RACI 640:6
worship the golden i. BIBL 91:19
imagery for their i. MCEW 501:14
images Bygone i. COLE 234:11
Fresh i. beget YEAT 853:10
garden of bright i. BRAM 149:8
I. split the truth LEVE 482:10
reflects i. ADAM 2:12
unpurged i. of day YEAT 853:8
imaginary i. relish SHAK 719:20
i. rights BENT 68:3
indistinguishable from the i. GIDE 346:11
make i. evils GOLD 355:18
imagination ages of i. BLAK 121:12
blow [dealt] to all i. DISR 275:18
car of the i. JAME 417:15
dream of our own i. BACO 46:5
exercising the i. GIRA 350:4
f—gg—g his i. BYRO 184:14
force of i. DRYD 288:25
hunting-grounds for the poetic i.

	ELIO 299:26

ideal of i. KANT 441:11
i. amend them SHAK 712:4
i. bodies forth SHAK 711:28
i. cold and barren BURK 166:19
i. droops her pinion BYRO 181:12
i. for his facts SHER 734:6
i. is not required JOHN 428:7
I., not invention CONR 240:24
i. of a boy KEAT 442:12
i. of man's heart BIBL 76:8
i. of their hearts BIBL 99:32
i. resembled MACA 498:24
i. sleeps CAMU 188:19
i. the rudder KEAT 445:26
i. to the proper pitch LACK 463:3
I., which in truth WORD 849:19
It is by i. SMIT 741:4
lava of the i. BYRO 184:4
nothing but his i. SHAW 725:18
of i. all compact SHAK 711:27
of moral good is the i. SHEL 732:14
primary i. COLE 233:21

save those that have no i. SHAW 727:19
shaping spirit of i. COLE 231:12
sweeten my i. SHAK 701:15
takes a lot of i. BAIL 49:17
Television contracts i. WOGA 843:7
truth of i. KEAT 446:1
Vision or I. BLAK 123:1
Where there is no i. DOYL 285:6
imaginations their own i. BOOK 134:1
imaginative function of i. literature

	EMPS 307:24

I. readers GRAV 360:12
imagine *buona i. paterna* DANT 256:2
I. there's no heaven LENN 480:12
people i. a vain thing BOOK 133:20
imagined i. such a device BOOK 134:25
imaginibus *Ex umbris et i.* EPIT 309:5
imaginings horrible i. SHAK 703:15
imitate i. the action SHAK 693:4
i. what is before him BAGE 49:2
Immature poets i. ELIO 303:28
never failed to i. them BALD 50:6
imitated can be i. by none CHAT 210:1
i. humanity SHAK 686:25
imitation art of I. LLOY 487:12
art of i. SIDN 736:15
child of i. REYN 646:5
i. in lines and colours POUS 609:12
I. is the sincerest form PROV 623:32
I. lies at the root FRAN 331:16
Were endless i. WORD 848:7
imitatores *O i., servum pecus* HORA 399:18
immanent I. Will HARD 372:14
Immanuel call his name I. BIBL 88:15
immaturity expression of human i.

	BRIT 151:19

immemorial in i. elms TENN 783:17
immense error is i. BOLI 126:9
immensity I. cloistered DONN 280:3
immolation i. so belied SASS 667:23
immoral art is i. WILD 836:1
good and i. CHUR 220:20
illegal, i., or fattening WOOL 845:16
moral or an i. book WILD 836:11
immorality i. is what they dislike

	WHIT 832:13

immortal death that is i. LUCR 495:18
do not seek i. life PIND 595:13
free and i. TRAH 797:13
I have I. longings SHAK 680:12
i. as they quote YOUN 857:2
i. hand or eye BLAK 122:19
i. in his own despite POPE 605:20
I., invisible SMIT 744:12
i. part of myself SHAK 713:23
i. spirit grows WORD 849:8
i. with a kiss MARL 513:4
race remains i. VIRG 815:5
sight of that i. sea WORD 848:13
Sire of an i. strain SHEL 728:14
soul is i. PLAT 597:17
soul is i. SOCR 745:7
With cold i. hands SWIN 768:15
immortalia *I. ne speres* HORA 402:12
immortality belief in i. DOST 282:17
cruel i. Consumes TENN 784:7
God, I., Duty ELIO 300:26
i. through my work ALLE 12:16
i. within His kingdom ZORO 859:20
just Ourselves— And I. DICK 272:22
lead me to i. UPAN 804:12
load of i. KEAT 446:14
Milk's leap toward i. FADI 314:2
Millions long for i. ERTZ 308:14
nothing for my i. SCHI 670:27
put on i. BIBL 108:11
they gave, their i. BROO 153:5
Imogen Iago as an I. KEAT 446:14
imp i. of fame SHAK 693:11
impaling I. worms COLM 236:5
impartial i. administration PEEL 590:14
neutrality of an i. judge BURK 169:8
pure i. hate THOR 793:19

impartiality i. is bias REIT 645:3
impatience i. would be so much fretted

	JOHN 429:19

one cardinal sin: i. KAFK 440:17
impatient growing i. to see him SMIT 743:5
never so i. BOOK 140:16
impavidum *I. ferient ruinae* HORA 401:14
impediment cause, or just i. BOOK 133:3
impenetrable dark i. wood SCOT 673:25
imperative i. is Categorical KANT 441:9
imperatur *non i.* BACO 46:18
imperfect i. man JEFF 420:5
use of an i. medium WILD 836:13
yet being i. BOOK 143:18
imperfections Dote on his i. EPHE 308:5
i. on my head SHAK 685:5
than i. ADDI 4:29
imperial act Of the i. theme SHAK 703:14
our great I. family ELIZ 305:1
imperialism I. is the monopoly stage

	LENI 480:3

I.'s face AUDE 36:3
wild-cat I. ROSE 654:19
imperialisms prey of rival i. KENY 449:15
imperium *I. et Libertas* DISR 276:21
impermanent consider what is i. PALI 583:6
impertinent ask an i. question BRON 152:6
ask i. questions DARW 257:17
privileged to be very i. FARQ 315:24
impious lift an i. hand BRON 152:9
implacable i. in hate DRYD 287:1
importance i. of a work of art FLAU 325:11
i. of the country HUXL 411:3
taking decisions of i. PARK 586:19
important being less i. MONT 544:8
i. book, the critic assumes WOOL 845:8
i. to be clever *about* MEDA 520:6
same as i. PRAT 610:8
trivial and the i. POTT 608:5
imports i. and exports ARIS 25:9
importunate no less i. MONT 544:8
importunes *sont pas moins i.* MONT 544:8
importunity ever-haunting i. LAMB 465:9
impossibilities i. enough in religion

	BROW 156:23

Probable i. ARIS 25:23
impossibility Upon I. MARV 515:10
impossible certain because it is i. TERT 786:2
Dream the i. DARI 256:16
eliminated the i. DOYL 285:1
i. shore ARNO 28:22
i. takes a little longer MILI 526:6
i. takes a little longer NANS 556:5
i. takes a little longer PROV 617:40
i.? that will be done CALO 186:5
i. to be silent BURK 169:3
i. to carry the heavy burden EDWA 296:12
i. to enjoy idling JERO 421:10
nothing is i. BISH 117:3
six i. things CARR 195:12
something is i. CLAR 225:2
That not i. she CRAS 250:19
'Tis a thing i. WORD 846:17
wish it were i. JOHN 433:8
impostors invented by i. GODW 352:4
treat those two i. KIPL 454:12
impotent i. people, sick THOM 791:3
imprecision Decay with i. ELIO 301:13
mess of i. of feeling ELIO 301:19
impresses i. me most about America

	EDWA 296:13

impression novel is an i. HARD 372:2
impressionable at an i. age SPAR 749:26
impressions First i. PROV 620:11
unweaving of false i. ELIO 300:21
imprint set it in i. CAXT 204:9
imprison Take me to you, i. me DONN 279:22
imprisoned taken or i. MAGN 506:4
imprisonment leaves his well-beloved i.

	DONN 280:3

improbability high degree of i. FISH 322:20
life is statistical i. DAWK 259:15
improbable i. possibilities ARIS 25:23

INSECURITY · **INVENT** 985

one is but an i. JOHN 427:13
'Tortis' is a i. PUNC 637:12
transformed into a gigantic i. KAFK 440:18
insecurity international i. NIEB 563:16
insensibility stark i. JOHN 427:6
inseparable one and i. WEBS 825:12
inside i. the tent pissing out JOHN 423:16
insight i. and the stretch BROW 158:10
insignificance of the utmost i. CURZ 254:10
sterling i. AUST 40:9
insignificant i. and is aware of it BECK 60:19
i. office ADAM 3:2
insincerity enemy of clear language i. ORWE 578:2
mark of i. of purpose BRAM 149:9
insinuating sly, i. Jacks SHAK 716:25
insolence flown with i. and wine MILT 531:21
i. is not invective DISR 275:15
i. of wealth JOHN 431:6
supports with i. JOHN 424:13
insomnia *mittunt i. Manes* VIRG 812:17
suffering from ideal i. JOYC 437:3
inspiration Genius is one per cent i. EDIS 296:5
inspire our souls i. BOOK 144:13
inspired i. by divine revelation BACO 42:17
inspissated i. gloom JOHN 429:5
instability mark of i. GALB 338:2
instant i. in season BIBL 110:30
instantaneous i. courage NAPO 556:17
instinct believe upon i. BRAD 148:18
coward on i. SHAK 690:13
healthy i. for it BUTL 177:1
intimate with by i. AUST 39:4
instincts i. and abilities BALZ 54:6
panders to i. BENN 67:10
true to your i. LAWR 474:24
institute on in the I. BETJ 72:16
institution change an i. TUSA 803:1
in a long term i. DURY 293:10
i. which does not suppose ROBE 650:6
It's an i. HUGH 407:14
place, person, or i. ARNO 30:17
transformed into an i. SART 667:14
institutional i. racism MACP 505:4
institutions acquiring their i. by chance HAIL 367:15
amending her own i. GODW 352:6
with their dirty i. THOR 793:10
instruct i. them AURE 38:11
when they might i. MORE 548:5
instructing same time as i. him HORA 398:13
instruction benefits of i. DEFO 261:5
better the i. SHAK 709:15
horses of i. BLAK 121:6
i. in the Law JAIN 416:10
I. is the pill RICH 647:18
needs no i. JAIN 416:5
no i. book came with it FULL 337:1
instructions AWAITING I. TELE 776:4
instrument i. of science JOHN 424:4
i. of Your peace FRAN 332:6
I tune the i. DONN 280:1
State is an i. STAL 754:1
instrumental i. to the brain SHAK 683:22
original or i. HOBB 390:11
instruments i. of their crooked designs GODW 352:4
with the aid of the i. HOLB 392:11
insubstantial this i. pageant SHAK 719:1
insufferable Oxford has made me i. BEER 63:2
insular i. country, subject to fogs DISR 277:10
insularum *Paene i.* CATU 202:16
insult blockhead's i. JOHN 426:12
i. to injuries MOOR 546:10
sooner forgotten than an i. CHES 214:24
threatened her with i. BURK 167:13
insulted never *hope* to get i. DAVI 259:5
insulting i. Christmas card GROS 365:7
insupportable i. labour STEE 754:16
insuppressible i. island KETT 450:8
insurance carry i. on those CHAN 207:13
form of moral i. BROD 152:1
National compulsory i. CHUR 221:17
intact is there, i. TRIM 798:17
intangible world i., we touch THOM 791:14
integer *I. vitae* HORA 400:17
integers God made the i. KRON 462:1
integral i. and differential calculus GILB 348:28
integration policy of European i. KOHL 459:2
integrity I. has no need of rules CAMU 188:14
i. of my intellect FARA 314:17
i. without knowledge JOHN 426:4
virgin white i. DONN 279:16
intellect highest i. MACA 498:10
integrity of my i. FARA 314:17
i. of man is forced to choose YEAT 853:11
march of i. SOUT 749:11
not i. but rather memory LEON 481:1
Our meddling i. WORD 850:13
put on I. BLAK 120:16
restless and versatile i. HUXL 412:4
scepticism of the i. NEWM 560:15
strengthening one's i. KEAT 447:3
tickle the i. LAMB 464:18
intellects hearts and i. EPIT 311:14
intellectual i. ability ARNO 30:14
i. All-in-all WORD 849:2
i., amongst the noblest CALV 186:10
i. bankruptcy HOLM 393:6
i. degradation MORE 548:6
I. disgrace Stares AUDE 35:6
i. eunuch Castlereagh BYRO 180:4
i. improvement JOHN 429:22
i. is someone whose mind CAMU 188:7
i. nature JOHN 425:7
'I.' suggests AUDE 35:14
i. sumo wrestling HARV 374:21
ladies i. BYRO 180:6
no i. superiority AUST 38:15
practical i. STRO 762:14
tear is an i. thing BLAK 120:11
to the i. world STER 757:8
intellectuals treachery of the i. BEND 66:9
intelligence arresting human i. LEAC 476:13
bewitchment of our i. WITT 842:7
endowed with i. DOST 283:8
I. is quickness to apprehend WHIT 832:12
people have little i. LA B 462:16
started at the i. SOUT 749:16
you pawn your i. CUMM 253:7
intelligencies we are The i. DONN 280:21
intelligent Every i. voter ADAM 2:4
most i. and most stupid CONF 238:10
Most i., very elegant BUCK 163:6
not necessarily i. CHAM 207:6
pleasing one i. man MAIM 507:16
rule of i. tinkering EHRL 297:7
so i. ELIO 303:15
intemperance brisk i. of youth GIBB 345:13
intend what I well i. SHAK 699:20
intensity full of passionate i. YEAT 855:12
intent first avowed i. BUNY 165:7
glorious great i. SPEN 751:17
i. is al CHAU 213:13
sides of my i. SHAK 704:7
told with bad i. BLAK 119:10
intention i. to keep my counsel GLAD 351:2
intentions devour second i. RABE 639:18
i. make blackguards LACL 463:5
only had good i. THAT 787:2
paved with good i. PROV 630:12
produced by their good i. WALP 819:20
inter hugger-mugger to i. him SHAK 688:10
interact do not i. at all UPDI 805:22
intercession made i. BIBL 90:5
interdependence closely knit i. HARD 372:7
interdependent everything is i. ZOHA 859:1
interest compete for her i. LEWI 484:1
i.'s on the dangerous edge BROW 158:16
i. that keeps peace CROM 252:4
its duty and its i. WASH 822:10
language of i. HELV 380:16
natural i. of money MACA 498:7
passion or i. LOCK 488:14
regard to their own i. SMIT 741:5
unbound by any i. HORA 400:1
interested i. him no more HART 374:17
i. in life CHAM 206:16
i. in the arts AYCK 41:4
i. in things CURI 254:3
only i. in art SHAW 727:26
interesting i. actions BAGE 48:12
i., but tough TWAI 803:4
proposition be i. WHIT 832:9
things and characters i. SCOT 674:27
Very i. . . . but CATC 201:30
interests Our i. are eternal PALM 584:19
pursue their respective i. JEVO 421:19
interjection is but an I. BYRO 182:2
interline diminish, i. SWIF 767:7
interlude present is an i. O'NE 573:14
intermission i. of pain SELD 676:10
internal i. attrition AURE 38:7
international dependable i. emotion ALSO 12:20
i. wrong AUDE 36:3
Internationale *L'I.* POTT 608:11
internationals Cambridge, Blackheath, and five I. DOYL 284:21
Internet I. is an élite CHOM 218:11
I., nobody knows you're a dog CART 198:7
thanks to the I. WILE 837:17
interpose i. my body STRA 762:3
interpretation lost in i. FROS 336:10
interpretations interpreting i. MONT 545:3
interpret i. DERR 265:7
interpreted i. the world MARX 517:1
interpreter i. is the hardest SHER 733:7
i. of nature WHEW 831:15
interpreters i. between us and the millions MACA 500:1
interrèd good is oft i. SHAK 697:21
intersecting i. monologues WEST 830:13
interstellar vacant i. spaces ELIO 301:17
interstice every i. of my body EDDI 295:5
interstices i. between the intersections JOHN 424:11
intervals lucid i. BACO 46:6
lucid intervals of i. WORD 846:9
intervening i. windings WHAR 831:2
interview strange and fatal i. DONN 279:10
interviewer i. allows you to say BENN 67:6
intestines product of the smaller i. CARL 192:2
intimacy avoid any i. KITC 457:14
determine i. AUST 40:10
every old i. LAMB 464:10
intimate i. with by instinct AUST 39:4
intimidation without i. ROBE 650:9
intolerable burden of them is i. BOOK 131:18
intolerance I. of groups FREU 334:2
intolerant not to tolerate the i. POPP 607:2
intoxicated God-i. man NOVA 565:20
i. with power BURK 166:3
when he is i. JOHN 431:13
intoxication best of life is but i. BYRO 180:22
intreat I. me not to leave thee BIBL 80:2
intrepid natural and i. WALP 818:18
intricated Poor i. soul DONN 282:12
intrigues I. half-gathered CRAB 248:29
intrinsicate knot i. Of life SHAK 680:14
introduce allow me to i. myself JAGG 415:17
introduced been i. to CARR 196:3
introduction i. to any literary work JOHN 427:19
pages of I. ELIO 300:24
introibo *I. at altare Dei* MISS 536:12
introitum *i. nobis ad vitam dedit* SENE 676:30
intruding rash, i. fool SHAK 687:22
intrusion I call it i. SPAR 749:28
invades first i. the ear DRYD 287:26
i. authors like a monarch DRYD 290:5
invalid i. called Bunbury WILD 835:13
invasion i. by an idea HUGO 407:17
invective insolence is not i. DISR 275:15
invent first i. the universe SAGA 663:2

of the stock of I.	BIBL 110:2	put there by J. Nastys	HUGH 407:11	J. is all the fun	JONG 434:13
out-casts of I.	BOOK 144:3	This J., joke	HOPK 397:7	j. is cruel as the grave	BIBL 87:22
prophet in I.	BIBL 82:6	**jackals** J. piss at their foot	FLAU 325:15	J. is feeling alone	BOWE 148:3
sweet psalmist of I.	BIBL 81:7	**jackdaw** J. sat on the Cardinal's chair		j. of rivals	ADAM 1:15
These be thy gods, O I.	BIBL 78:8		BARH 55:14	j. to the bride	BARR 57:6
waters of I.	BIBL 82:7	**jacket** short j.	EDWA 296:10	j. with a halo	WELL 828:18
Israelite Behold an I.	BIBL 102:26	thresh his old j.	COWP 248:25	No j. Was understood	MILT 533:14
Israelites I. passed over	BIBL 79:10	**jackknife** j. has Macheath	BREC 150:13	resting from all j.	BEAU 60:8
isst Der Mensch ist, was er i.	FEUE 317:4	**jacks** calls the knaves, J.	DICK 269:13	To j. nothing is more frighful	SAGA 663:4
issue happy i.	BOOK 129:19	**Jackson** J. with his Virginians	BEE 62:9	tyrant, tyrant J.	DRYD 288:29
honest madam's i.	SHAK 699:24	**Jacob** as the Angel did with J.	WALT 821:4	**Jeanie** J. with the light brown hair	
ist Der Mensch i., was er isst	FEUE 317:4	God of J.	BIBL 77:21		FOST 330:13
isthmus i. of a middle state	POPE 604:32	God of J.	BOOK 136:25	**jeans** blue j. and Coca-Cola	GREE 363:5
it It's just I.	KIPL 457:7	house of J.	BOOK 142:2	**jeepers** J. Creepers	MERC 522:9
Italia I.! oh Italia	BYRO 179:6	J. served seven years	BIBL 76:33	**jeering** laughing and j.	PEPY 592:3
Italian fair as an I. sun	BANV 54:19	J. was a plain man	BIBL 76:25	**jeers** flouts and j.	DISR 276:13
Proosian, Or perhaps I.	GILB 348:26	sold his birthright unto J.	BIBL 76:26	**Jeeves** J. shimmered out	WODE 842:17
to women I.	CHAR 209:13	traffic of J.'s ladder	THOM 791:16	**Jefferson** J.—still surv—	LAST 474:7
Italianato Inglese I.	ASCH 31:7	voice is J.'s voice	BIBL 76:28	**Jehovah** O thou great J.	WILL 838:9
Italie soleil d'I.	BANV 54:19	**jade** Go spin, you J.	SCOT 674:26	**Jehu** J., the son of Nimshi	BIBL 82:12
Italy after seeing I.	BURN 169:22	Let the galled j. wince	SHAK 687:7	**Jekyll** Dr J. and Mr Hyde	STEV 759:8
bought his doublet in I.	SHAK 708:27	**jades** pampered j.	MARL 513.26	**Jellicoe** J. was the only man on either side	
do I pursue I.	VIRG 812:4	pampered j. of Asia	SHAK 692:1		CHUR 222:17
first to hail, 'I.!'	VIRG 811:23	**Jael** J. Heber's wife	BIBL 79:16	**jellies** With j. soother	KEAT 443:2
has not been in I.	JOHN 430:21	**JAH** his name J.	BOOK 138:11	**jelly** blasted, j.-boned swines	LAWR 475:11
In I. under the Borgias	FILM 319:19	**jail** being in a j.	JOHN 427:23	J.-bellied Flag-flapper	KIPL 457:6
inside of it, 'I.'	BROW 159:6	dey gits you in j.	O'NE 573:8	Meaty j., too	DICK 271:19
I. is a geographical expression	METT 523:11	Go to j.	SAYI 669:22	nail currant j.	ROOS 654:9
made I. from designs	TWAI 803:15	patron, and the j.	JOHN 426:16	Out, vile j.	SHAK 701:5
Oh, my own I.	PETR 593:17	**jailbird** looks like a j.	BLOK 123:15	**jellybeans** way of eating j.	REAG 643:13
Paradise of exiles, I.	SHEL 729:16	**jails** emptied the British j.	DAY- 260:5	**Jena** J. came twenty years after	BISM 118:1
itch i. of literature	LOVE 493:12	**jam** j. to-morrow	CARR 195:10	**je-ne-sais-quoi** J. young man	GILB 348:16
poor i. of your opinion	SHAK 682:13	J. tomorrow	PROV 624:31	**Jenny** J. kissed me	HUNT 409:18
itching have an i. palm	SHAK 698:13	j. we thought was for	BENN 66:18	**jeopardy** in j. of their lives	BIBL 81:8
ite I. domum saturae	VIRG 814:11	**jamais** j. triste archy	MARQ 514:3	**jerks** bring me up by j.	DICK 269:15
I. missa est	MISS 539:11	**James** Bond. J. Bond	FILM 320:9	**Jerusalem** hills stand about J.	BOOK 142:2
iteration damnable i.	SHAK 689:23	Home J.	HILL 388:16	holy city, new J.	BIBL 114:16
i. of the nuptials	CONG 239:18	J. I, James II, and the Old Pretender		In that J.	SHAK 692:19
itself Everything is not i.	RILK 648:14		GUED 365:12	J. is built as a city	BOOK 142:18
Forever be I. again	GINS 349:14	J. James Morrison Morrison	MILN 527:21	J. the golden	NEAL 558:2
itur sic i. ad astra	VIRG 813:9	King J. stay behind	WHAR 831:5	J. thy sister calls	BLAK 120:14
Itylus half assuaged for I.	SWIN 767:25	**Jameson** RAID BY DR J.	TELE 776:3	Next year in J.	HAGG 367:5
iubeo sic i.	JUVE 439:20	**Jane** J., Jane, tall as a crane	SITW 738:14	O Jerusalem, J.	BIBL 98:12
iubes i. renovare dolorem	VIRG 811:9	you J.	MISQ 538:8	peace of J.	BOOK 142:19
ludaeus Credat I. Apella	HORA 403:10	**Janus** very J. of poets	DRYD 290:7	performed in J.	BOOK 138:5
iudice se I.	JUVE 440:13	**janvier** J. and Février	NICH 563:8	Till we have built J.	BLAK 121:15
sub i. lis est	HORA 398:4	**japan** J.'s advantage	HIRO 389:17	unto J.	BIBL 105:23
iunctura Reddiderit i. novum	HORA 398:1	**jar** does so j.	GASK 340:21	waste places of J.	BIBL 89:29
iurare i. in verba magistri	HORA 398:18	**jargon** from J. born to rescue Law		**jessamine** casement j. stirred	TENN 781:24
ivory as if done in i.	FULL 337:3		LLOY 487:11	j. faint	SHEL 731:15
belly is as bright i.	BIBL 87:16	j. of languages	DEFO 261:2	pale j.	MILT 530:8
cargo of i.	MASE 517:12	**jargons** clear of the j.	NIGH 564:14	**Jesse** stem of J.	BIBL 88:20
gleaming white i.	VIRG 812:17	**Jarndyce** J. and Jarndyce	DICK 267:13	**jesses** j. were my dear heart-strings	
in his i. tower	SAIN 663:7	Wards in J.	DICK 268:1		SHAK 713:28
i., and apes	BIBL 81:13	**Jason** J. hath received	BIBL 105:15	**jest** bitter is a scornful j.	JOHN 426:12
i. on which I work	AUST 40:18	**jasper** j. and a sardine stone	BIBL 113:7	cover of a j.	HORA 403:3
neck is as a tower of i.	BIBL 87:21	**jaundiced** yellow to the j. eye	POPE 604:14	fellow of infinite j.	SHAK 688:28
out of the i. gate	BROW 157:13	**javelin** hunter's j.	ARNO 28:15	good j. for ever	SHAK 690:1
upon an i. sled	MARL 513:17	**jaw** j.-jaw is always better	CHUR 222:3	j.'s prosperity	SHAK 702:24
ivy As creeping i. clings	COWP 247:12	let the j. go by	PROV 624:32	laughing at some j.	KIPL 454:3
holly and the i.	SONG 747:10	with the j. of an ass	BIBL 79:32	Life is a j.	EPIT 310:13
it was agony, I.	CATC 200:15	**jaws** gently smiling j.	CARR 194:1	poison in j.	SHAK 687:6
pluck an i. branch for me	ROSS 655:10	Into the j. of Death	TENN 776:15	that's no j.	RALE 641:4
yonder i.-mantled tow'r	GRAY 361:1	j. of hell	VIRG 812:12	true word spoken in j.	PROV 626:11
		j. of power	ADAM 3:6	world's a j.	STEP 755:20
		through the j. of death	LAUD 470:3	**jesting** talking, nor j.	BIBL 109:14
Jabberwock Beware the J., my son		**jay-bird** j. say ter der squinch-owl		**jests** He j. at scars	SHAK 717:15
	CARR 194:25		HARR 374:4	to his memory for his j.	SHER 734:6
jack about J. a Nory	NURS 567:12	**jazz** J. music is to be played	MORT 551:7	**Jesu** J., good above all other	DEAR 260:11
Damn you, J.	BONE 127:6	sunbathing and j.	WAUG 824:9	J., lover of my soul	WESL 828:26
Every J. has his Jill	PROV 619:10	**jealous** am a j. God	BIBL 78:1	J., the very thought	CASW 199:3
good J. makes a good Jill	PROV 621:10	Art is a j. mistress	EMER 306:19	**Jesuit** thing, a tool, a J.	KING 453:3
house that J. built	NURS 570:2	As thou Art j., Lord	DONN 279:25	**Jesus** another king, one J.	BIBL 105:15
J. and Jill	NURS 567:15	J. in honour	SHAK 681:11	at the name of J.	BIBL 109:25
J. as good as his master	PROV 624:29	one not easily j.	SHAK 714:30	At the name of J.	NOEL 565:6
J. became a gentleman	SHAK 716:26	to the j.	SHAK 713:31	blame J. for what was done	BENN 67:2
J. be nimble	NURS 567:16	tramp is j. of tramp	HESI 387:3	bon Sansculotte J.	DESM 265:14
J. of all trades	PROV 624:30	**jealousy** Anger and j.	ELIO 300:11	come, Lord J.	BIBL 114:25
J. shall have Jill	SHAK 711:19	beware, my lord, of j.	SHAK 713:27	cross of J.	BARI 56:4
J. Sprat could eat no fat	NURS 567:17	cold age, narrow j.	ROCH 651:4	disciple whom J. loved	BIBL 104:23
Little J. Horner	NURS 568:2	ear of j.	BIBL 92:20	Gentle J.	WESL 829:1
makes J. a dull boy	PROV 614:20	J. a human face	BLAK 122:22	If J. Christ were to come	CARL 193:5
news of my boy J.	KIPL 455:5	j. extinguishes love	MARG 512:5	J. Christ	BIBL 111:15

justice (*cont.*):
What use of J.   ANDR 14:10
which is the j.   SHAK 701:16
you have ravished j.   WEBS 826:8
justifiable j. act of war   BELL 64:12
j. to men   MILT 534:29
justification j. . . . . terms   ARNO 30:2
justified confessions of a j. sinner
  HOGG 392:10
no man living be j.   BOOK 143:22
Wisdom is j.   BIBL 96:26
justifies end j. the means   BUSE 174:20
end j. the means   PROV 618:41
justify j. God's ways   HOUS 405:2
j. the ways of God   MILT 531:6
men j. him   BIBL 93:15
justitia *Fiat j.*   MOTT 552:8
justly do j.   BIBL 92:9
justum *Dignum et j.*   MISS 536:23
juvenes *Gaudeamus igitur, J. dum sumus*
  ANON 21:17

K wear the Five Ks   SIKH 737:13
Kaaba My House [K.]   KORA 460:17
kaim siller k.   BALL 52:9
Kaiser put the kibosh on the K.   ELLE 305:10
Kalends pay at the Greek K.   AUGU 37:23
Kansas corny as K. in August   HAMM 370:10
K. had better stop raising corn   LEAS 478:1
not in K. any more   FILM 320:20
karma bad k. which he had   JAIN 416:16
Karshish K., the picker-up   BROW 159:8
Kaspar Old K.'s work was done   SOUT 748:17
Kate K. of my consolation   SHAK 718:12
Kiss me K.   SHAK 718:13
Kathleen K. Ni Houlihan   CARB 190:4
Kathleen Mavourneen K.! the grey dawn
  CRAW 250:20
Keats K.'s vulgarity   LEAV 478:4
Kedar habitation among the tents of K.
  BOOK 142:14
keel Joan doth k. the pot   SHAK 702:26
keener edged tool that grows k.   IRVI 414:4
with his k. eye   MARV 515:18
keep honour, and k. her   BOOK 133:8
Ideas won't k.   WHIT 832:11
If you can k. your head   KIPL 454:12
I k. away   WALL 818:12
intention to k. my counsel   GLAD 351:2
K. a thing seven years   PROV 624:35
k. me, King of Kings   KEN 448:7
k. the bridge with me   MACA 499:14
k. thee in all thy ways   BOOK 140:4
k. who can   WORD 849:25
k. your England   MUGA 553:6
many to k.   KING 452:22
shop will k. you   PROV 624:38
some day it'll k. you   WEST 830:2
ware that will not k.   HOUS 404:8
will not k. her long   SHAK 716:24
keeper Lord himself is thy k.   BOOK 142:16
my brother's k.   BIBL 75:28
keepers Finders k.   PROV 620:2
k. of the walls   BIBL 87:15
keepeth he that k. thee   BOOK 142:16
keepings Findings k.   PROV 620:3
keeps gave it us for k.   AYRE 41:11
Kelly K. from the Isle of Man   MURP 554:21
Kempenfeld When K. went down
  COWP 247:3
ken D'ye k. John Peel   GRAV 360:2
Kendal Mr K. is going to be confirmed
  TENN 785:1
kenne *k. mich auch nicht*   GOET 353:19
Kennedy you're no Jack K.   BENT 69:3
Kennedys Who killed the K.   JAGG 416:1
kennst *K. du das Land*   GOET 353:12
Kensal Green Paradise by way of K.
  CHES 216:11
Kent everybody knows K.   DICK 271:26
Kentish K. Sir Byng   BROW 160:5
Kentucky Long ago in K.   WARR 822:1

kept k. the faith   BIBL 111:1
k. them in thy name   BIBL 103:39
What wee k., wee lost   EPIT 311:16
kersey honest k. noes   SHAK 702:23
Ketch as Jack K.'s wife said   DRYD 290:14
kettle back to the tea-k.   DISR 275:11
filled with the k.'s breath   HILL 388:9
k. and the earthen pot   BIBL 93:14
Polly put the k.   NURS 569:4
speech is like a cracked k.   FLAU 324:22
Kew Go down to K.   NOYE 566:1
his Highness' dog at K.   POPE 602:21
key golden k. can open   PROV 621:3
I keep the k.   MONT 543:13
just hands on that golden k.   MILT 528:18
k. of India   DISR 276:22
k. of knowledge   BIBL 100:30
k. of the Union   CLAY 226:5
out of k. with his time   POUN 608:17
possession of the k.   PAIN 582:7
Turn the k.   KEAT 445:13
With this k. Shakespeare   WORD 849:26
keyboards people want k.   JOBS 422:2
keys half that's got my k.   GRAH 358:7
k. of all the creeds   TENN 778:30
k. of hell and of death   BIBL 112:30
k. of my prison   DONN 281:22
massy k. he bore   MILT 530:5
pattered with his k.   BYRO 183:18
keystone k. which closeth   STRA 762:5
Khatmandu to the north of K.   HAYE 376:7
kibosh put the k. on the Kaiser   ELLE 305:10
kick first k. I took   SPRI 753:10
get no k. from champagne   PORT 607:12
Got to k. at the darkness   COCK 229:22
great k. at misery   LAWR 475:12
k. against the pricks   BIBL 105:3
k. his wife out of bed   SURT 764:13
k. me downstairs   BICK 115:20
k. to come to the top   KEAT 446:11
k. you downstairs   CARR 194:5
kicked k. up stairs   HALI 369:10
no body to be k.   THUR 794:4
kicking flattering, kissing and k.   TRUM 801:6
K. you seems the common lot   BROW 161:30
running fast and k. something   FANT 314:13
kid comeback k.   CLIN 227:7
Here's looking at you, k.   FILM 319:10
lie down with the k.   BIBL 88:21
kiddies k. have crumpled the serviettes
  BETJ 72:7
kidding k., Mister Hitler   PERR 593:4
kidneys k. on a plate   HILL 388:14
liked grilled mutton k.   JOYC 437:19
kids don't have any k. yourself   LARK 469:3
how many k. did you kill   POLI 600:19
just a couple of k.   OPEN 575:2
kill able to k.   RUMS 658:10
as k. a good book   MILT 535:14
bombers to k. the babies   LE G 479:7
get out and k. something   LEAC 476:15
Guns don't k. people   SLOG 740:3
half-kisses k. me quite   DRAY 286:5
how many kids did you k.   POLI 600:19
in every war they k. you in a new way
  ROGE 652:20
Just how many did we k.   LEWI 483:17
k. a king   SHAK 687:21
k. all the lawyers   SHAK 694:20
k. a mockingbird   LEE 478:16
k. animals and stick in stamps   NICO 563:13
k. a wife with kindness   SHAK 718:14
k. care   SHAK 712:32
K. me to-morrow   SHAK 714:21
K. millions of men   ROST 656:16
K. not the moth   BLAK 119:9
k. sick people   MARL 513:14
k. them all   ARNA 26:20
k. the patient   BACO 44:16
k. us for their sport   SHAK 701:8
k. you if you quote it   BURG 165:19
K. your parents or relatives   I-HS 412:20
licence to k.   FLEM 326:10

licensed to k.   FILM 319:15
Licensed to k.   MISQ 538:6
not to k. anything   JAIN 416:18
or I k. you   CHAM 207:8
Otherwise k. me   MACN 504:20
prepared to k. one another   SHAW 725:28
something you k. for   BENN 67:3
they k. people   TAGL 771:12
Thou shalt not k.   BIBL 78:5
Thou shalt not k.   CLOU 229:5
time to k.   BIBL 85:32
we are going to k. it   POWE 609:17
won't k. me   COLL 235:7
would k. their church   TENN 782:3
killed Better be k.   SURT 764:19
Care k. the cat   PROV 616:24
Curiosity k. the cat   PROV 617:19
don't mind your being k.   KITC 457:15
I am the enemy you k.   OWEN 581:8
If hate k. men   BROW 161:12
I'm k., Sire   BROW 159:26
I was k.   LAST 472:17
k. in the war   POWE 610:4
k. with my own treachery   SHAK 689:10
King Harold was k.   ANON 22:9
kissed thee ere I k. thee   SHAK 715:2
so many people k.   AUST 40:14
(who k. him) thought   BELL 65:22
killer lover and k. are mingled   DOUG 283:18
killeth letter k.   BIBL 108:13
killing assert their manhood by k.
  WAUG 824:16
K. myself   SHAK 715:2
K. no murder   PROV 624:39
K. no murder   SEXB 677:12
k. time Is only the name   SITW 739:1
medal for k. two men   MATL 518:13
talk of k. time   BOUC 147:4
ways of k. a cat   PROV 631:45
ways of k. a dog   PROV 631:46
ways of k. a dog   PROV 631:47
kills grip that k. it   TAGO 770:16
k. all its pupils   BERL 70:7
k.. all known germs   ADVE 7:42
k. the thing he loves   WILD 836:29
pace that k.   PROV 624:15
pity k.   BALZ 54:9
suicide k. two people   MILL 527:2
that which k.   DE B 260:12
waking that k. us   BROW 157:11
Kiltartan My country is K. Cross   YEAT 854:15
kilted k. her green kirtle   BALL 53:8
kimonos girls in silk k.   YEAT 854:12
kin little more than k.   SHAK 683:23
makes the whole world k.   SHAK 719:24
one's own k. and kith   NASH 557:10
kind cruel only to be k.   SHAK 687:31
cruel to be k.   COMP 236:18
enjoy her while she's k.   DRYD 289:31
fordon the lawe of k.   CHAU 212:29
for my own k.   THOM 791:1
had been k.   JOHN 427:18
if ye be k. towards women   KORA 460:8
K. are her answers   CAMP 188:6
k. as she is fair   SHAK 721:23
K. hearts are more than coronets
  TENN 780:4
k. parent to man   PLIN 598:3
less than k.   SHAK 683:23
makes one wond'rous k.   GARR 340:4
People will always be k.   SASS 667:17
Too k., too kind   NIGH 564:16
kindergarten kind of k.   ROBI 650:16
kindest k. and the best   BURN 171:25
k. man   MALO 509:3
kindle And k. it   LITT 486:16
kindled K. he was, and blasted   BYRO 178:26
kindliness cool k. of sheets   BROO 153:6
kindling it only requires k.   PLUT 598:13
kindly k. fruits of the earth   BOOK 129:14
kindness breath of k.   ANON 18:5
generates k.   JOHN 427:5
good human behaviour is k.   ROOS 653:6

kill a wife with k. SHAK 718:14
k. and lies are worth GREE 362:12
K. in another's trouble GORD 356:17
k. in reserve POPE 602:30
k. to his Majesty HALL 369:15
milk of human k. GUED 365:11
milk of human k. SHAK 703:18
Of k. and of love WORD 847:7
on the k. of strangers WILL 839:11
spontaneous k. JOHN 431:28
tak a cup o' k. yet BURN 170:9
kindnesses thought of k. done CATU 203:5
kine seven fat k. BIBL 77:4
king a' for our rightfu' K. BURN 171:13
all the k.'s men NURS 567:10
another k., one Jesus BIBL 105:15
As to the K. CHAR 208:26
authority forgets a dying k. TENN 778:13
authority of a K. STRA 762:5
banners of the k. advance FORT 330:4
blessedness alone that makes a K.
TRAH 798:1
born K. of the Jews BIBL 94:5
but yesterday a K. BYRO 182:25
cat may look at a k. PROV 616:28
coming of the K. of Heaven ANON 20:6
Conscience as their K. TENN 777:20
constitutional k. BAGE 48:18
Cotton is K. CHRI 218:17
cotton is k. HUGO 407:19
cuts off his k.'s head SHAW 727:3
despised and dying k. SHEL 731:20
divinity doth hedge a k. SHAK 688:11
duty is the k.'s SHAK 693:16
every inch a k. SHAK 701:13
fight for its K. and Country GRAH 358:4
five kings did a k. to death THOM 789:11
follow the K. TENN 777:18
God bless the K. BYRO 177:19
God for K. Charles BROW 160:6
God save k. Solomon BIBL 81:9
God save our gracious k. SONG 747:7
God save the k. BIBL 80:11
God save the k. SHAK 716:7
God save the k. SONG 747:7
government without a k. BANC 54:13
great and mighty k. EPIT 309:14
greater than the K. PITT 596:4
hath eat of a k. SHAK 687:36
have served the K. WOLS 844:12
heaven's matchless k. MILT 532:23
He played the K. FIEL 317:10
He that plays the k. SHAK 685:25
Honour the k. BIBL 112:7
If the K. asks you ATTL 33:7
illiterate k. HENR 382:3
image of the K. TENN 777:24
in the K.'s throne BENT 68:6
kill a k. SHAK 687:21
K. and country need you MILI 526:19
K. asked the Queen MILN 528:2
K. can do no wrong BLAC 118:11
K. can do no wrong PROV 624:40
K. Charles's head DICK 268:16
K. David and King Solomon NAYL 557:23
k. delighteth to honour BIBL 82:24
K. enjoys his own again PARK 586:13
k. had given me Paris ANON 21:2
K. Harold was killed ANON 22:9
K. in Babylon HENL 381:17
k. indeed CHAP 208:10
k. is a thing men have made SELD 676:7
k. is but a man SHAK 693:14
k. is strongest BIBL 92:15
k. is truly *parens patriae* JAME 417:4
k. loved his people WILL 838:4
k. never dies BLAC 118:9
K., observing with judicious TRAP 798:4
K. of all these the dead HOME 394:16
k. of banks and stones KAVA 442:7
K. of England cannot enter PITT 596:2
K. of England's eyes LAST 473:2
K. of glory BOOK 135:6

K. of glory now NOEL 565:6
K. of Great Britain REED 644:12
K. of heaven LYTE 497:11
k. of infinite space SHAK 685:23
k. of intimate delights COWP 248:8
k. of kings BIBL 114:12
K. of love BAKE 50:2
k. of my own little island SMAL 739:12
k. of shreds and patches SHAK 687:27
k. of the castle NURS 567:14
K. OF THE JEWS BIBL 104:4
K. of tremendous majesty MISS 539:17
k. of Yvetot BÉRA 69:5
k. over himself SHEL 731:8
K. over the Water TOAS 796:5
K. refused a lesser sacrifice MARY 517:9
k. reigns THIE 788:1
k.'s a bawcock SHAK 693:11
King's a K. DRAY 285:21
k.'s chaff is worth PROV 624:41
K.'s daughter BOOK 136:22
k.'s daughter o' Noroway BALL 53:4
k.'s English SHAK 710:11
k. sits in Dunfermline BALL 53:3
k. sits in Dunfermline OPEN 574:30
K.'s life moving peacefully DAWS 259:19
K.'s Moll Reno'd NEWS 562:16
k.'s name SHAK 717:5
K. thought mair o' Marie BALL 52:17
K. to have things done as cheap PEPY 592:2
K. to Oxford sent BROW 157:14
K. was in his counting-house NURS 569:14
k. was much moved BIBL 81:5
K. was much pleased EDGE 296:4
lay on the k. SHAK 693:17
leave without the k. ELIZ 305:7
lessened my esteem of a k. PEPY 592:1
Lord is K. BOOK 140:6
loses the k. in the tyrant MAYH 519:15
man who would be k. KIPL 456:25
Moloch, horrid k. MILT 531:18
My dead k. JOYC 437:8
my K. and my God BOOK 139:15
my life to make you K. CHAR 209:8
neck of the last k. DIDE 273:17
No bishop, no K. JAME 417:2
no k. can govern ROCH 651:2
no k. in Israel BIBL 79:37
Northcliffe has sent for the K. ANON 16:7
not offended the k. LAST 474:3
not so much a k. SELL 676:22
Og the k. of Basan BOOK 143:10
once and future k. MALO 509:4
one eyed man is k. PROV 623:34
open The k.'s eyes SHAK 695:7
oure k. wes dede WYNT 852:17
Ozymandias, k. of kings SHEL 730:18
passing brave to be a k. MARL 513:20
rightwise K. MALO 508:18
Ruin seize thee, ruthless K. GRAY 360:20
sang a k. out of three kingdoms WHAR 831:6
shake hands with a k. HALL 369:15
sitting at the k.'s gate BIBL 82:22
smote the k. of Israel BIBL 81:34
speaks ill of your k. NELS 558:12
still am I k. of those SHAK 716:8
stomach of a k. ELIZ 304:7
stood for his K. BROW 160:5
thy k. is a child BIBL 86:18
To be a Pirate K. GILB 348:27
What is a K. PRIO 612:8
What must the k. do SHAK 715:26
whatsoever K. shall reign SONG 747:12
When I am k. NURS 567:19
With a k.'s son SURR 764:7
you must not be a k. CHAR 208:24
your K. and your Country RUBE 658:3
zeal I served my k. SHAK 695:16
kingdom but to mock the k. PYM 638:13
comest into thy k. BIBL 102:5
enter into the k. of heaven BIBL 94:25
found a k. MILT 534:18
His mind his k. COWP 248:23

into the k. of heaven BIBL 97:19
k. against kingdom BIBL 98:14
k. by the sea POE 598:18
k. for a little grave SHAK 716:2
k. for it was too small SHAK 691:13
k. of God BIBL 95:10
k. of God BIBL 97:27
k. of God BIBL 102:30
k. of God is within you BIBL 101:24
k. of heaven BIBL 94:20
k. of heaven BIBL 97:5
k. of heaven is at hand BIBL 94:9
k. of the shore SHAK 723:7
k. shall pass SWIN 768:23
k. stretch from shore to shore WATT 823:19
mind to me a k. is DYER 293:13
my k. for a horse SHAK 717:10
My k., safeliest DONN 279:13
of such is the k. of God BIBL 99:25
thine is the k. BIBL 95:3
Thy k. come BIBL 95:3
voice of the k. SWIF 765:7
kingdoms all the k. of the world BIBL 94:17
all the k. of the world BIBL 100:10
goodly states and k. KEAT 445:5
K. are clay SHAK 678:14
out of three k. WHAR 831:6
kingfish call me the K. LONG 489:15
kingfisher song of the k. VIRG 815:2
kingly K. conclaves stern SHEL 731:1
k. crop DAVI 258:4
kings all be as happy as k. STEV 760:3
All k. shall fall down BOOK 138:23
bind their k. in chains BOOK 144:8
captains and the k. KIPL 455:10
castles of k. HORA 400:5
Conquering k. CHAN 207:10
death of k. SHAK 715:23
dominion of k. changed PRIC 610:15
end of k. DEFO 261:28
five K. left FARO 315:6
heart of k. BIBL 85:2
keep even k. in awe D'AV 257:19
k. and counsellors BIBL 82:32
k. are not only God's lieutenants JAME 417:3
k. crept out again BROW 157:22
K.' daughters BOOK 136:21
k. haul up the lumps BREC 150:16
k. have cares GREE 362:23
K. have long arms PROV 624:42
K. have sat down BIBL 93:11
k. is mostly rapscallions TWAI 803:5
K. may be blest BURN 172:10
k. of the earth BIBL 113:15
k. of the earth BOOK 137:4
k. that fear SHAK 694:27
K. will be tyrants BURK 167:17
K. with their armies BOOK 138:12
K. would not play at COWP 248:12
last of the k. strangled MESL 523:7
laws or k. JOHN 426:14
laws or k. can cause GOLD 355:15
lays his icy hand on us SHIR 735:3
madness their k. commit HORA 399:3
Mad world! mad k. SHAK 699:2
meaner creatures k. SHAK 717:4
Of cabbages—and k. CARR 195:7
Physicians are like k. WEBS 825:27
poet k. KEAT 445:12
politeness of k. LOUI 492:13
prophets and k. have desired BIBL 100:21
puller down of k. SHAK 695:1
Right Divine of K. POPE 602:2
ruined sides of k. BEAU 60:6
ruin k. DRYD 286:18
Showers on her k. MILT 531:29
So many English k. SHAK 692:16
sport of k. D'AV 257:22
sport of k. SOME 745:21
sport of k. SURT 764:12
Vain the ambition of k. WEBS 825:19
walk with K. KIPL 454:13
War is the trade of k. DRYD 288:26

kinship crimson thread of k. PARK 586:15
kinsmen k. die ANON 22:12
Kipling K. and his views AUDE 35:7
Rudyards cease from k. STEP 756:1
kirtle kilted her green k. BALL 53:8
Near is my k. PROV 627:10
kiss Ae fond k. BURN 170:6
Close with her, k. her SWIN 769:8
clung into a k. BYRO 180:23
Colder thy k. BYRO 183:22
coward does it with a k. WILD 836:29
die upon a k. SHAK 715:2
Fain would I k. HERR 386:8
holy k. BIBL 107:1
I k. his dirty shoe SHAK 693:11
immortal with a k. MARL 513:4
k. a bonnie lass BURN 172:17
k. again with tears TENN 782:24
k., a sigh CRAS 250:18
k. but in the cup JONS 435:26
k. can be a comma MIST 540:4
k. is still a kiss HUPF 410:13
Kiss K. Bang Bang KAEL 440:16
k. me and never no more MALO 509:2
K. me, Hardy NELS 558:21
K. me Kate SHAK 718:13
k. my ass in Macy's window JOHN 423:15
k. of the sun for pardon GURN 365:20
k. on the hand ROBI 650:10
K. the book's outside COWP 246:11
k. the Managing Director WHIT 832:18
k. the place to make it well TAYL 774:15
k. the rod SHAK 721:20
last lamenting k. DONN 280:23
let me k. that hand SHAK 701:15
let us k. and part DRAY 285:23
O! a k. Long as my exile SHAK 682:24
rough male k. of blankets BROO 153:6
saw you take his k. PATM 588:15
she took the k. sedately TENN 781:20
sweetly did me k. WYAT 852:5
take occasion to k. SHAK 682:1
Then come k. me SHAK 720:16
wanting to k. me MACD 501:11
With one long k. TENN 776:22
Wouldst k. me pretty HART 374:14
kissed hasn't been k. MILI 526:14
k. each other BOOK 139:19
k. his sad Andromache CORN 243:9
k. thee ere I killed thee SHAK 715:2
k. the fiddler's wife BURN 172:1
K. the girls NURS 566:21
My lips k. dumb SWIN 769:5
never k. an ugly girl EPIT 310:3
wist, before I k. BALL 53:19
kisses fine romance with no k. FIEL 318:16
forgotten my k. SWIN 768:24
Give me a thousand k. CATU 202:14
k. are his daily feast LODG 489:8
k. of his mouth BIBL 87:2
Love's mart of k. CHAP 208:13
more than k. DONN 281:20
played At cards for k. LYLY 497:2
Stolen k. HUNT 409:19
sweet k., pigeon-wise DIAN 267:3
These poor half-k. DRAY 286:5
kissing I wasn't k. her MARX 516:8
K. don't last MERE 522:16
K. goes by favour PROV 624:43
k. had to stop BROW 161:23
k.'s out of fashion PROV 634:31
K. with golden face SHAK 723:2
k. your hand LOOS 491:19
like k. God BRUC 162:3
wonder who's k. her ADAM 2:3
kit have a K.-Kat ADVE 7:28
old k.-bag MILI 526:18
kitchen better mind the k. FITZ 323:18
brocades of the k. DAVI 258:3
get out of the k. PROV 623:14
get out of the k. TRUM 801:8
ghastly k. BERN 71:2
in the k. bred BYRO 183:6

K.-cabals, and nursery-mishaps CRAB 248:29
send me to eat in the k. HUGH 406:17
sitting in the k. sink OPEN 574:29
whip in k. cups STEV 757:21
kite not sufficient for a k.'s dinner
QUAR 638:18
kitten I had rather be a k. SHAK 690:23
kittens Three little k. NURS 570:6
Wanton k. make sober PROV 633:40
kitty K., a fair, but frozen maid GARR 340:7
Kjartan killed K. ANON 22:13
kleine eine k. Pause LAST 473:8
Klondike beer of a man in K. CHES 216:17
knappeth k. the spear in sunder
BOOK 136:26
knave epithet for a k. MACA 498:2
k. is not punished HALI 369:7
K. of Hearts he stole NURS 569:6
makes an honest man a k. DEFO 261:15
man must be supposed a k. HUME 409:7
slipper and subtle k. SHAK 713:20
To feed the titled k. BURN 173:2
knaves calls the k., Jacks DICK 269:13
fools and k. BUCK 163:8
k. in place DEFO 261:20
knee blude to the k. BALL 53:12
civility of my k. BROW 156:20
Every k. shall bow NOEL 565:6
every k. should bow BIBL 109:25
head on his k. BARH 56:1
little abune her k. BALL 53:8
kneel k. and adore him MONS 543:8
k. before him BOOK 138:23
k. before the Lord our Maker BOOK 140:10
k. for peace SHAK 718:17
kneeling meekly k. BOOK 131:17
knees body between your k. CORY 244:1
clasped in his hands his k. HOME 394:11
confirm the feeble k. BIBL 89:10
creeps rustling to her k. KEAT 442:21
I bow my k. BIBL 109:7
live on your k. IBAR 412:7
knell it is a k. SHAK 704:18
k. of parting day GRAY 360:24
like a rising k. BYRO 178:19
their k. is rung COLL 235:13
knew If you looked away, you k. SERE 677:4
I k. almost as much JOHN 428:14
I k. that once STEP 755:20
Johnny, I hardly k. ye BALL 52:8
k. it best BACO 43:21
K. YOU HAD IT IN YOU TELE 776:5
told what he k. AMIS 13:9
world k. him not BIBL 102:20
knife cannibal uses k. and fork LEC 478:8
deadly k. Long aimed FANS 314:10
k. is lost in it SHEL 729:23
k. see not the wound SHAK 703:21
k. that probes far deeper FORS 329:17
my oyster k. HURS 410:14
smylere with the k. CHAU 211:15
walk on a k. edge MONT 545:4
War to the k. PALA 583:2
will not use the k. HIPP 389:13
knight as the armèd k. ASKE 31:20
courteoust k. MALO 509:3
Fearless, blameless k. ANON 20:11
gentle k. was pricking SPEN 751:12
k. at arms KEAT 443:23
k.-errantry is religion CERV 205:11
k. like the young Lochinvar SCOT 673:19
K. of the Doleful Countenance CERV 205:9
k. was indeed a valiant Gent EVEL 313:1
monk and a k. HENR 382:8
new-slain k. BALL 53:15
red-cross k. for ever kneeled TENN 780:9
that was your k. CLOS 228:13
verray, parfit gentil k. CHAU 210:7
When a k. won his spurs STRU 762:17
knighthoods MBEs and your k. KEAT 442:9
knights ladies dead and lovely k.
SHAK 723:16
lances of ancient k. ROOT 654:17

knit k. together thine elect BOOK 131:2
life to k. me HOUS 404:15
knits k. man to man SICK 735:11
Sleep that k. up SHAK 704:24
knitter beautiful little k. SITW 738:19
knitters k. in the sun SHAK 720:25
knives night of the long k. HITL 389:24
knock k., and it shall be opened BIBL 95:15
K. as you please POPE 602:20
K. at a star HERR 385:17
k. at the door LAMB 464:15
k., breathe, shine DONN 279:21
k. him down first JOHN 430:18
k. is open wide SMAR 740:16
nice k.-down argument CARR 195:15
right to k. him down JOHN 431:17
stand at the door, and k. BIBL 113:6
when you k. COWP 246:10
knocked ruin that Cromwell k. about
BEDF 62:8
we k. the bastard off HILL 388:15
what they k. down FENT 316:11
knocker Tie up the k. POPE 602:23
knocking Here's a k., indeed SHAK 705:5
k. at Preferment's door ARNO 28:4
K. on the moonlit door DE L 263:2
K. on the moonlit door OPEN 574:21
knocks k. you down with the butt
GOLD 355:34
never k. twice PROV 629:8
knot crowned k. of fire ELIO 302:2
k. intrinsicate Of life SHAK 680:14
political k. BIER 116:3
So the k. be unknotted ELIO 301:8
knots pokers into true-love k. COLE 232:10
knotted Sat and k. SEDL 675:11
knotty moorish, and wild, and k.
BRON 152:14
know all I k. is what I read ROGE 652:19
all we k. WALL 818:14
all ye need to k. KEAT 444:15
Better the devil you k. PROV 615:28
dare to k. HORA 399:5
does not k. himself LA F 463:14
do not pretend to k. DARR 256:19
don't k. can't hurt you PROV 634:14
don't k. what I'm doing BRAU 150:2
fear, To be we k. not what DRYD 287:27
find out what you don't k. WELL 827:19
go we k. not where SHAK 708:10
hate any one that we k. HAZL 377:6
He must k. sumpin' HAMM 370:6
his place k. him BIBL 83:1
How do they k. PARK 586:8
How little do we k. BYRO 182:5
I do not k. myself GOET 353:19
I k. nothing SOCR 744:24
I k. not the Lord BIBL 77:23
I k. not the man BIBL 99:9
I k. thee not, old man SHAK 692:23
It's not what you k. SAYI 669:31
k. a man seven years PROV 636:9
k. a man who can ADVE 7:12
k., and not be known COLT 236:10
k. a thing or two MOLI 541:13
k. better what is good for people JAY 419:4
k. enough of hate FROS 335:14
k. everything MOLI 542:7
k. Him, love him CATE 199:7
k. more of mankind JOHN 432:11
k. not what they do BIBL 102:4
k. our will is free JOHN 429:4
k. that I am God BOOK 136:26
k. that my redeemer liveth BIBL 83:12
k. that you know not BACO 44:5
K. then thyself POPE 604:32
k. the place ELIO 301:25
k. the world YOUN 857:17
K. this to be thus JAIN 416:20
K. thyself PROV 624:44
k. to know no more MILT 533:9
K. what I mean, Harry BRUN 162:11
k. what I think WALL 818:4

k. what we are talking about RUSS 660:23
k. you're . . . God BARN 56:13
K. you the land GOET 353:12
let me k. mine end BOOK 136:4
master of those who k. DANT 255:17
men naturally desire to k. AUCT 34:12
merely k. more SAKI 663:19
More people k. Tom Fool PROV 626:42
never k. what you can do PROV 636:2
no one to k. ANON 15:14
not as we k. it MISQ 538:5
not k. what they have said CHUR 210:18
not k. where he is going LIN 486:11
nought did k. DAVI 258:8
say 'I don't k.' RUMS 658:8
say, 'I k. not' TALM 772:10
Tell me what you k. EMER 307:16
that kan hymselven k. CHAU 211:25
things they didn't k. POUN 608:16
those who do not wish to k. RALE 641:17
thought so once; but now I k. it EPIT 310:13
to k. a little BACO 45:25
To k. all is to forgive all PROV 633:10
To k. this only MILT 534:22
We must k. EPIT 311:13
What do I k. MONT 544:16
what should they k. of England KIPL 454:1
what we would, we k. ARNO 27:2
You k. more than you think SPOC 752:26
you k. who ADVE 8:13
you'll never k. ARMS 26:14
you'll never k. MISQ 538:7
you yourselves do k. SHAK 698:5
knowed all that there is to be k. GRAH 358:15
Knower How can the K. be known
UPAN 804:15
knowest k. all things BIBL 104:21
k. my down-sitting BOOK 143:14
thou k. not BIBL 85:12
knoweth k. not God BIBL 112:20
knowing Bewrapt past k. HARD 373:2
lust of k. FLEC 326:3
misfortune of knowing anything AUST 39:8
one who INSISTS on k. POUN 609:10
With a k. ignorance JOHN 422:10
knowingly Never k. undersold ADVE 8:6
knowledge After such k., what
forgiveness ELIO 302:4
all k. BIBL 107:25
all k. to be my province BACO 46:8
All our k. is POPE 605:13
bars To perfect k. BYRO 180:10
Benevolent K. BORG 145:5
bring home k. JOHN 431:5
by nature desire k. ARIS 25:11
communicate k. DE Q 264:21
Debarred from k. CHUD 219:8
desire more love and k. SHAK 680:21
dissemble sometimes your k. BACO 44:5
dotage of k. JACK 415:3
envied kind of k. ADAM 3:5
five ports of k. BROW 156:3
follow k. like a sinking star TENN 784:16
follow virtue and k. DANT 256:3
Friendship from k. BUSS 175:7
identical with his k. MAIM 507:18
increaseth k. BIBL 85:30
in the way of k. LOCK 488:6
key of k. BIBL 100:30
k. and wonder BACO 42:11
K. comes TENN 781:1
k. denied from senses SA'A 662:6
K. dwells In heads COWP 248:13
K. enormous KEAT 443:16
k. in mathematics BACO 47:5
k. in the making MILT 535:23
k. is a greater pleasure ARIS 25:19
k. is bought CLOU 227:18
k. is dangerous HUXL 411:17
K. is of two kinds JOHN 430:7
K. is power PROV 624:45
K. is proud COWP 248:14
K. is transmitted BLAK 121:14

k. itself is power BACO 46:10
k., it shall vanish away BIBL 107:25
K. may give weight CHES 215:13
k. of a lifetime WHIS 831:21
k. of causes BACO 46:13
k. of God LEIB 479:13
k. of good and evil BIBL 75:12
K. of good and evil COWP 247:14
k. of human nature AUST 39:6
k. of man is as the waters BACO 42:17
k. of nature HOLB 392:12
k. of nature WHEW 831:13
k. of nothing DICK 272:12
k. of the extinction PALI 583:9
k. of the Lord BIBL 88:22
k. of the world CHES 214:23
k. of truth BACO 45:32
k. puffeth up BIBL 107:16
k. shall be increased BIBL 91:26
k. that they are so OSBO 578:10
k. was divine TRAH 797:12
k. we have lost in information ELIO 303:2
k. when the day was done KEAT 443:19
k. which they cannot lose OPPE 573:18
k. without integrity JOHN 426:4
Language and k. SULL 763:10
Let k. grow TENN 778:21
literature of k. DE Q 265:3
little k. is dangerous PROV 625:26
make k. available BLAC 118:6
never better than k. FERM 317:3
no k. but I know it BEEC 62:16
No man's k. LOCK 488:9
objects of k. PLAT 597:14
organized k. SPEN 750:4
Out-topping k. ARNO 28:12
passeth k. BIBL 109:8
penetrate the land of k. SCHI 670:28
price for k. TICK 794:13
province of k. to speak HOLM 393:2
raising us to k. LEIB 479:14
show of k. DOUG 284:2
Sorrow is k. BYRO 182:20
spirit of k. BIBL 88:20
Such k. is too wonderful BOOK 143:15
touchstone of k. AUCT 34:15
tree of diabolical k. SHER 733:16
tree of the k. BIBL 75:13
Unto this k. DONN 280:24
What is all k. CARL 191:16
words without k. BIBL 83:20
You seek for k. SHEL 728:7
known all that is k. NEWM 560:19
child is k. by his doings BIBL 84:35
devil where he is k. JOHN 426:24
don't choose to have it k. CHES 215:16
even as also I am k. BIBL 107:25
hast thou not k. me BIBL 103:30
Have ye not k. BIBL 89:20
heard and k. BOOK 139:7
How can the Knower be k. UPAN 804:15
If you would be k. COLT 236:10
k. and the unknown PINT 595:16
k. by company he keeps PROV 626:1
k. no more than other men AUBR 33:16
k. too late SHAK 717:18
k. unto God EPIT 311:7
safer than a k. way HASK 375:2
then the end is k. SHAK 698:24
thy way may be k. BOOK 138:8
till I am k. JOHN 427:18
tree is k. by its fruit PROV 633:18
knows Every schoolboy k. MACA 498:15
has a mind and k. it SHAW 724:14
He k. nothing SHAW 725:27
if you k. of a better 'ole CART 198:11
knows about it all—HE k. FITZ 323:9
k. even his Bible ARNO 29:13
k. that all-highest Brahman UPAN 805:13
K. Things MILN 528:11
k. what he fights for CROM 251:13
less one k. LAO 467:15
sits in the middle and k. FROS 336:1

who k. does not speak LAO 468:2
knuckle k.-end of England SMIT 743:18
knucklebones harmless art of k. STEV 758:22
Kopf K. zum Greise MÜLL 553:21
Koran By the glorious K. KORA 461:8
K. was sent down KORA 459:12
not ponder the K. KORA 460:5
Korea doing in K. TRUM 801:7
Kosciuszko Freedom shrieked—as K. fell
CAMP 187:16
Kraken K. sleepeth TENN 780:1
Krorluppia Nasticreechia K. LEAR 477:10
Kruger killing K. with your mouth
KIPL 453:11
Kubla In Xanadu did K. Khan COLE 232:3
Kunst *In der K.* GOET 353:5
Kurtz Mistah K.—he dead CONR 240:17
Kyrie K. *eleison* MISS 536:15

label without a rag of a l. HUXL 411:13
labels l. serving to give a name TOLS 796:17
labor *hic l. est* VIRG 812:9
laborare L. est orare MOTT 552:10
laboratory guinea pigs in the l. of God
WILL 839:4
laborem *spectare l.* LUCR 495:14
laborious Studious of l. ease COWP 248:4
labour all his l. BIBL 85:25
all ye that l. BIBL 96:27
brow of l. BRYA 162:12
daily L. to pursue WESL 829:4
done to the L. Party TAWN 774:6
Don't let L. ruin it POLI 601:2
full of l. BIBL 85:27
Great is l. TALM 772:21
I l. for peace BOOK 142:15
In l. there is profit BIBL 84:20
insupportable l. STEE 754:16
l. against our own cure BROW 157:8
l. and not to ask IGNA 412:18
l. and sorrow BOOK 139:23
l. bears a lovely face DEKK 262:17
l. in his vocation SHAK 689:24
l.-intensive industry WILS 840:13
L. isn't working POLI 600:28
l. of love BIBL 110:15
l. of my hands THOR 793:7
l. of women in the house GILM 349:12
l. of your life MONT 544:3
L. Party owes more to Methodism
PHIL 595:2
L.'s call POLI 600:15
L.'s double whammy POLI 600:29
L. spin doctors CAMP 186:17
[L.] the natural party WILS 840:8
l. we delight in SHAK 705:8
L. without joy is base RUSK 659:26
life all l. be TENN 781:8
Love l. and hate mastery TALM 771:24
many still must l. BYRO 179:22
mental l. employed REYN 646:4
never visualised l. WEBB 824:24
New L., new danger POLI 601:3
reward for l. CARN 193:9
reward of l. is life MORR 549:20
right leader for the L. Party BEVA 73:16
Six days shalt thou l. BIBL 78:3
sore l.'s bath SHAK 704:24
spend your l. BIBL 90:6
their l. is but lost BOOK 143:1
to live without l. TAWN 774:4
true success is to l. STEV 759:20
Unremitting l. VIRG 814:13
We l. soon BURN 173:2
with difficulty and l. MILT 532:16
youth of l. GOLD 354:11
laboured fine, but as much l. WALP 819:19
l. more abundantly BIBL 108:2
labourer l. is worthy of his hire BIBL 100:19
l. to take his pension RUSK 660:26
l. worthy of hire PROV 624:46
labourers l. are few BIBL 96:12

labourers (cont.):
l. are idle · TALM 772:3
labouring l. man, that tills · OXFO 581:10
sleep of a l. man · BIBL 86:5
to the l. man · BUNY 164:24
women l. of child · BOOK 129:12
labours Children sweeten l. · BACO 45:5
completed l. are pleasant · CICE 223:8
line too l. · POPE 604:10
no l. tire · JOHN 426:17
rest from their l. · BIBL 114:4
laburnums L., dropping-wells of fire · TENN 779:15
labyrinth peopled l. of walls · SHEL 729:26
labyrinthical perplexed, l. soul · DONN 282:12
labyrinthine down the l. ways · THOM 791:7
l. buds the rose · BROW 161:15
lac *sine dolo l. concupiscite* · BIBL 115:18
lace l. my bodice blue · HUNT 410:10
Nottingham l. of the curtains · BETJ 72:2
lacessit *Nemo me impune l.* · MOTT 552:11
lack can I l. nothing · BOOK 135:3
lions do l. · BOOK 135:24
lacked questioning, If I l. any thing · HERB 384:13
lacking nothing is l. · LEON 481:4
lacrimae *Hinc illae l.* · TERE 785:4
Sunt l. rerum · VIRG 811:6
lacy l. sleeve with vitriol · WOOL 845:15
lad l. does not care · JOHN 428:25
l. that is gone · STEV 760:14
ladder behold a l. · BIBL 76:30
dropping down the l. · KIPL 454:7
l. of our vices · AUGU 37:18
l. of predictable progress · GOUL 357:11
path of the celestial l. · HEIK 379:10
traffic of Jacob's l. · THOM 791:16
Wiv a l. · BATE 58:9
ladders Crosses are l. · PROV 617:18
Holy One makes l. · MIDR 524:14
where all the l. start · YEAT 853:12
laden heavy l. · BIBL 96:27
ladies from a l.' seminary · GILB 347:24
Gentlemen and L. · DICK 273:11
good for l. · PROV 619:43
In praise of l. dead · SHAK 723:16
l. declare war on me · LOUI 492:9
l.' favours · SHAK 694:5
l., God bless them · SAYE 668:7
l. intellectual · BYRO 180:6
L., just a little · TREE 798:7
l. of St James's · DOBS 278:17
l. should ever sit down · MORE 548:5
l. to please · AUST 38:18
Ladies were l. · RAVE 642:16
lion among l. · SHAK 711:8
made the carlines l. · JAME 417:7
may the l. sit · BALL 53:6
remember the l. · ADAM 1:14
seminaries of young l. · KNOX 458:12
way the l. ride · NURS 570:3
worth any number of old l. · FAUL 316:5
young l. entered · SURT 764:22
ladles from the cooks' own l. · BROW 160:20
lads Come lasses and l. · SONG 747:3
Golden l. and girls · SHAK 683:8
l. in their hundreds · HOUS 404:12
l. that will never be old · HOUS 404:12
lady bird than a l. · RICH 647:12
called her his l. fair · KIPL 456:2
Here lies a l. · RANS 642:17
I met a l. · KEAT 443:25
Joan as my L. · HERR 386:5
l. doth protest too much · SHAK 687:5
l. fair · BALL 53:15
l. in a cage · CHES 216:15
L. Look owre · BALL 51:17
l. loved a swine · NURS 569:19
l. loves Milk Tray · ADVE 7:6
l. of a 'certain age' · BYRO 181:21
l. of Christ's College · AUBR 33:20
L. of Shalott · TENN 780:8
L. of Spain · REAV 643:18

l.'s in the case · GAY 341:27
l.-smocks all silver-white · SHAK 702:25
l.'s not for burning · FRY 336:12
l.'s not for turning · THAT 787:3
l. sweet and kind · ANON 19:8
l. that's known as Lou · SERV 677:10
L. with a Lamp · LONG 490:24
little l. comes by · GAY 342:14
lovely l., garmented · SHEL 732:8
My L. Bountiful · FARQ 315:8
ne'er wan A l. · BURN 172:23
Our L. of Pain · SWIN 768:11
our L. of the Snows · KIPL 455:7
saw my l. weep · ANON 17:1
talk like a l. · SHAW 727:12
To see a fine l. · NURS 569:8
why the l. is a tramp · HART 374:12
ladybird L., ladybird · NURS 567:18
Lafayette L., *nous voilà* · STAN 754:7
lag l.-end of my life · SHAK 691:4
laggard l. in love · SCOT 673:20
laid when I'm l. by thee · HERR 386:12
where they have l. him · BIBL 104:11
laily l. worm · BALL 52:9
lain There hath he l. for ages · TENN 780:2
laisser-faire *de l.* · QUES 639:6
L. · ARGE 24:19
laissez-faire L. · ANON 20:14
laity conspiracies against the l. · SHAW 725:4
tell the l. our love · DONN 281:17
lake l. water lapping · YEAT 854:18
slips into the l. of the lake · TENN 783:14
with a l. of fire · FLEC 326:4
lama Eli, Eli, l. sabachthani · BIBL 99:13
lamb Behold the L. of God · BIBL 102:24
fell down before the L. · BIBL 113:12
for a sheep as a l. · PROV 628:45
goes out like a l. · PROV 626:14
he who made the L. · BLAK 122:21
holy L. of God · BLAK 121:15
l. shall be without blemish · BIBL 77:28
l. to the slaughter · BIBL 90:3
leads me to the L. · COWP 246:28
Little L. who made thee · BLAK 122:5
Mary had a little l. · HALE 368:8
O L. of God, I come · ELLI 305:15
one little ewe l. · BIBL 80:32
Pipe a song about a L. · BLAK 121:26
provide himself a l. · BIBL 76:22
skin of an innocent l. · SHAK 694:21
tempers wind to shorn l. · PROV 621:1
to the shorn l. · STER 756:12
white in the blood of the L. · BIBL 113:19
wolf shall dwell with the l. · BIBL 88:21
Worthy the L. that died · WATT 823:13
wrath of the L. · BIBL 113:15
yoked with a l. · SHAK 698:19
lambs Feed my l. · BIBL 104:19
gather the l. · BIBL 89:18
l. who've lost our way · KIPL 454:6
lame feet was I to the l. · BIBL 83:16
L. dogs over stiles · KING 452:15
l. man · BIBL 89:11
Science without religion is l. · EINS 297:12
lamentation l., and weeping · BIBL 94:8
must be no l. · SAPP 666:16
lamented ye have not l. · BIBL 96:25
laments forest l. · CHUR 220:11
Lammastide fell about the L. · BALL 51:14
lamp Lady with a L. · LONG 490:24
l. is shattered · SHEL 729:24
l. of day · DOUG 283:14
lift my l. · LAZA 476:10
Slaves of the L. · ARNO 26:21
too strong of the l. · STER 756:22
unlit l. · BROW 161:17
lampada vitai l. · LUCR 495:15
lamp post leaning on a l. · GAY 342:14
lamp posts drunken man uses l. · LANG 466:12
lamprey surfeit by eating of a l. · FABY 313:20
lamps Heav'n's great l. · CAMP 187:23
l. are going out all over Europe · GREY 364:3
Life not a series of gig l. · WOOL 845:3

[monks] should live as l. · PALI 583:11
old l. for new · ARAB 23:16
women . . . who are the l. · LAWS 476:2
Lancashire L. merchants · CHES 216:17
Lancaster time-honoured L. · SHAK 715:4
Lancelot reading for pleasure about L. · DANT 255:19
land by sea as by l. · GILB 347:1
Ceres re-assume the l. · POPE 603:14
empire of the l. · RICH 648:2
Every l. has its own law · PROV 619:11
fat of the l. · BIBL 77:9
from l. to land · COLE 233:9
Grab this l. · MORR 550:11
heavenly l. from ours · WATT 823:18
house and l. are gone · PROV 634:22
if by l., one · REVE 645:14
Ill fares the l. · GOLD 354:10
I see l. · TENN 785:1
l. flowing with milk · BIBL 77:19
l. God gave to Cain · CART 197:7
l. of counterpane · STEV 760:4
l. of darkness · BIBL 83:2
L. of Heart's Desire · YEAT 854:19
L. of Hope and Glory · BENS 67:25
l. of lost content · HOUS 404:16
l. of my fathers · JAME 417:10
l. of my fathers · THOM 790:8
l. of pure delight · WATT 823:17
l. of the free · KEY 450:9
l. of the living · BIBL 90:4
l. of vainglory · BUNY 164:14
l. that I love · BERL 69:18
l. was ours before · FROS 335:15
L. where my fathers died · SMIT 742:18
l. . . . . where the light · BIBL 83:3
lane to the l. of the dead · AUDE 34:20
more precious than l. · SADA 662:13
nakedness of the l. · BIBL 77:7
no l. unhabitable · THOR 793:20
no yard of l. · ANON 22:10
one if by l. · LONG 491:5
One Law, one L. · KIPL 456:1
Ours is the l. · MAYA 519:12
piece of l. · HORA 403:14
possessed his l. · BIBL 78:18
prepared the dry l. · BOOK 140:10
ready by water as by l. · ELST 306:5
seems a moving l. · MILT 533:22
seen the promised l. · KING 452:6
splendid and a happy l. · GOLD 354:18
spy out the l. · BIBL 78:16
that pleasant l. · BOOK 141:14
There's the l., or cherry-isle · HERR 385:18
They love their l. · HALL 369:15
think there is no l. · BACO 42:18
This l. is your land · GUTH 366:5
to enjoy thy l. · SHAK 698:30
travel by l. or by water · BOOK 129:12
Unhappy the l. that needs heroes · BREC 150:6
we had the l. · GEOR 344:1
windy sea of l. · MILT 532:19
Woe to the l. · SHAK 716:29
landed Eagle has l. · ARMS 26:16
l. with an idea · BIRT 117:2
landing fight on the l. grounds · CHUR 221:8
successful l. in France · LIND 486:1
landlord l., fill the flowing bowl · SONG 747:2
paid to the l. · RICA 646:17
Sir Roger is l. · ADDI 4:26
landlords we're your l. · TINE 794:17
landlubbers l. lying down below · SONG 748:2
landmark Remove not the ancient l. · BIBL 84:41
lands Find other l. · THOM 792:13
sound is gone out into all l. · BOOK 134:20
take us l. away · DICK 273:2
though not of l. · WOTT 851:3
landscape gardening is but l.-painting · POPE 606:25
In Claude's l. · CONS 241:8
l. is deformed · THOR 793:1

l. of England	AUST 38:24
l. of the world	YOUN 857:16
part in a l.	CHEK 214:8
Who owns this l.	MCCA 500:4
landscapes abstract of several l.	BOWE 148:4
landslide pay for a l.	KENN 448:13
lane l. to the land of the dead	AUDE 34:20
long l. that has no turning	PROV 623:36
lanes streets and l. of the city	BIBL 101:8
lang For auld l. syne	BURN 170:9
How L., O Lord	BULL 163:17
language any l. you choose	GILB 347:16
best chosen l.	AUST 39:6
broke through l.	BROW 161:4
by means of l.	WITT 842:7
clear and beautiful l.	EMPS 307:26
cool web of l.	GRAV 360:6
dear l. that I spake	MACA 499:7
divided by a common l.	MISQ 537:12
enemy of clear l.	ORWE 578:2
enlargement of the l.	JOHN 424:5
entrance into the l.	BACO 45:28
everything else in our l.	MACA 498:23
except, of course, l.	WILD 835:10
from one l. to another	SHEL 732:13
from one l. to another	UNAM 804:10
hidden l. of the soul	GRAH 358:9
In l., the ignorant	DUPP 292:15
in l. there are only differences	SAUS 668:2
In such lovely l.	LAWR 475:10
l. all nations understand	BEHN 64:4
l. and ways of behaving	JUVE 439:14
l. an opera is sung in	APPL 23:13
l., by your skill made pliant	GAY 342:1
l. can be compared	SAUS 668:3
l. chiefly made by men	HARD 371:15
L. grows out of life	SULL 763:10
l. I have learned	SHAK 715:7
l. in her eye	SHAK 719:27
l. is a dialect with	WEIN 826:23
L. is a form of human reason	LÉVI 482:17
L. is called the garment	CARL 192:26
L. is fossil poetry	EMER 307:9
L. is only the instrument	JOHN 424:4
L. is the dress	JOHN 425:2
l. of another world	BYRO 182:22
l. of priorities	BEVA 73:10
l. of prose	WORD 850:24
l. of the age	GRAY 361:23
l. of the heart	POPE 603:1
l. of the heart	SHAD 677:20
l. of their own	SWIF 767:2
l. of the living	ELIO 301:21
l. of the unheard	KING 452:8
l. plain	COWP 246:7
L. tethers us	LIVE 487:4
L. was not powerful enough	DICK 270:24
laughter in a l.	GOLD 354:6
Life is a foreign l.	MORL 549:3
limits of my l.	WITT 842:13
Lovely enchanting l.	HERB 384:9
mathematical l.	GALI 338:10
merit of l. is clearness	GALE 338:8
mobilized the English l.	MURR 555:6
mystery of l.	KELL 447:18
no l. but a cry	TENN 779:7
not to be his l.	STAË 753:18
obscurity of a learned l.	GIBB 345:22
Political l. . . . . is designed	ORWE 578:4
refine our l.	JOHN 425:23
rich and delicate l.	WAUG 824:18
Sithe off our l.	LYDG 496:18
speech nor l.	BOOK 134:20
spoken in their own l.	BIBL 93:1
suicides have a special l.	SEXT 677:17
Under the tropic is our l.	WALL 818:15
very l. of men	WORD 850:23
world understands my l.	HAYD 376:5
You taught me l.	SHAK 718:24
languages between and across l.	CRAW 250:21
feast of l.	SHAK 702:21
knowledge of the ancient l.	BRIG 151:14
l. are the pedigree	JOHN 427:2
None of your live l.	DICK 269:6
silent in seven l.	BAGE 48:2
took and gave l.	PRIO 612:4
wit in all l.	DRYD 290:3
languors lilies and l.	SWIN 768:10
lantern l. on the stern	COLE 234:8
l. whereof tales are told	JONS 436:5
word is a l.	BOOK 142:13
lanterns show two l.	REVE 645:14
lap asked Carrie to sit on his l.	GROS 365:5
flowery l. of earth	ARNO 27:16
fresh l. of the crimson rose	SHAK 710:32
in the l. of the gods	HOME 394:9
l. of Earth	GRAY 361:8
strew the green l.	SHAK 716:13
lapdogs l. breathe their last	POPE 606:15
l. give themselves	POPE 606:4
lapidary In l. inscriptions	JOHN 430:10
lapping lake water l.	YEAT 854:18
lapwing Beatrice, like a l.	SHAK 712:20
lard l. their lean books	BURT 173:20
lards l. the lean earth	SHAK 690:2
large as l. as life	CARR 195:24
how l. a letter	BIBL 109:4
l.-brained woman	BROW 158:5
l.-hearted man	BROW 158:5
little volume, but l. book	CRAS 250:13
too l. to hang	ANON 19:14
we are at l.	JAME 417:15
larger L. than human	TENN 778:14
lark bell-swarmèd, l.-charmèd	HOPK 396:11
bisy l., messenger of day	CHAU 211:13
l. ascending	MERE 522:18
l. at break of day	SHAK 722:30
l. at heaven's gate sings	SHAK 682:30
l. becomes a sightless song	TENN 779:27
l. now leaves his wat'ry nest	D'AV 257:23
l.'s on the wing	BROW 160:22
merry l. her matins	SPEN 751:7
rise with the l.	BRET 150:25
sweet l. sing	FERG 316:18
larks catch l.	PROV 623:7
Four L. and a Wren	LEAR 477:3
hear the l.	HOUS 404:11
what l.	DICK 269:18
larkspur l. listens	TENN 781:26
Lars Porsena L. of Clusium	MACA 499:11
lasciate L. OGNI SPERANZA	DANT 255:13
lascivious l. gloating	STOP 761:6
long, l. reign	DEFO 261:25
lash blood drawn with the l.	LINC 485:11
l. that whore	SHAK 701:17
l. the age	POPE 603:28
rum, sodomy, prayers, and the l.	CHUR 222:1
lass every l. a queen	KING 453:1
It came with a l.	JAME 417:9
l. that loves a sailor	DIBD 267:8
lies A l. unparalleled	SHAK 680:16
lover and his l.	SHAK 682:6
O, gie me the l.	BURN 171:8
Sweet l. of Richmond Hill	SONG 748:8
lasses Come l. and lads	SONG 747:3
then she made the l.	BURN 171:7
lassie I love a l.	LAUD 470:6
love she's but a l.	BURN 171:28
What can a young l. do	BURN 173:7
last always the l. to know	PROV 622:39
birds in l. year's nest	PROV 631:48
cobbler stick to his l.	PROV 625:8
Don't wait for the l. judgement	CAMU 188:12
Free at l.	EPIT 309:7
give unto this l.	BIBL 98:3
has dawned is your l.	HORA 399:7
have been the l. cigarette	LAST 474:1
l. and best	MILT 534:2
l. article of my creed	GAND 339:7
l. best gift	MILT 533:12
l. breath of Julius Caesar	JEAN 419:6
L. came, and last did go	MILT 530:5
l. day of an era past	YELT 856:14
l. enemy	BORR 146:12
l. for ever	CONR 241:2
l. gasp	BIBL 94:4
l. gentleman in Europe	LEVE 482:9
l. great Englishman	TENN 782:14
l. my time	CARL 191:14
L. night I dreamt	OPEN 574:31
l. page is always latent	WHAR 831:2
l. person who has sat on him	HAIG 367:10
l. red leaf	TENN 778:28
l. rose of summer	MOOR 547:19
l. shall be first	BIBL 98:1
l. state of that man	BIBL 97:1
L.-supper-carved-on-a-peach-stone	LANC 465:21
l. taste of sweets	SHAK 715:12
l. thing I shall do	LAST 471:8
l. thing one knows	PASC 587:2
l. time I saw Paris	HAMM 370:4
l. while they last	DE G 262:10
l. words I should pronounce	REYN 646:9
laughs l.	PROV 621:41
laughs l., laughs longest	PROV 622:11
live and l.	CATU 202:10
Long foretold, long l.	PROV 625:38
Look thy l. on all things lovely	DE L 262:24
Nice guys finish l.	DURO 293:6
no l. nor first	BROW 160:23
this day as if thy l.	KEN 448:6
To the l. syllable	SHAK 707:14
Tristram Shandy did not l.	JOHN 430:12
We were the l. romantics	YEAT 853:14
without considering the l.	CLAU 225:16
won the l. war	ROOS 653:8
world's l. night	DONN 279:24
lasts Lets hope it l.	BONA 126:19
latch Cross-patch, Draw the l.	NURS 566:13
latchet shoe's l.	BIBL 102:23
late Better l. than never	PROV 615:25
borrows from the l. man	PROV 618:30
dread of being l.	BETJ 73:4
five minutes too l.	COWL 246:1
l. into the night	BYRO 183:8
never too l. to learn	PROV 624:8
never too l. to mend	PROV 624:9
not too l. to-morrow	ARMS 26:13
No, you were l.	LERN 481:17
offering even that too l.	NEVI 559:14
rather l. for me	LARK 468:12
This is a l. parrot	MONT 546:7
Too l. came I	AUGU 37:5
too l. into a world	MUSS 555:11
travel I'm too l.	RICH 647:21
years of human thought too l.	LA B 462:19
latent l. in my first	WHAR 831:2
later came l. in life	ASQU 32:3
l. it would be bitter	KIER 451:7
l. than you think	SERV 677:7
lateral l. thinking	DE B 260:16
latet L. anguis in herba	VIRG 813:22
lath l. of wood	BISM 118:3
Latin Devil knows L.	KNOX 458:10
half Greek, half L.	SCOT 672:15
he speaks L.	SHAK 694:24
L. for a whopping	ANST 23:4
L., ne of Greek	SPEN 752:13
L. word for Tea	BELL 65:29
No more L.	ANON 18:2
small L.	JONS 436:2
Then you understand L.	FARQ 315:14
latrine mouth had been used as a l.	AMIS 13:8
rotten seat of a l.	FLAU 325:7
latrone l. viator	JUVE 440:5
latter at the l. day	BIBL 83:12
former and the l.	BOOK 129:21
Lord blessed the l. end	BIBL 83:31
laudamus Te Deum l.	PRAY 611:7
laudant L. illa	MART 514:18
laudate L. Dominum, omnes gentes	BIBL 115:4
l. et superexaltate eum	BIBL 115:9
laudator l. temporis acti	HORA 398:11
laugh atheist-l.'s a poor exchange	BURN 171:1

laugh (*cont*.):
cannot make him l. — SHAK 692:14
decent people l. — MOLI 541:14
dismissed with a l. — HORA 403:12
do we not l. — SHAK 709:14
horse-l. in the reader — FIEL 318:11
l. all of the time — LOOS 491:20
l. and sing — BOOK 138:7
L. and the world laughs — PROV 624:48
L., and the world laughs — WILC 835:8
L. at all you trembled at — COWP 247:15
l. at any mortal thing — BYRO 181:13
l. at everything — BEAU 60:1
l. at human actions — SPIN 752:25
l. at live dragons — TOLK 796:9
l. at them — AUST 40:5
l. from the secret corner — HORA 400:12
l. like a loon — HARB 371:3
l. me to scorn — BOOK 134:27
L. no man to scorn — BIBL 93:7
l., to lie — ASCH 31:4
l. to scorn — SHAK 682:3
L. where we must — POPE 604:18
l. with me, or at me — STER 756:16
Let them l. that win — PROV 625:10
loud l. that spoke — GOLD 354:12
more unbecoming than to l. — CONG 238:15
must l. before we are happy — LA B 462:14
Others may be able to l. — RHYS 646:12
sillier than a silly l. — CATU 202:17
stupid will l. at him — I-HS 412:19
time to l. — BIBL 85:32
unextinguishable l. in heaven — BROW 155:16
laughable very l. things — JOHN 429:6
laughed first baby l. — BARR 57:2
honest man is l. at — HALI 369:7
l. at in the second — NAPO 556:9
l. him into patience — SHAK 679:12
l. with counterfeited glee — GOLD 354:15
one has not l. — CHAM 206:18
They all l. — GERS 344:10
they l. consumedly — FARQ 315:12
when he l. — AUDE 34:26
laughing Happiness is no l. matter
 — WHAT 813:8
hear you sweetly l. — CATU 202:20
killed while l. — KIPL 454:3
l. and jeering — PEPY 592:3
l. devil — BYRO 179:23
l. immoderately — SMIT 743:17
l. is heard on the hill — BLAK 122:7
l. queen — HUNT 409:17
l. sexily — SAPP 666:14
Minnehaha, L. Water — LONG 491:3
most fun I ever had without l. — ALLE 12:7
nothing worth l. at — HAZL 376:16
laughs l. at lovers' perjuries — TIBU 794:11
l. at lovers' perjury — DRYD 289:5
l. at lovers' perjury — PROV 624:33
l. at the time to come — BIBL 85:24
l. best who — PROV 621:41
l. last, laughs longest — PROV 622:11
l. to see the green man — HOFF 391:19
l. with a harvest — JERR 421:17
laughter audible l. — CHES 215:7
Even in l. — BIBL 84:19
faculty of l. — ADDI 5:11
gift of l. — SABA 662:7
grail of l. — CRAN 249:25
l. and ability — DICK 273:11
l. and sorrow — JOHN 425:15
l. and the love — BELL 65:28
l. for a month — SHAK 690:1
L. hath only a scornful — SIDN 736:19
L. holding both his sides — MILT 529:20
l. in a language — GOLD 354:6
L. is a refusal — VALÉ 806:7
L. is nothing else — HOBB 390:6
l. is pleasant — PEAC 590:3
L. is the best medicine — SAYI 670:2
l. of a fool — BIBL 86:6
L. . . . the most civilized music — USTI 806:2
L. would be bereaved — USTI 806:6

Laugh thy girlish l. — WATS 823:3
mouth filled with l. — BOOK 142:23
nothing more frightful than l. — SAGA 663:4
O Christ, the l. — MASE 517:14
Our sincerest l. — SHEL 731:29
peals of l. — POPE 602:24
present l. — SHAK 720:16
weeping and the l. — DOWS 284:7
weeping and with l. — MACA 499:20
launched l. a thousand ships — MARL 513:4
Laura Rose-cheeked L. — CAMP 188:5
laureate became Poet L. — TENN 784:24
laureateship offered the L. — SCOT 674:30
laurel Apollo's l. bough — MARL 513:7
Caesar's l. crown — BLAK 117:2
l. for the perfect prime — ROSS 655:10
that she might l. grow — MARV 515:15
laurels Birds on box and l. — SMAR 739:13
l. all are cut — ANON 20:18
l. to paeans — CICE 223:13
l. torn — SMOL 744:18
Once more, O ye l. — MILT 529:29
O ye l. — OPEN 576:4
worth all your l. — BYRO 183:10
lauriers l. sont coupés — ANON 20:18
lava in its l. I still find — WOOL 845:13
l. of the imagination — BYRO 184:4
L. quod es sordidum — LANG 467:1
lave Let the l. go by me — STEV 760:16
lavender cured with l. water — HEGE 379:2
l., mints — SHAK 722:4
L.'s blue — NURS 567:19
Lavinia L., therefore must be loved
 — SHAK 719:14
law according to the l. — BIBL 91:23
against the l. for generals — TRUM 801:13
army of unalterable l. — MERE 522:20
become a universal l. — KANT 441:8
books of l. — JOHN 423:10
Born under one l. — GREV 364:2
breaks the l. — PLAT 597:5
bringing them nigh to the L. — HILL 389:2
built with stones of L. — BLAK 121:4
but by the l. — BIBL 106:14
chief l. — CICE 223:9
child of l. — BENT 68:3
Common L. of England — HERB 383:15
Custom that is before all l. — DANI 255:4
Custom, that unwritten l. — D'AV 257:19
dead-level of l. and order — TAWN 774:1
end of l. is — LOCK 488:16
enonomic l. of motion — MARX 516:14
Every land has its own l. — PROV 619:11
fear of the L. — JOYC 437:5
fence around the L. — TALM 772:4
first is l. — DRYD 288:15
from Jargon born to rescue L. — LLOY 487:11
fulfilled the l. — BIBL 106:31
government above the l. — SCAR 668:11
had people not defied the l. — SCAR 668:9
Hard cases make bad l. — PROV 621:33
Hear my l. — BOOK 139:7
He that neglects the L. — TALM 772:7
I crave the l. — SHAK 709:27
Ignorance of the l. — PROV 623:29
Ignorance of the l. — SELD 676:4
in l.'s grave study — COKE 230:19
is a l. rational — CHAP 208:12
it is of no force in l. — COKE 230:14
judgement of the l. — JACK 415:7
keep this l. — BOOK 131:8
keystone of the rule of l. — DENN 264:11
laid His hand on Moses' l. — BLAK 120:2
l. and the prophets — BIBL 95:18
l. can take a purse — BUTL 176:21
l. doth give it — SHAK 709:31
l. floats in a sea of ethics — WARR 821:23
l. has made him equal — DARR 257:1
L. is a ass — DICK 271:15
L. is a bottomless pit — ARBU 24:6
l. is above you — DENN 264:10
L. is boldly — BURR 173:10
l. is contrary to liberty — BENT 68:9

l. is established — SIDN 735:18
l. is such an ass — CHAP 208:16
L. . . . is the perfection — COKE 230:16
L. is the true embodiment — GILB 347:10
l. is to be to restraint — MILT 535:17
L.: It has honoured us — WEBS 825:16
L. of Actions — MAIN 507:21
L. of the Jungle — KIPL 457:2
l. of the Yukon — SERV 677:8
l. of thy mouth — BOOK 142:12
l.'s delay — SHAK 686:10
L. to our selves — MILT 533:30
l. to weed it out — BACO 45:8
l. unto themselves — BIBL 106:2
lesser breeds without the L. — KIPL 455:12
life of the l. — COKE 230:15
madhouse there exists no l. — CLAR 224:6
majestic equality of the l. — FRAN 331:19
make a fence around the L. — TALM 771:22
make a scarecrow of the l. — SHAK 707:22
moral l. within me — KANT 441:6
Necessity has no l. — PUBL 636:16
Necessity hath no l. — CROM 252:5
Necessity knows no l. — PROV 627:13
nine points of the l. — PROV 629:28
No brilliance is needed in the l. — MORT 551:2
Nor l., nor duty — YEAT 854:16
not a l. at all — ROBE 650:5
Nothing is l. — POWE 610:6
No written l. more binding — CATT 199:20
of a common l. — JEFF 419:18
Of L. there can be no less — HOOK 395:18
old father antick, the l. — SHAK 689:22
one l. for all — BURK 169:7
One l. for the rich — PROV 628:41
One L., one Land — KIPL 456:1
People crushed by l. — BURK 168:19
perfection of our l. — ANON 16:4
principle of the English l. — DICK 267:23
purlieus of the L. — ETHE 312:3
purlieus of the l. — TENN 779:17
quillets of the l. — SHAK 694:9
Seven hours to l. — JONE 434:11
severity of the criminal l. — PEEL 590:14
study of l. — GIRA 350:4
sustained: by the L. — TALM 771:23
this is the royal l. — CORO 243:16
those by l. protected — BURN 171:18
touching the l., a Pharisee — BIBL 110:2
where no l. is — BIBL 106:6
whole of the L. — CROW 253:2
Who to himself is l. — CHAP 208:10
windward of the l. — CHUR 219:17
windy side of the l. — SHAK 721:13
Wrest once the l. — SHAK 709:28
lawful All things are l. for me — BIBL 107:21
L. as eating — SHAK 722:14
l. for me to do what I will — BIBL 98:3
their l. occasions — BOOK 144:11
lawk L. a mercy on me — NURS 567:4
lawn bird-haunted English l. — ARNO 27:19
Get your tanks off my l. — WILS 840:10
l. about the shoulders thrown — HERR 385:21
L. is full of south — DICK 273:13
on the l. I lie in bed — AUDE 35:19
saint in l. — POPE 603:18
lawned l. areas with paving — OFFI 572:15
lawns house with l. — STEV 760:19
laws are the l. of nature — SHAW 724:19
arranges l. — MACH 502:8
Bad l. — BURK 168:20
bad or obnoxious l. — GRAN 359:8
breaking of l. — MORE 547:24
broke the l. of God and man — EPIT 310:5
care who should make the l. — FLET 326:21
dole Unequal l. — TENN 784:13
dominion of l. — PRIC 610:15
do with the l. — HORS 403:18
facts governed by l. — WHEW 831:13
giving heed unto her l. — BIBL 92:29
government of l. — ADAM 2:20
Government of l. and not of men
 — FORD 328:11

Had l. not been — D'AV 257:21
If l. are needed — KHOM 451:1
l. and learning — MANN 511:2
L. are generally found to be nets — SHEN 732:24
L. are like cobwebs — SWIF 766:27
L. are silent — CICE 223:21
l. are their enemies — BURK 168:19
L. grind the poor — GOLD 355:14
L., like houses — BURK 168:12
l. of God will be suspended — SHAW 725:13
l. of most countries — MILL 525:15
l. of Nature — HUXL 411:18
l. of the land — CHAR 208:26
l. or kings — JOHN 426:14
l. or kings can cause — GOLD 355:15
L. were made to be broken — NORT 565:11
made so by l. — BOLI 126:11
more l. and orders — LAO 468:3
more l., the more thieves — PROV 626:41
more numerous the l. — TACI 770:8
Nature, and Nature's l. — POPE 603:27
neither l. made — JOHN 422:3
New lords, new l. — PROV 627:33
not a government of l. — WEBS 825:14
not judges of l. — PULT 637:3
observing God's l. — ELEA 298:19
override the l. of Heaven — SOPH 746:16
part of the l. of England — HALE 368:6
planted thick with l. — BOLT 126:15
prescribed l. to the learned — DUPP 292:15
rather than obey the l. — TOCQ 795:3
scientist's l. — QUIN 639:11
scrutiny of the l. — MONT 545:1
sweeps a room as for Thy l. — HERB 384:5
their l. approve — DRYD 288:20
two sorts of l. — DIDE 273:19
Written l. — ANAC 13:18
lawsuits engaged in l. — NEWT 561:16
lawyer eye iv a l. — DUNN 292:12
l. has no business — JOHN 426:23
l. interprets the truth — GIRA 350:4
l. tells me I may — BURK 166:24
l. with his briefcase — PUZO 638:11
own l. has a fool — PROV 626:9
to a corporate l. — COMM 236:15
lawyers crowd of l. — WYCH 852:15
kill all the l. — SHAK 694:20
l. can, with ease — GAY 342:1
L. may revere — FERG 316:20
l.' tongues — PROV 617:35
two l. the battledores — DICK 271:29
Woe unto you, l. — BIBL 100:30
lay Cleric before, and L. behind — BUTL 176:9
I l. me down to sleep — PRAY 611:5
l. down his life — BIBL 103:33
L. her i' the earth — SHAK 689:1
l. me down in peace — BOOK 133:25
l. mee downe — BALL 53:2
L. on, Macduff — SHAK 707:18
L.-overs for meddlers — PROV 624:49
L. your sleeping head — AUDE 35:11
layman neither cleric nor l. — BERN 70:13
lays constructing tribal l. — KIPL 454:14
Lazarus certain beggar named L. — BIBL 101:22
Come forth, L. — JOYC 437:21
L. mystified — HILL 388:8
laziness differs from l. — MARA 511:16
some from l. — EURI 312:16
lazy l. leaden-stepping hours — MILT 530:29
l., long, lascivious — DEFO 261:25
Long and l. — PROV 625:36
LBJ All the way with L. — POLI 600:2
Hey, L., how many kids — POLI 600:19
lead blind l. the blind — BIBL 97:12
child shall l. them — BIBL 88:21
easy to l. — BROU 154:13
evening l. — CHUR 222:8
gold wes changyd into l. — WYNT 852:17
l. a horticulture — PARK 586:10
L., kindly Light — NEWM 561:5
l. me in the right way — BOOK 135:14
l. those that are with young — BIBL 89:18

L. us, Heavenly Father — EDME 296:7
l. us not into temptation — BIBL 95:3
think we l. — BYRO 183:14
When the blind l. the blind — PROV 634:27
wherever it may l. — DOST 283:12
leadable is the Conservative Party l. — HESE 387:2
leaden voice revives the l. strings — CAMP 188:1
With l. foot — JAGO 416:2
leader fanatic is a great l. — BROU 154:18
I am their l. — LEDR 478:13
l. of the enterprise — VIRG 811:4
one people, one l. — POLI 600:14
Take me to your l. — CATC 201:28
test of a l. — LIPP 486:14
leaders l. of a revolution — CONR 240:25
leadership L. means making — CHRÉ 218:12
leaf And I were like the l. — SWIN 769:6
as an aspes l. — CHAU 213:6
days are in the yellow l. — BYRO 183:1
fade as a l. — BIBL 90:20
Falls with the l. — FLET 327:2
in tiny l. — BROW 159:17
last red l. — TENN 778:28
l., the bud, the flower — SPEN 751:25
light as l. on lynde — CHAU 211:6
sole remaining l. — WORD 845:17
where the dead l. fell — KEAT 443:10
wise man hide a l. — CHES 216:24
yellow l. — SHAK 707:8
league hadna sailed a l. — BALL 51:19
Half a l. onward — TENN 776:13
keep a l. till death — SHAK 716:11
leak One l. will sink — BUNY 165:2
leaks Little l. sink the ship — PROV 625:27
lean could eat no l. — NURS 567:17
if a man l. — BIBL 82:17
l. and hungry look — SHAK 696:12
l. as much to the contrary — HALI 368:12
l. on one another — BURK 168:12
l. over too far backward — THUR 793:26
l. to wild extremes — DURY 293:10
leaning l. all awry — FITZ 323:12
leap giant l. for mankind — ARMS 26:17
great l. in the dark — VANB 806:15
l. as an hart — BIBL 89:11
l. in the dark — LAST 471:19
l. into the dark — BROW 155:12
l. into the ocean — HUME 408:16
l. over the wall — BOOK 134:16
Look before you l. — PROV 625:39
methinks it were an easy l. — SHAK 689:29
leaped have I l. over a wall — BIBL 81:6
leaping l. from place to place — HARD 372:19
l. light — AUDE 35:10
so long as there is no l. — SURT 764:18
too broad for l. — HOUS 405:1
Walking, and l. — BIBL 104:30
learn but she can l. — SHAK 709:19
craft so long to l. — CHAU 212:26
don't want to l. — SELL 676:14
l., and inwardly digest — BOOK 130:1
l. how to be aged — BLYT 124:15
l. in suffering — SHEL 729:18
l. men from books — DISR 277:32
l. the world — CHES 214:25
L. to write well — BUCK 163:7
L. to write well — CLOS 228:18
live and l. — POMF 599:15
Live and l. — PROV 625:33
much desire to l. — MILT 535:23
never too late to l. — PROV 624:8
Never too old to l. — PROV 627:30
People must l. to hate — MAND 509:15
pleasure to l. — CONF 237:8
We l. so little — DAVI 258:7
while they teach, men l. — SENE 676:28
learned been l. has been forgotten — SKIN 739:11
l. anything from history — HEGE 379:3
l. well how to obey — THOM 788:8
L. without sense — CHUR 220:8

loads of l. lumber — POPE 604:16
much l. dust — COWP 247:32
obscurity of a l. language — GIBB 345:22
opinion with the l. — CONG 238:20
prescribed laws to the l. — DUPP 292:15
Things l. on earth — BROW 160:12
this l. man — MARL 513:7
learning alwayth a l. — DICK 269:20
and in l. rules — CRAB 249:5
a' the l. I desire — BURN 171:2
attain good l. — ASCH 31:1
commonwealth of l. — LOCK 488:6
cry both arts and l. — QUAR 639:5
deep l. little had he — SPEN 752:13
enough of l. to misquote — BYRO 182:9
Get l. — BIBL 94:2
l. is a process of remembering — PLAT 597:8
L. is better than house — PROV 624:50
l. is most excellent — PROV 634:22
l. lightly like a flower — TENN 779:29
l. many things — SOLO 745:12
l.'s crumbs — BROW 159:8
L. teacheth more — ASCH 31:5
L., that cobweb — BUTL 176:10
L. will be cast — BURK 167:18
little l. is a dangerous thing — POPE 604:2
loyal body wanted l. — TRAP 798:4
man of polite l. — DEFO 261:2
much l. doth make thee mad — BIBL 105:30
nonsense, and l. — GOLD 355:22
of a state, l. — BACO 45:35
of liberty, and of l. — DISR 276:10
pleasures that go with l. — SOCR 745:8
pursuit of l. — LAO 468:1
rights in l.'s world — EGER 297:5
royal road to l. — PROV 632:18
scraps of l. — YOUN 857:2
traitor to l. — JOHN 422:9
twins of l. — SHAK 695:22
Wear your l. — CHES 215:5
Whence is thy l. — GAY 341:25
will to l. — ASCH 31:2
written for our l. — BOOK 130:1
learnt forgotten nothing and l. nothing — DUMO 291:14
They have l. nothing — TALL 771:18
lease summer's l. — SHAK 722:24
leasehold l. for all — LUCR 495:17
least faithful in that which is l. — BIBL 101:21
l. government was the best — FEIN 316:10
l. of all seeds — BIBL 97:5
l. of these my brethren — BIBL 98:26
leather nothing like l. — PROV 632:19
leave for ever taking l. — RILK 648:15
If you can't l. in a taxi — FILM 319:14
Intreat me not to l. thee — BIBL 80:2
L. all things behind — BHAG 74:18
L. me, O Love — SIDN 736:12
L. not a rack behind — SHAK 719:1
L. not a stain — BIBL 93:25
L. off first — BIBL 93:23
l. spades alone — SITW 738:18
l. the outcome — CORN 243:5
l. the word of God — BIBL 104:31
l. things alone you leave them — CHES 217:5
l. without the King — ELIZ 305:7
moment during l.-taking — FLAU 325:6
Once I leave, I l. — BALD 50:19
ready to l. — MONT 544:1
shall a man l. his father — BIBL 75:17
we asked none l. to love — DONN 280:23
leaven l. leaveneth the whole lump — BIBL 107:10
l. of malice — BOOK 130:7
l. of malice and wickedness — BIBL 107:11
leaves burning of the l. — BINY 116:15
Crowned with calm l. — SWIN 768:15
flaps its glad green l. — HARD 372:9
laughing l. of the tree — SWIN 768:2
l. are falling — SHEL 730:12
l. behind a part of oneself — HARA 370:20
l. cover me — SWIN 769:4
l. dead Are driven — SHEL 730:7

leaves (*cont.*):
l. fall early — POUN 609:6
l. like light footfalls — SHEL 730:6
l. of the tree — BIBL 114:22
l. to a tree — KEAT 446:8
l. to the trees — HORA 402:11
noise among the l. — KEAT 443:21
stipple l. with sun — SACK 662:12
tender l. of hope — SHAK 695:11
Thick as autumnal l. — MILT 531:17
thou among the l. — KEAT 444:23
Very like l. — HOME 394:2
withered l. — ARNO 28:1
Words are like l. — DILL 274:8
leaving l. his country — FITZ 322:23
like the l. it — SHAK 703:17
Lebanon cedared L. — KEAT 443:2
cedars of L. — BIBL 79:27
Lebens L. goldner Baum — GOET 352:18
lecher small gilded fly Does l. — SHAK 701:14
lecherous l. as a sparwe — CHAU 210:26
rough and l. — SHAK 699:27
lechery L., sir, it provokes — SHAK 705:7
wars and l. — SHAK 719:29
lectorem L. delectando — HORA 398:13
lecture l., love, in love's philosophy — DONN 281:2
lecturer requisite to a l. — FARA 314:15
lectures l. or a little charity — WHIT 833:14
led we are most l. — BYRO 183:14
leek By this l. — SHAK 694:3
lees wine on the l. — BIBL 89:1
left better to be l. — CONG 239:10
but of my l. hand — MILT 536:3
everything is l. out — JAME 417:19
goats on the l. — BIBL 98:24
l. a lot o' little things — KIPL 453:12
L. hand down a bit — CATC 201:15
l.-handed marriage — WOLL 844:5
l. thy first love — BIBL 113:1
let not thy l. hand know — BIBL 95:1
O let them be l. — HOPK 396:17
other l. — BIBL 98:19
something l. to treat — MALL 508:16
leg does not resemble a l. — APOL 23:11
here I leave my second l. — HOOD 395:1
l. has often as much to do with it — HUNT 410:2
l. you shall put into your breeches — JOHN 428:16
lift a lawless l. — BURN 171:11
my Julia's dainty l. — HERR 386:8
legacy l. from a rich relative — SMIT 742:3
legally accomplishing small things l. — BALZ 54:10
lege Tolle l. — AUGU 37:4
legend before your l. ever did — JOHN 422:11
before your l. will — JOHN 422:14
fables in the l. — BACO 43:16
true l. — STAL 754:4
When the l. becomes fact — FILM 320:24
legends Men must have l. — MURR 555:4
Leger come back on St L. day — SAYI 670:12
leges l. inter arma — CICE 223:21
legibility dawn of l. — HAY 376:4
Legion My name is L. — BIBL 99:20
legions give me back my l. — AUGU 37:20
legislation imports and exports, l. — ARIS 25:9
possess divine l. — MEND 521:21
true basis of English l. — GLAD 351:11
legislator l. of mankind — JOHN 425:26
people is the true l. — BURK 168:13
legislators idea of hereditary l. — PAIN 582:18
unacknowledged l. — SHEL 732:17
legislature work for a L. — ELLI 306:4
legitimate l. warfare — NEWM 560:8
legs adorns my l. — HOUS 403:20
any man's l. — BOOK 144:4
born with your l. apart — ORTO 576:18
cannon-ball took off his l. — HOOD 394:26
dog's walking on his hinder l. — JOHN 428:19
four bare l. in a bed — PROV 632:3
Four l. good — ORWE 576:20

If you could see my l. — DICK 269:11
l. are as pillars of marble — BIBL 87:16
loves to fold his l. — JOHN 430:29
not for your bad l. — ELIZ 304:9
on their own two l. — CASS 198:16
stretches his l. — PROV 619:21
use of his l. — DICK 270:21
vast and trunkless l. — SHEL 730:16
Walk under his huge l. — SHAK 696:9
legunt sed ista l. — MART 514:18
Leicester Farewell, L. Square — JUDG 438:4
Here lies the Earl of L. — EPIT 310:1
Leicestershire finest run in L. — PAGE 581:15
leiden L. oder triumphieren — GOET 353:4
leisure At l. married — CONG 239:4
busiest have most l. — PROV 616:21
conspicuous l. — VEBL 808:8
detest at l. — BYRO 181:30
fill l. intelligently — RUSS 660:20
have l. to bother — SHAW 727:8
Idle have the least l. — PROV 622:41
improvement arises from l. — JOHN 429:22
increased l. — DISR 276:9
l. answers leisure — SHAK 708:17
L. with honour — CICE 223:23
life of l. — MORE 548:3
luck in l. — PROV 632:12
never at l. — JOHN 430:29
opportunity of l. — BIBL 93:28
polish it at l. — DRYD 289:35
Politicians also have no l. — ARIS 25:18
repent at l. — PROV 626:17
When I have l. — HILL 389:6
leman such l. — BALL 53:14
lemon in the squeezing of a l. — GOLD 355:24
l.-trees bloom — GOET 353:12
lemonade make l. — SAYI 669:26
lemons If life hans you l. — SAYI 669:26
Oranges and l. — NURS 568:19
lend l. me your ears — SHAK 697:21
L. you money and lose — PROV 625:2
men who l. — LAMB 464:13
lender borrower, nor a l. be — SHAK 684:19
lenders pen from l.' books — SHAK 700:25
lendeth merciful, and l. — BOOK 141:23
lendings Off, off, you l. — SHAK 700:26
lends Three things I never l. — SURT 764:16
length drags its dreary l. — DICK 267:13
drags its slow l. — POPE 604:8
in l. of days — BIBL 83:6
l. and breadth — BALL 52:2
L. begets loathing — PROV 625:3
L. of days — BIBL 83:34
what it lacks in l. — FROS 335:16
lengthens As the day l. — PROV 614:35
lengthy meaning of l. speech — SCHI 671:1
Lenore angels name L. — POE 599:6
lente Festina l. — AUGU 37:21
L. currite noctis equi — OVID 579:18
l., lente, currite — MARL 513:6
leoni vulpes aegroto cauta l. — HORA 399:2
Léonie Weep not for little L. — GRAH 358:5
leopard l. change his spots — BIBL 91:1
l. does not change — COMP 237:2
l. does not change — PROV 625:4
l. shall lie down — BIBL 88:21
leopards three white l. sat — ELIO 301:3
leper innocence is like a dumb l. — GREE 362:17
wash the l.'s wounds — TERE 785:13
leprosy skin was white as l. — COLE 232:21
lerne gladly wolde he l. — CHAU 210:18
Lesbia L. whom Catullus once loved — CATU 203:1
L. with her sparrow — MILL 526:21
Let us live, my L. — CATU 202:13
My sweetest L. — CAMP 187:23
lesbians l. often end up — PAGL 581:16
Lesley bonnie L. — BURN 170:16
less for nothing l. than thee — DONN 280:18
had he pleased us l. — ADDI 4:4
How l. what we may be — BYRO 182:5
L. is a bore — VENT 808:10
L. is more — PROV 625:5

l. likely to fall — GAY 341:22
L. than the dust — HOPE 396:9
l. we love her — PUSH 638:3
little l. — BROW 158:25
more and more about l. and less — BUTL 175:15
small Latin, and l. Greek — JONS 436:2
you can't take l. — CARR 194:11
lessen l. from day to day — CARR 194:16
lesser l. breeds — KIPL 455:12
l. to be chosen — THOM 788:14
lessons l. to be drawn — ELIZ 305:4
reason they're called l. — CARR 194:16
lest L. we forget — KIPL 455:10
let l. and hindered — BOOK 130:2
L. my people go — BIBL 77:26
L. my people go — SONG 748:10
L.'s go to work — FILM 320:1
l. them all to my elder — THOM 790:13
l. the sounds of music — SHAK 710:2
L. us with a gladsome mind — MILT 529:28
Lethe go not to L. — KEAT 444:16
waters of L. — GINS 349:18
Lethean drunken of things L. — SWIN 768:22
letter by speech than by l. — BACO 45:1
don't think this is a l. — RENO 645:9
how large a l. — BIBL 109:4
huge wordy l. — JUVE 440:6
l. by strange letter — HEAN 377:15
l. from his wife — CARR 196:14
l. killeth — BIBL 108:13
l. to my love — BALL 52:4
made this [l.] longer — PASC 587:1
my l. to the world — DICK 273:10
name and not the l. — PROV 616:32
scarlet l. — HAWT 375:17
Someone wants a l. — ADVE 8:14
thou unnecessary l. — SHAK 700:7
uncertain process of l.-writing — ELIO 300:21
used to start a l. — PLIN 598:8
very touch of the l. — NIN 564:17
were reading a l. — TALM 772:35
when he wrote a l. — BACO 43:30
letters burn your l. — ADAM 2:22
can't write l. — BISH 117:11
L. for the rich — AUDE 35:15
l. get in the wrong places — MILN 528:10
l. in the grave — JOHN 433:4
l., methinks, should be free — OSBO 578:11
l. mingle souls — DONN 281:20
L. of thanks — AUDE 35:16
l. to a non-existent — LEWI 483:10
like women's l. — HAZL 376:9
nat the l. space — CHAU 213:13
No arts; no l. — HOBB 390:16
professor of French l. — JOYC 437:23
than a man of l. — STER 757:14
twenty-two fundamental l. — SEFE 675:17
letting l. each other go — RILK 648:16
lettuce eating too much l. — POTT 608:3
letumque L. Labosque — VIRG 812:12
levee Drove my Chevy to the l. — MCLE 503:7
more alluring than a l. — CONG 239:15
level l. of provincial existence — ELIO 300:13
Those who attempt to l. — BURK 167:10
to one dead l. — POPE 602:3
leveller Death is the great l. — PROV 617:27
levellers l. wish to level *down* — JOHN 428:15
levelling cannot bear l. *up* — JOHN 428:15
leviathan draw out l. — BIBL 83:29
L., called a commonwealth — HOBB 390:7
L. Hugest of living creatures — MILT 533:22
l. retrieving pebbles — WELL 828:6
there is that L. — BOOK 141:10
levity little judicious l. — STEV 759:29
lewd certain l. fellows — BIBL 105:14
Lewley bricks to L. — BETJ 72:16
lex Salus populi suprema l. — SELD 676:9
suprema est l. — CICE 223:9
lexicographer L. A writer of dictionaries — JOHN 424:10
wake a l. — JOHN 424:6
lexicon Two men wrote a l. — WATE 822:15

lexicons We are walking l. LIVE 487:5
liar answered 'Little L.' BELL 65:3
best l. BUTL 176:25
every man a l. BIBL 106:3
he is a l. BIBL 103:12
l. should be outlawed HALI 368:14
l. to have good memory PROV 625:12
penalty of a l. TALM 772:29
proved l. HAIL 367:13
She's like a l. SHAK 714:24
liars All men are l. BOOK 142:7
fears may be l. CLOU 229:11
Income Tax made more L. ROGE 652:17
l. and swearers SHAK 706:21
L. ought to have good memories SIDN 735:15
Poets . . . though l. HUME 409:8
prove the greatest l. DRAY 285:22
libation pouring a l. SOCR 745.9
libel excessive wealth a l. SHEL 732:12
greater the l. PROV 621:17
l. in a frown SWIF 767:2
libellum *novum l.* CATU 199:22
liber *L. scriptus* MISS 539:16
liberal as distinguished from the L. BIER 116:5
damned l. majority IBSE 412:9
either a little L. GILB 347:12
first L. leader STEE 754:14
is a l. education STEE 755:1
l. education BANK 54:16
l. is a conservative who WOLF 843:20
l. of another man's BACO 45:10
panted for a l. profession COLM 236:3
liberality l. becomes a source BAED 47:7
liberals l. can understand BRUC 162:2
liberation l. of the human mind GOLD 354:8
liberavi *L. animam meam* BERN 70:14
libertas *Imperium et L.* DISR 276:21
L. et natale solum SWIF 767:20
Liberté *L.! Égalité* POLI 601:1
liberties give up their l. BURK 169:1
l. are taken in thy name GEOR 344:2
L. . . . depend on the silence HOBB 390:18
not to have l. PYM 638:13
libertine puffed and reckless l. SHAK 684:16
liberty ardour for l. PRIC 610:15
be light! said L. SHEL 729:10
Brightest in dungeons, L. BYRO 183:7
certainly destroys l. JOHN 432:3
chosen music, L. WORD 850:14
conceived in all l. LINC 485:7
contend for their l. HALI 369:4
contrary to l. BENT 68:9
dangers to l. lurk BRAN 149:13
delight with l. SPEN 752:12
desires in l. TOCQ 795:7
divests himself of natural l. LOCK 488:19
endanger the public l. ADAM 2:19
end to a woman's l. BURN 170:1
enemies of l. HUME 409:1
extremism in the defence of l. GOLD 356:2
full l. is not given COTT 244:8
given l. to man CURR 254:4
holy name of l. GAND 339:5
individual l. SALI 664:10
l. and equality ARIS 26:2
l. and prosperity JENY 421:2
l. and slavery CAMD 186:15
L. *and* Union WEBS 825:12
L. cannot be SUMN 764:2
L. cannot be preserved ADAM 3:5
l. cannot long exist BURK 166:11
l. consists in doing MILL 525:10
l. depends on freedom JEFF 419:11
l. doesn't even go to the trouble BALZ 54:10
L. is liberty, not BERL 70:4
L. is precious LENI 480:10
L. is to faction MADI 505:11
L. is, to the lowest rank JOHN 424:2
L. is unfinished business ANON 17:6
L. means responsibility SHAW 726:19
L. not a means ACTO 1:12

l. of the individual MILL 525:9
l. of the press JUNI 438:15
l., or give me death HENR 382:15
l. plucks justice SHAK 707:19
L.'s a glorious feast BURN 171:18
L.'s in every blow BURN 172:6
l. to be saucy HALI 369:5
l. to know, to utter MILT 535:24
L. too must be limited BURK 166:9
L., when it begins to take root WASH 822:12
l. which we can hope MILT 535:13
life, and l. JEFF 419:10
life, l. ANON 19:17
loudest yelps for l. JOHN 426:8
love is l. POPE 602:16
love of l. HAZL 376:14
mansion-house of l. MILT 535:22
notion of l. JOHN 428:2
of l., and of learning DISR 276:10
O l.! what crimes LAST 473:9
pinch the sea of its l. COTT 244:7
play not with my l. GODO 352:1
principate and l. TACI 769:21
proclaim l. to the captives BIBL 90:18
regulated l. BURK 167:5
right of l. TAFT 770:15
safeguards of l. FRAN 332:10
seek power and lose l. BACO 44:22
Shouted of l. LONG 490:25
so easy as l. ASTE 32:13
survival and the success of l. KENN 448:16
Sweet land of l. SMIT 742:18
symbol of constitutional l. GIBB 345:6
tree of l. JEFF 419:15
truth and l. SHEL 732:6
wait for l. MACA 498:4
what cannot be sold—l. GRAT 359:16
when they cry l. MILT 535:6
who ever gives, takes l. DONN 279:25
Wommen, of kynde, desiren l. CHAU 211:8
Liberty-Hall This is L., gentlemen GOLD 355:25
libraries circulating l. RUSK 659:21
l. of the Commons CHAN 208:4
library Alexandria's l. burned HUGH 407:6
choice of all my l. SHAK 719:15
circulating l. SHER 733:16
In his l. AUST 39:22
l. in every county town CARL 192:31
l. is thought in cold storage SAMU 665:10
lumber room of his l. DOYL 284:11
My l. Was dukedom SHAK 718:21
public l. BENN 67:5
public l. JOHN 425:22
sit in a l. FITZ 324:4
turn over half a l. JOHN 430:5
universe . . . others call the L. BORG 145:4
libro *Galeotto fu il l.* DANT 255:20
Libya L. about Cyrene BIBL 104:27
licence l. they mean MILT 535:6
l. to act like an asshole ZAPP 858:5
l. to kill FLEM 326:10
l. to print money THOM 792:22
love not freedom, but l. MILT 536:6
POETIC L. BANV 54:20
universal l. to be good COLE 231:2
license L. my roving hands DONN 279:13
licensed based upon l. premises O'BR 571:5
l. to kill FILM 319:15
L. to kill MISQ 538:6
licentious l. passages GIBB 345:22
l. soldiery BURK 168:25
Licht *Mehr L.* LAST 473:5
lick enemies shall l. the dust BOOK 138:23
l. it into form BURT 173:22
licking finger l. good ADVE 7:37
Liddell right part wrote L. WATE 822:15
this is Mrs L. SPRI 753:8
Liddesdale Eskdale and L. SCOT 674:15
lids Drops his blue-fringèd l. COLE 231:17
with eternal l. apart KEAT 442:11
lie Bodies never l. DE M 263:13
can't tell a l. WASH 822:11

definition of a l. ANON 14:18
dost thou l. so low SHAK 697:13
Every word she writes is a l. MCCA 500:9
fain wald l. down BALL 52:10
fall victim to a big l. HITL 389:23
give them both the l. RALE 641:2
Here L. I EPIT 309:13
home to a l. POUN 608:20
House of the L. ZORO 860:1
if a l. may do thee grace SHAK 691:18
I l. down alone HOUS 404:3
I mean you l. SWIF 766:9
Is a dream a l. SPRI 753:12
isn't told a l. KIPL 455:17
leads you to believe a l. BLAK 119:23
l. diagonally in his bed STER 757:11
l. direct SHAK 682:8
l. even when it is inconvenient VIDA 810:3
l. follows PROU 613:13
L. FOLLOWS BY POST TELE 776:11
L. heavy on him, Earth EPIT 311:12
l. in cold obstruction SHAK 708:10
l. in the soul JOWE 436:18
l. that makes us realize truth PICA 595:10
l. that sinketh in BACO 45:31
l. through centuries BROW 158:21
l. which is part a truth TENN 777:9
l. will go round the world SPUR 753:12
L. with me BIBL 77:3
Live and l. reclined TENN 781:9
make your bed, so you must l. PROV 614:39
May l. till seven CLAR 225:10
mixture of a l. BACO 45:30
noble l. PLAT 597:13
no worse l. JAME 418:21
obedient to their laws we l. EPIT 309:11
often a whole l. PROV 621:25
old L.: Dulce et decorum OWEN 581:4
possible to l. for the truth ADLE 5:19
readily can l. with art GAY 342:3
sent to l. abroad WOTT 851:8
that he should l. BIBL 78:20
undo the folded l. AUDE 36:4
what is a l. BYRO 181:26
when dead, l. as quietly EDWA 296:15
Whoever would l. usefully HERV 386:23
Who loves to l. with me SHAK 681:3
lieb *so herzlich l.* HEIN 380:2
lied because our fathers l. KIPL 453:18
l. to please the mob KIPL 454:2
lien have l. among the pots BOOK 138:12
lies Beats all the l. BLAK 119:10
believing their own l. ARBU 24:5
certain, and the rest is l. FITZ 323:6
delight is in l. BOOK 137:27
hear no l. PROV 614:42
Here l. a lady RANS 642:7
Here l. Groucho Marx EPIT 310:3
Here l. the Earl of Leicester EPIT 310:1
History is a pack of l. STUB 762:19
History, sir, will tell l. SHAW 725:1
kindness and l. are worth GREE 362:12
l. a man who never lived THOM 792:5
l. are like the father SHAK 690:10
l. are often told in silence STEV 759:27
L. are the mortar WELL 828:12
l. as will lie in thy sheet SHAK 721:5
l. beneath your spell HOPE 396:8
l., damned lies and statistics DISR 278:9
l. it lives on and propagates FOSD 330:6
l. of tongue and pen CHES 216:3
make l. sound truthful ORWE 587:4
Matilda told such Dreadful L. BELL 65:2
produces l. like sand ANON 21:7
reality and l. COCT 230:1
spring of endless l. COWP 247:14
telling l. about the Democrats STEV 758:12
There l. the Doctor AUBR 33:14
though I know she l. SHAK 723:29
Truth exists, l. are invented BRAQ 149:18
truth to cover l. CONG 238:18
Without l. humanity FRAN 331:20

lieto *Chi vuol esser l. sia* MEDI 520:9
lieutenants God's l. upon earth JAME 417:3
life accounted his l. madness BIBL 92:26
actor's l. for me WASH 822:13
afternoon of human l. JUNG 438:13
all human l. is there ADVE 7:3
all human l. is there JAME 417:22
All L. death does end HOPK 396:20
all part of l.'s rich pageant MARS 514:11
All present l. BYRO 182:2
all the days of my l. BOOK 135:4
answers to the meaning of l. DAWK 259:17
as large as l. CARR 195:24
Bankrupt of l. DRYD 286:22
believe in l. DU B 290:20
believe in the l. to come BECK 61:4
best days of l. VIRG 814:19
better to enjoy l. JOHN 424:15
betwixt l. and death WORD 850:4
bitterness of l. CARR 196:14
book of l. BIBL 113:3
Book of L. begins WILD 836:23
brisking about the l. SMAR 739:18
careful of the single l. TENN 779:8
changing scenes of l. TATE 773:13
Chaos often breeds l. ADAM 2:13
Chief nourisher in l.'s feast SHAK 704:24
clinging to l. ARNO 29:14
content to manufacture l. BERN 70:8
count l. just a stuff BROW 159:25
criticism of l. ARNO 29:24
crown of l. BIBL 111:19
crown of l. BIBL 113:2
day-to-day business l. is LAFO 463:17
death after l. SPEN 751:21
death in l. ANON 17:22
Death is not an event in l. WITT 842:12
death, nor l. BIBL 106:23
discovered the secret of l. CRIC 251:4
disease of modern l. ARNO 28:9
distinction of your l. TACI 770:6
Does thy l. destroy BLAK 122:14
doors to let out l. FLET 327:4
doors to let out l. MASS 518:5
drive l. into a corner THOR 793:12
escape the l.-sentence LAWR 475:17
essence of human l. MACD 501:3
essence of l. DAWK 259:15
everlasting l. BIBL 102:32
everlasting l. BIBL 103:6
evidence of l. after death SOPE 746:11
except my l. SHAK 685:20
fear love is to fear l. RUSS 660:22
fed full of l. LUCR 496:1
Fill me with l. anew HATC 375:3
findeth his l. BIBL 96:21
find l. in death COLE 231:10
finished A l. heroic MILT 535:2
following l. thro' creatures POPE 603:17
forfeit my l. BROW 155:7
for her l. he died STON 761:5
for l., not for lunch SAYI 669:29
former naughty l. BOOK 131:4
fountain of the water of l. BIBL 114:18
French for l.-jacket BARN 56:8
Friday I tasted l. DICK 273:13
from the dream of l. SHEL 728:22
Further sacrifice of l. DE V 266:2
gained in the university of l. BOTT 147:2
gave my l. for freedom EWER 313:8
genius into my l. WILD 837:8
give for his l. BIBL 82:28
giveth his l. for the sheep BIBL 103:17
giveth l. to the world BIBL 103:3
golden tree of actual l. GOET 352:18
Good l. be now my task DRYD 288:14
great l. if you don't weaken BUCH 162:18
had a happy l. LAST 474:13
hath a l. to live RAIN 640:15
His l. was gentle SHAK 698:29
honour and l. FRAN 332:4
hour of glorious l. MORD 547:23
Human l. BERN 71:5

human l. is, at the greatest TEMP 775:10
Human l. is everywhere JOHN 425:27
I bear a charmèd l. SHAK 707:16
If l. hands you lemons SAYI 669:26
if l. was bitter to thee SWIN 768:6
in l. as it is in ways BACO 43:3
in mourning for my l. CHEK 213:24
in our l. alone COLE 231:9
In the midst of l. BOOK 133:17
In the midst of l. MUMF 554:1
in the sea of l. ARNO 29:2
in this l. BIBL 108:3
Is it not l. BYRO 184:12
isn't l. a terrible thing THOM 790:6
It's l., Jim MISQ 538:5
I've had a wonderful l. LAST 473:20
journey of our l. DANT 255:12
jump the l. to come SHAK 704:3
lad of l. SHAK 693:11
lag-end of my l. SHAK 691:4
last of l. BROW 161:3
lay down his friends for his l. THOR 793:21
lay down his l. BIBL 103:33
leadeth unto l. BIBL 95:20
Lead me from death to l. KUMA 462:4
L., a Fury slinging flame TENN 779:4
l. a glorious cycle of song PARK 585:14
l. all labour be TENN 781:8
l. and death BIBL 79:1
l., and liberty JEFF 419:10
l. and loves of a she-devil WELD 827:6
l. and power FOX 331:7
l. at a pin's fee SHAK 684:27
l. began by flickering out GONC 356:8
L. begins at forty PITK 595:21
L. begins at forty PROV 625:13
l., being weary SHAK 696:20
l. beyond life MILT 535:15
l. eternal gave BYRO 178:10
L. exists in the universe JEAN 419:7
L. feeding death ALAB 9:12
L., force and beauty POPE 603:31
l. forget and death remember SWIN 769:1
L. for life BIBL 78:6
L., friends, is boring BERR 71:17
l. had been ruined BROO 154:3
l. has crept so long TENN 782:5
l. hath been one chain CLAR 224:4
L. imitates Art WILD 836:3
l. in another life ELIO 299:8
l. in miniature O'NE 573:11
l. in the village LEE 478:18
l. is 6 to 5 against RUNY 659:2
L. is a copiously branching GOUL 357:11
L. is a foreign language MORL 549:3
L. is a gamble STOP 761:16
L. is a great surprise NABO 555:16
L. is a horizontal fall COCT 230:2
L. is a jest EPIT 310:13
L. is all a VARIORUM BURN 171:19
L. is an incurable disease COWL 245:30
L. is an offensive WHIT 832:8
L. is a rainbow which YEVT 856:21
L. is a sexually SAYI 670:4
L. is as tedious SHAK 699:7
L. is a top GREV 364:1
L. is Colour and Warmth GREN 363:13
L. is doubt UNAM 804:9
L. is first boredom, then fear LARK 468:15
l. is given to none freehold LUCR 495:17
L. is just a bowl of cherries BROW 155:10
L. is just one damned HUBB 406:11
L. is made up of RICE 646:18
L. is mostly froth GORD 356:17
L. is not meant to be easy FRAS 333:5
L. is not meant to be easy SHAW 724:18
L. isn't finished CHEK 214:5
L. is real LONG 490:18
L. is short PROV 614:32
L. is short, the art long HIPP 389:9
L. is the desert YOUN 857:22
L. is the other way round LODG 489:6
l. is the thing SMIT 742:15

L. is too much like a pathless wood FROS 335:7
L. is too precious ELIO 300:21
l. is very short TAYL 775:2
l. is washed BARZ 57:20
L. itself BROW 156:1
l., its enemy ANOU 22:18
L., Joy, Empire SHEL 731:10
L. levels all men SHAW 726:29
l., liberty ANON 19:17
l. like a box of chocolates FILM 320:11
L., like a dome SHEL 729:2
l. may perfect be JONS 435:27
l. might be put on parade EULA 312:10
l. more than meat BIBL 95:7
L. not a series of gig lamps WOOL 845:3
l. of a man BIBL 76:10
l. of any important person PRIE 610:17
l. of his beast BIBL 84:13
l. of man, solitary, poor HOBB 390:16
l. of men on earth BEDE 62:7
l. of only one of them GODW 352:3
l. of the nation secure DOUG 284:4
l. of the world DOST 282:17
l. of wretchedness EURI 312:18
l. on the whole is far from gay LEAR 477:21
l. protracted JOHN 426:19
L. says: she did this BARN 56:9
L.'s better with POLI 601:2
L.'s but a walking shadow SHAK 707:14
l.'s dim windows BLAK 119:23
l.'s dull round SHEN 732:23
l. sentence goes on CONL 239:24
L.'s fitful fever SHAK 705:21
L.'s last scene JOHN 426:20
L.'s longing for itself GIBR 346:6
L.'s not just being alive MART 515:1
L. so fast doth fly DAVI 258:7
l. that breathes TENN 784:12
l. that I have MARK 512:10
L., the shadow of death SWIN 768:4
L., the Universe and Everything ADAM 2:2
l. time's fool SHAK 691:12
l. to a dream MONT 544:18
L., to be sure, is nothing much HOUS 404:4
L. too short to stuff a mushroom CONR 241:4
l. unto the bitter in soul BIBL 82:34
l. was duty HOOP 395:20
L. well spent is long LEON 481:2
L. went through with death FORT 330:14
l. will be sour grapes ASHF 31:16
L. without industry is guilt RUSK 659:11
l. without it were not ROWE 657:10
l. without theory DISR 277:7
L. would be tolerable LEWI 483:16
L. would be very pleasant SURT 764:20
L. would ring the bells GINS 349:14
live a l. half dead MILT 534:28
live out my l. talking VANZ 807:5
long as you have your l. JAME 417:14
looked at l. from both sides MITC 540:11
Lord and giver of l. BOOK 131:11
loss of l. HOWA 405:8
lost, except a little l. BYRO 182:28
love long l. better than figs SHAK 678:15
Mad from l.'s history HOOD 394:23
make l. happier MART 515:2
Man's l. BARN 56:18
matter of l. and death SHAN 724:7
measured out my l. with coffee spoons ELIO 302:15
medium of l. MANN 510:14
men confused with l. FRID 334:9
more a way of l. ANON 18:3
more of a l. CLAU 225:11
my l. is preserved BIBL 76:36
my l.'s a pain DAVI 258:9
my l. to make you King CHAR 209:8
my l. upon a cast SHAK 717:11
my whole l., long or short ELIZ 305:1
nauseous draught of l. ROCH 651:7
no l. of a man CARL 191:19

light (*cont.*):

speed far faster than l.	BULL 163:16
sudden gust of l.	MOTI 551:12
sweetness and l.	ARNO 29:8
sweetness and l.	SWIF 765:6
Teach l. to counterfeit a gloom	MILT 529:12
Thou art my l.	QUAR 639:1
through the realms of l.	GURN 366:3
thy l. and thy truth	BOOK 136:16
tried to mend the Electric L.	BELL 65:16
universal l.	POPE 603:31
upon the steps of the l.	MACD 501:7
waited for the l.	ROBI 650:15
Warmth and L.	GREN 363:13
when my l. is low	TENN 779:4
Wherefore is l. given	BIBL 82:34
where sweetness and l. failed	FORS 329:11
while the l. fails	ELIO 302:1
Will l. only shine	BERN 70:17
with a l. behind her	GILB 349:8
with Thee l.	BONH 127:8
Light Brigade Forward, the L.	TENN 776:14
lighten let thy mercy l. upon us	BOOK 128:2
L. our darkness	BOOK 128:20
l. with celestial fire	BOOK 144:13
lighter l. than vanity	BUNY 164:17
lightest feel the l. touch	REEV 644:13
l. things swim at the top	HALI 368:20
lighthouse Keeping a l. with his eyes	
	CAMP 187:4
sitivation at the l.	DICK 272:10
lightly l. as it comth	CHAU 212:6
unadvisedly, l., or wantonly	BOOK 133:5
lightness unbearable l. of being	KUND 462:6
lightning Art, and the summer l.	
	HERZ 386:25
bottled l.	DICK 271:2
chaos illuminated by l.	WILD 836:4
from Jove the l.	MANI 504:6
known the l.'s hour	DAY- 260:4
l. and lashed rod	HOPK 397:12
l. fall from heaven	BIBL 100:20
L. never strikes	PROV 625:16
loosed the fateful l.	HOWE 405:15
Shakespeare by flashes of l.	COLE 234:4
snatched the l.	TURG 802:13
to keep the l. out	ISHE 414:9
writing history with l.	WILS 840:16
lights all-the-l.-on man	REED 644:9
dimming of the l.	NICO 563:11
Father of l.	BIBL 111:20
Followed false l.	DRYD 288:13
glare of l.	CHRÉ 218:13
God made two great l.	BIBL 75:7
l. are dim and low	ORRE 576:12
l. around the shore	ROSS 656:8
may bear all l.	SHAF 678:6
northern l. astream	SMAR 740:18
Turn up the l.	LAST 474:8
watching the tail l.	CRAN 250:1
your l. burning	BIBL 101:2
ligno *Regnavit a l. Deus*	FORT 330:5
like but you'll l. it	CATC 202:5
company we don't greatly l.	WILL 838:13
do just what you l.	SHAW 725:11
don't l. this game	CATC 201:1
Do what you l.	RABE 639:17
I'd l. to get away	FROS 335:8
I L. Ike	POLI 600:20
l. and dislike the same	SALL 665:2
L. breeds like	PROV 625:17
L. cures like	MOTT 552:19
L. doth quit like	SHAK 708:17
l. everyone else	DE G 262:13
l. is not necessarily good	BELL 64:11
l. it the least	CHES 215:4
l., or at least tolerate	TREV 798:13
l. this sort of thing	LINC 485:14
l. what you get	SHAW 726:33
L. will to like	PROV 625:22
look upon his l. again	SHAK 684:10
made me l. him less	CONG 238:28
man I did not l.	AUST 40:12

man you don't l.	THOM 790:9
none of his friends l. him	WILD 837:10
nothing l. it	CARR 195:22
No wonder we l. them	AMIS 13:14
To be l. everyone else	SHIE 734:19
very, very l. me	STEV 760:5
wha's l. us	TOAS 796:3
whether we l. it or not	THOM 791:21
will much l.	AUST 40:21
liked feeling that one is not l.	SEI 675:18
l. it not, and died	WOTT 851:5
l. it so much	ADVE 7:33
l. whate'er She looked on	BROW 160:10
wish to be l.	RUSS 660:18
likely Not bloody l.	SHAW 727:16
likeness any l. of any thing	BIBL 77:37
in our image, after our l.	BIBL 75:8
l. in the Torah	KORA 461:7
l. of men	BIBL 105:10
made in the l. of men.	BIBL 109:24
likerous l. mouth	CHAU 212:15
likes does what he l. to do	GILL 349:10
likewise Go, and do thou l.	BIBL 100:25
liking Being alone and l. it	HASK 375:1
Friendships begin with l.	ELIO 299:13
lost me in your l.	SHAK 699:21
Not l. the person	THOM 790:18
lilac Kew in l.-time	NOYE 566:1
l. and the roses	ARAG 24:3
l. is in blossom	BROO 153:8
lilacs breeding L.	ELIO 303:7
l. last in the dooryard	WHIT 833:22
Lilian Airy, fairy L.	TENN 780:14
lilies braids of l. knitting	MILT 529:7
feedeth among the l.	BIBL 87:8
few l. blow	HOPK 396:16
give me l. in armfuls	VIRG 812:16
kingcups, and loved l.	SPEN 752:18
l. and languors	SWIN 768:10
l. by the rivers	BIBL 94:1
l. of the field	BIBL 95:9
L. that fester	SHAK 723:15
L. without	MARV 515:21
Lotos and l.	TENN 782:19
pale, lost l.	DOWS 284:6
peacocks and l.	RUSK 659:25
three l. in her hand	ROSS 655:19
Lilliburlero bars of L.	STER 756:20
L. Bullena-la	WHAR 831:4
lilting l., before dawn of day	ELLI 305:14
lily across the l. leven	BALL 53:11
Elaine, the l. maid	TENN 777:26
folds the l. all her sweetness up	TENN 783:14
l. of Florence	LONG 490:10
l. of the valleys	BIBL 87:5
l. on thy brow	KEAT 443:24
l. rears its gouged face	HILL 388:8
l.-white boys	SONG 747:11
little l.-handed baronet	TENN 783:18
paint the l.	BYRO 181:3
paint the l.	SHAK 699:10
pure as the l.	LAUD 470:6
trembles to a l.	DOBS 278:17
waved her l. hand	GAY 342:12
with a poppy or a l.	GILB 348:15
limb l. by limb	MILT 535:19
on every airth a l.	MONT 546:2
limber little child, a l. elf	COLE 231:7
limbo l. large and broad	MILT 532:20
limbs deck your lower l. in pants	
	NASH 557:18
great smooth marbly l.	BROW 158:20
life controls these l.	VIRG 812:3
l. of a poet	HORA 403:8
lime l.-tree bower my prison	COLE 233:13
limelight backing into the l.	BERN 71:6
limestone l. quarried near	YEAT 856:5
limit l. and isolate oneself	GOET 353:17
quiet l. of the world	TENN 784:7
limited Liberty too must be l.	BURK 166:9
whizzed the L.—	CRAN 250:1
limits l. of my language	WITT 842:13
l. prescribed by the law	LACL 463:8

stony l.	SHAK 717:23
limns l. the water	BACO 46:24
limousine All we want is a l.	MACN 504:15
One perfect l.	PARK 585:17
limp l. father of thousands	JOYC 437:20
Limpopo grey-green, greasy, L.	KIPL 456:17
Lincoln I am a Ford, not a L.	FORD 328:10
L. County Road or Armageddon	
	DYLA 294:14
L. shovelled into the tombs	SAND 665:18
L. went to New Orleans	HUGH 406:19
Linden On L., when the sun	CAMP 187:11
Linden Lea leän down low in L.	BARN 56:14
line active l. on a walk	KLEE 457:17
cancel half a l.	FITZ 323:10
carved not a l.	WOLF 843:12
combine to form a l.	LIND 486:2
cut, the style, the l.	LOES 489:11
direction of the right l.	NEWT 561:12
horizontal l.	WHEW 831:14
l. is a fuse	MAYA 519:9
l. is length without breadth	EUCL 312:8
l. too labours	POPE 604:10
l. upon line	BIBL 89:3
lives along the l.	POPE 604:28
Not a day without a l.	APEL 23:8
problem of the colour l.	DU B 290:21
thin red l.	RUSS 661:16
through colour and l.	MOND 542:19
lineaments l. of Gospel books	ROYD 658:1
linen Airing one's dirty l.	TRUF 801:3
did not love clean l.	JOHN 428:4
fair white l. cloth	BOOK 131:5
In blanchèd l.	KEAT 443:2
in l. like a gentleman	JOHN 424:20
Love is like l.	FLET 327:18
mad in white l.	SHER 733:10
purple and fine l.	BIBL 101:22
very fine l.	BRUM 162:8
wash your l.	STEV 760:12
lines face into more l.	SHAK 721:7
I plant l.	WALC 817:6
Just say the l.	COWA 245:14
l. and colours	POUS 609:12
l. are fallen unto me	BOOK 134:14
l. like these	CALV 186:6
l. (so loves) oblique	MARV 515:11
liquid l. mellifluously bland	BYRO 181:16
Prose is when all the l.	BENT 68:11
six l. written	RICH 647:19
town-crier spoke my l.	SHAK 686:21
walk on the l.	MILN 528:3
lingering alone sit l. here	VAUG 807:16
l., with boiling oil	GILB 348:7
lingua *Pange, l.*	FORT 330:3
Pange, l.	THOM 788:15
linguam *Et l. et mores*	JUVE 439:14
lining cloud has a silver l.	PROV 619:4
There's a silver l.	FORD 329:4
link weakest l.	PROV 616:30
You are the weakest l.	CATC 202:2
lin-lan-lone l. of evening bells	TENN 776:21
linnet l. born within the cage	TENN 778:31
linoleum shoot me through l.	BANK 54:17
linsy-woolsy lawless l. brother	BUTL 176:9
lion as a roaring l.	BIBL 112:15
better than a dead l.	PROV 625:35
bold as a l.	BIBL 85:16
buttocked like a l.	MALO 508:19
calf and the young l.	BIBL 88:21
dead l.	BIBL 86:13
desert l.	ARNO 28:15
gets the fattest l.	SAKI 663:15
hungry l. roars	SHAK 712:6
l. among ladies	SHAK 711:8
l. and adder	BOOK 140:4
L. and the Cock	GOGA 353:22
l. and the unicorn	NURS 567:20
l. shall eat straw	BIBL 88:22
l. to frighten the wolves	MACH 502:12
l. would cease to live	THOM 789:2
March comes in like a l.	PROV 626:14
mouse may help a l.	PROV 627:2

nation that had l.'s heart	CHUR 222:4
Rouse the l.	SCOT 674:24
said to the sick l.	HORA 399:2
Strong is the l.	SMAR 740:15
To rouse a l.	SHAK 689:28
wrath of the l.	BLAK 121:5
lions l. do lack	BOOK 135:24
L. led by donkeys	MILI 526:12
l., or Vanity-Fair	BUNY 165:4
l. roaring	BOOK 141:9
my darling from the l.	BOOK 135:27
on the other, l.	PATM 588:17
soul is among l.	BOOK 137:21
stronger than l.	BIBL 80:28
We are two l.	SHAK 697:5
lip 'twixt cup and l.	PROV 632:28
lips ashes on the l.	MOOR 547:21
beautiful l. in anger	RIMB 649:12
Eternity was in our l. and eyes	SHAK 678:21
ever at his l.	KFAT 444:19
Is it Lombard's l.	EWAR 313:7
keep the door of my l.	BOOK 143:20
l. cannot fail	BURG 166:1
l. drew near	BYRO 180:23
l. have spoken	SHEL 729:24
l. like a thread of scarlet	BIBL 87:10
l. of a strange woman	BIBL 83:38
l. of dying men	ARNO 28:16
l. of living men	BUTL 177:7
l. once sanctified	BROW 161:30
l. that laugh and hide	SWIN 768:2
l., that they speak no guile	BOOK 135:25
l. that touch liquor	YOUN 857:4
Loose l. sink ships	MILI 526:13
moisten poor Jim's l.	FARM 315:5
my Julia's l. do smile	HERR 385:18
My l. are sealed	BALD 50:17
My l. are sealed	MISQ 538:10
never come out of a lady's l.	FLEM 326:13
open my l.	BOOK 137:15
O take those l. away	SHAK 708:13
people of unclean l.	BIBL 88:11
put my l. to it	DICK 270:3
Read my l.	BUSH 174:23
roses of thy l.	LODG 489:9
round their narrow l.	ROSS 656:2
saw their starved l.	KEAT 443:29
shoot out their l.	BOOK 134:27
touched thy l.	BIBL 88:12
when I ope my l.	SHAK 708:21
lipstick bears a l.'s traces	MARV 516:7
liquefaction l. of her clothes	HERR 386:20
liquid Cats, no less l.	TESS 786:3
let their l. siftings fall	ELIO 303:6
l. lines mellifluously bland	BYRO 181:16
Thames is l. history	BURN 170:2
liquor Good l., I stoutly maintain	
	GOLD 355:22
lads for the l.	HOUS 404:12
lips that touch l.	YOUN 857:23
l. is quicker	NASH 557:15
Livelier l. than the Muse	HOUS 405:2
Love is that l.	HERB 383:19
other spiritual l.	BYRO 183:18
wanteth not l.	BIBL 87:20
lirra Tirra l.	TENN 780:11
lisped I l. in numbers	POPE 602:25
Somwhat he l.	CHAU 210:15
list I've got a little l.	GILB 347:21
List, list, O, l.	SHAK 684:31
snatched up the l.	AKHM 9:9
There is no l.	STRA 762:12
listen better not to l.	DELL 263:12
Darkling I l.	KEAT 444:27
l. all day	CARR 194:5
L., my children	LONG 491:4
l. the more	ZENO 858:7
only l. when I am unhappy	SMIT 742:21
privilege of wisdom to l.	HOLM 393:2
Stop-look-and-l.	OFFI 572:13
world should l. then	SHEL 732:1
listened he is not l. to	TALM 772:29
listener always be a mere l.	JUVE 439:6

l., who listens in the snow	STEV 758:7
listeners L. never hear any good	
	PROV 625:23
listening disease of not l.	SHAK 691:24
l., lying in wait	THOM 790:15
People hearing without l.	SIMO 738:4
listeth wind bloweth where it l.	BIBL 102:31
lit whole Fleet's l. up	WOOD 844:17
literal say a l. God	DONN 281:26
literary If I had to do l. work	SALI 664:12
improving l. taste	MCEL 501:13
l. and scientific	ARNO 29:20
l. cooks	MORE 548:1
l. man	DICK 271:17
l. prejudices	JOHN 425:5
l. productions	GIBB 345:3
Never l. attempt	HUME 409:6
Of all the l. scenes	PRES 610:12
parole of l. men	JOHN 431:25
unsuccessful l. man	BELL 65:13
with St Paul are l.	ARNO 30:2
literature function of imaginative l.	
	EMPS 307:24
great Cham of l.	SMOL 744:19
ideas to l.	BOUR 147:12
in l., the oldest	BULW 164:6
in the locks of l.	TENN 785:3
itch of l.	LOVE 493:12
life ruined by l.	BROO 154:3
like their l. clear and cold	LEWI 483:20
l. can and should do	BYAT 177:12
L. cannot be the business	SOUT 749:18
l. is a drug	BORR 145:12
L. is a luxury	CHES 216:20
l. is more dependable	BROD 152:1
l. is my mistress	CHEK 214:9
L. is news	POUN 609:9
l. mostly about having sex	LODG 489:6
l. of *power*	DE Q 265:3
L.'s always a good card	BENN 67:23
l. seeks to communicate	DE Q 264:21
l.'s performing flea	O'CA 571:10
L. the orchestration of platitudes	
	WILD 837:16
lover of l.	SOUT 749:12
Philistine of genius in l.	ARNO 30:6
profession of l.	JOHN 426:5
province of l.	MACA 499:1
Remarks are not l.	STEI 755:6
rest is l.	COLE 234:17
rest is l.	VALÉ 806:8
superior man studies l.	CONF 237:19
wash l. off	ARTA 30:19
lites *inter vos tantas componere l.*	VIRG 813:23
litigious l. lady	NEWT 561:16
littérature *tout le reste est l.*	VERL 808:15
little big words for l. matters	JOHN 428:21
by l. and little	BIBL 93:18
cry of the L. Peoples	LE G 479:6
eat up the l. ones	SHAK 715:3
Every l. helps	PROV 619:12
Ev'ry day a l. death	SOND 746:4
Go, l. bok	CHAU 213:14
had a l. gun	NURS 569:20
having too l.	COMP 236:20
here a l., and there a little	BIBL 89:3
hobgoblin of l. minds	EMER 307:5
how l. the mind	JOHN 430:4
how l. we think of the other	TWAI 803:20
l. and loud	PROV 625:36
L. boxes on the hillside	REYN 646:10
l. creep through	SHEN 732:24
L. drops of water	CARN 193:11
L. Englanders	ANON 17:8
l. fire kindleth	BIBL 111:26
l. fish are sweet	PROV 625:25
l. grey cells	CHRI 218:15
l. learning is a dangerous thing	POPE 604:2
little l. grave	SHAK 716:2
Little man, l. man	ELIZ 304:13
L. man, you've had a busy day	SIGL 736:23
L. Miss Muffet	NURS 568:3
l. more	BROW 158:25

L. one! Oh, little one	STEP 756:4
l. people pay taxes	HELM 380:13
l. pot is soon hot	PROV 625:29
l. saint	HERR 386:11
l. seemed to him great	MACA 498:14
l. ships of England	GUED 365:10
L. strokes fell great oaks	PROV 625:30
L. subject, little wit	CARE 191:6
L. things please	PROV 625:32
l. to say	SKEL 739:5
l. volume, but large book	CRAS 250:13
l. while	BIBL 103:37
l. woman who wrote	LINC 485:15
Love me l.	PROV 625:46
Man wants but l.	GOLD 355:1
Many a l.	PROV 626:8
no l. enemy	PROV 632:17
offering Germany too l.	NEVI 559:14
one of these l. ones	BIBL 96:22
our l. life	SHAK 719:1
Say l. and do much	SHAM 724:6
She gives but l.	YOUN 857:6
So l. done	LAST 473:17
so l. done	TENN 779:11
Thank heaven for l. girls	LERN 481:21
this l. world	SHAK 715:13
though she be but l.	SHAK 711:16
too l. or too much	BARR 56:20
very l. one	MARR 514:9
wants that l. strong	HOLM 393:5
with so l. stir	WHIT 832:17
littleness For the long l. of life	CORN 243:11
liturgy Popish l.	PITT 596:5
Publick L.	BOOK 127:11
live as if you were to l. for ever	EDMU 296:8
be, feel, l.	HERD 385:8
better l. as we think	BOUR 147:11
Bid me to l.	HERR 386:13
cannot l. with you	MART 515:3
Can these bones l.	BIBL 91:17
cease to l.	ARNO 29:5
Come l. with me	DONN 280:15
Come l. with me	MARL 513:16
Come l. with me	PROV 617:2
Could she not l.	BYRO 178:10
dangerous to l. long	THOM 788:11
Days are where we l.	LARK 468:14
desires to l. long	SWIF 766:25
Easy l. and quiet die	SCOT 674:5
Eat to l.	PROV 618:37
enable its citizens to l.	WEIL 826:22
find out why we l.	CHEK 214:5
forgets to l.	LA B 462:17
Glad did I l.	STEV 760:20
hast no more to l.	SWIN 768:6
he isn't fit to l.	KING 452:3
he shall l.	BOOK 139:1
He shall l. by them	TALM 772:15
he shall l. in them	BIBL 78:13
He shall not l.	SHAK 698:11
how long I have to l.	BOOK 136:4
If you don't l. it	PARK 585:13
I joy to see My self now l.	HERR 386:9
I l. not in myself	BYRO 178:25
in him we l., and move	BIBL 105:20
just shall l. by faith	BIBL 105:36
know how to l. right	HORA 399:24
let me l. to-night	SHAK 714:21
Let us l., my Lesbia	CATU 202:13
L. all you can	JAME 417:14
l. and last	CATU 202:10
l. and learn	POMF 599:15
L. and learn	PROV 625:33
L. and let live	PROV 625:34
L. and lie reclined	TENN 781:9
l. and take comfort	WORD 850:18
l. a novel	HARD 371:21
l. any longer in sin	BIBL 106:10
L. a thousand years	SHAK 697:14
l. beyond its income	BUTL 176:28
l. by bread alone	PROV 625:52
l. by sight	BUNY 165:11
l. cleanly	SHAK 691:19

live (cont.):
l. dog is better — PROV 625:35
l. in a fantasy world — MURD 554:18
L. in despite of murder — CHAP 208:11
l. in peace — ARIS 25:17
l. in society — ARIS 25:26
l. longest, see most — PROV 632:36
l., not as we wish — MENA 521:14
l. on this Crumpetty Tree — LEAR 477:21
l. on your knees — IBAR 412:7
l. or die wi' Charlie — HOGG 392:8
l. past years again — DRYD 287:28
l. their creeds — GUES 365:13
l. this long — BLAK 119:3
l. through someone else — FRIE 334:11
L. till tomorrow — COWP 246:21
l. to do that — MART 514:16
l. together as brothers — KING 452:5
l. too long — DANI 255:10
l. to please — JOHN 426:13
l. to study — BACO 46:11
l. under the shadow of a war — SPEN 751:1
l., unseen, unknown — POPE 605:32
l. well on nothing a year — THAC 786:18
L. with yourself — PERS 593:9
l. your life not as simple — PAST 588:3
long as ye both shall l. — BOOK 133:8
long to l. — BOOK 128:15
Man is born to l. — PAST 587:18
martyrdom to l. — BROW 156:10
means whereby I l. — SHAK 709:32
might as well l. — PARK 586:1
mortal millions l. alone — ARNO 29:2
must l. — ARGE 24:18
nations how to l. — MILT 536:1
never l. to be useless — WESL 829:21
no man see me and l. — BIBL 78:10
not l. to eat — MOLI 541:10
Sacco's name will l. — VANZ 807:4
see so much, nor l. so long — SHAK 702:9
short time to l. — BOOK 133:16
sometimes l. apart — SAKI 663:20
taught us how to l. — TICK 794:13
Teach me to l. — KEN 448:8
to l. dangerously — NIET 564:8
to l. is Christ — BIBL 109:22
To l. is like to love — BUTL 177:1
to l. is not — POMP 599:17
To l. without him — WOTT 851:5
to l. without labour — TAWN 774:4
To l. with thee — RALE 640:18
Too small to l. in — ANON 19:14
turn and l. with animals — WHIT 843:1
wanted to l. deep — THOR 793:12
way they have to l. — CATH 199:13
we bear to l. — POPE 605:8
We l., as we dream — CONR 240:14
We l. our lives — RILK 648:15
wouldn't l. under Niagara — CARL 193:3
would you l. for ever — FRED 333:6
lived Had we l. — SCOT 673:1
I have l. long enough — SHAK 707:8
lies a man who never l. — THOM 792:5
l. during the years around 1789 — TALL 771:17
l. in social intercourse — JOHN 429:15
l. light in the spring — ARNO 27:7
Mr Holmes where have you l. — DOYL 284:21
never loved, has never l. — GAY 341:21
Never to have l. is best — YEAT 854:9
say 'I have l.' — HORA 402:2
lively l. Oracles of God — CORO 243:16
true and l. Word — BOOK 131:15
liver l. is on the right — MOLI 542:1
L. of blaspheming Jew — SHAK 706:13
l. spotted — JONS 434:16
l.-wing of a fowl — TENN 784:24
open and notorious evil l. — BOOK 131:3
livered But I am pigeon-l. — SHAK 686:5
liveries summer l. — LANI 467:3
Liverpool folk that live in L. — CHES 216:8
livery in her sober l. all things clad — MILT 533:4

shadowed l. — SHAK 709:3
lives Careless talk costs l. — OFFI 572:1
Clarissa l. — RICH 647:14
Everything that l. — BLAK 119:18
evil that men do l. — SHAK 697:21
He l., he wakes — SHEL 728:24
He that l. upon hope — FRAN 332:15
he who l. more lives than one — WILD 837:1
how he l. — JOHN 429:7
how the other half l. — PROV 628:37
in jeopardy of their l. — BIBL 81:8
it's men's l. — SCOT 674:3
light wind l. or dies — KEAT 445:17
l. along the line — POPE 604:28
l. by the sword — PROV 622:12
l. long who lives well — PROV 621:42
l. of quiet desperation — THOR 793:4
l. to eat — SOCR 744:25
l. would grow together — SWIN 769:6
make our l. sublime — LONG 490:21
ninety l. have been taken — MCGO 501:16
passing their l. together — HUME 408:14
pleasant in their l. — BIBL 80:28
their l. before — SHAK 715:12
way to conduct our l. — PLAT 597:12
woman who l. for others — LEWI 483:7
liveth he that l. longest — HENS 382:17
know that my redeemer l. — BIBL 83:12
l. unto God — BIBL 106:12
name l. for evermore — BIBL 93:34
name l. for evermore — EPIT 311:8
that l., and was dead — BIBL 112:30
livid one l. smile — WALP 820:1
living affords a rule of l. — ADDA 3:18
appointed for all l. — BIBL 83:17
are you yet l. — SHAK 712:12
book of the l. — BOOK 138:18
Earned a precarious l. — ANON 15:19
envy of the l. — HOBB 391:2
even for the l. God — BOOK 136:11
fever called 'l.' — POE 599:4
fight for the l. — JONE 434:7
fillest all things l. — BOOK 143:25
for you to go on l. — SOCR 745:5
get mine own l. — BOOK 132:18
go on l. even after death — FRAN 332:9
hands of the l. God — BIBL 111:5
house is a machine for l. in — LE C 478:10
land of the l. — BIBL 90:4
land of the l. — WILD 837:14
language of the l. — ELIO 301:21
life is not worth l. — SOCR 745:3
L. and partly living — ELIO 302:23
l. at this hour — WORD 847:14
l. death — MILT 534:28
l. dog — BIBL 86:13
l. doll, everywhere you look — PLAT 596:18
l. in a time — BREC 150:18
l. in Philadelphia — EPIT 310:6
L. is abnormal — IONE 413:21
L. is an illness — CHAM 207:1
L. is my job — MONT 544:12
l. know No bounds — SHIR 735:6
l. man is the glory — IREN 414:2
l. need charity — ARNO 26:22
l. sacrifice — BIBL 106:25
L.? The servants will do that — VILL 810:10
l. to some purpose — PAIN 583:1
l. up to it is difficult — THAC 786:5
long habit of l. — BROW 156:11
machine for l. — TOLS 796:19
more alone while l. — CARR 193:14
more than the l. — BIBL 86:2
nets to catch the l. — WEBS 825:19
noble L. — WORD 849:17
no l. of its own — JENN 421:1
no l. people in it — CHEK 213:25
no l. with thee — ADDI 4:25
no man l. — BOOK 143:22
Plain l. and high thinking — WORD 848:18
reasons for l. — JUVE 440:4
respect to the l. — VOLT 816:11
riotous l. — BIBL 101:14

start by l. — ANOU 22:20
Summer time an' the l. is easy — HEYW 387:16
those who are l. — BURK 167:22
to go on l. — WOLF 843:8
too much love of l. — SWIN 768:17
well and l. in Paris — ANON 17:4
Who, l., had no roof — HEYW 388:1
Why seek ye the l. — BIBL 102:9
world does not owe us a l. — PHIL 594:10
you'll learn the art of l. — GOET 352:19
Livingstone Dr L., I presume — STAN 754:6
livres l. cadrent mal — MOLI 541:21
lizard L.'s leg — SHAK 706:12
llama L. is a sort of fleecy goat — BELL 65:13
Lloyd George L. knew my father — ANON 17:10
lo L.! He comes — WESL 829:9
L.! the poor Indian — POPE 604:23
load l. and bless With fruit — KEAT 445:14
L. every rift — KEAT 447:7
loaf Half a l. is better — PROV 621:23
l. with a field in the middle — WILD 837:6
slice off a cut l. — PROV 630:44
with a l. of bread — FITZ 323:2
loafing cricket as organized l. — TEMP 775:13
loan l. oft loses — SHAK 684:19
loathe l. all things held — CALL 186:2
loathing Length begets l. — PROV 625:3
loaves five barley l. — BIBL 103:1
lobster l. be any more ridiculous — NERV 559:9
seen the mailed l. rise — FRER 333:18
voice of the L. — CARR 194:19
local little l. difficulties — MACM 504:5
l., but prized elsewhere — AUDE 36:7
l. habitation and a name — SHAK 711:28
l. thing called Christianity — HARD 371:13
locally act l. — SLOG 740:12
Lochinvar young L. is come — SCOT 673:18
loci Geniumque l. — VIRG 812:18
lock broken the l. — AUDE 35:21
l. o' his gowden hair — BALL 53:15
why l. him in — SHAW 726:14
locked hand that l. her up — VAUG 808:2
locket Lucy L. lost — NURS 568:7
locks in the l. of literature — TENN 785:3
knotted and combinèd l. — SHAK 684:32
l. were like the raven — BURN 171:15
l. which are left you — SOUT 749:9
never shake Thy gory l. — SHAK 706:5
locksmiths Love laughs at l. — PROV 625:44
locust hath the l. eaten — BIBL 92:1
years that the l. hath eaten — BIBL 92:2
locusts l. and wild honey — BIBL 94:11
locuta Roma l. est — AUGU 37:17
lodestar he was the l. — LYDG 496:18
lodestone l. to the north — DAVI 258:11
lodge as a l. in a garden — BIBL 87:25
best to l. — SHAK 721:8
l. Him in the manger — ANON 20:6
lodged L. with me useless — MILT 535:7
lodging Hard was their l. — GART 340:11
lodgings l. in a head — BUTL 176:3
loft windy, untidy l. — CANN 189:14
lofty great and l. things — MONT 543:23
L. and sour — SHAK 695:21
log King L. — AESO 6:18
l.-cabin to White House — THAY 787:19
logic Good, too, L., of course — CLOU 227:17
l. and rhetoric — BACO 45:22
l. of our times — DAY- 260:6
overthrow of all his l. — STEV 759:6
Second L. then — ARIS 25:3
That's l. — CARR 195:5
logical L. consequences — HUXL 412:3
logically does not make them sound l. — HALD 367:18
logs Tom bears l. — SHAK 702:26
loin ungirt l. — BROW 161:17
loins girded up his l. — BIBL 81:25
Let your l. be girded — BIBL 101:2
shudder in the l. engenders — YEAT 854:21
thicker than my father's l. — BIBL 81:15
Loire L. more than the Latin Tiber — DU B 290:19

loitered l. my life away HAZL 376:11
loitering Alone and palely l. KEAT 443:23
palely l. OPEN 575:8
Lolita L., light of my life OPEN 574:32
Lombardy waveless plain of L. SHEL 729:25
London 1938 in L. MIDL 524:13
arch of L. Bridge MACA 498:18
best club in L. DICK 271:21
city much like L. SHEL 730:19
crowd flowed over L. Bridge ELIO 303:11
describes L. BAGE 49:9
foggy day in L. Town GERS 344:4
gazed at the L. skies BETJ 72:2
going to L. ELIO 300:10
gondola of L. DISR 277:20
in L. only is a trade DRYD 289:11
I've been to L. NURS 569:5
key of India is L. DISR 276:22
lies L.'s daughter THOM 789:16
L.: a nation DISR 277:19
L. Bridge is broken down NURS 568:6
L. doth pour out SHAK 694:1
L. is a fine town COLM 236:1
L. is a modern Babylon DISR 277:30
[L.] is become an overgrown SMOL 744:16
L. is to Paddington CANN 189:8
L. particular . . . A fog DICK 267:14
L., small and white and clean MORR 549:15
L. spread out in the sun LARK 469:6
L.'s towers BLAK 120:15
L., that great cesspool DOYL 285:4
L., that great sea SHEL 729:19
L., thou art of townes ANON 17:11
L., thou art the flower ANON 17:12
L. Transport diesel-engined FLAN 324:19
lungs of L. PITT 596:9
rainy Sunday in L. DE Q 264:19
tired of L. JOHN 430:27
vilest alleys in L. DOYL 284:10
Yankee Doodle came to L. COHA 230:8
lone From the l. shieling GALT 338:15
l. lorn creetur DICK 268:7
l. unhaunted place DONN 280:8
walking by his wild l. KIPL 456:15
loneliness bowery l. TENN 782:11
l. of the long-distance SILL 737:16
well of l. HALL 369:13
lonely All the l. people LENN 480:17
heart is a l. hunter BORR 146:11
mirrors are l. AUDE 36:1
None but the l. heart GOET 353:14
Only the l. ORBI 576:5
troubled with her l. life PEPY 592:4
lonesome on a l. road COLE 233:7
lonesomeness starlight lit my l. HARD 373:6
long be the day l. PROV 615:17
dangerous to live l. THOM 788:11
foot and a half l. HORA 398:5
For a l. time PROU 613:3
for such a l. time MOLI 541:16
fulfilled a l. time BIBL 92:25
How l. a time SHAK 715:8
how l. I have to live BOOK 134:4
how l. it takes to succeed MONT 545:8
How l. wilt thou forget me BOOK 134:9
if a man have l. hair BIBL 107:23
In the l. run KEYN 450:18
it hath very l. arms HALI 369:2
it sha'n't be l. CHES 214:17
lives l. who lives well PROV 621:42
live this l. BLAK 119:3
L. ago in Kentucky WARR 822:1
l., and lank, and brown COLE 232:24
L. and lazy PROV 625:36
l. and the short and the tall HUGH 406:16
l. as ye both shall live BOOK 133:8
l. day's task SHAK 679:23
l.-distance runner SILL 737:16
l. hot summer FILM 322:7
l. in city pent KEAT 445:22
L. is the way MILT 532:7
l., long thoughts LONG 490:15
l., long trail KING 452:10

loitered l. my life away HAZL 376:11
l.-nosed Etruscans LAWR 475:1
l.-suffering, and of great goodness BOOK 141:2
l.-suffering, and very pitiful BIBL 93:2
l. time ago TAGL 771:7
l. time deid MOTT 552:3
l. way to Tipperary JUDG 438:4
l. week-end FORS 329:12
l., withdrawing roar ARNO 27:3
Lord, how l. BIBL 88:14
love me l. ANON 17:13
love me l. PROV 625:46
make a l. prologue BIBL 94:3
man goeth to his l. home BIBL 86:25
night of the l. knives HITL 389:24
Nor wants that little l. GOLD 355:1
So l. as men can breathe SHAK 722:25
story need be l. THOR 792:27
week is a l. time in politics WILS 840:7
With l. life BOOK 140:5
wooing not l. a-doing PROV 621:32
your way be l. CAVA 203:15
longa Ars l., vita brevis HIPP 389:9
longer devolution takes l. CART 198:6
living lasts l. ANOU 22:20
l. than the wave BALL 52:19
no l. my own METH 523:8
wished l. by its readers JOHN 433:20
your l. life ELIZ 304:10
longest laughs last, laughs l. PROV 622:11
live l., see most PROV 632:36
l. day and shortest night PROV 615:1
l. journey SHEL 729:8
l. way round PROV 625:37
longeth l. my soul after thee BOOK 136:11
my flesh also l. BOOK 138:3
longing cast a l. eye JEFF 419:17
desire and l. BOOK 139:15
hopeless l. ARNO 27:9
longings I have Immortal l. SHAK 680:12
longitude l. with no platitude FRY 336:14
longtemps L., je me suis couché PROU 613:3
look afraid to l. upon God BIBL 77:18
at the l. of him BOOK 141:11
cat may l. at a king PROV 616:28
dares not l. behind BLAI 118:14
dares not l. behind SHEL 732:21
direct him, where to l. DONN 279:4
do we l. for another BIBL 96:23
full l. at the worst HARD 372:17
Hit l. lak sparrer-grass HARR 374:2
I l. at the senators HALE 368:5
l. after our people LAST 471:13
l., and pass on DANT 255:14
L. as much like home FRY 336:15
l. at things in bloom HOUS 404:7
L. back in anger OSBO 578:17
L. before you leap PROV 625:39
L. for me by moonlight NOYE 566:3
l. forward to the trip STIN 761:4
L. in my face TRAI 798:3
l. in thy heart and write SIDN 736:3
l. no way but downwards BUNY 165:1
l. on and help LAWR 475:14
l. on both indifferently SHAK 696:4
L., stranger AUDE 35:9
l. the East End in the face ELIZ 305:6
L. thy last on all things lovely DE L 262:24
l. to his bond SHAK 709:12
L. to it LINC 485:4
l. to other people UNAM 804:11
l. to the end ANON 22:3
L. to your Moat HALI 369:9
l. upon a monkey CONG 239:23
l. upon his like again SHAK 684:10
l. upon thee BIBL 87:18
L. with thine ears SHAK 701:16
One cannot l. at this GOYA 357:15
row one way and l. another BURT 174:1
sit and l. at it for hours JERO 421:14
Stop-l.-and-listen OFFI 572:13
'Tis very sweet to l. KEAT 445:22
We l. before and after SHEL 731:29

When I do l. on thee SIDN 736:13
looked If you l. away, you knew SERE 677:4
looked for a city BIBL 111:7
l. in this merciless glare WILL 839:9
l. upon Peter BIBL 102:2
more he l. inside MILN 527:16
She l. at me KEAT 443:26
lookers angels to be l. on BACO 42:21
l.-on see most PROV 625:40
looketh man l. on the outward BIBL 80:16
looking Here's l. at you FILM 319:10
keep l. over his shoulder BARU 57:19
l. at me like that ZOLA 859:6
l. back BIBL 100:18
l. for an honest man DIOG 274:19
l. one way, and rowing BUNY 164:19
l. together SAIN 663:10
May I be l. at you TIBU 794:9
no use l. beyond CHAM 206:6
someone may be l. MENC 521:18
stop other people from l. BLAC 118:6
looking glass cracked l. of a servant JOYC 437:15
looking-glass smiles, As in a l. SHAK 721:25
looking glasses plenty of l. ASHF 31:14
Women have served as l. WOOL 845:7
looks her l. went everywhere BROW 160:10
I have no proud l. BOOK 143:8
l. like a duck REUT 645:13
needs good l. TUCK 802:2
Second good l. ANON 21:10
Stolen l. HUNT 409:19
woman as old as she l. PROV 625:53
loom labours of the l. DYER 293:14
she left the l. TENN 780:12
loon cream-faced l. SHAK 707:7
laugh like a l. HARB 371:3
looney janitor in a l.-bin WODE 842:24
L. Tunes, and squalid criminals REAG 643:15
loophole l. through which the pervert BRON 152:7
loose all hell broke l. MILT 533:11
Every which way but l. FILM 322:5
I let you l. WESL 829:19
L. his beard GRAY 360:21
L. lips sink ships MILI 526:13
l. the bands of Orion BIBL 83:24
l. the bands of wickedness BIBL 90:14
l. the seals BIBL 113:11
L. types of things WORD 850:16
man who should l. me LOWE 493:17
loosed l. our heart in tears ARNO 27:16
looted All has been l. AKHM 9:6
lops l. the mouldered branch TENN 777:10
loquendi et ius et norma l. HORA 398:3
loquitur Cor ad cor l. MOTT 552:5
Lorca L. was killed, singing READ 643:3
lord acceptable year of the L. BIBL 90:18
Admit l. SHAF 678:3
And I replied, 'My L.' HERB 383:25
belong unto the l. BIBL 78:29
by the hand of the L. BIBL 77:36
come, L. Jesus BIBL 114:25
coming of the L. HOWE 405:15
day which the l. hath made BOOK 142:10
dwell in the house of the L. BOOK 135:4
earth is the l.'s BIBL 107:22
earth is the L.'s BOOK 135:5
Everybody loves a l. PROV 619:1
glory of the L. BIBL 89:16
Go, and the L. be with thee BIBL 80:20
great l. BEAU 60:3
Great l. of all things POPE 605:1
house of the L. BOOK 142:18
let a L. once own the happy lines POPE 604:11
L. and Father of mankind WHIT 834:4
L., deliver us BOOK 129:4
L., dismiss us BUCK 163:11
L., dost thou wash my feet BIBL 103:25
L. gave, and the Lord BIBL 82:27
L. has more truth yet ROBI 650:17
L., have mercy upon us BOOK 128:2

lord (*cont.*):

L. how it talk't	BEAU 60:10
L., how long	BIBL 88:14
L., I am coming	LAUD 470:3
L. in His mercy	CRAI 249:22
L. is a man of war	BIBL 77:35
L. is gracious	BIBL 112:4
L. is his name	MONS 543:8
L. is in this place	BIBL 76:31
L. is King	BOOK 140:6
L. is my light	BOOK 135:13
L. is my shepherd	BOOK 135:3
L. is One	SIDD 735:12
L. looketh on the heart	BIBL 80:16
L. make his face shine	BIBL 78:15
L. mighty in battle	BOOK 135:6
L., now lettest thou	BIBL 100:6
L. of all hopefulness	STRU 762:15
L. of all the world	SPEN 751:5
L. of himself	WOTT 851:3
L. of hosts	BOOK 135:7
L. Of life and death	CRAS 250:10
l. of lords	BIBL 114:12
L. of the Dance	CART 197:5
l. of the fowl and the brute	COWP 248:24
L. our God is one Lord	BIBL 78:26
L. Randal	BALL 52:10
L., remember me	BIBL 102:5
L.'s anointed temple	SHAK 705:10
L. shall raise me up	RALE 641:11
L.'s my shepherd	SCOT 675:4
L. survives the rainbow	LOWE 494:15
L. thy God	BIBL 77:37
L. thy God is with thee	BIBL 79:8
L., thy word abideth	BAKE 50:1
l. to leggen in his bedde	CHAU 211:22
L. Tomnoddy is thirty-four	BROU 154:10
L. turned, and looked	BIBL 102:2
L. was departed	BIBL 79:34
L. watch between	BIBL 76:34
L., what fools	SHAK 711:14
L. will be there	WHIT 833:15
L., ye know, is God	KETH 450:5
Love is our L.'s meaning	JULI 438:7
mouth of the L.	BIBL 89:16
My L. and my God	BIBL 104:16
My L. should take Frail flesh	CROS 252:18
my L. Tomnoddy	BARH 55:13
Name of the L.	BOOK 142:11
nor the servant above his l.	BIBL 96:17
nurture of the L.	BOOK 133:6
O L., to what a state	TERE 785:17
on the L.'s day	BIBL 112:26
own thee L.	PRAY 611:7
Praise the L.	FORG 329:5
Prepare ye the way of the L.	BIBL 94:10
Rejoice in the L.	BIBL 110:6
Rejoice, the L. is King	WESL 829:7
remembrance of his dying L.	SPEN 751:13
saying 'L. Jones Dead'	CHES 217:14
Seek ye the L.	BIBL 90:7
sing the L.'s song	BOOK 143:13
sought the L. aright	BURN 170:20
soul doth magnify the L.	BIBL 99:31
taken away my L.	BIBL 104:11
those who love the L.	HUNT 409:14
Up to a point, L. Copper	WAUG 824:11
wait upon the Lord	BIBL 89:21
way of the L.	BIBL 89:16
we battle for the L.	ROOS 654:13
Welcum the l. of lycht	DOUG 283:14
what hour your L. doth come	BIBL 98:20
when they crucified my L.	SONG 748:9
Whom the L. loveth	BIBL 111:11

lords admiring the House of L. | BAGE 48:7
from the House of L.	NORF 565:8
I made the carles l.	JAME 417:7
l. have their pleasures	MONT 545:9
L. in ermine	ROBI 650:21
l. of human kind	GOLD 355:13
l. o' the creation	BURN 173:4
l. who lay ye low	SHEL 731:17
l. whose parents were	DEFO 261:26

l. will alway	BARC 55:11
New l., new laws	PROV 627:33
one of the l. of life	LAWR 475:8
Scots l. at his feet	BALL 53:7
wit among L.	JOHN 427:14
with those L. I had gone so far	MORE 548:12

lordships good enough for their l.
| | ANON 19:12 |

lore l. its scholars need | KEBL 447:14
| volume of forgotten l. | POE 599:5 |

lose cannot fear to l. | ASTE 32:11
if you l., you lose nothing	PASC 587:11
is to l. it	ORWE 578:7
l. her as a friend	GLAD 351:12
l. his own soul	BIBL 99:23
l. one parent	WILD 835:16
l. the name of action	SHAK 686:12
l. the war in an afternoon	CHUR 222:17
l. to-morrow	ARNO 28:8
l. what he never had	WALT 820:24
l. what you never had	PROV 635:31
nothing much to l.	HOUS 404:4
nothing to l.	CLOS 228:20
nothing to l.	MARX 517:6
nothing to l. but our aitches	ORWE 577:26
shall l. it	BIBL 96:21
to l. thee were to lose	MILT 534:4
way to l. him	SHAK 678:19
we don't want to l. you	RUBE 658:3
What you l. on the swings	PROV 634:16
win or l. it all	MONT 546:3
wins if he does not l.	KISS 457:10
you l. a few	PROV 636:11

losers both should l. be | HERB 384:20
he shall be among the l.	KORA 459:21
l. weepers	PROV 620:2
no winners, but all are l.	CHAM 206:10

loses l. his misery | ARNO 28:11
| Who l., and who wins | SHAK 701:25 |

losest for fear thou l. all | HERB 385:1

losing conduct of a l. party | BURK 166:2
deem a l. gain	SOUT 749:21
Hath but a l. office	SHAK 691:22
l. everything Except	DURC 292:19
l. one pleased Cato	LUCA 494:24
l. trade	BORR 145:12
l. your brain	FOX 331:13
l. your sight	SASS 667:17

loss but from its l. | YOUN 857:9
counted l. for Christ	BIBL 110:3
deeper sense of her l.	GASK 340:18
do our country l.	SHAK 693:21
l. of innocence	HOWA 405:8
no great l. without	PROV 632:30
One man's l.	PROV 628:43
profit and l.	ELIO 303:22
text was l.	CUNN 253:19

lost All is l. save honour | MISQ 537:1
All is not l.	MILT 531:9
All love is l.	DUNB 292:4
all was l.	MILT 534:1
and we are l.	PYRR 638:14
Are you l. daddy	LARD 468:10
Balls will be l. always	BERR 71:15
better to have fought and l.	CLOU 229:9
better to have loved and l.	PROV 633:7
better to have loved and l.	TENN 779:1
country is l.	WILL 838:2
Die in the l., lost fight	CLOU 227:15
every day to be l.	JOHN 433:1
everything is l.	VOLT 816:14
found my sheep which was l.	BIBL 101:12
France has not l. the war	DE G 262:1
hesitates is l.	PROV 622:9
Home of l. causes	ARNO 29:15
I have l. a day	TITU 795:1
I once was l.	NEWT 563:4
land of l. content	HOUS 404:16
let it be l.	CATU 202:15
l. all the names	JOHN 431:27
l. an empire	ACHE 1:10
l. boyhood of Judas	Æ 6:2
l. chord	PROC 612:16

l. dog somewhere	ANOU 23:1
l. evermore in the main	TENN 784:4
l., except a little life	BYRO 182:28
l. generation	STEI 755:10
l. me in your liking	SHAK 699:21
l. sheep	BIBL 96:13
l., that is unsought	CHAU 212:30
l. their mittens	NURS 570:6
l. the only Playboy	CLOS 228:19
l. the only Playboy	SYNG 769:13
l. the world for love	DRYD 289:6
l. traveller's dream	BLAK 120:5
L., yesterday	MANN 510:7
never l. till won	CRAB 249:13
never to have l. at all	BUTL 176:26
Next to a battle l.	WELL 827:14
none of them is l.	BIBL 103:39
nothing be l.	BIBL 103:2
Not l. but gone before	NORT 565:16
not l. but sent before	CYPR 254:15
not that you won or l.	RICE 646:19
paradises we have l.	PROU 613:14
they're l. to us	MART 514:19
Vietnam was l. in	MCLU 503:16
was l., and is found	BIBL 101:18
what is l. in translation	FROS 336:10
wherever we're l.	FRY 336:15
who deliberates is l.	ADDI 4:11

lot l. is fallen unto me | BOOK 134:14
not a l. . . . but you'll like	CATC 202:2
policeman's l. is not a happy one	GILB 349:1
Remember L.'s wife	BIBL 101:25

Lothario gay L. | ROWE 657:8

Lothian West L. | DALY 255:2

lotos L. and lilies | TENN 782:19

lots cast l. upon my vesture | BOOK 135:2

lottery judgement is a mere l. | DRYD 290:6
l. is a taxation	FIEL 318:3
L., with weekly pay-out	ORWE 577:18
Marriage is a l.	PROV 626:15

lotus jewelled l. throne | MAHĀ 507:6
| plucks the l. without | TANT 773:6 |

Lou lady that's known as L. | SERV 677:10

loud upon the l. cymbals | BOOK 144:9

louder l. he talked of his honour | EMER 306:20

loungers l. and idlers | DOYL 285:4

lounging L. 'roun' en suffer'n' | HARR 374:6

louse l. and a flea | JOHN 432:7
| l. in the locks of literature | TENN 785:3 |

lousy *House Beautiful* is play l. | PARK 586:5
| L. but loyal | SLOG 740:8 |
| l. skin scabbed by cities | BUNT 164:9 |

lout l.'s game | WEST 830:10

Louvre You're the L. | PORT 607:19

love Absence is to l. | BUSS 175:8
acquainted with L.	JOHN 427:17
Ah, l., let us be true	ARNO 27:4
Ah! what is l.	GREE 362:23
Alas! the l. of women	BYRO 180:25
all did l. him once	SHAK 697:27
all for l.	SPEN 751:24
All l. at first	BUTL 176:20
All l. is lost	DUNB 292:4
All's fair in l. and war	PROV 614:14
All that matters is l. and work	FREU 334:6
Amazing l.	WESL 828:21
and be my l.	MARL 513:16
and be thy l.	RALE 640:18
and L. the night	DRYD 289:14
And yet I l. this false	EPHE 308:5
Anxiety l.'s greatest killer	NIN 564:18
Any kiddie in school can l.	NASH 557:14
arms of my true l.	TENN 782:2
as she did l.	KEAT 443:26
as to l. a husband	WYCH 852:13
bands of l.	BIBL 91:29
be wise and eke to l.	SPEN 752:17
be wise, and l.	SHAK 719:21
bid me take l. easy	YEAT 853:19
bridge is l.	WILD 837:14
bring those who l. Thee	TERE 785:17
brotherly l. continue	BIBL 111:13
burned with l.	VIRG 813:17

but one true l.   BALL 53:16
but to l. much   TERE 785:16
came I to l. thee   AUGU 37:5
cannot call it l.   SHAK 687:23
cannot l. a woman so well   ELIO 300:9
cantons of contemnèd l.   SHAK 720:13
car'st not whom I l.   DONN 279:25
caution in l.   RUSS 660:19
Christ's particular l.'s sake   BROW 161:8
come unto my l.   SPEN 751:9
commonly called l.   FIEL 318:9
constant l. deemed there   SIDN 736:5
corner in the thing I l.   SHAK 713:29
courage to l.   TROL 799:10
course of true l.   PROV 617:13
crime to l. too well   POPE 602:12
cruel madness of l.   TENN 781:17
dark secret l.   BLAK 122:18
daughterly l.   MORE 548:16
dearest l. in all the world   RODG 652:1
Dear l., for nothing less   DONN 280:18
Deep as first l.   TENN 783:5
desire more l. and knowledge   SHAK 680:21
disguise which can hide l.   LA R 469:11
doesn't l. a wall   FROS 335:18
done a great deal for l.   FRAN 331:18
do not l. thee, Dr Fell   BROW 155:13
earth could never living l.   EPIT 310:1
Earth's the right place for l.   FROS 335:8
every man's l. affair with America
   MAIL 507:11
experienced my greatest l.   PROU 613:6
failures in l.   MURD 554:13
faith and l.   BIBL 110:17
fall in l. today   GERS 344:5
fall in l. with me   SHAK 681:26
Farewell, L.   WYAT 852:1
fate of l. is   BARR 56:20
fear casteth out l.   CONN 240:7
fear l. is to fear life   RUSS 660:22
first virtues aroused by l.   BALZ 54:8
fit l. for gods   MILT 533:29
flag and sign of l.   SHAK 713:2
flowers and fruits of l.   BYRO 183:1
food is l. and fame   SHEL 729:9
food of l.   OPEN 574:15
fool of l.   HAZL 376:13
For ever wilt thou l.   KEAT 444:9
for the l. he had to her   BIBL 76:33
for us, it's l.   BOUS 147:13
fou o' l. divine   BURN 171:10
Friendship is L.   BYRO 182:18
from the l. of God   BIBL 106:23
gates unto my l.   SPEN 751:8
Gather the rose of l.   SPEN 751:26
gentleness And show of l.   SHAK 696:2
gin l. be bonnie   BALL 53:18
God is l., but   LEE 478:15
God of l.   HERB 385:2
God si L.   FORS 329:24
good man's l.   SHAK 681:25
got l. well weighed up   AMIS 13:13
Greater l. hath no man   BIBL 103:33
greater l. hath no man   THOR 793:21
Greater l. than this   JOYC 437:23
groans of l. to those of the dying
   LOWR 494:22
had a l. for Charlotte   THAC 786:22
half in l.   KEAT 444:27
hate all that don't l. me   FARQ 315:16
hate is conquered by l.   PALI 584:10
have not all thy l.   DONN 281:4
Hearts wound up with l.   SPEN 750:21
heart whose l. is innocent   BYRO 183:5
Hell is to l. no more   BERN 70:10
He was all for l.   DIBD 267:5
hidden l. of God   WESL 829:10
hid in the heart of l.   YEAT 855:5
hold l. out   SHAK 717:23
hold so fast, as l. can do   BURT 174:14
honeying and making l.   SHAK 687:25
how can he l. God   BIBL 112:22
how Christians l. one another   TERT 785:22

How do I l. thee   BROW 158:3
how I l. my country   LAST 473:10
how l. constrained him   DANT 255:19
How should I your true l. know   SHAK 688:5
hurt us that we l.   BEAU 60:7
I am sick of l.   BIBL 87:15
I do not l. the man   WATK 822:16
I don't l. you   MART 514:17
If I can't l. Hitler   MUST 555:13
If I l. you   GOET 353:13
If it be l. indeed   SHAK 678:13
if my l. were in my arms   ANON 19:19
If this be not l.   CONG 239:1
I hate and I l.   CATU 203:9
I knew it was l.   BYRO 183:11
I'll l. you   AUDE 34:19
I l. a lass   O'KE 572:19
I l., and know not why   EPHE 308:5
I l. but you alone   BALL 52:15
I l. my work   HILL 388:10
I l. you, honey   LAST 472:10
In l. alone we hate to find   WALS 820:12
in l., and in debt   BROM 152:3
in l. as in religion   COWL 245:25
In l., everything is true   CHAM 207:3
in l. to practise only this   RILK 648:16
in l. when he marries   BURN 169:21
in l. with a cold climate   SOUT 749:17
in l. with his fetters   BACO 43:11
in l. with night   SHAK 717:27
in the world is l.   BREN 150:20
I shall l. him   JOHN 427:8
is not in l.   SHAK 719:19
It's so simple, l.   PRÉV 610:13
jealousy extinguishes l.   MARG 512:5
joy of l. is too short   MALO 508:20
kind of l. called maintenance   FANT 314:12
King of l.   BAKE 50:2
knew thee but to l. thee   HALL 369:16
knowest that I l. thee   BIBL 104:21
know Him, l. him   CATE 199:7
labour of l.   BIBL 110:15
Land that I l.   BERL 69:18
lay aside long-cherished l.   CATU 203:6
lean over the soul we l.   GIDE 346:13
left thy first l.   BIBL 113:1
let me l.   DONN 280:17
Let me not l. Thee   HERB 383:18
let me sow l.   FRAN 332:6
Let's fall in l.   PORT 607:14
letter to my l.   BALL 52:4
Let those l. now   ANON 21:16
let us live and l.   CAMP 187:23
let us l.   CATU 202:13
lightly turns to thoughts of l.   TENN 780:15
little duty and less l.   SHAK 694:12
live with me, and be my l.   DONN 280:15
lost l. of mine   SCOT 673:22
lost the world for l.   DRYD 289:6
L., a child   WROT 851:18
L., all alike   DONN 281:13
L. alters not   SHAK 723:24
l., an abject intercourse   GOLD 355:17
L. and a cottage   COLM 235:17
L. and a cough cannot   PROV 625:41
l. and all its smart   BEDD 62:1
l. and beauty fail   ETHE 312:6
l. and be wise   PROV 628:30
L. and delight therein   DÜRE 293:3
l. and do what you will   AUGU 37:13
l. and fame   KEAT 445:25
L. and marriage   BYRO 180:27
l. and murder will out   CONG 238:17
l. and scandal   FIEL 318:4
l. a thing that can never go wrong
   PARK 585:14
L. bade me welcome   HERB 384:13
L. be controlled by advice   GAY 341:8
L. begets love   PROV 625:42
l. be younger than thyself   SHAK 720:24
l. boat has crashed   LAST 473:3
L. built on beauty   DONN 279:6
l. but only her   BYRO 179:16

L. ceases to be a pleasure   BEHN 63:19
l., cherish, and to obey   BOOK 133:9
L. comes from blindness   BUSS 175:7
L. comforteth like sunshine   SHAK 724:3
L. conquers all things   VIRG 814:10
L. consists in this   RILK 649:1
l. Creation's final law   TENN 779:10
L., curiosity, freckles, and doubt
   PARK 585:15
L. divine   WESL 829:8
l. does not consist   SAIN 663:10
L. doesn't just sit there   LE G 479:8
l. Flames for a year   LAMP 465:20
l. flies out of the window   PROV 634:26
l. for any place   ARNO 30:17
l. goes toward love   SHAK 717:26
l. grows diseased   ETHE 312:4
L. guards the roses   LODG 489:9
l. gushed from my heart   COLE 233:2
l. had been sae ill to win   BALL 53:19
l. has died for me to-day   BALL 51:13
L. has pitched his mansion   YEAT 853:16
l. her, comfort her   BOOK 133:8
l. her is a liberal education   STEE 755:1
l. her till I die   ANON 19:8
l. his country   SHAK 697:20
l., I do not go   DONN 281:11
l. in a cold climate   MITF 540:17
l. in a golden bowl   BLAK 119:17
L. in a hut   KEAT 444:1
l. in another's soul   LAYT 476:9
L. in a palace   KEAT 444:1
L. in desolation   SHEL 728:20
L. in dying   BARN 56:17
L.-in-idleness   SHAK 711:2
L. in my bosom   LODG 489:8
L., in the form   CHAM 207:4
L. in this part of the world   BYRO 184:9
L. is a beautiful image   MICH 524:2
L. is a boy   BUTL 176:12
L. is a child and naked   OVID 579:17
L. is a circle   HERR 386:3
L. is a growing   DONN 281:3
L. is ane fervent fire   SCOT 672:13
L. is a passion   HALI 368:11
L. is a spirit   SHAK 724:2
L. is a thing   PEEL 591:1
l. is a thing below a man   STER 757:10
L. is a universal migraine   GRAV 360:9
l. is better than wine   BIBL 87:2
L. is blind   ANON 20:15
l. is blind   PROV 625:43
l. is but discovery   SOUT 748:16
l. is here to stay   GERS 344:7
l. is he that alle thing   CHAU 212:29
L. is just a system   BARN 56:12
l. is liberty   POPE 602:16
L. is like any other luxury   TROL 800:15
L. is like linen   FLET 327:18
L. is longer than the wave   BALL 52:19
l. is Lord of all the world   SPEN 751:5
l. is maister   GOWE 357:13
l. is more cruel than lust   SWIN 768:12
L. is mor than gold   LYDG 496:21
L. is mutually feeding   HEAD 377:9
L. is never defeated   JOHN 422:16
L. is not love   SHAK 699:22
L. is not love   SHAK 723:22
l. is not secure   CHES 215:23
L. is of a birth as rare   MARV 515:10
L. is of the valley   TENN 783:16
L. is only one   JOHN 425:14
L. is our Lord's meaning   JULI 438:7
l. is slight   MARL 513:11
L. is so short   NERU 559:6
L. is strong as death   BIBL 87:22
L. is that liquor   HERB 383:19
L. is the delusion   MENC 521:15
L. is the discovery of reality   MURD 554:16
L. is the fart   SUCK 763:6
L. is the fire   SOUT 749:20
l. is the gift of oneself   ANOU 22:19
L. is the greatest mercy   WILB 835:7

love (cont.):

l. is the keeping of her laws | BIBL 92:29
l. is then our duty | GAY 341:16
l. is the wisdom of the fool | JOHN 433:16
l. is towards individuals | SWIF 766:5
l. it cannot return | ELIO 299:9
L. iz like the meazles | BILL 116:12
L. just makes it safer | ICE- 412:17
l. laughs at locksmiths | PROV 625:44
l. looks not with the eyes | SHAK 710:19
L. made me poet | EPIT 310:15
L. makes them dance | DAVI 258:10
L. makes the world go round | PROV 625:45
L. means not ever having | TAGL 771:8
l. me less | GODO 352:1
L. me little | ANON 17:13
L. me little | PROV 625:46
L. me, love my dog | PROV 625:47
l. men too little | BURK 167:27
L.? most natural painkiller | LAST 473:4
l., never strained | HORA 400:15
l. not man the less | BYRO 179:17
l. of Christ | BIBL 109:8
l. of finished years | ROSS 655:7
l. of friends | BELL 65:28
l. of God is shed abroad | BIBL 106:8
l. of liberty | HAZL 376:14
l. of money | BIBL 110:26
L. of our country | GODW 352:4
l. of savages | LERM 481:9
l. of Soul in the husband | UPAN 804:14
l. of the people | BURK 166:31
L. once possessed | MILT 534:31
l. one another | BIBL 106:31
l. one another or die | AUDE 36:4
l. one maiden only | TENN 777:21
L.'s a disease | MACA 497:15
L.'s always seen | COWL 245:23
l.'s a malady | DRYD 289:4
L.'s a man of war | HERB 384:1
l.'s a noble madness | DRYD 287:22
l. Scotland better | JOHN 424:21
L. seeketh not itself to please | BLAK 122:11
L. seeketh only Self to please | BLAK 122:12
l. seldom dies of hunger | LENC 480:2
L. set you going | PLAT 597:3
l.'s great artillery | CRAS 250:14
L.'s harbinger | MILT 534:9
l. she's but a lassie | BURN 171:28
l. slights it | BACO 44:2
L.'s like a red, red rose | BURN 172:4
L.'s like the measles | JERR 421:18
L.'s not Time's fool | SHAK 723:23
l. someone is to isolate | BAUD 59:4
L. sought is good | SHAK 721:3
L.'s passives | CRAS 250:8
l.'s philosophy | DONN 281:2
L.'s pleasure lasts but a moment | FLOR 327:20
l.'s proper exercise | DAVI 258:10
l.'s the noblest frailty | DRYD 288:22
L. still has something | SEDL 675:10
L.'s tongue is in the eyes | FLET 327:15
l.-story or an elopement | DOYL 284:23
L. supports his reign | SMAR 740:14
l.'s young dream | MOOR 547:16
l. that asks no question | SPRI 753:5
l. that can be reckoned | SHAK 678:13
L. . . . That cordial drop | ROCH 651:7
L. that dare not | DOUG 283:13
L., that doth reign | SURR 764:5
l. that endures for a breath | SWIN 768:4
l. that I have | MARK 512:10
l. that moves the sun | CLOS 228:2
l. that moves the sun | DANT 256:13
L. that never told can be | BLAK 121:25
l. the babe | SHAK 704:12
L. the Beloved Republic | FORS 330:2
l., the beloved Republic | SWIN 768:19
L. the brotherhood | BIBL 112:7
l. thee better after death | BROW 158:4
l. thee in prose | PRIO 612:1
L., the human form divine | BLAK 122:3

l. the Lord thy God | BIBL 98:8
l. the lovely bully | SHAK 693:11
L. the sinner | AUGU 37:16
L.-thirty, love-forty | BETJ 73:2
l. those who love you | VOLT 816:12
L., thou art absolute | CRAS 250:10
l. thy neighbour | BIBL 78:14
l. thy neighbour as thyself | BIBL 98:8
l. thyself last | SHAK 695:15
l. to hatred turned | CONG 238:30
L. to the loveless shown | CROS 252:18
l. toward thee | BOOK 130:14
l. up groweth | CHAU 213:16
l. was passion's essence | BYRO 178:26
l. were what the rose is | SWIN 769:6
l. . . . whatever that may | CHAR 209:14
l. what thou dost love | HATC 375:3
l. will find a way | PROV 625:48
l. will steer the stars | RADO 640:12
l. will yield to business | OVID 580:17
l. without the rhetoric | STOP 761:13
L. with unconfinèd wings | LOVE 493:4
L. wol nat been constreyned | CHAU 211:7
l. you because I need you | FROM 335:2
l. you gave her | ELIZ 305:5
l. you just the same | KIER 451:7
L. your enemies | BIBL 100:15
L. you ten years before | MARV 515:23
loving to l. | AUGU 36:25
make l. in a canoe | BERT 71:20
Make l. not war | SLOG 740:9
making l. all year round | BEAU 60:2
making l. to the Archbishop | SHER 734:8
Man's l. is of man's life | AMIS 13:12
Man's l. is of man's life | BYRO 180:15
Man's l. of God | MAIM 507:18
man, That l. my friend | SHAK 698:4
man you l. to hate | ADVE 8:2
man you l. to hate | FILM 320:5
marry them for l. | OSBO 578:13
may be crossed in l. | SHER 733:11
Men l. in haste | BYRO 181:30
met the L.-Talker | CARB 190:3
ministers of L. | COLE 232:9
money can't buy me l. | LENN 480:16
more of l. than matrimony | GOLD 355:32
Most people l. love | PAST 587:19
music be the food of l. | SHAK 720:3
my l. and I did meet | YEAT 853:19
My l. and I would lie | HOUS 404:11
My l. for Heathcliff | BRON 152:21
my l.'s in tune | PROV 634:29
My only l. | SHAK 717:18
My song is l. unknown | CROS 252:18
needs must l. the highest | TENN 777:23
never l. a stranger | BENS 68:1
never taint my l. | SHAK 714:15
new l. may get | WALS 820:11
no l. for such | THOM 790:25
no lyves creature Withouten l. | CHAU 213:3
none other I can l. | TENN 777:29
not enough to make us l. | SWIF 766:19
nothing but in l. | BACO 44:28
not that I l. you less | WALL 818:12
Now I know what L. is | VIRG 814:7
Now with his l. | CHAU 211:17
object of l. | LAMB 464:11
of connubial l. | MILT 533:8
office and affairs of l. | SHAK 712:15
off with the old l. | PROV 623:41
Of kindness and of l. | WORD 847:7
O L., O fire | TENN 776:22
O lyric L. | BROW 161:6
O my l. is slain | DONN 279:11
one jot of former l. | DRAY 285:23
one's absent l. | TROL 800:8
ones we choose to l. | HARR 374:8
Only by l. can men see me | BHAG 74:16
Only l. can apprehend | RILK 648:18
onset and waning of l. | LA B 462:15
Onstage I make l. | JOPL 436:12
opposite of l. | WIES 834:13
our l. hath no decay | DONN 280:14

over hir housbond as hir l. | CHAU 212:20
pangs of disprized l. | SHAK 686:10
passing the l. of women | BIBL 80:29
path of true l. | EWAR 313:6
perfect l. casteth out fear | BIBL 112:21
philosopher of l. | DRYD 288:28
Pity is akin to l. | PROV 629:24
pluck the rose And l. it | BROW 161:26
power and effect of l. | BURT 174:13
presume too much upon my l. | SHAK 698:15
price we pay for l. | SAYI 669:23
putting L. away | DICK 273:3
Queen's l. | BALL 51:17
quick-eyed L., observing | HERB 384:13
renewing is of l. | EDWA 297:3
right true end of l. | DONN 279:8
same as for l. | FROS 336:4
search for l. | WALE 817:7
secret l. | BIBL 85:13
Service and l. above all other | DUNB 292:1
She never told her l. | SHAK 720:29
shows of l. to other men | SHAK 696:3
some l. but little policy | SHAK 716:12
sports of l. | JONS 435:20
still their l. comes home to me | LAWL 470:15
successful without l. | TROL 799:2
support of the woman I l. | EDWA 296:12
survive of us is l. | LARK 468:13
sweet l.! was thought a crime | BLAK 122:15
take our fill of l. | BIBL 84:4
Tell l. it is but lust | RALE 641:3
tell the laity our l. | DONN 281:17
that they l. | WALL 818:14
them that l. God | BIBL 106:21
them which l. you | BIBL 94:32
there are those who l. it | WEBS 825:9
There is l. of course | ANOU 22:18
There is only l. | MCEW 501:15
there my l. will live | CLAR 224:8
They l. indeed | SIDN 736:7
They l. their land | HALL 369:15
They l. us for it | TENN 783:8
they're in l. | TAGL 771:12
think my l. as rare | SHAK 723:27
this spring of l. | SHAK 721:21
those who l. the Lord | HUNT 409:14
thought l. would adapt itself | WALK 817:9
thought that l. would last | AUDE 34:29
Through l., through hope | WORD 849:24
time to l. | BIBL 85:32
tired of L. | BELL 65:9
'tis the hour of l. | BYRO 181:11
To live is like to l. | BUTL 177:1
to l. and be loved | SAND 665:14
to l. and rapture's due | ROCH 651:5
To manage l. | BUTL 176:19
To see her is to l. her | BURN 170:16
to think but to l. | TERE 785:15
treason to our l. | THOR 793:19
true l. hath my heart | SIDN 736:2
true l. is a durable fire | RALE 641:9
true l. is, it showeth | DE P 264:16
'Twixt women's l., and men's | DONN 280:13
unity, and godly l. | BOOK 131:13
unlucky in l. | PROV 625:49
vegetable l. should grow | MARV 515:23
very few to l. | WORD 849:27
vividly gifted in l. | DUFF 291:7
was the song of l. | ROSS 656:1
waters cannot quench l. | BIBL 87:23
wayward is this foolish l. | SHAK 721:20
well-nourished l. | COLE 234:17
what is l. | RALE 640:19
What is l. | SHAK 720:16
What is L. | SHEL 732:18
What l. I bore to thee | WORD 847:4
When l. congeals | HART 374:11
When my l. swears | SHAK 723:29
where I cannot l. | BEHN 63:22
where l. is | BIBL 84:24
where the l. of God goes | LIGH 484:11
Where there is great love | CATH 199:9
where there is no l. | BACO 44:14

who l., time is eternity — VAN 806:21
who l. want wisdom — SHEL 731:2
Whom the gods l. — MENA 521:13
Whom the Gods l. — PROV 635:2
Whom the gods l. die young — BYRO 181:14
whom we l. most — ABEL 1:2
wilder shores of l. — BLAN 123:7
wi' L. o'ercome — BURN 171:17
winds were l.-sick — SHAK 679:3
wish I were in l. again — HART 374:11
with my true l. — RALE 641:8
withstand L.'s shock — GOGA 353:22
woman's l. for us increases — PUSH 638:3
woman wakes to l. — TENN 778:7
Women who l. the same man — BEER 63:6
Work is l. made visible — GIBR 346:8
world and l. were young — RALE 640:18
You can only l. one war — GELL 342:19
You may give them your l. — GIBR 346:5
'You must sit down,' says L. — HERB 384:14
your true l.'s coming — SHAK 720:15
loved all we l. of him — SHEL 728:19
And the l. one — BROW 160:11
better to have l. and lost — BUTL 176:26
better to have l. and lost — PROV 633:7
better to have l. and lost — TENN 779:1
Dante, who l. well — BROW 160:13
disciple whom Jesus l. — BIBL 104:23
feared than l. — MACH 502:10
God so l. the world — BIBL 102:32
him I l. the most — ANON 22:14
how much you were l. — CAVA 203:14
idols I have l. — FITZ 323:15
I have l. — SUCK 763:7
I l. a lass — WITH 842:6
I l. Ophelia — SHAK 689:4
I l. thee once — AYTO 41:11
I saw and l. — GIBB 345:16
king l. his people — WILL 838:4
Lavinia, therefore must be l. — SHAK 719:14
l. by the gods — PLAT 597:6
l. Caesar less — SHAK 697:18
l. each other beyond belief — HEIN 380:2
l. him so — BROW 160:3
l. him too much — RACI 640:2
L. I not honour more — LOVE 493:8
l. not at first sight — MARL 513:11
l. not at first sight — SHAK 681:27
l. the doctrine — DEFO 261:17
l. you, so I drew these tides — LAWR 475:19
men who have l. them — TROL 800:9
Might she have l. me — BROW 159:30
never be by woman l. — BLAK 119:8
never to have been l. — CONG 239:10
she l. much — BIBL 100:17
She who has never l. — GAY 341:21
Solomon l. many strange women — BIBL 81:14
thirst to be l. — RHYS 646:13
thrice had I l. thee — DONN 280:12
till we l. — DONN 280:26
To be l. as to love — FRAN 332:6
use him as though you l. him — WALT 820:25
We l., sir — BROW 159:3
who never l. before — ANON 21:16
wish I l. the Human Race — RALE 641:18
loveless Love to the l. shown — CROS 252:18
lovelier l. than your lovely mother — HORA 400:16
loveliness l. and perfection — MILT 535:19
l. I never knew — COLE 231:3
miracle of l. — GILB 348:6
portion of the l. — SHEL 729:1
weak from your l. — BETJ 73:2
woman of shining l. — YEAT 855:15
your l. — KEAT 446:22
lovely altogether l. — BIBL 87:16
Look thy last on all things l. — DE L 262:24
l. and pleasant — BIBL 80:28
l. at the beginning — PALI 584:3
l. boy — VIRG 813:18
L. enchanting language — HERB 384:9
l. is the rose — WORD 847:21
l. is thy dwelling-place — SCOT 675:5

l. woman stoops to folly — ELIO 303:21
l. woman stoops to folly — GOLD 355:33
more l. and more temperate — SHAK 722:24
once he made more l. — SHEL 729:1
She has a l. face — TENN 780:13
so be l. — GRAV 360:8
That they might l. be — CROS 252:18
what a l. war — LITT 487:2
whatsoever things are l. — BIBL 110:8
woods are l. — FROS 336:3
wouldn't it be l. — LERN 481:22
You have l. eyes — CHEK 214:7
lover affliction taught a l. — POPE 602:17
as true a l. — SHAK 681:2
Beauty is the l.'s gift — CONG 239:13
binds the l. — SANS 666:6
dividing l. and lover — SWIN 768:1
injured l.'s hell — MILT 533:14
l. and his lass — SHAK 682:6
l. and killer are mingled — DOUG 283:18
l., and the poet — SHAK 711:27
l. by lover — YEAT 856:7
l. of my soul — WESL 828:26
l.'s quarrel with the world — FROS 335:17
l. stole my rose — BURN 170:14
l. without indiscretion — HARD 371:16
prove a l. — SHAK 716:22
roaming l. — CALL 186:2
satisfied with her l.'s mind — TROL 800:8
she was a true l. — MALO 509:1
sighed as a l. — GIBB 345:17
some old l.'s ghost — DONN 281:5
truest l. — MALO 509:3
what is left of a l. — ROWL 657:11
Who could deceive a l. — VIRG 812:2
woman loves her l. — BYRO 180:26
woman says to her lusting l. — CATU 203:3
lovers Journeys end in l. meeting — SHAK 720:15
laughs at l.' perjuries — OVID 579:22
laughs at l.' perjuries — TIBU 794:11
laughs at l.' perjury — PROV 624:33
l.' declarations — AUDE 35:16
l.' perjury — DRYD 289:5
L., to bed — SHAK 712:5
l. were all untrue — DRYD 289:15
make two l. happy — POPE 605:30
old l. are soundest — WEBS 826:3
quarrel of l. — PROV 630:1
sleepless l. — POPE 606:4
star-crossed l. — SHAK 717:12
These l. fled away — KEAT 443:4
wonder if it's l. — MULD 553:17
loves all her l. around her — BYRO 182:17
all she l. is love — BYRO 180:26
baggage l. me — CONG 238:32
because God l. it — JULI 438:5
believe that God l. them — HUME 408:7
die to that which one l. — HARA 370:20
fooled by that which one l. — MOLI 542:10
For who l. that — MILT 535:6
He l. us not — SHAK 706:20
kills the thing he l. — WILD 836:29
lady l. Milk Tray — ADVE 7:6
life and l. of a she-devil — WELD 827:6
lines (so l.) oblique — MARV 515:11
l. his wife as himself — TALM 772:19
l. nothing but himself — SOUT 749:13
l. the fox less — SURT 764:15
l. what he is good at — SHAD 678:1
no creature l. me — SHAK 717:7
our l., must I remember them — APOL 23:10
reigned with your l. — ELIZ 304:11
son l. his sons — TALM 772:25
soul that l. is happy — GOET 352:11
who l. me must have — TENN 777:27
Who l. ya, baby — CATC 201:34
woman whom nobody l. — CORN 243:10
lovesome garden is a l. thing — BROW 155:11
lovest l. thou me more — BIBL 104:19
poor sinner, l. thou me — COWP 246:26
loveth he that l. another — BIBL 106:31
He that l. not — BIBL 112:20

him whom my soul l. — BIBL 87:9
prayeth well, who l. well — COLE 233:10
whom the Lord l. — BIBL 83:33
Whom the Lord l. — BIBL 111:11
loving Can't help l. dat man — HAMM 369:22
discharge for l. one — MATL 518:13
For l., and for saying so — DONN 281:15
heart be still as l. — BYRO 183:8
I ain't had no l. — NORW 565:17
l. and giving — PROV 626:28
l. himself better than all — COLE 233:17
l.-kindness and mercy — BOOK 135:4
l. longest — AUST 39:16
l. the land that has taught — MOOR 547:10
l. to love — AUGU 36:25
most l. mere folly — SHAK 681:15
wickedness that hinders l. — BROW 160:12
loving-kindness deeds of l. — TALM 771:23
low dost thou lie so l. — SHAK 697:13
exalted them of l. degree — BIBL 99:32
Had me l. and had me down — GERS 344:4
l. as where this earth — ROSS 655:21
l. estate of his handmaiden — BIBL 99:31
l. on whom assurance sits — ELIO 303:20
Malice is of a l. stature — HALI 369:2
Sweet and l. — TENN 782:26
That l. man — BROW 159:15
Too l. for envy — COWL 245:21
upper station of l. life — DEFO 261:9
lowbrow first militant l. — BERL 70:6
Lowells L. talk to the Cabots — BOSS 145:15
lower l. classes had such white — CURZ 254:11
l. orders don't set us a good — WILD 835:11
l. than the angels — BOOK 134:5
l. than vermin — BEVA 73:9
While there is a l. class — DEBS 260:18
lowest l. and most dejected — SHAK 701:6
take the l. room — BIBL 101:3
lowlands Highlands and ye L. — BALL 51:16
sails by the L. — SONG 748:4
lowliness l. become mine inner clothing — LITT 487:1
lowly l. air Of Seven Dials — GILB 347:11
meek and l. in heart — BIBL 96:27
loyal Lousy but l. — SLOG 740:8
l. to his own career — DALT 255:1
loyalties l. which centre upon number one — CHUR 222:14
tragic conflict of l. — HOWE 405:12
loyalty constitute l. — BOSW 146:22
I want l. — JOHN 423:15
learned body wanted l. — TRAP 798:4
L. the Tory's secret weapon — KILM 451:10
l. we feel to unhappiness — GREE 362:14
LSD L.? Nothing much happened — AUDE 36:19
L. reminds me of minks — GRAV 360:16
PC is the L. of the '90s — LEAR 477:23
Lucasta L., that bright northern star — LOVE 493:2
lucem ex fumo dare l. — HORA 398:9
lucid freqent l. intervals — CERV 205:12
l. intervals — BACO 46:6
l. intervals of life — WORD 846:9
Lucifer falls like L. — SHAK 695:12
L. arose — MERE 522:20
L., son of the morning — BIBL 88:24
luck believes in l. — STEA 754:13
devil's l. — PROV 617:36
Fools for l. — PROV 620:22
know about it [l.] — HART 374:18
l. in leisure — PROV 632:12
l. in odd numbers — PROV 632:13
l. of our name lost — HORA 402:10
mother of good l. — PROV 617:41
nae l. about the house — MICK 524:7
want their l. buttered — HARD 371:18
watching his l. — SERV 677:10
wished you good l. — BOOK 142:11
luckless What l. apple — MARV 516:5
lucky born l. than rich — PROV 623:43
L. at cards — PROV 625:49
l. if he gets out of it — FILM 319:21
l. to be born — WHIT 833:11

1010 LUCKY · MADMEN

lucky (*cont.*):
Third time l. PROV 632:40
lucrative so l. to cheat CLOU 229:7
lucre greedy of filthy l. BIBL 110:22
lucro *Fors dierum cumque dabit l.* HORA 400:11
Lucy L. ceased to be WORD 850:2
L. Locket lost NURS 568:7
Ludlow to L. come in HOUS 404:12
Luftwaffe With your L. PLAT 596:20
lug l. the guts SHAK 687:33
lugete *L., O Veneres* CATU 202:11
lugger Once aboard the l. MISQ 538:12
Luke honour unto L. Evangelist ROSS 656:4
lukewarm thou art l. BIBL 113:5
lukewarmness L. I account a sin COWL 245:25
lullaby dreamy l. GILB 347:19
I will sing a l. DEKK 262:18
Once in a l. HARB 371:4
lumber loads of learned l. POPE 604:16
l. of the schools SWIF 767:5
lumen *l. de lumine* MISS 536:20
luminous beating his l. wings ARNO 29:21
l. home of waters ARNO 28:18
with a l. nose LEAR 477:5
lump leaven leaveneth the whole l. BIBL 107:10
l. bred up in darkness KYD 462:9
L. the whole thing TWAI 803:15
lumps l. in it STEP 756:3
luna great Lord of L. MACA 499:16
in the vats of L. MACA 499:12
sol et l. AUGU 37:1
lunae *Tacitae per amica silentia l.* VIRG 811:14
lunatic l., the lover SHAK 711:27
lunatics lunatic asylum run by l. LLOY 487:20
l. have taken charge ROWL 657:14
lunch cork out of my l. FIEL 318:19
for life, not for l. SAYI 669:29
L. is for wimps FILM 320:2
no such thing as a free l. SAYI 670:15
unable to l. today PORT 607:15
luncheon Breakfast, supper, dinner, l. BROW 160:21
take soup at l. CURZ 254:12
lungs dangerous to the l. JAME 417:1
from froth-corrupted l. OWEN 581:4
l. of London PITT 596:9
l. of the tobacconist JONS 434:16
Lupercal on the L. I thrice SHAK 697:26
lupus *L. est homo homini* PLAU 597:20
lurcher half l. and half cur COWP 248:11
lurching L. to rag-time tunes SASS 667:16
lure l. it back FITZ 323:10
l. this tassel-gentle SHAK 717:27
lurk dangers to liberty l. BRAN 149:13
l. outside GRAC 357:17
lurks l. a politician ARIS 25:8
luscious l. woodbine SHAK 711:4
lusisti *l. satis* HORA 399:24
lust Delight in l. PETR 594:7
despair rather than l. READ 643:5
fash'd wi' fleshly l. BURN 171:11
generous in mere l. ROCH 651:10
horrible that l. and rage YEAT 855:20
hutch of tasty l. HOPK 396:15
into ashes all my l. MARV 516:2
love is more cruel than l. SWIN 768:12
l. and calls it advertising LAHR 464:3
l. in action SHAK 723:25
l. of knowing FLEC 326:3
Men, when they l. GREE 362:22
Tell love it is but l. RALE 641:3
to l. after it LEWI 483:12
lustily sing praises l. unto him BOOK 135:22
lustre bright l. of a court CECI 204:14
Where is thy l. now SHAK 701:5
lusts Abstain from fleshly l. BIBL 112:6
fulfil the l. thereof BIBL 106:33
l. of the flesh BOOK 132:13
l. of your father BIBL 103:12
lust'st Thou hotly l. SHAK 701:17
lusty seye Of l. folk CHAU 212:17
lute Apollo's l. MILT 529:2
harp with the l. BOOK 139:13
l. and harp BOOK 137:23
l. is broken SHEL 729:24
Orpheus with his l. SHAK 695:8
pleasing of a l. SHAK 716:19
rift within the l. TENN 778:5
to her l. Corinna sings CAMP 188:1
lutes l. of amber HERR 386:21
Luther beyond what L. saw ROBI 650:18
lux *l. perpetua* MISS 539:14
luxuries and which l. WRIG 851:11
l. of life MOTL 551:15
luxury height of l. TENN 785:2
like any other l. TROL 800:15
Literature is a l. CHES 216:20
l., not a necessity ANTH 23:6
l. of doing good CRAB 249:12
l., peace BAUD 58:14
l. was doing good GART 340:11
mainly a l. BRIG 151:14
Morality is a costly l. ADAM 2:15
Pessimism is a l. MEIR 520:11
swinish l. of the rich MORR 550:1
trust people is a l. FORS 329:14
Lycidas L. is dead MILT 529:30
lying branch of the art of l. CORN 243:14
express l. or falsehood SWIF 765:16
listening, l. in wait THOM 790:15
l., and slandering BOOK 132:17
l. into a universal principle KAFK 441:1
L. lips are abomination BIBL 84:14
L., on the other hand CAMU 188:20
l. till noon JOHN 426:25
One of you is l. PARK 586:3
smallest amount of l. BUTL 176:25
world is given to l. SHAK 691:17
Lyonnesse When I set out for L. HARD 373:6
lyre armour and my l. HORA 401:23
Make me thy l. SHEL 730:12
'Omer smote 'is bloomin' l. KIPL 456:6
lyric among the l. poets HORA 400:2
good l. should be GERS 344:11
lyricis *me l. vatibus inseres* HORA 400:2

Ma M.'s out, Pa's out FLAN 324:17
Mab M., the Mistress-Fairy JONS 435:3
Queen M. hath been with SHAK 717:15
macaroni called it M. SONG 748:11
Macaulay as Tom M. MELB 521:1
M.'s few pages ELIO 300:24
Macavity M. WASN'T THERE ELIO 302:27
Macbeth had Lady M. KNIG 458:4
harm M. SHAK 706:16
Little Nell and Lady M. WOOL 845:15
M. does murder sleep SHAK 704:24
M. shall never vanquished be SHAK 706:18
M. shall sleep no more SHAK 705:1
night I appeared as M. HARG 373:12
MacCorley Rody M. goes to die CARB 190:5
Macduff Lay on, M. SHAK 707:18
M. was from his mother's womb SHAK 707:17
mace fool's bauble, the m. CROM 252:3
Macedonia Come over into M. BIBL 105:12
MacGregor Where M. sits PROV 634:40
Macheath jack-knife has M. BREC 150:13
Machiavel murderous M. SHAK 694:29
machine body is a m. TOLS 796:19
desiccated calculating m. BEVA 73:16
Ghost in the M. RYLE 662:4
house is a m. for living in LE C 478:10
m. for converting CARL 192:1
m. for turning the red wine DINE 274:17
pulse of the m. WORD 850:4
sausage m. CHRI 218:16
machinery Age of M. CARL 191:24
m. of the night GINS 349:15
machines M. have less problems WARH 821:19
m. which had never been finished BABB 42:1
their survival m. DAWK 259:16
whether m. think SKIN 739:10
macht *Arbeit m. frei* ANON 21:5
mackerel like rotten m. RAND 642:4
m. of the sea BALL 52:9
Not so the m. FRER 333:17
mackintosh bit of black m. WELB 827:2
mad All poets are m. BURT 174:2
bad and m. it was BROW 159:3
believed him m. BEAT 59:10
called me m. LEE 479:1
Don't get m., get even SAYI 669:15
glad m. brother's name SWIN 768:7
half of the nation is m. SMOL 744:15
heroically m. DRYD 287:12
Hieronimo is m. again KYD 462:12
house for fools and m. SWIF 767:18
M. about the boy COWA 245:2
m. all in God's keeping KIPL 456:23
m. all my life JOHN 427:1
m. and furious DOST 283:8
m. and savage master SOPH 746:21
M., bad, and dangerous LAMB 464:9
M. dogs and Englishmen COWA 245:3
m. north-north-west SHAK 685:27
M. world! mad kings SHAK 699:2
Make m. the guilty SHAK 686:4
make poor females m. SHAK 711:18
makes men m. SHAK 714:22
man is m. BYRO 183:25
men that God made m. CHES 215:22
much learning doth make thee m. BIBL 105:30
nobly wild, not m. HERR 386:6
O fool! I shall go m. SHAK 700:13
old, m., blind SHEL 731:20
O! let me not be m. SHAK 700:6
pleasure sure, In being m. DRYD 289:21
saint run m. POPE 605:19
some did count him m. BUNY 165:5
they first make m. PROV 635:3
We all are born m. BECK 61:22
when a heroine goes m. SHER 733:9
Whom the m. would destroy LEVI 482:14
world was m. SABA 662:7
madam globe-trotting M. YEAT 856:2
M. I may not call you ELIZ 304:18
madame Ah, m.! truly it's not right CRAN 249:27
madding Far from the m. crowd's GRAY 361:7
m. crowd BORR 146:6
made All things were m. by him BIBL 102:16
almost m. for each other SMIT 743:11
Begotten, not m. BOOK 131:10
day which the Lord hath m. BOOK 142:10
earth and the world were m. BOOK 139:21
fearfully and wonderfully m. BOOK 143:17
God m. and eaten BROW 158:21
Here's one I m. earlier CATC 200:27
he that hath m. us BOOK 140:17
he who m. the Lamb BLAK 122:21
I m. it FILM 319:1
Little Lamb who m. thee BLAK 122:5
m. heaven and earth BOOK 132:20
m., like bread LE G 479:8
m. me thus BIBL 106:24
man was m. to mourn BURN 171:23
not born but m. JERO 421:8
Who m. you CATE 199:7
Madeira M., m'dear FLAN 324:15
madeleine little piece of m. PROU 613:4
Madelon *Ce n'est que M.* BOUS 147:13
mademoiselle M. from Armenteers MILI 526:14
madhouse don't want m. EMPS 307:22
m. there exists no law CLAR 224:6
madhouses M., prisons CLAR 224:4
madman If a m. were to come JOHN 430:18
m. shakes a dead geranium ELIO 303:1
m. who thought he was COCT 230:3
madmen M. in authority KEYN 450:17
none but m. know DRYD 289:21

What m. thinks of changing	TROL 800:4	ride m.	EMER 306:13	So m. worlds	TENN 779:11

What m. thinks of changing — TROL 800:4
What ought a m. to be — IBSE 412:15
when a m. should marry — BACO 44:33
When God at first made m. — HERB 384:19
when I became a m. — BIBL 107:25
who kills a m. — MILT 535:14
Who's master, who's m. — SWIF 767:3
Whoso would be a m. — EMER 307:4
woman was made for m. — STAN 754:10
woman without a m. — SAYI 670:23
You'll be a M., my son — KIPL 454:13
manage m. without butter — GOEB 352:7
managed disgracefully m. — FIRB 321:11
not a free press but a m. — RADC 640:10
management m. of a balance of power — KISS 457:9
M. that wants to change — TUSA 803:1
manager m. who gets the blame — LINE 486:7
No m. ever got fired — ADVE 8:8
managers m. of affairs of women — KORA 459:23
managing kiss the M. Director — WHIT 832:18
Manchester school of M. — DISR 278:8
What M. says today — PROV 634:7
mancipio Vitaque m. — LUCR 495:17
Mandalay come you back to M. — KIPL 454:21
road to M. — KIPL 455:1
mandarin M. style — CONN 240:4
mandate M. of Heaven — CONF 237:11
royal m. ran — BURN 171:3
Manderley went to M. again — OPEN 574:31
mandragora Give me to drink m. — SHAK 678:23
mandrake frightful as a M. — BYRO 183:25
Get with child a m. — DONN 281:9
this quiet m. — DONN 280:8
manes With draped m. — HUGH 407:7
manger babe was born in a m. — WHIT 832:17
in the rude m. lies — MILT 530:19
laid him in a m. — BIBL 100:2
lodge Him in the m. — ANON 20:6
m. for his bed — ALEX 11:8
mangle immense pecuniary m. — DICK 272:14
mangrove held together by m. roots — BISH 117:4
manhood ancient customs and its m. — ENNI 308:2
harsh and embittered m. — GOGO 354:1
M. a struggle — DISR 277:2
M. taken by the Son — NEWM 561:3
My m., long misled — DRYD 288:13
touching his M. — BOOK 129:2
manhoods hold their m. cheap — SHAK 693:24
manibus M. date lilia plenis — VIRG 812:16
manifesto first powerful plain m. — SPEN 750:18
manifestoes in the party m. — ROTH 656:21
manifold m. sins and wickedness — BOOK 127:13
sundry and m. changes — BOOK 130:8
manilla misery of m. folders — ROET 652:4
mankind all m. — BALL 52:15
countrymen are all m. — GARR 340:9
crucify m. — BRYA 162:12
Everything m. does — JUVE 439:10
giant leap for m. — ARMS 26:17
has not created m. — TOCQ 795:9
hate, m. — BYRO 178:24
How beauteous m. is — SHAK 719:7
in th'original perused m. — ARMS 26:11
legislator of m. — JOHN 425:26
M. always sets itself — MARX 516:12
m. and womankind — BAHA 49:12
M. has done more damage — COUS 244:13
M. is a dream — PIND 595:14
M. is on the move — SMUT 744:20
M. must put an end to war — KENN 449:3
M.'s moral test — KUND 462:7
no history of m. — POPP 607:4
not in Asia, was m. born — ARDR 24:13
one disillusion—m. — KEYN 450:11
proper study of m. — POPE 604:32
proper study of m. is books — HUXL 411:4

school of m. — BURK 168:16
slain m. altogether — KORA 460:11
manliness silent m. of grief — GOLD 354:19
manly than m. wise — MARL 513:25
manna Exalted m. — HERB 384:18
his tongue Dropped m. — MILT 531:30
loathe our m. — DRYD 289:1
m. of a day — GREE 362:6
rained down m. — BOOK 139:10
manned safeliest when with one man m. — DONN 279:13
manner after the m. of men — BIBL 108:6
all m. of thing — JULI 438:6
All m. of thing shall be well — ELIO 302:2
m. of his speech — SHAK 679:2
to the m. born — SHAK 684:24
manners As by his m. — SPEN 752:7
corrupt good m. — BIBL 108:7
corrupt good m. — PROV 619:25
droppings of the well of m. — BULW 164:2
English m. more frightening — JARR 419:1
evil m. live in brass — SHAK 695:20
for m.' sake — BIBL 93:23
gentleness of your m. — CLAI 224:1
good table m. — MIKE 524:23
had very good m. — SELL 676:18
lack of m. — HATH 375:4
M. maketh man — PROV 626:3
m. of a dancing master — JOHN 427:15
m. of a Marquis — GILB 349:3
Morals and m. — CHAM 206:5
not men, but m. — FIEL 318:1
Of m. gentle — POPE 603:28
Oh, the m. — CICE 223:16
Other times, other m. — PROV 629:9
polished m. — COWP 248:17
rectify m. — MILT 535:18
soften m., but corrupt — BYRO 182:14
thoughts and m. — JOHN 425:26
Manningtree roasted M. ox — SHAK 690:17
manoeuvre force with a m. — TROT 800:21
manque Un être seul vous m. — LAMA 464:7
mansion Back to its m. — GRAY 361:4
everlasting m. — SHAK 719:13
heavenly m., raging in the dark — YEAT 853:11
Love has pitched his m. — YEAT 853:16
m.-house of liberty — MILT 535:22
mansions dolorous m. — MILT 530:23
m. of the dead — CRAB 249:3
many m. — BIBL 103:28
man-slaying terrible, m. hands — HOME 394:11
mantle cast his m. upon him — BIBL 81:28
green m. — SHAK 700:28
her silver m. threw — MILT 533:5
in russet m. clad — SHAK 683:19
m. that covers all — CERV 205:16
purple m. to the light — RONS 653:4
twitched his m. blue — MILT 530:13
Mantovano salute thee, M. — TENN 784:11
mantras M. and tantras — TANT 773:5
Mantuan old M.! Who understandeth thee — SHAK 702:17
manufacture content to m. life — BERN 70:8
soul of every m. — SMIL 740:21
manunkind this busy monster, m. — CUMM 253:11
manure liquid m. from the West — SOLZ 745:20
Money, like m. — PROV 626:35
natural m. — JEFF 419:15
manuscript youth's sweet-scented m. — FITZ 323:16
many How m. things — SOCR 744:23
Just how m. did we kill — LEWI 483:17
makes so m. of them — LINC 485:8
m. are called — BIBL 98:5
m. are called — PROV 626:10
M. hands make light work — PROV 626:13
m.-headed monster — POPE 605:25
m.-splendoured thing — THOM 791:15
m. still must labour — BYRO 179:22
m. ways out — SENE 676:30
shed for you and for m. — BOOK 132:2

So m. worlds — TENN 779:11
so much owed by so m. to so few — CHUR 221:10
we are m. — BIBL 99:20
what are they among so m. — BIBL 103:1
map Does the m. remind you — TREV 798:15
in the new m. — SHAK 721:7
make a m. of it — JONE 434:8
m.-makers' colours — BISH 117:6
m. me no maps — FIEL 318:6
Roll up that m. — PITT 596:14
use a larger m. — SALI 664:4
mapmakers m. should place the Mississippi — BELL 66:1
maps Geography is about M. — BENT 68:12
in Afric-m. — SWIF 767:9
m. on a small scale — SALI 664:4
mar cannot m. — ARNO 27:15
marathon M. looks on the sea — BYRO 181:5
trivial skirmish fought near M. — GRAV 360:7
marble dreary m. halls — CALV 186:9
dwelt in m. halls — BUNN 164:8
Glowed on the m. — ELIO 303:12
I am m.-constant — SHAK 680:9
lasting m. seek — WALL 818:8
left it m. — AUGU 37:22
legs are as pillars of m. — BIBL 87:16
m. index of a mind — WORD 849:11
m., nor the gilded monuments — SHAK 723:5
m. not yet carved — MICH 524:1
m. to retain — BYRO 177:25
more than hard m. — DU B 290:19
mould from m. living faces — VIRG 812:15
placid m. — HUNT 410:1
marbly great smooth m. limbs — BROW 158:20
Marcellus M. exiled — POPE 605:10
Tu M. eris — VIRG 812:16
march Beware the ides of M. — SHAK 695:29
boundary of the m. of a nation — PARN 586:21
do not m. on Moscow — MONT 545:13
droghte of M. — CHAU 210:4
droghte of m. — OPEN 576:1
ides of M. are come — SHAK 697:8
in the front of M. — TENN 777:2
mad M. days — MASE 517:13
m. as an alternative — FITT 322:21
M. comes in like a lion — PROV 626:14
M., march, Ettrick — SCOT 674:15
m. my troops towards — GRIM 364:16
m. of intellect — SOUT 749:11
m. of mind — PEAC 589:14
m. on their stomachs — SELL 676:24
m. through rapine — GLAD 350:18
m. towards it — CALL 185:16
M., whan God first maked man — CHAU 212:2
m. with sovereign tread — BLOK 123:16
Men m. away — HARD 373:1
On the first of M. — PROV 628:25
peck of M. dust — PROV 629:18
So many mists in M. — PROV 631:5
take The winds of M. — SHAK 722:5
three hours' m. to dinner — HAZL 377:7
Truth is on the m. — ZOLA 859:9
marche congrès ne m. pas — LIGN 484:12
marched m. breast forward — BROW 158:11
M. them along — BROW 160:6
Märchen Ein M. aus alten Zeiten — HEIN 379:15
marches forced m., battles and death — GARI 339:15
Funeral m. to the grave — LONG 490:19
marching M. as to war — BARI 56:4
m., charging feet — JAGG 415:16
M. to the Promised Land — BARI 56:5
M. where it likes — ARNO 29:11
people m. on — MORR 549:12
soul is m. on — SONG 747:13
truth is m. on — HOWE 405:15
mare brought him a Flanders m. — HENR 382:6
grey m. is the better — PROV 621:21
lend me your grey m. — BALL 53:20
man shall have his m. — SHAK 711:19
Money makes the m. to go — PROV 626:38
qui trans m. currunt — HORA 399:10

Margaret It's me, M. BLUM 124:2
M. you mourn for HOPK 397:4
Merry M. SKEL 739:8
marge page having an ample m. TENN 778:8
margerain With m. gentle SKEL 739:7
Margery See-saw, M. Daw NURS 569:12
margin m. too narrow FERM 317:1
Maria Aunt M. flung herself GRAH 358:11
Ave M. PRAY 611:1
Ave M.! 'tis the hour BYRO 181:11
ex M. Virgine MISS 536:21
Mariana this dejected M. SHAK 708:11
Marie I am M. of Roumania PARK 585:14
Maries Queen had four M. BALL 52:18
marigold m., that goes to bed SHAK 722:4
marijuana experimented with m. CLIN 227:6
mariner It is an ancient M. COLE 232:11
m. with the gentleman DRAK 285:17
mariners rest ye, brother m. TENN 781:10
Ye M. of England CAMP 187:20
marjoram savory, m. SHAK 722:4
mark man's distinctive m. BROW 159:5
m., or the name of the beast BIBL 113:30
m. upon Cain BIBL 76:1
M. well her bulwarks BOOK 137:6
m. what is done amiss BOOK 143:6
no drowning m. SHAK 718:18
not a m. ROST 656:12
often hit the m. BUNY 164:12
press toward the m. BIBL 110:4
read, m., learn BOOK 130:1
would hit the m. LONG 490:6
market bought in the m. CLOU 227:18
enterprise of the m. ANON 15:13
Enthroned i' the m.-place SHAK 679:5
fast through the m. PROV 626:34
gathered in the m.-place CAVA 203:17
heart in the m.-place SHAK 712:29
marry a m.-gardener DICK 271:7
on m. research RODD 651:22
pig went to m. NURS 570:4
salutations in the m. BIBL 99:26
sold in the desolate m. BLAK 52:10
To m., to market NURS 570:9
Market Harborough AM IN M. TELE 776:1
marking malady of not m. SHAK 691:24
marks m. and scars I carry BUNY 165:9
m. of the beast HARD 371:19
marl Over the burning m. MILT 531:16
Marlborough Duke of M. MARL 512:12
From M.'s eyes JOHN 426:20
M.'s mighty soul ADDI 4:5
marmasyte Tullia's ape a m. ANON 16:10
marquis Abducted by a French M. GRAH 358:5
manners of a M. GILB 349:3
my lord the M. of Carabas PERR 593:2
marred man that's m. SHAK 678:10
young man m. PROV 636:5
marriage blessings of m. SHAW 726:14
by way of m. FIEL 318:12
Chains do not hold a m. SIGN 736:24
Christian m. MARG 512:3
Courtship to m. CONG 239:5
definition of m. SMIT 743:24
dictates before m. ELIO 299:25
drags the m. chain CENT 205:5
ended by a m. BYRO 180:29
every m. then is best in tune WATK 822:17
furnish forth the m. tables SHAK 684:8
get anywhere in a m. MURD 554:15
giving in m. BIBL 98:18
Hanging and m. FARQ 315:22
hear of a m. PROV 618:23
heart of m. is memories COSB 244:5
in companionship as in m. ADAM 2:8
In m., a man becomes slack STEV 759:21
joys of m. FORD 328:17
left-handed m. WOLL 844:5
live in a state of m. JOHN 429:14
long monotony of m. GIBB 346:3
Love and m. BYRO 180:27
m. as the sole object MART 515:5

M. a wonderful invention CONN 239:27
m. brings more joy EURI 312:11
m. for her was to be STAN 754:9
m. had always been her object AUST 39:24
M. has many pains JOHN 426:1
M. is a bribe WILD 837:15
M. is a lottery PROV 626:15
M. is like life STEV 759:24
M. is nothing but SELD 676:6
M. isn't a word FILM 320:7
M. is popular because SHAW 726:21
M. is the grave CAVE 204:3
M. is the waste-paper basket WEBB 825:2
m. makes man and wife CONG 238:16
M. may often be a stormy lake PEAC 590:1
m. of true minds SHAK 723:22
m. on the rocks MERR 523:2
m. than a ministry BAGE 48:11
M., to women ANTH 23:6
M. was all defeat TREV 798:14
m. with your mother SOPH 746:20
more to m. than four PROV 632:3
nor are given in m. SWIF 766:21
party is like a m. MCIN 502:15
prevents a bad m. SHAK 720:10
primal m. blessing KEBL 447:15
Reading and m. MOLI 541:21
retrieve his fortunes by m. DICK 269:23
so bent on m. AUST 40:11
So that is m. WOOL 845:9
think there is any in m. GAY 341:18
three of us in this m. DIAN 267:2
value of m. DE V 266:8
wo that is in m. CHAU 212:13
marriages All the unhappy m. WODE 842:15
few happy m. ASTE 32:15
few m. are happy SWIF 766:23
happiest m. on earth DE V 266:5
have no more m. SHAK 686:17
M. are made in heaven PROV 626:16
M. would in general JOHN 430:14
most m. selling one's soul MACK 502:17
present at their m. TROL 800:9
There are good m. LA R 469:14
thousands of m. LARK 468:19
married At leisure m. CONG 239:4
before he m. SWIF 767:19
can't get m. at all FILM 320:21
delight we m. people have PEPY 592:11
Each thirteenth year he m. MERR 523:1
getting m. in the morning LERN 481:15
going to be m. GOLD 355:21
going to be m. STER 757:11
honest man who m. GOLD 355:28
if ever we had been m. GAY 341:7
If m. life were all that MILL 525:15
imprudently m. the barber FOOT 328:6
in every m. couple FIEL 317:14
In m. life three is company WILD 835:14
let us be m. LEAR 477:16
like other m. couples SAKI 663:20
m. beneath me ASTO 32:19
M., charming, chaste BYRO 180:7
m. me with a ring RAIN 640:17
m. past redemption DRYD 288:34
m. to a poem KEAT 446:21
m. to a single life CRAS 250:15
m.—to be the more together MACN 504:17
Miss will soon be m. HAYW 376:8
Mocks the m. men SHAK 702:25
most m. man I ever saw WARD 821:12
One was never m. BURT 174:7
Reader, I m. him BRON 152:11
Trade Unionism of the m. SHAW 726:13
well-bred as if we were not m. CONG 239:16
wench who is just m. GAY 341:14
when they got m. OPEN 575:2
when you m. me SHER 733:27
young man m. PROV 636:5
young man m. SHAK 678:10
marries in love when he m. BURN 169:21
m. without any consideration OSBO 578:12
signify whom one m. ROGE 652:14

when a man m. PROV 627:14
When a man m. SHEL 729:22
marrow suck out all the m. THOR 793:12
marry advise no man to m. JOHN 433:19
better to m. than to burn BIBL 107:13
Better to m. than to burn PROV 615:31
Can't get away to m. you LEIG 479:18
Doänt thou m. for munny TENN 782:13
find it in my heart to m. thee CONG 239:6
How can a bishop m. SMIT 743:21
m. a man who hates his mother BENN 67:24
m. a market-gardener DICK 271:7
M. in haste PROV 626:17
M. in May PROV 626:18
m. Mr Collins AUST 39:23
M. my body to that dust KING 451:15
m. one another BUTL 176:27
m. whom she likes THAC 786:12
m. with his brother SHAK 687:21
may not m. his Mother BOOK 144:21
men we wanted to m. STEI 755:13
neither m., nor are given BIBL 98:7
never know who they may m. MITF 541:1
Never m. for money PROV 627:24
No artist should ever m. DELI 263:11
persons about to m. PUNC 637:4
taken in when they m. AUST 39:1
than m. a man AUST 40:12
they neither m. SWIF 766:21
To m. is to domesticate STEV 759:25
when a man should m. BACO 44:33
while ye may, go m. HERR 386:19
women m. off in haste ASTE 32:16
marrying m. in haste THOM 790:18
preventing men from m. TROL 800:14
Mars attack from M. SALI 664:14
Men are from M. GRAY 360:17
marshal m.'s baton LOUI 492:12
Martha M. was cumbered BIBL 100:26
martial m. airs of England WEBS 825:13
swashing and a m. outside SHAK 680:24
valiant and m. BACO 45:27
Martin Saint M.'s summer SHAK 694:7
Martini into a dry M. FILM 319:23
medium Vodka dry M. FLEM 326:9
Martinis Those dry M. ADE 5:16
martlet Like the m. SHAK 709:8
temple-haunting m. SHAK 704:2
martyr Glorious the m.'s gore SMAR 740:18
groan of the m.'s woe BLAK 120:11
if thow deye a m. CHAU 213:10
m. of the people CHAR 209:1
regarded as a m. KHOM 451:2
soul of a m. BAGE 47:11
martyrdom crown of m. WALP 819:24
M. is the test JOHN 431:17
m. must run its course AUDE 35:13
M. only way in which a man can SHAW 724:27
m. to live BROW 156:10
True m. is not determined AUGU 37:15
martyred shrouded oft our m. dead CONN 239:25
martyrs army of M. BOOK 127:20
blood of the m. PROV 616:6
graves of the m. STEV 760:15
love their m. DOST 283:5
no patience of m. THOM 789:2
stones and clouts make m. BROW 156:9
marvel m. at nothing HORA 399:8
m. my birthday away THOM 789:15
marvelled m. to see such things BOOK 137:4
marvellous Chatterton, the m. boy WORD 849:20
hath done m. things BOOK 140:13
m. demonstration FERM 317:1
m. in our eyes BOOK 142:10
towards the m. HUME 408:10
marvels to credit m. HEAN 377:20
workest great marvels BOOK 128:17
Marx blame M. for what was done BENN 67:2
illegitimate child of Karl M. ATTL 33:4

in M.'s pages SCHU 672:4
Marxism more to Methodism than to M.
PHIL 595:2
Marxist I am a M. SLOG 740:6
I am not a M. MARX 517:3
Marxiste *Je suis M.* SLOG 740:6
Mary Hail M. PRAY 611:1
M. Ambree BALL 52:14
M. had a little lamb HALE 368:8
M. hath chosen BIBL 100:27
M., quite contrary NURS 568:9
M.'s prayers FABE 313:13
M. was found in adulterous bed BLAK 120:1
Where the lady M. is ROSS 655:23
winking M.-buds SHAK 682:30
Mary Jane *What* is the matter with M.
MILN 528:4
Marylebone hanging garments of M.
JOYC 437:4
Mary Magdalene cometh M. early BIBL 104:9
Mary Magdalenes Madonnas or M.
WILL 839:2
mascot best m. is a good mechanic
EARH 294:22
masculine m. part, the poet in me
BEHN 63:20
mask had a m. like Castlereagh SHEL 730:3
like a M. dancing ACHE 1:8
loathsome m. has fallen SHEL 731:8
m. that eats into the face UPDI 805:21
No m. like open truth CONG 238:18
masochistic m. form of exhibitionism
OLIV 573:5
masons singing m. building SHAK 692:29
Where did the m. go BREC 150:16
masquerade m., a murdered peer ALCO 10:8
miss a m. POPE 606:9
truth in m. BYRO 181:26
mass activates the whole m. VIRG 812:14
blessed mutter of the m. BROW 158:21
listen to the B Minor M. TORK 797:3
M. is ended MISS 539:11
Meat and m. never hindered PROV 626:20
methods of m.-production LANC 465:22
Paris is well worth a m. HENR 382:1
rough and unordered m. OVID 580:8
two thousand years of m. HARD 372:11
Massachusetts denied in M. MILL 525:23
massacre not as sudden as a m. TWAI 803:7
masses bow, ye m. GILB 347:9
calling 'em the m. PRIE 611:9
huddled m. yearning LAZA 476:10
If it is for the m. SCHO 671:14
m. against the classes GLAD 351:4
m. conveying an emotion HEPW 382:19
m. get involved VOLT 816:14
sacrifices of M. BOOK 144:17
massy huge m. face MACA 498:1
mast m. Of some great admiral MILT 531:16
master allegiance to any m. HORA 398:18
be m. and win GOET 353:4
Caliban, Has a new m. SHAK 718:32
choice and m. spirits SHAK 697:14
Death is a m. from Germany CELA 205:3
disciple is not above his m. BIBL 96:17
dominion of the m. HUME 408:16
eye of a m. PROV 619:33
Jack as good as his m. PROV 624:29
Like m., like man PROV 625:19
love is m. GOWE 357:13
mad and savage m. SOPH 746:21
Man is the m. SWIN 768:20
m. a grief SHAK 712:24
M.-morality NIET 564:11
m. of his fate TENN 778:4
m. of my fate HENL 381:15
m. of none PROV 624:30
m. of the house cometh BIBL 99:28
m. of the Party HEAL 377:13
m. of those who know DANT 255:17
M., we have toiled BIBL 100:12
only the M. shall praise KIPL 456:5
slew his m. BIBL 82:14

This is our m. BROW 159:12
which is to be m. CARR 195:16
Who's m., who's man SWIF 767:3
Why eateth your M. BIBL 96:5
without m.-builders LOCK 488:6
masterly m. inactivity MACK 503:4
masterpiece Nature's great m. DONN 280:9
never makes for a m. TRUF 801:3
masterpieces in the midst of m. FRAN 332:1
masters anything but new m. HALI 369:4
ease of the m. SMIT 741:11
educate our m. MISQ 538:22
had two m. BEAV 60:17
m. of the Channel NAPO 556:8
m. of their fates SHAK 696:9
never wrong, the Old M. AUDE 35:12
people are the m. BURK 168:22
serve two m. BIBL 95:6
serve two m. PROV 627:40
spiritual pastors and m. BOOK 132:16
We are not the m. BLAI 118:17
We are the m. SHAW 727:28
We are the m. now MISQ 538:21
mastery m. of the thing HOPK 397:11
mastiff m.? the right hon. Gentleman's
poodle LLOY 487:13
mastodons like m. bellowing WODE 842:25
masturbation Don't knock m. ALLE 12:8
m. of war RAE 640:13
sort of mental m. BYRO 184:14
match Honour is like a m. PAGN 582:1
lighted m. BROW 160:7
love m. was the only thing EDGE 295:17
m. the world above ZOHA 859:2
matched m. us with His hour BROO 153:14
Thou wert never m. MALO 509:3
matches there he plays extravagant m.
GILB 348:5
with that stick of m. MADI 505:10
matchless m. deed's achieved SMAR 740:18
matchwood m., immortal diamond
HOPK 397:7
mate great artificer Made my m. STEV 760:13
mater *Stabat M. dolorosa* JACO 415:12
material bound by m. things CHUA 219:5
surpasses the m. OVID 580:9
materialism deteriorate into m. MOLT 542:17
materials I use simple m. LOWR 494:21
maternity m. a period of suffering
STAN 754:9
mathematical m. heads ASCH 31:3
m. language GALI 338:10
of m. celebrity DOYL 284:18
mathematician appear as a pure m.
JEAN 419:8
mathematicians beware of m. MISQ 537:15
mathematics avoid pregnancy by resort to
m. MENC 521:19
In m. you don't NEUM 559:12
knowledge in m. BACO 47:5
M. may be defined RUSS 660:23
M., rightly viewed RUSS 660:26
m., subtile BACO 45:22
mystical m. BROW 156:4
no place for ugly m. HARD 371:12
so like the m. WALT 820:14
study m. intensively HALD 368:3
used to love m. STEN 755:18
Matilda M. told such Dreadful Lies BELL 65:2
matrimony as that of m. TROL 799:12
critical period in m. HERB 383:13
in favour of m. AUST 40:19
joined together in holy M. BOOK 133:3
m. at its lowest STEV 759:22
more of love than m. GOLD 355:32
religion and m. CHES 214:19
safest in m. SHER 733:15
matron sober-suited m. SHAK 717:36
matter altering the position of m.
RUSS 660:21
away from the world of m. BAHA 49:13
between spirit and m. HEIN 380:3
dislike the m. SHAK 679:2

Does it m. SASS 667:17
if it is it doesn't m. GILB 349:5
inditing of a good m. BOOK 136:19
m. enough to save BROW 160:1
m. out of place GRAY 360:18
M., the wickedest offspring ROCH 651:18
More m. with less art SHAK 685:17
not fighting does m. STEP 756:5
root of the m. BIBL 83:13
speculations upon m. JOHN 425:7
sum of m. BACO 43:5
take away the m. BACO 45:12
this m. better in France STER 756:7
'twas no m. what he said BYRO 181:25
what does that m. GOET 353:13
What is M. PUNC 637:9
What is the m. with Mary Jane MILN 528:4
wretched m. and lame metre MILT 531:2
mattered one that m. GREG 363:8
matters big words for little m. JOHN 428:21
exercise myself in great m. BOOK 143:8
Most of what m. RUSH 659:4
Nobody that m. MILL 525:19
that's what m. most BROW 155:3
What can I do that m. SPEN 751:1
What m. is what works SAYI 670:19
Matthew M. Mark, Luke, and John
PRAY 611:4
mattress crack it open on a m. MILL 527:4
mattresses through twenty m. ANDE 14:3
mature M. love says FROM 335:2
m. women, *dancing* FRIE 334:17
maturing mind is m. late NASH 557:12
Maud into the garden, M. TENN 781:23
mausoleum as its m. AMIS 13:8
mawkish sweetly m. POPE 601:26
mawkishness thence proceeds m.
KEAT 442:12
Max happened to M. and Moritz BUSC 174:18
incomparable M. SHAW 727:24
maxim just political m. HUME 409:7
M. Gun BELL 65:12
will that my m. KANT 441:8
maxima *mea m. culpa* MISS 536:14
Maxwelton M. braes are bonnie
SONG 747:15
may bring forth M. flowers PROV 614:30
darling buds of M. SHAK 722:24
fressh as is the month of M. CHAU 210:8
I'm to be Queen o' the M. TENN 782:8
maids are M. SHAK 682:2
Marry in M. PROV 626:18
matter for a M. morning SHAK 721:12
M. chickens come cheeping PROV 626:19
M. is a pious fraud LOWE 494:5
M. month flaps its leaves HARD 372:9
M.'s new-fangled mirth SHAK 702:11
M. to December ANDE 14:7
meadow in M. BABE 42:8
merry month of M. BALL 51:12
merry month of M. BALL 53:1
month of M. MALO 509:1
month of M. Is comen CHAU 212:22
on a M. morning LANG 466:15
rose in M. CHAU 212:25
Sell in M. and go away SAYI 670:12
seventh of M. TROL 799:13
so many frosts in M. PROV 631:25
swarm in M. PROV 631:36
till M. be out PROV 627:16
what we m. be SHAK 688:7
will not when he m. PROV 621:52
world is white with M. TENN 777:17
Maya net of M. UPAN 805:11
maying let's go a-M. HERR 385:20
mayor tart who has married the M.
BAXT 59:7
maypole away to the M. hie SONG 747:3
M. in the Strand BRAM 149:10
organ and the m. JORD 436:13
maypoles I sing of M. HERR 385:16
Mazda in the soul as Lord M. ZORO 859:20

Mazda (*cont.*):
M.-worshipper — ZORO 859:14
maze m. wherein affection — RALE 641:1
mazes m. intricate — MILT 533:18
MBEs M. and your knighthoods — KEAT 442:9
McCarthyism M. is Americanism with — MCCA 500:6
McGregor Mr M.'s garden — POTT 608:4
McNamara M.'s War — MCNA 504:11
me Aim your weapons at m. — VIRG 813:6
For you but not for m. — MILI 526:15
M. Tarzan — MISQ 538:8
now in the M. Decade — WOLF 843:22
save thee and m. — OWEN 580:23
meadow m. in May — BABE 42:8
painted m. — ADDI 4:21
meadows M. trim with daisies pied — MILT 529:23
paint the m. — SHAK 702:25
meal gives a m. man-appeal — ADVE 8:9
handful of m. — BIBL 81:20
mean admires m. things — THAC 786:4
citizen of no m. city — BIBL 105:25
depends what you m. by — CATC 201:8
do a m. action — STER 756:9
Down these m. streets — CHAN 207:15
even if you don't m. it — TRUM 801:14
for m. or no uses — LOCK 488:8
Happy the golden m. — MASS 518:3
having a m. Court — BAGE 48:14
Know what I m., Harry — BRUN 162:11
loves the golden m. — HORA 401:4
M., Moody and Magnificent — TAGL 771:9
no m. of death — SHAK 697:14
nothing common did or m. — MARV 515:18
poem should not m. but be — MACL 503:10
say what you m. — CARR 194:9
They may not m. to — LARK 469:2
They m. well — DISR 277:16
whatever that may m. — CHAR 209:14
what we m., we say — ARNO 27:2
Meander M.'s margent green — MILT 528:23
meaner m. beauties of the night — WOTT 851:4
only m. things — ELIO 299:19
meaning emptied of m. — CAMU 188:19
Free from all m. — DRYD 287:12
get at his m. — RUSK 659:18
Is there a m. to music — COPL 242:17
Love is our Lord's m. — JULI 438:7
m. doesn't matter — GILB 348:13
m. to afford — CARY 197:12
mistake the m. — WESL 829:18
plain m. — SHAK 709:21
promises us m. — BELL 66:3
richest without m. — RUSK 659:23
take your m. — BROW 161:18
teems with hidden m. — GILB 349:4
To find its m. — BROW 159:11
to some faint m. make pretence — DRYD 288:31
What is the brief m. — SCHI 671:1
within the m. of the Act — ANON 18:9
meaningless almost m. — ANON 19:3
love m. generalizations — GREE 362:19
meanings two m. packed up — CARR 195:17
wrestle With words and m. — ELIO 301:15
meanly all m. wrapped — MILT 530:19
m. lose — LINC 485:6
meanness land of m., sophistry — BYRO 179:30
m. of opportunity — ELIO 299:23
publish its m. — THOR 793:12
means all m. are permitted — DAWS 259:18
between ends and scarce m. — ROBB 649:17
beyond our m. to pay — DOST 283:3
by the best m. — HUTC 410:18
die beyond my m. — WILD 837:7
end cannot justify the m. — HUXL 411:6
end justifies the m. — BUSE 174:20
end justifies the m. — PROV 618:41
end, never as m. — KANT 441:12
Increased m. — DISR 276:9
live within our m. — WARD 821:10
m. all he says — ADAM 2:17

m. just what I choose — CARR 195:15
m. of grace — BOOK 129:20
m. of rising — JOHN 430:8
m. to do ill deeds — SHAK 699:12
m. whereby I live — SHAK 709:32
my m. may lie — COWL 245:21
never know what it m. — SALI 664:6
persons of small m. — ELIO 300:19
politics by other m. — CLAU 225:17
Private M. is dead — SMIT 743:3
Whatever 'in love' m. — DUFF 291:7
wills also the m. — KANT 441:10
wills the m. — PROV 622:16
Without m. — BYRO 184:11
meant damned dots m. — CHUR 220:16
knew what it m. — BROW 162:1
knew what it m. — KLOP 458:1
more is m. — MILT 529:14
'w-a-t-e-r' m. the wonderful — KELL 447:18
what he m. by that — LOUI 492:15
measles Love's like the m. — JERR 421:18
m. of the human race — EINS 298:10
measure good m., pressed down — BIBL 100:16
If you cannot m. it — KELV 448:4
lead but one m. — SCOT 673:22
leave to heaven the m. — JOHN 426:22
Man is the m. — PROV 626:2
m. in all things — PROV 632:14
m. of all things — PROT 613:1
m. of movement — AUCT 34:17
m. of the universe — SHEL 731:6
M. still for Measure — SHAK 708:17
M. your mind's height — BROW 160:14
serves to grace my m. — PRIO 612:5
Shrunk to this little m. — SHAK 697:13
strength beyond due m. — EURI 312:20
With what m. ye mete — BIBL 99:19
measured dance is a m. pace — BACO 42:20
m. language lies — TENN 778:24
m. out my life with coffee spoons — ELIO 302:15
measureless caverns m. to man — COLE 232:3
over the m. whole — LUCR 495:9
measures in short m. — JONS 435:27
M. not men — CANN 189:9
M. not men — GOLD 355:20
Not men, but m. — BURK 168:9
meat all manner of m. — BOOK 141:17
appointed to buy the m. — SELD 676:7
but He sends m. — PROV 620:47
came forth m. — BIBL 79:29
dish of m. is too good — WALT 820:26
gavest m. or drink — BALL 52:13
get m. without violence — LAWS 475:24
givest them their m. — BOOK 143:25
God sends m. — PROV 620:49
have m. and cannot eat — BURN 171:20
Heaven sends us good m. — GARR 340:5
hungered, and ye gave me m. — BIBL 98:25
life more than m. — BIBL 95:7
M. and mass never hindered — PROV 626:20
m. in the hall — STEV 760:19
One man's m. — PROV 628:44
On our m., and on us all — HERR 385:15
Out-did the m. — HERR 386:7
seek their m. from God — BOOK 141:9
sent them m. enough — BOOK 139:10
solid m. for men — DRYD 290:11
taste my m. — HERB 384:14
Upon what m. — SHAK 696:10
meats funeral baked m. — SHAK 684:8
Meaulnes call le grand M. — ALAI 9:14
meazles Love iz like the m. — BILL 116:12
mechanic best mascot is a good m. — EARH 294:22
m. part of wit — ETHE 312:5
mechanical m. arts — BACO 45:35
méchant m. animal — MOLI 542:13
medal gold m. for poetry — GRAV 360:13
m. for killing two men — MATL 518:13
m. glitters — CHUR 221:14
meddle Do not m. in the affairs — TOLK 796:11

M. and muddle — DERB 265:5
meddlers Lay-overs for m. — PROV 624:49
meddles Minister that m. with art — MELB 520:17
meddling fool will be m. — BIBL 84:34
Medes M. and Persians — BIBL 91:23
media dealing with the modern m. — MORR 549:10
exposed to the m. — BOWI 148:11
m. It sounds like — STOP 761:9
medias in m. res — HORA 398:10
mediator M. and Advocate — BOOK 129:16
medical cocking their m. eyes — DICK 272:18
in advance of m. thought — WODE 843:1
medicinal M. discovery — AYRE 41:11
medicine desire to take m. — OSLE 579:7
doeth good like a m. — BIBL 84:30
ever m. thee — SHAK 714:1
Grief is itself a m. — COWP 246:5
it's late for m. — OVID 580:16
Laughter is the best m. — SAYI 670:2
m. for the sick — SHAN 724:8
M. for the soul — ANON 17:15
M. is my lawful wife — CHEK 214:9
m. of life — BIBL 93:6
m. the less — SHAK 683:6
m. to heal their sickness — BOOK 144:3
miserable have no other m. — SHAK 708:7
mistake m. for magic — SZAS 769:18
patent m. advertisement — JERO 421:13
practise m. — MOLI 542:1
Medicine Hat war-bonnet of M. — BENÉ 66:11
medicos m. marvelling — RANS 642:7
medicus plus sum quam m. — PLAU 597:22
medieval lily in your m. hand — GILB 348:15
medio M. de fonte leporum — LUCR 496:2
M. tutissimus ibis — OVID 580:10
mediocre Some men are born m. — HELL 380:9
Titles distinguish the m. — SHAW 726:22
mediocribus M. esse poetis — HORA 398:17
mediocritatem Auream quisquis m. — HORA 401:4
mediocrity M. knows nothing higher — DOYL 285:9
m. of her circumstances — SMIT 741:13
m. of the apparatus — TROT 800:20
m. thrust upon them — HELL 380:9
meditate m. on the lovely light — RIG 648:10
meditation abstracted m. — JOHN 424:27
happy tone Of m. — WORD 847:15
light with m. — DUNN 292:11
m. of my heart — BOOK 134:23
sage in m. found — SHEL 731:22
meditations enter infinite m. — MAHĀ 507:6
Mediterranean cooking of the m. — DAVI 258:2
M., where he lay — SHEL 730:9
taken from the M. — SHAF 678:2
medium insipid as a m. — BURN 169:16
m. because nothing's well done — ACE 1:7
m. is the message — MCLU 503:15
Roast Beef, M. — FERB 316:16
meek Blessed are the m. — BIBL 94:20
borne his faculties so m. — SHAK 704:5
m. and lowly in heart — BIBL 96:27
m. and quiet spirit — BIBL 112:10
m. shall inherit — SMIT 742:5
M. wifehood is no part — BRIT 151:18
meekly m. kneeling — BOOK 131:17
meet can never m. — MARV 515:11
Extremes m. — PROV 619:32
If I should m. thee — BYRO 183:23
If we do m. again — SHAK 698:23
make him an help m. — BIBL 75:14
m. and right so to do — BOOK 131:21
m. 'em on your way down — MIZN 541:4
m. thee in that hollow vale — KING 451:15
used to m. — BROW 159:3
very m., right — BOOK 131:22
When shall we three m. — SHAK 702:28

Where dead men m.   BUTL 177:7
meeting Journeys end in lovers m.
     SHAK 720:15
   m. where it likes   ARNO 29:11
meetings M. are held because   GALB 338:6
   m. made December June   TENN 779:20
meets than m. the ear   MILT 529:14
méfiez-vous Taisez-vous! M.   OFFI 572:14
megalith M.-still   HUGH 407:7
melancholy as lovely m.   FLET 327:6
   black sun of m.   NERV 559:8
   busy to avoid m.   BURT 173:19
   charm in m.   ROGE 652:13
   green and yellow m.   SHAK 720:29
   Hence, loathèd M.   MILT 529:17
   inherited a vile m.   JOHN 427:1
   m. fit shall fall   KEAT 444:18
   m. god protect thee   SHAK 720:27
   M. has her sovran shrine   KEAT 444:19
   m., long   ARNO 27:3
   M. marked him for her own   GRAY 361:8
   m. of human reflections   BAGE 48:25
   m.'s child   SHAK 698:25
   moping m.   MILT 534:8
   Most musical, most m.   MILT 529:11
   Naught so sweet as M.   BURT 173:18
   Pale M. sate retired   COLL 235:14
   recipe for m.   LAMB 463:3
   soothe her m.   GOLD 355:33
   suck m. out of a song   SHAK 681:4
   untroubled by m.   BANV 54:19
   villanous m.   SHAK 700:1
   what devil This m. is   FORD 328:20
Melchisedech order of M.   BOOK 141:21
meliora Video m.   OVID 580:13
mellificatis non vobis m. apes   VIRG 815:7
mellow m. fruitfulness   KEAT 445:14
   m. fruitfulness   OPEN 575:15
   too m. for me   MONT 543:9
melodie Luve's like the m.   BURN 172:4
melodies Heard m. are sweet   KEAT 444:8
melodious Melting m. words   HERR 386:21
melody ful of hevenyssh m.   CHAU 213:15
   M. is the essence   MOZA 553:1
   m. lingers   BERL 69:21
   m., which I've never   ALAI 10:4
   pretty girl is like a m.   BERL 69:20
   smale foweles maken m.   CHAU 210:5
   voice of m.   BOOK 137:1
melons Stumbling on m.   MARV 515:16
Melrose would'st view fair M.   SCOT 673:8
melt earth shall m. away   BOOK 136:25
   Let Rome in Tiber m.   SHAK 678:14
   m. with ruth   MILT 530:9
   So let us m.   DONN 281:17
   solid flesh would m.   SHAK 683:29
melted m. into air   SHAK 719:1
   M. to one vast Iris   BYRO 179:5
melting like m. wax   BOOK 135:1
   M.-Pot where all the races   ZANG 858:3
member every joint and m.   MILT 535:19
   I am not a m. of   FLEM 326:16
   m. of Christ   BOOK 132:12
   that will accept me as a m.   MARX 516:9
members m. one of another   BIBL 109:12
   very m. incorporate   BOOK 132:4
   were all my m. written   BOOK 143:18
membra Etiam disiecti m. poetae   HORA 403:8
même plus c'est la m. chose   KARR 441:17
meminisse Forsan et haec olim m. iuvabit
     VIRG 811:3
   Nec me m. pigebit Elissae   VIRG 812:3
memoirs M. are true and useful stars
     PEPY 592:17
   write one's m. is to speak ill   PÉTA 593:12
memor Dum m. ipse me   VIRG 812:3
memorable that m. scene   MARV 515:18
memorandum M. is written   ACHE 1:1
memorial have no m.   BIBL 93:34
   out of the M.   DICK 268:15

whole earth as their m.   PERI 592:23
memorials there are no m.   YEVT 856:18
memories dense melancholy of m.   BABE 42:5
   heart of marriage is m.   COSB 244:5
   m. are card-indexes   CONN 240:6
   m. are hunting horns   APOL 23:9
   M. are not shackles   BENN 67:11
   ought to have good m.   SIDN 735:15
memory comes o'er my m.   SHAK 714:9
   Everyone complains of his m.   LA R 469:13
   faculty of m.   DAVI 258:14
   Fond M. brings the light   MOOR 547:22
   Footfalls echo in the m.   ELIO 301:10
   grand m. for forgetting   STEV 759:3
   His m. is going   JOHN 432:5
   liar to have good m.   PROV 625:12
   like a m. lost   CLAR 224:11
   m. against forgetting   KUND 462:5
   m. be green   SHAK 683:20
   m. of a Macaulay   BARR 57:11
   m. of men   BROW 156:16
   m. of yesterday's pleasures   DONN 282:9
   m. remembers the happy things   LOVE 493:10
   m. revealed itself   PROU 613:4
   M. says: Want   RICH 647:5
   m. that only works backwards   CARR 195:11
   Midnight shakes the m.   ELIO 303:1
   mist of a m.   PARI 585:12
   my name and m.   LAST 471:14
   mystic chords of m.   LINC 485:3
   no force can abolish m.   ROOS 654:2
   No m. of having starred   FROS 335:22
   not intellect but rather m.   LEON 481:1
   Queen Elizabeth of most happy m.   BIBL 75:1
   sense them like a m.   MOSE 551:11
   silent m. of God   GIBR 346:7
   Some women'll stay in a man's m.
     KIPL 457:7
   stepmother to m., oblivion   JOHN 422:8
   Thanks for the m.   ROBI 650:11
   thy tablets, M.   ARNO 27:17
   to his m. for his jests   SHER 734:6
   Vibrates in the m.   SHEL 731:23
   while m. holds a seat   SHAK 685:6
men 200,000 m.   NAPO 557:2
   all m. are created equal   ANON 19:17
   all m. are rapists   FREN 333:13
   all things to all m.   ANON 17:7
   all things to all m.   BIBL 107:18
   best of m.   PROV 615:13
   between m. and women   THUR 794:1
   Bring forth m.-children   SHAK 704:13
   company of m.   CHEK 214:13
   conditions of m.   BOOK 129:17
   danger from all m.   ADAM 2:19
   daughters of m.   BIBL 76:5
   Destiny with M. for pieces   FITZ 323:8
   die like m.   BOOK 139:14
   finds too late that m. betray   GOLD 355:33
   fishers of m.   BIBL 94:19
   form Christian m.   ARNO 30:13
   generations of m.   HOME 394:2
   Good m. are scarce   PROV 621:11
   hell to m.   AESC 6:5
   how much m. hate them   GREE 363:4
   I eat m. like air   PLAT 599:7
   If m. could get pregnant   KENN 448:10
   imprudently m. engage   ASTE 32:15
   innocent m., women, and children
     JEFF 420:16
   in the catalogue ye go for m.   SHAK 705:18
   issue not towards m.   BACO 44:20
   learn m. from books   DISR 277:32
   likeness of m.   BIBL 105:10
   looking upon m. as virtuous   BOLI 126:11
   Measures not m.   CANN 189:9
   m. and mountains meet   BLAK 121:21
   m. and nations behave wisely   EBAN 294:24
   M. are April when they woo   SHAK 682:2
   M. are but children   DRYD 287:24
   m. are created equal   JEFF 419:10
   M. are so honest   LERN 481:15
   M. are vile   MONT 543:15

m. as trees, walking   BIBL 99:22
   M. at forty   JUST 439:2
   m. confused with life   FRID 334:9
   m. don most harm   LANG 466:17
   M. drawn by worth   PEMB 591:9
   M. eat Hogs   STEV 757:23
   m. from the barn   HOUS 404:12
   m. have got love   AMIS 13:13
   M. have had every advantage   AUST 39:15
   m. have precedency   BRAD 149:5
   m. have turned into women   XERX 852:19
   m. hurrying back   MULD 551:7
   m. in disguise   ABSE 1:3
   m. in shape and fashion   ASCH 31:7
   m. in women do require   BLAK 121:23
   men know so little of m.   DU B 291:1
   m., like satyrs   MARL 513:8
   M. lived like fishes   SIDN 735:16
   m. may come   TENN 775:19
   m. must work   KING 452:22
   M., my brothers   TENN 780:19
   m. naturally desire to know   AUCT 34.12
   m. naturally were born free   MILT 536:7
   m. of like passions   BIBL 105:11
   M. seldom make passes   PARK 585:16
   m.'s lack of manners   HATH 375:4
   m. that were boys when   BELL 65:23
   M.! the only animal to fear   LAWR 475:4
   M. were deceivers ever   SHAK 712:18
   m. we wanted to marry   STEI 755:13
   M., when they lust   GREE 362:22
   m. who have loved them   TROL 800:9
   M. who march away   HARD 373:1
   m. who will support me   MELB 521:6
   m. with the muck-rakes   ROOS 654:10
   m., women, and Herveys   MONT 543:18
   M. would be angels   POPE 604:25
   m. would be false   LYLY 497:1
   m. would be tyrants   ADAM 1:14
   Mocks married m.   SHAK 702:25
   more I see of m.   ROLA 653:1
   need of a world of m.   BROW 160:16
   not m., but manners   FIEL 318:1
   Not m., but measures   BURK 168:9
   not the m. in my life that counts
     WEST 830:4
   power over m.   WOLL 844:4
   proper young m.   BURN 171:16
   Rejoiced they were na m.   BURN 173:5
   schemes o' mice an' m.   BURN 172:22
   State is a relation of m.   WEBE 825:5
   studied books than m.   BACO 46:7
   think all m. mortal   YOUN 857:14
   to m. French   CHAR 209:13
   transform M. into monsters   FORD 328:20
   two strong m.   KIPL 453:15
   very language of m.   WORD 850:23
   wealth accumulates, and m. decay
     GOLD 354:10
   We are the hollow m.   ELIO 302:6
   What m. or gods   KEAT 444:7
   Women nicer than m.   AMIS 13:14
menace m. to be defeated   SCAR 668:11
mend Make do and m.   OFFI 572:10
   never too late to m.   PROV 624:9
   shine, and seek to m.   DONN 279:21
   we can't m. it   CLOU 227:20
mendax Splendide m.   HORA 401:20
mended all is m.   SHAK 712:8
   Least said, soonest m.   PROV 625:1
   nothing else but to be m.   BUTL 176:4
mendicus M. es   PLAU 597:22
mending ever want m.   PROV 635:15
mene M., TEKEL, UPHARSIN   BIBL 91:22
meningitis M. It was a word   DEAN 260:8
menpleasers with eyeservice, as m.
     BIBL 109:19
mens M. agitat molem   VIRG 812:14
   M. sana in corpore sano   JUVE 440:11
mensonge m. suit   PROU 613:13
mental cease from m. fight   BLAK 121:15
   day of m. alienation   RIEL 648:9

Middle Ages go and live in the M.
SMIT 743:2

middle class great English m.   ARNO 29:14
m. morality   SHAW 724:14
M. people are apt   SMIL 740:24
M. was quite prepared   BELL 65:1
Philistines proper, or m.   ARNO 29:10
sinking m.   ORWE 577:26
middle classes bow, ye lower m.   GILB 347:9
Middlesex acre in M.   MACA 498:9
Rural M. again   BETJ 72:13
midge like a fretful m.   ROSS 655:21
no bigger than a m.'s wing   PROV 627:1
Midian host of M.   BIBL 79:24
Midlands living in the M.   BELL 65:24
midnight a-bed after m.   SHAK 720:14
black, and m. hags   SHAK 706:15
budding morrow in m.   KEAT 445:20
came upon a m. clear   SEAR 675:8
cease upon the m.   KEAT 444:27
Cerberus, and blackest M.   MILT 529:17
chimes at m.   SHAK 692:8
consumed the m. oil   GAY 341:25
Holding hands at m.   GERS 344:8
hour's sleep before m.   PROV 628:40
iron tongue of m.   SHAK 712:5
Let's mock the m. bell   SHAK 679:17
m. never come   MARL 513:5
m. ride of Paul Revere   LONG 491:4
M. shakes the memory   ELIO 303:1
M. Without Pity   JOHN 423:1
our m. oil   QUAR 638:20
stroke of the m. hour   NEHR 558:3
'Tis the year's m.   DONN 281:6
upon a m. dreary   POE 599:5
upon a m. pillow   SHAK 681:2
woes at m. rise   LYLY 497:3
midst go up in the m. of thee   BIBL 78:9
In the m. of life   BOOK 133:17
there am I in the m.   BIBL 97:22
midsummer high M. pomps   ARNO 28:26
very m. madness   SHAK 721:10
midway M. along the path   OPEN 575:5
midwife fairies' m.   SHAK 717:15
midwinter In the bleak m.   ROSS 655:9
mie J'aime mieux ma m.   ANON 21:2
mieux m. est l'ennemi du bien   VOLT 815:14
tout est au m.   VOLT 815:8
might as our m. lessens   ANON 22:6
Britons alone use 'M.'   WAUG 824:15
counsel and m.   BIBL 88:20
do it with thy m.   BIBL 86:15
Exceeds man's m.   SHAK 719:21
It m. have been   HART 374:16
It m. have been   WHIT 834:5
M. is right   PROV 626:21
my name is M.-have-been   ROSS 656:5
right makes m.   LINC 485:1
Through the dear m.   MILT 530:11
mightier make thee m. yet   BENS 67:25
pen m. than the sword   BULW 164:5
mightiest m. in the mightiest   SHAK 709:25
mighty all that m. heart   WORD 846:7
bringeth m. things to pass   BOOK 142:9
how are the m. fallen   BIBL 80:27
Lord in m. battle   BOOK 135:6
Marlowe's m. line   JONS 436:1
m. God   BIBL 88:18
M. lak' a rose   STAN 754:11
m. man is he   LONG 491:8
m. man of valour   BIBL 79:22
m. Poets in their misery   WORD 849:22
m. working   BOOK 133:18
Nimrod the m. hunter   BIBL 76:13
put down the m.   BIBL 99:32
rushing m. wind   BIBL 104:26
things which are m.   BIBL 107:5
thou art m. yet   SHAK 698:26
through a m. hand   BIBL 78:25
mignonne M., allons voir   RONS 653:4
migraine Love is a universal m.   GRAV 360:9
migrations all our m.   GOLD 355:30
mild draw'd m.   DICK 270:5

m. and magnificent eye   BROW 160:3
prefer m. hale   SURT 764:17
milder Not m.   ARNO 27:26
mildest m. mannered man   BYRO 181:2
mile compel thee to go a m.   BIBL 94:30
miss is as good as a m.   PROV 626:26
walked a crooked m.   NURS 569:18
miles How many m.   NURS 567:9
m. to go before I sleep   FROS 336:3
milestones m. on the Dover Road
DICK 269:22
militant Christ's Church m.   BOOK 131:12
first m. lowbrow   BERL 70:6
militants m. like cleaning women   TRUF 801:4
militarism M. . . . . is fetish worship
TAWN 773:16
military disarm a m. capacity   COOK 242:3
entrust to m. men   CLEM 226:10
m. divisions   HAVE 375:7
M. force   MCNA 504:13
m. man approaches   SHAW 726:12
M. Two-step   GREN 363:12
order and m. discipline   MILI 526:5
milk Adversity's sweet m.   SHAK 717:38
buy wine and m.   BIBL 90:6
crying over spilt m.   PROV 624:10
drunk the m. of Paradise   COLE 232:8
end is moo, the other, m.   NASH 557:9
flowing with m. and honey   BIBL 77:19
Gin was mother's m.   SHAW 727:15
his mother's m.   SHAK 720:12
lady loves M. Tray   ADVE 7:6
M. and then just as it comes   BETJ 72:8
m. and the yoghurt   TRIL 798:16
m. comes frozen home   SHAK 702:26
m. is more likely   BUTL 177:2
m. is so cheap   PROV 635:7
m. my ewes and weep   SHAK 722:11
m. of human kindness   GUED 365:11
m. of human kindness   SHAK 703:18
m. of the word   BIBL 112:4
m. of the word   BIBL 115:18
M.'s leap toward immortality   FADI 314:2
M.-soup men call domestic   PATM 588:16
m. the bull   JOHN 428:12
m. the cow of the world   WILB 835:4
m.-white steed   BALL 53:10
Never cry over spilt m.   FIEL 318:23
putting m. into babies   CHUR 221:18
she gave him m.   BIBL 79:19
take my m. for gall   SHAK 703:20
trout in the m.   THOR 792:26
weyveth m. and flessh   CHAU 211:19
With m. and honey blessed   NEAL 558:2
milka Drinka Pinta M. Day   ADVE 7:19
milkmaid m. singeth blithe   MILT 529:22
milky M. Way, the bird of Paradise
HERB 384:18
steeped in stars, and m.   RIMB 649:6
mill at the m. with slaves   MILT 534:25
clappeth as a m.   CHAU 211:5
forge and the m.   HOUS 404:12
grist that comes to the m.   PROV 614:12
m. cannot grind with   PROV 626:22
neither a m.   HUNT 410:12
old m. by the stream   ARMS 26:10
mille Da mi basia m.   CATU 202:14
millennium after the m.   RAOU 642:9
calico m.   CARL 193:4
miller hackneyed jokes from M.   BYRO 182:9
jolly m.   BICK 115:21
milliner jewelled mass of m.   TENN 781:18
million aiming at a m.   BROW 159:15
Fifty m. Frenchmen   MILI 526:8
m. deaths a statistic   STAL 754:5
m. million spermatozoa   HUXL 411:10
m. of the mouthless dead   SORL 746:23
want to make a m.   ANON 16:18
millionaire And an old-fashioned m.
FISH 322:18
I am a M.   SHAW 725:23
m. who bought it   MCCA 500:4
silk hat on a Bradford m.   ELIO 303:20

millions I will be m.   EPIT 310:11
M. long for immortality   ERTZ 308:14
m. of strange shadows   SHAK 723:4
mortal m. live alone   ARNO 29:2
multiplying m.   O'SU 579:9
pour out m.   COLB 230:22
What m. died   CAMP 187:17
mills dark Satanic m.   BLAK 121:15
m. of God grind slowly   LONG 490:23
m. of God grind slowly   PROV 626:23
millstone m. round our necks   DISR 275:14
m. were hanged about his neck   BIBL 97:20
millstones eyes as big as m.   ANDE 14:6
Turned to m.   SHEL 730:4
Milton malt does more than M.   HOUS 405:2
M.! thou shouldst be living   WORD 847:14
M. was for us   BROW 160:3
morals hold Which M. held   WORD 847:3
mute inglorious M.   GRAY 361:5
mimic m. of the sun   CRAN 249:26
miminy Francesca di Rimini, m.   GILB 348:16
mimsy m. were the borogoves   CARR 194:25
minarets Fretted with m.   THWA 794:6
mince dined on m.   LEAR 477:18
mind absence of m.   SEEL 675:16
activity of his m.   HUNT 410:1
all in the m.   WOLF 843:16
And thou, my m.   SIDN 736:12
at the end of the m.   STEV 758:2
beat at your m.   HECH 379:1
blind in your ears and m.   SOPH 746:18
by the eternal m.   WORD 848:8
Cast your m. on other days   YEAT 856:4
change your m.   AURE 38:10
[Charles] Sumner's m.   ADAM 2:12
chords in the human m.   DICK 267:20
Come back into my m.   BELL 65:24
conformation of his m.   MACA 498:14
conjunction of the m.   MARV 515:11
could not make up his m.   OLIV 573:3
dagger of the m.   SHAK 704:16
damages his m.   ANON 21:11
don't m. if I do   CATC 201:2
empires of the m.   CHUR 221:19
enter into your own m.   VALÉ 806:11
exists merely in the m.   HUME 409:4
feeble, tiny m.   JUVE 440:14
female m.   IRWI 414:7
first destroys their m.   DRYD 288:21
fool uttereth all his m.   BIBL 85:11
forces of the m.   PROU 613:9
frailty of the m.   SHAD 677:21
frame of m.   HORA 399:10
furnished with a m. so rare   SHAK 682:28
generous and elevated m.   JOHN 426:9
gentle m. by gentle deeds   SPEN 752:7
Georgia on my m.   GORR 357:4
give a sex to the m.   WOLL 844:1
great regions of the m.   BROC 151:20
hand the cutting edge of the m.   BRON 152:5
has a m. and knows it   SHAW 724:14
His m. his kingdom   COWP 248:23
human m. in ruins   DAVI 258:17
index of a feeling m.   CRAB 249:14
infirmity of noble m.   MILT 530:2
in m., body, or estate   BOOK 129:19
In my m.'s eye   SHAK 684:9
innocent and quiet m.   STEV 759:23
in the m. of man   WORD 847:11
Keep violence in the m.   ALDI 10:12
know the m. of God   HAWK 375:15
liberation of the human m.   GOLD 354:8
losing your m.   FOX 331:13
love of the things of the m.   PERI 592:21
man's unconquerable m.   WORD 850:18
marble index of a m.   WORD 849:11
march of m.   PEAC 589:14
Measure your m.'s height   BROW 160:14
m. and hand went together   HEMI 381:3
m. and soul, according   TENN 778:21
m. at peace   BYRO 183:5
m. be a thoroughfare   KEAT 447:3
m. can make Substance   BYRO 182:7

mind (*cont.*):

m., did mind his grace	ROYD 658:2
m. diseased	BYRO 179:9
m. does not require filling	PLUT 598:13
m. has mountains	HOPK 396:19
M. has no sex	MISQ 538:9
M. in its purest play	WILB 835:5
m. is actually employed	JOHN 430:4
m. is a very opal	SHAK 720:27
m. is but a barren soil	REYN 646:6
m. is free	DRAY 285:21
m. is its own place	MILT 531:14
m. is like a mirror	CHUA 219:7
m. is maturing late	NASH 557:12
m. is not a bed	AGAT 6:22
m. loves the unknown	MAGR 506:6
Mind, m. alone	AKEN 9:4
m. moves upon silence	YEAT 854:22
M. my bike	CATC 201:18
m. of large general powers	JOHN 425:1
M. of Man	WORD 846:11
m. of the lower animals	DARW 257:15
m. of winter	STEV 758:6
m.'s construction	SHAK 703:17
m. serene for contemplation	GAY 342:4
m. shapes itself	WOLL 844:6
m. the least of possessions	WHIT 832:4
m. to me a kingdom is	DYER 293:13
m. was that of Lord Beaverbrook	ATTL 33:1
m. watches itself	CAMU 188:4
m. which cannot bear	MENG 521:22
m. which reveres details	LEWI 483:22
m. will very generally refuse	TROL 799:6
minister to a m. diseased	SHAK 707:9
moved was their own m.	HUI- 408:5
my m. a gap of danger	HEAN 378:4
my m. forbids to crave	DYER 293:13
My m. is stupefied	VILL 810:9
My m. may lose its force	BYRO 179:11
my m.'s unsworn	EURI 312:17
noble m.	DOYL 284:15
no blemish but the m.	SHAK 721:15
no deeply thinking m.	MELV 521:9
no female m.	GILM 349:13
not enough to have a good m.	DESC 265:10
nothing great but m.	HAMI 369:21
not in my perfect m.	SHAK 701:22
no way out of the m.	PLAT 596:19
ordinary m.	WOOL 845:2
outlaw of his own dark m.	BYRO 178:15
out of m.	PROV 629:12
out of m.	THOM 788:9
out of my m.	OPEN 574:13
O! what a noble m.	SHAK 686:18
padlock—on her m.	PRIO 612:2
padlock on the m.	POPE 602:1
persuaded in his own m.	BIBL 106:45
prepare the m. of the country	DISR 276:3
Reading is to the m.	STEE 755:2
recesses in my m.	BRON 152:10
remained, after his time, but m.	SMIT 743:10
robs the m.	BURK 167:3
sap the m. of the mind	LEON 481:3
seen is merely their own m.	MAHĀ 506:17
serve thee with a quiet m.	BOOK 130:18
sex in the m.	LAWR 475:3
so-called mortal m.	EDDY 295:9
sound m.	BIBL 110:28
sound m.	JUVE 440:11
subsistence without a m.	BERK 69:14
they're wrong. M. it	FORS 329:18
this m. be in you	BIBL 109:24
to one dead level ev'ry m.	POPE 602:3
travel broadens the m.	CHES 217:7
Travel broadens the m.	PROV 633:17
turn thy m. to the Lord	FOX 331:10
unbends the m. like them	GAY 341:15
unseemly exposure of the m.	HAZL 376:10
Until reeled the m.	GIBB 346:4
What is M.	PUNC 637:9
what one has in one's m.	PROU 613:9
with all thy m.	BIBL 98:8
without a m.	BACO 43:16

mindful m. of him	BOOK 134:5
M. of the Church's teaching	MARG 512:3
minds comfortable m.	CUMM 253:15
evil in young m.	ARNO 30:16
fairly developed m.	FORS 329:7
great empire and little m.	BURK 167:1
Great m. think alike	PROV 621:18
hearts and m.	BIBL 110:7
marriage of true m.	SHAK 723:22
M. are like parachutes	DEWA 266:11
m. comprehend all things	BYRO 181:17
M. innocent and quiet	LOVE 493:6
M. like beds always made up	WILL 839:12
m. made better	ELIO 300:20
m. me o' departed joys	BURN 170:15
m. of ordinary men	BRON 152:7
please little m.	PROV 625:32
poison and warp men's m.	BUCH 162:19
spur of all great m.	CHAP 208:19
weed their own m.	WALP 819:14
mine all that's m. is thine	BALL 52:7
but m. own	SHAK 682:7
If they are m. or no	HOUS 404:2
lovin' dat man of m.	HAMM 369:22
m. own familiar friend	BOOK 137:17
she is m. for life	SPAR 749:26
So be m., as I yours	GRAV 360:8
'Twas m., 'tis his	SHAK 713:26
What thou art is m.	MILT 534:4
with m. own	BIBL 98:3
minefield grief is like a m.	WARN 821:22
Life, if you're fat, is a m.	MARG 512:4
miner Dwelt a m.	MONT 546:5
mineral vegetable, animal, and m.	GILB 348:28
Minerva owl of M.	PAUL 589:5
mines m. reported in the fairway	KIPL 455:4
mineworkers National Union of M.	MACM 504:8
mingle In one spirit meet and m.	SHEL 730:2
mining m.-claims	BENÉ 66:11
minion morning's m.	HOPK 397:10
minister As m. of the Crown	PEEL 590:15
doobts aboot the m.	PUNC 637:20
God help the M.	MELB 520:17
m. kiss'd the fiddler's wife	BURN 172:1
m. to a mind diseased	SHAK 707:9
M., whoever he at any time	PAIN 582:21
m. who moves about	CHOI 218:7
Yes, M.! No, Minister	CROS 252:17
ministered Angels came and m.	BIBL 94:18
thousands m. unto him	BIBL 91:24
ministering m. angel	SHAK 689:1
m. angel thou	SCOT 673:24
ministers Angels and m. of grace	SHAK 684:25
grim Geneva m.	AYTO 41:14
group of Cabinet M.	CURZ 254:9
m. a flaming fire	BOOK 141:5
m. decide	THAT 787:13
m. of Christ	BIBL 108:20
M. of State	GILB 347:5
m. of the new testament	BIBL 108:13
my actions are my m.'	CHAR 209:11
passion-wingèd M.	SHEL 728:15
teaching m. to consult	SWIF 765:15
warning to all M.	WALP 820:10
you murdering m.	SHAK 703:20
ministries *Times* has made many m.	BAGE 47:19
ministry marriage than a m.	BAGE 48:11
m. of all the talents	ANON 17:16
performs its secret m.	COLE 231:18
secret m. of frost	COLE 231:23
work of the m.	BIBL 109:11
mink trick of wearing m.	BALM 54:5
minks LSD reminds me of m.	GRAV 360:16
Minnehaha M., Laughing Water	LONG 491:3
minnows death for the m.	TAWN 774:2
Triton of the m.	SHAK 682:16
minor change from major to m.	PORT 607:11

minorities M. . . . are almost always	SMIT 744:7
minority m. possess their equal rights	JEFF 420:1
not enough to make a m.	ALTM 12:21
smug m.	BERT 71:19
minstrel M. Boy to the war	MOOR 547:17
wandering m. I	GILB 347:19
mint m. which coined our misery	DRAY 286:2
m. with the hole	ADVE 8:4
tithes of m. and cumin	BIBL 98:9
mint-mark stamped with the m.	HORA 398:2
mints lavender, m.	SHAK 722:4
minuet constitutional m.	SCAR 668:10
minute cannot cage the m.	MACN 504:22
fill the unforgiving m.	KIPL 454:13
first m., after noon	DONN 281:3
good m. goes	BROW 161:26
in m. particulars	BLAK 120:12
sucker born every m.	BARN 56:19
minutes famous for fifteen m.	WARH 821:16
five m. too late	COWL 246:1
have the seven m.	COLL 235:6
m. hasten to their end	SHAK 723:6
rate of sixty m. an hour	LEWI 483:6
sixty diamond m.	MANN 510:7
take care of m.	CHES 215:3
Three m.' thought	HOUS 405:4
when the waves turn the m.	LIGH 484:11
white unblemished m.	THOM 792:6
Mirabeau Under M. Bridge	APOL 23:10
miracle m. in his own person	HUME 408:11
m. of a youth	EVEL 313:3
m. of our age	CARE 190:10
m. of rare device	COLE 232:5
seem a M.	DONN 282:10
miracles age of m.	PROV 614:8
age of m. hadn't passed	GERS 344:4
believe in m.	FOX 331:14
there are always m.	CATH 199:9
miraculous most m. organ	SHAK 686:7
Miranda Do you remember an Inn, M.	BELL 65:25
mire cast into the m.	BURK 167:18
m. and clay	BOOK 136:6
Sow returns to her M.	KIPL 454:9
mirk m., mirk night	BALL 53:12
mirror in the rear m.	RODD 651:22
live alone and smash his m.	ANON 20:16
mind is like a m.	CHUA 219:7
m. cracked from side to side	TENN 780:12
M., mirror on the wall	GRIM 364:14
m. of alle curteisye	CHAU 211:18
m. the image we cast there	GIDE 345:6
m. up to nature	SHAK 686:24
novel is like a m.	STEN 755:16
stand of m. bright	HUI- 408:3
sunlit m.	ABSE 1:5
mirrors m. and fatherhood are abominable	BORG 145:7
m. are lonely	AUDE 36:1
m. meant To glass the opulent	HARD 372:13
m. of the gigantic shadows	SHEL 732:17
m. of the sea are strewn	FLEC 326:5
mirth betray me to your m. or hate	FORD 329:1
I love such m.	WALT 820:22
M. is like a flash	ADDI 5:2
m.-subdual	GISS 350:6
must borrow its m.	WILC 835:8
Present m.	SHAK 720:16
song of the birds for m.	GURN 365:20
Than M. can do	ANON 17:1
misbeliever You call me m.	SHAK 709:2
misce M. *stultitiam consiliis*	HORA 403:1
mischance fil all this m.	CHAU 212:3
mischief evil and m.	BOOK 129:4
execute any m.	CLAR 224:16
if m. befall him	BIBL 77:8
In every deed of m.	GIBB 345:7
intended m. against thee	BOOK 134:25
it means m.	SHAK 687:4
m. then into the world	DRAY 286:2

m., thou art afoot SHAK 698:9
m. thou hast done NEWT 563:2
mother of m. PROV 627:1
no authority from God to do m.
MAYH 519:14
punishment is m. BENT 68:7
sown the world with m. BUCH 162:19
Spectatress of the m. ROWE 657:9
what m. is in hand BYRO 181:16
mischiefs heap m. upon them BIBL 79:4
misconceive hardly m. you BROW 161:18
misconduct no m. in anyone NELS 558:18
miscuit *qui m. utile dulci* HORA 398:13
misdoings these our m. BOOK 131:18
miserable make a man m. CHAR 209:5
Me m.! which way shall I fly MILT 532:24
M. comforters BIBL 83:9
m. have no other medicine SHAK 708:7
m. human being JAME 418:19
m. sinners BOOK 129:3
most m. things VIRG 811:10
of all men most m. BIBL 108:3
secret of being m. SHAW 727:8
so is it very m. TAYL 775:2
two people m. BUTL 176:27
miserande *Heu, m. puer* VIRG 812:16
miserere *m. nobis* MISS 539:9
miseria *Nella m.* DANT 255:18
miseries in shallows and in m. SHAK 698:21
miserrima *Quaeque ipse m. vidi* VIRG 811:10
miserum *Nec m. fieri* LUCR 495:18
misery bound in m. and iron BOOK 141:16
coined our m. DRAY 286:2
full of m. BOOK 133:16
great kick at m. LAWR 475:12
guilt and m. AUST 39:5
happiness and final m. MILT 532:9
loses his m. ARNO 28:11
Man hands on m. to man LARK 469:3
mighty Poets in their m. WORD 849:22
mine affliction and my m. BIBL 91:8
M. acquaints a man SHAK 718:31
m. is a battle gained WELL 827:14
M. loves company PROV 626:24
m. of being DRAB 285:14
m. of manilla folders ROET 652:4
m. which it is his duty LOWE 493:16
nothing but pure m. JOHN 431:20
Oppressed the m. CRAB 249:1
relation of distant m. GIBB 345:8
result m. DICK 268:14
splendid m. ROSS 655:17
to him that is in m. BIBL 82:34
vale of m. BOOK 139:16
when one is in m. DANT 255:18
misfits m., Looney Tunes, and criminals
REAG 643:15
misfortune after a recent m. MANZ 511:9
m. of our best friends LA R 469:21
m. to ourselves BIER 116:4
What a m. it is EDGE 296:2
misfortunes All the m. of men PASC 587:6
crimes and m. VOLT 816:5
crimes, follies, and m. GIBB 345:1
make m. more bitter BACO 45:5
M. never come singly PROV 626:25
m. of others LA R 469:10
talks of his m. JOHN 431:20
misgovernment cruelty, stupidity and m.
GLAD 351:12
misguided m. men KING 452:7
mislaid afterwards m. PAST 588:2
mislead mystify, m., and surprise JACK 415:8
one to m. the public ASQU 32:5
misleading bound to be m. WATS 822:18
m. thoughts SPEN 750:9
misled most have been m. DRYD 288:19
mislike M. me not for my complexion
SHAK 709:3
misnomer name of Epic's no m. BYRO 180:16
misquotation M. the privilege of the
learned PEAR 590:9

misquote enough of learning to m.
BYRO 182:9
misrepresentation some degree of m.
ELIO 300:21
misrule Thirteen years of Tory m. POLI 601:9
miss calls her 'M.' CHES 216:15
little m. HUME 408:15
m. but a tree BLAM 123:5
m. for pleasure GAY 342:13
m. is as good as a mile PROV 626:26
M. not the discourse BIBL 93:8
M. respectably unmarried CART 196:22
never had you never m. PROV 634:18
never m. the water PROV 636:3
so might I m. BROW 159:30
missa *Ite m. est* MISS 539:11
missed m. a good opportunity CHIR 218:3
m. the bus CHAM 206:14
m. the point completely ELIO 301:4
never would be m. GILB 347:21
No one would have m. her EPIT 310:2
Woman much m. HARD 373:3
misses m. family and friends EPIT 310:12
missing M. so much and so much
CORN 243:10
mission m. workers came out too early
RUNY 659:1
my duty and my m. SCHI 671:5
My m. is to pacify GLAD 350:14
sense of religious m. UPDI 805:24
missionaries eaten by m. SPOO 753:3
missionary I would eat a m. WILB 834:17
Mississippi place the m. BELL 66:1
singing of the M. HUGH 406:19
Missouri admit M. to the Union COBB 229:15
God has given us M. RAND 642:2
misspent thy m. time KEN 448:6
missus M., my Lord PUNC 637:19
mist air broke into a m. BROW 160:18
drizzling m. ASKE 31:20
Fuji through m. BASH 57:23
meanness, sophistry, and m. BYRO 179:30
m. and hum ARNO 28:17
m. in my face BROW 161:1
m. is dispelled GAY 341:14
mistake Among all forms of m. ELIO 300:1
have made a great m. MORS 550:16
made any such m. DICK 270:19
make a m. LA G 464:1
m. in the translation VANB 806:13
m. shall not be repeated EPIT 311:4
m. the meaning WESL 829:18
Nature's sole m. GILB 349:2
overlooks a m. HUXL 411:18
Shome m., shurely CATC 201:26
song and a m. OVID 580:18
under a m. SWIF 766:9
mistaken possible you may be m.
CROM 251:16
mistakes gives to their m. WILD 836:10
great men make m. CHUR 220:15
If he makes m. they must be covered
CHUR 222:14
If you don't make m. PROV 623:15
just created like m. EMEC 306:9
knows some of the worst m. HEIS 380:6
make no m. CONR 240:22
man who makes no m. PHEL 594:8
search for our m. POPP 607:6
mistress Art is a jealous m. EMER 306:19
court a m. JONS 435:25
deck her m.' head BYRO 183:6
In ev'ry port a m. GAY 342:11
literature is my m. CHEK 214:9
m. I am ashamed to call you ELIZ 304:18
m. in my own KIPL 455:7
m. of herself POPE 603:6
m. of the Earl OPEN 574:20
m. of the months SWIN 767:24
m. of the Party HEAL 377:13
m. or a friend SHEL 729:7
m. should be like WYCH 852:9
new m. now I chase LOVE 493:7

O m. mine SHAK 720:15
teeming m. POPE 603:4
worst m. BACO 43:7
mistresses I shall have m. GEOR 343:2
like all his other m. FLAU 325:2
m. with great smooth BROW 158:20
or your Lordship's m. WILK 837:19
Wives are young men's m. BACO 44:32
mists Season of m. KEAT 445:14
Season of m. OPEN 575:15
So many m. in March PROV 631:5
misty ful m. morwe CHAU 213:5
misunderstood people who remain m.
TURG 802:12
To be great is to be m. EMER 307:6
truth m. JAME 418:21
misuse m., then cast their toys away
COWP 246:15
misused m. words generate SPEN 750:9
mites threw in two m. BIBL 99:27
with m. of stars MAYA 519:8
Mithra M. of wide pastures ZORO 859:11
Mithridates M., he died old HOUS 405:3
mitre m. and a crown of martyrdom
WALP 819:24
mittens lost their m. NURS 570:6
mix M. a little foolishness HORA 403:1
m. her with me SWIN 769:8
m. them with my brains OPIE 573:16
mixen Better wed over the m. PROV 615:33
mixture m. of a lie BACO 45:30
strange m. of blood CEEV 251:2
Moab M. is my wash-pot BOOK 137:26
moan is not paid with m. THOM 791:6
made sweet m. KEAT 443:26
m. of doves TENN 783:17
moanday m., tearsday, wailsday JOYC 437:5
moaning no m. of the bar TENN 776:16
moat Look to your M. HALI 369:9
moated at the m. grange SHAK 708:11
lonely m. grange TENN 781:14
mob do what the m. do DICK 271:28
lied to please the m. KIPL 454:2
M., Parliament, Rabble COBB 229:18
remonstrative whisper to a m. HUNT 410:7
supreme governors, the m. WALP 818:17
Moby Dick Canadian did a M. ATWO 33:11
mock but to the kingdom PYM 638:13
m. at our accursed lot MCKA 502:16
m. on Voltaire BLAK 121:16
m. our eyes with air SHAK 679:22
mocked God is not m. BIBL 109:2
hand that m. them SHEL 730:17
mocker Wine is a m. BIBL 84:33
mocking great m. master DAVI 258:8
mockingbird kill a m. LEE 478:16
Out of the m.'s throat WHIT 833:6
mocks M. married men SHAK 702:25
model I am the very m. GILB 348:28
provide logical m. LÉVI 482:18
models pages of your Greek m. HORA 398:12
Rules and m. HAZL 376:20
moderate m. income DURH 293:4
white m. devoted to order KING 452:2
moderation astonished at my own m.
CLIV 227:11
M. in all things PROV 626:27
m. in everything HORA 403:5
m. in the pursuit of justice GOLD 356:2
m. in war is imbecility MACA 497:20
m. is a sort of treason BURK 166:7
perfect m. AUGU 37:14
playful m. in politics HUNT 410:7
term of m. BACO 43:8
modern All art was m. once SERO 677:5
disease of m. life ARNO 28:9
m. Babylon DISR 277:30
m. Major-General GILB 348:28
m. writers PLIN 598:1
spirit of m. life CLIF 227:2
writing a m. history RALE 641:13
modernity M. is the transition SACK 662:8
moderns m. without contempt CHES 215:6

modest M.? My word, no   REED 644:9
modesty M., or rather a fear   BALZ 54:8
modified M. rapture   GILB 347:25
modus Est m. in rebus   HORA 403:5
moenia flammantia m. mundi   LUCR 495:9
moi Madame Bovary, c'est m.   FLAU 325:17
moins m. des choses nouvelles   VOLT 815:9
mois m. des floraisons   ARAG 24:3
mole go ask the m.   BLAK 119:17
  m. cinque-spotted   SHAK 682:29
  Well said, old m.   SHAK 685:9
  working like a m.   HERB 384:10
molecule inhales one m. of it   JEAN 419:6
molecules cells and associated m.   CRIC 251:5
  without understanding m.   CRIC 251:6
molehills M. seem mountains   COTT 244:6
moles rudis indigestaque m.   OVID 580:8
moll King's M. Reno'd   NEWS 562:16
  Me and M. Maloney   GRAV 360:1
Moloch great M., national sovereignty   MEYE 523:16
  M., horrid king   MILT 531:18
mom place called M.'s   ALGR 11:15
mome m. raths outgrabe   CARR 194:25
moment decisive m.   RETZ 645:11
  Eternity was in that m.   CONG 239:2
  Every m. dies a man   BABB 42:2
  Exhaust the little m.   BROO 154:4
  fashion moves from the m.   KARA 441:15
  impulse of the m.   AUST 39:20
  in a m. of time   BIBL 100:10
  m. dies a man   TENN 784:21
  m. in childhood   GREE 362:16
  m. of madness   DAVI 258:16
  m. of my greatness flicker   ELIO 302:17
  m. spent in Paradise   SCHI 670:25
  one brief shining m.   LERN 481:14
momentary Beauty is m. in the mind   STEV 758:4
  pleasure is m.   CHES 215:17
moments evanescent of m.   JOYC 437:13
  m. big as years   KEAT 443:12
  Wagner has lovely m.   ROSS 656:10
Mona M. did researches in original sin   PLOM 598:11
monarch becomes The thronèd m.   SHAK 709:25
  hereditary m. was insane   BAGE 48:1
  merry m.   ROCH 651:14
  m. clothed with majesty   COWP 248:23
  m. of all I survey   COWP 248:24
  m. of the road   FLAN 324:19
  not so much a king as a M.   SELL 676:22
monarchical utility of m. power   BOSW 146:22
monarchies elective m.   GIBB 344:19
monarchs m. must obey   DRYD 288:30
  m. to choose favourites   SWIF 762:15
  righteous m.   BROO 153:4
monarchy absolute M.   PAIN 582:7
  constitutional m.   BAGE 48:17
  discontented under m.   HOBB 390:20
  essential to a true m.   BAGE 47:13
  m. and succession   PAIN 582:8
  M. is a labour-intensive   WILS 840:13
  m. is a merchantman   AMES 13:6
  M. is only   SHEL 732:20
  state of m.   JAME 417:3
  universal m. of wit   CARE 190:13
  US presidency a Tudor m.   BURG 165:17
monasteries So much decay of m.   SKEL 739:8
Monday Born on M.   NURS 569:15
  going to do on M.   YBAR 853:4
  M.'s child   NURS 568:10
  M.'s child is fair   PROV 626:28
monendo delectando pariterque m.   HORA 398:13
Monet M. is only an eye   CÉZA 209:5
money ain't got a barrel of m.   WOOD 844:18
  Bad m. drives out good   PROV 614:45
  bank will lend you m.   HOPE 396:9
  blessing that m. cannot buy   WALT 821:2
  Capitalism is using its m.   CAST 199:2

corrupted by m.   GREE 362:11
draining m. from the pockets   SMIT 741:12
enough courage—or m.   MITC 540:13
first thing to acquire is m.   HORA 398:21
fool and his m.   PROV 620:16
gay hym moore m.   CHAU 211:2
getting m.   JOHN 429:26
Give him the m., Barney   CATC 200:20
given his m. upon usury   BOOK 134:13
goä wheer m. is   TENN 782:13
haven't got the m.   RUTH 661:20
have to borrer the m.   WARD 821:10
He had m. as well   THAT 787:2
his private parts, his m.   BUTL 177:4
Hollywood m. isn't money   PARK 586:9
Honour, without m.   RACI 640:9
I fight for m.   PAPP 585:10
if you can count your m.   GETT 344:15
If you have m. you spend it   KENN 449:12
licence to print m.   THOM 792:22
listen to m. singing   LARK 468:20
long enough to get m. from   LEAC 476:13
love of m.   BIBL 110:26
man without m.   WYCH 852:15
m. answereth all things   BIBL 86:19
M. can't buy happiness   PROV 626:29
m. can't buy me love   LENN 480:16
M. couldn't buy friends   MILL 527:12
M. doesn't talk, it swears   DYLA 294:8
M. gives me pleasure   BELL 65:9
m.-grabbing cronies   HAGU 367:8
m. gushes into politics   WHIT 832:7
m. has a power above   BUTL 176:19
M. has no smell   PROV 626:30
M. has no smell   VESP 809:6
M. is indeed the most important   SHAW 725:15
M. is like a sixth sense   MAUG 518:20
M. is like muck   BACO 45:13
M. . . . is none of the wheels   HUME 408:13
M. isn't everything   PROV 626:31
m. I spend on advertising   LEVE 482:8
M. is power   PROV 626:32
M. is the root   PROV 626:33
M. is the sinews of love   FARQ 315:20
M. is the true fuller's earth   GAY 341:10
M., like manure   PROV 626:35
M. makes a man   PROV 626:36
M. makes money   PROV 626:37
M. makes the mare to go   PROV 626:38
m. of fools   HOBB 390:10
m. perish with thee   BIBL 105:1
M. speaks sense   BEHN 64:4
M. talks   PROV 626:39
m. the sinews of war   BACO 45:26
M. was exactly like sex   BALD 50:9
m. was not time   MERR 523:1
must put the m. in   BULL 163:15
natural interest of m.   MACA 498:7
Never marry for m.   PROV 627:24
No m.   RACI 640:8
No m., no Swiss   PROV 627:42
no one shall work for m.   KIPL 456:5
not spending m. alone   EISE 298:13
only interested in m.   SHAW 727:26
Papa! What's m.   DICK 269:5
pleasant it is to have m.   CLOU 229:2
plenty of m.   ANOU 22:15
poetry in m.   GRAV 360:14
poor know that it is m.   BREN 150:20
retreated back into their m.   FITZ 324:6
rich man without m.   USTI 806:4
rub up against m.   RUNY 658:15
see what m. will do   PEPY 592:14
somehow, make m.   HORA 399:1
spent all the m.   JOHN 431:27
Stealing m. is wrong   AYER 41:7
they have more m.   FITZ 323:20
They hired the m.   COOL 242:9
time is m.   FRAN 332:11
Time is m.   PROV 633:3
to get all that m.   CHES 217:13
unlimited m.   CICE 223:20

use the m. for the poor   PERÓ 592:25
Virtue does not come from m.   SOCR 745:1
voice is full of m.   FITZ 324:5
voter who uses his m.   SAMU 665:11
way the m. goes   MAND 509:12
What m. is better bestowed   THAC 786:7
When you have m., it's sex   DONL 279:3
Wherefore do ye spend m.   BIBL 90:6
without m. and without price   BIBL 90:6
wrote, except for m.   JOHN 430:20
You pays your m.   PROV 636:8
You pays your m.   PUNC 637:5
moneybag Aristocracy of the M.   CARL 192:10
moneyless m. man goes fast   PROV 626:34
moneys m. are for values   BACO 42:19
Mongols M. of our age   HUSS 410:17
mongoose motto of all the m. family   KIPL 456:12
mongrels continent of energetic m.   FISH 321:16
monk cowl does not make m.   PROV 617:15
  live as a m.   JAIN 416:13
  m. and a knight   HENR 382:8
  m. is still   PALI 584:18
  m. who shook the world   MONT 545:15
monkey attack the m.   BEVA 73:14
  descent from a m.   WILB 835:1
  higher the m. climbs   PROV 622:21
  look upon a m.   CONG 239:23
  make a m. of a man   BENC 66:6
  M. with lollipop paws   LEAR 477:9
  nothing but a painted m.   PARA 585:11
  softly, catchee m.   PROV 631:3
monkeys Cats and m.   JAME 417:22
  men and m.   JENY 421:3
  m. banging on typewriters   WILE 837:17
  m. strumming on typewriters   EDDI 295:3
  pay peanuts, get m.   PROV 623:20
  three wise m.   PROV 630:27
monks m. at Clonmacnoise   HEAN 377:21
monogamous Woman m.   JAME 418:24
monogamy M. is the same   ANON 15:8
monologue m. is not a decision   ATTL 33:6
monologues intersecting m.   WEST 830:13
monopolists Men are m.   MOOR 546:17
monopoly best of all m. profits   HICK 388:2
  m. stage of capitalism   LENI 480:3
monotonous it becomes m.   TROL 800:8
monotony eternal m. of passion   FLAU 325:2
  in its swarthy m.   HARD 371:22
  long m. of marriage   GIBB 346:3
Monroe M. Doctrine   MONR 543:4
  mouth of Marilyn M.   MITT 541:3
monster become a m.   NIET 564:9
  blunt m.   SHAK 691:21
  green-eyed m.   SHAK 713:27
  many-headed m.   POPE 605:25
  m. horrendous   VIRG 811:24
  m. unto many   BOOK 138:20
  m., which the Blatant beast   SPEN 752:6
  m. whom I had created   SHEL 728:8
  new kind of m.   HENR 382:8
  overgrown m.   SMOL 744:16
  this busy m., manunkind   CUMM 253:11
monsters in search of m. to destroy   ADAM 3:11
  reason produces m.   GOYA 357:16
  transform Men into m.   FORD 328:20
monstrosity numerous piece of m.   BROW 157:5
monstrous m. animal   FIEL 318:13
  m. carbuncle   CHAR 209:15
  M. carbuncles   SPEN 750:16
  m. regiment of women   KNOX 458:6
  this m. birth   SHAK 713:16
  Two evils, m. either one   RANS 642:8
  With m. head   CHES 215:24
monstrum M. horrendum   VIRG 811:24
montes Parturient m.   HORA 398:8
Montezuma halls of M.   MILI 526:9
  who imprisoned M.   MACA 498:15
month April is the cruellest m.   ELIO 303:7
  fressh as is the m. of May   CHAU 210:8

little m. SHAK 684:4
merry m. of May BALL 51:12
merry m. of May BALL 53:1
m. in which the world bigan CHAU 212:2
m. of metamorphoses ARAG 24:3
m. of tension LESS 482:3
This is the m. MILT 530:17
months for seven m. alone VIRG 815:6
mistress of the m. SWIN 767:24
Montreal no one ever leaves M. COHE 230:10
O God! O M. BUTL 177:8
road from Quebec to M. BROO 153:3
monument ask for his M. BARH 55:12
If you seek a m. EPIT 311:6
left some m. BURK 168:24
m. more lasting than bronze HORA 402:3
m. of the insufficiency JOHN 426:3
m. sticks like a fishbone LOWE 494:10
only m. the asphalt road ELIO 303:3
patience on a m. SHAK 720:29
shalt find thy m. SHAK 723:19
monumentum *Exegi m. aere perennius*
HORA 402:3
Si m. requiris, circumspice EPIT 311:6
moo One end is m. NASH 557:9
moocow m. coming down along the road
OPEN 575:10
mood no m. can be maintained MANN 511:1
moody Mean, M. and Magnificent
TAGL 771:9
moon auld m. in her arm BALL 53:5
bay the m. SHAK 698:14
beneath a waning m. COLE 232:4
Beneath the visiting m. SHAK 680:3
by the light of the m. LEAR 477:18
cold fruitless m. SHAK 710:15
danced in the m. CART 197:5
Daughter of the M. LONG 491:1
defend the m. SALI 664:14
Devil M. in your eyes HARB 371:3
Don't let's ask for the m. FILM 319:3
fair as the m. BIBL 87:17
fleeting m. SHAK 680:9
glimpses of the m. SHAK 684:26
hornèd M. COLE 232:23
horned m. WORD 845:18
in the m.'s eclipse SHAK 706:13
isle, a sickle m. FLEC 326:5
i' the cold o' the m. BROW 158:26
It is the m. BURN 173:8
jumped over the m. NURS 567:6
like the m. CHEK 214:11
looking at the full m. GINS 349:16
minions of the m. SHAK 689:19
m. belongs to everyone DE S 265:16
m. be still as bright BYRO 183:8
m. by night BOOK 142:16
m. doth shine NURS 566:9
m. in lonely alleys CRAN 249:25
M., in the valley of Ajalon BIBL 79:13
m. is in the seventh house RADO 640:12
m.'s an arrant thief SHAK 719:12
m. shines bright SHAK 709:35
m. shone bright on Mrs Porter ELIO 303:17
m. the stars TRUM 801:5
m. under her feet BIBL 113:27
m. walks the night DE L 263:7
m. was full TENN 778:12
mortals call the M. SHEL 729:4
No m., no man PROV 627:43
O more than m. DONN 281:19
only a paper m. HARB 371:2
Only you beneath the m. PORT 607:17
owl does to the m. complain GRAY 361:1
roses across the m. MORR 549:17
sad steps, O M. SIDN 736:4
Shaped like the crescent-m. WORD 848:20
shine on, harvest m. NORW 565:17
shining to the quiet m. COLE 231:23
silent as the m. MILT 534:27
sun and m. AUGU 37:1
Sun and M. should doubt BLAK 119:13
sun and m. to stand TOAS 796:2

unmask her beauty to the m. SHAK 684:15
very error of the m. SHAK 714:22
voyage to the m. LARD 468:9
wan m. sets BURN 172:2
when the m. shall rise WOTT 851:4
when the m. was blood CHES 215:24
moonlight How sweet the m. sleeps
SHAK 710:2
Ill met by m. SHAK 710:30
M. behind you COWA 245:6
of the soundless m. VIRG 811:14
visit it by the pale m. SCOT 673:8
Watch for me by m. NOYE 566:3
while there's m. and music BERL 69:19
moonlit Knocking on the m. door DE L 263:2
m. cedar ARNO 27:20
on the m. door OPEN 574:21
starlit or m. dome YEAT 853:9
moons m. make good their losses
HORA 402:14
m. shall wax and wane no more
WATT 823:19
moonshine everything as m. SCOT 675:1
find out m. SHAK 711:9
in pallid m. KEAT 442:19
Transcendental m. CARL 192:20
moonstruck m. madness MILT 534:8
moor M. has done his duty SCHI 671:4
m.-men win their hay BALL 51:14
moored island is m. only lightly BARR 57:10
moorish m., and wild, and knotty
BRON 152:14
moose strong as a bull m. ROOS 654:6
mops seven maids with seven m. CARR 195:6
moral accounting for the m. sense
CARL 191:23
attainment of m. good JOHN 422:5
Debasing the moral m. ELIO 299:22
detected in it by m. men ZOLA 859:8
drama onto the m. plane GIDE 346:12
Englishman thinks he is m. SHAW 726:8
Everything's got a m. CARR 194:13
form of m. effort LEAC 476:17
form of m. insurance BROD 152:1
good m. philosophy BACO 43:2
His m. pleases POPE 605:21
instrument of m. good SHEL 732:14
It *is* a m. issue NEWS 562:13
kind of m. eunuch SHEL 730:20
lower m. quality HARD 372:1
Mankind's m. test KUND 462:7
m. and intellectual MORE 548:6
m. as soon as one is unhappy PROU 613:7
M. courage is a rarer commodity
KENN 449:11
m. disapproval AYER 41:7
m. evil and of good WORD 850:12
m. flabbiness JAME 418:23
m. imperative DIDI 274:5
M. indignation is jealousy WELL 828:18
m. is not preaching DIMN 274:13
m. law within me KANT 441:6
m. or an immoral book WILD 836:11
m. power strong as sexual CONF 237:23
m. principles please MENG 522:4
M. science is better occupied THOM 788:17
m. virtues CHES 215:11
nature of m. sciences COND 237:7
O m. Gower CHAU 213:18
party is a m. crusade WILS 840:4
people act on m. convictions EMPS 307:24
point a m. JOHN 426:18
religious and m. principles ARNO 30:14
settling the m. ADAM 2:9
stage in m. culture DARW 257:3
State m. case JEFF 419:14
till all are m. SPEN 750:13
moralist gave to the m. AYER 41:8
problem for the m. RUSS 660:15
sturdy m. JOHN 424:21
moralists delight to m. RUSS 661:3
distinguishes m. THAC 786:20
Leave those vain m. ROUS 657:5

We are perpetually m. JOHN 425:7
morality Absolute m. SPEN 750:6
Dr Johnson's m. HAWT 375:16
fits of m. MACA 498:6
for our best m. AUST 39:2
Goodbye, m. HERB 383:8
know about m. CAMU 189:1
may be called M. KANT 441:9
middle-class m. SHAW 727:14
M. expires POPE 602:8
m. for morality's sake COUS 244:12
M. is a costly luxury ADAM 2:15
M. is the herd-instinct NIET 564:7
m. of art WILD 836:13
m. touched by emotion ARNO 30:3
national m. should have this SHAW 725:15
slave-m. NIET 564:11
some people talk of m. EDGE 295:14
system of m. HUME 409:11
What is m. WHIT 832:13
morally does nothing m. ELIO 300:23
morals either m. or principles GLAD 350:19
faith and m. hold WORD 847:3
Food first, then m. BREC 150:14
Have you no m. SHAW 727:13
lack of m. HATH 375:4
m. of a Methodist GILB 349:3
m. of a whore JOHN 427:15
pictured m. charm the mind EPIT 309:6
self-interest was bad m. ROOS 653:17
Why, man of m. COWL 245:18
morbo *Venienti occurrite m.* PERS 593:8
Mordecai I see M. the Jew BIBL 82:22
more For, I have m. DONN 280:2
I am m. BIBL 108:20
I want some m. DICK 271:9
Less is m. PROV 625:5
little m. BROW 158:25
m. and m. about less and less BUTL 175:15
m. equal than others ORWE 577:1
m. he has himself LAO 468:8
m. Piglet wasn't there MILN 527:16
m. than all NEWM 560:19
m. than Homer knew SWIF 767:8
m. than somewhat RUNY 658:16
m. the merrier PROV 626:43
m. things in heaven SHAK 685:10
M. will mean worse AMIS 13:16
m. you get PROV 626:44
Much would have m. PROV 627:4
no m. to say SHAK 720:2
O m. than moon DONN 281:19
take *m.* than nothing CARR 194:11
you get no m. of me DRAY 285:23
mores *Emollit m.* OVID 580:5
Et linguam et m. JUVE 439:14
O tempora, O m. CICE 223:16
morganatic m. alliance HARD 371:7
Morgen *M. sterb' ich* LESS 482:4
mori *In taberna m.* ANON 21:18
pro patria m. HORA 401:12
moriamur *M. et in media arma ruamus*
VIRG 811:19
moriar *Non omnis m.* HORA 402:4
moribus *M. antiquis res* ENNI 308:2
morituri *Ave Caesar, m. te salutant*
ANON 21:13
Moritz happened to Max and M. BUSC 174:18
morn But, look, the m. SHAK 683:19
Each m. a thousand roses FITZ 323:1
From m. to noon he fell MILT 531:27
m. Of bright carnations DRUM 286:13
new m. she saw not KEAT 443:19
Salute the happy m. BYRO 177:17
still m. went out MILT 530:12
this the happy m. MILT 530:17
morning arrested one fine m. OPEN 575:19
autumn arrives in the m. BOWE 147:17
before the m. watch BOOK 143:7
Come, lovely M. DAVI 259:2
danced in the m. CART 197:5
disasters in his m. face GOLD 354:15
Early in the m. HEBE 378:17

morning (cont.):
Early one m. — SONG 747:4
evening and the m. — BIBL 75:5
glad confident m. — BROW 160:4
Good m., sir — CATC 200:22
have the m. well-aired — BRUM 162:7
In the m. it is green — BOOK 139:22
joy cometh in the m. — BOOK 135:18
Lucifer, son of the m. — BIBL 88:24
many a glorious m. — SHAK 723:2
m. after — ADE 5:16
m. again in America — POLI 600:24
m. cometh — BIBL 88:25
M. dreams come true — PROV 626:46
m. gilds the skies — CASW 199:6
m. had been golden — CHUR 222:8
M. has broken — FARJ 315:2
M. in the bowl of night — FITZ 322:24
m. light creaks down again — SITW 738:14
m. of the world — SHEL 728:18
m. rose — KEAT 444:18
M.'s at seven — BROW 160:22
m.'s minion — HOPK 397:10
m.'s war — SHAK 694:26
Never m. wore — TENN 778:25
New every m. — KEBL 447:12
pay thy m. sacrifice — KEN 448:5
scent the m. air — SHAK 685:4
shining m. face — SHAK 681:10
take you in the m. — BALD 50:11
viewed the m. with alarm — GERS 344:4
What a glorious m. — ADAM 3:13
wings of the m. — BOOK 143:16
won't go home till m. — BUCK 163:12

Mornington present of M. Crescent
— HARG 373:12

Morocco we're M. bound — BURK 169:14
moron consumer isn't a m. — OGIL 571:14
See the happy m. — ANON 18:22
morphine m. or idealism — JUNG 438:11
Morris M. Minor prototype — NUFF 566:4
nine men's m. — SHAK 710:31
morrow bid the Devil good m. — PROV 627:17
Eagerly I wished the m. — POE 599:6
no thought for the m. — BIBL 95:11
mors Illi m. gravis incubat — SENE 677:3
Indignatio principis m. est — MORE 548:13
M. aurem vellens — ANON 22:2
M. stupebit — MISS 539:16
Mortalem vitam m. — LUCR 495:18
Nil igitur m. — LUCR 495:16
Pallida M. — HORA 400:5
morsel I found you as a m. — SHAK 679:16
morsels ice like m. — BOOK 144:5
mort La m. ne surprend — LA F 463:15
La m., sans phrases — SIEY 736:21
mortal gathers all things m. — SWIN 768:15
Her last disorder m. — GOLD 355:2
laugh at any m. thing — BYRO 181:13
m., and may err — SHIR 735:5
m. men, mortal men — SHAK 691:2
m. tongue — GURN 366:3
shuffled off this m. coil — SHAK 686:9
something m. — LUCR 495:16
think all men m. — YOUN 857:14
this m. life — BOOK 129:22
this m. life — BOOK 132:6
this m. must put on — BIBL 108:11
mortality emblem of m. — DISR 276:23
frail m. — BACO 46:24
m. touches the heart — VIRG 811:6
M. Weighs heavily on me — KEAT 445:7
Old m. — BROW 156:7
sad m. o'ersways — SHAK 723:8
sepulchres of m. — CREW 251:3
smells of m. — SHAK 701:15
mortals good that m. know — ADDI 4:22
not for m. — ARMS 26:12
not in m. — ADDI 4:8
startle Composing m. — AUDE 34:18
what fools these m. be — SHAK 711:14
mortar Lies are the m. — WELL 828:12

mortifications m. and humiliations
— WALP 820:2
mortifying m. reflections — CONG 239:23
Mortimer Are you Edmund M. — SELL 676:19
mortis Timor m. conturbat me — DUNB 292:2
morts Il n'y a pas de m. — MAET 505:15
mortuus Passer m. est — CATU 202:11
Moscow do not march on M. — MONT 545:13
If I lived in M. — CHEK 214:4
M.: those syllables — PUSH 638:5
Moses From M. to Moses — EPIT 309:8
Go down, M. — SONG 748:10
greater than M. — TALM 772:28
M. hid his face — BIBL 77:18
sitting in M.' chair — BLAK 120:2
Mosque from the Holy M. — KORA 460:14
mosquito just another m. — OKPI 572:22
moss gathers no m. — PROV 630:15
miles of golden m. — AUDE 34:27
mossy Happy field or m. cavern — KEAT 444:5
violet by a m. stone — WORD 850:1
mote m. that is in thy brother's eye
— BIBL 95:13
moth beetle, nor the death-m. — KEAT 444:17
Both m. and flame — ROET 652:8
candle singed the m. — SHAK 709:10
Kill not the m. — BLAK 119:9
like a m., the simple maid — GAY 341:5
m. and rust doth corrupt — BIBL 95:4
m. for the star — SHEL 731:24
mother all thy m.'s graces — CORB 243:3
artist man and the m. woman — SHAW 726:3
art thy m.'s glass — SHAK 722:23
As is the m. — BIBL 91:12
Behold thy m. — BIBL 104:6
by our m.'s dust — FORD 329:1
Can you hear me, m. — CATC 200:7
Christ and his m. — HOPK 397:6
church for his m. — CYPR 254:14
father was frightened of his m. — GEOR 343:13
for the m.'s sake — COLE 233:12
France, m. of arts — DU B 290:17
From whence his m. rose — SEDL 675:10
gave her m. forty whacks — ANON 17:9
Gentle Child of gentle M. — DEAR 260:11
great sweet m. — SWIN 769:8
happen to your m. — WALK 817:8
have a beautiful m. — WALK 817:12
heaviness of his m. — BIBL 84:8
Honour thy father and thy m. — BIBL 78:5
I arose a m. — BIBL 79:17
joyful m. — BOOK 142:1
leave his father and his m. — BIBL 75:17
Like m., like daughter — PROV 625:20
lovelier than your lovely m. — HORA 400:16
make love to the m. — PROV 629:36
marriage with your m. — SOPH 746:20
marry a man who hates his m. — BENN 67:24
may not marry his M. — BOOK 144:21
m. bids me bind — HUNT 410:10
m. bore me in the southern wild — BLAK 122:6
M. died today — OPEN 574:7
m., do not cry — FARM 315:5
M., give me the sun — IBSE 412:12
m. laid her baby — ALEX 11:8
m., make my bed — BALL 51:13
M. needs something today — JAGG 415:14
M. of Aeneas' race — LUCR 495:8
m. of all battles — HUSS 410:16
m. of all treachery — PAIS 583:2
M. OF HARLOTS — BIBL 114:9
m. of invention — PROV 627:12
m. of mankind — MILT 531:7
m. of Parliaments — BRIG 151:11
m. of sciences — BACO 46:16
M. of the Free — BENS 67:25
m. said I never should — NURS 568:11
m.'s grief — BRET 151:1
m.'s little helper — JAGG 415:14
m.'s safeguard — NAPO 556:12
m.'s yearning — ELIO 299:8
m. taught me as a boy — BERR 71:17
m. was glad to get asleep — EMER 307:17

m. who talks about her own — DISR 276:11
m. will be there — HERB 383:6
my father or my m. — STER 756:14
my m. and my brethren — BIBL 97:2
My m. groaned — BLAK 122:14
my m. I see in myself — FRID 334:8
never called me m. — WOOD 844:14
O M. blest — ALPH 12:19
O m., mother — SHAK 682:26
plans to resemble: her m. — BROO 154:1
recognize your m. — VIRG 814:3
rob his m. — FAUL 316:5
their Dacian m. — BYRO 179:12
to make it well? My M. — TAYL 774:15
Took great care of his M. — MILN 527:21
Upon his m.'s grave — WORD 849:1
mothers Come m. and fathers — DYLA 294:17
happy m. made — SHAK 717:14
m.-in-law and Wigan Pier — BRID 151:4
m. of large families — BELL 64:19
sorrows of the m. — FREN 333:12
women become like their m. — WILD 835:18
moths eaten by m. — SITW 738:17
motion alteration of m. — NEWT 561:12
Between the m. And the act — ELIO 302:7
Devoid of sense and m. — MILT 532:1
economic law of m. — MARX 516:14
God ordered m. — VAUG 807:7
m. of the wheels — HUME 408:13
perpetual m. — DICK 272:9
poetry in m. — KAUF 442:2
poetry of m. — GRAH 358:13
so many concepts of m. — RILK 649:2
time's eternal m. — FORD 329:3
uniform m. in a right line — NEWT 561:11
motions secret m. — BACO 46:13
motive m.-hunting of motiveless — COLE 233:25
motives better m. for all the trouble
— GREE 362:18
m. they act by — ASTE 32:15
motley made myself a m. — SHAK 723:20
M.'s the only wear — SHAK 681:8
motor heart's stalled m. — MAYA 519:11
motorcycle art of m. maintenance
— PIRS 595:19
motoribus Cincti Bis M. — GODL 351:19
motto Be that my m. — SWIF 767:14
motus Hi m. animorum — VIRG 815:3
mould broke the m. — ARIO 25:1
frozen in an out-of-date m. — JENK 420:21
m. falls close — ROSS 656:2
m. of a man's fortune — BACO 44:11
m. them into an immortal — MILT 535:19
moulded m. by the lips of man — TENN 784:11
m. out of faults — SHAK 708:18
mouldering many a m. heap — GRAY 361:2
Moulmein old M. Pagoda — KIPL 454:21
mount Mount, m., my soul — SHAK 716:17
m. up with wings — BIBL 89:21
Mount Abora Singing of M. — COLE 232:7
mountain all my holy m. — BIBL 88:22
alone on a great m. — KILV 451:12
bare m. tops — ARNO 29:25
climbed the highest m. — PETR 593:19
Climb ev'ry m. — HAMM 370:1
exceeding high m. — BIBL 94:17
Flatter the m.-tops — SHAK 723:2
from yonder m. height — TENN 783:15
gone on the m. — SCOT 673:5
go up to the m. — KING 452:6
gross as a m. — SHAK 690:10
In a m. greenery — HART 374:13
into a high m. — BIBL 100:10
misty m. tops — SHAK 718:2
m. and hill — BIBL 89:16
m. sheep are sweeter — PEAC 590:5
M.'s slumberous voice — SHEL 730:6
m. will not come to Mahomet — PROV 623:5
say unto this m., Remove — BIBL 97:18
shadows cast by the m. — VIRG 813:16
trees, And the m.-tops — SHAK 695:8
Up the airy m. — ALLI 12:18
mountainous m. sports girl — BETJ 72:15

mountains beautiful upon the m.   BIBL 89:28
broke up the towering m.   VIRG 814:15
Delectable M.   BUNY 164:23
delights in m.   CONF 237:18
Faith will move m.   PROV 619:41
From the m. to the prairies   BERL 69:18
like the tops of m.   MACA 498:10
men and m. meet   BLAK 121:21
m. also shall bring peace   BOOK 138:22
m. are a feeling   BYRO 178:25
M. are the beginning   RUSK 659:15
m. by the winter sea   TENN 778:11
m. gave back the sound   WORD 845:19
m. look on Marathon   BYRO 181:5
m. of Gilboa   BIBL 80:27
M. of Mourne   FREN 333:16
m. skipped like rams   BOOK 142:2
m. were brought forth   BOOK 139:21
M. will go into labour   HORA 398:8
One of the m.   WORD 850:14
river jumps over the m.   AUDE 34:19
rocks of the m.   BIBL 113:15
rose the m.   BYRO 178:17
scale the icy m.   MARL 513:17
so that I could remove m.   BIBL 107:25
mountebank m. and his zany   WALP 819:15
mourir *Partir c'est m. un peu*   HARA 370:20
mourn Blessed are they that m.   BIBL 94:20
comfort all that m.   BIBL 90:18
countless thousands m.   BURN 171:24
don't m. for me never   EPIT 309:15
each will m. her own   INGE 413:13
man was made to m.   BURN 171:23
Margaret you m. for   HOPK 397:4
M., hapless Caledonia   SMOL 744:18
m. in prison   MONT 543:13
m. with ever-returning spring   WHIT 833:22
M., you powers of Charm   CATU 202:11
No longer m. for me   SHAK 723:9
now can never m.   SHEL 728:23
sit and m.   BALL 53:16
time to m.   BIBL 85:32
Mourne Mountains of M.   FREN 333:16
mourned we have m. unto you   BIBL 96:25
Would have m. longer   SHAK 684:4
mourners let the m. come   AUDE 34:28
mournful m. Ever weeping Paddington   BLAK 120:8
mourning Don't waste time in m.   LAST 472:16
great m.   BIBL 94:8
in m. for my life   CHEK 213:24
M. becomes Electra   O'NE 573:12
oil of joy for m.   BIBL 90:19
very deep m.   AUST 40:13
widow bird sat m.   SHEL 729:3
mouse appetit hath he to ete a m.   CHAU 211:19
catch a m. or two   GRAY 361:24
except that damned M.   GEOR 343:11
free-born m.   BARB 55:4
invention of a m.   DISN 275:3
killing of a m. on Sunday   BRAT 149:19
little m. will be born   HORA 398:8
m. Kaught in a trappe   CHAU 210:12
m. may help a lion   PROV 627:2
m. ran up the clock   NURS 567:8
Not a m. Shall disturb   SHAK 712:7
Not a m. stirring   SHAK 683:13
not even a m.   MOOR 546:9
One for the m.   PROV 628:34
second m. that gets the cheese   SAYI 669:32
seen a m. go by the wal   CHAU 211:19
that damned M.   MAYE 519:13
mousetrap make a better m.   EMER 307:18
The M.   SHAK 687:6
mouth cometh out of the m.   BIBL 97:11
door and bar for thy m.   BIBL 93:21
Englishman to open his m.   SHAW 727:11
fills the m. pleasantly   JOIN 434:2
gift horse in the m.   PROV 627:23
God be in my m.   PRAY 611:3
God be in their m.   BOOK 144:8

in my m. sweet as honey   BIBL 113:26
Keep your m. shut   OFFI 572:14
kisses of his m.   BIBL 87:2
like chaff in my m.   KEAT 447:6
m. as greet was   CHAU 210:25
m. became the Brahmin   RIG 648:12
m. filled with laughter   BOOK 142:23
m. had been used as a latrine   AMIS 13:8
m. is most sweet   BIBL 87:16
m. is smoother than oil   BIBL 83:38
m. of Marilyn Monroe   MITT 541:3
m. of the dying day   AUDE 35:2
m. of the Lord   BIBL 89:16
m. of very babes   BOOK 134:4
m. speaketh   BIBL 96:31
my m. shall shew   BOOK 137:15
My m. went across   NERU 559:4
only one m.   ZENO 858:2
opened not his m.   BIBL 90:3
out of his m.   BIBL 112:29
out of the m. of God   BIBL 94:15
Out of thine own m.   BIBL 101:29
purple-stainèd m.   KEAT 444:22
shut m. catches no flies   PROV 630:38
silver foot in his m.   RICH 647:8
slap-dash down in the m.   CONG 239:3
spew thee out of my m.   BIBL 113:5
words of my m.   BOOK 134:23
z is keeping your m. shut   EINS 298:5
mouthful gold filling in a m. of decay   OSBO 578:23
mouths God never sends m.   PROV 620:47
made m. in a glass   SHAK 700:17
m., and speak not   BOOK 142:4
m. of babes   PROV 629:14
poet's m. be shut   YEAT 855:3
pork please our m.   MENG 522:4
stuffed their m. with gold   BEVA 73:19
moutons *Revenons à ces m.*   ANON 21:1
movable device of *M. Types*   CARL 192:23
Paris is a m. feast   HEMI 381:6
move Art has to m. you   HOCK 391:7
But it does m.   GALI 338:11
could m. a foot   SUGE 763:9
feel the earth m.   HEMI 381:5
great affair is to m.   STEV 759:11
in him we live, and m.   BIBL 105:20
m. the earth   ARCH 24:11
never should m.   BOOK 141:5
whichever way you m.   LUCA 495:4
moved earth be m.   BOOK 136:24
I do not like being m.   CLOU 227:14
king was much m.   BIBL 81:5
m. about like the wind   GERO 344:3
m. by what is not unusual   ELIO 300:6
m. to folly by a noise   LAWR 475:18
m. was their own mind   HUI- 408:5
suffer thy foot to be m.   BOOK 142:16
We shall not be m.   POLI 601:15
movement measure of m.   AUCT 34:17
picture equals a m.   CARR 193:15
right of free m.   JOHN 422:5
mover arrive at a prime m.   THOM 789:1
movere *Quieta m.*   SALL 665:3
movers m. and shakers   O'SH 579:1
moves If it m., salute it   MILI 526:10
m. with its own organs   SHAK 679:13
nothing m. in this world   MAIN 508:1
moveth all that m. doth   SPEN 752:9
movies M. should have a beginning   GODA 351:18
one thing that can kill the m.   ROGE 652:16
sexuality in the m.   DENE 264:2
moving m. accident is not my trade   WORD 846:23
m. finger writes   FITZ 323:10
m. from hence to there   SOCR 745:9
m. in opposite directions   SMIT 743:24
m. toyshop of the heart   POPE 606:5
Of m. accidents   SHAK 713:8
mower m. whets his scythe   MILT 529:22
Mozart Children are given M.   SCHN 671:13
when M. was my age   LEHR 479:11

MP Being an M.   PARR 586:23
MPs dull M. in close proximity   GILB 347:14
When in that House M. divide   GILB 347:13
Mrs M. respectably married   CART 196:22
Ms M. means nudge, nudge   CART 196:22
much how m. we think of ourselves   TWAI 803:20
just so m., no more   BROW 161:25
Missing so m. and so much   CORN 243:10
M. as you said you were   HARD 372:18
m. for my true-love   BALL 53:16
m. to hear   SKEL 739:5
M. would have more   PROV 627:4
not m. for them to be   COMP 236:19
Sing 'em m.   MELB 520:14
so m. owed by so many to so few   CHUR 221:10
so m. to do   LAST 473:17
so m. to do   TENN 779:11
too m. in anything   BACO 43:26
too m. of a good thing   PROV 635:26
muchness Much of a m.   VANB 806:12
muck Money is like m.   BACO 45:13
Where there's m.   PROV 634:43
muckle makes a m.   PROV 626:9
muckrake m. in his hand   BUNY 165:1
muckrakes men with the m.   ROOS 654:10
muckraking m. biographers   BENN 67:16
mucus excretion of m.   AURE 38:7
mud back in the m.   AUGI 36:22
builds on m.   MACH 502:11
crawled about in the m.   BECK 61:19
filled up with m.   SHAK 710:31
handful of m. against a wall   BLUN 124:9
M.! Glorious mud   FLAN 324:16
M.'s sister   HOUS 403:20
muddle beginning, a m.   LARK 469:7
Meddle and m.   DERB 265:5
m. through   BRIG 151:10
muddy almost always a m. horsepond   PEAC 590:1
M., ill-seeming   SHAK 718:15
m. understandings   BURK 167:15
muero *Muero porque no m.*   JOHN 422:9
Muffet Little Miss M.   NURS 568:3
muffin M. and Crumpet   DICK 270:13
mug graceful air and heavenly m.   FLEM 326:19
Muhammad M. is not the father   KORA 460:20
mulatto Grape is my m. mother   HUGH 407:10
mule m. of politics   DISR 277:3
Sicilian m. was to me   GLAD 351:7
mules m. of politics   POWE 610:7
mulier *m. formosa superne*   HORA 397:19
mullets We will eat our m.   JONS 434:15
Mulligan plump Buck M.   OPEN 575:20
multinational wealthy m. corporations   LEWI 483:14
multiplication M. is vexation   ANON 17:19
multiplicity m. of agreeable   JOHN 428:24
multiply Be fruitful, and m.   BIBL 75:10
Increase and m.   BOOK 130:12
m. my signs and my wonders   BIBL 77:24
multitude hoofs of a swinish m.   BURK 167:18
m. is in the wrong   DILL 274:12
m. of days   JOHN 426:19
m. of sins   BIBL 112:14
m. of the isles   BOOK 140:12
m., that numerous piece   BROW 157:5
m. the blind instruments   GODW 352:4
m., the *hoi polloi*   DRYD 290:6
m., which no man could number   BIBL 113:16
multitudes I contain m.   WHIT 833:16
m. in the valley of decision   BIBL 92:4
Pestilence-stricken m.   SHEL 730:7
Weeping, weeping m.   ELIO 301:6
mum oafish louts remember M.   BETJ 72:3
They fuck you up, your m. and dad   LARK 469:3
mumble When in doubt, m.   BORE 145:3
mumbled few m. cakes   HUNT 410:5
mummy dyed in m.   SHAK 714:8

munch m. on, crunch on · BROW 160:21
mundane grasp of m. matters · THOM 789:3
  in this m. life · MURA 554:10
mundi peccata m. · MISS 539:9
  Sic transit gloria m. · ANON 22:4
mundus pereat m. · MOTT 552:8
muneribus deorum M. sapiente uti · HORA 402:17
muove amor che m. il sole · DANT 256:13
  Eppur si m. · GALI 338:11
murder about a m. · ORWE 577:4
  battle and m. · BOOK 129:7
  decided to m. his wife · OPEN 574:26
  do no m. · BOOK 131:9
  do not contrived m. · SHAK 713:3
  Don't they m. the people · TROL 799:14
  I met M. on the way · SHEL 730:3
  indulges himself in m. · DE Q 265:2
  I wanted to m. · DOST 283:7
  Killing no m. · PROV 624:39
  Killing no m. · SEXB 677:12
  Live in despite of m. · CHAP 208:11
  love and m. will out · CONG 238:17
  Macbeth does m. sleep · SHAK 704:24
  Most sacrilegious m. · SHAK 705:10
  most unnatural m. · SHAK 685:1
  m. by the law · YOUN 857:6
  m. by the throat · LLOY 487:19
  m. cannot be hid long · SHAK 709:6
  M. considered · DE Q 265:1
  m. into the home · HITC 389:21
  m., like talent · LEWE 483:1
  m. men everywhere · FANO 314:8
  M. most foul · SHAK 685:2
  m. respectable · ORWE 577:4
  M.'s out of tune · SHAK 714:23
  m. the thinker · WESK 828:20
  m., though it have no tongue · SHAK 686:7
  m. to dissect · WORD 850:13
  m. whiles I smile · SHAK 694:28
  M. will out · PROV 627:5
  M. wol out · CHAU 212:1
  m. yet is but fantastical · SHAK 703:15
  One m. made a villain · PORT 607:20
  Sooner m. an infant · BLAK 121:9
  stick to m. and leave art · EPST 308:9
  story is about not m. · JAME 418:17
  to m., for the truth · ADLE 5:19
  Vanity, like m., will out · COWL 246:2
  We hear war called m. · MACD 501:10
  withered m. · SHAK 704:17
murdered Each one a m. self · ROSS 656:3
  m. peer · ALCO 10:8
  m. reputations · CONG 239:7
  Our royal master's m. · SHAK 705:12
  their m. man · KEAT 443:18
murderer help the escaping m. · STEV 759:6
  honourable m. · SHAK 714:29
  m. for fancy prose style · NABO 555:15
  m. from the beginning · BIBL 103:12
  tender m. · BROW 158:16
murderers m., and idolaters · BIBL 114:24
  m. of Jewish children · WIES 834:15
  m. take the first step · KARR 441:16
murderous m. hand a drowsy bench · CRAB 249:21
murders most hideous of m. · GISS 350:5
  m. and assaults · KOHL 459:3
murmur creeping m. · SHAK 693:7
  m. at his case · COWP 246:16
  m. of a summer's day · ARNO 28:3
murmured m. in their tents · BOOK 141:14
murmuring mazily m. · TENN 782:11
  m. of innumerable bees · TENN 783:17
murmurs hollow m. died away · COLL 235:15
  In the m. · SOND 746:4
  m. of self-will · BODE 125:4
Murphy M.'s Law · PROV 622:43
Murray slain the Earl of M. · BALL 51:16
mus nascetur ridiculus m. · HORA 398:8
muscle take the m. from bone · ELIO 302:25

muscles M. better and nerves more · CUMM 253:14
muscular His Christianity was m. · DISR 277:9
muse every conqueror creates a M. · WALL 818:11
  grace my barren m. · LANI 467:2
  like a tenth m. · ANON 16:9
  Livelier liquor than the M. · HOUS 405:2
  M. but served to ease · POPE 602:26
  M. forbids to die · HORA 402:15
  m. in silence sings · CLAR 224:8
  M. invoked · SWIF 767:7
  M. of fire · OPEN 575:7
  m. on dromedary trots · COLE 232:10
  O! for a M. of fire · SHAK 692:26
  tenth American m. · BRON 152:8
  tenth M. · TROL 800:12
  Tragic M. first trod the stage · POPE 606:2
  Why does my M. only speak · SMIT 742:21
mused m. a little space · TENN 780:13
muses charm of all the M. · TENN 784:10
  house that serves the M. · SAPP 666:16
  M.' garden with pedantic weeds · CARE 190:12
  M. made write verse · VIRG 814:9
  M. sing of happy swains · CRAB 249:16
museum ace caff with a nice m. · ADVE 7:2
  m. inside our heads · LIVE 487:5
mushroom I am . . . a m. · FORD 328:16
  Life too short to stuff a m. · CONR 241:4
  m. of a night's growth · DONN 282:7
  m. rich civilian · BYRO 183:20
  supramundane m. · LAUR 470:9
music accord all m. makes · SIDN 736:13
  aerial m.'s past · SHEN 732:22
  alive with the sound of m. · HAMM 370:8
  all kinds of m. · BIBL 91:19
  all m. is folk music · ARMS 26:15
  Beauty in m. · IVES 414:13
  beauty's Silent m. · CAMP 188:5
  body swayed to m. · YEAT 853:6
  built to m. · TENN 777:19
  but the m. there · POPE 604:7
  chosen m., liberty · WORD 850:14
  'classic' m. eliminates · STRA 762:8
  Classic m. is th'kind · HUBB 406:13
  come with your cold m. · BROW 161:21
  compulsion doth in m. lie · MILT 528:14
  condition of m. · PATE 588:10
  danceth without m. · HERB 385:7
  dance to the m. of time · POWE 609:14
  Darling of the m. halls · SMIT 742:4
  day the m. died · MCLE 503:6
  die in m. · SHAK 714:25
  essence of m. · MOZA 553:1
  Fading in m. · SHAK 709:16
  finds its food in m. · LILL 484:14
  Fled is that m. · KEAT 445:3
  From their own m. · CAMP 188:6
  frozen m. · SCHE 668:12
  Give me some m. · SHAK 679:10
  good m. · CECI 204:13
  honey-sweet m. from our lips · HOME 394:17
  how potent cheap m. is · COWA 245:11
  How sour sweet m. is · SHAK 716:15
  In sweet m. · SHAK 695:9
  I shall be made thy m. · DONN 280:1
  Is there a meaning to m. · COPL 242:17
  Let's face the m. and dance · BERL 69:19
  let the sounds of m. · SHAK 710:2
  Like softest m. · SHAK 717:28
  make the m. mute · TENN 778:5
  man that hath no m. · SHAK 710:5
  May make one m. · TENN 778:21
  most civilized m. · USTI 806:2
  M. alone with sudden charms · CONG 239:20
  M. and women · PEPY 592:13
  m. at the close · SHAK 715:12
  M. begins to atrophy · POUN 609:8
  m. be the food · OPEN 574:15
  m. be the food of love · SHAK 720:3
  M. breathing from her face · BYRO 178:3
  m. business is not · MORR 550:13

  m. by yonder springs · THEO 787:21
  m. could capture him so completely · KAFK 440:19
  M. has charms · CONG 238:29
  m. in the air · ELGA 299:3
  M. is essentially useless · SANT 666:10
  M. is feeling, then · STEV 758:3
  M. is not written in · MELB 520:13
  M. is your own experience · PARK 585:13
  m. of a distant drum · FITZ 323:3
  m. of a poem · SYNG 769:12
  m. of forfended spheres · PATM 588:17
  m. of men's lives · SHAK 716:15
  M. oft hath such a charm · SHAK 708:14
  m. of the Gospel · FABE 313:15
  m. of the spheres · BROW 157:7
  m. sent up to God · BROW 158:7
  M. shall untune the sky · DRYD 289:20
  m. that excels · FISH 322:17
  M. that gentlier on the spirit · TENN 781:6
  m. that I care to hear · HOPK 396:14
  m. the brandy of the damned · SHAW 726:6
  M., the greatest good · ADDI 4:22
  M., when soft voices die · SHEL 731:23
  My m. is best understood · STRA 762:9
  Of m. Dr Johnson used to say · JOHN 433:18
  passion cannot M. raise · DRYD 289:18
  perfected by m. · CONF 237:22
  practising your pastoral m. · VIRG 813:12
  seduction of martial m. · BURN 169:26
  silence sank Like m. · COLE 233:8
  sound of soft m. · DISR 277:34
  still, sad m. · WORD 847:10
  Susanna's m. · STEV 758:5
  thou hast thy m. too · KEAT 445:16
  uproar's your only m. · KEAT 446:5
  We are the m. makers · O'SH 579:1
  What then is m. · HEIN 380:3
  when I hear sweet m. · SHAK 710:4
  worth expressing in m. · DELI 263:10
musical found out m. tunes · BIBL 93:32
  Most m., most melancholy · MILT 529:11
  m. as is Apollo's lute · MILT 529:2
  Silence more m. · ROSS 655:14
  So m. a discord · SHAK 711:24
musician far below the m. · LEON 481:8
  m., if he's a messenger · HEND 381:11
  No better a m. · SHAK 710:7
musing M. full sadly · SPEN 751:20
  peace, and lonely m. · COLL 235:15
musk coming m.-rose · KEAT 444:26
  sweet m.-roses · SHAK 711:4
musket Sam, pick up tha' m. · HOLL 392:20
  shouldered a m. · LAUR 470:10
Muslim go into the M. mosque · JALA 416:23
  neither Hindu nor M. · SIKH 737:14
Muslims named you M. · KORA 460:8
  zealous M. to execute · KHOM 451:2
Muss M. es sein · BEET 63:10
mussels gaping m., left · CRAB 248:31
must forget because we m. · ARNO 27:1
  It m. be · BEET 63:10
  Must! Is m. a word · ELIZ 304:13
  Needs m. · PROV 627:15
  This year, the m. shall foam · MACA 499:12
  We m. know · EPIT 311:13
  What m. be, must be · PROV 634:8
  whispers low, Thou m. · EMER 306:16
  you m. go on · BECK 61:12
mustard faith as a grain of m. seed · BIBL 97:18
  grain of m. seed · BIBL 97:5
  Pass the m. · GILB 349:9
mutabile Varium et m. semper Femina · VIRG 812:5
mutability death, and m. · SHEL 731:8
  M. in them doth play · SPEN 752:8
  Nought may endure but M. · SHEL 730:5
mutant Caelum non animum m. · HORA 399:10
mutantur sputio m. · LUCR 495:15
mutato M. nomine de te · HORA 403:4
mutatus Quantum mutatus ab illo · VIRG 811:16
mute M. and magnificent · DRYD 289:23

m. recommendation PUBL 636:13
mutilate fold, spindle or m. SAYI 669:14
spindle or m. ANON 15:17
mutilated from m. egos PAGL 581:17
mutiny fear and m. SHAK 716:6
rise and m. SHAK 698:6
mutter blessed m. of the mass BROW 158:21
mutton make them into m.-pies CARR 195:27
object to eating a m. chop LIST 486:15
mutual meet a m. heart THOM 792:16
M. cowardice JOHN 431:9
my m.-lorded him THAC 786:13
Orthodoxy or M.-doxy CARL 192:7
sitting in m. chair SOUT 749:15
myriad Our m.-minded Shakespeare
COLE 233:23
There died a m. POUN 609:1
myrrh bundle of m. BIBL 87:4
frankincense, and m. BIBL 94:6
myrtle m. and turkey AUST 39:3
m. tree BIBL 90:9
myrtles Ye m. brown MILT 529:29
Ye m. brown OPEN 576:4
myself I celebrate m. WHIT 833:9
I do not know m. GOET 353:19
If I am not for m. HILL 389:4
love him as m. BOOK 132:15
Madame Bovary is m. FLAU 325:17
my mother I see in m. FRID 334:8
M. alone I seek to please GAY 342:2
such a thing as I m. SHAK 696:5
talking to m. BARN 56:13
thinking for m. GILB 348:23
When I give I give m. WHIT 833:14
mysteries most holy m. DION 274:22
m. in divinity BROW 156:23
m. of Hecate SHAK 699:18
m. of our religion HOBB 390:22
m. that are hidden HEIK 379:10
Stewards of the m. BIBL 107:7
mysterious moves in a m. way COWP 246:23
nothing m. or supernatural HUME 408:10
mystery burthen of the m. WORD 847:8
grasped the m. of the atom BRAD 148:22
heart of my m. SHAK 687:10
I shew you a m. BIBL 108:11
lose myself in a m. BROW 156:24
M., BABYLON THE GREAT BIBL 114:9
m. of the cross FORT 330:4
my tongue, the m. telling THOM 788:15
penetralium of m. KEAT 446:4
riddle wrapped in a m. CHUR 221:4
Your mystery, your m. SHAK 714:13
mystic m., wonderful TENN 777:15
mystical m. body of thy Son BOOK 132:4
m. mathematics BROW 156:4
m. way of Pythagoras BROW 156:26
mystify m., mislead, amd surprise JACK 415:8
myth m. not a fairy story RYLE 662:2
print the m. JOHN 423:3
purpose of m. LÉVI 482:18
thing itself and not the m. RICH 647:4
mythologies Out of old m. YEAT 853:13
myths Science must begin with m.
POPP 607:5
where m. Go when they die FENT 316:13

nabobs nattering n. AGNE 8:30
Naboth Ahab spake unto N. BIBL 81:30
nag gait of a shuffling n. SHAK 690:24
nagging N. is the repetition SUMM 764:1
nail blows his n. SHAK 702:26
I n. my pictures together SCHW 672:11
looks like a n. SAYI 670:21
n. currant jelly ROOS 654:9
n. into his temples BIBL 79:16
One n. drives out PROV 628:46
thrusting The final n. BLOK 123:13
want of a n. PROV 620:24
nailing n. his colours FIEL 317:11
nails blowing of his n. SHAK 694:26
My n. are drove EPIT 310:17

n. bitten and pared MACA 498:1
nineteen hundred and forty n. SITW 738:16
print of the n. BIBL 104:14
three cloves like n. HEAT 378:13
with his n. he'll dig WEBS 826:10
naive n. domestic Burgundy CART 198:2
n. forgive and forget SZAS 769:16
naked Half n., loving BYRO 180:24
left me n. to mine enemies SHAK 695:16
Love is a child and n. OVID 579:17
more enterprise In walking n. YEAT 853:13
my n. villainy SHAK 716:27
N., and ye clothed me BIBL 98:25
n. ape MORR 549:9
n. into the conference chamber BEVA 73:15
n. is the best disguise CONG 238:18
n. shingles of the world ARNO 27:3
n. to the hangman's noose HOUS 404:9
stark n. truth CLEL 226:9
starving hysterical n. GINS 349:15
When a' was n. SHAK 692:11
With n. foot WYAT 852:4
nakedness n. of the land BIBL 77:7
n. of the woman BLAK 121:5
not in utter n. WORD 848:5
only wealth is n. FUEN 336:21
namby-pamby N.'s little rhymes CARE 191:7
name above every n. BIBL 109:25
at the n. of Jesus BIBL 109:25
At the n. of Jesus NOEL 565:6
blot out his n. BIBL 113:3
Change the n. HORA 403:4
change the n. PROV 616:32
dare not speak its n. DOUG 283:13
deed without a n. SHAK 706:15
distain his n. BURN 171:22
fear my n. BIBL 92:14
filches from me my good n. SHAK 713:26
forgotten your n. SWIN 768:24
former n. Is heard no more MILT 533:19
gathered together in my n. BIBL 97:22
ghost of a great n. LUCA 495:1
gift of the divine N. SIKH 737:12
Give a dog a bad n. PROV 620:36
give them an everlasting n. BIBL 90:10
glory as an unsullied n. ELEA 298:19
glory in the n. of Briton GEOR 343:4
good n. BIBL 84:39
Grant that your n. remain SIKH 737:2
Halloo your n. SHAK 720:13
Hallowed be thy n. BIBL 95:3
his N. is great BOOK 139:5
his N. only is excellent BOOK 144:7
honour due unto his N. BOOK 140:11
I am become a n. TENN 784:14
I do not like her n. SHAK 681:22
ill n. is half hanged PROV 621:49
in a borrowed n. PRIO 612:5
In the n. of God, go AMER 13:5
In the n. of God, go CROM 252:2
In the N. of the Father MISS 536:11
In the N. of thy Lord KORA 461:13
its n. changed DANT 256:8
kept them in thy n. BIBL 103:39
king's n. SHAK 717:5
left a Corsair's n. BYRO 179:28
left a n. behind them BIBL 93:33
left the n. JOHN 426:18
Let me not n. it SHAK 714:19
liberties are taken in thy n. GEOR 344:2
local habitation and a n. SHAK 711:28
mark, or the n. of the beast BIBL 113:30
My Mary's n. to give CLAR 224:8
my n. and memory LAST 471:14
my n. is Jowett BEEC 62:16
My n. is Legion BIBL 99:20
My n. is Ozymandias SHEL 730:18
My n. is Used-to-was TRAI 798:3
My n. too will be linked OVID 580:3
my n. with a sign PARI 585:12
my new n. BIBL 113:4
my wife, and my n. SURT 764:16
n. Achilles assumed BROW 156:12

n. great in story BYRO 183:10
n. had been Edmund KEAT 447:4
n. is history THWA 794:6
n. is never heard BAYL 59:9
n. like yours CARR 195:13
n. liveth for ever SASS 667:23
n. liveth for evermore BIBL 93:34
n. liveth for evermore EPIT 311:8
n. made great HILL 389:3
n. of God in vain BIBL 78:2
N. of God is sweet SIKH 737:4
N. of God, the Merciful KORA 459:6
n. of—Michael Angelo REYN 646:9
n. of the Lord BOOK 132:20
N. of the Lord BOOK 142:11
n. of the Lord BOOK 142:21
N. of the Lord our God BOOK 134:24
n. shall be called BIBL 88:18
n. the names AKHM 9:9
n. to all succeeding ages curst DRYD 286:19
n. upon the strand SPEN 751:4
n. we give the people FLER 326:20
n. were not so terrible SHAK 691:28
no profit but the n. SHAK 688:1
nothing of a n. BYRO 179:21
one whose n. was writ EPIT 310:4
only differ in the n. CHUD 219:9
People you know, yet can't quite n.
LARK 469:1
perfect N. of God SIKH 737:5
power of Jesus' N. PERR 593:3
prefer a self-made n. HAND 370:14
problem that has no n. FRIE 334:10
problem that has no n. FRIE 334:12
provides us with n. and nation BUNT 164:9
spared the n. SWIF 767:17
spell my n. right COHA 230:9
Stamps God's own n. COWP 247:2
state with the prettiest n. BISH 117:4
thy n., thy nature know WESL 829:3
unto thy N. give the praise BOOK 142:3
What's in a n. SHAK 717:22
what was done in his n. BENN 67:2
whispering its n. COCT 230:6
Who gave you this N. BOOK 132:12
worshipped with spoken n. ZORO 859:11
worth an age without a n. MORD 547:23
writing our n. there HEAN 377:15
named N. is the mother LAO 467:4
n. you Muslims KORA 460:18
nameless intolerably n. names SASS 667:23
N. here for evermore POE 599:6
n. in worthy deeds BROW 156:15
N. is the origin LAO 467:4
n., unremembered, acts WORD 847:7
names All n. are shaken HORA 401:10
Called him soft n. KEAT 444:27
called them by wrong n. BROW 158:18
calleth them all by their n. BOOK 144:3
confused things with their n. SART 667:6
forget men's n. SHAK 699:1
in love with American n. BENÉ 66:11
lost all the n. JOHN 431:27
n. ignoble, born to be forgot COWP 247:4
N. Most Beautiful KORA 461:11
n. of all these particles FERM 317:2
n. of men TROL 800:6
n. of those who love HUNT 409:14
N. that should be CALV 186:7
n. to be mentioned AUST 40:4
No n., no pack-drill PROV 627:44
Not unholy n. DICK 270:1
naming N. of Cats ELIO 302:26
n. of parts REED 644:3
nap short n. at sermon ADDI 4:26
napalm smell of n. in the morning
FILM 319:18
nape n. caught in his bill YEAT 854:20
Napoleon N. of crime DOYL 284:18
N.'s armies SELL 676:24
thinks he is N. CLEM 226:13
Napoleons Caesars and N. HUXL 411:7

neighbours (cont.):
relying upon his n. — BAUD 59:2
sport for our n. — AUST 40:5
will the n. say — HARD 372:9
Nell Little N. and Lady Macbeth — WOOL 845:15
Pretty witty N. — PEPY 592:8
Nellie N. Dean — ARMS 26:10
Nelly Let not poor N. starve — LAST 472:18
Nelson N. touch — NELS 558:17
Nemo N. me impune lacessit — MOTT 552:11
neoclassical n. endogenous growth — BROW 155:1
Neptune stands As N.'s park — SHAK 683:2
Nereides gentlewomen, like the N. — SHAK 679:4
nerve after the n. has been extracted — ROWL 657:11
called a n. specialist — WODE 842:24
creep through every n. — BROW 161:21
do not lose my n. — NEHR 558:5
n. o'er which do creep — SHEL 729:17
nerves and the n. prick — TENN 779:4
his vitals and his n. — HUNT 410:2
Muscles better and n. more — CUMM 253:14
n. Shall never tremble — SHAK 706:6
nervous approaching n. breakdown — RUSS 660:16
n. force into phrases — CONR 241:3
they call it n. — KEAT 447:9
nervously sat n. before — RILK 648:13
nervousness only n. or death — LEBO 478:6
nest birds in last year's n. — PROV 631:48
fouls its own n. — PROV 624:17
he makes his n. — LODG 489:8
her soft and chilly n. — KEAT 442:22
I have no n.-eggs — LLOY 487:14
leaves his wat'ry n. — D'AV 257:23
my n. is made — TENN 783:7
n. of singing birds — JOHN 427:7
n. where she may lay — BOOK 139:15
theek our n. — BALL 53:15
nests birds build n. — VIRG 815:7
Birds in their little n. — PROV 615:42
Birds in their little n. agree — WATT 823:11
birds of the air have n. — BIBL 96:1
built their n. in my beard — LEAR 477:3
Made n. inside — BROW 160:20
net All fish that comes to n. — PROV 614:11
Heaven's n. is indeed vast — LAO 468:6
I will let down the n. — BIBL 100:12
laid a n. for my feet — BOOK 137:22
n. is spread — BIBL 83:32
n. is spread in the sight — PROV 623:35
n. of Maya — UPAN 805:11
play tennis with the n. down — FROS 336:9
too old to rush up to the n. — ADAM 2:5
nets holdeth fast the n. — OXFO 581:11
into their own n. — BOOK 143:21
Laws are generally found to be n. — SHEN 732:24
n. to catch the living — WEBS 825:19
time in making n. — SWIF 766:23
try to fly by those n. — JOYC 437:9
nettle gently touch a n. — PROV 623:18
Out of this n., danger — SHAK 690:3
Tender-handed stroke a n. — HILL 388:6
nettles dust on the n. — THOM 790:17
n. and brambles — BIBL 89:8
overrun with n. — WALP 819:14
network N. Anything reticulated — JOHN 424:11
neuroses Everyone has n. — ATWO 33:10
neurosis n. is a secret — TYNA 804:5
N. is a way of avoiding — TILL 794:15
neurotics come to us from n. — PROU 613:8
neuter aggressively n. — BETJ 72:14
neutral studiously n. — WILS 840:19
neutrality Armed n. is ineffectual — WILS 840:21
Just for a word 'n.' — BETH 72:1
N. helps the oppressor — WIES 834:14
n. of an impartial judge — BURK 169:8

neutralize White shall not n. — BROW 161:11
neutrinos N., they are very small — UPDI 805:22
never Better late than n. — PROV 615:25
come no more, N., never — SHAK 702:7
N. do to-day — PUNC 637:7
N. explain — FISH 322:15
N. explain — HUBB 406:10
n. go to sea — GILB 348:24
n. had it so good — MACM 504:4
n. home came she — KING 452:20
N. in the field of human conflict — CHUR 221:10
N. is a long time — PROV 627:21
N. knowingly undersold — ADVE 8:6
N. on Sunday — FILM 322:9
n. should move — BOOK 141:5
n. so impatient — BOOK 140:16
N. the time — BROW 160:11
n. thought of thinking — GILB 348:23
n. to have been loved — CONG 239:10
N. to have lived is best — YEAT 854:9
n. use a big, big D — GILB 348:20
She who has n. loved — GAY 341:21
This will n. do — JEFF 420:19
We n. closed — VAN 806:18
What, n. — GILB 348:19
You n. can tell — SHAW 727:22
nevermore Quoth the Raven, 'N.' — POE 599:8
new All appeared n. — TRAH 797:12
always old and always n. — BROW 161:7
beginning of a n. month — MANN 510:9
blessing of the N. — BACO 43:13
Brave n. world — BORR 146:2
brings something n. — PLIN 598:4
called the N. World — CANN 189:10
Emperor's n. clothes — ANDE 14:1
Few n. truths have ever won — BERL 70:5
find something n. — VOLT 815:9
hear some n. thing — BIBL 105:17
just a n. activity — DYSO 294:19
make all things n. — BIBL 114:17
make a n. acquaintance — JOHN 433:1
make n. acquaintance — JOHN 427:22
making n. enemies — VOLT 816:21
my n. found land — DONN 279:13
my n. name — BIBL 113:4
n. and untried — LINC 484:17
n.-bathed stars Emerge — ARNO 28:18
N. brooms sweep clean — PROV 627:32
n. deal for the American people — ROOS 653:11
N. every morning — KEBL 447:12
n. friend is as new wine — BIBL 93:10
n. heaven and a new earth — BIBL 114:16
n. heaven, new earth — SHAK 678:13
new heavens and a n. earth — BIBL 90:22
New Labour, n. danger — POLI 601:3
N. lords, new laws — PROV 627:33
n. man may be raised up — BOOK 132:10
N. men, strange faces — TENN 778:15
N. opinions are always suspected — LOCK 488:5
n. race is sent down — VIRG 814:2
n. wine in old bottles — PROV 635:43
n. wine into old bottles — BIBL 96:8
n. world order — BUSH 175:1
no n. thing under the sun — BIBL 85:28
nothing n. in dying — LAST 472:12
nothing n. under the sun — PROV 632:21
O brave n. world — SHAK 719:7
old lamps for n. — ARAB 23:16
on the nothing n. — BECK 61:9
put on the n. man — BIBL 110:12
require n. clothes — THOR 793:6
shock of the n. — DUNL 292:6
somehow always n. — HEIN 379:16
something n. out of Africa — PROV 632:6
songs for ever n. — KEAT 440:10
so quite n. a thing — CUMM 253:14
Tell not as n. — COWP 246:7
threshold of a n. house — ATWO 33:8
unto the Lord a n. song — BOOK 135:22

unto the Lord a n. song — BOOK 140:13
we'll find the n. — BAUD 58:16
What is n. cannot be true — PROV 634:6
wrote MAKE IT N. — POUN 608:14
Youth is something very n. — CHAN 208:2
newborn use of a n. child — FRAN 332:21
new-born n. bloom and thrive — HORA 398:2
Newcastle made of N. coal — WALP 819:4
newcomer O blithe n. — WORD 850:15
New England most serious charge against N. — KRUT 462:2
N. weather — TWAI 803:27
newest n. kind of ways — SHAK 692:18
n. works — BULW 164:6
newness walk in n. of life — BIBL 106:11
news bad n. infects — SHAK 678:17
Bad n. travels fast — PROV 614:46
bringer of unwelcome n. — SHAK 691:22
get the n. to you — TWAI 803:12
good day to bury bad n. — MISQ 537:16
good n. from a far country — BIBL 85:7
good n. from Ghent to Aix — BROW 159:22
good n. yet to hear — CHES 216:11
hear n. of home — PROV 620:42
HERE IS THE N. — HEAN 378:5
how much n. there is — DOUG 284:1
Ill n. hath wings — DRAY 285:20
it is an item of n. — TALL 771:15
love of n. — CRAB 249:8
n. and Prince of Peace — FLET 327:13
n. that's fit to print — ADVE 7:4
news that STAYS n. — POUN 609:9
n., the manna of a day — GREE 362:6
No n. is good news — PROV 627:45
only n. until he's read it — WAUG 824:14
that is n. — BOGA 125:8
What n. on the Rialto — SHAK 708:29
New South Wales govern N. — BELL 65:1
revive in N. — BANK 54:18
newspaper never to look into a n. — SHER 733:5
n. and journalistic activity — TOLS 797:1
N. editors — TROL 800:6
n. is a nation talking — MILL 527:9
seen in a n. — JEFF 420:8
newspapers n. I can't stand — STOP 761:10
read the n. — BEVA 73:18
writing for the n. — LEWI 484:1
Newspeak whole aim of N. — ORWE 577:16
newt Eye of n. — SHAK 706:12
Newton another N., a new Donne — HUXL 411:10
Let N. be — POPE 603:27
N. at Peru — WALP 819:9
N. in his garden — AUDE 35:17
N.'s sleep — BLAK 120:17
newts N., and blind-worms — SHAK 711:6
New York California to the N. Island — GUTH 366:5
gullet of N. — MILL 527:8
N.: building itself up — FUEN 336:20
N. is a catastrophe — LE C 478:11
New York, N. — COMD 236:13
present in N. — CHAP 208:21
three o'clock in N. — MIDL 524:13
New Zealanders When N. emigrate — MULD 553:18
next At forty-five, what n. — LOWE 494:12
n. to god america — CUMM 253:6
n. to Nature — LAND 466:2
used to be the n. president — GORE 357:1
nexus n. of man to man — CARL 191:12
Niagara wouldn't live under N. — CARL 193:3
Nicaragua dictator of N. — CARD 190:8
nice all that's n. — NURS 570:14
all the n. people — OPEN 575:1
Naughty but n. — FILM 322:8
N. but nubbly — KIPL 456:20
N. guys finish last — DURO 293:6
N. one, Cyril — ADVE 8:7
n. to people on your way up — MIZN 541:4
N. to see you — CATC 201:19
N. work if you can get it — GERS 344:8

NICELY · NOBLE 1031

thoroughly n. people PYM 638:12
Too n. for a statesman GOLD 355:5
nicely That'll do n. ADVE 7:5
nicens n. little boy OPEN 575:10
nicest nastiest thing in the n. way GOLD 354:4
niche your n. in creation HALL 369:14
Nicholas St N. soon would be there MOOR 546:9
nick improve the n. of time THOR 793:5
Satan, N., or Clootie BURN 170:3
nickname n. is the heaviest stone HAZL 376:18
Nicodemus N. saw such light VAUG 807:8
nidificatis *non vobis n. aves* VIRG 815:7
Nigeria daughter of N. EMEC 306:8
nigger n. of the world ONO 573:15
night acquainted with the n. FROS 335:6
after noon, is n. DONN 281:3
All n. long in the dark STEV 760:8
and Love the n. DRYD 289:14
armies clash by n. ARNO 27:5
bird of n. SHAK 696:18
black bat, n., has flown TENN 781:23
blue of the n. CROS 252:9
born to endless n. BLAK 119:15
borrower of the n. SHAK 705:17
breath Of the n.-wind ARNO 27:3
by n. in a pillar of fire BIBL 77:34
candles of the n. SHAK 710:8
carried His servant by n. KORA 460:14
Chaos and old N. MILT 531:23
cheek of n. SHAK 717:17
choose An everlasting n. DONN 279:27
city of dreadful n. THOM 792:19
Come, civil n. SHAK 717:36
come, dear n. CHAP 208:13
Come, thick n. SHAK 703:21
covered by the long n. HORA 402:16
curtain of the n. PUSH 638:7
dangers of this n. BOOK 128:20
dark and stormy n. OPEN 574:25
dark n. of the soul FITZ 324:7
dark n. of the soul MISQ 537:13
Dear N.! this world's defeat VAUG 807:10
dog in the n.-time DOYL 284:19
dusky n. rides down the sky FIEL 317:15
endure for a n. BOOK 135:18
Every n. and alle BALL 52:11
Farewell n. BUNY 165:8
fearful of the n. WILL 838:14
fit n. out for man or beast FIEL 318:20
forests of the n. BLAK 122:19
gentle into that good n. THOM 789:7
go bump in the n. PRAY 611:2
goes of a n. SHER 733:28
Greek models by n. HORA 398:12
hard day's n. LENN 480:19
Harry in the n. SHAK 693:9
Hecate and the n. SHAK 699:18
honeyed middle of the n. KEAT 442:18
horror of a deep n. RACI 640:3
horses of the n. OVID 579:18
in endless n. GRAY 361:19
infant crying in the n. TENN 779:7
in the n.-season also BOOK 134:26
I pass, like n. COLE 233:9
it was n. CHAU 211:9
journey into n. O'NE 573:10
know his God by n. VAUG 807:8
last out a n. in Russia SHAK 707:24
late into the n. BYRO 183:8
lovers' tongues by n. SHAK 717:28
machinery of the n. GINS 349:15
making n. do penance WORD 849:12
Making n. hideous SHAK 684:26
many a bad n. NIET 564:10
meaner beauties of the n. WOTT 851:4
mirk, mirk n. BALL 53:12
moon by n. BOOK 142:16
moon walks the n. DE L 263:7
Morning in the bowl of n. FITZ 322:24
n. admits no ray DRYD 288:31
N. and day BALL 52:6
n. and day, brother BORR 145:10
N. and day, you PORT 607:17
n. before Christmas MOOR 546:9
N. brings counsel PROV 627:34
N. came down VIRG 813:3
n. cometh BIBL 103:13
n. Darkens the streets MILT 531:21
n. has a thousand eyes BOUR 147:10
n. has been unruly SHAK 705:9
N. hath a thousand eyes LYLY 497:4
n. is far spent BIBL 106:32
N. Mail crossing the Border AUDE 35:15
N. makes no difference HERR 386:5
n. Of cloudless climes BYRO 183:4
n. of doubt BARI 56:5
n. of the long knives HITL 389:24
n. of time BROW 156:17
n. once more BECK 61:23
n.'s black agents SHAK 706:1
N.'s candles SHAK 718:2
n.'s starred face KEAT 445:24
n. stands like a black column BABE 42:6
n. starvation ADVE 7:31
n. succeeds thy little day EPIT 310:14
n.'s yawning peal SHAK 705:22
n. that he was betrayed BOOK 132:2
N., the shadow of light SWIN 768:4
n. to do with sleep MILT 528:21
n. will more than pay ARNO 27:9
one everlasting n. CATU 202:13
only for a n. WYCH 852:9
Out of the n. HENL 381:14
pass in the n. LONG 491:7
perfect day nor n. SHAK 694:26
perpetual n. JONS 435:18
Queen of silent n. BEST 71:21
returned on the previous n. BULL 163:16
revelry by n. BYRO 178:19
riding that n. LONG 491:6
rule the n. BIBL 75:7
Sable-vested N. MILT 532:14
shades of n. were falling LONG 490:9
sleep one ever-during n. CAMP 187:23
something of the n. WIDD 834:12
son of the sable N. DANI 255:7
Spirit of N. SHEL 732:3
Stay our all n. CHUR 220:1
such a n. as this SHAK 709:35
tender is the n. KEAT 444:25
terror by n. BOOK 140:3
that it may be n. BOOK 141:9
there shall be no n. BIBL 114:20
This ae n. BALL 52:11
This is the n. SHAK 714:18
Through the dim n. SHEL 731:9
tire the n. in thought QUAR 638:20
toiled all the n. BIBL 100:12
toiling upward in the n. LONG 490:13
under the lonely n. VIRG 812:11
vile contagion of the n. SHAK 696:27
visited all n. COLE 232:1
watch in the n. BOOK 139:22
Watchman, what of the n. BIBL 88:25
weary N.'s decline BLAK 120:5
witching time of n. SHAK 687:13
womb of uncreated n. MILT 532:1
world's last n. DONN 279:24
nighted cast thy n. colour off SHAK 683:25
nightgown in his n. NURS 570:13
nightingale ah, the N. ARNO 27:20
As a n. he sang VIRG 815:6
brown bright n. SWIN 767:25
describing a n. ANON 22:5
newe abaysed n. CHAU 213:7
n., and not the lark SHAK 718:1
n., if she should sing SHAK 710:7
n. in the sycamore STEV 760:19
n. when May is past CARE 191:2
ravished n. LYLY 497:3
roar you as 'twere any n. SHAK 710:24
nightingales n. are singing near ELIO 303:6
nightmare as it is in a n. VIRG 813:11
History is a n. JOYC 437:17
In the n. of the dark AUDE 35:6
long national n. is over FORD 328:11
nightmares Don't have n. CATC 200:13
nights chequerboard of n. and days FITZ 323:8
n. and feasts divine HORA 403:15
O ye N., and Days BOOK 128:6
nihil *Aut Caesar, aut n.* MOTT 552:2
N. est sine ratione LEIB 479:15
nil *N. actum credens* LUCA 495:2
N. admirari HORA 399:8
N. carborundum SAYI 670:6
N. desperandum HORA 400:9
N. posse creari LUCR 495:12
Nile my serpent of old N. SHAK 678:25
on the banks of the N. SHER 733:20
waters of the N. CARR 193:19
nimble Jack be n. NURS 567:16
nimini-pimini pronouncing to yourself n. BURG 166:1
Nimrod N. the mighty hunter BIBL 76:13
nine By the n. gods MACA 499:11
N. bean rows YEAT 854:17
N. days old NURS 569:2
n. men's morris SHAK 710:31
n. points of the law PROV 629:28
N. tailors make a man PROV 627:35
there be n. worthy CAXT 204:8
nineteenth n. century LAUR 470:11
ninety fears to speak of N.-Eight INGR 413:18
Leave the n. and nine BIBL 101:11
nurse of n. years TENN 783:10
Nineveh N. and Tyre KIPL 455:11
Quinquireme of N. MASE 517:12
Niobe Like N., all tears SHAK 684:4
nip n. him in the bud ROCH 651:3
nipping n. and an eager air SHAK 684:23
nipple plucked my n. SHAK 704:12
nirvana called N. because PALI 583:17
lead all beings to n. MAHĀ 506:11
leads to N. PALI 584:4
nisi *N. Dominus* BIBL 115:5
N. Dominus frustra MOTT 552:12
nives *Diffugere n.* HORA 402:11
nix Sticks n. hick pix NEWS 562:18
no everlasting N. CARL 192:28
I am also called N.-more ROSS 656:5
It's n. go the merrygoround MACN 504:15
Just say n. SLOG 740:7
land of the omnipotent N. BOLD 126:4
man who says n. CAMU 188:16
N. money RACI 640:8
n. more to say SHAK 720:2
N.! No! No THAT 787:15
N. sun—no moon HOOD 395:6
n. you always meant RUME 658:7
of Aye and N. NEWM 560:13
she said 'n.' ALLE 12:12
There is n. God BOOK 134:10
Noah gave N. the rainbow SONG 747:6
into N.'s ark COWP 247:18
N. he often said to his wife CHES 216:18
one poor N. HUXL 411:10
nobile *Par n. fratrum* HORA 403:13
nobility ancient n. BACO 45:2
flower of English n. ORDE 576:10
in others n. PAIN 582:17
N. has obligations LÉVI 482:15
N. is a graceful ornament BURK 167:23
N. of birth BACO 45:3
noble, save N. BYRO 178:7
one and only n. JUVE 440:3
order of n. BAGE 48:4
our old n. MANN 511:2
nobis *Non n., Domine* BIBL 115:3
noble Be n. to myself SHAK 680:6
days of the N. Savage BIKO 116:11
Do n. things KING 452:14
echo of a n. mind LONG 491:13
fredome is a n. thing BARB 55:10
Here all were n. BYRO 178:7
imagination, of n. grounds RUSK 659:12

noble (*cont.*):
Is this the n. nature   SHAK 714:12
know and understand to be n.   EURI 312:16
love's a n. madness   DRYD 287:22
Man is a n. animal   BROW 156:18
n. acts of chivalry   CAXT 204:9
n. and nude and antique   SWIN 768:9
n. grand book   GASK 340:21
n. heart, that harbours   SPEN 751:17
n. lie   PLAT 597:13
n. Living   WORD 849:17
n. mind   DOYL 284:15
n. savage ran   DRYD 287:30
O! what a n. mind   SHAK 686:18
silence is most n.   SWIN 768:5
than a n. death   EURI 312:18
What's brave, what's n.   SHAK 680:4
nobleman king may make a n.   BURK 169:10
Underrated N.   GILB 347:3
nobleness allied with perfect n.   ARNO 30:9
nobler Whether 'tis n. in the mind   SHAK 686:9
nobles n. by the right   MACA 498:5
n. with links of iron   BOOK 144:8
noblesse N. *oblige*   LÉVI 482:15
noblest honest man's the n. work   BURN 170:23
n. of mankind   CALV 186:10
n. prospect   JOHN 428:8
n. Roman of them all   SHAK 698:29
n. work of God   POPE 605:9
n. work of man   INGE 413:14
ruins of the n. man   SHAK 697:15
nobly I am n. born   DEKK 262:19
N., nobly Cape Saint Vincent   BROW 159:19
n. save   LINC 485:6
nobody care for n.   BICK 115:22
n. came   FILM 322:12
N. came   GINS 349:14
n. comes   BECK 61:17
n.'s going to stop 'em   BERR 71:9
n.'s perfect   FILM 320:21
n. walks much faster   CARR 195:23
n. will come   SAND 666:1
noctes *O n. cenaeque deum*   HORA 403:15
noctis *currite n. equi*   MARL 513:6
currite n. equi   OVID 579:18
nod dwelt in the land of N.   BIBL 76:2
n.'s as good as a wink   PROV 627:38
Old N., the shepherd   DE L 263:6
nodded n. with his darkish brows   HOME 393:20
nods excellent Homer n.   HORA 398:15
Homer sometimes n.   PROV 622:26
it n. a little   FARQ 315:23
N., and becks   MILT 529:19
noes honest kersey n.   SHAK 702:23
nohow for nothing. N.   CARR 195:4
noire *triste et n.*   BAUD 58:15
noise Go placidly amid the n.   EHRM 297:9
happy n. to hear   HOUS 404:11
little noiseless n.   KEAT 443:21
loud n. at one end   KNOX 458:11
make a cheerful n.   BOOK 139:13
melt, and make no n.   DONN 281:17
more n. they make   POPE 606:22
moved to folly by a n.   LAWR 475:18
n. is an effective means   GOEB 352:8
n. like that of a water-mill   SWIF 765:10
n., my dear   ANON 18:1
n. of battle rolled   TENN 778:11
Nursed amid her n.   LAMB 465:4
so little n.   LAWR 475:1
such n. that beast made   MALO 508:19
those who make the n.   BURK 167:19
till they make a n.   CRAB 249:15
wi' flichterin' n.   BURN 170:19
with a merry n.   BOOK 137:3
noiseless little n. noise   KEAT 443:21
n. tenor of their way   GRAY 361:7
noises isle is full of n.   SHAK 711:28
noisy into the n. crowd   TAGO 770:18
n. years seem moments   WORD 848:12

Nokomis wigwam of N.   LONG 491:1
noli *N. me tangere*   BIBL 115:17
N. *me tangere*   WYAT 852:8
nom de plume *n.* secures all   ELIO 300:22
nomen *Omne capax movet urna n.*   HORA 401:10
nominate n. a spade a spade   JONS 435:8
nominated will not accept if n.   SHER 734:18
nomination When you have got the n.   CARD 190:7
nominative her n. case   O'KE 572:19
nomine *In N. Patris*   MISS 536:11
nominis *magni n. umbra*   LUCA 495:1
non avoiding n.-being   TILL 794:15
comes from n.-being   LAO 467:8
no fury like a n.-combatant   MONT 543:20
n.-being into utility   LAO 467:7
n.-cooperation with evil   GAND 339:8
N.-violence is the first article   GAND 339:7
organization of n.-violence   BAEZ 47:9
saturam n. scribere   JUVE 439:7
nonconformist man must be a n.   EMER 307:4
N. conscience   WILD 836:8
none answer came there n.   CARR 195:8
answer came there n.   SCOT 673:2
answer made it n.   SHAK 684:11
malice toward n.   LINC 485:12
n. that doeth good   BOOK 134:10
This is n. of I   NURS 567:4
nonexistent obsolescent and n.   BREN 150:23
non-existent dead is to be n.   SOCR 745:4
nonsense His n. suits their nonsense   CHAR 209:7
lump of clotted n.   DRYD 290:12
n., and learning   GOLD 355:22
n. upon stilts   BENT 68:4
round the corner of n.   COLE 234:9
your damned n.   RICH 648:1
nook obscure n. for me   BROW 160:15
noon amid the blaze of n.   MILT 534:26
athwart the n.   COLE 231:17
Far from the fiery n.   KEAT 443:9
first minute, after n.   DONN 281:3
lying till n.   JOHN 426:25
returned before n.   SAIN 663:7
When n. is past   SHEL 729:15
noonday destroyeth in the n.   BOOK 140:3
no-one Duty is what n. else will do   FITZ 324:12
noose naked to the hangman's n.   HOUS 404:9
n. of light   FITZ 322:24
norfan N., both sides   WELL 828:10
Norfolk bear him up the N. sky   BETJ 72:5
Very flat, N.   COWA 245:10
normal n. and easy   JAME 418:4
normalcy not nostrums but n.   HARD 371:10
Norman like our N. King   KIPL 453:13
simple faith than N. blood   TENN 780:4
Normans If N. are disciplined   WILL 838:1
N. are a race   WILL 838:6
Noroway To N. o'er the faem   BALL 53:4
north against the people of the N.   LEE 479:3
Awake, O n. wind   BIBL 87:13
beauties of the n.   ADDI 4:10
heart of the N. is dead   LAWR 475:15
He was my N., my South   AUDE 34:29
mad n.-north-west   SHAK 685:27
n. of my lady's opinion   SHAK 721:4
N.-west passage   STER 757:8
n. wind doth blow   NURS 568:12
tender is the N.   TENN 783:6
to us the near n.   MENZ 522:6
triumph from the n.   MACA 499:5
True N. strong and free   WEIR 826:24
What answer from the N.   KIPL 456:1
wild N.-easter   KING 452:16
North African N. Empire
North America Mr and Mrs N.   WINC 841:3
Northcliffe N. has sent for the King   ANON 16:7
northern bright n. star   LOVE 493:2
constant as the n. star   SHAK 697:9

n. lights astream   SMAR 740:18
N. reticence, the tight gag   HEAN 378:6
Norval My name is N.   HOME 393:14
nose at the end of his n.   LEAR 477:16
cause of the human n.   COLE 234:1
Cleopatra's n. been shorter   PASC 587:7
cut off your n.   PROV 618:11
great hook n.   BLAK 119:19
hadde a semely n.   CHAU 212:11
hateful to the n.   JAME 417:1
insinuated n.   WATS 823:4
jolly red n.   BEAU 60:4
large n. is in fact the sign   ROST 656:11
lifts his n.   SWIF 767:1
n. and cheeks stand out   DRYD 290:13
n. May ravage with impunity   BROW 161:16
N. of Turk   SHAK 706:13
n.-painting, sleep   SHAK 705:7
n. was as sharp as a pen   SHAK 693:2
not a n. at all   WELL 828:14
plucks justice by the n.   SHAK 707:19
run up your n. dead against   BALD 51:1
That n., the hook   BYRO 177:20
thirty inches from my n.   AUDE 35:22
very shiny n.   MARK 512:9
wipe a bloody n.   GAY 341:28
with a luminous n.   LEAR 477:5
noses assaulting n.   MITC 540:7
n. cast is of the roman   FLEM 326:19
n. have they, and smell not   BOOK 144:4
slightly flatter n.   CONR 240:13
Where do the n. go   HEMI 381:4
nosethirles n. blake were   CHAU 210:25
nostalgia N. isn't what   SAYI 670:7
nostalgie *n. de la boue*   AUGI 36:22
noster *Pater n.*   MISS 539:7
nostrils breathed into his n.   BIBL 75:11
nostrums not n. but normalcy   HARD 371:10
not find out what you are n.   LOY 494:23
if this is n.   PALI 583:19
n. I, but the wind   LAWR 475:9
n.-incurious in God's handiwork   BROW 159:8
N. so much a programme   ANON 18:3
N. unto us, O Lord   BOOK 142:3
n. wisely but too well   SHAK 714:30
Thou shalt n. kill   BIBL 78:5
notable meet a n.   GERS 344:9
note living had no n.   GIBB 345:24
longest suicide n.   KAUF 442:1
n. I wanted   JAME 418:4
only the n. of a bird   SIMP 738:9
When found, make a n.   DICK 269:8
noted n. in thy book   BOOK 137:19
notes N. are often necessary   JOHN 425:19
n. I handle no better   SCHN 671:12
n. like little fishes   MACN 504:21
quality of the n.   SCHN 671:13
right n. at the right time   BACH 42:10
These rought n.   SCOT 673:1
thick-warbled n.   MILT 534:21
thinks two n. a song   DAVI 258:18
too many n.   JOSE 436:14
nothing better than n.   PROV 631:6
brought n. into this world   BIBL 110:25
but n. came   BYRO 178:4
Caesar or n.   MOTT 552:2
Death is n. to us   EPIC 308:8
desired to know n.   JOHN 430:3
doing n.   COWP 247:20
do n.   MELB 521:7
do n. for ever and ever   EPIT 309:15
do n. without it   BUTL 177:3
don't believe in n.   CHES 217:16
drawing n. up   COWP 248:1
Emperor has n. on   ANDE 14:2
Emperors can do n.   BREC 150:9
forgotten nothing and learnt n.   DUMO 291:14
get something for n.   PROV 636:1
gives to airy n.   SHAK 711:28
good man to do n.   MISQ 538:4
Goodness had n. to do with it   WEST 830:5

oafish o. louts remember Mum   BETJ 72:3
oafs muddied o. at the goals   KIPL 454:16
oak ashes of an O.   DONN 282:5
Beware of an o.   PROV 615:35
English o. and holly   HART 374:15
Heart of o.   GARR 340:2
Jove's stout o.   SHAK 719:3
juniper talks to the o.   PAUL 589:4
O., and Ash, and Thorn   KIPL 455:23
o.-cleaving. thunderbolts   SHAK 700:15
o. is before the ash   PROV 634:32
O. was round his breast   HORA 400:4
o. would sprout in Derry   HEAN 378:4
round that o. hangs   PUSH 638:6
thunders from her native o.   CAMP 187:21
oaks families last not three o.   BROW 156:14
hews down o. with rushes   SHAK 682:14
Little strokes fell great o.   PROV 625:30
o. from little acorns   PROV 621:19
O. that flourish   LEWE 483:3
Tall o., branch-charmèd   KEAT 443:13
oak-trees made the o. follow him   VIRG 815:6
oar heavy o. the pen is   FLAU 325:8
oatcakes o., and sulphur   SMIT 743:18
oath cheats with an o.   PLUT 598:17
good mouth-filling o.   SHAK 690:27
Hire gretteste o.   CHAU 210:10
man is not upon o.   JOHN 430:10
oaths Judges must follow their o.   ZOBE 858:13
o. are but words   BUTL 176:13
o. are straws   SHAK 693:3
soldier, Full of strange o.   SHAK 681:11
oats feeds the horse enough o.   GALB 338:5
O. A grain   JOHN 424:12
Oaxen *rapidum cretae veniemus O.*   VIRG 813:15
Obadiah O. Bind-their-kings   MACA 499:4
obedience o. of planetary influence   SHAK 699:26
o. to God   BRAD 149:2
soldier is o.   PROV 620:10
obedient o. to their laws we lie   EPIT 309:11
penitent, and o. heart   BOOK 127:13
Righteous women are o.   KORA 460:1
obeisance made o. to my sheaf   BIBL 76:38
obey cannot o. cannot command   PROV 621:43
duty is to o. orders   JACK 415:9
learned well how to o.   THOM 788:8
love, cherish, and to o.   BOOK 133:9
O. orders   PROV 628:16
o. them   HORS 403:18
To o. is better   BIBL 80:14
woman to o.   PEMB 591:9
obeyed o. as a son   GIBB 345:17
right to be o.   JOHN 422:3
She who must be o.   HAGG 367:7
obeying except by o.   BACO 46:18
obituary o. in serial form   CRIS 251:9
your own o.   BEHA 63:17
object My o. all sublime   GILB 348:4
no o. worth its constancy   SHEL 732:5
O. of Contempt   AUST 38:26
see the o.   ARNO 30:8
with his eye on the o.   ARNO 30:7
objectification o. of feeling   LANG 466:13
objectionable doubtless o.   ANON 19:3
objective have a great o.   CHIF 217:18
o. correlative   ELIO 303:27
oblation o. of himself   BOOK 132:1
oblations alms and o.   BOOK 131:13
obligation not always the sequel of o.   JOHN 425:11
o. is a pain   JOHN 425:21
o. which goes unrecognized   WEIL 826:12
obligations Nobility has o.   LÉVI 482:15
oblige *Noblesse o.*   LÉVI 482:15
obliteration policy is o.   BELL 64:12
oblivion from place to place over o.   HARD 372:19
iniquity of o.   BROW 156:16
journey towards o.   LAWR 475:6
love, and then o.   MCEW 501:15

mere o.   SHAK 681:13
O! my o. is a very Antony   SHAK 678:22
puts alms for o.   SHAK 719:22
sank unwept into o.   ELIO 299:23
stepmother to memory, o.   JOHN 422:8
To cold o.   SHEL 729:7
obnoxious I am o.   BRAD 149:4
obscene Sailing on o. wings   COLE 231:17
obscenity 'o.' not capable of exact definition   RUSS 661:4
obscure become o.   HORA 397:22
Deep and o.   LAO 467:10
o. nook for me   BROW 160:15
through the palpable o.   MILT 532:6
obscurely o. bright   BYRO 179:29
obscuri *Ibant o. sola sub nocte*   VIRG 812:11
obscurity man from o.   REYN 645:16
o. of a learned language   GIBB 345:22
rise out of o.   JUVE 439:17
obscurus *O. fio*   HORA 397:22
obsequies solemnized their o.   BROW 156:8
observation common sense, and o.   BROW 156:31
O. is a passive science   BERN 71:1
o. is concerned   PAST 588:6
o. of facts   COND 237:7
o. with extensive view   JOHN 426:15
observe o. the works of nature   GALE 338:9
You see, but you do not o.   DOYL 284:13
observed o. of all observers   SHAK 686:18
o. the golden rule   BLAK 121:18
observer for th'o.'s sake   POPE 603:16
He is a great o.   SHAK 696:13
keen o. of life   AUDE 35:14
observeth o. the wind   BIBL 86:22
obsolescence adolescence and o.   LINK 486:9
planned o.   STEV 757:18
obsolescent o. and nonexistent   BREN 150:23
obsolete Either war is o. or men are o.   FULL 336:25
obstinacy O. in a bad cause   BROW 156:29
o. in a bad one   STER 756:19
obstruct circumstances o.   JUVE 439:17
obstruction consecrated o.   BAGE 48:13
obtain o. effectually   BOOK 130:20
obvious in o. distress   BALF 51:6
Occam O.'s Razor   OCCA 571:11
occasion o. of all wars   FOX 331:7
o.'s forelock watchful   MILT 534:17
occasions o. do inform against me   SHAK 688:2
their lawful o.   BOOK 144:11
occidit *Occidit, o. Spes omnis*   HORA 402:10
occupation cure for it is o.   SHAW 727:8
diligent o.   MORE 548:3
o. for an idle hour   AUST 39:11
o. for an idle hour   OPEN 575:17
Othello's o.'s gone   SHAK 714:4
Waiting is still an o.   PAVE 589:7
occupations let us love our o.   DICK 268:2
occupy o. their business   BOOK 141:18
occurred never to have o.   BENT 68:17
ocean abandon the o.   CLAY 226:1
all great Neptune's o.   SHAK 705:3
all the O.'s sons   DENH 264:4
cause the o. to attend   BEST 71:21
day-star in the o. bed   MILT 530:10
deep and dark blue O.   BYRO 179:18
drop in the o.   TERE 785:10
Earth when it is clearly O.   CLAR 225:4
foliage of the o.   SHEL 730:10
great o. of truth   NEWT 561:16
In the o.'s bosom   MARV 515:6
leap into the o.   HUME 408:16
love you till the o.   AUDE 34:19
mighty o. deep   WHIT 832:22
o. as their road   WALL 818:7
O. forbidding separation   GRAT 359:17
o. has but one taste   PALI 584:8
o. of darkness   FOX 331:6
o. on a western beach   LANG 466:11
O.'s child   SHEL 730:1
o. sea   BARN 56:16

O.'s nursling, Venice   SHEL 729:26
On one side lay the O.   TENN 778:12
on the vast o.   HORA 400:10
Ransack the o.   MARL 513:1
rivers with the o.   SHEL 730:2
rolled the o.   BYRO 178:17
rolling on of o.   MORR 549:12
round o., and the living air   WORD 847:11
seen the hungry o.   SHAK 723:7
ship Upon a painted o.   COLE 232:19
thou, vast o.   MONT 545:16
oceanic his own o. mind   COLE 234:10
oceans compendious o.   CRAS 250:16
To the o. white with foam   BERL 69:18
octavos o. fill a spacious plain   CRAB 249:4
October O.'s strife   GURN 366:1
O., that ambiguous month   LESS 482:3
octopus dear o.   SMIT 741:16
odd But not so o.   BROW 155:14
divinity in o. numbers   SHAK 710:14
God must think it exceedingly o.   KNOX 458:9
How o. Of God   EWER 313:9
It's an o. job   MOLI 541:14
Nothing o. will do   JOHN 430:12
oddfellow desperate o. society   THOR 793:10
oddly eyes are o. made   HAMM 370:12
odds facing fearful o.   MACA 499:13
how am I to face the o.   HOUS 403:22
what o.   CRAS 250:17
oderint O., *dum metuant*   ACCI 1:6
odi O. *et amo*   CATU 203:9
O. *profanum vulgus*   HORA 401:9
odious Comparisons are o.   PROV 617:6
O.! in woollen   POPE 603:21
odium lived in the o.   BENT 68:14
odorous Comparisons are o.   SHAK 712:25
odours golden vials full of o.   BIBL 113:12
haste with o. sweet   MILT 530:18
o. tangle   DICK 273:13
Odysseus Like O., the President   KEYN 450:12
Odyssey thunder of the O.   LANG 466:11
oferēode *þæs o.*   ANON 22:8
off I want to be o. it   PAXM 589:9
O. with her head   CARR 194:12
O. with his head   CIBB 223:2
O. with his head   SHAK 716:31
offence best defence is a good o.   SAYI 669:3
conscience void of o.   BIBL 105:27
detest th'o.   POPE 602:18
for a rock of o.   BIBL 88:16
forgave the o.   DRYD 288:5
I was like to give o.   FROS 335:20
o. at a few faults   HORA 398:14
o. inspires less horror   GIBB 345:5
O! my o. is rank   SHAK 687:15
only defence is in o.   BALD 50:16
resented for an o.   SWIF 766:15
What dire o.   POPE 606:3
where the o. is   SHAK 688:15
offences o. of my youth   BOOK 135:8
offend doth o., when 'tis let loose   SUCK 763:6
freedom to o.   RUSH 659:5
offendar *non ego paucis O. maculis*   HORA 398:14
offended him have I o.   SHAK 697:20
not o. the king   LAST 474:3
shadows have o.   SHAK 712:8
offender hugged the o.   DRYD 288:5
love th'o.   POPE 602:18
offenders O. never pardon   PROV 628:18
society o.   GILB 347:21
offensive extremely o.   SMIT 742:6
Life is an o.   WHIT 832:8
offer close with the o.   HUXL 411:16
o. he can't refuse   PUZO 638:10
would refuse this o.   SCOT 674:30
offering o. too little   CANN 189:4
office campaigns for public o.   MORE 548:8
for o. boys   SALI 664:13
holding public o.   ACHE 1.9
in his o. wait   DODD 278:20
in o. but not in power   LAMO 465:18

insignificant o. — ADAM 3:2
insolence of the o. — SHAK 686:10
in which the o. is held — HUXL 411:3
man unfit for o. — FABI 313:18
no o. to go to — SHAW 725:16
O. builds up a man — BENN 67:1
o. party is not — WHIT 832:18
receives the seals of o. — ROSE 655:3
waters of o. — TROL 799:9
Whichever party is in o. — WILS 840:12
officer fear each bush an o. — SHAK 695:3
o. and a gentleman — MILI 526:3
official concept of the o. secret — WEBE 825:8
This high o., all allow — HERB 383:9
officialism Where there is o. — FORS 329:22
officials o. are the servants — GOWE 357:14
O. take different view — ROTH 656:20
offspring Time's noblest o. — BERK 69:15
wickedest o. of thy race — ROCH 651:18
oft as o. as ye shall drink it — BOOK 132:7
by o. falling — LATI 470:2
O. in danger — WHIT 832:2
o. was thought — POPE 604:5
often Vote early and vote o. — MILE 525:1
Og O. the king of Basan — BOOK 143:10
Ohioan black O. swan — WRIG 851:15
Ohrmazd O. was on high — ZORO 860:3
oil anointed my head with o. — BOOK 135:4
consumed the midnight o. — GAY 341:25
mix like o. and vinegar — GAIN 337:14
o. controlling American soil — DYLA 294:15
o. in a cruse — BIBL 81:20
o. into their ears — JONS 435:13
o. of gladness — BOOK 136:20
o. of joy for mourning — BIBL 90:19
o. to make him — BOOK 141:7
O., vinegar, sugar — GOLD 355:4
o. which renders — HUME 408:13
Scotland's o. — POLI 600:25
smoother than o. — BIBL 83:38
smoother than o. — BOOK 137:18
sound of o. wells — FISH 322:17
whose o. wellnigh would shine — KORA 460:19
with boiling o. in it — GILB 348:7
oiled in the o. wards — KEAT 445:13
O. his way around the floor — LERN 481:23
oily glib and o. art — SHAK 699:20
ointment o. might have been sold — BIBL 98:28
very precious o. — BIBL 98:27
Okie O. means you're scum — STEI 755:12
old adherence to the o. — LINC 484:17
Any o. iron — COLL 235:2
As with gladness men of o. — DIX 278:14
attendance on my o. age — YEAT 855:9
balance of the O. — CANN 189:10
Being an o. maid — FERB 316:15
being o. is having lighted rooms — LARK 469:1
better than the Good O. Days — BINC 116:13
blessing of the O. — BACO 43:13
boys of the o. Brigade — WEAT 824:22
catch o. birds with chaff — PROV 635:27
chilly and grown o. — BROW 161:24
considered the days of o. — BOOK 139:6
die before I get o. — TOWN 797:6
died in a good o. age — BIBL 82:19
Diseases and sad O. Age — VIRG 812:12
dreary o. age — VIRG 814:19
dressing o. words new — SHAK 723:11
ere thou grow o. — ROCH 651:16
foolish, fond o. man — SHAK 701:22
getting too o. — DISN 275:2
good o. age — BIBL 76:16
good o. Cause — MILT 536:2
Growing o. a bad habit — MAUR 519:2
Growing o. is like — POWE 609:16
Grow o. along with me — BROW 161:3
grow o. with a good grace — STEE 754:19
hard sentences of o. — BOOK 139:7
heart grows o. — YEAT 855:17
HOW O. CARY GRANT — TELE 776:7
I grow o. — SOLO 745:12
I grow o. . . . I grow old — ELIO 302:19
I'm growing o. — LOUI 492:9

instead of o. ones — PEEL 590:16
into a world too o. — MUSS 555:11
lads that will never be o. — HOUS 404:12
make an o. man young — TENN 777:3
make me conservative when o. — FROS 335:21
man is as o. as he feels — PROV 625:53
man who reviews the o. — CONF 237:12
Mithridates, he died o. — HOUS 405:3
my folks were growing o. — STEV 760:9
name thee O. Glory — DRIV 286:9
Never too o. to learn — PROV 627:30
no country for o. men — YEAT 855:8
no fool like an o. fool — PROV 632:29
no man would be o. — SWIF 766:25
not yet so o. — SHAK 709:19
now am not too o. — BLUN 124:5
now am o. — BOOK 136:1
off with the o. love — PROV 623:41
o. Adam in this Child — BOOK 132:10
o. age always fifteen years older — BARU 57:17
O. Age, and Experience — ROCH 651:12
O. Age a regret — DISR 277:2
O.-age, a second child — CHUR 219:21
o. age has brought to me — STEP 755:20
O. age hath yet his honour — TENN 784:18
O. age is the most unexpected — TROT 800:17
o. age of cards — POPE 603:5
O. age should burn — THOM 789:7
O. age, the last gap but one — WHIT 832:3
o. and faded — MARL 512:12
O. and young — STEV 759:19
o. before my time — ROSS 655:10
o. black magic — MERC 522:11
o. familiar faces — LAMB 464:21
O. friends are best — SELD 676:3
o. head on young shoulders — PROV 635:34
o. heads on your young shoulders — SPAR 749:25
o. in a second childhood — ARIS 25:4
o. is better — BIBL 100:13
O. King Cole — NURS 568:13
o. lamps for new — ARAB 23:16
o. Lie: Dulce et decorum — OWEN 581:4
o., mad, blind — SHEL 731:20
o. man does not care — JOHN 428:25
o. man in a dry month — ELIO 302:3
o. man in a hurry — CHUR 220:14
o. man of Thermopylae — LEAR 477:11
O. man river — HAMM 370:6
o. man's darling — PROV 615:21
o. man upon a winter's night — YEAT 855:3
o. man who said, 'Damn!' — HARE 373:10
o. men and children — BOOK 144:7
O. men and comets — SWIF 766:26
o. men from the chimney corner — SIDN 736:16
o. men must die — PROV 636:6
o. men shall dream dreams — BIBL 92:3
O. Mother Hubbard — NURS 568:14
old, o. survivors — SHAW 728:3
o. order changeth — TENN 778:16
O. soldiers never die — FOLE 327:24
o. too much — WALP 819:6
o. truth receives a new — WIGG 834:16
o., unhappy, far-off things — WORD 850:9
o., wild, and incomprehensible man — VICT 809:12
o. wine wholesomest — WEBS 826:3
o. wood best to burn — BACO 43:4
O, sir! you are o. — SHAK 700:10
planned by o. men — RICE 646:20
problem of growing o. — MORR 550:12
ruinous and o. — SPEN 751:16
sad o. age — TALL 771:20
Say I'm growing o. — HUNT 409:18
shift an o. tree — PROV 635:37
sing the o. songs — CLAR 224:20
so o. a head — SHAK 709:24
so o. a story — HEIN 379:16
story always o. — BROW 161:7
suppose an o. man decayed — JOHN 432:5
teach an o. dog new tricks — PROV 635:44
Tell me the o., old story — HANK 370:16

that horror—the o. woman — COLE 234:15
that's o. Europe — RUMS 658:11
They shall grow not o. — BINY 116:14
thinking of the o. 'un — DICK 268:9
though an o. man — JEFF 420:9
times begin to wax o. — BIBL 92:18
too o. to rush up to the net — ADAM 2:5
want an o.-fashioned house — FISH 322:18
warn you not to grow o. — KINN 453:8
wax o. as doth a garment — BOOK 140:19
well an o. age is out — DRYD 289:15
what an o. courtier is like — CHAM 206:19
When I am an o. woman — JOSE 436:17
when thou shalt be o. — BIBL 104:22
when 'tis o. — BALL 53:18
When you are very o. — RONS 653:5
you are o. and grey — YEAT 856:6
You are o., Father William — CARR 194:1
You are o., Father William — SOUT 749:9
young can do for the o. — SHAW 725:6
Young folks think o. folks — PROV 636:4
older Another day o. — TRAV 798:5
As we get o. — REED 644:2
O. men declare war — HOOV 396:2
o. than the rocks — PATE 588:9
so much o. then — DYLA 294:13
oldest o. hath borne most — SHAK 702:9
o. rule in the book — CARR 194:22
o. sins — SHAK 692:18
olet *Pecunia non o.* — VESP 809:6
oligarchy aristocracy, call it o. — HOBB 390:20
olive children like the o.-branches — BOOK 143:3
Olivet purple brows of O. — TENN 779:2
Olivia Cry out, 'O.!' — SHAK 720:13
eyes did see O. — SHAK 720:6
olla putrida what a clumsy o. — LAWR 475:16
ologies instructed in the 'o.' — CARL 192:16
olores *inter strepere anser o.* — VIRG 814:9
Olympian O. bolts — DISR 275:13
Olympus made great O. tremble — HOME 393:20
O. on top of Ossa — VIRG 814:15
Pelion on top of shady O. — HORA 401:16
om end of o. is silence — UPAN 805:15
Omega Alpha and O. — BIBL 112:25
omelette fuss about an o. — VOLT 816:20
make an o. without — PROV 635:32
o. all over our suits — BROK 152:2
omen gods avert this o. — CICE 223:19
Procul o. abesto — OVID 579:19
This is the one best o. — HOME 394:7
omens grievous o. — SUTT 765:1
omitted O., all the voyage — SHAK 698:21
omne *o. immensum peragravit* — LUCR 495:9
omnes *Laudate Dominum, o. gentes* — BIBL 115:4
omnia *Amor vincit o.* — CHAU 210:13
non o. possumus omnes — LUCI 495:7
Non o. possumus omnes — VIRG 814:8
O. vincit Amor — VIRG 814:10
omnibus man on the Clapham o. — BOWE 148:7
Ninety-seven horse power o. — FLAN 324:19
omnipotence proof of God's o. — DE V 266:7
omnipotent land of the o. No — BOLD 126:4
O. but friendless — SHEL 731:5
omnis *Non o. moriar* — HORA 402:4
omniscience o. his foible — SMIT 744:9
their o. — MARA 512:1
omnium Duke of O. — TROL 799:5
on O., on, on — LAST 473:12
Onan into the sin of O. — VOLT 816:13
once done but o. — DONN 282:10
I was adored o. — SHAK 720:21
oblation of himself o. offered — BOOK 132:1
O. a—, always a— — PROV 628:26
o. and future king — MALO 509:4
o. in a great while — PEPY 592:15
O. in royal David's city — ALEX 11:8
O. more unto the breach — SHAK 693:4
O. to every man — LOWE 494:3
O. upon a time — OPEN 575:9
through this world but o. — GREL 363:11

once (cont.):
You can only die o. — PROV 635:38
one All for o., one for all — DUMA 291:12
all is o. — ZOHA 859:2
all things and I are o. — CHUA 218:21
At o. fell swoop — SHAK 706:24
But the O. was Me — HUXL 411:10
doeth good, no not o. — BOOK 134:10
encompassed but o. man — SHAK 696:11
How to be o. up — POTT 608:8
Long-expected o.-and-twenty — JOHN 433:3
Lord is O. — SIDD 735:12
loyalties which centre upon number o. — CHUR 222:14
man not truly o. — STEV 759:9
o. being is wanting — LAMA 464:7
o. by one back — FITZ 323:8
o. day in thy courts — BOOK 139:17
o.-eyed man is king — ERAS 308:12
o.-eyed yellow idol — HAYE 376:7
O. flew east — NURS 568:17
o. for my baby — MERC 522:10
O. for sorrow — PROV 628:33
O. for the mouse — PROV 628:34
o. if by land — LONG 491:5
O. in Three — ALEX 11:9
o. man fewer — METT 523:12
O. man shall have one vote — CART 197:11
O. remains, the many change — SHEL 729:2
o. thing at once — SMIL 740:23
O., two, buckle — NURS 568:18
ought to be Number O. — CARR 194:22
she who but trifles with o. — GAY 341:22
square root of minus o. — BECK 61:28
Tao produced the O. — LAO 467:14
When I was o.-and-twenty — HOUS 404:10
oneself carefully at o. — MOLI 542:4
Hell is o. — ELIO 301:5
how to be o. — MONT 544:10
onion o. atoms lurk — SMIT 743:26
tears live in an o. — SHAK 678:18
onions o., and eek lekes — CHAU 210:27
only his o. begotten Son — BIBL 102:32
It's the o. thing — SAND 566:4
keep thee o. unto her — BOOK 133:8
o. begotten of the Father — BIBL 102:21
O. connect — FORS 329:16
O. the lonely — ORBI 576:5
To the o. begetter — SHAK 722:20
only-begotten o. Son of God — BOOK 131:10
onset o. and waning of love — LA B 462:15
onstage O. I make love — JOPL 436:12
ontogeny o. recapitulates — HAEC 366:11
onward O., Christian soldiers — BARI 56:4
O. goes the pilgrim band — BARI 56:5
ooze through the o. and slime — SMIT 742:11
oozing feel it o. out — SHER 733:25
O. charm from every pore — LERN 481:23
Time like a last o. — BECK 61:26
oozy sea-blooms and the o. woods — SHEL 730:10
opal mind is a very o. — SHAK 720:27
opals cream does look like o. — JONS 434:15
open either shut or o. — PROV 618:20
function when they are o. — DEWA 266:11
great o. spaces — MARQ 514:2
o. and notorious evil liver — BOOK 131:3
o. any door — PROV 621:3
O. covenants of peace — WILS 841:1
o. my lips — BOOK 137:15
O. not thine heart — BIBL 93:9
O. rebuke — BIBL 85:13
O. Sesame — ARAB 23:17
o. the Kingdom of Heaven — BOOK 128:1
o. the temple gates — SPEN 751:8
O. to me, my sister — BIBL 87:14
O., ye everlasting gates — MILT 533:23
Secret thoughts and o. countenance — ALBE 10:7
takc to the o. road — WHIT 833:19
opened bottle has just been o. — HESI 387:8
opera *Benedicite, omnia o. Domini* — BIBL 115:9
first rule of o. — MELB 520:12

language an o. is sung in — APPL 23:13
o. ain't over — SAYI 670:10
O. is when a guy gets stabbed — GARD 339:13
operas German text of French o. — WHAR 831:1
Soap o. sell — MCEL 501:13
operatic so romantic, so o. — PROU 613:11
operation end must direct the o. — WOTT 851:7
operations o. which we can perform — WHIT 832:15
opes *Fumum et o.* — HORA 402:1
golden o., the iron shuts — MILT 530:5
Magnas inter o. inops — HORA 401:22
Ophelia I loved O. — SHAK 689:4
opiate some dull o. — KEAT 444:20
opiates curing diverse maladies as o. — SYDE 769:10
opinion approve a private o. — HOBB 390:13
Backed his o. — PRIO 612:6
by prevalent o. — OLIV 573:2
fool gudgeon, this o. — SHAK 708:22
form a clear o. — BONH 127:9
Government and public o. — SHAW 726:7
independent of public o. — HEGE 379:9
man can brave o. — STAË 753:17
man of common o. — BAGE 47:10
north of my lady's o. — SHAK 721:4
of his own o. still — BUTL 176:17
o. and science — HUME 409:3
o. he held once — SHAK 696:25
o. in good men — MILT 535:23
o. of himself — BENN 67:17
o. one man entertains — PALM 585:4
o. with the learned — CONG 238:20
own o. still — PROV 621:45
Party is organized o. — DISR 275:20
plague of o. — SHAK 719:25
poor itch of your o. — SHAK 682:13
scorching world's o. — FLET 327:7
supported by popular o. — CATT 199:20
think the last o. right — POPE 604:12
vagrant o. — BIER 116:8
were of one o. — MILL 525:7
whole climate of o. — AUDE 35:1
opinions anger of men who have no o. — CHES 216:23
anyone's o. but your own — PERS 593:6
as many o. as people — TERE 785:8
by men's o. — FABI 313:18
conflict of o. — JOHN 433:12
delivers his o. — CICE 223:6
Golden o. — SHAK 704:8
halt ye between two o. — BIBL 81:21
killed with your hard o. — SHAK 692:25
New o. are always suspected — LOCK 488:5
public buys its o. — BUTL 177:2
Quebec does not have o. — LAUR 470:12
so bad as their o. — MACK 503:3
so many o. — PROV 631:4
Stiff in o. — DRYD 287:6
opium o.-dose for keeping beasts — KING 453:2
o. of the people — MARX 516:11
subtle, and mighty o. — DE Q 264:20
with an o. wand — PAIN 582:21
opponents o. eventually die — PLAN 596:17
opportunities one of those o. — GLAD 351:3
opportunity also a matter of o. — HIPP 389:16
God's o. — PROV 626:5
Ireland's o. — PROV 618:43
maximum of o. — SHAW 726:21
meanness of o. — ELIO 299:23
only requires o. — ELIO 300:18
o. is that wherein — HIPP 389:15
O. makes a thief — PROV 629:7
O. never knocks — PROV 629:8
o. to keep quiet — CHIR 218:3
strong seducer, o. — DRYD 288:2
unfettered o. — MADA 505:6
when he had the o. — ROWL 657:13
oppose o. everything — DERB 265:4
opposing by o. end them — SHAK 686:9
opposites o. are obviously absurd — BOHR 125:11
opposition duty of an O. — DERB 265:4

effective means of o. — GOEB 352:8
formidable O. — DISR 276:26
Her Majesty's O. — BAGE 47:18
His Majesty's O. — HOBH 391:3
O., on coming into power — BAGE 48:6
oppressed barbarously o. — LAST 473:1
let the o. go free — BIBL 90:14
o., and he was afflicted — BIBL 90:3
oppresseth enemy o. me — BOOK 136:14
oppressing o. city — BIBL 92:12
oppression behold o. — BIBL 88:6
mad with o. — TAYL 775:3
make o. bitter — SHAK 686:5
violate would be o. — JEFF 420:1
violence and o. — SOLZ 745:18
oppressions o. of this earth — SHEL 729:17
oppressor ends as an o. — CAMU 188:18
Neutrality helps the o. — WIES 834:14
o.'s wrong — SHAK 686:10
opprobrium term of o. — MOYN 551:18
optics o. of these eyes — BROW 157:2
optima O. *quaeque dies miseris* — VIRG 814:19
optimist o. is a guy — MARQ 513:28
o. proclaims that we live — CABE 184:17
opulent glass the o. — HARD 372:13
opus *Hic o., hic labor est* — VIRG 812:9
lamque o. exegi — OVID 580:15
superabat o. — OVID 580:9
orabunt *O. causas melius* — VIRG 812:15
oracle I am Sir O. — SHAK 708:21
when the o. has spoken — SALI 664:6
oracles earth's green o. — SUTT 765:1
lively O. of God — CORO 243:16
o. are dumb — MILT 530:25
oracular use of my o. tongue — SHER 733:19
oral o. contraception — ALLE 12:12
orange clockwork o. — BURG 165:15
future's O. — ADVE 7:24
in shades the o. bright — MARV 515:7
O. card — CHUR 220:12
o. flower perfumes the bower — SCOT 684:17
were an o.-tree — HERB 384:6
oranges Coffee and o. — STEV 758:8
O. and lemons — NURS 568:19
orang-outang o. or the tiger — BURK 168:24
orantes *Stabant o.* — VIRG 812:13
oration studied as an o. — OSBO 578:11
orator bring against an o. — DEMO 263:15
greatest o. — HUME 408:15
I am no o., as Brutus is — SHAK 698:4
o. ever made an impression — BAGE 47:15
without an o. — SHAK 722:17
orators play the o. — MARL 513:18
oratory first in o. — DEMO 263:19
orbed o. maiden — SHEL 729:4
orbis *Si fractus illabatur o.* — HORA 401:14
orchard on the o. bough — BROW 159:17
orchards new-planted o. — SHAK 698:7
orchestra golden rules for an o. — BEEC 62:12
orchestration o. of platitudes — WILD 837:16
Orci *in faucibus O.* — VIRG 812:12
ordained o. of God — BIBL 106:30
'Tis so o. — PRIO 612:9
order all in o. stand — CRAB 249:4
all is in o. — MANS 511:5
all that o. and beauty — NEWT 561:9
began in o. — BROW 156:4
best words in the best o. — COLE 234:3
cannot bring o. — MCNA 504:13
decently and in o. — BIBL 107:28
defined by the word 'o.' — METT 523:10
Father of O. — ZORO 859:19
Good o. is the foundation — BURK 167:29
harmony, o. or proportion — BROW 157:7
I o. it done — JUVE 439:20
more devoted to o. than justice — KING 452:2
new world o. — BUSH 175:1
not necessarily in that o. — GODA 351:18
old o. changeth — TENN 778:16
o. and beauty — BAUD 58:14
o. breeds habit — ADAM 2:13
o. in variety we see — POPE 606:17
o. of Melchisedech — BOOK 141:21

o. of the acts is planned — PAST 588:3
o. of your going — SHAK 706:7
O. reigns in Warsaw — ANON 20:17
o. to a peopled kingdom — SHAK 692:29
party of o. or stability — MILL 525:8
Peace, o., and good government — ANON 18:8
prejudice of good o. — MILI 526:5
restoration of o. — JAME 418:17
Set thine house in o. — BIBL 89:13
social o. destroyed — TOCQ 795:8
straining to. into tyranny — GODW 352:6
They o., said I — STER 756:7
war creates o. — BREC 150:7
wretched rage for o. — MAHO 507:10
ordered o. my goings — BOOK 136:6
ordering o. of the universe — ALFO 11:12
orders Almighty's o. to perform — ADDI 4:6
don't obey no o. — KIPL 453:21
duty is to obey o. — JACK 415:9
gave them their o. — WELL 828:3
Obey o. — PROV 628:16
ordinary learn to see the o. — BAIL 49:17
o. mind — WOOL 845:2
o. one seem original — HORA 398:1
see God in the o. things — AWDR 41:2
warn you not to be o. — KINN 453:8
ordure Every man's o. — MONT 544:19
ore dig the golden o. — CRAB 249:19
Load your subject with o. — KEAT 447:7
oremus O. — MISS 536:17
organ heaven's deep o. — MILT 530:21
mellering to the o. — DICK 271:19
one day at the o. — PROC 612:17
o. and the maypole — JORD 436:13
o. grinder is present — BEVA 73:14
o. of public opinion — DISR 275:13
o.-voice of England — TENN 782:10
playing of the merry o. — SONG 747:10
organic Be but o. harps — COLE 231:14
form the key to o. life — PAST 588:1
organization about the o. man — WHYT 834:10
o. of forms — CART 197:9
o. of hatreds — ADAM 2:7
o. of idolatry — SHAW 726:17
o. of non-violence — BAEZ 47:9
organize Don't waste time mourning—o. — LAST 472:16
organized it's got to be o. — HOCK 391:6
o. hypocrisy — DISR 275:10
Party is o. opinion — DISR 275:20
organizing Only an o. genius — BEVA 73:8
organs Loud o., his glory — BAKE 50:3
moves with its own o. — SHAK 679:13
o. of beasts and fowls — JOYC 437:19
other o. take their tone — GLAD 350:11
orgasm o. has replaced the Cross — MUGG 553:8
orgy o. has moved elsewhere — RICH 647:21
Oriens equis O. adflavit — VIRG 814:14
orient corn was o. — TRAH 797:14
origin Greek in its o. — MAIN 508:1
stamp of his lowly o. — DARW 257:6
original Behold the bright o. — GAY 342:5
gone from o. righteousness — BOOK 144:15
great and o. writer — WORD 851:2
great O. frame — ADDI 5:7
in th' o. perused mankind — ARMS 26:11
nothing o. in me — CAMP 187:1
ordinary one seem o. — HORA 398:1
o. face — HUI- 408:4
o. is unfaithful — BORG 145:6
o. or instrumental — HOBB 390:11
o. sin — MELV 521:9
o. writer — CHAT 210:1
returning to the o. — LAO 467:11
saves o. thinking — SAYE 668:6
To women their o. must owe — COLL 234:20
originality man without o. — SHAW 724:21
o. of your countenance — CLAI 224:1
originals do not admire the o. — PASC 587:5
few o. and many copies — TOCQ 795:6
origins Consider your o. — DANT 256:3
Orion bands of O. — BIBL 83:24

O. plunges prone — HOUS 404:3
orison mid his o. hears — DYER 294:1
Orlando Run, run, O. — SHAK 681:16
ornament deceived with o. — SHAK 709:18
Nobility is a graceful o. — BURK 167:23
o. of a meek and quiet spirit — BIBL 112:10
o. to her profession — BUNY 165:6
respecting all o. — RUSK 659:22
study's o. — MIDD 524:10
woman's finest o. — AUCT 34:16
ornaments Can a maid forget her o. — BIBL 90:23
lieu of many o. — SPEN 751:10
ornate o., and grotesque — BAGE 49:11
Orontes Syrian O. — JUVE 439:14
orphan defeat is an o. — CIAN 222:25
failure is an o. — PROV 631:31
O., both sides — WELL 828:10
Orpheus O. with his lute — SHAK 695:8
soul of O. sing — MILT 529:13
orthodoxy O. is my doxy — WARB 821:8
O. or My-doxy — CARL 192:7
ortolans die eating o. — DISR 277:34
Oscar assume that O. said it — PARK 585:18
You will, O. — WHIS 831:22
osprey o. to the fish — SHAK 682:22
Ossa pile O. on Pelion — VIRG 814:15
ossibus ex o. ultor — VIRG 812:6
ostentation use rather than o. — GIBB 345:3
ostentatious is not o. — REYN 646:7
ostrich wings of an o. — MACA 498:24
Othello O.'s occupation's gone — SHAK 714:4
other either to o. — BOOK 133:12
forsaking all o. — BOOK 133:8
happens to o. people — CART 196:21
I am not as o. men are — BIBL 101:27
o. Eden — SHAK 715:13
o. men's flowers — MONT 545:2
o. person is feeling — BURR 173:13
O. voices, other rooms — CAPO 189:17
Prudence is the o. woman — ANON 18:13
Were t'o. dear charmer away — GAY 341:20
wonderful for o. people — KERR 450:2
others Do unto o. as you would — PROV 618:22
judging o. — MOLI 542:4
man for o. — BONH 127:10
woman who lives for o. — LEWI 483:7
otherwise gods thought o. — VIRG 811:20
would wish o. — NEWS 562:21
otia deus nobis haec o. fecit — VIRG 813:13
Otis Miss O. regrets — PORT 607:15
otium Cum dignitate o. — CICE 223:23
ought connected with an o. — HUME 409:11
didn't o. never to have done it — BEVI 74:6
drew men as the o. to be — ARIS 25:24
hadn't o. to be — HART 374:16
o. to have done — BOOK 127:16
ounce o. of practice — PROV 629:10
our O. Father — BIBL 95:3
ours O. is the land — MAYA 519:12
they are o. — PERR 593:5
ourselves love of o. — HAZL 376:14
not we o. — BOOK 140:17
power of o. — BOOK 130:5
remedies oft in o. do lie — SHAK 683:8
ousel o. singing in the woods — THOM 790:22
out cannot o.-vote them — JOHN 431:1
counted them all o. — HANR 370:17
get o. and get under — CLAR 225:8
get o. while we're young — SPRI 753:11
include me o. — GOLD 356:3
left o. he would be dangerous — MELB 520:18
many ways o. — SENE 676:30
Mordre wol o. — CHAU 212:1
O.-babying Wordsworth — BULW 164:4
O., damned spot — SHAK 706:25
o.-glittering Keats — BULW 164:4
o.-herods Herod — SHAK 686:22
o. it wente — CHAU 213:9
o. of the body — BIBL 108:23
O. of the deep — BOOK 143:6
O. of this wood — SHAK 711:13
Out, o., brief candle — SHAK 707:14

O.-topping knowledge — ARNO 28:12
o. with the Stuarts — DISR 277:14
preserve thy going o. — BOOK 142:17
truth is o. there — CATC 201:29
will o.-argue them — JOHN 431:1
outcast beweep my o. state — SHAK 722:28
o. of the people — BOOK 134:27
o. on the world — HEWI 387:12
outcasts o. always mourn — WILD 837:2
o. of Israel — BOOK 144:3
outdated o. methods — WILS 840:6
outdoor system of o. relief — BRIG 151:8
outer o. life of telegrams — FORS 329:15
outflows o. extinguished — PALI 583:20
outgrabe mome raths o. — CARR 194:25
outlaw attacks from o. states — REAG 643:15
wandering o. — BYRO 178:15
outlawed liar should be o. — HALI 368:14
o. or exiled — MAGN 506:4
outlive o. this powerful rhyme — SHAK 723:5
outlived o. certain desires — WOOL 845:10
outlives o. this day — SHAK 693:22
outrage connive in civilised o. — HEAN 378:2
outrageous O. acts — STEI 755:14
outside just going o. — LAST 472:2
just going o. — MAHO 507:9
Kiss the book's o. — COWP 246:11
o. elements — GIDE 346:14
o. of the text — DERR 265:6
o. pissing in — JOHN 423:16
outsoared hath o. the shadow — SHEL 728:23
outstanding o. under pressure — GREG 363:8
outstretched o. beneath the tree — BLAK 122:17
outvoted they o. me — LEE 479:1
outward American-o.-bound — HOPK 397:13
In all her o. parts — COWL 245:23
man looketh on the o. — BIBL 80:16
on the o. wall — SHAK 709:8
O. and the Inward — KORA 461:10
o. and visible sign — BOOK 132:19
O. be fair — CHUR 219:2
o. show of things — SPEN 752:10
o. shows — SHAK 709:18
outwardly o. in our bodies — BOOK 130:5
serve God both o. — BAHY 49:15
Ovaltineys We are the O. — ADVE 8:21
over ain't o. till it's over — BERR 71:10
it is all o. — NORT 565:13
My war is o. — MCGU 502:6
opera ain't o. — SAYI 670:10
O. hill, over dale — SHAK 710:27
oversexed, and o. here — TRIN 798:19
O. the hills — GAY 341:12
O. the hills and far away — STEV 761:1
O. there — COHA 230:7
O. the sea to Skye — BOUL 147:7
They think it's all o. — WOLS 844:13
tyranny be o.-past — BOOK 137:20
overbearing o. and offensive — VICT 809:13
overbought thou hast o. So much — CRAS 250:6
overcame I came, saw, and o. — SHAK 692:13
overcoat my o. also — RIMB 649:9
put on your o. — LOWE 494:6
overcome Be not o. of evil — BIBL 106:29
never o. them — JUNG 438:9
o. the world — BIBL 103:38
We shall o. — POLI 601:16
overcomes Who o. By force — MILT 531:24
overlapping events o. each other — DURR 293:7
overlook knowing what to o. — JAME 418:20
overpaid grossly o. — HERB 383:9
O., overfed, oversexed — TRIN 798:19
overrated O., if you ask me — MILN 528:12
overrule threaten to o. him — PAXM 589:8
oversexed o., and over here — TRIN 798:19
overstated save by being o. — BERL 70:5
overthrown o. some of you — BIBL 92:7
overwhelm o. Myself in poesy — KEAT 445:10
overwrought Spirits o. — WORD 849:12
oves Inter o. — MISS 540:1
Ovid O. has sweetly — MONT 543:21
Venus clerk O. — CHAU 212:21

ovo *Ab o.* HORA 403:7
owe o. God a death SHAK 692:9
  O. no man anything BIBL 106:31
owed so much o. by so many to so few
  CHUR 221:10
owest o. God a death SHAK 691:7
oweth woman o. to her husband
  SHAK 718:16
owl bought an O. LEAR 477:9
  fat greedy o. RICH 647:9
  He respects O. MILN 527:18
  mousing o. SHAK 705:15
  O. and the Pussy-Cat LEAR 477:15
  O., and the Waverley pen ADVE 8:17
  o. does to the moon complain GRAY 361:1
  o., for all his feathers KEAT 442:15
  o., for all his feathers OPEN 575:14
  o. of Minerva HEGE 379:8
  o. of Minerva PAUL 589:5
  o. that is in the desert BOOK 140:18
  o. that shrieked SHAK 704:20
  sings the staring o. SHAK 702:26
owlet o. Atheism COLE 231:17
owls companion to o. BIBL 83:18
  couch when o. do cry SHAK 719:6
  court for o. BIBL 89:8
  eagle among blinking o. SHEL 729:20
  TWO BLACK O. TELE 776:4
  Two O. and a Hen LEAR 477:3
own All by my o.-alone HARR 374:3
  at least it is my o. MUSS 555:8
  but mine o. SHAK 682:7
  his o. received him not BIBL 102:20
  marked him for his o. WALT 821:4
  money and a room of her o. WOOL 845:6
  my words are my o. CHAR 209:11
  only to those who o. one LIEB 484:10
  recognize his o. ARNA 26:20
  that which is mine o. SHAK 709:2
  To each his o. ANON 21:6
owners if you break o. PROV 628:16
  o. reap the gains COLL 234:19
ownership common o. ANON 19:15
ox brother to the o. MARK 512:8
  eateth grass as an o. BIBL 83:26
  eat straw like the o. BIBL 88:22
  not covet his o. BIBL 78:5
  one o. or one cow ANON 22:10
  o. goeth to the slaughter BIBL 84:5
  o. is treading on my tongue AESC 6:3
  o. to wrath has moved BLAK 119:8
  o. would lurch against the gong
  HEAN 377:22
  roasted Manningtree o. SHAK 690:17
  stalled o. BIBL 84:24
  stalled o. where hate PROV 615:18
oxen breath of the o. HAGG 367:6
  great black o. YEAT 853:15
  hundred pair of o. HOWE 406:2
  Many o. are come about me BOOK 134:28
  Who drives fat o. JOHN 432:16
  with his own o. HORA 400:1
Oxenford Clerk there was of O. CHAU 210:16
Oxford academia in O. AUNG 38:1
  clever men at O. GRAH 358:15
  Half-Way House to Rome, O. PUNC 637:6
  heart was with the O. men LETT 482:7
  in O. made An art DRYD 289:11
  Ipswich and O. SHAK 695:22
  King to O. sent BROW 157:14
  O. has made me insufferable BEER 63:2
  O. is more attractive BAED 47:6
  O. is the last place SALI 664:12
  O. Street, stony-hearted DE Q 264:18
  secret in the O. sense FRAN 333:2
  sends his son to O. STEA 754:13
  stagecoach from London to O. HAZL 377:4
  To O. sent a troop TRAP 798:4
  To the University of O. GIBB 345:12
oxlips o. and the nodding violet SHAK 711:4
Oxonian impertinent, being an O.
  FARQ 315:24
oxygen o. of publicity THAT 787:10

oyster eye that can open an o. WODE 842:21
  first eat an o. SWIF 766:11
  my o. knife HURS 410:14
  o. may be crossed in love SHER 733:11
  world is an o. MILL 527:4
  world's mine o. SHAK 710:13
oysters Poverty and o. DICK 272:2
Ozymandias My name is O. SHEL 730:18

pace Creeps in this petty p. SHAK 707:14
  dance is a measured p. BACO 42:20
  nostra p. DANT 256:11
  not afraid of 'the p.' SURT 764:18
  p. that kills PROV 624:15
  requiescant in p. MISS 540:2
pacem *dona nobis p.* MISS 539:9
paces open an oyster at sixty p. WODE 842:21
pacific repose of a p. station ADAM 1:16
  stared at the P. KEAT 445:6
pacifist quietly p. peaceful WALK 817:11
pacify p. Ireland GLAD 350:14
pack changed the form of the p. TROT 800:18
  p. and label men for God THOM 791:13
  p., and take a train BROO 153:11
  p. the cards BACO 43:28
  p. up your troubles MILI 526:18
  Pay, p., and follow BURT 173:17
  running with the p. BUTL 175:19
  whole p. of you SHAK 721:17
packages small p. PROV 615:14
packaging brilliant p. SMIT 741:15
  my product and her p. RUBI 658:4
packdrill No names, no p. PROV 627:44
packhorses p., And hollow pampered
  jades SHAK 692:1
Paddington Ever weeping P. BLAK 120:8
  London is to P. CANN 189:8
paddle song my p. sings JOHN 423:18
paddling p. palms SHAK 721:25
paddocks Cold as p. HERR 385:15
paddy Come back, P. Reilly FREN 333:15
padlock p.—on her mind PRIO 612:2
  p. on the mind POPE 602:1
  Wedlock is a p. PROV 633:45
paeans laurels to p. CICE 223:13
paene *P. insularum* CATU 202:16
pagan p.—spoiled ZANG 858:2
  P. suckled in a creed outworn WORD 850:22
page allowed P. 3 to develop MURD 554:20
  foot of the first p. SAND 666:5
  p. having an ample marge TENN 778:8
  single p. of our life SAND 665:13
  turn the p. BROW 158:23
pageant all part of life's rich p. MARS 514:11
  p. of his bleeding heart ARNO 28:21
  this insubstantial p. SHAK 719:1
pagoda old Moulmein P. KIPL 454:21
paid attention must be p. MILL 527:5
  Judas was p. POWE 610:1
  p. for this microphone REAG 643:11
  p. the uttermost farthing BIBL 94:27
  we ha' p. in full KIPL 455:18
  well p. that is well satisfied SHAK 709:33
pain After great p. DICK 272:21
  almost to amount to p. HUNT 410:9
  any more p. BIBL 114:17
  beneath the aromatic p. WINC 841:9
  born in one another's p. THOM 791:6
  cost Ceres all that p. MILT 532:29
  cures all p. CLAR 224:7
  Eternal P. ARNO 27:21
  feel no p. ANON 16:17
  gain, not p. OXFO 581:10
  general drama of p. HARD 371:20
  hark—what p. ARNO 27:20
  I have no p., dear mother FARM 315:5
  intermission of p. SELD 676:10
  intoxication with p. BRON 152:7
  Joy always came after p. APOL 23:14
  long grief and p. TENN 782:2
  more joy than p. EURI 312:11
  my life's a p. DAVI 258:9

  never inflicts p. NEWM 560:16
  no greater p. DANT 255:18
  No p., no gain PROV 628:1
  No p., no palm PENN 591:15
  obligation is a p. JOHN 425:21
  Of p., darkness and cold BROW 161:2
  old age and p. sneak up VIRG 814:19
  Our Lady of P. SWIN 768:17
  p. and anguish wring the brow SCOT 673:24
  p. and grief BOOK 136:3
  p. of a new idea BAGE 48:24
  p. shall not be inflicted SPEN 750:6
  p. to the bear MACA 498:22
  physics p. SHAK 705:8
  pleasure after p. DRYD 287:15
  Pride feels no p. PROV 629:39
  redress Of all my p. WYAT 852:3
  rest from p. DRYD 288:24
  rose in aromatic p. POPE 604:27
  she hasn't a p. MILN 528:4
  sure she felt no p. BROW 160:25
  tender for another's p. GRAY 361:11
  to another's p. COWP 248:3
  travaileth in p. BIBL 106:20
  turns to pleasing p. SPEN 751:29
  vigil and all the p. SWIN 767:25
  with no p. KEAT 444:27
  without one p. TENN 781:13
  With some p. is fraught SHEL 731:29
painful p. as the other BACO 44:3
  p. pleasure SPEN 751:29
painkiller most natural p. LAST 473:4
pains capacity for taking p. PROV 620:35
  let our p. be less BROM 152:4
  Marriage has many p. JOHN 426:1
  no gains without p. STEV 758:13
  p. a man when 'tis kept close SUCK 763:6
  p. of hell BOOK 142:5
  pleasure in poetic p. COWP 247:29
  turned round in whirl of p. JAIN 416:5
paint can't pick it up, p. it MILI 526:10
  flinging a pot of p. RUSK 659:9
  I p. with my prick MISQ 538:3
  only showed the p. DRYD 288:7
  p. 'em truest ADDI 4:7
  p. my own reality KAHL 441:2
  p. objects as I think them PICA 595:7
  p. on the face of Existence BYRO 184:6
  p. the lily SHAK 699:10
  p. the meadows SHAK 702:25
  p. too much direct from nature GAUG 340:23
  price of the p. VAN 807:2
  should not p. the chair MUNC 554:9
  throws aside his p.-pots HORA 398:5
  wife needs no p. PROV 616:4
painted black as he is p. PROV 617:33
  fears a p. devil SHAK 705:2
  idle as a p. ship COLE 232:19
  Lift not the p. veil SHEL 731:19
  p. child of dirt POPE 602:31
  p. clay SHAK 715:5
  p. cunningly SPEN 751:16
  p. her face BIBL 82:13
  p. meadow ADDI 4:21
  p. on the wall BROW 160:9
  p. to look like iron BISM 118:3
  p. to the eyes DOBS 278:17
  took the p. thing BOCC 125:2
painter Farewell, great p. EPIT 309:6
  great sculptor or p. RUSK 659:10
  I am a p. SCHW 672:11
  I, too, am a p. CORR 243:17
  paintbrush in hands of p. PICA 595:3
  ranks far below the p. LEON 481:8
  scenes made me a p. CONS 241:6
  tea-tray p. BLUN 124:9
painters Good p. imitate nature CERV 205:18
  P. and poets HORA 397:20
painting amateur p. in water-colour
  STEV 759:23
  chapel I was p. MICH 524:3
  essence of p. MOND 542:19
  How vain p. is PASC 587:5

light is to p. BOUR 147:12
marvellous p. BACO 47:4
no matter what you're p. HOCK 391:6
p. and punctuality GAIN 337:14
P. became everything BROW 154:19
P. is saying 'Ta' SPEN 750:17
P. is silent poetry SIMO 738:7
p. not made to decorate PICA 595:4
poem is like a p. HORA 398:16
rudder of p. LEON 481:5
teachers of the Art of P. DÜRE 293:3
paintings I have heard of your p.
SHAK 686:16
p. can come to life CHAM 206:16
paints God the scenery HART 374:13
pair Sleep on Blest p. MILT 533:9
Take a p. of sparkling eyes GILB 347:6
palace Be thine own p. DONN 281:21
chalice from the p. FILM 320:15
if his p. were in flames GODW 352:3
keepeth his p. BIBL 100:28
Love in a p. KEAT 444:1
p. and a prison on each hand BYRO 179:3
p. for a hermitage SHAK 716:1
p. is more than a house COLE 234:5
p. is not safe DISR 278:5
straw cottage to a p. turns DYER 293:15
palaces dragons in their pleasant p.
BIBL 88:23
gorgeous p. SHAK 719:1
pleasures and p. PAYN 589:12
plenteousness with thy p. BOOK 142:19
saw in sleep old p. SHEL 730:9
paladin starry p. BROW 161:14
Palaeozoic In the P. time SMIT 742:11
palate P., the hutch of tasty lust
HOPK 396:15
steps down the p. OPEN 574:32
pale behold a p. horse BIBL 113:14
bond Which keeps me p. SHAK 706:1
P. as thy smock SHAK 714:27
P., beyond porch and portal SWIN 768:15
p. contented sort of discontent KEAT 444:2
p. fire she snatches SHAK 719:12
P. grew thy cheek BYRO 183:22
P. hands I loved HOPE 396:8
p.—is yet of gold CRAB 249:10
P. prime-roses SHAK 722:6
p., unripened beauties ADDI 4:10
p. young curate GILB 349:6
pink pills for p. people ADVE 7:20
turned p. SOUT 749:16
whiter shade of p. REID 644:16
Why so p. and wan SUCK 763:4
world grew p. JOHN 426:18
palely Alone and p. loitering KEAT 443:23
p. loitering OPEN 575:8
Palestine establishment in P. BALF 51:5
P. is the cement ARAF 24:2
To sweeten P. RUME 658:6
paletot Mon p. aussi RIMB 649:9
paling piece-bright p. HOPK 397:6
Palladium P. of all the civil JUNI 438:15
pallida P. Mors HORA 400:5
Palliser Plantagenet P. TROL 799:5
pallor of girls' brows OWEN 581:3
palls everything p. ANON 21:4
palm bear the p. alone SHAK 696:8
has won it bear the p. MOTT 552:14
have an itching p. SHAK 698:13
No pain, no p. PENN 591:15
p. at the end STEV 758:2
Turner's p. as itchy SCOT 674:25
winning the p. HORA 398:20
win the p. MARV 515:14
palmae sine pulvere p. HORA 398:20
palmerworm p. hath left BIBL 92:1
palms other p. are won WORD 848:15
p. before my feet CHES 215:25
p. of her hands BIBL 82:16
palmy most high and p. state SHAK 683:16
palpable poem should be p. MACL 503:8
very p. hit SHAK 689:9

paltry aged man is but a p. thing YEAT 855:9
Pam P., I adore you BETJ 72:15
pampered p. jades MARL 513:26
pan great god P. BROW 158:2
P. did after Syrinx speed MARV 515:15
panachaea p., or polygony SPEN 751:28
panache Mon p. ROST 656:12
Pancras P. and Kentish-town BLAK 120:10
pancreas adorable p. KERR 450:3
pandemonium P., the high capital
MILT 531:28
Pandora open that P.'s Box BEVI 74:5
P.'s box BURG 165:14
panem P. et circenses JUVE 440:7
pange P., lingua FORT 330:3
P., lingua THOM 788:15
pangs bitter p. SOUT 749:23
free of any p. CURT 254:7
panic p.'s in thy breastie BURN 172:20
wonderful p. HECH 379:1
Panjandrum grand P. himself FOOT 328:6
panoramic p. view of hell BYRO 180:16
pans If ifs and ands were pots and p.
PROV 622:48
pansies p., that's for thoughts SHAK 688:12
pansy p. at my feet WORD 848:4
pantaloon lean and slippered p. SHAK 681:12
panteth As the hart p. BOOK 136:11
panther Black P. Party NEWT 561:8
panting For ever p. KEAT 444:11
p. heart of Rome WISE 842:2
pants As p. the hart TATE 773:12
deck your lower limbs in p. NASH 557:18
in fast thick p. COLE 232:4
Panzer P.-man, panzer-man PLAT 596:20
papa word P., besides DICK 269:24
papacy p. is not other HOBB 391:1
paper All reactionaries are p. tigers
MAO 511:13
all the earth were p. LYLY 497:5
at a piece of tissue p. RUTH 661:19
built a p.-mill SHAK 694:23
By the evening p. MACN 504:17
he hath not eat p. SHAK 702:16
keep the p. work down ORTO 576:17
no more personality than a p. cup
CHAN 207:12
only a p. moon HARB 371:2
p. appears dull STEE 754:20
p. from the outside world KENO 449:14
p. hats and wooden swords USTI 806:5
plays with on unastonishing p. FANT 314:14
ran the p. for propaganda BEAV 60:14
scrap of p. BETH 72:1
sheet of p. SAUS 668:3
virtue of p. government BURK 166:17
worth the p. it is written on GOLD 356:5
papers He's got my p. PINT 595:15
reads p. FRIS 334:21
turns over your p. LAVA 470:13
what I read in the p. ROGE 652:19
Papist P., yet a Calvinist EPIT 310:7
parable open my mouth in a p. BOOK 139:7
parachutes Minds are like p. DEWA 266:11
parade life might be put on a p. EULA 312:10
p. of riches SMIT 741:7
parades produce victory p. HOBS 391:4
Paradise enjoy P. BECK 61:30
pass through P. COLE 233:19
paradise admit them to P. KORA 461:4
blundered into P. THOM 791:13
cannot catch the bird of p. KHRU 451:5
driven out of P. KAFK 440:17
drunk the milk of P. COLE 232:8
eastern side beheld Of P. MILT 534:14
gadget-filled p. NIEB 563:16
Gates of P. BLAK 120:4
keys of P. DE Q 264:20
moment spent in P. SCHI 670:25
P. by way of Kensal Green CHES 216:11
P. of exiles SHEL 729:16
P. of Fools MILT 532:20
p. of four seas MARV 516:5

p. of women PROV 618:42
p. within thee MILT 534:12
paved p. MITC 540:10
rudiments of P. SOUT 748:14
weave A p. KEAT 443:5
wilderness is p. enow FITZ 323:2
with me in p. BIBL 102:6
paradises true p. are PROU 613:14
paradox Man is an embodied p. COLT 236:11
paragon p. of animals SHAK 685:24
parallel North of the 49th p. ADAM 3:12
p. in the world above ZOHA 859:1
so truly p. MARV 515:11
parallelograms Princess of P. BYRO 184:1
parameters five free p. GAMO 339:1
paranoid Only the p. survive GROV 365:8
parapets of the ancient p. RIMB 649:8
parasites p. or sub-parasites JONS 435:17
parcelled hardships p. within them
BOLA 126:1
parcere P. subiectis et debellare VIRG 812:15
parch sun doth p. the green SURR 764:6
parchment should be made p. SHAK 694:21
parcus P. deorum cultor HORA 400:19
pardlike p. Spirit SHEL 728:20
pardon Alas but cannot p. AUDE 36:10
Bretful of p. CHAU 211:1
God may p. you ELIZ 304:12
God will p. me LAST 471:9
kiss of the sun for p. GURN 365:20
Offenders never p. PROV 628:18
P. all BUCK 163:11
p. and peace BOOK 130:18
P. me boy GORD 356:18
p., who have done the wrong DRYD 288:1
With a thousand Ta's and P.'s BETJ 72:13
pardoned praised than to be p. JONS 436:8
pardoning p. our offences BOOK 132:3
pardons P. him AUDE 35:7
parens king is truly p. patriae JAME 417:4
parent kind p. to man PLIN 598:3
lose one p. WILD 835:16
one child makes you a p. FROS 335:5
p. of settlement BURK 167:8
p. who could see his boy LEAC 476:12
put any p. mad FLEM 326:11
smile for your p. VIRG 814:4
parenthood means valuing p. TOYN 797:9
parents begin by loving their p. WILD 836:24
bondage to p. WOLL 844:8
girl needs good p. TUCK 802:2
Jewish man with p. alive ROTH 656:18
joys of p. BACO 45:4
judgment of your p. UPDI 805:19
lost to his p. BOWI 148:11
Of p. good SHAK 693:11
only illegitimate p. GLAD 350:8
Our p.' age HORA 401:19
P. can plant magic MACN 505:3
P. love their children AUCT 34:14
p. obey their children EDWA 296:13
p. take more care CAVE 204:5
p. were the Lord knows who DEFO 261:26
produce bad p. MORS 550:17
sacrifice and p.' tears MILT 531:24
sharp and severe p. GREY 364:4
stranger to one of your p. AUST 39:23
sue its p. WATS 822:19
parentum Aetas p. HORA 401:19
parfit verray, p. gentil knyght CHAU 210:7
paries p. cum proximus ardet HORA 399:15
Paris after they've seen P. LEWI 483:18
astonish P. with an apple CÉZA 206:2
Down and out in P. ORWE 577:5
go to P. APPL 23:14
Is P. burning HITL 390:4
king had given me P. ANON 21:2
last time I saw P. HAMM 370:4
P. is a movable feast HEMI 381:6
P. vaut bien une messe HENR 382:1
P. was French—and silent TUCH 802:1
poverty and P. SCHI 668:13
they go to P. WILD 836:20

Paris (cont.):
when they die go to P. — PROV 621:4
without me P. would be taken — ANON 20:13
parish all the world as my p. — WESL 829:17
p. of rich women — AUDE 35:3
pension from his p. — RUSK 660:6
park come out to the ball p. — BERR 71:9
gentleman's p. — CONS 241:7
p., a policeman — CHAP 208:5
Poisoning pigeons in the p. — LEHR 479:10
wandering round a stately p. — MAUG 518:14
within the new p. wall — DUFF 291:5
parking put up a p. lot — MITC 540:10
parks p. are the lungs of London — PITT 596:9
parles their treasonous p. — BROW 160:6
parley-voo Hinky, dinky, p. — MILI 526:14
parliament build your House of P. — WELL 828:5
crop-headed P. — BROW 160:5
enables P. to do things — SHAW 725:26
Irishmen in her P. — BALF 51:4
minuet danced by P. — SCAR 668:10
Mob, P., Rabble — COBB 229:18
[p.] a lot of hard-faced men — BALD 50:12
p. can do any thing — PEMB 591:12
P. itself would not exist — SCAR 668:9
P. of man — TENN 780:20
P. speaking through reporters — CARL 192:17
Scots p. — JOHN 433:23
Scottish P. — EWIN 313:10
Scottish p. — SALM 665:8
shall be a Scottish p. — ANON 19:10
shall be a Scottish p. — DEWA 266:9
united P. — FLET 326:22
parliamentarian safe pleasure for a p. — CRIT 251:10
parliamentary old P. hand — GLAD 351:2
p. eloquence — CARL 192:19
parliaments mother of P. — BRIG 151:11
parlour party in a p. — WORD 848:21
walk into my p. — HOWI 406:6
Parnassus my chief P. be — SIDN 736:10
Parnell Poor P. — JOYC 437:8
parochial he was p. — JAME 417:20
parody devil's walking p. — CHES 215:24
parole p. of literary men — JOHN 431:25
paroles confuses p. — BAUD 58:13
n'emploient les p. — VOLT 815:13
parrot This is a late p. — MONT 546:7
pars Et quorum p. magna fui — VIRG 811:10
parsley P. seed goes nine — PROV 629:15
parsnips butter no p. — PROV 620:5
parson If P. lost his senses — HODG 391:10
p. knows enough — COWP 248:19
P. left off conjuring — SELD 676:8
Whig in a p.'s gown — JOHN 427:3
parsons merriment of p. — JOHN 431:23
p. are the happiest men alive — LLOY 487:10
P. are very like men — CHES 214:22
p. do not care for truth — STUB 762:19
part chosen that good p. — BIBL 100:27
death p. thee and me — BIBL 80:2
every man must play a p. — SHAK 708:20
friends must p. — PROV 615:12
Friends p. forever — BASH 57:22
had but known one p. — SANA 665:12
if we were ever to p. — KIER 451:7
I was a major p. — VIRG 811:10
leaves behind a p. of oneself — HARA 370:20
let us kiss and p. — DRAY 285:23
more willingly p. withal — SHAK 685:20
My soul, bear thou thy p. — GURN 366:4
p. at last without a kiss — MORR 549:16
p. my garments — BOOK 135:2
p. to tear a cat in — SHAK 710:21
take your own p. — BORR 145:13
we know in p. — BIBL 107:25
What isn't p. of ourselves — HESS 387:9
parted Mine never shall be p. — MILT 534:3
When we two p. — BYRO 183:22
parterre nod on the p. — POPE 603:14
Parthians P., and Medes — BIBL 104:27
partial We grow more p. — POPE 603:16

partiality neither anger nor p. — TACI 770:7
particles names of all these p. — FERM 317:2
p. of light — BLAK 121:17
particular bright p. star — SHAK 678:7
Did nothing in p. — GILB 347:15
London p. . . . . A fog — DICK 267:14
particulars generals than in p. — HUME 409:3
in minute p. — BLAK 120:12
parties Like other p. — BYRO 184:7
P. must ever exist — BURK 166:28
p. 'playing politics' — WILS 840:15
warns the heads of p. — ARBU 24:5
parting Ere the p. hour go by — ARNO 27:17
In every p. — ELIO 300:17
P. is all we know — DICK 273:5
p. is such sweet sorrow — SHAK 717:29
p. of the ways — BIBL 91:15
p. was to die — TENN 779:20
rive not more in p. — SHAK 679:21
Speed the p. guest — POPE 605:15
this p. was well made — SHAK 698:23
partir P. c'est mourir un peu — HARA 370:20
partisan inferior man is p. — CONF 237:13
partitions thin p. — DRYD 286:21
partly Living and p. living — ELIO 302:23
partners change p. — BERL 69:16
partridge Always p. — ANON 21:3
p. sitteth on eggs — BIBL 91:4
parts above its p. — ARIS 25:12
dignified p. — BAGE 47:14
naming of p. — REED 644:3
P. of it are excellent — PUNC 637:24
p. of one stupendous whole — POPE 604:29
plays many p. — SHAK 681:9
refreshes the p. — ADVE 7:29
save all the p. — EHRL 297:7
sum of the p. — ANON 20:3
want of p. — JOHN 429:9
parturient P. montes — HORA 398:8
party Collapse of Stout P. — ANON 15:11
conduct of a losing p. — BURK 166:2
curse to p.-strife — WORD 846:9
educate our p. — DISR 276:3
Giving a p. — STRU 762:18
I believe that without a — DISR 276:7
in the p. manifestoes — ROTH 656:21
master of the P. — HEAL 377:13
nasty p. — MAY 519:6
natural p. of government — WILS 840:8
nature of a political p. — TROL 800:5
none was for a p. — MACA 499:15
Not a select p. — KEAT 447:3
not p. men — NEWM 560:13
office p. is not — WHIT 832:18
p. in a parlour — WORD 848:21
p. is but a kind of conspiracy — HALI 369:3
p. is like a marriage — MCIN 502:15
P. is organized opinion — DISR 275:20
p. not to be brought down — HAIL 367:13
p. of order or stability — MILL 525:8
p.'s over — COMD 236:14
p.'s over — CROS 252:12
P.-spirit, which at best is — POPE 606:18
p. which comes nearest — BAGE 49:5
p. which takes credit — MORR 550:15
passion and p. — COLE 234:8
political p. in power — SCAR 668:10
proud of my p. — JACK 415:2
save the P. we love — GAIT 337:17
sooner every p. breaks up — AUST 38:20
spirit of p. — WASH 822:9
Stick to your p. — DISR 277:36
stupidest p. — MILL 525:4
voted all my p.'s call — GILB 348:23
Whichever p. is in office — WILS 840:12
parva p. licet componere magnis — VIRG 815:4
pasarán No p. — IBAR 412:8
pass And this, too, shall p. away — SAYI 669:1
bringeth mighty things to p. — BOOK 142:9
Do not p. go — SAYI 669:22
let him p. for a man — SHAK 708:26
let this cup p. — BIBL 99:4
look, and p. on — DANT 255:14

must come to p. — BIBL 98:13
my words shall not p. — BIBL 98:17
O! let him p. — SHAK 702:8
p., and turn again — EMER 306:10
p. by me as the idle wind — SHAK 698:10
p. for forty-three — GILB 349:8
p. in a crowd — SWIF 765:19
p. in the night — LONG 491:7
P. it on — MORR 550:11
p. man's understanding — BOOK 130:14
p. the ammunition — FORG 329:5
P. the mustard — GILB 349:9
p. through this world — GREL 363:11
They shall not p. — IBAR 412:8
They shall not p. — MILI 526:11
with shining foot shall p. — FITZ 323:17
passage fret a p. through — FULL 337:7
long black p. — STEV 760:6
North-west p. — STER 757:8
p. from hand to hand — SICK 735:11
p. which is particularly fine — JOHN 429:24
passages imaginative or domestic p. — KEAT 446:6
passed p. by on the other side — BIBL 100:23
p. the time — BECK 61:20
That p. over — ANON 22:8
Timothy has p. — EPIT 311:9
passengers p. off in small boats — LAST 474:12
passer de laisser p. — QUES 639:6
P. mortuus est — CATU 202:11
passeront Ils ne p. pas — MILI 526:11
passes beauty p. — DE L 262:23
Everything p. — ANON 21:4
Men seldom make p. — PARK 585:16
p. the glory of the world — ANON 22:4
passeth p. all understanding — BIBL 110:7
p. knowledge — BIBL 109:8
passi O p. graviora — VIRG 811:2
passing did but see her p. by — ANON 19:8
p.-bells for these who die — OWEN 581:1
p. brave to be a king — MARL 513:20
p. of a day — SPEN 751:25
p. of the third floor — JERO 421:11
p. the love of women — BIBL 80:29
passion acknowledgement of a p. — KELL 447:21
all p. spent — MILT 535:4
commanding p. — SHER 734:7
consumptive p. — ETHE 312:4
Cows are my p. — DICK 269:10
earthly p. turn — LITT 486:16
eternal monotony of p. — FLAU 325:2
Eternal P. — ARNO 27:21
I have no p. for it — JOHN 428:4
image of p. — BART 57:14
In her first p. — BYRO 180:26
inspire hopeless p. — THAC 786:8
in such a p. about — SHAW 727:29
love was p.'s essence — BYRO 178:26
Man is a useless p. — SART 667:3
most insipid p. — ROCH 651:15
no good if a p. is in you — BLAK 119:13
No p. so effectually — BURK 167:3
of the tender p. — PUSH 638:2
one p. and another — STER 756:9
One p. doth expel another — CHAP 208:15
our p. is our task — JAME 417:23
O well-painted p. — SHAK 714:11
P. always goes — CHAN 207:19
P. and apathy — MILT 532:9
p. and party — COLE 234:8
p. and the power — BYRO 178:17
p. cannot Music raise — DRYD 289:18
p. could not shake — SHAK 714:12
p. for hunting — DICK 271:11
p. for words — MOOR 547:8
p. in the human soul — LILL 484:14
P., I see, is catching — SHAK 697:17
P. makes the world go — ICE- 412:17
p. or interest — LOCK 488:14
p. shall have spent — TENN 780:16
p.'s slave — SHAK 686:26
p. turn into respect — ETHE 312:6

prose and the p. FORS 329:16
remove p. by means of TANT 773:3
ruling p. conquers POPE 603:10
Search then the Ruling P. POPE 603:20
sick of an old p. DOWS 284:6
stubborn with his p. YEAT 853:7
vows his p. is infinite PARK 586:3
With all the p. EPHE 308:5
passionate full of p. intensity YEAT 855:12
passione P. interdum movemur THOM 788:12
passionless hopeless grief is p. BROW 157:25
P.?—no SHEL 731:8
passions acts from the p. DISR 277:5
concentrated p. HARD 372:7
diminishes commonplace p. LA R 469:18
experience of p. VOLT 816:8
his p. were expressed WALP 820:1
inferno of his p. JUNG 438:9
men of like p. BIBL 105:11
moderator of p. WALT 820:19
not his reason, but his p. STER 757:1
one of many p. JOHN 475:14
p. and resolutions HUME 408:15
p. are most like RALE 641:6
p. break not through PALI 584:11
p. come upon men EURI 312:20
p. of his fellow men HORA 401:13
slave of the p. HUME 409:9
two primal p. OSLE 579:6
passive Observation is a p. science BERN 71:1
p. and motionless CANN 189:1
passives Love's p. CRAS 250:8
Passover Christ our p. BIBL 107:11
come to our P. feast HAGG 367:1
it is the Lord's p. BIBL 77:30
passport My p.'s green HEAN 378:1
p. is sometimes asked for BAED 47:8
p. shall be made SHAK 693:22
past always praising the p. SMIT 743:2
atone for our p. CHEK 213:23
break with one's p. history WOOD 844:16
call on p. and future O'NE 573:14
cannot remember the p. SANT 666:8
change the p. AGAT 6:24
dead P. bury its dead LONG 490:20
dealing with the p. GRAS 359:13
deeds of the p. DAVI 259:11
designed to preserve the p. COHE 230:10
dossier on his p. HOWA 405:10
dote on p. achievement HAZL 376:22
funeral of the p. CLAR 224:13
Ghost of Christmas P. DICK 268:4
give me back my p. VIRG 813:4
God cannot alter the p. BUTL 176:22
knowledge of its p. DIEF 274:6
lament the p. BURK 168:3
last day of an era p. YELT 856:14
live p. years again DRYD 287:28
looking forward to the p. OSBO 578:21
Many a woman has a p. WILD 836:6
neither repeat his p. AUDE 36:15
nothing but the p. KEYN 450:14
nothing more than the p. BERG 69:6
p. as a watch BOOK 139:22
p., brittle with relics THOM 791:3
p. is a bucket of ashes SAND 665:21
p. is a foreign country HART 374:19
p. is a foreign country OPEN 575:12
p. is lost CHAP 208:21
p. is secure WEBS 825:10
p. is the only dead thing THOM 790:12
p. never dead FAUL 316:1
p. our dancing days SHAK 717:16
p., present and future EINS 298:9
plan the future by the p. BURK 166:5
Remembrance of things p. BORR 146:15
remembrance of things p. SHAK 723:1
soul of the whole P. CARL 192:13
things long p. SHAK 715:12
Things p. cannot be recalled PROV 632:38
Things p. redress SHAK 715:17
Time present and time p. ELIO 301:9
upon the p. has power DRYD 289:30

Utopia is a blessed p. KISS 457:13
What's p. is prologue SHAK 718:29
Who controls the p. ORWE 577:15
years that are p. BOOK 139:6
pastime take his p. therein BOOK 141:10
pastoral Cold P. KEAT 444:14
practising your p. music VIRG 813:12
pastors p. and teachers BIBL 109:11
P. she sends to help CHUR 219:20
some ungracious p. SHAK 684:16
spiritual p. and masters BOOK 132:16
pasture feed me in a green p. BOOK 135:3
people of his p. BOOK 140:10
sheep of his p. BOOK 140:17
pastures fresh woods, and p. new MILT 530:13
In p. green SCOT 675:4
Pipe me to p. HOPK 396:14
pat Now might I do it p. SHAK 687:16
P.-a-cake NURS 569:1
patch P. grief with proverbs SHAK 712:30
poor potsherd, p. HOPK 397:7
patches king of shreds and p. SHAK 687:27
thing of shreds and p. GILB 347:19
pate beat your p. POPE 602:20
p. of a politician SHAK 688:26
pâté de foie gras eating p. SMIT 744:8
pater P. noster MISS 539:7
paterna buona imagine p. DANT 256:2
P. rura HORA 400:1
paternal disclaim all my p. care SHAK 699:18
kindly p. image DANT 256:2
paternalism lessons of p. CLEV 226:17
paternoster No penny, no p. PROV 628:2
path beaten p. to his door EMER 307:18
Eightfold P. PALI 584:6
in the straight p. KORA 459:8
invisible p. PALI 584:12
long brown p. before me WHIT 833:19
Middle P. PALI 584:4
p. is narrow and difficult UPAN 805:9
p. of gold BROW 160:16
p. of the just BIBL 83:37
p. of true love EWAR 313:6
P. of Wickedness BALL 53:11
rough and thorny p. MONT 544:13
pathetic Is not p. WHIT 833:20
P. Fallacy RUSK 659:13
That's what it is. P. MILN 528:8
too p. for the feelings AUST 38:25
pathless pleasure in the p. woods BYRO 179:17
too much like a p. wood FROS 335:7
Truth is a p. land KRIS 461:18
pathos P., piety, courage FORS 329:21
paths all her p. are peace BIBL 83:35
all her p. are Peace SPRI 753:7
craggy p. of study JONS 435:15
light unto my p. BOOK 142:13
p. of glory GRAY 361:3
So many p. WILC 835:9
Thirty-two wondrous p. SEFE 675:17
pathway p. of a life unnoticed HORA 399:16
patience abuse our p. CICE 223:15
abusing of God's p. SHAK 710:11
aptitude for p. BUFF 163:14
burning p. RIMB 649:10
childhood had taught her p. COLE 234:14
deed, and eek hire p. CHAU 211:4
habits of peace and p. WALT 820:19
Have p., heart HOME 394:18
laughed him into p. SHAK 679:12
my p. is now at an end HITL 390:3
p., and shuffle the cards CERV 205:14
p. have her perfect work BIBL 111:18
P. is a virtue PROV 629:16
p. of Job BIBL 111:30
p. on a monument SHAK 720:29
p. to appreciate SANT 666:9
p. under their sufferings BOOK 129:19
p. will achieve BURK 167:26
pattern of all p. SHAK 700:18
preached up p. PRIO 612:6

preacheth p. HERB 383:22
patient fury of a p. man DRYD 287:11
kill the p. BACO 44:16
not so p. SHAK 691:25
P. continuance BIBL 106:1
P. endurance attains all TERE 785:18
p. etherized upon a table ELIO 302:12
p. etherized upon a table LEWI 483:9
patiently take it p. BIBL 112:8
waited p. for the Lord BOOK 136:6
patients hurry his p. along MOLI 542:5
poets are their own p. THOM 790:24
patines p. of bright gold SHAK 710:3
patria Died some, pro p. POUN 608:20
pro p. mori HORA 401:12
sed pro p. NEWB 560:4
patriarchal wi' p. grace BURN 170:22
patrician This is the P. DONN 282:6
patrie enfants de la p. ROUG 657:1
patries Europe des p. DE G 262:7
patrimony all his p. SABA 662:7
patriot honest p., in the full tide JEFF 420:2
p. of the world CANN 189:5
p. yet, but was a fool DRYD 287:10
Such is the p.'s boast GOLD 355:11
patriotism knock the p. out of the human race SHAW 727:7
larger p. ROSE 654:19
no Canadian p. BOUR 147:9
P. in the female sex ADAM 1:18
P. is a lively sense ALDI 10:11
P. is not enough CAVE 204:1
P. is the last refuge JOHN 430:6
p. run amok RATH 642:12
That kind of p. GASK 340:20
patriots all these country p. BYRO 177:21
blood of p. JEFF 419:15
P. are in the right WAUG 824:13
So to be p. BURK 168:11
True p. we CART 196:23
patron not a P., my Lord JOHN 427:18
p., and the jail JOHN 426:16
P. Commonly a wretch JOHN 424:13
patronage private p. ALBE 10:6
patrons great p. LUTY 496:16
patter rapid, unintelligible p. GILB 349:5
pattern Art is the imposing of a p. WHIT 832:14
Made him our p. BROW 160:3
p. informed by sensibility READ 643:2
p. in most lives WELD 827:4
p. of all patience SHAK 700:18
p. of the world BACO 46:5
shewed as a p. SWIF 765:8
trace the p. WOOL 845:4
web, then, or the p. STEV 758:25
patterns weaves algebraic p. LOVE 493:1
What are p. for LOWE 493:17
paucity p. of human pleasures JOHN 433:15
Paul If Saint P.'s day be fair PROV 623:3
with St P. are literary ARNO 30:2
Pauli P. [exclusion] principle GAMO 338:18
pauper He's only a p. NOEL 565:7
pauperiem Duramque callet p. HORA 402:17
paupertas infelix p. JUVE 439:16
pause dull it is to p. TENN 784:15
eine kleine P. LAST 473:8
I p. for a reply SHAK 697:20
p. in the day's occupations LONG 490:3
pauses happy p. BACO 46:6
p. between the notes SCHN 671:12
paved p. paradise MITC 540:10
streets are p. with gold COLM 236:1
pavement P. slippery ROBI 650:21
riches of heaven's p. MILT 531:25
pavilioned P. in splendour GRAN 359:3
paving lawned areas with p. OFFI 572:15
paw ear on its p. MAYA 519:8
pawn you p. your intelligence CUMM 253:7
pax in terra p. MISS 536:16
P. Domini MISS 539:8
P. Vobis BIBL 115:13
'P. vobiscum' will answer all SCOT 674:13

pay cannot p., let him pray PROV 621:44
Can't p., won't pay POLI 600:12
Crime doesn't p. PROV 617:17
devil to p. ANON 16:5
Equal P. ANTH 23:5
I can p. for the damage CLOU 227:20
No cure, no p. PROV 627:37
Not a penny off the p. COOK 241:16
p. any price KENN 448:16
p. at the Greek Kalends AUGU 37:23
P. beforehand PROV 629:17
p. for by one and one KIPL 455:21
P. given to a state hireling JOHN 424:14
p. glad life's arrears BROW 161:2
P., pack, and follow BURT 173:17
p. the blood price BLAI 119:1
p. us, pass us CHES 216:12
saved the sum of things for p. HOUS 404:1
sharper spur than p. GAY 341:26
two-thirds of a nation p. VOLT 816:16
unless you mean to p. them PROV 631:15
we are made to p. for FRIE 334:15
We won't p. FO 327:21
wonders what's to p. HOUS 403:23
paycock mornin' 'til night like a p.
O'CA 571:7
paying P. the Dane-geld KIPL 456:4
price well worth p. LAMO 465:17
payment passes for current p. BURN 169:20
pays Mon p. ce n'est pas un pays VIGN 810:5
p. the piper PROV 622:13
third time p. for all PROV 632:41
You p. your money PROV 636:8
You p. your money PUNC 637:5
PC P. is the LSD of the '90s LEAR 477:23
pea beautiful p.-green. boat LEAR 477:15
picking up a p. WELL 828:6
she had felt the p. ANDE 14:3
peace all her paths are p. BIBL 83:35
all her paths are P. SPRI 753:7
arch of p. morticed NICO 563:10
author of p. BOOK 128:12
banished p. SMOL 744:18
belong unto thy p. BIBL 101:31
blessing of p. BOOK 135:17
by judgement, and by p. TALM 772:1
call it p. TACI 770:3
came not to send p. BIBL 96:19
chastisement of our p. BIBL 90:3
[Christ] came and preached p. BIBL 109:5
cowardice keeps us in p. JOHN 431:9
exacts for granting p. EARH 294:21
for p. like retarded pygmies PEAR 590:11
Give p. a chance LENN 480:18
goods are in p. BIBL 100:28
good war, or a bad p. FRAN 332:8
Had Zimri p. BIBL 82:14
hard and bitter p. KENN 448:15
haunt of ancient P. TENN 782:21
have you known p. WEST 830:9
his p. and quiet SHAK 713:21
I find to p. PETR 593:18
If you want p. VEGE 808:9
I labour for p. BOOK 142:15
Imperishable p. HOUS 404:5
ingeminate the word P. CLAR 224:17
In His will is our p. DANT 256:11
inordinate demand for p. PEEL 590:17
In p.; goodwill CHUR 222:13
In p. there's nothing SHAK 693:4
instrument of Your p. FRAN 332:6
interest that keeps p. CROM 252:4
In the arts of p. SHAW 726:10
into the way of p. BIBL 99:33
in what p. a Christian can die LAST 473:16
Joy. P. PASC 587:17
just and lasting p. LINC 485:12
kneel for p. SHAK 718:17
lasting p. —cannot be secured LULA 496:5
lay me down in p. BOOK 133:25
Let p. fill our heart KUMA 462:4
Let us have p. GRAN 359:7

Let war yield to p. CICE 223:13
Love of p. COLL 235:15
loving p. and pursuing peace HILL 389:2
luxury, p. BAUD 58:14
Make it a green p. DARN 256:18
makes a good p. HERB 385:6
make your p. with authority MORR 550:9
may not be a just p. IZET 414:14
mountains also shall bring p. BOOK 138:22
My p. is gone GOET 352:20
never stable p. COTT 244:8
news and Prince of P. FLET 327:13
no p. unto the wicked BIBL 89:26
Nor p. within SHEL 731:22
Nor shall this p. sleep SHAK 695:25
no such thing as inner p. LEBO 478:6
not a p. treaty FOCH 327:23
no way to p. MUST 555:14
on earth p. BIBL 100:4
Open covenants of p. WILS 841:1
ordered ways upon a state of p. VIRG 812:15
Over all the mountain tops is p. GOET 353:10
pardon and p. BOOK 130:18
p. above all earthly dignities SHAK 695:13
p. and propagation WALP 819:12
p. at the last NEWM 561:2
P. been as a river BIBL 89:25
P. be to this house BOOK 133:13
P. between equals WILS 840:20
P. be unto you BIBL 115:13
P. Built on complacency GAUN 341:1
p. cannot be maintained RUSS 661:13
P., commerce JEFF 420:3
p. for our time CHAM 206:12
p. from freedom MALC 508:11
peaceful sloth, Not p. MILT 532:2
P. hath her victories MILT 535:11
p. I hope with honour DISR 276:17
P. I leave with you BIBL 103:32
p. in our time BOOK 128:11
p. in Shelley's mind SHEL 732:2
p. is a dream MOLT 542:17
P. is a very apoplexy SHAK 682:21
P. is indivisible LITV 487:3
P. is in the grave SHEL 731:3
P. is much more precious SADA 662:13
P. is poor reading HARD 371:14
'P.! it is I.' ANAT 13:19
P. its ten thousands PORT 607:21
P., n. In international affairs BIER 116:7
P. nothing but slovenliness BREC 150:7
p. of God BIBL 110:7
p. of God JAME 417:6
p. of Jerusalem BOOK 142:19
p. of the double-bed CAMP 187:2
p. of thine ARNO 27:15
p. of wild things BERR 71:12
P. on earth WESL 828:23
p. on the earth SEAR 675:8
P., order, and good government ANON 18:8
P.! Peace! Peace UPAN 805:4
P., perfect peace BICK 115:23
P., retrenchment, and reform BRIG 151:9
P., the human dress BLAK 122:3
p. there may be in silence EHRM 297:9
P. to corrupt MILT 534:10
P. to him that is far off BIBL 90:13
'P. upon earth!' was said HARD 372:11
p. which the world cannot give
BOOK 128:19
p. will guide the planets RADO 640:12
p. with honour CHAM 206:12
P. without Joy BUCH 162:17
people want p. so much EISE 298:16
plunging into a cold p. YELT 856:15
poor, and mangled P. SHAK 694:4
potent advocates of p. GEOR 343:9
prefers a negative p. KING 452:2
Prince of P. WESL 828:24
publisheth p. BIBL 89:28
righteousness and p. BOOK 130:19
rust in p. SOUT 748:15
seek p., and ensue it BOOK 135:25

servant depart in p. BIBL 100:6
sing The merry songs of p. SHAK 695:24
So enamoured on p. CLAR 224:18
soft phrase of p. SHAK 713:6
speak p. unto nation REND 645:7
tell me p. has broken out BREC 150:11
than to make p. CLEM 226:12
that we may live in p. ARIS 25:17
there is no p. BIBL 90:26
thousand years of p. TENN 779:24
time of p. BIBL 85:32
time of p. SHAK 716:21
universal p. TENN 777:7
want p., prepare for war PROV 623:25
war and p. in 21st century KOHL 459:2
War is p. ORWE 577:14
we cannot speak of p. BRAN 149:15
What hast thou to do with p. BIBL 82:11
White P. FANS 314:11
peaceably living p. BIBL 93:32
p. if we can CLAY 226:2
so p. ordered BOOK 130:13
peaceful made this p. life for us VIRG 813:13
quietly pacifist p. WALK 817:11
peacefully p. towards its close DAWS 259:19
peacemakers Blessed are the p. BIBL 94:20
peach dare to eat a p. ELIO 302:20
Last-supper-carved-on-a-p.-stone
LANC 465:21
nectarine, and curious p. MARV 515:16
woolly p. JONS 436:6
peaches What p. GINS 349:17
peacock Eyed like a p. KEAT 443:30
mornin' 'til night like a p. O'CA 571:7
pride of the p. BLAK 121:5
peacocks apes, and p. BIBL 81:13
p. and lilies RUSK 659:25
peak small things from the p. CHES 217:1
peal night's yawning p. SHAK 705:22
peanuts hate it as much as p. WELL 827:9
pay p., get monkeys PROV 623:20
pear And a golden p. NURS 567:11
Here we go round the prickly p. ELIO 302:7
pearl barbaric p. and gold MILT 531:29
orient p. MARL 513:1
p. in every cowslip's ear SHAK 710:28
p. of great price BIBL 97:6
splendid p. SEXT 677:15
threw a p. away SHAK 714:30
Too rich a p. BUTL 176:14
pearls Give p. away HOUS 404:10
He who would search for p. DRYD 287:21
p. before swine BIBL 95:14
p. fetch a high price WHAT 831:11
p. roll in all directions ORCH 576:6
p. that were his eyes SHAK 718:27
p. upon an Ethiop's arm DYER 293:17
p. were strung JAME 417:18
throw p. to swine PROV 618:5
to sea for p. SMAR 739:15
pears Walnuts and p. PROV 633:39
Pearse Tom P. BALL 53:20
Pearsean P. ghost in the eye O'BR 571:2
peartree p. leaves and blooms HOPK 397:1
peasan toe of the p. SHAK 688:27
peasant P. and a philosopher JOHN 428:24
rogue and p. slave SHAK 686:2
peasantry p. its pack animal TROT 800:18
p., their country's pride GOLD 354:10
peasants cricket with their p. TREV 798:11
p. now Resign their pipes CRAB 249:16
pease P. porridge hot NURS 569:2
pebble smoother p. NEWT 561:16
wise man hide a p. CHES 216:24
pebbles leviathan retrieving p. WELL 828:6
peccata p. mundi MISS 539:9
peccator Esto p. LUTH 496:7
peccavi P.—I have Sindh WINK 841:18
p. nimis cogitatione MISS 536:14
pecker p. in my pocket JOHN 423:15
pectora non mortalia p. cogis VIRG 811:22
peculiar Chosen and made p. ground
WATT 823:14

Funny-p. or funny ha-ha HAY 376:3
p. people BIBL 112:5
pecunia *P. non olet* VESP 809:6
pecuniary immense p. mangle DICK 272:14
pedant apothegmatical P. NASH 557:19
pedantic garden with p. weeds CARE 190:12
too p. for a gentleman CONG 238:27
pedantry P. is the dotage JACK 415:3
pedants learned p. much affect BUTL 175:22
peddle no shoddier than what they p. BECK 61:7
pede *nunc p. libero* HORA 400:20
pederasty Not flagellation, not p. RATT 642:14
pedestrians two classes of p. DEWA 266:12
pedigree languages are the p. JOHN 427:2
pee P., po, belly, bum, drawers FLAN 324:17
peel orange p. picked out RALE 641:19
p. me a grape WEST 830:3
peep Nevermore to p. again DE L 262:25
p. at such a world COWP 248:7
peepers where you get them p MERC 522:9
peeping sun Came p. in at morn HOOD 395:3
peepshow ticket for the p. MACN 504:15
peer hath not left his p. MILT 529:30
many a p. of England HOUS 405:2
murdered p. ALCO 10:8
p. is exalted PAIN 582:17
reluctant p. BENN 66:17
peerage p., or Westminster Abbey NELS 558:13
should study the P. WILD 836:26
When I want a p. NORT 565:15
peerless Buddha, p. among men PALI 583:18
Here lies that p. paper peer EPIT 310:5
unveiled her p. light MILT 533:5
peers *flattery of one's p.* LODG 489:7
House of P. GILB 347:15
judgement of his p. MAGN 506:4
Lord in the P. BROU 154:10
peewees p. crying STEV 760:15
Pegasus thought it P. KEAT 445:11
peignoir Complacencies of the p. STEV 758:8
peine *joie venait toujours après la p.* APOL 23:10
pelago *p. ratem* HORA 400:4
pelican bird is the p. MERR 523:3
p. in the wilderness BOOK 140:18
Pelion *P. imposuisse Olympo* HORA 401:16
pile Ossa on P. VIRG 814:15
pellet p. with the poison FILM 320:15
Pemberley shades of P. AUST 40:3
pen Before my p. has gleaned KEAT 445:23
bite his p. SWIF 767:16
Biting my truant p. SIDN 736:3
books and p. I will apply WHIT 834:2
female p. ALCO 10:8
fingers held the p. COWP 247:3
glorious by my p. MONT 546:4
heavy oar the p. is FLAU 325:8
holding a p. DICK 270:21
mightier than the p. HOGB 392:5
My tongue is the p. BOOK 136:19
needle and the p. LEWI 483:15
nose was as sharp as a p. SHAK 693:2
pain to p. the book OXFO 581:11
p. has been in their hands AUST 39:15
p. in his hand JOHN 427:10
p. in his hand JOHN 431:19
p., in our age LEWE 483:2
p. is mightier PROV 629:19
p. is worse than the sword BURT 174:5
p. mightier than the sword BULW 164:5
scratching of a p. LOVE 493:12
squat p. rests HEAN 377:19
Waverley p. ADVE 8:17
woman's p. BOOT 145:1
woman that attempts the p. WINC 841:6
penalty p. of Adam SHAK 680:25
penance making night do p. WORD 849:12
pence eternal want of p. TENN 784:22
Take care of the p. LOWN 494:20
Take care of the p. PROV 631:37

pencil coloured p. long enough CHES 217:8
p. of the Holy Ghost BACO 43:14
pencils feel for their blue p. ESHE 308:15
p. and what-not MILN 528:12
sadness of p. ROET 652:4
penetralium p. of mystery KEAT 446:4
peninsulas bright eye of p. CATU 202:16
penitent p., and obedient heart BOOK 127:13
p. drunkennesses RIMB 649:12
Restore thou them that are p. BOOK 127:17
penitus *p. toto divisos orbe* VIRG 813:15
pennant wind or the p. HUI- 408:5
pennies P. don't fall from heaven THAT 787:1
p. from heaven BURK 169:13
Pennsylvania leave the P. station GORD 356:18
penny bad p. always turns up PROV 614:47
In for a p. PROV 623:33
No p., no paternoster PROV 628:2
Not a p. off the pay COOK 241:16
One a p. NURS 568:16
one p. the worse BARH 55:17
p. plain and twopence coloured STEV 759:12
p. saved PROV 629:20
P. wise PROV 629:21
To turn a p. COWP 247:22
pens Let other p. dwell AUST 39:5
Penshurst Thou art not, P. JONS 436:5
pension made his p. jingle COWP 248:25
p. from his parish RUSK 660:6
p. list of the republic CLEV 226:16
P. Pay given JOHN 424:14
spend my p. on brandy JOSE 436:17
pensive Come, p. nun MILT 529:10
her p. soul COLL 235:14
vacant or in p. mood WORD 847:6
pent In the great city, p. COLE 231:21
pentagon P., that immense monument FRAN 333:1
penthouse his p. lid SHAK 703:6
Pentridge P. by the river BARN 56:15
peonies wealth of globèd p. KEAT 444:18
people afraid Of p. HAMM 370:12
All p. that on earth do dwell KETH 450:4
American p. have spoken CLIN 227:10
And the p. ANON 18:1
as if p. mattered SCHU 671:20
as many opinions as p. TERE 785:8
August for the p. AUDE 34:22
Before we were her p. FROS 335:15
bludgeoning of the p. WILD 837:5
builds on the p. MACH 502:11
by the p. PAGE 581:14
confidence of the p. CONF 238:4
debauch her p. JENY 421:2
die for the p. BIBL 103:23
dissolve the p. BREC 150:17
faces of p. going by PEPY 592:12
faith in the p. DICK 272:20
fiery, impulsive p. HOUS 405:7
fool all the p. LINC 485:16
full of p. BIBL 91:6
good of the p. CICE 223:9
Guns don't kill p. SLOG 740:3
I am myself the p. ROBE 650:2
indictment against an whole p. BURK 166:23
in favour of the p. BURK 168:4
is the p.'s choice SHER 733:13
I would be of the p. LA B 462:16
Let my p. go BIBL 77:26
Let my p. go SONG 748:10
Like p., like priest BIBL 91:27
Like p., like priest PROV 625:21
look after our p. LAST 471:13
love of the p. BURK 166:31
made for the p. WEBS 825:11
martyr of the p. CHAR 209:1
more than half the p. are right WHIT 832:1
Most p. ignore most poetry MITC 540:5
my p.'s happiness ELIZ 304:10
new p. takes the land CHES 216:13
no petty p. YEAT 856:11
Now, Sir, there are p. JOHN 431:22

one p., one leader POLI 600:14
opium of the p. MARX 516:11
p. are only human COMP 236:19
p. are the masters BLAI 118:17
p. are the masters BURK 168:22
p. arose as one BIBL 80:1
p. as a source of power SCAR 668:10
p. as base as itself PULI 637:2
P. die, but books never die ROOS 654:2
p. don't do such things IBSE 412:13
p. govern themselves THIE 788:1
p. hurting people MAIL 507:12
p. imagine a vain thing BOOK 133:20
p. is grass BIBL 89:17
p. is the true legislator BURK 168:13
p. made the Constitution MARS 514:13
p. marching on MORR 549:12
p. of his pasture BOOK 140:10
p. overlaid with taxes BACO 45:27
p.'s prayer DRYD 287:2
P.'s Princess BLAI 118:18
p.'s voice is odd POPE 605:22
p. that read SHEN 733:1
p. that walked in darkness BIBL 88:17
p. went up into the city BIBL 79:11
p. who got there first USTI 806:3
People who need p. MERR 522:26
P. you know, yet can't quite name LARK 469:1
Power to the p. POLI 601:6
Privileged and the P. DISR 277:25
same as if they was p. DURE 293:2
save the p. ELLI 305:18
strength unto his p. BOOK 135:17
support of the p. CLEV 226:17
suppose the p. good ROBE 650:6
than the p. their king WILL 838:4
thy p. shall be my people BIBL 80:2
thy p. which call upon thee BOOK 130:3
understanded of the p. BOOK 144:16
voice of the p. ALCU 10:10
voice of the p. PROV 633:37
we are the p. of England CHES 216:12
What is the city but the p. SHAK 682:17
world is bereft of p. LAMA 464:7
ye are the p. BIBL 83:5
peopled conquered and p. SEEL 675:16
peoples cry of the Little P. LE G 479:6
scripture of the p. JERO 421:9
Peoria play in P. POLI 600:23
pepper peck of pickled p. NURS 569:3
per P. ME SI VA DANT 255:13
perceive p. and know BOOK 130:3
percentage reasonable p. BECK 61:15
perception Agent of all human P. COLE 233:21
doors of p. BLAK 121:13
gates of p. MAIM 507:17
no p., appellation MAHĀ 506:9
perchance To sleep: p. to dream SHAK 686:9
perdition led to *p.* by a man WEST 830:16
P. catch my soul SHAK 713:25
son of p. BIBL 103:39
perdrix *Toujours p.* ANON 21:3
pereat *p. mundus* MOTT 552:8
P., qui crastina curat ANON 22:2
perenne *maneat p. saeclo* CATU 202:10
perennial Falsehood has a p. spring BURK 166:15
perennius *Exegi monumentum aere p.* HORA 402:3
perestroika restructuring [p.] GORB 356:15
started the process of p. GORB 356:16
pereunt *Qui nobis p.* MART 514:19
perfect being made p. BIBL 92:25
Be ye therefore p. BIBL 94:33
end of a p. day BOND 127:5
Entire and whole and p. SPRI 753:5
ever more p. eyes TEIL 775:9
Homage to thee, P. Wisdom MAHĀ 506:7
If thou wilt be p. BIBL 97:25
life may p. be JONS 435:27

1044 PERFECT · PETTY

perfect (*cont.*):
made p. BIBL 111:12
made p. in weakness BIBL 108:25
nobody's p. FILM 320:21
None of us are p. WILD 835:21
Nothing is p. STEP 756:3
One p. rose PARK 585:17
patience have her p. work BIBL 111:18
p. democracy BURK 167:21
P. fear casteth out CONN 240:7
P. God BOOK 129:2
p. in this world DONN 282:9
p. Name of God SIKH 737:5
p. use of an imperfect medium WILD 836:13
p. woman; nobly planned WORD 850:5
Practice makes p. PROV 629:34
service is p. freedom BOOK 128:12
that which is p. is come BIBL 107:25
They p. nature BACO 45:18
this one is p. PALI 584:17
unto the p. day BIBL 83:37
perfected p. by music CONF 237:22
p. your religion KORA 460:10
woman is p. PLAT 596:22
perfectibility P. most unequivocal GODW 352:2
perfection Dead p., no more TENN 781:16
loveliness and p. MILT 535:19
number of p. AUGU 36:23
p. is not the true basis GLAD 351:1
P. is the child HALL 369:12
p. of reason COKE 230:16
P. of the life YEAT 853:11
p. of wisdom MAHĀ 506:8
pictures of p. AUST 40:20
pursuit of p. ARNO 29:8
realise our p. WILD 835:28
road to p. JAIN 416:21
she did make defect p. SHAK 679:6
think of p. BURN 169:17
Trifles make p. MICH 524:4
true p. SHAK 710:7
very pink of p. GOLD 355:23
What's come to p. BROW 160:12
perfections where all p. keep ANON 17:1
with his sweet p. caught ROYD 658:2
perfectly p. love thee BOOK 131:6
P. pure and good BROW 160:24
small, but p. formed COOP 242:11
perfide *ah, la p. Angleterre* BOSS 145:16
perfidious p. Albion XIMÉ 852:20
p. friends MEDI 520:8
perform Almighty's orders to p. ADDI 4:6
not able to p. BOOK 134:25
p. without thinking WHIT 832:15
zeal will p. this BIBL 88:19
performance all words And no p. MASS 518:4
insipid and tedious p. WALP 818:22
p., as he is now SHAK 695:19
p. every thing HUNT 410:4
p. keeps no day CAMP 188:6
so many years outlive p. SHAK 692:3
takes away the p. SHAK 705:7
performed vow be p. BOOK 138:5
performing aroma of p. seals HART 374:11
perfume curious p. AUBR 34:3
p. on the violet SHAK 699:10
perfumes No p. BRUM 162:8
p. of Arabia SHAK 707:2
soaked in p. HORA 400:7
perhaps grand P. BROW 158:15
P. it may turn out a sang BURN 170:27
seek a great p. LAST 472:1
Perigord truffles, P. POPE 602:7
peril those in p. on the sea WHIT 832:22
perils defend us from all p. BOOK 128:20
in p. of waters BIBL 108:22
periphrastic p. study ELIO 301:15
perish England shall p. ELIZ 304:15
if I p., I perish BIBL 82:21
if it had to p. twice FROS 335:14
Let the day p. BIBL 82:31
Let them p. BOOK 134:1
money p. with thee BIBL 105:1
people p. BIBL 85:19
P. the thought CIBB 223:3
p. together as fools KING 452:5
p. with the sword BIBL 99:8
ready to p. BIBL 85:22
should not p. BIBL 102:32
single soul to p. TALM 771:21
speak again, and it will p. JOHN 426:7
They shall p. BOOK 140:19
They too shall p. LANG 466:10
though the world p. MOTT 552:8
To p. rather MILT 532:1
venal city ripe to p. SALL 665:5
world will p. BAKU 50:5
perished hope is p. BIBL 91:8
p., each alone COWP 246:4
perishes nothing really p. BACO 43:5
What's come to perfection p. BROW 160:12
peritis *decede p.* HORA 399:24
perjured p. Clarence SHAK 716:28
perjuries laughs at lovers' p. OVID 579:22
laughs at lovers' p. TIBU 794:11
perjury laughs at lovers' p. PROV 624:33
lovers' p. DRYD 289:5
permanent Suffering is p. WORD 846:4
permission p. of all-ruling heaven MILT 531:13
permitted p. to make all the ballads FLET 326:21
pernicious O most p. woman SHAK 685:7
P. weed COWP 246:9
perpendicular p. expression of horizontal SHAW 727:27
perpetrator thou shalt not be a p. BAUE 59:5
perpetua *lux p.* MISS 539:14
perpetual p. light MISS 539:14
p. motion DICK 272:9
p. night JONS 435:18
p. quarrel BURK 166:27
with p. motion SHAK 691:28
perplexes dull brain p. KEAT 444:25
persecute Why p. we him BIBL 83:13
persecuted I p. the church of God BIBL 108:1
merely because he is p. GOUL 357:10
persecutest Saul, why p. thou me BIBL 105:2
persecution no tyrannical p. THOM 789:2
P. is a bad and indirect way BROW 156:30
P. is not an original feature PAIN 582:19
P. produced its natural effect MACA 498:20
Religious p. BURK 169:2
some degree of p. SWIF 766:18
Persepolis through P. MARL 513:20
perseverance P., dear my lord SHAK 719:23
p. in a good cause STER 756:19
persevere Give us grace to p. DEAR 260:11
persevering no dignity in p. in error PEEL 590:18
Persia here and in P. ARIS 25:16
Persian hate all that P. gear HORA 400:21
Persians If the P. hide the sun HERO 385:13
Medes and P. BIBL 91:23
Truth-loving P. GRAV 360:7
Persicos *P. odi, puer, apparatus* HORA 400:21
persistence Hark, the dominant's p. BROW 161:19
take the place of p. COOL 242:10
person adornment of his p. THOM 791:22
frontier of my P. AUDE 35:22
most superior p. ANON 17:20
no more than a p. AUDE 35:1
P. from Porlock SMIT 743:5
p. on business from Porlock COLE 232:2
p. you and I took me for CARL 191:9
respect any p. BIBL 81:3
third p. was in the room POPE 606:27
personal No p. consideration GRAN 359:9
P. isn't the same PRAT 610:8
p. is political POLI 601:5
P. relations FORS 329:15
warm p. gesture GALB 338:4
what a p. gift is HEIN 379:11
personalities meeting of two p. JUNG 438:12
p. of the two sexes MEAD 519:18
personality From 35 to 55, good p. TUCK 802:2
no more p. than a paper cup CHAN 207:12
value on the p. market FROM 335:3
persons confounding the P. BOOK 128:22
no respecter of p. BIBL 105:8
things, not in p. CURI 254:3
perspective light, shade, and p. CONS 241:9
P. is the bridle LEON 481:5
perspiration ninety-nine per cent p. EDIS 296:5
perspire Gladstone may p. CHUR 220:11
perspiring city of p. dreads RAPH 642:11
persuade p. a multitude HOOK 395:17
persuaded p. in his own mind BIBL 106:35
p. of them BIBL 111:8
persuaders hidden p. PACK 581:12
persuadest Almost thou p. me BIBL 105:32
persuading By p. others JUNI 438:17
persuasion P. is the resource GIBB 345:9
p. only is to work MILT 535:17
p. that a a thing is so BLAK 121:12
persuasive p. argument FRAM 331:15
perturbation O polished p. SHAK 692:15
perturbations p. and calamities BACO 46:6
perturbed rest, p. spirit SHAK 685:12
Peru China to P. JOHN 426:15
perused in th'original p. mankind ARMS 26:11
perverse most p. creatures ADDI 5:1
P. and foolish BAKE 50:2
perversion War is the universal p. RAE 640:13
perversions of all the sexual p. HUXL 411:8
perversity p. of the human mind TROL 799:17
pervert loophole through which the p. BRON 152:7
pessimism p. is a luxury MEIR 520:11
pessimist know what a p. is SHAW 727:21
p. fears this is true CABE 184:17
p. waiting for rain COHE 230:12
pestered p. with a popinjay SHAK 689:26
pestilence breeds p. BLAK 120:24
p. and war MILT 532:12
p. that walketh in darkness BOOK 140:3
plague and p. NASH 557:22
purged the air of p. SHAK 720:6
pet p. theory of the universe EDDI 295:4
petal dropping a rose p. MARQ 514:5
Now sleeps the crimson p. TENN 783:12
petals peel all the p. off AYCK 41:5
P. on a wet, black bough POUN 609:2
petar Hoist with his own p. SHAK 687:32
Peter did outrun P. BIBL 104:10
government which robs P. SHAW 725:5
I'll call him P. SHAK 699:1
looked upon P. BIBL 102:2
P. Piper picked a peck NURS 569:3
P. wish himself within BYRO 183:18
Shock-headed P. HOFF 392:3
Simon P. saith unto them BIBL 104:18
Thou art P. BIBL 97:16
'twas P.'s drift SHEL 730:20
Where P. is AMBR 13:1
Petersburg P. the most abstract DOST 283:10
petis *Quod p. hic est* HORA 399:10
petitions desires and p. BOOK 128:18
petrifactions p. of a plodding brain BYRO 182:13
petrifies p. the feeling BURN 170:28
petrol price of p. has been increased CART 198:8
pets hate a word like 'p.' JENN 421:1
petticoat feet beneath her p. SUCK 763:5
keep down a single p. BYRO 184:13
out of the Realm in my p. ELIZ 304:4
petticoats hyena in p WALP 819:18
pettiness something to expiate: a p. LAWR 475:8
petty Creeps in this p. pace SHAK 707:14

Pilate (*cont.*):
Suffered under Pontius P.   BOOK 128:10
water like P.   GREE 362:8
pile Gaunt's embattled p.   MACA 499:3
P. it high   SLOG 740:10
p. Ossa on Pelion   VIRG 814:15
P. the bodies high   SAND 665:20
standst an ancient p.   JONS 436:5
piled p. in large cities   JEFF 419:16
pilfering quiet, p.   CLAR 224:10
pilgrim Forth, p.   CHAU 213:20
Onward goes the p. band   BARI 56:5
p. oft At dead of night   DYER 294:1
P. through this barren land   WILL 838:9
To be a p.   BUNY 165:7
pilgrimage I'll take my p.   RALE 641:5
proclaim the P.   KORA 460:17
quiet p.   CAMP 188:3
succeed me in my p.   BUNY 165:9
pilgrimages longen folk to goon on p.
   CHAU 210:5
pilgrims land of the p.   CUMM 253:6
Land of the p.' pride   SMIT 742:18
Like p. to th'appointed place   DRYD 289:8
p. on the earth   BIBL 111:8
We are all p.   RYDE 662:1
We are the P., master   FLEC 326:2
Pilgrim's Progress Crusoe, and P.
   JOHN 433:20
'P.', about a man   TWAI 803:4
pill any p. can be swallowed   TROL 799:9
Instruction is the p.   RICH 647:18
little yellow p.   JAGG 415:14
potion and his p.   HERR 386:1
sleeping p. is white   SEXT 677:15
women may take the p.   THOM 790:21
pillar became a p. of salt   BIBL 76:20
p. of a cloud   BIBL 77:34
p. of fire   BIBL 77:34
seemed A p. of state   MILT 532:4
triple p. of the world   SHAK 678:12
pillars hewn out her seven p.   BIBL 84:6
not one of its p.   ANON 16:8
p. bare like nude   SPEN 750:22
p. of government   BACO 45:11
seven p. of wisdom   BORR 146:17
Pillicock P. sat on Pillicock-hill   SHAK 700:24
pillow clean conscience is a good p.
   PROV 616:45
like a p. on a bed   DONN 280:20
like the feather p.   HAIG 367:10
softer p. than my heart   BYRO 184:16
upon a midnight p.   SHAK 681:2
upon the p.-hill   STEV 760:4
pillows endless p. rise   THOM 792:2
P. his chin   MILT 530:26
pills mountebank who sold p.   ADDI 5:14
p. and medicine   DEAN 260:9
p. for the sick   HOBB 390:22
pink p. for pale people   ADVE 7:20
pilot daring p. in extremity   DRYD 286:20
Dropping the p.   TENN 775:14
p. of the calm   BAGE 47:21
p. of the Galilean lake   MILT 530:5
See my p. face to face   TENN 776:17
pilots P. of the purple twilight   TENN 780:20
piminy Francesca di Rimini, miminy, p.
   GILB 348:16
Pimpernel demmed, elusive P.   ORCZ 576:9
pimples scratching of p. on the body
   WOOL 845:11
pin life at a p.'s fee   SHAK 684:27
p. up my hair with prose   CONG 239:12
See a p. and pick it up   PROV 630:24
siller p.   BALL 53:19
sin to steal a p.   PROV 624:19
with a little p.   SHAK 715:25
pinching p. fingers   SHAK 721:25
pine p. for what is not   SHEL 731:29
spray of Western p.   HART 374:15
whisper of the p.   THEO 787:21

pineapple p. of politeness   SHER 733:17
pines lofty p.   DRAY 286:2
pinguem p. et nitidum bene   HORA 399:7
pinion imagination droops her p.
   BYRO 181:12
pinions with p. skim the air   FRER 333:17
pink p. pills for pale people   ADVE 7:20
very p. of courtesy   SHAK 717:31
very p. of perfection   GOLD 355:23
pinkly p. bursts the spray   BETJ 72:12
pinko really p.-grey   FORS 329:19
pinnace p. like a fluttered bird   TENN 783:19
pinnacled p. dim   SHEL 731:8
pinprick p. of eternity   AURE 38:8
pins files of p. extend   POPE 606:6
mixed with a packet of p.   WELL 828:9
pinstripe come in a p. suit   FEIN 316:9
pint p. of plain   O'BR 571:6
p.—that's very nearly   GALT 338:16
quart into a p. pot   PROV 635:28
pinta Drinka P. Milka Day   ADVE 7:19
pioneers are simply p.   MURR 555:1
P.! O pioneers   WHIT 833:7
pios si qua p. respectant numina   VIRG 811:7
pious p. Aeneas   HORA 402:14
rarther p.   ASHF 31:13
pipe p. a simple song   WORD 846:23
p. Blown by surmises   SHAK 691:21
P. me to pastures   HOPK 396:14
P. might fall out   FORS 329:8
p. of half-awakened birds   TENN 783:5
p. with solemn interposing puff   COWP 246:8
piped We have p. unto you   BIBL 96:25
piper pays the p.   PROV 622:13
Peter P. picked a peck   NURS 569:3
Tom he was a p.'s son   NURS 570:10
Tom, Tom, the p.'s son   NURS 570:11
pipes on their scrannel p.   MILT 530:6
open the p.   BYRD 177:15
What p. and timbrels   KEAT 444:7
piping For ever p. songs   KEAT 444:10
Helpless, naked, p. loud   BLAK 122:14
P. songs of pleasant glee   BLAK 121:26
weak p. time   SHAK 716:21
Pippa P. passes   BEER 63:3
pips until the p. squeak   GEDD 342:15
pirate To be a P. King   GILB 348:27
piscem Desinat in p.   HORA 397:19
pismire p. is equally perfect   WHIT 833:12
piss May'st thou ne'er p.   ROCH 651:6
pitcher of warm p.   GARN 339:16
pissing inside the tent p. out   JOHN 423:16
pistol echo of a p.-shot   DURR 293:8
I reach for my p.   JOHS 434:1
p. in your pocket   WEST 830:7
p. on the wall   CHEK 214:15
p.-shot in the middle   STEN 755:17
pun is a p.   LAMB 464:18
when his p. misses fire   GOLD 355:34
pistols Have you your p.   WHIT 833:7
young ones carry p.   SHAW 724:15
piston steam and p. stroke   MORR 549:15
pistons black statement of p.   SPEN 750:18
pit digged a p. before me   BOOK 137:22
eagle know what is in the p.   BLAK 117:9
He that diggeth a p.   BIBL 86:17
Law is a bottomless p.   ARBU 24:6
monster of the p.   POPE 605:25
out of the horrible p.   BOOK 136:6
sulphurous p.   SHAK 701:15
pitch He that toucheth p.   BIBL 93:13
imagination to the proper p.   LACK 463:3
p. of grief   HOPK 396:18
p. or direction   HOPK 397:14
touches p. shall be defiled   PROV 621:51
pitcher p. be broken at the fountain
   BIBL 86:25
p. will go to the well   PROV 629:23
pitchers Little p. have large ears   PROV 625:28

pitchfork drive out nature with a p.
   HORA 399:9
nature with a p.   PROV 635:25
thrown on her with a p.   SWIF 766:10
use my wit as a p.   LARK 469:4
pith p. is in the postscript   HAZL 376:9
pitied Better envied than p.   PROV 615:22
pitieth p. his own children   BOOK 141:3
pitiful God be p.   BROW 157:24
long-suffering, and very p.   BIBL 93:2
'twas wondrous p.   SHAK 713:10
pitifulness p. of thy great mercy
   BOOK 129:16
pity by means of p. and fear   ARIS 25:20
cherish p.   BLAK 122:4
endure, then p.   POPE 605:3
full of p. and concerned   MAHĀ 506:10
Midnight Without P.   JOHN 423:1
no p. to myself   SHAK 717:7
O source of p.   MISS 539:17
P. a human face   BLAK 122:3
p. beyond all telling   YEAT 855:5
p. him afterwards   JOHN 430:18
p. his ignorance   DICK 270:22
P. is akin to love   PROV 629:24
p. kills   BALZ 54:9
p., like a naked new-born   SHAK 704:6
p. never ceases to be shown   DRYD 287:8
p. renneth soone   CHAU 211:14
P. the reapers   DUCK 291:2
p. this busy monster   CUMM 253:11
Poetry is in the p.   OWEN 580:24
saint took p. on   COLE 232:25
Scots deserve no p.   FLET 326:22
seas of p. lie   AUDE 35:6
she did p. them   SHAK 713:11
some to have p. on me   BOOK 138:16
some touch of p.   SHAK 716:23
yet the p. of it, Iago   SHAK 714:10
pix Sticks nix hick p.   NEWS 562:18
place all in one p.   BOIL 125:14
all other things give p.   GAY 341:27
and the p. thereof   BOOK 141:4
bourne of time and p.   TENN 776:17
could have no p.   BIBL 93:15
Ere time and p. were   ROCH 651:17
exalt us unto the same p.   BOOK 130:9
for one p. than another   SOUT 749:13
for the sake of the p.   HALI 368:19
gathered to the same p.   HORA 401:3
genius of the p.   POPE 603:12
Get p. and wealth   POPE 605:17
Gratitude of p.-expectants   WALP 820:9
his p. know him   BIBL 83:1
In p. of strife   CAST 198:18
keep in the same p.   CARR 195:2
know the p.   ELIO 301:25
lone unhaunted p.   DONN 280:8
Lord is in this p.   BIBL 76:31
love of p. and precedency   DONN 282:4
Men in great p.   BACO 44:21
no p. to go   WHIT 832:21
p. for everything   PROV 629:25
p. in the sun   BÜLO 164:1
p. in the sun   WILH 837:18
P., that great object   SMIT 741:3
p. within the meaning   ANON 18:9
p. without power   ROSE 654:18
prepare a p. for you   BIBL 103:28
right man in the right p.   JEFF 420:18
rising to great p.   BACO 44:25
rising unto p.   BACO 44:23
spirit of the p.   VIRG 812:18
stand in the holy p.   BIBL 98:15
thus with height of p.   WOTT 851:6
till there be no p.   BIBL 88:7
time and p.   JOHN 425:26
time and p. for   PROV 632:9
time and the p.   BROW 160:11
Time, P.   DRYD 290:7
woman's p. in the home   PROV 635:16
placem ut p. genus irritabile vatum
   HORA 399:23

placeo Quod spiro et p.　HORA 402:8
placere Nulla p. diu carmina possunt
　　HORA 399:17
places All p., all airs　BROW 157:4
all p. thou　MILT 534:13
all p. were alike to him　KIPL 456:14
father's fortunes, and his p.　CORB 243:3
longest distance between two p.　WILL 839:7
New p. you will not find　CAVA 203:19
p. that the eye of heaven　SHAK 715:10
P. where they sing　BOOK 128:14
Proper words in proper p.　SWIF 766:3
quietest p.　HOUS 404:20
placidly Go p. amid the noise　EHRM 297:9
plackets hand out of p.　SHAK 700:25
placuisse Principibus p. viris　HORA 399:13
plafond lignes du p.　ÉLUA 306:7
plagiaire l'état de p.　MUSS 555:8
plagiarism from one author, it's p.
　　MIZN 541.5
plagiarist situation of the p.　MUSS 555:8
plagiarize P.! Let no one else's work
　　LEHR 479:9
plague instruments to p. us　SHAK 702:2
p. and pestilence　NASH 557:22
p. come nigh thy dwelling　BOOK 140:4
p. making us cruel　PEPY 592:9
p. o' both your houses　SHAK 717:33
p. the inventor　SHAK 704:4
that's his p.　BURT 174:7
plagues Great p. remain　BOOK 135:21
of all p.　DEFO 261:27
omit those two main p.　BURT 174:4
plain best p. set　BACO 43:27
Books will speak p.　BACO 43:27
Cannot a p. man live　SHAK 716:25
darkling p.　ARNO 27:5
divine p. face　LAMB 465:8
Gromboolian p.　LEAR 477:6
make it p. upon tables　BIBL 92:11
Make thy way p.　BOOK 133:26
making things p.　HUXL 411:19
no p. women on television　FORD 328:8
penny p. and twopence coloured
　　STEV 759:12
pint of p.　O'BR 571:6
p., blunt man　SHAK 698:4
'p.' cooking cannot be entrusted
　　MORP 549:6
P. in thy neatness　HORA 400:8
p. Kate　SHAK 718:12
P. living and high thinking　WORD 848:18
p. meaning　SHAK 709:21
p. Michael Faraday　FARA 314:17
P. women he regarded　ELIO 300:2
pricking on the p.　SPEN 751:12
rough places p.　BIBL 89:16
truth for p. people　WESL 829:12
plainness Manifest p.　LAO 467:9
perfect p. of speech　ARNO 30:9
plains flowery p. of honour　JONS 435:15
ringing p. of windy Troy　TENN 784:14
plaintive p. treble　DISR 275:13
plaire n'est pas de p.　MOLI 541:15
plaisir P. d'amour　FLOR 327:20
plaister p. of the wall　BIBL 91:21
plan by his p. of attack　SASS 667:22
coherent p. to the universe　HOYL 406:9
cunning p.　CATC 201:4
no p. of operations reaches　MOLT 542:16
no p. survives first contact　MISQ 538:11
p. the future by the past　BURK 166:5
rest on its original p.　BURK 166:10
wagon of his 'P.'　PAST 588:5
plane It's a p.　ANON 15:25
only two emotions in a p.　WELL 827:10
planet born under a rhyming p.　SHAK 712:33
hanging from a round p.　EDDI 295:5
Jove's p.　BROW 159:20
new p. swims into his ken　KEAT 445:6
planetary p. influence　SHAK 699:26
planets chronicle of the p.　YEVT 856:20

people p. of its own　BYRO 182:7
p. circle other suns　POPE 604:19
p. in their stations　MILT 533:23
stars and all the p.　TRUM 801:5
plank landing on a p.　EDDI 295:5
planned order of the acts is p.　PAST 588:3
p. obsolescence　STEV 757:18
planning Failure of p.　HARE 373:8
p. is indispensable　EISE 298:17
plans p. are useless　EISE 298:17
plant Fame is no p.　MILT 530:4
I p. lines　WALC 817:6
p. for your heirs　PROV 633:39
p. of rapid growth　WASH 822:12
Sensitive P.　SHEL 731:14
That busy p.　HERB 384:6
time to p.　BIBL 85:32
What is a weed? A p.　EMER 307:10
Plantagenet where is P.　CREW 251:3
plantation still working on a p.　HOLI 392:16
planted I have p.　BIBL 107:6
What our forefathers p.　WITH 842:5
planter house of the p.　CLAR 225:6
Ulsterman, of p. stock　HEWI 387:13
planting p. my cabbages　MONT 544:2
plants as the young p.　BOOK 143:23
forced p.　JOHN 431:18
He that p. trees　FULL 337:8
p. suck in the earth　COWL 245:17
talk to the p.　CHAR 209:16
plasterer agog at the p.　HEAN 377:15
plasters p., pills, and ointment　LOCK 489:4
plastic cannot pass through p.　JOHN 422:7
plastics p., Picasso, sunbathing　WAUG 824:9
platinum bullets made of p.　BELL 64:18
eyebrows made of p.　FORS 329:6
platitude echo of a p.　BIER 116:2
longitude with no p.　FRY 336:14
p. is simply a truth repeated　BALD 50:13
stroke a p. until it purrs　MARQ 514:6
platitudes orchestration of p.　WILD 837:16
Plato attachment à la P.　GILB 348:14
be wrong with P.　CICE 223:24
P. is dear to me　ARIS 26:6
P.'s retirement　MILT 534:21
P., thou reason'st well　ADDI 4:15
p. told him: he couldn't　CUMM 253:10
series of footnotes to P.　WHIT 832:16
plaudits p. of the throng　LONG 490:17
plausible neat, p., and wrong　MENC 521:20
plausibly p. maintained　BURR 173:10
play all the p., the insight　BROW 158:10
All work and no p.　PROV 614:20
better at a p.　ANON 16:5
Better than a p.　CHAR 209:4
boys late at their p.　ARNO 28:1
cannot p. well　BACO 43:28
children at p.　MONT 544:5
come out to p.　NURS 566:9
Did that p. of mine send out　YEAT 854:23
Fair p.'s a jewel　PROV 619:40
game at which two can p.　BEER 63:7
Games people p.　BERN 71:4
good p. needs no epilogue　SHAK 682:11
holdeth children from p.　SIDN 736:16
I could p. Ercles rarely　SHAK 710:21
If you p. with fire　PROV 623:21
Judge not the p.　QUAR 638:19
Kings would not p. at　COWP 248:12
let me not p. a woman　SHAK 710:23
little victims p.　GRAY 361:10
may now sit and p.　ASTL 32:18
only to p. fair　LABO 462:13
our p. is played out　THAC 786:21
p. began to disgust　EVEL 313:4
p. in Peoria　POLI 600:23
P. it again, Sam　FILM 319:13
P. it again, Sam　MISQ 538:13
p. it over again　LAMB 465:13
p.'s the thing　SHAK 686:8
p. the game　NEWB 560:5

p. things as they are　STEV 757:25
p. with my cat　MONT 544:15
p. without a woman　KYD 462:11
p. with souls　BROW 160:1
p. with the gypsies　NURS 568:11
presents you with a p.　BOOT 145:1
rest of the p.　PASC 587:9
some foul p.　SHAK 684:13
than see a p.　BURT 174:12
very dull p.　CONG 239:5
work, rest and p.　ADVE 8:3
wouldst not p. false　SHAK 703:18
written a damned p.　REYN 645:16
y is p.　EINS 298:5
Your p.'s hard to act　CHEK 213:25
You would p. upon me　SHAK 687:10
playbills time to read p.　BURN 169:24
playboy lost the only P.　SYNG 769:13
P. of the Western World　CLOS 228:19
played He p. the King　FIEL 317:10
p. the fool　BIBL 80:26
playedst p. most foully for't　SHAK 705:16
player as strikes the p.　FITZ 323:9
p. on the other side　HUXL 411:18
poor p., That struts　SHAK 707:14
wrapped in a p.'s hide　GREE 362:24
players men and women merely p.
　　SHAK 681:9
P., Sir! I look　JOHN 430:9
see the p. well bestowed　SHAK 685:30
playing stood like a p. card　MAIL 507:13
won on the p. fields　WELL 828:1
work terribly hard at p.　MORT 551:1
plays English p. are like　VOLT 816:18
He that p. the king　SHAK 685:25
loves no p.　SHAK 696:14
Shaw's p.　AGAT 6:21
plaything child's a p.　LAMB 464:22
little p.-house　WALP 818:19
p. of the boy　BAGE 49:6
Plaza Toro Duke of P.　GILB 347:3
plea Though justice be thy p.　SHAK 709:26
without one p.　ELLI 305:15
pleasance Youth is full of p.　SHAK 722:15
pleasant abridgement of all that was p.
　　GOLD 355:6
completed labours are p.　CICE 223:8
do not find anything p.　VOLT 815:9
green and p. bowers　BLAK 120:15
green and p. land　BLAK 121:15
in p. places　BOOK 134:14
joyful and p. thing　BOOK 144:3
Life would be very p.　SURT 764:20
p. and clean work　RUSK 659:19
p. it is to have money　CLOU 229:2
P. to know Mr Lear　LEAR 477:13
something p. happens　MONT 546:1
that p. land　BOOK 141:14
pleasantness ways are ways of p.　BIBL 83:35
please can't p. everyone　PROV 635:42
circumstance to p. us　SWIF 767:15
do what I p.　FRED 333:8
ladies to p.　AUST 38:18
Little things p.　PROV 625:32
live to p.　JOHN 426:13
Myself alone I seek to p.　GAY 342:2
never fails to p.　SEDL 675:12
Nothing can p. many　JOHN 425:12
only Self to p.　BLAK 122:12
p. thee with my answer　SHAK 709:22
p. the touchy breed of poets　HORA 399:23
P. your eye　PROV 629:26
those whom I wished to p.　JOHN 427:21
To tax and to p.　BURK 166:16
'twas natural to p.　DRYD 286:17
pleased All seemed well p.　MILT 533:17
consists in being p.　HAZL 376:17
have p. leading men　HORA 399:13
in whom I am well p.　BIBL 94:14
more had p. us　ADDI 4:4
p. not the million　SHAK 685:29
p. with what he gets　SHAK 681:5

gentleman p. JOYC 437:18
grete p. of Ytaille CHAU 211:26
hate what every p. hates KAVA 442:7
have a p. able-bodied MACN 505:2
Honour the greatest p. DANT 255:16
Is this the great p. GARR 340:5
I was a p., I was young FLEC 326:6
lack their sacred p. HORA 402:16
Like a P. hidden SHEL 731:28
limbs of a p. HORA 403:8
lost on p.'s ear CLOS 228:10
Love made me p. EPIT 310:15
lover, and the p. SHAK 711:27
masculine part, the p. in me BEHN 63:20
modern p.'s fate HOOD 395:13
never be a p. DRYD 290:15
No p. ever interpreted GIRA 350:4
Not deep the P. sees ARNO 27:24
Now, children, the p. FANT 314:14
P. and Saint COWL 245:28
p. and the dreamer KEAT 443:6
p. and the theme COWP 248:23
p. image aught so fair THOM 792:18
p. includes a critic SHEN 733:2
p. is like the prince BAUD 58:11
p. is the priest STEV 757:19
p. kings KEAT 445:12
p. ranks far below the painter LEON 481:8
p. seems most himself YEAT 856:9
p.'s eye, in a fine frenzy SHAK 711:28
p.'s gift is to soothe YESE 856:16
p.'s hope: to be AUDE 36:7
p.'s inward pride DAY- 260:4
p.'s mouth be shut YEAT 855:3
p.'s pen, all scorn BRAD 149:4
p. spewed up a good lump DRYD 290:12
p. stubborn with his passion YEAT 853:7
p. will give up writing CELA 205:4
P. writes under one restriction WORD 850:25
poor p. named Clough SWIN 769:7
possess a p.'s brain DRAY 286:3
skilled p. PIND 595:12
starved p. LOCK 489:4
there is a p. indulging MAHO 507:10
Vex not thou the p.'s mind TENN 782:22
war p. whose right of honour GURN 366:1
was a true P. BLAK 120:21
what is left the p. here BYRO 181:6
poetae Etiam disiecti membra p. HORA 403:8
poète poète est semblable BAUD 58:11
poetic constitutes p. faith COLE 233:22
nurse for a p. child SCOT 673:13
P. Genius of my country BURN 173:9
P. Justice POPE 601:20
P. LICENCE BANV 54:20
poetical As to the p. character KEAT 446:16
claim to p. honours JOHN 425:5
poetis Mediocribus esse p. HORA 398:17
Pictoribus atque p. HORA 397:20
poetry best piece of p. JONS 435:23
bother about p. COCT 230:6
by no means rank p. BYRO 184:4
campaign in p. CUOM 254:1
car was p. and tragedy LEWI 483:21
cradled into p. by wrong SHEL 729:18
dead art Of p. POUN 608:17
drops into p. DICK 271:18
Emptied of its p. AUDE 35:5
give p. a proper flow BOIL 125:12
gold medal for p. GRAV 360:13
grand style arises in p. ARNO 30:10
I can repeat p. CARR 195:18
If p. comes not KEAT 446:8
Ireland hurt you into p. AUDE 35:3
It is not p. POPE 602:28
Language is fossil p. EMER 307:9
language of p. GRAY 361:23
mincing p. SHAK 690:24
misfortune of p. AUST 39:13
most p. ignores most people MITC 540:5
neither p. nor any thing else BYRO 184:14
no more define p. HOUS 405:5
p. administers to the effect SHEL 732:14

p. almost necessarily declines MACA 498:3
P. and Religion CARL 192:2
p. begins to atrophy POUN 609:8
p. belongs to those who use SKAR 739:4
p. in money GRAV 360:14
p. in motion KAUF 442:2
P., in the most comprehensive HUNT 410:3
P. is a subject as precise FLAU 325:12
P. is at bottom ARNO 29:24
P. is a way FROS 336:7
[P.] is capable of saving us RICH 647:10
P. is certainly something more COLE 234:5
P. is devil's wine AUGU 37:7
p. is eloquent painting SIMO 738:7
P. is in the pity OWEN 580:24
P. is more philosophical ARIS 25:22
P. is not most important THOM 790:10
P. is pre-eminently the medium FLAU 325:10
P. is the achievement SAND 666:2
P. is the breath WORD 851:1
P. is the record of the best SHEL 732:16
P. is the spontaneous overflow WORD 850:26
P. is the supreme fiction STEV 757:24
P. is what is lost FROS 336:10
P. is when some of them BENT 68:11
p. makes nothing happen AUDE 35:4
P. must be as well written POUN 609:11
p. of earth KEAT 445:8
p. of life GOET 353:6
p. of motion GRAH 358:13
p., prophecy, and religion RUSK 659:14
P.'s a mere drug FARQ 315:21
P.'s another word DURC 292:19
P. shall tune her sacred voice JOHN 426:10
P. should be great KEAT 446:7
P.'s the feverish fit WINC 841:5
p. = the best words COLE 234:3
P. there, is an art SIDN 736:15
P. Unearths from among the dead HILL 388:8
P. wants something DIDE 273:18
p., which is in Oxford DRYD 289:11
polar star of p. KEAT 445:26
quarrel with ourselves, p. YEAT 856:8
saying it and that is p. CAGE 185:9
saying so In whining p. DONN 281:15
She that with p. is won BUTL 176:11
Sir, what is p. JOHN 430:22
stimulated by p. CONF 237:22
That I make p. HORA 402:8
their p. is conceived ARNO 29:23
trying to say was p. OVID 580:20
turn to p. ARNO 29:22
We hate p. that has KEAT 446:7
What is p. RUSK 659:12
Writing a book of p. MARQ 514:5
poets All p. are mad BURT 174:2
amatory p. sing BYRO 181:16
for wits, then p. passed POPE 603:30
Greek, Latin p. CAVE 204:2
if there's room for p. BROW 157:18
impossible to hold the p. back GIRA 350:3
Irish p., learn your trade YEAT 856:3
mature p. steal ELIO 303:28
mighty P. in their misery WORD 849:22
No death has hurt p. more HEAN 378:8
only p. know COWP 247:29
Painters and p. HORA 397:20
P. are the hierophants SHEL 732:17
P. are their own patients THOM 790:24
p. being second-rate HORA 398:17
p. bicycle-pump the human heart AMIS 13:12
P.' food is love SHEL 729:9
P. must be difficult ELIO 303:31
p. only deliver a golden SIDN 736:14
P. that are sown WORD 846:12
P. that lasting marble seek WALL 818:8
P. . . . . though liars HUME 409:8
p. took their golden age THOM 792:6
p. witty BACO 45:22
powerful p. of the century ELIO 303:30
prince of p. BYRO 181:8

romantic p. LEAP 476:18
Souls of p. dead KEAT 444:5
Tenderest of Roman p. TENN 777:1
theft in other p. DRYD 290:5
think all p. were Byronic COPE 242:16
Three p. in an age SWIF 767:6
touchy breed of p. HORA 399:23
We p. in our youth WORD 849:21
who wants p. at all HÖLD 392:13
worst of p. ranks CATU 202:19
youthful p. dream MILT 529:27
point Aloof from the entire p. SHAK 699:22
different p. of view NAPO 556:10
from p. to point TENN 780:21
p. a moral JOHN 426:18
still p. of the turning world ELIO 301:12
That was the p. ELIO 301:4
upon a needle's p. CUDW 253:3
Up to a p., Lord Copper WAUG 824:11
You've hit the p. PLAU 597:22
points P. have no parts LIND 486:2
poising p. every weight MARV 515:13
poison administer a p. to anybody HIPP 389:12
another man's p. PROV 628:44
coward's weapon, p. FLET 327:19
food only a cover for p. BURK 168:7
got as far as p.-gas HARD 372:11
honey of p.-flowers TENN 781:17
if you p. us SHAK 709:14
p. in jest SHAK 687:6
p. the wells NEWM 560:8
p. the whole blood stream fills EMPS 307:23
p. wells MARL 513:14
put p. in your coffee CHUR 222:20
strongest p. ever known BLAK 119:12
tell them to drink the p. PLAT 597:9
Turning to p. KEAT 444:19
poisoned may have been p. FIEL 318:23
p. rat in a hole SWIF 766:6
poisoning P. pigeons LEHR 479:10
poisonous for its p. wine KEAT 444:16
p. reptiles to live in it GIRA 350:2
poisons p. all the rest WATT 823:5
well of p. GIRA 350:1
poke p. poor Billy GRAH 358:8
poker p. of whom every one is afraid MITF 540:16
pokers p. into true-love knots COLE 232:10
polar p. star of poetry KEAT 445:26
pole curses from p. to pole BLAK 120:2
from pole to p. COLE 233:3
top of the greasy p. DISR 278:2
polecat semi-house-trained p. FOOT 328:2
poles explored the P. JOHN 423:2
police among p. officers ORTO 576:17
citizen or the p. AUDE 36:4
friendship recognised by the p. STEV 759:22
p. can beat you SHAW 727:4
p. were to blame GRAN 359:1
policeman p. and a pretty girl CHAP 208:5
p.'s lot GILB 349:1
terrorist and the p. CONR 240:23
than a p. SALI 664:15
would not do for a p. NIGH 564:15
policy defend a bad p. SALI 664:16
English p. is to float SALI 664:3
foreign p. COOK 242:2
home p.: I wage war CLEM 226:11
Honesty is the best p. PROV 622:27
Honesty is the best p. WHAT 831:10
If the p. isn't hurting MAJO 508:3
My [foreign] p. BEVI 74:4
national p. BRIA 151:2
p. of the good neighbour ROOS 653:22
religion or p. RUSK 660:1
rugged brow of careful P. SPEN 751:6
some love but little p. SHAK 716:12
tyrants from p. BURK 167:17
polish contented to p. MORE 548:5
p. it at leisure DRYD 289:35
polished I p. up the handle GILB 348:22
O p. perturbation SHAK 692:15

polished (cont.):
p. corners of the temple — BOOK 143:23
p. dry with pumice — CATU 199:22
p. female friend — WHUR 834:9
polite no allies to be p. to — GEOR 343:14
p. meaningless words — YEAT 854:2
time to be p. — MONT 545:10
politeness glance of great p. — BYRO 183:19
pineapple of p. — SHER 733:17
p. of kings — LOUI 492:13
p. of princes — PROV 629:46
suave p. — KNOX 458:8
political fear of P. Economy — SELL 676:23
half your p. life — THAT 787:5
healthy state of p. life — MILL 525:8
highest p. end — ACTO 1:12
my p. creed — ADAM 3:4
nature of a p. party — TROL 800:5
personal is p. — POLI 601:5
points to a p. career — SHAW 725:27
p. animal — ARIS 25:25
p. Cave of Adullam — BRIG 151:12
p. consequences — MANS 511:6
p. economist — BAGE 48:21
p. genius — TAYL 774:13
p. intriguer — TROL 799:4
P. language . . . is designed — ORWE 578:4
p. lives end in failure — POWE 610:5
p. party is not capable — DISR 277:31
p. power of another — LOCK 488:18
p. speech and writing — ORWE 578:3
P. thought, in France — ARON 30:18
p. will — LYNN 497:7
Principles of P. Economy — BENT 68:15
schemes of p. improvement — JOHN 429:6
politician greatest art of a p. — BOLI 126:12
like a scurvy p. — SHAK 701:18
lurks a p. — ARIS 25:8
makes the p. wise — POPE 606:14
pate of a p. — SHAK 688:26
p. is a man — TRUM 801:10
p. is an arse upon — CUMM 253:9
p. is a statesman who — POMP 599:18
p. never believes what he says — DE G 262:9
p. ought to sacrifice — BURK 167:30
P.'s corpse — BELL 65:7
p. to complain about — POWE 610:3
p. tops his part — GAY 342:3
p. urges them to rebel — PERU 593:11
p. was a person — LLOY 488:1
popular p. — ARIS 25:7
when a p. does get an idea — MARQ 514:4
wise p. — OLIV 573:2
politicians die for p. — THOM 791:20
fault of our p. — TROL 799:25
Old p. chew — POPE 603:23
one of those p. — TROL 799:11
P. also have no leisure — ARIS 25:18
p. hear the word 'culture' — ESHE 308:15
P. often believe — ROTH 656:20
too serious to be left to p. — DE G 262:6
whole race of p. — SWIF 765:13
politics Confound their p. — SONG 747:8
continuation of p. — CLAU 225:17
first part of p. — MICH 524:5
From p., it was an easy step — AUST 39:9
In p., if you want anything — THAT 786:26
in p. the middle way — ADAM 2:21
In p., there is no use — CHAM 206:6
In p., what begins in fear — COLE 234:7
invisible hand in p. — FRIE 334:13
I taste no p. — SMIT 743:13
language of p. — DISR 275:17
Magnanimity in p. — BURK 167:1
mule of p. — DISR 277:3
no true friends in p. — CLAR 224:21
parties 'playing p.' — WILS 840:15
Philistine of genius in p. — ARNO 30:6
playful moderation in p. — HUNT 410:7
p. and equations — EINS 298:11
P. and the fate — CAMU 188:8
P. are now nothing more — JOHN 430:8
P., as a practice — ADAM 2:7

P. can only be — KEEN 447:17
P., executive expression — BRIT 151:19
p. grease — TAWN 773:17
P. has got to be fun — CLAR 224:23
P. in the middle — STEN 755:17
P. is not the art — GALB 338:7
p. is present history — FREE 333:10
P. is the art of preventing — VALÉ 806:10
P. is the Art of the Possible — BUTL 175:18
P. is the only profession — STEV 759:1
P. is war without bloodshed — MAO 511:11
p. like ours profess — GREE 362:4
P. makes strange — PROV 629:27
p. of happiness — HUMP 409:12
p. of the left — JENK 420:21
P. supposed to be — REAG 643:10
P. too serious a matter — DE G 262:6
practice of p. — DISR 277:8
science of p. — ARIS 25:14
secret of p. — BISM 117:13
solve that problem of p. — SCHI 671:7
than it has with p. — SHER 733:12
These are my p. — STEV 759:5
week is a long time in p. — WILS 840:7
will not close my p. — FOX 331:5
zeal in p. — JUNI 438:17
politique p. father — JAME 417:4
Polka see me dance the P. — GROS 365:2
polluted filthy and p. — BIBL 92:12
Pemberley thus p. — AUST 40:3
pollution engine of p., the dog — SPAR 750:2
p. of democracy — WHIT 832:7
Polly Little P. Flinders — NURS 568:4
Our P. is a sad slut — GAY 341:6
P. put the kettle on — NURS 569:4
polyanthus p. of unnumbered dyes — THOM 792:7
polygamous Man is p. — JAME 418:24
polygamy chaste p. — CARE 190:16
p. was made a sin — DRYD 286:15
polygony panachaea, or p. — SPEN 751:28
pomegranate from Browning some 'P.' — BROW 157:26
piece of a p. — BIBL 87:10
Pomeranian P. grenadier — BISM 117:17
pomp bright p. ascended — MILT 533:23
grinning at his p. — SHAK 715:24
p. and plenty — JOHN 433:3
p. and state — BEAU 60:6
p. of pow'r — GRAY 361:3
p. of waters — DANI 255:3
p. of yesterday — KIPL 455:11
Pride, p., and circumstance — SHAK 714:3
Take physic, p. — SHAK 700:23
tide of p. — SHAK 693:19
Pompey Knew you not P. — SHAK 695:28
P. the Great — SHAK 693:12
pompous p. in the grave — BROW 156:18
pomps high Midsummer p. — ARNO 28:26
p. and vanity — BOOK 132:13
pond have their stream and p. — BROO 153:7
Old p., leap-splash — BASH 58:1
ponder P. anew — WINK 841:17
pondered p. them in her heart — BIBL 100:5
ponies Five and twenty p. — KIPL 455:16
wretched, blind, pit p. — HODG 391:10
poodle right hon. Gentleman's p. — LLOY 487:13
pooh yawn, or 'P.' — BYRO 182:2
pool flies over this p. — SIKH 737:15
must first fill a p. — BACO 44:31
Walk across my swimming p. — RICE 647:2
pools p. are filled with water — BOOK 139:16
Where the p. are bright — HOGG 392:6
poop O p.-poop — GRAH 358:14
poor annals of the p. — GRAY 361:3
Blessed are the p. — BIBL 94:20
bring in hither the p. — BIBL 101:8
congregation of the p. — BOOK 139:3
cottages of the p. — HORA 400:5
dare to be p. — GAY 342:8
destruction of the p. — BIBL 84:9
feed with the p. — GARR 340:1

feel for the p. — LAND 466:1
found'st me p. at first — GOLD 354:21
give food to the p. — CAMA 186:13
given to the p. — BIBL 98:28
give to the p. — BIBL 97:25
Good to the p. — CARE 190:15
grind the faces of the p. — BIBL 88:3
help the many who are p. — KENN 448:17
how expensive it is to be p. — BALD 50:7
inconvenient to be p. — COWP 246:6
Laws grind the p. — GOLD 355:14
let the p., and Thou — HERB 385:3
live by robbing the p. — SHAW 726:5
makes me p. indeed — SHAK 713:26
murmuring p. — CRAB 249:7
My countrymen Kiltartan's p. — YEAT 854:15
nice people were p. — OPEN 575:1
no disgrace t'be p. — HUBB 406:14
no peasant in my kingdom so p. — HENR 381:19
not know how to be p. — AESC 6:6
not that men are p. — DU B 291:1
open to the p. and the rich — ANON 16:4
pastor for the p. — ZORO 860:2
Plenty has made me p. — OVID 580:11
p. always ye have — BIBL 103:24
p. and needy — BOOK 136:9
p. are Europe's blacks — CHAM 207:7
p. but she was honest — MILI 526:16
p. don't know that their function — SART 667:8
p. get children — KAHN 441:4
p. have cried — SHAK 697:25
p. have no right — RUSK 660:10
p. know that it is money — BREN 150:20
P. little rich girl — COWA 245:5
p. man at his gate — ALEX 11:7
p. man had nothing — BIBL 80:32
p. man loved the great — MACA 499:15
p. man's dearest friend — BURN 171:25
p. man slipped — BIBL 93:15
p. soul sat sighing — SHAK 714:16
p. who die — SART 666:20
p. wot gets the blame — MILI 526:16
propensity for being p. — AUST 40:19
realize that he was p. — USTI 806:4
Resolve not to be p. — JOHN 432:3
RICH AND THE P. — DISR 277:23
rich as well as the p. — FRAN 331:19
rich on the p. — JEFF 419:12
snatches senses from p. me — CATU 202:20
so p. to do him reverence — SHAK 697:28
Too p. for a bribe — GRAY 361:22
undeserving p. — SHAW 727:14
will be so p. — ELIO 300:10
your tired, your p. — LAZA 476:10
poorer for richer for p. — BOOK 133:9
poorest p. he that is in England — RAIN 640:15
p. man may in his cottage — PITT 596:2
poorly P. (poor man) he lived — FLET 327:16
pop P. goes the weasel — MAND 509:12
pope against the P. or the NUM — BALD 51:1
God bless our P. — WISE 842:2
P.! How many divisions — STAL 754:3
P. is quite satisfied — MICH 524:3
striving with the P. — PROV 624:6
to the P. afterwards — TOAS 796:4
popery danger of P. — ADDI 5:3
popinjay pestered with a p. — SHAK 689:26
popish P. liturgy — PITT 596:5
poplars p. are felled — COWP 247:8
poppies fume of p. — KEAT 445:15
In Flanders fields the p. blow — MCCR 500:17
pleasures are like p. — BURN 172:11
poppy not to wear a p. — MCAL 497:14
p., nor mandragora — SHAK 714:1
with a p. or a lily — GILB 348:15
populace Barbarians, Philistines, and P. — ARNO 29:7
clamours of the p. — ADAM 2:18
give the name of P. — ARNO 29:11
p. rise at once — WHIT 833:18
popular loved to be p. — JAME 418:13

nor ever shall be, p. LAND 466:8
p. politician ARIS 25:7
strong p. feeling TROL 799:21
popularity every difficulty except p.
WILD 837:9
population p., when unchecked MALT 509:9
talked of p. GOLD 355:28
populi *p., vox humbug* SHER 734:13
Salus p. CICE 223:9
Salus p. suprema lex SELD 676:9
Vox p. ALCU 10:10
porcelain dainty rogue in p. MERE 522:14
porcupines throw p. under you KHRU 451:6
pork p. please our mouths MENG 522:4
raw p. and opium BYRO 184:14
Porlock on business from P. COLE 232:2
Person from P. SMIT 743:5
pornographic p. show BLUN 124:9
pornography p. is really about SONT 746:9
p. of war RAE 640:13
P. the attempt to insult sex LAWR 474:22
porpentine quills upon the fretful p.
SHAK 684:32
porpoise p. close behind us CARR 194:17
porridge consistency of cold p. TURI 802:14
healsome p. BURN 170:21
like cold p. SHAK 718:28
Pease p. hot NURS 569:2
sand in the p. COWA 244:17
Porson Wordsworth drunk and P. sober
HOUS 405:6
port Any p. in a storm PROV 614:23
bent to make some p. ARNO 28:22
be p. if it could BENT 69:2
dissolved in p. POPE 601:27
In every p. a wife DIBD 267:7
In ev'ry p. a mistress GAY 342:11
little p. Had seldom seen CLOS 228:5
p., for men JOHN 431:12
p. is near WHIT 833:4
to which p. one is sailing SENE 676:27
portae *geminae Somni p.* VIRG 812:17
portal fitful tracing of a p. STEV 758:4
porter devil-p. it no further SHAK 705:6
moon shone bright on Mrs P. ELIO 303:17
p. of hell-gate SHAK 705:5
Portia P. is Brutus' harlot SHAK 697:1
portion p. for foxes BOOK 138:4
p. of a good man's life WORD 847:7
their p. to drink BOOK 134:8
portmanteau like a p. CARR 195:17
portrait Every time I paint a p. SARG 666:17
p. of a blinking idiot SHAK 709:9
p. of the artist JOYC 437:7
styles of p. painting DICK 270:20
portraits put up and take down p.
LICH 484:8
ports five p. of knowledge BROW 156:3
posies pocket full of p. NURS 569:9
position altering the p. of matter RUSS 660:21
only p. for women CARM 193:6
p. must be held to the last man HAIG 367:11
p. ridiculous CHES 215:17
positions p. of considerable emolument
GAIS 337:15
positive ac-cent-tchu-ate the p. MERC 522:8
energy into something p. IACO 412:6
most p. men POPE 606:24
power of p. thinking PEAL 590:6
possess you may p. it GOET 352:14
possessed in order to be p. BURK 166:9
Love once p. MILT 534:31
much p. by death ELIO 303:26
p. his land BIBL 78:18
possessing p. all things BIBL 108:17
too dear for my p. SHAK 723:13
possession in the glad p. JONS 435:12
just p. of truth BROW 156:22
Man's best p. EURI 312:24
never your p. BRIT 151:18
p. for all time THUC 793:22
P. is nine points PROV 629:28
p. of them both KEAT 446:22

right, title, and p. BOOK 144:20
possessions All my p. LAST 471:2
behind the great p. JAME 417:21
he had great p. BIBL 97:26
he who has many p. HORA 402:17
least of p. WHIT 832:4
multitude of p. SMAR 739:16
possibilities improbable p. ARIS 25:23
possibility deny the p. of anything
HUXL 412:5
p. of suicide CIOR 223:27
possible All things are p. with God
PROV 614:18
all things p. BACO 46:13
art of the p. BISM 117:14
Art of the P. BUTL 175:18
art of the p. GALB 338:7
as far as I think it p. COOK 242:1
best of all p. worlds BRAD 148:19
if a thing is p. CALO 186:5
p. you may be mistaken CROM 251:16
realm of the p. PIND 595:13
something is p. CLAR 225:2
with God all things are p. BIBL 97:28
possidentem *p. multa* HORA 402:17
possum said the Honourable P. BERR 71:18
possumus *Non omnia p. omnes* VIRG 814:8
possunt *p., quia posse videntur* VIRG 812:7
post driving briskly in a p.-chaise
JOHN 430:25
LIE FOLLOWS BY P. TELE 776:11
p. Allotted by the Gods TENN 781:12
P. coitum SAYI 670:11
p. of honour ADDI 4:14
p. of honour PROV 629:30
postal p. districts packed like squares of
wheat LARK 469:6
postcards p. of the hanging DYLA 294:4
posted p. presence of the watcher JAME 418:3
poster Kitchener is a great p. ASQU 32:6
p. a visual telegram CASS 198:14
posteri *Credite p.* HORA 401:8
posterity correspondent for p. BAGE 49:9
damage to p. WITH 842:5
go down to p. DISR 276:25
hope of p. POWE 610:7
looked upon by p. CLOS 228:14
look forward to p. BURK 167:9
P. as likely to be BROU 154:16
P. do something for us ADDI 5:12
P. is no more than CHAM 207:9
Think of your p. ADAM 3:9
To evoke p. GRAV 360:10
trustees of P. DISR 277:26
write for p. ADE 5:15
postern p. door makes a thief PROV 629:29
Present has latched its p. HARD 372:9
posters P. of the sea and land SHAK 703:7
Posthumus Ah! P., the years SMAR 740:19
Post-Impressionist P. pictures BLUN 124:9
postman p. always rings twice CAIN 185:10
think I am, a bloody p. BEHA 63:16
postscript but in her p. STEE 754:17
Here is yet a p. SHAK 721:1
most material in the p. BACO 43:30
pith is in the p. HAZL 376:9
posy I made a p. HERB 384:12
pot chicken in every p. HOOV 395:23
chicken in his p. HENR 381:19
death in the p. BIBL 82:5
flinging a p. of paint RUSK 659:9
Joan doth keel the p. SHAK 702:26
kettle and the earthen p. BIBL 93:14
Look at p. NASH 557:13
under a p. BIBL 86:6
watched p. never boils PROV 633:42
who the p. FITZ 323:13
potations dull and deep p. GIBB 345:13
potato bashful young p. GILB 348:14
p.-gatherers move KAVA 442:5
potency evidence of his p. DISR 278:4
potent how p. cheap music is COWA 245:11
potential p. you actually have BROW 155:2

potion p. and his pill HERR 386:1
Potomac All quiet along the P. BEER 63:9
quiet along the P. MCCL 500:11
potoribus *scribuntur aquae p.* HORA 399:17
pots have lien among the p. BOOK 138:12
potsherd Let the p. strive BIBL 89:23
poor p., patch HOPK 397:7
took him a p. BIBL 82:29
pottage mess of p. BIBL 76:24
potter hand then of the p. FITZ 323:12
Harry P. was an unusual boy OPEN 574:12
p. and clay endure BROW 161:5
p. power over the clay BIBL 106:24
p.'s vessel BOOK 133:21
Who *is* the p., pray FITZ 323:13
pottery P. is a practical COOP 242:13
pouch p. on side SHAK 681:12
poultry lives of the p. ELIO 299:16
pound any fool can do for a p. SHUT 735:10
in for a p. PROV 623:33
p. foolish PROV 629:21
p. here in Britain WILS 840:9
pounding Hard p. this WELL 827:13
pounds Give crowns and p. HOUS 404:10
how many p. JUVE 440:8
p. will take care LOWN 494:20
p. will take care of PROV 631:37
six hundred p. a-year SWIF 766:31
two hundred p. a year BUTL 176:16
pour P. into our hearts BOOK 130:14
p. out my spirit BIBL 92:3
poured p. into his clothes WODE 843:6
p. out like water BOOK 135:1
pouring make in p. it out POPE 606:22
pours never rains but it p. PROV 624:16
poverty cost of setting him up in p.
NAID 556:1
crime so shameful as p. FARQ 315:9
endure harsh p. HORA 402:17
Give me not p. DEFO 261:8
hunger and p. LARK 468:11
implication of dreary p. WEST 830:11
in his squadrons, P. FLAT 324:20
In honoured p. SHEL 732:6
In p., hunger, and dirt HOOD 395:11
misfortunes of p. JUVE 439:16
neither p. nor riches BIBL 85:20
P. a great evil AUST 40:11
p. and excess PENN 591:16
P. and oysters DICK 272:2
p. and Paris SCHI 668:13
P. is a great enemy JOHN 432:3
P. is a lot like childbirth ROWL 657:15
P. is no disgrace PROV 629:31
P. is not a crime PROV 629:32
p.'s catching BEHN 64:3
represent p. as no evil JOHN 428:11
struggled with p. BALD 50:7
their p. BIBL 84:9
When p. comes in at the door PROV 634:26
worse than p. TRAH 798:1
worst of crimes is p. SHAW 725:21
powder food for p. SHAK 691:2
keep your p. dry BLAC 118:7
keep your p. dry PROV 629:49
when your p.'s runnin' low NEWB 560:1
powdered Still to be p. JONS 435:4
power absolute p. ADAM 3:4
acquisition of p. RUSS 661:5
All p. to the Soviets POLI 600:1
another name for absolute p. WORD 849:19
art is of such p. SHAK 718:25
balance of p. KISS 457:9
balance of p. NICO 563:10
Beauty is p. ADVE 7:9
because we had p. BENÉ 66:14
Black P. CARM 193:7
breathless, p. breathe forth SHAK 679:6
certainty of p. DAY- 260:4
coming into p. BAGE 48:6
conceive a dominant p. HARD 372:2
corridors of p. SNOW 744:21
defy P. SHEL 731:10

power (cont.):

desire of p.	HOBB 390:12
desires to have—P.	BOUL 147:8
friend in p.	ADAM 2:11
from our hands have p.	WORD 849:24
good want to	SHEL 731:2
grace and p.	BOOK 130:3
greater the p.	BURK 168:17
have the p. to die	TENN 784:9
his p. and his love	GRAN 359:3
in office but not in p.	LAMO 465:18
intoxicated with p.	BURK 166:3
jaws of p.	ADAM 3:6
Knowledge is p.	PROV 624:45
knowledge itself is p.	BACO 46:10
life and p.	FOX 331:7
literature of p.	DE Q 265:3
live without a common p.	HOBB 390:14
love of p.	HAZL 376:14
maximal authority and minimal p.	
	SZAS 769:14
Money is p.	PROV 626:32
more contracted that p. is	JOHN 431:4
no hopes but from p.	BURK 168:19
not exempted from her p.	HOOK 395:18
notions about a superior p.	SWIF 765:4
only have p. over people	SOLZ 745:14
or p. more	BROM 152:4
outrun our spiritual p.	KING 452:7
O wad some P.	BURN 172:19
place without p.	ROSE 654:18
political p. of another	LOCK 488:18
P. a corrupter	SHEL 732:12
p., and the glory	BIBL 95:3
P. and War	KIPL 453:16
p. belongeth unto God	BOOK 138:2
p. can be rightfully exercised	MILL 525:6
P. corrupts	PROV 629:33
p. grows out of the barrel of a gun	
	MAO 511:12
p. in the day of death	BIBL 86:11
p. in trust	DRYD 287:3
P. is given only	DISR 277:33
P. is not a means	DOST 283:6
P. is so apt to be insolent	ORWE 577:21
P. is the great aphrodisiac	HALI 369:5
p. of a man	KISS 457:11
p. of Jesus' Name	HOBB 390:11
p. of suppress	PERR 593:3
p. of the crown	NORT 565:14
p. of the written word	BURK 168:5
p. over men	CONR 240:20
p. over nothing	WOLL 844:4
p. over other beings	HERO 385:14
p. should always be distrusted	FOST 330:10
P. tends to corrupt	JONE 434:10
p. that worketh	ACTO 1:13
p. to act according to discretion	BIBL 109:7
p. to be put forth	LOCK 488:21
p. to endanger	CANN 189:11
p. to tax	ADAM 2:19
P. to the people	MARS 514:12
p. Which erring men call chance	POLI 601:6
p. which stands on Privilege	MILT 529:5
P. without responsibility	BELL 65:19
remain the slaves of p.	KIPL 457:8
Responsibility without p.	WOLL 844:7
responsibility without p.	DORF 282:15
Restored to life, and p.	STOP 761:8
seek p. and lose liberty	KEBL 447:12
seeks to communicate p.	BACO 44:22
selves have given a p.	DE Q 264:21
shadow of some unseen P.	OSBO 578:14
some great P.	SHEL 729:14
source of p.	HUXL 411:16
strange p., After offence	MARS 514:15
stripped of p.	MILT 534:31
struggle of man against p.	SCOT 673:15
supreme p. must be arbitrary	KUND 462:5
take who have the p.	HALI 368:18
Too weak for p.	WORD 849:25
Treasury is in p.	LEAP 477:1
	WILS 840:12

unlimited p.	ADAM 1:14
Unlimited p.	PITT 596:3
upon the past has p.	DRYD 289:30
utility of monarchical p.	BOSW 146:22
want p. to execute	JOHN 426:7
What p. have you got	BENN 67:4
with Eternal God for p.	TENN 782:18
powerful fear is that we are p.	WILL 839:15
p. and free	TOCQ 795:9
P. women only succeed	LEE- 479:5
powerless p. to be born	ARNO 28:20
powers acquaintance with ruling p.	
	TALM 771:24
against p.	BIBL 109:21
Headmasters have p.	CHUR 222:10
high contracting p.	BRIA 151:2
non-resistance to the higher p.	MAYH 519:15
p. at work in this country	MISQ 537:9
p. that be	BIBL 106:30
principalities, nor p.	BIBL 106:23
principalities, or p.	BIBL 110:10
real separation of p.	DENN 264:11
ultimate p. of the society	JEFF 420:13
virtues, p.	MILT 533:16
we lay waste our p.	WORD 850:21
pox or of the p.	WILK 837:19
practical p. form of art	COOP 242:13
p. intellectual	STRO 762:14
we look at the p.	GLAD 351:1
practice ounce of p.	PROV 629:10
p. in being refused	DIOG 274:20
P. makes perfect	PROV 629:34
wear them out in p.	BEAU 59:14
practices bloody principles and p.	FOX 331:11
practise Go p. if you please	BROW 161:8
never to p. either	TWAI 803:9
p. in heaven	BROW 160:12
P. what you preach	PROV 629:35
p. without me	SHER 733:8
practised making p. smiles	SHAK 721:25
praemia P. *digna ferant*	VIRG 811:7
praemitti *non amitti sed p.*	CYPR 254:15
praestantissimum *Id quod est p.*	CICE 223:23
praevalet *Magna est veritas, et p.*	BIBL 115:19
pragmatism we need p.	RAFF 640:14
prairies From the mountains to the p.	
	BERL 69:18
praise against empty p.	POPE 601:20
All p. to thee	KEN 448:7
Apostles: p. thee	BOOK 127:20
as is p.	ASCH 31:2
chant hymns of p.	ZORO 859:15
countryman must have p.	BLYT 124:14
Damn with faint p.	POPE 602:29
girded with p.	GRAN 359:3
Give them not p.	SORL 746:23
highest p. of God	PROU 613:10
how to p.	AUDE 35:8
husband's first p.	BARB 55:8
idle smoke of p.	DANI 255:8
is p. indeed	MORT 551:9
lack tongues to p.	SHAK 723:17
let his just p. be given	WALT 821:6
little dust of p.	TENN 779:13
man worthy of p.	HORA 402:15
named thee but to p.	HALL 369:16
oblique p.	JOHN 431:7
Of p. a mere glutton	GOLD 355:8
p. at morning	POPE 604:12
P. belongs to God	KORA 459:7
P. be to Nero's Neptune	DYLA 294:5
p. 'em most	ADDI 4:7
p. famous men	BIBL 93:30
P. from Sir Hubert	MISQ 538:14
P. him, and magnify him	BOOK 128:5
P., laud, and bless his name	KETH 450:5
P. my soul	LYTE 497:11
p. of ancient authors	HOBB 391:2
p. of God	AUGU 37:19
P. the child	PROV 629:36
P. thee, God	PRAY 611:7
P. the green earth	BUNT 164:9
P. the Lord	BOOK 141:1

P. the Lord	FORG 329:5
P. the Lord, all nations	BIBL 115:4
P. the Lord, for he is kind	MILT 529:28
p. the tender feet	SAMB 665:9
P. they that will	HERR 386:9
p. those works	MART 514:18
p. to Mount Sion	BUNY 164:14
P. to the Holiest	NEWM 561:4
P. to the Lord	WINK 841:15
p. ye the Lord	BAKE 50:3
Self-p. no recommendation	PROV 630:28
shew thy p.	BOOK 137:15
thank, p., laud, glorify	HAGG 367:4
there were few to p.	WORD 849:27
they only want p.	MAUG 518:19
To their right p.	SHAK 710:7
unto thy Name give the p.	BOOK 142:3
utter all thy P.	ADDI 5:5
We p. thee, O God	BOOK 127:20
were no small p.	MILT 534:16
praised everybody p. the Duke	SOUT 749:2
God be p.	BROW 157:24
happy when being p.	BALF 51:10
more in him to be p.	JONS 436:8
p., and got rid of	CICE 223:26
p. him to his face	TENN 784:3
p. his fleas	YEAT 855:23
p. the dead	BIBL 86:2
praiser p. of past times	HORA 398:11
praises p. from the men	COWL 245:27
p. those who follow	HORA 403:2
These p. are not small	HEYW 387:19
with faint p.	WYCH 852:14
praising always p. the past	SMIT 743:2
doing one's p. for oneself	BUTL 176:24
P. all alike	GAY 342:6
pram p. in the hall	CONN 240:3
prata *sat p. biberunt*	VIRG 814:1
prater pert, prim p.	CHUR 220:6
pray as lief p. with Kit Smart	JOHN 428:4
best way to p.	BÜCH 163:3
came to scoff, remained to p.	GOLD 354:14
cannot pay, let him p.	PROV 621:44
fervently do we p.	LINC 485:11
I p. for the country	HALE 368:5
nor p. with you	SHAK 708:29
Often when I p.	LEWI 483:10
p. all day long	TALM 772:34
p., and not to faint	BIBL 101:26
P. for the dead	JONE 434:7
p. for them	LEE 479:3
P. for the repose of His soul	ROLF 653:2
p. for you at St Paul's	SMIT 744:5
p. in their distress	BLAK 122:2
p. to Him	BARN 56:13
P. without ceasing	BIBL 110:18
p. you, master Lieutenant	MORE 548:17
to Thee alone we p.	KORA 459:8
To work is to p.	MOTT 552:10
Watch and p.	BIBL 99:6
we do p. for mercy	SHAK 709:26
We p. for peace	GAUN 341:1
Work and p.	HILL 388:11
prayed P. aloud	AUBR 33:23
prayer Conservative Party at p.	ROYD 657:16
Father, hear the p.	WILL 839:17
Four spend in p.	COKE 230:19
hearest the p.	BOOK 138:5
house of p.	BIBL 90:11
house of p.	BIBL 98:4
lift up the hands in p.	HOPK 397:15
man of p.	SMAR 740:16
on a wing and a p.	ADAM 3:17
One p. absorbs all others	GLAD 351:5
people's p.	DRYD 287:2
perfect p.	LESS 482:5
p. at sinking of the sun	KORA 460:15
p. is only answered	TALM 772:18
p. never loses its value	TALM 772:34
p. of a righteous man	BIBL 112:1
p. reduces itself	TURG 802:11
p. the Church's banquet	HERB 384:17
things are wrought by p.	TENN 778:17

'tis the hour of p. BYRO 181:11
wish for p. is a prayer BERN 70:9
prayers addicted to p. ASHF 31:13
among my p. HORA 403:14
ask your prayers WILL 838:12
Christopher Robin is saying his p.
MILN 528:5
hear our p. BOOK 133:1
in my p. BIBL 105:34
mention of you in our p. BIBL 110:15
p. of saints BIBL 113:12
p. three hours a day POPE 603:25
recite one's p. TALM 772:35
three-mile p. BURN 173:1
your p. are wasted AESO 6:17
prayeth p. well, who loveth well COLE 233:10
praying Amelia was p. for George
THAC 786:16
No p. OTWA 579:13
now he is p. SHAK 687:16
past p. for SHAK 690:8
writing, or p. THOM 788:7
prays family that p. together SAYI 669:18
that faintly p. QUAR 639:2
preach could na p. for thinkin' o't
BURN 172:1
Practise what you p. PROV 629:35
p. among the Gentiles BIBL 109:6
P. not because you have WHAT 831:7
p. the gospel BIBL 99:29
preached p. to death by wild curates
SMIT 744:2
preacher Judge not the p. HERB 383:22
preachers best of all p. GUES 365:13
company of the p. BOOK 138:12
P. say, Do as I say SELD 676:12
preaching bad p. CECI 204:13
foolishness of p. BIBL 107:2
moral is not p. DIMN 274:13
woman's p. JOHN 428:19
precedency love of place and p. DONN 282:4
point of p. JOHN 432:7
precedent from p. LLOY 487:11
is a dangerous p. CORN 243:12
p. embalms a principle STOW 761:21
p. to precedent TENN 784:23
precept Example better than p. PROV 619:27
more efficacious than p. JOHN 426:2
p. must be upon precept BIBL 89:3
precepts We love the p. FARQ 315:18
precious Deserve the p. bane MILT 531:26
My P. TOLK 796:12
p. in our joys STER 756:13
so p. it must be rationed LENI 480:10
This p. stone SHAK 715:13
precipices from bogs and p. LOCK 488:16
p. show untrodden green KEAT 445:20
précis p. of life FRIE 334:16
precise when Art Is too p. HERR 385:21
precisely thinking too p. SHAK 688:3
predicament is the human p. QUIN 639:10
It is a p. BENN 67:15
predict always difficult to p. BERN 71:7
enable us to p. events HAWK 375:13
only p. things after IONE 413:22
pre-eminence hath no p. BIBL 86:1
Lord hath the p. BOOK 142:9
prefaces Shaw's p. AGAT 6:21
preference invidious p. LAMB 464:11
special p. for beetles HALD 368:2
preferment knocking at P.'s door ARNO 28:4
preferred ought to be p. GODW 352:3
pregnancies P. are damaging SADE 662:14
pregnancy avoid p. by resort to
mathematics MENC 521:19
pregnant elegant and p. texture STEV 758:25
If men could get p. KENN 448:10
p. bank swelled up DONN 280:20
prejudice P., n. A vagrant opinion BIER 116:8
p. of good order MILI 526:5
p. runs in favour of two DICK 270:15
Pride and p. BORR 146:14
PRIDE AND P. BURN 169:23

religious p. HUXL 412:4
when p. commands HELV 380:18
prejudices above national p. NORT 565:9
deposit of p. EINS 298:6
Drive out p. FRED 333:7
it p. a man so SMIT 744:6
one of its own p. HEGE 379:9
p. and habits GIBB 345:11
p. to rest on WOLL 844:2
proprietor's p. SWAF 765:3
prelate religion without a p. BANC 54:13
prelaty yoke of p. MILT 536:4
premature p. anti-Fascist ANON 20:8
premeditated abstract and p. city
DOST 283:10
p. sins TALM 772:16
premier great p. BAGE 49:4
premises based upon licenced p. O'BR 571:5
prentice Her p. han' she tried BURN 171:7
preparation no p. is thought necessary
STEV 759:1
prepare not to p. for life PAST 587:18
p. a place for you BIBL 103:28
p. for the worst PROV 622:30
p. to shed them now SHAK 698:1
P. VAULT FOR FUNERAL TELE 776:9
P. ye the way BIBL 89:16
P. ye the way of the Lord BIBL 94:10
prepared Be p. MOTT 552:4
favours only the p. PAST 588:6
p. for them that love thee BOOK 130:14
p. the dry land BOOK 140:10
world not yet p. DOYL 284:14
prerogative English subject's sole p.
DRYD 289:24
exert his p. JOHN 426:6
last p. DRYD 288:15
p. of the eunuch STOP 761:8
p. of the harlot KIPL 457:8
rotten as P. BURK 168:5
that which is called p. LOCK 488:21
presagers dumb p. SHAK 722:27
presbyter New P. is but old *Priest*
MILT 530:28
Presbytery let that [P.] go CHAR 209:6
prescription p. of a quick dip in bed
WESL 829:24
presence away from thy p. BOOK 137:13
beautified with his p. BOOK 133:5
before his p. with a song BOOK 140:17
come before his p. BOOK 140:9
conspicuous by its p. RUSS 661:14
made better by their p. ELIO 300:20
posted p. of the watcher JAME 418:3
p. on the field WELL 827:16
present Act in the living P. LONG 490:20
All p. and correct MILI 526:2
characteristic of the p. age DISR 275:21
clear and p. danger HOLM 393:10
Eternally p. within all SIKH 737:8
know nothing but the p. KEYN 450:14
live in the p. CHEK 213:23
many as are here p. BOOK 127:14
no p. in Wales THOM 791:3
no redress for the p. DISR 276:28
No time like the p. MANL 510:5
No time like the p. PROV 628:4
past, p. and future EINS 298:9
perpetuates the p. DE B 260:14
p. contains nothing more BERG 69:6
P. has latched its postern HARD 372:9
p. in New York CHAP 208:21
p. in spirit BIBL 107:9
p. is an age of talkers HAZL 376:22
p. is an interlude O'NE 573:14
p. is the funeral CLAR 224:13
p. joys are more DRYD 288:18
p. laughter SHAK 720:16
p. moment MANN 510:10
p. of Mornington Crescent HARG 373:12
p., past, and future, sees BLAK 122:9
p. scorn BEHN 63:21
p., yes, we are in it LOWE 494:19

p. your front to the world MOLI 541:9
things p., nor things to come BIBL 106:23
Time p. and time past ELIO 301:9
un-birthday p. CARR 195:14
very p. help in trouble BOOK 136:24
What if this p. DONN 279:24
who controls the p. ORWE 577:15
présentez P. toujours le devant MOLI 541:9
presents bring p. BOOK 140:11
Christmas without any p. OPEN 574:10
give p. BOOK 138:23
P., I often say, endear Absents LAMB 464:12
preservation our creation, p. BOOK 129:20
p. of their property LOCK 488:20
Self-p. is first law PROV 630:29
preservative p. from want AUST 39:24
preserve do not p. myself ORTE 576:13
Dr Strabismus (Whom God P.) MORT 551:6
give and p. to our use BOOK 129:14
p. and enlarge freedom LOCK 488:16
p.'s full of stones BETJ 72:8
p. thy going out BOOK 142:17
preserved my life is p. BIBL 76:36
need not be p. OMAR 573:6
Union: it must be p. JACK 414:16
preserver Destroyer and p. SHEL 730:7
presidency cancer close to the P. DEAN 260:7
heart-beat from the P. STEV 758:16
messenger-boy P. SCHL 671:8
Teflon-coated P. SCHR 671:17
US p. a Tudor monarchy BURG 165:17
vice-p. isn't worth a pitcher GARN 339:16
president All the P. is TRUM 801:6
anybody could become P. DARR 257:2
any boy may become P. STEV 758:14
As P., I have no eyes LINC 485:13
going to be your next p. CART 197:2
I'm P. BUSH 174:24
no criticism of the p. ROOS 654:16
P. is a crook NIXO 564:21
P. of the Immortals CLOS 228:17
P. of the Immortals HARD 372:5
P. should not wear MCAL 497:14
P.'s spouse BUSH 174:21
rather be right than be P. CLAY 226:4
security around the p. MAIL 507:14
used to be the next P. GORE 357:1
vote for the best P. PETE 593:14
We are the P.'s men KISS 456:7
When the P. does it NIXO 565:2
press be named P.-men ARNO 26:21
complain about the p. POWE 610:3
dead-born from the p. HUME 409:6
demagogic, corrupt p. PULI 637:2
depends on freedom of the p. JEFF 419:11
freedom of the p. JEFF 420:4
Freedom of the p. guaranteed LIEB 484:10
Freedom of the p. in Britain SWAF 765:3
Let's go to p. WINC 841:3
liberty of the p. JUNI 438:15
lose your temper with the P. PANK 585:6
not a free p. but a managed RADC 640:10
of our idolatry, the p. COWP 247:14
open and unshackled p. HOWE 405:14
Our Republic and its p. PULI 637:1
people from the p. TWAI 803:17
periodical p. TROL 800:12
popular p. is drinking MELL 521:8
power of the p. NORT 565:14
p. still hounded you JOHN 422:12
p. toward the mark BIBL 110:4
to th' p. to trudge BRAD 149:3
with you on the free p. STOP 761:10
You p. the button ADVE 8:2
pressed p. down my soul BOOK 137:22
p. out of shape FROS 336:2
worth two p. men PROV 629:3
pressure Grace under p. HEMI 381:8
presume Dr Livingstone, I p. STAN 754:6
P. not that I am SHAK 692:24
p. too much upon my love SHAK 698:15
presumption amused by its p. CART 198:2

presumptioun surquidrie and foul p.
CHAU 212:28
prêt toujours p. à partir LA F 463:15
pretence to some faint meaning make p.
DRYD 288:31
pretend We shall not p. NEWS 562:21
pretended p. friend is worse GAY 341:29
pretender blessing—the P. BYRO 177:19
James I, James II, and the Old P.
GUED 365:12
pretending p. to extraordinary revelations
BUTL 175:14
pretendy wee p. government CONN 240:1
pretension p. is nothing HUNT 410:4
pretentious P. quotations FOWL 330:18
pretexts Tyrants seldom want p. BURK 166:4
pretio Omnia Romae Cum p. JUVE 439:18
pretty all my p. chickens SHAK 706:24
all the maidens p. COLM 236:1
He is a very p. woeman FLEM 326:19
It is a p. thing GREE 362:23
lived in a p. how town CUMM 253:5
my p. maid NURS 570:15
policeman and a p. girl CHAP 208:5
p. and proud PROV 625:36
p. girl is like a melody BERL 69:20
P. is as pretty does PROV 629:37
p. maids all in a row NURS 568:9
p. to see what money will do PEPY 592:14
P. witty Nell PEPY 592:8
Puts on his p. looks SHAK 699:6
sex object if you're p. GIOV 349:19
prevail I believe man will p. FAUL 316:4
truth, and shall p. BROO 154:9
prevailed they have not p. BOOK 143:5
prevarication last dyke of p. BURK 169:4
prevent not knowing how to p. them
RUSS 661:11
P. us, O Lord BOOK 132:7
to p. war MCGU 502:6
try to p. it MILN 528:13
preventing grace p. us BOOK 130:6
p. people from taking part VALÉ 806:10
prevention P. is better PROV 629:38
prey bent on his p. MILT 532:19
destined p. SHAW 726:4
drive a p. BALL 51:14
greater p. upon the less GREE 362:4
p. of the rich JEFF 419:12
roaring after their p. BOOK 141:9
to hast'ning ills a p. GOLD 354:10
yet a p. to all POPE 605:1
preys only one that p. JAME 418:22
Priam P.'s sons of Troy SURR 764:7
price bought it at any p. CLAR 224:18
Courage is the p. EARH 294:21
Every man has his p. PROV 619:16
in Rome has its p. JUVE 439:18
love that pays the p. SPRI 753:5
pay any p. KENN 448:16
pay the blood p. BLAI 119:1
pearl of great p. BIBL 97:6
pearls fetch a high p. WHAT 831:11
p. is far above rubies BIBL 85:23
p. of admiralty KIPL 455:18
p. of a large turbot RUSK 659:20
p. of everything WILD 836:9
p. of justice BENN 67:19
p. of petrol has been increased CART 198:8
p. of the paint VAN 807:2
p. of wisdom BIBL 83:15
p. well worth paying LAMO 465:17
p. we pay for love SAYI 669:23
those men have their p. WALP 820:6
Too high a p. is asked DOST 283:3
What p. glory ANDE 14:8
without money and without p. BIBL 90:6
Wot p. Selvytion nah SHAW 725:25
prices contrivance to raise p. SMIT 741:6
High p. profit those CARR 196:13
paid the p. of life GURN 366:1
prick If you p. us SHAK 709:14
I paint with my p. MISQ 538:3

It is a p. PEEL 591:1
spur To p. the sides SHAK 704:7
pricking By the p. of my thumbs SHAK 706:14
p. on the plain SPEN 751:12
prickly Here we go round the p. pear
ELIO 302:7
pricks kick against the p. BIBL 105:3
pride contempt on all my p. WATT 823:15
family p. is something GILB 347:20
here have P. and Truth YEAT 855:4
He that is low no p. BUNY 165:3
I know thy p. BIBL 80:18
lacks a proper p. MACD 501:2
look backward to with p. FROS 335:11
maiden p., adieu SHAK 712:22
p. and high disdain SCOT 673:7
P. and pleasure JOHN 433:3
P. and prejudice BORR 146:14
P. AND PREJUDICE BURN 169:23
p., cruelty, and ambition RALE 641:14
P. feels no pain PROV 629:39
P. goes before a fall PROV 629:40
P. goeth before destruction BIBL 84:26
P. helps us ELIO 299:24
P. in their port GOLD 355:13
P. of Life HARD 372:12
p. of the peacock BLAK 121:5
P. ruled my will NEWM 561:6
P. still is aiming at the blest POPE 604:25
p. that apes humility COLE 231:13
rank p., and haughtiness ADDI 4:9
save its p. MEYE 523:16
soldier's p. BROW 159:26
will her p. deflower SPEN 751:26
pridie day that hath no p. DONN 282:7
priest As a p. COWP 248:20
fiddling p. COWP 247:9
great being a p. LINE 486:6
guts of the last p. DIDE 273:17
Like people, like p. BIBL 91:27
Like people, like p. PROV 625:21
listened to the p. BALL 52:17
New Presbyter is but old P. MILT 530:28
Once a p. PROV 628:27
p. continues DRYD 288:19
P. did offer Christ BOOK 144:17
p. doth reign MACA 499:9
P. for ever BOOK 141:21
p. of the invisible STEV 757:19
p. of the Muses HORA 401:9
p. persuades humble people PERU 593:11
religion from the p. GOLD 356:1
rid me of this turbulent p. HENR 382:4
'twixt the P. and Clerk HERR 386:5
priestcraft ere p. did begin DRYD 286:15
priesthood royal p. BIBL 112:5
priestlike at their p. task KEAT 442:11
priests beheaded p. HENR 382:7
dominion of p. PRIC 610:15
P., and Deacons BOOK 129:10
p. by the imposition MACA 498:5
p. have been enemies HUME 409:1
p. on their way to bury BOCC 124:16
treen p. JEWE 421:20
with the guts of p. MESL 523:7
priggish P. schoolgirl GRIG 364:10
prigs p. and pedants DISR 275:19
prime arrive at a p. mover THOM 789:1
having lost but once your p. HERR 386:19
My p. of youth TICH 794:12
One's p. is elusive SPAR 749:27
spent my youthfu' p. BURN 173:6
Prime Minister best P. we have BUTL 175:16
buried the Unknown P. ASQU 32:4
HOW DARE YOU BECOME P. TELE 776:6
model of a modern P. HENN 381:18
next P. but three BELL 65:1
No woman will be P. THAT 786:25
P. has resigned ANON 16:7
P. has to be a butcher BUTL 175:17
P. is like the banyan PATI 588:13
Prime Ministers P. and such as they
GILB 347:7

P. are wedded SAKI 663:20
P. have never yet been CHUR 222:10
wild flowers, and P. BALD 50:14
primerole She was a p. CHAU 211:22
primeval forest p. LONG 490:7
primitive p. nothing ROCH 651:17
primordial bit of p. chaos WELL 828:14
primrose go the p. way SHAK 705:6
P. first born child FLET 327:8
p. path of dalliance SHAK 684:16
p. that forsaken dies MILT 530:8
soft silken p. MILT 530:15
withered p. BOLT 126:17
Primrose Hill P. and Saint John's Wood
BLAK 120:9
primroses Pale p. SHAK 722:6
prince Advise the p. ELIO 302:18
bless the P. of Wales LINL 486:10
danced with the P. of Wales FARJ 315:3
dominion of a p. HUME 408:16
draws sword against p. PROV 635:5
Good-night, sweet p. SHAK 689:16
Gorgon, P. of darkness SPEN 751:14
great p. in prison lies DONN 280:22
Hamlet without the P. SCOT 674:23
in a p. the virtue MASS 518:1
news and P. of Peace FLET 327:13
p. among my own people BRAN 149:16
P. calls in the good old money LAMB 464:10
P. I am not DEKK 262:19
p. must be a fox MACH 502:12
p. of Aquitaine NERV 559:8
p. of darkness SHAK 700:29
p. of glory died WATT 823:15
P. of Peace BIBL 88:18
P. of Wales not a position BENN 67:15
p. sets himself up above the law
MAYH 519:15
p. who begins early BAGE 48:18
p. who gets a reputation NAPO 556:9
safer for a p. MACH 502:10
send the companion a better p. SHAK 691:26
Who made thee a p. BIBL 77:14
princedoms p., virtues MILT 533:16
princes death of p. SHAK 697:3
inform his p. BOOK 141:13
like one of the p. BOOK 139:14
mine were p. of the earth BENJ 66:16
P. and lords may flourish GOLD 354:10
p. are come home again SHAK 699:16
p. in all lands BOOK 136:23
trust in p. BOOK 143:26
princess People's P. BLAI 118:18
P. leave the Englishwoman BISM 117:12
P. of Parallelograms BYRO 184:1
P. of Wales AUST 40:15
see she was a real p. ANDE 14:3
principalities against p. BIBL 109:21
angels, nor p. BIBL 106:23
p., or powers BIBL 110:10
principate p. and liberty TACI 769:21
principibus P. placuisse viris HORA 399:13
principiis P. obsta OVID 580:16
principio In p. erat Verbum MISS 539:12
principis Indignatio p. mors est MORE 548:13
principle active P. WORD 846:18
does everything on p. SHAW 727:3
feel the p. of God FOX 331:10
little of the p. left REIT 645:2
precedent embalms a p. STOW 761:21
p. of all social progress FOUR 330:16
p. of the English law DICK 267:23
Protection is not a p. DISR 275:9
rebels from p. BURK 167:17
useful thing about a p. MAUG 518:15
principles bloody p. and practices
FOX 331:11
Damn your p. DISR 277:36
denies the first p. AUCT 34:5
either morals or p. GLAD 350:19
embrace your Lordship's p. WILK 837:19
fundamental p. are thirteen MAIM 507:15
he has good p. JOHN 428:6

projections other figures in it Merely p.
ELIO 301:5
projects fitter for new p. BACO 46:4
proletarian Sisyphus, p. CAMU 188:13
proletariat dictatorship of the p. MARX 517:2
prologue make a long p. BIBL 94:3
very witty p. CONG 239:5
What's past is p. SHAK 718:29
prologues happy p. SHAK 703:14
P. precede the piece GARR 340:6
Promethean true P. fire SHAK 702:18
promise broke no p. POPE 603:24
by p. BIBL 108:27
Eastern p. ADVE 7:23
eat the air, p.-crammed SHAK 687:1
ill keeper of p. BACO 43:23
P., large promise JOHN 424:18
p. made it a debt unpaid SERV 677:6
this p. which has stood HAGG 367:2
Whose p. none relies on EPIT 309:14
promised Marching to the P. Land BARI 56:5
O Jesus, I have p. BODE 125:3
P. from eternal years CASW 199:5
reach the p. land CALL 185:16
seen the p. land KING 452:6
weird women p. SHAK 705:16
promises According to thy p. BOOK 127:17
have p. to keep FROS 336:3
leave his p. unfulfilled JOHN 426:7
p. and panaceas ROTH 656:21
P., like pie-crust PROV 629:42
p. were, as he then was SHAK 695:19
received the p. BIBL 111:8
Vote for the man who p. least BARU 57:18
young man of p. BALF 51:9
promising first call p. CONN 240:2
promontory sat upon a p. SHAK 711:1
See one p. BURT 174:6
Stretched like a p. MILT 533:22
promotion none will sweat but for p.
SHAK 680:29
p. cometh neither from BOOK 139:4
p. to the blest DRYD 289:26
You'll get no p. HUGH 406:16
prone Orion plunges p. HOUS 404:3
position for women is p. CARM 193:6
pronounce better than they p. TWAI 803:14
could not frame to p. it BIBL 79:28
even to p. the word JOIN 434:2
pronounced p. the letter R AUBR 33:21
pronunciation p. Reigned tyrannically
HEAN 378:5
proof America is the p. MCCA 500:7
Come time of p. GOOG 356:12
lapped in p. SHAK 703:4
p. of the pudding PROV 629:43
proofs p. of holy writ SHAK 713:31
Prooshans others may be P. DICK 270:4
prop p. To our infirmity WORD 849:10
propaganda on p. CORN 243:14
P. is a soft weapon HELL 380:11
purely for p. BEAV 60:14
purpose of this war is p. WELL 828:17
propagate likely to p. understanding
JOHN 433:19
propagation peace and p. WALP 819:12
propensities natural p. BURK 168:15
propensity usual p. of mankind HUME 408:10
proper know our p. stations DICK 268:2
no p. time of day HOOD 395:6
noun, p. or improper FULL 336:26
p. man SHAK 710:25
P. words in proper places SWIF 766:3
p. young men BURN 171:16
properly never did anything p. LEAR 477:11
property degrees and kinds of p. MADI 505:12
dominion of p. GOLD 354:8
give me a little snug p. EDGE 295:14
makes it his p. LOCK 488:15
nature and p. BOOK 129:16
not p. but a trust FOX 331:3
preservation of their p. LOCK 488:20
preserve his p. LOCK 488:17

Private p. is a necessary TAWN 774:3
P. has its duties DRUM 286:11
p. is of greater value FRY 336:16
P. is theft PROU 613:2
p. of others SALL 665:1
p. of the rich RUSK 660:10
p. of thy fellow TALM 772:2
p. or honour MACH 502:13
p.-owning democracy SKEL 739:9
Propinquity and p. of blood SHAK 699:18
public p. JEFF 420:7
right of p. TAFT 770:15
Thieves respect p. CHES 217:2
through p. that we shall strike PANK 585:8
Where p. is in question SALI 664:10
prophecies p., they shall fail BIBL 107:25
verification of his own p. TROL 800:1
prophecy have the gift of p. BIBL 107:25
poetry, p., and religion RUSK 659:14
p. is the most gratuitous ELIO 300:1
prophesy man may p. SHAK 692:5
sons and daughters shall p. BIBL 92:3
prophet arise among you a p. BIBL 78:27
more than a p. BIBL 96:24
not as a p. MAND 509:14
p., his prophecy departs TALM 772:13
p. in Israel BIBL 82:6
p. is not without honour BIBL 97:7
p. not without honour PROV 629:44
p., to whose rapture THOM 792:18
p. who wishes to write HEIN 380:1
prophetic In her p. fury SHAK 714:8
O my p. soul SHAK 685:3
p. greeting SHAK 703:11
prophets Beware of false p. BIBL 95:21
Book, and the P. KORA 459:11
by the p. BIBL 111:3
ceased to pose as its p. POPP 607:1
fellowship of the P. BOOK 127:20
Is Saul also among the p. BIBL 80:10
knowledge from the p. SA'A 662:5
law and the p. BIBL 95:18
Men reject their p. DOST 283:5
p. and kings have desired BIBL 100:21
p. prophesy falsely BIBL 90:25
spake by the P. BOOK 131:11
propinquity P. and property of blood
SHAK 699:18
proportion harmony, order or p.
BROW 157:7
no p. kept SHAK 716:15
strangeness in the p. BACO 43:20
proportions by p. true MARV 515:13
proposes Man p. PROV 626:4
man p. THOM 788:6
proposition accept the p. AYER 41:6
copulations of p. HUME 409:11
expressing a genuine p. AYER 41:8
meaning of a p. SCHL 671:9
propositions General p. LOCK 488:7
propositum Meum est p. ANON 21:18
proprie p. communia dicere HORA 398:7
proprietor p.'s prejudices SWAF 765:3
propriety attention to p. WOLL 844:10
prose All that is not p. MOLI 541:11
as well written as p. POUN 609:11
but p. run mad POPE 602:28
differs in nothing from p. GRAY 361:23
for p. and verse CARE 190:10
Good p. like a window-pane ORWE 577:2
govern in p. CUOM 254:1
harmony of p. DRYD 290:8
in p. or rhyme MILT 531:5
language of p. WORD 850:24
love others in p. PRIO 612:1
Meredith's a p. Browning WILD 835:26
nearest p. DRYD 289:12
Not verse now, only p. BROW 158:23
pin up my hair with p. CONG 239:12
p. and the passion FORS 329:16
p. is verse BYRO 182:11
P. is when all the lines BENT 68:11
P. was born yesterday FLAU 325:10

P. = words in their best order COLE 234:3
shut me up in p. DICK 273:9
speaking p. without knowing it MOLI 541:12
Stein's p.-song LEWI 484:2
Proserpine P. gathering flowers MILT 532:29
prospect every p. pleases HEBE 378:16
noblest p. JOHN 428:8
prospects undetermined p. ADDI 5:4
prosper I grow, I p. SHAK 699:25
sinners' ways p. HOPK 397:8
Treason doth never p. HARI 373:15
prosperity day of p. BIBL 86:9
jest's p. SHAK 702:24
liberty and p. JENY 421:2
man to han ben in p. CHAU 213:8
man who can stand p. CARL 192:15
P. doth best BACO 43:15
P. doth bewitch men WEBS 826:15
P. is the blessing BACO 43:13
prosperous make a nation p. BACO 47:2
prostitute doormat or a p. WEST 830:14
puff the p. away DRYD 289:31
prostitutes small nations like p. KUBR 462:3
prostitution banking and p. WRIG 851:13
P. Selling one's body MACK 502:17
prostrating bowing, p. KORA 461:7
protect p. a working-girl SMIT 741:18
p. the writer ACHE 1:11
two solitudes p. RILK 649:1
protection calls mutely for p. GREE 362:17
Grant me p. SIKH 737:6
mercy and p. BOOK 133:14
p. against war BEVI 74:3
P. is not a principle DISR 275:9
protector appoint to us a p. KORA 460:3
Friend and P. BARB 55:8
God, the p. BOOK 130:12
p. of the believers KORA 459:15
protest lady doth p. too much SHAK 687:5
Protestant Hitler attacked the P. church
NIEM 563:18
I am the P. whore GWYN 366:6
live Thy P. to be HERR 386:13
preservation of the P. religion HAMP 370:13
P. counterpoint BEEC 62:13
p. ethic WEBE 825:3
P., if he wants aid DISR 277:18
P. Province of Ulster CARS 196:18
P. Religion CARL 192:3
P. with a horse BEHA 63:12
'tis a P. wind WHAR 831:5
Protestantism P., even the most cold
BURK 166:22
Protestants in the hands of P. PUGI 636:24
religion of P. CHIL 217:22
Proteus sight of P. rising WORD 850:22
protoplasmal p. primordial globule
GILB 347:20
protracted p. my work JOHN 427:21
p. woe JOHN 426:19
proud all the p. and mighty have
DYER 293:16
be an Indian and not be p. GAND 339:3
Death be not p. DONN 279:19
I have no p. looks BOOK 143:8
make death p. SHAK 680:4
makes him very p. MILN 528:7
mote ye lyve, and alle p. CHAU 213:1
p. and yet a wretched thing DAVI 258:9
proudest of the p. CHUR 220:6
p. if you'll be wise CHUD 219:10
p. in arms MILT 528:19
p. me no prouds SHAK 718:4
p. of the fact RUSS 660:14
scattered the p. BIBL 99:32
too p. for a wit GOLD 355:5
too p. to fight WILS 840:18
too p. to importune GRAY 361:22
prove chance to p. it MURR 555:2
I could p. everything PINT 595:15
O Lord, and p. me BOOK 135:10
P. all things BIBL 110:19
p. a lover SHAK 716:22

p. anything by figures CARL 191:10
p. me, and examine BOOK 143:19
p. our chance DRAY 286:6
to p. it I'm here CATC 201:11
proved God p. them BIBL 92:23
mighty soul was p. ADDI 4:5
p. me, and saw my works BOOK 140:10
p. most royally SHAK 689:18
you have p. to be HARD 372:18
Provence found it in P. WILL 839:14
proverb Israel shall be a p. BIBL 81:10
p. is one man's wit RUSS 661:15
proverbs Patch grief with p. SHAK 712:30
Solomon wrote the P. NAYL 557:23
proves exception p. the rule PROV 619:28
provide God will p. BIBL 76:22
goods the gods p. PROV 631:38
provided P. for DICK 268:24
providence assert eternal p. MILT 531:6
Behind a frowning p, COWP 246:25
inscrutable workings of P. SMIT 742:5
P. had sent a few men RUMB 658:5
P. has not created TOCQ 795:9
P. on the side PROV 629:45
p. so ordereth MATH 518:9
P. their guide MILT 534:15
way that P. dictates HITL 390:1
provident They are p. instead BOGA 125:7
province all knowledge to be my p. BACO 46:8
Ireland should be a p. GOOL 356:13
p. they have desolated GLAD 350:16
provinces defending those p. SMIT 741:13
provincial He was worse than p. JAME 417:20
level of p. existence ELIO 300:13
provincialism taken in p. HUXL 411:2
proving pleasure in p. their falseness DARW 257:4
provision p. for the flesh BIBL 106:33
provocation as in the p. BOOK 140:10
p. I have had POPE 605:28
provoke fathers, p. not BIBL 109:18
provoker Drink, sir, is a great p. SHAK 705:7
provokes No one p. me MOTT 552:11
proximus paries cum p. ardet HORA 399:15
prudence effect of p. on rascality SHAW 726:25
forced into p. AUST 39:12
P. bring thee back CHUR 220:1
P. is a rich, ugly BLAK 120:23
P. is the other woman ANON 18:13
prudent every p. act BURK 166:26
mercenary and the p. AUST 40:1
prudes p. for proctors TENN 782:23
prudhomme p. so grand JOIN 434:2
prunes p. and prism DICK 269:24
pruninghooks spears into p. BIBL 88:2
prurient p. curiosity STOP 761:6
Prussia military domination of P. ASQU 32:2
national industry of P. MIRA 536:8
Prussian P., Or perhaps Ital-ian GILB 348:26
psalm practising the hundredth p. BYRO 183:21
p. of thanksgiving BOOK 140:14
Take the p. BOOK 139:13
psalmist sweet p. of Israel BIBL 81:7
psalms David wrote the P. NAYL 557:23
with p. BOOK 140:9
psaltery p., dulcimer BIBL 91:19
pseudopodium lonely p. SHIP 734:22
Psyche Your mournful P. KEAT 444:17
psychiatrist man who goes to a p. GOLD 356:6
psychic manifests all p. powers MAHÃ 507:6
psychological P. flaws ANON 18:14
psychopath p. is the furnace RAYM 642:17
psychotherapy waste money on p. TORK 797:3
puberty p. assisted BYRO 180:12
pubic Hound that Caught the P. Hare BEHA 63:13
public as if I was a p. meeting VICT 809:14
assumes a p. trust JEFF 420:7

carry on great p. schemes BURK 169:12
complainers for the p. BURK 166:13
consult the p. good SWIF 765:15
Desolation in immaculate p. places ROET 652:4
English p. school WAUG 824:6
excites the p. odium CLAY 226:3
expense of p. interests TAYL 774:20
for the p. good LOCK 488:21
glorified p. relations man TRUM 801:6
hand into the p. purse PEEL 590:19
I and the p. know AUDE 36:2
Nor p. men YEAT 854:16
one p. which follows another CHAM 207:9
one to mislead the p. ASQU 32:5
precedence over p. relations FEYN 317:6
Private faces in p. places AUDE 35:18
p. and merited disgrace STEV 759:30
p. be damned VAND 806:19
p, Prayer in the Church BOOK 144:16
p. rallies around an idea ASIM 31:18
p. scandal that constitutes MOLI 542:12
p. school accent LEAV 478:4
P. schools are the nurseries FIEL 318:2
P. schools 'tis public folly COWP 248:18
p. seldom forgive LAVA 470:14
p. thinks long JOHN 424:24
respect p. opinion RUSS 660:17
servants of the p. GOWE 357:14
sound Of p. scorn MILT 534:6
tell the p. which way SULZ 763:16
vexes p. men TENN 784:22
what he thinks the p. wants REIT 645:1
wider p. life ELIO 299:15
publicans even the p. BIBL 94:32
p. and sinners BIBL 96:5
publications previous p. HILB 388:3
publicity Any p. is good publicity PROV 614:24
bad p. BEHA 63:17
channels of modern p. BUCH 162:19
eternal p. BENN 67:19
oxygen of p. THAT 787:10
publish P. and be damned WELL 827:15
p. it not BIBL 80:27
p., right or wrong BYRO 182:8
P. your message WESL 829:19
publisher Barabbas was a p. CAMP 187:22
makes everybody a p. MCLU 503:18
publishers numerous p. ADE 5:15
p. are not women ROBI 650:12
publishing p. faster than think PAUL 589:3
Puck streak of P. HENL 381:13
puck p. is going to be GRET 363:16
pudding chieftain o' the p.-race BURN 172:18
Mrs Carter, could make a p. JOHN 427:9
proof of the p. PROV 629:43
p. and pie NURS 566:21
p. in his belly SHAK 690:17
solid p. POPE 601:20
Take away that p. CHUR 222:24
puddings like their English p. VOLT 816:18
puddle shining into a p. PROV 631:34
puellis Vixi p. HORA 401:23
puerisque Virginibus p. canto HORA 401:9
puero p. reverentia JUVE 440:15
puff friends all united to p. SWIN 769:7
p. and get oneself puffed TROL 800:13
p.—and speak COWP 246:21
p. of a dunce GOLD 355:8
p. the prostitute away DRYD 289:31
puffs P., powders, patches POPE 606:6
pug O most charming p. FLEM 326:19
pugna P. magna victi sumus LIVY 487:8
puking infant, Mewling and p. SHAK 681:10
pulchrior p. evenit HORA 402:9
pull easier to p. down PROV 623:46
P. down thy VANITY POUN 609:5
puller p. down of kings SHAK 695:1
pulling Here p. down MARV 515:13
pulls p. a lady through MARQ 514:1
pulp p. my acquaintance TROL 800:16
p. so bitter THOM 791:10

pulpit such a bully p. ROOS 654:11
white glove p. REAG 643:9
pulsanda P. tellus HORA 400:20
pulse feeling a woman's p. STER 756:11
lost p. of feeling ARNO 27:2
My P., like a soft drum KING 451:16
p. begins to throb BRON 152:19
p. like a cannon EMER 306:21
p. of the machine WORD 850:4
two people with the one p. MACN 504:18
pulvere sine p. palmae HORA 398:20
pumice Beside a p. isle SHEL 730:9
polished dry with p. CATU 199:22
pumpkins early p. blow LEAR 477:4
pun make so vile a p. DENN 264:13
p. is a pistol LAMB 464:18
punch Some sipping p. WORD 848:21
punctuality painting and p. GAIN 337:14
P. is the politeness LOUI 492:13
P. is the politeness PROV 629:46
P. is the soul PROV 629:47
P. is the virtue of bores WAUG 824:19
punctuation concentrated on p. CORN 243:13
Punica P. fide SALL 665:6
punish God p. England FUNK 337:10
punished bodies to be p. PROV 617:11
p. everlastingly JOHN 432:14
[wickedness] is not p. COMP 237:3
punishing p. anyone who comes between SMIT 743:24
punishment cruel and unusual p. CONS 241:15
Does capital p. tend FRY 336:16
less horror than the p. GIBB 345:5
most terrible p. DOST 283:9
My p. is greater BIBL 75:30
object of p. MANN 510:6
p. fit the crime GILB 348:4
p. Is avarice JONS 435:14
p. is mischief BENT 68:7
p. is not for revenge FRY 336:17
restraint and p. MILT 535:17
suffer first p. CRAN 250:5
punishments charged with p. HENL 381:15
sanguinary p. PAIN 582:16
punk writings are p. ANON 16:16
punt better fun to p. than to be punted SAYE 668:5
punto cinco en p. de la tarde LORC 492:1
pupils kills all its p. BERL 70:7
pupped down to Brighton and p. SMIT 744:3
puppets God, whose p. BROW 160:23
p. in a play of shadows BHAG 74:17
shut up the box and the p. THAC 786:17
puppy p.-dogs' tails NURS 570:14
purblind whining, p., wayward boy SHAK 702:14
purchase p. of my wealth JONS 435:12
purchased p. with money BIBL 105:1
purchasing not worth p. REED 644:12
pure as p. as snow SHAK 686:15
Blessed are the p. in heart BIBL 94:20
Blessed are the p. in heart KEBL 447:11
led a p. life CATU 203:7
Live p., speak true TENN 777:18
more p. than his maker BIBL 82:36
my heart is p. TENN 784:5
Perfectly p. and good BROW 160:24
P. and ready to mount DANT 256:10
p. as the driven slush BANK 54:15
p. as the lily LAUD 470:6
p. deeds of the Bodhisattvas SHAN 724:11
P. religion and undefiled BIBL 111:24
To the p. all things PROV 633:15
truth is rarely p. WILD 835:12
Unto the p. BIBL 111:2
whatsoever things are p. BIBL 110:8
pureness p. of living and truth BOOK 130:7
purest O P. of Creatures FABE 313:17
p. thing there is JONG 434:12
purgation p. of such emotions ARIS 25:20
purgatorial black, p. rails KEAT 442:16

purgatory no other p. but a woman
BEAU 60:9
P. fire BALL 52:12
p. of servants PROV 618:42
purge I'll p., and leave sack SHAK 691:19
p. me with hyssop BOOK 137:12
purged p. the air of pestilence SHAK 720:6
purify p. My House KORA 460:17
p. the dialect of the tribe ELIO 301:24
puritan P. hated bear-baiting MACA 498:22
saw a P.-one BRAT 149:19
to the P. all things are impure LAWR 474:18
puritanism ecrudescence of P. RUSS 661:1
not P. but February KRUT 462:2
P. The haunting fear MENC 521:16
purity Except p. of heart DURC 292:19
Science lost its virgin p. GRAV 360:15
purlieus p. of the Law ETHE 312:3
p. of the law TENN 779:17
purling p. stream ADDI 4:21
to p. brooks POPE 603:25
purple colour p. WALK 817:13
deep p. falls PARI 585:12
in p. and gold BYRO 180:1
in the p. of Emperors KIPL 456:26
I shall wear p. JOSE 436:17
never saw a P. Cow BURG 165:18
p. and fine linen BIBL 101:22
p. brows of Olivet TENN 779:2
P. haze is in my brain HEND 381:10
p. mantle to the light RONS 653:4
p. patch or two HORA 397:21
p.-stainèd mouth KEAT 444:22
p. with love's wound SHAK 711:2
Ran p. to the sea MILT 531:20
yield much p. AESC 6:6
purpose any p. perverts art CONS 241:10
creature hath a p. KEAT 446:19
embrace the p. of God TENN 782:7
fits thy p. AURE 38:3
for an Irish p. DAVI 259:12
Infirm of p. SHAK 705:2
My p. is, indeed SHAK 720:20
one increasing p. TENN 780:2
politics of p. HUMP 409:12
p. of his life CHEK 214:3
p. of human existence JUNG 438:10
Shake my fell p. SHAK 703:19
speak and p. not SHAK 699:20
time to every p. BIBL 85:32
working his p. out AING 9:2
purpureus P. Adsuitur pannus HORA 397:21
purring p. at his heels BLAI 118:14
purrs p. like an epigram MARQ 514:4
purse as thy p. can buy SHAK 684:18
consumption of the p. SHAK 691:29
empty p. BRET 150:26
hand into the public p. PEEL 590:19
law can take a p. BUTL 176:21
silk p. out of sow's ear PROV 635:41
steals my p. SHAK 713:26
purses make heavy p. BACO 43:25
pursue fly it, it will p. JONS 435:25
I p. you as you run HORA 402:7
or knowing it, p. DRYD 289:32
road he wishes to p. TALM 772:30
thing we all p. BEAU 60:8
pursued p. a maiden SHEL 729:13
you who are the p. SHAW 726:4
pursueth flee when no man p. BIBL 85:16
pursuing Faint, yet p. BIBL 79:26
still p. LONG 490:22
pursuit common p. LEAV 478:2
p. of happiness ANON 19:17
p. of happiness JEFF 419:10
p. of perfection ARNO 29:8
p. of the uneatable WILD 836:21
What mad p. KEAT 444:22
pursy fatness of these p. times SHAK 687:29
purtenance with the p. thereof BIBL 77:29
purus scelerisque p. HORA 400:17
push one brave p. STEV 759:17
pushed and he p. LOGU 489:12

was he p. JAME 418:18
pussy I love little p. NURS 567:13
Owl and the P.-Cat LEAR 477:15
p. cat, where have you been NURS 569:5
P.'s in the well NURS 566:18
What a beautiful P. LEAR 477:15
put P. me to what you will METH 523:8
p. not your trust BOOK 143:26
p. on the new man BIBL 110:12
P. out the light SHAK 714:20
p. up with bad things TROL 799:24
up with which I will not p. CHUR 221:22
putrefaction preserve it from p. JOHN 432:19
puzzle Don't p. me STER 757:13
p. the devil BURN 172:7
Rule of Three doth p. me ANON 17:19
puzzles Nothing p. me more LAMB 465:5
pyjamas in p. for the heat LAWR 475:7
pylons P., those pillars bare SPEN 750:22
pyramid bottom of the economic p.
ROOS 653:10
pyramids not like children but like p.
FLAU 325:15
summit of these p. NAPO 556:6
Pyramus P. and Thisby SHAK 710:20
Pyrenees fleas that tease in the High P.
BELL 65:26
P. are no more LOUI 492:8
Pyrrha hugging you now, P. HORA 400:7
Pythagoras mystical way of P. BROW 156:26

quack potent q., long versed CRAB 249:21
q. of yesterday DOYL 285:7
quacks despicable q. JENY 421:2
quad No one about in the Q. KNOX 458:9
quadrangle triangle in a q. AUBR 33:17
quadrigis Q. petimus bene vivere HORA 399:10
quadrille q. in a sentry-box JAME 417:17
quadripedante Q. putrem VIRG 813:5
quadruped hairy q. DARW 257:5
quaffed jested, q., and swore DOYL 285:11
quaffing q., and unthinking DRYD 289:13
quail q. Whistle about us STEV 758:9
quailing No q., Mrs Gaskell BRON 153:2
quails we long for q. DRYD 289:1
quaint q. and curious war is HARD 372:22
quake q. to say they love SIDN 736:7
she gan to q. CHAU 213:6
qualis Non sum q. eram HORA 402:6
qualities great q. BAGE 47:20
Q. too elevated CHAM 207:2
such q. as would wear well GOLD 355:29
quality People of q. MOLI 542:7
persons of the best q. EVEL 313:2
q. of mercy SHAK 709:25
q. of the notes SCHN 671:13
q. which guarantees all CHUR 222:9
qualms cold q. SOUT 749:23
Quangle-Wangle Quee Said the Q.
LEAR 477:21
quanta O q. qualia ABEL 1:1
quantities ghosts of departed q. BERK 69:9
quantity q. of the notes SCHN 671:13
quantula Q. sint hominum corpuscula
JUVE 440:10
quantum q. o' the sin BURN 170:28
quarks Three q. for Muster Mark JOYC 437:6
quarrel find q. in a straw SHAK 688:4
hath his q. just SHAK 694:16
justice of my q. ANON 16:19
lover's q. with the world FROS 335:17
no q. with the Viet Cong ALI 12:3
perpetual q. BURK 166:27
q. in a far away country CHAM 206:11
q. is now between light and darkness
LAMB 465:15
q. of lovers PROV 630:1
q. with ourselves, poetry YEAT 856:8
takes one to make a q. INGE 413:8
two to make a q. PROV 624:27
very pretty q. SHER 733:24
quarrelled q. with my wife PEAC 590:4

quarrelling set them a q. HUME 409:5
surprised that they had been q. HUME 409:3
quarrels How many frivolous q. HUME 408:14
q. were hidden TRAH 797:13
q. with one's husband BONA 126:18
strained by nasty q. HORA 400:15
who in q. interpose GAY 341:28
quarry marked down q. SHAW 726:4
quart q. into a pint pot PROV 635:28
quarter for the remaining q. NAPO 556:13
quarterly nothing a-year, paid q.
SURT 764:24
quarters awful q. of an hour ROSS 656:10
quarto beautiful q. page SHER 733:26
quartos q. their ordered ranks maintain
CRAB 249:4
quatrains q. shovelled LOWE 494:18
quean flaunting, extravagant q. SHER 733:31
Quebec Long Live Free Q. DE G 262:11
Q. does not have opinions LAUR 470:12
road from Q. to Montreal BROO 153:3
Québecois I am a Q. LÉVE 482:12
queen Apparent q. MILT 533:5
Astarte, q. of heaven MILT 531:19
Cinara was my q. HORA 402:6
cold q. of England CHES 216:5
Ere you were Q. of Sheba SHIP 734:22
Famine Q. GONN 356:10
fought for Q. and Faith TENN 784:3
grace a summer q. SCOT 674:2
Hail holy q. PRAY 611:6
home life of our own dear Q. ANON 16:13
I have been to the Q. GLAD 351:7
I'm to be Q. o' the May TENN 782:8
Isabel the Q. MARL 513:9
laughing q. HUNT 409:17
Most Gracious Q. ANON 17:18
now our q. SHAK 683:21
Ocean's child, and then his q. SHEL 730:1
Q. and country THOM 791:20
Q. and huntress JONS 435:2
Q. had four Maries BALL 52:18
Q. has the quality PHIL 594:12
q. in a vesture of gold BOOK 136:21
q. in people's hearts DIAN 267:1
q. it no inch further SHAK 722:11
Q. must sign BAGE 48:15
q. of curds and cream SHAK 722:8
Q. of Hearts she made NURS 569:6
q. of Scots ELIZ 304:3
q. of Sheba BIBL 81:11
Q. of silent night BEST 71:21
Q. rose of the rosebud garden TENN 781:25
Q.'s luve BALL 51:17
q. was in the parlour NURS 569:14
Ruler of the Q.'s Navee GILB 348:22
to look at the q. NURS 569:5
To toast The Q. HEAN 378:1
weeping q. SHAK 716:5
your anointed Q. ELIZ 304:4
queens all the beautiful Q. DONN 282:7
all your acts are q. SHAK 722:7
Q. have died young NASH 557:21
Queensberry Duchess of Q. WALP 818:20
queer All the world is q. OWEN 580:23
here because we're q. BEHA 63:15
nowt so q. as folk PROV 632:34
q. sort of thing BARH 55:19
queerer universe q. than we suppose
HALD 367:17
quem Q. fugis VIRG 813:19
quench q. all the fiery darts BIBL 109:21
shall he not q. BIBL 89:22
waters cannot q. love BIBL 87:23
quenched What hath q. them SHAK 704:19
quest to whose winding q. VAUG 807:7
questing passes the q. vole WAUG 824:12
q. beast MALO 508:19
question Answer to the Great Q. ADAM 2:2
ask an impertinent q. BRON 152:6
Ask a silly q. PROV 614:41
asked any clear q. CAMU 188:9
ask him the same q. WEST 830:9

civil q. deserves	PROV 616:44	unravished bride of q.	KEAT 444:6	**radar** This is the writer's r.	HEMI 381:9

civil q. deserves — PROV 616:44
mere asking of a q. — FORS 329:20
not to q. other — KIPL 453:14
Others abide our q. — ARNO 28:12
q. is — CARR 195:16
q. is absurd — AUDE 36:12
q. why we died — KIPL 453:18
secretly changed the Q. — SELL 676:25
such a silly q. — STER 756:15
that is the q. — SHAK 686:9
To ask the hard q. — AUDE 36:11
two sides to every q. — PROV 632:2
unanswered q. — BELL 64:13
what is the q. — LAST 474:14
questioning Q. is not the mode — JOHN 430:16
questionings for those obstinate q. — WORD 848:11
questions *all* q. were stupid — WEIS 826:25
answered three q. — CARR 194:5
Ask no q. — PROV 614:42
ask q. of those who cannot tell — RALE 641:17
Fools ask q. — PROV 620:20
puzzling q. — BROW 156:12
q. the distempered part — ELIO 301:18
Them that asks no q. — KIPL 455:17
queue orderly q. of one — MIKE 524:24
quibble q. is to Shakespeare — JOHN 425:16
quick Come! q. as you can — DE L 262:20
Jack be q. — NURS 567:16
judge the q. and the dead — BOOK 128:10
q., and the dead — DEWA 266:12
q. could never rest — SURR 764:8
q. spirit — SHAK 696:1
q. to blame — AESC 6:10
quicken turn again, and q. us — BOOK 139:18
quickeneth spirit that q. — BIBL 103:17
quickly gives twice who gives q. — PROV 621:39
It were done q. — SHAK 704:3
Q. come, quickly go — PROV 630:2
That thou doest, do q. — BIBL 103:26
quickness q. of thought — ASTE 32:12
quicksands q., and the rocks — KEAT 446:15
Quicunque Q. vult — BOOK 128:21
quiddities quips and thy q. — SHAK 689:21
quidquid Q. *agunt homines* — JUVE 439:10
quies *Tempus erat quo prima q.* — VIRG 811:15
quiet All q. along the Potomac — BEER 63:9
alone with the q. day — JAME 418:8
Anythin' for a q. life — DICK 272:10
Anything for a q. life — MIDD 524:8
be q. and go a-Angling — WALT 821:3
determination of a q. man — SMIT 742:8
Easy live and q. die — SCOT 674:5
Fie upon this q. life — SHAK 690:5
harvest of a q. eye — WORD 849:3
hath a q. mind — VAUX 808:6
lain still and been q. — BIBL 82:32
lives of q. desperation — THOR 793:4
never have a q. world — SHAW 727:7
O for this q. — KEAT 447:8
opportunity to keep q. — CHIR 218:3
q. along the Potomac — MCCL 500:11
q. as a nun — WORD 847:2
q. flows the Don — SHOL 735:7
q. hours — SHAK 691:4
q. life — HICK 388:2
q. mind — SURR 764:4
q. mind is worse — TRAH 798:1
q. on the western front — REMA 645:4
q., pilfering — CLAR 224:10
Q. to quick bosoms — BYRO 178:23
serve thee with a q. mind — BOOK 130:18
sleepers in that q. earth — CLOS 228:16
Study to be q. — BIBL 110:16
quieta Q. *movere* — SALL 665:3
quieten q. your enemy by talking — CEAU 204:10
quieter q. retreat — AURE 38:2
quietest q. places — HOUS 404:20
quietly q. pacifist peaceful — WALK 817:11
Q. shining — COLE 231:23
quietness all godly q. — BOOK 130:13
bride of q. — OPEN 575:25

unravished bride of q. — KEAT 444:6
quietus q. make With a bare bodkin — SHAK 686:10
quillets q. of the law — SHAK 694:9
quills q. upon the fretful porpentine — SHAK 684:32
quilts Soft q. on quilts — THOM 792:2
quince slices of q. — LEAR 477:18
quincunx q. of heaven — BROW 156:3
quinquireme Q. of Nineveh — MASE 517:12
quintessence q. of dust — SHAK 685:24
quip q. modest — SHAK 682:8
quips q. and thy quiddities — SHAK 689:21
quires Q. and Places — BOOK 128:14
quis *q. custodiet ipsos Custodes* — JUVE 439:22
quit may not q. the post — TENN 781:12
q. for the next — SHAK 692:10
Q. yourselves like men — BIBL 80:7
quite not q. a gentleman — ASHF 31:12
quitter lighter not a q. — MAND 509:17
quiver hath his q. full — BOOK 143:2
quo Q. *vadis* — BIBL 115:14
quotable eminently q. — GERS 344:9
quotation always have a q. — SAYE 668:6
Every q. contributes — JOHN 424:5
get a happy q. anywhere — HOLM 393:12
good q. book — DAVI 258:14
q. what a speaker wants — BENN 67:6
quotations heaps of q. — DOUG 284:2
I hate q. — EMER 307:16
opinion with q. — PRIO 612:6
People who like q. — GREE 362:19
Pretentious q. — FOWL 330:18
read books of q. — CHUR 222:12
swathed himself in q. — KIPL 456:26
quote devil can q. Scripture — PROV 617:31
immortal as they q. — YOUN 857:2
kill you if you q. it — BURG 165:19
man is to q. him — BENC 66:6
quoted elegies And q. odes — TENN 782:25

R pronounced the letter R — AUBR 33:21
rabbit gone to get a r. skin — NURS 566:10
r. has a charming face — ANON 18:17
r. in a snare — STEP 756:4
rabble army would be a base r. — BURK 166:31
Mob, Parliament, R. — COBB 229:18
Rabelais soul of R. — COLE 234:6
race Another r. hath been — WORD 848:15
avails the sceptred r. — LAND 466:4
born like the rest of my r. — BLAK 120:18
melted into a new r. — CEEV 251:2
no matter what their r. — WILL 839:19
No r. can prosper — WASH 822:4
r. between education — WELL 828:13
r. is not to the swift — BIBL 86:16
r. is not to the swift — PROV 630:3
r. is to the swift — DAVI 258:5
r. remains immortal — VIRG 815:5
r. that is set before us — BIBL 111:10
r. that long in darkness — SCOT 675:7
run out thy r. — MILT 530:29
run the r. with Death — JOHN 432:20
Slow and steady wins the r. — PROV 630:45
they which run in a r. — BIBL 107:19
unprotected r. — CLAR 224:10
white r. *is* the cancer — SONT 746:10
racer melodist to a fine r. — MOZA 553:1
races darker to the lighter r. — DU B 290:21
so-called white r. — FORS 329:19
Some r. increase — LUCR 495:15
two distinct r. — LAMB 464:13
Rachel R. weeping — BIBL 94:8
served seven years for R. — BIBL 76:33
racism institutional r. — MACP 505:4
rack Leave not a r. behind — SHAK 719:1
r. of a too easy chair — POPE 602:6
r. of this tough world — SHAK 702:8
racked searched out and r. — ORCH 576:8
racket all a German r. — RIDL 648:6
rackets r. to these balls — SHAK 692:30
rackrent pleased with Castle R. — EDGE 296:4

radar This is the writer's r. — HEMI 381:9
radiance Stains the white r. — SHEL 729:2
radiances R. know him — BERR 71:14
radical never dared be r. when young — FROS 335:21
R. Chic . . . only radical in Style — WOLF 843:23
radio had the r. on — MONR 543:5
R. and television — SARR 666:19
r. expands it — WOGA 843:7
radish like a forked r. — SHAK 692:11
r. and an egg — COWP 248:5
raft discourse on dharma as a r. — MAHĀ 506:14
Parable of the R. — PALI 583:14
republic is a r. — AMES 13:6
rag foul r.-and-bone shop — YEAT 853:12
r. and a bone — KIPL 456:2
r. blown by the wind — WORD 845:11
Shakespeherian R. — ELIO 303:15
rage die here in a r. — SWIF 766:6
hard-favoured r. — SHAK 693:4
heathen so furiously r. — BOOK 133:20
Heaven has no r. — CONG 238:30
Heaven in a r. — BLAK 119:6
horrible that lust and r. — YEAT 855:20
r. against the dying of the light — THOM 789:7
r. of Caliban — WILD 836:12
replete with too much r. — SHAK 722:26
scholar in a r. — KIPL 457:3
temp'ring virtuous r. — POPE 603:28
wretched r. for order — MAHO 507:10
writing increaseth r. — DYER 293:12
rages weight of r. — SPOO 753:2
ragged pair of r. claws — ELIO 302:16
raggedness windowed r. — SHAK 700:22
raging r. in the dark — YEAT 853:11
r. of the sea — BOOK 138:6
strong drink is r. — BIBL 84:33
ragout fricassee, or a r. — SWIF 766:8
rags are as filthy r. — BIBL 90:20
r. and contempt — BUNY 164:20
r. and tatters — MOLI 541:14
r. of time — DONN 281:13
raid R. BY DR JAMESON — TELE 776:3
r. on the inarticulate — ELIO 301:19
rail r. at me — CONG 238:32
six young on the r. — BROW 159:28
railing R. at life — CHUR 219:21
railing for r. — BIBL 112:12
railroad Building that r. — VAN 807:3
enterprised a r. — RUSK 659:16
railway by r. timetables — TAYL 774:10
R. termini — FORS 329:13
with a r.-share — CARR 196:11
raiment body than r. — BIBL 95:7
man clothed in soft r. — BIBL 96:24
rain abundance of r. — BIBL 81:23
buried in the r. — MILL 526:20
clouds and wind without r. — BIBL 85:4
clouds return after the r. — BIBL 86:25
command the r. — PEPY 592:1
credit for the r. — MORR 550:15
cries against the r. — GASC 340:14
dead that the r. rains on — PROV 616:1
drop of r. maketh a hole — LATI 472:17
earth soaks up the r. — COWL 245:17
fall like r. — AUDE 36:13
February there be no r. — PROV 623:1
gentle r. from heaven — SHAK 709:25
glazed with r. water — WILL 839:13
had outwept its r. — SHEL 728:16
hard r.'s a gonna fall — DYLA 294:7
Hath the r. a father — BIBL 83:23
Jupiter the R.-giver — TIBU 794:10
latter r. — BOOK 129:21
like sunshine after r. — SHAK 724:3
out of the caverns of r. — SHEL 729:6
R. before seven — PROV 630:4
r. in Spain — LERN 481:19
r. is destroying his grain — HERB 383:7
r. is on our lips — SORL 746:22
r. is over and gone — BIBL 87:6

rain (cont.):
r. it raineth every day — SHAK 700:20
r. it raineth every day — SHAK 721:18
r., it raineth on the just — BOWE 148:9
r. of Dharma — MAHĀ 506:19
R., rain, go away — NURS 569:7
R.! Rain! Rain — KEAT 446:10
real sad r. — CASH 198:13
sendeth r. — BIBL 94:31
send my roots r. — HOPK 397:9
small drops of r. — BALL 53:16
small r. down can rain — ANON 19:19
smell the dew and r. — HERB 384:8
soft refreshing r. — CAMP 187:1
Still falls the r. — SITW 738:16
through the drizzling r. — TENN 778:27
wailing of the r. — LEDW 478:14
waiting for it to r. — COHE 230:12
waiting for r. — ELIO 302:3
wedding-cake in the r. — AUDE 36:20
rainbow another hue Unto the r. — SHAK 699:10
blessing of a r. — ABSE 1:5
colours in r. — BOOT 144:23
gave Noah the r. — SONG 747:6
Lord survives the r. — LOWE 494:15
melting r. — AKEN 9:5
r. and a cuckoo's song — DAVI 258:19
r. coalition — JACK 415:4
r. comes and goes — WORD 847:21
R. gave thee birth — DAVI 258:20
r. of the salt sand-wave — KEAT 444:18
r. round about the throne — BIBL 113:7
r.'s glory is shed — SHEL 729:24
r. which includes black — YEVT 856:21
Somewhere over the r. — HARB 371:4
when I behold A r. — WORD 847:16
rained r. down manna — BOOK 139:10
raineth R. drop and staineth slop — POUN 608:12
rainfall r. at morning — STEV 760:12
raining if it's r., apologizes — WELD 827:5
rains never r. but it pours — PROV 624:16
r. pennies from heaven — BURK 169:13
rainy r. day — BIBL 85:15
R. days — BASH 58:2
r. Pleiads wester — HOUS 404:3
r. Sunday in London — DE Q 264:19
strangers on a r. day — SMAR 740:13
wish him a r. evening — WALT 820:17
raise easier to r. the Devil — PROV 624:1
Lord shall r. me up — RALE 641:11
raised It is easily r. — FIEL 318:3
r. not a stone — WOLF 843:12
raising stop r. corn — LEAS 478:1
raison r. tonne en son cratère — POTT 608:11
rake r. in reading — MONT 543:17
ram r. caught in a thicket — BIBL 76:23
Rama In R. was there a voice — BIBL 94:8
Ramadan month of R. — KORA 459:12
ramas Verdes r. — LORC 492:2
rambling r. brat (in print) — BRAD 149:3
rampage On the R., Pip — DICK 269:17
rampart corse to the r. — WOLF 843:10
rams mountains skipped like r. — BOOK 142:2
than the fat r. — BIBL 80:14
Ramsbottom Mr and Mrs R. — EDGA 295:13
ran both r. together — BIBL 104:10
r. before Ahab — BIBL 81:25
they r. awa' — MCLE 503:11
They r., one fleeing — HOME 394:10
Who r. to help me — TAYL 774:15
Randal Lord R. — BALL 52:10
random word, at r. spoken — SCOT 673:14
rangers Eight for the eight bold r. — SONG 747:11
rank O! my offence is r. — SHAK 687:15
r. is but the guinea's stamp — BURN 171:4
r. me with whom you will — METH 523:8
Things r. and gross — SHAK 684:2
rankers Gentlemen-r. — KIPL 454:6
ranks glittering r. — MILT 530:20
In the r. of death — MOOR 547:17

r. of Tuscany — MACA 499:19
ransom world's r., blessèd Mary's Son — SHAK 715:14
ransomed R., healed — LYTE 497:11
rap r. at the ballot box — CHIL 217:20
rape procrastinated r. — PRIT 612:13
r.! a rape — WEBS 826:8
r., ultra-violence and Beethoven — TAGL 771:2
you r. it — DEGA 261:29
raped r. and speaks English — ANON 15:3
Raphael draw like R. — PICA 595:6
Raphaels talked of their R. — GOLD 355:9
rapid r., unintelligible patter — GILB 349:5
rapine march through r. — GLAD 350:18
rapist r. bothers to buy a bottle — DWOR 293:11
rapists all men are r. — FREN 333:13
rapping r. at my chamber door — POE 599:5
rapscallions kings is mostly r. — TWAI 803:5
rapture first fine careless r. — BROW 159:18
Modified r. — GILB 347:25
raptures high r. do infuse — WALL 818:11
r. and roses — SWIN 768:10
Rapunzel R., let down your hair — GRIM 364:15
rara R. avis — JUVE 439:19
rare man of culture r. — GILB 348:12
O r. Ben Jonson — EPIT 311:2
was indeed a r. one — WITH 842:6
rarely R., rarely, comest thou — SHEL 731:16
rarer r. than the unicorn — JONG 434:12
rari r. nantes in gurgite vasto — VIRG 810:18
rascal rather be called a r. — JOHN 430:23
you dirty r. — NURS 567:14
rascality effect of prudence on r. — SHAW 726:25
rascals R., would you live — FRED 333:6
rash Her r. hand — MILT 534:1
He was not r. — GRAH 358:11
too r., too unadvised — SHAK 717:25
Rasputin every R. has his Goethe — GRAS 359:15
Rast Ohne Hast, aber ohne R. — GOET 353:16
rat Anyone can r. — CHUR 220:22
Cat, the R., and Lovell — COLL 234:21
creeps like a r. — BOWE 148:2
giant r. of Sumatra — DOYL 284:14
How now! a r. — SHAK 687:20
poisoned r. in a hole — SWIF 766:6
r. swimming towards — CHUR 222:22
r. without a tail — SHAK 703:5
smell a r. — ROCH 651:3
terrier can define a r. — HOUS 405:5
You dirty r. — MISQ 539:5
rate cannot r. me very high — LACL 463:6
ratem pelago r. — HORA 400:4
rathe r. primrose that forsaken dies — MILT 530:8
ratio geometrical r. — MALT 509:9
inverse r. — HUXL 411:3
ratiocination pay with r. — BUTL 175:20
rationabile Sicut modo geniti infantes, r. — BIBL 115:18
rational call the r. soul — LEIB 479:14
irrational r. — STEV 758:1
What is r. is actual — HEGE 379:7
rationed so precious it must be r. — LENI 480:10
rats r.' alley — ELIO 303:14
R.! They fought the dogs — BROW 160:20
rattle education serves as a r. — ARIS 26:5
hearing 'em r. a little — FARQ 315:14
Pleased with a r. — POPE 605:5
R. his bones — NOEL 565:7
toy of man, his r. — WOLL 844:3
rattlesnake thought he saw a R. — CARR 196:15
raucle has a r. tongue — BURN 170:10
ravage nose May r. with impunity — BROW 161:16
ravaged R. and plundered — MORR 550:7
raved as I r. and grew more fierce — HERB 383:25
ravelling worn to a r. — POTT 608:2
raven grim and ancient r. — POE 599:7
Poe with this r. — LOWE 494:1

r. himself is hoarse — SHAK 703:19
r. o'er the infected house — SHAK 714:9
r., you do have a voice — AESO 6:15
saw a r. very high — WORD 845:19
With r.'s feather — SHAK 718:23
ravening r. wolves — BIBL 95:21
ravens acquitting the r. — JUVE 439:12
r. brought him bread — BIBL 81:19
seen the r. flock — AYTO 41:14
three r. — BALL 53:13
turbulently, like r. — PIND 595:12
ravish except you r. me — DONN 279:22
ravished transported and r. — TRAH 797:15
would have r. her — FIEL 317:17
you have r. justice — WEBS 826:8
ravishing dear r. thing — BEHN 63:18
ray r. of rays — DICK 267:21
r. of sunshine — WODE 842:16
razor hew blocks with a r. — POPE 606:20
mirror and a r. — OPEN 575:20
Occam's R. — OCCA 571:11
r. rusting — PLAT 596:23
reach could not r. it — SAPP 666:15
I r. for my pistol — JOHS 434:1
man's r. should exceed — BROW 158:9
My soul can r. — BROW 158:3
other beers cannot r. — ADVE 7:29
r. the brittle branches — VIRG 814:6
r. the promised land — CALL 185:16
things above his r. — OVER 579:16
reaching r. forth — BIBL 110:4
reaction can't get no girl r. — JAGG 415:15
if there is any r. — JUNG 438:12
opposed an equal r. — NEWT 561:13
reactionaries All r. are paper tigers — MAO 511:13
read be able to r. a building — ROGE 652:9
Being r. to by a boy — ELIO 302:3
bokes for to r. I me delyte — CHAU 212:22
but r. these — MART 514:18
cannot now r. a page — WALP 820:10
did not r. any more — DANT 255:20
even to r. his books — ISID 414:11
fast as they can r. — HAZL 377:1
has r. too widely — PEAR 590:9
his books were r. — BELL 65:21
In science, r. — BULW 164:6
I r., and sigh — HERB 383:17
I r. very hard — JOHN 428:14
man ought to r. — JOHN 428:9
Much had he r. — ARMS 26:11
none can r. the text — TENN 778:9
not r. Eliot, Auden — RICH 647:11
not that I ever r. them — SHER 733:5
only news until he's r. it — WAUG 824:14
others who can't r. — CHUR 219:20
people that r. — SHEN 733:1
people who can't r. — ZAPP 858:6
Pray, r., and work — MOTT 552:10
r. a book before reviewing it — SMIT 744:6
r., and censure — HEMI 381:2
r. a nod, a shrug — SWIF 767:2
r. any good books lately — CATC 200:24
r. as much as other men — AUBR 33:16
r. books through — JOHN 429:23
r. in the train — WILD 835:22
r., mark, learn — BOOK 130:1
r., much of the night — ELIO 303:8
R. my lips — BUSH 174:23
R. not to contradict — BACO 45:19
R. out my words — FLEC 326:6
R. somewhat seldomer — BROW 158:17
r. strange matters — SHAK 703:22
r. The Hunter's thoughts — AUDE 34:24
r. the life of any important — PRIE 610:17
r. without pleasure — JOHN 433:21
superfluous to r. — HILB 388:3
Take up and r. — AUGU 37:4
want to r. a novel — DISR 278:11
What do you r. — SHAK 685:18
what I r. in the papers — ROGE 652:19
who don't r. the books — BYAT 177:12
whom they never r. — CHUR 219:11

gave that thought r. WORD 848:1
r. of man's estate BACO 42:14
seek for kind r. BLAK 122:8
system of outdoor r. BRIG 151:8
relieve comfort and r. them BOOK 129:19
relieved By desperate appliances are r.
SHAK 687:34
religio Tantum r. potuit LUCR 495:10
religion act of duty and r. OSBO 578:14
affront her r. JENY 421:2
all of the same r. DISR 277:12
another r. than Islam KORA 459:21
Art and R. are two roads BELL 64:9
As if R. were intended BUTL 176:4
As to r. PAIN 582:10
become a popular r. INGE 413:6
born for the sake of r. LAWS 475:21
brothels with bricks of r. BLAK 121:4
but of one r. SHAF 678:4
can't talk r. to SHAW 725:24
Christianity was the r. SWIF 766:18
concerned with r. TEMP 775:12
cultivation of r. SADI 663:1
dominion of r. GOLD 354:8
establishment of r. CONS 241:13
Every dictator uses r. BHUT 74:19
feature of *any* r. PAIN 582:19
fox-hunting—the wisest r. HAIL 367:12
Freedom of r. JEFF 420:4
had only a little r. ANON 20:12
handmaid to r. BACO 43:2
impossibilities enough in r. BROW 156:23
increase in us true r. BOOK 130:15
in love as in r. COWL 245:25
innovation in r. MAEC 505:14
In their r. they are so uneven DEFO 261:22
just enough r. SWIF 766:19
Knight-errantry *is* r. CERV 205:11
matters of r. CHES 214:19
men's minds to r. BACO 43:17
more fierce in its r. NEWM 560:11
much wrong could r. induce LUCR 495:10
mysteries of our r. HOBB 390:22
No compulsion in r. KORA 459:14
no part of r. WESL 829:13
no r. but social WESL 829:11
on account of my r. BELL 65:30
One r. is as true BURT 174:17
only one r. SHAW 727:10
perfected your r. KORA 460:10
Philistine of genius in r. ARNO 30:6
Poetry and R. CARL 192:2
poetry, prophecy, and r. RUSK 659:14
politics as well as in r. JUNI 438:17
Pure r. and undefiled BIBL 111:24
r., and not atheism BURK 166:25
r. and philosophy ARNO 29:22
r., as a mere sentiment NEWM 560:12
r. at the lowest CHES 215:11
R. blushing POPE 602:8
r. but a childish toy MARL 513:12
r. for gentlemen CHAR 209:6
r. for religion's sake COUS 244:12
r. from the priest GOLD 356:1
r. has always been to me POTT 608:6
r. into after-dinner toasts TOAS 796:4
r. is allowed to invade MELB 521:3
R. is an all-important matter NAPO 556:12
R. is by no means CHES 214:20
r. is made MONT 544:14
r. is not circumambient FOST 330:9
r. is powerless to bestow FORB 328:7
R. is the sigh MARX 516:11
r. is to do good PAIN 582:23
r., justice, counsel BACO 45:11
r., knavery, and change BEHN 64:1
r. most prevalent BURK 166:22
r. of feeble minds BURK 167:24
r. of humanity PAIN 582:13
r. of Socialism BEVA 73:10
r. or policy RUSK 660:1
R. the frozen thought of men KRIS 461:17
r. weak SZAS 769:18

r. without a prelate BANC 54:13
r. without science is blind EINS 297:12
R.? Yes; but which BYRO 182:4
reproach to r. PENN 591:16
rum and true r. BYRO 180:19
some of r. EDGE 295:14
start your own r. ANON 16:18
system of r. PAIN 582:4
talks loudly against r. STER 757:1
That is my r. SHAW 725:23
that regards r. ADDI 5:6
They are for r. BUNY 164:20
too late to trust the old r. LOWE 494:17
tourism is their r. RUNC 658:13
true meaning of r. ARNO 30:3
true r. is Islam KORA 459:18
vice and r. SMIT 744:10
way to plant r. BROW 156:30
When I mention r. FIEL 318:7
religions R. are kept alive BREN 150:21
r. considered man as man TOCQ 795:5
sixty different r. CARA 190:2
they alone who found r. PROU 613:8
religiose r. And mystic DUNN 292:11
religious all r. revolution WEBE 825:7
but not r.-good HARD 372:6
dim r. light MILT 529:16
great r. art of the world CLAR 225:1
his r. opinions BUTL 177:4
hope I will be r. again FLEM 326:15
Old r. factions BURK 169:5
r. and moral principles ARNO 30:14
r. animal BURK 167:20
r. enquiries NEWM 560:15
R. persecution BURK 169:2
r. prejudice HUXL 412:4
seemeth to be r. BIBL 111:23
sense of r. mission UPDI 805:24
suspended my r. inquiries GIBB 345:15
relish one begins to have a r. HAYW 376:8
relished by which he is to be r. WORD 851:2
reluctance superstitious r. to sit JOHN 431:16
reluctant r. peer BENN 66:17
with r. feet LONG 490:14
rem *quocumque modo r.* HORA 399:1
R. *tene* CATO 199:19
remain fragments that r. BIBL 103:2
r. with you always BOOK 132:5
things have been, things r. CLOU 229:10
remains aught r. to do ROGE 652:10
r. of life WALP 819:2
remarkable anything r. about it PAST 587:19
nothing left r. SHAK 680:3
remarks R. are not literature STEI 755:6
said our r. before us DONA 279:1
remedies by violent r. MONT 545:5
desperate r. PROV 617:30
Extreme r. HIPP 389:10
r. oft in ourselves do lie SHAK 678:8
will not apply new r. BACO 44:27
remedy bestowed on mankind a r.
SYDE 769:10
dangerous r. FAWK 316:8
Force is not a r. BRIG 151:21
My dog! what r. remains COWP 247:1
no r. presents itself so soon DONN 281:22
r. for everything except PROV 632:8
r. is death CHAM 207:1
r. is worse than the disease BACO 45:14
r. our *enemies* have chosen SHER 734:16
r. our own KYD 462:8
Things without all r. SHAK 705:20
'Tis a sharp r. RALE 641:15
remember Body, r. not only CAVA 203:14
cannot r. the past SANT 666:8
Do you r. an Inn, Miranda BELL 65:25
if thou wilt, r. ROSS 655:16
I r., I remember HOOD 395:3
I r. it well LERN 481:17
Lord, r. me BIBL 102:5
man to r. me RUNY 659:3
R. LAST 473:15
r. a happy time DANT 255:18

r. and be sad ROSS 655:12
r. even these things VIRG 811:3
r. for ever WARN 821:20
R. me ROSS 655:11
R. me when I am dead DOUG 283:17
r. more than seven BELL 64:16
r. not past years NEWM 561:6
R. now thy Creator BIBL 86:25
r. sweet Alice ENGL 307:29
R. the Alamo SHER 734:11
r. the children you got BROO 154:5
R. thee BYRO 183:3
R. thee! Ay, thou poor ghost SHAK 685:6
r. the Fifth of November ANON 18:12
R. the sabbath day BIBL 78:3
r., whan it passed is CHAU 213:8
r. who I am VIRG 812:3
r. with advantages SHAK 693:23
thou r. and I forget SWIN 769:1
We will r. them BINY 116:14
what you can r. SELL 676:16
Yes; I r. Adlestrop THOM 790:11
yet never can, r. THOM 790:15
You must r. this HUPF 410:13
remembered blue r. hills HOUS 404:16
like to be r. POWE 610:4
r. around the world DISN 275:3
r. for a very long time MCGO 501:16
would have made myself r. KEAT 447:5
remembering learning is a process of r.
PLAT 597:8
R. without ceasing BIBL 110:15
remembrance arouse in them r. KORA 460:16
Do this in r. of me BOOK 132:2
everlasting r. BOOK 141:23
r. of a weeping queen SHAK 716:5
r. of his dying Lord SPEN 751:13
r. of them is grievous BOOK 131:18
R. of things past BORR 146:15
r. of things past SHAK 723:1
rosemary, that's for r. SHAK 688:12
Writ in r. more SHAK 715:12
remind R. me of you MARV 516:7
remission for the r. of sins BOOK 132:2
no r. BIBL 111:4
r. of pain or guilt BOOK 144:17
remnant smell my r. out HERB 384:12
remorse access and passage to r.
SHAK 703:19
rather feel r. THOM 788:2
R. is surely the most wasteful FORS 329:17
R., the fatal egg COWP 247:11
R.! Those dry Martinis ADE 5:16
remorseful blabbing, and r. day SHAK 694:17
remote r. enquiries JOHN 424:27
removals household r. BAUD 59:1
Three r. are as bad PROV 632:48
remove owl of the R. RICH 647:9
R. not the ancient landmark BIBL 84:41
say unto this mountain, R. BIBL 97:18
remover with the r. to remove SHAK 723:22
Remus descendants of R. CATU 203:1
On the left side goes R. MACA 499:21
renard Certain r. voulut LA F 463:16
renascentur Multa r. HORA 398:3
render r. The deeds of mercy SHAK 709:26
R. to all their dues BIBL 106:31
R. unto Caesar BIBL 98:6
rendezvous My r. is appointed WHIT 833:15
r. with Death SEEG 675:13
renew r. a right spirit BOOK 137:13
r. their strength BIBL 89:21
R. your brilliance GRAC 358:1
renewal r. of love PROV 630:1
renewing r. is of love EDWA 297:3
Reno King's Moll R.'d NEWS 562:16
renounce I r. war FOSD 330:6
r. the devil BOOK 132:13
renouncing r. his body JAIN 416:15
renown O vain r. DANT 256:7
r. on scraps of learning YOUN 857:2
rent r. is due TINE 794:17
R. is that portion RICA 646:17

results quick and effective r. BULL 163:15
than for r. BAGE 48:19
unless it achieves r. SHAC 677:19
resurrection by thy glorious R. BOOK 129:8
in the r. BIBL 98:7
on the Day of R. KORA 459:22
r., and the life BIBL 103:21
R. of the body BOOK 128:10
r. of the dead BIBL 108:4
r. of the dead BIBL 108:9
R. to eternal life BOOK 133:18
retained Him, they r. GERV 344:14
retaliate r. for a soul slain KORA 460:11
retard r. what we cannot repel JOHN 424:7
retentive r. to the strength SHAK 696:20
reticence Northern r., the tight gag
HEAN 378:6
R., in three volumes GLAD 351:10
reticulated *Network.* Anything r.
JOHN 424:11
retire r. from this station JEFF 420:5
retirement there must be no r. HAIG 367:11
retort r. courteous SHAK 682:8
retreat absolute r. WINC 841:8
make an honourable r. SHAK 681:18
more untroubled r. AURE 38:2
noblest station is r. LYTT 497:13
not r. a single inch GARR 340:8
This r., so sweet HORA 399:12
retreating Have you seen yourself r.
NASH 557:18
my right is r. FOCH 327:22
retrenchment Peace, r., and reform
BRIG 151:9
retrograde be not r. JONS 435:8
r. if it does not advance GIBB 345:10
retrorsum *nulla r.* HORA 399:2
return he shall not r. to me BIBL 81:2
I shall r. MACA 497:15
I will r. EPIT 310:11
not r. your blow SHAW 727:1
r. no more to his house BIBL 83:1
r. of democratic control STEE 754:15
r., O Shulamite BIBL 87:18
r. unto God BIBL 86:25
Should I never r. MANS 511:5
state I came, r. VAUG 807:15
They shall not r. to us KIPL 455:3
unto dust shalt thou r. BIBL 75:27
whence I shall not r. BIBL 83:2
returned r. on the previous night
BULL 163:16
returning R. were as tedious SHAK 706:9
returns r. to the sore tooth PROV 633:13
they say no one r. CATU 202:12
reveal like Nature, half r. TENN 778:23
r. Himself MILT 535:21
r. whatsoever He will KORA 461:2
revealed careless, when r. CENT 205:5
Lord shall be r. BIBL 89:16
nothing of r. religion MEND 521:21
what has been r. THOM 789:4
revelation except by r. KORA 461:2
first hole is a r. MOOR 546:15
inspired by divine r. BACO 42:17
Reason is natural r. LOCK 488:12
revelations ends with R. WILD 836:23
extraordinary r. BUTL 175:14
offers stupendous r. HOFF 392:4
revelry r. by night BYRO 178:19
revels Our r. now are ended SHAK 719:1
r. long o' nights SHAK 697:7
revenge deaths become r. by morning
MOTI 551:12
God's r. FOOT 328:4
gratitude is a species of r. JOHN 425:21
I will most horribly r. SHAK 694:3
man that studieth r. BACO 45:9
Punishment is not for r. FRY 336:17
ranging for r. SHAK 697:16
r. for slight injuries MACH 502:9
R. herself went down TENN 784:4
R. his foul SHAK 685:1

R. is a dish PROV 630:7
r. is a kind of wild justice BACO 45:8
r. is always the pleasure JUVE 440:14
R. is sweet PROV 630:8
r.! Timotheus cries DRYD 287:19
R. triumphs over death BACO 44:2
shall we not r. SHAK 709:14
spur my dull r. SHAK 688:2
study of r. MILT 531:9
Sweet is r. BYRO 180:13
sweet r. grows harsh SHAK 714:23
tribal, intimate r. HEAN 378:2
with envy and r. MILT 531:7
revenged I'll be r. SHAK 721:17
revenges brings in his r. SHAK 721:16
revenons R. à ces moutons ANON 21:1
revenue standing r. BURK 166:27
Thrift is a great r. PROV 632:50
reverence In deeper r. praise WHIT 834:4
mystic r. BAGE 47:13
R. for Life SCHW 672:9
r. the King TENN 777:20
so poor to do him r. SHAK 697:28
reverends Wrong R. of every Order
DICK 267:24
reveries r. so airy COWP 248:1
reversion r. in the sky POPE 602:13
review your r. before me REGE 644:14
reviewers indolent r. TENN 782:12
R. are usually people who COLE 233:27
reviewing read a book before r. it SMIT 744:6
revising power of r. GIDE 346:15
revisited r. ideas OLDF 572:23
revivalism rebellion and r. THOM 790:19
revivals history of r. BUTL 176:29
revive r. in New South Wales BANK 54:18
strive to r. PUGI 636:21
reviving r. the *castrati* REED 644:8
revolt It is a big r. LA R 469:23
r., disorder MORR 550:8
revolting r. and a rebellious heart BIBL 90:24
revolution After a r. HALI 368:16
after the r. AREN 24:16
age of r. JEFF 420:4
catalyst that sparks the r. DURY 293:10
commences a r. can rarely JEFF 420:15
crust over a volcano of r. ELLI 306:3
destroyed by a r. TOCQ 795:8
entered into this R. BROW 155:9
explain the French R. BAUD 59:1
French R. operated TOCQ 795:5
it is a big r. LA R 469:23
leaders of a r. CONR 240:25
not r., but restoration HARD 371:10
reform or r. BERL 70:2
R. a parent BURK 167:8
r. is the kicking down HEAN 378:7
R., like Saturn VERG 808:14
r. of rising expectations CLEV 226:18
r. without revolution ROBE 650:3
safeguard a r. ORWE 577:21
revolutionaries R. are more formalistic
CALV 186:12
r. potential Tories ORWE 577:8
revolutionary can't feel r. in a bathroom
LINK 486:8
Every r. ends CAMU 188:18
forge his r. spirit GUEV 365:14
revolutionists age fatal to R. DESM 265:14
revolutions All modern r. CAMU 188:17
main cause of r. INGE 413:5
R. are not made PROV 630:9
R. have never lightened SHAW 726:16
r. never go backward SEWA 677:11
r. with rosewater HEAL 377:14
share in two r. PAIN 583:1
revolver resembles a r. FANO 314:9
revolving with the r. year SHEL 728:17
reward in no wise lose his r. BIBL 96:22
nothing for r. SPEN 751:24
not to ask for any r. IGNA 412:18
only r. of virtue EMER 306:23
r. for labour CARN 193:9

r. is when we die RYDE 662:1
taken r. against the innocent BOOK 134:13
Virtue is its own r. PROV 633:36
what r. have ye BIBL 94:32
Work not for a r. BHAG 74:12
rewarded of thee be plenteously r.
BOOK 130:21
r. me evil for good BOOK 135:26
rewardest r. every man BOOK 138:2
rewards Crimes are their own r. FARQ 315:19
r. and Fairies CORB 242:18
rewrite is to r. it WILD 835:27
readers r. GRAV 360:12
rex r. quondam MALO 509:4
R. tremendae maiestatis MISS 539:17
Reynolds R. died BLAK 119:4
rhetoric aimless r. HUXL 412:4
Death, without r. SIEY 736:21
For r. he could not ope BUTL 175:21
logic and r. BACO 45:22
love without the r. STOP 761:13
quarrel with others, r. YEAT 856:8
[r.] doesn't involve expertise PLAT 597:7
rhetorician sophistical r. DISR 276:19
Rhine think of the R. BALD 50:16
rhinoceros armed r. SHAK 706:6
hide of a r. BARR 57:11
Rhodesia black majority rule in R.
SMIT 742:9
rhyme could not get a r. FLEM 326:19
hope and history r. HEAN 377:18
I'm fond of r. BYRO 180:17
in prose or r. MILT 531:5
I r. for fun BURN 172:24
many a musèd r. KEAT 444:27
mere knack of r. CHUR 220:3
outlive this powerful r. SHAK 723:5
R. being . . . but the invention MILT 531:2
r. is a barrel MAYA 519:9
R. is the rock DRYD 287:19
R. still the most effective drum GIRA 350:3
r. themselves SHAK 694:5
r. the rudder is BUTL 176:7
still more tired of R. BELL 65:9
stringing blethers up to r. BURN 173:6
rhymed r. conversation GERS 344:11
rhymes Namby-pamby's little r. CARE 191:7
ring out my mournful r. TENN 779:23
rhyming bondage of r. MILT 531:3
born under a r. planet SHAK 712:33
Thy drasty r. CHAU 212:12
rhythm I got r. GERS 344:6
sweet, soft, plenty r. MORT 551:7
rhythmical r. grumbling ELIO 304:1
rhythms r. for bears to dance FLAU 324:22
Rialto What news on the R. SHAK 708:29
riband Just for a r. BROW 160:2
r. in the cap SHAK 688:16
ribbon blue r. of the turf DISR 277:17
changing a typewriter r. BENC 66:5
road was a r. of moonlight NOYE 566:2
ribbons r. rare HUNT 410:10
ribs he took one of his r. BIBL 75:15
Ribstone Pippin Right as a R. BELL 65:8
rice r. field, ocean BASH 57:21
r. pudding for dinner again MILN 528:4
rich Beauty too r. for use SHAK 717:17
born lucky than r. PROV 623:43
by chance grow r. THOM 790:13
certain r. man BIBL 101:22
feed with the r. JOHN 429:3
fell from the r. man's table BIBL 101:22
Grow r. in that SIDN 736:12
Isn't it r. SOND 746:6
live by robbing the r. SHAW 726:5
maketh haste to be r. BIBL 85:17
making Gay r. JOHN 425:4
man who dies . . . r. CARN 193:8
neither r. nor rare POPE 602:27
never be too r. or too thin WIND 841:13
no sin, but to be r. SHAK 699:3
not really a r. man GETT 344:15
not r. enough REED 644:12

rich (*cont.*):
One law for the r.	PROV 628:41
open to the poor and the r.	ANON 16:4
parish of r. women	AUDE 35:3
Poor little r. girl	COWA 245:5
potentiality of growing r.	JOHN 431:24
R. AND THE POOR	DISR 277:23
r. are covetous	SMAR 739:16
r. are different from you and me	FITZ 323:20
r. are the scum of the earth	CHES 216:21
r. as well as the poor	FRAN 331:19
r. beyond the dreams	MOOR 546:11
r. enough to pay	HEAL 377:10
r. get rich	KAHN 441:4
r. have no right	RUSK 660:10
r. he hath sent empty away	BIBL 99:32
r. he hath sent empty away	BIBL 115:11
r. in a more precious treasure	MACA 498:5
r. in subjects	DEFO 261:13
r. man has his ice	PROV 630:10
r. man in his castle	ALEX 11:7
r. man is fallen	BIBL 93:15
r. man to enter	BIBL 97:27
r. man without money	USTI 806:4
R. men	BIBL 93:32
r. men rule the law	GOLD 355:14
r., not gaudy	SHAK 684:18
r. on the poor	JEFF 419:12
r., quiet, and infamous	MACA 498:16
r. wage war	SART 666:20
r. with forty pounds a year	GOLD 354:13
r. wot gets the gravy	MILI 526:16
save the few who are r.	KENN 448:17
seems it r. to die	KEAT 444:27
sincerely want to be r.	CORN 243:8
something r. and strange	SHAK 718:27
swinish luxury of the r.	MORR 550:1
Richard put down R.	SHAK 689:27
R.'s himself again	CIBB 223:4
richer for r. for poorer	BOOK 133:9
R. than all his tribe	SHAK 714:30
riches beggar amidst great r.	HORA 401:22
chosen than great r.	BIBL 84:39
deceitfulness of r.	BIBL 97:4
embarrassment of r.	ALLA 12:4
getteth r., and not by right	BIBL 91:4
gives r. to those	LUTH 496:14
gold or gret r.	LYDG 496:21
heapeth up r.	BOOK 136:5
Infinite r.	MARL 513:13
in her left hand r.	BIBL 83:34
looked upon r.	SWIF 766:4
neither poverty nor r.	BIBL 85:20
parade of r.	SMIT 741:7
R. are a good handmaid	BACO 43:7
R. are for spending	BACO 44:8
r. grow in hell	MILT 531:26
r. left, not got	SURR 764:4
r. of heaven's pavement	MILT 531:26
R., the dumb god	JONS 435:11
titled for r.	PEAR 590:10
unsearchable r. of Christ	BIBL 109:6
When r. do abound	GOOG 356:12
world's r., which dispersed lie	HERB 384:19
richest r. without meaning	RUSK 659:23
richly lady r. left	SHAK 708:23
Richmond Sweet lass of R. Hill	SONG 748:8
richness all in a rush With r.	HOPK 397:1
Here's r.	DICK 270:16
rid decorated, and got r. of	CICE 223:26
never get r. of	BARH 56:2
to be r. of thee	CONG 239:6
riddance die and be a r.	DICK 268:8
riddle dishcover the r.	CARR 196:4
found out my r.	BIBL 79:30
r. of the sands	CHIL 217:21
r. of the world	POPE 605:1
r. wrapped in a mystery	CHUR 221:4
riddles R. lie here	EPIT 310:7
ride if you cannot r. two horses	MAXT 519:3
know how to r.	BISM 117:14
R. a cock-horse	NURS 569:8
r. in triumph	MARL 513:20

r. of Paul Revere	LONG 491:4
R. on! ride on in majesty	MILM 527:15
She's got a ticket to r.	LENN 480:21
way the ladies r.	NURS 570:3
we r. them down	TENN 783:8
ridentem *Dulce* r.	HORA 400:18
rider r. and his horse	SURT 764:25
rideret r. *Democritus*	HORA 399:20
rides r. a tiger	PROV 622:14
r. upon the storm	COWP 246:23
rideth r. upon the heavens	BOOK 138:11
ridicule adulation and r.	LACL 463:4
r. in any subject	SHAF 678:6
r. is the best test	CHES 215:12
stand the test of r.	SHAF 678:5
ridiculos r. *homines facit*	JUVE 439:16
ridiculous heart of the r.	MAHO 507:9
makes men r.	JUVE 439:16
no spectacle so r.	MACA 498:6
position r.	CHES 215:17
r. and superficial	MURA 554:11
r. excess	SHAK 699:10
step above the r.	PAIN 582:5
sublime to the r.	NAPO 556:15
sublime to the r.	PROV 620:32
ridiculus *nascetur* r. *mus*	HORA 398:8
riding highwayman came r.	NOYE 566:2
man goes r. by	STEV 760:8
r. that night	LONG 491:6
Ridley good comfort, Master R.	LAST 471:4
rien *Ils n'ont* r. *appris*	TALL 771:18
je ne regrette r.	VAUC 807:6
R.	LOUI 492:11
rifle r. all the breathing spring	COLL 235:10
roll to your r.	KIPL 456:8
rift loaded every r.	SPEN 751:23
Load every r.	KEAT 447:7
r. within the lute	TENN 778:5
Rigby Eleanor R.	LENN 480:17
riggish Bless her when she is r.	SHAK 679:7
right All's r. with the world	BROW 160:22
almost always in the r.	SMIT 744:7
assert thy r.	BARB 55:6
convinced that they are r.	VAN 806:20
curst conceit o' bein' r.	MACD 501:1
customer is always r.	PROV 617:21
defend to the death your r.	MISQ 538:1
Do r. and fear no man	PROV 618:21
do what is r.	HUXL 411:16
everyone is r.	LA C 463:2
firmness in the r.	LINC 485:12
foot standeth r.	BOOK 135:12
forgive those who were r.	MACL 503:13
grounded on just and r.	MILT 533:26
heaven still guards the r.	SHAK 715:19
if r., to be kept right	SCHU 672:6
I had rather be r.	CLAY 226:4
indefeasible, divine r.	ADAM 3:5
individual r.	TAFT 770:15
in itself what is r.	VIRG 811:7
It must be r.	CRAB 248:30
Jack — I'm all r.	BONE 127:6
'just' or 'r.'	PLAT 597:11
majority never has r.	IBSE 412:10
Might is r.	PROV 626:21
more than half the people are r.	WHIT 832:1
my r. is retreating	FOCH 327:22
never r. to do wrong	SOCR 745:6
no more r. to consume	SHAW 724:22
no r. in the circus	MAXT 519:3
not all was r.	CRAB 249:11
of all the earth do r.	BIBL 76:19
of—them—is—r.	KIPL 454:14
our country, r. or wrong	DECA 261:1
questioned its r. to exist	SCHU 671:21
renew a r. spirit	BOOK 137:13
r., and our bounden duty	BOOK 131:22
R. as a Ribstone Pippin	BELL 65:8
R. but Repulsive	SELL 676:21
r. can be determined	HOBB 390:21
r. deed for the wrong reason	ELIO 302:24
R. Divine of Kings	POPE 602:2
r. hand of iniquity	BOOK 143:23

r. hand of the Majesty	BIBL 111:3
r. hands of fellowship	BIBL 108:26
R. . . . is the child	BENT 68:3
r. little, tight little Island	DIBD 267:10
r. makes might	LINC 485:1
r. man in the right place	JEFF 420:18
r. notes at the right time	BACH 42:10
r. of an excessive wrong	BROW 161:9
r. of the ignorant man	CARL 191:11
r. of trampling on them	CHIL 217:19
r. part of the country	FROS 336:8
r. that you have brought	SHEL 732:10
r. there is none to dispute	COWP 248:24
r. thought	PALI 584:6
r. to a fair portion	BURK 167:11
r. to be consulted	BAGE 48:17
r. to be obeyed	JOHN 422:3
r. which goes unrecognized	WEIL 826:19
r. wrong	TENN 777:18
scientists are probably r.	ASIM 31:18
Self-government is our r.	CASE 197:14
setting people r.	MOOR 547:5
sheep on his r. hand	BIBL 98:24
Sit thou on my r. hand	BOOK 141:20
that which they will, is r.	ADAM 2:9
that which was r.	BIBL 79:37
thing which is r.	BOOK 134:12
to be decorative and to do r.	FIRB 321:9
To do a great r.	SHAK 709:28
Two wrongs don't make a r.	PROV 633:31
Two wrongs don't make a r.	SZAS 769:19
vast r.-wing conspiracy	CLIN 227:5
Want to do r.	RICH 647:5
Whatever IS, is R.	POPE 604:31
What r. have they	DICK 271:16
what's r. and fair	HUGH 407:13
righteous godly, r., and sober life	BOOK 127:17
have seen the r. forsaken	BLUN 124:5
never the r. forsaken	BOOK 136:1
not come to call the r.	BIBL 96:7
prayer of a r. man	BIBL 112:1
r. are bold	BIBL 85:16
r. man	BIBL 84:13
r. perisheth	BIBL 90:12
r. shall be had	BOOK 141:23
souls of the r.	BIBL 92:23
righteousness breastplate of r.	BIBL 109:21
clouds rain down r.	BIBL 115:8
looked for r.	BIBL 88:6
loved r., and hated iniquity	BOOK 136:20
paths of r.	SCOT 675:4
pursue r.	PLAT 597:13
r. and peace	BOOK 139:19
r. as the waves of the sea	BIBL 89:25
R. exalteth a nation	BIBL 84:21
r. hath not been forgotten	BIBL 93:34
r. of the scribes	BIBL 94:25
Sun of r.	BIBL 92:14
Sun of R.	WESL 828:24
superior understands r.	CONF 237:16
thirst after r.	BIBL 94:20
what r. really is	ARNO 30:5
With r. shall he judge	BOOK 140:15
righteousnesses r. are as filthy rags	BIBL 90:20
rightful will to be r.	JEFF 420:1
rights all your r. become	CASE 198:12
as much r. as men	TRUT 801:18
asserting these r.	LAY 476:5
Bill of R.	COMM 236:15
coloured men getting r.	TRUT 801:19
duties as well as its r.	DRUM 286:11
equal in dignity and r.	ANON 15:1
extension of women's r.	FOUR 330:16
from the South its dearest r.	LEE 479:3
inalienable r.	ROBE 650:5
intruder on r. of men	WINC 841:6
Natural r.	BENT 68:4
of his natural r.	PRIE 611:13
r. are disregarded	BROW 155:7
r. inherent and inalienable	JEFF 419:10
r. in learning's world	EGER 297:5

blows so red The r. FITZ 323:4
English unofficial r. BROO 153:9
expectancy and r. SHAK 686:18
fading r. CARE 191:1
fayr as is the r. CHAU 212:25
fire and the r. are one ELIO 302:2
fresh lap of the crimson r. SHAK 710:32
Gather therefore the r. SPEN 751:26
gave Ruth a r. AYCK 41:5
ghost of a r. BROW 156:5
Go, lovely r. WALL 818:6
Goodbye, England's r. JOHN 422:13
I know the colour r. ABSE 1:4
inimitable r. WINC 841:10
Into the r.-garden ELIO 301:10
I r., went forth WESL 828:22
labyrinthine buds the r. BROW 161:15
last r. of summer MOOR 547:19
late r. may yet linger HORA 401:1
lovely is the r. WORD 847:21
love were what the r. is SWIN 769:6
luver stole my r. BURN 170:14
Luve's like a red, red r. BURN 172:4
Mighty lak' a r. STAN 754:11
morning r. KEAT 444:18
no more desire a r. SHAK 702:11
No thorns go as deep as a r.'s SWIN 768:12
One perfect r. PARK 585:17
Pluck a red r. SHAK 694:11
pluck a white r. SHAK 694:10
pluck the r. BROW 161:26
Queen r. of the rosebud garden TENN 781:25
ravage with impunity a r. BROW 161:16
r. again from the dead BOOK 128:10
r. By any other name SHAK 717:22
R.-cheeked Laura CAMP 188:5
r. distilled SHAK 710:16
r. in aromatic pain POPE 604:27
r. in dark and evil days INGR 413:17
R. is a rose STEI 755:9
R. of all my days YEAT 855:24
r. of Sharon BIBL 87:5
r. of yesterday FITZ 323:1
R. Of youth SHAK 679:15
r.-red city BURG 165:20
r.-red sissy PLOM 598:12
r. should shut KEAT 443:1
r.'s scent is bitterness THOM 791:5
R., thou art sick BLAK 122:18
r. to a pitch-black toad YESE 856:16
R., were you not PRIO 612:11
r. with all its sweetest leaves BYRO 182:3
r. without the thorn HERR 386:10
Roves back the r. DE L 262:21
secret and inviolate R. YEAT 855:14
sweet lovely r. SHAK 689:27
Sweet r., whose hue HERB 385:4
vanish with the r. FITZ 323:16
wavers to a r. DOBS 278:17
white r. of Scotland MACD 501:4
white r. weeps TENN 781:26
without thorn the r. MILT 532:28
yet a r. full-blown HERR 386:22

rosea *avertens r. cervice* VIRG 811:5
rosebud I did but touch the r. PHIL 594:16
R. is just a piece FILM 320:10
rosebuds crown ourselves with r. BIBL 92:21
Gather ye r. HERR 386:18
rosemary r. and rue SHAK 722:1
r., that's for remembrance SHAK 688:12
Rosencrantz R. and Guildenstern
SHAK 689:17
roses ash the burnt r. leave ELIO 301:22
criticism with r. D'IS 278:12
days of wine and r. DOWS 284:8
Each morn a thousand r. FITZ 323:1
Everything's coming up r. SOND 746:5
fields where r. fade HOUS 405:1
flower of r. BIBL 94:1
Flung r., roses DOWS 284:6
Honey of r. HERB 384:9
let fall a shower of r. TERE 785:20
like my r. to see you SHER 734:9

lilac and the r. ARAG 24:3
not a bed of r. STEV 759:24
on a bed of r. HORA 400:7
Plant thou no r. ROSS 655:16
raptures and r. SWIN 768:10
Ring-a-ring o'r. NURS 569:9
R. are flowering in Picardy WEAT 824:23
r. for the flush ROSS 655:10
R. have thorns SHAK 723:3
r. of thy lips LODG 489:9
roses, r., all the way BROW 160:17
r. within MARV 515:21
scent of the r. MOOR 547:14
smells like r. JOHN 423:15
soft as the r. BYRO 178:2
Treaties like girls and r. DE G 262:10
Two red r. MORR 549:17
rosewater made with r. PROV 630:9
revolutions with r. HEAL 377:14
rosy plain men have r. faces STEV 760:10
r.-fingered dawn HOME 394:14
rot in cold obstruction and to r. SHAK 708:10
one to r. PROV 628:34
r. in hospitals SOUT 748:15
we r. and rot SHAK 681:7
Rothschild R. and Baring GILB 347:18
rots Winter never r. PROV 635:12
rotted simply r. early NASH 557:12
rotten choice in r. apples PROV 631:1
good to feel r. YESE 856:17
hypocrite is really r. AREN 24:15
like r. mackerel RAND 642:4
r. apple injures PROV 630:17
r. boughs to climb WYAT 852:2
shines like r. wood RALE 641:2
Something is r. SHAK 684:29
Soon ripe, soon r. PROV 631:8
You r. swines CATC 202:6
rottenness r. begins in his conduct
JEFF 419:17
r. of eighty years BYRO 183:16
r. of our civilization READ 642:18
rotundity r. o' the world SHAK 700:15
rotundus *teres, atque r.* HORA 403:16
rough al r. and long yherd CHAU 211:23
like a r. diamond DEFO 261:4
r. and lecherous SHAK 699:27
r. and ready man BROW 158:17
R.-hew them how we will SHAK 689:5
r. magic I here abjure SHAK 719:4
r. places plain BIBL 89:16
R. winds do shake SHAK 722:24
roughness r. breedeth hate BACO 44:24
roughs among his fellow r. DOYL 285:11
round flat pretending to be r. FORS 329:10
in that little r. FORD 329:2
into the r. hole SMIT 743:11
Love makes the world go r. PROV 625:45
made the r. world so sure BOOK 140:6
R. and round the circle ELIO 301:8
Round and r. the garden NURS 569:10
r. as a ball JULI 438:5
R. both the shires HOUS 404:11
r. earth's imagined corners DONN 279:17
r., fat, oily man THOM 792:4
R. the world ARNO 27:13
r. unvarnished tale SHAK 713:7
R. up the usual suspects FILM 320:4
said the world was r. GERS 344:10
roundabouts gain on the r. PROV 634:19
rounded polished and well-r. HORA 403:16
r. with a sleep SHAK 719:1
Roundheads R. (Right but Repulsive)
SELL 676:21
rouse R. the lion SCOT 674:24
Rousseau ask Jean Jacques R. COWP 247:7
routine care more for r. BAGE 48:19
rove r. as well as you BEHN 63:23
rover blood's a r. HOUS 404:8
roving go no more a-r. BYRO 183:8
row R. after row with strict impunity
TATE 773:10
r. Of polished pillars JONS 436:5

r. one way and look another BURT 174:1
rowan r. leaves are dank BLOK 123:13
rowed All r. fast MISQ 537:2
rowing looking one way, and r. BUNY 164:19
Rowley 'Heigh-ho!' says R. NURS 566:20
royal needed no r. title SPEN 750:14
r. banners forward go FORT 330:4
r. captain of this ruined SHAK 693:8
r. priesthood BIBL 112:5
'r. road' to geometry EUCL 312:9
r. road to learning PROV 632:18
r. road to the unconscious MISQ 537:10
R. Society desires to confer FARA 314:7
r. throne of kings SHAK 715:13
this is the r. Law CORO 243:16
royalist more of a r. SAYI 669:28
royaliste *plus r.* SAYI 669:28
royally proved most r. SHAK 689:18
Royal Society proposed to the R. ARTS 30:21
royalties entertain four r. SALI 664:7
royalty R. is a government BAGE 48:12
r. is to be reverenced BAGE 48:16
r. of Albion's king SHAK 694:15
R. the gold filling OSBO 578:23
R. will be strong BAGE 48:12
when you come to R. DISR 277:37
rub ay, there's the r. SHAK 686:9
r. up against money RUNY 658:15
rubbers look out for r. PROV 632:44
rubbish cast as r. to the void TENN 779:6
r. of an Adam SOUT 748:14
some of the r. LOCK 488:6
What r. BLÜC 124:10
rubble crushed by the r. SOLZ 745:19
rubies above r. BIBL 83:15
pearls away and r. HOUS 404:10
price is far above r. BIBL 85:23
rubs fog that r. its back ELIO 302:14
Leave no r. nor botches SHAK 705:19
rudder heart was to thy r. tied SHAK 679:14
rhyme the r. is BUTL 176:7
r. broke off BARN 56:10
r. of painting LEON 481:5
ruled by the r. PROV 635:6
ruddier r. than the cherry GAY 341:4
ruddy r., and beautiful BIBL 80:17
rude let's talk r. FLAN 324:17
R. am I in my speech SHAK 713:6
r. and wild BELL 65:5
so r. to the good WORD 846:1
You have been very r. CHIR 218:2
rudest r. work that tells a story RUSK 659:23
Rudolph R., the Red-Nosed MARK 512:9
rue nought shall make us r. SHAK 699:16
rosemary and r. SHAK 722:1
R., even for ruth SHAK 716:5
There's r. for you SHAK 688:13
ruffian father r. SHAK 690:1
menaces of a r. JOHN 429:25
ruffle r. up your spirits SHAK 698:6
ruffled r. feathers sex can EWAR 313:6
rugby R. Union which is THOM 790:19
rugged harsh cadence of a r. line
DRYD 289:25
old r. cross BENN 67:7
r. verse I chose DRYD 289:12
steep and r. pathway WILL 839:17
system of r. individualism HOOV 395:22
rugs like a million bloody r. FITZ 324:8
Ruh *Meine R.' ist hin* GOET 352:20
Über allen Gipfeln Ist R.' GOET 353:10
Ruhm *Tat ist alles, nichts der R.* GOET 353:2
ruin God to r. has designed DRYD 288:21
its r. didst not share DODI 278:22
Majestic though in r. MILT 532:4
Resolved to r. DRYD 287:1
roving's been my r. SONG 747:1
r. himself in twelve months GEOR 343:10
r. of all happiness BURN 169:22
R. seize thee GRAY 360:20
r. that Cromwell knocked about BEDF 62:8
r. that it feeds upon COWP 247:12
r. that's romantic GILB 348:11

turn delight into a s.   HERB 383:21
sacrificed accuracy must be s.   JOHN 424:1
be s. to expediency   MAUG 518:15
slain and spent and s.   SWIN 768:8
sacrificers s., but not butchers   SHAK 696:23
sacrifices never forgive him for the s.   MAUG 518:17
such s., my Cordelia   SHAK 702:1
sacrilege consecrated s.   DISR 276:6
sacrilegious Most s. murder   SHAK 705:10
sad All my s. captains   SHAK 679:17
all their songs are s.   CHES 215:22
How s. and bad   BROW 159:3
mine a s. one   SHAK 708:20
of all s. words   WHIT 834:5
real s. rain   CASH 198:13
remember and be s.   ROSS 655:12
s. bad glad mad   SWIN 768:7
s., black isle   BAUD 58:15
s.-coloured sect   HOOD 395:15
s. old age   TALL 771:20
s. steps, O Moon   SIDN 736:4
s. tale's best for winter   SHAK 721:26
s. tires in a mile-a   SHAK 721:35
s. vicissitude of things   STER 757:17
So s., so fresh   TENN 783:4
tell s. stories   SHAK 715:23
very s. to find   BROW 161:18
why I am so s.   HEIN 379:15
why I am so s.   SHAK 708:19
world is s. and dreary   FOST 330:15
saddening unvaried, s. sound   CRAB 249:1
sadder s. and a wiser man   COLE 233:11
saddest telling the s. tale   SHAK 710:29
tell of s. thought   SHEL 731:29
saddle Boot, s., to horse   BROW 158:22
Germany in the s.   BISM 117:15
s. my horses   SCOT 674:21
Things are in the s.   EMER 306:13
saddled s. and bridled   RUMB 658:5
sadly take their pleasures s.   SULL 763:15
sadness diverter of s.   WALT 820:19
saeclum Solvet s. in favilla   MISS 539:15
saecula in s. saeculorum   MISS 536:13
saepibus S. in nostris parvam   VIRG 814:6
safe Better be s. than sorry   PROV 615:24
feeling s. with a person   ANON 18:5
made s. for democracy   WILS 840:22
S. bind, safe find   PROV 630:18
s., but ne'er will reach   DRYD 289:27
s. course for the defeated   VIRG 811:19
S. is spelled D-U-L-L   CLAR 224:23
s. lodging   NEWM 561:2
s. side   PROV 623:42
s. to be unpopular   STEV 758:15
see me s. up   MORE 548:17
thought it was s.   ANON 17:5
thought it was s.   TAGL 771:6
To fly is s.   COWP 248:5
will keep us s.   JOHN 429:17
world s. for hypocrisy   WOLF 843:17
safeguard s. of the West   WORD 848:19
safeliest s. when with one man manned   DONN 279:13
safely Thro' the world we s. go   BLAK 119:11
safer Love just makes it s.   ICE- 412:17
s. for a prince   MACH 502:10
s. than a known way   HASK 375:2
s. to be in a subordinate   THOM 788:5
world s. for children   LE G 479:7
safest when we are s.   BROW 158:14
safety every man shall eat in s.   SHAK 695:24
pluck this flower, s.   SHAK 690:3
s. and welfare of the American   HEAR 378:9
s. cometh from the Lord   SCOT 675:6
s., honour, and welfare   CHAR 209:10
s. in numbers   PROV 632:24
s. is in our speed   EMER 307:3
strike against public s.   COOL 242:4
sagacity resource-and-s.   KIPL 456:21
sagas frosty s.   CRAN 249:23
sage ne surprend point le s.   LA F 463:15
Newton, childlike s.   COWP 248:2

s. has the sun and moon   CHUA 219:1
s., his wisdom departs   TALM 772:13
sages all the s. can   WORD 850:12
into s. and cranks   QUIN 639:12
said all is done and s.   VAUX 808:6
as if I had s. it myself   SWIF 766:12
Everything has been s.   LA B 462:19
fool hath s. in his heart   BOOK 134:10
He himself s.   CICE 223:10
if you want anything s.   THAT 786:26
know who s. this   THOM 788:4
Least s., soonest mended   PROV 625:1
nobody had s. it before   TWAI 803:18
not been s. before   TERE 785:5
not know what they have s.   CHUR 220:18
s. on both sides   ADDI 4:27
s. our remarks before us   DONA 279:1
what the soldier s.   DICK 272:6
sail comes i' faith full s.   CONG 239:11
in a sieve I'll thither s.   SHAK 703:5
s. on, O Ship of State   LONG 490:2
sea-mark of my utmost s.   SHAK 714:26
To s. is necessary   POMP 599:17
sailed hadna s. a league   BALL 51:19
I have s. the seas   YEAT 855:10
s. away for a year and a day   LEAR 477:16
Saturday s. from Bremen   HOPK 397:13
you never s. with me   JACK 415:1
sailing failing occurred in the s.   CARR 196:9
S. over a cardboard sea   HARB 371:2
s. to the strand   BALL 53:6
to which port one is s.   SENE 676:27
sailor Home is the s.   STEV 760:20
lass that loves a s.   DIBD 267:8
No man will be a s.   JOHN 427:23
s.-boys were all up aloft   SONG 748:2
Soldier, S.   NURS 570:8
sailors children, s., and drunken men   PROV 622:18
s. but men   SHAK 708:28
s. who must rebuild   NEUR 559:13
tell thee, s., when away   GAY 342:11
sails Purple the s.   SHAK 679:3
S. ripped, seams op'ning   COWP 247:6
still the s. made on   COLE 233:6
saint able to corrupt a s.   SHAK 689:23
As with a s.   SHAK 707:20
became a S.   NEWM 560:19
call me a s.   CAMA 186:13
England and S. George   SHAK 693:5
greater the s.   PROV 621:16
little s.   HERR 386:11
make of me a s.   CONG 239:21
my late espousèd s.   MILT 535:9
neither s. nor sophist-led   ARNO 27:6
No one, except a s.   PÉGU 591:7
Poet and S.   COWL 245:28
reel out a s.   CHUR 220:1
s. in crape   POPE 603:18
S. Martin's summer   SHAK 694:7
s., n. A dead sinner   BIER 116:9
s. run mad   POPE 605:19
s. took pity on   COLE 232:25
seem a s.   SHAK 716:27
Sloane turned secular s.   BURC 165:13
to catch a s.   SHAK 708:4
Young s., old devil   PROV 636:7
sainted thing enskyed and s.   SHAK 707:20
saints Christ and His s.   ANON 22:11
Communion of S.   BOOK 128:10
death of his s.   BOOK 142:8
fearful s. fresh courage take   COWP 246:24
follow thy blessed S.   BOOK 131:2
his lot is among the s.   BIBL 92:26
least of all s.   BIBL 109:6
Let the s. be joyful   BOOK 144:8
prayers of s.   BIBL 113:12
s. have dwelt secure   WATT 823:20
s. immortal reign   WATT 823:17
S. should be judged guilty   ORWE 578:5
We are not s.   BECK 61:21
saisons Ô s.   RIMB 649:11
sake Art for art's s.   CONS 241:10

Art for art's s.   DIET 274:7
Christ's particular love's s.   BROW 161:8
for his country's s.   FITZ 322:23
loseth his life for my s.   BIBL 96:21
That for my s.   CROS 252:18
Saki like her, O S.   FITZ 323:17
salad chicken s.   JOHN 423:6
Our Garrick's a s.   GOLD 355:4
s. days   SHAK 679:1
s. from the brook   COWP 248:16
salary remembered that he had a s.   GIBB 345:14
s. of the chief executive   GALB 338:4
sales each equation would halve the s.   HAWK 375:12
salesman Death of a s.   MILL 527:3
s. is got to dream   MILL 527:6
salley by the s. gardens   YEAT 853:19
sally make a sudden s.   TENN 775:18
none like pretty S.   CARE 191:8
salmon s. sing in the street   AUDE 34:19
smoked s. and tinned   WILS 840:11
saloon in the last chance s.   MELL 521:8
salt adverbs the s.   JAME 418:12
became a pillar of s.   BIBL 76:20
grain of s.   PLIN 598:6
Help you to s.   PROV 622:20
how s. is the taste   DANT 256:12
s. of the earth   BIBL 94:21
s. rubbed into their wounds   WEST 830:12
s. tides seawards flow   ARNO 27:11
seasoned with s.   BIBL 110:14
unplumbed, s., estranging sea   ARNO 29:4
verge of the s. flood   SHAK 719:13
Salteena S. was an elderly man   ASHF 31:11
saltness sugar, and s.   GOLD 355:4
salus S. extra ecclesiam   AUGU 37:9
S. populi   CICE 223:9
S. populi suprema lex   SELD 676:9
salutant Ave Caesar, morituri te s.   ANON 21:13
salutations s. in the market   BIBL 99:26
salute If it moves, s. it   MILI 526:10
S. one another   BIBL 107:1
s. thee, Mantovano   TENN 784:11
S. the happy morn   BYRO 177:17
those about to die s. you   ANON 21:13
salutes see if anyone s. it   SAYI 670:3
salva S. me   MISS 539:17
salvaged ships have been s.   HALS 369:18
salvation bottle of s.   RABE 641:5
cannot be s.   CYPR 254:16
generally necessary to s.   BOOK 132:19
hope of s.   BIBL 110:17
my light, and my s.   BOOK 135:13
necessary to s.   BOOK 144:14
none of us Should see s.   SHAK 709:26
no s. outside the church   AUGU 37:9
Now is our s. nearer   BIBL 106:32
now is the day of s.   BIBL 108:16
publisheth s.   BIBL 89:28
s. of Europe   PITT 596:11
seeks her own s.   SHAK 688:21
shew him my s.   BOOK 140:5
strength of our s.   BOOK 140:9
Visit us with thy s.   WESL 829:8
Work out your own s.   BIBL 110:1
Wot prawce s. nah   SHAW 725:25
salve S., regina   PRAY 611:6
Sam nephew of my Uncle S.'s   COHA 230:8
Play it again, S.   FILM 319:13
Play it again, S.   MISQ 533:13
S., pick up tha' musket   HOLL 392:20
Samaritan remember the Good S.   THAT 787:2
Samarkand Golden Road to S.   FLEC 326:3
silken S.   KEAT 443:2
Samarra appointment with him in S.   MAUG 518:21
same all say the s.   MELB 521:2
but thou art the s.   BOOK 140:19
Ever the s.   MOTT 552:17
more they are the s.   KARR 441:17
much the s.   ANON 15:2

same (*cont.*):
s. yesterday, and to day — BIBL 111:15
would be all the s. — DICK 270:19
you are the s. — MART 515:3
samite Clothed in white s. — TENN 777:15
Sammy What makes S. run — SCHU 671:18
Samnites like S. — HORA 399:22
Samson binding S. with withes — HAMP 370:13
S. hath quit himself — MILT 535:2
Samuel Lord called S. — BIBL 80:4
sancta s. simplicitas — JERO 421:5
sanctified s. by the wife — BIBL 107:14
sanctify S. the Lord of hosts — BIBL 88:16
sanctions Baldwin denouncing s. — BEAV 60:11
sanctuary classes which need s. — BALD 50:14
Cunning is the dark s. — CHES 214:21
So much s.-breaking — SKEL 739:8
sanctus S., sanctus, sanctus — MISS 539:6
sand and a grain of s. — WHIT 833:12
die upon the s. — ARNO 28:15
house upon the s. — BIBL 95:25
Little grains of s. — CARN 193:11
on the edge of the s. — LEAR 477:18
quantities of s. — CARR 195:6
s. against the wind — BLAK 121:16
s. in the porridge — COWA 244:17
s.-strewn caverns — ARNO 27:12
world in a grain of s. — BLAK 119:5
sandal s. shoon — SHAK 688:5
sandals with s. grey — MILT 530:12
sandbank no s., thrown up — DAVI 259:10
sands Across the s. of Dee — KING 452:19
Come unto these yellow s. — SHAK 718:26
Footprints on the s. — LONG 490:21
lone and level s. — SHEL 730:18
riddle of the s. — CHIL 217:21
s., ignoble things — BEAU 60:6
s. upon the Red sea shore — BLAK 121:17
sandwich ask for a watercress s. — WILD 837:5
cheaper than a prawn s. — RATN 642:13
taste again that raw-onion s. — BARN 56:11
sane if he was s. he had to fly — HELL 380:8
remain s. — HALD 368:3
San Francisco left my heart in S. — CROS 252:14
sang morning stars s. — BIBL 83:22
Perhaps it may turn out a s. — BURN 170:27
s. a king out of three kingdoms — WHAR 831:6
s. his didn't he — CUMM 253:5
s. in my chains — THOM 789:8
s. within the bloody wood — ELIO 303:6
sanglots Les s. longs — VERL 808:6
Sangreal story of the S. — MALO 508:21
sanitary glorified s. engineer — STRA 762:2
sanitas S. sanitatum — MÉNA 521:12
sanitatum Sanitas s. — MÉNA 521:12
sanity ain't no S. Claus — FILM 319:22
sank s. my boat — KENN 449:7
Sighted sub, s. same — MASO 517:17
sano Mens sana in corpore s. — JUVE 440:11
sans sans singer, and—s. End — FITZ 323:5
S. teeth, sans eyes — SHAK 681:13
sansculotte bon S. Jésus — DESM 265:14
Santa Claus death or S. — BERN 71:5
there is a S. — NEWS 562:25
saoshyants truly shall be 's.' — ZORO 859:21
sap dried the s. of my veins — YEAT 854:8
world's whole s. is sunk — DONN 281:7
sapere s. aude — HORA 399:5
sapient s. head — ARNO 29:5
s. sutlers — ELIO 302:22
sapienti Dictum s. — PLAU 597:21
sapless s. foliage of the ocean — SHEL 730:10
saplings wind it plies the s. — HOUS 404:13
sapphire purer s. melts — TENN 781:22
sapphires ivory overlaid with s. — BIBL 87:16
Sappho Where burning S. loved — BYRO 181:4
Sarah ceased to be with S. — BIBL 76:18
sardine jasper and a s. stone — BIBL 113:7
sardines s. will be thrown — CANT 189:15
Sarum full upon S. plain — SHAK 720:8
sash s. my father wore — POLI 601:7
sashes one of his nice new s. — GRAH 358:8

Saskatchewan on the banks of the S. — LAUR 470:10
sassy I'm sickly but s. — HARR 374:4
sat everyone has s. except a man — CUMM 253:9
I s. down and wept — BORR 146:3
S. and knotted — SEDL 675:11
s. down under a juniper tree — BIBL 81:26
s. too long here — CROM 252:2
s. upon a promontory — SHAK 711:1
we s. down and wept — BOOK 143:12
Satan Auld Hornie, S. — BURN 170:3
beat down S. — BOOK 129:11
beheld S. — BIBL 100:20
casting out S. by Satan — SORL 748:13
Get thee behind me, S. — BIBL 97:17
high capital Of S. — MILT 531:28
Lord said unto S. — BIBL 82:25
S. cast out Satan — BIBL 99:16
S. exalted sat — MILT 531:29
S. finds some mischief still — WATT 823:7
S. met his ancient friend — BYRO 183:20
S., so call him now — MILT 533:19
S. stood Unterrified — MILT 532:12
S., thou art but a dunce — BLAK 120:5
Satanic dark S. mills — BLAK 121:15
satellite With s. TV — O'DO 571:13
satiable full of s. curtiosity — KIPL 456:16
satiety occasion of s. — BACO 43:26
satin ease a heart like a s. gown — PARK 586:2
mad in white s. — SHER 733:10
satire hard not to write s. — JUVE 439:7
let s. be my song — BYRO 182:8
S., being levelled at all — SWIF 766:15
s. indeed is entirely our own — QUIN 639:13
S. is a sort of glass — SWIF 765:5
S. is what closes Saturday — KAUF 441:18
S. or sense — POPE 602:31
s. out of time — CHUR 220:3
satiric one s. touch — SWIF 767:18
satirical sign of a s. wit — AUBR 33:21
satirist s. may laugh — GIBB 345:11
second English S. — HALL 369:11
satisfaction can't get no s. — JAGG 415:15
give you s. — GAY 341:18
murder, for my own s. — DOST 283:7
satisfied can't be s. — HUGH 407:2
fool s. — MILL 525:17
Never s. with having — WROT 851:18
well paid that is well s. — SHAK 709:33
satisfies where most she s. — SHAK 679:7
satisfieth that which s. not — BIBL 90:6
satisfy poorly s. our eyes — WOTT 851:4
will I s. him — BOOK 140:5
satisfying s. a voracious appetite — FIEL 318:9
satura S. quidem tota nostra est — QUIN 639:13
saturam s. non scribere — JUVE 439:7
Saturday closes S. night — KAUF 441:18
Glasgow Empire on a S. night — DODD 278:19
S.'s child — NURS 568:10
what he did on S. — YBAR 853:4
Saturn grey-haired S. — KEAT 443:9
Revolution, like S. — VERG 808:14
while S. whirls — TENN 782:20
Saturnia redeunt S. regna — VIRG 814:2
Saturnus S., with his frosty face — SACK 662:9
satyr Hyperion to a s. — SHAK 684:3
satyrs men, like s. — MARL 513:8
sauce Hunger is the best s. — PROV 622:36
only one s. — CARA 190:2
s. for the goose — PROV 634:11
Saul Is S. also among the prophets — BIBL 80:10
name was S. — BIBL 104:32
S. and Jonathan — BIBL 80:28
S. hath slain his thousands — BIBL 80:23
S. was consenting — BIBL 104:33
S., why persecutest thou me — BIBL 105:2
weep over S. — BIBL 80:28
sausage pig in a s. — TROL 800:16
s. machine — CHRI 218:16
savage days of the Noble S. — BIKO 116:11
dealing with the s. English — WILL 838:12
laws unto a s. race — TENN 784:13

mad and s. master — SOPH 746:21
noble s. ran — DRYD 287:30
not allow it to be s. — OVID 580:5
now the s. race — CHUR 219:20
s. wields his club — HUXL 411:15
sooth a s. breast — CONG 238:29
take some s. woman — TENN 781:2
savaged s. by a dead sheep — HEAL 377:11
savages love of s. — LERM 481:9
save destroy the town to s. it — ANON 17:2
exist in order to s. us — DE V 266:7
God's king Solomon — BIBL 81:9
God s. the king — SONG 747:7
helped s. the world — KEYN 450:19
himself he cannot s. — BIBL 99:12
rushed through life trying to s. — ROGE 652:21
s. five sous on unessential things — COLB 230:22
s. his soul — BIBL 91:14
s. me — MISS 539:17
Save me, oh, s. me — CANN 189:7
s. one's own — BROW 160:1
s. the Governor-General — WHIT 833:1
s. the people — ELLI 305:18
s. the Union — LINC 485:5
s. those that have no imagination — SHAW 727:19
s. time — BACO 44:7
S. us from our friends — PROV 630:20
To s. your world — AUDE 34:25
saved be s. in this World — HALI 369:9
could have s. sixpence — BECK 61:2
He s. others — BIBL 99:12
only s. the world — CHES 216:1
penny s. — PROV 629:20
s. alive a whole world — TALM 771:21
we are not s. — BIBL 90:27
What must I do to be s. — BIBL 105:13
Whosoever will be s. — BOOK 128:21
youthful hose well s. — SHAK 681:12
saving capable of s. us — RICH 647:10
s. of life must supersede — TALM 772:12
thy s. health — BOOK 138:8
saviour because I am the S. — JAIN 416:20
our S. dear — BASS 58:6
S.'s birth is celebrated — SHAK 683:18
s. spring to life — BIBL 115:8
savoir belle chose que de s. — MOLI 541:13
savory s., marjoram — SHAK 722:4
savour keep Seeming and s. — SHAK 722:1
salt have lost his s. — BIBL 94:21
saw do not s. the air — SHAK 686:21
He s., he sighed — GAY 341:23
I came, I s., I conquered — CAES 185:7
I came, I s., and overcame — SHAK 692:13
I s. and loved — GIBB 345:16
Saxon ancient S. phrase — LONG 490:11
say all s. the same — MELB 521:2
anything good to s. — LONG 491:16
could s. if I chose — CARR 194:15
Do as I s. — PROV 617:46
Do as I s. — SELD 676:12
don't s. nothin' — HAMM 370:6
find anything to s. — FLAU 325:6
Have something to s. — ARNO 30:11
I s., before the morning — BOOK 143:7
Lat thame s. — MOTT 552:21
many things to s. unto you — BIBL 103:36
more to s. when I am dead — ROBI 650:13
no more to s. — SHAK 720:2
nothing to s. — CAGE 185:9
nothing to s. — COLT 236:8
not much to s. — COMP 237:4
not s. what one thinks — EURI 312:23
S. I'm weary, say I'm sad — HUNT 409:18
S. it ain't so — ANON 18:19
S. it with flowers — ADVE 8:12
s. little and do much — SHAM 724:6
s. nowt — PROV 622:17
s. only the word — MISS 539:10
s. something — GOOD 356:11
s. something about me — COHA 230:9
s. the perfectly correct thing — SHAW 725:11

s. what they please FRED 333:8
s. what you mean CARR 194:9
s. what you think TACI 770:10
see what I s. WALL 818:4
shall not s. much MATH 518:9
someone else has got to s. GASK 340:19
some s. that we wan MCLE 503:11
something to s. WHAT 831:7
what circumstances we s. it HAVE 375:6
whatever you s. HEAN 378:6
wink wink, s. no more MONT 546:6
saying For loving, and for s. so DONN 281:15
not worth s. BEAU 59:15
were s. yesterday LUIS 496:4
sayings s. are like women's letters
HAZL 376:9
says not what he s. SMIT 742:17
What everybody s. PROV 634:3
What Manchester s. today PROV 634:7
Who s. A must say B PROV 635:4
scabbard threw away the s. CLAR 224:15
throw the s. away PROV 635:5
scabs Make yourselves s. SHAK 682:13
scaffold forever on the s. LOWE 494:4
s. and the doom AYTO 41:13
to a s. from a throne FANS 314:10
scale best s. for an experiment FISH 321:17
sufficiently large s. SPEN 750:11
with her lifted s. POPE 601:20
scales someone is practising s. MACN 504:21
scallop s.-shell of quiet RALE 641:5
scaly s. horror of his folded tail MILT 530:24
scan gently s. your brother man BURN 170:5
scandal In s., as in robbery CHES 214:18
Love and s. FIEL 318:4
no s. like rags FARQ 315:9
s. by a woman of easy virtue HAIL 367:13
s. that constitutes offence MOLI 542:12
tea and s. CONG 238:14
scandalous s. and poor ROCH 651:14
scapegoat Let him go for a s. BIBL 78:12
scar s. on the conscience BLAI 118:21
wears their going like a s. DUNN 292:13
scarce Good men are s. PROV 621:11
scarceness runagates continue in s.
BOOK 138:11
scare s. myself with my own desert
FROS 335:13
those footprints s. me HORA 399:2
scarecrow make a s. of the law SHAK 707:22
scarecrows mechanized s. KAVA 442:5
s. of fools HUXL 412:3
scared always been s. of *you* PLAT 596:20
scarf S. up the tender eye SHAK 706:1
scarlet apes, though clothed in s. JONS 435:9
clad in silk or s. PROV 614:25
Cowards in s. GRAN 359:11
His sins were s. BELL 65:21
line of s. thread BIBL 79:5
lips like a thread of s. BIBL 87:10
raise the s. standard CONN 239:26
s. letter HAWT 375:17
s. soldiers AUDE 35:20
sins be as s. BIBL 88:1
wear his s. coat WILD 836:27
scars He jests at s. SHAK 717:19
marks and s. I carry BUNY 165:9
show his s. SHAK 693:23
scattered enemies be s. BOOK 138:10
s. the proud BIBL 99:32
s. verses PETR 593:15
scatterest thou s. them BOOK 139:22
scelerisque s. purus HORA 400:17
scene life's last s. JOHN 426:20
lofty s. be acted o'er SHAK 697:12
Speaks a new s. QUAR 638:19
scenery among savage s. HOFF 392:4
end of all natural s. RUSK 659:15
God paints the s. HART 374:13
S. is fine KEAT 446:9

talk to me about s. BECK 61:19
scenes behind your s. JOHN 427:11
s. where man hath never CLAR 224:12
scent s. of the roses MOOR 547:14
s. survives their close THOM 791:5
s. the fair annoys COWP 246:9
s. the morning air SHAK 685:4
sweetest flower for s. SHEL 731:15
sceptered s. isle SHAK 715:13
sceptic s. could inquire for BUTL 176:1
too much of a s. HUXL 412:5
scepticism lead to s. BERK 69:12
s. kept her SART 667:9
s. of the intellect NEWM 560:15
sceptre His the s. DIX 278:13
s. and the ball SHAK 693:19
sceptred avails the s. race LAND 466:4
sceptreless S., free SHEL 731:8
schemes best-laid s. PROV 615.16
s. of political improvement JOHN 429:6
s. o' mice an' men BURN 172:22
scherzando S.! ma non troppo GILB 347:2
schizoid S. self-alienation FROM 335:4
schizophrenic you are a s. SZAS 769:17
Schleswig-Holstein S. question PALM 585:3
scholar before a great s. LOCK 489:2
gentleman and s. BURN 173:3
He was a s. SHAK 695:21
mere s. DEFO 261:2
s. all Earth's volumes carry CHAP 208:20
s. in a rage KIPL 457:3
s.'s life assail JOHN 426:16
Soldier, s., horseman YEAT 854:14
scholars philosophers and s. PASC 587:17
S. and gentlemen WORD 849:14
S. dispute HORA 398:4
school At s. I never minded MORT 551:1
been to a good s. SAKI 663:17
destroy every grammar s. CROS 252:11
erecting a grammar s. SHAK 694:23
every s. knows it TAYL 775:1
Experience keeps dear s. PROV 619:31
goeth to s. BACO 45:28
learned about in s. JARR 418:28
s. of Manchester DISR 278:8
s. of mankind BURK 168:16
s. of Stratford atte Bowe CHAU 210:11
sent to s. HUGH 407:12
tell tales out of s. PROV 627:29
Unwillingly to s. SHAK 681:10
vixen when she went to s. SHAK 711:16
schoolboy Every s. knows MACA 498:15
I see a s. YEAT 854:7
method that of a s. BLUN 124:9
Not the s. heat TENN 779:25
s.'s tip THAC 786:7
s. with a satchel BLAI 118:14
tell what every s. knows SWIF 767:1
whining s., with his satchel SHAK 681:10
schoolboys duly to delight s. JUVE 440:9
s. from their books SHAK 717:26
s. playing in the stream PEEL 591:2
schoolchildren What all s. learn AUDE 36:2
schoolgirl Pert as a s. GILB 347:23
priggish s. GRIG 364:10
s. complexion ADVE 7:41
schoolman no s.'s subtle art POPE 603:1
schoolmaster becoming a s. WAUG 824:5
s. is abroad BROU 154:12
so gentle a s. GREY 364:4
schoolmasters s. puzzle their brain
GOLD 355:22
schoolrooms s. for 'the boy' COOK 241:17
schools banished from the s. CHUD 219:8
hundred s. of thought contend MAO 511:14
in our great s. JOHN 430:11
in the maze of s. POPE 603:29
lumber of the s. SWIF 767:5
Oh wrangling s. DONN 280:24
some children, in some s. BLUN 124:7

schooner It was the s. Hesperus LONG 491:10
sciatica S.: he cured it AUBR 33:22
science aim of s. BREC 150:5
All s. physics or stamp collecting
RUTH 661:17
applications of s. PAST 588:7
beams of s. fall POPE 601:24
beginning of s. LEIB 479:13
countenance of all s. WORD 851:1
disease, not a s. MAIM 507:19
Dismal S. CARL 192:18
do s. in hell VAUG 808:4
essence of s. BRON 152:6
experimentation an active s. BERN 71:1
Fair S. frowned not GRAY 361:8
fear s. POLA 599:12
Geometry (which is the only s. HOBB 390:9
grand aim of all s. EINS 298:7
hand of s. AKEN 9:5
How s. dwindles YOUN 857:7
In s., read BULW 164:6
In s. the credit goes DARW 257:18
In s., we must be CURI 254:3
instrument of s. JOHN 424:4
investigated by s. ELIO 300:2
it is not s. KELV 448:4
opinion and s. HUME 409:3
plundered this new s. MCEW 501:14
redefined the task of s. HAWK 375:13
s. and everyday life FRAN 332:22
s. and nature will have charms FARA 314:15
S. appears WORD 849:10
S. finds ANON 18:21
S. is an edged tool EDDI 295:7
s. is at a loss CHOM 218:10
S. is built up of facts POIN 599:11
S. is for the cultivation SADI 663:1
S. is his forte SMIT 744:9
S. is nothing but trained HUXL 411:15
S. is organized knowledge SPEN 750:4
S. is part of culture GOUL 357:12
s. is satisfying the curiosity ARTS 30:20
s. is strong SZAS 769:18
s. is the right interpretation WHEW 831:15
S. lost its virgin purity GRAV 360:15
S. moves, but slowly TENN 780:21
S. must begin with myths POPP 607:5
S. offers best answers DAWK 259:17
s. of life BERN 71:2
s. of the tender passion PUSH 638:2
s. reassures BRAQ 149:17
S. the aggregate of all VALÉ 806:8
s. which pretends to lay open SMIT 741:2
s. will appear incomplete ARNO 29:22
S. without religion is lame EINS 297:12
separation of state and s. FEYE 317:5
tragedy of S. HUXL 411:14
triumph of modern s. WAUG 824:20
true s. and study CHAR 209:17
sciences advancing the s. LOCK 488:6
bent on these s. ASCH 31:3
Books must follow s. BACO 46:19
mother of s. BACO 46:16
Reason and the s. LEIB 479:14
Small s. BAGE 49:6
scientific as if they were s. terms ARNO 30:2
Death was but a s. fact WILD 836:30
empirical s. system POPP 606:28
importance of s. work HILB 388:3
Jesus the most s. EDDY 295:8
know the s. names GILB 348:28
new s. truth PLAN 596:11
on the most s. principles PEAC 589:14
plunges into s. questions HUXL 412:4
s. faith's absurd BROW 159:7
s. method doing one's damnedest
BRID 151:3
s. opinion ARNO 29:20
s. power has outrun KING 452:7
S. truth MAXW 519:5
scientis Signum s. AUCT 34:15
scientist elderly s. states CLAR 225:2
exercise for a research s. LORE 492:4

scientist (*cont.*):
not try to become a s. — EINS 298:8
s.'s laws — QUIN 639:11
s. thinks of a method — PERU 593:11
s. were to cut his ear — MEDA 520:4
scientists company of s. — AUDE 36:16
s. are probably right — ASIM 31:18
than most young s. — MEDA 520:6
scire s. *nefas* — HORA 400:13
scissor long, red-legged s.-man — HOFF 391:17
scoff fools, who came to s. — GOLD 354:14
scoffer product of a s.'s pen — WORD 846:15
scoffing S. his state — SHAK 715:24
scold what a s. you are — BULL 163:17
scones Over buttered s. — ELIO 301:6
tea-cakes and s. — BETJ 72:8
scope that man's s. — SHAK 722:29
score no matter what the s. — HORN 403:17
time required to s. 500 — COMP 236:16
scorer One Great S. — RICE 646:19
scores He shoots! He s. — CATC 200:28
scorn Disdain and s. — SHAK 712:21
Laugh no man to s. — BIBL 93:7
s. is alluring — CONG 239:14
S. not the Sonnet — WORD 849:26
s. their bodies — BAST 58:8
s. which mocked the smart — ARNO 28:21
sound Of public s. — MILT 534:6
surmounted by s. — CAMU 188:13
think foul s. — ELIZ 304:7
very s. of men — BOOK 134:27
what a deal of s. — SHAK 721:2
scorned fury, like a woman s. — CONG 238:30
was s. and died — GAY 341:23
scornful only a s. tickling — SIDN 736:19
seat of the s. — BOOK 133:19
scorpions chastise you with s. — BIBL 81:16
Scot Had Cain been S. — CLEV 227:1
Scotch as a S. banker — DAVI 258:15
inferior to the S. — NORT 565:9
into a S. understanding — SMIT 743:17
Mary, ma S. Bluebell — LAUD 470:6
scotched s. the snake — SHAK 705:20
Scotchman S. ever sees — JOHN 428:8
Scotia chief of S.'s food — BURN 170:21
old S.'s grandeur — BURN 170:23
Scotland fair S.'s spear — SCOT 674:1
fair S.'s strand — BURN 171:13
flower of S. — WILL 839:16
I do indeed come from S. — JOHN 428:1
inferior sort of S. — SMIT 743:12
in S. afore ye — SONG 748:3
in S. supports the people — JOHN 424:12
In S. we live between — CRAW 250:21
of S. — BYRO 179:30
our infinite S. — MACD 500:19
renewed in S. — DEWA 266:10
S. a raucle tongue — BURN 170:10
S. better than truth — JOHN 424:21
S., land of the omnipotent No — BOLD 126:4
S.'s oil — POLI 600:25
Stands S. — SHAK 706:22
white rose of S. — MACD 501:4
Scots S. deserve no pity — FLET 326:22
S. lords at his feet — BALL 53:7
S., wha hae wi' Wallace bled — BURN 172:5
six or seven dozen of S. — SHAK 690:5
Scotsman S. on the make — BARR 57:8
S. with a grievance — WODE 842:16
Scott half so flat as Walter S. — ANON 18:7
wrong part wrote S. — WATE 822:15
Scottish auld S. sang — BURN 170:18
S. Parliament — EWIN 313:10
S. parliament — SALM 665:8
shall be a S. parliament — ANON 19:10
shall be a S. parliament — DEWA 266:9
will of the S. people — SMIT 742:10
Scotty Beam me up, S. — MISQ 537:4
scoundrel over forty is a s. — SHAW 726:31

plea of the s. — BLAK 120:12
refuge of a s. — JOHN 430:6
to such a s. — SWIF 766:4
scoured s. to nothing — SHAK 691:28
scourge s. of small cords — BIBL 102:29
scout s. 'em, and flout 'em — SHAK 718:34
scrabble s. with all the vowels — ELLI 305:12
scrannel on their s. pipes — MILT 530:6
scrap s. of paper — BETH 72:1
scrape s. himself withal — BIBL 82:29
s. your strings darker — CELA 205:2
scraps stolen the s. — SHAK 702:21
scratch quick sharp s. — BROW 160:7
S. a Russian — PROV 630:21
S. the Christian — ZANG 858:2
s. the nurse — SHAK 721:20
scratching s. of a pen — LOVE 493:12
s. of my finger — HUME 409:10
s. of pimples on the body — WOOL 845:11
scream as a last resort, s. — SUGE 763:9
hilarity like a s. — GREE 362:15
no one can hear you s. — TAGL 771:5
s. in a low voice — BYRO 184:2
screw s. your courage — SHAK 704:12
to seek the right s. — HOLU 393:13
turn of the s. — JAME 418:7
scribblative babblative and s. — SOUT 749:10
scribble Always s., scribble, scribble — GLOU 351:15
scrawl, and s. — POPE 605:23
You who s. — WYCH 852:14
scribbled by a s. name — THOM 789:12
s. lines like fallen hopes — HOPE 396:7
scribbling mob of s. women — HAWT 376:1
s. fry — YOUN 857:5
scribendi S. *cacoethes* — JUVE 440:1
scribere *rapida* s. — CATU 203:3
saturam non s. — JUVE 439:7
scribes Beware of the s. — BIBL 99:26
s. and Pharisees — BIBL 94:25
s. and Pharisees, hypocrites — BIBL 98:9
scribimus S. *indocti doctique poemata* — HORA 399:19
scrip My s. of joy — RALE 641:5
with s. and scrippage — SHAK 681:18
scriptores *Cedite Romani* s. — PROP 612:23
scripture better it in S. — JAME 417:8
devil can cite S. — SHAK 709:1
devil can quote S. — PROV 617:31
Holy S. and nature — GALI 338:12
Holy S. containeth — BOOK 144:14
know more of the s. — TYND 804:6
S. moveth us — BOOK 127:13
s. of peoples — JERO 421:9
scriptures all holy S. — BOOK 130:1
Let us look at the s. — SELD 676:2
S. in the hands — PUGI 636:24
Search the s. — BIBL 102:38
scroll charged with punishments the s. — HENL 381:15
scrotumtightening s. sea — JOYC 437:14
scroungy all s. and bearded — CORS 243:18
scruple s. Of thinking too precisely — SHAK 688:3
scrupulosity oriental s. — JOHN 425:10
scrutamini s. *scripturas* — SELD 676:2
scullion Away, you s. — SHAK 691:30
sculptor great s. or painter — RUSK 659:10
sculpture like that of s. — RUSS 660:26
S. in stone — MOOR 546:14
s. the true school of modesty — PEAC 589:13
sculptured s. dead — KEAT 442:16
scum Okie means you're s. — STEI 755:12
rich are the s. of the earth — CHES 216:21
s. of the earth — WELL 827:17
scuttling S. across the floors of silent seas — ELIO 302:16
Scylla S. and Charybdis — NEWM 560:13
scythe mower whets his s. — MILT 529:22

sighs like s. — WALC 817:5
scythes shaking s. at cannon — HEAN 378:3
Scythia another group to S. — VIRG 813:15
se s. *Iudice* — JUVE 440:13
sea all the s. were ink — LYLY 497:5
Alone on a wide wide s. — COLE 232:25
around the glassy s. — HEBE 378:17
as good fish in the s. — PROV 631:44
As is the ribbed s.-sand — COLE 232:24
as the waters cover the s. — BIBL 88:22
beneath a rougher s. — COWP 246:4
best thing is—the s. — JERR 421:16
black s.-brute bulling — MERW 523:5
boat on the rough s. — HORA 400:4
burst Into that silent s. — COLE 232:18
clamorous whispering s. — HOME 393:18
cloud out of the s. — BIBL 81:24
cold grey stones, O S. — TENN 775:16
complaining about the s. — POWE 610:3
Death like a narrow s. — WATT 823:18
deep, deep s. — CONR 240:18
deeper than the s. — BALL 52:19
dominion of the s. — COVE 244:14
Down to a sunless s. — COLE 232:3
eating the s. — ROBE 650:1
ebbing s. — FORD 329:3
find another s. — CAVA 203:19
flowing s. — CUNN 253:17
forbear To teach the s. — DONN 281:19
gaping wretches of the s. — HUNT 409:16
garden front the s. — SWIN 768:13
go to s. for pleasure — PROV 622:4
gurly grew the s. — BALL 51:19
having been at s. — JOHN 431:2
headlong into the s. — KEAT 446:15
He divided the s. — BOOK 139:9
home from s. — STEV 760:20
houses are all gone under the s. — ELIO 301:16
if we gang to s. — BALL 53:5
if Ye take away the s. — KIPL 454:19
in a s. of glory — SHAK 695:11
In a solitude of the s. — HARD 372:12
in earth and air, And in the s. — SMAR 740:16
in my chains like the s. — THOM 789:8
in our s. of confusion — GAMO 338:18
in perils in the s. — BIBL 108:22
in the abysmal s. — TENN 780:1
in the s. of life — ARNO 29:2
Into a s. of dew — FIEL 317:9
into the midst of the s. — BOOK 136:24
like bathing in the s. — LEIG 479:20
London, that great s. — SHEL 729:19
looks s.-ward — BROW 159:28
lover of men, the s. — SWIN 769:8
machrel of the s. — BALL 52:9
melts into the s. — TENN 781:22
near to heaven by s. — GILB 347:1
never go to s. — GILB 348:24
of a sudden came the s. — BROW 160:16
one is of the s. — WORD 850:14
one s. to the other — BOOK 138:23
one that goes To s. — DONN 279:8
Over the s. to Skye — STEV 760:14
over the summer s. — TENN 784:1
Pieces of land and s. — WALP 820:3
pinch the s. of its liberty — COTT 244:7
Poem of the S. — RIMB 649:6
Put out to s. — MACN 505:1
Ran purple to the s. — MILT 531:20
rude s. grew civil — SHAK 711:1
sailed the wintry s. — LONG 491:10
S., and hill, and wood — COLE 231:19
s.-blooms and the oozy woods — SHEL 730:10
s.-change in politics — CALL 185:19
s. curling Star-climbed — MERW 523:6
s. gave up the dead — BIBL 114:15
s. hates a coward — O'NE 573:13
s. is his — BOOK 140:10
s. is not full — BIBL 85:26
s. itself floweth in your veins — TRAH 797:11
s.-mark of my utmost sail — SHAK 714:26
S. of Faith — ARNO 27:3
s. of glass — BIBL 113:8

s. of glass BIBL 114:5
s. refuses no river PROV 630:22
s. saw that, and fled BOOK 142:2
S. shall give up her dead BOOK 144:12
s.! the sea! XENO 852:18
s. to shining sea BATE 58:10
s. was made his tomb BARN 56:16
see nothing but s. BACO 42:18
serpent-haunted s. FLEC 326:1
set in the silver s. SHAK 715:13
ship in the midst of the s. BIBL 85:21
sight of that immortal s. WORD 848:13
slowly towards the s. CHES 216:13
smiling surface of the s. PLUT 598:16
snotgreen s. JOYC 437:14
something of the s. SEDL 675:10
spouts out a s. MILT 533:22
spread like a green s. SHEL 729:25
stillness of the central s. TENN 779:28
strawberries grow in the s. NURS 568:8
suffer a s.-change SHAK 718:27
sweet Star of the S. FABE 313:17
there was no more s. BIBL 114:16
those in peril on the s. WHIT 832:22
thousand furlongs of s. SHAK 718:19
tossed them to the foaming s. LAWL 470:15
to the English that of the s. RICH 648:2
to the s. in ships BOOK 141:18
two if by s. LONG 491:5
unplumbed, salt, estranging s. ARNO 29:4
Upon the slimy s. COLE 232:20
uttermost parts of the s. BOOK 143:16
walking on the s. BIBL 97:8
water in the rough rude s. SHAK 715:19
waves of the s. AESC 6:9
waves of the s. BOOK 140:7
waves on the great s. LUCR 495:14
went to s. LEAR 477:15
When I put out to s. TENN 776:16
Who hath desired the S. KIPL 455:15
who rush across the s. HORA 399:10
why the s. is boiling hot CARR 195:7
wider than all the s. NERU 559:3
willing foe and s. room TOAS 796:7
Winds somewhere safe to s. SWIN 768:17
wine-dark s. HOME 394:15
wrinkled s. beneath him TENN 776:20
your own s.-maws PROV 624:37
seagreen s. Incorruptible CARL 192:8
seagull I'm a s. CHEK 214:2
seagulls When s. follow a trawler
CANT 189:15
seal opened the seventh s. BIBL 113:22
S. her sweet eyes ROSS 655:13
s. is not yet fixed BYRO 184:3
s. of the Holy One TALM 772:11
S. of the Prophets KORA 460:20
s. upon thine heart BIBL 87:22
sealed My lips are s. BALD 50:17
My lips are s. MISQ 538:10
sealing wax ships—and s. CARR 195:7
seals loose the s. BIBL 113:11
receives the s. of office ROSE 655:3
seam sew a fine s. NURS 566:14
seaman s. tells stories of winds PROP 612:21
sear fall'n into the s. SHAK 707:8
search active s. for truth LESS 482:6
in s. of an author PIRA 595:18
S. the scriptures BIBL 102:38
travels the world in s. MOOR 546:13
searched thou hast s. me out BOOK 143:14
searching Canst thou by s. BIBL 83:4
seas dangers of the s. PARK 586:12
down to the s. again MASE 517:15
Draw not up s. DONN 281:19
foam Of perilous s. KEAT 445:1
hollow s., that roar MARV 515:8
multitudinous s. incarnadine SHAK 705:3
raging s. did roar SONG 748:2
Scuttling across the floors of silent s.
ELIO 302:16
s. colder than the Hebrides FLEC 325:18
s. do laugh WEBS 826:15

s. of life, like wine TRAH 798:2
s. roll over but the rocks remain
HERB 383:10
strange s. of thought WORD 849:11
such as pass on the s. BOOK 144:11
seashells She sells s. SULL 763:12
seashore boy on the s. NEWT 561:16
seasickness universal as s. SHAW 726:11
season by s. seasoned are SHAK 710:7
dry brain in a dry s. ELIO 302:5
In a summer s. LANG 466:14
in due s. BOOK 143:25
in s., out of season BIBL 110:30
man has every s. FOND 327:25
no s. knows, nor clime DONN 281:13
s. made for joys GAY 341:16
s. of all natures, sleep SHAK 706:10
s. of calm weather WORD 848:13
S. of mists KEAT 445:14
S. of mists OPEN 575:15
s. of snows and sins SWIN 768:1
there is a s. BIBL 85:32
time and s. AGES 8:28
word spoken in due s. BIBL 84:25
seasoned Like s. timber HERB 385:5
s. with salt BIBL 110:14
seasons four s. run their course CONF 238:11
lovers' s. run DONN 281:12
man for all s. BORR 146:13
man for all s. WHIT 834:7
O s., O castles RIMB 649:11
s. alter SHAK 710:32
s.' difference SHAK 680:25
s. shall be sweet COLE 231:22
s. such as these SHAK 700:22
seat Fasten your s.-belts FILM 319:6
into his s. SHAK 690:32
s. is the bosom of God HOOK 395:18
s. of Mars SHAK 715:13
s. of the scornful BOOK 133:19
seated looked wiser when he was s.
KEYN 450:12
S. one day at the organ PROC 612:17
seats fixed in our s. STEE 754:18
seawater salt s. passes TENN 778:29
seaworm s. crawls—grotesque HARD 372:13
seaworms Battening upon huge s.
TENN 780:2
second for my s. race VAUG 807:12
grow a s. tongue MONT 543:21
Habit is s. nature AUCT 34:4
many s.-rate ones BEEC 62:14
my s. best bed SHAK 724:5
Nor s. he GRAY 361:19
no s. acts FITZ 324:9
no s. knows MILT 534:32
no s. spring PHIL 594:14
not a s. on the day COOK 241:16
not your s. choice too LURI 496:6
s. at Rome CAES 185:4
s. best's a gay goodnight YEAT 854:9
s. childhood ARIS 25:4
s. childishness SHAK 681:13
s. mouse that gets the cheese SAYI 669:32
s. oldest profession REAG 643:10
S. thoughts are best PROV 630:23
things have s. birth WORD 849:15
truth 24 times per s. GODA 351:16
second-best anything but the s.-best
LESS 482:1
secrecy S. the human dress BLAK 122:22
secret alms may be in s. BIBL 95:1
bread eaten in s. BIBL 84:7
ceases to be a s. BEHN 63:19
concept of the official s. WEBE 825:8
discovered the s. of life CRIC 251:4
Et Vigny plus s. SAIN 663:7
girls that have no s. SPEN 750:22
gives charity in s. TALM 772:28
in s. sin CHUR 219:22
joys are s. BACO 45:4
knows the s. of God SIKH 737:9
know that's a s. CONG 238:23

laugh from the s. corner HORA 400:12
neurosis is a s. TYNA 804:5
no s. so close SURT 764:25
not one s. concealed KORA 461:12
photograph is a s. ARBU 24:4
s. and inviolate Rose YEAT 855:14
s. anniversaries LONG 490:12
s., black, and midnight hags SHAK 706:15
s. in the Oxford sense FRAN 333:2
s. love BIBL 85:13
s. magic of numbers BROW 156:26
s. ministry of frost COLE 231:23
s. of politics BISM 117:13
s. of the long-nosed Etruscans LAWR 475:1
s. of the Lord KEBL 447:11
s. parts of Fortune SHAK 685:21
S. sits in the middle FROS 336:1
s. sports betwixt us twain DIAN 267:3
s. things BIBL 78:29
S. thoughts and open countenance
ALBE 10:7
sin in s. MOLI 542:12
tender s. dwells BYRO 179:24
Three may keep a s. PROV 632:47
Vereker's s. JAME 417:18
secretary fate of the s. DORF 282:15
S. of Nature WALT 821:5
secretly entice thee s. BIBL 78:28
secrets no s. are hid BOOK 131:6
privacy and tawdry s. LEAC 476:11
s. are edged tools DRYD 289:16
s. of th' abyss GRAY 361:19
S. with girls CRAB 249:15
such things to be holy s. HIPP 389:14
throw their guilty s. PRIE 610:16
Trust not with s. LAVA 470:13
sect attached to that great s. SHEL 729:7
found them a s. MACA 498:20
into that ancient s. YEAT 855:21
loving his own s. COLE 233:17
paradise for a s. KEAT 443:5
sad-coloured s. HOOD 395:14
sectaries in a nation of s. DISR 277:4
sects diversity of s. SPEN 752:13
secular s. bird MILT 535:1
secure He is s. SHEL 728:23
past is s. WEBS 825:10
securities sooner trust to two s. CHES 215:11
security fear, otherwise styled s. MADA 505:8
make s. secure POPP 607:3
s. around the president MAIL 507:14
s. of Europe MITC 540:9
s. of free states DEMO 263:17
watchword is s. PITT 596:8
securus S. iudicat AUGU 37:8
sedentary s. humour MONT 543:17
sedge s. has withered KEAT 443:23
seditione de s. querentes JUVE 439:11
seditions way to prevent s. BACO 45:12
seducer strong s., opportunity DRYD 288:2
seduction delusive s. BURN 169:26
In s., the rapist DWOR 293:11
seductive some s. madness HORA 401:15
sedulous played the s. ape STEV 759:4
see All that we s. POE 599:3
And for to s. CHAU 212:17
by my form did s. me MAHĀ 506:15
complain we cannot s. BERK 69:13
eyes which s. BIBL 100:21
hold, but cannot s. WESL 829:2
I'll s. you again COWA 245:1
In all things Thee to s. HERB 384:3
into the wilderness to s. BIBL 96:24
I s. a voice SHAK 712:3
I s. dead people FILM 319:20
I s., not feel COLE 231:8
I shall never s. KILM 451:8
I was blind, now I s. BIBL 103:15
last s. your father YEAM 853:5
like my roses to s. you SHER 734:9
live longest, s. most PROV 632:36
make you s. CONR 240:20
more people s. than weigh CHES 215:13

Learned without s. CHUR 220:8
light of nature, s. ROCH 651:11
men of s. never tell SHAF 678:4
Money is like a sixth s. MAUG 518:20
motions of the s. SHAK 707:21
one grain of s. DRYD 288:3
pleasures of s. BHAG 74:13
Satire or s. POPE 602:31
s. for sense ALFR 11:13
s. is dim BEEC 62:15
servilely creeps after s. DRYD 289:27
Short gleams of s. CHUR 220:3
something more than good s. COLE 234:5
Take care of the s. CARR 194:14
talk s. to the American people STEV 758:13
to his own s. doth smell MONT 544:19
want of s. DILL 274:11
senseless kind of s. wit WILB 835:5
worse than s. things SHAK 695:28
senses by your s. five BLAK 121:11
horses are the s. UPAN 805:8
If Parson lost his s. HODG 391:10
knowledge denied from s. SA'A 662:6
not enslaved by the s. TANT 773:6
s. will never inform us SMIT 741:4
snatches away all the s. CATU 202:20
subtlety of the s. BACO 46:14
Unto our gentle s. SHAK 704:1
sensibilité equivalent to s. PALM 585:5
sensibility Dear s. STER 756:13
dissociation of s. ELIO 303:30
it is an immense s. JAME 418:1
pattern informed by s. READ 643:2
sensible All s. people are selfish EMER 306:18
S. men DISR 277:12
s. of his natural rights PRIE 611:13
This s. warm motion SHAK 708:10
sensitive s. being WORD 849:18
S. Plant SHEL 731:14
try to be s. MURA 554:11
sensual s. pleasure without vice JOHN 433:18
sensuality s. and strength FRIN 334:19
s., rebellion THOM 790:19
sent man s. from God BIBL 102:18
say I s. thee thither SHAK 695:4
s. before my time SHAK 716:20
sentence Give s. with me, O God
BOOK 136:15
isn't a word . . . it's a s. FILM 320:7
life s. goes on CONL 239:24
Makes half a s. COWP 246:8
No! No! S. first CARR 194:23
recording the s. VILL 810:9
s. is enough PLAU 597:21
s. is factually significant AYER 41:6
sentenced s. to death in my absence
BEHA 63:14
sentences Backward ran s. GIBB 346:4
half-finished s. EDGE 295:16
hard s. of old BOOK 139:7
sentiment corrupted by s. GREE 362:11
S. is what I am not FLEM 326:17
sentiments his words and his s. DEMO 263:15
my own s. BAGE 49:8
not have opinions, only s. LAUR 470:12
people of refined s. KELL 448:1
Them's my s. THAC 786:15
sentinel scarce worth the s. GOLD 355:31
S. of the grave TATE 773:11
sentinels s. to warn MARL 513:24
sentry quadrille in a s.-box JAME 417:17
stands a wingèd s. VAUG 807:11
separate able to s. us BIBL 106:23
can't s. peace MALC 508:11
s. and equal station JEFF 419:9
separated they cannot be s. SMIT 743:24
separately all hang s. FRAN 332:17
separateth s. very friends BIBL 84:28
separation impel them to the s. JEFF 419:9
prepare for a s. QUIN 639:9
prospect of an easy s. HUME 408:14
real s. of powers DENN 264:11
s., but fission and divorce SHIP 734:22

s. of state and science FEYE 317:5
that eternal s. STER 757:15
sept that damnable s. STAI 753:19
September days hath S. SAYI 670:16
S. blow soft PROV 630:30
When you reach S. ANDE 14:7
sepulchre first to the s. BIBL 104:10
living s. of life CLAR 224:13
No man knoweth of his s. BIBL 79:6
s. there by the sea POE 599:1
taken away from the s. BIBL 104:9
sepulchres s. BIBL 98:11
s. of mortality CREW 251:3
sepulcra Per s. regionum MISS 539:16
sequel natural s. AUST 39:12
sequestered one of those s. spots HARD 372:7
sera rosa S. moretur HORA 401:1
seraglio s. of eunuchs FOOT 328:1
seraphim bright s. in burning row
MILT 528:16
sworded s. MILT 530:20
seraphims Above it stood the s. BIBL 88:10
one of the s. BIBL 88:12
seraphin Cherubin, and S. BOOK 127:20
sere Now my s. fancy BYRO 181:12
serene from the s. Light HILD 388:5
s., That men call age BROO 153:9
serenity called the s. of age BLIS 123:9
serf another man's s. HOME 394:16
serfdom abolish s. ALEX 11:5
sergeant This fell s., death SHAK 689:11
serial obituary in s. form CRIS 251:9
serious joke's a s. thing CHUR 219:19
Murder is a s. business OPEN 574:26
s. and the smirk DICK 270:20
s.-minded activity MONT 544:5
War is too s. CLEM 226:10
seriously S., though CATC 201:25
sermon honest and painful s. PEPY 591:22
Perhaps, turn out a s. BURN 170:27
rejected the S. on the Mount BRAD 148:22
who is a s. flies HERB 383:21
sermons S. and soda-water BYRO 180:21
S. in stones SHAK 680:26
sero S. te amavi AUGU 37:5
serpent be the s. under't SHAK 703:22
biteth like a s. BIBL 85:1
infernal s. MILT 531:7
my s. of old Nile SHAK 678:25
Now the s. was more subtil BIBL 75:18
s. beguiled me BIBL 75:23
s., green in the mulberry bush TATE 773:11
s.-haunted sea FLEC 326:1
s. subtlest beast MILT 533:27
s. upon a rock BIBL 85:21
s., which is the Devil BIBL 114:13
sharper than a s.'s tooth DICK 271:23
sharper than a s.'s tooth SHAK 700:5
serpents wise as s. BIBL 96:16
servant as a humble s. MAND 509:14
become the s. of a man SHAW 725:8
born to be a s. TOCQ 795:7
carried his s. by night KORA 460:14
cracked lookingglass of a s. JOYC 437:15
Fire is a good s. PROV 620:7
form of a s. BIBL 109:24
good and faithful s. BIBL 98:21
Is thy s. a dog BIBL 82:10
judgement with thy s. BOOK 143:22
life of a s. of God NEWM 560:19
nor the s. above his lord BIBL 96:17
One s. worth a thousand gadgets
SCHU 672:5
sent down on Our s. KORA 459:10
s. depart in peace BIBL 100:6
S. of God, well done MILT 533:20
s. of the Living God SMAR 739:17
s. shall have small BARC 55:11
s. to the devil SISS 738:11
s. with this clause HERB 384:5
thou wast a s. BIBL 78:25
thy s. heareth BIBL 80:5
well enough for a s. CONG 238:27

Wife and S. CHUD 219:9
Your s.'s cut in half GRAH 358:7
servants Between them and s. BARC 55:11
equality in the s.' hall BARR 57:1
purgatory of s. PROV 618:42
s. of the public GOWE 357:14
s. of the sovereign BACO 44:21
s. will do that for us VILL 810:10
wife or your s. to read GRIF 364:8
Women and s. most difficult CONF 238:12
Ye s. of the Lord DODD 278:20
serve Fleet in which we s. BOOK 144:10
left me to s. alone BIBL 100:26
love to s. my country GIBR 346:5
not yet able to s. man CONF 238:2
s. and lose GOET 353:4
s. Him in this world CATE 199:7
s. in the wars BOOK 144:19
s. thee with a quiet mind BOOK 130:15
s. the Lord with gladness BOOK 140:17
s. two masters BIBL 95:6
s. two masters PROV 627:40
s. until my last breath GAND 339:4
s. your captives' need KIPL 456:7
than s. in heaven MILT 531:15
Thee only we s. KORA 459:8
They also s. MILT 535:8
will not s. if elected SHER 734:18
served first s. PROV 620:9
Had I but s. my God SHAK 695:16
s. her, perhaps mistakenly GLAD 351:8
s. to him course by course CHUR 221:3
well s. PROV 623:28
Worshipped and s. BIBL 105:37
Youth must be s. PROV 636:10
serveth as he that s. BIBL 101:34
service All s. ranks the same BROW 160:23
at the s. of the nation POMP 599:18
bounden duty and s. BOOK 132:3
devoted to your s. ELIZ 305:1
done the state some s. SHAK 714:30
Every kind of s. HALE 368:7
Hacked with constant s. SOUT 748:15
No s. RACI 640:8
Pressed into s. FROS 336:2
S. and love above all other DUNB 292:1
s. is perfect freedom BOOK 128:12
s. of my love SPRI 753:5
s.? The rent we pay CLAY 226:6
serviettes kiddies have crumpled the s.
BETJ 72:7
servile freed from s. bands WOTT 851:3
servilely s. creeps after sense DRYD 289:27
servility savage s. LOWE 494:9
serving cumbered about much s. BIBL 100:26
six honest s.-men KIPL 456:18
With s. still WYAT 852:3
servitude base laws of s. DRYD 287:30
Freedom and not s. BURK 166:25
servum O imitatores, s. pecus HORA 399:18
sesame Open S. ARAB 23:17
worm in a s. plant TALM 772:23
sesquipedalia s. verba HORA 398:5
sesquipedalian S. blackguard CLOU 227:16
sesquippedalian S. verboojuice WELL 828:8
sessions s. of sweet silent thought
SHAK 723:1
Sestos S. and Abydos of her breasts
DONN 279:9
set play a s. SHAK 692:30
s. fair BENN 67:17
s. himself doggedly to it JOHN 427:12
S. me whereas the sun SURR 764:6
s. one slip of them SHAK 722:3
s. our sins from us BOOK 141:3
S. thine house in order BIBL 89:13
would not have s. out CAVA 203:16
Setebos my dam's god, S. SHAK 718:25
S., Setebos BROW 158:26
sets sun never s. NORT 565:10
setter Proud s. up SHAK 695:1
setting against a s. sun SHAK 719:9
s. people right MOOR 547:5

setting (cont.):
time is s. with me — BURN 172:2
settled s. will — SMIT 742:10
s. will — STEE 754:15
settlement parent of s. — BURK 167:8
through the Act of S. — RICE 647:1
seven acts being s. ages — SHAK 681:9
first s. years — SAYI 669:21
have the s. minutes — COLL 235:6
hewn out her s. pillars — BIBL 84:6
Jacob served s. years — BIBL 76:33
Keep a thing s. years — PROV 624:35
lowly air Of S. Dials — GILB 347:11
man with s. wives — NURS 566:7
Rain before s. — PROV 630:4
remember more than s. — BELL 64:16
s. churches — BIBL 112:27
s. days are more than enough — AUST 40:10
s. fat kine — BIBL 77:4
s. feet of English ground — HARO 373:17
s. golden candlesticks — BIBL 112:28
s. maids with seven mops — CARR 195:6
s.-stone weakling — ADVE 7:40
S. types of ambiguity — EMPS 307:25
Until seventy times s. — BIBL 97:23
We are s. — WORD 850:19
sevenfold s. gifts impart — BOOK 144:13
seventeen Maud is not s. — TENN 781:20
seventh moon is in the s. house — RADO 640:12
opened the s. seal — BIBL 113:22
rested the s. day — BIBL 78:4
s. day is the sabbath — BIBL 78:3
seventies s. started 21st century — BOWI 148:12
seventy At s.-seven it is time — JOHN 424:22
Palmerston is now s. — DISR 278:6
s. years young — HOLM 393:8
Until s. times seven — BIBL 97:23
sever kiss, and then we s. — BURN 170:6
s. The chain — CORY 244:2
severae procul este, s. — OVID 579:20
several S. excuses — HUXL 411:9
severance their s. ruled — ARNO 29:3
severe man s. he was — GOLD 354:15
to nothing but herself s. — CARE 190:15
severity pure s. of perfect light — TENN 777:22
Severity breedeth s. — BACO 44:24
with its usual s. — COLE 234:12
Severn S.'s right of maker — GURN 366:2
thick on S. — HOUS 404:13
twice a day the S. fills — TENN 778:29
Seville these dogs of S. — TENN 783:20
sew It can s., it can cook — PLAT 596:18
s., sew, prick our fingers — BROW 157:16
sewer midst of this putrid s. — TOCQ 795:15
s. in a glass-bottomed boat — MIZN 541:6
sewers houses thick and s. — MILT 533:28
sewing job of s. on a button — BROU 154:15
sex attempt to insult s. — LAWR 474:22
because of my s. — BEHN 63:20
call you darling after s. — BARN 56:12
dies from lack of s. — ATWO 33:9
feathers s. can soothe — EWAR 313:6
for my own s. — AUST 39:16
give a s. to mind — WOLL 844:1
if s. rears its ugly head — AYCK 41:3
isn't s. but death — SONT 746:9
Is s. dirty — ALLE 12:9
men think. S., work — FISH 321:14
Mind has no s. — MISQ 538:9
Money was exactly like s. — BALD 50:9
mostly about having s. — LODG 489:6
no stronger than my s. — SHAK 697:2
not even have to s. it up — HOWA 405:10
of s. — ALLE 12:7
only unnatural s. act — KINS 453:10
portray this [s.] relation — ROBI 650:20
practically conceal its s. — NASH 557:7
S. and drugs and rock and roll — DURY 293:9
S. and taxes — JONE 434:9
s. business isn't worth — LAWR 475:3
s. in the mind — LAWR 475:3
S. never an obsession — BOY 148:15

s. object if you're pretty — GIOV 349:19
S. something I really don't understand — SALI 663:21
s. that brings forth — DE B 260:12
s. without emotion — PAGL 581:16
s. with someone I love — ALLE 12:8
soft, unhappy s. — BEHN 64:6
subordination of one s. — MILL 525:12
weaker s. — ALEX 11:11
When you have money, it's s. — DONL 279:3
sexes personalities of the two s. — MEAD 519:18
stronger, of the two s. — GIBB 345:2
there are three s. — SMIT 743:22
sexier make it s. — GILL 349:11
sexton s. tolled the bell — HOOD 395:2
that bald s., Time — SHAK 699:4
sexual car crash as a s. event — BALL 54:1
draws so oddly with the s. — GUNN 365:18
man's idea of his s. rights — STAN 754:10
moral power strong as s. — CONF 237:23
not have s. relations — CLIN 227:8
of all the s. perversions — HUXL 411:8
s. intercourse — AURE 38:7
S. intercourse began — LARK 468:12
s. subjects — GISS 350:5
shock of s. astonishment — WESL 829:24
sexuality relinquish their s. — WOLF 843:9
s. in the movies — DENE 264:2
when s. is repressed — AUGU 37:10
sexually s. transmitted disease — SAYI 670:4
shabby s. equipment always deteriorating — ELIO 301:19
shackles Memories are not s. — BENN 67:11
s. accidents — SHAK 680:5
shadblow Cowslip and s. — CRAN 249:24
shade battle will be in the s. — HERO 385:13
clutching the inviolable s. — ARNO 28:10
farewell to the s. — COWP 247:8
gentlemen of the s. — SHAK 689:19
his steadfast s. — TENN 782:20
image of a s. — SHEL 732:9
in a green s. — MARV 515:17
in s. of Tempe sit — SIDN 736:8
let it sleep in the s. — MOOR 547:18
light, s., and perspective — CONS 241:9
sitting in the s. — KIPL 454:8
sly s. of a Rural Dean — BROO 153:10
sweeter s. to shepherds — SHAK 694:27
whiter s. of pale — REID 644:16
windings and such s. — WINC 841:8
shades S. of the prison-house — WORD 848:5
till the s. lengthen — NEWM 561:2
shadow also casts a s. — CHUR 221:14
but the s. of heaven — MILT 533:15
cast their s. before — PROV 617:3
days on the earth are as a s. — BIBL 82:18
dream But of a s. — CHAP 208:9
dream of a s. — PIND 595:14
Falls the S. — ELIO 302:7
fleeth also as a s. — BIBL 83:8
Follow a s. — JONS 435:25
in the s. of death — BIBL 99:33
in the s. of the earth — BROW 157:12
Life's but a walking s. — SHAK 707:14
little s. that goes — STEV 760:5
little s. that runs — CROW 253:1
little s. that runs — HAGG 367:6
live under the s. of a war — SPEN 751:1
mere s. of death — LAUD 470:3
S. cloaked from head to foot — TENN 778:30
s. of a great rock — BIBL 89:7
s. of death — BIBL 83:2
s. of death — BIBL 88:17
s. of death — BOOK 141:16
s. of felicity — WALL 818:13
s. of God — BROW 156:1
s. of her even brows — SPEN 751:22
s. of our night — SHEL 728:23
s. of some unseen Power — SHEL 729:14
s. of the sun — RALE 641:1
s. of the Valois — CHES 216:5
s. of thy Throne — WATT 823:20
s. of turning — BIBL 111:20

s. stands over us — ALLI 12:17
s. will be shown — NIET 564:6
through the s. — VIRG 812:11
valley of the s. of death — BOOK 135:4
walketh in a vain s. — BOOK 136:5
shadowing employ any depth of s. — DRYD 290:13
shadowless s. like Silence — HOOD 395:8
shadows but s. — SHAK 712:4
cold white s. — WRIG 851:15
events cast their s. — CAMP 187:12
From s. and types — EPIT 309:5
half sick of s. — TENN 780:8
Individuals pass like s. — BURK 168:21
less liquid than their s. — TESS 786:3
longer fall the s. — VIRG 813:16
long s. on county grounds — MAJO 508:5
millions of strange s. — SHAK 723:4
Old sins cast long s. — PROV 628:21
Our fatal s. — FLET 327:5
puppets in a play of s. — BHAG 74:17
see only their own s. — PLAT 597:15
s. and twilights — Æ 6:2
s. flee away — BIBL 87:8
s. have offended — SHAK 712:8
s., not substantial things — SHIR 735:3
s. now so long do grow — COTT 244:6
s. of the clouds — WORD 846:2
s. of us men — JONS 435:25
s. to-night — SHAK 717:8
s. upon the sunbright walls — WORD 845:21
Types and s. — THOM 788:16
When the sun sets, s. — LEE 478:19
Shadrach S., Meshach, and Abed-nego — BIBL 91:20
shady s. trees — BIBL 83:28
shaft Lie like a s. of light — TENN 777:7
s., at random sent — SCOT 673:14
shafts Clear s. of day — LUCR 495:11
Its s. remain — ROET 652:3
shag common cormorant (or s.) — ISHE 414:9
shaggy S., and lean — COWP 248:11
shake Earth must s. — HORA 400:20
only S.-scene in a country — GREE 362:24
s. hands with a king — HALL 369:15
s. off the dust — BIBL 96:15
s. their heads — BOOK 134:27
this god did s. — SHAK 696:7
shaken is never s. — SHAK 723:22
S. and not stirred — FLEM 326:9
s. me by the hand — WESL 829:22
to be well s. — COLM 236:6
shakers movers and s. — O'SH 579:1
shakes is so my single state — SHAK 703:15
Shakespeare less S. he — BROW 159:21
Our myriad-minded S. — COLE 233:23
Our sweetest S. — MILT 529:27
reproduce works of S. — WILE 837:17
S., another Newton — HUXL 411:10
S. by flashes of lightning — COLE 234:2
S. is like bathing — LEIG 479:20
S. is of no age — COLE 234:10
S. one gets — AUST 39:4
S. unlocked his heart — WORD 849:26
S. was of us — BROW 160:3
S. would have grasped — MCEW 501:14
She had read S. — WELL 828:7
S.—the nearest thing — OLIV 573:4
talk of my being like S. — SCOT 674:29
When I read S. — LAWR 475:10
Shakespearean Dogs are S. — SCHW 672:7
That S. rag — BUCK 163:6
Shakespeherian S. Rag — ELIO 303:15
shaking entrusted to the s. hand — VICT 809:12
fall without s. — MONT 543:9
Shalimar loved beside the S. — HOPE 396:8
shall mark you His absolute 's.' — SHAK 682:16
picked the was of s. — CUMM 253:13
shallow S. brooks murmur — SIDN 735:19
s. in himself — MILT 534:23
s. murmur — RALE 641:6
shallows in s. and in miseries — SHAK 698:21
Shalott Lady of S. — TENN 780:8

shalt Thou s. have no other gods BIBL 77:37
sham real pain for my s. friends BACO 47:3
shame Ain't it all a bleedin' s. MILI 526:16
coward s. BURN 171:22
fruit of my vanity is s. PETR 593:16
glory is in their s. BIBL 110:5
mourn with her in s. EMEC 306:8
secret s. destroyed RICH 647:11
s. the devil PROV 631:43
s. unto him BIBL 107:23
terrible s. for me YOKO 856:22
waste of s. SHAK 723:25
shameless most s. thing BURK 167:21
What . . . can be more s. GODW 352:6
shamrock Apart from the s. MCAL 497:14
shamrocks watercresses or s. SPEN 752:22
Shandeism True S. STER 757:6
shank too wide For his shrunk s.
SHAK 681:12
Shannon green banks of S. CAMP 187:10
shantih S., shantih ELIO 303:25
shape might be any s. CARR 195:13
pressed out of s. FROS 336:2
s. of things to come WELL 828:15
Take any s. but that SHAK 706:6
wrought me into s. FITZ 323:14
shaped s., sir, like itself SHAK 679:13
shapen s. in wickedness BOOK 137:11
shapes Change s. with Proteus SHAK 694:29
shaping s. spirit of imagination COLE 231:12
share all persons alike s. ARIS 26:2
all that I have I s. BOOK 133:10
greater s. of honour SHAK 693:21
its ruin didst not s. DODI 278:22
s. no one's ideas TURG 802:6
s. the transport WORD 850:11
shared trouble s. PROV 633:19
shares Fair s. for all POLI 600:15
s. are a penny GILB 347:18
shark s. has pretty teeth BREC 150:13
sharks s. are circling ANON 17:5
s. circling, and waiting CLAR 224:21
Sharon rose of S. BIBL 87:5
sharp s. as a two-edged sword BIBL 83:38
so s. the conquerynge CHAU 212:26
'Tis a s. remedy RALE 641:15
sharpening s. my oyster knife HURS 410:14
sharper s. than a serpent's tooth DICK 271:23
s. than a serpent's tooth SHAK 700:5
s. the storm PROV 630:33
sharpness s. of death BOOK 128:1
sharps s. and flats BROW 160:20
shatter s. the vase MOOR 547:14
shaves s. and takes a train WHIT 831:24
Shaw S.'s plays AGAT 6:21
shawms trumpets also, and s. BOOK 140:14
she And then again S. does JAST 419:3
chaste, and unexpressive s. SHAK 681:16
life and loves of a s.-devil WELD 827:6
S. sells sea-shells SULL 763:12
S., she is dead DONN 279:5
S. who must be obeyed HAGG 367:7
S. who trifles with all GAY 341:22
That not impossible s. CRAS 250:19
sheaf made obeisance to my s. BIBL 76:38
shear good shepherd to s. his flock TIBE 794:7
shearers sheep before her s. BIBL 90:3
shears resembles a pair of s. SMIT 743:24
with th' abhorrèd s. MILT 530:3
sheathe s. the sword ASQU 32:2
sheaves bring his s. with him BOOK 142:24
s. of sacred fire CHAP 208:13
your s. stood BIBL 76:38
Sheba Another S. queen WITH 842:6
Ere you were Queen of S. SHIP 734:22
queen of S. BIBL 81:11
shed Burke under a s. JOHN 432:12
prepare to s. them now SHAK 698:1
shall his blood be s. BIBL 76:11
s. for you and for many BOOK 132:2
s. innocent blood BIBL 90:16
shedding Without s. of blood BIBL 111:4
sheen s. is the sonne LANG 466:21

sheep Among the s. MISS 540:1
as s. going astray BIBL 112:9
bleating s. loses bite PROV 615:44
care of s. DYER 293:14
craved the life of a s. LA F 463:16
ensample to his s. CHAU 210:22
Feed my s. BIBL 104:20
folds shall be full of s. BOOK 138:7
found my s. which was lost BIBL 101:12
get back to these s. ANON 21:1
giveth his life for the s. BIBL 103:17
hanged for a s. PROV 628:45
has lost her s. NURS 567:21
hills like young s. BOOK 142:2
His silly s. COWP 247:10
hungry s. look up MILT 530:6
in s.'s clothing BIBL 95:21
keep s. and cows OSBO 578:10
like lost s. BOOK 127:15
like s. have gone astray BIBL 90:3
little black s. KIPL 454:6
looking on their silly s. SHAK 694:27
lost s. BIBL 96:13
mere s.-herding POUN 609:10
mountain s. are sweeter PEAC 590:5
old half-witted s. STEP 755:21
Other s. I have BIBL 103:19
savaged by a dead s. HEAL 377:11
s. bear fleeces VIRG 815:7
s. before her shearers BIBL 90:3
s. born carnivorous FAGU 314:4
s. in sheep's clothing CHUR 222:23
s. in sheep's clothing GOSS 357:8
s. of his hand BOOK 140:10
s. on his right hand BIBL 98:24
s.'s in the meadow NURS 568:1
s. that have not a shepherd BIBL 81:32
s., that were wont to be MORE 548:7
s. to pass resolutions INGE 413:8
sickly s. infects the flock WATT 823:5
teeth are like a flock of s. BIBL 87:10
thousand years as a s. PROV 615:30
two hundred years like a s. TIPU 794:18
wolf in s.'s clothing AESO 6:19
sheeps s.' guts SHAK 712:17
sheet brought in the white s. LORC 492:1
England's winding s. BLAK 119:14
How at my s. THOM 789:10
s. knit at the four corners BIBL 105:6
s. were big enough SHAK 721:5
turn over the s. SAND 666:5
waters were his winding s. BARN 56:16
wet s. CUNN 253:17
sheets cool kindliness of s. BROO 153:6
s. with hay over JOHN 424:20
Shekinah rejoice in the S. ZOHA 859:3
shelf s. life of the modern TRIL 798:16
shell fired a 15-inch s. RUTH 661:19
gloomy s. ANON 17:22
prettier s. NEWT 561:16
thou s. of death MIDD 524:10
Shelley Burns, S., were with us BROW 160:3
did you once see S. BROW 160:8
peace in S.'s mind SHEL 732:2
shells choirs of wailing s. OWEN 581:2
shelter s. from the stormy blast WATT 823:20
shelves symmetry of s. LAMB 464:14
shepherd call you, S. ARNO 28:2
Dick the s. SHAK 702:26
God of love my S. is HERB 385:2
good s. BIBL 103:17
good s. to shear his flock TIBE 794:7
happy S. Boy WORD 848:3
like a s. BIBL 89:18
Lord is my s. BOOK 135:3
Lord's my s. SCOT 675:4
my s. is BAKE 50:2
Old Nod, the s. DE L 263:6
returned unto the S. BIBL 112:9
sheep that have not a s. BIBL 81:32
s., blowing of his nails SHAK 694:26
S., Corydon, burned with love VIRG 813:17
s. his sheep PROP 612:21

s.'s delight PROV 630:5
s. tells his tale MILT 529:22
shepherds s. abiding in the field BIBL 100:2
s. and butchers VOLT 816:9
s. call me also a poet VIRG 814:9
s. give a grosser name SHAK 688:18
s. watched their flocks TATE 773:14
sheriff I shot the s. MARL 512:14
Sheriffmuir at S. A battle MCLE 503:11
Sherman general (yes mam) s. CUMM 253:10
sherry s. flowing into second-rate whores
PLOM 598:10
shibboleth Say now S. BIBL 79:28
shield broken was her s. SCOT 674:1
efforts to s. children ADDA 4:2
faith shall be my s. ASKE 31:20
lady in his s. TENN 780:9
Our S. and Defender GRAN 359:3
s. against retribution TALM 772:8
s. and buckler BOOK 140:2
S. of Abraham SIDD 735:13
s. of British fair play AITK 9:3
s. of faith BIBL 109:21
trusty s. LUTH 496:11
shieling From the lone s. GALT 338:15
shift let me s. for myself MORE 548:1
s. in what the public wants CALL 185:15
shifted s. his trumpet GOLD 355:9
shilling sell for one s. Your ring LEAR 477:17
s. life will give you AUDE 36:5
shillings can do for ten s. SHUT 735:10
shimmered Jeeves s. out WODE 842:17
shine Arise, s. BIBL 90:17
Boy you can gimme a s. GORD 356:18
Let your light so s. BIBL 94:23
Lord make his face s. BIBL 78:15
s. all through the sphere VAUG 808:2
s., and run to and fro BIBL 92:24
s. in company SWIF 766:24
s. on, harvest moon NORW 565:17
shiners Nine for the nine bright s.
SONG 747:11
shines s. and stinks RAND 642:4
s. sae bright BURN 173:8
shingles naked s. of the world ARNO 27:3
shining I see it s. plain HOUS 404:16
s. from shook foil HOPK 396:12
s. into a puddle PROV 631:34
s. morning face SHAK 681:10
S. nowhere but in the dark VAUG 807:18
S. suspension CRAN 249:26
sun was s. everywhere GERS 344:4
with s. foot shall pass FITZ 323:17
woman of s. loveliness YEAT 855:15
ship all I ask is a tall s. MASE 517:15
being in a s. JOHN 427:23
build your s. of death LAWR 475:6
idle as a painted s. COLE 232:19
infantry or a fleet of s. SAPP 666:12
like a sinking s. WOOL 845:14
must rebuild their s. NEUR 559:13
one for the s. PROV 628:38
O S. of State LONG 490:2
S. and stores have gone SHAC 677:18
s., an isle FLEC 326:5
s. appeared in the air HEAN 377:21
s. has weathered every rack WHIT 833:4
s. I have got SONG 748:4
s. in a black storm WEBS 826:17
s. in the midst of the sea BIBL 85:21
S. me somewheres KIPL 455:2
s. on the sea LORC 492:2
s. substantial ASKE 31:20
s. was as still SOUT 749:4
s. would not travel CARR 196:9
Sink me the s., Master Gunner TENN 784:2
spoil the s. PROV 618:2
towards a sinking s. CHUR 222:22
What is a s. BURT 174:10
will sink a s. BUNY 165:2
woman and a s. ever want PROV 635:15
ships all the s. at sea WINC 841:3
Hell to s. AESC 6:5

ships (*cont.*):
launched a thousand s.   MARL 513:4
little s. of England   GUED 365:10
Loose lips sink s.   MILI 526:13
move with the moving s.   SWIN 769:9
Of shoes—and s.   CARR 195:7
S. are but boards   SHAK 708:28
S., dim-discovered   THOM 792:10
s. empty of men   NICI 563:9
s. have been salvaged   HALS 369:18
s. of the sea   BOOK 137:5
s. sail like swans asleep   FLEC 326:4
S. that pass in the night   LONG 491:7
S., towers, domes   WORD 846:6
something wrong with our bloody s.
   BEAT 59:13
Spanish s. of war   TENN 783:19
stately s. go on   TENN 775:17
There go the s.   BOOK 141:10
to the sea in s.   BOOK 141:18
we've got the s.   HUNT 409:13
wooden wall is your s.   THEM 787:20
shipwreck s. of time   BACO 42:15
suffered s.   BIBL 108:21
shire That s. which we may call   DRAY 286:1
shires bugles calling from sad s.   OWEN 581:2
Round both the s.   HOUS 404:11
shirt Near is my s.   PROV 627:11
Song of the S.   HOOD 395:11
shirtsleeves From s. to   PROV 620:31
shit chicken s.   JOHN 423:6
s. in a silk stocking   NAPO 557:6
s.-wiping stick   MUMO 554:7
shock-proof s. detector   HEMI 381:9
shiver praised and left to s.   JUVE 439:8
tremble and s.   HOOD 394:22
shivering like Augustine shivering
   WILL 838:12
shoal bank and s. of time   SHAK 704:3
s. of fools   CONG 239:11
shoals s. of herring   MACC 500:13
shock characterized by s.   FRAN 333:3
Future s.   TOFF 795:16
S. and Awe   ANON 18:10
S. and Awe   ULLM 804:7
S.-headed Peter   HOFF 392:3
s. of the new   DUNL 292:6
s. of your joy   HUGH 407:9
s. them and keep them up to date
   SHAW 725:6
short, sharp s.   GILB 348:1
sudden s. of joy   BLIS 123:9
we shall s. them   SHAK 699:16
shocked s. by this subject   BOHR 125:9
shocking looked on as something s.
   PORT 607:8
shocks s. the magistrate   RUSS 661:4
s. the mind of a child   PAIN 582:4
thousand natural s.   SHAK 686:9
twelve great s. of sound   TENN 779:1
shod All s. with steel   WORD 846:24
foot feel, being s.   HOPK 396:12
shoddier no s. than what they peddle
   BECK 61:7
shoe Buckle my s.   NURS 568:18
careless s.-string   HERR 385:21
cast out my s.   BOOK 137:26
embrace a woman's s.   KRAU 461:15
If the s. fits   PROV 623:6
I kiss his dirty s.   SHAK 693:11
Into a left-hand s.   CARR 196:1
lived in a s.   NURS 570:1
s.'s latchet   BIBL 102:23
want of a s.   PROV 620:24
shoemaker s.'s son always   PROV 630:34
shoes from the s.   GOLD 356:1
shoes call for his old s.   SELD 676:3
changing s.   BREC 150:19
dead men's s.   PROV 624:22
ere those s. were old   SHAK 684:4
I had no s.   SAYI 669:24
mind it wipes its s.   THOM 790:5
never tied my s.   PU Y 636:12

Of s.—and ships   CARR 195:7
Put off thy s.   BIBL 77:17
s. of his soldiers   BAGE 48:2
s. that were not fellows   DEFO 261:10
s. with broken high ideals   MCGO 502:2
thy feet with s.   BIBL 87:19
want of s.   SADI 662:15
shoeshine riding on a smile and a s.
   MILL 527:6
shook earth s.   BOOK 138:11
monk who s. the world   MONT 545:15
more it's s. it shines   HAMI 369:20
s. hands with time   FORD 328:19
Ten days that s. the world   REED 644:11
shoot can s., And can hit   HERB 384:1
he shall s. higher   SIDN 736:1
S., if you must   WHIT 834:3
s. me in my absence   BEHA 63:14
s. me through linoleum   BANK 54:17
s. out their lips   BOOK 134:27
s. the Hippopotamus   BELL 64:18
s. the hippopotamus   FORS 329:6
s. the pianist   ANON 18:11
s. the sleepy, green-coat man   HOFF 392:1
They s. horses don't they   MCCO 500:16
they shout and they s.   INGE 413:4
You'd s. a fellow down   HARD 372:22
young idea how to s.   THOM 792:8
shooting s. a gun   WILL 838:15
s.-stars attend thee   HERR 386:4
war minus the s.   ORWE 578:1
shoots green s. of recovery   MISQ 537:17
He s.! He scores   CATC 200:28
man who s. him gets caught   MAIL 507:14
shop ain't the s. for justice   DICK 271:14
back to the s.   LOCK 489:4
foul rag-and-bone s.   YEAT 853:12
little back s.   MONT 544:9
s. will keep you   PROV 624:38
shopkeepers nation of s.   ADAM 3:14
nation of s.   NAPO 557:4
nation of s.   PROV 618:44
nation of s.   SMIT 741:9
shopocracy abuse the s.   NORT 565:12
shopping main thing today is—s.   MILL 527:7
shore adieu! my native s.   BYRO 178:5
after-silence on the s.   BYRO 182:28
for the further s.   VIRG 812:13
high s. of this world   SHAK 693:19
impossible s.   ARNO 28:22
kingdom of the s.   SHAK 723:7
lights around the s.   ROSS 656:8
rapture on the lonely s.   BYRO 179:17
s. Of the wide world   KEAT 445:25
sounds by the s.   YEAT 854:18
stayed upon the green s.   KEAT 446:15
stretch s. to shore   WATT 823:19
To the other s.   PAUL 589:6
unknown and silent s.   LAMB 464:20
shored s. against my ruins   ELIO 303:24
shoreless s. watery wild   ARNO 29:2
shores around Desolate s.   KEAT 445:9
betwixt their s.   ARNO 29:4
on the s. of darkness   KEAT 445:20
recognize my s.   AKHM 9:7
wilder s. of love   BLAN 123:7
shorewards great winds s. blow   ARNO 27:11
shorn come home s.   PROV 626:12
green grass s.   BACO 44:18
priest all shaven and s.   NURS 570:2
sheep that are even s.   BIBL 87:10
tempers wind to s. lamb   PROV 621:1
short Anger is a s. madness   HORA 399:6
by s. grasses   PORT 607:23
Don't sell America s.   POLI 600:13
in a s. time   BIBL 92:25
it is well it is s.   TAYL 775:2
Life's s. span   HORA 400:6
long and the s. and the tall   HUGH 406:16
nasty, brutish, and s.   HOBB 390:16
not S.   DICK 271:9
s. and bandy-legged   ARCH 24:8
s. horse soon curried   PROV 630:35

s. in the story   BIBL 94:3
s. notice, soon past   PROV 625:38
s. of the glory of God   BIBL 106:5
S. reckonings   PROV 630:36
s., sharp shock   GILB 348:1
s. time to live   BOOK 133:16
s. time to stay   HERR 386:16
s. way   ASCH 31:6
Take s. views   SMIT 743:19
That lyf so s.   CHAU 212:26
When you're a s. actor   FOX 331:12
while to make it s.   THOR 792:27
shortcomings o'er its own s.   LITT 487:1
shorter s. by the head   ELIZ 304:6
time to make it s.   PASC 587:1
shortest longest day and s. night   PROV 615:1
s. way   BACO 43:3
s. way home   PROV 625:37
shorts Eat my s.   CATC 200:14
shot be s. at   HARD 373:7
Certain men the English s.   YEAT 854:23
fired the s.   BALL 52:6
I s. the sheriff   MARL 512:14
s. at for sixpence a-day   DIBD 267:6
s. heard round the world   EMER 306:12
s. mine arrow   SHAK 689:8
S.? so quick, so clean   HOUS 404:18
They've s. our fox   BIRC 116:17
shotgun blew his head off with a s.
   BLY 124:11
shots of the best s.   VOLT 816:10
shoulder giant's s. to mount on   COLE 233:24
government shall be upon his s.   BIBL 88:18
keep looking over his s.   BARU 57:19
left s.-blade   GILB 348:6
shifted it to another's s.   SHAW 726:16
stand s. to shoulder   BLAI 118:20
shoulders Borne on our s.   BROW 159:12
City of the Big S.   SAND 665:4
from her s. did fall   WYAT 852:5
grow beneath their s.   SHAK 713:9
lawn about the s.   HERR 385:21
old head on young s.   PROV 635:34
on the s. of giants   NEWT 561:15
on your young s.   SPAR 749:25
s. held the sky suspended   HOUS 404:1
s. of giants   BERN 70:11
shout hardly a s.   ARNO 28:1
shouted with a great s.   BIBL 79:11
S. round me, let me hear   WORD 848:3
s. that tore Hell's concave   MILT 531:23
S. with the largest   DICK 271:28
they s. and they shoot   INGE 413:4
shouted sons of God s.   BIBL 83:22
shouting thunder and the s.   BIBL 83:25
tumult and the s.   KIPL 455:10
shovelled quatrains s.   LOWE 494:18
shovelling S. white steam   AUDE 35:15
show business like s. business   BERL 69:22
learned not to s. it   ALCO 10:9
make a s. themselves   OVID 579:21
only a s.   GOET 352:13
s. any just cause   BOOK 133:7
s. business with blood   BRUN 162:10
s. him my salvation   BOOK 140:5
S. Must Go On   GERS 344:13
s. our simple skill   SHAK 712:1
s. that you have one   CHES 215:5
s. the light   BOOK 139:12
s. thy praise   BOOK 137:15
shower abundant s. of curates   BRON 152:12
coming s.   SWIF 766:29
have a summer s.   MACD 501:8
sweetness of a s.   THOM 790:17
showers After sharpest s.   LANG 466:21
April s. bring forth   PROV 614:30
land never pleads for s.   TIBU 794:10
S., and Dew   BOOK 128:5
with his s. soote   CHAU 210:4
with his s. soote   OPEN 576:1
showery S., Flowery, Bowery   ELLI 306:1
showeth true love is, it s.   DE P 264:16
showing worth s.   DANT 256:15

shows outward s. SHAK 709:18
shreds king of s. and patches SHAK 687:27
thing of s. and patches GILB 347:19
shrewd s. was that snatch BROW 158:19
shrewishly speaks very s. SHAK 720:12
Shrewsbury by S. clock SHAK 691:17
shriek hollow s. the steep MILT 530:25
short shrill s. COLL 235:11
shrieking Hooting and s. SHAK 696:18
s. and squeaking BROW 160:20
shrieks Not louder s. POPE 606:15
shrimp s. learns to whistle KHRU 451:3
s. of an author GRAY 362:1
shrimps s. to swim again JONS 434:15
shrine Erects a s. BYRO 182:10
fits a little s. HERR 386:11
shrined bower we s. to Tennyson
HARD 372:10
shrines mouldering s. removed BYRO 178:8
shrink all the boards did s. COLE 232.20
never make thee s. BALL 52:13
shroud April s. KEAT 444:18
stain the stiff dishonoured s. ELIO 303:6
striped s. THOM 790:20
whoever comes to s. me DONN 280:25
shrouds S. have no pockets PROV 630:37
shrug read a nod, a s. SWIF 767:2
with a patient s. SHAK 709:2
shrunk S. to this little measure SHAK 697:13
shudder I s. as I recall VIRG 811:13
s. at it beforehand DOST 283:9
s. in the loins engenders YEAT 854:21
shuffle All s. there YEAT 855:11
s. the cards CERV 205:14
shuffled reduced to a s. pack NERU 559:2
s. off this mortal coil SHAK 686:9
Shulamite return, O S. BIBL 87:18
shun let me s. that SHAK 700:21
s. that wretched state CHUD 219:10
shut either s. or open PROV 618:20
gates of it shall not be s. BIBL 114:20
Men s. their doors SHAK 719:9
ought to be s. up JOHN 428:4
s. mouth catches no flies PROV 630:38
s. the door POPE 602:23
s. the stable-door PROV 624:23
S. up he explained LARD 468:10
shuts When one door s. PROV 634:25
shutter before her on a s. THAC 786:23
click the s. EISE 298:18
shutters close the s. fast COWP 248:6
shuttle contingency for the space s.
ANON 15:15
Man is the s. VAUG 807:7
musical s. WHIT 833:6
swifter than a weaver's s. BIBL 82:38
shuttlecock Battledore and s. DICK 271:29
shy Once bitten, twice s. PROV 628:29
si S. possis recte HORA 399:1
Sibyl saw the S. at Cumae ROSS 656:9
Sibyllam Nam S. quidem Cumis PETR 594:5
Sicelides S. Musae VIRG 814:2
sick And I am s. at heart SHAK 683:12
Created s. GREV 364:2
devil was s. PROV 617:38
do not make me s. WHIT 833:13
do the s. no harm NIGH 564:13
extremely s. PRIO 612:11
half s. of shadows TENN 780:8
hired to watch the s. COWP 247:25
I am s., I must die NASH 557:21
I am s. of both JOHN 430:24
is Brutus s. SHAK 696:27
make him s. DONN 279:8
medicine for the s. SHAN 724:8
most s. and most healthy HA-L 368:9
Pass the s. bag, Alice CATC 201:23
Rose, thou art s. BLAK 122:18
s. and wicked AUST 40:20
s., and ye visited me BIBL 98:25
s. for home KEAT 445:1
s. hurry ARNO 28:9
s. in fortune SHAK 699:26

They are as s. SHAK 708:24
they that are s. BIBL 96:6
think we're s. WOLF 843:16
treatment to help the s. HIPP 389:12
when he is s. JOHN 432:4
sickened s. at all triumphs CHUR 220:5
sickle isle, a s. moon FLEC 326:5
s. in the fruitful field BLAK 121:24
sickly bloody war and a s. season TOAS 796:1
I'm s. but sassy HARR 374:4
kind of s. smile HART 374:17
s. sheep infects the flock WATT 823:5
sickness age, grief, or s. KING 451:15
falling s. SHAK 696:16
in s. and in health BOOK 133:9
medicine to heal their s. BOOK 144:3
s., or any other adversity BOOK 131:16
s. that destroyeth BOOK 140:3
Sid Tell S. ADVE 8:16
Sidcup get down to S. PINT 595.15
side bosom and half her s. COLE 231:6
Hear the other s. AUGU 37:11
my hand into his s. BIBL 104:14
on every s. BOOK 135:21
on our s. today MACA 499:10
on the other s. BUNY 165:10
on the s. of those ANOU 22:15
other s. of the hill WELL 827:19
over to the other s. REED 644:6
passed by on the other s. BIBL 100:23
S. by side WOOD 844:18
Which S. Are You On DYLA 294:5
which s. do they cheer for TEBB 775:7
Who is on my s. BIBL 82:15
sidelong s. would she bend KEAT 443:27
sidera Sublimi feriam s. vertice HORA 400:2
sides looked at life from both s. MITC 540:11
Norfan, both s. WELL 828:10
said on both s. ADDI 4:27
two s. to every question PROV 632:2
sidestreets down the s. GINS 349:16
siege My s. is over VERT 809:4
She kept the s. HILL 388:9
Siegfried washing on the S. Line
KENN 448:12
siesta Englishmen detest a s. COWA 245:3
sieve draws nectar in a s. COLE 233:16
in a s. I'll thither sail SHAK 703:5
went to sea in a S. LEAR 477:8
sifted s. a nation STOU 761:18
siftings let their liquid s. fall ELIO 303:6
sigh Born of the very s. KEAT 443:21
s. for thy repose WESL 829:10
s. in thanking BROW 157:15
s. is just a sigh HUPF 410:13
s. is the sword BLAK 120:11
s. like Tom o' Bedlam SHAK 700:1
s. no more, ladies SHAK 712:18
sighed S. and looked DRYD 287:18
S. and looked THOM 792:11
s. as a lover GIBB 345:17
s. his soul SHAK 709:35
sighing ability and S. DICK 273:11
poor soul sat s. SHAK 714:16
s. of a contrite heart BOOK 129:15
sighs on the Bridge of S. BYRO 179:3
sound of s. PETR 593:15
world of s. SHAK 713:10
sight all very well at first s. SHAW 726:15
at first s. STEE 754:18
deprived of sight VIRG 811:24
evil in thy s. BOOK 137:10
giveth s. to the blind BOOK 144:1
in the s. of God BOOK 133:4
in the s. of the Lord BOOK 142:8
in thy s. BOOK 143:22
My dying s. BLOK 123:13
neatly out of s. CRAN 250:1
Out of s. PROV 629:12
out of s. THOM 788:9
s. of means SHAK 699:12
s. to dream of COLE 231:6
s. to make an old man young TENN 777:3

s. was often puzzled BOCC 125:2
thousand years in thy s. BOOK 139:22
To feeling as to s. SHAK 704:16
triple s. in blindness KEAT 445:20
sights few more impressive s. BARR 57:8
s. as youthful poets dream MILT 529:27
sign If only God would give some s.
ALLE 12:14
if you s. this BRUG 162:5
In this s. shalt thou conquer CONS 241:11
Jews require a s. BIBL 107:3
outward and visible s. BOOK 132:19
Queen must s. BAGE 48:15
seeketh after a s. BIBL 96:33
signal do not see the s. NELS 558:14
Only a s. shown LONG 491:7
s.-elm ARNO 28:23
signals s. of the ancient flame DANT 256:9
signed hand that s. the paper THOM 789:11
I s. my death warrant COLL 235:5
What I have s. GRIF 364:6
significance s. of an event CART 197:9
s. of its own JUNG 438:13
signo In hoc s. vinces CONS 241:11
signposts s. to socialist Utopia CROS 252:10
signs merely conventional s. CARR 196:8
multiply my s. and my wonders BIBL 77:24
no 'white' or 'coloured' s. KENN 449:4
read s. of the times CHOI 218:7
s. and wonders BIBL 102:35
S. are the natural language SHAD 677:20
s. of the times BIBL 97:15
words are but the s. JOHN 424:4
Sikhs Grant to your S. SIKH 737:12
silence after-s. on the shore BYRO 182:28
answered best with s. JONS 435:16
but s. is golden PROV 631:16
chequered s. AKHM 9:10
clamour of s. TAGO 770:18
conspiracy of s. COMT 237:5
darkness again and a s. LONG 491:7
darkness and s. LEAR 477:6
Deep is the s. DRIN 286:8
easy step to s. AUST 39:9
end of OM is s. UPAN 805:15
eternal s. PASC 587:8
even darkness and s. KELL 447:19
flashes of s. SMIT 743:25
foster-child of s. KEAT 444:6
foster-child of s. OPEN 575:25
Gospel of S. MORL 549:4
Go to where the s. is GOOD 356:11
I kept s. BOOK 136:3
Indecency's conspiracy of s. SHAW 726:28
in that s. we the tempest DRYD 287:26
I shall state s. BECK 61:3
lies are often told in s. STEV 759:27
Lo! all in s. CRAB 249:4
mind moves upon s. YEAT 854:22
My gracious s., hail SHAK 682:15
Of the eternal S. WORD 848:12
other side of s. ELIO 300:5
period of s. on your part ATTL 33:2
rest is s. SHAK 689:15
shadowless like S. HOOD 395:8
sigh that s. heaves KEAT 443:21
s. all the airs MILT 535:18
S. alone is great VIGN 810:8
s. also does not ELIO 299:18
S. augmenteth grief DYER 293:12
s. deep as death CAMP 187:6
s., exile, and cunning JOYC 437:12
s. fell with the waking bird TENN 781:24
s. in heaven BIBL 113:22
s. in the hills TENN 778:29
S. is a woman's AUCT 34:16
S. is a woman's best PROV 630:39
S. is become his mother tongue GOLD 355:19
S. is deep as Eternity CARL 191:20
S. is golden PROV 630:40
s. is most noble SWIN 768:5
S. is the virtue BACO 43:9
S. like a cancer grows SIMO 738:4

silence (cont.):
S. means consent — PROV 630:41
S. more musical — ROSS 655:14
s. of a dream — ROSS 655:7
s. of the law — HOBB 390:18
s. sank Like music — COLE 233:8
S., sing to me — HOPK 396:14
s. surged softly backward — DE L 263:4
S. that dreadful bell — SHAK 713:22
S.! Voilà l'ennemi — COND 237:6
small change of s. — MERE 522:17
Sorrow and s. — LONG 490:8
stain upon the s. — BECK 61:27
Still-born S. — FLEC 326:7
talent pour le s. — CARL 192:12
Through the friendly s. — VIRG 811:14
trembles into s. — BYRO 179:24
twofold s. — ROSS 656:1
With s. and tears — BYRO 183:23
world of s. — EPIT 309:2
silenced because you have s. him
— MORL 549:5
silencing justified in s. — MILL 525:7
silent All s., and all damned — WORD 848:21
great ones are s. — SENE 677:1
Grey s. fragments — HUGH 407:7
impossible to be s. — BURK 169:3
into the s. land — ROSS 655:11
Laws are s. — CICE 223:21
mornings are strangely s. — CARS 196:20
one must be s. — WITT 842:10
Paris was French—and s. — TUCH 802:1
s. be — AUDE 35:10
s. in seven languages — BAGE 48:2
s. majority — NIXO 564:19
s. manliness of grief — GOLD 354:19
s. over Africa — BROW 159:20
s. touches of time — BURK 169:9
S., upon a peak — CLOS 228:21
S., upon a peak in Darien — KEAT 445:6
strong, s. man — MORL 549:4
t is s. — ASQU 32:7
unlocked her s. throat — GIBB 345:24
with the s. Virgin — HORA 402:5
silentia Tacitae per amica s. lunae — VIRG 811:14
silk breed the s. — SHAK 714:8
clad in s. or scarlet — PROV 614:25
he was shot s. — STRA 761:22
make a s. purse — MORT 551:4
make his couche of s. — CHAU 211:19
shit in a s. stocking — NAPO 557:6
s. hat on a Bradford millionaire — ELIO 303:20
s. makes the difference — FULL 337:9
s. purse out of sow's ear — PROV 635:41
s. stockings — JOHN 427:11
soft as s. remains — HILL 388:6
worn with a s. hat — EDWA 296:10
silken s. terms precise — SHAK 702:22
s. tie — SCOT 673:10
silks in fading s. compose — WINC 841:10
in s. my Julia goes — HERR 386:20
silkworm of s. size or immense — MOOR 546:18
s. expend her yellow labours — MIDD 524:12
silkworms s. droop — BASH 58:2
sillier s. than a silly laugh — CATU 202:17
silliest s. part of God's creation — ROCH 651:15
s. woman can manage a clever man
— KIPL 457:1
silly Ask a s. question — PROV 614:41
it's good to be s. — HORA 403:1
s. twisted boy — CATC 202:8
such a s. question — STER 756:15
'tis very s. — BYRO 181:3
You were s. like us — AUDE 35:3
silvae paulum s. super his — HORA 403:4
s. sint consule dignae — VIRG 814:2
silvam In s. . . . . ligna feras — HORA 403:11
silvas Habitarunt di quoque s. — VIRG 813:19
inter s. Academi — HORA 399:21
silver About a s. lining — COWA 245:8
all the Georgian s. — MACM 504:9
Between their s. bars — FLEC 326:5
bringing gold, and s. — BIBL 81:13

cloud has a s. lining — PROV 619:4
covered with s. wings — BOOK 138:12
for a handful of s. — BROW 160:2
gold and s. becks me — SHAK 699:5
in her s. shoon — DE L 263:7
pictures of s. — BIBL 85:3
Selling off the family s. — MISQ 538:16
S. and gold have I none — BIBL 104:29
s. apples of the moon — YEAT 855:19
s. cord be loosed — BIBL 86:25
s. foot in his mouth — RICH 647:8
s. link — SCOT 673:10
s. pin — BALL 53:19
s. plate on a coffin — CURR 254:5
s., snarling trumpets — KEAT 442:17
s.-sweet sound lovers' tongues — SHAK 717:28
Speech is s. — PROV 631:16
take s. or small change — CHAM 207:2
There's a s. lining — FORD 329:4
thirty pieces of s. — BEVA 73:13
thirty pieces of s. — BIBL 98:29
thousands of gold and s. — BOOK 142:12
time hath to s. turned — PEEL 591:3
silvery so s. is thy voice — HERR 386:21
silvestrem S. tenui Musam — VIRG 813:12
Silvia Who is S. — SHAK 721:22
similes play with s. — WORD 850:16
similia S. similibus curantur — MOTT 552:19
Simon real S. Pure — CENT 205:6
Simple S. met a pieman — NURS 569:13
simple and never s. — WILD 835:12
ask the hard question is s. — AUDE 36:11
beautiful and s. — HENR 382:12
C'est tellement s. — PRÉV 610:13
Everything is very s. in war — CLAU 225:15
I'm a s. man — LOWR 494:21
S. Simon met a pieman — NURS 569:13
s. truth must be abused — SHAK 716:25
smile with the s. — GARR 340:1
too clear, too s. — STEN 755:19
women are so s. — SHAK 718:17
simplicitas O sancta s. — HUSS 410:15
simplicity Cultivate s. — LAMB 465:2
elegant s. — STOW 761:20
Embrace s. — LAO 467:9
holy s. — JERO 421:5
O holy s. — HUSS 410:15
Pity my s. — WESL 829:1
s., a child — POPE 603:28
s. of the three per cents — DISR 277:13
simplify s. me when I'm dead — DOUG 283:17
S., simplify — THOR 793:13
Simpson I'm Bart S. — CATC 201:5
Simpsons less like the S. — BUSH 175:2
simulacrum dark s. — BROW 156:1
sin all the causes of s. — JAIN 416:3
And the s. I impute — BROW 161:17
bare the s. of many — BIBL 90:5
beauty is only s. deep — SAKI 663:16
brother s. against me — BIBL 97:23
brought s. and death — STAN 754:9
by making a s. of it — FRAN 331:18
By that s. fell the angels — SHAK 695:14
charity in s. — SHAK 708:6
dark world of s. — BICK 115:23
died unto s. once — BIBL 106:12
dreadful record of s. — DOYL 284:10
Excepting Original S. — CAMP 187:19
fall into no s. — BOOK 128:13
fall not in such s. — GILB 346:18
go, and s. no more — BIBL 103:10
go away and s. no more — ANON 17:18
hate the s. — AUGU 37:16
He that is without s. — BIBL 103:9
Ignorance excuses from s. — AUCT 34:7
I had not known s. — BIBL 106:14
in secret s. — CHUR 219:22
in s. hath my mother — BOOK 137:11
keep us this day without s. — BOOK 128:2
Lord imputeth no s. — BOOK 135:20
lose the s. — POPE 602:18
Lukewarmness I account a s. — COWL 245:25
made almost a s. — DRYD 287:29

My s., my soul — OPEN 574:32
no s. but ignorance — MARL 513:12
no s., but to be rich — SHAK 699:3
not innocence but s. — BROW 159:27
One s. will destroy — BUNY 165:2
only one real s. — LESS 482:1
original s. — MELV 521:9
physicists have known s. — OPPE 573:18
quantum o' the s. — BURN 170:28
rebellion is as the s. — BIBL 80:15
researches in original s. — PLOM 598:11
Shall we continue in s. — BIBL 106:10
s. blows quite away — HERB 384:25
s., death, and Hell — BUNY 165:4
single venial s. — NEWM 560:17
s. in secret — MOLI 542:12
S. is behovely — JULI 438:6
s. is ever before me — BOOK 137:10
s. not — BIBL 109:13
s. of public men — TAYL 774:20
S.'s a pleasure — BYRO 180:14
S.'s rotten trunk — COWP 247:12
s. tends to be addictive — AUDE 36:14
s. with caution — CENT 205:5
s. ye do by two and two — KIPL 455:21
Stand in awe, and s. not — BOOK 133:23
taketh away the s. — BIBL 102:24
triumph over death and s. — SPEN 751:3
wages of s. is death — BIBL 106:13
want of power to s. — DRYD 289:7
we have no s. — BIBL 112:18
what did he say about s. — COOL 242:8
Where s. abounded — BIBL 106:9
Which is my s. — DONN 280:2
worst s. towards our fellow — SHAW 724:26
Would you like to s. — ANON 20:5
your s. will find you out — BIBL 78:23
sincere Always be s. — TRUM 801:14
be as wholly s. — JUDA 438:1
be s. — MENG 522:5
friend s. enough — BULW 164:7
starkly s. — RHYS 646:14
sincerely s. want to be rich — CORN 243:8
sincerity be talked with in s. — SHAK 707:20
s. is a dangerous thing — WILD 836:2
unleavened bread of s. — BIBL 107:11
Sindh I have S. — WINK 841:18
sinecure no s. — BYRO 184:9
sinews Money is the s. of love — FARQ 315:20
money the s. of war — BACO 45:26
s. of the soul — FULL 337:5
s. of thy heart — BLAK 122:20
s. of war — CICE 223:20
Stiffen the s. — SHAK 693:24
very s. of virtue — WALT 820:20
sing Alleluia! s. to Jesus — DIX 278:13
bygynneth to s. — CHAU 213:7
can s. and won't sing — PROV 625:24
celebrate myself, and s. myself — WHIT 833:9
come, let us s. — BOOK 140:9
do what men may s. — PEMB 591:10
I came here to s. — NERU 559:5
I'll s. you twelve O — SONG 747:11
in thine heart to s. — SWIN 768:25
I s. of brooks — HERR 385:16
I s. the progress — DONN 280:6
I, too, s. America — HUGH 406:17
know ye s. well — FLET 327:10
laugh and s. — BOOK 137:1
never heard no horse s. — ARMS 26:15
O s. unto God — BOOK 137:1
people s. it — BEAU 59:15
Places where they s. — BOOK 128:14
Silence, s. to me — HOPK 396:14
S. a faery's song — KEAT 442:3
S. a song of sixpence — NURS 569:14
S. before breakfast — PROV 630:42
S. before him a new song — HAGG 367:4
S. both high and low — SHAK 720:15
S. 'em muck — MELB 520:14
s. in a hempen string — FLET 327:3
s. in the robber's face — JUVE 440:5
s. like birds i' the cage — SHAK 701:24

S. me a song STEV 760:14
S., my tongue FORT 330:3
S. no sad songs ROSS 655:16
s. nothing that is not attested CALL 186:4
s. praises unto his name BOOK 138:11
s. the ancient ways YEAT 855:24
s. the body electric WHIT 833:3
s. the Lord's song BOOK 143:13
s. the old songs CLAR 224:20
s. the sofa COWP 247:23
S. thou the songs of love GURN 366:4
s. to the harp BOOK 140:14
S. unto the Lord BOOK 135:22
s. unto the Lord BOOK 140:13
S. we merrily BOOK 139:13
S. whatever is well made YEAT 856:3
skilled to s. of time TENN 782:10
Soul clap its hands and s. YEAT 855:9
souls can s. openly SPEN 750:15
think that they will s. to me ELIO 302:20
thousand tongues to s. WESL 828:25
Who would not s. for Lycidas MILT 529:30
world in ev'ry corner s. HERB 383:20
singe it do s. yourself SHAK 695:5
S. my white head SHAK 700:15
singeing s. of the King of Spain's Beard
DRAK 285:16
singer sans s., and—sans End FITZ 323:5
s. not the song BORR 146:18
s. of an empty day MORR 549:13
S. of sweet Colonus ARNO 28:29
singers well-known s. REED 644:8
singing angels all were s. BYRO 183:15
exercise of s. BYRD 177:15
have a s. face FLET 327:10
hear mermaids s. DONN 281:9
like a s. bird ROSS 655:6
listen to money s. LARK 468:20
Lorca was killed, s. READ 643:3
nest of s. birds JOHN 427:7
once went s. southward CHES 216:6
s. in the wilderness FITZ 323:2
s. masons building SHAK 692:29
s. of birds BIBL 87:6
s. of foolish and bawdy healths TURN 802:19
S. so rarely SCOT 674:12
s. still dost soar SHEL 731:26
s. to the praise AUGU 37:19
s. will never be done SASS 667:21
six little s.-boys BARH 55:15
suddenly burst out s. SASS 667:20
waves of thy sweet s. SHEL 731:7
single but a s. thought CLOS 228:24
come not s. spies SHAK 688:9
dies, in s. blessedness SHAK 710:16
he who continued s. GOLD 355:28
married to a s. life CRAS 250:15
Nothing in the world is s. SHEL 730:2
s. completed action BOIL 125:14
s. in the field WORD 850:8
s. life doth well BACO 44:31
s. man in possession AUST 39:18
s. man in possession OPEN 574:22
s. soul to perish TALM 771:21
S. women AUST 40:19
with a s. hair DRYD 289:33
single-handedly perhaps be won s.
LULA 496:5
singly Misfortunes never come s.
PROV 626:25
sings fat lady s. SAYI 670:10
instead of bleeding, he s. GARD 339:13
s. each song twice over BROW 159:18
S. for his supper NURS 568:5
S. in the palm STEV 758:2
song my paddle s. JOHN 423:18
tell me what she s. WORD 850:9
why the caged bird s. DUNB 291:15
singular s. genius DIDE 274:3
s. in each particular SHAK 722:7
singularity S. is a clue DOYL 284:9
sinister strange and s. JAME 418:4
sink Little leaks s. the ship PROV 625:27

Not gross to s. SHAK 724:2
S. me the ship, Master Gunner TENN 784:2
sitting in the kitchen s. OPEN 574:29
sinking like a s. ship WOOL 845:14
that s. feeling ADVE 7:11
towards a s. ship CHUR 222:22
Sinn *Das kommt mir nicht aus dem S.*
HEIN 379:15
sinned all have s. BIBL 106:5
More s. against than sinning SHAK 700:19
people s. against COMP 237:1
s. against heaven BIBL 101:16
s. exceedingly MISS 536:14
sinner Be a s. LUTH 496:7
confessions of a justified s. HOGG 392:10
dead s. BIER 116:9
greater the s. PROV 621:16
Love the s. AUGU 37:16
Or I of her a s. CONG 239:21
poor s., lov'st thou me COWP 246:26
s. is at the heart PÉGU 591:7
s. that repenteth BIBL 101:13
to me a s. BIBL 101:28
who is that young s. HOUS 403:19
sinners early to catch any s. RUNY 659:1
favoured s. slain WESL 829:9
God and s. reconciled WESL 828:23
in the way of s. BOOK 133:19
miserable s. BOOK 129:3
publicans and s. BIBL 96:5
S.; of whom I am chief BIBL 110:21
s. to repentance BIBL 96:7
s.' ways prosper HOPK 397:8
sinneth s. before his Maker BIBL 93:27
sinning in good shape for more s. RUNY 659:1
More sinned against than s. SHAK 700:19
Sinns S. won in three years HEAL 377:14
sins Be all my s. remembered SHAK 686:13
chain of our s. BOOK 129:16
Compound for s. BUTL 176:5
covers a multitude of s. PROV 616:34
free from the bondage of s. BHAG 74:18
half the s. of mankind RUSS 660:15
Her s. are forgiven BIBL 100:17
His s. were scarlet BELL 65:21
manifold s. and wickedness BOOK 127:13
multitude of s. BIBL 112:14
not the s. of the fathers FREN 333:12
oldest s. SHAK 692:18
Old s. cast long shadows PROV 628:21
O remember not the s. BOOK 135:8
premeditated s. TALM 772:16
purged our s. BIBL 111:3
root of all s. JAME 416:24
set our s. from us BOOK 141:3
s. are attempts to fill WEIL 826:20
s. be as scarlet BIBL 88:1
s. of despair READ 643:5
s. of the fathers BOOK 131:7
s. or complaints TRAH 797:13
thinkin' on their s. BURN 171:9
two cardinal human s. KAFK 440:17
ways of committing s. JAIN 416:17
who s. most SHAK 708:3
sint S. *ut sunt* CLEM 226:14
Sion captivity of S. BOOK 142:23
gracious unto S. BOOK 137:15
praised in S. BOOK 138:5
praise to Mount S. BUNY 164:14
remembered thee, O S. BOOK 143:12
Walk about S. BOOK 137:6
sir S.-come-spy-see BARH 55:12
sire S. of an immortal strain SHEL 728:14
Still from the s. SCOT 674:1
sirens Blest pair of S. MILT 528:15
Sirmio S., bright eye CATU 202:16
Sisera fought against S. BIBL 79:18
sissy rose-red s. PLOM 598:12
sister done to our fair s. MORR 550:7
Had it been his s. EPIT 310:2
live a barren s. SHAK 710:15
my s. hath left me BIBL 100:26
my s., my spouse BIBL 87:12

no friend like a s. ROSS 655:8
Our sometime s. SHAK 683:21
s. and my sister's child COWP 246:19
s. throw up a lot WALK 817:8
s., thy first-begotten SWIN 769:2
trying to violate your s. STRA 762:3
sisterhood S. is powerful MORG 549:2
sisterly s. animosity SURT 764:22
sisters And so do his s. GILB 348:21
harmonious s. MILT 528:15
s. under their skins KIPL 454:18
twa s. sat in a bour BALL 51:15
weird s. SHAK 703:7
Sistine on the S. Chapel roof YEAT 856:2
Sisyphus imagine that S. is happy
CAMU 188:15
like the torture of S. DE B 260:14
S., proletarian CAMU 188:13
sit let us s. upon the ground SHAK 715:23
practically s. on it BISH 117:9
s. down on my botom FLEM 326:18
s. for a picture JOHN 431:16
S. thou on my right hand BOOK 141:20
So I did s. and eat HERB 384:14
Teach us to s. still ELIO 301:2
Though I s. down now DISR 275:4
sits I s. and thinks PUNC 637:26
Where MacGregor s. PROV 634:40
sitteth s. on the right hand of God
BOOK 128:10
sitting A-s. on a gate CARR 195:26
cheap s. as standing PROV 623:39
find Thee s. careless KEAT 445:15
s. comfortably CATC 200:4
s. in the kitchen sink OPEN 574:29
stay s. down CART 197:10
situation s. excellent FOCH 327:22
six on s. and sevene CHAU 213:10
Rode the s. hundred TENN 776:13
S. days shalt thou labour BIBL 78:3
s. honest serving-men KIPL 456:18
S. hundred threescore and six BIBL 113:31
S. is the number of perfection AUGU 36:23
s. little Singing-boys BARH 55:15
snowed for s. days THOM 790:1
sixpence bang—went s. PUNC 637:11
could have saved s. BECK 61:2
Finds s. in her shoe CORB 243:1
Nothing about s. BEVA 73:20
precious little for s. PUNC 637:13
Sing a song of s. NURS 569:14
s. given as change NESB 559:11
Whoso has s. CARL 192:25
sixpences two-and-forty s. JOHN 433:10
sixty past S. it's the young AUDE 36:6
rate of s. minutes an hour LEWI 483:6
When I'm s. four LENN 480:22
sixty-two in s. TAGL 771:14
size One s. does not fit all PROV 628:48
sizzling advertiser's 's.' PRIE 611:11
skate I s. to where GRET 363:16
skating S. across still water BLY 124:12
s. over thin ice EMER 307:3
skeletons s. copulating BEEC 62:10
ski still want to s. GREE 362:20
Skiddaw S. saw the fire MACA 499:3
skies born under other s. LE C 478:12
danced the s. MAGE 505:16
man whose god is in the s. SHAW 726:24
paint the sable s. DRUM 286:12
soaring claim the s. FRER 333:18
thou climb'st the s. SIDN 736:4
virgin-daughter of the s. DRYD 289:26
watcher of the s. KEAT 445:6
skill Short Time and Little S. HARI 373:13
S. comes so slow DAVI 258:7
skilled S. or unskilled HORA 399:19
skimming S. our gable HEAN 377:15
skin ask the Gods for a thick s. TROL 800:2
beauty being only s.-deep KERR 450:3
Beauty only s. deep PROV 615:5

sons of Edward s. — SHAK 717:1
such as s. o' nights — SHAK 696:12
suffer nobody to s. — ADDI 4:26
take their ease And s. — SHAK 695:26
that sweet s. — SHAK 714:1
Through s. and darkness — KEBL 447:12
time enough to s. — HOUS 404:8
time when first s. begins — VIRG 811:15
To die: to s. — SHAK 686:9
two gates of S. — VIRG 812:17
uninvaded s. — TENN 780:1
We shall not all s. — BIBL 108:11
We shall not s. — MCCR 500:18
We term s. a death — BROW 157:11
when you s. your remind me — SASS 667:19
will not s. — BOOK 142:16
sleeper never a quiet s. — TENN 782:4
sleepers seven s. den — DONN 280:26
s. in that quiet earth — CLOS 228:16
sleepeth not dead, but s. — RIRI 96:10
peradventure he s. — BIBL 81:22
sleeping art thou s. there below — NEWB 560:2
awakened a s. giant — FILM 319:12
cursed him in s. — BARH 55:16
fuss about s. together — WAUG 824:17
Lay your s. head — AUDE 35:11
Lest he find you s. — BIBL 99:28
Let s. dogs lie — PROV 625:6
like a S. Princess — LAWR 475:13
s. and the dead — SHAK 705:2
s., by a brother's hand — SHAK 685:5
s. hound to wake — CHAU 213:4
s. pill is white — SEXT 677:15
s. with an elephant — TRUD 801:2
smitten a s. enemy — YAMA 853:1
waking s. — MONT 544:18
sleepless S. as the river — CRAN 250:2
s. soul that perished — WORD 849:20
s. with cold commemorative — ROSS 656:6
sleeps Homer sometimes s. — BYRO 181:10
it s. obedience — PAIN 582:21
Now s. the crimson petal — TENN 783:12
wakes or s. — SHEL 728:21
while the world s. — NEHR 558:3
sleepwalker assurance of a s. — HITL 390:1
sleepy Contentment is a s. thing — TRAH 798:1
I'm not s. — DYLA 294:12
sleeve Ash on an old man's s. — ELIO 302:2
heart upon my s. — SHAK 712:35
lacy s. with vitriol — WOOL 845:15
no further than your s. — PROV 631:28
sleeves Americanism with its s. rolled — MCCA 500:6
language that rolls up its s. — SAND 666:3
Tie up my s. — HUNT 410:10
sleight perceive a juggler's s. — BUTL 176:15
slenderly s. known himself — SHAK 699:23
slepen s. al the nyght with open ye — CHAU 210:5
slept first fruits of them that s. — BIBL 108:4
he thought I s. — PATM 588:15
His saints s. — ANON 22:11
I should have s. — BIBL 82:32
s. with his fathers — BIBL 81:18
Whilst Adam s. — ANON 20:2
slew as he was ambitious, I s. him — SHAK 697:19
dead which he s. at his death — BIBL 79:36
s. his master — BIBL 82:14
s. mighty kings — BOOK 143:10
s. the slayer — MACA 499:9
slice S. him where you like — WODE 842:19
s. off a cut loaf — PROV 630:44
slight s. all that do — FARQ 315:16
slime daubed it with s. — BIBL 77:13
slimy hot s. channel — CRAB 248:31
s. things did crawl — COLE 232:20
thousand s. things — COLE 233:2
slings s. and arrows — SHAK 686:9
slip catch no s. by the way — BUNY 164:15
enemies that s. for ever — STER 756:18
gave us all the s. — BROW 161:27
many a s. 'twixt cup — PROV 632:28

set one s. of them — SHAK 722:3
s., slide, perish — ELIO 301:13
S., slop, slap — OFFI 572:11
slipper Old Mother S. Slopper — NURS 568:15
s. and subtle knave — SHAK 713:20
slippered lean and s. pantaloon — SHAK 681:12
slippers in his golden s. — BUNY 164:20
pair of s., sir — BROW 157:16
slippery standing is s. — BACO 44:23
slipping tail lights s. — CRAN 250:1
slit S. your girl's — KING 453:4
slits s. the thin-spun life — MILT 530:3
slitty all be s.-eyed — PHIL 594:11
sliver envious s. broke — SHAK 688:19
Sloane S. turned secular saint — BURC 165:13
sloe blacker than the s. — CARB 190:3
slogans instead of principles, s. — BENT 68:18
slogged s. up to Arras — SASS 667:22
slop coffee and other s.-kettle — COBB 229:16
Slip, s., slap — OFFI 572:11
woman with a s.-pail — HOPK 397:15
slopes butler's upper s. — WODE 843:5
sloth my own amazing s. — BISH 117:10
peaceful s., Not peace — MILT 532:2
Shake off dull s. — KEN 448:5
time in studies is s. — BACO 45:17
slouches S. towards Bethlehem — YEAT 855:13
slough friendly bombs, fall on S. — BETJ 72:17
s. was Despond — BUNY 164:13
slovenliness Peace nothing but s. — BREC 150:7
S. is no part of religion — WESL 829:13
slow come he s. — SCOT 673:17
comes ever s. — DRAY 285:20
S. and steady wins the race — PROV 630:45
S. but sure — PROV 630:46
s. of speech — BIBL 77:22
s. to anger — BIBL 84:27
s. to speak — BIBL 111:21
telling you to s. down — ANON 15:16
telling you to s. down — SAYI 669:11
Time is too s. — VAN 806:21
slower had to be s. — FRAS 333:4
slowly angel to pass, flying s. — FIRB 321:10
Architecture acts the most s. — DIMN 274:14
Make haste s. — AUGU 37:21
Make haste s. — PROV 625:50
mills of God grind s. — LONG 490:23
mills of God grind s. — PROV 626:23
Run s. — OVID 579:18
Science moves, but s. — TENN 780:21
twist s. in the wind — EHRL 297:8
slugabed Get up, sweet S. — HERR 385:19
sluggard foul s.'s comfort — CARL 191:14
s. is wiser — BIBL 85:11
thou s. — BIBL 84:1
voice of the s. — WATT 823:12
slughorn Dauntless the s. — BROW 159:2
sluices Close the s. — VIRG 814:1
sluicing browsing and s. — WODE 843:4
slum seen one city s. — AGNE 8:29
slumber little s. — BIBL 84:2
neither s. nor sleep — BOOK 142:16
s. did my spirit steal — WORD 850:6
s. is more sweet than toil — TENN 781:10
S.'s chain has bound me — MOOR 547:22
to soothing s. seven — JONE 434:11
slumbered you have but s. here — SHAK 712:8
slumbers Golden s. kiss your eyes — DEKK 262:18
has thou golden s. — DEKK 262:17
slums gay intimacy of the s. — WAUG 824:6
slurp s. into the barrels — FISH 322:17
slush pure as the driven s. — BANK 54:15
slut I am not a s. — SHAK 681:24
sluts foul s. in dairies — CORB 242:18
sly s. shade of a Rural Dean — BROO 153:10
small Better are s. fish — PROV 615:20
between the s. and great — COWP 248:21
big squadrons against the s. — BUSS 175:9
both great and s. — COLE 233:10
commonly thought s. — WOOL 845:4
day of s. nations — CHAM 206:8
grind exceeding s. — LONG 490:23

how s. the world is — GROS 365:4
In s. proportions — JONS 435:27
Microbe is so very s. — BELL 65:14
pictures that got s. — FILM 321:6
s., but perfectly formed — COOP 242:11
s. college — WEBS 825:9
S. is beautiful — SCHU 671:20
s. Latin — JONS 436:2
s. packages — PROV 615:14
S. sorrows speak — SENE 677:1
s. states—Israel, Athens — INGE 413:9
s.-talking world — FRY 336:14
s. things with great — VIRG 815:4
so s. a thing — ARNO 27:7
speaks s. like a woman — SHAK 710:10
Speech is the s. change — MERE 522:17
still s. voice — BIBL 81:27
that cannot reach the s. — SPEN 752:4
they are very s. — UPDI 805:22
Too s. to live in — ANON 19:14
Town s.-talk flows — CRAB 248:29
with s. men no great thing — MILL 525:11
smaller s. fleas to bite 'em — SWIF 767:11
s. than smallest atom — UPAN 805:9
smallest s. amount of lying — BUTL 176:25
s. room of my house — REGE 644:14
smaragdine green ribbons s. — TAYL 774:19
smart girls that are so s. — CARE 191:8
love and all its s. — BEDD 62:1
scorn which mocked the s. — ARNO 28:21
s. for it — BIBL 84:10
smash all s. and no grab — NICO 563:14
English never s. in a face — HALS 369:17
smashed s. it into because — CUMM 253:13
s. up things and creatures — FITZ 324:6
smatch some s. of honour — SHAK 698:28
smattering s. of everything — DICK 272:12
smell ancient and fish-like s. — SHAK 718:30
I s. the blood — SHAK 701:2
Money has no s. — PROV 626:30
Money has no s. — VESP 809:6
shares man's s. — HOPK 396:12
s. and hideous hum — GODL 351:19
s. a rat — ROCH 651:3
s. of napalm in the morning — FILM 319:18
s. too strong — STER 756:22
sweet keen s. — ROSS 656:8
Sweet s. of success — FILM 322:13
to his own sense doth s. — MONT 544:19
smelleth s. the battle afar off — BIBL 83:25
smells it s. to heaven — SHAK 687:15
s. like roses — JOHN 423:15
s. of mortality — SHAK 701:15
smile Asians could still s. — HEAD 377:8
call me that, s. — WIST 842:3
Cambridge people rarely s. — BROO 153:12
enchain him with a s. — CARY 197:12
has a nice s. — GROM 365:1
hear a s. — CROS 252:15
Is it Colman's s. — EWAR 313:7
kind of sickly s. — HART 374:17
murder whiles I s. — SHAK 694:18
my Julia's lips do s. — HERR 385:18
one livid s. — WALP 820:1
prison and a s. — WOTT 851:6
riding on a s. and a shoeshine — MILL 527:6
s., and be a villain — SHAK 685:7
S. at us, pay us — CHES 216:12
s. dwells a little longer — CHAP 208:7
s. his face — SHAK 721:7
s. his work to see — BLAK 122:21
s. of accomplishment — PLAT 596:22
s. of cosmic Cheshire cat — HUXL 411:12
s. of fate — DYER 293:14
s. on the face of the tiger — ANON 18:15
s., smile, smile — MILI 526:18
s. with the simple — GARR 340:1
s. with the wise — JOHN 429:3
tribute of a s. — CLOS 228:10
vain tribute of a s. — SCOT 673:9
why, we shall s. — SHAK 698:23
your mother with a s. — VIRG 814:3
smiled only the dead s. — AKHM 9:8

smiled (*cont.*):
Voltaire s. — HUGO 408:2
smiler s. with the knyf — CHAU 211:15
smiles charmed it with s. — CARR 196:11
daggers in men's s. — SHAK 705:14
greeted with s. — BROO 154:2
making practised s. — SHAK 721:25
robbed that s. — SHAK 713:13
smilest Thou s. and art still — ARNO 28:12
smiling hides a s. face — COWP 246:25
S. at grief — SHAK 720:29
s., damnèd villain — SHAK 685:7
s., destructive man — LEE 478:21
s. of Fortune — COCK 229:20
s. surface of the sea — PLUT 598:16
S. through her tears — HOME 394:5
S. wonder of a day — WRIG 851:16
smilingness Despair a s. assume — BYRO 178:18
smirk serious and the s. — DICK 270:20
smite ready to s. once — MILT 530:7
s. all the firstborn — BIBL 77:31
s. thee on thy right cheek — BIBL 94:29
without hands to s. — SWIN 768:4
smiteth to him that s. him — BIBL 91:10
smith by naming him S. — HOLM 393:3
Chuck it, S. — CHES 215:19
s., a mighty man is he — LONG 491:8
s. of his own fortune — CLAU 225:12
Smithfield Canterbury or S. — WALP 819:24
smithy village is stands — LONG 491:8
smitten bones are s. asunder — BOOK 136:14
s. a sleeping enemy — YAMA 853:1
smock nearer is my s. — PROV 627:10
smoke between clothes and s. — NERU 559:2
can't see their s. — FLEI 326:8
from the s. into the smother — SHAK 680:22
Gossip is a sort of s. — ELIO 299:10
her beloved s. — LAMB 465:4
hills, they shall s. — BOOK 141:11
idle s. of praise — DANI 255:8
light after s. — HORA 398:9
little s., in pallid moonshine — KEAT 442:19
No s. without fire — PROV 628:3
rise then as s. to the sky — CELA 205:2
s. and stir of this dim spot — MILT 528:17
s. and wealth — HORA 402:1
s.-filled room — SIMP 738:10
S. gets in your eyes — HARB 389:10
s. of their torment — BIBL 114:3
s. rises already — VIRG 813:16
Stygian s. — JAME 417:1
smoked s. salmon and tinned — WILS 840:11
smokeless in the s. air — WORD 846:6
smoking not found any s. guns — BLIX 123:11
S. can seriously damage — OFFI 572:12
s. flax — BIBL 89:22
smoky burnt-out ends of s. days — ELIO 302:28
smooth I am a s. man — BIBL 76:27
never did run s. — PROV 617:13
never did run s. — SHAK 710:17
s. the ice — SHAK 699:10
smoother s. than oil — BIBL 83:38
s. than oil — BOOK 137:18
smote Israel s. him — BIBL 78:18
s. divers nations — BOOK 143:10
s. him thus — SHAK 715:1
s. the king of Israel — BIBL 81:34
s. them hip and thigh — BIBL 79:31
smother from the smoke into the s. — SHAK 680:22
smudge wears man's s. — HOPK 396:12
smug s. minority — BERT 71:19
smut S. detected in it — ZOLA 859:6
snail creeping like s. — SHAK 681:10
said a whiting to a s. — CARR 194:17
seeing the s. — DONN 281:21
s.'s on the thorn — BROW 160:22
snails like s. after a rainstorm — VERG 808:11
snake doth like a s. renew — SHEL 729:11
like a wounded s. — POPE 604:8
move about like a s. — HELL 380:11
scotched the s. — SHAK 705:20
s. came to my water-trough — LAWR 475:7

s. hidden in the grass — VIRG 813:22
s. throws her enamelled skin — SHAK 711:5
snakes no s. to be met with — JOHN 431:3
S. eat Frogs — STEV 757:23
You spotted s. — SHAK 711:6
snakeskin s.-titles — BENÉ 66:11
snapper s.-up of unconsidered trifles — SHAK 721:34
snare mockery, and a s. — DENM 264:8
rabbit in a s. — STEP 756:4
s. of the fowler — BOOK 142:21
s. of the hunter — BOOK 140:2
world's great s. — SHAK 679:19
snares rain s. — BOOK 134:8
s. of death — BOOK 142:5
snaring s. the poor world — CRAN 249:27
Snark S. *was* a Boojum — CARR 196:12
snatch Shrewd was that s. — BROW 158:19
s. Bookie Bob — RUNY 658:17
s. me away — FROS 335:8
snatched s. from Jove — MANI 510:4
s. the lightning — TURG 802:13
snatching s. his victuals from the table — CHUR 221:3
sneaky snouty, s. mind — NICO 563:12
sneer devil in his s. — BYRO 179:23
refute a s. — PALE 583:5
teach the rest to s. — POPE 602:29
They s. at me — FITZ 323:12
with solemn s. — BYRO 179:1
sneering I was born s. — GILB 347:20
sneezed not to be s. at — SCOT 674:30
sneezes beat him when he s. — CARR 194:7
Coughs and s. — OFFI 572:3
sneezing people s. — ROBI 650:21
snicker hold my coat, and s. — ELIO 302:17
vorpal blade went s.-snack — CARR 194:26
snip S.! Snap! Snip — HOFF 391:18
snipe so wet you could shoot s. off him — POWE 609:15
snob admires mean things is a S. — THAC 786:4
snobbery bereaved if s. died — USTI 806:6
S. with Violence — BENN 67:13
snobbish s. and vulgar — VICT 809:13
snoring s., she disturbs — COWP 247:25
snorted not one s. — HUGH 407:7
Or s. we — DONN 280:26
snotgreen s. sea — JOYC 437:14
snout had as wise a s. on — FERG 316:19
in a swine's s. — BIBL 84:11
snouty s., sneaky mind — NICO 563:12
snow amid the winter's s. — CASW 199:5
architecture of the s. — EMER 306:15
as white as s. — BIBL 112:29
bloodless lay the untrodden s. — CAMP 187:11
chaste as unsunned s. — SHAK 683:1
congealed s. — PARK 586:9
dark over the s. — THOM 790:16
few acres of s. — VOLT 815:10
first fall of s. — PRIE 610:18
geese, like a s. cloud — RANS 642:6
giveth s. like wool — BOOK 144:5
Ice and s. — BOOK 128:6
I, this incessant s. — DE L 263:5
last long streak of s. — TENN 779:26
like the s. geese — OKPI 572:22
listens in the s. — STEV 758:7
little s.-white feet — YEAT 853:19
naked in December s. — SHAK 715:11
shivering in the s. — SOUT 749:19
skin was as white as s. — GRIM 364:13
s. and vapours — BOOK 144:6
s. before the summer sun — TECU 775:8
s. came flying — BRID 151:6
s. falling faintly — JOYC 436:21
s. flutters down — BLOK 123:14
s. in the mountains — OPEN 575:18
s. in winter — CAMP 187:1
s. of ferne yere — CHAU 213:12
S. on snow — ROSS 655:9
s. the leaves — HOUS 404:13
used to be S. White — WEST 830:8
we shall have s. — NURS 568:12

white as s. — BIBL 88:1
whiter than s. — BOOK 137:12
wish a s. — SHAK 702:11
wondrous strange s. — SHAK 711:30
wrapped in wild s. — BLOK 123:16
snowed s. for six days — THOM 790:1
snowflake crown of s. pearls — BLOK 123:16
snowflakes s. hurry — PUSH 638:1
snows our Lady of the S. — KIPL 455:7
s. have fled — HORA 402:11
s. of yesteryear — VILL 810:12
snowy S., Flowy, Blowy — ELLI 306:1
snuff only took s. — GOLD 355:9
You abuse s. — COLE 234:1
s. out by an article — BYRO 181:27
snuffed s. out by an article — BYRO 181:27
snug s. As a bug In a rug — EPIT 310:8
s. little Island — DIBD 267:10
so And s. do I — HARD 373:4
if it was s., it might be — CARR 195:5
soak expect a s. — PROV 634:32
soaked s. to the skin — COHE 230:12
soap of blood and s. — MITC 540:7
smiles and s. — CARR 196:11
S. and education — TWAI 803:7
S. operas sell — MCEL 501:13
What! no s. — FOOT 328:6
soapflakes sell Jack like s. — KENN 449:8
soar creep as well as s. — BURK 168:1
not to s. — MACA 498:24
Two of the wise who s. — WORD 850:17
soaring s. ever singest — SHEL 731:26
soars s. to match the sky — PROC 612:15
sobbing a-sighing and a-s. — NURS 570:16
sober at least not s. — JOHN 427:1
Be s., be vigilant — BIBL 112:15
compulsorily s. — MAGE 506:2
godly, righteous, and s. life — BOOK 127:17
go to bed s. — FLET 327:2
s. me up — FITZ 324:4
S., steadfast, and demure — MILT 529:10
To-morrow we'll be s. — SONG 747:2
to Philip s. — ANON 15:4
Wordsworth drunk and Porson s. — HOUS 405:6
sobs drawn-out s. — VERL 808:16
social judge at once of the s. position — TOCQ 795:13
no religion but s. — WESL 829:11
self-love and s. — POPE 605:7
s. and economic experiment — HOOV 395:21
s. contract — ROUS 657:3
S. Contract is nothing more — WELL 828:12
s. progress, order, security — JOHN 422:4
socialism Democracy and s. are means — NEHR 558:6
religion of S. — BEVA 73:10
S. can only arrive — VIER 810:4
S. does not mean — ORWE 577:24
s. would not lose its human face — DUBČ 290:16
socialist be a s. at twenty — SAYI 670:9
build a s. society — NYER 570:19
high-water mark of S. literature — ORWE 577:25
signposts to s. Utopia — CROS 252:10
socialists s. throw it away — CAST 199:2
We are all s. now — HARC 371:6
society action of s. upon itself — TOCQ 795:11
affluent s. — GALB 338:1
bonds of civil s. — LOCK 488:19
capital of polished s. — BURK 167:23
consolidates s. — JOHN 427:5
desperate oddfellow s. — THOR 793:10
Great S. — JOHN 423:12
happiness of s. — ADAM 3:7
influence in s. — LACL 463:4
in one s. — WORD 849:8
live in s. — ARIS 25:26
Man was formed for s. — BLAC 118:8
moves about in s. — CHOI 218:7
no letters; no s. — HOBB 390:16
no such thing as S. — THAT 787:11
One great s. — WORD 849:17

selects her own S. DICK 273:6
shape of s. ORWE 577:8
so-called affluent s. BEVA 73:17
S. became my glittering bride WORD 846:16
s. distributes itself ARNO 29:7
s. founded on trash SAYE 668:4
S. is built on MAIL 507:12
S. is indeed a contract BURK 167:22
S. is now one polished horde BYRO 181:33
s. is wonderfully delightful WILD 836:25
S. needs to condemn MAJO 508:4
s. of privacy RAND 642:1
s. where it is safe to be STEV 758:15
s., with all its combinations BURK 167:11
s. would be a hell upon earth MILL 525:15
three for s. THOR 793:11
unfit a man for s. CHAM 207:2
sock hole in a s. EINS 298:12
Jonson's learnèd s. MILT 529:27
socket Burn to the s. WORD 846:14
sockets candles burn the s. HOUS 403:23
s. of fine gold BIBL 87:16
socks inability to put on your s. GONC 356:9
Socrates contradict S. SOCR 745:10
S., I shall not accuse you PLAT 597:9
Socratic S. manner is not a game BEER 63:7
sod under my head a s. BALL 52:2
withered in the s. BRON 152:15
soda Sermons and s.-water BYRO 180:21
wash their feet in s. water ELIO 303:17
sodden s. and unkind BELL 65:24
sodium discovered S. BENT 68:14
Sodom S. and Gomorrah BIBL 92:7
sodomy rum, s., prayers, and the lash CHUR 222:1
sods s. with our bayonets turning WOLF 843:11
sofa accomplished s. last COWP 247:24
Alternately on a S. AUST 38:25
sing the s. COWP 247:23
s. upholstered in panther skin PLOM 598:11
under the s. HOLU 393:13
soft does not make us s. PERI 592:21
her s. and chilly nest KEAT 442:22
Ovid, the s. philosopher DRYD 288:18
s. and narrow BALL 51:13
s. answer BIBL 84:22
s. answer turneth PROV 631:1
s. as the dawn CART 198:4
s. as the dawn LOVE 493:13
s. can wear away the hard TALM 772:31
s. phrase of peace SHAK 713:6
s. under-belly of Europe MISQ 538:17
s., unhappy sex BEHN 64:6
s. was the sun LANG 466:14
turf that covers her s. bones MART 514:20
softer s. than butter BOOK 137:18
softest s. thing about him RUNY 658:17
softly Fair and s. PROV 619:38
go s. all my years BIBL 89:14
S. along the road DE L 263:6
s. and suddenly vanish CARR 196:10
S. come and softly go ORRE 576:12
Softly, s., catchee PROV 631:3
s. tread, said Christabel COLE 231:5
Tread s. YEAT 854:11
softness For s. she MILT 532:30
s. of my body will be guarded LOWE 493:17
whisper s. in chambers MILT 535:18
soggy s. little island UPDI 805:16
soil fertile s. BACO 47:2
Freedom's s. beneath our feet DRAK 285:19
grows in every s. BURK 166:29
powers of the s. RICA 646:17
regarding the s. as property THOR 793:7
s. Is bare now HOPK 396:12
s. which is soon exhausted REYN 646:6
tied to the s. HOME 394:16
sojourner discontented s. WORD 849:4
sojourners s., as were all our fathers BIBL 82:18
sol s. *et luna* AUGU 37:1
sold Never s. the truth TENN 782:18

ointment might have been s. BIBL 98:28
s. all that he had BIBL 97:6
s. his birthright BIBL 76:26
s. my reputation FITZ 323:15
what cannot be s.—liberty GRAT 359:16
soldier always tell an old s. SHAW 724:15
Ben Battle was a s. HOOD 394:25
British s. can stand up to SHAW 725:2
chocolate cream s. SHAW 724:16
death, who had the s. singled DOUG 283:18
Drinking is the s.'s pleasure DRYD 287:15
first duty of a s. PROV 620:10
For a s. I listed DIBD 267:6
German s. trying to violate STRA 762:3
go to your Gawd like a s. KIPL 456:8
great s.—of to-day BAGE 48:2
having been a s. JOHN 431:2
in the s. SHAK 708:2
iron-armed s. POLI 600:22
never expected a s. to think SHAW 724:28
s. a mere recreant SHAK 719:19
s. details his wounds PROP 612:21
s., Full of strange oaths SHAK 681:11
s. is better accommodated SHAK 692:6
s. is no more exempt STER 757:14
s. of the Great War EPIT 311:7
s. said isn't evidence PROV 634:13
S., Sailor NURS 570:8
S., scholar, horseman YEAT 854:14
s.'s life is terrible hard MILN 527:20
s.'s pole is fall'n SHAK 680:3
s.'s pride BROW 159:26
what the s. said DICK 272:8
soldiers believe the s. SALI 664:5
gives England her s. MERE 522:12
like s. may not quit TENN 781:12
Old s. never die FOLE 327:24
Old s. never die PROV 628:22
Onward, Christian s. BARI 56:4
our s. slighted QUAR 638:16
scarlet s. AUDE 35:20
S. are citizens of death's grey land SASS 667:18
s., mostly fools BIER 116:6
S. of Christ, arise WESL 829:5
S. of the ploughshare RUSK 660:8
S., this solitude DE L 263:5
s. under me BIBL 95:28
steel my s.' hearts SHAK 693:20
ten thousand s. SHAK 717:8
With twenty-six lead s. ANON 20:13
young Argentinian s. RUNC 658:12
soldiery Emperor's drunken s. YEAT 853:8
licentious s. BURK 168:25
sole *amor che muove il* s. DANT 256:13
nothing can be s. or whole YEAT 853:16
s. of her foot BIBL 76:7
solecism without a s. BROW 156:25
soleil *J'ai vu le* s. *bas* RIMB 649:7
s. *d'Italie* BANV 54:9
solemn Sapping a s. creed BYRO 179:1
upon our s. feast-day BOOK 139:13
soles S. *effugere atque abire sentit* MART 514:19
soliciting still-s. eye SHAK 699:21
solicitor only go to his s. DISR 277:18
solid s. for fluidity CHUR 221:1
solidity appearance of s. to pure wind ORWE 578:4
solitariness s. of our work FRIN 334:18
solitary Be not s. CLOS 228:6
ennui of a s. existence BONA 126:18
How doth the city sit s. BIBL 91:6
how s. they be ASCH 31:3
s., be not idle JOHN 431:15
s. confinement inside our own skins WILL 839:8
s. Highland lass! WORD 850:8
tedium of s. duties GALB 338:6
Their s. way CLOS 228:23
Their s. way MILT 534:15
till I am s. JOHN 427:18
solitude bliss of s. WORD 847:6
delighted in s. BACO 44:13

each protects the s. RILK 649:3
feel his s. more keenly VALÉ 806:9
harmless s. MOLL 542:15
In s. What happiness MILT 533:24
one for s. THOR 793:11
seclusion and s. MONT 544:9
self-sufficing power of S. WORD 849:9
s. of the sea HARD 372:12
s. Through which we go DE L 263:5
solitudes Two s. BORR 146:19
two s. protect RILK 649:1
solitudinem S. *faciunt pacem* TACI 770:3
Solomon all S.'s wisdom BIBL 81:1
anointed S. BIBL 81:9
felicities of S. BACO 43:14
greater than S. BIBL 96:34
S. Grundy NURS 569:15
S., I have vanquished JUST 439:11
S. in all his glory BIBL 95:9
S. loved many strange women BIBL 81:14
S. wrote the Proverbs NAYL 557:23
soluble art of the s. MEDA 520:5
solution always a well-known s. MENC 521:20
can't see the s. CHES 217:6
conditions for its s. MARX 516:12
either part of the s. CLEA 226:8
final s. HEYD 387:14
heterosexual love no s. DURA 292:18
kind of s. CAVA 203:18
part of the s. SAYI 669:27
total s. GOER 352:10
solutus S. *omni faenore* HORA 400:1
solve I did not come to s. anything NERU 559:5
solventur S. *risu tabulae* HORA 403:12
some fool s. of the people LINC 485:16
S. mishtake, shurely CATC 201:26
somebody brisk little s. BROW 158:13
S. has been sitting in SOUT 749:15
When every one is s. GILB 347:8
someday S. I'll find you COWA 245:6
someone it was s. else ROGE 652:14
necessary to s. EMER 306:17
s., somewhere, may be happy MENC 521:16
S. wants a letter ADVE 8:14
something get s. for nothing PROV 636:1
is that s. itself BECK 61:10
say s. about me COHA 230:9
s. cannot become nothing BÜCH 163:5
s. completely different CATC 200:2
s. for Posterity ADDI 5:12
S. is better than PROV 631:6
S. must be done MISQ 538:18
s. of the night WIDD 834:12
S. should be done EDWA 296:11
s. to forgive LEWI 483:5
s. to say WHAT 831:7
Time for a little s. MILN 528:9
was there s. CATC 200:22
sometime see me s. MISQ 539:4
woman is a s. thing HEYW 387:17
sometimes s. always RICH 648:1
somewhat more than s. RUNY 658:16
s. against thee BIBL 113:1
somewhere get s. else CARR 195:2
S. over the rainbow HARB 371:4
son bear a s. BIBL 88:15
bear our s. KYD 462:10
be called thy s. BIBL 101:16
brought forth her firstborn s. BIBL 100:2
coming of the S. of Man BIBL 98:18
Epicurus owene s. CHAU 210:20
Fitzdotterel's eldest s. BROU 154:10
Forgive your s. JOYC 437:25
good idea—s. CATC 200:21
hateth his s. BIBL 84:18
his only begotten S. BIBL 102:32
if his s. ask bread BIBL 95:17
leichter of a fair s. ELIZ 304:3
Like father, like s. PROV 625:18
little s. into his bosom FLET 327:17
my s. was dead BIBL 101:18

son (cont.):
O Absalom, my s., my son BIBL 81:5
s. loves his sons TALM 772:25
s. of Adam PRIO 612:3
s. of his old age BIBL 76:37
S. of man BIBL 96:1
S. of Morn in weary Night's decline
BLAK 120:5
S. of Saint Louis FIRM 321:12
s. shall hear SCOT 674:1
s. till he gets him a wife PROV 627:6
s. was killed KIPL 454:3
Take now thy s. BIBL 76:21
This is my beloved S. BIBL 94:14
This is my s. TENN 784:17
unto us a s. is given BIBL 88:18
unto us by his S. BIBL 111:3
what's a s. KYD 462:9
wise s. BIBL 84:8
With a king's s. SURR 764:7
Woman, behold thy s. BIBL 96:1
younger s. gathered all together BIBL 101:14
your s.'s tender years JUVE 440:15
song all this for a s. CECI 204:15
ane end of ane old s. OGIL 571:15
Assist our s. GURN 366:3
auld Scotish s. BURN 170:18
becomes a sightless s. TENN 779:27
before his presence with a s. BOOK 140:17
beyond a s. or a billet ETHE 312:5
burthen of his s. BICK 115:22
carcase of an old s. THOM 791:3
frame my s. CHES 214:17
glorious s. of old SEAR 675:8
hate a s. that has sold BERL 70:1
let satire be my s. BYRO 182:8
listen to our s. HOME 394:17
low lone s. CARP 193:13
made my s. a coat YEAT 853:13
My s. is love unknown CROS 252:18
my s. would come OVID 580:20
old and antique s. SHAK 720:22
old s. of Percy and Douglas SIDN 736:18
On wings of s. HEIN 379:14
play a s. for me DYLA 294:12
region of my s. WORD 846:11
Sans wine, sans s. FITZ 323:5
sing the Lord's s. BOOK 143:13
sold my reputation for a s. FITZ 323:15
s. and a mistake OVID 580:18
s. charms the sense MILT 532:8
s. is ended BERL 69:21
S. made in lieu SPEN 751:10
s. my paddle sings JOHN 423:18
s. of praise be sung POTT 607:24
s. of songs BIBL 87:2
s. of the birds for mirth GURN 365:20
s. of the kingfisher VIRG 815:2
S. of the Shirt HOOD 395:11
s. that echoes cheerly TENN 780:7
s. that found a path KEAT 445:1
s. that never ends GOET 352:17
s. the Syrens sang BROW 156:12
s. was wordless SASS 667:21
spur me into s. YEAT 855:20
start a s. VIRG 814:5
suck melancholy out of a s. SHAK 681:4
sung as it were a new s. BIBL 114:1
sung a s. of death BLAK 121:24
swallow-flights of s. TENN 779:3
thinks two notes a s. DAVI 258:18
Thy speech, thy s. JAME 417:11
till I end my s. SPEN 752:16
Time is our tedious s. MILT 530:27
trouble with a folk s. LAMB 465:13
unto the Lord a new s. BOOK 135:22
unto the Lord a new s. BOOK 140:13
was the s. of love ROSS 656:1
what they teach in s. SHEL 729:18
wine and s. LUTH 496:15
with the breeze of s. TENN 779:27
songs all their s. are sad CHES 215:22
For ever piping s. KEAT 444:10

I have s. of my own VIRG 814:9
lean and flashy s. MILT 530:6
Sing no sad s. ROSS 655:16
sing the old s. CLAR 224:20
Sing thou the s. of love GURN 366:4
S. consecrate to truth SHEL 732:6
s. never heard HORA 401:9
s. of Apollo SHAK 702:27
s. of expectation BARI 56:5
s. of gladness, praise SIKH 737:3
s. of peaceful Zion DIX 278:13
s. of pleasant glee BLAK 121:26
s. of Spring KEAT 445:16
s. were Ave Marys CORB 243:2
sweetest s. are those SHEL 731:29
with a few good s. FAIT 314:6
sonitu putrem s. quatit ungula VIRG 813:5
sonnet Scorn not the S. WORD 849:26
S.'s scanty plot WORD 847:18
sonneteer starved hackney s. POPE 604:11
sonneter I shall turn s. SHAK 702:12
sonnets written s. all his life BYRO 180:28
sons Bears all its s. away WATT 823:20
Clergymen's s. always PROV 616:47
cruel s. of Cain LE G 479:6
God's s. are things MADD 505:9
in war fathers bury their s. HERO 385:10
My s. ought to study mathematics
ADAM 3:1
s. and daughters of Life GIBR 346:6
s. and daughters shall prophesy BIBL 92:3
s. Of Belial, flown with insolence
MILT 531:21
s. of God BIBL 76:5
s. of God shouted BIBL 83:22
S. of the dark and bloody ground
O'HA 572:17
s. of the morning HEBE 378:14
That our s. may grow up BOOK 143:23
soon short notice, s. past PROV 625:38
S. can mean in one second BÖLL 126:13
S., too soon SHEL 732:4
to Eve: Be s. THOM 791:9
sooner make an end the s. BACO 44:6
s. begun PROV 631:7
s. every party breaks up AUST 38:20
soot in s. I sleep BLAK 122:1
sophist neither saint nor s.-led ARNO 27:6
sophistication product of s. FLAU 325:4
sophistry incline wits to s. BACO 46:9
s. and illusion HUME 408:9
s., cleaves close COWP 247:12
s. I can control ASTE 32:10
soporific lettuce is 's.' POTT 608:3
sops s. in wine SPEN 752:18
Sorbonne one day at the S. STEV 758:1
sorcerers s., and whoremongers BIBL 114:24
Sordello but the one 'S.' POUN 608:15
sore bear with a s. head MARR 514:8
we are s. let BOOK 130:2
soreness leave a little s. LAYT 476:8
sores dogs licked his s. BIBL 101:22
sorriness s. underlying HARD 372:8
sorrow and the s. thereof MALO 508:20
any sorrow like unto my s. BIBL 91:7
ate his bread in s. GOET 353:11
bee of s. BABE 42:7
beguile thy s. SHAK 719:15
doubt and s. BARI 56:5
forgather wi' S. BURN 170:18
From my books surcease of s. POE 599:6
from s. to joy HAGG 367:4
Give s. words SHAK 706:23
glut thy s. KEAT 444:18
help you to s. PROV 622:20
How small and selfish is s. ELIZ 305:8
increaseth s. BIBL 85:30
In s. thou shalt bring forth BIBL 75:25
in trouble, s. BOOK 131:16
labour and s. BOOK 139:23
Labour without s. RUSK 659:26
Love's s. lasts all through life FLOR 327:20
more in s. than in anger SHAK 684:12

not be in s. too BLAK 122:8
not sure of s. SWIN 768:16
One for s. PROV 628:33
s. and sighing BIBL 89:12
S. and silence LONG 490:8
s. comes with years BROW 157:23
S. in all lands SUTT 765:1
S. is knowledge BYRO 182:20
S. is tranquillity remembered PARK 586:4
S. proud to be exalted ANON 17:1
s.'s crown of sorrow TENN 780:17
s. unforeseen PHIL 594:16
sphere of our s. SHEL 731:24
such sweet s. SHAK 717:29
thou climbing s. SHAK 700:9
water this s. SHAK 678:18
whipping S. driveth GREV 364:1
with s. to the grave BIBL 77:8
Write s. on the bosom SHAK 715:22
sorrowful heart is s. BIBL 84:19
He went away s. BIBL 97:26
way to the s. city DANT 255:13
sorrowing borrowing, goes a s. PROV 621:48
sorrows age, Disease, or s. CLOU 229:3
carried our s. BIBL 90:2
costly in our s. STER 756:13
Half the s. of women ELIO 299:14
man of s. BIBL 90:2
Small s. speak SENE 677:1
soothes his s. NEWT 563:6
s. are at an end GAY 341:9
s. of the mothers FREN 333:12
When s. come SHAK 688:9
sorry Better be safe than s. PROV 615:24
having to say you're s. TAGL 771:8
heartily s. BOOK 131:18
I'm s., now, I wrote it BURG 165:19
S. CAN'T COME TELE 776:11
S. for itself LAWR 475:5
that I shall be s. for SHAK 698:15
sortem nemo, quam sibi s. HORA 403:2
sortir l'en faire s. LOUI 492:12
sorts all s. and conditions BOOK 129:17
takes all s. PROV 624:24
Sosostris Madame S. ELIO 303:10
sot s. savant MOLI 541:20
soteriological In s. terms FENT 316:12
soufflé cannot reheat a s. MCCA 500:10
sought Being, of all, least s. for CRAN 250:3
Love s. is good SHAK 721:3
never s. in vain BURN 170:20
s. it with thimbles CARR 196:11
soul adventures of his s. FRAN 332:1
assault and hurt the s. BOOK 130:5
believes in s. JAIN 416:3
bitterness of his s. BIBL 93:7
bitterness of my s. BIBL 89:14
brother's s. BARB 55:5
Call to the s. VAUG 808:1
call upon my s. SHAK 720:13
Calm s. of all things ARNO 27:15
captain of my s. HENL 381:15
casket of my s. KEAT 445:13
city of the s. BYRO 179:7
composed in the s. ARNO 29:23
confident concerning his s. SOCR 745:8
dark night of the s. FITZ 324:7
dark night of the s. MISQ 537:13
delivered my s. BOOK 142:6
depth of your s. ROUS 657:5
eager s., biting for anger FULL 337:7
engineers of the s. GORK 357:3
equal to the s.'s desires WORD 846:17
essence of a human s. CARL 193:1
every subject's s. SHAK 693:16
eyes are window of s. PROV 619:34
FIAT in my s. BEDD 62:3
fine point of his s. KEAT 446:3
flow of s. POPE 605:26
fortitude the S. contains DICK 272:24
freed my s. BERN 70:14
from the s. itself COLE 231:10
give his own s. BOLT 126:16

God rest his s.	SMIT 743:3	s. shall be required of thee	BIBL 101:1	**soundest** old lovers are s.	WEBS 826:3

God rest his s. — SMIT 743:3
good for the s. — PROV 617:8
half conceal the S. within — TENN 778:23
Half my own s. — HORA 400:3
Heart and s. do sing — SIDN 736:13
Heaven take my s. — SHAK 699:13
hidden language of the s. — GRAH 358:9
hurl my s. from heaven — SHAK 714:27
hurt of my s. — BOOK 138:4
if I have a s. — ANON 18:4
if your s. were — BIBL 83:10
into my very s. — SHAK 687:24
iron entered into his s. — BOOK 141:12
lean over the s. we love — GIDE 346:13
leave my s. in hell — BOOK 134:15
lie in the s. — JOWE 436:18
life unto the bitter in s. — BIBL 82:34
lift my s. to heaven — SHAK 695:6
like an infant's s. — TRAH 797:10
like s., my soul — SHAK 683:10
longeth my s. after thee — BOOK 136:11
lose his own s. — BIBL 99:23
love in another's s. — LAYT 476:9
love of S. in the husband — UPAN 804:14
lover of my s. — WESL 828:26
Marlbro's mighty s. — ADDI 4:5
Medicine for the s. — ANON 17:15
mind and s., according — TENN 778:21
My s., bear thou thy part — GURN 366:4
My s. can reach — BROW 158:3
My s. fleeth — BOOK 143:7
My s. in agony — COLE 232:25
my s. is white — BLAK 122:6
My s., like to a ship — WEBS 826:14
My s., there is a country — VAUG 807:11
my unconquerable s. — HENL 381:14
No coward s. is mine — BRON 152:18
no s. to be damned — THUR 794:4
not engineers of the s. — KENN 449:6
One s. inhabiting two bodies — ARIS 26:7
owe my s. to the company store — TRAV 798:5
Perdition catch my s. — SHAK 713:25
perfection of your s. — SOCR 744:26
Poor intricated s. — DONN 282:12
Pray for the repose of His s. — ROLF 653:2
pray the Lord my s. to take — PRAY 611:5
progress of a deathless s. — DONN 280:6
prophetic s. — SHAK 723:18
purest s. — CARE 190:14
Refined himself to s. — DRYD 287:29
require his sheep's s. — RADE 640:11
retreat in his own s. — AURE 38:2
save his s. — BIBL 91:14
saves her s. — BROW 158:16
selling one's s. — MACK 502:17
sighed his s. — SHAK 709:35
sinews of the s. — FULL 337:5
s. above buttons — COLM 236:3
S. and body part — CRAS 250:18
s., a spirit — FAUL 316:4
S. clap its hands and sing — YEAT 855:9
s. doth magnify the Lord — BIBL 99:31
s. has to itself decreed — KEAT 445:10
s. he doth restore — SCOT 675:4
s. in bliss — SHAK 701:21
s. is an enchanted boat — SHEL 731:7
s. is Christ's abode — KEBL 447:11
s. is form — SPEN 752:11
s. is immortal — PLAT 597:17
s. is immortal — SOCR 745:7
s. is marching on — SONG 747:13
s. is placed in the body — DEFO 261:4
S., leaving the body — UPAN 804:17
s. of a man is born — JOYC 437:9
s. of fire — JOHN 426:17
s. of our dear brother — BOOK 133:18
s. of pleasure — BEHN 64:2
s. of Rabelais — COLE 234:6
S. of the Age — JONS 435:28
s. of the same stature — MONT 543:23
s. of the whole Past — CARL 192:13
s.'s dark cottage — WALL 818:9
S. selects her own — DICK 273:6

s. shall be required of thee — BIBL 101:1
S. shall have her earthly freight — WORD 848:9
s., sit thou — QUAR 638:19
s.'s reduced to a shuffled — NERU 559:2
s. swooned slowly — JOYC 436:21
S. that rises with us — WORD 848:5
s. that should not have been born — HOUS 404:19
S., the Inner Controller — UPAN 804:16
S., thou hast much goods — BIBL 100:32
s. to feel the flesh — BRON 152:19
s. undergoes some sort — SOCR 745:4
sweet and virtuous S. — HERB 385:5
Tell out my s. — BIBL 99:31
than that one s. — NEWM 560:17
That S. is not this — UPAN 804:18
this s. of mine — LITT 486:16
this s.'s second inn — DONN 280:8
through thy own s. — BIBL 100:8
to an immortal s. — VICT 809:10
try the s.'s strength — BROW 159:25
two to bear my s. away — PRAY 611:4
vale of s.-making — KEAT 446:20
wake the soul by tender strokes — POPE 606:2
war against the s. — BIBL 112:6
What s. was his — WORD 846:13
windows of the s. — BLAK 119:23
with all thy s. — BIBL 98:8
with a Russian s. — LERM 481:13
with s. so dead — SCOT 673:11
women have no s. — ASTE 32:10
soulless when work is s. — CAMU 189:2
souls Bishop of your s. — BIBL 112:9
bodies but not their s. — GIBR 346:6
common men have s. — TAWN 774:5
damp s. of housemaids — ELIO 302:21
engineers of human s. — STAL 754:2
letters mingle s. — DONN 281:20
movements of s. — VIRG 815:3
neglecting our s. — WULF 851:19
open windows into men's s. — ELIZ 304:16
Our s. exult — BLAK 120:15
our waking s. — DONN 281:1
play with s. — BROW 160:1
price of s. — JONS 435:11
pure lovers' s. descend — DONN 280:22
s. do couch on flowers — SHAK 679:24
s. mounting up to God — ROSS 655:22
S. of poets dead — KEAT 444:5
s. of the brave — CLOU 227:15
s. of the righteous — BIBL 92:3
s. out of men's bodies — SHAK 712:17
s. to each other draw — POPE 602:16
s. who dwell in night — BLAK 119:16
sucks two s. — DONN 280:23
they have no s. — COKE 230:20
times that try men's s. — PAIN 582:11
Two s. — CLOS 228:24
Two s. dwell — GOET 352:15
two virtuous s. — BYRO 181:19
sound alive with the s. of music — HAMM 370:8
all is not s. — JONS 435:4
all things that give s. — BAKE 50:3
commanded to be s. — GREV 364:2
deep s. strikes — BYRO 178:19
feeling, then, not s. — STEV 758:3
form of s. words — BIBL 110:29
from the tombs a doleful s. — WATT 823:16
in a s. body — JUVE 440:11
other half is not very s. — SMOL 744:15
s. and fury — SHAK 707:14
s. and rumour — MORR 549:12
s. is gone out into all lands — BOOK 134:20
s. me from my lowest note — SHAK 687:10
s. mind — BIBL 110:28
s. must seem an echo — POPE 604:9
s. of abundance — BIBL 81:23
s. of surprise — BALL 54:4
s. the back — SAUS 668:3
trumpet give an uncertain s. — BIBL 107:26
what is that s. — AUDE 35:20
soundbite s. all an interviewer — BENN 67:6
sound bites not a time for s. — BLAI 118:19

soundest old lovers are s. — WEBS 826:3
s. thing in England — DOYL 284:22
sounding s. through the town — BALL 51:17
sounds better than it s. — NYE 570:17
concord of sweet s. — SHAK 710:5
let the s. of music — SHAK 710:2
S. and sweet airs — SHAK 718:36
s. will take care — CARR 194:14
sweetest s. I'll ever hear — RODG 652:1
soup blossom s. — BASH 58:3
cake of portable s. — BOSW 146:23
I won't have any s. today — HOFF 391:14
licked the s. — BROW 160:20
S. of the evening — CARR 194:20
take s. at luncheon — CURZ 254:12
soupe Je vis de bonne s. — MOLI 541:18
sour How s. sweet music is — SHAK 716:15
need any s. grapes — AESO 6:14
s. grapes — BIBL 91:13
s. grapes and ashes — ASHF 31:16
s., sober beverage — BYRO 180:27
source rise above its s. — PROV 631:27
s. of little visible delight — BRON 152:21
sourest sweetest things turn s. — SHAK 723:15
south fickle is the S. — TENN 783:6
full of the warm S. — KEAT 444:22
go s. in the winter — ELIO 303:8
hills of the S. Country — BELL 65:23
hills of the S. Country — BELL 65:24
I want to go s. — LAWR 475:15
Lawn is full of s. — DICK 273:13
nor yet from the s. — BOOK 139:4
rivers in the s. — BOOK 142:24
S. is avenged — BOOT 144:22
s.-wind rushing warm — TENN 780:20
wrest from the S. — LEE 479:3
Yes, but not in the S. — POTT 608:9
southern bore me in the s. wild — BLAK 122:6
S. trees bear strange — ALLE 12:6
southward once went singing s. — CHES 216:6
souvenirs s. sont cors de chasse — APOL 23:9
sovereign change for a s. — NESB 559:11
civilities with my S. — JOHN 429:1
has sixpence is s. — CARL 192:25
Here lies our s. lord — EPIT 309:14
he will have no s. — COKE 230:21
S. has — BAGE 48:17
s. Nation — PAGE 581:14
s. oppresses his people — JOHN 429:17
s. or state — BACO 44:21
subject and a s. — CHAR 208:26
to be a S. — ELIZ 304:5
sovereignest s. that any man — SKEL 739:5
sovereigns name ourselves its s. — BYRO 182:21
what s. are doing — NAPO 556:14
sovereignties addition of s. — MONN 543:2
sovereignty s. is an artificial soul — HOBB 390:7
s. of nature — SHAK 682:22
sovereynetee Wommen desiren to have s. — CHAU 212:20
soviet Communism is S. power — LENI 480:7
S. Union has indeed — FULB 336:24
soviets All power to the S. — POLI 600:1
sow As you s., so you reap — PROV 614:40
hath he s. by the right ear — HENR 382:5
old s. that eats her farrow — JOYC 437:10
shall not s. — BIBL 86:22
silk purse out of s.'s ear — PROV 635:41
S. dry and set wet — PROV 631:24
s. in tears — BOOK 142:24
s. may whistle — PROV 631:10
S. returns to her Mire — KIPL 454:9
s. the wind — PROV 632:37
they s. not — BIBL 95:7
went forth to s. — BIBL 97:3
sower s. went forth — BIBL 97:3
soweth whatsoever a man s. — BIBL 109:2
sown poets that are s. — WORD 846:12
s. the wind — BIBL 91:28
where thou hast not s. — BIBL 98:22
Ye have s. much — BIBL 92:13
space art of how to waste s. — JOHN 423:20

space (*cont.*):

Brahman is s.	UPAN 805:2
cantos of unvanquished s.	CRAN 249:23
contingency for the s. shuttle	ANON 15:15
Filling a s.	O'KE 572:18
filling the s.	WEST 830:15
head outward into s.	EDDI 295:5
Here is my s.	SHAK 678:14
In s., no one can hear you	TAGL 771:5
king of infinite s.	SHAK 685:23
more s. where nobody is	STEI 755:8
silent too as s.	BYRO 182:6
S. is blue	HEIS 380:7
S. isn't remote	HOYL 406:8
s. of life between	KEAT 442:12
s. you leave behind	COOP 242:14
time and s.	LAMB 465:5
untrespassed sanctity of s.	MAGE 506:1

spaces empty s. Between stars

	FROS 335:13
s. between the houses	FENT 316:11
s. in your togetherness	GIBR 346:7
vacant interstellar s.	ELIO 301:17

spaceship regarding S. Earth FULL 337:1

spade call a s. a spade

	BURT 173:21
fiddle, sir, and s.	SCOT 674:6
have never seen a s.	WILD 835:23
nominate a s. a spade	JONS 435:8

spades leave s. alone SITW 738:18

Let s. be trumps	POPE 606:13

Spain castels thanne in S.

	CHAU 212:27
King of S.'s daughter	NURS 567:11
Lady of S.	REAV 643:18
leave S.	JUAN 437:29
not into the hands of S.	TENN 784:2
permanence and unity of S.	JUAN 437:28
rain in S.	LERN 481:19

spake God s. once

	BOOK 138:2
no words he s.	GILB 346:18
s. wisely	BIBL 93:15

spam they offered s. MALA 508:8

span but a s.

	DAVI 258:9
Contract into a s.	HERB 384:19
Eternity shut in a s.	CRAS 250:12
Less than a s.	BACO 46:23

Spaniards not the power of the S.

	SCHU 671:19
S. seem wiser	BACO 45:15
thrash the S. too	DRAK 285:18

spanieled hearts That s. me SHAK 679:20

Spanish S. Ga-la-lee

	SONG 748:4
S. ships of war	TENN 783:19
To God I speak S.	CHAR 209:13

spare Brother can you s. a dime HARB 371:1

do in his s. time	GILL 349:10
S. all I have	FARQ 315:15
S. at the spigot	PROV 631:11
s. man	AUBR 33:19
s. the beechen tree	CAMP 187:8
S. the rod	PROV 631:12
s. those who have submitted	VIRG 812:15
S. us all word of the weapons	WILB 835:2
S. well and have to spend	PROV 631:13
s. your country's flag	WHIT 834:3
Woodman, s. that tree	MORR 549:11

spared better s. a better man SHAK 691:15

sufferings which thou art s.	ORCH 576:8

spares man that s. these stones EPIT 309:10

spareth s. his rod BIBL 84:18

spark shows a hasty s. SHAK 698:19

s. from heaven	ARNO 28:6
s.-gap is mightier	HOGB 392:5
s. of inextinguishable thought	SHEL 732:15
s. of that ancient flame	VIRG 812:1
s. o' Nature's fire	BURN 171:2
Vital s.	POPE 602:10
waitest for the s. from heaven	ARNO 28:8

sparkle s. out among the fern TENN 775:18

They s. still	SHAK 702:20

sparkles s. near the brim BYRO 178:16

sparks Ashes and s. SHEL 730:13

as the s. fly upward	BIBL 82:37
hide the s. of nature	SHAK 683:4
s. among the stubble	BIBL 92:24

sparrow am even as it were a s. BOOK 140:18

ef 'taint s.-grass	HARR 374:2
fall of a s.	SHAK 689:7
I, said the S.	NURS 570:16
lecherous as a s.	CHAU 210:26
Lesbia with her s.	MILL 526:21
My lady's s. is dead	CATU 202:11
or a s. fall	POPE 604:21
s. alight upon my shoulder	THOR 793:14
s. hath found her an house	BOOK 139:15
s. should fly swiftly	BEDE 62:7

sparrows five s. sold

	BIBL 100:31
of more value than many s.	BIBL 96:18
pass through for the s.	GALB 338:5
two s. sold	BIBL 96:18

Spartan remnant of our S. dead BYRO 181:7

Spartans Go, tell the S. EPIT 309:11

speak all I think or s. WESL 829:4

Books will s. plain	BACO 43:27
dare not s. its name	DOUG 283:13
didn't s. up	NIEM 563:18
difficult to s.	BURK 169:3
fears to s. of Ninety-Eight	INGR 413:18
grief that does not s.	SHAK 706:23
I'll do't before I s.	SHAK 699:20
I now s. for France	DE G 262:2
I only s. right on	SHAK 698:5
let him now s.	BOOK 133:7
Let us not s. of them	DANT 255:14
men shall s. well of you	BIBL 100:14
neither s. they	BOOK 142:4
one to s.	THOR 793:18
province of knowledge to s.	HOLM 393:2
slow to s.	BIBL 111:21
Small sorrows s.	SENE 677:1
s. afterwards	PROV 632:39
s. and purpose not	SHAK 699:20
speak, and to s. well	JONS 436:10
s. as the common people do	ASCH 31:9
s. as ye do	BIBL 83:10
S. as you find	PROV 631:14
S. for Britain	BOOT 145:2
S. for England	AMER 13:4
S. for himself	BIBL 103:14
s. ill of everybody except oneself	PÉTA 593:12
s. ill of the dead	PROV 627:28
s. in our tongues	BIBL 104:27
S., Lord	BIBL 80:5
S. low, if you speak love	SHAK 712:14
s. no evil	PROV 630:27
s. of eternity	BROW 156:25
S. Out	GRAS 359:12
S. roughly	CARR 194:7
S. softly	ROOS 654:7
s. their minds	BAGE 48:20
S. the speech	SHAK 686:21
S. to Him thou	TENN 777:12
s. to the wise	PIND 595:12
s. unto them therof	BOOK 142:15
s. when he is spoken to	STEV 760:7
s. with their enemies	BOOK 143:2
S. ye comfortably	BIBL 89:15
stop and s. to you	BROW 160:8
we shall s. of the somwhat	CHAU 213:2
when I think, I must s.	SHAK 681:20
whereof one cannot s.	WITT 842:10
You were better s. first	SHAK 682:1

speaker s. of fact PALI 583:13

speaketh s. things not to be spoken

	BIBL 93:15

speaking adepts in the s. trade CHUR 219:16

drowning their s.	BROW 160:20
heard for their much s.	BIBL 95:2
necessity for good s.	TROL 799:26
People talking without s.	SIMO 738:4
s. all their lives long	MATH 518:9
s. picture, with this end	SIDN 736:15
thy art of s.	SHER 734:10

speaks He s. to Me VICT 809:14

hides one thing and s. another	HOME 394:6
s. of a chair	BISH 117:9
s. small like a woman	SHAK 710:10
s. well of the bridge	PROV 619:20

who s. does not know	LAO 468:2

spear Bring me my s. BLAK 121:15

knappeth the s. in sunder	BOOK 136:26
s., to equal which the tallest	MILT 531:16
With a burning s.	ANON 20:4

spearmen s. still made good SCOT 673:25

spears sheen of their s. BYRO 180:1

s. into pruninghooks	BIBL 88:2
stars threw down their s.	BLAK 122:21

special all s. cases CAMU 188:10

by s. grace	BOOK 130:6

specials can't trust the 's.' COLL 235:3

species but a s. FIEL 318:1

characteristics of the human s.	GODW 352:2
not the individual, but the s.	JOHN 425:25
preys on its own s.	JAME 418:22

specimen brick as a s. JOHN 425:13

spectacle great s. of life ELIO 300:8

no s. so ridiculous	MACA 498:6
s. unto the world	BIBL 107:8

spectacles pair of s. SHAK 719:26

s. of books	DRYD 290:4
s. on nose	SHAK 681:12

spectantia *Omnia te adversum s.* HORA 399:2

spectatress S. of the mischief ROWE 657:9

spectatum *S. veniunt* OVID 579:21

spectre pale, and s.-thin KEAT 444:24

s. of Communism	MARX 517:4

spectres S. fly before it SMIL 741:1

speculate If you don't s. PROV 623:16

s. on the teachings	SA'A 662:5

speculations s. and subtleties BROW 156:31

s. upon matter	JOHN 425:7

speculative like a s. merchant BAGE 48:6

speech abridging the freedom of s.

	CONS 241:13
aspersion upon my parts of s.	SHER 733:18
deal by s.	BACO 45:1
forme of s. is chaunge	CHAU 212:32
freedom of s.	TWAI 803:9
freedom of the press's s.	TWAI 803:17
function of s. to free	BRAN 149:12
in one's s.	LA R 469:20
little other use of their s.	HALI 368:17
manner of his s.	SHAK 679:2
meaning of lengthy s.	SCHI 671:1
our concern was s.	ELIO 301:24
perfect plainness of s.	ARNO 30:9
quick of s.	WINT 841:19
rule of s.	HORA 398:3
slow of s.	BIBL 77:22
Speak the s.	SHAK 686:21
s. be alway with grace	BIBL 110:14
s. bewrayeth thee	BIBL 99:9
s. by Chamberlain	BEVA 73:20
s. created thought	SHEL 731:6
s. from Ernest Bevin	FOOT 327:26
S. happens not to be	STAË 753:18
S. is civilization itself	MANN 510:11
s. is comely	BIBL 87:10
s. is like a cracked kettle	FLAU 324:22
S. is often barren	ELIO 299:18
s. is shallow as Time	CARL 191:20
S. is silver	PROV 631:16
S. is the small change	MERE 522:17
s. nor language	BOOK 134:20
s. only to conceal	VOLT 815:13
s. they have resolved	ELIO 299:14
strange power of s.	COLE 233:9
true use of s.	GOLD 355:16
utterance, nor power of s.	SHAK 698:5
verse is a measured s.	BACO 42:20
what manner of s.	HOME 394:1
where s. is not	HOBB 390:8

speeches all the easy s. CHES 216:3

s. were fine	WALP 819:19

speechless from among the s. dead

	HILL 388:8
let it lie S. still	EPIT 310:7
s. Christ	SWIN 768:8
s. real	BARZ 57:20

speechmaking practising s. JUVE 440:9

speed More haste, less s. PROV 626:40

split (cont.):
make all s. — SHAK 710:21
s. Ireland — BRUG 162:5
when I s. an infinitive — CHAN 207:17
spoil been the s. of me — SHAK 690:30
divided the s. — BOOK 138:12
divide the s. — BIBL 88:17
s. it by trying to explain — SHER 733:24
s. the broth — PROV 633:14
s. the child — PROV 631:12
s. the ship — PROV 618:4
spoiled Better one house s. — PROV 615:26
s. the Egyptians — BIBL 77:33
s. the women's chats — BROW 160:20
Story the s. child of art — JAME 417:13
spoilers hands of s. — BIBL 79:15
spoils belong the s. — MARC 512:2
divideth his s. — BIBL 100:28
spoke blood S. in her cheeks — DONN 280:5
s., and the world was made — JOHN 426:7
spoken American people have s. — CLIN 227:10
Lord hath s. — BIBL 89:16
never been s. to like this — CHIR 218:2
never have s. yet — CHES 216:12
Rome has s. — AUGU 37:17
s. of thee — BOOK 139:20
s. unto us — BIBL 111:3
word fitly s. — BIBL 85:3
spongy Patrol the halls on s. shoes
— WILB 835:6
spontaneous S. joy and natural content
— YEAT 854:8
spoon ate with a runcible s. — LEAR 477:18
have a long s. — PROV 622:15
ran away with the s. — NURS 567:6
trifle with the s. — POPE 603:26
spoons counted our s. — EMER 306:20
let us count our s. — JOHN 428:10
world locks up its s. — SHAW 726:12
sport amateur s. — DOYL 284:22
Detested s. — COWP 248:3
ended his s. with Tess — CLOS 228:17
ended his s. with Tess — HARD 372:5
kill us for their s. — SHAK 701:8
owe to s. — CAMU 189:1
real love of your s. — GREE 362:20
Serious s. — ORWE 578:1
s. for our neighbours — AUST 40:5
s. of kings — D'AV 257:22
s. of kings — SOME 745:21
s. of kings — SURT 764:12
S. that wrinkled Care derides — MILT 529:20
s. with Amaryllis — MILT 530:2
s. would be as tedious — SHAK 689:25
sported s. on the green — SOUT 748:17
sports mountainous s. girl — BETJ 72:15
play Her cruel s. — SPEN 752:8
S. do not paint character — BROU 154:14
s. of love — JONS 435:20
sportsman fit to be called a s. — SURT 764:13
s. is a man who — LEAC 476:15
spot fellows we put on the s. — COLL 235:8
no s. in thee — BIBL 87:11
Out, damned s. — SHAK 706:25
sumpshous s. — ASHF 31:14
Tip me the black s. — STEV 759:14
with a s. I damn him — SHAK 698:11
spotless All things were s. — TRAH 797:13
spots change his s. — PROV 625:4
leopard change his s. — BIBL 91:1
s. rather a credit — COMP 237:2
spotted wants to have been s. — VIRG 813:21
You s. snakes — SHAK 711:6
spouse in s. occasion to complain
— CENT 205:5
my sister, my s. — BIBL 87:12
President's s. — BUSH 174:21
shuts the s. Christ home — HOPK 397:6
spout cataracts and hurricanoes s.
— SHAK 700:15
sprang s. to the stirrup — BROW 159:23
spray pinkly bursts the s. — BETJ 72:12
rime was on the s. — HARD 373:6

singis on the s. — DOUG 283:14
twirling in thy hand a withered s.
— ARNO 28:6
spread except it be s. — BACO 45:13
no good till it is s. — PROV 626:35
S. ALARM AND DESPONDENCY — PENI 591:14
s. my dreams under your feet — YEAT 854:11
sprightly first s. running — DRYD 287:28
spring Alas, that s. should vanish
— FITZ 323:16
as short a S. — HERR 386:16
azure sister of the s. — SHEL 730:7
beckoning to his S. Queen — JARR 418:27
bloom in the s. — GILB 348:9
Blossom by blossom the s. — SWIN 768:1
can S. be far behind — SHEL 730:14
commonly called the s. — COWP 248:26
easing the S. — REED 644:4
Falsehood has a perennial s. — BURK 166:15
first hour of s. — BOWE 147:17
hounds of s. — SWIN 767:25
In the s. a young man's fancy — TENN 780:15
in the s. to follow — SWIN 768:25
less quick to s. — ARNO 28:28
lived light in the s. — ARNO 27:7
new come s. — SHAK 716:13
no second s. — PHIL 594:14
No s., nor summer beauty — DONN 279:7
not s. until you can plant — PROV 624:11
only the right to s. — FOND 327:25
Pierian s. — DRAY 286:4
rifle all the breathing s. — COLL 235:10
songs of S. — KEAT 445:16
s. breaks through again — COWA 245:1
S. Flow down the woods — SACK 662:12
s. has gone out of the year — PERI 592:20
s. has kept in its folds — ARAG 24:3
s. is wound up tight — ANOU 22:16
s. now comes unheralded — CARS 196:20
s. of business — BAGE 47:16
s. of endless lies — COWP 247:14
s. of light — COLE 231:3
s. of the year — BIBL 94:1
S. restores balmy warmth — CATU 202:18
s. shut up, a fountain sealed — BIBL 87:12
s. summer autumn winter — CUMM 253:5
suddenly was changed to S. — SHEL 731:12
Sweet lovers love the s. — SHAK 682:6
Sweet s., full of sweet days — HERB 385:4
this s. of love — SHAK 721:21
trouble in the Balkans in the s. — KIPL 456:24
We need s. — GZOW 366:7
with ever-returning s. — WHIT 833:22
year's at the s. — BROW 160:22
springe woodcock to mine own s.
— SHAK 689:10
springes s. to catch woodcocks — SHAK 684:22
springlike limbs that fester are not s.
— ABSE 1:4
springs Fifty s. — HOUS 404:7
s. into the rivers — BOOK 141:6
Wastes without s. — CLAR 224:9
Where s. not fail — HOPK 396:16
springtime Ballinderry in the s. — FERG 316:17
Merry S.'s Harbinger — FLET 327:8
sprite fleeting, wav'ring s. — HADR 366:10
sprites s. and goblins — SHAK 721:26
sprouting S. despondently at area gates
— ELIO 302:21
spun s. twelve ells — ANON 22:13
spur Fame is the s. — MILT 530:2
I have no s. — SHAK 704:7
s. me into song — YEAT 855:20
s. of all great minds — CHAP 208:19
spurious s. brat, Tom Jones — RICH 647:17
spurs this day to wynne his s. — EDWA 296:9
When a knight won his s. — STRU 762:17
win his s. — EDWA 296:9
spy letters for a s. — KIPL 455:16
s. out the land — BIBL 78:16
s. who came in from the cold — LE C 478:9
squad awkward s. fire over me — LAST 471:11

squadrons big s. against the small
— BUSS 175:9
wingèd s. of the sky — MILM 527:15
square architects do s. and hew — MARV 515:12
I have not kept the s. — SHAK 679:8
S. deal afterwards — ROOS 654:8
s. on the hypotenuse — GILB 348:29
s. person has squeezed himself — SMIT 743:11
s. root of half a number — LONG 491:12
squares on the lines or s. — MILN 528:3
squat s. like a toad — MILT 533:10
s. pen rests — HEAN 377:19
urban, s., and packed with guile
— BROO 153:12
squats s. on the hearthstone — QUIL 639:8
squawking seven stars go s. — AUDE 34:19
squeak s. and gibber — SHAK 683:16
until the pips s. — GEDD 342:15
squeaking shrieking and s. — BROW 160:20
s. Cleopatra — SHAK 680:8
s. wheel gets — PROV 631:17
squeeze s. a right-hand foot — CARR 196:1
squeezing in the s. of a lemon — GOLD 355:24
squinch-owl jay-bird say ter der s.
— HARR 374:4
squint banish s. suspicion — MILT 528:25
squire s. and his relations — DICK 268:2
squires last sad s. ride — CHES 216:13
stab do I s. at thee — MELV 521:11
No iron can s. the heart — BABE 42:4
saw him s. — READ 643:4
stabant S. orantes — VIRG 812:13
stabat S. Mater dolorosa — JACO 415:12
stability natural s. of gold — SHAW 725:14
party of order or s. — MILL 525:8
s. or enlargement — JOHN 424:5
s. pact is stupid — PROD 612:19
stable born in a s. — PROV 626:5
nothing s. in the world — KEAT 446:5
stable-door shut the s. — PROV 624:23
stables S. are the centre — SHAW 725:12
stablish s. me with thy free Spirit
— BOOK 137:13
staff cockle hat and s. — SHAK 688:5
I'll break my s. — SHAK 719:5
s. of faith to walk upon — RALE 641:5
thy rod and thy s. — BOOK 135:4
trustest upon the s. — BIBL 82:17
stag lean as a rutting S. — BYRO 183:25
runnable s. — DAVI 258:4
stage All the world's a s. — SHAK 681:9
Don't put your daughter on the s.
— COWA 245:4
drown the s. with tears — SHAK 686:4
middle age of a s. — BACO 45:35
On the s. — GOLD 355:7
played upon a s. — SHAK 721:11
s. where every man must play — SHAK 708:20
this great s. of fools — SHAK 701:19
traffick of our s. — SHAK 717:13
wonder of our s. — JONS 435:28
stagecoach s. from London to Oxford
— HAZL 377:4
stages four s. of man — LINK 486:9
stagger s. like a drunken man — BOOK 141:19
stagnant fen Of s. waters — WORD 847:14
stagnation keeps life from s. — BURN 169:15
stain bright s. on the vision — GRAV 360:9
convict s. — HUGH 407:3
darkening like a s. — AUDE 36:13
s. in thine honour — BIBL 93:25
s. the stiff dishonoured shroud — ELIO 303:6
s. upon the silence — BECK 61:27
world's slow s. — SHEL 728:23
stained kick a hole in a s. glass window
— CHAN 207:11
s. with their own works — BOOK 141:15
stains Innumerable of s. — KEAT 442:20
s. the white radiance — SHEL 729:2
stair by a winding s. — BACO 44:25
falling from s. to stair — BAYL 59:8
stairs another man's s. — DANT 256:12
stake deep s. they have — BURK 166:31

starved (cont.):
s. poet — LOCK 489:4
starves steed s. — PROV 634:44
starving choice of working or s. — JOHN 424:2
s. hysterical naked — GINS 349:15
you have a s. population — DISR 275:6
state all were for the s. — MACA 499:15
Atlas of the s. — COWP 247:16
bosom of a single s. — DURH 293:5
defrauding of the S. — PENN 591:18
done the s. some service — SHAK 714:30
faithful to a s. — ELIZ 304:2
first duty of a S. — RUSK 660:2
Founding a firm s. — MARV 515:13
glories of our blood and s. — SHIR 735:3
Here's a s. of things — GILB 348:3
I am the S. — LOUI 492:5
in a free s. — CAVO 204:6
In that s. I came — VAUG 807:15
last s. of that man — BIBL 97:1
mine was the middle s. — DEFO 261:9
my glories and my s. — SHAK 716:8
no harm come to the s. — ANON 21:15
no such thing as the S. — AUDE 36:4
Only in the s. — HEGE 379:4
O Ship of S. — LONG 490:2
Our s. cannot be severed — MILT 534:4
put the s. to rights — ENNI 308:3
reinforcement of the s. — CAMU 188:17
ruin of the S. — BLAK 119:7
rule the s. — DRYD 287:1
Scoffing his s. — SHAK 715:24
separation of s. and science — FEYE 317:5
sovereign or s. — BACO 44:21
S. business is a cruel trade — HALI 369:8
s. can exist — CONF 238:4
S. for every Star — WINT 842:1
s. has no place — TRUD 800:23
S. in wonted manner keep — JONS 435:2
S. is an instrument — STAL 754:1
S. is a relation of men — WEBE 825:5
S. is not 'abolished' — ENGE 307:27
s. of life — BOOK 132:18
s. of the Union — CONS 241:12
s. to be endured — JOHN 425:27
S. which dwarfs its men — MILL 525:11
s. without the means — BURK 167:7
s. with the prettiest name — BISH 117:4
storms of s. — SHAK 695:17
sun begins his s. — MILT 529:21
to what a s. dost Thou bring — TERE 785:17
usurped the powers of the s. — GIBB 345:2
While the S. exists — LENI 480:5
stately She is tall and s. — TENN 781:20
S. as a galleon — GREN 363:12
S. Homes of England — COWA 245:7
s. homes of England — HEMA 381:5
S., plump Buck Mulligan — OPEN 575:20
with his s. stride — MACA 499:16
statement black s. of pistons — SPEN 750:18
s. that is quotable — GERS 344:9
woman makes the s. — MUIR 553:15
statements all previous s. inoperative — ZIEG 858:10
states goodly s. and kingdoms — KEAT 445:5
independent S. — ADAM 2:23
indestructible S. — CHAS 209:18
many sovereign S. — PAGE 581:14
rights of s. — BROW 155:9
S., like men, have their growth — LAND 466:7
s. unborn — SHAK 697:12
Union of these S. — WHIT 833:21
statesman chemist, fiddler, s. — DRYD 287:6
constitutional s. — BAGE 47:10
gift of any s. — METT 523:9
he was a s. — LLOY 488:1
set a s. right — YEAT 855:3
s. is a politician — TRUM 801:10
s. is a politician who — POMP 599:18
s. must wait — BISM 118:5
S., yet friend to Truth — POPE 603:24
Too nice for a s. — GOLD 355:5
statesmen faults of s. — WALP 819:20

government of s. — DISR 276:27
like great S. — GAY 341:19
station antique s. — BEER 63:4
By Grand Central S. — BORR 146:3
her s. keeping — JACO 415:12
private s. — ADDI 4:14
stations know our proper s. — DICK 268:2
statistic million deaths a s. — STAL 754:5
statistical life is s. improbability — DAWK 259:15
statistics experiment needs s. — RUTH 661:18
give plenty of s. — CARR 196:16
lies, damned lies and s. — DISR 278:9
uses s. as a drunken man — LANG 466:12
We are just s. — HORA 399:4
statuary form of s. — ANON 16:3
statue like a marble s. — SUGE 763:9
s. implicit in bronze — ARIS 26:8
statues Ep's s. are junk — ANON 16:16
stature cubit unto his s. — BIBL 95:8
Malice is of a low s. — HALI 369:2
of lofty s. — EINH 297:11
status *from* S. — MAIN 507:20
Human s. ought not to depend — TEMP 775:11
status quo restored the s. — SQUI 753:16
statutes keep my s. — BIBL 78:13
s. of the Lord — BOOK 134:21
staves comest to me with s. — BIBL 80:22
stay here I s. — MACM 503:19
If we can't s. here alive — MONT 545:12
love is here to s. — GERS 344:7
more care to s. — SHAK 718:3
S. a little — BACO 44:6
S. for me there — KING 451:11
S. out all night — CHUR 220:1
s. up all night — BRYS 162:13
things to s. as they are — LAMP 465:19
without thee here to s. — MILT 534:13
staying s. messengers — RILK 648:17
Tell the people I'm s. — PEDR 590:13
stays never s. too long — MACA 498:8
nothing s. — HERA 383:1
s. together — SAYI 669:18
stead in my soul's s. — BIBL 83:10
steadfast s. as thou art — KEAT 442:11
steady Full cup, s. hand — PROV 620:34
One thought more s. — FORD 329:3
Slow and s. wins the race — PROV 630:45
S., boys, steady — GARR 340:2
steak he wanted s. — MALA 508:8
not the meat of the s. — PRIE 611:11
steaks How many s. can one man — PAPP 585:10
smell of s. in passageways — ELIO 302:28
steal lest I s. — DEFO 261:8
One man may s. a horse — PROV 628:42
silently s. away — LONG 490:5
sin to s. a pin — PROV 624:19
s. a goose — POLI 601:12
s. bread — FRAN 331:19
s. from many, it's research — MIZN 541:5
S. from the world — POPE 605:32
s. more than a hundred men — PUZO 638:11
s. my Basil-pot — KEAT 443:20
s. my thunder — DENN 264:15
s. the very teeth — ARAB 24:1
thieves break through and s. — BIBL 95:4
Thou shalt not s. — BIBL 78:5
Thou shalt not s. — CLOU 229:7
stealing For de little s. — O'NE 573:8
hanged for s. horses — HALI 369:6
his s. steps — SHAK 688:25
picking and s. — BOOK 132:17
s. ducks — ARAB 23:19
S. money is wrong — AYER 41:7
steals s. my purse — SHAK 713:26
s. something — SHAK 713:13
stealth Do good by s. — POPE 605:27
good action by s. — LAMB 465:11
steam employ s. navigation — LARD 468:9
Shovelling white s. — AUDE 35:15
s.-engine in trousers — SMIT 743:23
traces the s.-engine — DISR 275:11
steamer s. from Harwich — GILB 347:17

steamers little holiday s. — PRIE 611:10
steaming wealth of s. phrases — SCHU 672:4
steamy Throws up a s. column — COWP 248:6
steed his s. was the best — SCOT 673:18
milk-white s. — BALL 53:10
set her on my pacing s. — KEAT 443:27
s. starves — PROV 634:44
s. That knows his rider — BYRO 178:14
steeds mounting barbèd s. — SHAK 716:19
steel All shod with s. — WORD 846:24
clad in complete s. — MILT 529:1
Give them the cold s. — ARMI 26:9
hoops of s. — SHAK 684:17
in complete s. — SHAK 684:26
long divorce of s. — SHAK 695:6
more than complete s. — ANON 16:19
s. canisters hurtling about — CASS 198:16
S.-true and blade-straight — STEV 760:13
with a line of s. — RUSS 661:16
worthy of their s. — SCOT 673:6
wounded surgeon plies the s. — ELIO 301:18
steep s. and rugged pathway — WILL 839:17
steeple lone religious s. — CAMP 187:4
North Church s. — REVE 645:14
three s.-house spires — FOX 331:8
steeples dreary S. of Fermanagh — CHUR 220:21
drenched our s. — SHAK 700:15
s. far and near — HOUS 404:11
steer s. their courses — BUTL 176:7
Stein family S. — ANON 16:16
stelle *muove il sole e l'altre s.* — DANT 256:13
riveder le s. — DANT 256:4
stem s. of Jesse — BIBL 88:20
Stendhal great secret of S. — GIDE 346:16
step first s. that is difficult — DU D 291:4
first s. that is difficult — PROV 624:13
not to take the first s. — CLAU 225:16
One more s. along — CART 197:6
one small s. for a man — ARMS 26:17
One s. at a time — PROV 628:49
one s. enough for me — NEWM 561:5
To s. aside is human — BURN 170:5
stepmother s. to memory, oblivion — JOHN 422:8
stony-hearted s. — DE Q 264:18
step-mother harsh s. — PLIN 598:3
stepped in blood S. in — SHAK 706:9
stepping rise on s.-stones — TENN 778:22
s. westward — WORD 850:10
s. where his comrade stood — SCOT 673:25
steps five s. from the table — ROBB 649:16
sad s., O Moon — SIDN 736:4
s. take hold on hell — BIBL 83:38
uneasy s. Over the burning marl — MILT 531:16
wandering s. and slow — CLOS 228:23
wandering s. and slow — MILT 534:15
sterbenden *einem s. Gotte* — HEIN 380:4
sterile s. promontory — SHAK 685:24
stern s. chase a long chase — PROV 631:18
S. daughter of the voice of God — WORD 848:17
sterner made of s. stuff — SHAK 697:25
sternest s. knight — MALO 509:3
steward commended the unjust s. — BIBL 101:19
stewards S. of the mysteries — BIBL 107:7
stewed S. in corruption — SHAK 687:25
stick carry a big s. — ROOS 654:7
fell like the s. — PAIN 582:14
I shall s. — SHAK 708:16
rattling of a s. inside — ORWE 578:9
s. and a string — SWIF 767:23
S. close to your desks — GILB 348:24
s. more close than a brother — KIPL 455:20
s. that he seizes — TORR 797:4
s. to beat a dog — PROV 624:3
tattered coat upon a s. — YEAT 855:9
sticketh friend that s. closer — BIBL 84:32
sticks S. and stones — PROV 631:19
S. nix hick pix — NEWS 562:18
stiff woman can be proud and s. — YEAT 853:16

stiffnecked thou art a s. people	BIBL 78:9	**stocks** hurt in the s.	BOOK 141:12	Sticks and s.	PROV 631:19
stiffness too much s. in refusing		**stoic** budge doctors of the s. fur	MILT 529:6	s. and clouts make martyrs	BROW 156:9
	BOOK 127:11	**stoical** s. scheme of supplying	SWIF 766:22	s. will teach you	BERN 70:12
stigma Any s. to beat a dogma	GUED 365:9	**stoicism** Romans call it s.	ADDI 4:9	s. would cry out	BIBL 101:30
stile lame dog over a s.	CHIL 217:23	**stole** I wonder where you s. 'em	SWIF 767:20	you are not s.	SHAK 697:29
still Because they liked me 's.'	DICK 273:9	son of a bitch s. my watch	FILM 320:17	You buy land, you buy s.	PROV 635:24
beside the s. waters	BOOK 135:3	**stolen** generation was s.	FREE 333:9	**stony** fell upon s. places	BIBL 97:3
best be s.	ARNO 27:14	had I s. the whole	STEV 760:18	morre s. than a shore	WILL 839:12
be s.	BOOK 133:23	s., be your apples	HUNT 409:19	s. limits	SHAK 717:23
Be s. and cool	FOX 331:10	S. fruit is sweet	PROV 631:23	S. outcrop of the Burren	BETJ 72:11
Be s. then, and know	BOOK 136:26	s. his wits away	DE L 262:22	**stood** should of s. in bed	JACO 415:11
do them s.	DONN 280:2	S. sweets are best	CIBB 223:5	s. against the world	SHAK 697:28
heart is lying s.	WORD 846:7	s. the scraps	SHAK 702:21	s. by me when I was crazy	SHER 734:15
monk is s.	PALI 584:18	S. waters are sweet	BIBL 84:7	s. four-square to all the winds	TENN 782:16
ship was as s.	SOUT 749:4	S. waters are sweet	PROV 631:24	**stools** Between two s.	PROV 615:34
S. crazy after all	SIMO 738:5	**stoles** nice white s.	BARH 55:15	necessity invented s.	COWP 247:24
S. falls the rain	SITW 738:16	**stolid** S. and stunned	MARK 512:8	**stoop** dares to s. and take it	DOST 283:6
S. glides the Stream	WORD 849:23	**stomach** army marches on its s.	NAPO 557:1	**stop** come to the end: then s.	CARR 194:21
s. it is not we	CHES 216:13	army marches on its s.	PROV 614:31	could not s. for Death	DICK 262:11
s., like air, I'll rise	ANGF 14:15	burst s. like a cave	DOUG 283:18	full s. at the right place	BABE 42:4
s. point of the turning world	ELIO 301:12	for thy s.'s sake	BIBL 110:24	impossible to s.	STRU 762:18
s., sad music	WORD 847:10	nor a stew-pan—but a s.	HUNT 410:12	kissing had to s.	BROW 161:21
s. small voice	BIBL 81:27	no s. to this fight	SHAK 693:22	Might s. a hole	SHAK 688:30
s. they gazed	GOLD 354:17	s. of a king	ELIZ 304:7	nobody's going to s. 'em	BERR 71:9
s. tongue makes wise head	PROV 631:20	s. of the country	GLAD 350:11	nothing will s. it	ZOLA 859:9
s.-vexed Bermoothes	SHAK 718:22	s. sets us to work	ELIO 299:20	so plain a s.	SHAK 691:21
S. waters run deep	PROV 631:21	through his s.	PROV 633:43	S. all the clocks	AUDE 34:28
s. we see thee lie	BROO 154:8	**stomacher** bird with the red s.	DONN 279:15	S. it at the start	OVID 580:16
'What gars ye rin sae s.?'	ANON 18:20	**stomachs** march on their s.	SELL 676:24	S.-look-and-listen	OFFI 572:13
stillness air a solemn s. holds	GRAY 360:24	**stone** against a s.	BOOK 140:4	S. me and buy one	ADVE 8:15
horrid s. first invades	DRYD 287:26	At his heels a s.	SHAK 688:6	S. the world	NEWL 560:6
modest s. and humility	SHAK 693:4	blossoming in s.	LONG 490:10	s. to busy fools	VAUG 807:10
present s.	WARR 822:2	bomb them back into the S. Age	LEMA 480:1	**stoppeth** s. one of three	COLE 232:11
s. in the midst of chaos	BELL 66:2	brass, nor s., nor earth	SHAK 723:8	**stops** buck s. here	TRUM 801:15
s. of the central sea	TENN 779:28	bronze and s.	RUNY 659:3	know my s.	SHAK 687:10
stilly Oft, in the s. night	MOOR 547:22	flung the s.	FITZ 322:24	**storage** thought in cold s.	SAMU 665:10
Stilton no end of S. Cheese	LEAR 477:9	for a s. of stumbling	BIBL 88:16	**store** amid thy s.	KEAT 445:15
stilts nonsense upon s.	BENT 68:4	get blood from a s.	PROV 635:29	in the s. we sell hope	REVS 645:15
stimulate s. the phagocytes	SHAW 725:3	give him s.	BIBL 95:17	**storehouse** rich s.	BACO 42:14
stimulation unnatural s.	MILL 525:13	give them the s.	MONT 543:19	**storey** crack in your upper s.	SMOL 744:17
sting death, where is thy s.	BIBL 108:12	hollows out a s.	OVID 580:7	**storied** S. of old	MILT 529:3
it is a s.	PEEL 591:1	jasper and a sardine s.	BIBL 113:7	**stories** beset him round With dismal s.	
s. like a bee	ALI 12:2	let him first cast a s.	BIBL 103:9		BUNY 165:7
s. you for your pains	PROV 623:18	Let them not make me a s.	MACN 504:20	S. to rede ar delitabill	BARB 55:9
where is thy s.-a-ling-a-ling	MILI 526:15	Like a rolling s.	DYLA 294:10	tell sad s.	SHAK 715:23
stingeth s. like an adder	BIBL 85:1	like a s. wall	BEE 62:9	**stork** S. from butter	ADVE 7:13
stings s. in their tails	BIBL 113:25	look honestly like s.	MOOR 546:14	**storm** After a s. comes a calm	PROV 614:5
s., The crowd, and buzz	COWL 245:26	make a s. of the heart	YEAT 854:4	Any port in a s.	PROV 614:23
s. you for your pains	HILL 388:6	mighty angel took up a s.	BIBL 114:10	carry you through the s.	EWAR 313:7
wanton s.	SHAK 707:21	nickname is the heaviest s.	HAZL 376:18	coming s.	GLAD 350:9
stink Fish and guests s.	PROV 620:15	not a s. Tell where I lie	POPE 605:32	directs the s.	ADDI 4:6
stinker Outrageous S.	KIPL 457:6	on sufferers from s.	HIPP 389:13	directs this s.	PAGE 581:13
stinks fish always s.	PROV 620:14	quiet as a s.	KEAT 443:9	fled away into the s.	KEAT 443:4
that s. and stings	POPE 602:31	Raise the s.	ANON 18:18	Head to the s.	KIPL 454:15
worse it s.	PROV 626:45	rolling s. gathers	PROV 630:15	pelting of this pitiless s.	SHAK 700:22
stir before you s. his fire	PROV 636:9	rolls back the restless s.	DUCK 291:3	pilot of the s.	BAGE 47:21
more you s. it	PROV 626:45	S.-dead hath no fellow	PROV 631:25	rides upon the s.	COWP 246:23
No s. in the air	SOUT 749:4	s. taken away	BIBL 104:9	sharper the s.	PROV 630:33
No s. of air was there	KEAT 443:10	s. the twenty-first	BROW 159:1	ship in a black s.	WEBS 826:14
smoke and s. of this dim spot	MILT 528:17	s. to beauty grew	EMER 306:14	S. and stress	KAUF 442:3
s. men's blood	SHAK 698:5	S. walls do not a prison make	LOVE 493:6	s.-clouds gather	LEAR 477:7
s. up undisputed matters	SALL 665:3	s. which he flings	TORR 797:4	S.-clouds whirl	PUSH 638:1
s. up, we beseech thee	BOOK 130:21	s. which the builders refused	BOOK 142:10	wind and s.	BOOK 144:6
s. without great argument	SHAK 688:4	sword out of this s.	MALO 508:18	**Stormont** Ulster Parliament at S.	GEOR 343:8
stirbt er s. ab	ENGE 307:27	take the s. from stone	ELIO 302:25	**storms** He sought the s.	DRYD 286:20
stirred Shaken and not s.	FLEM 326:9	This precious s.	SHAK 715:13	waves and s.	BOOK 136:13
something s.	SIMP 738:9	through a piece of s.	MOOR 546:15	**stormy** dark and s. night	OPEN 574:25
stirring s. the fire	AUST 39:21	Turn but a s.	THOM 791:15	O s. peple	CHAU 211:3
stirrup foot already in the s.	CERV 205:19	Under every s.	ARIS 25:8	S. weather	KOEH 458:14
sprang to the s.	BROW 159:23	under this little s.	FANS 314:10	to 'scape s. days	DONN 279:27
s. and the ground	EPIT 310:16	Virtue is like a rich s.	BACO 43:19	**story** about you, that s.	HORA 403:4
stirs Will that s. and urges	HARD 372:14	wears away a s.	PROV 617:10	dreaming s.	JARR 418:27
stitch s. in time saves	PROV 631:22	**Stonehenge** s. it deserves	HAWK 375:10	*Have you thought of a s.*	SHEL 728:6
S.! stitch! stitch	HOOD 395:11	**stones** chose him five smooth s.	BIBL 80:21	It's our *own* s.	CART 198:4
St Ives going to S.	NURS 566:7	Drive gently over the s.	PROV 618:26	name great in s.	BYRO 183:10
St James ladies of S.'s	DOBS 278:17	even the s. know you	VERG 808:13	novel tells a s.	FORS 329:9
stock s. that scents the garden	THOM 792:7	in pilèd s.	MILT 530:14	One s. is good	PROV 629:1
Woman s. is rising	CHIL 217:20	man that spares these s.	EPIT 309:10	picture tells a s.	ADVE 7:22
stocking glimpse of s.	PORT 607:8	move The s. of Rome	SHAK 698:6	picture tells a s.	PROV 619:22
silk s.'s hanging down	SELL 676:18	pile up s.	WULF 851:19	plot for a short s.	CHEK 214:2
stockings Golden s.	GOGA 353:21	scuttled under s.	ROET 652:6	read Richardson for the s.	JOHN 429:19
s. were hung	MOOR 546:9	Sermons in s.	SHAK 680:26	short in the s.	BIBL 94:3
thy yellow s.	SHAK 720:33	shouldn't throw s.	PROV 632:43	so old a s.	HEIN 379:16

story (cont.):
s. always old — BROW 161:7
s. and a byword — WINT 841:20
s. chronicled — MALO 508:21
s. need be long — THOR 792:27
s. of our days — RALE 641:11
S. the spoiled child of art — JAME 417:13
tell my s. — SHAK 689:14
tell you a s. — NURS 567:12
work that tells a s. — RUSK 659:23
stout Collapse of S. Party — ANON 15:11
s. heart to stey brae — PROV 629:48
St Pancras Towers of S. Station — BEEC 62:11
St Paul's ruins of S. — MACA 498:18
ruins of S. — WALP 819:9
Say I am designing S. — BENT 68:16
S. had slipped down — SMIT 744:3
Strachan Sir Richard S. — ANON 16:6
Strafford S., who was hurried hence — EPIT 310:7
straight crooked shall be made s. — BIBL 89:16
get it s. one day — STEV 758:1
line which is accurately s. — WHEW 831:14
make his paths s. — BIBL 94:10
makes a s.-cut ditch — THOR 792:25
no s. thing — KANT 441:13
nothing ever ran quite s. — GALS 338:13
street which is called S. — BIBL 105:4
unflexible as s. — LOCK 488:13
strain s. at a gnat — BIBL 98:10
s., Time's eunuch — HOPK 397:9
That s. again — SHAK 720:4
train take the s. — ADVE 7:43
Words s. — ELIO 301:13
strait S. is the gate — BIBL 95:20
straits echoing us between us — ARNO 29:2
strand fair Scotland's s. — BURN 171:13
Maypole in the S. — BRAM 149:10
name upon the s. — SPEN 751:4
never alone with a S. — ADVE 8:27
sailing to the s. — BALL 53:6
walk down the S. — HARG 373:11
walked along the S. — JOHN 433:6
strands last s. of man — HOPK 396:10
strange among the s. people — BOOK 142:2
everything that looks s. — PEPY 592:3
foul, s., and unnatural — SHAK 685:2
hand of s. children — BOOK 143:23
How s. it seems — BROW 160:8
in a s. land — BOOK 143:13
Let us be very s. — CONG 239:16
millions of s. shadows — SHAK 723:4
new and s. at first — TRAH 797:12
new men, s. faces — TENN 778:15
now wonder nyce and s. — CHAU 212:32
something rich and s. — SHAK 718:27
s. and sinister — JAME 418:4
'S. friend,' I said — OWEN 581:7
s. intelligence — SHAK 703:11
stranger in a s. land — BIBL 77:15
s. that one so young — BYRO 180:12
too s. a hand — SHAK 696:2
strangeness s. in the proportion — BACO 43:20
will die of s. — MURR 555:4
stranger by a complete s. — ANNE 14:17
entertain Him like a s. — ANON 20:6
entertain this starry s. — CRAS 250:11
gratitude of a s. — TOCQ 795:13
I am a s. grown — BURN 171:21
I, a s. and afraid — HOUS 403:22
I was a little s. — TRAH 797:12
Look, s. — AUDE 35:9
never love a s. — BENS 68:1
s. and alone — WOLF 843:15
s., and ye took me in — BIBL 98:25
s.? 'Eave 'arf a brick — PUNC 637:8
s. in a strange land — BIBL 77:15
S. than fiction — BYRO 182:1
s. than fiction — PROV 633:20
s. to my heart and me — SHAK 699:18
s. to one of your parents — AUST 39:23
S., unless with bedroom eyes — AUDE 35:22
surety for a s. — BIBL 84:10

wiles of the s. — NASH 557:10
You may see a s. — HAMM 370:7
strangers careth for the s. — BOOK 144:2
courteous to s. — BACO 44:19
entertain s. — BIBL 111:14
on the kindness of s. — WILL 839:11
s. and pilgrims — BIBL 111:8
s. in the Capitol — HEWI 387:12
s. of Rome — BIBL 104:27
s. on a rainy day — SMAR 740:13
we are s. before thee — BIBL 82:18
we may be better s. — SHAK 681:21
strangled And s. her — BROW 160:25
s. with the guts — MESL 523:7
strangling s. in a string — HOUS 404:9
S. is a very quiet death — WEBS 826:1
Stratford atte Bowe scole of S. — CHAU 210:11
strathspeys hornpipes and s. — BURN 170:26
straw all things as s. dogs — LAO 467:6
clutch at a s. — PROV 618:27
Headpiece filled with s. — ELIO 302:6
He gets the s. — OXFO 581:10
last s. that breaks — PROV 624:14
lion shall eat s. — BIBL 88:22
make bricks without s. — PROV 635:33
seems like s. — THOM 789:4
stumbles at a s. — SPEN 752:19
Take a s. and throw it up — SELD 676:5
strawberries s. grow in the sea — NURS 568:8
S. swimming in the cream — PEEL 591:2
strawberry Like s. wives — ELIZ 304:17
of the s. — BUTL 177:9
S. fields forever — LENN 480:20
Strawberry Hill [S.] is — WALP 818:19
strawed where thou hast not s. — BIBL 98:22
straws oaths are s. — SHAK 693:3
S. tell which way — PROV 631:26
stray If with me you'd fondly s. — GAY 341:12
what wonder if they s. — COWP 247:10
strayed erred, and s. from thy ways — BOOK 127:15
streak thin red s. — RUSS 661:16
stream change horses in mid s. — PROV 618:7
cool as a mountain s. — ADVE 7:14
Fish have their s. — BROO 153:7
like an ever-rolling s. — WATT 823:20
long-legged fly upon the s. — YEAT 854:22
old mill by the s. — ARMS 26:10
purling s. — ADDI 4:21
salt weed sways in the s. — ARNO 27:12
Still glides the S. — WORD 849:23
s. cannot rise above — PROV 631:27
streamers s. waving in the wind — GAY 342:10
streams cold Companionable s. — YEAT 856:7
Gilding pale s. — SHAK 723:2
hart for cooling s. — TATE 773:12
his crystàlline s. — SHEL 730:9
s. in the firmament — MARL 513:6
s. of dotage flow — JOHN 426:20
strebt so lang er s. — GOET 352:12
street almost a continued s. — BROO 153:3
don't do it in the s. — CAMP 187:3
inability to cross the s. — WOOL 845:10
jostling in the s. — BLAK 121:21
live in a s. — ELIO 300:10
long unlovely s. — TENN 778:26
On the bald s. — TENN 778:27
s. fighting man — JAGG 415:16
s. of the city was gold — BIBL 114:19
s. which is called Straight — BIBL 105:4
sunny side of the s. — FIEL 318:17
talking at s. corners — VANZ 807:5
where the long s. roars — TENN 779:28
streets children died in the s. — AUDE 34:26
Down these mean s. — CHAN 207:15
grass will grow in the s. — HOOV 396:1
negro s. at dawn — GINS 349:15
start in the s. — KENN 448:11
s. and lanes of the city — BIBL 101:8
s. are paved with gold — COLM 236:1
s. being paved with gold — LOUI 492:10
S. FLOODED — TELE 776:10
s. that no longer exist — FENT 316:11

strength as the s. of ten — TENN 784:5
Ephraim also is the s. — BOOK 137:25
Even if s. fail — PROP 612:22
exhausting its s. — MONT 545:5
from s. to strength — BOOK 139:16
giant's s. — SHAK 707:27
girded himself with s. — BOOK 140:6
His s. the more is — BUNY 165:7
is their s. then — BOOK 139:23
My s. and my hope — BIBL 91:8
ordained s. — BOOK 134:4
our hope and s. — BOOK 136:24
renew their s. — BIBL 89:21
roll all our s. — MARV 516:3
sensuality and s. — FRIN 334:19
S. and best security — TROL 799:11
S. and honour are her clothing — BIBL 85:24
s. is lacking — OVID 580:6
s. is made perfect — BIBL 108:25
s. of an horse — BOOK 144:4
s. of his spirit — LUCR 495:9
s. of spirit — SHAK 696:20
S. through joy — POLI 600:27
s. unto his people — BOOK 135:17
S. with his arm — BIBL 99:32
S. without hands to smite — SWIN 768:4
s. without insolence — BYRO 183:24
Sun in his s. — BIBL 75:2
that tower of s. — TENN 782:16
tower of s. — SHAK 717:5
try the soul's s. — BROW 159:25
Union is s. — PROV 633:33
yet would my s. be vain — SIKH 737:2
strengthen bread to s. man's heart — BOOK 141:7
S. me, O Lord — SIKH 737:7
s. such as do stand — BOOK 129:11
s. while one stands — ROSS 655:8
S. ye the weak hands — BIBL 89:10
strengtheneth Christ which s. me — BIBL 110:9
strengthens s. our nerves — BURK 167:25
strenua S. nos exercet inertia — HORA 399:10
strenuous s. life — ROOS 654:5
strepitumque opes s. Romae — HORA 402:1
stress Storm and s. — KAUF 442:3
times of s. and adversity — IACO 412:6
stretch insight and the s. — BROW 158:10
not always s. his bow — HORA 401:5
S. him out longer — SHAK 702:8
s. the human frame — SCAR 668:8
S. your arm no further — PROV 631:48
stretched by a s. out arm — BIBL 78:25
hand is s. out — BIBL 88:9
things he s. — TWAI 803:3
stretches s. his legs — PROV 619:21
stricken I was a s. deer — COWP 247:31
s. deer — SHAK 687:9
well s. in age — BIBL 76:18
stride At one s. comes the dark — COLE 232:22
strides Tarquin's ravishing s. — SHAK 704:17
strife double s. — BACO 46:25
In place of s. — CAST 198:18
Let there be no s. — BIBL 76:14
man of s. — BIBL 91:2
none was worth my s. — LAND 466:2
Of that stern s. — SCOT 674:1
step towards an end of s. — GEOR 343:8
s. and the discouragement — LONG 490:4
s. is o'er — POTT 607:20
void of s. — CHAL 206:4
strike in doubt, s. it out — TWAI 803:25
s. against public safety — COOL 242:4
S. him — CALI 185:14
s. his father's crown — SHAK 692:30
s. it in anger — SHAW 726:23
s. it out — JOHN 429:24
s. mine eyes — JONS 435:5
s. not awry — MORE 548:18
S. the tent — LAST 473:18
S. while the iron — PROV 631:29
thunder, S. flat — SHAK 700:15
yet afraid to s. — POPE 602:29
striker no s. — BIBL 110:22

strikes as s. the player FITZ 323:9
  Empire s. back FILM 322:4
  s. the same place twice PROV 625:16
string end of a golden s. BLAK 120:13
  one long yellow s. BROW 160:25
  strangling in a s. HOUS 404:9
  s. that ties SHEL 732:20
  s. that ties them MONT 545:2
  untune that s. SHAK 719:18
stringent s. execution GRAN 359:8
strings scrape your s. darker CELA 205:2
  s. . . . . in the human heart DICK 267:12
strip s. his sleeve SHAK 693:23
  S. thine own back SHAK 701:17
stripe s. for stripe BIBL 78:6
striped s. like a zebra KEAT 443:30
  s. shroud THOM 790:20
stripes forty s. save one BIBL 108:21
  with his s. we are healed BIBL 90:3
stripling s. Thames ARNO 28:5
strive need'st not s. CLOU 229:5
  s. on untiringly PALI 583:12
  s., to seek, to find TENN 784:20
strives err while yet he s. GOET 352:12
striving s. evermore for these GREN 363:13
stroke greater s. astonisheth CONS 241:5
  none so fast as s. MISQ 537:2
  s. of midnight ceases HOUS 404:3
strokes amorous of their s. SHAK 679:3
  Different s. SAYI 669:13
strong all s. enough LA R 469:10
  battle to the s. BIBL 86:16
  battle to the s. DAVI 258:5
  battle to the s. PROV 630:3
  Be s. and of a good courage BIBL 79:8
  keep the s. in awe SHAK 717:9
  men be so s. BOOK 139:23
  nature of s. people BONH 127:9
  only the S. shall thrive SERV 677:8
  out of the s. BIBL 79:29
  realize how s. she is REAG 643:8
  river Is a s. brown god ELIO 301:20
  Sorrow and silence are s. LONG 490:8
  s. drink BIBL 85:22
  s. drink is raging BIBL 84:33
  s. in the arm PROV 635:22
  S. is the lion SMAR 740:15
  s. man armed BIBL 100:28
  s. name of the Trinity ALEX 11:9
  s., silent man MORL 549:4
  wants that little s. HOLM 393:5
  weak overcomes the s. LAO 468:7
  without whom nothing is s. BOOK 130:12
stronger grows the s. STER 757:2
  interest of the s. PLAT 597:11
  no s. than my sex SHAK 697:2
  on the side of the s. TACI 770:13
  s. still, in earth and air SMAR 740:16
  s. than lions BIBL 80:28
  s. than Necessity EURI 312:13
strongest Wine is the s. BIBL 92:15
stronghold safe s. LUTH 496:11
strongly sin s. LUTH 496:7
strove s., and much repented BYRO 180:11
  s. with none LAND 466:2
struck Diogenes s. the father BURT 174:16
  I s. the board HERB 383:23
  s. regularly like gongs COWA 245:12
  they s. at my life FOX 331:8
structure good s. in a winding stair HERB 384:11
struggle alarms of s. and flight ARNO 27:5
  class s. MARX 517:2
  gods themselves s. SCHI 670:29
  Manhood a s. DISR 277:2
  s. between the artist man SHAW 726:3
  S. for Existence DARW 257:8
  s. for room MALT 509:10
  s. itself towards the heights CAMU 188:15
  s. naught availeth CLOU 229:10
  s. of man against power KUND 462:5
  tired of the s. GOET 353:9
  to-day the s. AUDE 36:9

What s. to escape KEAT 444:7
struggled s. against tyranny TUTU 803:2
struggles history of class s. MARX 517:5
struggling her s. ceases PUSH 638:3
strumpet Into a s.'s fool SHAK 678:12
  She was a s. HEIN 380:2
  true; she is a s. SHAK 685:21
struts s. and frets his hour SHAK 707:14
Stuart S. or Nassau PRIO 612:3
Stuarts out with the S. DISR 277:14
stubble sparks among the s. BIBL 92:24
stubborn Facts are s. things PROV 619:36
  faithless and s. generation BOOK 139:8
  too s. and too strange SHAK 696:2
Stubbs S. butters Freeman ROGE 652:15
stuck 'Amen' S. in my throat SHAK 704:23
  S. her with knives MORR 550:7
students not for the benefit of the s. SMIT 741:11
studied animal he s. less GOSS 357:7
  s. books than men BACO 46:7
studies air of delightful s. MILT 536:5
  Fred's s. ELIO 300:4
  some particular s. DRYD 290:1
  S. serve for delight BACO 45:16
  too much time in s. BACO 45:17
studieth man that s. revenge BACO 45:9
studio Sine ira et s. TACI 770:7
studious S. of elegance GAY 342:2
  S. of laborious ease COWP 248:4
studiously s. neutral WILS 840:19
study craggy paths of s. JONS 435:15
  I must s. politics and war ADAM 3:1
  leisure, I will s. HILL 389:6
  much s. is a weariness BIBL 86:26
  not s. to live BACO 46:11
  previous s. AUST 39:20
  proper s. of mankind POPE 604:32
  proper s. of mankind is books HUXL 411:4
  S. as if you were to live EDMU 296:8
  s. of Greek literature GAIS 337:15
  s. of man is man CHAR 209:17
  s.'s ornament MIDD 524:10
  S. to be quiet BIBL 110:16
studying I have been s. SHAK 716:14
stuff Life too short to s. a mushroom CONR 241:4
  made of sterner s. SHAK 697:25
  s. of life HOUS 404:15
  unrefinèd s. of mine BRAD 149:6
  Was there ever such s. GEOR 343:5
  write such s. JOHN 432:6
stuffed We are the s. men ELIO 302:6
stuffs S. out his vacant garments SHAK 699:6
stultitiam Misce s. consiliis HORA 403:1
stumbles how the strong man s. ROOS 654:12
  s. at a straw SPEN 752:19
stumbling for a stone of s. BIBL 88:16
  s. through my soul GORE 357:2
stumbling-block unto the Jews a s. BIBL 107:4
stung S. by the splendour BROW 159:4
stupefying s. incense-smoke BROW 158:21
stupid all questions were s. WEIS 826:25
  interesting . . . but s. CATC 201:30
  It's the economy, s. POLI 600:26
  most intelligent and most s. CONF 238:10
  on the part of the s. WARN 821:21
  stability pact is s. PROD 612:19
  s. enough to want it CHES 217:13
  s. is doing something SHAW 724:20
  s. neither forgive nor SZAS 769:16
  Would it be s. RUMS 658:10
stupidest s. party MILL 525:4
stupidity cruelty, s. and misgovernment GLAD 351:12
  excess of s. JOHN 428:17
  s. than depravity JOHN 429:9
  With s. the gods themselves SCHI 670:29
Sturm S. und Drang KAUF 442:3
'stute small 'S. Fish KIPL 456:20
sty Over the nasty s. SHAK 687:25

Stygian In S. cave forlorn MILT 529:17
  S. smoke JAME 417:1
style attain an English s. JOHN 424:25
  cut, the s., the line LOES 489:11
  definition of a s. SWIF 766:3
  forges one's s. ZOLA 859:7
  grand s. ARNO 30:10
  has no real s. PICA 595:8
  have his own s. MATH 518:7
  How the s. refines POPE 604:11
  Mandarin s. CONN 240:4
  murderer for fancy prose s. NABO 555:15
  only secret of s. ARNO 30:11
  own towering s. CHES 217:10
  see a natural s. PASC 587:3
  s. cannot be too clear STEN 755:19
  S. is life FLAU 325:13
  S. is the dress of thought WESL 830:1
  S. is the man BUFF 163:13
  s. is the man PROV 631:30
  that is s. STEV 758:25
  with his eye on his s. ARNO 30:7
styles All s. are good VOLT 816:2
suave S., mari magno LUCR 495:14
sub Sighted s., sank same MASO 517:17
subdue s. all things to himself BOOK 133:18
  s. the arrogant VIRG 812:15
  s. the people BOOK 137:2
subdued My nature is s. SHAK 723:21
subiectis Parcere s. VIRG 812:15
subject British s. I was born MACD 501:9
  Every s.'s duty SHAK 693:16
  Grasp the s. CATO 199:19
  honour is the s. SHAK 696:5
  Little s., little wit CARE 191:6
  shocked by this s. BOHR 125:9
  s. and a sovereign CHAR 208:26
  s. is not truth CHAP 208:18
  s. of all verse EPIT 311:11
  s. of almost equal importance BRAM 149:8
  s. of a novel MURA 554:10
  s. of conversation CHES 214:20
  We know a s. ourselves JOHN 430:7
  what it is to be a s. ELIZ 304:5
subjection bring it into s. BIBL 107:20
subjective any s. viewpoint CHUA 219:6
subjects good of s. DEFO 261:28
  most important s. ARIS 25:9
  rich in s. DEFO 261:13
  s. are rebels BURK 167:11
subjunctive hope to use the s. LEHR 479:12
sublime beauteous and s. AKEN 9:4
  egotistical s. KEAT 446:16
  essence of the true s. BYRO 182:11
  heart of the ridiculous, the s. MAHO 507:9
  My object all s. GILB 348:4
  step above the s. PAIN 582:5
  s. dashed to pieces COLE 234:9
  s. to the ridiculous NAPO 556:15
  s. to the ridiculous PROV 620:32
sublimity S. is the echo LONG 491:13
submerged s. tenth BOOT 144:24
submission appetite for s. ELIO 299:25
  s. of men's actions HOBB 390:31
  Yielded with coy s. MILT 533:1
submit Must he s. SHAK 715:26
  s. myself BOOK 132:16
  s. yourself CONR 240:19
subordinate in a s. position THOM 788:5
subordination s. of one sex MILL 525:12
subscribers list of s. JOHN 431:27
subsistence S. only increases MALT 509:9
  s. without a mind BERK 69:14
subsisting human flesh s. BOOK 129:2
substance dividing the S. BOOK 128:22
  eyes did see my s. BOOK 143:18
  mind can make S. BYRO 182:7
  persons of some s. WIND 841:12
  ruler of all his s. BOOK 141:13
  s. from the common earth FITZ 323:14
  s. of his house BIBL 87:23
  s. of ten thousand soldiers SHAK 717:8
  summed with all his s. CHAP 208:9

Upon a fearful s. SHAK 683:17
summum *S. bonum* CICE 223:11
Sumner [Charles] S.'s mind ADAM 2:12
sumpshous s. spot ASHF 31:14
sun against a setting s. SHAK 719:9
all, except their s., is set BYRO 181:4
At the going down of the s. BINY 116:14
aweary of the s. SHAK 707:15
Before you let the s. in THOM 790:5
behold the s. BIBL 86:23
beneath another s. THOM 792:13
best s. we have WALP 819:4
black s. of melancholy NERV 559:8
Born of the s. SPEN 750:20
bowled the s. TAYL 774:19
bride that s. shines on PROV 621:30
burnished s. SHAK 709:3
candle to the s. SIDN 735:17
candle to the s. YOUN 857:7
cannot make our s. Stand MARV 516:3
clear as the s. BIBL 87:17
countenance was as the s. BIBL 112:29
course of s. and stars ZORO 859:19
enjoyed the s. ARNO 27:7
especially Sir Brother S. FRAN 332:5
faded summer's s. BOLT 126:17
feel the s. BROW 157:22
flew between me and the s. BLUN 124:6
glorious S. uprist COLE 232:17
golden apples of the s. YEAT 855:19
Hath Britain all the s. SHAK 683:5
heat o' the s. SHAK 683:8
he beheld the s. WORD 846:13
hooting at the glorious s. COLE 231:17
I am too much i' the s. SHAK 683:24
If the Persians hide the s. HERO 385:13
Juliet is the s. SHAK 717:19
loves to live i' the s. SHAK 681:5
love that moves the s. CLOS 228:2
love that moves the s. DANT 256:13
maketh his sun to rise BIBL 94:31
maturing s. KEAT 445:14
Mother, give me the s. IBSE 412:12
never see the s. BROW 161:20
no new thing under the s. BIBL 85:28
nothing like the s. SHAK 723:26
nothing new under the s. PROV 632:21
no worship to the garish s. SHAK 717:37
old fool, unruly s. DONN 281:12
open face of the s. WESL 829:19
out in the midday s. COWA 245:3
place in the s. BÜLO 164:1
place in the s. WILH 837:18
places Under the s. HOUS 404:20
prayer at sinking of the s. KORA 460:15
ran the s. down with talk CALL 186:1
reign where'er the s. WATT 823:19
rising of the s. SONG 747:10
rising s. has first breathed VIRG 814:14
sacred radiance of the s. SHAK 699:18
seen the s. set RIMB 649:7
self-same s. SHAK 722:10
setting s. SHAK 715:12
shene is the s. LANG 466:21
shoots at the mid-day s. SIDN 736:1
soft was the s. LANG 466:14
stand out of my s. DIOG 274:18
staring at the s. BELL 64:20
s. also rises HEMI 381:7
s. and moon AUGU 37:1
S. and Moon should doubt BLAK 119:13
s. and moon to stand TOAS 796:2
s. begins his state MILT 529:21
s. does not set SCHI 670:26
s. doth parch the green SURR 764:6
S.-girt city SHEL 730:1
s. go down on your anger PROV 627:22
s. go down upon your wrath BIBL 109:13
s. grows cold TAYL 774:18
s. has gone in SMIT 742:16
S. himself cannot forget ANON 19:7
S. in his strength BIBL 75:2
s. is always setting NAIP 556:2

s. is laid to sleep JONS 435:2
s. is lost DONN 279:4
s. loses nothing PROV 631:34
s. loste his hewe CHAU 211:9
s. never sets NORT 565:10
s. now stands JOSE 436:15
s. of heaven prove a micher SHAK 690:15
S. of righteousness BIBL 92:14
S. of Righteousness WESL 828:24
s. of York SHAK 716:18
s. reigns supreme LE C 478:12
s. shall not burn thee BOOK 142:16
s. shone BECK 61:9
s. showing up the dust PERR 592:26
S.'s rim dips COLE 232:22
S., stand thou still BIBL 79:13
s. to me is dark MILT 534:27
S.-treader, life and light BROW 160:19
s. was shining everywhere GERS 344:4
S. wot won it NEWS 562:15
tired the s. with talking CORY 244:3
under the s. BIBL 85:25
Up roos the s. CHAU 211:16
when the s. in bed MILT 530:26
when the s. rise BLAK 123:2
where no s. shines THOM 789:13
while the s. shines PROV 625:51
woman clothed with the s. BIBL 113:27
yet I saw no s. TICH 794:12
sunbeam Jesus wants me for a s. TALB 770:19
s. in a winter's day DYER 293:16
sunbeams didst the stars and s. know
ARNO 28:13
s. out of cucumbers SWIF 765:14
sunbright upon the s. walls WORD 845:21
Sunday feeling of S. is the same RHYS 646:15
Here of a S. morning HOUS 404:11
killing of a mouse on S. BRAT 149:19
may be played on S. LEAC 476:17
Never on S. FILM 322:9
rainy S. afternoon ERTZ 308:14
rainy S. in London DE Q 264:19
She was the S. CLAR 225:7
S., bloody Sunday FILM 322:11
S. go-to-meeting clothes SHIE 734:20
this is S. morning MACN 504:21
working week and S. best AUDE 34:29
Sundays begin a journey on S. SWIF 766:13
sundial s., and I make a botch BELL 65:20
sundry s. and manifold changes BOOK 130:8
sunflower S.! weary of time BLAK 122:10
sung s. as it were a new song BIBL 114:1
s. from noon to noon MORR 549:17
sunk s. beneath the wave COWP 247:2
sunless Down to a s. sea COLE 232:3
to the s. land WORD 846:19
sunlight s. on the garden MACN 504:22
sunnier s. side of doubt TENN 775:15
sunny Candlemas day be s. and bright
PROV 622:46
leaps S. Jim ADVE 7:30
lived in a warm, s. climate COWA 245:9
s. pleasure-dome COLE 232:5
s. side of the street FIEL 318:17
sunrise Eternity's s. BLAK 121:22
suns light of setting s. WORD 847:11
planets circle other s. POPE 604:19
process of the s. TENN 780:22
S. can set and come CATU 202:13
S., that set JONS 435:18
sunset make a fine s. MADA 505:7
sail beyond the s. TENN 784:19
S. and evening star TENN 776:15
S. breezes shiver NEWB 560:3
s. of my life REAG 643:17
S. ran BROW 159:19
s.-seas ALDR 11:1
there's a s.-touch BROW 158:14
sunsets Autumn s. exquisitely dying
HUXL 411:11
horror of s. PROU 613:11
sunshine Digressions are the s. STER 756:21
in the s. and with applause BUNY 164:20

like s. after rain SHAK 724:3
ray of s. WODE 842:16
s. in the shady place SPEN 751:15
s. is a glorious birth WORD 847:21
s. of the heart CONS 241:8
s. to the sunless land WORD 846:19
sunt *Sint ut s.* CLEM 226:14
sup liveth longest doth but s. HENS 382:17
s. with my Lord Jesus Christ BRUC 162:4
superbos *et debellare s.* VIRG 812:15
superficial ridiculous and s. MURA 554:11
superfluities must have s. GAY 342:7
superfluity barren s. of words GART 340:12
superfluous in the poorest thing s.
SHAK 700:10
nothing is s. LEON 481:4
s., a very necessary thing VOLT 816:7
s. in me ADAM 2:1
S., superfluous TURG 802:4
superhuman S. effort isn't worth
SHAC 677:19
superior being s. to time JOHN 425:26
embarrass the s. SHAW 726:22
most s. person ANON 17:20
no-one to be their s. TOCQ 795:14
notions about a s. power SWIF 765:4
s. man is broadminded CONF 237:13
S. people never make long visits
MOOR 547:3
superman I teach you the s. NIET 564:1
It's S. ANON 15:25
supernatural nothing mysterious or s.
HUME 408:10
s. source of evil CONR 241:1
superstition character of a s. CHOM 218:9
main source of s. RUSS 661:7
species of s. HUME 409:5
s. in avoiding superstition BACO 45:23
S. is the poetry of life GOET 353:6
S. is the religion BURK 167:24
s. sets the whole world VOLT 815:16
s. to enslave a philosophy INGE 413:6
superstitions end as s. HUXL 412:1
s. of the human mind VOLT 816:6
superstitious he is s. grown SHAK 696:25
in all things ye are too s. BIBL 105:18
more s., more bigoted NEWM 560:11
s. reluctance to sit JOHN 431:16
superwoman I am not S. BLAI 118:13
supped Hobson has s. MILT 531:1
s. full with horrors SHAK 707:13
supper after s. walk a mile PROV 614:6
consider s. as a turnpike EDWA 297:2
good s. at night ANST 23:2
Last-s.-carved-on-a-peach-stone
LANC 465:21
leaned on his breast at s. BIBL 104:23
Sings for his s. NURS 568:5
S. of the Lord BOOK 132:19
suppliant s. for his own BYRO 182:26
thus the s. prays JOHN 426:19
supplications make our common s.
BOOK 128:18
supplies just bought fresh s. BREC 150:11
support depend on the s. of Paul SHAW 725:5
help and s. of the woman EDWA 296:12
no invisible means of s. BUCH 162:20
s. him after SHAK 719:8
s. me when I am in the wrong MELB 521:6
s. of the people CLEV 226:17
s. us all the day long NEWM 561:2
swears that he will s. it JACK 414:17
visible means of s. BIER 116:8
without the s. of all LULA 496:5
supports s. with insolence JOHN 424:13
suppose universe queerer than we s.
HALD 367:17
suppress power of s. NORT 565:14
supramundane s. mushroom LAUR 470:9
supreme in none s. ARNO 29:1
S. God EMPS 307:20
s. *power must be arbitrary* HALI 368:18
sups s. with the Devil PROV 622:15

surcease catch With his s. success
    SHAK 704:3
sure joy was never s.   SWIN 768:16
  made the round world so s.   BOOK 140:6
  Slow but s.   PROV 630:46
  What nobody is s. about   BELL 65:15
surely Shome mishtake, s.   CATC 201:26
surety s. for a stranger   BIBL 84:10
surf s. floods over the reeds   PAST 588:4
surface looks dingy on the s.   PIRS 595:20
surfeit s. by eating of a lamprey   FABY 313:20
  s. of our own behaviour   SHAK 699:26
  s. with too much   SHAK 708:24
surge s. and thunder   LANG 466:11
  thine aëry s.   SHEL 730:8
  turbulent s. shall cover   SHAK 719:13
surgeon not call the s.   DICK 273:12
  There can be no s.   PARA 585:11
  wounded s. plies the steel   ELIO 301:18
surges s. lash the sounding shore
    POPE 604:10
surmise smothered in s.   SHAK 703:15
  with a wild s.   KEAT 445:6
surprise Life is a great s.   NABO 555:16
  Live frugally on s.   WALK 817:10
  mystify, mislead, and s.   JACK 415:8
  no little s.   BARH 55:17
  No s. for the writer   FROS 336:5
  Respect was mingled with s.   SCOT 673:6
  sound of s.   BALL 54:4
  wise man by s.   LA F 463:15
surprised guilty thing s.   WORD 848:11
  S. by joy   WORD 850:11
  S. by unjust force   MILT 529:5
surprises millions of s.   HERB 384:24
  S. are foolish things   AUST 38:21
surprising everything is s.   BYAT 177:11
surquidry s. and foul presumpcioun
    CHAU 212:28
surrender die but do not s.   CAMB 186:14
  entire s.   BELH 64:7
  I s. to you   GERO 344:3
  No s.   POLI 601:4
  to Him we s.   KORA 459:20
  unconditional and immediate s.   GRAN 359:4
  we shall never s.   CHUR 221:8
surrendered never s. her soul   DE V 266:4
surroundings I plus my s.   ORTE 576:13
sursum S. corda   MISS 536:22
survey monarch of all I s.   COWP 248:24
  s. of all the world   SHAK 691:12
  s. the wondrous cross   WATT 823:15
survival s. game   CHRÉ 218:13
  s. is all there is   FULL 337:2
  S. of the Fittest   DARW 257:9
  s. of the fittest   SPEN 750:8
  their s. machines   DAWK 259:16
  without victory, there is no s.   CHUR 221:7
survive Dare hope to s.   HUXL 411:10
  expect to s.   JEAN 419:5
  know they can s.   HART 374:9
  Only the paranoid s.   GROV 365:8
  s. of us is love   LARK 468:13
  s. to consume   VANE 807:1
survived I s.   SIEY 736:22
  know how I s.   SIMO 738:8
survivors more the s.' affair   MANN 510:13
  old, old s.   SHAW 728:3
Susan black-eyed S. came aboard   GAY 342:10
susceptible s. to draughts   WILD 835:21
suspect Always s. everybody   DICK 271:8
  makes a man s. much   BACO 45:25
suspected New opinions are always s.
    LOCK 488:5
suspects Round up the usual s.   FILM 320:4
suspended s. my religious inquiries
    GIBB 345:15
suspenders not forget the s.   KIPL 456:19
suspension Shining s.   CRAN 249:26
  willing s. of disbelief   COLE 233:22
suspicion above s.   CAES 185:13
  above s.   PROV 616:21
  against despots—s.   DEMO 263:18

banish squint s.   MILT 528:25
  S. always haunts   SHAK 695:3
  s. that more than half   WHIT 832:1
suspicions S. amongst thoughts   BACO 45:24
Sussex S. won't be druv   PROV 631:35
sustaining our s. corn   SHAK 701:11
sutlers sapient s.   ELIO 302:22
swaddling wrapped him in s. clothes
    BIBL 100:2
swagman Once a jolly s.   PATE 588:12
swains all our s. commend her   SHAK 721:22
swallow and the s. a nest   BOOK 139:15
  before the s. dares   SHAK 722:5
  O summer s.   SWIN 769:2
  speed of a s.   BETJ 73:2
  s. a camel   BIBL 98:10
  s. does not make summer   PROV 629:2
  s.-flights of song   TENN 779:3
  S., flying, flying South   TENN 783:6
  s. has set her six young   BROW 159:28
  S., my sister   SWIN 768:25
  s. the cow   PROV 624:5
swallowed soon to be s.   BLY 124:12
  s. by way of viaticum   GLAD 350:20
  They had s. us up quick   BOOK 142:20
swallows gathering s. twitter   KEAT 445:18
  watching the s.   WORD 845:21
swamp botanize in the s.   CHES 217:9
swamps across primeval s.   WODE 842:25
swan black Ohioan s.   WRIG 851:15
  hatched from a s.'s egg   ANDE 14:4
  I will play the s.   SHAK 714:25
  Leda's goose a s.   ANON 16:10
  like a sleeping s.   SHEL 731:7
  silver s.   GIBB 345:24
  some full-breasted s.   TENN 778:19
  so much as a black s.   JUVE 439:19
  Sweet S. of Avon   JONS 436:4
  this pale s.   SHAK 722:19
Swanee down upon the S. River   FOST 330:14
swanlike He makes a s. end   SHAK 709:16
Swann no more talk of S.   PROU 613:5
swans amongst tuneful s.   VIRG 814:9
  Dumb s., not chattering pies   SIDN 736:7
  I saw two s.   SPEN 752:15
  ships sail like s. asleep   FLEC 326:4
  s. are geese   ARNO 27:14
  s. of others are geese   WALP 819:16
swap s. horses when crossing   LINC 485:10
swarm s. in May   PROV 631:36
  S. over, death   BETJ 72:17
swarthy in its s. monotony   HARD 371:22
swashing s. and a martial outside
    SHAK 680:24
swath thy hook Spares the next s.
    KEAT 445:15
sway little rule, a little s.   DYER 293:16
swaying s. sound of the sea   AUDE 35:10
sways So s. she level   SHAK 720:23
swear And s. No where   DONN 281:10
  s. by Apollo the physician   HIPP 389:11
  s. like a comfit-maker's wife   SHAK 690:26
  s. not at all   BIBL 94:28
  s. not by the moon   SHAK 717:24
  when very angry, s.   TWAI 803:24
swearers and s. swear   BURN 171:11
  liars and s.   SHAK 706:21
sweareth s. unto his neighbour   BOOK 134:13
swearing let me alone for s.   SHAK 721:14
swears Money doesn't talk, it s.   DYLA 294:8
sweat Blood, s., and tear-wrung   BYRO 177:22
  blood, toil, tears and s.   CHUR 221:5
  die of a s.   SHAK 692:25
  In the s. of thy face   BIBL 75:26
  none will s. but for promotion   SHAK 680:29
  placed the s. of our brows   HESI 387:7
  spend our midday s.   QUAR 638:20
  s. of an enseamèd bed   SHAK 687:25
  s. of its labourers   EISE 298:13
  work by the s. of his brow   CHEK 214:3
sweats Falstaff s. to death   SHAK 690:2
  wild regrets, and the bloody s.   WILD 837:1
sweep he'd s. the country   DISR 278:6

Mountains of Mourne s. down   FREN 333:16
  s. his own door-step   PROV 622:47
  s. the dust   SHAK 712:7
  your chimneys I s.   BLAK 122:1
sweeping S. up the Heart   DICK 273:3
sweeps beats as it s.   ADVE 7:35
  s. a room as for Thy laws   HERB 384:5
sweet All is not s.   JONS 435:4
  as a s. morsel   HENR 382:10
  buried in so s. a place   SHEL 728:12
  dead thing that smells s.   THOM 790:12
  Home, s. home   PAYN 589:11
  how it was s.   BROW 159:3
  How s. the moonlight sleeps   SHAK 710:2
  if TO-DAY be s.   FITZ 323:7
  in my mouth s. as honey   BIBL 113:26
  kiss me, s. and twenty   SHAK 720:16
  Life is very s.   BORR 145:10
  light is s.   BIBL 86:23
  Pyramus is a s.-faced man   SHAK 710:25
  seasons shall be s.   COLE 231:22
  Sleep is s.   BUNY 164:24
  Stolen waters are s.   BIBL 84:7
  such s. sorrow   SHAK 717:29
  such s. thunder   SHAK 711:24
  S. and low   TENN 782:26
  S. are the uses of adversity   SHAK 680:26
  s. as summer   SHAK 695:21
  s. day, so cool   HERB 385:4
  S. is revenge   BYRO 180:13
  s. is the whisper of the pine   THEO 787:21
  s. o' the year   SHAK 721:32
  s. peas, on tip-toe   KEAT 443:22
  s. reasonableness of Jesus   ARNO 30:5
  S. smell of success   FILM 322:13
  S., soft, plenty rhythm   MORT 551:7
  s. the name of Jesus   NEWT 563:6
  s. water and bitter   BIBL 111:28
  technically s.   OPPE 573:19
  Tell me not, s.   LOVE 493:7
  Things s. to taste   SHAK 715:9
  'Tis not so s. now   SHAK 720:5
  took s. counsel   BOOK 137:17
  wit enough to keep it s.   JOHN 432:19
sweeteners s. of tea   FIEL 318:4
sweeter mountain sheep are s.   PEAC 590:5
  s. also than honey   BOOK 134:22
  s. and a healthier one   DOYL 284:22
  s. than the berry   GAY 341:4
  those unheard Are s.   KEAT 444:8
sweetest From the s. wine   PROV 620:43
  Success is counted s.   DICK 273:7
  s. girl I know   JUDG 438:4
  s. sounds I'll ever hear   RODG 652:1
sweetheart Blanch, and S.   SHAK 701:3
  Like the s. of the sun   HOOD 395:10
sweetly Lalage, who laughs so s.
    HORA 400:18
sweetmeats pyramids of s.   DRYD 290:11
  s. and sugar-plums   TROL 799:8
sweetness came forth s.   BIBL 79:29
  O how great the sum Of s.   SMAR 740:13
  s. and light   ARNO 29:8
  s. and light   SWIF 765:6
  s. of Anjou   DU B 290:19
  s. of a shower   THOM 790:17
  waste its s.   GRAY 361:5
  where s. and light failed   FORS 329:11
sweets bag of boiled s.   CRIT 251:10
  brought'st Thy s.   HERB 384:2
  discandy, melt their s.   SHAK 679:20
  last taste of s.   SHAK 715:12
  Stolen s.   HUNT 409:19
  Stolen s. are best   CIBB 223:5
  s. compacted lie   HERB 385:4
  S. into your list   HUNT 409:18
  s. of place with power   ROSE 654:18
  S. to the sweet   SHAK 689:2
sweetshop pressed to a s. window
    YEAT 854:7
swell deep sea s.   ELIO 303:22
  s. a progress   ELIO 302:18
  Thou s.! Thou witty   HART 374:14

What a s. party PORT 607:18
swelling s. act SHAK 703:14
swept empty, s., and garnished BIBL 96:35
I s. the floor GILB 348:22
S. it for half a year CARR 195:6
swift Be s. to hear BIBL 111:21
Cousin S. DRYD 290:15
Love is s. of foot HERB 384:1
race is not to the s. BIBL 86:16
race is not to the s. PROV 630:3
race is to the s. DAVI 258:5
S. expires a driv'ler JOHN 426:20
swifter s. than a weaver's shuttle BIBL 82:38
s. than eagles BIBL 80:28
swiftness O s. never ceasing PEEL 591:3
prizes for s. of foot HOME 394:10
swim learn how to s. PROV 618:12
s., so hard of heart HORA 402:9
swimmer s. in his agony BYRO 180:20
swimmers s. into cleanness leaping BROO 153:14
swimming Come softly s. SPEN 752:15
few figures s. VIRG 810:18
S. for his life GLAD 350:15
S. from tree to tree LOWE 494:13
s. in the air EDWA 296:14
s. under water FITZ 324:11
swindles all truly great s. HENR 382:12
swine husks that the s. did eat BIBL 101:15
in a s.'s snout BIBL 84:11
lady loved a s. NURS 569:19
Nor yet feed the s. NURS 566:14
pearls before s. BIBL 95:14
s. cheweth not the cud BIBL 78:11
throw pearls to s. PROV 618:5
turkeys, geese and s. PROV 628:24
whole herd of s. BIBL 96:3
swines You rotten s. CATC 202:6
swing ain't got that s. MILL 527:14
s. for it KING 453:4
S. low, sweet chariot SONG 748:6
s. our ungirded hips SORL 746:22
Swing, s. together CORY 244:1
want to s. a cat DICK 268:26
swings What you lose on the s. PROV 634:16
Swiss No money, no S. PROV 627:42
switching sanction of s. off EYRE 313:11
Swithun Saint S.'s day PROV 630:19
Switzerland I look upon S. SMIT 743:12
In S. they had FILM 319:19
swoop all at one s. WEBS 826:4
At one fell s. SHAK 706:24
sword brave man with a s. WILD 836:29
but a s. BIBL 96:19
draws s. against prince PROV 635:5
edge of the s. BOOK 138:4
fallen by the edge of the s. BIBL 93:20
famous by my s. MONT 546:4
first drew the s. CLAR 224:15
His father's s. he has MOOR 547:17
I gave them a s. NIXO 565:3
lives by the s. PROV 622:12
make his s. BIBL 83:27
mightier than the s. PROV 629:19
My s., I give BUNY 165:9
nation shall not lift up s. BIBL 88:2
pen is worse than the s. BURT 174:5
pen mightier than the s. BULW 164:5
perish with the s. BIBL 99:8
put to the s. CROM 251:15
Put up thy s. BIBL 103:40
sharp as a two-edged s. BIBL 83:38
sheathe the s. ASQU 32:2
sigh is the s. BLAK 120:11
s., a horse, a shield LOVE 493:7
s. of a Norman Baron LEWE 483:2
s. of truth AITK 9:3
s. out of this stone MALO 508:18
s. shall pierce BIBL 100:8
s. sleep in my hand BLAK 121:15
s. sung on the barren heath BLAK 121:24
s. the axis of the world DE G 262:12
s. was in the sheath COWP 247:3

terrible swift s. HOWE 405:15
two-edged s. BIBL 112:29
two-edged s. BOOK 144:8
watery if not flaming s. MARV 516:5
wield the s. of France DE G 262:3
with the edge of the s. BIBL 78:18
swords books are either dreams or s. LOWE 493:18
Keep up your bright s. SHAK 713:4
s. In our own proper entrails SHAK 698:26
s. into plowshares BIBL 88:2
s. shall play the orators MARL 513:18
ten thousand s. leapt BURK 167:13
yet they be very s. BOOK 137:18
swore armies s. terribly STER 757:3
My tongue s. EURI 312:17
when the son s. BURT 174:16
sworn had I so s. as you SHAK 704:12
sycamore nightingale in the s. STEV 760:19
sycophants s. and flatterers HARD 371:7
syllable chase A panting s. COWP 247:18
To the last s. SHAK 707:14
syllables light s. leaped ROET 652:5
S. govern the world SELD 676:11
syllogism conclusion of your s. O'BR 571:5
sylph only s. I ever saw DICK 271:1
symbol Five for the s. at your door SONG 747:11
S. or energy ADAM 2:16
symboles forêts de s. BAUD 58:13
symbolic s. expression MAXW 519:5
symbolical works of women are s. BROW 157:16
symbols forests of s. BAUD 58:13
s. of a high romance KEAT 445:24
symmetry fearful s. BLAK 122:19
S. is tedious HUGO 407:18
s. of his body EINH 297:11
sympathetic s. wife EURI 312:24
sympathies enlarge men's s. ELIO 300:23
sympathy give or take s. RHYS 646:14
messages of s. AYCK 41:4
secret s. SCOT 673:10
s. is cold GIBB 345:8
Tea and s. ANDE 14:9
symphony angelic s. MILT 530:21
Ninth S. will remain BAKU 50:5
s. like the world MAHL 507:8
symptoms hundred good s. POPE 606:26
synagogues chief seats in the s. BIBL 99:26
syne For auld lang s. BURN 170:9
synod S. of Cooks JOHN 428:20
Syrens song the S. sang BROW 156:12
Syria S. isn't on it STRA 762:12
Syrian S. damsels to lament his fate MILT 531:20
S. Orontes JUVE 439:14
syrops lucent s. KEAT 443:2
system cannot be a true s. PAIN 582:4
must create a s. BLAK 120:7
rocked the s. ROBI 650:22
s. into system runs POPE 604:19
s. of Government GLAD 350:10
s. of outdoor relief BRIG 151:8
systems little s. have their day TENN 778:20
s. into ruin hurled POPE 604:21

T t is silent ASQU 32:7
ta saying 'T.' to God SPEN 750:17
tabby Demurest of the t. kind GRAY 361:13
tabernacle dwell in thy t. BOOK 134:12
t. were dissolved BIBL 108:15
tabernacles t. of thy grace SCOT 675:5
tabernas pauperum t. HORA 400:5
table behave mannerly at t. STEV 760:7
biforn his fader at the t. CHAU 210:9
cannot make a t. JOHN 428:5
fall from their masters' t. BIBL 97:13
fell from the rich man's t. BIBL 101:22
five steps from the t. ROBB 649:16
on a t.?—and under it BYRO 184:12
patient etherized upon a t. ELIO 302:12

prepare a t. before me BOOK 135:4
round about thy t. BOOK 143:3
T., at the Communion-time BOOK 131:5
takes the t. clean away BARN 56:18
tableau t. of crimes VOLT 816:5
tables make it plain upon t. BIBL 92:11
serve t. BIBL 104:31
tablet keep taking The T. THOM 790:21
tablets thy t., Memory ARNO 27:17
taboo t.'d by anxiety GILB 347:16
tabret bring hither the t. BOOK 139:13
tabulae Solventur risu t. HORA 403:12
tache sans une t. ROST 656:12
tactful t. in audacity COCT 230:4
tactics art of t. BAGE 48:2
tadpole When you were a t. SMIT 742:11
taedium vitae keep off the t. JOHN 428:2
taffeta doublet of changeable t. SHAK 720:27
T. phrases SHAK 702:22
Taffy T. was a Welshman NURS 569:16
tail choke on the t. PROV 624:5
Improve his shining t. CARR 193:19
more he shows his t. PROV 622:21
O! thereby hangs a t. SHAK 713:24
rat without a t. SHAK 703:5
scaly horror of his folded t. MILT 530:24
sensations of its "t." DISR 275:10
t. hangs down behind KIPL 456:13
t. that wagged WATS 823:4
treading on my t. CARR 194:17
tailor coat from the t. GOLD 356:1
ninth part even of a t. CARL 191:15
t. in Gloucester POTT 608:1
t. make thy doublet SHAK 720:27
Tinker, T. NURS 570:8
tailors eighteen t. CARL 192:30
Nine t. make a man PROV 627:35
tails bring their t. behind them NURS 567:21
stings in their t. BIBL 113:25
taint never t. my love SHAK 714:15
tainted t. wether of the flock SHAK 709:23
taisez-vous T.! Méfiez-vous OFFI 572:14
take big enough to t. away everything FORD 328:9
Give and t. fair play PROV 620:39
O t. those lips away SHAK 708:13
something people t. BALD 50:8
T. a pair of sparkling eyes GILB 347:6
t. a thing PROV 620:38
T., eat BIBL 99:1
T., eat, this is my Body BOOK 132:2
T. me to your leader CATC 201:28
t. my life FARQ 315:15
t. my life and all SHAK 709:32
t. not thy holy Spirit BOOK 137:13
T. now thy son BIBL 76:21
t. the nasty soup away HOFF 391:14
T. up the White Man's Burden KIPL 456:7
t. who have the power WORD 849:25
t. you in the morning BALD 50:11
taken Lord hath t. away BIBL 82:27
much is t., much abides TENN 784:19
One shall be t. BIBL 98:19
shall be t. away BIBL 98:23
she was t. out of Man BIBL 75:16
t. away my Lord BIBL 104:11
t. in when they marry AUST 39:1
When t. COLM 236:6
takes if it t. all summer GRAN 359:5
t. just like a woman DYLA 294:9
that it t. away BYRO 183:9
taketh t. away the sin BIBL 102:24
taking t. life by the throat FROS 336:7
we're t. over MORR 550:5
tale adorn a t. JOHN 426:18
fortunate for t.-tellers SCOT 674:16
had a t. to tell SCOT 673:1
I could a t. unfold SHAK 684:32
mere t. of a tub WEBS 826:6
most tremendous t. of all BETJ 72:3
plain t. shall put you down SHAK 690:12
round unvarnished t. SHAK 713:7
sad t.'s best for winter SHAK 721:26

tale (*cont*.):
t. never loses in telling — PROV 631:39
t. should be judicious — COWP 246:7
t. Told by an idiot — SHAK 707:14
t. which holdeth children — SIDN 736:16
telling the saddest t. — SHAK 710:29
Tell t. tit — NURS 569:17
thereby hangs a t. — SHAK 681:7
Trust the t. — LAWR 474:23
twice-told t. — SHAK 699:7
talent into my works is my t. — WILD 837:8
Murder, like t. — LEWE 483:1
no t. for writing — BENC 66:8
sister of t. — CHEK 214:10
T. develops in quiet places — GOET 353:7
T. does what it can — MERE 522:24
t. instantly recognizes genius — DOYL 285:9
t. of a liar — BYRO 184:10
t. pour le silence — CARL 192:12
t. to amuse — COWA 244:18
t. which is death to hide — MILT 535:7
tomb of a mediocre t. — SMIT 742:14
talents career open to the t. — NAPO 557:3
If you have great t. — REYN 646:1
ministry of all the t. — ANON 17:16
virtue and t. — JEFF 420:10
Whate'er the t. — POPE 602:1
tales Dead men tell no t. — PROV 617:25
idle t. — BIBL 102:10
increased with t. — BACO 44:1
tell t. out of school — PROV 627:29
tali *t. auxilio nec defensoribus* — VIRG 811:21
talk Can they t. — BENT 68:8
Careless t. costs lives — OFFI 572:1
do not t. of ourselves — TROL 799:16
good to t. — ADVE 7:38
gotta use words when I t. to you — ELIO 303:5
have out his t. — JOHN 430:29
If you t. to God — SZAS 769:17
I long to t. — DONN 281:5
It can t., talk, talk — PLAT 596:18
It would t. — BEAU 60:10
let the people t. — DANT 256:6
Money doesn't t., it swears — DYLA 294:8
Most English t. — JAME 417:17
Must t. — SMIT 741:17
no more t. of Swann — PROU 613:5
No use to t. to me — HOUS 404:10
people who can't t. — ZAPP 858:6
ran the sun down with t. — CALL 186:1
t. about the rest of us — ANON 19:9
t. but a tinkling cymbal — BACO 44:14
T. is cheap — PROV 631:40
t. like a lady — SHAW 727:12
t. of many things — CARR 195:7
t. of the child — TALM 772:17
T. of the Devil — PROV 631:41
t. of wills — SHAK 715:22
t. on for ever — HAZL 376:10
t. six times — BYRO 181:28
t. the less — ZENO 858:7
t. too much — DRYD 287:5
t. to the plants — CHAR 209:16
They always t. — PRIO 612:12
very easy to t. — DICK 270:23
ways of making you t. — CATC 201:32
we had a good t. — BOSW 146:25
world may t. of hereafter — COLL 234:22
talked I believe they t. of me — FARQ 315:12
least t. about by men — PERI 592:24
not being t. about — WILD 836:14
t. like poor Poll — GARR 340:3
t. of their Raphaels — GOLD 355:9
t. shop — ANON 16:9
t. with us by the way — BIBL 102:12
talkers present is an age of t. — HAZL 376:22
ten thousand t. — DYLA 294:7
talking foolish t. — BIBL 109:14
He is t. — BIBL 81:22
know what we are t. about — RUSS 660:23
leaves off t. — BUTL 177:6
nation t. to itself — MILL 527:9
People t. without speaking — SIMO 738:4

quieten your enemy by t. — CEAU 204:10
redtape t.-machine — CARL 192:19
stop people t. — ATTL 33:5
T. and eloquence — JONS 436:10
t., Signior Benedick — SHAK 712:12
t. to myself — BARN 56:13
tired the sun with t. — CORY 244:3
talks Garbo t. — TAGL 771:3
Money t. — PROV 626:39
t. it so very fast — FARQ 315:14
t. of Arthur's death — SHAK 699:11
t. of his misfortunes — JOHN 431:20
tall all I ask is a t. ship — MASE 517:15
divinely t. — TENN 776:19
don't look t. — PORT 607:23
exceeding t. men — BACO 46:20
for this the clay grew t. — OWEN 581:5
long and the short and the t. — HUGH 406:16
t. as a crane — SITW 738:14
'Tis a t. building — CRAB 248:27
taller t. by almost the breadth — SWIF 765:9
t. than other men — HARO 373:17
Talmuds rotted T. of my childhood — BABE 42:5
Tam T. was glorious — BURN 172:10
tambourine Mr T. Man — DYLA 294:12
play the t. — DICK 271:1
tame tongue can no man t. — BIBL 111:27
taming T. my wild heart — SHAK 712:22
Tam Lin ken this night, T. — BALL 53:9
tamper never want to t. — AUDE 35:4
Tandy met wid Nappy T. — POLI 600:21
tangere *Noli me t.* — BIBL 115:17
tangle odors t. — DICK 273:13
t. me no more — WYAT 852:1
tangled t. web we weave — SCOT 673:23
tangles t. of Neaera's hair — MILT 530:2
tango Takes two to t. — HOFF 391:12
takes two to t. — PROV 624:28
tank T. come down the stalls — SASS 667:16
tiger in your t. — ADVE 8:11
tanks Get your t. off my lawn — WILS 840:10
tanstaafl T. — SAYI 670:15
tantae *T. molis erat* — VIRG 810:17
tantras Mantras and t. — TANT 773:5
tantum *T. ergo sacramentum* — THOM 788:16
T. religio potuit — LUCR 495:10
Tao not the eternal T. — LAO 467:4
one is near T. — CHUA 218:19
T. has reality and evidence — CHUA 219:4
Therefore T. is great — LAO 467:11
tap t. being turned off — KIPL 457:4
taper Out went the t. — KEAT 442:19
t. to the outward room — DONN 280:4
with t. light To seek — SHAK 699:10
tapestry earth in so rich t. — SIDN 736:14
Turkey t. — HOWE 406:1
tapping suddenly there came a t. — POE 599:5
tar ha'porth of t. — PROV 618:4
T.-baby ain't sayin' nuthin' — HARR 374:7
T. water — BERK 69:10
Tara through T.'s halls — MOOR 547:15
when T. rose so high — LAND 466:3
taratantara *t. dixit* — ENNI 308:4
tarde *cinco en punto de la t.* — LORC 492:1
tares but a field of t. — TICH 794:12
t. of mine own brain — BROW 156:31
tarnished neither t. nor afraid — CHAN 207:15
Tarquin great house of T. — MACA 499:11
T.'s ravishing strides — SHAK 704:17
tarried too long he t. — SWIF 767:19
too long we have t. — LEAR 477:16
tarry Boatman, do not t. — CAMP 187:13
t. till I come — BIBL 104:24
why t. the wheels — BIBL 79:21
You may for ever t. — HERR 386:19
tarrying make no long t. — BOOK 136:8
tart t. cathartic virtue — EMER 306:24
t. who has married the Mayor — BAXT 59:7
tartar find a T. — PROV 630:21
T.'s lips — SHAK 706:13
tarts action of two t. — MACM 504:7
stole the t. — NURS 569:6
Tarzan Me T. — MISQ 538:8

task completed the t. — TALM 772:24
long day's t. — SHAK 679:23
thy worldly t. hast done — SHAK 683:8
what he reads as a t. — JOHN 428:9
with weary t. fordone — SHAK 712:6
tasks have been my t. — KOLL 459:4
tassel lure this t.-gentle — SHAK 717:27
tassie fill it in a silver t. — BURN 171:26
taste arbiter of t. — TACI 770:9
bad t. — HOPK 397:16
bad t. of the smoker — ELIO 299:10
bouquet is better than the t. — POTT 608:7
common sense and good t. — SHAW 724:21
create the t. — WORD 851:2
difference of t. in jokes — ELIO 299:11
Every man to his t. — PROV 619:18
forgot the t. of fears — SHAK 707:12
ghastly good t. — BETJ 73:6
good sense and good t. — LA B 462:18
Good t. and humour — MUGG 553:10
I did but t. a little honey — BIBL 80:13
last t. of sweets — SHAK 715:12
never t. who always drink — PRIO 612:12
nobody has any t. for them — VOLT 816:18
No! let me t. — BROW 161:2
no t. when you married — SHER 733:27
nothing for good t. — TOLS 796:18
nowhere worse t. — JOWE 436:19
ocean has but one t. — PALI 584:8
t. and see — BOOK 135:23
T. is the feminine — FITZ 323:19
t. it but sparingly — AUST 39:13
t. my meat — HERB 384:14
t. or genius — REYN 646:3
Things sweet to t. — SHAK 715:9
undoubtedly wanted t. — WALP 819:1
tasted books are to be t. — BACO 45:20
so be ye have t. — BIBL 112:4
tastes if it t. good, it's bad — ASIM 31:19
no accounting for t. — PROV 632:16
strongest t. were negative — WAUG 824:9
T. differ — PROV 631:42
t. greatly alter — JOHN 428:25
tasting T. of Flora — KEAT 444:21
Tat *T. ist alles, nichts der Ruhm* — GOET 353:2
Tathagata called T. — PALI 583:13
tattered t. coat upon a stick — YEAT 855:9
wars have t. his ears — HUGH 407:4
tatters rags and t. — MOLI 541:19
taught afterward he t. — CHAU 210:22
as if you t. them not — POPE 604:15
Cristes loore He t. — CHAU 210:24
got to be carefully t. — HAMM 370:12
t. anything — MOLI 542:7
t. by the enemy — OVID 580:12
t. me first to beg — SHAK 709:34
t. them as one having authority — BIBL 95:26
t. to any purpose — REYN 645:17
what we call highly t. — ELIO 300:8
what we have t. her — GAY 341:6
You t. me language — SHAK 718:24
taunting grave, and not t. — BACO 44:24
tavern hostess of the t. — SHAK 689:20
in a t. drinking — ANON 21:18
'So is the London T.' — ANON 16:4
t. for his friends — DOUG 283:21
t. in the town — SONG 748:7
t. or inn — JOHN 430:13
tax Excise. A hateful t. — JOHN 424:30
I t. not you, you elements — SHAK 700:16
power to t. — MARS 514:12
soon be able to t. it — FARA 314:18
To t. and to please — BURK 166:16
taxation art of t. consists — COLB 230:23
Inflation one form of t. — FRIE 334:14
lottery is a t. — FIEL 318:3
T. and representation — CAMD 186:15
T. without representation — OTIS 579:11
taxed world should be t. — BIBL 100:1
taxes as true . . . as t. — DICK 268:19
death and t. — DEFO 261:6
death and t. — FRAN 332:19
death and t. — PROV 628:8

shouting fire in a t. HOLM 393:10
t. of man's life BACO 42:21
t. of the world MARY 517:10
This House today is a t. BALD 50:18
theatres domes, t., temples WORD 846:6
theatrical t. writers SCOT 674:16
thee Dreamin' of t. WALL 817:15
save t. and me OWEN 580:23
theek t. our nest BALL 53:15
theft clever t. was praiseworthy SPEN 750:11
Property is t. PROU 613:2
t. in other poets DRYD 290:5
theist offer the t. AYER 41:8
them Lat t. say MOTT 552:21
theme Fools are my t. BYRO 182:8
it has no t. CHUR 222:24
t. For reason DONN 280:18
t. Too high doth seem GURN 366:3
themselves did not do things t. RAVE 642:16
laid violent hands upon t. BOOK 133:15
law unto t. BIBL 106:2
theologians believe the t. SALI 664:5
t. have employed ARNO 30:2
theology golden rule in t. MILT 535:20
schools of t. DIDE 274:2
theorem binomial t. GILB 348:29
Theorie Grau ist alle T. GOET 352:18
theories let our false t. die POPP 607:6
T. pass ROST 656:14
theorist t. could fit GAMO 339:1
theorize capital mistake to t. DOYL 285:5
theory All t., dear friend, is grey GOET 352:18
Died of a T. DAVI 259:4
life without t. DISR 277:7
sometimes t. MACA 499:1
t. against the second law EDDI 295:4
therapy T., tenth American muse
BRON 152:8
there Because it's t. MALL 508:17
be t. when it happens ALLE 12:13
cry over me, T., there BOOK 138:19
I am not t. ANON 15:18
MACAVITY WASN'T T. ELIO 302:27
met a man who wasn't t. MEAR 520:2
Over t. COHA 230:7
T. but for the grace of God BRAD 148:17
T. you go again REAG 643:12
thou art t. BOOK 143:16
Were you t. SONG 748:9
you were not t. HENR 381:20
thereby O! t. hangs a tail SHAK 713:24
therein all that t. is BOOK 135:5
thereof and the place t. BOOK 141:4
thermodynamics second law of t. EDDI 295:4
Thermopylae make a new T. BYRO 181:7
old man of T. LEAR 477:11
Thersites T.' body SHAK 683:7
they t. are not they WAUG 824:2
thick ask the Gods for a t. skin TROL 800:2
lay it on so t. BUTL 176:24
thcream till I'm t. CROM 251:11
t. on Severn HOUS 404:13
t. skin a gift ADEN 5:18
t. with corn BOOK 138:7
thickens now the plot t. BUCK 163:10
thicker History gets t. TAYL 774:9
little finger shall be t. BIBL 81:15
thicket ram caught in a t. BIBL 76:23
thief embrace the impenitent t. STEV 759:6
first cries stop t. CONG 238:24
Hang a t. when he's young PROV 621:28
he was a t. HEIN 380:2
honest t. BROW 158:16
I come as a t. BIBL 114:6
Opportunity makes a t. PROV 629:7
postern door makes a t. PROV 629:29
Set a t. to catch PROV 630:32
something from the t. SHAK 713:13
subtle t. of youth MILT 535:5
Taffy was a t. NURS 569:16
t. doth fear SHAK 759:6
t. of time YOUN 857:12
t. to business DEFO 261:3

thought as bad as the t. CHES 214:18
which is the t. SHAK 701:16
thieves den of t. BIBL 98:4
fell among t. BIBL 100:22
Her t. are never hung FERG 316:20
honour among t. PROV 632:11
Little t. are hanged PROV 625:31
more laws, the more t. PROV 626:41
more t. and bandits LAO 468:3
no receivers, no t. PROV 623:8
One of the t. BECK 61:15
t. break through and steal BIBL 95:4
T. respect property CHES 217:2
When t. fall out PROV 634:35
thievish Time's t. progress SHAK 723:12
thigh smote them hip and t. BIBL 79:31
thighs from her loosening t. YEAT 854:20
his t. the People RIG 648:12
thimbles sought it with t. CARR 196:11
thin as t. as the shell KENO 449:14
become unnaturally t. WOLF 843:9
never be too rich or too t. WIND 841:13
pale and t. ones PLUT 598:15
t. ears devoured BIBL 77:5
t. man inside every fat man ORWE 577:3
t. one wildly signalling CONN 240:5
t. red line RUSS 661:16
T. red line of 'eroes KIPL 455:22
thine continue t. for ever BOOK 133:2
not my will, but t., be done BIBL 102:1
t. is the kingdom BIBL 95:3
thing draw the T. as he sees It KIPL 456:5
great To do that t. SHAK 680:5
ill-favoured t., sir SHAK 682:7
is it not the t. BYRO 184:12
one damned t. after another HUBB 406:11
one t. at once SMIL 740:23
play's the t. SHAK 686:8
Roman Conquest was a Good T. SELL 676:17
sort of t. they like LINC 485:14
that a t. is so BLAK 121:12
t. enskyed and sainted SHAK 707:20
t. itself and not the myth RICH 647:4
t. of beauty KEAT 442:13
t. of beauty OPEN 575:24
thingish Thing which seemed very T.
MILN 527:19
things all t. through Christ BIBL 110:9
all t. to all men BIBL 107:18
confused t. with their names SART 667:6
God's sons are t. MADD 505:9
how t. did MORR 550:12
infection of t. gone LOWE 494:19
just one of those t. PORT 607:13
people don't do such t. IBSE 412:13
quick bright t. SHAK 710:18
tears shed for t. VIRG 811:6
T. ain't what they used to be PERS 593:10
T. are in the saddle EMER 306:13
t. are the sons of heaven JOHN 424:4
t. are wrought by prayer TENN 778:17
T. can only get better PETR 594:2
T. can only get better POLI 601:8
T. fall apart YEAT 855:12
t. in heaven and earth SHAK 685:10
t. that are not SHAK 698:25
t. they didn't know POUN 608:16
think on these t. BIBL 110:8
Very excellent t. BOOK 139:20
think all I t. or speak WESL 829:4
attains to t. right JOHN 424:24
because I t. him so SHAK 721:19
better live as we t. BOUR 147:11
can't make her t. PARK 586:10
capacity to t. TERE 785:15
comedy to those that t. WALP 819:11
don't t. I'll fall in love GERS 344:5
don't t. much of it LAST 472:5
Don't t. twice DYLA 294:6
don't t. you can't INGE 413:3
do something besides t. LOOS 491:18
easier to act than to t. AREN 24:17
fun you t. they had JONG 434:13

greatly t. POPE 602:13
Great minds t. alike PROV 621:18
Haply I t. on thee SHAK 722:30
hurts to t. HOUS 405:2
I can't t. for you DYLA 294:18
impulse to t. independently PLUT 598:13
I t., therefore I am DESC 265:11
know what I t. WALL 818:4
might very well t. that CATC 202:4
more clearly than you t. BOHR 125:10
never expected a soldier to t. SHAW 724:28
not here to t. HERD 385:8
not so t. as you drunk SQUI 753:14
not to t. much but TERE 785:16
now—I t. it STEP 755:20
paint objects as I t. them PICA 595:7
people that t. SHEN 733:1
publishing faster than t. PAUL 589:3
refusal to t. VALÉ 806:7
spirit that would t. HUGO 408:1
t. alike who think at all PAIN 582:24
t. as wise men do ASCH 31:9
T. first and speak PROV 632:39
t. globally SLOG 740:12
T. like a wise man YEAT 856:12
t. like other people SHEL 728:11
t. of England SAYI 669:7
T. of your forefathers ADAM 3:9
t. only this of me BROO 153:15
t. only this of me OPEN 574:14
t. on these things BIBL 110:8
t. perhaps even less BROW 158:17
t. too little DRYD 287:5
t. what is true HUXL 411:16
t. what other people think YEAT 855:11
t. what you like TACI 770:10
t. with my hands HODG 391:8
t. with our wombs LUCE 495:6
t. without his hat BECK 61:18
t. yourself above BAGE 49:10
time to t. before I speak DARW 257:17
we've got to t. RUTH 661:20
Whatever you t. of your friend MIDR 524:16
what I must do then, t. now DONN 280:1
What the Bandar-log t. KIPL 456:10
when I t., I must speak SHAK 681:20
whether machines t. SKIN 739:10
who never t. PRIO 612:12
You know more than you t. SPOC 752:26
Young folks t. old folks PROV 636:4
young t. too little WALP 819:6
thinker murder the t. WESK 828:20
thinking ain't t. about it TROL 799:19
All t. for themselves GILB 347:14
can't prevent myself from t. SART 667:11
Every t. man ADAM 2:4
gentleman's way of t. ANON 21:18
he is a t. reed PASC 587:13
in t. to be spent VAUX 808:6
lateral t. DE B 260:16
modes of t. are different JOHN 432:1
much drinking, little t. SWIF 766:2
not t. accurately HOLM 393:11
our modes of t. EINS 298:4
own way of t. NAPO 556:10
Plain living and high t. WORD 848:18
power of positive t. PEAL 590:6
saves original t. SAYE 668:6
song for t. hearts WORD 846:23
t. for myself GILB 348:23
t. makes it so SHAK 685:22
t. man's crumpet MUIR 553:13
t. of the old 'un DICK 268:9
t. on it continually NEWT 563:3
t. what nobody has thought SZEN 769:20
thinks as unhappy as one t. LA R 469:22
drinks beer, t. beer PROV 621:46
He t. too much SHAK 696:12
If any man t. he slays UPAN 805:6
I sits and t. PUNC 637:26
man t. he slays BHAG 74:9
not say what one t. EURI 312:23
t. he knows everything SHAW 725:27

thinks (*cont.*):
what she t. — ROBI 650:12
third passing of the t. floor — JERO 421:11
second and a t. time — TALM 773:2
t. day he rose again — BOOK 128:10
T. time lucky — PROV 632:40
t. time pays for all — PROV 632:41
t. who walks always — ELIO 303:23
third-rate t. foreign conductors — BEEC 62:14
Third World T. is an artificial — NAIP 556:2
thirst I t. — BIBL 104:7
man can raise a t. — KIPL 455:2
neither t. any more — BIBL 113:20
offer you hunger, t. — GARI 339:15
provocation of t. — SWIF 765:17
shall never t. — BIBL 103:4
soul is a t. for God — BOOK 136:11
t. after righteousness — BIBL 94:20
T. of wealth — WINC 841:4
thirsteth every one that t. — BIBL 90:6
thirsty cold waters to a t. soul — BIBL 85:7
Drinking when we are not t. — BEAU 60:2
t. and ye gave me drink — BIBL 98:25
when I was t. — BOOK 138:16
thirteen striking t. — OPEN 574:24
T. years of Tory misrule — POLI 601:9
thirtieth t. year to heaven — THOM 789:14
thirty At t. a man suspects — YOUN 857:13
at t., the wit — FRAN 332:14
I am past t. — ARNO 30:1
I shall soon be t. — BRON 152:16
remained t.-five for years — WILD 835:24
T. days hath — SAYI 670:16
t. pieces of silver — BEVA 73:13
t. pieces of silver — BIBL 98:29
this T. happy breed of men — SHAK 715:13
T. was a man — SHAK 698:29
thistles figs of t. — BIBL 95:22
Thomas On Saint T. the Divine — PROV 628:24
ta'en true T. — BALL 53:10
T., because thou hast seen — BIBL 104:17
thorn creep under the t. — PROV 615:35
Instead of the t. — BIBL 90:9
left the t. wi' me — BURN 170:14
Oak, and Ash, and T. — KIPL 455:23
one t. out of many — HORA 399:24
rose without the t. — HERR 386:10
snail's on the t. — BROW 160:22
t. in Charles's side — FOX 331:2
t. in the flesh — BIBL 108:24
t. removed by a thorn — TANT 773:3
without t. the rose — MILT 532:28
thorns crackling of t. — BIBL 86:6
crown of t. — BEVA 73:13
crown of t. — BRYA 162:12
grapes of t. — BIBL 95:22
some fell among t. — BIBL 97:3
t. shall come up — BIBL 89:8
upon the t. of life — SHEL 730:11
thorough more desirable than a t. grasp — THOM 789:3
thoroughfare t. for all thoughts — KEAT 447:3
thou t. art not he or she — WAUG 824:2
T. ART THAT — UPAN 805:3
T. art the man — BIBL 81:1
t. shalt have no other gods — BIBL 77:37
T. swell! Thou witty — HART 374:14
Through the T. a person becomes I — BUBE 162:12
thought beautiful clean t. — LAWR 474:25
Beyond the last t. — STEV 758:2
bound of human t. — TENN 784:16
by taking t. — BIBL 95:8
carry all that t. — HUNT 410:1
dress of t. — JOHN 425:2
dress of t. — POPE 604:6
enemy of t. — CONR 240:21
father, Harry, to that t. — SHAK 692:17
forced into a state of t. — GALS 338:14
form Of every t. — MICH 524:1
for want of t. — DRYD 288:4
garment of t. — CARL 192:26
gave that t. relief — WORD 848:1

Grave without t. — CHUR 220:2
harbours virtuous t. — SPEN 751:17
he t. I slept — PATM 588:15
inextinguishable t. — SHEL 732:15
In the light of t. — SHEL 731:28
life-blood of t. — FLAU 325:13
Ministers of t. — SHEL 728:15
modes of t. — MILL 525:3
mystery beyond t. — UPAN 805:14
My t. is *me* — SART 667:11
never t. of thinking — GILB 348:23
no t. for the morrow — BIBL 95:11
oft was t. — POPE 604:5
one that was never t. of — BIBL 93:11
One t. more steady — FORD 329:3
pale cast of t. — SHAK 686:12
Perish the t. — CIBB 223:3
put t. in a concentration camp — ROOS 654:2
rear the tender t. — THOM 792:8
Religion the frozen t. of men — KRIS 461:17
right t. — PALI 584:6
Roman t. hath struck him — SHAK 678:16
single grateful t. — LESS 482:5
speech created t. — SHEL 731:6
strange seas of t. — WORD 849:11
sudden t. — BROW 159:4
sweet silent t. — SHAK 723:1
tease us out of t. — KEAT 444:14
t. and resolution — TROL 800:10
T. can with difficulty visit — SHEL 732:21
t. charged with emotion — GIDE 346:16
T. does not crush — ROET 652:3
t.-executing fires — SHAK 700:15
t. in cold storage — SAMU 665:10
T. is free — PROV 632:45
T. is free — SHAK 718:34
T. is the child of Action — DISR 277:32
t. is the front — SAUS 668:3
t. is viscous — ADAM 2:17
T. shall be the harder — ANON 22:6
t. so once; but now I know it — EPIT 310:13
t.'s the slave of life — SHAK 691:12
thought the t. — BALL 52:6
t., word, and deed — MISS 536:14
Three minutes' t. — HOUS 405:4
To a green t. — MARV 515:17
very t. of Thee — CASW 199:3
want of t. — HOOD 395:4
what he t., he uttered — HEMI 381:3
while, celestial t. — VAUG 807:12
wish is father to the t. — PROV 635:13
working-house of t. — SHAK 694:1
years of human t. too late — LA B 462:19
thoughtcrime t. literally impossible — ORWE 577:16
thoughts all evil t. — BOOK 130:5
As man's own t. — WEBS 826:13
bring my t. to an end — SMIT 743:5
Cleanse the t. of our hearts — BOOK 131:6
conceal their t. — VOLT 815:13
examine my t. — BOOK 143:19
First t. are best — PROV 620:13
Good t. — CAMP 188:3
have bloody t. — SHAK 719:2
Hunter's waking t. — AUDE 34:24
in a shroud Of t. — BYRO 179:4
in the t. of children — LOCK 488:7
long, long t. — LONG 490:15
misleading t. — SPEN 750:9
my bloody t. — SHAK 714:6
my t. are not your thoughts — BIBL 90:8
ought to control our t. — DARW 257:3
pansies, that's for t. — SHAK 688:12
present t. build our life — PALI 584:9
rather than of t. — KEAT 446:2
Second t. are best — PROV 630:23
secret t. — ALBE 10:7
Staled are my t. — DYER 293:12
thoroughfare for all t. — KEAT 447:3
t. and manners — JOHN 425:26
t. are legible in the eye — ROYD 658:1
T., boundless, deep — BYRO 182:6
t. of a prisoner — SOLZ 745:17

t. of men are widened — TENN 780:22
t. of other men — COWP 248:13
t. that arise in me — TENN 775:16
T., that breathe — GRAY 361:20
T. that do often lie — WORD 848:15
t. within the breasts — KORA 460:21
Words without t. — SHAK 687:18
your love but not your t. — GIBR 346:6
thousand better than a t. — BOOK 139:17
blotted a t. — JONS 436:8
cattle upon a t. hills — BOOK 137:8
Death has a t. doors — MASS 518:5
Empire lasts for a t. years — CHUR 221:9
first t. days — KENN 449:1
Give me a t. kisses — CATU 202:14
had five t. a year — THAC 786:19
night has a t. eyes — BOUR 147:10
Night hath a t. eyes — LYLY 497:4
not in a t. years — SMIT 742:9
possessing ten t. eyes — ZORO 859:11
ten t. — BIBL 91:24
ten t. things — LAO 467:14
t. ages in Thy sight — WATT 823:20
t. doors open on to it — SENE 677:2
t. shall fall — BOOK 140:3
t. thousand slimy things — COLE 233:1
t. tongues to sing — WESL 828:25
t. years in thy sight — BOOK 139:22
t. years of history — GAIT 337:18
thousands limp father of t. — JOYC 437:20
t. equally were meant — SWIF 767:17
t. of gold and silver — BOOK 142:12
thraldom single t. — BACO 46:25
thrall Thee hath in t. — KEAT 443:28
thread crimson t. of kinship — PARK 586:15
line of scarlet t. — BIBL 79:9
tied, With a silken t. — KEAT 443:17
with a twined t. — BURT 174:14
threads hundreds of tiny t. — SIGN 736:24
threaten t. to overrule him — PAXM 589:8
threatened t., a lion — CHAP 208:8
t. its life — CARR 196:11
t. men live long — PROV 632:46
threats no terror, Cassius, in your t.
— SHAK 698:16
something of t. — KORA 460:16
t. unexecuted — JOHN 426:7
three at t. years old — LEON 481:7
confessing the T. — PATR 588:19
divided into t. parts — CAES 185:1
divided into t. parts — OPEN 574:11
give him t. sides — MONT 545:7
grant but t. — BYRO 181:7
strike out t. — BOIL 125:15
tell you t. times — CARR 196:5
than T. in One — DRYD 288:14
Though he was only t. — MILN 527:21
T. acres and a cow — POLI 601:10
T. bags full — NURS 566:8
T. blind mice — NURS 570:5
t. corners of the world — SHAK 699:16
t. events in his life — LA B 462:17
t. for a wedding — PROV 628:33
t.-fourths of our life — ARNO 30:4
t. gentlemen at once — SHER 733:23
T. hours a day — TROL 799:3
T. in One — ALEX 11:9
t. is a houseful — SAYI 669:5
t. is company — WILD 835:14
T. may keep a secret — PROV 632:47
t. merry boys are we — FLET 327:3
T. minutes' thought — HOUS 405:4
t. o'clock in the morning — FITZ 324:7
t.-o-clock in the morning — THOR 793:9
t. of us in this marriage — DIAN 267:2
t.-pipe problem — DOYL 284:12
t. ravens — BALL 53:13
T. whole days together — SUCK 763:7
T. wise men of Gotham — NURS 570:7
two or t. are gathered — BOOK 128:18
When shall we t. meet — SHAK 702:28
where t. ways meet — SOPH 746:19
where two or t. — BIBL 97:22

time (*cont.*):

It saves t.	CARR 195:1
Keeping t., time, time	POE 599:2
last my t.	CARL 191:14
leave exactly on t.	MUSS 555:12
long t. with you	BIBL 103:30
loved the t. too well	CLAR 224:3
Love's not T.'s fool	SHAK 723:23
may be some t.	LAST 472:2
money was not t.	MERR 523:1
mus'd on wasted t.	BURN 173:6
my world as in my t.	CHAU 212:16
night of t.	BROW 156:17
no enemy but t.	YEAT 854:13
no note of T.	YOUN 857:9
No t. like the present	MANL 510:5
No t. like the present	PROV 628:4
not the t. to falter	BLAI 119:2
now doth t. waste me	SHAK 716:16
now is the accepted t.	BIBL 108:16
O aching t.	KEAT 443:12
old common arbitrator, T.	SHAK 719:28
Old T. the clock-setter	SHAK 699:4
Once upon a t.	OPEN 575:9
on the sands of t.	LONG 490:21
O t. too swift	PEEL 591:3
passed the t.	BECK 61:20
peace for our t.	CHAM 206:12
peace in our t.	BOOK 128:11
possession for all t.	THUC 793:22
productions of t.	BLAK 121:1
puzzles me more than t.	LAMB 465:5
rags of t.	DONN 281:13
ravages of t.	HORA 401:19
recorded t.	SHAK 707:14
Redeeming the t.	BIBL 109:16
ringing grooves of t.	TENN 781:4
save t.	BACO 44:7
sent before my t.	SHAK 716:20
she's on t.	AUDE 35:15
shipwreck of t.	BACO 42:15
shook hands with t.	FORD 328:19
Short T. and Little Skill	HARI 373:13
silent touches of t.	BURK 169:9
speech is shallow as T.	CARL 191:20
spend more t. with family	THAT 787:14
stitch in t. saves	PROV 631:22
strain, T.'s eunuch	HOPK 397:9
Sun-flower! weary of t.	BLAK 122:10
talk of killing t.	BOUC 147:4
Tell t. it metes but motion	RALE 641:3
tether t. or tide	BURN 172:12
thief of t.	PROV 629:41
thief of t.	YOUN 857:12
This day T. winds	BURN 172:8
T., a maniac scattering dust	TENN 779:4
t. and place for	PROV 632:9
t. and season	AGES 8:28
T. and the hour	SHAK 703:16
t. and the place	BROW 160:11
t. and the present moment	MANN 510:10
T. and tide wait	PROV 632:52
t. and times are done	YEAT 855:9
T. an endless song	YEAT 854:19
t. by heart-throbs	BAIL 49:18
T. cools	MANN 511:1
t. cracks into furious flower	BROO 154:6
t. creeps along	JAGO 416:2
T. did beckon	HERB 384:12
t. enough to sleep	HOUS 404:8
T. flies	PROV 633:1
T. for a little something	MILN 528:9
t. for everything	PROV 632:10
t. for such a word	SHAK 707:14
t. for you to go	HORA 399:24
t. has been properly spent	TAYL 774:17
t. has come	CARR 195:7
T. has no divisions	MANN 510:9
T. has shaken me	WESL 829:22
T. has three dimensions	HOPK 397:14
T. has too much credit	COMP 236:17
T. has transfigured them	LARK 468:13
T. hath, my lord, a wallet	SHAK 719:22

T. held me green	THOM 789:8
T. in hours, days, years	VAUG 808:3
T. is a great healer	PROV 633:2
T. is a great teacher	BERL 70:7
T. is a violent torrent	AURE 38:4
t. is fleeing	HORA 400:14
T. is fleeting	LONG 490:19
t. is flying	VIRG 815:1
t. is money	FRAN 332:11
t. is money	HUGO 407:19
T. is money	PROV 633:3
T. is on our side	GLAD 350:13
T. is our tedious song	MILT 530:27
t. is out of joint	SHAK 685:13
t. is running out	KOES 458:16
t. is setting with me	BURN 172:2
T. is that wherein	HIPP 389:15
t. is the greatest innovator	BACO 44:27
T. is the great physician	DISR 277:15
T. is the measure	AUCT 34:17
t. is the medium	MANN 510:14
T. is too slow	VAN 806:21
T. like a last oozing	BECK 61:26
T., like an ever-rolling stream	WATT 823:20
T. makes these decay	CARE 190:11
T., not Corydon	ARNO 28:27
t. of asking	BOOK 133:3
t. of darkness	BREC 150:18
t. of our tribulation	BOOK 129:9
T., Place	DRYD 290:2
T. present and time past	ELIO 301:9
t. remembered	SWIN 768:1
t. runs	MARL 513:6
t.'s arrow	EDDI 295:2
T.'s devouring hand	BRAM 149:10
t.'s eternal motion	FORD 329:3
T.'s glory is to calm	SHAK 722:18
T. shall throw a dart	EPIT 311:11
T.'s iron feet	MONT 545:16
T.'s noblest offspring	BERK 69:15
T. spent on any item	PARK 586:18
T. stays, we go	DOBS 278:18
T.'s thievish progress	SHAK 723:12
T.'s wheel runs back or stops	BROW 161:5
T.'s winged chariot	MARV 516:1
t. that shall surely be	AING 9:2
T. that's lost	BUCK 163:11
t., that takes survey	SHAK 691:12
T., the avenger	BYRO 179:10
T. the devourer	OVID 580:14
t. the longest distance	WILL 839:7
T. the subtle thief	MILT 535:5
t. to be in earnest	JOHN 424:22
t. to every purpose	BIBL 85:32
t. to learn the technology	DYSO 294:20
t. to read play-bills	BURN 169:24
t. to think before I speak	DARW 257:17
t. to win this game	DRAK 285:18
T. travels in divers paces	SHAK 681:23
T. was away and somewhere else	
	MACN 504:18
t. was out of joint	STRA 762:1
T. we may comprehend	BROW 156:25
T. which destroys all things	BHAG 74:15
t., which is the author	BACO 42:12
t. will come	DISR 275:4
T. will doubt of Rome	BYRO 181:15
T. will run back	MILT 530:22
T. will tell	PROV 633:4
T. with a gift of tears	SWIN 768:3
T. works wonders	PROV 633:5
t. ylost	CHAU 213:11
T., you old gipsy man	HODG 391:11
T., you thief	HUNT 409:18
to fill the t. available	PARK 586:17
To it comes T.	BARN 56:18
took t. to consider	ASTE 32:16
to sell t.	TAWN 774:4
to the church on t.	LERN 481:15
triumphed over t.	RALE 641:12
uncertain balance of proud t.	GREE 362:21
unconscionable t. dying	CHAR 209:12
unthinking t.	DRYD 289:13

use your t.	HERR 386:19
very good t. it was	OPEN 575:10
waste of t. and effort	VEBL 808:8
ways By which T. kills us	SITW 739:1
When t. is broke	SHAK 716:15
whips and scorns of t.	SHAK 686:10
whirligig of t.	SHAK 721:16
with his own t.	AUST 40:8
womb of t.	HEIN 380:5
world enough, and t.	MARV 515:22
timely t. compliance	FIEL 317:17
t. utterance	WORD 848:1
timeo t. *Danaos et dona ferentes*	VIRG 811:11
times bad t. just around	COWA 245:8
best of t.	OPEN 574:28
blissful old t.	BLAM 123:5
coldness of the t.	TENN 779:23
five t. did I say	WORD 846:3
It was the best of t.	DICK 272:13
nature of the t. deceased	SHAK 692:5
Oh, the t.	CICE 223:16
one year's experience 30 t.	CARR 193:16
Other t., other manners	PROV 629:9
praiser of past t.	HORA 398:11
signs of the t.	BIBL 97:15
t. begin to wax old	BIBL 92:18
T. change	PROV 633:6
T. go by turns	SOUT 749:22
T. has made many ministries	BAGE 47:19
t. in which a genius	ADAM 1:16
t. past	HERR 386:9
t. that try men's souls	PAIN 582:11
t. they are a-changin'	DYLA 294:16
t. will not mend	PARK 586:13
Top people take *The T.*	ADVE 8:19
timet flagitium t.	HORA 402:17
timetables by railway t.	TAYL 774:10
timing t. of your death	TACI 770:6
timor T. *mortis conturbat me*	DUNB 292:2
Timothy T. has passed	EPIT 311:9
T. Winters comes to school	CAUS 203:13
tin cat on a hot t. roof	WILL 839:5
cheap t. trays	MASE 517:13
corrugated t. roof	BEEC 62:10
tincture Actions receive their t.	DEFO 261:19
t. in the blood	DEFO 261:18
ting bells of Hell go t.-a-ling	MILI 526:15
tingle ears shall t.	BIBL 80:6
tingling It's t. fresh	ADVE 7:39
tinker don't matter a t.'s cuss	SHIN 734:21
T., Tailor	NURS 570:8
to t. with his car	MACN 504:21
tinkering rule of intelligent t.	EHRL 297:7
tinkers no work for t.' hands	PROV 622:48
tinklings t. lull the distant folds	GRAY 360:24
tinned smoked salmon and t.	WILS 840:11
tintinnabulation To the t.	POE 599:2
tiny My t. watching eye	DE L 263:8
Your t. hand is frozen	GIAC 344:17
tip depends on the t.	FILM 321:2
Within the nether t.	COLE 232:23
Tippecanoe soldier of T.	POLI 600:22
T. and Tyler, too	POLI 601:11
Tipperary It's in T.	TROL 799:14
long way to T.	JUDG 438:4
notorious county of T.	KOHL 459:3
tipple Fishes, that t.	LOVE 493:5
tippled Have ye t. drink	KEAT 444:5
tiptoe Dance t., bull	BUNT 164:10
jocund day Stands t.	SHAK 718:2
stand a t.	SHAK 693:22
sweet peas, on t.	KEAT 443:22
tired Give me your t., your poor	LAZA 476:10
heart gets t. too	VERG 808:12
He was so t.	ROLF 653:2
I'm t.	LAST 472:11
Thou art t.	ARNO 27:14
t. her head	BIBL 82:13
t. of Bath	AUST 39:7
t. of being a woman	SEXT 677:13
t. of London	JOHN 430:27
t. of Love	BELL 65:9
t. of the struggle	GOET 353:9

t. of the world — WALP 819:2
t. the sun with talking — CORY 244:3
woman who always was t. — EPIT 309:15
Tiresias T., old man with wrinkled dugs — ELIO 303:19
tiresome except the t. — VOLT 816:2
tiring T. thy wits — DANI 255:8
tirra T. lirra — TENN 780:11
tissue beautiful feminine t. — HARD 372:3
Titan like thy glory, T. — SHEL 731:10
titanic furniture on the deck of the T. — MORT 551:8
T. sails at dawn — DYLA 294:5
t. wars had groined — OWEN 581:6
Tite *O T. tute Tati* — ENNI 308:1
tithes t. of mint and cumin — BIBL 98:9
Titian at heart about T. — RUSK 660:5
title farcèd t. — SHAK 693:19
feel his t. Hang loose — SHAK 707:5
gained no t. — POPE 603.24
needed no royal t. — SPEN 750:14
right, t., and possession — BOOK 144:20
t. from a better man I stole — STEV 760:18
whatever t. suit thee — BURN 170:3
titles rich for t. — PEAR 590:10
their t. take — CHAN 207:10
T. are shadows — DEFO 261:28
T. are tinsel — SHEL 732:12
T. distinguish the mediocre — SHAW 726:22
T. thou hast given away — SHAK 700:2
tittle t. tattle. prittle prattle — BURN 169:27
titwillow Willow, t. — GILB 348:10
Tityre T., *tu patulae recumbans* — VIRG 813:12
toad Give me your arm, old t. — LARK 469:5
let the t. work — LARK 469:4
like the t., ugly — SHAK 680:26
not so old as the t. — THOM 790:22
rather be a t. — SHAK 713:29
rose to a pitch-black t. — YESE 856:16
squat like a t. — MILT 533:10
t. beneath the harrow — KIPL 455:8
toads imaginary gardens with real t. — MOOR 547:2
inconstant t. — MONT 543:15
toast Let the t. pass — SHER 733:31
My t. would be — ADAM 3:10
never had a piece of t. — PAYN 589:10
t. that pleased the most — DIBD 267:8
toasted cheese—t., mostly — STEV 759:16
his enemies, 'T.-cheese' — CARR 196:7
tobacco divine t. were — SPEN 751:28
For thy sake, T. — LAMB 464:19
leave off t. — LAMB 465:6
lives without t. — MOLI 541:17
that tawney weed t. — JONS 434:19
tobacconist lungs of the t. — JONS 434:16
tocsin t. of the soul — BYRO 181:18
today get where I am t. without — CATC 200:29
if T. be sweet — FITZ 323:7
I have lived t. — DRYD 289:29
let us do something t. — COLL 234:22
live t. — MART 514:16
never jam t. — CARR 195:10
Not of t. Or yesterday — SOPH 746:16
standing here t. — JOHN 423:9
t. I am fifty-five — REED 644:2
T. if ye will hear — BOOK 140:10
T. is the last day — YELT 856:14
t. I suffer — LESS 482:4
T. shalt thou be with me — BIBL 102:6
t. the struggle — AUDE 36:9
T. we have naming of parts — REED 644:3
T. you; tomorrow me — PROV 633:8
to-morrow as t. — SHAK 721:24
we gave our t. — EPIT 311:17
What Manchester says t. — PROV 634:7
what you can do t. — PROV 627:26
will not hang myself t. — CHES 215:20
toe big t. ends up making a hole — EINS 298:12
clerical, printless t. — BROO 153:10
light fantastic t. — MILT 529:20
t. of the peasant — SHAK 688:27
toes Pobble who has no t. — LEAR 477:19

toff Saunter along like a t. — HARG 373:11
together all that believed were t. — BIBL 104:28
keep them t. — JOHN 429:14
lived comfortably so long t. — GAY 341:7
persons acting t. — ARAB 23:18
togetherness spaces in your t. — GIBR 346:7
toil bleared, smeared with t. — HOPK 396:12
blood, t., tears and sweat — CHUR 221:5
day in t. — QUAR 638:20
Death and T. — VIRG 812:12
Double, double t. and trouble — SHAK 706:11
Horny-handed sons of t. — SALI 664:11
horny hands of t. — LOWE 494:2
mock their useful t. — GRAY 361:3
slumber is more sweet than t. — TENN 781:10
strong t. of grace — SHAK 680:17
they t. not — BIBL 95:9
they waste their t. — CLOS 228:10
t. after virtue — LAMB 465:12
t. and not to seek for rest — IGNA 412:18
T., envy, want — JOHN 426:16
t. in other men's extremes — KYD 462:8
unrequited t. — LINC 485:11
with t. of breath — COLE 231:16
toiled Master, we have t. — BIBL 100:12
toiling t. upward in the night — LONG 490:13
toils poorly recompense their t. — COLL 234:19
token t. of a covenant — BIBL 76:12
t. snatched from her arm — HORA 400:12
tokens Words are the t. — BACO 42:19
Tolbooth-gate resistance of the T. — SCOT 674:11
told half was not t. me — BIBL 81:12
I t. you so — EPIT 309:9
not what we were formerly t. — BLUN 124:5
our fathers have t. us — BOOK 136:18
phrase, 'I t. you so.' — BYRO 181:34
plato t. him: he couldn't — CUMM 253:10
t. my wrath — BLAK 122:16
t. you from the beginning — BIBL 89:20
Toledo T. trusty — BUTL 176:6
tolerable Life would be t. — LEWI 483:16
tolerance such a thing as t. — WILS 840:23
T. the essential — PHIL 594:12
tolerate like, or at least t. — TREV 798:13
not to t. the intolerant — POPP 607:2
toleration t. produced mutual indulgence — GIBB 344:18
toll T. for the brave — COWP 247:2
t. me back from thee — KEAT 445:2
tolle T. *lege* — AUGU 37:4
tollis t. *peccata mundi* — MISS 539:9
tolls For whom the bell t. — BORR 146:7
for whom the bell t. — DONN 282:2
Tom Ground control to Major T. — BOWI 148:10
Poor T.'s a-cold — SHAK 701:1
spurious brat, T. Jones — RICH 647:17
T. he was a piper's son — NURS 570:10
T. Pearse — BALL 53:20
T., Tom, the piper's son — NURS 570:11
Uncle T. Cobbleigh — BALL 53:20
tomatoes babies in the t. — GINS 349:17
tomb blossom on the t. — CRAB 248:28
confined into a t. — VAUG 808:2
empty in thy t. — KING 451:15
fair Fidele's grassy t. — COLL 235:10
in the silent t. — WORD 850:11
like what it is—a t. — SHEL 729:21
mother to the t. — MACA 499:21
sea make me his t. — BARN 56:16
tell the lover's t. — THOM 789:10
this side the t. — BYRO 178:18
threefold, fourfold t. — BASS 58:7
t. by the side of the sea — POE 599:1
t. of a mediocre talent — SMIT 742:14
t. of wit — CAVE 204:3
tombs from the t. a doleful sound — WATT 823:16
in the cool t. — SAND 665:18
t. of all regions — MISS 539:16
tombstone end of the fight is a t. — KIPL 455:6
t. where he lies — LONG 490:16
written on its t. — DAVI 259:4

tomcat t. lies stretched flat — HUGH 407:4
Tommy Little T. Tucker — NURS 568:5
T. this, an' Tommy that — KIPL 455:22
Tomnoddy my Lord T. — BARH 55:13
tomorrow Boast not thyself of t. — BIBL 85:12
build our life of t. — PALI 584:9
for t. we die — PROV 618:36
For your t. we gave — EPIT 311:17
Here today—in next week t. — GRAH 358:13
jam t. — CARR 195:10
Jam t. — PROV 624:31
Leave t. behind — COWA 244:15
Never put off till t. — PROV 627:26
no dividend from time's t. — SASS 667:18
put off till t. — PUNC 637:7
This, no t. hath — DONN 280:14
Today you; t. me — PROV 633:8
T., and to-morrow — SHAK 707:14
t. as to-day — SHAK 721:24
T. do thy worst — DRYD 289:29
T. for the young — AUDE 36:9
t. I die — LESS 482:4
t. is another day — CLOS 228:1
T. is another day — PROV 633:11
T. never comes — PROV 633:12
t.'s life's too late — MART 514:16
t. there's no knowing — MEDI 520:9
t. to be brave — ARMS 26:13
t. we shall die — BIBL 88:26
T. we shall sail again — HORA 400:10
Unborn T. — FITZ 323:7
we thought was for t. — BENN 66:18
what t. may bring — HORA 400:11
tomtit little t. Sang — GILB 348:10
tone t. of the company — CHES 215:5
tones t. are remembered not — SHEL 729:24
tongs taken with the t. — BIBL 88:12
t. and the bones — SHAK 711:20
tongue become his mother t. — GOLD 355:19
Bite out the t. — ROBE 650:1
bridleth not his t. — BIBL 111:23
each carping t. — BRAD 149:4
Englissh sweete upon his t. — CHAU 210:15
eye, and such a t. — SHAK 699:21
fallen by the t. — BIBL 93:20
fellows of infinite t. — SHAK 694:5
give dust a t. — HERB 383:26
grow a second t. — MONT 543:21
has a raucle t. — BURN 170:10
him whose strenuous t. — KEAT 444:19
his t. Dropped manna — MILT 531:30
hold your t. — DONN 280:17
I held my t. — BOOK 136:3
I must hold my t. — SHAK 684:6
in the vulgar t. — BOOK 132:9
iron t. of midnight — SHAK 712:5
I would feel my t. — HEAN 377:22
Keep thy t. from evil — BOOK 135:25
Kepe wel they t. — CHAU 211:20
Let thy t. acquire — TALM 772:10
lies of t. and pen — CHES 216:3
Love's t. is in the eyes — FLET 327:15
my t. could utter — TENN 775:16
my t. from evil-speaking — BOOK 132:17
My t. is the pen — BOOK 136:19
My t. swore — EURI 312:17
my t. the mystery telling — THOM 788:15
nor t. to speak — LENT 480:25
of a slow t. — BIBL 77:22
our t. with joy — BOOK 142:23
ox is treading on my t. — AESC 6:3
rolls it under his t. — HENR 382:10
senates hang upon thy t. — THOM 792:12
sharp t. — IRVI 414:4
Sing, my t. — FORT 330:3
still t. makes wise head — PROV 631:20
tip of the t. — OPEN 574:32
t. always returns — PROV 633:13
t. a sharp sword — BOOK 137:21
t. can no man tame — BIBL 111:27
t. freezes into silence — SAPP 666:14
t. In every wound — SHAK 698:6
t. is the clapper — SHAK 712:23

tongue (*cont.*):
t. not understood   BOOK 144:16
t. of the dumb   BIBL 89:11
t. shall be slit   NURS 569:17
t. That Shakespeare spake   WORD 847:3
t. to conceive   SHAK 711:26
t. to persuade   CLAR 224:16
t. Won't work at all   VIRG 813:11
treasure of our t.   DANI 255:9
use of my oracular t.   SHER 733:19
voice and t.   AUGU 37:3
while I held my t.   BOOK 135:20
yield to the t.   BIER 116:3
tongued t. with fire   ELIO 301:21
tongueless t. vigil   SWIN 767:25
tongues Hush your t.   HORA 401:9
lack t. to praise   SHAK 723:17
nor spoke with t. of gold   RICH 647:7
painted full of t.   SHAK 691:20
speak in our t.   BIBL 104:27
thousand t. to sing   WESL 828:25
time in the t.   SHAK 720:9
t. in trees   SHAK 680:26
t. like as of fire   BIBL 104:26
t. of living flame   AUBE 33:13
t. of men and of angels   BIBL 107:25
t., they shall cease   BIBL 107:25
t. were all broken   DYLA 294:7
Walls have t.   SWIF 767:12
tonic Hatred is a t.   BALZ 54:9
tonight Not t., Josephine   NAPO 557:5
tons Sixteen t.   TRAV 798:5
too T. kind, too kind   NIGH 564:16
we are t. menny   HARD 371:17
took 'E went an' t.   KIPL 456:6
t. a man's life with him   CARL 191:22
tool edged t. that grows keener IRVI 414:4
Man is a t.-making animal   FRAN 332:20
Man is a t.-using animal   CARL 192:24
Science is an edged t.   EDDI 295:7
tooled t. in a post-chaise   BYRO 184:12
tools bad workman blames his t.
                                 PROV 614:49
Give us the t.   CHUR 221:12
quarrel with their t.   BYRO 180:17
secrets are edged t.   DRYD 289:16
t. to him that can handle them   CARL 191:21
Toome On the Bridge of T.   CARB 190:5
tooth danger of her former t. SHAK 705:20
hadde alwey a coltes t.   CHAU 212:18
red in t. and claw   TENN 779:10
returns to the sore t.   PROV 633:8
sharper than a serpent's t.   SHAK 700:5
t. for tooth   BIBL 78:6
where each t.-point goes   KIPL 455:8
toothache endure the t.   SHAK 712:31
Venerable Mother T.   HEAT 378:13
toothpaste t. is out of the tube HALD 368:4
top always room at the t.   PROV 632:5
always room at the t.   WEBS 825:18
I shall die at the t.   SWIF 767:22
Life is a t.   GREV 364:1
t. of it reached to heaven   BIBL 76:30
T. of the world   FILM 319:1
T. people   ADVE 8:19
t. thing in the world   KEAT 447:1
You're the t.   PORT 607:19
toper Lo! the poor t.   CRAB 249:2
topics providing t. of amusement SWIF 765:4
two t., yourself and me   JOHN 430:24
topless t. towers of Ilium   MARL 513:4
topmost on the t. twig   ROSS 655:18
topography T. displays no favourites
                                 BISH 117:6
Torah found in the T.   ELEA 298:20
garments of the T.   ZOHA 859:5
only through the T.   ZOHA 858:16
T. are likened to fire   MIDR 524:17
T., hard like iron   TALM 772:31
T. in Edom   MIDR 524:18
Turn it [T.]   TALM 772:9
torch t. borne in the wind   CHAP 208:9
t. of life   LUCR 495:15

t. passed to a new generation   KENN 448:15
Truth, like a t.   HAMI 369:20
we throw The t.   MCCR 500:18
torches Lighting our little t. COKA 230:13
teach the t.   SHAK 717:17
torchlight t. procession   O'SU 579:10
Tories both T.   BOSW 146:22
revolutionaries potential T.   ORWE 577:8
T. born wicked   ANON 17:14
T. own no argument   BROW 157:14
torment measure of our t.   KIPL 454:7
More grievous t.   KEAT 444:1
most hateful t. for men   HERO 385:14
no t. touch them   BIBL 92:23
smoke of their t.   BIBL 114:3
tormenting t. the people   NAPO 556:18
torments many t. lie   CIBB 223:1
t. also may in length of time   MILT 532:3
T. not moved   ALAB 9:12
tornado set off a t. in Texas LORE 492:3
torpedo becomes a t.   JOHN 427:10
torpedoes Damn the t.   FARR 315:26
torrent Time is a violent t. AURE 38:4
t. of his fate   JOHN 426:21
torrents t. of her myriad universe
                                 TENN 781:11
torrid t. or the frozen zone CARE 190:17
torso remain only a t.   ERHA 308:13
tortoise How t.-like   MARV 516:6
'T.' is a insect   PUNC 637:12
torture tire T. and Time   BYRO 179:11
t. one poor word   DRYD 288:32
t. them, into believing   NEWM 560:18
t. to death   DOST 283:4
tortured T. with the telephone generator
                                 BLY 124:11
torturer t.'s horse scratches AUDE 35:13
Tory deep burning hatred for the T. Party
                                 BEVA 73:9
Loyalty the T.'s secret weapon   KILM 451:10
Thirteen years of T. misrule   POLI 601:9
to like T. MPs   CAMP 186:17
T. and Whig in turns   SMIT 743:13
T. Corps d'Armée   GLAD 350:17
T. men and Whig measures   DISR 277:1
wise T.   JOHN 432:1
tossed t. to and fro   BIBL 109:11
you t. and gored   BOSW 146:25
total t. solution   GOER 352:10
totalitarianism under the name of t.
                                 GAND 339:5
totter t. into vogue   WALP 819:3
totters Who t. forth   SHEL 732:7
totus *et in se ipso t.*   HORA 403:16
touch t. exquisite t.   SCOT 674:27
feel the lightest t.   REEV 644:13
gently t. a nettle   PROV 623:18
little t. of Harry   SHAK 693:9
men who first t. with words   SKAR 739:3
Nelson t.   NELS 558:17
nothing, Can t. him further   SHAK 705:21
One t. of nature   SHAK 719:24
puts it not unto the t.   MONT 546:3
T.— for there is a spirit   WORD 847:19
T. me not   BIBL 104:13
T. not the cat   SCOT 674:7
t. of earthly years   WORD 850:6
t. the hills   BOOK 141:11
very t. of the letter   NIN 564:17
wants the natural t.   SHAK 706:20
touched t. none that he did not adorn
                                 EPIT 311:1
t. thy lips   BIBL 88:12
Who t. my clothes   BIBL 99:21
touches Each of us t. one place JALA 416:22
silent t. of time   BURK 169:9
t. of sweet harmony   SHAK 710:2
Who t. this touches a man   WHIT 833:8
toucheth He that t. pitch   BIBL 93:13
tough in t. joints   RUNY 658:16
T., and devilish sly   DICK 269:4
t. get going   KENN 449:9
T. on crime   BLAI 118:15

When the going gets t.   PROV 634:30
toughness T. doesn't have to come
                                 FEIN 316:9
tourism t. is their religion RUNC 658:13
What an odd thing t. is   BRYS 162:14
tourist loathsome is the British t. KILV 451:11
t. of wars   GELL 342:18
whisper to the t.   BEER 63:4
tourmente *l'infini me t.*   MUSS 555:9
tout *capable de t.*   VOLT 816:19
T. passe   ANON 21:4
toves slithy t.   CARR 194:25
tower build a t.   BIBL 101:10
Child Roland to the dark t.   SHAK 701:2
fall'n at length that t.   TENN 782:16
Fighting in the captain's t.   DYLA 294:5
Giotto's t.   LONG 490:10
Julius Caesar's ill-erected t.   SHAK 716:10
prisoner in the T.   FABY 314:1
to the Dark T. came   BROW 159:2
t. of David   BIBL 87:10
t. of nine storeys begins   LAO 468:5
t. of strength   SHAK 717:5
watchman on the lonely t.   SCOT 673:15
with a t. and bells   CRAB 248:27
with the blasted t.   NERV 559:8
towered t. cities please us MILT 529:26
towering own t. style   CHES 217:10
towers branchy between t.   HOPK 396:11
cloud-capped t.   SHAK 719:1
from a hundred t.   TENN 777:6
tell the t. thereof   BOOK 137:6
Whispering from her t.   ARNO 29:15
ye antique t.   GRAY 361:9
towery T. city   HOPK 396:11
town Country in the t.   MART 515:4
country t. is my detestation   BURN 169:27
destroy the t. to save it   ANON 17:2
Dirty old t.   MACC 500:12
haunted t. it is to me   LANG 466:9
leave your own t.   VERG 808:13
little t. of Bethlehem   BROO 154:8
lived in a pretty how t.   CUMM 253:5
man made the t.   COWP 247:26
man made the t.   PROV 620:45
never go down to the end of the t.
                                 MILN 527:21
retreat near the t.   WYCH 852:9
sounding through the t.   BALL 51:17
spreading of the hideous t.   MORR 549:15
studies it in t.   COWP 247:17
tavern in the t.   SONG 748:7
t.-crier spoke my lines   SHAK 686:21
way that takes the t.   HERB 383:16
towns London, thou art of t. ANON 17:11
Seven wealthy t.   ANON 19:1
too long in country t.   CATH 199:12
toy be the t. of man   WOLL 844:3
foolish thing was but a t.   SHAK 721:18
toys brooches and t.   STEV 760:11
Deceive boys with t.   LYSA 497:8
misuse, then cast their t. away COWP 246:15
toyshop moving t. of the heart POPE 606:5
trace t. unusual things   WINC 841:10
traces on winter's t.   SWIN 767:25
tracing fitful t. of a portal STEV 758:4
track flying on our t.   THOM 792:20
T. twenty nine   GORD 356:18
tracks hungry on the t.   CRAN 250:1
staring at its own t.   MAND 510:2
tract left a little t.   WILD 836:30
trade all is seared with t. HOPK 396:12
articles of t.   ALBE 10:6
arts of t.   DYER 293:14
autocrat: that's my t.   CATH 199:15
Every man to his t.   PROV 619:19
from the vulgar t.   MARL 513:13
great t.   BURK 166:14
in London only is a t.   DRYD 289:11
in the way of t.   COWP 247:22
Irish poets, learn you t.   YEAT 856:3
It is his t.   LAST 471:9
People of the same t.   SMIT 741:6

There isn't any T.	HERB 383:9
T. follows the flag	PROV 633:16
t. to make tables	JOHN 428:5
tricks in every t.	PROV 632:1
Two of a t. never agree	PROV 633:30
us that t. in love	SHAK 679:10
War is the t. of kings	DRYD 288:26
wheels of t.	HUME 408:13
traders into the hands of t.	GRAV 360:15
trades Jack of all t.	PROV 624:30
live by twa t.	SCOT 674:6
tradesmen bow, ye t.	GILB 347:9
trade unionism t. of the married	
	SHAW 726:13
trade unionist British T.	BEVI 74:1
trading t. on the blood	LEE 479:4
tradition revolting against their t.	
	GRAN 359:2
t. Approves	CLOU 229:8
t. is a fence	TALM 772:4
T. is entirely different	STRA 762:7
T. means giving votes to	CHES 217:3
t. objects to their being disqualified	
	CHES 217:4
traditions those barbarous t.	FINK 321:7
traduced t. Joseph K.	OPEN 575:19
traffic Hushing the latest t.	BRID 151:6
means of t.	MARL 513:13
roar of London's t.	CATC 201:22
trade and t.	PUSH 638:7
t. of Jacob's ladder	THOM 791:16
two hours' t.	SHAK 717:13
trafficking permitted t.	KORA 459:16
tragedies All t. are finished	BYRO 180:29
t. of antiquity	STOP 761:12
tragedy blustering about Imperial T.	
	BROW 155:6
comedy is t. that happens	CART 196:21
composition of a t.	VOLT 816:17
convenient in t.	ANOU 22:16
element of t.	ELIO 300:6
Fate wrote her a t.	BEER 63:8
first time as t.	BARN 56:11
first time as t.	MARX 516:16
go, litel myn t.	CHAU 213:14
it is a t.	AUST 38:23
I will write you a t.	FITZ 324:3
out of it simply a t.	WILD 836:25
That is their t.	WILD 835:18
t., comedy, history	SHAK 685:28
T. is clean	ANOU 22:17
t. is thus an imitation	ARIS 25:20
t. of a man	OLIV 573:3
t. of a man who has found	BARR 57:9
t. of Science	HUXL 411:14
t. of the age	DU B 291:1
t. of the classical languages	MADA 505:5
T. ought to be a great kick	LAWR 475:12
t. to those that feel	WALP 819:11
weak, washy way of true t.	KAVA 442:6
what t. means	STOP 761:15
You *may* abuse a t.	JOHN 428:5
tragic I acted so t.	HARG 373:12
t. and passionate	FLAU 325:5
t. consciousness	FUEN 336:22
t. failure	ELIO 299:23
T. Muse first trod the stage	POPE 606:2
tragical Merry and t.	SHAK 711:30
trahison t. des clercs	BEND 66:9
trahit T. sua quemque voluptas	VIRG 813:20
trail long, long t.	KING 452:10
t. has its own stern code	SERV 677:6
trailing t. clouds of glory	WORD 848:5
train biggest electric t.	WELL 827:8
charge of the clattering t.	BEAV 60:18
express-t. drew up there	THOM 790:11
headlight of an oncoming t.	DICK 273:16
light of the oncoming t.	LOWE 494:16
like a runaway t.	CONL 239:24
pack, and take a t.	BROO 153:11
read in the t.	WILD 835:22
Runs the red electric t.	BETJ 72:13
rush in the t.	THOM 792:20

shaves and takes a t.	WHIT 831:24
Shaw is like a t.	LEIG 479:20
t. filled the temple	BIBL 88:10
t. is arriving on time	MUSS 555:12
t. of events	AMER 13:3
t. take the strain	ADVE 7:43
T. up a child	BIBL 84:40
waited for the t.	TENN 777:4
trained We t. hard	MISQ 539:1
trains Noting the numbers of t.	MAXW 519:4
traitor hate the t.	DANI 255:11
shot dead the household t.	HOUS 404:19
t. to learning	JOHN 422:8
traitors fears do make us t.	SHAK 706:19
form of our t.	WEST 830:10
hate t. and the treason love	DRYD 288:20
tram not even a bus, I'm a t.	HARE 373:10
trammel t. up the consequence	SHAK 704:3
tramp why the lady is a t.	HART 374:12
trample t. the very values	RATH 642:12
t. the vices	AUGU 37:18
trampling right of t. on them	CHIL 217:19
trance fell into a t.	BIBL 105:6
tranced t. summer-night	KEAT 443:13
trances t. of the blast	COLE 231:23
tranquil Farewell the t. mind	SHAK 714:2
man of humanity is t.	CONF 237:18
tranquillity chaos remembered in t.	
	THUR 794:3
divine T.	TENN 781:13
Fame and t.	MONT 544:11
feeling of inward t.	FORB 328:7
moments of t.	VOLT 816:8
overcomes male by t.	LAO 468:4
recollected in t.	WORD 850:26
T. Base here	ARMS 26:16
t. remembered in emotion	PARK 586:4
tranquillized t. Fifties	LOWE 494:11
transcendental of a t. kind	GILB 348:13
T. moonshine	CARL 192:20
transformed t. into a gigantic insect	
	KAFK 440:18
transgression keeps himself from t.	
	TALM 773:2
there is no t.	BIBL 106:6
transgressions wounded for our t.	BIBL 90:3
transgressors numbered with the t.	
	BIBL 90:5
way of t.	BIBL 84:16
transient t. is the smile	DYER 293:16
T. lustre	WRIG 851:16
transit O quam cito t. gloria mundi	
	THOM 788:3
Sic t. gloria mundi	ANON 22:4
transitory this t. life	BOOK 131:16
translate such as cannot write, t.	
	DENH 264:7
t. Epictetus	JOHN 427:9
translated bless thee! thou art t.	SHAK 711:11
T. Daughter, come	AUDE 34:18
t. into another tongue	BIBL 93:1
t. into Italian	WHAR 831:1
translation mistake in the t.	VANB 806:13
t. is no translation	SYNG 769:12
T. it is that openeth	BIBL 75:3
t. of the Bible	WHAT 831:12
t. thief	MARV 516:4
unfaithful to the t.	BORG 145:6
vanity of t.	SHEL 732:13
what is lost in t.	FROS 336:10
translations hold t. not unlike	HOWE 406:1
transmigrates elements once out of it, it t.	
	SHAK 679:13
transmit t. but do not create	CONF 237:20
transmutations delighted with t.	
	NEWT 561:10
transport share the t.	WORD 850:11
transported t. and ravished	TRAH 797:15
trapeze on the flying t.	LEYB 484:5
trappings t. and the suits of woe	
	SHAK 683:28
traps recognize the t.	MACH 502:12
trash society founded on t.	SAYE 668:4

steals t.	SHAK 713:26
traurig ich so t. bin	HEIN 379:15
travaileth t. in pain	BIBL 106:20
travel books of t.	ELIO 300:12
in a moment t. thither	WORD 848:13
Men t. faster now	CATH 199:10
obliged to t. again	CHAR 209:9
preserve all that t.	SWIF 766:13
real way to t.	GRAH 358:13
Some minds improve by t.	HOOD 395:9
T. broadens the mind	PROV 633:17
t. broadens the mind; but	CHES 217:7
t. by land or by water	BOOK 129:12
t. for travel's sake	STEV 759:11
t. from Dan to Beersheba	STER 756:8
t. hopefully	PROV 623:45
t. hopefully is a better thing	STEV 759:20
t. I'm too late	RICH 647:21
t. in the direction of our fear	BERR 71:16
T., in the younger sort	BACO 45:28
T. light	JUVE 440:5
T. them	HABI 366:8
two classes of t.	BENC 66:7
travelled care which way he t.	BEAV 60:12
took the one less t.	FROS 335:23
t. a good deal in Concord	THOR 793:2
t. among unknown men	WORD 847:4
traveller fellow t.	ANON 19:7
good t. is one	LIN 486:11
lost t.'s dream	BLAK 120:5
No t. returns	SHAK 686:11
O thou T. unknown	WESL 829:2
said the T.	DE L 263:2
said the T.	OPEN 574:21
spurs the lated t.	SHAK 706:7
t. betwixt life and death	WORD 850:4
t. from an antique land	SHEL 730:16
t. need have no scruple	BAED 47:7
travellers returning t.	BYAT 177:10
t. must be content	SHAK 681:1
t. of eternity	BASH 58:5
travelling t. at twenty miles a second	
	EDDI 295:5
T. is the ruin	BURN 169:22
travels t. fastest	PROV 622:5
t. the fastest	KIPL 454:20
t. the world in search	MOOR 546:13
trawler When seagulls follow a t.	
	CANT 189:15
tray T., Blanch	SHAK 701:3
treachery fear their subjects' t.	SHAK 694:27
killed with my own t.	SHAK 689:10
mother of all t.	PAIS 583:2
not an absolution for t.	ASHC 31:10
ready for any t.	WILL 838:1
t. cannot trust	JUNI 438:19
t. of the intellectuals	BEND 66:9
t. or meanness	DISR 277:31
tread Doth close behind him t.	COLE 233:7
face with an undaunted t.	STEV 760:6
May we t. rejoicingly	WILL 839:17
so airy we t.	TENN 782:1
softly t., said Christabel	COLE 231:5
t. on classic ground	ADDI 4:20
T. softly	YEAT 854:11
t. the verge of Jordan	WILL 838:10
Where'er you t.	POPE 606:1
treason bloody t. flourished	SHAK 698:3
condoned high t.	DISR 276:6
[corporations] cannot commit t.	
	COKE 230:20
Gunpowder T. and Plot	ANON 18:12
hate traitors and the t. love	DRYD 288:20
In trust I have found t.	MISQ 538:2
last temptation is the greatest t.	ELIO 302:24
love the t.	DANI 255:11
moderation is a sort of t.	BURK 166:7
none dare call it t.	HARI 373:15
popular humanity is t.	ADDI 4:12
t. a matter	TALL 771:19
t. can but peep	SHAK 688:11
T. has done his worst	SHAK 705:21
t. is not owned	DRYD 289:2

truth (cont.):
in spirit and in t.	BIBL 102:34
irreconcilable foes to t.	BUCK 163:8
is such a thing as t.	BAGE 47:11
Is there in t. no beauty	HERB 384:11
just possession of t.	BROW 156:22
just tell the t.	TRUM 801:9
keep t. safe in its hand	TAGO 770:16
knew T. put to the worse	MILT 535:25
know the t. at last	EPIT 311:3
lawyer interprets the t.	GIRA 350:4
least touch of t.	BYRO 184:6
lie which is part a t.	TENN 777:9
Lord has more t. yet	ROBI 650:17
mainly he told the t.	TWAI 803:3
May t. be embodied	ZORO 859:18
Mercy and t.	BOOK 139:19
mistook disenchantment for t.	SART 667:5
neither T. nor Falsehood	HOBB 390:8
Never sold the t.	TENN 782:18
new scientific t.	PLAN 596:17
noble end of glorious t.	IRWI 414:8
Noble T. of Suffering	PALI 584:5
No mask like open t.	CONG 238:18
not maintained for the t.	SWIF 765:15
not only t.	RUSS 660:26
no t. in him	BIBL 103:12
old t. receives a new	WIGG 834:16
plain t. for plain people	WESL 829:12
positive in error as in t.	LOCK 488:13
possible to lie for the t.	ADLE 5:19
rooted in t.	HUNT 410:3
sad friends of T.	MILT 535:19
Scotland better than t.	JOHN 424:21
seal of Holy One is t.	TALM 772:11
seekers after t.	AUCT 34:13
seek for t.	HORA 399:21
she is made of t.	SHAK 723:29
should he even tell the t.	TALM 772:29
simple t. must be abused	SHAK 716:25
simply a t. repeated	BALD 50:13
sincerity and t.	BIBL 107:11
speaketh the t.	BOOK 134:12
speak the t.	HAZL 376:12
spirit of t.	BOOK 131:13
stark naked t.	CLEL 226:9
Statesman, yet friend to T.	POPE 603:24
stop telling the t.	STEV 758:12
strife of T. with Falsehood	LOWE 494:3
subject is not t.	CHAP 208:18
sword of t.	AITK 9:3
Tell the t. and shame	PROV 631:43
test of t.	CRAB 248:30
that portion of t.	LOCK 488:12
thy light and thy t.	BOOK 136:16
trusted to speak the t.	BALF 51:2
T. and honour	CHAU 210:6
t. and liberty	SHEL 732:6
t. and untruth	BACO 44:13
T. beareth away the victory	BIBL 92:15
t., beauty, and goodness	WEIL 826:21
T. can never be told	BLAK 121:10
T. exists, lies are invented	BRAQ 149:18
T. forever on the scaffold	LOWE 494:4
T. from his lips prevailed	GOLD 354:14
t. has no special time	SCHW 672:10
t. has such a face	DRYD 288:12
t. in action	DISR 275:12
t. in masquerade	BYRO 181:26
t. in whores	WRIG 851:17
t. in wine	PROV 632:25
t. is always strange	BYRO 182:1
T. is a pathless land	KRIS 461:18
t. is marching on	HOWE 405:15
T. is never undone	ROET 652:3
t. is not in us	BIBL 112:18
T. is now her painted toy	YEAT 855:18
T. is on the march	ZOLA 859:9
t. is out there	CATC 201:29
t. is pulling its boots on	SPUR 753:13
t. is rarely pure	WILD 835:12
T. is stranger than	PROV 633:20
T. is the cry	BERK 69:11

t. is the first	SAYI 670:22
t. is the hyeste thyng	CHAU 211:10
T. is the most valuable thing	TWAI 803:8
T. itself becomes suspicious	JEFF 420:8
t., justice, and humanity	GLAD 351:4
t., justice and the American way	ANON 15:25
T. lies at the bottom	PROV 633:21
t. lies somewhere	COWP 246:17
T. lies within a little	BOLI 126:9
T., like a torch	HAMI 369:20
T., like the light, blinds	CAMU 188:20
T.-loving Persians	GRAV 360:7
t. makes men free	AGAR 6:20
T. makes the Devil blush.	PROV 633:22
t. misunderstood	JAME 418:21
T. not be impress'd	HORA 403:3
T. not merely what we are thinking	HAVE 375:6
t. of imagination	KEAT 446:1
t. serve as a stalking-horse	BOLI 126:6
t. shall make you free	BIBL 103:11
T., Sir, is a cow	JOHN 428:12
T. sits upon the lips	ARNO 28:16
T. stands	DONN 280:10
t. that has lost its temper	GIBR 346:9
t. that's told with bad intent	BLAK 119:10
t. thee shal delivere	CHAU 213:20
t. then be thy dower	SHAK 699:18
T., 'tis supposed	SHAF 678:6
t. universally acknowledged	AUST 39:18
t. universally acknowledged	OPEN 574:22
T. was buried deep below	DAVI 258:8
t. which you cannot contradict	SOCR 745:10
T. will come to light	SHAK 709:6
T. will out	PROV 633:23
t. with gold she weighs	POPE 601:20
two to speak the t.	THOR 793:18
ultimate t.	NAGA 555:19
utter what he thinks t.	JOHN 431:17
very few lovers of t.	LOCK 488:11
War told me t.	GURN 366:2
way, the t., and the life	BIBL 103:29
wedded to the t.	SAKI 663:20
we owe only t.	VOLT 816:11
What is t.	BACO 45:29
What is t.	BIBL 104:1
white star of T.	ARNO 28:19
truths all t. are half-truths	WHIT 832:10
disagreeable t.	BULW 164:7
eternal t.	LEIB 479:14
fate of new t.	HUXL 412:1
Few new t. have ever won	BERL 70:5
Flat and flexible t.	BROW 156:2
Irrationally held t.	HUXL 412:2
lies are worth a thousand t.	GREE 362:12
profound t. recognized	BOHR 125:11
repetition of unpalatable t.	SUMM 764:1
t. begin as blasphemies	SHAW 724:13
t. being in and out of favour	FROS 335:9
t. he can impart	WORD 849:3
T. that become old	OUSP 579:15
t. that wake	WORD 848:12
t. to be self-evident	ANON 19:17
Two t. are told	SHAK 703:14
We hold these t.	JEFF 419:10
try can do till you t.	PROV 636:2
t. him afterwards	MOLI 542:6
T. me, O God	BOOK 143:19
t. out my reins	BOOK 135:10
t., try, try again	PROV 622:45
We t. harder	ADVE 8:22
trying I am t. to be	SMIT 742:6
just goes on t.	PICA 595:8
succeed in business without really t.	MEAD 520:1
tsar no t., but the slaves remain	ZAMY 858:1
T-shirt got the T.	SAYI 669:2
tu *Et t., Brute?*	SHAK 697:10
T.-whit, tu-who	SHAK 702:26
tua *Nam t. res agitur*	HORA 399:15
tub Every t. must stand	PROV 619:24
mere tale of a t.	WEBS 826:6

tuba *T. mirum spargens sonum*	MISS 539:16
t. terribili sonitu	ENNI 308:4
tube artificial inlet—a t.	FOST 330:9
toothpaste is out of the t.	HALD 368:4
tuberose sweet t.	SHEL 731:15
tucker Little Tommy T.	NURS 568:5
Tudor US presidency a T. monarchy	BURG 165:17
tue *je te* t.	CHAM 207:8
Tuesday spelling T.	MILN 527:18
T.'s child	NURS 568:10
tuffet Sat on a t.	NURS 568:3
tug then comes the t. of war	PROV 634:21
then was the t. of war	LEE 478:20
tulgey whiffling through the t. wood	CARR 194:26
tumble t. headlong down	MARL 513:10
tumbled might is t. down	COLE 231:4
tumbler t., and a corkscrew	DICK 271:2
tumour aspirin for a brain t.	CHAN 207:14
ripens in a t.	ABSE 1:4
tumult t. and the shouting	KIPL 455:10
t. dwindled to a calm	BYRO 183:21
tun t. of man is thy companion	SHAK 690:16
tune all the t. that he could play	NURS 570:10
calls the t.	PROV 622:13
dances to an ill t.	PROV 621:50
good t. played on	PROV 632:27
guy who could carry a t.	EPIT 310:9
I t. the instrument	DONN 280:1
keep thinkin'll turn into a t.	HUBB 406:13
out of t. and harsh	SHAK 686:19
sweetly play'd in t.	BURN 172:4
turn on, t. in and drop out	LEAR 477:22
tunes devil have all the best t.	PROV 635:9
found out musical t.	BIBL 93:32
have all the good t.	HILL 388:13
Heft Of Cathedral T.	DICK 273:8
t. of Handel	SITW 739:2
tunnel back down the time t.	KEAT 442:9
light at the end of the t.	DICK 273:16
light at the end of the t.	LOWE 494:16
some profound dull t.	OWEN 581:6
tuppence wouldn't give you t.	COLL 235:2
turbot (by way of t.) an archdeacon	SMIT 743:16
price of a large t.	RUSK 659:20
T., Sir	WELB 827:2
turbulent rid me of this t. priest	HENR 382:4
turd nat worth a t.	CHAU 212:12
turf blue ribbon of the t.	DISR 277:17
grass-green t.	SHAK 688:6
Green be the t. above thee	HALL 369:16
green t. beneath my feet	HAZL 377:7
on the dappled t.	WORD 850:16
t. that covers her soft bones	MART 514:20
Where heaves the t.	GRAY 361:2
Turk French, or T.	GILB 348:26
Nose of T.	SHAK 706:13
turkey It *was* a t.	DICK 268:6
myrtle and t.	AUST 39:3
T., heresy, hops	PROV 633:24
T. is a dying man	NICH 563:7
turkeys kill all t., geese	PROV 628:24
t. vote for Christmas	CALL 185:18
Turkish English, not the T. court	SHAK 692:20
Turks Let the T. now carry	GLAD 350:16
turn and quickly t. away	YEAT 854:9
Because I do not hope to t.	ELIO 301:1
Even a worm will t.	PROV 618:49
my t. now	NELS 558:11
One good t. deserves	PROV 628:36
pass, and t. again	EMER 306:10
T. about is fair play	PROV 633:25
t. again, and quicken us	BOOK 139:18
t. down an empty glass	FITZ 323:17
t. of the screw	JAME 418:7
t. on, tune in and drop out	LEAR 477:22
T. our captivity, O Lord	BOOK 142:24
t. over a new life	FLEM 326:14
t. over the sheet	SAND 666:5
T. that off	WILL 839:9

unsad U. and evere untrewe   CHAU 211:3
unsafe u. at *any* speed   KEAT 447:10
   U. at any speed   NADE 555:18
unsatisfied leaves one u.   WILD 836:16
unscathed u. tourist of wars   GELL 342:18
unseamed Till he u. him   SHAK 703:3
unsearchable heart of kings is u.   BIBL 85:2
   u. riches of Christ   BIBL 109:6
unseen born to blush u.   GRAY 361:5
   effect, itself u.   REYN 646:7
   God knows the U.   KORA 460:21
   Greet the u.   BROW 158:12
   O friend u.   FLEC 326:6
   Thou art u.   SHEL 731:27
   u. among us   SHEL 729:14
   u. things above   HANK 370:16
   walk the earth U.   MILT 533:7
unsex U. me here   SHAK 703:19
unshackled open and u. press   HOWE 405:14
unshook u. amidst a bursting world   POPE 602:24
unsifted like a green girl, U.   SHAK 684:21
unsoiled delicately and u.   CHUR 222:7
unsolicited u. advice   COOL 242:7
unsought lost, that is u.   CHAU 212:30
unspeakable come to those u. joys   BOOK 131:2
   joy u.   BIBL 112:2
   u. in full pursuit   WILD 836:21
unspoken fond words left u.   STRU 762:16
unspotted keep himself u.   BIBL 111:24
unstable absolutely u.   ARTS 30:21
   U. as water   BIBL 77:12
unsubstantial u. realms of Hades   VIRG 812:11
unsung unhonoured, and u.   SCOT 673:12
untalented product of the u.   CAPP 190:1
untaught U. the noble end   IRWI 414:8
untender So young, and so u.   SHAK 699:18
unterrified Satan stood U.   MILT 532:12
unthinking u. time   DRYD 289:13
untilled land u.   IRWI 414:7
untimely came I so u. forth   WALL 818:13
   U. ripped   SHAK 707:17
unto give u. this last   BIBL 98:3
   u. us a child is born   BIBL 88:18
untravelled Gleams that u. world   TENN 784:15
untried difficult; and left u.   CHES 217:11
   new and u.   LINC 484:17
untrodden among the u. ways   WORD 849:27
   through an u. forest   MURR 555:1
untroubled u. where I lie   CLAR 224:12
untrue man who's u. to his wife   AUDE 35:14
   Unsad and evere u.   CHAU 211:3
untruth one wilful u.   NEWM 560:17
   truth and u.   BACO 44:13
untune Music shall u. the sky   DRYD 289:20
untwisted U. all the shining robe   THOM 792:17
unusual cruel and u. punishment   CONS 241:15
   Harry Potter was an u. boy   OPEN 574:12
   moved by what is not u.   ELIO 300:6
unutterable looked u. things   THOM 792:11
unvarnished round u. tale   SHAK 713:7
unwanted feeling of being u.   TERE 785:12
unwary all u.   GILB 347:24
unwashed lean u. artificer   SHAK 699:11
unwearied U. still, lover by lover   YEAT 856:7
unwept U., unhonoured   SCOT 673:12
   Upon his watery bier U.   MILT 529:31
unwholesome not u.   AUST 38:16
unwilling committee is a group of the u.   ANON 17:1
   group of the u.   SAYI 669:8
   u. or unable   WILL 839:12
unwillingly U. to school   SHAK 681:10
unwise sight of the u.   BIBL 92:23
   to the wise, and to the u.   BIBL 105:35
unworthiness for our u. we dare not   BOOK 132:8
unworthy fear of being u.   BALZ 54:8

unwritten Custom, that u. law   D'AV 257:19
   U. and unchanging   SOPH 746:16
up be u. betimes   SHAK 720:14
   Is notwithstanding u.   SHAK 697:7
   nice to people on your way u.   MIZN 541:4
   U. and down   MAND 509:12
   u. go we   QUAR 639:5
   U. Guards and at them   WELL 827:12
   u.-hill all the way   ROSS 655:15
   U., lad   HOUS 404:8
   U., Lord   BOOK 134:6
   U. to a point, Lord Copper   WAUG 824:11
   U. with your damned nonsense   RICH 648:1
   What goes u. must come down   PROV 634:4
upharsin MENE, TEKEL, U.   BIBL 91:22
upper butler's u. slopes   WODE 843:5
   large u. room   BIBL 101:33
   Like many of the U. Class   BELL 55:1
   man have the u. hand   BOOK 134:6
   prove the u. classes   COWA 245:7
   tempt the u. classes   SMIT 741:18
   u. station of low life   DEFO 261:9
upright God hath made man u.   BIBL 86:10
   stand u. in the winds   BOLT 126:15
   that is, u.   THOM 790:3
   we walk u.   GAND 339:2
uprightness born with u.   CONF 237:17
uprising mine u.   BOOK 143:14
   Our wakening and u.   KEBL 447:12
uproar set all the city on an u.   BIBL 105:14
   u.'s your only music   KEAT 446:5
upside turneth it u. down   BOOK 144:2
   world u. down   BIBL 105:15
upstairs kicked u.   HALI 369:10
   u. into the world   CONG 238:22
upstanding clean u. chap like you   KING 453:4
upward Eternal Woman draws us u.   GOET 353:3
   Woman draws us u.   CLOS 228:8
upwards car could go straight u.   HOYL 406:8
uranium element u. may be turned   EINS 298:3
urban u., squat, and packed with guile   BROO 153:12
urbe *Rus in u.*   MART 515:4
urge Always the procreant u.   WHIT 833:10
   u. for destruction   BAKU 50:4
urgent Why is it now so u.   COOK 242:3
urges Will that stirs and u.   HARD 372:14
Uriah Set ye U. in the forefront   BIBL 80:31
Uricon ashes under U.   HOUS 404:14
Urim U. and the Thummim   BIBL 78:7
urine red wine of Shiraz into u.   DINE 274:17
   sleep, and u.   SHAK 705:7
   tang of faintly scented u.   JOYC 437:19
   u. is congealed ice   SHAK 708:12
urn darling in an u.   CARE 190:18
   loud-hissing u.   COWP 248:6
   Pit's long-broken u.   WILD 837:2
   storied u.   GRAY 361:4
urna *Omne capax movet u. nomen*   HORA 401:10
urns u. and sepulchres   CREW 251:3
ursa major nativity was under u.   SHAK 699:27
us he is u.   CART 198:9
   Not unto u., O Lord   BOOK 142:3
USA Born in the U.   SPRI 753:9
usage if u. so choose   HORA 398:3
use Beauty too rich for u.   SHAK 717:17
   let u. be preferred   BACO 43:24
   main thing is to u. it well   DESC 265:10
   Poetry belongs to those who u.   SKAR 739:4
   such as cannot u. them   JONS 435:7
   true u. of speech   GOLD 355:16
   u. alone that sanctifies   POPE 603:15
   u. a poor maiden so   SONG 747:4
   U. every man after his desert   SHAK 686:1
   u. him as though you loved him   WALT 820:25
   u. of a new-born child   FRAN 332:21
   u. rather than ostentation   GIBB 345:3

worn away by u.   OVID 580:7
used buy a u. car   POLI 601:17
   get u. to them   NEUM 559:12
   My name is U.-to-was   TRAI 798:3
   Things ain't what they u. to be   PERS 593:10
useful be a Really U. Engine   AWDR 41:1
   know to be u.   MORR 549:19
   magistrate, as equally u.   GIBB 344:18
   some u. work   THOM 788:7
   way to what is u.   COUS 244:12
useless absolutely, completely u.   DOST 283:9
   are the most u.   RUSK 659:25
   essentially u.   SANT 666:10
   Lodged with me u.   MILT 535:7
   never live to be u.   WESL 829:21
   plans are u.   EISE 298:17
   U.! useless   LAST 474:9
usquebae Wi' u., we'll face   BURN 172:13
USSR Back in the U.   LENN 480:15
usual Business carried on as u.   CHUR 220:19
usura With u. hath no man a house   POUN 608:13
usury forbidden u.   KORA 459:16
   given his money upon u.   BOOK 134:13
   u. is contrary to Scripture   TAWN 774:4
usus *si volet u.*   HORA 398:3
uti *deorum Muneribus sapienter u.*   HORA 402:17
utile *qui miscuit u. dulci*   HORA 398:13
utility non-being into u.   LAO 467:7
   u. to its conditions   SANT 666:10
Utopia Not in U.   WORD 849:16
   possibly be attained in U.   GLAD 351:1
   principality in U.   MACA 498:9
   signposts to socialist U.   CROS 252:10
   U. is a blessed past   KISS 457:13
Utopias all the static U.   INGE 413:5
utterance timely u.   WORD 848:1
   u. of the early gods   KEAT 443:11
utterly should u. have fainted   BOOK 135:15
uttermost u. parts of the sea   BOOK 143:16
U-turn media catchphrase, the U.   THAT 787:3

V with a "V" or a "W"   DICK 272:5
vacancies v. to be obtained   JEFF 420:6
vacancy another v. soon   PRIE 611:12
vacant spoke the v. mind   GOLD 354:12
   Stuffs out his v. garments   SHAK 699:6
   V. heart and hand   SCOT 674:5
   v. interstellar spaces   ELIO 301:17
   v. or in pensive mood   WORD 847:6
vacations No extras, no v.   DICK 270:14
vacuous be absolutely v.   CHUA 219:6
vacuum from behind the v. cleaner   GREE 363:7
   Nature abhors a v.   PROV 627:7
   Nature abhors a v.   RABE 639:16
   v. a hell of a lot better   WILL 839:6
   nature spore   DESC 265:13
vadis *Quo v.*   BIBL 115:14
vae *V. victis*   LIVY 487:7
vagabond is a v.   GOLD 355:27
vagabonds So many v.   SKEL 739:8
vagrancy instructed v.   ELIO 300:12
vague don't be v.   ADVE 7:17
   V. and eluding   LAO 467:10
vagueness no hypocrisy and no v.   STEN 755:18
vain deceive you with v. words   BIBL 109:15
   disquieteth himself in v.   BOOK 136:5
   knowledge that he lived in v.   BYRO 178:18
   name of God in v.   BIBL 78:2
   people imagine a v. thing   BOOK 133:20
   this man's religion is v.   BIBL 111:23
   v., ill-natured   DEFO 261:23
   V. man, said she   SPEN 751:4
   v. repetitions   BIBL 95:2
   V. the ambition of kings   WEBS 825:19
   V. wisdom all   MILT 532:9
   watchman waketh but in v.   BOOK 143:1
vainglory land of v.   BUNY 164:14
vainly V. begot   GREV 364:2

v. men themselves amaze	MARV 515:14	fruit of my v.	PETR 593:16	V., deep-brooding	SCOT 673:7
vale *ave atque v.*	CATU 203:10	lighter than v.	BOOK 138:1	V.! Forgyve be in nevere	LANG 466:20
cool sequestered v. of life	GRAY 361:7	lions, or V.-Fair	BUNY 165:4	V. is mine	BIBL 106:28
in that hollow v.	KING 451:15	mouth talketh of v.	BOOK 143:23	**veni** V., *Sancte Spiritus*	LANG 466:22
shady sadness of a v.	KEAT 443:9	name of the *Golden V.*	SONG 748:4	V., *vidi, vici*	CAES 185:7
this v. of tears	PRAY 611:6	name of V.-Fair	BUNY 164:17	**veniam** *v. petimusque damusque vicissim*	
v. of misery	BOOK 139:14	pomps and v.	BOOK 132:13		HORA 397:20
v. of soul-making	KEAT 446:20	Pull down thy v.	POUN 609:5	**Venice** Ocean's nursling, V.	SHEL 729:26
valentine Hail, Bishop V.	DONN 279:14	revenge against v.	FOOT 328:4	stood in V.	BYRO 179:3
thank you for a V.	LOCH 488:4	v. and vexation of spirit	BIBL 85:29	V.' pride is nought	COLE 231:4
valere *sed v. vita est*	MART 515:1	v. in years	SHAK 690:17	what V. earned	BROW 161:2
vales lily-silver'd v.	POPE 602:4	V. is as ill at ease	ELIO 299:9	**venit** *Benedictus qui v.*	MISS 539:6
thy hills and v.	JAME 417:11	V., like murder, will out	COWL 246:2	**venite** v., *adoremus Dominum*	ANON 21:12
valet hero to his v.	CORN 243:15	v. of human hopes	JOHN 425:22	**venomous** no being so v.	TROL 799:22
hero to his v.	PROV 627:41	v. of others	AUST 39:8	v. as the poison	BOOK 137:24
to his very v. seemed	BYRO 177:24	V. of vanities	BIBL 85:25	**vento** *In v. et rapida*	CATU 203:3
valiant As he was v., I honour him		v. the great passion	SHER 734:7	**ventriloquizing** V. for the unborn	
	SHAK 697:19	ye that work v.	BOOK 134:3		GRAV 360:10
He who would v. be	DEAR 260:10	**vanquish** I will v.	NEWM 560:9	**venture** drew a bow at a v.	BIBL 81:34
v. Jack Falstaff	SHAK 690:19	**vanquished** I have v. thee	JUST 439:4	Each v. Is a new beginning	ELIO 301:19
v. never taste of death	SHAK 697:4	Valiantly v.	SHAK 680:2	Nothing v.	PROV 628:14
valley great things from the v.	CHES 217:1	**vapour** deceitful v.	SMOL 744:17	Nothing v.	PROV 628:15
How green was my v.	LLEW 487:9	I absorb the v.	GLAD 351:9	**ventured** You have deeply v.	BYRO 182:24
in the v. below	SONG 744:6	It is even a v.	BIBL 111:29	**ventus** *nullus suus v. est*	SENE 676:27
in the v. of Death	TENN 776:13	v. sometime like a bear	SHAK 679:22	**Venus** V. clerk Ovide	CHAU 212:21
Love is of the v.	TENN 783:16	**vapours** congregation of v.	SHAK 685:24	V. here will choose her dwelling	
multitudes in the v. of decision	BIBL 92:4	snow and v.	BOOK 144:6		DRYD 288:27
V. and lowland, sing	OAKL 571:1	v. weep their burthen	TENN 784:7	*V. tout entière*	RACI 640:5
v. full of bones	BIBL 91:16	**variable** love prove likewise v.	SHAK 717:24	women are from V.	GRAY 360:17
v. of Humiliation	BUNY 164:15	**variableness** with whom is no v.	BIBL 111:20	*ver v. egelidos*	CATU 202:18
v. of the shadow of death	BOOK 135:4	**variation** admitting any v.	BOOK 127:11	**vera** *v. incessu patuit dea*	VIRG 811:5
v. shall be exalted	BIBL 89:16	**variety** order in v. we see	POPE 606:17	**veracity** tell us with v.	GRAY 362:2
valleys down the v. wild	BLAK 121:26	source of pleasure is v.	JOHN 424:26	**verb** V. is God	HUGO 407:15
lily of the v.	BIBL 87:5	stale Her infinite v.	SHAK 679:7	v. not a noun	FULL 336:26
v. also shall stand	BOOK 138:7	V. is the soul	BEHN 64:2	word is the V.	HUGO 407:15
v., groves, hills	MARL 513:16	V. is the spice of life	PROV 633:35	**verba** *iurare in v. magistri*	HORA 398:18
Vallombrosa V., where the Etrurian		V.'s the very spice	COWP 247:30	*Nullius in v.*	MOTT 552:13
shades	MILT 531:17	**variorum** Life is all a v.	BURN 171:19	*v. sequentur*	CATO 199:19
Valois shadow of the V.	CHES 216:5	**various** constant as v.	GRAV 360:8	**verbal** v. contract isn't worth	GOLD 356:5
valorous childish v.	MARL 513:25	man so v.	DRYD 287:6	v. rusticitas	JERO 421:5
valour better part of v.	PROV 617:43	so be v.	GRAV 360:8	**verbooJuice** Sesquippledan v.	WELL 828:8
better part of v.	SHAK 691:16	**varium** *V. et mutabile semper Femina*		**verbosa** *V. et grandis epistula*	JUVE 440:6
For contemplation he and v.	MILT 532:30		VIRG 812:5	v. rusticitas	JERO 421:5
For v., is not love	SHAK 702:19	**Varus** V., give me back my legions		**verbosity** crude v.	DISR 276:19
men of great v.	WILL 838:1		AUGU 37:20	exuberance of his own v.	DISR 276:19
mighty man of v.	BIBL 79:22	**vase** not a v. to be filled	RABE 639:19	**verbrennt** *wo man Bücher V.*	HEIN 379:13
much care and v.	SHAK 693:13	Sèvres v. in the hands	WAUG 824:18	**verbum** *In principio erat V.*	MISS 539:12
My v. is certainly going	SHER 733:25	shatter the v.	MOOR 547:14	V. CARO FACTUM EST	MISS 539:12
true v. see	BUNY 165:7	**vast** v. right-wing conspiracy	CLIN 227:5	*V. infans*	ANDR 14:11
valuable Truth is the most v. thing		**vasty** v. hall of death	ARNO 27:23	*V. sapienti*	PLAU 597:21
	TWAI 803:8	**vate** *carent quia v. sacro*	HORA 402:16	*volat irrevocabile v.*	HORA 399:14
value Four things of paramount v.		**vats** boilers and v.	JOHN 431:24	**verde** *V. que te quiero verde*	LORC 492:2
	JAIN 416:10	purple in the v.	TENN 783:16	**verdict** v. afterwards	CARR 194:23
little v. of fortune	STEE 755:3	**vatum** *genus irritabile v.*	HORA 399:23	v. of the world	AUGU 37:8
Nothing has v.	FORS 329:21	**vaulted** v. with such ease	SHAK 690:32	**Verdun** being shipped to V.	GRAS 359:14
of more v. than many sparrows	BIBL 96:18	**vaulting** V. ambition	SHAK 704:7	**Vereker** V.'s secret	JAME 417:18
prayer never loses its v.	TALM 772:34	V. the sea	CRAN 250:2	**verge** get to the v.	DULL 291:10
v. a virtuous	LOCK 489:2	**veal** Bellamy's v. pies	LAST 473:10	**verger** erudite V.	BARH 55:12
v. of life	MONT 544:4	**vécu** *J'ai v.*	SIEY 736:22	**verifiability** criterion of v.	AYER 41:6
v. of nothing	WILD 836:9	**veels** V. vithin veels	DICK 272:8	not the v.	POPP 606:28
v. on the personality market	FROM 335:3	**Vega** V. conspicuous overhead	AUDE 35:19	**verification** method of its v.	SCHL 671:9
V. yourselves	CHUD 219:10	**vegetable** v., animal, and mineral		v. of his own prophecies	TROL 800:1
values authentic and pure v.	WEIL 826:21		GILB 348:28	**verify** v. your references	ROUT 657:6
moneys are for v.	BACO 42:19	v. love should grow	MARV 515:23	**verily** v., I say unto you	BIBL 103:6
Victorian v.	THAT 787:7	**vehicles** no triad of v.	MAHĀ 507:2	**verisimilitude** artistic v.	GILB 348:8
van Follow the v.	COLL 235:3	**veil** from behind a v.	KORA 461:2	fine isolated v.	KEAT 446:4
Vandyke V. is of the company	LAST 474:11	Lift not the painted v.	SHEL 731:19	**veritas** *magis amica v.*	ARIS 26:6
vanish making men v. like that	DORF 282:16	wrapped in a gauzy veil	SHEL 732:7	*Magna est v., et praevalet*	BIBL 115:19
softly and suddenly v.	CARR 196:10	**vein** not in the giving v.	SHAK 716:32	**veritatem** *Ex umbris in v.*	EPIT 309:5
v. with the rose	FITZ 323:16	than the jugular v.	KORA 461:9	**vermilion** V.-spotted, golden	KEAT 443:30
vanished This time it v.	CARR 194:8	tyrant's v.	SHAK 710:22	**vermin** lower than v.	BEVA 73:9
this v. being	HAWK 375:11	**veins** fury and the mire of human v.		**Vermont** so goes V.	FARL 315:4
touch of a v. hand	TENN 775:17		YEAT 853:9	**vermouth** gin and v.	DE V 266:5
v. before the white man	TECU 775:8	**vellera** *non vobis v. oves*	VIRG 815:7	**vernal** from a v. wood	WORD 850:12
v. like a dream	CARL 192:13	**velvet** one in a v. gown	NURS 567:3	**vero** *Se non è v.*	SAYI 670:13
vanisheth and then v.	BIBL 111:29	**venal** v. city ripe to perish	SALL 665:5	**verre** *je bois dans mon v.*	MUSS 555:8
vanishings Fallings from us, v.	WORD 848:11	**venerable** what v. creatures	TRAH 797:16	**Versailles** lady at the court of V.	VOLT 816:15
vanitas Ah! *V. Vanitatum*	THAC 786:21	**veneration** object of universal v.	IRVI 414:6	**verse** accomplishment of v.	WORD 846:12
V. vanitatum	BIBL 115:7	**Veneres** *V. Cupidinesque*	CATU 202:11	all that is not v.	MOLI 541:11
vanities bonfire of the v.	WOLF 843:19	**vengeance** day of v.	BIBL 90:18	as soon write free v.	FROS 336:9
vanity all is v.	BIBL 85:25	stay the hands of v.	JACK 415:7	book of v.—and Thou	FITZ 323:2
feeds your v.	PARR 586:23	sudden v. waits	POPE 602:15	by v. seek fame	SIDN 736:11
forbidden v.	GREV 364:2	swift v.	LANG 466:18	could not v. immortal save	BYRO 178:10

foxes, that spoil the v. — BIBL 87:7
vineyard Give me thy v. — BIBL 81:30
v., which was in Jezreel — BIBL 81:29
well-beloved hath a v. — BIBL 88:4
who planteth a v. — BIBL 107:17
vintage O, for a draught of v. — KEAT 444:21
trampling out the v. — HOWE 405:15
vinum call poesy v. daemonum — BACO 43:1
violate v. would be oppression — JEFF 420:1
violations no end to the v. — BOWE 148:1
violence do v. to own nature — MENG 522:1
get meat without v. — LAWS 475:24
Keep v. in the mind — ALDI 10:12
legitimate v. — WEBE 825:5
not by v. — LATI 470:2
organization of v. — BAEZ 47:9
rape, ultra-v. and Beethoven — TAGL 771:2
slain, nor treated with v. — JAIN 416:8
Snobbery with V. — BENN 67:13
source of all v. — SART 667:12
Thus with v. — BIBL 114:10
v. is necessary — BROW 155:4
violent All v. feelings — RUSK 659:13
laid v. hands upon themselves — BOOK 133:15
violently v. if they must — QUIN 639:9
violet At the v. hour — ELIO 303:18
oxlips and the nodding v. — SHAK 711:4
perfume on the v. — SHAK 699:10
v. by a mossy stone — WORD 850:1
v.-embroidered vale — MILT 528:23
v. into a crucible — SHEL 732:13
v. smells to him — SHAK 693:14
v.'s reclining head — DONN 280:20
violets By ashen roots the v. blow — TENN 779:26
daisies pied and v. blue — SHAK 702:25
Fast fading v. — KEAT 444:26
I would give you some v. — SHAK 688:13
Who are the v. now — SHAK 716:13
violin v. so much wood and catgut — PRIE 610:19
violins sobs of autumn's v. — VERL 808:16
vipers O generation of v. — BIBL 94:12
plays with his v. — CELA 205:1
vir Beatus v. qui timet Dominum — BIBL 115:2
vires Quod si deficiant v. — PROP 612:22
Ut desint v. — OVID 580:6
Virgil have only glimpsed V. — OVID 580:1
V. at Mexico — WALP 819:9
virgin In a V.'s womb once dwelling — THOM 788:15
v. girls and boys — HORA 401:9
v. goddess returns — VIRG 814:2
V. had acted — ADAM 2:16
v. mother born — MILT 530:17
v. renowned for ever — HORA 401:20
v. shall conceive — BIBL 88:15
V. shrouded in snow — BLAK 122:10
v. white integrity — DONN 279:16
v., yet a bride — CARE 190:16
was a v. once — BLAK 120:5
withering on the v. thorn — SHAK 710:16
with the silent V. — HORA 402:5
virgined my true lip Hath v. it — SHAK 682:24
Virginian I am not a V. — HENR 382:14
virginibus V. puerisque canto — HORA 401:9
virginity for my v. — PRIO 612:11
little more v. — TREE 798:7
long preserved v. — MARV 516:2
v. could be a virtue — VOLT 816:6
virgins holy v. in their ecstasies — TENN 777:25
v. are soft — BYRO 178:2
virgo Iam redit et v. — VIRG 814:2
virisque stat Romana v. — ENNI 308:2
virtue accommodating sort of v. — MOLI 542:2
Assume a v. — SHAK 687:30
beginning of v. — HORA 398:19
best discover v. — BACO 43:15
blundered on some v. unawares — CHUR 220:7
call v. there ungratefulness — SIDN 736:5
excellence or v. — ARIS 25:15
Few men have v. to withstand — WASH 822:7
flattered into v. — SURT 764:9

follow v. and knowledge — DANT 256:3
form of every v. at the testing point — LEWI 483:11
governs his state by v. — CONF 237:10
in a prince the v. — MASS 518:1
instrument of v. — MORE 548:3
is a soverayn v. — LANG 466:18
lilies and languors of v. — SWIN 768:10
Loss of v. in a female — AUST 40:2
my v.'s guide — MONT 543:10
no v. like necessity — SHAK 715:10
O infinite v. — SHAK 679:19
one v., and a thousand crimes — BYRO 179:28
only reward of v. — EMER 306:23
Patience is a v. — PROV 629:16
really possesses v. — LAO 467:12
recognize v. — PERS 593:7
Self-denial is not a v. — SHAW 726:25
stops the growth of v. — WOLL 844:10
tart cathartic v. — EMER 306:24
'tis some v. — CONG 239:22
'tis some v. — CONG 239:23
toil after v. — LAMB 465:12
to the cause of v. — BOLI 126:12
true v. of human beings — MILL 525:16
very sinews of v. — WALT 820:20
vice pays to v. — LA R 469:15
virginity could be a v. — VOLT 816:6
v. and talents — JEFF 420:10
v. and vice — JOHN 428:10
V. could see to do — MILT 528:24
V. does not come from money — SOCR 745:1
v. had gone out of him — BIBL 99:21
V. is its own reward — PROV 633:36
V. is like a rich stone — BACO 43:19
v. is made of the vice — VOLT 816:13
V. is the essence — ROBE 650:7
V. is the fount — MARL 513:22
V. is the one and only — JUVE 440:3
V. itself of vice must — SHAK 687:29
v. knows to a farthing — WALP 820:4
V. may be assailed — MILT 529:5
v. of bores — WAUG 824:19
v. of fools — BACO 43:9
V. she finds too painful — POPE 603:2
V. shuns ease — MONT 544:13
v. which requires — GOLD 355:31
What is v. — SHAW 726:13
without v. — ROBE 650:9
woman of easy v. — HAIL 367:13
Young men have more v. — JOHN 428:13
virtues all the v. of Man — BYRO 183:24
Curse on his v. — ADDI 4:12
makes some v. impracticable — JOHN 432:3
moral v. — CHES 215:11
necessities call out v. — ADAM 1:16
plant whose v. — EMER 307:10
rural v. leave — GOLD 354:20
vices and v. of mankind — TOCQ 795:2
vices with his v. — JONS 436:8
v. made or crimes — DEFO 261:19
V. neglected — CRAB 248:28
v. very kind — PRIO 612:2
v. were his arts — BURK 169:11
v. We write in water — SHAK 695:20
v. Will plead — SHAK 704:5
virtuous because thou art v. — SHAK 720:19
looking upon men as v. — BOLI 126:11
men grow v. — POPE 606:23
value a v. — LOCK 489:2
v. woman — BIBL 85:23
v. woman is a crown — BIBL 84:12
virtute Macte nova v. — VIRG 813:7
vis V. consili expers mole — HORA 401:17
visibilium v. omnium — MISS 536:19
visible all things v. and invisible — BOOK 131:10
darkness v. — MILT 531:8
it makes v. — KLEE 457:16
outward and v. sign — BOOK 132:19
representation of v. things — LEON 481:8
Work is love made v. — GIBR 346:8
vision art is but a v. of reality — YEAT 854:6

Bedlam v. — BYRO 184:14
Bright the v. — MANT 511:8
by the v. splendid — WORD 848:6
fabric of this v. — SHAK 719:1
In v. beatific — MILT 531:25
Saw the v. of the world — TENN 780:20
single central v. — BERL 70:3
Single v. and Newton's sleep — BLAK 120:17
v. and the faculty — WORD 846:12
v. flies — SHEN 732:22
V. of Christ — BLAK 119:19
V. or Imagination — BLAK 123:1
v. thing — BUSH 174:22
Was it a v. — KEAT 445:3
Where there is no v. — BIBL 85:19
Write the v. — BIBL 92:11
young men's v. — DRYD 287:2
visionary Whither is fled the v. gleam — WORD 848:4
visioned V. One sees all — PALI 583:18
visions Cecilia, appear in v. — AUDE 34:18
shades send deceptive v. — VIRG 812:17
these v. did appear — SHAK 712:8
what v. have I seen — SHAK 711:23
young men shall see v. — BIBL 92:3
visit Christ came to v. us — BOOK 129:22
v. the fatherless and widows — BIBL 111:24
visitation time of their v. — BIBL 92:24
visited sick, and ye v. me — BIBL 98:25
visitest thou v. him — BOOK 134:5
visiting ordinary v.-card — BAED 47:8
v. acquaintance — SHER 733:21
v. the iniquity — BIBL 78:1
visitor travel as a v. — HORA 398:18
visits Superior people never make long v. — MOOR 547:3
visual v. telegram — CASS 198:14
vita Ars longa, v. brevis — HIPP 389:9
cammin del nostra v. — OPEN 575:5
cammin di nostra v. — DANT 255:12
vitae Integer v. — HORA 400:17
V. summa brevis — HORA 400:6
vitai v. lampada — LUCR 495:15
vital V. spark — POPE 602:10
v. spirit — BERG 69:7
vitality v. enough to preserve it — JOHN 432:19
V. in a woman — SHAW 726:2
vitam Si v. puriter egi — CATU 203:7
vitriol sleeve with bottle of v. — WOOL 845:15
vivacity v. of an idle man — BAGE 49:4
vivam sapientis dicere 'V.' — MART 514:16
vivamus V., mea Lesbia — CATU 202:13
vive v. la bagatelle — STER 756:10
vivendi vitam v. perdere causas — JUVE 440:4
vivere Nec tecum possum v. — MART 515:3
Quadrigis petimus bene v. — HORA 399:10
vivid left the v. air signed — SPEN 750:20
v. rather than happy — LOVE 493:10
vivite 'v.' ait — ANON 22:2
vivre V.? les serviteurs feront cela — VILL 810:10
vixen v. when she went to school — SHAK 711:16
vixi Dixisse V. — HORA 402:2
vobis Pax V. — BIBL 115:13
vobiscum Dominus v. — MISS 536:10
sit semper v. — MISS 539:8
vocabula nunc sunt in honore v. — HORA 398:3
vocabulary v. of 'Bradshaw' — DOYL 285:8
vocation art is a comparable v. — FRIN 334:18
As if his whole v. — WORD 848:7
labour in his v. — SHAK 689:24
test of a v. — SMIT 742:13
v. of unhappiness — SIME 738:1
worthy of the v. — BIBL 109:10
vodka medium V. dry Martini — FLEM 326:9
vogue totter into v. — WALP 819:3
voi Siete v. qui — DANT 256:1
voice All I have is a v. — AUDE 36:4
daughter of the v. of God — WORD 848:17
far-away tentative v. — ALAI 10:4
followed me by my v. — MAHA 506:15
great v. as of a trumpet — BIBL 112:26
her v. the harmony — HOOK 395:18

voice (cont.):

Her v. was ever soft	SHAK 702:6
horrible v.	ARIS 25:7
humble v.	BOOK 127:14
I have lost my v.	WEBS 826:16
inexhaustible v.	FAUL 316:4
In Rama was there a v.	BIBL 94:8
I see a v.	SHAK 712:3
I've lost my v.	MORR 550:4
lift up your v.	WESL 829:7
Lord, hear my v.	BOOK 143:6
No v.; but oh	COLE 233:8
Only a look and a v.	LONG 491:7
people's v. is odd	POPE 605:22
raven. you do have a v.	AESO 6:15
scream in a low v.	BYRO 184:2
so silvery is thy v.	HERR 386:21
sound of a v. that is still	TENN 775:17
still small v.	BIBL 81:27
supplicating v.	JOHN 426:22
Thunder is the v. of God	MATH 518:10
tune her sacred v.	JOHN 426:10
v. and nothing more	ANON 22:5
V., and Verse	MILT 528:15
v. as the sound of many waters	BIBL 112:29
v. from heaven	BIBL 114:1
v. is full of money	FITZ 324:5
v. is Jacob's voice	BIBL 76:28
v. of a nation	RUSS 661:12
v. of Doris Day	FISH 322:17
v. of my beloved	BIBL 87:14
v. of one crying	BIBL 94:10
v. of Rome	JONS 434:18
v. of the Bard	BLAK 122:9
v. of the charmer	BOOK 137:24
v. of the dead	TENN 777:4
v. of the kingdom	SWIF 765:7
v. of the Lobster	CARR 194:19
v. of the Lord	BOOK 135:16
v. of the Lord God	BIBL 75:20
v. of the people	ALCU 10:10
v. of the people	PROV 633:37
v. of the sluggard	WATT 823:12
v. of the turtle	BIBL 87:6
v. of thy brother's blood	BIBL 75:29
v. revives the leaden strings	CAMP 188:1
v. that breathed o'er Eden	KEBL 447:15
v. was that of Mr Churchill	ATTL 33:1
v. will run	KEAT 445:8

voices Ancestral v. prophesying war

	COLE 232:6
Other v., other rooms	CAPO 189:17
Two v. are there	STEP 755:21
Two V. are there	WORD 850:14
v. of children	BLAK 122:7
when soft v. die	SHEL 731:23

void conscience v. of offence

	BIBL 105:27
habitation be v.	BOOK 138:17
infinite V.	PALI 584:12
without form, and v.	BIBL 75:4

voids attempts to fill v.	WEIL 826:20
vol suspend ton v.	LAMA 464:8
volat v. irrevocabile verbum	HORA 399:14
volatile v. spirits	SANT 666:9

volcano crust over a v. of revolution

	ELLI 306:3
dancing not on a v.	FLAU 325:7
volcanoes range of exhausted v.	DISR 276:8
v. burnt out	BURK 169:5
vole passes the questing v.	WAUG 824:12
volenti V. non fit iniuria	ULPI 804:8
Volk ein V.	POLI 600:14

Volkswagen V. parked in the gap

	MULD 553:17
volley v. of the sun	WILB 835:7
v. we have just heard	COLL 235:4
volo Hoc v.	JUVE 439:20
volontade E'n la sua v.	DANT 256:11
Voltaire V. in the Bastille	DE G 262:14

V.'s *Candide* had come off the press

	GRAN 359:2
volousse in magnis et v. sat est	PROP 612:22
volume in one v. octavo	SMIT 743:10

In the v. of the book	BOOK 136:7
take in our hand any v.	HUME 408:9
volumes all Earth's v.	CHAP 208:20
creators of odd v.	LAMB 464:14
thirty fine v.	MORL 549:4
whole v. in folio	SHAK 702:12
voluntary Composing's not v.	BIRT 117:2
v. spies	AUST 39:10
voluntas *fiat v.*	MISS 539:7
sit pro ratione v.	JUVE 439:20
tamen est laudanda v.	OVID 580:6
volunteer One v. is worth	PROV 629:3
voluptas *Trahit sua quemque v.*	VIRG 813:20
voluptuous V. as the first	BYRO 182:17
vomit dog is turned to his own v.	BIBL 112:17
dog returneth to his v.	BIBL 85:9
Dog returns to his V.	KIPL 454:9
dog returns to its v.	PROV 617:49
returning to one's own v.	POWE 610:2
Vorsprung V. *durch Technik*	ADVE 8:20
votaress imperial v.	SHAK 711:2
vote always v. *against*	FIEL 318:22
brute v.	BAGE 48:3
Don't buy a single v. more	KENN 448:13
One man shall have one v.	CART 197:11
turkeys v. for Christmas	CALL 185:18
v. against somebody	ADAM 2:6
V. early and vote often	MILE 525:1
v. for the best President	PETE 593:14
V. for the man who promises least	
	BARU 57:18
v. just as their leaders tell 'em	GILB 347:13
voted only have v. for myself	BAUD 58:17
v. at my party's call	GILB 348:23
v. cent per cent	BYRO 177:22
voter Every intelligent v.	ADAM 2:4
votes V. for women	POLI 601:13
v. to get the things done	SAMU 665:11
voting If v. changed anything	LIVI 487:6
not the v. that's democracy	STOP 761:7
votis *Hoc erat in v.*	HORA 403:14
vouchsafe V., O Lord: to keep us	BOOK 128:2
voulu *Vous l'avez v.*	MOLI 541:23
vow v. be performed	BOOK 138:5
v. to thee, my country	SPRI 753:5
vowels U green, O blue: v.	RIMB 649:12
with all the v. missing	ELLI 305:12
vows cancel all our v.	DRAY 285:23
first v. sworn	DIDE 273:20
pay my v. now	BOOK 142:8
v. made in wine	SHAK 681:26
vox V. *et praeterea nihil*	ANON 22:5
v. humbug	SHER 734:13
V. populi	ALCU 10:10
voyage in for Hobbes's v.	VANB 806:15
make the v. over	VIRG 812:13
take my last v.	LAST 471:19
v. not a harbour	TOYN 797:7
v. of their life	SHAK 698:21
v. to the moon	LARD 468:9
voyages v. of the starship *Enterprise*	
	RODD 651:20

voyaging V. through strange seas

	WORD 849:11
vulgar great v., and the small	COWL 245:20
in the v. tongue	BOOK 132:9
it's v.	PUNC 637:16
let the v. stuff alone	BELL 65:29
money-spending always 'v.'	GASK 340:17
takes place with the v.	BACO 43:8
trivial and v. way	BROW 157:6
upon the v. with fine sense	POPE 606:20
v. expression	CONG 238:15
vulpes v. *aegroto cauta leoni*	HORA 399:2

W with a "V" or a "W"	DICK 272:5
wabe gimble in the w.	CARR 194:25
wade should I w. no more	SHAK 706:9
waded w. thro' red blude	BALL 53:12
wafer men's faiths are w.-cakes	SHAK 693:3
Waffen *Wehr und W.*	LUTH 496:11
wag ambition to be a w.	JOHN 433:9

W. as it will	BYRO 177:16
Wood, the Weed, the W.	RALE 641:7
wage give themselves for w.	YEAT 855:4
home policy: I w. war	CLEM 226:11
wager lost the w.	SHAK 682:28
wagering w. that God is	PASC 587:11
wages better w. and shorter hours	
	ORWE 577:24
earneth w.	BIBL 92:13
neither honours nor w.	GARI 339:15
paid in full your w.	KORA 459:22
ta'en thy w.	SHAK 683:8
took their w.	HOUS 404:1
w. of sin is death	BIBL 106:13
wagged tail that w.	WATS 823:4
Wagner W. has lovely moments	ROSS 656:10
W.'s music	NYE 570:17
wagon Hitch your w. to a star	EMER 307:12
w. of his 'Plan'	PAST 588:5
wail nothing to w.	MILT 535:3
wrynge, and w.	CHAU 211:6
wailing w. for her demon-lover	COLE 232:4
wains hangs heavy from the w.	GIBB 346:1
wainscot In w. tubs	DRAY 286:2
waist live about her w.	SHAK 685:21
waistcoat open your w.	HUNT 410:6
yolk runs down the w.	DICK 270:23
wait All things come to those who w.	
	PROV 614:19
having nothing to w. for	PAVE 589:7
laid great w. for me	BOOK 136:10
Time and tide w.	PROV 632:52
too slow for those who w.	VAN 806:21
w. and see	ASQU 32:1
w. a wee	BURN 173:8
w. for ever	MACA 498:4
W. for me	SIMO 738:8
w. for what will come	ROBI 650:14
wait upon the Lord	BIBL 89:21
we won't w.	ANON 19:18
who only stand and w.	MILT 535:8
waited w. patiently for the Lord	BOOK 136:6
waiter myself and a dam' good head w.	
	GULB 365:16
waiting nearly kept w.	LOUI 492:6
w. for Godot	BECK 61:16
w. for something	GRIF 364:9
w. for the Earl of Chatham	ANON 16:6
W. for the end	EMPS 307:21
W. is still an occupation	PAVE 589:7
w. means hurrying on	MANN 510:10
w. seven hundred years	COLL 235:6
w. somewhere for me	RODG 652:1
What are we w. for	CAVA 203:17
wake do I w. or sleep	KEAT 445:3
slepyng hound to w.	CHAU 213:4
w. in a fright	BARH 55:16
w. the soul by tender strokes	POPE 606:2
W. up, England	GEOR 343:7
we w. eternally	DONN 279:20
waked You have w. me too soon	
	WATT 823:12
wakening Our w. and uprising	KEBL 447:12
wakes breed one work that w.	HOPK 397:9
Hock-carts, wassails, w.	HERR 385:16
w. or sleeps	SHEL 728:21
w. them himself	ADDI 4:26
What angel w. me	SHAK 711:12
Wordsworth sometimes w.	BYRO 181:10
waking I lay broad w.	WYAT 852:6
w., no such matter	SHAK 723:14
w. that kills us	BROW 157:11
Wales bless the Prince of W.	LINL 486:10
live ever in W.	JAME 417:11
no present in W.	THOM 791:3
Princess of W.	AUST 40:15
Side and W. Gate	GURN 366:2
still parts of W.	THOM 790:20
whole world . . . But for W.	BOLT 126:16
womanhood of W.	ELLI 306:4
walet His w., biforn him in his lappe	
	CHAU 211:1
walk after supper w. a mile	PROV 614:6

Can two w. together | BIBL 92:5
closer w. with God | COWP 246:28
machine that would w. | APOL 23:11
men must w. | POPE 605:16
never w. alone | HAMM 370:11
no easy w.-over to freedom | NEHR 558:7
not easy to w. on ways | JAIN 416:19
take up thy bed, and w. | BIBL 102:36
taking a w. that day | OPEN 575:23
time to w. round me | BALZ 54:12
upon which the people w. | CRAZ 250:22
W. about Sion | BOOK 137:6
w. abroad o' nights | MARL 513:14
W. across my swimming pool | RICE 647:2
w. a little faster | CARR 194:17
w. before we can run | PROV 633:48
W. cheerfully over the world | FOX 331:9
w. circumspectly | BIBL 109:16
w. humbly with thy God | BIBL 92:9
w. in fear and dread | COLE 233:7
w. in newness of life | BIBL 106:11
w. o'er the western wave | SHEL 732:3
w. on the wild side | ALGR 11:14
w. the night | SHAK 684:30
W. under his huge legs | SHAK 696:9
W. upon England's mountains green | BLAK 121:15
w. within the purlieus | ETHE 312:3
w. ye | BIBL 89:6
Where'er you w. | POPE 606:1
Yea, though I w. | BOOK 135:4

walked He w. by himself | KIPL 456:14
people that w. in darkness | BIBL 88:17
slowly w. away | BURT 173:14
W. day and night | LOGU 489:13
w. through the wilderness | OPEN 574:5

walkedst w. whither thou wouldest | BIBL 104:22

walkers Six for the six proud w. | SONG 747:11

walketh w. in a vain shadow | BOOK 136:5
w. upon the wings | BOOK 141:5

walking craves wary w. | SHAK 696:21
empire w. very slowly | FITZ 324:8
fingers do the w. | ADVE 8:1
Lord God w. in the garden | BIBL 75:20
men as trees, w. | BIBL 99:22
W., and leaping | BIBL 104:30
w. by his wild lone | KIPL 456:15
w. every day | COWL 245:29
w. in an air of glory | VAUG 807:17
w. on the sea | BIBL 97:8
w. up and down | BIBL 82:25
wings prevent him from w. | BAUD 58:11

walks Gibbon levelled w. | COLM 236:4
left you all his w. | SHAK 698:7
nobody w. much faster | CARR 195:23
She w. in beauty | BYRO 183:4
w. always beside you | ELIO 303:23
w. put on their summer liveries | LANI 467:3

wall against a w. of stone | WILB 835:5
close the w. up | SHAK 693:4
doesn't love a w. | FROS 335:18
have I leaped over a w. | BIBL 81:6
leap over the w. | BOOK 134:18
like a stone w. | BEE 62:9
look like a w. | DUNN 292:12
on the outward w. | SHAK 709:8
plaister of the w. | BIBL 91:21
w. fell down flat | BIBL 79:11
w. next door catches fire | HORA 399:15
W. Street lays an egg | NEWS 562:20
w. to a layman | COMM 236:15
Watch the w., my darling | KIPL 455:16
weakest go to the w. | PROV 633:44
With our backs to the w. | HAIG 367:11
Without a city w. | ALEX 11:10
wooden w. is your ships | THEM 787:20

Wallace hae wi' W. bled | BURN 172:5

wallet Time hath, my lord, a w. | SHAK 719:22
w. and a woeful end | GASC 340:13

wallflower yellow w. | THOM 792:7

walling What I was w. in | FROS 335:20

wallow w. In glorious mud | FLAN 324:16
w. in our victory | PRES 610:11

walls angels on the w. | MARL 513:24
not in w. | NICI 563:9
Stone w. do not a prison make | LOVE 493:6
these w. thy sphere | DONN 281:14
Thy w. defaced | BYRO 178:8
W. have ears | PROV 633:38
W. have tongues | SWIF 767:12
w. of Eden | BYRO 178:4
w. of stone or brass | COTT 244:7
within thy w. | BOOK 142:19
wooden w. are the best | COVE 244:14

walnut woman, dog, and w. tree | PROV 635:14

walnuts W. and pears | PROV 633:39

walrus W. and the Carpenter | CARR 195:6

Walsingham holy land Of W. | RALE 641:8

Waltons more like the W. | BUSH 175:2

waltz dance a second w. | SHIE 734:20
zest goes out of a beautiful w. | GREN 363:12

waltzing You'll come a-w., Matilda | PATE 588:12

waly w., waly | BALL 53:17

wan Why so pale and w. | SUCK 763:4

wander love to w. | CASS 198:15
Nor forced him w. | CLEV 227:1
w. in the ways of men | BURN 171:21
w. like a breeze | COLE 231:21
Whither shall I w. | NURS 567:1
will not w. more | TENN 781:10

wandered w. far and wide | HOME 394:13
w. far and wide | OPEN 575:22
w. lonely as a cloud | WORD 847:5

wanderer do not we, W., await it too | ARNO 28:8
w. from the narrow way | COWP 247:10

wandering but a w. voice | WORD 850:15
by long w. | ASCH 31:6
I'm just w. | MURD 554:19
W. between two worlds | ARNO 28:20
w. minstrel I | GILB 347:19
w. outlaw | BYRO 178:15
Werchynge and w. | LANG 466:16

waning onset and w. of love | LA B 462:15

want don't w. him | MILN 527:17
feel the w. of it | COLE 233:18
get what you w. in life | LURI 496:6
in w. of a wife | AUST 39:18
I shall not w. | BOOK 135:3
I w. some more | DICK 271:9
more you w. | PROV 626:44
preservative from w. | AUST 39:24
probably won't w. | HOPE 396:3
Ring out the w. | TENN 779:23
that people know what they w. | MENC 521:17
third is freedom from w. | ROOS 653:20
Though much I w. | DYER 293:13
Toil, envy, w. | JOHN 426:16
w. it the most | CHES 215:4
w. no manner of thing | BOOK 135:24
w. of a nail | PROV 620:24
w. of decency | DILL 274:11
W. one only of five giants | BEVE 73:22
Waste not, w. not | PROV 633:41
weep with w. | TAYL 775:3
we w. it now | MORR 550:7
What can I w. or need | HERB 385:2
What does a woman w. | FREU 334:5
what I really really w. | ROWB 657:7
Wilful waste makes woeful w. | PROV 635:11

wanted no man is w. much | EMER 307:8
w. everything | HAZL 376:11
w. nothing but death | AUST 40:22
w. simply you | HÉLO 380:14

wanting found w. | BIBL 91:22

wanton do but w. in the South | TENN 783:7
W. kittens make sober | PROV 633:40
w. stings | SHAK 707:21
wightly w. | SHAK 702:15

wantonly unadvisedly, lightly, or w. | BOOK 133:5

wantonness in clothes a w. | HERR 385:21

wants Man w. but little | GOLD 355:1
physical w. | BAGE 47:15
provide for human w. | BURK 167:12
scheme of supplying our w. | SWIF 766:22
what he thinks the public w. | REIT 645:1
who w. poets at all | HÖLD 392:13

wanwood worlds of w. leafmeal | HOPK 397:3

war able to make w. with him | BIBL 113:29
After each w. | ATKI 32:20
ain't gonna be no w. | MACM 504:2
Alas, it is w. | CLAU 225:13
All's fair in love and w. | PROV 614:14
Ancestral voices prophesying w. | COLE 232:6
another w. in Europe | BISM 118:2
at w. with Germany | CHAM 206:13
better than to w.-war | CHUR 222:3
blast of w. | SHAK 693:4
blood-red blossom of w. | TENN 782:6
bloody w. and a sickly season | TOAS 796:1
bungled, unwise w. | PLOM 598:9
business of w. | WELL 827:19
but it is not w. | BOSQ 145:14
calamities of w. | JOHN 424:17
clamour for w. | PEEL 590:17
cold w. | BARU 57:16
cold w. warrior | THAT 786:27
condition which is called w. | HOBB 390:14
Councils of w. never fight | PROV 617:12
cruellest and most terrible w. | LLOY 487:17
cudgel of the people's w. | TOLS 796:18
day w. broke out | CATC 200:9
delays are dangerous in w. | DRYD 289:28
desolation of w. | GEOR 343:9
determined without w. | HOBB 390:21
devil's madness—w. | SERV 677:9
done very well out of the w. | BALD 50:12
Don John of Austria is going to the w. | CHES 216:7
easier to make w. | CLEM 226:12
Either w. is obsolete or men are | FULL 336:25
enable it to make w. | WEIL 826:22
endless w. still breed | MILT 530:16
essence of w. is violence | MACA 497:20
European w. might do it | REDM 644:1
Everything is very simple in w. | CLAU 225:15
except the British W. Office | SHAW 725:2
first invented w. | MARL 513:19
first w. fought without | WEST 830:18
First World W. had begun | TAYL 774:10
France has not lost the w. | DE G 262:1
furnish the w. | HEAR 378:10
garland of the w. | SHAK 680:3
gone wrong since the W. | AMIS 13:7
Grim-visaged w. | SHAK 716:19
guarantee success in w. | CHUR 221:11
hand of w. | SHAK 715:13
his father's great w. helm | HOME 394:4
home policy: I wage w. | CLEM 226:11
I am for w. | RED 643:19
I am the tongue of w. | VOZN 817:1
if someone gave a w. | GINS 349:14
I hate w. | ROOS 653:19
I have seen w. | ROOS 653:15
Image of w. | SOME 745:21
I must study politics and w. | ADAM 3:1
In a civil w. | REED 644:6
in every w. they kill you in a new way | ROGE 652:20
in the trade of w. | SHAK 713:3
in w. fathers bury their sons | HERO 385:14
In w. it is necessary | BONA 127:2
In w., no winners | CHAM 206:10
In w.; resolution | CHUR 222:13
in w. the two cardinal virtues | HOBB 390:17
In w., three-quarters turns | NAPO 556:13
I renounce w. | FOSD 330:6
justifiable act of w. | BELL 64:12
killed in the w. | POWE 610:4
ladies declare w. on me | LOUI 492:9
lead this people into w. | WILS 840:23

war (*cont.*):

Let me have w.	SHAK 682:21
let slip the dogs of w.	SHAK 697:16
Let w. stay abroad	AESC 6:8
Let w. yield to peace	CICE 223:13
liking for w.	BENN 67:10
live under the shadow of a w.	SPEN 751:1
looks on w. as all glory	SHER 734:17
Lord is a man of w.	BIBL 77:35
lose the w. in an afternoon	CHUR 222:17
made this great w.	LINC 485:15
Make love not w.	SLOG 740:9
makes a good w.	HERB 385:6
make w. that we may live	ARIS 25:17
Mankind must put an end to w.	KENN 449:3
McNamara's W.	MCNA 504:11
money the sinews of w.	BACO 45:26
morning's w.	SHAK 694:26
My w. is over	MCGU 502:6
nature of w.	HOBB 390:15
neither shall they learn w.	BIBL 88:2
never met anyone who wasn't against w.	LOW 493:15
never was a good w.	FRAN 332:18
no declaration of w.	EDEN 295:10
no discharge in that w.	BIBL 86:11
Older men declare w.	HOOV 396:2
Only in w.	MAND 510:3
page 1 of the book of w.	MONT 545:13
pattern called a w.	LOWE 493:17
pestilence and w.	MILT 532:12
Power and W.	KIPL 453:16
prepare for w.	VEGE 808:9
protection against w.	BEVI 74:3
provoke a new civil w.	JUAN 437:29
quaint and curious w. is	HARD 372:22
race inured to w.	WILL 838:6
recourse to w.	BRIA 151:2
rich wage w.	SART 666:20
seek no wider w.	JOHN 423:13
seven days w.	MUIR 553:12
silent in time of w.	CICE 223:21
sinews of w.	CICE 223:20
soon as w. is declared	GIRA 350:3
state of w. by nature	SWIF 767:10
steel couch of w.	SHAK 713:15
subject is W.	OWEN 580:24
Suppose they gave a w.	FILM 322:12
talk of a just w.	SORL 748:13
tell us all about the w.	SOUT 749:1
tempered by w.	KENN 448:15
then comes the tug of w.	PROV 634:21
they'll give a w.	SAND 666:1
third world w.	TRUM 801:7
this is w.	ADAM 2:1
this w. on terrorism	BUSH 175:5
time of w.	BIBL 85:32
to the w. is gone	MOOR 547:17
To w. and arms	LOVE 493:7
two nations have been at w.	VOLT 815:10
used to w.'s alarms	HOOD 394:25
wage a pitiless w.	GREE 362:10
wage w. against a monstrous tyranny	CHUR 221:6
want peace, prepare for w.	PROV 623:25
W. always finds a way	BREC 150:10
w., an' a debt	LOWE 493:20
w. and peace	ARIS 25:9
w. and peace in 21st century	KOHL 459:2
w. between men	THUR 794:1
w. creates order	BREC 150:7
w., dearth, age, agues	DONN 279:18
w.-gamed against	WALL 818:2
w. has its laws	NEWM 560:8
w. has used up words	JAME 418:11
W. hath no fury	MONT 543:20
W., he sung, is toil	DRYD 287:17
w. in heaven	BIBL 113:28
w. in his heart	BOOK 137:18
w. is a necessary part	MOLT 542:17
W. is capitalism with	STOP 761:17
W. is continuation of politics	CLAU 225:17
W. is hell, and all that	HAY 376:2

w. is over	GRAN 359:6
W. is peace	ORWE 577:14
w. is politics with bloodshed	MAO 511:11
w. is so terrible	LEE 479:2
W. is the national industry	MIRA 536:8
W. is the remedy	SHER 734:16
W. is the trade of kings	DRYD 288:26
W. is the universal perversion	RAE 640:13
W. is too serious	CLEM 226:10
W. its thousands slays	PORT 607:21
W. makes good history	HARD 371:14
w. minus the shooting	ORWE 578:1
w. of nature	DARW 257:10
w. poet whose right of honour	GURN 366:1
w.'s a game	COWP 248:12
W.'s annals will cloud	HARD 372:21
W.'s glorious art	YOUN 857:6
w. situation	HIRO 389:17
w. that drags on	WAUG 824:13
w. that will end war	WELL 828:16
w. that would not boil	TAYL 774:12
W. the most exciting thing	DAYA 260:2
W. told me truth	GURN 366:2
W. to the knife	PALA 583:3
w. to waste	MILT 534:10
w. which existed in order to	HOBS 391:4
W. will cease	POLI 601:14
w. without an enemy	WALL 818:16
w. without its guilt	SURT 764:12
waste of God, W.	STUD 763:1
way of ending a w.	ORWE 578:7
weapons of w.	BIBL 80:29
We hear w. called murder	MACD 501:10
we prepare for w.	PEAR 590:11
what a lovely w.	LITT 487:2
what did you do in the W.	SAYI 669:10
When w. enters a country	ANON 21:7
When w. is declared	SAYI 670:22
win an atomic w.	BRAD 148:21
win a w. is as disastrous	CHRI 218:14
with himself at w.	SHAK 696:3
without having won the w.	YOKO 856:22
won the last w.	ROOS 653:8
You can only love one w.	GELL 342:19
warble W., child	SHAK 702:13
warbler Attic w. pours	GRAY 361:17
warder w. silent on the hill	SCOT 673:16
wardrobe dalliance in the w. lies	
	SHAK 692:31
open your w.	WELD 827:7
wards W. in Jarndyce	DICK 268:1
ware Breath's a w.	HOUS 404:8
for the bed of W.	SHAK 721:5
warfare Armed w. must be	ZINO 858:11
legitimate w.	NEWM 560:8
true method of w.	MAZZ 519:16
w. is accomplished	BIBL 89:15
Who goeth a w.	BIBL 107:17
Waring What's become of W.	BROW 161:27
warlord concubine of a w.	OPEN 574:6
warm For ever w.	KEAT 444:11
lived in a w., sunny climate	COWA 245:9
man who's w. to understand	SOLZ 745:16
O! she's w.	SHAK 722:14
too w. work, Hardy	NELS 558:20
W. beds	JOYC 437:22
w., but pure	BYRO 182:12
w. courage	BUSH 175:4
w. courage	ROOS 653:14
w. kind world	CORY 244:4
W., live, improvident	BROW 157:17
W. what is cold	LANG 467:1
winters and keeps w.	CARE 191:2
warmed heart strangely w.	WESL 829:16
warming w. the teapot	MANS 511:3
warmth awful load of w.	KEAT 446:14
more w.	SORL 748:12
Spring restores balmy w.	CATU 202:18
vigorous w.	DRYD 286:16
W. and Light	GREN 363:13
yearned for w. and colour	TENN 777:22
warn All a poet can do is w.	OWEN 580:25
right to w.	BAGE 48:17

w., to comfort, and command	WORD 850:5
w. you not to be ordinary	KINN 453:8
warning carry a Government w.	MITC 540:6
ruin in spite of a w.	JUDA 438:2
w. from another's wound	JERO 421:4
w. to the world	SHAK 723:9
With horrid w.	KEAT 443:29
warp Weave the w.	GRAY 360:22
warrant not a sufficient w.	MILL 525:6
warring two nations w.	DURH 293:5
W. in heaven	MILT 532:23
warrior cold war w.	THAT 786:27
Here lies a valiant w.	EPIT 310:1
Home they brought her w.	TENN 783:9
This is the happy w.	READ 643:4
Who is the happy W.	WORD 846:5
wars all their w. are merry	CHES 215:22
at home while they fight w.	EURI 312:19
came to an end all w.	LLOY 487:17
end to the beginnings of all w.	ROOS 654:4
History littered with the w.	POWE 609:20
how do w. start	KRAU 461:14
into any foreign w.	ROOS 653:18
its w. are over	HORA 401:23
maketh w. to cease	BOOK 136:26
My w. were global	REED 644:5
not armaments that cause w.	MADA 505:8
occasion of all w.	FOX 331:7
serve in the w.	BOOK 144:19
thousand w. of old	TENN 779:24
tourist of w.	GELL 342:18
w. and lechery	SHAK 719:29
w. and rumours of wars	BIBL 98:13
w. brought nothing about	DRYD 289:15
w., horrible wars	VIRG 812:8
w. planned by old men	RICE 646:20
Warsaw Order reigns in W.	ANON 20:17
warts w. and all	MISQ 538:20
Warwick impudent and shameless W.	
	SHAK 695:1
wary craves w. walking	SHAK 696:21
was picked the w. of shall	CUMM 253:13
Thinks what ne'er w.	POPE 604:4
wash Lord, dost thou w. my feet	BIBL 103:25
Moab is my w.-pot	BOOK 137:26
thou shalt w. me	BOOK 137:12
w. literature off	ARTA 30:19
W. me throughly	BOOK 137:10
w. my hands in innocency	BOOK 135:11
w. one's dirty linen	PROV 628:31
w. out a word of it	FITZ 323:10
w. that man right outa	HAMM 370:2
w. the balm	SHAK 715:19
w. their feet in soda water	ELIO 303:15
w. the wind	ELIO 302:25
W. what is dirty	LANG 467:1
washed He w. himself	JOHN 431:16
never w. my own feet	PU Y 636:12
w. his hands	BIBL 99:10
w. in the blood of the Lamb	LIND 486:4
w. their robes	BIBL 113:19
washerman w. removes the grime	
	TANT 773:3
washes Happiness w. away many things	
	BÖLL 126:14
One hand w. the other	PROV 628:39
Persil w. whiter	ADVE 8:10
washing came up from the w.	BIBL 87:10
country w.	BRUM 162:8
previously w. the hands	TALM 772:22
taking in one another's w.	ANON 15:19
w. on the Siegfried Line	KENN 448:12
Where w. ain't done	EPIT 309:15
Washington come to W. to be loved	
	GRAM 358:18
Government at W. lives	GARF 339:14
wasp everything about the w.	THOM 790:2
wasps w. and hornets break through	
	SWIF 766:27
wassails Hock-carts, w., wakes	HERR 385:16
waste art of how to w. space	JOHN 423:20
Don't w. time in mourning	LAST 472:16
file your w. basket-paper	BENN 67:5

waxworks If you think we're w. — CARR 195:4
way all gone out of the w. — BOOK 134:11
All the w. with LBJ — POLI 600:2
broad is the w. — BIBL 95:19
by w. of Beachy Head — CHES 216:10
every one to his own w. — BIBL 90:3
Every which w. — FILM 322:5
flowers to strew Thy w. — HERB 384:2
going the w. of all the earth — BIBL 79:14
I did it my w. — ANKA 14:16
If w. to the Better there be — HARD 372:17
In each thing give him w. — SHAK 678:19
long w. to Tipperary — JUDG 438:4
Love will find a w. — PROV 625:48
make the W. great — CONF 238:7
Make thy w. plain — BOOK 133:26
more a w. of life — ANON 18:3
no w. out of the mind — PLAT 596:19
one w. in to life — SENE 676:30
Prepare ye the w. of the Lord — BIBL 94:10
Set your will on the W. — CONF 237:21
She did it the hard w. — EPIT 311:5
shortest w. — BACO 43:3
Teach me thy w., O Lord — BOOK 135:14
there was a w. to Hell — BUNY 164:25
This is the w. — BIBL 89:6
Thou art my w. — QUAR 639:1
thy w. may be known — BOOK 138:8
War always finds a w. — BREC 150:10
W. down upon the Swanee — FOST 330:14
w. of a man with a maid — BIBL 85:21
W. of our Master — CONF 237:15
w. of seeing — KEEN 447:17
w. of taking life — FROS 336:7
w. of the Lord — BIBL 89:16
w. of transgressors — BIBL 84:16
W. that can be told of — LAO 467:4
w., the truth, and the life — BIBL 103:29
w. to dusty death — SHAK 707:14
w. to skin a cat — PROV 632:15
w. to the stars — VIRG 813:7
wilful man must have his w. — PROV 635:10
will there's a w. — PROV 634:42
your w. be long — CAVA 203:15
ways in His w. with men — TENN 778:10
in whose heart are thy w. — BOOK 139:16
justify the w. of God — MILT 531:6
keep them in all thy w. — BOOK 140:4
Let me count the w. — BROW 158:3
maintain mine own w. — BIBL 83:7
neither are your w. my ways — BIBL 90:8
of the w. of God — BIBL 83:27
parting of the w. — BIBL 91:15
vindicate the w. of God — POPE 604:18
wander in the w. of men — BURN 171:21
w. are ways of pleasantness — BIBL 83:35
w. be unconfined — PRIO 612:2
w. of making you talk — CATC 201:32
where three w. meet — SOPH 746:19
wayside seeds fell by the w. — BIBL 97:3
wayward w. is this foolish love — SHAK 721:20
we still it is not w. — CHES 216:13
W. are seven — WORD 850:19
W.'re here — MILI 526:17
W. shall not pretend — NEWS 562:21
weak concessions of the w. — BURK 166:18
flesh is w. — BIBL 99:6
found him w. in chemistry — WELL 828:7
help the w.-hearted — BOOK 129:11
Like all w. men — MAUG 518:18
nature has made w. — JOHN 424:19
refuge of w. minds — CHES 215:10
Strengthen ye the w. hands — BIBL 89:10
virtue of w. minds — DRYD 288:23
w. alone repent — BYRO 179:25
w. always have to decide — BONH 127:9
w. from your loveliness — BETJ 73:2
w. in the head — PROV 635:22
W. men must fall — SHAK 715:19
w. overcomes the strong — LAO 468:7
w. piping time — SHAK 716:21
W. shall perish — SERV 677:8
w. things of the world — BIBL 107:5

weaken great life if you don't w. — BUCH 162:18
weakening w. the will — SPEN 750:23
weaker to the w. side inclined — BUTL 176:18
unto the w. vessel — BIBL 112:11
w. sex — ALEX 11:11
weakest w. go to the wall — PROV 633:44
w. kind of fruit — SHAK 709:23
w. link — PROV 616:30
You are the w. link — CATC 202:2
weakling seven-stone w. — ADVE 7:40
weakness made perfect in w. — BIBL 108:25
makes our w. weaker — BALZ 54:9
w. of our mortal nature — BOOK 130:11
weal according to the common w. — JAME 417:5
wealth acquisition of w. — SOCR 744:26
consume w. without producing — SHAW 724:22
excessive w. a libel — SHEL 732:12
gave the little w. he had — SWIF 767:18
get w. and place — POPE 605:17
greater the w. — GALB 338:3
health and w. — HUNT 409:18
I'm a man of w. — JAGG 415:17
In Eden the only w. — FUEN 336:21
in health and w. — BOOK 128:15
insolence of w. — JOHN 431:6
no increase in material w. — TAWN 774:5
no w. but life — RUSK 660:11
Outshone the w. of Ormuz — MILT 531:29
prevents the rule of w. — BAGE 48:4
promoting the w. — BURK 167:2
purchase of my w. — JONS 435:12
road to w. — TROL 799:12
squandering w. — DRYD 287:7
third honest w. — ANON 21:10
Thirst of w. — WINC 841:4
w. accumulates, and men decay — GOLD 354:10
w. and commerce — MANN 511:2
w. and din of Rome — HORA 402:1
w. around them makes them — CRAB 249:19
w. a well-spent age — CAMP 188:3
w. is a sacred thing — FRAN 331:17
W. I seek not — STEV 760:17
w. of you beside me — GAND 339:3
w. ye find — SHEL 731:18
wealthy business of the w. man — BELL 65:16
healthy, w., and wise — PROV 618:31
some people are very w. — ARIS 26:3
w. curlèd darlings — SHAK 713:5
w. in a religious diving-bell — FOST 330:9
weaned w. on a pickle — ANON 19:13
were we not w. — DONN 280:26
weapon art is not a w. — KENN 449:6
bayonet is a w. — POLI 600:6
held a w. — BIBL 82:20
his w. wit — EPIT 310:10
Innocence no earthly w. — HILL 388:10
Loyalty the Tory's secret w. — KILM 451:10
offensive and dangerous w. — PICA 595:4
shield and w. — LUTH 496:11
weapons books are w. — ROOS 654:2
fightings with outward w. — FOX 331:11
Spare us all word of the w. — WILB 835:2
w. of war — BIBL 80:29
w. will be our words — TRIM 798:18
wear w. — BOOK 144:19
wear better to w. out — CUMB 253:4
qualities as would w. well — GOLD 355:29
w. him In my heart's core — SHAK 686:26
w. of winning — BELL 65:28
w. out than to rust out — PROV 615:32
w. out to nought — SHAK 701:15
w. them out in practice — BEAU 59:14
what you are going to w. — WELD 827:5
wearies you say it w. you — SHAK 708:19
weariest even the w. river — SWIN 768:17
weariness For w. of thee — DONN 281:11
for w. of-walked — LANG 466:15
much study is a w. — BIBL 86:26
pale for w. — SHEL 732:5

w. May toss him to My breast — HERB 384:21
w., the fever — KEAT 444:23
w. treads on desire — PETR 594:7
wearing w. armchairs tight about the hips — WODE 843:3
w. o' the Green — POLI 600:21
wherefore is he w. — HOUS 403:19
wears so w. she to him — SHAK 720:23
w. itself out — HAZL 376:16
w. man's smudge — HOPK 396:12
weary got the W. Blues — HUGH 407:2
How w., stale, flat — SHAK 684:1
not be w. in well doing — BIBL 109:3
run, and not be w. — BIBL 89:21
sae w. fu' o' care — BURN 170:12
Waukin still and w. — BURN 170:12
w. be at rest — BIBL 82:33
w. of my groaning — BOOK 134:2
w. warl goes round — BLAM 123:4
w. wi' hunting — BALL 52:10
with w. task fordone — SHAK 712:6
weasel as a w. sucks eggs — SHAK 681:4
Pop goes the w. — MAND 509:12
w. under the cocktail cabinet — PINT 595:17
w. word — ROOS 654:15
weather blue unclouded w. — TENN 780:10
Builds in the w. — SHAK 709:8
care what the w. was like — CHEK 214:4
first talk is of the w. — JOHN 424:16
hard grey w. — KING 452:17
Jolly boating w. — CORY 244:1
most extraordinary w. — GOGA 353:20
not in fine w. — CLOU 227:17
sad or singing w. — SWIN 769:6
Some are w.-wise — FRAN 332:12
Stormy w. — KOEH 458:14
w. gynneth clere — CHAU 212:31
w. is always doing something — TWAI 803:27
w. the cuckoo likes — HARD 373:4
w. turned around — THOM 789:15
will be fair w. — BIBL 97:14
winter and rough w. — SHAK 681:3
you won't hold up the w. — MACN 504:16
weave tangled web we w. — SCOT 673:23
W. the warp — GRAY 360:22
weaver swifter than a w.'s shuttle — BIBL 82:38
weaving my own hand's w. — KEAT 443:17
web cool w. of language — GRAV 360:6
She left the w. — TENN 780:12
tangled w. we weave — SCOT 673:23
weaving of the w. — HEIK 379:10
W. is exciting for two reasons — JOBS 422:1
w., then, or the pattern — STEV 758:25
wove a w. in childhood — BRON 152:15
Webb W. from Dawley — BETJ 72:16
webs By the dark w. — YEAT 854:20
like spiders' w. — ANAC 13:18
Webster Like W.'s Dictionary — BURK 169:14
wed Better w. over the mixen — PROV 615:33
December when they w. — SHAK 682:2
for any good yeman to w. — CHAU 211:22
I w. again — CLAR 224:5
Som Cristen man shall w. me — CHAU 212:14
think to w. it — SHAK 678:7
w. the fair Ellen — SCOT 673:20
With this Ring I thee w. — BOOK 133:10
wedded I have w. fyve — CHAU 212:14
No w. man so hardy be — CHAU 211:4
w. to the truth — SAKI 663:20
w. wife — BOOK 133:8
wedding as she did her w. gown — GOLD 355:29
earliest w.-day — KEBL 447:15
face looks like a w.-cake — AUDE 36:20
O God, and the w. — CORS 243:18
One w. brings another — PROV 629:4
small circle of a w.-ring — CIBB 223:1
to a w. — BIBL 101:3
w. clothes — ADDI 5:9
w. dresses ready — BYRO 181:28
W.-Guest here beat — COLE 232:14
wedlock in holy w. — BOOK 133:12
W., indeed, hath oft — DAVI 258:6

W. is a padlock	PROV 633:45
w.'s the devil	BYRO 183:13
Wednesday W.'s child	NURS 568:10
weds Egghead w. hourglass	NEWS 562:6
wee cried, W.-wee-wee	NURS 570:4
expectant w.-things	BURN 170:19
w. pretendy government	CONN 240:1
W., sleekit, cow'rin'	BURN 172:20
w. wifie waitin'	MORR 550:10
W. Willie Winkie	NURS 570:13
weed honey from the w.	SHAK 693:10
Ignorance is an evil w.	BEVE 73:21
law to w. it out	BACO 45:8
Pernicious w.	COWP 246:9
salt w. sways in the stream	ARNO 27:12
w. that grows	BURK 166:29
w. their own minds	WALP 819:14
What is a w.? A plant	EMER 307:10
Wood, the W., the Wag	RALE 641:7
weeded W. and worn	TENN 781:14
weeding seven years w.	PROV 629:6
weeds all the idle w.	SHAK 701:11
bred among the w.	BROW 156:31
come up like w.	WALK 817:9
coronet w.	SHAK 688:19
grubbing w. from gravel paths	KIPL 454:8
Ill w. grow apace	PROV 623:31
Long live the w.	HOPK 396:17
smell far worse than w.	SHAK 723:15
w. spontaneous rise	IRWI 414:7
week accomplished in a w.	STEV 759:17
die in my w.	JOPL 436:11
Middle of Next W.	CARR 196:15
Sunday In every w.	CLAR 225:7
w. after next	CARR 196:2
w. a long time in politics	WILS 840:7
w. of death	DONN 281:24
weekend long w.	FORS 329:12
w. starts here	CATC 201:31
weep Doth w. full sore	SPEN 751:18
Fair daffodils, we w.	HERR 386:15
fear of having to w.	BEAU 60:1
If you want me to w.	HORA 398:6
I may not w.	BYRO 181:13
I w. for Adonais	SHEL 728:13
make the angels w.	SHAK 708:1
milk my ewes and w.	SHAK 722:11
pale, and wan, and w.	CLAU 225:14
saw my lady w.	ANON 17:1
scarcely cry 'w.! weep!'	BLAK 122:1
She wolde w.	CHAU 210:12
sit down and w.	WALP 819:10
That he should w. for her	SHAK 686:3
time to w.	BIBL 85:32
w. and know why	HOPK 397:3
w., and wrynge	CHAU 211:6
w. and you weep alone	PROV 624:48
W., and you weep alone	WILC 835:8
w. as a woman	AYES 41:10
W., children	NERV 559:7
W. me not dead	DONN 281:19
W. not for little Léonie	GRAH 358:5
w. on your own grave	GRAV 360:10
w. or she will die	TENN 783:9
w. over Saul	BIBL 80:28
weep with them that w.	BIBL 106:26
W. you no more	ANON 19:16
women must w.	KING 452:22
weepers losers w.	PROV 620:2
weepest Woman, why w. thou	BIBL 104:12
weeping full cause of w.	SHAK 700:13
goeth on his way w.	BOOK 142:24
hear the children w.	BROW 157:23
two w. motions	CRAS 250:16
w. and gnashing	BIBL 95:30
w. and the laughter	DOWS 284:7
W. and watching	GOET 353:11
w. and with laughter	MACA 499:20
w. for her children	BIBL 94:8
W. queen	SHAK 716:5
weeps w. with loathing	LITT 487:1
Weib W. und Gesang	LUTH 496:15
Weibliche Das Ewig-W.	CLOS 228:8

weigh more people see than w.	CHES 215:13
w. and consider	BACO 45:19
w. it down on one side	HALI 368:12
w. thy words	BIBL 93:21
weighed w. in the balances	BIBL 91:22
weighing not w. our merits	BOOK 132:3
weight bear the w. of Antony	SHAK 678:24
heavy and the weary w.	WORD 847:8
w. of rages	SPOO 753:2
words are of less w.	BACO 43:29
weights system of w. and measures	NAPO 556:18
weilest wo w. du	WAGN 817:3
Wein W., Weib und Gesang	LUTH 496:15
weird w. sisters	SHAK 703:7
w. women promised	SHAK 705:16
welcome Advice is seldom w.	CHES 215:4
be w. back again	BURN 172:17
good evening, and w.	CATC 200:25
Love bade me w.	HERB 384:13
warmest w., at an inn	SHEN 732:23
W., all wonders	CRAS 250:12
w. day	BUNY 165:8
W. the coming	POPE 605:15
W. the sixte	CHAU 212:14
W. to your gory bed	BURN 172:5
welcomes w. at once all the world	ANST 23:3
welcomest w. when they are gone	SHAK 694:8
welfare anxious for its w.	BURK 166:13
concerned with the w.	MAHĀ 506:10
corporate w. bums	LEWI 483:13
W. became a term	MOYN 551:18
W. is for the needy	LEWI 483:14
w. of this realm	CHAR 209:10
welkin all the w. rings	WESL 828:23
well alive and w.	ANON 17:4
all shall be w.	ELIO 302:2
all shall be w.	JULI 438:6
All's w. that ends well	PROV 614:16
at the bottom of a w.	PROV 633:21
being w.	MART 515:1
deep as a w.	SHAK 717:32
Didn't she do w.	CATC 200:10
does himself extremely w.	ANON 17:22
Do sleep w.	CATC 200:13
drink from every w.	CALL 186:2
foolish thing w. done	JOHN 429:21
handsome, w.-shaped. man	AUBR 34:2
have the morning w.-aired	BRUM 162:7
Is it w. with the child	BIBL 82:4
It is not done w.	JOHN 428:19
Let w. alone	PROV 625:11
Like a w.-conducted person	THAC 786:23
looking. w. can't move her	SUCK 763:4
men shall speak w. of you	BIBL 100:14
never speaks w. of me	CONG 238:32
not feeling very w.	PUNC 637:22
not wisely but too w.	SHAK 714:30
one who meant w.	STEV 758:24
pitcher will go to the w.	PROV 629:23
Pussy's in the w.	NURS 566:18
rare as a w.-spent one	CARL 191:18
sense of being w.-dressed	FORB 328:7
shall be w. again	ARNO 27:9
spent one whole day w.	THOM 788:10
that's as w. said	SWIF 766:12
till the w. runs dry	PROV 636:3
use it for a w.	BOOK 139:16
want a thing done w.	PROV 623:24
want to do something w.	BISH 117:10
W. begun is half done	PROV 633:46
w.-beloved hath a vineyard	BIBL 88:4
w.-born and unhappy woman	ELIO 299:17
w.-bred as if we were not married	CONG 239:16
w.-bred resignation	TURG 802:7
W. done	BIBL 98:21
w.-informed mind	AUST 39:8
w. of English undefiled	SPEN 752:2
w. of loneliness	HALL 369:13
w. of love	COLE 231:3

w. of poisons	GIRA 350:1
w.-tuned cymbals	BOOK 144:9
w.-written Life	CARL 191:18
when ye do w.	BIBL 112:8
would do very w.	WALP 819:5
wellbeloved my w. unto me	BIBL 87:4
Wellesley fat with W.'s glory	BYRO 181:23
wells poison the w.	NEWM 560:8
poison w.	MARL 513:14
Welsh devil understands W.	SHAK 690:25
Welshman Taffy was a W.	NURS 569:16
valour in this W.	SHAK 693:13
Weltgeschichte W. ist das Weltgericht	SCHI 671:3
wen great w. of all	COBB 229:19
Wenceslas Good King W.	NEAL 558:1
wench O ill-starred w.	SHAK 714:27
w. is dead	MARL 513:15
wenches many young w.	OSBO 578:10
Wenlock On W. Edge	HOUS 404:13
went He w. forth conquering	BIBL 113:13
wept He w. beneath a crag	VIRG 815:6
I sat down and w.	BORR 146:3
Jesus w.	BIBL 103:22
No one w. for the dead	AGNO 8:31
sometimes w.	MUSS 555:10
w. for want of more Worlds	WATT 824:1
W. over her	TENN 781:19
we sat down and w.	BOOK 143:12
would have w.	MALO 509:2
Werther W. had a love for Charlotte	THAC 786:22
west Cincinnatus of the W.	BYRO 182:27
come out of the w.	SCOT 673:18
daughter of the W.	TENN 777:11
east is from the w.	BOOK 141:3
East, w., home's best	PROV 618:33
face neither East nor W.	NKRU 565:5
gardens of the W.	CONN 240:8
Go W., young man	GREE 362:3
Go W., young man	NEWS 562:10
Islam and the W.	STRA 762:11
liquid manure from the W.	SOLZ 745:20
nor from the w.	BOOK 139:4
O wild W. Wind	SHEL 730:7
safeguard of the W.	WORD 848:19
sailing away to the w.	KING 452:21
travel due W.	CARR 196:9
W. is West	KIPL 453:15
w. is west	PROV 618:32
W. Lothian	DALY 255:2
W. of these out to seas	FLEC 325:18
W.'s awake	DAVI 259:9
where the W. begins	CHAP 208:7
wester rainy Pleiads w.	HOUS 404:3
western delivered by W. Union	GOLD 356:7
Go to the w. gate	ROBI 650:14
o'er the w. wave	SHEL 732:3
Playboy of the W. World	CLOS 228:19
Playboy of the W. World	SYNG 769:13
quiet on the w. front	REMA 645:4
spray of W. pine	HART 374:15
When you've seen one W.	WHIT 832:19
Wind of the w. sea	TENN 782:26
Westerners W. have aggressive	KAUN 442:4
Westminster peerage, or W. Abbey	NELS 558:18
westward stepping w.	WORD 850:10
w., look, the land	CLOU 229:12
W. the course of empire	BERK 69:15
wet out of these w. clothes	FILM 319:23
Sow dry and set w.	PROV 631:9
so w. you could shoot snipe off him	POWE 609:15
w. and wildness	HOPK 396:17
w. sheet	CUNN 253:17
would not w. her feet	PROV 616:29
wether tainted w. of the flock	SHAK 709:23
whacks gave her mother forty w.	ANON 17:9
whale point of view of the w.	ATWO 33:11
prophet with the w.	DICK 270:8
Save the w.	SLOG 740:11
unconquering w.	MELV 521:11

whose W. finger — NEWS 562:23
whoso W. doeth these things — BOOK 134:13
whosoever W. will be saved — BOOK 128:21
why about the wasp, except w. — THOM 790:2
but also w., to whom — HAVE 375:6
can't tell you w. — MART 514:17
finding only w. — CUMM 253:13
For every w. he had a wherefore — BUTL 176:1
W., Edward, tell me why — WORD 846:3
W. not? Why not? Yeah — LAST 474:16
Would this man ask w. — AUDE 34:25
vibrated better not be w. — DICK 267:12
wicked all the world w. — BURK 168:6
August is a w. month — O'BR 571:4
deceitful and w. man — BOOK 136:15
desperately w. — BIBL 91:3
fiery darts of the w. — BIBL 109:21
no peace unto the w. — BIBL 89:26
not that men are w. — DU B 291:1
pretending to be w. — WILD 835:20
sick and w. — AUST 40:20
Something w. this way comes — SHAK 706:14
tender mercies of the w. — BIBL 84:13
Tories born w. — ANON 17:14
what is more w. — BALL 52:19
w. and moral — CHUR 220:20
w. cease from troubling — BIBL 82:33
w. flee — BIBL 85:16
w. pack of cards — ELIO 303:10
worse than w. — PUNC 637:16
wickedness abhorrence for w. — THAC 786:20
bands of w. — BIBL 90:14
capable of every w. — CONR 241:1
Hated w. — BROW 160:13
malice and w. — BOOK 130:7
manifold sins and w. — BOOK 127:13
Path of W. — BALL 53:11
shapen in w. — BOOK 137:11
than human w. — TAYL 774:11
turneth away from his w. — BIBL 91:4
w. in high places — BIBL 109:21
[w.] is not punished — COMP 237:3
W. is the root — ROBE 650:7
wicket flannelled fools at the w. — KIPL 454:16
Widdicombe Fair want for to go to W.
— BALL 53:20
wide how w. also the east is — BOOK 141:3
I am very w. — BALZ 54:12
Poet sees, but w. — ARNO 27:24
w. as a church door — SHAK 717:32
W. is the gate — BIBL 95:19
wideness w. in God's mercy — FABE 313:16
wider seek no w. war — JOHN 423:13
w. still and wider — BENS 67:25
widow certain poor w. — BIBL 99:27
fatherless and w. — BOOK 144:2
French w. in every bedroom — HOFF 392:4
Molly Stark's w. — STAR 754:12
old grey W.-maker — KIPL 454:11
retired w. — BAGE 48:10
virgin-w., and a *mourning bride* — DRYD 289:9
w. bird sat mourning — SHEL 729:3
w. of fifty — SHER 733:31
W. The word consumes itself — PLAT 597:4
widowhood comfortable estate of w.
— GAY 341:11
widows cause of the w. — BOOK 138:11
devour w.' houses — BIBL 99:26
fatherless children, and w. — BOOK 129:13
These w., Sir — ADDI 5:1
visit the fatherless and w. — BIBL 111:24
w. whose husbands are alive — BERN 70:16
wife as a w. is — MILL 525:14
as his w. — BRON 152:10
blind man's w. needs — PROV 616:4
blind w. — PROV 617:26
Brutus took to w. — SHAK 697:2
Caesar's w. — CAES 185:3
Caesar's w. — PROV 616:21
cleave unto his w. — BIBL 75:17
come in on the w.'s side — LAMB 464:10
covet thy neighbour's w. — BIBL 78:5

decided to murder his w. — OPEN 574:26
Despair had a w. — BUNY 164:22
divorces his first w. — TALM 772:26
dwindle into a w. — CONG 239:17
happy for a week take a w. — PROV 623:27
have no w. — BACO 46:25
his [Lot's] w. looked back — BIBL 76:20
honour unto the w. — BIBL 112:11
husband and w. — FIEL 318:13
I'd have no w. — CRAS 250:15
If I were your w. — CHUR 222:20
I have a w. — CONG 239:8
I have a w. — LUCA 495:3
I have married a w. — BIBL 101:7
in want of a w. — AUST 39:18
in want of a w. — OPEN 574:22
keeps up a w.'s spirits — GAY 341:11
kick his w. out of bed — SURT 764:13
kill a w. with kindness — SHAK 718:14
lay down his w. for his friend — JOYC 437:23
Like Caesar's w. — ANON 17:7
look out for a w. — SURT 764:21
love his w. as himself — TALM 772:19
Man and W. — BOOK 133:12
man who's untrue to his w. — AUDE 35:14
Medicine is my lawful w. — CHEK 214:9
moral centaur, man and w. — BYRO 181:19
my sonne's w., Elizabeth — INGE 413:13
my w., and my name — SURT 764:16
My w., who, poor wretch — PEPY 592:4
My w. won't let me — LEIG 479:18
Petrarch's w. — BYRO 180:28
quarrelled with my w. — PEAC 590:4
Remember Lot's w. — BIBL 101:25
riding to and from his w. — WHIT 831:24
she is your w. — OGIL 571:14
some friend, not w. — POPE 602:26
sympathetic w. — EURI 312:24
Thane of Fife had a w. — SHAK 707:1
There's my w. — SPRI 753:8
thrive must first ask his w. — PROV 622:1
took from me my w. — CLAR 224:5
to suit his w. — TROL 800:4
true and honourable w. — SHAK 697:1
wedded w. — BOOK 133:8
w. and children — BACO 44:30
W. and Servant — CHUD 219:9
w. for breed — GAY 342:13
w. has ever taken — SHAF 678:2
w. in bondage — LEAP 477:1
w. is May — WATK 822:17
w. or your servants to read — GRIF 364:8
w. shall be as the fruitful vine — BOOK 143:3
w. talks Greek — JOHN 433:17
w. who looks out of door — WELD 827:5
wind is my w. — KEAT 446:17
with a w. — SHAK 692:6
world and his w. — ANST 23:3
wifehood Meek w. is no part — BRIT 151:18
wig w. with the scorched foretop
— MACA 498:1
Wigan mothers-in-law and W. Pier
— BRID 151:4
wights descriptions of the fairest w.
— SHAK 723:16
wigwam w. of Nokomis — LONG 491:1
wild brought forth w. grapes — BIBL 88:5
call of the w. — LOND 489:14
gone w. into his grave — SHAK 692:21
grew more fierce and w. — HERB 383:25
never saw a w. thing — LAWR 475:5
nobly w., not mad — HERR 386:6
not a more fearful w.-fowl — SHAK 711:8
O Caledonia! stern and w. — SCOT 673:13
peace of w. things — BERR 71:12
three w. lads were we — SCOT 674:9
walk on the w. side — ALGR 11:14
waving his w. tail — KIPL 456:15
w. for to hold — WYAT 852:8
w. geese are flighting — KIPL 454:15
w. with all regret — TENN 783:5
wilder w. shores of love — BLAN 123:7
wilderness crieth in the w. — BIBL 89:16

crying in the w. — BIBL 94:10
day's journey into the w. — BIBL 81:26
dwellings of the w. — BOOK 138:7
grain into the w. — STOU 761:18
in perils in the w. — BIBL 108:22
in the w. — BIBL 101:11
into the w. — BIBL 78:12
into the w. to see — BIBL 96:24
savage w. — BURK 167:2
singing in the w. — FITZ 323:2
temptation in the w. — BOOK 140:10
They make a w. — TACI 770:3
To the w. I wander — ANON 20:4
walked through the w. — OPEN 574:5
weeds and the w. — HOPK 396:17
w. of idea — BUTL 176:31
Women have no w. — BOGA 125:7
world's wide w. — WATT 823:14
wildness wet and w. — HOPK 396:17
wilful w. man must have his way
— PROV 635:10
Wilhelmine little grandchild W. — SOUT 748:17
will according to the common w. — JAME 417:5
cause is in my w. — SHAK 697:6
complies against his w. — BUTL 176:17
complies against his w. — PROV 621:45
death with one's w. — JAIN 416:11
except a *good* w. — KANT 441:7
general w. rules — ROBE 650:4
Immanent W. — HARD 372:14
In His w. is our peace — DANT 256:11
knowing that we do Thy w. — IGNA 412:18
know our w. is free — JOHN 429:4
let my w. replace — JUVE 439:20
not because we w. — ARNO 27:1
not my w., but thine, be done — BIBL 102:1
Not of my own free w. — VIRG 812:4
One single w. — ROBE 650:8
political w. — LYNN 497:7
resigning up one's w. — OSBO 578:14
settled w. — SMIT 742:10
settled w. — STEE 754:15
their w. — ADAM 2:9
Thy w. be done — BIBL 95:3
to have had the w. — PROP 612:22
torrent of a woman's w. — ANON 20:1
Where there's a w. — PROV 634:42
w. against enjoyment — HARD 372:4
W. in over-plus — SHAK 723:28
w. not when he may — PROV 621:52
w. of even common man — CONF 238:1
w. of the majority — JEFF 420:1
w. or decision — CHOM 218:10
w. reigns — FRAN 332:14
w. that my maxim — KANT 441:8
w. to carry on — LIPP 486:14
w. to go — SHAK 718:3
W. you, won't you — CARR 194:18
wind's w. — LONG 490:15
wrote my w. across the sky — LAWR 475:19
You w., Oscar — WHIS 831:22
willed only a w. gentleness — THOM 790:25
William You are old, Father W. — CARR 194:4
Willie Wee W. Winkie — NURS 570:13
willing Barkis is w. — DICK 268:10
spirit indeed is w. — BIBL 99:6
w. suspension of disbelief — COLE 233:22
willingness w. is commendable — OVID 580:6
willow green w. is my garland — HEYW 387:18
Make me a w. cabin — SHAK 720:13
Sing all a green w. — SHAK 714:16
Stood Dido with a w. — SHAK 710:1
w. grows aslant a brook — SHAK 688:17
w. must be my garland — SHAK 714:17
W., titwillow — GILB 348:10
willows runs away into the w. — VIRG 813:21
w. of the brook — BIBL 83:28
w., old rotten planks — CONS 241:6
W. whiten, aspens quiver — TENN 780:6
wills talk of w. — SHAK 715:22
w. the end — PROV 622:16
wilt Do what thou w. — CROW 253:2

Wimbledon Spill your guts at W.
CONN 240:11

wimps Lunch is for w. FILM 320:2

win can't w. them all PROV 635:46
From w. and lose MITC 540:11
Greetings, we w. LAST 471:17
if only you w. BREC 150:4
know how to w. POLY 599:14
Let them laugh that w. PROV 625:10
spend it, and w. KENN 449:12
that's to w. MALR 509:6
To w. in Vietnam SPOC 753:1
w. an atomic war BRAD 148:21
w. a war is as disastrous CHRI 218:14
w. his spurs EDWA 296:9
W. just one for the Gipper GIPP 349:20
w. or lose it all MONT 546:3
would greatly w. BYRO 182:24
yet wouldst wrongly w. SHAK 703:18
You w. a few PROV 636:11

wince rather w. DICK 273:12

wind All-powerful as the w. AUBE 33:13
answer is blowin' in the w. DYLA 294:3
appearance of solidity to pure w.
ORWE 578:4
as the idle w. SHAK 698:16
available with an east w. LOWE 494:6
Awake, O north w. BIBL 87:13
bleak w. of March HOOD 394:22
Blow, blow, thou winter w. SHAK 681:14
Blow, thou w. of God KING 452:18
boy's will is the w.'s LONG 490:15
candle in the w. JOHN 422:11
candles in the w. MERE 522:13
chiding of the winter's w. SHAK 680:25
clouds and w. without rain BIBL 85:4
east w. made flesh APPL 23:15
every w. of doctrine BIBL 109:11
feather for each w. SHAK 721:29
flare up in a w. FRAN 332:7
Freshly blows the w. WAGN 817:3
Frosty w. made moan ROSS 655:9
gentle w. does move BLAK 121:25
God tempers the w. STER 756:12
gone with the w. DOWS 284:6
hey, ho, the w. and the rain SHAK 700:20
His hammer of w. THOM 791:19
how the w. doth ramm POUN 608:12
ill w. that blows PROV 624:18
impatient as the w. WORD 850:11
let her down the w. SHAK 713:28
light w. lives or dies KEAT 445:17
like the w., that shifts DANT 256:8
Lord was not in the w. BIBL 81:27
moved about like the w. GERO 344:3
north w. doth blow NURS 568:12
not I, but the w. LAWR 475:9
Not with this w. blowing KIPL 455:5
no w. is favourable SENE 676:27
observeth the w. BIBL 86:22
O wild West W. SHEL 730:7
O w., the weder gynneth clere CHAU 212:31
piffle before the w. ASHF 31:15
rag blown by the w. WORD 845:17
reed before the w. PROV 630:6
reed shaken with the w. BIBL 96:24
rude w. Blows in your face SHAK 701:9
rushing mighty w. BIBL 104:26
sand against the w. BLAK 121:16
sown the w. BIBL 91:28
sow the w. PROV 632:37
stood the w. for France DRAY 286:6
substance is but only w. WYAT 852:7
tempers w. to shorn lamb PROV 621:1
thaw w. PROV 630:14
'tis a Protestant w. WHAR 831:5
torch borne in the w. CHAP 208:9
twist slowly in the w. EHRL 297:8
Unhelped by any w. COLE 231:18
wash the w. ELIO 302:25
way the w. blows PROV 631:26
Western w. ANON 19:19
western w. was wild KING 452:19

Whenever the w. is high STEV 760:8
when the w. is southerly SHAK 685:27
wherever the w. takes me HORA 398:18
which way the w. is SELD 676:5
w. and storm BOOK 144:6
w. and swift-flowing water CATU 203:3
w. and the rain SHAK 721:18
w. and wave and oar TENN 781:10
w. blew due East CARR 196:9
w. bloweth where it listeth BIBL 102:31
w. blow the earth SHAK 700:14
w. doth blow BALL 53:16
w. extinguishes candles LA R 469:18
w. goeth over it BOOK 141:4
w. in that corner SHAK 712:19
w. is in the east PROV 634:33
w. is to fire BUSS 175:8
w. it into a ball BLAK 120:13
w. it plies the saplings HOUS 404:13
w. of change is blowing MACM 504:6
W. of the western sea TENN 782:26
w. or the pennant HUI- 408:5
w. plays up BLOK 123:14
w.'s feet shine SWIN 769:4
w.'s in the east DICK 267:16
wings of the w. BOOK 134:16
wings of the w. BOOK 141:5
Woord is but w. LYDG 496:20

windbags W. can be right FENT 316:14

winder w., a casement DICK 270:18

winding by a w. stair BACO 44:25
England's w. sheet BLAK 119:14
good structure in a w. stair HERB 384:11
have w. sheet DONN 281:23
waters were his w. sheet BARN 56:16
w.-sheet of Edward's GRAY 360:22

windings w. and such shade WINC 841:8
w. of the grove BEAT 59:12

window appears at a w. BEER 63:3
argument of the broken w. PANK 585:9
clapte the w. to CHAU 211:23
doggie in the w. MERR 522:25
eyes are w. of soul PROV 619:34
Good prose like a w.-pane ORWE 577:2
has not one w. JAME 418:3
kick a hole in a stained glass w.
CHAN 207:11
kiss my ass in Macy's w. JOHN 423:15
little w. where the sun HOOD 395:3
looked out at a w. BIBL 82:13
openeth the w. BIBL 75:3
return through the w. FRED 333:7
rubs its back upon the w.-panes ELIO 302:14
through thrown w. breaks SHAK 717:19
throw it out of the w. BECK 61:8
Waits at the w. LENN 480:17

windows breaking of w. MORE 547:24
life's dim w. BLAK 119:23
open the w. of the Church JOHN 422:6
open w. into men's souls ELIZ 304:16
storied w. MILT 529:16
then the W. failed DICK 273:1
thought of high w. LARK 468:17
thus, Through w. DONN 281:12
without looking through w. LAO 467:15

winds all the w. of doctrine MILT 535:25
Blow, w., and crack SHAK 700:15
great w. shorewards blow ARNO 27:11
howling w. drive COWP 247:6
O ye W. of God BOOK 128:5
stormy w. did blow SONG 748:2
take The w. of March SHAK 722:5
w. come to me WORD 848:2
w. do blow HERB 384:15
w. of heaven SHAK 684:3
w. that would blow BOLT 126:15
w. were love-sick SHAK 679:3

windscreen through the w. DONN 292:7
windvane w. changabil huf puffe VIRG 812:5
windward w. of the law CHUR 219:17
windy ringing plains of w. Troy TENN 784:14
w. side of the law SHAK 721:13

wine be not drunk with w. BIBL 109:17

best fits my little w. HERR 386:11
blood and w. WILD 836:27
Botticelli isn't a w. PUNC 637:23
buy w. and milk BIBL 90:6
can with w. dispense CRAB 249:2
castaway w.-pots CLOU 227:13
days of w. and roses DOWS 284:8
do crush their w. MARV 515:16
doesn't get into the w. CHES 216:18
Drinking the blude-red w. BALL 53:3
Drinking the blude-red w. OPEN 574:30
drink one cup of w. SCOT 673:22
drunk old w. BIBL 100:13
flask of w. FITZ 323:2
flown with insolence and w. MILT 531:21
From the sweetest w. PROV 620:33
Good w. needs no bush PROV 621:13
have w. and women BYRO 180:21
he drinks no w. SHAK 692:14
I as w. HERB 383:19
I'll not look for w. JONS 435:26
in w. we steep LOVE 493:5
kept the good w. BIBL 102:28
last companion, W. BELL 65:10
like generous w. Ferments BUTL 176:20
Look not thou upon the w. BIBL 85:1
love is better than w. BIBL 87:2
mine host's Canary w. KEAT 444:5
new friend is as new w. BIBL 93:10
new w. in old bottles PROV 635:43
new w. into old bottles BIBL 96:8
Not given to w. BIBL 110:22
old w. wholesomest WEBS 826:3
out-did the frolic w. HERR 386:7
pint o' w. BURN 171:26
Poetry is devil's w. AUGU 37:7
red sweet w. of youth BROO 153:5
red w. of Shiraz into urine DINE 274:17
refreshed with w. BOOK 139:11
rinsed with w. HOPK 396:15
Sans w., sans song FITZ 323:5
seas of life, like w. TRAH 798:2
take a glass of w. SHER 734:5
that is without w. BIBL 93:24
truth in w. PROV 632:25
vows made in w. SHAK 681:26
When the w. is in PROV 634:34
w. and women BURT 174:4
w.-dark sea HOME 394:15
w. for thy stomach's sake BIBL 110:24
W. is a mocker BIBL 84:33
W. is the strongest BIBL 92:15
W. maketh merry BIBL 86:19
W. may well be considered PAST 588:8
W., not water SANS 666:6
w. on the lees BIBL 89:1
w., reed as blood CHAU 210:27
w. that maketh glad BOOK 141:7
w. unto those of heavy hearts BIBL 85:22
w. with a merry heart BIBL 86:14
woman, w. and song LUTH 496:15
Women and w. GAY 341:13

wines Soused in high-country w.
JONS 434:15

wing flits by on leathern w. COLL 235:11
joy is ever on the w. MILT 534:24
knowst'ou w. from tail POUN 609:5
lark's on the w. BROW 160:22
never flew on one w. PROV 615:41
on a w. and a pray'r ADAM 3:17
so long on a broken w. TENN 782:5

winged Time's w. chariot MARV 516:1
w. life destroy BLAK 121:22
w. squadrons of the sky MILM 527:15
W. words HOME 393:19

wings beating his luminous w. ARNO 29:21
beating of his w. BRIG 151:7
Beteth his w. CHAU 211:7
brought beneath His w. MIDR 524:15
Clap her broad w. FRER 333:18
clip an Angel's w. KEAT 444:4
covered with silver w. BOOK 138:12
defend thee under his w. BOOK 140:2

dip Their w. in tears TENN 779:3
eagle's w., Unseen KEAT 443:14
envy birds their w. CLAR 224:6
Fear gave w. to his feet VIRG 813:2
giant's w. BAUD 58:11
great w. beating YEAT 854:20
Grief has no w. QUIL 639:8
healing in his w. BIBL 92:14
if I have w. to fly KAHL 441:3
Ill news hath w. DRAY 285:20
in her dusky w. VIRG 813:3
Love without his w. BYRO 182:18
mount up with w. BIBL 89:21
O, for a horse with w. SHAK 683:3
on extended w. STEV 758:9
on laughter-silvered w. MAGE 505:16
On w. of song HEIN 379:14
own almighty w. KEN 448:7
shadow of thy w. BOOK 137:20
spread his w. on the blast BYRO 180:2
spreads her downy w. FANS 314:11
viewless w. of Poesy KEAT 444:25
Waft your w. together NURS 567:2
w. like a dove BOOK 137:16
w. of the morning BOOK 143:16
w. of the wind BOOK 134:16
w. of the wind BOOK 141:5
with ah! bright w. HOPK 396:13
with unconfinèd w. LOVE 493:4
wingy w. mysteries BROW 156:23
wink nod's as good as a w. PROV 627:38
w. a reputation down SWIF 767:2
wink w., say no more MONT 546:6
Winkie Wee Willie W. NURS 570:13
winners no w., but all are losers
CHAM 206:10
winning glory of the w. MERE 522:19
wear of w. BELL 65:28
w. cause pleased the gods LUCA 494:24
w. isn't anything SAND 666:4
winnowing by the w. wind KEAT 445:15
wins Who dares w. MOTT 552:22
w. if he does not lose KISS 457:10
winter all the w. long SHAK 722:1
amid the w.'s snow CASW 199:5
by the w. sea TENN 778:11
English w. BYRO 181:32
furious w. blowing RANS 642:8
furious w.'s rages SHAK 683:8
go south in the w. ELIO 303:8
If W. comes SHEL 730:14
in the Middle of W. ADDI 4:28
In w. I get up at night STEV 760:2
It was the w. wild MILT 530:19
mind of the w. STEV 758:6
my age is as a lusty w. SHAK 680:28
not a country, it is w. VIGN 810:5
of autumn and w. cometh CLAR 224:14
old man upon a w.'s night YEAT 855:3
on w.'s traces SWIN 767:25
Our severest w. COWP 248:26
perils of w. TROL 799:13
sad tale's best for w. SHAK 721:26
sluggish W. comes running HORA 402:13
summer or w. CHEK 214:4
very dead of W. ANDR 14:12
very dead of w. ELIO 302:9
W. Afternoons DICK 273:8
w. and rough weather SHAK 681:3
W. comes to rule the varied year
THOM 792:14
W. is come and gone SHEL 728:17
W. is icummen in POUN 608:12
w. is past BIBL 87:6
W. lies too long CATH 199:12
W. never rots PROV 635:12
w. of discontent CALL 185:17
W. of discontent NEWS 562:24
w. of our discontent SHAK 716:18
w. of this year ALAI 10:2
w., plague and pestilence NASH 557:22
w.'s rains and ruins SWIN 768:1
W. suddenly was changed SHEL 731:12

winters When forty w. shall besiege
SHAK 722:22
w. and keeps warm CARE 191:2
wipe Gives it a w. HOOD 395:13
Let me w. it first SHAK 701:15
w. away all tears BIBL 113:21
w. away all tears BIBL 114:17
wiped w. out of the book BOOK 138:18
wire Along the electric w. ANON 15:2
Resemble copper w. HOOD 395:9
wires If hairs be w. SHAK 723:26
wisdom all men's w. RUSS 661:15
all Solomon's w. BIBL 81:11
apply our hearts unto w. BOOK 140:1
Authority without w. BRAD 149:7
beginning of w. BOOK 141:22
beginning of w. HORA 398:19
contrivance of human w. BURK 167:12
door to infinite w. BREC 150:5
ends in w. FROS 336:4
evidences of our w. TROL 799:23
Experience father of w. PROV 619:30
Greeks seek after w. BIBL 107:3
his is a serene w. BHAG 74:13
Homage to thee, Perfect W. MAHĀ 506:7
How can he get w. BIBL 93:29
how little w. OXEN 581:9
infallible criterion of w. BURK 166:2
Mere cleverness is not w. EURI 312:14
perfection of w. MAHĀ 506:8
price of w. BIBL 83:15
privilege of w. to listen HOLM 393:2
quintessence of w. JAIN 416:18
righteousness with w. PLAT 597:17
seven pillars of w. BORR 146:17
teach Eternal W. how to rule POPE 605:2
teach his senators w. BOOK 141:13
To die in w. CERV 205:17
to the palace of w. BLAK 120:22
we had w. BENÉ 66:14
what is bettre than w. CHAU 211:21
where shall w. be found BIBL 83:14
w. and truth SOCR 744:26
w. and understanding BIBL 88:20
W. and Wit BRER 150:24
w. as many of us have TROL 800:10
w. be put in a silver rod BLAK 119:17
w. comes at the price AESC 6:4
W. denotes the pursuing HUTC 410:18
W. excelleth folly BIBL 85:31
w. has no perplexities CONF 238:5
W. hath builded her house BIBL 84:6
w. in Edom MIDR 524:18
W. in minds attentive COWP 248:13
W. is humble COWP 248:14
W. is justified BIBL 96:26
W. is not the purchase PAIN 582:12
W. is sold in the desolate market BLAK 120:6
W. is the principal thing BIBL 83:36
w. lingers TENN 781:1
W. of the crocodiles BACO 46:3
w. of the fool JOHN 433:16
W. say another BURK 167:31
w. shall die with you BIBL 83:5
w. we have lost in knowledge ELIO 303:2
With the ancient is w. BIBL 83:6
wise art of being w. JAME 418:20
Astrologers or three w. men LONG 491:14
beacons of w. men HUXL 412:3
become w. BIBL 93:28
being darkly w. POPE 604:32
be w. and eke to love SPEN 752:17
be w., and love SHAK 719:21
Be w. to-day YOUN 857:11
Be w. with speed YOUN 857:4
confound the w. BIBL 107:5
consider her ways, and be w. BIBL 84:1
cunning man pass for w. BACO 43:31
deemed him wondrous w. BEAT 59:10
enough for the w. PLAU 597:21
errors of a w. man BLAK 121:20
follies of the w. JOHN 426:20
fool may give w. man PROV 620:18

fortunate than w. WEBS 826:12
Ful w. is he CHAU 211:25
have gone the few w. men LUIS 496:3
healthy, wealthy, and w. PROV 618:31
heard a w. man say HOUS 404:10
love and be w. PROV 628:30
man w. in his own conceit BIBL 85:10
more w. when he had JOHN 431:19
Nature is always w. THUR 794:5
Nor ever did a w. one EPIT 309:14
not always w. BIBL 83:19
only wretched are the w. PRIO 612:10
or a w. man LOCK 489:2
Penny w. PROV 629:21
proud if you'll be w. CHUD 219:10
smile with the w. JOHN 429:3
So w. so young SHAK 716:30
speak to the w. PIND 595:12
still tongue makes w. head PROV 631:20
than manly w. MARL 513:25
that a w. man sees BLAK 120:25
think as w. men do ASCH 31:9
Three w. men of Gotham NURS 570:7
'Tis folly to be w. GRAY 361:12
to the w., and to the unwise BIBL 105:35
What all the w. men promised MELB 521:4
w. after the event PROV 624:2
w. as serpents BIBL 96:16
w. father that knows SHAK 709:5
w., for cure DRYD 288:8
w. forgive but do not forget SZAS 769:16
w. in his own conceit BIBL 85:8
w. in your own conceits BIBL 106:27
w. man or a fool BLAK 120:16
w. men from the east BIBL 94:5
w. men only are the better FRAN 332:16
w. son BIBL 84:8
w. want love SHEL 731:2
word to the w. is enough PROV 635:19
wisecracking w. and wit PARK 586:7
wisely Be w. worldly QUAR 638:21
nations behave w. EBAN 294:24
not w. but too well SHAK 714:30
spake w. BIBL 93:15
wiser French are w. BACO 45:15
guided by the w. CARL 191:11
he is w. today POPE 606:21
in their generation w. BIBL 101:19
looked w. when he was seated KEYN 450:12
not the w. grow POMF 599:15
on his way a w. man HOME 394:17
sadder and a w. man COLE 233:11
w. in his own conceit BIBL 85:11
wisest been noght w. men CHAU 212:8
first and w. of them MILT 534:22
Seems w., virtuousest MILT 533:25
w. and justest PLAT 597:10
w. fool in Christendom HENR 382:2
w. man can answer COLT 236:9
w. of all moral men DAVI 258:8
wish believe what they w. CAES 185:2
If otherwise w. I SHAW 728:1
live, not as we w. MENA 521:16
Whoever hath her w. SHAK 723:28
w. for prayer is a prayer BERN 70:9
w. I loved the Human Race RALE 641:18
w. is father to the thought PROV 635:13
w. I were in love again HART 374:11
w. was father, Harry SHAK 692:17
wished Much w., hoped little TASS 773:8
wishes compliance with my w. after
reasonable discussion CHUR 222:16
exact to my w. EPIT 309:15
If w. were horses PROV 623:10
w. it were MALR 509:7
wist w., before I kist BALL 53:19
wit accepted w. has but to say GILB 349:9
age is in, the w. is out SHAK 712:26
at their w.'s end BOOK 141:19
at thirty, the w. FRAN 332:14
Brevity is the soul of w. PROV 616:14
Brevity is the soul of w. SHAK 685:15
but a little w. ANON 19:20

wit (cont.):
Devise, w.; write, pen	SHAK 702:12
fancy w. will come	POPE 602:20
heart did do it, And not my w.	EPIT 310:15
his weapon w.	EPIT 310:10
His w. invites you	COWP 246:10
How the w. brightens	POPE 604:11
In w., a man	POPE 603:28
little tiny w.	SHAK 700:20
mechanic part of w.	ETHE 312:5
mingled with a little w.	DRYD 288:17
nature by her mother w.	SPEN 752:3
neither w., nor words	SHAK 698:5
no free and splendid w.	MILT 536:4
no pick-purse of another's w.	SIDN 736:9
nor all thy piety nor w.	FITZ 323:10
not his pointed w.	POPE 605:21
o'erflowing of unbounded w.	WINC 841:5
Old Mother W.	DENH 264:6
only idea of w.	SMIT 743:17
past the w. of man	SHAK 711:25
proverb is one man's w.	RUSS 661:15
ready and pleasant smooth w.	AUBR 34:2
sharpen a good w.	ASCH 31:2
shoots his w.	SHAK 682:10
Some beams of w.	DRYD 288:31
Staircase w.	DIDE 274:1
steal their w.	CAVE 204:2
takes more than w.	LA B 463:1
tomb of w.	CAVE 204:3
too proud for a w.	GOLD 355:5
True w. is Nature	POPE 604:5
universal monarchy of w.	CARE 190:13
use my w. as a pitchfork	LARK 469:4
Wisdom and W.	BRER 150:24
w. among Lords	JOHN 427:14
w. and humour	AUST 39:6
w. enough to keep it sweet	JOHN 432:19
W. has truth in it	PARK 586:7
w. in all languages	DRYD 290:3
w. is out	PROV 634:34
w. its soul	COLE 231:15
w. Makes such a wound	SHEL 729:23
W.'s empire	EGER 297:5
w.'s the noblest frailty	SHAD 677:21
W. will shine	DRYD 289:25
w. with dunces	POPE 601:28
witch Aroint thee, w.	SHAK 703:5
witchcraft as the sin of w.	BIBL 80:15
no w. charm thee	SHAK 683:9
W. celebrates	SHAK 704:17
w., there has been	WALP 819:17
witches burnt at the stake as w.	SMIT 743:2
Men feared w.	BRAN 149:12
witching w. time of night	SHAK 687:13
with He that is not w. me	BIBL 96:28
I am w. you alway	BIBL 99:14
Lord of hosts is w. us	BOOK 136:25
withdrawing long, w. roar	ARNO 27:3
withdrawn yawn and be w.	DURY 293:10
withdrew departed, he w.	CICE 223:17
wither Age cannot w. her	SHAK 679:7
w. and perish	SMIT 744:14
w. slowly in thine arms	TENN 784:7
withered are w. away	COCK 229:21
dried up, and w.	BOOK 139:2
O! w. is the garland	SHAK 680:3
So w. and so wild	SHAK 703:9
w. in the sod	BRON 152:15
withereth grass w.	BIBL 112:3
rose Fast w. too	KEAT 443:24
withers it w. away	ENGE 307:27
our w. are unwrung	SHAK 687:7
within kingdom of God is w. you	BIBL 101:24
oh, he never went w.	COWL 245:23
that w. which passeth show	SHAK 683:28
they that are w.	DAVI 258:6
without forasmuch as w. thee	BOOK 130:17
get where I am today w.	CATC 200:29
I can do w.	SOCR 744:23
no good thing w. thee	BOOK 130:11
they that are w.	DAVI 258:6
with you—or w. you	MART 515:3

withstand w. in the evil day	BIBL 109:21
witness bear false w.	BIBL 78:5
bear w. of that Light	BIBL 102:19
w. against you	BIBL 78:24
witnessed worst thing I've ever w.	MORR 550:4
witnesses cloud of w.	BIBL 111:10
w. against mankind	KORA 460:18
w. laid down their clothes	BIBL 104:32
w. to the desolation of war	GEOR 343:9
wits composed in their w.	ARNO 29:23
for w., then poets passed	POPE 603:30
Great w.	DRYD 286:21
Great w. may sometimes	POPE 604:1
stolen his w. away	DE L 262:22
Tiring thy w.	DANI 255:8
warming his five w.	TENN 784:6
W. are gamecocks	GAY 341:26
wittles live on broken w.	DICK 268:11
witty dull men w.	BACO 46:22
fancy myself mighty w.	FARQ 315:23
It shall be w.	CHES 214:17
of the w. devil	GRAV 360:5
Thou swell! Thou w.	HART 374:14
w. in myself	SHAK 691:23
wives And sklendre w.	CHAU 211:5
divides the w. of aldermen	SMIT 741:3
Husbands, love your w.	BIBL 110:13
man with seven w.	NURS 566:7
profane and old w.' fables	BIBL 110:23
several chilled w.	MERR 523:1
when they are w.	SHAK 682:2
W. are young men's mistresses	BACO 44:32
W. in the avocados	GINS 349:17
wiving Hanging and w.	PROV 621:29
wizards affairs of W.	TOLK 796:11
star-led w.	MILT 530:18
wobbly spelling is W.	MILN 528:10
woe and all my w.	GOLD 354:21
Companions of our w.	WALS 820:12
deep, unutterable w.	AYTO 41:15
discover sights of w.	MILT 531:8
Europe made his w. her own	ARNO 28:21
feel another's w.	POPE 606:16
full of w.	PROV 626:28
gave signs of w.	MILT 534:1
oft in w.	WHIT 832:2
protracted w.	JOHN 426:19
see another's w.	BLAK 122:8
source of softer w.	SCOT 673:7
suits of w.	SHAK 683:28
W. is me	BIBL 88:11
w. that is in marriage	CHAU 212:13
W. to her that is filthy	BIBL 92:12
W. to the bloody city	BIBL 92:10
W. to thee, O land	BIBL 86:18
W. to the land	SHAK 716:29
w. unto them	BIBL 88:7
woes direful spring of w.	OPEN 574:2
Of w. unnumbered	POPE 605:14
self-consumer of my w.	CLAR 224:11
What is the worst of w.	BYRO 178:13
w. which Hope thinks infinite	SHEL 731:10
wolf his sentinel, the w.	SHAK 704:17
Hunger drives the w.	PROV 622:35
keep the w. far thence	WEBS 826:10
like the w. on the fold	BYRO 180:1
no w. has ever craved	LA F 463:16
there really was a w.	AESO 6:12
w. behowls the moon	SHAK 712:6
w. by the ears	JEFF 420:12
w. in sheep's clothing	AESO 6:19
w. of a different opinion	INGE 413:8
w. shall dwell with the lamb	BIBL 88:21
W. that shall keep it	KIPL 457:2
w. to another man	PLAU 597:20
wolfsbane twist W., tight-rooted	KEAT 444:16
Wolsey W.'s home town	NEWS 562:16
wolves eat like w.	SHAK 693:6
frighten the w.	MACH 502:12
howling of Irish w.	SHAK 682:5

ravening w.	BIBL 95:21
woman aren't I a w.	TRUT 801:17
artist man and the mother w.	SHAW 726:3
As you are w.	GRAV 360:8
A w. sat	HOOD 395:11
bad w.	ADDI 4:17
beautiful w. on top	HORA 397:19
bettre than a good w.	CHAU 211:21
body of a weak and feeble w.	ELIZ 304:7
born a w.	EDGE 296:2
born of a w.	BIBL 83:8
brawling w.	BIBL 84:38
broken-hearted w.	HAYE 376:7
business of a w.'s life	SOUT 749:18
But what is w.	COWL 246:3
cannot love a w. so well	ELIO 300:9
changeable thing always is w.	VIRG 812:5
Christ wasn't a w.	TRUT 801:17
Come to my w.'s breasts	SHAK 703:20
contentious w.	BIBL 85:15
could be a good w.	THAC 786:19
dead w. bites not	GRAY 360:19
dear deluding w.	BURN 172:25
done, ask a w.	THAT 786:26
Do you not know I am a w.	SHAK 681:20
Each thought on the w.	KING 452:21
embrace a w.'s shoe	KRAU 461:15
end to a w.'s liberty	BURN 170:1
Eternal W. draws us	CLOS 228:8
Eternal W. draws us upward	GOET 353:3
Every w. adores a Fascist	PLAT 596:21
excellent thing in w.	SHAK 702:6
fair w. without discretion	BIBL 84:11
fat white w.	CORN 243:10
Frailty, thy name is w.	SHAK 684:4
fury, like a w. scorned	CONG 238:30
greatest glory of a w.	PERI 592:24
hair of a w.	HOWE 406:2
Here lies a poor w.	EPIT 309:15
honest w. of her word	SHAK 709:11
I am a w. of the world	SHAW 725:11
if a w. have long hair	BIBL 107:23
I grant I am a w.	SHAK 697:2
in a w. all defects excuse	LANI 467:2
in a w.'s hide	SHAK 694:25
inconstant w.	GAY 342:9
injured w.	BARB 55:6
In w.'s eye	BYRO 179:26
Is to a w.	DONN 280:16
just like a w.	DYLA 294:9
large-brained w.	BROW 158:5
leader of the enterprise a w.	VIRG 811:4
let me not play a w.	SHAK 710:23
Let us look for the w.	DUMA 291:11
Like to a constant w.	FORD 328:17
lips of a strange w.	BIBL 83:38
little w. who wrote	LINC 485:15
Love a w.	ROCH 651:15
lovely w.	HUNT 409:20
lovely w. stoops to folly	GOLD 355:33
made he a w.	BIBL 75:15
make a man a w.	PEMB 591:12
man's desire is for the w.	COLE 234:4
Man that is born of a w.	BOOK 133:16
Many a w. has a past	WILD 836:6
nakedness of the w.	BLAK 121:5
never be by w. loved	BLAK 119:8
never trust a w.	WILD 836:22
never yet fair w.	SHAK 700:17
no, nor w. neither	SHAK 685:24
no other purgatory but a w.	BEAU 60:9
not inspired by a w.	JUVE 439:21
No w. can be a beauty	FARQ 315:11
No w. will be Prime Minister	THAT 786:25
O most pernicious w.	SHAK 685:7
One is not born a w.	DE B 260:13
one of w. born	SHAK 707:16
one young w. and another	SHAW 725:29
only way for a w.	SHAW 727:5
perfect w.; nobly planned	WORD 850:5
play without a w.	KYD 462:11
post-chaise with a pretty w.	JOHN 430:25
pretty w. as was ever seen	BYRO 178:1

prime truth of w.	CHES 217:12	w.'s friendship ever ends	GAY 341:24	joined a w.'s group	STEV 758:20
Prudence is the other w.	ANON 18:13	w.'s noblest station	LYTT 497:13	labour of w. in the house	GILM 349:12
she *is* a w.	AUST 40:15	w. sober	PEPY 592:5	like w.'s letters	HAZL 376:9
She is a w.	SHAK 694:13	w.'s pen	BOOT 145:1	managers of affairs of w.	KORA 459:23
she's a w.	RACI 640:4	w.'s place in the home	PROV 635:16	many w., and many children	JOHN 428:3
she shall be called W.	BIBL 75:16	w.'s preaching	JOHN 428:19	mature w., *dancing*	FRIE 334:17
sort of bloom on a w.	BARR 57:7	w.'s reason	SHAK 721:19	men have turned into w.	XERX 852:19
stages in a w.'s life	KELL 447:21	W. stock is rising	CHIL 217:20	men, w., and Herveys	MONT 543:18
suffered over *such* a w.	HOME 393:21	w.'s whole existence	BYRO 180:15	mere persons of w.	MORE 548:6
sweeter w. ne'er drew breath	INGE 413:13	w.'s workhouse	SHAW 726:30	mob of scribbling w.	HAWT 376:1
takes a very clever w.	KIPL 457:1	w.'s work is never done	PROV 635:17	Music and w.	PEPY 592:13
take some savage w.	TENN 781:2	w. take An elder	SHAK 720:23	no plain w. on television	FORD 328:8
that ever loved w.	MALO 509:3	w. taken in adultery	BIBL 103:8	not w. truly then	JONS 435:25
that horror—the old w.	COLE 234:15	w. that attempts the pen	WINC 841:6	now called the nature of w.	MILL 525:13
that one w. differs from another		W. the nigger of the world	ONO 573:15	other w. cloy The appetites	SHAK 679:7
	MENC 521:15	w. think him an angel	THAC 786:6	our chilly w.	BYRO 177:26
There was an old w.	NURS 570:1	w. to define her feelings	HARD 371:15	paradise of w.	PROV 618:42
this Man and this W.	BOOK 133:4	w. to obey	PEMB 591:9	passing the love of w.	BIBL 80:29
tired of being a w.	SEXT 677:13	w. under her father's control	LAWS 476:1	Plain w. he regarded	ELIO 300:2
torrent of a w.'s will	ANON 20:1	w. wakes to love	TENN 778:7	position for w. Is prone	CARM 193.6
unbecoming to a w.	WILD 836:8	w. was full of good works	BIBL 105:5	Powerful w. only succeed	LEE- 479:5
victory by a w.	WEST 830:16	W. was God's second blunder	NIET 564:4	proper function of w.	ELIO 300:15
virtuous w.	BIBL 85:23	w. watches her body uneasily	COHE 230:11	publishers are not w.	ROBI 650:12
virtuous w. is a crown	BIBL 84:12	W., what have I to do	BIBL 102:27	regiment of w.	KNOX 458:6
Vitality in a w.	SHAW 726:2	w. who deliberates	ADDI 4:11	Righteous w. are obedient	KORA 460:1
warst w.	BALL 52:9	w. who did not care	KIPL 456:2	'rights' of w.	NIGH 564:14
weep as a w.	AYES 41:10	w. who didn't appeal to me	PROU 613:6	should w. be denied	DEFO 261:9
well-born and unhappy w.	ELIO 299:17	w. who lives for others	LEWI 483:7	simple w. only fit	LEWI 483:15
What does a w. want	FREU 334:5	w. whom thou gavest	BIBL 75:21	Single w.	AUST 40:19
What is a w.	KIPL 454:11	W., why weepest thou	BIBL 104:12	Solomon loved many strange w.	BIBL 81:14
when a w. appears	GAY 341:14	w., wine and song	LUTH 496:15	Some w.'ll stay in a man's memory	
where w. never smiled	CLAR 224:12	w. with a slop-pail	HOPK 397:15		KIPL 457:7
whistling w. and a crowing hen	PROV 635:1	w. with fair opportunities	THAC 786:12	sorrows of w.	ELIO 299:14
who cheats a w.	GAY 341:17	w. without a man	SAYI 670:23	spoiled the w.'s chats	BROW 160:20
Why can't a w. be	LERN 481:16	writer first and a w. after	MANS 511:4	tide in the affairs of w.	BYRO 181:20
wisest w. in Europe	ELIO 303:10	**womanhead** learnt that w.	DONN 281:8	To please w.	FLAU 325:5
w. and a ship ever want	PROV 635:15	**womanhood** Heroic w.	LONG 490:24	to w. as to men	ANTH 23:6
W., a pleasing but a short-lived	LEAP 477:1	**womankind** mankind and w.	BAHA 49:12	to w. Italian	CHAR 209:13
w. as old as she looks	PROV 625:53	packs off its w.	SHAW 726:12	To w. their original must owe	COLL 234:20
W., behold thy son	BIBL 104:6	think better of w.	KEAT 446:13	Votes for w.	POLI 601:13
w. brought sin and death	STAN 754:9	w.'s in every state a slave	EGER 297:4	way with the w.	DICK 272:7
w. can be proud and stiff	YEAT 853:16	**womb** cloistered in thy dear w.	DONN 280:3	weird w. promised	SHAK 705:16
w. can forgive a man	MAUG 518:17	from his mother's w.	SHAK 707:17	Whatever w. do	WHIT 834:8
w. can hardly ever choose	ELIO 299:19	fruit of thy w.	PRAY 611:1	when w. were the defeated	TREV 798:14
w. clothed with the sun	BIBL 113:27	in our mother's w.	DONN 281:23	wine and w.	BURT 174:4
w., coloured ill	SHAK 723:30	O w.! O bely	CHAU 212:5	With many w. I doubt	TROL 799:20
w. dictates	ELIO 299:25	teeming w. of royal kings	SHAK 715:14	w. and care and trouble	WARD 821:15
w., dog, and walnut tree	PROV 635:14	w. of time	HEIN 380:5	W., and Champagne	BELL 65:9
w. especially	AUST 39:8	w. of uncreated night	MILT 532:1	W. and fortune	WYCH 852:11
w. forget her sucking child	BIBL 89:27	**wombs** think with our w.	LUCE 495:6	W. and Horses	KIPL 453:16
w. has given you her heart	VANB 806:16	**women** about the coloured w.	TRUT 801:19	W. and servants most difficult	CONF 238:12
W.! in our hours of ease	SCOT 673:24	after the manner of w.	BIBL 76:18	W. and wine	GAY 341:13
w. in this humour	SHAK 716:24	Alas! the love of w.	BYRO 180:25	w. are born slaves	ASTE 32:14
w. is a sometime thing	HEYW 387:17	American w. shoot	FORS 329:6	w. are from Venus	GRAY 360:17
w. is his game	TENN 783:8	between men and w.	THUR 794:1	w. are like tricks	CONG 238:25
w. is like a teabag	REAG 643:8	blessed art thou among w.	BIBL 99:30	w. are not educated	CAVE 204:5
w. is so hard	TENN 783:11	Certain w. should be struck	COWA 245:12	W. are only children	CHES 215:8
W. *is the equal of man*	LOY 494:23	Charming w.	FARQ 315:18	w. are so simple	SHAK 718:17
W. is the great unknown	HARD 371:8	choose your w. or linen	PROV 627:18	W. are strongest	BIBL 92:15
w., let her be as good	ELIO 300:7	claim our right as w.	PANK 585:7	w.-authors	COOP 242:12
w. loves her lover	BYRO 180:26	comfortable w.	STRI 762:13	w. become like their mothers	WILD 835:18
w. makes the statement	MUIR 553:15	conduct of the w.	MORE 548:4	w. become unnaturally thin	WOLF 843:9
w. moved	SHAK 718:15	designs to please w.	CLIF 222:7	w. born slaves	WOLL 844:9
W. much missed	HARD 373:3	dream of fair w.	TENN 776:18	w. can't forgive failure	CHEK 214:1
w. must have money	WOOL 845:6	drives the w. out of their minds	DORF 282:16	w. come and go	ELIO 302:13
w. must submit to it	STAE 753:17	Equality for w. demands	TOYN 797:9	w. come out to cut up	KIPL 456:8
w. must wear chains	FARQ 315:10	especially to w.	BYRO 180:13	w. come to see the show	OVID 579:21
w. of education	AUST 40:11	Even w. and children	SA'A 662:6	W. deprived of the company	CHEK 214:13
w. of mean understanding	AUST 39:19	extension of w.'s rights	FOUR 330:16	W. desiren to have sovereynetee	
w. of real genius	FITZ 323:18	feelings of w. in a drawing-room			CHAU 212:20
w. of shining loveliness	YEAT 855:15		WOOL 845:8	W. do not find it difficult	MACK 503:1
w. once was	BALL 52:19	fight to get w. out	GREE 363:7	W. don't seem to think	AMIS 13:13
w. only the right to spring	FOND 327:25	Free w. are not women	COLE 234:16	W. enjoyed	SUCK 763:3
w. possessed of a common share	ADAM 1:15	From w.'s eyes	SHAK 702:18	w., God help us	SAYE 668:7
W.'s at best a contradiction	POPE 603:7	From w.'s eyes	SHAK 702:20	W. have a positive moral sense	ADAM 2:9
w. says to her lusting lover	CATU 203:3	going to w.	NIET 564:2	W. have no soul	ASTE 32:10
w.'s best garment	PROV 630:39	Good w. always think	BROO 153:17	W. have no wilderness	BOGA 125:7
w. scorned	PROV 622:19	greatly troubled by w.	JAIN 416:6	W. have served as looking-glasses	
W.'s cully made	CONG 238:33	happiest w.	ELIO 300:14		WOOL 845:7
W.'s degradation	STAN 754:10	have wine and w.	BYRO 180:21	W. have very little idea	GREE 363:4
w. seldom asks advice	ADDI 5:9	hops, and w.	DICK 271:26	w. in a state of ignorance	KNOX 458:13
w. seldom writes her mind	STEE 754:17	if ye be kind towards w.	KORA 460:8	W. in furious secret rebellion	SHAW 725:8
w.'s finest ornament	AUCT 34:16	I must have w.	GAY 341:15	w. in men require	BLAK 121:23

women (*cont.*):
w. labouring of child — BOOK 129:12
w. marry off in haste — ASTE 32:16
w. marry them for love — OSBO 578:13
w. must weep — KING 452:22
w. need to be helped — TRUT 801:17
W. never have young minds — DELA 263:9
W. never look so well — SURT 764:23
w. never so fair — LYLY 497:1
W. nicer than men — AMIS 13:14
W., of kynde, desiren libertee — CHAU 211:8
W.—one half the human race — WOLL 844:7
w. remain the slaves of power — WOLL 844:7
W. reminded him of lilies — MITC 540:7
w. were first at the Cradle — SAYE 668:7
W. what they are — BRAD 149:5
w. . . . who are the lamps — LAWS 476:2
W. who love the same man — BEER 63:6
w. who write — DURA 292:17
works of w. — BROW 157:16
writ by w. — CENT 205:8
you grim w. — OVID 579:20
zeal of w. themselves — MILL 525:18
won EVERYBODY has w. — CARR 194:2
field is w. — MORE 548:14
ground w. to-day — ARNO 28:8
has w. it bear the palm — MOTT 552:14
in this humour w. — SHAK 716:24
I w. the count — SOMO 746:1
never lost till w. — CRAB 249:13
never w. fair lady — PROV 619:37
No one w. — ROOS 653:8
not that you w. or lost — RICE 646:9
not to have w. — COUB 244:9
Sun wot w. it — NEWS 562:15
Things w. are done — SHAK 719:17
Where you will never w. — BALL 52:1
woman, therefore may be w. — SHAK 719:14
woman, therefore to be w. — SHAK 694:13
wonder boneless w. — CHUR 220:23
eyes to w. — SHAK 723:17
great w. in heaven — BIBL 119:43
I w. any man alive — GAY 341:6
I w. by my troth — DONN 280:26
knowledge and w. — BACO 42:11
moon-washed apples of w. — DRIN 286:8
One can only w. — BENT 68:17
Smiling w. of a day — WRIG 851:16
state of w. — GOUL 357:9
still the w. grew — GOLD 354:17
To work a w. — HERR 386:22
transcendent w. — CARL 192:11
W. . . . and not any expectation — SMIT 741:2
w. of our age — DYER 293:12
w. of our stage — JONS 435:28
w. that would be — TENN 780:20
w. who's kissing her — ADAM 2:3
wonderful God, how w. Thou art — FABE 313:14
I've had a w. life — LAST 473:20
many w. things — SOPH 746:15
most w. wonderful — SHAK 681:19
strange and w. — TRAH 797:15
too w. and excellent — BOOK 143:15
too w. for me — BIBL 85:21
too w. to be true — FARA 314:16
W., Counsellor — BIBL 88:18
w. works of God — BIBL 104:27
Yes, w. things — CART 197:1
wonderfully fearfully and w. made — BOOK 143:17
wonders Everything has its w. — KELL 447:19
His w. to perform — COWP 246:23
multiply my signs and my w. — BIBL 77:24
signs and w. — BIBL 102:35
Time works w. — PROV 633:5
Welcome, all w. — CRAS 250:12
w. in the deep — BOOK 144:18
w. we seek without us — BROW 156:27
W. will never cease — PROV 635:18
wondrous all thy w. works — BOOK 135:11
survey the w. cross — WATT 823:15
won't administrative w. — LYNN 497:7

if she w., she won't — ANON 20:1
woo Come, w. me, woo me — SHAK 681:28
Men are April when they w. — SHAK 682:2
wood behind the little w. — TENN 781:15
Bows down to w. and stone — HEBE 378:16
bows down to w. and stone — KIPL 453:21
cleave the w. — ANON 18:18
deep and gloomy w. — WORD 847:9
hewers of w. — BIBL 79:12
In a dark w. I saw — ROET 652:6
native w.-notes wild — MILT 529:27
out of the w. — PROV 618:13
Out of this w. — SHAK 711:13
set out to plant a w. — SWIF 766:31
within a dark w. — DANT 255:12
w. of English bows — DOYL 285:10
w.'s in trouble — HOUS 404:13
W. the Weed, the Wag — RALE 641:7
You are not w. — SHAK 697:29
woodbine luscious w. — SHAK 711:4
woodcock Spirits of well-shot w. — BETJ 72:5
w. near the gin — SHAK 720:31
w. to mine own springe — SHAK 689:10
woodcocks springes to catch w. — SHAK 684:22
wooden Sailed off in a w. shoe — FIEL 317:9
with a w. leg — DICK 271:17
Within this w. O — SHAK 692:27
w. wall is your ships — THEM 787:20
w. walls are the best — COVE 244:14
woodland bit of w. — HORA 403:14
stands about the w. ride — HOUS 404:6
woodlanded by w. ways — BETJ 73:3
woodlands About the w. I will go — HOUS 404:7
woodman W., spare that tree — MORR 549:11
w., spare the beechen tree — CAMP 187:8
woods Enter these enchanted w. — MERE 522:23
found dead in the w. — KELL 447:20
fresh w., and pastures new — MILT 530:13
go down in the w. today — BRAT 149:20
gods have lived in the w. — VIRG 813:19
Love-whisp'ring w. — POPE 602:5
never knew the summer w. — TENN 778:31
once a road through the w. — KIPL 456:3
pleasure in the pathless w. — BYRO 179:17
senators of mighty w. — KEAT 443:13
spirit in the w. — WORD 847:19
We'll to the w. no more — ANON 20:18
Wet Wild W. — KIPL 456:15
w. against the world — BLUN 124:4
w. and groves — WITH 842:4
w. are lovely — FROS 336:3
w. decay and fall — TENN 784:7
w. have ears — PROV 619:49
w. More free from peril — SHAK 680:25
w. of consular dignity — VIRG 814:2
woodshed Something nasty in the w. — GIBB 346:2
wooed therefore to be w. — SHAK 694:13
woman, therefore may be w. — SHAK 719:14
wooer knight to be their w. — BALL 51:15
woof weave the w. — GRAY 360:22
wooing my w. mind — SHAK 702:23
w. not long a-doing — PROV 621:32
would a-w. go — NURS 566:20
wool giveth snow like w. — BOOK 144:5
go out for w. — PROV 626:12
hairs are white like w. — BIBL 112:29
Have you any w. — NURS 566:8
like the pure w. — BIBL 91:24
Much cry and little w. — PROV 627:3
Woolf afraid of Virginia W. — ALBE 10:5
woollen Odious! in w. — POPE 603:21
woolly w. peach — JONS 436:6
Woolworth visit to W.'s — BEVA 73:20
Wops Huns or W. — MITF 541:2
word action to the w. — SHAK 686:23
be ye doers of the w. — BIBL 111:22
By water and the w. — STON 761:5
captive with a gentle w. — CARY 197:12
choke the w. — BIBL 97:4
comfort of thy holy W. — BOOK 130:1

Englishman's w. — PROV 618:46
engrafted w. — BIBL 111:21
Every idle w. — BIBL 96:32
Every w. she writes is a lie — MCCA 500:9
every w. that proceedeth — BIBL 94:15
flowering in a lonely w. — TENN 784:10
for whom the w. 'fuck' — TYNA 804:3
fulfilling his w. — BOOK 144:6
Greeks had a w. — AKIN 9:11
honour? A w. — SHAK 691:9
honour his own w. — TENN 777:20
I kept my w. — DE L 263:3
In the beginning was the W. — BIBL 102:15
In the beginning was the W. — OPEN 574:19
in w. mightier — MILT 533:20
leave the w. of God — BIBL 104:31
lies in one little w. — SHAK 715:8
Lord gave the w. — BOOK 138:12
Lord, thy w. abideth — BAKE 50:1
milk of the w. — BIBL 112:4
milk of the w. — BIBL 115:18
nat o w. wol he faille — CHAU 211:26
no w. in their language — SWIF 765:16
out of his holy w. — ROBI 650:17
packed up into one w. — CARR 195:17
Perhaps we have not the w. — ARNO 29:18
power of the written w. — CONR 240:20
repugnant to the W. of God — BOOK 144:16
single w. even may be — SHEL 732:15
time for such a w. — SHAK 707:14
To-day I pronounced a w. — FLEM 326:13
torture one poor w. — DRYD 288:32
truth of thy holy W. — BOOK 131:13
understanding of thy W. — BOOK 129:10
wash out a w. of it — FITZ 323:10
weasel w. — ROOS 654:15
what the w. did make it — ELIZ 304:20
When I use a w. — CARR 195:15
whose eternal W. — MARR 514:7
w., at random spoken — SCOT 673:14
w. fitly spoken — BIBL 85:3
w. for word — ALFR 11:13
w. is a lantern — BOOK 142:13
W. is but wynd — LYDG 496:20
w. is enough — PLAU 597:21
w. is the Verb — HUGO 407:15
w. of Caesar — SHAK 697:28
w. preserves contact — MANN 510:11
w. spoken in due season — BIBL 84:25
w. takes wing — HORA 399:14
w. to the wise is enough — PROV 635:19
W. was made flesh — BIBL 102:21
W. WAS MADE FLESH — MISS 539:13
W. without a word — ANDR 14:11
wordless poem should be w. — MACL 503:9
words Actions speak louder than w. — PROV 614:2
adequately expressed in w. — BERG 69:8
all w. And no performance — MASS 518:4
artillery of w. — SWIF 767:4
barren superfluity of w. — GART 340:12
big w. for little matters — JOHN 428:21
But for your w. — SHAK 698:22
coiner of sweet w. — ARNO 28:14
comfortable w. — BOOK 131:19
conceal a fact with w. — MACH 502:7
confused w. — BAUD 58:13
deceive you with vain w. — BIBL 109:15
doctrines without w. — LAO 467:5
dreamed out in w. — MURR 555:3
dressing old w. new — SHAK 723:11
Fair w. enough — WYAT 852:7
fear those big w. — JOYC 437:16
few w. of my own — EDWA 296:12
Fine w. — PROV 620:5
fond w. left unspoken — STRU 762:16
food and not fine w. — MOLI 541:18
form of sound w. — BIBL 110:29
four w. I write — BOIL 125:15
frying pan of your w. — FLAU 325:9
Give 'em w. — JONS 435:13
Give sorrow w. — SHAK 706:23
Good w. do not last long — JOSE 436:16

w. i' the bud   SHAK 720:29
w., the canker, and the grief   BYRO 183:1
worms Among the hungry w.   BALL 51:18
convocation of politic w.   SHAK 687:35
diet of w.   FENT 316:12
eaten of w.   BIBL 105:9
Flies, w., and flowers   WATT 823:8
Impaling w.   COLM 236:5
set on me in W.   LUTH 496:9
with vilest w. to dwell   SHAK 723:9
w. destroy this body   BIBL 83:12
w. shall try   MARV 516:2
w. were hallowed   SHAK 714:8
wormwood bitter as w.   BIBL 83:38
star is called W.   BIBL 113:43
w. and the gall   BIBL 91:8
worn one so w.   CRAB 249:10
When we're w.   SOUT 748:15
worried may not be w. into being   FROS 336:6
w. about Jim   CATC 201:7
worry humanity has no w.   CONF 238:5
kills, but w.   PROV 624:12
worrying What's the use of w.   MILI 526:18
W. the carcase   THOM 791:3
worse Defend the bad against the w.   DAY- 260:6
follow the w.   OVID 580:13
for better for w.   BOOK 133:9
For fear of finding something w.   BELL 64:22
from w. to better   HOOK 395:19
from w. to better   JOHN 424:3
Go further and fare w.   PROV 620:43
If my books had been any w.   CHAN 207:16
is it something w.   SPRI 753:12
make the w. appear   MILT 531:30
Many w., better few   LOCK 489:5
mean the W. one   ARIS 25:3
might have been w.   PROV 628:11
More will mean w.   AMIS 13:16
one penny the w.   BARH 55:17
something even w.   AESO 6:18
We make them w.   GOET 353:15
w. off for having known   STEP 756:6
w. than a crime   BOUL 147:5
w. than the first   BIBL 97:1
worst are no w.   SHAK 712:4
worship earth doth w. thee   BOOK 127:20
ignorantly w.   BIBL 105:18
O w. the King   GRAN 359:3
O w. the Lord   BOOK 140:11
second is freedom to w.   ROOS 653:20
Some w. stones   SIKH 737:9
various modes of w.   GIBB 344:18
we w. thy Name   BOOK 128:2
who w. the beast   BIBL 114:3
with my body I thee w.   BOOK 133:10
w. and fall down   BOOK 140:10
w. her by years   TENN 777:21
w. him in spirit   BIBL 102:34
W. is transcendent wonder   CARL 192:11
w. the Lord   MONS 543:8
worshipped W. and served   BIBL 105:37
worships w. in his way   SMAR 739:17
worst best and the w. of this   SWIN 768:24
did the w. to him   ANON 22:14
full look at the w.   HARD 372:17
good in the w. of us   ANON 19:9
His w. is better   HAZL 377:1
inn's w. room   POPE 603:11
it was the w. of times   DICK 272:13
knew the w. too young   KIPL 454:7
know the w.   BRAD 148:20
No w., there is none   HOPK 396:18
prepare for the w.   PROV 622:30
This is the w.   SHAK 701:7
To-morrow do thy w.   DRYD 289:29
When things are at the w.   PROV 634:36
While the w. are full   YEAT 855:12
world's w. wound   SASS 667:23
w. form of Government   CHUR 221:21
w. is death   SHAK 715:21
w. is yet to come   JOHN 423:19

w. of times   OPEN 574:28
w. thing I've ever witnessed   MORR 550:4
w. time of the year   ANDR 14:12
w. time of the year   ELIO 302:9
w. woman   BALL 52:9
worth Because I'm w. it   ADVE 7:10
calculate the w. of a man   FLAU 325:11
If a thing's w. doing   PROV 622:44
more w. than his chambermaid   GODW 352:3
nor words, nor w.   SHAK 698:5
not w. going to see   JOHN 431:14
not w. reading   AUST 38:23
not w. the dust   SHAK 701:9
trifles were w. something   CATU 202:9
turned out w. anything   SCOT 675:3
W. a guinea a box   ADVE 8:25
w. a load of hay   PROV 631:36
w. and spiritual reality   HEGE 379:4
w. doing badly   CHES 217:12
w. of a thing is what   PROV 635:21
worthiness for the w. of thy Son   BOOK 132:8
Worthington daughter on the stage, Mrs W.   COWA 245:4
worthless this false, this w. man   EPHE 308:5
worthy am no more w.   BIBL 101:16
I am not w.   MISS 539:10
labourer is w. of his hire   BIBL 100:19
Lord I am not w.   BIBL 95:27
nameless in w. deeds   BROW 156:15
not w. to unloose   BIBL 102:23
there be nine w.   CAXT 204:8
world was not w.   BIBL 111:9
w. of their steel   SCOT 673:6
w. of the vocation   BIBL 109:10
W. the Lamb that died   WATT 823:13
w. to open the book   BIBL 113:11
wotthehell w. archy   MARQ 514:3
would evil which I w. not   BIBL 106:15
He w., wouldn't he   RICE 647:3
w. they should do unto me   BOOK 132:15
wouldest whither thou w. not   BIBL 104:22
wound Earth felt the w.   MILT 534:1
heal me of my grievous w.   TENN 778:18
Hearts w. up with love   SPEN 750:21
help to w. itself   SHAK 699:16
keep the w. open   GRAS 359:13
knife see not the w.   SHAK 703:21
never felt a w.   SHAK 717:19
purple with love's w.   SHAK 711:2
tongue In every w.   SHAK 698:6
warning from another's w.   JERO 421:4
Willing to w.   POPE 602:29
wit Makes such a w.   SHEL 729:23
world's worst w.   SASS 667:23
w. for wound   BIBL 78:6
w. had been for Ireland   LAST 474:17
w., not the bandage   POTT 608:6
wounded escapes being w.   PUGI 636:20
like a w. snake   POPE 604:8
w. and left   KIPL 456:8
w. for our transgressions   BIBL 90:3
w. spirit   BIBL 84:31
You're w.   BROW 159:26
Wounded Knee Bury my heart at W.   BENÉ 66:12
wounding w. heart   CRAS 250:8
wounds bind up the nation's w.   LINC 485:12
keeps his own w. green   BACO 45:9
not to heed the w.   IGNA 412:18
old w. bleed anew   WALL 818:12
salt rubbed into their w.   WEST 830:12
soldier details his w.   PROP 612:21
These w. I had   SHAK 693:23
to heal the mortal w.   PETR 593:17
w. of a friend   BIBL 85:14
w. thou madest   DANI 255:6
woven w. them a garment   AKHM 9:9
Wragg W. is in custody   ARNO 29:16
wrangle shall we begin to w.   ANON 19:2
wrap w. me in a gown   HERB 383:16
wrapped all meanly w.   MILT 530:19
w. him in swaddling clothes   BIBL 100:2

wrath cometh the w. of God   BIBL 109:15
day of his w. is come   BIBL 113:15
day of w.   MISS 539:15
dragon and his w.   SHAK 699:19
Envy and w.   BIBL 93:22
flee from the w. to come   BIBL 94:12
grapes of w.   BORR 146:10
grapes of w.   HOWE 405:15
neither w. of Jove   OVID 580:15
provoke not your children to w.   BIBL 109:18
sun go down upon your w.   BIBL 109:13
turneth away w.   BIBL 84:22
turneth away w.   PROV 631:2
tygers of w.   BLAK 121:6
w. did end   BLAK 122:16
w. of the Lamb   BIBL 113:15
wreathed becks, and w. smiles   MILT 529:19
wreaths laurel w. entwine   HART 374:15
wreck on which thou art to w.   DRYD 287:13
w. and not the story   RICH 647:4
wrecks Vomits its w.   SHEL 729:19
Wrekin W. heaves   HOUS 404:13
wren Four Larks and a W.   LEAR 477:3
hurt the little w.   BLAK 119:8
Mr Christopher W.   EVEL 313:3
musician than the w.   SHAK 710:7
robin and the w.   PROV 630:13
Sir Christopher W.   BARH 55:12
Sir Christopher W.   BENT 68:16
w. goes to't   SHAK 701:14
youngest w. of nine   SHAK 721:6
wrest W. once the law   SHAK 709:28
wrestle w. not against flesh   BIBL 109:21
w. With words and meanings   ELIO 301:15
wrestled w. for perhaps too long   HOWE 405:12
w. with him   WALT 821:4
wrestles He that w. with us   BURK 167:25
wrestling intellectual sumo w.   HARV 374:21
W., I will not let thee go   WESL 829:3
wretch w. that dares not die   BURN 171:22
wretched all men hate the w.   SHEL 728:9
only w. are the wise   PRIO 612:10
proud and yet a w. thing   DAVI 258:9
w. men are cradled   SHEL 729:18
wretchedness O! the fierce w.   SHAK 719:11
w. is irremediable   EDGE 296:2
wretches feel what w. feel   SHAK 700:23
How shall w. live   GODL 351:19
Poor naked w.   SHAK 700:22
wring soon w. their hands   WALP 820:5
wrings at last w. its neck   RUSS 660:27
wrinkle stamps the w. deeper   BYRO 178:13
wrinkled w. sea beneath him   TENN 776:20
wrinkles w. will devour   NASH 557:20
wrist With gyves upon his w.   HOOD 394:24
writ censure this mysterious w.   DRYD 288:17
I never w.   SHAK 723:24
name was w. in water   EPIT 310:4
write angel should w.   MOOR 547:11
baseness to w. fair   SHAK 689:6
best to w. in wind   CATU 203:3
compulsion to w.   LARK 469:9
die while I w.   PETR 594:1
Ek gret effect men w.   CHAU 213:13
four words I w.   BOIL 125:15
hate all who w.   WYCH 852:14
I w. of melancholy   BURT 173:19
I w. one   DISR 278:11
I w. them   PUNC 637:17
Learn to w. well   BUCK 163:7
Learn to w. well   CLOS 228:18
little more I have to w.   HERR 386:2
look in thy heart and w.   SIDN 736:3
love to w. them   BISH 117:11
make me w. too much   DANI 255:10
man ought to w.   TROL 799:3
men w. for profit   WALP 819:13
not enough for me to w.   LYLY 497:5
nothing to w. about   PLIN 598:8
people that w.   SHEN 733:1
people who can't w.   ZAPP 858:6
reading, in order to w.   JOHN 430:5

touch of earthly y. WORD 850:6
two hundred y. like a sheep TIPU 794:18
two thousand y. of hope WEIZ 827:1
y. are slipping by HORA 401:6
y. like great black oxen YEAT 853:15
y. of desolation JEFF 420:14
Y. steal Fire from the mind BYRO 178:16
y. that the locust hath eaten BIBL 92:2
y. to come YEAT 854:16
yeas russet y. SHAK 702:23
yell angry spirit's y. BEAT 59:12
yellow Come unto these y. sands
  SHAK 718:26
expend her yellow y. MIDD 524:12
falls into the y. Leaf BYRO 181:12
Follow the y. brick road HARB 371:5
Goodbye y. brick road JOHN 422:15
one long y. string BROW 160:25
paved with y. brick BAUM 59:6
sparkled on the y. field TENN 780:9
thy y. stockings SHAK 720:33
With a y. petticoat NURS 566:16
Y., and black, and pale SHEL 730:7
Y. God forever gazes HAYE 376:7
y. leaf SHAK 707:8
y. like ripe corn ROSS 655:20
yelps loudest y. for liberty JOHN 426:8
yeoman did me y.'s service SHAK 689:6
yes getting the answer y. CAMU 188:9
I did say y. O at lightning HOPK 397:12
never hear the word 'y.' WEST 830:9
Y., but not in the South POTT 608:9
'Y.,' I answered you BROW 158:1
Y. it hurt POLI 601:18
Y., Minister! No, Minister CROS 252:17
Y., Virginia NEWS 562:25
y. you don't mean RUME 658:7
yesterday authority of the eternal y.
  WEBE 825:6
but as y. BOOK 139:22
but y. a King BYRO 182:25
dead y. FITZ 323:7
give me y. JONE 434:5
keeping up with y. MARQ 513:27
O! call back y. SHAK 715:20
perhaps it was y. OPEN 574:7
rose of y. FITZ 323:1
same y., and to day BIBL 111:15
thoughts of y. PALI 584:9
were saying y. LUIS 496:4
y. doth not usher it in DONN 282:7
Y. I loved LESS 482:4
Y.'s men POLI 601:19
yesterdays all our y. SHAK 707:14
yesteryear snows of y. VILL 810:12
yet as y. there were none BOOK 143:18
but not y. AUGU 37:2
young man not y. BACO 44:33
yew Of true wood, of y. wood DOYL 285:10
slips of y. SHAK 706:13
YHVH image of Y. ZOHA 859:4
yid PUT THE ID BACK IN Y. ROTH 656:19
yield and not to y. TENN 784:20
just to y. to it GRAH 358:3
yin carry the y. LAO 467:14
yo Y.-ho-ho, and a bottle of rum STEV 759:13
yoga Y. is evenness of mind BHAG 74:12
yogi y. has gone to the root TANT 773:6
yoke bear the y. in his youth BIBL 91:9
break every y. BIBL 90:14
hath received our y. WALL 818:15
my y. is easy BIBL 96:27
y. of prelaty MILT 536:4
yoked y. with a lamb SHAK 698:19
yolk y. runs down the waistcoat DICK 270:23
Yonghy-Bonghy-Bó Lived the Y. LEAR 477:4
Yorick Alas, poor Y. SHAK 688:28
Yorkshire Y. born PROV 635:22
you cannot live with y. MART 515:3
For y. but not for me MILI 526:15
It could be y. ADVE 7:36
it was y. and me JAGG 416:1
wanted simply y. HÉLO 380:14

Y.'ll never walk HAMM 370:11
Y. too, Brutus CAES 185:8
Y.'ve got to be carefully taught
  HAMM 370:12
'Y.' your joys and sorrows CRIC 251:5
young artist as a y. man JOYC 437:7
Being y. is overestimated QUAN 638:15
censor of the y. HORA 398:11
country of y. men EMER 307:14
crime of being a y. man PITT 596:1
defrauded y. KIPL 454:2
dies y. MENA 521:13
evil in y. minds ARNO 30:16
for ever y. KEAT 444:11
get out while we're y. SPRI 753:11
Gods love die y. PROV 635:2
good die y. PROV 621:6
Hang a thief when he's y. PROV 621:28
Hip y. gunslinger ANON 16:12
If I were y. MARL 512:12
I have been y. BLUN 124:5
I have been y. BOOK 136:1
I'll die y. BRUC 162:3
in the will of a y. gentleman ASCH 31:8
I was a poet, I was y. FLEC 326:6
knew the worst too y. KIPL 454:7
lead those that are with y. BIBL 89:18
look y. till forty DRYD 288:33
love's y. dream MOOR 547:16
make an old man y. TENN 777:3
Old and y. STEV 759:19
on your y. shoulders SPAR 749:25
O y., fresshe folkes CHAU 213:16
proper y. men BURN 171:16
resolute, the y. KIPL 455:3
seventy years y. HOLM 393:8
So wise so y. SHAK 716:30
so y. a body SHAK 709:24
So y., and so untender SHAK 699:18
They're y. TAGL 771:12
too y. to fall asleep for ever SASS 667:19
too y. to take up golf ADAM 2:5
What can a y. lassie do BURN 173:7
what the world would call y. men
  PEEL 590:16
When thou wast y. BIBL 104:22
While we are y. ANON 21:17
Whom the gods love die y. BYRO 181:14
Women never have y. minds DELA 263:9
y. and foolish YEAT 853:19
y. are quick of speech WINT 841:19
Y. blood must have its course KING 453:1
y. can do for the old SHAW 725:6
Y. folks think old folks PROV 636:4
y., gifted and black HANS 370:18
Y., gifted and black IRVI 414:3
y. man married PROV 636:5
y. man married SHAK 678:10
y. man not yet BACO 44:33
y. man's slave PROV 615:21
Y. men and maidens BOOK 144:7
Y. men are fitter BACO 46:4
y. men glittering TRAH 797:16
y. men have more virtue JOHN 428:13
y. men may die PROV 636:6
y. men shall see visions BIBL 92:3
y. men's vision DRYD 287:2
y. men think it is HOUS 404:4
Y. saint, old devil PROV 636:7
y. think too little WALP 819:6
y. was very heaven WORD 846:20
y. whom I hope to bother AUDE 36:6
younger love be y. than thyself SHAK 720:24
y. race succeeds DILL 274:8
y. son gathered all together BIBL 101:14
y. than she SHAK 717:14
y. than that now DYLA 294:13
youngster You're going out a y. FILM 321:4
yours never y., Augustus DICK 270:12
no hands but y. SAYI 669:6
y. and yours MARK 512:10
Y. till Hell freezes FISH 322:16
yourself DO IT Y. BARH 56:3

do it y. PROV 623:24
see to everything y. MELB 520:12
yourselve make honey not for y. VIRG 815:7
youth April of your y. HERB 383:5
bear the yoke in his y. BIBL 91:9
cap of y. SHAK 688:16
Crabbed age and y. SHAK 722:15
days of our y. BYRO 183:10
days of thy y. BIBL 86:25
evil from his y. BIBL 76:8
flattering y. defy ROCH 651:16
flower of their y. VIRG 814:5
from my y. BOOK 143:4
How beautiful is y. MEDI 520:9
If y. knew ESTI 312:2
I have y. WEBS 825:20
In lusty y. SURR 764:6
in the days of thy y. BIBL 86:24
it is y. who must fight HOOV 396:2
miracle of a y. EVEL 313:3
My prime of y. TICH 794:12
noble y. did dress SHAK 691:32
offences of my y. BOOK 135:8
promises of y. JOHN 425:24
red sweet wine of y. BROO 153:5
remember my y. CONR 241:2
remembreth me Upon my y. CHAU 212:16
rose Of y. SHAK 679:15
seized my y. ARNO 28:19
shake their wicked sides at y. YEAT 855:4
sign of an ill-spent y. ROUP 657:2
spice-islands of Y. COLE 234:11
subtle thief of y. MILT 535:5
tender years of y. GOGO 354:1
things Y. needed not WORD 850:7
thoughts of y. are long LONG 490:15
To y. and age in common ARNO 29:6
unemployed y. BAGE 48:10
Where y. grows pale KEAT 444:24
world has lost his y. BIBL 92:18
Y. and Pleasure meet BYRO 178:20
y., I do adore thee SHAK 722:16
Y. is a blunder DISR 277:2
Y. is not an absolution ASHC 31:10
Y. is something very new CHAN 208:2
Y. is vivid LOVE 493:10
Y. must be served PROV 636:10
Y. of a Nation DISR 277:26
y. of a state BACO 45:35
y. of England SHAK 692:31
y. of frolics POPE 603:5
y. of his generation FITZ 324:10
y. of labour GOLD 354:11
y. of the realm SHAK 694:23
y. of the world BACO 43:6
Y. on the prow GRAY 360:23
Y. pined away BLAK 122:10
y. replies, I can EMER 306:16
Y.'s a stuff SHAK 720:16
y.'s sweet-scented manuscript FITZ 323:16
Y.'s the season GAY 341:16
y. to fortune GRAY 361:3
y. to the gallows PAIN 582:22
y. unkind BAST 58:8
Y., what man's age is like DENH 264:5
Y., which is forgiven SHAW 726:32
Y. would be an ideal state ASQU 32:3
Yule green Y. makes PROV 621:20
yuppie y. version of bulimia EHRE 297:6
Yvetot king of Y. BÉRA 69:5

Zadok Z. the priest BIBL 81:9
Zaire Z. is the trigger FANO 314:9
zany mountebank and his z. WALP 819:15
Zanzibar count the cats in Z. THOR 793:15
Zarathustra follower of Z. ZORO 859:14
Zauber Deine Z. binden wieder SCHI 668:16
zeal all z., Mr Easy MARR 514:10
by men of Z. BRAN 149:13
holy mistaken z. JUNI 438:17
not the slightest z. TALL 771:16
take it for z. THOM 788:12

zeal (*cont.*):
Tell z. it wants devotion   RALE 641:3
tempering bigot z.   KNOX 458:8
z. of the Lord   BIBL 88:19
z. of thine house   BOOK 138:15
z. of women themselves   MILL 525:18
zealous z. citizen   BURK 167:28
zed Thou whoreson z.   SHAK 700:7
Zen Z. and the art   PIRS 595:19

zenith from the z. like a falling star
                                            MILT 531:27
zephyr Odes to every z.   KING 452:16
zephyrs cold melts in the Z.   HORA 402:13
Zephyrus Sweet breathing Z.   SPEN 752:14
zest z. goes out of a beautiful waltz
                                            GREN 363:12
Zimbabwe keep my z.   MUGA 553:6
Zion daughter of Z.   BIBL 87:25

songs of peaceful Z.   DIX 278:13
Z., city of our God   NEWT 563:5
Zionism Z., be it right or wrong   BALF 51:7
zipless z. fuck   JONG 434:12
Zitronen *Land, wo die Z. blühn*   GOET 353:12
zone torrid or the frozen z.   CARE 190:17
zoo human z.   MORR 549:8
Zuleika Such was Z.   BYRO 178:3
Zurich gnomes in Z.   WILS 840:3